NomosGesetze

Prof. Dr. Kerstin von der Decken

Kulturgüterrecht

2. Auflage

Die Deutsche Nationalbibliothek verzeichnet diese Publikation in der Deutschen Nationalbibliografie; detaillierte bibliografische Daten sind im Internet über http://dnb.d-nb.de abrufbar.

ISBN 978-3-8487-3647-8

2. Auflage 2020
© Nomos Verlagsgesellschaft, Baden-Baden 2020. Gedruckt in Deutschland. Alle Rechte, auch die des Nachdrucks von Auszügen, der fotomechanischen Wiedergabe und der Übersetzung, vorbehalten.

Vorwort zur 2. Auflage

Kulturgüter sind „körperliche Gegenstände, beweglich oder unbeweglich, Einzelstücke oder Sammlungen/Ensembles, vom Menschen geschaffen, verändert, geprägt oder seine kulturelle Entwicklung widerspiegelnd, denen ein historischer, künstlerischer, wissenschaftlicher, architektonischer, archäologischer oder sonstiger kultureller Wert unterschiedlicher Dimension zukommt."[1] Vereinfacht gesagt, handelt es sich also um Gegenstände von kulturellem Wert.

Kulturgüter sind diversen Gefährdungen ausgesetzt. Die primäre Gefährdung betrifft ihre Substanz. Kulturgüter können zerstört, beschädigt, verändert, vernachlässigt oder dem Verfall preisgegeben werden. Die sekundäre Gefährdung betrifft ihre kulturellen Bindungen. Ein Gegenstand wird erst dadurch zum Kulturgut, das ihm eine bestimmte Gesellschaft einen kulturellen Wert beimisst. Jedes Kulturgut hat daher eine kulturelle Bindung an die Gesellschaft, die es als kulturell wertvoll einstuft und schätzt. Ein Kulturgut kann in einem Staat von höchster kultureller Bedeutung sein, während das gleiche Objekt in einem anderen Staat einen folkloristischen, einen exotischen oder aber gar keinen kulturellen Wert haben kann. Weitere Gefährdungen von Kulturgütern betreffen ihre Zugänglichkeit für die Allgemeinheit, ihre Nutzung und ihre wissenschaftliche Erforschung.

Das Kulturgüterrecht verfolgt das Ziel, Kulturgüter vor allen genannten Gefahren zu schützen. Das dazu entwickelte Normensystem ist komplex und auf allen Normebenen angesiedelt. Auf nationaler Ebene, also im deutschen Recht, ist der Schutz der Substanz eine Aufgabe der Länder, die diese insbesondere durch ihr Denkmal- und Archivrecht wahrnehmen. Der Schutz der kulturellen Bindungen, also der Schutz vor Abwanderung deutschen Kulturguts ins Ausland und die Rückgabe illegal eingeführten ausländischen Kulturguts, ist hingegen primäre Aufgabe des Bundes. Die weiteren Schutzziele werden wiederum in erster Linie von den Ländern im Rahmen ihrer allgemeinen Kulturkompetenz wahrgenommen. Das deutsche Recht ist allerdings nicht autonom. Es unterliegt zahlreichen völker- und europarechtlichen Vorgaben und Rahmenbedingungen, die alle Schutzziele in unterschiedlicher Weise beeinflussen.

Ziel dieser Normensammlung ist es, alle für Deutschland relevanten, unmittelbaren kulturgüterrechtlichen Normen auf Bundes- und Landes- sowie auf völker- und europarechtlicher Ebene zusammen zu tragen. Keine Aufnahme gefunden haben spezial- bzw. mittelbar einschlägige Normen, wie etwa diejenigen aus dem Steuerrecht. Die Sammlung konzentriert sich auf verbindliche Normen; von den zahlreichen unverbindlichen Leitlinien, Grundsätzen etc.[2] wurden nur die wichtigsten aufgenommen. Die Zusammenstellung aller unmittelbar kulturgüterschützenden Normen soll das hochkomplexe und sehr spannende Rechtsgebiet des Kulturgüterrechts erschließen. Diesem Ziel dienen auch die zahlreichen Fußnoten mit Verweisen zwischen den Normen. Sie sollen ihre systematische Zusammengehörigkeit sichtbar machen. Die Normen sind grundsätzlich in deutscher Sprache wiedergegeben. Das gilt auch für völkerrechtliche Verträge, die von Deutschland ratifiziert worden sind. Nicht ratifizierte Verträge sowie völkerrechtliche Umsetzungsnormen, die nicht auf Deutsch verfügbar sind, sind hingegen in englischer Sprache abgedruckt.

Für eine Neuauflage dieser Normensammlung wurde es dringend Zeit. Seit dem Erscheinen der ersten Auflage im Jahr 2006 sind 14 Jahre vergangen. In diesem Zeitraum hat es zahlreiche Entwicklungen auf allen Normebenen gegeben. Erwähnt seien insbesondere die Ratifikation des UNESCO-Übereinkommens über Maßnahmen zum Verbot und zur Verhütung der unzulässigen Einfuhr, Ausfuhr und Übereignung von Kulturgut von 1970 durch Deutschland, der Erlass neuer europarechtlicher Richtlinien und Verordnungen sowie die teilweise weitreichenden Reformen des Denkmalrechts auf Landesebene. Dass die Neuauflage erst jetzt erscheint, hängt vor allem damit zusammen, dass der sich seit längerem abzeichnende Erlass des neuen Kulturgutschutzgesetzes von 2016 und die damit einhergehende Aufhebung bzw. Änderung zahlreicher weiterer Normen abgewartet werden sollten. Da zur Umsetzung des Kulturgutschutzgesetzes der Erlass von Landesnormen erforderlich ist, war auch dieser Schritt abzuwarten. Die entsprechenden Landesnormen sind, bis auf zwei,[3] mittlerweile erlassen, so dass die Neuauflage veröffentlicht werden kann. Die Normensammlung befindet sich auf dem Stand

---

[1] Odendahl, Kulturgüterschutz, 2005, S. 387.
[2] Für einen Gesamtüberblick über die unverbindlichen Normen vgl. *Strobl*, Kulturgüterrelevante Verhaltenskodizes. Bestand, Analyse und rechtliche Bedeutung, 2018.
[3] Es handelt sich um die Landesnormen von Thüringen und dem Saarland. Beide Länder arbeiten noch mit den alten Normen; neue Normen bzw. Überarbeitungen der bisherigen Normen sind in Arbeit, vgl. die entsprechenden Fußnoten.

Vorwort

von Juni 2020. Konkret anstehende neue Entwicklungen wurden durch entsprechende Fußnotenhinweise berücksichtigt.

Die Neuauflage wäre ohne die engagierte und gewissenhafte Arbeit zahlreicher Mitarbeiterinnen und Mitarbeiter meines Kieler Lehrstuhls, die das Projekt während der letzten Jahre begleitet haben, nicht möglich gewesen. Ich bin allen zu großem Dank verpflichtet. In erster Linie möchte ich meinen Wissenschaftlichen Mitarbeiter Felix Telschow erwähnen, der alle Fäden in der Hand gehalten, die studentischen Hilfskräfte koordiniert und selbst recherchiert sowie alle Texte durchgesehen hat. Die studentischen Mitarbeiterinnen und Mitarbeiter, die über mehrere Jahre in dem Projekt mitgewirkt haben, sind Joschka Peters-Wunnenberg, Charlotte Gaschke, Marvin Schwope, Nora Harder sowie in besonders großem Umfang – vor allem in der sehr anstrengenden Schlussphase – Tom Wittke. Auch meine Sekretärin, Samira Wagner, hat durch Formatierungsarbeiten das Projekt unterstützt. Ihnen allen gebühren großer Dank und Anerkennung!

Trotz aller Unterstützung bleibe jedoch ich allein für den Inhalt und die Auswahl der Normen verantwortlich. Sollten sich Fehler eingeschlichen haben oder aber Normen übersehen worden sein, so freue ich mich über entsprechende Hinweise! Dasselbe gilt für Anregungen zur Aufnahme weiterer Normen in der nächsten Auflage. Nachrichten erreichen mich elektronisch über decken@wsi.uni-kiel.de oder über die folgende Adresse:

Walther-Schücking-Institut für Internationales Recht
Christian-Albrechts-Universität zu Kiel
Westring 400
24118 Kiel

Kiel, im Juli 2020

Kerstin von der Decken

Inhaltsverzeichnis

A: Völkerrecht

A.I: Schutz von Kulturgütern in bewaffneten Konflikten

A.I.1	Konvention zum Schutz von Kulturgut bei bewaffneten Konflikten, v. 14.05.1954 (inkl. Ausführungsbestimmungen)	25
A.I.1a	Rules Established by the Director-General of the United Nations Educational, Scientific and Cultural Organization, concerning the International Register of Cultural Property under Special Protection, v. 18.08.1956	40
A.I.1b	Zweites Protokoll zur Haager Konvention von 1954 zum Schutz von Kulturgut bei bewaffneten Konflikten, v. 26.03.1999	43
A.I.1c	Guidelines for the Implementation of the 1999 Second Protocol to the Hague Convention of 1954 for the Protection of Cultural Property in the Event of Armed Conflict, v. 16.12.2019	55
A.I.2	Zusatzprotokoll zu den Genfer Abkommen vom 12. August 1949 über den Schutz der Opfer internationaler bewaffneter Konflikte (Protokoll I) (Auszüge), v. 08.06.1977	78
A.I.3	Zusatzprotokoll zu den Genfer Abkommen vom 12. August 1949 über den Schutz der Opfer nicht internationaler bewaffneter Konflikte (Protokoll II) (Auszüge), v. 08.06.1977	79
A.I.4	Resolution 2199 (2015), verabschiedet auf der 7379. Sitzung des Sicherheitsrats (Auszüge), v. 12.02.2015	80
A.I.5	Resolution 2295 (2016), verabschiedet auf der 7727. Sitzung des Sicherheitsrats (Auszüge), v. 29.06.2016	83
A.I.6	Resolution 2347 (2017), verabschiedet auf der 7907. Sitzung des Sicherheitsrats, v. 24.03.2017	90

A.II: Schutz von Kulturgütern allgemein

A.II.1	Übereinkommen zum Schutz des Kultur- und Naturerbes der Welt, v. 23.11.1972	96
A.II.1a	Operational Guidelines for the Implementation of the World Heritage Convention, v. 12.07.2017	105
A.II.2	Seerechtsübereinkommen der Vereinten Nationen (Auszüge), v. 10.12.1982	169
A.II.3	Convention on the Protection of the Underwater Cultural Heritage, v. 06.11.2001	170
A.II.4	Europäisches Kulturabkommen, v. 19.12.1954	182
A.II.5	Übereinkommen zum Schutz des architektonischen Erbes Europas, v. 03.10.1985	185
A.II.6	Europäisches Übereinkommen zum Schutz des archäologischen Erbes (revidiert), v. 16.01.1992	191
A.II.7	Internationale Charta über die Konservierung und Restaurierung von Denkmälern und Ensembles, v. 1965	197
A.II.8	Internationale Charta zur Denkmalpflege in historischen Städten, v. Okt. 1987	201

Inhaltsverzeichnis

A.II.9	Charta für den Schutz und die Pflege des archäologischen Erbe, v. 1990	203
A.II.10	Charta zu Schutz und Pflege des Unterwasser-Kulturerbes, v. Okt. 1996	207
A.II.11	Ethische Grundsätze des Internationalen Rats für Denkmalpflege, v. 2014	211

A.III: Ein- und Ausfuhr von Kulturgütern sowie Rückgabefragen

A.III.1	Protokoll zur Konvention zum Schutz von Kulturgut bei bewaffneten Konflikten, v. 14.05.1954	217
A.III.2	Übereinkommen über Maßnahmen zum Verbot und zur Verhütung der unzulässigen Einfuhr, Ausfuhr und Übereignung von Kulturgut, v. 14.11.1970	219
A.III.2a	Operational Guidelines for the Implementation of the Convention on the Means of Prohibiting and Preventing the Illicit Import, Export and Transfer of Ownership of Cultural Property, v. 1970	225
A.III.3	UNIDROIT Convention on Stolen or Illegally Exported Cultural Objects, v. 24.06.1995	245
A.III.4	Abkommen über die Einfuhr von Gegenständen erzieherischen, wissenschaftlichen oder kulturellen Charakters, v. 22.11.1950	252
A.III.4a	Protokoll zum Abkommen über die Einfuhr von Gegenständen erzieherischen, wissenschaftlichen oder kulturellen Charakters, v. 26.11.1976	258
A.III.5	Grundsätze der Washingtoner Konferenz in Bezug auf Kunstwerke, die von den Nationalsozialisten beschlagnahmt wurden, v. 03.12.1998	266
A.III.6	ICOM Recommendations concerning the Return of Works of Art Belonging to Jewish Owners, v. 14.01.1999	267
A.III.7	International Code of Ethics for Dealers in Cultural Property, v. Nov. 1999	268
A.III.8	Ethische Richtlinien für Museen von ICOM, v. 08.10.2004	269

A.IV: (Völker-)Strafrecht

A.IV.1	Statute of the International Criminal Tribunal for the former Yugoslavia (Auszüge), v. 25.05.1993	284
A.IV.2	Statute of the International Criminal Tribunal for Rwanda (Auszüge), v. 08.11.1994	285
A.IV.3	Statute of the International Residual Mechanism for Criminal Tribunals (Auszüge), v. 22.12.2010	286
A.IV.4	Römisches Statut des Internationalen Strafgerichtshofs (Auszüge), v. 17.07.1998	287
A.IV.5	Council of Europe Convention on Offences relating to Cultural Property, v. 19.05.2017	289

B: Europarecht

B.I: Einfuhr von Kulturgütern

B.I.1	Vertrag über die Arbeitsweise der Europäischen Union (Auszüge), v. 13.12.2007	299
B.I.2	Verordnung (EG) Nr. 1210/2003 des Rates v. 07.07.2003 über bestimmte spezifische Beschränkungen in den wirtschaftlichen und finanziellen Beziehungen zu Irak und zur Aufhebung der Verordnung (EG) Nr. 2465/1996	302
B.I.3	Verordnung (EU) Nr. 36/2012 des Rates v. 18.01.2012 über restriktive Maßnahmen angesichts der Lage in Syrien und zur Aufhebung der Verordnung (EU) Nr. 442/2011 (Auszüge)	309
B.I.4	Verordnung (EU) 2019/880 des Europäischen Parlaments und des Rates v. 17.04.2019 über das Verbringen und die Einfuhr von Kulturgütern	310

B.II: Ausfuhr und Rückgabe von Kulturgütern

B.II.1	Vertrag über die Arbeitsweise der Europäischen Union (Auszüge), v. 13.12.2007	323
B.II.2	Verordnung (EG) Nr. 116/2009 des Rates v. 18.12.2008 über die Ausfuhr von Kulturgütern	326
B.II.2a	Durchführungsverordnung (EU) Nr. 1081/2012 der Kommission v. 09.11.2012 zu der Verordnung (EG) Nr. 116/2009 des Rates über die Ausfuhr von Kulturgütern	332
B.II.2b	Liste der Behörden, die bevollmächtigt sind, Ausfuhrgenehmigungen für Kulturgüter auszustellen, veröffentlicht gemäß Artikel 3 Absatz 2 der Verordnung (EG) Nr. 116/2009 des Rates	338
B.II.2c	Liste der Zollstellen, die für die Erfüllung der Ausfuhrzollformalitäten für Kulturgüter zuständig sind, veröffentlicht gemäß Artikel 5 Absatz 2 der Verordnung (EG) Nr. 116/09 des Rates	359
B.II.3	Richtlinie 2014/60/EU des Europäischen Parlaments und des Rates v. 15.05.2014 über die Rückgabe von unrechtmäßig aus dem Hoheitsgebiet eines Mitgliedstaats verbrachten Kulturgütern und zur Änderung der Verordnung (EU) Nr. 1024/2012	363
B.II.3a	Liste der von den Mitgliedstaaten benannten zentralen Stellen für die Rückgabe unrechtmäßig aus dem Hoheitsgebiet eines Mitgliedstaats verbrachter Kulturgüter gemäß Artikel 4 der Richtlinie 2014/60/EU	372

B.III: Kulturförderung

B.III.1	Vertrag über die Europäische Union (Auszüge), v. 13.12.2007	385
B.III.2	Vertrag über die Arbeitsweise der Europäischen Union (Auszüge), v. 13.12.2007	386
B.III.3	Charta der Grundrechte der Europäischen Union (Auszüge), v. 12.12.2007	388
B.III.4	Verordnung (EU) Nr. 1295/2013 des Europäischen Parlaments und des Rates v. 11.12.2013 zur Einrichtung des Programms Kreatives Europa (2014-2020) und zur Aufhebung der Beschlüsse Nr. 1718/2006/EG, Nr. 1855/2006/EG und Nr. 1041/2009/EG	389

Inhaltsverzeichnis

B.III.5	Beschluss Nr. 1194/2011/EU des Europäischen Parlaments Und des Rates v. 16.11.2011 zur Schaffung einer Maßnahme der Europäischen Union für das Europäische Kulturerbe-Siegel	407

C: Bundesrecht

C.I: Ein- und Ausfuhr von Kulturgütern sowie Rückgabefragen

C.I.1	Grundgesetz für die Bundesrepublik Deutschland (Auszüge), v. 23.05.1949	416
C.I.2	Gesetz zum Schutz von Kulturgut, v. 31.07.2016	417
C.I.3	Erste Eckpunkte zum Umgang mit Sammlungsgut aus kolonialen Kontexten der Staatsministerin des Bundes für Kultur und Medien, der Staatsministerin im Auswärtigen Amt für internationale Kulturpolitik, der Kulturministerinnen und Kulturminister der Länder und der kommunalen Spitzenverbände, v. 13.03.2019	446

C.II: Zivilschutz

C.II.1	Gesetz über den Zivilschutz und die Katastrophenhilfe des Bundes, v. 25.03.1997	450

C.III: Archivrecht

C.III.1	Gesetz über die Nutzung und Sicherung von Archivgut des Bundes, v. 10.03.2017	459
C.III.1a	Verordnung über die Benutzung von Archivgut beim Bundesarchiv, v. 29.10.1993	466

C.IV: Kulturförderung

C.IV.1	Bekanntmachung des Organisationserlasses des Bundeskanzlers (Auszüge), v. 27.10.1998	467
C.IV.2	Fördergrundsätze für das Denkmalpflegeprogramm „National wertvolle Kulturdenkmäler" der Beauftragten der Bundesregierung für Kultur und Medien (BKM), v. 01.09.2015	468
C.IV.3	Gesetz zur Errichtung einer Stiftung „Preußischer Kulturbesitz" und zur Übertragung von Vermögenswerten des ehemaligen Landes Preußen auf die Stiftung, v. 25.07.1957	470
C.IV.3a	Satzung der Stiftung „Preußischer Kulturbesitz", v. 06.09.1961	474
C.IV.4	Satzung der Kulturstiftung des Bundes, i.d.F. v. 18.10.2011	478
C.IV.5	Gesetz über die Angelegenheiten der Vertriebenen und Flüchtlinge (Auszüge), v. 19.05.1953	483
C.IV.6	Vertrag zwischen der Bundesrepublik Deutschland, vertreten durch den Bundeskanzler, und dem Zentralrat der Juden in Deutschland, v. 27.01.2003	484

C.V: Strafrecht

C.V.1	Strafgesetzbuch (Auszüge), i.d.F. v. 13.11.1998	486
C.V.2	Völkerstrafgesetzbuch (Auszüge), v. 26.6.2002	489

Inhaltsverzeichnis

D: Landesrecht

D1: Baden-Württemberg

D1	Verfassung des Landes Baden-Württemberg (Auszüge), v. 11.11.1953	490

D1.I: Denkmalrecht

D1.I.1	Gesetz zum Schutz der Kulturdenkmale, i.d.F. v. 06.12.1983	491
D1.I.1a	Verordnung des Kultusministeriums über die Entschädigung und den Reisekostenersatz für die Beauftragten der Denkmalschutzbehörden, v. 12.01.1973	499
D1.I.1b	Verwaltungsvorschrift des Finanz- und Wirtschaftsministeriums für das Verfahren zum Vollzug des Denkmalschutzgesetzes für Baden-Württemberg, v. 22.12.2014	500
D1.I.1c	Verwaltungsvorschrift des Wirtschaftsministeriums für die Erfassung von Kulturdenkmalen in einer Liste, v. 26.04.2018	504

D1.II: Archivrecht

D1.II.1	Gesetz über die Pflege und Nutzung von Archivgut, v. 27.07.1987	509
D1.II.1a	Verordnung der Landesregierung über die Benutzung des Landesarchivs Baden-Württemberg, v. 10.04.2006	514

D.1.III: Kulturförderung

D1.III.1	Verwaltungsvorschrift des Wirtschaftsministeriums für die Gewährung von Zuwendungen zur Erhaltung und Pflege von Kulturdenkmalen, v. 28.11.2019	517
D1.III.2	Satzung der Denkmalstiftung Baden-Württemberg	528
D1.III.2a	Richtlinien für die satzungsgemäße Vergabe und Verwendung der Zuwendungen der Denkmalstiftung Baden-Württemberg, v. 12.05.2015	531

D1.IV: Umsetzung Kulturgutschutzgesetz des Bundes

D1.IV.1	Verordnung der Landesregierung und des Wissenschaftsministeriums über die Zuständigkeiten nach dem Kulturgutschutzgesetz, v. 08.11.2016	534

D2: Bayern

D2	Verfassung des Freistaates Bayern (Auszüge), i.d.F. v. 15.12.1998	535

D2.I: Denkmalrecht

D2.I.1	Gesetz zum Schutz und zur Pflege der Denkmäler, v. 25.06.1973	537
D2.I.1a	Vollzug des Denkmalschutzgesetzes und baurechtlicher Vorschriften im Bereich der Bayerischen Verwaltung der staatlichen Schlösser, Gärten und Seen, v. 24.03.1975	546
D2.I.1b	Flurbereinigung und Denkmalpflege, v. 06.06.1978	547
D2.I.1c	Vollzug des Denkmalschutzgesetzes und baurechtlicher Vorschriften, v. 27.06.1984	552

Inhaltsverzeichnis

D2.I.1d	Denkmalpflegerische Maßnahmen an kirchlichen Gebäuden im Zusammenhang mit der Durchführung von Arbeiten, die der staatlichen Baulast unterfallen, v. 03.05.1990	565
D2.I.1e	Grundsätze für die Inventarisation der Kunst- und Geschichtsdenkmäler Bayerns, v. 06.09.1990	567
D2.I.1f	Verwaltungsverfahren bei der Inanspruchnahme des Entschädigungsfonds nach dem Gesetz zum Schutz und zur Pflege der Denkmäler, v. 13.05.2011	574
D2.I.1g	Vollzug des DSchG; hier: Prüfung der Zumutbarkeit im Erlaubnisverfahren nach Art. 6 DSchG	577
D2.I.1h	Wirtschaftlichkeitsprüfung, Zumutbarkeit mit Prüfungsverfahren (s. Nr. 3.3.3)	581
D2.I.1i	Empfehlungen des Bayerischen Landesdenkmalrates für Baumaßnahmen innerhalb oder in der Nähe von Ensembles im Sinne des Denkmalschutzgesetzes sowie in der Nähe von Einzelbaudenkmälern v. 14. 02. 1977	585

D2.II: Archivrecht

D2.II.1	Bayerisches Archivgesetz, v. 22.12.1989	588
D2.II.1a	Benützungsordnung für die staatlichen Archive Bayerns, v. 16.01.1990	593

D2.III: Kulturförderung

D2.III.1	Verleihung einer Denkmalschutzmedaille, v. 18.05.1987	597
D2.III.2	Richtlinien zur Vergabe von Zuwendungen an nichtstaatliche Museen in Bayern	598

D2.IV: Zivilschutz

D2.IV.1	Vollzug der Haager Konvention zum Schutz von Kulturgut bei bewaffneten Konflikten; hier: Anbringung der Kennzeichen der Konvention gemäß Art. 6, 16 und 17 der Haager Konvention, v. 16.10.1984	601

D2.V: Umsetzung Kulturgutschutzgesetz des Bundes

D2.V.1	Zuständigkeitsgesetz (Auszüge), v. 07.05.2013	604

D3: Berlin

D3	Verfassung von Berlin (Auszüge), v. 23.11.1995	606

D3.I: Denkmalrecht

D3.I.1	Gesetz zum Schutz von Denkmalen in Berlin, v. 24.04.1995	607
D3.I.1a	Errichtung des Landesdenkmalamtes Berlin, v. 02.08.1995	614
D3.I.1b	Ausführungsvorschriften zu § 6 Absatz 5 Satz 1 Denkmalschutzgesetz (DSchG Bln) über die Beteiligung des Landesdenkmalamtes an den Entscheidungen der unteren Denkmalschutzbehörden, v. 01.07.2019	615

D3.II: Archivrecht

D3.II.1	Gesetz über die Sicherung und Benutzung von Archivgut des Landes Berlin, v. 14.03.2016	617
D3.II.1a	Ordnung für die Benutzung von Archivgut im Landesarchiv Berlin, v. 04.03.2008	622

D3.III: Kulturförderung

D3.III.1	Richtlinie über die Gewährung von Zuwendungen zur Erhaltung, Unterhaltung und Wiederherstellung von Denkmalen sowie sonstigen Anlagen von denkmalpflegerischem Interesse, v. 01.01.2019	625

D3.IV: Umsetzung Kulturgutschutzgesetz des Bundes

D3.IV.1	Gesetz über die Zuständigkeiten in der Allgemeinen Berliner Verwaltung, mit Anlage (Auszüge), i.d.F. v. 22.07.1996	630

D4: Brandenburg

D4	Verfassung des Landes Brandenburg (Auszüge), v. 20.08.1992	631

D4.I: Denkmalrecht

D4.I.1	Gesetz über den Schutz und die Pflege der Denkmale im Land Brandenburg, v. 24.05.2004	632
D4.I.1a	Verordnung über das Grabungsschutzgebiet „Siedlungs- und Ritualraum Königsgrab Seddin", v. 12.07.2016	641
D4.I.1b	VwV des Ministeriums für Wissenschaft, Forschung und Kultur zur Prüfung der Zumutbarkeit im Rahmen von Erlaubnisverfahren und ordnungsrechtlichen Verfahren nach dem Brandenburgischen Denkmalschutzgesetz, v. 16.04.2009	643
D4.I.2	Ordnungsbehördliche Verordnung zum Schutz von Kriegsstätten, v. 31.03.2014	648

D4.II: Archivrecht

D4.II.1	Gesetz über die Sicherung und Nutzung von öffentlichem Archivgut im Land Brandenburg, v. 07.04.1994	650
D4.II.1a	Verordnung über die Benutzung von Archivgut im Brandenburgischen Landeshauptarchiv, v. 17.02.2000	657

D4.III: Kulturförderung

D4.III.1	Fördergrundsätze des Ministeriums für Wissenschaft, Forschung und Kultur für das Jahr 2019, v. 20.08.2018	659

D4.IV: Umsetzung Kulturgutschutzgesetz des Bundes

D4.IV.1	Verordnung über die Zuständigkeit nach dem Kulturgutschutzgesetz für das Land Brandenburg, v. 13.03.2017	662

Inhaltsverzeichnis

D5: Bremen

D5   Landesverfassung der Freien Hansestadt Bremen (Auszüge), i.d.F. v. 12.08.2019   663

D5.I: Denkmalrecht

D5.I.1   Bremisches Gesetz zur Pflege und zum Schutz der Kulturdenkmäler, v. 20.12.2018   664

D5.I.1a   Verordnung über die Zusammensetzung und die Tätigkeit des Denkmalrates, v. 30.04.2019   671

D5.I.1b   Verordnung über die Unterschutzstellung von Kulturdenkmälern und das Eintragungs- und Löschungsverfahren, v. 30.04.2019   673

D5.II: Archivrecht

D5.II.1   Gesetz über die Sicherung und Nutzung öffentlichen Archivguts im Lande Bremen, v. 07.05.1991   675

D5.II.1a   Verordnung über die Benutzung des Staatsarchivs, v. 30.10.2013   682

D5.III: Umsetzung Kulturgutschutzgesetz des Bundes

D5.III.1   Verordnung über die zuständigen Behörden nach dem Kulturgutschutzgesetz, v. 18.09.2018   686

D6: Hamburg

D6.I: Denkmalrecht

D6.I.1   Denkmalschutzgesetz, v. 05.04.2013   687

D6.I.1a   Anordnung zur Durchführung des Denkmalschutzgesetzes, v. 08.04.2014   695

D6.II: Archivrecht

D6.II.1   Hamburgisches Archivgesetz, v. 21.01.1991   696

D6.II.1a   Verwaltungsvorschrift über die Benutzung von Archivgut im Staatsarchiv der Freien und Hansestadt Hamburg, 01.06.2004   700

D6.III: Umsetzung Kulturgutschutzgesetz des Bundes

D6.III.1   Anordnung über die Zuständigkeiten auf dem Gebiet des Kulturgutschutzes, v. 07.11.2017   703

D7: Hessen

D7   Verfassung des Landes Hessen (Auszüge), v. 01.12.1946   705

D7.I: Denkmalrecht

D7.I.1   Hessisches Denkmalschutzgesetz, v. 28.11.2016   706

D7.I.1a   Verordnung über Zuständigkeiten nach dem Hessischen Denkmalschutzgesetz, v. 21.06.2018   714

D7.II: Archivrecht

D7.II.1	Hessisches Archivgesetz vom 26.11.2012	715
D7.II.1a	Nutzungsordnung für die Hessischen Staatsarchive, v. 13.12.2013	722

D7.III: Kulturförderung

D7.III.1	Richtlinie des Hessischen Ministeriums für Wissenschaft und Kunst für die Bewilligung von Zuwendungen für Kulturdenkmäler, v. 10.09.2008	725
D7.III.2	Verfassung der Hessischen Kulturstiftung, v. 2017	730
D7.III.3	Hessische Kulturstiftung, Richtlinien für die Antragstellung	733

D7.IV: Umsetzung Kulturgutschutzgesetz des Bundes

D7.IV.1	Verordnung zur Benennung der zuständigen Behörde nach dem Kulturgutschutzgesetz, v. 24.10.2016	734

D8: Mecklenburg-Vorpommern

D8	Verfassung des Landes Mecklenburg-Vorpommern (Auszüge), v. 23.05.1993	735

D8.I: Denkmalrecht

D8.I.1	Gesetz zum Schutz und zur Pflege der Denkmale im Lande Mecklenburg-Vorpommern, i.d.F. v. 06.01.1998	736
D8.I.1a	Verwaltungsvorschrift über die ehrenamtlichen Denkmalpfleger, v. 12.05.1997	744
D8.I.1b	Bußgeldkatalog für die Ahndung von Verstößen gegen das Denkmalschutzgesetz Mecklenburg-Vorpommern, v. 20.10.1999	745

D8.II: Archivrecht

D8.II.1	Archivgesetz für das Land Mecklenburg-Vorpommern, v. 07.07.1997	748
D8.II.1a	Verordnung über die Benutzung des staatlichen Archivs in Mecklenburg-Vorpommern, v. 21.08.2006	753

D8.III: Kulturförderung

D8.III.1	Richtlinie für die Bewilligung finanzieller Zuwendungen zur Erhaltung von Denkmalen in Mecklenburg-Vorpommern, v. 29.10.1994	757
D8.III.2	Richtlinie über die Gewährung von Zuwendungen im kulturellen Bereich in Mecklenburg-Vorpommern, 05.10.2017	760

D8.IV: Umsetzung Kulturgutschutzgesetz des Bundes

D8.IV.1	Landesverordnung über die zuständigen Behörden nach dem Kulturgutschutzgesetz, v. 04.07.2017	767

Inhaltsverzeichnis

D9: Niedersachsen

D9	Niedersächsische Verfassung (Auszüge), v. 19.05.1993	768

D9.I: Denkmalrecht

D9.I.1	Niedersächsisches Denkmalschutzgesetz, v. 30.05.1978	769
D9.I.1a	Verordnung über die Aufwandsentschädigung der Beauftragten für die Bau- und Kunstdenkmalpflege und der Beauftragten für die archäologische Denkmalpflege, v. 22.08.1979	780
D9.I.1b	Richtlinie zur Durchführung des § 22 des Niedersächsischen Denkmalschutzgesetzes (Beauftragte für die Denkmalpflege), v. 12.11.2019	781

D9.II: Archivrecht

D9.II.1	Gesetz über die Sicherung und Nutzung von Archivgut in Niedersachsen, v. 25.05.1993	784
D9.II.1a	Benutzungsordnung für das Niedersächsische Landesarchiv, v. 23.06.2008	788
D9.II.1b	Verwaltungsvorschriften zum Niedersächsischen Archivgesetz, v. 24.10.2006	794

D9.III: Kulturförderung

D9.III.1	Richtlinie über die Gewährung von Zuwendungen zur Erhaltung und Pflege von Kulturdenkmalen, v. 11.12.2018	800

D9.IV: Umsetzung Kulturgutschutzgesetz des Bundes

D9.IV.1	Verordnung über Zuständigkeiten im Bereich des Kulturgutschutzes, v. 29.08.2017	804

D10: Nordrhein-Westfalen

D10	Verfassung des Landes Nordrhein-Westfalen (Auszüge), v. 28.06.1950	805

D10.I: Denkmalrecht

D10.I.1	Gesetz zum Schutz und zur Pflege der Denkmäler im Lande Nordrhein-Westfalen, v. 11.03.1980	806
D10.I.1a	Verordnung über die Führung der Denkmalliste, v. 13.03.2015	816
D10.I.1b	Verfahren bei Übernahmeverlangen gemäß § 31 DSchG, v. 16.03.1984	819
D10.I.1c	Denkmalplakette des Landes Nordrhein-Westfalen, v. 05.05.1988	820
D10.I.1d	Verwaltungsvorschrift zur Ausführung des Gesetzes zum Schutz und zur Pflege der Denkmäler im Lande Nordrhein-Westfalen, v. 11.04.2014	821
D10.I.1e	Berücksichtigung des Bodendenkmalschutzes bei der Umweltverträglichkeitsprüfung in Verfahren zur Zulassung oder Genehmigung von Abgrabungen und in bergrechtlichen Planfeststellungsverfahren (Gewinnung nicht-energetischer oberflächennaher Rohstoffe), v. 01.02.2016	830

D10.II: Archivrecht

D10.II.1 Gesetz über die Sicherung und Nutzung öffentlichen Archivguts im Lande Nordrhein-Westfalen, v. 16.03.2010 — 832

D10.II.1a Verordnung über die Nutzung und die Gebührenerhebung des Landesarchivs Nordrhein-Westfalen, v. 29.05.2015 — 838

D10.III: Kulturförderung

D10.III.1 Gesetz zur Förderung und Entwicklung der Kultur, der Kunst und der kulturellen Bildung in Nordrhein-Westfalen (Kulturfördergesetz NRW), v. 18.12.2014 — 844

D10.III.2 Allgemeine Richtlinie zur Förderung von Projekten und Einrichtungen auf dem Gebiet der Kultur, der Kunst und der kulturellen Bildung, v. 30.12.2014 — 852

D10.III.3 Richtlinien über die Gewährung von Zuwendungen für Denkmalschutz und Denkmalpflege, v. 16.05.2019 — 854

D10.IV: Umsetzung Kulturgutschutzgesetz des Bundes

D10.IV.1 Verordnung über Zuständigkeiten im Bereich des Kulturgutschutzes, v. 30.04.2019 — 863

D11: Rheinland-Pfalz

D11 Verfassung für Rheinland-Pfalz (Auszüge), v. 18.05.1947 — 864

D11.I: Denkmalrecht

D11.I.1 Denkmalschutzgesetz, v. 23.03.1978 — 865

D11.I.1a Landesverordnung über Aufgaben, Berufung und Entschädigung ehrenamtlicher Denkmalpfleger, v. 22.03.1982 — 879

D11.I.1b Landesverordnung über die Berufung und Entschädigung der Mitglieder des Landesbeirats für Denkmalpflege, v. 30.12.1978 — 881

D11.II: Archivrecht

D11.II.1 Landesarchivgesetz, v. 05.10.1990 — 883

D11.II.1a Landesarchiv-Benutzungsverordnung, v. 08.12.2004 — 888

D11.III: Kulturförderung

D11.III.1 Zuwendungen des Landes Rheinland-Pfalz zur Erhaltung von nichtstaatlichen Kulturdenkmälern, v. 25.11.2015 — 892

D11.III.2 Errichtung „Generaldirektion Kulturelles Erbe", v. 02.02.2007 — 901

D11.IV: Umsetzung Kulturgutschutzgesetz des Bundes

D11.IV.1 Landesverordnung über Zuständigkeiten nach dem Kulturgutschutzgesetz, v. 14.02.2017 — 903

Inhaltsverzeichnis

D12: Saarland

D12	Verfassung des Saarlandes (Auszüge), v. 15.12.1947	904

D12.I: Denkmalrecht

D12.I.1	Saarländisches Denkmalschutzgesetz, v. 13.06.2018	905

D12.II: Archivrecht

D12.II.1	Saarländisches Archivgesetz, v. 23.09.1992	916
D12.II.1a	Verordnung über die Benutzung von Archivgut beim Landesarchiv, v. 10.12.2001	921
D12.II.1b	Benutzersaalordnung des Landesarchivs Saarbrücken, v. 23.04.2002	924
D12.II.1c	Verordnung über den Erlass des Besonderen Gebührenverzeichnisses für das Landesarchiv, v. 28.05.2002	926

D12.III: Kulturförderung

D12.III.1	Richtlinie für die Gewährung von Zuwendungen des Landes aus Mitteln der Denkmalpflege zur Erhaltung und Instandsetzung von Kulturdenkmälern, v. 15.04.2002	929
D12.III.2	Gesetz über die Stiftung Saarländischer Kulturbesitz, v. 24.04.2013	936
D12.III.2a	Satzung der Stiftung Saarländischer Kulturbesitz, v. 31.05.2016	940

D12.IV: Umsetzung Kulturgutschutzgesetz des Bundes

D12.IV.1	Zweite Verordnung über Zuständigkeit nach dem Gesetz zum Schutz deutschen Kulturgutes gegen Abwanderung, v. 20.09.1961	945
D12.IV.2	Verordnung über das Antragsrecht gemäß § 3 Abs. 1 und § 11 Abs. 2 des Gesetzes zum Schutz deutschen Kulturgutes gegen Abwanderung vom 06.08.1955, v. 18.12.1958	946
D12.IV.3	Verordnung über Anträge auf Eintragung von Archivbeständen in das „Verzeichnis national wertvollen Archivgutes", v. 24.10.1961	947

D13: Sachsen

D13	Verfassung des Freistaates Sachsen (Auszüge), v. 27.05.1992	948

D13.I: Denkmalrecht

D13.I.1	Gesetz zum Schutz und zur Pflege der Kulturdenkmale im Freistaat Sachsen, v. 03.03.1993	949
D13.I.1a	Verordnung des Sächsischen Staatsministeriums des Innern über die Entschädigung und den Reisekostenersatz für die ehrenamtlichen Beauftragten für Denkmalpflege, v. 04.04.2015	961
D13.I.1b	Verwaltungsvorschrift des Sächsischen Staatsministeriums des Innern über die ehrenamtlichen Beauftragten für Denkmalpflege und zur Aufhebung einer Verwaltungsvorschrift, v. 04.04.2015	963

Inhaltsverzeichnis

D13.I.1c	Verwaltungsvorschrift des Sächsischen Staatsministerium des Innern über die Geschäftsordnung für den Denkmalrat, v.15.09.1993	966
D13.I.1d	Verwaltungsvorschrift des Sächsischen Staatsministeriums des Innern für die Erfassung von Kulturdenkmalen in öffentlichen Verzeichnissen, v. 08.09.2016	968
D13.I.1e	Verwaltungsvorschrift des Sächsischen Staatsministeriums des Innern zur Herstellung des Einvernehmens gemäß § 4 Abs. 2 SächsDSchG zwischen den unteren Denkmalschutzbehörden und dem Landesamt für Denkmalpflege Sachsen, v. 12.03.2001	972
D13.I.1f	Gemeinsame Verwaltungsvorschrift des Sächsischen Staatsministeriums des Innern und des Sächsischen Staatsministeriums für Wissenschaft und Kunst zur Zuständigkeit des Landesamtes für Denkmalpflege und des Landesamtes für Archäologie, v. 18.06.2003	974

D13.II: Archivrecht

D13.II.1	Archivgesetz für den Freistaat Sachsen, v. 17.05.1993	975
D13.II.1a	Verordnung des Sächsischen Staatsministeriums des Innern über die Benutzung der staatlichen Archive, v. 24.02.2003	982
D13.II.1b	Verordnung des Sächsischen Staatsministeriums des Innern über die Benutzungsgebühren des Sächsischen Staatsarchivs, v. 23.05.2006	984

D13.III: Kulturförderung

D13.III.1	Verwaltungsvorschrift des Sächsischen Staatsministeriums des Innern über die Gewährung von Zuwendungen zur Erhaltung und Pflege von sächsischen Kulturdenkmalen und zur Aus- und Fortbildung der Denkmalpflege, v. 20.12.1996	988

D13.IV: Umsetzung Kulturgutschutzgesetz des Bundes

D13.IV.1	Verordnung der Sächsischen Staatsregierung und des Sächsischen Staatsministeriums für Wissenschaft und Kunst über Zuständigkeiten nach dem Kulturgutschutzgesetz, v. 22.06.2017	995

D14: Sachsen-Anhalt

D14	Verfassung des Landes Sachsen-Anhalt (Auszüge), v. 16.07.1992	996

D14.I: Denkmalrecht

D14.I.1	Denkmalschutzgesetz des Landes Sachsen-Anhalt, v. 21.10.1991	997
D14.I.1a	Verordnung über Tätigkeit und Entschädigung ehrenamtlicher Beauftragter für die Denkmalpflege und für archäologische Denkmalpflege, v. 03.02.1994	1007
D14.I.1b	Verordnung über die Tätigkeit und die Kostenerstattung der Mitglieder des Denkmalrates, v. 18.08.1994	1009
D14.I.1c	Richtlinien zur Durchführung des § 6 des Denkmalschutzgesetzes des Landes Sachsen-Anhalt; Bestellung der ehrenamtlichen Beauftragten, v. 05.07.1994	1010

Inhaltsverzeichnis

D14.I.1d	Zusammensetzung, Berufung und Organisation des Denkmalrates, v. 25.04.2014	1012
D14.I.1e	Verordnung über Umfang, Inhalt und Form des Antrags auf denkmalrechtliche Genehmigung, v. 27.08.2018	1014
D14.I.2	Gesetz zur Neuordnung der Landesverwaltung (Auszüge), v. 17.12.2003	1016
D14.I.3	Übertragung der Funktion einer unteren Denkmalschutzbehörde auf Kulturstiftungen, v. 22.01.2004	1017
D14.I.4	Übertragung der Aufgaben der unteren Denkmalschutzbehörde auf das Bistum Magdeburg, v. 05.03.2003	1018

D14.II: Archivrecht

D14.II.1	Archivgesetz Sachsen-Anhalt, v. 28.06.1995	1020
D14.II.1a	Benutzungsordnung des Landesarchivs Sachsen-Anhalt, v. 2016	1027

D14.III: Kulturförderung

D14.III.1	Beschluß der Landesregierung über die Stiftung des öffentlichen Rechts „Kulturstiftung Dessau-Wörlitz" in Dessau, i.d.F. v. 19.11.1996	1029
D14.III.1a	Satzung der Kulturstiftung Dessau-Wörlitz, v. 02.05.2016	1030
D14.III.2	Beschluss der Landesregierung zur Errichtung der Stiftung Schlösser, Burgen und Gärten des Landes Sachsen-Anhalt, i.d.F. v. 10.02.1996	1034
D14.III.3	Richtlinie über die kumulierte Anwendung von Förderprogrammen, v. 24.11.1997	1037
D14.III.4	Richtlinie über die Gewährung von Zuwendungen zur Förderung von Maßnahmen zur Erhaltung, Pflege und Erschließung von Kulturdenkmalen, v. 27.07.2017	1038

D14.IV: Umsetzung Kulturgutschutzgesetz des Bundes

D14.IV.1	Verordnung über Zuständigkeiten nach dem Kulturgutschutzgesetz, v. 22.11.2016	1042
D14.IV.2	Verordnung zur Übertragung von Verordnungsermächtigungen im Bereich der Justiz (Auszüge), i.d.F. v. 22.05.2018	1043

D15: Schleswig-Holstein

D15	Verfassung des Landes Schleswig-Holstein (Auszüge), i.d.F. v. 02.12.2014	1044

D15.I: Denkmalrecht

D15.I.1	Gesetz zum Schutz der Denkmale, v. 30.12.2014	1045
D15.I.1a	Landesverordnung über den Denkmalrat, v. 10.06.2015	1055
D15.I.1b	Landesverordnung über die Vertrauensleute für Kulturdenkmale, v. 10.06.2015	1058
D15.I.1c	Landesverordnung über das Verfahren zur Ausweisung von Denkmalbereichen und Grabungsschutzgebieten, v. 10.06.2015	1059
D15.I.1d	Landesverordnung über die Einführung des Zustimmungsvorbehalts bei Genehmigungsverfahren betreffend Gründenkmale, v. 10.06.2015	1060

D15.I.1e	Landesverordnung über die Denkmallisten der Kulturdenkmale, v. 10.06.2015	1061

D15.II: Archivrecht

D15.II.1	Gesetz über die Sicherung und Nutzung öffentlichen Archivgutes in Schleswig-Holstein, v. 11.08.1992	1063
D15.II.2	Gesetz für die Bibliotheken in Schleswig-Holstein, v. 30.08.2016 (Auszüge)	1070

D15.III: Kulturförderung

D15.III.1	Gesetz zur Umwandlung der Kulturstiftung des Landes Schleswig-Holstein in eine Stiftung des öffentlichen Rechts, v. 30.05.1995	1075

D15.IV: Umsetzung Kulturgutschutzgesetz des Bundes

D15.IV.1	Landesverordnung über die zuständige Behörde nach dem Kulturgutschutzgesetz, v. 11.10.2016	1077

D16: Thüringen

D16	Verfassung des Freistaats Thüringen (Auszüge), v. 25.10.1993	1078

D16.I: Denkmalrecht

D16.I.1	Thüringer Gesetz zur Pflege und zum Schutz der Kulturdenkmale, i.d.F. v. 14.04.2004	1079
D16.I.1a	Thüringer Verordnung zur Verleihung der Zuständigkeit als untere Denkmalschutzbehörde, v. 02.06.1994	1090
D16.I.1b	Satzung des Thüringer Landesdenkmalrates, v. 27.10.1993	1091
D16.I.1c	Anordnung über die Organisation der gemeinsamen Verwaltung des Landesamtes für Denkmalpflege und Archäologie und des Landesarchivs, v. 29.12.2016	1094
D16.I.1d	Verwaltungsvorschrift zu einem verkürzten Verfahren entsprechend § 14 Abs. 3 ThürDSchG zwischen den Unteren Denkmalschutzbehörden und dem Thüringischen Landesamt für Denkmalpflege und Archäologie, i.d.F. v. 30.03.2017	1096

D16.II: Archivrecht

D16.II.1	Thüringer Gesetz über die Sicherung und Nutzung von Archivgut, v. 29.06.2018	1099
D16.II.1a	Thüringer Verordnung über die Benutzung der Staatsarchive, v. 26.02.1993	1108
D16.II.1b	Abgabe amtlicher Veröffentlichungen an Bibliotheken und das Hauptstaatsarchiv, v. 19.11.2008	1111

Inhaltsverzeichnis

D16.III: Kulturförderung

D16.III.1	Thüringer Gesetz über die Errichtung der Kulturstiftung des Freistaats Thüringen, v. 19.05.2004	1112
D16.III.2	Richtlinie zur Förderung von Kultur und Kunst, i.d.F. v. 17.08.2015	1115
D16.III.3	Richtlinie für die Bewilligung von Zuwendungen für Denkmalschutz und Denkmalpflege, i.d.F. v. 06.06.2016	1120
D16.III.4	Thüringer Gesetz über die Errichtung der „Stiftung Thüringer Schlösser und Gärten", v. 10.03.1994	1124

D16.IV: Umsetzung Kulturgutschutzgesetz des Bundes

D16.IV.1	Zuständigkeit der einzelnen Ministerien nach Artikel 76 Abs. 2 Satz 1 der Verfassung des Freistaats Thüringen, Beschluss der Thüringer Landesregierung (Auszüge), v. 31.03.2015	1128

D17: Gemeinsame Normen des Bundes und/oder der Länder

D17.I: Umsetzung völkerrechtlicher Verträge

D17.I.1	Anzahl der in der Bundesrepublik Deutschland nach der Haager Konvention zum Schutz von Kulturgut bei bewaffneten Konflikten zu schützenden Objekte (ohne Denkmäler der Vor- und Frühgeschichte, Museen, Bibliotheken und Archive), v. 26.06.1998	1130
D17.I.2	Fortschreibung der deutschen Tentativliste und Verfahren zur Nominierung von Welterbestätten, v. 04.03.2010	1131
D17.I.3	UNESCO-Weltkulturerbe, Fortschreibung der deutschen Liste, 12.06.2014	1132
D17.I.4	Empfehlung der Kultusministerkonferenz zur Durchführung des Europäischen Übereinkommens zum Schutz archäologischen Kulturguts vom 6. Mai 1969, v. 05.11.1976	1133

D17.II: Kriegsbedingt verlagerte Kulturgüter

D17.II.1	Gemeinsame Länderposition zur Frage der kriegsbedingt verlagerten Kulturgüter, v. 12.04.1996	1134
D17.II.1a	Ergänzung der Länderposition zur Frage der kriegsbedingt verlagerten Kulturgüter, v. 08.05.2003	1135

D17.III: NS-verfolgungsbedingt entzogenes Kulturgut

D17.III.1	Erklärung der Bundesregierung, der Länder und der kommunalen Spitzenverbände zur Auffindung und zur Rückgabe NS-verfolgungsbedingt entzogenen Kulturgutes, insbesondere aus jüdischem Besitz, v. 09.12.1999	1136
D17.III.2	Absprache zwischen Bund, Ländern und kommunalen Spitzenverbänden zur Einsetzung einer Beratenden Kommission im Zusammenhang mit der Rückgabe NS-verfolgungsbedingt entzogenen Kulturguts, insbesondere aus jüdischem Besitz, i.d.F. v. 08.12.2016	1138
D17.III.3	Satzung der Stiftung „Deutsches Zentrum Kulturgutverluste"	1139

D17.IV: Kulturstiftung der Länder

D17.IV.1	Abkommen zur Errichtung der Kulturstiftung der Länder, i.d.F. v. 25.10.1991	1145
D17.IV.2	Abkommen über die Mitwirkung des Bundes an der Kulturstiftung der Länder, i.d.F. v. 25.11.1993	1146
D17.IV.3	Satzung der Kulturstiftung der Länder, i.d.F. v. 22.06.2016	1148

D17.V: Stiftung Preußische Schlösser und Gärten Berlin-Brandenburg

D17.V.1	Staatsvertrag über die Errichtung einer „Stiftung Preußische Schlösser und Gärten Berlin-Brandenburg", v. 23.08.1994	1151
D17.V.2	Abkommen über die gemeinsame Finanzierung der „Stiftung Preußische Schlösser und Gärten Berlin-Brandenburg", v. 23.08. 1994	1156
D17.V.3	Satzung der Stiftung Preußische Schlösser und Gärten Berlin-Brandenburg, v. 18.02.1998	1157
D17.V.4	Ordnungsbehördliche Verordnung zur Abwehr von Gefahren für die im Vermögen der Stiftung Preußische Schlösser und Gärten Berlin-Brandenburg befindlichen baulichen und gärtnerischen Anlagen, v. 21.09.2006	1160

D17.VI: Gemeinsames Vorgehen auf Landesebene

D17.VI.1	Vertrag über die gemeinnützige Verwendung der gemäß § 20 b Parteiengesetz der DDR in Verbindung mit Buchstabe d) Satz 3 Anlage II Kapitel II Sachgebiet A Abschnitt III des Einigungsvertrages unter treuhänderischer Verwaltung stehenden Kunstwerke der Parteien und der mit ihnen verbundenen Organisationen, juristischen Personen und Massenorganisationen der DDR, v. 18.05.1995	1167
D17.VI.2	Bericht und Empfehlungen der Kultusministerkonferenz zur Erhaltung und Pflege jüdischen Kulturguts in Deutschland, v. 06.12.1996	1171
D17.VI.3	Grundsätze für die Beschäftigung von Volontären/Volontärinnen in der Denkmalpflege, v. 26.06.1998	1176

Konvention zum Schutz von Kulturgut bei bewaffneten Konflikten
Vom 14. Mai 1954[1]) (BGBl. 1967 II S. 1233, 1235)

(Übersetzung)
Die Hohen Vertragsparteien –
IN DER ERKENNTNIS, daß während der letzten bewaffneten Konflikte das Kulturgut ernsten Schaden gelitten hat und infolge der Entwicklung der Kriegstechnik in zunehmendem Maße der Vernichtungsgefahr ausgesetzt ist;
IN DER ÜBERZEUGUNG, daß jede Schädigung von Kulturgut, gleichgültig welchem Volke es gehört, eine Schädigung des kulturellen Erbes der ganzen Menschheit bedeutet, weil jedes Volk seinen Beitrag zur Kultur der Welt leistet;
IN DER ERWÄGUNG, daß die Erhaltung des kulturellen Erbes für alle Völker der Welt von großer Bedeutung ist und daß es wesentlich ist, dieses Erbe unter internationalen Schutz zu stellen;
GELEITET von den Grundsätzen für den Schutz des Kulturgutes bei bewaffneten Konflikten, die in den Haager Abkommen von 1899 und 1907 und im Washingtoner Vertrag vom 15. April 1935 niedergelegt wurden;
IN DER ERWÄGUNG, daß dieser Schutz nur dann wirksam sein kann, wenn sowohl nationale als auch internationale Maßnahmen ergriffen werden, um ihn schon in Friedenszeiten zu organisieren;
ENTSCHLOSSEN, alle zum Schutz des Kulturgutes möglichen Maßnahmen zu treffen –
SIND WIE FOLGT ÜBEREINGEKOMMEN:

Kapitel I
Allgemeine Schutzbestimmungen

Artikel 1[2]) **Begriffsbestimmung des Kulturguts**
Kulturgut im Sinne dieser Konvention sind, ohne Rücksicht auf Herkunft oder Eigentumsverhältnisse:
a) [3]) bewegliches oder unbewegliches Gut, das für das kulturelle Erbe aller Völker von großer Bedeutung ist, wie z.B. Bau-, Kunst- oder geschichtliche Denkmale religiöser oder weltlicher Art, archäologische Stätten, Gebäudegruppen, die als Ganzes von historischem oder künstlerischem Interesse sind, Kunstwerke, Manuskripte, Bücher und andere Gegenstände von künstlerischem, historischem oder archäologischem Interesse sowie wissenschaftliche Sammlungen und bedeutende Sammlungen von Büchern, Archivalien oder Reproduktionen des oben bezeichneten Kulturguts;
b) Baulichkeiten, die in der Hauptsache und tatsächlich der Erhaltung oder Ausstellung des unter a) bezeichneten beweglichen Gutes dienen, wie z.B. Museen, größere Bibliotheken, Archive sowie Bergungsorte, in denen im Falle bewaffneter Konflikte das unter a) bezeichnete bewegliche Kulturgut in Sicherheit gebracht werden soll;
c) Orte, die in beträchtlichem Umfange Kulturgut im Sinne der Unterabsätze a) und b) aufweisen und als „Denkmalsorte" bezeichnet sind.

Artikel 2 Schutz des Kulturguts
Der Schutz des Kulturguts im Sinne dieser Konvention umfaßt die Sicherung und Respektierung solchen Gutes.

Artikel 3 Sicherung des Kulturguts
Die Hohen Vertragsparteien verpflichten sich, schon in Friedenszeiten die Sicherung des auf ihrem Gebiet befindlichen Kulturguts gegen die absehbaren Folgen eines bewaffneten Konflikts vorzubereiten, indem sie alle Maßnahmen treffen, die sie für geeignet erachten.

---
1) Zu den übrigen Geltungsbereichen siehe die Übersicht in der Anlage.
2) Siehe hierzu auch das Kulturgut-Schutzkonvention-AusführungsG v. 18.5.2007 (BGBl. I S. 757, 762).
3) Der Beschluss der Kultusministerkonferenz über die Anzahl der in der Bundesrepublik Deutschland nach der Haager Konvention zu schützenden Objekte ist abgedruckt als Nr. D17.I.1.

Artikel 4 Respektierung des Kulturguts

1. Die Hohen Vertragsparteien verpflichten sich, das auf ihrem eigenen Gebiet oder auf dem Gebiet anderer Hoher Vertragsparteien befindliche Kulturgut zu respektieren, indem sie es unterlassen, dieses Gut und seine unmittelbare Umgebung sowie die zu seinem Schutz bestimmten Einrichtungen für Zwecke zu benutzen, die es im Falle bewaffneter Konflikte der Vernichtung oder Beschädigung aussetzen könnten, und indem sie von allen gegen dieses Gut gerichteten feindseligen Handlungen Abstand nehmen.
2. Die im Absatz 1 dieses Artikels erwähnten Verpflichtungen sind nur in denjenigen Fällen nicht bindend, in denen die militärische Notwendigkeit dies zwingend erfordert.
3. ¹Die Hohen Vertragsparteien verpflichten sich ferner, jede Art von Diebstahl, Plünderung oder anderer widerrechtlicher Inbesitznahme von Kulturgut sowie jede sinnlose Zerstörung solchen Gutes zu verbieten, zu verhindern und nötigenfalls zu unterbinden. ²Sie nehmen davon Abstand, bewegliches Kulturgut, das sich auf dem Hoheitsgebiet einer anderen Hohen Vertragspartei befindet, zu beschlagnahmen.
4. Sie enthalten sich jeder Repressalie gegenüber Kulturgut.
5. Keine Hohe Vertragspartei kann sich den ihr nach diesem Artikel obliegenden Verpflichtungen gegenüber einer anderen Hohen Vertragspartei mit der Begründung entziehen, daß letztere die in Artikel 3 genannten Sicherungsmaßnahmen nicht getroffen hat.

Artikel 5 Besetzung

1. Jede Hohe Vertragspartei, die das Gebiet einer anderen Hohen Vertragspartei ganz oder zum Teil besetzt hält, hat, soweit wie möglich, die zuständigen nationalen Behörden des besetzten Landes bei der Sicherung und Erhaltung seines Kulturguts zu unterstützen.
2. Sollte es erforderlich sein, Maßnahmen zur Erhaltung von Kulturgut zu treffen, das sich im besetzten Gebiet befindet und durch militärische Handlungen beschädigt worden ist, und sollten die zuständigen nationalen Behörden dazu nicht imstande sein, so hat die Besatzungsmacht, soweit wie möglich, in enger Zusammenarbeit mit diesen Behörden die notwendigsten Erhaltungsmaßnahmen zu treffen.
3. Jede Hohe Vertragspartei, deren Regierung von den Angehörigen einer Widerstandsbewegung als ihre legitime Regierung angesehen wird, hat, wenn möglich, die Angehörigen der Widerstandsbewegung auf die Verpflichtung hinzuweisen, diejenigen Artikel des Abkommens, die die Respektierung von Kulturgut zum Gegenstand haben, zu beachten.

Artikel 6 Kennzeichnung des Kulturguts

Kulturgut kann nach den Bestimmungen des Artikels 16 mit einem Kennzeichen versehen werden, das seine Feststellung erleichtert.

Artikel 7 Militärische Maßnahmen

1. Die Hohen Vertragsparteien verpflichten sich, schon in Friedenszeiten in ihre militärischen Dienstvorschriften oder -anweisungen Bestimmungen aufzunehmen, um die Einhaltung dieser Konvention zu gewährleisten, und den Mitgliedern ihrer Streitkräfte Achtung vor der Kultur und dem Kulturgut aller Völker einzuflößen.
2. Die Hohen Vertragsparteien verpflichten sich, bereits in Friedenszeiten Dienststellen oder Fachpersonal bei ihren Streitkräften vorzusehen oder bereitzustellen, deren Aufgabe darin besteht, über die Respektierung des Kulturguts zu wachen und mit den für seine Sicherung verantwortlichen zivilen Behörden zusammenzuarbeiten.

Kapitel II
Sonderschutz

Artikel 8 Gewährung des Sonderschutzes

1. Eine begrenzte Anzahl von Bergungsorten zur Sicherung beweglichen Kulturguts bei bewaffneten Konflikten, von Denkmalsorten und anderen unbeweglichen Kulturgütern von sehr hoher Bedeutung kann unter Sonderschutz gestellt werden, vorausgesetzt,
   a) daß diese sich in ausreichender Entfernung von einem großen Industriezentrum oder einem wichtigen militärischen Ziel, das einen gefährdeten Punkt darstellt, befinden, wie zum Beispiel ein

Flugplatz, ein Rundfunksender, ein für die Landesverteidigung arbeitender Betrieb, ein verhältnismäßig bedeutender Hafen oder Bahnhof oder ein Hauptverkehrsweg,
b) daß sie nicht zu militärischen Zwecken benutzt werden.
2. Ein Bergungsort für bewegliches Kulturgut kann ohne Rücksicht auf seine Lage ebenfalls unter Sonderschutz gestellt werden, wenn er so gebaut ist, daß er aller Wahrscheinlichkeit nach bei Bombardierungen nicht beschädigt werden kann.
3. ¹Ein Denkmalsort gilt als zu militärischen Zwecken benutzt, wenn er, sei es auch nur im Durchgangsverkehr, für die Beförderung von Militärpersonal oder Kriegsmaterial verwendet wird. ²Das gleiche gilt in allen Fällen, in denen innerhalb des Denkmalsorts unmittelbar mit den militärischen Operationen, der Stationierung von Militärpersonal oder der Herstellung von Kriegsmaterial zusammenhängende Handlungen durchgeführt werden.
4. Die Bewachung des in Absatz 1 dieses Artikels bezeichneten Kulturguts durch bewaffnetes Wachpersonal, das hierzu besonders befugt ist, oder die Anwesenheit von Polizeikräften, die normalerweise für die Aufrechterhaltung der öffentlichen Ordnung verantwortlich sind, in der Umgebung solchen Kulturguts gilt nicht als Benutzung zu militärischen Zwecken.
5. ¹Befindet sich in Absatz 1 dieses Artikels bezeichnetes Kulturgut in der Nähe eines wichtigen militärischen Zieles im Sinne desselben Absatzes, so kann es trotzdem unter Sonderschutz gestellt werden, wenn die diesen Schutz beantragende Hohe Vertragspartei sich verpflichtet, im Falle eines bewaffneten Konflikts das Ziel nicht zu benutzen und insbesondere, falls es sich um einen Hafen, Bahnhof oder Flugplatz handelt, jeden Verkehr davon abzuleiten. ²In diesem Falle muß die Umleitung schon in Friedenszeiten vorbereitet werden.
6. ¹Die Verleihung des Sonderschutzes erfolgt durch Eintragung in das „Internationale Register für Kulturgut unter Sonderschutz".[1]) ²Diese Eintragung darf nur in Übereinstimmung mit den Bestimmungen dieser Konvention und unter den in den Ausführungsbestimmungen vorgesehenen Bedingungen vorgenommen werden.

Artikel 9 Unverletzlichkeit des Kulturguts unter Sonderschutz
Die Hohen Vertragsparteien verpflichten sich, die Unverletzlichkeit des unter Sonderschutz stehenden Kulturguts zu gewährleisten, indem sie vom Zeitpunkt der Eintragung in das Internationale Register an jede gegen solches Gut gerichtete feindselige Handlung und, außer in den in Absatz 5 des Artikels 8 vorgesehenen Fällen, jede Benutzung dieses Guts oder seiner unmittelbaren Umgebung zu militärischen Zwecken unterlassen.

Artikel 10 Kennzeichnung und Überwachung
Während eines bewaffneten Konflikts ist das unter Sonderschutz stehende Kulturgut mit dem in Artikel 16 beschriebenen Kennzeichen zu versehen und einer internationalen Überwachung gemäß den Ausführungsbestimmungen zu dieser Konvention zugänglich zu machen.

Artikel 11 Aufhebung der Unverletzlichkeit
1. ¹Begeht eine der Hohen Vertragsparteien bezüglich eines unter Sonderschutz stehenden Kulturguts eine Verletzung der in Artikel 9 festgelegten Verpflichtungen, so ist die gegnerische Partei, solange die Verletzung fortbesteht, von ihrer Verpflichtung zur Gewährleistung der Unverletzlichkeit dieses Kulturguts befreit. ²Jedoch hat die gegnerische Partei, soweit möglich, zunächst dazu aufzufordern, die Verletzung innerhalb einer angemessenen Frist einzustellen.
2. ¹Abgesehen von dem in Absatz 1 dieses Artikels vorgesehenen Falle darf die Unverletzlichkeit von unter Sonderschutz stehendem Kulturgut nur in Ausnahmefällen unausweichlicher militärischer Notwendigkeit, und nur solange diese Notwendigkeit fortbesteht, aufgehoben werden. ²Das Vorliegen einer solchen Notwendigkeit kann nur durch den Kommandeur einer militärischen Einheit festgestellt werden, die der Größe nach einer Division oder einer höheren Einheit entspricht. ³Sofern die Umstände es erlauben, ist die Entscheidung, die Unverletzlichkeit aufzuheben, eine angemessene Zeit vorher der gegnerischen Partei zu notifizieren.
3. Die Partei, die die Unverletzlichkeit aufhebt, hat dies, sobald wie möglich, dem in den Ausführungsbestimmungen zu dieser Konvention vorgesehenen Generalkommissar für Kulturgut unter Angabe der Gründe schriftlich mitzuteilen.

---

1) Siehe hierzu die aktuelle Fassung des Registers vom 23.07.2015, abrufbar unter: http://www.unesco.org/new/fileadmin/MULTIMEDIA/HQ/CLT/pdf/Register2015EN.pdf.

Kapitel III
Transporte von Kulturgut

Artikel 12 Transporte unter Sonderschutz

1. Transporte, die ausschließlich der Verlagerung von Kulturgut innerhalb eines Hoheitsgebietes oder in ein anderes Hoheitsgebiet dienen, können auf Antrag der betreffenden Hohen Vertragspartei unter den in den Ausführungsbestimmungen vorgesehenen Bedingungen unter Sonderschutz stattfinden.
2. Transporte unter Sonderschutz erfolgen unter der in den erwähnten Ausführungsbestimmungen vorgesehenen internationalen Aufsicht und führen das in Artikel 16 beschriebene Kennzeichen.
3. Die Hohen Vertragsparteien unterlassen jede feindselige Handlung gegen Transporte, die unter Sonderschutz stehen.

Artikel 13 Transporte in dringenden Fällen

1. [1]Ist eine der Hohen Vertragsparteien der Auffassung, daß die Sicherheit bestimmter Kulturgüter deren Verlagerung erfordert und die Angelegenheit so dringlich ist, daß insbesondere zu Beginn eines bewaffneten Konflikts das in Artikel 12 vorgesehene Verfahren nicht eingehalten werden kann, so kann der Transport das in Artikel 16 beschriebene Kennzeichen führen, sofern nicht bereits ein Antrag auf Unverletzlichkeit gemäß Artikel 12 gestellt und abgelehnt wurde. [2]Soweit möglich, sollen die gegnerischen Parteien von der Verlagerung benachrichtigt werden. [3]Ein Transport von Kulturgut nach dem Gebiet eines anderen Landes darf jedoch das Kennzeichen keinesfalls führen, sofern ihm nicht die Unverletzlichkeit ausdrücklich verliehen worden ist.
2. Die Hohen Vertragsparteien werden nach Möglichkeit die erforderlichen Vorkehrungen treffen, um feindselige Handlungen gegen Transporte im Sinne des Absatzes 1 dieses Artikels, die das Kennzeichen führen, zu vermeiden.

Artikel 14 Unverletzlichkeit in Bezug auf Beschlagnahme, Wegnahme und Ausübung des Prisenrechts

1. Der Beschlagnahme, Wegnahme und der Ausübung des Prisenrechts unterliegen nicht:
a) Kulturgut, das unter dem in Artikel 12 oder Artikel 13 vorgesehenen Schutz steht;
b) Transportmittel, die ausschließlich der Verlagerung solchen Kulturguts dienen.
2. Die Bestimmungen dieses Artikels beschränken in keiner Weise das Recht zur Durchsuchung und Kontrolle.

Kapitel IV
Personal

Artikel 15 Personal

Das mit dem Schutz von Kulturgut betraute Personal ist, soweit mit den Erfordernissen der Sicherheit vereinbar, im Interesse dieses Gutes zu respektieren; fällt es in die Hände der gegnerischen Partei, so darf es seine Tätigkeit weiter ausüben, sofern das von ihm betreute Kulturgut ebenfalls in die Hände der gegnerischen Partei gefallen ist.

Kapitel V
Das Kennzeichen

Artikel 16 Das Kennzeichen

1. Das Kennzeichen der Konvention besteht aus einem nach unten hin spitzen Schild in Ultramarinblau und Weiß; (der Schild wird aus einem ultramarinblauen Quadrat, dessen eine Ecke die Spitze des Schildes darstellt, und aus einem oberhalb des Quadrats befindlichen ultramarinblauen Dreieck gebildet, wobei der verbleibende Raum auf beiden Seiten von je einem weißen Dreieck ausgefüllt wird).
2. Unter den in Artikel 17 festgelegten Bedingungen wird das Kennzeichen entweder einzeln oder dreifach in Dreiecksanordnung wiederholt (ein Schild unten) angewandt.

Artikel 17 Verwendung des Kennzeichens
1. Das Kennzeichen in dreifacher Wiederholung darf nur angewendet werden:
a) für unbewegliches Kulturgut unter Sonderschutz;
b) für Transporte von Kulturgut unter den in Artikel 12 und 13 vorgesehenen Bedingungen;
c) für improvisierte Bergungsorte unter den in Artikel 11 der Ausführungsbestimmungen vorgesehenen Bedingungen.
2. Das einfache Kennzeichen darf nur angewendet werden zur Kennzeichnung
a) von nicht unter Sonderschutz stehendem Kulturgut,
b) der gemäß den Ausführungsbestimmungen zu dieser Konvention mit Aufgaben der Überwachung beauftragten Personen,
c) von mit dem Schutz von Kulturgut betrautem Personal,
d) für die in den Ausführungsbestimmungen vorgesehenen Ausweise.
3. Während eines bewaffneten Konflikts ist die Verwendung des Kennzeichens für andere als die in den vorangehenden Absätzen vorgesehenen Fälle, sowie die Verwendung eines dem Kennzeichen ähnlichen Zeichens, für irgendwelche Zwecke verboten.
4. Das Kennzeichen darf nur dann zur Identifizierung von unbeweglichem Kulturgut verwendet werden, wenn zugleich eine von der zuständigen Behörde der Hohen Vertragspartei ausgestellte ordnungsgemäß datierte und unterzeichnete Genehmigung angebracht wird.

Kapitel VI
Anwendungsbereich der Konvention

Artikel 18 Anwendung der Konvention
1. Abgesehen von den Bestimmungen, die schon in Friedenszeiten wirksam werden, findet diese Konvention Anwendung im Falle eines erklärten Krieges oder eines anderen bewaffneten Konflikts, der zwischen zwei oder mehreren Hohen Vertragsparteien entsteht, selbst wenn der Kriegszustand von einer oder mehreren von ihnen nicht anerkannt wird.
2. Die Konvention findet auch in allen Fällen teilweiser oder vollständiger Besetzung des Gebietes einer der Hohen Vertragsparteien Anwendung, selbst wenn diese Besetzung auf keinen bewaffneten Widerstand stößt.
3. ¹Ist eine der an dem Konflikt beteiligten Mächte nicht Vertragspartei dieser Konvention, so bleiben die Mächte, die Parteien der Konvention sind, trotzdem in ihren gegenseitigen Beziehungen durch diese Konvention gebunden. ²Sie sind ferner durch die Konvention auch gegenüber der erwähnten Macht gebunden, wenn diese erklärt hat, daß sie die Bestimmungen der Konvention annimmt, und solange sie selbst diese anwendet.

Artikel 19 Konflikte nicht-internationalen Charakters
1. Im Falle eines bewaffneten Konflikts, der keinen internationalen Charakter hat und innerhalb des Gebietes einer der Hohen Vertragsparteien entsteht, ist jede in den Konflikt verwickelte Partei verpflichtet, mindestens diejenigen Bestimmungen dieser Konvention anzuwenden, die die Respektierung von Kulturgut betreffen.
2. Die an diesem Konflikt beteiligten Parteien werden bestrebt sein, durch Sondervereinbarungen auch die anderen Bestimmungen dieser Konvention ganz oder teilweise in Kraft zu setzen.
3. Die Organisation der Vereinten Nationen für Erziehung, Wissenschaft und Kultur kann den an dem Konflikt beteiligten Parteien ihre Dienste anbieten.
4. Die Anwendung der vorstehenden Bestimmungen läßt die Rechtsstellung der in den Konflikt verwickelten Parteien unberührt.

Kapitel VII
Durchführung der Konvention

Artikel 20 Ausführungsbestimmungen
Das Verfahren zur Anwendung dieser Konvention wird in den Ausführungsbestimmungen festgelegt, die einen Bestandteil dieser Konvention bilden.

A.I.1 Haager Konvention

Artikel 21 Schutzmächte
Diese Konvention und ihre Ausführungsbestimmungen werden unter Mitwirkung der Schutzmächte angewandt, die mit der Wahrnehmung der Interessen der an dem Konflikt beteiligten Parteien betraut sind.

Artikel 22 Schlichtungsverfahren
1. Die Schutzmächte stellen ihre guten Dienste in allen Fällen zur Verfügung, in denen sie dies im Interesse des Kulturguts für angezeigt erachten, insbesondere wenn zwischen den an dem Konflikt beteiligten Parteien über die Anwendung oder Auslegung der Bestimmungen dieser Konvention oder ihrer Ausführungsbestimmungen Meinungsverschiedenheiten bestehen.
2. [1]Zu diesem Zweck kann jede der Schutzmächte entweder auf Einladung einer Partei oder des Generaldirektors der Organisation der Vereinten Nationen für Erziehung, Wissenschaft und Kultur oder von sich aus den am Konflikt beteiligten Parteien eine Zusammenkunft ihrer Vertreter und insbesondere der für den Schutz des Kulturguts verantwortlichen Behörden vorschlagen, gegebenenfalls auf einem passend gewählten neutralen Gebiet. [2]Die am Konflikt beteiligten Parteien sind gehalten, den ihnen für die Zusammenkunft gemachten Vorschlägen Folge zu leisten. [3]Die Schutzmächte schlagen den an dem Konflikt beteiligten Parteien eine einer neutralen Macht angehörende oder vom Generaldirektor der Organisation der Vereinten Nationen für Erziehung, Wissenschaft und Kultur benannte Persönlichkeit zur Genehmigung vor; diese wird aufgefordert, an dieser Zusammenkunft als Vorsitzender teilzunehmen.

Artikel 23 Unterstützung durch UNESCO
1. [1]Die Hohen Vertragsparteien können um die technische Unterstützung der Organisation der Vereinten Nationen für Erziehung, Wissenschaft und Kultur bei der Organisierung des Schutzes ihres Kulturgutes oder in Zusammenhang mit jedem anderen Problem, das sich aus der Anwendung dieser Konvention oder ihrer Ausführungsbestimmungen ergibt, nachsuchen. [2]Die Organisation gewährt diese Unterstützung im Rahmen ihrer Zielsetzung und ihrer Mittel.
2. Die Organisation kann in dieser Hinsicht den Hohen Vertragsparteien von sich aus Vorschläge unterbreiten.

Artikel 24 Sondervereinbarungen
1. Die Hohen Vertragsparteien können Sondervereinbarungen über alle Fragen treffen, deren besondere Regelung ihnen zweckmäßig erscheint.
2. Sondervereinbarungen, die den Schutz verringern, den diese Konvention dem Kulturgut und dem mit seinem Schutz betrauten Personal gewährt, dürfen nicht getroffen werden.

Artikel 25 Verbreitung der Konvention
[1]Die Hohen Vertragsparteien verpflichten sich, in Friedenszeiten sowie in Zeiten eines bewaffneten Konflikts dem Wortlaut dieser Konvention und ihrer Ausführungsbestimmungen in ihren Ländern die weitestmögliche Verbreitung zu verschaffen. [2]Insbesondere verpflichten sie sich, ihre Behandlung in die militärischen und, wenn möglich, zivilen Ausbildungspläne aufzunehmen, so daß die Gesamtheit der Bevölkerung und insbesondere die Streitkräfte und das mit dem Schutz des Kulturguts betraute Personal mit ihren Grundsätzen vertraut gemacht werden.

Artikel 26 Übersetzung und Berichte
1. Die Hohen Vertragsparteien stellen sich gegenseitig durch Vermittlung des Generaldirektors der Organisation der Vereinten Nationen für Erziehung, Wissenschaft und Kultur die amtlichen Übersetzungen dieser Konvention und ihrer Ausführungsbestimmungen zu.
2. Außerdem übersenden sie dem Generaldirektor mindestens alle vier Jahre einen Bericht mit den ihnen geeignet erscheinenden Angaben über die von ihren Behörden zur Durchführung dieser Konvention und ihrer Ausführungsbestimmungen getroffenen, vorbereiteten oder in Aussicht genommenen Maßnahmen.

Artikel 27 Tagungen
1. [1]Der Generaldirektor der Organisation der Vereinten Nationen für Erziehung, Wissenschaft und Kultur kann mit Zustimmung des Exekutivrats Tagungen von Vertretern der Hohen Vertragsparteien einberufen. [2]Er muß dies tun, wenn mindestens ein Fünftel der Hohen Vertragsparteien es wünscht.

2. Unbeschadet anderer ihr durch diese Konvention übertragener Aufgaben dient die Tagung dem Zweck, Fragen der Anwendung der Konvention und ihrer Ausführungsbestimmungen zu untersuchen und diesbezügliche Empfehlungen auszuarbeiten.
3. Die Tagung kann ferner, sofern die Mehrheit der Hohen Vertragsparteien vertreten ist, nach Maßgabe der Bestimmungen des Artikels 39 eine Abänderung der Konvention oder ihrer Ausführungsbestimmungen vornehmen.

Artikel 28 Strafmaßnahmen
Die Hohen Vertragsparteien verpflichten sich, im Rahmen ihrer Strafgerichtsbarkeit alle erforderlichen Maßnahmen zu treffen, um Personen jeder Staatsangehörigkeit, die sich einer Verletzung dieser Konvention schuldig machen oder den Befehl zu einer solchen geben, zu verfolgen und strafrechtlich oder disziplinarisch zu bestrafen.

Schlußbestimmungen

Artikel 29 Sprachen
1. Diese Konvention ist in englischer, französischer, russischer und spanischer Sprache abgefaßt; alle vier Fassungen sind in gleicher Weise maßgeblich.
2. Die Organisation der Vereinten Nationen für Erziehung, Wissenschaft und Kultur läßt Übersetzungen der Konvention in die anderen Amtssprachen ihrer Hauptversammlung anfertigen.

Artikel 30 Unterzeichnung
Diese Konvention trägt das Datum des 14. Mai 1954 und liegt bis zum 31. Dezember 1954 für alle zu der Haager Konferenz vom 21. April bis 14. Mai 1954 eingeladenen Staaten zur Unterzeichnung auf.

Artikel 31 Ratifikation
1. Diese Konvention bedarf der Ratifikation durch die Unterzeichnerstaaten nach Maßgabe ihrer eigenen verfassungsmäßigen Verfahren.
2. Die Ratifikationsurkunden sind beim Generaldirektor der Organisation der Vereinten Nationen für Erziehung, Wissenschaft und Kultur zu hinterlegen.

Artikel 32 Beitritt
[1]Vom Zeitpunkt ihres Inkrafttretens an steht diese Konvention allen Staaten zum Beitritt offen, die in Artikel 30 erwähnt sind und nicht unterzeichnet haben, sowie allen anderen Staaten, die vom Exekutivrat der Organisation der Vereinten Nationen für Erziehung, Wissenschaft und Kultur zum Beitritt eingeladen werden. [2]Der Beitritt erfolgt durch Hinterlegung einer Beitrittsurkunde beim Generaldirektor der Organisation der Vereinten Nationen für Erziehung, Wissenschaft und Kultur.

Artikel 33 Inkrafttreten
1. Diese Konvention tritt drei Monate nach Hinterlegung von fünf Ratifikationsurkunden in Kraft.[1)2)]
2. Späterhin tritt sie für jede Hohe Vertragspartei drei Monate nach Hinterlegung ihrer Ratifikations- oder Beitrittserklärungen in Kraft.
3. [1]Tritt die in Artikel 18 und 19 vorgesehene Lage ein, so treten die vor oder nach Beginn der Feindseligkeiten oder der Besetzung von in den Konflikt verwickelten Parteien hinterlegten Ratifikations- und Beitrittserklärungen mit sofortiger Wirkung in Kraft. [2]In diesen Fällen macht der Generaldirektor der Organisation der Vereinten Nationen für Erziehung, Wissenschaft und Kultur auf dem schnellsten Wege die in Artikel 38 vorgesehenen Mitteilungen.

Artikel 34 Wirksame Durchführung
1. Jeder Staat, der bei Inkrafttreten dieser Konvention Vertragspartei ist, hat alle erforderlichen Maßnahmen zu treffen, um ihre wirksame Durchführung binnen sechs Monaten nach Inkrafttreten zu gewährleisten.

---

1) Die Konvention ist für die Bundesrepublik Deutschland am **11.11.1967** in Kraft getreten; vgl. hierzu die Bek. v. 26.10.1967 (DGDl. II S. 2471).
2) Für das Inkrafttreten des Übereinkommens in den anderen Vertragsstaaten siehe die Übersicht in der Anlage.

2. Für diejenigen Staaten, die ihre Ratifikations- oder Beitrittsurkunden nach dem Inkrafttreten der Konvention hinterlegen, beträgt die Frist sechs Monate, vom Tage der Hinterlegung der Ratifikations- oder Beitrittsurkunden gerechnet.

Artikel 35 Ausdehnung des Geltungsbereichs der Konvention
[1]Jede der Hohen Vertragsparteien kann bei der Ratifikation oder beim Beitritt oder zu jedem späteren Zeitpunkt durch Notifikation an den Generaldirektor der Organisation der Vereinten Nationen für Erziehung, Wissenschaft und Kultur erklären, daß diese Konvention sich auf alle oder einige der Gebiete erstreckt, deren internationale Beziehungen sie wahrnimmt. [2]Diese Notifikation wird drei Monate nach dem Tage ihres Eingangs wirksam.

Artikel 36 Zusammenhang mit früheren Abkommen
1. In den Beziehungen zwischen Mächten, die durch die Haager Abkommen betreffend die Gesetze und Gebräuche des Landkrieges (IV)[1)] und betreffend die Beschießung durch Seestreitkräfte in Kriegszeiten (IX) – sei es vom 29. Juli 1899 oder vom 18. Oktober 1907 – gebunden und Vertragsparteien dieser Konvention sind, ergänzt diese Konvention das vorgenannte Abkommen (IX) und die dem vorgenannten Abkommen (IV) als Anlage beigefügte Ordnung; es ersetzt das in Artikel 5 des vorgenannten Abkommens (IX) beschriebene Zeichen durch das in Artikel 16 dieser Konvention beschriebene Kennzeichen in den Fällen, in denen diese Konvention und ihre Ausführungsbestimmungen die Verwendung dieses Kennzeichens vorsehen.
2. In den Beziehungen zwischen Mächten, die durch den Vertrag von Washington vom 15. April 1935 über den Schutz künstlerischer und wissenschaftlicher Einrichtungen und geschichtlicher Denkmale (Roerich-Pakt) gebunden und Vertragsparteien dieser Konvention sind, ergänzt diese Konvention den Roerich-Pakt und ersetzt die in Artikel III des Paktes beschriebene Flagge durch das Kennzeichen gemäß Artikel 16 dieser Konvention in allen Fällen, in denen diese Konvention und ihre Ausführungsbestimmungen die Verwendung dieses Kennzeichens vorsehen.

Artikel 37 Kündigung
1. Jede der Hohen Vertragsparteien kann diese Konvention für sich selbst oder für Gebiete, deren internationale Beziehungen sie wahrnimmt, kündigen.
2. Die Kündigung erfolgt durch eine schriftliche Erklärung, die beim Generaldirektor der Organisation der Vereinten Nationen für Erziehung, Wissenschaft und Kultur zu hinterlegen ist.
3. [1]Die Kündigung wird ein Jahr nach Eingang der Kündigungserklärung wirksam. [2]Ist jedoch die kündigende Partei beim Ablauf dieser Frist in einen bewaffneten Konflikt verwickelt, so wird die Kündigung erst nach Einstellung der Feindseligkeiten oder nach Abschluß der Rückführung des Kulturguts wirksam, je nachdem, welcher Zeitpunkt der spätere ist.

Artikel 38 Notifikationen
Der Generaldirektor der Organisation der Vereinten Nationen für Erziehung, Wissenschaft und Kultur benachrichtigt die in Artikel 30 und 32 bezeichneten Staaten und die Vereinten Nationen von der Hinterlegung aller in Artikel 31, 32 und 39 vorgesehenen Ratifikations- und Beitrittsurkunden oder Annahmeerklärungen sowie von den in Artikel 35, 37 und 39 vorgesehenen Notifikationen und Kündigungen.

Artikel 39 Abänderung der Konvention und ihrer Ausführungsbestimmungen
1. [1]Jede der Hohen Vertragsparteien kann Abänderungen dieser Konvention oder ihrer Ausführungsbestimmungen vorschlagen. [2]Abänderungsvorschläge sind dem Generaldirektor der Organisation der Vereinten Nationen für Erziehung, Wissenschaft und Kultur mitzuteilen, der ihren Wortlaut allen Hohen Vertragsparteien mit der Bitte übermittelt, ihn innerhalb von vier Monaten wissen zu lassen,
a) ob sie wünschen, daß eine Konferenz einberufen wird, um die vorgeschlagenen Abänderungsvorschläge zu erörtern; oder
b) ob sie für die Annahme der vorgeschlagenen Abänderungsvorschläge ohne Abhaltung einer Konferenz eintreten;

---
1) **Amtl. Anm.:** Die römischen Zahlen beziehen sich auf die Haager Abkommen vom 18. Oktober 1907.

oder
c) ob sie für die Ablehnung der vorgeschlagenen Abänderung ohne Abhaltung einer Konferenz eintreten.
2. Der Generaldirektor übermittelt die gemäß Absatz 1 dieses Artikels bei ihm eingegangenen Antworten allen Hohen Vertragsparteien.
3. ¹Haben sämtliche Hohen Vertragsparteien gemäß Absatz 1, Unterabsatz b) dieses Artikels dem Generaldirektor der Organisation der Vereinten Nationen für Erziehung, Wisschenschaft und Kultur innerhalb der vorgeschriebenen Frist ihre Meinung mitgeteilt und ihn davon unterrichtet, daß sie für die Annahme des Abänderungsvorschlages ohne Abhaltung einer Konferenz eintreten, so wird diese Entscheidung durch den Generaldirektor gemäß Artikel 38 bekanntgemacht. ²Die Abänderung wird 90 Tage nach dem Tage dieser Notifikation gegenüber allen Hohen Vertragsparteien wirksam.
4. Der Generaldirektor hat eine Konferenz der Hohen Vertragsparteien zur Erörterung des Abänderungsvorschlags einzuberufen, wenn mehr als ein Drittel der Hohen Vertragsparteien dies verlangt.
5. Abänderungsvorschläge zu dieser Konvention oder zu ihren Ausführungsbestimmungen, die nach dem im vorangehenden Absatz festgelegten Verfahren behandelt werden, treten erst in Kraft, nachdem sie von den auf der Konferenz vertretenen Hohen Vertragsparteien einstimmig beschlossen und von allen Hohen Vertragsparteien angenommen worden sind.
6. Die Annahme von Abänderungsvorschlägen zu dieser Konvention oder zu ihren Ausführungsbestimmungen, die von der in Absatz 4 und 5 erwähnten Konferenz angenommen worden sind, durch die Hohen Vertragsparteien erfolgt durch Hinterlegung einer förmlichen Erklärung beim Generaldirektor der Organisation der Vereinten Nationen für Erziehung, Wissenschaft und Kultur.
7. Nach Inkrafttreten von Abänderungen dieser Konvention oder ihrer Ausführungsbestimmungen steht nur der so abgeänderte Text der Konvention oder ihrer Ausführungsbestimmungen zur Ratifikation und zum Beitritt offen.

Artikel 40 Eintragung
Gemäß Artikel 102 der Satzung der Vereinten Nationen wird diese Konvention auf Ersuchen des Generaldirektors der Organisation der Vereinten Nationen für Erziehung, Wissenschaft und Kultur beim Sekretariat der Vereinten Nationen eingetragen.

ZU URKUND DESSEN haben die gehörig bevollmächtigten Unterzeichneten diese Konvention unterschrieben.

GESCHEHEN zu Den Haag, am 14. Mai 1954 in einem einzigen Exemplar, das in den Archiven der Organisation der Vereinten Nationen für Erziehung, Wissenschaft und Kultur hinterlegt wird und von dem beglaubigte Ausfertigungen allen in Artikel 30 und 32 bezeichneten Staaten sowie den Vereinten Nationen übermittelt werden.

Ausführungsbestimmungen zur Konvention zum Schutz von Kulturgut bei bewaffneten Konflikten

(Übersetzung)

Kapitel I Überwachung

Artikel 1 Internationales Personenverzeichnis
¹Nach dem Inkrafttreten der Konvention stellt der Generaldirektor der Organisation der Vereinten Nationen für Erziehung, Wissenschaft und Kultur ein internationales Verzeichnis aller Personen auf, die von den Hohen Vertragsparteien als für das Amt eines Generalkommissars für Kulturgut geeignet benannt worden sind. ²Auf Veranlassung des Generaldirektors der Organisation der Vereinten Nationen für Erziehung, Wissenschaft und Kultur wird dieses Verzeichnis in gewissen Zeitabständen auf Grund der von den Hohen Vertragsparteien gestellten Anträge berichtet.

Artikel 2 Organisation der Überwachung
Sobald eine Hohe Vertragspartei in einen bewaffneten Konflikt, auf den Artikel 18 der Konvention Anwendung findet, verwickelt wird
a) ernennt sie einen Vertreter für das auf ihrem Gebiet befindliche Kulturgut und, falls sie ein anderes Gebiet besetzt hält, einen besonderen Vertreter für das dort befindliche Kulturgut;

b) ernennt die Schutzmacht jeder Partei, die sich mit dieser Hohen Vertragspartei im Konflikt befindet, bei letzterer gemäß Artikel 3 dieser Ausführungsbestimmungen einen Delegierten;
c) wird bei dieser Hohen Vertragspartei gemäß Artikel 4 dieser Ausführungsbestimmungen ein Generalkommissar für Kulturgut ernannt.

Artikel 3 Ernennung von Delegierten der Schutzmächte
Die Schutzmacht ernennt ihre Delegierten aus dem Kreis der Angehörigen ihres diplomatischen oder konsularischen Dienstes oder, mit Zustimmung der Partei, bei der sie tätig sein sollen, aus einem anderen Personenkreis.

Artikel 4 Ernennung des Generalkommissars
1. Der Generalkommissar für Kulturgut wird von der Partei, bei der er tätig sein soll, und den Schutzmächten der gegnerischen Parteien aus dem internationalen Personenverzeichnis im gegenseitigen Einvernehmen ausgewählt.
2. Gelingt es den Parteien nicht, sich innerhalb von drei Wochen nach Beginn ihrer Erörterungen über diese Frage zu einigen, so ersuchen sie den Präsidenten des Internationalen Gerichtshofes, den Generalkommissar zu ernennen, der jedoch seine Tätigkeit erst dann aufnimmt, wenn die Partei, bei der er tätig sein soll, seine Ernennung gebilligt hat.

Artikel 5 Aufgaben der Delegierten
[1]Die Delegierten der Schutzmächte stellen Verletzungen der Konvention fest, untersuchen mit Genehmigung der Partei, bei der sie tätig sind, die Umstände, unter denen Verletzungen erfolgt sind, erheben an Ort und Stelle Vorstellungen zu ihrer Beseitigung und machen dem Generalkommissar davon erforderlichenfalls Mitteilung. [2]Sie halten ihn über ihre Tätigkeit auf dem laufenden.

Artikel 6 Aufgaben des Generalkommissars
1. Der Generalkommissar für Kulturgut behandelt zusammen mit dem Vertreter der Partei, bei der er tätig ist, und mit den beteiligten Delegierten alle Angelegenheiten, mit denen er hinsichtlich der Anwendung der Konvention befaßt ist.
2. Er ist befugt, in den in diesen Ausführungsbestimmungen angegebenen Fällen Entscheidungen zu treffen und Ernennungen vorzunehmen.
3. Mit Zustimmung der Partei, bei der er tätig ist, ist er berechtigt, eine Untersuchung anzuordnen oder selbst durchzuführen.
4. Er erhebt bei den Konfliktsparteien oder ihren Schutzmächten die Vorstellungen, die er zur Anwendung der Konvention für zweckmäßig erachtet.
5. [1]Er verfaßt die etwa erforderlichen Berichte über die Anwendung der Konvention und übermittelt sie den beteiligten Parteien und ihren Schutzmächten. [2]Er übersendet Abschriften an den Generaldirektor der Organisation der Vereinten Nationen für Erziehung, Wissenschaft und Kultur, der nur von den darin enthaltenen technischen Angaben Gebrauch machen darf.
6. Ist keine Schutzmacht vorhanden, so übernimmt der Generalkommissar die durch die Artikel 21 und 22 der Konvention der Schutzmacht übertragenen Aufgaben.

Artikel 7 Inspektoren und Sachverständige
1. [1]Wenn der Generalkommissar für das Kulturgut auf Ersuchen der beteiligten Delegierten oder nach Beratung mit ihnen dies für erforderlich hält, schlägt er der Partei, bei der er tätig ist, zur Durchführung eines Sonderauftrages einen Inspektor für das Kulturgut zur Genehmigung vor. [2]Der Inspektor ist nur dem Generalkommissar verantwortlich.
2. Der Generalkommissar, die Delegierten und die Inspektoren können Sachverständige hinzuziehen, die ebenfalls der im vorstehenden Absatz erwähnten Partei zur Genehmigung vorzuschlagen sind.

Artikel 8 Erfüllung der Überwachungsaufgaben
[1]Die Generalkommissare für Kulturgut, die Delegierten der Schutzmächte, die Inspektoren und Sachverständigen dürfen keinesfalls die Grenzen ihres Auftrages überschreiten. [2]Sie haben insbesondere den Sicherheitsbedürfnissen der Hohen Vertragspartei, bei der sie tätig sind, Rechnung zu tragen und unter allen Umständen auf die Erfordernisse der militärischen Lage, wie sie ihnen von der betreffenden Hohen Vertragspartei zur Kenntnis gebracht wird, Rücksicht zu nehmen.

Artikel 9 Stellvertretung der Schutzmacht
[1]Stehen einer der Konfliktsparteien die Dienste einer Schutzmacht nicht oder nicht mehr zur Verfügung, so kann ein neutraler Staat ersucht werden, diejenigen Aufgaben einer Schutzmacht zu übernehmen, die die Ernennung eines Generalkommissars für Kulturgut nach dem im vorstehenden Artikel 4 festgelegten Verfahren betreffen. [2]Der auf diese Weise ernannte Generalkommissar betraut erforderlichenfalls In-

spektoren mit den in diesen Ausführungsbestimmungen festgelegten Aufgaben der Delegierten der Schutzmächte.

Artikel 10 Kosten
[1]Besoldung und Ausgaben des Generalkommissars für Kulturgut, der Inspektoren und Sachverständigen sind von der Partei zu tragen, bei der sie tätig sind. [2]Besoldung und Ausgaben der Delegierten der Schutzmächte werden durch eine Vereinbarung zwischen diesen Mächten und den Staaten, deren Interessen sie wahrnehmen, geregelt.

Kapitel II Sonderschutz

Artikel 11 Improvisierte Bergungsorte
1. Sieht sich eine Hohe Vertragspartei während eines bewaffneten Konfliktes durch unvorhergesehene Umstände veranlaßt, einen improvisierten Bergungsort einzurichten, und möchte sie ihn unter Sonderschutz stellen, so hat sie den bei ihr tätigen Generalkommissar für Kulturgut unverzüglich davon in Kenntnis zu setzen.
2. [1]Ist der Generalkommissar der Auffassung, daß eine solche Maßnahme durch die Umstände und durch die Bedeutung des in diesem improvisierten Bergungsort untergebrachten Kulturguts gerechtfertigt ist, so kann er die Hohe Vertragspartei ermächtigen, den Bergungsort mit dem in Artikel 16 der Konvention vorgesehenen Kennzeichen zu versehen. [2]Er hat seine Entscheidung unverzüglich den beteiligten Delegierten der Schutzmächte mitzuteilen, von denen jeder innerhalb von 30 Tagen die sofortige Zurückziehung des Kennzeichens anordnen kann.
3. Sobald diese Delegierten ihre Zustimmung ausgedrückt haben oder wenn innerhalb der Frist von dreißig Tagen keiner der beteiligten Delegierten Einspruch erhoben hat, und wenn nach Auffassung des Generalkommissars der Bergungsort den in Artikel 8 der Konvention aufgeführten Bedingungen entspricht, ersucht der Generalkommissar den Generaldirektor der Organisation der Vereinten Nationen für Erziehung, Wissenschaft und Kultur, den Bergungsort in das Internationale Register für Kulturgut unter Sonderschutz einzutragen.

Artikel 12 Internationales Register für Kulturgut unter Sonderschutz
1. Es ist ein „Internationales Register für Kulturgut unter Sonderschutz" einzurichten.[1)]
2. [1]Das Register wird vom Generaldirektor der Organisation der Vereinten Nationen für Erziehung, Wissenschaft und Kultur geführt. [2]Er übersendet Abschriften an den Generalsekretär der Vereinten Nationen und an die Hohen Vertragsparteien.
3. [1]Das Register ist in Abteilungen zu gliedern, und zwar ist für jede der Hohen Vertragsparteien eine Abteilung vorzusehen. [2]Jede Abteilung ist in drei Unterabteilungen zu gliedern mit den Überschriften: Bergungsorte, Denkmalsorte, sonstiges unbewegliches Kulturgut. [3]Der Generaldirektor bestimmt die Einzelheiten innerhalb jeder Abteilung.

Artikel 13 Anträge auf Eintragung
1. [1]Jede Hohe Vertragspartei kann beim Generaldirektor der Organisation der Vereinten Nationen für Erziehung, Wissenschaft und Kultur beantragen, bestimmte auf ihrem Gebiet gelegene Bergungsorte, Denkmalsorte oder sonstige unbewegliche Kulturgüter in das Internationale Register einzutragen. [2]Der Antrag muß eine Beschreibung der Lage des betreffenden Kulturguts enthalten und bescheinigen, daß es die Bedingungen des Artikels 8 der Konvention erfüllt.
2. Im Falle der Besetzung eines Gebietes ist die Besatzungsmacht für die Stellung dieses Antrages zuständig.
3. Der Generaldirektor der Organisation der Vereinten Nationen für Erziehung, Wissenschaft und Kultur hat unverzüglich jeder der Hohen Vertragsparteien Abschriften der Anträge auf Eintragung zu übersenden.

Artikel 14 Einsprüche
1. [1]Jede Hohe Vertragspartei kann mit einem an den Generaldirektor der Organisation der Vereinten Nationen für Erziehung, Wissenschaft und Kultur gerichteten Schreiben gegen die Eintragung von Kulturgut Einspruch erheben. [2]Dieses Schreiben muß innerhalb von vier Monaten nach dem Tage, an dem der Generaldirektor eine Abschrift des Antrags auf Eintragung abgesandt hat, bei ihm eingegangen sein.
2. Der Einspruch muß begründet sein; er kann nur darauf gestützt werden, daß
a) das Gut kein Kulturgut ist;
b) die in Artikel 8 der Konvention angeführten Bedingungen nicht erfüllt sind.

---
1) Siehe hierzu die aktuelle Fassung des Registers vom 23.07.2015, abrufbar unter: http://www.unesco.org/new/fileadmin/MULTIMEDIA/HQ/CLT/pdf/Register2015EN.pdf.

A.I.1 Haager Konvention

3. ¹Der Generaldirektor hat den Hohen Vertragsparteien unverzüglich eine Abschrift des Einspruchs zu übermitteln. ²Er hat erforderlichenfalls die Stellungnahme des „Internationalen Ausschusses für Denkmale, künstlerische und geschichtliche Stätten und archäologische Ausgrabungen" sowie, wenn er es für angebracht hält, sonstiger geeigneter Organisationen oder Persönlichkeiten einzuholen.
4. Der Generaldirektor oder die die Eintragung beantragende Hohe Vertragspartei kann bei der Hohen Vertragspartei, die den Einspruch erhoben hat, alle für notwendig erachteten Schritte unternehmen, um die Rücknahme des Einspruchs zu erwirken.
5. Wird eine Hohe Vertragspartei, die in Friedenszeiten einen Antrag auf Eintragung gestellt hat, in einen bewaffneten Konflikt verwickelt, bevor die Eintragung erfolgt ist, so hat der Generaldirektor das betreffende Kulturgut sofort vorläufig in das Register einzutragen, vorbehaltlich der Bestätigung, Zurückziehung oder Streichung noch zu erhebender oder bereits erhobener Einsprüche.
6. Hat der Generaldirektor nicht binnen sechs Monaten nach Eingang des Einspruchs von der Hohen Vertragspartei, die Einspruch erhoben hat, eine Mitteilung dahingehend erhalten, daß der Einspruch zurückgezogen ist, so kann die Hohe Vertragspartei, die die Eintragung beantragt hat, ein Schiedsverfahren gemäß dem im folgenden Absatz geregelten Verfahren beantragen.
7. ¹Der Antrag auf ein Schiedsverfahren ist innerhalb eines Jahres nach Eingang des Einspruchs beim Generaldirektor zu stellen. ²Jede der beiden am Streitfall beteiligten Parteien ernennt einen Schiedsrichter. ³Ist mehr als ein Einspruch gegen einen Antrag auf Eintragung erhoben worden, so ernennen die Hohen Vertragsparteien, die die Einsprüche erhoben haben, in gegenseitigem Einvernehmen einen einzigen Schiedsrichter. ⁴Die beiden Schiedsrichter wählen einen Oberschiedsrichter aus dem in Artikel 1 dieser Ausführungsbestimmungen erwähnten internationalen Verzeichnis. ⁵Einigen sich die Schiedsrichter bei der Wahl nicht, so ersuchen sie den Präsidenten des Internationalen Gerichtshofs, einen Oberschiedsrichter zu bestimmen, der nicht notwendigerweise aus dem internationalen Verzeichnis ausgewählt zu werden braucht. ⁶Das auf diese Weise gebildete Schiedsgericht bestimmt selbst sein Verfahren. ⁷Gegen seine Entscheidungen kann kein Rechtsmittel eingelegt werden.
8. ¹Jede der Hohen Vertragsparteien kann bei Entstehung eines Streitfalls, in dem sie Partei ist, erklären, daß sie die Anwendung des im vorangehenden Absatz vorgesehenen Schiedsverfahrens nicht wünscht. ²In diesem Falle hat der Generaldirektor den Einspruch gegen einen Antrag auf Eintragung den Hohen Vertragsparteien vorzulegen. ³Der Einspruch kann nur dann bestätigt werden, wenn die Hohen Vertragsparteien dies mit einer Zweidrittelmehrheit der sich an der Abstimmung beteiligenden Hohen Vertragsparteien beschließen. ⁴Die Abstimmung erfolgt schriftlich, sofern nicht der Generaldirektor der Organisation der Vereinten Nationen für Erziehung, Wissenschaft und Kultur es für unerläßlich erachtet, auf Grund der ihm gemäß Artikel 27 der Konvention zustehenden Befugnisse eine Tagung einzuberufen. ⁵Entscheidet der Generaldirektor, daß die Abstimmung auf schriftlichem Wege durchgeführt werden soll, so fordert er die Hohen Vertragsparteien auf, ihre Stimme innerhalb von sechs Monaten, vom Tage der Aufforderung an gerechnet, in einem versiegelten Schreiben abzugeben.

Artikel 15 Eintragung
1. Der Generaldirektor der Organisation der Vereinten Nationen für Erziehung, Wissenschaft und Kultur veranlaßt, daß jedes Kulturgut, für das ein Antrag auf Eintragung gestellt worden ist, unter einer Ordnungsnummer in das Register eingetragen wird, sofern nicht innerhalb der in Artikel 14 Absatz 1 dieser Ausführungsbestimmungen vorgesehenen Frist ein Einspruch erhoben worden ist.
2. Ist ein Einspruch erhoben worden, dann darf der Generaldirektor, unbeschadet der Bestimmung des Artikels 14 Absatz 5, Kulturgut nur dann in das Register eintragen, wenn der Einspruch zurückgezogen oder nach dem in Absatz 7 oder Absatz 8 des Artikels 14 dieser Ausführungsbestimmungen vorgesehenen Verfahren nicht bestätigt worden ist.
3. In dem in Artikel 11 Absatz 3 vorgesehenen Fall nimmt der Generaldirektor die Eintragung auf Ersuchen des Generalkommissars für Kulturgut vor.
4. ¹Der Generaldirektor übersendet eine beglaubigte Abschrift jeder Eintragung in das Register unverzüglich an den Generalsekretär der Vereinten Nationen, an die Hohen Vertragsparteien und, auf Ersuchen der die Eintragung beantragenden Partei, an alle anderen in Artikel 30 und 32 der Konvention bezeichneten Staaten. ²Die Eintragung wird dreißig Tage nach Absendung dieser Abschriften wirksam.

Artikel 16 Streichung
1. Der Generaldirektor der Organisation der Vereinten Nationen für Erziehung, Wissenschaft und Kultur veranlaßt die Streichung der Eintragung von Kulturgut
   a) auf Antrag der Hohen Vertragspartei, auf deren Gebiet sich das Kulturgut befindet;
   b) im Falle der Kündigung der Konvention durch die Hohe Vertragspartei, die die Eintragung beantragt hatte, sobald die Kündigung wirksam geworden ist;
   c) in dem in Artikel 14 Absatz 5 dieser Ausführungsbestimmungen vorgesehenen Sonderfalle, wenn ein Einspruch nach dem in Artikel 14 Absatz 7 oder 8 vorgesehenen Verfahren bestätigt worden ist.

2. ¹Der Generaldirektor übersendet dem Generalsekretär der Vereinten Nationen sowie allen Staaten, die eine Abschrift der Eintragung ins Register erhalten haben, unverzüglich eine beglaubigte Abschrift der Streichungsverfügung. ²Die Streichung wird dreißig Tage nach Absendung dieser Abschriften wirksam.

Kapitel III Transporte von Kulturgut

Artikel 17 Verfahren zur Erlangung der Unverletzlichkeit

1. ¹Der Antrag gemäß Artikel 12 Absatz 1 der Konvention ist an den Generalkommissar für Kulturgut zu richten. ²Der Antrag muß begründet sein und die ungefähre Zahl und die Bedeutung der zu verlagernden Kulturgüter, ihre derzeitige Unterbringung, die in Aussicht genommene Unterbringung, die vorgesehenen Transportmittel, den beabsichtigten Reiseweg und den für die Verlagerung vorgeschlagenen Tag sowie alle sonstigen einschlägigen Angaben angeben.
2. ¹Ist der Generalkommissar nach Einholung der von ihm als zweckmäßig erachteten Stellungnahmen der Auffassung, daß diese Verlagerung gerechtfertigt ist, so hat er sich mit den beteiligten Delegierten der Schutzmächte wegen der für die Durchführung in Aussicht genommenen Maßnahmen ins Benehmen zu setzen. ²Danach hat er den in Frage kommenden Konfliktsparteien die Verlagerung mitzuteilen, wobei die Mitteilung alle zweckmäßigen Angaben enthalten muß.
3. ¹Der Generalkommissar ernennt einen oder mehrere Inspektoren, die sich zu vergewissern haben, daß nur das in dem Antrag angeführte Kulturgut verlagert wird und daß der Transport auf die genehmigte Art und Weise erfolgt und das Kennzeichen führt. ²Der Inspektor oder die Inspektoren begleiten das Kulturgut bis an den Bestimmungsort.

Artikel 18 Transport ins Ausland

Erfolgt die unter Sonderschutz stehende Verlagerung in das Gebiet eines anderen Landes, so finden nicht nur Artikel 12 der Konvention und Artikel 17 dieser Ausführungsbestimmungen Anwendung, sondern auch die nachstehenden weiteren Bestimmungen:
a) Solange sich das Kulturgut auf dem Gebiet eines anderen Staates befindet, ist dieser Staat Verwahrer des Kulturguts und er hat darauf dieselbe Sorgfalt zu verwenden wie auf eigenes Kulturgut von vergleichbarer Bedeutung.
b) Der Verwahrerstaat gibt das Kulturgut erst nach Beendigung des Konflikts zurück; die Rückgabe hat innerhalb von sechs Monaten nach dem Tage, an dem ein entsprechendes Ersuchen gestellt worden ist, zu erfolgen.
c) Während der verschiedenen Phasen der Verlagerung und solange sich das Kulturgut im Gebiet eines anderen Staates befindet, ist es beschlagnahmefrei und es kann darüber weder vom Hinterleger noch vom Verwahrer verfügt werden. Jedoch kann der Verwahrer das Kulturgut, wenn es dessen Sicherheit erfordert, mit Zustimmung des Hinterlegers in das Gebiet eines dritten Landes unter den in diesem Artikel bezeichneten Voraussetzungen transportieren lassen.
d) In dem Antrag auf Sonderschutz ist anzugeben, daß der Staat, in dessen Gebiet das Kulturgut verlagert werden soll, die Bestimmungen dieses Artikels annimmt.

Artikel 19 Besetztes Gebiet

In allen Fällen, in denen eine Hohe Vertragspartei, die das Gebiet einer anderen Hohen Vertragspartei besetzt hält, Kulturgut in einen an anderer Stelle innerhalb dieses Gebiets gelegenen Bergungsort verlagert, ohne in der Lage zu sein, das in Artikel 17 dieser Ausführungsbestimmungen geregelte Verfahren zu befolgen, gilt die in Betracht kommende Verlagerung nicht als unrechtmäßige Aneignung im Sinne des Artikels 4 der Konvention, sofern der Generalkommissar für Kulturgut nach Befragung des ordentlichen Verwaltungspersonals schriftlich bestätigt, daß diese Verlagerung durch die Umstände geboten war.

Kapitel IV Das Kennzeichen

Artikel 20 Anbringung des Kennzeichens

1. ¹Die Anbringung des Kennzeichens und der Grad seiner Sichtbarkeit liegen im Ermessen der zuständigen Behörden jeder Hohen Vertragspartei. ²Es kann auf Flaggen oder Armbinden gezeigt werden; es kann auf einen Gegenstand aufgemalt oder in jeder anderen geeigneten Form dargestellt werden.
2. ¹Unbeschadet einer etwa möglichen deutlicheren Kennzeichnung ist das Kennzeichen im Fall eines bewaffneten Konflikts und in den in den Artikeln 12 und 13 der Konvention erwähnten Fällen auf den Transportfahrzeugen so anzubringen, daß es bei Tageslicht aus der Luft ebenso wie vom Boden aus deutlich erkennbar ist. ²Das Kennzeichen muß vom Boden aus sichtbar sein
a) in regelmäßigen Abständen, die ausreichend klar den Umkreis des unter Sonderschutz stehenden Denkmalsorts erkennen lassen;
b) am Zugang zu sonstigem unter Sonderschutz stehendem unbeweglichen Kulturgut.

A.I.1 Haager Konvention

Artikel 21 Kennzeichnung von Personen

1. Die in Artikel 17 Absatz 2 b) und c) der Konvention bezeichneten Personen können eine von den zuständigen Behörden ausgegebene und abgestempelte Armbinde mit dem Erkennungszeichen tragen.

2. [1]Diese Personen haben eine besondere mit dem Erkennungszeichen versehene Identitätskarte bei sich zu führen. [2]Diese Karte muß mindestens den Familien- und Vornamen, das Geburtsdatum, den Titel oder Rang und die Funktion des Inhabers angeben. [3]Die Karte muß ein Lichtbild des Inhabers und dessen Unterschrift oder Fingerabdrücke oder beides enthalten. [4]Sie muß den Stempel der zuständigen Behörden in Prägedruck tragen.

3. [1]Jede Hohe Vertragspartei stellt ihre eigenen Identitätskarten aus, wobei sie sich nach dem diesen Ausführungsbestimmungen beispielsweise angefügtem Muster richtet. [2]Die Hohen Vertragsparteien tauschen jeweils einen Vordruck des von ihnen verwendeten Musters aus. [3]Die Identitätskarten sind möglichst jeweils in mindestens zwei Ausfertigungen auszustellen, wovon die eine von der ausstellenden Macht aufbewahrt wird.

4. Den erwähnten Personen darf die Identitätskarte oder das Recht zum Tragen der Armbinde nicht ohne berechtigten Grund entzogen werden.

Haager Konvention A.I.1

(Vorderseite)

**Identitätskarte
für mit dem Schutz von
Kulturgut betrautes Personal**

Nachname ....
Vorname ....
Geburtstag ....
Titel oder Rang ....
Tätigkeit ....

ist Inhaber dieser Karte gemäß den Bestimmungen der Haager Konvention über den Schutz von Kulturgut bei bewaffneten Konflikten vom 14. Mai 1954.

Tag der Ausstellung   Nr. der Karte

....

(Rückseite)

| Photographie des Inhabers | Unterschrift oder Fingerabdrücke oder beides |

Stempel der ausstellenden Behörde im Prägedruck

| Größe: | Augen: | Haare: |

Andere Kennzeichen

....
....
....
....
....

A.I.1a Rules for the Register of Special Protection

Rules Established by the Director-General of the United Nations Educational, Scientific and Cultural Organization, concerning the International Register of Cultural Property under Special Protection

Paris, 18 August 1956 (CL/1136(G), Annex I, September 1956)

Whereas Article 8 of the Convention for the protection of cultural property in the event of armed conflict provides that, subject to certain conditions, a limited numer of "refuges intended to shelter movable cultural property in the event of armed conflict", "centres containing monuments", and "other immovable cultural property of very great importance" may be placed under special protection and that this special protection shall be granted by the entry of the said property in the "International Register of Cultural Property und Special Protection";

Whereas Article 12 of the Regulations for the Execution of the Convention states that the Director-General of the United Nations Educational, Scientific and Cultural Organization shall maintain this Register and shall determine what details each section shall contain;

Considering Chapter II of the afore-mentioned Regulations for the Execution of the Convention, The Director-General of Unesco establishes the following rules:

Article 1
The International Register of Cultural Property under Special Protection shall be kept in French. Proper names and references to geographical features[1] and administrative units[2] shall, however, be given in the language of the country concerned in Latin characters, and shall be followed where applicable by a French translation in brackets.

Article 2
The Register shall take the form of a bound book, all the pages of which, consisting of lined paper, shall be numbered and initialled by the Director-General. Each page shall be marked "Chapitre…" (Section) and shall be divided into five columns headed as follows: (1) No. (2) "Indication du bien culturel" (Description of the cultural property). (3) "Date d'inscription" (Date of registration). (4) "Envoi des copies de l'inscription" (Despatch of copies of the entry). (5) "Radiation" (Cancellation).

Article 3
The Register shall be divided into sections, which shall not be numbered. Each section shall bear the name of the territory of a High Contracting Party, or the name of a territory for whose international relations a High Contracting Party is responsible, followed, in brackets, by the name of the High Contracting Party concerned.

Article 4
Each section shall be sub-divided into three paragraphs headed: "Refuges", "Centres monumentaux" (Centres containing monuments), "Autres biens culturels immeubles" (Other immovable cultural property).

Article 5
In column (1) shall be shown a serial number for each item of cultural property registered. In each paragraph, numbering shall begin with the figure 1.

Article 6
In column (2) shall be shown the following details, in order, for each item of cultural property accepted for entry in the Register:
1. The name, underlined, of the place where the cultural property is situated[3] followed by the names of the series of administrative units to which it pertains.[4]

---

1) For example: mountain, lake, forest.
2) For example: county, parish.
3) For example: the name of the town, village, hamlet, forest, etc.
4) For example: in France, commune, canton, département; in the United Kingdom, county, city, borough, urban district or parish; in Germany, Gemeinde, Kreis, Regierungspräsidium, etc.

2. The name, underlined, by which the cultural property is locally known;[1)] in the case of "other immovable cultural property", the character of that cultural property[2)] shall be specified, after the name.
3. The details necessary to enable the cultural property to be easily located; these to include:
   (a) in the case of a "centre containing monuments", precise indications of the boundaries of such centre, and details of the main cultural property contained therein, as defined in paragraphs (a) and (b) of Article 1 of the Convention; in the case of a "refuge" or "other immovable cultural property", where appropriate, the name of the district, and the street in which it is situated, and the number in the street;
   (b) the approximate surface area of the property, in square metres;
   (c) its approximate distance, in metres, from the seat of the smallest administrative unit (town hall) and its situation in relation thereto; any other indication helpful for locating it may also be given;[3)]
   (d) the longitude an latitude, the former in relation to the Greenwich meridian, in seconds.

Article 7
In cases within the meaning of Article 8, paragraph 5, of the Convention, the entry in column (2) shall be followed by a mention of the important military objective near which the cultural property is situated, and a note that the High Contracting Party concerned has undertaken, in the event of armed conflict, to make no use of the objective; where a port, railway station or aerodrome is concerned, there shall, in addition, be a note to the effect that the High Contracting Party has undertaken to make preparations, in time of peace, to divert all traffic therefrom in the event of armed conflict.

Article 8
In cases within the meaning of paragraph 3 of Article 11 of the Regulations for the Execution of the Convention, it shall be noted, at the end of the entry in column (2), that the registration has been made at the request of the competent Commissioner-General for Cultural Property.

Article 9
In cases where the details entered in column (2) do not fill up the entire line, the blank space remaining shall be filled in by an unbroken stroke, in ink, so as to ensure that no subsequent addition can be made. The same shall be done if there is any blank space remaining at the foot of column (2).

Article 10
In column (3) shall be shown the date of entry in the Register, for each item of cultural property.
In the case mentioned in paragraph 5 of Article 14 of the Regulations for the Execution of the Convention, the word "provisoire" (provisional) shall also be entered in column (3). If no objection has been lodged within the period stipulated in the Regulations, if an objection has been withdrawn or cancelled, or if it has failed to be confirmed following the procedure laid down in either paragraph 7 of paragraph 8 of Article 14, then the words "inscription définitive" (final registration) shall be added under the word "provisoire" together with the date.

Article 11
In column (4) shall be shown the dates of despatch of a certified copy of the entry, in the Register, of an item of cultural property, or of a series of entries in the same section of the Register; and also, where applicable, the dates of despatch of a certified copy of the declaration stating that a provisional registration has become final:
   (a) to the Secretary-General of the United Nations and to the High Contracting Parties;
   (b) where appropriate at the request of the High Contracting Party which applied for registration, to the other States mentioned in Articles 30 and 32 of the Convention;
   (c) to all States which have become High Contracting Parties after the date of despatch to the parties mentioned under (a).

---

1) For example: Refuge d'oeuvres d'art A.X.; Vieille ville, Quartier du Marché, Castel Sant'Angelo, Yeni Valide Cami, Nordisk Museet, Borobudur, Hotel Sully.
2) For example: tell, excavation site, old fortifications, castle, museum, town hall, public baths, temple, church, mosque, stupa, monastery, private house, etc.
3) For example: in the western part of the forest of...; at a height of 500 metres on the north slope of the mountain...; in the centre of the only copse in the region, etc...

A.I.1a Rules for the Register of Special Protection

Article 12

In column (5) shall be shown the dates:
(a) of any cancellation of an entry in the Register, or of a series of entries in the same section of the Register, with the reason therefor;
(b) of the despatch by registered letter, of certified copies of the record of cancellation to the Secretary-General of the United Nations and to all States which received copies of the entry in the Register.

Article 13

For all entries, amendments or cancellations made in the Register, or for all series of entries, amendments or cancellations in the same section of the Register, a record shall be drawn up containing all relevant details of the procedure followed. These records shall be signed by the Director-General, and kept in the Secretariat of Unesco.

Article 14

In the copies of the Register, furnished to the Secretary-General of the United Nations and to the High Contracting Parties in accordance with Article 12, paragraph 2, of the Regulations for the Execution of the Convention, the sections shall be published in alphabetical order by names of countries, regardless of the order of registration. Within each section, entries shall be published in the order of the paragraphs and shall follow the numbering of the entries.

The first copy of the complete Register shall be furnished two years after the date of the first entry in the Register.

Zweites Protokoll[1] zur Haager Konvention von 1954 zum Schutz von Kulturgut bei bewaffneten Konflikten

Vom 26. März 1999 (BGBl. 2009 II S. 717) (BGBl. 2012 II S. 54)

(Übersetzung)

Die Vertragsparteien –

im Bewusstsein der Notwendigkeit, den Schutz von Kulturgut bei bewaffneten Konflikten zu verbessern und ein verstärktes Schutzsystem für besonders bezeichnetes Kulturgut zu schaffen;

in Bekräftigung der Bedeutung der Bestimmungen der am 14. Mai 1954 in Den Haag beschlossenen Konvention zum Schutz von Kulturgut bei bewaffneten Konflikten und unter Hinweis auf die Notwendigkeit, diese Bestimmungen durch Maßnahmen zur verstärkten Durchführung zu ergänzen;

in dem Wunsch, den Hohen Vertragsparteien der Konvention eine Möglichkeit zu bieten, sich eingehender mit dem Schutz von Kulturgut bei bewaffneten Konflikten zu befassen, indem geeignete Verfahren geschaffen werden;

in der Erwägung, dass die Vorschriften über den Schutz von Kulturgut bei bewaffneten Konflikten die Entwicklungen des Völkerrechts widerspiegeln sollen;

in Bekräftigung des Grundsatzes, dass die Sätze des Völkergewohnheitsrechts weiterhin für Fragen gelten, die in diesem Protokoll nicht geregelt sind –

sind wie folgt übereingekommen:

Kapitel 1
Einleitung

Artikel 1 Begriffsbestimmungen
Im Sinne dieses Protokolls bedeutet
a) „Vertragspartei" einen Staat, der Vertragspartei dieses Protokolls ist;
b) „Kulturgut" Kulturgut im Sinne des Artikels 1 der Konvention;
c) „Konvention" die am 14. Mai 1954 in Den Haag beschlossene Konvention zum Schutz von Kulturgut bei bewaffneten Konflikten;
d) „Hohe Vertragspartei" einen Staat, der Vertragspartei der Konvention ist;
e) „verstärkter Schutz" das durch die Artikel 10 und 11 geschaffene System des verstärkten Schutzes;
f) „militärisches Ziel" ein Objekt, das auf Grund seiner Beschaffenheit, seines Standorts, seiner Zweckbestimmung oder seiner Verwendung wirksam zu militärischen Handlungen beiträgt und dessen gänzliche oder teilweise Zerstörung, dessen Inbesitznahme oder Neutralisierung unter den in dem betreffenden Zeitpunkt gegebenen Umständen einen eindeutigen militärischen Vorteil darstellt;
g) „unerlaubt" durch Zwangsausübung oder anderweitig unter Verstoß gegen die anwendbaren Vorschriften des innerstaatlichen Rechts des besetzten Gebiets oder des Völkerrechts;
h) „Liste" die nach Artikel 27 Absatz 1 Buchstabe b erstellte Internationale Liste des unter verstärktem Schutz stehenden Kulturguts;
i) „Generaldirektor" den Generaldirektor der UNESCO;
j) „UNESCO" die Organisation der Vereinten Nationen für Erziehung, Wissenschaft und Kultur;
k) „Erstes Protokoll" das am 14. Mai 1954 in Den Haag beschlossene Protokoll zum Schutz von Kulturgut bei bewaffneten Konflikten.

Artikel 2 Verhältnis zur Konvention
Dieses Protokoll ergänzt die Konvention in den Beziehungen zwischen den Vertragsparteien.

---

[1] Das Erste Haager Protokoll von 1954 befasst sich mit Restitutionsfragen und ist demnach unter „Ein- und Ausfuhr von Kulturgütern sowie Rückgabefragen" abgedruckt als Nr. A.III.1.

Artikel 3 Anwendungsbereich

(1) Zusätzlich zu den Bestimmungen, die in Friedenszeiten Anwendung finden, findet dieses Protokoll in den in Artikel 18 Absätze 1 und 2 der Konvention und in Artikel 22 Absatz 1 bezeichneten Situationen Anwendung.

(2) ¹Ist eine der an einem bewaffneten Konflikt beteiligten Parteien nicht durch dieses Protokoll gebunden, so bleiben dessen Vertragsparteien in ihren gegenseitigen Beziehungen durch das Protokoll gebunden. ²Sie sind durch das Protokoll auch gegenüber einem an dem Konflikt beteiligten Staat gebunden, der nicht durch das Protokoll gebunden ist, sofern er dessen Bestimmungen annimmt und solange er sie anwendet.

Artikel 4 Verhältnis von Kapitel 3 zu anderen Bestimmungen der Konvention und dieses Protokolls

Die Anwendung des Kapitels 3 dieses Protokolls berührt nicht
a) die Anwendung des Kapitels I der Konvention und des Kapitels 2 dieses Protokolls;
b) die Anwendung des Kapitels II der Konvention, außer dass zwischen den Vertragsparteien dieses Protokolls oder zwischen einer Vertragspartei und einem Staat, der dieses Protokoll nach Artikel 3 Absatz 2 annimmt und anwendet, nur die Bestimmungen über verstärkten Schutz Anwendung finden, wenn Kulturgut sowohl Sonderschutz als auch verstärkter Schutz gewährt wurde.

Kapitel 2
Allgemeine Schutzbestimmungen

Artikel 5 Sicherung des Kulturguts

Die nach Artikel 3 der Konvention in Friedenszeiten getroffenen Vorbereitungsmaßnahmen zur Sicherung des Kulturguts gegen die absehbaren Folgen eines bewaffneten Konflikts umfassen gegebenenfalls die Erstellung von Verzeichnissen, die Planung von Notfallmaßnahmen zum Schutz gegen Feuer oder Gebäudeeinsturz, die Vorbereitung der Verlagerung von beweglichem Kulturgut oder die Bereitstellung von angemessenem Schutz solchen Gutes an Ort und Stelle sowie die Bezeichnung der für die Sicherung des Kulturguts zuständigen Behörden.

Artikel 6 Respektierung des Kulturguts

Um die Respektierung des Kulturguts nach Artikel 4 der Konvention zu gewährleisten,
a) kann, wenn eine feindselige Handlung gegen Kulturgut gerichtet werden soll, eine Abweichung von den Verpflichtungen auf Grund der zwingenden militärischen Notwendigkeit nach Artikel 4 Absatz 2 der Konvention nur geltend gemacht werden, sofern und solange
  i) dieses Kulturgut durch seine Funktion zu einem militärischen Ziel gemacht worden ist und
  ii) keine andere praktische Möglichkeit besteht, einen vergleichbaren militärischen Vorteil zu erlangen, wie er sich bietet, wenn eine feindselige Handlung gegen dieses Ziel gerichtet wird;
b) kann, wenn Kulturgut für Zwecke verwendet werden soll, die es möglicherweise der Zerstörung oder Beschädigung aussetzen, eine Abweichung von den Verpflichtungen auf Grund der zwingenden militärischen Notwendigkeit nach Artikel 4 Absatz 2 der Konvention nur geltend gemacht werden, sofern und solange keine Möglichkeit besteht, zwischen dieser Verwendung des Kulturguts und einer anderen praktisch möglichen Methode zur Erlangung eines vergleichbaren militärischen Vorteils zu wählen;
c) ist die Entscheidung, eine zwingende militärische Notwendigkeit geltend zu machen, nur vom Kommandeur einer militärischen Einheit zu treffen, die der Größe nach einem Bataillon oder einer höheren Einheit oder, wenn die Umstände nichts anderes erlauben, einer kleineren Einheit entspricht;
d) muss im Fall eines Angriffs auf Grund einer nach Buchstabe a getroffenen Entscheidung eine wirksame Warnung vorausgehen, sofern die Umstände es erlauben.

Artikel 7 Vorsichtsmaßnahmen beim Angriff

Unbeschadet der durch das humanitäre Völkerrecht erforderlichen anderen Vorsichtsmaßnahmen bei der Durchführung militärischer Operationen hat jede an einem Konflikt beteiligte Vertragspartei
a) alles praktisch Mögliche zu tun, um sicherzugehen, dass die Angriffsziele kein nach Artikel 4 der Konvention geschütztes Kulturgut darstellen;

b) bei der Wahl der Angriffsmittel und -methoden alle praktisch möglichen Vorsichtsmaßnahmen zu treffen, um eine damit verbundene Beschädigung von nach Artikel 4 der Konvention geschütztem Kulturgut zu vermeiden und in jedem Fall auf ein Mindestmaß zu beschränken;
c) von jedem Angriff Abstand zu nehmen, bei dem damit zu rechnen ist, dass er auch eine Beschädigung von nach Artikel 4 der Konvention geschütztem Kulturgut verursacht, die in keinem Verhältnis zu dem erwarteten konkreten und unmittelbaren militärischen Vorteil steht, und
d) einen Angriff endgültig oder vorläufig einzustellen, wenn sich erweist,
   i) dass das Ziel nach Artikel 4 der Konvention geschütztes Kulturgut darstellt;
   ii) dass damit zu rechnen ist, dass der Angriff auch eine Beschädigung von nach Artikel 4 der Konvention geschütztem Kulturgut verursacht, die in keinem Verhältnis zu dem erwarteten konkreten und unmittelbaren militärischen Vorteil steht.

Artikel 8 Vorsichtsmaßnahmen gegen die Wirkungen von Feindseligkeiten
Soweit dies praktisch irgend möglich ist, werden die an einem Konflikt beteiligten Vertragsparteien
a) bewegliches Kulturgut aus der Umgebung militärischer Ziele entfernen oder für angemessenen Schutz an Ort und Stelle sorgen;
b) es vermeiden, militärische Ziele in der Nähe von Kulturgut anzulegen.

Artikel 9 Schutz von Kulturgut in besetztem Gebiet
(1) Unbeschadet der Artikel 4 und 5 der Konvention verbietet und verhindert eine Vertragspartei, die das Hoheitsgebiet einer anderen Vertragspartei ganz oder zum Teil besetzt hält, in Bezug auf das besetzte Gebiet Folgendes:
a) jede unerlaubte Ausfuhr oder sonstige Entfernung von Kulturgut oder die unerlaubte Übertragung des Eigentums an diesem Kulturgut;
b) jede archäologische Ausgrabung, außer wenn sie unumgänglich ist, um Kulturgut zu sichern, zu erfassen oder zu erhalten;
c) jede Veränderung von Kulturgut oder die Änderung seiner Verwendung mit dem Ziel, kulturelle, historische oder wissenschaftliche Belege zu verbergen oder zu zerstören.
(2) Archäologische Ausgrabungen, Veränderungen von Kulturgut oder Änderungen seiner Verwendung in besetztem Gebiet werden, außer wenn die Umstände es nicht erlauben, in enger Zusammenarbeit mit den zuständigen nationalen Behörden des besetzten Gebiets vorgenommen.

Kapitel 3
Verstärkter Schutz

Artikel 10 Verstärkter Schutz
Kulturgut kann unter verstärkten Schutz gestellt werden, sofern es die folgenden drei Voraussetzungen erfüllt:
a) Es handelt sich um kulturelles Erbe von höchster Bedeutung für die Menschheit;
b) es wird durch angemessene innerstaatliche Rechts- und Verwaltungsmaßnahmen geschützt, mit denen sein außergewöhnlicher kultureller und historischer Wert anerkannt und das höchste Maß an Schutz gewährleistet wird;
c) es wird weder für militärische Zwecke noch für den Schutz militärischer Anlagen verwendet, und die Vertragspartei, unter deren Kontrolle sich das Kulturgut befindet, hat in einer Erklärung bestätigt, dass es nicht dafür verwendet werden wird.

Artikel 11 Gewährung des verstärkten Schutzes
(1) Jede Vertragspartei soll dem Ausschuss eine Liste des Kulturguts vorlegen, für das sie die Gewährung des verstärkten Schutzes zu beantragen beabsichtigt.
(2) [1]Die Vertragspartei, unter deren Hoheitsgewalt oder Kontrolle sich das Kulturgut befindet, kann beantragen, dass es in die nach Artikel 27 Absatz 1 Buchstabe b zu erstellende Liste aufgenommen wird. [2]Dieser Antrag muss alle notwendigen Angaben zu den in Artikel 10 genannten Kriterien enthalten. [3]Der Ausschuss kann eine Vertragspartei auffordern, die Aufnahme eines Kulturguts in die Liste zu beantragen.
(3) [1]Andere Vertragsparteien, das Internationale Komitee vom Blauen Schild und andere nichtstaatliche Organisationen mit einschlägiger Erfahrung können dem Ausschuss ein bestimmtes Kulturgut

empfehlen. ²In diesen Fällen kann der Ausschuss beschließen, eine Vertragspartei aufzufordern, die Aufnahme dieses Kulturguts in die Liste zu beantragen.

(4) Die Rechte der Streitparteien werden weder von dem Antrag auf Aufnahme eines Kulturguts, das sich in einem Gebiet befindet, über das von mehr als einem Staat Souveränität oder Hoheitsgewalt beansprucht wird, noch von seiner Aufnahme in die Liste berührt.

(5) ¹Hat der Ausschuss einen Antrag auf Aufnahme in die Liste erhalten, so unterrichtet er alle Vertragsparteien davon. ²Die Vertragsparteien können dem Ausschuss innerhalb von sechzig Tagen ihre Einwände gegen diesen Antrag zuleiten. ³Diese Einwände dürfen nur auf der Grundlage der Kriterien des Artikels 10 erhoben werden. ⁴Sie müssen bestimmt sein und sich auf Tatsachen beziehen. ⁵Der Ausschuss prüft die Einwände, wobei er der die Aufnahme beantragenden Vertragspartei ausreichend Gelegenheit zur Antwort gibt, bevor er einen Beschluss fasst. ⁶Liegen dem Ausschuss solche Einwände vor, so bedürfen Beschlüsse über die Aufnahme in die Liste unbeschadet des Artikels 26 der Vierfünftelmehrheit der anwesenden und abstimmenden Mitglieder.

(6) Bei der Beschlussfassung über einen Antrag soll der Ausschuss den Rat von staatlichen und nichtstaatlichen Organisationen sowie von einzelnen Sachverständigen einholen.

(7) Ein Beschluss über die Gewährung oder Ablehnung des verstärkten Schutzes darf nur auf der Grundlage der Kriterien des Artikels 10 gefasst werden.

(8) Kommt der Ausschuss zu dem Ergebnis, dass die die Aufnahme in die Liste beantragende Vertragspartei die Kriterien des Artikels 10 Buchstabe b nicht erfüllen kann, so kann der Ausschuss in Ausnahmefällen beschließen, den verstärkten Schutz zu gewähren, sofern die beantragende Vertragspartei einen Antrag auf internationale Unterstützung nach Artikel 32 stellt.

(9) ¹Mit Beginn der Feindseligkeiten kann eine an dem Konflikt beteiligte Vertragspartei in dringenden Fällen für Kulturgut unter ihrer Hoheitsgewalt oder Kontrolle den verstärkten Schutz beantragen, indem sie den Antrag dem Ausschuss zuleitet. ²Der Ausschuss übermittelt diesen Antrag unverzüglich allen an dem Konflikt beteiligten Vertragsparteien. ³In diesem Fall prüft der Ausschuss die Einwände der betroffenen Vertragsparteien in einem beschleunigten Verfahren. ⁴Der Beschluss über die vorläufige Gewährung des verstärkten Schutzes wird so bald wie möglich gefasst; er bedarf unbeschadet des Artikels 26 der Vierfünftelmehrheit der anwesenden und abstimmenden Mitglieder. ⁵Der vorläufige verstärkte Schutz kann vom Ausschuss gewährt werden, bevor das Ergebnis des normalen Verfahrens zur Gewährung des verstärkten Schutzes feststeht, sofern Artikel 10 Buchstaben a und c eingehalten wird.

(10) Kulturgut wird vom Ausschuss der verstärkte Schutz gewährt, sobald es in die Liste aufgenommen worden ist.

(11) Der Generaldirektor notifiziert dem Generalsekretär der Vereinten Nationen und allen Vertragsparteien unverzüglich jeden Beschluss des Ausschusses über die Aufnahme von Kulturgut in die Liste.

Artikel 12 Unverletzlichkeit des Kulturguts unter verstärktem Schutz

Die an einem Konflikt beteiligten Vertragsparteien gewährleisten die Unverletzlichkeit des unter verstärktem Schutz stehenden Kulturguts, indem sie dieses Gut weder zum Ziel eines Angriffs machen noch das Gut oder seine unmittelbare Umgebung zur Unterstützung militärischer Handlungen verwenden.

Artikel 13 Verlust des verstärkten Schutzes

(1) Kulturgut unter verstärktem Schutz verliert diesen nur,
a) sofern der Schutz nach Artikel 14 ausgesetzt oder aufgehoben wird oder
b) sofern und solange das Gut auf Grund seiner Verwendung ein militärisches Ziel geworden ist.

(2) Unter den Umständen des Absatzes 1 Buchstabe b darf das Gut nur dann Ziel eines Angriffs sein,
a) wenn der Angriff das einzige praktisch mögliche Mittel ist, die in Absatz 1 Buchstabe b bezeichnete Verwendung zu unterbinden;
b) wenn bei der Wahl der Angriffsmittel und -methoden alle praktisch möglichen Vorsichtsmaßnahmen getroffen werden, um diese Verwendung zu unterbinden und eine Beschädigung des Kulturguts zu vermeiden oder in jedem Fall auf ein Mindestmaß zu beschränken;
c) wenn – sofern die Umstände es nicht auf Grund der Erfordernisse der unmittelbaren Selbstverteidigung verbieten –

i) der Angriff auf der höchsten Befehlsebene angeordnet wird,
ii) eine wirksame Warnung an die gegnerischen Streitkräfte vorausgegangen ist, in der die Beendigung der in Absatz 1 Buchstabe b bezeichneten Verwendung verlangt wird, und
iii) den gegnerischen Streitkräften ausreichend Zeit eingeräumt wird, die Verwendung aufzugeben.

Artikel 14 Aussetzen oder Aufheben des verstärkten Schutzes
(1) Erfüllt Kulturgut die Kriterien des Artikels 10 nicht mehr, so kann der Ausschuss den Status des verstärkten Schutzes aussetzen oder aufheben, indem er das Kulturgut von der Liste streicht.
(2) ¹Bei einem schweren Verstoß gegen Artikel 12 durch die Verwendung von Kulturgut unter verstärktem Schutz zur Unterstützung militärischer Handlungen kann der Ausschuss den Status des verstärkten Schutzes aussetzen. ²Sind diese Verstöße anhaltend, so kann der Ausschuss den Status des verstärkten Schutzes ausnahmsweise aufheben, indem er das Kulturgut von der Liste streicht.
(3) Der Generaldirektor notifiziert dem Generalsekretär der Vereinten Nationen und allen Vertragsparteien dieses Protokolls unverzüglich jeden Beschluss des Ausschusses über die Aussetzung oder Aufhebung des verstärkten Schutzes.
(4) Bevor der Ausschuss einen solchen Beschluss fasst, gibt er den Vertragsparteien Gelegenheit zur Stellungnahme.

Kapitel 4
Strafrechtliche Verantwortlichkeit und Gerichtsbarkeit

Artikel 15 Schwere Verstöße gegen dieses Protokoll
(1) Eine Straftat im Sinne dieses Protokolls begeht, wer vorsätzlich und unter Verstoß gegen die Konvention oder dieses Protokoll
a) Kulturgut unter verstärktem Schutz zum Ziel eines Angriffs macht;
b) Kulturgut unter verstärktem Schutz oder seine unmittelbare Umgebung zur Unterstützung militärischer Handlungen verwendet;
c) Kulturgut, das nach der Konvention und diesem Protokoll geschützt ist, in großem Ausmaß zerstört oder sich aneignet;
d) Kulturgut, das nach der Konvention und diesem Protokoll geschützt ist, zum Ziel eines Angriffs macht oder
e) Kulturgut, das nach der Konvention geschützt ist, stiehlt, plündert, unterschlägt oder böswillig beschädigt.
(2) ¹Jede Vertragspartei trifft die notwendigen Maßnahmen, um die in diesem Artikel genannten Straftaten nach innerstaatlichem Recht als Straftaten zu umschreiben und um diese Straftaten mit angemessenen Strafen zu bedrohen. ²Dabei beachten die Vertragsparteien allgemeine Rechtsgrundsätze und das Völkerrecht einschließlich der Vorschriften, welche die individuelle strafrechtliche Verantwortlichkeit auf Personen ausdehnen, welche die Handlung nicht unmittelbar verübt haben.

Artikel 16 Gerichtsbarkeit
(1) Unbeschadet des Absatzes 2 trifft jede Vertragspartei die notwendigen gesetzgeberischen Maßnahmen, um ihre Gerichtsbarkeit über die in Artikel 15 genannten Straftaten in den folgenden Fällen zu begründen:
a) wenn die Straftat im Hoheitsgebiet dieses Staates begangen wird;
b) wenn die verdächtige Person eine Angehörige dieses Staates ist;
c) wenn sich bei den in Artikel 15 Absatz 1 Buchstaben a bis c genannten Straftaten die verdächtige Person in ihrem Hoheitsgebiet befindet.
(2) Im Hinblick auf die Ausübung der Gerichtsbarkeit und unbeschadet des Artikels 28 der Konvention
a) schließt dieses Protokoll weder aus, dass nach anwendbarem innerstaatlichen Recht oder Völkerrecht individuelle strafrechtliche Verantwortlichkeit begründet oder Gerichtsbarkeit ausgeübt wird, noch berührt es die Ausübung der Gerichtsbarkeit nach dem Völkergewohnheitsrecht;
b) entsteht für die Mitglieder der Streitkräfte und die Angehörigen eines Nichtvertragsstaats, mit Ausnahme derjenigen seiner Staatsangehörigen, die in den Streitkräften eines Vertragsstaats Dienst tun, nach diesem Protokoll keine individuelle strafrechtliche Verantwortlichkeit, und

macht dieses Protokoll es nicht zur Pflicht, die Gerichtsbarkeit über solche Personen zu begründen oder sie auszuliefern; dies gilt nicht, wenn ein Staat, der nicht Vertragspartei dieses Protokolls ist, dessen Bestimmungen nach Artikel 3 Absatz 2 annimmt und anwendet.

Artikel 17 Strafverfolgung

(1) Die Vertragspartei, in deren Hoheitsgebiet sich die Person, die einer der in Artikel 15 Absatz 1 Buchstaben a bis c genannten Straftat verdächtigt wird, befindet, unterbreitet den Fall, wenn sie diese Person nicht ausliefert, ausnahmslos und unverzüglich ihren zuständigen Behörden zum Zweck der strafrechtlichen Verfolgung in einem Verfahren nach ihrem innerstaatlichen Recht oder nach den einschlägigen Regeln des Völkerrechts, falls diese anwendbar sind.

(2) Unbeschadet der einschlägigen Regeln des Völkerrechts, sofern anwendbar, werden jeder Person, gegen die ein Verfahren im Zusammenhang mit der Konvention oder diesem Protokoll eingeleitet wird, in allen Verfahrensstufen faire Behandlung und ein faires Gerichtsverfahren in Übereinstimmung mit dem innerstaatlichen Recht und dem Völkerrecht gewährleistet; keinesfalls genießt eine solche Person weniger vorteilhafte Garantien, als ihr durch das Völkerrecht zuerkannt werden.

Artikel 18 Auslieferung

(1) ¹Die in Artikel 15 Absatz 1 Buchstaben a bis c genannten Straftaten gelten als in jeden zwischen Vertragsparteien vor dem Inkrafttreten dieses Protokolls geschlossenen Auslieferungsvertrag einbezogene auslieferungsfähige Straftaten. ²Die Vertragsparteien verpflichten sich, diese Straftaten in jeden künftig zwischen ihnen zu schließenden Auslieferungsvertrag aufzunehmen.

(2) Erhält eine Vertragspartei, welche die Auslieferung vom Bestehen eines Vertrags abhängig macht, ein Auslieferungsersuchen von einer anderen Vertragspartei, mit der sie keinen Auslieferungsvertrag hat, so steht es der ersuchten Vertragspartei frei, dieses Protokoll als Rechtsgrundlage für die Auslieferung in Bezug auf die in Artikel 15 Absatz 1 Buchstaben a bis c genannten Straftaten anzusehen.

(3) Vertragsparteien, welche die Auslieferung nicht vom Bestehen eines Vertrags abhängig machen, anerkennen unter sich die in Artikel 15 Absatz 1 Buchstaben a bis c genannten Straftaten als auslieferungsfähige Straftaten vorbehaltlich der im Recht der ersuchten Vertragspartei vorgesehenen Bedingungen.

(4) Die in Artikel 15 Absatz 1 Buchstaben a bis c genannten Straftaten werden für die Zwecke der Auslieferung zwischen den Vertragsparteien nötigenfalls so behandelt, als seien sie nicht nur an dem Ort, an dem sie sich ereignet haben, begangen worden, sondern auch in den Hoheitsgebieten der Vertragsparteien, die ihre Gerichtsbarkeit nach Artikel 16 Absatz 1 begründet haben.

Artikel 19 Rechtshilfe

(1) Die Vertragsparteien gewähren einander die weitestgehende Hilfe im Zusammenhang mit Ermittlungen sowie Straf- und Auslieferungsverfahren, die in Bezug auf die in Artikel 15 genannten Straftaten eingeleitet werden, einschließlich der Hilfe bei der Beschaffung der ihnen zur Verfügung stehenden und für das Verfahren erforderlichen Beweismittel.

(2) ¹Die Vertragsparteien erfüllen ihre Verpflichtungen nach Absatz 1 im Einklang mit den zwischen ihnen bestehenden Verträgen oder sonstigen Übereinkünften über Rechtshilfe. ²In Ermangelung solcher Verträge oder Übereinkünfte gewähren die Vertragsparteien einander Rechtshilfe nach ihrem innerstaatlichen Recht.

Artikel 20 Gründe für die Verweigerung der Rechtshilfe

(1) ¹Für die Zwecke der Auslieferung werden die in Artikel 15 Absatz 1 Buchstaben a bis c genannten Straftaten und für die Zwecke der Rechtshilfe die in Artikel 15 genannten Straftaten nicht als politische Straftaten, als mit politischen Straftaten zusammenhängende oder als auf politischen Beweggründen beruhende Straftaten angesehen. ²Folglich darf ein Ersuchen um Auslieferung oder Rechtshilfe, das auf solchen Straftaten beruht, nicht allein mit der Begründung verweigert werden, dass es sich um eine politische Straftat, um eine mit einer politischen Straftat zusammenhängende oder um eine auf politischen Beweggründen beruhende Straftat handle.

(2) Dieses Protokoll ist nicht so auszulegen, als enthalte es eine Verpflichtung zur Auslieferung oder Rechtshilfe, wenn die ersuchte Vertragspartei ernstliche Gründe für die Annahme hat, dass das Auslieferungsersuchen wegen der in Artikel 15 Absatz 1 Buchstaben a bis c genannten Straftaten oder das Ersuchen um Rechtshilfe in Bezug auf die in Artikel 15 genannten Straftaten gestellt worden ist, um eine Person wegen ihrer Rasse, ihrer Religion, ihrer Staatsangehörigkeit, ihrer ethnischen Herkunft

oder ihrer politischen Anschauungen zu verfolgen oder zu bestrafen, oder dass die Lage dieser Person aus einem dieser Gründe erschwert werden könnte, wenn dem Ersuchen stattgegeben würde.

Artikel 21 Maßnahmen bezüglich anderer Verstöße
Unbeschadet des Artikels 28 der Konvention trifft jede Vertragspartei die notwendigen gesetzgeberischen sowie Verwaltungs- und Disziplinarmaßnahmen, um folgende Handlungen, wenn vorsätzlich verübt, zu unterbinden:
a) jede Verwendung von Kulturgut unter Verstoß gegen die Konvention oder dieses Protokoll;
b) jede unerlaubte Ausfuhr oder sonstige Entfernung von Kulturgut oder die unerlaubte Übertragung des Eigentums an Kulturgut aus besetztem Gebiet unter Verstoß gegen die Konvention oder dieses Protokoll.

Kapitel 5
Schutz von Kulturgut bei bewaffneten Konflikten nicht internationalen Charakters

Artikel 22 Bewaffnete Konflikte nicht internationalen Charakters
(1) Dieses Protokoll findet im Fall eines bewaffneten Konflikts, der keinen internationalen Charakter hat und im Hoheitsgebiet einer Vertragspartei stattfindet, Anwendung.
(2) Dieses Protokoll findet nicht auf Fälle innerer Unruhen und Spannungen wie Tumulte, vereinzelt auftretende Gewalttaten und andere ähnliche Handlungen Anwendung.
(3) Dieses Protokoll darf nicht zur Beeinträchtigung der Souveränität eines Staates oder der Verantwortung der Regierung herangezogen werden, mit allen rechtmäßigen Mitteln die öffentliche Ordnung im Staat aufrechtzuerhalten oder wiederherzustellen oder die nationale Einheit und territoriale Unversehrtheit des Staates zu verteidigen.
(4) Dieses Protokoll berührt nicht den Vorrang der Gerichtsbarkeit der Vertragspartei, in deren Hoheitsgebiet ein bewaffneter Konflikt stattfindet, der keinen internationalen Charakter hat, über die in Artikel 15 genannten Verstöße.
(5) Dieses Protokoll darf nicht zur Rechtfertigung einer wie immer begründeten unmittelbaren oder mittelbaren Einmischung in den bewaffneten Konflikt oder in die inneren oder äußeren Angelegenheiten der Vertragspartei herangezogen werden, in deren Hoheitsgebiet dieser Konflikt stattfindet.
(6) Die Anwendung dieses Protokolls auf die in Absatz 1 bezeichnete Situation berührt nicht die Rechtsstellung der an einem Konflikt beteiligten Parteien.
(7) Die UNESCO kann den an dem Konflikt beteiligten Parteien ihre Dienste anbieten.

Kapitel 6
Institutionelle Fragen

Artikel 23 Tagungen der Vertragsparteien
(1) Die Tagung der Vertragsparteien wird zur selben Zeit einberufen wie die Generalkonferenz der UNESCO und in Abstimmung mit der Tagung der Hohen Vertragsparteien, wenn eine solche vom Generaldirektor einberufen worden ist.
(2) Die Tagung der Vertragsparteien gibt sich eine Geschäftsordnung.
(3) Die Tagung der Vertragsparteien hat folgende Aufgaben:
a) Wahl der Mitglieder des Ausschusses nach Artikel 24 Absatz 1;
b) Billigung der vom Ausschuss nach Artikel 27 Absatz 1 Buchstabe a erstellten Richtlinien;
c) Bereitstellung von Richtlinien für die Verwendung des Fonds durch den Ausschuss und Überwachung der Verwendung;
d) Prüfung des vom Ausschuss nach Artikel 27 Absatz 1 Buchstabe d vorgelegten Berichts;
e) Erörterung von Problemen im Zusammenhang mit der Anwendung dieses Protokolls und gegebenenfalls Abgabe von Empfehlungen.
(4) Auf Antrag von mindestens einem Fünftel der Vertragsparteien hat der Generaldirektor eine außerordentliche Tagung der Vertragsparteien einzuberufen.

A.I.1b Zweites Haager Protokoll

Artikel 24 Ausschuss für den Schutz von Kulturgut bei bewaffneten Konflikten
(1) ¹Hiermit wird der Ausschuss für den Schutz von Kulturgut bei bewaffneten Konflikten eingesetzt. ²Ihm gehören zwölf Vertragsparteien an; sie werden von der Tagung der Vertragsparteien gewählt.
(2) Der Ausschuss tritt einmal im Jahr zu einer ordentlichen Sitzung zusammen und immer dann, wenn er es für notwendig erachtet, zu außerordentlichen Sitzungen.
(3) Bei der Festlegung der Zusammensetzung des Ausschusses sind die Vertragsparteien bemüht, eine ausgewogene Vertretung der verschiedenen Regionen und Kulturen der Welt zu gewährleisten.
(4) Die Vertragsparteien, die Mitglieder des Ausschusses sind, wählen zu ihren Vertretern Personen, die Sachverständige auf dem Gebiet des Kulturerbes, der Verteidigung oder des Völkerrechts sind, und sie sind bestrebt, in gegenseitiger Abstimmung zu gewährleisten, dass im Ausschuss insgesamt angemessener Sachverstand auf allen diesen Gebieten vereinigt ist.

Artikel 25 Amtszeit
(1) Eine Vertragspartei wird für vier Jahre in den Ausschuss gewählt; eine unmittelbare Wiederwahl ist einmal zulässig.
(2) ¹Unbeschadet des Absatzes 1 endet die Amtszeit der Hälfte der bei der ersten Wahl gewählten Mitglieder mit Ablauf der ersten ordentlichen Tagung der Vertragsparteien nach der Tagung, auf der sie gewählt wurden. ²Diese Mitglieder werden vom Präsidenten der Tagung nach der ersten Wahl durch das Los ermittelt.

Artikel 26 Geschäftsordnung
(1) Der Ausschuss gibt sich eine Geschäftsordnung.
(2) ¹Der Ausschuss ist beschlussfähig, wenn die Mehrheit der Mitglieder anwesend ist. ²Die Beschlüsse des Ausschusses bedürfen der Zweidrittelmehrheit seiner abstimmenden Mitglieder.
(3) Die Mitglieder dürfen an der Abstimmung über Beschlüsse im Zusammenhang mit Kulturgut, das von einem bewaffneten Konflikt berührt wird, an dem sie beteiligt sind, nicht teilnehmen.

Artikel 27 Aufgaben
(1) Der Ausschuss hat folgende Aufgaben:
a)   Erstellung von Richtlinien zur Durchführung dieses Protokolls;¹⁾
b)   Gewährung, Aussetzung oder Aufhebung des verstärkten Schutzes für Kulturgut und Erstellung, Aktualisierung und Förderung der Liste des Kulturguts unter verstärktem Schutz;²⁾
c)   Beobachtung und Überwachung der Durchführung dieses Protokolls und Förderung der Erfassung von Kulturgut unter verstärktem Schutz;
d)   Prüfung der Berichte der Vertragsparteien und Stellungnahme dazu, erforderlichenfalls deren Klärung und Erstellung eines eigenen Berichts über die Durchführung dieses Protokolls für die Tagung der Vertragsparteien;
e)   Entgegennahme und Prüfung von Anträgen auf internatio nale Unterstützung nach Artikel 32;
f)   Festlegung der Verwendung des Fonds;
g)   Wahrnehmung anderer Aufgaben, die ihm von der Tagung der Vertragsparteien zugewiesen werden.
(2) Die Aufgaben des Ausschusses werden in Zusammenarbeit mit dem Generaldirektor wahrgenommen.
(3) ¹Der Ausschuss arbeitet mit internationalen und nationalen staatlichen und nichtstaatlichen Organisationen zusammen, die ähnliche Ziele verfolgen wie die Konvention, das Erste Protokoll und dieses Protokoll. ²Zur Unterstützung der Wahrnehmung seiner Aufgaben kann der Ausschuss bedeutende Fachorganisationen wie etwa solche, die formelle Beziehungen zur UNESCO unterhalten, einschließlich des Internationalen Komitees vom Blauen Schild (ICBS) und der Organisationen, aus denen es gebildet wird, einladen, in beratender Eigenschaft an seinen Sitzungen teilzunehmen. ³Vertreter der Internationalen Studienzentrale für die Erhaltung und Restaurierung von Kulturgut (Römische Zentrale) ICCROM) und des Internationalen Komitees vom Roten Kreuz (IKRK) können ebenfalls eingeladen werden, in beratender Eigenschaft teilzunehmen.

---

1) Die Guidelines sind abgedruckt als Nr. A.I.1c.
2) Siehe hierzu die aktuelle Liste der Objekte unter verstärktem Schutz aus 2019, abrufbar unter: http://www.unesco.org/new/en/culture/themes/armed-conflict-and-heritage/protection/enhanced-protection/.

Artikel 28 Sekretariat
Dem Ausschuss steht das Sekretariat der UNESCO zur Seite, das die Dokumentation des Ausschusses und die Tagesordnung seiner Sitzungen vorbereitet und für die Durchführung seiner Beschlüsse verantwortlich ist.

Artikel 29 Fonds für den Schutz von Kulturgut bei bewaffneten Konflikten
(1) Hiermit wird ein Fonds für die folgenden Zwecke errichtet:
a) Bereitstellung finanzieller oder anderer Hilfe zur Unterstützung von vorbereitenden und sonstigen Maßnahmen, die in Friedenszeiten unter anderem nach Artikel 5, Artikel 10 Buchstabe b und Artikel 30 getroffen werden, und
b) Bereitstellung finanzieller oder anderer Hilfe im Zusammenhang mit Notfallmaßnahmen oder vorläufigen oder sonstigen Maßnahmen, die getroffen werden, um Kulturgut während eines bewaffneten Konflikts oder während der Bergung und Sicherung unmittelbar nach Ende der Feindseligkeiten unter anderem nach Artikel 8 Buchstabe a zu schützen.

(2) Der Fonds stellt ein Treuhandvermögen im Sinne der Finanzordnung der UNESCO dar.
(3) [1]Die Auszahlungen aus dem Fonds werden nur für die vom Ausschuss nach den Richtlinien im Sinne des Artikels 23 Absatz 3 Buchstabe c beschlossenen Zwecke verwendet. [2]Der Ausschuss kann Beiträge entgegennehmen, die nur für ein bestimmtes Programm oder Vorhaben verwendet werden sollen, sofern er die Durchführung dieses Programms oder Vorhabens beschlossen hat.
(4) Die Mittel des Fonds bestehen aus
a) freiwilligen Beiträgen der Vertragsparteien;
b) Beiträgen, Spenden oder Vermächtnissen
    i) anderer Staaten,
    ii) der UNESCO oder anderer Organisationen des Systems der Vereinten Nationen,
    iii) sonstiger zwischenstaatlicher oder nichtstaatlicher Organisationen und
    iv) von Einrichtungen des öffentlichen oder privaten Rechts oder von Einzelpersonen;
c) den für den Fonds anfallenden Zinsen;
d) Mitteln, die durch Sammlungen und Einnahmen aus Veranstaltungen zu Gunsten des Fonds aufgebracht werden, und
e) allen sonstigen Mitteln, die durch die auf den Fonds anzuwendenden Richtlinien genehmigt sind.

Kapitel 7
Verbreitung von Informationen und internationale Unterstützung

Artikel 30 Verbreitung
(1) Die Vertragsparteien bemühen sich unter Einsatz geeigneter Mittel, insbesondere durch Erziehungs- und Informationsprogramme, die Würdigung und Respektierung von Kulturgut durch ihre gesamte Bevölkerung zu stärken.
(2) Die Vertragsparteien verbreiten dieses Protokoll so weit wie möglich, und zwar sowohl in Friedenszeiten als auch in Zeiten eines bewaffneten Konflikts.
(3) [1]Die militärischen oder zivilen Dienststellen, die in Zeiten eines bewaffneten Konflikts Verantwortlichkeiten bei der Anwendung dieses Protokolls zu übernehmen haben, müssen mit seinem Wortlaut voll und ganz vertraut sein. [2]Zu diesem Zweck werden die Vertragsparteien gegebenenfalls
a) Richtlinien und Anweisungen zum Schutz von Kulturgut in ihre Militärvorschriften aufnehmen;
b) in Zusammenarbeit mit der UNESCO und einschlägigen staatlichen und nichtstaatlichen Organisationen Ausbildungs- und Erziehungsprogramme in Friedenszeiten entwickeln und durchführen;
c) einander über den Generaldirektor Informationen über die nach den Buchstaben a und b erlassenen Gesetze oder Verwaltungsvorschriften und die nach den Buchstaben a und b getroffenen Maßnahmen übermitteln;
d) einander über den Generaldirektor so bald wie möglich die Gesetze und Verwaltungsvorschriften übermitteln, die sie zur Sicherstellung der Anwendung dieses Protokolls erlassen werden.

Artikel 31   Internationale Zusammenarbeit
Die Vertragsparteien verpflichten sich, im Fall schwerer Verstöße gegen dieses Protokoll gemeinsam durch den Ausschuss oder einzeln in Zusammenarbeit mit der UNESCO und den Vereinten Nationen und im Einklang mit der Charta der Vereinten Nationen zu handeln.

Artikel 32   Internationale Unterstützung
(1) Eine Vertragspartei kann beim Ausschuss internationale Unterstützung für Kulturgut unter verstärktem Schutz und Unterstützung für die Vorbereitung, Entwicklung oder Durchführung der in Artikel 10 bezeichneten Gesetze, Verwaltungsvorschriften und Maßnahmen beantragen.

(2) Eine an dem Konflikt beteiligte Partei, die nicht Vertragspartei dieses Protokolls ist, aber nach Artikel 3 Absatz 2 dessen Bestimmungen annimmt und anwendet, kann beim Ausschuss geeignete internationale Unterstützung beantragen.

(3) Der Ausschuss beschließt Vorschriften über das Antragsverfahren in Bezug auf internationale Unterstützung und bestimmt die Form, welche die Unterstützung annehmen kann.

(4) Die Vertragsparteien werden ermutigt, über den Ausschuss den Vertragsparteien oder den an einem Konflikt beteiligten Parteien, die darum ersuchen, technische Unterstützung aller Art zu gewähren.

Artikel 33   Unterstützung durch die UNESCO
(1) [1]Die Vertragsparteien können um die technische Unterstützung der UNESCO bei der Organisierung der Schutzmaßnahmen für ihr Kulturgut, wie etwa Vorbereitungen zur Sicherung von Kulturgut, vorbeugende und organisatorische Maßnahmen für Notfälle und nationale Verzeichnisse des Kulturguts, oder in Zusammenhang mit jedem anderen Problem, das sich aus der Anwendung dieses Protokolls ergibt, nachsuchen. [2]Die UNESCO gewährt diese Unterstützung im Rahmen ihrer Zielsetzung und ihrer Mittel.

(2) Die Vertragsparteien werden ermutigt, technische Unterstützung auf zwei- oder mehrseitiger Ebene zu gewähren.

(3) Die UNESCO kann in dieser Hinsicht den Vertragsparteien von sich aus Vorschläge unterbreiten.

Kapitel 8
Durchführung dieses Protokolls

Artikel 34   Schutzmächte
Dieses Protokoll wird unter Mitwirkung der Schutzmächte angewandt, die mit der Wahrnehmung der Interessen der an dem Konflikt beteiligten Vertragsparteien betraut sind.

Artikel 35   Schlichtungsverfahren
(1) Die Schutzmächte stellen ihre guten Dienste in allen Fällen zur Verfügung, in denen sie dies im Interesse des Kulturguts für angezeigt erachten, insbesondere wenn zwischen den an dem Konflikt beteiligten Vertragsparteien über die Anwendung oder Auslegung dieses Protokolls Meinungsverschiedenheiten bestehen.

(2) [1]Zu diesem Zweck kann jede der Schutzmächte entweder auf Einladung einer Vertragspartei oder des Generaldirektors oder von sich aus den an dem Konflikt beteiligten Vertragsparteien eine Zusammenkunft ihrer Vertreter und insbesondere der für den Schutz des Kulturguts verantwortlichen Behörden vorschlagen, gegebenenfalls im Hoheitsgebiet eines Staates, der nicht an dem Konflikt beteiligt ist. [2]Die an dem Konflikt beteiligten Vertragsparteien sind gehalten, den ihnen gemachten Vorschlägen von Zusammenkünften Folge zu leisten. [3]Die Schutzmächte schlagen den an dem Konflikt beteiligten Vertragsparteien eine Persönlichkeit, die einem Staat angehört, der nicht an dem Konflikt beteiligt ist, oder eine vom Generaldirektor bezeichnete Persönlichkeit zur Genehmigung vor; diese wird aufgefordert, an der Zusammenkunft als Vorsitzender teilzunehmen.

Artikel 36   Schlichtung ohne Schutzmächte
(1) In einem Konflikt, bei dem keine Schutzmächte bestellt sind, kann der Generaldirektor seine guten Dienste anbieten oder durch eine andere Art der Schlichtung oder Vermittlung handeln, um die Meinungsverschiedenheit beizulegen.

(2) Auf Einladung einer Vertragspartei oder des Generaldirektors kann der Vorsitzende des Ausschusses den an einem Konflikt beteiligten Vertragsparteien eine Zusammenkunft ihrer Vertreter und ins-

besondere der für den Schutz des Kulturguts verantwortlichen Behörden vorschlagen, gegebenenfalls im Hoheitsgebiet eines Staates, der nicht an dem Konflikt beteiligt ist.

Artikel 37 Übersetzung und Berichte
(1) Die Vertragsparteien übersetzen dieses Protokoll in ihre Amtssprachen und übermitteln dem Generaldirektor diese amtlichen Übersetzungen.
(2) Die Vertragsparteien legen dem Ausschuss alle vier Jahre einen Bericht über die Durchführung dieses Protokolls vor.

Artikel 38 Verantwortung der Staaten
Die Bestimmungen dieses Protokolls über die individuelle strafrechtliche Verantwortlichkeit berühren nicht die völkerrechtliche Verantwortung der Staaten, einschließlich der Pflicht, Reparationen zu leisten.

Kapitel 9
Schlussbestimmungen

Artikel 39 Sprachen
Dieses Protokoll ist in arabischer, chinesischer, englischer, französischer, russischer und spanischer Sprache abgefasst, wobei jeder Wortlaut gleichermaßen verbindlich ist.

Artikel 40 Unterzeichnung
[1]Dieses Protokoll trägt das Datum des 26. März 1999. [2]Es liegt vom 17. Mai 1999 bis zum 31. Dezember 1999 in Den Haag für alle Hohen Vertragsparteien zur Unterzeichnung auf.

Artikel 41 Ratifikation, Annahme oder Genehmigung
(1) Dieses Protokoll bedarf der Ratifikation, Annahme oder Genehmigung durch die Hohen Vertragsparteien, die dieses Protokoll unterzeichnet haben, nach Maßgabe ihrer eigenen verfassungsrechtlichen Verfahren.
(2) Die Ratifikations-, Annahme- oder Genehmigungsurkunden werden beim Generaldirektor hinterlegt.

Artikel 42 Beitritt
(1) Dieses Protokoll steht den anderen Hohen Vertragsparteien ab dem 1. Januar 2000 zum Beitritt offen.
(2) Der Beitritt erfolgt durch Hinterlegung einer Beitrittsurkunde beim Generaldirektor.

Artikel 43 Inkrafttreten
(1) Dieses Protokoll tritt drei Monate nach Hinterlegung von zwanzig Ratifikations-, Annahme-, Genehmigungs- oder Beitrittsurkunden in Kraft.
(2) Danach tritt es für jede Vertragspartei drei Monate nach Hinterlegung ihrer Ratifikations-, Annahme-, Genehmigungsoder Beitrittsurkunde in Kraft[1)2)].

Artikel 44 Inkrafttreten während bewaffneter Konflikte
[1]Die in den Artikeln 18 und 19 der Konvention bezeichneten Situationen bewirken, dass die vor oder nach Beginn der Feindseligkeiten oder der Besetzung von an dem Konflikt beteiligten Parteien hinterlegten Ratifikations-, Annahme-, Genehmigungsund Beitrittserklärungen mit sofortiger Wirkung in Kraft treten. [2]In diesen Fällen macht der Generaldirektor auf dem schnellsten Weg die in Artikel 46 vorgesehenen Mitteilungen.

Artikel 45 Kündigung
(1) Jede der Vertragsparteien kann dieses Protokoll kündigen.
(2) Die Kündigung wird durch eine Urkunde notifiziert, die beim Generaldirektor hinterlegt wird.
(3) [1]Die Kündigung wird ein Jahr nach Eingang der Kündigungsurkunde wirksam. [2]Ist jedoch die kündigende Vertragspartei bei Ablauf dieser Frist an einem bewaffneten Konflikt beteiligt, so wird die

---

1) Das Protokoll ist für die Bundesrepublik Deutschland am **25.2.2010** in Kraft getreten; siehe hierzu die Bekanntmachung über das Inkrafttreten des Zweiten Protokolls zur Haager Konvention vom 14. Mai 1954 zum Schutz von Kulturgut bei bewaffneten Konflikten v. 14.1.2011 (BGBl. II S. 486, ber. S. 1357).
2) Liste der Vertragsstaaten und Ratifikationen: http://www.unesco.org/eri/la/convention.asp?KO-13637&language=E.

A.I.1b Zweites Haager Protokoll

Kündigung erst nach Einstellung der Feindseligkeiten oder nach Abschluss der Rückführung des Kulturguts wirksam, je nachdem, welcher Zeitpunkt der spätere ist.

Artikel 46 Notifikationen
Der Generaldirektor benachrichtigt alle Hohen Vertragsparteien und die Vereinten Nationen von der Hinterlegung aller in den Artikeln 41 und 42 vorgesehenen Ratifikations-, Annahme-, Genehmigungs- und Beitrittsurkunden sowie von den in Artikel 45 vorgesehenen Kündigungen.

Artikel 47 Registrierung bei den Vereinten Nationen
Dieses Protokoll wird auf Ersuchen des Generaldirektors nach Artikel 102 der Charta der Vereinten Nationen beim Sekretariat der Vereinten Nationen registriert.

Zu Urkund dessen haben die gehörig befugten Unterzeichneten dieses Protokoll unterschrieben. Geschehen zu Den Haag am 26. März 1999 in einer Urschrift, die im Archiv der UNESCO hinterlegt wird; beglaubigte Abschriften werden allen Hohen Vertragsparteien übermittelt.

Guidelines for the Implementation of the 1999 Second Protocol to the Hague Convention of 1954 for the Protection of Cultural Property in the Event of Armed Conflict

Paris, 16 December 2019[1)]

I INTRODUCTION

I.A The Guidelines for the Implementation of the 1999 Second Protocol to the Hague Convention of 1954 for the Protection of Cultural Property in the Event of Armed Conflict

1. The main purpose of the present document (hereinafter "the Guidelines") is to provide a concise and practical tool to facilitate the implementation of the Second Protocol to the Hague Convention of 1954 for the Protection of Cultural Property in the Event of Armed Conflict (hereinafter "the Second Protocol") by its Parties and to provide guidance to the Committee for the Protection of Cultural Property in the Event of Armed Conflict (hereinafter "the Committee") and the Secretariat of UNESCO (hereinafter "the Secretariat") for the fulfilment of their functions as established by the Second Protocol.
2. The Guidelines attempt to embody the best practices in the implementation of the Second Protocol.
3. In accordance with Article 27(1)(a) of the Second Protocol, the Guidelines are developed by the Committee. Following Article 23(3)(b) of the Second Protocol, they are subsequently endorsed by the Meeting of the Parties. The Guidelines may be revised to reflect the decisions and recommendations adopted by the Meeting of the Parties and the Committee.

Article 27(1)(a) of the Second Protocol
Article 23(3)(b) of the Second Protocol

I.B Scope of application of the Second Protocol

4. The Second Protocol, which entered into force on 9 March 2004, is an international agreement supplementing the Hague Convention of 1954 for the Protection of Cultural Property in the Event of Armed Conflict (hereinafter "the Convention") in relations between the Parties. It aims to improve the protection of cultural property in the event of armed conflict as defined by the Convention. Thus, for the purposes of the Second Protocol, the term "cultural property" covers, irrespective of origin or ownership:
   a. Movable or immovable property of great importance to the cultural heritage of every people, such as monuments of architecture, art or history, whether religious or secular; archaeological sites; groups of buildings which, as a whole, are of historical or artistic interest; works of art; manuscripts, books and other objects of artistic, historical or archaeological interest; as well as scientific collections and important collections of books or archives or of reproductions of the property defined above;
   b. Buildings whose main and effective purpose is to preserve or exhibit the movable cultural property defined in sub-paragraph (a) such as museums, large libraries and depositories of archives, and refuges intended to shelter, in the event of armed conflict, the movable cultural property defined in sub-paragraph (a);

Article 2 of the Second Protocol
Article 1(b) of the Second Protocol and

Article 1 of the Convention

---

1) Quelle: http://www.unesco.org/new/fileadmin/MULTIMEDIA/HQ/CLT/pdf/1999-SecondProtocol_Guidelines_2019_En g.pdf. Von einem Abdruck der Anlagen wurde aus technischen Gründen abgesehen.

	c. Centres containing a large amount of cultural property as defined in sub-paragraphs (a) and (b), to be known as "centres containing monuments".	
5.	In addition to the provisions which shall be implemented in time of peace, the Second Protocol applies: a. In the event of declared war or of any other armed conflict which may arise between two or more of the Parties, even if the state of war is not recognized by one or more of them. b. To all cases of partial or total occupation of the territory of a Party, even if the said occupation meets with no armed resistance. c. In the event of an armed conflict not of an international character, occurring within the territory of one of the Parties.	Article 3(1) of the Second Protocol
6.	The Second Protocol supplements the Convention by reinforcing the provisions related to the safeguarding of and respect for cultural property in the event of armed conflict.	Articles 5 – 9 of the Second Protocol
7.	The Second Protocol introduces a regime of enhanced protection. It stipulates that cultural property of the greatest importance for humanity can be placed under enhanced protection. Enhanced protection is granted to the cultural property from the moment of its entry in the List of Cultural Property under Enhanced Protection (hereinafter "the List") as decided by the Committee.	Articles 10 – 14 of the Second Protocol
8.	The Second Protocol defines serious violations and obliges Parties to adopt appropriate legislation to make these violations to the Second Protocol criminal offences under their national law, notwithstanding the responsibility of States under international law. It also covers other obligations of Parties related to criminal responsibility and jurisdiction.	Articles 15 – 21 of the Second Protocol
9.	The Second Protocol establishes the Committee composed of twelve Parties, which is essentially responsible for the management of enhanced protection, the monitoring and supervision of the implementation of the Second Protocol and the granting of international assistance. It also establishes the Fund for the Protection of Cultural Property in the Event of Armed Conflict (hereinafter "the Fund"). Finally, the Second Protocol provides for periodic meetings of the Parties.	Chapter 6 of the Second Protocol

I.C Relationship between the Convention and the Second Protocol

10.	Only the High Contracting Parties to the Convention may become Parties to the Second Protocol. The Second Protocol supplements the Convention in mutual relations between the Parties. As an exception, however, if the cultural property has been granted both special protection as defined in the Convention and enhanced protection, the provisions of special protection will be replaced by the provisions of enhanced protection.	Articles 2 and 4(b) of the Second Protocol
11.	The Second Protocol does not affect the rights and obligations of the High Contracting Parties to the Convention.[1] In mutual relations between the High Contracting Parties to the Convention, the Parties remain bound by the Convention alone. In mutual relations between States Parties to the Convention and the Second Protocol, they are bound by both instruments. In mutual relations between a State Party to the Convention and the Second Protocol and a High Contracting	Article 34 of the 1969 Vienna Convention on the Law of Treaties Article 30(4) of the 1969 Vienna Convention on the Law of Treaties

---

1) Final Act of the Diplomatic Conference on the Second Protocol to the Hague Convention for the Protection of Cultural Property in the Event of Armed Conflict, Summary report, Annex 1, para 11, http://unesdoc.unesco.org/images/0013/001332/133243eo.pdf.

Party to the Convention, they are bound only by the provisions of the Convention.

I.D Key actors of the Second Protocol

12. The key actors of the Second Protocol are:
    a. Parties;
    b. the Meeting of the Parties;
    c. the Committee; and,
    d. UNESCO.
13. The key actors of the Second Protocol are encouraged to ensure the participation of a wide variety of stakeholders, including international and national governmental and non- governmental organizations having objectives similar to those of the Convention and its two Protocols. In particular, such participation may address, amongst other issues related to the Second Protocol, the national implementation, awareness-raising and dissemination of the Second Protocol both within target groups and the general public, offering technical advice related to safeguarding of cultural property or, in case of the constitutent bodies of the International Committee of the Blue Shield, on providing advice with regard to the granting of enhanced protection.

Parties

14. The High Contracting Parties to the Convention are encouraged to become Parties to the Second Protocol by depositing an instrument of ratification, acceptance, approval or accession with the Director-General of UNESCO (hereinafter "the Director-General"). Model instruments for that are provided by the Secretariat. — *Articles 41 and 42 of the Second Protocol*
15. The Second Protocol enters into force for each new Party three months after the deposit of its instrument of ratification, acceptance, approval or accession. As an exception to the three-month rule, situations of armed conflict, both of an international or non-international character, give immediate effect to ratifications, acceptances, approvals or accessions to the Second Protocol deposited by the parties to the conflict either before or after the beginning of hostilities or occupation. — *Articles 43 and 44 of the Second Protocol*
16. The list of Parties is available online at the following address: www.unesco.org.

Meeting of the Parties

17. The Meeting of the Parties is the highest body established by the Second Protocol in order to promote its implementation. Its functions are: — *Article 23 of the Second Protocol*
    a. to elect the Members of the Committee;
    b. to endorse the Guidelines developed by the Committee;
    c. to provide guidelines for and supervise the use of the Fund by the Committee;
    d. to consider the reports submitted by the Committee;
    e. to discuss any problem related to the application of the Second Protocol, and make recommendations, as appropriate; and,
    f. to assign to the Committee functions other than those mentioned in Article 27 (1) (a – f) of the Second Protocol.
18. The Meeting of the Parties is convened at the same time as the General Conference of UNESCO, and in co-ordination with the Meeting of the High Contracting Parties to the Convention, if such a meeting has been

called by the Director-General. At the request of at least one-fifth of the Parties, the Director-General convenes an Extraordinary Meeting of the Parties.

The Committee

19. The Committee is the intergovernmental executive body entitled by the Second Protocol to perform, in co-operation with the Director-General, the following functions: ⎯ Articles 24 – 27 of the Second Protocol
    a. to develop Guidelines for the implementation of the Second Protocol;
    b. to grant, suspend or cancel enhanced protection for cultural property and to establish, maintain and promote the List;
    c. to monitor and supervise the implementation of the Second Protocol and to promote the identification of cultural property under enhanced protection;
    d. to consider and comment on reports of the Parties, to seek clarifications as required, and to prepare its own report on the implementation of the Second Protocol for the Meeting of the Parties;
    e. to receive and consider requests for international assistance from Parties as provided by the Second Protocol;
    f. to determine the use of the Fund; and,
    g. to execute other functions assigned to it by the Meeting of the Parties.

20. In addition to its functions, the Committee adopts rules for the submission of requests for international assistance. It also defines the forms this international assistance may take. The Committee also conveys technical assistance provided by Parties or parties to a given conflict. ⎯ Article 32(3) of the Second Protocol / Article 32(4) of the Second Protocol

21. The Committee is composed of twelve Parties which, paying due regard to equitable geographical distribution, are elected by the Meeting of the Parties for four-year terms. Immediate re-election of a Party is possible only once. Parties that are members of the Committee choose as their representatives persons qualified in the fields of cultural heritage, defence or international law, and they endeavour, in consultation with one another, to ensure that the Committee as a whole contains adequate expertise in all these fields. ⎯ Article 24 of the Second Protocol

22. The Committee meets once a year in ordinary session and in extraordinary sessions whenever it deems necessary. The Committee conducts its business in accordance with its Rules of Procedure. ⎯ Article 24 of the Second Protocol

23. The Committee adopts and updates its own Rules of Procedure. The Committee may define its internal annual working schedule as well as provide other relevant guidance concerning the practical conduct of business under these Rules. Guidance provided by the Rules of Procedure and concerning Parties will be distributed through the Secretariat. ⎯ Article 26(1) of the Second Protocol

24. The Committee also co-operates with international and national governmental and non-governmental organizations having objectives similar to those of the Convention and its two Protocols. To assist in the implementation of its functions, the Committee may invite to its meetings, and consult within the framework of granting enhanced protection, in an advisory capacity, eminent professional organizations such as those which have formal relations with UNESCO, including the International Committee of the Blue Shield (ICBS) and its constituent bodies (the Co-ordinating Council of Audiovisual Archi- ⎯ Article 27(3) of the Second Protocol

ves Associations (CCAAA), the International Council on Archives (ICA), the International Council of Museums (ICOM), the International Council on Monuments and Sites (ICOMOS) and the International Federation of Library Associations and Institutions (IFLA)). Representatives of the International Centre for the Study of the Preservation and Restoration of Cultural Property (Rome Centre) (ICCROM) and of the International Committee of the Red Cross (ICRC) may also be invited to attend in an advisory capacity.

UNESCO

25. The Committee is assisted by the Secretariat which prepares the Committee's documentation and the agenda for its meetings and has the responsibility for the implementation of its decisions. The Secretariat receives, translates and distributes all official documents of the Committee and arranges interpretation as needed. The Secretariat also performs other necessary functions so that the Committee may perform its work properly. — Article 28 of the Second Protocol
Rules of Procedure of the Committee

26. In addition, UNESCO provides technical assistance to the Parties in organizing the protection of their cultural property. The nature and terms of such assistance are described in detail in Chapter VI. — Article 33 of the Second Protocol

II. GENERAL PROVISIONS REGARDING PROTECTION
II.A Safeguarding of cultural property

27. Preparatory measures taken in time of peace for the safeguarding of cultural property against the foreseeable effects of an armed conflict pursuant to Article 3 of the Convention include, as appropriate: — Article 5 of the Second Protocol
    – the preparation of inventories;
    – the planning of emergency measures for protection against fire or structural collapse;
    – the preparation for the removal of movable cultural property or the provision for adequate in situ protection of such property; and,
    – the designation of competent authorities responsible for the safeguarding of cultural property.

    As the above list of preparatory measures is not exhaustive, Parties are also encouraged to consider other appropriate preparatory measures consistent with the purposes of the Second Protocol.

28. The Committee encourages the Parties to cooperate both at international and national level with the competent non-governmental organisations as well as to exchange information on national safeguarding policies and practices.

29. In order to harmonise the documentation related to all cultural property protected under the Second Protocol, the Committee encourages the Parties to apply, as appropriate, the relevant provisions of the Guidelines regarding the nomination dossier for enhanced protection to documentation of all cultural property protected under the Second Protocol.

II.B Precautions against the effects of hostilities

30. The Parties are obliged, to the maximum extent feasible: — Article 8 of the Second Protocol

- to remove movable cultural property from the vicinity of military objectives or to provide adequate in situ protection; and,
- to avoid locating military objectives near cultural property.

III. ENHANCED PROTECTION
III.A The granting of enhanced protection
Criteria

31. The Committee may place cultural property under enhanced protection provided that it meets the three criteria laid down in the Second Protocol. — Article 10 of the Second Protocol

Greatest importance for humanity

32. While considering whether cultural property is of greatest importance for humanity, the Committee will evaluate, case by case, its exceptional cultural significance, and/or its uniqueness, and/or if its destruction would lead to irretrievable loss for humanity. — Article 10(a) of the Second Protocol

33. Cultural property of national, regional or universal value may have exceptional cultural significance. This significance may be deduced from the following indicative criteria:
    - it is an exceptional cultural property bearing testimony to one or more periods of the development of humankind at the national, regional or global level;
    - it represents a masterpiece of human creativity;
    - it bears an exceptional testimony to a cultural tradition or to a civilization which is living or which has disappeared;
    - it exhibits an important interchange of human achievements, over a span of time or within a cultural area of the world on developments in arts and sciences;
    - it has a central significance to the cultural identity of societies concerned.

34. Cultural property is considered to be unique if there is no other comparable cultural property that is of the same cultural significance. The unique character may be deduced from a variety of indicative criteria including:
    a. age;
    b. history;
    c. community;
    d. representativity;
    e. location;
    f. size and dimension;
    g. shape and design;
    h. purity and authenticity in style;
    i. integrity;
    j. context;
    k. artistic craftsmanship;
    l. aesthetic value;
    m. scientific value.

35. The criterion of irretrievable loss for humanity is met if the damage or destruction of the cultural property in question would result in the impoverishment of the cultural diversity or cultural heritage of humankind.

36. It is presumed that the Committee, subject to other relevant considerations, will consider that immovable cultural property inscribed on the World Heritage List satisfies the condition of greatest importance for humanity.
37. In the case of documentary heritage, the Committee will consider the fact that the cultural property is inscribed on UNESCO's Memory of the World Register.

Adequate domestic legal and administrative measures of protection

38. The cultural property is protected by adequate domestic legal and administrative measures recognizing its exceptional cultural and historic value and ensuring the highest level of protection. The protection accorded to cultural property of exceptional value takes into account the obligations of the Parties under Article 12 of the Second Protocol. *Articles 10(b) and 12 of the Second Protocol*
39. Such measures ensure that the cultural property is protected adequately against any kind of negligence, decay or destruction even in time of peace. In evaluating whether cultural property is protected by adequate domestic legal and administrative measures recognizing its exceptional cultural and historic value and ensuring the highest level of protection, the Committee considers, in particular, national measures intended for:
    - the identification and safeguarding of cultural property proposed for enhanced protection in accordance with Article 5 of the Second Protocol;
    - due consideration of the protection of the cultural property proposed for enhanced protection in military planning and military training programs; and,
    - appropriate criminal legislation providing for the repression of, and jurisdiction over, offenses committed against cultural property under enhanced protection within the meaning of, and in accordance with, Chapter 4 of the Second Protocol.
40. The domestic legal and administrative measures of protection are only adequate if they are effective in practice. The Committee therefore examines, inter alia, whether they are based on a coherent system of protection and achieve the expected results. *Article 32(1) of the Second Protocol*
41. A Party may request international assistance from the Committee in the preparation, development or implementation of the laws, administrative provisions and other measures to be fulfilled.

No military use

42. The cultural property concerned must not be used for military purposes or to shield military sites. The Party which has control over the cultural property has to make a declaration confirming that the cultural property will not be used for military purposes or to shield military sites. In accordance with Article 3 of the Second Protocol, these provisions also apply in times of peace. *Article 10(c) of the Second Protocol*
43. The guarding of cultural property by armed custodians specially empowered to do so, or the presence, in the vicinity of such cultural property, of police forces normally responsible for the maintenance of public order, is not deemed "use for military purposes". *Article 8(4) of the Convention*

Procedure for granting enhanced protection

44. The Parties are entitled and encouraged to submit to the Committee requests for the granting of enhanced protection to cultural property

A.I.1c Guidelines Zweites Haager Protokoll

under their jurisdiction or control. The Committee, which establishes and maintains the List, decides in each particular case whether the criteria set out above are met. To facilitate the granting of enhanced protection, the Secretariat prepared an enhanced protection request form (Annex I).

45. The request for the granting of enhanced protection is sent by the Permanent Delegation to UNESCO of the Party to the Committee through the Secretariat. Requests need to be received by the Secretariat by 1 March of each year at the latest in order to be considered at the upcoming meeting of the Committee. Requests received after this deadline will be considered during the next meeting of the Committee. The above-mentioned date does not apply to requests for provisional enhanced protection.

46. The Secretariat acknowledges the receipt, checks for completeness and registers the request. The Secretariat requests any additional information from the Party, as appropriate, and all such information must be received, preferably, in a single submission of one complete file within two months of the date of the request from the Secretariat. The Secretariat forwards complete requests to the Bureau for prima facie consideration together with a review of completeness prepared by the Secretariat.

47. The Bureau may consult organisations with relevant expertise for evaluation of the request. The Bureau will forward the request (including the evaluation) to the Committee and may propose a decision. — Article 11(5) of the Second Protocol

48. Once the Committee has received a request, it informs all Parties of the request for inclusion in the List. Parties may submit a representation concerning the request to the Committee within 60 days. These representations may only be made on the basis of the criteria mentioned in Article 10 and will be specific and related to facts. — Article 11(5) of the Second Protocol

49. The Committee considers the representations, providing the requesting Party with a reasonable opportunity to respond before making a decision.

50. In exceptional cases, if the cultural property does not meet the criteria laid down in Article 10(b), the Committee requires the Party which has control or jurisdiction over the cultural property to submit a request for international assistance under Article 32. — Articles 11(2) and (8) of the Second Protocol; Article 32(1) of the Second Protocol

51. The Committee may decide to invite a Party to request inclusion of cultural property in the List. Other Parties as well as ICBS and other NGO's with relevant expertise may recommend cultural property to the Committee for inclusion in the List. In such cases, the Committee may decide to invite the Party concerned to request inclusion of that property in the List.

Tentative lists

52. For the purposes of the Guidelines the term "tentative list" means a list of cultural property for which a Party intends to request the granting of enhanced protection. Parties are encouraged to submit tentative lists in order to facilitate the Committee's maintenance and update of the List as well as the management of requests for international assistance. Parties may amend their tentative lists as appropriate. However, the fact that cultural property has not been included in the tentative — Article 11(1) of the

list does not prevent the Party from requesting the granting of enhanced protection for such cultural property.

53. The tentative list, which contains a brief description of the cultural property, is submitted by the Party to the Committee through the Secretariat.

Second Protocol

Content of a request

54. A request submitted by a Party meets the following requirements in order to be considered by the Committee:

Article 11(2) of the Second Protocol

a. Identification of the cultural property

55. The boundaries of an immovable cultural property and, as appropriate, its immediate surroundings are clearly defined, and the Universal Transverse Mercator ("UTM") co-ordinates of the boundaries of such property are marked on the map(s) attached to the request. Maps are sufficiently detailed to determine precisely which area of land and/or building(s) are nominated. Movable cultural property is identified by its detailed descriptions and sufficient images.

56. The location of the cultural property (including shelters or other storage for movable cultural property) should be indicated by reference to its geographical location. At a minimum, the approximate central point of each cultural property should be indicated by a pair of coordinates in the Universal Transverse Mercator system. Boundaries of a wider property could be indicated by providing a list of coordinates indicating the course of the property boundary. In case of movable cultural property this information refers to the location where this cultural property is stored or intended to be stored.

b. Description of the cultural property

57. The Party provides the relevant information and documentation on the cultural property concerned, including those on the present state of conservation, the appearance of the cultural property, as well as its history and development. This includes a description on how the cultural property has reached its present form and the significant changes that it has undergone. The information provides the facts needed to support and substantiate the argument that the cultural property meets the criterion of being of greatest importance for humanity under Article 10(a).

c. Protection of the cultural property

58. The Party includes a list of the legal and administrative measures regarding the adequate protection and maintenance of the cultural property. It provides a detailed analysis with regard to the practical implementation of the protection measures and the safeguarding of the highest level of protection. Legislative, regulatory, and/or institutional texts, or an abstract of the texts, are attached to the request. The information provides the facts needed to support and substantiate the argument that the cultural property meets the criterion of being adequately protected under Article 10(b).

d. Use of the cultural property

59. The Party describes the use of the cultural property. It provides all relevant information to establish that the property is not used for military purposes or to shield military sites. In addition, a declaration,

A.I.1c Guidelines Zweites Haager Protokoll 64

issued by the national authority which has been authorized by the State concerned as competent for this matter, confirms that the cultural property and, as appropriate, its immediate surroundings will not be used for military purposes or to shield military sites is attached to the request. The information provides the facts needed to support and substantiate the argument that the cultural property meets the criterion laid down in Article 10(c).

e. Information regarding responsible authorities

60. Detailed contact information of responsible authorities is provided in the request.

f. Signature on behalf of the Party

61. The request is duly signed by the Party's competent authorities.

g. Format of the request

62. Parties are invited to submit their requests both in paper and electronic format provided by the Secretariat. Requests may be submitted in one of the two working languages of the Secretariat.

Emergency request

63. If a Party submits a request upon the outbreak of hostilities the request is to be considered as an "emergency request" under Article 11 (9). The emergency request has to meet the requirements a., b., d., e., f. and g. as set forth in paragraphs 54 – 62.	Article 11(9) of the Second Protocol

Withdrawal of a request

64. A Party may withdraw in writing a request it has submitted at any time prior to the Committee's session at which it is scheduled to be examined. The Party can resubmit a request for the cultural property, which will be considered as a new request.

Information about a change of situation

65. The Party informs the Committee of any change affecting the cultural property concerned to meet the criteria set out in Article 10 in order to allow an update and, where appropriate, a reconsideration of the status of enhanced protection and/or a new decision by the Committee.

Decisions of the Committee on Enhanced Protection

66. The Committee decides by a majority of two-thirds of its members present and voting whether a cultural property shall be granted or denied enhanced protection or whether the request should be referred or deferred. In two exceptional cases, a majority of four-fifths of the members of the Committee present and voting is needed: i) when Parties make a representation to the Committee on the basis of another Party's request for inclusion in the List; and ii) when a Party requests enhanced protection on an emergency basis.	Article 26(2) of the Second Protocol Rules of Procedure of the Committee Article 11(5) and 11(9) of the Second Protocol
67. Members of the Committee may not participate in the voting on any decisions relating to cultural property affected by an armed conflict to which they are parties.	Article 26(3) of the Second Protocol

68. When deciding to grant enhanced protection to a cultural property, the Committee adopts a "Statement of Inclusion of the Property on the List of Cultural Property under Enhanced Protection" (hereinafter "the Statement"). The Statement confirms that all criteria laid down in Article 10 are met. Therefore, a summary of the Committee's reasoning regarding the questions whether the cultural property is of greatest importance for humanity, including the assessments of its adequate domestic protection and its non-military use, are included. The Statement is the basis for the further protection of the cultural property. At the time of decision, the Committee may also make other recommendations concerning the protection of the cultural property. Enhanced protection is granted from the moment of the entry of the cultural property in the List.
69. The Committee immediately informs the Director-General of its decision to include cultural property in the List. The Director-General in turn notifies without delay the Secretary- General of the United Nations and all Parties to the Second Protocol of the decision of the Committee.   Article 11(11) of the Second Protocol
70. If the Committee decides to deny enhanced protection to a cultural property, it will generally not accept an identical request.
71. Requests which the Committee decides to refer back to the Party for additional information and/or documentation may be resubmitted to the Committee for examination. A referred request which is not presented to the Committee within three years following the original decision of the Committee will be considered as a new request when it is resubmitted for examination, following the regular procedure.
72. The Committee may decide to defer a request for more in- depth assessment, study or a substantial revision by the Party. If the Party decides to resubmit the revised request, this request will then be re-valuated according to the regular procedure.

Decision on enhanced protection in exceptional cases

73. The Committee may grant enhanced protection in exceptional cases to a cultural property which does not meet the criteria laid down in Article 10(b) provided that the Party submits a request for international assistance under Article 32 of the Second Protocol. The Committee may advise the Party concerned with regard to the compliance with Article 10(b). To grant enhanced protection in such cases, the Committee follows the procedure outlined in paragraphs 66 – 72. However, the Statement points out that the criteria laid down in Article 10(a) and 10(c) are met and that the Party has already submitted a request.   Article 11(8) of the Second Protocol
74. If the criteria set forth in Article 10(b) are not met within a given period of time by the Party, the enhanced protection may be suspended by the Committee.

Decision on provisional enhanced protection

75. Upon the outbreak of hostilities, the decision on provisional enhanced protection on an emergency basis is taken by the Committee as soon as possible. Such a decision can only grant provisional enhanced protection pending the outcome of the regular procedure. The provisional enhanced protection will only be granted if the criteria laid down in Article 10(a) and 10(c) are met. When deciding to grant provisional enhanced protection to a cultural property, the Committee adopts   Article 11(9) of the Second Protocol

a "Statement of Provisional Inclusion of the Property on the List of Cultural Property under Enhanced Protection". This statement summarizes the Committee's reasoning regarding the question whether the outbreak of hostilities does not allow for a regular procedure and whether the cultural property meets the criteria of Article 10(a) and 10(c). Provisional enhanced protection is granted from the moment of the entry of the cultural property in the List.

III.B The List

76. The Committee establishes, maintains and promotes the List. The List consists of two divisions:
    a. Division 1: Cultural property under enhanced protection; and
    b. Division 2: Cultural property under provisional enhanced protection.

    Article 27(1)(b) of the Second Protocol

77. Each cultural property is inscribed in one of the two divisions. Information about the cultural property and the scope of its protection is provided as follows:
    a. name and identification of the cultural property;
    b. description of the cultural property;
    c. location, boundaries and, as appropriate, immediate surroundings of the cultural property;
    d. other relevant information.
78. The information provided for in the above-mentioned paragraph (d) includes, inter alia, the date of entry in the List, descriptions of an exceptional or emergency situation, decisions and recommendations made by the Committee, and conditions set forth by the Committee such as time periods, as well as suspensions or cancellations.
79. The List is made available by the Secretariat through appropriate media.

III.C The loss of enhanced protection

80. Cultural property loses its enhanced protection under any of the three below-mentioned conditions:
    a. the enhanced protection is suspended by the Committee;
    b. the enhanced protection is cancelled by the Committee;
    c. the cultural property has become, by its use, a military objective.

    Article 13(1)(a) and (1)(b) of the Second Protocol

81. While the third condition does not need any further clarification, since the notion of "military objective" is defined in Article 1(f), the conditions of suspension and cancellation are to be set forth by the Committee.

    Article 1(f) of the Second Protocol

Suspension

82. The suspension is a provisional measure which does not result in a permanent loss of the enhanced protection but in an interruption of the protection when the criteria for granting it are no longer met. When the criteria are met again, the Committee will decide whether to resume the enhanced protection.

    Article 14 of the Second Protocol

83. The Committee may suspend the enhanced protection under two conditions:

    Article 14(1) and (2) of the Second Protocol

a. if the cultural property does no longer meet any of the criteria laid down in Article 10; or
　　b. if there is a serious violation of Article 12 in relation to cultural property under enhanced protection arising from its use in support of military action.
84. Since the suspension is a provisional measure, the Committee may only suspend the enhanced protection if the criteria laid down in Article 10, which are no longer met at the time of decision, may be fulfilled again at a later date. This applies to the criteria laid down in Articles 10(b) and (c), since the criteria of both adequate domestic protection and the non-military use may not be established for a certain period of time, but may be re-established at a later stage.
85. The Committee may suspend the enhanced protection if the cultural property or its immediate surroundings are used in support of military action.

Cancellation

86. Cancellation is a definitive measure. It leads to the permanent loss of the enhanced protection. The Committee may cancel enhanced protection under two conditions: Article 14(1) and (2) of the Second Protocol
　　a. the cultural property no longer meets any of the criteria laid down in Article 10; or,
　　b. there is a continuous and serious violation of Article 12 in relation to cultural property under enhanced protection arising from its use in support of military action.
87. Since cancellation is a definitive measure, the Committee may only cancel the enhanced protection if the criteria laid down in Article 10, which are no longer met, cannot be fulfilled at a later date.   Article 14(1) of the Second Protocol
88. The Committee may exceptionally cancel the enhanced protection if the cultural property is continuously used in support of military action. The condition of "continuity" is met if the use exceeds the time period of six months and if there is no evidence that such use will end.   Article 14(2) of the Second Protocol

III.D Procedure on suspension and cancellation

89. Before suspending or cancelling the enhanced protection, the Committee informs the Party of its intention to suspend or cancel the enhanced protection and provides its reasons. The Committee sets forth a time period for the reply of the Party. This period does not exceed three months.
90. The Committee immediately informs the Director-General on its decision to suspend or cancel the enhanced protection of cultural property. The Director-General informs, without any delay, the Secretary-General of the United Nations and all Parties to the Protocol of the Committee's decision to suspend or cancel the enhanced protection of cultural property.   Article 14(3) of the Second Protocol

Suspension

91. If the Committee suspends the enhanced protection, the cultural property is not removed from the List. However, the suspension is duly noted in the List.
92. The Committee will decide whether to re-establish the enhanced protection if the Party proves that the criteria laid down in Articles 10(b)

or (c) are met again or that the cultural property is no longer used for military purposes or to shield military sites. The re-establishment of the enhanced protection is duly noted in the List.

Cancellation

93. If the Committee cancels the enhanced protection, the cultural property is deleted from the List. The Party may only submit a new request for enhanced protection following the regular procedure.

III.E The Distinctive Emblem for cultural property under enhanced protection and modalities for its use

94. Without prejudice to the provisions of the 1954 Hague Convention and the Regulations for its execution relating to the marking of cultural property under general protection and to the marking of cultural property under special protection, a distinctive emblem (hereinafter the "Distinctive Emblem") is created for the exclusive marking of cultural property under enhanced protection.
95. "Marking of cultural property under enhanced protection" means marking as defined ratione materiae in paragraph 103 of these Guidelines.
96. The considerations related to the visibility of the Distinctive Emblem guide the Parties in their choice of modalities for placing of the Distinctive Emblem.

Modalities for using the Distinctive Emblem

97. The Distinctive Emblem should be used in accordance with the modalities for its use, as set out below. Under these Guidelines, the expression "modalities for using the Distinctive Emblem" covers the basic principles relating to the Distinctive Emblem, the modalities for its use and measures protecting it from misuse.

Basic principles relating to the Distinctive Emblem

98. The Distinctive Emblem is intended to ensure the recognition and identification of cultural property under enhanced protection, particularly during the conduct of hostilities, in order to ensure the effectiveness of the provisions of the Second Protocol and, more particularly, to contribute to the effectiveness of Article 12 on the "Immunity of cultural property under enhanced protection". The Distinctive Emblem is also intended to ensure legal certainty with regard to criminal responsibility of belligerents in order to ensure reasonable implementation of Article 15 (1) of the Second Protocol. Under these Guidelines, "reasonable implementation" means establishing as criminal offences under domestic criminal law of the Parties serious violations of the Second Protocol as set forth in Article 15 (2) of the Second Protocol.
99. The marking of cultural property under enhanced protection is declaratory of the enhanced protection granted for cultural property pursuant to a decision taken by the Committee. The marking of cultural property, while contributing to the effectiveness of enhanced protection, has no constitutive effect.
100. On account of its use for protective purposes and in order to ensure its visibility, the Distinctive Emblem – without prejudice to the use of

other relevant emblems, in particular the World Heritage emblem, to mark cultural property – should be affixed alone without any other logo and/or emblem, due consideration being taken of a combatant's field of vision when directing an attack, be it from the land, sea or air, during hostilities.
101. The Distinctive Emblem must be used in accordance with the relevant rules of international humanitarian law and the modalities ratione materiae and ratione temporis for its use specified in these Guidelines. All use of the Distinctive Emblem that is inconsistent with observance of the prescribed rules should be considered to be misuse.
102. When the Committee grants enhanced protection for cultural property under the normal procedure, it encourages the Party that has jurisdiction or control over that cultural property to mark it by using the Distinctive Emblem for cultural property under enhanced protection. When the Committee is requested to grant enhanced protection under the emergency procedure, it requests the Party that has jurisdiction or control over the cultural property to mark the property.

Modalities for using the Distinctive Emblem

Use ratione materiae
103. The Distinctive Emblem should be used only to mark cultural property under enhanced protection. It may not be used for purposes – e.g. commercial, non-commercial – other than those specified in these Guidelines.
104. The use of the Distinctive Emblem for cultural property under enhanced protection is without prejudice to the provisions of the 1954 Hague Convention and the Regulation for its execution with regard to the application of the "transport under special protection".

Use ratione temporis
105. In peacetime, Parties that have jurisdiction or control over cultural property under enhanced protection may make preparations to mark such property by using the Distinctive Emblem.
106. In times of armed conflict – i.e. from the outbreak of hostilities leading to the advent of the armed conflict until the end of the armed conflict, including occupation – the Parties to the conflict are encouraged to mark cultural property under enhanced protection by using the Distinctive Emblem.
107. Without prejudice to Article 17 paragraph (2) of the 1954 Hague Convention, in the event of suspension or cancellation of enhanced protection by the Committee, Parties that have jurisdiction or control over the cultural property concerned by said suspension or cancellation should remove the Distinctive Emblem that had been used to mark the property.

Modalities for placing the Distinctive Emblem

108. The Distinctive Emblem should be placed and the extent of its visibility determined at the discretion of the Parties' competent authorities.
109. As cultural property under enhanced protection is primarily part and parcel of heritage that is of the greatest importance to humanity, the Distinctive Emblem should be placed on the cultural property in a manner benefitting the property.

110. The Parties' resources permitting, technological developments will determine the means used – in times of peace and in times of armed conflict – to place the Distinctive Emblem on cultural property, including movable property, under enhanced protection.

Protection of the Distinctive Emblem from misuse

111. Use of the Distinctive Emblem that does not comply with principles set out in these Guidelines should be avoided.
112. The Parties are encouraged to disseminate the information concerning the Distinctive Emblem and the modalities for its use both within their civilian population and among military personnel.
113. The Parties are encouraged to enact legislation on the protection of the Distinctive Emblem and the modalities for its use and/or take other measures, as appropriate, on the protection of the Distinctive Emblem and the modalities for its use.

IV. DISSEMINATION

114. The Second Protocol requires Parties to disseminate as widely as possible its provisions in time of peace and in time of armed conflict. Parties undertake by appropriate means to strengthen appreciation and respect for cultural property by their entire population. Particular attention should be paid to encouraging educational and informational programmes. Article 30 of the Second Protocol
115. Any military or civilian authority which, in time of armed conflict, assumes responsibilities with respect to the application of the Second Protocol, has to be fully acquainted with the text thereof. To this end, the Parties are required to, as appropriate:
    - incorporate guidelines and instructions on the protection of cultural property in their military regulations, doctrine and training materials,
    - develop and implement, in cooperation with UNESCO and relevant governmental and non-governmental organizations, peacetime training and educational programmes,
    - communicate to one another, through the Director-General, information on laws, administrative provisions and measures taken under the preceding paragraphs, and
    - communicate to one another, as soon as possible, through the Director-General, the laws and administrative provisions which they have adopted to ensure the application of the Second Protocol.

V. MONITORING THE IMPLEMENTATION OF THE SECOND PROTOCOL

116. The Second Protocol strengthens the protection of cultural property by establishing a monitoring mechanism for its implementation. According to the Second Protocol, the Parties are required to report to the Committee on measures taken by them to implement the Protocol. The Committee will in turn consider and comment on these reports and prepare its own report to the Meeting of the Parties. Article 27(1)(d) of the Second Protocol

V.A Periodic Reports of the Parties

117. As High Contracting Parties to the Convention and Parties to the Second Protocol are required to report every four years on the implementation of the named instruments, Parties to the Second Protocol are invited to follow the same four-year reporting period as for the Convention.[1]) While reports concerning the implementation of the Convention are addressed to the Director-General, periodic reports on the Second Protocol are addressed to the Committee through the Secretariat.
   Article 26(2) of the Convention
   Article 37(2) of the Second Protocol

118. In order to facilitate the implementation of the provisions of the Second Protocol by the Parties, the Committee encourages Parties to submit their reports on the implementation of the Second Protocol together with their report on the implementation of the Convention. The periodic reports duly inform on the legal, administrative and practical implementation measures adopted by the Parties.

119. The Committee requests Parties to cover the following items in their periodic reports on the implementation of the Second Protocol:
   - Implementation of general provisions regarding protection
     - To inform on peacetime preparatory measures for the safeguarding of cultural property undertaken or envisaged to be undertaken.
     - Parties which are occupying powers, to inform how the provisions of the Protocol concerning the protection of cultural property in occupied territory are complied with.

   Chapter 2 of the Second Protocol

   - Implementation of provisions regarding enhanced protection
     - To inform whether the Party intends to request the inclusion of cultural property in the List.
     - To inform on the use of the emblem, as stated in Chapter III.E of the Guidelines.

   Chapter 3 of the Second Protocol

   - Implementation of provisions regarding criminal responsibility
     - To inform on national legislation concerning criminal responsibility for serious violations within the meaning of the Second Protocol.
     - To inform on national legislative, administrative or disciplinary measures to suppress other violations.

   Chapter 4 of the Second Protocol
   Article 15 and 21 of the Second Protocol

   - Implementation of provisions regarding dissemination
     - To inform on the measures taken concerning dissemination.

   Chapter 7 of the Second Protocol

   - Implementation of provisions regarding technical assistance
     - Any other activities relating to the Second Protocol, including activities at bi- or multilateral level, in order to share their experiences or best practices, as referred to in paragraph 151 of the Guidelines.

120. Parties to the Second Protocol should also provide the Secretariat with the name and address of a single national focal point for all official documents and correspondence related to the implementation of the Second Protocol by their relevant authorities. Unless a Party requests otherwise, the presumed focal point would be its Permanent Delegation to UNESCO. The Secretariat will make a list of these addresses available on its website.

121. The Parties are also invited to inform the Committee through the Secretariat, on a voluntary basis, of all legislative, judicial or other mat-

---

1) The High Contracting Parties, which are Parties to the Second Protocol, were asked by the Director-General of UNESCO to forward their first reports on the implementation of the Second Protocol by 1 July 2008.

ters relevant to the Parties' implementation of the Second Protocol. The Secretariat will register this information in a database.

V.B Reports of the Committee to the Meeting of the Parties

122. An important function of the Committee is to monitor and supervise the implementation of the Second Protocol, and to promote the identification of cultural property under enhanced protection. The Committee is entitled to consider and comment on the reports of the Parties, to seek clarification as required, and to prepare its own report on the implementation of the Second Protocol to the Meeting of the Parties. In fulfilling its functions, the Committee makes recommendations, as appropriate.   Article 27(1)(c) of the Second Protocol
Article 27(1)(d) of the Second Protocol

123. The Committee will, with the assistance of the Secretariat, keep under review all aspects of the implementation of the Second Protocol. The Committee will make full use, to the extent possible, of the periodic reports, representations and other communications from Parties. The Committee may also make use of information and advice from stakeholders, as referred to in paragraph 13 of the Guidelines, as well as of the information and documentation services of UNESCO.

124. The Committee takes, at a minimum, the following issues into account in its report:
    – Parties' requests for inclusion of cultural property in the List;
    – Parties' requests for international assistance;
    – International cooperation; and,
    – The use of the Fund.

VI. INTERNATIONAL ASSISTANCE

125. In order to strengthen protection of cultural property, the Second Protocol distinguishes the following forms of assistance: Articles 29, 32 and 33 of the Second Protocol
   a. International assistance provided by the Committee (Article 32 of the Second Protocol), including financial and other assistance from the Fund (Article 29 of the Second Protocol);
   b. Technical assistance provided by the Parties through the Committee (Article 32 of the Second Protocol);
   c. Technical assistance provided by the Parties at bi- or multilateral level (Article 33 of the Second Protocol); and,
   d. Technical assistance provided by UNESCO (Article 33 of the Second Protocol).

   Examples of forms of assistance and a procedural matrix are listed in Table 1 of Annex III.

126. The granting of international assistance is not, however, automatic and depends on compliance with the conditions set forth by the Second Protocol and the relevant parts of the Guidelines, as well as on available means.

VI.A International assistance provided by the Committee, including financial and other assistance from the Fund

Scope of international assistance provided by the Committee

127. International assistance provided by the Committee may be requested by: Articles 32 and 3(2) of the Second Protocol

- a Party at any time or
- a party to a conflict which is not a Party to the Second Protocol but which accepts and applies provisions in accordance with Article 3(2) of the Second Protocol during the conflict.

128. International assistance provided by the Committee may be requested for:
    — cultural property under enhanced protection;
    — cultural property submitted for inclusion in the List provided that the Committee has concluded that the criteria of Article 10(b) cannot be fulfilled; and,
    — cultural property in support of measures referred to in Article 29(1).
    Articles 11(8), 29(1) and 32(1) of the Second Protocol

129. International assistance provided by the Committee is in principle complementary to national measures taken by an applicant for the protection of its cultural property.

130. The Committee may use the Fund for financing international assistance provided by the Committee. *Articles 29(1) and (3) of the Second Protocol*

Forms of international assistance provided by the Committee

131. The Committee assesses the requests for international assistance and, in case of approval, co-ordinates this assistance.

132. International assistance provided by the Committee may be of technical or consultative character, covering in particular legal, administrative, military and practical aspects of the protection of cultural property. *Article 32 of the Second Protocol*

133. International assistance provided by the Committee may, in accordance with the available means, be granted for the following purposes:
    a. preparatory measures;
    b. emergency measures; and,
    c. recovery measures.

134. Preparatory measures are in principle taken in times of peace:
    a. to support Parties' overall domestic sustainable efforts related to cultural property;
    b. to contribute to the preparation and development of administrative or institutional measures, provisions and structures for the safeguarding of cultural property; and,
    c. to contribute to the preparation, development or implementation of the laws, administrative provisions and measures recognizing the exceptional cultural and historic value and ensuring the highest level of protection of cultural property to be nominated for enhanced protection. Examples of possible measures are listed in Table 2 of Annex III.
    Article 5 of the Second Protocol
    Article 10(b) of the Second Protocol

135. Emergency measures are, in principle, taken during an armed conflict. Their essential purpose is to ensure the adequate protection of the cultural property concerned and to prevent its deterioration, destruction or looting. Examples of possible measures are listed in Table 2 of Annex III. *Article 10(b) of the Second Protocol*

136. Recovery measures are, in principle, taken after a conflict. Their essential purpose is to ensure the preservation and conservation of cultural property damaged in connection with the conflict as well as the return of the cultural property which has been removed. Examples of possible measures are listed in Table 2 of Annex III. *Article 5 of the Second Protocol*

A.I.1c Guidelines Zweites Haager Protokoll

Priorities and principles for granting international assistance provided by the Committee

137. While considering requests for international assistance, and taking into account special needs of applicants that are developing countries, priority is given bearing in mind the emergency or the preventive nature of the request. Emergency measures are of the highest priority.
138. The Committee's decisions in granting international assistance may be, among others, guided by the following considerations:
    a. the probability that the assistance will have a catalytic and multiplier effect ("seed money") and promote financial and technical contributions from other sources;
    b. whether the legislative, administrative and, wherever possible, financial commitment of the recipient is available to the activity;
    c. the exemplary value of the activity; and,
    d. the cost efficiency of the activity.
139. Further guidance for requests concerning international assistance and description of the process of considering requests for international assistance provided by the Committee is provided in detail below in Chapter VI.E of the Guidelines.

Monitoring and evaluation of international assistance provided by the Committee

140. The Secretariat assists in the monitoring of the implementation of the international assistance provided by the Committee and regularly informs it of outcomes of its monitoring.
141. The recipient of the international assistance provided by the Committee submits to the Secretariat the final report on the implementation of that assistance within three months of the completion of projects carried out. The Secretariat presents this report to the Committee.

VI.B Technical assistance provided by the Parties through the Committee

142. Parties are encouraged to provide all kinds of technical assistance through the Committee to those Parties or parties to the conflict who request it.   *Article 32(4) of the Second Protocol*
143. Assistance provided by the Parties through the Committee may concern all cultural property and it may be applied at any time. Forms of technical assistance are defined by the Parties offering assistance. The Meeting of the Parties and the Committee may also give recommendations concerning such technical assistance.
144. A party to an armed conflict which is not Party to the Second Protocol but which accepts and applies the provisions of the Second Protocol in accordance with its Article 3(2), may request technical assistance only during the conflict.   *Article 32(2) of the Second Protocol*
145. Parties providing technical assistance are responsible for its funding.
146. Requests concerning technical assistance are addressed to the Committee through the Secretariat, which will transfer the information to the national focal points of the Parties for their consideration.
147. Parties in a position to provide technical assistance are invited to inform the Committee of the possibilities of providing such assistance.
148. The Committee, through the Secretariat, informs the requesting Parties or parties to a conflict accordingly.
149. After giving such information, it is incumbent upon the providing Parties and the requesting Parties or parties to a conflict to proceed and convene directly the provision of such assistance.

VI.C Technical assistance provided by the Parties directly at bi- or multilateral level

150. Parties are encouraged to provide technical assistance at bi- or multilateral level. Such assistance is at their discretion. For this purpose, Parties are invited to be in direct contact with each other through their national focal points. *Article 33(2) of the Second Protocol*
151. The Parties having activities at bi- or multilateral level are invited to inform the Committee, through the Secretariat, in their periodic reports, of their activities in order to share their experiences or best practices.

VI.D Technical assistance provided by UNESCO

152. A Party may call upon UNESCO for technical assistance in organizing the protection of its cultural property, such as preparatory action to safeguard cultural property, preventive and organizational measures for emergency situations and compilation of national inventories of cultural property, or in connection with any other problem arising out of the application of the Second Protocol. UNESCO may also provide its services in accordance with Articles 33(3) and 22(7) of the Second Protocol. *Article 33(1) of the Second Protocol* *Articles 33(3) and 22(7) of the Second Protocol*
153. Examples of possible measures of technical assistance provided by UNESCO are listed in Table 3 of Annex III.
154. The Secretariat will provide the Committee during its sessions with the relevant information concerning the technical assistance provided to the Parties.

VI.E Process of considering requests for international assistance provided by the Committee, including financial and other assistance from the Fund

155. The Committee will work in close co-operation as appropriate with the Parties, the relevant eminent international and national governmental and non- governmental organisations, and the Secretariat in order to ensure the proper handling of requests for different categories of assistance so that the assistance is provided in the most adequate manner in order to advance the aims of the Second Protocol. *Article 27(3) of the Second Protocol*
156. In particular, they keep each other informed, as appropriate, of the requests submitted and the assistance provided in order to avoid the duplication of efforts, time and resources. The transmission of information is to be carried out, among others, through the reports of the Committee to the Meeting of the Parties.

Requests concerning international assistance provided by the Committee

157. The Parties may submit to the Committee requests for international assistance provided by the Committee. Also a party to a conflict which is not a Party to the Second Protocol but which accepts and applies the provisions of the Second Protocol may submit requests for international assistance during the conflict. Requests also may be submitted jointly by two or more Parties concerned. *Articles 32(1), 32(2), 11(8) and 3(2) of the Second Protocol*
158. The Committee examines each particular case to determine whether the priorities and principles adopted by the Committee concerning international assistance provided by the Committee are met. The Committee may also make reservations or set conditions for the assistance depending on the particular conditions of each case. It may

A.I.1c Guidelines Zweites Haager Protokoll

also suggest to the applicant other forms than originally requested if it considers it appropriate.

159. The Committee may decide not to grant assistance if the applicant has not accepted the form of assistance proposed by the Committee.
160. If necessary, the Committee may request the applicant to provide additional information.
161. The Committee may also defer the request if more in-depth assessment, study or substantial revision is required.
162. While examining requests for international assistance, the Committee may also study the possibility of obtaining technical assistance from the Parties. The Committee may also consult the Secretariat in order to ascertain whether the applicant previously requested assistance from UNESCO for the same purpose.
163. Requests for all forms of international assistance provided by the Committee have to be submitted to the Committee by or in cooperation with the Permanent Delegation of the Party to UNESCO, where appropriate, through the Secretariat, which acknowledges the receipt, verifies the completeness of the request and, if incomplete, requests the applicant to provide the missing information required as listed in Annex II. Only duly completed requests are registered by the Secretariat. The Secretariat informs the applicant of the registration of its request when it is completed. A copy of the form to request international assistance for cultural property provided by the Committee is attached in Annex II.
164. Requests registered by the Secretariat at least six months before the ordinary meeting of the Committee are forwarded to the Bureau of the Committee for its prima facie consideration together with a review of completeness prepared by the Secretariat.
165. The Bureau may consult eminent international and national governmental and non-governmental organisations with the professional expertise for evaluation of the request and, in cases where technical assistance is required, consult Parties offering such assistance.   *Article 27(3) of the Second Protocol*
166. After evaluation, the Bureau will forward the request to the Committee for consideration and appropriate decision. The Bureau may offer any relevant observations. For the above purpose, the Committee assigns the Bureau to prepare the ordinary meeting of the Committee.
167. The Committee will consider requests in its meetings. It decides by a majority of two-thirds of its members present and voting on the requests for international assistance.   *Article 26(2) of the Second Protocol*
168. The Committee communicates its decision through the Secretariat to the recipient of the international assistance within two weeks following the decision. If the international assistance is granted, the Secretariat concludes an agreement with the recipient of the international assistance as appropriate.
169. Requests for emergency measures may be submitted at any time. As an exception to the six-month deadline set forth in paragraph 164, in view of the urgency, the Committee will consider as soon as possible these requests on an ad hoc basis.
170. The granted international assistance is subject to appropriate monitoring and evaluation by the Committee.
171. Applicants shall submit their requests in writing, by using the application form attached in Annex II, and if possible, in an electronic format provided by the Secretariat. Requests may be submitted in one of the two working languages of the Secretariat.

172. Applicants shall provide all the information requested by the application form. They may submit additional information as appropriate.

VI.F Requests for assistance provided by UNESCO

173. Parties may apply for assistance provided by UNESCO at any time. Following the receipt of the request for such assistance, the Secretariat verifies whether an identical request has not already been submitted for international assistance. If necessary, the Secretariat may request additional information. The Secretariat informs the Committee of the request. If necessary, the Secretariat may consult eminent international and national governmental and non-governmental organizations with the relevant professional expertise for evaluation of the request.   Article 33 (1) of the Second Protocol

A.I.2 Erstes Genfer Zusatzprotokoll

Zusatzprotokoll zu den Genfer Abkommen vom 12. August 1949 über den Schutz der Opfer internationaler bewaffneter Konflikte (Protokoll I)[1][2]

Vom 8. Juni 1977 (BGBl. 1990 II S. 1550, 1551)
zuletzt geändert durch Art. 1 ÄndG vom 17. Juli 1997 (BGBl. 1993 II S. 1366)
– Auszug –

Teil IV
Zivilbevölkerung

Abschnitt I
Allgemeiner Schutz vor den Auswirkungen von Feindseligkeiten

Kapitel III
Zivile Objekte

Artikel 53 Schutz von Kulturgut und Kultstätten
Unbeschadet der Bestimmungen der Haager Konvention vom 14. Mai 1954 zum Schutz von Kulturgut bei bewaffneten Konflikten und anderer einschlägiger internationaler Übereinkünfte ist es verboten,
a) feindselige Handlungen gegen geschichtliche Denkmäler, Kunstwerke oder Kultstätten zu begehen, die zum kulturellen oder geistigen Erbe der Völker gehören,
b) solche Objekte zur Unterstützung des militärischen Einsatzes zu verwenden oder
c) solche Objekte zum Gegenstand von Repressalien zu machen.

Teil V
Durchführung der Abkommen und dieses Protokolls

Abschnitt II
Ahndung von Verletzungen der Abkommen und dieses Protokolls

Artikel 85 Ahndung von Verletzungen dieses Protokolls
[...]
(4) Als schwere Verletzungen dieses Protokolls gelten außer den in den vorstehenden Absätzen und in den Abkommen bezeichneten schweren Verletzungen folgende Handlungen, wenn sie vorsätzlich und unter Verletzung der Abkommen oder des Protokolls begangen werden:
[...]
d) weitgehende Zerstörungen verursachende Angriffe, die gegen eindeutig erkannte geschichtliche Denkmäler, Kunstwerke oder Kultstätten gerichtet sind, welche zum kulturellen oder geistigen Erbe der Völker gehören und denen auf Grund einer besonderen Vereinbarung, zum Beispiel im Rahmen einer zuständigen internationalen Organisation, besonderer Schutz gewährt wurde, wenn keine Anzeichen dafür vorliegen, daß die gegnerische Partei Artikel 53 Buchstabe b verletzt hat und wenn die betreffenden geschichtlichen Denkmäler, Kunstwerke und Kultstätten nicht in unmittelbarer Nähe militärischer Ziele gelegen sind;
[...]

---

1) Liste der Vertragsstaaten: https://www.eda.admin.ch/eda/de/home/aussenpolitik/voelkerrecht/internationale-vertraege/datenbank-staatsvertraege/detailansicht-staatsvertrag.ggst0_51.contract19770112.html?_charset_=UTF-8
Zu den Genfer Abkommen vom 12. August 1949 vgl. die vier Genfer Rotkreuz-Abkommen: das Genfer Abkommen zur Verbesserung des Loses der Verwundeten und Kranken der Streitkräfte im Felde, das Genfer Abkommen zur Verbesserung des Loses der Verwundeten, Kranken und Schiffbrüchigen der Streitkräfte zur See, das Genfer Abkommen über die Behandlung der Kriegsgefangenen und das Genfer Abkommen zum Schutze von Zivilpersonen in Kriegszeiten.
2) Vgl. hierzu auch das Zusatzprotokoll über die Annahme eines zusätzlichen Schutzzeichens (Protokoll III, BGBl. 2009 II S. 223).

Zusatzprotokoll zu den Genfer Abkommen vom 12. August 1949 über den Schutz der Opfer nicht internationaler bewaffneter Konflikte (Protokoll II)[1)2)]

Vom 8. Juni 1977 (BGBl. 1990 II S. 1637)

– Auszug –

Teil IV
Zivilbevölkerung

Artikel 16 Schutz von Kulturgut und Kultstätten
Unbeschadet der Bestimmungen der Haager Konvention vom 14. Mai 1954 zum Schutz von Kulturgut bei bewaffneten Konflikten ist es verboten, feindselige Handlungen gegen geschichtliche Denkmäler, Kunstwerke oder Kultstätten zu begehen, die zum kulturellen oder geistigen Erbe der Völker gehören, und sie zur Unterstützung des militärischen Einsatzes zu verwenden.

---

1) Liste der Vertragsstaaten: https://www.eda.admin.ch/eda/de/home/aussenpolitik/voelkerrecht/internationale-vertraege/datenbank-staatsvertraege/detailansicht-staatsvertrag.ggst0_51.contract19770113.html?_charset_=UTF-8.
Zu den Genfer Abkommen vom 12. August 1949 vgl. die vier Genfer Rotkreuz-Abkommen: das Genfer Abkommen zur Verbesserung des Loses der Verwundeten und Kranken der Streitkräfte im Felde, das Genfer Abkommen zur Verbesserung des Loses der Verwundeten, Kranken und Schiffbrüchigen der Streitkräfte zur See, das Genfer Abkommen über die Behandlung der Kriegsgefangenen und das Genfer Abkommen zum Schutze von Zivilpersonen in Kriegszeiten.
2) Vgl. hierzu auch das Zusatzprotokoll über die Annahme eines zusätzlichen Schutzzeichens (Protokoll III, BGBl. 2009 II S. 223).

A.I.4 UNSR-Resolution 2199 (2015)

Vereinte Nationen
Sicherheitsrat
Resolution 2199 (2015)

Verabschiedet auf der 7379. Sitzung des Sicherheitsrats am 12. Februar 2015, S/RES/2199 (2015)

Der Sicherheitsrat,

in Bekräftigung seiner Hauptverantwortung für die Wahrung des Weltfriedens und der internationalen Sicherheit im Einklang mit der Charta der Vereinten Nationen,

bekräftigend, dass der Terrorismus in allen seinen Arten und Erscheinungsformen eine der schwersten Bedrohungen des Weltfriedens und der internationalen Sicherheit darstellt und dass alle terroristischen Handlungen verbrecherisch und nicht zu rechtfertigen sind, ungeachtet ihrer Beweggründe und gleichviel wann und von wem sie begangen werden,

in Bekräftigung der Notwendigkeit, Bedrohungen des Weltfriedens und der internationalen Sicherheit durch terroristische Handlungen mit allen Mitteln, im Einklang mit der Charta der Vereinten Nationen und dem Völkerrecht, einschließlich der anwendbaren internationalen Normen auf dem Gebiet der Menschenrechte, des Flüchtlingsrechts und des humanitären Rechts, zu bekämpfen, und in diesem Zusammenhang die wichtige Rolle hervorhebend, die den Vereinten Nationen bei der Führung und Koordinierung dieser Anstrengungen zukommt,

betonend, dass Sanktionen ein wichtiges in der Charta der Vereinten Nationen vorgesehenes Instrument zur Wahrung und Wiederherstellung des Weltfriedens und der internationalen Sicherheit, einschließlich der Terrorismusbekämpfung, sind, und *unterstreichend,* wie wichtig die umgehende und wirksame Durchführung der einschlägigen Resolutionen, insbesondere der Resolutionen des Sicherheitsrats 1267 (1999) und 1989 (2011), als Schlüsselinstrument im Kampf gegen den Terrorismus ist,

unter Hinweis auf seine Resolutionen 1267 (1999), 1989 (2011), 2161 (2014), 2170 (2014) und 2178 (2014) und die Erklärungen seines Präsidenten vom 28. Juli 2014 und 19. November 2014, namentlich seine erklärte Absicht, zusätzliche Maßnahmen zu erwägen, um den Handel mit Erdöl, den der Islamische Staat in Irak und der Levante (ISIL, auch bekannt als „Daesh"), die Al-Nusra-Front (ANF) und alle anderen mit Al-Qaida verbundenen Personen, Gruppen, Unternehmen und Einrichtungen zum Zweck der Terrorismusfinanzierung betreiben, zu unterbinden,

in der Erkenntnis, dass finanziellen Sanktionen eine wichtige Rolle dabei zukommt, die Aktivitäten des ISIL, der ANF und aller anderen mit Al-Qaida verbundenen Personen, Gruppen, Unternehmen und Einrichtungen zu unterbinden, sowie *betonend,* dass für die vollständige Zerschlagung des ISIL und der ANF ein umfassender Ansatz notwendig ist, der multilaterale Strategien mit Maßnahmen der Mitgliedstaaten auf nationaler Ebene kombiniert,

in Bekräftigung der Unabhängigkeit, Souveränität, Einheit und territorialen Unversehrtheit der Republik Irak und der Arabischen Republik Syrien und ferner in Bekräftigung der Ziele und Grundsätze der Charta der Vereinten Nationen,

sowie bekräftigend, dass der Terrorismus nicht mit einer bestimmten Religion, Nationalität oder Zivilisation in Verbindung gebracht werden kann und soll,

betonend, dass der Terrorismus nur durch einen nachhaltigen und umfassenden Ansatz besiegt werden kann, mit der aktiven Beteiligung und Zusammenarbeit aller Staaten und internationalen und regionalen Organisationen, um die terroristische Bedrohung zu behindern, zu schwächen, zu isolieren und auszuschalten,

in dieser Hinsicht *mit dem Ausdruck* seines tief empfundenen Dankes für die Resolution 7804 der Arabischen Liga (7. September 2014), die Pariser Erklärung (15. September 2014), die Erklärung der Arbeitsgruppe „Finanzielle Maßnahmen" über die Bekämpfung der Finanzierung des ISIL (24. Oktober 2014) und die Erklärung von Manama über die Bekämpfung der Terrorismusfinanzierung (9. November 2014),

in Bekräftigung seiner Resolution 1373 (2001) und insbesondere seiner Beschlüsse, wonach alle Staaten die Finanzierung terroristischer Handlungen verhüten und bekämpfen und es unterlassen müssen, Einrichtungen oder Personen, die an terroristischen Handlungen beteiligt sind, in irgendeiner Form aktiv oder passiv zu unterstützen, indem sie namentlich die Anwerbung von Mitgliedern terroristischer Gruppen unterbinden und die Belieferung von Terroristen mit Waffen beendigen,

in der Erkenntnis, dass erheblicher Bedarf besteht, die Kapazitäten der Mitgliedstaaten zur Bekämpfung des Terrorismus und der Terrorismusfinanzierung auszubauen,
erneut seine tiefe Besorgnis darüber zum Ausdruck bringend, dass Ölfelder und die dazugehörige Infrastruktur sowie weitere Infrastruktur wie Staudämme und Kraftwerke, die von dem ISIL, der ANF und möglicherweise anderen mit Al-Qaida verbundenen Personen, Gruppen, Unternehmen und Einrichtungen kontrolliert werden, neben Erpressung, privaten Spenden aus dem Ausland, Lösegeldern aus Entführungen und gestohlenem Geld aus dem von ihnen kontrollierten Gebiet einen bedeutenden Anteil der Einkünfte der Gruppen erzeugen, die ihre Anwerbungsbemühungen unterstützen und ihre operative Fähigkeit zur Organisation und Durchführung von Terroranschlägen stärken,
unter entschiedenster *Verurteilung* der Entführungen von Frauen und Kindern, *mit dem Ausdruck seiner Empörung* über ihre Ausbeutung und ihren Missbrauch, darunter Vergewaltigung, sexueller Missbrauch und Zwangsverheiratung, die von dem ISIL, der ANF und anderen mit Al-Qaida verbundenen Personen, Gruppen, Unternehmen und Einrichtungen begangen werden, und alle staatlichen und nichtstaatlichen Akteure, denen diesbezügliche Beweise vorliegen, ermutigend, diese Beweise sowie alle Informationen über eine mögliche finanzielle Unterstützung der Täter durch Menschenhandel dem Rat zur Kenntnis zu bringen,
bekräftigend, dass die Mitgliedstaaten verpflichtet sind, Gelder und sonstige finanzielle Vermögenswerte oder wirtschaftliche Ressourcen von Personen, die terroristische Handlungen begehen, zu begehen versuchen oder sich an deren Begehung beteiligen oder diese erleichtern, von Einrichtungen, die unmittelbar oder mittelbar im Eigentum oder unter der Kontrolle dieser Personen stehen, und von Personen und Einrichtungen, die im Namen oder auf Anweisung dieser Personen und Einrichtungen handeln, unverzüglich einzufrieren, einschließlich der Gelder, die aus Vermögen stammen oder hervorgehen, das unmittelbar oder mittelbar im Eigentum oder unter der Kontrolle dieser Personen und mit ihnen verbundener Personen und Einrichtungen steht,
mit dem Ausdruck seiner Besorgnis darüber, dass wirtschaftliche Ressourcen wie Erdöl, Erdölprodukte, modulare Raffinerien und dazugehöriges Material, andere natürliche Ressourcen, darunter Edelmetalle wie Gold, Silber und Kupfer, Diamanten und andere Vermögenswerte dem ISIL, der ANF und anderen mit Al-Qaida verbundenen Personen, Gruppen, Unternehmen und Einrichtungen zur Verfügung gestellt werden, und darauf hinweisend, dass der direkte oder indirekte Handel mit dem ISIL und der ANF mit diesen Materialien einen Verstoß gegen die mit Resolution 2161 (2014) auferlegten Verpflichtungen darstellen könnte,
alle Staaten an ihre Verpflichtung *erinnernd*, sicherzustellen, dass alle Personen, die an der Finanzierung, Planung, Vorbereitung oder Begehung terroristischer Handlungen oder an deren Unterstützung mitwirken, vor Gericht gestellt werden,
in Bekräftigung seiner Resolution 2133 (2014) und *erneut feststellend*, dass Lösegeldzahlungen an terroristische Gruppen eine der Einnahmequellen sind, die ihre Anwerbungsbemühungen unterstützen, ihre operative Fähigkeit zur Organisation und Durchführung von Terroranschlägen stärken und Anreize für weitere Entführungen zur Erpressung von Lösegeld schaffen,
mit dem Ausdruck der Besorgnis darüber, dass die neuen Informations- und Kommunikationstechnologien, insbesondere das Internet, in einer globalisierten Gesellschaft von Terroristen und ihren Unterstützern verstärkt zur Erleichterung terroristischer Handlungen benutzt werden und dass sie dazu benutzt werden, zu terroristischen Handlungen aufzustacheln, dafür anzuwerben, sie zu finanzieren oder sie zu planen,
mit dem Ausdruck seiner ernsten Besorgnis über die Zunahme der vom ISIL begangenen Entführungen *und* Geiselmorde und unter Verurteilung dieser abscheulichen und feigen Morde, die deutlich machen, dass der Terrorismus eine Geißel für die gesamte Menschheit ist und sich gegen Menschen aus allen Regionen und Angehörige aller Religionen oder Weltanschauungen richtet, unter Begrüßung des am 14. November 2014 veröffentlichten Berichts des Teams für analytische Unterstützung und Sanktionsüberwachung über die ANF und den ISIL und Kenntnis nehmend von seinen Empfehlungen,
mit Besorgnis Kenntnis nehmend von der anhaltenden Bedrohung des Weltfriedens und der internationalen Sicherheit, die von dem ISIL, der ANF und allen anderen mit Al-Qaida verbundenen Personen, Gruppen, Unternehmen und Einrichtungen nach wie vor ausgeht, und in Bekräftigung seiner Entschlossenheit, gegen alle Aspekte dieser Bedrohung anzugehen,
tätig werdend nach Kapitel VII der Charta der Vereinten Nationen,

[...]
Kulturelles Erbe
15. *verurteilt* die Zerstörung kulturellen Erbes in Irak und Syrien, insbesondere durch den ISIL und die ANF, gleichviel ob unbeabsichtigt oder beabsichtigt, namentlich die gezielte Zerstörung religiöser Stätten und Gegenstände;
16. *stellt mit Besorgnis fest,* dass der ISIL, die ANF und andere mit Al-Qaida verbundene Personen, Gruppen, Unternehmen und Einrichtungen durch die direkte oder indirekte Beteiligung an der Plünderung und dem Schmuggel von Gegenständen kulturellen Erbes von archäologischen Stätten, aus Museen, Bibliotheken, Archiven und von anderen Stätten in Irak und Syrien Einkünfte erzeugen, das zur Unterstützung ihrer Anwerbungsbemühungen und zur Stärkung ihrer operativen Fähigkeit zur Organisation und Durchführung von Terroranschlägen verwendet wird;
17. *bekräftigt* seinen Beschluss in Ziffer 7 der Resolution 1483 (2003) und *beschließt,* dass alle Mitgliedstaaten geeignete Schritte unternehmen, um den Handel mit irakischem und syrischem Kulturgut und anderen Gegenständen von archäologischer, historischer, kultureller und religiöser Bedeutung und wissenschaftlichem Seltenheitswert, die seit dem 6. August 1990 aus Irak und seit dem 15. März 2011 aus Syrien unrechtmäßig entfernt wurden, zu verhüten, namentlich durch ein Verbot des grenzüberschreitenden Handels mit solchen Gegenständen, und so ihre spätere sichere Rückgabe an das irakische und das syrische Volk zu ermöglichen, und *fordert* die Organisation der Vereinten Nationen für Erziehung, Wissenschaft und Kultur, die INTERPOL und andere internationale Organisationen *auf,* gegebenenfalls bei der Durchführung dieses Beschlusses Hilfe zu leisten;
[...]
Berichterstattung
29. *fordert* die Mitgliedstaaten *auf,* dem Ausschuss innerhalb von 120 Tagen über die Maßnahmen Bericht zu erstatten, die sie zur Befolgung der in dieser Resolution verhängten Maßnahmen getroffen haben;
30. *ersucht* das Team für analytische Unterstützung und Sanktionsüberwachung, in enger Zusammenarbeit mit den anderen für die Terrorismusbekämpfung zuständigen Organen der Vereinten Nationen eine Bewertung der Wirkung dieser neuen Maßnahmen durchzuführen und dem Ausschuss nach den Resolutionen 1267 (1999) und 1989 (2011) innerhalb von 150 Tagen Bericht zu erstatten und danach die Berichterstattung über die Wirkung dieser neuen Maßnahmen in ihre Berichte an den Ausschuss aufzunehmen, um den Stand der Umsetzung zu verfolgen und unbeabsichtigte Folgen und unerwartete Herausforderungen aufzuzeigen sowie zur Erleichterung etwaig erforderlicher weiterer Anpassungen beizutragen, und ersucht ferner den Ausschuss nach den Resolutionen 1267 (1999) und 1989 (2011), den Sicherheitsrat im Rahmen seiner regelmäßigen mündlichen Berichte an den Rat über den Stand der allgemeinen Arbeit des Ausschusses und des Überwachungsteams über die Durchführung dieser Resolution unterrichtet zu halten;
31. *beschließt,* mit der Angelegenheit aktiv befasst zu bleiben.

**Vereinte Nationen
Sicherheitsrat
Resolution 2295 (2016)**

Verabschiedet auf der 7727. Sitzung des Sicherheitsrats am 29. Juni 2016, S/RES/2295 (2016)

Der Sicherheitsrat,
unter Hinweis auf seine früheren Resolutionen, insbesondere die Resolutionen 2227 (2015) und 2100 (2013), die Erklärung seines Präsidenten vom 6. Februar 2015 (S/PRST/2015/5) sowie seine Presseerklärungen, unter anderem vom 12. Januar 2016, betreffend die Situation in Mali,
in Bekräftigung seines nachdrücklichen Bekenntnisses zur Souveränität, Einheit und territorialen Unversehrtheit Malis, *hervorhebend*, dass die malischen Behörden die Hauptverantwortung für die Gewährleistung der Stabilität und der Sicherheit im gesamten Hoheitsgebiet Malis haben, und *unterstreichend*, wie wichtig es ist, dass Friedens- und Sicherheitsinitiativen unter nationaler Eigenverantwortung stehen,
in Bekräftigung der Grundprinzipien der Friedenssicherung, darunter die Zustimmung der Parteien, die Unparteilichkeit und die Nichtanwendung von Gewalt außer zur Selbstverteidigung und zur Verteidigung des Mandats, und feststellend, dass das Mandat jeder Friedenssicherungsmission auf die Bedürfnisse und die Situation des jeweiligen Landes zugeschnitten ist, *sowie unter Hinweis* auf die Erklärung seines Präsidenten vom 25. November 2015 (S/PRST/2015/22),
in Anerkennung des legitimen Strebens aller malischen Bürger nach dauerhaftem Frieden und dauerhafter Entwicklung,
in der Erkenntnis, dass das Abkommen für Frieden und Aussöhnung in Mali („Abkommen"), das 2015 von der Regierung Malis, der Koalition bewaffneter Gruppen „Plateforme" und der Koalition bewaffneter Gruppen „Coordination des mouvements de l'Azawad" unterzeichnet wurde, eine historische Chance zur Herbeiführung eines dauerhaften Friedens in Mali darstellt,
die Auffassung vertretend, dass das Abkommen ausgewogen und umfassend ist und zum Ziel hat, die Krise in Mali in ihren politischen und institutionellen Dimensionen sowie in den Dimensionen der Regierungsführung, der Sicherheit, der Entwicklung und der Aussöhnung anzugehen, unter Achtung der Souveränität, Einheit und territorialen Unversehrtheit des malischen Staates,
unterstreichend, dass die vollständige und wirksame Durchführung des Abkommens, die unter malischer Führung und Eigenverantwortung erfolgen muss, Aufgabe der Regierung Malis und der Koalitionen bewaffneter Gruppen „Plateforme" und „Coordination" ist und dass sie entscheidend zu einem dauerhaften Frieden in Mali beiträgt, da dabei die Lehren aus früheren Friedensabkommen berücksichtigt werden,
unter Begrüßung der positiven Schritte, die die Regierung Malis und die Koalitionen bewaffneter Gruppen „Plateforme" und „Coordination" zur Durchführung des Abkommens unternommen haben, jedoch gleichzeitig *mit dem Ausdruck* seiner ernsten Besorgnis über die weiteren Verzögerungen bei seiner Durchführung, sowie *unter Begrüßung* dessen, dass die Waffenruhe seit August 2015 geachtet wird, was eine wichtige und konkrete Geste des guten Willens der malischen Parteien darstellt,
es begrüßend, dass die Regierung Malis und die Koalitionen bewaffneter Gruppen „Plateforme" und „Coordination" am 19. Juni 2016 die Vereinbarung über die Interimsbehörden und andere damit zusammenhängende Regelungen unterzeichnet haben und dass der Präsident Malis, Herr Ibrahim Boubacar Keita, am 15. Juni 2016 beschlossen hat, Herrn Mahamadou Diagouraga zu seinem Hohen Beauftragten für die Durchführung des Abkommens zu ernennen,
es begrüßend, dass die Regierung Malis im Januar 2016 den zweiten Nationalen Aktionsplan Malis für die Durchführung der Resolution 1325 (2000) des Sicherheitsrats angenommen hat, und in dieser Hinsicht *ferner begrüßend*, dass die Regierung Malis im Dezember 2015 ein Gesetz erlassen hat, das eine Frauenquote von 30 Prozent in den staatlichen Institutionen vorschreibt,
in Bekräftigung seiner Absicht, die Durchführung des Abkommens zu erleichtern, zu unterstützen und genau zu beobachten, und *in Würdigung* der Rolle Algeriens und anderer Mitglieder des internationalen Vermittlungsteams bei der Unterstützung der malischen Parteien bei der Durchführung des Abkommens,

A.I.5 UNSR-Resolution 2295 (2016)

es begrüßend, dass die Regierung Malis am 12. April 2016 angekündigt hat, dass am 25. September 2016 Kommunalwahlen abgehalten werden, dass im November 2016 ein Verfassungsreferendum stattfinden wird, in dessen Verlauf die Bildung eines Senats vorgeschlagen werden soll, und dass im ersten Halbjahr 2017 Regionalwahlen stattfinden werden, und *mit der Forderung*, alle Seiten in diese Prozesse einzuschließen,

mit dem Ausdruck seiner Besorgnis über die prekäre Sicherheitslage, insbesondere die jüngste Ausweitung terroristischer und anderer krimineller Aktivitäten auf das Zentrum und den Süden Malis, sowie über die Verschärfung der Gewalt zwischen den Volksgruppen im Zentrum Malis,

feststellend, dass die schleppenden Fortschritte bei der Durchführung des Abkommens, insbesondere seiner Verteidigungs- und Sicherheitsbestimmungen, sowie die verzögerte Umstrukturierung des Sicherheitssektors die Anstrengungen zur Wiederherstellung der Sicherheit im Norden Malis behindert haben, und *betonend*, dass die Regierung Malis und die Koalitionen bewaffneter Gruppen „Plateforme" und „Coordination" die Hauptverantwortung für die beschleunigte Durchführung des Abkommens tragen, mit dem Ziel, die Sicherheitslage in ganz Mali zu verbessern und Versuche terroristischer Gruppen zu vereiteln, die Durchführung des Abkommens zum Scheitern zu bringen,

unter nachdrücklicher Verurteilung der Aktivitäten terroristischer Organisationen in Mali und der Sahel-Region, namentlich Al-Qaidas im islamischen Maghreb, Al-Murabituns, Ansar Eddines und der ihnen angeschlossenen Organisationen wie der Massina-Befreiungsfront, die nach wie vor in Mali operieren und eine Bedrohung des Friedens und der Sicherheit in der Region und darüber hinaus darstellen, sowie der von terroristischen Gruppen in Mali und in der Region begangenen Menschenrechtsverletzungen und Gewalthandlungen gegenüber Zivilpersonen, namentlich Frauen und Kindern,

unter Verurteilung der nach wie vor von terroristischen Gruppen begangenen Angriffe auf die Mehrdimensionale integrierte Stabilisierungsmission der Vereinten Nationen in Mali (MINUSMA), die malische Verteidigungs- und Sicherheitskräfte, die Ausbildungsmission der Europäischen Union in Mali (EUTM Mali) und die französischen Truppen,

betonend, dass der Terrorismus nur durch einen nachhaltigen und umfassenden Ansatz besiegt werden kann, bei dem alle Staaten und die regionalen und internationalen Organisationen sich aktiv beteiligen und zusammenarbeiten, um die terroristische Bedrohung einzudämmen, zu schwächen und zu isolieren, und *erneut erklärend*, dass der Terrorismus nicht mit einer bestimmten Religion, Nationalität oder Zivilisation in Verbindung gebracht werden kann und soll,

unter Hinweis auf die Aufnahme der Bewegung für die Einheit und den Dschihad in Westafrika, der Organisation Al-Qaida im islamischen Maghreb, Ansar Eddines und ihres Anführers Iyad Ag Ghali sowie Al-Murabituns in die von dem ISIL (Daesh)- und Al-Qaida-Sanktionsausschuss nach den Resolutionen 1267 (1999), 1989 (2011) und 2253 (2015) aufgestellte Al-Qaida-Sanktionsliste und *erneut seine Bereitschaft bekundend*, im Rahmen des genannten Regimes Sanktionen gegen weitere Personen, Gruppen, Unternehmen und Einrichtungen zu verhängen, die mit Al-Qaida und anderen gelisteten Einrichtungen und Personen, einschließlich Al-Qaidas im islamischen Maghreb, Al-Murabituns und Ansar Eddines, verbunden sind, im Einklang mit den festgelegten Kriterien für die Aufnahme in die Liste,

die Maßnahmen *begrüßend*, die die französischen Truppen auf Ersuchen und in Unterstützung der malischen Behörden weiter zur Abschreckung der terroristischen Bedrohung im Norden Malis durchführen,

betonend, dass die Sicherheit und Stabilität in Mali unauflöslich mit denen der Sahel-Region und der Region Westafrika sowie mit der Situation in Libyen und in der Region Nordafrika verbunden sind,

mit dem Ausdruck seiner anhaltenden Besorgnis über die grenzüberschreitende Dimension der terroristischen Bedrohung in der Sahel-Region sowie über die ernsten Herausforderungen, die von der grenzüberschreitenden organisierten Kriminalität in der Sahel-Region ausgehen, unter anderem vom illegalen Waffen- und Drogenhandel, von der Schleusung von Migranten und vom Menschenhandel, und über ihre in einigen Fällen zunehmenden Verbindungen zum Terrorismus, *unterstreichend*, dass den Ländern der Region die Verantwortung für das Vorgehen gegen diese Bedrohungen und Herausforderungen zukommt, in diesem Zusammenhang *unter Begrüßung* der Anstrengungen der Gruppe der Fünf für den Sahel (G5 Sahel), darunter die Schaffung eines Rahmens zur Stärkung der regionalen Sicherheitszusammenarbeit sowie zur Durchführung gemeinsamer grenzüberschreitender Militäreinsätze, und des Prozesses von Nouakchott der Afrikanischen Union *sowie unter Begrüßung* des Beschlusses der Verteidigungsminister der Sahel- und Saharastaaten vom 24. und 25. März 2016, ihre regionale Zusammenarbeit zur Terrorismusbekämpfung zu verstärken und ein neues Zentrum für Terrorismusbekämpfung mit Sitz in Kairo einzurichten, und *unter Begrüßung* der Maßnahmen, die die französischen Truppen durchführen, um die Mitgliedstaaten der G5 Sahel bei der Verstärkung der regionalen Zusammenarbeit zur Terrorismusbekämpfung zu unterstützen,

unter nachdrücklicher Verurteilung der Fälle von Entführungen und Geiselnahmen, die mit dem Ziel begangen werden, Mittel zu beschaffen oder politische Zugeständnisse zu erwirken, *von neuem* seine Entschlossenheit *bekundend*, Entführungen und Geiselnahmen in der Sahel-Region im Einklang mit dem anwendbaren Völkerrecht zu verhindern, *unter Hinweis* auf seine Resolutionen 2133 (2014) und 2253 (2015) und insbesondere seine Aufforderung an alle Mitgliedstaaten, zu verhindern, dass Terroristen unmittelbar oder mittelbar von Lösegeldzahlungen oder politischen Zugeständnissen profitieren, und die sichere Freilassung von Geiseln zu erwirken, und in dieser Hinsicht *unter Hinweis* auf das von dem Globalen Forum Terrorismusbekämpfung veröffentlichte Memorandum von Algier über bewährte Verfahren zur Verhütung von Entführungen zur Erpressung von Lösegeld durch Terroristen und zur Beseitigung der damit verbundenen Vorteile,

unter nachdrücklicher Verurteilung aller Menschenrechtsübergriffe und -verletzungen und Verstöße gegen das humanitäre Völkerrecht, insbesondere der außergerichtlichen und summarischen Hinrichtungen, der willkürlichen Festnahmen und Inhaftierungen und der Misshandlung von Gefangenen, der sexuellen und geschlechtsspezifischen Gewalt sowie der Tötungen und Verstümmelungen, der Einziehung und des Einsatzes von Kindern und der Angriffe auf Schulen und Krankenhäuser, *mit der Aufforderung* an alle Parteien, den zivilen Charakter von Schulen im Einklang mit dem humanitären Völkerrecht zu achten und die rechtswidrige und willkürliche Inhaftierung von Kindern zu beenden, und *mit der Aufforderung* an alle Parteien, diesen Verstößen und Rechtsverletzungen ein Ende zu setzen und ihren Verpflichtungen nach dem anwendbaren Völkerrecht nachzukommen,

in dieser Hinsicht *erneut erklärend*, dass alle diejenigen, die solche Handlungen begangen haben, zur Rechenschaft gezogen werden müssen und dass einige der im vorstehenden Absatz genannten Handlungen möglicherweise Verbrechen nach dem Römischen Statut darstellen, davon *Kenntnis nehmend*, dass die Anklägerin des Internationalen Strafgerichtshofs am 16. Januar 2013 aufgrund der Unterbreitung durch die Übergangsbehörden Malis vom 13. Juli 2012 Ermittlungen wegen der seit Januar 2012 im Hoheitsgebiet Malis angeblich begangenen Verbrechen aufgenommen hat, in dieser Hinsicht *ferner davon Kenntnis nehmend*, dass der Gerichtshof am 1. März 2016 im ersten beim Gerichtshof anhängigen Verfahren wegen des mutmaßlichen Kriegsverbrechens der vorsätzlichen Angriffe auf religiöse und geschichtliche Denkmäler in Timbuktu die Verhandlung betreffend die Bestätigung der Anklagepunkte eröffnet hat, und *unter Hinweis* darauf, wie wichtig die Unterstützung des Gerichtshofs und die Zusammenarbeit mit ihm durch alle betroffenen Parteien sind,

unterstreichend, wie wichtig es ist, dass die malischen Verteidigungs- und Sicherheitskräfte ziviler malischer Kontrolle und Aufsicht unterstehen und weiter konsolidiert werden, um die langfristige Sicherheit und Stabilität Malis zu gewährleisten und das Volk von Mali zu schützen,

in Würdigung der Rolle der EUTM Mali bei der Ausbildung und Beratung der malischen Verteidigungs- und Sicherheitskräfte, einschließlich ihres Beitrags zur Stärkung der Zivilgewalt und der Achtung der Menschenrechte, und der Rolle der Mission der Europäischen Union für Kapazitätsaufbau (EUCAP Sahel Mali) bei der strategischen Beratung und Ausbildung der Polizei, der Gendarmerie und der Nationalgarde in Mali,

betonend, dass alle Parteien die humanitären Grundsätze der Menschlichkeit, der Neutralität, der Unparteilichkeit und der Unabhängigkeit wahren und achten müssen, um die fortgesetzte Bereitstellung humanitärer Hilfe, die Sicherheit und den Schutz der Zivilpersonen, die Hilfe erhalten, und die Sicherheit des in Mali tätigen humanitären Personals zu gewährleisten, und *hervorhebend*, wie wichtig es ist, dass die humanitäre Hilfe auf der Grundlage der Bedürfnisse bereitgestellt wird,

nach wie vor ernsthaft besorgt über die anhaltende gravierende Nahrungsmittel- und humanitäre Krise in Mali und über die herrschende Unsicherheit, die den humanitären Zugang behindert und die durch die Anwesenheit bewaffneter Gruppen, terroristischer und krimineller Netzwerke und deren Aktivitäten, das Vorhandensein von Landminen sowie die fortgesetzte unerlaubte Verbreitung von Waffen aus der Region selbst und von außerhalb, die den Frieden, die Sicherheit und die Stabilität der Staaten in dieser Region bedroht, noch verschlimmert wird, und die Angriffe auf humanitäres Personal *verurteilend*,

mit dem Ausdruck seiner nachdrücklichen Unterstützung für den Sonderbeauftragten des Generalsekretärs für Mali und für die MINUSMA, die den malischen Behörden und dem malischen Volk bei ihren Bemühungen behilflich sind, ihrem Land auf Dauer Frieden und Sicherheit zu bringen, eingedenk der Hauptverantwortung der malischen Behörden für den Schutz der Bevölkerung, und *unter Begrüßung* der stabilisierenden Wirkung der internationalen Präsenz, einschließlich der MINUSMA, in Mali, *in Würdigung* des Beitrags der Länder, die Truppen und Polizei für die MINUSMA stellen, *mit dem Ausdruck seiner Hochachtung* für die Friedenssicherungskräfte, die hier ihr Leben riskieren und hingeben, *unter nachdrücklicher Verurteilung* der Angriffe auf Friedenssicherungskräfte und *unterstreichend*, dass gezielte Angriffe auf Friedenssicherungskräfte Kriegsverbrechen nach dem Völkerrecht darstellen können,

mit dem Ausdruck seiner ernsten Besorgnis darüber, dass der MINUSMA weiter wesentliche Einsatzmittel fehlen, unter Betonung der Notwendigkeit, die Kapazitäten der MINUSMA zu stärken, damit sie ihr Mandat in einem komplexen Sicherheitsumfeld, das unter anderem durch asymmetrische Bedrohungen gekennzeichnet ist, erfüllen kann, und *betonend*, dass die Gewährleistung der Sicherheit des Personals der MINUSMA in dieser Hinsicht von äußerster Wichtigkeit ist,

betonend, wie wichtig es ist, dass die MINUSMA für die möglichst wirksame Verwendung und Dislozierung ihrer Truppen und Einsatzmittel sorgt und dabei den Prioritäten der in ihrem Mandat enthaltenen Aufgaben folgt,

feststellend, dass die Situation in Mali nach wie vor eine Bedrohung des Weltfriedens und der internationalen Sicherheit darstellt,

tätig werdend nach Kapitel VII der Charta der Vereinten Nationen,
[…]

Mandat der MINUSMA

14. *beschließt*, das Mandat der MINUSMA bis zum 30. Juni 2017 zu verlängern;
15. *beschließt*, die Kräfte der MINUSMA bis zu einer Obergrenze von 13.289 Soldaten und 1.920 Polizisten zu erhöhen, und *ersucht* den Generalsekretär, die notwendigen Schritte zu unternehmen, um die Mobilisierung von Kräften und Ausrüstung sowie die Dislozierung zu beschleunigen, wie unter anderem in Ziffer 41 festgelegt;
16. *beschließt*, dass die strategische Priorität der MINUSMA darin besteht, die Durchführung des Abkommens für Frieden und Aussöhnung in Mali, insbesondere seiner Bestimmungen betreffend die schrittweise Wiederherstellung und Ausweitung der staatlichen Autorität, durch die Regierung und die Koalitionen bewaffneter Gruppen „Plateforme" und „Coordination" sowie anderer in Betracht kommender malischer Interessenträger zu unterstützen;
17. *ermächtigt* die MINUSMA, alle erforderlichen Mittel einzusetzen, um ihr Mandat im Rahmen ihrer Möglichkeiten und in ihren Einsatzgebieten durchzuführen;
18. *ersucht* die MINUSMA, eine proaktivere und robustere Position zur Durchführung ihres Mandats einzunehmen;
19. *beschließt*, dass das Mandat der MINUSMA die folgenden vorrangigen Aufgaben umfasst:
    a) *Unterstützung für die Durchführung des Abkommens für Frieden und Aussöhnung in Mali*
       i) die Durchführung der im Abkommen, insbesondere in Teil II, vorgesehenen politischen und institutionellen Reformen zu unterstützen und insbesondere die Anstrengungen der Regierung zur wirksamen Wiederherstellung und Ausweitung der staatlichen Autorität und der Rechtsstaatlichkeit im gesamten Hoheitsgebiet zu unterstützen, unter anderem durch die Unterstützung der wirksamen Einsetzung von Interimsverwaltungen im Norden Malis unter den im Abkommen festgelegten Bedingungen;
       ii) die Durchführung der im Abkommen, insbesondere seinem Teil III und seinem Anhang 2, vorgesehenen Verteidigungs- und Sicherheitsmaßnahmen zu unterstützen, namentlich

- die Waffenruhe zu unterstützen, zu beobachten und zu überwachen und dem Sicherheitsrat etwaige Verstöße zu melden;
- die Neudislozierung der reformierten und neu konstituierten malischen Verteidigungs- und Sicherheitskräfte, insbesondere im Zentrum und im Norden Malis, zu unterstützen;
- die Kantonierung, Entwaffnung, Demobilisierung und Wiedereingliederung der bewaffneten Gruppen zu unterstützen, unter anderem durch die Eingliederung von Elementen der bewaffneten Gruppen, die das Abkommen unterzeichnet haben, in die malischen Verteidigungs- und Sicherheitskräfte, als Interimsmaßnahme, im Rahmen der Sicherheitssektorreform und unbeschadet der voraussichtlichen Pläne der Kommissionen für Demobilisierung, Entwaffnung und Wiedereingliederung beziehungsweise Eingliederung;
- für die Kohärenz der internationalen Anstrengungen zu sorgen und dabei eng mit anderen bilateralen Partnern, Gebern und internationalen Organisationen, einschließlich der Europäischen Union, die auf diesen Gebieten tätig sind, zusammenzuarbeiten, um den malischen Sicherheitssektor innerhalb des durch das Abkommen vorgegebenen Rahmens wiederaufzubauen;

iii) die Durchführung der Aussöhnung und Gerechtigkeit betreffenden Maßnahmen des Abkommens, insbesondere in Teil V, namentlich die Einsetzung einer internationalen Untersuchungskommission, in Absprache mit den Parteien zu unterstützen und die Operationalisierung der Kommission für Wahrheit, Gerechtigkeit und Aussöhnung zu unterstützen;

iv) im Rahmen ihrer Mittel und innerhalb ihrer Einsatzgebiete die Abhaltung inklusiver, freier, fairer und transparenter Kommunalwahlen sowie die Abhaltung eines Verfassungsreferendums zu unterstützen, namentlich durch die Bereitstellung der entsprechenden logistischen Hilfe und Sicherheitsregelungen, gemäß dem Abkommen;

v) die besonderen Bedürfnisse der mit bewaffneten Gruppen verbundenen Frauen zu berücksichtigen und für ihren uneingeschränkten Zugang zu Entwaffnungs-, Demobilisierungs- und Wiedereingliederungsprogrammen zu sorgen, unter anderem im Benehmen mit Frauenorganisationen;

b) *Gute Dienste und Aussöhnung*
durch Gute Dienste, Vertrauensbildung und Moderation auf nationaler und lokaler Ebene den auf Aussöhnung und sozialen Zusammenhalt gerichteten Dialog mit und zwischen allen Interessenträgern zu unterstützen, Anstrengungen zur Verringerung von Spannungen zwischen den Volksgruppen eingedenk der Hauptverantwortung der malischen Behörden zu unterstützen und die vollständige Durchführung des Abkommens durch die Regierung Malis und die Koalitionen bewaffneter Gruppen „Plateforme" und „Coordination" zu fördern und zu unterstützen, unter anderem durch die Förderung der Mitwirkung der Zivilgesellschaft, einschließlich Frauen- sowie Jugendorganisationen;

c) *Schutz von Zivilpersonen und Stabilisierung, einschließlich des Schutzes vor asymmetrischen Bedrohungen*

i) unbeschadet der Hauptverantwortung der malischen Behörden Zivilpersonen vor drohender körperlicher Gewalt zu schützen;

ii) zur Unterstützung der malischen Behörden die wichtigsten Bevölkerungszentren und andere Gebiete, in denen Zivilpersonen Gefahren ausgesetzt sind, namentlich im Norden und im Zentrum Malis, zu stabilisieren und in diesem Zusammenhang die Frühwarnung zu verbessern, Bedrohungen, einschließlich asymmetrischer Bedrohungen, vorauszusehen, von ihnen abzuschrecken und sie zu bekämpfen und robuste und aktive Schritte zum Schutz von Zivilpersonen zu unternehmen, unter anderem durch aktive und wirksame Patrouillen in Gebieten, in denen Zivilpersonen Gefahr droht, und die Rückkehr bewaffneter Elemente in diese Gebiete zu verhindern und Direkteinsätze nur dann zu führen, wenn schwere und glaubwürdige Bedrohungen vorliegen;

iii) Frauen und Kindern, die von bewaffneten Konflikten betroffen sind, spezifischen Schutz zu gewähren, einschließlich durch Kinderschutz- und Frauenschutzberater, und

den Bedürfnissen der Opfer sexueller und geschlechtsspezifischer Gewalt in bewaffneten Konflikten Rechnung zu tragen;
- d) *Vorgehen gegen asymmetrische Angriffe in aktiver Verteidigung des Mandats der MINUSMA*

  in Verfolgung ihrer Prioritäten und in aktiver Verteidigung ihres Mandats Bedrohungen vorauszusehen, von ihnen abzuschrecken und robuste und aktive Schritte gegen asymmetrische Angriffe auf Zivilpersonen oder Personal der Vereinten Nationen zu unternehmen, rasche und wirksame Gegenmaßnahmen zu gewährleisten, wenn Zivilpersonen Gewalt droht, und eine Rückkehr bewaffneter Elemente in diese Gebiete zu verhindern und Direkteinsätze nur dann zu führen, wenn schwere und glaubwürdige Bedrohungen vorliegen;
- e) *Schutz und Sicherheit des Personals der Vereinten Nationen*

  das Personal, insbesondere das uniformierte Personal, die Einrichtungen und die Ausrüstung der Vereinten Nationen zu schützen und die Sicherheit und Bewegungsfreiheit des Personals der Vereinten Nationen und des beigeordneten Personals zu gewährleisten;
- f) *Förderung und Schutz der Menschenrechte*
  - i) den malischen Behörden bei ihren Anstrengungen zur Förderung und zum Schutz der Menschenrechte behilflich zu sein, insbesondere auf dem Gebiet der Gerechtigkeit und der Aussöhnung, und soweit möglich und angebracht die malischen Behörden unbeschadet ihrer Verantwortlichkeiten dabei zu unterstützen, diejenigen, die für schwere Menschenrechtsübergriffe oder -verletzungen oder Verstöße gegen das humanitäre Völkerrecht, insbesondere Kriegsverbrechen und Verbrechen gegen die Menschlichkeit in Mali, verantwortlich sind, vor Gericht zu stellen, unter Berücksichtigung dessen, dass die Übergangsbehörden Malis die seit Januar 2012 in ihrem Land herrschende Situation dem Internationalen Strafgerichtshof unterbreitet haben;
  - ii) in ganz Mali begangene Verstöße gegen das humanitäre Völkerrecht und Menschenrechtsverletzungen und -übergriffe, einschließlich aller Formen von sexueller und geschlechtsspezifischer Gewalt und Rechtsverletzungen und Missbrauchshandlungen an Frauen und Kindern, zu beobachten, untersuchen zu helfen und dem Sicherheitsrat und gegebenenfalls der Öffentlichkeit Bericht zu erstatten und zu den Maßnahmen zur Verhütung solcher Rechtsverletzungen und Verstöße beizutragen;
- g) *Humanitäre Hilfe*

  in Unterstützung der malischen Behörden dazu beizutragen, ein sicheres Umfeld für die sichere, unter ziviler Führung und im Einklang mit humanitären Grundsätzen erfolgende Erbringung humanitärer Hilfe und für die freiwillige Rückkehr der Binnenvertriebenen und Flüchtlinge in Sicherheit und Würde oder ihre Integration vor Ort oder Neuansiedlung in enger Abstimmung mit den humanitären Akteuren zu schaffen;

20. *ermächtigt* die MINUSMA ferner, ihre vorhandenen Kapazitäten zu nutzen, um bei der Durchführung der folgenden Aufgaben behilflich zu sein:
    - a) *Stabilisierungsprojekte*

      in Unterstützung der malischen Behörden zur Schaffung eines sicheren Umfelds für Projekte mit dem Ziel der Stabilisierung des Nordens Malis, einschließlich Projekten mit rascher Wirkung, beizutragen;
    - b) *Verwaltung der Bestände an Waffen und Munition*

      den malischen Behörden bei der Beseitigung und Zerstörung von Minen und anderen Sprengkörpern und bei der Verwaltung der Bestände an Waffen und Munition behilflich zu sein;
    - c) *Unterstützung für die Erhaltung des Kulturguts*

      den malischen Behörden nach Bedarf und soweit durchführbar dabei behilflich zu sein, die kulturellen und historischen Stätten in Mali in Zusammenarbeit mit der Organisation der Vereinten Nationen für Erziehung, Wissenschaft und Kultur vor Angriffen zu schützen;
    - d) *Zusammenarbeit mit dem ISIL (Daesh)- und Al-Qaida-Sanktionsausschuss nach den Resolutionen 1267 (1999), 1989 (2011) und 2253 (2015)*

      im Rahmen ihrer Möglichkeiten und in ihren Einsatzgebieten und unbeschadet ihres Mandats dem ISIL (Daesh)- und Al-Qaida-Sanktionsausschuss nach den Resolutionen 1267 (1999),

1989 (2011) und 2253 (2015) und dem mit Resolution 1526 (2004) eingesetzten Team für analytische Unterstützung und Sanktionsüberwachung behilflich zu sein, unter anderem indem sie Informationen weiterleitet, die für die Durchführung der in Ziffer 2 der Resolution 2253 (2015) vorgesehenen Maßnahmen von Belang sind;
[...]

Umweltauswirkungen der Einsätze der MINUSMA

39. *ersucht* die MINUSMA, bei der Erfüllung ihrer mandatsmäßigen Aufgaben die Umweltauswirkungen ihrer Einsätze zu berücksichtigen und in diesem Zusammenhang diese Auswirkungen je nach Bedarf und im Einklang mit den anwendbaren und einschlägigen Resolutionen der Generalversammlung und Vorschriften und Regeln der Vereinten Nationen unter Kontrolle zu halten und in der Nähe kultureller und historischer Stätten achtsam vorzugehen;
[...]

Berichte des Generalsekretärs

46. *ersucht* den Generalsekretär, dem Sicherheitsrat alle drei Monate nach Verabschiedung dieser Resolution über die Durchführung dieser Resolution und dabei insbesondere über den Stand der Durchführung des Abkommens für Frieden und Aussöhnung in Mali und die diesbezüglichen Unterstützungsbemühungen der MINUSMA Bericht zu erstatten, und *ersucht* den Generalsekretär in dieser Hinsicht, in seinen Bericht für Dezember die in Ziffer 12 genannten Zielmarken und Zeitpläne aufzunehmen und dann in seinen regelmäßigen Berichten über diese Zielmarken Bericht zu erstatten;

47. *beschließt*, mit der Angelegenheit aktiv befasst zu bleiben.

A.I.6 UNSR-Resolution 2347 (2017)

Vereinte Nationen
Sicherheitsrat
Resolution 2347 (2017)

Verabschiedet auf der 7907. Sitzung des Sicherheitsrats am 24. März 2017, S/RES/2347 (2017)

Der Sicherheitsrat,

unter Hinweis auf seine Resolutionen 1267 (1999), 1373 (2001), 1483 (2003), 1546 (2004), 2056 (2012), 2071 (2012), 2085 (2012), 2100 (2013), 2139 (2014), 2170 (2014), 2195 (2014), 2199 (2015)[1], 2249 (2015), 2253 (2015) und 2322 (2016) sowie die Erklärung seines Präsidenten S/PRST/2012/26,

Kenntnis nehmend von der Resolution 38 C/48 der Generalkonferenz der Organisation der Vereinten Nationen für Erziehung, Wissenschaft und Kultur (UNESCO), mit der die Mitgliedstaaten die Strategie für die Verstärkung der Maßnahmen der UNESCO zum Schutz der Kultur und zur Förderung des kulturellen Pluralismus bei bewaffneten Konflikten verabschiedeten und die Generaldirektorin baten, einen Aktionsplan zur Umsetzung der Strategie auszuarbeiten,

in Bekräftigung seiner Hauptverantwortung für die Wahrung des Weltfriedens und der internationalen Sicherheit gemäß der Charta der Vereinten Nationen und *ferner in Bekräftigung* der Ziele und Grundsätze der Charta der Vereinten Nationen,

bekräftigend, dass der Terrorismus in allen seinen Arten und Erscheinungsformen eine der schwersten Bedrohungen des Weltfriedens und der internationalen Sicherheit darstellt und dass alle terroristischen Handlungen verbrecherisch und nicht zu rechtfertigen sind, ungeachtet ihrer Beweggründe und gleichviel wann und von wem sie begangen werden,

betonend, dass die rechtswidrige Zerstörung von Kulturerbe und die Plünderung und der Schmuggel von Kulturgut bei bewaffneten Konflikten, namentlich durch terroristische Gruppen, und der Versuch, in diesem Kontext historische Wurzeln und kulturelle Vielfalt zu leugnen, Konflikte schüren und verschärfen und die nationale Aussöhnung nach Konflikten behindern können, wodurch die Sicherheit, die Stabilität, die Staatsführung und die soziale, wirtschaftliche und kulturelle Entwicklung der betroffenen Staaten untergraben werden,

mit großer Sorge Kenntnis nehmend von der Beteiligung nichtstaatlicher Akteure, namentlich terroristischer Gruppen, an der Zerstörung von Kulturerbe, dem illegalen Handel mit Kulturgut und damit verbundenen Straftaten, insbesondere von der anhaltenden Bedrohung des Weltfriedens und der internationalen Sicherheit durch die Organisation Islamischer Staat in Irak und der Levante (ISIL, auch bekannt als Daesh), Al-Qaida und mit ihnen verbundene Personen, Gruppen, Unternehmen und Einrichtungen, und seine Entschlossenheit *bekräftigend*, gegen alle Aspekte dieser Bedrohung anzugehen,

sowie mit Besorgnis feststellend, dass die Organisation Islamischer Staat in Irak und der Levante (ISIL, auch bekannt als Daesh), Al-Qaida und mit ihnen verbundene Personen, Gruppen, Unternehmen und Einrichtungen durch die direkte oder indirekte Beteiligung an der illegalen Ausgrabung, der Plünderung und dem Schmuggel von Kulturgut von archäologischen Stätten, aus Museen, Bibliotheken, Archiven und von anderen Stätten Einkünfte erzeugen, die zur Unterstützung ihrer Anwerbungsbemühungen und zur Stärkung ihrer operativen Fähigkeit zur Organisation und Durchführung von Terroranschlägen verwendet werden,

mit großer Sorge Kenntnis nehmend von der ernsthaften Bedrohung des Kulturerbes durch Landminen und nicht zur Wirkung gelangte explosive Kampfmittel,

zutiefst besorgt über die Verbindungen zwischen den Aktivitäten von Terroristen und organisierten kriminellen Gruppen, die in manchen Fällen kriminelle Aktivitäten erleichtern, darunter den illegalen Handel mit Kulturgut, illegale Einnahmen und Finanzströme sowie Geldwäsche, Bestechung und Korruption,

unter Hinweis auf die Resolution 1373 (2001) des Sicherheitsrats, wonach alle Staaten die Finanzierung terroristischer Handlungen verhüten und bekämpfen müssen und es unterlassen müssen, Personen, Gruppen, Unternehmen oder Einrichtungen, die an terroristischen Handlungen beteiligt sind, in irgendeiner Form aktiv oder passiv zu unterstützen, und auf andere Resolutionen, die die Notwendigkeit

---

[1] Die Resolution 2199 (2015) ist abgedruckt als Nr. A.I.4.

betonen, dass die Mitgliedstaaten auch weiterhin Wachsamkeit in Bezug auf einschlägige Finanztransaktionen üben und im Einklang mit dem anwendbaren Völkerrecht über die zuständigen Behörden bessere Kapazitäten und Verfahrensweisen für den Informationsaustausch innerhalb der Regierungen und zwischen ihnen schaffen,

in Anerkennung der unverzichtbaren Rolle der internationalen Zusammenarbeit bei Maßnahmen der Verbrechensverhütung und Strafrechtspflege zur umfassenden und wirksamen Bekämpfung des illegalen Handels mit Kulturgut und damit zusammenhängender Straftaten, *betonend*, dass die Schaffung und Aufrechterhaltung fairer und wirksamer Strafjustizsysteme Teil jeder Strategie zur Bekämpfung von Terrorismus und grenzüberschreitender organisierter Kriminalität sein sollte, und in dieser Hinsicht an die Bestimmungen des Übereinkommens der Vereinten Nationen gegen die grenzüberschreitende organisierte Kriminalität und der dazugehörigen Protokolle *erinnernd*,

unter Hinweis auf die Konvention vom 14. Mai 1954 zum Schutz von Kulturgut bei bewaffneten Konflikten und die dazugehörigen Protokolle vom 14. Mai 1954 und vom 26. März 1999, das Übereinkommen vom 14. November 1970 über Maßnahmen zum Verbot und zur Verhütung der rechtswidrigen Einfuhr, Ausfuhr und Übereignung von Kulturgut, das Übereinkommen vom 16. November 1972 zum Schutz des Kultur- und Naturerbes der Welt, das Übereinkommen von 2003 zur Erhaltung des immateriellen Kulturerbes und das Übereinkommen von 2005 über den Schutz und die Förderung der Vielfalt kultureller Ausdrucksformen,

Kenntnis nehmend von den laufenden Anstrengungen des Ausschusses des Europarats betreffend Straftaten im Zusammenhang mit Kulturgut in Bezug auf einen rechtlichen Rahmen zur Bekämpfung des illegalen Handels mit Kulturgut,

in Würdigung der von Mitgliedstaaten unternommenen Anstrengungen zum Schutz und zur Erhaltung des Kulturerbes bei bewaffneten Konflikten und *Kenntnis nehmend* von der Erklärung, die die an der Internationalen Konferenz „Kultur als Mittel des Dialogs zwischen den Völkern" vom 31. Juli bis 1. August 2015 in Mailand (Italien) teilnehmenden Minister für Kultur abgaben, sowie von der Internationalen Konferenz über die Opfer ethnisch und religiös motivierter Gewalt im Nahen Osten, die am 8. September 2015 in Paris stattfand, und von der Konferenz zur Erhaltung des bedrohten Kulturerbes, die am 3. Dezember 2016 in Abu Dhabi stattfand, und der dort abgegebenen Erklärung,

unter Begrüßung der zentralen Rolle, die die UNESCO beim Schutz des Kulturerbes und bei der Förderung der Kultur als Mittel zur Annäherung von Menschen und zur Erweiterung des Dialogs spielt, unter anderem durch die #Unite4Heritage-Kampagne, und der zentralen Rolle des Büros der Vereinten Nationen für Drogen- und Verbrechensbekämpfung und der Internationalen Kriminalpolizeilichen Organisation – INTERPOL bei der Verhütung und Bekämpfung aller Arten und Aspekte des illegalen Handels mit Kulturgut und damit zusammenhängender Straftaten, unter anderem durch die Förderung einer umfassenden polizeilichen und justiziellen Zusammenarbeit, und bei der Förderung des Bewusstseins für diesen illegalen Handel,

sowie in Anerkennung der Rolle des Teams für analytische Unterstützung und Sanktionsüberwachung des ISIL (Daesh) und Al-Qaida-Sanktionsausschusses nach den Resolutionen 1267 (1999), 1989 (2011) und 2253 (2015) bei der Identifizierung und stärkeren Bewusstmachung der Herausforderungen im Kontext des illegalen Handels mit Kulturgut im Zusammenhang mit der Terrorismusfinanzierung gemäß den Resolutionen 2199 (2015) und 2253 (2015) und *unter Begrüßung* der Leitlinien der Arbeitsgruppe „Finanzielle Maßnahmen" (FATF) zu Empfehlung 5 über die Unterstrafestellung der Terrorismusfinanzierung zu jedem Zweck, im Einklang mit den genannten Resolutionen,

in dieser Hinsicht mit dem Ausdruck seiner Besorgnis darüber, dass die neuen Informations- und Kommunikationstechnologien, insbesondere das Internet, in einer globalisierten Gesellschaft von Terroristen und ihren Unterstützern nach wie vor zur Erleichterung terroristischer Handlungen benutzt werden, und unter Verurteilung ihrer Benutzung zu dem Zweck, terroristische Handlungen über den illegalen Handel mit Kulturgut zu finanzieren,

unterstreichend, wie wichtig es ist, dass alle zuständigen Institutionen der Vereinten Nationen bei der Durchführung ihres jeweiligen Mandats ihre Anstrengungen abstimmen,

davon Kenntnis nehmend, dass der Internationale Strafgerichtshof in einem kürzlich ergangenen Urteil erstmals eine Person verurteilte, die des Kriegsverbrechens vorsätzlicher Angriffe auf dem Gottesdienst gewidmete Gebäude und geschichtliche Denkmäler und Gebäude angeklagt war,

A.I.6 UNSR-Resolution 2347 (2017)

1. *missbilligt und verurteilt* die rechtswidrige Zerstörung von Kulturerbe, darunter die Zerstörung religiöser Stätten und Artefakte, sowie die Plünderung und den Schmuggel von Kulturgut von archäologischen Stätten, aus Museen, Bibliotheken, Archiven und von anderen Stätten bei bewaffneten Konflikten, namentlich durch terroristische Gruppen;
2. *erinnert* an seine Verurteilung jeder Beteiligung am direkten oder indirekten Handel mit ISIL, der Al-Nusra-Front und allen anderen mit Al-Qaida verbundenen Personen, Gruppen, Unternehmen und Einrichtungen und *weist erneut darauf hin*, dass eine solche Beteiligung eine finanzielle Unterstützung für von dem ISIL (Daesh) und Al-Qaida-Sanktionsausschuss nach den Resolutionen 1267 (1999), 1989 (2011) und 2253 (2015) benannte Einrichtungen darstellen und zu weiteren Listungen durch den Ausschuss führen könnte;
3. *verurteilt außerdem* die systematischen Kampagnen zur illegalen Ausgrabung und die Plünderung von Kulturerbe, insbesondere diejenigen, die von ISIL, Al-Qaida und mit ihnen verbundenen Personen, Gruppen, Unternehmen und Einrichtungen begangen werden;
4. *erklärt*, dass gezielte rechtswidrige Angriffe auf Stätten und Gebäude, die dem Gottesdienst, der Erziehung, der Kunst, der Wissenschaft oder der Wohltätigkeit gewidmet sind, oder auf geschichtliche Denkmäler unter gewissen Umständen und nach dem Völkerrecht ein Kriegsverbrechen darstellen können und dass diejenigen, die solche Angriffe begehen, vor Gericht gestellt werden müssen;
5. *betont*, dass den Mitgliedstaaten die Hauptverantwortung für den Schutz ihres Kulturerbes zukommt und dass die Anstrengungen zum Schutz des Kulturerbes bei bewaffneten Konflikten im Einklang mit der Charta, einschließlich ihrer Ziele und Grundsätze, und dem Völkerrecht stehen und die Souveränität aller Staaten achten sollen;
6. *bittet* in dieser Hinsicht die Vereinten Nationen und alle anderen zuständigen Organisationen, den Mitgliedstaaten auch weiterhin auf deren Antrag und auf der Grundlage ihrer ermittelten Bedürfnisse jede notwendige Unterstützung zur Verfügung zu stellen;
7. *ermutigt* alle Mitgliedstaaten, die die Konvention vom 14. Mai 1954 zum Schutz von Kulturgut bei bewaffneten Konflikten und die dazugehörigen Protokolle sowie andere einschlägige internationale Übereinkommen noch nicht ratifiziert haben, dies zu erwägen;
8. *ersucht* die Mitgliedstaaten, geeignete Schritte zu unternehmen, um den illegalen Handel mit Kulturgut und anderen Gegenständen von archäologischer, historischer, kultureller und religiöser Bedeutung und wissenschaftlichem Seltenheitswert, die einem Kontext bewaffneten Konflikts entstammen und insbesondere von terroristischen Gruppen kommen, zu verhüten und zu bekämpfen, unter anderem indem sie den grenzüberschreitenden Handel mit diesen unerlaubten Gegenständen verbieten, wenn Staaten den begründeten Verdacht hegen, dass diese Gegenstände einem Kontext bewaffneten Konflikts entstammen und insbesondere von terroristischen Gruppen kommen, und wenn ihre Herkunft nicht klar dokumentiert und bescheinigt ist, um letztendlich ihre sichere Rückgabe zu ermöglichen, insbesondere Gegenstände, die seit dem 6. August 1990 aus Irak und seit dem 15. März 2011 aus Syrien illegal entfernt wurden, und *erinnert* in dieser Hinsicht daran, dass die Staaten sicherzustellen haben, dass keine Gelder, anderen finanziellen Vermögenswerte oder anderen wirtschaftlichen Ressourcen von ihren Staatsangehörigen oder von in ihrem Hoheitsgebiet befindlichen Personen direkt oder indirekt zugunsten von ISIL und mit ISIL oder Al-Qaida verbundenen Personen, Gruppen, Unternehmen und Einrichtungen zur Verfügung gestellt werden, im Einklang mit den einschlägigen Resolutionen;
9. *fordert* die Mitgliedstaaten *nachdrücklich auf*, nach Bedarf und im Einklang mit den Verpflichtungen nach dem Völkerrecht und den innerstaatlichen Rechtsinstrumenten wirksame nationale Maßnahmen auf gesetzgeberischer und operativer Ebene einzuführen, um den illegalen Handel mit Kulturgut und damit zusammenhängende Straftaten zu verhüten und zu bekämpfen, und dabei auch zu erwägen, Handlungen, die organisierten kriminellen Gruppen, Terroristen oder terroristischen Gruppen zugute kommen könnten, als schwere Straftaten gemäß Artikel 2 Buchstabe b des Übereinkommens der Vereinten Nationen gegen die grenzüberschreitende organisierte Kriminalität zu umschreiben;
10. *ermutigt* die Mitgliedstaaten, ISIL, Al-Qaida und mit ihnen verbundene Personen, Gruppen, Unternehmen und Einrichtungen, die am illegalen Handel mit Kulturgut beteiligt sind und die in den Resolutionen 1267 (1999), 1989 (2011) und 2253 (2015) dargelegten Benennungskriterien er-

füllen, für eine Listung vorzuschlagen, die vom ISIL (Daesh) und Al-Qaida-Sanktionsausschuss nach den Resolutionen 1267 (1999), 1989 (2011) und 2253 (2015) zu prüfen ist;
11. *legt* den Mitgliedstaaten *eindringlich nahe*, auf Anfrage unter anderem auch mit Unterstützung durch das Büro der Vereinten Nationen für Drogen- und Verbrechensbekämpfung und gegebenenfalls in Zusammenarbeit mit der UNESCO und der INTERPOL eine umfassende polizeiliche und justizielle Zusammenarbeit bei der Verhütung und Bekämpfung aller Arten und Aspekte des illegalen Handels mit Kulturgut und damit zusammenhängender Straftaten, die organisierten kriminellen Gruppen, Terroristen oder terroristischen Gruppen zugute kommen oder zugute kommen könnten, zu entwickeln;
12. *fordert* die Mitgliedstaaten *auf*, bei Ermittlungen, Strafverfolgungen, Beschlagnahmen und Einziehungen sowie bei der Rückgabe, Rückerstattung oder Repatriierung von illegal ein- oder ausgeführtem, gestohlenem, geplündertem, illegal ausgegrabenem oder illegal gehandeltem Kulturgut und bei Gerichtsverfahren über geeignete Kanäle und im Einklang mit der jeweiligen innerstaatlichen Rechtsordnung, dem Übereinkommen der Vereinten Nationen gegen die grenzüberschreitende organisierte Kriminalität und den dazugehörigen Protokollen und den einschlägigen regionalen, subregionalen und bilateralen Übereinkünften die Zusammenarbeit zu suchen und zu gewähren;
13. *begrüßt* die Aktivitäten der UNESCO im Rahmen ihres Mandats zur Bewahrung und Erhaltung des bedrohten Kulturerbes sowie ihre Aktivitäten zum Schutz der Kultur und zur Förderung des kulturellen Pluralismus bei bewaffneten Konflikten und *ermutigt* die Mitgliedstaaten, diese Aktivitäten zu unterstützen;
14. *ermutigt* die Mitgliedstaaten, nach Bedarf die bilaterale, subregionale und regionale Zusammenarbeit durch gemeinsame Initiativen im Rahmen der einschlägigen Programme der UNESCO zu stärken;
15. *nimmt Kenntnis* von dem Kulturerbe-Notfonds der UNESCO sowie von dem am 3. Dezember 2016 in Abu Dhabi angekündigten internationalen Fonds für den Schutz bedrohten Kulturerbes in bewaffneten Konflikten und von anderen diesbezüglichen Initiativen und *ermutigt* die Mitgliedstaaten, finanzielle Beiträge zu leisten, um im Geiste der Grundsätze der Übereinkommen der UNESCO Präventiv- und Nothilfemaßnahmen zu unterstützen, den illegalen Handel mit Kulturgut zu bekämpfen und alle geeigneten Anstrengungen zur Wiedererlangung von Kulturerbe zu unternehmen;
16. *ermutigt* die Mitgliedstaaten *außerdem*, Präventivmaßnahmen zur Erhaltung ihres in nationalem Eigentum stehenden Kulturguts und ihres sonstigen Kulturguts von nationaler Bedeutung bei bewaffneten Konflikten zu ergreifen, unter anderem gegebenenfalls durch die Dokumentierung und Konsolidierung ihres Kulturguts in einem Netzwerk „sicherer Orte" in ihrem eigenen Hoheitsgebiet, um ihr Kulturgut zu schützen, und dabei die kulturellen, geografischen und historischen Besonderheiten ihres schutzbedürftigen Kulturerbes zu berücksichtigen, und nimmt Kenntnis von dem Entwurf des Aktionsplans der UNESCO, der mehrere Anregungen zur Erleichterung dieser Maßnahmen enthält;
17. *fordert* die Mitgliedstaaten *auf*, zur Verhütung und Bekämpfung des illegalen Handels mit Kulturgut, das bei bewaffneten Konflikten unrechtmäßig in Besitz genommen und ausgeführt wurde, namentlich durch terroristische Gruppen, in Bezug auf dieses Kulturgut die folgenden Maßnahmen zu erwägen:
    a) lokale und nationale Bestandsverzeichnisse für Kulturerbe und Kulturgut einzuführen oder zu verbessern, nach Möglichkeit auch durch digitalisierte Informationen, und diese nach Bedarf den zuständigen Behörden und Organisationen leicht zugänglich zu machen;
    b) geeignete und wirksame Vorschriften für die Aus- und Einfuhr von Kulturgut zu erlassen, gegebenenfalls einschließlich der Bescheinigung der Herkunft, entsprechend den internationalen Standards;
    c) die Nomenklatur und die Einreihung der Waren im Harmonisierten System der Weltzollorganisation zu unterstützen und zu ihrer Aktualisierung beizutragen;
    d) im Einklang mit den innerstaatlichen Rechtsvorschriften und Verfahren gegebenenfalls in den zentralen und lokalen Verwaltungsbehörden spezialisierte Einheiten einzurichten und

in den Zoll- und Strafverfolgungsbehörden spezielles Personal einzusetzen und dieses sowie die Staatsanwälte mit wirksamen Mitteln auszustatten und ausreichend zu schulen;

e) Verfahren und gegebenenfalls Datenbanken zur Sammlung von Informationen über kriminelle Tätigkeiten im Zusammenhang mit Kulturgut sowie über illegal ausgegrabenes, aus- oder eingeführtes oder illegal gehandeltes, gestohlenes oder verschwundenes Kulturgut einzurichten;

f) zur Datenbank der INTERPOL über gestohlene Kunstwerke, zur UNESCO-Datenbank nationaler Kulturgutschutzgesetze und zur ARCHEO-Plattform der Weltzollorganisation und zu einschlägigen aktuellen nationalen Datenbanken beizutragen und sie zu verwenden sowie gegebenenfalls sachdienliche Daten und Angaben zu Ermittlungen und Strafverfolgungen und deren Ergebnissen bei einschlägigen Straftaten für das „SHERLOC"-Portal des Büros der Vereinten Nationen für Drogen- und Verbrechensbekämpfung und zur Beschlagnahme von Kulturgut für das Team für analytische Unterstützung und Sanktionsüberwachung zur Verfügung zu stellen;

g) mit Museen, relevanten Wirtschaftsverbänden und Akteuren auf dem Antiquitätenmarkt über Standards für die Herkunftsdokumentierung, differenzierte Maßnahmen zur Erfüllung der Sorgfaltspflicht und alle Maßnahmen zur Verhütung des Handels mit gestohlenem oder illegal gehandeltem Kulturgut in Dialog zu treten;

h) den in ihrem Hoheitsgebiet tätigen relevanten Interessenträgern und Verbänden in der Branche Verzeichnisse, sofern vorhanden, von archäologischen Stätten, Museen und Lagern für Grabungsfunde zur Verfügung zu stellen, die sich in Gebieten befinden, die von ISIL oder anderen Gruppen kontrolliert werden, die auf der Liste des ISIL (Daesh) und Al-Qaida-Sanktionsausschusses nach den Resolutionen 1267 (1999), 1989 (2011) und 2253 (2015) verzeichnet sind;

i) auf allen Ebenen Aufklärungsprogramme über den Schutz von Kulturerbe zu schaffen und die Öffentlichkeit stärker für den illegalen Handel mit Kulturgut und seine Verhütung zu sensibilisieren;

j) geeignete Maßnahmen zur Verzeichnung von Kulturgut und anderen Gegenständen von archäologischer, historischer, kultureller und religiöser Bedeutung und wissenschaftlichem Seltenheitswert, die aus Gebieten bewaffneter Konflikte widerrechtlich entfernt, übertragen oder verbracht wurden, durchzuführen und sich mit den zuständigen Institutionen der Vereinten Nationen und internationalen Akteuren abzustimmen, um die sichere Rückgabe aller verzeichneten Gegenstände zu gewährleisten;

18. *ermutigt* die Mitgliedstaaten, die zuständigen Institutionen der Vereinten Nationen im Einklang mit ihrem bestehenden Mandat und internationale Akteure, die dazu in der Lage sind, auf Ersuchen der betroffenen Staaten Hilfe bei der Minenräumung an kulturellen Stätten und Objekten zu leisten;

19. *erklärt*, dass das Mandat von Friedenssicherungseinsätzen der Vereinten Nationen, im Einklang mit ihren Einsatzregeln und wenn der Sicherheitsrat diesbezüglich ein konkretes Mandat erteilt hat, gegebenenfalls umfassen kann, den zuständigen Behörden auf Ersuchen und in Zusammenarbeit mit der UNESCO dabei behilflich zu sein, Kulturerbe vor Zerstörung, illegaler Ausgrabung, Plünderung und Schmuggel bei bewaffneten Konflikten zu schützen, und dass die Friedenssicherungseinsätze in der Umgebung kultureller und historischer Stätten behutsam vorgehen sollen;

20. *fordert* die UNESCO, das Büro der Vereinten Nationen für Drogen- und Verbrechensbekämpfung, die INTERPOL, die Weltzollorganisation und andere zuständige internationale Organisationen auf, sofern erforderlich und im Rahmen ihres bestehenden Mandats den Mitgliedstaaten bei ihren Anstrengungen behilflich zu sein, die Zerstörung und Plünderung von Kulturgut aller Art sowie den illegalen Handel damit zu verhüten und zu bekämpfen;

21. *ersucht* das Team für analytische Unterstützung und Sanktionsüberwachung des ISIL (Daesh) und Al-Qaida-Sanktionsausschusses nach den Resolutionen 1267 (1999), 1989 (2011) und 2253 (2015), im Rahmen seines bestehenden Mandats dem Ausschuss auch weiterhin sachdienliche Informationen betreffend den illegalen Handel mit Kulturgut zur Verfügung zu stellen;

22. *ersucht* den Generalsekretär *außerdem*, mit Unterstützung des Büros der Vereinten Nationen für Drogen- und Verbrechensbekämpfung, der UNESCO und des Teams für analytische Unterstüt-

zung und Sanktionsüberwachung des ISIL (Daesh) und Al-Qaida-Sanktionsausschusses nach den Resolutionen 1267 (1999), 1989 (2011) und 2253 (2015) sowie anderer zuständiger Organe der Vereinten Nationen dem Rat vor Jahresende einen Bericht über die Durchführung dieser Resolution vorzulegen;
23. *beschließt*, mit der Angelegenheit aktiv befasst zu bleiben.

A.II.1 Welterbe-Übereinkommen

Übereinkommen zum Schutz des Kultur- und Naturerbes der Welt[1)]
Vom 23. November 1972 (BGBl. 1977 II S. 215)

Die Generalkonferenz der Organisation der Vereinten Nationen für Erziehung, Wissenschaft und Kultur, die vom 17. Oktober bis 21. November 1972 in Paris zu ihrer 17. Tagung zusammengetreten ist –
im Hinblick darauf, daß das Kulturerbe und das Naturerbe zunehmend von Zerstörung bedroht sind, nicht nur durch die herkömmlichen Verfallsursachen, sondern auch durch den Wandel der sozialen und wirtschaftlichen Verhältnisse, der durch noch verhängnisvollere Formen der Beschädigung oder Zerstörung die Lage verschlimmert;
in der Erwägung, daß der Verfall oder der Untergang jedes einzelnen Bestandteils des Kultur- oder Naturerbes eine beklagenswerte Schmälerung des Erbes aller Völker der Welt darstellt;
in der Erwägung, daß der Schutz dieses Erbes auf nationaler Ebene wegen der Höhe der erforderlichen Mittel und der unzureichenden wirtschaftlichen, wissenschaftlichen und technischen Hilfsquellen des Landes, in dem sich das zu schützende Gut befindet, oft unvollkommen ist;
eingedenk der Tatsache, daß die Satzung der Organisation vorsieht, daß sie Kenntnisse aufrechterhalten, vertiefen und verbreiten wird, und zwar durch Erhaltung und Schutz des Erbes der Welt sowie dadurch, daß sie den beteiligten Staaten die diesbezüglich erforderlichen internationalen Übereinkünfte empfiehlt;
in der Erwägung, daß die bestehenden internationalen Übereinkünfte, Empfehlungen und Entschließungen über Kultur- und Naturgut zeigen, welche Bedeutung der Sicherung dieses einzigartigen und unersetzlichen Gutes, gleichviel welchem Volk es gehört, für alle Völker der Welt zukommt;
in der Erwägung, daß Teile des Kultur- oder Naturerbes von außergewöhnlicher Bedeutung sind und daher als Bestandteil des Welterbes der ganzen Menschheit erhalten werden müssen;
in der Erwägung, daß es angesichts der Größe und Schwere der drohenden neuen Gefahren Aufgabe der internationalen Gemeinschaft als Gesamtheit ist, sich am Schutz des Kultur- und Naturerbes von außergewöhnlichem universellem Wert zu beteiligen, indem sie eine gemeinschaftliche Unterstützung gewährt, welche die Maßnahmen des betreffenden Staates zwar nicht ersetzt, jedoch wirksam ergänzt;
in der Erwägung, daß es zu diesem Zweck erforderlich ist, neue Bestimmungen in Form eines Übereinkommens zur Schaffung eines wirksamen Systems des gemeinschaftlichen Schutzes des Kultur- und Naturerbes von außergewöhnlichem universellem Wert zu beschließen, das als ständige Einrichtung nach modernen wissenschaftlichen Methoden aufgebaut wird;
nach dem auf ihrer 16. Tagung gefaßten Beschluss, diese Frage zum Gegenstand eines internationalen Übereinkommens zu machen –
beschließt am 16. November 1972 dieses Übereinkommen.

I.
Begriffsbestimmung des Kultur- und Naturerbes

Artikel 1
Im Sinne dieses Übereinkommens gelten als „Kulturerbe"
Denkmäler: Werke der Architektur, Großplastik und Monumentalmalerei, Objekte oder Überreste archäologischer Art, Inschriften, Höhlen und Verbindungen solcher Erscheinungsformen, die aus geschichtlichen, künstlerischen oder wissenschaftlichen Gründen von außergewöhnlichem universellem Wert sind;
Ensembles: Gruppen einzelner oder miteinander verbundener Gebäude, die wegen ihrer Architektur, ihrer Geschlossenheit oder ihrer Stellung in der Landschaft aus geschichtlichen, künstlerischen oder wissenschaftlichen Gründen von außergewöhnlichem universellem Wert sind;
Stätten: Werke von Menschenhand oder gemeinsame Werke von Natur und Mensch sowie Gebiete einschließlich archäologischer Stätten, die aus geschichtlichen, ästhetischen, ethnologischen oder anthropologischen Gründen von außergewöhnlichem universellem Wert sind.

---

1) Liste der Vertragsstaaten: http://www.unesco.org/eri/la/convention.asp?KO=13055&language=E&order=alpha.

Artikel 2
Im Sinne diese Übereinkommens gelten als „Naturerbe"
Naturgebilde, die aus physikalischen und biologischen Erscheinungsformen oder -gruppen bestehen, welche aus ästhetischen oder wissenschaftlichen Gründen von außergewöhnlichem universellem Wert sind;
geologische und physiographische Erscheinungsformen und genau abgegrenzte Gebiete, die den Lebensraum für bedrohte Pflanzen- und Tierarten bilden, welche aus wissenschaftlichen Gründen oder ihrer Erhaltung wegen von außergewöhnlichem universellem Wert sind;
Naturstätten oder genau abgegrenzte Naturgebiete, die aus wissenschaftlichen Gründen oder ihrer Erhaltung oder natürlichen Schönheit wegen von außergewöhnlichem universellem Wert sind.

Artikel 3
Es ist Sache jedes Vertragsstaats, die in seinem Hoheitsgebiet befindlichen, in den Artikeln 1 und 2 bezeichneten Güter zu erfassen und zu bestimmen.

II.
Schutz des Kultur- und Naturerbes auf nationaler und internationaler Ebene

Artikel 4
Jeder Vertragsstaat erkennt an, daß es in erster Linie seine eigene Aufgabe ist, Erfassung, Schutz und Erhaltung in Bestand und Wertigkeit des in seinem Hoheitsgebiet befindlichen, in den Artikeln 1 und 2 bezeichneten Kultur- und Naturerbes sowie seine Weitergabe an künftige Generationen sicherzustellen. Er wird hierfür alles in seinen Kräften Stehende tun, unter vollem Einsatz seiner eigenen Hilfsmittel und gegebenenfalls unter Nutzung jeder ihm erreichbaren internationalen Unterstützung und Zusammenarbeit, insbesondere auf finanziellem, künstlerischem, wissenschaftlichem und technischem Gebiet.

Artikel 5
Um zu gewährleisten, daß wirksame und tatkräftige Maßnahmen zum Schutz und zur Erhaltung in Bestand und Wertigkeit des in seinem Hoheitsgebiet befindlichen Kultur- und Naturerbes getroffen werden, wird sich jeder Vertragsstaat bemühen, nach Möglichkeit und im Rahmen der Gegebenheiten seines Landes
a) eine allgemeine Politik zu verfolgen, die darauf gerichtet ist, dem Kultur- und Naturerbe eine Funktion im öffentlichen Leben zu geben und den Schutz dieses Erbes in erschöpfende Planungen einzubeziehen;
b) in seinem Hoheitsgebiet, sofern Dienststellen für den Schutz und die Erhaltung des Kultur- und Naturerbes in Bestand und Wertigkeit nicht vorhanden sind, eine oder mehrere derartige Dienststellen einzurichten, die über geeignetes Personal und die zur Durchführung ihrer Aufgaben erforderlichen Mittel verfügen;
c) wissenschaftliche und technische Untersuchungen und Forschungen durchzuführen und Arbeitsmethoden zu entwickeln, die es ihm ermöglichen, die seinem Natur- und Kulturerbe drohenden Gefahren zu bekämpfen,
d) geeignete rechtliche, wissenschaftliche, technische, Verwaltungs- und Finanzmaßnahmen zu treffen, die für Erfassung, Schutz, Erhaltung in Bestand und Wertigkeit sowie Revitalisierung dieses Erbes erforderlich sind, und
e) die Errichtung oder den Ausbau nationaler oder regionaler Zentren zur Ausbildung auf dem Gebiet des Schutzes und der Erhaltung des Natur- und Kulturerbes in Bestand und Wertigkeit zu fördern und die wissenschaftliche Forschung in diesem Bereich zu unterstützen.

Artikel 6
(1) Unter voller Achtung der Souveränität der Staaten, in deren Hoheitsgebiet sich das in den Artikeln 1 und 2 genannte Kultur- und Naturerbe befindet, und unbeschadet der durch das innerstaatliche Recht gewährten Eigentumsrechte erkennen die Vertragsstaaten an, daß dieses Erbe ein Welterbe darstellt, zu dessen Schutz die internationale Staatengemeinschaft als Gesamtheit zusammenarbeiten muß.
(2) Die Vertragsstaaten verpflichten sich, im Einklang mit diesem Übereinkommen bei Erfassung, Schutz und Erhaltung des in Artikel 11 Absätze 2 und 4 bezeichneten Kultur- und Naturerbes in Bestand

und Wertigkeit Hilfe zu leisten, wenn die Staaten, in deren Hoheitsgebiet sich dieses Erbe befindet, darum ersuchen.
(3) Jeder Vertragsstaat verpflichtet sich, alle vorsätzlichen Maßnahmen zu unterlassen, die das in den Artikeln 1 und 2 bezeichnete, im Hoheitsgebiet anderer Vertragsstaaten befindliche Kultur- und Naturerbe mittelbar oder unmittelbar schädigen könnten.

Artikel 7
Im Sinne dieses Übereinkommens bedeutet internationaler Schutz des Kultur- und Naturerbes der Welt die Einrichtung eines Systems internationaler Zusammenarbeit und Hilfe, das die Vertragsstaaten in ihren Bemühungen um die Erhaltung und Erfassung dieses Erbes unterstützen soll.

III.
Zwischenstaatliches Komitee für den Schutz des Kultur- und Naturerbes der Welt

Artikel 8
(1) Hiermit wird innerhalb der Organisation der Vereinten Nationen für Erziehung, Wissenschaft und Kultur ein Zwischenstaatliches Komitee für den Schutz des Kultur- und Naturerbes von außergewöhnlichem universellem Wert mit der Bezeichnung „Komitee für das Erbe der Welt" errichtet. Ihm gehören 15 Vertragsstaaten an; sie werden von den Vertragsstaaten gewählt, die während der ordentlichen Tagung der Generalkonferenz der Organisation der Vereinten Nationen für Erziehung, Wissenschaft und Kultur zu einer Hauptversammlung zusammentreten. Die Zahl der dem Komitee angehörenden Mitgliedsstaaten wird auf 21 erhöht, sobald eine ordentliche Tagung der Generalkonferenz nach dem Zeitpunkt stattfindet, an dem das Übereinkommen für mindestens 40 Staaten in Kraft tritt.
(2) Bei der Wahl der Komiteemitglieder ist eine ausgewogene Vertretung der verschiedenen Regionen und Kulturen der Welt zu gewährleisten.
(3) Je ein Vertreter der Internationalen Studienzentrale für die Erhaltung und Restaurierung von Kulturgut (Römische Zentrale), des Internationalen Rates für Denkmalpflege (ICOMOS) und der Internationalen Union zur Erhaltung der Natur und der natürlichen Hilfsquellen (IUCN) sowie auf Verlangen der Vertragsstaaten, die während der ordentlichen Tagungen der Generalkonferenz der Organisation der Vereinten Nationen für Erziehung, Wissenschaft und Kultur zu einer Hauptversammlung zusammentreten, weitere Vertreter anderer zwischenstaatlicher oder nichtstaatlicher Organisationen mit ähnlichen Zielen können in beratender Eigenschaft an den Sitzungen des Komitees teilnehmen.

Artikel 9
(1) Die Amtszeit der Mitgliedstaaten des Komitees für das Erbe der Welt beginnt mit Ablauf der ordentlichen Tagung der Generalkonferenz, auf der sie gewählt wurden, und endet mit Ablauf der dritten darauffolgenden ordentlichen Tagung.
(2) Die Amtszeit eines Drittels der bei der ersten Wahl bestellten Mitglieder endet jedoch mit Ablauf der ersten ordentlichen Tagung der Generalkonferenz nach der Tagung, auf der sie gewählt wurden; die Amtszeit eines weiteren Drittels der zur selben Zeit bestellten Mitglieder endet mit Ablauf der zweiten ordentlichen Tagung der Generalkonferenz nach der Tagung, auf der sie gewählt wurden. Die Namen dieser Mitglieder werden vom Präsidenten der Generalkonferenz der Organisation der Vereinten Nationen für Erziehung, Wissenschaft und Kultur nach der ersten Wahl durch das Los ermittelt.
(3) Die Mitgliedsstaaten des Komitees wählen zu ihren Vertretern Personen, die Sachverständige auf dem Gebiet des Kulturerbes oder des Naturerbes sind.

Artikel 10
(1) Das Komitee für das Erbe der Welt gibt sich eine Geschäftsordnung.
(2) Das Komitee kann jederzeit Organisationen des öffentlichen oder privaten Rechts oder Einzelpersonen einladen, zur Konsultation über Einzelfragen an seinen Sitzungen teilzunehmen.
(3) Das Komitee kann beratende Gremien einsetzen, die es zur Wahrnehmung seiner Aufgaben für erforderlich hält.

Artikel 11
(1) Jeder Vertragsstaat legt dem Komitee für das Erbe der Welt nach Möglichkeit ein Verzeichnis des Gutes vor, das zu dem in seinem Hoheitsgebiet befindlichen Kultur- und Naturerbe gehört und für eine

Aufnahme in die in Absatz 2 vorgesehene Liste geeignet ist. Dieses Verzeichnis, das nicht als erschöpfend anzusehen ist, muss Angaben über Lage und Bedeutung des betreffenden Gutes enthalten.
(2) Das Komitee wird auf Grund der von den Staaten nach Absatz 1 vorgelegten Verzeichnisse unter der Bezeichnung „Liste des Erbes der Welt" eine Liste der zu dem Kultur- und Naturerbe im Sinne der Artikel 1 und 2 gehörenden Güter, die nach seiner Auffassung nach den von ihm festgelegten Maßstäben von außergewöhnlichem universellem Wert sind, aufstellen, auf dem neuesten Stand halten und veröffentlichen. Eine auf den neuesten Stand gebrachte Liste wird mindestens alle zwei Jahre verbreitet.[1]
(3) Die Aufnahme eines Gutes in die Liste des Erbes der Welt bedarf der Zustimmung des betreffenden Staates. Die Aufnahme eines Gutes, das sich in einem Gebiet befindet, über das von mehr als einem Staat Souveränität oder Hoheitsgewalt beansprucht wird, berührt nicht die Rechte der Streitparteien.
(4) Das Komitee wird unter der Bezeichnung „Liste des gefährdeten Erbes der Welt" nach Bedarf eine Liste des in der Liste des Erbes der Welt aufgeführten Gutes, zu dessen Erhaltung umfangreiche Maßnahmen erforderlich sind und für das auf Grund dieses Übereinkommens Unterstützung angefordert wurde, aufstellen, auf dem neuesten Stand halten und veröffentlichen. Diese Liste hat einen Voranschlag der Kosten für derartige Maßnahmen zu enthalten. In die Liste darf nur solches zu dem Kultur- und Naturerbe gehörendes Gut aufgenommen werden, das durch ernste und spezifische Gefahren bedroht ist, z. B. Gefahr des Untergangs durch beschleunigten Verfall, öffentliche oder private Großvorhaben oder rasch vorangetriebene städtebauliche oder touristische Entwicklungsvorhaben; Zerstörung durch einen Wechsel in der Nutzung des Grundbesitzes oder im Eigentum daran; größere Veränderungen auf Grund unbekannter Ursachen; Preisgabe aus irgendwelchen Gründen; Ausbruch oder Gefahr eines bewaffneten Konflikts; Natur- und sonstige Katastrophen; Feuersbrünste, Erdbeben, Erdrutsche; Vulkanausbrüche; Veränderungen des Wasserspiegels, Überschwemmungen und Sturmfluten.[2] Das Komitee kann, wenn dies dringend notwendig ist, jederzeit eine neue Eintragung in die Liste des gefährdeten Erbes der Welt vornehmen und diese Eintragung sofort bekannt machen.
(5) Das Komitee bestimmt die Maßstäbe, nach denen ein zum Kultur- oder Naturerbe gehörendes Gut in eine der in den Absätzen 2 und 4 bezeichneten Listen aufgenommen werden kann.[3]
(6) Bevor das Komitee einen Antrag auf Aufnahme in eine der beiden in den Absätzen 2 und 4 bezeichneten Listen ablehnt, konsultiert es den Vertragsstaat, in dessen Hoheitsgebiet sich das betreffende Kultur- oder Naturgut befindet.
(7) Das Komitee koordiniert und fördert im Einvernehmen mit den betreffenden Staaten die Untersuchungen und Forschungen, die zur Aufstellung der in den Absätzen 2 und 4 bezeichneten Listen erforderlich sind.

Artikel 12
Ist ein zum Kultur- oder Naturerbe gehörendes Gut in keine der in Artikel 11 Absätze 2 und 4 bezeichneten Listen aufgenommen worden, so bedeutet das nicht, daß dieses Gut nicht für andere als die sich aus der Aufnahme in diese Listen ergebenden Zwecke von außergewöhnlichem universellem Wert ist.

Artikel 13
(1) Das Komitee für das Erbe der Welt nimmt die von Vertragsstaaten für in ihrem Hoheitsgebiet befindliches, zum Kultur- und Naturerbe gehörendes Gut, das in die Artikel 11 Absätze 2 und 4 bezeichneten Listen aufgenommen oder möglicherweise für eine Aufnahme geeignet ist, gestellten Anträge auf internationale Unterstützung entgegen und prüft sie. Derartige Anträge können gestellt werden, um den Schutz, die Erhaltung in Bestand und Wertigkeit oder die Revitalisierung dieses Gutes zu sichern.
(2) Anträge auf internationale Unterstützung nach Absatz 1 können auch die Erfassung von Kultur- oder Naturgut im Sinne der Artikel 1 und 2 zum Gegenstand haben, wenn Voruntersuchungen gezeigt haben, daß weitere Untersuchungen gerechtfertigt wären.

---

1) Siehe hierzu die aktuelle Liste des Erbes der Welt, abrufbar unter: http://whc.unesco.org/en/list/.
2) Siehe hierzu die aktuelle Liste des gefährdeten Erbes der Welt, abrufbar unter: http://whc.unesco.org/pg.cfm?cid=86.
3) Die "Operational Guidelines for the Implementation of the World Heritage Convention" sind abgedruckt als Nr. A.II.1a.

A.II.1 Welterbe-Übereinkommen

(3) Das Komitee entscheidet über die hinsichtlich dieser Anträge zu treffenden Maßnahmen, bestimmt gegebenenfalls Art und Ausmaß seiner Unterstützung und genehmigt den Abschluß der in seinem Namen mit der beteiligten Regierung zu treffenden erforderlichen Vereinbarungen.

(4) Das Komitee legt eine Rangordnung seiner Maßnahmen fest. Dabei berücksichtigt es die Bedeutung des schutzbedürftigen Gutes für das Kultur- und Naturerbe der Welt, die Notwendigkeit, internationale Unterstützung für das Gut zu gewähren, das die natürliche Umwelt oder die schöpferische Kraft und die Geschichte der Völker der Welt am besten verkörpert, ferner die Dringlichkeit der zu leistenden Arbeit, die Mittel, die den Staaten, in deren Hoheitsgebiet sich das betreffende Gut befindet, zur Verfügung stehen, und insbesondere das Ausmaß, in dem sie dieses Gut mit eigenen Mitteln sichern können.

(5) Das Komitee wird eine Liste des Gutes, für das internationale Unterstützung gewährt wurde, aufstellen, auf dem neuesten Stand halten und veröffentlichen.

(6) Das Komitee entscheidet über die Mittel des nach Artikel 15 errichteten Fonds. Es erkundet Möglichkeiten, diese Mittel zu erhöhen, und trifft dazu alle zweckdienlichen Maßnahmen.

(7) Das Komitee arbeitet mit internationalen und nationalen staatlichen und nichtstaatlichen Organisationen zusammen, deren Ziele denen dieses Übereinkommens gleichen. Zur Durchführung seiner Programme und Vorhaben kann das Komitee die Hilfe derartiger Organisationen, insbesondere der Internationalen Studienzentrale für die Erhaltung und Restaurierung von Kulturgut (Römische Zentrale), des Internationalen Rates für Denkmalpflege (ICOMOS) und der Internationalen Union zur Erhaltung der Natur und der natürlichen Hilfsquellen (ICUN) sowie sonstiger Einrichtungen des öffentlichen und privaten Rechts und von Einzelpersonen in Anspruch nehmen.

(8) Die Beschlüsse des Komitees bedürfen der Zweidrittelmehrheit seiner anwesenden und abstimmenden Mitglieder. Das Komitee ist beschlussfähig, wenn die Mehrheit der Mitglieder anwesend ist.

Artikel 14

(1) Dem Komitee für das Erbe der Welt steht ein Sekretariat zur Seite, das vom Generaldirektor der Organisation der Vereinten Nationen für Erziehung, Wissenschaft und Kultur bestellt wird.

(2) Der Generaldirektor der Organisation der Vereinten Nationen für Erziehung, Wissenschaft und Kultur bereitet unter möglichst weitgehender Nutzung der Dienste der Internationalen Studienzentrale für die Erhaltung und Restaurierung von Kulturgut (Römische Zentrale), des Internationalen Rates für Denkmalpflege (ICOMOS) und der Internationalen Union zur Erhaltung der Natur und der natürlichen Hilfsquellen (ICUN) in ihrem jeweiligen Zuständigkeits- und Fachbereich die Dokumentation des Komitees und die Tagesordnung seiner Sitzungen vor und ist für die Durchführung seiner Beschlüsse verantwortlich.

IV.
Fonds für den Schutz des Kultur- und Naturerbes der Welt

Artikel 15

(1) Hiermit wird ein Fonds für den Schutz des Kultur- und Naturerbes der Welt von außergewöhnlichem universellem Wert errichtet; er wird als „Fonds für das Erbe der Welt" bezeichnet.

(2) Der Fonds stellt ein Treuhandvermögen im Sinne der Finanzordnung der Organisation der Vereinten Nationen für Erziehung, Wissenschaft und Kultur dar.

(3) Die Mittel des Fonds bestehen aus
a) Pflichtbeiträgen und freiwilligen Beiträgen der Vertragsstaaten
b) Beiträgen, Spenden und Vermächtnissen
   i) anderer Staaten
   ii) der Organisationen der Vereinten Nationen für Erziehung, Wissenschaft und Kultur, anderer Organisationen des Systems der Vereinten Nationen, insbesondere des Entwicklungsprogramms der Vereinten Nationen, sowie sonstiger zwischenstaatlicher Organisationen.
   iii) von Einrichtungen des öffentlichen oder privaten Rechts oder von Einzelpersonen;
c) den für die Mittel des Fonds anfallenden Zinsen
d) Mitteln, die durch Sammlungen und Einnahmen aus Veranstaltungen zugunsten des Fonds aufgebracht werden, und

e) allen sonstigen Mitteln, die durch die vom Komitee für das Erbe der Welt für den Fonds aufgestellten Vorschriften genehmigt sind.

(4) Beiträge an den Fonds und sonstige dem Komitee zur Verfügung gestellten Unterstützungsbeiträge dürfen nur für die vom Komitee bestimmten Zwecke verwendet werden. Das Komitee kann Beiträge entgegennehmen, die nur für ein bestimmtes Programm oder Vorhaben verwendet werden sollen, sofern es die Durchführung dieses Programms oder Vorhabens beschlossen hat. An die dem Fonds gezahlten Beiträge dürfen keine politischen Bedingungen geknüpft werden.

Artikel 16

(1) Unbeschadet etwaiger zusätzlicher freiwilliger Beiträge verpflichten sich die Vertragsstaaten, regelmäßig alle zwei Jahre an den Fonds für das Erbe der Welt Beiträge zu zahlen, deren Höhe nach einem einheitlichen, für alle Staaten geltenden Schlüssel errechnet und von der Generalversammlung der Vertragsstaaten festgesetzt wird, die während der Tagungen der Generalkonferenz der Organisation der Vereinten Nationen für Erziehung, Wissenschaft und Kultur zusammentritt. Dieser Beschluß der Generalversammlung bedarf der Mehrheit der anwesenden und abstimmenden Vertragsstaaten, die nicht die in Absatz 2 genannte Erklärung abgegeben haben. Der Pflichtbeitrag der Vertragsstaaten darf 1 v. H. des Beitrags zum ordentlichen Haushalt der Organisation der Vereinten Nationen für Erziehung, Wissenschaft und Kultur nicht überschreiten.

(2) Ein in Artikel 31 und 32 genannter Staat kann jedoch bei Hinterlegung seiner Ratifikations-, Annahme- oder Beitrittsurkunde erklären, daß er durch Absatz 1 des vorliegenden Artikels nicht gebunden ist.

(3) Ein Vertragsstaat, der die in Absatz 2 genannte Erklärung abgegeben hat, kann diese jederzeit durch eine an den Generaldirektor der Organisation der Vereinten Nationen für Erziehung, Wissenschaft und Kultur gerichtete Notifikation zurücknehmen. Die Rücknahme der Erklärung wird jedoch für den Pflichtbeitrag des betreffenden Staates erst mit dem Zeitpunkt der nächsten Generalversammlung der Vertragsstaaten wirksam.

(4) Um dem Komitee die wirksame Planung seiner Tätigkeit zu ermöglichen, sind die Beiträge von Vertragsstaaten, welche die in Absatz 2 genannte Erklärung abgegeben haben, regelmäßig, mindestens jedoch alle zwei Jahre zu entrichten; sie sollen nicht niedriger sein als die Beiträge, die sie zu zahlen hätten, wenn Absatz 1 für sie gelten würde.

(5) Ein Vertragsstaat, der mit der Zahlung seiner Pflichtbeiträge oder seiner freiwilligen Beiträge für das laufende Jahr und das unmittelbar vorangegangene Kalenderjahr im Rückstand ist, kann nicht Mitglied des Komitees für das Erbe der Welt werden; dies gilt jedoch nicht für die erste Wahl. Die Amtszeit eines solchen Staates, der bereits Mitglied des Komitees ist, endet im Zeitpunkt der in Artikel 8 Absatz 1 vorgesehenen Wahl.

Artikel 17

Die Vertragsstaaten erwägen oder fördern die Errichtung nationaler Stiftungen oder Vereinigungen des öffentlichen und privaten Rechts, die den Zweck haben, Spenden für den Schutz des Kultur- und Naturerbes im Sinne der Artikel 1 und 2 anzuregen.

Artikel 18

Die Vertragsstaaten unterstützen die unter der Schirmherrschaft der Organisation der Vereinten Nationen für Erziehung, Wissenschaft und Kultur zugunsten des Fonds für das Erbe der Welt durchgeführten Werbemaßnahmen zur Aufbringung von Mitteln. Sie erleichtern die Sammlungen, die von den in Artikel 15 Absatz 3 bezeichneten Einrichtungen für diesen Zweck durchgeführt werden.

V.

Voraussetzungen und Maßnahmen internationaler Unterstützung

Artikel 19

Jeder Vertragsstaat kann internationale Unterstützung für in seinem Hoheitsgebiet befindliches und zum Kultur- und Naturerbe von außergewöhnlichem universellem Wert gehörendes Gut beantragen. Mit seinem Antrag hat er alle in Artikel 21 genannten Informationen und Unterlagen vorzulegen, über die er verfügt und die das Komitee benötigt, um einen Beschluß zu fassen.

A.II.1 Welterbe-Übereinkommen

Artikel 20

Vorbehaltlich des Artikels 13 Absatz 2, des Artikels 22 Buchstabe c und des Artikels 23 kann die in diesem Übereinkommen vorgesehene internationale Unterstützung nur für solches zum Kultur- und Naturerbe gehörendes Gut gewährt werden, dessen Aufnahme in eine der in Artikel 11 Absätze 2 und 4 bezeichneten Listen vom Komitee für das Erbe der Welt beschlossen wurde oder künftig beschlossen wird.

Artikel 21

(1) Das Komitee für das Erbe der Welt bestimmt das Verfahren, nach dem die ihm unterbreiteten Anträge auf internationale Unterstützung zu behandeln sind und schreibt die Einzelheiten des Antrags vor, der die erwogene Maßnahme, die erforderliche Arbeit, die voraussichtlichen Kosten, den Dringlichkeitsgrad und die Gründe, warum die Eigenmittel des antragstellenden Staates nicht zur Deckung aller Kosten ausreichen, umfassen soll. Den Anträgen sind, sofern irgend möglich, Sachverständigengutachten beizufügen.

(2) Anträge auf Grund von Natur- oder sonstigen Katastrophen sollen vom Komitee wegen der gegebenenfalls erforderlichen dringlichen Arbeiten sofort und vorrangig erörtert werden; es soll für derartige Notfälle über einen Reservefonds verfügen.

(3) Bevor das Komitee einen Beschluss fasst, führt es alle Untersuchungen und Konsultationen durch, die es für erforderlich hält.

Artikel 22

Unterstützung durch das Komitee für das Erbe der Welt kann in folgender Form gewährt werden:

a) Untersuchungen über die künstlerischen, wissenschaftlichen und technischen Probleme, die der Schutz, die Erhaltung in Bestand und Wertigkeit und die Revitalisierung des Kultur- und Naturerbes im Sinne des Artikels 11 Absätze 2 und 4 aufwerfen;

b) Bereitstellung von Sachverständigen, Technikern und Facharbeitern, um sicherzustellen, daß die genehmigte Arbeit richtig ausgeführt wird;

c) Ausbildung von Personal und Fachkräften aller Ebenen auf dem Gebiet der Erfassung, des Schutzes, der Erhaltung in Bestand und Wertigkeit und der Revitalisierung des Kultur- und Naturerbes;

d) Lieferung von Ausrüstungsgegenständen, die der betreffende Staat nicht besitzt oder nicht erwerben kann.

e) Darlehen mit niedrigem Zinssatz oder zinslose Darlehen, die langfristig zurückgezahlt werden können;

f) in Ausnahmefällen und aus besonderen Gründen Gewährung verlorener Zuschüsse.

Artikel 23

Das Komitee für das Erbe der Welt kann auch internationale Unterstützung für nationale und regionale Zentren zur Ausbildung von Personal und Fachkräften aller Ebenen auf dem Gebiet der Erfassung, des Schutzes, der Erhaltung in Bestand und Wertigkeit und Revitalisierung des Kultur- und Naturerbes gewähren.

Artikel 24

Einer großangelegten internationalen Unterstützung müssen eingehende wissenschaftliche, wirtschaftliche und technische Untersuchungen vorausgehen. Diesen Untersuchungen müssen die fortschrittlichsten Verfahren für Schutz, Erhaltung in Bestand und Wertigkeit und Revitalisierung des Natur- und Kulturerbes zugrunde liegen; sie müssen den Zielen dieses Übereinkommens entsprechen. Die Untersuchungen müssen auch Mittel und Wege erkunden, die in dem betreffenden Staat vorhandenen Hilfsquellen rationell zu nutzen.

Artikel 25

In der Regel wird nur ein Teil der Kosten für die erforderliche Arbeit von der internationalen Gemeinschaft getragen. Der Beitrag des Staates, dem die internationale Unterstützung zuteil wird, muss einen wesentlichen Teil der für jedes Programm oder Vorhaben aufgewendeten Mittel darstellen, es sei denn, seine Mittel erlauben dies nicht.

Artikel 26

Das Komitee für das Erbe der Welt und der Empfängerstaat legen in dem von ihnen zu schließenden Abkommen die Bedingungen für die Durchführung eines Programms oder Vorhabens fest, für das nach diesem Übereinkommen internationale Unterstützung gewährt wird. Es ist Aufgabe des Staates, der die internationale Unterstützung erhält, das betreffende Gut danach im Einklang mit diesem Übereinkommen zu schützen sowie in Bestand und Wertigkeit zu erhalten.

VI.
Erziehungsprogramme

Artikel 27
(1) Die Vertragsstaaten bemühen sich unter Einsatz aller geeigneten Mittel, insbesondere durch Erziehungs- und Informationsprogramme, die Würdigung und Achtung des in den Artikeln 1 und 2 bezeichneten Kultur- und Naturerbes durch ihre Völker zu stärken.
(2) Sie verpflichten sich, die Öffentlichkeit über die diesem Erbe drohenden Gefahren und die Maßnahmen aufgrund dieses Übereinkommens umfassend zu unterrichten.

Artikel 28
Die Vertragsstaaten, die internationale Unterstützung aufgrund dieses Übereinkommens erhalten, treffen geeignete Maßnahmen, um die Bedeutung sowohl des Gutes, für das Unterstützung empfangen wurde, als auch der Unterstützung bekanntzumachen.

VII.
Berichte

Artikel 29
(1) Die Vertragsstaaten machen in den Berichten, die sie der Generalkonferenz der Organisation der Vereinten Nationen für Erziehung, Wissenschaft und Kultur zu den von dieser festgesetzten Terminen in der von ihr bestimmten Weise vorlegen, Angaben über die von ihnen erlassenen Rechts- und Verwaltungsvorschriften und über sonstige Maßnahmen, die sie zur Anwendung dieses Übereinkommens getroffen haben, sowie über Einzelheiten der auf diesem Gebiet gesammelten Erfahrungen.
(2) Die Berichte sind dem Komitee für das Erbe der Welt zur Kenntnis zu bringen.
(3) Das Komitee legt auf jeder ordentlichen Tagung der Generalkonferenz der Organisation der Vereinten Nationen für Erziehung, Wissenschaft und Kultur einen Tätigkeitsbericht vor.

VIII.
Schlussbestimmungen

Artikel 30
Diese Übereinkommen ist in arabischer, englischer, französischer, russischer und spanischer Sprache abgefasst, wobei jeder Wortlaut gleichermaßen verbindlich ist.

Artikel 31
(1) Dieses Übereinkommen bedarf der Ratifikation oder Annahme durch die Mitgliedstaaten der Organisation der Vereinten Nationen für Erziehung, Wissenschaft und Kultur nach Maßgabe ihrer verfassungsrechtlichen Verfahren.
(2) Die Ratifikations- oder Annahmeurkunden werden beim Generaldirektor der Organisation der Vereinten Nationen für Erziehung, Wissenschaft und Kultur hinterlegt.

Artikel 32
(1) Dieses Übereinkommen liegt für alle Nichtmitgliedstaaten der Organisation der Vereinten Nationen für Erziehung, Wissenschaft und Kultur, die von der Generalkonferenz der Organisation hierzu aufgefordert werden, zum Beitritt auf.
(2) Der Beitritt erfolgt durch Hinterlegung einer Beitrittsurkunde beim Generaldirektor der Organisation der Vereinten Nationen für Erziehung, Wissenschaft und Kultur.

Artikel 33
Dieses Übereinkommen tritt drei Monate nach Hinterlegung der zwanzigsten Ratifikations-, Annahme- oder Beitrittsurkunde in Kraft, jedoch nur für die Staaten, die bis zu diesem Tag ihre Ratifikations-, Annahme- oder Beitrittsurkunde hinterlegt haben. Für jeden anderen Staat tritt es drei Monate nach Hinterlegung seiner Ratifikations-, Annahme- oder Beitrittsurkunde in Kraft.

A.II.1 Welterbe-Übereinkommen

Artikel 34
Folgende Bestimmungen gelten für die Vertragsstaaten, die ein bundesstaatliches oder nicht einheitsstaatliches Verfassungssystem haben:
a) Hinsichtlich derjenigen Bestimmungen dieses Übereinkommens, deren Durchführung in die Zuständigkeit des Bundes- oder Zentral-Gesetzgebungsorgans fällt, sind die Verpflichtungen der Bundes- oder Zentralregierung dieselben wie für diejenigen Vertragsstaaten, die nicht Bundesstaaten sind;
b) hinsichtlich derjenigen Bestimmungen des Übereinkommens, deren Durchführung in die Zuständigkeit eines einzelnen Gliedstaats, einer Provinz oder eines Kantons fällt, die nicht durch das Verfassungssystem des Bundes verpflichtet sind, gesetzgeberische Maßnahmen zu treffen, unterrichtet die Bundesregierung die zuständigen Stellen dieser Staaten, Länder, Provinzen oder Kantone von den genannten Bestimmungen und empfiehlt ihnen ihre Annahme.

Artikel 35
(1) Jeder Vertragsstaat kann dieses Übereinkommen kündigen.
(2) Die Kündigung wird durch eine Urkunde notifiziert, die beim Generaldirektor der Organisation der Vereinten Nationen für Erziehung, Wissenschaft und Kultur hinterlegt wird.
(3) Die Kündigung wird zwölf Monate nach Eingang der Kündigungsurkunde wirksam. Sie lässt die finanziellen Verpflichtungen des kündigenden Staates bis zu dem Tag unberührt, an dem der Rücktritt wirksam wird.

Artikel 36
Der Generaldirektor der Organisation der Vereinten Nationen für Erziehung, Wissenschaft und Kultur unterrichtet die Mitgliedsstaaten der Organisation, die in Artikel 32 bezeichneten Nichtmitgliedsstaaten der Organisation sowie die Vereinten Nationen von der Hinterlegung aller Ratifikations-, Annahme- oder Beitrittsurkunden nach den Artikeln 31 und 32 und von den Kündigungen nach Artikel 35.

Artikel 37
(1) Dieses Übereinkommen kann von der Generalkonferenz der Organisation der Vereinten Nationen für Erziehung, Wissenschaft und Kultur revidiert werden. Jede Revision ist jedoch nur für diejenigen Staaten verbindlich, die Vertragsparteien des Revisionsübereinkommens werden.
(2) Beschließt die Generalkonferenz ein neues Übereinkommen, das dieses Übereinkommen ganz oder teilweise revidiert, so liegt dieses Übereinkommen, sofern nicht das neue Übereinkommen etwas anderes bestimmt, vom Tag des Inkrafttretens des neuen Revisionsübereinkommens an nicht mehr zur Ratifikation, zur Annahme oder zum Beitritt auf.

Artikel 38
Auf Ersuchen des Generaldirektors der Organisation der Vereinten Nationen für Erziehung, Wissenschaft und Kultur wird dieses Übereinkommen nach Artikel 102 der Charta der Vereinten Nationen beim Sekretariat der Vereinten Nationen registriert.

GESCHEHEN zu Paris am 23. November 1972 in zwei Urschriften, die mit den Unterschriften des Präsidenten der 17. Tagung der Generalkonferenz und des Generaldirektors der Organisation der Vereinten Nationen für Erziehung, Wissenschaft und Kultur versehen sind und im Archiv der Organisation der Vereinten Nationen für Erziehung, Wissenschaft und Kultur hinterlegt werden; allen in den Artikeln 31 und 32 bezeichneten Staaten sowie den Vereinten Nationen werden beglaubigte Abschriften übermittelt.

Operational Guidelines for the Implementation of the World Heritage Convention[1)]

Vom 19. Juli 2019, WHC.19/01

ACRONYMS AND ABBREVIATIONS

DoCoMoMo	International Committee for the Documentation and Conservation of Monuments and Sites of the Modern Movement
ICCROM	International Centre for the Study of the Preservation and Restoration of Cultural Property
ICOMOS	International Council on Monuments and Sites
IFLA	International Federation of Landscape Architects
IUCN	International Union for Conservation of Nature and Natural Resources
IUGS	International Union of Geological Sciences
MAB	Man and the Biosphere Programme of UNESCO
NGO	Non-governmental organization
TICCIH	International Committee for the Conservation of the Industrial Heritage
UNEP	United Nations Environment Programme
UNEP-WCMC	World Conservation Monitoring Centre (UNEP)
UNESCO	United Nations Educational, Scientific and Cultural Organization

I Introduction
I.A The *Operational Guidelines*

1. The *Operational Guidelines for the Implementation of the World Heritage Convention* (hereinafter referred to as the *Operational Guidelines*) aim to facilitate the implementation of the *Convention concerning the Protection of the World Cultural and Natural Heritage* (hereinafter referred to as "the *World Heritage Convention*" or "the *Convention*"), by setting forth the procedures for:
   a) the inscription of properties on the World Heritage List and the List of World Heritage in Danger;
   b) the protection and conservation of World Heritage properties;
   c) the granting of International Assistance under the World Heritage Fund; and
   d) the mobilization of national and international support in favor of the *Convention*.

2. The *Operational Guidelines* are periodically revised to reflect the decisions of the World Heritage Committee.

3. The key users of the *Operational Guidelines* are:
   a) the States Parties to the *World Heritage Convention*;
   b) the Intergovernmental Committee for the Protection of the Cultural and Natural Heritage of Outstanding Universal Value, hereinafter referred to as "the World Heritage Committee" or "the Committee";
   c) the UNESCO World Heritage Centre as Secretariat to the World Heritage Committee, hereinafter referred to as "the Secretariat";

The historical development of the *Operational Guidelines* is available at: https://whc.unesco.org/en/guidelines/

---

1) Quelle: http://whc.unesco.org/en/guidelines/.

A.II.1a Operational Guidelines Welterbe-Übereinkommen

d) the Advisory Bodies to the World Heritage Committee;
e) site managers, stakeholders and partners in the protection of World Heritage properties.

I.B The *World Heritage Convention*

4. The cultural and natural heritage is among the priceless and irreplaceable assets, not only of each nation, but of humanity as a whole. The loss, through deterioration or disappearance, of any of these most prized assets constitutes an impoverishment of the heritage of all the peoples of the world. Parts of this heritage, because of their exceptional qualities, can be considered to be of "Outstanding Universal Value" and as such worthy of special protection against the dangers which increasingly threaten them.

5. To ensure, as far as possible, the proper identification, protection, conservation and presentation of the world's heritage, the Member States of UNESCO adopted the World Heritage Convention in 1972. The Convention foresees the establishment of a "World Heritage Committee" and a "World Heritage Fund". Both the Committee and the Fund have been in operation since 1976.

6. Since the adoption of the Convention in 1972, the international community has embraced the concept of "sustainable development". The protection and conservation of the natural and cultural heritage constitute a significant contribution to sustainable development.

7. The Convention aims at the identification, protection, conservation, presentation and transmission to future generations of cultural and natural heritage of Outstanding Universal Value.

8. The criteria and conditions for the inscription of properties on the World Heritage List have been developed to evaluate the Outstanding Universal Value of properties and to guide States Parties in the protection and management of World Heritage properties.

9. When a property inscribed on the World Heritage List is threatened by serious and specific dangers, the Committee considers placing it on the List of World Heritage in Danger. When the Outstanding Universal Value of the property which justified its inscription on the World Heritage List is lost, the Committee considers deleting the property from the World Heritage List.

I.C The States Parties to the *World Heritage Convention*

10. States are encouraged to become party to the *Convention*. Model instruments for ratification/acceptance and accession are included as Annex 1. The original signed version should be sent to the Director-General of UNESCO.

11. The list of States Parties to the *Convention* is available at: https://whc.unesco.org/en/statesparties

12. States Parties to the *Convention* are encouraged to adopt a human-rights based approach, and ensure gender-balanced participation of a wide variety of stakeholders and rights-holders, including site managers, local and regional governments, local communities, indigenous peoples, non-governmental organizations (NGOs) and other interested parties and partners in the identification, nomination, management and protection processes of World Heritage properties.

Decision 43 COM 11A

13.	States Parties to the *Convention* should provide the Secretariat with the names and contact details of the governmental organization(s) primarily responsible as national focal point(s) for the implementation of the *Convention*, so that copies of all official correspondence and documents can be sent by the Secretariat to these national focal points as appropriate.	Decision 43 COM 11A
14.	States Parties are encouraged to bring together their cultural and natural heritage experts at regular intervals to discuss the implementation of the *Convention*. States Parties may wish to involve representatives of the Advisory Bodies and other experts and partners as appropriate.	Decision 43 COM 11A
14bis.	States Parties are encouraged to mainstream into their programmes and activities related to the *World Heritage Convention* the principles of the relevant policies adopted by the World Heritage Committee, the General Assembly of States Parties to the *Convention* and the UNESCO Governing Bodies, such as the Policy Document for the Integration of a Sustainable Development Perspective into the Processes of the *World Heritage Convention* and the UNESCO policy on engaging with indigenous peoples, as well as other related policies and documents, including the 2030 Agenda for Sustainable Development and international human rights standards.	Decision 43 COM 11A
15.	While fully respecting the sovereignty of the States on whose territory the cultural and natural heritage is situated, States Parties to the *Convention* recognize the collective interest of the international community to cooperate in the protection of this heritage. States Parties to the *World Heritage Convention*, have the responsibility to:	Article 6(1) of the *World Heritage Convention*. Decision 43 COM 11A
	a) ensure the identification, nomination, protection, conservation, presentation, and transmission to future generations of the cultural and natural heritage found within in their territory, and give help in these tasks to other States Parties that request it;	Article 4 and 6(2) of the *World Heritage Convention*.
	b) adopt general policies to give the heritage a function in the life of the community;	Article 5 of the *World Heritage Convention*.
	c) integrate heritage protection into comprehensive planning programmes and coordination mechanisms, giving consideration in particular to the resilience of socio-ecological systems of properties;	
	d) establish services for the protection, conservation and presentation of the heritage;	
	e) develop scientific and technical studies to identify actions that would counteract the dangers that threaten the heritage;	
	f) take appropriate legal, scientific, technical, administrative and financial measures to protect the heritage;	
	g) foster the establishment or development of national or regional centres for training in the protection, conservation and presentation of the heritage and encourage scientific research in these fields;	

h)	not take any deliberate measures that directly or indirectly damage their heritage or that of another State Party to the *Convention*;	Article 6(3) of the *World Heritage Convention*.
i)	submit to the World Heritage Committee an inventory of properties suitable for inscription on the World Heritage List (referred to as a Tentative List);	Article 11(1) of the *World Heritage Convention*.
j)	make regular contributions to the World Heritage Fund, the amount of which is determined by the General Assembly of States Parties to the *Convention*;	Article 16(1) of the *World Heritage Convention*.
k)	consider and encourage the establishment of national, public and private foundations or associations to facilitate donations for the protection of World Heritage;	Article 17 of the *World Heritage Convention*.
l)	give assistance to international fundraising campaigns organized for the World Heritage Fund;	Article 18 of the *World Heritage Convention*.
m)	use educational and information programmes to strengthen appreciation and respect by their peoples of the cultural and natural heritage defined in Articles 1 and 2 of the *Convention*, and to keep the public informed of the dangers threatening this heritage;	Article 27 of *the World Heritage Convention*.
n)	provide information to the World Heritage Committee on the implementation of the *World Heritage Convention* and the state of conservation of properties; and	Article 29 of the **World Heritage Convention.** Resolution adopted by the 11th General Assembly of States Parties (1997)
o)	contribute to and comply with the sustainable development objectives, including gender equality, in the World Heritage processes and in their heritage conservation and management systems.	

16. States Parties are encouraged to attend sessions of the World Heritage Committee and its subsidiary bodies.

Rule 8.1 of the Rules of Procedure of the World Heritage Committee.

I.D The General Assembly of States Parties to the *World Heritage Convention*

17. The General Assembly of States Parties to the *World Heritage Convention* meets during the sessions of the General Conference of UNESCO. The General Assembly manages its meetings according to its Rules of Procedure, available at: https://whc.unesco.org/en/ga

Article 8(1), of the *World Heritage Convention*, Rule 49 of the Rules of Procedure of the World Heritage Committee.

18. The General Assembly determines the uniform percentage of contributions to the World Heritage Fund applicable to all States Parties and elects members to the World Heritage Committee. Both the General Assembly and General Conference of UNESCO receive a report from the World Heritage Committee on its activities.

Articles 8(1), 16(1) and 29 of the *World Heritage Convention* and Rule 49 of the Rules of Procedure of the World Heritage Committee.

I.E The World Heritage Committee

19. The World Heritage Committee is composed of 21 members and meets at least once a year (June/July). It establishes its Bureau, which meets during the sessions of the Committee as frequently

The World Heritage Committee can be contacted through its Secreta-

	as deemed necessary. The composition of the Committee and its Bureau is available at: https://whc.unesco.org/en/committee	riat, the World Heritage Centre.
20.	The Committee manages its meetings according to its Rules of Procedure, available at: https://whc.unesco.org/en/committee	
21.	The term of office of Committee members is six years but, in order to ensure equitable representation and rotation, States Parties are invited by the General Assembly to consider voluntarily reducing their term of office from six to four years and are discouraged from seeking consecutive terms of office.	Article 8(2) of the *World Heritage Convention* and the Resolutions of the 7th (1989), 12th (1999) and 13th (2001) General Assembly of States Parties to the *World Heritage Convention*. Article 9(1) of the *World Heritage Convention*.
22.	At each election, due consideration shall be given to the election of at least one State Party which has never served as a Member of the World Heritage Committee.	Rule 14.1 of the Rules of Procedure of the General Assembly of States Parties. Decision 43 COM 11A
23.	Committee decisions are based on objective and scientific considerations, and any appraisal made on its behalf must be thoroughly and responsibly carried out. The Committee recognizes that such decisions depend upon: a) carefully prepared documentation; b) thorough and consistent procedures; c) evaluation by qualified experts; and d) if necessary, the use of expert referees.	
24.	The main functions of the Committee are, in cooperation with States Parties, to:	
	a) identify, on the basis of Tentative Lists and nominations submitted by States Parties, cultural and natural properties of Outstanding Universal Value which are to be protected under the *Convention* and to inscribe those properties on the World Heritage List;	Articles 11(2) and 11(7) of the *World Heritage Convention*.
	b) examine the state of conservation of properties inscribed on the World Heritage List through processes of Reactive Monitoring (see Chapter IV) and Periodic Reporting (see Chapter V);	Article 29 of the *World Heritage Convention*.
	c) decide which properties inscribed on the World Heritage List are to be inscribed on, or removed from the List of World Heritage in Danger;	Article 11(4) and 11(5) of the *World Heritage Convention*.
	d) decide whether a property should be deleted from the World Heritage List (see Chapter IV);	
	e) define the procedure by which requests for International Assistance are to be considered and carry out studies and consultations as necessary before coming to a decision (see Chapter VII);	Article 21(1) and 21(3) of the *World Heritage Convention*.
	f) determine how the resources of the World Heritage Fund can be used most advantageously to assist States Parties	Article 13(6) of the *World Heritage Convention*.

in the protection of their properties of Outstanding Universal Value;

g) seek ways to increase the World Heritage Fund;

h) submit a report on its activities every two years to the General Assembly of States Parties and to the UNESCO General Conference;

Article 29(3) of the World Heritage Convention and Rule 49 of the Rules of procedure of the World Heritage Committee.

i) review and evaluate periodically the implementation of the *Convention*;

j) revise and adopt the *Operational Guidelines*.

25. In order to facilitate the implementation of the *Convention*, the Committee develops Strategic Objectives; they are periodically reviewed and revised to define the goals and objectives of the Committee to ensure that new threats placed on World Heritage are addressed effectively.

The first 'Strategic Orientations' adopted by the Committee in 1992 are contained in Annex II of document WHC-92/CONF.002/12

26. The current Strategic Objectives (also referred to as "the 5 Cs") are the following:
   1. Strengthen the **Credibility** of the World Heritage List;
   2. Ensure the effective **Conservation** of World Heritage Properties;
   3. Promote the development of effective **Capacity building** in States Parties;
   4. Increase public awareness, involvement and support for World Heritage through **Communication**;
   5. Enhance the role of **Communities** in the implementation of the *World Heritage Convention*.

In 2002 the World Heritage Committee revised its Strategic Objectives. The *Budapest Declaration on World Heritage* (2002) is available at the following Web address: https://whc.unesco.org/en/budapestdeclaration

Decision 31 COM 13B

I.F The Secretariat to the World Heritage Committee (World Heritage Centre)

UNESCO World Heritage Centre 7, place de Fontenoy 75352 Paris 07 SP France https://whc.unesco.org/

27. The World Heritage Committee is assisted by a Secretariat appointed by the Director-General of UNESCO. The function of the Secretariat is currently assumed by the World Heritage Centre, established in 1992 specifically for this purpose. The Director-General designated the Director of the World Heritage Centre as Secretary to the Committee. The Secretariat assists and collaborates with the States Parties and the Advisory Bodies. The Secretariat works in close cooperation with other sectors and field offices of UNESCO.

Article 14 of the World Heritage Convention. Rule 43 of Rules of Procedure of the World Heritage Committee. Circular Letter 16 of 21 October 2003 https://whc.unesco.org/circs/circ03-16e.pdf

28. The Secretariat's main tasks are:

a) the organization of the meetings of the General Assembly and the Committee;

Decision 39 COM 11
Decision 43 COM 11A

Article 14(2) of the World Heritage Convention.

b) the implementation of decisions of the World Heritage Committee and resolutions of the General Assembly and reporting on their execution;

Article 14(2) of the World Heritage Convention and the Budapest Declaration on World Heritage (2002)

c) the receipt, registration, checking the completeness, archiving and transmission to the relevant Advisory Bodies of nominations to the World Heritage List;

d) the co-ordination of studies and activities as part of the Global Strategy for a Representative, Balanced and Credible World Heritage List;

e) the organization of Periodic Reporting;

f) coordination and conduct of Reactive Monitoring, including Reactive Monitoring missions[1], as well coordination of and participation in Advisory missions[2], as appropriate;

g) the coordination of International Assistance;

h) the mobilization of extra-budgetary resources for the conservation and management of World Heritage properties;

i) the assistance to States Parties in the implementation of the Committee's programmes and projects; and

j) the promotion of World Heritage and the *Convention* through the dissemination of information to States Parties, the Advisory Bodies and the general public.

29. These activities follow the decisions and Strategic Objectives of the Committee and the resolutions of the General Assembly of the States Parties and are conducted in close cooperation with the Advisory Bodies.

I.G   The Advisory Bodies to the World Heritage Committee

30. The Advisory Bodies to the World Heritage Committee are ICCROM (the International Centre for the Study of the Preservation and Restoration of Cultural Property), ICOMOS (the Inter-

Article 8(3) of the World Heritage Convention

---

1) Reactive Monitoring missions are part of the statutory reporting by the Secretariat and the Advisory Bodies to the World Heritage Committee on the state of conservation of specific properties that are under threat (see Paragraph 169). They are requested by the World Heritage Committee to ascertain, in consultation with the State Party concerned, the condition of the property, the dangers to the property and the feasibility of adequately restoring the property or to assess progress made in implementing such corrective measures, and include a reporting back to the Committee on the findings of the mission (see Paragraph 176.e). The terms of reference of Reactive Monitoring missions are proposed by the World Heritage Centre, in line with the decision adopted by the World Heritage Committee, and consolidated in consultation with the State Party and the relevant Advisory Body(ies). Experts for such missions shall not be nationals of the country where the property is located. It is however encouraged that, where possible, they be from the same region as the property. The costs of the Reactive Monitoring missions are borne by the World Heritage Fund.

2) Advisory missions are not *stricto sensu* of the statutory and mandatory processes, as they are voluntarily initiated by States Parties and depend on the considerations and judgement of the States Parties requesting them. Advisory missions are to be understood as missions providing expert advice to a State Party on specific matters. They can concern provision of "upstream" support and advice on identification of sites, Tentative Lists or nomination of sites for inscription on the World Heritage List or alternatively, they can relate to the state of conservation of properties and provide advice in evaluating possible impact of a major development project on the Outstanding Universal Value of the property, advice in the preparation/revision of a management plan, or in the progress achieved in the implementation of specific mitigation measures, etc. The terms of reference of Advisory missions are proposed by the State Party itself, and consolidated in consultation with the World Heritage Centre and the relevant Advisory Bod(ies), other organization(s) or experts. Experts for such missions shall not be nationals of the country where the property is located. It is however encouraged that, where possible, they be from the same region as the property. The entire costs of Advisory missions are borne by the State Party inviting the mission, except where the State Party is eligible for relevant International Assistance or funding from the new budget line for Advisory missions approved by Decision 38 COM 12.

national Council on Monuments and Sites), and IUCN (the International Union for Conservation of Nature).

31. The roles of the Advisory Bodies are to:

a)	advise on the implementation of the *World Heritage Convention* in the field of their expertise;	Article 13(7) of the *World Heritage Convention*.
b)	assist the Secretariat, in the preparation of the Committee's documentation, the agenda of its meetings and the implementation of the Committee's decisions;	Decision 39 COM 11
c)	assist with the development and implementation of the Global Strategy for a Representative, Balanced and Credible World Heritage List, the World Heritage Capacity Building Strategy, Periodic Reporting, and the strengthening of the effective use of the World Heritage Fund;	
d)	monitor the state of conservation of World Heritage properties (including through Reactive Monitoring missions at the request of the Committee and Advisory missions at the invitation of the States Parties) and review requests for International Assistance;	Article 14(2) of the *World Heritage Convention*.
e)	in the case of ICOMOS and IUCN, evaluate properties nominated for inscription on the World Heritage List, in consultation and dialogue with nominating States Parties, and present evaluation reports to the Committee; and	
f)	attend meetings of the World Heritage Committee and the Bureau in an advisory capacity.	Article 8(3) of the *World Heritage Convention*.

ICCROM

32. ICCROM (the International Centre for the Study of the Preservation and Restoration of Cultural Property) is an international intergovernmental organization with headquarters in Rome, Italy. Established by UNESCO in 1956, ICCROM's statutory functions are to carry out research, documentation, technical assistance, training and public awareness programmes to strengthen conservation of immovable and moveable cultural heritage.

ICCROM
Via di S. Michele, 13
I-00153 Rome, Italy
Tel: +39 06 585531
Fax: +39 06 5855 3349
Email: iccrom@iccrom.org
http://www.iccrom.org/

33. The specific role of ICCROM in relation to the *Convention* includes: being the priority partner in training for cultural heritage, monitoring the state of conservation of World Heritage cultural properties, reviewing requests for International Assistance submitted by States Parties, and providing input and support for capacity building activities.

ICOMOS

34.	ICOMOS (the International Council on Monuments and Sites) is a non-governmental organization with headquarters in Charenton-le-Pont, France. Founded in 1965, its role is to promote the application of theory, methodology and scientific techniques to the conservation of the architectural and archaeological heritage. Its work is based on the principles of the 1964 International Charter on the Conservation and Restoration of Monuments and Sites (the Venice Charter).	**ICOMOS** 1 rue du Séminaire de Conflans 94220 Charenton-le-Pont France Tel: +33 (0)1 41 94 17 59 Fax: +33 (0)1 48 93 19 16 E-mail: secretariat@icomos.org http://www.icomos.org/
35.	The specific role of ICOMOS in relation to the *Convention* includes: evaluation of properties nominated for inscription on the World Heritage List, monitoring the state of conservation of World Heritage cultural properties, reviewing requests for International Assistance submitted by States Parties, and providing input and support for capacity building activities.	

IUCN

36.	IUCN – The International Union for Conservation of Nature was founded in 1948 and brings together national governments, NGOs, and scientists in a worldwide partnership. IUCN has its headquarters in Gland, Switzerland. Its mission is to influence, encourage and assist societies throughout the world to conserve the integrity and diversity of nature and to ensure that any use of natural resources is equitable and ecologically sustainable.	**IUCN – The International Union for Conservation of Nature** rue Mauverney 28 CH-1196 Gland, Switzerland Tel: + 41 22 999 0001 Fax: +41 22 999 0010 E-Mail: mail@hq.iucn.org http://www.iucn.org
37.	The specific role of IUCN in relation to the *Convention* includes: evaluation of properties nominated for inscription on the World Heritage List, monitoring the state of conservation of World Heritage natural properties, reviewing requests for International Assistance submitted by States Parties, and providing input and support for capacity building activities.	

I.H Other organizations

38.	The Committee may call on other international and non-governmental organizations with appropriate competence and expertise to assist in the implementation of its programmes and projects, including for Reactive Monitoring missions.	Decision 39 COM 11

I.I Partners in the protection of World Heritage

39.	A partnership approach, underpinned by inclusive, transparent and accountable decision-making, to nomination, management and monitoring provides a significant contribution to the protection of World Heritage properties and the implementation of the *Convention*.	Decision 43 COM 11A
40.	Partners in the protection and conservation of World Heritage can be those individuals and other stakeholders, especially local communities, indigenous peoples, governmental, non-governmental and private organizations and owners who have an interest and involvement in the conservation and management of a World Heritage property.	United Nations Declaration on the Rights of Indigenous Peoples (2007) Decision 39 COM 11

A.II.1a Operational Guidelines Welterbe-Übereinkommen 114

I.J Other Conventions, Recommendations and Programmes

41. The World Heritage Committee recognizes the benefits of closer coordination of its work with other UNESCO programmes and their relevant conventions. For a list of relevant global conservation instruments, conventions and programmes see paragraph 44.

42. The World Heritage Committee with the support of the Secretariat will ensure appropriate coordination and information-sharing between the *World Heritage Convention* and other conventions, programmes and international organizations related to the conservation of cultural and natural heritage.

43. The Committee may invite representatives of the intergovernmental bodies under related conventions to attend its meetings as observers. It may appoint a representative to observe meetings of the other intergovernmental bodies upon receipt of an invitation.

44. **Selected global conventions and programmes relating to the protection of cultural and natural heritage**
UNESCO conventions and programmes
Convention for the Protection of Cultural Property in the Event of Armed Conflict (1954)
Protocol I (1954)
Protocol II (1999)
http://www.unesco.org/new/en/culture/themes/armed-conflict-and-heritage/convention-and-protocols/
Convention on the Means of Prohibiting and Preventing the Illicit Import, Export and Transfer of Ownership of Cultural Property (1970)
http://www.unesco.org/new/en/culture/themes/illicit-trafficking-of-cultural-property/1970-convention
Convention concerning the Protection of the World Cultural and Natural Heritage (1972)
https://whc.unesco.org/en/conventiontext
Convention on the Protection of the Underwater Cultural Heritage (2001)
https://unesdoc.unesco.org/ark:/48223/pf0000126065
Convention for the Safeguarding of the Intangible Cultural Heritage (2003)
https://unesdoc.unesco.org/ark:/48223/pf0000132540
Convention on the Protection and Promotion of the Diversity of Cultural Expressions (2005)
https://unesdoc.unesco.org/ark:/48223/pf0000142919
Man and the Biosphere (MAB) Programme
http://www.unesco.org/new/en/natural-sciences/environment/ecological-sciences/man-and-biosphere-programme/
International Geoscience and Geoparks Programme (IGGP)
http://www.unesco.org/new/en/natural-sciences/environment/earth-sciences/international-geoscience-and-geoparks-programme/
International Hydrological Programme (IHP)
https://en.unesco.org/themes/water-security/hydrology
Other conventions
International Whaling Commission (IWC) (1946)
https://iwc.int

International Plant Protection Convention (IPPC) (1951)
https://www.ippc.int
Convention on Wetlands of International Importance especially as Waterfowl Habitat (Ramsar) (1971)
http://www.ramsar.org
Convention on International Trade in Endangered Species of Wild Fauna and Flora (CITES) (1973)
http://www.cites.org
Convention on the Conservation of Migratory Species of Wild Animals (CMS) (1979)
http://www.cms.int
United Nations Convention on the Law of the Sea (UNCLOS) (1982)
https://www.un.org/Depts/los/convention_agreements/convention_overview_convention.htm
Convention on Biological Diversity (1992)
http://www.cbd.int
UNIDROIT Convention on Stolen or Illegally Exported Cultural Objects (Rome, 1995)
https://www.unidroit.org/cultural-property#Convention1995
United Nations Framework Convention on Climate Change (New York, 1992)
http://unfccc.int
International Treaty on Plant Genetic Resources for Food and Agriculture (2001)
http://www.fao.org/plant-treaty/en/

II The World Heritage List
II.A Definition of World Heritage
Cultural and Natural Heritage

45. Cultural and natural heritage are defined in Articles 1 and 2 of the *World Heritage Convention*.

Article 1
For the purposes of this Convention, the following shall be considered as "cultural heritage";
– monuments: architectural works, works of monumental sculpture and painting, elements or structures of an archaeological nature, inscriptions, cave dwellings and combinations of features, which are of Outstanding Universal Value from the point of view of history, art or science;
– groups of buildings: groups of separate or connected buildings which, because of their architecture, their homogeneity or their place in the landscape, are of Outstanding Universal Value from the point of view of history, art or science;
– sites: works of man or the combined works of nature and of man, and areas including archaeological sites which are of Outstanding Universal Value from the historical, aesthetic, ethnological or anthropological points of view.

Article 2
For the purposes of this Convention, the following shall be considered as "natural heritage":

- *natural features consisting of physical and biological formations or groups of such formations, which are of Outstanding Universal Value from the aesthetic or scientific point of view;*
- *geological and physiographical formations and precisely delineated areas which constitute the habitat of threatened species of animals and plants of Outstanding Universal Value from the point of view of science or conservation;*
- *natural sites or precisely delineated natural areas of Outstanding Universal Value from the point of view of science, conservation or natural beauty.*

Mixed Cultural and Natural Heritage

46. Properties shall be considered as "mixed cultural and natural heritage" if they satisfy a part or whole of the definitions of both cultural and natural heritage laid out in Articles 1 and 2 of the *Convention*.

Cultural landscapes

47. Cultural landscapes are cultural properties and represent the "combined works of nature and of man" designated in Article 1 of the *Convention*. They are illustrative of the evolution of human society and settlement over time, under the influence of the physical constraints and/or opportunities presented by their natural environment and of successive social, economic and cultural forces, both external and internal.

Annex 3

Movable Heritage

48. Nominations of immovable heritage which are likely to become movable will not be considered.

Outstanding Universal Value

49. Outstanding Universal Value means cultural and/or natural significance which is so exceptional as to transcend national boundaries and to be of common importance for present and future generations of all humanity. As such, the permanent protection of this heritage is of the highest importance to the international community as a whole. The Committee defines the criteria for the inscription of properties on the World Heritage List.

50. States Parties are invited to submit nominations of properties of cultural and/or natural value considered to be of "Outstanding Universal Value" for inscription on the World Heritage List.

51. At the time of inscription of a property on the World Heritage List, the Committee adopts a Statement of Outstanding Universal Value (see paragraph 154) which will be the key reference for the future effective protection and management of the property.

52. The *Convention* is not intended to ensure the protection of all properties of great interest, importance or value, but only for a select list of the most outstanding of these from an international viewpoint. It is not to be assumed that a property of national and/or regional importance will automatically be inscribed on the World Heritage List.

53. Nominations presented to the Committee shall demonstrate the full commitment of the State Party to preserve the heritage concerned, within its means. Such commitment shall take the form of appropriate policy, legal, scientific, technical, administrative

and financial measures adopted and proposed to protect the property and its Outstanding Universal Value.

II.B A Representative, Balanced and Credible World Heritage List

54. The Committee seeks to establish a representative, balanced and credible World Heritage List in conformity with the four Strategic Objectives it adopted at its 26th session (Budapest, 2002).

<ins>The Global Strategy for a Representative, Balanced and Credible World Heritage List</ins>

55. The Global Strategy for a Representative, Balanced and Credible World Heritage List is designed to identify and fill the major gaps in the World Heritage List. It does this by encouraging more countries to become States Parties to the *Convention* and to develop Tentative Lists as defined in paragraph 62 and nominations of properties for inscription on the World Heritage List (see https://whc.unesco.org/en/globalstrategy).

56. States Parties and the Advisory Bodies are encouraged to participate in the implementation of the Global Strategy in cooperation with the Secretariat and other partners. Regional and thematic Global Strategy meetings and comparative and thematic studies are organized for this purpose. The results of these meetings and studies are available to assist States Parties in preparing Tentative Lists and nominations. The reports of the expert meetings and studies presented to the World Heritage Committee are available at: https://whc.unesco.org/en/globalstrategy.

57. All efforts should be made to maintain a reasonable balance between cultural and natural heritage on the World Heritage List.

58. No formal limit is imposed on the total number of properties to be inscribed on the World Heritage List.

<ins>Other measures</ins>

59. To promote the establishment of a representative, balanced and credible World Heritage List, States Parties are requested to consider whether their heritage is already well represented on the List and if so, to slow down their rate of submission of further nominations by:
    a) spacing voluntarily their nominations according to conditions that they will define, and/or;
    b) proposing only properties falling into categories still under-represented, and/or;
    c) linking each of their nominations with a nomination presented by a State Party whose heritage is under-represented; or
    d) deciding, on a voluntary basis, to suspend the presentation of new nominations.

60. States Parties whose heritage of Outstanding Universal Value is under-represented on the World Heritage List are requested to:
    a) give priority to the preparation of their Tentative Lists and nominations;
    b) initiate and consolidate partnerships at the regional level based on the exchange of technical expertise;

Budapest Declaration on World Heritage (2002) at https://whc.unesco.org/en/budapestdeclaration

The report of the Expert Meeting on the "Global Strategy" and thematic studies for a representative World Heritage List (20-22 June 1994) was adopted by the World Heritage Committee at its 18th session (Phuket, 1994).

The Global Strategy was initially developed with reference to cultural heritage. At the request of the World Heritage Committee, the Global Strategy was subsequently expanded to also include reference to natural heritage and combined cultural and natural heritage.

Resolution adopted by the 12th General Assembly of States Parties (1999).

Resolution adopted by the 12th General Assembly of States Parties (1999).

A.II.1a Operational Guidelines Welterbe-Übereinkommen 118

c) encourage bilateral and multilateral cooperation so as to increase their expertise and the technical capacities of institutions in charge of the protection, safeguarding and management of their heritage; and,
d) participate, as much as possible, in the sessions of the World Heritage Committee.

61. The Committee has decided to apply the following mechanism: **As from 2 February 2018:**
    a) examine one complete nomination per State Party,
    b) set at 35 the annual limit on the number of nominations it will review, inclusive of nominations deferred and referred by previous sessions of the Committee, extensions (except minor modifications of limits of the property), transboundary and serial nominations,
    c) the following order of priorities will be applied in case the overall annual limit of 35 nominations is exceeded:
    i) nominations of properties submitted by States Parties with no properties inscribed on the List,
    ii) nominations of properties submitted by States Parties having up to 3 properties inscribed on the List,
    iii) resubmitted referred nominations that were not transmitted to the relevant Advisory Bodies for evaluation further to the application of paragraph 61.b)[1],
    iv) nominations of properties that have been previously excluded due to the annual limit of 35 nominations and the application of these priorities,
    v) nominations of properties for natural heritage,
    vi) nominations of properties for mixed heritage,
    vii) nominations of transboundary/transnational properties,
    viii) nominations from States Parties in Africa, the Pacific and the Caribbean,
    ix) nominations of properties submitted by States Parties having ratified the *World Heritage Convention* during the last twenty years,
    x) nominations of properties submitted by States Parties that have not submitted nominations for five years or more,
    xi) nominations of States Parties, former Members of the Committee, who accepted on a voluntary basis not to have a nomination reviewed by the Committee during their mandate. This priority will be applied for 4 years after the end of their mandate on the Committee,
    xii) when applying this priority system, date of receipt of full and complete nominations by the World Heritage Centre shall be used as a secondary factor to determine the priority be-

Decision 24 COM VI. 2.3.3,
Decision 28 COM 13.1 and 7 EXT.COM 4B.1
Decision 29 COM 18A
Decision 31 COM 10
Decision 35 COM 8B.61
Decision 40 COM 11
Decision 43 COM 11A

---

[1] This provision also applies in case the resubmitted referred nomination is received in the third year following the referral decision.

d) the States Parties co-authors of a transboundary or transnational serial nomination can choose, amongst themselves and with a common understanding, the State Party which will be bearing this nomination; and this nomination can be registered exclusively within the ceiling of the bearing State Party.

This decision will be implemented on a trial basis for 4 years and takes effect on 2 February 2018, in order to ensure a smooth transition period for all States Parties. The impact of this decision will be evaluated at the Committee's 46th session (2022).

II.C Tentative Lists
Procedure and Format

62. A Tentative List is an inventory of those properties situated on its territory which each State Party considers suitable for nomination to the World Heritage List. States Parties should therefore include, in their Tentative Lists, details of those properties which they consider to be of potential Outstanding Universal Value and which they intend to nominate during the following years.

    Articles 1, 2 and 11(1) of the World Heritage Convention.
    Decision 39 COM 11

63. Nominations to the World Heritage List are not considered unless the nominated property has already been included on the State Party's Tentative List.

    Decision 24 COM para. VI.2.3.2

64. States Parties are encouraged to prepare their Tentative Lists with the full, effective and gender-balanced participation of a wide variety of stakeholders and rights-holders, including site managers, local and regional governments, local communities, indigenous peoples, NGOs and other interested parties and partners. In the case of sites affecting the lands, territories or resources of indigenous peoples, States Parties shall consult and cooperate in good faith with the indigenous peoples concerned through their own representative institutions in order to obtain their free, prior and informed consent before including the sites on their Tentative List.

    Decision 43 COM 11A

65. States Parties shall submit Tentative Lists to the Secretariat, at least one year prior to the submission of any nomination. States Parties are encouraged to re-examine and re-submit their Tentative List at least every ten years.

66. States Parties are requested to submit their Tentative Lists in English or French using the standard formats in Annex 2A and Annex 2B (for transnational and transboundary future nominations), containing the name of the properties, their geographical location, a brief description of the properties, and justification of their Outstanding Universal Value.

    Decision 39 COM 11

67. The original duly signed version of the completed Tentative List shall be submitted by the State Party, to:
    UNESCO World Heritage Centre
    7, place de Fontenoy
    75352 Paris 07 SP
    France
    Tel: +33 (0) 1 4568 1136
    E-mail: wh-tentativelists@unesco.org

68.	Upon reception of the Tentative Lists from the States Parties, the World Heritage Centre checks for compliance of the documentation with Annex 2. If the documentation is not considered in compliance with Annex 2, the World Heritage Centre refers it back to the State Party. When all information has been provided, the Tentative List is registered by the Secretariat and transmitted to the relevant Advisory Bodies for information. A summary of all Tentative Lists is presented annually to the Committee. The Secretariat, in consultation with the States Parties concerned, updates its records, in particular by removing from the Tentative Lists the inscribed properties and nominated properties which were not inscribed.	Decision 7 EXT.COM 4A
	The Tentative Lists of States Parties are published by the World Heritage Centre on its website and/or in working documents in order to ensure transparency, access to information and to facilitate harmonization of Tentative Lists at regional and thematic levels. The sole responsibility for the content of each Tentative List lies with the State Party concerned. The publication of the Tentative Lists does not imply the expression of any opinion whatsoever of the World Heritage Committee or of the World Heritage Centre or of the Secretariat of UNESCO concerning the legal status of any country, territory, city or area or of its boundaries.	Decision 41 COM 11
69.	The Tentative Lists of States Parties are available at : https://whc.unesco.org/en/tentativelists	Decision 27 COM 8A

Tentative Lists as a planning and evaluation tool

70.	Tentative Lists are a useful and important planning tool for States Parties, the World Heritage Committee, the Secretariat, and the Advisory Bodies, as they provide an indication of future nominations.	
71.	Tentative Lists should be established selectively and on the basis of evidence that supports potential Outstanding Universal Value. States Parties are encouraged to consult the analyses of both the World Heritage List and Tentative Lists prepared at the request of the Committee by ICOMOS and IUCN to identify the gaps in the World Heritage List. These analyses could enable States Parties to compare themes, regions, geo-cultural groupings and bio-geographic provinces for prospective World Heritage properties. States Parties are encouraged to seek as early as possible upstream advice from the Advisory Bodies during the development of their Tentative Lists as appropriate.	Decision 24 COM para. VI.2.3.2(ii) Decision 39 COM 11 Documents WHC-04/28.COM/13.B I and II https://whc.unesco.org/document/5297 (ICOMOS) and https://whc.unesco.org/document/5298 (IUCN)
72.	In addition, States Parties are encouraged to consult the specific thematic studies carried out by the Advisory Bodies (see paragraph 147). These studies are informed by a review of the Tentative Lists submitted by States Parties and by reports of meetings on the harmonization of Tentative Lists, as well as by other technical studies performed by the Advisory Bodies and qualified organizations and individuals. A list of studies already completed is available at: https://whc.unesco.org/en/globalstrategy	Thematic studies are different than the comparative analysis to be prepared by States Parties when nominating properties for inscription in the World Heritage List (see paragraph 132).
73.	States Parties are encouraged to harmonize their Tentative Lists at regional and thematic levels. Harmonization of Tentative Lists is the process whereby States Parties, with the assistance of the Advisory Bodies, collectively assess their respective Tentative	Decision 43 COM 11A

List to review gaps and identify common themes. The harmonization has considerable potential to generate fruitful dialogue between States Parties and different cultural communities, promoting respect for common heritage and cultural diversity and can result in improved Tentative Lists, new nominations from States Parties and cooperation amongst groups of States Parties in the preparation of nominations.

<u>Assistance and Capacity Building for States Parties in the preparation of Tentative Lists</u>

74. To implement the Global Strategy, cooperative efforts in capacity building and training for diverse groups of beneficiaries may be necessary to assist States Parties in acquiring and/or consolidating expertise in the preparation, updating and harmonization of their Tentative List and the preparation of nominations.

   Decision 43 COM 11A

75. International Assistance may be requested by States Parties for the purpose of preparing, updating and harmonizing Tentative Lists (see Chapter VII).

76. The Advisory Bodies and the Secretariat will use the opportunity of evaluation missions to hold regional training workshops to assist under-represented States in the methods of preparation of their Tentative List and nominations.

   Decision 24 COM VI. 2.3.5(ii)

II.D Criteria for the assessment of Outstanding Universal Value

77. The Committee considers a property as having Outstanding Universal Value (see paragraphs 49-53) if the property meets one or more of the following criteria. Nominated properties shall therefore:

   (i) represent a masterpiece of human creative genius;
   (ii) exhibit an important interchange of human values, over a span of time or within a cultural area of the world, on developments in architecture or technology, monumental arts, town-planning or landscape design;
   (iii) bear a unique or at least exceptional testimony to a cultural tradition or to a civilization which is living or which has disappeared;
   (iv) be an outstanding example of a type of building, architectural or technological ensemble or landscape which illustrates (a) significant stage(s) in human history;
   (v) be an outstanding example of a traditional human settlement, land-use, or sea-use which is representative of a culture (or cultures), or human interaction with the environment especially when it has become vulnerable under the impact of irreversible change;
   (vi) be directly or tangibly associated with events or living traditions, with ideas, or with beliefs, with artistic and literary works of outstanding universal significance. (The Committee considers that this criterion should preferably be used in conjunction with other criteria);
   (vii) contain superlative natural phenomena or areas of exceptional natural beauty and aesthetic importance;
   (viii) be outstanding examples representing major stages of earth's history, including the record of life, significant on-going geological processes in the development of

   These criteria were formerly presented as two separate sets of criteria – criteria (i) – (vi) for cultural heritage and (i) – (iv) for natural heritage. The 6th extraordinary session of the World Heritage Committee decided to merge the ten criteria (Decision 6 EXT.COM 5.1)

A.II.1a Operational Guidelines Welterbe-Übereinkommen

landforms, or significant geomorphic or physiographic features;

(ix) be outstanding examples representing significant ongoing ecological and biological processes in the evolution and development of terrestrial, fresh water, coastal and marine ecosystems and communities of plants and animals;

(x) contain the most important and significant natural habitats for in-situ conservation of biological diversity, including those containing threatened species of Outstanding Universal Value from the point of view of science or conservation.

78. To be deemed of Outstanding Universal Value, a property must also meet the conditions of integrity and/or authenticity and must have an adequate protection and management system to ensure its safeguarding.

II.E Authenticity and/or integrity

Authenticity

79. Properties nominated under criteria (i) to (vi) must meet the conditions of authenticity. Annex 4, which includes the Nara Document on Authenticity, provides a practical basis for examining the authenticity of such properties and is summarized below.

80. The ability to understand the value attributed to the heritage depends on the degree to which information sources about this value may be understood as credible or truthful. Knowledge and understanding of these sources of information, in relation to original and subsequent characteristics of the cultural heritage, and their meaning as accumulated over time, are the requisite bases for assessing all aspects of authenticity.

Decision 39 COM 11

81. Judgments about value attributed to cultural heritage, as well as the credibility of related information sources, may differ from culture to culture, and even within the same culture. The respect due to all cultures requires that cultural heritage must be considered and judged primarily within the cultural contexts to which it belongs.

82. Depending on the type of cultural heritage, and its cultural context, properties may be understood to meet the conditions of authenticity if their cultural values (as recognized in the nomination criteria proposed) are truthfully and credibly expressed through a variety of attributes including:
    - form and design;
    - materials and substance;
    - use and function;
    - traditions, techniques and management systems;
    - location and setting;
    - language, and other forms of intangible heritage;
    - spirit and feeling; and
    - other internal and external factors.

83. Attributes such as spirit and feeling do not lend themselves easily to practical applications of the conditions of authenticity, but nevertheless are important indicators of character and sense of place, for example, in communities maintaining tradition and cultural continuity.

84. The use of all these sources permits elaboration of the specific artistic, historic, social, and scientific dimensions of the cultural heritage being examined. "Information sources" are defined as all physical, written, oral, and figurative sources, which make it possible to know the nature, specificities, meaning, and history of the cultural heritage.

85. When the conditions of authenticity are considered in preparing a nomination for a property, the State Party should first identify all of the applicable significant attributes of authenticity. The statement of authenticity should assess the degree to which authenticity is present in, or expressed by, each of these significant attributes.

86. In relation to authenticity, the reconstruction of archaeological remains or historic buildings or districts is justifiable only in exceptional circumstances. Reconstruction is acceptable only on the basis of complete and detailed documentation and to no extent on conjecture.

Integrity

87. All properties nominated for inscription on the World Heritage List shall satisfy the conditions of integrity.   Decision 20 COM IX.13

88. Integrity is a measure of the wholeness and intactness of the natural and/or cultural heritage and its attributes. Examining the conditions of integrity, therefore requires assessing the extent to which the property:
    a) includes all elements necessary to express its Outstanding Universal Value;
    b) is of adequate size to ensure the complete representation of the features and processes which convey the property's significance;
    c) suffers from adverse effects of development and/or neglect.

    This should be presented in a statement of integrity.

89. For properties nominated under criteria (i) to (vi), the physical fabric of the property and/or its significant features should be in good condition, and the impact of deterioration processes controlled. A significant proportion of the elements necessary to convey the totality of the value conveyed by the property should be included. Relationships and dynamic functions present in cultural landscapes, historic towns or other living properties essential to their distinctive character should also be maintained.

    Examples of the application of the conditions of integrity to properties nominated under criteria (i) – (vi) are under development.

90. For all properties nominated under criteria (vii) – (x), bio-physical processes and landform features should be relatively intact. However, it is recognized that no area is totally pristine and that all natural areas are in a dynamic state, and to some extent involve contact with people. Biological diversity and cultural diversity can be closely linked and interdependent and human activities, including those of traditional societies, local communities and indigenous peoples, often occur in natural areas. These activities may be consistent with the Outstanding Universal Value of the area where they are ecologically sustainable.

    Decision 43 COM 11A

91. In addition, for properties nominated under criteria (vii) to (x), a corresponding condition of integrity has been defined for each criterion.

92. Properties proposed under criterion (vii) should be of Outstanding Universal Value and include areas that are essential for maintaining the beauty of the property. For example, a property whose scenic value depends on a waterfall, would meet the conditions of integrity if it includes adjacent catchment and downstream areas that are integrally linked to the maintenance of the aesthetic qualities of the property.

93. Properties proposed under criterion (viii) should contain all or most of the key interrelated and interdependent elements in their natural relationships. For example, an "ice age" area would meet the conditions of integrity if it includes the snow field, the glacier itself and samples of cutting patterns, deposition and colonization (e.g. striations, moraines, pioneer stages of plant succession, etc.); in the case of volcanoes, the magmatic series should be complete and all or most of the varieties of effusive rocks and types of eruptions be represented.

94. Properties proposed under criterion (ix) should have sufficient size and contain the necessary elements to demonstrate the key aspects of processes that are essential for the long term conservation of the ecosystems and the biological diversity they contain. For example, an area of tropical rain forest would meet the conditions of integrity if it includes a certain amount of variation in elevation above sea level, changes in topography and soil types, patch systems and naturally regenerating patches; similarly a coral reef should include, for example, seagrass, mangrove or other adjacent ecosystems that regulate nutrient and sediment inputs into the reef.

95. Properties proposed under criterion (x) should be the most important properties for the conservation of biological diversity. Only those properties which are the most biologically diverse and/or representative are likely to meet this criterion. The properties should contain habitats for maintaining the most diverse fauna and flora characteristic of the bio-geographic province and ecosystems under consideration. For example, a tropical savannah would meet the conditions of integrity if it includes a complete assemblage of co-evolved herbivores and plants; an island ecosystem should include habitats for maintaining endemic biota; a property containing wide ranging species should be large enough to include the most critical habitats essential to ensure the survival of viable populations of those species; for an area containing migratory species, seasonal breeding and nesting sites, and migratory routes, wherever they are located, should be adequately protected.

II.F Protection and management

96. Protection and management of World Heritage properties should ensure that their Outstanding Universal Value, including the conditions of integrity and/or authenticity at the time of inscription, are sustained or enhanced over time. A regular review of the general state of conservation of properties, and thus also their Outstanding Universal Value, shall be done within a framework of monitoring processes for World Heritage properties, as specified within the *Operational Guidelines*[1].

---

1) The processes of monitoring specified in the *Operational Guidelines* are Reactive Monitoring (see paragraphs 169-176) and Periodic Reporting (see paragraphs 199-210).

97. All properties inscribed on the World Heritage List must have adequate long-term legislative, regulatory, institutional and/or traditional protection and management to ensure their safeguarding. This protection should include adequately delineated boundaries. Similarly States Parties should demonstrate adequate protection at the national, regional, municipal, and/or traditional level for the nominated property. They should append appropriate texts to the nomination with a clear explanation of the way this protection operates to protect the property.

Legislative, regulatory and contractual protection measures

98. Legislative and regulatory measures at national and local levels should assure the protection of the property from social, economic and other pressures or changes that might negatively impact the Outstanding Universal Value, including the integrity and/or authenticity of the property. States Parties should also assure the full and effective implementation of such measures. — Decision 39 COM 11

Boundaries for effective protection

99. The delineation of boundaries is an essential requirement in the establishment of effective protection of nominated properties. Boundaries should be drawn to incorporate all the attributes that convey the Outstanding Universal Value and to ensure the integrity and/or authenticity of the property. — Decision 39 COM 11

100. For properties nominated under criteria (i) – (vi), boundaries should be drawn to include all those areas and attributes which are a direct tangible expression of the Outstanding Universal Value of the property, as well as those areas which, in the light of future research possibilities, offer potential to contribute to and enhance such understanding.

101. For properties nominated under criteria (vii) – (x), boundaries should reflect the spatial requirements of habitats, species, processes or phenomena that provide the basis for their inscription on the World Heritage List. The boundaries should include sufficient areas immediately adjacent to the area of Outstanding Universal Value in order to protect the property's heritage values from direct effects of human encroachments and impacts of resource use outside of the nominated area.

102. The boundaries of the nominated property may coincide with one or more existing or proposed protected areas, such as national parks or nature reserves, biosphere reserves or protected cultural or historic districts or other areas and territories. While such established areas for protection may contain several management zones, only some of those zones may satisfy requirements for inscription. — Decision 39 COM 11

Buffer zones

103. Wherever necessary for the proper protection of the property, an adequate buffer zone should be provided.

104. For the purposes of effective protection of the nominated property, a buffer zone is an area surrounding the nominated property which has complementary legal and/or customary restrictions placed on its use and development in order to give an added layer of protection to the property. This should include the immediate setting of the nominated property, important views and other areas or attributes that are functionally important as a sup-

A.II.1a Operational Guidelines Welterbe-Übereinkommen

port to the property and its protection. The area constituting the buffer zone should be determined in each case through appropriate mechanisms. Details on the size, characteristics and authorized uses of a buffer zone, as well as a map indicating the precise boundaries of the property and its buffer zone, should be provided in the nomination.

105. A clear explanation of how the buffer zone protects the property should also be provided.

106. Where no buffer zone is proposed, the nomination should include a statement as to why a buffer zone is not required.

107. Although buffer zones are not part of the nominated property, any modifications to or creation of buffer zones subsequent to inscription of a property on the World Heritage List should be approved by the World Heritage Committee using the procedure for a minor boundary modification (see paragraph 164 and Annex 11). The creation of buffer zones subsequent to inscription is normally considered to be a minor boundary modification[1].

<u>Management systems</u>

108. Each nominated property should have an appropriate management plan or other documented management system which must specify how the Outstanding Universal Value of a property should be preserved, preferably through participatory means.

109. The purpose of a management system is to ensure the effective protection of the nominated property for present and future generations.

110. An effective management system depends on the type, characteristics and needs of the nominated property and its cultural and natural context. Management systems may vary according to different cultural perspectives, the resources available and other factors. They may incorporate traditional practices, existing urban or regional planning instruments, and other planning control mechanisms, both formal and informal. Impact assessments for proposed interventions are essential for all World Heritage properties.

111. In recognizing the diversity mentioned above, common elements of an effective management system could include:
    a) a thorough shared understanding of the property, its universal, national and local values and its socio-ecological context by all stakeholders, including local communities and indigenous peoples;
    b) a respect for diversity, equity, gender equality and human rights and the use of inclusive and participatory planning and stakeholder consultation processes;
    c) a cycle of planning, implementation, monitoring, evaluation and feedback;
    d) an assessment of the vulnerabilities of the property to social, economic, environmental and other pressures and changes, including disasters and climate change, as well as the monitoring of the impacts of trends and proposed interventions;

Decision 39 COM 11
Decision 43 COM 11A

---

[1] With regards to transnational/transboundary properties, any modification will need the agreement of all States Parties concerned.

e) the development of mechanisms for the involvement and coordination of the various activities between different partners and stakeholders;
f) the allocation of necessary resources;
g) capacity building;
h) an accountable, transparent description of how the management system functions.

112. Effective management involves a cycle of short, medium and long-term actions to protect, conserve and present the nominated property. An integrated approach to planning and management is essential to guide the evolution of properties over time and to ensure maintenance of all aspects of their Outstanding Universal Value. This approach goes beyond the property to include any buffer zone(s), as well as the broader setting. The broader setting may relate to the property's topography, natural and built environment, and other elements such as infrastructure, land use patterns, spatial organization, and visual relationships. It may also include related social and cultural practices, economic processes and other intangible dimensions of heritage such as perceptions and associations. Management of the broader setting is related to its role in supporting the Outstanding Universal Value. Its effective management may also contribute to sustainable development, through harnessing the reciprocal benefits for heritage and society. Decision 39 COM 11
Decision 43 COM 11A

113. Moreover, in the context of the implementation of the *Convention*, the World Heritage Committee has established a process of Reactive Monitoring (see Chapter IV) and a process of Periodic Reporting (see Chapter V).

114. In the case of serial properties, a management system or mechanisms for ensuring the coordinated management of the separate components are essential and should be documented in the nomination (see paragraphs 137-139).

115. [Deleted] Decision 39 COM 11

116. Where the intrinsic qualities of a nominated site are threatened by human action and yet meet the criteria and the conditions of authenticity or integrity set out in paragraphs 78-95, an action plan outlining the corrective measures required should be submitted with the nomination file. Should the corrective measures submitted by the nominating State Party not be taken within the time proposed by the State Party, the property will be considered by the Committee for delisting in accordance with the procedure adopted by the Committee (see Chapter IV.C). Decision 39 COM 11

117. States Parties are responsible for implementing effective management activities for a World Heritage property. States Parties should do so in close collaboration with property managers, the agency with management authority and other partners, local communities and indigenous peoples, rights-holders and stakeholders in property management, by developing, when appropriate, equitable governance arrangements, collaborative management systems and redress mechanisms. Decision 43 COM 11A

118. The Committee recommends that States Parties include disaster, climate change and other risk preparedness as an element in their World Heritage site management plans and training strategies. Decision 43 COM 11A

A.II.1a Operational Guidelines Welterbe-Übereinkommen

118bis. Notwithstanding Paragraphs 179 and 180 of the *Operational Guidelines*, States Parties shall ensure that Environmental Impact Assessments, Heritage Impact Assessments, and/or Strategic Environmental Assessments be carried out as a pre-requisite for development projects and activities that are planned for implementation within or around a World Heritage property. These assessments should serve to identify development alternatives, as well as both potential positive and negative impacts on the Outstanding Universal Value of the property and to recommend mitigation measures against degradation or other negative impacts on the cultural or natural heritage within the property or its wider setting. This will ensure the long-term safeguarding of the Outstanding Universal Value, and the strengthening of heritage resilience to disasters and climate change. *(Decision 43 COM 11A)*

Sustainable use

119. World Heritage properties may sustain biological and cultural diversity and provide ecosystem services and other benefits, which may contribute to environmental and cultural sustainability. Properties may support a variety of ongoing and proposed uses that are ecologically and culturally sustainable and which may enhance the quality of life and well-being of communities concerned. The State Party and its partners must ensure their use is equitable and fully respects the Outstanding Universal Value of the property. For some properties, human use would not be appropriate. Legislation, policies and strategies affecting World Heritage properties should ensure the protection of the Outstanding Universal Value, support the wider conservation of natural and cultural heritage, and promote and encourage the effective, inclusive and equitable participation of the communities, indigenous peoples and other stakeholders concerned with the property as necessary conditions to its sustainable protection, conservation, management and presentation. *(Decision 43 COM 11A)*

III Process for the inscription of properties on the World Heritage List

III.A Preparation of Nominations

120. The nomination document is the primary basis on which the Committee considers the inscription of properties on the World Heritage List. All relevant information should be included in the nomination document and it should be cross-referenced to the source of information.

121. Annex 3 provides guidance to States Parties in preparing nominations of specific types of properties.

122. Before States Parties begin to prepare a nomination of a property for inscription on the World Heritage List, they should become familiar with the nomination cycle, described in Paragraph 168. It is desirable to carry out initial preparatory work to establish that a property has the potential to justify Outstanding Universal Value, including integrity or authenticity, before the development of a full nomination dossier which could be expensive and time-consuming. Such preparatory work might include the collection of available information on the property, thematic studies, scoping studies on the potential for demonstrating Outstanding Universal Value, including integrity or authenticity, or an

Decision 34 COM 12 (III) Report of the Expert meeting on Upstream Processes to Nominations: Creative Approaches in the Nomination Process" (Phuket: 2010)
Decision 36 COM 13.I
Decision 39 COM 11
Decision 43 COM 11A

initial comparative study of the property in its wider global or regional context, including an analysis in the context of the Gap Studies produced by the Advisory Bodies. This first phase of work will help to establish the feasibility of a possible nomination and avoid the use of resources in the preparation of nominations that may be unlikely to succeed. States Parties are encouraged to seek upstream advice[1)] from the relevant Advisory Body(ies) for this first phase as well as to contact the World Heritage Centre at the earliest opportunity in considering nominations to seek information and guidance.

123. Effective and inclusive participation in the nomination process of local communities, indigenous peoples, governmental, non-governmental and private organizations and other stakeholders is essential to enable them to have a shared responsibility with the State Party in the maintenance of the property. States Parties are encouraged to prepare nominations with the widest possible participation of stakeholders and shall demonstrate, as appropriate, that the free, prior and informed consent of indigenous peoples has been obtained, through, inter alia, making the nominations publicly available in appropriate languages and public consultations and hearings.   Decision 39 COM 11
Decision 43 COM 11A

124. Preparatory Assistance, as described in Chapter VII.E, may be requested by States Parties for the preparation of nominations.

125. States Parties are encouraged to contact the Secretariat, which can provide assistance throughout the nomination process.

126. The Secretariat can also provide:
   a) assistance in identifying appropriate maps and photographs and the national agencies from which these may be obtained;
   b) examples of successful nominations, of management and legislative provisions;
   c) guidance for nominating different types of properties, such as Cultural Landscapes, Towns, Canals, and Heritage Routes (see Annex 3);
   d) guidance for nominating serial and transboundary properties (see paragraphs 134-139).

127. States Parties may submit draft nominations to the Secretariat for comment and review at any time during the year. However, States Parties are strongly encouraged to transmit to the Secretariat by **30 September** of the preceding year (see paragraph 168), the draft nominations that they wish to submit by the 1 February deadline. This submission of a draft nomination should include maps showing the boundaries for the proposed site. Draft   Decision 37 COM 12.II

---

1) Upstream Process: In relation to the nomination of sites for inscription on the World Heritage List, the "Upstream Process" comprises advice, consultation and analysis that occurs prior to the preparation of a nomination and is aimed at reducing the number of nominations that experience significant problems during the evaluation process. The basic principle of the Upstream Process is to enable the Advisory Bodies and the World Heritage Centre to provide guidance and capacity building directly to States Parties, throughout the whole process leading up to the preparation of a possible World Heritage nomination. For the upstream support to be effective, it should be undertaken from the earliest stage in the nomination process, at the moment of the preparation or revision of the States Parties' Tentative Lists.
The purpose of the advice given in the context of a nomination is limited to providing guidance on the technical merit of the nomination and the technical framework needed, in order to offer the State(s) Party(ies) the essential tools that enable it(them) to assess the feasibility and/or actions necessary to prepare a possible nomination.
Requests for the Upstream Process shall be submitted using the official format (Annex 15 of the *Operational Guidelines*). Should the number of requests exceed the capacity, then the prioritization system as per paragraph 61.c will be applied.

A.II.1a Operational Guidelines Welterbe-Übereinkommen

nominations could be submitted either in electronic format or in printed version (only in 1 copy without annexes except for maps). In both cases they should be accompanied by a cover letter.

128. Nominations may be submitted **at any time during the year**, but only those nominations that are "**complete**" (see paragraph 132 and Annex 5) and received by the Secretariat on or before **1 February**[1] will be considered for inscription on the World Heritage List by the World Heritage Committee during the following year. Only nominations of properties included in the State Party's Tentative List will be examined by the Committee (see paragraphs 63 and 65).

Decision 37 COM 12.II
Decision 39 COM 11

III.B Format and content of nominations

129. Nominations of properties for inscription on the World Heritage List should be prepared in accordance with the format set out in Annex 5.

130. The format includes the following sections:
 1. Identification of the Property
 2. Description of the Property
 3. Justification for Inscription
 4. State of conservation and factors affecting the property
 5. Protection and Management
 6. Monitoring
 7. Documentation
 8. Contact Information of responsible authorities
 9. Signature on behalf of the State Party(ies)

131. Nominations to the World Heritage List are evaluated on content rather than on appearance.

132. For a nomination to be considered as "**complete**", the following requirements (see format in Annex 5) are to be met:

Decision 37 COM 12.II
Decision 39 COM 11
Decision 43 COM 11A

Executive Summary
An Executive Summary shall include essential information (see Annex 5) extracted from the main text of the nomination including a reduced size version of the map(s) indicating the boundaries of the nominated property and of the buffer zone (where appropriate) and the draft Statement of Outstanding Universal Value (the same text presented in Section 3.3 of the nomination).

 1. Identification of the property
 The boundaries of the property being proposed shall be clearly defined, unambiguously distinguishing between the nominated property and any buffer zone (when present) (see paragraphs 103-107). Maps shall be sufficiently detailed (see Explanatory Note of section 1.e in Annex 5) to determine precisely which area of land and/ or water is nominated. Officially up-to-date published topographic maps of the State Party annotated to show the property boundaries and any buffer zone (when present) shall be provided if available in printed version. A nomination shall be considered "incomplete" if it does not include clearly defined boundaries.

 2. Description of the property
 The Description of the property shall include the identification of the property and an overview of its history

---
[1] If 1 February falls on a weekend, the nomination must be received by 17h00 GMT the preceding Friday.

and development. All component parts that are mapped shall be identified and described. In particular, where serial nominations are proposed, each of the component parts shall be clearly described.

The History and Development of the property shall describe how the property has reached its present form and the significant changes that it has undergone. This information shall provide the important facts needed to support and give substance to the argument that the property meets the criteria of Outstanding Universal Value and conditions of integrity and/or authenticity.

3. Justification for inscription

This section must make clear why the property is considered to be of Outstanding Universal Value.

The text in sections from 3.1.a to 3.1.e should contain more detailed information to support the text of the proposed Statement of Outstanding Universal Value (section 3.3).

Section 3.1.b shall indicate the World Heritage criteria (see Paragraph 77) under which the property is proposed, together with a clearly stated argument for the use of each criterion. Statements of integrity and (when cultural criteria are proposed) of authenticity shall be included and shall demonstrate how the property satisfies the conditions outlined in paragraphs 78-95.

In section 3.2, a comparative analysis of the property in relation to similar properties, whether or not on the World Heritage List, both at the national and international levels, shall be provided. The comparative analysis shall explain the importance of the nominated property in its national and international context.

In section 3.3, a proposed Statement of Outstanding Universal Value (see paragraphs 49–53 and 155) of the property prepared by the State Party shall make clear why the property is considered to merit inscription on the World Heritage List.

The comparative analyses prepared by States Parties when nominating properties for inscription in the World Heritage List should not be confused with the thematic studies prepared by the Advisory Bodies at the request of the Committee (paragraph 148 below) Decision 7 EXT.COM 4A

4. State of conservation and factors affecting the property

This section shall include accurate information on the present state of conservation of the property (including information on its physical condition of the property and conservation measures in place). It shall also include a description of the factors affecting the property (including threats). Information provided in this section constitutes the baseline data which are necessary to monitor the state of conservation of the nominated property in the future.

5. Protection and management

Protection: Section 5 shall include the list of the legislative, regulatory, contractual, planning, institutional and/or traditional measures most relevant to the protection of the property and provide a detailed analysis of the way in which this protection actually operates. Legislative, regulatory, contractual planning and/or insti-

A.II.1a Operational Guidelines Welterbe-Übereinkommen

tutional texts, or an abstract of the texts, shall also be attached in English or French.

Management: An appropriate management plan or other management system is essential and shall be provided in the nomination. Assurances of the effective implementation of the management plan or other management system are also expected. Sustainable development principles should be integrated into the management system, for all types of natural, cultural and mixed properties, including their buffer zones and wider setting.

A copy of the management plan or documentation of the management system shall be annexed to the nomination. If the management plan exists only in a language other than English or French, an English or French detailed description of its provisions shall be annexed.

A detailed analysis or explanation of the management plan or a documented management system shall be provided in Section 5.e of the nomination.

A nomination which does not include the above-mentioned documents is considered incomplete unless other documents guiding the management of the property until the finalization of the management plan are provided.

6. Monitoring

States Parties shall include the key indicators in place and/or proposed to measure and assess the state of conservation of the property, the factors affecting it, conservation measures at the property, the periodicity of their examination, and the identity of the responsible authorities.

7. Documentation

All documentation necessary to substantiate the nomination shall be provided. In addition to what is indicated above, this shall include a) images of a quality suitable for printing (digital photographs at 300 dpi minimum, and if essential, supplementary film, video or other audio visual material); and b) image/audiovisual inventory and authorization form (see Annex 5, point 7.a). The text of the nomination shall be transmitted in printed form as well as in electronic format (Word and/or PDF format preferred).

8. Contact information of responsible authorities

Detailed contact information of responsible authorities shall be provided.

9. Signature on behalf of the State Party

The nomination shall conclude with the original signature of the official empowered to sign it on behalf of the State Party.

10. Number of printed copies required (including annexed maps)

Nominations of cultural and natural properties (excluding cultural landscapes): 2 identical copies

Nominations of mixed properties and cultural landscapes: 3 identical copies

11. Paper and electronic formats
Nominations shall be presented on A4-size paper and in electronic format (Word and/or PDF format).
12. Sending
States Parties shall submit the nomination in English or French duly signed, to:
UNESCO World Heritage Centre
7, place de Fontenoy
75352 Paris 07 SP
France
Tel: +33 (0) 1 4568 1136
E-mail: wh-nominations@unesco.org

133. The Secretariat will retain all supporting documentation (maps, plans, photographic material, etc.) submitted with the nomination.

III.C Requirements for the nomination of different types of properties

Transboundary properties

134. A nominated property may occur: Decision 7 EXT.COM 4A
    a) on the territory of a single State Party, or
    b) on the territory of all concerned States Parties having adjacent borders (transboundary property).
135. Wherever possible, transboundary nominations should be prepared and submitted by States Parties jointly in conformity with Article 11.3 of the *Convention*. It is highly recommended that the States Parties concerned establish a joint management committee or similar body to oversee the management of the whole of a transboundary property.
136. Extensions to an existing World Heritage property located in one State Party may be proposed to become transboundary properties.

Serial properties

137. Serial properties will include two or more component parts related by clearly defined links:
    a) Component parts should reflect cultural, social or functional links over time that provide, where relevant, landscape, ecological, evolutionary or habitat connectivity.
    b) Each component part should contribute to the Outstanding Universal Value of the property as a whole in a substantial, scientific, readily defined and discernible way, and may include, inter alia, intangible attributes. The resulting Outstanding Universal Value should be easily understood and communicated.
    c) Consistently, and in order to avoid an excessive fragmentation of component parts, the process of nomination of the property, including the selection of the component parts, should take fully into account the overall manageability and coherence of the property (see paragraph 114).

and provided the series <u>as a whole</u> – and not necessarily its individual component parts–is of Outstanding Universal Value.

138. A serial nominated property may occur:
   a) on the territory of a single State Party (<u>serial national property</u>); or
   b) within the territory of different States Parties, which need not be contiguous and is nominated with the consent of all States Parties concerned (<u>serial transnational property</u>).

   Decision 7 EXT.COM 4A

139. Serial nominations, whether from one State Party or multiple States, may be submitted for evaluation over several nomination cycles, provided that the first property nominated is of Outstanding Universal Value in its own right. States Parties planning serial nominations phased over several nomination cycles are encouraged to inform the Committee of their intention in order to ensure better planning.

III.D Registration of nominations

140. On receipt of nominations from States Parties, the Secretariat will acknowledge receipt, check for completeness and register nominations. The Secretariat will forward complete nominations to the relevant Advisory Bodies for evaluation. The Secretariat will also make available the electronic format of the text of the nominations to the Members of the Committee on the World Heritage Centre's website. The Secretariat will request any additional information from the State Party and when required by Advisory Bodies. The timetable for registration and processing of nominations is detailed in paragraph 168.

   Decision 39 COM 11

141. The Secretariat establishes and submits at each Committee session a list of all nominations received, including the date of reception, an indication of their status "complete" or "incomplete", as well as the date at which they are considered as "complete" in conformity with paragraph 132 and Annex 5.

   Decisions 26 COM 14
   Decision 28 COM 14B. 57
   Decision 39 COM 11

142. A nomination passes through a cycle between the time of its submission and the decision by the World Heritage Committee. This cycle normally lasts one and a half years between submission in February of Year 1 and the decision of the Committee in June of Year 2.

III.E Evaluation of nominations by the Advisory Bodies

143. The Advisory Bodies will evaluate whether or not properties nominated by States Parties have Outstanding Universal Value, meet the conditions of integrity and (when relevant) of authenticity and meet the requirements of protection and management. The procedures and format of ICOMOS and IUCN evaluations are described in Annex 6.

   Decision 39 COM 11

144. Evaluations of cultural heritage nominations will be carried out by ICOMOS.

145. Evaluations of natural heritage nominations will be carried out by IUCN.

146. In the case of nominations of cultural properties in the category of "cultural landscapes", the evaluation will be carried out by ICOMOS in consultation with IUCN, as appropriate. For mixed properties, the evaluation will be carried out jointly by ICOMOS and IUCN.

147. As requested by the World Heritage Committee or as necessary, ICOMOS and IUCN will carry out thematic studies to evaluate

proposed World Heritage properties in their regional, global or thematic context. These studies should be informed by a review of the Tentative Lists submitted by States Parties and by reports of meetings on the harmonization of Tentative Lists, as well as by other technical studies performed by the Advisory Bodies and qualified organizations and individuals. A list of those studies already completed may be found in section III of Annex 3, and on the Web addresses of the Advisory Bodies. These studies should not be confused with the comparative analysis to be prepared by States Parties in nominating properties for inscription on the World Heritage List (see paragraph 132).

148. The following principles must guide the evaluations and presentations of ICOMOS and IUCN. The evaluations and presentations should:
   a) adhere to the *World Heritage Convention* and the relevant *Operational Guidelines* and any additional policies set out by the Committee in its decisions;
   b) be objective, rigorous and scientific including in considering all information provided to the Advisory Bodies regarding a nomination;
   c) be conducted to a consistent standard of professionalism, equity and transparency throughout the evaluation process in consultation and dialogue with nominating States Parties;
   d) comply to standard format, both for evaluations and presentations, to be agreed with the Secretariat and include the names of all experts who participated in the evaluation process, except desk reviewers who provide confidential reviews, and, in an annex, a detailed breakdown of all costs and expenses related to the evaluation;
   e) involve regional experts familiar with the subject;
   f) indicate clearly and separately whether the property has Outstanding Universal Value, meets the conditions of integrity and/or authenticity, a management plan/system and legislative protection;
   g) evaluate each property systematically according to all relevant criteria, including its state of conservation, relatively, that is, by comparison with that of other properties of the same type, both inside and outside the State Party's territory;
   h) include references to Committee decisions and requests concerning the nomination under consideration;
   i) not take into account or include any information submitted by the State Party after **28 February**, in the year in which the nomination is considered. The State Party should be informed when information has arrived after the deadline and is not being taken into account in the evaluation. This deadline should be rigorously enforced; and
   j) provide a justification for their views through a list of references (literature) consulted, as appropriate.

Decision 28 COM 14B. 57
Decision 30 COM 13
Decision 39 COM 11

149. The Advisory Bodies are requested to forward to States Parties, with copy to the World Heritage Centre for distribution to the Chair of the World Heritage Committee, by **31 January** of each

Decision 7 EXT.COM 4B.1
Decision 39 COM 11

A.II.1a Operational Guidelines Welterbe-Übereinkommen

year, a short interim report outlining the status and any issues relevant to evaluations, and detailing any requests for supplementary information, in one of the two working languages of the *Convention*.

150. Letters from the concerned States Parties, submitted in the appropriate form in Annex 12, detailing the factual errors that might have been identified in the evaluation of their nomination made by the Advisory Bodies, must be received by the World Heritage Centre no later than 14 days before the opening of the session of the Committee with copies to the relevant Advisory Bodies. The letters shall be made available as an annex to the documents for the relevant agenda item, and no later than the first day of the Committee session. The World Heritage Centre and the Advisory Bodies may add their comments to the letters, in the relevant section of the form, before they are made available.
    Decision 7 EXT.COM 4B.1
    Decision 37 COM 12.II

151. ICOMOS and IUCN make their recommendations under three categories:
    a) properties which are **recommended for inscription** without reservation;
    b) properties which are **not recommended** for inscription;
    c) nominations which are recommended for **referral** or **deferral**.

III.F Withdrawal of nominations

152. A State Party may **withdraw** a nomination it has submitted at any time prior to the Committee session at which it is scheduled to be examined. The State Party should inform the Secretariat in writing of its intention to withdraw the nomination. If the State Party so wishes it can resubmit a nomination for the property, which will be considered as a new nomination according to the procedures and timetable outlined in paragraph 168.

III.G Decision of the World Heritage Committee

153. The World Heritage Committee decides whether a property should or should not be inscribed on the World Heritage List, referred or deferred.

Inscription

154. When deciding to inscribe a property on the World Heritage List, the Committee, guided by the Advisory Bodies, adopts a Statement of Outstanding Universal Value for the property.

155. The Statement of Outstanding Universal Value should include a summary of the Committee's determination that the property has Outstanding Universal Value, identifying the criteria under which the property was inscribed, including the assessments of the conditions of integrity, and, for cultural and mixed properties, authenticity. It should also include a statement on the protection and management in force and the requirements for protection and management for the future. The Statement of Outstanding Universal Value shall be the basis for the future protection and management of the property.
    Decision 39 COM 11

Where necessary, the protection and management part of the Statement of Outstanding Universal Value may be updated by the World Heritage Committee, in consultation with the State Party and further to a review by the Advisory Bodies. Such updates could be made periodically further to the outcomes of Periodic Reporting cycles, or at any Committee session, if required.

The World Heritage Centre will automatically keep the Statements of Outstanding Universal Value updated further to subsequent decisions taken by the Committee concerning a change of name of the property and change of surface further to minor boundary modifications and correct any factual errors as agreed with the relevant Advisory Bodies.

In the framework of the Gender Equality Priority of UNESCO, the use of gender-neutral language in the preparation of Statements of Outstanding Universal Value is encouraged.

156. At the time of inscription, the Committee may also make other recommendations concerning the protection and management of the World Heritage property.

157. The Statement of Outstanding Universal Value (including the criteria for which a specific property is inscribed on the World Heritage List) will be set out by the Committee in its reports and publications.

Decision not to inscribe

158. If the Committee decides that a property should **not be inscribed** on the World Heritage List, the nomination may not be presented to the Committee again except in exceptional circumstances. These exceptional circumstances may include new discoveries, new scientific information about the property, or different criteria not presented in the original nomination. In these cases, a new nomination shall be submitted.

Referral of Nominations

159. Nominations which the Committee decides **to refer** back to the State Party for additional information may be resubmitted to the following Committee session for examination. The additional information must be received by the Secretariat by **1 February**[1)] of the year in which examination by the Committee is desired. The Secretariat will immediately transmit it to the relevant Advisory Bodies for evaluation. A referred nomination which is not presented to the Committee within three years of the original Committee decision will be considered as a new nomination when it is resubmitted for examination, following the procedures and timetable outlined in paragraph 168. States Parties might seek advice from the relevant Advisory Body(ies) and/or the World Heritage Centre to discuss how the recommendations of the Committee might be addressed.

Decision 39 COM 11

Deferral of Nominations

160. The Committee may decide **to defer** a nomination for more in-depth assessment or study, or a substantial revision by the State Party. Should the State Party decide to resubmit the deferred nomination in any subsequent year, it must be received by the Secretariat by **1 February**[1)]. These nominations will then be reevaluated (evaluated again) by the relevant Advisory Bodies during the course of the full year and a half evaluation cycle including an evaluation mission according to the procedures and timetable outlined in paragraph 168. States Parties are encouraged to seek advice from the relevant Advisory Body and/or the World Heritage Centre to discuss how the recommendations of the

Decision 39 COM 11

---

1) If 1 February falls on a weekend, the nomination must be received by 17h00 GMT the preceding Friday.

Committee might be addressed. Where required, the States Parties may wish to consider inviting an Advisory mission.

III.H Nominations to be processed on an emergency basis

161. The normal timetable and definition of completeness for the submission and processing of nominations will not apply in the case of properties which would be in Danger, as a result of having suffered damage or facing serious and specific dangers from natural events or human activities, which would constitute an emergency situation for which an immediate decision by the Committee is necessary to ensure their safeguarding, and which, according to the report of the relevant Advisory Bodies, may unquestionably justify Outstanding Universal Value. Such nominations will be processed on an emergency basis and their examination is included in the agenda of the next Committee session. These properties may be inscribed on the World Heritage List. They shall, in that case, be simultaneously inscribed on the List of World Heritage in Danger (see paragraphs 177-191). *Decision 37 COM 12.II*

162. The procedure for nominations to be processed on an emergency basis is as follows: *Decision 37 COM 12.II*

   a) A State Party presents a nomination with the request for processing on an emergency basis. The State Party shall have already included, or immediately include, the property on its Tentative List.

   b) The nomination shall:

   i) describe the property and identify precisely its boundaries;

   ii) justify its Outstanding Universal Value according to the criteria;

   iii) justify its integrity and/or authenticity;

   iv) describe its protection and management system;

   v) describe the nature of the emergency, and the nature and extent of the damage or specific danger and show that immediate action by the Committee is necessary to ensure the safeguarding of the property.

   c) The Secretariat immediately transmits the nomination to the relevant Advisory Bodies, requesting an assessment of the qualities of the property which may justify its Outstanding Universal Value, of the nature of the danger and the urgency of a decision by the Committee. A field visit may be necessary if the relevant Advisory Bodies consider it appropriate and if the time allows.

   d) When reviewing the nomination the Committee will also consider:

   vi) allocation of International Assistance to complete the nomination; and

   vii) follow-up missions as necessary by the Secretariat and the relevant Advisory Bodies as soon as possible after inscription to fulfil the Committee's recommendations.

III.I Modifications to the boundaries, to the criteria used to justify inscription or to the name of a World Heritage property

<u>Minor modifications to the boundaries</u>

163. A minor modification is one which does not have a significant impact on the extent of the property nor affects its Outstanding Universal Value.

164. If a State Party wishes to request a minor modification to the boundaries of a property already on the World Heritage List, it must be prepared in compliance with the format of Annex 11 and must be received by **1 February**[1] by the Committee through the Secretariat, which will seek the evaluation of the relevant Advisory Bodies on whether this can be considered a minor modification or not. The Secretariat shall then submit the Advisory Bodies' evaluation to the World Heritage Committee. The Committee may approve such a modification, or it may consider that the modification to the boundary is sufficiently significant as to constitute a significant boundary modification of the property, in which case the procedure for new nominations will apply. *Decision 39 COM 11*

Significant modifications to the boundaries

165. If a State Party wishes to significantly modify the boundary of a property already on the World Heritage List, the State Party shall submit this proposal as if it were a new nomination (including the requirement to be previously included on the Tentative List – see paragraph 63 and 65). This re-nomination shall be presented by **1 February**[1] and will be evaluated in the full year and a half cycle of evaluation according to the procedures and timetable outlined in paragraph 168. This provision applies to extensions, as well as reductions. *Decision 39 COM 11*

Modifications to the criteria used to justify inscription on the World Heritage List

166. Where a State Party wishes to have the property inscribed under additional, fewer or different criteria other than those used for the original inscription, it shall submit this request as if it were a new nomination (including the requirement to be previously included on the Tentative List – see paragraphs 63 and 65). This re-nomination must be received by **1 February**[1] and will be evaluated in the full year and a half cycle of evaluation according to the procedures and timetable outlined in paragraph 168. Properties recommended will only be evaluated under the new criteria and will remain on the World Heritage List even if unsuccessful in having additional criteria recognized. *Decision 39 COM 11*

Modification to the name of a World Heritage property

167. A State Party [2] may request that the Committee authorize a modification to the name of a property already inscribed on the World Heritage List. A request for a modification to the name shall be received by the Secretariat **at least 3 months prior to the meeting of the Committee.**

III.J   Timetable – overview

168. *Decision 39 COM 11*

---

1) If 1 February falls on a weekend, the nomination must be received by 17h00 GMT the preceding Friday.
2) In case of transnational/transboundary properties, any modification will need the agreement of all States Parties concerned.

A.II.1a Operational Guidelines Welterbe-Übereinkommen

Timetable	Procedures
30 September (before Year 1)	Voluntary deadline for receipt of <u>draft</u> nominations from States Parties by the Secretariat.
15 November (before Year 1)	Secretariat to respond to the nominating State Party concerning the completeness of the draft nomination, and, if incomplete, to indicate the missing information required to make the nomination complete.
1 February Year 1	Deadline by which <u>complete</u> nominations must be received by the Secretariat to be transmitted to the relevant Advisory Bodies for evaluation. Nominations shall be received by 17h00 GMT, or, if the date falls on a weekend by 17h00 GMT the preceding Friday. Nominations received after this date will be examined in a future cycle.
1 February – 1 March Year 1	Registration, assessment of completeness and transmission to the relevant Advisory Bodies. The Secretariat registers each nomination, acknowledges receipt to the nominating State Party and inventories its contents. The Secretariat will inform the nominating State Party whether or not the nomination is complete. Nominations that are <u>not complete</u> (see paragraph 132) will not be transmitted to the relevant Advisory Bodies for evaluation. If a nomination is incomplete, the State Party concerned will be advised of information required to complete the nomination by the deadline of 1 February of the following year in order for the nomination to be examined in a future cycle. Nominations that are <u>complete</u> are transmitted to the relevant Advisory Bodies for evaluation. The Secretariat will also make available the electronic format of the text of the nominations to the Members of the Committee on the World Heritage Centre's website.
1 March Year 1	Deadline by which the Secretariat informs the State Party of the receipt of a Nomination, whether it is considered complete and whether it has been received by 1 February.
March Year 1 – May Year 2	Evaluation by the Advisory Bodies
31 January Year 2	The Advisory Bodies are requested to forward to States Parties, with copy to the World Heritage Centre for distribution to the Chair of the World Heritage Committee, by **31 January** of Year 2 a short interim report outlining the status of and any issues relevant to evaluations, and detailing any requests for supplementary information, in one of the two working languages of the *Convention*.
28 February Year 2	Deadline by which additional information requested by the relevant Advisory Bodies shall be submitted by the State Party to them via the Secretariat. Additional information shall be submitted in the same number of copies and electronic formats as specified in Paragraph 132 to the Secretariat. To avoid confusing new and old texts, if the additional information submitted concerns changes to the main text of the nomination, the State Party shall submit these changes in an amended version of the original text. The chan-

Timetable	Procedures
	ges shall be clearly identified. An electronic version (CD-ROM or USB Flash Drive) of this new text shall accompany the paper version.
Six weeks prior to the annual World Heritage Committee session Year 2	The relevant Advisory Bodies deliver their evaluations and recommendations to the Secretariat for transmission to the World Heritage Committee as well as to States Parties.
At least 14 working days before the opening of the annual World Heritage Committee session Year 2	Correction of factual errors by States Parties. The concerned States Parties can send, at least 14 working days before the opening of the session of the Committee, a letter to the Chairperson, with copies to the Advisory Bodies, detailing the factual errors they might have identified in the evaluation of their nomination made by the Advisory Bodies.
Annual session of the World Heritage Committee (June/July) Year 2	The Committee examines the nominations and makes its decisions.
Immediately following the annual session of the World Heritage Committee	Notification to the States Parties
The Secretariat notifies all States Parties whose nominations have been examined by the Committee of the relevant decisions of the Committee.
Following the decision of the World Heritage Committee to inscribe a property on the World Heritage List, the Secretariat writes to the State Party and site managers providing a map of the area inscribed and the Statement of Outstanding Universal Value (to include reference to the criteria met).
Immediately following the annual session of the World Heritage Committee	The Secretariat publishes the updated World Heritage List every year following the annual session of the Committee. The name of the States Parties having nominated the properties inscribed on the World Heritage List are presented in the published form of the List under the following heading: "Contracting State having submitted the nomination of the property in accordance with the *Convention*".
In the month following the closure of the annual session of the World Heritage Committee	The Secretariat forwards the published report of all the decisions of the World Heritage Committee to all States Parties.

III.K Financing of evaluation of nominations

168bis. States Parties submitting new nominations are expected to make voluntary contributions towards funding evaluation of nominations by the Advisory Bodies, taking into account the average costs of evaluations as indicated by the Secretariat in the document related to the World Heritage Fund presented at each Committee session. The modalities are as follows: Decision 43 COM 11A
Decision 43 COM 14

    a)   The contributions shall be made to a dedicated sub-account of the World Heritage Fund;

    b)   No contributions would be expected from Least Developed Countries or Low-Income Economies (as defined by the United Nations Economic and Social Council's Committee for Development Policy), Lower Middle-Income Countries as defined by the World Bank, Small Island Developing States and States Parties in conflict or post conflict situations;

c) The contributions are expected to be made after the nomination enters the evaluation cycle upon a positive outcome of the completeness check;

d) This mechanism shall not impact the objective evaluation of sites by the Advisory Bodies, nor the order of priority as defined in the *Operational Guidelines* to be used when handling nominations.

IV Process for monitoring the State of conservation of World Heritage Properties

IV.A Reactive Monitoring

Definition of Reactive Monitoring

169. Reactive Monitoring is the reporting by the Secretariat, other sectors of UNESCO and the Advisory Bodies to the Committee on the state of conservation of specific World Heritage properties that are under threat. To this end, the States Parties shall submit specific reports and impact studies each time exceptional circumstances occur or work is undertaken which may have an impact on the Outstanding Universal Value of the property or its state of conservation.

Reactive Monitoring is also foreseen in reference to properties inscribed, or to be inscribed, on the List of World Heritage in Danger as set out in paragraphs 177-191. Reactive Monitoring is also foreseen in the procedures for the eventual deletion of properties from the World Heritage List as set out in paragraphs 192-198.

These reports shall be submitted to the World Heritage Committee through the Secretariat, using the standard format in Annex 13, in English or French:

a) by 1 December of the year preceding the examination of the property by the Committee, for the properties inscribed on the World Heritage List,

b) by 1 February of the year of examination of the property by the Committee, for the properties inscribed on the List of World Heritage in Danger, and for specific cases of utmost urgency.

Decision 39 COM 11

Objective of Reactive Monitoring

170. When adopting the process of Reactive Monitoring, the Committee was particularly concerned that all possible measures should be taken to prevent the deletion of any property from the List and was ready to offer technical cooperation as far as possible to States Parties in this connection.

171. The Committee recommends that States Parties cooperate with the Advisory Bodies which have been asked by the Committee to carry out monitoring and reporting on its behalf on the progress of work undertaken for the preservation of properties inscribed on the World Heritage List.

Information received from States Parties and/or other sources

172. The World Heritage Committee invites the States Parties to the *Convention* to inform the Committee, through the Secretariat, of their intention to undertake or to authorize in an area protected under the *Convention* major restorations or new constructions which may affect the Outstanding Universal Value of the property. Notice should be given as soon as possible (for instance,

Article 4 of the Convention:
"Each State Party to this Convention recognizes that the duty of ensuring the identification, protection, conservation, presentation and transmission to future generations of the cultural and natural heritage referred to in Articles 1 and 2 and situated on its territory, belongs primarily to that State...".

173. The World Heritage Committee requests that reports of missions to review the state of conservation of the World Heritage properties include:
    a) an indication of threats or significant improvement in the conservation of the property since the last report to the World Heritage Committee;
    b) any follow-up to previous decisions of the World Heritage Committee on the state of conservation of the property;
    c) information on any threat or damage to or loss of Outstanding Universal Value, integrity and/or authenticity for which the property was inscribed on the World Heritage List.

    Decision 27 COM 7B. 106

before drafting basic documents for specific projects) and before making any decisions that would be difficult to reverse, so that the Committee may assist in seeking appropriate solutions to ensure that the Outstanding Universal Value of the property is fully preserved.

174. When the Secretariat receives information that a property inscribed has seriously deteriorated, or that the necessary corrective measures have not been taken within the time proposed, from a source other than the State Party concerned, it will, as far as possible, verify the source and the contents of the information in consultation with the State Party concerned and request its comments.

Decision by the World Heritage Committee

175. The Secretariat will request the relevant Advisory Bodies to forward comments on the information received.

176. The information received, together with the comments of the State Party and the Advisory Bodies, will be brought to the attention of the Committee in the form of a state of conservation report for each property, which may take one or more of the following steps:

    Decision 39 COM 11
    Decision 43 COM 11A

    a) it may decide that the property has not seriously deteriorated and that no further action should be taken;
    b) when the Committee considers that the property has seriously deteriorated, but not to the extent that its restoration is impossible, it may decide that the property be maintained on the List, provided that the State Party takes the necessary measures to restore the property within a reasonable period of time. The Committee may also decide that technical cooperation be provided under the World Heritage Fund for work connected with the restoration of the property, proposing to the State Party to request such assistance, if it has not already been done; in some circumstances States Parties may wish to invite an Advisory mission by the relevant Advisory Body(ies) or other organization(s) or expert(s) to seek advice on necessary measures to reverse deterioration and address threats;
    c) when the requirements and criteria set out in paragraphs 177-182 are met, the Committee may decide to inscribe the property on the List of World Heritage in Danger

A.II.1a Operational Guidelines Welterbe-Übereinkommen 144

               according to the procedures set out in paragraphs 183-189;

    d)   when there is evidence that the property has deteriorated to the point where it has irretrievably lost those characteristics which determined its inscription on the List, the Committee may decide to delete the property from the List. Before any such action is taken, the Secretariat will inform the State Party concerned. Any comments which the State Party may make will be brought to the attention of the Committee;

    e)   when the information available is not sufficient to enable the Committee to take one of the measures described in a), b), c) or d) above, the Committee may decide that the Secretariat be authorized to take the necessary action to ascertain, in consultation with the State Party concerned, the present condition of the property, the dangers to the property and the feasibility of adequately restoring the property. Such measures may include the sending of a Reactive Monitoring mission or the consultation of specialists, or through an Advisory mission. The Secretariat shall report to the Committee on the results of its action. In case an emergency action is required, the Committee may authorize its financing from the World Heritage Fund through an emergency assistance request.

IV.B The List of World Heritage in Danger

Guidelines for the inscription of properties on the List of World Heritage in Danger

177.   In accordance with Article 11, paragraph 4, of the *Convention*, the Committee may inscribe a property on the List of World Heritage in Danger when the following requirements are met:

    a)   the property under consideration is on the World Heritage List;

    b)   the property is threatened by serious and specific danger;

    c)   major operations are necessary for the conservation of the property;

    d)   assistance under the *Convention* has been requested for the property; the Committee is of the view that its assistance in certain cases may most effectively be limited to messages of its concern, including the message sent by inscription of a property on the List of World Heritage in Danger and that such assistance may be requested by any Committee member or the Secretariat.

Criteria for the inscription of properties on the List of World Heritage in Danger

178.   A World Heritage property – as defined in Articles 1 and 2 of the *Convention* – can be inscribed on the List of World Heritage in Danger by the Committee when it finds that the condition of the property corresponds to at least one of the criteria in either of the two cases described below.

179.   In the case of <u>cultural properties</u>:

    a)   <u>ASCERTAINED DANGER</u> – The property is faced with specific and proven imminent danger, such as:

- i) serious deterioration of materials;
- ii) serious deterioration of structure and/or ornamental features;
- iii) serious deterioration of architectural or town-planning coherence;
- iv) serious deterioration of urban or rural space, or the natural environment;
- v) significant loss of historical authenticity;
- vi) important loss of cultural significance.

b) POTENTIAL DANGER – The property is faced with threats which could have deleterious effects on its inherent characteristics. Such threats are, for example:
- i) modification of juridical status of the property diminishing the degree of its protection;
- ii) lack of conservation policy;
- iii) threatening effects of regional planning projects;
- iv) threatening effects of town planning;
- v) outbreak or threat of armed conflict;
- vi) threatening impacts of climatic, geological or other environmental factors.

180. In the case of <u>natural properties</u>:   Decision 39 COM 11

a) ASCERTAINED DANGER The property is faced with specific and proven imminent danger, such as:
- i) A serious decline in the population of the endangered species or the other species of Outstanding Universal Value for which the property was legally established to protect, either by natural factors such as disease or by human-made factors such as poaching.
- ii) Severe deterioration of the natural beauty or scientific value of the property, as by human settlement, construction of reservoirs which flood important parts of the property, industrial and agricultural development including use of pesticides and fertilizers, major public works, mining, pollution, logging, firewood collection, etc.
- iii) Human encroachment on boundaries or in upstream areas which threaten the integrity of the property.

b) POTENTIAL DANGER The property is faced with major threats which could have deleterious effects on its inherent characteristics. Such threats are, for example:
- i) a modification of the legal protective status of the area;
- ii) planned resettlement or development projects within the property or so situated that the impacts threaten the property;
- iii) outbreak or threat of armed conflict;

A.II.1a Operational Guidelines Welterbe-Übereinkommen

      iv)   the management plan or management system is lacking or inadequate, or not fully implemented.
      v)   threatening impacts of climatic, geological or other environmental factors.

181. In addition, the threats and/or their detrimental impacts on the integrity of the property must be those which are amenable to correction by human action. In the case of cultural properties, both natural factors and human-made factors may be threatening, while in the case of natural properties, most threats will be human-made and only very rarely a natural factor (such as an epidemic disease) will threaten the integrity of the property. In some cases, the threats and/or their detrimental impacts on the integrity of the property may be corrected by administrative or legislative action, such as the cancelling of a major public works project or the improvement of legal status.   *Decision 39 COM 11*

182. The Committee may wish to bear in mind the following supplementary factors when considering the inclusion of a cultural or natural property in the List of World Heritage in Danger:
    a) Decisions which affect World Heritage properties are taken by Governments after balancing all factors. The advice of the World Heritage Committee can often be decisive if it can be given <u>before</u> the property becomes threatened.
    b) Particularly in the case of <u>ascertained danger</u>, the physical or cultural deteriorations to which a property has been subjected should be judged according to the <u>intensity</u> of its effects and analyzed case by case.
    c) Above all, in the case of <u>potential danger</u> to a property, one should consider that:
        i) the threat should be appraised according to the normal evolution of the social and economic framework in which the property is situated;
        ii) it is often impossible to assess certain threats such as the threat of armed conflict as to their effect on cultural or natural properties;
        iii) some threats are not imminent in nature, but can only be anticipated, such as demographic growth.
    d) Finally, in its appraisal, the Committee should take into account <u>any cause of unknown or unexpected origin</u> which endangers a cultural or natural property.

Procedure for the inscription of properties on the List of World Heritage in Danger

183. When considering the inscription of a property on the List of World Heritage in Danger, the Committee shall develop, and adopt, as far as possible, in consultation with the State Party concerned, a "Desired state of conservation for the removal of the property from the List of World Heritage in Danger", and a programme for corrective measures.

184. In order to develop the programme of corrective measures referred to in the previous paragraph, the Committee shall request the Secretariat to ascertain, as far as possible in cooperation with the State Party concerned, the present condition of the property,   *Decision 39 COM 11*

the dangers to the property and the feasibility of undertaking corrective measures. The Committee may further decide to send a Reactive Monitoring mission from the relevant Advisory Bodies or other organizations to visit the property, evaluate the nature and extent of the threats and propose the measures to be taken. In some circumstances, the State Party may wish to invite an Advisory mission to provide advice and guidance.

185. The information received, together with the comments as appropriate of the State Party and the relevant Advisory Bodies or other organizations, will be brought to the attention of the Committee by the Secretariat.

186. The Committee shall examine the information available and take a decision concerning the inscription of the property on the List of World Heritage in Danger. Any such decision shall be taken by a majority of two-thirds of the Committee members present and voting. The Committee will then define the programme of corrective action to be taken. This programme will be proposed to the State Party concerned for immediate implementation.

187. The State Party concerned shall be informed of the Committee's decision and public notice of the decision shall immediately be issued by the Committee, in accordance with Article 11.4 of the *Convention*.

188. The Secretariat publishes the updated List of World Heritage in Danger in printed form and is also available at: https://whc.unesco.org/en/danger

189. The Committee shall allocate a specific, significant portion of the World Heritage Fund to financing of possible assistance to World Heritage properties inscribed on the List of World Heritage in Danger.

Regular review of the state of conservation of properties on the List of World Heritage in Danger

190. The Committee shall review annually the state of conservation of properties on the List of World Heritage in Danger. This review shall include such monitoring procedures and expert missions as might be determined necessary by the Committee.

191. On the basis of these regular reviews, the Committee shall decide, in consultation with the State Party concerned, whether:
   a) additional measures are required to conserve the property;
   b) to delete the property from the List of World Heritage in Danger if the property is no longer under threat;
   c) to consider the deletion of the property from both the List of World Heritage in Danger and the World Heritage List if the property has deteriorated to the extent that it has lost those characteristics which determined its inscription on the World Heritage List, in accordance with the procedure set out in paragraphs 192-198.

IV.C Procedure for the eventual deletion of properties from the World Heritage List

192. The Committee adopted the following procedure for the deletion of properties from the World Heritage List in cases: Decision 39 COM 11
   a) where the property has deteriorated to the extent that it has lost those characteristics which determined its inclusion in the World Heritage List; and

A.II.1a Operational Guidelines Welterbe-Übereinkommen 148

b) where the intrinsic qualities of a World Heritage property were already threatened at the time of its nomination by human action and where the necessary corrective measures as outlined by the State Party at the time, have not been taken within the time proposed (see paragraph 116).

193. When a property inscribed on the World Heritage List has seriously deteriorated, or when the necessary corrective measures have not been taken within the time proposed, the State Party on whose territory the property is situated should so inform the Secretariat.

194. When the Secretariat receives such information from a source other than the State Party concerned, it will, as far as possible, verify the source and the contents of the information in consultation with the State Party concerned and request its comments.

195. The Secretariat will request the relevant Advisory Bodies to forward comments on the information received.

196. The Committee will examine all the information available and will take a decision. Any such decision shall, in accordance with Article 13 (8) of the *Convention*, be taken by a majority of two-thirds of its members present and voting. The Committee shall not decide to delete any property unless the State Party has been consulted on the question.

197. The State Party shall be informed of the Committee's decision and public notice of this decision shall be immediately given by the Committee.

198. If the Committee's decision entails any modification to the World Heritage List, this modification will be reflected in the next updated List that is published.

V Periodic Reporting on the implementation of the *World Heritage Convention*
V.A Objectives

199. States Parties are requested to submit reports to the UNESCO General Conference through the World Heritage Committee, on the legislative and administrative provisions they have adopted and other actions which they have taken for the application of the *Convention*, including the state of conservation of the World Heritage properties located on their territories.

Article 29 of the *World Heritage Convention* and Resolutions of the 11th session of the General Assembly of States Parties (1997) and the 29th session of the UNESCO General Conference.

Decision 41 COM 11

200. Periodic Reporting is a self-reporting process and should be led as far as possible by the States Parties in each region. The Secretariat coordinates and facilitates the Periodic Reporting Process at the global level. States Parties may request expert advice from the Advisory Bodies and the Secretariat, which may also (with agreement of the States Parties concerned) commission further expert advice.

201. Periodic Reporting serves four main purposes:
   a) to provide an assessment of the application of the *World Heritage Convention* by the State Party;
   b) to provide an assessment as to whether the Outstanding Universal Value of the properties inscribed on the World Heritage List is being maintained over time;
   c) to provide up-dated information about the World Heritage properties to record the changing circumstances and state of conservation of the properties;
   d) to provide a mechanism for regional cooperation and exchange of information and experiences between States Parties concerning the implementation of the *Convention* and World Heritage conservation.

202. Periodic Reporting is important for more effective long term conservation of the properties inscribed, as well as to strengthen the credibility of the implementation of the *Convention*. It is also an important tool for assessing the implementation by States Parties and World Heritage properties of policies adopted by the World Heritage Committee and the General Assembly.   Decision 41 COM 11

V.B Procedure and Format

203. Every six years, States Parties submit periodic reports for examination by the World Heritage Committee. During the six-year Periodic Reporting cycle, States Parties report region by region in the following order: Decision 22 COM VI.7 / Decision 41 COM 11
   – Arab States
   – Africa
   – Asia and the Pacific
   – Latin America and the Caribbean
   – Europe and North America

204. The sixth year of each cycle is a period for reflection and evaluation. This pause allows the Periodic Reporting mechanism to be assessed and revised as appropriate before a new cycle is initiated. The World Heritage Committee may also decide to use the reflection to initiate the development and publication of a Global World Heritage Report.   Decision 41 COM 11

205. At appropriate intervals, and whenever deemed necessary, the World Heritage Committee adopts and revises Monitoring Indicators and an Analytical Framework for Periodic Reporting.

205bis. The Periodic Reporting process is used as an opportunity for regional exchange and cooperation and to enhance active coordination and synchronization between States Parties, particularly in the case of transboundary and transnational properties.   Decision 41 COM 11

206. The Periodic Reporting questionnaire is an online tool to be completed by the respective National Focal Points and Site Managers of the World Heritage properties, as appropriate.
   a) **Section I** refers to the legislative and administrative provisions which the State Party has adopted and other actions which it has taken for the application of the *Convention*, together with details of the experience acquired in this field. This particularly concerns the general obligations defined in specific articles of the *Convention*.

The format of this questionnaire was reviewed further to the second cycle of Periodic Reporting and was adopted by the World Heritage Committee at its 41st session (Krakow, 2017).
Decision 41 COM 10A

A.II.1a Operational Guidelines Welterbe-Übereinkommen

	b)	Section II refers to the state of conservation of specific World Heritage properties located on the territory of the State Party concerned. This Section should be completed for each World Heritage property.	
206bis.	The Periodic Reporting format may be reviewed following each cycle of Periodic Reporting. An outline of the format is contained in Annex 7 to the *Operational Guidelines*.	Decision 41 COM 11
207.	In order to facilitate management and analysis of information, States Parties are requested to submit reports, in English or French, using the online tool provided on the website of the World Heritage Centre. The online tool of the full questionnaire can be accessed here: https://whc.unesco.org/en/periodicreporting/	Decision 41 COM 11

V.C Evaluation and Follow Up

208.	The Secretariat and the Advisory Bodies facilitate the States Parties to consolidate national reports into Regional State of the World Heritage reports, which are available in electronic format at https://whc.unesco.org/en/publications and in paper version (World Heritage Paper series).	Decision 41 COM 11
209.	The World Heritage Committee carefully reviews issues raised in Periodic Reports and advises the States Parties of the regions concerned on matters arising from them.	
210.	States Parties, working in partnership with the Secretariat and the Advisory Bodies, develop long-term regional follow-up programmes structured according to the Committee's Strategic Objectives and submit them for examination. These programmes are adopted as follow-up to Periodic Reports and regularly reviewed by the Committee based on the needs of States Parties identified in Periodic Reports. They should accurately reflect the needs of World Heritage in the region and facilitate the granting of International Assistance.	Decision 36 COM 13.I Decision 41 COM 11

VI Encouraging support for the *World Heritage Convention*

VI.A Objectives

211.	The objectives are: a) to enhance capacity building and research; b) to raise the general public's awareness, understanding and appreciation of the need to preserve cultural and natural heritage; c) to enhance the function of World Heritage in the life of the community; and d) to increase equitable, inclusive and effective participation of local and national populations, including indigenous peoples, in the protection and presentation of heritage.	Article 27 of the *World Heritage Convention* Decision 43 COM 11A Article 5(a) of the *World Heritage Convention*

VI.B Capacity building and research

212.	The Committee seeks to develop capacity building within the States Parties in conformity with its Strategic Objectives and the World Heritage Capacity Building Strategy adopted by the Committee. <u>The World Heritage Capacity Building Strategy</u>	Budapest Declaration on World Heritage (2002) Decision 43 COM 11A

213.	Recognizing the high level of skills and multidisciplinary approach necessary for the protection, conservation, and presentation of the World Heritage, the Committee has adopted the World Heritage Capacity Building Strategy. The definition of capacity building identifies three broad areas where capacities reside and for which audiences for capacity building need targeting: practitioners, institutions, and communities and networks. The World Heritage Capacity Building Strategy provides a framework of action, and orients actors at the international, regional, or national levels to create regional and national capacity building strategies in addition to individual capacity building activities. The actions can be taken up by the many actors who currently provide or could provide capacity building activities for the benefit of World Heritage. The primary goal of the Capacity Building Strategy is to ensure that necessary skills are developed by a wide range of actors for better implementation of the *Convention*. In order to avoid overlap and effectively implement the Strategy, the Committee will ensure links to other initiatives such as the Global Strategy for a Representative, Balanced and Credible World Heritage List and Periodic Reporting. The Committee will annually review relevant capacity building issues, assess capacity building needs, review annual reports on capacity building initiatives, and make recommendations for future capacity building initiatives.	World Heritage Capacity Building Strategy adopted by the World Heritage Committee at its 35th session (UNESCO, 2011) (see Document WHC-11/35.COM/9B). Decision 43 COM 11A

National capacity building strategies and regional co-operation

214.	States Parties are encouraged to ensure that there is a gender-balanced representation of their professionals and specialists at all levels and that they are adequately trained. To this end, States Parties are encouraged to develop national capacity building strategies and include regional cooperation for training as part of their strategies. Development of such regional and national strategies can be assisted by the Advisory Bodies and the various UNESCO Category 2 Centres related to World Heritage, taking into consideration the World Heritage Capacity Building Strategy.	Decision 43 COM 11A
214bis.	States Parties are encouraged to develop educational and capacity building programmes that harness the reciprocal benefits of the *Convention* for heritage and society. The programmes may be based on innovation and local entrepreneurship, and aimed in particular at medium/small/micro scale levels, to promote sustainable and inclusive economic benefits for local communities and indigenous peoples and to identify and promote opportunities for public and private investment in sustainable development projects, including those that promote use of local materials and resources and foster local cultural and creative industries and safeguarding intangible heritage associated with World Heritage properties.	Decision 43 COM 11A

Research

215.	The Committee develops and coordinates international cooperation in the area of research needed for the effective implementation of the *Convention*. States Parties are also encouraged to make resources available to undertake research, since knowledge and understanding are fundamental to the identification, ma-	Decision 43 COM 11A

nagement, and monitoring of World Heritage properties. States Parties are encouraged to support scientific studies and research methodologies, including traditional and indigenous knowledge held by local communities and indigenous peoples, with all necessary consent. Such studies and research are aimed at demonstrating the contribution that the conservation and management of World Heritage properties, their buffer zones and wider setting make to sustainable development, such as in conflict prevention and resolution, including, where relevant, by drawing on traditional ways of dispute resolution that may exist within communities.

International Assistance

216. Training and Research Assistance may be requested by States Parties from the World Heritage Fund (see Chapter VII).

VI.C Awareness-raising and education
Awareness-raising

217. States Parties are encouraged to raise awareness of the need to preserve World Heritage in their own countries. In particular, they should ensure that World Heritage status is adequately marked and promoted on-site.

218. The Secretariat provides assistance to States Parties in developing activities aimed at raising public awareness of the *Convention* and informing the public of the dangers threatening World Heritage. The Secretariat advises States Parties regarding the preparation and implementation of on-site promotional and educational projects to be funded through International Assistance. The Advisory Bodies and appropriate State agencies may also be solicited to provide advice on such projects.

Education

219. The World Heritage Committee encourages and supports the development of educational materials, activities and programmes.

International Assistance

220. States Parties are encouraged to develop quality educational activities related to World Heritage through a variety of learning environments tailored to each audience with, wherever possible, the participation of schools, universities, museums and other local and national educational authorities.

Article 27(1) of the World Heritage Convention

Decision 43 COM 11A

221. The Secretariat, in cooperation with the UNESCO Education Sector and other partners, produces and publishes a World Heritage Educational Resource Kit, "World Heritage in Young Hands", for use in secondary schools around the world. The Kit is adaptable for use at other educational levels.

"World Heritage in Young Hands" is available at https://whc.unesco.org/en/wheducation/

222. International Assistance may be requested by States Parties from the World Heritage Fund for the purpose of developing and implementing awareness-raising and educational activities or programmes (see Chapter VII).

VII The World Heritage Fund and International Assistance
VII.A The World Heritage Fund

223. The World Heritage Fund is a trust fund, established by the *Convention* in conformity with the provisions of the Financial Regulations of UNESCO. The resources of the Fund consist of compulsory and voluntary contributions made by States Parties

Article 15 of the World Heritage Convention

to the *Convention*, and any other resources authorized by the Fund's regulations.

224. The financial regulations for the Fund are set out in document WHC/7 available at https://whc.unesco.org/en/financialregulations

VII.B Mobilization of other technical and financial resources and partnerships in support of the *World Heritage Convention*

225. To the extent possible, the World Heritage Fund should be used to mobilize additional funds for International Assistance from other sources.

226. The Committee decided that contributions offered to the World Heritage Fund for international assistance campaigns and other UNESCO projects for any property inscribed on the World Heritage List shall be accepted and used as International Assistance pursuant to Section V of the *Convention*, and in conformity with the modalities established for carrying out the campaign or project.

227. States Parties are invited to provide support to the *Convention* in addition to obligatory contributions paid to the World Heritage Fund. This voluntary support can be provided through additional contributions to the World Heritage Fund or direct financial and technical contributions to properties.   *Article 15(3) of the World Heritage Convention*

228. States Parties are encouraged to participate in international fundraising campaigns launched by UNESCO and aimed at protecting World Heritage.

229. States Parties and others who anticipate making contributions towards these campaigns or other UNESCO projects for World Heritage properties are encouraged to make their contributions through the World Heritage Fund.

230. States Parties are encouraged to promote the establishment of national, public and private foundations or associations aimed at raising funds to support World Heritage conservation efforts.   *Article 17 of the World Heritage Convention*

231. The Secretariat provides support in mobilizing financial and technical resources for World Heritage conservation and actively engages in resource mobilization, including through developing partnerships with public and private institutions in conformity with the decisions and the strategies adopted by the World Heritage Committee and UNESCO regulations.   "Comprehensive Partnership Strategy" including "Separate strategies for engagement with individual categories of partners" 192 EX/5.INF
Decision 43 COM 11A
Decision 39 COM 11

232. The Secretariat should refer to UNESCO's "Comprehensive Partnership Strategy" to govern external fundraising in favour of the World Heritage Fund. This document is available at http://en.unesco.org/partnerships

VII.C International Assistance

233. The *Convention* provides International Assistance to States Parties for the protection of the world cultural and natural heritage located on their territories and inscribed, or potentially suitable for inscription on the World Heritage List. International Assistance should be seen as supplementary to national efforts for the conservation and management of World Heritage and Tentative List properties when adequate resources cannot be secured at the national level.   See Articles 13 (1)(2) and Articles 19-26 of the *World Heritage Convention*

234.	International Assistance is primarily financed from the World Heritage Fund, established under the *World Heritage Convention*. The Committee determines the budget for International Assistance on a biennial basis.	Section IV of the *World Heritage Convention*
235.	The World Heritage Committee coordinates and allocates types of International Assistance in response to State Party requests. These types of International Assistance, described in the summary table set out below, in order of priority are: a) Emergency assistance; b) Conservation and Management assistance (incorporating assistance for training and research, technical cooperation and promotion and education); c) Preparatory assistance.	Decision 30 COM 14A Decision 36 COM 13.I

VII.D Principles and priorities for International Assistance

236.	Priority is given to International Assistance for properties inscribed on the List of World Heritage in Danger. The Committee created a specific budget line to ensure that a significant portion of assistance from the World Heritage Fund is allocated to properties inscribed on the List of World Heritage in Danger.	Article 13(1) of the *World Heritage Convention*
237.	States Parties in arrears of payment of their compulsory or voluntary contributions to the World Heritage Fund are not eligible for International Assistance, it being understood that this provision does not apply to requests for emergency assistance.	Decision 13 COM XII. 34
238.	To support its Strategic Objectives, the Committee also allocates International Assistance in conformity with the priorities set out in its decisions and in the Regional Programmes it adopts as a follow-up to Periodic Reports (see para. 210).	Decision 26 COM 17.2 Decision 26 COM 20 Decision 26 COM 25.3 Decision 36 COM 13.I

239.	In addition to the priorities outlined in paragraphs 236-238 above, the following considerations govern the decisions of the Committee in granting International Assistance:
	a) the likelihood that the assistance will have a catalytic and multiplier effect ("seed money") and promote financial and technical contributions from other sources;
	b) when funds available are limited and a selection has to be made, preference is given to:
	   – a Least Developed Country or Low Income Economy as defined by the United Nations Economic and Social Council's Committee for Development Policy, or
	   – a Lower Middle Income Country as defined by the World Bank, or
	   – a Small Island Developing State (SIDS), or
	   – a State Party in a post-conflict situation;
	c) the urgency of the protective measures to be taken at World Heritage properties;
	d) whether the legislative, administrative and, wherever possible, financial commitment of the recipient State Party is available to the activity;
	e) the impact of the activity on furthering the Strategic Objectives or on the implementation of policies adopted by the Committee, such as the Policy Document for the Integration of a Sustainable Development Perspective into
		Decision 43 COM 11A
		
		Decision 31 COM 18B
		
		Paragraph 26 of *Operational Guidelines*

		the Processes of the World Heritage Convention or the Policy Document on the Impact of Climate Change on World Heritage properties;	
	f)	the degree to which the activity responds to needs identified through the reactive monitoring process and/or the analysis of regional Periodic Reports;	Decision 20 COM XII
	g)	the exemplary value of the activity in respect to scientific research and the development of cost-effective conservation techniques;	
	h)	the cost of the activity and expected results;	65 % of the total International Assistance budget is set aside for cultural properties and 35 % for natural properties
	i)	the educational value both for the training of experts and for the general public; and	
	j)	the inclusive nature of the activity, in particular as concerns gender equality and the involvement of local communities and indigenous peoples.	
			Decision 31 COM 18B
240.		A balance will be maintained in the allocation of resources between cultural and natural heritage and between Conservation and Management and Preparatory Assistance. This balance is reviewed and decided upon on a regular basis by the Committee and during the second year of each biennium by the Chairperson or the World Heritage Committee.	Decision 36 COM 13.I Decision 37 COM 12.II

VII.E Summary Table

241.

Decision 36 COM 13.I
Decision 30 COM 13.13
Decision 43 COM 11A

Type of international assistance	Purpose	Budget ceilings per request	Deadline for submission of request	Authority for approval
Emergency Assistance	This assistance may be requested to address ascertained or potential threats facing properties included on the List of World Heritage in Danger and the World Heritage List which have suffered severe damage or are in imminent danger of severe damage due to sudden, unexpected phenomena. Such phenomena may include land subsidence, extensive fires, explosions, flooding or human-made disasters including war. This assistance does not concern cases of damage or deterioration caused by gradual processes of decay, pollution or erosion. It addresses emergency situations strictly relating to the conservation of a World Heritage property (see Decision 28 COM 10B 2.c). It may be made available, if necessary, to more than one World Heritage property in a single State Party (see Decision 6 EXT. COM 15.2). The budget ceilings relate to a single World Heritage property.	Up to US$ 5.000 Between US$ 5.001 and 75.000	At any time At any time	Director of the World Heritage Centre Chairperson of the Committee

A.II.1a Operational Guidelines Welterbe-Übereinkommen

Type of international assistance	Purpose	Budget ceilings per request	Deadline for submission of request	Authority for approval
	The assistance may be requested to: (i) undertake emergency measures for the safeguarding of the property; (ii) draw up an emergency plan for the property.			
Preparatory assistance	This assistance may be requested to (in order of priority): (i) prepare or update national Tentative Lists of properties suitable for inscription on the World Heritage List; a commitment will be required from the State Party to nominate in priority on these lists sites recognized in approved thematic advice, such as the thematic studies prepared by the Advisory Bodies, as corresponding to gaps on the List; (ii) organize meetings for the harmonization of national Tentative Lists within the same geo-cultural area; (iii) prepare nominations of properties for inscription on the World Heritage List, including preparatory work such as collection of basic information, scoping studies of the potential for demonstration of Outstanding Universal Value, including integrity or authenticity, comparative studies of the property in relation to other similar properties (see 3.2 of Annex 5), including analysis in the context of the Gap Studies produced by the Advisory Bodies. Priority will be given to requests for sites recognized in approved thematic advice as corresponding to gaps on the List and/or for sites where preliminary investigations have shown that further inquiries would be justified, especially in the case of States Parties whose heritage is unrepresented or underrepresented on the World Heritage List; (iv) prepare requests for Conservation & Management assistance for consideration by the World Heritage Committee.	Up to US$ 5.000 Between US$ 5.001 and 30.000	At any time 31 October	Director of the World Heritage Centre Chairperson of the Committee

Type of international assistance	Purpose	Budget ceilings per request	Deadline for submission of request	Authority for approval
Conservation and Management Assistance (incorporating Training and Research assistance, Technical co-operation assistance and Promotion and education assistance)	This assistance may be requested for: (i) the training of staff and specialists at all levels in the fields of identification, monitoring, conservation, management and presentation of World Heritage, with an emphasis on group training;	Only for requests falling under items (i) to (vi):	Only for requests falling under items (i) to (vi):	Only for requests falling under items (i) to (vi)
	(ii) scientific research benefiting World Heritage properties or studies on the scientific and technical problems of conservation, management, and presentation of World Heritage properties;	Up to US$ 5.000	At any time	Director of the World Heritage Centre
	(iii) establishment/revision of national policies or legal frameworks on heritage preservation benefiting World Heritage properties; Note: Requests for support for individual training courses from UNESCO should be submitted on the standard "Application for fellowship" form available from the Secretariat.	Between US$ 5.001 and 30.000	31 October	Chairperson of the Committee
	(iv) provision of experts, technicians and skilled labour for the conservation, management, and presentation of properties inscribed on the List of World Heritage in Danger and the World Heritage List;	Over US$ 30.000	31 October	Committee
	(v) supply of equipment which the State Party requires for the conservation, management, and presentation of properties inscribed on the List of World Heritage in Danger and the World Heritage List;			
	(vi) low-interest or interest-free loans for undertaking activities for the conservation, management, and presentation of properties inscribed on the List of World Heritage in Danger and the World Heritage List, which may be repayable on a long-term basis;			
	(vii) At the regional and international levels for programmes, activities and the holding of meetings that could:	Only for requests fal-	Only for requests falling	Only for requests fal-

A.II.1a Operational Guidelines Welterbe-Übereinkommen 158

Type of international assistance		Purpose	Budget ceilings per request	Deadline for submission of request	Authority for approval
		– help to create interest in the *Convention* within the countries of a given region;	ling under items (vii) and (viii):	under items (vii) and (viii):	ling under items (vii) and (viii):
		– create a greater awareness of the different issues related to the implementation of the *Convention* to promote more active involvement in its application;	Up to US$ 5,000	At any time	Director of the World Heritage Centre
		– be a means of exchanging experiences;			
		– stimulate joint education, information and promotional programmes and activities, especially when they involve the participation of young people in World Heritage conservation activities;	Between US$ 5,001 and 10,000	31 October	Chairperson of the Committee
	(viii)	At the national level for:			
		– meetings specifically organized to make the *Convention* better known, especially amongst young people, or for the creation of national World Heritage associations, in accordance with Article 17 of the *Convention*;			
		– the preparation and discussion of education and information material (such as brochures, publications, exhibitions, films, multimedia tools) for the general promotion of the *Convention* and the World Heritage List and not for the promotion of a particular property, and especially for young people.			

VII.F Procedure and format

242. All States Parties submitting requests for international assistance are encouraged to consult the Secretariat and the Advisory Bodies during the conceptualization, planning and elaboration of each request. To facilitate States Parties' work, examples of successful international assistance requests may be provided upon request.

243. The application form for International Assistance is presented in Annex 8 and the types, amounts, deadlines for submission and the authorities responsible for approval are outlined in the summary table in Chapter VII.E.

244.	The request should be submitted in English or French, duly signed and transmitted by the National Commission for UNESCO, the State Party Permanent Delegation to UNESCO and/or appropriate governmental Department or Ministry to the following address: **UNESCO World Heritage Centre** 7, place de Fontenoy 75352 Paris 07 SP France Tel: +33 (0) 1 4568 12 76 E-mail: wh-intassistance@unesco.org	
245.	Requests for international assistance may be submitted by electronic mail by the State Party or by filling the online format on the World Heritage Centre's website at: https://whc.unesco.org; they must be accompanied by an officially signed copy.	Decision 43 COM 11A
246.	It is important that all information requested in this application form is provided. If appropriate or necessary, requests may be supplemented by additional information, reports, etc.	

VII.G Assessment of International Assistance requests

247.	Provided they are complete, all requests are assessed by the Secretariat irrespective of the amount requested. In addition, requests with a budget above US$ 30,000 are assessed as follows: a) By ICOMOS for requests for cultural heritage (all types of assistance) and ICCROM (all types of assistance except Preparatory assistance); b) By IUCN for requests for natural heritage; c) By ICOMOS and IUCN for requests for mixed heritage (all types of assistance) and ICCROM (all types of assistance except Preparatory assistance). The Secretariat processes requests for Emergency assistance within up to 10 working days. Whenever necessary, the Secretariat may consult the Advisory Bodies, for the assessment of requests with a budget under US$ 30,000. ICOMOS, IUCN and ICCROM will be consulted on all requests which specifically demand the involvement of one or more Advisory Bodies in the respective project.	Decision 43 COM 11A
248.	[Deleted]	Decision 43 COM 11A
249.	[Deleted]	Decision 43 COM 11A
250.	[Deleted]	Decision 43 COM 11A
251.	The criteria used for the assessment of international assistance requests are outlined in Annex 9.	Decision 31 COM 18B Decision 43 COM 11A
252.	A panel composed of representatives of the World Heritage Centre Regional Desks and the Advisory Bodies, and if possible, the Chairperson of the World Heritage Committee or, in observer capacity, a person designated by the Chairperson, meets once or twice a year to examine the International Assistance requests of more than US$ 5,000, except those for Emergency Assistance, and to make recommendations to the Chairperson and/or the Committee.	Decision 31 COM 18B Decision 36 COM 13.I Decision 43 COM 11A

A.II.1a Operational Guidelines Welterbe-Übereinkommen

253. The Chairperson is not authorized to approve requests submitted by his/her own country. These will be examined by the Committee.

254. All requests for Preparatory Assistance or Conservation and Management Assistance of more than US$ 5,000 should be received by the Secretariat on or before **31 October**. Incomplete forms which do not come back duly completed by 30 November will be sent back to the States Parties for submission to a next cycle. Complete requests are examined by a first panel held in January. Requests for which the panel issues a positive or a negative recommendation will be submitted to the Chairperson/Committee for decision. A second panel may be held at least eight weeks before the Committee session for requests which were revised since the first panel. Requests sent back for a substantial revision will be examined by the panel depending on their date of receipt. Requests requiring only minor revision and no further examination by the panel must come back within the year when they were examined first; otherwise they will be sent again to a next panel. The chart detailing the submission process is attached in Annex 8.

Decision 36 COM 13.I
Decision 43 COM 11A

VII.H Contractual Arrangements

255. Agreements are established between UNESCO and the concerned State Party or its representative(s) for the implementation of the approved International Assistance requests in conformity with UNESCO regulations, following the work plan and budget breakdown described in the originally approved request.

VII.I Evaluation and follow-up of International Assistance

256. The monitoring and evaluation of the implementation of the International Assistance requests will take place within 3 months of the activities' completion. The results of these evaluations will be collated and maintained by the Secretariat in collaboration with the Advisory Bodies and examined by the Committee on a regular basis.

257. The Committee reviews the implementation, evaluation and follow-up of International Assistance in order to evaluate the International Assistance effectiveness and to redefine its priorities.

VIII The World Heritage Emblem
VIII.A Preamble

258. At its second session (Washington, 1978), the Committee adopted the World Heritage Emblem which had been designed by Mr. Michel Olyff. This Emblem symbolizes the interdependence of cultural and natural properties: the central square is a form created by humans and the circle represents nature, the two being intimately linked. The Emblem is round, like the world, but at the same time it is a symbol of protection. It symbolizes the *Convention*, signifies the adherence of States Parties to the *Convention*, and serves to identify properties inscribed in the World Heritage List. It is associated with public knowledge about the *Convention* and is the imprimatur of the *Convention*'s credibility and prestige. Above all, it is a representation of the universal values for which the *Convention* stands.

Decision 43 COM 11A

259. The Committee decided that the Emblem proposed by the artist could be used, in any colour or size, depending on the use, the

technical possibilities and considerations of an artistic nature. The Emblem should always carry the text "WORLD HERITAGE. PATRIMOINE MONDIAL". The space occupied by "PATRIMONIO MUNDIAL" can be used for its translation into the national language of the country where the Emblem is to be used.

260. In order to ensure the Emblem benefits from as much visibility as possible while preventing improper uses, the Committee at its twenty-second session (Kyoto, 1998) adopted "Guidelines and Principles for the Use of the World Heritage Emblem" as set out in the following paragraphs. In addition, a "Table of Uses" (Annex 14) provides complementary guidance.

Decision 39 COM 11

261. Although there is no mention of the Emblem in the *Convention*, its use has been promoted by the Committee to identify properties protected by the *Convention* and inscribed on the World Heritage List since its adoption in 1978.

262. The World Heritage Committee is responsible for determining the use of the World Heritage Emblem and for making policy prescriptions regarding how it may be used. Since the adoption by the UNESCO General Conference in October 2007 of the *Directives concerning the Use of the Name, Acronym, Logo and Internet Domain Names of UNESCO*[1], it is strongly encouraged to use the World Heritage Emblem as part of a linked logo block accompanied by UNESCO's logo, whenever feasible. The use of the World Heritage Emblem alone remains however possible, in line with the present Guidelines and with the Table of Uses (Annex 14).

Decision 39 COM 11

263. As requested by the Committee at its 26th session (Budapest, 2002), the World Heritage Emblem, with and without its surrounding text, has been notified and accepted on 21 May 2003 by the Paris Union Member states under Article 6ter of the Paris *Convention* for the Protection of Industrial Property, adopted in 1883 and revised at Stockholm in 1967. Therefore UNESCO has recourse to Paris Convention Member States' domestic systems to prevent the use of the World Heritage Emblem where such use falsely suggests a connection with UNESCO, the *World Heritage Convention*, or any other abusive use.

Decision 26 COM 15
Decision 39 COM 11

264. The Emblem also has fund-raising potential that can be used to enhance the marketing value of products with which it is associated. A balance is needed between the Emblem's use to further

---

1) The most recent version of the *Directives concerning the Use of the Name, Acronym, Logo and Internet Domain Names of UNESCO* is found in the annex to Resolution 86 of the 34th session of the General Conference (34 C/Resolution 86) or at http://unesdoc.unesco.org/images/0015/001560/156046e.pdf.

the aims of the *Convention* and optimize knowledge of the *Convention* worldwide and the need to prevent its abuse for inaccurate, inappropriate, and unauthorized commercial or other purposes.

265. The Guidelines and Principles for the Use of the Emblem and modalities for quality control should not become an obstacle to cooperation for promotional activities. Authorities responsible for reviewing and deciding on uses of the Emblem may base their decisions on the parameters developed below and those contained in the Table of Uses (Annex 14).   Decision 39 COM 11

VIII.B Applicability

266. The Guidelines and Principles proposed herein cover all proposed uses of the Emblem by: Decision 39 COM 11
    a) The World Heritage Centre;
    b) The UNESCO Division of Public Information and other UNESCO offices;
    c) Agencies or National Commissions, responsible for implementing the *Convention* in each State Party;
    d) World Heritage properties;
    e) Other contracting parties, especially those operating for predominantly commercial purposes.

VIII.C Responsibilities of States Parties

267. States Parties to the *Convention* should take all possible measures to prevent the use of the Emblem in their respective countries by any group or for any purpose not explicitly recognized by the Committee. States Parties are encouraged to make full use of national legislation including Trade Mark Laws.

VIII.D Increasing proper uses of the World Heritage Emblem

268. Properties inscribed on the World Heritage List should be marked with the emblem jointly with the UNESCO logo, which should, however, be placed in such a way that they do not visually impair the property in question.

Production of plaques to commemorate the inscription of properties on the World Heritage List

269. Once a property is inscribed on the World Heritage List, the State Party should place a plaque, whenever possible, to commemorate this inscription. These plaques are designed to inform the public of the country concerned and foreign visitors that the property visited has a particular value which has been recognized by the international community. In other words, the property is exceptional, of interest not only to one nation, but also to the whole world. However, these plaques have an additional function which is to inform the general public about the *World Heritage Convention,* or at least about the World Heritage concept and the World Heritage List.

270. The Committee has adopted the following Guidelines for the production of these plaques:
    a) the plaque should be so placed that it can easily be seen by visitors, without disfiguring the property;
    b) the World Heritage Emblem should appear on the plaque;
    c) the text should mention the property's Outstanding Universal Value; in this regard it might be useful to give a short description of the property's outstanding charac-

d) the text should make reference to the *World Heritage Convention* and particularly to the World Heritage List and to the international recognition conferred by inscription on this List (however, it is not necessary to mention at which session of the Committee the property was inscribed); it may be appropriate to produce the text in several languages for properties which receive many foreign visitors.

271. The Committee proposes the following text as an example: "(Name of property) has been inscribed upon the World Heritage List of the *Convention concerning the Protection of the World Cultural and Natural Heritage*. Inscription on this List confirms the Outstanding Universal Value of a cultural or natural property which deserves protection for the benefit of all humanity."

272. This text could be then followed by a brief description of the property concerned.

273. Furthermore, the national authorities should encourage World Heritage properties to make a broad use of the Emblem such as on their letterheads, brochures and staff uniforms.

274. Third parties which have received the right to produce communication products related to the *World Heritage Convention* and World Heritage properties must give the Emblem proper visibility. They should avoid creating a different Emblem or logo for that particular product.

VIII.E Principles on the use of the World Heritage Emblem

275. The responsible authorities are henceforth requested to use the following principles in making decisions on the use of the Emblem: Decision 39 COM 11

a) The Emblem should be utilized for all projects substantially associated with the work of the *Convention*, including, to the maximum extent technically and legally possible, those already approved and adopted, in order to promote the *Convention*.

b) A decision to approve use of the Emblem should be linked strongly to the quality and content of the product with which it is to be associated, not on the volume of products to be marketed or the financial return expected. The main criterion for approval should be the educational, scientific, cultural, or artistic value of the proposed product related to World Heritage principles and values. Approval should not routinely be granted to place the Emblem on products that have no, or extremely little, educational value, such as cups, T-shirts, pins, and other tourist souvenirs. Exceptions to this policy will be considered for special events, such as meetings of the Committee and ceremonies at which plaques are unveiled.

c) Any decision with respect to authorizing the use of the Emblem must be completely unambiguous and in keeping with the explicit and implicit goals and values of the *World Heritage Convention*.

A.II.1a   Operational Guidelines Welterbe-Übereinkommen 164

d) Except when authorized in accordance with these principles, it is not legitimate for commercial entities to use the Emblem directly on their own material to show their support for World Heritage. The Committee recognizes, however, that any individual, organization, or company is free to publish or produce whatever they consider to be appropriate regarding World Heritage properties, but official authorization to do so under the World Heritage Emblem remains the exclusive prerogative of the Committee, to be exercised as prescribed in these Guidelines and Principles and in the Table of Uses.

e) Use of the Emblem by other contracting parties should normally only be authorized when the proposed use deals directly with World Heritage properties. Such uses may be granted after approval by the national authorities of the countries concerned.

f) In cases where no specific World Heritage properties are involved or are not the principal focus of the proposed use, such as general seminars and/or workshops on scientific issues or conservation techniques, use may be granted only upon express approval in accordance with these Guidelines and Principles and with the Table of Uses. Requests for such uses should specifically document the manner in which the proposed use is expected to enhance the work of the *Convention*.

g) Permission to use the Emblem should not be granted to travel agencies, airlines, or to any other type of business operating for predominantly commercial purposes, except under exceptional circumstances and when manifest benefit to the World Heritage generally or particular World Heritage properties can be demonstrated. Requests for such use should require approval in accordance with these Guidelines and Principles and with the Table of Uses. Such requests should be approved by the national authorities concerned, and be defined within the framework of specific partnership agreements with UNESCO/World Heritage Centre.

"Comprehensive Partnership Strategy" including "Separate strategies for engagement with individual categories of partners" 192 EX/5.INF and PACT Strategy (Document WHC-13/37.COM/5D) Decision 37 COM 5D

The Secretariat is not to accept any advertising, travel, or other promotional considerations from travel agencies or other, similar companies in exchange or in lieu of financial remuneration for use of the Emblem.

h) When commercial benefits are anticipated, the Secretariat should ensure that the World Heritage Fund receives a fair share of the revenues and conclude a contract or other agreement that documents the nature of the understandings that govern the project and the arrangements for provision of income to the Fund. In all cases of commercial use, any staff time and related costs for personnel assigned by the Secretariat or other reviewers, as appropriate, to any initiative, beyond the nominal, must be fully covered by the party requesting authorization to use the Emblem.

National authorities are also called upon to ensure that their properties or the World Heritage Fund receive a fair share of the revenues and to document the nature of the understandings that govern the project and the distribution of any proceeds.

i) If sponsors are sought for manufacturing products whose distribution the Secretariat considers necessary, the choice of partner or partners should be consistent, at a minimum, with the criteria set forth in the "Comprehensive Partnership Strategy" including "Separate strategies for engagement with individual categories or partners" 192 EX/5.INF and PACT Strategy (Document WHC-13/37.COM/5D) and with such further fund-raising guidance as the Committee may prescribe. The necessity for such products should be clarified and justified in written presentations that will require approval in such manner as the Committee may prescribe.

j) The sale of goods or services bearing the name, acronym, logo and/or Internet domain name of UNESCO combined with the World Heritage Emblem chiefly for profit shall be regarded as "commercial use" for the purpose of the *Operational Guidelines*. Such use must be expressly authorized by the Director-General, under a specific contractual arrangement (definition adapted from 2007 UNESCO Logo Directives. Art III.2.1.3).

VIII.F Authorization procedure for the use of the World Heritage Emblem

Simple agreement of the national authorities

276. National authorities may grant the use of the Emblem to a national entity, provided that the project, whether national or international, involves only World Heritage properties located on the same national territory. National authorities' decision should be guided by the Guidelines and Principles and by the Table of Uses.
Decision 39 COM 11

277. States Parties are invited to provide the Secretariat with the names and addresses of the authorities in charge of managing the use of the Emblem.
Circular letter dated 14 April 1999. https://whc.unesco.org/circs/circ99-4e.pdf

Agreement requiring quality control of content

278. Any other request for authorization to use the Emblem should adopt the following procedure:
Decision 39 COM 11

a) A request indicating the objective of the use of the Emblem, its duration and territorial validity, should be addressed to the Director of the World Heritage Centre.

b) The Director of the World Heritage Centre has the authority to grant the use of the Emblem in accordance with the Guidelines and Principles. For cases not covered, or not sufficiently covered, by the Guidelines and Principles and by the Table of Uses, the Director refers the matter to the Chairperson who, in the most difficult cases, might wish to refer the matter to the Committee for final decision. A yearly report on the authorized uses of the Emblem will be submitted to the World Heritage Committee.

c) Authorization to use the Emblem in major products to be widely distributed over an undetermined period of time is conditional upon obtaining the manufacturer's commitment to consult with countries concerned and secure their endorsement of texts and images illustrating properties situated in their territory, at no cost to the Secretariat, together with the proof that this has been done. The text to be approved should be provided in either one of the official languages of the Committee or in the language of the country concerned. A draft model to be used by States Parties to authorize the use of the Emblem to third parties appears below.

Content Approval Form:

[Name of responsible national body], officially identified as the body responsible for approving the content of the texts and photos relating to the World Heritage properties located in the territory of **[name of country]**, hereby confirms to **[name of producer]** that the text and the images that it has submitted for the **[name of property(ies)]** World Heritage property(ies) are **[approved] [approved subject to the following changes requested] [are not approved]**

(delete whatever entry does not apply, and provide, as needed, a corrected copy of the text or a signed list of corrections).

Notes:

It is recommended that the initials of the responsible national official be affixed to each page of text.

The National Authorities are given one month from their acknowledged receipt in which to authorize the content, following which the producers may consider that the content has been tacitly approved, unless the responsible National Authorities request in writing a longer period. Texts should be supplied to the National Authorities in one of the two official languages of the Committee, or in the official language (or in one of the official languages) of the country in which the properties are located, at the convenience of both parties.

    d)   After having examined the request and considered it as acceptable, the Secretariat may establish an agreement with the partner.

    e)   If the Director of the World Heritage Centre judges that a proposed use of the Emblem is not acceptable, the Secretariat informs the requesting party of the decision in writing.

VIII.G Right of States Parties to exert quality control

279. Authorization to use the Emblem is inextricably linked to the requirement that the national authorities may exert quality control over the products with which it is associated.

    a)   The States Parties to the *Convention* are the only parties authorized to approve the content (images and text) of any distributed product appearing under the World Heritage Emblem with regard to the properties located in their territories.

    b)   States Parties that protect the Emblem legally must review these uses.

c) Other States Parties may elect to review proposed uses or refer such proposals to the Secretariat. States Parties are responsible for identifying an appropriate national authority and for informing the Secretariat whether they wish to review proposed uses or to identify uses that are inappropriate. The Secretariat maintains a list of responsible national authorities.

IX Information Sources

IX.A Information archived by the Secretariat

280. The Secretariat maintains a database of all documents of the World Heritage Committee and the General Assembly of States Parties to the *World Heritage Convention*. This database is available at: https://whc.unesco.org/en/documents

281. The Secretariat ensures that copies of Tentative Lists, World Heritage nominations, including copies of maps and relevant information received from States Parties are archived in hard copy and in electronic format where possible. The Secretariat also arranges for the archiving of relevant information relating to inscribed properties, including evaluations and other documents developed by the Advisory Bodies, any correspondence and reports received from States Parties (including Reactive Monitoring and Periodic Reports) and correspondence and material from the Secretariat and World Heritage Committee.

282. Archived material will be kept in a form appropriate to long-term storage. Provisions will be made for the storage of paper copies and electronic copies, as relevant. Provision will be made for copies to be provided to States Parties as requested.

283. Nomination dossiers of those properties inscribed on the World Heritage List by the Committee will be made available for consultation. States Parties are urged to upload a copy of the nomination on their own websites and inform the Secretariat of this action. States Parties preparing nominations may wish to use such information as guides for identifying and elaborating nomination of properties within their own territories.

284. Advisory Body evaluations and Committee decisions concerning each inscribed property are available on the World Heritage Centre's website on the page dedicated to each property of the World Heritage List. For the sites not inscribed on the List, the Advisory Body evaluation is available on the World Heritage Centre's website on the page dedicated to the Committee session when the nomination was examined.

Decision 43 COM 11A

IX.B Specific Information for World Heritage Committee members and other States Parties

285. The Secretariat maintains two electronic mailing lists: one for Committee members (wh-committee@unesco.org) and one for all States Parties (wh-states@unesco.org). States Parties are requested to supply all appropriate email addresses for the establishment of these lists. These electronic mailing lists, which supplement but do not replace the traditional means of notifying States Parties, allow the Secretariat to communicate, in a timely manner, announcements about the availability of documents, changes to meeting schedules, and other issues relevant to Committee members and other States Parties.

A.II.1a   Operational Guidelines Welterbe-Übereinkommen

286.	Specific information targeted at Committee members, other States Parties and Advisory Bodies is available on the World Heritage Centre's website (https://whc.unesco.org) with restricted access.	Decision 43 COM 11A
287.	The Secretariat also maintains a database of decisions of the Committee and resolutions of the General Assembly of States Parties. These are available at: https://whc.unesco.org/en/decisions	Decision 28 COM 9

IX.C Information and publications available to the public

288. The Secretariat provides access to information labelled as publicly available and copyright free on World Heritage properties and other relevant matters, wherever possible.

289. Information on issues related to World Heritage is available on the Secretariat's website (https://whc.unesco.org), on the websites of the Advisory Bodies and in libraries. A list of online databases and links to relevant webpages can be found in the Bibliography.

290. The Secretariat produces a wide variety of World Heritage publications, including the World Heritage List, the List of World Heritage in Danger, Brief Descriptions of World Heritage properties, World Heritage Paper series, newsletters, brochures and information kits. In addition, other information materials aimed specifically at experts and the general public are also developed. The list of World Heritage publications can be found in the Bibliography or at: https://whc.unesco.org/en/publications

These information materials are distributed to the public directly or through the national and international networks established by States Parties or by World Heritage partners.

Seerechtsübereinkommen der Vereinten Nationen[1]

Vom 10. Dezember 1982 (BGBl. 1994 II S. 1798)

– Auszug –

Teil XI:
Das Gebiet

Abschnitt 2
Für das Gebiet geltende Grundsätze

Artikel 149 Archäologische und historische Gegenstände
Alle im Gebiet gefundenen Gegenstände archäologischer oder historischer Art werden zum Nutzen der gesamten Menschheit bewahrt oder verwendet, wobei die Vorzugsrechte des Ursprungsstaats oder -lands, des Staates des kulturellen Ursprungs oder des Staates des historischen oder archäologischen Ursprungs besonders zu beachten sind.

Teil XVI:
Allgemeine Bestimmungen

Artikel 303 Im Meer gefundene archäologische und historische Gegenstände
(1) Die Staaten haben die Pflicht, im Meer gefundene Gegenstände archäologischer oder historischer Art zu schützen, und arbeiten zu diesem Zweck zusammen.
(2) Um den Verkehr mit diesen Gegenständen zu kontrollieren, kann der Küstenstaat in Anwendung des Artikels 33 davon ausgehen, daß ihre ohne seine Einwilligung erfolgende Entfernung vom Meeresboden innerhalb der in jenem Artikel bezeichneten Zone zu einem Verstoß gegen die in jenem Artikel genannten Gesetze und sonstigen Vorschriften in seinem Hoheitsgebiet oder in seinem Küstenmeer führen würde.
(3) Dieser Artikel berührt nicht die Rechte feststellbarer Eigentümer, das Bergungsrecht oder sonstige seerechtliche Vorschriften sowie Gesetze und Verhaltensweisen auf dem Gebiet des Kulturaustausches.
(4) Dieser Artikel berührt nicht andere internationale Übereinkünfte und Regeln des Völkerrechts über den Schutz von Gegenständen archäologischer oder historischer Art.

---

1) Liste der Vertragsstaaten: https://treaties.un.org/Pages/ViewDetailsIII.aspx?src=TREATY&mtdsg_no=XXI-6&chapter=21&Temp=mtdsg3&clang=_en.

Convention on the Protection of the Underwater Cultural Heritage[1]
Vom 6. November 2001, ILM 41 (2002), S. 40

The General Conference of the United Nations Educational, Scientific and Cultural Organization, meeting in Paris from 15 October to 3 November 2001, at its 31st session,
Acknowledging the importance of underwater cultural heritage as an integral part of the cultural heritage of humanity and a particularly important element in the history of peoples, nations, and their relations with each other concerning their common heritage,
Realizing the importance of protecting and preserving the underwater cultural heritage and that responsibility therefor rests with all States,
Noting growing public interest in and public appreciation of underwater cultural heritage,
Convinced of the importance of research, information and education to the protection and preservation of underwater cultural heritage,
Convinced of the public's right to enjoy the educational and recreational benefits of responsible non-intrusive access to *in situ* underwater cultural heritage, and of the value of public education to contribute to awareness, appreciation and protection of that heritage,
Aware of the fact that underwater cultural heritage is threatened by unauthorized activities directed at it, and of the need for stronger measures to prevent such activities,
Conscious of the need to respond appropriately to the possible negative impact on underwater cultural heritage of legitimate activities that may incidentally affect it,
Deeply concerned by the increasing commercial exploitation of underwater cultural heritage, and in particular by certain activities aimed at the sale, acquisition or barter of underwater cultural heritage,
Aware of the availability of advanced technology that enhances discovery of and access to underwater cultural heritage,
Believing that cooperation among States, international organizations, scientific institutions, professional organizations, archaeologists, divers, other interested parties and the public at large is essential for the protection of underwater cultural heritage,
Considering that survey, excavation and protection of underwater cultural heritage necessitate the availability and application of special scientific methods and the use of suitable techniques and equipment as well as a high degree of professional specialization, all of which indicate a need for uniform governing criteria,
Realizing the need to codify and progressively develop rules relating to the protection and preservation of underwater cultural heritage in conformity with international law and practice, including the UNESCO Convention on the Means of Prohibiting and Preventing the Illicit Import, Export and Transfer of Ownership of Cultural Property of 14 November 1970, the UNESCO Convention for the Protection of the World Cultural and Natural Heritage of 16 November 1972 and the United Nations Convention on the Law of the Sea of 10 December 1982,
Committed to improving the effectiveness of measures at international, regional and national levels for the preservation *in situ* or, if necessary for scientific or protective purposes, the careful recovery of underwater cultural heritage,
Having decided at its twenty-ninth session that this question should be made the subject of an international convention,
Adopts this second day of November 2001 this Convention.

---

[1] Eine Ratifikation durch Deutschland ist noch nicht erfolgt; dies ist allerdings geplant laut Koalitionsvertrag der 18. Legislaturperiode vom 27. November 2013, S. 122; für die Vertragsstaaten trat der Vertrag am 2. Januar 2009 in Kraft; eine Liste der Vertragsstaaten und Ratifikationen findet sich unter: http://www.unesco.org/eri/la/convention.asp?KO=13520&language=E&order=alpha.

Article 1 – Definitions

For the purposes of this Convention:
1. (a) "Underwater cultural heritage" means all traces of human existence having a cultural, historical or archaeological character which have been partially or totally under water, periodically or continuously, for at least 100 years such as:
    (i) sites, structures, buildings, artefacts and human remains, together with their archaeological and natural context;
    (ii) vessels, aircraft, other vehicles or any part thereof, their cargo or other contents, together with their archaeological and natural context; and
    (iii) objects of prehistoric character.
   (b) Pipelines and cables placed on the seabed shall not be considered as underwater cultural heritage.
   (c) Installations other than pipelines and cables, placed on the seabed and still in use, shall not be considered as underwater cultural heritage.
2. (a) "States Parties" means States which have consented to be bound by this Convention and for which this Convention is in force.
   (b) This Convention applies *mutatis mutandis* to those territories referred to in Article 26, paragraph 2(b), which become Parties to this Convention in accordance with the conditions set out in that paragraph, and to that extent "States Parties" refers to those territories.
3. "UNESCO" means the United Nations Educational, Scientific and Cultural Organization.
4. "Director-General" means the Director-General of UNESCO.
5. "Area" means the seabed and ocean floor and subsoil thereof, beyond the limits of national jurisdiction.
6. "Activities directed at underwater cultural heritage" means activities having underwater cultural heritage as their primary object and which may, directly or indirectly, physically disturb or otherwise damage underwater cultural heritage.
7. "Activities incidentally affecting underwater cultural heritage" means activities which, despite not having underwater cultural heritage as their primary object or one of their objects, may physically disturb or otherwise damage underwater cultural heritage.
8. "State vessels and aircraft" means warships, and other vessels or aircraft that were owned or operated by a State and used, at the time of sinking, only for government non-commercial purposes, that are identified as such and that meet the definition of underwater cultural heritage.
9. "Rules" means the Rules concerning activities directed at underwater cultural heritage, as referred to in Article 33 of this Convention.

Article 2 – Objectives and general principles

1. This Convention aims to ensure and strengthen the protection of underwater cultural heritage.
2. States Parties shall cooperate in the protection of underwater cultural heritage.
3. States Parties shall preserve underwater cultural heritage for the benefit of humanity in conformity with the provisions of this Convention.
4. States Parties shall, individually or jointly as appropriate, take all appropriate measures in conformity with this Convention and with international law that are necessary to protect underwater cultural heritage, using for this purpose the best practicable means at their disposal and in accordance with their capabilities.
5. The preservation *in situ* of underwater cultural heritage shall be considered as the first option before allowing or engaging in any activities directed at this heritage.
6. Recovered underwater cultural heritage shall be deposited, conserved and managed in a manner that ensures its long-term preservation.
7. Underwater cultural heritage shall not be commercially exploited.
8. Consistent with State practice and international law, including the United Nations Convention on the Law of the Sea, nothing in this Convention shall be interpreted as modifying the rules of international law and State practice pertaining to sovereign immunities, nor any State's rights with respect to its State vessels and aircraft.
9. States Parties shall ensure that proper respect is given to all human remains located in maritime waters.

10. Responsible non-intrusive access to observe or document *in situ* underwater cultural heritage shall be encouraged to create public awareness, appreciation, and protection of the heritage except where such access is incompatible with its protection and management.
11. No act or activity undertaken on the basis of this Convention shall constitute grounds for claiming, contending or disputing any claim to national sovereignty or jurisdiction.

Article 3 – Relationship between this Convention and the United Nations Convention on the Law of the Sea

Nothing in this Convention shall prejudice the rights, jurisdiction and duties of States under international law, including the United Nations Convention on the Law of the Sea. This Convention shall be interpreted and applied in the context of and in a manner consistent with international law, including the United Nations Convention on the Law of the Sea.

Article 4 – Relationship to law of salvage and law of finds

Any activity relating to underwater cultural heritage to which this Convention applies shall not be subject to the law of salvage or law of finds, unless it:
(a) is authorized by the competent authorities, and
(b) is in full conformity with this Convention, and
(c) ensures that any recovery of the underwater cultural heritage achieves its maximum protection.

Article 5 – Activities incidentally affecting underwater cultural heritage

Each State Party shall use the best practicable means at its disposal to prevent or mitigate any adverse effects that might arise from activities under its jurisdiction incidentally affecting underwater cultural heritage.

Article 6 – Bilateral, regional or other multilateral agreements

1. States Parties are encouraged to enter into bilateral, regional or other multilateral agreements or develop existing agreements, for the preservation of underwater cultural heritage. All such agreements shall be in full conformity with the provisions of this Convention and shall not dilute its universal character. States may, in such agreements, adopt rules and regulations which would ensure better protection of underwater cultural heritage than those adopted in this Convention.
2. The Parties to such bilateral, regional or other multilateral agreements may invite States with a verifiable link, especially a cultural, historical or archaeological link, to the underwater cultural heritage concerned to join such agreements.
3. This Convention shall not alter the rights and obligations of States Parties regarding the protection of sunken vessels, arising from other bilateral, regional or other multilateral agreements concluded before its adoption, and, in particular, those that are in conformity with the purposes of this Convention.

Article 7 – Underwater cultural heritage in internal waters, archipelagic waters and territorial sea

1. States Parties, in the exercise of their sovereignty, have the exclusive right to regulate and authorize activities directed at underwater cultural heritage in their internal waters, archipelagic waters and territorial sea.
2. Without prejudice to other international agreements and rules of international law regarding the protection of underwater cultural heritage, States Parties shall require that the Rules be applied to activities directed at underwater cultural heritage in their internal waters, archipelagic waters and territorial sea.
3. Within their archipelagic waters and territorial sea, in the exercise of their sovereignty and in recognition of general practice among States, States Parties, with a view to cooperating on the best methods of protecting State vessels and aircraft, should inform the flag State Party to this Convention and, if applicable, other States with a verifiable link, especially a cultural, historical or archaeological link, with respect to the discovery of such identifiable State vessels and aircraft.

Article 8 – Underwater cultural heritage in the contiguous zone

Without prejudice to and in addition to Articles 9 and 10, and in accordance with Article 303, paragraph 2, of the United Nations Convention on the Law of the Sea, States Parties may regulate and authorize activities directed at underwater cultural heritage within their contiguous zone. In so doing, they shall require that the Rules be applied.

Article 9 – **Reporting and notification in the exclusive economic zone and on the continental shelf**

1. All States Parties have a responsibility to protect underwater cultural heritage in the exclusive economic zone and on the continental shelf in conformity with this Convention. Accordingly:
    (a) a State Party shall require that when its national, or a vessel flying its flag, discovers or intends to engage in activities directed at underwater cultural heritage located in its exclusive economic zone or on its continental shelf, the national or the master of the vessel shall report such discovery or activity to it;
    (b) in the exclusive economic zone or on the continental shelf of another State Party:
        (i) States Parties shall require the national or the master of the vessel to report such discovery or activity to them and to that other State Party;
        (ii) alternatively, a State Party shall require the national or master of the vessel to report such discovery or activity to it and shall ensure the rapid and effective transmission of such reports to all other States Parties.
2. On depositing its instrument of ratification, acceptance, approval or accession, a State Party shall declare the manner in which reports will be transmitted under paragraph 1(b) of this Article.
3. A State Party shall notify the Director-General of discoveries or activities reported to it under paragraph 1 of this Article.
4. The Director-General shall promptly make available to all States Parties any information notified to him under paragraph 3 of this Article.
5. Any State Party may declare to the State Party in whose exclusive economic zone or on whose continental shelf the underwater cultural heritage is located its interest in being consulted on how to ensure the effective protection of that underwater cultural heritage. Such declaration shall be based on a verifiable link, especially a cultural, historical or archaeological link, to the underwater cultural heritage concerned.

Article 10 – **Protection of underwater cultural heritage in the exclusive economic zone and on the continental shelf**

1. No authorization shall be granted for an activity directed at underwater cultural heritage located in the exclusive economic zone or on the continental shelf except in conformity with the provisions of this Article.
2. A State Party in whose exclusive economic zone or on whose continental shelf underwater cultural heritage is located has the right to prohibit or authorize any activity directed at such heritage to prevent interference with its sovereign rights or jurisdiction as provided for by international law including the United Nations Convention on the Law of the Sea.
3. Where there is a discovery of underwater cultural heritage or it is intended that activity shall be directed at underwater cultural heritage in a State Party's exclusive economic zone or on its continental shelf, that State Party shall:
    (a) consult all other States Parties which have declared an interest under Article 9, paragraph 5, on how best to protect the underwater cultural heritage;
    (b) coordinate such consultations as "Coordinating State", unless it expressly declares that it does not wish to do so, in which case the States Parties which have declared an interest under Article 9, paragraph 5, shall appoint a Coordinating State.
4. Without prejudice to the duty of all States Parties to protect underwater cultural heritage by way of all practicable measures taken in accordance with international law to prevent immediate danger to the underwater cultural heritage, including looting, the Coordinating State may take all practicable measures, and/or issue any necessary authorizations in conformity with this Convention and, if necessary prior to consultations, to prevent any immediate danger to the underwater cultural heritage, whether arising from human activities or any other cause, including looting. In taking such measures assistance may be requested from other States Parties.

A.II.3 Convention on the Underwater Cultural Heritage

5. The Coordinating State:
   (a) shall implement measures of protection which have been agreed by the consulting States, which include the Coordinating State, unless the consulting States, which include the Coordinating State, agree that another State Party shall implement those measures;
   (b) shall issue all necessary authorizations for such agreed measures in conformity with the Rules, unless the consulting States, which include the Coordinating State, agree that another State Party shall issue those authorizations;
   (c) may conduct any necessary preliminary research on the underwater cultural heritage and shall issue all necessary authorizations therefor, and shall promptly inform the Director-General of the results, who in turn will make such information promptly available to other States Parties.
6. In coordinating consultations, taking measures, conducting preliminary research and/or issuing authorizations pursuant to this Article, the Coordinating State shall act on behalf of the States Parties as a whole and not in its own interest. Any such action shall not in itself constitute a basis for the assertion of any preferential or jurisdictional rights not provided for in international law, including the United Nations Convention on the Law of the Sea.
7. Subject to the provisions of paragraphs 2 and 4 of this Article, no activity directed at State vessels and aircraft shall be conducted without the agreement of the flag State and the collaboration of the Coordinating State.

Article 11 – Reporting and notification in the Area

1. States Parties have a responsibility to protect underwater cultural heritage in the Area in conformity with this Convention and Article 149 of the United Nations Convention on the Law of the Sea. Accordingly when a national, or a vessel flying the flag of a State Party, discovers or intends to engage in activities directed at underwater cultural heritage located in the Area, that State Party shall require its national, or the master of the vessel, to report such discovery or activity to it.
2. States Parties shall notify the Director-General and the Secretary-General of the International Seabed Authority of such discoveries or activities reported to them.
3. The Director-General shall promptly make available to all States Parties any such information supplied by States Parties.
4. Any State Party may declare to the Director-General its interest in being consulted on how to ensure the effective protection of that underwater cultural heritage. Such declaration shall be based on a verifiable link to the underwater cultural heritage concerned, particular regard being paid to the preferential rights of States of cultural, historical or archaeological origin.

Article 12 – Protection of underwater cultural heritage in the Area

1. No authorization shall be granted for any activity directed at underwater cultural heritage located in the Area except in conformity with the provisions of this Article.
2. The Director-General shall invite all States Parties which have declared an interest under Article 11, paragraph 4, to consult on how best to protect the underwater cultural heritage, and to appoint a State Party to coordinate such consultations as the "Coordinating State". The Director-General shall also invite the International Seabed Authority to participate in such consultations.
3. All States Parties may take all practicable measures in conformity with this Convention, if necessary prior to consultations, to prevent any immediate danger to the underwater cultural heritage, whether arising from human activity or any other cause including looting.
4. The Coordinating State shall:
   (a) implement measures of protection which have been agreed by the consulting States, which include the Coordinating State, unless the consulting States, which include the Coordinating State, agree that another State Party shall implement those measures; and
   (b) issue all necessary authorizations for such agreed measures, in conformity with this Convention, unless the consulting States, which include the Coordinating State, agree that another State Party shall issue those authorizations.
5. The Coordinating State may conduct any necessary preliminary research on the underwater cultural heritage and shall issue all necessary authorizations therefore, and shall promptly inform the Director-General of the results, who in turn shall make such information available to other States Parties.

6. In coordinating consultations, taking measures, conducting preliminary research, and/or issuing authorizations pursuant to this Article, the Coordinating State shall act for the benefit of humanity as a whole, on behalf of all States Parties. Particular regard shall be paid to the preferential rights of States of cultural, historical or archaeological origin in respect of the underwater cultural heritage concerned.
7. No State Party shall undertake or authorize activities directed at State vessels and aircraft in the Area without the consent of the flag State.

Article 13 – Sovereign immunity

Warships and other government ships or military aircraft with sovereign immunity, operated for non-commercial purposes, undertaking their normal mode of operations, and not engaged in activities directed at underwater cultural heritage, shall not be obliged to report discoveries of underwater cultural heritage under Articles 9, 10, 11 and 12 of this Convention. However States Parties shall ensure, by the adoption of appropriate measures not impairing the operations or operational capabilities of their warships or other government ships or military aircraft with sovereign immunity operated for non-commercial purposes, that they comply, as far as is reasonable and practicable, with Articles 9, 10, 11 and 12 of this Convention.

Article 14 – Control of entry into the territory, dealing and possession

States Parties shall take measures to prevent the entry into their territory, the dealing in, or the possession of, underwater cultural heritage illicitly exported and/or recovered, where recovery was contrary to this Convention.

Article 15 – Non-use of areas under the jurisdiction of States Parties

States Parties shall take measures to prohibit the use of their territory, including their maritime ports, as well as artificial islands, installations and structures under their exclusive jurisdiction or control, in support of any activity directed at underwater cultural heritage which is not in conformity with this Convention.

Article 16 – Measures relating to nationals and vessels

States Parties shall take all practicable measures to ensure that their nationals and vessels flying their flag do not engage in any activity directed at underwater cultural heritage in a manner not in conformity with this Convention.

Article 17 – Sanctions

1. Each State Party shall impose sanctions for violations of measures it has taken to implement this Convention.
2. Sanctions applicable in respect of violations shall be adequate in severity to be effective in securing compliance with this Convention and to discourage violations wherever they occur and shall deprive offenders of the benefit deriving from their illegal activities.
3. States Parties shall cooperate to ensure enforcement of sanctions imposed under this Article.

Article 18 – Seizure and disposition of underwater cultural heritage

1. Each State Party shall take measures providing for the seizure of underwater cultural heritage in its territory that has been recovered in a manner not in conformity with this Convention.
2. Each State Party shall record, protect and take all reasonable measures to stabilize underwater cultural heritage seized under this Convention.
3. Each State Party shall notify the Director-General and any other State with a verifiable link, especially a cultural, historical or archaeological link, to the underwater cultural heritage concerned of any seizure of underwater cultural heritage that it has made under this Convention.
4. A State Party which has seized underwater cultural heritage shall ensure that its disposition be for the public benefit, taking into account the need for conservation and research; the need for reassembly of a dispersed collection; the need for public access, exhibition and education; and the interests of any State with a verifiable link, especially a cultural, historical or archaeological link, in respect of the underwater cultural heritage concerned.

Article 19 – Cooperation and information-sharing

1. States Parties shall cooperate and assist each other in the protection and management of underwater cultural heritage under this Convention, including, where practicable, collaborating in the investigation, excavation, documentation, conservation, study and presentation of such heritage.
2. To the extent compatible with the purposes of this Convention, each State Party undertakes to share information with other States Parties concerning underwater cultural heritage, including discovery of heritage, location of heritage, heritage excavated or recovered contrary to this Convention or otherwise in violation of international law, pertinent scientific methodology and technology, and legal developments relating to such heritage.
3. Information shared between States Parties, or between UNESCO and States Parties, regarding the discovery or location of underwater cultural heritage shall, to the extent compatible with their national legislation, be kept confidential and reserved to competent authorities of States Parties as long as the disclosure of such information might endanger or otherwise put at risk the preservation of such underwater cultural heritage.
4. Each State Party shall take all practicable measures to disseminate information, including where feasible through appropriate international databases, about underwater cultural heritage excavated or recovered contrary to this Convention or otherwise in violation of international law.

Article 20 – Public awareness

Each State Party shall take all practicable measures to raise public awareness regarding the value and significance of underwater cultural heritage and the importance of protecting it under this Convention.

Article 21 – Training in underwater archaeology

States Parties shall cooperate in the provision of training in underwater archaeology, in techniques for the conservation of underwater cultural heritage and, on agreed terms, in the transfer of technology relating to underwater cultural heritage.

Article 22 – Competent authorities

1. In order to ensure the proper implementation of this Convention, States Parties shall establish competent authorities or reinforce the existing ones where appropriate, with the aim of providing for the establishment, maintenance and updating of an inventory of underwater cultural heritage, the effective protection, conservation, presentation and management of underwater cultural heritage, as well as research and education.
2. States Parties shall communicate to the Director-General the names and addresses of their competent authorities relating to underwater cultural heritage.

Article 23 – Meetings of States Parties

1. The Director-General shall convene a Meeting of States Parties within one year of the entry into force of this Convention and thereafter at least once every two years. At the request of a majority of States Parties, the Director-General shall convene an Extraordinary Meeting of States Parties.
2. The Meeting of States Parties shall decide on its functions and responsibilities.
3. The Meeting of States Parties shall adopt its own Rules of Procedure.
4. The Meeting of States Parties may establish a Scientific and Technical Advisory Body composed of experts nominated by the States Parties with due regard to the principle of equitable geographical distribution and the desirability of a gender balance.
5. The Scientific and Technical Advisory Body shall appropriately assist the Meeting of States Parties in questions of a scientific or technical nature regarding the implementation of the Rules.

Article 24 – Secretariat for this Convention

1. The Director-General shall be responsible for the functions of the Secretariat for this Convention.
2. The duties of the Secretariat shall include:
   (a) organizing Meetings of States Parties as provided for in Article 23, paragraph 1; and
   (b) assisting States Parties in implementing the decisions of the Meetings of States Parties.

Article 25 – Peaceful settlement of disputes

1. Any dispute between two or more States Parties concerning the interpretation or application of this Convention shall be subject to negotiations in good faith or other peaceful means of settlement of their own choice.

2. If those negotiations do not settle the dispute within a reasonable period of time, it may be submitted to UNESCO for mediation, by agreement between the States Parties concerned.
3. If mediation is not undertaken or if there is no settlement by mediation, the provisions relating to the settlement of disputes set out in Part XV of the United Nations Convention on the Law of the Sea apply *mutatis mutandis* to any dispute between States Parties to this Convention concerning the interpretation or application of this Convention, whether or not they are also Parties to the United Nations Convention on the Law of the Sea.
4. Any procedure chosen by a State Party to this Convention and to the United Nations Convention on the Law of the Sea pursuant to Article 287 of the latter shall apply to the settlement of disputes under this Article, unless that State Party, when ratifying, accepting, approving or acceding to this Convention, or at any time thereafter, chooses another procedure pursuant to Article 287 for the purpose of the settlement of disputes arising out of this Convention.
5. A State Party to this Convention which is not a Party to the United Nations Convention on the Law of the Sea, when ratifying, accepting, approving or acceding to this Convention or at any time thereafter shall be free to choose, by means of a written declaration, one or more of the means set out in Article 287, paragraph 1, of the United Nations Convention on the Law of the Sea for the purpose of settlement of disputes under this Article. Article 287 shall apply to such a declaration, as well as to any dispute to which such State is party, which is not covered by a declaration in force. For the purpose of conciliation and arbitration, in accordance with Annexes V and VII of the United Nations Convention on the Law of the Sea, such State shall be entitled to nominate conciliators and arbitrators to be included in the lists referred to in Annex V, Article 2, and Annex VII, Article 2, for the settlement of disputes arising out of this Convention.

Article 26 – Ratification, acceptance, approval or accession
1. This Convention shall be subject to ratification, acceptance or approval by Member States of UNESCO.
2. This Convention shall be subject to accession:
   (a) by States that are not members of UNESCO but are members of the United Nations or of a specialized agency within the United Nations system or of the International Atomic Energy Agency, as well as by States Parties to the Statute of the International Court of Justice and any other State invited to accede to this Convention by the General Conference of UNESCO;
   (b) by territories which enjoy full internal self-government, recognized as such by the United Nations, but have not attained full independence in accordance with General Assembly resolution 1514 (XV) and which have competence over the matters governed by this Convention, including the competence to enter into treaties in respect of those matters.
3. The instruments of ratification, acceptance, approval or accession shall be deposited with the Director-General.

Article 27 – Entry into force
This Convention shall enter into force three months after the date of the deposit of the twentieth instrument referred to in Article 26, but solely with respect to the twenty States or territories that have so deposited their instruments. It shall enter into force for each other State or territory three months after the date on which that State or territory has deposited its instrument.

Article 28 – Declaration as to inland waters
When ratifying, accepting, approving or acceding to this Convention or at any time thereafter, any State or territory may declare that the Rules shall apply to inland waters not of a maritime character.

Article 29 – Limitations to geographical scope
At the time of ratifying, accepting, approving or acceding to this Convention, a State or territory may make a declaration to the depositary that this Convention shall not be applicable to specific parts of its territory, internal waters, archipelagic waters or territorial sea, and shall identify therein the reasons for such declaration. Such State shall, to the extent practicable and as quickly as possible, promote conditions under which this Convention will apply to the areas specified in its declaration, and to that end shall also withdraw its declaration in whole or in part as soon as that has been achieved.

Article 30 – Reservations
With the exception of Article 29, no reservations may be made to this Convention.

Article 31 – Amendments

1. A State Party may, by written communication addressed to the Director-General, propose amendments to this Convention. The Director-General shall circulate such communication to all States Parties. If, within six months from the date of the circulation of the communication, not less than one half of the States Parties reply favourably to the request, the Director-General shall present such proposal to the next Meeting of States Parties for discussion and possible adoption.
2. Amendments shall be adopted by a two-thirds majority of States Parties present and voting.
3. Once adopted, amendments to this Convention shall be subject to ratification, acceptance, approval or accession by the States Parties.
4. Amendments shall enter into force, but solely with respect to the States Parties that have ratified, accepted, approved or acceded to them, three months after the deposit of the instruments referred to in paragraph 3 of this Article by two thirds of the States Parties. Thereafter, for each State or territory that ratifies, accepts, approves or accedes to it, the amendment shall enter into force three months after the date of deposit by that Party of its instrument of ratification, acceptance, approval or accession.
5. A State or territory which becomes a Party to this Convention after the entry into force of amendments in conformity with paragraph 4 of this Article shall, failing an expression of different intention by that State or territory, be considered:
   (a) as a Party to this Convention as so amended; and
   (b) as a Party to the unamended Convention in relation to any State Party not bound by the amendment.

Article 32 – Denunciation

1. A State Party may, by written notification addressed to the Director-General, denounce this Convention.
2. The denunciation shall take effect twelve months after the date of receipt of the notification, unless the notification specifies a later date.
3. The denunciation shall not in any way affect the duty of any State Party to fulfil any obligation embodied in this Convention to which it would be subject under international law independently of this Convention.

Article 33 – The Rules

The Rules annexed to this Convention form an integral part of it and, unless expressly provided otherwise, a reference to this Convention includes a reference to the Rules.

Article 34 – Registration with the United Nations

In conformity with Article 102 of the Charter of the United Nations, this Convention shall be registered with the Secretariat of the United Nations at the request of the Director-General.

Article 35 – Authoritative texts

This Convention has been drawn up in Arabic, Chinese, English, French, Russian and Spanish, the six texts being equally authoritative.

Annex Rules concerning activities directed at underwater cultural heritage

I. General principles

Rule 1. The protection of underwater cultural heritage through *in situ* preservation shall be considered as the first option. Accordingly, activities directed at underwater cultural heritage shall be authorized in a manner consistent with the protection of that heritage, and subject to that requirement may be authorized for the purpose of making a significant contribution to protection or knowledge or enhancement of underwater cultural heritage.

Rule 2. The commercial exploitation of underwater cultural heritage for trade or speculation or its irretrievable dispersal is fundamentally incompatible with the protection and proper management of underwater cultural heritage. Underwater cultural heritage shall not be traded, sold, bought or bartered as commercial goods.
This Rule cannot be interpreted as preventing:
(a) the provision of professional archaeological services or necessary services incidental thereto whose nature and purpose are in full conformity with this Convention and are subject to the authorization of the competent authorities;

(b) the deposition of underwater cultural heritage, recovered in the course of a research project in conformity with this Convention, provided such deposition does not prejudice the scientific or cultural interest or integrity of the recovered material or result in its irretrievable dispersal; is in accordance with the provisions of Rules 33 and 34; and is subject to the authorization of the competent authorities.

Rule 3. Activities directed at underwater cultural heritage shall not adversely affect the underwater cultural heritage more than is necessary for the objectives of the project.

Rule 4. Activities directed at underwater cultural heritage must use non-destructive techniques and survey methods in preference to recovery of objects. If excavation or recovery is necessary for the purpose of scientific studies or for the ultimate protection of the underwater cultural heritage, the methods and techniques used must be as non-destructive as possible and contribute to the preservation of the remains.

Rule 5. Activities directed at underwater cultural heritage shall avoid the unnecessary disturbance of human remains or venerated sites.

Rule 6. Activities directed at underwater cultural heritage shall be strictly regulated to ensure proper recording of cultural, historical and archaeological information.

Rule 7. Public access to *in situ* underwater cultural heritage shall be promoted, except where such access is incompatible with protection and management.

Rule 8. International cooperation in the conduct of activities directed at underwater cultural heritage shall be encouraged in order to further the effective exchange or use of archaeologists and other relevant professionals.

II. Project design

Rule 9. Prior to any activity directed at underwater cultural heritage, a project design for the activity shall be developed and submitted to the competent authorities for authorization and appropriate peer review.

Rule 10. The project design shall include:
(a) an evaluation of previous or preliminary studies;
(b) the project statement and objectives;
(c) the methodology to be used and the techniques to be employed;
(d) the anticipated funding;
(e) an expected timetable for completion of the project;
(f) the composition of the team and the qualifications, responsibilities and experience of each team member;
(g) plans for post-fieldwork analysis and other activities;
(h) a conservation programme for artefacts and the site in close cooperation with the competent authorities;
(i) a site management and maintenance policy for the whole duration of the project;
(j) a documentation programme;
(k) a safety policy;
(l) an environmental policy;
(m) arrangements for collaboration with museums and other institutions, in particular scientific institutions;
(n) report preparation;
(o) deposition of archives, including underwater cultural heritage removed; and
(p) a programme for publication.

Rule 11. Activities directed at underwater cultural heritage shall be carried out in accordance with the project design approved by the competent authorities.

Rule 12. Where unexpected discoveries are made or circumstances change, the project design shall be reviewed and amended with the approval of the competent authorities.

Rule 13. In cases of urgency or chance discoveries, activities directed at the underwater cultural heritage, including conservation measures or activities for a period of short duration, in particular site stabilization, may be authorized in the absence of a project design in order to protect the underwater cultural heritage.

III. Preliminary work

Rule 14. The preliminary work referred to in Rule 10 (a) shall include an assessment that evaluates the significance and vulnerability of the underwater cultural heritage and the surrounding natural environment to damage by the proposed project, and the potential to obtain data that would meet the project objectives.

Rule 15. The assessment shall also include background studies of available historical and archaeological evidence, the archaeological and environmental characteristics of the site, and the consequences of any potential intrusion for the long-term stability of the underwater cultural heritage affected by the activities.

IV. Project objective, methodology and techniques
Rule 16. The methodology shall comply with the project objectives, and the techniques employed shall be as non-intrusive as possible.

V. Funding
Rule 17. Except in cases of emergency to protect underwater cultural heritage, an adequate funding base shall be assured in advance of any activity, sufficient to complete all stages of the project design, including conservation, documentation and curation of recovered artefacts, and report preparation and dissemination.
Rule 18. The project design shall demonstrate an ability, such as by securing a bond, to fund the project through to completion.
Rule 19. The project design shall include a contingency plan that will ensure conservation of underwater cultural heritage and supporting documentation in the event of any interruption of anticipated funding.

VI. Project duration – timetable
Rule 20. An adequate timetable shall be developed to assure in advance of any activity directed at underwater cultural heritage the completion of all stages of the project design, including conservation, documentation and curation of recovered underwater cultural heritage, as well as report preparation and dissemination.
Rule 21. The project design shall include a contingency plan that will ensure conservation of underwater cultural heritage and supporting documentation in the event of any interruption or termination of the project.

VII. Competence and qualifications
Rule 22. Activities directed at underwater cultural heritage shall only be undertaken under the direction and control of, and in the regular presence of, a qualified underwater archaeologist with scientific competence appropriate to the project.
Rule 23. All persons on the project team shall be qualified and have demonstrated competence appropriate to their roles in the project.

VIII. Conservation and site management
Rule 24. The conservation programme shall provide for the treatment of the archaeological remains during the activities directed at underwater cultural heritage, during transit and in the long term. Conservation shall be carried out in accordance with current professional standards.
Rule 25. The site management programme shall provide for the protection and management *in situ* of underwater cultural heritage, in the course of and upon termination of fieldwork. The programme shall include public information, reasonable provision for site stabilization, monitoring, and protection against interference.

IX. Documentation
Rule 26. The documentation programme shall set out thorough documentation including a progress report of activities directed at underwater cultural heritage, in accordance with current professional standards of archaeological documentation.
Rule 27. Documentation shall include, at a minimum, a comprehensive record of the site, including the provenance of underwater cultural heritage moved or removed in the course of the activities directed at underwater cultural heritage, field notes, plans, drawings, sections, and photographs or recording in other media.

X. Safety
Rule 28. A safety policy shall be prepared that is adequate to ensure the safety and health of the project team and third parties and that is in conformity with any applicable statutory and professional requirements.

XI. Environment
Rule 29. An environmental policy shall be prepared that is adequate to ensure that the seabed and marine life are not unduly disturbed.

XII. Reporting
Rule 30. Interim and final reports shall be made available according to the timetable set out in the project design, and deposited in relevant public records.
Rule 31. Reports shall include:
(a) an account of the objectives;
(b) an account of the methods and techniques employed;

(c) an account of the results achieved;
(d) basic graphic and photographic documentation on all phases of the activity;
(e) recommendations concerning conservation and curation of the site and of any underwater cultural heritage removed; and
(f) recommendations for future activities.

XIII. Curation of project archives
Rule 32. Arrangements for curation of the project archives shall be agreed to before any activity commences, and shall be set out in the project design.
Rule 33. The project archives, including any underwater cultural heritage removed and a copy of all supporting documentation shall, as far as possible, be kept together and intact as a collection in a manner that is available for professional and public access as well as for the curation of the archives. This should be done as rapidly as possible and in any case not later than ten years from the completion of the project, in so far as may be compatible with conservation of the underwater cultural heritage.
Rule 34. The project archives shall be managed according to international professional standards, and subject to the authorization of the competent authorities.

XIV. Dissemination
Rule 35. Projects shall provide for public education and popular presentation of the project results where appropriate.
Rule 36. A final synthesis of a project shall be:
(a) made public as soon as possible, having regard to the complexity of the project and the confidential or sensitive nature of the information; and
(b) deposited in relevant public records.

Done in Paris this 6 day of November 2001 in two authentic copies bearing the signature of the President of the thirty-first session of the General Conference and of the Director-General of the United-Nations Educational, Scientific and Cultural Organization, which shall be deposited in the archives of the United-Nations Educational, Scientific and Cultural Organization and certified true copies of which shall be delivered to all the States and territories referred to in Article 26 as well as to the United Nations.

The foregoing is the authentic text of the Convention duly adopted by the General Conference of the United Nations Educational, Scientific and Cultural Organization during its thirty-first session, which was held in Paris and declared closed the 6 day of November 2001.
IN WITNESS WHEREOF we have appended our signature this 6 day of November 2001.

The President of the General Conference
The Director-General

A.II.4 Europäisches Kulturabkommen

Europäisches Kulturabkommen[1]

Vom 19. Dezember 1954 (BGBl. 1955 II S. 1128)

DIE UNTERZEICHNETEN REGIERUNGEN der Mitglieder des Europarates,
IN DER ERWÄGUNG, daß der Europarat die Herstellung einer engeren Verbindung zwischen seinen Mitgliedern zur Aufgabe hat, insbesondere um die Ideale und Grundsätze, die ihr gemeinsames Erbe bilden, zu wahren und zu fördern;
IN DER ERWÄGUNG, daß ein besseres gegenseitiges Verständnis zwischen den europäischen Völkern es ermöglichen würde, diesem Ziel näher zu kommen;
IN DER ERWÄGUNG, daß es deshalb wünschenswert ist, nicht nur zweiseitige Kulturabkommen zwischen den Mitgliedern des Europarates abzuschließen, sondern auch gemeinsam zu handeln, um die europäische Kultur zu wahren und ihre Entwicklung zu fördern;
IN DEM ENTSCHLUSS, ein allgemeines europäisches Kulturabkommen abzuschließen, um unter den Staatsangehörigen aller Mitglieder des Europarates und derjenigen anderen europäischen Staaten, die diesem Abkommen beitreten, das Studium der Sprachen, der Geschichte und der Zivilisation der anderen Vertragsparteien sowie auch ihrer gemeinsamen Kultur zu fördern,
SIND wie folgt übereingekommen:

Artikel 1
Jede Vertragspartei trifft geeignete Maßnahmen zum Schutz und zur Mehrung ihres Beitrags zum gemeinsamen kulturellen Erbe Europas.

Artikel 2
Jede Vertragspartei wird, soweit wie möglich,
(a) bei ihren Staatsangehörigen das Studium der Sprachen, der Geschichte und der Zivilisation der anderen Vertragsparteien fördern und diesen Vertragsparteien auf ihrem Gebiet Erleichterungen für die Ausgestaltung solcher Studien gewähren;
(b) bestrebt sein, das Studium ihrer Sprache oder Sprachen, ihrer Geschichte und ihrer Zivilisation im Gebiet der anderen Vertragsparteien zu fördern und deren Staatsangehörigen die Möglichkeit zu geben, sich solchen Studien auf ihrem Gebiet zu widmen.

Artikel 3
Die Vertragsparteien konsultieren sich im Rahmen des Europarates, um ihr Vorgehen zur Förderung der im europäischen Interesse liegenden kulturellen Maßnahmen aufeinander abzustimmen.

Artikel 4
Zwecks Durchführung der Artikel 2 und 3 erleichtert jede Vertragspartei soweit wie möglich die Bewegungsfreiheit und den Austausch von Personen und Kulturgütern.

Artikel 5
Jede Vertragspartei betrachtet die europäischen Kulturgüter, die sich unter ihrer Kontrolle befinden, als Bestandteil des gemeinsamen europäischen kulturellen Erbes, trifft die erforderlichen Maßnahmen zu ihrem Schutz und erleichtert den Zugang zu ihnen.

Artikel 6
1. Vorschläge zur Anwendung und Fragen der Auslegung dieses Abkommens werden auf den Tagungen des Ausschusses der Kultursachverständigen des Europarates geprüft.
2. Jeder Staat, der nicht Mitglied des Europarates ist, aber diesem Abkommen gemäß Artikel 9 Abs. 4 beigetreten ist, kann einen oder mehrere Vertreter zu den in Absatz 1 vorgesehenen Tagungen entsenden.
3. Die auf den in Absatz 1 vorgesehenen Tagungen gefaßten Beschlüsse werden dem Ministerkomitee des Europarates als Empfehlungen vorgelegt, es sei denn, daß es sich um Entscheidungen handelt, die als Verwaltungsangelegenheiten, welche keine zusätzlichen Ausgaben erfordern, in die Zuständigkeit des Ausschusses der Kultursachverständigen fallen.

---

[1] Liste der Vertragsstaaten: https://www.coe.int/en/web/conventions/full-list/-/conventions/treaty/018/signatures?p_auth=n Rhxm23G.

4. Der Generalsekretär des Europarates bringt den Mitgliedern des Rates sowie den Regierungen aller Staaten, die diesem Abkommen beigetreten sind, jede darauf bezügliche Entscheidung, die vom Ministerkomitee oder vom Ausschuß der Kultursachverständigen getroffen wird, zur Kenntnis.
5. Jede Vertragspartei notifiziert dem Generalsekretär des Europarates zu gegebener Zeit jede Maßnahme, die sie auf Grund der Entscheidungen des Ministerkomitees oder des Ausschusses der Kultursachverständigen zur Durchführung dieses Abkommens trifft.
6. Sind bestimmte Vorschläge zur Durchführung dieses Abkommens nur für eine beschränkte Anzahl von Vertragsparteien von Interesse, so können sie gemäß Artikel 7 behandelt werden, sofern ihre Verwirklichung keine Ausgaben für den Europarat zur Folge hat.

Artikel 7
Wünschen zwei oder mehr Vertragsparteien zur Förderung der Ziele dieses Abkommens am Sitz des Europarates andere Tagungen abzuhalten als in Artikel 6 Abs. 1 vorgesehen, so gewährt ihnen der Generalsekretär des Europarates jede erforderliche Verwaltungshilfe.

Artikel 8
Keine Bestimmung dieses Abkommens darf so ausgelegt werden,
(a) daß sie die Bestimmungen eines von einer Vertragspartei bereits unterzeichneten zweiseitigen Kulturabkommens beeinträchtigt oder den künftigen Abschluß eines solchen weniger erstrebenswert macht, oder
(b) daß sie die Pflicht einer Person zur Beachtung der im Hoheitsgebiet einer Vertragspartei geltenden Rechtsvorschriften über die Einreise, den Aufenthalt und die Ausreise von Ausländern berührt.

Artikel 9
1. Dieses Abkommen wird zur Unterzeichnung durch die Mitglieder des Europarates aufgelegt. Es bedarf der Ratifizierung; die Ratifikationsurkunden werden beim Generalsekretär des Europarates hinterlegt.
2. Dieses Abkommen tritt, sobald drei Unterzeichnerregierungen ihre Ratifikationsurkunden hinterlegt haben, für diese Regierungen in Kraft.
3. Für jede Unterzeichnerregierung, die dieses Abkommen in der Folge ratifiziert, tritt es mit der Hinterlegung ihrer Ratifikationsurkunde in Kraft.
4. Das Ministerkomitee des Europarates kann durch einstimmigen Beschluß und unter den ihm zweckmäßig erscheinenden Bedingungen jeden europäischen Staat, der nicht Mitglied des Europarates ist, einladen, diesem Abkommen beizutreten. Jeder Staat, der eine Einladung erhält, kann dem Abkommen durch Hinterlegung seiner Beitrittsurkunde beim Generalsekretär des Europarates beitreten; der Beitritt wird mit dem Eingang dieser Urkunde wirksam.
5. Der Generalsekretär des Europarates notifiziert allen Mitgliedern des Rates sowie den beigetretenen Staaten die Hinterlegung aller Ratifikations- und Beitrittsurkunden.

Artikel 10
Jede Vertragspartei kann diejenigen Hoheitsgebiete, auf die dieses Abkommen Anwendung finden soll, durch eine an den Generalsekretär des Europarates zu richtende Erklärung bestimmen; diese Erklärung bringt der Generalsekretär allen anderen Vertragsparteien zur Kenntnis.

Artikel 11
1. Nach Ablauf von fünf Jahren, von seinem Inkrafttreten an gerechnet, kann dieses Abkommen jederzeit von jeder Vertragspartei gekündigt werden. Die Kündigung erfolgt durch schriftliche Notifizierung an den Generalsekretär des Europarates; dieser setzt die anderen Vertragsparteien davon in Kenntnis.
2. Die Kündigung wird für die betreffende Vertragspartei mit Ablauf von sechs Monaten nach dem Tag ihres Eingangs beim Generalsekretär des Europarates wirksam.

A.II.4 Europäisches Kulturabkommen

ZU URKUND DESSEN haben die von ihren Regierungen hierzu gehörig beglaubigten Unterzeichneten dieses Abkommen unterschrieben.

GESCHEHEN zu Paris am 19. Dezember 1954 in englischer und französischer Sprache, wobei beide Fassungen in gleicher Weise maßgebend sind, in einer Urschrift, die im Archiv des Europarates hinterlegt wird. Der Generalsekretär übermittelt den unterzeichneten und den beigetretenen Regierungen beglaubigte Abschriften.

# Granada-Übereinkommen A.II.5

Übereinkommen zum Schutz des architektonischen Erbes Europas[1]

Vom 3. Oktober 1985 (BGBl. 1987 II S. 624)

Die Mitgliedstaaten des Europarats, die dieses Übereinkommen unterzeichnen –
von der Erwägung geleitet, daß es das Ziel des Europarats ist, eine engere Verbindung zwischen seinen Mitgliedern herbeizuführen, um insbesondere die Ideale und Grundsätze, die ihr gemeinsames Erbe bilden, zu wahren und zu fördern;
in der Erkenntnis, daß das architektonische Erbe einen unersetzlichen Ausdruck des Reichtums und der Vielfalt des europäischen Kulturerbes darstellt, auf unschätzbare Weise Zeugnis von unserer Vergangenheit ablegt und ein gemeinsames Erbe aller Europäer ist;
im Hinblick auf das am 19. Dezember 1954 in Paris unterzeichnete Europäische Kulturabkommen, insbesondere auf dessen Artikel 1;
im Hinblick auf die am 26. September 1975 vom Ministerkomitee des Europarats angenommene Europäische Charta des architektonischen Erbes und die am 14. April 1976 angenommene Entschließung (76) 28 über die Anpassung von Gesetzen und sonstigen Vorschriften an die Erfordernisse einer integrierten Erhaltung des architektonischen Erbes;
im Hinblick auf die Empfehlung 880 (1979) der Parlamentarischen Versammlung des Europarats über die Erhaltung des architektonischen Erbes Europas;
im Hinblick auf die Empfehlung Nr. R (80) 16 des Ministerkomitees an die Mitgliedstaaten über die Fachausbildung von Architekten, Städteplanern, Ingenieuren und Landschaftsplanern sowie die am 1. Juli 1981 angenommene Empfehlung Nr. R (81) 13 des Ministerkomitees über Maßnahmen zur Unterstützung bestimmter vom Untergang bedrohter Handwerkszweige im Rahmen der Tätigkeit im Bereich des Handwerks;
eingedenk dessen, daß es wichtig ist, den künftigen Generationen ein System kultureller Bezugspunkte zu hinterlassen, die städtische und ländliche Umwelt zu verbessern und auf diese Weise die wirtschaftliche, soziale und kulturelle Entwicklung von Staaten und Regionen zu fördern;
in Anerkennung dessen, daß es wichtig ist, sich über die Hauptrichtung einer gemeinsamen Politik zur Erhaltung und Aufwertung des architektonischen Erbes zu einigen –
sind wie folgt übereingekommen:

Bestimmung des Begriffs „architektonisches Erbe"

Artikel 1
Der Ausdruck „architektonisches Erbe" im Sinne dieses Übereinkommens umfaßt folgende ortsfeste Güter:
1. Denkmäler: alle Bauwerke von herausragender geschichtlicher, archäologischer, künstlerischer, wissenschaftlicher, sozialer oder technischer Bedeutung, einschließlich ihres Zubehörs und ihrer unbeweglichen Ausstattung;
2. Ensembles: geschlossene Gruppen städtischer oder ländlicher Gebäude von herausragender geschichtlicher, archäologischer, künstlerischer, wissenschaftlicher, sozialer oder technischer Bedeutung, die genügend zusammenhängen, um topographisch abgrenzbare Einheiten zu bilden;
3. Stätten: gemeinsame Werke von Mensch und Natur, bei denen es sich um teilweise bebaute Gebiete handelt, die genügend charakteristisch und geschlossen sind, um topographisch abgrenzbar zu sein, und die von herausragender geschichtlicher, archäologischer, künstlerischer, wissenschaftlicher, sozialer oder technischer Bedeutung sind.

Erfassung der zu schützenden Güter

Artikel 2
Um die Denkmäler, Ensembles und Stätten, die geschützt werden sollen, genau zu erfassen, verpflichtet sich jede Vertragspartei, Inventare zu führen und in Fällen, in denen den betreffenden Gütern Gefahr droht, so früh wie möglich eine geeignete Dokumentation vorzubereiten.

---

[1] Liste der Vertragsstaaten: https://www.coe.int/de/web/conventions/full-list/-/conventions/treaty/121/signatures?p_auth=9 mVHX56d

A.II.5 Granada-Übereinkommen

Gesetzliche Schutzverfahren

Artikel 3

Jede Vertragspartei verpflichtet sich,
1. gesetzliche Maßnahmen zum Schutz des architektonischen Erbes zu treffen;
2. im Rahmen dieser Maßnahmen auf eine für jeden Staat oder jede Region spezifische Art und Weise Vorsorge für den Schutz der Denkmäler, Ensembles und Stätten zu treffen.

Artikel 4

Jede Vertragspartei verpflichtet sich,
1. die für den rechtlichen Schutz der betreffenden Güter erforderlich werdenden geeigneten Überwachungs- und Genehmigungsverfahren durchzuführen;
2. zu verhindern, daß geschützte Güter verunstaltet, dem Verfall anheimgegeben oder zerstört werden. Zu diesem Zweck verpflichtet sich jede Vertragspartei, falls dies noch nicht geschehen ist, Rechtsvorschriften einzuführen,
   a) die vorsehen, daß jedes Vorhaben der Zerstörung oder Änderung von Denkmälern, die bereits geschützt sind oder für die ein Schutzverfahren eingeleitet worden ist, sowie jedes Vorhaben, das ihre Umgebung berührt, einer zuständigen Behörde vorzulegen ist;
   b) die vorsehen, daß jedes Vorhaben, das ein Ensemble oder einen Teil davon oder eine Stätte berührt und das
      – die Zerstörung von Gebäuden,
      – die Errichtung neuer Gebäude,
      – den Charakter des Ensembles oder der Stätte beeinträchtigende wesentliche Änderungen

      bedingt, einer zuständigen Behörde vorzulegen ist;
   c) die es den Behörden ermöglichen, von dem Eigentümer eines geschützten Gutes die Durchführung von Arbeiten zu verlangen oder diese Arbeiten selbst durchzuführen, wenn der Eigentümer dies unterläßt;
   d) welche die Enteignung eines geschützten Gutes erlauben.

Artikel 5

Jede Vertragspartei verpflichtet sich, die vollständige oder teilweise Versetzung eines geschützten Denkmals an eine andere Stelle zu verhindern, es sei denn, daß die materielle Sicherung dieses Denkmals die Versetzung unbedingt erforderlich macht. In einem derartigen Fall trifft die zuständige Behörde die erforderlichen Sicherheitsmaßnahmen für den Abbau des Denkmals, seine Verbringung und seinen Wiederaufbau an einer geeigneten Stelle.

Begleitende Maßnahmen

Artikel 6

Jede Vertragspartei verpflichtet sich,
1. in ihrem Hoheitsgebiet entsprechend den gesamtstaatlichen, regionalen und kommunalen Zuständigkeiten und im Rahmen der verfügbaren Haushaltsmittel durch die Behörden finanzielle Unterstützung für die Unterhaltung und Wiederherstellung des architektonischen Erbes zu gewähren;
2. erforderlichenfalls zu steuerlichen Maßnahmen zu greifen, um die Erhaltung dieses Erbes zu erleichtern;
3. private Initiativen zur Unterhaltung und Wiederherstellung des architektonischen Erbes zu fördern.

Artikel 7

Jede Vertragspartei verpflichtet sich, in der Umgebung von Denkmälern, innerhalb von Ensembles und innerhalb von Stätten Maßnahmen zur allgemeinen Verbesserung der Umwelt einzuführen.

Artikel 8
Zur Begrenzung der Gefahren des physischen Verfalls des architektonischen Erbes verpflichtet sich jede Vertragspartei,
1. wissenschaftliche Forschungen zu unterstützen, welche die schädlichen Auswirkungen der Umweltverschmutzung ermitteln und analysieren und Mittel und Wege zur Verringerung oder Beseitigung dieser Auswirkungen aufzeigen;
2. bei Maßnahmen gegen die Umweltverschmutzung die besonderen Probleme der Erhaltung des architektonischen Erbes zu berücksichtigen.

Sanktionen

Artikel 9
Jede Vertragspartei verpflichtet sich, im Rahmen ihrer Befugnisse sicherzustellen, daß bei Verstößen gegen Gesetze zum Schutz des architektonischen Erbes von der zuständigen Behörde sachdienliche und angemessene Gegenmaßnahmen getroffen werden. Diese Maßnahmen können gegebenenfalls dazu führen, daß der Gesetzesübertreter verpflichtet wird, ein neu errichtetes Gebäude, das den Anforderungen nicht entspricht, abzubrechen oder ein geschütztes Gut in seinen früheren Zustand zurückzuversetzen.

Erhaltungsmaßnahmen

Artikel 10
Jede Vertragspartei verpflichtet sich, integrierte Erhaltungsmaßnahmen zu treffen,
1. die den Schutz des architektonischen Erbes als wesentliches Ziel der Raumordnung und des Städtebaus umfassen und sicherstellen, daß diese Forderung sowohl bei der Aufstellung von Bauleitplänen als auch bei den Genehmigungsverfahren für Bauarbeiten in jeder Phase berücksichtigt wird;
2. die Programme zur Wiederherstellung und Unterhaltung des architektonischen Erbes fördern;
3. welche die Erhaltung, Förderung und Aufwertung des architektonischen Erbes zu einem wesentlichen Aspekt der Kultur-, Umwelt- und Raumordnungspolitik machen;
4. die beim Planungsprozeß im Rahmen der Raumordnung und des Städtebaus, wann immer dies möglich ist, die Erhaltung und Nutzung bestimmter Gebäude erleichtern, deren Eigenbedeutung keinen Schutz im Sinne des Artikels 3 Nummer 1 rechtfertigen würde, die aber im Hinblick auf ihre Lage in der städtischen oder ländlichen Umgebung und auf die Lebensqualität von Interesse sind;
5. welche die Anwendung und Entwicklung traditioneller Fertigkeiten und Werkstoffe wegen ihrer wesentlichen Bedeutung für die Zukunft des architektonischen Erbes fördern.

Artikel 11
Jede Vertragspartei verpflichtet sich,
– die Nutzung geschützter Güter entsprechend den Bedürfnissen des heutigen Lebens;
– soweit angängig die Anpassung alter Gebäude an neue Nutzungsarten
unter gebührender Beachtung des architektonischen und geschichtlichen Charakters des Erbes zu fördern.

Artikel 12
Ohne den Wert des Zugangs der Allgemeinheit zu geschützten Gütern zu verkennen, verpflichtet sich jede Vertragspartei, die erforderlichen Maßnahmen zu treffen, um sicherzustellen, daß die Folgen der Zugänglichmachung, insbesondere bauliche Maßnahmen, den architektonischen und geschichtlichen Charakter dieser Güter und ihrer Umgebung nicht beeinträchtigen.

Artikel 13
Um die Durchführung der Erhaltungsmaßnahmen zu erleichtern, verpflichtet sich jede Vertragspartei, im Rahmen ihrer politischen und verwaltungsmäßigen Ordnung auf allen Ebenen eine wirksame Zusammenarbeit zwischen Denkmalpflege, Kulturarbeit, Umweltschutz und Raumordnung zu fördern.

A.II.5 Granada-Übereinkommen

Mitwirkung und Vereinigungen

Artikel 14

Um die Wirkung der behördlichen Maßnahmen zur Erfassung, zum Schutz, zur Wiederherstellung, zur Unterhaltung, zur Verwaltung und zur Förderung des architektonischen Erbes zu verstärken, verpflichtet sich jede Vertragspartei,

1. in den verschiedenen Phasen des Entscheidungsprozesses die organisatorischen Voraussetzungen für die wechselseitige Information, Konsultation und Zusammenarbeit zwischen Staat, Gebietskörperschaften, kulturellen Einrichtungen und Vereinigungen und der Öffentlichkeit zu schaffen;
2. die Entwicklung des Mäzenatentums und von auf diesem Gebiet tätigen, nicht auf Gewinn gerichteten Vereinigungen zu fördern.

Information und Ausbildung

Artikel 15

Jede Vertragspartei verpflichtet sich,

1. das Bewußtsein der Öffentlichkeit für den Wert der Erhaltung des architektonischen Erbes sowohl als Teil der kulturellen Identität als auch als Quelle der Inspiration und Kreativität für heutige und künftige Generationen zu stärken;
2. zu diesem Zweck Maßnahmen zur Verbreitung von Informationen und zur Entwicklung eines verstärkten Bewußtseins insbesondere unter Verwendung moderner Techniken der Kommunikation und der Öffentlichkeitsarbeit zu fördern, die namentlich darauf abzielen,
   a) schon vom Schulalter an das Interesse der Öffentlichkeit am Schutz des Erbes, an der Qualität der gebauten Umwelt und der Architektur zu wecken oder zu steigern;
   b) die Einheit des Kulturerbes und die Zusammenhänge zu verdeutlichen, die zwischen Architektur, Kunst, Brauchtum und Lebensweisen bestehen, sei es auf europäischer, nationaler oder regionaler Ebene.

Artikel 16

Jede Vertragspartei verpflichtet sich, die Ausbildung in den verschiedenen Berufen und Handwerken, die mit der Erhaltung des architektonischen Erbes befaßt sind, zu fördern.

Abstimmung der Erhaltungsmaßnahmen auf europäischer Ebene

Artikel 17

Die Vertragsparteien verpflichten sich, Informationen über ihre Erhaltungsmaßnahmen auszutauschen, beispielsweise über

1. die Methoden der Erfassung, des Schutzes und der Erhaltung von Gütern unter Berücksichtigung der historischen Entwicklung und des ständigen Anwachsens des architektonischen Erbes;
2. die Art und Weise, in der die Notwendigkeit, das architektonische Erbe zu schützen, am besten mit den Bedürfnissen des heutigen wirtschaftlichen, sozialen und kulturellen Lebens vereinbart werden kann;
3. die durch neue Technologien gebotenen Möglichkeiten zur Erfassung und Aufzeichnung des architektonischen Erbes und zur Bekämpfung des Verfalls von Material sowie im Bereich der wissenschaftlichen Forschung, der Restaurierung und der Methoden der Verwaltung und Förderung des Erbes;
4. Mittel und Wege zur Förderung des architektonischen Schaffens als Beitrag unseres Zeitalters zum europäischen Erbe.

Artikel 18

Die Vertragsparteien verpflichten sich, einander bei Bedarf technische Unterstützung durch Austausch von Erfahrungen und Sachverständigen auf dem Gebiet der Erhaltung des architektonischen Erbes zu gewähren.

Artikel 19

Die Vertragsparteien verpflichten sich, im Rahmen der einschlägigen innerstaatlichen Rechtsvorschriften oder der völkerrechtlichen Übereinkünfte, durch die sie gebunden sind, den Austausch von

Fachleuten für die Erhaltung des architektonischen Erbes einschließlich derjenigen, die für Weiterbildung zuständig sind, auf europäischer Ebene zu fördern.

Artikel 20
Für die Zwecke dieses Übereinkommens wird ein vom Ministerkomitee des Europarats nach Artikel 17 der Satzung des Europarats eingesetzter Sachverständigenausschuß die Anwendung des Übereinkommens überwachen und insbesondere
1. dem Ministerkomitee des Europarats regelmäßig über den Stand der Maßnahmen zur Erhaltung des architektonischen Erbes in den Vertragsstaaten des Übereinkommens, über die Anwendung der in dem Übereinkommen niedergelegten Grundsätze und über seine eigenen Tätigkeiten berichten;
2. dem Ministerkomitee des Europarats Maßnahmen zur Durchführung des Übereinkommens vorschlagen, einschließlich multilateraler Tätigkeiten, der Revision oder Änderung des Übereinkommens und der Unterrichtung der Öffentlichkeit über den Zweck des Übereinkommens;
3. dem Ministerkomitee des Europarats Vorschläge hinsichtlich der Einladung von Nichtmitgliedstaaten des Europarats zum Beitritt zu dem Übereinkommen unterbreiten.

Artikel 21
Dieses Übereinkommen läßt die Anwendung günstigerer einschlägiger Bestimmungen über den Schutz der in Artikel 1 beschriebenen Güter unberührt, wie sie in folgenden Übereinkünften enthalten sind:
– Übereinkommen vom 16. November 1972 zum Schutz des Kultur- und Naturerbes der Welt;
– Europäisches Übereinkommen vom 6. Mai 1969 zum Schutz archäologischen Kulturguts.

Schlußklauseln

Artikel 22
(1) Dieses Übereinkommen liegt für die Mitgliedstaaten des Europarats zur Unterzeichnung auf. Es bedarf der Ratifikation, Annahme oder Genehmigung. Die Ratifikations-, Annahme- oder Genehmigungsurkunden werden beim Generalsekretär des Europarats hinterlegt.
(2) Dieses Übereinkommen tritt am ersten Tag des Monats in Kraft, der auf einen Zeitabschnitt von drei Monaten nach dem Tag folgt, an dem drei Mitgliedstaaten des Europarats nach Absatz 1 ihre Zustimmung ausgedrückt haben, durch das Übereinkommen gebunden zu sein.
(3) Für jeden Mitgliedstaat, der später seine Zustimmung ausdrückt, durch das Übereinkommen gebunden zu sein, tritt es am ersten Tag des Monats in Kraft, der auf einen Zeitabschnitt von drei Monaten nach Hinterlegung der Ratifikations-, Annahme- oder Genehmigungsurkunde folgt.

Artikel 23
(1) Nach Inkrafttreten dieses Übereinkommens kann das Ministerkomitee des Europarats durch einen mit der in Artikel 20 Buchstabe d der Satzung des Europarats vorgesehenen Mehrheit und mit einhelliger Zustimmung der Vertreter der Vertragsstaaten, die Anspruch auf einen Sitz im Komitee haben, gefaßten Beschluß jeden Nichtmitgliedstaat des Rates und die Europäische Wirtschaftsgemeinschaft einladen, dem Übereinkommen beizutreten.
(2) Für jeden beitretenden Staat oder, falls sie beitritt, die Europäische Wirtschaftsgemeinschaft tritt das Übereinkommen am ersten Tag des Monats in Kraft, der auf einen Zeitabschnitt von drei Monaten nach Hinterlegung der Beitrittsurkunde beim Generalsekretär des Europarats folgt.

Artikel 24
(1) Jeder Staat kann bei der Unterzeichnung oder bei der Hinterlegung seiner Ratifikations-, Annahme-, Genehmigungs- oder Beitrittsurkunde einzelne oder mehrere Hoheitsgebiete bezeichnen, auf die dieses Übereinkommen Anwendung findet.
(2) Jeder Staat kann jederzeit danach durch eine an den Generalsekretär des Europarats gerichtete Erklärung die Anwendung dieses Übereinkommens auf jedes weitere in der Erklärung bezeichnete Hoheitsgebiet erstrecken. Das Übereinkommen tritt für dieses Hoheitsgebiet am ersten Tag des Monats in Kraft, der auf einen Zeitabschnitt von drei Monaten nach Eingang der Erklärung beim Generalsekretär folgt.
(3) Jede nach den Absätzen 1 und 2 abgegebene Erklärung kann in bezug auf jedes darin bezeichnete Hoheitsgebiet durch eine an den Generalsekretär gerichtete Notifikation zurückgenommen werden.

A.II.5 Granada-Übereinkommen

Die Rücknahme wird am ersten Tag des Monats wirksam, der auf einen Zeitabschnitt von sechs Monaten nach Eingang der Notifikation beim Generalsekretär folgt.

Artikel 25
(1) Jeder Staat kann bei der Unterzeichnung oder bei der Hinterlegung seiner Ratifikations-, Annahme-, Genehmigungs- oder Beitrittsurkunde erklären, daß er sich das Recht vorbehält, die Bestimmungen des Artikels 4 Buchstaben c und d insgesamt oder teilweise nicht einzuhalten. Weitere Vorbehalte sind nicht zulässig.

(2) Jeder Vertragsstaat, der einen Vorbehalt nach Absatz 1 angebracht hat, kann ihn durch eine an den Generalsekretär des Europarats gerichtete Notifikation ganz oder teilweise zurücknehmen. Die Rücknahme wird mit dem Eingang der Notifikation beim Generalsekretär wirksam.

(3) Eine Vertragspartei, die einen Vorbehalt zu der in Absatz 1 genannten Bestimmung angebracht hat, kann nicht verlangen, daß eine andere Vertragspartei diese Bestimmung anwendet; sie kann jedoch, wenn es sich um einen Teilvorbehalt oder einen bedingten Vorbehalt handelt, die Anwendung der betreffenden Bestimmung insoweit verlangen, als sie selbst sie angenommen hat.

Artikel 26
(1) Jede Vertragspartei kann dieses Übereinkommen jederzeit durch eine an den Generalsekretär des Europarats gerichtete Notifikation kündigen.

(2) Die Kündigung wird am ersten Tag des Monats wirksam, der auf einen Zeitabschnitt von sechs Monaten nach Eingang der Notifikation beim Generalsekretär folgt.

Artikel 27
Der Generalsekretär des Europarats notifiziert den Mitgliedstaaten des Europarats, jedem Staat, der diesem Übereinkommen beigetreten ist, und der Europäischen Wirtschaftsgemeinschaft, falls sie beigetreten ist,
a) jede Unterzeichnung;
b) jede Hinterlegung einer Ratifikations-, Annahme-, Genehmigungs- oder Beitrittsurkunde;
c) jeden Zeitpunkt des Inkrafttretens dieses Übereinkommens nach den Artikeln 22, 23 und 24;
d) jede andere Handlung, Notifikation oder Mitteilung im Zusammenhang mit diesem Übereinkommen.

Zu Urkund dessen haben die hierzu gehörig befugten Unterzeichneten dieses Übereinkommen unterschrieben.

Geschehen zu Granada am 3. Oktober 1985 in englischer und französischer Sprache, wobei jeder Wortlaut gleichermaßen verbindlich ist, in einer Urschrift, die im Archiv des Europarats hinterlegt wird. Der Generalsekretär des Europarats übermittelt allen Mitgliedstaaten des Europarats und allen Staaten oder der Europäischen Wirtschaftsgemeinschaft, die zum Beitritt zu diesem Übereinkommen eingeladen werden, beglaubigte Abschriften.

Europäisches Übereinkommen zum Schutz des archäologischen Erbes (revidiert)[1)]

Valletta, 16. Januar 1992 (BGBl. 2002 II S. 2710)
Inkrafttreten: 25. Mai 1995

Präambel

Die Mitgliedstaaten des Europarats und die anderen Staaten, Vertragsparteien des Europäischen Kulturabkommens, die dieses Übereinkommen unterzeichnen –
von der Erwägung geleitet, dass es das Ziel des Europarats ist, eine enge Verbindung zwischen seinen Mitgliedern herbeizuführen, um insbesondere die Ideale und Grundsätze, die ihr gemeinsames Erbe bilden, zu wahren und zu fördern;
im Hinblick auf das am 19. Dezember 1954 in Paris unterzeichnete Europäische Kulturabkommen, insbesondere auf dessen Artikel 1 und 5;
im Hinblick auf das am 3. Oktober 1985 in Granada unterzeichnete Übereinkommen zum Schutz des architektonischen Erbes Europas;
im Hinblick auf das am 23. Juni 1985 in Delphi unterzeichnete Europäische Übereinkommen über Straftaten im Zusammenhang mit Kulturgut;
im Hinblick auf die Empfehlungen der Parlamentarischen Versammlung über Archäologie, insbesondere die Empfehlungen 848 (1978), 921 (1981) und 1072 (1988);
im Hinblick auf die Empfehlung Nr. R (89) 5 betreffend den Schutz und die Förderung des archäologischen Erbes im Rahmen der Städteplanung und Raumordnung;
eingedenk der Tatsache, dass das archäologische Erbe wesentlich zur Kenntnis der Menschheitsgeschichte beiträgt;
in der Erkenntnis, dass das europäische archäologische Erbe, das von der frühesten Geschichte Zeugnis ablegt, durch die wachsende Zahl groß angelegter Planungsvorhaben, natürliche Gefahren, heimliche oder unwissenschaftliche Ausgrabungen und unzulängliches öffentliches Bewusstsein ernsthaft von Zerstörung bedroht ist;
in Bekräftigung der Tatsache, dass es wichtig ist, geeignete verwaltungsmäßige und wissenschaftliche Überwachungsverfahren einzuführen, soweit sie noch nicht vorhanden sind, und dass es notwendig ist, den Schutz des archäologischen Erbes in Städtebau und Raumordnung sowie in der Kulturentwicklungspolitik fest zu verankern;
unter Hinweis darauf, dass die Verantwortung für den Schutz des archäologischen Erbes nicht nur dem unmittelbar betroffenen Staat, sondern allen europäischen Staaten obliegen soll, damit die Gefahr der Zerstörung verringert und die Erhaltung durch Förderung des Austauschs von Sachverständigen und Erfahrungen verbessert wird;
in Anbetracht der Notwendigkeit, infolge der Entwicklung der Planungspolitik in europäischen Ländern die in dem am 6. Mai 1969 in London unterzeichneten Europäischen Übereinkommen zum Schutz archäologischen Kulturguts niedergelegten Grundsätze zu vervollständigen –
sind wie folgt übereingekommen:

Bestimmung des Begriffs archäologisches Erbe

Artikel 1

(1) Ziel dieses (revidierten) Übereinkommens ist es, das archäologische Erbe als Quelle gemeinsamer europäischer Erinnerung und als Instrument für historische und wissenschaftliche Studien zu schützen.
(2) Zu diesem Zweck gelten als Elemente des archäologischen Erbes alle Überreste und Gegenstände sowie alle aus vergangenen Epochen herrührenden sonstigen Spuren des Menschen,
   i) deren Bewahrung und Untersuchung dazu beitragen, die Geschichte des Menschen und seiner Beziehung zur natürlichen Umwelt zurückzuverfolgen;
   ii) für die Ausgrabungen oder Funde und andere Methoden der Erforschung des Menschen und seiner jeweiligen Umwelt als hauptsächliche Informationsquellen dienen;
   iii) die sich in einem beliebigen Gebiet unter der Hoheitsgewalt der Vertragsparteien befinden.

---
1) Liste der Vertragsstaaten: http://conventions.coe.int/treaty/EN/cadreprincipal.htm.

(3) Das archäologische Erbe umfasst Bauwerke, Gebäude, Ensembles, erschlossene Stätten, bewegliche Gegenstände, Denkmäler jeder Art sowie ihre Umgebung, gleichviel ob an Land oder unter Wasser.

Erfassung des Erbes und Schutzmaßnahmen

Artikel 2

Jede Vertragspartei verpflichtet sich, durch die dem betreffenden Staat geeignet erscheinenden Mittel ein Rechtssystem zum Schutz des archäologischen Erbes einzuführen und dabei Folgendes vorzusehen:
i) Sie führt ein Inventar ihres archäologischen Erbes und bezeichnet geschützte Denkmäler und geschütztes Gelände;
ii) sie schafft archäologische Schutzzonen auch dort, wo auf der Erdoberfläche oder unter Wasser keine Überreste sichtbar sind, um die von künftigen Generationen zu untersuchenden Zeugnisse der Vergangenheit zu erhalten;
iii) sie verpflichtet den Entdecker eines zufälligen Fundes von Elementen archäologischen Erbes, den Fund den zuständigen Behörden zu melden, und stellt den Fund zu Untersuchungszwecken zur Verfügung.

Artikel 3

Zur Bewahrung des archäologischen Erbes und um die wissenschaftliche Bedeutung archäologischer Forschungsarbeit zu gewährleisten, verpflichtet sich jede Vertragspartei,
i) Verfahren zur Genehmigung und Überwachung von Ausgrabungen und sonstigen archäologischen Tätigkeiten so anzuwenden,
   a) dass jede unerlaubte Ausgrabung oder Beseitigung von Elementen des archäologischen Erbes verhindert wird,
   b) dass archäologische Ausgrabungen und Erkundungen in wissenschaftlicher Weise und mit der Maßgabe vorgenommen werden,
      – dass soweit möglich zerstörungsfreie Untersuchungsmethoden angewandt werden;
      – dass die Elemente des archäologischen Erbes nicht freigelegt werden oder während oder nach der Ausgrabung freigelegt bleiben, ohne dass für ihre sachgemäße Bewahrung, Erhaltung und Behandlung Vorkehrungen getroffen worden sind;
ii) sicherzustellen, dass Ausgrabungen und andere möglicherweise zerstörende technische Verfahren nur von fachlich geeigneten, besonders ermächtigten Personen durchgeführt werden;
iii) den Einsatz von Metalldetektoren und anderen Suchgeräten oder von Verfahren für archäologische Forschungsarbeiten von einer vorherigen Sondergenehmigung abhängig zu machen, soweit das innerstaatliche Recht des Staates dies vorsieht.

Artikel 4

Jede Vertragspartei verpflichtet sich, Maßnahmen zum physischen Schutz des archäologischen Erbes zu ergreifen, indem sie je nach den Umständen Folgendes vorsieht:
i) Erwerb oder anderweitiger geeigneter Schutz von Gelände seitens der Behörden, das für die Schaffung archäologischer Schutzgebiete vorgesehen ist;
ii) Erhaltung und Pflege des archäologischen Erbes, vornehmlich an Ort und Stelle;
iii) Schaffung geeigneter Aufbewahrungsorte für archäologische Überreste, die von ihrem Ursprungsort entfernt wurden.

Integrierte Erhaltung des archäologischen Erbes

Artikel 5

Jede Vertragspartei verpflichtet sich,
i) danach zu streben, die jeweiligen Erfordernisse der Archäologie und der Erschließungspläne miteinander in Einklang zu bringen und zu verbinden, indem sie dafür Sorge trägt, dass Archäologen beteiligt werden:
   a) an einer Raumordnungspolitik, die auf ausgewogene Strategien zum Schutz, zur Erhaltung und zur Förderung der Stätten von archäologischem Interesse ausgerichtet ist, und
   b) an den verschiedenen Stadien der Erschließungspläne;

ii) für eine systematische Konsultation zwischen Archäologen, Städteplanern und Raumplanern Sorge zu tragen,
   a) damit Erschließungspläne, die sich auf das archäologische Erbe wahrscheinlich nachteilig auswirken, geändert werden können;
   b) damit genügend Zeit und Mittel für eine geeignete wissenschaftliche Untersuchung der Stätte und für die Veröffentlichung der Ergebnisse zur Verfügung gestellt werden können;
iii) sicherzustellen, dass bei Umweltverträglichkeitsprüfungen und den sich daraus ergebenden Entscheiden die archäologischen Stätten und ihr Umfeld in vollem Umfang berücksichtigt werden;
iv) dafür zu sorgen, dass im Zuge von Erschließungsarbeiten gefundene Elemente des archäologischen Erbes soweit praktisch möglich an Ort und Stelle erhalten bleiben;
v) sicherzustellen, dass die Öffnung archäologischer Stätten für die Öffentlichkeit, insbesondere notwendige bauliche Vorkehrungen für die Aufnahme großer Besucherzahlen, den archäologischen und wissenschaftlichen Charakter der Stätten und ihrer Umgebung nicht nachteilig beeinflusst.

Finanzierung der archäologischen Forschung und Erhaltung

Artikel 6
Jede Vertragspartei verpflichtet sich,
i) für die öffentliche finanzielle Unterstützung der archäologischen Forschung durch die gesamtstaatlichen, regionalen und kommunalen Behörden entsprechend der jeweiligen Zuständigkeit zu sorgen;
ii) die materiellen Mittel für archäologische Rettungsmaßnahmen zu erhöhen,
   a) indem sie geeignete Maßnahmen trifft, um sicherzustellen, dass die Deckung der Gesamtkosten etwaiger notwendiger archäologischer Arbeiten im Zusammenhang mit groß angelegten öffentlichen oder privaten Erschließungsvorhaben aus Mitteln der öffentlichen Hand beziehungsweise der Privatwirtschaft vorgesehen ist;
   b) indem sie im Haushalt dieser Vorhaben eine vorausgehende archäologische Untersuchung und Erkundung, eine wissenschaftliche Zusammenfassung sowie die vollständige Veröffentlichung und Aufzeichnung der Funde ebenso vorsieht wie die als Vorsorgemaßnahmen in Bezug auf Umwelt und Regionalplanung erforderlichen Verträglichkeitsprüfungen.

Sammlung und Verbreitung wissenschaftlicher Informationen

Artikel 7
Zur Erleichterung des Studiums und der Verbreitung von Kenntnissen über archäologische Funde verpflichtet sich jede Vertragspartei,
i) Vermessungspläne, Inventare und Karten archäologischer Stätten in dem Gebiet unter ihrer Hoheitsgewalt anzufertigen oder auf den neuesten Stand zu bringen;
ii) alle durchführbaren Maßnahmen zu ergreifen, um nach Abschluss der archäologischen Arbeiten vor der notwendigen vollständigen Veröffentlichung der Spezialuntersuchungen eine zur Veröffentlichung geeignete wissenschaftliche Zusammenfassung zu erwirken.

Artikel 8
Jede Vertragspartei verpflichtet sich,
i) den nationalen und internationalen Austausch von Elementen des archäologischen Erbes für akademisch-wissenschaftliche Zwecke zu erleichtern und gleichzeitig geeignete Schritte zu unternehmen, um zu verhindern, dass der kulturelle und wissenschaftliche Wert dieser Elemente durch die Weitergabe beeinträchtigt wird;
ii) die zentrale Erfassung von Informationen über bereits laufende archäologische Forschungs- und Ausgrabungsarbeiten zu fördern und zur Aufstellung internationaler Forschungsprogramme beizutragen.

A.II.6 Valletta-Übereinkommen

Förderung des öffentlichen Bewusstseins

Artikel 9

Jede Vertragspartei verpflichtet sich,
i) bildungspolitische Maßnahmen mit dem Ziel durchzuführen, in der Öffentlichkeit das Bewusstsein für den Wert des archäologischen Erbes zum Verständnis der Vergangenheit sowie für die Gefahren, die dieses Erbe bedrohen, zu wecken und weiterzuentwickeln,
ii) den öffentlichen Zugang zu wichtigen Elementen ihres archäologischen Erbes, insbesondere Ausgrabungsstätten, zu fördern und die öffentliche Ausstellung ausgewählter archäologischer Gegenstände anzuregen.

Verhinderung der unerlaubten Weitergabe von Elementen des archäologischen Erbes

Artikel 10

Jede Vertragspartei verpflichtet sich,
i) den Informationsaustausch zwischen den zuständigen Behörden und den wissenschaftlichen Einrichtungen über festgestellte Ausgrabungen zu veranlassen;
ii) die zuständigen Stellen des Herkunftsstaats, der Vertragspartei dieses (revidierten) Übereinkommens ist, von jedem angebotenen Gegenstand zu unterrichten, bei dem der Verdacht besteht, dass er aus einer unerlaubten Ausgrabung stammt oder bei einer amtlichen Ausgrabung entwendet wurde, sowie alle notwendigen Einzelheiten darüber zu beschaffen;
iii) die notwendigen Schritte zu unternehmen, um zu verhindern, dass Museen und ähnliche Einrichtungen, deren Ankäufe staatlicher Aufsicht unterstehen, Elemente des archäologischen Erbes erwerben, bei denen der Verdacht besteht, dass sie aus unüberwachten Funden oder unerlaubten Ausgrabungen stammen oder bei amtlichen Ausgrabungen entwendet wurden,
iv) in Bezug auf Museen und ähnliche Einrichtungen, die sich im Hoheitsgebiet einer Vertragspartei befinden, deren Ankäufe jedoch nicht staatlicher Aufsicht unterstehen,
   a) diesen Museen und Einrichtungen den Wortlaut dieses (revidierten) Übereinkommens zu übermitteln;
   b) keine Mühe zu scheuen, um sicherzustellen, dass die genannten Museen und Einrichtungen die in Absatz 3 dargelegten Grundsätze beachten;
v) so weit wie möglich durch bildungspolitische Maßnahmen, Aufklärung, Wachsamkeit und Zusammenarbeit die Übertragung von Elementen des archäologischen Erbes zu unterbinden, die aus unüberwachten Funden oder unerlaubten Ausgrabungen stammen oder bei amtlichen Ausgrabungen entwendet wurden.

Artikel 11

Dieses (revidierte) Übereinkommen greift geltenden oder künftigen zwei- oder mehrseitigen Verträgen zwischen Vertragsparteien über die unerlaubte Weitergabe von Elementen des archäologischen Erbes oder deren Rückgabe an den rechtmäßigen Eigentümer nicht vor.

Gegenseitige technische und wissenschaftliche Hilfe

Artikel 12

Die Vertragsparteien verpflichten sich,
i) einander technische und wissenschaftliche Hilfe zu leisten durch den Austausch von Erfahrungen und Sachverständigen in Angelegenheiten betreffend das archäologische Erbe;
ii) im Rahmen der einschlägigen innerstaatlichen Rechtsvorschriften oder der für sie verbindlichen internationalen Übereinkünfte den Austausch von Fachleuten auf dem Gebiet der Erhaltung des archäologischen Erbes, einschließlich der für Weiterbildung Verantwortlichen, zu fördern.

Überwachung der Anwendung des (revidierten) Übereinkommens

Artikel 13

Für die Zwecke dieses (revidierten) Übereinkommens wird ein vom Ministerkomitee des Europarats nach Artikel 17 der Satzung des Europarats eingesetzter Sachverständigenausschuss die Anwendung des (revidierten) Übereinkommens überwachen und insbesondere

i) dem Ministerkomitee des Europarats regelmäßig über den Stand der in den Vertragsstaaten des (revidierten) Übereinkommens verfolgten Politik zum Schutz des archäologischen Erbes und über die Anwendung der in dem (revidierten) Übereinkommen niedergelegten Grundsätze berichten;
ii) dem Ministerkomitee des Europarats Maßnahmen zur Durchführung des (revidierten) Übereinkommens vorschlagen, darunter auch mehrseitige Tätigkeiten, eine Revision oder Änderung des (revidierten) Übereinkommens und die Information der Öffentlichkeit über den Zweck des (revidierten) Übereinkommens;
iii) dem Ministerkomitee des Europarats Empfehlungen hinsichtlich der Einladung an Nichtmitgliedstaaten des Europarats zum Beitritt zu dem (revidierten) Übereinkommen unterbreiten.

Schlussklauseln

Artikel 14
(1) Dieses (revidierte) Übereinkommen liegt für die Mitgliedstaaten des Europarats und die anderen Staaten, die Vertragsparteien des Europäischen Kulturabkommens sind, zur Unterzeichnung auf. Es bedarf der Ratifikation, Annahme oder Genehmigung. Die Ratifikations-, Annahme- oder Genehmigungsurkunden werden beim Generalsekretär des Europarates hinterlegt.
(2) Ein Staat, der Vertragspartei des am 6. Mai 1969 in London beschlossenen Europäischen Übereinkommens zum Schutz archäologischen Kulturguts ist, kann seine Ratifikations-, Annahme- oder Genehmigungsurkunde nur hinterlegen, wenn er das genannte Übereinkommen bereits gekündigt hat oder gleichzeitig kündigt.
(3) Dieses (revidierte) Übereinkommen tritt sechs Monate nach dem Tag in Kraft, an dem vier Staaten, darunter mindestens drei Mitgliedstaaten des Europarats, nach den Absätzen 1 und 2 ihre Zustimmung ausgedrückt haben, durch das (revidierte) Übereinkommen gebunden zu sein.
(4) Wird im Einzelfall in Anwendung der Absätze 2 und 3 die Kündigung des Übereinkommens vom 6. Mai 1969 nicht gleichzeitig mit dem Inkrafttreten des vorliegenden (revidierten) Übereinkommens wirksam, so kann der Vertragsstaat bei Hinterlegung seiner Ratifikations-, Annahme- oder Genehmigungsurkunde erklären, dass er das Übereinkommen vom 6. Mai 1969 bis zum Inkrafttreten dieses (revidierten) Übereinkommens anwenden wird.
(5) Für jeden Unterzeichnerstaat, der später seine Zustimmung ausdrückt, durch dieses (revidierte) Übereinkommen gebunden zu sein, tritt es sechs Monate nach Hinterlegung der Ratifikations-, Annahme- oder Genehmigungsurkunde in Kraft.

Artikel 15
(1) Nach Inkrafttreten dieses (revidierten) Übereinkommens kann das Ministerkomitee des Europarats durch einen mit der in Artikel 20 Buchstabe d der Satzung des Europarats vorgesehenen Mehrheit und mit einhelliger Zustimmung der Vertreter der Vertragsstaaten, die Anspruch auf einen Sitz im Komitee haben, gefassten Beschluss jeden Staat, der nicht Mitglied des Rates ist, und die Europäische Wirtschaftsgemeinschaft einladen, dem (revidierten) Übereinkommen beizutreten.
(2) Für jeden beitretenden Staat oder für die Europäische Wirtschaftsgemeinschaft, falls sie beitritt, tritt dieses (revidierte) Übereinkommen sechs Monate nach Hinterlegung der Beitrittsurkunde beim Generalsekretär des Europarats in Kraft.

Artikel 16
(1) Jeder Staat kann bei der Unterzeichnung oder bei der Hinterlegung seiner Ratifikations-, Annahme-, Genehmigungs- oder Beitrittsurkunde einzelne oder mehrere Hoheitsgebiete bezeichnen, auf die dieses (revidierte) Übereinkommen Anwendung findet.
(2) Jeder Staat kann jederzeit danach durch eine an den Generalsekretär des Europarats gerichtete Erklärung die Anwendung dieses (revidierten) Übereinkommens auf jedes weitere in der Erklärung bezeichnete Hoheitsgebiet erstrecken. Das (revidierte) Übereinkommen tritt für dieses Hoheitsgebiet sechs Monate nach Eingang der Erklärung beim Generalsekretär in Kraft.
(3) Jede nach den Absätzen 1 und 2 abgegebene Erklärung kann in Bezug auf jedes darin bezeichnete Hoheitsgebiet durch eine an den Generalsekretär gerichtete Notifikation zurückgenommen werden. Die Rücknahme wird sechs Monate nach Eingang der Notifikation beim Generalsekretär wirksam.

A.II.6 Valletta-Übereinkommen

Artikel 17
(1) Jede Vertragspartei kann dieses (revidierte) Übereinkommen jederzeit durch eine an den Generalsekretär des Europarats gerichtete Notifikation kündigen.
(2) Die Kündigung wird sechs Monate nach Eingang der Notifikation beim Generalsekretär wirksam.

Artikel 18
Der Generalsekretär des Europarats notifiziert den Mitgliedstaaten des Europarats, den anderen Staaten, die Vertragsparteien des Europäischen Kulturabkommens sind, sowie jedem Staat und der Europäischen Wirtschaftsgemeinschaft, die diesem Übereinkommen beigetreten sind oder eingeladen wurden, dem (revidierten) Übereinkommen beizutreten,
i) jede Unterzeichnung;
ii) jede Hinterlegung einer Ratifikations-, Annahme-, Genehmigungs- oder Beitrittsurkunde;
iii) jeden Zeitpunkt des Inkrafttretens dieses (revidierten) Übereinkommens nach den Artikeln 14, 15 und 16;
iv) jede andere Handlung, Notifikation oder Mitteilung im Zusammenhang mit diesem (revidierten) Übereinkommen.

Zu Urkund dessen haben die hierzu gehörig befugten Unterzeichneten dieses (revidierte) Übereinkommen unterschrieben.

Geschehen zu Valletta am 16. Januar 1992 in englischer und französischer Sprache, wobei jeder Wortlaut gleichermaßen verbindlich ist, in einer Urschrift, die im Archiv des Europarats hinterlegt wird. Der Generalsekretär des Europarats übermittelt allen Mitgliedstaaten des Europarats, den anderen Staaten, die Vertragsparteien des Europäischen Kulturabkommens sind, sowie allen Nichtmitgliedstaaten oder der Europäischen Wirtschaftsgemeinschaft, die zum Beitritt zu diesem (revidierten) Übereinkommen eingeladen werden, beglaubigte Abschriften.

Internationale Charta zur Konservierung und Restaurierung von Denkmälern und Ensembles

II. Internationaler Kongress der Architekten und Techniker in der Denkmalpflege, Venedig 1964, verabschiedet von ICOMOS 1965

Fundstelle: Internationale Grundsätze und Richtlinien der Denkmalpflege, Monumenta I, ICOMOS Deutschland, Luxemburg, Österreich, Schweiz (Hrsg.), Stuttgart 2012, 47-51

Als lebendige Zeugnisse jahrhundertelanger Traditionen der Völker vermitteln die Denkmäler der Gegenwart eine geistige Botschaft der Vergangenheit. Die Menschheit, die sich der universellen Geltung menschlicher Werte mehr und mehr bewusst wird, sieht in den Denkmälern ein gemeinsames Erbe und fühlt sich kommenden Generationen gegenüber für ihre Bewahrung gemeinsam verantwortlich. Sie hat die Verpflichtung, ihnen die Denkmäler im ganzen Reichtum ihrer Authentizität weiterzugeben.

Es ist daher wesentlich, dass die Grundsätze, die für die Konservierung und Restaurierung der Denkmäler maßgebend sein sollen, gemeinsam erarbeitet und auf internationaler Ebene formuliert werden, wobei jedes Land für die Anwendung im Rahmen seiner Kultur und seiner Tradition verantwortlich ist.

Indem sie diesen Grundprinzipien eine erste Form gab, hat die Charta von Athen von 1931 zur Entwicklung einer breiten internationalen Bewegung beigetragen, die insbesondere in nationalen Dokumenten, in den Aktivitäten von ICOM und UNESCO und in der Gründung des "Internationalen Studienzentrums für die Erhaltung und Restaurierung der Kulturgüter" Gestalt angenommen hat. Wachsendes Bewusstsein und kritische Haltung haben sich immer komplexeren und differenzierteren Problemen zugewandt; so scheint es an der Zeit, die Prinzipien jener Charta zu überprüfen, um sie zu vertiefen und in einem neuen Dokument aufeine breitere Basis zu stellen.

Daher hat der vom 25.–31. Mai 1964 in Venedig versammelte II. Internationale Kongress der Architekten und Techniker der Denkmalpflege den folgenden Text gebilligt:

Definitionen

Artikel 1
Der Denkmalbegriff umfasst sowohl das einzelne Denkmal als auch das städtische oder ländliche Ensemble (Denkmalbereich), das von einer ihm eigentümlichen Kultur, einer bezeichnenden Entwicklung oder einem historischen Ereignis Zeugnis ablegt. Er bezieht sich nicht nur auf große künstlerische Schöpfungen, sondern auch auf bescheidene Werke, die im Lauf der Zeit eine kulturelle Bedeutung bekommen haben.

Artikel 2
Konservierung und Restaurierung der Denkmäler bilden eine Disziplin, welche sich aller Wissenschaften und Techniken bedient, die zur Erforschung und Erhaltung des kulturellen Erbes beitragen können.

Zielsetzung

Artikel 3
Ziel der Konservierung und Restaurierung von Denkmälern ist ebenso die Erhaltung des Kunstwerks wie die Bewahrung des geschichtlichen Zeugnisses.

Konservierung

Artikel 4
Die Erhaltung der Denkmäler erfordert zunächst ihre dauernde Pflege.

A.II.7 Charta von Venedig

Artikel 5
Die Erhaltung der Denkmäler wird immer begünstigt durch eine der Gesellschaft nützliche Funktion. Ein solcher Gebrauch ist daher wünschenswert, darf aber Struktur und Gestalt der Denkmäler nicht verändern. Nur innerhalb dieser Grenzen können durch die Entwicklung gesellschaftlicher Ansprüche und durch Nutzungsänderungen bedingte Eingriffe geplant und bewilligt werden.

Artikel 6
Zur Erhaltung eines Denkmals gehört die Bewahrung eines seinem Maßstab entsprechenden Rahmens, Wenn die überlieferte Umgebung noch vorhanden ist, muss sie erhalten werden, und es verbietet sich jede neue Baumaßnahme, jede Zerstörung, jede Umgestaltung, die das Zusammenwirken von Bauvolumen und Farbigkeit verändern könnte.

Artikel 7
Das Denkmal ist untrennbar mit der Geschichte verbunden, von der es Zeugnis ablegt, sowie mit der Umgebung, zu der es gehört. Demzufolge kann eine Translozierung des ganzen Denkmals oder eines Teiles nur dann geduldet werden, wenn dies zu seinem Schutz unbedingt erforderlich ist oder bedeutende nationale oder internationale Interessen dies rechtfertigen.

Artikel 8
Werke der Bildhauerei, der Malerei oder der dekorativen Ausstattung, die integraler Bestandteil eines Denkmals sind, dürfen von ihm nicht getrennt werden; es sei denn, diese Maßnahme ist die einzige Möglichkeit, deren Erhaltung zu sichern.

Restaurierung

Artikel 9
Die Restaurierung ist eine Maßnahme, die Ausnahmecharakter behalten sollte. Ihr Ziel ist es, die ästhetischen und historischen Werte des Denkmals zu bewahren und zu erschließen. Sie gründet sich auf die Respektierung des überlieferten Bestandes und auf authentische Dokumente. Sie findet dort ihre Grenze, wo die Hypothese beginnt. Wenn es aus ästhetischen oder technischen Gründen notwendig ist, etwas wiederherzustellen, von dem man nicht weiß, wie es ausgesehen hat, wird sich das ergänzende Werk vom baulichen Kontext abheben und den Stempel unserer Zeit tragen. Zu einer Restaurierung gehören vorbereitende und begleitende archäologische, kunst- und geschichtswissenschaftliche Untersuchungen.

Artikel 10
Wenn sich die traditionellen Techniken als unzureichend erweisen, können zur Sicherung eines Denkmals alle modernen Konservierungs- und Konstruktionstechniken herangezogen werden, deren Wirksamkeit wissenschaftlich nachgewiesen und durch praktische Erfahrung erprobt ist.

Artikel 11
Die Beiträge aller Epochen zu einem Denkmal müssen respektiert werden: Stileinheit ist kein Restaurierungsziel. Wenn ein Werk verschiedene sich überlagernde Zustände aufweist, ist eine Aufdeckung verdeckter Zustände nur dann gerechtfertigt, wenn das zu Entfernende von geringer Bedeutung ist, wenn der aufzudeckende Bestand von hervorragendem historischen, wissenschaftlichen oder ästhetischen Wert ist und wenn sein Erhaltungszustand die Maßnahme rechtfertigt. Das Urteil über den Wert der zur Diskussion stehenden Zustände und die Entscheidung darüber, was beseitigt werden darf, dürfen nicht allein von dem für das Projekt Verantwortlichen abhängen.

Artikel 12
Die Elemente, welche fehlende Teile ersetzen sollen, müssen sich dem Ganzen harmonisch einfügen und vom Originalbestand unterscheidbar sein, damit die Restaurierung den Wert des Denkmals als Kunst und Geschichtsdokument nicht verfälscht.

Artikel 13
Hinzufügungen können nur geduldet werden, soweit sie alle interessanten Teile des Denkmals, seinen überlieferten Rahmen, die Ausgewogenheit seiner Komposition und sein Verhältnis zur Umgebung respektieren.

Denkmalstätten

Artikel 14
Denkmalstätten müssen Gegenstand besonderer Sorge sein, um ihre Integrität zu bewahren und zu sichern, dass sie saniert und in angemessener Weise präsentiert werden. Die Erhaltungs- und Restaurierungsarbeiten sind so durchzuführen, dass sie eine sinngemäße Anwendung der Grundsätze der vorstehenden Artikel darstellen.

Ausgrabungen

Artikel 15
Ausgrabungen müssen dem wissenschaftlichen Standard entsprechen und gemäß der UNESCO-Empfehlungen von 1956 durchgeführt werden, welche internationale Grundsätze für archäologische Ausgrabungen formuliert. Erhaltung und Erschließung der Ausgrabungsstätten sowie die notwendigen Maßnahmen zum dauernden Schutz der Architekturelemente und Fundstücke sind zu gewährleisten. Außerdem muss alles getan werden, um das Verständnis für das ausgegrabene Denkmal zu erleichtern, ohne dessen Aussagewert zu verfälschen. Jede Rekonstruktionsarbeit soll von vornherein ausgeschlossen sein; nur die Anastylose kann in Betracht gezogen werden, das heißt, das Wiederzusammensetzen vorhandener, jedoch aus dem Zusammenhang gelöster Bestandteile. Neue Integrationselemente müssen erkennbar sein und sollen sich auf das Minimum beschränken, das zur Erhaltung des Bestandes und zur Wiederherstellung des Formzusammenhanges notwendig ist.

Dokumentation und Publikation

Artikel 16
Alle Arbeiten der Konservierung, Restaurierung und archäologischen Ausgrabungen müssen immer von der Erstellung einer genauen Dokumentation in Form analytischer und kritischer Berichte, Zeichnungen und Photographien begleitet sein. Alle Arbeitsphasen sind hier zu verzeichnen: Freilegung, Bestandssicherung, Wiederherstellung und Integration sowie alle im Zuge der Arbeiten festgestellten technischen und formalen Elemente. Diese Dokumentation ist im Archiv einer öffentlichen Institution zu hinterlegen und der Wissenschaft zugänglich zu machen. Eine Veröffentlichung wird empfohlen. Mitglieder der Redaktionskommission für die Internationale Charta über die Konservierung und Restaurierung von Denkmälern waren:

- Piero Gazzola (Italien), Präsident
- Raymond Lemaire (Belgien), Berichterstatter
- José Bassegoda Nonell (Spanien)
- Luis Benavente (Portugal)
- Djurdje Boscovic (Jugoslawien)
- Hirsoshi Daifuku (UNESCO)
- P. L. de Vrieze (Niederlande)
- Harald Langberg (Dänemark)
- Mario Matteucci (Italien)
- Jean Merlet (Frankreich)
- Carlos Flores Marini (Mexico)
- Roberto Pane (Italien)
- S. C. J. Pavel (Tschechoslowakei)
- Paul Philippot (ICCROM)
- Victor Pimentel (Peru)
- Harold Plenderleith (ICCROM)
- Deoclecio Redig de Campos (Vatikan)
- Jean Sonnier (Frankreich)
- François Sorlin (Frankreich)
- Eustathios Stikas (Griechenland)
- Gertrud Tripp (Österreich)

A.II.7 Charta von Venedig

- Jan Zachwatovicz (Polen)
- Mustafa S. Zbiss (Tunesien)

Deutsche Übersetzung auf der Grundlage des französischen und englischen Originaltextes und vorhandener deutscher Fassungen durch:
- Ernst Bacher (Präsident des ICOMOS Nationalkomitees Österreich)
- Ludwig Deiters (Präsident des ICOMOS Nationalkomitees Deutsche Demokratische Republik)
- Michael Petzet (Präsident des ICOMOS Nationalkomitees Bundesrepublik Deutschland) und
- Alfred Wyss (Vizepräsident des ICOMOS Nationalkomitees Schweiz), Chorin, 14. April 1989

Internationale Charta zur Denkmalpflege in historischen Städten (1987)[1)]

Verabschiedet bei der ICOMOS-Generalkonferenz in Washington, Oktober 1987

Präambel und Definitionen
Alle städtischen Gemeinwesen, die allmählich gewachsenen wie die planmäßig geschaffenen, sind Ausdruck vielfältiger gesellschaftlicher Entwicklungen im Lauf der Geschichte.
Die vorliegende Charta betrifft historische städtische Bereiche, große wie kleine Städte, Stadtkerne oder Stadtteile samt ihrer natürlichen und der vom Menschen geschaffenen Umwelt. Über ihre Rolle als Geschichtszeugnisse hinaus verkörpern sie die Werte traditioneller städtischer Kultur. Doch als Folge der Stadtentwicklung, wie sie die Industrialisierung allenthalben mit sich bringt, sind heute viele dieser Bereiche bedroht, verfallen, beschädigt oder sogar der Zerstörung preisgegeben.
Angesichts dieser dramatischen Situation, die oft zu nicht wieder gutzumachenden kulturellen, sozialen und sogar wirtschaftlichen Verlusten führt, hält es der International Council on Monuments and Sites (ICO-MOS) für notwendig, eine internationale Charta zur Denkmalpflege in historischen Städten abzufassen, welche die „Internationale Charta über die Konservierung und Restaurierung von Denkmälern und Ensembles" (Charta von Venedig, 1964) ergänzen soll. Die neue Charta definiert Grundsätze, Ziele und Methoden zur Denkmalpflege in historischen Städten und städtischen Bereichen. Damit soll auch die Harmonie des individuellen und gemeinschaftlichen Lebens in diesen Bereichen begünstigt und der gesamte kulturelle Besitz, selbst in seinen bescheidensten Formen, als historisches Erbe der Menschheit auf Dauer gesichert werden.
Wie in der UNESCO-Empfehlung zum Schutz historischer Ensembles und zu ihrer Rolle im heutigen Leben (Warschau-Nairobi, 1976) und in verschiedenen anderen internationalen Dokumenten sind unter Denkmalpflege in historischen Städten und städtischen Bereichen jene Maßnahmen zu verstehen, die für deren Schutz, Erhaltung und Restaurierung wie auch deren Entwicklung und harmonische Anpassung an das heutige Leben notwendig sind.

Grundsätze und Ziele
1. Die Denkmalpflege in historischen Städten und städtischen Bereichen muss, um wirksam zu sein, in eine kohärente Politik der wirtschaftlichen und sozialen Entwicklung integriert sein und in der städtischen und regionalen Planung auf allen Ebenen Berücksichtigung finden.
2. Zu den Werten, die es zu bewahren gilt, gehören der historische Charakter der Stadt und alle jene materiellen und geistigen Elemente, in denen sich dieser Charakter ausdrückt, insbesondere:
    a) die Anlage einer Stadt, wie sie durch Parzellen und Straßennetz bestimmt ist;
    b) die Beziehungen zwischen Bauwerken, Grünflächen und Freiflächen;
    c) die innere und äußere Erscheinungsform von Bauwerken, wie sie durch Struktur und Stil, Maßstab und Volumen, Konstruktion und Materialien, Farbe und Dekor gegeben ist;
    d) die Beziehungen zwischen der Stadt oder dem städtischen Bereich und der natürlichen und vom Menschen geschaffenen Umgebung;
    e) die verschiedenen Funktionen, die die Stadt oder der städtische Bereich im Lauf der Zeit übernommen hat.
    Jede Bedrohung dieser Werte stellt eine Gefahr für die Authentizität der historischen Stadt oder des städtischen Bereichs dar.
3. Teilnahme und Einbeziehung der Bewohner sind wesentlich für eine erfolgreiche Stadterhaltung und sollten gefördert werden. Man sollte nie vergessen, dass die Bewahrung historischer Städte und städtischer Bereiche in erster Linie deren Bewohner betrifft.
4. Die Denkmalpflegemaßnahmen in einer historischen Stadt oder einem städtischen Bereich erfordern reifliche Überlegung, Methodik und Fachwissen. Dabei sollte jeder Dogmatismus vermieden werden, weil im Einzelfall spezifische Probleme zu berücksichtigen sind.

---
1) Quelle: http://www.dnk.de/International/n2370.

A.II.8 Charta von Washington

Methoden und Mittel

5. Die Planung für die Erhaltung historischer Städte und städtischer Bereiche soll in multidisziplinärer Zusammenarbeit vorbereitet werden. Dabei muss unter Berücksichtigung aller relevanten Faktoren wie Archäologie, Geschichte, Architektur, Technik, Soziologie und Wirtschaft von einer Analyse der Gegebenheiten ausgegangen werden. Die Hauptziele der Erhaltungsplanung sollten ebenso klar definiert werden wie die gesetzlichen, administrativen und finanziellen Mittel, die zu ihrer Verwirklichung notwendig sind. Die Erhaltungsplanung sollte um ein ausgewogenes Verhältnis zwischen den historischen Stadtbereichen und der Stadt als Ganzes bemüht sein. Sie sollte Gebäude und Gebäudegruppen nennen, die zu erhalten oder unter bestimmten Bedingungen zu erhalten sind, unter Umständen auch Gebäude, auf die man im Ausnahmefall verzichten könnte. Vor jeglichem Eingriff muss der Vorzustand genauestens dokumentiert werden. Die Erhaltungsplanung sollte von den Stadtbewohnern mitgetragen werden.
6. Unabhängig vom Stand einer Erhaltungsplanung sind alle notwendigen denkmalpflegerischen Maßnahmen gemäß den Grundsätzen und Zielen der vorliegenden Charta und der Charta von Venedig durchzuführen.
7. Die laufende Instandhaltung ist eine entscheidende Voraussetzung für die Bewahrung historischer Städte und städtischer Bereiche.
8. Neue Funktionen und Aktivitäten sowie die Einrichtung einer zum heutigen Leben gehörenden Infrastruktur müssen mit dem Charakter der historischen Stadt oder des städtischen Bereichs vereinbar sein.
9. Die Verbesserung der Wohnverhältnisse sollte zu den grundlegenden Zielen der Stadterhaltung gehören.
10. Falls es notwendig sein sollte, Gebäude neu zu errichten oder umzubauen, muss die bestehende räumliche Struktur, besonders Parzellenteilung und Maßstab, respektiert werden. Zeitgenössische Elemente können eine Bereicherung sein, soweit sie sich in das Ensemble einfügen.
11. Das Verständnis der Vergangenheit der historischen Städte sollte durch archäologische Untersuchungen und eine angemessene Präsentation der Ergebnisse der Stadtarchäologie vertieft werden.
12. Der Fahrzeugverkehr innerhalb einer historischen Stadt oder eines historischen Bereichs muss eingeschränkt werden; Areale zum Parken sind so anzulegen, dass sie weder ihre Umgebung noch die Stadtstruktur beeinträchtigen.
13. Das in der Stadt- oder Regionalplanung vorgesehene Netz von Hauptverkehrsstraßen sollte die Zugangsmöglichkeiten verbessern, ohne in die historische Stadt einzugreifen.
14. Vorsorgliche Maßnahmen zum Schutz der historischen Städte gegen Naturkatastrophen und Umweltschäden (Luftverschmutzung, Erschütterungen u. a.) müssen ebenso im Interesse der Sicherheit und des Wohlbefindens der Bewohner wie zur Bewahrung des historischen Erbes getroffen werden. Vorsorgliche Maßnahmen beziehungsweise Reparaturmaßnahmen müssen unabhängig von der Natur drohender oder bereits eingetretener Katastrophen und Schäden dem besonderen Charakter der betroffenen Kulturgüter angepasst sein.
15. Teilnahme und Einbeziehung der Stadtbewohner sollen durch ein allgemeines Informationsprogramm, das bereits in der Schule einsetzt, gefördert und die Aktivitäten von Vereinigungen für Heimat- und Denkmalschutz ermutigt werden. Es sind Maßnahmen zur ausreichenden Finanzierung der Denkmalpflege zu beschließen.
16. Für alle an Denkmalpflege und Stadterhaltung beteiligten Berufe sollte die Möglichkeit einer speziellen fachlichen Ausbildung vorgesehen werden.

Deutsche Übersetzung auf der Grundlage des englischen und französischen Originaltextes durch Ernst Bacher (Präsident des ICOMOS Nationalkomitees Österreich), Ludwig Deiters (Präsident des ICOMOS Nationalkomitees Deutsche Demokratische Republik), Michael Petzet (Präsident des ICOMOS Nationalkomitees Bundesrepublik Deutschland) und Alfred Wyss (Vizepräsident des ICOMOS Nationalkomitees Schweiz), Basel, 3. November 1989.

Charta für den Schutz und die Pflege des archäologischen Erbes (1990)[1)]

Vom International Committee for the Management of Archaeological Heritage (ICAHM) erarbeitet und 1990 von der 9. ICOMOS-Generalversammlung in Lausanne beschlossen

Präambel
Das Wissen um Ursprung und Entwicklung der menschlichen Gesellschaften ist nach allgemeiner Auffassung von wesentlicher Bedeutung für die Menschheit auf der Suche nach ihren kulturellen und gesellschaftlichen Wurzeln.
Das archäologische Erbe stellt das grundlegende Zeugnis menschlicher Tätigkeiten in der Vergangenheit dar. Sein Schutz und seine sachgemäße Pflege sind daher notwendig, um Archäologen und andere Wissenschaftler in die Lage zu versetzen, es zum Nutzen gegenwärtiger und künftiger Generationen zu erforschen und zu interpretieren.
Zum Schutz dieses Erbes sind nicht allein archäologische Techniken gefordert, sondern auch eine breitere Basis an fachlichen und wissenschaftlichen Kenntnissen und Fertigkeiten. Es gibt Elemente des archäologischen Erbes, die Bestandteile von Architektur sind. Für deren Schutz gelten die Kriterien, wie sie 1964 in der Charta von Venedig über die Konservierung und Restaurierung von Denkmälern und Ensembles festgelegt wurden. Andere Elemente des archäologischen Erbes sind Teil der lebendigen Traditionen autochthoner Völker. Für Schutz und Erhaltung solcher historischer Stätten und Denkmäler ist die Teilnahme lokaler Volksgruppen von Bedeutung.
Aus diesen und anderen Gründen muss der Schutz des archäologischen Erbes auf der engen Zusammenarbeit von Fachleuten aus einer Reihe unterschiedlicher Disziplinen beruhen. Erforderlich ist auch die Mitarbeit von staatlichen Stellen, Wissenschaftlern, privaten oder öffentlichen Unternehmen sowie der allgemeinen Öffentlichkeit. In der vorliegenden Charta sind daher Grundsätze zu den verschiedenen Aspekten des Umgangs mit dem archäologischen Erbe festgehalten. Dazu gehört die Verantwortung von Behörden und Gesetzgebern, Grundsätze für die fachgerechte Durchführung von Inventarisation, Prospektion, Ausgrabung, Dokumentation, Forschung, Erhaltung, Instandhaltung, Konservierung, Rekonstruktion, Information und Präsentation, für die öffentliche Zugänglichkeit und Nutzung des archäologischen Erbes sowie für die erforderliche Qualifikation der mit dem Schutz dieses Erbes befassten Fachleute.
Die Charta wurde angeregt durch den Erfolg der in der Charta von Venedig verkörperten Ideen in Verwaltung und Politik, Wissenschaft und Praxis.
Die Charta soll grundlegende Prinzipien und Richtlinien von weltweiter Geltung enthalten. Sie kann daher die speziellen Probleme und Möglichkeiten einzelner Regionen oder Länder nicht berücksichtigen. Deshalb soll sie auf regionaler und nationaler Ebene durch weitere Grundsätze und Richtlinien ergänzt werden.

Artikel 1 – Begriffsbestimmung
Das „archäologische Erbe" ist jener Teil des materiellen Erbes, über den archäologische Methoden grundlegende Erkenntnisse liefern. Es umfasst alle Spuren menschlicher Existenz und besteht aus Stätten, an denen sich menschliche Tätigkeiten manifestieren, verlassenen Baustrukturen, Befunden und Überresten aller Art über und unter der Erde sowie unter Wasser und den damit verbundenen beweglichen kulturellen Hinterlassenschaften.

Artikel 2 – Integrierter Schutz
Das archäologische Erbe ist ein empfindliches und nicht erneuerbares Kulturgut. Die Nutzung des Bodens muss daher einer Kontrolle unterliegen und so gesteuert werden, dass möglichst keine Zerstörung des archäologischen Erbes eintritt.
Maßnahmen zum Schutz des archäologischen Erbes sollen integrierter Bestandteil aller Planungen zur Erschließung und Nutzung des Bodens sowie der Kultur-, Umwelt- und Bildungspolitik sein. Die Politik zum Schutz des archäologischen Erbes soll ständig überprüft werden, damit sie auf dem neuesten Stand bleibt. Die Schaffung archäologischer Schutzzonen (Reservate) soll Teil dieser Politik sein.

---

1) Quelle: https://www.bak.admin.ch/bak/de/home/kulturerbe/heimatschutz-und-denkmalpflege/grundlagen/bundesgesetzgebung--internationale-konventionen-und-charten.html.

A.II.9 Charta von Lausanne

Der Schutz des archäologischen Erbes soll auf internationaler, nationaler, regionaler und lokaler Ebene in die Planungspolitik integriert werden.

Die aktive Teilnahme der breiten Öffentlichkeit muss Teil der Politik zum Schutz des archäologischen Erbes sein. Dies ist wichtig, wenn es um das Erbe der autochthonen Völker geht. Eine Mitwirkung ist ohne Zugang zu dem für die Entscheidungsfindung erforderlichen Wissen nicht möglich. Öffentlichkeitsinformation ist daher wesentliches Element eines integrierten archäologischen Denkmalschutzes.

Artikel 3 – Gesetzgebung

Der Schutz des archäologischen Erbes ist als moralische Verpflichtung aller Menschen und als ein gemeinsamer öffentlicher Auftrag zu betrachten. Diese Verpflichtung muss erfüllt werden durch eine entsprechende Gesetzgebung sowie durch die Bereitstellung ausreichender finanzieller Mittel für eine effektive archäologische Denkmalpflege.

Das archäologische Erbe gehört der ganzen Menschheit. Es ist daher die Pflicht eines jeden Landes, die Bereitstellung der erforderlichen finanziellen Mittel zum Schutz dieses Erbes zu gewährleisten.

Die Gesetzgebung soll dem archäologischen Erbe einen Schutz bieten, der die Gegebenheiten, die Geschichte und die Traditionen eines jeden Landes und jeder Region berücksichtigt, die Erhaltung in situ sicherstellt sowie den Bedürfnissen der Forschung entgegenkommt.

Die Gesetzgebung soll vom Konzept des archäologischen Erbes als Erbe der ganzen Menschheit und Erbe von Bevölkerungsgruppen ausgehen und darf nicht auf Einzelpersonen oder Nationen zugeschnitten sein.

Die Gesetzgebung soll Zerstörung, Beeinträchtigung oder Veränderung durch Eingriffe in archäologische Stätten und Denkmäler oder deren Umgebung verbieten, wenn sie ohne Zustimmung der zuständigen archäologischen Behörden erfolgen.

Die Gesetzgebung soll in all jenen Fällen, in denen die Zerstörung eines Denkmals genehmigt wird, eine vollständige archäologische Untersuchung und Dokumentation verlangen.

Die Gesetzgebung soll eine angemessene Instandhaltung, Pflege und Erhaltung des archäologischen Erbes vorsehen und fordern.

Für Verstöße gegen die Gesetze zum Schutz des archäologischen Erbes müssen entsprechende gesetzliche Sanktionen vorgesehen sein.

Schützt die Gesetzgebung nur jene Elemente des archäologischen Erbes, die als Auswahl in ein Verzeichnis oder ein amtliches Inventar aufgenommen worden sind, muss Vorsorge für einen vorläufigen Schutz von ungeschützten oder neu entdeckten Stätten und Denkmälern getroffen werden, bis eine archäologische Begutachtung erstellt ist.

Erschließungs- und Bauvorhaben sind eine der größten Bedrohungen für das archäologische Erbe. Die entsprechenden Gesetze sollen daher die Maßnahmenträger verpflichten, schon im Planungsstadium Verträglichkeitsstudien hinsichtlich des archäologischen Erbes zu erstellen, mit der Bedingung, dass die Kosten dieser Studien Bestandteil der Projektkosten sind. Es soll auch der Grundsatz gesetzlich verankert werden, Bauvorhaben so zu planen, dass Auswirkungen auf das archäologische Erbe möglichst vermieden werden.

Artikel 4 – Bestandsaufnahme

Der archäologische Denkmalschutz muss auf möglichst vollständigen Kenntnissen über Umfang und Beschaffenheit beruhen. Eine umfassende Bestandsaufnahme der archäologischen Quellen ist daher ein wesentliches Arbeitsinstrument bei der Entwicklung von Strategien zum Schutz des archäologischen Erbes. Aus diesem Grund ist die Aufnahme des archäologischen Bestands im Rahmen von Denkmalschutz und Denkmalpflege eine grundlegende Verpflichtung.

Gleichzeitig sind Inventare die wichtigsten Unterlagen für wissenschaftliche Studien und Forschung. Die Erstellung von Inventaren ist daher als andauernder dynamischer Prozess zu betrachten. Daraus folgt, dass Inventare Informationen von unterschiedlicher Wichtigkeit und Verlässlichkeit enthalten können; auch lückenhaftes Wissen kann als Ausgangspunkt für Schutzmaßnahmen dienen.

Artikel 5 – Archäologische Untersuchungen

Archäologisches Wissen basiert vor allem auf wissenschaftlichen Untersuchungen des archäologischen Erbes. Solche Untersuchungen umfassen alle anwendbaren Methoden, von zerstörungsfreien Techniken über Sondierungen bis zur vollständigen Ausgrabung.

Als Grundprinzip muss gelten, dass bei der Sammlung von Informationen über das archäologische Erbe nicht mehr archäologische Zeugnisse zerstört werden dürfen, als dies für die Erreichung der angestrebten konservatorischen oder wissenschaftlichen Zielsetzungen der Untersuchung erforderlich ist. Zerstörungsfreie Techniken wie Prospektion aus der Luft oder im Gelände und Sondierungen sollten in allen Fällen ermutigt werden und sind der vollständigen Ausgrabung vorzuziehen.
Ausgrabungen sind immer mit der Notwendigkeit verbunden, unter den zu dokumentierenden und zu bewahrenden Zeugnissen eine Auswahl zu treffen, und zwar unter Inkaufnahme des Verlusts weiterer Informationen, womöglich sogar der totalen Zerstörung des Denkmals oder der archäologischen Stätte. Die Entscheidung, eine Ausgrabung zu unternehmen, darf daher nur nach gründlicher Überlegung getroffen werden.
An archäologischen Stätten und Denkmälern, die von Erschließungs- und Bauvorhaben, Nutzungsänderung, Plünderung oder natürlichem Verfall bedroht sind, müssen Ausgrabungen vorgenommen werden.
In Ausnahmefällen können an nicht bedrohten archäologischen Stätten Ausgrabungen durchgeführt werden, um wissenschaftliche Fragen zu klären oder eine verbesserte Präsentation für die Öffentlichkeit zu erzielen. In diesen Fällen muss der Ausgrabung eine gründliche wissenschaftliche Bewertung der archäologischen Stätte vorausgehen. Die Ausgrabung soll nur einen Teil der Stätte betreffen und einen anderen Teil für zukünftige Untersuchungen unberührt lassen.
Der Wissenschaft soll ein dem Stand der Forschung angemessener Bericht zur Verfügung stehen, der innerhalb einer angemessenen Frist nach Abschluss der Grabungsarbeiten in Verbindung mit dem entsprechenden Inventar veröffentlicht werden soll.
Ausgrabungen sollen in Übereinstimmung mit den Grundsätzen der UNESCO-Empfehlungen von 1956 (Empfehlung zur Festlegung internationaler Prinzipien bei archäologischen Ausgrabungen) und gemäß den anerkannten internationalen und nationalen fachlichen Maßstäben durchgeführt werden.

Artikel 6 – Erhaltung und Konservierung
Die grundlegende Zielsetzung bei der Pflege des archäologischen Erbes muss die Erhaltung von Denkmälern und archäologischen Stätten in situ (an Ort und Stelle) sein, und zwar einschließlich ihrer langfristig gesicherten Konservierung und der Sorge für alle dazugehörenden Aufzeichnungen, Sammlungen usw. Jede Übertragung von Elementen des archäologischen Erbes an einen anderen Ort verletzt den Grundsatz, nach dem das Erbe in seinem ursprünglichen Kontext zu erhalten ist. Dieser Grundsatz unterstreicht die Notwendigkeit von Erhaltung, Sicherung und Konservierung in angemessener Form. Daraus folgt auch das Prinzip, dass das archäologische Erbe weder freigelegt noch nach Abschluss der Grabung im freigelegten Zustand belassen werden soll, wenn seine angemessene Erhaltung und Pflege nicht gewährleistet ist.
Engagement und Teilnahme der örtlichen Bevölkerung müssen ermutigt werden, weil auf diese Weise die Erhaltung des archäologischen Erbes gefördert werden kann. Dieser Grundsatz ist vor allem dann wichtig, wenn es sich um das archäologische Erbe einer autochthonen Bevölkerung oder lokaler Bevölkerungsgruppen handelt. In manchen Fällen kann es ratsam sein, diesen die Verantwortung für Schutz und Pflege von archäologischen Stätten und Denkmälern zu übertragen.
Angesichts der unvermeidlichen Begrenztheit der verfügbaren Mittel werden sich Aktivitäten der archäologischen Denkmalpflege auf eine Auswahl beschränken. Diese Auswahl sollte aufgrund einer wissenschaftlichen Einschätzung der Bedeutung und des repräsentativen Charakters typische Beispiele aus der Vielfalt der archäologischen Stätten und Denkmäler betreffen, nicht nur bemerkenswerte und spektakuläre Denkmäler.
Die entsprechenden Grundsätze der UNESCO-Empfehlungen von 1956 sollen bei Erhaltung und Konservierung des archäologischen Erbes angewandt werden.

Artikel 7 – Präsentation, Information, Rekonstruktion
Die Präsentation des archäologischen Erbes für die allgemeine Öffentlichkeit ist ein wesentliches Mittel zur Förderung des Verständnisses für Ursprung und Entwicklung der modernen Gesellschaften. Zugleich ist sie das wichtigste Mittel, um begreiflich zu machen, dass das archäologische Erbe geschützt werden muss.

A.II.9 Charta von Lausanne

Präsentation und Information sollen als eine allgemein verständliche Darstellung auf dem jeweiligen Wissensstand aufgefasst werden und bedürfen daher ständiger Aktualisierung. Sie sollen die vielfältigen Möglichkeiten nützen, um Geschichtsverständnis zu wecken.

Rekonstruktionen können zwei wichtige Funktionen erfüllen: experimentelle Forschung und Interpretation. Sie sollten jedoch mit großer Vorsicht ausgeführt werden, um jede Störung vorhandener archäologischer Befunde zu vermeiden. Um größtmögliche Authentizität zu erreichen, sind Zeugnisse und Quellen aller Art heranzuziehen. Wo es möglich und angemessen ist, sollen Rekonstruktionen nicht unmittelbar auf den archäologischen Überresten errichtet werden, und sie müssen als Rekonstruktionen erkennbar sein.

Artikel 8 – Fachliche Qualifikation

Für die Pflege des archäologischen Erbes ist ein hohes wissenschaftliches Niveau in den verschiedenen Disziplinen unumgänglich. Die Ausbildung einer entsprechenden Zahl qualifizierter Fachleute in den betreffenden Fachgebieten ist daher ein wichtiges Ziel der Bildungspolitik jedes Landes. Das notwendige Fachwissen in gewissen hoch spezialisierten Bereichen verlangt internationale Zusammenarbeit. Standards für Berufsausbildung und Berufsethik müssen festgelegt und aufrechterhalten werden.

Die Ausbildung zum Archäologen auf Universitätsebene soll dem inzwischen eingetretenen Wandel in der Politik archäologischer Denkmalpflege Rechnung tragen, wonach die Erhaltung in situ der Ausgrabung vorzuziehen ist. Sie sollte auch berücksichtigen, dass das Studium der Geschichte der einheimischen Völker für Schutz und Verständnis des archäologischen Erbes ebenso wichtig ist wie das Studium herausragender Denkmäler und archäologischer Stätten.

Der Schutz des archäologischen Erbes ist ein andauernder dynamischer Prozess. Deshalb soll den in diesem Bereich tätigen Fachleuten Gelegenheit gegeben werden, ihr Wissen auf den neuesten Stand zu bringen. Im Rahmen der Postgraduierten-Ausbildung sollte ein Schwerpunkt auf Schutz und Pflege des archäologischen Erbes gelegt werden.

Artikel 9 – Internationale Zusammenarbeit

Das archäologische Erbe ist gemeinsames Erbe der ganzen Menschheit. Bei der Entwicklung und Aufrechterhaltung von Standards für den Umgang mit diesem Erbe kommt es daher wesentlich auf internationale Zusammenarbeit an.

Es ist dringlich, Möglichkeiten für den Austausch von Informationen und Erfahrungen unter den Fachleuten auf dem Gebiet der archäologischen Denkmalpflege zu schaffen. Dies erfordert die Organisation von Konferenzen, Seminaren, Arbeitsgruppen usw. auf weltweiter und regionaler Ebene sowie die Einrichtung von regionalen Zentren für Postgraduierten-Studien. Der Internationale Rat für Denkmalpflege (ICOMOS) sollte in seinen zuständigen Arbeitsgruppen diesem Aspekt in seiner mittel- und langfristigen Planung Rechnung tragen.

Der internationale Austausch von Fachleuten soll zur Hebung der Maßstäbe im Umgang mit dem archäologischen Erbe gefördert werden.

Technische Hilfsprogramme im Bereich der archäologischen Denkmalpflege sollten unter der Schirmherrschaft von ICOMOS abgewickelt werden.

Die vorliegende deutsche Übersetzung auf der Grundlage des englischen Originaltextes besorgten Christa Farke, Erwin Keller, Michael Petzet und Alfred Wyss für das Deutsche, Österreichische und Schweizerische Nationalkomitee von ICOMOS; München, 3. Dezember 1991.

Charta zu Schutz und Pflege des Unterwasser-Kulturerbes (1996)[1)]

Verabschiedet durch die 11. Generalversammlung von ICOMOS in Sofia, Oktober 1996

Einleitung

Diese Charta soll zu Schutz und Pflege des unter Wasser befindlichen Kulturerbes in Binnen- und Küstengewässern, im flachen offenen Meer und in den Tiefen des Ozeans ermutigen. Sie behandelt seine besonderen Eigenschaften und Umstände und sollte als Ergänzung zur ICOMOS-Charta für Schutz und Pflege des archäologischen Erbes von 1990 verstanden werden. Die Charta von 1990 definiert „archäologisches Erbe" als denjenigen Teil des materiellen Kulturerbes, über den archäologische Methoden grundlegende Erkenntnisse liefern; es umfasst alle Spuren menschlicher Aktivitäten und besteht aus Stätten, an denen sich menschliche Tätigkeiten manifestieren, wie verlassene Strukturen, Überreste und Befunde aller Art sowie die damit in Zusammenhang stehenden beweglichen kulturellen Hinterlassenschaften. Im Rahmen der vorliegenden Charta versteht sich das Unterwasser-Kulturerbe als dasjenige archäologische Erbe, das sich unter Wasser befindet oder aus dem Wasser geborgen wurde. Es umfasst versunkene Fundstätten und Strukturen, Fundstellen von Schiffswracks und aus dem Verband gelöste Teile sowie deren archäologischen und natürlichen Kontext.

Seinem Charakter entsprechend ist das Unterwasser-Kulturerbe eine internationale Ressource. Ein großer Teil des Unterwasser-Kulturerbes befindet sich in internationalen Gewässern und hat seinen Ursprung im internationalen Handel und Austausch, bei dem Schiffe und ihre Ladungen in weiter Ferne von Heimat- und Zielhafen untergegangen sind.

Archäologie ist in den Umweltschutz eingebunden; in der Sprache des Ressourcenmanagements bedeutet dies: Das Unterwasser-Kulturerbe ist endlich und nicht erneuerbar. Wenn das Unterwasser-Kulturerbe in Zukunft zur Wertschätzung unserer Umwelt beitragen soll, dann haben wir jetzt und heute individuelle und kollektive Verantwortung für seinen anhaltenden Fortbestand zu übernehmen.

Archäologie ist eine Sache der Öffentlichkeit. Jeder hat das Recht, aus der Quelle der Vergangenheit zu schöpfen, um sein Leben zu bereichern, und jeder Versuch, die Kenntnis der Vergangenheit zu schmälern, beschneidet die Autonomie und Selbstentfaltung des Einzelnen. Das Unterwasser-Kulturerbe trägt zur Bildung von Identität bei und kann für den Gemeinschaftssinn der Menschen wichtig sein. Behutsam verwaltet, kann Unterwasser-Kulturerbe in der Entwicklung von Freizeitgestaltung und Tourismus eine positive Rolle spielen.

Archäologie wird durch Forschung getragen; sie vermehrt die Kenntnisse über die Vielfalt menschlicher Kultur über Jahrtausende und eröffnet neue Perspektiven des Lebens in der Vergangenheit. Diese Kenntnisse und Vorstellungen tragen dazu bei, das heutige Leben zu verstehen und Herausforderungen der Zukunft zu begegnen.

Viele Tätigkeiten unter Wasser, die an sich nutzbringend und erwünscht sein mögen, können für das Unterwasser-Kulturerbe unglückliche Konsequenzen haben, wenn ihre Auswirkungen nicht berücksichtigt werden.

Das Unterwasser-Kulturerbe kann durch Bautätigkeit gefährdet werden, die Ufer und Meeresboden oder Strömungen, Ablagerungen und Verunreinigungen verändern. Das Unterwasser-Kulturerbe kann auch von unbedachter Ausbeutung lebender und toter Ressourcen bedroht werden. Ebenso können ungeeignete Formen des Zugangs und die ständig steigende Zahl der vom Fundort entfernten „Souvenirs" verheerende Folgen haben.

Viele dieser Gefahren können beseitigt oder merklich vermindert werden, wenn Archäologen um Rat gefragt und Maßnahmen zur Schadenbegrenzung ergriffen werden. Die vorliegende Charta soll zu einem hohen Standard der archäologischen Expertisen beitragen, um solchen Gefahren für das Unterwasser-Kulturerbe rasch und wirksam entgegenzutreten.

Das Unterwasser-Kulturerbe ist auch durch Tätigkeiten bedroht, die gänzlich unerwünscht sind, da sie einigen Wenigen auf Kosten Vieler Profit bringen. Kommerzielle Ausbeutung des Unterwasser-Kulturerbes zu Handels- und Spekulationszwecken ist grundsätzlich nicht vereinbar mit dessen Schutz und Management. Die vorliegende Charta will sicherstellen, dass alle Untersuchungen bezüglich Ziel-

---

1) Quelle: https://www.unesco.de/sites/default/files/2018-03/2001_%C3%9Cbereinkommen %C3%BCber_%20den_Schutz_des_Unterwasser_0.pdf.

A.II.10 Charta Unterwasser-Kulturerbe

setzung, Methodik und zu erwartender Ergebnisse deutlich formuliert sind, sodass die Absicht jedes Projekts für jedermann transparent wird.

Artikel 1 – Grundprinzipien

Die Erhaltung von Unterwasser-Kulturgut ‚in situ' ist vorrangig. Der öffentliche Zugang soll gefördert werden.

Zerstörungsfreie Untersuchungstechniken, störungsfreie Bestandsaufnahmen und die Entnahme von Proben sind der Ausgrabung vorzuziehen.

Untersuchungen dürfen das Unterwasser-Kulturerbe nicht weiter beeinträchtigen, als es Schutzmaßnahmen oder Forschungsziele des Projekts erfordern.

Untersuchungen dürfen menschliche Überreste und Kultstätten nicht unnötig stören. Untersuchungen müssen von angemessener Dokumentation begleitet werden.

Artikel 2 – Projektdesign

Vor jeder Untersuchung ist ein Projekt auszuarbeiten, das folgende Programmpunkte festlegt:
- Schutz- oder Forschungsziele,
- anzuwendende Methoden und einzusetzende Techniken,
- Finanzierungsplan,
- Zeitplan bis zum Abschluss des Projektes,
- Zusammensetzung, Qualifikation, Verantwortung und Erfahrung des Forschungsteams,
- Konservierung des Fundmaterials,
- Management und Instandhaltung der archäologischen Stätte,
- Übereinkünfte über Zusammenarbeit mit Museen und anderen Institutionen,
- die Dokumentation,
- Gesundheit und Sicherheit,
- Verfassen des Berichts,
- Archivierung der Dokumentation und Aufbewahrung der während der Untersuchung geborgenen Unterwasser-Kulturgüter,
- Vorlage der Forschungsergebnisse, einschließlich der Vermittlung an die Öffentlichkeit.

Das Programm sollte je nach Umständen revidiert und modifiziert werden. Die archäologischen Untersuchungen müssen entsprechend dem Programm in Übereinstimmung mit dem Projektdesign durchgeführt werden. Das Programm sollte der archäologischen Fachwelt zugänglich sein.

Artikel 3 – Finanzierung

Eine angemessene Finanzierung muss vor Beginn der Untersuchung gesichert sein, damit alle Phasen des Programms, einschließlich der Konservierung, der Vorbereitung des Berichts und der Vermittlung der Forschungsergebnisse realisiert werden. Das Programm soll Pläne enthalten, die notfalls die Konservierung des Unterwasser-Kulturguts und die zugehörige Dokumentation sicherstellen, wenn vorgesehene Finanzierungen ausfallen.

Die Finanzierung des Projekts darf nicht auf dem Verkauf von Unterwasser-Kulturgut oder anderen Strategien beruhen, die Unterwasser-Kulturgut und zugehörige Dokumentationen unwiederbringlich zerstreuen.

Artikel 4 – Zeitplan

Vor Beginn der archäologischen Untersuchung muss die notwendige Zeit gesichert sein, um alle Phasen des Programms, einschließlich Konservierung, Vorbereitung des Berichts und Verbreitung der Forschungsergebnisse abzuschließen. Das Programm sollte Ersatzlösungen vorsehen, um die Konservierung des Unterwasser-Kulturguts und die zugehörige Dokumentation sicherzustellen, wenn der vorgesehene Zeitplan Unterbrechungen erfährt.

Artikel 5 – Forschungsziele, Methoden und Techniken

Forschungsziele sowie Einzelheiten der anzuwendenden Methoden und Techniken müssen im Programm festgelegt werden. Die Methoden sollten im Einklang mit den Forschungszielen stehen und die angewandten Techniken sollten so zerstörungsfrei wie möglich sein.

Nach der Feldforschung müssen unabdingbar die Analyse der Funde und Auswertung der Befunde erfolgen; entsprechende Planungen der Auswertungsarbeiten sind im Programm vorzusehen.

Artikel 6 – Qualifikation, Verantwortung und Erfahrungsschatz
Alle Mitarbeiter des Forschungsteams müssen für ihre Aufgabe hinreichend qualifiziert und erfahren sein. Sie müssen über ihre Aufgabe gut instruiert werden und ihre Arbeit verstehen.
Jeder untersuchende Eingriff in Unterwasser-Kulturgut soll unter Leitung und Kontrolle eines namhaften Unterwasser-Archäologen durchgeführt werden, der über anerkannte Qualifikationen und Erfahrungen verfügt, die der geplanten Untersuchung entsprechen.

Artikel 7 – Voruntersuchungen
Jedem untersuchenden Eingriff in Unterwasser-Kulturgut muss eine Beurteilung der Fundstätte vorangehen, welche deren Verletzlichkeit, Bedeutung und Potential bewertet und zugrunde legt.
Die Beurteilung einer Fundstätte muss folgende Aspekte enthalten: ein gründliches Studium der verfügbaren historischen und archäologischen Quellen, der archäologischen und natürlichen Charakteristiken der Fundstätte sowie eine Abwägung der Folgen von Eingriffen für die langfristige Stabilität des von den Untersuchungen betroffenen Gebietes.

Artikel 8 – Dokumentation
Jede Untersuchung muss gründlich dokumentiert werden, in Übereinstimmung mit den jeweiligen Standards archäologischer Dokumentation.
Die Dokumentation muss umfangreiche Aufzeichnungen über die archäologische Stätte enthalten, die über die Herkunft der Unterwasser-Kulturgüter Auskunft geben sollen, die im Verlauf der Untersuchung freigelegt, bewegt oder geborgen wurden; sie enthält Feldnotizen, Pläne und Skizzen, Photographien und jede andere Form der Dokumentation.

Artikel 9 – Konservierung des Materials
Das Programm der Fundkonservierung muss eine Versorgung der geborgenen Objekte während der Untersuchung, beim Transport und auf lange Sicht vorsehen.
Die Konservierung muss jeweiligen professionellen Standards entsprechen.

Artikel 10 – Management und Instandhaltung von Fundstätten
Ein Programm zum Management der Fundstätten muss vorbereitet sein; Maßnahmen für Schutz und Management von Unterwasser-Kulturgut ‚in situ' müssen im Hinblick auf den Abschluss der Feldforschung ausführlich dargestellt sein. Das Programm soll die Information der Öffentlichkeit enthalten, ebenso wie begründete Vorkehrungen zur Sicherung der Fundstätte, für ihre Überwachung und ihren Schutz gegen Störungen. Der öffentliche Zugang zu Unterwasser-Kulturgut ‚in situ' soll gefördert werden, sofern sich der Zugang mit dem Schutz und dem Management der Fundstätte vereinbaren lässt.

Artikel 11 – Gesundheit und Sicherheit
Die Gesundheit und Sicherheit des Forschungsteams und von Dritten steht über allem. Alle Personen des Forschungsteams müssen gemäß den Sicherheitsvorschriften arbeiten, die den geltenden Statuten und professionellen Vorschriften entsprechen und im Programm festgelegt sind.

Artikel 12 – Berichte
Zwischenberichte sollen gemäß einem im Programm festgelegten Zeitplan vorgelegt werden und in anerkannten öffentlichen Berichtsorganen vorgelegt werden.
Die Berichte sollen enthalten:
– eine Beschreibung der Zielsetzung,
– eine Beschreibung der angewandten Methoden und eingesetzten Techniken,
– eine Beschreibung der erzielten Ergebnisse,
– Empfehlungen für zukünftige Forschungen, das Management der Fundstätte und den fürsorglichen Umgang mit den Unterwasser-Kulturgütern, die während der Untersuchung geborgen wurden.

Artikel 13 – Archivierung
Das Projektarchiv enthält das während der Untersuchung geborgene Unterwasser-Kulturgut und eine Kopie aller zugehörigen Dokumente und muss in einer Institution hinterlegt werden, die einen öffentlichen Zugang und dauerhafte Unterbringung und Pflege gewährleisten kann. Vereinbarungen für die Deponierung der Dokumentation sollten vor Beginn der Untersuchung getroffen werden und im Programm festgehalten sein. Das Archiv sollte nach gängigen professionellen Standards arbeiten.

A.II.10 Charta Unterwasser-Kulturerbe

Die wissenschaftliche Integrität des Projektarchivs muss sichergestellt sein; befindet sich die Dokumentation in mehreren Institutionen, darf eine künftige Zusammenführung nicht ausgeschlossen werden, um weitere Forschungen zu ermöglichen. Unterwasser-Kulturgüter dürfen nicht kommerziell gehandelt werden.

Artikel 14 – Vermittlung an die Öffentlichkeit

Die öffentliche Wahrnehmung der Forschungsergebnisse und der Bedeutung des Unterwasser-Kulturerbes soll durch populäre Präsentationen in den Medien gefördert werden. Die Möglichkeit, an solchen Präsentationen teilzuhaben, sollte nicht durch hohe Gebühren beeinträchtigt werden.

Die Zusammenarbeit mit lokalen Vereinigungen und Gruppen ist ebenso zu fördern, wie die Zusammenarbeit mit Vereinigungen und Gruppen, die dem Unterwasser-Kulturerbe besonders verbunden sind. Es ist zu wünschen, dass Untersuchungen unter Zustimmung und mit Befürwortung solcher Vereinigungen und Gruppen durchgeführt werden.

Das Forschungsteam soll versuchen, Vereinigungen und Interessengruppen in dem Maße in die Untersuchungen einzubeziehen, wie dies mit dem Schutz und dem Management zu vereinbaren ist. Wo es sinnvoll erscheint, sollte das Forschungsteam der Öffentlichkeit Möglichkeiten bieten, durch Training und Ausbildung archäologische Fertigkeiten zu erwerben.

Die Zusammenarbeit mit Museen und anderen Institutionen sollte ermutigt werden. Vor den archäologischen Eingriffen sollte man sich die Ergebnisse früherer Untersuchungen und die Berichte der beteiligten Institutionen besorgen und Vorkehrungen für die Besuche der archäologischen Stätte treffen.

Ein zusammenfassender Schlussbericht muss unter Berücksichtigung der Komplexität der Forschung so schnell wie möglich verfügbar sein und in anerkannten öffentlichen Berichtsorganen vorgelegt werden.

Artikel 15 – Internationale Zusammenarbeit

Internationale Zusammenarbeit ist für den Schutz und das Management von Unterwasser-Kulturgut von grundlegender Bedeutung und sollte im Interesse hoher Standards bei der Untersuchung und Forschung gefördert werden. Internationale Kooperation sollte ermutigt werden, um die Kompetenz von Archäologen und anderen Fachleuten zu nutzen, die auf die Untersuchungen von Unterwasser-Kulturerbe spezialisiert sind. Austauschprogramme für Fachleute sollten als ein Mittel verstanden werden, ‚best practice-Beispiele' bekannt zu machen.

Ethische Grundsätze des Internationalen Rats für Denkmalpflege (ICOMOS)
(ICOMOS Ethical Principles)[1)]

Die vorliegenden Ethischen Grundsätze wurden von der 18. Generalversammlung (Florenz 2014) verabschiedet und ersetzen die Erklärung zum ethischen Verhalten, die von der 13. Generalversammlung (Madrid 2002) verabschiedet worden war.

Präambel
Der Internationale Rat für Denkmalpflege (ICOMOS) ist eine Nichtregierungsorganisation (NGO), deren Ziel es ist, die Bewahrung des kulturellen Erbes (Denkmale, Ensembles und historische Stätten) mit seinen materiellen und immateriellen Aspekten und in seiner ganzen Vielfalt und Authentizität zu fördern.
ICOMOS erreicht seine Ziele durch sein Netzwerk aus Mitgliedern und Komitees, durch seine Tätigkeiten und durch die Zusammenarbeit mit anderen Organisationen. Die Mitglieder von ICOMOS teilen gemeinsame Grundsätze. Zugleich vertreten sie die Vielfalt der Fachrichtungen und Kompetenzen im Bereich der Erhaltung des kulturellen Erbes.
Die Ethischen Grundsätze definieren die Verantwortung der ICOMOS-Mitglieder und der Gremien bei der Erhaltung des kulturellen Erbes und gegenüber ICOMOS.

Artikel 1: Gültigkeit
a) Die Ethischen Grundsätze gelten für alle Mitglieder von ICOMOS. Sie gelten darüber hinaus für alle Nationalkomitees, Internationalen Wissenschaftlichen Komitees und sonstigen Gremien von ICOMOS. Bestimmungen für die „Mitglieder" betreffen daher auch – mit den notwendigen und angemessenen Änderungen – die Komitees und sonstigen Gremien;
b) Indem sie ICOMOS beitreten und ihre Mitgliedschaft aufrechterhalten, bestätigen die Mitglieder, dass sie die Ethischen Grundsätze beachten.

Artikel 2: Ethische Grundsätze in Bezug auf das kulturelle Erbe
a) Im Einklang mit den Zielen von ICOMOS verteidigen und fördern dessen Mitglieder die Erhaltung des kulturellen Erbes und dessen Weitergabe an kommende Generationen.
b) Die Mitglieder von ICOMOS verteidigen und fördern den Respekt vor dem kulturellen Erbe. Sie setzen sich mit allen Kräften dafür ein, dass die Nutzung des kulturellen Erbes und mögliche Eingriffe in dieses respektvoll erfolgen.
c) Die Mitglieder von ICOMOS erkennen die wirtschaftliche, soziale und kulturelle Rolle des Erbes als treibende Kraft für eine nachhaltige Entwicklung auf lokaler und globaler Ebene.
d) Die Mitglieder von ICOMOS erkennen und respektieren die verschiedenen materiellen und immateriellen Werte des kulturellen Erbes, welche die menschliche Kultur bereichern und unterschiedliche Bedeutungen für verschiedene Gruppen und Gemeinschaften besitzen können.
e) Wo immer kulturelles Erbe unmittelbar gefährdet oder bedroht ist, bieten die Mitglieder von ICOMOS jede mögliche und angemessene Hilfe an, soweit sie damit nicht ihre eigene Gesundheit und Sicherheit oder die anderer Personen gefährden.

Artikel 3: Ethische Grundsätze in Bezug auf die Öffentlichkeit und die lokale Bevölkerung
a) Die Mitglieder von ICOMOS erkennen an, dass sie eine generelle moralische Verpflichtung zur Erhaltung und Weitergabe des kulturellen Erbes an die heutige sowie an nachfolgende Generationen haben. Eine besondere Verpflichtung haben sie für Tätigkeiten, die unter ihrer Leitung durchgeführt werden.
b) Im Rahmen ihrer Möglichkeiten unternehmen Mitglieder von ICOMOS alles, damit bei Entscheidungen bezüglich des kulturellen Erbes dem öffentlichen Interesse Rechnung getragen wird.
c) Die Mitglieder von ICOMOS erkennen den Wert der Einbindung der lokalen Bevölkerung in die Erhaltung des kulturellen Erbes an. Sie arbeiten mit den Personen und Körperschaften zusammen, die mit dem kulturellen Erbe verbunden sind.

---

1) Quelle: https://www.icomos.de/admin/ckeditor/plugins/alphamanager/uploads/pdf/ethische_grundsaetze_ICOMOS_2014_deutsch.pdf.

A.II.11 Ethische Grundsätze ICOMOS

d) Die Mitglieder von ICOMOS erkennen die Koexistenz kultureller Werte an, vorausgesetzt, dass diese weder gegen die Menschenrechte noch gegen grundlegende Prinzipien der Freiheit verstoßen, die in der Allgemeinen Erklärung der Menschenrechte oder anderen internationalen Vereinbarungen festgelegt sind.

e) Die Mitglieder von ICOMOS fördern auf lokaler und globaler Ebene alle Tätigkeiten zur Sensibilisierung der Öffentlichkeit für das kulturelle Erbe, insbesondere jene, die zu seiner Wertschätzung beitragen, die Zugänglichkeit fördern und seine Erhaltung unterstützen.

Artikel 4: Ethische Grundsätze für das Qualitätsmanagement in der Praxis

a) Bei der Erhaltung des kulturellen Erbes bieten die Mitglieder von ICOMOS in ihrem jeweiligen Kompetenzbereich die bestmöglichen Ratschläge und Dienste an.

b) Die Mitglieder von ICOMOS müssen die durch die Generalversammlung von ICOMOS verabschiedeten Grundsatzdokumente zur Kenntnis nehmen. Sie machen sich ferner kundig über Konventionen, Empfehlungen und Richtlinien zum Erhalt des kulturellen Erbes, die von der UNESCO und anderen internationalen Organisationen verabschiedet worden sind und die ihre Tätigkeiten betreffen.

c) Die Mitglieder von ICOMOS führen ihre Tätigkeiten professionell aus und sind für Zusammenarbeit offen.

1. Die Mitglieder von ICOMOS sind objektiv, gründlich und wissenschaftlich in ihrem methodischen Vorgehen.
2. Die Mitglieder von ICOMOS pflegen, verbessern und aktualisieren ihren Wissensstand bezüglich der Erhaltung des kulturellen Erbes.
3. Die Mitglieder von ICOMOS erkennen an, dass die Erhaltung des kulturellen Erbes einen interdisziplinären Ansatz erfordert. Sie fördern die Zusammenarbeit von multidisziplinären Expertenteams mit den Entscheidungsträgern und allen weiteren betroffenen Interessensvertretern.
4. Die Mitglieder von ICOMOS respektieren die kulturelle und sprachliche Vielfalt.
5. Die Mitglieder von ICOMOS vergewissern sich, dass der Umfang und das Umfeld ihrer eigenen Tätigkeiten, auch Zwänge jeglicher Art, hinreichend offen gelegt werden.
6. Die Mitglieder von ICOMOS vergewissern sich, dass umfassende, altersbeständige und allgemein zugängliche Dokumentationen über die unter ihrer Leitung vorgenommenen Konservierungsmaßnahmen angelegt werden. Sie sorgen dafür, dass diese Dokumentationen unverzüglich in öffentlichen Archiven abgelegt werden, soweit sich dies mit den jeweiligen kulturellen und konservatorischen Zielsetzungen vereinbaren lässt.

d) Wenn Mitglieder von ICOMOS aufgefordert sind, sich für das kulturelle Erbe zu engagieren, wenden sie ihre ganze Sorgfalt, ihre Kompetenz und ihren Fleiß auf, um sicherzustellen, dass alle Entscheidungen zum Erhalt des kulturellen Erbes gut begründet und nachvollziehbar sind.

1. Die Mitglieder von ICOMOS stellen sicher, dass ihre Entscheidungen bezüglich der Erhaltung des kulturellen Erbes auf fundierten Kenntnissen und angemessenen Untersuchungen basieren und den neuesten Standards entsprechen.
2. Die Mitglieder von ICOMOS tun alles in ihrer Macht Stehende, um sicherzustellen, dass verschiedene in Frage kommende Optionen untersucht und die gewählten Vorgehensweisen angemessen begründet werden.
3. Die Mitglieder von ICOMOS tun alles in ihrer Macht Stehende, damit wichtige Entscheidungen bei Projekten zur Erhaltung des kulturellen Erbes nicht nur von der Projektleitung getroffen werden, sondern das Ergebnis von gemeinsamen interdisziplinären Überlegungen sind.

Artikel 5: Ethisches Verhalten

a) Die Mitglieder von ICOMOS führen ihre Tätigkeiten im Geist der Offenheit, Toleranz, Rechtschaffenheit, Unabhängigkeit, Unparteilichkeit und Verantwortung aus.

1. Die Mitglieder von ICOMOS müssen jeden augenscheinlichen oder tatsächlichen Interessenskonflikt, der den unabhängigen, unparteiischen und objektiven Charakter ihrer Arbeit kompromittieren könnte, vermeiden oder gegebenenfalls offenlegen. Mitglieder und Komitees von ICOMOS dürfen keine Geschenke, Vergünstigungen oder andere Anreize, welche

Ethische Grundsätze ICOMOS A.II.11

ihre Unabhängigkeit gefährden oder auch nur diesen Eindruck erwecken könnten, annehmen oder anbieten.
2. Die Mitglieder von ICOMOS müssen es vermeiden, über ihre eigene Arbeit zu urteilen: Wenn sie als Gutachter zu einer bestimmten historischen Stätte gerufen werden, aber gleichzeitig auf lokaler oder nationaler Ebene einer in dieser Angelegenheit beratenden oder entscheidenden Institution angehören, dürfen sie sich nicht an Entscheidungen beteiligen, die diese Stätte betreffen.
3. Die Mitglieder von ICOMOS müssen den gegebenenfalls vertraulichen Charakter von Daten und Informationen jeglicher Art respektieren, einschließlich der Dokumente, Meinungen und Diskussionen, zu denen sie in Ausübung ihrer Tätigkeiten Zugang hatten.
b) Die Mitglieder von ICOMOS respektieren und erkennen die intellektuelle Arbeit anderer an. Die intellektuellen, materiellen und praktischen Beiträge anderer sind präzise und getreu zu zitieren, nachzuweisen und zu publizieren.
c) Die Mitglieder von ICOMOS müssen klarstellen, ob die fachlichen Ansichten und Meinungen, die sie äußern, ihre persönlichen Ansichten darstellen oder die der Institution, die sie vertreten.
d) Die Mitglieder von ICOMOS lehnen verfälschende Präsentationen des kulturellen Erbes ab, ebenso Fehlinformationen über dieses und über Konservierungsmaßnahmen. Sie lehnen jede Unterschlagung oder Manipulation von Daten und Forschungsergebnissen ab.

Artikel 6: Ethische Grundsätze in Bezug auf ICOMOS und seine Mitglieder
a) Die Mitglieder von ICOMOS handeln kollegial, loyal und rücksichtsvoll gegenüber anderen Mitgliedern.
b) Die Mitglieder von ICOMOS fördern den Wissensaustausch durch das Teilen von Informationen und Erfahrungen innerhalb des Verbands, und zwar besonders auf internationaler Ebene.
c) Die Mitglieder von ICOMOS handeln als Mentoren der jungen KollegInnen und lassen sie im Geist der Solidarität zwischen den Generationen an ihren Kenntnissen und Erfahrungen teilhaben.
d) Die Mitglieder von ICOMOS dürfen weder ihre Stellung innerhalb des Verbands noch vertrauliche Informationen, die sie durch ihre Arbeit für ICOMOS erhalten haben, zu ihrem persönlichen Vorteil nutzen.
e) Die Mitglieder von ICOMOS, die von ICOMOS mit einer Mission betraut werden, müssen sich nach den speziell anwendbaren und gegebenenfalls vom ICOMOS-Vorstand für diese Mission präzisierten Grundsätzen richten. So müssen sich die Mitglieder von ICOMOS, die im Auftrag von ICOMOS an einer Tätigkeit im Zusammenhang mit dem Übereinkommen zum Schutz des Kultur- und Naturerbes der Welt (1972) beteiligt sind, nach den „Richtlinien für die Umsetzung des ICOMOS-Welterbemandats" (siehe S. 6ff.) und deren Aktualisierungen richten.
f) Die Mitglieder von ICOMOS handeln verantwortlich gegenüber ihrem Verband und stützen dessen Ruf und Fortbestand.
1. Die Mitglieder von ICOMOS müssen die Statuten von ICOMOS, die ihres Nationalkomitees sowie die Bestimmungen ihrer Internationalen Wissenschaftlichen Komitees beachten.
2. Die Mitglieder von ICOMOS dürfen der Finanzlage von ICOMOS oder der seiner Komitees nicht schaden.
3. Die Mitglieder von ICOMOS müssen sich bewusst sein, dass der Name ICOMOS und das ICOMOS-Logo ICOMOS gehören.
4. Die Mitglieder von ICOMOS dürfen nicht ohne Zustimmung des Verbandes oder des direkt betroffenen Gremiums im Namen von ICOMOS handeln oder sprechen. Wenn diese Zustimmung vorliegt, müssen sie sich strikt am institutionellen Standpunkt ausrichten.
5. Anwärter auf Ämter innerhalb von ICOMOS dürfen mit den Mitteln, die allen Mitgliedern von ICOMOS zugänglich sind, eine Wahlkampagne führen; sie dürfen aber nicht ihr Land oder öffentliche oder private Organisationen mobilisieren, damit diese zu ihren Gunsten Wahlkampf betreiben.

Artikel 7: Inkrafttreten und Änderungen
a) Die Nationalkomitees und die Internationalen Wissenschaftlichen Komitees von ICOMOS verbreiten die Ethischen Grundsätze unter ihren Mitgliedern und stellen deren Umsetzung sicher.

A.II.11 Ethische Grundsätze ICOMOS

b) Das Nichtbefolgen der Ethischen Grundsätze kann als Verstoß gewertet werden. Vermutete Verstöße werden geprüft und mit dem betreffenden Mitglied diskutiert; sie können zu Sanktionen führen, wie sie Artikel 7 der ICOMOS-Statuten vorsieht.
c) Die Nationalkomitees und die Internationalen Wissenschaftlichen Komitees von ICOMOS können weitere ethische Grundsätze beschließen, sofern sie nicht im Widerspruch zu den Statuten von ICOMOS, den vorliegenden Ethischen Grundsätzen oder allen anderen ICOMOS-Grundsatzdokumenten stehen.
d) Die Ethischen Grundsätze werden mindestens alle sechs Jahre vom ICOMOS-Vorstand geprüft. Dieser erstattet gemäß Artikel 10 der Statuten Bericht an die Generalversammlung. Jegliche Änderung der Ethischen Grundsätze von ICOMOS wird von der ICOMOS-Generalversammlung auf Antrag des Vorstands verabschiedet.

Übersetzt von Georg Germann (Bern), Ursula Schädler-Saub (München) und John Ziesemer (München), Januar–April 2015, auf der Grundlage der englischen und französischen Fassungen.
Im September 2015 Abstimmung und Bestätigung der deutschen Fassung durch die Vorstände der ICOMOS-Nationalkomitees von Deutschland, Luxemburg, Österreich und der Schweiz.
Stand: 18. September 2015

Richtlinien für die Umsetzung des ICOMOS-Welterbemandats
(Policy for the Implementation of the ICOMOS World Heritage Mandate)

ICOMOS ist mit dem Ziel in die Welterbekonvention eingebunden, höchstqualifiziertes Fachwissen bei der Beurteilung von Welterbeanträgen und bei anderen Aspekten für die Umsetzung der Welterbekonvention zur Verfügung zu stellen.
Dieses Dokument will daher sicherstellen, dass die Glaubwürdigkeit von ICOMOS bei der Ausführung dieser Aufgaben außer Frage steht. Dazu trägt es eine Vielzahl von anerkannten Regeln und Entscheidungen zusammen.
Darüber hinaus ist ICOMOS sich der Tatsache bewusst, dass bei jeder Art von Tätigkeit in diesem Bereich alle Situationen, die den Eindruck von Interessenskonflikten erwecken könnten, genauso schädlich für die Glaubwürdigkeit seiner Arbeit sind wie Situationen, in denen in der Tat ein derartiger Konflikt besteht. Die vorliegenden Richtlinien wollen dazu beitragen, beide Situationen zu vermeiden, sowohl solche, in denen ein falscher Eindruck entstehen könnte, als auch solche, in denen die Gültigkeit fachlicher Urteile tatsächlich in Frage gestellt werden könnte.
Zu den Fachleuten im ICOMOS-Welterbesystem gehören alle Personen, die am Bewertungsverfahren von Anträgen, an Berichten zum Erhaltungszustand, am reaktiven Monitoring und anderen Missionen und Programmen beteiligt sind. Dies schließt u.a. mit ein: ExpertInnen, die von ICOMOS konsultiert werden, das World Heritage Panel (d.h. das Gremium, das vom Exekutivkomitee von ICOMOS beauftragt wird, die Arbeit der Organisation im Bereich des Welterbes und der Welterbe-Arbeitsgruppe [WHWG] zu beurteilen), ExpertInnen, die dem Panel und dem Welterbekomitee Anträge und Berichte zum Erhaltungszustand vorstellen, ExpertInnen, die Evaluierungsmissionen durchführen, und andere Vertreter der Organisation.
Um mögliche Interessenskonflikte zu vermeiden, gilt das Folgende:
1. ICOMOS gründet seine Beurteilungen und weitere Stellungnahmen auf Forschung und Begutachtung durch unabhängige FachkollegInnen (*peer review*).
2. Während es gängige Praxis ist, dass ICOMOS die Nationalkomitees konsultiert, die mit dem zu bewertenden kulturellen Erbe befasst sind, greift ICOMOS in allen anderen Belangen nur auf ExpertInnen zurück, die aus anderen Ländern als dem betroffenen Vertragsstaat kommen.
3. ICOMOS greift bei seiner Bewertung eines kulturellen Erbes, bei zugehörigen Zustandsberichten oder bei der Beurteilung von Bedrohungen nicht auf Fachleute zurück, die an der Vorbereitung des Antragsdokuments, der Entwicklung des Managementsystems oder –plans, einer anderen Studie oder eines vom Vertragsstaat eingereichten Zustandsberichts beteiligt gewesen sind.
4. Wenn es um die Förderung des Antrags für ein kulturelles Erbe geht, so werden ExpertInnen, die an der Welterbearbeit von ICOMOS beteiligt sind, aufgefordert, ICOMOS über alle Ratschläge, die zu einem bestimmten Antragsdokument gegeben worden sind, Auskunft zu erteilen, einschließlich der besonderen Umstände für diese Dienstleistung. Dies gilt für Fachleute, die an Missionen teilnehmen, Personen, die das Antragsdokument bewerten, BeraterInnen, Mitglieder des World Heritage Panel sowie für Mitglieder der Welterbe-Arbeitsgruppe. Dies gilt nicht für wissenschaftliche Kommentare allgemeiner Art. Nationalkomitees und Internationale Wissenschaftliche Komitees

werden gebeten, jegliche Form der Beteiligung an Welterbeanträgen bekannt zu geben, ebenso die Tätigkeiten von Einzelmitgliedern, die an solcher Arbeit beteiligt sind. Mitglieder des World Heritage Panel und der Welterbe-Arbeitsgruppe dürfen sich nicht an Diskussionen zu Anträgen bzw. an SOC [= state of conservation] Reports beteiligen, die sich auf ihr eigenes Land beziehen.

5. Alle Fachleute und Mitglieder, die an der Vorbereitung von Antragsdokumenten beteiligt sind (einschließlich Beratung, Empfehlungen oder Förderung eines Antrags in irgendeiner Form; ausgenommen ist jedoch jede wissenschaftliche Arbeit, die nicht mit einem spezifischen Antrag in Verbindung steht), dürfen nicht an Diskussionen zum Antrag beim World Heritage Panel oder bei der Welterbe-Arbeitsgruppe teilnehmen. Auch dürfen sie keine Missionen oder schriftliche Gutachten für diese Anträge durchführen.
6. ICOMOS setzt für seine Bewertungen vor Ort keine Fachleute ein, die derzeit ihr Land im Welterbekomitee vertreten.
7. Allen Fachleuten werden die Ethischen Grundsätze von ICOMOS zur Kenntnis gebracht. Sie werden aufgefordert, sich an diese Grundsätze zu halten.
8. Um sicher zu gehen, dass alle Anträge und Zustandsberichte gleichberechtigt behandelt werden, vertraut ICOMOS externe Missionen nicht Personen an, die in seinem Sekretariat beschäftigt sind oder in anderer Eigenschaft Welterbeanträge bearbeiten. Auch werden keine Personen beteiligt, die im World Heritage Panel, in der Welterbe-Arbeitsgruppe oder im internationalen Exekutivkomitee tätig sind.
9. Während der Diskussion eines Berichts oder einer Situation, die ihr eigenes Land betrifft, müssen Mitglieder der Welterbe-Arbeitsgruppe wie auch des World Heritage Panel der Diskussion und den Entscheidungsprozessen fernbleiben.
10. Die Empfehlungen an das Welterbekomitee, welche vom ICOMOS World Heritage Panel oder von einer Arbeitsgruppe verabschiedet worden sind, die das Mandat hat, zusätzliche Informationen zu beurteilen, sind endgültig und dürfen nur vom Panel geändert oder berichtigt werden.
11. Wenn neue Informationen zu einem Antrag von einem Vertragsstaat vor dem 28. Februar eingereicht werden, wird dem World Heritage Panel oder einer Arbeitsgruppe, die zu diesem Zweck zusammengestellt worden ist, eine überarbeitete Beurteilung vorgelegt. So kann, falls angemessen, die Empfehlung an das Welterbekomitee berichtet werden. Neue Informationen, die nach dem 28. Februar eingehen, werden erst für die Einreichung zur Welterbesitzung im darauf folgenden Jahr durchgesehen.
12. Die Empfehlungen und Stellungnahmen der ICOMOS-ExpertInnen, der Welterbe-Arbeitsgruppe und des World Heritage Panel sind vertraulich. Eingeweihte Fachleute haben Schweigepflicht gegenüber den Medien, den Vertretern des Vertragsstaates und allen Einzelpersonen oder Organisationen, die möglicherweise ein Interesse am betroffenen kulturellen Erbe haben könnten. Des Weiteren dürfen ICOMOS-Funktionäre und Mitglieder der Welterbe-Arbeitsgruppe und des World Heritage Panel anderen Personen oder Organisationen, die nicht an den Diskussionen teilgenommen haben, nichts über den Inhalt der Diskussionen im Panel mitteilen.
13. Falls ein Mitglied der Welterbe-Arbeitsgruppe oder des World Heritage Panel oder eine Fachperson, die in den ICOMOS-Welterbeangelegenheiten tätig ist, einen Aspekt dieser Richtlinien nicht umsetzen sollte, kommen Sanktionen zur Anwendung. Diese Sanktionen werden vom ICOMOS-Exekutivkomitee festgelegt oder von einem seiner Subkomitees, das dazu berechtigt worden ist. Die Sanktionen richten sich nach der Schwere der Rechtsverletzung. In Fällen, in denen anzunehmen ist, dass die Glaubwürdigkeit von ICOMOS als objektiver und unparteiischer Berater des Welterbekomitees und der UNESCO kompromittiert worden ist, soll die betroffene Person allerdings automatisch von der weiteren Teilnahme an allen ICOMOS-Tätigkeiten in Welterbeangelegenheiten ausgeschlossen werden, ebenso von allen anderen relevanten Bereichen der ICOMOS-Arbeit, bei denen die Organisation einen unparteiischen Eindruck vermitteln muss.
14. Für den Fall, dass es Beweise dafür gibt, dass ein/e Angestellte/r der Organisation gegen diese Richtlinien verstoßen hat, wird ein entsprechendes Disziplinarverfahren eingeleitet.
15. Jede Person, die bei ICOMOS angestellt ist oder anderweitig von ICOMOS bezahlt wird, sei es im Sekretariat oder in einer anderen Zuständigkeit, bei der es um die Bearbeitung von Welterbeanträgen geht, sowie alle Teilnehmer des World Heritage Panel müssen eine Ausfertigung dieser Stellungnahme unterschreiben und dem Sekretariat vorlegen, bevor sie ihre Tätigkeiten aufnehmen.
16. Eine Ausfertigung dieser Richtlinien ist auch allen anderen Personen vorzulegen, die offiziell an der ICOMOS-Welterbearbeit beteiligt werden. Sie müssen im Voraus bezeugen, dass sie die Richtlinien verstanden haben und sich nach ihnen richten werden.

A.II.11 Ethische Grundsätze ICOMOS

Zur Umsetzung genehmigt ICOMOS-Exekutivkomitee
17. Januar 2006, überarbeitet im November 2007, Oktober 2010 und Oktober 2012

Ich (vollständiger Name) … erkläre, dass ich das Obige gelesen habe, es verstehe und mich danach richten werde in allen Bereichen meiner Beteiligung an der Arbeit von ICOMOS in Welterbeangelegenheiten. Ich verstehe, dass ein Verstoß dazu führen kann, von solchen Zuständigkeitsbereichen ausgeschlossen zu werden.

Datum Unterschrift

Übersetzung von John Ziesemer (München), Georg Germann (Bern) und Ursula Schädler-Saub (München), August 2015, auf der Grundlage der englischen und französischen Fassungen.
Im September 2015 Abstimmung und Bestätigung der deutschen Fassung durch die Vorstände der ICOMOS-Nationalkomitees von Deutschland, Luxemburg, Österreich und der Schweiz.
Stand: 18. September 2015

Protokoll zur Konvention zum Schutz von Kulturgut bei bewaffneten Konflikten[1)]

Vom 14. Mai 1954 (BGBl. 1967 II S. 1301)

Die Hohen Vertragsparteien sind wie folgt übereingekommen:

I.
1. Jede Hohe Vertragspartei verpflichtet sich, die Ausfuhr von Kulturgut im Sinne von Artikel 1 der am 14. Mai 1954 in Den Haag unterzeichneten Konvention zum Schutz von Kulturgut bei bewaffneten Konflikten aus dem von ihr während eines bewaffneten Konflikts besetzten Gebiete zu verhindern.
2. Jede Hohe Vertragspartei verpflichtet sich, Kulturgut, das mittelbar oder unmittelbar aus einem besetzten Gebiet in ihr Gebiet eingeführt wird, in Gewahrsam zu nehmen. Dies hat entweder von Amts wegen bei der Einfuhr des Kulturguts zu erfolgen, oder, falls dies nicht geschehen ist, auf Verlangen der Behörden des betreffenden besetzten Gebiets.
3. Jede Hohe Vertragspartei verpflichtet sich, bei Beendigung der Feindseligkeiten auf ihrem Gebiet befindliches Kulturgut den zuständigen Behörden des früher besetzten Gebiets zurückzugeben, sofern dieses Gut unter Verletzung des in Ziffer 1 dieses Protokolls niedergelegten Grundsatzes ausgeführt worden ist. In keinem Fall darf solches Gut für Reparationszwecke zurückgehalten werden.
4. Die Hohe Vertragspartei, die verpflichtet war, die Ausfuhr von Kulturgut aus dem von ihr besetzten Gebiet zu verhindern, hat den gutgläubigen Besitzer von Kulturgut, das gemäß der vorstehenden Ziffer dieses Protokolls zurückzugeben ist, zu entschädigen.

II.
5. Kulturgut aus dem Gebiet einer Hohen Vertragspartei, das von dieser in dem Gebiet einer anderen Hohen Vertragspartei deponiert wurde, um es gegen die Gefahren eines bewaffneten Konflikts zu schützen, ist von dieser nach Beendigung der Feindseligkeiten an die zuständige Behörde des Herkunftsgebietes zurückzugeben.

III.
6. Dieses Protokoll trägt das Datum des 14. Mai 1954 und liegt bis zum 31. Dezember 1954 für alle zu der vom 21. April bis 14. Mai 1954 abgehaltenen Haager Konferenz eingeladenen Staaten zur Unterzeichnung auf.
7. a) Dieses Protokoll bedarf der Ratifikation durch die Unterzeichnerstaaten nach Maßgabe ihrer eigenen verfassungsmäßigen Verfahren.
    b) Die Ratifikationsurkunden sind beim Generaldirektor der Organisation der Vereinten Nationen für Erziehung, Wissenschaft und Kultur zu hinterlegen.
8. Vom Zeitpunkt seines Inkrafttretens an steht dieses Protokoll allen Staaten zum Beitritt offen, die in Ziffer 6 erwähnt sind und nicht unterzeichnet haben, sowie allen anderen Staaten, die von dem Exekutivrat der Organisation der Vereinten Nationen für Erziehung, Wissenschaft und Kultur zum Beitritt eingeladen werden. Der Beitritt erfolgt durch Hinterlegung einer Beitrittsurkunde beim Generaldirektor der Organisation der Vereinten Nationen für Erziehung, Wissenschaft und Kultur.
9. Die in den Ziffern 6 und 8 genannten Staaten können bei der Unterzeichnung, der Ratifikation oder dem Beitritt eine Erklärung abgeben, nach der sie entweder durch die Bestimmungen in Abschnitt I oder die Bestimmungen in Abschnitt II dieses Protokolls nicht gebunden sind.
10. a) Dieses Protokoll tritt drei Monate nach Hinterlegung von fünf Ratifikationsurkunden in Kraft.
    b) Späterhin tritt es für jede Hohe Vertragspartei drei Monate nach Hinterlegung ihrer Ratifikations- oder Beitrittsurkunde in Kraft.
    c) Tritt die in Artikel 18 und 19 der in Den Haag am 14. Mai 1954 unterzeichneten Konvention zum Schutz von Kulturgut bei bewaffneten Konflikten vorgesehene Lage ein, so werden die vor oder nach Beginn der Feindseligkeiten oder der Besetzung hinterlegten Ratifikations-

---

[1)] Liste der Vertragsstaaten: http://www.unesco.org/eri/la/convention.asp?KO=13637&language=E.

A.III.1 Erstes Haager Protokoll

oder Beitrittsurkunden der an dem Konflikt beteiligten Parteien sofort wirksam. In diesen Fällen macht der Generaldirektor der Organisation der Vereinten Nationen für Erziehung, Wissenschaft und Kultur auf dem schnellsten Wege die in Ziffer 14 vorgesehenen Mitteilungen.

11. a) Jeder Staat, der mit Inkrafttreten dieses Protokolls Vertragspartei wird, hat binnen sechs Monaten alle erforderlichen Maßnahmen zu treffen, um seine wirksame Durchführung zu gewährleisten.

    b) Für diejenigen Staaten, die ihre Ratifikations- oder Beitrittsurkunden nach dem Inkrafttreten des Protokolls hinterlegen, beträgt die Frist sechs Monate, vom Tage der Hinterlegung der Ratifikations- oder Beitrittsurkunde an gerechnet.

12. Jede der Hohen Vertragsparteien kann bei der Ratifizierung oder beim Beitritt oder zu jedem späteren Zeitpunkt durch Notifikation an den Generaldirektor der Organisation der Vereinten Nationen für Erziehung, Wissenschaft und Kultur erklären, daß dieses Protokoll sich auf alle oder einige der Gebiete erstreckt, deren internationale Beziehungen sie wahrnimmt. Diese Notifikation wird drei Monate nach dem Tage ihres Eingangs wirksam.

13. a) Jede der Hohen Vertragsparteien kann dieses Protokoll für sich selbst oder für Gebiete, deren internationale Beziehungen sie wahrnimmt, kündigen.

    b) Die Kündigung hat durch schriftliche Erklärung zu erfolgen, die beim Generaldirektor der Organisation der Vereinten Nationen für Erziehung, Wissenschaft und Kultur zu hinterlegen ist.

    c) Die Kündigung wird ein Jahr nach Eingang der Kündigungsurkunde wirksam. Ist jedoch die kündigende Partei beim Ablauf dieser Frist in einen bewaffneten Konflikt verwickelt, so wird die Kündigung erst nach Beendigung der Feindseligkeiten oder nach Abschluß der Rückführung des Kulturguts wirksam, je nachdem, welcher Zeitpunkt der spätere ist.

14. Der Generaldirektor der Organisation der Vereinten Nationen für Erziehung, Wissenschaft und Kultur benachrichtigt die in den Ziffern 6 und 8 bezeichneten Staaten und die Vereinten Nationen von der Hinterlegung aller in Ziffern 7, 8 und 15 vorgesehenen Ratifikations- und Beitrittsurkunden oder Annahmeerklärungen sowie von den in Ziffern 12 und 13 vorgesehenen Notifikationen und Kündigungen.

15. a) Dieses Protokoll kann abgeändert werden, wenn die Abänderung von mehr als einem Drittel der Hohen Vertragsparteien verlangt wird.

    b) Zu diesem Zweck hat der Generaldirektor der Organisation der Vereinten Nationen für Erziehung, Wissenschaft und Kultur eine Konferenz einzuberufen.

    c) Abänderungen dieses Protokolls treten erst in Kraft, wenn sie von den auf der Konferenz vertretenen Hohen Vertragsparteien einstimmig beschlossen und von allen Hohen Vertragsparteien angenommen worden sind.

    d) Die Annahme von Abänderungen dieses Protokolls, die von der in Absatz b) und c) erwähnten Konferenz durch die Hohen Vertragsparteien beschlossen worden sind, erfolgt durch Hinterlegung einer förmlichen Erklärung beim Generaldirektor der Organisation der Vereinten Nationen für Erziehung, Wissenschaft und Kultur.

    e) Nach dem Inkrafttreten von Abänderungen dieses Protokolls steht nur der so abgeänderte Text des Protokolls zur Ratifikation oder zum Beitritt offen.

Gemäß Artikel 102 der Satzung der Vereinten Nationen wird dieses Protokoll auf Ersuchen des Generaldirektors der Organisation der Vereinten Nationen für Erziehung, Wissenschaft und Kultur beim Sekretariat der Vereinten Nationen eingetragen.

ZU URKUND DESSEN haben die ordnungsgemäß bevollmächtigten Unterzeichneten dieses Protokoll unterschrieben.

GESCHEHEN zu Den Haag, am 14. Mai 1954, in englischer, französischer, russischer und spanischer Sprache, wobei alle vier Texte in gleicher Weise maßgeblich sind, in einem einzigen Exemplar, das in den Archiven der Organisation der Vereinten Nationen für Erziehung, Wissenschaft und Kultur hinterlegt wird; beglaubigte Ausfertigungen desselben werden allen in den Ziffern 6 und 8 bezeichneten Staaten sowie den Vereinten Nationen übermittelt.

UNESCO-Übereinkommen Ein- und Ausfuhr von Kulturgut A.III.2

Übereinkommen über Maßnahmen zum Verbot und zur Verhütung der rechtswidrigen Einfuhr, Ausfuhr und Übereignung von Kulturgut[1)]

Vom 14.11.1970 (BGBl. 2007 II S. 627)

Die Generalkonferenz der Organisation der Vereinten Nationen für Erziehung, Wissenschaft und Kultur, die vom 12. Oktober bis zum 14. November 1970 in Paris zu ihrer 16. Tagung zusammengetreten ist –

im Hinblick auf die Bedeutung der Bestimmungen der von der Generalkonferenz auf ihrer 14. Tagung angenommenen Erklärung über die Grundsätze der internationalen kulturellen Zusammenarbeit,

in der Erwägung, dass der Austausch von Kulturgut unter den Nationen zu wissenschaftlichen, kulturellen und erzieherischen Zwecken das Wissen über die menschliche Zivilisation vertieft, das kulturelle Leben aller Völker bereichert und die gegenseitige Achtung und Wertschätzung unter den Nationen fördert,

in der Erwägung, dass das Kulturgut zu den wesentlichen Elementen der Zivilisation und Kultur der Völker gehört und dass sein wahrer Wert nur im Zusammenhang mit einer möglichst umfassenden Unterrichtung über seinen Ursprung, seine Geschichte und seinen traditionellen Hintergrund erfasst werden kann,

in der Erwägung, dass es jedem Staat obliegt, das in seinem Hoheitsgebiet vorhandene Kulturgut vor den Gefahren des Diebstahls, der unerlaubten Ausgrabung und der rechtswidrigen Ausfuhr zu schützen,

in der Erwägung, dass es zur Abwendung dieser Gefahren unerlässlich ist, dass sich jeder Staat in zunehmendem Maße der moralischen Verpflichtung zur Achtung seines kulturellen Erbes und desjenigen aller Nationen bewusst wird,

in der Erwägung, dass Museen, Bibliotheken und Archive als kulturelle Einrichtungen dafür Sorge zu tragen haben, dass ihre Sammlungen nach weltweit anerkannten moralischen Grundsätzen aufgebaut werden,

in der Erwägung, dass die rechtswidrige Einfuhr, Ausfuhr und Übereignung von Kulturgut der Verständigung zwischen den Nationen im Wege steht, die zu fördern Aufgabe der Unesco ist, etwa indem sie interessierten Staaten den Abschluss internationaler Übereinkünfte zu diesem Zweck empfiehlt,

in der Erwägung, dass der Schutz des kulturellen Erbes nur wirksam sein kann, wenn er sowohl auf nationaler als auch auf internationaler Ebene durch enge Zusammenarbeit zwischen den Staaten gestaltet wird,

in der Erwägung, dass die Generalkonferenz der Unesco zu diesem Zweck im Jahre 1964 eine Empfehlung angenommen hat,

angesichts weiterer Vorschläge über Maßnahmen zum Verbot und zur Verhütung der rechtswidrigen Einfuhr, Ausfuhr und Übereignung von Kulturgut, eine Frage, die als Punkt 19 auf der Tagesordnung der Tagung steht,

nach dem auf ihrer 15. Tagung gefassten Beschluss, diese Frage zum Gegenstand eines internationalen Übereinkommens zu machen –

nimmt dieses Übereinkommen am 14. November 1970 an.

Artikel 1

Im Sinne dieses Übereinkommens gilt als Kulturgut das von jedem Staat aus religiösen oder weltlichen Gründen als für Archäologie, Vorgeschichte, Geschichte, Literatur, Kunst oder Wissenschaft besonders bedeutsam bezeichnete Gut, das folgenden Kategorien angehört:

a) seltene Sammlungen und Exemplare der Zoologie, Botanik, Mineralogie und Anatomie sowie Gegenstände von paläontologischem Interesse;
b) Gut, das sich auf die Geschichte einschließlich der Geschichte von Wissenschaft und Technik sowie der Militär- und Sozialgeschichte, das Leben nationaler Führungspersönlichkeiten, Denker, Wissenschaftler und Künstler und Ereignisse von nationaler Bedeutung bezieht;
c) Ergebnisse archäologischer Ausgrabungen (sowohl vorschriftsmäßiger als auch unerlaubter) oder archäologischer Entdeckungen;

---

1) Liste der Vertragsstaaten: http://www.unesco.org/eri/la/convention.asp?KO=13039&language=E.

d) Teile künstlerischer oder geschichtlicher Denkmäler oder archäologischer Stätten, deren Zusammenhang zerstört ist;
e) Antiquitäten, die mehr als hundert Jahre alt sind, wie Inschriften, Münzen und gravierte Siegel;
f) Gegenstände von ethnologischem Interesse;
g) Gut von künstlerischem Interesse wie
   i) Bilder, Gemälde und Zeichnungen, die ausschließlich von Hand auf einem beliebigen Träger und aus einem beliebigen Material angefertigt sind (ausgenommen industrielle Entwürfe und handbemalte Manufakturwaren);
   ii) Originalwerke der Bildhauerkunst und der Skulptur aus einem beliebigen Material;
   iii) Originalgravuren, -drucke und -lithographien;
   iv) Originale von künstlerischen Zusammenstellungen und Montagen aus einem beliebigen Material;
h) seltene Manuskripte und Inkunabeln, alte Bücher, Dokumente und Publikationen von besonderem Interesse (historisch, künstlerisch, wissenschaftlich, literarisch usw.), einzeln oder in Sammlungen;
i) Briefmarken, Steuermarken und Ähnliches, einzeln oder in Sammlungen;
j) Archive einschließlich Phono-, Foto- und Filmarchive;
k) Möbelstücke, die mehr als hundert Jahre alt sind, und alte Musikinstrumente.

Artikel 2

(1) Die Vertragsstaaten erkennen an, dass die rechtswidrige Einfuhr, Ausfuhr und Übereignung von Kulturgut eine der Hauptursachen für die Verluste am kulturellen Erbe der Ursprungsländer darstellen und dass die internationale Zusammenarbeit eines der wirksamsten Mittel zum Schutz des Kulturguts jedes Landes gegen alle sich daraus ergebenden Gefahren ist.

(2) Zu diesem Zweck verpflichten sich die Vertragsstaaten, mit den ihnen zur Verfügung stehenden Mitteln diese Praktiken zu bekämpfen, indem sie insbesondere ihre Ursachen beseitigen, ihre Ausübung beenden und zu den erforderlichen Wiedergutmachungen beitragen.

Artikel 3

Die Einfuhr, Ausfuhr und Übereignung von Kulturgut gelten als rechtswidrig, wenn sie im Widerspruch zu den Bestimmungen stehen, die von den Vertragsstaaten auf Grund dieses Übereinkommens angenommen worden sind.

Artikel 4

Die Vertragsstaaten erkennen an, dass im Sinne dieses Übereinkommens das zu folgenden Kategorien gehörende Gut Teil des kulturellen Erbes jedes Staates ist:
a) Kulturgut, das durch die individuelle oder kollektive Schöpferkraft von Angehörigen des betreffenden Staates entstanden ist, und für den betreffenden Staat bedeutsames Kulturgut, das in seinem Hoheitsgebiet von dort ansässigen Ausländern oder Staatenlosen geschaffen wurde;
b) im Staatsgebiet gefundenes Kulturgut;
c) durch archäologische, ethnologische oder naturwissenschaftliche Missionen mit Zustimmung der zuständigen Behörden des Ursprungslands erworbenes Kulturgut;
d) Kulturgut, das auf Grund freier Vereinbarung ausgetauscht worden ist;
e) Kulturgut, das als Geschenk entgegengenommen oder mit Zustimmung der zuständigen Behörden des Ursprungslands rechtmäßig gekauft wurde.

Artikel 5

Um den Schutz ihres Kulturguts vor rechtswidriger Einfuhr, Ausfuhr oder Übereignung sicherzustellen, verpflichten sich die Vertragsstaaten, je nach den Gegebenheiten ihres Landes in ihren Hoheitsgebieten zum Schutz des kulturellen Erbes eine oder mehrere Dienststellen einzurichten, soweit solche nicht bereits vorhanden sind, die mit qualifiziertem und zahlenmäßig ausreichendem Personal ausgestattet sind, das in der Lage ist, folgende Aufgaben wirksam zu erfüllen:
a) Mitwirkung bei der Ausarbeitung von Gesetzentwürfen und sonstigen Rechtsvorschriften zum Schutz des kulturellen Erbes und insbesondere zur Verhütung der rechtswidrigen Einfuhr, Ausfuhr und Übereignung bedeutsamen Kulturguts;

b) auf der Grundlage eines nationalen Bestandsverzeichnisses des zu schützenden Gutes Aufstellung und Führung eines Verzeichnisses des bedeutsamen öffentlichen und privaten Kulturguts, dessen Ausfuhr für das nationale kulturelle Erbe einen merklichen Verlust bedeuten würde;
c) Förderung des Ausbaus oder der Errichtung wissenschaftlicher und technischer Einrichtungen (Museen, Bibliotheken, Archive, Laboratorien, Werkstätten usw.), die zur Erhaltung und Ausstellung von Kulturgut notwendig sind;
d) Einrichtung der Überwachung archäologischer Ausgrabungen, Gewährleistung der Konservierung bestimmten Kulturguts „in situ" und Schutz bestimmter Gebiete, die künftigen archäologischen Forschungen vorbehalten sind;
e) Aufstellung von Vorschriften für die betroffenen Personen (Kuratoren, Sammler, Antiquitätenhändler usw.) entsprechend den ethischen Grundsätzen dieses Übereinkommens und Überwachung der Einhaltung dieser Vorschriften;
f) Durchführung von Bildungsmaßnahmen, um die Achtung vor dem kulturellen Erbe aller Staaten zu wecken und zu entwickeln, und Verbreitung der Kenntnis der Bestimmungen dieses Übereinkommens;
g) Vorsorge dafür, dass jedes Verschwinden von Kulturgut angemessen in der Öffentlichkeit bekannt gemacht wird.

Artikel 6
Die Vertragsstaaten verpflichten sich,
a) eine geeignete Bescheinigung einzuführen, durch die der ausführende Staat bescheinigt, dass die Ausfuhr des betreffenden Kulturguts genehmigt ist. Jedes vorschriftsmäßig ausgeführte Kulturgut muss von einer solchen Bescheinigung begleitet sein;
b) die Ausfuhr von Kulturgut aus ihrem Hoheitsgebiet zu verbieten, sofern die oben genannte Ausfuhrbescheinigung nicht vorliegt;
c) dieses Verbot auf geeignete Weise in der Öffentlichkeit bekannt zu machen, insbesondere bei Personen, die für die Ausfuhr oder Einfuhr von Kulturgut in Frage kommen.

Artikel 7
Die Vertragsstaaten verpflichten sich,
a) im Rahmen der innerstaatlichen Rechtsvorschriften die erforderlichen Maßnahmen zu ergreifen, um Museen und ähnliche Einrichtungen in ihrem Hoheitsgebiet am Erwerb von Kulturgut zu hindern, das aus einem anderen Vertragsstaat stammt und nach Inkrafttreten dieses Übereinkommens für die betreffenden Staaten widerrechtlich ausgeführt worden ist. Soweit möglich unterrichten sie einen Ursprungsstaat, der Vertragspartei ist, wenn solches Kulturgut angeboten wird, das nach Inkrafttreten dieses Übereinkommens für beide Staaten widerrechtlich aus jenem Staat entfernt worden ist;
b) i) die Einfuhr von Kulturgut, das nach Inkrafttreten dieses Übereinkommens für die betreffenden Staaten aus einem Museum oder einem religiösen oder weltlichen öffentlichen Baudenkmal oder einer ähnlichen Einrichtung in einem anderen Vertragsstaat gestohlen worden ist, zu verbieten, sofern nachgewiesen werden kann, dass dieses Gut zum Bestand jener Einrichtung gehört;
ii) auf Ersuchen des Ursprungsstaats, der Vertragspartei ist, geeignete Maßnahmen zur Wiedererlangung und Rückgabe solchen Kulturguts zu ergreifen, das nach Inkrafttreten dieses Übereinkommens für beide betreffenden Staaten eingeführt wurde, mit der Maßgabe, dass der ersuchende Staat einem gutgläubigen Erwerber oder einer Person mit einem gültigen Rechtsanspruch an dem Gut eine angemessene Entschädigung zahlt. Ersuchen um Wiedererlangung und Rückgabe sind auf diplomatischem Weg zu übermitteln. Der ersuchende Staat stellt auf seine Kosten die Unterlagen und Nachweise zur Verfügung, die zur Feststellung seines Anspruchs auf Wiedererlangung und Rückgabe erforderlich sind. Die Vertragsstaaten erheben auf das nach diesem Artikel zurückgegebene Gut weder Zölle noch sonstige Abgaben. Alle Kosten im Zusammenhang mit der Rückgabe und Zustellung des Kulturguts werden von dem ersuchenden Staat getragen.

A.III.2 UNESCO-Übereinkommen Ein- und Ausfuhr von Kulturgut

Artikel 8
Die Vertragsstaaten verpflichten sich, gegen jeden, der für einen Verstoß gegen die in Artikel 6 Buchstabe b und Artikel 7 Buchstabe b genannten Verbote verantwortlich ist, Kriminal- oder Ordnungsstrafen zu verhängen.

Artikel 9
Jeder Vertragsstaat, dessen kulturelles Erbe durch Plünderung archäologischen oder ethnologischen Gutes gefährdet ist, kann sich an andere betroffene Vertragsstaaten wenden. Die Vertragsstaaten verpflichten sich, in diesen Fällen an einer konzertierten internationalen Aktion teilzunehmen mit dem Ziel, die erforderlichen konkreten Maßnahmen festzulegen und durchzuführen, einschließlich der Überwachung der Ausfuhr, der Einfuhr und des internationalen Handels mit dem betroffenen spezifischen Gut. Bis zu einer Vereinbarung ergreift jeder betroffene Staat im Rahmen des Möglichen einstweilige Maßnahmen, um zu verhindern, dass dem kulturellen Erbe des ersuchenden Staates nicht wieder gutzumachender Schaden zugefügt wird.

Artikel 10
Die Vertragsstaaten verpflichten sich,
a) durch Erziehung, Information und aufmerksame Beobachtung den Verkehr mit Kulturgut, das aus einem Vertragsstaat widerrechtlich entfernt worden ist, einzuschränken und je nach den Gegebenheiten des Landes die Antiquitätenhändler unter Androhung von Kriminal- oder Ordnungsstrafen zu verpflichten, ein Verzeichnis zu führen, aus dem der Ursprung jedes einzelnen Kulturguts, Name und Anschrift des Lieferanten sowie die Beschreibung und der Preis jedes verkauften Gegenstands hervorgehen, und den Käufer des Kulturguts über das dafür möglicherweise bestehende Ausfuhrverbot zu unterrichten;
b) sich zu bemühen, durch erzieherische Maßnahmen in der Öffentlichkeit das Verständnis für den Wert des Kulturguts sowie für seine Gefährdung durch Diebstahl, unerlaubte Ausgrabungen und rechtswidrige Ausfuhr zu wecken und zu entwickeln.

Artikel 11
Die erzwungene Ausfuhr und Übereignung von Kulturgut, die sich unmittelbar oder mittelbar aus der Besetzung eines Landes durch eine fremde Macht ergeben, gelten als rechtswidrig.

Artikel 12
Die Vertragsstaaten achten das kulturelle Erbe in den Hoheitsgebieten, deren internationale Beziehungen sie wahrnehmen, und ergreifen alle geeigneten Maßnahmen, um die rechtswidrige Einfuhr, Ausfuhr und Übereignung von Kulturgut in diesen Hoheitsgebieten zu verbieten und zu verhüten.

Artikel 13
Die Vertragsstaaten verpflichten sich ferner im Rahmen ihrer innerstaatlichen Rechtsordnung,
a) mit allen geeigneten Mitteln Übereignungen von Kulturgut zu verhüten, durch die eine rechtswidrige Einfuhr oder Ausfuhr desselben begünstigt werden könnte;
b) dafür zu sorgen, dass ihre zuständigen Dienststellen zusammenarbeiten, um eine möglichst baldige Rückgabe des rechtswidrig ausgeführten Kulturguts an den rechtmäßigen Eigentümer zu erleichtern;
c) Verfahren zur Wiedererlangung verloren gegangenen oder gestohlenen Kulturguts zuzulassen, die vom rechtmäßigen Eigentümer oder in seinem Namen angestrengt werden;
d) das unantastbare Recht jedes Vertragsstaats anzuerkennen, bestimmtes Kulturgut als unveräußerlich einzustufen und zu erklären, das daher ipso facto nicht ausgeführt werden darf, und die Wiedererlangung solchen Gutes durch den betreffenden Staat in Fällen zu erleichtern, in denen es ausgeführt worden ist.

Artikel 14
Zur Verhütung der rechtswidrigen Ausfuhr und zur Einhaltung der aus der Durchführung dieses Übereinkommens entstehenden Verpflichtungen soll jeder Vertragsstaat im Rahmen seiner Möglichkeiten seine innerstaatlichen Dienststellen, die für den Schutz seines kulturellen Erbes verantwortlich sind, mit ausreichenden Mitteln ausstatten und, soweit erforderlich, zu diesem Zweck einen Fonds schaffen.

Artikel 15
Dieses Übereinkommen hindert die Vertragsstaaten nicht, untereinander Sonderabkommen zu schließen oder bereits geschlossene Abkommen weiter anzuwenden, welche die Rückgabe von Kulturgut zum Inhalt haben, das aus irgendwelchen Gründen vor Inkrafttreten dieses Übereinkommens für die betreffenden Staaten aus dem Ursprungsland entfernt worden ist.

Artikel 16
Die Vertragsstaaten geben in ihren regelmäßigen Berichten, die sie der Generalkonferenz der Organisation der Vereinten Nationen für Erziehung, Wissenschaft und Kultur zu den von der Generalkonferenz festzulegenden Zeitpunkten und in einer von ihr anzugebenden Weise vorlegen, Auskunft über die von ihnen erlassenen Rechts- und Verwaltungsvorschriften und sonstige von ihnen zur Anwendung dieses Übereinkommens ergriffene Maßnahmen sowie ihre auf diesem Gebiet gewonnenen Erfahrungen.

Artikel 17
(1) Die Vertragsstaaten können die technische Hilfe der Organisation der Vereinten Nationen für Erziehung, Wissenschaft und Kultur in Anspruch nehmen, insbesondere in folgenden Belangen:
a) Information und Erziehung;
b) Beratung und Sachverständigengutachten;
c) Koordinierung und gute Dienste.
(2) Die Organisation der Vereinten Nationen für Erziehung, Wissenschaft und Kultur kann von sich aus über Fragen im Zusammenhang mit dem rechtswidrigen Verkehr von Kulturgut Forschungsarbeiten durchführen und Untersuchungen veröffentlichen.
(3) Zu diesem Zweck kann sich die Organisation der Vereinten Nationen für Erziehung, Wissenschaft und Kultur mit der Bitte um Zusammenarbeit auch an jede sachverständige nichtstaatliche Organisation wenden.
(4) Die Organisation der Vereinten Nationen für Erziehung, Wissenschaft und Kultur kann von sich aus den Vertragsstaaten Vorschläge für die Durchführung des Übereinkommens unterbreiten.
(5) Auf Ersuchen von wenigstens zwei Vertragsstaaten, zwischen denen eine Streitigkeit über die Durchführung des Übereinkommens entstanden ist, kann die Unesco ihre guten Dienste für eine Beilegung anbieten.

Artikel 18
Dieses Übereinkommen ist in englischer, französischer, russischer und spanischer Sprache abgefasst, wobei jeder Wortlaut gleichermaßen verbindlich ist.

Artikel 19
(1) Dieses Übereinkommen bedarf der Ratifikation oder Annahme durch die Mitgliedstaaten der Organisation der Vereinten Nationen für Erziehung, Wissenschaft und Kultur nach Maßgabe ihrer verfassungsrechtlichen Verfahren.
(2) Die Ratifikations- oder Annahmeurkunden werden beim Generaldirektor der Organisation der Vereinten Nationen für Erziehung, Wissenschaft und Kultur hinterlegt.

Artikel 20
(1) Dieses Übereinkommen liegt für alle Nichtmitgliedstaaten der Organisation der Vereinten Nationen für Erziehung, Wissenschaft und Kultur, die vom Exekutivrat der Organisation hierzu aufgefordert werden, zum Beitritt auf.
(2) Der Beitritt erfolgt durch Hinterlegung einer Beitrittsurkunde beim Generaldirektor der Organisation der Vereinten Nationen für Erziehung, Wissenschaft und Kultur.

Artikel 21
Dieses Übereinkommen tritt drei Monate nach Hinterlegung der dritten Ratifikations-, Annahme- oder Beitrittsurkunde in Kraft, jedoch nur für die Staaten, die bis zu diesem Zeitpunkt ihre Urkunden hinterlegt haben. Für jeden anderen Staat tritt es drei Monate nach Hinterlegung seiner Ratifikations-, Annahme- oder Beitrittsurkunde in Kraft.

Artikel 22
Die Vertragsstaaten erkennen an, dass das Übereinkommen nicht nur auf ihre Mutterländer anzuwenden ist, sondern auch auf alle Hoheitsgebiete, deren internationale Beziehungen sie wahrnehmen; sie

verpflichten sich, nötigenfalls die Regierungen oder sonstigen zuständigen Behörden jener Hoheitsgebiete vor oder bei der Ratifikation, der Annahme oder dem Beitritt zu konsultieren, damit die Anwendung des Übereinkommens auf diese Gebiete gewährleistet ist, und dem Generaldirektor der Organisation der Vereinten Nationen für Erziehung, Wissenschaft und Kultur die Hoheitsgebiete zu notifizieren, auf die das Übereinkommen Anwendung findet; die Notifikation wird drei Monate nach ihrem Eingang wirksam.

Artikel 23
(1) Jeder Vertragsstaat kann dieses Übereinkommen für sich selbst oder für ein Hoheitsgebiet, dessen internationale Beziehungen er wahrnimmt, kündigen.
(2) Die Kündigung wird durch eine schriftliche Urkunde notifiziert, die beim Generaldirektor der Organisation der Vereinten Nationen für Erziehung, Wissenschaft und Kultur hinterlegt wird.
(3) Die Kündigung wird zwölf Monate nach Eingang der Kündigungsurkunde wirksam.

Artikel 24
Der Generaldirektor der Organisation der Vereinten Nationen für Erziehung, Wissenschaft und Kultur unterrichtet die Mitgliedstaaten der Organisation, die in Artikel 20 bezeichneten Nichtmitgliedstaaten der Organisation sowie die Vereinten Nationen von der Hinterlegung aller Ratifikations-, Annahme- und Beitrittsurkunden nach den Artikeln 19 und 20 und von den Notifikationen und Kündigungen nach den Artikeln 22 bzw. 23.

Artikel 25
(1) Dieses Übereinkommen kann von der Generalkonferenz der Organisation der Vereinten Nationen für Erziehung, Wissenschaft und Kultur revidiert werden. Jede Revision ist jedoch nur für diejenigen Staaten verbindlich, die Vertragsparteien des Revisionsübereinkommens werden.
(2) Nimmt die Generalkonferenz ein neues Übereinkommen an, das dieses Übereinkommen ganz oder teilweise revidiert, so liegt dieses Übereinkommen, sofern das neue Übereinkommen nichts anderes bestimmt, vom Tag des Inkrafttretens des neuen Revisionsübereinkommens an nicht mehr zur Ratifikation, zur Annahme oder zum Beitritt auf.

Artikel 26
Auf Ersuchen des Generaldirektors der Organisation der Vereinten Nationen für Erziehung, Wissenschaft und Kultur wird dieses Übereinkommen nach Artikel 102 der Charta der Vereinten Nationen beim Sekretariat der Vereinten Nationen registriert.

Geschehen zu Paris am 17. November 1970 in zwei Urschriften, die mit den Unterschriften des Präsidenten der 16. Tagung der Generalkonferenz und des Generaldirektors der Organisation der Vereinten Nationen für Erziehung, Wissenschaft und Kultur versehen sind und im Archiv der Organisation der Vereinten Nationen für Erziehung, Wissenschaft und Kultur hinterlegt werden; allen in den Artikeln 19 und 20 bezeichneten Staaten sowie den Vereinten Nationen werden beglaubigte Abschriften übermittelt.

Dieses ist der verbindliche Wortlaut des Übereinkommens, das von der Generalkonferenz der Organisation der Vereinten Nationen für Erziehung, Wissenschaft und Kultur auf ihrer in Paris abgehaltenen und am 14. November 1970 für beendet erklärten 16. Tagung ordnungsgemäß angenommen wurde.

Zu Urkund dessen haben wir am 17. November 1970 das Übereinkommen mit unseren Unterschriften versehen.

Operational Guidelines for the Implementation of the Convention on the Means of Prohibiting and Preventing the Illicit Import, Export and Transfer of Ownership of Cultural Property[1)]

UNESCO, Paris, 1970

Introduction

1. Cultural heritage is among the priceless and irreplaceable inheritance, not only of each nation, but also of humanity as a whole. The loss, through theft, damage, clandestine excavations, illicit transfer or trade, of its invaluable and exceptional contents constitutes an impoverishment of the cultural heritage of all nations and peoples of the world and infringes upon the fundamental human rights to culture and development.
2. To ensure, as far as possible, the protection of their cultural heritage against the illicit import, export and transfer of ownership, the Member States of UNESCO adopted the Convention on the Means of Prohibiting and Preventing the Illicit Import, Export and Transfer of Ownership of Cultural Property (hereafter referred to as the "1970 Convention" or the "Convention") on 14 November 1970, at the 16th Session of the General Conference of UNESCO. The 1970 Convention constituted a step forward to stop and reverse the erosion of the cultural heritage by, inter-alia, damage, theft, clandestine excavation, and illicit transfer and trade. It raised hopes that cultural heritage and traditions would be duly protected for the benefit of all nations and peoples of the world and for the better education of all. However, the number of Sates Parties has increased slowly and its effective implementation has been lacking. Moreover, worrisome trends, such as the proliferation of pillage and clandestine excavations of archaeological and paleontological sites and related sales on Internet, are posing further challenges to the protection of cultural heritage. At the same time, during the last decades new approaches and attitudes for strengthened partnership to protect cultural heritage have evolved, creating the potential of higher forms of understanding and international cooperation to combat the illicit traffic of cultural property. To date, more than 125 UNESCO Member States have become Parties to the Convention and thus it can be considered as generally accepted by the international community. However, further efforts are needed to increase its acceptance as well as to strengthen its implementation by its States Parties.
3. The first Meeting of States Parties to the 1970 Convention took place in October 2003 in order to examine issues concerning the effective implementation of the Convention (CLT-2003/CONF/207/5). In accordance with 187 EX/Decision 43 and in consideration of the discussions held at the meeting held on the occasion of the 40th anniversary of the 1970 Convention, the Executive Board convened a second Meeting of States Parties to examine in depth the impact of measures taken by States Parties to the Convention to optimize its implementation, appraise its effectiveness with particular regard to new trends in trafficking in cultural property, and reflect on possible modalities for ensuring its effective and regular application and follow-up.
4. The Second Meeting of States Parties took place in June 2012. At that occasion, the Meeting of States Parties decided to convene its meetings every two years. The Meeting of States Parties adopted its own Rules of Procedure. The Meeting of States Parties also decided to establish a Subsidiary Committee of the Meeting of the States Parties of the Convention of 1970 to support the strengthening of the implementation of the Convention (hereafter referred to as the "Subsidiary Committee"), to be convened every year.
5. Following that Second Meeting of States Parties, UNESCO's Executive Board approved the holding of an Extraordinary Meeting of States Parties in 2013, to proceed with the establishment of the Subsidiary Committee (190 EX 190/43). At the Extraordinary Meeting, held on 1 July 2013, the Subsidiary Committee was duly elected. The Subsidiary Committee held its First Meeting on 2-3 July 2013 and adopted its own Rules of Procedure.
6. In accordance with Article 14.6 of its Rules of Procedure, the functions of the Subsidiary Committee are:

---

1) Quelle: http://www.unesco.org/new/fileadmin/MULTIMEDIA/HQ/CLT/pdf/OPERATIONAL_GUIDELINES_EN_FINAL_FINAL.pdf.

A.III.2a Operational Guidelines

- To promote the purposes of the Convention, as set forth in the Convention;
- To review national reports presented to the General Conference by the States Parties to the Convention;
- To exchange best practices, and prepare and submit to the Meeting of the States Parties recommendations and guidelines that may contribute to the implementation of the Convention;
- To identify problem areas arising from the implementation of the Convention, including issues relating to the protection and return of cultural property;
- To initiate and maintain co-ordination with the Intergovernmental Committee for Promoting the Return of Cultural Property to its Countries of Origin or its Restitution in case of Illicit Appropriation (hereafter referred to as the "ICPRCP") in relation to capacity building measures combating illicit traffic in cultural property;
- To report to the Meeting of States Parties on the activities it has carried out.

7. In accordance to its mandate, and with the commitment of fully supporting the achievement of higher forms of understanding and international cooperation to combat the illicit traffic of cultural property, the Subsidiary Committee submitted these Operational Guidelines for the implementation of the UNESCO 1970 Convention by States Parties, for their adoption at the Third Meeting of States Parties of the Convention in 2015. The present guidelines may be subsequently amended by the Meeting of States Parties either on the recommendation of the Subsidiary Committee or on its own initiative.

Purpose of these guidelines

8. The Operational Guidelines of the UNESCO 1970 Convention (hereafter referred to as the Operational Guidelines) aim to strengthen and facilitate the implementation of the Convention to minimize risks related to disputes over the interpretation of the Convention as well as to litigation, and thus to contribute towards international understanding. The Convention was adopted by the General Conference on 14 November 1970. Building upon improved shared understandings and experience, the Operational Guidelines are intended to assist States Parties in implementing the provisions of the Convention, including by learning from the best practices of States Parties geared to enhance the effective implementation of the Convention, and also to identify ways and means to further the achievement of the goals of the Convention through strengthened international cooperation.

Purpose of the Convention

9. The reciprocal responsibilities and obligations agreed in the Convention have the purpose of enabling the international community to protect cultural property against damage, theft, clandestine excavations, illicit import, export and transfer of ownership, trafficking, to implement preventive measures and raise awareness of the importance thereof, to establish a moral and ethical code for the acquisition of cultural property to provide a platform among State Parties to the Convention for facilitating the recovery and return of stolen, illicitly excavated or illicitly exported cultural property, and to promote international cooperation and assistance.

10. The Preamble to the Convention proclaims that the exchange of cultural property among nations for scientific, cultural and educational purposes increases the knowledge of the civilization of humanity; enriches the cultural life of all peoples and inspires mutual respect and appreciation among nations; that cultural property constitutes one of the basic elements of civilization and national culture and that its true value can be appreciated only in relation to the fullest possible information regarding its origin, history and traditional setting; that it is incumbent upon every State to protect the cultural property existing within its territory against the dangers of damage, theft, clandestine excavation, and illicit export; that, to avert these dangers, it is essential for every State Party to become increasingly alive to the moral obligations to respect its own cultural heritage and that of all nations; that, as cultural institutions, museums, libraries and archives should ensure that their collections are built up in accordance with universally recognized moral principles; that the illicit import, export and transfer of ownership of cultural property is an obstacle to that understanding between nations which it is part of UNESCO's mission to promote by recommending to concerned States, international conventions to this end; and that the protection of cultural heritage can be effective only if organized both nationally and internationally among

States working in close cooperation. These agreed general principles should guide the interpretation of the provisions of the Convention.

Definition of cultural property for the purposes of the Convention (Article 1)

11. In drafting the 1970 Convention, UNESCO Member States concluded that it was desirable for all States Parties to apply a common definition of cultural property for the purposes of the Convention, in order to adequately address the issue of exports and imports of such property. Thus, Article 1 states that, for the purposes of the Convention, the term "cultural property" means property which, on religious or secular grounds, is specifically designated by each State as being of importance for archaeology, prehistory, history, literature, art or science and which belongs to the categories identified in the same Article.

12. States Parties are encouraged to keep such designation up to date. Among the categories of cultural property, as enumerated in Article 1 of the Convention, three categories pose special challenges in terms of their specific designation, as follows:

<u>Products of archaeological and paleontological clandestine excavations:</u> Regarding archaeological and paleontological finds clandestinely excavated, States are unable to produce any specific inventories. To avoid the problem of specifically identifying an object of archaeological or paleontological significance, it has been demonstrated that one useful approach is to make a clear assertion of State ownership of undiscovered objects, so that the State Party can request its return under the provisions of the 1970 Convention and/or by recourse to any other relevant means. This is particularly important in the case of an undisturbed archaeological site that has not yet been looted: every object in that site, still to be found, is important for the preservation of cultural heritage and the understanding and knowledge of the archaeological site's full meaning and context. Consequently, States Parties are encouraged to follow best practice in designating the cultural property that is protected under their national law in accordance with these characteristics and all States Parties are encouraged to recognize this sovereign assertion for the purposes of the Convention.

<u>Elements of artistic or historical monuments or archaeological sites which have been dismembered:</u> The specific designation of objects severed or torn from artistic or historical monuments or archaeological sites which have not yet been inventoried also pose a serious challenge. States Parties are invited to define these types of objects that are susceptible to pillage.

<u>Objects of ethnological interest and items of indigenous communities:</u> A special concern is posed by the increasing traffic of objects of ethnological interest that have special anthropological significance in festive or ritual customs and traditions, among others. State Parties are invited to draw and appropriately update lists by type of such significant objects in order to support the fight against their illicit traffic. Another important concern is the return of objects from indigenous communities whose absence has deprived them of significant cultural items necessary for the continuance of their culture, education of their children and respect for their traditions. Items of spiritual importance in all cultures have also been the subject of increased concern. For instance, while human remains are not necessarily covered under the 1970 Convention, many indigenous communities feel strongly about the return of human remains originating in their communities for traditional burial or other ceremonies in their home country. These returns are not regarded as taking place in accordance with the 1970 Convention, since it uses the phrase "cultural property" and most indigenous communities do not accept that human remains can be regarded as "property". States Parties are encouraged to take this into full account and thus to establish legislation, where necessary, that provides for the return of grave objects associated with burials, in view of the anthropological knowledge on the importance of burial practices to such communities and to conform with the wishes of those communities in accordance with the principles of the United Nations Declaration on the Rights of Indigenous Peoples 2007 and the Principles & Guidelines for the Protection of the Heritage of Indigenous People (drafted 1993 and revised 2000).

Fundamental principles of the Convention (Articles 2; 3)

13. Article 2 and 3 state the fundamental principles of the Convention. The first principle is the recognition of "illicit import, export and transfer of ownership of cultural property" as "one of the main causes of the impoverishment of the cultural heritage of the countries of origin of such

A.III.2a Operational Guidelines

property and that international cooperation constitutes one of the most efficient means of protecting each country's cultural property" against these dangers. The second principle is a solemn undertaking by States Parties to fight these practices with the means at their disposal, and particularly by removing their causes, putting a stop to current practices and by helping to make necessary reparations.

14. Trafficking of cultural property has many causes. Ignorance and poor ethics are at its very root and therefore the critical role of education and awareness raising must not be disregarded. Lack of capacity to protect cultural heritage is an important weakness in many countries, which also has to be remedied as much as possible, taking into account that in many instances it is materially impossible to adopt exhaustive measures of physical security and surveillance of all relevant cultural heritage, particularly regarding archaeological and paleontological sites. Moreover, the market has to be better regulated. Law enforcement and customs controls both at export and import points require to be strengthened with rigorous and efficient mechanisms, as well as educating and utilizing an active judiciary in order to confer effective protection to cultural heritage. Moreover, information on trade exchanges should be fully and readily available to States Parties concerned, to enabling them to better confront illicit trafficking. As long as demand remains high there will be an incentive to supply any goods. The trade of archaeological and paleontological objects not only trivializes the invaluable nature of such objects but also may create incentives for looting. In direct relation to the aforementioned, it should be further noticed that objects of recent manufacture are regularly introduced into the market and sold at high prices as genuine archaeological artifacts. This circumstance may further incentivize pillaging and trafficking. Special attention is required in these regards.
15. Clandestine excavations of archaeological sites are among the most pernicious practices within the cycle of illicit trafficking. The damage caused by clandestine excavations of archaeological sites goes well beyond the theft of important archaeological pieces, as it destroys the unity of meaning of the whole archaeological monument and archaeological context of the site, depriving the nations and peoples of the world of the opportunity to understand and learn from their irreplaceable cultural heritage. This pernicious practice should be fully stopped.
16. The recovery and return of stolen, illicitly excavated and illicitly exported cultural property, to countries of origin remains a top priority. All efforts should be made to proceed with this required reparation in fairness to the affected nations and peoples of the world.
17. To advance on all these fronts, States Parties are encouraged to reinforce the promotion of the effective implementation of the fundamental principles of the Convention through appropriate legislation and their full enforcement, as well as through education and awareness raising, capacity building and a strengthened international cooperation.

Link between heritage and State (Article 4)

18. Article 4 (a) to (e) sets out categories of cultural property that can form part of the cultural heritage of a State, either owned by the State itself or a private individual. States Parties to the Convention are required to recognize a link between those categories and the relevant State where the object concerned has been created by an individual or by the "collective genius" of nationals, foreign nationals or stateless persons resident within its territory; found within its national territory; acquired by archaeological, ethnological or natural science missions with the consent of the competent authorities of that country; the subject of a freely agreed exchange; or received as a gift or legally purchased with the consent of the competent authorities of that country.
19. The Convention does not attempt to establish priorities where more than one State may regard a cultural object as part of its cultural heritage. Competing claims to such items, if they cannot be settled by negotiations between the States or their relevant institutions or by special agreement (see paras. 113-115 below), they should be regulated by out of court resolution mechanisms, such as mediation (see para. 104 below) or good offices, or by arbitration. There is no strong tradition for the judicial settlement of such differences in cultural matters. State practice would suggest a preference for mechanisms that allow consideration for legal, as well as cultural, historical and other relevant factors. States Parties are encouraged to exhaust all options provided by the Convention before entering into arbitration or litigation. States Parties are encouraged to cooperate to ensure that appropriate arrangements are established to allow the interested States to realize

their interests in a compatible way through, *inter alia*, loans, temporary exchange of objects for scientific, cultural and educational purposes, temporary exhibitions, joint activities of research and restoration.

National services for the protection of cultural heritage (Article 5, 13(a; b), 14)

20. To ensure the effective implementation of the Convention, Article 5 requires that States Parties undertake, as appropriate for each country, to set up one or more national services for the protection of cultural heritage, with sufficient staff and adequate budget to carry out the following functions:
    - Contributing to the drafting of legislation (Art. 5(a); paras. 24-32 below);
    - Establishing and updating a list of cultural property whose export would constitute an impoverishment of the cultural heritage of the country (Art. 5(b); paras. 33-38 below);
    - Promoting the development or the establishment of scientific and technical institutions required to ensure preservation and presentation of that cultural property (Art. 5(c); paras. 39-41 below);
    - Organizing the supervision of archaeological excavations and ensuring the preservation *in situ* of certain cultural property (Art. 5(d); paras. 42-48 below);
    - Establishing rules "in conformity with the ethical principles set forth in this Convention" and taking steps to ensure their observance (Art. 5(e), paras. 49-51);
    - Taking educational measures to develop respect for the cultural heritage of all States and spreading knowledge of the principles of the Convention (Art. 5(f); paras. 52-53 below);
    - Arranging appropriate publicity for the disappearance of any item of cultural property (Art. 5(g) paras. 54-55 below);

21. States Parties should also ensure that their national services support adequately other functions entrusted to them, such as the ones stipulated in Article 13(a; b):
    - Preventing transfers of ownership of cultural property likely to promote the illicit import or export of such property
    - Ensuring cooperation between their competent services to facilitate restitution of illicitly exported cultural property to its rightful owner.

22. In this context, since previous experiences have proven their efficacy, States Parties are also encouraged to create "specialized police and customs units" or "law enforcement agencies" such as a pool of prosecutors or experts specialized in art-crime investigations, dedicated to the protection of cultural property and the recovery of stolen cultural property under constant cooperation with all the relevant authorities from the different branches and levels of government of the States Parties. States Parties should promote cooperation between such units created in different States, as well as with UNODC, INTERPOL and WCO, and are encouraged to exchange good practice and if possible technical support on all the relevant means and methods used for the prohibition and prevention of the illicit import, export and transfer of cultural property, with special attention to the fight against clandestine excavations of archaeological sites. States Parties are encouraged to enhance police activities to prevent illicit excavations or research in archaeological, paleontological and underwater sites, adopting for their surveillance, in accordance with the particular situations, the appropriate physical and technological measures. States Parties should also promote the exchanges of police and law enforcement experiences, taking into account the relevant investigating experience by specialized units having multi-year practice in the specific sector.

23. Article 14 states that each State Party should, as far as it is able, provide the national services responsible for the protection of its cultural heritage with an adequate budget. If necessary a fund should be set up for this purpose. States Parties are encouraged to ensure that their national services support adequately all of the functions given to them. States Parties are also encouraged to strengthen international cooperation in support of these national efforts.

Legislation (Article 5(a))

24. Article 5(a) requires States Parties to adopt appropriate legislation for the protection of the cultural heritage and particularly prevention of the illicit import, export and transfer of ownership of cultural property. States Parties may seek assistance or advice for the making of such legislation

A.III.2a Operational Guidelines

from UNESCO. States Parties are encouraged to review their legislation periodically to ensure that it integrates the relevant international legal framework and best practice.

25. In fulfilling their duty to protect cultural heritage, several States have enacted explicit laws on State ownership of certain cultural property, even when it remains officially undiscovered or is otherwise unrecorded. State ownership laws constitute the first barrier against looting and should prevent laundering and international trade in undocumented cultural property.

26. State ownership laws cannot fulfill their protective purpose or facilitate the return of cultural property if the removal of the relevant cultural property from the territory of the concerned State without its express consent as rightful owner is not internationally regarded as theft of public property. Thus, when a State has declared ownership of certain cultural property, States Parties are, in the spirit of the Convention, encouraged to consider the illicit removal of that cultural property from the territory of the dispossessed State as theft of public property, where such demonstration of ownership is necessary in order to allow for its return.

27. In this context, it is important to recall that, following the UNESCO Recommendation on International Principles Applicable to Archaeological Excavations (1956) and the ECOSOC Resolution 2008/23 on the need for States to assert State ownership of the archaeological subsoil, and as requested by the ICPRCP at its 16th session in 2010, the UNESCO and UNIDROIT Secretariats convened a group of experts from all different regions of the world and mandated them to draft a text that would appropriately address the subject. The document was finalized and adopted at the ICPRCP at its 17th session in 2011.

28. These Model Provisions are intended to assist domestic legislative bodies in the establishment of a legislative framework for heritage protection, in States concerned, in order to adopt effective legislation for the establishment and recognition of the State's ownership of undiscovered cultural objects with a view to facilitating return in case of unlawful removal and to ensure that courts will have full knowledge of the relevant legal provisions abroad. The Model Provisions and their explanatory guidelines are included in Annex 1.

29. Consequently, States Parties may consider, as appropriate for each country, to apply in their legislation the six Model Provisions on State ownership drafted by the UNESCO/UNIDROIT Working Group and adopted by the UNESCO/ICPRCP in 2011.

30. States Parties are encouraged to also consider becoming Parties of the UNIDROIT Convention on Stolen or Illicitly Exported Cultural Objects 1995. Significant provisions which complement the 1970 Convention are among others a duty to return a stolen object, a clear test for due diligence in checking provenance and specific provisions for the return of illegally exported cultural objects.

31. It is important that all relevant national legislation be appropriately publicized so that collectors, dealers, museums and other concerned stakeholders with the movement of cultural objects are fully aware of the precise national provisions they should comply with. To ensure, as far as possible, this publicity and visibility of the laws/rules concerning the protection of cultural property, UNESCO has established a Database of National Cultural Heritage Laws, a source of information easily and freely accessible (hereafter referred to as the "UNESCO Database"). The development of this innovative tool was approved by the UNESCO General Conference in 2003 and launched in 2005 by the 13th session of the ICPRCP.

32. The UNESCO database encompasses numerous types of national standard-setting instruments and related materials as well as information on the national authorities responsible for the protection of the cultural heritage and addresses of the official national websites dedicated to the protection of the cultural heritage. States Parties are encouraged to provide all relevant legislation, including their export and import laws and the legislation on criminal and administrative sanctions, to the UNESCO Secretariat translated into English or French which are the working languages of UNESCO, for inclusion on the UNESCO Database and especially to keep it updated.

Inventories, inalienability and State ownership (Article 5(b))

33. A key step in the protection of States Parties' cultural property against illicit import, export and transfer of ownership is establishing and keeping up to date, on the basis of a national inventory

of protected cultural property, a list of important public and private cultural property whose export would constitute an impoverishment of the national cultural heritage.
34. These lists can include cultural property identified either by individual description or by category, considering that, in developing and recognizing inventories of such protected cultural property inventories, States Parties should bear in mind the specific characteristics of cultural property, as defined in Article 1, in particular regarding clandestinely excavated archaeological sites and other cultural property that poses special challenges in terms of their specific designation (see para. 12 above).
35. States Parties have the indefeasible right to classify and declare certain cultural property as inalienable and, to enact State ownership laws on cultural property. In the spirit of the Convention and unless evidence of the contrary, States Parties are encouraged, for restitution purposes after the entry into force of the Convention as appropriate, to consider cultural property forming part of the cultural heritage of a State as appertaining to the relevant official inventory of the owner State. There is a need to develop a common methodology based on existing methods and databases to ensure that such inventories are fully integrated into the international procedures now available for tracking lost and stolen cultural objects in support of full compliance with and enforcement of the Convention. This common methodology may allow for the granting of a unique identity number not only to every object found in archaeological and paleontological sites and displayed or stored in museums but also to categories of types of cultural objects claimed by a State Party to be deriving from clandestine excavations, which may be categorized by region and epoch or any other suitable archaeological or paleontological reference.
36. Regarding movable cultural property in museums and religious or secular public monuments or similar institutions, including legally excavated archaeological sites and objects of ethnological interest, the usage of the Object-ID Standard is recommended. The Object-ID Standard facilitates rapid transmission of basic information on lost and stolen cultural objects. The Standard provides for eight key identifying elements which, together with a photograph, make the identification of an object and its tracking much simpler. States Parties which do not have extensive inventories and need to elaborate them quickly to make use of the international procedures now available for tracking cultural objects are encouraged to use the Object-ID Standard. Other methods may be proposed, as appropriate, in order to facilitate the use of the international procedures now available for tracking lost and stolen cultural objects in support of full compliance with and enforcement of the Convention. States Parties which have communities which, on religious or other grounds, are unwilling to photograph items used in sacred rituals are encouraged to discuss this issue with a view to improving the recovery of religious objects.
37. To facilitate the work of customs officers dealing with the import of cultural objects, it is imperative that they have precise information about protected cultural property and export bans in other States Parties. This can be done in two ways: either by means of an itemized list in case of documented protected cultural property or, in case of protected cultural property that cannot be itemized, by means of a list of categories with descriptive explanations with as much detail as possible. Such list(s) should be made readily available for the customs authorities of other States Parties and other relevant authorities and entities.
38. The UNESCO database should be the first point of call for a customs service supervising imports because it will provide them with the legislation on the definition of what is a controlled export, what is an illegal export, and what needs to be discussed with the authorities of the country of export. It is therefore important to also have the legislation in an accessible language. National heritage services should be encouraged to publicize their protected cultural property nationally as well as to other States Parties so as to facilitate cooperation.

Expert institutions (Article 5(c))

39. In accordance to Article 5(c), States Parties have undertaken to promote the development or the establishment of scientific and technical institutions (museums, libraries, archives, laboratories, workshops, etc.) required to ensure the preservation and presentation of cultural property.

A.III.2a Operational Guidelines

40. States Parties are encouraged to establish national specialized institutions where circumstances permit or to make arrangements for access to specialist institutions outside their own country where necessary. Such institutions should be well staffed, well funded and well provisioned with appropriate infrastructure, including security infrastructure.
41. States Parties are also encouraged to cooperate in the development or the establishment of scientific and technical institutions, including training workshops, capacity-building programs and infrastructure projects and share specialized scientific and technical expertise related to the protection of cultural property through methods such as trainings, internships and publication researches.

Archaeology and protected areas (Article 5(d))

42. States Parties are encouraged to protect by legislation and, if necessary, by other specific measures, sites of archaeological interest, including their movable items. Concerning the legislation, the relevant provisions of the section "Legislation" (see paras. 24-32 above) should be followed.
43. Specific activities should be established to protect the archaeological heritage in accordance with the principles contained in the UNESCO Recommendation on International Principles Applicable to Archaeological Excavations (1956), as appropriate. The following principles of that Recommendation are relevant to efforts to prevent clandestine excavation:
    - The purpose of archaeological research lies in the public interest from the point of view of history or art or science. Excavation should not take place for other purposes, except in the case of the extraordinary circumstances described in the UNESCO Recommendation concerning the Preservation of Cultural Property Endangered by Public or Private Works (1968) and subject to the preventive and corrective measures prescribed in para. 8 of that Recommendation.
    - Protection should be extended to all objects belonging to a given period or of the minimum age fixed by law.
    - Each State Party should make archaeological explorations and excavation subject to prior authorization of the competent heritage authority.
    - Authority to carry out excavations should be granted only to institutions represented by qualified archaeologists or to persons offering unimpeachable scientific, moral and financial guarantees that the excavations will be completed in accordance with the terms of the contract.
    - The contract should include provision for guarding, maintenance, restoration and conservation of both the objects recovered and the site during and on completion of work.
    - An excavator or finder and the subsequent holders should be required to declare any object of archaeological character whether movable or immovable.
    - Objects recovered during the course of the work should be immediately photographed, registered and kept in a secure structure.
44. State Parties are encouraged, within the framework of applicable rules and existing mechanisms, to conduct archaeological surface surveys for different purposes, including for preventive purposes, and to enhance the inventory of national archaeological sites.
45. States Parties are also encouraged to establish provisions on the use of methods of ground-penetrating analysis such as the use of metal detectors. States are encouraged to prohibit, as appropriate, unauthorized use of such equipment for purposes of undertaking clandestine excavations on archaeological sites.
46. States directly affected are also encouraged to carefully guard archaeological sites and all States Parties are encouraged to take sanctions against any person involved in theft and clandestine excavations of such sites.
47. States Parties should acknowledge that participation by individuals or groups of individuals belonging to local communities in unauthorized excavations and looting of sites cannot be considered in isolation from the larger socio-economic conditions that those communities find themselves in. In protecting known archaeological sites from unauthorised excavation and pillage, States Parties are invited to encourage local communities, as appropriate, to cooperate in the protection

of cultural heritage. State Parties are encouraged to raise awareness among local communities of the importance of safeguarding the cultural heritage as well as emphasizing to those communities the potential long-term economic benefits of such preservation – through such means as cultural tourism – over the short-term, limited economic benefits of participating in unauthorised excavation activities.

48. States Parties are encouraged to establish specific means to protect underwater archaeological remains from looting and illicit traffic, including the reporting of discoveries to the competent authorities and the regulation of salvage and accidental finds. States Parties are encouraged to cooperate in providing technical capacity in this regard.

Rules in conformity with the ethical principles set forth in the Convention (Article 5(e))

49. In accordance with Article 5(e), States Parties have undertaken to set up national services which have as a function establishing, for the benefit of those concerned (curators, collectors, antique dealers, etc.) rules in conformity with the ethical principles set forth in the Convention; and taking steps to ensure the observance of those rules.

50. Such rules may be developed on a national, regional, international, or professional level. Anthropologists, archaeologists, auctioneers, conservators, curators, dealers, restorers and all professional staff working with cultural objects are obliged to conform to these rules based on ethical principles which refuse service for cultural objects whose provenance appears faulty or dubious and should notify relevant authorities of this kind of artefacts when they have been asked to provide such service. The rules to be developed regarding acquisitions should be equally applied to collectors, dealers, curators, and others involved in the trade in cultural property so as not to disadvantage or exempt any single group. Also, such rules should be internationally standardized to ensure maximum effectiveness.

51. In this regard, States Parties are encouraged to use codes of ethics developed by national and international bodies. These include the International Code of Ethics for Dealers in Cultural Property adopted by the ICPRCP in 1999. This Code incorporates the principles developed in the 1970 Convention and subsequently in the UNIDROIT Convention on Stolen or Illegally Exported Cultural Objects (1995). This Code also takes into account the experience of various national codes, the Code of the Confédération Internationale des Négociants d'Oeuvres d'Art (CINOA) as well as the Code of Professional Ethics of the International Council of Museums (ICOM). States Parties are encouraged to ensure that all dealers abide by this Code, both by imposing appropriate compulsory measures and by offering incentives to those dealers who do undertake to abide by its provisions, such as tax concessions. States Parties are encouraged to monitor the success of such efforts and to continue developing, strengthening and enforcing appropriate rules for the benefit of curators, collectors, antique dealers, and others concerned, in conformity with the ethical principles set forth in this Convention.

Education (Articles 5(f); 10)

52. In accordance with Article 10, States Parties should use all appropriate means to prevent the movement of cultural property illegally removed from any State Party through education, awareness rising, information and vigilance. In particular, educational means and awareness rising and should be used to help local communities and the public in general to appreciate the value of cultural heritage and the threat to it from theft, clandestine excavations and illicit trafficking as well as its relation to the cultural identity and history of the local communities and mankind.

53. In accordance with Article 5(f) the national services for the protection of the cultural heritage should take educational measures to stimulate and develop respect for the cultural heritage of all States and should also spread knowledge of the provisions of the Convention. In particular, States Parties are encouraged to strengthen educational measures within their countries, with the cooperating services and with the public in other countries This includes adequate coordination with educational institutions at primary, secondary, tertiary level and lifelong learning programs to include teaching and research on cultural heritage issues in their own curricula; through

A.III.2a Operational Guidelines

awareness-raising, capacity building and training programs targeted at judges, prosecutors, customs officers, police, museums, dealers and others concerned; and through mass-media, museum, library, and other outreach programs.

Publicizing the disappearance of cultural objects (Article 5(g))

54. In accordance with Article 5(g), the national services for the protection of the cultural heritage should see that appropriate publicity is given to the disappearance of cultural property. Publicity through mass communication can help investigation efforts, make an object untradeable, and can result directly in its recovery. Recognizing this situation, States Parties should publicize thefts and other forms of illegal conduct against cultural property and to make use of the mass media to publicize lost and stolen cultural objects.
55. States Parties are encouraged to support and use databases and other mechanisms that have been established to share information internationally about stolen works of art, including the INTERPOL Stolen Works of Art Database. States Parties are also encouraged to disseminate ICOM Red Lists to all stakeholders involved in the protection of cultural property, especially police and customs services.

Prohibition and Prevention of Illicit Import, Export, and Transfer of Ownership of Cultural Property (Articles 6, 7(a, b (i)), 8, 10(a); 13(a))

Export certificates (Article 6(a, b))

56. In accordance with Article 6(a), States Parties have undertaken to introduce an appropriate certificate in which the exporting State would specify that the export of an item of cultural property is authorized, which should accompany all items of cultural property exported in accordance with the relevant legislation. In accordance to Article 6(b), States Parties have also undertaken to prohibit the exportation of any cultural property from their territory unless accompanied by such a certificate. Customs authorities should check the export certificate both at the moment of export and import.
57. The certificate is an official document issued by the exporting country certifying that it has authorized the export of the cultural object. This document is essential for effective control, and implies cooperation between national services for the protection of cultural heritage and customs authorities of all countries involved in the movement of protected cultural property, including countries of transit. States Parties that apply import certificates should distribute such import certificates only for the cultural objects that have export certificates. Holding an import certificate without a corresponding export certificate should not be considered as a proof of good faith or title of ownership.
58. To ensure that such export certificates fulfill their intended purpose, in the spirit of the Convention State Parties should prohibit the entering into their territory of cultural property, to which the Convention applies, that are not accompanied by such export certificate. Consequently, the prohibition of the export of cultural property without its corresponding export certificate should make illicit the import of that cultural property into another State Party, as the cultural property has not been exported legally from the country affected.
59. Export certificates should carry at least the following information: the name of the owner if appropriate; photographs of the item; a description of the item; its dimensions; its characteristics; the validity period of the export certificate; the State of destination; and the signature of the competent authorities. States Parties issuing export certificates should maintain searchable records of such certificates, in the event that forgeries or unauthorized alterations are identified during import in a foreign State, and the issuing state is called upon to confirm whether the permit is genuine and accurate. In order to avoid forgeries States Parties are encouraged to make available model forms of their export certificates to the relevant authorities of other states as well as to send, whenever feasible, copies of the issued export certificates to the relevant authorities of other States Parties. The States concerned are encouraged to establish the appropriate channel of communication.

60. All cultural objects forming part of the cultural heritage of a State according to its legislation appearing in the art market of another State, exported from the territory of the former and imported into the territory of the latter after the entry into force of the Convention for both States, have to have an export certificate issued by the State of origin. In these cases, the exportation of said cultural objects without an export certificate will be considered illicit and as the basis for reporting to the competent authorities of the State of origin.
61. States Parties may also introduce special provisions for certificates for temporary export. Such temporary export certificates may be issued for exhibitions and return, for study by specialized research institutions or for any other reason such as conservation or restoration purposes. An export in violation of the conditions provided in a temporary export certificate should be considered as an illicit export.
62. States Parties are encouraged to give particular attention to the issue, form and security of the export certificate and to ensure close liaison between the customs authorities, heritage managers and police officers for its control and reliability. The Model Export Certificate for Cultural Objects, developed jointly by the UNESCO and the WCO Secretariats, is a useful operational tool for the fight against illicit trafficking of cultural property (Annex 2). It has been specially adapted to the growing phenomenon of cross-border movements of cultural objects and is useful to the law enforcement agencies and customs services, enabling them to combat trafficking in cultural property more effectively. States Parties are encouraged to use or adapt the model export certificate and to consider whether a temporary export certificate would suit their protective scheme. The Model Export Certificate may be improved if need be.

Prohibition of importing stolen cultural property (Article 7(b)(i))

63. In accordance with Article 7(b)(i), States Parties have undertaken to prohibit the import of cultural property stolen from a museum or a religious or secular public monument or similar institution in another State Party to this Convention after the entry into force of this Convention for the States concerned, provided that such property is documented as appertaining to the inventory of that institution.
There are two important considerations to be made regarding this prohibition:
First, evidently, the implementation of this prohibition could be facilitated by making compulsory the requirement of an export certificate from the State of origin in order to make licit the import of any cultural property (see paras. 56-62 above). Moreover, States Parties are encouraged to collaborate, especially via their customs authorities, as required and to diligently revise all their relevant regulations in accordance with best practice to ensure effective import controls best practice at all entry points to protect cultural heritage items and prevent smuggling. Furthermore, to assist State Parties to effectively implement this prohibition, it is important that all known thefts and other forms of illegal conduct against cultural property are promptly publicized and reported to relevant law enforcement agencies as well as to INTERPOL.
Second, this prohibition should recall the specific characteristics of cultural property, as defined in Article 1, especially in regard to clandestinely excavated archaeological sites and other cultural property that poses special challenges in terms of their specific designation (see para. 12 above). In these cases, States Parties' right to classify and declare certain cultural property inalienable which should therefore not be exported (as stated in Article 13(d)), should be fully respected.

Penalties and administrative sanctions (Articles 6(b), 7(b); 8)

64. In accordance with Article 8, States Parties undertake to impose penalties or administrative sanctions on any person responsible for infringing the prohibitions referred to under Articles 6(b) and 7(b) of the Convention. In any such case, if documentary proof of legal export cannot be provided to the competent authorities for cultural property to which the Convention applies, such a cultural property should be retained by such authorities and returned to the State Party concerned, according to the relevant national legal procedures.

A.III.2a Operational Guidelines

65. As the Convention does not specify what sort of sanctions are to be applied, States Parties are encouraged to introduce in their national legislation, as appropriate, specific penal or administrative sanctions against all those who commit acts prohibited by the Convention. In addition, States Parties are encouraged to penalize offences against cultural property, committed in violation of the Convention, by introducing penal sanctions against the perpetrators of such offences. The said national legislations should be included and timely updated in the UNESCO database.
66. States Parties to the 1970 Convention that are also States Parties to the UN Convention against Transnational Organized Crime (UNTOC) are encouraged to make offences related to trafficking in cultural property a serious crime, as defined in article 2 of the UNTOC, in particular with regard to the relevant penalties.
67. Due to their relevance for the development and strengthening of crime prevention and criminal justice policies, strategies, legislation and cooperation mechanisms to prevent and combat trafficking in cultural property and related offences in all situations, States Parties are encouraged to duly take into consideration, in implementing the 1970 Convention, the International Guidelines for Crime Prevention and Criminal Justice Responses with Respect to Trafficking in Cultural Property and Other Related Offences, as submitted to the United Nations General Assembly, following an intergovernmental process facilitated by the United Nations Office on Drugs and Crime (UNODC) in consultation with Member States and in close cooperation with UNESCO, UNIDROIT and other relevant international organizations.

Sales on internet

68. At the time of the drafting of the 1970 Convention, Internet was not a channel for sales. The exponential growth of the use of the Internet to sell or traffic cultural objects which are stolen, clandestinely excavated from archaeological sites, or illegally exported or imported cultural objects, is a matter of serious concern and constitutes a major threat to cultural heritage.
69. Some States Parties are not sufficiently organized to supervise and quickly follow-up offers on the Internet that appear to be advertising protected cultural property. Most national cultural administrations do not have sufficient resources to continually check offers on the Internet. Further, such websites advertise cultural property for a limited time, sometimes only a few hours, hence hindering the ability of the owner States to track such cultural property and to take the necessary actions. In addition, some websites play the role of intermediary in selling cultural property and consequently, they are not in possession of the cultural property offered for sale and cannot verify the validity of the documentation envisaged under the Convention for such cultural property. There is a need to explore ways and means to thoroughly screen all websites throughout the world to determine where offers of cultural property falling under the scope of the protection of the 1970 Convention are made and create an alert method of notifying the relevant State Parties on a daily basis. National authorities are encouraged to marshal the support of all Internet providers and promote the supervision by the public (specialists or other individuals interested in particular cultures) to be vigilant concerning Internet offers and to inform the administration when it appears that an object of national heritage not previously known is being offered on a website or when an object of foreign heritage origin is offered with a local address. Such notifications should be examined immediately by the cultural administration; if necessary, using experts (from universities, museums, libraries and other institutions) to verify the nature and importance of the item(s) being offered. In all the above-mentioned efforts, special attention should be given to the screening of Internet auctions. When the evidence justifies it, the national authorities should undertake prosecutions and enforce all appropriate provisions of the 1970 Convention and national legislation.
70. Following a recommendation adopted by the third annual meeting of the INTERPOL Expert Group on Stolen Cultural Property (7-8 March 2006, INTERPOL General Secretariat), INTERPOL, UNESCO and ICOM have developed a list of Basic Actions to counter the Increasing Illicit Sale of Cultural Objects through the Internet. States Parties are encouraged to incorporate the Basic Actions as a tool within their national context. The Basic Actions currently developed are presented in Annex 3. There is a need to consider ways and means to keep improving the Basic

Actions, in order to ensure the effective implementation of the Convention, in coordination with the ICPRCP, or exploring other ways to contribute to countering the illicit sale of cultural property through the Internet.

Sales in auctions

71. Sales in auctions of cultural property claimed to have been subject to illicit trafficking have greatly affected the cultural heritage of many countries whose requests for return have not been met and have sometimes been used as a means to launder cultural property of illicit provenance. States where auctions are held are encouraged to give special attention to such sales, including by introducing national legislation, where appropriate, to ensure that the cultural property involved has been licitly imported, as documented by a legally issued export certificate, to inform the State of origin of the properties of any doubts in this regard, and to put in place the appropriate interim measures. In addition, on the petition of affected States, when an auction of protected cultural property is intended to take place, the Director General of UNESCO is invited to consider issuing a public statement concerning such commercial activity, highlighting the negative effects of such practices for the protection of world cultural heritage.

Preventing transfers of ownership likely to promote illicit import or export, controlling trade by registers, and establishment of rules in conformity with ethical principles (Articles 13(a); 10(a); 7(a); 5(e))

72. Although this is a basic aim of the Convention described by the 1969 Preliminary Report on the Means of Prohibiting and Preventing the Illicit Import, Export, and Transfer of Ownership (SCH/MD/3), there is no information in the Convention itself as to which such transfers are likely to promote illicit import or export of cultural property. However, it is illuminating to recall that the 1969 Report indicated that lack of information about the origin of the item, the names and addresses of the supplier, description and price of each item sold, as well as lack of information provided to the purchaser about an object's possible export prohibition, might well be a transaction likely to promote illicit trafficking of cultural property. In accordance with Article 10(a), the States Parties to this Convention undertake, as appropriate for each country, to oblige antique dealers, subject to penal or administrative sanctions, to maintain a register recording such essential information. Control of such registers by the national services for the protection of cultural heritage would make it possible to follow up an item of cultural property and perhaps retrace an item that has disappeared after being lost or stolen.

73. The drafters of the preliminary version of the Convention text in 1969 also pointed out: "It is essential that the new rules to be worked out for acquisitions shall place collectors and dealers on the same footing as curators; otherwise museums would be restrained for the sole benefit of illicit trade in cultural property." States Parties are encouraged to ensure that equally constraining rules, whether legislative or ethical, include the same provisions for collectors and dealers as those being observed by museums or other similar institutions, particularly those concerning the provenance of the cultural property.

74. In accordance with Article 7(a), States Parties undertake to take the necessary measures, consistent with national legislation, to prevent museums and similar institutions within their territories from acquiring cultural property originating in another State Party which has been illegally exported after the entry into force of the Convention in the States concerned and, whenever possible, to inform the State of origin Party to the Convention of an offer of such cultural property illegally removed from that State after the entry into force of the Convention in both States.

75. States Parties establishing tax incentive regimes, benefits or government subsidies to encourage the acquisition of cultural property by public institutions should take appropriate steps to ensure that such measures do not inadvertently facilitate the private collection, and subsequent acquisition by institutions, of material that has been the subject of illicit activity as defined by the provisions of the Convention.

A.III.2a Operational Guidelines 238

76. In accordance with Article 5(e), States Parties are also required to establish ethical rules and ensure their observance by curators, collectors, dealers and other similar actors.
77. Consequently, States Parties are encouraged to strengthen the supervision of the activities of dealers and museums through effective policies and regulations and to use all appropriate means to prevent illicit transactions.
78. States Parties are encouraged to explore further possible avenues for preventing transfers of ownership likely to promote illicit import or export. For instance, specific regulations can be enacted to ensure that cultural property such as archaeological objects that are claimed by the States of origin or that are subject to inalienability laws may not be transferred by purchase or assignment from public museums and institutions to private collectors, museums, institutions or businesses.
79. States Parties are also encouraged to undertake studies on the size and nature of illicit activities in the field of cultural property, and establish risk analysis with customs to prevent the illicit import and export of cultural property, as well as exchange information and best practices among each other.
80. States are encouraged as well to make further use of all existing controls over markets and fairs where items of cultural property may be transferred and subsequently exported and to strengthen such controls as necessary to ensure the fulfilment of the purposes of the Convention.
81. The true value of cultural property remains to some degree unrecognized. This fact, added to dissociation from the cause-effect relationship between an ever-increasing demand for numerous types of cultural property and its trafficking, as well as lack of knowledge of the adverse effects of trafficking, hampers protective efforts. Therefore, different educational strategies may also be put in use to diminish the looting, trafficking and the demand for archaeological and paleontological objects, such as education in museums and exhibitions to explain the importance of the damage done to the heritage by clandestine excavation, illicit trade and theft. With a view towards restitution, the States Parties are encouraged to adopt appropriate national legal and policy frameworks to ensure that museums and other cultural institutions, whether public or private, do not exhibit or keep for other purposes imported cultural property that do not have a clear provenance and place of origin. The stylistic or aesthetic qualities of a cultural property can never compensate the loss of its context.

Cooperation on recovery and return of cultural property (Articles 7(b)(ii); 13(b, c, d); 15)

82. In accordance with Article 7(b)(ii), the States Parties have undertaken, at the request of the State Party of origin, to take appropriate steps to recover and return any stolen cultural property imported after the entry into force of this Convention in both States concerned, provided, however, that the requesting State shall pay just compensation to an innocent purchaser or to a person who has valid title to that property. Requests for recovery and return shall be made through diplomatic offices and shall be furnished, at the expense of the requesting Party, with the documentation and other evidence necessary to establish the corresponding claim.
83. Also, in accordance with Article 13 (b,c,d), the States Parties have undertaken, consistent with laws of each State, to ensure that their competent services cooperate in facilitating the earliest possible restitution of illicitly exported cultural property to its rightful owner; to admit actions for recovery of lost or stolen items of cultural property brought by or on behalf of the rightful owners; and to recognize the indefeasible right of each State Party to this Convention to classify and declare certain cultural property as inalienable which should therefore not be exported, and to facilitate recovery of such property by the State concerned in cases where it has been exported.
84. Furthermore, Article 15 provides that nothing in this Convention shall prevent States Parties thereto from concluding special agreements among themselves or from continuing to implement agreements already concluded regarding the restitution of cultural property removed, whatever the reason, from its territory of origin, before the entry into force of this Convention for the States concerned.
85. The above-referred provisions indicate the actions that States Parties should pursue for the restitution, recovery and return after an illicit import, export or transfer of ownership has taken place in spite of prohibition and prevention efforts. A number of issues should be clarified:
    – Request of State Party
    – Evidence to establish a claim

- Just compensation and due diligence
- Cooperation for earliest possible restitution
- Admission of legal actions for recovery of lost or stolen cultural property
- Non-retroactivity of the 1970 Convention, entry into force of the Convention, and resolution of claims
- Intergovernmental Committee for Promoting the Return of Cultural Property to its Countries of Origin or its Restitution in case of Illicit Appropriation (ICPRCP)

Request of State Party (Article 7(b)(ii))

86. In accordance with Article 7(b)(ii), the request of a State Party to recover cultural property and have it returned under the provisions of the 1970 Convention shall be made through diplomatic offices. This is without prejudice to any other recourse that may contribute to the recovery or return under other relevant legal instruments or any other procedures for international legal assistance, which may be used in the course of criminal law proceedings. In this regard, States Parties should consider providing each other with the widest possible legal assistance in investigations, prosecutions and judicial proceedings in relation to cultural property offences, also in order to ensure effectiveness and speediness in the procedures. The provision of spontaneous information between the competent authorities should be encouraged.

Evidence to establish a claim (Article 7(b)(ii))

87. Also in accordance with Article 7(b)(ii), requests for recovery and return shall be furnished, at the expense of the requesting State Party, with the documentation and other evidence necessary to establish the corresponding claim. In this regard, States Parties should bear in mind the specific characteristics of cultural property protected by the requesting State, as defined in Article 1, in particular regarding clandestinely excavated archaeological and paleontological sites and other cultural property that poses special challenges in terms of their specific designation and their implications in terms of inventories (see paras. 12; 24-30; 33-35; 37; 100-103; 108).
88. The considerations made regarding the prohibition of importing stolen cultural property stipulated in Article 7(b)(i) and in the spirit of Article 2 are also fully relevant for the request of States Parties for recovery and return (see para. 63 above).
89. States Parties should bear in mind the implications of the prohibition of the export of a cultural property without its corresponding export certificate. The import of that object should be considered illicit, as it has not been exported legally from the country affected. Consequently, a State Party should be able to introduce a request for items of cultural property that have been clandestinely excavated from archaeological and paleontological sites or which pose special challenges in terms of their specific designation where the possessor or holder does not provide the necessary export certificate of the cultural objects exported after the entry into force of the Convention for both States concerned.
90. When a State has enacted laws on State ownership of certain cultural property in the spirit of the Convention, States Parties are, for recovery and restitution purposes, encouraged to duly take into account these laws.
91. States Parties may support their requests for the recovery and return of cultural property which is unlawfully excavated or lawfully excavated but unlawfully retained in another State Party to the Convention, with reasonable scientific reports, results of scientific analysis or experts' evaluations on provenance of the unlawfully excavated property. Considering the difficulties of conducting research for retrospective evidence, States Parties are strongly encouraged to consider accredited scientific studies and analysis as evidence.
92. Furthermore, States Parties sharing a particular culture with archaeological remains in more than one country are encouraged to consider joint actions for recovery. All States Parties are encouraged to consider such cooperative efforts positively. Requesting States sharing a particular culture are encouraged to reach appropriate agreements on the cultural property recovered, considering solutions such as loans, exchanges of properties, etc.

A.III.2a Operational Guidelines

Just compensation and due diligence (Article 7(b)(ii))

93. The question of compensation is one area where there has been a significant development of approaches. The 1970 Convention stipulates (Art. 7 (b) (ii)) "that the requesting State shall pay just compensation to an innocent purchaser or to a person who has valid title to that property." Developments since then have demonstrated that many States appreciate further the relevance of returning cultural property. They are also aware that States of origin very much resent requirements to pay for objects that they regard as owned by them and that many of them are unable to pay large sums for their return. In addition, States are now much more aware of the importance of cultural matters in their foreign relations. Recent practice suggests little use of the compensation provision of the Convention. Some States Parties have made reservations which, among others, exempt other States Parties from having to pay just compensation. It is also important to note that the issue of compensation is not mentioned in Article 9 of the 1970 Convention and in many States it has not been raised in the context of illegally imported cultural objects.

94. In the spirit of the Convention, States Parties should use the criteria of due diligence in assessing purchaser innocence and validity of titles. In this regard, States Parties which seek compensation are encouraged to adopt recent best practice which can include the UNIDROIT standard of due diligence. Article 4.1 of the 1995 UNIDROIT Convention on Stolen or Illegally Exported Cultural Objects stipulates that the possessor of a stolen cultural object required to return it shall be entitled, at the time of its restitution, to payment of fair and reasonable compensation provided that the possessor neither knew nor ought reasonably to have known that the object was stolen and can prove that it exercised due diligence when acquiring the object.

Cooperation for earliest possible restitution (Article 13(b))

95. In accordance with Article 13(b), States Parties have undertaken, consistent with laws of each State, to ensure that their competent services cooperate in facilitating the earliest possible restitution of illicitly exported cultural property to its rightful owner.

96. In this context, and also considering the provision contained in Article 13(d), when a State Party, including those that have enacted laws on State ownership, is dispossessed of cultural property and seeks to recover it, States Parties are encouraged to resort to and to exhaust all means at their disposal to provide the fullest cooperation. In order to expeditiously grant requests for the restitution of stolen public property to its rightful owner, such cooperation should include pondering, as appropriate, the requesting State's ownership laws. Moreover, due to the clandestine nature of the pillage of cultural property, States Parties are encouraged to take into consideration that it may be materially impossible for dispossessed States to offer concrete data concerning thefts of State-owned cultural property. Therefore, State Parties are encouraged to attempt as far as possible to facilitate restitutions of State-owned cultural property even when the plundered sites remain unknown.

97. When it is impossible to furnish documentation and evidence concerning theft of State-owned cultural property, and without prejudice to the considerations presented above, State Parties are encouraged to explore the possibility of reaching an agreement by diplomatic channels concerning the expeditious admissibility and processing of the relevant restitution requests.

98. If the States concerned by the recovery have a specialized law enforcement unit in charge of the protection of cultural heritage, this unit should play an essential role in international cooperation, in particular through the National Central Bureaux of INTERPOL.

Admission of legal actions for recovery of list or stolen cultural property (Article 13 (c))

99. In accordance with Article 13(c), consistent with the laws of each State, the States Parties are required to admit actions for recovery of lost or stolen items of cultural property brought by or on behalf of the rightful owner(s). If no such action is available in a State Party, this Article requires it to create one. States Parties are therefore encouraged to check that there exists, in their national system, a legal proceeding available to an owner of lost or stolen items of cultural pro-

perty, and, if there is none, to institute one. The relevant information should be incorporated in a timely manner and kept updated in the UNESCO database.

Non-retroactivity of the 1970 Convention, entry into force of the Convention and resolution of claims (Article 21)

100. The general rule of public international law embodied in Article 28 of the Vienna Convention on the Law of Treaties does not provide for retroactive application of treaties. The provisions of the 1970 Convention entered into force on 24 April 1972, three months after the date of deposit of the third instrument of ratification, acceptance or accession. For the other Signatory States, the Convention entered into force three months after the deposit of the instrument of ratification, acceptance or accession.
101. In accordance with the provisions of the 1970 Convention, especially Article 7, a State Party can seek the recovery and return of any illegally exported, illegally removed or stolen cultural property imported into another State Party only after the entry into force of this Convention in both States concerned.
102. However, the Convention does not in any way legitimize any illicit transaction of whatever nature which has taken place before the entry into force of this Convention nor limit any right of a State or other person to make a claim under specific procedures or legal remedies available outside the framework of this Convention for the restitution or return of a cultural object stolen or illegally exported before the entry into force of this Convention.
103. For items of illegally exported, illegally removed or stolen cultural property imported into another State Party before the entry into force of the Convention for any of the States Parties concerned, States Parties are encouraged to find a mutually acceptable agreement which is in accordance with the spirit and the principles of the Convention, taking into account all the relevant circumstances. States Parties may also call on the technical assistance of the Secretariat, particularly good offices, to help reaching a solution mutually acceptable by them.

Intergovernmental Committee for Promoting the Return of Cultural Property to its Countries of Origin or its Restitution in case of Illicit Appropriation (ICPRCP)

104. In cases where neither the 1970 UNESCO Convention nor any bilateral or multilateral agreement can be applied and the bilateral discussions have failed or are suspended, UNESCO Member States may submit a request to the ICPRCP for the return or restitution of cultural property of "fundamental significance from the point of view of the spiritual values and cultural heritage of the people of a Member State or Associate Member of UNESCO and which has been lost as a result of colonial or foreign occupation or as a result of illicit appropriation" (ICPRCP Statute Article 3(2)), that they consider as having been wrongfully taken. In order to resolve disputes on cultural property, States may also use the Rules of Procedure for Mediation and Conciliation procedure adopted by the ICPRCP at its 16th session in 2010.

Pillage of Archaeological and Ethnological materials (Article 9)

105. In accordance with Article 9, any State Party to this Convention whose cultural patrimony is in jeopardy from pillage of archaeological or ethnological materials may call upon other States Parties who are affected. The States Parties to this Convention undertake, in these circumstances, to participate in a concerted international effort to determine and to carry out the necessary concrete measures, including the control of exports and imports and international commerce in the specific materials concerned. Pending agreement each State concerned shall take provisional measures to the extent feasible to prevent irremediable injury to the cultural heritage of the requesting State. UNESCO and all relevant cooperating partners may also contribute, upon same request, to such a concerted international effort.
106. It is important to note that the conclusion of a bilateral or multilateral agreement is not required for a State Party to call upon another State Party for assistance. Such special agreements are not in any way a precondition for the fulfillment of the obligations arising under the Convention but may be entered into following a request for assistance under Article 9. States Parties, UNESCO

and all relevant cooperating partners are encouraged to respond expeditiously, with all possible means, to the call of the requesting State Party whose cultural property is in jeopardy. In particular, States Parties shall take provisional measures to the extent feasible to prevent irremediable injury to the cultural heritage of the requesting State. This obligation should be adequately incorporated into national laws and best practices. The relevant information should be incorporated into the UNESCO database.

107. In applying Article 9, State Parties should consider, as appropriate, categorical lists as representing the protected cultural patrimony of another State Party. A categorical or representative list describes general types of cultural patrimony rather than specific objects. Categorical lists are particularly useful for describing types of objects that are typically found in clandestine excavation, trafficked, and therefore not documented in their country of origin.

108. As a complementary measure and without prejudice to the above, bilateral or multilateral agreements may be reached to stimulate more effective and broad collaborative responses based on a better understanding of the pillaged States Parties' particular situation, as well as to enhance support and financial and technical assistance to improve capacity-building, training and protection on site. There is a need to explore ways and means to strengthen international cooperation in the implementation of Article 9.

109. States Parties are encouraged to make full use of the provisions of Article 9 in addressing the challenges posed by clandestine excavations of their archaeological sites or in cases of natural disasters or conflict.

Occupation (Article 11)

110. Article 11 of the Convention specifies that the export and transfer of ownership of cultural property under compulsion arising directly or indirectly from the occupation of a country by a foreign power shall be regarded as illicit. States Parties must apply this principle when implementing provisions of the Convention and if required under their respective system of national laws, States Parties should make this obligation clear in their legislation. The relevant information should be incorporated in the UNESCO Database.

111. As appropriate, synergies should be explored with the efforts undertaken under the Hague Convention of 1954, its First and Second Protocols and by the Committee established by the Second Protocol.

Special agreements (Article 15)

112. In accordance with Article 15, nothing in the 1970 Convention prevents States from concluding special agreements among themselves on the restitution of cultural property removed, for whatever the reason, or from continuing implementing agreements already established before the Convention was adopted. The increasing globalization of offences that affect cultural heritage calls for a stronger and more systematic regional and interregional cooperation.

113. States Parties are encouraged to incorporate into bilateral or regional agreements the highest level of protection developed in the 1970 UNESCO Convention, the 1995 UNIDROIT Convention, the 2001 Convention on the Protection of the Underwater Cultural Heritage and in the 2000 UN Convention against Transnational Organized Crime so as to ensure that such agreements embody the best protection for their cultural objects.

114. As indicated in para. 101 above, bilateral or multilateral agreements may be reached to achieve strengthened international cooperation in the implementation of Article 9.

Reports by States Parties (Article 16)

115. States Parties are required to submit reports to the UNESCO General Conference on the legislative and administrative provisions they have adopted and other action they have taken for the application of the Convention, including the details of the experience acquired in this field.

116. Periodic reporting is valuable for the exchange of information on the manner in which different national systems are dealing with the question of illicit traffic and can assist other States Parties in implementing the provisions of the Convention. Periodic reporting also serves the important function of strengthening the credibility of the implementation of the Convention.

117. Reports on the implementation of the 1970 Convention must be submitted every four years. To assist the national authorities, a simplified and practical questionnaire is at the disposal of the

UNESCO Member States to ensure that their reports contain sufficiently precise information on the ratification process and legal and operational implementation of the 1970 Convention.
118. In order to facilitate assessment of information, States Parties shall submit reports in English or French. States parties are encouraged, whenever possible, to submit their reports in both languages. These reports have to be sent in electronic as well as in printed form to:
Secretariat of the 1970 Convention 7, place de Fontenoy
75352 Paris 07 SP
France
E-mail: convention1970@unesco.org

Secretariat to the 1970 Convention and to the Subsidiary Committee (Article 17)
119. The Secretariat of the 1970 Convention is appointed by the Director-General of UNESCO and is provided by the Organization's Culture Sector. The Secretariat assists and collaborates with the States Parties, the Meeting of States Parties and the Subsidiary Committee to the Meeting of States Parties. The Secretariat works in close cooperation with other Sectors and Field Offices of UNESCO, as well as with other international partners in the fight against the illicit traffic of cultural and archaeological property.
120. States Parties are encouraged to seek advice and assistance from the Secretariat in the implementation of the Convention, particularly with regard to information and training; consultation and expert advice; coordination and good offices.
121. Among other contributions, the Secretariat may assist the State Parties by creating standard procedures to be followed when informed about clandestine excavations, illicit import, export and transfer of cultural property. These standard procedures may include the immediate publication of the incident and the cultural property involved on UNESCO's website. The Secretariat may also assist the State Parties by creating mechanisms of direct communication with the art market in order to prevent trafficking of cultural property (e.g. auction houses, e-commerce). If necessary, States Parties may call for the technical assistance of the Secretariat to support the presentation of requests for recovery and restitution of cultural property.
122. At the request of at least two States Parties that are engaged in a dispute over the implementation of the Convention, the Secretariat may extend its good offices to reach a settlement between them. Such good offices may include technical assistance, negotiations, checking due diligence, etc. In the case in which it is only one of the States which asks for support, the Secretariat will offer its assistance to that State and may send a written request to the other State party to ask for its acquiescence or refusal for the Secretariat to exercise good offices for the settlement of the dispute. The good offices of the Secretariat also may be brought to bear in disputes over the implementation of the Convention with auction houses and e-commerce sponsors. It may also seek to enhance dialogue and cooperation with the art market in the fight against the illicit traffic of all kinds of cultural property, with special concern for objects of archaeological and ethnological significance.
123. The Secretariat's main tasks are:
   − Organizing of the statutory meetings;
   − Providing legal and technical assistance to States Parties in the implementation of the 1970 Convention;
   − Promoting the 1970 Convention through advocacy and good offices, the organization of policy and prospective dialogues and forums, the dissemination of information to States Parties, the specialized public and the general public, and through the organization of capacity-building programs (regional or national);
   − Cooperating with partner Organizations; and,
   − Assisting in the preservation of movable cultural heritage in case of emergency situations caused by natural disaster or conflict, upon the request of the concerned State(s).

124. The Secretariat may, on its own initiative or on the initiative of the Committee:
    - Conduct research and publish studies on matters relevant to the illicit traffic of cultural property;
    - Call on the cooperation of any competent, and recognized by UNESCO and State Parties, non-governmental organization; and,
    - Make proposals to States Parties for the implementation of the Convention.

States Parties to the 1970 Convention (Articles 20 and 24)

125. UNESCO Member States are encouraged to become Parties to the Convention. Model instruments for ratification/acceptance and accession are included as Annex 4. The original signed version of the instrument shall be deposited with to the Director-General of UNESCO.
126. The Director General is invited to highlight the information about new ratifications/acceptances and accessions and to actively promote the broadest participation in the Convention.

Reservations

127. A "reservation" means a unilateral statement, however phrased or named, made by a State when signing, ratifying, accepting, approving or acceding to a treaty, whereby it purports to exclude or to modify the legal effect of certain provisions of the treaty in their application to that State (Vienna Convention on the Law of Treaties 1969 (Art. 2 (d)).
128. States Parties which have lodged reservations to the Convention are encouraged to withdraw any kind of reservations.

Cooperating partners in the fight against illicit trafficking of cultural property

129. Partners for the fight against illicit trafficking of cultural property may be intergovernmental or non-governmental organizations which have an interest, involvement and appropriate competence and expertise in the protection of cultural objects and are formally recognized by UNESCO as having specialized appropriate skills and proven track records. These partners include INTERPOL, UNIDROIT, UNODC, WCO and ICOM. Relevant information on each of these five cooperating partners and its specific links to the 1970 Convention is provided in Annex 5.
130. States Parties are invited to make use of the tools offered by all international partners, as possible, in the implementation of the 1970 Convention in the fight against the illicit traffic of cultural and archaeological property and against the clandestine excavations of archaeological sites.
131. Other partners may include local, regional or international organizations such as ICOMOS, ICCROM, Europol and national specialized police and customs bodies.

Conventions relating to the protection of cultural property

132. The 1970 Convention has important complementary relationship with other UNESCO Culture Conventions, as well as to the UNIDROIT Convention on Stolen or Illegally Exported Cultural Objects and the United Nations Convention against Transnational Organized Crime. Relevant information on each of these Conventions and its specific links to the 1970 Convention is provided in Annex 6.
133. States Parties are encouraged to actively strengthen the synergies of these instruments in support of the fight against the illicit traffic of cultural property and against the clandestine excavations of archaeological and paleontological sites.

UNIDROIT Convention on Stolen or Illegally Exported Cultural Objects[1)]
Vom 24. Juni 1995, ILM 34 (1995), S. 1330.

THE STATES PARTIES TO THIS CONVENTION,
ASSEMBLED in Rome at the invitation of the Government of the Italian Republic from 7 to 24 June 1995 for a Diplomatic Conference for the adoption of the draft Unidroit Convention on the International Return of Stolen or Illegally Exported Cultural Objects,
CONVINCED of the fundamental importance of the protection of cultural heritage and of cultural exchanges for promoting understanding between peoples, and the dissemination of culture for the well-being of humanity and the progress of civilisation,
DEEPLY CONCERNED by the illicit trade in cultural objects and the irreparable damage frequently caused by it, both to these objects themselves and to the cultural heritage of national, tribal, indigenous or other communities, and also to the heritage of all peoples, and in particular by the pillage of archaeological sites and the resulting loss of irreplaceable archaeological, historical and scientific information,
DETERMINED to contribute effectively to the fight against illicit trade in cultural objects by taking the important step of establishing common, minimal legal rules for the restitution and return of cultural objects between Contracting States, with the objective of improving the preservation and protection of the cultural heritage in the interest of all,
EMPHASISING that this Convention is intended to facilitate the restitution and return of cultural objects, and that the provision of any remedies, such as compensation, needed to effect restitution and return in some States, does not imply that such remedies should be adopted in other States,
AFFIRMING that the adoption of the provisions of this Convention for the future in no way confers any approval or legitimacy upon illegal transactions of whatever kind which may have taken place before the entry into force of the Convention,
CONSCIOUS that this Convention will not by itself provide a solution to the problems raised by illicit trade, but that it initiates a process that will enhance international cultural co-operation and maintain a proper role for legal trading and inter- State agreements for cultural exchanges,
ACKNOWLEDGING that implementation of this Convention should be accompanied by other effective measures for protecting cultural objects, such as the development and use of registers, the physical protection of archaeological sites and technical co-operation,
RECOGNISING the work of various bodies to protect cultural property, particularly the 1970 UNESCO Convention on illicit traffic and the development of codes of conduct in the private sector,
HAVE AGREED as follows:

CHAPTER I
SCOPE OF APPLICATION AND DEFINITION

Article 1
This Convention applies to claims of an international character for:
(a) the restitution of stolen cultural objects;
(b) the return of cultural objects removed from the territory of a Contracting State contrary to its law regulating the export of cultural objects for the purpose of protecting its cultural heritage (hereinafter "illegally exported cultural objects").

Article 2
For the purposes of this Convention, cultural objects are those which, on religious or secular grounds, are of importance for archaeology, prehistory, history, literature, art or science and belong to one of the categories listed in the Annex to this Convention.

---
1) Liste der Vertragsstaaten: https://www.unidroit.org/status-cp.

CHAPTER II
RESTITUTION OF STOLEN CULTURAL OBJECTS

Article 3

(1) The possessor of a cultural object which has been stolen shall return it.

(2) For the purposes of this Convention, a cultural object which has been unlawfully excavated or lawfully excavated but unlawfully retained shall be considered stolen, when consistent with the law of the State where the excavation took place.

(3) Any claim for restitution shall be brought within a period of three years from the time when the claimant knew the location of the cultural object and the identity of its possessor, and in any case within a period of fifty years from the time of the theft.

(4) However, a claim for restitution of a cultural object forming an integral part of an identified monument or archaeological site, or belonging to a public collection, shall not be subject to time limitations other than a period of three years from the time when the claimant knew the location of the cultural object and the identity of its possessor.

(5) Notwithstanding the provisions of the preceding paragraph, any Contracting State may declare that a claim is subject to a time limitation of 75 years or such longer period as is provided in its law. A claim made in another Contracting State for restitution of a cultural object displaced from a monument, archaeological site or public collection in a Contracting State making such a declaration shall also be subject to that time limitation.

(6) A declaration referred to in the preceding paragraph shall be made at the time of signature, ratification, acceptance, approval or accession.

(7) For the purposes of this Convention, a "public collection" consists of a group of inventoried or otherwise identified cultural objects owned by:
(a) a Contracting State
(b) a regional or local authority of a Contracting State;
(c) a religious institution in a Contracting State; or
(d) an institution that is established for an essentially cultural, educational or scientific purpose in a Contracting State and is recognised in that State as serving the public interest.

(8) In addition, a claim for restitution of a sacred or communally important cultural object belonging to and used by a tribal or indigenous community in a Contracting State as part of that community's traditional or ritual use, shall be subject to the time limitation applicable to public collections.

Article 4

(1) The possessor of a stolen cultural object required to return it shall be entitled, at the time of its restitution, to payment of fair and reasonable compensation provided that the possessor neither knew nor ought reasonably to have known that the object was stolen and can prove that it exercised due diligence when acquiring the object.

(2) Without prejudice to the right of the possessor to compensation referred to in the preceding paragraph, reasonable efforts shall be made to have the person who transferred the cultural object to the possessor, or any prior transferor, pay the compensation where to do so would be consistent with the law of the State in which the claim is brought.

(3) Payment of compensation to the possessor by the claimant, when this is required, shall be without prejudice to the right of the claimant to recover it from any other person.

(4) In determining whether the possessor exercised due diligence, regard shall be had to all the circumstances of the acquisition, including the character of the parties, the price paid, whether the possessor consulted any reasonably accessible register of stolen cultural objects, and any other relevant information and documentation which it could reasonably have obtained, and whether the possessor consulted accessible agencies or took any other step that a reasonable person would have taken in the circumstances.

(5) The possessor shall not be in a more favourable position than the person from whom it acquired the cultural object by inheritance or otherwise gratuitously.

CHAPTER III
RETURN OF ILLEGALLY EXPORTED CULTURAL OBJECTS

Article 5
(1) A Contracting State may request the court or other competent authority of another Contracting State to order the return of a cultural object illegally exported from the territory of the requesting State.
(2) A cultural object which has been temporarily exported from the territory of the requesting State, for purposes such as exhibition, research or restoration, under a permit issued according to its law regulating its export for the purpose of protecting its cultural heritage and not returned in accordance with the terms of that permit shall be deemed to have been illegally exported.
(3) The court or other competent authority of the State addressed shall order the return of an illegally exported cultural object if the requesting State establishes that the removal of the object from its territory significantly impairs one or more of the following interests:
(a) the physical preservation of the object or of its context;
(b) the integrity of a complex object;
(c) the preservation of information of, for example, a scientific or historical character;
(d) the traditional or ritual use of the object by a tribal or indigenous community,
or establishes that the object is of significant cultural importance for the requesting State.
(4) Any request made under paragraph 1 of this article shall contain or be accompanied by such information of a factual or legal nature as may assist the court or other competent authority of the State addressed in determining whether the requirements of paragraphs 1 to 3 have been met.
(5) Any request for return shall be brought within a period of three years from the time when the requesting State knew the location of the cultural object and the identity of its possessor, and in any case within a period of fifty years from the date of the export or from the date on which the object should have been returned under a permit referred to in paragraph 2 of this article.

Article 6
(1) The possessor of a cultural object who acquired the object after it was illegally exported shall be entitled, at the time of its return, to payment by the requesting State of fair and reasonable compensation, provided that the possessor neither knew nor ought reasonably to have known at the time of acquisition that the object had been illegally exported.
(2) In determining whether the possessor knew or ought reasonably to have known that the cultural object had been illegally exported, regard shall be had to the circumstances of the acquisition, including the absence of an export certificate required under the law of the requesting State.
(3) Instead of compensation, and in agreement with the requesting State, the possessor required to return the cultural object to that State may decide:
(a) to retain ownership of the object; or
(b) to transfer ownership against payment or gratuitously to a person of its choice residing in the requesting State who provides the necessary guarantees.
(4) The cost of returning the cultural object in accordance with this article shall be borne by the requesting State, without prejudice to the right of that State to recover costs from any other person.
(5) The possessor shall not be in a more favourable position than the person from whom it acquired the cultural object by inheritance or otherwise gratuitously.

Article 7
(1) The provisions of this Chapter shall not apply where:
(a) the export of a cultural object is no longer illegal at the time at which the return is requested; or
(b) the object was exported during the lifetime of the person who created it or within a period of fifty years following the death of that person.
(2) Notwithstanding the provisions of sub-paragraph (b) of the preceding paragraph, the provisions of this Chapter shall apply where a cultural object was made by a member or members of a tribal or indigenous community for traditional or ritual use by that community and the object will be returned to that community.

CHAPTER IV
GENERAL PROVISIONS

Article 8
(1) A claim under Chapter II and a request under Chapter III may be brought before the courts or other competent authorities of the Contracting State where the cultural object is located, in addition to the courts or other competent authorities otherwise having jurisdiction under the rules in force in Contracting States.

(2) The parties may agree to submit the dispute to any court or other competent authority or to arbitration.

(3) Resort may be had to the provisional, including protective, measures available under the law of the Contracting State where the object is located even when the claim for restitution or request for return of the object is brought before the courts or other competent authorities of another Contracting State.

Article 9
(1) Nothing in this Convention shall prevent a Contracting State from applying any rules more favourable to the restitution or the return of stolen or illegally exported cultural objects than provided for by this Convention.

(2) This article shall not be interpreted as creating an obligation to recognise or enforce a decision of a court or other competent authority of another Contracting State that departs from the provisions of this Convention.

Article 10
(1) The provisions of Chapter II shall apply only in respect of a cultural object that is stolen after this Convention enters into force in respect of the State where the claim is brought, provided that:
(a) the object was stolen from the territory of a Contracting State after the entry into force of this Convention for that State; or
(b) the object is located in a Contracting State after the entry into force of the Convention for that State.

(2) The provisions of Chapter III shall apply only in respect of a cultural object that is illegally exported after this Convention enters into force for the requesting State as well as the State where the request is brought.

(3) This Convention does not in any way legitimise any illegal transaction of whatever nature which has taken place before the entry into force of this Convention or which is excluded under paragraphs (1) or (2) of this article, nor limit any right of a State or other person to make a claim under remedies available outside the framework of this Convention for the restitution or return of a cultural object stolen or illegally exported before the entry into force of this Convention.

CHAPTER V
FINAL PROVISIONS

Article 11
(1) This Convention is open for signature at the concluding meeting of the Diplomatic Conference for the adoption of the draft Unidroit Convention on the International Return of Stolen or Illegally Exported Cultural Objects and will remain open for signature by all States at Rome until 30 June 1996.

(2) This Convention is subject to ratification, acceptance or approval by States which have signed it.

(3) This Convention is open for accession by all States which are not signatory States as from the date it is open for signature.

(4) Ratification, acceptance, approval or accession is subject to the deposit of a formal instrument to that effect with the depositary.

Article 12
(1) This Convention shall enter into force on the first day of the sixth month following the date of deposit of the fifth instrument of ratification, acceptance, approval or accession.

(2) For each State that ratifies, accepts, approves or accedes to this Convention after the deposit of the fifth instrument of ratification, acceptance, approval or accession, this Convention shall enter into force

in respect of that State on the first day of the sixth month following the date of deposit of its instrument of ratification, acceptance, approval or accession.

Article 13
(1) This Convention does not affect any international instrument by which any Contracting State is legally bound and which contains provisions on matters governed by this Convention, unless a contrary declaration is made by the States bound by such instrument.
(2) Any Contracting State may enter into agreements with one or more Contracting States, with a view to improving the application of this Convention in their mutual relations. The States which have concluded such an agreement shall transmit a copy to the depositary.
(3) In their relations with each other, Contracting States which are Members of organisations of economic integration or regional bodies may declare that they will apply the internal rules of these organisations or bodies and will not therefore apply as between these States the provisions of this Convention the scope of application of which coincides with that of those rules.

Article 14
(1) If a Contracting State has two or more territorial units, whether or not possessing different systems of law applicable in relation to the matters dealt with in this Convention, it may, at the time of signature or of the deposit of its instrument of ratification, acceptance, approval or accession, declare that this Convention is to extend to all its territorial units or only to one or more of them, and may substitute for its declaration another declaration at any time.
(2) These declarations are to be notified to the depositary and are to state expressly the territorial units to which the Convention extends.
(3) If, by virtue of a declaration under this article, this Convention extends to one or more but not all of the territorial units of a Contracting State, the reference to:
(a) the territory of a Contracting State in Article 1 shall be construed as referring to the territory of a territorial unit of that State;
(b) a court or other competent authority of the Contracting State or of the State addressed shall be construed as referring to the court or other competent authority of a territorial unit of that State;
(c) the Contracting State where the cultural object is located in Article 8 (1) shall be construed as referring to the territorial unit of that State where the object is located;
(d) the law of the Contracting State where the object is located in Article 8 (3) shall be construed as referring to the law of the territorial unit of that State where the object is located; and
(e) a Contracting State in Article 9 shall be construed as referring to a territorial unit of that State.
(4) If a Contracting State makes no declaration under paragraph 1 of this article, this Convention is to extend to all territorial units of that State.

Article 15
(1) Declarations made under this Convention at the time of signature are subject to confirmation upon ratification, acceptance or approval.
(2) Declarations and confirmations of declarations are to be in writing and to be formally notified to the depositary.
(3) A declaration shall take effect simultaneously with the entry into force of this Convention in respect of the State concerned. However, a declaration of which the depositary receives formal notification after such entry into force shall take effect on the first day of the sixth month following the date of its deposit with the depositary.
(4) Any State which makes a declaration under this Convention may withdraw it at any time by a formal notification in writing addressed to the depositary. Such withdrawal shall take effect on the first day of the sixth month following the date of the deposit of the notification.

Article 16
(1) Each Contracting State shall at the time of signature, ratification, acceptance, approval or accession, declare that claims for the restitution, or requests for the return, of cultural objects brought by a State under Article 8 may be submitted to it under one or more of the following procedures:

(a) directly to the courts or other competent authorities of the declaring State;
(b) through an authority or authorities designated by that State to receive such claims or requests and to forward them to the courts or other competent authorities of that State;
(c) through diplomatic or consular channels.

(2) Each Contracting State may also designate the courts or other authorities competent to order the restitution or return of cultural objects under the provisions of Chapters II and III.

(3) Declarations made under paragraphs 1 and 2 of this article may be modified at any time by a new declaration.

(4) The provisions of paragraphs 1 to 3 of this article do not affect bilateral or multilateral agreements on judicial assistance in respect of civil and commercial matters that may exist between Contracting States.

Article 17
Each Contracting State shall, no later than six months following the date of deposit of its instrument of ratification, acceptance, approval or accession, provide the depositary with written information in one of the official languages of the Convention concerning the legislation regulating the export of its cultural objects. This information shall be updated from time to time as appropriate.

Article 18
No reservations are permitted except those expressly authorised in this Convention.

Article 19
(1) This Convention may be denounced by any State Party, at any time after the date on which it enters into force for that State, by the deposit of an instrument to that effect with the depositary.

(2) A denunciation shall take effect on the first day of the sixth month following the deposit of the instrument of denunciation with the depositary. Where a longer period for the denunciation to take effect is specified in the instrument of denunciation it shall take effect upon the expiration of such longer period after its deposit with the depositary.

(3) Notwithstanding such a denunciation, this Convention shall nevertheless apply to a claim for restitution or a request for return of a cultural object submitted prior to the date on which the denunciation takes effect.

Article 20
The President of the International Institute for the Unification of Private Law (Unidroit) may at regular intervals, or at any time at the request of five Contracting States, convene a special committee in order to review the practical operation of this Convention.

Article 21
(1) This Convention shall be deposited with the Government of the Italian Republic.
(2) The Government of the Italian Republic shall:
(a) inform all States which have signed or acceded to this Convention and the President of the International Institute for the Unification of Private Law (Unidroit) of:
  (i) each new signature or deposit of an instrument of ratification, acceptance, approval or accession, together with the date thereof;
  (ii) each declaration made in accordance with this Convention;
  (iii) the withdrawal of any declaration;
  (iv) the date of entry into force of this Convention;
  (v) the agreements referred to in Article 13;
  (vi) the deposit of an instrument of denunciation of this Convention together with the date of its deposit and the date on which it takes effect;
(b) transmit certified true copies of this Convention to all signatory States, to all States acceding to the Convention and to the President of the International Institute for Unification of Private Law (Unidroit);
(c) perform such other functions customary for depositaries.

IN WITNESS WHEREOF the undersigned plenipotentiaries, being duly authorised, have signed this Convention.

DONE at Rome, this twenty-fourth day of June, one thousand nine hundred and ninety-five, in a single original, in the English and French languages, both texts being equally authentic.

Annex
(a) Rare collections and specimens of fauna, flora, minerals and anatomy, and objects of palaeontological interest;
(b) property relating to history, including the history of science and technology and military and social history, to the life of national leaders, thinkers, scientists and artists and to events of national importance;
(c) products of archaeological excavations (including regular and clandestine) or of archaeological discoveries;
(d) elements of artistic or historical monuments or archaeological sites which have been dismembered;
(e) antiquities more than one hundred years old, such as inscriptions, coins and engraved seals;
(f) objects of ethnological interest;
(g) property of artistic interest, such as:
    (i) pictures, paintings and drawings produced entirely by hand on any support and in any material (excluding industrial designs and manufactured articles decorated by hand);
    (ii) original works of statuary art and sculpture in any material;
    (iii) original engravings, prints and lithographs;
    (iv) original artistic assemblages and montages in any material;
(h) rare manuscripts and incunabula, old books, documents and publications of special interest (historical, artistic, scientific, literary, etc.) singly or in collections;
(i) postage, revenue and similar stamps, singly or in collections;
(j) archives, including sound, photographic and cinematographic archives;
(k) articles of furniture more than one hundred years old and old musical instruments.

A.III.4 Abkommen von Florenz

Abkommen über die Einfuhr von Gegenständen erzieherischen, wissenschaftlichen oder kulturellen Charakters[1)]

22. November 1950 (BGBl. 1957 II S. 171)

Präambel

DIE VERTRAGSCHLIESSENDEN STAATEN,

IN DER ERWÄGUNG, daß der freie Austausch von Ideen und Wissen und ganz allgemein die möglichst weite Verbreitung der verschiedenen kulturellen Ausdrucksformen unerläßliche Voraussetzungen sowohl für den geistigen Fortschritt als auch für die internationale Verständigung sind und deshalb zur Erhaltung des Friedens in der Welt beitragen;

IN DER ERWÄGUNG, daß dieser Austausch hauptsächlich durch die Vermittlung von Büchern, Veröffentlichungen und Gegenständen erzieherischen, wissenschaftlichen oder kulturellen Charakters zustande kommt;

IN DER ERWÄGUNG, daß die Satzung der Organisation der Vereinten Nationen für Erziehung, Wissenschaft und Kultur die Zusammenarbeit zwischen den Nationen auf allen Gebieten des Geisteslebens und insbesondere den Austausch „von Veröffentlichungen und Gegenständen von künstlerischem oder wissenschaftlichem Interesse und anderem Informationsmaterial befürwortet" und ferner vorsieht, daß die Organisation dabei mitwirkt, „das gegenseitige Sichkennenlernen und Verstehen der Völker durch alle Massen-Informationsmittel zu fördern" und daß sie „zu diesem Zweck internationale Vereinbarungen empfiehlt, die für die freie Verbreitung von Ideen durch Wort und Bild gegebenenfalls erforderlich sind";

ERKENNEN AN, daß eine internationale Vereinbarung zur Förderung der freien Verbreitung von Büchern, Veröffentlichungen und Gegenständen erzieherischen, wissenschaftlichen oder kulturellen Charakters ein wirksames Mittel zur Erreichung dieser Ziele darstellt und

SIND daher wie folgt übereingekommen:

Artikel I

1. Die Vertragschließenden Staaten verpflichten sich, keine Zölle oder sonstigen Abgaben zu erheben bei oder anläßlich der Einfuhr von
   (a) Büchern, Veröffentlichungen und Dokumenten, die im Anhang A dieses Abkommens aufgeführt sind;
   (b) Gegenständen erzieherischen, wissenschaftlichen oder kulturellen Charakters, die in den Anhängen B, C, D und E dieses Abkommens aufgeführt sind,
   sofern diese den in diesen Anhängen aufgeführten Voraussetzungen entsprechen und Erzeugnisse eines anderen Vertragschließenden Staates sind.

2. Die Bestimmungen des Absatzes 1 dieses Artikels hindern einen Vertragsschließenden Staat nicht, für die eingeführten Gegenstände
   (a) anläßlich der Einfuhr oder später Steuern oder sonstige innere Abgaben irgendwelcher Art zu erheben, vorausgesetzt, daß diese nicht höher sind als die Abgaben, die direkt oder indirekt für gleichartige einheimische Erzeugnisse erhoben werden;
   (b) durch Verwaltungsbehörden bei oder anläßlich der Einfuhr Gebühren oder Abgaben zu erheben, die keine Zölle sind, vorausgesetzt, daß sie ungefähr den Kosten der geleisteten Dienste entsprechen und daß sie nicht eine mittelbare Schutzmaßnahme für einheimische Erzeugnisse oder eine Abgabe bei der Einfuhr darstellen.

Artikel II

1. Die Vertragschließenden Staaten verpflichten sich, für die Einfuhr der nachstehenden Gegenstände die erforderlichen Devisen- bzw. Einfuhrgenehmigungen zu erteilen:
   (a) Bücher und Veröffentlichungen, die für öffentliche Bibliotheken und Sammlungen sowie für Bibliotheken und Sammlungen öffentlicher, dem Unterrichtswesen, der Forschung oder kulturellen Zwecken dienender Institutionen bestimmt sind;
   (b) amtliche, im Ursprungsland veröffentlichte Dokumente der Parlamente, Regierungen und Verwaltungen;

[1)] Liste der Vertragsstaaten:https://www.eda.admin.ch/eda/de/home/aussenpolitik/voelkerrecht/internationale-vertraege/datenbank-staatsvertraege/detailansicht-staatsvertrag.ggst0_63.contract19500286.html?_charset_=UTF-8.

- (c) Bücher und Veröffentlichungen der Vereinten Nationen und ihrer Sonderorganisationen;
- (d) Bücher und Veröffentlichungen, die bei der Organisation der Vereinten Nationen für Erziehung, Wissenschaft und Kultur eingehen und die von ihr oder unter ihrer Aufsicht unentgeltlich verteilt werden;
- (e) Veröffentlichungen, die für den Fremdenverkehr im Ausland werben und unentgeltlich versandt und verteilt werden;
- (f) für Blinde bestimmte Gegenstände:
  - (i) in Blindenschrift hergestellte Bücher, Veröffentlichungen und Dokumente aller Art;
  - (ii) andere, besonders für die erzieherische, wissenschaftliche oder kulturelle Weiterbildung der Blinden hergerichtete Gegenstände, sofern sie durch Blindeninstitutionen oder Blinden-Hilfswerke, die von den zuständigen Behörden des Einfuhrlandes zur zollfreien Einfuhr solcher Gegenstände ermächtigt worden sind, unmittelbar eingeführt werden.
2. Sofern Vertragschließende Staaten mengenmäßige Beschränkungen vornehmen und Devisenvorschriften erlassen, verpflichten sie sich, im Rahmen des Möglichen auch für die Einfuhr anderer Gegenstände erzieherischen, wissenschaftlichen oder kulturellen Charakters, insbesondere der in den Anhängen zu diesem Abkommen aufgeführten Gegenstände, die erforderlichen Devisen- oder Einfuhrgenehmigungen zu erteilen.

Artikel III

1. Die Vertragschließenden Staaten verpflichten sich, für Gegenstände erzieherischen, wissenschaftlichen oder kulturellen Charakters, die ausschließlich eingeführt werden, um auf einer von den zuständigen Behörden des Einfuhrlandes zugelassenen öffentlichen Ausstellung ausgestellt zu werden und die später wieder ausgeführt werden sollen, alle möglichen Einfuhrerleichterungen zu gewähren. Diese Erleichterungen sollen umfassen: die Erteilung der erforderlichen Einfuhrbewilligungen, die Befreiung von Zöllen, Steuern und anderen, anläßlich der Einfuhr erhobenen inneren Abgaben mit Ausnahme von Gebühren und Abgaben, die den ungefähren Kosten von geleisteten Diensten entsprechen.
2. Die Bestimmungen dieses Artikels hindern die Behörden des Einfuhrlandes nicht, die Maßnahmen zu treffen, die erforderlich sind, um die Wiederausfuhr der betreffenden Gegenstände nach Schluß der Ausstellung sicherzustellen.

Artikel IV

Die Vertragschließenden Staaten verpflichten sich im Rahmen des Möglichen
- (a) ihre gemeinsamen Anstrengungen fortzusetzen, um mit allen Mitteln die freie Verbreitung von Gegenständen erzieherischen, wissenschaftlichen und kulturellen Charakters zu fördern und alle Beschränkungen der freien Verbreitung, die in diesem Abkommen nicht vorgesehen sind, aufzuheben oder zu verringern;
- (b) das mit der Einfuhr von Gegenständen erzieherischen, wissenschaftlichen oder kulturellen Charakters verbundene Verwaltungsverfahren zu vereinfachen;
- (c) für eine schnelle umsichtige Zollabfertigung der Gegenstände erzieherischen, wissenschaftlichen und kulturellen Charakters zu sorgen.

Artikel V

Keine Bestimmung dieses Abkommens berührt das Recht der Vertragschließenden Staaten, in Übereinstimmung mit ihren Rechtsvorschriften Maßnahmen zu treffen, um die Einfuhr oder spätere Verbreitung bestimmter Gegenstände zu verbieten oder einzuschränken, sofern diese Maßnahmen aus unmittelbaren Gründen der nationalen Sicherheit, der öffentlichen Ordnung oder Sittlichkeit des Vertragschließenden Staates nötig werden.

Artikel VI

Dieses Abkommen beeinträchtigt oder ändert Rechtsvorschriften eines Vertragschließenden Staates oder irgendwelche von ihm angenommene internationale Verträge, Übereinkommen, Abkommen, Vereinbarungen oder Erklärungen betreffend den Schutz des Urheberrechts oder des Schutzes des gewerblichen Eigentums einschließlich der Patente und Warenzeichen nicht.

A.III.4 Abkommen von Florenz

Artikel VII

Unbeschadet früherer vertraglicher Abmachungen, die sie gegebenenfalls zur Regelung von Streitigkeiten getroffen haben, verpflichten sich die Vertragschließenden Staaten, alle Streitigkeiten über die Auslegung oder Anwendung dieses Abkommens auf dem Verhandlungswege oder durch ein Vergleichsverfahren zu regeln.

Artikel VIII

Im Falle einer Meinungsverschiedenheit zwischen Vertragschließenden Staaten über den erzieherischen, wissenschaftlichen oder kulturellen Charakter eines eingeführten Gegenstandes können die beteiligten Parteien in gemeinsamem Einvernehmen ein Gutachten von dem Generaldirektor der Organisation der Vereinten Nationen für Erziehung, Wissenschaft und Kultur anfordern.

Artikel IX

1. Dieses Abkommen, dessen englischer und französischer Wortlaut in gleicher Weise maßgebend sind, trägt das heutige Datum und steht allen Mitgliedstaaten der Organisation der Vereinten Nationen für Erziehung, Wissenschaft und Kultur, allen Mitgliedstaaten der Vereinten Nationen sowie allen Nichtmitgliedstaaten, die vom Exekutivrat der Organisation der Vereinten Nationen für Erziehung, Wissenschaft und Kultur dazu eingeladen worden sind, zur Unterzeichnung offen.
2. Das Abkommen bedarf der Ratifizierung durch die Unterzeichnerstaaten im Einklang mit dem in ihren Verfassungen vorgeschriebenen Verfahren.
3. Die Ratifikationsurkunden sind beim Generalsekretär der Vereinten Nationen zu hinterlegen.

Artikel X

Die in Artikel IX Abs. 1 erwähnten Staaten können diesem Abkommen vom 22. November 1950 an beitreten. Der Beitritt erfolgt durch Hinterlegung einer formellen Urkunde beim Generalsekretär der Organisation der Vereinten Nationen.

Artikel XI

Dieses Abkommen tritt mit dem Tage in Kraft, an dem die Ratifikations- oder Beitrittsurkunden von zehn Staaten bei dem Generalsekretär der Vereinten Nationen eingegangen sind.

Artikel XII

1. Jeder Staat, der am Tag des Inkrafttretens Partner des Abkommens ist, trifft innerhalb von sechs Monaten alle Maßnahmen, die für die praktische Durchführung des Abkommens erforderlich sind.
2. Für Staaten, die ihre Ratifikations- oder Beitrittsurkunde nach dem Inkrafttreten des Abkommens hinterlegen, beträgt diese Frist drei Monate vom Zeitpunkt der Hinterlegung an.
3. Spätestens einen Monat nach Ablauf der in den Absätzen 1 und 2 dieses Artikels vorgesehenen Fristen legen die Vertragschließenden Staaten der Organisation der Vereinten Nationen für Erziehung, Wissenschaft und Kultur einen Bericht über die Maßnahmen vor, die sie zur vollwirksamen Anwendung des Abkommens getroffen haben.
4. Dieser Bericht wird von der Organisation der Vereinten Nationen für Erziehung, Wissenschaft und Kultur allen Unterzeichnerstaaten des Abkommens sowie der Internationalen Handelsorganisation (vorläufig deren Interimsausschuß) übermittelt.

Artikel XIII

Jeder Vertragschließende Staat kann bei der Unterzeichnung oder der Hinterlegung der Ratifikations- oder Beitrittsurkunde oder zu jedem späteren Zeitpunkt in einer an den Generalsekretär der Vereinten Nationen zu richtenden förmlichen Mitteilung erklären, daß dieses Abkommen sich auch auf Gebiete erstreckt, deren internationale Beziehungen der Vertragschließende Staat wahrnimmt.

Artikel XIV

1. Zwei Jahre nach dem Inkrafttreten dieses Abkommens kann jeder Vertragschließende Staat das Abkommen für sich selbst oder ein Gebiet, dessen internationale Beziehungen er wahrnimmt, durch eine beim Generalsekretär der Vereinten Nationen zu hinterlegende Urkunde kündigen.
2. Die Kündigung wird ein Jahr nach Empfang der Erklärung wirksam.

Artikel XV

Der Generalsekretär der Vereinten Nationen teilt den in Artikel IX Abs. 1 erwähnten Staaten, der Organisation der Vereinten Nationen für Erziehung, Wissenschaft und Kultur und der Internationalen

Abkommen von Florenz A.III.4

Handelsorganisation (vorläufig deren Interimsausschuß) die Hinterlegung aller in den Artikeln IX und X aufgeführten Ratifikations- oder Beitrittsurkunden sowie die in den Artikeln XIII und XIV vorgesehenen Erklärungen und Kündigungen mit.

Artikel XVI
Auf Verlangen eines Drittels der Vertragschließenden Staaten setzt der Generaldirektor der Organisation der Vereinten Nationen für Erziehung, Wissenschaft und Kultur die Frage der Einberufung einer Konferenz für die Revision dieses Abkommens auf die Tagesordnung der nächsten Tagung der Generalkonferenz dieser Organisation.

Artikel XVII
Die Anhänge A, B, C, D und E sowie das beigefügte Protokoll bilden integrierende Bestandteile dieses Abkommens.

Artikel XVIII
1. In Übereinstimmung mit Artikel 102 der Satzung der Vereinten Nationen wird dieses Abkommen am Tage seines Inkrafttretens vom Generalsekretär der Vereinten Nationen eingetragen.
2. ZU URKUND DESSEN haben die ordnungsgemäß bevollmächtigten Unterzeichneten namens ihrer Regierungen dieses Abkommen unterschrieben.

GESCHEHEN in Lake Success, New York, am zweiundzwanzigsten November neunzehnhundertundfünfzig in einer einzigen Ausfertigung, die im Archiv der Vereinten Nationen hinterlegt wird. Beglaubigte Abschriften werden allen in Artikel IX Abs. 1 erwähnten Staaten sowie der Organisation der Vereinten Nationen für Erziehung, Wissenschaft und Kultur und der Internationalen Handelsorganisation (vorläufig deren Interimsausschuß) übermittelt.

Anhang A
Bücher, Veröffentlichungen und Dokumente
1. Gedruckte Bücher;
2. Zeitungen und periodische Druckschriften;
3. Bücher und Dokumente, die durch andere Vervielfältigungsverfahren als der Druck hergestellt wurden;
4. amtliche, im Ursprungsland veröffentlichte Dokumente der Parlamente, Regierungen und Verwaltungen;
5. Plakate und Veröffentlichungen für den Fremdenverkehr, die für Reisen außerhalb des Einfuhrlandes werben: Broschüren, Führer, Fahrpläne, Prospekte und ähnliche Veröffentlichungen, mit oder ohne Illustrationen, einschließlich der von privaten Unternehmen herausgegebenen;
6. Veröffentlichungen, die für ein Studium im Auslande werben;
7. Manuskripte und maschinengeschriebene Dokumente;
8. Kataloge von Büchern und Veröffentlichungen, die von einem außerhalb des Einfuhrlandes ansässigen Verleger oder Buchhändler zum Kauf angeboten werden;
9. Kataloge von Filmen, Tonaufnahmen oder jeglichem sonstigem Bild- oder Tonmaterial erzieherischen, wissenschaftlichen oder kulturellen Charakters, die von den oder für die Rechnung der Vereinten Nationen oder einer ihrer Sonderorganisationen hergestellt wurden;
10. Noten, handgeschrieben, gedruckt oder durch sonstige Vervielfältigungsverfahren herge- stellt;
11. geographische, hydrographische und astronomische Karten;
12. Bauzeichnungen oder Pläne und Zeichnungen industriellen oder technischen Charakters und deren Kopien, die für das Studium in einem von den zuständigen Behörden des Einfuhrlandes zur zollfreien Einfuhr solcher Gegenstände ermächtigten wissenschaftlichen Institut bzw. Lehrinstitut bestimmt sind.

Die in diesem Anhang A vorgesehenen Vergünstigungen finden keine Anwendung auf folgende Gegenstände:
(a) Schreibwaren;
(b) Bücher, Veröffentlichungen und Dokumente (mit Ausnahme der oben bezeichneten Kataloge und Fremdenverkehrsplakate und -veröffentlichungen), die hauptsächlich der kommerziellen Werbung dienen und von einem privaten Unternehmen oder für dessen Rechnung herausgegeben werden;
(c) Zeitungen und periodische Druckschriften, in denen der Reklameteil mehr als 70 % des Raumes einnimmt.

A.III.4 Abkommen von Florenz

(d) alle anderen Gegenstände (mit Ausnahme der oben bezeichneten Kataloge), in denen der Reklameteil mehr als 25 % des Raumes einnimmt. Bei Plakaten und Veröffentlichungen für den Fremdenverkehr umfaßt dieser Prozentsatz nur die privaten Geschäftsanzeigen.

Anhang B
Kunstgegenstände und Sammlungsstücke erzieherischen, wissenschaftlichen oder kulturellen Charakters

1. Gemälde und Zeichnungen einschließlich Kopien, vollständig mit der Hand gearbeitet, ausgenommen fabrikmäßig hergestellte verzierte Gegenstände;
2. Handdrucke, die vom Künstler signiert und numeriert und von Stein, Platten oder anderem vollständig handgearbeitetem Material abgezogen sind;
3. Originalerzeugnisse der Bildhauerkunst, Plastiken, Hoch- oder Tiefreliefs, ausgenommen serienweise hergestellte Reproduktionen und kunsthandwerkliche Gegenstände kommerziellen Charakters;
4. Sammlungsstücke und Kunstgegenstände, die für Museen, Galerien und andere von den zuständigen Behörden des Einfuhrlandes zur zollfreien Einfuhr dieser Gegenstände ermächtigte öffentliche Institute bestimmt sind, unter der Bedingung, daß sie nicht verkauft werden dürfen;
5. wissenschaftliche Sammlungen und Sammlungsgegenstände, insbesondere auf den Gebieten der Anatomie, Zoologie, Botanik, Mineralogie, Paläontologie, Archäologie und Ethnographie beziehen, sofern sie nicht kommerziellen Zwecken dienen;
6. über 100 Jahre alte Antiquitäten.

Anhang C
Bild- und Hörmaterial mit erzieherischem, wissenschaftlichem oder kulturellem Charakter

1. Filme, Filmstreifen, Mikrofilme und Diapositive erzieherischen, wissenschaftlichen oder kulturellen Charakters, die von den durch die zuständigen Behörden des Einfuhrlandes zur zollfreien Einfuhr ermächtigten Organisationen (nach Ermessen des Einfuhrlandes auch Rundfunkgesellschaften) eingeführt werden. Die Gegenstände dürfen nur von diesen Organisationen oder von anderen öffentlichen oder privaten Instituten oder Vereinigungen erzieherischen, wissenschaftlichen oder kulturellen Charakters vorgeführt werden, die von den genannten Behörden dazu ermächtigt sind;
2. Wochenschauen (mit oder ohne Ton), die zur Zeit ihrer Einfuhr aktuell sind. Sie können zum Zwecke der Wiedergabe in der Form von Negativen, belichtet und entwickelt, oder von Positiven, kopiert und entwickelt, eingeführt werden unter Vorbehalt einer möglichen Beschränkung der zollfreien Einfuhr auf zwei Kopien; dies gilt nur für Wochenschauen, die von den durch die zuständigen Behörden des Einfuhrlandes zur zollfreien Einfuhr ermächtigten Organisationen (nach Ermessen des Einfuhrlandes auch Rundfunkgesellschaften) eingeführt werden;
3. Tonaufnahmen erzieherischen, wissenschaftlichen oder kulturellen Charakters, die ausschließlich für die von den zuständigen Behörden des Einfuhrlandes zur zollfreien Einfuhr dieses Materials ermächtigten öffentlichen oder privaten Institutionen erzieherischen, wissenschaftlichen oder kulturellen Charakters bestimmt sind (nach Ermessen des Einfuhrlandes auch Rundfunkgesellschaften);
4. Filme, Filmbildstreifen, Mikrofilme und Tonaufnahmen erzieherischen, wissenschaftlichen oder kulturellen Charakters, die von den Vereinten Nationen oder einer ihrer Sonderorganisationen hergestellt worden sind;
5. Modelle, Skizzen, Wandbilder, die ausschließlich zu Vorführungs- und Unterrichtszwecken in öffentlichen oder privaten Instituten erzieherischen, wissenschaftlichen oder kulturellen Charakters dienen; diese müssen von den zuständigen Behörden des Einfuhrlandes zur zollfreien Einfuhr dieses Materials ermächtigt sein.

Anhang D
Wissenschaftliche Instrumente und Apparate

Wissenschaftliche Instrumente und Apparate, die ausschließlich zu Unterrichtszwecken oder zur rein wissenschaftlichen Forschung bestimmt sind, mit Vorbehalt:

(a) daß die betreffenden wissenschaftlichen Instrumente und Apparate für öffentliche oder private wissenschaftliche oder Lehranstalten bestimmt sind, die von den zuständigen Behörden des Einfuhrlandes dazu ermächtigt sind, diese Gegenstände zollfrei einzuführen. Die Gegenstände müssen unter der Aufsicht und Verantwortung dieser Anstalten verwendet werden;
(b) daß zur Zeit keine Instrumente oder Apparate von gleichem wissenschaftlichem Wert im Einfuhrland hergestellt werden.

Abkommen von Florenz A.III.4

Anhang E
Gegenstände für Blinde
1. Bücher, Veröffentlichungen und Dokumente aller Art in Blindenschrift;
2. sonstige, besonders für die erzieherische, wissenschaftliche oder kulturelle Weiterbildung der Blinden hergerichtete Gegenstände, die unmittelbar von ihren eigenen Institutionen oder von den von den zuständigen Behörden des Einfuhrlandes zur zollfreien Einfuhr dieses Materials ermächtigten Blinden-Hilfsorganisationen eingeführt werden.

Zusatzprotokoll zu dem Abkommen über die Einfuhr von Gegenständen erzieherischen, wissenschaftlichen oder kulturellen Charakters

DIE VERTRAGSCHLIESSENDEN STAATEN;
IN DEM BESTREBEN; den Beitritt der Vereinigten Staaten von Amerika zu dem Abkommen über die Einfuhr von Gegenständen erzieherischen, wissenschaftlichen oder kulturellen Charakters zu erleichtern, SIND wie folgt übereingekommen:

1. Die Vereinigten Staaten von Amerika können dieses Abkommen mit dem nachstehend aufgeführten Vorbehalt gemäß Artikel IX ratifizieren oder ihr gemäß Artikel X beitreten.
2. Falls die Vereinigten Staaten von Amerika dem Abkommen mit dem in Nummer 1 vorgesehenen Vorbehalt beitreten und Vertragspartei werden, können sie sich gegenüber jedem Staat, der Partei dieses Abkommens ist, auf die Bestimmungen des Vorbehalts berufen; desgleichen kann sich auch jeder Vertragsschließende Staat den Vereinigten Staaten von Amerika gegenüber auf diese berufen. Keine im Hinblick auf diesen Vorbehalt getroffene Maßnahme darf einen diskriminierenden Charakter haben.
(Wortlaut des Vorbehalts)
 (a) Falls es sich herausstellen sollte, daß – infolge der von einem Vertragsschließenden Staat gemäß diesem Abkommen eingegangenen Verpflichtungen – die Einfuhr eines in diesem Abkommen erwähnten Erzeugnisses in diesen Staat unverhältnismäßig zunimmt oder unter solchen Bedingungen geschieht, daß die einheimischen Hersteller ähnlicher oder konkurrierender Erzeugnisse dadurch bedroht werden oder bedroht werden könnten, so ist es dem Vertragsschließenden Staat freigestellt, unter Beachtung der in Ziffer 2 enthaltenen Bestimmungen für den in Frage stehenden Gegenstand in dem Ausmaß und so lange, wie es zur Verhinderung oder Wiedergutmachung eines solchen Schadens nötig ist, die er mit diesem Abkommen übernommen hat, ganz oder teilweise auszusetzen.
 (b) Bevor ein Vertragsstaat eine der unter Buchstabe a vorgesehenen Maßnahmen trifft, gibt er davon so frühzeitig wie möglich der Organisation der Vereinten Nationen für Erziehung, Wissenschaft und Kultur schriftlich Kenntnis und ermöglicht ihr und den Vertragschließenden Staaten, die Parteien dieses Abkommens sind, mit ihm die in Aussicht genommene Maßnahme zu erörtern.
 (c) In dringenden Fällen, in denen ein verspätetes Eingreifen schwer wiedergutzumachende Nachteile mit sich bringen würde, können auf Grund von Buchstabe a dieses Protokolls ohne vorherige Rückfragen, aber unter der Bedingung, daß unverzüglich danach Konsultationen stattfinden, einstweilige Schutzmaßnahmen getroffen werden.

A.III.4a Nairobi-Protokoll

Protokoll zum Abkommen über die Einfuhr von Gegenständen erzieherischen, wissenschaftlichen oder kulturellen Charakters[1]

26. November 1976 (BGBl. 1989 II S. 491)

Die Vertragsstaaten, die Vertragsparteien des von der Generalkonferenz der Organisation der Vereinten Nationen für Erziehung, Wissenschaft und Kultur auf ihrer fünften Tagung in Florenz im Jahr 1950 angenommenen Abkommens über die Einfuhr von Gegenständen erzieherischen, wissenschaftlichen oder kulturellen Charakters sind –

unter Bekräftigung der Grundsätze, auf denen das Abkommen, im folgenden als „Abkommen" bezeichnet, beruht;

in der Erwägung, daß sich das Abkommen als wirksames Instrument zum Abbau der Zollschranken und zur Verringerung sonstiger wirtschaftlicher Beschränkungen, die den Austausch von Ideen und Wissen behindern, erwiesen hat;

in der Erwägung jedoch, daß sich in dem Vierteljahrhundert, das auf die Annahme des Abkommens folgte, die Methoden der Übermittlung von Informationen und Wissen, die das Hauptziel dieses Abkommens ist, durch den technischen Fortschritt geändert haben;

in der Erwägung ferner, daß die Entwicklung des internationalen Handels in diesem Zeitraum allgemein zu einer größeren Freizügigkeit des Handels geführt hat;

in der Erwägung, daß sich die internationale Lage seit der Annahme des Abkommens infolge der Entwicklung der internationalen Gemeinschaft grundlegend gewandelt hat, vor allem weil zahlreiche Staaten ihre Unabhängigkeit erlangt haben;

in der Erwägung, daß den Bedürfnissen und Anliegen der Entwicklungsländer Rechnung getragen werden sollte, um ihnen einen leichteren und weniger kostspieligen Zugang zu Erziehung, Wissenschaft, Technologie und Kultur zu ermöglichen;

eingedenk des von der Generalkonferenz der UNESCO im Jahr 1970 angenommenen Übereinkommens über Maßnahmen zum Verbot und zur Verhütung der unerlaubten Einfuhr, Ausfuhr und Übereignung von Kulturgut sowie des von der Generalkonferenz im Jahr 1972 angenommenen Übereinkommens zum Schutz des Kultur- und Naturerbes der Welt;

eingedenk ferner der unter der Schirmherrschaft des Rates für die Zusammenarbeit auf dem Gebiet des Zollwesens unter Mitwirkung der Organisation der Vereinten Nationen für Erziehung, Wissenschaft und Kultur abgeschlossenen Zollabkommen über die vorübergehende Einfuhr von Gegenständen erzieherischen, wissenschaftlichen oder kulturellen Charakters;

überzeugt, daß neue Bestimmungen getroffen werden sollten und daß diese Bestimmungen noch wirksamer zur Entwicklung der Erziehung, Wissenschaft und Kultur, welche die wesentlichen Grundlagen des wirtschaftlichen und sozialen Fortschritts darstellen, beitragen werden;

eingedenk der von der Generalkonferenz der UNESCO auf ihrer achtzehnten Tagung angenommenen Entschließung 4.112 –

sind wie folgt übereingekommen:

I.

(1) Die Vertragsstaaten verpflichten sich, auf Gegenstände, die in den Anhängen A, B, D und E sowie, sofern die betreffenden Anhänge nicht Gegenstand einer in Absatz 16 Buchstabe a vorgesehenen Erklärung sind, in den Anhängen C.1, F, G und H dieses Protokolls aufgeführt sind, die Befreiung von Zöllen und sonstigen bei oder anläßlich ihrer Einfuhr erhobenen Abgaben nach Artikel I Absatz 1 des Abkommens auszudehnen, sofern diese Gegenstände den in diesen Anhängen festgelegten Voraussetzungen entsprechen und Erzeugnisse eines anderen Vertragsstaats sind.

(2) Absatz 1 dieses Protokolls hindert einen Vertragsstaat nicht, auf eingeführte Gegenstände

a) anläßlich der Einfuhr oder später Steuern oder sonstige inländische Abgaben irgendwelcher Art zu erheben, vorausgesetzt, daß sie nicht höher sind als die Abgaben, die direkt oder indirekt auf gleichartige einheimische Erzeugnisse erhoben werden;

---

[1] Liste der Vertragsstaaten: http://portal.unesco.org/en/ev.php-URL_ID=15224&URL_DO=DO_TOPIC&URL_SECTION=201.html.

b) durch Regierungs- oder Verwaltungsbehörden bei oder anläßlich der Einfuhr Gebühren oder Abgaben zu erheben, die keine Zölle sind, vorausgesetzt, daß sie ungefähr den Kosten der geleisteten Dienste entsprechen und daß sie nicht eine mittelbare Schutzmaßnahme für einheimische Erzeugnisse oder eine Abgabe zur Erzielung von Einnahmen bei der Einfuhr darstellen.

II.
(3) Abweichend von Absatz 2 Buchstabe a verpflichten sich die Vertragsstaaten, anläßlich der Einfuhr oder später auf die nachstehend angeführten Gegenstände keine Steuern oder sonstigen inländischen Abgaben irgendwelcher Art zu erheben:
a) Bücher und Veröffentlichungen, die für die in Absatz 5 bezeichneten Bibliotheken bestimmt sind;
b) amtliche, im Ursprungsland veröffentlichte Dokumente der Parlamente und Verwaltungen;
c) Bücher und Veröffentlichungen der Vereinten Nationen und ihrer Sonderorganisationen;
d) Bücher und Veröffentlichungen, die bei der Organisation der Vereinten Nationen für Erziehung, Wissenschaft und Kultur eingehen und von ihr oder unter ihrer Aufsicht unentgeltlich verteilt werden;
e) Veröffentlichungen, die für den Fremdenverkehr außerhalb des Einfuhrlandes werben und unentgeltlich versandt und verteilt werden;
f) für Blinde und sonstige körperlich oder geistig Behinderte bestimmte Gegenstände:
   i) in Blindenschrift hergestellte Bücher, Veröffentlichungen und Dokumente aller Art,
   ii) andere eigens für die erzieherische, wissenschaftliche oder kulturelle Weiterbildung der Blinden und sonstigen körperlich oder geistig Behinderten gestaltete Gegenstände, die unmittelbar von den mit der Erziehung oder Unterstützung der Blinden und sonstigen körperlich oder geistig Behinderten befaßten und durch die zuständigen Behörden des Einfuhrlandes zur zollfreien Einfuhr dieser Gegenstände ermächtigten Institutionen oder Organisationen eingeführt werden.

III.
(4) Die Vertragsstaaten verpflichten sich, bei oder anläßlich der Ausfuhr auf die in den Anhängen dieses Protokolls angeführten Gegenstände und Materialien keine Zölle oder Abgaben und keine sonstigen inländischen Abgaben irgendwelcher Art zu erheben, die auf diese Gegenstände und Materialien erhoben werden, wenn sie für die Ausfuhr nach anderen Vertragsparteien bestimmt sind.

IV.
(5) Die Vertragsstaaten verpflichten sich, die in Artikel II Absatz 1 des Abkommens vorgesehene Gewährung der erforderlichen Genehmigungen und/oder die Freigabe der erforderlichen Devisen auf die Einfuhr der folgenden Gegenstände auszudehnen:
a) Bücher und Veröffentlichungen, die für Bibliotheken von öffentlichem Interesse bestimmt sind, wie
   i) Staatsbibliotheken und sonstige größere, der Forschung dienende Bibliotheken,
   ii) Allgemein- und Fachbibliotheken der Hochschulen, einschließlich der Universitätsbibliotheken, der College-Bibliotheken, der Institutsbibliotheken und der der Öffentlichkeit zugänglichen Hochschulbibliotheken,
   iii) öffentliche Bibliotheken,
   iv) Schulbibliotheken,
   v) Fachbibliotheken für einen bestimmten Leserkreis mit besonderen und feststellbaren Interessengebieten, wie Bibliotheken von Regierungsstellen, öffentlichen Verwaltungen, Wirtschaftsunternehmen und Berufsverbänden,
   vi) Bibliotheken für Behinderte und für Personen, die sich nicht frei bewegen können, wie Bibliotheken für Blinde, Krankenhausbibliotheken und Gefängnisbibliotheken,
   vii) Bibliotheken für Musikwerke einschließlich Diskotheken;
b) in Hochschulen als Lehrbücher zugelassene oder empfohlene und von diesen eingeführte Bücher;
c) fremdsprachige Bücher mit Ausnahme von Büchern in der oder den hauptsächlichen Landessprachen des Einfuhrlandes;
d) Filme, Diapositive, Videobänder und Tonaufnahmen erzieherischen, wissenschaftlichen oder kulturellen Charakters, die von den durch die zuständigen Behörden des Einfuhrlandes zur zollfreien Einfuhr dieser Gegenstände ermächtigten Organisationen eingeführt werden.

A.III.4a Nairobi-Protokoll

V.

(6) Die Vertragsstaaten verpflichten sich, die Gewährung der in Artikel III des Abkommens vorgesehenen Erleichterungen auf Material und Ausstattungsgegenstände auszudehnen, die ausschließlich zur Ausstellung auf einer von den zuständigen Behörden des Einfuhrlandes zugelassenen öffentlichen Ausstellung von Gegenständen erzieherischen, wissenschaftlichen oder kulturellen Charakters eingeführt und später wieder ausgeführt werden.

(7) Absatz 6 hindert die Behörden des Einfuhrlandes nicht, die Maßnahmen zu treffen, die erforderlich sind, um die tatsächliche Wiederausfuhr des betreffenden Materials und der betreffenden Ausstattungsgegenstände nach Schluß der Ausstellung sicherzustellen.

VI.

(8) Die Vertragsstaaten verpflichten sich,
a) Artikel IV des Abkommens auf die Einfuhr der von diesem Protokoll erfassten Gegenstände auszudehnen;
b) durch geeignete Maßnahmen die Verbreitung und Verteilung der in den Entwicklungsländern hergestellten Gegenstände und Materialien erzieherischen, wissenschaftlichen oder kulturellen Charakters zu fördern.

VII.

(9) Dieses Protokoll berührt nicht das Recht der Vertragsstaaten, in Übereinstimmung mit ihren Rechtsvorschriften Maßnahmen zu treffen, um die Einfuhr oder die spätere Verbreitung bestimmter Gegenstände zu verbieten oder einzuschränken, sofern diese Maßnahmen unmittelbar aus Gründen der nationalen Sicherheit, der öffentlichen Ordnung oder Sittlichkeit des Vertragsstaats nötig werden.

(10) Ungeachtet der sonstigen Bestimmungen dieses Protokolls kann ein Entwicklungsland, das nach den feststehenden Gepflogenheiten der Generalversammlung der Vereinten Nationen als solches definiert ist und das Vertragspartei des Protokolls ist, sich aus diesem Protokoll ergebenden Verpflichtungen im Zusammenhang mit der Einfuhr von Gegenständen oder Materialien aussetzen oder einschränken, wenn diese Einfuhr die einheimische Industrie dieses Entwicklungslandes ernstlich schädigt oder zu schädigen droht. Das betreffende Land hat diese Maßnahme in nicht diskriminierender Weise durchzuführen. Es unterrichtet den Generaldirektor der Organisation der Vereinten Nationen für Erziehung, Wissenschaft und Kultur über jede Maßnahme dieser Art, soweit möglich vor ihrem Inkrafttreten, und der Generaldirektor der Organisation der Vereinten Nationen für Erziehung, Wissenschaft und Kultur unterrichtet alle Vertragsparteien des Protokolls.

(11) Dieses Protokoll ändert oder beeinträchtigt nicht die Gesetze und sonstigen Rechtsvorschriften eines Vertragsstaats oder irgendwelche von ihm angenommenen internationalen Verträge, Übereinkommen, Abkommen oder Erklärungen betreffend den Schutz des Urheberrechts oder des gewerblichen Eigentums einschließlich der Patente und Warenzeichen.

(12) Unbeschadet früherer vertraglicher Abmachungen, die sie gegebenenfalls zur Regelung von Streitfällen getroffen haben, verpflichten sich die Vertragsstaaten, alle Streitfälle über die Auslegung oder Anwendung dieses Protokolls auf dem Verhandlungsweg oder durch ein Vergleichsverfahren zu regeln.

(13) Im Fall einer Meinungsverschiedenheit zwischen Vertragsstaaten über den erzieherischen, wissenschaftlichen oder kulturellen Charakter eines eingeführten Gegenstands können die beteiligten Parteien in gemeinsamem Einvernehmen ein Gutachten von dem Generaldirektor der Organisation der Vereinten Nationen für Erziehung, Wissenschaft und Kultur anfordern.

VIII.

(14)
a) Dieses Protokoll, dessen englischer und französischer Wortlaut gleichermaßen verbindlich ist, trägt das heutige Datum und liegt für alle Staaten, die Vertragsparteien des Abkommens sind, sowie für Zoll- oder Wirtschaftsunionen zur Unterzeichnung auf, sofern alle ihre Mitgliedstaaten ebenfalls Vertragsparteien des Protokolls sind.
Der in diesem Protokoll oder in dem in Absatz 18 genannten Protokoll verwendete Begriff „Staat" oder „Land" bezieht sich, wenn es sich aus dem Zusammenhang ergibt, auch auf die Zoll- oder Wirtschaftsunionen und bei allen in ihre Zuständigkeit fallenden Fragen des Anwendungsbereichs

dieses Protokolls auf die Gesamtheit der Hoheitsgebiete der Mitgliedstaaten dieser Zoll- oder Wirtschaftsunionen, nicht aber auf das Hoheitsgebiet jedes einzelnen dieser Staaten. Es wird davon ausgegangen, daß diese Zoll- oder Wirtschaftsunionen, wenn sie Vertragspartei dieses Protokolls werden, auch die Bestimmungen des Abkommens auf derselben Grundlage anwenden, wie sie im vorstehenden Absatz für das Protokoll vorgesehen ist.

b) Dieses Protokoll bedarf der Ratifikation oder der Annahme durch die Unterzeichnerstaaten in Übereinstimmung mit ihren verfassungsrechtlichen Verfahren.

c) Die Ratifikations- oder Annahmeurkunden sind beim Generalsekretär der Vereinten Nationen zu hinterlegen.

(15)
a) Die in Absatz 14 Buchstabe a erwähnten Staaten, die dieses Protokoll nicht unterzeichnet haben, können ihm beitreten.

b) Der Beitritt erfolgt durch Hinterlegung einer formellen Urkunde beim Generalsekretär der Vereinten Nationen.

(16)
a) Die in Absatz 14 Buchstabe a erwähnten Staaten können zum Zeitpunkt der Unterzeichnung, der Ratifikation, der Annahme oder des Beitritts erklären, daß sie durch Teil II, Teil IV, Anhang C. 1, Anhang F, Anhang G und Anhang H oder irgendeinen dieser Teile oder Anhänge nicht gebunden sind. Sie können ebenfalls erklären, daß sie hinsichtlich des Anhangs C. 1 nur gegenüber Vertragsstaaten gebunden sind, die diesen Anhang ihrerseits angenommen haben.

b) Jeder Vertragsstaat, der eine solche Erklärung abgegeben hat, kann sie jederzeit ganz oder teilweise durch eine an den Generalsekretär der Vereinten Nationen zu richtende Notifikation unter genauer Angabe des Zeitpunkts, zu dem die Zurücknahme wirksam wird, zurücknehmen.

c) Staaten, die nach Buchstabe a erklärt haben, daß für sie Anhang C. 1 nicht verbindlich ist, sind zwangsläufig durch Anhang C. 2 gebunden. Diejenigen Staaten, die erklärt haben, daß für sie Anhang C. 1 nur gegenüber Vertragsstaaten verbindlich ist, die diesen Anhang ihrerseits angenommen haben, sind zwangsläufig gegenüber den Vertragsstaaten, die Anhang C.1 nicht angenommen haben, durch Anhang C. 2 gebunden.

(17)
a) Dieses Protokoll tritt sechs Monate nach dem Tag der Hinterlegung der fünften Ratifikations-, Annahme- oder Beitrittsurkunde beim Generalsekretär der Vereinten Nationen in Kraft.

b) Für jeden anderen Staat tritt es sechs Monate nach dem Tag der Hinterlegung seiner Ratifikations-, Annahme- oder Beitrittsurkunde in Kraft.

c) Innerhalb eines Monats nach Ablauf der in den Buchstaben a und b vorgesehenen Fristen übermitteln die Vertragsstaaten dieses Protokolls der Organisation der Vereinten Nationen für Erziehung, Wissenschaft und Kultur einen Bericht über die Maßnahmen, die sie getroffen haben, um dem Protokoll volle Wirksamkeit zu verleihen.

d) Die Organisation der Vereinten Nationen für Erziehung, Wissenschaft und Kultur übermittelt diese Berichte allen Staaten, die Vertragsparteien dieses Protokolls sind.

(18) Das dem Abkommen beigefügte Protokoll, das nach Artikel XVII des Abkommens Bestandteil desselben ist, ist ebenfalls Bestandteil dieses Protokolls und findet auf die sich aus diesem Protokoll ergebenden Verpflichtungen sowie auf die von ihm erfaßten Erzeugnisse Anwendung.

(19)
a) Zwei Jahre nach Inkrafttreten dieses Protokolls kann jeder Vertragsstaat dieses Protokoll durch eine beim Generalsekretär der Vereinten Nationen zu hinterlegende schriftliche Urkunde kündigen.

b) Die Kündigung wird ein Jahr nach Eingang der Kündigungsurkunde wirksam.

c) Die Kündigung des Abkommens nach seinem Artikel XIV bewirkt auch die Kündigung dieses Protokolls.

(20) Der Generalsekretär der Vereinten Nationen unterrichtet die in Absatz 14 Buchstabe a erwähnten Staaten und die Organisation der Vereinten Nationen für Erziehung, Wissenschaft und Kultur über die Hinterlegung aller in den Absätzen 14 und 15 aufgeführten Ratifikations-, Annahme- oder Beitrittsurkunden, über die nach Absatz 16 abgegebenen oder zurückgenommenen Erklärungen, über das In-

A.III.4a Nairobi-Protokoll

krafttreten dieses Protokolls nach Absatz 17 Buchstaben a und b und über die in Absatz 19 vorgesehenen Kündigungen.

(21)
a) Dieses Protokoll kann von der Generalkonferenz der Organisation der Vereinten Nationen für Erziehung, Wissenschaft und Kultur revidiert werden. Eine solche Revision ist jedoch nur für Staaten verbindlich, die Vertragsparteien des Revisionsprotokolls werden.
b) Nimmt die Generalkonferenz ein neues Protokoll an, durch das dieses Protokoll ganz oder teilweise revidiert wird, und sieht das neue Protokoll nichts anderes vor, so liegt dieses Protokoll vom Tag des Inkrafttretens des neuen revidierten Protokolls an nicht mehr zur Unterzeichnung, zur Ratifikation, zur Annahme oder zum Beitritt auf.

(22) Das Abkommen wird durch dieses Protokoll nicht geändert.

(23) Die Anhänge A, B, C. 1, C. 2, D, E, F, G und H sind Bestandteil dieses Protokolls.

(24) In Übereinstimmung mit Artikel 102 der Charta der Vereinten Nationen wird dieses Protokoll am Tag seines Inkrafttretens vom Generalsekretär der Vereinten Nationen registriert.

Zu Urkund dessen haben die hierzu gehörig befugten Unterzeichneten dieses Protokoll im Namen ihrer Regierungen unterschrieben.

Anhang A
Bücher, Veröffentlichungen und Dokumente
i) Gedruckte Bücher, ungeachtet der Sprache, in der sie gedruckt sind, und der für Illustrationen verwendeten Fläche, einschließlich
   a) Luxusausgaben,
   b) Bücher, die im Ausland nach dem Manuskript eines Autors gedruckt wurden, der im Einfuhrland wohnt,
   c) Zeichen- und Malbücher für Kinder,
   d) Übungshefte für Schüler, die neben einem gedruckten Text leere Felder zum Ausfüllen enthalten,
   e) Kreuzworträtselhefte mit gedrucktem Text,
   f) einzelne Illustrationen und Druckseiten in Form von losen oder gebundenen Blättern und Druckvorlagen oder Reproduktionsfilme für die Herstellung von Büchern;
ii) gedruckte Dokumente oder Berichte nichtkommerziellen Charakters;
iii) Mikrowiedergaben der unter den Ziffern i und ii dieses Anhangs und unter den Ziffern 1 bis 6 des Anhangs A des Abkommens aufgeführten Gegenstände;
iv) Kataloge von Filmen, Tonaufnahmen oder jeglichem sonstigen Bild- und Tonmaterial erzieherischen, wissenschaftlichen oder kulturellen Charakters;
v) kartographische Erzeugnisse für wissenschaftliche Bereiche wie Geologie, Zoologie, Botanik, Mineralogie, Paläontologie, Archäologie, Ethnologie, Meteorologie, Klimatologie und Geophysik sowie meteorologische und geophysikalische Diagramme;
vi) Bauzeichnungen und -pläne oder Zeichnungen und Pläne industriellen oder technischen Charakters und deren Kopien;
vii) bibliographisches Informationsmaterial, das zur unentgeltlichen Verteilung bestimmt ist.

Anhang B
Kunstwerke und Sammlungsgegenstände erzieherischen, wissenschaftlichen oder kulturellen Charakters
i) Gemälde und Zeichnungen, ungeachtet des Materials, auf dem sie vollständig mit der Hand geschaffen worden sind, einschließlich der mit der Hand geschaffenen Kopien, jedoch ausgenommen fabrikmäßig hergestellte verzierte Gegenstände;
ii) Originalkunstgegenstände aus keramischen Stoffen und Mosaik auf Holz;
iii) Sammlungsstücke und Kunstgegenstände, die für Galerien, Museen und sonstige von den zuständigen Behörden des Einfuhrlandes zur zollfreien Einfuhr dieser Gegenstände ermächtigte Institute bestimmt sind, unter der Bedingung, daß sie nicht verkauft werden.

Nairobi-Protokoll A.III.4a

Anhang C. 1
Bild- und Tonmaterial
i) Filme,[1)] Filmbildstreifen, Mikrowiedergaben und Diapositive;
ii) Tonaufnahmen;
iii) Modelle, Skizzen und Wandbilder erzieherischen, wissenschaftlichen oder kulturellen Charakters, ausgenommen Spielzeugmodelle;
iv) sonstiges Bild- und Tonmaterial wie
   a) Videobänder, Kinescope, Videoplatten, Videoprogramme und andere Bild- und Tonträger,
   b) Mikrokarten, Mikroplanfilme (Mikrofiches), Magnetbänder oder sonstige Datenträger, die von rechnergesteuerten Informations- und Dokumentationsdiensten verwendet werden,
   c) Material für programmierten Unterricht, auch in Form von Zusammenstellungen, mit dem entsprechenden gedruckten Material, einschließlich Bild- und Tonkassetten,
   d) Diafolien, einschließlich derjenigen für die unmittelbare Projektion oder für Lese- geräte,
   e) Hologramme für die Laserprojektion,
   f) Modelle oder bildliche Darstellungen von abstrakten Begriffen wie Molekularstrukturen oder mathematischen Formeln,
   g) Multimediensätze,
   h) Material zur Förderung des Fremdenverkehrs, einschließlich des von privaten Unternehmen hergestellten Materials, das die Öffentlichkeit zu Reisen außerhalb des Einfuhrlandes anregen soll.

(Die in diesem Anhang vorgesehenen Befreiungen finden keine Anwendung auf
a) gelöschte und unbenutzte Träger für Mikrowiedergaben und gelöschte und unbenutzte Bild- und Tonaufnahmeträger sowie deren besondere Verpackung wie Kassetten, Patronen, Spulen;
b) Bild- und Tonaufnahmen, ausgenommen Material zur Förderung des Fremdenverkehrs nach Ziffer iv Buchstabe h, die durch oder für ein privates Handelsunternehmen hauptsächlich für Werbezwecke hergestellt worden sind;
c) Bild- und Tonaufnahmen, bei denen die Werbung mehr als 25 v. H. der Laufzeit einnimmt. Bei Material zur Förderung des Fremdenverkehrs nach Ziffer iv Buchstabe h gilt dieser Hundertsatz nur für die private kommerzielle Werbung.)

Anhang C. 2
Bild- und Tonmaterial erzieherischen, wissenschaftlichen oder kulturellen Charakters
Bild- und Tonmaterial erzieherischen, wissenschaftlichen oder kulturellen Charakters, das von Organisationen (nach Ermessen des Einfuhrlandes auch Rundfunk- und Fernsehgesellschaften) oder sonstigen öffentlichen oder privaten Institutionen oder Vereinigungen, die durch die zuständigen Behörden des Einfuhrlandes zur zollfreien Einfuhr dieses Materials ermächtigt sind, eingeführt oder von den Vereinten Nationen oder einer ihrer Sonderorganisationen hergestellt worden ist, wie
i) Filme, Filmbildstreifen, Mikrofilme und Diapositive;
ii) Filme (mit oder ohne Ton), die zur Zeit der Einfuhr aktuelle Ereignisse darstellen und entweder in Form von Negativen, belichtet und entwickelt, oder von Positiven, kopiert und entwickelt, für Kopierzwecke eingeführt werden, wobei die zollfreie Einfuhr auf zwei Kopien je Thema beschränkt werden kann;
iii) archivarisches Filmmaterial (mit oder ohne Ton), das zur Verwendung mit Filmen aktuellen Inhalts bestimmt ist;
iv) Unterhaltungsfilme, die sich besonders für Kinder und Jugendliche eignen;
v) Tonaufnahmen;
vi) Videobänder, Kinescope, Videoplatten, Videogramme und andere Bild- und Tonträger;
vii) Mikrokarten, Mikroplanfilme (Mikrofiches) und Magnetbänder oder sonstige Datenträger, die von rechnergesteuerten Informations- und Dokumentationsdiensten verwendet werden;
viii) Material für programmierten Unterricht, auch in Form von Zusammenstellungen, mit dem entsprechenden gedruckten Material, einschließlich Bild- und Tonkassetten;
ix) Diafolien, einschließlich derjenigen für die unmittelbare Projektion oder für Lesegeräte;
x) Hologramme für die Laserprojektion;
xi) Modelle oder bildliche Darstellungen von abstrakten Begriffen wie Molekularstrukturen oder mathematischen Formeln;
xii) Multimediensätze.

---

1) Die zollfreie Einfuhr von belichteten und entwickelten kinematographischen Filmen zum Zweck der öffentlichen kommerziellen Vorführung oder des öffentlichen Verkaufs kann auf Negative beschränkt werden, vorausgesetzt, daß diese Beschränkung nicht auf Filme (einschließlich Filme aktuellen Inhalts) Anwendung findet, die nach Anhang C. 2 dieses Protokolls zollfrei zugelassen sind.

Anhang D
Wissenschaftliche Instrumente, Apparate und Geräte
i) Wissenschaftliche Instrumente, Apparate und Geräte unter der Voraussetzung,
    a) daß sie für die von den zuständigen Behörden des Einfuhrlandes zur zollfreien Einfuhr dieser Gegenstände ermächtigten öffentlichen oder privaten wissenschaftlichen Institute oder Lehranstalten bestimmt sind und unter der Aufsicht und Verantwortung dieser Institute oder Anstalten für nichtkommerzielle Zwecke verwendet werden;
    b) daß zur Zeit keine Instrumente, Apparate oder Geräte von gleichem wissenschaftlichem Wert im Einfuhrland hergestellt werden;
ii) eigens zu wissenschaftlichen Instrumenten, Apparaten und Geräten passende Ersatzteile, Bestandteile oder Zubehörteile unter der Voraussetzung, daß diese Ersatzteile, Bestandteile oder Zubehörteile zur gleichen Zeit wie diese Instrumente, Apparate und Geräte eingeführt werden oder daß im Fall der späteren Einfuhr erkennbar ist, daß sie für Instrumente, Apparate und Geräte bestimmt sind, die früher zollfrei eingeführt worden sind oder zollfrei eingeführt werden durften;
iii) Werkzeuge für die Instandhaltung, Prüfung, Einstellung oder Instandsetzung wissenschaftlicher Instrumente unter der Voraussetzung, daß diese Werkzeuge zur gleichen Zeit wie diese Instrumente, Apparate und Geräte eingeführt werden oder daß im Fall der späteren Einfuhr erkennbar ist, daß sie für Instrumente, Apparate und Geräte bestimmt sind, die früher zollfrei eingeführt worden sind oder zollfrei eingeführt werden durften, sowie unter der Voraussetzung, daß Werkzeuge von gleichem wissenschaftlichem Wert zur Zeit nicht im Einfuhrland hergestellt werden.

Anhang E
Gegenstände für Blinde und sonstige Behinderte
i) Alle eigens für die erzieherische, wissenschaftliche oder kulturelle Weiterbildung der Blinden gestalteten Gegenstände, die unmittelbar von den mit der Erziehung oder Unterstützung von Blinden befaßten und von den zuständigen Behörden des Einfuhrlandes zur zollfreien Einfuhr dieser Gegenstände ermächtigten Institutionen oder Organisationen eingeführt werden, einschließlich
    a) Hörbücher (Schallplatten, Kassetten oder sonstige Tonwiedergaben) und Bücher in Großdruck;
    b) eigens für Blinde und sonstige Behinderte gestaltete oder angepaßte und für das Abspielen der Hörbücher erforderliche Plattenspieler und Kassettenrecorder;
    c) Apparate, die es den Blinden und Sehschwachen ermöglichen, normal gedruckte Texte zu lesen, wie elektronische Lesegeräte, Fernsehbildvergrößerer und optische Hilfsmittel;
    d) Ausrüstungen für die mechanische oder rechnergesteuerte Herstellung von Blindenschriftmaterial und aufgezeichnetem Material, wie Punziergeräte (Stereotypiergeräte), elektronische Geräte zum Übertragen und Drucken in Blindenschrift, Computer-Terminals mit Blindenschriftanzeige;
    e) Blindenschriftpapier, Magnetbänder und Kassetten für die Herstellung von Blindenschrift- und Hörbüchern;
    f) Hilfsmittel zur Verbesserung der Mobilität der Blinden wie elektronische Orientierungsgeräte und elektronische Geräte zur Feststellung von Hindernissen sowie weiße Blindenstöcke;
    g) technische Hilfsmittel für die Erziehung, Rehabilitation, berufliche Ausbildung und Beschäftigung von Blinden, wie Blindenuhren, Blindenschriftschreibmaschinen, Lehr- und Lernmittel, Spiele und sonstige eigens für die Verwendung durch Blinde gestaltete Geräte;
ii) alle eigens für die Erziehung, Beschäftigung und soziale Weiterbildung anderer körperlich oder geistig Behinderter gestaltete Gegenstände, die unmittelbar von den mit der Erziehung oder Unterstützung dieser Personen befassten und von den zuständigen Behörden des Einfuhrlandes zur zollfreien Einfuhr dieser Gegenstände ermächtigten Institutionen oder Organisationen eingeführt werden, unter der Voraussetzung, daß zur Zeit gleichwertige Gegenstände im Einfuhrland nicht hergestellt werden.

Anhang F
Sportausrüstungen
Sportausrüstungen, die ausschließlich für von den zuständigen Behörden des Einfuhrlandes zur zollfreien Einfuhr dieser Gegenstände ermächtigten Amateursportvereinigungen oder Amateursportgruppen bestimmt sind, unter der Voraussetzung, daß zur Zeit gleichwertige Gegenstände im Einfuhrland nicht hergestellt werden.

Nairobi-Protokoll A.III.4a

Anhang G
Musikinstrumente und sonstige Musikausrüstungen
Musikinstrumente und sonstige Musikausrüstungen, die ausschließlich für von den zuständigen Behörden des Einfuhrlandes zur zollfreien Einfuhr dieser Gegenstände ermächtigte kulturelle Institutionen oder Musikschulen bestimmt sind, unter der Voraussetzung, daß zur Zeit gleichwertige Instrumente und sonstige Ausrüstungen im Einfuhrland nicht hergestellt werden.

Anhang H
Zur Herstellung von Büchern, Veröffentlichungen und Dokumenten verwendete Materialien und Maschinen
i) Zur Herstellung von Büchern, Veröffentlichungen und Dokumenten verwendetes Material (Papierhalbstoffe, wiedergewonnenes Papier, Zeitungsdruckpapier und anderes Druckpapier, Druckfarbe, Klebstoffe usw.);
ii) Maschinen zur Be- und Verarbeitung von Papierhalbstoff und Papier sowie Druck- und Buchbindemaschinen unter der Voraussetzung, daß zur Zeit Maschinen von gleicher technischer Qualität im Einfuhrland nicht hergestellt werden.

A.III.5 Washingtoner Erklärung

Grundsätze der Washingtoner Konferenz in Bezug auf Kunstwerke, die von den Nationalsozialisten beschlagnahmt wurden[1]

Veröffentlicht im Zusammenhang mit der Washingtoner Konferenz über Vermögenswerte aus der Zeit des Holocaust, Washington, D.C., 3. Dezember 1998.

Im Bestreben, eine Einigung über nicht bindende Grundsätze herbeizuführen, die zur Lösung offener Fragen und Probleme im Zusammenhang mit den durch die Nationalsozialisten beschlagnahmten Kunstwerken beitragen sollen, anerkennt die Konferenz die Tatsache, dass die Teilnehmerstaaten unterschiedliche Rechtssysteme haben und dass die Länder im Rahmen ihrer eigenen Rechtsvorschriften handeln.

1. Kunstwerke, die von den Nationalsozialisten beschlagnahmt und in der Folge nicht zurückerstattet wurden, sollten identifiziert werden.
2. Einschlägige Unterlagen und Archive sollten der Forschung gemäß den Richtlinien des International Council on Archives zugänglich gemacht werden.
3. Es sollten Mittel und Personal zur Verfügung gestellt werden, um die Identifizierung aller Kunstwerke, die von den Nationalsozialisten beschlagnahmt und in der Folge nicht zurückerstattet wurden, zu erleichtern.
4. Bei dem Nachweis, dass ein Kunstwerk durch die Nationalsozialisten beschlagnahmt und in der Folge nicht zurückerstattet wurde, sollte berücksichtigt werden, dass aufgrund der verstrichenen Zeit und der besonderen Umstände des Holocaust Lücken und Unklarheiten in der Frage der Herkunft unvermeidlich sind.
5. Es sollten alle Anstrengungen unternommen werden, Kunstwerke, die als durch die Nationalsozialisten beschlagnahmt und in der Folge nicht zurückerstattet identifiziert wurden, zu veröffentlichen, um so die Vorkriegseigentümer oder ihre Erben ausfindig zu machen.
6. Es sollten Anstrengungen zur Einrichtung eines zentralen Registers aller diesbezüglichen Informationen unternommen werden.
7. Die Vorkriegseigentümer und ihre Erben sollten ermutigt werden, ihre Ansprüche auf Kunstwerke, die durch die Nationalsozialisten beschlagnahmt und in der Folge nicht zurückgegeben wurden, anzumelden.
8. Wenn die Vorkriegseigentümer von Kunstwerken, die durch die Nationalsozialisten beschlagnahmt und in der Folge nicht zurückgegeben wurden, oder ihre Erben ausfindig gemacht werden können, sollten rasch die nötigen Schritte unternommen werden, um eine gerechte und faire Lösung zu finden, wobei diese je nach den Gegebenheiten und Umständen des spezifischen Falls unterschiedlich ausfallen kann.
9. Wenn bei Kunstwerken, die nachweislich von den Nationalsozialisten beschlagnahmt und in der Folge nicht zurückgegeben wurden, die Vorkriegseigentümer oder deren Erben nicht ausfindig gemacht werden können, sollten rasch die nötigen Schritte unternommen werden, um eine gerechte und faire Lösung zu finden.
10. Kommissionen oder andere Gremien, welche die Identifizierung der durch die Nationalsozialisten beschlagnahmten Kunstwerke vornehmen und zur Klärung strittiger Eigentumsfragen beitragen, sollten eine ausgeglichene Zusammensetzung haben.
11. Die Staaten werden dazu aufgerufen, innerstaatliche Verfahren zur Umsetzung dieser Richtlinien zu entwickeln. Dies betrifft insbesondere die Einrichtung alternativer Mechanismen zur Klärung strittiger Eigentumsfragen.

---

[1] Quelle: http://www.lostart.de/stelle/grundsaetzewashington.php3?lang=german.

ICOM Recommendations concerning the Return of Works of Art Belonging to Jewish Owners[1)]

14 January 1999

During its last meeting, held in Paris in December 1998, the Executive Council of the International Council of Museums (ICOM) discussed the issue of works of art confiscated from Jewish owners during the Second World War and kept in museums or public collections.
According to ICOM's Code of Professional Ethics, the Executive Council wished to reiterate that *In all activities, museum employees must act with integrety and in accordance with the most stringent ethical principles as well as the highest standards of objectivity.*
Concerning the confiscation of Jewish works of art, the Executive Council of ICOM made the following recommendations to museum professionals around the world:

– To actively investigate and identify all acquisitions of a museum, especially those acquired during or just after the Second World War, that might be regarded as of dubious provenance (notably objects once belonging to Jewish owners and stolen, looted or removed forcibly).
– To make such relevant information accessible to facilitate the research and identification of objects of doubtful provenance by potential rightful owners or their heirs.
– To actively address and participate in drafting and establishing procedures, nationally and internationally, for disseminating information on these objects and facilitating their rightful return.
– To actively address the return of all objects of art that formerly belonged to Jewish owners or any other owner, and that are now in the possession of museums, to their rightful owners or their heirs, according to national legislation and where the legitimate ownership of these objects can clearly be established.

Created in 1946, ICOM is the international organisation of museums and professional museum workers. Composed of 15 000 members from around the world, ICOM is devoted to the promotion and development of museums and the museum profession.
In 1986, ICOM adopted a Code of Professional Ethics that every museum professional agrees to respect upon joining the Organisation. This Code, now translated in more than 20 languages, lays down precise rules governing the acquisition and de-accessioning of collections, and personal responsibility towards the collections, the public and the profession.
The Executive Council is ICOM's governing body. It is composed of 10 members elected triennially and chaired by Jacques Perot (France), President of ICOM.

---

1) Quelle: http://archives.icom.museum/worldwar2.html.

A.III.7 UNESCO Code of Ethics

International Code of Ethics for Dealers in Cultural Property[1]
November 1999

Members of the trade in cultural property recognize the key role that trade has traditionally played in the dissemination of culture and in the distribution to museums and private collectors of foreign cultural property for the education and inspiration of all peoples.

They acknowledge the world wide concern over the traffic in stolen, illegally alienated, clandestinely excavated and illegally exported cultural property and accept as binding the following principles of professional practice intended to distinguish cultural property being illicitly traded from that in licit trade and they will seek to eliminate the former from their professional activities.

ARTICLE 1
Professional traders in cultural property will not import, export or transfer the ownership of this property when they have reasonable cause to believe it has been stolen, illegally alienated, clandestinely excavated or illegally exported.

ARTICLE 2
A trader who is acting as agent for the seller is not deemed to guarantee title to the property, provided that he makes known to the buyer the full name and address of the seller. A trader who is himself the seller is deemed to guarantee to the buyer the title to the goods.

ARTICLE 3
A trader who has reasonable cause to believe that an object has been the product of a clandestine excavation, or has been acquired illegally or dishonestly from an official excavation site or monument will not assist in any further transaction with that object, except with the agreement of the country where the site or monument exists. A trader who is in possession of the object, where that country seeks its return within a reasonable period of time, will take all legally permissible steps to co-operate in the return of that object to the country of origin.

ARTICLE 4
A trader who has reasonable cause to believe that an item of cultural property has been illegally exported will not assist in any further transaction with that item, except with the agreement of the country of export. A trader who is in possession of the item, where the country of export seeks its return within a reasonable period of time, will take all legally permissible steps to co-operate in the return of that object to the country of export.

ARTICLE 5
Traders in cultural property will not exhibit, describe, attribute, appraise or retain any item of cultural property with the intention of promoting or failing to prevent its illicit transfer or export. Traders will not refer the seller or other person offering the item to those who may perform such services.

ARTICLE 6
Traders in cultural property will not dismember or sell separately parts of one complete item of cultural property.

ARTICLE 7
Traders in cultural property undertake to the best of their ability to keep together items of cultural heritage that were originally meant to be kept together.

ARTICLE 8
Violations of this Code of Ethics will be rigorously investigated by (a body to be nominated by participating dealers). A person aggrieved by the failure of a trader to adhere to the principles of this Code of Ethics may lay a complaint before that body, which shall investigate that complaint before that body, which shall investigate that complaint. Results of the complaint and the principles applied will be made public.

Adopted by the UNESCO intergovernmental Committee for Promoting the Return of Cultural Property to its Countries of Origin or its Restitution in Case of Illicit Appropriation at its Tenth Session, January 1999 and endorsed by the 30th General Conference of UNESCO, November 1999.

---

[1] Quelle: https://unesdoc.unesco.org/ark:/48223/pf0000121320.

Ethische Richtlinien für Museen von ICOM[1)]

ICOM – Internationaler Museumsrat

Die ethischen Richtlinien wurden am 4. November 1986 auf der 15. ICOM-Vollversammlung in Buenos Aires, Argentinien, einstimmig angenommen, am 6. Juli 2001 auf der 20. ICOM-Vollversammlung in Barcelona, Spanien, ergänzt und am 8. Oktober 2004 auf der 21. ICOM-Vollversammlung in Seoul, Südkorea, revidiert.

Diese Übersetzung ist von den Präsidenten der Nationalkomitees von Deutschland, Österreich und der Schweiz autorisiert.

Dieser Publikation liegt die schweizerische Orthographie zugrunde, weshalb auf die Verwendung des Buchstabens «ß» verzichtet wurde.

Die «Ethischen Richtlinien für Museen von ICOM» bilden die Grundlage der professionellen Arbeit von Museen und Museumsfachleuten. Bei der Aufnahme in die Organisation verpflichten sich die Mitglieder, diesen Kodex zu befolgen.

ICOM – Conseil international des musées
Maison de l'UNESCO
1, rue Miollis
F-75732 Paris Cedex 15
Tél. +33 1 47 34 05 00
Fax +33 1 43 06 78 62
secretariat@icom.museum www.icom.museum

Präambel

Der Status der «Ethischen Richtlinien für Museen von ICOM»

Die «Ethischen Richtlinien für Museen von ICOM» wurden vom Internationalen Museumsrat erarbeitet. Sie beinhalten die Berufsethik für Museen, auf die in den ICOM-Statuten Bezug genommen wird. Die «Ethischen Richtlinien» spiegeln Prinzipien wider, die in der internationalen Museumswelt allgemein anerkannt sind. Die Mitgliedschaft bei ICOM und die Zahlung der jährlichen Beiträge an ICOM gelten als Anerkennung der «Ethischen Richtlinien für Museen von ICOM».

Mindeststandards für Museen

Die ICOM-Richtlinien stellen einen Mindeststandard für Museen dar. Sie präsentieren eine Reihe von Grundsätzen, die durch Verhaltensrichtlinien innerhalb der beruflichen Praxis ergänzt werden. In einigen Ländern/Staaten sind gewisse Mindeststandards durch Gesetze oder staatliche Vorschriften geregelt. In anderen können Orientierung an und Beurteilung von fachlichen Mindeststandards in Form von Akkreditierung, Registrierung oder äquivalenten Einstufungsverfahren die Einhaltung gewährleisten. Wo keine entsprechenden Standards festgelegt sind, können das ICOM-Sekretariat oder ein zuständiges nationales bzw. entsprechendes internationales ICOM-Komitee weiterhelfen. Ein weiteres Ziel ist es, dass Einzelstaaten und museumsbezogene Fachorganisationen auf Grundlage dieser Richtlinien zusätzliche Standards entwickeln.

Übersetzungen der «Ethischen Richtlinien für Museen von ICOM»

Die «Ethischen Richtlinien für Museen von ICOM» wurden in den drei offiziellen Arbeitssprachen der Organisation herausgegeben: Englisch, Französisch und Spanisch. ICOM begrüsst die Übersetzung der Richtlinien in weitere Sprachen. Allerdings wird eine Übersetzung nur dann als «offiziell» anerkannt, wenn sie von mindestens einem Nationalkomitee gebilligt wurde, in dessen Land diese Sprache

---

1) Quelle: https://icom-deutschland.de/de/component/abook/book/2-icom-publikationen/6-ethische-richtlinien-fuer-museen-von-icom.html.

A.III.8 Ethische Richtlinien für Museen von ICOM

gesprochen wird, normalerweise als Hauptsprache. Ist die Sprache auch in anderen Staaten Landessprache, sollen nach Möglichkeit auch deren Nationalkomitees konsultiert werden. Sprachliche Kompetenz und Fachkenntnisse im Museumsberuf sind für die Erstellung offizieller Übersetzungen unabdingbar. Die der Übersetzung zugrunde liegende Sprachfassung und die involvierten Nationalkomitees sind anzugeben. Diese Bedingungen beschränken nicht die vollständige oder auszugsweise Übersetzung der «Ethischen Richtlinien für Museen» zu Lehr- oder Studienzwecken.

Einführung

Diese Fassung der «Ethischen Richtlinien für Museen von ICOM» (ICOM Code of Ethics for Museums) ist das Resultat einer sechs Jahre dauernden Überarbeitung. Nach eingehender Überprüfung des Regelwerks unter Berücksichtigung aktueller Museumspraxis, wurde 2001 eine revidierte und nach dem Vorbild der früheren Ausgabe strukturierte Fassung herausgegeben. Wie seinerzeit geplant, wurde die jetzige Version vollkommen neu strukturiert, um den Museumsberuf zeitgemäss zu repräsentieren. Sie basiert auf den Grundprinzipien der beruflichen Praxis und wurde zur Schaffung allgemeiner ethischer Orientierung zu einem generellen ethischen Leitfaden weiterentwickelt. Die «Ethischen Richtlinien» waren Gegenstand einer dreimaligen Mitgliederumfrage. Im Jahr 2004 wurden sie von der 21. ICOM-Vollversammlung in Seoul per Akklamation verabschiedet.

Das gesamte Ethos des Dokuments bleibt das des Dienstes an der Gesellschaft, des Gemeinwesens, der Öffentlichkeit und ihrer unterschiedlichen Gruppierungen sowie der Professionalität von Museumsmitarbeiter/innen. Die neue Struktur des Dokuments, die Betonung von Schwerpunkten und kürzere Paragraphen führten zwar durchwegs zu anderen Gewichtungen, jedoch ist nur weniges völlig neu. Die neuen Themen finden sich im Paragraph 2.11 und den in den Abschnitten 3, 5 und 6 umrissenen Prinzipien.

Die «Ethischen Richtlinien für Museen» dienen als Werkzeug zur beruflichen Selbstkontrolle in einem Bereich der öffentlichen Dienstleistung, in dem nationale Gesetzgebungen variieren und nur selten übereinstimmen. Sie setzen Mindeststandards für Verhalten und Arbeit, die Museumsmitarbeiter/innen auf der ganzen Welt vernünftigerweise anstreben können. Weiter legen die «Ethischen Richtlinien» dar, was die Öffentlichkeit von Museen, deren Mitarbeiter/innen und deren Berufsstand realistischerweise erwarten darf.

1970 veröffentlichte ICOM seine «Ethics of Acquisition» [Ethik der Sammlungsbeschaffung] und 1986 den ersten vollständigen «Code of Professional Ethics». Die vorliegende Fassung – sowie das Übergangsdokument von 2001 – beruht in ihren Grundzügen auf diesem Ausgangswerk. Die Hauptaufgabe der Überarbeitung und Neustrukturierung fiel jedoch den Mitgliedern des Ethikausschusses zu. Für ihre persönlichen oder in elektronischer Form gelieferten Beiträge und ihre Entschlossenheit, zielgerichtet und planmäss mitzuarbeiten, gebührt ihnen Dank. Ihre Namen werden an anderer Stelle aufgeführt.

Nachdem wir unsere Aufgabe erfüllt haben, übertragen wir die Verantwortung für die «Ethischen Richtlinien» an die weitgehend neuen Mitglieder des von Bernice Murphy geleiteten Ethikausschusses. Bernice Murphy bringt ihr gesammeltes Wissen und ihre Erfahrungen als ehemalige ICOM-Vizepräsidentin und früheres Mitglied des Ethikausschusses ein.

Wie die Vorläufer gibt der vorliegende Kodex einen globalen Mindeststandard vor, den nationale und fachliche Gruppierungen entsprechend ihren individuellen Erfordernissen ausgestalten können. ICOM unterstützt die Entwicklung nationaler und fachspezifischer Ethikrichtlinien und würde sich sehr über die Überlassung entsprechender Exemplare freuen. Bitte diese an folgende Adresse senden:
Secrétaire général de l'ICOM, Maison de l'UNESCO, 1, rue Miollis, 75732 Paris Cedex 15, Frankreich,
E-Mail: secretariat@icom.museum

Geoffrey Lewis
Vorsitzender des ICOM-Ethikausschusses (1997–2004) Präsident von ICOM (1983–1989)

Ethische Richtlinien für Museen von ICOM   A.III.8

Der ICOM-Ethikausschuss für den Zeitraum 2001–2004

Vorsitz:
Geoffrey Lewis (Grossbritannien)
Mitglieder:
Gary Edson (USA)
Per Kåks (Schweden)
Byung-mo Kim (Republik Korea)
Pascal Makambila (Kongo)
Jean-Yves Marin (Frankreich)
Bernice Murphy (Australien)
Tereza Scheiner (Brasilien)
Shaje'a Tshiluila (Demokratische Republik Kongo)
Michel Van-Praët (Frankreich)
Ethische Fragen, die den ICOM-Ethikausschuss betreffen und/oder von ihm geprüft werden sollen, können per E-Mail an seinen Vorsitz gerichtet werden: ethics@icom.museum

1. Museen bewahren, zeigen, vermitteln und fördern das Verständnis für das Natur- und Kulturerbe der Menschheit.

Grundsatz

Museen sind für das materielle und immaterielle Natur- und Kulturerbe verantwortlich. Museumsträger und jene, die mit der strategischen Richtungsweisung und Aufsicht von Museen befasst sind, haben in erster Linie die Verantwortung, dieses Erbe zu schützen und zu fördern. Dazu zählen auch personelle, materielle und finanzielle Ressourcen, die zu diesem Zweck zur Verfügung stehen.

Statuten und Leitbilder für Museen

1.1 Grundsatzdokument
Der Museumsträger hat sicherzustellen, dass das Museum über eine schriftliche und publizierte Satzung, ein Statut oder ein anderes allgemein veröffentlichtes Dokument verfügt, das seinen rechtlichen Status, seinen Auftrag, seine Dauerhaftigkeit und seine Gemeinnützigkeit – in Übereinstimmung mit nationalen Gesetzen – klar darlegt.

1.2 Aufgabenbeschreibung, Ziele und Vorgehensweisen
Der Träger soll eine eindeutige Erklärung über Aufgaben, Ziele und Vorgehensweisen des Museums und über seine eigene Rolle und Zusammensetzung ausarbeiten und veröffentlichen. Diese Erklärung soll dem Träger als Richtlinie dienen.

Sachmittel

1.3 Räumlichkeiten
Der Träger soll sowohl angemessene Räumlichkeiten, als auch ein geeignetes Umfeld für das Museum gewährleisten, sodass es die seinem Auftrag entsprechenden Grundfunktionen erfüllen kann.

1.4 Zugänglichkeit
Der Träger soll gewährleisten, dass das Museum und seine Sammlungen allen Interessierten zu angemessenen, regelmässigen Zeiten zugänglich sind. Besonderes Augenmerk ist auf Personen mit körperlichen Beeinträchtigungen zu richten.

1.5 Gesundheit und Sicherheit
Der Träger soll gewährleisten, dass die Standards der Institution bezüglich Gesundheit, Sicherheit und Zugänglichkeit gegenüber Personal und Besuchern eingehalten werden.

1.6 Katastrophenschutz
Der Träger soll Massnahmen treffen, um Publikum, Personal, Sammlungen und andere Ressourcen vor Naturkatastrophen und von Menschen verursachte Schäden nachhaltig zu schützen.

A.III.8 Ethische Richtlinien für Museen von ICOM

1.7 Sicherheitsanforderungen
Der Träger soll geeignete Sicherheitsmassnahmen ergreifen, um die Sammlungen in Ausstellungsräumen, Depots und Arbeitsräumen sowie während des Transports vor Diebstahl und Beschädigung zu schützen.

1.8 Versicherungen und Entschädigungen
Soweit Versicherungen in Anspruch genommen werden, soll der Träger sicherstellen, dass die Risiken ausreichend abgedeckt sind und Transitgüter, Leihgaben und andere Gegenstände einschliesst, für die das Museum haftet. Für Gegenstände, die sich nicht im Eigentum des Museums befinden, ist für eine ausreichende Entschädigungsleistung im Schadensfall zu sorgen.

Finanzmittel

1.9 Finanzierung
Der Träger soll sicherstellen, dass ausreichende finanzielle Mittel zur Verfügung stehen, um den Betrieb des Museums zu ermöglichen und weiter zu entwickeln. Über sämtliche Finanzen ist professionell Buch zu führen (Buchhaltungspflicht).

1.10 Gewinnorientierte Tätigkeiten
Der Träger soll über Einkünfte die er durch Aktivitäten selbst generiert oder die ihm aus externen Quellen zufliessen, nach genau festgelegten Regeln verfügen. Ungeachtet der Quelle der Einkünfte sollen Museen eine Selbstkontrolle über Inhalt und Rechtschaffenheit ihrer Programme, Ausstellungen und Aktivitäten ausüben. Gewinnorientierte Tätigkeiten dürfen nicht die Museumseinrichtung oder deren Besucher kompromittieren (siehe 6.6).

Personal

1.11 Personalpolitik
Der Träger soll sicherstellen, dass sämtliche personellen Massnahmen im Einklang mit den Grundsätzen des Museums stehen und nach Recht und Gesetz erfolgen.

1.12 Ernennung des/der Direktors/in oder Leiters/in
Die Stelle des/der Museumsdirektors/in bzw. -leiters/in stellt eine Schlüsselposition des Museums dar. Bei der Ernennung soll der Träger die Kenntnisse und Fähigkeiten berücksichtigen, die zur effektiven Ausübung dieser Stellung erforderlich sind. Diese Eigenschaften sollen angemessene intellektuelle Fähigkeiten und Fachkenntnisse einschliessen, ergänzt durch einen hohen Grad ethischen Verhaltens.

1.13 Zugang zu Trägern
Der/die Museumsdirektor/in bzw. -leiter/in soll den zuständigen Trägern unmittelbar verantwortlich sein und sich direkt an sie wenden können.

1.14 Kompetenz des Museumspersonals
Die Anstellung qualifizierter Mitarbeiter/innen mit den für sämtliche Aufgaben erforderlichen Fachkenntnissen ist unerlässlich (siehe auch 2.19; 2.24; 8.11).

1.15 Weiterbildung des Personals
Geeignete Möglichkeiten zur beruflichen Aus-, Fort- und Weiterbildung aller Museumsmitarbeiter/innen sind sicherzustellen, um Fachwissen und Kompetenz der Belegschaft zu erhalten und auszubauen.

1.16 Ethische Konflikte
Der Träger darf von Museumsmitarbeiter/innen niemals Handlungen verlangen, die als Verletzung der «Ethischen Richtlinien für Museen von ICOM», nationaler Gesetze oder fachspezifischer Ethikrichtlinien betrachtet werden können.

1.17 Museumspersonal und ehrenamtliche Mitarbeiter/innen
Der Träger soll bezüglich der Mitarbeit ehrenamtlicher Mitarbeiter/innen über schriftlich festgelegte Regeln verfügen, die eine positive Beziehung zwischen diesen und den Museumsangestellten fördern.

1.18 Ehrenamtliche Mitarbeiter/innen und museale Berufsethik
Der Träger soll sicherstellen, dass ehrenamtliche Mitarbeiter/innen bei ihren Museums- und Privataktivitäten vollständig mit den «Ethischen Richtlinien für Museen von ICOM» und anderen anwendbaren Regelwerken und Gesetzen vertraut sind.

2. Museen, die Sammlungen unterhalten, bewahren diese treuhänderisch zum Nutzen und zum Fortschritt der Gesellschaft.

Grundsatz
Museen haben die Aufgabe, ihre Sammlungen als Beitrag zum Schutz des natürlichen, kulturellen und wissenschaftlichen Erbes zu erwerben, zu bewahren und fortzuentwickeln. Museumssammlungen sind ein bedeutendes Erbe der Gemeinschaft, haben in der Rechtsordnung einen besonderen Stellenwert und sind durch die internationale Gesetzgebung geschützt. Diese Verpflichtung der Öffentlichkeit gegenüber macht Museen zu Verwaltern, die für den rechtmässigen Besitz der in ihrer Obhut befindlichen Objekte, für den dauerhaften Charakter ihrer Sammlungen, für deren Dokumentation und Zugänglichkeit sowie für eine verantwortungsvolle Aussonderungspolitik verantwortlich sind.

Erwerb von Sammlungen
2.1 Sammlungspolitik
Der Museumsträger soll für jedes Museum die Sammlungspolitik schriftlich festlegen und veröffentlichen, die sich mit dem Erwerb, der Pflege und der Verwendung der Sammlungen befasst. Dieses Dokument soll auch über alle Materialien Klarheit schaffen, die nicht katalogisiert, aufbewahrt oder ausgestellt werden (siehe 2.7; 2.8).
2.2 Gültige Rechtstitel
Objekte oder Exemplare dürfen nur dann gekauft, geliehen, getauscht oder als Geschenk bzw. Legat angenommen werden, wenn das entgegennehmende Museum überzeugt ist, dass ein gültiger Rechtstitel besteht. Der Beleg rechtsgültigen Eigentums in einem Land ist nicht notwendigerweise ein gültiger Rechtstitel.
2.3 Provenienz und Sorgfaltspflicht
Vor einem Erwerb muss jede Anstrengung unternommen werden, um sicherzustellen, dass die zum Kauf, zur Leihe, zum Tausch, als Geschenk bzw. als Legat angebotenen Objekte oder Exemplare nicht gesetzeswidrig in ihrem Ursprungsland erlangt oder aus ihm bzw. aus einem dritten Land (einschliesslich dem des Museums) ausgeführt wurden, in dem sie möglicherweise in legalem Besitz waren. In dieser Hinsicht muss mit aller gebotenen Sorgfalt versucht werden, die vollständige Provenienz des betreffenden Objekts zu ermitteln und zwar von seiner Entdeckung oder Herstellung an.
2.4 Objekte und Exemplare aus nicht genehmigten oder unwissenschaftlichen Feldforschungen
Museen sollen keine Objekte in ihren Besitz bringen, bei denen der begründete Verdacht besteht, dass ihre Entdeckung mit behördlich nicht genehmigten und unwissenschaftlichen Aktivitäten einherging oder mutwillige Zerstörung oder Beschädigung von Denkmälern, archäologischen oder geologischen Stätten bzw. natürlichen Lebensräumen oder Tier- und Pflanzenarten nach sich zog. Dies gilt auch für Funde, bei denen es versäumt wurde, diese dem Eigentümer oder Besitzer des Grundstückes oder den zuständigen Rechts- bzw. Regierungsbehörden zu melden.
2.5 Kulturell sensible Gegenstände und Materialien
Sammlungen, die menschliche Überreste oder Gegenstände von religiöser Bedeutung enthalten, sollen nur angenommen werden, wenn sie sicher untergebracht und respektvoll behandelt werden können. Dies muss in einer Art und Weise erfolgen, die vereinbar ist mit professionellen Standards und den Interessen und Glaubensgrundsätzen der Gemeinschaft, ethnischer oder religiöser Gruppen, denen die Objekte entstammen und soweit diese bekannt sind (siehe auch 3.7; 4.3).

A.III.8 Ethische Richtlinien für Museen von ICOM

2.6 Geschützte biologische oder geologische Exemplare
Museen sollen keine biologischen oder geologischen Exemplare erwerben, die unter Verstoss gegen lokale, regionale, nationale oder internationale Artenschutz- oder Naturschutzgesetze oder -abkommen gesammelt, verkauft oder auf andere Weise weitergegeben wurden.

2.7 Lebende Sammlungen
Wenn die Sammlungen lebende botanische oder zoologische Exemplare enthalten, sind bezüglich ihrer ursprünglichen, natürlichen und sozialen Umgebung besondere Rücksichtnahmen erforderlich. Weiterhin sind auch hier lokale, regionale, nationale oder internationale Artenschutz- und Naturschutzgesetze oder -abkommen zu beachten.

2.8 Arbeitssammlungen
Die Sammlungspolitik kann Sonderregelungen für bestimmte Arten von Arbeitssammlungen enthalten, bei denen der Schwerpunkt eher auf der Bewahrung kultureller, wissenschaftlicher oder technischer Prozesse als auf der Bewahrung der Objekte liegt oder bei denen Objekte oder Exemplare zu praktischen Übungs- oder Lehrzwecken zusammengestellt wurden (siehe auch 2.1).

2.9 Erwerb ausserhalb der Sammlungspolitik
Der Erwerb von Objekten oder Exemplaren soll nur in Ausnahmefällen ausserhalb der geltenden Sammlungspolitik erfolgen. Der Träger soll den Rat von Fachleuten und die Standpunkte aller beteiligten Interessenten berücksichtigen. Auch die Bedeutung des Objekts oder Exemplars im Kontext des kulturellen oder natürlichen Erbes, aus dem es stammt, sowie die Interessen anderer Museen, die derartiges Material sammeln, sind zu beachten. Aber selbst unter solchen Umständen sollen keinesfalls Objekte ohne gültigen Rechtstitel erworben werden (siehe auch 3.4).

2.10 Erwerbungen, wenn diese von Mitgliedern der Trägerschaft und des Museumspersonals angeboten werden
Besondere Vorsicht ist geboten, wenn Mitglieder der Trägerschaft, des Personals oder deren Familienangehörige oder ihnen nahestehende Personen Gegenstände zum Kauf, als Schenkung oder als abzugsberechtigte Spende anbieten.

2.11 Aufbewahrungsort
Die vorliegenden «Ethischen Richtlinien» sollen unter keinen Umständen ein Museum daran hindern, als autorisierter Aufbewahrungsort für illegal gesammelte oder geborgene Objekte und Exemplare oder solche ohne Herkunftsnachweis aus dem Bereich zu fungieren, für das es gesetzlich zuständig ist.

Aussonderung von Sammlungen

2.12 Gesetzlich oder anderweitig geregelte Aussonderungsbefugnisse
Ein Museum, das zu Aussonderungen rechtlich befugt ist oder das Objekte erworben hat, die Aussonderungsbedingungen unterliegen, muss die gesetzlichen und anderen Vorschriften und Verfahren voll und ganz einhalten. Wo der ursprüngliche Erwerb bindenden oder anderen Beschränkungen unterworfen ist, müssen diese Bedingungen eingehalten werden, es sei denn, es ist klar zu belegen, dass das Festhalten an diesen Beschränkungen unmöglich oder dem Wohl der Einrichtung in hohem Masse abträglich ist. Falls erforderlich, kann das Museum den Rechtsweg beschreiten, um sich von derartigen Beschränkungen entbinden zu lassen.

2.13 Aussonderung aus Museumssammlungen
Die Aussonderung eines Objekts oder Exemplars aus einer Museumssammlung darf nur bei vollem Verständnis für die Bedeutung des Gegenstandes, seines Charakters (erneuerbar oder nicht erneuerbar), seiner rechtlichen Stellung und unter Erwägung des öffentlichen Vertrauensverlustes erfolgen, den ein derartiges Vorgehen möglicherweise nach sich zieht.

2.14 Verantwortung für Aussonderungen
Die Entscheidung zur Aussonderung soll in der Verantwortung des Museumsträgers liegen. Dabei hat dieser in Abstimmung mit der Direktion des Museums und der Kuratorin oder dem Kurator der betreffenden Sammlung zu handeln. Für Arbeitssammlungen können Sondervereinbarungen getroffen werden (siehe 2.7; 2.8).

2.15 Veräusserung von ausgesonderten Objekten
Jedes Museum soll über Richtlinien verfügen, in denen die erlaubten Vorgehensweisen für die dauerhafte Entfernung von Objekten aus seinen Sammlungen durch Schenkung, Übereignung, Tausch, Verkauf, Rückführung oder Vernichtung definiert sind. Diese Regeln sollten auch die uneingeschränkte Übertragung von Rechtstiteln an den Empfänger umfassen. Über sämtliche Aussonderungsentscheidungen, die betreffenden Objekte und deren Verbleib ist genauestens Buch zu führen. Ein ausgesondertes Stück soll zuerst einem anderen Museum angeboten werden.

2.16 Einkünfte aus der Veräusserung von Sammlungen
Museumssammlungen werden für die Öffentlichkeit treuhänderisch verwaltet und dürfen nicht als Aktivvermögen behandelt werden. Gelder oder Ersatzleistungen, die durch Aussonderung und Veräusserung von Objekten oder Exemplaren aus einer Museumssammlung erlangt wurden, sind ausschliesslich zum Nutzen der Sammlung – im Regelfall für Neuerwerbungen eben dieser – zu verwenden.

2.17 Erwerb von ausgesonderten Sammlungen
Museumspersonal, Mitgliedern der Trägerschaft sowie deren Familienangehörigen oder deren engerem Umfeld ist der Erwerb von ausgesonderten Objekten einer Sammlung für die sie mitverantwortlich sind, nicht zu gestatten.

Pflege von Sammlungen

2.18 Kontinuität der Sammlungen
Das Museum soll Richtlinien festlegen und anwenden, die sicherstellen, dass alle (vorübergehend oder dauerhaft) in seinem Besitz befindlichen Sammlungen und zugehörigen Informationen ordnungsgemäss dokumentiert werden, für gegenwärtigen Gebrauch verfügbar bleiben und an zukünftige Generationen weitergegeben werden und zwar in einem unter Berücksichtigung heutiger Kenntnisse und Mittel möglichst guten und sicheren Zustand.

2.19 Übertragung der Sammlungsverantwortung
Fachliche Verantwortlichkeiten in Bezug auf die Pflege der Sammlungen sollen an Personen übertragen werden, die über entsprechende Kenntnisse und Fähigkeiten verfügen oder die angemessen beaufsichtigt werden (siehe auch 8.11).

2.20 Dokumentation der Sammlungen
Museumssammlungen sollen nach allgemein anerkannten professionellen Standards dokumentiert werden. Diese Dokumentation soll eine vollständige Kennzeichnung und Beschreibung jedes Stückes beinhalten, über sein Umfeld, seine Herkunft, seinen Zustand, seine Behandlung sowie seinen gegenwärtigen Standort Auskunft geben. Diese Sammlungsdaten sollen sicher verwahrt und so katalogisiert werden, dass ein Zugriff durch das Museumspersonal und andere Berechtigte gewährleistet ist.

2.21 Schutz vor Katastrophen
Grösste Aufmerksamkeit soll der Ausarbeitung von Regeln gewidmet werden, die die Sammlungen während bewaffneter Konflikte sowie vor anderen von Menschen verursachten oder natürlichen Katastrophen schützen.

2.22 Datensicherheit
Das Museum soll sicherstellen, dass keine sensiblen persönlichen Daten oder anderen vertraulichen Informationen preisgegeben werden, wenn Sammlungsdaten der Allgemeinheit zugänglich sind.

2.23 Vorbeugende Konservierung
Vorbeugende Konservierung ist ein wichtiges Element der Museumstätigkeit und der Sammlungspflege. Es ist eine wesentliche Verantwortung der Museumsmitarbeiter/innen, ein schützendes Umfeld für die in ihrer Obhut befindlichen Sammlungen zu schaffen und zu erhalten, sei es im Depot, bei der Präsentation oder beim Transport.

2.24 Konservierung und Restaurierung der Sammlungen
Das Museum soll den Zustand seiner Sammlungen sorgfältig beobachten, um zu entscheiden, wann ein Objekt oder Exemplar Konservierungs- oder Restaurierungsarbeiten benötigt und den Einsatz eines qualifizierten Konservators/Restaurators erforderlich macht. Das eigentliche Ziel soll darin liegen, den Zustand des Objekts oder Exemplars zu stabilisieren. Alle Konservierungsverfahren müssen doku-

A.III.8 Ethische Richtlinien für Museen von ICOM

mentiert werden und so weit wie möglich reversibel sein; sämtliche Veränderungen am ursprünglichen Objekt oder Exemplar sollen deutlich erkennbar sein.

2.25 Das Wohl lebender Tiere
Ein Museum, das lebende Tiere hält, übernimmt für deren Gesundheit und Wohlergehen die volle Verantwortung. Das Museum muss von einer tiermedizinischen Fachkraft anerkannte Sicherheitsvorschriften zum Schutz von Personal, Besuchern und Tieren ausarbeiten und umsetzen. Genetische Veränderungen sollen klar erkennbar sein.

2.26 Persönlicher Gebrauch von Museumssammlungen
Museumspersonal und Mitgliedern der Trägerschaft bzw. deren Familienangehörigen oder dem engeren Umfeld ist die – auch nur vorübergehende – Aneignung von Gegenständen aus den Sammlungen des Museums zum persönlichen Gebrauch nicht gestattet.

3. Museen bewahren elementare Zeugnisse zur Gewinnung und Erweiterung von Wissen.

Grundsatz

Museen tragen eine besondere Verantwortung für Pflege, Präsentation, Zugänglichkeit (auch im Depot) und Erforschung der gesammelten elementaren Zeugnisse, die sich in ihren Sammlungen befinden.

Elementare Zeugnisse

3.1 Sammlungen als elementare Zeugnisse
Die Sammlungspolitik eines Museums soll die Bedeutung von Sammlungen als elementare Zeugnisse klar zum Ausdruck bringen. Sie darf nicht allein von aktuellen, geistigen Trends oder gegenwärtigen Museumsgepflogenheiten beherrscht sein.

3.2 Verfügbarkeit der Sammlungen
Museen fällt die besondere Aufgabe zu, ihre Sammlungen und alle wichtigen Informationen so frei wie möglich verfügbar zu machen, wobei Einschränkungen aus Gründen der Vertraulichkeit und Sicherheit zu beachten sind.

Museales Sammeln und Forschung

3.3 Aufsammlungen
Museen, die Aufsammlungen in Feldforschung vornehmen, sollten Richtlinien entwickeln, die im Einklang mit wissenschaftlichen Standards sowie zutreffenden nationalen und internationalen Gesetzen und Abkommen stehen. Feldforschung soll nur unter respektvoller Rücksichtnahme auf die Anschauungen lokaler Gemeinschaften, auf ihre natürlichen Ressourcen und kulturellen Gepflogenheiten und zur besseren Würdigung des kulturellen und natürlichen Erbes erfolgen.

3.4 Sammlung von elementaren Zeugnissen unter besonderen Umständen
Unter besonderen Umständen kann ein Stück ohne Herkunftsnachweis von derart überragender wissenschaftlicher Bedeutung sein, dass seine Bewahrung im öffentlichen Interesse liegt. Über die Aufnahme eines derartigen Stückes in eine Museumssammlung sollen Fachleute aus dem betreffenden Fachgebiet ohne nationale oder internationale Parteinahme entscheiden (siehe auch 2.11).

3.5 Forschung
Forschungen von Museumsmitarbeiter/innen sollen im Zusammenhang mit dem Auftrag und den Zielen des Museums stehen und der bestehenden rechtlichen, ethischen und akademischen Praxis entsprechen.

3.6 Zerstörende Untersuchung
Wenn zerstörende Untersuchungsverfahren angewendet werden, sollen vollständige Aufzeichnungen über das untersuchte Material, das Untersuchungsergebnis und daraus resultierende Forschungen und Veröffentlichungen in die permanenten Aufzeichnungen über das Objekt eingehen.

3.7 Menschliche Überreste und Gegenstände von religiöser Bedeutung
Wissenschaftliche Untersuchungen an menschlichen Überresten und Gegenständen von religiöser Bedeutung müssen unter Einhaltung professioneller Standards erfolgen und den Interessen und Glau-

bensgrundsätzen der gesellschaftlichen, ethnischen oder religiösen Gruppen, denen die Objekte entstammen, Rechnung tragen, soweit diese bekannt sind (siehe auch 2.5; 4.3).

3.8 Eigentumsrechte
Sofern Museumsmitarbeiter/innen Materialien zur Präsentation oder zur Dokumentation von Feldforschungen aufbereiten, sind klare Übereinkünfte mit dem finanzierenden Museum bezüglich sämtlicher Rechte an ihrer Arbeit zu treffen.

3.9 Der Austausch von Fachkenntnissen
Museumsmitarbeiter/innen sind verpflichtet, ihr Wissen und ihre Erfahrung mit Kolleg/innen, Forschenden und Studierenden ihrer Fachrichtungen zu teilen. Sie sollen diejenigen, von denen sie ihr Wissen erlangt haben, respektieren und anerkennen und neue Methoden und Erfahrungen weitergeben, die für andere von Nutzen sein könnten.

3.10 Zusammenarbeit zwischen Museen und anderen Einrichtungen
Museumsmitarbeiter/innen sollen die Notwendigkeit zur Zusammenarbeit und Absprache zwischen Einrichtungen mit ähnlichen Interessen und Sammelmethoden anerkennen und dafür eintreten. Dies gilt besonders für Bildungsinstitutionen und bestimmte öffentliche Einrichtungen, in denen im Rahmen von Forschungstätigkeiten wichtige Sammlungen entstehen können, für die es keine langfristige Sicherheit gibt.

4. Museen schaffen Voraussetzungen für die Wertschätzung, das Verständnis und die Förderung von Natur- und Kulturerbe.

Grundsatz
Museen haben die wichtige Aufgabe, ihre bildungspolitische Funktion weiterzuentwickeln und ein immer breiteres Publikum aus der Gesellschaft, der örtlichen Gemeinschaft oder der Zielgruppe, für die sie eingerichtet sind, anzuziehen. Die Wechselbeziehung des Museums mit der Gesellschaft und die Förderung ihres Erbes sind unmittelbarer Bestandteil des Bildungsauftrages eines Museums.

Dauer- und Sonderausstellungen

4.1 Dauer- und Sonderausstellungen und besondere Aktivitäten
Dauer- und Sonderausstellungen, ob materiell oder in elektronischer Form, sollen mit dem erklärten Auftrag, den Richtlinien und den Zielen des Museums in Einklang stehen. Sie dürfen weder die Qualität noch die notwendige Pflege und Erhaltung der Sammlungen in Mitleidenschaft ziehen.

4.2 Interpretation von Ausstellungsstücken
Museen sollen sicherstellen, dass die in Dauer- und Sonderausstellungen präsentierten Informationen fundiert und korrekt sind und die repräsentierten Gruppen oder Glaubensrichtungen angemessen beachtet werden.

4.3 Ausstellung sensibler Objekte
Die Ausstellung von menschlichen Überresten und Gegenständen von religiöser Bedeutung muss unter Einhaltung professioneller Standards erfolgen und, soweit bekannt, den Interessen und Glaubensgrundsätzen der gesellschaftlichen, ethnischen oder religiösen Gruppen, denen die Objekte entstammen, Rechnung tragen. Die Objekte sind mit Taktgefühl und Achtung vor den Gefühlen der Menschwürde, die alle Völker haben, zu präsentieren.

4.4 Entfernung aus öffentlichen Ausstellungen
Wünschen betroffener Gruppen nach der Entfernung von menschlichen Überresten oder Gegenständen von religiöser Bedeutung aus der öffentlichen Ausstellung muss umgehend und mit Respekt und Sensibilität begegnet werden. Auf Anfragen bezüglich der Rückgabe solcher Gegenstände ist entsprechend zu reagieren. Museen sollen für die Beantwortung solcher Anfragen klare Richtlinien definieren.

4.5 Ausstellung von Objekten ohne Herkunftsnachweis
Museen sollten vermeiden, Gegenstände fragwürdigen Ursprungs oder solche ohne Herkunftsnachweis auszustellen oder auf andere Weise zu nutzen. Sie müssen sich bewusst sein, dass dies als Duldung und Förderung des illegalen Handels mit Kulturgütern aufgefasst werden kann.

A.III.8 Ethische Richtlinien für Museen von ICOM

Andere Aktivitäten

4.6 Publikationen
Die von Museen auf welche Weise auch immer veröffentlichten Informationen sollen fundiert und korrekt sein und die präsentierten wissenschaftlichen Disziplinen, Gesellschaften oder Glaubensrichtungen verantwortungsvoll behandeln. Museumspublikationen sollen die Standards der Einrichtung nicht beeinträchtigen.

4.7 Reproduktionen und Nachbildungen
Museen sollen bei der Anfertigung von Nachbildungen, Reproduktionen oder Kopien von Sammlungsgegenständen die Integrität des Originals respektieren. Alle Kopien sollen dauerhaft als Faksimile gekennzeichnet sein.

5. Museen verfügen über Mittel, die weitere öffentliche Dienstleistungen und Vorteile ermöglichen.

Grundsatz

Museen nutzen ein breites Spektrum an Spezialwissen, Fertigkeiten und materiellen Ressourcen, die auch ausserhalb des Museums von Nutzen sein können. Daher bieten sich die Teilung von Ressourcen und die Bereitstellung von Dienstleistungen als Erweiterung der Museumsaktivitäten an. Diese sollen so organisiert werden, dass sie den festgelegten Auftrag des Museums nicht beeinträchtigen.

Gutachterdienste

5.1 Identifizierung illegal oder unerlaubt erworbener Objekte
Wo Museen den Service der Identifizierung anbieten, sollen sie sich keinesfalls dem Verdacht aussetzen, von solcherlei Aktivitäten direkt oder indirekt zu profitieren. Die Identifizierung und Echtheitsbestätigung von Objekten, bei denen man glaubt oder vermutet, dass sie illegal oder unerlaubt erworben, übertragen, ein- oder ausgeführt wurden, sollte erst bekannt gemacht werden, wenn die zuständigen Behörden informiert wurden.

5.2 Echtheitsnachweise und Schätzungen (Begutachtungen)
Zu Versicherungszwecken können Schätzungen von Museumssammlungen durchgeführt werden. Gutachten über den finanziellen Wert von anderen Objekten sollten nur auf offizielle Anfrage von Museen, zuständigen Rechts-, Regierungs- oder anderen verantwortlichen, öffentlichen Stellen erstellt werden. Wenn allerdings das Museum selbst vom Ergebnis profitieren könnte, muss die Begutachtung eines Objektes oder Gegenstandes von unabhängiger Seite erfolgen.

6. Museen arbeiten sowohl mit den Gemeinschaften, aus denen ihre Sammlungen stammen, als auch mit denen, welchen sie dienen, eng zusammen.

Grundsatz

Museumssammlungen spiegeln das kulturelle und natürliche Erbe der Gemeinschaften wider, aus denen sie stammen. Somit reicht ihr Charakter über jenen von gewöhnlichem Eigentum hinaus, da enge Bindungen an nationale, regionale, lokale, ethnische, religiöse oder politische Identitäten bestehen können. Es ist daher wichtig, dass die Museumstätigkeit diesen Umständen aufgeschlossen gegenübersteht.

Herkunft von Sammlungen

6.1 Zusammenarbeit
Museen sollen den Austausch von Wissen, Dokumenten und Sammlungen mit Museen und Kulturorganisationen in deren Herkunftsländern und -gemeinschaften fördern. Die Möglichkeit des Aufbaus von Partnerschaften mit Museen in Ländern oder Gebieten, die einen bedeutenden Teil ihres Erbes verloren haben, ist zu prüfen.

6.2 Rückgabe von Kulturgütern
Museen sollen bereit sein, in einen Dialog bezüglich der Rückgabe von Kulturgütern an ihre Herkunftsländer oder -völker zu treten. Der Dialog sollte unparteiisch und auf der Basis wissenschaftlicher, professioneller und humanitärer Prinzipien sowie unter Berücksichtigung lokaler, nationaler und internationaler Gesetze geführt werden. Diese Vorgehensweise ist Massnahmen auf politischer oder Regierungsebene vorzuziehen.

6.3 Rückführung von Kulturgütern
Wenn ein Herkunftsland oder -volk die Rückgabe eines Objekts oder Gegenstandes erbittet, von dem belegbar ist, dass es/er unter Verletzung der Prinzipien internationaler und nationaler Abkommen exportiert oder auf anderem Wege übereignet wurde und es/er zum kulturellen oder natürlichen Erbe dieses Landes oder Volkes gehört, sollte das betroffene Museum umgehend verantwortungsvolle Schritte einleiten, um bei der Rückgabe zu kooperieren, sofern es rechtlich dazu befugt ist.

6.4 Kulturgüter aus besetzten Ländern
Museen sollen Abstand davon nehmen, Kulturgüter aus besetzten Ländern oder Gebieten zu erwerben oder anzunehmen und sich voll und ganz an alle Gesetze und Abkommen halten, die Einfuhr, Ausfuhr und Übereignung von Kultur- und Naturgütern regeln.

Respekt vor den Gemeinschaften, denen die Museen dienen

6.5 Bestehende Gemeinschaften
Soweit Museumsaktivitäten eine bestehende Gemeinschaft oder ihr Erbe betreffen, sollen Erwerbungen nur auf der Grundlage gegenseitiger Information und Zustimmung erfolgen, ohne den Eigentümer oder die Gewährsleute auszunutzen. Es ist überaus wichtig, den Wertvorstellungen und Bedürfnissen der beteiligten Gemeinschaft mit Respekt zu begegnen.

6.6 Finanzierung von Einrichtungen für bestehende Gemeinschaften
Bei der Suche nach finanzieller Unterstützung für Tätigkeiten, von denen eine bestehende Gemeinschaft betroffen ist, sollte nicht gegen deren Interessen gehandelt werden (siehe 1.10).

6.7 Nutzung von Sammlungen aus bestehenden Gemeinschaften
Die musale Nutzung von Sammlungen aus bestehenden Gemeinschaften erfordert Respekt vor der Würde des Menschen sowie vor den Traditionen und Kulturen, in denen die enthaltenen Gegenstände Verwendung finden. Derartige Sammlungen sollen genutzt werden, um durch das Eintreten für soziale, kulturelle und sprachliche Vielfalt das Wohlergehen der Menschen, soziale Entwicklung, Toleranz und Respekt zu fördern (siehe 4.3).

6.8 Förderorganisationen
Museen sollen für die Unterstützung durch die Gemeinschaft (z. B. «Freunde des Museums» und andere unterstützende Organisationen) günstige Voraussetzungen schaffen, ihren Beitrag anerkennen und eine harmonische Beziehung zwischen Gemeinschaft und Museumspersonal fördern.

7. Museen halten sich an Recht und Gesetz.

Grundsatz
Museen müssen sich voll und ganz an internationale, nationale, regionale und lokale Gesetze und an vertragliche Pflichten halten. Ausserdem muss der Träger rechtsverbindliche Abkommen und Bedingungen jeglicher Art einhalten, die mit dem Museum, seinen Sammlungen und seiner Funktion in Zusammenhang stehen.

Rechtlicher Rahmen

7.1 Nationales und lokales Recht
Museen sollen sich an nationales und lokales Recht halten und die Gesetze anderer Staaten respektieren, soweit diese Einfluss auf ihre Arbeit haben.

A.III.8 Ethische Richtlinien für Museen von ICOM

7.2 Internationales Recht
Museumspolitik soll die folgenden internationalen Regelwerke anerkennen, die als ein Massstab für die Auslegung der «Ethischen Richtlinien für Museen von ICOM» dienen:
- Haager Konvention zum Schutz von Kulturgut bei bewaffneten Konflikten (UNESCO Convention for the Protection of Cultural Property in the Event of Armed Conflict, erstes Protokoll 1954 und zweites Protokoll 1999);
- UNESCO-Konvention über Massnahmen zum Verbot und zur Verhütung der unzulässigen Einfuhr, Ausfuhr und Übereignung von Kulturgut (UNESCO Convention on the Means of Prohibiting and Preventing the Illicit Import, Export and Transfer of Ownership of Cultural Property, 1970);
- Washingtoner Artenschutzabkommen CITES (Convention on International Trade in Endangered Species of Wild Fauna and Flora, 1973);
- UNO-Konvention über die biologische Vielfalt (UN Convention on Biological Diversity, 1992);
- Unidroit-Konvention über gestohlene und illegal ausgeführte Kulturgüter (Unidroit Convention on Stolen and Illegally Exported Cultural Objects, 1995);
- Übereinkommen zum Schutz des Unterwasserkulturerbes (UNESCO Convention on the Protection of the Underwater Cultural Heritage, 2001);
- Übereinkommen zur Bewahrung des immateriellen Kulturerbes (UNESCO Convention for the Safeguarding of the Intangible Cultural Heritage, 2003).

8. Museen arbeiten professionell.

Grundsatz
Museumsmitarbeiter/innen müssen anerkannte Standards und Gesetze beachten und die Würde und Ehre ihres Berufsstandes wahren. Sie sollen die Gesellschaft vor illegalem oder unethischem Verhalten schützen. Jede Möglichkeit ist wahrzunehmen, die Öffentlichkeit über Ziele, Zweck und Anspruch ihres Berufsstandes zu informieren und aufzuklären, um mehr öffentliches Verständnis für den gesellschaftlichen Beitrag von Museen zu erreichen.

Verhalten von Museumsmitarbeiter/innen

8.1 Vertrautheit mit einschlägigen Gesetzen
Museumsmitarbeiter/innen sollen mit einschlägigen internationalen, nationalen und lokalen Gesetzen sowie den Bedingungen ihrer Anstellung vertraut sein. Sie müssen Situationen vermeiden, in denen ihr Verhalten als unangebracht ausgelegt werden kann.

8.2 Berufliche Verantwortlichkeit
Museumsmitarbeiter/innen sind verpflichtet, die Handlungs- und Verhaltensregeln der Institution, bei der sie beschäftigt sind, zu befolgen. Sie dürfen jedoch zu Recht widersprechen, wenn sie Praktiken als schädlich für ein Museum oder ihren Berufsstand und dessen Ethos einstufen.

8.3 Professionelles Verhalten
Loyalität gegenüber Kolleginnen und Kollegen und dem sie beschäftigendem Museum ist unabdingbar und muss auf der Treue zu den grundlegenden ethischen Prinzipien des Berufsstandes basieren. Museumsmitarbeiter/innen sollen sich an die Bestimmungen der «Ethischen Richtlinien für Museen von ICOM» halten und auch alle anderen für die Museumsarbeit relevanten Grundsätze und Richtlinien kennen.

8.4 Akademische und wissenschaftliche Verantwortung
Museumsmitarbeiter/innen sollen die Gewinnung, Erhaltung und Anwendung von Informationen, die den Sammlungen innewohnen, fördern. Daher sollen sie jegliche Tätigkeiten oder Umstände vermeiden, die den Verlust von wissenschaftlichen Informationen zur Folge haben könnten.

8.5 Illegaler Handel
Museumsmitarbeiter/innen dürfen weder direkt noch indirekt den illegalen Handel mit Natur- und Kulturgütern unterstützen.

8.6 Vertraulichkeit
Vertrauliche Informationen, die Museumsmitarbeiter/innen im Rahmen ihrer Arbeit erlangen, dürfen nicht preisgegeben werden. Ausserdem sind Informationen über Gegenstände vertraulich, die dem Museum zur Bestimmung übergeben werden; sie dürfen ohne ausdrückliche Zustimmung des Eigentümers nicht veröffentlicht oder an andere Institutionen oder Personen weitergegeben werden.

8.7 Museums- und Sammlungssicherheit
Informationen über die Sicherheitsvorkehrungen des Museums oder privater Sammlungen und anderer Ausstellungsorte, die im Rahmen ihrer offiziellen Tätigkeit aufgesucht werden, sind von Museumsmitarbeiter/innen streng vertraulich zu behandeln.

8.8 Ausnahme von der Pflicht zur Vertraulichkeit
Vertraulichkeit wird durch die rechtliche Verpflichtung eingeschränkt, der Polizei oder anderen zuständigen Behörden bei der Untersuchung möglicherweise gestohlener, illegal erworbener oder unrechtmässig übereigneter Gegenstände behilflich zu sein.

8.9 Persönliche Unabhängigkeit
Zwar steht den Angehörigen jedes Berufsstandes ein gewisses Mass an persönlicher Unabhängigkeit zu, ihnen muss jedoch klar sein, dass kein Privatgeschäft oder berufliches Interesse völlig von ihrer Dienststelle zu trennen ist.

8.10 Berufliche Beziehungen
Museumsmitarbeiter/innen pflegen innerhalb und ausserhalb des Museums, in dem sie beschäftigt sind, berufliche Beziehungen zu vielen anderen Menschen. Man erwartet von ihnen, dass sie diesen ihre professionellen Dienste wirkungsvoll und auf hohem Niveau zur Verfügung stellen.

8.11 Berufliche Konsultation
Es besteht die berufliche Verpflichtung, externe Berufskolleg/innen hinzuzuziehen, wenn die Fachkenntnisse im Museum nicht ausreichen, um eine gute Entscheidungsfindung sicherzustellen.

Interessenkonflikte

8.12 Geschenke, Gefälligkeiten, Darlehen oder andere persönliche Vorteile
Museumsmitarbeiter/innen dürfen keine Geschenke, Gefälligkeiten und Darlehen annehmen oder andere persönliche Vorteile akzeptieren, die ihnen im Zusammenhang mit ihren Museumsaufgaben angeboten werden. Gelegentlich kann es die berufliche Höflichkeit erfordern, Geschenke zu überreichen oder anzunehmen; dies soll jedoch stets im Namen der betreffenden Einrichtung erfolgen.

8.13 Berufliche oder geschäftliche Interessen ausserhalb des Museums
Auch wenn ihnen das Recht auf ein gewisses Mass an persönlicher Unabhängigkeit zusteht, müssen sich Museumsmitarbeiter/innen bewusst sein, dass kein Privatgeschäft oder berufliches Engagement völlig von der Institution, bei der sie beschäftigt sind, zu trennen ist. Sie sollen keine weiteren bezahlten Tätigkeiten über- oder Aufträge von ausserhalb annehmen, die den Interessen des Museums zuwiderlaufen oder als solche wahrgenommen werden könnten.

8.14 Handel mit Natur- oder Kulturerbe
Museumsmitarbeiter/innen dürfen sich weder direkt noch indirekt am Handel (gewinnorientiertem Kauf oder Verkauf) mit Natur- oder Kulturerbe beteiligen.

8.15 Umgang mit Händlern
Museumsmitarbeiter/innen dürfen keine Geschenke, Gefälligkeiten oder sonstige Gegenleistungen von Händlern, Auktionatoren oder anderen Personen als Anreiz nehmen, einen Kauf oder Verkauf von Museumsstücken einzuleiten oder um offizielle Massnahmen zu ergreifen oder zu unterlassen. Ausserdem sollen sie Dritten gegenüber keine bestimmten Händler, Auktionatoren oder Sachverständige empfehlen.

8.16 Privates Sammeln
Museumsmitarbeiter/innen sollen weder beim Erwerb von Objekten noch mit einer privaten Sammeltätigkeit mit ihrer Einrichtung in Konkurrenz treten. Zwischen Mitarbeiter/innen und dem Träger ist eine Vereinbarung bezüglich jeglicher Form von privatem Sammeln zu treffen und genauestens einzuhalten.

A.III.8 Ethische Richtlinien für Museen von ICOM

8.17 Verwendung des Namens und des Logos von ICOM
Name, Abkürzung und Logo der Organisation dürfen nicht zur Bewerbung oder Aufwertung einer gewinnorientierten Tätigkeit oder eines kommerziellen Produktes genutzt werden.

8.18 Andere Interessenkonflikte
Im Falle eines anderen Interessenkonflikts zwischen dem Museum und einer Einzelperson muss das Museumsinteresse den Vorrang haben.

Ethische Richtlinien für Museen von ICOM A.III.8

Glossar

Begutachtung (Schätzungen): Die Bestätigung der Echtheit und Ermittlung eines Schätzwerts eines Objektes oder Gegenstandes. In bestimmten Ländern wird der Begriff für eine unabhängige Schätzung eines vorgesehenen Geschenks zum Zwecke von Steuerbegünstigungen verwendet.

Gemeinnützige Organisation: Ein als natürliche oder juristische Person rechtlich anerkanntes Organ, dessen Einkommen (einschliesslich aller Überschüsse und Gewinne) ausschliesslich zum Nutzen dieses Organs und seiner Funktion verwendet wird. Der Ausdruck «Nicht gewinnorientiert» hat die gleiche Bedeutung.

Gewinnorientierte Aktivitäten: Tätigkeiten zur Erzielung finanzieller Vorteile oder Gewinne zugunsten der Institution.

Gültiger (Rechts-)Titel: Das durch vollständigen Herkunftsnachweis von der Entdeckung oder Herstellung eines Gegenstandes an unzweifelhaft festgestellte Eigentumsrecht an einer Sache.

Handel: Kauf und Verkauf von Gegenständen zum persönlichen oder institutionellen Vorteil.

Herkunftsnachweis (Provenienz): Die vollständige Dokumentation eines Gegenstandes und seiner Besitzverhältnisse vom Zeitpunkt seiner Entdeckung oder Schöpfung bis in die Gegenwart, wodurch Echtheit und Eigentumsansprüche festgestellt werden.

Interessenkonflikt: Eine durch persönliche oder private Interessen verursachte Kollision von Prinzipien in einer Arbeitssituation, die die Objektivität eines Entscheidungsprozesses dem Anschein nach oder tatsächlich beeinträchtigt.

Konservator/Restaurator: Angestellte oder selbstständige Personen, die befähigt sind, Kulturgüter technisch zu untersuchen, zu erhalten, zu konservieren und zu restaurieren (für weiterführende Informationen siehe ICOM News, Bd. 39, Nr. 1 (1986), S. 5 f.).

Kulturerbe: Alle Ideen und Dinge, die als ästhetisch, historisch, wissenschaftlich oder geistig bedeutsam erachtet werden.

Mindeststandard: Ein Standard, der nach realistischem Ermessen von allen Museen und deren Mitarbeiter/innen erwartet werden kann. Manche Länder haben eigene Mindeststandards festgelegt.

Museum: Ein Museum ist eine gemeinnützige, auf Dauer angelegte, der Öffentlichkeit zugängliche Einrichtung im Dienste der Gesellschaft und ihrer Entwicklung, die zum Zwecke des Studiums, der Bildung und des Erlebens materielle und immaterielle Zeugnisse von Menschen und ihrer Umwelt beschafft, bewahrt, erforscht, bekannt macht und ausstellt.

Naturerbe: Jede natürliche Sache, jede Idee oder Erscheinung, die von wissenschaftlicher oder geistiger Bedeutung ist.

Provenienz → siehe «Herkunftsnachweis»

Qualifiziertes Museumspersonal[1]**:** Qualifiziertes Museumspersonal bezeichnet alle entgeltlich oder ehrenamtlich beschäftigten Mitarbeiter/innen von Museen oder der Definition in Artikel 2, Absatz 1 und 2 der ICOM Statuten entsprechenden Einrichtungen, die in einem für die Leitung oder Funktion eines Museums relevanten Bereich ausgebildet wurden oder über entsprechende Berufserfahrung verfügen, sowie Selbstständige, die die «Ethischen Richtlinien für Museen von ICOM» anerkennen und für Museen oder im oben zitierten Statut definierte Einrichtungen tätig sind. Dies gilt nicht für Personen, die mit für Museen und deren Dienstleistungen benötigten kommerziellen Produkten und Ausstattungen Handel treiben oder für sie werben.

Rechtstitel: Das gesetzlich verankerte Eigentumsrecht an einer Sache im betroffenen Land. In manchen Ländern kann dies ein verliehenes Recht sein, das nicht ausreicht, um der Sorgfaltspflicht zu genügen.

Sorgfaltspflicht: Die Verpflichtung, alle Anstrengungen zu unternehmen, um die Fakten eines Vorganges zu ermitteln, bevor man über das weitere Verfahren entscheidet, insbesondere die Feststellung von Ursprung und Geschichte eines zum Erwerb oder zur Nutzung angebotenen Gegenstandes vor seiner Anschaffung.

Träger(schaft): Die Personen oder Organisationen, die laut Museumssatzung für Fortbestand, Weiterentwicklung und Finanzierung des Museums verantwortlich sind.

---

1) Es soll darauf hingewiesen werden, dass die Bezeichnungen «Museum» und «Museumsmitarbeiterin und -mitarbeiter» vorläufige Definitionen zur Interpretation der «Ethischen Richtlinien für Museen von ICOM» sind. Die Definitionen von «Museum» und «professioneller Museumsmitarbeiterin und professionellem Museumsmitarbeiter», wie sie in den ICOM Statuten verwendet werden, bleiben in Kraft, bis die Überarbeitung dieser Statuten abgeschlossen ist.

A.IV.1 Statut des Jugoslawientribunals

Statute of the International Criminal Tribunal for the former Yugoslavia (Auszüge)

Geschaffen durch Resolution des Sicherheitsrates am 25. Mai 1993, S/RES/827 (1993); zuletzt geändert durch S/Res/1877 (2009).

Article 1 Competence of the International Tribunal

The International Tribunal shall have the power to prosecute persons responsible for serious violations of international humanitarian law committed in the territory of the former Yugoslavia since 1991 in accordance with the provisions of the present Statute.

Article 3 Violations of the laws or customs of war

The International Tribunal shall have the power to prosecute persons violating the laws or customs of war. Such violations shall include, but not be limited to:

[...]
(b) wanton destruction of cities, towns or villages, or devastation not justified by military necessity;
(c) attack, or bombardment, by whatever means, of undefended towns, villages, dwellings, or buildings;
(d) seizure of, destruction or wilful damage done to institutions dedicated to religion, charity and education, the arts and sciences, historic monuments and works of art and science;
(e) plunder of public or private property.

Statute of the International Criminal Tribunal for Rwanda (Auszüge)

Geschaffen durch Resolution des Sicherheitsrates am 08. November 1994, S/RES/955 (1994); zuletzt geändert durch S/RES/1901 (2009).

Article 4: Violations of Article 3 Common to the Geneva Conventions and of Additional Protocol II

The International Tribunal for Rwanda shall have the power to prosecute persons committing or ordering to be committed serious violations of Article 3 common to the Geneva Conventions of 12 August 1949 for the Protection of War Victims, and of Additional Protocol II thereto of 8 June 1977. These violations shall include, but shall not be limited to:

[...]
(f) Pillage;
[...]
(h) Threats to commit any of the foregoing acts.

Statute of the International Residual Mechanism for Criminal Tribunals (Auszug)

Geschaffen durch Resolution des Sicherheitsrates am 22. Dezember 2010, S/RES/1966 (2010); am 1. Juli 2012 Beginn der Arbeit unter der Gerichtsbarkeit des ICTR; am 1. Juli 2013 Beginn der Arbeit unter der Gerichtsbarkeit des ICTY.

Article 1: Competence of the Mechanism

1. The Mechanism shall continue the material, territorial, temporal and personal jurisdiction of the ICTY and the ICTR as set out in Articles 1 to 8 of the ICTY Statute and Articles 1 to 7 of the ICTR Statute, as well as the rights and obligations, of the ICTY and the ICTR, subject to the provisions of the present Statute.

   [...]

Römisches Statut des Internationalen Strafgerichtshofs[1)]

Vom 17. Juli 1998 (BGBl. 2000 II S. 1394)

– Auszug –

Teil 2
Gerichtsbarkeit, Zulässigkeit und anwendbares Recht

Artikel 5 Der Gerichtsbarkeit des Gerichtshofs unterliegende Verbrechen

¹Die Gerichtsbarkeit des Gerichtshofs ist auf die schwersten Verbrechen beschränkt, welche die internationale Gemeinschaft als Ganzes berühren. ²Die Gerichtsbarkeit des Gerichtshofs erstreckt sich in Übereinstimmung mit diesem Statut auf folgende Verbrechen:

[...]
c) Kriegsverbrechen;
[...]

Artikel 8 Kriegsverbrechen

[...]

(2) Im Sinne dieses Statuts bedeutet „Kriegsverbrechen"

a) schwere Verletzungen der Genfer Abkommen vom 12. August 1949, nämlich jeder der folgenden Handlungen gegen die nach dem jeweiligen Genfer Abkommen geschützten Personen oder Güter:

   [...]
   iv) Zerstörung und Aneignung von Eigentum in großem Ausmaß, die durch militärische Erfordernisse nicht gerechtfertigt sind und rechtswidrig und willkürlich vorgenommen werden;
   [...]

b) andere schwere Verstöße gegen die innerhalb des feststehenden Rahmens des Völkerrechts im internationalen bewaffneten Konflikt anwendbaren Gesetze und Gebräuche, nämlich jede der folgenden Handlungen:

   [...]
   ii) vorsätzliche Angriffe auf zivile Objekte, das heißt auf Objekte, die nicht militärische Ziele sind;
   [...]
   v) der Angriff auf unverteidigte Städte, Dörfer, Wohnstätten oder Gebäude, die nicht militärische Ziele sind, oder deren Beschießung, gleichviel mit welchen Mitteln;
   [...]
   ix) vorsätzliche Angriffe auf Gebäude, die dem Gottesdienst, der Erziehung, der Kunst, der Wissenschaft oder der Wohltätigkeit gewidmet sind, auf geschichtliche Denkmäler, Krankenhäuser und Sammelplätze für Kranke und Verwundete, sofern es nicht militärische Ziele sind;
   [...]
   xiii) die Zerstörung oder Beschlagnahme feindlichen Eigentums, sofern diese nicht durch die Erfordernisse des Krieges zwingend geboten ist;
   [...]
   xvi) die Plünderung einer Stadt oder Ansiedlung, selbst wenn sie im Sturm genommen wurde;
   [...]

e) andere schwere Verstöße gegen die innerhalb des feststehenden Rahmens des Völkerrechts anwendbaren Gesetze und Gebräuche im bewaffneten Konflikt, der keinen internationalen Charakter hat, nämlich jede der folgenden Handlungen:

   [...]
   iv) vorsätzliche Angriffe auf Gebäude, die dem Gottesdienst, der Erziehung, der Kunst, der Wissenschaft oder der Wohltätigkeit gewidmet sind, auf geschichtliche Denkmäler, Kran-

---

1) Liste der Vertragsstaaten: https://treaties.un.org/Pages/ViewDetails.aspx?src=TREATY&mtdsg_no=XVIII-10&chapter=18&lang=en.

A.IV.4 IStGH-Statut

kenhäuser und Sammelplätze für Kranke und Verwundete, sofern es nicht militärische Ziele sind;

v) die Plünderung einer Stadt oder Ansiedlung, selbst wenn sie im Sturm genommen wurde;

[…]

Council of Europe Convention on Offences relating to Cultural Property

Vom 19. Mai 2017, Council of Europe Treaty Series – No. 221.

Preamble
The member States of the Council of Europe and the other signatories to this Convention, Considering that the aim of the Council of Europe is to achieve a greater unity between its members;
Being convinced that the diverse cultural property belonging to peoples constitutes a unique and important testimony of the culture and identity of such peoples, and forms their cultural heritage;
Concerned that offences related to cultural property are growing and that such offences, to an increasing extent, are leading to the destruction of the world's cultural heritage;
Considering that unlawfully excavated and illicitly exported or imported cultural property is increasingly being sold in many different ways, including through antique shops and auction houses, and over the internet;
Considering that organised crime is involved in the trafficking of cultural property;
Concerned that terrorist groups are involved in the deliberate destruction of cultural heritage and use the illicit trade of cultural property as a source of financing;
Convinced of the need for a new Council of Europe Convention on Offences relating to Cultural Property which sets out criminal sanctions in this regard and which will replace the European Convention on Offences relating to Cultural Property (ETS No. 119), opened for signature in Delphi on 23 June 1985;
Having regard to the European Cultural Convention (ETS No. 18, 1954), the European Convention on the Protection of the Archaeological Heritage (ETS No. 66, 1969; ETS No. 143, revised in 1992), the Convention for the Protection of the Architectural Heritage of Europe (ETS No. 121, 1985)[1]) and the Council of Europe Framework Convention on the Value of Cultural Heritage for Society (CETS No. 199, 2005);
Having regard to the European Convention on Mutual Assistance in Criminal Matters (ETS No. 30, 1959) and the European Convention on Extradition (ETS No. 24, 1957);
Bearing in mind Resolution 2199 (2015) adopted by the Security Council of the United Nations at its 7379th meeting, on 12 February 2015, and in particular paragraphs 15, 16 and 17; Resolution 2253 (2015) adopted by the Security Council of the United Nations at its 7587th meeting, on 17 December 2015, and in particular paragraphs 14 and 15; Resolution 2322 (2016) adopted by the Security Council of the United Nations at its 7831st meeting, on 12 December 2016, and in particular paragraph 12; Resolution 2347 (2017) adopted by the Security Council of the United Nations at its 7907th meeting, on 24 March 2017;
Bearing in mind also the 1954 Hague Convention for the Protection of Cultural Property in the Event of Armed Conflict, its First Protocol of 1954 and Second Protocol of 1999; the 1970 UNESCO Convention on the Means of Prohibiting and Preventing the Illicit Import, Export and Transfer of Ownership of Cultural Property and its Operational Guidelines adopted in 2015 by the third Meeting of States Parties; the 1972 UNESCO Convention concerning the Protection of the World Cultural and Natural Heritage; the 1995 UNIDROIT Convention on Stolen or Illegally Exported Cultural Objects; the 2000 United Nations Convention against Transnational Organized Crime and the 2001 UNESCO Convention on the Protection of the Underwater Cultural Heritage;
Also bearing in mind Resolution 2057 (2015) on cultural heritage in crisis and post-crisis situations, adopted by the Standing Committee of the Parliamentary Assembly of the Council of Europe on 22 May 2015;
Taking into consideration the International Guidelines for Crime Prevention and Criminal Justice Responses with Respect to Trafficking in Cultural Property and Other Related Offences, adopted by the General Assembly of the United Nations with its Resolution 69/196 of 18 December 2014;
Considering that the purpose of this Convention is to protect cultural property through the prevention of and the fight against criminal offences relating to cultural property;
Recognising that, to efficiently combat cultural property crimes, close international co-operation between Council of Europe member States and non-member States alike should be encouraged,

---
1) Die Delphi Konvention trat nie in Kraft.

Have agreed as follows:

Chapter I –
Purpose, scope, use of terms

Article 1 – Purpose of the Convention

¹The purpose of this Convention is to:
a) prevent and combat the destruction of, damage to, and trafficking of cultural property by providing for the criminalisation of certain acts;
b) strengthen crime prevention and the criminal justice response to all criminal offences relating to cultural property;
c) promote national and international co-operation in combating criminal offences relating to cultural property;
and thereby protect cultural property.
²In order to ensure effective implementation of its provisions by the Parties, this Convention sets up a follow-up mechanism.

Article 2 – Scope and use of terms

¹This Convention applies to the prevention, investigation, and prosecution of the criminal offences referred to in this Convention relating to movable and immovable cultural property.
²For the purposes of this Convention the term "cultural property" shall mean:
a) in respect of movable property, any object, situated on land or underwater or removed therefrom, which is, on religious or secular grounds, classified, defined or specifically designated by any Party to this Convention or to the 1970 UNESCO Convention on the Means of Prohibiting and Preventing the Illicit Import, Export and Transfer of Ownership of Cultural Property, as being of importance for archaeology, prehistory, ethnology, history, literature, art or science, and which belongs to the following categories:
   (a) rare collections and specimens of fauna, flora, minerals and anatomy, and objects of palaeontological interest;
   (b) property relating to history, including the history of science and technology and military and social history, to the life of national leaders, thinkers, scientists and artists and to events of national importance;
   (c) products of archaeological excavations (including regular and clandestine) or of archaeological discoveries;
   (d) elements of artistic or historical monuments or archaeological sites which have been dismembered;
   (e) antiquities more than one hundred years old, such as inscriptions, coins and engraved seals;
   (f) objects of ethnological interest;
   (g) property of artistic interest, such as:
      (i) pictures, paintings and drawings produced entirely by hand on any support and in any material (excluding industrial designs and manufactured articles decorated by hand);
      (ii) original works of statuary art and sculpture in any material;
      (iii) original engravings, prints and lithographs;
      (iv) original artistic assemblages and montages in any material;
   (h) rare manuscripts and incunabula, old books, documents and publications of special interest (historical, artistic, scientific, literary, etc.) singly or in collections;
   (i) postage, revenue and similar stamps, singly or in collections;
   (j) archives, including sound, photographic and cinematographic archives;
   (k) articles of furniture more than one hundred years old and old musical instruments;
b) in respect of immovable property, any monument, group of buildings, site or structure of any other kind, whether situated on land or underwater, which is, on religious or secular grounds, defined or specifically designated by any Party to this Convention or by any Party to the 1970 UNESCO Convention as being of importance for archaeology, prehistory, ethnology, history, art or science or listed in accordance with Article 1 and Article 11 (paragraphs 2 or 4) of the 1972 UNESCO Convention concerning the Protection of the World Cultural and Natural Heritage.

Chapter II –
Substantive criminal law

Article 3 – Theft and other forms of unlawful appropriation
Each Party shall ensure that the offence of theft and other forms of unlawful appropriation as set out in their domestic criminal law apply to movable cultural property.

Article 4 – Unlawful excavation and removal
¹Each Party shall ensure that the following conducts constitute a criminal offence under its domestic law, when committed intentionally:
a) the excavation on land or under water in order to find and remove cultural property without the authorisation required by the law of the State where the excavation took place;
b) the removal and retention of movable cultural property excavated without the authorisation required by the law of the State where the excavation took place;
c) the unlawful retention of movable cultural property excavated in compliance with the authorisation required by the law of the State where the excavation took place.

²Any State may, at the time of signature or when depositing its instrument of ratification, acceptance, approval or accession, by a declaration addressed to the Secretary General of the Council of Europe, declare that it reserves the right to provide for non-criminal sanctions, instead of criminal sanctions for the conduct described in paragraph 1 of this article.

Article 5 – Illegal importation
¹Each Party shall ensure that, when committed intentionally, the importation of movable cultural property, the importation of which is prohibited pursuant to its domestic law on the grounds that it has been:
a) stolen in another State;
b) excavated or retained under circumstances described in Article 4 of this Convention; or
c) exported in violation of the law of the State that has classified, defined or specifically designated such cultural property in accordance with Article 2 of this Convention, constitutes a criminal offence under its domestic law where the offender knew that the cultural property had been stolen, excavated or exported in violation of the law of that other State.

²Any State may, at the time of signature or when depositing its instrument of ratification, acceptance, approval or accession, by a declaration addressed to the Secretary General of the Council of Europe, declare that it reserves the right to provide for non-criminal sanctions, instead of criminal sanctions for the conduct described in paragraph 1 of the present article.

Article 6 – Illegal exportation
¹Each Party shall ensure that the exportation of movable cultural property, if the exportation is prohibited or carried out without authorisation pursuant to its domestic law, constitutes a criminal offence under its domestic law, when committed intentionally.

²Each Party shall consider taking the necessary measures to apply paragraph 1 of the present article also in respect of movable cultural property that had been illegally imported.

Article 7 – Acquisition
¹Each Party shall ensure that the acquisition of movable cultural property that has been stolen in accordance with Article 3 of this Convention or has been excavated, imported or exported under circumstances described in Articles 4, 5 or 6 of this Convention constitutes a criminal offence under its domestic law where the person knows of such unlawful provenance.

²Each Party shall consider taking the necessary measures to ensure that the conduct described in paragraph 1 of the present article constitutes a criminal offence also in the case of a person who should have known of the cultural property's unlawful provenance if he or she had exercised due care and attention in acquiring the cultural property.

Article 8 – Placing on the market
¹Each Party shall ensure that the placing on the market of movable cultural property that has been stolen in accordance with Article 3 of this Convention or has been excavated, imported or exported under circumstances described in Articles 4, 5 or 6 of this Convention constitutes a criminal offence under its domestic law where the person knows of such unlawful provenance.

[2]Each Party shall consider taking the necessary measures to ensure that the conduct described in paragraph 1 of this article constitutes a criminal offence also in the case of a person who should have known of the cultural property's unlawful provenance if he or she had exercised due care and attention in placing the cultural property on the market.

Article 9 – Falsification of documents
Each Party shall ensure that the making of false documents and the act of tampering with documents relating to movable cultural property constitute criminal offences under its domestic law, where these actions are intended to present the property as having licit provenance.

Article 10 – Destruction and damage
[1]Each Party shall ensure that the following conducts constitute a criminal offence under its domestic law, when committed intentionally:
a) the unlawful destruction or damaging of movable or immovable cultural property, regardless of the ownership of such property;
b) the unlawful removal, in whole or in part, of any elements from movable or immovable cultural property, with a view to importing, exporting or placing on the market these elements under the circumstances described in Articles 5, 6 and 8 of this Convention.

[2]Any State may, at the time of signature or when depositing its instrument of ratification, acceptance, approval or accession, by a declaration addressed to the Secretary General of the Council of Europe, declare that it reserves the right not to apply paragraph 1 of the present article, or to apply it only in specific cases or conditions in cases where the cultural property has been destroyed or damaged by the owner of the cultural property or with the owner's consent.

Article 11 – Aiding or abetting and attempt
[1]Each Party shall ensure that the intentional aiding or abetting the commission of a criminal offence referred to in this Convention also constitutes a criminal offence under its domestic law.

[2]Each Party shall ensure that the intentional attempt to commit any of the criminal offences referred to in this Convention with the exception of those defined in Article 4, paragraph 1, sub-paragraph a and in Article 8 also constitutes a criminal offence under its domestic law.

[3]Any State may, at the time of signature or when depositing its instrument of ratification, acceptance, approval or accession, by a declaration addressed to the Secretary General of the Council of Europe, declare that it reserves the right not to apply, or to apply only in specific cases or conditions, the provision of paragraph 1 of the present article in respect of offences defined in Article 4, paragraph 1, sub-paragraph a.

Article 12 – Jurisdiction
[1]Each Party shall take the necessary measures to establish jurisdiction over the criminal offences referred to in this Convention, when the offence is committed:
a) in its territory;
b) on board a ship flying the flag of that Party;
c) on board an aircraft registered under the laws of that Party; or
d) by one of its nationals.

[2]Each Party shall take the necessary measures to establish jurisdiction over any criminal offence referred to in this Convention, when the alleged offender is present in its territory and cannot be extradited to another State, solely on the basis of his or her nationality.

[3]Each State may, at the time of signature or when depositing its instrument of ratification, acceptance, approval or accession, by a declaration addressed to the Secretary General of the Council of Europe, declare that it reserves the right not to apply, or to apply only in specific cases or conditions, the jurisdiction rules laid down in paragraph 1, sub-paragraph d of the present article.

[4]Where more than one Party claims jurisdiction over an alleged offence in accordance with this Convention, the Parties concerned shall, where appropriate, consult each other with a view to determining the most appropriate jurisdiction for prosecution.

[5]Without prejudice to the general rules of international law, this Convention shall not exclude any criminal jurisdiction exercised by a Party in accordance with its domestic law.

Article 13 – Liability of legal persons

¹Each Party shall ensure that legal persons can be held liable for criminal offences referred to in this Convention, when committed for their benefit by any natural person, acting either individually or as part of an organ of the legal person, who has a leading position within that legal person, based on:
a) a power of representation of the legal person;
b) an authority to take decisions on behalf of the legal person;
c) an authority to exercise control within the legal person.

²Apart from the cases provided for in paragraph 1 of the present article, each Party shall ensure that a legal person can be held liable where the lack of supervision or control by a natural person referred to in paragraph 1 of the present article has made possible the commission of a criminal offence referred to in this Convention for the benefit of that legal person by a natural person acting under its authority.

³Subject to the legal principles of the Party, the liability of a legal person may be criminal, civil or administrative.

⁴Such liability shall be without prejudice to the criminal liability of a natural person who has committed the offence.

Article 14 – Sanctions and measures

¹Each Party shall ensure that the criminal offences referred to in this Convention, when committed by natural persons, are punishable by effective, proportionate and dissuasive sanctions, which take into account the seriousness of the offence. These sanctions shall include, except for offences defined in Article 4, paragraph 1, sub-paragraph a and in Article 5, paragraph 1, sub-paragraphs b and c of this Convention, penalties involving deprivation of liberty that may give rise to extradition.

²Each Party shall ensure that legal persons held liable in accordance with Article 13 of this Convention are subject to effective, proportionate and dissuasive sanctions, which shall include criminal or non-criminal monetary sanctions, and could include other measures, such as:
a) temporary or permanent disqualification from exercising commercial activity;
b) exclusion from entitlement to public benefits or aid;
c) placing under judicial supervision;
d) a judicial winding-up order.

³Each Party shall take the necessary legislative and other measures, in accordance with domestic law, to permit seizure and confiscation of the:
a) instrumentalities used to commit criminal offences referred to in this Convention;
b) proceeds derived from such offences, or property whose value corresponds to such proceeds.

⁴Each Party shall, where cultural property has been seized in the course of criminal proceedings but is no longer required for the purposes of these proceedings, undertake to apply, where appropriate, its criminal procedural law, other domestic law or applicable international treaties when deciding to hand over that property to the State that had specifically designated, classified or defined it as cultural property in accordance with Article 2 of this Convention.

Article 15 – Aggravating circumstances

Each Party shall ensure that the following circumstances, in so far as they do not already form part of the constituent elements of the offence, may, in conformity with the relevant provisions of domestic law, be taken into consideration as aggravating circumstances in determining the sanctions in relation to the criminal offences referred to in this Convention:
a) the offence was committed by persons abusing the trust placed in them in their capacity as professionals;
b) the offence was committed by a public official tasked with the conservation or the protection of movable or immovable cultural property, if he or she has intentionally refrained from properly performing his or her duties with a view to obtaining an undue advantage or a prospect thereof;
c) the offence was committed in the framework of a criminal organisation;
d) the perpetrator has previously been convicted of the offences referred to in this Convention.

Article 16 – Previous sentences passed by another Party
Each Party shall take the necessary measures to provide for the possibility to take into account final sentences passed by another Party in relation to the criminal offences referred to in this Convention when determining the sanctions.

Chapter III –
Investigation, prosecution and procedural law

Article 17 – Initiation of proceedings
Each Party shall take the necessary legislative and other measures to ensure that investigations or prosecution of criminal offences referred to in this Convention should not be subordinate to a complaint.

Article 18 – Investigations
Each Party shall consider taking legislative and other measures to ensure that persons, units or services in charge of investigations are specialised in the field of combating the trafficking of cultural property or that persons are trained for this purpose.

Article 19 – International co-operation in criminal matters
^{1}The Parties shall co-operate with each other, in accordance with the provisions of this Convention and in pursuance of relevant applicable international and regional instruments and arrangements agreed on the basis of uniform legislation or reciprocity and their domestic law, to the widest extent possible, for the purpose of investigations or proceedings concerning the criminal offences referred to in this Convention, including seizure and confiscation.

^{2}If a Party that makes extradition or mutual legal assistance in criminal matters conditional on the existence of a treaty receives a request for extradition or legal assistance in criminal matters from a Party with which it has no such a treaty, it may, acting in full compliance with its obligations under international law and subject to the conditions provided for by the domestic law of the requested Party, consider this Convention as the legal basis for extradition or mutual legal assistance in criminal matters in respect of the offences referred to in this Convention and may apply, *mutatis mutandis*, Articles 16 and 18 of the United Nations Convention on Transnational Organized Crime to this effect.

Chapter IV –
Preventive measures and other administrative measures

Article 20 – Measures at domestic level
Each Party should, taking into account its obligations under applicable international treaties, consider taking the legislative and other necessary measures to:
a) establish or develop inventories or databases of its cultural property defined under Article 2, paragraph 2, of this Convention;
b) introduce import and export control procedures, in accordance with the relevant international instruments, including a system whereby the importation and exportation of movable cultural property are subject to the issuance of specific certificates;
c) introduce due diligence provisions for art and antiquity dealers, auction houses and others involved in the trade in cultural property, and introduce an obligation to establish records of their transactions. These records should be made available to the competent authorities in accordance with domestic law;
d) establish a central national authority or empower existing authorities and putting in place other mechanisms for co-ordinating the activities related to the protection of cultural property;
e) enable the monitoring and reporting of suspicious dealings or sales on the internet;
f) enable the mandatory reporting to the competent authorities of the discovery by chance of cultural property of the archaeological heritage;
g) promote awareness-raising campaigns addressed to the general public about the protection of cultural property and the dangers posed by the crimes against it;

h)   ensure that museums and similar institutions whose acquisition policy is under State control do not acquire illicitly removed cultural property, and provide information and training for the relevant officials on the prevention of and fight against cultural property-related crimes;
i)   encourage museums and similar institutions, whose acquisition policy is not under State control, to comply with existing ethical rules on the acquisition of movable cultural property and report to law enforcement authorities any suspected trafficking of cultural property;
j)   encourage internet service providers, internet platforms and web-based sellers to co-operate in preventing the trafficking of cultural property by participating in the elaboration and implementation of relevant policies;
k)   prevent free ports from being used for the purpose of trafficking of cultural property either through legislative measures or by encouraging them to establish and effectively implement internal norms through self-regulation;
l)   improve the dissemination of information relating to any cultural property that has been the subject of an offence as defined by this Convention to its customs and police authorities in order to prevent the trafficking of this cultural property.

Article 21 – Measures at international level
Each Party shall co-operate to the widest extent possible for the purpose of preventing and fighting the intentional destruction of, damage to, and trafficking of cultural property. In particular, the States Parties should:
a)   promote consultation and exchange of information as regards the identification, seizure and confiscation of cultural property that has been the subject of an offence defined by this Convention and that has been recovered within their territory;
b)   contribute to international data collection on trafficking of movable cultural property by sharing or interconnecting national inventories or databases on cultural property that has been the subject of an offence defined by this Convention, and/or contributing to international inventories or databases, such as the Interpol database on stolen works of art;
c)   facilitate co-operation for the purpose of also protecting and preserving cultural property in times of instability or conflict.

Chapter V –
Follow-up mechanism

Article 22 – Committee of the Parties
¹The Committee of the Parties shall be composed of representatives of the Parties to the Convention.
²The Committee of the Parties shall be convened by the Secretary General of the Council of Europe. Its first meeting shall be held within a period of one year following the entry into force of this Convention for the tenth signatory having ratified it. It shall subsequently meet whenever at least one third of the Parties or the Secretary General so requests.
³The Committee of the Parties shall adopt its own rules of procedure.
⁴The Committee of the Parties shall be assisted by the Secretariat of the Council of Europe in carrying out its functions.
⁵The Committee of the Parties may propose to the Committee of Ministers appropriate ways to engage relevant expertise in support of the effective implementation of this Convention.

Article 23 – Other representatives
¹The Parliamentary Assembly of the Council of Europe, the European Committee on Crime Problems (CDPC) and the Steering Committee for Culture, Heritage and Landscape (CDCPP) shall each appoint a representative to the Committee of the Parties in order to contribute to a multisectoral and multidisciplinary approach.
²The Committee of Ministers may invite other Council of Europe bodies to appoint a representative to the Committee of the Parties, after consultation with the committee.
³Representatives of relevant international bodies may be admitted as observers to the Committee of the Parties following the procedure established by the relevant rules of the Council of Europe.

⁴Representatives of relevant official bodies of the Parties may be admitted as observers to the Committee of the Parties following the procedure established by the relevant rules of the Council of Europe.
⁵Representatives of civil society, and in particular non-governmental organisations, may be admitted as observers to the Committee of the Parties following the procedure established by the relevant rules of the Council of Europe.
⁶In the appointment of representatives under paragraphs 2 to 5 of the present article, a balanced representation of the different sectors and disciplines shall be ensured.
⁷Representatives appointed in accordance with paragraphs 1 to 5 of this article shall participate in meetings of the Committee of the Parties without the right to vote.

Article 24 – Functions of the Committee of the Parties

¹The Committee of the Parties shall monitor the implementation of this Convention. Its rules of procedure shall determine the procedure for evaluating the implementation of this Convention.
²The Committee of the Parties shall also facilitate the collection, analysis and exchange of information, experience and good practice between States to improve their capacity to prevent and combat trafficking in cultural property. The committee may avail itself of the expertise of other relevant Council of Europe committees and bodies.
³Furthermore, the Committee of the Parties shall, where appropriate:
a) facilitate the effective use and implementation of this Convention, including the identification of any problems that may arise and the effects of any declaration or reservation made under this Convention;
b) express an opinion on any question concerning the application of this Convention and facilitate the exchange of information on significant legal, policy or technological developments;
c) make specific recommendations to Parties concerning the implementation of this Convention.
⁴The European Committee on Crime Problems and the Steering Committee for Culture, Heritage and Landscape shall be kept periodically informed about the activities mentioned in paragraphs 1, 2 and 3 of this article.

Chapter VI –
Relationship with other international instruments

Article 25 – Relationship with other international instruments

¹This Convention shall not affect the rights and obligations arising from the provisions of other international instruments to which Parties to the present Convention are Parties or shall become Parties and which contain provisions on matters governed by this Convention. However, where Parties establish their relations in respect of the matters dealt with in the present Convention other than as regulated therein, they shall do so in a manner that is not inconsistent with the Convention's objectives and principles.
²The Parties to the Convention may conclude bilateral or multilateral agreements with one another on the matters dealt with in this Convention, for purposes of supplementing or strengthening its provisions or facilitating the application of the principles embodied in it.

Chapter VII –
Amendments to the Convention

Article 26 – Amendments

¹Any proposal for an amendment to this Convention presented by a Party shall be communicated to the Secretary General of the Council of Europe and forwarded by him or her to the member States of the Council of Europe, the non-member States which have participated in its elaboration and to any State which has acceded to, or has been invited to accede to this Convention in accordance with the provisions of Article 28.
²Any amendment proposed by a Party shall be communicated to the European Committee on Crime Problems and the Steering Committee for Culture, Heritage and Landscape, which shall submit to the Committee of the Parties their opinions on that proposed amendment.

³The Committee of Ministers of the Council of Europe shall consider the proposed amendment and the opinion submitted by the Committee of Parties and, after having consulted the Parties to this Convention that are not members of the Council of Europe, may adopt the amendment by the majority provided for in Article 20.d of the Statute of the Council of Europe.
⁴The text of any amendment adopted by the Committee of Ministers in accordance with paragraph 3 of this article shall be forwarded to the Parties for acceptance.
⁵Any amendment adopted in accordance with paragraph 3 of this article shall enter into force on the first day of the month following the expiration of a period of one month after the date on which all Parties have informed the Secretary General that they have accepted it.

Chapter VIII –
Final clauses

Article 27 – Signature and entry into force
¹This Convention shall be open for signature by the member States of the Council of Europe and the non-member States which have participated in its elaboration.
²This Convention is subject to ratification, acceptance or approval. Instruments of ratification, acceptance or approval shall be deposited with the Secretary General of the Council of Europe.
³This Convention shall enter into force on the first day of the month following the expiration of a period of three months after the date on which five Signatories, including at least three member States of the Council of Europe, have expressed their consent to be bound by the Convention in accordance with the provisions of the preceding paragraph.
⁴In respect of any Signatory which subsequently expresses its consent to be bound by it, the Convention shall enter into force, in its respect, on the first day of the month following the expiration of a period of three months after the date of the deposit of its instrument of ratification, acceptance or approval.

Article 28 – Accession to the Convention
¹After the entry into force of this Convention, the Committee of Ministers of the Council of Europe may, after consulting the Contracting States to this Convention and obtaining their unanimous consent, invite any non-member State of the Council of Europe which has not participated in the elaboration of the Convention to accede to this Convention by a decision taken by the majority provided for in Article 20 d of the Statute of the Council of Europe, and by unanimous vote of the representatives of the Contracting States entitled to sit on the Committee of Ministers.
²In respect of any acceding State, the Convention shall enter into force on the first day of the month following the expiration of a period of three months after the date of deposit of the instrument of accession with the Secretary General of the Council of Europe.

Article 29 – Territorial application
¹Any State may, at the time of signature or when depositing its instrument of ratification, acceptance, approval or accession, specify the territory or territories to which this Convention shall apply.
²Any State may, at any later date, by a declaration addressed to the Secretary General of the Council of Europe, extend the application of this Convention to any other territory specified in the declaration and for whose international relations it is responsible or on whose behalf it is authorised to give undertakings. In respect of such territory, the Convention shall enter into force on the first day of the month following the expiration of a period of three months after the date of receipt of such declaration by the Secretary General.
³Any declaration made under the two preceding paragraphs may, in respect of any territory specified in any such declaration, be withdrawn by a notification addressed to the Secretary General of the Council of Europe. The withdrawal shall become effective on the first day of the month following the expiration of a period of three months after the date of receipt of such notification by the Secretary General.

Article 30 – Reservations
¹Any State may, at the time of signature or when depositing its instrument of ratification, acceptance, approval or accession, declare that it avails itself of one or more of the reservations provided for in

A.IV.5 Nicosia Convention

Articles 4, 5, 10, 11 and 12, paragraph 3, of this Convention. No other reservation may be made in respect of any provision of this Convention.

²Each Party which has made a reservation may, at any time, withdraw it entirely or partially by a notification addressed to the Secretary General of the Council of Europe. The withdrawal shall take effect from the date of the receipt of such notification by the Secretary General.

³A Party which has made a reservation in respect of a provision of this Convention may not claim the application of that provision by any other Party; it may, however, if the reservation is partial or conditional, claim the application of that provision in so far as it has itself accepted it.

Article 31 – Denunciation

¹Any Party may, at any time, denounce this Convention by means of a notification addressed to the Secretary General of the Council of Europe.

²Such denunciation shall become effective on the first day of the month following the expiration of a period of six months after the date of receipt of the notification by the Secretary General.

Article 32 – Notifications

The Secretary General of the Council of Europe shall notify the member States of the Council of Europe, the non-member States which have participated in its elaboration, any Signatory, any Contracting State and any other State which has been invited to accede to this Convention of:
a) any signature;
b) the deposit of any instrument of ratification, acceptance, approval or accession;
c) any date of entry into force of this Convention in accordance with Article 27, paragraphs 3 and 4; Article 28, paragraph 2, and Article 29, paragraph 2;
d) any amendment adopted in accordance with Article 26 and the date on which such an amendment enters into force;
e) any reservation and withdrawal of reservation made in pursuance of Article 30;
f) any denunciation made in pursuance of Article 31;
g) any other act, declaration, notification or communication relating to this Convention.

In witness whereof the undersigned, being duly authorised thereto, have signed this Convention.

Done at Nicosia, this 19th day of May 2017, in English and in French, both texts being equally authentic, in a single copy which shall be deposited in the archives of the Council of Europe. The Secretary General of the Council of Europe shall transmit certified copies to each member State of the Council of Europe, to the non-member States which have participated in the elaboration of this Convention, and to any State invited to accede to this Convention.

Vertrag über die Arbeitsweise der Europäischen Union

In der Fassung der Bekanntmachung vom 9. Mai 2008[1]) (ABl. C 115 S. 47) (ABl. 2010 C 83 S. 47) (ABl. 2012 C 326 S. 47) (ABl. 2016 C 202 S. 47, ber. ABl. C 400 S. 1) zuletzt geändert durch Art. 2 ÄndBeschl. 2012/419/EU vom 11. Juli 2012 (ABl. L 204 S. 131)
– Auszug –

Dritter Teil
Die internen Politiken und Maßnahmen der Union

Titel V
Der Raum der Freiheit, der Sicherheit und des Rechts

Kapitel 1
Allgemeine Bestimmungen

Artikel 67 [Grundsätze]
(1) Die Union bildet einen Raum der Freiheit, der Sicherheit und des Rechts, in dem die Grundrechte und die verschiedenen Rechtsordnungen und -traditionen der Mitgliedstaaten geachtet werden.
(2) ¹Sie stellt sicher, dass Personen an den Binnengrenzen nicht kontrolliert werden, und entwickelt eine gemeinsame Politik in den Bereichen Asyl, Einwanderung und Kontrollen an den Außengrenzen, die sich auf die Solidarität der Mitgliedstaaten gründet und gegenüber Drittstaatsangehörigen angemessen ist. ²Für die Zwecke dieses Titels werden Staatenlose den Drittstaatsangehörigen gleichgestellt.
(3) Die Union wirkt darauf hin, durch Maßnahmen zur Verhütung und Bekämpfung von Kriminalität sowie von Rassismus und Fremdenfeindlichkeit, zur Koordinierung und Zusammenarbeit von Polizeibehörden und Organen der Strafrechtspflege und den anderen zuständigen Behörden sowie durch die gegenseitige Anerkennung strafrechtlicher Entscheidungen und erforderlichenfalls durch die Angleichung der strafrechtlichen Rechtsvorschriften ein hohes Maß an Sicherheit zu gewährleisten.
(4) Die Union erleichtert den Zugang zum Recht, insbesondere durch den Grundsatz der gegenseitigen Anerkennung gerichtlicher und außergerichtlicher Entscheidungen in Zivilsachen.
[...]

Artikel 75 [Maßnahmen gegen Terrorismusfinanzierung]
Sofern dies notwendig ist, um die Ziele des Artikels 67 in Bezug auf die Verhütung und Bekämpfung von Terrorismus und damit verbundener Aktivitäten zu verwirklichen, schaffen das Europäische Parlament und der Rat gemäß dem ordentlichen Gesetzgebungsverfahren durch Verordnungen einen Rahmen für Verwaltungsmaßnahmen in Bezug auf Kapitalbewegungen und Zahlungen, wozu das Einfrieren von Geldern, finanziellen Vermögenswerten oder wirtschaftlichen Erträgen gehören kann, deren Eigentümer oder Besitzer natürliche oder juristische Personen, Gruppierungen oder nichtstaatliche Einheiten sind.
Der Rat erlässt auf Vorschlag der Kommission Maßnahmen zur Umsetzung des in Absatz 1 genannten Rahmens.
In den Rechtsakten nach diesem Artikel müssen die erforderlichen Bestimmungen über den Rechtsschutz vorgesehen sein.

---

1) Konsolidierte Fassung des Vertrags zur Gründung der Europäischen Gemeinschaft v. 25.3.1957 (BGBl. II S. 766). Die Bundesrepublik Deutschland hat dem Vertrag von Lissabon mit G. v. 8.10.2008 (BGBl. II S. 1038) zugestimmt; Inkrafttreten am 1.12.2009, siehe Bek. v. 13.11.2009 (BGBl. II S. 1223).

Fünfter Teil
Das auswärtige Handeln der Union

Titel II
Gemeinsame Handelspolitik

Artikel 207 [Grundsätze der gemeinsamen Handelspolitik]

(1) ¹Die gemeinsame Handelspolitik wird nach einheitlichen Grundsätzen gestaltet; dies gilt insbesondere für die Änderung von Zollsätzen, für den Abschluss von Zoll- und Handelsabkommen, die den Handel mit Waren und Dienstleistungen betreffen, und für die Handelsaspekte des geistigen Eigentums, die ausländischen Direktinvestitionen, die Vereinheitlichung der Liberalisierungsmaßnahmen, die Ausfuhrpolitik sowie die handelspolitischen Schutzmaßnahmen, zum Beispiel im Fall von Dumping und Subventionen. ²Die gemeinsame Handelspolitik wird im Rahmen der Grundsätze und Ziele des auswärtigen Handelns der Union gestaltet.

(2) Das Europäische Parlament und der Rat erlassen durch Verordnungen[1]) gemäß dem ordentlichen Gesetzgebungsverfahren die Maßnahmen, mit denen der Rahmen für die Umsetzung der gemeinsamen Handelspolitik bestimmt wird.

(3) Sind mit einem oder mehreren Drittländern oder internationalen Organisationen Abkommen auszuhandeln und zu schließen, so findet Artikel 218 vorbehaltlich der besonderen Bestimmungen dieses Artikels Anwendung.

¹Die Kommission legt dem Rat Empfehlungen vor; dieser ermächtigt die Kommission zur Aufnahme der erforderlichen Verhandlungen. ²Der Rat und die Kommission haben dafür Sorge zu tragen, dass die ausgehandelten Abkommen mit der internen Politik und den internen Vorschriften der Union vereinbar sind.

¹Die Kommission führt diese Verhandlungen im Benehmen mit einem zu ihrer Unterstützung vom Rat bestellten Sonderausschuss und nach Maßgabe der Richtlinien, die ihr der Rat erteilen kann. ²Die Kommission erstattet dem Sonderausschuss sowie dem Europäischen Parlament regelmäßig Bericht über den Stand der Verhandlungen.

(4) Über die Aushandlung und den Abschluss der in Absatz 3 genannten Abkommen beschließt der Rat mit qualifizierter Mehrheit.

Über die Aushandlung und den Abschluss eines Abkommens über den Dienstleistungsverkehr, über Handelsaspekte des geistigen Eigentums oder über ausländische Direktinvestitionen beschließt der Rat einstimmig, wenn das betreffende Abkommen Bestimmungen enthält, bei denen für die Annahme interner Vorschriften Einstimmigkeit erforderlich ist.

Der Rat beschließt ebenfalls einstimmig über die Aushandlung und den Abschluss von Abkommen in den folgenden Bereichen:

a) Handel mit kulturellen und audiovisuellen Dienstleistungen, wenn diese Abkommen die kulturelle und sprachliche Vielfalt in der Union beeinträchtigen könnten;
b) Handel mit Dienstleistungen des Sozial-, des Bildungs- und des Gesundheitssektors, wenn diese Abkommen die einzelstaatliche Organisation dieser Dienstleistungen ernsthaft stören und die Verantwortlichkeit der Mitgliedstaaten für ihre Erbringung beinträchtigen könnten.

(5) Für die Aushandlung und den Abschluss von internationalen Abkommen im Bereich des Verkehrs gelten der Dritte Teil Titel VI sowie Artikel 218.

(6) Die Ausübung der durch diesen Artikel übertragenen Zuständigkeiten im Bereich der gemeinsamen Handelspolitik hat keine Auswirkungen auf die Abgrenzung der Zuständigkeiten zwischen der Union und den Mitgliedstaaten und führt nicht zu einer Harmonisierung der Rechtsvorschriften der Mitgliedstaaten, soweit eine solche Harmonisierung in den Verträgen ausgeschlossen wird.

[...]

---

1) Siehe dazu z.B. Verordnung (EU) 2019/880 des Europäischen Parlaments und des Rates v. 17. April 2019 über das Verbringen und die Einfuhr von Kulturgütern, abgedruckt als Nr. B.I.4.

Titel IV
Restriktive Maßnahmen

Artikel 215 [Wirtschaftsembargo; Beschlussfassung; Rechtsschutz]
(1) ¹Sieht ein nach Titel V Kapitel 2 des Vertrags über die Europäische Union erlassener Beschluss die Aussetzung, Einschränkung oder vollständige Einstellung der Wirtschafts- und Finanzbeziehungen zu einem oder mehreren Drittländern vor, so erlässt der Rat die erforderlichen Maßnahmen mit qualifizierter Mehrheit auf gemeinsamen Vorschlag des Hohen Vertreters der Union für Außen- und Sicherheitspolitik und der Kommission. ²Er unterrichtet hierüber das Europäische Parlament.
(2) Sieht ein nach Titel V Kapitel 2 des Vertrags über die Europäische Union erlassener Beschluss dies vor, so kann der Rat nach dem Verfahren des Absatzes 1 restriktive Maßnahmen gegen natürliche oder juristische Personen sowie Gruppierungen oder nichtstaatliche Einheiten erlassen.
(3) In den Rechtsakten nach diesem Artikel müssen die erforderlichen Bestimmungen über den Rechtsschutz vorgesehen sein.

B.I.2 Verordnung (EG) 1210/2003

Verordnung (EG) Nr. 1210/2003 des Rates vom 7. Juli 2003 über bestimmte spezifische Beschränkungen in den wirtschaftlichen und finanziellen Beziehungen zu Irak und zur Aufhebung der Verordnung (EG) Nr. 2465/1996

(ABl. L 169 vom 8.7.2003, S. 6)

Zuletzt geändert durch: Durchführungsverordnung (EU) 2020/37 der Kommission vom 16. Januar 2020, L 13/13 vom 17.1.2020

Artikel 1
Im Sinne dieser Verordnung bezeichnet der Ausdruck
1. „Sanktionsausschuss" den gemäß Ziffer 6 der Resolution 661 (1990) eingesetzte Ausschuss des Sicherheitsrates der Vereinten Nationen;
2. „Gelder" finanzielle Vermögenswerte und wirtschaftliche Vorteile jeder Art einschließlich von – aber nicht beschränkt auf
    a) Bargeld, Schecks, Geldforderungen, Wechsel, Geldanweisungen oder andere Zahlungsmittel;
    b) Guthaben bei Finanzinstituten oder anderen Einrichtungen, Guthaben auf Konten, Schulden und Schuldverschreibungen;
    c) öffentlich und privat gehandelte Wertpapiere und Schuldtitel einschließlich Aktien und Anteile, Wertpapierzertifikate, Obligationen, Schuldscheine, Optionsscheine, Pfandbriefe und Derivatverträge;
    d) Zinserträge, Dividenden oder andere Einkünfte oder Wertzuwächse aus Vermögenswerten;
    e) Kredite, Rechte auf Verrechnung, Bürgschaften, Vertragserfüllungsgarantien oder andere finanzielle Zusagen;
    f) Akkreditive, Konnossemente, Sicherungsübereignungen;
    g) Dokumente zur Verbriefung von Anteilen an Fondsvermögen oder anderen Finanzressourcen;
    h) jedes andere Finanzierungsinstrument für Ausfuhren;
3. „wirtschaftliche Ressourcen" Vermögenswerte jeder Art, unabhängig davon, ob sie materiell oder immateriell, beweglich oder unbeweglich sind, bei denen es sich nicht um Gelder handelt, die aber für den Erwerb von Geldern, Waren oder Dienstleistungen verwendet werden können;
4. „Einfrieren von Geldern" die Verhinderung jeglicher Form von Bewegung, Transfer, Veränderung oder Handel mit Geldern, wodurch das Volumen, die Beträge, die Belegenheit, das Eigentum, der Besitz, die Eigenschaften oder die Zweckbestimmung der Gelder verändert oder sonstige Veränderungen bewirkt werden und somit eine Nutzung der Mittel einschließlich der Vermögensverwaltung ermöglicht wird;
5. „Einfrieren wirtschaftlicher Ressourcen" die Verhinderung ihrer Verwendung für den Erwerb von Geldern, Waren oder Dienstleistungen, einschließlich von – aber nicht beschränkt auf – den Verkauf, das Vermieten oder das Verpfänden dieser Ressourcen;
6. „Entwicklungsfonds für Irak" den von der irakischen Zentralbank geführten Entwicklungsfonds für Irak.

Artikel 2
Sämtliche Einnahmen aus Exportverkäufen von Erdöl, Erdölprodukten und Erdgas aus Irak gemäß der in Anhang I aufgeführten Liste werden ab dem 22. Mai 2003 entsprechend den in der UNSC-Resolution 1483 (2003), insbesondere in den Nummern 20 und 21, festgelegten Bedingungen in den Entwicklungsfonds für Irak eingezahlt.

Artikel 3
(1) Es ist untersagt, irakische Kulturgüter und andere Gegenstände von archäologischer, historischer, kultureller, besonderer wissenschaftlicher und religiöser Bedeutung, einschließlich der in Anhang II aufgelisteten Gegenstände,
a) in das Gebiet der Gemeinschaft einzuführen oder zu verbringen,
b) aus dem Gebiet der Gemeinschaft auszuführen oder zu verbringen und

c) mit ihnen zu handeln,
  i) wenn sie illegal von irakischen Orten entfernt wurden, insbesondere, wenn diese Gegenstände entweder Teil öffentlicher Sammlungen sind, die in den Bestandsverzeichnissen von irakischen Museen, Archiven oder besonderen Sammlungen von Bibliotheken oder aber in den Bestandsverzeichnissen religiöser Einrichtungen Iraks aufgeführt sind, oder
  ii) ein begründeter Verdacht besteht, dass die Kulturgüter ohne Zustimmung des rechtmäßigen Besitzers aus Irak oder aber unter Verstoß gegen die einschlägigen irakischen Gesetze und Bestimmungen aus Irak verbracht wurden.

(2) Dieses Verbot gilt nicht, wenn nachgewiesen wird, dass
a) die Kulturgüter vor dem 6. August 1990 aus Irak ausgeführt wurden, oder
b) die Kulturgüter den irakischen Einrichtungen gemäß dem in Absatz 7 der UNSC-Resolution 1483 (2003) beschriebenen Ziel der sicheren Rückgabe zurückgegeben werden.

Artikel 4
(1) Alle Gelder und wirtschaftlichen Ressourcen der früheren irakischen Regierung oder der vom Sanktionsausschuss benannten und in Anhang III aufgeführten staatlichen Organe, Unternehmen (einschließlich privatrechtlicher Unternehmen, in denen öffentliche Stellen über eine Mehrheits- oder Kontrollbeteiligung verfügen) oder Einrichtungen dieser Regierung, die am 22. Mai 2003 außerhalb des Irak belegen waren, werden eingefroren.
(2) Alle Gelder und wirtschaftlichen Ressourcen, die im Eigentum der folgenden vom Sanktionsausschuss benannten und in Anhang IV aufgeführten Personen stehen oder sich in deren Besitz befinden, werden eingefroren:
a) des ehemaligen Präsidenten Saddam Hussein;
b) hoher Amtsträger seines Regimes;
c) ihrer unmittelbaren Familienangehörigen oder
d) juristischer Personen, Einrichtungen oder Organisationen, die den unter den Buchstaben a), b) und c) genannten Personen oder in ihrem Namen oder auf ihre Anweisung handelnden natürlichen oder juristischen Personen gehören oder von diesen direkt oder indirekt kontrolliert werden.
(3) Den in Anhang IV aufgeführten natürlichen oder juristischen Personen, Einrichtungen oder Organisationen dürfen Gelder oder wirtschaftliche Ressourcen weder direkt noch indirekt zur Verfügung gestellt werden noch sonstwie zugute kommen.

Artikel 4a
Die betreffenden natürlichen und juristischen Personen oder Organisationen können im Zusammenhang mit dem Verbot nach Artikel 4 Absatz 3 nicht haftbar gemacht werden, wenn sie nicht wussten und keinen Grund zu der Annahme hatten, dass sie mit ihrem Handeln gegen das Verbot verstoßen.

Artikel 5
(1) Artikel 4 hindert Finanz- und Kreditinstitute nicht daran, Gelder, die von Dritten auf das Konto einer in der Liste geführten Person, Einrichtung oder Organisation überwiesen werden, auf den eingefrorenen Konten gutzuschreiben, sofern die auf diesen Konten gutgeschriebenen Beträge ebenfalls eingefroren sind. Die Finanz- und Kreditinstitute unterrichten die zuständigen Behörden über diese Transaktionen ohne Verzögerung.
(2) Abweichend von Artikel 4 Absatz 3 können die auf den Websites in Anhang V aufgeführten zuständigen Behörden die Freigabe von Geldern oder wirtschaftlichen Ressourcen unter ihnen geeignet erscheinenden Bedingungen genehmigen, wenn sie festgestellt haben, dass die betreffenden Gelder oder wirtschaftlichen Ressourcen
a) zur Deckung der Grundbedürfnisse der in Anhang IV aufgeführten natürlichen oder juristischen Personen, Einrichtungen oder Organisationen und der unterhaltsberechtigten Familienangehörigen solcher natürlicher Personen, einschließlich für die Bezahlung von Nahrungsmitteln, Mieten oder Hypotheken, Medikamenten und medizinischer Behandlung, Steuern, Versicherungsprämien und Gebühren öffentlicher Versorgungseinrichtungen, erforderlich sind;
b) ausschließlich der Bezahlung angemessener Honorare und der Erstattung von Ausgaben im Zusammenhang mit der Erbringung von Rechtsdienstleistungen dienen,
c) ausschließlich der Bezahlung von Gebühren oder Kosten für die routinemäßige Verwahrung oder Verwaltung eingefrorener Gelder oder wirtschaftlicher Ressourcen dienen oder

d) für die Bezahlung außerordentlicher Ausgaben erforderlich sind, sofern die zuständige Behörde den zuständigen Behörden der anderen Mitgliedstaaten und der Kommission mindestens zwei Wochen vor der Genehmigung die Gründe dafür mitteilt, weshalb sie der Auffassung ist, dass eine Sondergenehmigung erteilt werden sollte.

(3) Die betreffenden Mitgliedstaaten unterrichten die anderen Mitgliedstaaten und die Kommission von jeder Genehmigung, die sie nach Maßgabe dieses Artikels erteilt haben.

Artikel 6

(1) Abweichend von Artikel 4 können die auf den Websites in Anhang V angegebenen zuständigen Behörden der Mitgliedstaaten die Freigabe eingefrorener Gelder oder wirtschaftlicher Ressourcen genehmigen, wenn alle nachstehenden Bedingungen erfüllt sind:
a) die Gelder oder die wirtschaftlichen Ressourcen waren bereits vor dem 22. Mai 2003 Gegenstand eines Pfandrechts oder einer Entscheidung, die von einem Gericht, einer Verwaltungsstelle oder einem Schiedsgericht begründet bzw. erlassen wurden;
b) die Gelder oder die wirtschaftlichen Ressourcen werden ausschließlich für die Erfüllung von Forderungen verwendet, die durch ein solches Pfandrecht gesichert sind oder durch eine solche Entscheidung als gültig anerkannt wurden, wobei die Gesetze und sonstigen Rechtsvorschriften, die die Rechte der solche Forderungen geltend machenden Personen begründen, einzuhalten sind;
c) die Erfüllung der Forderung stellt keinen Verstoß gegen die Verordnung (EG) Nr. 3541/92 dar;
d) die Anerkennung des Pfandrechts oder der Entscheidung steht nicht im Widerspruch zur öffentlichen Ordnung des betreffenden Mitgliedstaats.

(2) In allen anderen Fällen dürfen die gemäß Artikel 4 eingefrorenen Gelder, wirtschaftlichen Ressourcen und Einnahmen aus wirtschaftlichen Ressourcen nur zum Zweck ihres Transfers an die Nachfolgeregelungen des Entwicklungsfonds für Irak, die die irakische Regierung gemäß den in den Resolutionen 1483 (2003) und 1956 (2010) des Sicherheitsrates der Vereinten Nationen festgelegten Bedingungen eingeführt hat, freigegeben werden.

Artikel 7

(1) Die wissentliche und vorsätzliche Beteiligung an Maßnahmen, deren Ziel oder Folge direkt oder indirekt die Umgehung des Artikels 4 oder die Förderung der in den Artikeln 2 und 3 genannten Transaktionen ist, ist untersagt.

(2) Informationen darüber, dass die Bestimmungen dieser Verordnung umgangen werden oder wurden, sind den auf den Websites in Anhang V angegebenen zuständigen Behörden der Mitgliedstaaten und der Kommission direkt oder über diese zuständigen Behörden zu übermitteln.

Artikel 8

(1) Unbeschadet der für die Berichterstattung, Vertraulichkeit und das Berufsgeheimnis geltenden Bestimmungen und unbeschadet des Artikels 284 des Vertrags sind natürliche und juristische Personen, Organisationen und Einrichtungen verpflichtet,
a) den auf den Websites in Anhang V angegebenen zuständigen Behörden der Mitgliedstaaten, in denen sie ihren Sitz oder eine Niederlassung haben, sowie der Kommission – direkt oder über diese zuständigen Behörden – unverzüglich alle Informationen zu übermitteln, die die Einhaltung dieser Verordnung erleichtern würden, z. B. über gemäß Artikel 4 eingefrorene Konten und Guthaben;
b) mit den auf den Websites in Anhang V angegebenen zuständigen Behörden bei der Überprüfung dieser Angaben zusammenzuarbeiten.

(2) Die gemäß diesem Artikel übermittelten oder erhaltenen Informationen dürfen nur für die Zwecke verwendet werden, für die sie übermittelt oder entgegengenommen wurden.

Artikel 9

Weder die natürlichen oder juristischen Personen oder Organisationen, die Gelder und wirtschaftliche Ressourcen in dem guten Glauben einfrieren, dass derartige Handlungen mit dieser Verordnung im Einklang stehen, noch deren Direktoren oder Beschäftigte können auf irgendeine Weise hierfür haftbar gemacht werden, sofern das Einfrieren der Gelder und wirtschaftlichen Ressourcen nicht erwiesenermaßen auf Nachlässigkeit zurückzuführen ist.

Artikel 10
(1) Folgendes genießt Immunität von Gerichtsverfahren und unterliegt keiner Form von Pfändung, Forderungspfändung oder Zwangsvollstreckung:
a) Erdöl, Erdölprodukte und Erdgas mit Ursprung in Irak, bis diese Waren in das Eigentum eines Käufers übergegangen sind;
b) Erlöse und Verpflichtungen aus Verkäufen von Erdöl, Erdölprodukten und Erdgas mit Ursprung in Irak, einschließlich der für diese Waren fälligen Beträge, die in den von der irakischen Zentralbank geführten Entwicklungsfonds für Irak eingezahlt werden;
c) gemäß Artikel 4 eingefrorene Gelder und wirtschaftliche Ressourcen;
d) der von der irakischen Zentralbank geführte Entwicklungsfonds für Irak.
(2) Abweichend von Absatz 1 gilt für die Erlöse und Verpflichtungen aus dem Verkauf von Erdöl, Erdölprodukten und Erdgas mit Ursprung in Irak und für den Entwicklungsfonds für Irak keine Immunität, wenn Forderungen auf der Grundlage der Haftung Iraks für Schäden in Verbindung mit Umweltunfällen, die nach dem 22. Mai 2003 erfolgen, geltend gemacht werden.
(3) Absatz 1 Buchstaben a), b) und d) gelten weder für Gerichtsverfahren bezüglich vertraglicher Verpflichtungen, die Irak – einschließlich insbesondere seiner Interimsregierung, der irakischen Zentralbank und des Entwicklungsfonds für Irak – nach dem 30. Juni 2004 eingegangen ist noch für aufgrund solcher vertraglicher Verpflichtungen ergangene rechtskräftige Urteile.

Artikel 11
Die Kommission wird ermächtigt,
a) Anhang II erforderlichenfalls zu ändern,
b) die Anhänge III und IV auf der Grundlage von Entscheidungen des Sicherheitsrates der Vereinten Nationen oder des Sanktionsausschusses zu ändern oder zu ergänzen und
c) Anhang V anhand der von den Mitgliedstaaten übermittelten Informationen zu ändern.

Artikel 12
Unbeschadet der Rechte und Pflichten der Mitgliedstaaten nach der Charta der Vereinten Nationen unterhält die Kommission die für die wirksame Durchführung dieser Verordnung erforderlichen Kontakte zum Sanktionsausschuss.

Artikel 13
Die Kommission und die Mitgliedstaaten unterrichten einander unverzüglich über die gemäß dieser Verordnung ergriffenen Maßnahmen. Sie tauschen die ihnen im Zusammenhang mit dieser Verordnung vorliegenden sachdienlichen Informationen aus, insbesondere gemäß Artikel 8 eingegangene Informationen und Informationen über Verstöße gegen diese Verordnung, Probleme bei ihrer Durchsetzung und Urteile nationaler Gerichte.

Artikel 14
Diese Verordnung gilt ungeachtet etwaiger Rechte und Pflichten, die sich aus vor ihrem Inkrafttreten unterzeichneten internationalen Übereinkünften, geschlossenen Verträgen oder erteilten Lizenzen oder Genehmigungen ergeben.

Artikel 15
(1) Die Mitgliedstaaten erlassen Vorschriften über Sanktionen für Verstöße gegen diese Verordnung und ergreifen alle erforderlichen Maßnahmen um sicherzustellen, dass sie durchgeführt werden. Die vorgesehenen Sanktionen müssen wirksam, verhältnismäßig und abschreckend sein.
(2) Bis zur Annahme gegebenenfalls erforderlicher entsprechender Rechtsvorschriften werden im Fall von Verstößen gegen diese Verordnung gegebenenfalls Sanktionen verhängt, die von den Mitgliedstaaten in Einklang mit Artikel 7 Absatz 3 der Verordnung (EG) Nr. 2465/1996 festgelegt wurden.
(3) Jeder Mitgliedstaat ist dafür verantwortlich, gegen alle natürlichen oder juristischen Personen, Gruppen oder Organisationen vorzugehen, die seiner Rechtshoheit unterliegen und die gegen die in dieser Verordnung erlassenen Verbote verstoßen haben.

Artikel 15a
(1) Die Mitgliedstaaten benennen die in den Artikeln 6, 7 und 8 dieser Verordnung genannten zuständigen Behörden und stellen alle diesbezüglichen Informationen auf den oder über die in Anhang V genannten Websites zur Verfügung.

(2) Die Mitgliedstaaten teilen der Kommission bis zum 15. März 2008 ihre zuständigen Behörden mit und setzen sie von allen späteren Änderungen in Kenntnis.

Artikel 16
Diese Verordnung gilt
a) im Gebiet der Gemeinschaft, einschließlich ihres Luftraums,
b) an Bord jedes Luft- oder Wasserfahrzeugs, das der Hoheitsgewalt eines Mitgliedstaats unterliegt,
c) für jede Person, die die Staatsangehörigkeit eines Mitgliedstaats besitzt und sich innerhalb oder außerhalb des Gebiets der Gemeinschaft aufhält,
d) für jede nach dem Recht eines Mitgliedstaats gegründete oder eingetragene juristische Person, Organisation oder Einrichtung und
e) für jede juristische Person, Organisation oder Einrichtung in Bezug auf Geschäfte, die ganz oder teilweise in der Gemeinschaft getätigt werden.

Artikel 17
Die Verordnung (EG) Nr. 2465/96 wird aufgehoben.

Artikel 18
(1) Diese Verordnung tritt am Tag nach ihrer Veröffentlichung im Amtsblatt der Europäischen Union in Kraft.
(2) Mit Ausnahme der Artikel 4 und 6 gilt die Verordnung ab dem 23. Mai 2003.
(3) Die Artikel 2 und 10 gelten bis zum 30. Juni 2011.
Diese Verordnung ist in allen ihren Teilen verbindlich und gilt unmittelbar in jedem Mitgliedstaat.

ANHANG II Liste der Waren nach Artikel 3

ex KN-Code		Warenbeschreibung
9705 00 00 9706 00 00	1.	Mehr als 100 Jahre alte archäologische Gegenstände aus – Grabungen und archäologischen Funden zu Lande oder unter Wasser, – archäologischen Stätten, – archäologischen Sammlungen
9705 00 00 9706 00 00	2.	Bestandteile von Kunst- und Baudenkmälern oder religiösen Denkmälern, die aus deren Aufteilung stammen und älter sind als 100 Jahre
9701	3.	Bilder und Gemälde, die nicht unter die Kategorie 3A oder 4 fallen, die vollständig von Hand und auf allen Stoffen hergestellt sind, älter als 50 Jahre und nicht ihren Urhebern gehörend
9701	3A.	Aquarelle, Gouachen und Pastelle, die vollständig von Hand auf allen Stoffen hergestellt sind, älter als 50 Jahre und nicht ihren Urhebern gehörend
6914 9701	4.	Mosaike, die vollständig von Hand und aus allen Materialien hergestellt sind und nicht unter die Kategorie 1 oder 2 fallen, und Zeichnungen, die vollständig von Hand und auf allen Stoffen hergestellt sind, älter als 50 Jahre und nicht ihren Urhebern gehörend
Kapitel 49 9702 00 00 8442 50 99	5.	Original-Radierungen, -Stiche, -Serigrafien und -Lithografien und lithografische Matrizen sowie Original-Plakate, älter als 50 Jahre und nicht ihren Urhebern gehörend
9703 00 00	6.	Nicht unter die Kategorie 1 fallende Originalerzeugnisse der Bildhauerkunst und Kopien, die auf dieselbe Weise wie das Original hergestellt worden sind, älter als 50 Jahre und nicht ihren Urhebern gehörend
3704 3705 3706 4911 91 80	7.	Fotografien, Filme und die dazugehörigen Negative, älter als 50 Jahre und nicht ihren Urhebern gehörend

Verordnung (EG) 1210/2003 B.I.2

ex KN-Code	Warenbeschreibung
9702 00 00 9706 00 00 4901 10 00 4901 99 00 4904 00 00 4905 91 00 4905 99 00 4906 00 00	8. Wiegendrucke und Handschriften, einschließlich Landkarten und Partituren, als Einzelstücke oder Sammlung, älter als 50 Jahre und nicht ihren Urhebern gehörend
9705 00 00 9706 00 00	9. Bücher, die älter sind als 100 Jahre, als Einzelstücke oder Sammlung
9706 00 00	10. Gedruckte Landkarten, die älter sind als 200 Jahre
3704 3705 3706 4901 4906 9705 00 00 9706 00 00	11. Archive aller Art, mit Archivalien, die älter sind als 50 Jahre, auf allen Trägern
9705 00 00 9705 00 00	12. a) Sammlungen im Sinne des Urteils des Gerichtshofes in der Rechtssache 252/84[1]) und Einzelexemplare aus zoologischen, botanischen, mineralogischen oder anatomischen Sammlungen b) Sammlungen im Sinne des Urteils des Gerichtshofes in der Rechtssache 252/84 von historischem, paläontologischem, ethnografischem oder numismatischem Wert
9705 00 00 Kapitel 86-89	13. Verkehrsmittel, die älter sind als 75 Jahre
Kapitel 95 7013 7114 Kapitel 94 Kapitel 90 Kapitel 92 Kapitel 91 Kapitel 44 Kapitel 69 5805 00 00 Kapitel 57 4814 Kapitel 93 9706 00 00	14. Sonstige, nicht unter den Kategorien 1 bis 13 genannte Antiquitäten, a) die 50 bis 100 Jahre alt sind: – Spielzeug, Spiele – Glaswaren – Gold- und Silberschmiedewaren – Möbel – Optische, fotografische und kinematografische Instrumente – Musikinstrumente – Uhrmacherwaren und Teile davon – Holzwaren – Keramische Waren – Tapisserien – Teppiche – Papiertapeten – Waffen b) Antiquitäten, mehr als 100 Jahre alt

---

1) Sammlungsstücke im Sinne der Position 97.05 des Gemeinsamen Zolltarifs sind Gegenstände, die geeignet sind, in eine Sammlung aufgenommen zu werden, das heißt Gegenstände, die verhältnismäßig selten sind, normalerweise nicht ihrem ursprünglichen Verwendungszweck gemäß benutzt werden, Gegenstand eines Spezialhandels außerhalb des üblichen Handels mit ähnlichen Gebrauchsgegenständen sind und einen hohen Wert haben.

B.I.2 Verordnung (EG) 1210/2003

ANHANG V Websites mit Informationen über die in den Artikeln 5, 6, 7 und 8 genannten zuständigen Behörden und Anschrift für Notifikationen an die Europäische Kommission

A.
Zuständige Behörden der Mitgliedstaaten:

DEUTSCHLAND
http://www.bmwi.de/DE/Themen/Aussenwirtschaft/aussenwirtschaftsrecht,did=404888.html

B.
Anschrift für Notifikationen an die Europäische Kommission:

Europäische Kommission
Dienst für außenpolitische Instrumente (FPI)
Büro EEAS 07/99
B-1049 Brüssel, BelgienE-Mail: relex-sanctions@ec.europa.eu.

Verordnung (EU) Nr. 36/2012 des Rates vom 18. Januar 2012 über restriktive Maßnahmen angesichts der Lage in Syrien und zur Aufhebung der Verordnung (EU) Nr. 442/2011 (Auszüge)

(ABl. L 16/1 v. 19.1.2012, S. 1, zuletzt geändert durch Durchführungsverordnung des Rates (EU) Nr. 2019/350 des Rates vom 4. März 2019, ABl. L 631/1 v. 4.3.2019)

– Auszug –

Kapitel II
Ausfuhr- und Einfuhrbeschränkungen

Artikel 11c
(1) Es ist verboten, Kulturgüter, die zum kulturellen Eigentum Syriens gehören, sowie sonstige Gegenstände von archäologischer, historischer, kultureller, besonderer wissenschaftlicher oder von religiöser Bedeutung, einschließlich derjenigen, die in Anhang XI aufgeführt sind, einzuführen, auszuführen, weiterzugeben oder dazugehörige Vermittlungsdienste bereitzustellen, sofern Grund zu der Annahme besteht, dass die Güter ohne Einwilligung ihrer rechtmäßigen Eigentümer oder unter Verstoß gegen syrisches Recht oder Völkerrecht aus Syrien entfernt wurden, insbesondere wenn die Güter zu öffentlichen Sammlungen gehören, die in den Bestandsverzeichnissen der erhaltenswürdigen Bestände syrischer Museen, Archive oder Bibliotheken oder in den Bestandsverzeichnissen religiöser Einrichtungen Syriens aufgeführt sind.
(2) Das Verbot in Absatz 1 gilt nicht, wenn die Güter nachweislich
a) vor dem 15. März 2011 aus Syrien ausgeführt wurden oder
b) auf sichere Weise an ihre rechtmäßigen Besitzer in Syrien zurückgegeben werden.

B.I.4 Verordnung (EU) 2019/880

Verordnung (EU) 2019/880 des Europäischen Parlaments und des Rates vom 17. April 2019 über das Verbringen und die Einfuhr von Kulturgütern

Das Europäische Parlament und der Rat der Europäischen Union —
gestützt auf den Vertrag über die Arbeitsweise der Europäischen Union, insbesondere auf Artikel 207 Absatz 2, auf Vorschlag der Europäischen Kommission,
nach Zuleitung des Entwurfs des Gesetzgebungsakts an die nationalen Parlamente, gemäß dem ordentlichen Gesetzgebungsverfahren[1)],
in Erwägung nachstehender Gründe:

(1) Im Licht der Schlussfolgerungen des Rates vom 12. Februar 2016 zur Bekämpfung der Terrorismusfinanzierung, der Mitteilung der Kommission an das Europäische Parlament und den Rat vom 2. Februar 2016 über einen Aktionsplan für ein intensiveres Vorgehen gegen Terrorismusfinanzierung und der Richtlinie (EU) 2017/541 des Europäischen Parlaments und des Rates[2)] sollten gemeinsame Vorschriften für den Handel mit Drittländern erlassen werden, um so einen wirksamen Schutz vor dem illegalen Handel mit Kulturgütern, ihrem Verlust oder ihrer Zerstörung, die Erhaltung des kulturellen Erbes der Menschheit und die Verhinderung von Terrorismusfinanzierung und Geldwäsche durch den Verkauf von geraubten Kulturgütern an Abnehmer in der Union sicherzustellen.

(2) Die Ausbeutung von Völkern und Gebieten kann zum illegalen Handel mit Kulturgütern führen, insbesondere wenn ein solcher illegaler Handel vor dem Hintergrund eines bewaffneten Konflikts erfolgt. Mit Blick darauf sollte in dieser Verordnung regionalen und lokalen Merkmalen von Völkern und Gebieten und nicht dem Marktwert der Kulturgüter Rechnung getragen werden.

(3) Kulturgüter sind Teil des Kulturerbes und häufig von wesentlicher kultureller, künstlerischer, historischer und wissenschaftlicher Bedeutung. Das kulturelle Erbe ist eines der wesentlichen Elemente der Zivilisation, hat unter anderem symbolischen Wert und gehört zum kulturellen Gedächtnis der Menschheit. Es bereichert das kulturelle Leben aller Völker und eint die Menschen im Wissen um dieses gemeinsame Gedächtnis und durch die gemeinsame Entwicklung der Zivilisation. Es sollte daher vor unrechtmäßiger Aneignung und Plünderung geschützt werden. Archäologische Stätten werden seit jeher geplündert, aber inzwischen hat dieses Phänomen gewerbsmäßige Ausmaße angenommen und ist zusammen mit dem Handel mit illegal ausgegrabenen Kulturgütern ein schwerwiegendes Verbrechen, durch das den direkt und indirekt Betroffenen erhebliches Leid zugefügt wird. Der illegale Handel mit Kulturgütern trägt in vielen Fällen zu einer aufgezwungenen kulturellen Homogenisierung oder zum aufgezwungenen Verlust von kultureller Identität bei, während die Plünderung von Kulturgütern unter anderem zur Desintegration von Kulturen führt. Solange der Handel mit Kulturgütern aus illegalen Ausgrabungen lukrativ und gewinnbringend bleibt und keine nennenswerten Risiken birgt, wird es auch Raubgrabungen und Plünderungen geben. Aufgrund der wirtschaftlichen und künstlerischen Bedeutung der Kulturgüter ist die Nachfrage auf dem internationalen Markt hoch. Die Tatsache, dass es auf internationaler Ebene keine durchgreifenden rechtlichen Maßnahmen gibt und dass diejenigen Maßnahmen, die es gibt, nicht wirksam durchgesetzt werden, führt dazu, dass diese Güter in die Schattenwirtschaft überführt werden. Die Union sollte dementsprechend die Verbringung von aus Drittländern illegal ausgeführten Kulturgütern in das Zollgebiet der Union verbieten, mit besonderem Augenmerk auf Kulturgütern aus Drittländern, die von bewaffneten Konflikten betroffen sind, vor allem wenn diese Kulturgüter durch terroristische oder andere kriminelle Organisationen illegal gehandelt wurden. Dieses allgemeine Verbot hat zwar keine systematischen Kontrollen zur Folge, doch sollte es den Mitgliedstaaten gestattet sein, bei Vorliegen von Informationen über verdächtige Sendungen einzugreifen und alle geeigneten Maßnahmen zu treffen, um unzulässig ausgeführte Kulturgüter abzufangen.

---

1) Standpunkt des Europäischen Parlaments vom 12. März 2019 (noch nicht im Amtsblatt veröffentlicht) und Beschluss des Rates vom 9. April 2019.
2) Richtlinie (EU) 2017/541 des Europäischen Parlaments und des Rates vom 15. März 2017 zur Terrorismusbekämpfung und zur Ersetzung des Rahmenbeschlusses 2002/475/JI des Rates und zur Änderung des Beschlusses 2005/671/JI des Rates (ABl. L 88 vom 31.3.2017, S. 6).

(4) Angesichts der unterschiedlichen Vorschriften, die in den Mitgliedstaaten für die Einfuhr von Kulturgütern in das Zollgebiet der Union gelten, sollten Maßnahmen getroffen werden, um insbesondere sicherzustellen, dass bestimmte Einfuhren von Kulturgütern in das Zollgebiet der Union einheitlichen Kontrollen auf der Grundlage bestehender Prozesse, Verfahren und Verwaltungsinstrumente unterzogen werden, durch die eine einheitliche Durchführung der Verordnung (EU) Nr. 952/2013 des Europäischen Parlaments und des Rates[1] erreicht werden soll.

(5) Der Schutz von Kulturgütern, die als nationales Kulturgut der Mitgliedstaaten gelten, wird bereits von der Verordnung (EG) Nr. 116/2009 des Rates[2] und der Richtlinie 2014/60/EU des Europäischen Parlaments und des Rates[3] abgedeckt. Daher sollte die vorliegende Verordnung nicht für Kulturgüter gelten, die im Zollgebiet der Union geschaffen oder entdeckt wurden. Die durch die vorliegende Verordnung eingeführten gemeinsamen Vorschriften sollten für die zollrechtliche Behandlung von Nicht-Unions-Kulturgütern, die in das Zollgebiet der Union verbracht werden, gelten. Für die Zwecke der vorliegenden Verordnung sollte das relevante Zollgebiet das Zollgebiet der Union zum Zeitpunkt der Einfuhr sein.

(6) Die einzuführenden Kontrollmaßnahmen, die Freizonen und sogenannte Freihäfen betreffen, sollten hinsichtlich der betroffenen Zollverfahren einen möglichst breiten Anwendungsbereich haben, damit eine Umgehung dieser Verordnung durch Ausnutzung dieser Freizonen, die für eine anhaltende Ausbreitung des illegalen Handels genutzt werden können, verhindert wird. Deshalb sollten diese Kontrollmaßnahmen nicht nur Kulturgüter betreffen, die zum zollrechtlich freien Verkehr überlassen werden, sondern auch Kulturgüter, die in ein besonderes Zollverfahren übergeführt werden. Allerdings sollte der Anwendungsbereich nicht über das Ziel, eine Verbringung unzulässig ausgeführter Kulturgüter in das Zollgebiet der Union zu verhindern, hinausgehen. Während die systematischen Kontrollmaßnahmen die Überlassung zum zollrechtlich freien Verkehr und einige der besonderen Zollverfahren, in die Güter beim Eingang in das Zollgebiet der Union übergeführt werden können, betreffen, sollte das Versandfahren ausgeschlossen sein.

(7) Viele Drittländer und die meisten Mitgliedstaaten sind mit den Begriffsbestimmungen vertraut, die in dem am 14. November 1970 in Paris unterzeichneten Unesco-Übereinkommen über die Maßnahmen zum Verbot und zur Verhütung der unzulässigen Einfuhr, Ausfuhr und Übereignung von Kulturgut (im Folgenden „Unesco-Übereinkommen von 1970") dessen Vertragspartei zahlreiche Mitgliedstaaten sind, und in dem am 24. Juni 1995 in Rom unterzeichneten UNIDROIT-Übereinkommen über gestohlene oder unrechtmäßig ausgeführte Kulturgüterverwendet werden. Aus diesem Grunde beruhen die in dieser Verordnung verwendeten Begriffsbestimmungen auf den dort verwendeten Begriffsbestimmungen.

(8) Die Rechtmäßigkeit der Ausfuhr von Kulturgütern sollte vor allem auf der Grundlage der Rechts- und Verwaltungsvorschriften der Länder geprüft werden, in denen diese Kulturgüter geschaffen oder entdeckt wurden. Um allerdings den legalen Handel nicht unangemessen zu beeinträchtigen, sollte einer Person, die die Kulturgüter in das Zollgebiet der Union einführen möchte, in bestimmten Fällen ausnahmsweise gestattet werden, stattdessen nachzuweisen, dass die Kulturgüter aus dem anderen Drittland, in dem sie sich vor ihrer Absendung in die Union befanden, rechtmäßig ausgeführt wurden. Diese Ausnahme sollte in Fällen gelten, in denen das Land, in denen die Kulturgüter geschaffen oder entdeckt wurden, nicht verlässlich bestimmt werden kann oder die Ausfuhr der betreffenden Kulturgüter vor dem Inkrafttreten des Unesco-Übereinkommens von 1970 am 24. April 1972 erfolgte. Um die Umgehung dieser Verordnung zu verhindern, indem unzulässig ausgeführte Kulturgüter vor ihrer Einfuhr in die Union einfach in ein anderes Drittland geschickt werden, sollten diese Ausnahmen gelten, wenn sich die Kulturgüter für einen Zeitraum von mehr als fünf Jahren zu anderen Zwecken als die vorübergehende Verwendung, Durchfuhr, Wiederausfuhr oder Umladung in einem Drittland befanden. Werden diese Bedingungen von

---

[1] Verordnung (EU) Nr. 952/2013 des Europäischen Parlaments und des Rates vom 9. Oktober 2013 zur Festlegung des Zollkodex der Union (ABl. L 269 vom 10.10.2013, S. 1).

[2] Verordnung (EG) Nr. 116/2009 des Rates vom 18. Dezember 2008 über die Ausfuhr von Kulturgütern (ABl. L 39 vom 10.2.2009, S. 1).

[3] Richtlinie 2014/60/EU des Europäischen Parlaments und des Rates vom 15. Mai 2014 über die Rückgabe von unrechtmäßig aus dem Hoheitsgebiet eines Mitgliedstaats verbrachten Kulturgütern und zur Änderung der Verordnung (EU) Nr. 1024/2012 (ABl. L 159 vom 28.5.2014, S. 1).

B.I.4 Verordnung (EU) 2019/880

mehr als einem Land erfüllt, sollte das letzte dieser Länder, in dem sich die Kulturgüter vor ihrem Verbringen in das Zollgebiet der Union befanden, relevant sein.

(9) Artikel 5 des Unesco-Übereinkommens von 1970 fordert die Vertragsstaaten auf, eine oder mehrere nationale Dienststellen einzurichten, um Kulturgüter vor unzulässiger Einfuhr, Ausfuhr und Übereignung zu schützen. Diese nationalen Dienststellen sollten mit qualifiziertem und zahlenmäßig ausreichendem Personal ausgestattet sein, um diesen Schutz gemäß dem Übereinkommen sicherzustellen und die erforderliche aktive Zusammenarbeit zwischen den zuständigen Behörden der Mitgliedstaaten, die Vertragsparteien dieses Übereinkommens sind, im Bereich der Sicherheit und der Bekämpfung der unzulässigen Einfuhr von Kulturgütern, insbesondere aus Ländern, die von bewaffneten Konflikten betroffen sind, zu ermöglichen.

(10) Um den grenzüberschreitenden Handel mit Kulturgütern über die Außengrenzen der Union nicht unverhältnismäßig zu beeinträchtigen, sollte diese Verordnung nur für Kulturgüter oberhalb einer bestimmten Altersgrenze gelten, die in dieser Verordnung festgelegt ist. Zudem erscheint es angebracht, einen Mindestwert festzulegen, um Kulturgüter von geringerem Wert von den Bedingungen und Verfahren für die Einfuhr von Kulturgütern in das Zollgebiet der Union auszuschließen. Durch diese Schwellenwerte wird sichergestellt, dass sich die in dieser Verordnung vorgesehenen Maßnahmen auf diejenigen Kulturgüter konzentrieren, auf die es Plünderer in Konfliktgebieten aller Wahrscheinlichkeit nach abgesehen haben dürften, ohne andere Güter auszuschließen, deren Kontrolle mit Blick auf den Schutz des kulturellen Erbes notwendig ist.

(11) Der illegale Handel mit geplünderten Kulturgütern wurde im Rahmen der supranationalen Bewertung der Risiken der Geldwäsche und der Terrorismusfinanzierung für den Binnenmarkt als mögliche Quelle für Terrorismusfinanzierung und Geldwäsche ermittelt.

(12) Da bestimmte Kategorien von Kulturgütern, namentlich archäologische Gegenstände und Teile von Denkmälern, für Plünderungen und Zerstörungen besonders anfällig sind, erscheint es notwendig, eine Regelung verstärkter Kontrollen vorzusehen, bevor die Güter in das Zollgebiet der Union verbracht werden dürfen. Eine solche Regelung sollte vorsehen, dass vor der Überlassung dieser Güter zum zollrechtlich freien Verkehr in die Union oder ihrer Überführung in ein besonderes Zollverfahren mit Ausnahme des Versandverfahrens eine von der zuständigen Behörde eines Mitgliedstaats erteilte Einfuhrgenehmigung vorzulegen ist. Personen, die eine solche Genehmigung beantragen, sollten die rechtmäßige Ausfuhr aus dem Land, in dem die Kulturgüter geschaffen oder entdeckt wurden, anhand geeigneter Unterlagen und Nachweise, wie etwa Ausfuhrbescheinigungen Eigentumsnachweise, Rechnungen, Kaufverträge, Versicherungsunterlagen, Beförderungspapiere und Sachverständigengutachten, belegen können. Die zuständigen Behörden der Mitgliedstaaten sollten auf der Grundlage von vollständigen und korrekten Anträgen unverzüglich über die Erteilung einer Lizenz entscheiden. Sämtliche Einfuhrgenehmigungen sollten in einer elektronischen Datenbank gespeichert werden.

(13) Eine „Ikone" ist eine Darstellung einer Persönlichkeit der Religion oder eines religiösen Ereignisses. Sie kann auf verschiedenen Trägermaterialien und in verschiedenen Größen angefertigt sein, entweder als Teil eines Denkmals oder in tragbarer Form. Wenn sie einst, entweder frei stehend oder als Teil der architektonischen Ausstattung, beispielsweise einer Ikonostase oder eines Ikonenständers, z. B. zum Innenraum einer Kirche, eines Klosters oder einer Kapelle gehörte, ist sie ein grundlegendes und untrennbares Element der göttlichen Verehrung und des liturgischen Lebens und sollte als fester Bestandteil eines religiösen Denkmals, das nicht mehr vollständig ist, betrachtet werden. Auch in Fällen, in denen das spezifische Denkmal, zu dem die Ikone gehörte, unbekannt ist, es jedoch Anhaltspunkte dafür gibt, dass sie einst fester Bestandteil eines Denkmals war, insbesondere wenn Spuren oder Elemente vorhanden sind, die darauf hinweisen, dass sie einst Teil einer Ikonostase oder eines Ikonenständers gewesen ist, sollte die Ikone auch weiterhin unter die Kategorie „Teile künstlerischer oder geschichtlicher Denkmäler oder archäologischer Stätten, die nicht mehr vollständig sind" im Anhang fallen.

(14) Angesichts des besonderen Charakters der Kulturgüter spielen die Zollbehörden eine äußerst wichtige Rolle und sie sollten erforderlichenfalls in der Lage sein, zusätzliche Informationen von den Anmeldern anzufordern und die Kulturgüter im Wege einer Beschau zu untersuchen.

(15) Bei Kategorien von Kulturgütern, für deren Einfuhr keine Einfuhrgenehmigung benötigt wird, sollten die Personen, die solche Güter in das Zollgebiet der Union einführen möchten, mittels

einer Erklärung deren rechtmäßige Ausfuhr aus dem Drittland bestätigen und die Verantwortung dafür übernehmen sowie mit Blick auf eine Identifizierung durch die Zollbehörden ausreichende Informationen über diese Kulturgüter bereitstellen. Zur Vereinfachung des Verfahrens und aus Gründen der Rechtssicherheit sollten die Informationen über die Kulturgüter mithilfe eines Standarddokuments bereitgestellt werden. Für die Beschreibung der Kulturgüter kann der von der Unesco empfohlene Objektidentifizierungsstandard verwendet werden. Der Besitzer der Güter sollte diese Einzelheiten in einem elektronischen System registrieren, um die Identifizierung durch die Zollbehörden zu erleichtern, Risikoanalysen und gezielte Kontrollen zu ermöglichen und die Rückverfolgbarkeit der Kulturgüter auf dem Binnenmarkt sicherzustellen.

(16) Im Rahmen des EU Single Window — Umfeld für den Zoll sollte die Kommission dafür zuständig sein, ein zentrales elektronisches System für die Einreichung von Anträgen auf Einfuhrgenehmigung und die Einreichung von Erklärungen der Einführer und für den Austausch von Informationen zwischen den Behörden der Mitgliedstaaten, insbesondere über Einfuhrgenehmigungen und Erklärungen der Einführer, einzurichten.

(17) Die Datenverarbeitung gemäß dieser Verordnung sollte auch die Verarbeitung personenbezogener Daten umfassen können, und diese Verarbeitung sollte im Einklang mit dem Unionsrecht erfolgen. Die Mitgliedstaaten und die Kommission sollten personenbezogene Daten nur für die Zwecke dieser Verordnung oder in wohlbegründeten Fällen für die Zwecke der Verhütung, Ermittlung, Aufdeckung oder Verfolgung von Straftaten oder der Strafvollstreckung, was den Schutz vor und die Abwehr von Gefahren für die öffentliche Sicherheit einschließt, verarbeiten. Für jede Sammlung, Weitergabe, Übertragung, Kommunikation und sonstige Verarbeitung personenbezogener Daten innerhalb des Anwendungsbereichs dieser Verordnung sollten die Anforderungen der Verordnungen (EU) 2016/679[1]) und (EU) 2018/1725[2]) des Europäischen Parlaments und des Rates gelten. Die Verarbeitung personenbezogener Daten für die Zwecke dieser Verordnung sollte auch im Einklang mit dem Recht auf Achtung des Privat- und Familienlebens gemäß Artikel 8 der Konvention zum Schutz der Menschenrechte und Grundfreiheiten des Europarats und dem Recht auf Achtung des Privat- und Familienlebens und dem Recht auf Schutz personenbezogener Daten gemäß Artikel 7 bzw. 8 der Charta der Grundrechte der Europäischen Union erfolgen.

(18) Für Kulturgüter, die nicht im Zollgebiet der Union geschaffen oder entdeckt, jedoch als Unionswaren ausgeführt wurden, sollte keine Einfuhrgenehmigung oder Erklärung des Einführers erforderlich sein, wenn sie in dieses Gebiet als Rückwaren im Sinne der Verordnung (EU) Nr. 952/2013 wieder eingeführt werden.

(19) Für die vorübergehende Verwendung von Kulturgütern zu Zwecken der Bildung, der Wissenschaft, der Konservierung, der Restaurierung, der Ausstellung, der Digitalisierung, der darstellenden Künste, der Forschung akademischer Einrichtungen oder der Zusammenarbeit zwischen Museen oder ähnlichen Einrichtungen sollte keine Einfuhrgenehmigung oder Erklärung des Einführers erforderlich sein.

(20) Die Lagerung von Kulturgütern aus Ländern, die von bewaffneten Konflikten oder Naturkatastrophen betroffen sind, mit dem ausschließlichen Ziel, ihre sichere Aufbewahrung und ihren Erhalt durch eine Behörde oder unter der Aufsicht einer Behörde zu gewährleisten, sollte nicht der Vorlage einer Einfuhrgenehmigung oder einer Erklärung des Einführers unterliegen.

(21) Um die Präsentation von Kulturgütern auf kommerziellen Kunstmessen zu erleichtern, sollte keine Einfuhrgenehmigung erforderlich sein, wenn sich die Kulturgüter in vorübergehender Verwendung im Sinne des Artikels 250 der Verordnung (EU) Nr. 952/2013 befinden und statt der Einfuhrgenehmigung eine Erklärung des Einführers vorgelegt wurde. Allerdings sollte eine die Vorlage einer Einfuhrgenehmigung erforderlich sein, wenn solche Kulturgüter im Anschluss an die Kunstmesse in der Union verbleiben sollen.

---

1) Verordnung (EU) 2016/679 des Europäischen Parlaments und des Rates vom 27. April 2016 zum Schutz natürlicher Personen bei der Verarbeitung personenbezogener Daten, zum freien Datenverkehr und zur Aufhebung der Richtlinie 95/46/EG (Datenschutz-Grundverordnung) (ABl. L 119 vom 4.5.2016, S. 1).

2) Verordnung (EU) 2018/1725 des Europäischen Parlaments und des Rates vom 23. Oktober 2018 zum Schutz natürlicher Personen bei der Verarbeitung personenbezogener Daten durch die Organe, Einrichtungen und sonstigen Stellen der Union, zum freien Datenverkehr und zur Aufhebung der Verordnung (EG) Nr. 45/2001 und des Beschlusses Nr. 1247/2002/EG (ABl. L 295 vom 21.11.2018, S. 39).

B.I.4 Verordnung (EU) 2019/880

(22) Um einheitliche Bedingungen für die Durchführung dieser Verordnung zu gewährleisten, sollten der Kommission Durchführungsbefugnisse für die Annahme detaillierter Regelungen übertragen werden, und zwar für als Rückwaren wieder eingeführte Kulturgüter, oder die vorübergehende Verwendung von Kulturgütern im Zollgebiet der Union und deren sichere Verwahrung, die Muster für Einfuhrgenehmigungsanträge und Einfuhrgenehmigungsformulare, die Muster der Erklärung des Einführers und die begleitenden Dokumente sowie weitere Verfahrensvorschriften für deren Vorlage und Bearbeitung. Außerdem sollten der Kommission Durchführungsbefugnisse übertragen werden, damit sie Vorkehrungen für die Einrichtung eines elektronischen Systems für die Einreichung von Anträgen auf Erteilung einer Einfuhrgenehmigung und die Abgabe der Erklärung des Einführers sowie für die Speicherung von Informationen und den Austausch von Informationen zwischen den Mitgliedstaaten treffen kann. Diese Befugnisse sollten im Einklang mit der Verordnung (EU) Nr. 182/2011 des Europäischen Parlaments und des Rates[1] ausgeübt werden.

(23) Um eine wirksame Koordinierung sicherzustellen und Doppelarbeit zu vermeiden, wenn Schulungen, Maßnahmen zum Kapazitätsaufbau und Sensibilisierungskampagnen organisiert werden, und um gegebenenfalls einschlägige Forschungsarbeiten und die Ausarbeitung von Normstandards in Auftrag zu geben, sollten die Kommission und die Mitgliedstaaten mit internationalen Organisationen und Einrichtungen zusammenarbeiten, etwa Unesco, Interpol, Europol, der Weltzollorganisation, der Internationalen Studienzentrale für die Erhaltung und Restaurierung von Kulturgut und dem Internationalen Museumsrat (ICOM).

(24) Es sollten sachdienliche Informationen über die Handelsströme von Kulturgütern auf elektronischem Wege zusammengetragen und zwischen den Mitgliedstaaten und der Kommission ausgetauscht werden, um die effiziente Durchführung dieser Verordnung zu unterstützen und die Grundlage für ihre künftige Bewertung zu schaffen. Im Interesse der Transparenz und der öffentlichen Kontrolle sollten möglichst viele Informationen veröffentlicht werden. Handelsströme von Kulturgütern können nicht allein anhand ihres Wertes oder Gewichts wirksam überwacht werden. Es ist von grundlegender Bedeutung, Informationen über die Anzahl der angemeldeten Gegenstände auf elektronischem Wege zusammenzutragen. Da in der Kombinierten Nomenklatur keine zusätzliche Maßeinheit für Kulturgüter aufgeführt ist, ist es notwendig zu verlangen, dass die Anzahl der Gegenstände angemeldet wird.

(25) Mit der Strategie und dem Aktionsplan der EU für das Zollrisikomanagement sollen — unter anderem — die Kapazitäten der Zollbehörden ausgebaut und die Reaktionsfähigkeit bei Risiken im Bereich Kulturgüter verbessert werden. Der in der Verordnung (EU) Nr. 952/2013 festgelegte gemeinsame Rahmen für das Risikomanagement sollte Anwendung finden und es sollten sachdienliche Informationen zwischen den Zollbehörden ausgetauscht werden.

(26) Um das Fachwissen der internationalen Organisationen und Einrichtungen, die im Kulturbereich tätig sind, und ihre Erfahrungen im Zusammenhang mit dem illegalen Handel mit Kulturgütern nutzbringend einzusetzen, sollten im gemeinsamen Rahmen für das Risikomanagement die Empfehlungen und Leitlinien dieser Organisationen und Einrichtungen berücksichtigt werden, wenn die mit Kulturgütern verbundenen Risiken ermittelt werden. Bei der Ermittlung der Drittländer, deren kulturelles Erbe am stärksten gefährdet ist, und der Gegenstände, die von dort häufiger im Rahmen des illegalen Handels ausgeführt werden, sollten insbesondere die von ICOM veröffentlichten Roten Listen als Leitlinien dienen.

(27) Es ist notwendig, Sensibilisierungskampagnen durchzuführen, die sich an die Käufer von Kulturgütern richten und die mit dem illegalen Handel verbundenen Risiken betreffen, und die Marktakteure bezüglich der Auslegung und der Anwendung dieser Verordnung zu unterstützen. Die Mitgliedstaaten sollten die einschlägigen nationalen Kontaktstellen und andere Informationsdienste bei der Verbreitung dieser Informationen einbeziehen.

(28) Die Kommission sollte dafür sorgen, dass Kleinstunternehmen sowie kleine und mittlere Unternehmen („KMU") von geeigneter technischer Unterstützung profitieren, und sie sollte die Bereitstellung von Information an diese erleichtern, damit diese Verordnung wirksam durchgeführt

---

[1] Verordnung (EU) Nr. 182/2011 des Europäischen Parlaments und des Rates vom 16. Februar 2011 zur Festlegung der allgemeinen Regeln und Grundsätze, nach denen die Mitgliedstaaten die Wahrnehmung der Durchführungsbefugnisse durch die Kommission kontrollieren (ABl. L 55 vom 28.2.2011, S. 13).

wird. In der Union niedergelassene KMU, die Kulturgüter einführen, sollten daher von den bestehenden und künftigen Unionsprogrammen zur Förderung der Wettbewerbsfähigkeit von kleineren und mittleren Unternehmen profitieren.
(29) Um die Einhaltung der Vorschriften zu fördern und vor deren Umgehung abzuschrecken, sollten die Mitgliedstaaten bei Nichtbeachtung der Bestimmungen dieser Verordnung wirksame, verhältnismäßige und abschreckende Sanktionen einführen und der Kommission diese Sanktionen mitteilen. Die von den Mitgliedstaaten gegen Verstöße gegen diese Verordnung eingeführten Sanktionen sollten in der gesamten Union eine vergleichbare abschreckende Wirkung entfalten.
(30) Die Mitgliedstaaten sollten sicherstellen, dass sich die Zollbehörden und die zuständigen Behörden auf Maßnahmen nach Artikel 198 der Verordnung (EU) Nr. 952/2013 einigen. Die Einzelheiten dieser Maßnahmen sollten dem nationalen Recht unterliegen.
(31) Die Kommission sollte unverzüglich Durchführungsbestimmungen zu dieser Verordnung annehmen, insbesondere in Bezug auf die geeigneten elektronischen Standardformulare, die zur Beantragung einer Einfuhrgenehmigung oder zur Vorbereitung einer Erklärung des Einführers zu verwenden sind, und anschließend das elektronische System in möglichst kurzer Zeit einrichten. Der Geltungsbeginn der Bestimmungen über die Einfuhrgenehmigung und die Erklärung des Einführers sollte entsprechend verschoben werden.
(32) Gemäß dem Grundsatz der Verhältnismäßigkeit ist es zur Erreichung der grundlegenden Ziele dieser Verordnung erforderlich und angemessen, Vorschriften über das Verbringen, sowie über die Voraussetzungen und das Verfahren für die Einfuhr, von Kulturgütern in das Zollgebiet der Union festzulegen. Die vorliegende Verordnung geht im Einklang mit Artikel 5 Absatz 4 des Vertrags über die Europäische Union nicht über das für die Verwirklichung dieser Ziele erforderliche Maß hinaus —

HABEN FOLGENDE VERORDNUNG ERLASSEN:

Artikel 1 Gegenstand und Anwendungsbereich
(1) Diese Verordnung enthält die Voraussetzungen für das Verbringen von Kulturgütern sowie die Voraussetzungen und Verfahren für ihre Einfuhr zum Schutze des kulturellen Erbes der Menschheit und der Verhinderung des illegalen Handels mit Kulturgütern, insbesondere wenn dieser illegale Handel zur Terrorismusfinanzierung beitragen kann.
(2) Diese Verordnung gilt nicht für Kulturgüter, die im Zollgebiet der Union geschaffen oder entdeckt wurden.

Artikel 2 Begriffsbestimmungen
Für die Zwecke dieser Verordnung bezeichnet der Ausdruck
1. „Kulturgüter" alle im Anhang aufgeführten Gegenstände, die für Archäologie, Vorgeschichte, Geschichte, Literatur, Kunst oder Wissenschaft von Bedeutung sind;
2. „Verbringen von Kulturgütern" den Eingang von Kulturgütern in das Zollgebiet der Union, die der zollamtlichen Überwachung oder Zollkontrollen im Zollgebiet der Union gemäß der Verordnung (EU) Nr. 952/2013 unterliegen;
3. „Einfuhr von Kulturgütern"
   a) die Überlassung von Kulturgütern zum zollrechtlich freien Verkehr gemäß Artikel 201 der Verordnung (EU) Nr. 952/2013 oder
   b) die Überführung von Kulturgütern in eines der folgenden besonderen Verfahren gemäß Artikel 210 der Verordnung (EU) Nr. 952/2013:
      i) die Lagerung, die das Zolllager und Freizonen umfasst,
      ii) die Verwendung, die die vorübergehende Verwendung und die Endverwendung umfasst,
      iii) die aktive Veredelung;
4. „Besitzer der Waren" den Besitzer der Waren gemäß Artikel 5 Nummer 34 der Verordnung (EU) Nr. 952/2013;
5. „zuständige Behörden" die von den Mitgliedstaaten benannten Behörden, die für die Erteilung der Einfuhrgenehmigungen zuständig sind.

Artikel 3 Verbringen und Einfuhr von Kulturgütern

(1) Das Verbringen von in Teil A des Anhangs genannten Kulturgütern ist verboten, wenn sie aus dem Hoheitsgebiet eines Landes, in dem sie geschaffen oder entdeckt worden sind, unter Verstoß gegen dessen Rechts- und Verwaltungsvorschriften entfernt wurden. Die Zollbehörden und die zuständigen Behörden ergreifen alle geeigneten Maßnahmen, wenn versucht wird, Kulturgüter gemäß Unterabsatz 1 zu verbringen.

(2) Die Einfuhr von in den Teilen B und C des Anhangs aufgeführten Kulturgütern ist nur zulässig nach Vorlage entweder

a) einer Einfuhrgenehmigung gemäß Artikel 4 oder
b) einer Erklärung des Einführers gemäß Artikel 5.

(3) Die in Absatz 2 des vorliegenden Artikels genannte Einfuhrgenehmigung oder Erklärung des Einführers ist den Zollbehörden gemäß Artikel 163 der Verordnung (EU) Nr. 952/2013 vorzulegen. Werden die Kulturgüter in das Freizonenverfahren übergeführt, so hat der Besitzer der Waren die Einfuhrgenehmigung oder die Erklärung des Einführers bei der Gestellung der Güter gemäß Artikel 245 Absatz 1 Buchstaben a und b der Verordnung (EU) Nr. 952/2013 vorzulegen.

(4) Absatz 2 des vorliegenden Artikels gilt nicht für

a) als Rückwaren wieder eingeführte Kulturgüter im Sinne des Artikels 203 der Verordnung (EU) Nr. 952/2013;
b) die Einfuhr von Kulturgütern zum alleinigen Zweck, ihre sichere Verwahrung durch eine Behörde oder unter der Aufsicht einer Behörde zu gewährleisten und in der Absicht, diese Kulturgüter zurückzugeben, sobald die Situation dies zulässt;
c) die vorübergehende Verwendung von Kulturgütern im Sinne des Artikels 250 der Verordnung (EU) Nr. 952/2013 im Zollgebiet der Union zum Zwecke der Bildung, der Wissenschaft, der Konservierung, der Restaurierung, der Ausstellung, der Digitalisierung, der darstellenden Künste, der Forschung akademischer Einrichtungen oder der Zusammenarbeit zwischen Museen oder ähnlichen Einrichtungen.

(5) Eine Einfuhrgenehmigung ist nicht erforderlich für Kulturgüter in vorübergehender Verwendung im Sinne des Artikels 250 der Verordnung (EU) Nr. 952/2013, wenn diese Kulturgüter auf kommerziellen Kunstmessen präsentiert werden sollen. In diesen Fällen ist die Erklärung des Einführers gemäß dem Verfahren des Artikels 5 der vorliegenden Verordnung vorzulegen. Werden diese Kulturgüter jedoch anschließend in ein anderes in Artikel 2 Absatz 3 der vorliegenden Verordnung genanntes Zollverfahren übergeführt, so ist eine gemäß Artikel 4 der vorliegenden Verordnung erteilte Einfuhrgenehmigung erforderlich.

(6) Die Kommission legt im Wege von Durchführungsrechtsakten die Einzelheiten für als Rückwaren wieder eingeführte Kulturgüter für die Einfuhr von Kulturgütern zum Zwecke ihrer sicheren Verwahrung und für die vorübergehende Verwendung von Kulturgütern gemäß den Absätzen 4 und 5 des vorliegenden Artikels fest. Diese Durchführungsrechtsakte werden gemäß dem in Artikel 13 Absatz 2 genannten Prüfverfahren erlassen.

(7) Absatz 2 des vorliegenden Artikels gilt unbeschadet anderer Maßnahmen, die die Union im Einklang mit Artikel 215 des Vertrags über die Arbeitsweise der Europäischen Union verabschiedet.

(8) Bei Vorlage einer Zollanmeldung für die Einfuhr von in den Teilen B und C des Anhangs aufgeführten Kulturgütern ist die Anzahl der Gegenstände unter Verwendung der im Anhang festgelegten besonderen Maßeinheiten anzugeben. Werden die Kulturgüter in das Freizonenverfahren übergeführt, so hat Besitzer der Waren die Anzahl der Gegenstände bei der Gestellung der Güter gemäß Artikel 245 Absatz 1 Buchstaben a und b der Verordnung (EU) Nr. 952/2013 anzugeben.

Artikel 4 Einfuhrgenehmigung

(1) Für die Einfuhr von in Teil B des Anhangs aufgeführten Kulturgütern, die keine Kulturgüter gemäß Artikel 3 Absätze 4 und 5 sind, ist eine Einfuhrgenehmigung erforderlich. Diese Einfuhrgenehmigung wird von der zuständigen Behörde des Mitgliedstaats erteilt, in dem die Kulturgüter zum ersten Mal in eines der in Artikel 2 Nummer 3 genannten Zollverfahren übergeführt werden.

(2) Einfuhrgenehmigungen, die von den zuständigen Behörden eines Mitgliedstaats gemäß dem vorliegenden Artikel erteilt werden, gelten in der gesamten Union.

(3) Eine gemäß diesem Artikel erteilte Einfuhrgenehmigung gilt nicht als Nachweis einer rechtmäßigen Herkunft der betreffenden Kulturgüter oder eines rechtmäßigen Eigentums an diesen.
(4) Der Besitzer der Waren beantragt bei der zuständigen Behörde des Mitgliedstaats gemäß Absatz 1 des vorliegenden Artikels eine Einfuhrgenehmigung über das elektronische System gemäß Artikel 8. Dem Antrag sind alle Unterlagen und Informationen beizufügen, die belegen, dass die jeweiligen Kulturgüter aus dem Land, in dem sie geschaffen oder entdeckt worden waren, im Einklang mit den Rechts- und Verwaltungsvorschriften dieses Landes ausgeführt wurden oder dass es zu dem Zeitpunkt, zu dem sie aus seinem Hoheitsgebiet verbracht wurden, solche Rechts- und Verwaltungsvorschriften nicht gab.
Abweichend von Unterabsatz 1 können in folgenden Fällen dem Antrag stattdessen Unterlagen und Informationen beigefügt werden, die belegen, dass die Kulturgüter im Einklang mit den Rechts- und Verwaltungsvorschriften des letzten Landes ausgeführt wurden, in dem sie sich für einen Zeitraum von mehr als fünf Jahren und für andere Zwecke als vorübergehende Verwendung, Durchfuhr, Wiederausfuhr oder Umladung befanden:
a) Das Land, in dem die Kulturgüter geschaffen oder entdeckt wurden, kann nicht verlässlich bestimmt werden, oder
b) die Kulturgüter wurden aus dem Land, in dem sie geschaffen oder entdeckt wurden, vor dem 24. April 1972 entfernt.
(5) Der Nachweis, dass die betreffenden Kulturgüter im Einklang mit Absatz 4 ausgeführt wurden, ist in Form von Ausfuhrbescheinigungen oder Ausfuhrgenehmigungen zu erbringen, sofern im betreffenden Land solche Dokumente für die Ausfuhr von Kulturgütern zum Zeitpunkt der Ausfuhr vorgesehen sind.
(6) Die zuständige Behörde prüft die Vollständigkeit des Antrags. Sie fordert den Antragsteller auf, alle fehlenden oder zusätzlichen Informationen oder Unterlagen innerhalb von 21 Tagen nach Eingang des Antrags vorzulegen.
(7) Innerhalb von 90 Tagen nach Eingang des vollständigen Antrags prüft die zuständige diesen und entscheidet über die Erteilung der Einfuhrgenehmigung oder über die Ablehnung des Antrags.
Die zuständige Behörde lehnt den Antrag ab, wenn
a) sie Informationen oder hinreichende Gründe für die Annahme hat, dass die Kulturgüter unter Verstoß gegen die Rechts- und Verwaltungsvorschriften des Landes, auf dessen Hoheitsgebiet sie geschaffen oder entdeckt wurden, von dort entfernt wurden;
b) die gemäß Absatz 4 erforderlichen Nachweise nicht vorgelegt wurden;
c) sie Informationen oder hinreichende Gründe für die Annahme hat, dass der Besitzer der Waren diese nicht rechtmäßig erworben hat, oder
d) sie darüber unterrichtet wurde, dass für diese Kulturgüter anhängige Rückgabeforderungen seitens der Behörden des Landes bestehen, in sie geschaffen oder entdeckt wurden.
(8) Bei Ablehnung des Antrags wird die Verwaltungsentscheidung gemäß Absatz 7 mit einer Begründung und mit Informationen über Rechtsbehelfe versehen und dem betreffenden Antragsteller unverzüglich übermittelt.
(9) Wird eine Einfuhrgenehmigung für Kulturgüter beantragt, für die ein gleichartiger Antrag bereits früher abgelehnt worden ist, so hat der Antragsteller die mit dem Antrag befasste zuständige Behörde über die frühere Ablehnung zu unterrichten.
(10) Lehnt ein Mitgliedstaat einen Antrag ab, so werden diese Ablehnung und die Gründe, auf denen sie beruht, den anderen Mitgliedstaaten und der Kommission über das elektronische System gemäß Artikel 8 mitgeteilt.
(11) Die Mitgliedstaaten bestimmt unverzüglich die zuständigen Behörden, die für die Erteilung von Einfuhrgenehmigungen gemäß diesem Artikel zuständig sind. Die Mitgliedstaaten unterrichten die Kommission über die Einzelheiten zu den zuständigen Behörden und alle diesbezüglichen Änderungen.
Die Kommission veröffentlicht die Einzelheiten zu den zuständigen Behörden sowie alle Änderungen im *Amtsblatt der Europäischen Union* Reihe C.
(12) Die Kommission legt im Wege von Durchführungsrechtsakten das Muster und das Format für den Antrag auf die Einfuhrgenehmigung fest und gibt die möglichen Unterlagen für den Nachweis der rechtmäßigen Herkunft der betreffenden Kulturgüter und die Verfahrensvorschriften für die Einrei-

chung und die Bearbeitung eines solchen Antrags an. Bei der Festlegung dieser Elemente strebt die Kommission eine einheitliche Anwendung der Einfuhrgenehmigungsverfahren durch die zuständigen Behörden an. Diese Durchführungsrechtsakte werden gemäß dem in Artikel 13 Absatz 2 genannten Prüfverfahren erlassen.

Artikel 5 Erklärung des Einführers
(1) Für die Einfuhr der in Teil C des Anhangs aufgeführten Kulturgüter ist eine Erklärung des Einführers erforderlich, die der Besitzer der Waren über das elektronische System gemäß Artikel 8 vorlegt.

(2) Die Erklärung des Einführers besteht aus
a) einer vom Besitzer der Waren unterzeichneten Erklärung, aus der hervorgeht, dass die Kulturgüter aus dem Land, in dem sie geschaffen oder entdeckt wurden im Einklang mit dessen zum Zeitpunkt der Entfernung aus dem Hoheitsgebiet geltenden Rechts- und Verwaltungsvorschriften ausgeführt wurden, und
b) einem Standarddokument, in dem die betreffenden Kulturgüter so detailliert beschrieben sind, dass sie von den Behörden identifiziert und Risikoanalysen und gezielte Kontrollen durchgeführt werden können.

Abweichend von Unterabsatz 1 Buchstabe a kann in folgenden Fällen die Erklärung stattdessen beinhalten, dass die Kulturgüter im Einklang mit den Rechts- und Verwaltungsvorschriften des letzten Landes ausgeführt wurden, in dem sie sich für einen Zeitraum von mehr als fünf Jahren und für andere Zwecke als vorübergehende Verwendung, Durchfuhr, Wiederausfuhr oder Umladung befanden:
a) Das Land, in dem die Kulturgüter geschaffen oder entdeckt wurden, kann nicht verlässlich bestimmt werden, oder
b) die Kulturgüter wurden aus dem Land, in dem sie geschaffen oder entdeckt wurden, vor dem 24. April 1972 entfernt.

(3) Die Kommission legt im Wege von Durchführungsrechtsakten das Standardmuster und das Format für die Erklärung des Einführers sowie die Verfahrensvorschriften für ihre Vorlage fest und gibt die möglichen Unterlagen für den Nachweis der rechtmäßigen Herkunft der betreffenden Kulturgüter an, die sich im Besitz des Besitzers der Waren befinden sollten, sowie die Vorschriften über die Bearbeitung der Erklärung des Einführers. Diese Durchführungsrechtsakte werden gemäß dem in Artikel 13 Absatz 2 genannten Prüfverfahren erlassen.

Artikel 6 Zuständige Zollstellen
Die Mitgliedstaaten können die Anzahl der Zollstellen, die für die Bearbeitung der Einfuhr von unter diese Verordnung fallende Kulturgüter zuständig sind, begrenzen. Wenden die Mitgliedstaaten diese Begrenzung an, so teilen sie der Kommission die Einzelheiten zu diesen Zollstellen sowie alle diesbezüglichen Änderungen mit.

Die Kommission veröffentlicht die Einzelheiten zu den zuständigen Zollstellen sowie alle Änderungen im *Amtsblatt der Europäischen Union* Reihe C.

Artikel 7 Verwaltungszusammenarbeit
Zur Durchführung dieser Verordnung gewährleisten die Mitgliedstaaten die Zusammenarbeit zwischen ihren Zollbehörden und mit den zuständigen Behörden gemäß Artikel 4.

Artikel 8 Verwendung eines elektronischen Systems
(1) Die Speicherung und der Austausch von Informationen zwischen den Behörden der Mitgliedstaaten, insbesondere zu Einfuhrgenehmigungen und zu Erklärungen des Einführers, erfolgt mithilfe eines zentralen elektronischen Systems.

Fällt das elektronische System vorübergehend aus, so können vorübergehend andere Mittel für die Speicherung und den Austausch von Informationen genutzt werden.

(2) Die Kommission legt im Wege von Durchführungsrechtsakten Folgendes fest:
a) die Maßnahmen bezüglich Einführung, Anwendung und Pflege des elektronischen Systems gemäß Absatz 1;
b) die Einzelheiten für die Bereitstellung, Verarbeitung, Speicherung und den Austausch von Informationen zwischen den Behörden der Mitgliedstaaten mithilfe des elektronischen Systems oder anderer Mittel gemäß Absatz 1.

Diese Durchführungsrechtsakte werden bis zum 28. Juni 2021 gemäß dem in Artikel 13 Absatz 2 genannten Prüfverfahren erlassen.

Artikel 9 Einrichtung eines elektronischen Systems
Die Kommission richtet das in Artikel 8 genannte elektronische System ein. Das elektronische System ist spätestens vier Jahre nach Inkrafttreten des ersten der Durchführungsrechtsakte gemäß Artikel 8 Absatz 2 einsatzbereit.

Artikel 10 Schutz personenbezogener Daten und Datenspeicherfristen
(1) Die Zollbehörden und die zuständigen Behörden der Mitgliedstaaten sind die Verantwortlichen für die personenbezogenen Daten, die sie gemäß den Artikeln 4, 5 und 8 erhalten haben.
(2) Die Verarbeitung personenbezogener Daten auf der Grundlage dieser Verordnung darf nur für die in Artikel 1 Absatz 1 bestimmten Zwecke erfolgen.
(3) Die gemäß den Artikeln 4, 5 und 8 erhaltenen personenbezogenen Daten dürfen nur von ordnungsgemäß bevollmächtigten Mitarbeitern der Behörden abgerufen werden und müssen angemessen gegen unbefugten Zugriff und unbefugte Weitergabe geschützt werden. Die Daten dürfen nicht ohne ausdrückliche schriftliche Genehmigung der Behörde, die die Informationen ursprünglich erhalten hat, offengelegt oder weitergegeben werden. Diese Genehmigung ist jedoch nicht erforderlich, wenn die Behörden gehalten sind, diese Informationen nach in dem betreffenden Mitgliedstaat geltenden Rechtsvorschriften, insbesondere im Zusammenhang mit Gerichtsverfahren, offenzulegen oder weiterzugeben.
(4) Die Behörden speichern personenbezogene Daten, die sie gemäß den Artikeln 4, 5 und 8 erhalten haben, für einen Zeitraum von 20 Jahren ab dem Zeitpunkt des Erhalts der Daten. Am Ende dieses Zeitraums werden diese personenbezogenen Daten gelöscht.

Artikel 11 Sanktionen
Die Mitgliedstaaten legen die Vorschriften für Sanktionen fest, die bei Verstößen gegen diese Verordnung Anwendung finden und sie ergreifen alle erforderlichen Maßnahmen, um sicherzustellen, dass sie umgesetzt werden. Die vorgesehenen Sanktionen müssen wirksam, verhältnismäßig und abschreckend sein.
Bis zum 28. Dezember 2020 setzen die Mitgliedstaaten die Kommission über die Vorschriften für Sanktionen und die damit zusammenhängenden Maßnahmen in Kenntnis, die auf ein nach Artikel 3 Absatz 1 verbotswidriges Verbringen von Kulturgütern anwendbar sind,
Bis zum 28. Juni 2025 setzen die Mitgliedstaaten die Kommission über die Vorschriften für Sanktionen und die damit zusammenhängenden Maßnahmen im Falle anderer Verstöße gegen diese Verordnung, insbesondere im Falle falscher Erklärungen oder der Vorlage falscher Informationen, sowie über die entsprechenden Maßnahmen, in Kenntnis,
Die Mitgliedstaaten teilen der Kommission unverzüglich alle nachfolgenden Änderungen dieser Vorschriften mit.

Artikel 12 Zusammenarbeit mit Drittländern
Die Kommission kann für in ihren Tätigkeitsbereich fallende Angelegenheiten, und soweit dies für die Erfüllung ihrer Aufgaben im Rahmen dieser Verordnung erforderlich ist, in Zusammenarbeit mit den Mitgliedstaaten Schulungen und Maßnahmen zum Kapazitätsaufbau für Drittländer organisieren.

Artikel 13 Ausschussverfahren
(1) Die Kommission wird von dem mit Artikel 8 der Verordnung (EG) Nr. 116/2009 des Rates eingesetzten Ausschuss unterstützt. Dabei handelt es sich um einen Ausschuss im Sinne der Verordnung (EU) Nr. 182/2011.
(2) Wird auf diesen Absatz Bezug genommen, so gilt Artikel 5 der Verordnung (EU) Nr. 182/2011.

Artikel 14 Berichterstattung und Bewertung
(1) Die Mitgliedstaaten stellen der Kommission Informationen über die Umsetzung dieser Verordnung zur Verfügung.
Die Kommission übermittelt den Mitgliedstaaten zu diesem Zweck entsprechende Fragebogen. Die Mitgliedstaaten haben nach Eingang des Fragebogens sechs Monate Zeit, um der Kommission die angeforderten Informationen zu übermitteln.
(2) Innerhalb von drei Jahren nach dem Tag, an dem diese Verordnung in Ihrer Gesamtheit anwendbar wird, und danach alle fünf Jahre legt die Kommission dem Europäischen Parlament und dem Rat einen Bericht über die Durchführung dieser Verordnung vor. Dieser Bericht ist öffentlich zugänglich und

enthält einschlägige statistische Informationen sowohl auf Unionsebene als auch auf nationaler Ebene wie etwa die Anzahl der erteilten Einfuhrgenehmigungen, der abgelehnten Anträge und der vorgelegten Erklärungen der Einführer. Er enthält eine Prüfung der praktischen Durchführung, einschließlich der Auswirkungen auf die Wirtschaftsbeteiligten der Union, insbesondere KMU.

(3) Bis zum 28. Juni 2020 und danach alle zwölf Monate, bis das elektronische System gemäß Artikel 9 eingerichtet worden ist, legt die Kommission dem Europäischen Parlament und dem Rat einen Bericht über die Fortschritte bei der Annahme der Durchführungsrechtsakte gemäß Artikel 8 Absatz 2 und bei der Einrichtung des elektronischen Systems gemäß Artikel 9 vor.

Artikel 15 Inkrafttreten
Diese Verordnung tritt am zwanzigsten Tag nach ihrer Veröffentlichung im *Amtsblatt der Europäischen Union* in Kraft.

Artikel 16 Geltung
(1) Diese Verordnung gilt ab dem Tag ihres Inkrafttretens.
(2) Ungeachtet des Absatzes 1
a) gilt Artikel 3 Absatz 1 ab dem 28. Dezember 2020;
b) gelten Artikel 3 Absätze 2 bis 5, Absatz 7 und 8, Artikel 4 Absätze 1 bis 10, Artikel 5 Absätze 1 und 2 und Artikel 8 Absatz 1 ab dem Tag, an dem das elektronische System gemäß Artikel 8 einsatzbereit ist, oder spätestens ab dem 28. Juni 2025. Die Kommission veröffentlicht das Datum, an dem die Bedingungen dieses Absatzes erfüllt sind, im *Amtsblatt der Europäischen Union* Reihe C.

Diese Verordnung ist in allen ihren Teilen verbindlich und gilt unmittelbar in jedem Mitgliedstaat.
Geschehen zu Straßburg 17. April 2019 am.

Im Namen des Europäischen Parlaments *Im Namen des Rates*
Der Präsident *Der Präsident*
A. TAJANI **G. CIAMBA**

Teil A. Kulturgüter gemäß Artikel 3 Absatz 1
a) Seltene Sammlungen und Exemplare der Zoologie, Botanik, Mineralogie und Anatomie sowie Gegenstände von paläontologischem Interesse;
b) Gut, das sich auf die Geschichte einschließlich der Geschichte von Wissenschaft und Technik sowie der Militär- und Sozialgeschichte, das Leben nationaler Anführer, Denker, Wissenschaftler und Künstler und Ereignisse von nationaler Bedeutung bezieht;
c) Ergebnisse archäologischer Ausgrabungen (sowohl vorschriftsmäßiger als auch unerlaubter) oder archäologischer Entdeckungen zu Lande oder unter Wasser;
d) Teile künstlerischer oder geschichtlicher Denkmäler oder archäologischer Stätten, die nicht mehr vollständig sind[1)];
e) Antiquitäten, die mehr als hundert Jahre alt sind, wie Inschriften, Münzen und gravierte Siegel;
f) Gegenstände von ethnologischem Interesse;
g) Gegenstände von künstlerischem Interesse wie:
    i) Bilder, Gemälde und Zeichnungen, die ausschließlich von Hand auf einem beliebigen Träger und aus einem beliebigen Material angefertigt sind (ausgenommen industrielle Entwürfe und handbemalte Manufakturwaren);
    ii) Originalwerke der Bildhauerkunst und der Skulptur aus einem beliebigen Material;
    iii) Originalgravuren, -drucke und -lithographien;
    iv) Originale von künstlerischen Assemblagen und Montagen aus einem beliebigen Material;
h) seltene Manuskripte und Inkunabeln;
i) alte Bücher, Dokumente und Publikationen von besonderem Interesse (historisch, künstlerisch, wissenschaftlich, literarisch usw.), einzeln oder in Sammlungen;
j) Briefmarken, Steuermarken und Ähnliches, einzeln oder in Sammlungen;
k) Archive einschließlich Phono-, Foto- und Filmarchive;
l) Möbelstücke, die mehr als hundert Jahre alt sind, und alte Musikinstrument

---

1) Liturgische Ikonen und Statuen, selbst wenn sie freistehend sind, sind als Kulturgüter zu betrachten, die unter diese Kategorie fallen.

Verordnung (EU) 2019/880 B.I.4

Teil B. Kulturgüter gemäß Artikel 4

Kategorien von Kulturgütern gemäß Teil A	Kombinierte Nomenklatur (KN), Kapitel, Position oder Unterposition	Mindestalter	Mindestwert (Zollwert)	Besondere Maßeinheiten
c) Ergebnisse archäologischer Ausgrabungen (sowohl vorschriftsmäßiger als auch unerlaubter), oder archäologischer Entdeckungen zu Lande oder unter Wasser;	ex 9705; ex 9706	über 250 Jahre alt	wertunabhängig	Anzahl Stück (p/st)
d) Teile künstlerischer oder geschichtlicher Denkmäler oder archäologischer Stätten, die nicht mehr vollständig sind[1)];	ex 9705; ex 9706	über 250 Jahre alt	wertunabhängig	Anzahl Stück (p/st)

Teil C. Kulturgüter gemäß Artikel 5

Kategorien von Kulturgütern gemäß Teil A	Kombinierte Nomenklatur (KN), Kapitel, Position oder Unterposition	Mindestalter	Mindestwert (Zollwert)	Besondere Maßeinheiten
a) Seltene Sammlungen und Exemplare der Zoologie, Botanik, Mineralogie und Anatomie sowie Gegenstände von paläontologischem Interesse;	ex 9705	über 200 Jahre alt	18 000 EUR pro Stück oder mehr	Anzahl Stück (p/st)
b) Gut, das sich auf die Geschichte einschließlich der Geschichte von Wissenschaft und Technik sowie der Militär- und Sozialgeschichte, das Leben nationaler Anführer, Denker, Wissenschaftler und Künstler und Ereignisse von nationaler Bedeutung bezieht;	ex 9705	über 200 Jahre alt	18 000 EUR pro Stück oder mehr	Anzahl Stück (p/st)
e) Antiquitäten wie Inschriften, Münzen und gravierte Siegel;	ex 9706	über 200 Jahre alt	18 000 EUR pro Stück oder mehr	Anzahl Stück (p/st)
f) Gegenstände von ethnologischem Interesse;	ex 9705	über 200 Jahre alt	18 000 EUR pro Stück oder mehr	Anzahl Stück (p/st)
g) Gegenstände von künstlerischem Interesse wie:				
i) Bilder, Gemälde und Zeichnungen, die ausschließlich von Hand auf einem beliebigen Träger und aus einem beliebigen Material angefertigt sind (ausgenommen industrielle Entwürfe und handbemalte Manufakturwaren);	ex 9701	über 200 Jahre alt	18 000 EUR pro Stück oder mehr	Anzahl Stück (p/st)
ii) Originalwerke der Bildhauerkunst und der Skulptur aus einem beliebigen Material;	ex 9703	über 200 Jahre alt	18 000 EUR pro Stück oder mehr	Anzahl Stück (p/st)

---

1) Liturgische Ikonen und Statuen, selbst wenn sie frei stehend sind, sind als Kulturgüter zu betrachten, die unter diese Kategorie fallen.

B.I.4 Verordnung (EU) 2019/880

Kategorien von Kulturgütern gemäß Teil A	Kombinierte Nomenklatur (KN), Kapitel, Position oder Unterposition	Mindestalter	Mindestwert (Zollwert)	Besondere Maßeinheiten
iii) Originalgravuren, -drucke und -lithographien;	ex 9702;	über 200 Jahre alt	18 000 EUR pro Stück oder mehr	Anzahl Stück (p/st)
iv) Originale von künstlerischen Assemblagen und Montagen aus einem beliebigen Material;	ex 9701	über 200 Jahre alt	18 000 EUR pro Stück oder mehr	Anzahl Stück (p/st)
h) seltene Manuskripte und Inkunabeln	ex 9702; ex 9706	über 200 Jahre alt	18 000 EUR pro Stück oder mehr	Anzahl Stück (p/st)
i) alte Bücher, Dokumente und Publikationen von besonderem Interesse (historisch, künstlerisch, wissenschaftlich, literarisch usw.), einzeln oder in Sammlungen;	ex 9705; ex 9706	über 200 Jahre alt	18 000 EUR pro Stück oder mehr	Anzahl Stück (p/st)

Vertrag über die Arbeitsweise der Europäischen Union (Auszüge)

In der Fassung der Bekanntmachung vom 9.5.2008

ABl. Nr. C 115/47, ABl. 2010 Nr. C 83/47, ABl. 2012 Nr. C 326/47, ABl. 2016 Nr. C 202/47, ber. ABl. Nr. C 400/1; amtliche deutsche Fundstelle: BGBl. 2008 II S. 1038, ber. durch BGBl. 2010 II S. 151; zuletzt geändert durch BGBl. 2013 II S. 586.

– Auszug –

Dritter Teil
Die internen Politiken und Maßnahmen der Union

Titel II
Der freie Warenverkehr

Kapitel 3
Verbot von mengenmäßigen Beschränkungen zwischen den Mitgliedstaaten

Artikel 34 (ex-Artikel 28 EGV)
Mengenmäßige Einfuhrbeschränkungen sowie alle Maßnahmen gleicher Wirkung sind zwischen den Mitgliedstaaten verboten.

Artikel 35 (ex-Artikel 29 EGV)
Mengenmäßige Ausfuhrbeschränkungen sowie alle Maßnahmen gleicher Wirkung sind zwischen den Mitgliedstaaten verboten.

Artikel 36 (ex-Artikel 30 EGV)
Die Bestimmungen der Artikel 34 und 35 stehen Einfuhr-, Ausfuhr- und Durchfuhrverboten oder -beschränkungen nicht entgegen, die aus Gründen der öffentlichen Sittlichkeit, Ordnung und Sicherheit, zum Schutze der Gesundheit und des Lebens von Menschen, Tieren oder Pflanzen, des nationalen Kulturguts von künstlerischem, geschichtlichem oder archäologischem Wert oder des gewerblichen und kommerziellen Eigentums gerechtfertigt sind.[1)] Diese Verbote oder Beschränkungen dürfen jedoch weder ein Mittel zur willkürlichen Diskriminierung noch eine verschleierte Beschränkung des Handels zwischen den Mitgliedstaaten darstellen.

Titel VII
Gemeinsame Regeln betreffend Wettbewerb, Steuerfragen und Angleichung der Rechtsvorschriften

Kapitel 3
Angleichung der Rechtsvorschriften

Artikel 114 (ex-Artikel 95 EGV)
(1) Soweit in den Verträgen nichts anderes bestimmt ist, gilt für die Verwirklichung der Ziele des Artikels 26 die nachstehende Regelung. Das Europäische Parlament und der Rat erlassen gemäß dem ordentlichen Gesetzgebungsverfahren und nach Anhörung des Wirtschafts- und Sozialausschusses die Maßnahmen zur Angleichung der Rechts- und Verwaltungsvorschriften der Mitgliedstaaten, welche die Errichtung und das Funktionieren des Binnenmarkts zum Gegenstand haben.
(2) Absatz 1 gilt nicht für die Bestimmungen über die Steuern, die Bestimmungen über die Freizügigkeit und die Bestimmungen über die Rechte und Interessen der Arbeitnehmer.
(3) Die Kommission geht in ihren Vorschlägen nach Absatz 1 in den Bereichen Gesundheit, Sicherheit, Umweltschutz und Verbraucherschutz von einem hohen Schutzniveau aus und berücksichtigt dabei insbesondere alle auf wissenschaftliche Ergebnisse gestützten neuen Entwicklungen. Im Rahmen ihrer jeweiligen Befugnisse streben das Europäische Parlament und der Rat dieses Ziel ebenfalls an.

---

1) Siehe dazu auch Art. 10 Verordnung (EU) 2015/479 des Europäischen Parlaments und des Rates vom 11. März 2015 über eine gemeinsame Ausfuhrregelung und Art. 24 Abs. 2 lit. a Verordnung (EU) 2015/478 des Europäischen Parlaments und des Rates vom 11. März 2015 über eine gemeinsame Einfuhrregelung.

(4) Hält es ein Mitgliedstaat nach dem Erlass einer Harmonisierungsmaßnahme durch das Europäische Parlament und den Rat beziehungsweise durch den Rat oder die Kommission für erforderlich, einzelstaatliche Bestimmungen beizubehalten, die durch wichtige Erfordernisse im Sinne des Artikels 36 oder in Bezug auf den Schutz der Arbeitsumwelt oder den Umweltschutz gerechtfertigt sind, so teilt er diese Bestimmungen sowie die Gründe für ihre Beibehaltung der Kommission mit.

(5) Unbeschadet des Absatzes 4 teilt ferner ein Mitgliedstaat, der es nach dem Erlass einer Harmonisierungsmaßnahme durch das Europäische Parlament und den Rat beziehungsweise durch den Rat oder die Kommission für erforderlich hält, auf neue wissenschaftliche Erkenntnisse gestützte einzelstaatliche Bestimmungen zum Schutz der Umwelt oder der Arbeitsumwelt aufgrund eines spezifischen Problems für diesen Mitgliedstaat, das sich nach dem Erlass der Harmonisierungsmaßnahme ergibt, einzuführen, die in Aussicht genommenen Bestimmungen sowie die Gründe für ihre Einführung der Kommission mit.

(6) Die Kommission beschließt binnen sechs Monaten nach den Mitteilungen nach den Absätzen 4 und 5, die betreffenden einzelstaatlichen Bestimmungen zu billigen oder abzulehnen, nachdem sie geprüft hat, ob sie ein Mittel zur willkürlichen Diskriminierung und eine verschleierte Beschränkung des Handels zwischen den Mitgliedstaaten darstellen und ob sie das Funktionieren des Binnenmarkts behindern.

Erlässt die Kommission innerhalb dieses Zeitraums keinen Beschluss, so gelten die in den Absätzen 4 und 5 genannten einzelstaatlichen Bestimmungen als gebilligt.

Die Kommission kann, sofern dies aufgrund des schwierigen Sachverhalts gerechtfertigt ist und keine Gefahr für die menschliche Gesundheit besteht, dem betreffenden Mitgliedstaat mitteilen, dass der in diesem Absatz genannte Zeitraum gegebenenfalls um einen weiteren Zeitraum von bis zu sechs Monaten verlängert wird.

(7) Wird es einem Mitgliedstaat nach Absatz 6 gestattet, von der Harmonisierungsmaßnahme abweichende einzelstaatliche Bestimmungen beizubehalten oder einzuführen, so prüft die Kommission unverzüglich, ob sie eine Anpassung dieser Maßnahme vorschlägt.

(8) Wirft ein Mitgliedstaat in einem Bereich, der zuvor bereits Gegenstand von Harmonisierungsmaßnahmen war, ein spezielles Gesundheitsproblem auf, so teilt er dies der Kommission mit, die dann umgehend prüft, ob sie dem Rat entsprechende Maßnahmen vorschlägt.

(9) In Abweichung von dem Verfahren der Artikel 258 und 259 kann die Kommission oder ein Mitgliedstaat den Gerichtshof der Europäischen Union unmittelbar anrufen, wenn die Kommission oder der Staat der Auffassung ist, dass ein anderer Mitgliedstaat die in diesem Artikel vorgesehenen Befugnisse missbraucht.

(10) Die vorgenannten Harmonisierungsmaßnahmen sind in geeigneten Fällen mit einer Schutzklausel verbunden, welche die Mitgliedstaaten ermächtigt, aus einem oder mehreren der in Artikel 36 genannten nicht wirtschaftlichen Gründe vorläufige Maßnahmen zu treffen, die einem Kontrollverfahren der Union unterliegen.

Fünfter Teil
Das auswärtige Handeln der Union

Titel II
Gemeinsame Handelspolitik

Artikel 207 (ex-Artikel 133 EGV)

(1) Die gemeinsame Handelspolitik wird nach einheitlichen Grundsätzen gestaltet; dies gilt insbesondere für die Änderung von Zollsätzen, für den Abschluss von Zoll- und Handelsabkommen, die den Handel mit Waren und Dienstleistungen betreffen, und für die Handelsaspekte des geistigen Eigentums, die ausländischen Direktinvestitionen, die Vereinheitlichung der Liberalisierungsmaßnahmen, die Ausfuhrpolitik sowie die handelspolitischen Schutzmaßnahmen, zum Beispiel im Fall von Dumping und Subventionen. Die gemeinsame Handelspolitik wird im Rahmen der Grundsätze und Ziele des auswärtigen Handelns der Union gestaltet.

(2) Das Europäische Parlament und der Rat erlassen durch Verordnungen gemäß dem ordentlichen Gesetzgebungsverfahren die Maßnahmen, mit denen der Rahmen für die Umsetzung der gemeinsamen Handelspolitik bestimmt wird.[1)]

(3) Sind mit einem oder mehreren Drittländern oder internationalen Organisationen Abkommen auszuhandeln und zu schließen, so findet Artikel 218 vorbehaltlich der besonderen Bestimmungen dieses Artikels Anwendung.

Die Kommission legt dem Rat Empfehlungen vor; dieser ermächtigt die Kommission zur Aufnahme der erforderlichen Verhandlungen. Der Rat und die Kommission haben dafür Sorge zu tragen, dass die ausgehandelten Abkommen mit der internen Politik und den internen Vorschriften der Union vereinbar sind.

Die Kommission führt diese Verhandlungen im Benehmen mit einem zu ihrer Unterstützung vom Rat bestellten Sonderausschuss und nach Maßgabe der Richtlinien, die ihr der Rat erteilen kann. Die Kommission erstattet dem Sonderausschuss sowie dem Europäischen Parlament regelmäßig Bericht über den Stand der Verhandlungen.

(4) Über die Aushandlung und den Abschluss der in Absatz 3 genannten Abkommen beschließt der Rat mit qualifizierter Mehrheit.

Über die Aushandlung und den Abschluss eines Abkommens über den Dienstleistungsverkehr, über Handelsaspekte des geistigen Eigentums oder über ausländische Direktinvestitionen beschließt der Rat einstimmig, wenn das betreffende Abkommen Bestimmungen enthält, bei denen für die Annahme interner Vorschriften Einstimmigkeit erforderlich ist.

Der Rat beschließt ebenfalls einstimmig über die Aushandlung und den Abschluss von Abkommen in den folgenden Bereichen:
a) Handel mit kulturellen und audiovisuellen Dienstleistungen, wenn diese Abkommen die kulturelle und sprachliche Vielfalt in der Union beeinträchtigen könnten;
b) Handel mit Dienstleistungen des Sozial-, des Bildungs- und des Gesundheitssektors, wenn diese Abkommen die einzelstaatliche Organisation dieser Dienstleistungen ernsthaft stören und die Verantwortlichkeit der Mitgliedstaaten für ihre Erbringung beeinträchtigen könnten.

(5) Für die Aushandlung und den Abschluss von internationalen Abkommen im Bereich des Verkehrs gelten der Dritte Teil Titel VI sowie Artikel 218.

(6) Die Ausübung der durch diesen Artikel übertragenen Zuständigkeiten im Bereich der gemeinsamen Handelspolitik hat keine Auswirkungen auf die Abgrenzung der Zuständigkeiten zwischen der Union und den Mitgliedstaaten und führt nicht zu einer Harmonisierung der Rechtsvorschriften der Mitgliedstaaten, soweit eine solche Harmonisierung in den Verträgen ausgeschlossen wird.

---

1) Siehe z.B. Verordnung (EG) Nr. 116/2009 des Rates vom 18. Dezember 2008 über die Ausfuhr von Kulturgütern, abgedruckt als Nr. B.II.2

Verordnung (EG) Nr. 116/2009 des Rates vom 18. Dezember 2008 über die Ausfuhr von Kulturgütern (kodifizierte Fassung)

(ABl. 2009 L 39 S. 1)[1]

DER RAT DER EUROPÄISCHEN UNION –
gestützt auf den Vertrag zur Gründung der Europäischen Gemeinschaft, insbesondere auf Artikel 133,
auf Vorschlag der Kommission,
in Erwägung nachstehender Gründe:

(1) Die Verordnung (EWG) Nr. 3911/92 des Rates vom 9. Dezember 1992 über die Ausfuhr von Kulturgütern[2] ist mehrfach und in wesentlichen Punkten geändert worden[3]. Aus Gründen der Übersichtlichkeit und Klarheit empfiehlt es sich, die genannte Verordnung zu kodifizieren.

(2) Um den Binnenmarkt aufrechtzuerhalten, müssen im Warenverkehr mit Drittländern Vorschriften erlassen werden, die den Schutz von Kulturgütern gewährleisten.

(3) Es erscheint angezeigt, insbesondere Maßnahmen vorzusehen, welche eine einheitliche Kontrolle der Ausfuhr von Kulturgütern an den Außengrenzen der Gemeinschaft sicherstellen.

(4) Eine derartige Regelung sollte darin bestehen, dass vor der Ausfuhr der unter diese Verordnung fallenden Kulturgüter eine von den zuständigen Mitgliedstaaten ausgestellte Ausfuhrgenehmigung vorzulegen ist. Dies setzt eine genaue Festlegung des sachlichen Anwendungsbereichs dieser Maßnahmen einschließlich ihrer Durchführungsmodalitäten voraus. Die Durchführung der Regelung sollte so einfach und wirksam wie möglich gestaltet werden.

(5) Die zur Durchführung dieser Verordnung erforderlichen Maßnahmen sollten gemäß dem Beschluss 1999/468/EG des Rates vom 28. Juni 1999 zur Festlegung der Modalitäten für die Ausübung der der Kommission übertragenen Durchführungsbestimmungen[4] erlassen werden.

(6) Angesichts der eingehenden Erfahrungen der Behörden der Mitgliedstaaten bei der Anwendung der Verordnung (EG) Nr. 515/97 des Rates vom 13. März 1997 betreffend die gegenseitige Unterstützung der Verwaltungsbehörden der Mitgliedstaaten und die Zusammenarbeit dieser Behörden mit der Kommission, um die ordnungsgemäße Anwendung der Zoll- und der Agrarregelung zu gewährleisten[5] sollte jene Verordnung auch auf diesen Sachbereich Anwendung finden.

(7) Mit Anhang I dieser Verordnung sollen die Kategorien von Kulturgütern eindeutig festgelegt werden, die im Handel mit Drittländern eines besonderen Schutzes bedürfen; den Mitgliedstaaten bleibt es jedoch unbenommen, festzulegen, welche Gegenstände als nationales Kulturgut im Sinne des Artikels 30 des Vertrags einzustufen sind –

HAT FOLGENDE VERORDNUNG ERLASSEN:

Artikel 1 Definition
Unbeschadet der Befugnisse der Mitgliedstaaten nach Artikel 30 des Vertrages gelten als „Kulturgüter" im Sinne dieser Verordnung die im Anhang I aufgeführten Güter.

Artikel 2 Ausfuhrgenehmigung
(1) Die Ausfuhr von Kulturgütern aus dem Zollgebiet der Gemeinschaft darf nur erfolgen, wenn eine Ausfuhrgenehmigung vorliegt.
(2) Die Ausfuhrgenehmigung wird auf Antrag des Beteiligten erteilt:
a) von einer zuständigen Behörde des Mitgliedstaats, in dessen Hoheitsgebiet sich das betreffende Kulturgut am 1. Januar 1993 rechtmäßig und endgültig befunden hat;
b) oder, nach dem genannten Datum, von einer zuständigen Behörde des Mitgliedstaats, in dessen Hoheitsgebiet es sich nach rechtmäßiger und endgültiger Verbringung aus einem anderen Mitgliedstaat oder nach der Einfuhr aus einem Drittland oder der Wiedereinfuhr aus einem Drittland nach rechtmäßiger Verbringung aus einem Mitgliedstaat in dieses Land befindet.

Unbeschadet des Absatzes 4 ist jedoch der nach Buchstaben a oder b des Unterabsatzes 1 zuständige Mitgliedstaat ermächtigt, keine Ausfuhrgenehmigungen für die im Anhang I unter dem ersten und

---

[1] Veröffentlicht am 10.2.2009.
[2] **Amtl. Anm.:** ABl. L 395 vom 31.12.1992, S. 1.
[3] **Amtl. Anm.:** Siehe Anhang II.
[4] **Amtl. Anm.:** ABl. L 184 vom 17.7.1999, S. 23.
[5] **Amtl. Anm.:** ABl. L 82 vom 22.3.1997, S. 1.

zweiten Gedankenstrich der Kategorie A.1 aufgeführten Kulturgüter zu verlangen, wenn diese von archäologisch oder wissenschaftlich beschränktem Wert sind, vorausgesetzt, dass sie nicht unmittelbar aus Grabungen, archäologischen Funden und archäologischen Stätten in einem Mitgliedstaat stammen oder dass der Handel mit ihnen rechtmäßig ist.

Die Ausfuhrgenehmigung kann im Hinblick auf die Ziele dieser Verordnung dann verweigert werden, wenn die betreffenden Kulturgüter unter eine Rechtsvorschrift zum Schutz nationalen Kulturguts von künstlerischem, geschichtlichem oder archäologischem Wert in dem betreffenden Mitgliedstaat fallen. Erforderlichenfalls tritt die unter dem Buchstaben b des Unterabsatzes 1 genannte Behörde mit den zuständigen Behörden des Mitgliedstaats, aus dem das betreffende Kulturgut stammt, in Verbindung, insbesondere mit den nach der Richtlinie 93/7/EWG des Rates[1] vom 15. März 1993 über die Rückgabe von unrechtmäßig aus dem Hoheitsgebiet eines Mitgliedstaats verbrachten Kulturgütern zuständigen Behörden.

(3) Die Ausfuhrgenehmigung gilt in der gesamten Gemeinschaft.

(4) Unbeschadet der Absätze 1, 2 und 3 unterliegt die direkte Ausfuhr von nationalem Kulturgut von künstlerischem, geschichtlichem oder archäologischem Wert, das kein Kulturgut im Sinne dieser Verordnung ist, aus dem Zollgebiet der Gemeinschaft den innerstaatlichen Rechtsvorschriften des Ausfuhrmitgliedstaats.

Artikel 3 Zuständige Behörden

(1) Die Mitgliedstaaten übermitteln der Kommission ein Verzeichnis der Behörden, die für die Erteilung der Ausfuhrgenehmigungen für Kulturgüter zuständig sind.

(2) Die Kommission veröffentlicht das Verzeichnis dieser Behörden[2] sowie sämtliche Änderungen des Verzeichnisses im *Amtsblatt der Europäischen Union*, Reihe C.

Artikel 4 Vorlegen der Genehmigung

Die Ausfuhrgenehmigung ist der für die Annahme der Zollerklärung zuständigen Zollstelle bei der Erfüllung der Ausfuhrzollförmlichkeiten als Beleg für die Zollerklärung vorzulegen.

Artikel 5 Beschränkung der zuständigen Zollstellen

(1) Die Mitgliedstaaten können die Zahl der Zollstellen beschränken, die für die Erfüllung der Ausfuhrzollförmlichkeiten für Kulturgüter zuständig sind.

(2) Machen die Mitgliedstaaten von der Möglichkeit nach Absatz 1 Gebrauch, so teilen sie der Kommission die ermächtigten Zollstellen mit.

Die Kommission veröffentlicht diese Mitteilungen im *Amtsblatt der Europäischen Union*, Reihe C.[3]

Artikel 6 Zusammenarbeit der Verwaltungen

Zur Durchführung dieser Verordnung gelten die Vorschriften der Verordnung (EG) Nr. 515/97, insbesondere die Vorschriften über die Vertraulichkeit der Auskünfte, entsprechend.

Über die in Absatz 1 vorgesehene Zusammenarbeit hinaus treffen die Mitgliedstaaten im Rahmen ihrer gegenseitigen Beziehungen alle zweckdienlichen Vorkehrungen für eine Zusammenarbeit zwischen den Zollverwaltungen und den zuständigen Behörden nach Artikel 4 der Richtlinie 93/7/EWG.

Artikel 7 Durchführungsvorschriften

Die zur Durchführung dieser Verordnung erforderlichen Maßnahmen,[4] insbesondere die Vorschriften über den zu verwendenden Vordruck (z.B. das Muster und die technischen Einzelheiten) werden nach dem in Artikel 8 Absatz 2 genannten Verfahren erlassen.

---

1) **Amtl. Anm.:** ABl. L 74 vom 27.3.1993, S. 74.
2) Die Liste der Behörden, die bevollmächtigt sind, Ausfuhrgenehmigungen für Kulturgüter auszustellen, ist abgedruckt als Nr. B.II.2b.
3) Die Liste der Zollstellen, die für die Erfüllung der Ausfuhrzollformalitäten für Kulturgüter zuständig sind, ist abgedruckt als Nr. B.II.2c
4) Siehe dazu insbesondere Durchführungsverordnung (EU) Nr. 1081/2012 der Kommission v. 09.11.2012 zu der Verordnung (EG) Nr. 116/2009 des Rates über die Ausfuhr von Kulturgütern, abgedruckt unter Nr. D.II.2a.

Artikel 8 Ausschuss

(1) Die Kommission wird von einem Ausschuss unterstützt.

(2) Wird auf diesen Absatz Bezug genommen, so gelten die Artikel 3 und 7 des Beschlusses 1999/468/EG.

Artikel 9 Sanktionen

Die Mitgliedstaaten legen die Sanktionen fest, die bei einem Verstoß gegen diese Verordnung zu verhängen sind und treffen alle geeigneten Maßnahmen, um deren Durchsetzung zu gewährleisten. Die Sanktionen müssen wirksam, verhältnismäßig und abschreckend sein.

Artikel 10 Berichterstattung

(1) Die Mitgliedstaaten unterrichten die Kommission über die zur Durchführung dieser Verordnung getroffenen Maßnahmen.

Die Kommission teilt diese Informationen den anderen Mitgliedstaaten mit.

(2) Die Kommission legt dem Europäischen Parlament, dem Rat und dem Europäischen Wirtschafts- und Sozialausschuss alle drei Jahre einen Bericht über die Durchführung dieser Verordnung vor. Der Rat überprüft auf Vorschlag der Kommission alle drei Jahre die im Anhang I genannten Beträge und bringt sie gegebenenfalls entsprechend den wirtschaftlichen und monetären Daten in der Gemeinschaft auf den neuesten Stand.

Artikel 11 Aufhebung

Die Verordnung (EWG) Nr. 3911/92, geändert durch die in Anhang II aufgeführten Verordnungen, wird aufgehoben.

Bezugnahmen auf die aufgehobene Verordnung gelten als Bezugnahmen auf die vorliegende Verordnung und sind nach Maßgabe der Entsprechungstabelle in Anhang III zu lesen.

Artikel 12 Inkrafttreten

Diese Verordnung tritt am zwanzigsten Tag nach ihrer Veröffentlichung im *Amtsblatt der Europäischen Union* in Kraft.

Diese Verordnung ist in allen ihren Teilen verbindlich und gilt unmittelbar in jedem Mitgliedstaat. Geschehen zu Brüssel am 18. Dezember 2008.

Anhang I Kategorien von Kulturgütern nach Artikel 1

A. 1. Mehr als 100 Jahre alte archäologische Gegenstände aus
   - Grabungen und archäologischen Funden zu Lande oder unter Wasser — 9705 00 00
   - archäologischen Stätten — 9706 00 00
   - archäologischen Sammlungen

2. Bestandteile von Kunst- und Baudenkmälern oder religiösen Denkmälern, die aus deren Aufteilung stammen und älter sind als 100 Jahre — 9705 00 00 / 9706 00 00

3. Bilder und Gemälde, die nicht unter die Kategorien 4 oder 5 fallen, aus jeglichem Material und auf jeglichem Träger vollständig von Hand hergestellt[1] — 9701

4. Aquarelle, Gouachen und Pastelle, auf jeglichem Träger vollständig von Hand hergestellt[2] — 9701

5. Mosaike, die nicht unter die Kategorien 1 oder 2 fallen, aus jeglichem Material vollständig von Hand hergestellt, und Zeichnungen, aus jeglichem Material und auf jeglichem Träger vollständig von Hand hergestellt[2] — 6914 / 9701

6. Original-Radierungen, -Stiche, -Serigraphien, und -Lithographien und lithographische Matrizen sowie Original-Plakate[2] — Kapitel 49 / 9702 00 00 / 8442 50 99

---

1) **Amtl. Anm.:** Die älter sind als 50 Jahre und nicht ihren Urhebern gehören.

2) **Amtl. Anm.:** Im Sinne des Urteils des Gerichtshofs in der Rechtssache 252/84: „Sammlungsstücke im Sinne der Tarifnummer 9705 des GZT sind Gegenstände, die geeignet sind, in eine Sammlung aufgenommen zu werden, das heißt Gegenstände, die verhältnismäßig selten sind, normalerweise nicht ihrem ursprünglichen Verwendungszweck gemäß benutzt werden, Gegenstand eines Spezialhandels außerhalb des üblichen Handels mit ähnlichen Gebrauchsgegenständen sind und einen hohen Wert haben."

7.	Nicht unter die Kategorie 1 fallende Originalerzeugnisse der Bildhauerkunst und Kopien, die auf dieselbe Weise wie das Original hergestellt worden sind[1]	9703 00 00
8.	Photographien, Filme und die dazugehörigen Negative[1]	3704 3705 3706 4911 91 80
9.	Wiegendrucke und Handschriften, einschließlich Landkarten und Partituren, als Einzelstücke oder Sammlung[1]	9702 00 00 9706 00 00 4901 10 00 4901 99 00 4904 00 00 4905 91 00 4905 99 00 4906 00 00
10.	Bücher, die älter sind als 100 Jahre, als Einzelstücke oder Sammlung	9705 00 00 9706 00 00
11.	Gedruckte Landkarten, die älter sind als 200 Jahre	9706 00 00
12.	Archive aller Art, mit Archivalien, die älter sind als 50 Jahre, auf allen Trägern	3704 3705 3706 4901 4906 9705 00 00 9706 00 00
13. a)	Sammlungen[1] und Einzelexemplare aus zoologischen, botanischen, mineralogischen oder anatomischen Sammlungen	9705 00 00
b)	Sammlungen[1] von historischem, paläontologischem, ethnographischem oder numismatischem Wert	9705 00 00
14.	Verkehrsmittel, die älter sind als 75 Jahre	9705 00 00 Kapitel 86–89
15.	Sonstige Antiquitäten, die nicht unter die Kategorien A1 bis A14 fallen	
a)	zwischen 50 und 100 Jahre alte Antiquitäten	
	Spielzeug, Spiele	Kapitel 95
	Gegenstände aus Glas	7013
	Gold- und Silberschmiedearbeiten	7114
	Möbel und Einrichtungsgegenstände	Kapitel 94
	optische, photographische und kinematographische Instrumente	Kapitel 90
	Musikinstrumente	Kapitel 92
	Uhrmacherwaren	Kapitel 91
	Holzwaren	Kapitel 44
	keramische Waren	Kapitel 69
	Tapisserien	5805 00 00
	Teppiche	Kapitel 57
	Tapeten	4814
	Waffen	Kapitel 93
b)	über 100 Jahre alte Antiquitäten	9706 00 00

---

1) **Amtl. Anm.:** Im Sinne des Urteils des Gerichtshofs in der Rechtssache 252/84: „Sammlungsstücke im Sinne der Tarifnummer 9705 des GZT sind Gegenstände, die geeignet sind, in eine Sammlung aufgenommen zu werden, das heißt Gegenstände, die verhältnismäßig selten sind, normalerweise nicht ihrem ursprünglichen Verwendungszweck gemäß benutzt werden, Gegenstand eines Spezialhandels außerhalb des üblichen Handels mit ähnlichen Gebrauchsgegenständen sind und einen hohen Wert haben."

B.II.2 Verordnung (EG) 116/2009

Die Kulturgüter, die unter die Kategorien A.1 bis A.15 fallen, wurden von der vorliegenden Verordnung nur erfasst, wenn ihr Wert mindestens den in Teil B aufgeführten Wertgruppen entspricht.

B. Wertgruppen, die bestimmten in Teil A genannten Kategorien entsprechen
(in Euro)

Wert:

Wertunabhängig
- 1 (archäologische Gegenstände)
- 2 (Aufteilung von Denkmälern)
- 9 (Wiegendrucke und Handschriften)
- 12 (Archive)

15 000
- 5 (Mosaike und Zeichnungen)
- 6 (Radierungen)
- 8 (Photographien)
- 11 (gedruckte Landkarten)

30 000
- 4 (Aquarelle, Gouachen und Pastelle)

50 000
- 7 (Bildhauerkunst)
- 10 (Bücher)
- 13 (Sammlungen)
- 14 (Verkehrsmittel)
- 15 (sonstige Gegenstände)

150 000
- 3 (Bilder)

Die Erfüllung der Voraussetzungen im Hinblick auf den finanziellen Wert ist bei Einreichung des Antrags auf Erteilung einer Ausfuhrgenehmigung zu beurteilen. Der finanzielle Wert ist der Wert des Kulturgutes in dem in Artikel 2 Absatz 2 genannten Mitgliedstaat.

Für die Mitgliedstaaten, in denen der Euro nicht die Währung ist, werden die in Anhang I aufgeführten und in Euro ausgedrückten Wertgruppen in die jeweilige Landeswährung umgerechnet und in dieser Währung ausgedrückt, und zwar zu dem Umrechnungskurs vom 31. Dezember 2001, der im *Amtsblatt der Europäischen Gemeinschaften* veröffentlicht wurde. Diese Beträge in der jeweiligen Landeswährung werden mit Wirkung vom 31. Dezember 2001 alle zwei Jahre überprüft. Die Berechnung stützt sich auf das Mittel der Tageswerte dieser Währungen ausgedrückt in Euro, während der 24 Monate, die am letzten Tag des Monats August enden, der der Überprüfung mit Wirkung vom 31. Dezember vorausgeht. Diese Berechnungsmethode wird auf Vorschlag der Kommission vom Beratenden Ausschuss für Kulturgüter grundsätzlich zwei Jahre nach der ersten Anwendung überprüft. Bei jeder Überprüfung werden die in Euro ausgedrückten Wertgruppen und die entsprechenden Beträge in Landeswährung regelmäßig in den ersten Tagen des Monats November, der dem Zeitpunkt vorausgeht, zu dem die Überprüfung wirksam wird, im *Amtsblatt der Europäischen Union* veröffentlicht.

Anhang II Aufgehobene Verordnung mit ihren nachfolgenden Änderungen

Verordnung (EWG) Nr. 3911/92 des Rates
(ABl. L 395 vom 31.12.1992, S. 1)

Verordnung (EG) Nr. 2469/96 des Rates
(ABl. L 335 vom 24.12.1996, S. 9)

Verordnung (EG) Nr. 947/2001 des Rates
(ABl. L 137 vom 19.5.2001, S. 10)

Verordnung (EG) Nr. 806/2003 des Rates   nur Anhang I Nr. 2
(ABl. L 122 vom 16.5.2003, S. 1)

Anhang III Entsprechungstabelle

Verordnung (EWG) Nr. 3911/92	Vorliegende Verordnung
Artikel 1	Artikel 1
Artikel 2 Absatz 1	Artikel 2 Absatz 1
Artikel 2 Absatz 2 Unterabsatz 1 einleitende Worte	Artikel 2 Absatz 2 Unterabsatz 1 einleitende Worte
Artikel 2 Absatz 2 Unterabsatz 1 erster Gedankenstrich	Artikel 2 Absatz 2 Unterabsatz 1 Buchstabe a
Artikel 2 Absatz 2 Unterabsatz 1 zweiter Gedankenstrich	Artikel 2 Absatz 2 Unterabsatz 1 Buchstabe b
Artikel 2 Absatz 2 Unterabsatz 2	Artikel 2 Absatz 2 Unterabsatz 2
Artikel 2 Absatz 2 Unterabsatz 3	Artikel 2 Absatz 2 Unterabsatz 3
Artikel 2 Absatz 2 Unterabsatz 4	Artikel 2 Absatz 2 Unterabsatz 4
Artikel 2 Absatz 3	Artikel 2 Absatz 3
Artikel 2 Absatz 4	Artikel 2 Absatz 4
Artikel 3 bis 9	Artikel 3 bis 9
Artikel 10 Absatz 1	Artikel 10 Absatz 1 Unterabsatz 1
Artikel 10 Absatz 2	Artikel 10 Absatz 1 Unterabsatz 2
Artikel 10 Absatz 3	Artikel 10 Absatz 2 Unterabsatz 1
Artikel 10 Absatz 4	–
Artikel 10 Absatz 5	Artikel 10 Absatz 2 Unterabsatz 2
–	Artikel 11
Artikel 11	Artikel 12
Anhang Teil A.1, A.2 und A.3	Anhang I Teil A.1, A.2 und A.3
Anhang Teil A.3 Buchstabe a	Anhang I Teil A.4
Anhang Teil A.4	Anhang I Teil A.5
Anhang Teil A.5	Anhang I Teil A.6
Anhang Teil A.6	Anhang I Teil A.7
Anhang Teil A.7	Anhang I Teil A.8
Anhang Teil A.8	Anhang I Teil A.9
Anhang Teil A.9	Anhang I Teil A.10
Anhang Teil A.10	Anhang I Teil A.11
Anhang Teil A.11	Anhang I Teil A.12
Anhang Teil A.12	Anhang I Teil A.13
Anhang Teil A.13	Anhang I Teil A.14
Anhang Teil A.14	Anhang I Teil A.15
Anhang Teil B	Anhang I Teil B
–	Anhang II
–	Anhang III

Durchführungsverordnung (EU) Nr. 1081/2012 der Kommission vom 9. November 2012 zu der Verordnung (EG) Nr. 116/2009 des Rates über die Ausfuhr von Kulturgütern

(ABl. Nr. L 324 S. 1, ber. ABl. 2014 Nr. L 93 S. 86)[1)]

DIE EUROPÄISCHE KOMMISSION –
gestützt auf den Vertrag über die Arbeitsweise der Europäischen Union,
gestützt auf die Verordnung (EG) Nr. 116/2009 des Rates vom 18. Dezember 2008 über die Ausfuhr von Kulturgütern[2)], insbesondere auf Artikel 7,
in Erwägung nachstehender Gründe:
(1) Die Verordnung (EWG) Nr. 752/93 der Kommission vom 30. März 1993 zur Durchführung der Verordnung (EWG) Nr. 3911/92 des Rates über die Ausfuhr von Kulturgütern[3)] ist mehrfach und in wesentlichen Punkten geändert worden[4)]. Aus Gründen der Übersichtlichkeit und Klarheit empfiehlt es sich daher, die genannte Verordnung zu kodifizieren.
(2) Es sind Durchführungsbestimmungen zu der Verordnung (EG) Nr. 116/2009 erforderlich, die insbesondere eine Ausfuhrgenehmigungspflicht für die in Anhang I der Verordnung aufgeführten Kategorien von Kulturgütern vorsieht.
(3) Um die Einheitlichkeit des Vordrucks für die in der Verordnung vorgesehene Ausfuhrgenehmigung zu gewährleisten, sind die Einzelheiten der Ausstellung, Erteilung und Verwendung dieses Papiers zu regeln. Dazu ist ein Muster für die Genehmigung festzulegen.
(4) Zum Abbau unnötigen Verwaltungsaufwands ist es zweckmäßig, für die vorübergehende Ausfuhr von Kulturgütern zur Verwendung und/oder Ausstellung durch verantwortungsvolle Personen oder Organisationen in Drittländern das Konzept offener Genehmigungen beizubehalten.
(5) Die Mitgliedstaaten, die von dieser Möglichkeit Gebrauch machen wollen, sollten dies in Bezug auf die Kulturgüter, Personen und Organisationen, für die sie zuständig sind, tun können. Die dafür zu erfüllenden Voraussetzungen sind von einem Mitgliedstaat zum anderen unterschiedlich. Die Mitgliedstaaten sollten daher die Möglichkeit haben, sich für oder gegen die Verwendung offener Genehmigungen zu entscheiden und die Voraussetzungen ihrer Erteilung festzulegen.
(6) Die Ausfuhrgenehmigung sollte in einer der Amtssprachen der Union erteilt werden.
(7) Die in dieser Verordnung vorgesehenen Maßnahmen entsprechen der Stellungnahme des in Artikel 8 der Verordnung (EG) Nr. 116/2009 genannten Ausschusses –
HAT FOLGENDE VERORDNUNG ERLASSEN:

Abschnitt I
Vordruck

Artikel 1 [Genehmigungen]
(1) Für die Ausfuhr von Kulturgütern gibt es drei Arten von Genehmigungen, die nach Maßgabe der Verordnung (EG) Nr. 116/2009 und der vorliegenden Verordnung erteilt und verwendet werden:
a) die normale Genehmigung;
b) die spezifische offene Genehmigung;
c) die allgemeine offene Genehmigung.
(2) Die Verpflichtungen hinsichtlich der Ausfuhrförmlichkeiten und der entsprechenden Papiere werden durch die Verwendung einer Ausfuhrgenehmigung in keiner Weise berührt.
(3) Der Ausfuhrgenehmigungsvordruck muss auf Anfrage bei der (den) in Artikel 2 Absatz 2 der Verordnung (EG) Nr. 116/2009 genannten zuständigen Behörde(n) erhältlich sein.

---

1) Veröffentlicht am 22.11.2012.
2) **Amtl. Anm.:** ABl. L 39 vom 10.2.2009, S. 1, abgedruckt als Nr. B.II.2.
3) **Amtl. Anm.:** ABl. L 77 vom 31.3.1993, S. 24.
4) **Amtl. Anm.:** Siehe Anhang IV.

Artikel 2 [Anwendungsbereich der einzelnen Genehmigungen]

(1) Eine normale Genehmigung wird grundsätzlich für alle der Verordnung (EG) Nr. 116/2009 unterworfenen Ausfuhren verwendet.
Jedoch bleibt es jedem Mitgliedstaat überlassen, ob er statt dessen die spezifischen oder allgemeinen offenen Genehmigungen erteilt, die unter den besonderen Voraussetzungen der Artikel 10 oder 13 möglich sind.

(2) Eine spezifische offene Genehmigung berechtigt eine bestimmte Person oder Organisation nach Maßgabe des Artikels 10 zur mehrmaligen vorübergehenden Ausfuhr eines bestimmten Kulturguts.

(3) Eine allgemeine offene Genehmigung berechtigt nach Maßgabe des Artikels 13 zu jeglicher vorübergehenden Ausfuhr von Kulturgütern, die Teil der ständigen Sammlung eines Museums oder einer anderen Einrichtung sind.

(4) [1]Ein Mitgliedstaat kann eine spezifische oder allgemeine offene Genehmigung jederzeit widerrufen, wenn die Voraussetzungen, unter denen sie erteilt wurde, nicht mehr erfüllt sind. [2]Er informiert die Kommission unverzüglich, wenn er die von ihm erteilte Genehmigung nicht zurückerhält und folglich ihren unrechtmäßigen Gebrauch nicht ausschließen kann. [3]Die Kommission unterrichtet daraufhin unverzüglich die anderen Mitgliedstaaten.

(5) Die Mitgliedstaaten können alle notwendigen Maßnahmen erlassen, die sie für die Überwachung der Verwendung der von ihnen erteilten offenen Genehmigungen in ihrem Hoheitsgebiet für erforderlich halten.

Abschnitt II
Die normale Genehmigung

Artikel 3 [Vordrucke]

(1) [1]Normale Genehmigungen werden auf Vordrucken nach dem Muster in Anhang I erteilt. [2]Für den Ausfuhrgenehmigungsvordruck ist weißes holzfreies geleimtes Schreibpapier mit einem Gewicht von mindestens 55 Gramm/m^2 zu verwenden.

(2) Die Vordrucke haben das Format 210 mm × 297 mm.

(3) Der Vordruck ist in einer von den zuständigen Behörden des ausstellenden Mitgliedstaats bezeichneten Amtssprache der Union zu drucken oder elektronisch zu erstellen und auszufüllen.
[1]Die zuständigen Behörden des Mitgliedstaats, in dem das Dokument vorgelegt wird, können eine Übersetzung in die oder eine Amtssprache dieses Mitgliedstaats verlangen. [2]In diesem Fall trägt der Genehmigungsinhaber die Kosten der Übersetzung.

(4) Es obliegt den Mitgliedstaaten,
a) die Vordrucke zu drucken oder drucken zu lassen. Sie sind mit dem Namen und der Anschrift der Druckerei zu versehen oder müssen ihr Kennzeichen tragen;
b) Vorbeugemaßnahmen gegen deren Fälschung zu treffen. Die zu diesem Zweck von den Mitgliedstaaten festgelegte Art und Weise der Nämlichkeitsfeststellung ist der Kommission anzuzeigen, damit sie den zuständigen Behörden der anderen Mitgliedstaaten mitgeteilt werden kann.

(5) Der Vordruck ist vorzugsweise auf mechanischem oder elektronischem Wege auszufüllen; er kann jedoch auch handschriftlich mit Tinte in Großbuchstaben leserlich ausgefüllt werden.
Bei allen Verfahren dürfen die Vordrucke weder Radierungen noch Übermalungen oder sonstige Änderungen aufweisen.

Artikel 4 [Getrennte Ausfuhrgenehmigung; „Sendung"]

(1) Unbeschadet des Absatzes 3 wird für jede Sendung von Kulturgütern eine getrennte Ausfuhrgenehmigung erteilt.

(2) Im Sinne des Absatzes 1 bedeutet „Sendung" ein einzelnes Kulturgut oder mehrere Kulturgüter.

(3) Handelt es sich um eine Sendung mit mehreren Kulturgütern, so bleibt es den zuständigen Behörden überlassen, ob für eine solche Sendung die Ausstellung einer oder mehrerer Genehmigungen zweckmäßig erscheint.

Artikel 5 [Umfang des Vordrucks]
Der Vordruck umfasst drei Blätter:
a) Blatt 1 ist das Antragsformular und trägt die Nummer 1;
b) Blatt 2 ist für den Inhaber bestimmt und trägt die Nummer 2;
c) Blatt 3, das an die ausstellende Behörde zurückgeschickt werden muss, trägt die Nummer 3.

Artikel 6 [Ausfüllen des Vordrucks, Anlagen, Vorlage]
(1) Der Antragsteller füllt die Felder 1, 3, 6 bis 21, 24 sowie gegebenenfalls 25 des Antragsformulars auf allen Blättern aus, mit Ausnahme des Feldes bzw. der Felder, deren Vorabdruck genehmigt worden ist.
Die Mitgliedstaaten können jedoch bestimmen, dass nur das Antragsformular auszufüllen ist.
(2) Dem Antrag sind beizufügen:
a) Unterlagen mit allen zweckdienlichen Angaben über das Kulturgut bzw. die Kulturgüter und seine bzw. ihre Rechtslage zum Zeitpunkt des Antrages sowie gegebenenfalls entsprechende Belege (Rechnungen, Gutachten usw.);
b) eine oder gegebenenfalls auf Verlangen der zuständigen Behörden mehrere beglaubigte Schwarz-Weiß- oder Farbfotografien (Mindestformat 8 cm × 12 cm) des bzw. der Kulturgüter.
Statt der Fotografie kann mit Zustimmung der zuständigen Behörden gegebenenfalls auch eine detaillierte Liste des bzw. der Kulturgüter vorgelegt werden.
(3) Die zuständigen Behörden können zur Erteilung der Ausfuhrgenehmigung die körperliche Vorführung des bzw. der auszuführenden Kulturgüter verlangen.
(4) Die durch die Anwendung der Absätze 2 und 3 entstehenden Kosten trägt derjenige, der die Ausfuhrgenehmigung beantragt.
(5) [1]Der für die Erteilung der Ausfuhrgenehmigung ordnungsgemäß ausgefüllte Vordruck ist den von den Mitgliedstaaten in Anwendung von Artikel 2 Absatz 2 der Verordnung (EG) Nr. 116/2009 bezeichneten zuständigen Behörden vorzulegen. [2]Erteilen diese die Genehmigung, so behalten sie Blatt Nr. 1 ein. [3]Die übrigen Blätter werden dem Antragsteller ausgehändigt, der damit Inhaber der Ausfuhrgenehmigung wird, bzw. seinem Stellvertreter.

Artikel 7 [Exemplar für den Inhaber und die ausstellende Behörde]
Die Blätter der Ausfuhrgenehmigung, die zusammen mit der Ausfuhranmeldung vorgelegt werden müssen, sind:
a) das Blatt für den Inhaber;
b) das Blatt, das an die ausstellende Behörde zurückgeschickt wird.

Artikel 8 [Aufgaben der Zollstelle]
(1) Die für die Annahme der Ausfuhranmeldung zuständige Zollstelle überzeugt sich davon, dass die Angaben der Ausfuhranmeldung mit denen der Ausfuhrgenehmigung oder gegebenenfalls des Carnets ATA übereinstimmen und dass in Feld 44 der Ausfuhranmeldung oder auf dem entsprechenden Abschnitt des Carnets ATA auf die Ausfuhrgenehmigung verwiesen wird.
[1]Die Zollstelle ergreift die notwendigen Maßnahmen zur Nämlichkeitssicherung. [2]Diese können im Anbringen eines Zollverschlusses oder eines Stempelabdruckes der Zollstelle bestehen. [3]Dem Exemplar Nr. 3 des Einheitspapiers wird das an die ausstellende Behörde zurückzusendende Blatt der Ausfuhrgenehmigung beigeheftet.
(2) Nach Ausfüllen des Feldes 23 auf den Blättern 2 und 3 übergibt die für die Annahme der Ausfuhranmeldung zuständige Zollstelle dem Zollbeteiligten oder seinem Stellvertreter das für den Inhaber der Genehmigung bestimmte Blatt.
(3) Das Blatt der Genehmigung, das an die ausstellende Behörde zurückzusenden ist, begleitet die Sendung bis zur Zollstelle des Ausgangs aus dem Zollgebiet der Gemeinschaft.
Die Zollstelle setzt ihren Dienststempelabdruck in Feld 26 dieses Blatts und sendet es an die ausstellende Behörde zurück.

Artikel 9 [Gültigkeitsdauer]
(1) Die Gültigkeitsdauer einer Ausfuhrgenehmigung beträgt höchstens zwölf Monate ab dem Ausstellungsdatum.

(2) Wird eine vorübergehende Ausfuhrgenehmigung beantragt, so können die zuständigen Behörden eine Frist für die Wiedereinfuhr für das/die Kulturgut/Kulturgüter in den Mitgliedstaat der Ausfuhr setzen.
(3) Ist eine nicht verwendete Ausfuhrgenehmigung abgelaufen, so werden die Blätter, die sich im Besitz des Inhabers befinden, von diesem unverzüglich an die ausstellende Behörde zurückgesandt.

Abschnitt III
Spezifische offene Genehmigungen

Artikel 10 [Erteilung; Gültigkeitsdauer]
(1) [1]Spezifische offene Genehmigungen können für bestimmtes Kulturgut erteilt werden, dessen regelmäßige vorübergehende Ausfuhr aus der Union zur Verwendung und/oder Ausstellung in einem Drittland wahrscheinlich ist. [2]Das Kulturgut muss Eigentum oder rechtmäßiger Besitz der Person oder Organisation sein, die es verwendet oder ausstellt.
(2) Eine Genehmigung kann nur erteilt werden, wenn die Behörden davon überzeugt sind, dass die betreffende Person oder Organisation alle erforderlichen Sicherheiten für eine Rückkehr der Waren in die Union in gutem Zustand bieten, und die Güter so beschrieben oder gekennzeichnet werden können, dass die Übereinstimmung der Warenbezeichnung in der spezifischen offenen Genehmigung mit der Warenbezeichnung in der spezifischen offenen Genehmigung mit der vorübergehend ausgeführten Ware im Zeitpunkt der Ausfuhr keinen Zweifeln unterliegt.
(3) Die Gültigkeitsdauer einer Genehmigung darf fünf Jahre nicht überschreiten.

Artikel 11 [Vorlage]
Die Genehmigung ist für Prüfzwecke auf Verlangen zusammen mit einer schriftlichen Ausfuhranmeldung oder in anderen Fällen zusammen mit den Kulturgütern vorzulegen.
[1]Die zuständigen Behörden des Mitgliedstaats, in dem die Genehmigung vorgelegt wird, können eine Übersetzung in die Landessprache oder eine der Amtssprachen dieses Mitgliedstaats verlangen. [2]Der Genehmigungsinhaber hat die Kosten einer solchen Übersetzung zu tragen.

Artikel 12 [Prüfung durch die Zollstelle, Beifügung zu den Papieren]
(1) Die für die Annahme der Ausfuhranmeldung zuständige Zollstelle prüft, ob die gestellten Waren mit der Beschreibung in der Ausfuhranmeldung übereinstimmen und ob bei schriftlicher Zollanmeldung im Feld 44 auf die Ausfuhrgenehmigung Bezug genommen wird.
(2) [1]Ist eine schriftliche Zollanmeldung vorgeschrieben, so wird die Genehmigung dem Exemplar Nr. 3 des Einheitspapiers beigefügt und begleitet die Waren zu der Zollstelle, bei der sie das Zollgebiet der Union verlassen. [2]Wird Exemplar Nr. 3 des Einheitspapiers dem Ausführer oder seinem Vertreter ausgehändigt, ist ihm der Gebrauch der Genehmigung auch für eine spätere Verwendung zu ermöglichen.

Abschnitt IV
Allgemeine offene Genehmigungen

Artikel 13 [Erteilung; Geltungsdauer]
(1) Allgemeine offene Genehmigungen können Museen oder anderen Einrichtungen zur vorübergehenden Ausfuhr aller Teile ihrer ständigen Sammlung erteilt werden, die regelmäßig für eine vorübergehende Ausfuhr aus der Union für eine Ausstellung in einem Drittland in Frage kommen.
(2) [1]Eine Genehmigung kann nur erteilt werden, wenn die zuständigen Behörden davon überzeugt sind, dass die Einrichtung die erforderliche Gewähr dafür bietet, dass die Waren in gutem Zustand wieder in die Union zurückkehren. [2]Die Genehmigung kann für jede vorübergehende Ausfuhr von Waren der ständigen Sammlung in beliebiger Zusammenstellung verwendet werden. [3]Sie gilt auch für mehrere verschiedene Zusammenstellungen von Waren, die nacheinander oder gleichzeitig ausgeführt werden.
(3) Die Geltungsdauer einer solchen Genehmigung darf fünf Jahre nicht überschreiten.

Artikel 14 [Vorlage]
Die Genehmigung ist zusammen mit der Ausfuhranmeldung vorzulegen.

B.II.2a Durchführungsverordnung zur VO (EG) 116/2009

[1]Die zuständigen Behörden des Mitgliedstaats, in dem die Genehmigung vorgelegt wird, können eine Übersetzung in die oder in eine Amtssprache dieses Mitgliedstaats verlangen. [2]Der Genehmigungsinhaber hat die Kosten einer solchen Übersetzung zu tragen.

Artikel 15 [Verbindung mit dem Warenverzeichnis; Beifügung zu den Papieren]
(1) [1]Die zur Annahme der Ausfuhranmeldung befugte Zollstelle stellt sicher, dass die Genehmigung zusammen mit einem Verzeichnis der Waren, die ausgeführt und in der Ausfuhranmeldung beschrieben werden, vorgelegt wird. [2]Dieses Verzeichnis ist auf Papier mit dem Briefkopf der Einrichtung zu erstellen, und jede Seite ist von einem auf der Genehmigung namentlich angegebenen Mitarbeiter der Einrichtung zu unterzeichnen. [3]Außerdem muss jede Seite wie die Genehmigung selbst den Stempelabdruck der Einrichtung tragen. [4]In Feld 44 der Ausfuhranmeldung ist auf die Genehmigung Bezug zu nehmen.
(2) [1]Die Genehmigung ist dem Exemplar Nr. 3 des Einheitspapiers beizufügen und muss die Warensendung bis zu der Zollstelle begleiten, bei der sie das Zollgebiet der Union verlässt. [2]Wird Exemplar Nr. 3 des Einheitspapiers dem Ausführer oder seinem Vertreter ausgehändigt, wird ihm der Gebrauch der Genehmigung auch bei späterer Verwendung ermöglicht.

Abschnitt V
Vordrucke für offene Genehmigungen

Artikel 16
(1) Eine spezifische offene Genehmigung wird auf dem Vordruck nach dem Muster in Anhang II erteilt.
(2) Eine allgemeine offene Genehmigung wird auf einem Vordruck nach dem Muster in Anhang III erteilt.
(3) Der Genehmigungsvordruck wird in einer der Amtssprachen der Union gedruckt oder elektronisch erstellt.
(4) Der Vordruck für die Genehmigung hat das Format 210 × 297 mm, wobei die Länge höchstens 5 mm weniger oder 8 mm mehr betragen darf.
[1]Es ist weißes holzfreies, geleimtes Schreibpapier mit einem Gewicht von mindestens 55 Gramm je Quadratmeter zu verwenden. [2]Die Vorderseite des Originals ist mit einem hellblauen guillochierten Überdruck zu versehen, auf dem jede mechanisch oder chemisch vorgenommene Fälschung sichtbar wird.
(5) Das zweite, nicht mit guillochiertem Überdruck zu versehende Blatt der Genehmigung, ist dem Ausführer für seine eigenen Zwecke oder Unterlagen vorbehalten.
Der Vordruck für den Antrag wird von den jeweiligen Mitgliedstaaten vorgeschrieben.
(6) Die Mitgliedstaaten können sich den Druck der Vordrucke vorbehalten oder ihn Druckereien überlassen, die sie hierzu ermächtigen.
[1]Im letzteren Fall muss in jedem Vordruck auf die Ermächtigung hingewiesen werden. [2]Jeder Vordruck muss den Namen und die Anschrift oder das Kennzeichen der Druckerei enthalten. [3]Es trägt ferner zur Kennzeichnung eine eingedruckte oder gestempelte Seriennummer.
(7) Es obliegt den Mitgliedstaaten, Vorbeugemaßnahmen gegen die Fälschung von Genehmigungen zu treffen.
Die zu diesem Zweck von den Mitgliedstaaten festgelegte Art und Weise der Nämlichkeitsfeststellung ist der Kommission anzuzeigen, damit diese sie den zuständigen Behörden der anderen Mitgliedstaaten mitteilen kann.
(8) [1]Die Genehmigungen sind auf mechanischem oder elektronischem Wege auszufüllen. [2]In Ausnahmefällen können sie auch mit schwarzem Kugelschreiber in Großbuchstaben ausgefüllt werden. In keinem Fall dürfen sie Radierungen, Übermalungen oder sonstige Änderungen aufweisen.

Abschnitt VI
Schlussbestimmungen

Artikel 17 [Aufhebung]
Die Verordnung (EWG) Nr. 752/93 wird aufgehoben.

Bezugnahmen auf die aufgehobene Verordnung gelten als Bezugnahmen auf die vorliegende Verordnung und sind nach Maßgabe der Entsprechungstabelle in Anhang V zu lesen.

Artikel 18 [Inkrafttreten]
Diese Verordnung tritt am zwanzigsten Tag nach ihrer Veröffentlichung im *Amtsblatt der Europäischen Union* in Kraft.
Diese Verordnung ist in allen ihren Teilen verbindlich und gilt unmittelbar in jedem Mitgliedstaat.
Brüssel, den 9. November 2012

Anhang I Mustervordruck einer normalen Ausfuhrgenehmigung

[hier nicht wiedergegeben]

Anhang II Muster des Vordrucks für die spezifischen offenen Genehmigungen und ihre Blätter

[hier nicht wiedergegeben]

Anhang III Muster für die Vordrucke für die allgemeinen offenen Genehmigungen und ihre Blätter

[hier nicht wiedergegeben]

Anhang IV Aufgehobene Verordnung mit Liste ihrer nachfolgenden Änderungen

[hier nicht wiedergegeben]

Anhang V Entsprechungstabelle

[hier nicht wiedergegeben]

B.II.2b Ausfuhrgenehmigungsbehörden nach VO (EG) 116/2009

Liste der Behörden, die bevollmächtigt sind, Ausfuhrgenehmigungen für Kulturgüter auszustellen, veröffentlicht gemäß Artikel 3 Absatz 2 der Verordnung (EG) Nr. 116/2009 des Rates[1)]

(2014/C 72/07)

Mitgliedstaat	Zuständige Behörden
BELGIEN	**Vlaamse Gemeenschap** Ministerie van de Vlaamse Gemeenschap Administratie Cultuur Afdeling Beeldende Kunst en Musea Parochiaansstraat 15 1000 Brussel BELGIË **Communauté française** Ministère de la Communauté française Direction générale de la culture Service général du patrimoine culturel et des arts plastiques Boulevard Léopold II 44 1080 Bruxelles BELGIQUE **Deutschsprachige Gemeinschaft** Ministerium der Deutschsprachigen Gemeinschaft Abteilung Kulturelle Angelegenheiten Gospertstrasse 1 4700 Eupen BELGIQUE/BELGIË
BULGARIEN	**Ministry of Culture** DG Inspectorate for Protection of Cultural Heritage Alexander Stamboliyski 17 1040 Sofia BULGARIA **Министерство на културата** ГД „Инспекторат за опазване на културното наследство" бул. „Александър Стамболийски" № 17 1040 София/Sofia БЪЛГАРИЯ/BULGARIA
TSCHECHISCHE REPUBLIK	Ministerstvo kultury ČR Maltézské náměstí 471/1 118 01 Praha 1 ČESKÁ REPUBLIKA Ministerstvo vnitra ČR (zuständig für Archive) Milady Horákové 133 166 21 Praha 6 ČESKÁ REPUBLIKA

---

1) ABl. L 39 vom 10.2.2009, S. 1. Die Verordnung ist abgedruckt als Nr. B.II.2.

Mitgliedstaat	Zuständige Behörden
DÄNEMARK	Kulturværdiudvalget Sekretariat Kulturarvsstyrelsen Slotsholmsgade 1, 3. sal 1216 København K DANMARK
DEUTSCHLAND	Zuständige Behörde auf Landesebene **Baden-Württemberg** Direktion des Badischen Landesmuseums Karlsruhe Schloss 76131 Karlsruhe DEUTSCHLAND **Bayern** Bayerische Staatsgemäldesammlungen Barer Straße 29 80799 München DEUTSCHLAND **Berlin** Der Regierende Bürgermeister von Berlin Senatskanzlei — Kulturelle Angelegenheiten Referat Grundsatzangelegenheiten Brunnenstr. 188-190 10119 Berlin DEUTSCHLAND **Brandenburg** Ministerium für Wissenschaft, Forschung und Kultur des Landes Brandenburg Abteilung 3/Referat 31 Dortustraße 36 14467 Potsdam DEUTSCHLAND **Freie und Hansestadt Bremen** Der Senator für Kultur Referat 11 Altenwall 15/16 28195 Bremen DEUTSCHLAND **Freie und Hansestadt Hamburg** Freie und Hansestadt Hamburg Kulturbehörde — Staatsarchiv Grundsatzangelegenheiten des Archivwesens und des Kulturgutschutzes (ST121) Kattunbleiche 19 22041 Hamburg DEUTSCHLAND

B.II.2b Ausfuhrgenehmigungsbehörden nach VO (EG) 116/2009

Mitgliedstaat	Zuständige Behörden
	Hessen Hessisches Ministerium für Wissenschaft und Kunst Referat IV 5 Rheinstraße 23-25 65185 Wiesbaden DEUTSCHLAND **Mecklenburg-Vorpommern** Ministerium für Bildung, Wissenschaft und Kultur des Landes Mecklenburg-Vorpommern Abteilung Kultur Referat 420 Werderstraße 124 19055 Schwerin DEUTSCHLAND **Niedersachsen** *Für Kulturgut* Niedersächsisches Landesmuseum Hannover Willy-Brandt-Allee 5 30169 Hannover DEUTSCHLAND *Für Archivgut* Niedersächsische Staatskanzlei Abteilung 2/Referat 201 Planckstraße 2 30169 Hannover DEUTSCHLAND **Nordrhein-Westfalen** Ministerium für Familie, Kinder, Jugend, Kultur und Sport des Landes Nordrhein- Westfalen Abteilung IV — Kultur Referat 412 Haroldstr. 4 40213 Düsseldorf DEUTSCHLAND **Rheinland-Pfalz** Ministerium für Bildung, Wissenschaft, Weiterbildung und Kultur Abteilung Allgemeine Kulturpflege Mittlere Bleiche 61 55116 Mainz DEUTSCHLAND **Saarland** Ministerium für Bildung und Kultur Referat E 6 Am Ludwigsplatz 6-7 66117 Saarbrücken DEUTSCHLAND

Mitgliedstaat	Zuständige Behörden
	Sachsen *Für Kulturgut* Staatliche Kunstsammlungen Dresden Residenzschloss Taschenberg 2 01067 Dresden DEUTSCHLAND *Für Archivgut* Sächsisches Staatsministerium des Innern Referat 15 Wilhelm-Buck-Str. 2 01097 Dresden DEUTSCHLAND
	Sachsen-Anhalt *Für Kulturgut* Kultusministerium Sachsen-Anhalt Abteilung Kultur Referat 46 Turmschanzenstr. 32 39114 Magdeburg DEUTSCHLAND *Für Archivgut* Ministerium für Inneres und Sport des Landes Sachsen-Anhalt Referat 15 Halberstädter Straße 2/Am „Platz des 17. Juni" 39112 Magdeburg DEUTSCHLAND
	Schleswig-Holstein Ministerium für Justiz, Kultur und Europa des Landes Schleswig-Holstein Kulturabteilung Referat II 42 Postfach 7145 24105 Kiel DEUTSCHLAND
	Thüringen Thüringer Ministerium für Bildung, Wissenschaft und Kultur Abteilung 5/Referat 53 Werner-Seelenbinder-Straße 7 99096 Erfurt DEUTSCHLAND
ESTLAND	**Muinsuskaitseamet** (National Heritage Board) Uus 18 10 111 Tallinn EESTI/ESTONIA
IRLAND	**Department of Arts, Heritage and the Gaeltacht** New Road Killarney Co. Kerry IRELAND

B.II.2b Ausfuhrgenehmigungsbehörden nach VO (EG) 116/2009

Mitgliedstaat	Zuständige Behörden
GRIECHENLAND	**Hellenic Ministry of Culture** Directorate of Museums, Exhibitions and Educational Programmes Department for non-State Archaeological Museums and Collections for Antique Shops and for the Fight against Illicit Traffic of Antiquities Bouboulinas Street 20 101 86 Athens GREECE **Hellenic Ministry of Culture, Ephorate for Antique Shops and Private Archaeological Collections** Polygnotou Str. 13 105 55 Athens GREECE
SPANIEN	**Ministerio de Cultura** Dirección General de Bellas Artes y Bienes Culturales Subdirección General de Protección del Patrimonio Histórico Español Plaza del Rey, 1 28071 Madrid ESPAÑA
FRANKREICH	**Ministère de la culture et de la communication** Direction générale des patrimoines Service des musées de France 6 rue des Pyramides 75001 Paris FRANCE
	Ministère de la culture et de la communication Direction générale des médias et des industries culturelles Service du livre et de la lecture 182 rue Saint-Honoré 75001 Paris FRANCE
	Ministère de la culture et de la communication Direction générale des patrimoines Service du patrimoine 182 rue Saint-Honoré 75001 Paris FRANCE
	Ministère de la culture et de la communication Direction générale des patrimoines Service interministériel des archives de France 60 rue des Francs-Bourgeois 75003 Paris FRANCE

KROATIEN	1. **Ministry of Culture**
	    Directorate for the Protection of Cultural Heritage
	    Conservation Department in Dubrovnik
	    C. Zuzorić 6

Ausfuhrgenehmigungsbehörden nach VO (EG) 116/2009 B.II.2b

Mitgliedstaat	Zuständige Behörden
	HR-20000 Dubrovnik CROATIA
	2. **Ministry of Culture** Directorate for the Protection of Cultural Heritage Conservation Department in Karlovac A. Vraniczanyja 6 HR-47000 Karlovac CROATIA
	3. **Ministry of Culture** Directorate for the Protection of Cultural Heritage Conservation Department in Osijek Kuhačeva 27 HR-31000 Osijek CROATIA
	4. **Ministry of Culture** Directorate for the Protection of Cultural Heritage Conservation Department in Pula Ul. Grada Graza 2 HR-52000 Pula CROATIA
	5. **Ministry of Culture** Directorate for the Protection of Cultural Heritage Conservation Department in Varaždin Gundulićeva 2 HR-42000 Varaždin CROATIA
	6. **Ministry of Culture** Directorate for the Protection of Cultural Heritage Conservation Department in Split Porinova bb HR-21000 Split CROATIA
	7. **Ministry of Culture** Directorate for the Protection of Cultural Heritage Conservation Department in Šibenik J. Čulinovića 1/3 HR-22000 Šibenik CROATIA
	8. **Ministry of Culture** Directorate for the Protection of Cultural Heritage Conservation Department in Rijeka Užarska 26 HR-51000 Rijeka CROATIA
	9. **Ministry of Culture** Directorate for the Protection of Cultural Heritage Conservation Department in Zadar I. Smiljanića 3 HR-23000 Zadar CROATIA

B.II.2b Ausfuhrgenehmigungsbehörden nach VO (EG) 116/2009

Mitgliedstaat	Zuständige Behörden
	10. **Ministry of Culture** Directorate for the Protection of Cultural Heritage Conservation Department in Zagreb Mesnička 49 HR-10000 Zagreb CROATIA
	11. **Ministry of Culture** Directorate for the Protection of Cultural Heritage Conservation Department in Požega M. Peića 3 HR-34000 Požega CROATIA
	12. **Ministry of Culture** Directorate for the Protection of Cultural Heritage Conservation Department in Bjelovar Trg E. Kvaternika 6 HR-43000 Bjelovar CROATIA
	13. **Ministry of Culture** Directorate for the Protection of Cultural Heritage Conservation Department in Gospić Budačka 12 HR-53000 Gospić CROATIA
	14. **Ministry of Culture** Directorate for the Protection of Cultural Heritage Conservation Department in Trogir Gradska 41 HR-21220 Trogir CROATIA
	15. **Ministry of Culture** Directorate for the Protection of Cultural Heritage Conservation Department in Krapina Magistratska 12 HR-49000 Krapina CROATIA
	16. **Ministry of Culture** Directorate for the Protection of Cultural Heritage Conservation Department in Sisak I. Meštrovića 28 HR-44000 Sisak CROATIA
	17. **Ministry of Culture** Directorate for the Protection of Cultural Heritage Conservation Department in Imotski A. Starčevića 7 HR-21260 Imotski CROATIA
	18. **Ministry of Culture** Directorate for the Protection of Cultural Heritage

Mitgliedstaat	Zuständige Behörden
	Conservation Department in Slavonski Brod A. Starčevića 43 HR-35000 Slavonski Brod CROATIA
	19. **Ministry of Culture** Directorate for the Protection of Cultural Heritage Conservation Department in Vukovar Županijska 5 HR-32000 Vukovar CROATIA
	20. **City of Zagreb** City Institute for the Protection of Cultural Monuments and Nature Kuševićeva 2 HR-10000 Zagreb CROATIA
ITALIEN	UFFICIO ESPORTAZIONE DI BOLOGNA Viale delle Belle Arti 56 40126 Bologna BO ITALIA
	UFFICIO ESPORTAZIONE DI CAGLIARI Via Cesare Battisti 2 09123 Cagliari CA ITALIA
	UFFICIO ESPORTAZIONE DI FIRENZE Piazza Pitti 1 50122 Firenze FI ITALIA
	UFFICIO ESPORTAZIONE DI GENOVA Via Balbi 10 16126 Genova GE ITALIA
	UFFICIO ESPORTAZIONE DI MILANO Via Brera 28 20121 Milano MI ITALIA
	UFFICIO ESPORTAZIONE DI NAPOLI Via Tito Angelini 20 — Castel S. Elmo 80129 Napoli NA ITALIA
	UFFICIO ESPORTAZIONE DI PALERMO Via P. Calvi 13 90139 Palermo PA ITALIA
	UFFICIO ESPORTAZIONE DI PISA Lungarno Pacinotti 46 56126 Pisa PI ITALIA

B.II.2b Ausfuhrgenehmigungsbehörden nach VO (EG) 116/2009

Mitgliedstaat	Zuständige Behörden
	UFFICIO ESPORTAZIONE DI ROMA Via Cernaia 1 00185 Roma RM ITALIA
	UFFICIO ESPORTAZIONE DI TORINO Via Accademia delle Scienze 5 10123 Torino TO ITALIA
	UFFICIO ESPORTAZIONE DI VENEZIA Piazza San Marco 63 30124 Venezia VE ITALIA
	UFFICIO ESPORTAZIONE DI VERONA Via Corte Dogana 2/4 37121 Verona VR ITALIA
ZYPERN	The Director of the Department of Antiquities of the Ministry of Communications and Works Museum Street 1 1516 Nicosia CYPRUS
	The Director of the Cultural Services of the Ministry of Education and Culture Kimonos and Thoukididou Street 1434 Nicosia CYPRUS
	The Registrar of the Public Records Office of the Ministry of Justice and Public Order State Archives 1461 Nicosia CYPRUS
	The Director of the Department of Geological Studies of the Ministry of Agriculture, Natural Resources and Environment Cyprus Geological Survey 1415 Nicosia CYPRUS
	The Director of the Department of Environment of the Ministry of Agriculture, Natural Resources and Environment Environment Service 1498 Nicosia CYPRUS
	The Director of the State Library of the Ministry of Education and Culture Cyprus Library 1011 Nicosia CYPRUS
LETTLAND	Valsts kultūras pieminekļu aizsardzības inspekcija State Inspection for Heritage Protection Maza Pils iela 19 Rīga, LV-1050 LATVIJA

Ausfuhrgenehmigungsbehörden nach VO (EG) 116/2009 B.II.2b

Mitgliedstaat	Zuständige Behörden
LITAUEN	Kulturos paveldo departamentas prie Kultūros ministerijos Department of Cultural Heritage under Ministry of Culture Snipiskiu g. 3 Snipiskiu st. 3 LT-09309 Vilnius LIETUVA/LITHUANIA
LUXEMBURG	Ministère de la culture 4, bd Roosevelt 2450 Luxembourg LUXEMBOURG
UNGARN	Forster Gyula Nemzeti Örökséggazdálkodási és Szolgáltatási Központ – Műtárgyfelügyeleti Iroda (Gyula Forster National Centre for Cultural Heritage Management – Inspectorate of Cultural Goods) Budapest Táncsics M. u. 1. 1014 MAGYARORSZÁG/HUNGARY
MALTA	The Superintendence of Cultural Heritage 173, St Christopher Street Valletta VLT 2000 MALTA
NIEDERLANDE	Ministry of Education, Culture and Science Cultural Heritage Inspectorate PO Box 16478 (IPC 3500) 2500 BL The Hague NEDERLAND Customs Administration Central licensing office for import and export PO Box 30003 9700 RD Groningen NEDERLAND
ÖSTERREICH	Bundesdenkmalamt Hofburg, Säulenstiege 1010 Wien ÖSTERREICH *Für Archive:* Österreichisches Staatsarchiv Nottendorferstraße 2 1030 Wien ÖSTERREICH
POLEN	Muzeum Narodowe we Wrocławiu pl. Powstańców 5 50-153 Wrocław POLSKA/POLAND

B.II.2b Ausfuhrgenehmigungsbehörden nach VO (EG) 116/2009

Mitgliedstaat	Zuständige Behörden
	Wojewódzki Urząd Ochrony Zabytków we Wrocławiu Delegatura w Jeleniej Górze ul. 1 Maja 23 58-500 Jelenia Góra POLSKA/POLAND
	Wojewódzki Urząd Ochrony Zabytków we Wrocławiu Delegatura w Legnicy ul. Zamkowa 2 59-220 Legnica POLSKA/POLAND
	Wojewódzki Urząd Ochrony Zabytków we Wrocławiu Delegatura w Wałbrzychu ul. Zamkowa 3 58-300 Wałbrzych POLSKA/POLAND
	Wojewódzki Urząd Ochrony Zabytków w Toruniu ul. Łazienna 8 87-100 Toruń POLSKA/POLAND
	Wojewódzki Urząd Ochrony Zabytków w Toruniu Delegatura w Bydgoszczy ul. Jezuicka 2 85-102 Bydgoszcz POLSKA/POLAND
	Wojewódzki Urząd Ochrony Zabytków w Toruniu Delegatura we Włocławku ul. Łęgska 42 87-800 Włocławek POLSKA/POLAND
	Wojewódzki Urząd Ochrony Zabytków w Lublinie ul. Archidiakońska 4 20-113 Lublin POLSKA/POLAND
	Wojewódzki Urząd Ochrony Zabytków w Lublinie Delegatura w Białej Podlaskiej ul. Janowska 27/29 21-500 Biała Podlaska POLSKA/POLAND
	Wojewódzki Urząd Ochrony Zabytków w Lublinie Delegatura w Chełmie pl. Niepodległości 1, Blok E 22-100 Chełm POLSKA/POLAND
	Wojewódzki Urząd Ochrony Zabytków w Lublinie Delegatura w Zamościu ul. Staszica 29 22-400 Zamość POLSKA/POLAND

Mitgliedstaat	Zuständige Behörden
	Wojewódzki Urząd Ochrony Zabytków w Zielonej Górze ul. Kopernika 1 65-063 Zielona Góra POLSKA/POLAND
	Wojewódzki Urząd Ochrony Zabytków w Zielonej Górze Delegatura w Gorzowie Wlkp. ul. Kosynierów Gdyńskich 75 66-400 Gorzów Wlkp. POLSKA/POLAND
	Wojewódzki Urząd Ochrony Zabytków w Łodzi ul. Piotrkowska 99 90-425 Łódź POLSKA/POLAND
	Wojewódzki Urząd Ochrony Zabytków w Łodzi Delegatura w Piotrkowie Trybunalskim ul. Farna 8 97-300 Piotrków Trybunalski POLSKA/POLAND
	Wojewódzki Urząd Ochrony Zabytków w Łodzi Delegatura w Sieradzu ul. Kościuszki 3 98-200 Sieradz POLSKA/POLAND
	Wojewódzki Urząd Ochrony Zabytków w Łodzi Delegatura w Skierniewicach ul. Trzcińska 18 96-100 Skierniewice POLSKA/POLAND
	Wojewódzki Urząd Ochrony Zabytków w Krakowie ul. Kanonicza 24 31-002 Kraków POLSKA/POLAND
	Wojewódzki Urząd Ochrony Zabytków w Krakowie Delegatura w Nowym Sączu ul. Wiśniowieckiego 127 33-300 Nowy Sącz POLSKA/POLAND
	Wojewódzki Urząd Ochrony Zabytków w Krakowie Delegatura w Nowym Targu ul. Jana Kazimierza 22 34-400 Nowy Targ POLSKA/POLAND
	Wojewódzki Urząd Ochrony Zabytków w Krakowie Delegatura w Tarnowie ul. Konarskiego 15 33-100 Tarnów POLSKA/POLAND

B.II.2b Ausfuhrgenehmigungsbehörden nach VO (EG) 116/2009

Mitgliedstaat	Zuständige Behörden
	Wojewódzki Urząd Ochrony Zabytków w Warszawie ul. Nowy Świat 18/20 00-373 Warszawa POLSKA/POLAND
	Wojewódzki Urząd Ochrony Zabytków w Warszawie Delegatura w Ciechanowie ul. Strażacka 6 06-400 Ciechanów POLSKA/POLAND
	Wojewódzki Urząd Ochrony Zabytków w Warszawie Delegatura w Ostrołęce ul. Kościuszki 16 07-400 Ostrołęka POLSKA/POLAND
	Wojewódzki Urząd Ochrony Zabytków w Warszawie Delegatura w Płocku ul. Zduńska 13a 09-400 Płock POLSKA/POLAND
	Wojewódzki Urząd Ochrony Zabytków w Warszawie Delegatura w Radomiu ul. Żeromskiego 53 26-600 Radom POLSKA/POLAND
	Wojewódzki Urząd Ochrony Zabytków w Warszawie Delegatura w Siedlcach ul. Bema 4a 08-110 Siedlce POLSKA/POLAND
	Wojewódzki Urząd Ochrony Zabytków w Opolu ul. Piastowska 14 45-082 Opole POLSKA/POLAND
	Muzeum Śląska Opolskiego w Opolu ul. Św. Wojciecha 13 45-023 Opole POLSKA/POLAND
	Wojewódzki Urząd Ochrony Zabytków w Przemyślu ul. Jagiellońska 29 37-700 Przemyśl POLSKA/POLAND
	Wojewódzki Urząd Ochrony Zabytków w Przemyślu Delegatura w Krośnie ul. Bieszczadzka 1 38-400 Krosno POLSKA/POLAND

Ausfuhrgenehmigungsbehörden nach VO (EG) 116/2009 B.II.2b

Mitgliedstaat	Zuständige Behörden
	Wojewódzki Urząd Ochrony Zabytków w Przemyślu Delegatura w Rzeszowie ul. Mickiewicza 7 35-064 Rzeszów POLSKA/POLAND
	Wojewódzki Urząd Ochrony Zabytków w Przemyślu Delegatura w Tarnobrzegu ul. 1 Maja 4 39-400 Tarnobrzeg POLSKA/POLAND
	Wojewódzki Urząd Ochrony Zabytków w Białymstoku ul. Dojlidy Fabryczne 23 15-554 Białystok POLSKA/POLAND
	Wojewódzki Urząd Ochrony Zabytków w Białymstoku Delegatura w Łomży ul. Nowa 2 18-400 Łomża POLSKA/POLAND
	Wojewódzki Urząd Ochrony Zabytków w Białymstoku Delegatura w Suwałkach ul. Sejneńska 13 16-400 Suwałki POLSKA/POLAND
	Wojewódzki Urząd Ochrony Zabytków w Gdańsku ul. Kotwiczników 20 80-881 Gdańsk POLSKA/POLAND
	Wojewódzki Urząd Ochrony Zabytków w Gdańsku Delegatura w Słupsku ul. Jaracza 6 76-200 Słupsk POLSKA/POLAND
	Wojewódzki Urząd Ochrony Zabytków w Katowicach ul. Francuska 12 40-015 Katowice POLSKA/POLAND
	Wojewódzki Urząd Ochrony Zabytków w Katowicach Delegatura w Bielsku-Białej ul. Powstańców Śląskich 6 43-300 Bielsko-Biała POLSKA/POLAND
	Wojewódzki Urząd Ochrony Zabytków w Katowicach Delegatura w Częstochowie ul. Mirowska 8 42-217 Częstochowa POLSKA/POLAND

B.II.2b Ausfuhrgenehmigungsbehörden nach VO (EG) 116/2009

Mitgliedstaat	Zuständige Behörden
	Wojewódzki Urząd Ochrony Zabytków w Kielcach ul. Zamkowa 5 25-009 Kielce POLSKA/POLAND
	Wojewódzki Urząd Ochrony Zabytków w Olsztynie ul. Podwale 1 10-076 Olsztyn POLSKA/POLAND
	Wojewódzki Urząd Ochrony Zabytków w Olsztynie Delegatura w Elblągu ul. Św. Ducha 19 82-300 Elbląg POLSKA/POLAND
	Wojewódzki Urząd Ochrony Zabytków w Olsztynie Delegatura w Ełku ul. Mickiewicza 11 19-300 Ełk POLSKA/POLAND
	Wojewódzki Urząd Ochrony Zabytków w Poznaniu ul. Gołębia 2 61-834 Poznań POLSKA/POLAND
	Wojewódzki Urząd Ochrony Zabytków w Poznaniu Delegatura w Kaliszu ul. Tuwima 10 62-800 Kalisz POLSKA/POLAND
	Wojewódzki Urząd Ochrony Zabytków w Poznaniu Delegatura w Koninie al. 1 Maja 7, pokoje 308–314 62-510 Konin POLSKA/POLAND
	Wojewódzki Urząd Ochrony Zabytków w Poznaniu Delegatura w Lesznie pl. Komeńskiego 6 64-100 Leszno POLSKA/POLAND
	Wojewódzki Urząd Ochrony Zabytków w Poznaniu Delegatura w Pile ul. Śniadeckich 46 64-920 Piła POLSKA/POLAND
	Wojewódzki Urząd Ochrony Zabytków w Szczecinie ul. Wały Chrobrego 4 70-502 Szczecin POLSKA/POLAND

Ausfuhrgenehmigungsbehörden nach VO (EG) 116/2009 B.II.2b

Mitgliedstaat	Zuständige Behörden
	Wojewódzki Urząd Ochrony Zabytków w Szczecinie Delegatura w Koszalinie ul. Władysława Andersa 34 75-626 Koszalin POLSKA/POLAND
	Narodowy Instytut Muzealnictwa i Ochrony Zbiorów ul. Goraszewska 7 02-910 Warszawa POLSKA/POLAND
	Biblioteka Narodowa al. Niepodległości 213 02-086 Warszawa POLSKA/POLAND
	Naczelna Dyrekcja Archiwów Państwowych ul. Rakowiecka 2D 02-517 Warszawa POLSKA/POLAND
PORTUGAL	Para as espécies bibliográficas Biblioteca Nacional de Portugal Campo Grande 83.º 1749-081 Lisboa PORTUGAL
	Para os bens do património arquivístico e fotográfico Direção-Geral de Arquivos Alameda da Universidade 1649-010 Lisboa PORTUGAL
	Para os bens do património audiovisual Cinemateca Portuguesa — Museu do Cinema, I.P. Rua Barata Salgueiro 39.º 1269-059 Lisboa PORTUGAL
	Para os restantes bens culturais Direção-Geral do Património Cultural Palácio Nacional da Ajuda 1349-021 Lisboa PORTUGAL
RUMÄNIEN	1. Direcţia Judeţeană pentru Cultură Alba (D.J.C. Alba) Str. Regina Maria nr. 20 510103 Alba Iulia ROMÂNIA
	2. Direcţia Judeţeană pentru Cultură Arad (D.J.C. Arad) Str. Gheorghe Lazăr nr. 21 310126 Arad ROMÂNIA
	3. Direcţia Judeţeană pentru Cultură Argeş (D.J.C. Argeş) Piaţa Vasile Milea nr. 1 110053 Piteşti

B.II.2b Ausfuhrgenehmigungsbehörden nach VO (EG) 116/2009   354

Mitgliedstaat	Zuständige Behörden
	ROMÂNIA
	4. **Direcția Județeană pentru Cultură Bacău (D.J.C. Bacău)** Str. Vasile Alecsandri nr. 41, etaj IV 600011 Bacău ROMÂNIA
	5. **Direcția Județeană pentru Cultură Bihor (D.J.C. Bihor)** Str. Moscovei nr. 25 4110001 Oradea ROMÂNIA
	6. **Direcția Județeană pentru Cultură Bistrița-Năsăud (D.J.C. Bistrița-Năsăud)** Str. Eremia Grigorescu nr. 6 420018 Bistrița ROMÂNIA
	7. **Direcția Județeană pentru Cultură Botoșani (D.J.C. Botoșani)** Str. Unirii nr. 10 710221 Botoșani ROMÂNIA
	8. **Direcția Județeană pentru Cultură Brașov (D.J.C. Brașov)** Str. Michael Weiss nr. 22 500031 Brașov ROMÂNIA
	9. **Direcția Județeană pentru Cultură Brăila (D.J.C. Brăila)** Str. Mihai Eminescu nr. 10-12 810024 Brăila ROMÂNIA
	10. **Direcția Județeană pentru Cultură Buzău (D.J.C. Buzău)** Bd. Nicolae Bălcescu nr. 48 120525 Buzău ROMÂNIA
	11. **Direcția Județeană pentru Cultură Caraș-Severin (D.J.C. Caraș-Severin)** Piața 1 Decembrie 1918 nr. 30-31 320067 Reșița ROMÂNIA
	12. **Direcția Județeană pentru Cultură Călărași (D.J.C. Călărași)** Str. 13 Decembrie nr. 9 A 910014 Călărași ROMÂNIA
	13. **Direcția Județeană pentru Cultură Cluj (D.J.C. Cluj)** Piața Unirii nr. 1 400133 Cluj-Napoca ROMÂNIA
	14. **Direcția Județeană pentru Cultură Constanța (D.J.C. Constanța)** Str. Mircea cel Bătrân nr. 106 900663 Constanța

Ausfuhrgenehmigungsbehörden nach VO (EG) 116/2009 B.II.2b

Mitgliedstaat	Zuständige Behörden
	ROMÂNIA
	15. **Direcția Județeană pentru Cultură Covasna** (D.J.C. Covasna) Str. Gabor Aron nr. 1 520003 Covasna ROMÂNIA
	16. **Direcția Județeană pentru Cultură Dâmbovița** (D.J.C. Dâmbovița) Piața Tricolorului nr. 1 130140 Târgoviște ROMÂNIA
	17. **Direcția Județeană pentru Cultură Dolj** (D.J.C. Dolj) Str. M. Viteazu nr. 14 200417 Craiova ROMÂNIA
	18. **Direcția Județeană pentru Cultură Galați** (D.J.C. Galați) Str. Domnească nr. 84, bl. Miorița, sc. 1, ap. 2, et. I-II 800215 Galați ROMÂNIA
	19. **Direcția Județeană pentru Cultură Giurgiu** (D.J.C. Giurgiu) Str. Livezilor nr. 3 080246 Giurgiu ROMÂNIA
	20. **Direcția Județeană pentru Cultură Gorj** (D.J.C. Gorj) Calea Eroilor nr. 15-17 210135 Târgu-Jiu ROMÂNIA
	21. **Direcția Județeană pentru Cultură Harghita** (D.J.C. Harghita) Piata Libertății nr. 5 530140 Miercurea-Ciuc ROMÂNIA
	22. **Direcția Județeană pentru Cultură Hunedoara** (D.J.C. Hunedoara) Str. Octavian Goga nr. 1 330018 Deva ROMÂNIA
	23. **Direcția Județeană pentru Cultură Ialomița** (D.J.C. Ialomița) Str. Matei Basarab nr. 26 920055 Slobozia ROMÂNIA
	24. **Direcția Județeană pentru Cultură Iași** (D.J.C. Iași) Str. Ștefan cel Mare și Sfânt nr. 69 70075 Iași ROMÂNIA
	25. **Direcția Județeană pentru Cultură Maramureș** (D.J.C. Maramureș) Str. Pictorilor nr. 4

B.II.2b Ausfuhrgenehmigungsbehörden nach VO (EG) 116/2009

Mitgliedstaat	Zuständige Behörden
	430145 Baia Mare ROMÂNIA 26. **Direcția Județeană pentru Cultură Mehedinți (D.J.C. Mehedinți)** Aleea Mihai Gusita nr. 6, etaj 3 220055 Drobeta Turnu-Severin ROMÂNIA 27. **Direcția Județeană pentru Cultură Mureș (D.J.C. Mureș)** Str. Mărăști nr. 8 540328 Târgu-Mureș ROMÂNIA 28. **Direcția Județeană pentru Cultură Neamț (D.J.C. Neamț)** Bd. Traian nr. 17, bl. A4, etaj I 610136 Piatra-Neamț ROMÂNIA 29. **Direcția Județeană pentru Cultură Olt (D.J.C. Olt)** Str. Dinu Lipatti nr. 6 230086 Slatina ROMÂNIA 30. **Direcția Județeană pentru Cultură Prahova (D.J.C. Prahova)** Str. Nicolae Iorga nr. 18 100537 Ploiești ROMÂNIA 31. **Direcția Județeană pentru Cultură Satu Mare (D.J.C. Satu Mare)** Piața 25 Octombrie nr. 1 440026 Satu Mare ROMÂNIA 32. **Direcția Județeană pentru Cultură Sălaj (D.J.C. Sălaj)** Piața Iuliu Maniu nr. 13 450016 Zalău ROMÂNIA 33. **Direcția Județeană pentru Cultură Sibiu (D.J.C. Sibiu)** Str. Tribunei nr. 6 550176 Sibiu ROMÂNIA 34. **Direcția Județeană pentru Cultură Suceava (D.J.C. Suceava)** Str. Mihai Viteazu nr. 27 720061 Suceava ROMÂNIA 35. **Direcția Județeană pentru Cultură Teleorman (D.J.C. Teleorman)** Str. Dunării nr. 222, bl. 911, sc. E, ap. 40 140065 Alexandria ROMÂNIA 36. **Direcția Județeană pentru Cultură Timiș (D.J.C. Timiș)** Str. Episcop Augustin Pacha nr. 8 300055 Timișoara

Mitgliedstaat	Zuständige Behörden
	ROMÂNIA
	37. **Direcția Județeană pentru Cultură Tulcea (D.J.C. Tulcea)** Str. Isaccei nr. 20 820241 Tulcea ROMÂNIA
	38. **Direcția Județeană pentru Cultură Vaslui (D.J.C. Vaslui)** Str. Ștefan cel Mare nr. 79 730168 Vaslui ROMÂNIA
	39. **Direcția Județeană pentru Cultură Vâlcea (D.J.C. Vâlcea)** Str. Tudor Vladimirescu nr. 1 240168 Râmnicu-Vâlcea ROMÂNIA
	40. **Direcția Județeană pentru Cultură Vrancea (D.J.C. Vrancea)** Str. Nicolae Titulescu nr. 1 620018 Focșani ROMÂNIA
	41. **Direcția Județeană pentru Cultură Ilfov (D.J.C. Ilfov)** Str. Studioului nr. 1 070000 Buftea ROMÂNIA
	42. **Direcția pentru Cultură București (D.C. București)** Str. Sfântul Ștefan nr. 3, sector 2 023996 București ROMÂNIA
SLOWENIEN	**Ministrstvo za kulturo Republike Slovenije** The ministry of culture of The Republic of Slovenia Maistrova 10 SI-1000 Ljubljana SLOVENIA
SLOWAKEI	**Ministerstvo kultúry Slovenskej republiky/Ministry of Culture of the Slovak Republic** sekcia kultúrneho dedičstva/Section of Cultural Heritage Námestie SNP 33 813 31 Bratislava SLOVENSKO/SLOVAKIA
	Ministerstvo vnútra Slovenskej republiky/Ministry of the Interior of the Slovak Republic sekcia verejnej správy/Section of Public Administration odbor archívov/Department of archives Križkova 7 811 04 Bratislava SLOVENSKO/SLOVAKIA
FINNLAND	**Museovirasto (National Board of Antiquities)** PL 913 FI-00101 Helsinki SUOMI/FINLAND

B.II.2b Ausfuhrgenehmigungsbehörden nach VO (EG) 116/2009

Mitgliedstaat	Zuständige Behörden
	Kansallisgalleria (National Gallery) Kaivokatu 2 FI-00100 Helsinki SUOMI/FINLAND
SCHWEDEN	**The Swedish National Heritage Board** Riksantikvarieämbetet Box 5405 SE-114 84 Stockholm SVERIGE **National Library of Sweden** Kungliga biblioteket Box 5039 SE-102 41 Stockholm SVERIGE **National Archives** Riksarkivet Box 12541 SE-102 29 Stockholm SVERIGE **Nationalmuseum med Prins Eugens Waldemarsudde** Box 161 76 SE-103 24 Stockholm SVERIGE **Nordiska museet** Box 27820 SE-115 93 Stockholm SVERIGE
VEREINIGTES KÖNIGREICH	Arts Council, England Export Licensing Unit 21 Bloomsbury Street London WC1B 3HF UNITED KINGDOM E-Mail: elu@artscouncil.org.uk Internet: http://www.artscouncil.org.uk/what-we-do/supporting-museums/cultural-property/export-controls/export-licensing/

Liste der Zollstellen, die für die Erfüllung der Ausfuhrzollformalitäten für Kulturgüter zuständig sind, veröffentlicht gemäß Artikel 5 Absatz 2 der Verordnung (EG) Nr. 116/09 des Rates[1]

(2009/C 134/05)

Mitgliedstaat	Name der Zollstelle	(gegebenenfalls) Region
BELGIEN	Alle Zollstellen	
BULGARIEN	Териториално митническо управление Бургас Customs house Bourgas (BG001000) Митнически пункт Летище Бургас Border point Letishte Bourgas (BG001002) Митнически пункт Малко Търново Border point Malko Tarnovo (BG1003) Териториално митническо управление Варна Customs house Varna (BG002000) Митнически пункт Летище Варна Border point Letishte Varna (BG002003) Митнически пункт Пристанище Варна Border point Pristanishte Varna (BG002005) Териториално митническо управление Пловдив Customs house Plovdiv (BG003000) Митническо бюро Международен пловдивски панаир Customs office Mejdunaroden plovdivski panair (BG003003) Митнически пункт Капитан Андреево Border point Kapitan Andreevo (BG003103) Териториално митническо управление Русе Customs house Rousse (BG004000) Митническо бюро Русе Customs office Rousse (BG004003) Териториално митническо управление Видин Customs house Vidin (BG004100) Териториално митническо управление Свищов Customs house Svishtov (BG004300) Митническо бюро Горна Оряховица Customs office Gorna Oryahovitza (BG4302) Териториално митническо управление Силистра Customs house Silistra (BG004400) Териториално митническо управление София Customs house Sofia (BG005000) Териториално митническо управление Аерогара София Customs house Aerogara Sofia (BG005100) Митнически пункт Летище София Border point Letishte Sofia (BG005106)	

---

[1] ABl. L 39 vom 10.2.2009, S. 1. Die Verordnung ist abgedruckt als Nr. B.II.2.

B.II.2c Zollstellen nach VO (EG) 116/2009

	Териториално митническо управление Благоевград Customs house Blagoevgrad (BG005200) Митнически пункт Калотина Border point Kalotina (BG005304) Териториално митническо управление Кулата Customs house Kulata (BG005400) Териториално митническо управление Кюстендил Customs house (BG005500) Митнически пункт Гюешево Border point Gjueshevo (BG005501) Териториално митническо управление Перник Customs house Pernik (BG5600)	
TSCHECHISCHE REPUBLIK	Alle Zollstellen	
DÄNEMARK	Alle Zollstellen	
DEUTSCHLAND	Alle Zollstellen	
ESTLAND	Alle Zollstellen	
GRIECHENLAND	Customs Offices of Athens 4th Customs Office of Thessalonica	
SPANIEN	Aduana provincial de Cádiz Aduana de Algeciras Aduana provincial de Málaga Aduana del aeropuerto de Málaga Aduana provincial de Sevilla Aduana provincial de Zaragoza Aduana del aeropuerto de Zaragoza Aduana provincial de Baleares Aduana del aeropuerto de Palma de Mallorca Aduana provincial de Las Palmas Aduana del aeropuerto de Las Palmas Aduana provincial de Santa Cruz de Tenerife Aduana del aeropuerto de Santa Cruz de Tenerife-Reina Sofía Aduana del aeropuerto de Santa Cruz de Tenerife-Los Ro deos Aduana provincial de Barcelona Aduana de Barcelona-marítima Aduana de Barcelona-carretera Aduana del aeropuerto de Barcelona-El Prat Aduana provincial de A Coruña Aduana del aeropuerto de Santiago de Compostela Aduana Provincial de Madrid Aduana de Madrid-carretera Aduana del aeropuerto de Madrid-Barajas	

	Aduana de Madrid-ferrocarril	
	Recinto habilitado CTM (Centro de Transportes de Madrid)	
	Aduana provincial de Vizcaya	
	Aduana de Bilbao-marítima	
	Aduana del aeropuerto de Bilbao	
	Aduana de Bilbao-carretera-Apárcabisa	
	Aduana provincial de Alicante	
	Aduana del aeropuerto de Alicante	
	Aduana provincial de Valencia	
	Aduana de Valencia-marítima	
	Aduana del aeropuerto de Valencia-Manises	
FRANKREICH	Alle Zollstellen	
IRLAND	Alle Zollstellen	
ITALIEN	Alle Zollstellen	
ZYPERN	District Customs House of Nicosia	Nicosia
	District Customs House of Larnaca	Larnaca
	District Customs House of Limassol	Limassol
LETTLAND	Alle Zollstellen	
LITAUEN	Alle Zollstellen	
LUXEMBURG	Bureau des douanes et accises	
	Luxembourg airport	
	Boîte postale 61	
	L-6905 Niederanven	
	Centre douanier	
	Croix de Gasperich	
	Boîte postale 1122	
	L-1352 Luxembourg	
UNGARN	South-Pest Regional Main Customs Office	Budapest
	Buda-Regional Main Customs Office	County Pest
	Main Customs Office Nr 17	Non-commercial traffic
	Customs Office Letenye	Croatian border section
	Customs Office Gyékényes	Croatian border section
	Customs Office Röszke	Serbian border section
	Customs Office Tompa	Serbian border section
	Customs Office Záhony	Ukrainian border section
	Airport Customs Office Nr 1 Ferihegy Airport (Budapest)	Air traffic
	Main Customs Office Győr	Győr-Moson-Sopron County
	Main Customs Office Szombathely	Vas County
	Main Customs Office Zalaegerszeg	Zala County
	Main Customs Office Veszprém	Veszprém
	Main Customs Office Tatabánya	Komárom-Esztergom County
	Main Customs Office Székesfehérvár	Fejér County

B.II.2c Zollstellen nach VO (EG) 116/2009

	Main Customs Office Szekszárd	Tolna County
	Main Customs Office Kaposvár	Somogy County
	Main Customs Office Pécs	Baranya County
	Main Customs Office Salgótarján	Nógrád County
	Main Customs Office Eger	Heves County
	Main Customs Office Miskolc	Borsod-Abaúj-Zempéln County
	Main Customs Office Nyíregyháza	Szabolcs-Szatmár-Bereg County
	Main Customs Office Debrecen	Hajdú-Bihar County
	Main Customs Office Szolnok	Jász-Nagykun-Szolnok County
	Main Customs Office Békéscsaba	Békés County
	Main Customs Office Szeged	Csongrád County
	Main Customs Office Kecskemét	Bács-Kiskun County
MALTA	Customs Economic Procedures Unit Lascaris Wharf, Valletta VLT 1920	
NIEDERLANDE	Alle Zollstellen	
ÖSTERREICH	Alle Zollstellen	
POLEN	Alle Zollstellen	
PORTUGAL	Alfândega Marítima de Lisboa	
	Alfândega do Aeroporto de Lisboa Alfândega de Alverca	
	Alfândega de Leixões	
	Alfândega do Aeroporto de Sá Carneiro (Porto)	
	Alfândega do Funchal	
	Alfândega de Ponta Delgada	
RUMÄNIEN	Alle Zollstellen	
SLOWENIEN	Alle Zollstellen	
SLOWAKEI	Alle Zollstellen	
FINNLAND	Alle Zollstellen	
SCHWEDEN	Alle Zollstellen	
VEREINIGTES KÖNIGREICH	Alle großen Zollstellen im Vereinigten Königreich	

Richtlinie 2014/60/EU des Europäischen Parlaments und des Rates vom 15. Mai 2014 über die Rückgabe von unrechtmäßig aus dem Hoheitsgebiet eines Mitgliedstaats verbrachten Kulturgütern und zur Änderung der Verordnung (EU) Nr. 1024/2012 (Neufassung)

(ABl. Nr. L 159 S. 1[1]); berichtigt in ABl. L 147 vom 12.6.2015, S. 24)

DAS EUROPÄISCHE PARLAMENT UND DER RAT DER EUROPÄISCHEN UNION –
gestützt auf den Vertrag über die Arbeitsweise der Europäischen Union, insbesondere auf Artikel 114,
auf Vorschlag der Europäischen Kommission,
nach Zuleitung des Entwurfs des Gesetzgebungsakts an die nationalen Parlamente,
gemäß dem ordentlichen Gesetzgebungsverfahren[2],
in Erwägung folgender Gründe:

(1) Die Richtlinie 93/7/EWG des Rates[3] ist durch die Richtlinien 96/100/EG[4] und 2001/38/EG[5] des Europäischen Parlaments und des Rates in wesentlichen Punkten geändert worden. Da nunmehr weitere Änderungen vorgenommen werden sollen, empfiehlt sich aus Gründen der Klarheit eine Neufassung.

(2) Der Binnenmarkt umfasst einen Raum ohne Binnengrenzen, in dem der freie Verkehr von Waren, Personen, Dienstleistungen und Kapital gemäß dem Vertrag über die Arbeitsweise der Europäischen Union gewährleistet ist (AEUV). Gemäß Artikel 36 AEUV stehen die einschlägigen Bestimmungen über den freien Warenverkehr Einfuhr-, Ausfuhr- und Durchfuhrverboten oder -beschränkungen nicht entgegen, die zum Schutz des nationalen Kulturgutes von künstlerischem, geschichtlichem oder archäologischem Wert gerechtfertigt sind.

(3) Aufgrund und im Rahmen von Artikel 36 AEUV haben die Mitgliedstaaten das Recht, ihre nationalen Kulturgüter zu bestimmen und die notwendigen Maßnahmen zu deren Schutz zu treffen. Dennoch spielt die Union eine wertvolle Rolle, indem sie die Zusammenarbeit zwischen den Mitgliedstaaten beim Schutz des kulturellen Erbes von europäischer Bedeutung fördert, zu dem das genannte nationale Kulturgut gehört.

(4) Mit der Richtlinie 93/7/EWG wurde eine Rückgaberegelung eingeführt, die es den Mitgliedstaaten ermöglicht, die Rückgabe von Kulturgütern in ihr Hoheitsgebiet zu erreichen, die im Sinne von Artikel 36 AEUV als nationales Kulturgut eingestuft sind, das unter die gemeinsamen Kategorien von Kulturgütern gemäß dem Anhang dieser Richtlinie fällt, und die in Verletzung der nationalen Vorschriften oder der Verordnung (EG) Nr. 116/2009 des Rates[6] aus ihrem Hoheitsgebiet verbracht wurden. Diese Richtlinie erfasste auch Kulturgüter, die als nationales Kulturgut eingestuft wurden und zu öffentlichen Sammlungen gehören oder im Bestandsverzeichnis kirchlicher Einrichtungen aufgeführt sind und nicht unter diese gemeinsamen Kategorien fallen.

(5) Aufgrund der Richtlinie 93/7/EWG arbeiten die Mitgliedstaaten auf Verwaltungsebene in Fragen ihres nationalen Kulturgutes zusammen, und zwar in enger Verbindung mit ihrer Zusammenarbeit mit Interpol und anderen zuständigen Stellen in Bezug auf gestohlene Kunstwerke, wobei insbesondere verlorengegangene, gestohlene oder unrechtmäßig verbrachte Kulturgüter,

---
1) Veröffentlicht am 28.5.2014.
2) **Amtl. Anm.:** Standpunkt des Europäischen Parlaments vom 16. April 2014 (noch nicht im Amtsblatt veröffentlicht) und Beschluss des Rates vom 8. Mai 2014.
3) **Amtl. Anm.:** Richtlinie 93/7/EWG des Rates vom 15. März 1993 über die Rückgabe von unrechtmäßig aus dem Hoheitsgebiet eines Mitgliedstaats verbrachten Kulturgütern (ABl. L 74 vom 27.3.1993, S. 74).
4) **Amtl. Anm.:** Richtlinie 96/100/EG des Europäischen Parlaments und des Rates vom 17. Februar 1997 zur Änderung des Anhangs der Richtlinie 93/7/EWG über die Rückgabe von unrechtmäßig aus dem Hoheitsgebiet eines Mitgliedstaats verbrachten Kulturgütern (ABl. L 60 vom 1.3.1997, S. 59).
5) **Amtl. Anm.:** Richtlinie 2001/38/EG des Europäischen Parlaments und des Rates vom 5. Juni 2001 zur Änderung des Anhangs der Richtlinie 93/7/EWG über die Rückgabe von unrechtmäßig aus dem Hoheitsgebiet eines Mitgliedstaats verbrachten Kulturgütern (ABl. L 187 vom 10.7.2001, S. 43).
6) **Amtl. Anm.:** Verordnung (EG) Nr. 116/2009 des Rates vom 18. Dezember 2008 über die Ausfuhr von Kulturgütern (ABl. L 39 vom 10.2.2009, S. 1).

die Teil des nationalen Kulturgutes und der öffentlichen Sammlungen der Mitgliedstaaten sind, zu erfassen sind.

(6) Das in der Richtlinie 93/7/EWG vorgesehene Rückgabeverfahren stellte einen ersten Schritt auf dem Wege zu einer Zusammenarbeit zwischen den Mitgliedstaaten auf dem Gebiet des Schutzes der Kulturgüter im Rahmen des Binnenmarktes dar, mit dem Ziel der weiteren gegenseitigen Anerkennung der einschlägigen nationalen Rechtsvorschriften.

(7) Die Verordnung (EG) Nr. 116/2009 – zusammen mit Richtlinie 93/7/EWG – führte eine Regelung auf Unionsebene zum Schutz der Kulturgüter der Mitgliedstaaten ein.

(8) Das Ziel der Richtlinie 93/7/EWG bestand darin, die materielle Rückgabe der Kulturgüter an den Mitgliedstaat sicherzustellen, aus dessen Hoheitsgebiet sie unrechtmäßig verbracht wurden – ungeachtet der an diesen Kulturgütern bestehenden Eigentumsrechten. Die Anwendung dieser Richtlinie hat jedoch die Grenzen der Regelung zur Rückgabe dieser Kulturgüter aufgezeigt. Die Berichte über die Umsetzung der Richtlinie haben aufgezeigt, dass die Richtlinie insbesondere aufgrund ihres begrenzten Anwendungsbereichs, der auf die im Anhang dieser Richtlinie festgelegten Bedingungen zurückzuführen ist, sowie aufgrund des kurzen Zeitraums für die Einleitung von Rückgabeverfahren und der mit diesen Verfahren verbundenen Kosten selten angewendet wurde.

(9) Der Geltungsbereich der vorliegenden Richtlinie sollte auf jedes Kulturgut ausgeweitet werden, das von einem Mitgliedstaat nach den nationalen Rechtsvorschriften oder Verwaltungsverfahren im Sinne des Artikels 36 AEUV als nationales Kulturgut von künstlerischem, geschichtlichem oder archäologischem Wert eingestuft oder definiert wurde. Die vorliegende Richtlinie sollte somit Gegenstände von historischem, paläontologischem, ethnographischem, numismatischem Interesse oder wissenschaftlichem Wert erfassen, unabhängig davon, ob es sich dabei um einen Teil einer öffentlichen oder sonstiger Sammlungen oder ein Einzelstück handelt und ob diese Gegenstände aus regulären oder unerlaubten Grabungen stammen, sofern sie als nationales Kulturgut eingestuft oder definiert sind. Des Weiteren sollten als nationales Kulturgut eingestufte oder definierte Kulturgüter nicht länger bestimmten Kategorien angehören und keine Alters- bzw. Wertgrenzen einhalten müssen, um für eine Rückgabe im Rahmen dieser Richtlinie in Frage zu kommen.

(10) In Artikel 36 AEUV wird die Vielfalt der nationalen Regelungen zum Schutz der nationalen Kulturgüter anerkannt. Um gegenseitiges Vertrauen, Bereitschaft zur Zusammenarbeit und Verständnis zwischen den Mitgliedstaaten zu fördern, sollte die Bedeutung des Begriffs "nationales Kulturgut" im Rahmen des Artikels 36 AEUV definiert werden. Die Mitgliedstaaten sollten zudem die Rückgabe von Kulturgütern an den Mitgliedstaat, aus dessen Hoheitsgebiet diese Güter unrechtmäßig verbracht wurden, ungeachtet des Zeitpunkts des Beitritts jenes Mitgliedstaats erleichtern und dafür sorgen, dass die Rückgabe solcher Güter keine unverhältnismäßigen Kosten verursacht. Es sollte den Mitgliedstaaten möglich sein, die Rückgabe von Kulturgütern unter Einhaltung der betreffenden Bestimmungen des AEUV zu veranlassen, die nicht als nationale Kulturgüter des AEUV eingestuft oder definiert sind, sowie von Kulturgütern, die vor dem 1. Januar 1993 unrechtmäßig verbracht wurden.

(11) Die Zusammenarbeit der Mitgliedstaaten auf der Verwaltungsebene sollte verstärkt werden, um eine wirksamere und einheitlichere Anwendung dieser Richtlinie zu fördern. Daher sollten die zentralen Stellen ersucht werden, wirksam untereinander zusammenzuarbeiten und Informationen über unrechtmäßig verbrachte Kulturgüter auszutauschen und hierzu das Binnenmarktinformationssystem ("IMI") gemäß der Verordnung (EU) Nr. 1024/2012 des Europäischen Parlaments und des Rates zu nutzen[1]). Im Hinblick auf eine bessere Umsetzung dieser Richtlinie sollte ein spezifisches Modul des IMI-Systems für Kulturgüter entwickelt werden. Es ist wünschenswert, dass auch die übrigen zuständigen Stellen der Mitgliedstaaten sich gegebenenfalls dieses Systems bedienen.

(12) Damit der Schutz personenbezogener Daten gewährleistet ist, sollten bei der administrativen Zusammenarbeit und beim Informationsaustausch zwischen den zuständigen Stellen die Re-

---

1) **Amtl. Anm.:** Verordnung (EU) Nr. 1024/2012 des Europäischen Parlaments und des Rates vom 25. Oktober 2012 über die Verwaltungszusammenarbeit mit Hilfe des Binnenmarkt-Informationssystems und zur Aufhebung der Entscheidung 2008/49/EG der Kommission (ABl. L 316 vom 14.11.2012, S. 1).

geln eingehalten werden, die in der Richtlinie 95/46/EG des Europäischen Parlaments und des Rates[1]) und, soweit das IMI eingesetzt wird, in der Verordnung (EU) Nr. 1024/2012 festgelegt sind. Die Begriffsbestimmungen der Richtlinie 95/46/EG und der Verordnung (EG) Nr. 45/2001 des Europäischen Parlaments und des Rates[2]) sollten auch für die Zwecke der vorliegenden Richtlinie gelten.

(13) Die Frist, innerhalb deren zu prüfen ist, ob das in einem anderen Mitgliedstaat aufgefundene Kulturgut ein Kulturgut im Sinne der Richtlinie 93/7/EWG darstellt, wurde für die Praxis als zu kurz erachtet. Daher sollte sie auf sechs Monate verlängert werden. Eine längere Frist sollte den Mitgliedstaaten ermöglichen, die Maßnahmen zu ergreifen, die notwendig sind, um das Kulturgut zu bewahren und gegebenenfalls zu verhindern, dass es dem Rückgabeverfahren entzogen wird.

(14) Die Frist für eine Rückgabeklage muss ebenfalls auf drei Jahre nach dem Zeitpunkt, zu dem der Mitgliedstaat, aus dessen Hoheitsgebiet das Kulturgut unrechtmäßig verbracht wurde, von dem Ort der Belegenheit des Kulturgutes und der Identität seines Eigenbesitzers oder Fremdbesitzers Kenntnis erhält, verlängert werden. Die Verlängerung dieses Zeitraums sollte die Rückgabe erleichtern und der unrechtmäßigen Verbringung nationaler Kulturgüter entgegenwirken. Der Eindeutigkeit halber sollte klargestellt werden, dass die Verjährungsfrist ab dem Zeitpunkt der Kenntnisnahme durch die zentrale Stelle des Mitgliedstaats, aus dessen Hoheitsgebiet das Kulturgut unrechtmäßig verbracht wurde, läuft.

(15) Gemäß der Richtlinie 93/7/EWG erlosch der Rückgabeanspruch 30 Jahre nach dem Zeitpunkt, zu dem das Kulturgut unrechtmäßig aus dem Hoheitsgebiet des Mitgliedstaats verbracht wurde. Im Fall von Kulturgütern, die zu öffentlichen Sammlungen gehören, sowie von Kulturgütern, die im Bestandsverzeichnis kirchlicher Einrichtungen in Mitgliedstaaten aufgeführt sind, in denen sie nach den nationalen Rechtsvorschriften besonderen Schutzregelungen unterliegen, gilt allerdings unter bestimmten Umständen eine längere Frist für den Rückgabeanspruch. Da Mitgliedstaaten nach den nationalen Rechtsvorschriften möglicherweise besondere Schutzregelungen für religiöse Einrichtungen anwenden, die keine kirchlichen Einrichtungen sind, sollte diese Richtlinie auch für diese anderen religiösen Einrichtungen gelten.

(16) In seinen Schlussfolgerungen über die Prävention und Bekämpfung des unrechtmäßigen Handels mit Kulturgütern vom 13./14. Dezember 2011 hat der Rat die Notwendigkeit von Maßnahmen zur wirksameren Prävention und Bekämpfung von Straftaten betreffend Kulturgüter anerkannt. Er empfahl, dass die Kommission zur Prävention und Bekämpfung des unrechtmäßigen Handels mit Kulturgütern die Mitgliedstaaten beim wirksamen Schutz von Kulturgütern unterstützt und gegebenenfalls ergänzende Maßnahmen fördert. Darüber hinaus empfahl der Rat, dass die Mitgliedstaaten die Ratifizierung des am 17. November 1970 in Paris unterzeichneten Unesco-Übereinkommens über die Maßnahmen zum Verbot und zur Verhütung der unzulässigen Einfuhr, Ausfuhr und Übereignung von Kulturgut und des am 24. Juni 1995 in Rom unterzeichneten UNIDROIT-Übereinkommens über gestohlene oder rechtswidrig ausgeführte Kulturgüter erwägen.

(17) Es sollte daher sichergestellt werden, dass alle Marktteilnehmer beim Handel mit Kulturgütern die erforderliche Sorgfalt walten lassen. Der Erwerb eines Kulturgutes mit illegaler Herkunft hat nur dann wirklich abschreckende Folgen, wenn der Eigenbesitzer des Gegenstandes neben der Zahlung einer Entschädigung auch dazu verpflichtet ist, nachzuweisen, dass er mit der erforderlichen Sorgfalt vorgegangen ist. Zur Verwirklichung der Ziele der Union auf dem Gebiet der Prävention und Bekämpfung des unrechtmäßigen Handels mit Kulturgütern sollte daher in dieser Richtlinie festgelegt werden, dass der Eigenbesitzer nur dann eine Entschädigung erhalten kann, wenn er nachweist, dass er beim Erwerb des Kulturgutes mit der gebotenen Sorgfalt vorgegangen ist.

---

1) **Amtl. Anm.:** Richtlinie 95/46/EG des Europäischen Parlaments und des Rates vom 24. Oktober 1995 zum Schutz natürlicher Personen bei der Verarbeitung personenbezogener Daten und zum freien Datenverkehr (ABl. L 281 vom 23.11.1995, S. 74).

2) **Amtl. Anm.:** Verordnung (EG) Nr. 45/2001 des Europäischen Parlaments und des Rates vom 18. Dezember 2000 zum Schutz natürlicher Personen bei der Verarbeitung personenbezogener Daten durch die Organe und Einrichtungen der Gemeinschaft und zum freien Datenverkehr (ABl. L 8 vom 12.1.2001, S. 1).

B.II.3 Richtlinie 2014/60/EU

(18) Es wäre ebenfalls für jede Person und insbesondere für jeden Marktteilnehmer hilfreich, einen leichten Zugang zu den öffentlichen Informationen über die von den Mitgliedstaaten als nationale Kulturgüter eingestuften oder definierten Kulturgüter zu haben. Die Mitgliedstaaten sollten sich darum bemühen, dass der Zugang zu diesen öffentlichen Informationen vereinfacht wird.

(19) Zur Erleichterung einer einheitlichen Auslegung des Begriffs der erforderlichen Sorgfalt sollten in dieser Richtlinie nicht erschöpfende Kriterien festgelegt werden, die bei der Entscheidung, ob der Eigenbesitzer beim Erwerb des Kulturgutes mit der gebotenen Sorgfalt vorgegangen ist, zu berücksichtigen sind.

(20) Da das Ziel dieser Richtlinie, nämlich die Ermöglichung der Rückgabe von als "nationales Kulturgut" eingestuften oder definierten Kulturgütern, die unrechtmäßig aus dem Hoheitsgebiet eines Mitgliedstaats verbracht wurden, von den Mitgliedstaaten nicht ausreichend verwirklicht werden kann, sondern vielmehr wegen seines Umfangs und seiner Folgen auf Unionsebene besser zu verwirklichen ist, kann die Union im Einklang mit dem in Artikel 5 des Vertrags über die Europäische Union verankerten Subsidiaritätsprinzip tätig werden. Entsprechend dem im demselben Artikel genannten Grundsatz der Verhältnismäßigkeit geht diese Richtlinie nicht über das für die Verwirklichung dieses Ziels erforderliche Maß hinaus.

(21) Da die Aufgaben des mit der Verordnung (EG) Nr. 116/2009 eingesetzten Ausschusses durch die Streichung des Anhangs der Richtlinie 93/7/EWG wegfallen, sind die Bezugnahmen auf diesen Ausschuss dementsprechend zu streichen. Um die Plattform für den Austausch von Erfahrungen und bewährten Praktiken mit bzw. bei der Umsetzung dieser Richtlinie zwischen den Mitgliedstaaten beizubehalten, sollte die Kommission eine Sachverständigengruppe einsetzen, die aus Experten aus den für die Umsetzung dieser Richtlinie zuständigen zentralen Stellen der Mitgliedstaaten besteht und unter anderem in die Entwicklung eines spezifischen Moduls des IMI-Systems für Kulturgüter eingebunden werden sollte.

(22) Da der Anhang der Verordnung (EU) Nr. 1024/2012 eine Liste der Bestimmungen über die Verwaltungszusammenarbeit enthält, die in Rechtsakten der Union enthalten sind und mit Hilfe des IMI umgesetzt werden, ist dieser Anhang zu ändern und die vorliegende Richtlinie aufzunehmen.

(23) Die Verpflichtung zur Umsetzung der vorliegenden Richtlinie in nationales Recht muss auf die Bestimmungen beschränkt bleiben, die inhaltliche Änderungen gegenüber den vorherigen Richtlinien darstellen. Die Verpflichtung zur Umsetzung der unveränderten Bestimmungen ergibt sich aus der früheren Richtlinie.

(24) Die Pflichten der Mitgliedstaaten hinsichtlich der Fristen zur Umsetzung der in Anhang I Teil B aufgeführten Richtlinien in nationales Recht dürfen durch diese Richtlinie nicht berührt werden –

HABEN FOLGENDE RICHTLINIE ERLASSEN:

Artikel 1 [Anwendung]

Diese Richtlinie findet Anwendung auf die Rückgabe von Kulturgütern, die von einem Mitgliedstaat als "nationales Kulturgut" im Sinne des Artikels 2 Nummer 1 eingestuft oder definiert und unrechtmäßig aus dem Hoheitsgebiet dieses Mitgliedstaats verbracht wurden.

Artikel 2 [Begriffsbestimmungen]

Im Sinne dieser Richtlinie bezeichnet der Ausdruck

1. "Kulturgut" einen Gegenstand, der vor oder nach der unrechtmäßigen Verbringung aus dem Hoheitsgebiet eines Mitgliedstaats nach den nationalen Rechtsvorschriften oder Verwaltungsverfahren im Sinne des Artikels 36 AEUV von diesem Mitgliedstaat als "nationales Kulturgut von künstlerischem, geschichtlichem oder archäologischem Wert" eingestuft oder definiert wurde;

2. "unrechtmäßig aus dem Hoheitsgebiet eines Mitgliedstaats verbracht"
   a) jede Verbringung aus dem Hoheitsgebiet eines Mitgliedstaats entgegen dessen Rechtsvorschriften für den Schutz nationaler Kulturgüter oder entgegen der Verordnung (EG) Nr. 116/2009 oder
   b) jede nicht erfolgte Rückgabe nach Ablauf der Frist für eine vorübergehende rechtmäßige Verbringung bzw. jeder Verstoß gegen eine andere Bedingung für diese vorübergehende Verbringung;

3. "ersuchender Mitgliedstaat" den Mitgliedstaat, aus dessen Hoheitsgebiet das Kulturgut unrechtmäßig verbracht wurde;
4. "ersuchter Mitgliedstaat" den Mitgliedstaat, in dessen Hoheitsgebiet sich ein Kulturgut befindet, das unrechtmäßig aus dem Hoheitsgebiet eines anderen Mitgliedstaats verbracht wurde;
5. "Rückgabe" die materielle Rückgabe des Kulturgutes in das Hoheitsgebiet des ersuchenden Mitgliedstaats;
6. "Eigenbesitzer" die Person, die die tatsächliche Sachherrschaft über das Kulturgut für sich selbst ausübt;
7. "Fremdbesitzer" die Person, die die tatsächliche Sachherrschaft über das Kulturgut für andere ausübt;
8. "öffentliche Sammlungen" diejenigen Sammlungen, die nach der Rechtsordnung dieses Mitgliedstaats als öffentlich gelten, und die im Eigentum dieses Mitgliedstaats, einer lokalen oder einer regionalen Behörde innerhalb dieses Mitgliedstaats oder einer im Hoheitsgebiet dieses Mitgliedstaats gelegenen Einrichtung stehen, wobei dieser Mitgliedstaat oder eine lokale oder regionale Behörde entweder Eigentümer dieser Einrichtung ist oder sie zu einem beträchtlichen Teil finanziert.

Artikel 3 [Rückgabemodalitäten]
Die unrechtmäßig aus dem Hoheitsgebiet eines Mitgliedstaats verbrachten Kulturgüter werden nach den in dieser Richtlinie vorgesehenen Verfahren und Bedingungen zurückgegeben.

Artikel 4 [Zentrale Stelle]
Jeder Mitgliedstaat benennt eine oder mehrere zentrale Stellen, die die in dieser Richtlinie vorgesehenen Aufgaben wahrnehmen.[1)]
Die Mitgliedstaaten haben der Kommission die zentralen Stellen mitzuteilen, die sie gemäß diesem Artikel benennen.
Die Kommission veröffentlicht eine Liste dieser zentralen Stellen sowie spätere Änderungen im *Amtsblatt der Europäischen Union* Reihe C.

Artikel 5 [Zusammenarbeit und Abstimmung; Aufgaben der Behörden]
[1]Die zentralen Stellen der Mitgliedstaaten arbeiten zusammen und fördern eine Abstimmung zwischen den zuständigen nationalen Behörden der Mitgliedstaaten. [2]Diese erfüllen insbesondere folgende Aufgaben:
1. auf Antrag des ersuchenden Mitgliedstaats Nachforschungen nach einem bestimmten Kulturgut, das unrechtmäßig aus seinem Hoheitsgebiet verbracht wurde, und nach der Identität seines Eigenbesitzers und/oder Fremdbesitzers. Diesem Antrag sind alle erforderlichen Angaben, insbesondere über den tatsächlichen oder vermutlichen Ort der Belegenheit des Kulturgutes, zur Erleichterung der Nachforschungen beizufügen;
2. Unterrichtung der betroffenen Mitgliedstaaten im Fall des Auffindens eines Kulturgutes in ihrem Hoheitsgebiet, wenn begründeter Anlass für die Vermutung besteht, dass das Kulturgut unrechtmäßig aus dem Hoheitsgebiet eines anderen Mitgliedstaats verbracht wurde;
3. Erleichterung der Überprüfung durch die zuständigen Behörden des ersuchenden Mitgliedstaats, ob der betreffende Gegenstand ein Kulturgut darstellt, sofern die Überprüfung innerhalb von sechs Monaten nach der Unterrichtung gemäß Nummer 2 erfolgt. Wird diese Überprüfung nicht innerhalb der festgelegten Frist durchgeführt, so sind die Nummern 4 und 5 nicht mehr anwendbar;
4. in Zusammenarbeit mit dem betroffenen Mitgliedstaat erforderlichenfalls Erlass der notwendigen Maßnahmen für die physische Erhaltung des Kulturgutes;
5. Erlass der erforderlichen vorläufigen Maßnahmen, um zu verhindern, dass das Kulturgut dem Rückgabeverfahren entzogen wird;
6. Wahrnehmung der Rolle eines Vermittlers zwischen dem Eigenbesitzer und/oder Fremdbesitzer und dem ersuchenden Mitgliedstaat in der Frage der Rückgabe. Zu diesem Zweck können die zuständigen Behörden des ersuchten Mitgliedstaats unbeschadet des Artikels 6 zunächst die Einleitung eines Schiedsverfahrens gemäß den nationalen Rechtsvorschriften des ersuchten Mit-

---
1) Die Liste der von den Mitgliedstaaten benannten zentralen Stellen für die Rückgabe unrechtmäßig aus dem Hoheitsgebiet eines Mitgliedstaats verbrachter Kulturgüter ist abgedruckt als Nr. B.II.3a.

gliedstaats erleichtern, sofern der ersuchende Mitgliedstaat sowie der Eigenbesitzer oder Fremdbesitzer ihre förmliche Zustimmung erteilen.

¹Im Hinblick auf die Zusammenarbeit und die Abstimmung untereinander nutzen die zentralen Stellen der Mitgliedstaaten ein auf Kulturgüter abgestimmtes spezifisches Modul des mit der Verordnung (EU) Nr. 1024/2012 eingeführten Binnenmarktinformationssystems ("IMI"). ²Sie können das IMI auch für die Verbreitung einschlägiger fallbezogener Informationen über Kulturgüter, die gestohlen oder unrechtmäßig aus ihrem Hoheitsgebiet verbracht wurden, nutzen. ³Die Mitgliedstaaten entscheiden, ob auch die sonstigen zuständigen Stellen das IMI für die Zwecke der vorliegenden Richtlinie nutzen.

Artikel 6 [Klage auf Rückgabe]
Der ersuchende Mitgliedstaat kann gegen den Eigenbesitzer und ersatzweise gegen den Fremdbesitzer bei dem zuständigen Gericht des ersuchten Mitgliedstaats Klage auf Rückgabe eines Kulturgutes erheben, das sein Hoheitsgebiet unrechtmäßig verlassen hat.

Die Klage auf Rückgabe ist nur dann zulässig, wenn der Klageschrift Folgendes beigefügt ist:
a) ein Dokument mit der Beschreibung des Gutes, das Gegenstand der Klage ist, und der Erklärung, dass es sich dabei um ein Kulturgut handelt;
b) eine Erklärung der zuständigen Stellen des ersuchenden Mitgliedstaats, wonach das Kulturgut unrechtmäßig aus seinem Hoheitsgebiet verbracht wurde.

Artikel 7 [Unterrichtung der zentralen Stelle]
Die zuständige zentrale Stelle des ersuchenden Mitgliedstaats setzt die zuständige zentrale Stelle des ersuchten Mitgliedstaats unverzüglich von der Erhebung der Rückgabeklage in Bezug auf das betreffende Gut in Kenntnis.

Die zuständige zentrale Stelle des ersuchenden Mitgliedstaats unterrichtet unverzüglich die zentrale Stelle der anderen Mitgliedstaaten.

Der Informationsaustausch erfolgt über das IMI im Einklang mit den rechtlichen Bestimmungen zum Schutz personenbezogener Daten und der Privatsphäre, unbeschadet der Möglichkeit der zuständigen zentralen Stellen, neben dem IMI auf andere Informationsmedien zurückzugreifen.

Artikel 8 [Erlöschen des Rückgabeanspruchs]
(1) Die Mitgliedstaaten sehen in ihren Rechtsvorschriften vor, dass der Rückgabeanspruch gemäß dieser Richtlinie drei Jahre nach dem Zeitpunkt erlischt, zu dem die zuständige zentrale Stelle des ersuchenden Mitgliedstaats von dem Ort der Belegenheit des Kulturgutes und der Identität seines Eigenbesitzers oder Fremdbesitzers Kenntnis erhält.

In jedem Fall erlischt der Rückgabeanspruch 30 Jahre nach dem Zeitpunkt, zu dem das Kulturgut unrechtmäßig aus dem Hoheitsgebiet des ersuchenden Mitgliedstaats verbracht wurde. Handelt es sich jedoch um Kulturgüter, die zu öffentlichen Sammlungen im Sinne des Artikels 2 Nummer 8 gehören, sowie um Kulturgüter, die im Bestandsverzeichnis kirchlicher oder anderer religiöser Einrichtungen in den Mitgliedstaaten aufgeführt sind, in denen sie nach den innerstaatlichen Rechtsvorschriften besonderen Schutzregelungen unterliegen, so erlischt der Rückgabeanspruch nach 75 Jahren; hiervon ausgenommen sind die Mitgliedstaaten, in denen der Rückgabeanspruch unverjährbar ist, sowie bilaterale Abkommen zwischen Mitgliedstaaten, in denen eine Verjährungsfrist von über 75 Jahren festgelegt ist.

(2) Die Rückgabeklage ist unzulässig, wenn das Verbringen des Kulturgutes aus dem Hoheitsgebiet des ersuchenden Mitgliedstaats zu dem Zeitpunkt, zu dem die Klage erhoben wird, nicht mehr unrechtmäßig ist.

Artikel 9 [Gerichtliche Anordnung]
Vorbehaltlich der Artikel 8 und 14 wird die Rückgabe des Kulturgutes von dem zuständigen Gericht angeordnet, wenn erwiesen ist, dass es sich dabei um ein Kulturgut im Sinne des Artikels 2 Nummer 1 handelt und die Verbringung aus dem Hoheitsgebiet unrechtmäßig war.

Artikel 10 [Entschädigung]
Wird die Rückgabe angeordnet, so gewährt das zuständige Gericht des ersuchten Mitgliedstaats dem Eigenbesitzer eine dem jeweiligen Fall angemessene Entschädigung, sofern der Eigenbesitzer nachweist, dass er beim Erwerb des Kulturgutes mit der erforderlichen Sorgfalt vorgegangen ist.

Bei der Entscheidung, ob der Eigenbesitzer mit der erforderlichen Sorgfalt vorgegangen ist, werden alle Umstände des Erwerbs berücksichtigt, insbesondere die Unterlagen über die Herkunft des Kulturgutes, die nach dem Recht des ersuchenden Mitgliedstaats erforderlichen Ausfuhrgenehmigungen, die jeweiligen Eigenschaften der Beteiligten, der gezahlte Preis, die Einsichtnahme des Eigenbesitzers in die zugänglichen Verzeichnisse entwendeter Kulturgüter, alle einschlägigen Informationen, die er mit zumutbarem Aufwand hätte erhalten können, oder jeder andere Schritt, den eine vernünftige Person unter denselben Umständen unternommen hätte.

Im Fall einer Schenkung oder Erbschaft darf die Rechtsstellung des Eigenbesitzers nicht günstiger sein als die des Schenkers oder Erblassers.

Der ersuchende Mitgliedstaat hat die Entschädigung bei der Rückgabe zu zahlen.

Artikel 11 [Kostentragung]
¹Die Ausgaben, die sich aus dem Vollzug der Entscheidung ergeben, mit der die Rückgabe des Kulturgutes angeordnet wird, gehen zu Lasten des ersuchenden Mitgliedstaats. ²Gleiches gilt für die Kosten der Maßnahmen gemäß Artikel 5 Nummer 4.

Artikel 12 [Zahlung der Entschädigung]
Die Zahlung der angemessenen Entschädigung gemäß Artikel 10 und der Ausgaben gemäß Artikel 11 steht dem Recht des ersuchenden Mitgliedstaats nicht entgegen, die Erstattung dieser Beträge von den Personen zu fordern, die für die unrechtmäßige Verbringung des Kulturgutes aus seinem Hoheitsgebiet verantwortlich sind.

Artikel 13 [Frage des Eigentums]
Die Frage des Eigentums an dem Kulturgut nach erfolgter Rückgabe bestimmt sich nach dem Recht des ersuchenden Mitgliedstaats.

Artikel 14 [Stichtag]
Diese Richtlinie gilt nur in Fällen, in denen Kulturgüter ab dem 1. Januar 1993 unrechtmäßig aus dem Hoheitsgebiet eines Mitgliedstaats verbracht werden.

Artikel 15 [Weitergehende Anwendung]
(1) Jeder Mitgliedstaat kann die in dieser Richtlinie vorgesehenen Regelungen auf die Rückgabe anderer als in Artikel 2 Absatz 1 definierter Kulturgüter anwenden.
(2) Jeder Mitgliedstaat kann die in dieser Richtlinie vorgesehene Regelung auf Anträge auf Rückgabe von Kulturgütern anwenden, die vor dem 1. Januar 1993 unrechtmäßig aus dem Hoheitsgebiet anderer Mitgliedstaaten verbracht wurden.

Artikel 16 [Zivil- oder strafrechtliche Maßnahmen]
Diese Richtlinie lässt zivil- oder strafrechtliche Maßnahmen unberührt, die dem ersuchenden Mitgliedstaat und/oder dem Eigentümer eines entwendeten Kulturgutes aufgrund der nationalen Rechtsvorschriften der Mitgliedstaaten zur Verfügung stehen.

Artikel 17 [Bericht]
(1) Bis zum 18. Dezember 2020 und anschließend alle fünf Jahre übermitteln die Mitgliedstaaten der Kommission einen Bericht über die Anwendung dieser Richtlinie.
(2) ¹Alle fünf Jahre legt die Kommission dem Europäischen Parlament, dem Rat und dem Europäischen Wirtschafts- und Sozialausschuss einen Bericht mit einer Bewertung der Anwendung und der Wirksamkeit dieser Richtlinie vor. ²Dieser Bericht kann erforderlichenfalls von geeigneten Vorschlägen begleitet sein.

Artikel 18 [Änderung der Verordnung (EU) Nr. 1024/2012]
Im Anhang der Verordnung (EU) Nr. 1024/2012 wird folgende Nummer hinzugefügt:
"8. Richtlinie 2014/60/EU des Europäischen Parlaments und des Rates vom 15. Mai 2014 über die Rückgabe von unrechtmäßig aus dem Hoheitsgebiet eines Mitgliedstaats verbrachten Kulturgütern sowie zur Änderung der Verordnung (EU) Nr. 1024/2012[1]) Artikel 5 und 7.

---

1) **Amtl. Anm.:** ABl. L 159 vom 28.5.2014, S. 1.".

B.II.3 Richtlinie 2014/60/EU

Artikel 19 [Umsetzung]

(1) Die Mitgliedstaaten setzen die Rechts- und Verwaltungsvorschriften in Kraft, die erforderlich sind, um Artikel 2 Nummer 1, Artikel 5 Absatz 1 Nummer 3, Artikel 5 Absatz 2, Artikel 7 Absatz 3, Artikel 8 Absatz 1, Artikel 10 Absätze 1 und 2 und Artikel 17 Absatz 1 dieser Richtlinie bis zum 18. Dezember 2015 nachzukommen.

Sie übermitteln der Kommission unverzüglich den Wortlaut dieser Vorschriften.

[1]Bei Erlass dieser Vorschriften nehmen die Mitgliedstaaten in den Vorschriften selbst oder durch einen Hinweis bei der amtlichen Veröffentlichung auf die vorliegende Richtlinie Bezug. [2]In diese Vorschriften fügen sie die Erklärung ein, dass Bezugnahmen in den geltenden Rechts- und Verwaltungsvorschriften auf die durch die vorliegende Richtlinie aufgehobene(n) Richtlinie(n) als Bezugnahmen auf die vorliegende Richtlinie gelten. [3]Die Mitgliedstaaten regeln die Einzelheiten dieser Bezugnahme und die Formulierung dieser Erklärung.

(2) Die Mitgliedstaaten teilen der Kommission den Wortlaut der wichtigsten nationalen Rechtsvorschriften mit, die sie auf dem unter diese Richtlinie fallenden Gebiet erlassen.

Artikel 20 [Aufhebung]

Die Richtlinie 93/7/EWG, in der Fassung der in Anhang I Teil A aufgeführten Richtlinien, wird unbeschadet der Verpflichtung der Mitgliedstaaten hinsichtlich der in Anhang I Teil B genannten Fristen für die Umsetzung in nationales Recht mit Wirkung vom 19. Dezember 2015 aufgehoben.

Bezugnahmen auf die aufgehobene Richtlinie gelten als Bezugnahmen auf die vorliegende Richtlinie und sind nach Maßgabe der Entsprechungstabelle in Anhang II zu lesen.

Artikel 21 [Inkrafttreten]

Diese Richtlinie tritt am zwanzigsten Tag nach ihrer Veröffentlichung im *Amtsblatt der Europäischen Union* in Kraft.

Artikel 2 Nummern 2 bis 8, Artikel 3, Artikel 4, Artikel 5 Absatz 1 Nummern 1, 2 und 4 bis 6, Artikel 6, Artikel 7 Absätze 1 und 2, Artikel 8 Absatz 2, Artikel 9, Artikel 10 Absätze 3 und 4 sowie Artikel 11 bis 16 gelten ab dem 19. Dezember 2015.

Artikel 22 [Adressaten]

Diese Richtlinie ist an die Mitgliedstaaten gerichtet.

Geschehen zu Brüssel am 15. Mai 2014.

Anhang I

TEIL A Aufgehobene Richtlinie mit Liste ihrer nachfolgenden Änderungen (gemäß Artikel 20)

Richtlinie 93/7/EWG des Rates (ABl. L 74 vom 27.3.1993, S. 74)

Richtlinie 96/100/EG des Europäischen Parlaments und des Rates (ABl. L 60 vom 1.3.1997, S. 59)

Richtlinie 2001/38/EG des Europäischen Parlaments und des Rates (ABl. L 187 vom 10.7.2001, S. 43)

TEIL B Fristen für die Umsetzung in nationales Recht (gemäß Artikel 20)

Richtlinie	Umsetzungsfrist
93/7/EWG	15.12.1993 (15.3.1994 für Belgien, Deutschland und die Niederlande)
(96/100/EG)	1.9.1997
(2001/38/EG)	31.12.2001

Anhang II Entsprechungstabelle

Richtlinie 93/7/EWG	Vorliegende Richtlinie
–	Artikel 1
Artikel 1 Nummer 1 erster Gedankenstrich	Artikel 2 Nummer 1
Artikel 1 Nummer 1 zweiter Gedankenstrich einleitender Teil	–
Artikel 1 Nummer 1 zweiter Gedankenstrich erster Untergedankenstrich Satz 1	–
Artikel 1 Nummer 1 zweiter Gedankenstrich erster Untergedankenstrich Satz 2	Artikel 2 Nummer 8
Artikel 1 Nummer 1 zweiter Gedankenstrich zweiter Untergedankenstrich	–
Artikel 1 Nummer 2 erster Gedankenstrich	Artikel 2 Nummer 2 Buchstabe a
Artikel 1 Nummer 2 zweiter Gedankenstrich	Artikel 2 Nummer 2 Buchstabe b
Artikel 1 Nummern 3 bis 7	Artikel 2 Nummern 3 bis 7
Artikel 2	Artikel 3
Artikel 3	Artikel 4
Artikel 4 einleitender Teil	Artikel 5 Absatz 1 einleitender Teil
Artikel 4 Nummern 1 und 2	Artikel 5 Absatz 1 Nummern 1 und 2
Artikel 4 Nummer 3	Artikel 5 Absatz 1 Nummer 3
Artikel 4 Nummern 4 bis 6	Artikel 5 Absatz 1 Nummern 4 bis 6
–	Artikel 5 Absatz 2
Artikel 5 Absatz 1	Artikel 6 Absatz 1
Artikel 5 Absatz 2 erster Gedankenstrich	Artikel 6 Absatz 2 Buchstabe a
Artikel 5 Absatz 2 zweiter Gedankenstrich	Artikel 6 Absatz 2 Buchstabe b
Artikel 6 Absatz 1	Artikel 7 Absatz 1
Artikel 6 Absatz 2	Artikel 7 Absatz 2
–	Artikel 7 Absatz 3
Artikel 7 Absätze 1 und 2	Artikel 8 Absätze 1 und 2
Artikel 8	Artikel 9
Artikel 9 Absatz 1	Artikel 10 Absatz 1
Artikel 9 Absatz 2	–
–	Artikel 10 Absatz 2
Artikel 9 Absätze 3 und 4	Artikel 10 Absätze 3 und 4
Artikel 10 bis 15	Artikel 11 bis 16
Artikel 16 Absätze 1 und 2	Artikel 17 Absätze 1 und 2
Artikel 16 Absatz 3	–
Artikel 16 Absatz 4	–
Artikel 17	Artikel 18
–	Artikel 19 Absatz 1
Artikel 18	Artikel 20
–	Artikel 21
–	Artikel 22
Artikel 19	–
Anhang	Anhang I
–	Anhang II

B.II.3a Zentrale Stellen nach Richtlinie 2014/60/EU

Liste der von den Mitgliedstaaten benannten zentralen Stellen für die Rückgabe unrechtmäßig aus dem Hoheitsgebiet eines Mitgliedstaats verbrachter Kulturgüter gemäß Artikel 4 der Richtlinie 2014/60/EU[1)]
(2016/C 160/02)

Mitgliedstaat	Zentrale Stelle
Belgien	Service Public Fédéral Justice/Federale Overheidsdienst Justitie Service de droit de la procedure civile et droit patrimonial/Dienst burgerlijk procesrecht en vermogensrecht Boulevard de Waterloo/Waterloolaan 115 1000 Bruxelles/Brussel BELGIQUE/BELGIË Kontaktperson: Herr Jean-Christophe Boulet Tel. +32 25426597 Fax +32 25427006 E-Mail: jean-christophe.boulet@just.fgov.be
Bulgarien	Ministry of Culture DG Inspectorate for Protection of Cultural Heritage 17 Al. Stamboliyski Blvd. 1040 Sofia BULGARIA Kontaktperson: Frau Petya Ganchovska Tel. +359 29400879 Fax +359 29871434 E-Mail: p.ganchovska@mc.government.bg Frau Mariya Todorova-Simova Tel. +359 29400972 E-Mail: m.todorova@mc.government.bg
Tschechische Republik	Ministerstvo kultury Maltézské nám. 1 118 11 Praha 1 ČESKÁ REPUBLIKA Kontaktperson: Frau Magda Němcová Tel. +420 257085454 Fax +420 602623699 E-Mail: Magda.Nemcova@mkcr.cz Ministerstvo vnitra (responsible for archives) Milady Horákové 133 166 21 Praha 6 ČESKÁ REPUBLIKA Kontaktperson: Herr PhDr. Pavel Šimůnek odbor archivní správy a spisové služby Tel. +420 974847606 Fax +420 974835032 E-Mail: pavel.simunek@mvcr.cz

---

1) ABl. L 159 vom 28.5.2014, S. 1 und Berichtigung im ABl. L 147 vom 12.6.2015, S. 24. Die Richtlinie ist abgedruckt als Nr. B.II.3.

Zentrale Stellen nach Richtlinie 2014/60/EU B.II.3a

Mitgliedstaat	Zentrale Stelle
Dänemark	Kulturværdiudvalget Nationalmuseet Frederiksholms Kanal 12 1220 København K DANMARK Tel. +45 33745185 Fax +45 33745101 E-Mail: kulturvaerdier@natmus.dk Kontaktperson: Herr Jan B. Jans Tel. +45 33744500/+45 33744514 Fax +45 40786818
Deutschland	FÜR DIE BUNDESREGIERUNG Die Beauftragte der Bundesregierung für Kultur und Medien Referat K 42 Graurheindorfer Str. 198 53117 Bonn DEUTSCHLAND Kontaktperson: Herr Ministerialrat Frithjof Berger Tel. +49 228996813657 Fax +49 2289968153657 E-Mail: K42@bkm.bund.de Internet: www.kulturstaatsministerin.de FÜR DIE LÄNDER Ministerium für Wissenschaft, Forschung und Kunst Baden-Württemberg Königstraße 46 70173 Stuttgart DEUTSCHLAND Kontaktperson: Herr Leitender Ministerialrat Joachim Uhlmann Tel. +49 7112792980 Fax +49 7112793213 E-Mail: joachim.uhlmann@mwk.bwl.de Internet: www.mwk.baden-wuerttemberg.de Bayerisches Staatsministerium für Bildung und Kultus, Wissenschaft und Kunst Abteilung B Referat B 3 Salvatorstraße 2 80333 München DEUTSCHLAND Kontaktperson: Herr Ministerialrat Dr. Burkhard von Urff Tel. +49 8921862369 Fax +49 8921862842 E-Mail: burkhard.urff@stmbkwk.bayern.de Internet: www.stmbkwk.bayern.de

B.II.3a Zentrale Stellen nach Richtlinie 2014/60/EU

Mitgliedstaat	Zentrale Stelle
	Der Regierende Bürgermeister von Berlin Senatskanzlei — Kulturelle Angelegenheiten Brunnenstraße 188-190 10119 Berlin DEUTSCHLAND Kontaktperson: Frau Regierungsdirektorin Liane Rybczyk Tel. +49 3090228410 Fax +49 3090228456 E-Mail: liane.rybczyk@kultur.berlin.de Internet: www.berlin.de/senatskanzlei Ministerium für Wissenschaft, Forschung und Kultur des Landes Brandenburg Dortustraße 36 14467 Potsdam Kontaktperson: Herr Ministerialrat Dr. Philipp Riecken Tel.: +49 3318664910 Fax +49 3318664998 E-Mail: Philipp.Riecken@mwfk.brandenburg.de Internet: www.mwfk.brandenburg.de Der Senator für Kultur Altenwall 15/16 28195 Bremen DEUTSCHLAND Kontaktperson: Herr Referatsleiter Dr. Andreas Mackeben Tel. +49 42136119541/4213612749 Fax +49 4213616025 E-Mail: Andreas.Mackeben@Kultur.Bremen.de Kirsten.Paffhausen@Kultur.Bremen.de Internet: www.kultur.bremen.de Freie und Hansestadt Hamburg Kulturbehörde — Staatsarchiv Kattunbleiche 19 22041 Hamburg DEUTSCHLAND Kontaktperson: Frau Dr. Christine Axer Tel. +49 40428313132 Fax +49 40427916001 E-Mail: christine.axer@staatsarchiv.hamburg.de

Zentrale Stellen nach Richtlinie 2014/60/EU B.II.3a

Mitgliedstaat	Zentrale Stelle
	Hessisches Ministerium für Wissenschaft und Kunst Rheinstraße 23-25 65185 Wiesbaden DEUTSCHLAND Kontaktperson: Herr Dr. Reinhard Dietrich Tel. +49 611323463 Fax +49 611323499 E-Mail: Reinhard.Dietrich@HMWK.Hessen.de Internet: www.HMWK.Hessen.de Ministerium für Bildung, Wissenschaft und Kultur Mecklenburg-Vorpommern Werderstraße 124 19055 Schwerin DEUTSCHLAND Kontaktperson: Herr Ministerialrat Ulf Tielking Tel. +49 3855887420 Fax +49 3855887087 E-Mail: U.Tielking@bm.mv-regierung.de Niedersächsisches Ministerium für Wissenschaft und Kultur Leibnizufer 9 30169 Hannover DEUTSCHLAND Kontaktperson: Herr Lars Augath Tel. +49 5111202596 Fax +49 511120992596 E-Mail: lars.augath@mwk.niedersachsen.de Internet: www.mwk.niedersachsen.de Ministerium für Familie, Kinder, Jugend, Kultur und Sport des Landes Nordrhein-Westfalen Abteilung IV — Kultur Haroldstr. 4 40213 Düsseldorf DEUTSCHLAND Kontaktperson: Herr Ministerialrat Johannes Lierenfeld Tel. +49 2118374391 Fax +49 211837664391 E-Mail: Johannes.Lierenfeld@mfkjks.nrw.de Internet: www.mfkjks.nrw.de

B.II.3a Zentrale Stellen nach Richtlinie 2014/60/EU

Mitgliedstaat	Zentrale Stelle
	Ministerium für Bildung, Wissenschaft, Weiterbildung und Kultur des Landes Rheinland-Pfalz Mittlere Bleiche 61 55116 Mainz DEUTSCHLAND Kontaktperson: Frau Hedda Frank Tel. +49 6131165451 Fax +49 6131164151 E-Mail: Hedda.Frank@mbwwk.rlp.de Internet: www.mbwwk.rlp.de Der Minister für Bildung und Kultur Trierer Straße 33 66111 Saarbrücken DEUTSCHLAND Kontaktperson: Herr Jörg Sämann Tel. +49 6815017458 Fax +49 6815017227 E-Mail: J.saemann@kultur.saarland.de Internet: www.saarland.de Sächsisches Staatsministerium für Wissenschaft und Kunst Wigardstraße 17 01097 Dresden DEUTSCHLAND Kontaktperson: Frau Uta Volkmann Tel. +49 3515646211 Fax +49 3515646099 E-Mail: uta.volkmann@smwk.sachsen.de Internet: www.smwk.sachsen.de Kultusministerium des Landes Sachsen-Anhalt Turmschanzenstraße 32 39114 Magdeburg DEUTSCHLAND Kontaktperson: Herr Ingo Mundt Tel. +49 3915673635 Fax +49 3915673695 E-Mail: ingo.mundt@mk.sachsen-anhalt.de Zuständiger Referent Kontaktperson: Herr Felix Meister E-Mail: felix.meister@mk.sachsen.anhalt.de Internet: www.mk.sachsen-anhalt.de Ministerium für Justiz Kultur und Europa des Landes Schleswig-Holstein Kulturabteilung, Referat II 42

Zentrale Stellen nach Richtlinie 2014/60/EU B.II.3a

Mitgliedstaat	Zentrale Stelle
	Reventlouallee 2-4 24105 Kiel DEUTSCHLAND Kontaktperson: Frau Anne Nilges Tel. +49 4319885845 Fax +49 4319886125845 E-Mail: anne.nilges@jumi.landsh.de Thüringer Staatskanzlei Referat 43 Werner-Seelenbinder-Straße 7 99096 Erfurt DEUTSCHLAND Kontaktperson: Herr Ministerialrat Stefan Biermann Tel. +49 3613794120 Fax +49 3613794008 E-Mail: stefan.biermann@tsk.thueringen.de Internet: www.thueringen.de
Estland	Kultuuriministeerium Muinsuskaitseamet Uus, 18 10 111 Tallinn EESTI/ESTONIA Kontaktperson: Frau Linda Lainvoo Tel. +372 6403018 Fax +372 6403060 E-Mail: linda.lainvoo@muinas.ee
Irland	Department of Arts, Heritage and the Gaeltacht Cultural Institutions Unit New Road Killarney Co. Kerry IRELAND Kontaktperson: Frau Orlaith Gleeson Tel. +353 646627337 E-Mail: Orlaith.gleeson@ahg.gov.ie Kontaktperson: Frau Angela Byrne Tel. +353646627355 E-Mail: angela.byrne@ahg.gov.ie
Griechenland	Hellenic Ministry of Culture & General Directorate of Antiquities and Culture Property Directorate for the Documentation & Protection of Cultural Goods Ag. Assomaton 33 str.

B.II.3a Zentrale Stellen nach Richtlinie 2014/60/EU

Mitgliedstaat	Zentrale Stelle
	10 553 Αθήνα/Athens ΕΛΛΑΔΑ/GREECE Kontaktperson: Frau Katerina Voutsa Herr Kosta Nikolentzos Tel. +30 2103238877/+30 2103238870 Fax +30 2103238874 E-Mail: dtppa@culture.gr
Spanien	Ministerio de Educación, Cultura y Deporte Dirección General de Bellas Artes y Bienes Culturales y de Archivos y Bibliotecas Plaza del Rey, 1 28004 Madrid ESPAÑA Kontaktperson: Herr Carlos González-Barandiarán y de Muller, Consejero Tecnico E-Mail: carlos.gonzalez@mecd.es Kontaktperson: Frau Elisa de Cabo de la Vega, Subdirectora General de Protección del Patrimonio Histórico E-Mail: elisa.decabo@mecd.es Kontaktperson: Herr Miguel Ángel Recio Crespo, Director General de Bellas Artes y Bienes Culturales y de Archivos y Bibliotecas E-Mail: secretaria.bellasartes@mecd.es Tel. +34 917017040/917017035 Fax +34 917017381
Frankreich	Office central de lutte contre le trafic illicite de biens culturels (OCBC) 101 rue des trois Fontanot 92000 Nanterre FRANCE Tel. +33 147449863 Fax +33 147449866 E-Mail: ocbc-doc.dcpjac@interieur.gouv.fr
Kroatien	Ministarstvo kulture Runjaninova 2 HR — 10 000 Zagreb HRVATSKA Kontaktperson: Herr Nives Milinković Tel. +385 14866255 Fax +385 14866280 E-Mail: nives.milinkovic@min-kulture.hr

Zentrale Stellen nach Richtlinie 2014/60/EU B.II.3a

Mitgliedstaat	Zentrale Stelle
Italien	Ministero dei beni e delle attività culturali e del turismo Segretario Generale Via del Collegio Romano, 27 00186 Roma ITALIA Central authority: Segretario Generale Arch. Antonia Pasqua Recchia Tel. +39 0672320022433 Fax +39 0667232705 E-Mail: sg@beniculturali.it Kontaktstelle: Ministero dei beni e delle attività culturali e del turismo Segretario Generale — Servizio I, Coordinamento e studi Via del Collegio Romano, 27 00186 Roma ITALIA Kontaktperson: Herr Dott. Vitantonio Bruno Tel. +39 0667232098 Fax +39 0667232547 E-Mail: vitantonio.bruno@beniculturali.it
	Sonstige Kontaktpersonen: Frau Dott. ssa Loredana Rossigno Ufficio legislativo Via del Collegio Romano, 27 00186 Roma ITALIA Tel. +39 0667232699 Fax +39 0667232290 E-Mail: loredana.rossigno@beniculturali.it Frau Dott.ssa Jeannette Papadopoulos Direzione generale Archeologia — Servizio III Via di San Michele, 22 00153 Roma ITALIA Tel. +39 0658434689 Fax +39 0658434721 E-Mail: jeannette.papadopoulos@beniculturali.it
Zypern	Ministry of Transport, Communications and Works Department of Antiquities 1 Museum Street, 1516 Nicosia CYPRUS Kontaktperson: Herr Dr. Despo Pilides, (Curator of Antiquities) Tel. +357 22865800/22865806 Fax +357 22303148 E-Mail: antiquitiesdept@da.mcw.gov.cy

B.II.3a Zentrale Stellen nach Richtlinie 2014/60/EU

Mitgliedstaat	Zentrale Stelle
Lettland	Valsts kultūras pieminekļu aizsardzības inspekcija Mazā Pils iela 19 Rīga, LV — 1050 LATVIJA Kontaktperson: Frau Liāna Liepa Tel. +371 67229272 Fax +371 67228808 E-Mail: Liana.Liepa@mantojums.lv, vkpai@mantojums.lv
Litauen	Kultūros ministerija J. Basanavičiaus st. 5 LT — 01118 Vilnius LIETUVA/LITHUANIA Saugomų teritorijų ir paveldo apsaugos skyrius Kontaktperson: Herr Mindaugas Žolynas Tel. +370 52193460 Fax +370 52623120 E-mail: m.zolynas@lrkm.lt
Luxemburg	Ministère de la Justice Direction des affaires pénales et judiciaires Centre administratif Pierre Werner 13, rue Erasme 1468 Luxembourg LUXEMBOURG Kontaktperson: Frau Catherine Trierweiler Tel. +352 24788534 Fax +352 24784026 E-Mail: Catherine.trierweiler@mj.etat.lu
Ungarn	Forster Gyula Nemzeti Örökséggazdálkodási és Szolgáltatási Központ — Műtárgyfelügyeleti Iroda Szentháromság tér 6. III. emelet Budapest, Táncsics M.u.1. 1014 MAGYARORSZÁG/HUNGARY Kontaktperson: Herr Dr. Péter Buzinkay Tel. +36 12254980 Fax +36 12254985 E-Mail: mutargy@forsterkozpont.hu peter.buzinkay@forsterkozpont.hu
Malta	Superintendence of Cultural Heritage 173, St. Christopher Street Valletta VLT 2000 MALTA Kontaktperson: Herr Nathaniel Cutajar Tel. +356 23950503/23950100 Fax +356 23950444 E-Mail: nathaniel.cutajar@gov.mt

Zentrale Stellen nach Richtlinie 2014/60/EU B.II.3a

Mitgliedstaat	Zentrale Stelle
Niederlande	Ministerie van Onderwijs, Cultuur en Wetenschap Erfgoedinspectie Rijnstraat 50 Postbus 16478 2500 BL Den Haag NEDERLAND Kontaktperson: Frau M.M.C. van Heese Tel. +31 652367793 Fax +31 704124014 E-Mail: vanheese@erfgoedinspectie.nl Internet: www.erfgoedinspectie.nl
Österreich	Bundesdenkmalamt Hofburg, Säulenstiege 1010 Wien ÖSTERREICH Kontaktperson: Frau Dr. Brigitte Faszbinder-Brückler Tel. +43 153415105 Fax +43 1534155107 Kontaktperson: Frau Dr. Ulrike Emberger Tel. +43 153415108 Fax +43 1534155107 E-Mail: ausfuhr@bda.at recht@bda.at
	Österreichisches Staatsarchiv Nottendorfergasse 2 1030 Wien ÖSTERREICH Kontaktperson: Herr Mag. Erwin Wolfslehner Tel. +43 79540150 E-Mail: Erwin.wolfslehner@oesta.gv.at Minoritenplatz 1 1010 Wien ÖSTERREICH Kontaktperson: Mag. Thomas Just Tel. +43 79540800 E-Mail: thomas.just@oesta.gv.at
Polen	Ministry of Culture and National Heritage National Institute for Museums and Public Collections ul. Goraszewska 7 02-910 Warszawa POLSKA/POLAND Kontaktperson: Frau Maria Romanowska-Zadrożna Tel. +48 222569613 Fax +48 222569650 E-Mail: mromanowska@nimoz.pl Herr Olgierd Jakubowski Tel. +48 222569619 Fax +48 222569650 E-Mail: ojakubowski@nimoz.pl

B.II.3a Zentrale Stellen nach Richtlinie 2014/60/EU

Mitgliedstaat	Zentrale Stelle
Portugal	Direção-Geral do Património Cultural Palácio Nacional da Ajuda 1349-021, Lisboa PORTUGAL Kontaktpersonen: Frau Dra. Maria Ramalho, Frau Dra. Deolinda Folgado, Frau Dra. Maria João Zagalo Tel. +351 213614200 Fax +351 213637047 E-Mail: dgpc@dgpc.pt mramalho@dgpc.pt dfolgado@dgpc.pt mzagalo@dgpc.pt Direção-Geral do Livro, Arquivos e Bibliotecas Edifício da Torre do Tombo Alameda da Universidade 1649-010 Lisboa PORTUGAL Kontaktperson: Herr Dr. José Cortês Tel. +351 217811500 Fax +351 217937230 E-Mail: secretariado@dglab.gov.pt Biblioteca Nacional de Portugal Campo Grande, no 83 1749-081 Lisboa PORTUGAL Kontaktperson: Frau Dra. Maria Inês Cordeiro Tel. +351 217982000 Fax +351 217982140 E-Mail: bn@bnportugal.pt
	Cinemateca Portuguesa-Museu do Cinema Rua Barata Salgueiro, no 39 1269-059 Lisboa PORTUGAL Kontaktperson: Herr Dr. José Manuel Costa Tel. +351 213596200 Fax +351 213523180 E-Mail: cinemateca@cinemateca.pt
Rumänien	Ministerul Culturii Bulevardul Unirii, nr. 22 O.P. 4, C.P. 15, Sector 3 030833 București ROMÂNIA Kontaktperson: Herr Dl. Daniel-Lucian Ene Direcția Patrimoniu Cultural Tel. +402 12244421 Fax +402 12233157 E-Mail: daniel.ene@cultura.ro

Zentrale Stellen nach Richtlinie 2014/60/EU B.II.3a

Mitgliedstaat	Zentrale Stelle
Slowenien	Ministry of Culture Maistrova 10 SI — 1000 Ljubljana SLOVENIJA Kontaktperson: Frau Marija Brus Tel. +386 13695917 Fax +386 13695902 E-Mail: marija.brus@gov.si
Slowakische Republik	Ministerstvo vnútra Odbor archívov a registratúr Križkova 7 811 04 Bratislava 1 SLOVENSKO/SLOVAKIA Kontaktperson: Frau Mária Španková Tel. +421 257283226 Fax +421 252494530 E-Mail: maria.spankova@mvsr.vs.sk Ministerstvo kultúry SR sekcia kultúrneho dedičstva Nám. SNP 33 813 33 Bratislava 1 SLOVENSKO/SLOVAKIA Kontaktperson: Frau Ing. Iveta Kodoňová Tel. +421 220482414 Fax +421 220482476 E-Mail: skd@culture.gov.sk
Finnland	Ministry of Education and Culture P.O. Box 29 FI-00023 Government, Finland SUOMI/FINLAND Kontaktperson: Frau Merja Leinonen Tel. +358 295330269 E-Mail: merja.leinonen@minedu.fi Weitere Kontaktperson: Frau Mirva Mattila Tel. +358 295330269 E-Mail: mirva.mattila@minedu.fi
	National Board of Antiquities P.O. Box 913 FI-00101 Helsinki SUOMI/FINLAND Kontaktperson: Frau Tiina Tähtinen Tel. +358 295336033 E-Mail: tiina.tahtinen@museovirasto.fi Weitere Kontaktperson: Frau Raila Kataja Tel. +358 295336388 E-Mail: raila.kataja@kansallismuseo.fi

B.II.3a Zentrale Stellen nach Richtlinie 2014/60/EU

Mitgliedstaat	Zentrale Stelle
Schweden	Swedish National Heritage Board Riksantikvarieämbetet Box 5405 SE — 114 84 Stockholm SVERIGE Kontaktperson: Frau Maria Adolfsson Tel. +46 851918179 E-Mail: maria.adolfsson@raa.se
Vereinigtes Königreich	Department for Culture, MEDIA and Sport 4th Floor, 100 Parliament Street London SW1A 2BQ UNITED KINGDOM Kontaktperson: Herr James Pender Tel. +44 2072116491 E-Mail: james.pender@culture.gsi.gov.uk Kontaktperson: Herr Dominic Lake Tel. +44 2072116957 E-Mail: dominic.lake@culture.gsi.gov.uk

Vertrag über die Europäische Union

Vom 13. Dezember 2007 (ABl. C 306 S. 1, ber. ABl. 2008 C 111 S. 56, ABl. 2009 C 290 S. 1, ABl. 2011 C 378 S. 3) (ABl. 2010 C 83 S. 13) (ABl. 2012 C 326 S. 13) (ABl. 2016 C 202 S. 13) zuletzt geändert durch Art. 13, 14 Abs. 1 EU-Beitrittsakte 2013 vom 9. Dezember 2011 (ABl. 2012 L 112 S. 21)

– Auszug –

[...]
SCHÖPFEND aus dem kulturellen, religiösen und humanistischen Erbe Europas, aus dem sich die unverletzlichen und unveräußerlichen Rechte des Menschen sowie Freiheit, Demokratie, Gleichheit und Rechtsstaatlichkeit als universelle Werte entwickelt haben,
[...]
IN DEM WUNSCH, die Solidarität zwischen ihren Völkern unter Achtung ihrer Geschichte, ihrer Kultur und ihrer Traditionen zu stärken,

Titel I
Gemeinsame Bestimmungen

Artikel 3 [Ziel der Union]
[...]
(3)
[...]
Sie wahrt den Reichtum ihrer kulturellen und sprachlichen Vielfalt und sorgt für den Schutz und die Entwicklung des kulturellen Erbes Europas.
[...]

Vertrag über die Arbeitsweise der Europäischen Union

In der Fassung der Bekanntmachung vom 9. Mai 2008 (ABl. C 115 S. 47) (ABl. 2010 C 83 S. 47) (ABl. 2012 C 326 S. 47) (ABl. 2016 C 202 S. 47, ber. ABl. C 400 S. 1) zuletzt geändert durch Art. 2 ÄndBeschl. 2012/419/EU vom 11. Juli 2012 (ABl. L 204 S. 131)
– Auszug –

Erster Teil
Grundsätze

Titel I
Arten und Bereiche der Zuständigkeit der Union

Artikel 6 [Unterstützungs-, Koordinierungs- und Ergänzungsmaßnahmen]
¹Die Union ist für die Durchführung von Maßnahmen zur Unterstützung, Koordinierung oder Ergänzung der Maßnahmen der Mitgliedstaaten zuständig. ²Diese Maßnahmen mit europäischer Zielsetzung können in folgenden Bereichen getroffen werden:
[...]
c) Kultur,
[...]

Titel II
Allgemein geltende Bestimmungen

Artikel 8 [Gleichstellung; Querschnittsklausel]
Bei allen ihren Tätigkeiten wirkt die Union darauf hin, Ungleichheiten zu beseitigen und die Gleichstellung von Männern und Frauen zu fördern.

Artikel 13 [Tierschutz; Querschnittsklausel]
Bei der Festlegung und Durchführung der Politik der Union in den Bereichen Landwirtschaft, Fischerei, Verkehr, Binnenmarkt, Forschung, technologische Entwicklung und Raumfahrt tragen die Union und die Mitgliedstaaten den Erfordernissen des Wohlergehens der Tiere als fühlende Wesen in vollem Umfang Rechnung; sie berücksichtigen hierbei die Rechts- und Verwaltungsvorschriften und die Gepflogenheiten der Mitgliedstaaten insbesondere in Bezug auf religiöse Riten, kulturelle Traditionen und das regionale Erbe.

Dritter Teil
Die internen Politiken und Maßnahmen der Union

Titel VII
Gemeinsame Regeln betreffend Wettbewerb, Steuerfragen und Angleichung der Rechtsvorschriften

Kapitel 1
Wettbewerbsregeln

Abschnitt 2
Staatliche Beihilfen

Artikel 107 [Beihilfeverbot; Ausnahmen]
(1) Soweit in den Verträgen nicht etwas anderes bestimmt ist, sind staatliche oder aus staatlichen Mitteln gewährte Beihilfen gleich welcher Art, die durch die Begünstigung bestimmter Unternehmen oder Produktionszweige den Wettbewerb verfälschen oder zu verfälschen drohen, mit dem Binnenmarkt unvereinbar, soweit sie den Handel zwischen Mitgliedstaaten beeinträchtigen.
[...]

(3) Als mit dem Binnenmarkt vereinbar können angesehen werden:
[...]
d) Beihilfen zur Förderung der Kultur und der Erhaltung des kulturellen Erbes, soweit sie die Handels- und Wettbewerbsbedingungen in der Union nicht in einem Maß beeinträchtigen, das dem gemeinsamen Interesse zuwiderläuft;
[...]

Titel XIII
Kultur

Artikel 167 [Beitrag der Union unter Wahrung und Förderung der Kulturvielfalt]
(1) Die Union leistet einen Beitrag zur Entfaltung der Kulturen der Mitgliedstaaten unter Wahrung ihrer nationalen und regionalen Vielfalt sowie gleichzeitiger Hervorhebung des gemeinsamen kulturellen Erbes.
(2) Die Union fördert durch ihre Tätigkeit die Zusammenarbeit zwischen den Mitgliedstaaten und unterstützt und ergänzt erforderlichenfalls deren Tätigkeit in folgenden Bereichen:
– Verbesserung der Kenntnis und Verbreitung der Kultur und Geschichte der europäischen Völker,
– Erhaltung und Schutz des kulturellen Erbes von europäischer Bedeutung,
– nichtkommerzieller Kulturaustausch,
– künstlerisches und literarisches Schaffen, einschließlich im audiovisuellen Bereich.
(3) Die Union und die Mitgliedstaaten fördern die Zusammenarbeit mit dritten Ländern und den für den Kulturbereich zuständigen internationalen Organisationen, insbesondere mit dem Europarat.
(4) Die Union trägt bei ihrer Tätigkeit aufgrund anderer Bestimmungen der Verträge den kulturellen Aspekten Rechnung, insbesondere zur Wahrung und Förderung der Vielfalt ihrer Kulturen.
(5) Als Beitrag zur Verwirklichung der Ziele dieses Artikels
– erlassen das Europäische Parlament und der Rat gemäß dem ordentlichen Gesetzgebungsverfahren und nach Anhörung des Ausschusses der Regionen Fördermaßnahmen unter Ausschluss jeglicher Harmonisierung der Rechts- und Verwaltungsvorschriften der Mitgliedstaaten.
– erlässt der Rat auf Vorschlag der Kommission Empfehlungen.

Charta der Grundrechte der Europäischen Union

Vom 12. Dezember 2007 (ABl. C 303 S. 1) (BGBl. 2008 II S. 1165) (ABl. 2010 C 83 S. 389) (ABl. 2012 C 326 S. 391) (ABl. 2016 C 202 S. 389)

– Auszug –

Präambel

Die Völker Europas sind entschlossen, auf der Grundlage gemeinsamer Werte eine friedliche Zukunft zu teilen, indem sie sich zu einer immer engeren Union verbinden.
[...]
[1]Die Union trägt zur Erhaltung und zur Entwicklung dieser gemeinsamen Werte unter Achtung der Vielfalt der Kulturen und Traditionen der Völker Europas sowie der nationalen Identität der Mitgliedstaaten und der Organisation ihrer staatlichen Gewalt auf nationaler, regionaler und lokaler Ebene bei. [2]Sie ist bestrebt, eine ausgewogene und nachhaltige Entwicklung zu fördern und stellt den freien Personen-, Dienstleistungs-, Waren- und Kapitalverkehr sowie die Niederlassungsfreiheit sicher.

Titel III
Gleichheit

Artikel 22 Vielfalt der Kulturen, Religionen und Sprachen
Die Union achtet die Vielfalt der Kulturen, Religionen und Sprachen.

Verordnung (EU) Nr. 1295/2013 des Europäischen Parlaments und des Rates vom 11. Dezember 2013 zur Einrichtung des Programms Kreatives Europa (2014–2020) und zur Aufhebung der Beschlüsse Nr. 1718/2006/EG, Nr. 1855/2006/EG und Nr. 1041/2009/EG

(Text von Bedeutung für den EWR)
(ABl. L 347 S. 221, ber. ABl. 2014 L 189 S. 260)[1]
zuletzt geändert durch VO (EU) 2018/596 des EP und des Rates vom 18. April 2018 (ABl. L 103 S. 1)

DAS EUROPÄISCHE PARLAMENT UND DER RAT DER EUROPÄISCHEN UNION –
gestützt auf den Vertrag über die Arbeitsweise der Europäischen Union, insbesondere auf Artikel 166 Absatz 4, Artikel 167 Absatz 5 erster Gedankenstrich und Artikel 173 Absatz 3,
auf Vorschlag der Europäischen Kommission,
nach Zuleitung des Entwurfs des Gesetzgebungsakts an die nationalen Parlamente,
nach Stellungnahme des Europäischen Wirtschafts- und Sozialausschusses[2],
nach Stellungnahme des Ausschusses der Regionen[3],
gemäß dem ordentlichen Gesetzgebungsverfahren[4],
in Erwägung nachstehender Gründe:

(1) Der Vertrag über die Arbeitsweise der Europäischen Union (AEUV) strebt die Schaffung eines immer engeren Zusammenschlusses der europäischen Völker an und überträgt der Union u.a. die Aufgabe, zur Entfaltung der Kulturen der Mitgliedstaaten unter Wahrung ihrer nationalen und regionalen Vielfalt beizutragen und gleichzeitig dafür zu sorgen, dass die für die Wettbewerbsfähigkeit der Industrie der Union notwendigen Voraussetzungen gegeben sind. In dieser Hinsicht unterstützt und ergänzt die Union, wo nötig, die Maßnahmen der Mitgliedstaaten zur Wahrung der kulturellen und sprachlichen Vielfalt gemäß Artikel 167 AEUV und dem UNESCO-Übereinkommen zum Schutz und zur Förderung der Vielfalt kultureller Ausdrucksformen aus dem Jahr 2005 (im Folgenden „UNESCO-Übereinkommen von 2005"), zur Stärkung der Wettbewerbsfähigkeit des Kultur- und Kreativsektors und um die Anpassung an die industriellen Wandlungsprozesse zu erleichtern.

(2) Die Unterstützung der Union für den Kultur- und Kreativsektor beruht hauptsächlich auf den Erfahrungen, die mit den durch folgende Beschlüsse eingerichteten Unionsprogrammen gesammelt wurden: Beschluss Nr. 1718/2006/EG des Europäischen Parlaments und des Rates[5] (im Folgenden „Programm MEDIA"), Beschluss Nr. 1855/2006/EG des Europäischen Parlaments und des Rates[6] (im Folgenden „Programm Kultur") und Beschluss Nr. 1041/2009/EG des Europäischen Parlaments und des Rates[7] (im Folgenden „Programm MEDIA Mundus"). Beschluss Nr. 1622/2006/EG des Europäischen Parlaments und des Rates[8] (im Folgenden „Initiative Kulturhauptstadt Europas") und Beschluss Nr. 1194/2011/EU des Europäischen

---

1) Veröffentlicht am 20.12.2013.
2) **Amtl. Anm.:** ABl. C 181 vom 21.6.2012, S. 35.
3) **Amtl. Anm.:** ABl. C 277 vom 13.9.2012, S. 156.
4) **Amtl. Anm.:** Standpunkt des Europäischen Parlaments vom 19. November 2013 (noch nicht im Amtsblatt veröffentlicht) und Beschluss des Rates vom 5. Dezember 2013.
5) **Amtl. Anm.:** Beschluss Nr. 1718/2006/EG des Europäischen Parlaments und des Rates vom 15. November 2006 zur Umsetzung eines Förderprogramms für den europäischen audiovisuellen Sektor (MEDIA 2007) (ABl. L 327 vom 24.11.2006, S. 12).
6) **Amtl. Anm.:** Beschluss Nr. 1855/2006/EG des Europäischen Parlaments und des Rates vom 12. Dezember 2006 über das Programm Kultur (2007–2013) (ABl. L 372 vom 27.12.2006, S. 1).
7) **Amtl. Anm.:** Beschluss Nr. 1041/2009/EG des Europäischen Parlaments und des Rates vom 21. Oktober 2009 über ein Programm für die Zusammenarbeit mit Fachkräften aus Drittländern im audiovisuellen Bereich (MEDIA Mundus) (ABl. L 288 vom 4.11.2009, S. 10).
8) **Amtl. Anm.:** Beschluss Nr. 1622/2006/EG des Europäischen Parlaments und des Rates vom 24. Oktober 2006 über die Einrichtung einer Gemeinschaftsaktion zur Förderung der Veranstaltung Kulturhauptstadt Europas für die Jahre 2007 bis 2019 (ABl. L 304 vom 3.11.2006, S. 1).

B.III.4 Programm Kreatives Europa

Parlaments und des Rates[1] (im Folgenden „Initiative Kulturerbe-Siegel") tragen ebenfalls zur Förderung des Kultur- und Kreativsektors durch die Union bei.

(3) In der Mitteilung der Kommission über eine „europäische Kulturagenda im Zeichen der Globalisierung", die der Rat in seiner Entschließung vom 16. November 2007[2] und das Europäische Parlament in seiner Entschließung vom 10. April 2008[3] billigte, sind die Zielsetzungen für zukünftige Aktivitäten der Union für den Kultur- und Kreativsektor festgelegt. Die Agenda soll die kulturelle Vielfalt und den interkulturellen Dialog, die Kultur als Katalysator für Kreativität innerhalb des Rahmens für Wachstum und Beschäftigung und als wesentliches Element in den internationalen Beziehungen der Union fördern.

(4) Im Hinblick auf die Charta der Grundrechte der Europäischen Union und vor allem die Artikel 11, 21 und 22 leistet der Kultur- und Kreativsektor einen wichtigen Beitrag im Kampf gegen jede Form der Diskriminierung, darunter Rassismus und Fremdenfeindlichkeit, und ist eine wichtige Plattform für die Freiheit der Meinungsäußerung und die Förderung der Achtung der Vielfalt der Kulturen und Sprachen.

(5) Im UNESCO-Übereinkommen von 2005, das am 18. März 2007 in Kraft getreten ist und dem die Union als Vertragspartei angehört, wird betont, dass kulturelle Aktivitäten, Waren und Dienstleistungen sowohl eine wirtschaftliche als auch eine kulturelle Natur haben, da sie Träger von Identitäten, Werten und Sinn sind, und daher nicht so behandelt werden dürfen, als hätten sie nur einen kommerziellen Wert. Das Übereinkommen dient der Stärkung der internationalen Zusammenarbeit, einschließlich internationaler Vereinbarungen über Koproduktion und gemeinsamen Vertrieb, sowie der internationalen Solidarität, um die kulturellen Ausdrucksformen aller Länder und Einzelpersonen zu fördern. Im Übereinkommen wird auch festgelegt, dass die besonderen Bedingungen und Bedürfnisse von verschiedenen gesellschaftlichen Gruppen, einschließlich der Personen, die Minderheiten angehören, gebührend zu berücksichtigen sind. Dementsprechend sollte die kulturelle Vielfalt auf internationaler Ebene im Einklang mit diesem Übereinkommen durch ein Programm zur Unterstützung des Kultur- und Kreativsektors gefördert werden.

(6) Die Förderung des materiellen und immateriellen Kulturerbes unter anderem im Lichte des UNESCO-Übereinkommens zum Schutz des immateriellen Kulturerbes von 2003 und des UNESCO-Übereinkommens zum Schutz des Kultur- und Naturerbes der Welt von 1972 sollte auch zur Steigerung des Werts der relevanten Standorte beitragen und den Völkern ein Gefühl der Teilhabe am kulturellen und historischen Wert solcher Standorte vermitteln.

(7) Die Mitteilung der Kommission mit dem Titel „Europa 2020 – Eine Strategie für intelligentes, nachhaltiges und integratives Wachstum" (im Folgenden "Strategie Europa 2020") umreißt eine Strategie, mit der die Union zu einem intelligenten, nachhaltigen und inklusiven Wirtschaftsraum, der einen hohen Grad an Beschäftigung, Produktivität und sozialem Zusammenhalt liefert, werden soll. In dieser Mitteilung merkte die Kommission an, dass die Union attraktivere Rahmenbedingungen für Innovation und Kreativität schaffen muss. In diesem Zusammenhang ist der Kultur- und Kreativsektor eine Quelle innovativer Ideen, die zur Schaffung von Produkten und Dienstleistungen führen können, die Wachstum und Beschäftigung schaffen und dazu beitragen, auf Veränderungen in der Gesellschaft einzugehen. Darüber hinaus sind hohe Kompetenz und Wettbewerbsfähigkeit in diesem Sektor hauptsächlich das Ergebnis der Bemühungen von Künstlern, Kulturschaffenden und anderen professionellen Kulturakteuren, die gefördert werden müssen. Zu diesem Zweck sollte der Zugang zu Finanzierungen für den Kultur- und Kreativsektor verbessert werden.

(8) In seinen Schlussfolgerungen zu mobilitätsspezifischen Informationsdiensten für Künstler und Kulturschaffende[4] bestätigte der Rat die Bedeutung der Mobilität von Künstlern und Kulturschaffenden für die Union und für das Erreichen ihrer Ziele im Rahmen der Strategie Europa 2020 und ersuchte die Mitgliedstaaten und die Kommission, im Rahmen ihrer jeweiligen Zu-

---

1) **Amtl. Anm.:** Beschluss Nr. 1194/2011/EU des Europäischen Parlaments und des Rates vom 16. November 2011 zur Schaffung einer Maßnahme der Europäischen Union für das Europäische Kulturerbe-Siegel (ABl. L 303 vom 22.11.2011, S. 1).
2) **Amtl. Anm.:** ABl. C 287 vom 29.11.2007, S. 1.
3) **Amtl. Anm.:** ABl. C 247 E vom 15.10.2009, S. 32.
4) **Amtl. Anm.:** ABl. C 175 vom 15.6.2011, S. 5.

ständigkeiten und unter Wahrung des Subsidiaritätsprinzips die Bereitstellung umfassender und genauer Informationen für mobilitätswillige Künstler und Kulturschaffende in der Union zu erleichtern.

(9) Als Beitrag zur Verstärkung eines gemeinsamen Kulturraums ist es wichtig, die länderübergreifende Mobilität der Kultur- und Kreativakteure und die länderübergreifende Verbreitung kultureller und kreativer Werke, einschließlich audiovisueller Werke und Produkte, zu unterstützen und somit den kulturellen Austausch und den interkulturellen Dialog zu fördern.

(10) Die Programme MEDIA, Kultur und MEDIA Mundus waren Gegenstand regelmäßigen Monitorings und regelmäßiger externer Bewertung und es fanden öffentliche Konsultationen zu ihrer zukünftigen Gestaltung statt, bei denen sich gezeigt hat, dass die Programme MEDIA, Kultur und MEDIA Mundus eine sehr wichtige Rolle für den Schutz und die Förderung der kulturellen und sprachlichen Vielfalt Europas spielen. Diese Monitoring-, Bewertungs- und Konsultationsaktivitäten sowie verschiedene unabhängige Studien, vor allem die Studie „Study on the Entrepreneurial Dimension of Cultural and Creative Industries" zeigen, dass der Kultur- und Kreativsektor vor gemeinsamen Herausforderungen steht – nämlich einem schnellen Wandel aufgrund von Digitalisierung und Globalisierung, Marktfragmentierung im Zusammenhang mit sprachlicher Vielfalt, Problemen beim Zugang zu Finanzierungen, komplexen Verwaltungsverfahren und dem Mangel an vergleichbaren Daten – die alle ein Aktivwerden auf Unionsebene erfordern.

(11) Der europäische Kultur- und Kreativsektor ist von Natur aus diversifiziert, und zwar entlang der nationalen und sprachlichen Grenzen, was zu einer kulturell reichhaltigen und sehr unabhängigen Kulturlandschaft führt und den vielen verschiedenen Kulturtraditionen Europas Erbes eine Stimme verleiht. Eine solche Diversifizierung führt jedoch auch zum Entstehen einer Reihe von Hindernissen, die das reibungslose länderübergreifende Zirkulieren von kulturellen und kreativen Werken erschweren sowie die Mobilität von Kultur- und Kreativakteuren innerhalb und außerhalb der Union behindern, was zu geografischen Unausgewogenheiten und in der Folge zu eingeschränkten Wahlmöglichkeiten für die Konsumenten führen kann.

(12) Da der europäische Kultur- und Kreativsektor durch sprachliche Vielfalt gekennzeichnet ist, die in einigen Bereichen zu einer Fragmentierung entlang der sprachlichen Grenzen führt, sind Untertitelung, Synchronisierung und Audiobeschreibung entscheidend für die Verbreitung kultureller und kreativer Werke, einschließlich audiovisueller Werke.

(13) Die Digitalisierung hat sehr starken Einfluss auf die Art, wie kulturelle und kreative Produkte und Dienstleistungen hergestellt, verbreitet, konsumiert und monetär genutzt werden, sowie darauf, wie der Zugriff erfolgt. Auch wenn anerkanntermaßen ein neues Gleichgewicht zwischen der zunehmenden Zugänglichkeit von kulturellen und kreativen Werken, der fairen Entlohnung von Künstlern und Schaffenden und dem Entstehen neuer Geschäftsmodelle gefunden werden muss, bieten die Veränderungen aufgrund der Digitalisierung große Chancen für den europäischen Kultur- und Kreativsektor und für die europäische Gesellschaft im Allgemeinen. Niedrigere Vertriebskosten, neue Vertriebskanäle, das Potenzial für ein neues und größeres Publikum und neue Chancen für Nischenprodukte können den Zugang erleichtern und die Verbreitung von kulturellen und kreativen Werken weltweit erhöhen. Der Kultur- und Kreativsektor muss, um diese Chancen vollständig zu nutzen und sich an die Rahmenbedingungen der Digitalisierung und Globalisierung anzupassen, neue Kompetenzen entwickeln; sie benötigt besseren Zugang zu Finanzierungen, um ihre technische Ausrüstung auf den neusten Stand zu bringen, neue Produktions- und Vertriebsmethoden zu entwickeln und ihre Geschäftsmodelle entsprechend anzupassen.

(14) Die derzeitige Verleihpraxis stützt das Filmfinanzierungssystem. Es besteht jedoch zunehmend die Notwendigkeit, attraktive legale Online-Angebote und Innovationen zu unterstützen. Daher gilt es, neue Vertriebswege zu fördern, damit neue Geschäftsmodelle entstehen können.

(15) Die Digitalisierung von Kinos ist aufgrund der hohen Kosten der digitalen Ausrüstung seit längerem ein Problem für viele kleine Kinobetreiber, insbesondere solche mit nur einer Leinwand. Auch wenn für Kultur in erster Linie die Mitgliedstaaten zuständig sind und diese daher weiterhin je nach Bedarf auf nationaler, regionaler und lokaler Ebene dieses Problem angehen

B.III.4 Programm Kreatives Europa

sollten, gibt es Potenzial für Finanzierung aus Programmen und Mitteln der Union, insbesondere solche, die für lokale und regionale Entwicklung bestimmt sind.

(16) Um neue Publikumskreise zu erreichen, insbesondere junge Menschen, sind zielgerichtete Anstrengungen der Union insbesondere zur Förderung der Film- und Medienkompetenz erforderlich.

(17) Eine der größten Herausforderungen für den Kultur- und Kreativsektor – vor allem für Kleinst-, kleine und mittlere Unternehmen (KMU) und Kleinst-, kleine und mittlere Organisationen, einschließlich gemeinnützigen und Nichtregierungsorganisationen – ist das Problem des Zugangs zu Finanzmitteln, damit sie ihre Aktivitäten finanzieren, wachsen, wettbewerbsfähig bleiben und wettbewerbsfähiger werden und international tätig werden können. Obwohl KMU ganz allgemein vor diesem Problem stehen, ist die Lage in des Kultur- und Kreativsektors noch deutlich schwieriger, weil viele ihrer Vermögenswerte immaterieller Natur sind, ihre Aktivitäten Prototyp-Charakter haben und die Unternehmen, um Innovationen zu tätigen, grundsätzlich risikobereit und experimentierfreudig sein müssen. Eine solche Risikobereitschaft muss auch vom Finanzsektor verstanden und unterstützt werden.

(18) Als Pilotprojekt ist die Europäische Allianz der Kreativwirtschaft eine sektorübergreifende Initiative, die den Kreativsektor vor allem auf politischer Ebene unterstützt. Die Allianz soll eine Hebelwirkung auf zusätzliche Finanzmittel für den Kreativsektor entfalten und die Nachfrage anderer Branchen und Sektoren nach Dienstleistungen des Kreativsektors ankurbeln. Zur besseren Unterstützung von Innovationen im Kreativsektor sollen neue Instrumente erprobt werden und in eine politische Lernplattform einfließen, die sich aus europäischen, nationalen und regionalen Interessenträgern zusammensetzt.

(19) Die Zusammenfassung der derzeit laufenden Einzelprogramme für den Kultur- und Kreativsektor MEDIA, Kultur und MEDIA Mundus in einem einzigen umfassenden Rahmenprogramm (im Folgenden „Programm") würde KMU sowie Kleinst-, kleinen und mittleren Organisationen mehr Unterstützung in ihren Anstrengungen bieten, damit sie die Chancen der Digitalisierung und Globalisierung nutzen sowie Probleme in Angriff nehmen können, die zur aktuellen Marktfragmentierung führen. Damit das Programm erfolgreich sein kann, sollten die jeweiligen Charakteristika der beiden verschiedenen Sektoren, ihre unterschiedlichen Zielgruppen und ihre besonderen Bedürfnisse mithilfe maßgeschneiderter Konzepte im Rahmen von zwei unabhängigen Unterprogrammen und einem sektorübergreifenden Aktionsbereich berücksichtigt werden. Auf der Durchführungsebene ist besonders auf Synergien zwischen dem Programm und den nationalen und regionalen Strategien für eine intelligente Spezialisierung zu achten. Zu diesem Zweck sollte das Programm eine kohärente Unterstützungsstruktur für die verschiedenen Kultur- und Kreativbranchen enthalten, die aus einer Finanzhilferegelung und einem ergänzenden Finanzierungsinstrument besteht.

(20) Das Programm sollte der Doppelnatur der Kultur und der kulturellen Aktivitäten Rechnung tragen und somit zum einen den Eigenwert und künstlerischen Wert von Kultur und zum anderen den wirtschaftlichen Wert des Sektors – einschließlich seines umfassenderen gesellschaftlichen Beitrags zu Kreativität, Innovation und sozialer Inklusion – anerkennen.

(21) Bei der Umsetzung des Programms sollten der intrinsische Wert von Kultur und die Charakteristika des Kultur- und Kreativsektors berücksichtigt werden, einschließlich der Bedeutung von gemeinnützigen Organisationen und Projekten im Rahmen eines Unterprogramms für Kultur.

(22) Ein eigenständiges Finanzinstrument, die Bürgschaftsfazilität für den Kultur- und Kreativsektor (im Folgenden „Bürgschaftsfazilität") sollte es dem Kultur- und Kreativsektor allgemein ermöglichen, zu wachsen, und insbesondere eine ausreichende Hebelwirkung für neue Aktionen und Möglichkeiten schaffen. Ausgewählte Finanzmittler sollten im Sinne von Kultur- und Kreativprojekten handeln, um in Bezug auf geografische Abdeckung und Vertretung der Sektoren ein ausgewogenes Kreditportfolio sicherzustellen. Außerdem spielen öffentliche und private Organisationen in diesem Zusammenhang eine wichtige Rolle, um einen breit angelegten Ansatz im Rahmen der Bürgschaftsfazilität zu erzielen.

(23) Es sollten auch Mittel für die Maßnahme Kulturhauptstädte Europas und für die Verwaltung der Maßnahme Europäisches Kulturerbe-Siegel bereitgestellt werden, da sie dazu beitragen,

das Zugehörigkeitsgefühl zu einem gemeinsamen Kulturraum zu stärken, interkulturellen Dialog und gegenseitiges Verständnis anzuregen und den Wert des kulturellen Erbes steigern.

(24) Abgesehen von Mitgliedstaaten und überseeischen Ländern und Gebieten, die gemäß Artikel 58 des Beschlusses des Rates Nr. 2001/822/EG[1]) berechtigt sind, am Programm teilzunehmen, sollten vorbehaltlich gewisser Bedingungen auch Länder der Europäischen Freihandelsgemeinschaft (im Folgenden „EFTA"), die Mitglieder des Abkommens über den europäischen Wirtschaftsraum (im Folgenden "EWR"), und die Schweizerische Eidgenossenschaft am Programm teilnehmen können. Beitritts-, Kandidaten- und potenzielle Kandidatenländer, die von einer Heranführungsstrategie profitieren, und Länder, die von der Europäischen Nachbarschaftspolitik erfasst werden, sollten ebenfalls am Programm – mit Ausnahme der Bürgschaftsfazilität – teilnehmen können.

(25) Darüber hinaus sollte das Programm im Einvernehmen mit den betreffenden Parteien und auf der Grundlage noch festzulegender zusätzlicher Mittel und spezifischer Regelungen für bilaterale oder multilaterale Kooperationsaktionen mit anderen Drittstaaten geöffnet werden.

(26) Die Zusammenarbeit im Kultur- und audiovisuellen Bereich zwischen dem Programm und internationalen Organisationen wie der UNESCO, dem Europarat, der Organisation für wirtschaftliche Zusammenarbeit und Entwicklung (OECD) und der Weltorganisation für geistiges Eigentum (WIPO) sollte gestärkt werden.

(27) Der europäische Mehrwert aller im Rahmen des Programms durchgeführten Maßnahmen und Aktionen, ihre Komplementarität mit den Aktivitäten der Mitgliedstaaten sowie ihre Übereinstimmung mit Artikel 167 Absatz 4 AEUV und ihre Kohärenz mit anderen Tätigkeiten der Union, vor allem in den Bereichen Bildung, Beschäftigung, Binnenmarkt, Unternehmen, Jugend, Gesundheit, Bürgerschaft und Justiz, Forschung und Innovation, Industrie- und Kohäsionspolitik, Tourismus und Außenbeziehungen, Handel und Entwicklung und der digitalen Agenda ist zu gewährleisten.

(28) Unter Einhaltung der Grundsätze für die leistungsbezogene Bewertung sollten die Monitoring- und Bewertungsverfahren für das Programm detaillierte jährliche Berichte einschließen und sollten sich auf spezifische, messbare, erreichbare, relevante und zeitgebundene Ziele und Indikatoren beziehen, einschließlich qualitativer Verfahren für das Monitoring und die Bewertung haben die Arbeit der einschlägigen Akteure wie Eurostat und die Befunde des Projekts ESSnet-Kultur und des Statistikinstituts der UNESCO zu berücksichtigen. In diesem Zusammenhang sollte, soweit der audiovisuelle Sektor betroffen ist, die Union Mitglied der Europäischen Audiovisuellen Informationsstelle (im Folgenden „Informationsstelle") bleiben.

(29) Zur Gewährleistung eines optimalen Monitoring und einer optimalen Bewertung des Programms während seiner gesamten Laufzeit sollte der Kommission die Befugnis übertragen werden, Rechtsakte gemäß Artikel 290 AEUV bezüglich der Annahme zusätzlicher qualitativer und quantitativer Indikatoren zu erlassen. Insbesondere muss die Kommission bei ihren Vorarbeiten angemessene Konsultationen auch auf der Ebene von Sachverständigen durchführen. Bei der Vorbereitung und Ausarbeitung delegierter Rechtsakte sollte die Kommission gewährleisten, dass die einschlägigen Dokumente dem Europäischen Parlament und dem Rat gleichzeitig, rechtzeitig und auf angemessene Weise übermittelt werden.

(30) Wie im Bericht der Kommission vom 30. Juli 2010 über die Wirkung der Beschlüsse des Europäischen Parlaments und des Rates zur Änderung der Rechtsgrundlagen der europäischen Programme in den Bereichen lebenslanges Lernen, Kultur, Jugend und Bürgerschaft festgestellt, hat die deutliche Verkürzung der Fristen für die Verwaltungsverfahren die Programmeffizienz erhöht. Es sollte besonders darauf geachtet werden, dass Verwaltungs- und Finanzverfahren weiter vereinfacht werden, auch durch die Nutzung robuster, objektiver und regelmäßig aktualisierter Systeme zur Bestimmung von Pauschalbeträgen, Stückkostensätzen und Pauschalfinanzierungen.

(31) Um einheitliche Bedingungen für die Durchführung dieser Verordnung zu gewährleisten, sollten der Kommission Durchführungsbefugnisse übertragen werden. Diese Befugnisse sollten

---

[1] **Amtl. Anm.:** Beschlusses des Rates Nr. 2001/822/EG vom 27. November 2001 über die Assoziation der überseeischen Länder und Gebiete mit der Europäischen Gemeinschaft („Übersee-Assoziationsbeschluss") ABl. L 314 vom 30.11.2001, S. 1.

im Einklang mit der Verordnung (EU) Nr. 182/2011 des Europäischen Parlaments und des Rates[1], ausgeübt werden.

(32) Gemäß der Verordnung (EG) Nr. 58/2003 des Rates[2], hat die Kommission die Exekutivagentur Bildung, Audiovisuelles und Kultur seit 2009 mit der Durchführung von Verwaltungsaufgaben für Maßnahmen der Union in den Bereichen Bildung, Audiovisuelles und Kultur betraut. Daher kann die Kommission – gemäß der genannten Verordnung – für die Durchführung des Programms auf der Grundlage einer Kosten-Nutzen-Analyse auf eine bereits bestehende Exekutivagentur zurückgreifen.

(33) Mit dieser Verordnung wird für die gesamte Laufzeit des Programms die Finanzausstattung festgelegt, die für das Europäische Parlament und den Rat im Rahmen des jährlichen Haushaltsverfahrens den vorrangigen Bezugsrahmen im Sinne der Nummer 7 der Interinstitutionellen Vereinbarung vom 2. Dezember 2013 zwischen dem Europäischen Parlament, dem Rat und der Kommission über die Haushaltsdisziplin, die Zusammenarbeit im Haushaltsbereich und die wirtschaftliche Haushaltsführung[3] darstellt.

(34) Die finanziellen Interessen der Union sollten während des gesamten Ausgabenzyklus durch angemessene Maßnahmen geschützt werden; dazu gehören unter anderem Maßnahmen zur Prävention, Aufdeckung und Untersuchung von Unregelmäßigkeiten, die Rückforderung entgangener, zu Unrecht gezahlter oder nicht widmungsgemäß verwendeter Mittel und gegebenenfalls verwaltungsrechtliche und finanzielle Sanktionen gemäß der Verordnung (EU, Euratom) Nr. 966/2012 des Europäischen Parlaments und des Rates[4] (im Folgenden „Haushaltsordnung").

(35) Im Hinblick auf das Europäische Amt für Betrugsbekämpfung (im Folgenden „OLAF") und gemäß der Verordnung (Euratom, EG) Nr. 2185/96 des Rates[5] und der Verordnung (EU, Euratom) Nr. 883/2013 des Europäischen Parlaments und des Rates[6] sollten geeignete Maßnahmen ausgearbeitet und umgesetzt werden, um Betrug zu verhindern und entgangene, zu Unrecht überwiesene oder nicht widmungsgemäß verwendete Mittel zurückzufordern.

(36) Da die Ziele dieser Verordnung, nämlich der Schutz, die Entwicklung und die Förderung der europäischen kulturellen und linguistischen Vielfalt und die Förderung des kulturellen Erbes Europas und die Stärkung der Wettbewerbsfähigkeit des europäischen Kultur- und Kreativsektors, insbesondere des audiovisuellen Sektors, von den Mitgliedstaaten angesichts des länderübergreifenden und internationalen Charakters des Programms nicht in ausreichendem Maße verwirklicht werden können, sondern vielmehr wegen seiner Größenordnung und der erwarteten Wirkung auf Unionsebene besser verwirklicht werden können, kann die Union im Einklang mit dem in Artikel 5 des Vertrags über die Europäische Union niedergelegten Subsidiaritätsprinzip tätig werden. Gemäß dem im selben Artikel festgelegten Grundsatz der Verhältnismäßigkeit geht diese Verordnung nicht über das zur Verwirklichung dieser Ziele erforderliche Ausmaß hinaus,

(37) Die Beschlüsse Nr. 1718/2006/EG, Nr. 1855/2006/EG und Nr. 1041/2009/EG sollten daher aufgehoben werden.

---

1) **Amtl. Anm.:** Verordnung (EU) Nr. 182/2011 des Europäischen Parlaments und des Rates vom 16. Februar 2011 zur Festlegung der allgemeinen Regeln und Grundsätze, nach denen die Mitgliedstaaten die Wahrnehmung der Durchführungsbefugnisse durch die Kommission kontrollieren (ABl. L 55 vom 28.2.2011, S. 13).
2) **Amtl. Anm.:** Verordnung (EG) Nr. 58/2003 des Rates vom 19. Dezember 2002 zur Festlegung des Statuts der Exekutivagenturen, die mit bestimmten Aufgaben bei der Verwaltung von Gemeinschaftsprogrammen beauftragt werden (ABl. L 11 vom 16.1.2003, S. 1).
3) **Amtl. Anm.:** ABl. C 420 vom 20.12.2013, S. 1.
4) **Amtl. Anm.:** Verordnung (EU, Euratom) Nr. 966/2012 des Europäischen Parlaments und des Rates vom 25. Oktober 2012 über die Haushaltsordnung für den Gesamthaushaltsplan der Union und zur Aufhebung der Verordnung (EG, Euratom) Nr. 1605/2002 (ABl. L 298 vom 26.10.2012, S. 1).
5) **Amtl. Anm.:** Verordnung (Euratom, EG) Nr. 2185/96 des Rates vom 11. November 1996 betreffend die Kontrollen und Überprüfungen vor Ort durch die Kommission zum Schutz der finanziellen Interessen der Europäischen Gemeinschaften vor Betrug und anderen Unregelmäßigkeiten (ABl. L 292 vom 15.11.1996, S. 2).
6) **Amtl. Anm.:** Verordnung (EU, Euratom) Nr. 883/2013 des Europäischen Parlaments und des Rates vom 11. September 2013 über die Untersuchungen des Europäischen Amtes für Betrugsbekämpfung (OLAF) und zur Aufhebung der Verordnung (EG) Nr. 1073/1999 des Europäischen Parlaments und des Rates und der Verordnung (Euratom) Nr. 1074/1999 des Rates (ABl. L 248 vom 18.9.2013, S. 1).

(38) Für den Übergang von den Programmen MEDIA, Kultur und MEDIA Mundus zum Programm sollten Übergangsbestimmungen vorgesehen werden.
(39) Um die Kontinuität der im Rahmen des Programms gewährten finanziellen Förderung zu gewährleisten, sollte die Kommission die Möglichkeit haben, die direkt mit der Durchführung der geförderten Maßnahmen und Aktivitäten zusammenhängenden Kosten als förderfähig einzustufen, auch wenn diese Kosten dem Empfänger bereits vor der Einreichung des Finanzhilfeantrags entstanden sind.
(40) Um die Kontinuität der im Rahmen des Programms gewährten finanziellen Förderung zu gewährleisten, sollte diese Verordnung ab dem 1. Januar 2014 gelten. Aus Gründen der Dringlichkeit sollte diese Verordnung sobald wie möglich nach ihrer Veröffentlichung im Amtsblatt der Europäischen Union in Kraft treten –
HABEN FOLGENDE VERORDNUNG ERLASSEN:

Kapitel I
Allgemeine Bestimmungen

Artikel 1 Auflegung des Programms und Laufzeit
(1) Mit dieser Verordnung wird das Förderprogramm Kreatives Europa für den europäischen Kultur- und Kreativsektor (im Folgenden „Programm") eingerichtet.
(2) Die Durchführung des Programms beginnt am 1. Januar 2014 und endet am 31. Dezember 2020.

Artikel 2 Begriffsbestimmungen
Für die Zwecke dieser Verordnung gelten folgende Begriffsbestimmungen:
1. „Kultur- und Kreativsektor": alle Sektoren, deren Aktivitäten auf kulturellen Werten und/oder künstlerischen und anderen kreativen Ausdrucksformen beruhen, unabhängig davon, ob diese Aktivitäten marktorientiert sind oder nicht, und unabhängig von der Art der Einrichtung, die sie durchführt, sowie unabhängig davon, wie diese Einrichtung finanziert wird; zu diesen Aktivitäten zählen Entwicklung, Entwurf, Produktion, Verbreitung und Erhaltung von Waren und Dienstleistungen, die für kulturelle, künstlerische oder andere kreative Ausdrucksformen stehen, sowie damit verbundene Funktionen wie Ausbildung oder Management; zum Kultur- und Kreativsektor zählen unter anderem Architektur, Archive, Bibliotheken und Museen, Kunsthandwerk, der audiovisuelle Bereich (einschließlich Film, Fernsehen, Videospiele und Multimedia), das materielle und immaterielle Kulturerbe, Design, Festivals, Musik, Literatur, darstellende Kunst, Verlagswesen, Radio und bildende Kunst;
2. „KMU": Kleinstunternehmen sowie kleine und mittlere Unternehmen im Sinne der Empfehlung 2003/361/EG der Kommission[1];
3. „teilnehmende Finanzmittler": Finanzmittler nach Artikel 139 Absatz 4 Unterabsatz 2 der Haushaltsordnung, die im Rahmen der Bürgschaftsfazilität im Einklang mit der Haushaltsordnung und Anhang I der vorliegenden Verordnung Folgendes anbieten oder anzubieten planen:
   a) Darlehen für KMU sowie Kleinst-, kleine und mittlere Organisationen des Kultur- und Kreativsektors (Bürgschaften des Europäischen Investitionsfonds (im Folgenden „EIF")) oder
   b) Darlehensbürgschaften für andere Finanzmittler, die Darlehen an KMU sowie Kleinst-, kleine und mittlere Organisationen des Kultur- und Kreativsektors vergeben (Rückbürgschaften des EIF).
4. „Dienstleister für Kapazitätsaufbau": Einrichtungen, die gemäß Anhang I Fachwissen zur Verfügung stellen können, mit dem sie teilnehmenden Finanzmittlern ermöglichen, die Besonderheiten und Risiken im Zusammenhang mit KMU sowie Kleinst-, kleinen und mittleren Organisationen im Kultur- und Kreativsektor und ihren Projekten wirksam zu bewerten.

---

1) **Amtl. Anm.:** Empfehlung 2003/361/EG der Kommission vom 6. Mai 2003 betreffend die Definition der Kleinstunternehmen sowie der kleinen und mittleren Unternehmen (ABl. L 124 vom 20.5.2003, S. 36).

B.III.4 Programm Kreatives Europa

Artikel 3 Allgemeine Ziele
Die allgemeinen Ziele des Programms lauten:
a) Wahrung, Entwicklung und Förderung der kulturellen und sprachlichen Vielfalt Europas und Förderung des kulturellen Erbes Europas;
b) Stärkung der Wettbewerbsfähigkeit des europäischen Kultur- und Kreativsektors, insbesondere des audiovisuellen Sektors, um intelligentes, nachhaltiges und integratives Wachstum zu fördern.

Artikel 4 Einzelziele
Die Einzelziele des Programms lauten:
a) Förderung der Fähigkeit des europäischen Kultur- und Kreativsektors, länderübergreifend und international zu arbeiten;
b) Förderung der länderübergreifenden Zirkulation kultureller und kreativer Werke und der länderübergreifenden Mobilität der Kultur- und Kreativakteure, insbesondere Künstler, sowie Erschließung neuer und größerer Publikumsschichten und Verbesserung des Zugangs zu kulturellen und kreativen Werken in der Union und darüber hinaus, mit besonderem Schwerpunkt auf Kindern, Jugendlichen, Menschen mit Behinderungen und unzureichend vertretenen Gruppen;
c) Stärkung der Finanzkraft von KMU sowie Kleinst-, kleinen und mittleren Organisationen im Kultur- und Kreativsektor auf nachhaltige Weise bei gleichzeitigem Bestreben, eine ausgewogene geografische Erfassung und eine ausgewogene Vertretung der Sektoren zu gewährleisten;
d) Förderung von Politikgestaltung, Innovation, Kreativität, Publikumsentwicklung und neuen Geschäfts- und Managementmodellen durch Unterstützung der länderübergreifenden politischen Zusammenarbeit.

Artikel 5 Europäischer Mehrwert
(1) ¹In Anerkennung des Eigenwertes und des wirtschaftlichen Wertes der Kultur unterstützt das Programm Maßnahmen und Aktivitäten mit einem europäischen Mehrwert im Kultur- und Kreativsektor. ²Es trägt zur Erreichung der Ziele der Strategie Europa 2020 sowie ihrer Leitinitiativen bei.
(2) Der europäische Mehrwert wird durch eines oder mehrere der folgenden Merkmale gewährleistet:
a) den länderübergreifenden Charakter der Maßnahmen und Aktivitäten, die regionale, nationale, internationale und andere Unionsprogramme und -maßnahmen ergänzen, sowie die Auswirkungen dieser Maßnahmen und Aktivitäten auf den Kultur- und Kreativsektor sowie die Bürger und deren Kenntnisse über andere Kulturen als ihre eigene;
b) Entwicklung und Förderung der länderübergreifenden Zusammenarbeit zwischen Kultur- und Kreativakteuren einschließlich Künstlern, audiovisuellen Fachkräften, kulturellen und kreativen Organisationen und audiovisuellen Akteuren mit einem Schwerpunkt auf der Anregung zu umfassenderen, rascheren, wirksameren und langfristigeren Reaktionen auf globale Herausforderungen;
c) die Skaleneffekte und die kritische Masse, die die Unterstützung durch die Union fördert, wodurch eine Hebelwirkung für zusätzliche Mittel entsteht,
d) die Gewährleistung von vergleichbareren Ausgangsbedingungen im europäischen Kultur- und Kreativsektor dadurch, dass Länder mit niedriger Produktionskapazität und/oder Länder oder Regionen, die einen geografisch und/oder sprachlich eingeschränkten Raum umfassen, berücksichtigt werden.

Artikel 6 Programmstruktur
Das Programm besteht aus:
a) einem Unterprogramm MEDIA,
b) einem Unterprogramm Kultur,
c) einem sektorübergreifenden Aktionsbereich.

Artikel 7 Logos der Unterprogramme
(1) Die Kommission gewährleistet die Sichtbarkeit des Programms durch den Einsatz von Logos, die für jedes der Unterprogramme kennzeichnend sind.
(2) ¹Die Empfänger des Unterprogramms MEDIA verwenden das Logo, das in Anhang II angeführt ist. ²Die Kommission legt Einzelheiten zur Verwendung dieses Logos fest und teilt diese den Empfängern mit.

(3) ¹Die Empfänger des Unterprogramms Kultur verwenden ein Logo, das von der Kommission festgelegt wird. ²Die Kommission legt Einzelheiten zu Verwendung dieses Logos fest und teilt diese den Empfängern mit.
(4) Die Kommission und die in Artikel 16 genannten „Kreatives-Europa"-Desks dürfen auch die Logos der Unterprogramme verwenden.

Artikel 8 Zugang zum Programm
(1) Das Programm fördert die kulturelle Vielfalt auf internationaler Ebene gemäß dem UNESCO-Übereinkommen von 2005.
(2) Die Teilnahme an dem Programm steht den Mitgliedstaaten offen.
(3) Unbeschadet des Absatzes 4 können ferner folgende Länder an dem Programm teilnehmen, sofern sie zusätzliche Mittel einbringen und sofern sie – für das Unterprogramm MEDIA – die Bedingungen der Richtlinie 2010/13/EU des Europäischen Parlaments und des Rates[1] erfüllen:
a) Beitritts-, Kandidaten- und potenzielle Kandidatenländer, die von einer Heranführungsstrategie profitieren, im Einklang mit den allgemeinen, in Rahmenabkommen, Assoziationsratsbeschlüssen oder ähnlichen Übereinkünften festgelegten Grundsätzen und Bedingungen für die Teilnahme dieser Länder an Unionsprogrammen;
b) Länder der EFTA, die Mitglied des EWR-Abkommens sind, gemäß jenem Abkommen;
c) die Schweizerische Eidgenossenschaft gemäß einem bilateralen Abkommen;
d) Länder, die von der Europäischen Nachbarschaftspolitik abgedeckt werden, gemäß den Verfahren, die in den Rahmenvereinbarungen für die Teilnahme an Unionsprogrammen mit diesen Ländern festgelegt wurden.
(4) Die unter Absatz 3 Buchstaben a und d genannten Länder sind von der Teilnahme an der Bürgschaftsfazilität ausgeschlossen.
(5) Im Rahmen des Programms können auf der Grundlage von seitens dieser Länder oder Regionen eingebrachten zusätzlichen Mittel und von mit diesen Ländern oder Regionen zu vereinbarenden besonderen Regelungen bilaterale oder multilaterale Kooperationsmaßnahmen durchgeführt werden, die sich auf diese Länder oder Regionen beziehen.
(6) Im Rahmen des Programms sind Kooperations- und gemeinsame Maßnahmen mit nicht teilnehmenden Ländern und mit internationalen Organisationen zulässig, die im Kultur- und Kreativsektor aktiv sind, wie UNESCO, Europarat, die OECD oder die WIPO, und zwar auf der Basis gemeinsamer Beiträge für die Realisierung der Programmziele.

Kapitel II
Unterprogramm MEDIA

Artikel 9 Prioritäten des Unterprogramms MEDIA
(1) Prioritäten für die Stärkung der Kapazitäten des europäischen audiovisuellen Sektors im Hinblick auf länderübergreifende Aktivitäten:
a) Förderung des Erwerbs und der Verbesserung von Kompetenzen und Qualifikationen von audiovisuellen Fachkräften und des Aufbaus von Netzwerken, einschließlich des Einsatzes von Digitaltechnik, um die Anpassung an die Marktentwicklung zu gewährleisten, Erprobung neuer Konzepte für die Publikumsentwicklung sowie neuer Geschäftsmodelle;
b) Erhöhung der Kapazität von audiovisuellen Akteuren, europäische audiovisuelle Werke zu entwickeln, die das Potenzial zur Verbreitung inner- und außerhalb der Union haben; Förderung der europäischen und internationalen Koproduktion – auch mit Fernsehsendern;
c) Förderung des Austausches zwischen Unternehmen durch besseren Zugang zu Märkten und unternehmerischen Instrumenten für audiovisuelle Akteure, damit ihre Projekte auf den Unions- und internationalen Märkten stärker wahrgenommen werden.

---
1) **Amtl. Anm.:** Richtlinie 2010/13/EU des Europäischen Parlaments und des Rates vom 10. März 2010 zur Koordinierung bestimmter Rechts- und Verwaltungsvorschriften der Mitgliedstaaten über die Bereitstellung audiovisueller Mediendienste (Richtlinie über audiovisuelle Mediendienste) (ABl. L 95 vom 15.4.2010, S. 1).

B.III.4 Programm Kreatives Europa

(2) Prioritäten für die länderübergreifende Verbreitung:
a) Förderung des Kinoverleihs dadurch, dass audiovisuelle Werke länderübergreifend vermarktet, gekennzeichnet, verliehen und vorgeführt werden;
b) Förderung der länderübergreifenden Vermarktung, Kennzeichnung und des Vertriebs von audiovisuellen Werken auf allen anderen Plattformen abgesehen vom Kino;
c) Förderung der Publikumsentwicklung – vor allem mittels Werbung, Veranstaltungen, Filmkompetenz und Festivals – als eine Möglichkeit, das Interesse an europäischen audiovisuellen Werken zu beleben und den Zugang dazu zu verbessern;
d) Förderung neuer Vertriebswege, damit neue Geschäftsmodelle entstehen können.

Artikel 10 Fördermaßnahmen im Unterprogramm MEDIA

Im Hinblick auf die Umsetzung der in Artikel 9 genannten Prioritäten wird im Unterprogramm MEDIA Folgendes gefördert:
a) Entwicklung einer umfassenden Palette an Aus- und Weiterbildungsmaßnahmen zur Förderung des Erwerbs und der Verbesserung von Qualifikationen und Kompetenzen durch audiovisuelle Fachkräfte, der gemeinsamen Nutzung von Wissen und der Vernetzung, einschließlich der Integration digitaler Technik;
b) Entwicklung europäischer audiovisueller Werke, insbesondere Film- und Fernsehproduktionen wie Spielfilme, Dokumentarfilme, Kinder- und Trickfilme, sowie interaktiver Werke wie Videospiele und Multimedia mit starkem Potenzial für die grenzüberschreitende Verbreitung;
c) Aktivitäten zur Unterstützung europäischer audiovisueller Produktionsgesellschaften, insbesondere unabhängiger Produktionsgesellschaften, im Hinblick auf die Erleichterung europäischer und internationaler Koproduktionen von audiovisuellen Werken, einschließlich Fernsehproduktionen;
d) Aktivitäten, die europäische und internationale Koproduktionspartner zusammenbringen und/oder indirekte Unterstützung für koproduzierte audiovisuelle Werke bieten, indem internationale Koproduktionsfonds mit Sitz in einem am Programm teilnehmenden Land unterstützt werden;
e) besserer Zugang zu audiovisuellen Fachmessen und -Märkten sowie stärkerer Einsatz von Online-Instrumenten für den Geschäftsverkehr inner- und außerhalb der Union;
f) Einrichtung von Fördersystemen für den Verleih nicht-nationaler europäischer Filme durch Kinoverleih und auf anderen Plattformen sowie für internationale Vertriebstätigkeiten, insbesondere Untertitelung, Synchronisierung und Audiobeschreibung audiovisueller Werke;
g) die Erleichterung der Verbreitung europäischer Filme weltweit und von internationalen Filmen in der Union – auf allen Vertriebsplattformen über internationale Kooperationsprojekte im audiovisuellen Sektor;
h) ein Netzwerk europäischer Kinobetreiber, die einen signifikanten Anteil nicht-nationaler europäischer Filme zeigen;
i) Initiativen, die die Vielfalt europäischer audiovisueller Werke, einschließlich Kurzfilmen, präsentieren und fördern, wie Festivals und sonstige Förderveranstaltungen;
j) Aktivitäten, die die Filmkompetenz fördern und den Kenntnisstand und das Interesse des Publikums an europäischen audiovisuellen Werken, einschließlich des audiovisuellen und kinematographischen Erbes, erhöhen, insbesondere beim jungen Publikum;
k) innovative Maßnahmen für das Testen neuer Geschäftsmodelle und Instrumente in Bereichen, auf die sich die Einführung und den Einsatz von Digitaltechnik wahrscheinlich auswirken werden.

Artikel 11 Europäische Audiovisuelle Informationsstelle

(1) Die Union ist für die Laufzeit des Programms ein Mitglied der Informationsstelle.
(2) Die Beteiligung der Union an der Informationsstelle trägt zur Erreichung der Prioritäten des Unterprogramms MEDIA bei, indem:
a) die Transparenz und die Schaffung gleicher Bedingungen bezüglich der Zugänglichkeit von rechtlichen und finanzmarktbezogenen Informationen sowie die Vergleichbarkeit rechtlicher und statistischer Informationen gefördert werden;
b) Daten und Marktanalysen, die bei der Ausarbeitung der Aktionslinien des Unterprogramms MEDIA sowie für die Auswertung ihrer Auswirkungen auf den Markt nützlich sind, bereitgestellt werden.

(3) Die Kommission vertritt die Union in ihren Beziehungen zur Informationsstelle.

Kapitel III
Unterprogramm Kultur

Artikel 12 Prioritäten des Unterprogramms Kultur
(1) Prioritäten für die Stärkung der Kapazitäten des Kultur- und Kreativsektors im Hinblick auf länderübergreifende Aktivitäten sind Folgende:
a) Förderung von Maßnahmen, die den Kultur- und Kreativakteuren Fertigkeiten, Kompetenzen und Know-how vermitteln, die zur Stärkung des Kultur- und Kreativsektors beitragen, darunter Impulsgebung für die Anpassung an die Digitaltechnik, Erprobung innovativer Ansätze für die Publikumsentwicklung und Erprobung neuer Geschäfts- und Managementmodelle;
b) Förderung von Maßnahmen, die die Kultur- und Kreativakteure bei ihrer internationalen Zusammenarbeit und beim Aufbau einer internationalen Karriere und internationaler Aktivitäten inner- und außerhalb der Union unterstützen, wenn möglich auf der Grundlage langfristiger Strategien;
c) Stärkung der europäischen Kultur- und Kreativorganisationen sowie der internationalen Vernetzung, um den Zugang zu beruflichen Chancen zu erleichtern.
(2) Prioritäten für die länderübergreifende Verbreitung und Mobilität sind Folgende:
a) Unterstützung für internationale Tourneen, Veranstaltungen, Ausstellungen und Festivals;
b) Förderung der Verbreitung europäischer Literatur mit dem Ziel einer möglichst weitreichenden Verfügbarkeit;
c) Förderung der Publikumsentwicklung als eine Möglichkeit, das Interesse an europäischen kulturellen und kreativen Werken und materiellem und immateriellem kulturellem Erbe zu beleben und den Zugang dazu zu verbessern.

Artikel 13 Fördermaßnahmen im Unterprogramm Kultur
(1) Im Hinblick auf die Umsetzung der in Artikel 12 genannten Prioritäten wird im Unterprogramm Kultur Folgendes gefördert:
a) Projekte der länderübergreifenden Zusammenarbeit von Kultur- und Kreativorganisationen aus verschiedenen Ländern, um sektorspezifische oder sektorübergreifende Aktivitäten durchzuführen;
b) Aktivitäten europäischer Netzwerke von Kultur- und Kreativorganisationen verschiedener Länder;
c) Aktivitäten von Organisationen mit europaweiter Ausrichtung, die die Entwicklung junger Talente fördern und die länderübergreifende Mobilität von Kultur- und Kreativakteuren sowie die Verbreitung von Werken fördern, mit dem Potenzial, den Kultur- und Kreativsektor umfassend zu beeinflussen und eine dauerhafte Wirkung zu erzielen;
d) literarische Übersetzung und ihre weitere Förderung;
e) besondere Maßnahmen, die den Reichtum und die Vielfalt der europäischen Kulturen deutlicher sichtbar machen und den interkulturellen Dialog sowie das gegenseitige Verstehen fördern, darunter Kulturpreise der Union, die Initiative Kulturhauptstadt Europas und die Initiative Europäisches Kulturerbe-Siegel;
f) Kosten im Zusammenhang mit Aktivitäten des Jugendorchesters der Europäischen Union, die zur Mobilität von Musikern, zur grenzüberschreitenden Verbreitung europäischer Werke und zur internationalen Ausrichtung der Karrieren junger Musiker beitragen.
(2) Mit den in Absatz 1 dargelegten Maßnahmen werden insbesondere gemeinnützige Projekte unterstützt.

Kapitel IV
Sektorübergreifender Aktionsbereich

Artikel 14 Bürgschaftsfazilität für den Kultur- und Kreativsektor
(1) Die Kommission richtet eine auf den Kultur- und Kreativsektor zielende Bürgschaftsfazilität ein.

B.III.4 Programm Kreatives Europa

Die Bürgschaftsfazilität arbeitet als eigenständiges Instrument und wird gemäß Titel VIII der Haushaltsordnung eingerichtet und verwaltet.

(2) Für die Bürgschaftsfazilität gelten folgende Prioritäten:
a) Erleichterung des Zugangs zu Finanzierungen für KMU und Kleinst-, kleine und mittlere Organisationen im gesamten Kultur- und Kreativsektor;
b) Verbesserung der Fähigkeit teilnehmender Finanzmittler, die Risiken im Zusammenhang mit KMU sowie Kleinst-, kleinen und mittleren Organisationen im Kultur- und Kreativsektor und ihren Projekten zu bewerten, unter anderem durch fachliche Unterstützung, Wissensaufbau und Vernetzungsmaßnahmen.

Die Umsetzung der Prioritäten erfolgt gemäß Anhang I.

(3) Gemäß Artikel 139 Absatz 4 der Haushaltsordnung setzt die Kommission die Bürgschaftsfazilität im Wege der indirekten Mittelverwaltung um, indem sie dem EIF Aufgaben gemäß Artikel 58 Absatz 1 Buchstabe c Ziffer iii der genannten Verordnung – vorbehaltlich einer Vereinbarung zwischen der Kommission und dem EIF – überträgt.

Artikel 15 Länderübergreifende politische Zusammenarbeit

(1) Zur Förderung der länderübergreifenden politischen Zusammenarbeit ist im sektorübergreifenden Aktionsbereich Unterstützung für Folgendes vorgesehen:
a) länderübergreifender Austausch von Erfahrungen und Know-how für neue Geschäfts- und Managementmodelle, Peer Learning und Vernetzung von Kultur- und Kreativorganisationen und Politikverantwortlichen im Zusammenhang mit der Weiterentwicklung des Kultur- und Kreativsektors, gegebenenfalls unter Förderung der digitalen Vernetzung;
b) Erhebung von Marktdaten, Studien, Analysen von Arbeitsmarkt- und Qualifikationsbedarf, Analyse der europäischen und nationalen Kulturpolitik und statistische Erhebungen auf der Grundlage von sektorspezifischen Instrumenten und Kriterien sowie Bewertungen einschließlich Messung aller Aspekte der Auswirkungen des Programms;
c) Entrichtung des Mitgliedsbeitrags der Union für die Informationsstelle zur Förderung der Erhebung von Daten und Analysen im audiovisuellen Bereich;
d) Erprobung neuer, sektorübergreifender Unternehmenskonzepte für die Finanzierung, den Vertrieb und die Monetarisierung der geschaffenen Werke;
e) Konferenzen, Seminare und politischer Dialog, auch im Bereich der Kultur- und Medienkompetenz, wobei gegebenenfalls die digitale Vernetzung gefördert werden sollte;
f) die in Artikel 16 genannten „Kreatives-Europa"-Desks und die Durchführung ihrer Aufgaben;
g) das Jugendorchester der Europäischen Union im Hinblick auf Kosten, die nicht unter die Förderung nach Artikel 13 Absatz 1 Buchstabe f fallen.

(2) Bis 30. Juni 2014 führt die Kommission eine Machbarkeitsstudie durch, in der die Möglichkeit zur Erhebung und Analyse von Daten im Kultur- und Kreativsektor – ausgenommen im audiovisuellen Bereich – untersucht wird, und stellt die Ergebnisse der Studie dem Europäischen Parlament und dem Rat vor.

Abhängig von den Ergebnissen der Machbarkeitsstudie kann die Kommission einen entsprechenden Vorschlag zur Änderung dieser Verordnung vorlegen.

Artikel 16 „Kreatives-Europa"-Desks

(1) Die am Programm teilnehmenden Länder richten in Zusammenarbeit mit der Kommission die „Kreatives-Europa"-Desks im Einklang mit nationalem Recht und nationalen Gepflogenheiten ein ("Kreatives-Europa"-Desks).

(2) Die Kommission unterstützt ein Netzwerk von „Kreatives-Europa"-Desks.

(3) Die „Kreatives-Europa"-Desks führen die folgenden Aufgaben aus, wobei die besonderen Eigenschaften jedes Sektors berücksichtigt werden:
a) Bereitstellen von Informationen über das und Förderung des Programms in ihren Ländern;
b) Hilfestellung für den Kultur- und Kreativsektor im Zusammenhang mit dem Programm und grundlegende Informationen über die sonstigen einschlägigen Möglichkeiten der Unterstützung, die im Rahmen der Unionspolitik zur Verfügung stehen;
c) Förderung der grenzüberschreitenden Zusammenarbeit innerhalb des Kultur- und Kreativsektors;

Programm Kreatives Europa B.III.4

d) Unterstützung der Kommission im Hinblick auf den Kultur- und Kreativsektor in den am Programm teilnehmenden Ländern, z.b. durch die Bereitstellung verfügbarer Daten zu diesem Sektor;
e) Unterstützung der Kommission, damit die Ergebnisse und die Wirkung des Programms in geeigneter Form kommuniziert bzw. verbreitet werden;
f) Sicherstellung der Kommunikation und Verbreitung von Informationen zu den von der Union gewährten Fördermitteln und den erzielten Ergebnissen in ihren Ländern.

(4) Die Kommission stellt die Qualität und die Ergebnisse der Dienstleistungen der „Kreatives-Europa"-Desks gemeinsam mit den Mitgliedstaaten durch regelmäßiges und unabhängiges Monitoring und Bewertung sicher.

Kapitel V
Leistungsbezogene Ergebnisse und Verbreitung

Artikel 17 Kohärenz und Komplementarität

(1) In Zusammenarbeit mit den Mitgliedstaaten sorgt die Kommission für die Kohärenz und Komplementarität des Programms mit
a) der relevanten Politik der Union, wie z.B. in den Bereichen Bildung, Beschäftigung, Gesundheit, Binnenmarkt, digitale Agenda, Jugend, Bürgerschaft, Außenbeziehungen, Handel, Forschung und Innovation, Unternehmen, Tourismus, Justiz, Erweiterung und Entwicklung;
b) anderen relevanten Finanzquellen der Union im Bereich der Kultur- und Medienpolitik, vor allem dem Europäischen Sozialfonds, dem Europäischen Fonds für regionale Entwicklung und den Programmen Forschung und Innovation, den Finanzinstrumenten für die Bereiche Justiz und Bürgerschaft, den Programmen für die Zusammenarbeit mit Drittländern und den Heranführungsinstrumenten.

(2) Diese Verordnung gilt und wird angewendet unbeschadet der internationalen Verpflichtungen der Union.

Artikel 18 Monitoring und Bewertung

(1) Die Kommission sorgt für regelmäßiges Monitoring und regelmäßige externe Bewertung des Programms anhand der folgenden qualitativen und quantitativen Leistungsindikatoren:
a) Indikatoren für die allgemeinen Ziele nach Artikel 3:
   i) Niveau, Veränderung und Anteil des Kultur- und Kreativsektors an der Beschäftigung und am Bruttoinlandsprodukt;
   ii) Anzahl der Menschen, die auf europäische kulturelle und kreative Werke zugreifen, darunter, wenn möglich, Werke aus anderen Ländern als aus ihrem eigenen.
b) Indikatoren für das Einzelziel nach Artikel 4 Buchstabe a:
   i) Umfang der internationalen Aktivitäten von Kultur- und Kreativorganisationen und Anzahl der ins Leben gerufenen länderübergreifenden Partnerschaften;
   ii) Anzahl der durch das Programm unterstützten Lernerfahrungen und -aktivitäten, die die Qualifikationen der Kultur- und Kreativakteure, einschließlich audiovisuellen Fachkräften, verbessert und ihre Beschäftigungsfähigkeit erhöht haben;
c) Indikatoren für das Einzelziel nach Artikel 4 Buchstabe b im Hinblick auf das Unterprogramm MEDIA:
   i) Besucherzahlen für nicht-nationale europäische Filme in Europa und europäische Filme weltweit (zehn wichtigste nicht-europäische Märkte) in Kinos;
   ii) Prozentsatz europäischer audiovisueller Werke in Kinos, im Fernsehen und auf digitalen Plattformen;
   iii) Anzahl der Menschen in den Mitgliedstaaten, die auf nicht-nationale europäische audiovisuelle Werke zugreifen, und Anzahl der Menschen in den Ländern, die am Programm teilnehmen, die auf europäische audiovisuelle Werke zugreifen;
   iv) Anzahl der in der Union sowie in den am Programm teilnehmenden Ländern hergestellten europäischen Videospiele;
d) Indikatoren für das Einzelziel nach Artikel 4 Buchstabe b im Hinblick auf das Unterprogramm Kultur:

B.III.4 Programm Kreatives Europa

 i) Anzahl der Menschen, die direkt und indirekt mit über das Programm geförderten Projekten erreicht wurden;
 ii) Anzahl der an Kinder, Jugendliche und unzureichend vertretene Gruppen gerichteten Projekte und geschätzte Anzahl der erreichten Menschen.
e) Indikatoren für das Einzelziel nach Artikel 4 Buchstabe c:
 i) Volumen der im Rahmen der Bürgschaftsfazilität garantierten Darlehen, aufgeschlüsselt nach nationaler Herkunft, Größe und Sektor der KMU sowie Kleinst-, kleinen und mittleren Organisationen;
 ii) Volumen der durch teilnehmende Finanzmittler bewilligten Darlehen, aufgeschlüsselt nach nationaler Herkunft;
 iii) Anzahl und geografische Verteilung der teilnehmenden Finanzmittler;
 iv) Anzahl der von der Bürgschaftsfazilität profitierenden KMU sowie Kleinst-, kleinen und mittleren Organisationen, aufgeschlüsselt nach nationaler Herkunft, Größe und Sektor;
 v) durchschnittliche Ausfallquote der Darlehen;
 vi) erreichte Hebelwirkung der garantierten Darlehen im Verhältnis zur indikativen Hebelwirkung (1:5,7).
f) Indikatoren für das Einzelziel nach Artikel 4 Buchstabe d:
 i) Anzahl der Mitgliedstaaten, die die Ergebnisse der offenen Methode der Koordinierung für ihre nationale Politikgestaltung nutzen;
 ii) Anzahl neuer Initiativen und Politikergebnisse.

(2) Die Ergebnisse des Monitorings und der Bewertung werden bei der Durchführung des Programms berücksichtigt.

(3) Zusätzlich zum regelmäßigen Monitoring des Programms erstellt die Kommission einen Halbzeitbericht auf der Grundlage einer externen und unabhängigen Bewertung, die

a) qualitative und quantitative Elemente umfasst, um zu bewerten, wie wirksam das Programm darin ist, seine Ziele zu erreichen, sowie die Effizienz des Programms sowie seinen europäischen Mehrwert zu bewerten;
b) mögliche Vereinfachungen des Programms sowie seine interne und externe Kohärenz, die Aktualität aller seiner Ziele sowie den Beitrag, den die Maßnahmen zu den Prioritäten der Union für intelligentes, nachhaltiges und integratives Wachstum leisten, thematisiert;
c) Bewertungsergebnisse zu den langfristigen Auswirkungen der Beschlüsse Nr. 1718/2006/EG, Nr. 1855/2006/EG und Nr. 1041/2009/EG berücksichtigt.

(4) Die Kommission legt dem Europäischen Parlament und dem Rat bis zum 31. Dezember 2017 den in Absatz 3 genannten Halbzeitbericht vor.

(5) [1]Auf der Grundlage einer abschließenden externen und unabhängigen Bewertung erstellt die Kommission einen abschließenden Bewertungsbericht, in dem die langfristigeren Auswirkungen und die nachhaltige Wirkung des Programms auf der Grundlage der ausgewählten quantitativen und qualitativen Indikatoren bewertet werden. [2]Im Hinblick auf das in Artikel 4 Buchstabe c genannte Einzelziel bewertet die Kommission ferner die Wirkungen der Bürgschaftsfazilität auf den Zugang zu Bankdarlehen und die damit verbundenen Kosten für KMU sowie Kleinst-, kleine und mittlere Organisationen des Kultur- und Kreativsektors.

(6) Die Kommission legt dem Europäischen Parlament und dem Rat bis zum 30. Juni 2022 den in Absatz 5 genannten Abschlussbewertungsbericht vor.

Artikel 19 Kommunikation und Verbreitung

(1) Die Kommission unterrichtet die am Programm teilnehmenden Länder über die von der Union geförderten Projekte und übermittelt ihnen die entsprechenden Auswahlentscheidungen innerhalb von zwei Wochen, nachdem diese Entscheidungen getroffen wurden.

(2) Die Empfänger der im Rahmen des Programms vergebenen Projektförderungen sorgen dafür, dass die erzielten Ergebnisse und Angaben zu den Unionsmitteln, die sie erhalten haben, kommuniziert und verbreitet werden.

(3) Die Kommission stellt die Verbreitung der einschlägigen Informationen an die „Kreatives-Europa"-Desks sicher.

Kapitel VI
Delegierte Rechtsakte

Artikel 20 Befugnisübertragung an die Kommission
Der Kommission wird die Befugnis übertragen, gemäß Artikel 21 in Bezug auf die Ergänzung der in Artikel 18 Absatz 1 festgelegten quantitativen und qualitativen Leistungsindikatoren delegierte Rechtsakte zu erlassen.

Artikel 21 Ausübung der Befugnisübertragung
(1) Die Befugnis zum Erlass delegierter Rechtsakte wird der Kommission unter den in diesem Artikel festgelegten Bedingungen übertragen.
(2) Die Befugnis zum Erlass delegierter Rechtsakte gemäß Artikel 20 wird der Kommission für die Dauer des Programms übertragen.
(3) [1]Die Befugnisübertragung gemäß Artikel 20 kann vom Europäischen Parlament oder vom Rat jederzeit widerrufen werden. [2]Ein Beschluss über den Widerruf beendet die Übertragung der in diesem Beschluss genannten Befugnis. [3]Er wird am Tag nach seiner Veröffentlichung im *Amtsblatt der Europäischen Union* oder zu einem im Beschluss über den Widerruf angegebenen späteren Zeitpunkt wirksam. [4]Die Gültigkeit von delegierten Rechtsakten, die bereits in Kraft sind, wird von dem Beschluss über den Widerruf nicht berührt.
(4) Sobald die Kommission einen delegierten Rechtsakt erlässt, übermittelt sie ihn gleichzeitig dem Europäischen Parlament und dem Rat.
(5) [1]Ein delegierter Rechtsakt, der gemäß Artikel 20 erlassen wurde, tritt nur in Kraft, wenn weder das Europäische Parlament noch der Rat innerhalb einer Frist von zwei Monaten nach Übermittlung dieses Rechtsakts an das Europäische Parlament und den Rat Einwände erhoben haben oder wenn vor Ablauf dieser Frist das Europäische Parlament und der Rat beide der Kommission mitgeteilt haben, dass sie keine Einwände erheben werden. [2]Auf Initiative des Europäischen Parlaments oder des Rates wird diese Frist um zwei Monate verlängert.

Kapitel VII
Durchführungsbestimmungen

Artikel 22 Programmdurchführung
(1) Bei der Durchführung des Programms beachtet die Kommission die Bestimmungen der Haushaltsordnung.
(2) [1]Die Kommission nimmt mittels Durchführungsrechtsakten ein jährliches Arbeitsprogramm in Bezug auf Unterprogramme und den sektorübergreifenden Aktionsbereich an. [2]Im jährlichen Arbeitsprogramm stellt die Kommission sicher, dass die in Artikel 3 und 4 genannten allgemeinen und Einzelziele sowie die in Artikel 9 und 12 genannten Prioritäten jährlich auf konsistente Art umgesetzt werden, und legt die erwarteten Ergebnisse, die Umsetzungsmethode und den Gesamtbetrag des Finanzplans fest. [3]Darüber hinaus enthält das jährliche Arbeitsprogramm eine Beschreibung der zu finanzierenden Maßnahmen, die Höhe der Mittelzuweisung für jede Maßnahme und einen vorläufigen Zeitplan für die Durchführung.
[1]Für Finanzhilfen enthält das jährliche Arbeitsprogramm die Prioritäten, die Förderfähigkeits-, Auswahl- und Vergabekriterien und die maximale Kofinanzierungsrate. [2]Der finanzielle Beitrag des Programms beträgt maximal 80 % der Kosten der unterstützten Maßnahmen.
Für die Bürgschaftsfazilität enthält das jährliche Arbeitsprogramm die Förderfähigkeits- und Auswahlkriterien für die Finanzmittler, die Ausschlusskriterien in Bezug auf den Inhalt der den teilnehmenden Finanzmittlern vorgelegten Projekte, die jährliche Mittelzuweisung an den EIF sowie die Förderfähigkeits-, Auswahl- und Vergabekriterien für die Dienstleister für den Kapazitätsaufbau.
Solche Durchführungsrechtsakte werden nach dem in Artikel 23 Absatz 4 genannten Prüfverfahren erlassen.
(3) Die Kommission erlässt die allgemeinen Leitlinien zur Durchführung des Programms gemäß dem Beratungsverfahren nach Artikel 23 Absatz 3.

B.III.4 Programm Kreatives Europa

Artikel 23 Ausschussverfahren

(1) ¹Die Kommission wird von einem Ausschuss (dem Ausschuss „Kreatives Europa") unterstützt. ²Dabei handelt es sich um einen Ausschuss im Sinne der Verordnung (EU) Nr. 182/2011.

(2) Der Ausschuss „Kreatives Europa" kann in spezifischen Zusammensetzungen tagen, um konkrete Fragen in Bezug auf die Unterprogramme und die sektorübergreifende Aktion zu behandeln.

(3) Wird auf diesen Absatz Bezug genommen, so gilt Artikel 4 der Verordnung (EU) Nr. 182/2011.

(4) Wird auf diesen Absatz Bezug genommen, so gilt Artikel 5 der Verordnung (EU) Nr. 182/2011.

Artikel 24 Finanzbestimmungen

(1) Die Finanzausstattung für die Durchführung des Programms wird für den Zeitraum vom 1. Januar 2014 bis zum 31. Dezember 2020 auf 1 462 724 000 EUR zu jeweiligen Preisen festgesetzt.

Die jährlichen Mittel werden vom Europäischen Parlament und dem Rat in den Grenzen des mehrjährigen Finanzrahmens bewilligt.

(2) Die in Absatz 1 genannte Finanzausstattung wird wie folgt zugewiesen:
a) mindestens 56 % für das Unterprogramm MEDIA,
b) mindestens 31 % für das Unterprogramm Kultur,
c) maximal 13 % für den sektorübergreifenden Aktionsbereich, wobei mindestens 4 % den in Artikel 15 genannten länderübergreifenden Kooperationsmaßnahmen und den „Kreatives-Europa"-Desks zugewiesen werden.

(3) Die Verwaltungskosten hinsichtlich der Umsetzung des Programms bilden einen Teil der Zuweisung nach Absatz 2 und der Gesamtbetrag dieser Kosten darf 7 % des Programmhaushalts nicht überschreiten, wovon 5 % der Durchführung des Unterprogramms MEDIA und 2 % der Durchführung des Unterprogramms Kultur zugewiesen werden.

(4) Die in Absatz 1 genannte Finanzausstattung kann Ausgaben im Zusammenhang mit Vorbereitungs-, Monitoring-, Kontroll-, Prüfungs- und Bewertungsaktivitäten abdecken, die für die Programmverwaltung und die Erreichung der Ziele unmittelbar notwendig sind; insbesondere Studien, Expertensitzungen, Informations- und Kommunikationsaktivitäten – einschließlich der institutionellen Kommunikation zu den politischen Prioritäten der Union, sofern diese mit den allgemeinen Zielen des Programms zusammenhängen – Ausgaben in Verbindung mit IT-Netzwerken für die Verarbeitung und den Austausch von Informationen sowie alle anderen Ausgaben für administrative und technische Unterstützung, die der Kommission bei der Verwaltung des Programms entstehen.

(5) Die in Absatz 1 genannte Finanzausstattung kann Ausgaben für die technische und administrative Unterstützung abdecken, die für den Übergang zwischen den auf der Grundlage der Beschlüsse Nr. 1718/2006/EG, Nr. 1855/2006/EG und Nr. 1041/2009/EG verabschiedeten Maßnahmen und dieser Verordnung erforderlich sind.

Falls notwendig, können Mittel auch über das Jahr 2020 hinaus ins Budget eingestellt werden, um vergleichbare Ausgaben für die Verwaltung von Maßnahmen abzudecken, die zum 31. Dezember 2020 noch nicht abgeschlossen sind.

(6) Gemäß Artikel 130 Absatz 1 der Haushaltsordnung kann die Kommission in entsprechend gerechtfertigten Fällen direkt mit der Umsetzung der geförderten Maßnahmen und Aktivitäten zusammenhängenden Kosten als förderfähig einstufen, auch wenn sie dem Empfänger bereits vor der Einreichung des Finanzhilfeantrags entstanden sind.

Artikel 25 Schutz der finanziellen Interessen der Union

(1) Die Kommission ergreift geeignete Maßnahmen, um bei der Durchführung der im Rahmen dieser Verordnung finanzierten Maßnahmen den Schutz der finanziellen Interessen der Union durch Präventivmaßnahmen gegen Betrug, Korruption und sonstige rechtswidrige Handlungen, durch wirksame Überprüfungen und Kontrollen und – bei Feststellung von Unregelmäßigkeiten – Rückforderung zu Unrecht gezahlter Beträge sowie gegebenenfalls durch wirksame, verhältnismäßige und abschreckende verwaltungsrechtliche und finanzielle Sanktionen zu gewährleisten.

(2) Die Kommission oder ihre Vertreter und der Rechnungshof sind befugt, bei allen Empfängern, Auftragnehmern und Unterauftragnehmern, die Unionsmittel aus dem Programm erhalten haben, Rechnungsprüfungen anhand von Unterlagen sowie durch Überprüfungen und Kontrollen vor Ort durchzuführen.

(3) Gemäß den in der Verordnung (Euratom, EG) Nr. 2185/96 und der Verordnung (EU, Euratom) Nr. 883/2013 festgelegten Bestimmungen und Verfahren darf das OLAF bei allen direkt oder indirekt von diesen Finanzierungen betroffenen Wirtschaftstreibenden Untersuchungen, einschließlich Überprüfungen vor Ort und Kontrollen, durchführen, um festzustellen, ob im Zusammenhang mit einer Finanzhilfevereinbarung, einem Finanzhilfebeschluss oder einem durch das Programm finanzierten Vertrag ein Betrugs- oder Korruptionsdelikt oder eine sonstige rechtswidrige Handlung zum Nachteil der finanziellen Interessen der Union vorliegt.
(4) Unbeschadet der Absätze 1, 2 und 3 ist der Kommission, dem Rechnungshof und dem OLAF in Kooperationsabkommen mit Drittstaaten und internationalen Organisationen, in Verträgen, Finanzhilfevereinbarungen und Finanzhilfebeschlüssen, die sich aus der Umsetzung dieser Verordnung ergeben, ausdrücklich die Befugnis zu erteilen, Rechnungsprüfungen und Untersuchungen im Rahmen ihrer jeweiligen Zuständigkeiten durchzuführen.

Kapitel VIII
Schlussbestimmungen

Artikel 26 Aufhebung und Übergangsbestimmungen
(1) Die Beschlüsse Nr. 1718/2006/EG, Nr. 1855/2006/EG und Nr. 1041/2009/EG werden mit Wirkung 1. Januar 2014 aufgehoben.
(2) Aktivitäten, die vor dem 31. Dezember 2013 auf der Grundlage der in Absatz 1 genannten Beschlüsse angelaufen sind, werden, bis sie beendet sind, gemäß den genannten Beschlüssen verwaltet.

Artikel 27 Inkrafttreten
Diese Verordnung tritt am Tag nach ihrer Veröffentlichung im *Amtsblatt der Europäischen Union* in Kraft.
Sie gilt ab 1. Januar 2014.
Diese Verordnung ist in allen ihren Teilen verbindlich und gilt unmittelbar in jedem Mitgliedstaat.
Geschehen zu Straßburg am 11. Dezember 2013.

Anhang I Durchführungsbestimmungen zur Bürgschaftsfazilität für den Kultur- und Kreativsektor
Die durch die Bürgschaftsfazilität bereitgestellte finanzielle Unterstützung ist für KMU sowie für Kleinst-, kleine und mittlere Organisationen des Kultur- und Kreativsektors vorgemerkt; sie ist an die speziellen Bedürfnisse des Sektors angepasst und als solche erkennbar.
1. Aufgaben
   Die Bürgschaftsfazilität soll
   a) teilnehmenden Finanzmittlern aus allen an der Bürgschaftsfazilität teilnehmenden Ländern Bürgschaften bieten;
   b) teilnehmenden Finanzmittlern zusätzliches Fachwissen bieten, um die Risikobewertung von KMU und Kleinst-, kleinen und mittleren Organisationen und ihren Projekten im Kultur- und Kreativbereich vorzunehmen.
2. Auswahl der teilnehmenden Finanzmittler
   Der EIF wählt die teilnehmenden Finanzmittler nach marktüblichen Grundsätzen und den in Artikel 4 Buchstabe c genannten Einzelzielen aus. Die Auswahlkriterien umfassen insbesondere:
   a) das Volumen der Fremdfinanzierungen, die KMU sowie Kleinst-, kleinen und mittleren Organisationen zur Verfügung gestellt werden,
   b) die Grundsätze für das Risikomanagement bei der Darlehensvergabe, insbesondere in Bezug auf Kultur- und Kreativprojekte;
   c) die Fähigkeit zum Aufbau eines diversifizierten Darlehensportfolios und zum Vorschlagen eines regionen- und sektorübergreifenden Marketing- und Absatzförderungsplans für KMU sowie Kleinst-, kleine und mittlere Organisationen.
3. Laufzeit der Bürgschaftsfazilität
   Die Laufzeit einzelner Bürgschaften kann bis zu zehn Jahre betragen.
   Gemäß Artikel 21 Absatz 3 Ziffer i der Haushaltsordnung werden durch die Bürgschaften generierte Rückzahlungen für einen Zeitraum, der die Dauer des Verpflichtungszeitraums plus zehn Jahre nicht überschreiten darf, der Bürgschaftsfazilität zugewiesen. Rückzahlungen, die gemäß den Bestimmungen einschlägiger Übertragungsvereinbarungen durch die Maßnahmen des vor 2014 eingerichteten MEDIA-Produktionsgarantiefonds generiert wurden, sind der Bürgschaftsfazilität im Zeit-

B.III.4 Programm Kreatives Europa

raum 2014–2020 zuzuordnen. Die Kommission informiert die Mitgliedstaaten durch den Ausschuss „Kreatives Europa" über Zuordnungen dieser Art.

4. Kapazitätenaufbau
Im Rahmen der Bürgschaftsfazilität betrifft der Kapazitätenaufbau die Bereitstellung von Fachwissen für teilnehmende Finanzmittler, um deren Verständnis des Kultur- und Kreativsektors (in Bezug auf Aspekte wie die immaterielle Natur von als Sicherheit geltenden Vermögenswerten, die Größe des Marktes, dem die kritische Masse fehlt, und den Prototypcharakter der Produkte und Dienstleistungen) zu verbessern und jedem teilnehmenden Finanzmittler zusätzliches Fachwissen beim Aufbau von Portfolios und der Risikobewertung im Zusammenhang mit Kultur- und Kreativprojekten zur Verfügung zu stellen.

Die für den Kapazitätenaufbau zugewiesenen Mittel sind auf 10 % des Haushalts der Bürgschaftsfazilität beschränkt.

Der EIF wählt die Anbieter von Dienstleistungen für den Kapazitätenaufbau im Auftrag der Bürgschaftsfazilität und unter Aufsicht der Kommission in einem öffentlichen und offenen Vergabeverfahren aus, auf der Grundlage von Kriterien wie Erfahrung mit Finanzierungen im Kultur- und Kreativsektor, Fachkompetenz, geografische Reichweite, Leistungsfähigkeit und Marktkenntnis.

5. Budget
Die Mittelzuweisung deckt die Gesamtkosten der Bürgschaftsfazilität ab, einschließlich Zahlungsverpflichtungen gegenüber teilnehmenden Finanzmittlern, wie z.B. Ausfallzahlungen, Gebühren für die Verwaltung der Ressourcen der Union durch den EIF sowie alle sonstigen förderfähigen Kosten oder Ausgaben.

6. Publizität und Sensibilisierung
Der EIF trägt zur Bekanntmachung der Bürgschaftsfazilität im europäischen Bankensektor bei. Darüber hinaus stellen jeder teilnehmende Finanzmittler und der EIF sicher, dass der Unterstützung im Rahmen der Bürgschaftsfazilität die angemessene Sichtbarkeit und Transparenz zukommt, indem sie KMU sowie Kleinst-, kleine und mittlere Organisationen, die die Zielgruppe bilden, über die Finanzierungsmöglichkeiten Informationen bereitstellen.

Zu diesem Zweck stellt die Kommission u.a. dem Netz der „Kreatives-Europa"-Desks die zur Erfüllung ihrer Aufgaben erforderlichen Informationen zur Verfügung.

7. Arten von Darlehen
Arten von Darlehen, die von der Bürgschaftsfazilität abgedeckt sind, umfassen insbesondere:
a) Investitionen in materielle und immaterielle Vermögenswerte;
b) Unternehmensübertragungen;
c) Umlaufmittel (wie z.B. Vorfinanzierung, Lückenfinanzierung, Cashflow, Kreditlinien).

Anhang II Logo des Unterprogramms MEDIA

Das Logo des Unterprogramms MEDIA sieht folgendermaßen aus:

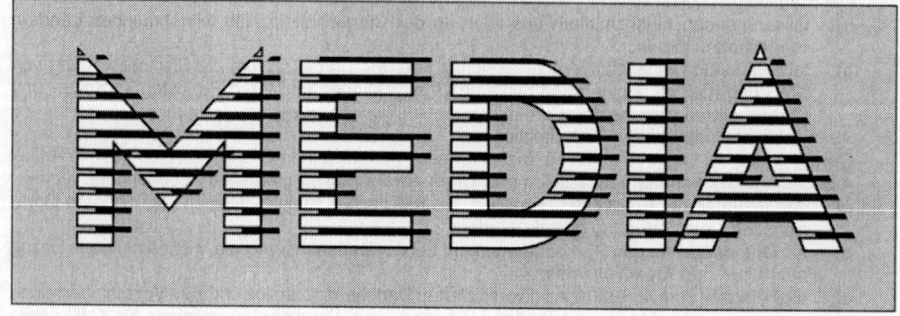

Beschluss Nr. 1194/2011/EU des Europäischen Parlaments und des Rates vom 16. November 2011 zur Schaffung einer Maßnahme der Europäischen Union für das Europäische Kulturerbe-Siegel

(ABl. L 303 S. 1)[1])

DAS EUROPÄISCHE PARLAMENT UND DER RAT DER EUROPÄISCHEN UNION –
gestützt auf den Vertrag über die Arbeitsweise der Europäischen Union, insbesondere auf Artikel 167 Absatz 5 erster Gedankenstrich,
auf Vorschlag der Europäischen Kommission,
nach Zuleitung des Entwurfs des Gesetzgebungsakts an die nationalen Parlamente,
nach Stellungnahme des Ausschusses der Regionen[2]),
gemäß dem ordentlichen Gesetzgebungsverfahren[3]),
in Erwägung nachstehender Gründe:

(1) Der Vertrag über die Arbeitsweise der Europäischen Union (AEUV) strebt eine immer engere Union der Völker Europas an und überträgt der Union u.a. die Aufgabe, einen Beitrag zur Entfaltung der Kulturen der Mitgliedstaaten unter Wahrung ihrer nationalen und regionalen Vielfalt bei gleichzeitiger Hervorhebung des gemeinsamen kulturellen Erbes zu leisten. In dieser Hinsicht unterstützt und ergänzt die Union erforderlichenfalls die Maßnahmen der Mitgliedstaaten zur Verbesserung der Kenntnis und der Verbreitung der Kultur und der Geschichte der Völker Europas.

(2) Wenn die Bürgerinnen und Bürger und insbesondere junge Menschen ihr gemeinsames und zugleich vielfältiges Kulturerbe besser kennen und schätzen lernen, trägt dies zur Stärkung des Zugehörigkeitsgefühls zur Union bei und regt den interkulturellen Dialog an. Deshalb ist es wichtig, für einen breiteren Zugang zum Kulturerbe zu sorgen und dessen europäische Dimension besser herauszustellen.

(3) Der AEUV führt auch die Unionsbürgerschaft ein, die die nationale Staatsbürgerschaft der einzelnen Mitgliedstaaten ergänzt und ein wichtiges Element für die Sicherung und Stärkung des europäischen Einigungsprozesses ist. Damit die Bürgerinnen und Bürger die europäische Einigung uneingeschränkt unterstützen, sollten ihre gemeinsamen Werte sowie ihre gemeinsame Geschichte und Kultur als zentrale Elemente ihrer Zugehörigkeit zu einer Gesellschaft, die auf den Grundsätzen der Freiheit, der Demokratie, der Achtung der Menschenrechte, der kulturellen und sprachlichen Vielfalt, der Toleranz und der Solidarität aufbaut, stärker hervorgehoben werden.

(4) Am 28. April 2006 haben mehrere Mitgliedstaaten in Granada, Spanien, eine zwischenstaatliche Initiative zum Europäischen Kulturerbe-Siegel (im Folgenden „zwischenstaatliche Initiative") ins Leben gerufen.

(5) Der Rat hat am 20. November 2008 Schlussfolgerungen[4]) angenommen, in denen er die Absicht bekundet, diese zwischenstaatliche Initiative in eine Maßnahme der Union (im Folgenden „Maßnahme") umzuwandeln, und die Kommission auffordert, einen Vorschlag für die Schaffung eines Europäischen Kulturerbe-Siegels (im Folgenden "Siegel") durch die Union zu unterbreiten und die praktischen Modalitäten für die Durchführung dieses Projekts festzulegen.

(6) Die Kommission hat hierzu eine öffentliche Konsultation sowie eine Folgenabschätzung durchgeführt, die den Wert der zwischenstaatlichen Initiative bestätigten, allerdings darauf hinwiesen, dass die Initiative weiterentwickelt werden muss, um ihr Potenzial vollumfänglich zu entfalten, und dass die Einbindung der Union einen eindeutigen Mehrwert generieren könnte und der Initiative einen qualitativen Schritt nach vorn ermöglichen würde.

---

1) Veröffentlicht am 22.11.2011.
2) **Amtl. Anm.:** ABl. C 267 vom 1.10.2010, S. 52.
3) **Amtl. Anm.:** Standpunkt des Europäischen Parlaments vom 16. Dezember 2010 (noch nicht im Amtsblatt veröffentlicht) und Standpunkt des Rates in erster Lesung vom 19. Juli 2011. Standpunkt des Europäischen Parlaments vom 16. November 2011.
4) **Amtl. Anm.:** ABl. C 319 vom 13.12.2008, S. 11.

B.III.5 Europäisches Kulturerbe-Siegel

(7) Das Siegel sollte von den mit der zwischenstaatlichen Initiative gemachten Erfahrungen profitieren.

(8) Das Siegel sollte einen Mehrwert anstreben und andere Initiativen zu ergänzen suchen, z.B. die Unesco-Liste des Welterbes, die Repräsentative Unesco-Liste des immateriellen Kulturerbes der Menschheit und die Initiative des Europarats „Europäische Kulturwege". Sein Mehrwert sollte auf dem Beitrag der ausgewählten Stätten zur Geschichte und Kultur Europas, einschließlich des Aufbaus der Union, auf einer klar definierten Bildungskomponente, die die Bürgerinnen und Bürger und insbesondere junge Menschen ansprechen soll, sowie auf der Vernetzung der Stätten untereinander zum Austausch von Erfahrungen und bewährter Verfahren beruhen. Im Mittelpunkt der Maßnahme sollte nicht die Erhaltung der Stätten stehen, die bereits durch bestehende Schutzregelungen gewährleistet sein sollte, sondern die Bekanntmachung der Stätten, die Verbesserung des Zugangs zu ihnen sowie die Qualität der angebotenen Informationen und Aktivitäten.

(9) Die Maßnahme der Union dürfte nicht nur das Zugehörigkeitsgefühl der europäischen Bürgerinnen und Bürger zur Union stärken und den interkulturellen Dialog anregen, sondern könnte auch zu einer Aufwertung und größeren Ausstrahlung des Kulturerbes, zur Stärkung der Rolle des Kulturerbes bei der wirtschaftlichen und nachhaltigen Entwicklung der Regionen, insbesondere durch den Kulturtourismus, zur Förderung von Synergien zwischen Kulturerbe und zeitgenössischer künstlerischer und kreativer Arbeit und – allgemein – zur Förderung der demokratischen Werte und der Menschenrechte, die das Fundament der europäischen Integration bilden, beitragen.

(10) Diese Ziele stehen vollständig im Einklang mit denen, die die Kommission in ihrer Mitteilung mit dem Titel „Eine europäische Kulturagenda im Zeichen der Globalisierung" aufgeführt hat, zu denen unter anderem die Förderung der kulturellen Vielfalt und des interkulturellen Dialogs sowie der Kultur als Katalysator für Kreativität gehört.

(11) Es ist von entscheidender Bedeutung, dass das Siegel auf der Grundlage gemeinsamer, eindeutiger und transparenter Kriterien und Verfahren verliehen wird; dies gilt auch für die ersten beiden Jahre der Auswahl, in denen Übergangsregeln gelten.

(12) Das Verfahren zur Auswahl von Stätten im Rahmen der Maßnahme sollte in zwei Phasen durchgeführt werden. Zunächst sollte auf nationaler Ebene eine Vorauswahl der Stätten stattfinden. Gegebenenfalls können die Mitgliedstaaten dabei lokale und regionale Behörden einbinden. Die Auswahl sollte dann auf Ebene der Union erfolgen. Jede Stätte, der das Siegel zuerkannt wurde, sollte kontrolliert werden, um sicherzustellen, dass die Kriterien, die für das Siegel aufgestellt wurden, fortlaufend erfüllt werden.

(13) Im Laufe der ersten Evaluierung der Maßnahme sollte die geografische Ausweitung der Maßnahme geprüft werden.

(14) Besteht eine klare thematische Verbindung zwischen mehreren in einem Mitgliedstaat befindlichen Stätten, so sollte die Maßnahme gemeinsame Bewerbungen zulassen. Solche gemeinsamen Bewerbungen sollten eine angemessene Anzahl teilnehmender Stätten zum Gegenstand haben und im Vergleich zu Einzelbewerbungen bezüglich derselben Stätten einen europäischen Mehrwert nachweisen.

(15) Ebenso sollte die Maßnahme aus Gründen der länderübergreifenden Dimension bestimmter Stätten gemeinsame Bewerbungen sowohl im Fall von in verschiedenen Mitgliedstaaten befindlichen Stätten, die ein bestimmtes Thema als Schwerpunkt haben, als auch im Fall einer Stätte, die sich im Hoheitsgebiet von mindestens zwei Mitgliedstaaten befindet, zulassen.

(16) Zur Gewährleistung einheitlicher Bedingungen für die Durchführung dieses Beschlusses und insbesondere der Bestimmungen zur Benennung der Stätten, denen das Siegel verliehen werden soll, zur Aberkennung des Siegels und zur Formalisierung des Verzichts auf das Siegel sollten der Kommission Durchführungsbefugnisse übertragen werden.

(17) Die Verwaltungsvorschriften für das Siegel sollten im Einklang mit dem Subsidiaritätsprinzip einfach und flexibel sein.

(18) Da die Ziele dieses Beschlusses auf Ebene der Mitgliedstaaten nicht ausreichend verwirklicht werden können und insbesondere wegen der Notwendigkeit neuer gemeinsamer, klarer und transparenter Kriterien und Verfahren für das Siegel sowie wegen der Notwendigkeit einer

verstärkten Koordinierung zwischen den Mitgliedstaaten daher besser auf Unionsebene zu verwirklichen sind, kann die Union im Einklang mit dem in Artikel 5 des Vertrags über die Europäische Union niedergelegten Subsidiaritätsprinzip tätig werden. Entsprechend dem in demselben Artikel genannten Grundsatz der Verhältnismäßigkeit geht der vorliegende Beschluss nicht über das zur Erreichung dieser Ziele erforderliche Maß hinaus –
HABEN FOLGENDEN BESCHLUSS ERLASSEN:

Artikel 1 Gegenstand
Mit diesem Beschluss wird eine Maßnahme der Europäischen Union (im Folgenden „Maßnahme") mit dem Titel "Europäisches Kulturerbe-Siegel" (im Folgenden "Siegel") geschaffen.

Artikel 2 Begriffsbestimmungen
Für die Zwecke dieses Beschlusses bezeichnet der Ausdruck:
1. „Stätten" Denkmäler, natürliche Stätten, Unterwasser- und archäologische Stätten, Industriestätten, Stätten im städtischen Raum, Kulturlandschaften, Gedenkstätten, Kulturgüter und -gegenstände sowie mit einem Ort verbundenes immaterielles Kulturerbe, einschließlich zeitgenössischen Kulturerbes;
2. „länderübergreifende Stätten"
   a) mehrere, in verschiedenen Mitgliedstaaten befindliche Stätten, die ein bestimmtes Thema als Schwerpunkt haben, um eine gemeinsame Bewerbung einzureichen, oder
   b) eine Stätte, die sich im Hoheitsgebiet von mindestens zwei Mitgliedstaaten befindet;
3. „nationale thematische Stätten" mehrere in demselben Mitgliedstaat befindliche Stätten, die ein bestimmtes Thema als Schwerpunkt haben, um eine gemeinsame Bewerbung einzureichen.

Artikel 3 Ziele
(1) Die Maßnahme trägt zu folgenden allgemeinen Zielen bei:
a) Stärkung des Zugehörigkeitsgefühls der europäischen Bürgerinnen und Bürger, insbesondere von jungen Menschen, zur Union auf der Grundlage gemeinsamer Werte und Elemente der europäischen Geschichte und des Kulturerbes sowie einer Würdigung des Stellenwerts der nationalen und regionalen Vielfalt;
b) Förderung des interkulturellen Dialogs.
(2) Um die in Absatz 1 genannten Ziele zu erreichen, zielt die Maßnahme mittelfristig darauf ab,
a) den symbolischen Wert von Stätten hervorzuheben und besser bekannt zu machen, die in der Geschichte und Kultur Europas und/oder beim Aufbau der Union eine bedeutende Rolle gespielt haben;
b) die europäischen Bürgerinnen und Bürger eingehender mit der Geschichte Europas und dem Aufbau der Union sowie mit ihrem gemeinsamen und zugleich vielfältigen Kulturerbe vertraut zu machen, insbesondere unter Bezugnahme auf die demokratischen Werte und die Menschenrechte, die das Fundament der europäischen Integration bilden.
(3) Die Stätten selbst dienen dazu, die folgenden konkreten Ziele zu erreichen:
a) Hervorhebung ihrer europäischen Bedeutung;
b) Sensibilisierung der Bürgerinnen und Bürger Europas, insbesondere junger Menschen, für das gemeinsame Kulturerbe;
c) Erleichterung des Austauschs von Erfahrungen und bewährter Verfahren in der gesamten Union;
d) Verbesserung und/oder Ausweitung des Zugangs für alle und insbesondere für junge Menschen;
e) Vertiefung des interkulturellen Dialogs, insbesondere unter jungen Menschen, durch künstlerische, kulturelle und geschichtliche Bildung;
f) Ausschöpfung der Synergien zwischen dem Kulturerbe einerseits und zeitgenössischer künstlerischer und kreativer Arbeit andererseits;
g) Leistung eines Beitrags zur Attraktivität und zur wirtschaftlichen Erschließung und nachhaltigen Entwicklung der Regionen, insbesondere durch den Kulturtourismus.

Artikel 4 Teilnahme an der Maßnahme
An der Maßnahme können die Mitgliedstaaten auf freiwilliger Basis teilnehmen.

B.III.5 Europäisches Kulturerbe-Siegel

Artikel 5 Mehrwert und Komplementarität der Maßnahme im Verhältnis zu anderen Initiativen

Die Kommission und die Mitgliedstaaten gewährleisten, dass die Maßnahme im Verhältnis zu anderen Initiativen im Bereich Kulturerbe, beispielsweise der Unesco-Liste des Welterbes, der repräsentativen Unesco-Liste des immateriellen Kulturerbes der Menschheit und der „Kulturwege Europas" des Europarates, einen Mehrwert bietet und diese ergänzt.

Artikel 6 Auswahlfähigkeit

Das Siegel kann Stätten im Sinne des Artikels 2 zuerkannt werden.

Artikel 7 Kriterien

(1) Die Zuerkennung des Siegels erfolgt auf Grundlage der nachstehenden Kriterien (im Folgenden „Kriterien"):

a) Die Bewerberstätten für das Siegel müssen einen symbolischen europäischen Wert aufweisen und eine bedeutende Rolle in der Geschichte und Kultur Europas und/oder beim Aufbau der Union gespielt haben. Sie müssen daher eine oder mehrere der folgenden Eigenschaften nachweisen:
 i) ihren grenzübergreifenden oder europaweiten Charakter: die Art und Weise, in der der Einfluss und die Anziehungskraft, die von der Stätte ausgingen und weiter von ihr ausgehen, über die Grenzen eines Mitgliedstaats hinausreichen;
 ii) ihre Stellung und Rolle in der europäischen Geschichte und im europäischen Integrationsprozess sowie ihre Verbindung zu maßgeblichen europäischen Ereignissen, Persönlichkeiten oder Bewegungen;
 iii) ihre Stellung und Rolle im Rahmen der Entwicklung und Förderung der gemeinsamen Werte, die das Fundament der europäischen Integration bilden.

b) Die Bewerberstätten für das Siegel müssen ein Projekt vorlegen, mit dessen Umsetzung spätestens am Ende des Jahres der Zuerkennung begonnen werden muss und das alle folgenden Elemente umfasst:
 i) Sensibilisierung für die europäische Bedeutung der Stätte, insbesondere mittels geeigneter Informationsaktivitäten, Ausschilderung und Schulungen für das Personal;
 ii) Organisation von Bildungsmaßnahmen, insbesondere für junge Menschen, um die Bürgerinnen und Bürger besser mit der gemeinsamen Geschichte Europas und ihrem gemeinsamen und zugleich vielfältigen Kulturerbe vertraut zu machen und ihr Zugehörigkeitsgefühl zu einem gemeinsamen Kulturraum zu fördern;
 iii) Förderung der Mehrsprachigkeit und Erleichterung des Zugangs zu der Stätte durch die Nutzung mehrerer Sprachen der Union;
 iv) Teilnahme an den Aktivitäten der Netzwerke der mit dem Siegel ausgezeichneten Stätten, um Erfahrungen auszutauschen und gemeinsame Projekte anzustoßen;
 v) Steigerung der Ausstrahlung und der Attraktivität der Stätte auf europäischer Ebene, unter anderem durch die Nutzung der Möglichkeiten neuer Technologien sowie digitaler und interaktiver Mittel und indem Synergien mit anderen europäischen Initiativen angestrebt werden.

Sofern der spezifische Charakter der Stätte dies erlaubt, ist die Ausrichtung künstlerischer und kultureller Aktivitäten zu begrüßen, die die Mobilität europäischer Kulturschaffender, Künstler und Sammlungen unterstützen, den interkulturellen Dialog stimulieren und Verknüpfungen zwischen dem Kulturerbe und zeitgenössischer künstlerischer und kreativer Arbeit fördern.

c) Die Bewerberstätten für das Siegel müssen ein Arbeitsprogramm vorlegen, das alle folgenden Elemente umfasst:
 i) Gewährleistung des soliden Managements der Stätte, einschließlich der Festlegung von Zielen und Indikatoren;
 ii) Gewährleistung der Erhaltung der Stätte für künftige Generationen im Einklang mit den einschlägigen Schutzregelungen;
 iii) Gewährleistung einer qualitativ hochwertigen Besucherinfrastruktur, wie geschichtliche Darstellung, Besucherinformationen und Ausschilderung;
 iv) Gewährleistung der Zugänglichkeit der Stätte für ein möglichst breites Publikum, unter anderem durch bauliche Anpassungen und Schulung des Personals;

v) besondere Berücksichtigung junger Menschen, insbesondere indem ihnen beim Zugang zur Stätte Vorrang gewährt wird;
vi) Bekanntmachung der Stätte als nachhaltiges touristisches Ziel;
vii) Entwicklung einer kohärenten und umfassenden Kommunikationsstrategie, die die europäische Bedeutung der Stätte hervorhebt;
viii) Gewährleistung, dass die Stätte in möglichst umweltfreundlicher Weise verwaltet wird.
(2) Bezüglich der in Absatz 1 Buchstaben b und c genannten Kriterien wird jede Stätte unter Berücksichtigung ihrer jeweiligen besonderen Merkmale in angemessener Weise bewertet.

Artikel 8 Europäische Jury
(1) ¹Es wird eine europäische Jury aus unabhängigen Experten eingerichtet (im Folgenden „europäische Jury"), die die Auswahl und Kontrolle auf Ebene der Union durchführt. ²Die Jury stellt sicher, dass die Kriterien seitens der Stätten in sämtlichen Mitgliedstaaten ordnungsgemäß angewandt werden.
(2) ¹Die europäische Jury besteht aus 13 Mitgliedern; gemäß ihren jeweiligen Verfahren ernennen das Europäische Parlament, der Rat und die Kommission jeweils vier Mitglieder und der Ausschuss der Regionen ein Mitglied. ²Die europäische Jury benennt ihren Vorsitz.
(3) ¹Bei den Mitgliedern der europäischen Jury handelt es sich um unabhängige Experten, die über umfassende Erfahrungen und Fachkenntnisse in den für die Ziele der Maßnahme relevanten Bereichen verfügen. ²Die Organe und Einrichtungen bemühen sich sicherzustellen, dass die Kompetenzen der von ihnen ernannten Experten sich so weit wie möglich ergänzen und dass diese Experten ein ausgewogenes geografisches Spektrum abbilden.
(4)
Die Mitglieder der europäischen Jury werden für drei Jahre ernannt.
Im Jahr 2012 gilt jedoch, dass das Europäische Parlament vier Mitglieder für zwei Jahre, der Rat vier Mitglieder für drei Jahre, die Kommission vier Mitglieder für ein Jahr und der Ausschuss der Regionen ein Mitglied für drei Jahre ernennen.
(5) ¹Die Mitglieder der europäischen Jury müssen auf jeden tatsächlichen oder potenziellen Interessenkonflikt in Bezug auf eine bestimmte Stätte hinweisen. ²Wird eine solche Erklärung durch ein Mitglied abgegeben oder stellt sich ein solcher Interessenkonflikt heraus, so nimmt dieses Mitglied nicht an der Bewertung der Stätte oder jeder anderen Stätte aus dem betreffenden Mitgliedstaat/den betreffenden Mitgliedstaaten teil.
(6) Sämtliche Berichte, Empfehlungen und Mitteilungen der europäischen Jury werden von der Kommission veröffentlicht.

Artikel 9 Bewerbungsformular
Um die Verfahren so straff und einfach wie möglich zu gestalten, erstellt die Kommission ein von allen Bewerberstätten zu verwendendes einheitliches Bewerbungsformular (im Folgenden „Bewerbungsformular"), das sich auf die Kriterien stützt.

Artikel 10 Vorauswahl auf nationaler Ebene
(1) Für die Vorauswahl der Stätten für die Zuerkennung des Siegels sind die Mitgliedstaaten zuständig.
(2) Jeder Mitgliedstaat kann alle zwei Jahre bis zu zwei Stätten in die Vorauswahl aufnehmen.
(3) Die Vorauswahl erfolgt auf Grundlage der Kriterien und des Bewerbungsformulars.
(4) ¹Gemäß dem Subsidiaritätsprinzip legt jeder teilnehmende Mitgliedstaat seine Verfahren und seinen Zeitplan für die Vorauswahl der Stätten selbst fest, wobei die Verwaltungsvorschriften so einfach und flexibel wie möglich zu halten sind. ²Die Mitgliedstaaten übermitteln der Kommission gemäß dem im Anhang aufgeführten Zeitplan die Bewerbungsformulare für die in die Vorauswahl aufgenommenen Stätten bis zum 1. März des Jahres, in dem das Auswahlverfahren stattfindet.
(5) Die Kommission veröffentlicht die vollständige Liste der in die Vorauswahl aufgenommenen Stätten und setzt das Europäische Parlament, den Rat und den Ausschuss der Regionen unverzüglich nach Abschluss der Vorauswahlphase davon in Kenntnis, so dass das Europäische Parlament, der Rat, der Ausschuss der Regionen, die Mitgliedstaaten oder jede sonstige Person oder Einrichtung der Kommission Bemerkungen vorlegen können, die Auswirkungen auf die Auswahl dieser Stätten haben könnten.

B.III.5 Europäisches Kulturerbe-Siegel

Artikel 11 Auswahl auf Unionsebene
(1) Die Auswahl von Stätten für die Zuerkennung des Siegels wird von der europäischen Jury unter der Verantwortung der Kommission vorgenommen.
(2) [1]Die europäische Jury bewertet die Bewerbungen für die in die Vorauswahl aufgenommenen Stätten und wählt höchstens eine Stätte pro Mitgliedstaat aus. [2]Erforderlichenfalls können zusätzliche Informationen angefordert und Besuche bei den Stätten durchgeführt werden.
(3) [1]Die Auswahl erfolgt auf Grundlage der Kriterien und des Bewerbungsformulars. [2]Die europäische Jury berücksichtigt in gebührender Form die in Artikel 10 Absatz 5 genannten Bemerkungen.
(4) [1]Die europäische Jury legt bis spätestens Ende des Jahres, in dem das Auswahlverfahren stattfindet, einen Bericht über die in die Vorauswahl aufgenommenen Stätten vor; sie leitet diesen Bericht der Kommission zu. [2]Dieser Bericht enthält eine Empfehlung, welchen Stätten das Siegel zuerkannt werden sollte, sowie eine begleitende Begründung für ihre Schlussfolgerungen bezüglich der Stätten, die ausgewählt werden und bezüglich der Stätten, die nicht ausgewählt werden. [3]Die Kommission leitet diesen Bericht informationshalber unverzüglich an das Europäische Parlament, den Rat und den Ausschuss der Regionen weiter.
(5) Bewerberstätten, die nicht ausgewählt werden, können in den Folgejahren erneut eine Bewerbung für die Vorauswahl auf nationaler Ebene einreichen.

Artikel 12 Länderübergreifende Stätten
(1) Für die Zuerkennung des Siegels an eine länderübergreifende Stätte muss diese sämtliche folgenden Bedingungen erfüllen:
a) vollständige Erfüllung der Kriterien durch jede teilnehmende Stätte;
b) Benennung einer der teilnehmenden Stätten als Koordinator, die als einzige Kontaktstelle für die Kommission dient;
c) Bewerbung unter einem gemeinsamen Namen;
d) gegebenenfalls Nachweis einer klaren thematischen Verbindung.
(2) [1]Für Bewerbungen hinsichtlich länderübergreifender Stätten gilt das gleiche Verfahren wie für andere Stätten. [2]Im Anschluss an eine Konsultation zwischen den teilnehmenden Stätten unter Beteiligung der zuständigen nationalen Behörden füllt jede teilnehmende Stätte ein Bewerbungsformular aus, das dem Koordinator zugeleitet wird. [3]Die Vorauswahl länderübergreifender Stätten erfolgt durch den Mitgliedstaat des Koordinators im Rahmen der in Artikel 10 Absatz 2 vorgesehenen Höchstzahl von Stätten, und die Stätten werden im Namen aller betreffenden Mitgliedstaaten nach deren Zustimmung vorgeschlagen.
(3) Wird eine länderübergreifende Stätte ausgewählt, so wird das Siegel der länderübergreifenden Stätte als Ganzes und unter dem gemeinsamen Namen zuerkannt.
(4) Erfüllt eine länderübergreifende Stätte sämtliche Kriterien, so wird ihr bei der Auswahl Priorität eingeräumt.

Artikel 13 Nationale thematische Stätten
(1) Für die Zuerkennung des Siegels an eine nationale thematische Stätte muss diese sämtliche folgenden Bedingungen erfüllen:
a) Nachweis des europäischen Mehrwerts einer gemeinsamen Bewerbung im Vergleich zu einzelnen Bewerbungen;
b) Nachweis einer klaren thematischen Verbindung;
c) vollständige Einhaltung der Kriterien durch jede teilnehmende Stätte;
d) Benennung einer teilnehmenden Stätte als Koordinator, die als einzige Kontaktstelle für die Kommission dient;
e) Bewerbung unter einem gemeinsamen Namen.
(2) [1]Für Bewerbungen hinsichtlich nationaler thematischer Stätten gilt das gleiche Verfahren wie für andere Stätten. [2]Jede teilnehmende Stätte füllt ein Bewerbungsformular aus, das dem Koordinator zugeleitet wird. [3]Die Vorauswahl nationaler thematischer Stätten erfolgt durch den betreffenden Mitgliedstaat im Rahmen der in Artikel 10 Absatz 2 vorgesehenen Höchstzahl von Stätten.
(3) Wird eine nationale thematische Stätte ausgewählt, so wird das Siegel der nationalen thematischen Stätte als Ganzes und unter dem gemeinsamen Namen zuerkannt.

Artikel 14 Zuerkennung

(1) ¹Unter gebührender Berücksichtigung der Empfehlungen der europäischen Jury benennt die Kommission die Stätten, denen das Siegel zuerkannt wird. ²Die Kommission unterrichtet das Europäische Parlament, den Rat und den Ausschuss der Regionen über die Zuerkennung.

(2) Vorbehaltlich der Bedingungen nach Artikel 15 und der Weiterführung der Maßnahme sowie unbeschadet des Artikels 16 wird das Siegel den Stätten auf unbegrenzte Zeit zuerkannt.

Artikel 15 Kontrolle

(1) Jede Stätte, der das Siegel zuerkannt wurde, wird regelmäßig kontrolliert, um zu gewährleisten, dass die Stätte die Kriterien dauerhaft erfüllt und dem Projekt und dem Arbeitsprogramm, die mit der Bewerbung eingereicht wurden, nachkommt.

(2) ¹Die Mitgliedstaaten sind für die Kontrolle sämtlicher Stätten zuständig, die sich in ihrem jeweiligen Hoheitsgebiet befinden. ²Für die Kontrolle einer länderübergreifenden Stätte ist der Mitgliedstaat des Koordinators zuständig.

(3) ¹Die Mitgliedstaaten tragen alle benötigten Informationen zusammen und erstellen gemäß dem im Anhang aufgeführten Zeitplan alle vier Jahre einen Bericht. ²Die Mitgliedstaaten übermitteln der Kommission diesen Bericht bis zum 1. März des Jahres, in dem das Kontrollverfahren stattfindet. ³Die Kommission legt den Bericht der europäischen Jury zur Prüfung vor.

(4) Die europäische Jury legt bis zum Ende des Jahres, in dem das Kontrollverfahren stattfindet, einen Bericht über den Zustand der mit dem Siegel ausgezeichneten Stätten vor; dieser Bericht enthält erforderlichenfalls Empfehlungen, die im folgenden Kontrollzeitraum zu berücksichtigen sind.

(5) Um ein kohärentes Vorgehen beim Kontrollverfahren zu gewährleisten, legt die Kommission in Zusammenarbeit mit der europäischen Jury gemeinsame Indikatoren für die Mitgliedstaaten fest.

Artikel 16 Aberkennung des Siegels oder Verzicht

(1) Stellt die europäische Jury fest, dass eine Stätte die Kriterien nicht mehr erfüllt oder dem mit ihrer Bewerbung eingereichten Projekt und Arbeitsprogramm nicht mehr nachkommt, so leitet sie über die Kommission einen Dialog mit dem betreffenden Mitgliedstaat ein, um die erforderlichen Anpassungsmaßnahmen bei der Stätte zu unterstützen.

(2) ¹Wurden 18 Monate nach Beginn des Dialogs die erforderlichen Anpassungsmaßnahmen bei der Stätte nicht durchgeführt, so teilt die europäische Jury diese Tatsache der Kommission mit. ²Dieser Mitteilung wird eine Begründung beigefügt und sie enthält praktische Empfehlungen zur Verbesserung der Situation.

(3) Wurden die praktischen Empfehlungen 18 Monate, nachdem die Mitteilung gemäß Absatz 2 erfolgte, nicht umgesetzt, so gibt die europäische Jury der Kommission gegenüber eine Empfehlung ab, der betreffenden Stätte das Siegel abzuerkennen.

(4) ¹Stellt die europäische Jury fest, dass eine Stätte, die an einer länderübergreifenden Stätte oder einer nationalen themenbezogenen Stätte beteiligt ist, die Kriterien nicht mehr erfüllt oder dem mit ihrer Bewerbung eingereichten Projekt und Arbeitsprogramm nicht mehr nachkommt, so gilt das Verfahren gemäß den Absätzen 1, 2 und 3. ²Die Aberkennung gemäß dem vorliegenden Absatz gilt für die gesamte länderübergreifende Stätte bzw. die gesamte nationale themenbezogene Stätte. ³Allerdings kann in Fällen, in denen die Kohärenz der länderübergreifenden bzw. der nationalen themenbezogenen Stätte nicht beeinträchtigt wird, die europäische Jury empfehlen, die Aberkennung auf die fragliche teilnehmende Stätte zu beschränken.

(5) ¹Unter gebührender Berücksichtigung der in Absatz 3 genannten Empfehlung trifft die Kommission die Entscheidung über die Aberkennung des Siegels. ²Die Kommission unterrichtet das Europäische Parlament, den Rat und den Ausschuss der Regionen über die Aberkennung.

(6) ¹Eine Stätte kann jederzeit auf das Siegel verzichten. ²In diesem Fall teilt sie dies den betreffenden Mitgliedstaaten mit, die ihrerseits die Kommission über den Verzicht unterrichten. ³Die Kommission formalisiert den Verzicht und unterrichtet das Europäische Parlament, den Rat und den Ausschuss der Regionen entsprechend.

Artikel 17 Praktische Modalitäten

(1) ¹Die Kommission setzt die Maßnahme um. ²Sie hat insbesondere folgende Aufgaben:
a) Gewährleistung der Gesamtkohärenz und der Qualität der Maßnahme;
b) Gewährleistung der Koordination zwischen den Mitgliedstaaten und der europäischen Jury;

c) im Lichte der Ziele und Kriterien Aufstellung von Leitlinien zur Unterstützung bei den Auswahl- und Kontrollverfahren in enger Zusammenarbeit mit der europäischen Jury;
d) Unterstützung der europäischen Jury.

(2) ¹Die Kommission ist auf Ebene der Union für die Kommunikation im Zusammenhang mit dem Siegel und die Gewährleistung seiner Öffentlichkeitswirksamkeit zuständig; insbesondere erstellt und unterhält sie hierzu eine eigene Website. ²Die Kommission stellt ferner sicher, dass ein Logo für die Maßnahme gestaltet wird.

(3) Die Kommission fördert die Vernetzung der mit dem Siegel ausgezeichneten Stätten.

(4) Die in den Absätzen 2 und 3 dieses Artikels genannten Maßnahmen und die durch die europäische Jury anfallenden Kosten werden aus der in Artikel 20 vorgesehenen Finanzausstattung finanziert.

Artikel 18 Evaluierung

(1) ¹Die Kommission veranlasst die externe und unabhängige Evaluierung der Maßnahme. ²Bei einer solchen Evaluierung, die gemäß dem Zeitplan im Anhang alle sechs Jahre stattfindet, werden sämtliche relevanten Aspekte untersucht, einschließlich der Effizienz der bei der Umsetzung der Maßnahme angewandten Verfahren, der Anzahl der Stätten, der Wirkung der Maßnahme, der Ausweitung ihres geografischen Geltungsbereichs, der Möglichkeiten zu ihrer Verbesserung und der Frage, ob sie weitergeführt werden sollte.

(2) Die Kommission legt dem Europäischen Parlament, dem Rat und dem Ausschuss der Regionen innerhalb von sechs Monaten nach Abschluss der Evaluierung nach Absatz 1 einen Evaluierungsbericht, gegebenenfalls zusammen mit geeigneten Vorschlägen, vor.

Artikel 19 Übergangsbestimmungen

(1) Mitgliedstaaten, die nicht an der zwischenstaatlichen Initiative zum Europäischen Kulturerbe-Siegel von 2006 (im Folgenden „zwischenstaatliche Initiative") teilgenommen haben, können im Jahr 2013 bis zu vier Stätten für die Zuerkennung des Siegels in die Vorauswahl aufnehmen.

(2) ¹Mitgliedstaaten, die an der zwischenstaatlichen Initiative teilgenommen haben, können im Jahr 2014 bis zu vier Stätten für die Zuerkennung des Siegels in die Vorauswahl aufnehmen. ²Sie können Stätten vorschlagen, denen bereits im Rahmen der zwischenstaatlichen Initiative ein Siegel zuerkannt wurde.

(3) Alle in den Absätzen 1 und 2 genannten Stätten werden von der europäischen Jury nach denselben Kriterien bewertet wie alle anderen Stätten, und sie durchlaufen auch dasselbe Verfahren, das für die übrigen Stätten gilt.

(4) ¹Erfüllt eine der in den Absätzen 1 und 2 genannten Stätten nicht die Kriterien oder werden zusätzliche Informationen benötigt, so leitet die europäische Jury über die Kommission einen Dialog mit dem betreffenden Mitgliedstaat ein, um zu prüfen, ob die Bewerbung vor einer Entscheidung verbessert werden kann. ²Erforderlichenfalls können Besuche bei der betreffenden Stätte durchgeführt werden.

Artikel 20 Finanzbestimmungen

(1) Die Finanzausstattung für die Durchführung der Maßnahme im Zeitraum vom 1. Januar 2012 bis zum 31. Dezember 2013 wird auf 650 000 EUR festgesetzt.

(2) Die jährlichen Mittel werden von der Haushaltsbehörde in den Grenzen des mehrjährigen Finanzrahmens bewilligt.

Artikel 21 Inkrafttreten

Dieser Beschluss tritt am Tag nach seiner Veröffentlichung im *Amtsblatt der Europäischen Union* in Kraft.

Geschehen zu Straßburg am 16. November 2011.

Anhang Zeitplan

Jahr	
2011	Inkrafttreten des Beschlusses Vorarbeiten
2012	Vorarbeiten
2013	Erste Auswahl von Stätten für die Mitgliedstaaten, die nicht an der zwischenstaatlichen Initiative teilgenommen haben
2014	Erste Auswahl von Stätten für die Mitgliedstaaten, die an der zwischenstaatlichen Initiative teilgenommen haben
2015	Auswahl
2016	Kontrolle
2017	Auswahl
2018	Evaluierung des Siegels
2019	Auswahl
2020	Kontrolle
2021	Auswahl
2022	–
2023	Auswahl
2024	Kontrolle Evaluierung des Siegels
2025	Auswahl
...	...

C.I.1 Grundgesetz

Grundgesetz für die Bundesrepublik Deutschland
Vom 23. Mai 1949 (BGBl. S. 1)
(BGBl. III/FNA 100-1)
zuletzt geändert durch Art. 1 ÄndG (Art. 72, 105 und 125b) vom 15. November 2019 (BGBl. I S. 1546)
– Auszug –

VII.
Die Gesetzgebung des Bundes

Artikel 73 [Gegenstände der ausschließlichen Gesetzgebung]
(1) Der Bund hat die ausschließliche Gesetzgebung über:
1. die auswärtigen Angelegenheiten sowie die Verteidigung einschließlich des Schutzes der Zivilbevölkerung;
[...]
5. die Einheit des Zoll- und Handelsgebietes, die Handels- und Schiffahrtsverträge, die Freizügigkeit des Warenverkehrs und den Waren- und Zahlungsverkehr mit dem Auslande einschließlich des Zoll- und Grenzschutzes;
5a. den Schutz deutschen Kulturgutes gegen Abwanderung ins Ausland;
[...]

Artikel 74 [Gegenstände der konkurrierenden Gesetzgebung]
(1) Die konkurrierende Gesetzgebung erstreckt sich auf folgende Gebiete:
1. das bürgerliche Recht, das Strafrecht, die Gerichtsverfassung, das gerichtliche Verfahren (ohne das Recht des Untersuchungshaftvollzugs), die Rechtsanwaltschaft, das Notariat und die Rechtsberatung;
[...]
11. das Recht der Wirtschaft (Bergbau, Industrie, Energiewirtschaft, Handwerk, Gewerbe, Handel, Bank- und Börsenwesen, privatrechtliches Versicherungswesen) ohne das Recht des Ladenschlusses, der Gaststätten, der Spielhallen, der Schaustellung von Personen, der Messen, der Ausstellungen und der Märkte;
[...]

Gesetz zum Schutz von Kulturgut (Kulturgutschutzgesetz – KGSG)[1)]

Vom 31. Juli 2016 (BGBl. I S. 1914)
(FNA 224-26)
zuletzt geändert durch Art. 40 des Gesetzes vom 20. November 2019 (BGBl. I S. 1626)

Inhaltsübersicht

Kapitel 1
Allgemeine Bestimmungen

- § 1 Anwendungsbereich
- § 2 Begriffsbestimmungen
- § 3 Zuständige Behörden
- § 4 Internetportal zum Kulturgutschutz

Kapitel 2
Schutz von Kulturgut vor Abwanderung

Abschnitt 1
Unterschutzstellen des nationalen Kulturgutes

- § 5 Grundsatz
- § 6 Nationales Kulturgut
- § 7 Eintragung in ein Verzeichnis national wertvollen Kulturgutes
- § 8 Nachträgliche Eintragung
- § 9 Kulturgut im Eigentum der Kirchen und Religionsgemeinschaften
- § 10 Ausnahmen zur Eintragung von Kulturgut bei Leihgaben aus dem Ausland und nach Rückkehr in das Bundesgebiet
- § 11 Ortswechsel von eingetragenem Kulturgut
- § 12 Steuerliche Begünstigung von national wertvollem Kulturgut, Ausgleich bei Verkauf infolge wirtschaftlicher Notlage
- § 13 Löschung der Eintragung

Abschnitt 2
Verfahren und Mitwirkungspflichten; Veröffentlichung

- § 14 Eintragungsverfahren
- § 15 Mitwirkungspflichten während des Eintragungsverfahrens
- § 16 Führung und Veröffentlichung der Verzeichnisse national wertvollen Kulturgutes
- § 17 Öffentliche Bekanntmachung

Abschnitt 3
Beschädigungsverbot und Mitteilungspflicht

- § 18 Beschädigungsverbot
- § 19 Mitteilungspflichten

Kapitel 3
Kulturgutverkehr

Abschnitt 1
Grundsatz

- § 20 Kulturgutverkehrsfreiheit

Abschnitt 2
Ausfuhr

- § 21 Ausfuhrverbot
- § 22 Genehmigung der vorübergehenden Ausfuhr von nationalem Kulturgut
- § 23 Genehmigung der dauerhaften Ausfuhr von nationalem Kulturgut
- § 24 Genehmigungspflichtige Ausfuhr von Kulturgut; Verordnungsermächtigung
- § 25 Allgemeine offene Genehmigung
- § 26 Spezifische offene Genehmigung
- § 27 Genehmigung der Ausfuhr von kirchlichem Kulturgut

Abschnitt 3
Einfuhr

- § 28 Einfuhrverbot
- § 29 Ausnahmen vom Einfuhrverbot
- § 30 Nachweis der Rechtmäßigkeit der Einfuhr

Abschnitt 4
Unrechtmäßiger Kulturgutverkehr

- § 31 Unrechtmäßige Ausfuhr von Kulturgut
- § 32 Unrechtmäßige Einfuhr von Kulturgut
- § 33 Sicherstellung von Kulturgut
- § 34 Verwahrung sichergestellten Kulturgutes
- § 35 Aufhebung der Sicherstellung
- § 36 Herausgabe sichergestellten Kulturgutes
- § 37 Einziehung sichergestellten Kulturgutes
- § 38 Folgen der Einziehung; Entschädigung
- § 39 Kosten für Sicherstellung, Verwahrung, Erhaltung und Herausgabe

Kapitel 4
Pflichten beim Inverkehrbringen von Kulturgut

- § 40 Verbot des Inverkehrbringens
- § 41 Allgemeine Sorgfaltspflichten
- § 42 Sorgfaltspflichten beim gewerblichen Inverkehrbringen
- § 43 Erleichterte Sorgfaltspflichten beim gewerblichen Inverkehrbringen
- § 44 Erhöhte Sorgfaltspflichten beim gewerblichen Inverkehrbringen
- § 45 Aufzeichnungs- und Aufbewahrungspflichten
- § 46 Auskunftspflicht
- § 47 Rechtsfolge bei Verstößen
- § 48 Einsichtsrechte des Käufers

---

1) Verkündet als Art. 1 G v. 31.7.2016 (BGBl. I S. 1914); Inkrafttreten gem. Art. 10 dieses Gesetzes am 6.8.2016.

C.I.2 Kulturgutschutzgesetz

Kapitel 5
Rückgabe unrechtmäßig eingeführten Kulturgutes

Abschnitt 1
Rückgabeanspruch

- § 49 Öffentlich-rechtliche Rückgabeansprüche
- § 50 Rückgabeanspruch eines Mitgliedstaates
- § 51 Rückgabeanspruch wegen Verstoßes gegen das Recht der Europäischen Union
- § 52 Rückgabeanspruch eines Vertragsstaates
- § 53 Rückgabeanspruch nach der Haager Konvention
- § 54 Anzuwendendes Zivilrecht
- § 55 Befristung und Verjährung des Rückgabeanspruchs
- § 56 Beginn der Verjährung
- § 57 Hemmung und Neubeginn der Verjährung und Erlöschensfristen

Abschnitt 2
Rückgabeverfahren

- § 58 Grundsatz der Rückgabe
- § 59 Rückgabeersuchen
- § 60 Kollidierende Rückgabeersuchen
- § 61 Aufgaben der Länder
- § 62 Aufgaben der obersten Bundesbehörden
- § 63 Zulässigkeit der Klage auf Rückgabe
- § 64 Kosten der behördlichen Sicherstellung
- § 65 Kosten der Rückgabe und Erhaltungsmaßnahmen

Abschnitt 3
Entschädigung und Erstattungsanspruch

- § 66 Entschädigung bei Rückgabe
- § 67 Höhe der Entschädigung
- § 68 Erstattungsanspruch des ersuchenden Mitglied- oder Vertragsstaates

Kapitel 6
Rückgabe unrechtmäßig ausgeführten Kulturgutes

- § 69 Rückgabeanspruch gegenüber Mitgliedstaaten
- § 70 Rückgabeanspruch gegenüber Vertragsstaaten
- § 71 Kosten

- § 72 Eigentum an zurückgegebenem Kulturgut

Kapitel 7
Rückgabezusage im internationalen Leihverkehr

- § 73 Rechtsverbindliche Rückgabezusage
- § 74 Erteilung der rechtsverbindlichen Rückgabezusage
- § 75 Verlängerung
- § 76 Wirkung

Kapitel 8
Datenschutz, gemeinsames Verfahren, Zoll

- § 77 Verarbeitung von Informationen einschließlich personenbezogener Daten
- § 78 Übermittlung von Informationen einschließlich personenbezogener Daten an die zuständige Behörde
- § 79 Gemeinsames Verfahren von Bund und Ländern
- § 80 Übermittlung von Informationen einschließlich personenbezogener Daten an Mitgliedstaaten und Vertragsstaaten
- § 81 Mitwirkung der Zollbehörden, Anhaltung von Kulturgut
- § 82 Anmeldepflicht bei Ein- und Ausfuhr im Kulturgutverkehr mit Drittstaaten

Kapitel 9
Straf- und Bußgeldvorschriften

- § 83 Strafvorschriften
- § 84 Bußgeldvorschriften
- § 85 Einziehung
- § 86 Besondere Voraussetzung der Verwertung von Kulturgut
- § 87 Aufgaben und Befugnisse der Zollbehörden
- § 88 Straf- und Bußgeldverfahren

Kapitel 10
Evaluierung, Übergangs- und Ausschlussvorschriften

- § 89 Evaluierung
- § 90 Fortgeltung und Befristung bisherigen Abwanderungsschutzes
- § 91 Ausschluss abweichenden Landesrechts

Kapitel 1
Allgemeine Bestimmungen

§ 1 Anwendungsbereich

Das Gesetz regelt
1. den Schutz nationalen Kulturgutes gegen Abwanderung,
2. die Ein- und Ausfuhr von Kulturgut,
3. das Inverkehrbringen von Kulturgut,
4. die Rückgabe unrechtmäßig eingeführten Kulturgutes,
5. die Rückgabe unrechtmäßig ausgeführten Kulturgutes und
6. die Rückgabezusage im internationalen Leihverkehr.

§ 2 Begriffsbestimmungen

(1) Im Sinne dieses Gesetzes ist oder sind

1. „archäologisches Kulturgut" bewegliche Sachen oder Sachgesamtheiten, die von Menschen geschaffen oder bearbeitet wurden oder Aufschluss über menschliches Leben in vergangener Zeit geben, sich im Boden oder in einem Gewässer befinden oder befunden haben oder bei denen aufgrund der Gesamtumstände dies zu vermuten ist,
2. „Ausfuhr" die Verbringung von Kulturgut aus dem Bundesgebiet,
3. „Drittstaat" jeder Staat, der kein Mitgliedstaat der Europäischen Union ist,
4. „Eigenbesitzer" die Person, die die tatsächliche Sachherrschaft über das Kulturgut für sich selbst ausübt,
5. „Einfuhr" die Verbringung von Kulturgut in das Bundesgebiet,
6. „Fremdbesitzer" die Person, die die tatsächliche Sachherrschaft über das Kulturgut für andere ausübt,
7. „Haager Konvention" die Haager Konvention vom 14. Mai 1954 zum Schutz von Kulturgut bei bewaffneten Konflikten (BGBl. 1967 II S. 1233, 1235),
8. „Herkunftsstaat" ein Mitgliedstaat oder Vertragsstaat, in dem das Kulturgut entstanden ist oder der eine so enge Beziehung zu dem Kulturgut hat, dass er es zum Zeitpunkt der Verbringung aus seinem Hoheitsgebiet als nationales Kulturgut unter Schutz gestellt hat,
9. „Inverkehrbringen" von Kulturgut das Anbieten, das Verkaufen, die Vermittlung, der Vertrieb, das Absetzen, die unentgeltliche Weiter- oder Abgabe zum Zweck der wirtschaftlichen Verwertung oder die wirtschaftliche Verwertung in sonstiger Weise im eigenen oder fremden Namen,
10. „Kulturgut" jede bewegliche Sache oder Sachgesamtheit von künstlerischem, geschichtlichem oder archäologischem Wert oder aus anderen Bereichen des kulturellen Erbes, insbesondere von paläontologischem, ethnographischem, numismatischem oder wissenschaftlichem Wert,
11. „Kulturgut bewahrende Einrichtung" jede Einrichtung im Bundesgebiet, deren Hauptzweck die Bewahrung und Erhaltung von Kulturgut und die Sicherung des Zugangs der Öffentlichkeit zu diesem Kulturgut ist, insbesondere Museen, Bibliotheken und Archive,
12. „Mitgliedstaat" jeder Mitgliedstaat der Europäischen Union außer der Bundesrepublik Deutschland,
13. „Protokoll zur Haager Konvention" das Protokoll zur Konvention vom 14. Mai 1954 zum Schutz von Kulturgut bei bewaffneten Konflikten (BGBl. 1967 II S. 1233, 1300),
14. „rechtswidrig ausgegraben" ein Kulturgut, wenn es unter Verstoß gegen eine inländische oder ausländische Rechtsvorschrift zum Schutz von archäologischem oder paläontologischem Kulturgut, insbesondere ohne eine nach einer solchen Rechtsvorschrift erforderliche Genehmigung, ausgegraben worden ist,
15. „Rückgabe" die Verbringung des Kulturgutes in das Hoheitsgebiet des ersuchenden Staates zur Erfüllung eines Rückgabeanspruchs,
16. „Sachgesamtheit" mehrere zusammengehörige Kulturgüter, insbesondere Archivbestände, Bibliotheksbestände, Nachlässe, Sammlungen oder Teile davon,
17. „UNESCO-Übereinkommen" das Übereinkommen über Maßnahmen zum Verbot und zur Verhütung der rechtswidrigen Einfuhr, Ausfuhr und Übereignung von Kulturgut (BGBl. 2007 II S. 626, 627),
18. die Verbringung von Kulturgut
    a) „vorübergehend", wenn sie für einen von Anfang an befristeten Zeitraum von höchstens fünf Jahren erfolgt,
    b) „dauerhaft", wenn sie für einen Zeitraum von mehr als fünf Jahren erfolgt,
19. „Vertragsstaat" jeder andere Staat außer der Bundesrepublik Deutschland, für den das UNESCO-Übereinkommen bindend ist,
20. „Verzeichnis national wertvollen Kulturgutes" ein Verzeichnis eines Landes, in das es Kulturgut als national wertvoll einträgt.

(2) Keine Ein- und Ausfuhr im Sinne dieses Gesetzes ist

1. die Herausgabe von Kulturgut durch Rechtshilfe im Sinne des § 66 des Gesetzes über die internationale Rechtshilfe in Strafsachen in der Fassung der Bekanntmachung vom 27. Juni 1994

C.I.2 Kulturgutschutzgesetz

(BGBl. I S. 1537), das zuletzt durch Artikel 163 der Verordnung vom 31. August 2015 (BGBl. I S. 1474) geändert worden ist,
2. die Rückgabe von unrechtmäßig verbrachtem Kulturgut nach Kapitel 5 und
3. die Rückgabe von Kulturgut an einen anderen Staat oder aus einem ausländischen Staat aufgrund bilateraler völkerrechtlicher Vereinbarungen.

§ 3 Zuständige Behörden

(1) [1]Zuständige Behörden im Sinne dieses Gesetzes sind die zuständigen Behörden der Länder, soweit in diesem Gesetz nichts anderes bestimmt ist. [2]Die Länder benennen die zuständigen Behörden durch Gesetz oder Rechtsverordnung.[1)]

(2) Die zentrale Stelle der Bundesrepublik Deutschland im Sinne des Artikels 4 der Richtlinie 2014/60/EU des Europäischen Parlaments und des Rates vom 15. Mai 2014 über die Rückgabe von unrechtmäßig aus dem Hoheitsgebiet eines Mitgliedstaats verbrachten Kulturgütern und zur Änderung der Verordnung (EU) Nr. 1024/2012 (Neufassung) (ABl. L 159 vom 28.5.2014, S. 1), die durch die Berichtigung der Richtlinie 2014/60/EU des Europäischen Parlaments und des Rates vom 15. Mai 2014 über die Rückgabe von unrechtmäßig aus dem Hoheitsgebiet eines Mitgliedstaats verbrachten Kulturgütern und zur Änderung der Verordnung (EU) Nr. 1024/2012 (ABl. L 147 vom 12.6.2015, S. 24) berichtigt worden ist, für die Kontaktaufnahme und Zusammenarbeit zwischen den Mitgliedstaaten ist die für Kultur und Medien zuständige oberste Bundesbehörde.

§ 4 Internetportal zum Kulturgutschutz

(1) [1]Die für Kultur und Medien zuständige oberste Bundesbehörde ist verpflichtet, ein zentrales Internetportal zum Kulturgutschutz zu errichten und zu unterhalten. [2]Das Internetportal dient insbesondere der Unterrichtung der Öffentlichkeit und der Herstellung von Transparenz im Kulturgutschutz, namentlich durch die
1. Darstellung der Aufgaben und Ziele des Kulturgutschutzes,
2. Darstellung der nationalen und internationalen Rechtsgrundlagen des Kulturgutschutzes,
3. Unterstützung der Verwaltungsverfahren etwa durch Bereitstellung von Formularen und Leitfäden,
4. Datenbank zur Dokumentation geschützten Kulturgutes und
5. Information über zuständige Behörden und Ansprechpartner.

(2) Die Datenbereitstellung im Internet erfolgt durch die für Kultur und Medien zuständige oberste Bundesbehörde und die zuständigen obersten Landesbehörden in deren jeweiliger Verantwortlichkeit.

(3) [1]Bund und Länder richten einen Verwaltungsausschuss zur koordinierten Erfüllung der maßgeblichen Aufgaben nach diesem Gesetz und zur Gewährleistung der einheitlichen Verwaltungspraxis der Länder ein, insbesondere zur
1. Beschlussfassung über Grundsätze der Veröffentlichung der Verzeichnisse national wertvollen Kulturgutes nach § 16,
2. Beschlussfassung über Grundsätze des gemeinsamen Verfahrens nach § 79 und
3. Zusammenarbeit zwischen Bund und Ländern.

[2]Der Verwaltungsausschuss berät darüber hinaus die oberste für Kultur und Medien zuständige Bundesbehörde bei dem Betrieb des Internetportals. [3]Ihm gehören zwei Vertreter oder Vertreterinnen der für Kultur und Medien zuständigen obersten Bundesbehörde und ein Vertreter oder eine Vertreterin jedes Landes an.

(4) [1]Der Verwaltungsausschuss trifft seine Beschlüsse mit der Mehrheit der abgegebenen Stimmen. [2]Bei Entscheidungen über Fragen, die nicht die Aufgaben der Länder nach diesem Gesetz betreffen, kann ein Beschluss nicht gegen die Stimmen der Vertreter der für Kultur und Medien zuständigen obersten Bundesbehörde getroffen werden. [3]Die Beschlüsse sind verbindlich für alle Länder, wenn sie mit einer Mehrheit von drei Vierteln der abgegebenen Stimmen getroffen werden. [4]Ein Mehrheitsbeschluss im schriftlichen Verfahren ist möglich, wenn nicht drei Viertel der Mitglieder des Verwaltungsausschusses dem widersprechen.

(5) Zur Klärung weiterer Verfahrensfragen und zur Regelung der Aufgaben im Einzelnen gibt sich der Verwaltungsausschuss eine Geschäftsordnung.

---
1) Die Zuständigkeitsregelungen der Länder nach dem KGSG sind abgedruckt im jeweiligen Abschnitt D, unter dem Punkt „Umsetzung Kulturgutschutzgesetz des Bundes".

Kapitel 2
Schutz von Kulturgut vor Abwanderung

Abschnitt 1
Unterschutzstellen des nationalen Kulturgutes

§ 5 Grundsatz
Nationales Kulturgut unterliegt als Teil des kulturellen Erbes Deutschlands dem Schutz gegen Abwanderung aus dem Bundesgebiet nach diesem Gesetz.

§ 6 Nationales Kulturgut
(1) Nationales Kulturgut ist Kulturgut, das
1. in ein Verzeichnis national wertvollen Kulturgutes eingetragen ist,
2. sich in öffentlichem Eigentum und im Bestand einer öffentlich-rechtlichen Kulturgut bewahrenden Einrichtung befindet,
3. sich im Eigentum und im Bestand einer Kulturgut bewahrenden Einrichtung befindet, die überwiegend durch Zuwendungen der öffentlichen Hand finanziert wird, oder
4. Teil einer Kunstsammlung des Bundes oder der Länder ist.

(2) [1]Nur mit Zustimmung des Verleihers oder Deponenten gegenüber der zuständigen Behörde gilt Kulturgut in einer öffentlich-rechtlichen Kulturgut bewahrenden Einrichtung oder einer solchen, die überwiegend durch Zuwendungen der öffentlichen Hand finanziert wird, für die Dauer des Leih- oder Depositalvertrages vorübergehend ebenfalls als nationales Kulturgut. [2]Der Verleiher oder der Deponent kann seine Zustimmung jederzeit widerrufen. [3]Die Einrichtung hat den Verleiher oder Deponenten über die Rechtsfolgen des Verzichts auf den Schutz als nationales Kulturgut nach den §§ 69 und 70 zu unterrichten. [4]Dieser Schutz endet mit der Kündigung oder mit dem Ablauf des Leih- oder Depositalvertrages.

§ 7 Eintragung in ein Verzeichnis national wertvollen Kulturgutes
(1) [1]Kulturgut ist von der obersten Landesbehörde in ein Verzeichnis national wertvollen Kulturgutes einzutragen, wenn
1. es besonders bedeutsam für das kulturelle Erbe Deutschlands, der Länder oder einer seiner historischen Regionen und damit identitätsstiftend für die Kultur Deutschlands ist und
2. seine Abwanderung einen wesentlichen Verlust für den deutschen Kulturbesitz bedeuten würde und deshalb sein Verbleib im Bundesgebiet im herausragenden kulturellen öffentlichen Interesse liegt.

[2]Werke lebender Urheber oder Hersteller dürfen nur mit deren Zustimmung eingetragen werden.
(2) [1]Eine Sachgesamtheit ist auch dann nach Absatz 1 in ein Verzeichnis national wertvollen Kulturgutes einzutragen, wenn die Sachgesamtheit als solche, nicht aber zwingend ihre einzelnen Bestandteile die Kriterien nach Absatz 1 erfüllen. [2]Einer Eintragung steht nicht entgegen, wenn eine Sachgesamtheit
1. teilweise zerstört ist,
2. an unterschiedlichen Orten im Inland aufbewahrt ist oder
3. teilweise im Ausland aufbewahrt ist.

(3) [1]Zuständig für die Eintragung in ein Verzeichnis national wertvollen Kulturgutes ist die oberste Landesbehörde des Landes, in dem sich das Kulturgut zum Zeitpunkt der Einleitung des Eintragungsverfahrens befindet. [2]Die Zuständigkeit bleibt bestehen, bis die Entscheidung über die Eintragung unanfechtbar geworden ist.
(4) Die Eintragung von Kulturgut im Eigentum der Kirchen und der als Körperschaften des öffentlichen Rechts anerkannten Religionsgemeinschaften richtet sich nach § 9.

§ 8 Nachträgliche Eintragung
(1) Ist Kulturgut unter Verstoß gegen § 24 ausgeführt worden, so kann es von der zuständigen obersten Landesbehörde auch nach der Ausfuhr in ein Verzeichnis national wertvollen Kulturgutes eingetragen werden, wenn die Voraussetzungen nach § 7 Absatz 1 und 2 erfüllt sind.
(2) [1]Die örtliche Zuständigkeit für die Eintragung richtet sich nach dem Ort der letzten dauerhaften Belegenheit im Bundesgebiet. [2]Ist dieser Ort nicht feststellbar, bestimmt die für Kultur und Medien zuständige oberste Bundesbehörde die zuständige oberste Landesbehörde. [3]Dabei hat sie die besondere

Verbindung des Kulturgutes mit einem Land aus historischen oder anderen Gründen zu berücksichtigen.
(3) Die Befugnis zur nachträglichen Eintragung in ein Verzeichnis national wertvollen Kulturgutes endet, wenn die zuständige oberste Landesbehörde das Eintragungsverfahren nicht innerhalb eines Jahres eingeleitet hat, nachdem sie von der unrechtmäßigen Ausfuhr und dem Ort der neuen Belegenheit Kenntnis erlangt hat.
(4) Mit der Einleitung des Eintragungsverfahrens gilt das Kulturgut nach Absatz 1 als nationales Kulturgut, bis die Entscheidung über die Eintragung unanfechtbar geworden ist.

§ 9 Kulturgut im Eigentum der Kirchen und Religionsgemeinschaften
(1) ¹Die Kirchen und die als Körperschaften des öffentlichen Rechts anerkannten Religionsgemeinschaften können bei der zuständigen obersten Landesbehörde beantragen, dass Kulturgut, das sich in ihrem Eigentum befindet, in ein Verzeichnis national wertvollen Kulturgutes eingetragen wird. ²§ 7 Absatz 1 und 2 ist entsprechend anzuwenden.
(2) ¹Bei einer nachträglichen Eintragung nach § 8 kann der Antrag nur innerhalb der Frist nach § 8 Absatz 3 gestellt werden. ²Die zuständige oberste Landesbehörde unterrichtet unverzüglich die Kirche oder die als Körperschaft des öffentlichen Rechts anerkannte Religionsgemeinschaft, wenn sie von Umständen Kenntnis erhält, die einen Antrag nach Absatz 1 ermöglichen.
(3) Die Kirchen und die als Körperschaften des öffentlichen Rechts anerkannten Religionsgemeinschaften können bei den obersten Landesbehörden beantragen, dass für einzelne Sachgesamtheiten ihrer Kulturgut bewahrenden Einrichtungen und für das Inventar ihrer liturgischen Räume § 6 Absatz 1 Nummer 3 entsprechend anzuwenden ist mit der Maßgabe, dass an die Stelle der Finanzierung durch die öffentliche Hand die Finanzierung durch die Kirchen oder Religionsgemeinschaften tritt.

§ 10 Ausnahmen zur Eintragung von Kulturgut bei Leihgaben aus dem Ausland und nach Rückkehr in das Bundesgebiet
(1) Für ehemals im Bundesgebiet belegenes Kulturgut, das sich mehr als fünf Jahre vor dem 6. August 2016 außerhalb des Bundesgebietes befunden hat und nach dem 6. August 2016 wieder in das Bundesgebiet eingeführt werden soll, kann die zuständige oberste Landesbehörde, wenn eine Eintragung nach § 7 in Betracht kommt, auf Antrag einer Kulturgut bewahrenden Einrichtung vor der Einfuhr dem Eigentümer des Kulturgutes zusichern, dass das Kulturgut nicht nach § 7 in ein Verzeichnis national wertvollen Kulturgutes eingetragen wird, sofern der Eigentümer die Gewähr dafür bietet, dass das Kulturgut für mindestens fünf Jahre
1. sich ohne Unterbrechung im Bundesgebiet befinden wird und
2. bei der antragstellenden Einrichtung als Leihgabe öffentlich ausgestellt oder für die Forschung zugänglich gemacht wird.

(2) Die oberste Landesbehörde kann die Zusicherung davon abhängig machen, dass die Kulturgut bewahrende Einrichtung nach Absatz 1 mit dem Eigentümer des Kulturgutes einen Vertrag über einen möglichen Ankauf des Kulturgutes schließt.
(3) ¹Die Zusicherung nach Absatz 1 ist von der zuständigen obersten Landesbehörde mit Nebenbestimmungen zu versehen, die sicherstellen, dass die Voraussetzungen nach Absatz 1 Nummer 1 und 2 eingehalten werden. ²Weitere Nebenbestimmungen sind zulässig.
(4) Die zuständige oberste Landesbehörde kann über die Zusicherung nach Absatz 1 auch einen öffentlich-rechtlichen Vertrag mit dem Eigentümer schließen.
(5) Wird Kulturgut nach Ablauf des vereinbarten Zeitraums nach Absatz 1 ausgeführt, so unterliegt es nicht der Genehmigungspflicht nach § 24 Absatz 1 Nummer 2.
(6) ¹Wird Kulturgut unter Verstoß gegen die Nebenbestimmungen zur Zusicherung nach Absatz 1 oder gegen den nach Absatz 4 geschlossenen öffentlich-rechtlichen Vertrag ausgeführt, gilt das Kulturgut als unrechtmäßig ausgeführt. ²Dies gilt auch dann, wenn der Eigentümer bei der Ausfuhr gegen eine Vereinbarung verstößt, die er mit der zuständigen Behörde oder mit einer Kulturgut bewahrenden Einrichtung nach Absatz 1 getroffen hat.
(7) ¹Wird ein Leihvertrag zwischen einem Verleiher mit nicht nur vorübergehendem Wohnsitz oder Sitz im Ausland und einer Kulturgut bewahrenden Einrichtung im Inland abgeschlossen, so kann die zuständige oberste Landesbehörde außer in den Fällen einer Rückkehr des Kulturgutes nach Absatz 1 auf Antrag des Entleihers dem Verleiher vor der Einfuhr des Kulturgutes schriftlich zusichern, dass

für die Dauer von bis zu sechs Monaten nach Ende des Leihvertrages kein Verfahren zur Eintragung in ein Verzeichnis national wertvollen Kulturgutes eingeleitet wird. ²Auf Kulturgut, das sich vor dem 6. August 2016 auf der Grundlage eines Leihvertrages im Sinne des Satzes 1 im Inland befindet, findet § 7 Absatz 1 und 2 ebenfalls für die Dauer von bis zu sechs Monaten nach Ablauf des Leihvertrages keine Anwendung. ³Die Ausfuhr bis zu sechs Monate nach Beendigung eines Leihvertrages nach den Sätzen 1 und 2 unterliegt nicht der Genehmigungspflicht nach § 24 Absatz 1 Nummer 2.

§ 11 Ortswechsel von eingetragenem Kulturgut
(1) Wird Kulturgut, das in ein Verzeichnis national wertvollen Kulturgutes eingetragen ist, für weniger als ein Jahr von einem Land in ein anderes Land verbracht, so behält die Eintragung in das Verzeichnis national wertvollen Kulturgutes ihre Wirkung.
(2) ¹Wird Kulturgut, das in ein Verzeichnis national wertvollen Kulturgutes eingetragen ist, für mehr als ein Jahr in ein anderes Land verbracht, so wird es in das Verzeichnis national wertvollen Kulturgutes des Landes übertragen, in das es verbracht worden ist. ²Der unmittelbare Besitzer hat den Ortswechsel und den Zeitpunkt des Ortswechsels der nunmehr zuständigen obersten Landesbehörde schriftlich oder elektronisch mitzuteilen.

§ 12 Steuerliche Begünstigung von national wertvollem Kulturgut, Ausgleich bei Verkauf infolge wirtschaftlicher Notlage
(1) Kulturgut, das in ein Verzeichnis national wertvollen Kulturgutes eingetragen ist, wird bei der Heranziehung zu Steuern begünstigt nach
1. § 13 Absatz 1 Nummer 2 Buchstabe b Doppelbuchstabe bb des Erbschaftsteuer- und Schenkungsteuergesetzes in der Fassung des Artikels 8 des Gesetzes vom 31. Juli 2016 (BGBl. I S. 1914) sowie
2. § 10g des Einkommensteuergesetzes in der Fassung des Artikels 7 des Gesetzes vom 31. Juli 2016 (BGBl. I S. 1914).

(2) Wird die Genehmigung zur dauerhaften Ausfuhr nach § 23 rechtskräftig versagt und ist der Eigentümer national wertvollen Kulturgutes infolge wirtschaftlicher Notlage zum Verkauf gezwungen, so hat die oberste Landesbehörde des Landes, in dem sich das Kulturgut befindet, im Einvernehmen mit der für Kultur und Medien zuständigen obersten Bundesbehörde auf einen billigen Ausgleich unter Berücksichtigung der Steuervorteile nach Absatz 1 hinzuwirken.

§ 13 Löschung der Eintragung
(1) Haben sich die das Kulturgut betreffenden Umstände, die zur Eintragung des Kulturgutes in ein Verzeichnis national wertvollen Kulturgutes geführt haben, wesentlich verändert, so kann die Eintragung von Amts wegen oder auf Antrag des Eigentümers von der obersten Landesbehörde gelöscht werden.
(2) Eine Änderung wesentlicher Umstände nach Absatz 1 ist stets gegeben, wenn rechtskräftig oder durch eine abschließende Regelung der Beteiligten im Hinblick auf einen Entzug festgestellt ist, dass das Kulturgut zwischen dem 30. Januar 1933 und dem 8. Mai 1945 aufgrund der Verfolgung durch den Nationalsozialismus einem früheren Eigentümer entzogen worden ist[1)] und es aus dem Bundesgebiet ausgeführt werden soll, um es an außerhalb des Bundesgebietes lebende ursprüngliche Eigentümer oder deren dort lebende Rechtsnachfolger zurückzugeben.
(3) Ist Kulturgut nach § 11 Absatz 2 in das Verzeichnis eines anderen Landes übertragen worden, so gibt die oberste Landesbehörde vor ihrer Entscheidung über die Löschung der ursprünglich für die Eintragung zuständigen obersten Landesbehörde die Gelegenheit zur Stellungnahme.
(4) Für das Verfahren zur Löschung der Eintragung ist § 14 Absatz 1 bis 5 entsprechend anzuwenden.

---

1) Siehe dazu auch die Grundsätze der Washingtoner Konferenz in Bezug auf Kunstwerke, die von den Nationalsozialisten beschlagnahmt wurden, abgedruckt als A.III.5.

Abschnitt 2
Verfahren und Mitwirkungspflichten; Veröffentlichung
§ 14 Eintragungsverfahren

(1) ¹Die Einleitung des Verfahrens auf Eintragung in ein Verzeichnis national wertvollen Kulturgutes erfolgt von Amts wegen oder auf Antrag des Eigentümers. ²Der Antrag ist an die oberste Landesbehörde zu richten und muss folgende Angaben enthalten
1. die Bezeichnung des Kulturgutes,
2. den Namen und die Anschrift des Eigentümers und des Besitzers,
3. die Belegenheit zum Zeitpunkt der Antragstellung und
4. die Begründung der Eintragungsvoraussetzungen nach § 7 Absatz 1 Satz 1 Nummer 1 und 2.

(2) ¹Die obersten Landesbehörden berufen Sachverständigenausschüsse, die keiner Weisung unterliegen. ²Diese bestehen aus fünf Sachverständigen und werden für die Dauer von fünf Jahren berufen, wobei Wiederberufungen möglich sind. ³Bei der Berufung sind sachkundige Personen aus dem Kreis der Kulturgut bewahrenden Einrichtungen, der Wissenschaft, des Kunsthandels und Antiquariats sowie der privaten Sammlerinnen und Sammler zu berücksichtigen. ⁴Verbände und Organisationen aus diesen Bereichen können Vorschläge für die Berufung einreichen. ⁵Eine der sachkundigen Personen ist auf Vorschlag der für Kultur und Medien zuständigen obersten Bundesbehörde zu berufen. ⁶Die Zusammensetzung der Sachverständigenausschüsse der Länder ist im Internetportal nach § 4 zu veröffentlichen. ⁷Die Ausschüsse können vor ihrer Entscheidung auch externe sachkundige Personen anhören.

(3) ¹Kulturgut darf nur im Benehmen mit dem Sachverständigenausschuss eingetragen werden. ²Die zuständige oberste Landesbehörde hat nach Herstellung des Benehmens mit dem Sachverständigenausschuss und vor ihrer Sachentscheidung den Eigentümer des Kulturgutes zu hören.

(4) Die zuständige oberste Landesbehörde gibt vor ihrer Entscheidung über die Eintragung in ihr Verzeichnis national wertvollen Kulturgutes anderen Ländern die Gelegenheit zur Stellungnahme, sofern das Kulturgut zu diesen Ländern insbesondere aus historischen Gründen eine besondere Verbindung hat.

(5) Zur Wahrung eines gesamtstaatlichen Interesses kann auch die für Kultur und Medien zuständige oberste Bundesbehörde die Eintragung in ein Verzeichnis national wertvollen Kulturgutes beantragen.

(6) ¹Das Eintragungsverfahren endet mit der Entscheidung der zuständigen obersten Landesbehörde über die Eintragung. ²Erfolgt diese Entscheidung nicht binnen sechs Monaten nach Einleitung des Verfahrens, so gilt das Verfahren als ohne Eintragung beendet. ³Verhandlungen des Eigentümers mit der zuständigen obersten Landesbehörde, Rechtsmittel des Eigentümers im Verfahren sowie in begründeten Ausnahmefällen bei der Einholung externen Sachverstands nach Absatz 2 Satz 7 hemmen die Frist. ⁴Die Frist ist ferner gehemmt, wenn der Eigentümer seinen Mitwirkungspflichten nach § 15 nicht nachkommt oder das Verfahren sonst verzögert. ⁵Ist das Verfahren ohne Eintragung beendet und die Beendigung nach § 17 bekannt gemacht worden, so kann ein erneutes Verfahren zur Eintragung, auch in einem anderen Land, nur eingeleitet werden, wenn sich die Umstände, die zur Beendigung des Verfahrens geführt haben, wesentlich verändert haben.

(7) ¹Der Eigentümer kann, sofern er nachweist, dass das Kulturgut die Alters- und Wertgrenzen der in § 24 Absatz 1 Nummer 1 in Bezug genommenen Verordnung übersteigt, entsprechend Absatz 1 auch unter Darlegung seines berechtigten Interesses und der Versicherung der Vollständigkeit und Wahrheit seiner Angaben beantragen, dass die zuständige Behörde verbindlich feststellt, dass die Voraussetzungen der Eintragung in das Verzeichnis national wertvollen Kulturgutes nicht vorliegen. ²Die zuständige Behörde kann den nach Absatz 2 berufenen Sachverständigenausschuss beteiligen. ³Die Absätze 4 und 6 Satz 5 gelten entsprechend. ⁴Die Ausfuhr von Kulturgut, für das eine solche verbindliche Feststellung vorliegt, unterliegt nicht der Genehmigungspflicht nach § 24 Absatz 1 Nummer 2.

§ 15 Mitwirkungspflichten während des Eintragungsverfahrens

(1) ¹Im Verfahren zur Eintragung in ein Verzeichnis national wertvollen Kulturgutes ist der Eigentümer, hilfsweise der unmittelbare Besitzer, verpflichtet, der obersten Landesbehörde
1. die zur eindeutigen Identifizierung des Kulturgutes erforderlichen Angaben, die Eigentumsverhältnisse und den Aufbewahrungsort mitzuteilen,

2. geeignete Abbildungen des Kulturgutes zur Verfügung zu stellen oder deren Herstellung durch die zuständige oberste Landesbehörde oder eines oder einer durch sie Beauftragten zu gestatten und
3. nicht ausschließliche, zeitlich unbefristete, weltweite Rechte zur Vervielfältigung und öffentlichen Zugänglichmachung der identifizierenden Angaben sowie der Abbildungen zur Nutzung für das Verzeichnis national wertvollen Kulturgutes einzuräumen oder zu übertragen.
²Urheberrechtliche Vorschriften bleiben unberührt.
(2) Der Eigentümer, hilfsweise der unmittelbare Besitzer, ist während des Eintragungsverfahrens verpflichtet, jede Änderung der mitgeteilten Angaben nach Absatz 1 Satz 1 Nummer 1 unverzüglich der obersten Landesbehörde mitzuteilen.

§ 16 Führung und Veröffentlichung der Verzeichnisse national wertvollen Kulturgutes
(1) Die Länder führen ihre Verzeichnisse national wertvollen Kulturgutes[1] in dem gemeinsamen Verfahren nach § 79 Absatz 1 Satz 1 und veröffentlichen sie zentral und länderübergreifend im Internetportal nach § 4.
(2) ¹Personenbezogene Daten des Eigentümers oder des Besitzers und der Ort der Belegenheit des eingetragenen Kulturgutes dürfen nicht veröffentlicht werden. ²Dies gilt nicht, soweit diese Angaben für die eindeutige Bezeichnung des Kulturgutes erforderlich sind.
(3) Die für Kultur und Medien zuständige oberste Bundesbehörde hat bei der Veröffentlichung durch organisatorische und dem jeweiligen Stand der Technik entsprechende technische Maßnahmen sicherzustellen, dass die Eintragungen während ihrer Veröffentlichung unversehrt, vollständig sowie aktuell bleiben und jederzeit ihrem Ursprung nach zugeordnet werden können.
(4) Für den Zugang zu einer Veröffentlichung ist § 15 Absatz 2 Satz 1 bis 3 des E-Government-Gesetzes entsprechend anzuwenden.
(5) Einzelheiten der Führung und Veröffentlichung der Verzeichnisse werden durch für alle Länder verbindliche Beschlüsse des Verwaltungsausschusses nach § 4 Absatz 4 geregelt.

§ 17 Öffentliche Bekanntmachung
(1) Die zuständige oberste Landesbehörde hat jede Einleitung und jede Beendigung eines Verfahrens zur Eintragung, jede Eintragung, jede Löschung oder jede sonstige Änderung einer Eintragung in ein Verzeichnis national wertvollen Kulturgutes öffentlich im Bundesanzeiger bekannt zu machen und den Beteiligten mitzuteilen.
(2) § 16 Absatz 2 ist entsprechend anzuwenden.

Abschnitt 3
Beschädigungsverbot und Mitteilungspflicht

§ 18 Beschädigungsverbot
(1) ¹Es ist verboten, Kulturgut, das in ein Verzeichnis national wertvollen Kulturgutes eingetragen ist, zu zerstören, zu beschädigen oder dessen Erscheinungsbild nicht nur unerheblich und nicht nur vorübergehend zu verändern, sofern dieses nicht zur fachgerechten Konservierung und Restaurierung oder zur Forschung nach anerkannten wissenschaftlichen Standards erfolgt. ²§ 304 Absatz 1 und 2 des Strafgesetzbuches bleibt unberührt.
(2) Absatz 1 gilt auch, wenn für ein Kulturgut das Verfahren zur Eintragung in ein Verzeichnis national wertvollen Kulturgutes eingeleitet ist.

§ 19 Mitteilungspflichten
(1) ¹Der unmittelbare Besitzer eines Kulturgutes, das in ein Verzeichnis national wertvollen Kulturgutes eingetragen ist, ist verpflichtet, der zuständigen obersten Landesbehörde unverzüglich das Abhandenkommen, die Zerstörung, die Beschädigung oder die nicht nur unerhebliche und nicht nur vorübergehende Veränderung des Erscheinungsbildes des Kulturgutes mitzuteilen. ²Bei Besitzwechsel ist der neue, hilfsweise der frühere unmittelbare Besitzer, zur Mitteilung verpflichtet.
(2) Sind der Eigentümer und der unmittelbare Besitzer des Kulturgutes nicht dieselbe Person, so gilt die Mitteilungspflicht nach Absatz 1 hilfsweise auch für den Eigentümer.

---

1) Die Länderverzeichnisse national wertvollen Kulturgutes sind abrufbar unter: http://www.kulturgutschutz-deutschland.de/DE/3_Datenbank/LVnationalWertvollenKulturguts/lvnationalwertvollenkulturguts_node.html.

C.I.2 Kulturgutschutzgesetz

(3) Bei einem Eigentumswechsel ist der neue Eigentümer des Kulturgutes, hilfsweise der frühere Eigentümer, verpflichtet, der zuständigen obersten Landesbehörde diesen Eigentumswechsel unverzüglich mitzuteilen.

(4) Die Absätze 1 bis 3 sind entsprechend anzuwenden, wenn für ein Kulturgut das Verfahren zur Eintragung in ein Verzeichnis national wertvollen Kulturgutes eingeleitet ist.

Kapitel 3
Kulturgutverkehr

Abschnitt 1
Grundsatz

§ 20 Kulturgutverkehrsfreiheit
Kulturgut kann ein- oder ausgeführt sowie in Verkehr gebracht werden, soweit nicht dieses Gesetz oder andere Rechtsvorschriften, insbesondere unmittelbar geltende Rechtsakte der Europäischen Union, Verbote oder Beschränkungen vorsehen.

Abschnitt 2
Ausfuhr

§ 21 Ausfuhrverbot
Die Ausfuhr von Kulturgut ist verboten, wenn
1. für das Kulturgut das Verfahren zur Eintragung in ein Verzeichnis national wertvollen Kulturgutes eingeleitet worden ist und die Entscheidung über die Eintragung noch nicht unanfechtbar geworden ist,
2. für das Kulturgut keine nach den §§ 22, 23, 24, 27 Absatz 1 bis 3 erforderliche Genehmigung vorliegt oder nach den §§ 25, 26 oder § 27 Absatz 4 erteilt worden ist,
3. das Kulturgut nach § 32 Absatz 1 unrechtmäßig eingeführt worden ist,
4. das Kulturgut nach § 33 Absatz 1 sichergestellt ist oder
5. das Kulturgut nach § 81 Absatz 4 angehalten wird.

§ 22 Genehmigung der vorübergehenden Ausfuhr von nationalem Kulturgut
(1) Genehmigungspflichtig ist die vorübergehende Ausfuhr von nationalem Kulturgut nach § 6 in einen Mitgliedstaat oder Drittstaat.
(2) Die Genehmigung ist zu erteilen, wenn der Antragsteller die Gewähr dafür bietet, dass das zur Ausfuhr bestimmte Kulturgut in unbeschadetem Zustand und fristgerecht in das Bundesgebiet wieder eingeführt wird.
(3) ¹Zuständig für die Erteilung der Genehmigung ist die oberste Landesbehörde des Landes, in dessen Verzeichnis national wertvollen Kulturgutes das Kulturgut nach § 6 Absatz 1 Nummer 1 eingetragen ist oder in dem sich das Kulturgut nach § 6 Absatz 1 Nummer 2 und 3 zum Zeitpunkt der Antragstellung befindet. ²Ist der Antragsteller eine juristische Person mit mehreren Sitzen, so ist sein Hauptsitz im Bundesgebiet für die örtliche Zuständigkeit maßgeblich. ³Die oberste Landesbehörde kann die Zuständigkeit nach Maßgabe des Landesrechts auf eine andere Landesbehörde übertragen.
(4) Die Ausfuhrgenehmigung kann der Eigentümer oder ein bevollmächtigter Dritter beantragen.
(5) Eine durch Drohung, Bestechung oder Kollusion erwirkte oder durch unrichtige oder unvollständige Angaben erschlichene Genehmigung ist nichtig.

§ 23 Genehmigung der dauerhaften Ausfuhr von nationalem Kulturgut
(1) Genehmigungspflichtig ist die dauerhafte Ausfuhr von nationalem Kulturgut nach § 6 in einen Mitgliedstaat oder einen Drittstaat.
(2) Die Genehmigung ist zu versagen, wenn bei Abwägung der Umstände des Einzelfalls wesentliche Belange des deutschen Kulturgutbesitzes überwiegen.
(3) Die Genehmigung ist zu erteilen, wenn rechtskräftig oder durch eine abschließende Regelung der Beteiligten im Hinblick auf einen Entzug festgestellt ist, dass das Kulturgut zwischen dem 30. Januar 1933 und dem 8. Mai 1945 einem früheren Eigentümer aufgrund der Verfolgung durch den National-

sozialismus entzogen worden ist[1]) und es aus dem Bundesgebiet ausgeführt werden soll, um es an außerhalb des Bundesgebietes lebende ursprüngliche Eigentümer oder deren dort lebende Rechtsnachfolger zurückzugeben.

(4) [1]Zuständig für die Erteilung der Genehmigung ist die für Kultur und Medien zuständige oberste Bundesbehörde. [2]Vor der Entscheidung hört sie die zuständige oberste Landesbehörde und einen Sachverständigenausschuss an. [3]Hinsichtlich der Zusammensetzung des Sachverständigenausschusses ist § 14 Absatz 2 entsprechend anzuwenden. [4]Im Falle eines Ortswechsels nach § 11 Absatz 2 ist auch die ursprünglich für die Eintragung zuständige oberste Landesbehörde anzuhören.

(5) [1]Mit der Genehmigung der dauerhaften Ausfuhr endet die Unterschutzstellung nach § 6 Absatz 1. [2]Eingetragenes Kulturgut ist nach der Ausfuhr von der zuständigen obersten Landesbehörde aus dem Verzeichnis national wertvollen Kulturgutes zu löschen.

(6) [1]Wird die Genehmigung zur dauerhaften Ausfuhr von eingetragenem Kulturgut abgelehnt, so unterrichtet die oberste für Kultur und Medien zuständige Bundesbehörde die nach Absatz 4 angehörten obersten Landesbehörden. [2]Auf Antrag des Eigentümers klären die oberste für Kultur und Medien zuständige Bundesbehörde und die nach Satz 1 unterrichteten Landesbehörden unter organisatorischer Leitung der Kulturstiftung der Länder binnen zwölf Monaten die nach Abwägung der beteiligten Interessen angemessenen Bedingungen für einen möglichen Ankauf des Kulturgutes durch oder für eine Kulturgut bewahrende Einrichtung im Bundesgebiet, die das Kulturgut der Öffentlichkeit zugänglich macht. [3]Zur Klärung dieser Bedingungen gehören insbesondere
1. die Klärung, zum Bestand welcher Kulturgut bewahrenden Einrichtung das Kulturgut passen würde,
2. die Festlegung eines angemessenen Preises unter Berücksichtigung der Steuervorteile des Eigentümers nach § 12 Absatz 1 oder sonstiger Vorteile des Eigentümers,
3. die Klärung,[2]) ob und gegebenenfalls wann und in welcher Höhe eine Kulturgut bewahrende Einrichtung nach Nummer 1 Fördermittel für einen Ankauf aus öffentlichen und privaten Mitteln erhalten könnte,
4. die sonstigen Modalitäten eines möglichen Ankaufes.

[4]Für die Festlegung eines angemessenen Preises nach Satz 3 Nummer 2 zieht die Kulturstiftung der Länder externen Sachverstand heran.

(7) [1]Sind die Bedingungen eines Ankaufes nach Absatz 6 geklärt, kann eine Kulturgut bewahrende Einrichtung nach Absatz 6 Nummer 1 dem Eigentümer auf dieser Basis und sofern die Finanzierung gesichert ist, ein Ankaufsangebot machen. [2]Weist der Eigentümer nach, dass er den Ausfuhrantrag aufgrund einer wirtschaftlichen Notlage gestellt hat, wirken die beteiligten Bundes- und Landesbehörden darauf hin, dass die Finanzierung eines Ankaufes gesichert ist, und die Kulturgut bewahrende Einrichtung ein Ankaufsangebot unterbreitet. [3]§ 12 Absatz 2 bleibt unberührt.

(8) [1]Der Eigentümer kann das Angebot nach Absatz 7 binnen sechs Monaten annehmen. [2]Kommt ein Ankauf nicht zustande, kann ein neuer Ausfuhrantrag erst nach einer Frist von fünf Jahren nach Ablehnung des vorhergehenden Antrages gestellt werden.

(9) [1]In besonderen Einzelfällen kann auf Antrag des Landes die für Kultur und Medien zuständige oberste Bundesbehörde die Genehmigung nach Absatz 1 auch für eine erst zukünftige Ausfuhr anlässlich eines öffentlich-rechtlichen Vertrages zwischen dem Eigentümer und der obersten Landesbehörde erteilen, wenn die Voraussetzungen nach § 10 Absatz 1 Nummer 1 und 2 für mindestens 15 Jahre vorliegen. [2]Die für Kultur und Medien zuständige oberste Bundesbehörde soll diese Zustimmung davon abhängig machen, dass die Einrichtung im Bundesgebiet mit dem Eigentümer des Kulturgutes einen Vertrag über einen möglichen Ankauf des Kulturgutes trifft. [3]Weitere Nebenbestimmungen sind zulässig.

(10) § 22 Absatz 4 und 5 ist entsprechend anzuwenden.

---

1) Siehe dazu auch die Grundsätze der Washingtoner Konferenz in Bezug auf Kunstwerke, die von den Nationalsozialisten beschlagnahmt wurden, abgedruckt als A.III.5.
2) Zeichensetzung nichtamtlich.

C.I.2 Kulturgutschutzgesetz

§ 24 Genehmigungspflichtige Ausfuhr von Kulturgut; Verordnungsermächtigung
(1) Genehmigungspflichtig ist die Ausfuhr von Kulturgut
1. in einen Drittstaat nach der unmittelbar geltenden Verordnung (EG) Nr. 116/2009 des Rates vom 18. Dezember 2008 über die Ausfuhr von Kulturgütern (kodifizierte Fassung) (ABl. L 39 vom 10.2.2009, S. 1),
2. in einen Mitgliedstaat, sofern das Kulturgut den Kriterien nach Absatz 2 bei Ausfuhr in den Binnenmarkt unterfällt und nicht Eigentum des Urhebers oder Herstellers ist.

(2) [1]Für die Ausfuhr in den Binnenmarkt sind die Altersuntergrenzen und das Doppelte der Wertuntergrenzen nach Anhang I der Verordnung (EG) Nr. 116/2009 mit der Maßgabe anzuwenden, dass bei den nachstehenden Kategorien folgende weiter heraufgesetzte Mindestuntergrenzen bei Kulturgut nach Anhang I Kategorie A gelten:
1. Nummer 3: 75 Jahre und 300 000 Euro;
2. die Nummern 4 und 7: 75 Jahre und 100 000 Euro;
3. die Nummern 5, 6, 8 und 9: 75 Jahre und 50 000 Euro;
4. Nummer 12: 50 Jahre und 50 000 Euro;
5. Nummer 14: 150 Jahre und 100 000 Euro;
6. Nummer 15: 100 Jahre und 100 000 Euro.

[2]Münzen gelten nicht als archäologische Gegenstände nach Kategorie 1 des Anhangs I der Verordnung (EG) Nr. 116/2009, wenn es sie in großer Stückzahl gibt, sie für die Archäologie keinen relevanten Erkenntniswert haben und nicht von einem Mitgliedstaat als individualisierbare Einzelobjekte unter Schutz gestellt sind. [3]Im Übrigen sind die Kategorien nach Absatz 2 Satz 1 im Lichte der Auslegung der Kategorien des Anhangs I der Verordnung (EG) Nr. 116/2009 anzuwenden.

(3) Das für Kultur und Medien zuständige Mitglied der Bundesregierung wird ermächtigt, die Wertgrenzen zur Anpassung an die Preisentwicklungen in den für die in Absatz 2 Satz 1 genannten Kategorien relevanten Märkten in einer Rechtsverordnung,[1]) die der Zustimmung des Bundesrates bedarf, anzuheben.

(4) Der für die Genehmigungspflicht nach Absatz 1 maßgebliche finanzielle Wert des Kulturgutes ist der innerhalb der letzten drei Jahre gezahlte Preis bei einem An- oder Verkauf, in sonstigen Fällen ein begründeter inländischer Schätzwert zum Zeitpunkt der Antragstellung.

(5) Die Genehmigung ist zu erteilen, wenn zum Zeitpunkt der Entscheidung über den Antrag kein Ausfuhrverbot nach § 21 Nummer 1, 3, 4 und 5 besteht.

(6) [1]Zuständig für die Erteilung der Genehmigung nach Absatz 1 ist die oberste Landesbehörde des Landes, in dem sich das Kulturgut zum Zeitpunkt der Antragstellung befindet, sofern sich in Fällen des Absatzes 1 Nummer 1 keine andere Zuständigkeit aus Artikel 2 der Verordnung (EG) Nr. 116/2009 ergibt. [2]Als Ort der Belegenheit wird der Wohnort oder Sitz des Antragstellers widerleglich vermutet. [3]§ 22 Absatz 3 Satz 2 ist entsprechend anzuwenden.

(7) [1]Über den Antrag auf Erteilung der Genehmigung hat die oberste Landesbehörde innerhalb von zehn Arbeitstagen nach Einreichung der vollständigen Antragsunterlagen zu entscheiden. [2]Diese Landesbehörde kann die Zuständigkeit nach Maßgabe des Landesrechts auf eine andere Landesbehörde übertragen.

(8) [1]Die Genehmigungspflicht nach Absatz 1 Nummer 2 entfällt, wenn das Kulturgut sich nachweisbar nur vorübergehend bis zu zwei Jahren im Bundesgebiet befindet. [2]Dies gilt nicht für Kulturgut, das
1. unrechtmäßig eingeführt wurde (§ 28) oder
2. zuvor ohne Genehmigung nach Absatz 1 ausgeführt wurde.

(9) § 22 Absatz 4 und 5 ist entsprechend anzuwenden.

§ 25 Allgemeine offene Genehmigung
(1) [1]Für die vorübergehende Ausfuhr von Kulturgut kann die zuständige oberste Landesbehörde einer Kulturgut bewahrenden Einrichtung auf Antrag eine zeitlich befristete generelle Genehmigung (allgemeine offene Genehmigung) erteilen, wenn diese Einrichtung regelmäßig Teile ihrer Bestände vorübergehend für öffentliche Ausstellungen, Restaurierungen oder Forschungszwecke ausführt. [2]Die allgemeine offene Genehmigung kann mit Nebenbestimmungen versehen werden.

---
1) Die Bundesregierung hat noch keine entsprechende Verordnung erlassen.

(2) ¹Die allgemeine offene Genehmigung kann erteilt werden für die Ausfuhr in Mitgliedstaaten oder Drittstaaten. ²Beide Genehmigungen können in einem Bescheid erteilt werden.
(3) Der Antragsteller muss die Gewähr dafür bieten, dass das zur Ausfuhr bestimmte Kulturgut in unbeschadetem Zustand und fristgerecht wiedereingeführt wird.
(4) ¹Die Geltungsdauer einer allgemeinen offenen Genehmigung darf fünf Jahre nicht überschreiten. ²Die zuständige oberste Landesbehörde veröffentlicht im Internetportal zum Kulturgutschutz nach § 4 diejenigen Kulturgut bewahrenden Einrichtungen, denen eine allgemeine offene Genehmigung erteilt worden ist.
(5) Teile des Bestandes einer Kulturgut bewahrenden Einrichtung können von der allgemeinen offenen Genehmigung durch die zuständige oberste Landesbehörde ausgenommen werden.

§ 26 Spezifische offene Genehmigung
(1) Für die regelmäßige vorübergehende Ausfuhr von Kulturgut kann die zuständige oberste Landesbehörde dem Eigentümer oder rechtmäßigen unmittelbaren Besitzer auf Antrag eine zeitlich befristete, auf ein bestimmtes Kulturgut bezogene Genehmigung (spezifische offene Genehmigung) erteilen, wenn das Kulturgut im Ausland wiederholt verwendet oder ausgestellt werden soll.
(2) ¹Die spezifische offene Genehmigung kann erteilt werden für die Ausfuhr in Mitgliedstaaten oder Drittstaaten. ²Beide Genehmigungen können in einem Bescheid erteilt werden.
(3) Die Genehmigung darf nur erteilt werden, wenn der Antragsteller die Gewähr dafür bietet, dass das zur vorübergehenden Ausfuhr bestimmte Kulturgut in unbeschadetem Zustand und fristgerecht wiedereingeführt wird.
(4) Die Geltungsdauer einer spezifischen offenen Genehmigung darf fünf Jahre nicht überschreiten.

§ 27 Genehmigung der Ausfuhr von kirchlichem Kulturgut
(1) Für die vorübergehende Ausfuhr von nationalem Kulturgut, das sich im Eigentum einer Kirche oder einer als Körperschaft des öffentlichen Rechts anerkannten Religionsgemeinschaft befindet, erteilt die Kirche oder Religionsgemeinschaft die Genehmigung nach § 22 im Benehmen mit der zuständigen Landesbehörde.
(2) ¹Bei einem Verfahren zur Genehmigung nach § 23 für die dauerhafte Ausfuhr von nationalem Kulturgut nach § 6 Absatz 1 Nummer 1 in Verbindung mit § 9 Absatz 1 wird bei Kulturgut, das sich im Eigentum einer Kirche oder einer als Körperschaft des öffentlichen Rechts anerkannten Religionsgemeinschaft befindet, abweichend von § 23 Absatz 4 Satz 2 ausschließlich die betroffene Kirche oder die als Körperschaft des öffentlichen Rechts anerkannte Religionsgemeinschaft angehört. ²Sofern es sich um nationales Kulturgut nach § 9 Absatz 3 handelt, erteilt die Kirche oder Religionsgemeinschaft die Genehmigung im Benehmen mit der zuständigen obersten Landesbehörde.
(3) ¹Die Kirchen und die als Körperschaften des öffentlichen Rechts anerkannten Religionsgemeinschaften können beantragen, dass für Kulturgut, das sich in ihrem Eigentum befindet, die Genehmigung für die Ausfuhr in einen Mitgliedstaat nach § 24 Absatz 1 Nummer 2 nicht erforderlich ist. ²In diesem Falle ist eine nachträgliche Eintragung in ein Verzeichnis national wertvollen Kulturgutes nach § 8 ausgeschlossen.
(4) Die §§ 25 und 26 sind für Kirchen und die als Körperschaft des öffentlichen Rechts anerkannten Religionsgemeinschaften sowie für die von ihnen beaufsichtigten Einrichtungen und Organisationen mit der Maßgabe entsprechend anzuwenden, dass die Genehmigung nur im Einvernehmen mit der zuständigen Kirche oder Religionsgemeinschaft erteilt werden kann.

Abschnitt 3
Einfuhr

§ 28 Einfuhrverbot
Die Einfuhr von Kulturgut ist verboten, wenn es
1. von einem Mitgliedstaat oder Vertragsstaat als nationales Kulturgut eingestuft oder definiert worden ist und unter Verstoß gegen dessen Rechtsvorschriften zum Schutz nationalen Kulturgutes aus dessen Hoheitsgebiet verbracht worden ist,
2. unter Verstoß gegen im Amtsblatt der Europäischen Union veröffentlichte unmittelbar geltende Rechtsakte der Europäischen Union, die die grenzüberschreitende Verbringung von Kulturgut einschränken oder verbieten, verbracht worden ist oder

3. unter Verstoß gegen Abschnitt I Nummer 1 des Protokolls zur Haager Konvention aufgrund eines bewaffneten Konflikts verbracht worden ist.

§ 29 Ausnahmen vom Einfuhrverbot
Das Einfuhrverbot ist nicht anzuwenden auf Kulturgut, das
1. sich zum 6. August 2016 rechtmäßig im Bundesgebiet befunden hat, soweit nicht unmittelbar geltende Rechtsakte der Europäischen Union Abweichendes anordnen, oder
2. zum Schutz vor den Gefahren eines bewaffneten Konflikts im Sinne des Abschnitts II Nummer 5 des Protokolls zur Haager Konvention im Bundesgebiet deponiert werden soll, um es zeitweilig zu verwahren.

§ 30 Nachweis der Rechtmäßigkeit der Einfuhr
¹Wer Kulturgut einführt, hat, sofern es von einem Mitgliedstaat oder Vertragsstaat als nationales Kulturgut eingestuft oder definiert worden ist, zum Nachweis der Rechtmäßigkeit der Ausfuhr aus dem Herkunftsstaat im Sinne von § 28 Nummer 1 entsprechende Unterlagen mitzuführen. ²Ein solcher Nachweis sind Ausfuhrgenehmigungen des Herkunftsstaates sowie sonstige Bestätigungen des Herkunftsstaates, dass das Kulturgut rechtmäßig ausgeführt werden konnte.

Abschnitt 4
Unrechtmäßiger Kulturgutverkehr

§ 31 Unrechtmäßige Ausfuhr von Kulturgut
(1) Die Ausfuhr von Kulturgut ist unrechtmäßig, wenn sie unter Verstoß gegen die §§ 21 bis 27 erfolgt oder unter Verstoß gegen Verordnungen der Europäischen Union, die die grenzüberschreitende Verbringung von Kulturgut ausdrücklich einschränken oder verbieten.
(2) Einer unrechtmäßigen Ausfuhr stehen auch jede nicht erfolgte Rückkehr nach Ablauf der Frist für eine vorübergehende rechtmäßige Ausfuhr und jeder Verstoß gegen eine Nebenbestimmung zur Genehmigung der vorübergehenden Ausfuhr gleich.

§ 32 Unrechtmäßige Einfuhr von Kulturgut
(1) Die Einfuhr von Kulturgut ist unrechtmäßig,
1. wenn das Kulturgut bei der Ausfuhr aus einem anderen Staat entgegen den in diesem Staat geltenden Rechtsvorschriften zum Schutz nationalen Kulturgutes verbracht worden ist
   a) nach dem 31. Dezember 1992 aus dem Hoheitsgebiet eines anderen Mitgliedstaates oder
   b) nach dem 26. April 2007 aus dem Hoheitsgebiet eines Vertragsstaates,
2. wenn die Einfuhr gegen § 28 verstößt oder
3. wenn die Einfuhr gegen sonstige in der Bundesrepublik Deutschland geltende Rechtsvorschriften verstößt.
(2) Kann die Herkunft von Kulturgut in mehreren heutigen Staaten liegen und lässt sich keine eindeutige Zuordnung vornehmen, so ist das Kulturgut unrechtmäßig eingeführt, wenn das Kulturgut nach dem Recht jedes in Frage kommenden Staates nicht ohne Ausfuhrgenehmigung hätte ausgeführt werden dürfen und eine solche Ausfuhrgenehmigung nicht vorliegt.

§ 33 Sicherstellung von Kulturgut
(1) Die zuständige Behörde hat Kulturgut sicherzustellen,
1. wenn der hinreichende Verdacht besteht, dass es
   a) entgegen einem Verbot nach § 21 ausgeführt werden soll oder
   b) entgegen einem Verbot nach § 28 eingeführt worden ist, oder
2. wenn bei der Einfuhr die nach § 30 erforderlichen Unterlagen nicht vorgelegt werden.
(2) ¹Nach Sicherstellung des Kulturgutes ist dem bisherigen Gewahrsamsinhaber eine Bescheinigung auszuhändigen, die das sichergestellte Kulturgut und den Grund der Sicherstellung nennt. ²Kann eine Bescheinigung nicht ausgehändigt werden, so ist über die Sicherstellung eine Niederschrift aufzunehmen, die auch erkennen lässt, warum eine Bescheinigung nicht ausgestellt worden ist.
(3) ¹Widerspruch und Anfechtungsklage gegen die Sicherstellung des Kulturgutes haben keine aufschiebende Wirkung. ²Die Sicherstellung hat die Wirkung eines Veräußerungsverbots im Sinne des § 136 des Bürgerlichen Gesetzbuches; das Verbot umfasst auch andere Verfügungen als Veräußerungen.

(4) Die Sicherstellung des Kulturgutes ist durch die zuständige Behörde unverzüglich der für Kultur und Medien zuständigen obersten Bundesbehörde zur Erfüllung der Aufgaben nach § 62 mitzuteilen.
(5) Es ist verboten, sichergestelltes Kulturgut zu zerstören, zu beschädigen oder dessen Erscheinungsbild nicht nur unerheblich und nicht nur vorübergehend zu verändern.

§ 34 Verwahrung sichergestellten Kulturgutes
(1) ¹Sichergestelltes Kulturgut ist von der zuständigen Behörde in Verwahrung zu nehmen. ²Sie kann das Kulturgut, sofern der Zweck der Sicherstellung dadurch nicht gefährdet ist, durch die Person, der der Gewahrsam entzogen worden ist, oder durch einen Dritten verwahren lassen. ³In diesem Fall darf das Kulturgut nur mit schriftlicher oder elektronisch übermittelter Zustimmung der zuständigen Behörde an andere Personen oder Einrichtungen weitergegeben werden.
(2) Zu Beginn und nach Ende der Verwahrung soll der Erhaltungszustand des sichergestellten Kulturgutes von der zuständigen Behörde oder einem von ihr beauftragten Dritten festgehalten werden.
(3) Die zur Erhaltung des Kulturgutes erforderlichen Maßnahmen werden von der zuständigen Behörde getroffen oder veranlasst.

§ 35 Aufhebung der Sicherstellung
(1) Die Sicherstellung des Kulturgutes ist von der zuständigen Behörde aufzuheben, wenn
1. der hinreichende Verdacht nach § 33 Absatz 1 Nummer 1 entfallen ist,
2. die Voraussetzungen des § 33 Absatz 1 Nummer 1 Buchstabe a entfallen sind,
3. im Falle des § 33 Absatz 1 Nummer 1 Buchstabe b
   a) die Voraussetzungen des Rückgabeanspruchs nach Kapitel 5 dieses Gesetzes offensichtlich nicht vorliegen oder
   b) die Verjährung des Rückgabeanspruchs nach Kapitel 5 dieses Gesetzes eingetreten ist,
4. im Falle des § 33 Absatz 1 Nummer 1 Buchstabe b die Sicherstellung im Hinblick auf einen Anspruch aus § 50 oder § 52 erfolgt ist
   a) nicht innerhalb von sechs Kalendermonaten nach Unterrichtung nach § 62 Absatz 1 Nummer 1 oder Absatz 2 Nummer 1 um eine Rückgabe nach § 50 oder § 52 ersucht worden ist,
   b) eine gütliche Einigung zwischen dem ersuchenden Mitgliedstaat oder Vertragsstaat und dem Rückgabeschuldner erzielt worden ist oder
   c) die Entscheidung über die Klage auf Rückgabe rechtskräftig geworden ist,
5. im Falle des § 33 Absatz 1 Nummer 1 Buchstabe b die Sicherstellung im Hinblick auf einen Anspruch aus § 51 erfolgt ist und eine Rückgabe erfolgen soll,
6. im Falle des § 33 Absatz 1 Nummer 1 Buchstabe b die Sicherstellung im Hinblick auf einen Anspruch aus § 53 Absatz 1 erfolgt ist und eine Rückgabe erfolgen soll oder,[1)]
7. sobald sich im Falle des § 33 Absatz 1 Nummer 2 kein hinreichender Verdacht ergibt, dass das Kulturgut unrechtmäßig eingeführt worden ist.
(2) Hat ein Mitgliedstaat oder Vertragsstaat ein Rückgabeersuchen nach § 59 bereits gestellt oder ist geklärt, welcher Mitgliedstaat oder Vertragsstaat ein solches Ersuchen stellen könnte, so kann die Sicherstellung nur mit Zustimmung dieses Mitgliedstaates oder Vertragsstaates aufgehoben werden, es sei denn, der Anlass der Sicherstellung ist zwischenzeitlich entfallen.

§ 36 Herausgabe sichergestellten Kulturgutes
(1) Ist die Sicherstellung aufgehoben worden, so ist das Kulturgut herauszugeben
1. in den Fällen des § 35 Absatz 1 Nummer 1 bis 3, 4 Buchstabe a und Nummer 7 an den Eigenbesitzer,
2. in den Fällen des § 35 Absatz 1 Nummer 4 Buchstabe b und c an den Berechtigten,
3. in den Fällen des § 35 Absatz 1 Nummer 5 an den betreffenden Mitgliedstaat oder Vertragsstaat oder
4. in den Fällen des § 35 Absatz 1 Nummer 6 an die jeweils zuständige Behörde des Herkunftsgebiets.
(2) ¹In den Fällen der Herausgabe an den Eigenbesitzer ist diesem eine Mitteilung über eine Frist zur Abholung zuzustellen. ²Die Frist ist ausreichend zu bemessen. ³Die Mitteilung hat den Hinweis zu enthalten, dass das Kulturgut eingezogen wird, wenn es nicht innerhalb der Frist abgeholt wird.

---

1) Richtig wohl: „soll, oder".

§ 37 Einziehung sichergestellten Kulturgutes

(1) ¹Sichergestelltes Kulturgut soll von der zuständigen Behörde eingezogen werden, wenn es in den Fällen des § 36 Absatz 1 Nummer 1 nicht an den Eigenbesitzer herausgegeben werden kann, weil
1. der Eigenbesitzer nicht bekannt ist und nicht mit einem vertretbaren Aufwand zu ermitteln ist oder
2. der Eigenbesitzer das Kulturgut nicht innerhalb der Frist nach § 36 Absatz 2 Satz 2 abholt.

²Die Anordnung der Einziehung ist nach Landesrecht öffentlich bekannt zu machen und im Internetportal nach § 4 zu veröffentlichen. ³Sie ist unverzüglich der für Kultur und Medien zuständigen obersten Bundesbehörde zur Erfüllung der Aufgaben nach § 62 mitzuteilen.

(2) Die zuständige Behörde kann das eingezogene Kulturgut einer Kulturgut bewahrenden Einrichtung in Verwahrung geben.

§ 38 Folgen der Einziehung; Entschädigung

(1) ¹Wird sichergestelltes Kulturgut eingezogen, so gehen der Besitz an dem Kulturgut mit der Anordnung der Einziehung und das Eigentum an dem Kulturgut mit der Bestandskraft der Anordnung auf das Land über. ²Rechte Dritter erlöschen mit der Bestandskraft der Anordnung.

(2) Der Eigentümer, dessen Recht an dem Kulturgut durch die Entscheidung erloschen ist, wird von dem Land, in dessen Eigentum das Kulturgut übergegangen ist, unter Berücksichtigung des Verkehrswertes angemessen in Geld entschädigt, es sei denn, es wird rückübereignet, Zug um Zug gegen den Ersatz einer möglichen Entschädigung an den Dritten nach Absatz 3.

(3) War das Kulturgut mit dem Recht eines Dritten belastet, das durch die Einziehung erloschen ist, so wird auch der Dritte von dem Land, in dessen Eigentum das Kulturgut übergegangen ist, unter Berücksichtigung des Verkehrswertes angemessen in Geld entschädigt.

(4) ¹In den Fällen des Absatzes 2 wird eine Entschädigung nicht gewährt, wenn
1. der Eigentümer mindestens leichtfertig dazu beigetragen hat, dass die Voraussetzungen der Sicherstellung und die Voraussetzungen der Einziehung des Kulturgutes vorlagen,
2. der Eigentümer das Kulturgut in Kenntnis der Umstände, die die Sicherstellung zugelassen haben, erworben hat oder
3. es nach den Umständen, welche die Sicherstellung und Einziehung begründet haben, aufgrund anderer gesetzlicher Vorschriften zulässig wäre, das Kulturgut dem Eigentümer ohne Entschädigung dauernd zu entziehen.

²Satz 1 ist nicht anzuwenden, soweit die Nichtgewährung der Entschädigung eine unbillige Härte wäre.

(5) ¹In den Fällen des Absatzes 3 wird eine Entschädigung nicht gewährt, wenn
1. der Dritte wenigstens leichtfertig dazu beigetragen hat, dass die Voraussetzungen der Sicherstellung des Kulturgutes vorlagen,
2. der Dritte das Recht an dem Kulturgut in Kenntnis der Umstände, die die Einziehung zugelassen haben, erworben hat oder
3. es nach den Umständen, die die Sicherstellung und Einziehung begründet haben, aufgrund anderer gesetzlicher Vorschriften zulässig wäre, das Recht an dem Kulturgut dem Dritten ohne Entschädigung dauernd zu entziehen.

²Satz 1 ist nicht anzuwenden, soweit die Nichtgewährung der Entschädigung eine unbillige Härte wäre.

(6) Der Anspruch auf Entschädigung nach den Absätzen 2 oder 3 erlischt 30 Jahre nach der Bekanntmachung der Anordnung der Einziehung.

§ 39 Kosten für Sicherstellung, Verwahrung, Erhaltung und Herausgabe

¹Die notwendigen Kosten und Auslagen für die Sicherstellung, Verwahrung, Erhaltung und Herausgabe des Kulturgutes trägt die Person, der der Gewahrsam entzogen worden ist. ²Die §§ 66 bis 68 bleiben unberührt. ³Die zuständige Behörde setzt den zu erstattenden Betrag durch Bescheid fest.

Kapitel 4
Pflichten beim Inverkehrbringen von Kulturgut

§ 40 Verbot des Inverkehrbringens

(1) Verboten ist das Inverkehrbringen von Kulturgut, das abhandengekommen ist, rechtswidrig ausgegraben oder unrechtmäßig eingeführt worden ist.

(2) Verpflichtungs- und Verfügungsgeschäfte, die nach Absatz 1 verboten sind, sind nichtig.
(3) Verpflichtungs- und Verfügungsgeschäfte über Kulturgut, das entgegen § 21 ausgeführt worden ist, sind verboten.
(4) ¹Derjenige, der das Kulturgut unter Verstoß gegen das Verbot in Absatz 1 in Verkehr gebracht hat, ist dem Erwerber zum Ersatz des Schadens unter Einschluss des Ersatzes der Aufwendungen anlässlich des Erwerbs und der Aufwendungen zur Erhaltung des Kulturgutes verpflichtet. ²Dies gilt nicht, wenn derjenige, der das Kulturgut in Verkehr gebracht hat, nachweist, dass er den Verstoß nicht zu vertreten hat.

§ 41 Allgemeine Sorgfaltspflichten
(1) Wer Kulturgut in Verkehr bringt, ist verpflichtet, zuvor mit der erforderlichen Sorgfalt zu prüfen, ob das Kulturgut
1. abhandengekommen ist,
2. unrechtmäßig eingeführt worden ist oder
3. rechtswidrig ausgegraben worden ist.

(2) ¹Die allgemeine Sorgfaltspflicht nach Absatz 1 ist von der Person, die Kulturgut in Verkehr bringt, anzuwenden, wenn sich einer vernünftigen Person die Vermutung aufdrängen müsste, dass einer der in Absatz 1 genannten Tatbestände in Betracht kommt. ²Diese Vermutung ist insbesondere anzunehmen, wenn bei einem früheren Erwerb des Kulturgutes, das in Verkehr gebracht werden soll,
1. ein außergewöhnlich niedriger Preis ohne nähere Begründung gefordert worden ist oder
2. der Verkäufer bei einem Kaufpreis von mehr als 5 000 Euro Barzahlung verlangt hat.

(3) Die erforderliche Sorgfalt umfasst die Prüfung einschlägiger Informationen, die mit zumutbarem Aufwand zu beschaffen sind, oder jede andere Prüfung, die eine vernünftige Person unter denselben Umständen des Inverkehrbringens von Kulturgut unternehmen würde.

§ 42 Sorgfaltspflichten beim gewerblichen Inverkehrbringen
(1) ¹Wer in Ausübung seiner gewerblichen Tätigkeit Kulturgut in Verkehr bringt, ist verpflichtet, zuvor zusätzlich zu den Pflichten nach § 41
1. Name und Anschrift des Veräußerers, des Einlieferers, des Erwerbers oder des Auftraggebers festzustellen,
2. eine Beschreibung und eine Abbildung anzufertigen, die geeignet sind, die Identität des Kulturgutes festzustellen,
3. die Provenienz des Kulturgutes zu prüfen,
4. Dokumente, die eine rechtmäßige Ein- und Ausfuhr belegen, zu prüfen,
5. Verbote und Beschränkungen zur Ein- und Ausfuhr sowie zum Handel zu prüfen,
6. zu prüfen, ob das Kulturgut in öffentlich zugänglichen Verzeichnissen und Datenbanken eingetragen ist, und
7. eine schriftliche oder elektronisch übermittelte Erklärung des Einlieferers oder Veräußerers einzuholen, dass dieser berechtigt ist, über das Kulturgut zu verfügen.

²Die Pflichten nach Satz 1 Nummer 2 lassen urheberrechtliche Vorschriften unberührt. ³Die Pflichten nach Satz 1 Nummer 3 bis 6 sind nach Maßgabe des zumutbaren Aufwandes, insbesondere der wirtschaftlichen Zumutbarkeit, zu erfüllen.

(2) Die zusätzlichen Sorgfaltspflichten nach Absatz 1 sind nicht anzuwenden
1. für den gewerblichen Buchhandel mit Ausnahme des Antiquariatshandels und
2. für den gewerblichen Handel mit Bild- und Tonträgern.

(3) ¹Die zusätzlichen Sorgfaltspflichten nach Absatz 1 sind ferner nicht anzuwenden für Kulturgut,
1. das kein archäologisches Kulturgut ist und
2. dessen Wert 2 500 Euro nicht übersteigt.

²Münzen gelten nicht als archäologisches Kulturgut im Sinne des Satzes 1 Nummer 1, wenn es sie in großer Stückzahl gibt und sie für die Archäologie keinen relevanten Erkenntniswert haben. ³Maßgeblicher Wert ist bei einem Kauf der gezahlte Preis, in sonstigen Fällen ein begründeter inländischer Schätzwert.

C.I.2 Kulturgutschutzgesetz

§ 43 Erleichterte Sorgfaltspflichten beim gewerblichen Inverkehrbringen
¹Erleichterte Sorgfaltspflichten gelten, wenn
1. der Urheber oder Hersteller des Kulturgutes dieses in Verkehr bringt oder
2. jemand das Kulturgut unmittelbar von dessen Urheber oder Hersteller erworben hat und es in Verkehr bringt oder
3. jemand für den Urheber oder Hersteller das von diesem geschaffene Kulturgut in Verkehr bringt.

²Die erleichterten Sorgfaltspflichten umfassen zusätzlich zu den Pflichten nach § 41 nur diejenigen nach § 42 Absatz 1 Nummer 1 und 2. ³§ 42 Absatz 2 und 3 ist entsprechend anzuwenden.

§ 44 Erhöhte Sorgfaltspflichten beim gewerblichen Inverkehrbringen
¹Beim gewerblichen Inverkehrbringen ist der Maßstab des zumutbaren Aufwandes nach § 42 Absatz 1 Satz 3 nicht für Kulturgut anzuwenden,
1. bei dem nachgewiesen oder zu vermuten ist, dass es zwischen dem 30. Januar 1933 und dem 8. Mai 1945 aufgrund der Verfolgung durch den Nationalsozialismus entzogen worden ist,¹⁾ es sei denn, das Kulturgut ist an seinen ursprünglichen Eigentümer oder dessen Erben zurückgegeben worden oder diese haben eine andere abschließende Regelung im Hinblick auf den Entzug getroffen,
2. das aus einem Mitgliedstaat oder Vertragsstaat stammt, für den der Internationale Museumsrat eine Rote Liste gefährdeter Kulturgüter veröffentlicht hat, oder
3. für das ein Verbot zur Ein- oder Ausfuhr sowie zum Inverkehrbringen nach einer Verordnung der Europäischen Union maßgebend ist.

²Auf Kulturgut nach Satz 1 ist § 42 Absatz 3 nicht anzuwenden.

§ 45 Aufzeichnungs- und Aufbewahrungspflichten
(1) ¹Wer in Ausübung einer gewerblichen Tätigkeit Kulturgut in Verkehr bringt, ist verpflichtet, über die Prüfungen und Feststellungen nach § 42 Aufzeichnungen zu führen. ²Die Aufzeichnungen und die Sicherung entsprechender Unterlagen können in elektronischer Form erfolgen.

(2) ¹Die Aufzeichnungen nach Absatz 1 sind mit den dazugehörigen Unterlagen und Nachweisen vom Aufzeichnungspflichtigen 30 Jahre lang aufzubewahren. ²Absatz 1 Satz 2 ist entsprechend anzuwenden.

(3) ¹Aufzeichnungen nach anderen Rechtsvorschriften stehen den Aufzeichnungen nach Absatz 1 gleich, sofern sie den Prüfungen und Feststellungen nach § 42 entsprechen und die in diesem Gesetz geforderte Feststellung der Identität des Kulturgutes nach § 42 Absatz 1 Nummer 2 ermöglichen. ²Für die Aufbewahrungsfrist ist Absatz 2 Satz 1 anzuwenden.

§ 46 Auskunftspflicht
(1) ¹Wer in Ausübung einer gewerblichen Tätigkeit Kulturgut in Verkehr bringt, ist verpflichtet, der zuständigen Behörde auf Verlangen
1. die Aufzeichnungen nach § 45 vorzulegen oder
2. Auskunft über die nach § 41 Absatz 1 über ein Kulturgut gewonnenen Informationen zu erteilen.

²Die nach Satz 1 vorzulegenden Aufzeichnungen und zu erteilenden Auskünfte beschränken sich auf die Informationen, die für die zuständigen Behörden zur Durchführung ihrer Aufgaben nach diesem Gesetz erforderlich sind.

(2) § 29 der Gewerbeordnung bleibt unberührt.

§ 47 Rechtsfolge bei Verstößen
Hat die zuständige Behörde belegbare Erkenntnisse darüber, dass wiederholt gegen Aufzeichnungs-, Aufbewahrungs- und Auskunftspflichten nach den §§ 45 und 46 Absatz 1 verstoßen worden ist, so teilt sie diese Erkenntnisse der Gewerbeaufsicht zur Prüfung der Zuverlässigkeit im Sinne des § 35 der Gewerbeordnung mit.

§ 48 Einsichtsrechte des Käufers
(1) Wird ein Erwerber eines Kulturgutes gerichtlich nach diesem Gesetz oder aufgrund zivilrechtlicher Vorschriften auf Herausgabe des Kulturgutes in Anspruch genommen, so hat er gegenüber demjenigen,

---

1) Siehe dazu auch die Grundsätze der Washingtoner Konferenz in Bezug auf Kunstwerke, die von den Nationalsozialisten beschlagnahmt wurden, abgedruckt als A.III.5.

der das Kulturgut nach den §§ 42 bis 44 in Verkehr gebracht hat, einen Anspruch auf Einsicht in die Aufzeichnungen nach § 45, wenn er das Kulturgut nach dem 6. August 2016 erworben hat.
(2) Absatz 1 ist auch anzuwenden im Falle der außergerichtlichen Inanspruchnahme bei Geltendmachung
1. eines Rückgabeanspruchs eines Mitgliedstaates oder Vertragsstaates oder
2. eines Entzuges dieses Kulturgutes aufgrund der Verfolgung durch den Nationalsozialismus.[1]

Kapitel 5
Rückgabe unrechtmäßig eingeführten Kulturgutes

Abschnitt 1
Rückgabeanspruch

§ 49 Öffentlich-rechtliche Rückgabeansprüche
(1) ¹Ansprüche auf Rückgabe von Kulturgut nach diesem Abschnitt sind öffentlich-rechtliche Ansprüche. ²Zivilrechtliche Ansprüche bleiben davon unberührt.
(2) Rückgabeschuldner ist der unmittelbare Eigenbesitzer, hilfsweise der unmittelbare Fremdbesitzer.

§ 50 Rückgabeanspruch eines Mitgliedstaates
Auf Ersuchen eines Mitgliedstaates ist Kulturgut zurückzugeben, wenn es
1. nach dem 31. Dezember 1992 aus dem Hoheitsgebiet eines Mitgliedstaates unter Verstoß gegen dortige Rechtsvorschriften verbracht worden ist und
2. vor oder nach der Verbringung von dem ersuchenden Mitgliedstaat durch nationale Rechtsvorschriften oder durch Verwaltungsverfahren als nationales Kulturgut von künstlerischem, geschichtlichem oder archäologischem Wert im Sinne des Artikels 36 des Vertrags über die Arbeitsweise der Europäischen Union eingestuft oder definiert worden ist.

§ 51 Rückgabeanspruch wegen Verstoßes gegen das Recht der Europäischen Union
Ist Kulturgut entgegen einem im Amtsblatt der Europäischen Union veröffentlichten, unmittelbar geltenden Rechtsakt der Europäischen Union unrechtmäßig eingeführt worden, so ist es an den betreffenden Staat zurückzugeben.

§ 52 Rückgabeanspruch eines Vertragsstaates
(1) Auf Ersuchen eines Vertragsstaates ist Kulturgut zurückzugeben, wenn es
1. einer der in Artikel 1 des UNESCO-Übereinkommens genannten Kategorien angehört,
2. aus dessen Hoheitsgebiet nach dem 26. April 2007 unter Verstoß gegen dortige Rechtsvorschriften verbracht worden ist,
3. vor der Ausfuhr von dem ersuchenden Vertragsstaat als bedeutsam nach Artikel 1 des UNESCO-Übereinkommens oder im Sinne des Artikels 13 Buchstabe d des UNESCO-Übereinkommens als unveräußerlich eingestuft oder erklärt worden ist und
4. hinsichtlich seiner Herkunft dem ersuchenden Vertragsstaat zuzuordnen ist, insbesondere wenn es zum Bestand einer Einrichtung im Vertragsstaat gehört oder eine Einigung nach § 60 vorliegt.
(2) ¹Lässt sich nicht klären, ob das Kulturgut nach dem 26. April 2007 verbracht worden ist, so wird widerleglich vermutet, dass das Kulturgut nach diesem Tag aus dem Hoheitsgebiet des Vertragsstaates verbracht worden ist. ²Diese Vermutung kann nur durch den Nachweis widerlegt werden, dass sich das Kulturgut schon vor diesem Tag im Bundesgebiet, im Binnenmarkt oder in einem Drittstaat befunden hat. ³Die Abgabe einer Versicherung an Eides statt ist zur Erbringung des Nachweises nach Satz 2 zulässig gemäß § 27 Absatz 1 des Verwaltungsverfahrensgesetzes sowie gemäß der Verwaltungsverfahrensgesetze der Länder. ⁴Für die Abnahme zuständig sind im Rahmen des behördlichen Vermittlungsverfahrens die in § 61 Absatz 1 Nummer 5 und § 62 Absatz 2 genannten Behörden.
(3) Wird der Nachweis erbracht, dass sich das Kulturgut vor dem 6. August 2016 im Bundesgebiet oder im Binnenmarkt befunden hat, so sind abweichend von Absatz 1 für den Rückgabeanspruch des Vertragsstaates § 6 Absatz 2 und für die Entschädigung § 10 des Kulturgüterrückgabegesetzes vom 18. Mai 2007 (BGBl. I S. 757, 2547) in der bis zum 5. August 2016 geltenden Fassung anzuwenden.

---

[1] Siehe dazu auch die Grundsätze der Washingtoner Konferenz in Bezug auf Kunstwerke, die von den Nationalsozialisten beschlagnahmt wurden, abgedruckt als A.III.5.

§ 53 Rückgabeanspruch nach der Haager Konvention

(1) Kulturgut nach Kapitel I Artikel 1 der Haager Konvention, das entgegen § 28 Nummer 3 aufgrund eines bewaffneten Konflikts eingeführt worden ist, ist nach Beendigung des bewaffneten Konflikts an die jeweils zuständige Behörde des Herkunftsgebiets nach Abschnitt I Nummer 3 des Protokolls zur Haager Konvention zurückzugeben, wenn
1. es nach dem 11. November 1967 verbracht worden ist und
2. die jeweils zuständige Behörde des Herkunftsgebiets um Rückgabe ersucht.

(2) Kulturgut, das im Sinne von Abschnitt II Nummer 5 des Protokolls zur Haager Konvention deponiert worden ist, ist nach Beendigung des bewaffneten Konflikts zurückzugeben, ohne dass die Voraussetzungen des Absatzes 1 Nummer 1 und 2 erfüllt sein müssen.

§ 54 Anzuwendendes Zivilrecht

(1) Wer Eigentümer des Kulturgutes ist, das nach den Bestimmungen dieses Gesetzes in das Hoheitsgebiet eines anderen Mitgliedstaates oder Vertragsstaates zurückgegeben worden ist, bestimmt sich nach den Sachvorschriften dieses Mitgliedstaates oder Vertragsstaates.

(2) Rechte, die aufgrund rechtsgeschäftlicher Verfügung oder durch Zwangsvollstreckung oder Arrestvollziehung erworben worden sind, stehen der Rückgabepflicht nicht entgegen.

§ 55 Befristung und Verjährung des Rückgabeanspruchs

(1) ¹Rückgabeansprüche unterliegen nicht der Verjährung, wenn sie auf die Rückgabe von Kulturgut gerichtet sind, das
1. zu öffentlichen Sammlungen nach Artikel 2 Nummer 8 der Richtlinie 2014/60/EU gehört oder
2. in einem Bestandsverzeichnis kirchlicher oder anderer religiöser Einrichtungen in den Mitgliedstaaten aufgeführt ist, in denen es nach den in diesem Mitgliedstaat geltenden Rechtsvorschriften besonderen Schutzregelungen unterliegt.

²Die Ansprüche nach Satz 1 erlöschen 75 Jahre nach ihrem Entstehen. ³Ein Anspruch erlischt nicht nach Satz 2, wenn der ersuchende Mitgliedstaat in seinem Recht bestimmt, dass solche Rückgabeansprüche nicht erlöschen.

(2) Rückgabeansprüche verjähren außer in den Fällen des Absatzes 1 ohne Rücksicht auf die Kenntnis in 30 Jahren ab dem Zeitpunkt der unrechtmäßigen Verbringung des Kulturgutes aus dem Hoheitsgebiet des ersuchenden Mitgliedstaates oder Vertragsstaates.

(3) Alle anderen Ansprüche auf Rückgabe von Kulturgut nach diesem Abschnitt verjähren nach drei Jahren.

§ 56 Beginn der Verjährung

Die Verjährungsfrist beginnt mit dem Zeitpunkt, in dem der ersuchende Mitgliedstaat oder Vertragsstaat von dem Ort der Belegenheit des Kulturgutes und von der Identität des Rückgabeschuldners Kenntnis erlangt.

§ 57 Hemmung und Neubeginn der Verjährung und Erlöschensfristen

(1) Auf die Verjährung und auf die Frist nach § 55 Absatz 1 Satz 2 sind die Vorschriften über die Hemmung der Verjährung nach den §§ 204, 206 und 209 des Bürgerlichen Gesetzbuches und über den Neubeginn der Verjährung nach § 212 des Bürgerlichen Gesetzbuches entsprechend anzuwenden.

(2) Die Verjährung und die Frist nach § 55 Absatz 1 Satz 2 sind wegen höherer Gewalt insbesondere auch gehemmt, solange der ersuchende Mitgliedstaat oder Vertragsstaat durch innere Unruhen, bewaffnete Konflikte oder vergleichbare Umstände gehindert ist, seine Ansprüche geltend zu machen.

Abschnitt 2
Rückgabeverfahren

§ 58 Grundsatz der Rückgabe

Die Rückgabe kann durch eine gütliche Einigung im behördlichen Vermittlungsverfahren erreicht werden oder mit einer Klage auf Rückgabe des ersuchenden Staates verfolgt werden.

§ 59 Rückgabeersuchen
Das Rückgabeersuchen ist zu stellen für
1. den Rückgabeanspruch eines Mitgliedstaates nach § 50 bei der für Kultur und Medien zuständigen obersten Bundesbehörde oder
2. Ansprüche nach den §§ 51 bis 53 auf diplomatischem Weg beim Auswärtigen Amt.

§ 60 Kollidierende Rückgabeersuchen
Stellen zu demselben Kulturgut mehrere Mitgliedstaaten oder Vertragsstaaten Rückgabeersuchen und lässt sich nicht klären, welchem Mitgliedstaat oder Vertragsstaat das Kulturgut zuzuordnen ist, so ist es erst zurückzugeben, wenn die Einigung der betroffenen Mitgliedstaaten oder Vertragsstaaten schriftlich festgehalten und der für Kultur und Medien zuständigen obersten Bundesbehörde sowie dem Auswärtigen Amt mitgeteilt worden ist.

§ 61 Aufgaben der Länder
(1) Die zuständige Behörde eines Landes hat insbesondere folgende Aufgaben:
1. Nachforschungen nach Kulturgut, bei dem der Verdacht besteht, dass es unrechtmäßig verbracht worden ist oder unrechtmäßig in Verkehr gebracht worden ist,
2. Nachforschungen nach dem Eigentümer oder dem unmittelbaren Besitzer des betreffenden Kulturgutes,
3. Unterstützung der Nachforschungen des ersuchenden Mitgliedstaates oder Vertragsstaates, insbesondere nach dem Eigentümer oder dem unmittelbaren Besitzer des betreffenden Kulturgutes,
4. Durchführung oder Veranlassung von Maßnahmen zur Erhaltung des sichergestellten Kulturgutes,
5. Durchführung von Maßnahmen, die verhindern, dass das Kulturgut der Rückgabe entzogen wird,
6. Durchführung des behördlichen Vermittlungsverfahrens zwischen dem ersuchenden Mitgliedstaat und dem Rückgabeschuldner und
7. Unterstützung des Bundes bei der Rückgabe von Kulturgut.

(2) ¹Zur Unterstützung nach Absatz 1 Nummer 3 ist die zuständige Behörde nur verpflichtet, wenn ein Mitgliedstaat innerhalb von sechs Monaten nach Unterrichtung nach § 62 Absatz 1 Nummer 1 der zuständigen Behörde mitteilt, dass es sich um ein Kulturgut im Sinne des Artikels 2 Nummer 1 der Richtlinie 2014/60/EU handelt. ²Lässt ein Mitgliedstaat diese Frist ohne diese Mitteilung verstreichen, so ist die zuständige Behörde nicht mehr verpflichtet, Maßnahmen nach Absatz 1 Nummer 4 und 5 zu ergreifen.

§ 62 Aufgaben der obersten Bundesbehörden
(1) Die für Kultur und Medien zuständige oberste Bundesbehörde hat folgende Aufgaben:
1. Unterrichtung des betroffenen Mitgliedstaates über das Auffinden und die Sicherstellung von Kulturgut, bei dem der Verdacht besteht, dass es unrechtmäßig eingeführt worden ist,
2. Unterstützung des behördlichen Vermittlungsverfahrens zwischen dem ersuchenden Mitgliedstaat und dem Rückgabeschuldner und
3. Mitteilung an die zentralen Stellen der anderen Mitgliedstaaten, wenn der ersuchende Mitgliedstaat Klage auf Rückgabe erhoben hat.

(2) Das Auswärtige Amt hat in Zusammenarbeit mit der für Kultur und Medien zuständigen obersten Bundesbehörde folgende Aufgaben:
1. Unterrichtung des betroffenen Vertragsstaates über das Auffinden und die Sicherstellung von Kulturgut, bei dem der Verdacht besteht, dass es unrechtmäßig eingeführt worden ist, und
2. Durchführung des behördlichen Vermittlungsverfahrens zwischen dem ersuchenden Vertragsstaat und dem Rückgabeschuldner.

§ 63 Zulässigkeit der Klage auf Rückgabe
(1) Die Klage eines ersuchenden Mitgliedstaates oder Vertragsstaates auf Rückgabe ist nur dann zulässig, wenn der Klageschrift folgende Unterlagen beigefügt sind:
1. eine geeignete Beschreibung des Kulturgutes mit Angaben über
   a) die Identität und Herkunft,
   b) den tatsächlichen oder mutmaßlichen Zeitpunkt der Verbringung und
   c) den tatsächlichen oder mutmaßlichen Ort der Belegenheit im Bundesgebiet,

2. eine Erklärung, dass es sich um ein nach nationalen Rechtsvorschriften oder Verwaltungsverfahren des ersuchenden Mitgliedstaates oder Vertragsstaates nationales Kulturgut handelt, und
3. eine Erklärung des ersuchenden Mitgliedstaates oder Vertragsstaates, dass das Kulturgut unrechtmäßig aus seinem Hoheitsgebiet ausgeführt worden ist.

(2) Die Klage auf Rückgabe ist unzulässig, wenn das Verbringen des Kulturgutes aus dem Hoheitsgebiet des ersuchenden Mitgliedstaates oder Vertragsstaates zu dem Zeitpunkt, zu dem die Klage erhoben wird, nicht mehr unrechtmäßig ist.

§ 64 Kosten der behördlichen Sicherstellung

Hat die zuständige Behörde das Kulturgut, über dessen Rückgabe das Gericht zu entscheiden hat, nach § 33 sichergestellt, so ist in der gerichtlichen Entscheidung über die Rückgabe auch über die Kosten zu entscheiden, die der zuständigen Behörde durch die Sicherstellung entstanden sind.

§ 65 Kosten der Rückgabe und Erhaltungsmaßnahmen

(1) Die Kosten, die sich aufgrund der Rückgabe ergeben, gehen zu Lasten des ersuchenden Mitgliedstaates oder Vertragsstaates.

(2) ¹Die Kosten, die durch Durchführung oder Veranlassung von notwendigen Maßnahmen zur Erhaltung des sichergestellten Kulturgutes entstehen, gehen zu Lasten des ersuchenden Mitgliedstaates oder Vertragsstaates. ²§ 64 ist entsprechend anzuwenden.

Abschnitt 3
Entschädigung und Erstattungsanspruch

§ 66 Entschädigung bei Rückgabe

(1) Ist der unmittelbare Eigenbesitzer beim Erwerb des Kulturgutes mit der erforderlichen Sorgfalt vorgegangen, so kann er die Rückgabe des Kulturgutes verweigern, bis der ersuchende Mitgliedstaat oder Vertragsstaat eine angemessene Entschädigung geleistet hat.

(2) ¹Bei einer unentgeltlichen Rechtsnachfolge muss die erforderliche Sorgfalt beim Erwerb sowohl vom Rechtsvorgänger als auch vom Rechtsnachfolger beachtet worden sein. ²Beim Erwerb durch Erbschaft muss der Erbe oder Vermächtnisnehmer die mangelnde Sorgfalt des Erblassers gegen sich gelten lassen.

(3) Bei der Entscheidung, ob der unmittelbare Eigenbesitzer mit der erforderlichen Sorgfalt vorgegangen ist, werden alle Umstände beim Erwerb des Kulturgutes berücksichtigt, insbesondere
1. die Unterlagen über die Herkunft des Kulturgutes,
2. die nach dem Recht des ersuchenden Mitgliedstaates oder Vertragsstaates erforderliche Ausfuhrgenehmigung,
3. die jeweiligen Eigenschaften der beim Erwerb des Kulturgutes Beteiligten,
4. der Kaufpreis,
5. die Einsichtnahme des unmittelbaren Eigenbesitzers in die zugänglichen Verzeichnisse entwendeten Kulturgutes und das Einholen einschlägiger Informationen, die er mit zumutbarem Aufwand erhalten konnte, und
6. jeder andere Schritt, den eine vernünftige Person unter denselben Umständen unternommen hätte.

(4) § 52 Absatz 3 bleibt unberührt.

§ 67 Höhe der Entschädigung

(1) ¹Die Höhe der Entschädigung bestimmt sich unter Berücksichtigung der entstandenen Aufwendungen des Rückgabeschuldners für
1. den Erwerb des Kulturgutes und
2. die notwendigen Maßnahmen zur Erhaltung des Kulturgutes.

²Die Entschädigung darf die Aufwendungen nicht übersteigen. ³Für entgangenen Gewinn ist keine Entschädigung zu zahlen.

(2) Bleibt das Kulturgut auch nach der Rückgabe Eigentum des Rückgabeschuldners, so hat der ersuchende Mitgliedstaat oder Vertragsstaat dem Rückgabeschuldner abweichend von Absatz 1 nur die Aufwendungen zu erstatten, die dem Rückgabeschuldner daraus entstanden sind, dass er darauf vertraut hat, das Kulturgut im Bundesgebiet belassen zu dürfen.

§ 68 Erstattungsanspruch des ersuchenden Mitglied- oder Vertragsstaates
(1) ¹Der ersuchende Mitgliedstaat oder Vertragsstaat kann von den Personen, die Kulturgut unrechtmäßig verbracht haben oder die die unrechtmäßige Verbringung von Kulturgut veranlasst haben, Erstattung der aus dem Rückgabeverfahren entstandenen Kosten fordern. ²§ 840 Absatz 1 des Bürgerlichen Gesetzbuches ist entsprechend anzuwenden.
(2) Der Anspruch nach Absatz 1 ist vor den ordentlichen Gerichten geltend zu machen.

Kapitel 6
Rückgabe unrechtmäßig ausgeführten Kulturgutes

§ 69 Rückgabeanspruch gegenüber Mitgliedstaaten
(1) ¹Den Anspruch auf Rückgabe von Kulturgut, das unrechtmäßig in das Hoheitsgebiet eines Mitgliedstaates ausgeführt worden ist, macht im jeweiligen Mitgliedstaat nach dessen Vorschriften die für Kultur und Medien zuständige oberste Bundesbehörde im Benehmen mit der zuständigen obersten Landesbehörde des Landes, in dem sich das Kulturgut vor der unrechtmäßigen Ausfuhr dauerhaft befand, geltend. ²Ist der Ort der letzten dauerhaften Belegenheit des Kulturgutes im Bundesgebiet nicht feststellbar, so macht die für Kultur und Medien zuständige oberste Bundesbehörde den Anspruch geltend.
(2) Die für Kultur und Medien zuständige oberste Bundesbehörde setzt die zuständige zentrale Stelle des ersuchten Mitgliedstaates unverzüglich davon in Kenntnis, dass sie Klage auf Rückgabe des betreffenden Kulturgutes erhoben hat.

§ 70 Rückgabeanspruch gegenüber Vertragsstaaten
(1) Den Anspruch auf Rückgabe von Kulturgut, das unrechtmäßig in das Hoheitsgebiet eines Vertragsstaates ausgeführt worden ist, macht das Auswärtige Amt im Einvernehmen mit der für Kultur und Medien zuständigen obersten Bundesbehörde geltend.
(2) Bevor die für Kultur und Medien zuständige oberste Bundesbehörde den Rückgabeanspruch geltend macht, stellt sie das Benehmen her mit der zuständigen obersten Landesbehörde des Landes, in dem sich das Kulturgut vor der unrechtmäßigen Ausfuhr dauerhaft befand.

§ 71 Kosten
(1) ¹Die notwendigen Kosten und Auslagen, die durch die Geltendmachung des Rückgabeanspruchs entstanden sind, trägt derjenige, der das Kulturgut unrechtmäßig ausgeführt hat. ²§ 840 Absatz 1 des Bürgerlichen Gesetzbuches ist entsprechend anzuwenden.
(2) Die Bundesbehörde, die den Rückgabeanspruch nach den §§ 69, 70 geltend macht, setzt den zu erstattenden Betrag durch Bescheid fest.

§ 72 Eigentum an zurückgegebenem Kulturgut
Wer Eigentümer des Kulturgutes ist, das unrechtmäßig ausgeführt worden ist und in das Bundesgebiet zurückgegeben worden ist, bestimmt sich nach den deutschen Sachvorschriften.

Kapitel 7
Rückgabezusage im internationalen Leihverkehr

§ 73 Rechtsverbindliche Rückgabezusage
(1) ¹Wird Kulturgut aus dem Ausland für eine öffentliche Ausstellung oder für eine andere Form der öffentlichen Präsentation, einschließlich einer vorherigen Restaurierung für diesen Zweck, oder für Forschungszwecke an eine Kulturgut bewahrende oder wissenschaftliche Einrichtung im Bundesgebiet vorübergehend ausgeliehen, so kann die oberste Landesbehörde im Benehmen mit der für Kultur und Medien zuständigen obersten Bundesbehörde eine rechtsverbindliche Rückgabezusage für die Aufenthaltsdauer des Kulturgutes im Bundesgebiet erteilen. ²Die Rückgabezusage darf höchstens für zwei Jahre erteilt werden.
(2) ¹Für die Erteilung der rechtsverbindlichen Rückgabezusage ist die oberste Landesbehörde des Landes zuständig, in dem der Entleiher seinen Hauptsitz hat. ²Bei mehreren Leihorten ist die Behörde des ersten Leihortes zuständig.

C.I.2 Kulturgutschutzgesetz

§ 74 Erteilung der rechtsverbindlichen Rückgabezusage
(1) ¹Auf Antrag des Entleihers kann die oberste Landesbehörde im Benehmen mit der für Kultur und Medien zuständigen obersten Bundesbehörde dem Verleiher vor der Einfuhr des Kulturgutes die Rückgabezusage erteilen. ²Der Antrag kann schriftlich oder elektronisch übermittelt werden.
(2) Die Rückgabezusage erfolgt schriftlich und unter Gebrauch der Worte „rechtsverbindliche Rückgabezusage".

§ 75 Verlängerung
(1) ¹Die rechtsverbindliche Rückgabezusage kann von der obersten Landesbehörde im Einvernehmen mit der für Kultur und Medien zuständigen obersten Bundesbehörde auf Antrag des Entleihers verlängert werden. ²Die Höchstdauer von zwei Jahren soll auch durch eine Verlängerung nicht überschritten werden. ³In begründeten Ausnahmefällen kann die Frist für einen Aufenthalt im Bundesgebiet auf bis zu vier Jahre verlängert werden.
(2) § 73 Absatz 2 ist entsprechend anzuwenden.

§ 76 Wirkung
(1) ¹Die rechtsverbindliche Rückgabezusage bewirkt, dass
1. dem Rückgabeanspruch des Verleihers keine Rechte entgegengehalten werden können, die Dritte an dem Kulturgut geltend machen, und
2. kein Verfahren zur Eintragung in ein Verzeichnis national wertvollen Kulturgutes eingeleitet werden kann.

²Die Rückgabezusage kann nicht aufgehoben, zurückgenommen oder widerrufen werden und ist für die Aufenthaltsdauer des Kulturgutes im Bundesgebiet sofort vollziehbar.
(2) Bis zur Rückgabe des Kulturgutes an den Verleiher, höchstens jedoch für die Dauer der erteilten Rückgabezusage, sind gerichtliche Klagen auf Herausgabe, Arrestverfügungen, Pfändungen und Beschlagnahmen des Kulturgutes sowie behördliche Vollstreckungsmaßnahmen oder Sicherstellungen nach diesem Gesetz oder anderen Rechtsvorschriften nicht zulässig.
(3) Die Ausfuhr nach Ablauf des Leihvertrages unterliegt nicht der Genehmigungspflicht nach § 24.

Kapitel 8
Datenschutz, gemeinsames Verfahren, Zoll

§ 77 Verarbeitung von Informationen einschließlich personenbezogener Daten
(1) Die für die Ausführung dieses Gesetzes zuständigen Behörden des Bundes und der Länder dürfen Informationen einschließlich personenbezogener Daten verarbeiten, soweit dies erforderlich ist
1. zur Erfüllung ihrer Aufgaben nach diesem Gesetz, nach landesrechtlichen Regelungen zum Schutz beweglichen Kulturgutes, nach unmittelbar geltenden Rechtsakten der Europäischen Union und der Europäischen Gemeinschaft, die Verbote und Beschränkungen enthalten, sowie
2. zur Erfüllung ihrer Aufgaben nach der aufgrund dieses Gesetzes erlassenen Rechtsverordnung.

(2) Die Vorschriften zum Schutz personenbezogener Daten bleiben unberührt.

§ 78 Übermittlung von Informationen einschließlich personenbezogener Daten an die zuständige Behörde
(1) Öffentliche Stellen im Sinne des § 2 des Bundesdatenschutzgesetzes dürfen Informationen einschließlich personenbezogener Daten der nach diesem Gesetz zuständigen Behörde des Bundes und der Länder übermitteln, soweit dies erforderlich ist, damit diese Behörde ihre in § 77 genannten Aufgaben erfüllen kann.
(2) Öffentliche Stellen haben unverzüglich die zuständigen Behörden des Bundes und der Länder zu unterrichten, wenn sie im Zusammenhang mit der Erfüllung ihrer Aufgaben Kenntnis davon erlangen, dass Kulturgut unter Verstoß gegen die Einfuhr- und Ausfuhrbestimmungen ein- oder ausgeführt worden ist oder werden soll.
(3) ¹Die für die Einleitung und Durchführung eines Straf- oder eines Bußgeldverfahrens zuständigen Stellen haben die nach diesem Gesetz zuständigen Behörden des Bundes und der Länder unverzüglich über die Einleitung und die Erledigung eines auf Kulturgut bezogenen Straf- oder Bußgeldverfahrens bei der Staatsanwaltschaft, bei Gericht oder bei der für die Verfolgung und Ahndung der Ordnungswidrigkeit zuständigen Verwaltungsbehörde unter Angabe der gesetzlichen Vorschriften zu unterrich-

ten. ²Satz 1 ist nicht für Verfahren wegen einer Ordnungswidrigkeit anzuwenden, die nur mit einer Geldbuße bis zu tausend Euro geahndet werden kann.
(4) ¹Bei Eingang eines Rechtshilfeersuchens eines anderen Mitgliedstaates oder Vertragsstaates ist Absatz 3 entsprechend anzuwenden mit der Maßgabe, dass auch die für Kultur und Medien zuständige oberste Bundesbehörde unterrichtet wird. ²Diese unterrichtet in Fällen eines Rechtshilfeersuchens eines Vertragsstaates das Auswärtige Amt.

§ 79 Gemeinsames Verfahren von Bund und Ländern
(1) ¹Zum umfassenden Schutz nationalen Kulturgutes führen Bund und Länder ein gemeinsames Verfahren im Sinne des § 11 des E-Government-Gesetzes. ²Sie sind befugt, Informationen einschließlich personenbezogener Daten in dem gemeinsamen Verfahren zu verarbeiten. ³§ 16 Absatz 2 bleibt unberührt.
(2) Die am gemeinsamen Verfahren beteiligten Behörden des Bundes und der Länder sind jeweils für die Rechtmäßigkeit der von ihnen vorgenommenen Datenverarbeitung verantwortlich.
(3) ¹Die am gemeinsamen Verfahren beteiligten Behörden des Bundes und der Länder unterliegen, soweit sie an dem gemeinsamen Verfahren teilnehmen, dem Bundesdatenschutzgesetz. ²Die zuständige Kontrollstelle im Sinne des § 11 Absatz 4 Satz 2 des E-Government-Gesetzes für die Einhaltung der Datenschutzvorschriften mit Bezug auf das gemeinsame Verfahren ist die oder der Bundesbeauftragte für den Datenschutz und die Informationsfreiheit. ³Die Zuständigkeit der oder des Bundesbeauftragten für den Datenschutz und die Informationsfreiheit lässt die Zuständigkeit der oder des Landesbeauftragten für den Datenschutz im Übrigen unberührt.
(4) ¹Im Rahmen des gemeinsamen Verfahrens werden neben den Daten zur Identifikation des Kulturgutes auch die personenbezogenen Daten der Eigentümer und soweit erforderlich der Besitzer des nationalen Kulturgutes nach Maßgabe von Absatz 1 verarbeitet. ²Dies sind insbesondere deren Namen und Adressen.
(5) Einzelheiten des gemeinsamen Verfahrens, insbesondere die jeweils verantwortliche Stelle für die Festlegung, Änderung, Fortentwicklung und Einhaltung von fachlichen und technischen Vorgaben nach § 11 Absatz 3 Satz 1 des E-Government-Gesetzes, werden durch für alle Länder verbindliche Beschlüsse des Verwaltungsausschusses nach § 4 Absatz 4 geregelt.

§ 80 Übermittlung von Informationen einschließlich personenbezogener Daten an Mitgliedstaaten und Vertragsstaaten
(1) ¹Die für Kultur und Medien zuständige oberste Bundesbehörde erteilt den zuständigen zentralen Stellen eines Mitgliedstaates auf begründetes Ersuchen,
1. soweit es für deren Prüfung erforderlich ist, Auskunft, ob
   a) die Voraussetzungen für ein Rückgabeersuchen oder eine Klage auf Rückgabe gegeben sind oder
   b) die Voraussetzungen für die Erteilung einer Ausfuhrgenehmigung nach der Verordnung (EG) Nr. 116/2009 gegeben sind, sowie
2. Auskünfte, die zur Auffindung und Rückgabe von gestohlenem oder unrechtmäßig in das Bundesgebiet eingeführtem Kulturgut beitragen können.

²Die Auskunftserteilung nach Satz 1 Nummer 1 und 2 umfasst neben nichtpersonenbezogenen Daten den Namen und die ladungsfähige Anschrift der derzeitigen oder vorherigen Eigentümer oder Besitzer, soweit dies für die Prüfung der zuständigen Stelle des anderen Mitgliedstaates erforderlich ist.
(2) Das Auswärtige Amt erteilt einem Vertragsstaat auf begründetes Ersuchen
1. soweit es für dessen Prüfung erforderlich ist, Auskunft, ob die Voraussetzungen für ein Rückgabeersuchen oder eine Klage auf Rückgabe gegeben sind, sowie
2. Auskünfte, die zur Auffindung und Rückgabe von gestohlenem oder unrechtmäßig in das Bundesgebiet eingeführtem Kulturgut beitragen können.

(3) ¹Personenbezogene Daten dürfen an Stellen in Mitgliedstaaten und Vertragsstaaten nur übermittelt werden, wenn deren Kenntnis für die Rechtsverfolgung von Rückgabeansprüchen nach diesem Gesetz erforderlich ist.

§ 81 Mitwirkung der Zollbehörden, Anhaltung von Kulturgut
(1) ¹Die Zollbehörden wirken im Rahmen ihrer Zuständigkeit bei der Überwachung der Ein- und Ausfuhr von Kulturgut mit, für das Verbote oder Beschränkungen nach diesem Gesetz oder einer

C.I.2 Kulturgutschutzgesetz

aufgrund dieses Gesetzes erlassenen Rechtsverordnung gelten. ²Soweit es zur Durchführung dieses Gesetzes und der aufgrund dieses Gesetzes erlassenen Rechtsverordnungen erforderlich ist, dürfen die Zollbehörden die im Rahmen ihrer zollamtlichen Überwachung gewonnenen Informationen, auch soweit sie dem Steuergeheimnis unterliegen, den zuständigen Behörden übermitteln.
(2) Die für Kultur und Medien zuständige oberste Bundesbehörde kann der zuständigen zentralen Stelle der Zollverwaltung konkrete länder-, waren- oder personenbezogene Risikohinweise übermitteln.
(3) Ergeben sich bei der zollamtlichen Überwachung Anhaltspunkte für einen Verstoß gegen dieses Gesetz oder gegen eine aufgrund dieses Gesetzes erlassene Rechtsverordnung, so unterrichten die Zollbehörden unverzüglich die zuständige Behörde des Landes, in dem sich das Kulturgut bei der Anhaltung befindet.
(4) ¹Im Falle des Absatzes 3 halten die Zollbehörden die Waren, deren Beförderungs- und Verpackungsmittel sowie die beigefügten Unterlagen auf Kosten und Gefahr des Verfügungsberechtigten an. ²Sie können die angehaltenen Waren sowie deren Beförderungs- und Verpackungsmittel auch durch einen Dritten verwahren lassen. ³§ 39 ist entsprechend anzuwenden.
(5) Die Zollbehörde gibt das angehaltene Kulturgut, die Beförderungs- und Verpackungsmittel sowie die beigefügten Unterlagen frei, wenn die sonstigen Anforderungen und Förmlichkeiten für eine Freigabe erfüllt sind und
1. die zuständige Behörde mitgeteilt hat, dass sie das Kulturgut nach § 33 sichergestellt hat,
2. die zuständige Behörde mitgeteilt hat, dass das Kulturgut nicht sichergestellt wird, oder
3. nach Ablauf von drei Arbeitstagen seit der Unterrichtung nach Absatz 3 keine Mitteilung der zuständigen Behörde zum weiteren Vorgehen vorliegt oder
4. nach Ablauf von zehn Arbeitstagen seit der Unterrichtung nach Absatz 3 keine Mitteilung der zuständigen Behörde über die Sicherstellung des Kulturgutes nach § 33 vorliegt.
(6) Es ist verboten, nach Absatz 4 angehaltenes Kulturgut zu beschädigen, zu zerstören oder dessen Erscheinungsbild nicht nur unerheblich und nicht nur vorübergehend zu verändern.

§ 82 Anmeldepflicht bei Ein- und Ausfuhr im Kulturgutverkehr mit Drittstaaten
(1) Bei der zuständigen Zollstelle ist Kulturgut anzumelden, das
1. unmittelbar aus einem Drittstaat eingeführt werden soll und zur Ausfuhr aus dem Herkunftsstaat einer Genehmigung durch diesen Staat bedarf oder
2. in einen Drittstaat ausgeführt werden soll und zur Ausfuhr aus dem Binnenmarkt einer Genehmigung nach diesem Gesetz oder nach einem im Amtsblatt der Europäischen Union veröffentlichten, unmittelbar geltenden Rechtsakt der Europäischen Union bedarf.
(2) ¹Die Anmeldung hat die Person vorzunehmen, die das Kulturgut einführt oder ausführt. ²Bei der Anmeldung sind die für die Einfuhr oder Ausfuhr erforderlichen Genehmigungen oder sonstigen Dokumente vorzulegen.
(3) Auf Verlangen der zuständigen Zollstelle ist das anmeldepflichtige Kulturgut vorzuführen.

Kapitel 9
Straf- und Bußgeldvorschriften

§ 83 Strafvorschriften
(1) Mit Freiheitsstrafe bis zu fünf Jahren oder mit Geldstrafe wird bestraft, wer
1. entgegen § 21 Nummer 1, 2, 4 oder 5 Kulturgut ausführt,
2. entgegen § 21 Nummer 3 Kulturgut ausführt, von dem er weiß, dass es nach § 32 Absatz 1 Nummer 1 oder 2 unrechtmäßig eingeführt wurde,
3. entgegen § 28 Kulturgut einführt, von dem er weiß, dass es unter Verstoß gegen eine dort genannte Rechtsvorschrift verbracht worden ist,
4. entgegen § 40 Absatz 1 Kulturgut in Verkehr bringt, das abhandengekommen ist oder von dem er weiß, dass es rechtswidrig ausgegraben oder nach § 32 Absatz 1 Nummer 1 oder 2 unrechtmäßig eingeführt worden ist, oder
5. entgegen § 40 Absatz 3 ein Verpflichtungs- oder Verfügungsgeschäft über Kulturgut abschließt, das durch eine in Nummer 1 oder 2 bezeichnete Handlung ausgeführt worden ist.

(2) Ebenso wird bestraft, wer entgegen Artikel 2 Absatz 1 der Verordnung (EG) Nr. 116/2009 des Rates vom 18. Dezember 2008 über die Ausfuhr von Kulturgütern (kodifizierte Fassung) (ABl. L 39 vom 10.2.2009, S. 1) Kulturgut ausführt.
(3) Mit Freiheitsstrafe bis zu drei Jahren oder mit Geldstrafe wird bestraft, wer entgegen § 18 Absatz 1, auch in Verbindung mit Absatz 2, Kulturgut beschädigt, zerstört oder verändert.
(4) Der Versuch ist strafbar.
(5) Mit Freiheitsstrafe von einem Jahr bis zu zehn Jahren wird bestraft, wer in den Fällen des Absatzes 1 Nummer 4
1. gewerbsmäßig handelt oder
2. als Mitglied einer Bande handelt, die sich zur fortgesetzten Begehung solcher Taten verbunden hat.
(6) Mit Freiheitsstrafe bis zu drei Jahren oder mit Geldstrafe wird bestraft, wer in den Fällen des Absatzes 1 Nummer 1 oder des Absatzes 2 in Ausübung einer gewerblichen Tätigkeit fahrlässig handelt.
(7) Das Gericht kann in den Fällen des Absatzes 1 Nummer 1 die Strafe nach § 49 Absatz 1 des Strafgesetzbuches mildern oder von Strafe absehen, wenn der Täter das Kulturgut unverzüglich in das Bundesgebiet zurückbringt.

§ 84 Bußgeldvorschriften
(1) Ordnungswidrig handelt, wer
1. entgegen § 15 Absatz 2 eine Mitteilung nicht, nicht richtig, nicht vollständig oder nicht rechtzeitig macht,
2. entgegen § 42 Absatz 1 Satz 1 Nummer 1 Name oder Anschrift einer dort genannten Person nicht oder nicht rechtzeitig feststellt,
3. entgegen § 42 Absatz 1 Satz 1 Nummer 2 eine Beschreibung oder eine Abbildung nicht oder nicht rechtzeitig anfertigt oder
4. entgegen § 42 Absatz 1 Satz 1 Nummer 7 eine dort genannte Erklärung nicht oder nicht rechtzeitig einholt.
(2) Ordnungswidrig handelt, wer vorsätzlich oder fahrlässig
1. entgegen § 30 Satz 1 bei der Einfuhr von Kulturgut, von dem er weiß oder hätte wissen müssen, dass es von einem Mitgliedstaat oder Vertragsstaat als nationales Kulturgut eingestuft oder definiert worden ist, eine dort verlangte Unterlage nicht mit sich führt oder
2. entgegen § 82 Absatz 3 Kulturgut nicht oder nicht rechtzeitig vorführt.
(3) Die Ordnungswidrigkeit kann in den Fällen des Absatzes 1 Nummer 2 bis 4 mit einer Geldbuße bis zu dreißigtausend Euro, in den übrigen Fällen mit einer Geldbuße bis zu hunderttausend Euro geahndet werden.

§ 85 Einziehung
¹Ist eine Straftat nach § 83 oder eine Ordnungswidrigkeit nach § 84 Absatz 1 oder 2 begangen worden, so können folgende Gegenstände eingezogen werden:
1. Gegenstände, auf die sich die Straftat oder Ordnungswidrigkeit bezieht, oder
2. Gegenstände, die durch sie hervorgebracht oder zu ihrer Begehung oder Vorbereitung gebraucht worden oder bestimmt gewesen sind.
²§ 74a des Strafgesetzbuches und § 23 des Gesetzes über Ordnungswidrigkeiten sind anzuwenden.

§ 86 Besondere Voraussetzung der Verwertung von Kulturgut
(1) Kulturgut, das der Einziehung unterliegt, darf nur mit Zustimmung der zuständigen Behörde verwertet werden.
(2) ¹Die Zustimmung kann versagt werden. ²Sie ist im Regelfall zu versagen für Kulturgut,
1. das der genehmigungspflichtigen Ausfuhr nach § 24 unterliegt und dessen Eintragung in ein Verzeichnis national wertvollen Kulturgutes noch nicht abschließend geprüft worden ist,
2. das einem Rückgabeanspruch nach Kapitel 5 unterliegen könnte und für das die Verjährungsfrist für den Rückgabeanspruch noch nicht abgelaufen oder der Anspruch noch nicht erloschen ist oder
3. dessen Inverkehrbringen nach § 40 verboten ist oder für dessen Inverkehrbringen eine erhöhte Sorgfaltspflicht nach § 44 besteht.

(3) Vor der Verwertung von Kulturgut ausländischer Staaten sind das Auswärtige Amt und die für Kultur und Medien zuständige oberste Bundesbehörde anzuhören.
(4) Die Absätze 1 bis 3 sind auch bei Einziehung nach anderen Rechtsvorschriften anzuwenden.
(5) Eine Verwertung von Kulturgut, das die zuständige Behörde nach diesem Gesetz eingezogen hat, ist erst möglich, wenn die Voraussetzungen nach Absatz 2 abschließend geprüft sind.

§ 87 Aufgaben und Befugnisse der Zollbehörden
(1) ¹Die Staatsanwaltschaft kann bei Straftaten und Ordnungswidrigkeiten nach den §§ 83 und 84 Ermittlungen nach § 161 Absatz 1 Satz 1 der Strafprozessordnung in den Fällen des § 83 Absatz 1 Nummer 1, 2 oder 3 in Verbindung mit den Absätzen 4 und 6 sowie im Fall des § 83 Absatz 2 in Verbindung mit Absatz 4 auch durch die Hauptzollämter oder die Zollfahndungsämter vornehmen lassen. ²Die nach § 36 Absatz 1 Nummer 2 oder Absatz 2 des Gesetzes gegen Ordnungswidrigkeiten zuständige Verwaltungsbehörde kann in den Fällen des Satzes 1 Ermittlungen auch durch die Hauptzollämter oder die Zollfahndungsämter vornehmen lassen.
(2) § 21 Absatz 3 des Außenwirtschaftsgesetzes vom 6. Juni 2013 (BGBl. I S. 1482), das durch Artikel 297 der Verordnung vom 31. August 2015 (BGBl. I S. 1474) geändert worden ist, ist entsprechend anzuwenden.

§ 88 Straf- und Bußgeldverfahren
¹Soweit für Straftaten nach § 83 das Amtsgericht sachlich zuständig ist, liegt die örtliche Zuständigkeit bei dem Amtsgericht, in dessen Bezirk das örtlich zuständige Landgericht seinen Sitz hat. ²Die Landesregierung kann durch Rechtsverordnung die örtliche Zuständigkeit des Amtsgerichts abweichend regeln, soweit dies mit Rücksicht auf die Wirtschafts- oder Verkehrsverhältnisse, den Aufbau der Verwaltung oder andere örtliche Bedürfnisse zweckmäßig erscheint. ³Die Landesregierung kann diese Ermächtigung auf die Landesjustizverwaltung übertragen.[1]

Kapitel 10
Evaluierung, Übergangs- und Ausschlussvorschriften

§ 89 Evaluierung
Das für Kultur und Medien zuständige Mitglied der Bundesregierung unterrichtet den Deutschen Bundestag und den Bundesrat über die Anwendung des Gesetzes fünf Jahre und vorab zum Umfang des Verwaltungsaufwandes zwei Jahre nach Inkrafttreten des Gesetzes.

§ 90 Fortgeltung und Befristung bisherigen Abwanderungsschutzes
(1) Bestandteil des Verzeichnisses national wertvollen Kulturgutes ist Kulturgut, das aufgrund des Gesetzes zum Schutz deutschen Kulturgutes gegen Abwanderung in der Fassung der Bekanntmachung vom 8. Juli 1999 (BGBl. I S. 1754), das zuletzt durch Artikel 2 des Gesetzes vom 18. Mai 2007 (BGBl. I S. 757) geändert worden ist, eingetragen worden ist in
1. ein Verzeichnis national wertvollen Kulturgutes oder
2. ein Verzeichnis national wertvoller Archive eines Landes.
(2) Die Ausfuhr bleibt genehmigungspflichtig, längstens bis zum Ablauf des 31. Dezember 2025
1. von Kunstwerken, die aufgrund der Verordnung über die Ausfuhr von Kunstwerken der Reichsregierung vom 11. Dezember 1919 (RGBl. S. 1961), die zuletzt durch die Verordnung vom 20. Dezember 1932 (RGBl. I S. 572) verlängert worden ist, in das Verzeichnis der national wertvollen Kunstwerke eingetragen waren und über deren Eintragung in ein Verzeichnis national wertvollen Kulturgutes noch nicht entschieden worden ist, und
2. von registriertem Kulturgut nach dem Kulturgutschutzgesetz vom 3. Juli 1980 (GBl. I Nr. 20 S. 191) und über dessen Eintragung in ein Verzeichnis national wertvollen Kulturgutes noch nicht entschieden worden ist.

---

[1] Siehe hierzu für Sachsen-Anhalt § 1 Nr. 3a Verordnung zur Übertragung von Verordnungsermächtigungen im Bereich der Justiz vom 28. März 2008 (GVBl. S. 137), zuletzt geändert am 22. Mai 2018 (GVBl. S. 62); siehe für Schleswig-Holstein § 1 Abs. 1 Nr. 19 Landesverordnung zur Übertragung von Ermächtigungen zum Erlaß von Rechtsverordnungen im Bereich der Rechtspflege Justizermächtigungsübertragungsverordnung vom 4. Dezember 1996 (GVOBl. S. 720), zuletzt geändert am 15. November 2019 (GVOBl. S. 546).

(3) Für Verfahren, die bis 6. August 2016 eingeleitet und bekannt gemacht worden sind, gelten die Vorschriften des Gesetzes zum Schutz deutschen Kulturgutes gegen Abwanderung in der Fassung der Bekanntmachung vom 8. Juli 1999 (BGBl. I S. 1754), das zuletzt durch Artikel 2 des Gesetzes vom 18. Mai 2007 (BGBl. I S. 757, 2547) geändert worden ist, bis zum Abschluss des Verfahrens fort.

§ 91 Ausschluss abweichenden Landesrechts
Von den in den §§ 7 bis 17, 22 bis 27 und 73 bis 76 getroffenen Regelungen des Verwaltungsverfahrens kann durch Landesrecht nicht abgewichen werden.

C.I.3 Eckpunkte Kolonialgut

Erste Eckpunkte zum Umgang mit Sammlungsgut aus kolonialen Kontexten der Staatsministerin des Bundes für Kultur und Medien, der Staatsministerin im Auswärtigen Amt für internationale Kulturpolitik, der Kulturministerinnen und Kulturminister der Länder und der kommunalen Spitzenverbände[1]

Stand: 13.03.2019

Präambel

Wir, die Staatsministerin des Bundes für Kultur und Medien, die Staatsministerin im Auswärtigen Amt für internationale Kulturpolitik, die Kulturministerinnen und Kulturminister der Länder und die kommunalen Spitzenverbände, stellen uns der historischen Verantwortung im Zusammenhang mit dem deutschen Kolonialismus und der Verantwortung, die sich aus von kolonialem Denken geprägten Handlungen ergeben hat. Das während der Zeit des Kolonialismus geschehene Unrecht und seine zum Teil bis heute nachwirkenden Folgen dürfen nicht vergessen werden.

Die Aufarbeitung der deutschen Kolonialgeschichte als Teil unserer gemeinsamen gesellschaftlichen Erinnerungskultur gehört zum demokratischen Grundkonsens in Deutschland und ist über die Politik hinaus eine Aufgabe für alle Bereiche der Gesellschaft, auch für Kultur, Bildung, Wissenschaft und Zivilgesellschaft. Dies stellt uns vor große historische, ethische und politische Herausforderungen. Der aufrichtige, glaubwürdige und sensible Umgang hiermit ist eine gesamtgesellschaftliche Aufgabe. Sie soll getragen sein von partnerschaftlichem Dialog, Verständigung und Versöhnung mit den vom Kolonialismus betroffenen Gesellschaften.

Nach unserem Verständnis sollten alle Menschen die Möglichkeit haben, in ihren Herkunftsstaaten und Herkunftsgesellschaften ihrem reichen materiellen Kulturerbe zu begegnen, sich damit auseinanderzusetzen und es an zukünftige Generationen weiterzugeben. Deutschland erkennt die Bedeutung von Kulturgütern für die kulturelle Identität der Herkunftsstaaten und den betroffenen Zivilgesellschaften an und hat unter anderem deshalb 2007 das UNESCO-Übereinkommen zum Kulturgutschutz von 1970 ratifiziert und umgesetzt.

Wir wollen in engem Austausch mit den Herkunftsstaaten und den betroffenen Herkunftsgesellschaften verantwortungsvoll mit Sammlungsgut aus kolonialen Kontexten umgehen. Wir wollen dabei die Voraussetzungen für Rückführungen von menschlichen Überresten schaffen und für Rückführungen von Kulturgütern aus kolonialen Kontexten, deren Aneignung in rechtlich und/oder ethisch heute nicht mehr vertretbarer Weise erfolgte. Wir werden gemeinsam mit den betroffenen Einrichtungen Rückführungsverfahren mit der erforderlichen Dringlichkeit und Sensibilität behandeln.

Das Sammlungsgut aus kolonialen Kontexten stammt nicht nur aus ehemaligen deutschen Kolonialgebieten, sondern auch aus anderen Teilen der Welt. Durch gewaltsame Aneignung von Kulturgütern im Zuge des europäischen Kolonialismus wurden vielen betroffenen Gesellschaften Kulturgüter geraubt, die für ihre Geschichte und ihre kulturelle Identität prägend sind. Kulturgüter vergegenwärtigen Zusammenhänge, die für das kulturelle Selbstverständnis der Gesellschaft, aus der sie stammen, von fundamentaler Bedeutung sind.

Wir erkennen die Notwendigkeit an, das Bewusstsein für und das Wissen um die Kolonialgeschichte und ihre Auswirkungen bis in die Gegenwart zu schärfen und zu vermehren. Eine wichtige Rolle nehmen dabei all jene Einrichtungen ein, die Sammlungsgut aus kolonialen Kontexten bewahren.

Die Staatsministerin des Bundes für Kultur und Medien, die Staatsministerin im Auswärtigen Amt für internationale Kulturpolitik, die Kulturministerinnen und Kulturminister der Länder und die kommunalen Spitzenverbände verstehen die Aufarbeitung von Sammlungsgut aus kolonialen Kontexten als einen klar von der Aufarbeitung NS-verfolgungsbedingt entzogenen Kulturguts zu trennenden Sachverhalt. Sie wird nicht zu einer Reduzierung der Bemühungen und Maßnahmen zur Aufarbeitung des NS-Unrechts führen. Der Holocaust ist präzedenzlos und unvergleichbar.

---

1) https://www.kmk.org/fileadmin/pdf/PresseUndAktuelles/2019/2019-03-25_Erste-Eckpunkte-Sammlungsgut-koloniale-Kontexte_final.pdf.

Wir stehen für Dialog und Transparenz. Den Einbezug von Menschen aus Herkunftsstaaten und den Herkunftsgesellschaften ehemals kolonisierter Gebiete sehen wir als Voraussetzung an, um überkommene Deutungshoheiten und eine eurozentrische Perspektive zu überwinden und zu einem partnerschaftlichen Austausch zu finden. Dies schließt auch Menschen aus Herkunftsstaaten und den betroffenen Herkunftsgesellschaften ein, die heute in Deutschland oder Europa leben.

Der angemessene Umgang mit Sammlungsgut aus kolonialen Kontexten ist ein zentrales kulturpolitisches Handlungsfeld und ein wichtiger Beitrag zu unserer gemeinsamen postkolonialen Erinnerungskultur. Zu diesem Sammlungsgut in kulturgutbewahrenden Einrichtungen und wissenschaftlichen Institutionen gehören ethnologische, naturkundliche, historische, kunst- und kulturhistorische Objekte und Schriftgut. Zu dem Sammlungsgut gehören auch menschliche Überreste.

Viele deutsche Kultureinrichtungen stehen bei der Aufarbeitung von Sammlungsgut aus kolonialen Kontexten nicht am Anfang und können auf Erfahrungen aus bereits abgeschlossenen oder noch laufenden Projekten aufbauen. Wir begrüßen, dass sich die deutschen Museen Richtlinien und Empfehlungen für einen sensiblen Umgang mit Kulturgutarten wie auch mit menschlichen Überresten gegeben haben. Dies sind auf internationaler Ebene die „Ethischen Richtlinien für Museen" des Internationalen Museumsrats (ICOM) sowie auf nationaler Ebene die „Empfehlungen zum Umgang mit menschlichen Überresten in Museen und Sammlungen" und der „Leitfaden zum Umgang mit Sammlungsgut aus kolonialen Kontexten" des Deutschen Museumsbundes. Wir begrüßen die Einrichtung eines neuen Förderbereichs „Kulturgüter aus kolonialen Kontexten" beim Deutschen Zentrum Kulturgutverluste, die Planungen zum Aufbau einer „Agentur für die internationale Museumskooperation" im Auswärtigen Amt sowie Initiativen von Ländern, Kommunen und Bund zur Digitalisierung ihrer Sammlungen und zum Aufbau von online-Plattformen.

Für den Handel mit Sammlungsgut aus kolonialen Kontexten gelten seit dessen Inkrafttreten die Vorschriften des Kulturgutschutzgesetzes.

Wir verständigen uns auf nachfolgende Handlungsfelder und Ziele. Diese bedürfen in wesentlichen Punkten noch einer Konkretisierung und werden in einem weiteren Arbeitsprozess gemeinsam und unter Hinzuziehung von nationalen und internationalen Expertinnen und Experten, insbesondere dem Deutschen Museumsbund, dem Internationalen Museumsrat ICOM sowie den Kulturstiftungen des Bundes und der Länder – und unter Beteiligung der Herkunftsstaaten und der betroffenen Herkunftsgesellschaften – weiterentwickeln und zu einer abschließenden Positionierung ausarbeiten.

Wir fordern alle öffentlichen Träger von Einrichtungen und Organisationen, in deren Beständen sich Sammlungsgut aus kolonialen Kontexten befinden, aber auch nichtstaatliche Museen, Sammlerinnen und Sammler sowie den Kunsthandel dazu auf, im Sinne dieser Eckpunkte an der Aufarbeitung der Herkunftsgeschichte von Sammlungsgut aus kolonialen Kontexten aktiv mitzuwirken und die jeweils erforderlichen Maßnahmen hierfür zu ergreifen.

Handlungsfelder und Ziele

Transparenz und Dokumentation

1.) Voraussetzung für einen verantwortungsvollen Umgang mit Sammlungsgut aus kolonialen Kontexten und die damit verbundene Aufarbeitung ist größtmögliche Transparenz, denn Transparenz ermöglicht weltweite Teilhabe.

Für eine umfassende Aufarbeitung der Herkunftsgeschichte von Sammlungsgut aus kolonialen Kontexten ist es erforderlich, entsprechendes Sammlungsgut, das sich in Deutschland befindet, zu dokumentieren und zu veröffentlichen. Durch die Veröffentlichung der entsprechenden Bestände wird ein Diskurs mit Herkunftsstaaten und den betroffenen Herkunftsgesellschaften über diese möglich sein. Wir erkennen daher die Bedeutung der Inventarisierung und Digitalisierung von Sammlungsgut aus kolonialen Kontexten an und prüfen Handlungsoptionen zur Unterstützung von Einrichtungen, die derartiges Sammlungsgut bewahren. Wir werden prüfen, ob die Einstellung von digitalisierten Beständen durch die Einrichtungen in die Deutsche Digitale Bibliothek hierfür ein geeignetes Instrument ist.

2.) Vorrang bei der Aufarbeitung des Sammlungsgutes kommt menschlichen Überresten aus kolonialen Kontexten zu. Bei den Kulturgütern ist im Hinblick auf kurz- und mittelfristig durchzuführende Maßnahmen angesichts der hohen Zahl eine Priorisierung notwendig. Besonders relevant sind aufgrund

C.I.3 Eckpunkte Kolonialgut

ihrer Erwerbungsumstände diejenigen Kulturgüter, die im Rahmen formaler Kolonialherrschaften des Deutschen Reiches aus ihren Gesellschaften entfernt und nach Deutschland verbracht wurden, sowie Kulturgüter aus anderen Kolonialherrschaften, für die Rückgabeersuchen vorliegen.

3.) Insbesondere Menschen und Institutionen aus den Herkunftsstaaten und den betroffenen Herkunftsgesellschaften werden wir die Möglichkeit eröffnen, sich über Bestände von Sammlungsgut aus kolonialen Kontexten in Deutschland zu informieren und konkrete Beratung, auch hinsichtlich möglicher Rückführungen und Kooperationen, zu erhalten.

Um den Zugang zu diesen Informationen deutlich zu erleichtern und zu verbessern, werden wir einen Vorschlag zur Errichtung und Ausgestaltung einer Anlaufstelle erarbeiten. Die rechtlichen Voraussetzungen, Einblicke in die Bestände öffentlicher Sammlungen zu erlangen, sind durch die Informationsfreiheitsgesetze des Bundes und der Länder gewährleistet. Wir begrüßen Schritte zur Veröffentlichung von Archivgut zur Kolonialgeschichte und zu Sammlungsgut aus kolonialen Kontexten, beispielsweise die bereits erfolgte digitale Veröffentlichung der Akten des Reichskolonialamtes durch das Bundesarchiv.

Provenienzforschung

4.) Die Provenienzforschung bildet die Grundlage zur Beurteilung der Herkunft des Sammlungsgutes und der Erwerbungsumstände.

Mit der Erforschung der Herkunft von Sammlungsgut aus kolonialen Kontexten soll auch ergründet werden, ob eine Aneignung gewaltsam oder ohne Zustimmung des Berechtigten erfolgte. Dabei ist zu berücksichtigen, dass nicht alle Kulturgüter aus kolonialen Kontexten unmittelbar gewaltsam entzogen wurden und die Dokumentationslage im Hinblick auf die tatsächlichen Erwerbungsumstände von Sammlungsgut aus kolonialen Kontexten in vielen Fällen unzureichend ist. Umso notwendiger ist es, die Voraussetzungen dafür zu schaffen, eine fundierte Beurteilung der jeweiligen Erwerbungsumstände durchführen zu können.

5.) Die Einrichtungen in Deutschland, welche Sammlungsgut aus kolonialen Kontexten bewahren, sind aufgefordert, ihre Bestände zu erforschen.

Bei der Aufarbeitung der Provenienzen von menschlichen Überresten einerseits und Kulturgut aus kolonialen Kontexten andererseits werden wir die deutschen kulturgutbewahrenden Einrichtungen nachhaltig unterstützen.

Bund, Länder und Kommunen als Träger der Museen und Sammlungen haben sich in den letzten Jahren bereits vielfältig engagiert und Projekte zur Sammlungserschließung und Provenienzforschung gefördert.

Präsentation und Vermittlung

6.) Wir fordern die kulturbewahrenden Einrichtungen und wissenschaftlichen Institutionen dazu auf, die Erwerbungsumstände von Sammlungsgut aus kolonialen Kontexten transparent darzustellen und angemessene Formate für eine zielgruppengerechte Vermittlung der in diesem Zusammenhang relevanten Sachverhalte, Fragestellungen und Lösungsansätze zu entwickeln. Die Erfüllung dieser Aufgaben ist von zentraler Bedeutung.

Rückführung

7.) Die generelle Bereitschaft zur Rückführung von Sammlungsgut aus kolonialen Kontexten, insbesondere von menschlichen Überresten, in die Herkunftsstaaten und Herkunftsgesellschaften ist wichtig für den von uns angestrebten partnerschaftlichen Dialog und eine aufrichtige Verständigung.

Kulturgüter aus kolonialen Kontexten zu identifizieren, deren Aneignung in rechtlich und/oder ethisch heute nicht mehr vertretbarer Weise erfolgte, und deren Rückführung zu ermöglichen, entspricht einer ethisch-moralischen Verpflichtung und ist eine wichtige politische Aufgabe unserer Zeit. Menschliche Überreste aus kolonialen Kontexten sind zurückzuführen.

8.) Rückführungsersuchen von Sammlungsgut aus kolonialen Kontexten sind zeitnah zu bearbeiten. Gleichzeitig sind die kulturgutbewahrenden Einrichtungen aufgerufen, selbstständig und proaktiv

Sammlungsgut zu identifizieren, für das eine Rückführung in Frage kommt, auch ohne dass ein vorheriges Rückführungsersuchen vorliegt.

9.) Rückführungen werden grundsätzlich nur im Einvernehmen mit den Herkunftsstaaten und den betroffenen Herkunftsgesellschaften erfolgen.

10.) In Deutschland steht die überwiegende Zahl von Einrichtungen, in deren Beständen sich Sammlungsgut aus kolonialen Kontexten befindet, in der Trägerschaft und Zuständigkeit der Länder und Kommunen.

Die rechtlichen Voraussetzungen für eine mögliche Rückführung von Sammlungsgut aus kolonialen Kontexten sind abhängig vom jeweils für die Einrichtungen geltenden Bundes-, Landes- und Organisationsrecht, insbesondere den Haushaltsordnungen des Bundes, der Länder und der Kommunen. Danach sind Rückgaben grundsätzlich möglich. Sofern rechtlicher Handlungsbedarf besteht, um die Rückführung von Sammlungsgut aus kolonialen Kontexten zu ermöglichen, wird dem nachgekommen.

Kulturaustausch, internationale Kooperationen

11.) Der verantwortungsvolle Umgang mit Sammlungsgut aus kolonialen Kontexten setzt den Dialog, den Austausch und die Kooperation mit den Herkunftsstaaten und den betroffenen Herkunftsgesellschaften sowie ihrer in Deutschland lebenden Diaspora voraus. Wichtig ist hierbei insbesondere der Erfahrungs- und Wissensaustausch.

Wir beabsichtigen, entsprechende internationale Kooperationen sowie den Kulturaustausch zu stärken. Dies kann etwa durch Stipendienprogramme für Kuratorinnen und Kuratoren, die Finanzierung gemeinsamer Projekte für die Forschung oder den Kapazitätsaufbau kultureller Infrastruktur erfolgen. Die Bundesregierung, ihre Mittlerorganisationen und die Kulturstiftung des Bundes engagieren sich bereits jetzt in diesem Bereich. Auch die Länder sind im Rahmen von wissenschaftlichen und kulturellen Austauschbeziehungen vielfach engagiert und haben ihre Aktivitäten verstärkt.

Ebenso wichtig ist es, bei der Erforschung und Präsentation von Kulturgut in deutschen Museen, Bibliotheken, Archiven und wissenschaftlichen Sammlungen frühzeitig den unmittelbaren Austausch mit den Herkunftsstaaten und den betroffenen Herkunftsgesellschaften zu suchen. Hier ist ein enger Dialog und partnerschaftlicher Austausch zu führen. Einseitig eurozentrische Deutungshoheiten sind nicht mehr zeitgemäß.

Wissenschaft und Forschung

12.) Die vielfach gewaltsame Aneignung von einerseits menschlichen Überresten und andererseits Kulturgut aus kolonialen Kontexten als Teil der deutschen und europäischen Kolonialgeschichte und ihre Auswirkungen bis in die Gegenwart bedürfen einer breit angelegten Erforschung, die sich vielfältigen Fragestellungen, von den Erwerbungsumständen und der Geschichte von Sammlungsgut über die ethischen und rechtlichen Rahmenbedingungen bis hin zu den gesellschaftlichen Folgen der deutschen Kolonialvergangenheit widmet. Dies erfordert Kompetenzen aus verschiedenen Wissenschaftsbereichen und die gleichberechtigte Zusammenarbeit von Wissenschaftlerinnen und Wissenschaftlern aus Deutschland mit den Herkunftsstaaten und den betroffenen Herkunftsgesellschaften.

C.II.1 Zivilschutz- und Katastrophenhilfegesetz

Gesetz über den Zivilschutz und die Katastrophenhilfe des Bundes (Zivilschutz- und Katastrophenhilfegesetz – ZSKG)[1]

Vom 25. März 1997 (BGBl. I S. 726)
(FNA 215-12)
zuletzt geändert durch Art. 2 Nr. 1 Erstes G zur Änd. des G zur Regelung der Rechtsverhältnisse der Helfer der Bundesanstalt Technisches Hilfswerk vom 29. Juli 2009 (BGBl. I S. 2350)

Nichtamtliche Inhaltsübersicht

Erster Abschnitt
Allgemeine Bestimmungen
- § 1 Aufgaben des Zivilschutzes
- § 2 Auftragsverwaltung
- § 3 Völkerrechtliche Stellung
- § 4 Zuständigkeit des Bundes für den Schutz der Zivilbevölkerung

Zweiter Abschnitt
Selbstschutz
- § 5 Selbstschutz

Dritter Abschnitt
Warnung der Bevölkerung
- § 6 Warnung der Bevölkerung

Vierter Abschnitt
Schutzbau
- § 7 Öffentliche Schutzräume
- § 8 Hausschutzräume
- § 9 Baulicher Betriebsschutz

Fünfter Abschnitt
Aufenthaltsregelung
- § 10 Aufenthaltsregelung

Sechster Abschnitt
Katastrophenschutz im Zivilschutz und Katastrophenhilfe des Bundes
- § 11 Einbeziehung des Katastrophenschutzes
- § 12 Grundsatz der Katastrophenhilfe
- § 13 Ausstattung
- § 14 Aus- und Fortbildung
- § 15 Aufgaben der Katastrophenschutzbehörde

Siebter Abschnitt
Maßnahmen zum Schutz der Gesundheit
- § 16 Koordinierungsmaßnahmen; Ressourcenmanagement
- § 17 Datenerhebung und -verwendung
- § 18 Zusammenarbeit von Bund und Ländern
- § 19 Schutzkommission
- § 20 Unterstützung des Ehrenamtes
- § 21 Planung der gesundheitlichen Versorgung
- § 22 Erweiterung der Einsatzbereitschaft
- § 23 Sanitätsmaterialbevorratung
- § 24 Erste-Hilfe-Ausbildung und Ausbildung von Pflegehilfskräften

Achter Abschnitt
Maßnahmen zum Schutz von Kulturgut
- § 25 Kulturgutschutz

Neunter Abschnitt
Organisationen, Helferinnen und Helfer
- § 26 Mitwirkung der Organisationen
- § 27 Rechtsverhältnisse der Helferinnen und Helfer
- § 28 Persönliche Hilfeleistung

Zehnter Abschnitt
Kosten des Zivilschutzes
- § 29 Kosten

Elfter Abschnitt
Bußgeldvorschriften
- § 30 Bußgeldvorschriften

Zwölfter Abschnitt
Schlußbestimmungen
- § 31 Einschränkungen von Grundrechten
- § 32 Stadtstaatenklausel

Der Bundestag hat mit Zustimmung des Bundesrates das folgende Gesetz beschlossen:

---

[1] Verkündet als Art. 1 ZivilschutzneuordnungsG v. 25 3. 1997 (BGBl. I S. 726); Inkrafttreten gem. Art. 7 Abs. 1 dieses G am 4.4.1997.

Erster Abschnitt
Allgemeine Bestimmungen

§ 1 Aufgaben des Zivilschutzes
(1) ¹Aufgabe des Zivilschutzes ist es, durch nichtmilitärische Maßnahmen die Bevölkerung, ihre Wohnungen und Arbeitsstätten, lebens- oder verteidigungswichtige zivile Dienststellen, Betriebe, Einrichtungen und Anlagen sowie das Kulturgut vor Kriegseinwirkungen zu schützen und deren Folgen zu beseitigen oder zu mildern. ²Behördliche Maßnahmen ergänzen die Selbsthilfe der Bevölkerung.
(2) Zum Zivilschutz gehören insbesondere
1. der Selbstschutz,
2. die Warnung der Bevölkerung,
3. der Schutzbau,
4. die Aufenthaltsregelung,
5. der Katastrophenschutz nach Maßgabe des § 11,
6. Maßnahmen zum Schutz der Gesundheit,
7. Maßnahmen zum Schutz von Kulturgut.

§ 2 Auftragsverwaltung
(1) ¹Soweit die Ausführung dieses Gesetzes den Ländern einschließlich der Gemeinden und Gemeindeverbände obliegt, handeln sie im Auftrage des Bundes. ²Wenn nichts anderes bestimmt ist, richten sich die Zuständigkeit der Behörden und das Verwaltungsverfahren nach den für den Katastrophenschutz geltenden Vorschriften der Länder.
(2) ¹Die Landesregierungen werden ermächtigt, durch Rechtsverordnung zu bestimmen, daß mehrere Gemeinden, kommunale Zusammenschlüsse oder Gemeindeverbände alle oder einzelne Aufgaben des Zivilschutzes gemeinsam wahrnehmen und wer für die Leitung zuständig ist. ²Die Landesregierungen können diese Ermächtigung auf oberste Landesbehörden übertragen.

§ 3 Völkerrechtliche Stellung
(1) Einheiten, Einrichtungen und Anlagen, die für den Zivilschutz eingesetzt werden, haben den Voraussetzungen des Artikels 63 des IV. Genfer Abkommens vom 12. August 1949 zum Schutz von Zivilpersonen in Kriegszeiten (BGBl. 1954 II S. 781) und des Artikels 61 des Zusatzprotokolls zu den Genfer Abkommen vom 12. August 1949 über den Schutz der Opfer internationaler bewaffneter Konflikte (Protokoll I) (BGBl. 1990 II S. 1550) zu entsprechen.
(2) Die Stellung des Deutschen Roten Kreuzes als anerkannte nationale Gesellschaft vom Roten Kreuz sowie die der anderen freiwilligen Hilfsgesellschaften und ihres Personals nach dem humanitären Völkerrecht bleiben unberührt.

§ 4 Zuständigkeit des Bundes für den Schutz der Zivilbevölkerung
(1) Der Bund unterhält ein Bundesamt für Zivilschutz als Bundesoberbehörde; es untersteht dem Bundesministerium des Innern.
(2) ¹Die Verwaltungsaufgaben des Bundes nach diesem Gesetz werden dem Bundesamt für Bevölkerungsschutz und Katastrophenhilfe zugewiesen. ²Dem Bundesamt für Bevölkerungsschutz und Katastrophenhilfe obliegen insbesondere
1. die Unterstützung der fachlich zuständigen obersten Bundesbehörden bei einer einheitlichen Zivilverteidigungsplanung,
2. a) die Unterweisung des mit Fragen der zivilen Verteidigung befaßten Personals sowie die Ausbildung von Führungskräften und Ausbildern des Katastrophenschutzes im Rahmen ihrer Zivilschutzaufgaben,
   b) die Entwicklung von Ausbildungsinhalten des Zivilschutzes, einschließlich des Selbstschutzes,
   c) die Unterstützung der Gemeinden und Gemeindeverbände bei der Erfüllung der Aufgaben nach § 5 Abs. 1 dieses Gesetzes,
3. die Mitwirkung bei der Warnung der Bevölkerung,
4. die Information der Bevölkerung über den Zivilschutz, insbesondere über Schutz- und Hilfeleistungsmöglichkeiten,

C.II.1 Zivilschutz- und Katastrophenhilfegesetz

5. die Aufgabenstellung für technisch-wissenschaftliche Forschung im Benehmen mit den Ländern, die Auswertung von Forschungsergebnissen sowie die Sammlung und Auswertung von Veröffentlichungen auf dem Gebiet der zivilen Verteidigung,
6. die Prüfung von ausschließlich oder überwiegend für den Zivilschutz bestimmten Geräten und Mitteln sowie die Mitwirkung bei der Zulassung, Normung und Qualitätssicherung dieser Gegenstände.

(3) Die der Bundesregierung nach Artikel 85 Abs. 4 des Grundgesetzes auf dem Gebiet des Zivilschutzes zustehenden Befugnisse werden auf das Bundesamt für Bevölkerungsschutz und Katastrophenhilfe übertragen.

Zweiter Abschnitt
Selbstschutz

§ 5 Selbstschutz

(1) Aufbau, Förderung und Leitung des Selbstschutzes der Bevölkerung sowie Förderung des Selbstschutzes der Behörden und Betriebe gegen die besonderen Gefahren, die im Verteidigungsfall drohen, obliegen den Gemeinden.

(2) Für die Unterrichtung und Ausbildung der Bevölkerung sowie in den sonstigen Angelegenheiten des Selbstschutzes können die Gemeinden sich der nach § 26 mitwirkenden Organisationen bedienen.

(3) Die Maßnahmen der kreisangehörigen Gemeinden werden durch die Behörden der allgemeinen Verwaltung auf der Kreisstufe unterstützt.

(4) [1]Im Verteidigungsfall können die Gemeinden allgemeine Anordnungen über das selbstschutzmäßige Verhalten der Bevölkerung bei Angriffen treffen. [2]Die Anordnungen bedürfen keiner besonderen Form.

Dritter Abschnitt
Warnung der Bevölkerung

§ 6 Warnung der Bevölkerung

(1) Der Bund erfaßt die besonderen Gefahren, die der Bevölkerung in einem Verteidigungsfall drohen.

(2) [1]Die für die Warnung bei Katastrophen zuständigen Behörden der Länder warnen im Auftrage des Bundes auch vor den besonderen Gefahren, die der Bevölkerung in einem Verteidigungsfall drohen. [2]Soweit die für den Katastrophenschutz erforderlichen Warnmittel für Zwecke des Zivilschutzes nicht ausreichen, ergänzt der Bund das Instrumentarium.

(3) Die Bundesregierung wird ermächtigt, zur Ausführung dieses Gesetzes das Verfahren für die Warnung der Bevölkerung in einem Verteidigungsfall, insbesondere den Informationsaustausch zwischen Bund und Ländern sowie die Gefahrendurchsage einschließlich der Anordnung vor Verhaltensmaßregeln durch Rechtsverordnung mit Zustimmung des Bundesrates näher zu regeln.

Vierter Abschnitt
Schutzbau

§ 7 Öffentliche Schutzräume

(1) [1]Öffentliche Schutzräume sind die mit Mitteln des Bundes wiederhergestellten Bunker und Stollen sowie die als Mehrzweckbauten in unterirdischen baulichen Anlage errichteten Schutzräume zum Schutz der Bevölkerung. [2]Sie werden von den Gemeinden verwaltet und unterhalten. [3]Einnahmen aus einer friedensmäßigen Nutzung der Schutzräume stehen den Gemeinden zu. [4]Bildet der öffentliche Schutzraum mit anderen Anlagen eine betriebliche Einheit, so kann dem Grundstückseigentümer die Verwaltung und Unterhaltung des Schutzraumes und seiner Ausstattung übertragen werden. [5]Die Kosten sind ihm von der Gemeinde zu erstatten.

(2) [1]An dem Grundstück und den Baulichkeiten dürfen ohne Zustimmung der nach Landesrecht zuständigen Behörde keine Veränderungen vorgenommen werden, die die Benutzung des öffentlichen Schutzraums beeinträchtigen könnten. [2]Bei Bauten im Eigentum des Bundes erteilt die Zustimmung das Bundesministerium des Innern.

(3) Die Absätze 1 und 2 gelten auch für Schutzräume in dem in Artikel 3 des Einigungsvertrages genannten Gebiet, die vom Bundesministerium des Innern als öffentliche Schutzräume anerkannt worden sind, sowie für die Bestandserhaltung der bisher zum Zwecke der gesundheitlichen Versorgung der Bevölkerung im Verteidigungsfall errichteten Schutzbauwerke.

§ 8 Hausschutzräume
(1) ¹Hausschutzräume, die mit Zuschüssen des Bundes oder steuerlich begünstigt gebaut wurden, sind vom Eigentümer oder Nutzungsberechtigten in einem ihrer Bestimmung entsprechenden Zustand zu erhalten. ²Veränderungen, die die Benutzung des Schutzraumes beeinträchtigen könnten, dürfen ohne Zustimmung der nach Landesrecht zuständigen Behörde nicht vorgenommen werden.
(2) Der Eigentümer oder Nutzungsberechtigte hat bei Gefahr den Personen, für die der Schutzraum bestimmt ist, die Mitbenutzung zu gestatten.

§ 9 Baulicher Betriebsschutz
Zum Schutz lebens- oder verteidigungswichtiger Anlagen und Einrichtungen können die obersten Bundesbehörden jeweils für ihren Geschäftsbereich Regelungen für bauliche Schutzmaßnahmen treffen.

Fünfter Abschnitt
Aufenthaltsregelung

§ 10 Aufenthaltsregelung
(1) Zum Schutze vor den besonderen Gefahren, die der Bevölkerung im Verteidigungsfall drohen, oder für Zwecke der Verteidigung können die obersten Landesbehörden oder die von ihnen bestimmten oder nach Landesrecht zuständigen Stellen nach Maßgabe des Artikels 80a des Grundgesetzes anordnen, daß
1. der jeweilige Aufenthaltsort nur mit Erlaubnis verlassen oder ein bestimmtes Gebiet nicht betreten werden darf,
2. die Bevölkerung besonders gefährdeter Gebiete vorübergehend evakuiert wird.

(2) ¹Die Länder, Gemeinden und Gemeindeverbände sind verpflichtet, die zur Durchführung der Evakuierung sowie zur Aufnahme und Versorgung der evakuierten Bevölkerung erforderlichen Vorbereitungen und Maßnahmen zu treffen. ²Die zuständigen Bundesbehörden leisten die erforderliche Unterstützung.

Sechster Abschnitt
Katastrophenschutz im Zivilschutz und Katastrophenhilfe des Bundes

§ 11 Einbeziehung des Katastrophenschutzes
(1) ¹Die nach Landesrecht im Katastrophenschutz mitwirkenden Einheiten und Einrichtungen nehmen auch die Aufgaben zum Schutz der Bevölkerung vor den besonderen Gefahren und Schäden, die im Verteidigungsfall drohen, wahr. ²Sie werden zu diesem Zwecke ergänzend ausgestattet und ausgebildet. ³Das Bundesministerium des Innern legt Art und Umfang der Ergänzung im Benehmen mit der zuständigen obersten Landesbehörde fest.
(2) Die Einheiten und Einrichtungen der Bundesanstalt Technisches Hilfswerk verstärken im Verteidigungsfall den Katastrophenschutz bei der Wahrnehmung der Aufgaben nach Absatz 1.

§ 12 Grundsatz der Katastrophenhilfe
Die Vorhaltungen und Einrichtungen des Bundes für den Zivilschutz stehen den Ländern auch für ihre Aufgaben im Bereich des Katastrophenschutzes zur Verfügung.

§ 13 Ausstattung
(1) Der Bund ergänzt die Ausstattung des Katastrophenschutzes in den Aufgabenbereichen Brandschutz, ABC-Schutz, Sanitätswesen und Betreuung.
(2) ¹Die ergänzende Ausstattung wird vom Bund zur Verfügung gestellt. ²Die Länder teilen die Ausstattung auf die für den Katastrophenschutz zuständigen Behörden auf. ³Diese können die Ausstattung an die Träger der Einheiten und Einrichtungen weitergeben.
(3) Die vom Bund den Ländern für den Zivilschutz zur Verfügung gestellte ergänzende Ausstattung steht den Ländern zusätzlich für Aufgaben im Bereich des Katastrophenschutzes zur Verfügung.

C.II.1 Zivilschutz- und Katastrophenhilfegesetz

(4) Helferinnen und Helfer in Einheiten und Einrichtungen des Katastrophenschutzes, die für eine Verwendung in den in Absatz 1 genannten Aufgabenbereichen vorgesehen sind, erhalten bei ihrer Ausbildung eine ergänzende Zivilschutzausbildung für die Wahrnehmung der Aufgaben nach § 11.

§ 14 Aus- und Fortbildung

¹Die Aus- und Fortbildungsmaßnahmen des Bundesamtes für Bevölkerungsschutz und Katastrophenhilfe nach § 4 Abs. 1 Satz 2 Nr. 2 Buchstabe a dienen zugleich den Ländern für die Vorbereitung ihrer Entscheidungsträger, Führungskräfte und sonstigen Fachkräfte auf die Bewältigung von Katastrophen und Unglücksfällen und umfassen insbesondere auch die Planung, Durchführung und Auswertung von ressort- und länderübergreifenden Krisenmanagementübungen. ²Die Aus- und Fortbildungsmaßnahmen des Bundes bauen auf der Ausbildung der Länder im Bereich des Katastrophenschutzes auf und ergänzen diese.

§ 15 Aufgaben der Katastrophenschutzbehörde

¹Die für den Katastrophenschutz zuständige Behörde leitet und koordiniert alle Hilfsmaßnahmen in ihrem Bereich. ²Sie beaufsichtigt die Einheiten und Einrichtungen des Katastrophenschutzes bei der Durchführung der Aufgaben nach diesem Gesetz. ³Sie kann den Trägern der Einheiten in ihrem Bereich Weisungen zur Durchführung von Veranstaltungen zur ergänzenden Aus- und Fortbildung sowie zur Unterbringung und Pflege der ergänzenden Ausstattung erteilen. ⁴Bei Einsätzen und angeordneten Übungen nach diesem Gesetz unterstehen ihr auch die Einheiten und Einrichtungen der Bundesanstalt Technisches Hilfswerk, die nach § 1 Absatz 2 Nummer 1 des THW-Gesetzes in der jeweils geltenden Fassung beauftragt und ermächtigt ist, technische Hilfe im Zivilschutz zu leisten.

Siebter Abschnitt
Maßnahmen zum Schutz der Gesundheit

§ 16 Koordinierungsmaßnahmen; Ressourcenmanagement

(1) Die Einrichtungen und Vorhaltungen des Bundesamtes für Bevölkerungsschutz und Katastrophenhilfe, insbesondere im Bereich Lageerfassung und -bewertung sowie Nachweis und Vermittlung von Engpassressourcen, können auch im Rahmen der Amtshilfe nach Artikel 35 Abs. 1 des Grundgesetzes zur Unterstützung eines Landes verwendet werden.
(2) ¹Die Unterstützung nach Absatz 1 umfasst auch die Koordinierung von Hilfsmaßnahmen durch den Bund, wenn das betroffene Land oder die betroffenen Länder darum ersuchen. ²Die Festlegung, welche Maßnahmen vom Bund koordiniert werden, trifft der Bund im Einvernehmen mit dem betroffenen Land oder den betroffenen Ländern.
(3) Die Zuständigkeit der Länder für das operative Krisenmanagement bleibt unberührt.
(4) ¹Der Bund hält Koordinierungsinstrumente vor. ²Der Aufruf bundeseigener Krisenmanagementstrukturen für die Erfüllung seiner eigenen Aufgaben bleibt unberührt.

§ 17 Datenerhebung und -verwendung

(1) ¹Soweit es zur Erfüllung seiner Aufgaben nach § 16 erforderlich ist, darf das Bundesamt für Bevölkerungsschutz und Katastrophenhilfe Angaben, einschließlich personenbezogener Daten, über Hilfeleistungspotenziale und über Objekte und infrastrukturelle Einrichtungen, die für den Zivil- und Katastrophenschutz relevant sind, erheben und verwenden. ²Hierzu zählen insbesondere Angaben über
1. personelle, materielle und infrastrukturelle Potenziale der allgemeinen Gefahrenabwehr,
2. Betriebe, Einrichtungen und Anlagen, von denen bei einer Schadenslage zusätzliche Gefahren ausgehen können (Risikopotenziale),
3. Infrastrukturen, bei deren Ausfall die Versorgung der Bevölkerung erheblich beeinträchtigt wird (kritische Infrastrukturen), und
4. Objekte, die aufgrund ihrer Symbolkraft oder Dimension als mögliche Ziele von Angriffen in Betracht kommen (gefährdete Objekte).

(2) ¹Die nach Absatz 1 erhobenen personenbezogenen Daten dürfen nur an die im Zivil- und Katastrophenschutz mitwirkenden öffentlichen und nichtöffentlichen Stellen übermittelt werden und nur, soweit die Kenntnis der Daten aus Sicht des Bundesamtes für Bevölkerungsschutz und Katastrophenhilfe für Zwecke der Lageerfassung oder -bewertung oder zum Nachweis oder zur Vermittlung von Engpassressourcen erforderlich ist. ²Eines Ersuchens dieser Stellen um Übermittlung bedarf es nicht.

(3) ¹Das Nähere regelt das Bundesministerium des Innern durch Rechtsverordnung mit Zustimmung des Bundesrates. ²Dabei sind insbesondere die Datenarten, die erhoben und verwendet werden dürfen, sowie Fristen für die Löschung der Daten zu bestimmen.

§ 18 Zusammenarbeit von Bund und Ländern
(1) ¹Der Bund erstellt im Zusammenwirken mit den Ländern eine bundesweite Risikoanalyse für den Zivilschutz. ²Das Bundesministerium des Innern unterrichtet den Deutschen Bundestag über die Ergebnisse der Risikoanalyse nach Satz 1 ab 2010 jährlich. ³Im Jahr ihrer Fertigstellung unterrichtet es den Deutschen Bundestag darüber hinaus über die von der Schutzkommission erstellten Gefahrenberichte.
(2) Der Bund berät und unterstützt die Länder im Rahmen seiner Zuständigkeiten beim Schutz kritischer Infrastrukturen.
(3) Im Benehmen mit den Ländern entwickelt der Bund Standards und Rahmenkonzepte für den Zivilschutz, die den Ländern zugleich als Empfehlungen für ihre Aufgaben im Bereich des Katastrophenschutzes dienen, sofern diese für ein effektives gesamtstaatliches Zusammenwirken der für den Katastrophenschutz zuständigen Behörden auch bei Naturkatastrophen und besonders schweren Unglücksfällen erforderlich sind.

§ 19 Schutzkommission
(1) Beim Bundesministerium des Innern besteht eine Kommission zum Schutz der Zivilbevölkerung.
(2) Sie berät die Bundesregierung ehrenamtlich in wissenschaftlichen und technischen Fragen des Zivilschutzes und der Katastrophenhilfe.
(3) Die organisatorische Betreuung der Kommission obliegt dem Bundesamt für Bevölkerungsschutz und Katastrophenhilfe.

§ 20 Unterstützung des Ehrenamtes
Der Bund unterstützt das Ehrenamt als Grundlage des Zivil- und Katastrophenschutzes.

§ 21 Planung der gesundheitlichen Versorgung
(1) ¹Die nach Landesrecht zuständigen Behörden haben ergänzende Maßnahmen zur gesundheitlichen Versorgung der Bevölkerung im Verteidigungsfall zu planen. ²Sie ermitteln insbesondere die Nutzungs- und Erweiterungsmöglichkeiten der vorhandenen Einrichtungen sowie den voraussichtlichen personellen und materiellen Bedarf und melden ihn an die für die Bedarfsdeckung zuständigen Behörden. ³Mit den für das Gesundheits- und Sanitätswesen der Bundeswehr zuständigen Stellen ist eng zusammenzuarbeiten. ⁴Soweit die zuständigen Behörden nach Satz 1 nicht die Gesundheitsämter sind, ist deren Mitwirkung bei der Planung sicherzustellen.
(2) Die gesetzlichen Berufsvertretungen der Ärzte, Zahnärzte, Tierärzte und Apotheker, die Kassenärztlichen und Kassenzahnärztlichen Vereinigungen sowie die Träger der Einrichtungen der gesundheitlichen Versorgung und ihre Verbände wirken bei der Planung und Bedarfsermittlung mit und unterstützen die Behörden.
(3) ¹Für Zwecke der Planung nach Absatz 1 haben die Träger von Einrichtungen der gesundheitlichen Versorgung auf Verlangen Auskünfte zu erteilen und das Betreten ihrer Geschäfts- und Betriebsräume während der üblichen Geschäfts- und Betriebszeiten zu dulden. ²Die hierbei gewonnenen Informationen dürfen nur insoweit verwertet werden, als dies für Zwecke dieses Gesetzes oder für die Erfüllung von Katastrophenschutzaufgaben erforderlich ist.
(4) Die zuständigen Behörden können anordnen, daß
1. die Träger von Krankenhäusern Einsatz- und Alarmpläne für die gesundheitliche Versorgung,
2. die Veterinärämter Pläne für die Tierseuchenbekämpfung
aufstellen und fortschreiben.

§ 22 Erweiterung der Einsatzbereitschaft
(1) Nach Freigabe durch die Bundesregierung können die nach Landesrecht zuständigen Behörden anordnen, daß
1. Einrichtungen der gesundheitlichen Versorgung ihre Leistungsfähigkeit auf die Anforderungen im Verteidigungsfall umzustellen, zu erweitern und ihre Einsatzbereitschaft herzustellen haben,
2. den für den Katastrophenschutz zuständigen Behörden die Rettungsleitstellen ihres Bereiches unterstellt werden und daß diese die ihnen zugeordneten Dienste in ständiger Einsatzbereitschaft

C.II.1 Zivilschutz- und Katastrophenhilfegesetz

zu halten und unter ärztlicher Leitung die Belegung von stationären Einrichtungen zu regeln haben,
3. jede der stationären Behandlung dienende Einrichtung der zuständigen Rettungsleitstelle anzuschließen ist.

(2) ¹Zur Sicherstellung von Arbeitsleistungen in Einrichtungen der gesundheitlichen Versorgung wird die Bundesregierung ermächtigt, durch Rechtsverordnung zu bestimmen, daß sich Wehrpflichtige und Frauen, die nach § 2 Nr. 2 und 3 des Arbeitssicherstellungsgesetzes in ein Arbeitsverhältnis verpflichtet werden können, bei der zuständigen Agentur für Arbeit zu melden haben, soweit sie als Angehörige der Heil- und Heilhilfsberufe im Zeitpunkt des Eintritts der Meldepflicht seit weniger als zehn Jahren nicht in ihrem Beruf tätig sind. ²Die Rechtsverordnung regelt insbesondere den Beginn der Meldepflicht, die meldepflichtigen Berufsgruppen und die für die Verpflichtung erforderlichen meldepflichtigen Angaben sowie den Schutz von personenbezogenen Informationen unter Berücksichtigung des Grundsatzes der Zweckbindung.

(3) ¹Die Rechtsverordnung nach Absatz 2 darf nur erlassen werden, wenn und soweit der Bedarf an Arbeitskräften nicht mehr auf freiwilliger Grundlage gedeckt werden kann. ²Sie ist aufzuheben, wenn Bundestag und Bundesrat es verlangen. ³Satz 2 gilt entsprechend für die Anordnungen nach Absatz 1.

§ 23 Sanitätsmaterialbevorratung

(1) ¹Der Bund stellt den Ländern für die gesundheitliche Versorgung der Bevölkerung im Verteidigungsfall ergänzend Sanitätsmaterial zur Verfügung. ²Dieses steht den Ländern für ihre Aufgaben im Bereich des Katastrophenschutzes zusätzlich zur Verfügung. ³Die Länder können das Sanitätsmaterial in ihre Katastrophenschutzvorsorge einplanen.

(2) ¹Das Bundesministerium des Innern kann im Einvernehmen mit dem Bundesministerium für Gesundheit durch Rechtsverordnung mit Zustimmung des Bundesrates anordnen, dass nach Maßgabe des Artikels 80a des Grundgesetzes ausreichend Sanitätsmaterial von Herstellungsbetrieben, Großhandlungen sowie öffentlichen und Krankenhausapotheken vorgehalten wird, um die Deckung von zusätzlichem Bedarf im Verteidigungsfall sicherzustellen. ²Die §§ 4, 8 und 13 bis 16 des Wirtschaftssicherstellungsgesetzes in der Fassung vom 31. Oktober 2006 sind entsprechend anzuwenden.

§ 24 Erste-Hilfe-Ausbildung und Ausbildung von Pflegehilfskräften

Der Bund fördert die Ausbildung der Bevölkerung durch die nach § 26 Abs. 1 mitwirkenden privaten Organisationen
1. in Erster Hilfe mit Selbstschutzinhalten und
2. zu Pflegehilfskräften.

Achter Abschnitt
Maßnahmen zum Schutz von Kulturgut

§ 25 Kulturgutschutz

Die Maßnahmen zum Schutz von Kulturgut richten sich nach dem Gesetz zu der Konvention vom 14. Mai 1954 zum Schutz von Kulturgut bei bewaffneten Konflikten (BGBl. 1967 II S. 1233), geändert durch Artikel 1 des Gesetzes vom 10. August 1971 (BGBl. II S. 1025).

Neunter Abschnitt
Organisationen, Helferinnen und Helfer

§ 26 Mitwirkung der Organisationen

(1) ¹Die Mitwirkung der öffentlichen und privaten Organisationen bei der Erfüllung der Aufgaben nach diesem Gesetz richtet sich nach den landesrechtlichen Vorschriften für den Katastrophenschutz. ²Für die Mitwirkung geeignet sind insbesondere der Arbeiter-Samariter-Bund, die Deutsche Lebensrettungsgesellschaft, das Deutsche Rote Kreuz, die Johanniter-Unfall-Hilfe und der Malteser-Hilfsdienst.

(2) Die mitwirkenden öffentlichen und privaten Organisationen bilden die erforderliche Zahl von Helferinnen und Helfern aus, sorgen für die sachgerechte Unterbringung und Pflege der ergänzenden Ausstattung und stellen die Einsatzbereitschaft ihrer Einheiten und Einrichtungen sicher.

(3) ¹Die mitwirkenden privaten Organisationen erhalten nach Maßgabe des § 29 Mittel zur Wahrnehmung ihrer Aufgaben nach diesem Gesetz. ²Sie können die ihnen zugewiesene ergänzende Ausstattung

für eigene Zwecke nutzen, soweit hierdurch die Aufgaben des Katastrophenschutzes und des Zivilschutzes nicht beeinträchtigt werden.
(4) ¹Die Mitwirkung von anderen Behörden, Stellen und Trägern öffentlicher Aufgaben bestimmt sich nach dem Katastrophenschutzrecht des Landes. ²Die Behörden und Stellen des Bundes sowie die seiner Aufsicht unterstehenden juristischen Personen des öffentlichen Rechts sind zur Mitwirkung verpflichtet.

§ 27 Rechtsverhältnisse der Helferinnen und Helfer
(1) Rechte und Pflichten der im Zivilschutz mitwirkenden Helferinnen und Helfer richten sich nach den landesrechtlichen Vorschriften für den Katastrophenschutz, soweit durch dieses Gesetz oder andere Rechtsvorschriften des Bundes nichts anderes bestimmt ist.
(2) Für den ehrenamtlichen Dienst im Zivil- und Katastrophenschutz vom Wehrdienst oder Zivildienst freigestellte Helfer sind zur Mitwirkung im Zivil- und Katastrophenschutz verpflichtet.

§ 28 Persönliche Hilfeleistung
(1) ¹Die für den Katastrophenschutz zuständige Behörde kann Männer und Frauen vom vollendeten 18. bis zum vollendeten 60. Lebensjahr verpflichten, bei der Bekämpfung der besonderen Gefahren und Schäden, die im Verteidigungsfall drohen, Hilfe zu leisten, wenn die vorhandenen Kräfte im Einsatzfall nicht ausreichen. ²Die zur Hilfeleistung Herangezogenen oder die freiwillig mit Einverständnis der zuständigen Stellen bei der Hilfeleistung Mitwirkenden haben für die Dauer der Hilfeleistung die Rechtsstellung einer Helferin oder eines Helfers. ³Bei der Verpflichtung ist auf den Bedarf von Behörden und Betrieben mit lebens- oder verteidigungswichtigen Aufgaben Rücksicht zu nehmen.
(2) ¹Die Verpflichteten können als Helferinnen oder Helfer den nach § 26 Abs. 1 mitwirkenden Organisationen zugewiesen werden. ²Diese können den Einsatz ablehnen, wenn die Zugewiesenen als Helferinnen oder Helfer für die Fachaufgaben ungeeignet sind oder andere berechtigte Gründe gegen ihren Einsatz in der Organisation sprechen.
(3) Die Verpflichtung darf einen Zeitraum von zehn Werktagen im Vierteljahr nicht überschreiten.

Zehnter Abschnitt
Kosten des Zivilschutzes

§ 29 Kosten
(1) Der Bund trägt die Kosten, die den Ländern, Gemeinden und Gemeindeverbänden durch dieses Gesetz, durch die allgemeinen Verwaltungsvorschriften auf Grund dieses Gesetzes und durch Weisungen der zuständigen Bundesbehörden entstehen; personelle und sächliche Verwaltungskosten werden nicht übernommen.
(2) ¹Die Ausgaben sind für Rechnung des Bundes zu leisten; die damit zusammenhängenden Einnahmen sind an den Bund abzuführen. ²Auf diese Ausgaben und Einnahmen sind die Vorschriften über das Haushaltsrecht des Bundes anzuwenden. ³Die für die Durchführung des Haushaltes verantwortlichen Bundesbehörden können ihre Befugnisse auf die zuständigen obersten Landesbehörden übertragen und zulassen, daß auf diese Ausgaben und Einnahmen die landesrechtlichen Vorschriften über die Kassen- und Buchführung der zuständigen Landes- und Gemeindebehörden angewandt werden.
(3) ¹Der Bund trägt die planmäßigen fahrzeug- und helferbezogenen Kosten nach § 13 ab dem Jahr 2010 nach folgenden Maßgaben: Pauschal erstattet werden die Kosten für
1. die Unterbringung der Fahrzeuge und der persönlichen ABC-Schutzausrüstung,
2. die ärztliche Untersuchung und die Ausbildung der Helferinnen und Helfer und
3. die Gewährleistung der jederzeitigen Einsatzbereitschaft der Analytischen Task Forces zur Unterstützung der örtlichen Einsatzleitung mit Spezialtechnik bei komplexen ABC-Lagen.

²Die Kosten der Wartung und Instandsetzung der ergänzenden Ausstattung werden gegen Nachweis erstattet. ³Im Verhältnis zwischen den für den Katastrophenschutz zuständigen Behörden und den privaten Organisationen richtet sich der Nachweis der Ausgaben und die Belegpflicht nach den Bestimmungen der Bundeshaushaltsordnung und den dazu erlassenen Verwaltungsvorschriften über das Nachweisverfahren bei Zuwendungen.
(4) Die Kosten, die dem Bund durch Verwendung von ihm finanzierter Ausstattung und Anlagen des Zivilschutzes bei Katastrophen und Unglücksfällen entstehen, sind ihm von dem Aufgabenträger zu

erstatten, es sei denn, der Einsatz dient gleichzeitig überwiegend zivilschutzbezogenen Ausbildungszwecken.
(5) Kosten, die für Maßnahmen nach § 22 Abs. 1 anfallen, sind dem Pflichtigen zu ersetzen.

Elfter Abschnitt
Bußgeldvorschriften

§ 30 Bußgeldvorschriften
(1) Ordnungswidrig handelt, wer vorsätzlich oder fahrlässig einer vollziehbaren Anordnung nach § 5 Abs. 4 Satz 1, § 10 Abs. 1, § 21 Abs. 4 oder § 22 Abs. 1 zuwiderhandelt.
(2) Ordnungswidrig handelt, wer vorsätzlich oder fahrlässig
1. einer Rechtsverordnung nach § 22 Abs. 2 Satz 1, soweit sie für ein bestimmten Tatbestand auf diese Bußgeldvorschrift verweist,
2. einer Vorschrift des § 27 Abs. 2 über die Mitwirkung oder
3. einer vollziehbaren Anordnung nach § 28 Abs. 1 Satz 1

zuwiderhandelt.
(3) Die Ordnungswidrigkeit kann in den Fällen des Absatzes 1 mit einer Geldbuße bis zu zehntausend Euro, in den Fällen des Absatzes 2 mit einer Geldbuße bis zu tausend Euro geahndet werden.
(4) Verwaltungsbehörde im Sinne des § 36 Abs. 1 Nr. 1 des Gesetzes über Ordnungswidrigkeiten ist
1. in den Fällen des Absatzes 1 die Behörde, welche die Anordnung erlassen hat,
2. in den Fällen des Absatzes 2 Nr. 1 die Agentur für Arbeit,
3. in den Fällen des Absatzes 2 Nr. 2 die Bundesanstalt Technisches Hilfswerk für ihre Helfer, im übrigen und in den Fällen des Absatzes 2 Nr. 3 die für den Katastrophenschutz zuständige Behörde.

Zwölfter Abschnitt
Schlußbestimmungen

§ 31 Einschränkungen von Grundrechten
Die Grundrechte der körperlichen Unversehrtheit (Artikel 2 Abs. 2 Satz 1 des Grundgesetzes), der Freiheit der Person (Artikel 2 Abs. 2 Satz 2 des Grundgesetzes), der Freizügigkeit (Artikel 11 Abs. 1 des Grundgesetzes) und der Unverletzlichkeit der Wohnung (Artikel 13 des Grundgesetzes) werden nach Maßgabe dieses Gesetzes eingeschränkt.

§ 32 Stadtstaatenklausel
Die Senate der Länder Berlin, Bremen und Hamburg werden ermächtigt, entsprechend dem besonderen Verwaltungsaufbau ihrer Länder die Zuständigkeit von Behörden abweichend von den Vorschriften dieses Gesetzes zu regeln und insbesondere zu bestimmen, welche Stellen die Aufgaben der Gemeinden und Gemeindeverbände nach Maßgabe dieses Gesetzes wahrzunehmen haben.

Gesetz über die Nutzung und Sicherung von Archivgut des Bundes (Bundesarchivgesetz – BArchG)[1)2)]

Vom 10. März 2017 (BGBl. I S. 410)
(FNA 224-28)
zuletzt geändert durch Art. 2 G zum Erlass und zur Änd. bundesrechtl. Vorschriften in Bezug auf die Übernahme der Angehörigenbenachrichtigungs-Aufgabenübertragung vom 4. Dezember 2018 (BGBl. I S. 2257 iVm Bek v. 12.4.2019, BGBl. I S. 496)

§ 1 Begriffsbestimmungen

Im Sinne dieses Gesetzes ist oder sind
1. Angehörige: Ehegatten, Lebenspartner sowie Kinder, Enkelkinder, Großeltern, Eltern und Geschwister der Betroffenen;
2. Archivgut des Bundes: Unterlagen von bleibendem Wert, die das Bundesarchiv nach Ablauf der Aufbewahrungsfristen dauerhaft übernommen hat; Unterlagen aus dem Zwischenarchiv des Bundesarchivs, deren Aufbewahrungsfristen bereits abgelaufen sind, deren bleibender Wert jedoch noch nicht festgestellt worden ist, werden wie Archivgut des Bundes behandelt;
3. Betroffene: bestimmte oder bestimmbare natürliche Personen, zu denen Informationen vorliegen;
4. deutsche Kinofilme: Kinofilme, deren Hersteller ihren Wohnsitz, Sitz oder eine Niederlassung in Deutschland haben; im Fall einer Koproduktion muss einer der Hersteller seinen Wohnsitz, seinen Sitz oder eine Niederlassung in Deutschland haben;
5. Entstehung: der Zeitpunkt der letzten inhaltlichen Bearbeitung der Unterlagen eines Vorgangs;
6. Kinofilme: Filmwerke,
   a) die für eine öffentliche Aufführung in einem Kino bestimmt sind oder auf einem national oder international bedeutsamen Festival oder bei einer national oder international bedeutsamen Preisverleihung öffentlich aufgeführt werden und
   b) bei denen nicht im Sinne von § 3 Absatz 4 des Gesetzes über die Deutsche Nationalbibliothek vom 22. Juni 2006 (BGBl. I S. 1338), das durch Artikel 15 Absatz 62 des Gesetzes vom 5. Februar 2009 (BGBl. I S. 160) geändert worden ist, die Musik im Vordergrund steht;
7. national oder international bedeutsame Festivals und Preisverleihungen: die Festivals und Preisverleihungen, einschließlich sämtlicher Festivalreihen, die genannt werden in der jeweils geltenden Fassung
   a) des Filmförderungsgesetzes vom 23. Dezember 2016 (BGBl. I S. 3413) und
   b) der zum Filmförderungsgesetz gehörenden Richtlinien;
8. öffentliche Stellen des Bundes: die Verfassungsorgane des Bundes, die Behörden und Gerichte des Bundes, die bundesunmittelbaren Körperschaften, Anstalten und Stiftungen des öffentlichen Rechts und die sonstigen Stellen des Bundes;
9. Unterlagen: Aufzeichnungen jeder Art, unabhängig von der Art ihrer Speicherung;
10. Unterlagen von bleibendem Wert: Unterlagen,
    a) denen insbesondere wegen ihrer politischen, rechtlichen, wirtschaftlichen, sozialen oder kulturellen Inhalte besondere Bedeutung zukommt
       aa) für die Erforschung und das Verständnis von Geschichte und Gegenwart, auch im Hinblick auf künftige Entwicklungen,
       bb) für die Sicherung berechtigter Interessen der Bürger und Bürgerinnen oder
       cc) für die Gesetzgebung, vollziehende Gewalt oder Rechtsprechung, oder
    b) die nach einer Rechtsvorschrift oder Vereinbarung dauerhaft aufzubewahren sind;
11. Zwischenarchivgut des Bundes: Unterlagen, die das Bundesarchiv vor Ablauf der Aufbewahrungsfristen vorläufig übernommen hat und in einem Zwischenarchiv oder digitalen Zwischenarchiv verwahrt.

---

1) Verkündet als Art. 1 G v. 10.3.2017 (BGBl. I S. 410); Inkrafttreten gem. Art. 6 dieses G am 16.3.2017.
2) Siehe bis zum 15.3.2017 das Bundesarchivgesetz v. 6.1.1988 (BGBl. I S. 62).

C.III.1 Bundesarchivgesetz

§ 2 Organisation des Bundesarchivs
Der Bund unterhält ein Bundesarchiv als selbstständige Bundesoberbehörde, die der Dienst- und Fachaufsicht der für Kultur und Medien zuständigen obersten Bundesbehörde untersteht.

§ 3 Aufgaben des Bundesarchivs
(1) ¹Das Bundesarchiv hat die Aufgabe, das Archivgut des Bundes auf Dauer zu sichern, nutzbar zu machen und wissenschaftlich zu verwerten. ²Es gewährleistet den Zugang zum Archivgut des Bundes unter Wahrung des Schutzes privater oder öffentlicher Belange. ³Dies kann auch durch Digitalisierung und öffentliche Zugänglichmachung im Internet geschehen.

(2) ¹Das Bundesarchiv verwahrt Unterlagen der folgenden Stellen als Archivgut des Bundes, wenn es den bleibenden Wert dieser Unterlagen festgestellt hat:
1. Unterlagen der öffentlichen Stellen des Bundes,
2. Unterlagen der Stellen des Deutschen Reiches und des Deutschen Bundes,
3. Unterlagen der Stellen der Besatzungszonen,
4. Unterlagen der Stellen der Deutschen Demokratischen Republik,
5. Unterlagen der Sozialistischen Einheitspartei Deutschlands, der mit dieser Partei verbundenen Organisationen und juristischen Personen sowie der Massenorganisationen der Deutschen Demokratischen Republik und
6. Unterlagen der anderen Parteien und der mit diesen Parteien verbundenen Organisationen und juristischen Personen der Deutschen Demokratischen Republik.

²Das Bundesarchiv stellt den bleibenden Wert der Unterlagen im Benehmen mit der anbietenden Stelle fest.

(3) Das Bundesarchiv kann auch Unterlagen anderer als der in § 1 Nummer 8 genannten öffentlichen Stellen sowie Unterlagen nichtöffentlicher Einrichtungen und natürlicher Personen als Archivgut des Bundes übernehmen oder erwerben, wenn ihm diese Unterlagen angeboten werden und es den bleibenden Wert dieser Unterlagen festgestellt hat.

(4) ¹Das Bundesarchiv berät die öffentlichen Stellen des Bundes im Rahmen seiner Zuständigkeit bei der Verwaltung und Sicherung ihrer Unterlagen. ²Bei der Einführung neuer Systeme der Informationstechnologie insbesondere zur Führung elektronischer Akten gemäß § 6 des E-Government-Gesetzes vom 25. Juli 2013 (BGBl. I S. 2749) oder bei der wesentlichen Änderung solcher Systeme ist das Bundesarchiv rechtzeitig zu informieren, wenn hierbei anbietungspflichtige Unterlagen entstehen können.

(5) Die Bundesregierung kann dem Bundesarchiv andere als in diesem Gesetz oder in anderen Gesetzen genannte Aufgaben des Bundes übertragen, wenn
1. diese Aufgaben in unmittelbarem sachlichem Zusammenhang mit dem Archivwesen des Bundes oder mit der Erforschung der deutschen Geschichte anhand des Archivguts des Bundes stehen und
2. es erforderlich ist, dass diese Aufgaben zentral durch das Bundesarchiv wahrgenommen werden.

(6) Rechtsvorschriften des Bundes, durch die anderen Stellen Archivaufgaben übertragen sind, bleiben unberührt.

§ 3a Wahrnehmung besonderer Aufgaben
(1) ¹Die Aufgaben der aufgelösten „Deutschen Dienststelle für die Benachrichtigung der nächsten Angehörigen von Gefallenen der ehemaligen deutschen Wehrmacht (WASt)" werden vom Bundesarchiv wahrgenommen. ²Das Bundesarchiv verwahrt deren Unterlagen zum Schicksal von Militärpersonen und diesen in personenstandsrechtlicher Hinsicht gleichgestellten Personen infolge des Ersten und Zweiten Weltkrieges und führt die anhängigen Verwaltungsverfahren fort.

(2) ¹Das Bundesarchiv verwahrt die in Absatz 1 bezeichneten Unterlagen im öffentlichen Interesse. ²Es nimmt darüber hinaus insbesondere folgende Aufgaben wahr:
1. Klärung von Einzelschicksalen,
2. Kriegssterbefallanzeigen,
3. Kriegsgräberangelegenheiten und
4. Erteilung sonstiger personenbezogener Auskünfte.

³Zur Erfüllung seiner Aufgaben nach Satz 2 erteilt das Bundesarchiv mündliche und schriftliche Auskünfte einschließlich erforderlicher Bescheinigungen oder Stellungnahmen an Betroffene, Angehörige, öffentliche und nicht öffentliche Stellen.

(3) ¹Ergänzend zu Absatz 2 gelten für die Unterlagen die Zugangsvorschriften der §§ 10 bis 16 entsprechend. ²Soweit in Absatz 1 bezeichnete Unterlagen nicht mehr bearbeitet werden und ihnen bleibender Wert zukommt, können sie als Archivgut gewidmet werden.

§ 4 Stiftung „Archiv der Parteien und Massenorganisationen der DDR"

(1) Die „Stiftung Archiv der Parteien und Massenorganisationen der DDR" ist eine unselbständige Stiftung des öffentlichen Rechts im Bundesarchiv.

(2) ¹Die Stiftung hat die Aufgabe, Unterlagen von Stellen nach § 3 Absatz 2 Nummer 5 und 6 als Archivgut des Bundes zu übernehmen, auf Dauer zu sichern, nutzbar zu machen und zu ergänzen. ²Dies gilt auch für Bibliotheksbestände zur deutschen Geschichte, insbesondere für solche, die in historischem oder sachlichem Zusammenhang mit der deutschen und internationalen Arbeiterbewegung stehen. ³§ 3 Absatz 1 Satz 2 ist entsprechend anzuwenden.

(3) Die in § 11 Absatz 1 genannte Schutzfrist ist nicht auf die Bestände der Stiftung anzuwenden.

(4) Einzelheiten zu Organisation, Aufgaben und Vermögen der Stiftung werden durch die für Kultur und Medien zuständige oberste Bundesbehörde geregelt.

§ 5 Anbietung und Abgabe von Unterlagen

(1) ¹Die öffentlichen Stellen des Bundes haben dem Bundesarchiv oder, im Fall des § 7, dem zuständigen Landes- oder Kommunalarchiv alle Unterlagen, die bei ihnen vorhanden sind, in ihr Eigentum übergegangen sind oder ihnen zur Nutzung überlassen worden sind, zur Übernahme anzubieten, wenn

1. sie die Unterlagen zur Erfüllung ihrer öffentlichen Aufgaben einschließlich der Wahrung der Sicherheit der Bundesrepublik Deutschland oder eines ihrer Länder nicht mehr benötigen und
2. ihnen die weitere Aufbewahrung der Unterlagen nicht durch besondere Rechtsvorschriften gestattet ist.

²Vorbehaltlich des Satzes 1 sollen Unterlagen spätestens 30 Jahre nach ihrer Entstehung dem Bundesarchiv angeboten werden.

(2) ¹Zur Feststellung des bleibenden Werts ist den Mitarbeitern des Bundesarchivs im Einvernehmen mit der zuständigen öffentlichen Stelle des Bundes Einsicht in die nach Maßgabe des Absatzes 1 anzubietenden Unterlagen und die dazugehörigen Registraturhilfsmittel zu gewähren. ²Wird der bleibende Wert der Unterlagen festgestellt, hat die anbietende öffentliche Stelle die Unterlagen mit Ablieferungsverzeichnissen an das Bundesarchiv abzugeben. ³Das Bundesarchiv kann auf die Anbietung und Abgabe von Unterlagen ohne bleibenden Wert verzichten.

(3) ¹Werden elektronische Unterlagen zur Übernahme angeboten, legt das Bundesarchiv den Zeitpunkt der Übermittlung vorab im Einvernehmen mit der anbietenden öffentlichen Stelle des Bundes fest. ²Die Form der Übermittlung und das Datenformat richten sich nach dem für die Bundesverwaltung verbindlich festgelegten Standards. ³Sofern für die Form der Übermittlung und das Datenformat kein Standard für die Bundesverwaltung verbindlich festgelegt wurde, sind diese im Einvernehmen mit der abgebenden öffentlichen Stelle des Bundes festzulegen. ⁴Stellt das Bundesarchiv den bleibenden Wert der elektronischen Unterlagen fest, hat die anbietende öffentliche Stelle des Bundes nach Ablauf der Aufbewahrungsfrist die bei ihr verbliebenen Kopien dieser Unterlagen nach dem Stand der Technik zu löschen, es sei denn, sie benötigt die Kopien noch für Veröffentlichungen; über die Löschung ist ein Nachweis zu fertigen. ⁵Elektronische Unterlagen, die einer laufenden Aktualisierung unterliegen, sind unter den Voraussetzungen der Sätze 1 bis 3 zu bestimmten, einvernehmlich zwischen Bundesarchiv und abgebender Stelle festzulegenden Stichtagen ebenfalls anzubieten. ⁶Satz 5 ist nicht auf Unterlagen anzuwenden, die nach § 6 Absatz 1 Satz 2 und Absatz 2 von der Anbietungspflicht ausgenommen sind.

(4) Die gesetzgebenden Körperschaften entscheiden in eigener Zuständigkeit, ob sie dem Bundesarchiv Unterlagen anbieten und als Archivgut des Bundes abgeben.

(5) Die Verarbeitung personenbezogener Daten für archivische Zwecke ist zulässig, wenn schutzwürdige Belange Betroffener nicht beeinträchtigt werden.

C.III.1 Bundesarchivgesetz

§ 6 Anbietung und Abgabe von Unterlagen, die einer Geheimhaltungs-, Vernichtungs- oder Löschungspflicht unterliegen

(1) ¹Die öffentlichen Stellen des Bundes haben dem Bundesarchiv oder, im Fall des § 7, dem zuständigen Landes- oder Kommunalarchiv auch Unterlagen zur Übernahme anzubieten, die den Rechtsvorschriften des Bundes über die Geheimhaltung oder § 30 der Abgabenordnung in der Fassung der Bekanntmachung vom 1. Oktober 2002 (BGBl. I S. 3866; 2003 I S. 61), die zuletzt durch Artikel 19 Absatz 12 des Gesetzes vom 23. Dezember 2016 (BGBl. I S. 3234) geändert worden ist, unterliegen. ²Unterlagen der Nachrichtendienste sind anzubieten, wenn sie deren Verfügungsberechtigung unterliegen und zwingende Gründe des nachrichtendienstlichen Quellen- und Methodenschutzes sowie der Schutz der Identität der bei ihnen beschäftigten Personen einer Abgabe nicht entgegenstehen.
(2) Von der Anbietungspflicht ausgenommen sind
1. Unterlagen, deren Offenbarung gegen das Brief-, Post- oder Fernmeldegeheimnis verstößt, sowie
2. Unterlagen, die nach gesetzlichen Vorschriften vernichtet oder gelöscht werden müssen und die nach diesen gesetzlichen Vorschriften nicht ersatzweise den zuständigen öffentlichen Archiven angeboten werden dürfen.
(3) ¹Das Bundesarchiv hat vom Zeitpunkt der Übernahme an
1. die Geheimhaltungsvorschriften im Sinne von Absatz 1 sowie der Verschlusssachenanweisung vom 31. März 2006 in der Fassung vom 26. April 2010 (GMBl S. 846) und der Allgemeinen Verwaltungsvorschrift des Bundesministeriums des Innern zur Ausführung des Gesetzes über die Voraussetzungen und das Verfahren von Sicherheitsüberprüfungen des Bundes vom 29. April 1994 in der Fassung vom 31. Januar 2006 (GMBl S. 339) anzuwenden und
2. die schutzwürdigen Belange Betroffener in gleicher Weise zu beachten wie die abgebende Stelle.
²Amtsträger und für den öffentlichen Dienst besonders Verpflichtete in öffentlichen Archiven unterliegen allen für die Bediensteten der abgebenden Stellen geltenden Geheimhaltungsvorschriften.
(4) Unterlagen, die den Rechtsvorschriften des Bundes über die Geheimhaltung oder dem Steuergeheimnis nach § 30 der Abgabenordnung unterliegen oder Angaben über Verhältnisse eines anderen oder fremde Betriebs- oder Geschäftsgeheimnisse enthalten, dürfen dem Bundesarchiv oder, im Fall des § 7, dem zuständigen Landes- oder Kommunalarchiv auch von anderen Stellen als den öffentlichen Stellen des Bundes zur Archivierung angeboten und abgegeben werden.

§ 7 Anbietung und Abgabe von Unterlagen an Landes- oder Kommunalarchive

Die öffentlichen Stellen des Bundes haben Unterlagen von nachgeordneten Stellen des Bundes, deren örtliche Zuständigkeit sich nicht auf den gesamten Geltungsbereich dieses Gesetzes erstreckt, auf Vorschlag des Bundesarchivs mit Zustimmung der zuständigen obersten Bundesbehörde dem zuständigen Landes- oder Kommunalarchiv zur Übernahme anzubieten und abzugeben, wenn die Vorgaben der §§ 6 und 10 bis 14 durch Landesgesetze oder kommunale Satzungen sichergestellt sind.

§ 8 Zwischenarchiv und digitales Zwischenarchiv

(1) ¹Das Bundesarchiv unterhält das Zwischenarchiv für die nicht elektronischen Unterlagen der obersten Bundesbehörden und der Verfassungsorgane. ²Das Bundesarchiv unterhält zudem das digitale Zwischenarchiv für die elektronischen Unterlagen aller Einrichtungen der Bundesverwaltung.
(2) ¹Das Bundesarchiv verwahrt das Zwischenarchivgut des Bundes im Auftrag der anbietenden öffentlichen Stelle des Bundes oder ihres Rechts- und Funktionsnachfolgers. ²Bis zur Übernahme als Archivgut des Bundes beschränkt sich die Verantwortung des Bundesarchivs auf die notwendigen technischen und organisatorischen Maßnahmen zur Verwahrung und Sicherung der Unterlagen. ³Die Bewertung des Zwischenarchivguts des Bundes nach Maßgabe von § 3 Absatz 2 Satz 2 durch das Bundesarchiv ist zulässig; § 5 Absatz 5 ist entsprechend anzuwenden.
(3) ¹Auf die Abgabe elektronischer Unterlagen an das digitale Zwischenarchiv sind die für die Bundesverwaltung verbindlich festgelegten Standards anzuwenden. ²Sofern für die Form der Übermittlung und für das Datenformat kein Standard für die Bundesverwaltung verbindlich festgelegt wurde, sind diese im Einvernehmen mit der abgebenden öffentlichen Stelle festzulegen.

§ 9 Veräußerungsverbot

Archivgut des Bundes ist unveräußerlich.

§ 10 Nutzung von Archivgut des Bundes
(1) ¹Jeder Person steht nach Maßgabe dieses Gesetzes auf Antrag das Recht zu, Archivgut des Bundes zu nutzen. ²Regelungen in anderen Rechtsvorschriften über die Nutzung von Unterlagen sowie besondere Vereinbarungen zugunsten von Eigentümern Archivguts privater Herkunft bleiben unberührt.
(2) Die Nutzung kann zum Schutz öffentlicher Belange und zur Wahrung schutzwürdiger Interessen Betroffener mit Auflagen verbunden oder unter dem Vorbehalt des Widerrufs genehmigt werden.
(3) Verlangen die Antragsteller eine bestimmte Art der Nutzung, so darf eine andere Art der Nutzung nur aus wichtigem Grund bestimmt werden.

§ 11 Schutzfristen
(1) ¹Die allgemeine Schutzfrist für Archivgut des Bundes beträgt 30 Jahre, sofern durch Rechtsvorschrift nichts anderes bestimmt ist. ²Sie beginnt mit der Entstehung der Unterlagen.
(2) ¹Nach Ablauf der Schutzfrist des Absatzes 1 darf Archivgut des Bundes, das sich seiner Zweckbestimmung oder seinem wesentlichen Inhalt nach auf eine oder mehrere natürliche Personen bezieht, frühestens zehn Jahre nach dem Tod der jeweiligen Person genutzt werden. ²Ist das Todesjahr nicht oder nur mit unverhältnismäßigem Aufwand festzustellen, endet die Schutzfrist 100 Jahre nach der Geburt der Personen. ³Kann auch der Geburtstag nicht oder nur mit unvertretbarem Aufwand festgestellt werden, endet die Schutzfrist 60 Jahre nach der Entstehung der Unterlagen.
(3) Archivgut des Bundes, das aus Unterlagen besteht, die der Geheimhaltungspflicht nach § 6 Absatz 1 Satz 1 und Absatz 4 unterliegen, darf erst 60 Jahre nach seiner Entstehung genutzt werden.
(4) Die Schutzfristen nach Absatz 2 sind nicht auf Archivgut des Bundes anzuwenden, das sich auf Amtsträger in Ausübung ihrer Ämter und auf Personen der Zeitgeschichte bezieht, es sei denn ihr schutzwürdiger privater Lebensbereich ist betroffen.
(5) Die Schutzfristen der Absätze 1 bis 3 sind nicht auf Archivgut des Bundes anzuwenden,
1. das aus Unterlagen besteht, die bereits bei ihrer Entstehung zur Veröffentlichung bestimmt waren, oder
2. soweit es aus Unterlagen besteht, die vor der Übergabe an das Bundesarchiv bereits einem Informationszugang nach einem Informationszugangsgesetz offengestanden haben.

(6) Auf die Nutzung von Unterlagen, die älter als 30 Jahre sind und noch der Verfügungsgewalt der öffentlichen Stellen des Bundes unterliegen, sind die Absätze 1 bis 5 und die §§ 10, 12 und 13 entsprechend anzuwenden.

§ 12 Verkürzungen und Verlängerungen der Schutzfristen
(1) Das Bundesarchiv kann die Schutzfrist nach § 11 Absatz 1 verkürzen, soweit dem keine Einschränkungs- und Versagungsgründe gemäß § 13 entgegenstehen.
(2) ¹Das Bundesarchiv kann die Schutzfristen nach § 11 Absatz 2 verkürzen, wenn die Einwilligung der Betroffenen vorliegt. ²Liegt keine Einwilligung vor, kann das Bundesarchiv die Schutzfristen nach § 11 Absatz 2 verkürzen, wenn
1. die Nutzung für ein wissenschaftliches Forschungs- oder Dokumentationsvorhaben oder zur Wahrnehmung berechtigter Belange unerlässlich ist, die im überwiegenden Interesse einer anderen Person oder Stelle liegen, und
2. eine Beeinträchtigung schutzwürdiger Belange Betroffener oder ihrer Angehörigen durch angemessene Maßnahmen wie die Vorlage anonymisierter Reproduktionen oder das Einholen von Verpflichtungserklärungen ausgeschlossen werden kann.

(3) Das Bundesarchiv kann die Schutzfrist nach § 11 Absatz 3 um höchstens 30 Jahre verkürzen oder verlängern, wenn dies im öffentlichen Interesse liegt.
(4) ¹Ist das Archivgut des Bundes bei einer öffentlichen Stelle des Bundes entstanden, bedarf die Verkürzung oder Verlängerung der Schutzfristen nach den Absätzen 1 bis 3 der Einwilligung dieser Stelle. ²Die Einwilligung ist entbehrlich, soweit dies durch eine vorherige allgemeine Vereinbarung mit der abgebenden Stelle festgelegt worden ist.

§ 13 Einschränkungs- und Versagungsgründe
(1) ¹Das Bundesarchiv hat die Nutzung nach den §§ 10 bis 12 einzuschränken oder zu versagen, wenn
1. Grund zu der Annahme besteht, dass durch die Nutzung das Wohl der Bundesrepublik Deutschland oder eines ihrer Länder gefährdet würde,

C.III.1 Bundesarchivgesetz

2. Grund zu der Annahme besteht, dass der Nutzung schutzwürdige Interessen Betroffener oder ihrer Angehörigen entgegenstehen oder
3. durch die Nutzung Rechtsvorschriften des Bundes über die Geheimhaltung verletzt würden.

²Bei der Abwägung der in Satz 1 Nummer 2 genannten Belange ist insbesondere zu berücksichtigen, ob die Informationserhebung erkennbar auf einer Menschenrechtsverletzung beruht.
(2) Im Übrigen kann das Bundesarchiv die Nutzung einschränken oder versagen, wenn durch die Nutzung
1. der Erhaltungszustand des Archivguts des Bundes gefährdet würde oder
2. ein unverhältnismäßiger Verwaltungsaufwand entstünde.

(3) Die Nutzung von Archivgut des Bundes, das aus Unterlagen besteht, die der Geheimhaltungspflicht nach § 203 Absatz 1, 2 oder 4 des Strafgesetzbuches unterlagen, kann vom Bundesarchiv eingeschränkt oder versagt werden, soweit dies zur Wahrung schutzwürdiger Interessen Betroffener erforderlich ist.

§ 14 Rechte der Betroffenen

(1) ¹Den Betroffenen steht auf Antrag das Recht zu, Auskunft über die im Archivgut des Bundes zu ihrer Person enthaltenen Unterlagen zu erhalten, soweit das Archivgut des Bundes durch den Namen der Person erschlossen ist oder Angaben gemacht werden, die das Auffinden des betreffenden Archivguts des Bundes mit vertretbarem Verwaltungsaufwand ermöglichen. ²Auf die Einsichtnahme ist § 10 Absatz 3 entsprechend anzuwenden.
(2) Nach dem Tod der Betroffenen stehen die Rechte nach Absatz 1 den Angehörigen zu, wenn diese ein berechtigtes Interesse geltend machen und die Betroffenen keine andere Verfügung hinterlassen haben oder ihr entgegenstehender Wille sich nicht aus anderen Umständen eindeutig ergibt.
(3) ¹Der Anspruch auf Auskunft oder Einsichtnahme kann aus den in § 13 Absatz 1 genannten Gründen eingeschränkt werden. ²In diesem Fall ist dem Antrag in dem Umfang stattzugeben, in dem der Zugang ohne Preisgabe der nach Maßgabe von § 13 Absatz 1 zu schützenden Informationen und ohne unverhältnismäßigen Verwaltungsaufwand möglich ist.
(4) ¹Bestreiten die Betroffenen die Richtigkeit von Unterlagen mit personenbezogenen Daten, so ist ihnen die Möglichkeit einer Gegendarstellung einzuräumen. ²Die Möglichkeit einer Gegendarstellung ist auch den Angehörigen verstorbener Betroffener einzuräumen, wenn sie ein berechtigtes Interesse daran geltend machen. ³Das Bundesarchiv ist verpflichtet, die Gegendarstellungen den Unterlagen hinzuzufügen.

§ 15 Nutzung von Archivgut des Bundes durch die abgebenden Stellen

(1) ¹Die abgebenden Stellen und ihre Rechts- oder Funktionsnachfolger haben gegen Ersatz der Auslagen im Bundesarchiv jederzeit gebührenfreien Zugang zu Archivgut des Bundes, das sie abgegeben haben, wenn sie dieses zur Erfüllung ihrer Aufgaben benötigen. ²In Ausnahmefällen wird der Zugang bei der abgebenden Stelle gewährt.
(2) ¹Das Nutzungsrecht nach Absatz 1 ist nicht auf Unterlagen mit personenbezogenen Daten anzuwenden, die vor einer Vernichtung oder Löschung an das Bundesarchiv abgegeben worden sind. ²In diesen Fällen besteht das Zugangsrecht nur nach Maßgabe der §§ 10 bis 13, jedoch nicht zu dem Zweck, zu welchem die personenbezogenen Daten ursprünglich gespeichert worden sind.

§ 16 Übermittlung von Vervielfältigungen von Archivgut des Bundes vor Ablauf der Schutzfristen

(1) Das Bundesarchiv kann Archiven, Bibliotheken und Museen sowie Forschungs- und Dokumentationsstellen Vervielfältigungen von Archivgut des Bundes vor Ablauf der Schutzfristen übermitteln, wenn ein besonderes öffentliches Interesse besteht, dass ihnen dieses Archivgut zur Wahrnehmung ihrer jeweiligen Aufgaben zur Verfügung steht; § 12 Absatz 4 ist entsprechend anzuwenden.
(2) Die Vervielfältigung und die Übermittlung von Unterlagen mit personenbezogenen Daten sind nur zulässig, wenn
1. die empfangende Stelle ausreichend Gewähr für die Wahrung schutzwürdiger Interessen Betroffener und der Ausübung der damit verbundenen Rechte bietet und
2. die empfangende Stelle sich in einer schriftlichen Vereinbarung mit dem Bundesarchiv verpflichtet, § 6 Absatz 3 und die §§ 11 bis 14 entsprechend anzuwenden und die Unterlagen nur für eigene Zwecke zu nutzen.

(3) Der Vervielfältigung und Übermittlung dürfen andere Rechtsvorschriften nicht entgegenstehen.

§ 17 Pflichtregistrierung für deutsche Kinofilme

(1) ¹Die Hersteller und Mithersteller deutscher Kinofilme haben diese Filme in einer Datenbank beim Bundesarchiv nach Satz 2 zu registrieren. ²Die Registrierung ist binnen zwölf Monaten nach der ersten öffentlichen Aufführung in einem Kino, auf einem national oder international bedeutsamen Festival, bei einer national oder international bedeutsamen Preisverleihung oder nach einer öffentlichen Auszeichnung bei einer solchen national oder international bedeutsamen Veranstaltung vorzunehmen.

(2) ¹Die Hersteller und Mithersteller von Kinofilmen im Sinne des Absatzes 1 haben bei der Registrierung, spätestens jedoch binnen zwölf Monaten danach beim Bundesarchiv bekannt zu machen, an welchem Ort sich eine technisch einwandfreie archivfähige Kopie des Kinofilms befindet. ²Änderungen in Bezug auf den Lagerungsort einer Kinofilmkopie sind dem Bundesarchiv unverzüglich mitzuteilen.

(3) Nicht programmfüllende Kinofilme, die eine Vorführdauer von weniger als 79 Minuten oder bei Kinderfilmen von weniger als 59 Minuten haben, sind nur dann zu registrieren, wenn sie entweder öffentlich aufgeführt oder mit öffentlichen Mitteln gefördert worden sind oder eine öffentliche Auszeichnung auf einem national oder international bedeutsamen Festival oder bei einer national oder international bedeutsamen Preisverleihung erhalten haben.

§ 18 Bußgeldvorschriften

(1) Ordnungswidrig handelt, wer
1. entgegen § 17 Absatz 1 einen Kinofilm nicht, nicht richtig oder nicht rechtzeitig registriert oder
2. entgegen § 17 Absatz 2 eine Bekanntmachung nicht oder nicht rechtzeitig vornimmt.

(2) Ordnungswidrig handelt, wer eine in Absatz 1 bezeichnete Handlung als gewerblich tätige registrierungspflichtige Person fahrlässig begeht.

(3) Die Ordnungswidrigkeit kann mit einer Geldbuße bis zu zehntausend Euro geahndet werden.

(4) Verwaltungsbehörde im Sinne des § 36 Absatz 1 Nummer 1 des Gesetzes über Ordnungswidrigkeiten ist das Bundesarchiv.

§ 19 Verordnungsermächtigung

Das für Kultur und Medien zuständige Mitglied der Bundesregierung wird ermächtigt, durch Rechtsverordnung ohne Zustimmung des Bundesrates
1. nähere Einzelheiten der Nutzung von Archiv- und Bibliotheksgut des Bundesarchivs zu regeln[1]) und
2. Verfahren und Form der Pflichtregistrierung von Kinofilmen festzulegen.

---

1) Die Verordnung über die Benutzung von Archivgut beim Bundesarchiv ist abgedruckt als Nr. C.III.1a.

C.III.1a Bundesarchiv–Benutzungsverordnung

Verordnung über die Benutzung von Archivgut beim Bundesarchiv (Bundesarchiv–Benutzungsverordnung – BArchBV)

Vom 29. Oktober 1993 (BGBl. I S. 1857)
(BGBl. III / FNA 224–8–1)

Auf Grund des § 6 Satz 1 Nr. 1 des Bundesarchivgesetzes vom 6. Januar 1988 (BGBl. I S. 62) verordnet das Bundesministerium des Innern:

§ 1 Benutzungsrecht
Archivgut beim Bundesarchiv steht jedermann auf Antrag nach den Vorschriften des Bundesarchivgesetzes und dieser Verordnung zur Benutzung offen.

§ 2 Benutzungsart
(1) [1]Archivgut wird zur Benutzung im Original oder in Kopie vorgelegt, als Kopie 1 abgegeben, oder es werden Auskünfte über seinen Inhalt erteilt. [2]Über die Art der Benutzung entscheidet das Bundesarchiv.

(2) [1]Archivgut wird im Original grundsätzlich nur im Bundesarchiv vorgelegt. [2]Über Ausnahmen entscheidet der Präsident.

§ 3 Benutzungsvoraussetzungen
(1) Der Benutzungsantrag ist unter genauer Angabe von Thema und Zweck der Nachforschung schriftlich zu stellen.

(2) [1]Über den Benutzungsantrag entscheidet das Bundesarchiv. [2]Es kann die Genehmigung mit Auflagen erteilen.

(3) Der Antragsteller hat sich auf Verlangen des Bundesarchivs schriftlich zu verpflichten, bei der Verwertung von Erkenntnissen aus Archivgut Persönlichkeits- und Urheberrechte sowie schutzwürdige Belange Dritter zu beachten und bei Verstößen das Bundesarchiv von der Haftung freizustellen.

(4) [1]Die Mitwirkung von Hilfskräften bei der Benutzung ist besonders zu beantragen. [2]Die Namen der Hilfskräfte sind im Benutzungsantrag anzugeben; Absatz 3 gilt entsprechend.

(5) Sollen aus dem Archivgut gewonnene Erkenntnisse für andere als im Benutzungsantrag genannte Themen oder Zwecke verwendet werden, ist ein neuer Antrag erforderlich.

§ 4 Sorgfaltspflicht des Benutzers
Der Benutzer ist verpflichtet, das Archivgut in den Benutzerräumen zu belassen, die innere Ordnung des Archivgutes zu bewahren, es nicht zu beschädigen, zu verändern oder in seinem Erhaltungszustand zu gefährden.

§ 5 Ausschluß von der Benutzung
Verstößt ein Benutzer gröblich gegen Vorschriften des Bundesarchivgesetzes oder gegen die nach § 6 des Bundesarchivgesetzes erlassenen Rechtsverordnungen, wird er von Benutzungen beim Bundesarchiv ausgeschlossen.

§ 6 Nutzung durch Stellen des Bundes
[1]Eine der in § 2 Abs. 1 Satz 1 des Bundesarchivgesetzes oder der in § 1 Abs. 2 und § 2 des Gesetzes über die zentrale Archivierung der Unterlagen aus dem Bereich des Kriegsfolgenrechts vom 6. Januar 1988 (BGBl. I S. 65) bezeichneten Stellen kann jederzeit auf das bei ihr oder ihrem Rechtsvorgänger entstandene Archivgut für die Zwecke zurückgreifen, für die diese Unterlagen vor Abgabe an das Bundesarchiv verwendet werden durften. [2]Die §§ 1 bis 5 dieser Verordnung finden insoweit keine Anwendung.

§ 7 Inkrafttreten
Diese Verordnung tritt am Tage nach der Verkündung[1] in Kraft.

---

1) Verkündet am 10.11.1993.

Organisationserlass 1998 C.IV.1

Bekanntmachung des Organisationserlasses des Bundeskanzlers[1)]

Vom 27. Oktober 1998 (BGBl. I S. 3288)
(FNA 1103-4-15)
zuletzt geändert durch Organisationserlass 2002 vom 22. Oktober 2002 (BGBl. I S. 4206)
– Auszug –

Nachstehend mache ich den Organisationserlaß des Bundeskanzlers vom 27. Oktober 1998 bekannt, der mit Wirkung vom 27. Oktober 1998 in Kraft tritt:

„Gemäß § 9 der Geschäftsordnung der Bundesregierung ordne ich mit sofortiger Wirkung an:

IV.
[Beauftragter der Bundesregierung für Angelegenheiten der Kultur und der Medien]

Es wird ein Beauftragter der Bundesregierung für Angelegenheiten der Kultur und der Medien bestellt; dies geschieht unter Wahrung der Kulturhoheit der Länder und soweit der Bund zuständig ist.[2)] Der Beauftragte untersteht dem Bundeskanzler unmittelbar.
Dem Beauftragten werden übertragen
1. aus dem Geschäftsbereich des Bundesministeriums des Innern die Zuständigkeiten für
   a) Kultur und Medien (außer der Zuständigkeit für Kirchen und Religionsgemeinschaften); eingeschlossen ist die Zuständigkeit für die Pflege des Kulturguts für Vertriebene und Flüchtlinge (§ 96 Bundesvertriebenengesetz) sowie die kulturelle Betreuung für heimatlose Ausländer und fremde Volksgruppen;
   b) Gedenkstätten;
2. aus dem Geschäftsbereich des Bundesministeriums für Wirtschaft und Technologie die Zuständigkeit für Medien- und Filmwirtschaft, Verlagswesen;
3. aus dem Geschäftsbereich des Bundesministeriums für Verkehr, Bau- und Wohnungswesen die Zuständigkeiten für
   a) Hauptstadtkulturförderung in Berlin;
   b) kulturelle Angelegenheiten im Blick auf die Region der Bundesstadt Bonn;
4. aus dem Geschäftsbereich des Bundesministeriums für Bildung und Forschung die Zuständigkeit für Medienpolitik.

[1]Der Beauftragte führt seine inneren Verwaltungsangelegenheiten selbständig. [2]In seinem Geschäftsbereich vertritt er die Bundesrepublik Deutschland gerichtlich und außergerichtlich.
[…]"

---

1) Siehe auch Organisationserlass des Bundeskanzlers v. 22.10.2002 (BGBl. I S. 4206).
2) Vgl. dazu die Bek. der Bezeichnung der Beauftragten der Bundesregierung für Kultur und Medien v. 9.12.2003: „Die durch Ziffer IV des Organisationserlasses vom 27. Oktober 1998 (BGBl. I S. 3288) geschaffene oberste Bundesbehörde im Geschäftsbereich des Bundeskanzlers führt seit dem 22. Oktober 2002 die Bezeichnung „Die Beauftragte der Bundesregierung für Kultur und Medien"."

C.IV.2 BKM-Förderung national wertvoller Kulturdenkmäler

**Fördergrundsätze
für das Denkmalpflegeprogramm „National wertvolle Kulturdenkmäler"
der Beauftragten der Bundesregierung für Kultur und Medien (BKM)**[1]
Stand: 01.09.2015

Allgemeine Voraussetzungen

1.1 Gefördert werden **unbewegliche** Kulturdenkmäler (Baudenkmäler, historische Parks und Gärten, Bodendenkmäler) von **nationaler** Bedeutung. Hierzu zählen Denkmäler, in denen sich beispielhaft architektonische, städtebauliche, wissenschaftliche, geschichtliche oder politische Leistungen abbilden. Die nationale Bedeutung des Denkmals kann sich weiterhin daraus ergeben, dass das Objekt maßgeblich zur Entwicklung einer Kulturlandschaft oder des Gesamtstaates als Kulturnation beigetragen hat.

1.2 Weitere Fördervoraussetzungen sind, dass

a) sich die Länder an den aus Bundesmitteln zu fördernden Maßnahmen mit gleichhohen, mindestens aber angemessenen Haushaltsmitteln beteiligen. In begründeten Einzelfällen kann die BKM Ausnahmen zulassen,

b) der/die Landeskonservator/in vor der erstmaligen Beantragung von Bundesmitteln zu der für eine Bundesförderung notwendigen **nationalen** Bedeutung des Kulturdenkmals im Sinne von Ziffer 1.1 positiv Stellung nimmt und die geplanten denkmalpflegerischen Maßnahmen aus fachlicher Sicht befürwortet. Die nationale Bedeutung des Kulturdenkmals, insbesondere im Vergleich zu anderen Objekten dieser Art, ist zur Begründung der Förderwürdigkeit durch Hinweis auf das Spezifikum bzw. Alleinstellungsmerkmal des Objekts besonders herauszustellen. Am Ende der Stellungnahme sollen die wesentlichen Gründe für die nationale Bedeutung des Kulturdenkmals als Punktation dargestellt werden. Detaillierte Ausführungen, zum Beispiel zur allgemeinen Baugeschichte etc., sind hingegen nicht erforderlich.

1.3 Die BKM entscheidet über die Förderwürdigkeit eines Kulturdenkmals unter Berücksichtigung der Stellungnahme des Landeskonservators/der Landeskonservatorin und nach Anhörung von externen Sachverständigen. Weiterhin entscheidet sie sowohl bei Erstanträgen als auch bei Fortsetzungsanträgen je Haushaltsjahr über die Höhe der Bundeszuwendung unter Berücksichtigung der von dem/von der Landeskonservator/in befürworteten Maßnahmen.

1.4 Gefördert werden können nur vom Landesdenkmalamt im Sinne der Denkmalpflegepraxis des Landes anerkannte denkmalpflegerische Maßnahmen, die der Substanzerhaltung und Restaurierung von Kulturdenkmälern einschließlich ihrer wesentlichen Bestandteile dienen. Renovierungsarbeiten sowie Umbau- und nutzungsbezogene Modernisierungsmaßnahmen sind nicht zuwendungsfähig. Maßnahmen zur Barrierefreiheit sollen mit geprüft und soweit möglich berücksichtigt werden, sind jedoch grundsätzlich nicht zuwendungsfähig.

1.5 Kulturdenkmäler im unmittelbaren Eigentum der Länder sind grundsätzlich von der Bundesförderung ausgeschlossen.

1.6 Privateigentümer des Kulturdenkmals haben grundsätzlich einen etwaigen Erstattungsanspruch des Bundes bei einer Gesamtzuwendung ab 51.000 Euro abzusichern. Dies erfolgt in aller Regel durch Eintragung einer Buchgrundschuld in Höhe der Bundeszuwendung zugunsten der Bundesrepublik Deutschland.

Besondere Voraussetzungen

2.1 Die Bundesmittel werden im Rahmen der **jährlich** zur Verfügung stehenden Haushaltsmittel nach den einschlägigen haushaltsrechtlichen Bestimmungen für grundsätzlich längstens **5 Jahre** (alte Länder) beziehungsweise **7 Jahre** (neue Länder einschließlich Berlin-Ost) vergeben. Bei mehrjährigen Maßnahmen ist eine jährliche Antragstellung erforderlich.

2.2 Laufende oder bereits abgeschlossene Maßnahmen können nicht mit Bundesmitteln nachfinanziert werden. Mit den Vorhaben darf daher vor Antragstellung noch nicht begonnen worden sein. Im Vorfeld erforderliche Planungen und Bodenuntersuchungen gelten nicht als Beginn eines Vorhabens, soweit

---

[1] Quelle: https://www.bundesregierung.de/breg-de/bundesregierung/staatsministerin-fuer-kultur-und-medien/kultur/kunst-kulturfoerderung/foerderbereiche/denkmalschutz-und-baukultur.

sie nicht alleiniger Zweck der Zuwendung sind. In begründeten Fällen kann auf Antrag ein förderunschädlicher vorzeitiger Maßnahmebeginn zugelassen werden.

2.3 Die Finanzierungsart des Bundes folgt als Anteilfinanzierung in der Regel derjenigen des Landes. Der Antragsteller muss zunächst seine eigene Finanzkraft im Rahmen des Zumutbaren ausschöpfen. Er hat zu versichern, dass das Projekt ohne Fördermittel nicht finanziert werden kann. Auf Verlangen des BVA sind die Angaben durch geeignete Unterlagen zu belegen.

2.4 Aufgrund dieser Fördergrundsätze gewährte Zuwendungen sind in der Regel staatliche Beihilfen im Sinne von Artikel 107 des Vertrags über die Arbeitsweise der Europäischen Union (AEUV).

2.5 Die Zuwendungen erfolgen nach Art. 53 der Verordnung (EU) Nr. 651/2014 der Europäischen Kommission vom 17. Juni 2014 zur Feststellung der Vereinbarkeit bestimmter Gruppen von Beihilfen mit dem Binnenmarkt in Anwendung der Art. 107 und 108 des Vertrages über die Arbeitsweise der Europäischen Union („Allgemeine Gruppenfreistellungsverordnung" – AGVO; ABl. EU L 187 vom 26. Juni 2014, S.1 ff.) Danach sind diese Fördergrundsätze und die auf ihrer Grundlage gewährten Zuwendungen von der ansonsten geltenden Anmeldepflicht gegenüber der Kommission freigestellt (Art. 3).

2.6 Unternehmen bzw. Einrichtungen die einer Rückforderungsanordnung aufgrund eines früheren Beschlusses der Europäischen Kommission zur Feststellung der Rechtswidrigkeit und Unvereinbarkeit einer Beihilfe mit dem Binnenmarkt nicht nachgekommen sind, dürfen keine Einzelbeihilfen gewährt werden (Art. 1 Nr. 4a AGVO). Wer eine entsprechende Anordnung nicht befolgt hat, ist von einer Förderung aufgrund dieser Fördergrundsätze ausgeschlossen.

2.7 Jede ab dem 1. Juli 2016 aufgrund dieser Fördergrundsätze gewährte Förderung über 500.000 € wird wegen europarechtlicher Maßgaben veröffentlicht (Art. 9 Absatz 1 c) AGVO).

Hinweise zum Verfahren

Das **Bundesverwaltungsamt (BVA) – Außenstelle Stuttgart** ist für die verwaltungsmäßige Abwicklung des Denkmalpflegeprogramms der BKM zuständig. Der Antrag auf Förderung aus dem Denkmalpflegeprogramm ist bis spätestens 31. Oktober für das **Folgejahr** auf dem entsprechenden Vordruck zu stellen. Nach dem 31. Oktober eingehende Anträge werden nicht berücksichtigt. Erst- und Folgeanträge sind ausschließlich beim **Bundesverwaltungsamt (BVA) – Außenstelle Stuttgart** einzureichen.

a) Erstanträge
Erstanträge sind in **7-facher Ausfertigung beim BVA – Außenstelle Stuttgart** wie folgt vorzulegen:
   – Antragsvordruck mit ausführlicher Maßnahmenbeschreibung
   – Baupläne und geeignetes Bildmaterial (in beschränktem Umfang), Lageplan, Grundriss, Gesamt- und Innenansicht – bitte nicht in gebundener Form
   – Aufstellung der voraussichtlichen Kosten und deren Finanzierung bis zum Abschluss der Maßnahme, getrennt nach Jahresscheiben
   – Positive Stellungnahme des/der zuständigen Landeskonservators/in zur nationalen Bedeutung des Kulturdenkmals mit fachlicher Befürwortung der geplanten Maßnahmen (siehe 1.2 b)
   – Nachweis über die Beantragung von Landesmitteln (z. B. Antragskopie, Bewilligungsbescheid oder ggf. Ablehnungsbescheid)

b) Folgeanträge
Folgeanträge sind in **2-facher Ausfertigung** beim **BVA – Außenstelle Stuttgart** wie folgt vorzulegen:
   – Antragsvordruck mit Maßnahmenbeschreibung und Kostenaufstellung
   – Der Antrag ist gleichzeitig dem zuständigen Landesdenkmalamt und – sofern die Bauverwaltung zu beteiligen ist – auch der zuständigen Baufachbehörde des Landes zur fachlichen Stellungnahme vorzulegen.

Antragsvordrucke können unter: http://bva.bund.de (Suchbegriff: BKM / Kulturförderung – Formularcenter – Denkmalpflegeprogramm der BKM) heruntergeladen oder unter den oben angegebenen Telefonnummern sowie per E-Mail beim BVA angefordert werden.

C.IV.3 Errichtung der Stiftung Preußischer Kulturbesitz

Gesetz zur Errichtung einer Stiftung „Preußischer Kulturbesitz" und zur Übertragung von Vermögenswerten des ehemaligen Landes Preußen auf die Stiftung

Vom 25. Juli 1957 (BGBl. I S. 841)
(BGBl. III/FNA 224-3)
zuletzt geändert durch Art. 15 Abs. 59 DienstrechtsneuordnungsG vom 5. Februar 2009 (BGBl. I S. 160, ber. S. 462)

Der Bundestag hat das folgende Gesetz beschlossen:

§ 1 [Die Stiftung]
(1) Unter dem Namen „Preußischer Kulturbesitz" wird eine rechtsfähige Stiftung des öffentlichen Rechts mit Sitz in Berlin errichtet, die mit dem Inkrafttreten dieses Gesetzes als entstanden gilt.
(2) Die Stiftung führt ein Dienstsiegel.

§ 2 [Substanz]
(1) Eigentum und sonstige Vermögensrechte des ehemaligen Landes Preußen, die sich auf Gegenstände erstrecken, welche bis zum 9. Mai 1945 im Amtsbereich des Reichs- und Preußischen Ministers für Wissenschaft, Erziehung und Volksbildung oder im Amtsbereich des Preußischen Ministerpräsidenten verwaltet wurden, gehen mit dem Inkrafttreten dieses Gesetzes auf die Stiftung über, soweit es sich handelt
1. um Kulturgüter; hierzu gehören insbesondere Archiv-, Bibliotheks-, Museumsbestände und sonstige Kunstsammlungen oder wissenschaftliche Sammlungen einschließlich Inventar;
2. um Grundstücke, die überwiegend zur Unterbringung dieser Kulturgüter bestimmt waren oder dienten.

(2) Die Vorschriften des Absatzes 1 finden keine Anwendung
1. auf die Bestände der Bibliotheken und sonstigen Sammlungen der Hochschulen und staatlichen Lehranstalten sowie auf die dazugehörigen Grundstücke;
2. auf die Grundstücke, die der Verwaltung der preußischen staatlichen Schlösser und Gärten unterstanden;
3. auf das zu den unter Nummer 2 fallenden Grundstücken gehörige Inventar, soweit es nicht im einzelnen Bestandteil einer selbständigen Sammlung war oder ist;
4. auf Archivbestände, die nur von regionaler Bedeutung für das Land sind, in welchem sie sich befinden;
5. auf die Bestände der Staatlichen Kunstsammlungen in Kassel.

(3) Die Stiftung ist verpflichtet, auf sie nach Absatz 1 übergegangene Vermögenswerte, die nur von regionaler kultureller Bedeutung für ein bestimmtes Land sind, auf dieses Land zu übertragen.

§ 3 [Zweck]
(1) Die Stiftung hat den Zweck, bis zu einer Neuregelung nach der Wiedervereinigung die ihr übertragenen preußischen Kulturgüter für das deutsche Volk zu bewahren, zu pflegen und zu ergänzen, unter Beachtung der Tradition den sinnvollen Zusammenhang der Sammlungen zu erhalten und eine Auswertung dieses Kulturbesitzes für die Interessen der Allgemeinheit in Wissenschaft und Bildung und für den Kulturaustausch zwischen den Völkern zu gewährleisten.
(2) Die Stiftung ist verpflichtet, die auf sie übergegangenen, aus kriegsbedingten Gründen aus Berlin verlagerten Kulturgüter alsbald zurückzuführen.
(3) Die Stiftung kann die Verwaltung zusammengehöriger Bestände der Kulturgüter anderen geeigneten Dienststellen oder sonstigen Einrichtungen auf deren Antrag übertragen.
(4) Die Stiftung kann sich die treuhänderische Verwaltung von Kulturgut übertragen lassen, das sich nicht in der Obhut des Berechtigten befindet.

§ 4 [Satzung]
Die Stiftung erhält eine Satzung, die die Bundesregierung mit Zustimmung des Bundesrates errichtet und die sie in gleicher Weise ändern und ergänzen kann.

§ 5 [Organe]
Organe der Stiftung sind
1. der Stiftungsrat; ihm obliegt die Leitung der Stiftung;
2. der Präsident; er hat die Beschlüsse des Stiftungsrates auszuführen und die laufenden Angelegenheiten der Stiftung wahrzunehmen;
3. der Beirat; er hat den Stiftungsrat und den Präsidenten zu beraten.

§ 6 [Stiftungsrat]
[1]Der Stiftungsrat besteht aus Vertretern des Bundes und der in der Satzung zu bezeichnenden Länder. [2]Das Nähere regelt die Satzung.

§ 7 [Präsident]
Der Präsident wird auf Vorschlag des Stiftungsrates vom Bundespräsidenten bestellt oder ernannt.

§ 8 [Beirat]
[1]Die Mitglieder des Beirates sind vom Stiftungsrat aus dem Kreis von Sachverständigen zu berufen. [2]Das Nähere regelt die Satzung.

§ 9 [Aufsicht]
Die Stiftung untersteht der Aufsicht des Beauftragten der Bundesregierung für Angelegenheiten der Kultur und der Medien.

§ 10 [Haushaltsplan]
(1) [1]Die Stiftung hat rechtzeitig vor Beginn eines jeden Geschäftsjahres einen Haushaltsplan aufzustellen. [2]Der Haushaltsplan bedarf der Genehmigung des Beauftragten der Bundesregierung für Angelegenheiten der Kultur und der Medien. [3]Das Nähere regelt die Satzung.
(2) Die Haushalts- und Wirtschaftsführung der Stiftung unterliegt der Prüfung durch den Bundesrechnungshof.

§ 11 [Fehlbeträge und Überschüsse]
(1) [1]Die nach dem Haushaltsplan zum Ausgleich etwaiger Fehlbeträge erforderlichen Mittel werden anteilig entsprechend dem satzungsmäßigen Stimmrecht vom Bund und von den in der Satzung bezeichneten Ländern zur Verfügung gestellt. [2]Hierbei trägt jedes dieser Länder, soweit nichts anderes unter ihnen vereinbart ist, einen gleichen Teilbetrag. [3]Die zur Verfügung zu stellenden Zuschüsse sind im Haushaltsplan in den Einnahmen nachzuweisen.
(2) Überschüsse sind dem Absatz 1 entsprechend anteilig an den Bund und die Länder bis zur Höhe der von diesen zur Verfügung gestellten Beträge abzuführen und in den Ausgaben nachzuweisen.
(3) [1]Der Stiftungsrat wird ermächtigt, die Benutzung von Einrichtungen der Stiftung durch Benutzungsordnung zu regeln. [2]In den Benutzungsordnungen kann die Erhebung von Kosten (Gebühren und Auslagen) vorgesehen werden. [3]Die Gebührensätze sind so zu bemessen, daß das geschätzte Gebührenaufkommen den auf die Amtshandlungen entfallenden durchschnittlichen Personal- und Sachaufwand nicht übersteigt.

§ 12 [Arbeitskräfte]
(1) Die Geschäfte der Stiftung werden in der Regel durch Arbeitskräfte wahrgenommen, die durch privatrechtlichen Dienstvertrag angestellt sind.
(2) Planstellen für Beamte dürfen nur in dem Umfange eingerichtet werden, als sie für eine dauernde Tätigkeit zur Erfüllung hoheitsrechtlicher Aufgaben erforderlich sind.

§ 13 [Beamte]
(1) Die Beamten der Stiftung sind Bundesbeamte.
(2) [1]Der Präsident und sein ständiger Vertreter sind, wenn sie nicht mit dem Ziele der Ernennung zu Beamten auf Lebenszeit berufen oder durch privatrechtlichen Dienstvertrag angestellt werden, auf die Dauer von zwölf Jahren zu berufen; Wiederernennung ist zulässig. [2]Werden sie auf Zeit ernannt, so finden auf sie die für Beamte auf Lebenszeit geltenden Vorschriften des Bundesbeamtengesetzes entsprechende Anwendung.
(3) Oberste Dienstbehörde ist, soweit nicht die Zuständigkeit des Beauftragten der Bundesregierung für Angelegenheiten der Kultur und der Medien begründet ist, für den Präsidenten und seinen ständigen Vertreter der Vorsitzende des Stiftungsrates, für die übrigen Beamten der Präsident.

§ 14 [Ernennungsrecht]
[1]Mit Ausnahme des Präsidenten werden die Beamten der Stiftung von der Besoldungsgruppe A 15 an aufwärts vom Vorsitzenden des Stiftungsrates ernannt. [2]Die Beamten der Besoldungsgruppe A 2 bis A 14 werden vom Präsidenten ernannt.

§ 15 [Angestellte und Arbeiter]
Auf das Dienstverhältnis der Angestellten und Arbeiter der Stiftung finden die für die Angestellten und Arbeiter des Bundes jeweils geltenden gesetzlichen Vorschriften, Tarif- und Dienstordnungen sowie Tarifvereinbarungen und Tarifverträge Anwendung.

§ 16 [Einschränkung des § 2]
Die Vorschriften des § 2 Abs. 1 dieses Gesetzes gelten nicht für Eigentum und sonstige Vermögensrechte, die nach dem 30. Januar 1933 einer Gewerkschaft, Genossenschaft, politischen Partei oder sonstigen demokratischen Organisation weggenommen worden sind.

§ 17 [Ausweitung des § 2]
Unter die Vorschriften des § 2 Abs. 1 dieses Gesetzes fallen auch Eigentum und sonstige Vermögensrechte, die durch Gesetz für unübertragbar oder nur auf Grund besonderer Vereinbarung für übertragbar erklärt worden sind.

§ 18 [Fortbestand dinglicher Rechte]
Dingliche Rechte an Grundstücken und sonstigen Sachen und Rechten, auf die die Vorschriften des § 2 Abs. 1 dieses Gesetzes Anwendung finden, bleiben bestehen.

§ 19 [Fortgeltung rechtsgeschäftlicher Verfügungen]
[1]Die Wirksamkeit rechtsgeschäftlicher Verfügungen, die vor dem Inkrafttreten dieses Gesetzes über Eigentum und sonstige Vermögensrechte der in § 2 Abs. 1 dieses Gesetzes bezeichneten Art getroffen worden sind, bleibt unberührt. [2]Das gleiche gilt für Rechtsänderungen kraft Gesetzes, die vor dem 20. April 1949 eingetreten sind.

§ 20 [Auseinandersetzung zwischen Stiftung und Ländern]
Soweit zwischen den Beteiligten nichts anderes vereinbart wird, gilt für die Auseinandersetzung zwischen der Stiftung und den Ländern folgendes:
1. [1]Ein Ersatz für Aufwendungen und Verwendungen, die bis zum Inkrafttreten dieses Gesetzes von den Ländern in bezug auf Eigentum und sonstige Vermögensrechte gemacht worden sind, auf die die Vorschriften des § 2 Abs. 1 dieses Gesetzes Anwendung finden, wird nicht geleistet. [2]Den Ländern verbleiben bis zu diesem Zeitpunkt erzielte Nutzungen.
2. [1]Aufwendungen und Verwendungen, die nach dem Inkrafttreten dieses Gesetzes in bezug auf Eigentum und sonstige Vermögensrechte gemacht worden sind, auf die die Vorschriften des § 2 Abs. 1 dieses Gesetzes Anwendung finden, sind von der Stiftung nach Maßgabe der Vorschriften des bürgerlichen Rechts zu erstatten. [2]Nach diesem Zeitpunkt erzielte Nutzungen sind an die Stiftung abzuführen.
3. Unbeschadet der Vorschrift der Nummer 1 Satz 2 sind an die Stiftung ferner abzuführen alle sonstigen Vorteile, die ein Land auf Grund eines Vermögenswertes, auf den die Vorschriften des § 2 Abs. 1 dieses Gesetzes Anwendung finden, oder als Ersatz für die Zerstörung, Beschädigung oder Entziehung eines solchen Vermögenswertes oder durch ein Rechtsgeschäft erworben hat, das sich auf einen solchen Vermögenswert bezieht.

§ 21 [Auskunftsrecht]
[1]Der Beauftragte der Bundesregierung für Angelegenheiten der Kultur und der Medien und der Präsident der Stiftung sind berechtigt, von allen Stellen, die seit dem 9. Mai 1945 mit der Verwaltung des unter die Vorschriften dieses Gesetzes fallenden Eigentums oder der unter die Vorschriften dieses Gesetzes fallenden sonstigen Vermögensrechte befaßt waren, Auskunft zu verlangen und Einsicht in die Akten und Unterlagen zu nehmen. [2]Das gleiche Recht hat der Bundesrechnungshof.

§ 22 [Antragsberechtigung]
(1) [1]Steht das Eigentum an einem Grundstück nach diesem Gesetz der Stiftung zu, so ist der Antrag auf Berichtigung des Grundbuchs von der Stiftung zu stellen. [2]Der Antrag muß von dem Präsidenten oder seinem Vertreter unterschrieben und mit dem Siegel oder Stempel der Stiftung versehen sein.

³Zum Nachweis des Eigentums gegenüber dem Grundbuchamt genügt die in den Antrag aufzunehmende Erklärung, daß das Grundstück zum Vermögen der Stiftung gehört.
(2) Dies gilt entsprechend für sonstige im Grundbuch eingetragene Rechte.

§ 23 [Kosten bei Rechtsstreit]
¹Soweit sich ein anhängiger Rechtsstreit durch dieses Gesetz erledigt, trägt jede Partei ihre außergerichtlichen Kosten und die Hälfte der gerichtlichen Auslagen. ²Die Gerichtsgebühren werden nicht erhoben.

§ 24 [Gerichtsgebühren]
¹Gerichtsgebühren und andere Abgaben, die aus Anlaß und in Durchführung dieses Gesetzes entstehen, werden nicht erhoben. ²Bare Auslagen bleiben außer Ansatz.

§ 25 [Berlin-Klausel]
[gegenstandslos]

§ 26 [Inkrafttreten]
Dieses Gesetz tritt am Tage nach seiner Verkündung¹⁾ in Kraft.

---

1) Verkündet am 5.8.1957.

Satzung der Stiftung „Preußischer Kulturbesitz"[1)]

Vom 6. September 1961 (BGBl. 1961 I S. 1709)
(BGBl. III/FNA 224-3-1)
zuletzt geändert durch Art. 1 Dritte ÄndVO vom 15. April 2014 (BGBl. I S. 347)

Die Stiftung „Preußischer Kulturbesitz" erhält folgende Satzung:
Satzung der Stiftung „Preußischer Kulturbesitz"

§ 1 [Organe der Stiftung]
(1) Die Stiftung wird durch ihre Organe verwaltet.
(2) Organe der Stiftung sind
  der Stiftungsrat,
  der Präsident,
  der Beirat.
(3) Die Stiftung führt ein Dienstsiegel, über dessen Ausgestaltung der Stiftungsrat mit Zustimmung des Beauftragten der Bundesregierung für Angelegenheiten der Kultur und der Medien beschließt.

§ 2 [Mitglieder; Stimmenverteilung]
(1) Mitglieder des Stiftungsrates sind zwei Vertreter des Bundes, zwei Vertreter des Landes Berlin, zwei Vertreter des Landes Nordrhein-Westfalen und je ein Vertreter der Länder Baden-Württemberg, Bayern, Brandenburg, Bremen, Hamburg, Hessen, Mecklenburg-Vorpommern, Niedersachsen, Rheinland-Pfalz, Saarland, Sachsen, Sachsen-Anhalt, Schleswig-Holstein und Thüringen.
(2) [1]Für jedes Mitglied ist ein Stellvertreter zu bestellen. [2]Sind ein Mitglied und dessen Stellvertreter verhindert, so können sie zu der betreffenden Sitzung einen Bevollmächtigten entsenden.
(3) [1]Der Bund hat hundertundzwanzig Stimmen. [2]Die Länder haben achtzig Stimmen, die sich wie folgt verteilen:

Baden-Württemberg	neun Stimmen,
Bayern	eine Stimme,
Berlin	dreiundzwanzig Stimmen,
Brandenburg	zwei Stimmen,
Bremen	eine Stimme,
Hamburg	zwei Stimmen,
Hessen	fünf Stimmen,
Mecklenburg-Vorpommern	eine Stimme,
Niedersachsen	sechs Stimmen,
Nordrhein-Westfalen	sechzehn Stimmen,
Rheinland-Pfalz	drei Stimmen,
Saarland	eine Stimme,
Sachsen	vier Stimmen,
Sachsen-Anhalt	zwei Stimmen,
Schleswig-Holstein	zwei Stimmen,
Thüringen	zwei Stimmen.

(4) Die Stimmen des Bundes und jedes einzelnen Landes können nur einheitlich abgegeben werden.
(5) Kann ein Land in einer Stiftungsratssitzung nicht vertreten sein, so kann es sein Stimmrecht dem Vertreter eines anderen Landes zur Wahrnehmung in der Sitzung übertragen.

§ 3 [Wahl des Vorsitzenden]
(1) [1]Der Stiftungsrat wählt den Vorsitzenden und stellvertretende Vorsitzende auf die Dauer von drei Jahren; Wiederwahl ist zulässig. [2]Er gibt sich eine Geschäftsordnung.
(2) Die Geschäftsordnung soll insbesondere Bestimmungen enthalten über die Einberufung, den Gang der Verhandlung und die Beurkundung der Beschlüsse des Stiftungsrates.

---

1) Verkündet als Art. 1 VO v. 6.9.1961 (BGBl. I S. 1709); Inkrafttreten gem. Art. 3 dieses G am 16.9.1961.

§ 4 [Beschlußfähigkeit]

(1) Der Stiftungsrat ist beschlußfähig, wenn je ein Mitglied des Bundes, des Landes Berlin und des Landes Nordrhein-Westfalen sowie mindestens sieben der übrigen Mitglieder anwesend oder vertreten sind.

(2) Einer Mehrheit, die die Mehrheit der abgegebenen Länderstimmen einschließt, bedürfen Beschlüsse des Stiftungsrates über
a) den Vorschlag zur Bestellung oder Ernennung des Präsidenten,
b) den Vorschlag zur Bestellung oder Ernennung des ständigen Vertreters des Präsidenten,
c) den Vorschlag zur Bestellung oder Ernennung des Generaldirektors der Staatlichen Museen, des Generaldirektors der Staatsbibliothek sowie der Direktoren des Geheimen Staatsarchivs, des Ibero-Amerikanischen Instituts und des Staatlichen Instituts für Musikforschung,
d) die Feststellung des Stiftungshaushaltsplans – ausgenommen den Abschnitt für Neubauten und ihre Ersteinrichtung einschließlich des Grunderwerbs –, die Bewilligung über- und außerplanmäßiger Ausgaben, soweit sie nicht durch Einsparungen im laufenden Stiftungshaushaltsplan abgedeckt werden können, sowie die Entlastung des Präsidenten,
e) die Übertragung der Verwaltung von Vermögenswerten auf eine andere Dienststelle oder Einrichtung,
f) die Veränderung des Standortes einer Sammlung,
g) den Erlaß und die Änderung seiner Geschäftsordnung.

(3) ¹Über Grunderwerb für Neubauten und über die Errichtung von Neubauten einschließlich ihrer Ersteinrichtung sowie über den entsprechenden Abschnitt des Stiftungshaushaltsplans beschließen der Bund und das Land Berlin allein mit gleichem Stimmrecht. ²Beschlüsse hierüber werden nicht wirksam, wenn ihnen nach Maßgabe näherer Bestimmungen in der Geschäftsordnung mit zwei Dritteln der abgegebenen Stimmen der übrigen Länder im Hinblick auf die von ihnen mitzutragenden Folgekosten widersprochen wird.

(4) Im übrigen faßt der Stiftungsrat seine Beschlüsse mit der einfachen Mehrheit der abgegebenen Stimmen, nicht jedoch gegen zwei Drittel der abgegebenen Länderstimmen.

§ 5 [Aufgaben des Stiftungsrates]

(1) Der Stiftungsrat ist zuständig für die Willensbildung der Stiftung, soweit es sich nicht um die Erledigung der laufenden Angelegenheiten handelt.

(2) ¹Der Stiftungsrat kann Richtlinien beschließen, nach denen die Stiftung zu verwalten ist. ²Er kann dem Präsidenten Weisungen erteilen.

(3) ¹Der Stiftungsrat überwacht die Geschäftsführung der Stiftung. ²Er erteilt dem Präsidenten Entlastung und kann von ihm jederzeit Auskunft und Bericht sowie die Vorlage der Akten und Bücher verlangen.

(4) ¹Der Stiftungsrat bildet einen geschäftsführenden Ausschuß, dem nach näherer Bestimmung in der Geschäftsordnung alle Angelegenheiten des Stiftungsrates mit Ausnahme der in § 4 Abs. 2 und 3 genannten übertragen werden können. ²Der Ausschuß setzt sich zusammen aus je zwei Stiftungsratsmitgliedern des Bundes, des Landes Berlin und des Landes Nordrhein-Westfalen sowie aus drei Stiftungsratsmitgliedern, die für jeweils drei Jahre von den übrigen Ländern benannt werden. ³Auch stellvertretende Stiftungsratsmitglieder können zu Ausschußmitgliedern bestellt werden. ⁴Für jedes Ausschußmitglied ist ein Stellvertreter zu bestellen. ⁵Sind ein Mitglied und dessen Stellvertreter verhindert, so können sie zu der betreffenden Sitzung einen Bevollmächtigten entsenden. ⁶Der Vorsitzende und die stellvertretenden Vorsitzenden werden vom Stiftungsrat aus dem Kreis der Ausschußmitglieder für drei Jahre bestellt. ⁷Der Ausschuß ist beschlußfähig, wenn mindestens je ein Vertreter des Bundes, des Landes Berlin und des Landes Nordrhein-Westfalen sowie zwei der drei Vertreter der übrigen Länder anwesend sind. ⁸Der Bund hat sechs Stimmen, das Land Berlin und das Land Nordrhein-Westfalen haben je eine Stimme, die übrigen Länder haben zusammen drei Simmen. ⁹Die Stimmen des Bundes können nur einheitlich abgegeben werden. ¹⁰Beschlüsse werden mit einfacher Mehrheit der abgegebenen Stimmen gefaßt, nicht jedoch gegen zwei Drittel der abgegebenen Länderstimmen.

§ 6 [Aufgaben des Präsidenten]

(1) Der Präsident hat die Beschlüsse des Stiftungsrates auszuführen und die laufenden Angelegenheiten der Stiftung wahrzunehmen.

(2) Zu den laufenden Angelegenheiten der Stiftung gehören insbesondere
a) die mit der Verwaltung der Stiftung verbundenen, regelmäßig wiederkehrenden Rechtsgeschäfte,
b) die mit der Durchführung und Abwicklung von Dauerverträgen verbundenen Rechtsgeschäfte,
c) die Ernennung von Beamten bis einschließlich Besoldungsgruppe A 14 und die Einstellung von Referendaren,
d) der Abschluß von Arbeitsverträgen mit Tarifbeschäftigten der Entgeltgruppen 1 bis 14 des Tarifvertrags für den öffentlichen Dienst.
(3) Zu den laufenden Angelegenheiten gehören nicht
a) alle Geschäfte, die die Stiftung zu einer Ausgabe von mehr als 500 000 DM verpflichten, es sei denn, der Stiftungsrat hat eine besondere Ermächtigung erteilt,
b) die Aufnahme von Darlehen, die Übernahme von Bürgschaften und der Abschluß von Gewährverträgen,
c) Verträge über Grundstücke und grundstücksgleiche Rechte,
d) alle sonstigen Geschäfte, über die der Stiftungsrat sich die Beschlußfassung vorbehält.

§ 7 [Vetretung der Stiftung]
(1) Der Präsident vertritt die Stiftung gerichtlich und außergerichtlich.
(2) Gegenüber dem Präsidenten wird die Stiftung durch den Vorsitzenden des Stiftungsrates vertreten.

§ 8 [Ausschluss der Vertreter]
Der Präsident und sein ständiger Vertreter können nicht Mitglieder des Stiftungsrates oder deren Stellvertreter sein.

§ 9 [Zusammensetzung des Beirates]
(1) ¹Der Beirat besteht aus nicht mehr als fünfzehn sachverständigen Mitgliedern, die vom Stiftungsrat unter Berücksichtigung der verschiedenen Zweige der Verwaltung des ehemals preußischen Kulturbesitzes jeweils auf fünf Jahre berufen werden. ²Vorschlagsberechtigt sind die Bundesregierung und die Regierung jedes an der Stiftung beteiligten Landes.
(2) Die Geschäftsordnung für den Beirat erläßt der Stiftungsrat.

§ 10 [Aufgaben des Beirates]
¹Der Beirat und seine einzelnen Mitglieder beraten den Stiftungsrat und den Präsidenten. ²Der Beirat und jedes seiner Mitglieder können dem Stiftungsrat und dem Präsidenten Vorschläge und Anregungen unterbreiten.

§ 11 [Kostenerstattung]
(1) ¹Die Mitglieder des Beirates werden ehrenamtlich tätig. ²Die Stiftung erstattet ihnen die notwendigen baren Auslagen, entschädigt sie für entgangenen Verdienst, für notwendige Stellvertretungskosten und dergleichen durch eine Sitzungsvergütung und zahlt ihnen bei Dienstreisen eine Reisekostenvergütung. ³Dabei gelten die Vorschriften für die Abfindung der Mitglieder von Beiräten, Ausschüssen, Kommissionen und dergleichen in der Bundesverwaltung.
(2) Für Erstattung schriftlicher Gutachten können Vergütungen vereinbart werden.

§ 12 [Verschwiegenheitspflicht]
Die Mitglieder der Organe der Stiftung sind verpflichtet, über Angelegenheiten, deren Geheimhaltung durch Gesetz, Organbeschluß oder besondere Anordnung vorgeschrieben ist, Verschwiegenheit zu bewahren.

§ 13 [Geschäftsjahr]
Das Geschäftsjahr der Stiftung ist das Kalenderjahr.

§ 14 [Haushaltsplan; Rechnungsprüfung]
(1) Für das Haushalts-, Kassen- und Rechnungswesen sowie für die Rechnungslegung der Stiftung finden die für die Bundesverwaltung geltenden Bestimmungen entsprechende Anwendung.
(2) Der Haushaltsplan der Stiftung ist alljährlich rechtzeitig vor Beginn des Geschäftsjahres von dem Präsidenten im Entwurf aufzustellen, von dem Stiftungsrat festzustellen und von dessen Vorsitzenden dem Beauftragten der Bundesregierung für Angelegenheiten der Kultur und der Medien zur Genehmigung vorzulegen.

(3) ¹Die jährliche Prüfung der Rechnung sowie der Haushalts- und Wirtschaftsführung erfolgt im Sinne des § 109 Absatz 2 der Bundeshaushaltsordnung durch die für Kultur zuständige oberste Bundesbehörde. ²Diese kann mit der Prüfung eine geeignete Stelle oder einen Abschlussprüfer beauftragen. ³Abschlussprüfer können Wirtschaftsprüfer oder Wirtschaftsprüfungsgesellschaften sein. ⁴Die jährliche Prüfung erfolgt unbeschadet einer Prüfung durch den Bundesrechnungshof nach § 111 der Bundeshaushaltsordnung.
(4) ¹Das Ergebnis der Prüfung ist dem Bundesrechnungshof vorzulegen. ²Auf der Grundlage des Ergebnisses der jährlichen Prüfung entscheidet der Stiftungsrat über die Entlastung des Präsidenten oder der Präsidentin der Stiftung. ³Die Entlastung bedarf der Genehmigung der für Kultur zuständigen obersten Bundesbehörde und des Bundesministeriums der Finanzen.

§ 15 [Übergangsbestimmungen]

(1) ¹Die Stiftung übernimmt mit dem Ersten des Monats, der dem Inkrafttreten dieser Satzung folgt, die Beamten, die bei Errichtung der Stiftung ganz oder überwiegend für die auf die Stiftung übergegangenen Vermögenswerte beschäftigt waren; die Vorschriften der §§ 129 und 130 des Beamtenrechtsrahmengesetzes vom 1. Juli 1957 (BGBl. I S. 667) sind anzuwenden. ²Die nach Errichtung der Stiftung von den Treuhänder-Dienstherren für Zwecke der Stiftung in das Beamtenverhältnis berufenen Personen werden nach Maßgabe des § 123 des Beamtenrechtsrahmengesetzes in den Dienst der Stiftung versetzt; dies gilt auch für Beamte, denen ein Amt noch nicht verliehen ist.
(2) ¹Die im Zeitpunkt der Errichtung der Stiftung ganz oder überwiegend für die auf die Stiftung übergegangenen Vermögenswerte beschäftigten und die nach diesem Zeitpunkt für Zwecke der Stiftung eingestellten Arbeitnehmer sind mit dem Ersten des Monats, der dem Inkrafttreten dieser Satzung folgt, in den Dienst der Stiftung zu übernehmen. ²Soweit die für diese Arbeitnehmer maßgebenden Arbeitsbedingungen günstiger sind als diejenigen, die sich aus dem Tarifrecht der Stiftung ergeben, gelten die günstigeren Arbeitsbedingungen weiter, solange sie nicht durch andere tarifvertragliche oder arbeitsvertragliche Abmachungen ersetzt werden.
(3) Den nach Absatz 2 übernommenen Arbeitnehmern sowie ihren Hinterbliebenen wird abweichend von dem für die Stiftung geltenden Tarifrecht die Alters- und Hinterbliebenenversorgung einschließlich der zusätzlichen Alters- und Hinterbliebenenversorgung nach dem für sie bisher geltenden Recht gewährt.
(4) Der Präsident regelt mit Zustimmung des Stiftungsrates und im Einvernehmen mit den betroffenen Ländern die Erstattung der Versorgungsaufwendungen für die Beamten, Angestellten und Arbeiter, wenn diese bei Eintritt des Versorgungsfalles für die auf die Stiftung übergegangenen Vermögenswerte ganz oder überwiegend beschäftigt gewesen sind und der Versorgungsfall vor dem Übernahmezeitpunkt (Absatz 1 und 2) eingetreten ist, sowie für deren Hinterbliebene.

C.IV.4 Satzung der Kulturstiftung des Bundes

Die Satzung der Kulturstiftung des Bundes
In der Fassung vom 18. Oktober 2011[1)]

§ 1 – Name, Sitz, Rechtsform
Die Stiftung führt den Namen „Kulturstiftung des Bundes". Sie ist eine rechtsfähige Stiftung des Bürgerlichen Rechts und hat ihren Sitz in Halle/Saale.

§ 2 – Stiftungszweck
(1) Zweck der Stiftung ist die Förderung von Kunst und Kultur im Rahmen der Zuständigkeit des Bundes. Ein Schwerpunkt soll die Förderung innovativer Programme und Projekte im internationalen Kontext sein.
(2) Die Stiftung strebt eine Zusammenarbeit mit der „Kulturstiftung der Länder" an.
(3) Die Stiftung soll ein eigenständiges Förderprofil entwickeln. Leistungen der Stiftung werden in der Regel als Projektförderung gewährt. Institutionelle Förderungen von Einrichtungen sind grundsätzlich ausgeschlossen.
(4) Auf die Förderung durch Stiftungsmittel besteht kein Rechtsanspruch. Die Leistungen der Stiftung richten sich nach Maßgabe der ihr zur Verfügung stehenden Mittel.

§ 3 – Gemeinnützigkeit
(1) Die Stiftung verfolgt ausschließlich und unmittelbar gemeinnützige und mildtätige Zwecke im Sinne des Abschnitts „Steuerbegünstigte Zwecke" der Abgabenordnung.
(2) Die Stiftung ist selbstlos tätig. Sie verfolgt nicht in erster Linie eigenwirtschaftliche Zwecke.
(3) Mittel der Stiftung dürfen nur für die satzungsmäßigen Zwecke verwendet werden. Es darf keine Person durch Ausgaben, die dem Zweck der Stiftung fremd sind, oder durch unverhältnismäßig hohe Vergütungen begünstigt werden.
(4) Die Stiftung erfüllt ihre Aufgaben selbst oder durch eine Hilfsperson im Sinne des § 57 Abs. 1 Satz 2 der Abgabenordnung (AO), sofern sie nicht im Wege der Mittelbeschaffung gemäß § 58 Nr. 1 AO tätig wird. Die Stiftung kann zur Verwirklichung des Stiftungszwecks Zweckbetriebe unterhalten.

§ 4 – Stiftungsvermögen
(1) Die Stiftung ist mit einem Grundstockvermögen ausgestattet, dessen Höhe im Stiftungsgeschäft näher bestimmt ist. Zur Erfüllung des Stiftungszweckes erhält die Stiftung einen jährlichen Zuschuss des Bundes nach Maßgabe des jeweiligen Haushaltsgesetzes und der verfügbaren Haushaltsmittel.
(2) Das Stiftungsvermögen kann durch Zustiftungen (Geldbeträge, Rechte und sonstige Gegenstände) des Stifters sowie Dritter erhöht werden. Zuwendungen Dritter dürfen nicht mit Auflagen verbunden sein, die die Erfüllung des Stiftungszwecks beeinträchtigen. Werden Zuwendungen nicht ausdrücklich zum Vermögen gewidmet, so dienen diese ausschließlich und unmittelbar der Erfüllung des Stiftungszwecks.
(3) Zuwendungen Dritter können auch mit der Maßgabe erbracht werden, dass aus diesen Mitteln eine unselbständige Stiftung oder ein Sonderfonds gebildet wird, der einen vom Spender festgelegten Namen trägt und im Rahmen der allgemeinen Aufgabenstellung der Stiftung zweckgebunden ist; hierzu bedarf es der Zustimmung des Stiftungsrates. Die treuhändlerische Verwaltung und die Kosten dafür können in diesen Fällen von der Stiftung übernommen werden, damit die Mittel ungeschmälert den vom Zuwendenden festgelegten kulturellen Zwecken zu Gute kommen.
(4) Das Vermögen der Stiftung ist grundsätzlich in seinem Bestand zu erhalten. Ein Rückgriff auf das Stiftungsvermögen ist nur zulässig, wenn der Stiftungszweck anders nicht zu verwirklichen ist und der Bestand der Stiftung nicht gefährdet erscheint, insbesondere das Stiftungsvermögen in den folgenden Jahren auf seinen vollen Wert wieder aufgefüllt werden kann. Es darf nur veräußert oder belastet werden, wenn von dem Erlös gleichwertiges Vermögen erworben wird.
(5) Die Stiftung ist nicht befugt, Kredite aufzunehmen.

§ 5 – Verwendung der Stiftungsmittel
(1) Die Erträge des Stiftungsvermögens und die ihm nicht zuwachsenden Zuwendungen sind zur Erfüllung des Stiftungszwecks zu verwenden.

---
1) Fundstelle: https://www.kulturstiftung-des-bundes.de/de/stiftung/satzung.html.

(2) Die Stiftung kann ihre Mittel ganz oder teilweise einer Rücklage zuführen, soweit dies erforderlich ist, um ihre steuerbegünstigten satzungsmäßigen Zwecke nachhaltig erfüllen zu können, und soweit für die Verwendung der Rücklage konkrete Ziel- und Zeitvorstellungen bestehen.
(3) Freie Rücklagen zur Werterhaltung dürfen gebildet werden, soweit die Vorschriften des steuerlichen Gemeinnützigkeitsrechts dies zulassen. Sie können dem Stiftungsvermögen zugeführt werden.

§ 6 – Organe der Stiftung
(1) Organe der Stiftung sind
1. der Stiftungsrat;
2. der Vorstand;
3. der Stiftungsbeirat.

(2) Die Mitglieder der Stiftungsgremien sind mit Ausnahme des Vorstands ehrenamtlich für die Stiftung tätig. Sie haben Anspruch auf Ersatz der ihnen entstandenen Auslagen und Aufwendungen entsprechend den für die unmittelbare Bundesverwaltung geltenden Bestimmungen.

§ 7 – Stiftungsrat
(1) Der Stiftungsrat besteht aus vierzehn Mitgliedern:
1. Dem/die Beauftragte(n) der Bundesregierung für Angelegenheiten der Kultur und der Medien sowie je einem Vertreter des Auswärtigen Amtes und des Bundesministeriums der Finanzen;
2. drei vom Deutschen Bundestag entsandten Vertretern;
3. zwei Vertretern der Länder, die von der Ständigen Konferenz der Kultusminister der Länder entsandt werden;
4. zwei Vertretern der Kommunen, die durch die Bundesvereinigung der kommunalen Spitzenverbände benannt werden;
5. dem/der Vorsitzenden des Stiftungsrates der „Kulturstiftung der Länder";
6. drei Persönlichkeiten aus dem Bereich von Kunst und Kultur, die von der Bundesregierung berufen werden.

(2) Der/Die Vorsitzende des Stiftungsbeirats nimmt beratend an den Sitzungen des Stiftungsrates teil.
(3) Die Stiftungsratsmitglieder gemäß Absatz 1 Nr. 1 und 3 werden von ihren ständigen Vertretern im Amt vertreten. Für die Mitglieder nach Absatz 1 Nr. 2, 4 und 5 soll ein Vertreter benannt werden. Ein Mitglied, das als Inhaber eines öffentlichen Amtes entsandt ist, scheidet mit Beendigung dieses Amtes aus dem Stiftungsrat aus. Jedes Mitglied kann sein Amt durch schriftliche Erklärung gegenüber dem/der Vorsitzenden des Stiftungsrates niederlegen.
(4) Die Amtszeit der Mitglieder des Stiftungsrates und einer Stellvertretung beträgt fünf Jahre. Scheidet jemand vorher aus, ist unverzüglich ein neues Mitglied oder eine neue Stellvertretung für den Rest der Amtsperiode zu bestellen. Solange von einem Entsendungsrecht nach Absatz 1 Ziff. 3 bis 5 kein Gebrauch gemacht wird, bleibt dieser Stiftungsratssitz unbesetzt.
(5) Der/die Beauftragte der Bundesregierung für Angelegenheiten der Kultur und der Medien ist Vorsitzende(r) des Stiftungsrates und wird auch in dieser Funktion durch seinen/ihren ständigen Vertreter im Amt vertreten.

§ 8 – Aufgaben des Stiftungsrates
(1) Dem Stiftungsrat obliegt die Entscheidung in allen Angelegenheiten, die für die Stiftung und ihre Entwicklung von grundsätzlicher oder besonderer Bedeutung sind. Seine Aufgabe ist insbesondere:
1. die Festlegung von Leitlinien und Förderrichtlinien für die Arbeit der Stiftung;
2. die Bestimmung der Schwerpunkte der Förderung (Programme);
3. die Beschlussfassung über den Wirtschaftsplan (einschließlich Stellenplan);
4. die Kontrolle der gewissenhaften und sparsamen Verwaltung des Stiftungsvermögens und der sonstigen Mittel;
5. die Entgegennahme der Jahresrechnung, die Bestellung eines Rechnungsprüfers/in und die Entlastung des Vorstands;
6. die Billigung des Jahresberichts über die Tätigkeit der Stiftung.

(2) Der Stiftungsrat kann dem Vorstand Weisung erteilen und überwacht die Geschäftsführung der Stiftung. Er kann vom Vorstand jederzeit Auskunft und Bericht sowie die Vorlage der Akten und Bücher verlangen.

C.IV.4 Satzung der Kulturstiftung des Bundes

§ 9 – Beschlussfassung des Stiftungsrates

(1) Die Mitglieder des Stiftungsrates gemäß § 7 Abs. 1 Ziff. 1 und 2 führen jeweils zwei Stimmen, die übrigen Mitglieder gemäß § 7 Abs. 1 Ziff. 3 bis 6 jeweils eine Stimme. Beschlüsse werden, soweit nicht die Satzung eine andere Regelung vorsieht, mit einfacher Mehrheit der abgegebenen Stimmen gefasst. Bei Stimmengleichheit geben die Stimmen des/der Vorsitzenden den Ausschlag. Entscheidungen über Haushalts- und Personalangelegenheiten bedürfen der Zustimmung der Vertreter der Bundesregierung (§ 7 Abs. 1 Ziff. 1), wobei in diesen Angelegenheiten deren Stimmen nur einheitlich abgegeben werden können.

(2) Der Stiftungsrat entscheidet in der Regel in Sitzungen, die der Vorstand im Auftrag der/des Vorsitzende(n) nach Bedarf, jedoch mindestens zweimal im Jahr einberuft. Auf Antrag von mindestens einem Drittel der Mitglieder muss eine Sitzung einberufen werden.

(3) Die Einladung zur Stiftungssitzung erfolgt schriftlich oder fernschriftlich unter Angabe der Tagesordnung, wobei zwischen dem Tag der Absendung der Ladung und dem Tag der Sitzung – beide nicht mitgezählt – 14 Tage liegen müssen. Auf Form und Frist zur Ladung kann durch Beschluss von zwei Dritteln der Stimmen im Stiftungsrat verzichtet werden. Der Stiftungsrat ist beschlussfähig, wenn zu der Sitzung ordnungsgemäß eingeladen wurde.

(4) An den Sitzungen des Stiftungsrates nehmen die beiden Vorstandsmitglieder mit Rederecht teil, soweit der Stiftungsrat im Einzelfall nichts anderes beschließt. Der Vorstand ist berechtigt, Anträge zu stellen.

(5) Eine Beschlussfassung im schriftlichen oder fernschriftlichen Umlaufverfahren ist zulässig, wenn eine Mehrheit von zwei Dritteln der Stimmen im Stiftungsrat sich mit diesem Verfahren schriftlich oder fernschriftlich einverstanden erklärt hat.

(6) Über die Sitzungen des Stiftungsrates ist eine Niederschrift anzufertigen, die von der Sitzungsleitung zu unterzeichnen ist. Beschlüsse sind im Wortlaut festzuhalten. Die Stiftungsratsmitglieder und der/die Vorsitzende des Stiftungsbeirates erhalten Abschriften der Sitzungsniederschriften.

(7) Weitere Regelungen über den Geschäftsgang des Stiftungsrates kann eine von diesem mit einer Mehrheit von zwei Dritteln der Stimmen zu erlassende Geschäftsordnung enthalten.

§ 10 – Vorstand

(1) Der Stiftungsrat bestellt auf die Dauer von bis zu fünf Jahren eine(n) Künstlerische(n) Direktor/in und eine(n) Verwaltungsdirektor/in zum Vorstand im Sinne der §§ 86, 26 BGB. Diese können nicht gleichzeitig Mitglieder des Stiftungsrates oder des Stiftungsbeirates sein. Erneute Berufung ist zulässig. Nach einer ununterbrochenen Amtszeit von 10 Jahren kann die Berufung der Mitglieder des Vorstands bis zum Erreichen der Altersgrenze für den gesetzlichen Ruhestand von Tarifbeschäftigten im öffentlichen Dienst erfolgen.

(2) Der Vorstand führt die laufenden Geschäfte der Stiftung unbeschadet der Rechte der anderen Organe und nach durch den Stiftungsrat in einer Geschäftsordnung festgelegten Richtlinien. Jedes Vorstandsmitglied vertritt die Stiftung gerichtlich und außergerichtlich. Im Innenverhältnis sind sie gehalten, jeweils nur im Rahmen ihrer in der Geschäftsordnung abgegrenzten Zuständigkeitsbereiche tätig zu werden. Für Rechtsgeschäfte, welche die Stiftung im Einzelfall mit mehr als 10.000 Euro verpflichten, sind die Vorstandsmitglieder nur gemeinschaftlich zur Vertretung der Stiftung berechtigt.

(3) Die Stiftung wird gegenüber dem Vorstand durch den/die Vorsitzende(n) des Stiftungsrates vertreten.

(4) Der Stiftungsrat kann ein Mitglied des Vorstandes aus wichtigem Grund abberufen. Hierzu bedarf es eines Beschlusses von mehr als zwei Dritteln der Stimmen im Stiftungsrat.

(5) Der Vorstand beruft die Sitzungen der Stiftungsgremien im Einvernehmen mit dem/der jeweiligen Vorsitzenden ein, bereitet diese vor, nimmt an ihnen ohne Stimmrecht teil und führt ihre Beschlüsse aus.

(6) Der Vorstand stellt die Entwürfe des Wirtschaftsplans sowie der mittelfristigen Finanzplanung auf und erstellt die Jahresrechnung und den Jahresbericht.

§ 11 – Stiftungsbeirat

(1) Der Stiftungsbeirat besteht aus Persönlichkeiten, die in den unterschiedlichen Sparten der Kunst und des Kulturlebens tätig sind. Sie werden vom Stiftungsrat berufen, der zuvor Voten von Fachverbänden einholen kann.

(2) Die Mitglieder des Stiftungsbeirats werden auf die Dauer von fünf Jahren bestellt. Wiederbestellung ist zulässig. § 7 Abs. 3 Satz 3 und Abs. 4 Satz 2 gelten entsprechend.
(3) Der Stiftungsbeirat wählt für die Dauer der Amtszeit aus seiner Mitte jeweils eine Person in den Vorsitz und in den stellvertretenden Vorsitz. Wiederwahl ist zulässig.

§ 12 – Rechte und Pflichten des Stiftungsbeirats
(1) Der Stiftungsbeirat berät und unterstützt den Stiftungsrat und den Vorstand bei ihrer Tätigkeit. Er erörtert die inhaltlichen Schwerpunkte der Stiftungstätigkeit und gibt hierzu Empfehlungen ab.
(2) Der Stiftungsbeirat soll einmal im Jahr zu einer ordentlichen Sitzung zusammentreffen. Eine außerordentliche Sitzung ist einzuberufen, wenn mindestens ein Drittel der Mitglieder oder der Stiftungsrat dies verlangen. Die Stiftungsratsmitglieder können, der Vorstand soll an den Sitzungen des Stiftungsbeirats beratend teilnehmen.
(3) Für die Einberufung und Beschlussfassung des Stiftungsbeirats gelten § 9 Abs. 2 bis 4, 6 und 7 entsprechend.

§ 13 – Fachbeiräte
(1) Die Stiftung kann Fachbeiräte einrichten. Diese beraten den Stiftungsrat und den Vorstand bei der Festlegung der Förderschwerpunkte (Programme) und geben Empfehlungen für die Auswahl der zu fördernden oder durch die Stiftung selbst durchzuführenden Projekte ab.
(2) Zu Mitgliedern der Fachbeiräte beruft der Stiftungsrat, nachdem dieser Vorschläge des/der Künstlerischen Direktors/in eingeholt hat, für einen befristeten Zeitraum Persönlichkeiten, die sich durch besondere Leistungen in der Kunst und Kultur überregional und möglichst auch international ausgezeichnet haben. Außerdem können an den Sitzungen der Fachbeiräte jeweils ein Vertreter der Behörde des/der Beauftragte(n) der Bundesregierung für Angelegenheiten der Kultur und der Medien ohne Stimmrecht teilnehmen.
(3) Das Nähere wird in einem vom Stiftungsrat zu beschließenden Organisationsstatut festgelegt.

§ 14 – Zusammenwirken mit anderen kulturellen Einrichtungen
Die Stiftung erfüllt ihre Aufgaben in engem Zusammenwirken mit anderen vergleichbaren in- und ausländischen kulturellen Einrichtungen.

§ 15 – Aufsicht, Haushalt, Rechnungsprüfung
(1) Für die Aufstellung und Ausführung des Wirtschaftsplans gelten die Bestimmungen der Bundeshaushaltsordnung entsprechend.
(2) Das Geschäftsjahr der Stiftung ist das Kalenderjahr. Innerhalb der ersten fünf Monate eines jeden Jahres hat der Vorstand eine Jahresrechnung für das abgelaufene Kalenderjahr aufzustellen. Die Rechnung kann jährlich durch eine(n) Wirtschaftsprüfer/in oder eine Wirtschaftsprüfungsgesellschaft geprüft werden, die vom Stiftungsrat im Einvernehmen mit dem Bundesrechnungshof bestellt werden. Sie haben nach Richtlinien zu prüfen, die vom Stiftungsrat im Einvernehmen mit dem Bundesrechnungshof zu erlassen sind.
(3) Die Haushalts- und Wirtschaftsführung der Stiftung unterliegt der Prüfung durch den Bundesrechnungshof gemäß § 104 Abs. 1 Nr. 4 BHO.
(4) Die Stiftung darf ihre Beschäftigten nicht besser stellen als vergleichbare Bundesbedienstete. Ausnahmen bedürfen der Zustimmung des/der Beauftragte(n) der Bundesregierung für Angelegenheiten der Kultur und der Medien und des Bundesministeriums der Finanzen.
(5) Ausnahmen im Sinne von § 2 Abs. 3 Satz 2 und 3 sind nur zulässig, wenn hierzu eine Ermächtigung im Haushaltsplan des Bundes besteht.

§ 16 – Berichterstattung
Die Stiftung legt jährlich einen öffentlich zugänglichen Bericht über ihre bisherige Tätigkeit und ihre Vorhaben vor.

§ 17 – Satzungsänderungen, Änderung des Stiftungszwecks, Zusammenlegung mit einer anderen Stiftung, Auflösung
(1) Änderungen der Satzung sind durch Beschluss des Stiftungsrates zulässig, wenn die Anpassung an veränderte Verhältnisse notwendig erscheint oder die Änderung sonst nach Einschätzung des Stiftungsrates einer Verbesserung der Stiftungsarbeit dient.

(2) Der Stiftungsrat kann Änderungen des Stiftungszwecks, die Zusammenlegung mit einer anderen Stiftung oder die Auflösung der Stiftung beschließen, wenn die Erfüllung des Stiftungszwecks unmöglich wird oder dem Stiftungsrat die Erfüllung des Stiftungszwecks mit der bisherigen Zweckbeschreibung oder in der bisherigen Organisationsstruktur nicht mehr sinnvoll erscheint.

(3) Der Stiftungsrat kann jederzeit eine Zusammenlegung oder institutionelle Verschränkung mit der „Kulturstiftung der Länder" beschließen, wenn deren Stiftungsgremien gleichlautende Entscheidungen treffen.

(4) Beschlüsse des Stiftungsrates nach Abs. 1–3 bedürfen einer Mehrheit von zwei Dritteln der Stimmen sowie der Zustimmung des Stifters; sie werden erst nach Genehmigung durch die zuständige Stiftungsbehörde wirksam. Eine Beschlussfassung im Umlaufverfahren ist nicht möglich.

(5) Beschlüsse über Satzungsänderungen oder über eine Zusammenlegung dürfen die Steuerbegünstigung der Stiftung nicht beeinträchtigen.

§ 18 – Stiftungsbehörde

(1) Die Stiftung unterliegt der staatlichen Aufsicht nach Maßgabe des jeweils im Lande Sachsen-Anhalt geltenden Stiftungsrechts. Zuständige Stiftungsbehörde ist das Regierungspräsidium in Halle/Saale.

(2) Der Stiftungsbehörde sind Änderungen in der Zusammensetzung der Stiftungsorgane sowie Haushaltsplan, Jahresrechnung und Tätigkeitsbericht unaufgefordert vorzulegen.

§ 19 – Anfallberechtigung

Im Falle der Aufhebung der Stiftung oder bei Wegfall des gemeinnützigen Zwecks fällt deren Vermögen an die Bundesrepublik Deutschland, die es unmittelbar und ausschließlich zugunsten des bisherigen Stiftungszweckes verwenden soll.

§ 20 – Inkrafttreten

Die Satzung tritt mit dem Tage der Zustellung der Genehmigungsurkunde in Kraft.

Gesetz über die Angelegenheiten der Vertriebenen und Flüchtlinge (Bundesvertriebenengesetz – BVFG)

In der Fassung der Bekanntmachung vom 10. August 2007[1] (BGBl. I S. 1902) (FNA 240-1)
zuletzt geändert durch Art. 3 Terminservice- und VersorgungsG vom 6. Mai 2019 (BGBl. I S. 646)
– Auszug –

Sechster Abschnitt
Kultur, Forschung und Statistik

§ 96 Pflege des Kulturgutes der Vertriebenen und Flüchtlinge und Förderung der wissenschaftlichen Forschung

¹Bund und Länder haben entsprechend ihrer durch das Grundgesetz gegebenen Zuständigkeit das Kulturgut der Vertreibungsgebiete in dem Bewusstsein der Vertriebenen und Flüchtlinge, des gesamten deutschen Volkes und des Auslandes zu erhalten, Archive, Museen und Bibliotheken zu sichern, zu ergänzen und auszuwerten sowie Einrichtungen des Kunstschaffens und der Ausbildung sicherzustellen und zu fördern. ²Sie haben Wissenschaft und Forschung bei der Erfüllung der Aufgaben, die sich aus der Vertreibung und der Eingliederung der Vertriebenen und Flüchtlinge ergeben, sowie die Weiterentwicklung der Kulturleistungen der Vertriebenen und Flüchtlinge zu fördern. ³Die Bundesregierung berichtet jährlich dem Bundestag über das von ihr Veranlasste.

---

[1] Neubekanntmachung des BVFG idF der Bek. v. 2.6.1993 (BGBl. I S. 829) in der ab 24.5.2007 geltenden Fassung.

C.IV.6 Vertrag mit dem Zentralrat der Juden

Vertrag zwischen der Bundesrepublik Deutschland, vertreten durch den Bundeskanzler, und dem Zentralrat der Juden in Deutschland

Vom 27. Januar 2003[1]) (BGBl. I S. 1597)
zuletzt geändert durch Art. 1 ÄndVertrag vom 6. Juli 2018[2]) (BGBl. I S. 2235)

Präambel

Im Bewusstsein der besonderen geschichtlichen Verantwortung des deutschen Volkes für das jüdische Leben in Deutschland, angesichts des unermesslichen Leides, das die jüdische Bevölkerung in den Jahren 1933 bis 1945 erdulden musste, geleitet von dem Wunsch, den Wiederaufbau jüdischen Lebens in Deutschland zu fördern und das freundschaftliche Verhältnis zu der jüdischen Glaubensgemeinschaft zu verfestigen und zu vertiefen, schließt die Bundesrepublik Deutschland mit dem Zentralrat der Juden in Deutschland folgenden Vertrag:

Artikel 1 Zusammenwirken

¹Die Bundesregierung und der Zentralrat der Juden in Deutschland, Körperschaft des öffentlichen Rechts, der nach seinem Selbstverständnis für alle Richtungen innerhalb des Judentums offen ist, vereinbaren eine kontinuierliche und partnerschaftliche Zusammenarbeit in den Bereichen, die die gemeinsamen Interessen berühren und in der Zuständigkeit der Bundesregierung liegen. ²Die Bundesregierung wird zur Erhaltung und Pflege des deutsch-jüdischen Kulturerbes, zum Aufbau einer jüdischen Gemeinschaft und zu den integrationspolitischen und sozialen Aufgaben des Zentralrats in Deutschland beitragen. ³Dazu wird sie den Zentralrat der Juden in Deutschland bei der Erfüllung seiner überregionalen Aufgaben sowie den Kosten seiner Verwaltung finanziell unterstützen.

Artikel 2 Staatsleistung

(1) Zu den in Artikel 1 genannten Zwecken zahlt die Bundesrepublik Deutschland an den Zentralrat der Juden in Deutschland jährlich einen Betrag von 13 000 000 Euro, beginnend – unabhängig vom Inkrafttreten des Vertrages – mit dem Haushaltsjahr 2018.

(2) ¹Die Vertragsschließenden werden sich nach Ablauf von jeweils fünf Jahren – beginnend im Jahr 2008 – hinsichtlich einer Anpassung der Leistung nach Absatz 1 verständigen. ²Sie sind sich darüber einig, dass die Entwicklung der Zahl der vom Zentralrat repräsentierten Gemeindemitglieder ein wichtiges Kriterium bei der Berechnung der Leistungsanpassung darstellt.

Artikel 3 Zahlungsmodalitäten

Die Leistung wird 2003 in einer Summe, ab 2004 mit je einem Viertel des Jahresbetrages jeweils zum 15. Februar, 15. Mai, 15. August und 15. November gezahlt.

Artikel 4 Prüfung der Verwendung der Mittel

¹Der Zentralrat der Juden in Deutschland weist die Verwendung der Zahlung jährlich durch eine von einem unabhängigen vereidigten Wirtschaftsprüfer geprüfte Rechnung nach. ²Die Rechnung und der Bericht des Wirtschaftsprüfers sind der Bundesregierung vorzulegen.

Artikel 5 Weitere Einrichtungen des Zentralrats

(1) Der Bund wird darüber hinaus auch zukünftig die bisher geförderten Einrichtungen des Zentralrats der Juden in Deutschland – Hochschule für Jüdische Studien und Zentralarchiv zur Erforschung der Geschichte der Juden in Deutschland, beide mit Sitz in Heidelberg – auf freiwilliger Basis unterstützen.

(2) Die Förderung der Hochschule für Jüdische Studien erfolgt derzeit mit einem Bundesanteil von 30 Prozent im Einvernehmen mit den Ländern.

(3) Das Zentralarchiv wird vom Bund institutionell gefördert auf der Grundlage der vorgelegten Wirtschaftspläne.

(4) In beiden Fällen handelt es sich um vom Bund jährlich festzulegende Zuwendungen im Sinne des Bundeshaushaltsrechts nach den Vorgaben des Haushaltsgesetzgebers.

---

1) Der Vertrag wurde von der Bundesrepublik Deutschland ratifiziert durch G v. 10.8.2003 (BGBl. I S. 1597).
2) Der Änderungsvertrag wurde für die Bundesrepublik Deutschland ratifiziert durch G v. 29.11.2018 (BGBl. I S. 2235).

Artikel 6 Ausschluss weiterer Leistungen
(1) Der Zentralrat der Juden in Deutschland wird über die in Artikel 2 und 5 gewährten Leistungen hinaus keine weiteren finanziellen Forderungen an die Bundesrepublik Deutschland herantragen.
(2) Auf besonderer Grundlage mögliche oder bestehende Leistungen an die jüdische Gemeinschaft auf Bundesebene bleiben durch diesen Vertrag unberührt, insbesondere staatliche Leistungen für die Integration jüdischer Zuwanderer aus den GUS-Staaten und für die Pflege verwaister jüdischer Friedhöfe auf der Grundlage der Vereinbarung zwischen dem Bund und den Ländern vom 21. Juni 1957.

Artikel 7 Vertragsanpassung
[1]Die Vertragsschließenden sind sich bewusst, dass die Festlegung der finanziellen Leistungen dieses Vertrages auf der Grundlage der derzeitigen Verhältnisse erfolgt. [2]Bei einer wesentlichen Veränderung der Verhältnisse werden sich die Vertragsschließenden um eine angemessene Anpassung bemühen.

Artikel 8 Freundschaftsklausel
Die Vertragsschließenden werden etwa in Zukunft auftretende Meinungsverschiedenheiten über die Auslegung dieses Vertrages in freundschaftlicher Weise beseitigen.

Artikel 9 Zustimmung des Deutschen Bundestages, Inkrafttreten
(1) Der Vertrag bedarf der Zustimmung des Deutschen Bundestages durch ein Bundesgesetz.
(2) Er tritt am Tag des Inkrafttretens des Gesetzes, mit dem diesem Vertrag zugestimmt wird,[1)] in Kraft.

---

1) ZustimmungsG v. 10.8.2003 (BGBl. I S. 1597), verkündet am 14.8.2003 und nach seinem Art 3 in Kraft getreten am 15.8.2003.

C.V.1 Strafgesetzbuch

Strafgesetzbuch (StGB)

In der Fassung der Bekanntmachung vom 13. November 1998[1] (BGBl. I S. 3322) (FNA 450-2)

zuletzt geändert durch Art. 62 Zweites Datenschutz-Anpassungs- und Umsetzungsgesetz EU vom 20. November 2019 (BGBl. I S. 1626)

– Auszug –

Neunzehnter Abschnitt
Diebstahl und Unterschlagung

§ 242 Diebstahl

(1) Wer eine fremde bewegliche Sache einem anderen in der Absicht wegnimmt, die Sache sich oder einem Dritten rechtswidrig zuzueignen, wird mit Freiheitsstrafe bis zu fünf Jahren oder mit Geldstrafe bestraft.

(2) Der Versuch ist strafbar.

§ 243 Besonders schwerer Fall des Diebstahls

(1) ¹In besonders schweren Fällen wird der Diebstahl mit Freiheitsstrafe von drei Monaten bis zu zehn Jahren bestraft. ²Ein besonders schwerer Fall liegt in der Regel vor, wenn der Täter

[…]

4. aus einer Kirche oder einem anderen der Religionsausübung dienenden Gebäude oder Raum eine Sache stiehlt, die dem Gottesdienst gewidmet ist oder der religiösen Verehrung dient,
5. eine Sache von Bedeutung für Wissenschaft, Kunst oder Geschichte oder für die technische Entwicklung stiehlt, die sich in einer allgemein zugänglichen Sammlung befindet oder öffentlich ausgestellt ist,

[…]

(2) In den Fällen des Absatzes 1 Satz 2 Nr. 1 bis 6 ist ein besonders schwerer Fall ausgeschlossen, wenn sich die Tat auf eine geringwertige Sache bezieht.

§ 246[2] Unterschlagung

(1) Wer eine fremde bewegliche Sache sich oder einem Dritten rechtswidrig zueignet, wird mit Freiheitsstrafe bis zu drei Jahren oder mit Geldstrafe bestraft, wenn die Tat nicht in anderen Vorschriften mit schwererer Strafe bedroht ist.

(2) Ist in den Fällen des Absatzes 1 die Sache dem Täter anvertraut, so ist die Strafe Freiheitsstrafe bis zu fünf Jahren oder Geldstrafe.

(3) Der Versuch ist strafbar.

Einundzwanzigster Abschnitt
Begünstigung und Hehlerei

§ 259 Hehlerei

(1) Wer eine Sache, die ein anderer gestohlen oder sonst durch eine gegen fremdes Vermögen gerichtete rechtswidrige Tat erlangt hat, ankauft oder sonst sich oder einem Dritten verschafft, sie absetzt oder absetzen hilft, um sich oder einen Dritten zu bereichern, wird mit Freiheitsstrafe bis zu fünf Jahren oder mit Geldstrafe bestraft.

(2) Die §§ 247 und 248a gelten sinngemäß.

(3) Der Versuch ist strafbar.

---

1) Neubekanntmachung des StGB idF der Bek. v. 10.3.1987 (BGBl. I S. 945, 1160) in der seit 1.1.1999 geltenden Fassung.
2) Beachte auch §§ 34 ff. DepotG.

Siebenundzwanzigster Abschnitt
Sachbeschädigung

§ 303 Sachbeschädigung
(1) Wer rechtswidrig eine fremde Sache beschädigt oder zerstört, wird mit Freiheitsstrafe bis zu zwei Jahren oder mit Geldstrafe bestraft.
(2) Ebenso wird bestraft, wer unbefugt das Erscheinungsbild einer fremden Sache nicht nur unerheblich und nicht nur vorübergehend verändert.
(3) Der Versuch ist strafbar.

§ 303c Strafantrag
In den Fällen der §§ 303, 303a Abs. 1 und 2 sowie 303b Abs. 1 bis 3 wird die Tat nur auf Antrag verfolgt, es sei denn, daß die Strafverfolgungsbehörde wegen des besonderen öffentlichen Interesses an der Strafverfolgung ein Einschreiten von Amts wegen für geboten hält.

§ 304 Gemeinschädliche Sachbeschädigung
(1) Wer rechtswidrig Gegenstände der Verehrung einer im Staat bestehenden Religionsgesellschaft oder Sachen, die dem Gottesdienst gewidmet sind, oder Grabmäler, öffentliche Denkmäler, Naturdenkmäler, Gegenstände der Kunst, der Wissenschaft oder des Gewerbes, welche in öffentlichen Sammlungen aufbewahrt werden oder öffentlich aufgestellt sind, oder Gegenstände, welche zum öffentlichen Nutzen oder zur Verschönerung öffentlicher Wege, Plätze oder Anlagen dienen, beschädigt oder zerstört, wird mit Freiheitsstrafe bis zu drei Jahren oder mit Geldstrafe bestraft.
(2) Ebenso wird bestraft, wer unbefugt das Erscheinungsbild einer in Absatz 1 bezeichneten Sache oder eines dort bezeichneten Gegenstandes nicht nur unerheblich und nicht nur vorübergehend verändert.
(3) Der Versuch ist strafbar.

§ 305 Zerstörung von Bauwerken
(1) Wer rechtswidrig ein Gebäude, ein Schiff, eine Brücke, einen Damm, eine gebaute Straße, eine Eisenbahn oder ein anderes Bauwerk, welche fremdes Eigentum sind, ganz oder teilweise zerstört, wird mit Freiheitsstrafe bis zu fünf Jahren oder mit Geldstrafe bestraft.
(2) Der Versuch ist strafbar.

Achtundzwanzigster Abschnitt
Gemeingefährliche Straftaten

§ 306 Brandstiftung
(1) Wer fremde
1. Gebäude oder Hütten,
2. Betriebsstätten oder technische Einrichtungen, namentlich Maschinen,
3. Warenlager oder -vorräte,
4. Kraftfahrzeuge, Schienen-, Luft- oder Wasserfahrzeuge,
5. Wälder, Heiden oder Moore oder
6. land-, ernährungs- oder forstwirtschaftliche Anlagen oder Erzeugnisse

in Brand setzt oder durch eine Brandlegung ganz oder teilweise zerstört, wird mit Freiheitsstrafe von einem Jahr bis zu zehn Jahren bestraft.
(2) In minder schweren Fällen ist die Strafe Freiheitsstrafe von sechs Monaten bis zu fünf Jahren.

§ 306a Schwere Brandstiftung
(1) Mit Freiheitsstrafe nicht unter einem Jahr wird bestraft, wer
1. ein Gebäude, ein Schiff, eine Hütte oder eine andere Räumlichkeit, die der Wohnung von Menschen dient,
2. eine Kirche oder ein anderes der Religionsausübung dienendes Gebäude oder
3. eine Räumlichkeit, die zeitweise dem Aufenthalt von Menschen dient, zu einer Zeit, in der Menschen sich dort aufzuhalten pflegen,

in Brand setzt oder durch eine Brandlegung ganz oder teilweise zerstört.

C.V.1 Strafgesetzbuch

(2) Ebenso wird bestraft, wer eine in § 306 Abs. 1 Nr. 1 bis 6 bezeichnete Sache in Brand setzt oder durch eine Brandlegung ganz oder teilweise zerstört und dadurch einen anderen Menschen in die Gefahr einer Gesundheitsschädigung bringt.

(3) In minder schweren Fällen der Absätze 1 und 2 ist die Strafe Freiheitsstrafe von sechs Monaten bis zu fünf Jahren.

Völkerstrafgesetzbuch (VStGB)[1)]

Vom 26. Juni 2002 (BGBl. I S. 2254)
(FNA 453-21)
zuletzt geändert durch Art. 1 G zur Änd. des Völkerstrafgesetzbuches vom 22. Dezember 2016
(BGBl. I S. 3150)
– Auszug –

Teil 2
Straftaten gegen das Völkerrecht

Abschnitt 2
Kriegsverbrechen

§ 9 Kriegsverbrechen gegen Eigentum und sonstige Rechte
(1) Wer im Zusammenhang mit einem internationalen oder nichtinternationalen bewaffneten Konflikt plündert oder, ohne dass dies durch die Erfordernisse des bewaffneten Konflikts geboten ist, sonst in erheblichem Umfang völkerrechtswidrig Sachen der gegnerischen Partei, die der Gewalt der eigenen Partei unterliegen, zerstört, sich aneignet oder beschlagnahmt, wird mit Freiheitsstrafe von einem Jahr bis zu zehn Jahren bestraft.
[…]

§ 11 Kriegsverbrechen des Einsatzes verbotener Methoden der Kriegsführung
(1) ¹Wer im Zusammenhang mit einem internationalen oder nichtinternationalen bewaffneten Konflikt
[…]
2. mit militärischen Mitteln einen Angriff gegen zivile Objekte richtet, solange sie durch das humanitäre Völkerrecht als solche geschützt sind, namentlich Gebäude, die dem Gottesdienst, der Erziehung, der Kunst, der Wissenschaft oder der Wohltätigkeit gewidmet sind, geschichtliche Denkmäler, Krankenhäuser und Sammelplätze für Kranke und Verwundete, unverteidigte Städte, Dörfer, Wohnstätten oder Gebäude oder entmilitarisierte Zonen sowie Anlagen und Einrichtungen, die gefährliche Kräfte enthalten,
[…]
wird mit Freiheitsstrafe nicht unter drei Jahren bestraft. ²In minder schweren Fällen der Nummer 2 ist die Strafe Freiheitsstrafe nicht unter einem Jahr.
[…]

---

1) Verkündet als Art. 1 Völkerstrafgesetzbuch-EinführungsG v. 26. 6. 2002 (BGBl. I S. 2254); Inkrafttreten gem. Art. 8 dieses G am 30. 6. 2002.

D1 Verfassung Baden-Württemberg

Verfassung des Landes Baden-Württemberg

Vom 11. November 1953 (GBl. S. 173)
(BWGültV Sachgebiet 100)
zuletzt geändert durch ÄndG vom 1. Dezember 2015 (GBl. S. 1032)
– Auszug –

Erster Hauptteil
Vom Menschen und seinen Ordnungen

I.
Mensch und Staat

Artikel 3c [Kultur- und Sportförderung; Landschafts- und Denkmalschutz]
(1) Der Staat, die Gemeinden und die Gemeindeverbände fördern den ehrenamtlichen Einsatz für das Gemeinwohl, das kulturelle Leben und den Sport unter Wahrung der Autonomie der Träger.
(2) Die Landschaft sowie die Denkmale der Kunst, der Geschichte und der Natur genießen öffentlichen Schutz und die Pflege des Staates und der Gemeinden.

Gesetz zum Schutz der Kulturdenkmale (Denkmalschutzgesetz – DSchG)

In der Fassung vom 6. Dezember 1983[1]) (GBl. S. 797)
(BWGültV Sachgebiet 2139)
zuletzt geändert durch Art. 37 9. AnpassungsVO vom 23. Februar 2017 (GBl. S. 99)

Nichtamtliche Inhaltsübersicht

1. Abschnitt
Denkmalschutz und Denkmalpflege
§ 1   Aufgabe

2. Abschnitt
Gegenstand und Organisation des Denkmalschutzes
§ 2   Gegenstand des Denkmalschutzes
§ 3   Denkmalschutzbehörden
§ 3a   Landesamt für Denkmalpflege
§ 4   Denkmalrat
§ 5   Entschädigungen

3. Abschnitt
Allgemeine Schutzvorschriften
§ 6   Erhaltungspflicht
§ 7   Maßnahmen und Zuständigkeit der Denkmalschutzbehörden
§ 8   Allgemeiner Schutz von Kulturdenkmalen
§ 9   Sammlungen
§ 10   Auskunfts- und Duldungspflichten
§ 11   Kulturdenkmale, die dem Gottesdienst dienen

4. Abschnitt
Zusätzlicher Schutz für eingetragene Kulturdenkmale
§ 12   Kulturdenkmale von besonderer Bedeutung
§ 13   Eintragungsverfahren
§ 14   Denkmalbuch

§ 15   Wirkung der Eintragung
§ 16   Anzeigepflichten
§ 17   Vorläufiger Schutz
§ 18   Besonderer Schutz bei Katastrophen

5. Abschnitt
Gesamtanlagen
§ 19   Gesamtanlagen

6. Abschnitt
Fund von Kulturdenkmalen
§ 20   Zufällige Funde
§ 21   Nachforschungen
§ 22   Grabungsschutzgebiete
§ 23   Schatzregal

7. Abschnitt
Entschädigung
§ 24   Entschädigung

8. Abschnitt
Förmliche Enteignung
§ 25   Voraussetzungen der Enteignung
§ 26   Enteignung beweglicher Sachen

9. Abschnitt
Ordnungswidrigkeiten und Schlußbestimmungen
§ 27   Ordnungswidrigkeiten
§ 28   Übergangsbestimmungen
§ 29   Inkrafttreten

1. Abschnitt
Denkmalschutz und Denkmalpflege

§ 1 Aufgabe
(1) Es ist Aufgabe von Denkmalschutz und Denkmalpflege, die Kulturdenkmale zu schützen und zu pflegen, insbesondere den Zustand der Kulturdenkmale zu überwachen sowie auf die Abwendung von Gefährdungen und die Bergung von Kulturdenkmalen hinzuwirken.
(2) Diese Aufgabe wird vom Land und im Rahmen ihrer Leistungsfähigkeit von den Gemeinden erfüllt.

2. Abschnitt
Gegenstand und Organisation des Denkmalschutzes

§ 2 Gegenstand des Denkmalschutzes
(1) Kulturdenkmale im Sinne dieses Gesetzes sind Sachen, Sachgesamtheiten und Teile von Sachen, an deren Erhaltung aus wissenschaftlichen, künstlerischen oder heimatgeschichtlichen Gründen ein öffentliches Interesse besteht.[2])

---
1) Neubekanntmachung des DSchG v. 25.5.1971 (GBl. S. 209) in der ab 1.1.1984 geltenden Fassung. Die VwV zum Vollzug des DSchG ist abgedruckt als Nr. D1.I.1b.
2) Siehe dazu auch die VwV-Kulturdenkmalliste, abgedruckt als Nr. D1.I.1c.

D1.I.1 Denkmalschutzgesetz Baden-Württemberg 492

(2) Zu einem Kulturdenkmal gehört auch das Zubehör, soweit es mit der Hauptsache eine Einheit von Denkmalwert bildet.
(3) Gegenstand des Denkmalschutzes sind auch
1. die Umgebung eines Kulturdenkmals, soweit sie für dessen Erscheinungsbild von erheblicher Bedeutung ist (§ 15 Abs. 3), sowie
2. Gesamtanlagen (§ 19).

§ 3 Denkmalschutzbehörden
(1) Denkmalschutzbehörden sind
1. das Wirtschaftsministerium als oberste Denkmalschutzbehörde,
2. die Regierungspräsidien als höhere Denkmalschutzbehörden,
3. die unteren Baurechtsbehörden als untere Denkmalschutzbehörden,
4. das Landesamt für Denkmalpflege,
5. das Landesarchiv als Landesoberbehörde für den Denkmalschutz im Archivwesen.

(2) Die oberste Denkmalschutzbehörde entscheidet über alle grundsätzlichen Angelegenheiten des Denkmalschutzes und der Denkmalpflege sowie über andere wichtige Angelegenheiten von landesweiter Bedeutung, insbesondere über die Aufstellung des Denkmalförderprogramms.
(3) [1]Die den Gemeinden und Verwaltungsgemeinschaften nach Absatz 1 Nr. 3 übertragenen Aufgaben der unteren Denkmalschutzbehörde sind Pflichtaufgaben nach Weisung; das Weisungsrecht ist nicht beschränkt. [2]Für die Erhebung von Gebühren und Auslagen gilt das Kommunalabgabengesetz.
(4) [1]Die unteren Denkmalschutzbehörden entscheiden nach Anhörung des Landesamtes für Denkmalpflege nach Absatz 1 Nr. 4. [2]Will die untere Denkmalschutzbehörde von der Äußerung des Landesamtes für Denkmalpflege abweichen, so hat sie dies der höheren Denkmalschutzbehörde rechtzeitig vorher mitzuteilen. [3]Im Bereich des Archivwesens tritt an die Stelle des Landesamtes für Denkmalpflege das Landesarchiv.
(5) Ist das Land als Eigentümer oder Besitzer betroffen, entscheidet die untere Denkmalschutzbehörde im Einvernehmen mit der für die Verwaltung des Kulturdenkmals zuständigen Landesbehörde.
(6) [1]Leistet eine Denkmalschutzbehörde einer ihr erteilten Weisung innerhalb der gesetzten Frist keine Folge, so kann an ihrer Stelle jede Fachaufsichtsbehörde die erforderlichen Maßnahmen auf Kosten des Kostenträgers der Denkmalschutzbehörde treffen. [2]§ 129 Abs. 5 der Gemeindeordnung gilt entsprechend.

§ 3a Landesamt für Denkmalpflege
[1]Das Landesamt für Denkmalpflege im Regierungspräsidium Stuttgart ist zuständige Behörde für die fachliche Denkmalpflege. [2]Es unterstützt die Denkmalschutzbehörden in allen Angelegenheiten der fachlichen Denkmalpflege bei der Ausführung dieses Gesetzes. [3]Dabei hat es im Rahmen der Vorgaben der obersten Denkmalschutzbehörde insbesondere die Aufgabe,
1. fachliche Grundlagen und Leitlinien für Methodik und Praxis der Denkmalpflege zu erarbeiten und deren landeseinheitliche Umsetzung sicherzustellen,
2. die Aufstellung von Denkmalförderprogrammen vorzubereiten und abzuwickeln,
3. Kulturdenkmale und Gesamtanlagen in Listen zu erfassen, zu dokumentieren und zu erforschen,
4. Dritte, insbesondere die Eigentümer und Besitzer von Kulturdenkmalen, denkmalfachlich zu beraten,
5. die zentrale denkmalfachliche Öffentlichkeitsarbeit durchzuführen und das vom Denkmalschutz umfasste kulturelle Erbe des Landes und die Maßnahmen zu seinem Erhalt in der Öffentlichkeit zu vermitteln,
6. zentrale Fachbibliotheken, Dokumentationen, Fachdatenbanken sowie sonstige zentrale Dienstleistungen zu unterhalten und
7. Steuerbescheinigungen nach § 10g des Einkommensteuergesetzes zu erteilen, soweit keine Zuständigkeit des Landesarchivs besteht.

§ 4 Denkmalrat
(1) [1]Bei der obersten Denkmalschutzbehörde wird ein Denkmalrat gebildet. [2]Der Denkmalrat soll von der obersten Denkmalschutzbehörde bei allen Entscheidungen von grundsätzlicher Bedeutung gehört werden.

(2) ¹Die Mitglieder des Denkmalrats werden von der obersten Denkmalschutzbehörde auf die Dauer von fünf Jahren berufen. ²Die Mitgliederzahl kann bis zu 40 Personen betragen. ³Dem Denkmalrat sollen insbesondere Vertreter der Denkmalschutzbehörden, der staatlichen Hochbauverwaltung, der Kirchen, der kommunalen Landesverbände und der Kulturdenkmaleigentümer sowie weitere Personen angehören, die mit den Fragen des Denkmalschutzes vertraut sind. ⁴Dem Denkmalrat sollen Personen aus allen Regierungsbezirken angehören.
(3) ¹In den Sitzungen führt die oberste Denkmalschutzbehörde den Vorsitz. ²Die Mitglieder des Denkmalrats sind ehrenamtlich tätig.
(4) ¹Die oberste Denkmalschutzbehörde erläßt eine Geschäftsordnung für den Denkmalrat, die auch das Berufungsverfahren und das Vorschlagsrecht regelt. ²Die Geschäftsordnung kann bestimmen, daß der Denkmalrat Fachausschüsse bildet, an die Aufgaben delegiert werden können.

§ 5 Entschädigungen
¹Die oberste Denkmalschutzbehörde kann mit Zustimmung des Finanzministeriums durch Rechtsverordnung[1]) die Entschädigung und den Reisekostenersatz für die Beauftragten der Denkmalschutzbehörden regeln. ²Dabei können Durchschnittssätze festgesetzt werden.

3. Abschnitt
Allgemeine Schutzvorschriften

§ 6 Erhaltungspflicht
¹Eigentümer und Besitzer von Kulturdenkmalen haben diese im Rahmen des Zumutbaren zu erhalten und pfleglich zu behandeln. ²Das Land trägt hierzu durch Zuschüsse nach Maßgabe der zur Verfügung stehenden Haushaltsmittel bei.[2])

§ 7 Maßnahmen und Zuständigkeit der Denkmalschutzbehörden
(1) ¹Die Denkmalschutzbehörden haben zur Wahrnehmung ihrer Aufgaben diejenigen Maßnahmen zu treffen, die ihnen nach pflichtgemäßem Ermessen erforderlich erscheinen. ²Die Vorschriften der §§ 6, 7 und 9 des Polizeigesetzes finden sinngemäß Anwendung.
(2) Soweit ein Vorhaben einer Genehmigung nach diesem Gesetz bedarf, kann diese mit Bedingungen oder Auflagen verknüpft werden.
(3) Bedarf ein Vorhaben nach anderen Vorschriften einer Genehmigung, tritt die Zustimmung der Denkmalschutzbehörde an die Stelle der Genehmigung nach diesem Gesetz.
(4) ¹Soweit nicht etwas Abweichendes bestimmt ist, ist die untere Denkmalschutzbehörde zuständig. ²Erscheint bei Gefahr im Verzug ein rechtzeitiges Tätigwerden der zuständigen Denkmalschutzbehörde nicht erreichbar, so kann das Landesamt für Denkmalpflege oder im Bereich des Archivwesens das Landesarchiv oder, falls diese nicht rechtzeitig tätig werden können, die höhere Denkmalschutzbehörde oder, falls auch diese nicht rechtzeitig tätig werden kann, der Polizeivollzugsdienst die erforderlichen vorläufigen Maßnahmen treffen. ³Die zuständige Behörde ist unverzüglich zu unterrichten.
(5) Ist als Eigentümer oder Besitzer eine kommunale Körperschaft betroffen, so entscheidet
1. die höhere Denkmalschutzbehörde
bei Stadt- und Landkreisen, Großen Kreisstädten sowie Verwaltungsgemeinschaften nach § 17 des Landesverwaltungsgesetzes, die der Rechtsaufsicht des Regierungspräsidiums unterstehen, und den ihnen angehörenden Gemeinden,
2. das Landratsamt als untere Denkmalschutzbehörde
bei Verwaltungsgemeinschaften nach § 17 des Landesverwaltungsgesetzes, die der Rechtsaufsicht des Landratsamts unterstehen, und den ihnen angehörenden Gemeinden, bei sonstigen Gemeinden mit Baurechtszuständigkeit sowie bei sonstigen Verwaltungsgemeinschaften mit Baurechtszuständigkeit und den ihnen angehörenden Gemeinden.

---
1) Die Denkmalschutz-ReisekostenVO ist abgedruckt als Nr. D1.I.1a.
2) Die VwV-Denkmalförderung ist abgedruckt als Nr. D1.III.1.

D1.I.1 Denkmalschutzgesetz Baden-Württemberg

§ 8 Allgemeiner Schutz von Kulturdenkmalen
(1) Ein Kulturdenkmal darf nur mit Genehmigung der Denkmalschutzbehörde
1. zerstört oder beseitigt werden,
2. in seinem Erscheinungsbild beeinträchtigt werden oder
3. aus seiner Umgebung entfernt werden, soweit diese für den Denkmalwert von wesentlicher Bedeutung ist.

(2) Dies gilt für bewegliche Kulturdenkmale nur, wenn sie allgemein sichtbar oder zugänglich sind.

§ 9 Sammlungen
[1]Von den Genehmigungspflichten nach diesem Gesetz sind Kulturdenkmale ausgenommen, die von einer staatlichen Sammlung verwaltet werden. [2]Die oberste Denkmalschutzbehörde kann andere Sammlungen von den Genehmigungspflichten ausnehmen, soweit sie fachlich betreut werden.

§ 10 Auskunfts- und Duldungspflichten
(1) Eigentümer und Besitzer sind verpflichtet, Auskünfte zu erteilen, die zur Erfüllung der Aufgaben des Denkmalschutzes notwendig sind.

(2) [1]Die Denkmalschutzbehörden oder ihre Beauftragten sind berechtigt, Grundstücke und zur Verhütung dringender Gefahr für Kulturdenkmale Wohnungen zu betreten und Kulturdenkmale zu besichtigen, soweit es zur Erfüllung der Aufgaben des Denkmalschutzes erforderlich ist. [2]Sie sind zu den erforderlichen wissenschaftlichen Erfassungsmaßnahmen – wie der Inventarisation – berechtigt; insbesondere können sie in national wertvolle oder landes- oder ortsgeschichtlich bedeutsame Archive oder entsprechende andere Sammlungen Einsicht nehmen. [3]Artikel 13 des Grundgesetzes wird insoweit eingeschränkt.

(3) [1]Kirchen, die nicht dauernd für die Öffentlichkeit zugänglich sind, dürfen nur mit Zustimmung betreten werden. [2]Öffentliche Kirchenräume dürfen nur außerhalb des Gottesdienstes besichtigt werden.

§ 11 Kulturdenkmale, die dem Gottesdienst dienen
(1) [1]Die Denkmalschutzbehörden haben bei Kulturdenkmalen, die dem Gottesdienst dienen, die gottesdienstlichen Belange, die von der oberen Kirchenbehörde oder der entsprechenden Stelle der betroffenen Religionsgemeinschaft festzustellen sind, vorrangig zu beachten. [2]Vor der Durchführung von Maßnahmen setzen sich die Denkmalschutzbehörden mit der oberen Kirchenbehörde oder der entsprechenden Stelle der betroffenen Religionsgemeinschaft ins Benehmen.

(2) [1]§ 7 Abs. 1, § 8 sowie § 15 Abs. 1 und 2 finden keine Anwendung auf Kulturdenkmale, die im kirchlichen Eigentum stehen, soweit sie dem Gottesdienst dienen und die Kirchen im Einvernehmen mit der obersten Denkmalschutzbehörde eigene Vorschriften zum Schutz dieser Kulturdenkmale erlassen. [2]Vor der Durchführung von Vorhaben im Sinne der erwähnten Bestimmungen ist die höhere Denkmalschutzbehörde zu hören. [3]Kommt eine Einigung mit der höheren Denkmalschutzbehörde nicht zustande, so entscheidet die obere Kirchenbehörde im Benehmen mit der obersten Denkmalschutzbehörde.

(3) Der 8. Abschnitt dieses Gesetzes ist auf kircheneigene Kulturdenkmale nicht anwendbar.

4. Abschnitt
Zusätzlicher Schutz für eingetragene Kulturdenkmale

§ 12 Kulturdenkmale von besonderer Bedeutung
(1) Kulturdenkmale von besonderer Bedeutung genießen zusätzlichen Schutz durch Eintragung in das Denkmalbuch.

(2) Bewegliche Kulturdenkmale werden nur eingetragen,
1. wenn der Eigentümer die Eintragung beantragt oder
2. wenn sie eine überörtliche Bedeutung haben oder zum Kulturbereich des Landes besondere Beziehungen aufweisen oder
3. wenn sie national wertvolles Kulturgut darstellen oder
4. wenn sie national wertvolle oder landes- oder ortsgeschichtlich bedeutsame Archive darstellen oder
5. wenn sie auf Grund internationaler Empfehlungen zu schützen sind.

(3) Die Eintragung ist zu löschen, wenn ihre Voraussetzungen nicht mehr vorliegen.

§ 13 Eintragungsverfahren
(1) Für die Eintragung und Löschung ist die höhere Denkmalschutzbehörde zuständig.
(2) Bei einem unbeweglichen Kulturdenkmal ist die Gemeinde zu hören, in deren Gebiet es sich befindet.
(3) Bestehen aus tatsächlichen oder rechtlichen Gründen erhebliche Zweifel, wer Eigentümer eines Kulturdenkmals ist, so können Verwaltungsakte der Denkmalschutzbehörden öffentlich bekanntgegeben werden.
(4) Die Eintragung wirkt für und gegen den Rechtsnachfolger.

§ 14 Denkmalbuch
(1) Das Denkmalbuch wird von der höheren Denkmalschutzbehörde geführt.
(2) Die Einsicht in das Denkmalbuch ist jedermann gestattet, der ein berechtigtes Interesse darlegt.

§ 15 Wirkung der Eintragung
(1) ¹Ein eingetragenes Kulturdenkmal darf nur mit Genehmigung der Denkmalschutzbehörde
1. wiederhergestellt oder instand gesetzt werden,
2. in seinem Erscheinungsbild oder seiner Substanz verändert werden,
3. mit An- oder Aufbauten, Aufschriften oder Werbeeinrichtungen versehen werden,
4. von seinem Stand- oder Aufbewahrungsort insoweit entfernt werden, als bei der Eintragung aus Gründen des Denkmalschutzes verfügt wird, das Kulturdenkmal dürfe nicht entfernt werden.

²Einer Genehmigung bedarf auch die Aufhebung der Zubehöreigenschaft im Sinne von § 2 Abs. 2.
(2) ¹Aus einer eingetragenen Sachgesamtheit, insbesondere aus einer Sammlung, dürfen Einzelsachen nur mit Genehmigung der Denkmalschutzbehörde entfernt werden. ²Die höhere Denkmalschutzbehörde kann allgemein genehmigen, daß Einzelsachen im Rahmen der ordnungsgemäßen Verwaltung entfernt werden.
(3) ¹Bauliche Anlagen in der Umgebung eines eingetragenen Kulturdenkmals, soweit sie für dessen Erscheinungsbild von erheblicher Bedeutung ist, dürfen nur mit Genehmigung der Denkmalschutzbehörde errichtet, verändert oder beseitigt werden. ²Andere Vorhaben bedürfen dieser Genehmigung, wenn sich die bisherige Grundstücksnutzung ändern würde. ³Die Genehmigung ist zu erteilen, wenn das Vorhaben das Erscheinungsbild des Denkmals nur unerheblich oder nur vorübergehend beeinträchtigen würde oder wenn überwiegende Gründe des Gemeinwohls unausweichlich Berücksichtigung verlangen.

§ 16 Anzeigepflichten
(1) Eigentümer und Besitzer haben Schäden oder Mängel, die an eingetragenen Kulturdenkmalen auftreten und die ihre Erhaltung gefährden können, unverzüglich einer Denkmalschutzbehörde anzuzeigen.
(2) Wird ein eingetragenes Kulturdenkmal veräußert, so haben Veräußerer und Erwerber den Eigentumswechsel innerhalb von einem Monat einer Denkmalschutzbehörde anzuzeigen.

§ 17 Vorläufiger Schutz
¹Die höhere Denkmalschutzbehörde kann anordnen, daß Sachen, Sachgesamtheiten oder Teile von Sachen, mit deren Eintragung als Kulturdenkmal in das Denkmalbuch zu rechnen ist, vorläufig als eingetragen gelten. ²Die Anordnung tritt außer Kraft, wenn die Eintragung nicht binnen eines Monats eingeleitet und spätestens nach sechs Monaten bewirkt wird. ³Bei Vorliegen wichtiger Gründe kann diese Frist um höchstens drei Monate verlängert werden.

§ 18 Besonderer Schutz bei Katastrophen
(1) ¹Die oberste Denkmalschutzbehörde wird ermächtigt, durch Rechtsverordnung die zum Schutz eingetragener Kulturdenkmale für den Fall von Katastrophen erforderlichen Vorschriften zu erlassen. ²Dabei können insbesondere die Eigentümer und Besitzer verpflichtet werden,
1. den Aufbewahrungsort von Kulturdenkmalen zu melden,
2. Kulturdenkmale mit den in internationalen Verträgen vorgesehenen Kennzeichen versehen zu lassen,

D1.I.1 Denkmalschutzgesetz Baden-Württemberg

3. Kulturdenkmale zu bergen, besonders zu sichern, bergen oder besonders sichern zu lassen oder sie zum Zwecke der vorübergehenden Verwahrung an Bergungsorten auf Anordnung der Denkmalschutzbehörde abzuliefern,
4. die wissenschaftliche Erfassung von Kulturdenkmalen oder sonstige zu ihrer Dokumentierung, Sicherung oder Wiederherstellung von der Denkmalschutzbehörde angeordnete Maßnahmen zu dulden.

³Soweit in der Rechtsverordnung eine Ablieferungspflicht vorgesehen wird, ist anzuordnen, daß die abgelieferten Sachen unverzüglich den Berechtigten zurückzugeben sind, sobald die weitere Verwahrung an einem Bergungsort zum Schutz der Kulturdenkmale nicht mehr erforderlich ist.

(2) Die Ermächtigung nach Absatz 1 kann von der obersten Denkmalschutzbehörde durch Rechtsverordnung auf die nachgeordneten Denkmalschutzbehörden übertragen werden.

5. Abschnitt
Gesamtanlagen

§ 19 [Gesamtanlagen]

(1) Die Gemeinden können Gesamtanlagen, insbesondere Straßen-, Platz- und Ortsbilder, an deren Erhaltung aus wissenschaftlichen, künstlerischen oder heimatgeschichtlichen Gründen ein besonderes öffentliches Interesse besteht, im Benehmen mit dem Landesamt für Denkmalpflege durch Satzung unter Denkmalschutz stellen.

(2) ¹Veränderungen an dem geschützten Bild der Gesamtanlage bedürfen der Genehmigung der unteren Denkmalschutzbehörde. ²Die Genehmigung ist zu erteilen, wenn die Veränderung das Bild der Gesamtanlage nur unerheblich oder nur vorübergehend beeinträchtigen würde oder wenn überwiegende Gründe des Gemeinwohls unausweichlich Berücksichtigung verlangen. ³Die Denkmalschutzbehörde hat vor ihrer Entscheidung die Gemeinde zu hören.

6. Abschnitt
Fund von Kulturdenkmalen

§ 20 Zufällige Funde

(1) ¹Wer Sachen, Sachgesamtheiten oder Teile von Sachen entdeckt, von denen anzunehmen ist, daß an ihrer Erhaltung aus wissenschaftlichen, künstlerischen oder heimatgeschichtlichen Gründen ein öffentliches Interesse besteht, hat dies unverzüglich einer Denkmalschutzbehörde oder der Gemeinde anzuzeigen. ²Der Fund und die Fundstelle sind bis zum Ablauf des vierten Werktages nach der Anzeige in unverändertem Zustand zu erhalten, sofern nicht die Denkmalschutzbehörde mit einer Verkürzung der Frist einverstanden ist. ³Diese Verpflichtung besteht nicht, wenn damit unverhältnismäßig hohe Kosten oder Nachteile verbunden sind und die Denkmalschutzbehörde es ablehnt, hierfür Ersatz zu leisten.

(2) Das Landesamt für Denkmalpflege und seine Beauftragten sind berechtigt, den Fund auszuwerten und, soweit es sich um bewegliche Kulturdenkmale handelt, zu bergen und zur wissenschaftlichen Bearbeitung in Besitz zu nehmen.

(3) Die Gemeinden sind verpflichtet, die ihnen bekanntwerdenden Funde unverzüglich dem Landesamt für Denkmalpflege mitzuteilen.

§ 21 Nachforschungen

¹Nachforschungen, insbesondere Grabungen, mit dem Ziel, Kulturdenkmale zu entdecken, bedürfen der Genehmigung. ²Die Genehmigung erteilt das Landesamt für Denkmalpflege im Benehmen mit der höheren Denkmalschutzbehörde.

§ 22 Grabungsschutzgebiete

(1) Die untere Denkmalschutzbehörde ist ermächtigt, Gebiete, die begründeter Vermutung nach Kulturdenkmale von besonderer Bedeutung bergen, durch Rechtsverordnung zu Grabungsschutzgebieten zu erklären.

(2) ¹In Grabungsschutzgebieten dürfen Arbeiten, durch die verborgene Kulturdenkmale zutage gefördert oder gefährdet werden können, nur mit Genehmigung vorgenommen werden. ²Die Genehmigung

erteilt das Landesamt für Denkmalpflege im Benehmen mit der höheren Denkmalschutzbehörde. [3]Die bisherige land- und forstwirtschaftliche Nutzung bleibt unberührt.

§ 23 Schatzregal

Bewegliche Kulturdenkmale, die herrenlos sind oder die so lange verborgen gewesen sind, daß ihr Eigentümer nicht mehr zu ermitteln ist, werden mit der Entdeckung Eigentum des Landes, wenn sie bei staatlichen Nachforschungen oder in Grabungsschutzgebieten entdeckt werden oder wenn sie einen hervorragenden wissenschaftlichen Wert haben.

7. Abschnitt
Entschädigung

§ 24 [Entschädigung]

(1) [1]Soweit Maßnahmen auf Grund dieses Gesetzes enteignende Wirkung haben, ist eine angemessene Entschädigung zu leisten. [2]§§ 7 bis 13 des Landesenteignungsgesetzes gelten entsprechend.

(2) Kommt eine Einigung über die Entschädigung nicht zustande, so entscheidet die höhere Denkmalschutzbehörde.

8. Abschnitt
Förmliche Enteignung

§ 25 Voraussetzungen der Enteignung

(1) Die Enteignung ist zulässig, soweit die Erhaltung eines eingetragenen Kulturdenkmals oder seines Erscheinungsbildes oder die Erhaltung einer geschützten Gesamtanlage auf andere zumutbare Weise nicht gesichert werden kann.

(2) Die Enteignung ist außerdem zulässig
1. bei Funden, soweit auf andere Weise nicht sicherzustellen ist, daß ein Kulturdenkmal wissenschaftlich ausgewertet werden kann oder allgemein zugänglich ist,
2. bei Kulturdenkmalen, soweit auf andere Weise nicht sicherzustellen ist, daß sie wissenschaftlich erfaßt werden können.

(3) Zum Zwecke von planmäßigen Nachforschungen ist die Enteignung zulässig, wenn eine begründete Vermutung dafür besteht, daß durch die Nachforschung Kulturdenkmale entdeckt werden.

§ 26 Enteignung beweglicher Sachen

(1) [1]Ist Gegenstand der Enteignung eine bewegliche Sache, ein Recht an einer beweglichen Sache oder ein Recht, das zum Erwerb, Besitz oder zur Nutzung der beweglichen Sache berechtigt oder den Verpflichteten in der Nutzung der beweglichen Sache beschränkt, gelten §§ 4, 5, 7 bis 13, 17, § 22 Abs. 1, 3 und 4, §§ 23, 27 bis 36, 39, 40, 42 und 43 des Landesenteignungsgesetzes entsprechend. [2]In der Ausführungsanordnung können der Eigentümer und der Besitzer verpflichtet werden, die Sache an den Enteignungsbegünstigten herauszugeben.

(2) [1]Ist zur Erhaltung, wissenschaftlichen Erfassung oder Auswertung eines Kulturdenkmals die sofortige Herausgabe an den Antragsteller dringend geboten, kann die Enteignungsbehörde den Eigentümer oder Besitzer verpflichten, die Sache an den Antragsteller herauszugeben. [2]Im übrigen gelten § 37 Abs. 2 bis 5 und § 38 Abs. 2 und 3 des Landesenteignungsgesetzes entsprechend.

9. Abschnitt
Ordnungswidrigkeiten und Schlußbestimmungen

§ 27 Ordnungswidrigkeiten

(1) Ordnungswidrig handelt, wer vorsätzlich oder fahrlässig
1. ohne Genehmigung der Denkmalschutzbehörde die in § 8, § 15 Abs. 1, Abs. 2 Satz 1, Abs. 3 Sätze 1 und 2, § 21, § 22 Abs. 2 Satz 1 bezeichneten Handlungen vornimmt oder den in Genehmigungen enthaltenen vollziehbaren Auflagen zuwiderhandelt,
2. den ihn nach § 16, § 20 Abs. 1 treffenden Pflichten zuwiderhandelt,
3. den Maßnahmen der Denkmalschutzbehörden nach § 7 Abs. 1 oder 4 zuwiderhandelt, sofern die Behörde auf diese Bußgeldvorschrift verweist.

4. den Vorschriften einer nach § 18 erlassenen Rechtsverordnung zuwiderhandelt, soweit die Rechtsverordnung auf diese Bußgeldvorschrift verweist,
5. ohne Genehmigung der Denkmalschutzbehörde entgegen § 19 Abs. 2 Satz 1 Veränderungen an dem geschützten Bild einer Gesamtanlage vornimmt oder den in Genehmigungen enthaltenen vollziehbaren Auflagen zuwiderhandelt, soweit die Gesamtanlage durch Rechtsverordnung nach § 19 Abs. 1 dieses Gesetzes in der bis zum 31. Dezember 1983 geltenden Fassung unter Denkmalschutz gestellt wurde,
6. den Vorschriften einer nach § 19 Abs. 1 erlassenen Satzung zuwiderhandelt, soweit die Satzung für einen bestimmten Tatbestand auf diese Bußgeldvorschrift verweist.

(2) Die Ordnungswidrigkeit kann mit einer Geldbuße bis zu 250 000 Euro, in besonders schweren Fällen bis zu 500 000 Euro geahndet werden.

(3) Gegenstände, auf die sich die Ordnungswidrigkeit nach Absatz 1 Nr. 1, 3 oder 4 bezieht, können eingezogen werden.

(4) Verwaltungsbehörde im Sinne des § 36 Abs. 1 Nr. 1 des Gesetzes über Ordnungswidrigkeiten ist die untere Denkmalschutzbehörde.

§ 28 Übergangsbestimmungen

(1) Als Eintragung in das Denkmalbuch gemäß § 12 gilt die Eintragung in
1. das Denkmalbuch und das Buch der Bodenaltertümer nach dem bad. Landesgesetz zum Schutz der Kulturdenkmale,
2. das auf Grund von Artikel 97 Abs. 7 der württ. Bauordnung angelegte Landesverzeichnis der Baudenkmale,
3. das auf Grund von § 34 der bad. Landesbauordnung angelegte Verzeichnis der Baudenkmale,
4. das Verzeichnis der Denkmäler nach Artikel 8 und 10 des hess. Gesetzes den Denkmalschutz betreffend vom 16. Juli 1902 (RegBl. S. 275),
5. das Denkmalverzeichnis gemäß Verfügung des württ. Ministeriums des Kirchen- und Schulwesens, betreffend den Schutz von Denkmalen und heimatlichem Kunstbesitz, vom 25. Mai 1920 (RegBl. S. 317).

(2) Die Eintragungen nach Absatz 1 sollen in das nach diesem Gesetz anzulegende Denkmalbuch nach den für Neueintragungen geltenden Bestimmungen übertragen werden.

(3) ¹Straßen-, Platz- und Ortsbilder, die nach dem bad. Denkmalschutzgesetz geschützt waren, behalten diese Eigenschaft gemäß § 19, soweit der Schutz im Einvernehmen mit der Gemeinde verfügt worden ist. ²Gebiete, die nach dem bad. Denkmalschutzgesetz zu Grabungsschutzgebieten erklärt waren, werden Grabungsschutzgebiete gemäß § 22.

(4) Kulturdenkmale im Eigentum des Staates und öffentlich-rechtliche Körperschaften, Anstalten oder Stiftungen, die nicht in das Denkmalbuch eingetragen sind, aber eine besondere Bedeutung besitzen, stehen bis zum Ablauf von zehn Jahren nach Inkrafttreten dieses Gesetzes den eingetragenen Kulturdenkmalen gleich.

(5) ¹Maßnahmen, die im Zusammenhang mit der Fideikommißauflösung zum Schutz von Gegenständen und Sachgesamtheiten von besonderem künstlerischen, wissenschaftlichen, geschichtlichen oder heimatlichen Wert getroffen sind, werden durch dieses Gesetz nicht berührt. ²Solche Maßnahmen können geändert, an die Vorschriften dieses Gesetzes angepaßt oder aufgehoben werden. ³Zuständig hierfür sind die höheren Denkmalschutzbehörden. ⁴Sie haben auch die zur Durchsetzung der Maßnahmen erforderlichen Anordnungen zu treffen. ⁵Soweit zur Wirksamkeit eines Rechtsgeschäftes oder zur Vornahme einer Handlung die Genehmigung des Fideikommißgerichts erforderlich war, geht die Genehmigungszuständigkeit auf die höhere Denkmalschutzbehörde über.

§ 29 Inkrafttreten

(1) Dieses Gesetz tritt am 1. Januar 1972 in Kraft.[1]
(2) Gleichzeitig treten alle diesem Gesetz entsprechenden oder widersprechenden Vorschriften außer Kraft, insbesondere *[hier nicht wiedergegeben]*.

---

[1] Amtl. Anm.: Die Vorschrift betrifft das Gesetz in der ursprünglichen Fassung vom 25. Mai 1971 (GBl. S. 209).

Verordnung des Kultusministeriums über die Entschädigung und den Reisekostenersatz für die Beauftragten der Denkmalschutzbehörden – Denkmalschutz-Reisekosten-Verordnung –

Vom 12. Januar 1973 (GBl. S. 21)

Geänd. d. Art. 2 G. v. 18.7.1983 (GBl. S. 378)

Auf Grund von § 5 des Gesetzes zum Schutz der Kulturdenkmale (Denkmalschutzgesetz) vom 25. Mai 1971 (GBl. S. 209) wird mit Zustimmung des Finanzministeriums verordnet:

§ 1
(1) Beauftragte der Denkmalschutzbehörden erhalten auf Antrag eine Reisekostenvergütung in sinngemäßer Anwendung des Landesreisekostengesetzes. Dabei ist die Reisekostenstufe B zugrunde zu legen; für Strecken, die mit einem privateigenen Kraftfahrzeug zurückgelegt wurden, wird als Auslagenersatz eine Wegstrecken- und Mitnahmeentschädigung nach § 6 Abs. 1 Satz und Abs. 3 des Landesreisekostengesetzes gewährt.

(2) Absatz 1 gilt nicht, soweit einem Beauftragten dadurch keine zusätzlichen Aufwendungen entstehen, daß er denkmalpflegerische Aufgaben in Verbindung mit einer dienstlichen Tätigkeit wahrnimmt.

§ 2
Diese Verordnung tritt am Tage nach ihrer Verkündung in Kraft.

D1.I.1b VwV Vollzug Denkmalschutzgesetz

Verwaltungsvorschrift des Finanz- und Wirtschaftsministeriums für das Verfahren zum Vollzug des Denkmalschutzgesetzes für Baden-Württemberg (VwV Vollzug DSchG)[1)]

Vom 22.12.2014 – Az.: 6-2550.0-1/6 – (GABl. 2015 S. 4)

Zur Durchführung des Gesetzes zum Schutz der Kulturdenkmale (Denkmalschutzgesetz – DSchG –) in der Fassung vom 6. Dezember 1983 (GBl. S. 797), zuletzt geändert durch das Gesetz vom 9. Dezember 2014 (GBl. S. 686) wird im Einvernehmen mit dem Wissenschaftsministerium bestimmt:

1 Aufgaben des Landesamtes für Denkmalpflege (§ 3a DSchG)

Das Landesamt für Denkmalpflege im Regierungspräsidium Stuttgart ist Denkmalschutzbehörde nach § 3 DSchG und zuständige Behörde für die fachliche Denkmalpflege. Es unterstützt die Denkmalschutzbehörden in allen Angelegenheiten der fachlichen Denkmalpflege bei der Ausführung des Denkmalschutzgesetzes.

§ 3a Satz 3 DSchG enthält eine Beschreibung der Aufgaben des Landesamtes für Denkmalpflege. Danach hat es im Rahmen der Vorgaben der obersten Denkmalschutzbehörde insbesondere die Aufgabe,

a) fachliche Grundlagen und Leitlinien für Methodik und Praxis der Denkmalpflege zu erarbeiten und deren landeseinheitliche Umsetzung sicherzustellen (§ 3a Satz 3 Nummer 1 DSchG). Zur Wahrnehmung dieser Aufgabe finden auch regelmäßige Dienstbesprechungen zwischen dem Landesamt für Denkmalpflege und den Denkmalschutzbehörden nach § 3 Absatz 1 Nummer 2 DSchG statt.

b) die Aufstellung von Denkmalförderprogrammen vorzubereiten und abzuwickeln (§ 3a Satz 3 Nummer 2 DSchG). Die Aufstellung des Denkmalförderprogramms des Landes erfolgt im Bereich der Zuwendungen durch die oberste Denkmalschutzbehörde nach der Verwaltungsvorschrift des Finanz- und Wirtschaftsministeriums für die Gewährung von Zuwendungen zur Erhaltung und Pflege von Kulturdenkmalen. Bei Projekten mit nationaler oder internationaler Denkmalförderung, die nicht eine überwiegend regionale Zielsetzung verfolgen, sowie bei Projekten mit überwiegender Förderung durch Dritte (sogenannte Drittmittelprojekte) erfolgen Koordinierung, Steuerung und abschließende Stellungnahme gegenüber den Finanzierungsträgern nach Abstimmung mit der obersten Denkmalschutzbehörde durch das Landesamt für Denkmalpflege.

c) Kulturdenkmale und Gesamtanlagen in Listen zu erfassen, zu dokumentieren und zu erforschen (§ 3a Satz 3 Nummer 3 DSchG). Dazu erstellt das Landesamt für Denkmalpflege auch Denkmaltopografien sowie archäologische Stadtkataster. Das Landesamt für Denkmalpflege führt eine landesweite Denkmaldatenbank (ADAB), das Verzeichnis der national wertvollen Kulturdenkmale sowie der Kulturdenkmale, die nach der Haager Konvention geschützt sind.

d) Dritte, insbesondere die Eigentümer und Besitzer von Kulturdenkmalen, denkmalfachlich zu beraten (§ 3a Satz 3 Nummer 4 DSchG).

e) in Abstimmung mit der obersten Denkmalschutzbehörde die zentrale denkmalfachliche Öffentlichkeitsarbeit durchzuführen und das vom Denkmalschutz umfasste kulturelle Erbe des Landes und die Maßnahmen zu seinem Erhalt in der Öffentlichkeit zu vermitteln (§ 3a Satz 3 Nummer 5 DSchG). Die zentrale denkmalfachliche Öffentlichkeitsarbeit umfasst die Durchführung von Fachtagungen und die Koordination und Herausgabe fachlicher Publikationen.

f) zentrale Fachbibliotheken, Dokumentationen, Fachdatenbanken sowie sonstige zentrale Dienste zu unterhalten (§ 3a Satz 3 Nummer 6 DSchG). Aufgabe des Landesamtes für Denkmalpflege ist auch die Koordination der paläontologischen Schutzgebiete in Kooperation mit den staatlichen Museen für Naturkunde.

g) Steuerbescheinigungen nach § 10g des Einkommensteuergesetzes zu erteilen, soweit keine Zuständigkeit des Landesarchivs besteht (§ 3a Satz 3 Nummer 7 DSchG).

[1)] Die VwV **tritt zum 31.12.2021 außer Kraft**, vgl. Nr. 12 Satz 2.

2 Denkmalschutzrechtliche Zustimmungen oder Beteiligungen (§ 7 Absatz 3 DSchG)

2.1

Die untere Denkmalschutzbehörde leitet das Ersuchen einer Genehmigungsbehörde auf Zustimmung nach § 7 Absatz 3 DSchG innerhalb von zehn Arbeitstagen an das Landesamt für Denkmalpflege weiter. Sie setzt für dessen Äußerung nach § 3 Absatz 4 DSchG eine angemessene Frist. Denkmalschutzbehörden sind gehalten, den Eintritt der gesetzlichen Zustimmungsfiktion nach § 54 Absatz 3 Satz 3 der Landesbauordnung für Baden-Württemberg (LBO) durch fristgerechte Bearbeitung oder ausnahmsweise durch Fristverlängerungsantrag zu vermeiden.

2.2

Ist die Baurechtsbehörde als Genehmigungsbehörde mit der zuständigen Denkmalschutzbehörde identisch, entfällt das Zustimmungsverfahren. Für die Anhörung des Landesamtes für Denkmalpflege durch die Baurechtsbehörde gelten dann die Regelungen des § 54 Absatz 3 Satz 1 und 2 LBO.

2.3

Die Denkmalschutzbehörden sind stets zu beteiligen, wenn es Anhaltspunkte dafür gibt, dass Belange des Denkmalschutzes berührt sein könnten, insbesondere wenn
a) Veränderungen an einem Kulturdenkmal vorgenommen werden,
b) in der Umgebung eines eingetragenen Kulturdenkmals, soweit sie für dessen Erscheinungsbild von erheblicher Bedeutung ist, bauliche Anlagen errichtet, verändert oder beseitigt werden,
c) Baumaßnahmen im Bereich einer Gesamtanlage durchgeführt werden,
d) Bodendenkmale vermutet werden.
Dies gilt neben den Fällen nach § 7 Absatz 3 DSchG auch immer dann, wenn ihr Aufgabenbereich in einem Verfahren nach anderen Vorschriften berührt wird.

2.4

Die untere Denkmalschutzbehörde übermittelt dem Landesamt für Denkmalpflege eine Mehrfertigung ihrer Entscheidung.

3 Denkmalschutzrechtliche Genehmigungen (§§ 8, 15 und 19 Absatz 2 DSchG)

3.1

Die untere Denkmalschutzbehörde leitet den Antrag auf Erteilung einer denkmalschutzrechtlichen Genehmigung innerhalb von zehn Arbeitstagen an das Landesamt für Denkmalpflege weiter. Sie setzt eine angemessene Äußerungsfrist nach § 3 Absatz 4 Satz 1 DSchG.

3.2

Nach Eingang der Unterlagen prüft das Landesamt für Denkmalpflege in der Regel innerhalb von fünf Arbeitstagen, ob diese ausreichend sind. Hält es die Unterlagen nicht für ausreichend, hat es dies unter genauer Bezeichnung der noch beizubringenden Unterlagen unverzüglich der unteren Denkmalschutzbehörde mitzuteilen. Diese entscheidet, welche Unterlagen in welcher Weise und in welcher Frist noch beizubringen sind. Verzögert sich die Vorlage entscheidungserheblicher Unterlagen aus Gründen, die das Landesamt für Denkmalpflege nicht zu vertreten hat, so ist die Dauer der Verzögerung nicht auf die nach Nummer 3.1 gesetzte Äußerungsfrist anzurechnen.

3.3

An die Stelle des Landesamtes für Denkmalpflege tritt im Bereich des Archivwesens das Landesarchiv.

3.4

Die untere Denkmalschutzbehörde übermittelt dem Landesamt für Denkmalpflege oder dem Landesarchiv eine Mehrfertigung ihrer Entscheidung.

3.5

Für Verfahren, die nach § 7 Absatz 5 Nummer 1 DSchG in die Zuständigkeit der höheren Denkmalschutzbehörde fallen, gelten die Nummern 3.1 bis 3.4 entsprechend.

4 Abweichung von der Äußerung der fachlichen Denkmalpflege (§ 3 Absatz 4 DSchG)

Will die untere Denkmalschutzbehörde von der Äußerung des Landesamtes für Denkmalpflege oder des Landesarchivs abweichen, so hat sie dies unter Angabe der Gründe der höheren Denkmalschutzbehörde nach § 3 Absatz 1 Nummer 2 DSchG schriftlich mitzuteilen. Eine Mehrfertigung dieses Schreibens ist dem Landesamt für Denkmalpflege zuzuleiten. Die höhere Denkmalschutzbehörde prüft innerhalb von zwei Wochen nach Eingang des Schreibens der unteren Denkmalschutzbehörde, ob sie von ihrem Fachaufsichtsrecht Gebrauch macht oder nicht und benachrichtigt davon die untere Denkmalschutzbehörde. Die Entscheidung der höheren Denkmalschutzbehörde erfolgt im Benehmen mit dem Landesamt für Denkmalpflege. Will die untere Denkmalschutzbehörde vor Ablauf dieser Frist eine Entscheidung in der Angelegenheit treffen, muss sie sich bei der höheren Denkmalschutzbehörde darüber vergewissern, dass vom Fachaufsichtsrecht nicht Gebrauch gemacht wird. Soll vom Fachaufsichtsrecht Gebrauch gemacht werden, ist die Entscheidung der höheren Denkmalschutzbehörde abzuwarten. Dabei sind die Fristen des § 54 LBO einzuhalten.

5 Verfahrensweise bei der Eintragung und Löschung von Kulturdenkmalen von besonderer Bedeutung (§ 13 DSchG)

Vor der Eintragung oder Löschung von Kulturdenkmalen von besonderer Bedeutung (§§ 12 und 28 DSchG) ist das Landesamt für Denkmalpflege anzuhören.

6 Beteiligung des Landesamtes für Denkmalpflege in Widerspruchs- oder Gerichtsverfahren

In Widerspruchs- oder Gerichtsverfahren ist dem Landesamt für Denkmalpflege Gelegenheit zur Stellungnahme gegenüber der zuständigen Behörde zu geben.

7 Veräußerung eingetragener Kulturdenkmale (§ 16 Absatz 2 DSchG)

Die Behörde, die die Anzeige des Eigentumswechsels entgegennimmt, hat unverzüglich die höhere Denkmalschutzbehörde zu unterrichten. Die höhere Denkmalschutzbehörde unterrichtet den Erwerber eines eingetragenen Kulturdenkmals über die für das Kulturdenkmal maßgebenden denkmalschutzrechtlichen Bestimmungen. Sie prüft, ob zum Schutz des Kulturdenkmals Weiteres zu veranlassen ist und informiert die untere Denkmalschutzbehörde darüber.

8 Vorläufiger Schutz bei Eintragung von Kulturdenkmalen (§ 17 DSchG)

Die höhere Denkmalschutzbehörde unterrichtet den Eigentümer mit der Bekanntgabe der Anordnung über die Rechtsfolgen einer Anordnung nach § 17 DSchG. Bei unbeweglichen Kulturdenkmalen ist auch die Gemeinde zu unterrichten.

9 Nachforschungen (§ 21 DSchG)

Die Genehmigung zu Nachforschungen, insbesondere für Grabungen mit dem Ziel, Kulturdenkmale zu entdecken, darf nur fachlich geeigneten Personen erteilt werden. Die Entscheidung erfolgt durch das Landesamt für Denkmalpflege. Die untere Denkmalschutzbehörde, der Eigentümer und die Gemeinde sind vorher zu hören. Sie sind über die Entscheidung zu unterrichten.

10 Grabungsschutzgebiete (§ 22 Absatz 1 DSchG)

10.1

Das Landesamt für Denkmalpflege schlägt der unteren Denkmalschutzbehörde den Erlass der Rechtsverordnung im Sinne von § 22 Absatz 1 DSchG vor. Der Vorschlag ist zu begründen.

10.2

Vor Erlass der Rechtsverordnung soll die untere Denkmalschutzbehörde
a) die Gemeinde,
b) die Behörde, die für die Verwaltung der Grundstücke zuständig ist, die einer juristischen Person des öffentlichen Rechts gehören und unter den Schutz fallen würden,
c) etwa sonst fachlich berührte amtliche Stellen
anhören und betroffene Grundstückseigentümer in geeigneter Weise informieren.

11 Zuweisung von Sachen, an denen das Land Eigentum erlangt (§§ 23, 25, 27 Absatz 3 DSchG)

Über die Zuweisung von Sachen, an denen das Land nach § 23 DSchG das Eigentum erwirbt oder die enteignet (§ 25 DSchG) oder eingezogen (§ 27 Absatz 3 DSchG) werden, entscheidet das Landesamt für Denkmalpflege, bei Archivgut das Landesarchiv, nach Anhörung der höheren Denkmalschutzbehörde. Bewegliche Sachen sind dem zentralen Fundarchiv des Archäologischen Landesmuseums, Archivalien einem Archiv, Bibliotheksgut einer Bibliothek zuzuweisen. Vor der Zuweisung an nichtstaatliche Museen, Archive oder Bibliotheken ist die zuständige staatliche Stelle (Museum oder Landesbibliothek) zu hören. In Zweifelsfällen ist die Entscheidung der obersten Denkmalschutzbehörde herbeizuführen.

12 Inkrafttreten

Diese Verwaltungsvorschrift tritt am Tage nach der Bekanntmachung[1] in Kraft. Sie tritt zum 31. Dezember 2021 außer Kraft.

---

1) Bekannt gemacht am 28.1.2015.

Verwaltungsvorschrift des Wirtschaftsministeriums für die Erfassung von Kulturdenkmalen in einer Liste (VwV-Kulturdenkmalliste)[1)]

Vom 26. April 2018 – Az.: 5-2555.1-0/4 – (GABl. S. 318)

1
Vorbemerkung

1.1
Zweck der Erfassung

Kulturdenkmale im Sinne des Denkmalschutzgesetzes (DSchG) werden vom Landesamt für Denkmalpflege im Regierungspräsidium Stuttgart aus Gründen der Transparenz in der Kulturdenkmalliste (Denkmalliste) erfasst. Damit soll insbesondere ermöglicht werden,
- Eigentümerinnen und Eigentümer von Kulturdenkmalen zu informieren;
- Planungsunterlagen (zum Beispiel für die Landes- und Regionalplanung, die kommunalen Bauleitplanungen, die Flurbereinigung, Infrastrukturprojekte oder Umweltverträglichkeitsprüfungen) zu erstellen sowie
- die Arbeit der Denkmalschutzbehörden zu rationalisieren.

Die Eintragung von Kulturdenkmalen von besonderer Bedeutung in das Denkmalbuch gemäß §§ 12 ff DSchG bleibt davon unberührt.

1.2
Rechtliche Bedeutung der Denkmalliste

Die Aufnahme in die Denkmalliste beinhaltet die denkmalfachliche Bewertung, dass es sich um ein Kulturdenkmal nach den Bestimmungen des Denkmalschutzgesetzes handelt. Die Aufnahme hat deklaratorische Bedeutung und dient den oben genannten Zwecken.

Der Schutz nach dem Denkmalschutzgesetz ist nicht davon abhängig, dass Kulturdenkmale in die Denkmalliste eingetragen sind. Aus der fehlenden Aufnahme eines Gegenstandes in die Denkmalliste kann nicht geschlossen werden, dass es sich dabei nicht um ein Kulturdenkmal handelt.

Die rechtsverbindliche Feststellung der Denkmaleigenschaft erfolgt inzident im Rahmen eines denkmalschutzrechtlichen Genehmigungs- oder Zustimmungsverfahrens oder im Rahmen eines Feststellungsverfahrens auf Antrag des Eigentümers durch die zuständige untere beziehungsweise höhere Denkmalschutzbehörde.

2
Gegenstand der Erfassung

2.1

In der Denkmalliste werden Kulturdenkmale im Sinne des Denkmalschutzgesetzes erfasst. Danach sind Kulturdenkmale bewegliche und unbewegliche Sachen, Sachgesamtheiten und Teile von Sachen, an deren Erhaltung
- aus wissenschaftlichen, künstlerischen oder heimatgeschichtlichen Gründen (Denkmalfähigkeit)
- ein öffentliches Interesse (Denkmalwürdigkeit) besteht.

Zu einem Kulturdenkmal gehört auch das Zubehör, soweit es mit der Hauptsache eine Einheit von Denkmalwert bildet (§ 2 Absatz 2 DSchG).

Kulturdenkmale können zum Beispiel sein: Bauwerke, Teile von Bauwerken, Gebäudegruppen, historische Gärten und Parks, Elemente der Kulturlandschaft wie Hohlwege, Alleen, Weinberge sowie Bodendenkmale der Vor- und Frühgeschichte, des Mittelalters und der Neuzeit und der Naturkunde, Werke der Kunst, des Kunsthandwerks und der Technik, Sachgüter der Volkskunde sowie Urkunden, Archivalien und anderes Schriftgut.

[1)] Die VwV **tritt mit Ablauf des 31.12.2024 außer Kraft**, vgl. Nr. 6.

2.2

Denkmalfähig ist eine Sache, wenn wissenschaftliche, künstlerische oder heimatgeschichtliche Schutzgründe vorliegen:
- Wissenschaftliche Gründe sind insbesondere solche, die die Bedeutung einer Sache für die Wissenschaft oder einen Wissenschaftszweig dokumentieren;
- künstlerische Gründe sind insbesondere vom kunsthistorischen Interesse bestimmt, gehen aber auch über dieses hinaus. Das Merkmal der künstlerischen Bedeutung verlangt eine gesteigerte ästhetische oder gestalterische Qualität;
- heimatgeschichtliche Gründe liegen insbesondere vor, wenn durch das Schutzobjekt geschichtliche oder spezifisch heimatgeschichtliche Entwicklungen anschaulich gemacht werden (Aussagewert), ihm als Wirkungsstätte namhafter Personen oder Schauplatz historischer Ereignisse ein bestimmter Erinnerungswert beizumessen ist oder es einen im Bewusstsein der Bevölkerung vorhandenen Bezug zu bestimmten politischen, kulturellen oder sozialen Verhältnissen seiner Zeit herstellt (Assoziationswert).

2.3

Denkmalwürdig ist eine Sache, wenn ein (von den Interessen des Eigentümers oder Besitzers unabhängiges) öffentliches Interesse besteht, das die auf einem gesetzlichen Schutzgrund beruhende Erhaltung der Sache rechtfertigt.

2.3.1

Die Erhaltung eines Kulturdenkmals im öffentlichen Interesse setzt voraus, dass die Denkmaleigenschaft einer Sache und die Notwendigkeit ihrer Erhaltung in das Bewusstsein der Bevölkerung oder mindestens eines breiten Kreises von Sachverständigen eingegangen sind.

2.3.2

Wegen der Korrektivfunktion, die dem Merkmal des öffentlichen Interesses in Bezug auf die weit gefassten Voraussetzungen der Denkmalfähigkeit zukommt, bedarf es im Blick auf das konkrete Schutzobjekt einer Bewertung des Ranges seiner denkmalpflegerischen Bedeutung.
Bei dieser wertenden Entscheidung sind insbesondere die folgenden Kriterien zu berücksichtigen:
- der Seltenheitswert des Schutzobjekts gegenüber anderen vergleichbaren Objekten;
- seine Bedeutung für die Umgebung (Ortsbild, Kulturlandschaft);
- sein wissenschaftlich-dokumentarischer und exemplarischer Wert;
- seine Vorbildhaftigkeit für eine Tradition;
- sein Alter;
- das Maß seiner Originalität und Integrität;
- sein künstlerischer Rang;
- das Gewicht der einschlägigen Schutzgründe.

2.4
Erfassungstiefe

Die fachlich-konservatorische Bewertung der Denkmaleigenschaft (Denkmalfähigkeit und Denkmalwürdigkeit) ist wissenschaftlich abzusichern und als Ergebnis in der Denkmalliste gegliedert zu dokumentieren. Diese Dokumentationen bestehen aus
- einer Darstellung des Schutzgutumfangs;
- einer Beschreibung des Gegenstandes unter Nennung denkmalkonstituierender Teile;
- der Benennung und Begründung der Schutzgründe und
- der Begründung des öffentlichen Interesses an seiner Erhaltung.

2.5

Ohne Belang für die Bewertung der Denkmaleigenschaft ist,
- in welchem Erhaltungszustand (zum Beispiel vernachlässigt) ein Gegenstand angetroffen wird, es sei denn, dass der Gegenstand nicht unter Wahrung seiner denkmalkonstituierenden Teile erhalten werden kann,
- ob im Fall eines Konflikts mit anderen öffentlichen Belangen oder privaten Interessen ein Kulturdenkmal tatsächlich unverändert oder verändert erhalten werden kann oder soll,
- ob und in welcher Höhe Mittel für die Erhaltung von Kulturdenkmalen zur Verfügung stehen.

3
Einteilung und Inhalt der Denkmalliste

3.1
Allgemeines

Die Denkmalliste wird für jede Gemeinde gesondert angelegt. Sie besteht aus
- Teil A 1: Unbewegliche Bau- und Kunstdenkmale;
- Teil A 2: Unbewegliche Bodendenkmale aus dem Bereich der Vor- und Frühgeschichte, des Mittelalters und der Neuzeit sowie der Naturkunde;
- Teil B 1: Bewegliche Bau- und Kunstdenkmale;
- Teil B 2: Bewegliche Bodendenkmale.

Werden Objekte in verschiedenen Teilen der Denkmalliste erfasst, sind die Eintragungen aufeinander abzustimmen; auf die Eintragung im jeweils anderen Listenteil ist zu verweisen.

3.2
Einteilung

Die Denkmalliste ist den Vorgaben dieser Verwaltungsvorschrift entsprechend im Fachinformationssystem der Denkmalpflege in Baden-Württemberg (ADABweb) darzustellen.

3.3
Inhalt der Denkmalliste

Die Denkmalliste enthält folgende Angaben:
- Grundstücksbezeichnung: Landkreis, Gemeinde, Ortsteil, Gemarkung, Straße, Hausnummer, Flurstücksnummer (nur A 1 und A 2);
- Bezeichnung des Objekts: zum Beispiel Kirche, Rathaus, Wohnhaus oder jungsteinzeitliche Siedlung, merowingerzeitlicher Friedhof, Grabhügel;
- Angaben zum Denkmalstatus: Kulturdenkmal nach §§ 2, 12 oder 28 DSchG (Entfernungsverbote nach § 15 Absatz 1 Nummer 4 DSchG sind aufzunehmen); Gesamtanlage nach § 19 DSchG; Grabungsschutzgebiet nach § 22 DSchG; Objekte, bei denen die Kulturdenkmaleigenschaft noch nicht abschließend geprüft ist, werden als Prüffälle geführt;
- gegebenenfalls Darstellung der Lage eines Kulturdenkmals in der Kern- oder Pufferzone einer Welterbestätte;
- Beschreibung und fachlich-konservatorische Bewertung gemäß Nummer 2.4;
- Kartierung der Denkmalflächen und
- Fotos, soweit vorhanden.

3.4

Bei Bodendenkmalen ist deren Ausdehnung häufig nicht exakt feststellbar. Zur Sicherung eines angemessenen Schutzes kann, wenn die Lage des Bodendenkmals noch nicht genau bekannt ist, vorsorglich eine ausreichend große Fläche angegeben werden (Parzellenunschärfe). Die Flächengröße ist zu begründen.

3.5

Mehrere Zubehörstücke sind möglichst einzeln anzugeben; sofern dies nach der Zahl der Zubehörstücke nicht leistbar ist, genügt die pauschale Benennung des Zubehörs. Wichtige Zubehörstücke sind jedoch stets ausdrücklich aufzuführen.

4
Verfahren

4.1

Das Landesamt für Denkmalpflege erarbeitet die Liste mit den oben genannten Angaben. Grundlage sind dabei insbesondere Ortsbegehungen, Fachliteratur und Nachforschungen in Archiven.

4.2

Die Denkmalschutzbehörden unterstützen die Listenerfassung im Rahmen der Amtshilfe.

4.3

Den zuständigen Denkmalschutzbehörden, den Eigentümerinnen und Eigentümern und sonstigen im Einzelfall Betroffenen soll Gelegenheit zur Äußerung und zur Teilnahme an Ortsbegehungen gegeben werden.

4.4

Die Entscheidung über die Aufnahme eines Kulturdenkmals in die Liste obliegt dem Landesamt für Denkmalpflege.

4.5

Die Liste ist dem denkmalfachlichen Bedarf entsprechend zu aktualisieren und fortzuschreiben.

5
Benachrichtigung und Auskunftserteilung

5.1

Das Landesamt für Denkmalpflege benachrichtigt die Eigentümerinnen und Eigentümer schriftlich über die Aufnahme ihres Kulturdenkmals in die Denkmalliste und fügt die fachlich-konservatorische Bewertung gemäß Nummer 2.4 bei.

5.2

Das Landesamt für Denkmalpflege stellt die Denkmalliste mit Ausnahme des Teils B 1 – bewegliche Bau- und Kunstdenkmale – über das Fachinformationssystem der Denkmalpflege in Baden-Württemberg (ADABweb) den zuständigen Denkmalschutzbehörden zur Verfügung und weist diese auf Veränderungen der Denkmalliste (Neueintragungen, Streichungen) hin.

5.3

Gemeinden erhalten vom Landesamt für Denkmalpflege auf Anfrage einen auf ihr Gemeindegebiet bezogenen Auszug der aktuellen Denkmalliste.

D1.I.1c VwV-Kulturdenkmalliste

6
Inkrafttreten

Diese Verwaltungsvorschrift tritt am Tag nach ihrer Veröffentlichung[1] in Kraft und am 31. Dezember 2024 außer Kraft.

---

[1] Veröffentlicht am 30.5.2018.

Gesetz über die Pflege und Nutzung von Archivgut (Landesarchivgesetz – LArchG)[1)2)]

Vom 27. Juli 1987 (GBl. S. 230)
(BWGültV Sachgebiet 116)
zuletzt geändert durch Art. 2 G zur Einführung der Informationsfreiheit vom 17. Dezember 2015 (GBl. S. 1201)

Nichtamtliche Inhaltsübersicht

1. Abschnitt:
Staatliches Archivgut

§ 1 Organisation der staatlichen Archivverwaltung
§ 2 Zuständigkeit und Aufgaben
§ 3 Übernahme des Archivguts
§ 4 Sicherung des Archivguts
§ 5 Recht auf Auskunft und Gegendarstellung
§ 6 Nutzung des Archivguts
§ 6a Unterlagen von Stellen des Bundes, bundesrechtliche Geheimhaltungsvorschriften

2. Abschnitt:
Kommunales und sonstiges öffentliches Archivgut

§ 7 Kommunales Archivgut
§ 8 Sonstiges öffentliches Archivgut

3. Abschnitt:
Schlussbestimmungen

§ 9 Änderung des Denkmalschutzgesetzes
§ 10 Ausnahmen vom Geltungsbereich
§ 11 Inkrafttreten

Der Landtag hat am 1. Juli 1987 das folgende Gesetz beschlossen:

1. Abschnitt:
Staatliches Archivgut

§ 1 Organisation der staatlichen Archivverwaltung

(1) Zuständige Fachbehörde für alle Aufgaben des staatlichen Archivwesens einschließlich der Ausbildung ist das Landesarchiv Baden-Württemberg mit seinen Standorten Staatsarchiv Freiburg, Generallandesarchiv Karlsruhe, Staatsarchiv Ludwigsburg, Staatsarchiv Sigmaringen, Hauptstaatsarchiv Stuttgart und Staatsarchiv Wertheim.

(2) Den Sitz der Leitung des Landesarchivs und die Verteilung der Aufgaben regelt ein Organisationsstatut.

§ 2 Zuständigkeit und Aufgaben

(1) ¹Das Landesarchiv verwahrt, erhält und erschließt als Archivgut alle Unterlagen, die von den Behörden, Gerichten und sonstigen Stellen des Landes, deren Funktionsvorgängern oder von Rechtsvorgängern des Landes übernommen worden sind und die bleibenden Wert haben; es macht das Archivgut allgemein nutzbar. ²Das Landesarchiv erfasst die Unterlagen bei den Behörden, Gerichten und sonstigen Stellen des Landes und kann diese bei der Verwaltung von Schriftgut und anderen Unterlagen beraten.

(2) ¹Unterlagen im Sinne von Absatz 2[3)] sind insbesondere Schriftstücke, Akten, Karteien, Karten, Pläne, Bild-, Film- und Tonmaterialien sowie sonstige Informationsträger und maschinenlesbar auf diesen gespeicherte Informationen und Programme. ²Bleibenden Wert haben Unterlagen, denen historischer Wert zukommt oder die auf Grund von Rechtsvorschriften oder von Verwaltungsvorschriften der jeweils zuständigen obersten Landesbehörde zur Sicherung berechtigter Belange der Bürger oder zur Bereitstellung von Informationen für Gesetzgebung, Verwaltung oder Rechtspflege dauernd aufzubewahren sind. ³Der bleibende Wert von Unterlagen, die nicht aufgrund von Rechtsvorschriften oder von Verwaltungsvorschriften der jeweils zuständigen obersten Landesbehörde dauernd aufzubewahren sind, wird durch die Archivare festgestellt.

(3) Das Landesarchiv kann auch Archivgut anderer Stellen und Privater mit deren Einvernehmen erfassen, verwahren, erhalten, erschließen und allgemein nutzbar machen sowie andere Stellen und Pri-

---
1) Änderungen vor dem 1.4.1997 sind nicht in Fußnoten nachgewiesen.
2) Vgl. die LandesarchivgebührenO.
3) Nach den Änderungen durch G v. 1.7.2004 (GBl. S. 469) wohl richtig: „Absatz 1".

D1.II.1 Landesarchivgesetz Baden-Württemberg

vate bei der Wahrnehmung dieser Aufgaben unterstützen, soweit daran ein öffentliches Interesse besteht.

(4) Die Landesregierung kann dem Landesarchiv durch Rechtsverordnung[1)] weitere Aufgaben übertragen, die mit dem Archivwesen zusammenhängen; sie kann insbesondere bestimmen, daß das Landesarchiv im Auftrag der in Absatz 1 genannten Stellen von diesen noch nicht gemäß § 3 Abs. 1 Sätze 1 und 2 anzubietende Unterlagen verwahren.

§ 3 Übernahme des Archivguts

(1) [1]Die Behörden, Gerichte und sonstigen Stellen des Landes bieten alle Unterlagen, die sie zur Erfüllung ihrer Aufgaben nicht mehr benötigen, dem Landesarchiv an. [2]Unabhängig davon sind alle Unterlagen jedoch spätestens 30 Jahre nach ihrer Entstehung dem Landesarchiv anzubieten, sofern durch Rechtsvorschriften oder durch Verwaltungsvorschriften der obersten Landesbehörden nicht längere Aufbewahrungsfristen vorgesehen sind. [3]Anzubieten sind auch Unterlagen, die durch Rechtsvorschriften über Geheimhaltung geschützt sind, wenn die abgebende Stelle im Benehmen mit dem Landesarchiv festgestellt hat, daß schutzwürdige Belange des Betroffenen durch geeignete Maßnahmen unter Abwägung aller Umstände des Einzelfalls angemessen berücksichtigt werden. [4]Die erforderlichen Maßnahmen müssen bereits vor der Übergabe durchgeführt oder festgelegt werden. [5]Unterlagen, die durch § 203 Abs. 1 Nr. 4 und 4a des Strafgesetzbuches geschützt sind, dürfen nur in anonymisierter Form übergeben werden.

(2) [1]Das Landesarchiv entscheidet im Benehmen mit der anbietenden Stelle über die Übernahme von Unterlagen, denen historischer Wert zukommt. [2]Auswahl und Form der Übernahme maschinenlesbar gespeicherter Informationen und Programme vereinbart das Landesarchiv mit der anbietenden Stelle. [3]Wenn das Landesarchiv die Übernahme ablehnt oder nicht innerhalb eines Jahres über die Übernahme entschieden hat, sind die Unterlagen zu vernichten, wenn kein Grund zu der Annahme besteht, daß durch die Vernichtung schutzwürdige Belange des Betroffenen beeinträchtigt werden. [4]Vorher dürfen Unterlagen nur mit Zustimmung des Landesarchivs vernichtet werden.

(3) [1]In Ausnahmefällen können im Einvernehmen mit dem Landesarchiv Unterlagen einem anderen Archiv übergeben werden, solange die Einhaltung der in den §§ 4 bis 6 getroffenen Bestimmungen gewährleistet ist und die archivfachlichen Ansprüche hierfür insbesondere in personeller, baulicher und einrichtungsmäßiger Hinsicht erfüllt sind. [2]Unter den Voraussetzungen des Satzes 1 sollen die Landratsämter als untere Verwaltungsbehörden Unterlagen dem Archiv des Landkreises anbieten und übergeben.

§ 4 Sicherung des Archivguts

[1]Das Archivgut ist durch die erforderlichen technischen und organisatorischen Maßnahmen vor unbefugter Nutzung, vor Beschädigung oder Vernichtung zu schützen. [2]Die Verknüpfung personenbezogener Daten ist innerhalb der in § 6 genannten Sperrfristen nur zulässig, wenn die schutzwürdigen Belange des Betroffenen angemessen berücksichtigt sind. [3]Unterlagen, denen kein bleibender Wert zukommt, sind zu vernichten.

§ 5 Recht auf Auskunft und Gegendarstellung

(1) [1]Das Auskunftsrecht gemäß § 12[2)] des Landesdatenschutzgesetzes bleibt unberührt. [2]§ 12[2)] Landesdatenschutzgesetz gilt entsprechend für personenbezogene Daten, die nicht in Dateien gespeichert sind, soweit sie mit vertretbarem Aufwand zu ermitteln sind; statt einer Auskunft kann Einsicht in das Archivgut gewährt werden.

(2) [1]Wer die Richtigkeit von Angaben zu seiner Person bestreitet, kann verlangen, daß dem Archivgut seine Gegendarstellung beigefügt wird, wenn er ein berechtigtes Interesse daran glaubhaft macht. [2]Nach seinem Tod steht dieses Recht dem Ehegatten, dem Lebenspartner, den Kindern oder den Eltern zu.

(3) [1]Rechtsansprüche auf Berichtigung personenbezogener Angaben bleiben unberührt, richten sich jedoch gegen die Stelle, bei der die Unterlagen entstanden sind. [2]Löschungsansprüche gemäß § 13 Abs. 3[3)] des Landesdatenschutzgesetzes sind nach Übergabe der Unterlagen an das Landesarchiv ausgeschlossen.

---

1) Siehe die AuftragsverwahrungsO.
2) Jetzt geregelt in § 21 LDSG.
3) Jetzt geregelt in § 23 Abs. 1 LDSG.

§ 6 Nutzung des Archivguts

(1) Jedermann hat nach Maßgabe der Benutzungsordnung das Recht, das Archivgut nach Ablauf der Sperrfristen zu nutzen, soweit sich aus Rechtsvorschriften oder Vereinbarungen mit derzeitigen oder früheren Eigentümern des Archivguts nichts anderes ergibt.

(2) ¹Archivgut darf nicht vor Ablauf von 30 Jahren seit Entstehung der Unterlagen genutzt werden. ²Unterlag Archivgut Rechtsvorschriften über Geheimhaltung, darf es frühestens 60 Jahre nach Entstehung der Unterlagen genutzt werden. ³Bezieht es sich nach seiner Zweckbestimmung auf eine natürliche Person, so darf es frühestens 10 Jahre nach deren Tod genutzt werden; kann der Todestag nicht oder nur mit unvertretbarem Aufwand festgestellt werden, endet die Sperrfrist 90 Jahre nach der Geburt.

(3) Die Sperrfristen nach Absatz 2 gelten nicht für solche Unterlagen, die schon bei ihrer Entstehung zur Veröffentlichung bestimmt oder der Öffentlichkeit zugänglich waren.

(4) ¹Das Landesarchiv kann Sperrfristen um höchstens 20 Jahre verlängern, wenn dies im öffentlichen Interesse liegt oder wenn schutzwürdige Belange des Betroffenen dies erfordern. ²Das Landesarchiv kann Sperrfristen verkürzen, wenn schutzwürdige Belange des Betroffenen nicht entgegenstehen. ³Eine Verkürzung der Sperrfrist nach Absatz 2 Satz 3 ist nur zulässig, wenn die Person, auf die sich das Archivgut bezieht, oder im Falle ihres Todes ihr Ehegatte, ihr Lebenspartner, ihre Kinder oder ihre Eltern eingewilligt haben oder wenn die Nutzung zu wissenschaftlichen Zwecken oder zur Wahrnehmung berechtigter Belange, die im überwiegenden Interesse einer anderen Person oder Stelle liegen, unerläßlich ist und durch Anonymisierung oder durch andere Maßnahmen die schutzwürdigen Belange des Betroffenen angemessen berücksichtigt werden. ⁴Bei einer Nutzung zu wissenschaftlichen Zwecken kann von einer Anonymisierung abgesehen werden, wenn das wissenschaftliche Interesse an der Offenbarung wegen der Bedeutung des Forschungsvorhabens die schutzwürdigen Belange des Betroffenen erheblich überwiegt und das Forschungsvorhaben sonst nicht durchgeführt werden könnte.

(5) ¹Für die Nutzung von Archivgut durch Behörden, Gerichte und sonstige Stellen des Landes, bei denen es entstanden ist oder die es abgegeben haben, gelten die Sperrfristen der Absätze 2 und 4 nicht, es sei denn, daß das Archivgut durch diese Stellen auf Grund von Rechtsvorschriften *hätten*[1] gesperrt oder vernichtet werden müssen. ²§ 13 Abs. 2 Satz 3 Halbsatz 2[2] des Landesdatenschutzgesetzes bleibt unberührt.

(6) ¹Die Nutzung ist einzuschränken oder zu versagen, soweit
1. Grund zu der Annahme besteht, daß das Wohl der Bundesrepublik Deutschland oder eines ihrer Länder gefährdet würde oder
2. Grund zu der Annahme besteht, daß schutzwürdige Belange Dritter entgegenstehen oder
3. der Erhaltungszustand des Archivguts gefährdet würde oder
4. ein nicht vertretbarer Verwaltungsaufwand entstehen würde oder
5. Vereinbarungen mit derzeitigen oder früheren Eigentümern entgegenstehen.

²Die Nutzung kann aus anderen wichtigen Gründen eingeschränkt oder versagt werden. ³Die Entscheidung über die Einschränkung oder Versagung der Nutzung trifft das Landesarchiv. ⁴Das Nähere über die Nutzung des Archivguts, insbesondere über das Antrags- und Genehmigungsverfahren, über die Sorgfaltspflichten bei der Nutzung, über die Versendung von Archivgut, über die Ablieferung von Belegexemplaren und über die Herstellung von Kopien und Reproduktionen, regelt die Landesregierung durch Rechtsverordnung (Benutzungsordnung).[3]

(7) ¹Der Nutzer ist verpflichtet, von einem Druckwerk im Sinne von § 2 Abs. 1 des Pflichtexemplargesetzes, das er unter wesentlicher Verwendung von Archivgut des Landesarchivs verfaßt oder erstellt hat, nach Erscheinen des Druckwerkes der Archivverwaltung unaufgefordert ein Belegexemplar unentgeltlich abzuliefern. ²Ist dem Nutzer die unentgeltliche Ablieferung eines Belegexemplares insbesondere wegen der niedrigen Auflage oder der hohen Kosten des Druckwerkes nicht zumutbar, kann er der Archivverwaltung entweder ein Exemplar des Druckwerkes zur Herstellung einer Vervielfältigung für einen angemessenen Zeitraum überlassen oder eine Entschädigung bis zur Höhe des halben Ladenpreises verlangen. ³Wenn ein Ladenpreis nicht besteht, kann der Nutzer eine Entschädigung bis zur Höhe der halben Herstellungskosten des Belegexemplars verlangen. ⁴Sätze 1 bis 3 gelten entspre-

---
1) Richtig wohl: „hätte".
2) Die Nutzung gesperrter personenbezogener Daten ist jetzt in § 24 Abs. 4 LDSG geregelt.
3) Die Landesarchivbenutzungsordnung ist abgedruckt als Nr. D1.II.1a.

chend für Veröffentlichungen des Nutzers in Sammelwerken oder Zeitschriften sowie für Schriftwerke, die nicht veröffentlicht sind. [5]Ohne Zustimmung des Nutzers dürfen nichtveröffentlichte Schriftwerke von der Archivverwaltung nur zur Erschließung von Archivgut verwendet werden; anderen Personen darf keine Einsicht in nichtveröffentlichte Schriftwerke gewährt werden. [6]Satz 5 findet keine Anwendung, wenn das Urheberrecht erloschen ist.

§ 6a Unterlagen von Stellen des Bundes, bundesrechtliche Geheimhaltungsvorschriften
(1) Für Archivgut, das gemäß § 2 Abs. 3 Satz 1 des Bundesarchivgesetzes von Stellen des Bundes dem Staatsarchiv übergeben worden ist, gelten § 2 Abs. 4 Satz 2 sowie §§ 4 und 5 Abs. 1 bis 7 und 9 des Bundesarchivgesetzes entsprechend.

(2) Für Archivgut, das Rechtsvorschriften des Bundes über die Geheimhaltung im Sinne der §§ 10 oder 11 des Bundesarchivgesetzes unterliegt und das von anderen als den in § 2 Abs. 1 des Bundesarchivgesetzes genannten Stellen öffentlichen Archiven übergeben woden ist, gelten § 2 Abs. 4 Satz 2 und § 5 Abs. 1 bis 7 und 9 des Bundesarchivgesetzes entsprechend.

2. Abschnitt:
Kommunales und sonstiges öffentliches Archivgut

§ 7 Kommunales Archivgut
(1) [1]Die Gemeinden und Landkreise verwahren, erhalten und erschließen Unterlagen von bleibendem Wert im Sinne von § 2 Abs. 3 mit den entsprechenden Amtsdrucksachen als Archivgut in eigenen Archiven; sie sollen das Archivgut nutzbar machen. [2]Dies gilt auch für Unterlagen, die gemäß § 3 Abs. 3 Satz 2 vom Archiv des Landkreises übernommen worden sind.
(2) [1]Die Gemeinden und Landkreise überprüfen alle Unterlagen, die sie zur Aufgabenerfüllung nicht mehr benötigen. [2]Sind die überprüften Unterlagen von bleibendem Wert, so sind sie in das Archiv zu übernehmen; anderenfalls sind sie zu vernichten, wenn kein Grund zu der Annahme besteht, daß durch die Vernichtung schutzwürdige Belange der Betroffenen beeinträchtigt werden. [3]§ 3 Abs. 1 Sätze 3 bis 5 gelten entsprechend; anstelle des Landesarchivs entscheiden die Gemeinden und Landkreise.
(3) [1]Die Gemeinden und Landkreise erlassen eine Archivordnung als Satzung. [2]In der Satzung kann eine Verpflichtung zur Ablieferung von Belegexemplaren bestimmt werden; § 6 Abs. 7 gilt entsprechend. [3]Beruht das Druckwerk oder nichtveröffentlichte Schriftwerk nur zum Teil auf der Verwendung von Archivgut des kommunalen Archivs, kann bestimmt werden, daß eine Vervielfältigung der entsprechenden Seiten dem kommunalen Archiv zu überlassen ist. [4]§§ 4, 5, 6 Abs. 2 bis 5 und Abs. 6 Satz 1 und 2 sowie § 6a Abs. 2 gelten entsprechend. [5]Über die Verlängerung oder Verkürzung von Sperrfristen (§ 6 Abs. 4, § 6a Abs. 2) sowie über die Einschränkung oder Versagung der Nutzung (§ 6 Abs. 6 Satz 1 und 2, § 6a Abs. 2) entscheiden die Gemeinden und Landkreise. [6]Rechtsansprüche auf Einsichtnahme, die sich aus kommunalrechtlichen Bestimmungen ergeben, bleiben unberührt.
(4) Absätze 1 bis 3 gelten für Gemeindeverwaltungsverbände, Zweckverbände, Nachbarschaftsverbände und kommunale Stiftungen entsprechend.

§ 8 Sonstiges öffentliches Archivgut
(1) [1]Körperschaften, Anstalten und Stiftungen des öffentlichen Rechts, die der Aufsicht des Landes unterstehen und über kein eigenes Archiv verfügen, das archivfachlichen Ansprüchen genügt, haben Unterlagen, die sie zur Erfüllung ihrer Aufgaben nicht mehr benötigen, dem Landesarchiv anzubieten. [2]Eine Anbietungspflicht gegenüber dem Landesarchiv besteht nicht, wenn die Unterlagen einer für Archivierungszwecke geschaffenen Gemeinschaftseinrichtung oder einem anderen Archiv angeboten und übergeben werden, solange diese archivfachlichen Ansprüchen genügen und die Einhaltung der in §§ 4 bis 6 getroffenen Bestimmungen gewährleistet ist. [3]Das Landesarchiv stellt fest, ob ein Archiv archivfachlichen Ansprüchen im Sinne von § 3 Abs. 3 genügt. [4]Das Landesarchiv kann das angebotene Archivgut übernehmen, verwahren, erhalten, erschließen und allgemein nutzbar machen. [5]Die übergebende Stelle hat ein Rücknahmerecht für den Fall, daß sie selbst ein Archiv im Sinne des Satzes 1 einrichtet und unterhält. [6]§ 3 Abs. 1 Sätze 3 bis 5 und Absätze 2 und 3 sowie § 6 Abs. 5 gelten entsprechend.
(2) [1]Für die in Absatz 1 genannten Stellen, die eigene Archive unterhalten und für die keine besonderen gesetzlichen Regelungen bestehen, gelten § 2 Abs. 2 und 3, § 3 Abs. 1 und 2, §§ 4, 5, 6 und 6a Abs. 2 entsprechend. [2]Über die Verlängerung oder Verkürzung von Sperrfristen (§ 6 Abs. 4, § 6a

Abs. 2) sowie über die Einschränkung oder Versagung der Nutzung (§ 6 Abs. 6 Satz 1 und 2, § 6a Abs. 2) entscheidet der Träger des Archivs; dieser erläßt auch die Benutzungsordnung (§ 6 Abs. 6 Satz 4).

3. Abschnitt:
Schlußbestimmungen

§ 9 Änderung des Denkmalschutzgesetzes
[hier nicht wiedergegeben]

§ 10 Ausnahmen vom Geltungsbereich
(1) Der Landtag entscheidet in eigener Zuständigkeit, ob Unterlagen, die zur Erfüllung der Aufgaben nicht mehr benötigt werden, dem Landesarchiv angeboten werden.
(2) Dieses Gesetz gilt nicht für die öffentlich-rechtlichen Rundfunkanstalten und für öffentlich-rechtliche Unternehmen mit eigener Rechtspersönlichkeit, die am Wettbewerb teilnehmen, und deren Zusammenschlüsse, mit Ausnahme von Zweckverbänden.
(3) Bestehende Eigentums- und sonstige Rechtsverhältnisse am Archivgut werden durch dieses Gesetz nicht berührt.

§ 11 Inkrafttreten
(1) Dieses Gesetz tritt am Tage nach seiner Verkündung[1]) in Kraft.
(2) *[nicht wiedergegebene Aufhebungsvorschrift]*

---

1) Verkündet am 31.7.1987.

D1.II.1a Landesarchivbenutzungsordnung

Verordnung der Landesregierung über die Benutzung des Landesarchivs Baden-Württemberg (Landesarchivbenutzungsordnung – LArchBO)

Vom 10. April 2006 (GBl. S. 110)

Auf Grund von § 6 Abs. 6 Satz 4 des Landesarchivgesetzes vom 27. Juli 1987 (GBl. S. 230), geändert durch Gesetz vom 12. März 1990 (GBl. S. 89) und vom 1. Juli 2004 (GBl. S. 469), wird verordnet:

§ 1 Art der Nutzung

(1) Archivgut wird grundsätzlich durch Einsichtnahme genutzt.

(2) [1]Das Landesarchiv kann die Nutzung auch durch Beantwortung von schriftlichen oder mündlichen Anfragen, durch Vorlage oder Abgabe von Reproduktionen, durch Versendung oder durch Ausleihe von Archivgut ermöglichen. [2]Die Beantwortung von schriftlichen oder mündlichen Anfragen beschränkt sich grundsätzlich auf Hinweise zu einschlägigem Archivgut.

(3) Die für die Nutzung von Archivgut getroffenen Bestimmungen gelten für die Nutzung von nicht publizierten Findmitteln, sonstigen Hilfsmitteln und Reproduktionen entsprechend.

§ 2 Nutzungsvoraussetzungen

(1) Für die Nutzung des Archivguts im Landesarchiv ist ein gültiger Nutzerausweis erforderlich, der bei jeder Nutzung vorzulegen ist.

(2) Abweichend von Absatz 1 kann bei Nutzungen nach § 1 Abs. 2 und 3, insbesondere bei schriftlichen oder mündlichen Anfragen, auf die Ausstellung eines Nutzerausweises verzichtet werden.

(3) [1]Der Nutzerausweis ist schriftlich bei einer Archivgut verwahrenden Abteilung des Landesarchivs für das gesamte Landesarchiv zu beantragen. [2]Im Antrag sind Name, Vorname und Anschrift des Antragstellers anzugeben. [3]Auf Verlangen hat sich der Antragsteller auszuweisen.

(4) Der Nutzerausweis wird fünf Jahre nach der letzten Nutzung in einem Lesesaal des Landesarchivs ungültig.

(5) [1]Der Nutzerausweis ist nicht übertragbar. [2]Sein Verlust ist dem Landesarchiv unverzüglich anzuzeigen.

(6) Vor der Bestellung von Archivgut zur Einsichtnahme ist einmalig für jedes Nutzungsvorhaben Folgendes anzugeben:
1. Nutzungsvorhaben (Thema der Arbeit) mit möglichst präziser zeitlicher und sachlicher Eingrenzung,
2. Name, Vorname und Anschrift des Auftraggebers, wenn die Nutzung im Auftrag eines Dritten erfolgt, und
3. Nutzungszweck.

(7) Der Nutzer ist verpflichtet, Urheberrechte, Persönlichkeitsrechte sowie schutzwürdige Belange Dritter zu beachten.

§ 3 Verkürzung der Sperrfristen

[1]Eine Verkürzung der Sperrfristen wird vom Nutzer bei der das betreffende Archivgut verwahrenden Abteilung des Landesarchivs schriftlich beantragt. [2]Die Entscheidung über den Antrag trifft deren Abteilungsleiter. [3]Über die in § 2 genannten Angaben hinaus hat der Antragsteller dem Antrag auf Nutzung von Unterlagen, die sich nach ihrer Zweckbestimmung auf eine natürliche Person beziehen, entweder die schriftliche Einwilligung des Betroffenen oder seiner Angehörigen im Sinne von § 6 Abs. 4 Satz 3 des Landesarchivgesetzes beizufügen oder im Antrag eingehend zu begründen, warum eine Verkürzung der Sperrfrist unerlässlich ist. [4]Soll bei einer Nutzung zu wissenschaftlichen Zwecken von der Anonymisierung personenbezogener Angaben abgesehen werden, so hat der Antragsteller außerdem zu begründen, warum das wissenschaftliche Interesse an der Offenbarung wegen der Bedeutung des Forschungsvorhabens die schutzwürdigen Belange des Betroffenen erheblich überwiegt und das Forschungsvorhaben sonst nicht durchgeführt werden kann. [5]Auf Verlangen der das Archivgut verwahrenden Abteilung des Landesarchivs sind dem Antrag ergänzende Angaben und Unterlagen, bei Hochschularbeiten insbesondere Stellungnahmen der akademischen Lehrer, beizufügen.

§ 4 Einschränkung, Versagung und Entzug des Rechts auf Nutzung

(1) Das Landesarchiv kann außer aus den in § 6 Abs. 6 Satz 1 des Landesarchivgesetzes genannten Gründen die Nutzung des Archivguts aus anderen wichtigen Gründen einschränken oder versagen, insbesondere wenn
1. der Nutzer wiederholt oder schwerwiegend gegen diese Benutzungsordnung oder gegen die Lesesaalordnung (§ 5 Abs. 1 Satz 2) verstößt oder ihm erteilte Auflagen nicht einhält,
2. der Erhaltungszustand oder der Ordnungszustand des Archivguts eine Nutzung nicht zulässt,
3. Archivalien aus dienstlichen Gründen oder wegen gleichzeitiger amtlicher oder anderweitiger Nutzung nicht verfügbar sind oder
4. der Nutzungszweck anderweitig, insbesondere durch Einsichtnahme in Druckwerke oder in Reproduktionen, hinlänglich erreicht werden kann.

(2) Das Landesarchiv kann den Nutzerausweis einziehen oder für ungültig erklären, wenn
1. nachträgliche Gründe bekannt werden, die zur Versagung der Nutzung geführt hätten,
2. der Nutzer wiederholt oder schwerwiegend gegen diese Benutzungsordnung oder gegen die Lesesaalordnung verstößt oder ihm erteilte Auflagen nicht einhält oder
3. der Nutzer Urheber- und Persönlichkeitsrechte sowie schutzwürdige Belange Dritter nicht beachtet.

§ 5 Nutzung des Archivguts im Lesesaal

(1) ¹Archivgut wird grundsätzlich in den Lesesälen des Landesarchivs zur Nutzung vorgelegt. ²Regelungen, die dem Schutz des Archivguts und einem geordneten Ablauf der Nutzung dienen, werden in einer Verwaltungsvorschrift des Landesarchivs (Lesesaalordnung) bestimmt.

(2) ¹Das vorgelegte Archivgut, die vorgelegten Reproduktionen sowie Findmittel und sonstige Hilfsmittel sind mit aller Sorgfalt zu behandeln. ²Insbesondere ist es nicht gestattet,
1. den Ordnungszustand des Archivguts zu verändern,
2. Bestandteile des Archivguts wie insbesondere Blätter, Zettel, Umschläge, Siegel, Stempelabdrucke und Briefmarken zu entfernen,
3. Vermerke im Archivgut anzubringen oder vorhandene zu tilgen oder
4. Archivgut als Schreib- oder Durchzeichnungsunterlage zu verwenden.

(3) ¹Das Landesarchiv kann auch die Nutzung von Archivgut ermöglichen, das von anderen Archiven oder sonstigen Stellen zur Nutzung durch Dritte übersandt wurde. ²Soweit die versendende Stelle nichts anderes verfügt hat, gelten die Vorschriften dieser Benutzungsordnung und der Lesesaalordnung entsprechend.

§ 6 Versendung und Ausleihe von Archivgut

(1) ¹Auf die Versendung von Archivgut zur Einsichtnahme außerhalb des Lesesaals der das betreffende Archivgut verwahrenden Abteilung des Landesarchivs besteht kein Anspruch. ²Die Versendung kann nur in begründeten Ausnahmefällen und nur in sehr beschränktem Umfang zur Nutzung in hauptamtlich verwalteten Archiven in der Bundesrepublik Deutschland erfolgen, sofern sich diese verpflichten, das Archivgut in den Diensträumen unter ständiger fachlicher Aufsicht nur dem Antragsteller vorzulegen, es diebstahl- und feuersicher zu verwahren, keine Kopien oder Reproduktionen anzufertigen und das Archivgut nach Ablauf der vom Landesarchiv bestimmten Ausleihfrist, die zwei Monate nicht überschreiten soll, in der von diesem bestimmten Versendungsart zurückzusenden.

(2) ¹Zur Begrenzung des Versendungsrisikos soll der Antragsteller das in Frage kommende Archivgut im Lesesaal der das Archivgut verwahrenden Abteilung des Landesarchivs durchsehen und auf die Archivalieneinheiten reduzieren, deren Nutzung in der verwahrenden Abteilung des Landesarchivs nicht zumutbar erscheint. ²Vor der Versendung ist zu prüfen, ob der Nutzungszweck nicht durch die Übersendung von Reproduktionen erreicht werden kann. ³Eine Sendung soll höchstens zehn Archivalieneinheiten umfassen.

(3) ¹Auf die Ausleihe von Archivalien zu Ausstellungszwecken besteht kein Anspruch. ²Eine Ausleihe ist nur möglich, wenn gewährleistet ist, dass das ausgeliehene Archivgut wirksam vor Verlust, Beschädigung und unbefugter Nutzung geschützt wird und der Ausstellungszweck nicht durch Reproduktionen oder Nachbildungen erreicht werden kann. ³Das Landesarchiv stellt die Sicherheit und Erhaltung des zu Ausstellungszwecken ausgeliehenen Archivguts durch die erforderlichen Auflagen

sicher. ⁴Die Herstellung von Reproduktionen von ausgestelltem Archivgut durch Dritte bedarf der Zustimmung der verwahrenden Abteilung des Landesarchivs.

§ 7 Reproduktionen und Nachbildungen von Archivgut

(1) ¹Reproduktionen aller Art von Archivgut werden im Rahmen der bestehenden Möglichkeiten von den im Landesarchiv bestehenden Werkstätten grundsätzlich selbst hergestellt. ²Sind diese dazu technisch nicht in der Lage, dürfen Reproduktionen in begründeten Ausnahmefällen mit Zustimmung der das Archivgut verwahrenden Abteilung des Landesarchivs bei einer von dieser benannten Stelle hergestellt werden, wenn sich der Nutzer verpflichtet, dem Landesarchiv die Vervielfältigungsträger zu überlassen. ³Das Landesarchiv kann außerdem verlangen, dass die Reproduktionen unter seiner Aufsicht hergestellt werden, und es kann dem Auftraggeber die dadurch entstehenden Kosten in Rechnung stellen.

(2) Reproduktionen dürfen nur mit Zustimmung der das betreffende Archivgut verwahrenden Abteilung des Landesarchivs, nur zu dem angegebenen Zweck und nur unter Angabe der verwahrenden Abteilung und der von dieser festgelegten Signatur sowie unter Hinweis auf die dem Landesarchiv zustehenden Veröffentlichungs- und Vervielfältigungsrechte vervielfältigt oder an Dritte weitergegeben werden.

(3) ¹Reproduktionen von Archivgut werden nur hergestellt, soweit dabei eine Gefährdung oder Schädigung des Archivguts ausgeschlossen werden kann. ²Über die jeweils geeigneten Reproduktionsverfahren entscheidet die das Archivgut verwahrende Abteilung des Landesarchivs. ³Aufnahmefilme und sonstige Reproduktionsvorlagen mit Ausnahme der zur unmittelbaren Abgabe bestimmten Bildträger wie Mikrofilme oder Diapositive verbleiben dem Landesarchiv. ⁴Die Herstellung oder Abgabe von Reproduktionen kann auch versagt oder eingeschränkt werden, wenn sich Archivgut wegen seines Formats nicht zur Reproduktion eignet.

(4) Für Siegelabgüsse, Siegelabdrücke, Faksimiles und sonstige Nachbildungen aller Art von Archivgut gelten die Absätze 1 bis 3 entsprechend.

§ 8 Nutzung durch abgebende Stellen

¹Für die Nutzung von Archivgut durch Behörden, Gerichte und sonstige Stellen des Landes, bei denen es entstanden ist oder die es abgegeben haben, finden die Vorschriften dieser Benutzungsordnung keine Anwendung. ²Die Art und Weise der Nutzung wird zwischen der abgebenden Stelle und der das Archivgut verwahrenden Abteilung des Landesarchivs im Einzelfall vereinbart. ³Dabei ist sicherzustellen, dass das Archivgut gegen Verlust, Beschädigung und unbefugte Nutzung geschützt und innerhalb eines angemessenen Zeitraums zurückgegeben wird.

§ 9 Gebühren

Die Erhebung von Gebühren richtet sich nach der Verordnung des Ministeriums für Wissenschaft, Forschung und Kunst über die Gebühren des Landesarchivs (Gebührenverordnung Landesarchiv – GebVOLArch) in der jeweils geltenden Fassung.

§ 10 Inkrafttreten

¹Diese Verordnung tritt am Tage nach ihrer Verkündung[1]) in Kraft. ²Gleichzeitig tritt die Archivbenutzungsordnung vom 29. August 1988 (GBl. S. 250) außer Kraft.

---

1) Verkündet am 28.4.2006.

Verwaltungsvorschrift des Wirtschaftsministeriums für die Gewährung von Zuwendungen zur Erhaltung und Pflege von Kulturdenkmalen (VwV-Denkmalförderung)

Vom 28. November 2019 – Az.: 5-2552.1/9 – (GABl. S. 377)

Inhaltsübersicht

Einleitung

Abschnitt 1:
Allgemeine Zuwendungsbestimmungen
1 Rechtsgrundlage und Zuwendungszweck
2 Zuwendungsempfänger
3 Zuwendungsvoraussetzungen
4 Art und Umfang der Zuwendung
5 Sonderfälle
6 Besondere Nebenbestimmungen zum Zuwendungsbescheid
7 Beihilfehöchstintensität und beihilfefähige Kosten im Sinne von Artikel 7 AGVO

Abschnitt 2:
Verfahren, Auszahlung
8 Antragsfrist, Antragsunterlagen
9 Antragsprüfung und Programmvorschläge
10 Verwaltungsmäßige Abwicklung
Abschnitt 3:
Schlussbestimmungen
11 Inkrafttreten/Geltungsdauer

Einleitung

Denkmale der Kunst und der Geschichte genießen öffentlichen Schutz und Pflege des Staates und der Gemeinden (Artikel 3c Absatz 2 Landesverfassung). Rechtliche Grundlage für die Erfüllung des Verfassungsauftrages bildet das Denkmalschutzgesetz Baden-Württemberg (DSchG). Danach entscheidet das Wirtschaftsministerium als oberste Denkmalschutzbehörde über alle grundsätzlichen Angelegenheiten des Denkmalschutzes und der Denkmalpflege, insbesondere über die Aufstellung des Denkmalförderprogramms.

Abschnitt 1
Allgemeine Zuwendungsbestimmungen

1 Rechtsgrundlage und Zuwendungszweck

1.1

Das Land gewährt Zuwendungen zu Maßnahmen, die der Erhaltung und Pflege von Kulturdenkmalen dienen auf Grund des § 6 DSchG nach Maßgabe
– dieser Verwaltungsvorschrift,
– der §§ 23 und 44 der Landeshaushaltsordnung (LHO) sowie der Allgemeinen Verwaltungsvorschrift (VV) zur Landeshaushaltsordnung Baden-Württemberg (VV-LHO),
– der maßgeblichen Bestimmungen des Landesverwaltungsverfahrensgesetzes,
– der Artikel 4 Absatz 1z und 53 der Allgemeinen Gruppenfreistellungsverordnung (EU) Nummer 651/2014 der Kommission (AGVO) vom 17. Juni 2014 zur Feststellung der Vereinbarkeit bestimmter Gruppen von Beihilfen mit dem Binnenmarkt in Anwendung der Artikel 107 und 108 des Vertrages über die Arbeitsweise der Europäischen Union (ABl. L 187 vom 26.6.2014, S. 1, L 283, S. 65), die zuletzt durch Artikel 1 ÄndVO (EU) 2017/1084 vom 14.6.2017 (ABl. L 156, S. 1) geändert worden ist.

1.2

Die Zuwendungen, die ausschließlich für investive Projekte der Denkmalpflege zur Verfügung stehen, sollen den Eigentümer oder Besitzer bei der Erfüllung der sich nach § 6 DSchG aus der Sozialbindung des Eigentums ergebenden Pflichten unterstützen. Das Land beteiligt sich unbeschadet bestehender Verpflichtungen an den Kosten des Denkmalschutzes und der Denkmalpflege. Ein Rechtsanspruch auf Gewährung einer Zuwendung besteht nicht. Das Wirtschaftsministerium entscheidet nach pflichtgemäßem Ermessen im Rahmen der verfügbaren Haushaltsmittel.

2 Zuwendungsempfänger

2.1
Eine Zuwendung kann auf Antrag erhalten der Eigentümer, Besitzer oder sonstige Bauunterhaltungspflichtige eines Kulturdenkmals. Der Bauunterhaltungspflichtige hat die Unterhaltungspflicht für mindestens weitere zehn Jahre zu übernehmen. Eine Zuwendung kann ebenso der Erwerber eines Grundstücks erhalten, das ein besonders bedeutsames Bodendenkmal (§ 22 Absatz 1 DSchG) birgt (Nummer 2.8).

2.2
Zuwendungen werden nicht gewährt an den Bund (einschließlich Sondervermögen), ein Bundesland, einen ausländischen Staat sowie deren Körperschaften, Anstalten und Stiftungen des öffentlichen Rechts.

2.3
Von der Förderung ausgeschlossen sind Unternehmen beziehungsweise Sektoren in den Fällen des Artikel 1 Absatz 2 bis 5 AGVO.

2.4
Einem Unternehmen, das einer Rückforderungsanordnung aufgrund eines früheren Beschlusses der Kommission zur Feststellung der Unzulässigkeit einer Beihilfe und ihrer Unvereinbarkeit mit dem Binnenmarkt nicht nachgekommen ist, dürfen keine Einzelbeihilfen gewährt werden; ausgenommen sind Beihilferegelungen zur Bewältigung der Folgen bestimmter Naturkatastrophen.

2.5
Den Gemeinden, Gemeindeverbänden, Zweckverbänden, Landkreisen und Kirchen als Zuwendungsempfänger gleichgestellt sind deren Körperschaften, Anstalten und Stiftungen des öffentlichen Rechts.

2.6
Den unter den Nummern 2.2 und 2.5 genannten öffentlich-rechtlichen Einrichtungen werden die von diesen mit mehrheitlicher Beteiligung gebildeten juristischen Personen des Privatrechts gleichgestellt.

2.7
Den Kirchen sind die sonstigen, als Körperschaften des öffentlichen Rechts anerkannten Religions- und Weltanschauungsgemeinschaften sowie deren Untergliederungen und Mitgliedsverbände und die ihnen zugeordneten Einrichtungen, Anstalten und Stiftungen gleichgestellt.

2.8
Zuwendungen zum Erwerb von Grundstücken, die ein besonders bedeutsames Bodendenkmal bergen, werden nur gewährt an Gemeinden und Kirchen sowie an sonstige Körperschaften, Anstalten und Stiftungen des öffentlichen Rechts und juristische Personen des Privatrechts, die als gemeinnützig anerkannt sind.

3 Zuwendungsvoraussetzungen

3.1
Abstimmung der Maßnahme

Die Maßnahme muss den denkmalpflegerischen Erfordernissen des Denkmalschutzgesetzes entsprechen und mit dem bewilligenden Landesamt für Denkmalpflege im Regierungspräsidium Stuttgart (LAD) abgestimmt sein.

3.2
Baubeginn

Die Maßnahme darf vor der Bewilligung der Zuwendung nicht begonnen sein. Eine Maßnahme ist begonnen, sobald dafür entsprechende Lieferungs- oder Leistungsverträge abgeschlossen sind. Ist eine Entscheidung über die Bewilligung noch nicht möglich, kann das LAD bei Maßnahmen, die aus sachlichen oder wirtschaftlichen Gründen keinen Aufschub dulden oder gottesdienstliche Belange berühren, im Einzelfall auf schriftlichen Antrag nach Maßgabe der VV Nummer 1.2 zu § 44 LHO einen vorzeitigen Baubeginn schriftlich zulassen. Die Zustimmung zum vorzeitigen Baubeginn ersetzt nicht die bau- oder denkmalschutzrechtliche Genehmigung und begründet keinen Rechtsanspruch auf eine Zuwendung.

3.3
Bagatellgrenzen

Zuwendungen an den Eigentümer werden nur gewährt, wenn die zuwendungsfähigen Ausgaben
- bei Gemeinden, Gemeindeverbänden, Zweckverbänden, Landkreisen sowie Kirchen 30 000 Euro,
- bei sonstigen Personen 3 000 Euro übersteigen.

Werden Zuwendungen an den Besitzer oder Bauunterhaltspflichtigen gewährt, ist die für den Antragsteller des jeweiligen Kulturdenkmals maßgebliche Bagatellgrenze anzuwenden.

3.4
Höchstgrenzen

Zuwendungen werden bis zu einem Höchstbetrag von 500 000 Euro je Objekt, Kalenderjahr und Förderempfänger gewährt. Die Bildung von Bauabschnitten bleibt davon unberührt. Das Wirtschaftsministerium kann grundsätzlich eine Gesamthöchstgrenze je Objekt festlegen.

4 Art und Umfang der Zuwendung

4.1
Zuwendungsart

Zuwendungen werden als Projektförderung im Wege der Anteilsfinanzierung in Form von Zuschüssen gewährt.

4.2
Zuwendungsfähige Ausgaben

Zuwendungsfähig sind Ausgaben nach Maßgabe der Liste der förderfähigen Ausgaben des Wirtschaftsministeriums (Anlage 1), die zu Schutz und Pflege eines Kulturdenkmals im Sinne des Denkmalschutzgesetzes erforderlich sind.

4.3
Nicht zuwendungsfähige Ausgaben

Ausgaben für denkmalpflegerische Maßnahmen in Sanierungsgebieten sind dann nicht zuwendungsfähig, soweit für sie Mittel aus der Städtebauförderung eingesetzt werden. Dies gilt auch für Maßnahmen an Kulturdenkmalen, die Museumsgut sind oder werden sollen.

4.4
Anrechnung von Eigenleistungen

Die Anrechnung von Eigenleistungen ist nach Maßgabe der Bestimmungen in Anlage 2 zulässig.

4.5
Höhe der Zuwendung

Die Zuwendung orientiert sich am Interesse des Landes an der Durchführung der Maßnahme (Punktebewertung). Der Fördersatz beträgt bei Zuwendungen an Private die Hälfte und bei Zuwendungen an Gemeinden, Gemeindeverbände, Zweckverbände, Landkreise, Kirchen und die sonstigen als Körperschaften des öffentlichen Rechts anerkannten Religions- und Weltanschauungsgemeinschaften ein Drittel der zuwendungsfähigen Ausgaben. Werden Zuwendungen an den Besitzer oder Bauunterhaltungspflichtigen gewährt, ist der für den Antragsteller des jeweiligen Kulturdenkmals maßgebliche Fördersatz anzuwenden.

4.6
Nachfinanzierung

Die Zuwendung darf nur erhöht werden (Nachfinanzierung), wenn die Zuwendungsvoraussetzungen weiter vorhanden sind, eine anderweitige Finanzierung unzumutbar ist, ein entsprechender Bewilligungsrahmen noch verfügbar ist und die Zuwendungsempfänger die Umstände, die zur Nachfinanzierung führen, nicht zu vertreten hat. Ein Rechtsanspruch auf Nachfinanzierung besteht nicht.

5 Sonderfälle

Von den Vorgaben in den Nummern 3.3, 3.4, 4.3 Satz 2, 4.5 und 4.6 kann in begründeten Einzelfällen mit Zustimmung des Wirtschaftsministeriums abgewichen werden.

6 Besondere Nebenbestimmungen zum Zuwendungsbescheid

Abweichend von den VV Nummern 3.2.1.1, 3.2.1.2 und 4.2.7 zu § 44 LHO ist ein auf die Gesamtmaßnahme bezogener Kosten- und Finanzierungsplan vorzulegen. Der Kosten- und Finanzierungsplan ist der Bewilligung zu Grunde zu legen.

7 Beihilfehöchstintensität und beihilfefähige Kosten im Sinne von Artikel 7 AGVO

Nach Artikel 7 AGVO werden für die Berechnung der Beihilfeintensität und der beihilfefähigen Kosten die Beträge vor Abzug von Steuern und sonstigen Abgaben herangezogen. Die beihilfefähigen Kosten sind durch schriftliche Unterlagen zu belegen, die klar, spezifisch und aktuell sein müssen.

Abschnitt 2
Verfahren, Auszahlung

8 Antragsfrist, Antragsunterlagen

Zuwendungsanträge sind unter Verwendung der beim LAD erhältlichen Vordrucke[1] unter Beifügung der dort genannten Unterlagen (insbesondere Baupläne, beschriftete Fotos, bau- oder denkmalschutzrechtliche Genehmigungen, Maßnahme- und Leistungsbeschreibungen, Bauzeitenplan, gewerkebezogene Kostenberechnungen, Kosten- und Finanzierungsplan der Gesamtmaßnahme) vor Beginn der Maßnahme beim LAD einzureichen. Das Wirtschaftsministerium kann Regelungen zu einem Antragsstichtag treffen.

9 Antragsprüfung und Programmvorschläge

9.1

Das LAD prüft die Anträge in der Regel innerhalb von 15 Arbeitstagen auf das Vorliegen der formalen Zuwendungsvoraussetzungen (unter anderem Vollständigkeit, Fördervoraussetzungen, Kostenberech-

---

[1] **Amtl. Anm.:** Das LAD verwendet Vordrucke zum Zuwendungsantrag, Zuwendungsbescheid, Verwendungsnachweis und den jeweils erforderlichen Anlagen entsprechend dem vom Wirtschaftsministerium vorgegebenen Muster.

nung, Kosten- und Finanzierungsplan). Es übersendet danach dem Antragsteller eine Eingangsbestätigung, gegebenenfalls unter Anforderung fehlender Unterlagen und setzt für eine erforderliche Ergänzung der Antragsunterlagen eine angemessene Frist.

9.2

Das LAD führt die konservatorische Prüfung der Anträge durch und bewertet die denkmalpflegerische Priorität, Dringlichkeit und Zweckmäßigkeit der Vorhaben nach den vom Wirtschaftsministerium vorgegebenen Kriterien. Bei Vorhaben mit einer hinreichenden denkmalpflegerischen Wertigkeit für eine Einbeziehung in die Programmvorschläge ermittelt das LAD die voraussichtliche Zuwendungshöhe.

9.3

Das Nähere zu den Programmvorschlägen wird vom Wirtschaftsministerium festgelegt.

10 Verwaltungsmäßige Abwicklung

10.1

Dem LAD obliegt die verwaltungsmäßige Abwicklung des Denkmalförderprogramms, vor allem die Bewilligung, Auszahlung und Abrechnung der Zuwendungen.

10.2

Die Verwendung der Zuwendung ist dem LAD innerhalb von sechs Monaten nach Durchführung der Maßnahme unter Verwendung des dort erhältlichen Vordrucks[1] nachzuweisen. Wird ein Bauträger, Baubetreuer, Generalunternehmer oder ähnliches mit der Durchführung der Maßnahmen beauftragt, hat der Zuwendungsempfänger mit dem Verwendungsnachweis zusätzlich auch die spezifizierten Rechnungsbelege der Handwerker, Subunternehmer und Lieferanten an den Bauträger sowie einen detaillierten Einzelnachweis über Vergütungen für dessen eigene Leistungen (falls erforderlich die Originalkalkulation) vorzulegen. Zur Sicherstellung dieser Vorgabe wird eine entsprechende vertragliche Regelung zwischen Bauherrn (Zuwendungsempfänger) und Bauträger oder ähnliches empfohlen.

10.3

Nach dieser Förderrichtlinie gewährte Förderungen können kumuliert werden mit anderen staatlichen Beihilfen, sofern diese Maßnahmen unterschiedliche bestimmbare beihilfefähige Kosten betreffen, sowie mit anderen staatlichen Beihilfen für dieselben, sich teilweise oder vollständig überschneidenden beihilfefähigen Kosten, jedoch nur, wenn diese Kumulierung die höchste nach der AGVO für diese Beihilfen geltende Beihilfenintensität beziehungsweise der höchste nach der AGVO für diese Beihilfen geltende Beihilfebetrag nach Artikel 4 Absatz 1z AGVO nicht überschritten wird.

10.4

Es wird darauf hingewiesen, dass Informationen über jede Einzelbeihilfe von über 500 000 Euro auf einer ausführlichen Beihilfe-Website gemäß Artikel 9 AGVO veröffentlicht werden.

10.5

Erhaltene Förderungen können im Einzelfall gemäß Artikel 12 AGVO von der Europäischen Kommission geprüft werden.

---

1) **Amtl. Anm.:** Das LAD verwendet Vordrucke zum Zuwendungsantrag, Zuwendungsbescheid, Verwendungsnachweis und den jeweils erforderlichen Anlagen entsprechend dem vom Wirtschaftsministerium vorgegebenen Muster.

Abschnitt 3
Schlussbestimmungen

11 Inkrafttreten/Geltungsdauer

11.1

Die Verwaltungsvorschrift tritt am Tag nach ihrer Verkündung[1] in Kraft.

11.2

Die Laufzeit dieser Förderrichtlinie ist bis zum noch zu beschließenden Zeitpunkt des Auslaufens der AGVO zuzüglich einer Anpassungsperiode von sechs Monaten, frühestens bis zum 30. Juni 2021 befristet. Sollte die zeitliche Anwendung der AGVO ohne die Beihilferegelung betreffende relevante inhaltliche Veränderungen verlängert werden, verlängert sich die Laufzeit dieser Förderrichtlinie entsprechend, aber nicht über den 31. Dezember 2023 hinaus. Sollte die AGVO nicht verlängert und durch eine neue AGVO ersetzt werden, oder sollten relevante inhaltliche Veränderungen der derzeitigen AGVO vorgenommen werden, wird eine den dann geltenden Freistellungsbestimmungen entsprechende Nachfolge-Förderrichtlinie bis mindestens 31. Dezember 2023 in Kraft gesetzt werden.

Anlage 1
(zu Nummer 4.2 VwV-Denkmalförderung)

Liste der förderfähigen Ausgaben des Wirtschaftsministeriums im Rahmen der Denkmalförderung des Landes

Vorwort

Die allgemeinen Zuwendungsbestimmungen finden Sie in der VwV-Denkmalförderung. Die nachfolgende Zusammenstellung basiert auf diesen Vorgaben und dient der Ermittlung der zuwendungsfähigen Ausgaben. Zuwendungsfähige Ausgaben sind Ausgaben, die im Rahmen von Sicherungs-, Konservierungs- und Reparaturmaßnahmen an Kulturdenkmalen anfallen. Ziel dieser Zuwendungen ist es, schwerpunktmäßig Maßnahmen zu fördern, die dem Erhalt denkmalwerter Substanz dienen und ihren historischen Bestand sichern. In Einzelfällen können diese auch auf den Erhalt beziehungsweise die Wiederherstellung eines besonders schützenswerten Erscheinungsbildes ausgerichtet sein.

Ausgaben für üblichen Bauunterhalt, Nutzungserweiterungen und -änderungen sowie deren Folgeausgaben sind nicht zuwendungsfähig. Ebenso wenig sind Abbruch- und Entsorgungsarbeiten, Reinigung und Dämmung zuwendungsfähig. Entsalzung und Entfeuchtung sowie Schwammbekämpfung sind nur unter Position 16 zuwendungsfähig.

Grundsätzlich können nur Maßnahmen anerkannt werden, die auf fachlichen Anforderungen des LAD beruhen beziehungsweise mit diesem abgestimmt sind. Voraussetzung für einen Zuschussantrag ist eine denkmalschutzrechtliche Genehmigung für die anfallenden Maßnahmen.

Maßgeblich ist, dass qualifizierte, denkmalerfahrene Planer, Handwerker und Fachrestauratoren zum Einsatz kommen, die die Denkmalsubstanz unter Einsatz reparierender Konzepte und konservierender Verfahren weitestgehend erhalten und gegebenenfalls nach denkmalfachlichen Vorgaben des LAD wieder ablesbar machen.

Ermittlungsgrundlage für die Zuwendungen sind detaillierte gewerkebezogene Kostenberechnungen (Anlage 2 zum Zuwendungsantrag). Pauschalangebote, Angebote von Generalunternehmern und sonstige pauschale Angaben wie Unvorhergesehenes, Regiestunden und ähnliches werden nicht berücksichtigt. Werden Zuwendungen für Restaurierungs- oder Natursteinarbeiten beantragt, sind detaillierte gewerkebezogene Kostenvoranschläge durch Fachrestauratoren beziehungsweise Steinmetzbetriebe vorzulegen.

Leistungsbereiche
1. Gerüstbauarbeiten
2. Maurerarbeiten
3. Beton- und Stahlbetonarbeiten
4. Natur- und Kunstwerksteinarbeiten
5. Zimmermannsarbeiten
6. Stahl- und Metallbauarbeiten
7. Dachdeckungsarbeiten
8. Klempnerarbeiten

---

[1] Verkündet am 27.11.2019.

9. Putz- und Stuckarbeiten
10. Belagsarbeiten an Wand und Boden
11. Schreinerarbeiten
12. Schlosserarbeiten
13. Fensterarbeiten
14. Statische Sicherungsarbeiten
15. Schutzbauten
16. Konservierungs- und Restaurierungsmaßnahmen
17. Orgelwerke, Glocken und Uhrwerke
18. Technische Kulturdenkmale
19. Archäologische Kulturdenkmale
20. Gartendenkmale
21. Maßnahmen an Archivgut
22. Kulturdenkmale ohne bzw. mit untergeordneter Nutzung
23. Voruntersuchungen und Dokumentation
24. Baunebenkosten

Art der zuwendungsfähigen Ausgaben	Anteil an Gesamt-ausgaben in %
1. Gerüstbauarbeiten	
1.1. Mehrausgaben bei längerer Standzeit, höherer Tragfähigkeit des Gerüstes (Steinmetzarbeiten) oder bauwerksbezogenen beziehungsweise topographischen Erschwernissen	20
1.2. Ausgaben für Gerüstbauarbeiten, die ausschließlich im Zusammenhang mit Restaurierungsarbeiten an denkmalrelevanter Ausstattung stehen	40
2. Maurerarbeiten	
Sichtmauerwerk und Lehmbaukonstruktionen (zum Beispiel Flechtwerk mit Lehmbewurf, Lehmwickel): Reparatur	40
3. Beton- und Stahlbetonarbeiten	
Sichtbetonflächen und Zierelemente: Reparatur auf der Grundlage einer Materialanalyse	60
4. Natur- und Kunstwerksteinarbeiten	
Natur- und Kunstwerksteine: Reparatur	60
5. Zimmermannsarbeiten	
5.1. Holzkonstruktionen: Reparatur	
5.2. Holzschindelfassaden: Reparatur, Ergänzung und Wiederherstellung nach vorhandenem Bestand	60
5.3. Zierelemente: Reparatur	
6. Stahl- und Metallbauarbeiten	
Stahl- und Eisentragwerke: Reparatur einschließlich Oberflächenbehandlung	40
7. Dachdeckungsarbeiten	
7.1. Dachdeckungen: Erhaltung und Ergänzung	80
7.2. Naturschiefer, Mönch- und Nonnenziegel, glasierte Ziegel, Sonderdachdeckungen, Sonderformate: Reparatur, Ergänzung und Wiederherstellung nach vorhandenem Bestand	
8. Klempnerarbeiten	
Zier- und profilierte Werkstücke: Reparatur	60
9. Putz- und Stuckarbeiten	
9.1. Putz an Sichtfachwerk oder Putz nach besonderer historischer Handwerkstechnik, Materialzusammensetzung oder Oberflächenstruktur: Reparatur	20
9.2. Putz- und Stuckgliederungen: Reparatur	60

D1.III.1 VwV-Denkmalförderung

Art der zuwendungsfähigen Ausgaben	Anteil an Gesamtausgaben in %
10. Belagsarbeiten an Wand und Boden	
Fliesen, Platten, Mosaik, Estrich und Terrazzo, Linoleum, Holzböden und Parkett: Reparatur	60
11. Schreinerarbeiten	
Holzausstattungen: Reparatur einschließlich Oberflächenbehandlung	80
12. Schlosserarbeiten	
Bauelemente: Reparatur einschließlich Oberflächenbehandlung	60
13. Fensterarbeiten	
13.1. Fensterbestand: Reparatur einschließlich Oberflächenbehandlung	100
13.2. Fenster: Ergänzung zu Kastenfenstern im Zuge einer Reparatur gemäß Position 13.1	40
13.3. Fensterbestand: Reparatur und bauphysikalische Verbesserung einschließlich Oberflächenbehandlung	60
13.4. Neue Fenster, soweit sie für das geschützte Erscheinungsbild von herausragender Bedeutung sind und denkmalfachlichen Vorgaben entsprechen (ohne Ein- und Ausbau)	40
13.5. Schutzverglasungen von Fensterscheiben mit besonderer Bedeutung	40
14. Statische Sicherungsarbeiten	
Statische Sicherung, auf Grundlage einer denkmalfachlich abgestimmten statischen Voruntersuchung	40
15. Schutzbauten	
Schutzbauten, Schutzdächer, Einhausungen in angemessenem Umfang, die ausschließlich dem Erhalt des Kulturdenkmals dienen	40
16. Konservierungs- und Restaurierungsmaßnahmen	
16.1. Natur- und Kunstwerkstein, Putz, Stuck, Fassungen (innen wie außen), Wandmalereien, Holz (Intarsien, veredelte Holzoberflächen), Gemälde und Ausstattungsteile, Tapeten, Textilien, Gläser, Glasmalerei, Kacheln, Mosaike, Fliesen, Metall: Konservierung und Restaurierung durch Fachrestaurator Typische Maßnahmen sind: – Befunderhebung, Bestandsuntersuchung – Substanzfestigung, -stabilisierung, Korrosionsschutz – Entsalzung innerhalb des zu konservierenden Bereichs – Hinterspritzen und Wiederbefestigen hohlliegender Bereiche – Niederlegen, Festigen von Malschichten – Differenzierte Reinigungen – Reduzierung und Abnahme von Schichten (Überzüge, Übermalungen, Überputzungen) – Kittung, kleinteilige plastische Ergänzungen – Farbergänzung, Retusche – Bekämpfung von Schädlingen und Mikroorganismen am zu konservierenden Objekt – Reversible Schutzbeschichtungen Oberflächen	100
16.2. Wartung und Pflege auf der Grundlage von denkmalfachlich geforderten Wartungsverträgen	100
16.3. Maßnahmen zur Klimastabilisierung und Einhausungen sowie fachgerechter Deponierung, die ausschließlich zum Schutz der Substanz erforderlich sind	60
16.4. Maßnahmen zur Mauerwerksentfeuchtung und -entsalzung, die ausschließlich zum Schutz der bedeutenden Substanz (wie Wandmalereien, mittelalterliche Mörtel) erforderlich sind	60

Art der zuwendungsfähigen Ausgaben	Anteil an Gesamt-ausgaben in %
16.5. Schädlingsbekämpfungsmaßnahmen zum Schutz von Ausstattung	40
Anmerkungen: Handwerkliche Leistungen wie Maler-, Putz-, Schreiner- und Schlosserarbeiten, die von Restauratoren erbracht werden, werden nicht nach Position 16 behandelt. Bewegliche Ausstattungen sind nur zuwendungsfähig, wenn 1. es sich um ein im Denkmalbuch eingetragenes Kulturdenkmal (§§ 12 und 28 DSchG) handelt und/oder 2. sie als Zubehör mit der Hauptsache eine Einheit beim Denkmalwert bilden.	
17. **Orgelwerke, Glocken und Uhrwerke** Orgelwerke, Glocken und Uhrenwerke: Reparatur	60
Anmerkungen: Die Erweiterung von Orgelwerken, der Nachguss von Glocken und die Modernisierung von Uhrwerken sind nicht zuwendungsfähig.	
18. **Technische Kulturdenkmale** Technische Kulturdenkmale: Grundsätzlich für Reparatur und Sicherungsmaßnahmen Darüber hinaus bedürfen Maßnahmen an technischen Kulturdenkmalen abhängig von den Erhaltungsforderungen und der vorgesehenen Nutzung einer Einzelfallentscheidung.	60
Anmerkungen: Bewegliche technische Kulturdenkmale sind nur zuwendungsfähig, wenn sie in das Denkmalbuch (§§ 12 und 28 DSchG) eingetragen sind.	
19. **Archäologische Kulturdenkmale** 19.1. Sicherung und Erhaltung 19.2. Schutzbauten in angemessenem Umfang, die nur dem Erhalt archäologischer Befunde dienen 19.3. Angemessene Darstellung der denkmalpflegerischen Bedeutung eines archäologischen Kulturdenkmals am Befund oder in seiner Umgebung	100
Anmerkungen: Rekonstruktionen und bauliche Maßnahmen, die der Zugänglichkeit der archäologischen Befunde dienen, sind nicht zuwendungsfähig.	
20. **Gartendenkmale** Voraussetzung für eine Förderung ist, dass die Maßnahmen auf der Grundlage eines mit dem LAD abgestimmten Parkpflegewerks respektive Voruntersuchung erfolgen.	
20.1. Besonders wertvoller Pflanzenbestand: aufwendige Erhaltungs- und Pflegemaßnahmen	80
20.2. Gartenarchitektonische und bauliche Bestandteile des Gartendenkmals (Treppen, Wege): Reparatur	40
20.3. Turnusmäßige Pflegemaßnahmen bei Gartendenkmalen von besonderer Bedeutung (§§ 12 und 28 DSchG) auf der Grundlage eines Parkpflegewerks	40
21. **Maßnahmen an Archivgut** Privat- und Kirchenarchivgut: Restaurierung und Konservierung, einschließlich dessen fachgerechter Lagerung, sowie Maßnahmen zur Erschließung des Archivguts	100
Anmerkungen: • Nutzungsbedingte Ausgaben (Schutzverfilmungen et cetera) sind nicht förderfähig.	

D1.III.1 VwV-Denkmalförderung

Art der zuwendungsfähigen Ausgaben	Anteil an Gesamtausgaben in %
• Maßnahmen an Archivgut, das dem Landesarchivgesetz unterliegt, sowie Maßnahmen, die eine anderweitige Förderung des Landes mit archivpflegerischer Zielsetzung erfahren, sind nicht zuwendungsfähig.	
22. Kulturdenkmale ohne beziehungsweise mit untergeordneter Nutzung	
22.1. Sicherungsmaßnahmen an Kulturdenkmalen, die nicht nutzbar sind (zum Beispiel Burgruinen)	80
22.2. Sicherungsmaßnahmen an Kulturdenkmalen, die nicht genutzt werden beziehungsweise nur einer untergeordneten Nutzung dienen und in einem Zeitraum von mindestens zehn Jahren nach Sicherung keiner Nutzung beziehungsweise nur einer untergeordneten Nutzung zugeführt werden (zum Beispiel ungenutzte Scheune)	60
Anmerkungen: Mauern mit Funktion siehe Position 2, Maurerarbeiten	
23. Voruntersuchungen und Dokumentation	
23.1. Bauaufnahmen entsprechend denkmalfachlicher Vorgaben	
Genauigkeitsstufe II	40
Genauigkeitsstufe III	80
Genauigkeitsstufe IV	100
23.2. Dokumentation und Raumbuch entsprechend denkmalfachlicher Vorgaben	100
23.3. Gutachten entsprechend denkmalfachlicher Vorgaben	100
23.4. Statische Voruntersuchungen entsprechend denkmalfachlicher Vorgaben	60
23.5. Gutachten zur energetischen Sanierung von Kulturdenkmalen: Voraussetzung hierfür ist ein energetisches Gesamtkonzept, das sämtliche Bauteile des Gebäudes und die Haustechnik umfasst sowie von einem Energieberater für Baudenkmale erstellt wird.	60
23.6. Materialanalysen entsprechend denkmalfachlicher Vorgaben	40
24. Baunebenkosten	
Leistungen von Architekten und Statikern werden grundsätzlich anteilig anerkannt, **maximal zusammen jedoch 8 Prozent der zuwendungsfähigen Ausgaben.**	

Anlage 2
(zu Nummer 4.4 VwV-Denkmalförderung)

Anrechnung von Eigenleistungen

I. Definition von Eigenleistungen:
Eigenleistungen sind Leistungen zur Bauplanung, Bauleitung und Bauausführung, die vom Zuwendungsempfänger selbst oder den unter den Nummern 1. bis 3. genannten Personen erbracht werden.
1. Privat:
   - **Privatpersonen**
   Zusätzlich zu den Leistungen des Zuwendungsempfängers können auch Leistungen seines im Haushalt lebenden Ehegatten beziehungsweise Lebenspartners als Eigenleistungen angegeben werden. Unentgeltliche Leistungen von Verwandten im Sinne des § 1589 BGB (außer den oben genannten) und Nachbarn sind keine Eigenleistungen.
   - **Trägervereine**
   Bei Trägervereinen, die zur Erhaltung eines Kulturdenkmals gegründet wurden und denen die Bauunterhaltungspflicht für das geförderte Kulturdenkmal auf mindestens zehn Jahre übertragen worden ist, können Leistungen der Vereinsmitglieder als Eigenleistungen angegeben werden.

- **Eigenleistungen im Rahmen des eigenen Geschäftsbetriebs**
  Bauunternehmer, Handwerker, Restauratoren, Architekten, Ingenieure und Statiker, die bei Eigenleistungen im Rahmen ihres Geschäftsbetriebs tätig werden, können die ortsüblichen Entgelte innerhalb der gestellten Rechnungen als Eigenleistungen angeben.
- **Private Bauhöfe**
  Bei privaten Bauhöfen kann der tatsächliche Lohn (Lohn und Lohnnebenkosten) der eingesetzten Arbeitskräfte für Leistungen des Bauhofes für Bauplanung, Bauleitung und Bauausführung als Eigenleistung angegeben werden.
2. Politische Gemeinden:
   Bei politischen Gemeinden kann der Tariflohn der eingesetzten Arbeitskräfte für Leistungen des gemeindeeigenen Bauamtes beziehungsweise Bauhofes für Bauplanung, Bauleitung und Bauausführung als Eigenleistung angegeben werden. Leistungen der Mitglieder einer politischen Gemeinde sind keine Eigenleistungen.
3. Kirchliche Gemeinden:
   Bei Kirchengemeinden kann der Tariflohn der eingesetzten Arbeitskräfte für Leistungen der kirchlichen Bauämter für Bauplanung und Bauleitung als Eigenleistung angegeben werden. Leistungen der Mitglieder einer kirchlichen Gemeinde sind keine Eigenleistungen.

II. Anerkennung von Eigenleistungen:
Eigenleistungen können gemäß der „Liste der förderfähigen Ausgaben des Wirtschaftsministeriums im Rahmen der Denkmalförderung des Landes" (Anlage 1) berücksichtigt werden.
Die Eigenleistung kann nur anerkannt werden, wenn zuwendungsfähige Leistungen insgesamt in mehr als 150 Stunden erbracht werden. Sie ist grundsätzlich durch eine Bestätigung des Architekten glaubhaft zu machen.
Die absolute Grenze der Förderung liegt bei der Summe der tatsächlich entstandenen Ausgaben, wobei bei der Förderhöhe ausgehend vom Grundsatz der Subsidiarität der Landeszuwendung nach § 23 LHO alle übrigen Finanzierungsmittel des Projekts (zum Beispiel Spenden, Stiftungsmittel, Zuwendungen anderer Träger) zu berücksichtigen sind, um eine Überfinanzierung der Maßnahme auszuschließen.
1. Private:
   - **Privatpersonen**
     Die vom Zuwendungsempfänger und den unter Nummer I.1. genannten Privatpersonen geleistete Arbeitszeit für die Eigenleistung wird nach einem Stundensatz in Höhe von 12 Euro bei den Gesamtausgaben für die Maßnahme angerechnet und gemäß der Anlage 1 gegebenenfalls ganz oder teilweise anerkannt. Das vom Zuwendungsempfänger selbst bereitgestellte Material wird zum Einkaufspreis angerechnet. Der Einsatz von Geräten und Fahrzeugen von Privaten ist nicht zuwendungsfähig.
   - **Trägervereine**
     Siehe Nummer II.1. (Privatpersonen).
   - **Eigenleistungen im Rahmen des eigenen Geschäftsbetriebs**
     Bei Unternehmern, Handwerkern und Restauratoren, die bei Eigenleistungen im Rahmen ihres Geschäftsbetriebs tätig werden, werden die förderfähigen Ausgaben abzüglich eines pauschalierten Gewinnanteils von 25 Prozent anerkannt. Diese Regelung gilt auch für Architekten, Ingenieure und Baustatiker bis zu einem Höchstbetrag von 10 Prozent der Gesamtausgaben für die Maßnahme.
   - **Private Bauhöfe**
     Bei privaten Bauhöfen werden die förderfähigen Ausgaben aus dem tatsächlichen Lohn (Lohn und Lohnnebenkosten) der eingesetzten Arbeitskräfte ermittelt. Beim Einsatz hofeigener Baufahrzeuge und Baumaschinen können maximal bis zu 15 Prozent der anerkannten Lohnkosten als förderfähig berücksichtigt werden.
2. Politische Gemeinden:
   Bei politischen Gemeinden werden die förderfähigen Ausgaben aus dem Tariflohn der eingesetzten Arbeitskräfte mit einem pauschalen Abzug von 25 Prozent ermittelt. Beim Einsatz gemeindeeigener Baufahrzeuge und Baumaschinen kann ein angemessener Stundensatz abzüglich eines Gemeindeanteils von 25 Prozent anerkannt werden.
3. Kirchliche Gemeinden:
   Bei Kirchengemeinden werden die förderfähigen Ausgaben für Bauplanung und Bauleitung aus dem Tariflohn der eingesetzten Arbeitskräfte mit einem pauschalen Abzug von 25 Prozent ermittelt.

D1.III.2 Satzung der Denkmalstiftung Baden-Württemberg

Satzung der Denkmalstiftung Baden-Württemberg[1)]

§ 1 Name, Sitz und Rechtsform
Die Denkmalstiftung Baden-Württemberg ist eine rechtsfähige Stiftung des bürgerlichen Rechts. Sie hat ihren Sitz in Stuttgart.

§ 2 Zweck der Stiftung
(1) Die Stiftung hat die Aufgabe, zur Erhaltung von Kulturdenkmalen im Sinne des Denkmalschutzgesetzes beizutragen. Dieser Zweck soll vorrangig durch die Förderung privater Initiativen auf dem Gebiet der Denkmalpflege verwirklicht werden. Die Stiftung wird insbesondere dort tätig, wo staatliche Denkmalpflege nicht oder nur in beschränktem Umfang wirkt.

(2) Zur Erfüllung ihrer Aufgaben kann die Stiftung Zuschüsse gewähren, vorrangig an
- private Eigentümer von Kulturdenkmalen, soweit diese erhöhte Erhaltungskosten zu tragen haben; die Förderung darf nicht eigenwirtschaftlichen Zwecken des Eigentümers dienen,
- gemeinnützige Bürgervereine und Bürgeraktionen zur Erhaltung und Pflege von Kulturdenkmalen.

Zuschüsse können auch für Erhaltungsmaßnahmen an Kulturdenkmalen durch andere Träger oder Institutionen, z.B. Kommunen und anerkannte Religionsgemeinschaften gewährt werden, soweit diese erhöhte Erhaltungskosten zu tragen haben.

(3) In begründeten Einzelfällen können zinslose Darlehen bis zu einem Höchstbetrag von 50.000 Euro gewährt werden. Die Anzahl noch nicht restlos abgewickelter Einzelkredite darf höchstens 20, deren Darlehenssumme zusammen höchstens 500.000 EUR betragen.

(4) Die Stiftung kann gefährdete, besonders bedeutsame Kulturdenkmale selbst erwerben, wenn dies für deren Erhaltung erforderlich oder hilfreich ist. Gleiches gilt für Grundstücke, die bedeutsame archäologische Denkmale bergen. Erworbene Kulturdenkmale oder Grundstücke sollen nach Möglichkeit an private, gemeinnützige oder öffentliche Träger übertragen werden, wenn der Erhaltungszweck erfüllt oder seine Erfüllung gewährleistet ist.

(5) Die Stiftung soll die Bedeutung des Denkmalschutzes einer breiten Öffentlichkeit in Baden-Württemberg vermitteln und über ihre Tätigkeit informieren. Sie kann Publikationen fördern oder herausgeben, durch die der Stiftungszweck unterstützt wird.

§ 3 Gemeinnützigkeit
(1) Die Stiftung verfolgt ausschließlich und unmittelbar Zwecke im Sinne des Abschnitts „steuerbegünstigte Zwecke" der Abgabenordnung; sie ist selbstlos tätig und verfolgt nicht überwiegend eigenwirtschaftliche Zwecke.

(2) Die Mittel der Stiftung dürfen nur für die satzungsgemäßen Zwecke verwendet werden. Es darf keine Person durch Ausgaben, die dem Zweck der Stiftung fremd sind, oder durch unverhältnismäßig hohe Vergütungen begünstigt werden. Die Mitgliedschaft in Vorstand und Kuratorium ist ehrenamtlich; Aufwandsentschädigungen werden nicht gewährt.

§ 4 Stifter, Stiftungsvermögen
Das Stiftungsvermögen besteht aus dem vom Land Baden-Württemberg (Stifter) und anderer Seite (Zustiftern) erbrachten Leistungen.

§ 5 Mittelverwendung
(1) Die Stiftung erfüllt ihre Aufgaben aus den Erträgen des Stiftungsvermögens und aus dazu bestimmten Zuwendungen des Landes Baden-Württemberg oder Dritter.

(2) Der Vorstand informiert das Kuratorium zeitnah über die aktuellen Anlagerichtlinien zum Stiftungsvermögen.

(3) Das Stiftungsvermögen ist in seinem Bestand zu erhalten, soweit die Zuwendenden nichts anderes bestimmt haben.

§ 6 Stiftungsorgane
Organe der Stiftung
1. der Vorstand
2. das Kuratorium

---

1) Fundstelle: http://denkmalstiftung-baden-wuerttemberg.de/stiftung/satzung/.

§ 7 Vorstand

(1) Der Vorstand der Stiftung besteht aus fünf Mitgliedern.
(2) Ein Mitglied des Vorstandes wird von der Landesregierung, die übrigen Mitglieder werden vom Kuratorium auf die Dauer von vier Jahren bestellt. Soweit Mitglieder des Kuratoriums zu Mitgliedern des Vorstandes bestellt werden, scheiden sie aus dem Kuratorium aus. Wiederholte Bestellung ist möglich.
(3) Wird ein neuer Vorstand nicht unmittelbar nach Beendigung der Amtszeit des bisherigen Vorstandes gebildet, so verlängert sich dessen Amtszeit bis zur Bildung des neuen Vorstands, längstens jedoch um ein Jahr.
(4) Für ein vorzeitig ausscheidendes Mitglied des Vorstandes kann ein Nachfolger nur für den Rest der Amtszeit bestellt werden.
(5) Der Vorstand wählt aus seiner Mitte einen Vorsitzenden und seinen Stellvertreter.
(6) Der Vorstand ist beschlussfähig, wenn mehr als die Hälfte seiner Mitglieder anwesend ist. Der Vorstand beschließt mit einfacher Mehrheit der abgegebenen Stimmen. Bei Stimmengleichheit entscheidet die Stimme des Vorsitzenden. Der Vorstand kann eilbedürftige Beschlüsse im schriftlichen Verfahren fassen, wenn alle Mitglieder diesem Verfahren zustimmen.
(7) Das Nähere kann durch eine Geschäftsordnung geregelt werden.

§ 8 Aufgaben des Vorstandes

(1) Der Vorstand führt die Geschäfte der Stiftung. Beschlüsse über Einzelvorhaben, an denen die Stiftung mit einem Gesamtbetrag von mehr als 250.000 Euro beteiligt ist, bedürfen der Zustimmung des Kuratoriums. Der Vorstand kann einen Geschäftsführer bestellen. Der Geschäftsführer kann nicht Mitglied des Vorstandes sein.
(2) Die Stiftung wird gerichtlich und außergerichtlich durch den Vorsitzenden des Vorstandes oder seinen Stellvertreter vertreten.
(3) Der Vorstand betreut Stifter und Förderer, hierzu kann er einen Förderkreis bilden.

§ 9 Zusammensetzung und Amtsdauer des Kuratoriums

(1) Dem Kuratorium sollen Stifter, Vertreter der Wirtschaft, Wissenschaft und Kunst, der auf dem Gebiet der Denkmalpflege tätigen Verbände und Bürgergruppen, der Kirchen, kommunalen Körperschaften und der staatlichen Denkmalpflege sowie der Eigentümer von Kulturdenkmalen angehören.
(2) Dem Kuratorium gehören an:
1. ein Vertreter der obersten Denkmalschutzbehörde,
2. ein Vertreter des Landesamtes für Denkmalpflege im Regierungspräsidium Stuttgart, der vom für die Denkmalpflege zuständigen Ministerium berufen wird,
3. ein Vertreter aus dem Ministerium, das für Schlösser und Gärten, Kulturliegenschaften zuständig ist,
4. je ein Vertreter des Landkreistages, Städtetages und Gemeindetages,
5. je ein Vertreter der evangelischen und der katholischen Kirche sowie der israelitischen Religionsgemeinschaft,
6. höchstens sieben Mitglieder, die von der Landesregierung Baden-Württemberg bestellt werden,
7. höchstens sieben weitere Mitglieder, die vom Kuratorium aufgrund von Vorschlägen des Vorstandes bestellt werden.

(3) Die Amtszeit des Kuratoriums entspricht der Dauer der Legislaturperiode des Landtages von Baden-Württemberg. Für ein vorzeitig ausscheidendes Mitglied kann ein Nachfolger nur für den Rest der Amtszeit bestellt werden. Wiederholte Bestellung ist möglich. Für die Mitglieder nach Absatz 2 Nr. 1 bis 5 können Vertreter entsandt werden. Die Mitglieder nach Absatz 2 Nr. 6 und 7 können Vertreter benennen, die im Fall der Nummer 6 von der Landesregierung, im Fall der Nummer 7 vom Kuratorium bestellt werden können.
(4) Das Kuratorium wählt aus seiner Mitte einen Vorsitzenden und seinen Stellvertreter.
(5) Wird ein neues Kuratorium nicht unmittelbar nach Beendigung der Amtszeit des bisherigen Kuratoriums gebildet, verlängert sich dessen Amtszeit bis zum Zusammentritt des neuen Kuratoriums, längstens jedoch um ein Jahr.

§ 10 Aufgaben des Kuratoriums

(1) Das Kuratorium legt Richtlinien für die Arbeit der Stiftung, insbesondere für die Vergabe und für die satzungsgemäße Verwendung der Zuwendungen fest. Die Mitglieder des Kuratoriums sollen insbesondere Wirtschaft und Bevölkerung zu aktiver ideeller, finanzieller und eigenhändiger Mithilfe bei der Denkmalpflege anregen.

Das Kuratorium unterstützt den Vorstand bei der Erfüllung seiner Aufgaben und überwacht die Rechtmäßigkeit, Zweckmäßigkeit und die Wirtschaftlichkeit der Führung der Stiftungsgeschäfte.

(2) Das Kuratorium hat ferner folgende Aufgaben:
1. Bestellung des Vorstandes gemäß § 7 Abs. 2 Satz 1,
2. Feststellung des Haushalts- und Wirtschaftsplans,
3. Zustimmung zu Beschlüssen über Einzelvorhaben, an denen die Stiftung mit einem Gesamtbetrag von mehr als 250.000 Euro beteiligt ist,
4. Entgegennahme der Jahresrechnung und des Tätigkeitsberichtes des Vorstandes, erforderlichenfalls unter der Mitwirkung eines Rechnungsprüfers,
5. Entlastung des Vorstandes,
6. Änderung der Satzung und des Stiftungszwecks.

(3) Das Kuratorium kann die von ihm bestellten Mitglieder des Vorstandes aus wichtigem Grund abberufen.

(4) Sitzungen des Kuratoriums finden nach Bedarf, mindestens jedoch einmal jährlich statt. Das Kuratorium ist einzuberufen, wenn mindestens ein Viertel der Mitglieder dies verlangen. Es ist beschlussfähig, wenn mindestens ein Drittel seiner Mitglieder anwesend sind. Entscheidungen werden, soweit nichts anderes bestimmt ist, mit Stimmenmehrheit der anwesenden Mitglieder gefasst; bei Stimmengleichheit gibt die Stimme des Vorsitzenden den Ausschlag.

(5) Das Nähere kann durch eine Geschäftsordnung geregelt werden.

§ 11 Haushalts-, Kassen- und Rechnungswesen

(1) Die Mittel der Stiftung sind nach wirtschaftlichen Gesichtspunkten sparsam zu verwenden.

(2) Über die Einnahmen und Ausgaben sowie über das Vermögen der Stiftung ist nach Ablauf eines Geschäftsjahres durch den Vorstand Rechnung zu legen. Geschäftsjahr ist das Kalenderjahr.

(3) Der Rechnungshof ist berechtigt, die Haushalts- und Wirtschaftsführung der Stiftung gemäß § 104 Abs. 1 Nr. 4 der Landeshaushaltsordnung zu prüfen.

§ 12 Satzungsänderung, Aufhebung der Stiftung

(1) Beschlüsse über Satzungsänderungen und der Beschluss über die Aufhebung der Stiftung sowie über eine Änderung des Stiftungszwecks bedürfen einer Zweidrittel-Mehrheit der Mitglieder des Kuratoriums. Beschlüsse können auch im schriftlichen Umlaufverfahren gefasst werden. Der Vorstand ist vorher zu hören. Der Beschluss über eine Änderung des Stiftungszwecks bedarf der Zustimmung der Landesregierung. Die Beschlüsse werden erst mit Genehmigung der Stiftungsbehörde rechtswirksam.

(2) Bei Aufhebung der Stiftung fällt das Stiftungsvermögen an das Land Baden-Württemberg. Es darf nur für Zwecke der Denkmalpflege verwendet werden.

§ 13 Inkrafttreten

Die Satzung tritt mit dem Tag der Genehmigung in Kraft.

Richtlinien für die satzungsgemäße Vergabe und Verwendung der Zuwendungen der Denkmalstiftung Baden-Württemberg

Stand: Beschluss des Kuratoriums vom 12.5.2015[1)]

1. Förderzweck

Die Denkmalstiftung fördert die Erhaltung von Kulturdenkmalen im Sinne des Denkmalschutzgesetzes. Sie fördert vorrangig private Initiativen auf dem Gebiet der Denkmalpflege.

Die Stiftung wird insbesondere dort tätig, wo die staatliche Denkmalpflege nicht oder nur in beschränktem Umfang wirkt.

2. Förderempfänger

Die Denkmalstiftung kann gem. § 2 Abs. 2 und 3 der Satzung Zuschüsse gewähren vorrangig an private Eigentümer von Kulturdenkmalen soweit diese denkmalschutzbedingte Mehrkosten zu tragen haben und an gemeinnützige Bürgervereine und Bürgeraktionen.

Zuwendungen kann die Stiftung auch an andere Träger oder Institutionen wie Kommunen und anerkannte Religionsgemeinschaften gewähren, soweit diese denkmalschutzbedingte Mehrkosten zu tragen haben.

3. Eigenbeteiligung

Zuwendungen werden nur gewährt, wenn die Zuwendungsempfänger ihrerseits zur Erhaltung des Kulturdenkmals angemessen beitragen, z. B. durch Eigenmittel, eigene Arbeitsleistung, Übernahme der Unterhaltungslast für die Zukunft.

Sofern das Kulturdenkmal nicht öffentlich zugänglich ist sollen Zuwendungsempfänger gewährleisten, dass es in angemessener Form, z.B. am Tag des offenen Denkmals, der Öffentlichkeit vorgestellt werden kann. In begründeten Ausnahmefällen kann diese Verpflichtung entfallen.

4. Förderfähige Aufwendungen

4.1. Förderfähig sind insbesondere

4.1.1. bei Maßnahmen von gemeinnützigen Bürgeraktionen Aufwendungen, die zur Erhaltung, Pflege und denkmalverträglichen Nutzung des Kulturdenkmals erforderlich sind, insbesondere Sicherungs-, Instandsetzungs- und Unterhaltungsmaßnahmen sowie Aufwendungen für die Wiederherstellung von teilzerstörten Kulturdenkmalen;

4.1.2. bei Erhaltungsmaßnahmen an Kulturdenkmalen, die von privaten, nichtgemeinnützigen Trägern durchgeführt werden, nur die erhöhten Erhaltungskosten; dies sind die Mehraufwendungen, die im Rahmen von Sicherungs-, Instandsetzungs- und Unterhaltungsmaßnahmen an Kulturdenkmalen allein oder überwiegend aus Gründen der Denkmalpflege erforderlich werden, soweit sie den üblichen Aufwand bei vergleichbaren nichtgeschützten Objekten übersteigen (denkmalbedingte Mehraufwendungen);

4.1.3. Kosten des Erwerbs von Grundstücken, sofern dies für die Erhaltung eines besonders bedeutsamen Kulturdenkmals erforderlich oder hilfreich ist;

4.2. Nicht förderfähig sind

4.2.1. Aufwendungen, die eigenwirtschaftlichen Zwecken dienen; der Eigentümer eines Kulturdenkmals darf gegenüber dem Eigentümer eines vergleichbaren Altbaus ohne Denkmaleigenschaft nicht besser gestellt werden;

4.2.2. in der Regel Kosten der Umgebungsarbeiten, soweit die Umgebung nicht denkmalgeschützt ist.

5. Verhältnis zur staatlichen Denkmalförderung

Die Denkmalstiftung kann neben der staatlichen Denkmalförderung ergänzend fördern. Eine Förderung kommt insbesondere dort in Betracht, wo die staatliche Denkmalförderung nicht oder nicht ausreichend fördern kann.

Vor einer Förderzusage holt die Stiftung eine fachliche Stellungnahme des Landesamtes für Denkmalpflege zur Förderwürdigkeit des Kulturdenkmals und zur fachlichen Qualität der Erhaltungsmaßnahme ein.

---

1) Fundstelle: http://denkmalstiftung-baden-wuerttemberg.de/denkmale/foerderrichtlinien/.

D1.III.2a Richtlinien der Denkmalstiftung Baden-Württemberg

6. Höhe und Form der Förderung

Die Höhe der Förderung wird von der Stiftung nach den Erfordernissen des Einzelfalls festgesetzt. Sie richtet sich danach, was für die Erfüllung des Förderzwecks notwendig ist, abzüglich der Leistungen Dritter und einer angemessenen Eigenbeteiligung.

Die Förderung wird als verlorener Zuschuss oder in begründeten Einzelfällen als zinsloses Darlehen bis zu einem Höchstbetrag von 50.000 Euro gewährt. Über die Förderung wird ein Zuwendungsvertrag geschlossen.

Die verbindliche Förderzusage an den Antragsteller setzt die Förderwürdigkeit des Objekts, die fachliche Qualität der Erhaltungsmaßnahme, eine nachvollziehbare Kostenermittlung und einen Finanzierungsplan voraus.

Liegt ein Finanzierungsplan noch nicht vor, kann die Stiftung eine Förderung unter dem Vorbehalt in Aussicht stellen, dass ein tragfähiger Finanzierungsplan erstellt wird. Dies kommt insbesondere in Betracht, wenn damit bei Objekten mit hoher Förderwürdigkeit die Chance der Gesamtfinanzierung für den Träger der Erhaltungsmaßnahme erhöht werden kann.

7. Auszahlung

Bei Baumaßnahmen werden bis zu 90 % der Zuwendung entsprechend dem Baufortschritt in einem Betrag oder mehreren Teilbeträgen ausbezahlt, die restlichen 10 % nach Nachweis der zweckbestimmten Verwendung.

Bei sonstigen Maßnahmen wird die Zuwendung in der Regel nach Nachweis der zweckbestimmten Verwendung ausbezahlt.

In begründeten Fällen sind vorherige Teilzahlungen möglich.

Soweit erforderlich wird der Auszahlungsmodus im Einzelfall bei der Bewilligung geregelt.

8. Nachweis der Verwendung

Der Zuwendungsempfänger hat nach Abschluss der Maßnahme schriftlich zu bestätigen, dass die Zuwendung bestimmungsgemäß verwendet worden ist. Er hat der Erklärung eine Zusammenstellung der Kosten und der Finanzierung beizufügen (Verwendungsnachweis). Dieser Verwendungsnachweis ist in der Regel innerhalb eines Jahres einzureichen.

Die Denkmalstiftung kann zusätzlich die Bestätigung einer öffentlichen Stelle (z. B. Gemeinde) oder die Vorlage weiterer Nachweise fordern.

9. Rückforderung

Die Zuwendung ist unverzüglich zurückzuzahlen, wenn
- sie nicht für ihren bestimmten Zweck oder nicht innerhalb der gesetzten Frist verwendet worden ist,
- mit der Zuwendung verbundene Auflagen nicht oder nicht innerhalb der gesetzten Frist erfüllt worden sind, oder
- die für die Zuwendung maßgebenden Voraussetzungen nachträglich weggefallen sind.

Die Zuwendung ist außerdem insoweit zurückzuzahlen, als aufgrund von Angaben des Zuwendungsempfängers mehr ausbezahlt worden ist, als nach den tatsächlich angefallenen gewerkebezogenen Gesamtkosten hätte ausbezahlt werden dürfen.

10. Verfahren

Die Zuwendung ist auf dem jeweils aktuellen Antragsformular der Denkmalstiftung zu beantragen. Mit dem Antrag sind grundsätzlich vorzulegen:
- denkmalschutzrechtliche Genehmigung
- eine Beschreibung der Maßnahmen,
- Pläne und Abbildungen, soweit zur Beurteilung des Vorhabens erforderlich,
- eine Kostenvoranschlag,
- ein Finanzierungsplan mit Angabe anderer Zuwendungen,
- ein Zeitplan über die Abwicklung,
- vorhandene fachliche Stellungnahmen der staatlichen Denkmalpflege; die Stiftung kann von sich aus weitere fachliche Stellungnahmen anfordern oder beiziehen.

12. Bewertung der Eigenarbeit von Bürgerinitiativen und Vereinen
Für die Bewertung der Arbeitsleistung von Bürgerinitiativen und Vereinen, die für eigene Baudenkmale oder für Baudenkmale Dritter aufgebracht wird, gelten analog die Bestimmungen der Verwaltungsvorschrift für die Gewährung von Zuwendungen zur Erhaltung und Pflege von Kulturdenkmalen des Landes Baden-Württemberg in ihrer jeweils gültigen Fassung.

D1.IV.1 KGSG-Zuständigkeitsverordnung

Verordnung der Landesregierung und des Wissenschaftsministeriums über die Zuständigkeiten nach dem Kulturgutschutzgesetz

Vom 8. November 2016 (GBl. S. 599)

Es wird verordnet auf Grund von
1. § 3 Absatz 1 Satz 2 und § 22 Abs. 3 Satz 3, auch in Verbindung mit § 24 Abs. 6 Satz 3 des Kulturgutschutzgesetzes (KGSG) vom 31. Juli 2016 (BGBl. I S. 1914) und
2. § 4 Absatz 1 des Landesverwaltungsgesetzes vom 14. Oktober 2008 (GBl. S. 313, 314), das zuletzt durch Artikel 10 des Gesetzes vom 23. Juni 2015 (GBl S. 585, 614) geändert worden ist:

§ 1 [Zuständige Landesbehörde iSd § 27 Abs. 1 KGSG]
Zuständige Landesbehörde im Sinne des § 27 Absatz 1 KGSG ist das Badische Landesmuseum Karlsruhe.

§ 2 [Genehmigung der vorübergehenden Ausfuhr von nationalem Kulturgut]
Die Zuständigkeiten zur Genehmigung der vorübergehenden Ausfuhr von nationalem Kulturgut im Sinne des § 22 KGSG sowie zur Genehmigung der Ausfuhr von Kulturgut im Sinne des § 24 KGSG werden auf das Badische Landesmuseum Karlsruhe übertragen.

§ 3 [Übrige Zuständigkeiten]
In allen übrigen Fällen ist zuständige Behörde im Sinne des Kulturgutschutzgesetzes das Wissenschaftsministerium.

§ 4 [Inkrafttreten]
Diese Verordnung tritt am Tag nach ihrer Verkündung[1] in Kraft.

---

1) Verkündet am 25.11.2016.

Verfassung des Freistaates Bayern

In der Fassung der Bekanntmachung vom 15. Dezember 1998[1] (GVBl. S. 991, 992) (BayRS 100-1-I)
zuletzt geändert durch § 1 ÄndG vom 11. November 2013 (GVBl. S. 642)
– Auszug –

Erster Hauptteil
Aufbau und Aufgaben des Staates

1. Abschnitt
Die Grundlagen des Bayerischen Staates

Artikel 3 [Rechts-, Kultur- und Sozialstaatlichkeit]
(1) ¹Bayern ist ein Rechts-, Kultur- und Sozialstaat. ²Er dient dem Gemeinwohl.
(2) ¹Der Staat schützt die natürlichen Lebensgrundlagen und die kulturelle Überlieferung. ²Er fördert und sichert gleichwertige Lebensverhältnisse und Arbeitsbedingungen in ganz Bayern, in Stadt und Land.

Artikel 11 [Gemeinden]
[...]
(2) ¹Die Gemeinden sind ursprüngliche Gebietskörperschaften des öffentlichen Rechts. ²Sie haben das Recht, ihre eigenen Angelegenheiten im Rahmen der Gesetze selbst zu ordnen und zu verwalten, insbesonders ihre Bürgermeister und Vertretungskörper zu wählen.
[...]

7. Abschnitt
Die Verwaltung

Artikel 83 [Gemeinden und Gemeindeverbände]
(1) In den eigenen Wirkungskreis der Gemeinden (Art. 11 Abs. 2) fallen insbesondere die Verwaltung des Gemeindevermögens und der Gemeindebetriebe; der örtliche Verkehr nebst Straßen- und Wegebau; die Versorgung der Bevölkerung mit Wasser, Licht, Gas und elektrischer Kraft; Einrichtungen zur Sicherung der Ernährung; Ortsplanung, Wohnungsbau und Wohnungsaufsicht; örtliche Polizei, Feuerschutz; örtliche Kulturpflege; Volks- und Berufsschulwesen und Erwachsenenbildung; Vormundschaftswesen und Wohlfahrtspflege; örtliches Gesundheitswesen; Ehe- und Mütterberatung sowie Säuglingspflege; Schulhygiene und körperliche Ertüchtigung der Jugend; öffentliche Bäder; Totenbestattung; Erhaltung ortsgeschichtlicher Denkmäler und Bauten.
[...]
(4) ¹Die Gemeinden unterstehen der Aufsicht der Staatsbehörden. ²In den Angelegenheiten des eigenen Wirkungskreises der Gemeinden wacht der Staat nur über die Erfüllung der gesetzlichen Pflichten und die Einhaltung der gesetzlichen Vorschriften durch die Gemeinden. ³In den Angelegenheiten des übertragenen Wirkungskreises sind die Gemeinden überdies an die Weisungen der übergeordneten Staatsbehörden gebunden. ⁴Der Staat schützt die Gemeinden bei Durchführung ihrer Aufgaben.
[...]

Zweiter Hauptteil
Grundrechte und Grundpflichten

Artikel 108 [Freiheit von Kunst und Wissenschaft]
Die Kunst, die Wissenschaft und ihre Lehre sind frei.

---

1) Neubekanntmachung der Bayerischen Verfassung in der in der Bayerischen Rechtssammlung (100-1-S) veröffentlichten bereinigten Fassung in der ab 1.12.1998 geltenden Fassung. Die Bayerische Verfassung nennt keinen Zeitpunkt für ihr Inkrafttreten. Nach einer Feststellung des Ministerrats vom 4. Dezember 1946 (StAnz. Nr. 28) trat sie mit ihrer Veröffentlichung im Bayerischen Gesetz-und Verordnungsblatt am 8. Dezember 1946 in Kraft (Nr. 23 S. 333).

Dritter Hauptteil
Das Gemeinschaftsleben

2. Abschnitt
Bildung und Schule, Schutz der natürlichen Lebensgrundlagen und der kulturellen Überlieferung

Artikel 140 [Förderung von Kunst, Wissenschaft, kulturellem Leben und Sport]
(1) Kunst und Wissenschaft sind von Staat und Gemeinde zu fördern.
(2) Sie haben insbesonders Mittel zur Unterstützung schöpferischer Künstler, Gelehrter und Schriftsteller bereitzustellen, die den Nachweis ernster künstlerischer oder kultureller Tätigkeit erbringen.
(3) Das kulturelle Leben und der Sport sind von Staat und Gemeinden zu fördern.

Artikel 141 [Schutz der natürlichen Lebensgrundlagen und der Denkmäler; Recht auf Naturgenuss]
[...]
(2) Staat, Gemeinden und Körperschaften des öffentlichen Rechts haben die Aufgabe,
  die Denkmäler der Kunst, der Geschichte und der Natur sowie die Landschaft zu schützen und zu pflegen,[1)]
  herabgewürdigte Denkmäler der Kunst und der Geschichte möglichst ihrer früheren Bestimmung wieder zuzuführen,
  die Abwanderung deutschen Kunstbesitzes ins Ausland zu verhüten.
[...]

---

1) Siehe dazu auch die VwV Flurbereinigung und Denkmalpflege, abgedruckt als Nr. D2.I.1b.

Gesetz zum Schutz und zur Pflege der Denkmäler (Bayerisches Denkmalschutzgesetz – BayDSchG)

Vom 25. Juni 1973 (BayRS IV S. 354)[1)]
(BayRS 2242-1-WK)
zuletzt geändert durch § 1 Abs. 255 V zur Anpassung des Landesrechts an die geltende Geschäftsverteilung vom 26. März 2019 (GVBl. S. 98)

Teil 1
Allgemeine Bestimmungen

Artikel 1 Begriffsbestimmungen
(1) Denkmäler sind von Menschen geschaffene Sachen oder Teile davon aus vergangener Zeit, deren Erhaltung wegen ihrer geschichtlichen, künstlerischen, städtebaulichen, wissenschaftlichen oder volkskundlichen Bedeutung im Interesse der Allgemeinheit liegt.
(2) ¹Baudenkmäler[2)] sind bauliche Anlagen oder Teile davon aus vergangener Zeit, soweit sie nicht unter Absatz 4 fallen, einschließlich dafür bestimmter historischer Ausstattungsstücke und mit der in Absatz 1 bezeichneten Bedeutung. ²Auch bewegliche Sachen können historische Ausstattungsstücke sein, wenn sie integrale Bestandteile einer historischen Raumkonzeption oder einer ihr gleichzusetzenden historisch abgeschlossenen Neuausstattung oder Umgestaltung sind. ³Gartenanlagen, die die Voraussetzungen des Absatzes 1 erfüllen, gelten als Baudenkmäler.
(3) Zu den Baudenkmälern kann auch eine Mehrheit von baulichen Anlagen (Ensemble)[3)] gehören, und zwar auch dann, wenn keine oder nur einzelne dazugehörige bauliche Anlagen die Voraussetzungen des Abs. 1 erfüllen, das Orts-, Platz- oder Straßenbild aber insgesamt erhaltenswürdig ist.
(4) Bodendenkmäler sind bewegliche und unbewegliche Denkmäler, die sich im Boden befinden oder befanden und in der Regel aus vor- oder frühgeschichtlicher Zeit stammen.

Artikel 2 Denkmalliste
(1) ¹Die Baudenkmäler und die Bodendenkmäler sollen nachrichtlich in ein Verzeichnis (Denkmalliste) aufgenommen werden. ²Die Eintragung erfolgt durch das Landesamt für Denkmalpflege von Amts wegen im Benehmen mit der Gemeinde. ³Der Berechtigte und der zuständige Heimatpfleger können die Eintragung anregen. ⁴Die Eintragung ist im Bebauungsplan kenntlich zu machen. ⁵Die Liste kann von jedermann eingesehen werden.
(2) Auf Antrag des Berechtigten und in besonders wichtigen Fällen können bewegliche Denkmäler, soweit sie nicht nach Absatz 1 eingetragen sind, in das Verzeichnis eingetragen werden.

Artikel 3 Gemeindliche Rücksichtnahme
Die Gemeinden nehmen bei ihrer Tätigkeit, vor allem im Rahmen der Bauleitplanung, auf die Belange des Denkmalschutzes und der Denkmalpflege, insbesondere auf die Erhaltung von Ensembles, angemessen Rücksicht.

Teil 2
Baudenkmäler

Artikel 4 Erhaltung von Baudenkmälern
(1) ¹Die Eigentümer und die sonst dinglich Verfügungsberechtigten von Baudenkmälern haben ihre Baudenkmäler instandzuhalten, instandzusetzen, sachgemäß zu behandeln und vor Gefährdung zu schützen, soweit ihnen das zuzumuten ist. ²Ist der Eigentümer oder der sonst dinglich Verfügungsberechtigte nicht der unmittelbare Besitzer, so gilt Satz 1 auch für den unmittelbaren Besitzer, soweit dieser die Möglichkeit hat, entsprechend zu verfahren.
(2) ¹Die in Absatz 1 genannten Personen können verpflichtet werden, bestimmte Erhaltungsmaßnahmen ganz oder zum Teil durchzuführen, soweit ihnen das insbesondere unter Berücksichtigung ihrer sonstigen Aufgaben und Verpflichtungen zumutbar ist; soweit sie die Maßnahmen nicht selbst durch-

---
1) Siehe auch die VwV Vollzug DSchG, abgedruckt als Nr. D2.I.1c.
2) Siehe dazu auch die VwV Wirtschaftlichkeitsprüfung, abgedruckt als Nr. D2.I.1h.
3) Siehe dazu auch die Empfehlungen zu Ensembles, abgedruckt als Nr. D2.I.1i.

D2.I.1 Bayerisches Denkmalschutzgesetz

zuführen haben, können sie zur Duldung der Maßnahmen verpflichtet werden. ²Entscheidungen, durch die der Bund oder die Länder verpflichtet werden sollen, bedürfen der vorherigen Zustimmung der Obersten Denkmalschutzbehörde.

(3) ¹Macht der Zustand eines Baudenkmals Maßnahmen zu seiner Instandhaltung, Instandsetzung oder zu seinem Schutz erforderlich, ohne daß eine vollstreckbare Entscheidung nach Absatz 2 vorliegt, so kann die zuständige Denkmalschutzbehörde die Maßnahmen durchführen oder durchführen lassen. ²Die dinglich und obligatorisch Berechtigten können zur Duldung der Maßnahmen verpflichtet werden. ³Die Kosten der Maßnahmen tragen die in Absatz 1 genannten Personen, soweit sie nach Absatz 2 zur Durchführung der Maßnahmen verpflichtet wurden oder hätten verpflichtet werden können, im übrigen der Entschädigungsfonds[1] (Art. 21 Abs. 2).

(4) Handlungen, die ein Baudenkmal schädigen oder gefährden, können untersagt werden.

Artikel 5 Nutzung von Baudenkmälern

¹Baudenkmäler sollen möglichst entsprechend ihrer ursprünglichen Zweckbestimmung genutzt werden. ²Werden Baudenkmäler nicht mehr entsprechend ihrer ursprünglichen Zweckbestimmung genutzt, so sollen die Eigentümer und die sonst dinglich oder obligatorisch zur Nutzung Berechtigten eine der ursprünglichen gleiche oder gleichwertige Nutzung anstreben. ³Soweit dies nicht möglich ist, soll eine Nutzung gewählt werden, die eine möglichst weitgehende Erhaltung der Substanz auf die Dauer gewährleistet. ⁴Sind verschiedene Nutzungen möglich, so soll diejenige Nutzung gewählt werden, die das Baudenkmal und sein Zubehör am wenigsten beeinträchtigt. ⁵Staat, Gemeinden und sonstige Körperschaften des öffentlichen Rechts sollen Eigentümer und Besitzer unterstützen. ⁶Die Eigentümer und die sonst dinglich oder obligatorisch zur Nutzung Berechtigten können bei Vorliegen der Voraussetzungen des Art. 4 Abs. 2 verpflichtet werden, eine bestimmte Nutzungsart durchzuführen; soweit sie nicht zur Durchführung verpflichtet werden, können sie zur Duldung einer bestimmten Nutzungsart verpflichtet werden.

Artikel 6 Maßnahmen an Baudenkmälern

(1) ¹Wer
1. Baudenkmäler beseitigen, verändern oder an einen anderen Ort verbringen oder
2. geschützte Ausstattungsstücke beseitigen, verändern, an einen anderen Ort verbringen oder aus einem Baudenkmal entfernen

will, bedarf der Erlaubnis.[2] ²Der Erlaubnis bedarf auch, wer in der Nähe von Baudenkmälern Anlagen errichten, verändern oder beseitigen will, wenn sich dies auf Bestand oder Erscheinungsbild eines der Baudenkmäler auswirken kann. ³Wer ein Ensemble verändern will, bedarf der Erlaubnis nur, wenn die Veränderung eine bauliche Anlage betrifft, die für sich genommen ein Baudenkmal ist, oder wenn sie sich auf das Erscheinungsbild des Ensembles auswirken kann.[3]

(2) ¹Die Erlaubnis kann im Fall des Abs. 1 Satz 1 Nrn. 1 und 2 versagt werden, soweit gewichtige Gründe des Denkmalschutzes für die unveränderte Beibehaltung des bisherigen Zustands sprechen.[4] ²Im Fall des Absatzes 1 Satz 2 kann die Erlaubnis versagt werden, soweit das Vorhaben zu einer Beeinträchtigung des Wesens, des überlieferten Erscheinungsbilds oder der künstlerischen Wirkung eines Baudenkmals führen würde und gewichtige Gründe des Denkmalschutzes für die unveränderte Beibehaltung des bisherigen Zustands sprechen.

(3) ¹Ist eine Baugenehmigung oder an ihrer Stelle eine bauaufsichtliche Zustimmung oder abgrabungsaufsichtliche Genehmigung erforderlich, entfällt die Erlaubnis. ²Für denkmaltypische Bauprodukte, die in Baudenkmälern verwendet werden sollen, erteilt die zuständige untere Bauaufsichtsbehörde die Zustimmung im Einzelfall nach Art. 20 der Bayerischen Bauordnung (BayBO). ³Ist in den Fällen des Satzes 2 keine Baugenehmigung oder bauaufsichtliche Zustimmung, jedoch eine durch die Denkmaleigenschaft bedingte Abweichung nach Art. 63 Abs. 1 Satz 1 BayBO erforderlich, schließt die Erlaubnis nach diesem Gesetz die Zustimmung im Einzelfall nach Art. 20 BayBO und die Abweichung nach Art. 63 Abs. 1 Satz 1 BayBO mit ein.

---

1) Siehe dazu auch die VwV Inanspruchnahme Entschädigungsfonds, abgedruckt als Nr. D2.I.1f.
2) Siehe dazu auch die VwV Vollzug DSchG staatliche Schlösser, abgedruckt als Nr. D2.I.1a.
3) Siehe dazu auch die Empfehlungen zu Ensembles, abgedruckt als Nr. D2.I.1i.
4) Siehe zum Abbruch eines Baudenkmals wegen wirtschaftlicher Unzumutbarkeit der Erhaltung die VwV Vollzug DSchG (Zumutbarkeit nach Art. 6 DSchG), abgedruckt als Nr. D2.I.1g; siehe auch die VwV Wirtschaftlichkeitsprüfung, abgedruckt als Nr. D2.I.1h.

(4) Bei Entscheidungen nach den Abs. 1 bis 3 sind auch die Belange von Menschen mit Behinderung und von Menschen mit sonstigen Mobilitätsbeeinträchtigungen zu berücksichtigen.

Teil 3
Bodendenkmäler

Artikel 7 Ausgraben von Bodendenkmälern, Verordnungsermächtigung
(1) [1]Wer auf einem Grundstück nach Bodendenkmälern graben oder zu einem anderen Zweck Erdarbeiten auf einem Grundstück vornehmen will, obwohl er weiß oder vermutet oder den Umständen nach annehmen muß, daß sich dort Bodendenkmäler befinden, bedarf der Erlaubnis. [2]Die Erlaubnis kann versagt werden, soweit dies zum Schutz eines Bodendenkmals erforderlich ist.
(2) [1]Die Bezirke können durch Rechtsverordnung bestimmte Grundstücke, in oder auf denen Bodendenkmäler zu vermuten sind, zu Grabungsschutzgebieten erklären. [2]In einem Grabungsschutzgebiet bedürfen alle Arbeiten, die Bodendenkmäler gefährden können, der Erlaubnis. [3]Art. 6 Abs. 2 Satz 2 und Abs. 3 gelten entsprechend. [4]Grabungsschutzgebiete sind im Flächennutzungsplan kenntlich zu machen.
(3) Absatz 1 und Absatz 2 Satz 2 gelten nicht für Grabungen, die vom Landesamt für Denkmalpflege oder unter seiner Mitwirkung vorgenommen oder veranlaßt werden.
(4) [1]Wer in der Nähe von Bodendenkmälern, die ganz oder zum Teil über der Erdoberfläche erkennbar sind, Anlagen errichten, verändern oder beseitigen will, bedarf der Erlaubnis, wenn sich dies auf Bestand oder Erscheinungsbild eines dieser Bodendenkmäler auswirken kann. [2]Art. 6 Abs. 2 Satz 2 und Abs. 3 gelten entsprechend.
(5) [1]Soll eine Grabung auf einem fremden Grundstück erfolgen, so kann der Eigentümer verpflichtet werden, die Grabung zuzulassen, wenn das Landesamt für Denkmalpflege festgestellt hat, daß ein besonderes öffentliches Interesse an der Grabung besteht. [2]Der Inhaber der Grabungsgenehmigung hat den dem Eigentümer entstehenden Schaden zu ersetzen.

Artikel 8 Auffinden von Bodendenkmälern
(1) [1]Wer Bodendenkmäler auffindet, ist verpflichtet, dies unverzüglich der Unteren Denkmalschutzbehörde oder dem Landesamt für Denkmalpflege anzuzeigen. [2]Zur Anzeige verpflichtet sind auch der Eigentümer und der Besitzer des Grundstücks sowie der Unternehmer und der Leiter der Arbeiten, die zu dem Fund geführt haben. [3]Die Anzeige eines der Verpflichteten befreit die übrigen. [4]Nimmt der Finder an den Arbeiten, die zu dem Fund geführt haben, auf Grund eines Arbeitsverhältnisses teil, so wird er durch Anzeige an den Unternehmer oder den Leiter der Arbeiten befreit.
(2) Die aufgefundenen Gegenstände und der Fundort sind bis zum Ablauf von einer Woche nach der Anzeige unverändert zu belassen, wenn nicht die Untere Denkmalschutzbehörde die Gegenstände vorher freigibt oder die Fortsetzung der Arbeiten gestattet.
(3) Die Absätze 1 und 2 gelten nicht bei Arbeiten, die vom Landesamt für Denkmalpflege oder unter seiner Mitwirkung vorgenommen oder veranlaßt werden.
(4) Eigentümer, dinglich Verfügungsberechtigte und unmittelbare Besitzer eines Grundstücks, auf dem Bodendenkmäler gefunden werden, können verpflichtet werden, die notwendigen Maßnahmen zur sachgemäßen Bergung des Fundgegenstands sowie zur Klärung der Fundumstände und zur Sicherung weiterer auf dem Grundstück vorhandener Bodendenkmäler zu dulden.
(5) Aufgefundene Gegenstände sind dem Landesamt für Denkmalpflege oder einer Denkmalschutzbehörde unverzüglich zur Aufbewahrung zu übergeben, wenn die Gefahr ihres Abhandenkommens besteht.

Artikel 9 Auswertung von Funden
Der Eigentümer eines beweglichen Bodendenkmals, die dinglich Verfügungsberechtigten und die unmittelbaren Besitzer können verpflichtet werden, dieses dem Landesamt für Denkmalpflege befristet zur wissenschaftlichen Auswertung und Dokumentation zu überlassen.

Teil 4
Eingetragene bewegliche Denkmäler

Artikel 10 Erlaubnispflicht

(1) ¹Wer ein eingetragenes bewegliches Denkmal beseitigen, verändern oder an einen anderen Ort verbringen will, bedarf der Erlaubnis. ²Die Erlaubnis kann versagt werden, soweit dies zum Schutz des Denkmals erforderlich ist.

(2) ¹Die Veräußerung eines eingetragenen beweglichen Denkmals ist dem Landesamt für Denkmalpflege unverzüglich anzuzeigen. ²Zur Anzeige sind der Veräußerer und der Erwerber verpflichtet.

Teil 5
Verfahrensbestimmungen

Artikel 11 Denkmalschutzbehörden

(1) ¹Untere Denkmalschutzbehörden sind die Kreisverwaltungsbehörden. ²Soweit kreisangehörigen Gemeinden die Aufgaben der Unteren Bauaufsichtsbehörden übertragen sind oder übertragen werden, gilt diese Übertragung auch für die Aufgaben der Unteren Denkmalschutzbehörden. ³Art. 115 Abs. 2 der Gemeindeordnung gilt entsprechend.

(2) Höhere Denkmalschutzbehörden sind die Regierungen.

(3) Oberste Denkmalschutzbehörde ist das Staatsministerium für Wissenschaft und Kunst (Staatsministerium).

(4) ¹Soweit nichts anderes bestimmt ist, sind die Unteren Denkmalschutzbehörden für den Vollzug dieses Gesetzes zuständig. ²In den Fällen des Art. 73 Abs. 1 BayBO treten die Höheren an die Stelle der Unteren Denkmalschutzbehörden.

(5) Die Aufgaben der Denkmalschutzbehörden sind Staatsaufgaben; für die Gemeinden sind sie übertragene Aufgaben.

Artikel 12 Landesamt für Denkmalpflege

(1) ¹Das Landesamt für Denkmalpflege ist die staatliche Fachbehörde für alle Fragen des Denkmalschutzes und der Denkmalpflege. ²Es ist dem Staatsministerium unmittelbar nachgeordnet.

(2) ¹Dem Landesamt für Denkmalpflege obliegen die Denkmalpflege und die Mitwirkung beim Denkmalschutz. ²Die Denkmalpflege umfasst auch die Erforschung der Denkmäler, soweit solche Vorhaben mit den sonstigen Aufgaben des Landesamts für Denkmalpflege in unmittelbarem Zusammenhang stehen und mit diesen vereinbar sind. ³Insbesondere hat es folgende Aufgaben:
1. Mitwirkung beim Vollzug dieses Gesetzes und anderer einschlägiger Vorschriften nach Maßgabe der hierzu ergangenen und ergehenden Bestimmungen;
2. Herausgabe von Richtlinien zur Pflege der Denkmäler unter Beteiligung der kommunalen Spitzenverbände;
3. Erstellung und Fortführung der Inventare[1]) und der Denkmalliste;
4. Konservierung und Restaurierung von Denkmälern, soweit die Konservierung und die Restaurierung nicht von anderen dafür zuständigen staatlichen Stellen durchgeführt werden;
5. fachliche Beratung und Erstattung von Gutachten in allen Angelegenheiten des Denkmalschutzes und der Denkmalpflege;
6. Überwachung der Ausgrabungen sowie die Überwachung und Erfassung der anfallenden beweglichen Bodendenkmäler;
7. Fürsorge für Heimatmuseen und ähnliche Sammlungen, soweit diese nicht vom Staat verwaltet werden.

⁴Das Staatsministerium kann dem Landesamt für Denkmalpflege weitere einschlägige Aufgaben zuweisen.

(3) Die bisherigen Aufgaben der Bayerischen Verwaltung der staatlichen Schlösser, Gärten und Seen bleiben unberührt.

Artikel 13 Heimatpfleger

(1) ¹Die Heimatpfleger beraten und unterstützen die Denkmalschutzbehörden und das Landesamt für Denkmalpflege in den Fragen der Denkmalpflege und des Denkmalschutzes. ²Ihnen ist durch die

---
1) Siehe dazu auch die VwV Grundsätze für die Inventarisation, abgedruckt als Nr. D2.I.1e.

Denkmalschutzbehörden in den ihren Aufgabenbereich betreffenden Fällen rechtzeitig Gelegenheit zur Äußerung zu geben.
(2) Die Denkmalschutzbehörden und das Landesamt für Denkmalpflege sollen sich in geeigneten Fällen der Unterstützung kommunaler Stellen sowie privater Initiativen bedienen.

Artikel 14 Landesdenkmalrat
(1) ¹Der Landesdenkmalrat berät die Staatsregierung in allen wichtigen Fragen der Denkmalpflege. ²Er wirkt an der Festlegung von Ensembles mit.
(2) ¹In den Landesdenkmalrat werden folgende Mitglieder jeweils für die Dauer der Legislaturperiode entsandt:
1. sechs von den Fraktionen des Bayerischen Landtags gemäß ihren Besetzungsrechten nach dem Verfahren Sainte-Laguë/Schepers,
2. je zwei von der Katholischen Kirche und der Evangelisch-Lutherischen Landeskirche,
3. je eines
   a) von den israelitischen Kultusgemeinden in Bayern,
   b) vom Verein zur Erhaltung privater Baudenkmäler und sonstiger Kulturgüter in Bayern e.V.,
   c) von der Deutschen Burgenvereinigung, Landesgruppe Bayern,
   d) vom Landesverband der Bayerischen Haus- und Grundbesitzer e.V.,
   e) vom Familienbetriebe Land und Forst Bayern e.V.,
   f) von der Bayerischen Akademie der Schönen Künste,
   g) von der Bayerischen Architektenkammer,
   h) von der Deutschen Akademie für Städtebau und Landesplanung, Landesgruppe Bayern,
   i) vom Bayerischen Landesverein für Heimatpflege,
   j) vom Bayerischen Bauernverband,
   k) von der Arbeitsgemeinschaft der Bayerischen Handwerkskammern,
   l) vom Bayerischen Gemeindetag,
   m) vom Bayerischen Städtetag,
   n) vom Bayerischen Landkreistag,
   o) vom Bayerischen Bezirketag,
4. bis zu sieben vom Staatsministerium.

²Es wird entsprechend Satz 1 jeweils ein Stellvertreter bestimmt. ³Die Mitglieder und ihre Stellvertreter werden vom Landtag bestellt, in den Fällen des Satzes 1 Nr. 2 bis 4 auf Vorschlag der jeweiligen entsendenden Stelle.
(3) ¹Die Mitglieder sind ehrenamtlich tätig. ²Sie erhalten Reisekosten nach den Vorschriften des Bayerischen Reisekostengesetzes und ist ein Ehrenbeamter.
(4) ¹Der Landesdenkmalrat wählt aus seiner Mitte mit einfacher Mehrheit der anwesenden Mitglieder ein vorsitzendes Mitglied und einen Stellvertreter. ²Der Landesdenkmalrat gibt sich im Übrigen eine Geschäftsordnung. ³Das Staatsministerium führt seine Geschäfte.
(5) Ohne Stimmrecht nehmen an den Beratungen des Landesdenkmalrats bei Bedarf Sachverständige nach Einladung des Landesdenkmalrats teil.

Artikel 15 Erlaubnisverfahren und Wiederherstellung
(1) ¹Der Antrag auf Erteilung einer Erlaubnis nach Art. 6, 7 und 10 Abs. 1 und auf Verpflichtung des Eigentümers nach Art. 7 Abs. 5 ist schriftlich bei der Gemeinde einzureichen, die ihn mit ihrer Stellungnahme unverzüglich der Unteren Denkmalschutzbehörde vorlegt. ²Art. 75 und 76 BayBO gelten in den Fällen der Art. 6, 7 und 8 Abs. 2 entsprechend.
(2) ¹Die Untere Denkmalschutzbehörde soll vor einer Entscheidung nach den Teilen 2 bis 4 das Landesamt für Denkmalpflege hören. ²Art. 65 Abs. 1 Satz 3 BayBO gilt entsprechend.
(3) Für eine Erlaubnis nach den Teilen 2 bis 4 gilt Art. 69 BayBO entsprechend.
(4) Werden Handlungen nach Art. 6, 7, 8 Abs. 2 oder Art. 10 Abs. 1 ohne die erforderliche Erlaubnis, Baugenehmigung oder abgrabungsaufsichtliche Genehmigung durchgeführt, so kann die Untere Denkmalschutzbehörde verlangen, daß der ursprüngliche Zustand wieder hergestellt wird, soweit dies noch möglich ist, oder daß Bau- und Bodendenkmäler und eingetragene bewegliche Denkmäler auf andere Weise wieder instandgesetzt werden.

D2.I.1 Bayerisches Denkmalschutzgesetz

(5) Wer widerrechtlich Bau- oder Bodendenkmäler oder eingetragene bewegliche Denkmäler vorsätzlich oder grob fahrlässig zerstört oder beschädigt, ist unabhängig von der Verhängung einer Geldbuße zur Wiedergutmachung des von ihm angerichteten Schadens bis zu dessen vollem Umfang verpflichtet.

(6) Die zuständige Behörde kann die Entscheidung über einen Antrag auf Erlaubnis, Baugenehmigung, baurechtliche Zustimmung oder abgrabungsaufsichtliche Genehmigung auf höchstens zwei Jahre aussetzen, soweit dies zur Klärung der Belange des Denkmalschutzes, insbesondere für Untersuchungen des Baudenkmals und seiner Umgebung, erforderlich ist.

Artikel 16 Betretungs- und Auskunftsrecht

(1) Die Denkmalschutzbehörden und das Landesamt für Denkmalpflege sind berechtigt, im Vollzug dieses Gesetzes Grundstücke auch gegen den Willen der Betroffenen zu betreten, soweit das zur Erhaltung eines Bau- oder Bodendenkmals oder eines eingetragenen beweglichen Denkmals dringend erforderlich erscheint.

(2) Eigentümer und Besitzer von Bau- und Bodendenkmälern und von eingetragenen beweglichen Denkmälern und sonstige Berechtigte sind verpflichtet, den Denkmalschutzbehörden und dem Landesamt für Denkmalpflege alle zum Vollzug dieses Gesetzes erforderlichen Auskünfte zu erteilen.

Artikel 17 Kostenfreiheit

[1]Für Amtshandlungen nach diesem Gesetz werden Kosten nicht erhoben. [2]Schließt die Erlaubnis gemäß Art. 6 Abs. 3 Satz 3 die Zustimmung im Einzelfall nach Art. 20 BayBO oder die Abweichung nach Art. 63 Abs. 1 Satz 1 BayBO ein, werden für die Zustimmung oder die Abweichung Kosten nach dem Kostengesetz erhoben.

Teil 6
Enteignung

Artikel 18 Zulässigkeit der Enteignung

(1) [1]Kann eine Gefahr für den Bestand oder die Gestalt eines Bau- oder Bodendenkmals oder eines eingetragenen beweglichen Denkmals auf andere Weise nicht nachhaltig abgewehrt werden, so ist die Enteignung zugunsten des Staates oder einer anderen juristischen Person des öffentlichen Rechts zulässig. [2]Zugunsten einer juristischen Person des Privatrechts ist die Enteignung dann zulässig, wenn die dauernde Erhaltung des Bau- oder Bodendenkmals oder des eingetragenen beweglichen Denkmals zu den satzungsmäßigen Aufgaben der juristischen Person gehört und bei Berücksichtigung aller Umstände gesichert erscheint.

(2) [1]Zugunsten des Staates ist die Enteignung außerdem zulässig bei beweglichen Bodendenkmälern, an deren Erhaltung für die Öffentlichkeit ein besonderes Interesse besteht. [2]Im Fall des Satzes 1 kann der Antrag nur gestellt werden, wenn dem Landesamt für Denkmalpflege im Zeitpunkt der Antragstellung die vollständige Bergung des Bodendenkmals nicht länger als ein Jahr bekannt war.

(3) bis (5) *[aufgehoben]*

Artikel 19 Vorkaufsrecht

(1) [1]Dem Freistaat Bayern steht beim Kauf historischer Ausstattungsstücke, die nach Art. 1 Abs. 2 zusammen mit Baudenkmälern geschützt und in die Denkmalliste eingetragen sind, und beim Kauf von eingetragenen beweglichen Denkmälern ein Vorkaufsrecht zu. [2]Das Vorkaufsrecht darf nur ausgeübt werden, wenn das Wohl der Allgemeinheit dies rechtfertigt, insbesondere wenn die Ausstattungsstücke oder die eingetragenen beweglichen Denkmäler der Öffentlichkeit zugänglich gemacht oder in ihrer Gesamtheit erhalten werden sollen. [3]Das Vorkaufsrecht ist ausgeschlossen, wenn der Eigentümer Ausstattungsstücke oder eingetragene bewegliche Denkmäler an seinen Ehegatten oder an eine Person veräußert, die mit ihm in gerader Linie verwandt oder verschwägert oder in der Seitenlinie bis zum dritten Grad verwandt ist. [4]Das Vorkaufsrecht beim Kauf historischer Ausstattungsstücke ist ausgeschlossen, wenn diese mit dem Baudenkmal veräußert werden und in dem Baudenkmal verbleiben sollen.

(2) [1]Das Vorkaufsrecht kann nur binnen drei Monaten nach Mitteilung des Kaufvertrags an das Landesamt für Denkmalpflege durch das Landesamt für Denkmalpflege ausgeübt werden. [2]§§ 463 bis 468 Abs. 1, 469 Abs. 1, § 471 des Bürgerlichen Gesetzbuchs sind anzuwenden. [3]Das Vorkaufsrecht ist nicht übertragbar. [4]Es geht unbeschadet bundesrechtlicher Vorschriften allen anderen Vorkaufsrechten im

Rang vor. ⁵Bei einem Eigentumserwerb auf Grund der Ausübung des Vorkaufsrechts erlöschen rechtsgeschäftliche Vorkaufsrechte.

Artikel 20 Enteignende Maßnahmen
(1) ¹Soweit der Vollzug dieses Gesetzes eine über den Rahmen der Sozialgebundenheit des Eigentums (Art. 14 Abs. 2 des Grundgesetzes, Art. 103 Abs. 2 und Art. 158 der Verfassung) hinausgehende Wirkung hat, ist dem Betroffenen nach den Vorschriften des Bayerischen Gesetzes über die entschädigungspflichtige Enteignung Entschädigung in Geld zu gewähren. ²Steuervorteile, die auf die Denkmaleigenschaft zurückzuführen sind, sind in allen Fällen in angemessenem Umfang auf die Entschädigung anzurechnen.
(2) ¹Die Kreisverwaltungsbehörde setzt auf Antrag des Betroffenen die Entschädigung fest. ²Die Vorschriften des Bayerischen Gesetzes über die entschädigungspflichtige Enteignung über die Festsetzung der Entschädigung gelten sinngemäß.
(3) ¹Ergeht auf einen neuen Antrag hin eine Entscheidung, die für den Entschädigungsberechtigten günstiger ist als die der Entschädigungsfestsetzung nach Absatz 1 zugrunde liegende Entscheidung, so ist in allen Fällen die Entschädigung auf die Höhe herabzusetzen, die der entstandenen Beeinträchtigung entspricht. ²Absatz 2 gilt entsprechend. ³Ein überzahlter Betrag ist zurückzuerstatten, soweit der Entschädigungsberechtigte noch bereichert ist.

Artikel 21 Entschädigungsaufwand
(1) ¹Der Freistaat Bayern und die Gemeinden haben die Entschädigung grundsätzlich gemeinsam zu tragen. ²Die Ansprüche des Berechtigten sind gegen den Freistaat Bayern zu richten. ³Der Entschädigungsfonds[1]) erstattet dem Freistaat Bayern auf Antrag der örtlich zuständigen Regierung die dem Betroffenen gewährten Entschädigungsleistungen.
(2) ¹Die Oberste Denkmalschutzbehörde unterhält und verwaltet einen Entschädigungsfonds als staatliches Sondervermögen. ²Der Freistaat Bayern und die Gemeinden tragen den Fonds durch Beiträge von je 13,5 Millionen Euro jährlich.
(3) ¹Die staatlichen Beiträge sind in zwei gleichen Teilbeträgen im Januar und im Juli zahlbar. ²Die von den Gemeinden zu tragenden Einzelbeiträge errechnen sich nach dem Verhältnis der jeweiligen gemeindlichen Umlagegrundlagen für die Kreisumlage oder die Bezirksumlage. ³Sie werden jährlich vom Landesamt für Statistik berechnet und sollen entsprechend bis 31. März des jeweiligen Beitragsjahres gegenüber den Gemeinden durch Beitragsbescheid festgesetzt werden. ⁴Die Beiträge werden mit der Auszahlung der Schlüsselzuweisungen für das dritte Vierteljahr fällig, staatlicherseits einbehalten und an den Fonds abgeführt. ⁵Soweit Gemeinden keine Schlüsselzuweisungen erhalten, zahlen sie die Beiträge bis zum 15. September an die Staatsoberkasse.
(4) Erfolgt eine Enteignung zugunsten einer juristischen Person des öffentlichen Rechts, die nicht Gebietskörperschaft ist, oder zugunsten einer juristischen Person des Privatrechts, so hat diese die Entschädigung zu tragen.

Teil 7
Finanzierung

Artikel 22 Leistungen
(1) ¹Der Freistaat Bayern beteiligt sich unbeschadet bestehender Verpflichtungen in Höhe der jeweils im Staatshaushalt ausgewiesenen Mittel an den Kosten des Denkmalschutzes und der Denkmalpflege, insbesondere an den Kosten der Instandsetzung, Erhaltung, Sicherung und Freilegung von Denkmälern. ²Die Höhe der Beteiligung richtet sich nach der Bedeutung und der Dringlichkeit des Falls und nach der Leistungsfähigkeit des Eigentümers.
(2) Die kommunalen Gebietskörperschaften beteiligen sich im Rahmen ihrer Leistungsfähigkeit in angemessenem Umfang an den Kosten der in Absatz 1 genannten Maßnahmen.

---

1) Siehe dazu auch die VwV Inanspruchnahme Entschädigungsfonds, abgedruckt als Nr. D2.I.1f.

Teil 8
Ordnungswidrigkeiten

Artikel 23 Ordnungswidrigkeiten
(1) Mit Geldbuße bis zu zweihundertfünfzigtausend Euro kann belegt werden, wer vorsätzlich oder fahrlässig
1. Handlungen nach Art. 4 Abs. 4 vornimmt, obwohl ihm dies durch vollziehbare Anordnung untersagt wurde,
2. ohne die nach Art. 6 Abs. 1, Art. 7 Abs. 4 Satz 1 oder Art. 10 Abs. 1 erforderliche Erlaubnis oder die an ihre Stelle tretende baurechtliche oder abgrabungsaufsichtliche Genehmigung Maßnahmen an einem Denkmal durchführt,
3. ohne die nach Art. 7 Abs. 1 erforderliche Erlaubnis nach Bodendenkmälern gräbt oder zu einem anderen Zweck Erdarbeiten auf einem Grundstück vornimmt oder wer ohne die nach Art. 7 Abs. 2 erforderliche Erlaubnis Arbeiten in einem Grabungsschutzgebiet durchführt, die Bodendenkmäler gefährden können,
4. die gemäß Art. 8 Abs. 1 oder Art. 10 Abs. 2 erforderliche Anzeige nicht unverzüglich erstattet,
5. die aufgefundenen Gegenstände und den Fundort nicht gemäß Art. 8 Abs. 2 unverändert läßt,
6. seiner Übergabepflicht gemäß Art. 8 Abs. 5 nicht unverzüglich nachkommt.

(2) Die Verfolgung der Ordnungswidrigkeiten verjährt in fünf Jahren.

Teil 9
Allgemeine Bestimmungen und Schlussbestimmungen

Artikel 24 Grundrechtseinschränkung
Die Grundrechte der Unverletzlichkeit der Wohnung (Art. 13 des Grundgesetzes, Art. 106 Abs. 3 der Verfassung), der freien Entfaltung der Persönlichkeit (Art. 2 Abs. 1 des Grundgesetzes, Art. 101 der Verfassung) und des Eigentums (Art. 14 des Grundgesetzes, Art. 103 der Verfassung) werden durch dieses Gesetz eingeschränkt.

Artikel 25 Erteilung von Bescheinigungen für steuerliche Zwecke
Bescheinigungen für die Erlangung von Steuervergünstigungen werden vorbehaltlich anderweitiger Bestimmungen vom Landesamt für Denkmalpflege erteilt.

Artikel 26 Kirchliche Denkmäler
(1) Art. 10 §§ 3 und 4 des Konkordats mit dem Heiligen Stuhl vom 29. März 1924[1]) und Art. 18 und 19 des Vertrags zwischen dem Freistaat Bayern und der Evangelisch-Lutherischen Kirche in Bayern rechts des Rheins vom 15. November 1924[2]) bleiben unberührt.
(2) [1]Sollen Entscheidungen über Bau- oder Bodendenkmäler oder über eingetragene bewegliche Denkmäler getroffen werden, die unmittelbar gottesdienstlichen Zwecken der Katholischen Kirche oder der Evangelisch-Lutherischen Kirche dienen, so haben die Denkmalschutzbehörden die von den zuständigen kirchlichen Oberbehörden festgestellten kirchlichen Belange zu berücksichtigen. [2]Die

---

1) Art. 10 §§ 3 und 4 des Bayerischen Konkordats vom 29. März 1924 (GVBl. 1925. S. 53) haben folgenden Wortlaut:
„§ 3: Die staatlichen Gebäude und Grundstücke, die zur Zeit unmittelbar oder mittelbar Zwecken der Kirche einschließlich der Orden oder religiösen Kongregationen dienen, bleiben diesen Zwecken auch fernerhin unter Berücksichtigung etwa bestehender Verträge überlassen.
§ 4: Die Güter der Seminarien, Pfarreien, Benefizien, Kirchenfabriken und aller übrigen Kirchenstiftungen werden innerhalb der Schranken des für alle geltenden Gesetzes gewährleistet und können ohne Zustimmung der zuständigen kirchlichen Obrigkeit nicht veräußert werden. Die Kirche hat das Recht neues Besitztum zu erwerben und als Eigentum zu haben. Dieses so erworbene Eigentum soll in gleicher Weise unverletzlich sein."
2) Art. 18 und 19 des Vertrages zwischen dem Bayerischen Staate und der Evangelisch-Lutherischen Kirche Bayern rechts des Rheins vom 15. November 1924 (GVBl. 1925, S. 61) haben folgenden Wortlaut:
„Art. 18: Die staatlichen Gebäude und Grundstücke, die zur Zeit unmittelbar oder mittelbar Zwecken der Kirche einschließlich der kirchlich anerkannten Diakonen- und Diakonissenanstalten dienen, bleiben diesen Zwecken auch fernerhin unter Berücksichtigung etwa bestehender Verträge überlassen.
Art. 19: Die Güter der Gesamtkirche, der Kirchen- und Pfründestiftungen, der Kirchengemeinden und der Gesamtkirchengemeinden werden innerhalb der Schranken des für alle geltenden Gesetzes gewährleistet und können ohne Zustimmung der zuständigen kirchlichen Obrigkeit nicht veräußert werden. Die Kirche hat das Recht neues Besitztum zu erwerben und als Eigentum zu haben. Dieses so erworbene Eigentum soll in gleicher Weise unverletzlich sein."

Kirchen sind am Verfahren zu beteiligen.[1] ³Die zuständige kirchliche Oberbehörde entscheidet im Benehmen mit der Obersten Denkmalschutzbehörde, falls die Untere und Höhere Denkmalschutzbehörde die geltend gemachten kirchlichen Belange nicht anerkennen. ⁴Gegenüber anderen Religionsgemeinschaften, die Körperschaften des öffentlichen Rechts sind, gelten die Sätze 1 bis 3 sinngemäß.

Artikel 27 Inkrafttreten, Außerkrafttreten
(1) Dieses Gesetz tritt am 1. Oktober 1973 in Kraft[2].
(2) Art. 26a tritt mit Ablauf des 31. Dezember 2018 außer Kraft.

---

1) Siehe dazu auch die VwV Maßnahmen an kirchlichen Gebäuden, abgedruckt als Nr. D2.I.1d
2) **Amtl. Anm.:** Betrifft die ursprüngliche Fassung vom 25. Juni 1973 (GVBl S. 328).

D2.I.1a VwV Vollzug DSchG staatliche Schlösser

Vollzug des Denkmalschutzgesetzes und baurechtlicher Vorschriften im Bereich der Bayerischen Verwaltung der staatlichen Schlösser, Gärten und Seen[1)]

Vom 24. März 1975 (KWMBl. I 1975 S. 1181 MABl. 1975 S. 447)
(BayVV Gliederungsnummer 2242-WK)

Gemeinsame Bekanntmachung der Staatsministerien des Innern, für Unterricht und Kultus[2)] und der Finanzen vom 24. März 1975 Nr. IV/2-7/46 998, Nr. II B 4-9130/1-64, Az. 45-VV 2534-7/100-20382

An die Höheren und Unteren Denkmalschutzbehörden,
die Gemeinden,
die Bayerische Verwaltung der staatlichen Schlösser, Gärten und Seen,
das Bayerische Landesamt für Denkmalpflege

1. Bei Bauvorhaben der Bayerischen Verwaltung der staatlichen Schlösser, Gärten und Seen, die einer Zustimmung (Art. 103 BayBO) bedürfen, ist die Beteiligung des Landesamts für Denkmalpflege als Träger öffentlicher Belange wie folgt durchzuführen:
Die Schlösserverwaltung stimmt die anstehenden Bauvorhaben mindestens zweimal jährlich jeweils vor Einleitung des Zustimmungsverfahrens mit dem Landesamt für Denkmalpflege ab. Eine nochmalige Einschaltung des Landesamtes für Denkmalpflege nach Einreichung des Zustimmungsantrages kann dann entfallen. Die Entscheidungsbefugnis der Regierungen als Zustimmungsbehörden wird hierdurch nicht berührt.
Bei Meinungsverschiedenheiten zwischen der Schlösserverwaltung und dem Landesamt für Denkmalpflege entscheidet auf Antrag des Landesamtes für Denkmalpflege das Staatsministerium für Unterricht und Kultus im Einvernehmen mit dem Staatsministerium der Finanzen.
2. Für Maßnahmen der Schlösserverwaltung, die nicht einer baurechtlichen Zustimmung, sondern der Erlaubnis nach Art. 6 DSchG bedürfen, wird hiermit generell die Erlaubnis nach Art. 6 DSchG erteilt. Die Schlösserverwaltung unterrichtet das Landesamt für Denkmalpflege mindestens zweimal jährlich über die beabsichtigten Maßnahmen.

[1)] Fortgeltung ab 1.1.2016 gem. VwVWBek v. 31.5.2016 (AllMBl. S. 1555).
[2)] **Amtl. Anm.:** jetzt: Bayerisches Staatsministerium des Innern, für Bau und Verkehr und Bayerisches Staatsministerium für Bildung und Kultus, Wissenschaft und Kunst

Flurbereinigung und Denkmalpflege[1)]

Vom 06. Juni 1978 (LMBl 1978 S. 204)
(BayVV Gliederungsnummer 7815-L)
Gemeinsame Bekanntmachung der Bayerischen Staatsministerien des Innern, für Unterricht und Kultus und für Ernährung, Landwirtschaft und Forsten vom 6. Juni 1978
Az.: II B 4 – 9130/1-170, IV/2 – 7/171 456 und N 3 – 5671/71

I. Allgemeines

1 – Die Verfassung des Freistaates Bayern bestimmt in Art. 141, dass die Denkmäler der Kunst, der Geschichte und der Natur sowie die Landschaft öffentlichen Schutz und die Pflege des Staates, der Gemeinden und der Körperschaften des öffentlichen Rechts genießen. Die Flurbereinigungsdirektionen[2)] und die Teilnehmergemeinschaften haben nach § 37 Abs. 2 des Flurbereinigungsgesetzes (FlurbG) in der Fassung der Bekanntmachung vom 16. März 1976 (BGBl I S. 546) bei der Neuordnung im ländlichen Raum durch Flurbereinigung auch den Erfordernissen der Raumordnung, der Landesplanung und des Umweltschutzes, des Naturschutzes und der Landschaftspflege sowie der Gestaltung des Orts- und Landschaftsbildes Rechnung zu tragen. Dem Schutz und der Pflege von Bau- und Bodendenkmälern ist dabei im Hinblick auf das Gesetz zum Schutz und zur Pflege der Denkmäler (Denkmalschutzgesetz– DSchG) vom 25. Juni 1973 (GVBl S. 328) ebenfalls Rechnung zu tragen.
Um die Belange der Denkmalpflege und des Denkmalschutzes im möglichen Umfang bei der Durchführung der Flurbereinigung beachten zu können, ist eine enge Zusammenarbeit der Flurbereinigungsdirektion, des Vorstands der Teilnehmergemeinschaft und der Stellen der Denkmalpflege und des Denkmalschutzes erforderlich.
Zur Sicherung der Zusammenarbeit wird bestimmt:

II. Einleitung der Flurbereinigung

2 – Regierung und Flurbereinigungsdirektion stellen gemeinsam alljährlich für jeweils fünf Jahre Arbeitsprogramme nach der GemBek vom 20. Juni 1977 (MABl S. 551, LMBl S. 132) auf; damit soll eine frühzeitige Koordinierung der Planungen und Maßnahmen aller öffentlichen Planungsträger in den geplanten Neuordnungsgebieten der Flurbereinigung gewährleistet werden. An der jährlichen Arbeitsprogrammbesprechung, die an der Regierung unter Vorsitz des Regierungspräsidenten oder seines Stellvertreters stattfindet, nehmen auch die Leiter der Abteilungen/Sachgebiete der Regierungen teil, die für die Belange der Denkmalpflege und des Denkmalschutzes zuständig sind.
Das Landesamt für Denkmalpflege erhält von der Regierung nach Nummer 3.2 der GemBek vom 20. Juni 1977 die Niederschrift über das Ergebnis der Besprechung. Denkmalschutzbehörden und Landesamt für Denkmalpflege werden somit frühzeitig von den Arbeitsprogrammen der Flurbereinigungsdirektionen in Kenntnis gesetzt und können erforderliche Erhebungen rechtzeitig in Angriff nehmen.
3 – Das Landesamt für Denkmalpflege überprüft und vervollständigt die Denkmalliste bevorzugt in den Gemeinden, die in den Zeitstufen 1 und 2 des Arbeitsprogramms aufgeführt sind. Spätestens zur Aufstellung der Neugestaltungsgrundsätze (vgl. Nr. 6) soll die Denkmalliste der Flurbereinigungsdirektion vorliegen.
Bis zur Aufstellung der Denkmalliste treten an deren Stelle die Entwürfe; dies gilt auch für den Fall der Aufstellung der Neugestaltungsgrundsätze.
4 – Vor der Anordnung eines Verfahrens nach dem Flurbereinigungsgesetz beteiligt die Flurbereinigungsdirektion nach § 5 Abs. 2 und 3 FlurbG das Landesamt für Denkmalpflege (vgl. Nr. 2.4 der LMBek vom 7. März 1977, LMBl S. 69, geändert durch LMBek vom 7. März 1978, LMBl S. 89). Dieses hat der Flurbereinigungsdirektion rechtzeitig die das voraussichtliche Flurbereinigungsgebiet berührenden beabsichtigten oder bereits feststehenden Planungen der Denkmalpflege und des Denkmalschutzes mitzuteilen; die Stellungnahmen zu den Bereichen Denkmalpflege und Denkmalschutz sind nach Möglichkeit zu einem Beitrag zusammenzufassen.

[1)] Fortgeltung ab 1.1.2016 gem. VwVWBek v. 31.5.2016 (AllMBl. S. 1555).
[2)] **Amtl. Anm.:** nichtamtlicher Hinweis: nunmehr (im gesamten Text) Direktion für Ländliche Entwicklung

III. Neugestaltungsgrundsätze

5 – Bei der Aufstellung der allgemeinen Grundsätze für die zweckmäßige Neugestaltung des Flurbereinigungsgebietes nach § 38 FlurbG – Neugestaltungsgrundsätze – hat die Flurbereinigungsdirektion auch die Erfordernisse der Denkmalpflege und des Denkmalschutzes zu beachten. Der Aufstellung der Neugestaltungsgrundsätze kommt besondere Bedeutung zu, weil diese Grundsätze
- die übergeordnete Neuordnungskonzeption darstellen, die als Grundlage für die parzellenscharfen und rechtsverbindlichen Planungen und Maßnahmen der Teilnehmergemeinschaft zur Neugestaltung des Flurbereinigungsgebietes dient, und
- im Benehmen mit allen beteiligten Behörden und Stellen aufgestellt werden; dabei soll nicht nur die Koordinierung und Abstimmung der für das Flurbereinigungsgebiet raumbedeutsamen Planungen und Maßnahmen aller öffentlichen Planungsträger sichergestellt, sondern auch gewährleistet werden, dass die Belange der Denkmalpflege und des Denkmalschutzes bei der Neugestaltung des Flurbereinigungsgebietes im möglichen Umfange berücksichtigt werden.

6 – Die Flurbereinigungsdirektion stellt im Benehmen mit dem Landesamt für Denkmalpflege und den sonstigen beteiligten Stellen die Neugestaltungsgrundsätze auf; die Beteiligung des Heimatpflegers (Kreis- und Stadtheimatpfleger) kann sich in einzelnen Fällen als notwendig erweisen.
Ist auf Grund der Mitteilung gemäß § 5 Abs. 3 FlurbG oder der Denkmalliste zu erwarten, dass Belange der Denkmalpflege und des Denkmalschutzes durch Planungen der Flurbereinigung oder anderer Planungsträger berührt werden, sollen die anstehenden Probleme in Einzelterminen vorher abgeklärt werden.

IV. Dorferneuerungsplan

7 – Die Dorferneuerung ist eine wirkungsvolle Maßnahme zur integralen Verbesserung der Agrarstruktur und der Lebensverhältnisse auf dem Lande, sowie ein Beitrag zur Landentwicklung. Bei den Maßnahmen der Dorferneuerung ist im Rahmen der Ordnungsmaßnahmen neben der Erhaltung und Sicherung einzelner Bauten vor allem auf die Gestaltung und Erhaltung des Ortsbildes zu achten.
Bei einer umfassenden Dorferneuerung wird vom Vorstand der Teilnehmergemeinschaft gemeinsam mit der Gemeinde unter rechtzeitiger Beteiligung der Träger öffentlicher Belange, die durch die Maßnahmen berührt sein können, ein Dorferneuerungsplan aufgestellt. Dieser dient auch der gegenseitigen Abstimmung der Maßnahmen zur Verbesserung der Agrarstruktur und der städtebaulichen Maßnahmen sowie anderer Vorhaben öffentlicher und privater Träger im Ortsbereich. Im Dorferneuerungsplan sollen die agrarstrukturell begründeten Neugestaltungsmaßnahmen mit den städtebaulich begründeten Ordnungs- und Gestaltungsmaßnahmen der Gemeinde im Sinne eines städtebaulichen Rahmenkonzeptes verbunden werden, das Grundlage für die verbindliche Bauleitplanung ist.
Bei der Aufstellung des Dorferneuerungsplans hat der Vorstand der Teilnehmergemeinschaft auch das Landesamt für Denkmalpflege und den Heimatpfleger frühzeitig im Planungsstadium zu beteiligen. Die Beteiligung soll in der Regel durch die Teilnahme an gemeinsamen Ortsterminen geschehen; sie kann sich nur in einfach gelagerten Fällen auf einen schriftlichen Beitrag zur Aufstellung der Neugestaltungsgrundsätze bzw. auf die Teilnahme am Erörterungstermin nach § 41 Abs. 2 FlurbG beschränken.
Die Stellen der Denkmalpflege und des Denkmalschutzes sollen ihre Mitwirkung nicht nur auf den Schutz von Baudenkmälern abstellen, sondern auch Vorschläge zur Gestaltung der Baudenkmäler unter Berücksichtigung des Ortsbildes sowie zur Instandhaltung und Instandsetzung der Baudenkmäler und deren funktionsgerechte Verwendung unterbreiten. Sie beteiligen sich bei der Abstimmung der Planungen.
Maßnahmen der Dorferneuerung, deren Träger die Teilnehmergemeinschaft ist, werden in den Plan über die gemeinschaftlichen und öffentlichen Anlagen bzw. in den Flurbereinigungsplan aufgenommen.

V. Plan über die gemeinschaftlichen und öffentlichen Anlagen

8 – Der Vorstand der Teilnehmergemeinschaft stellt auf der Grundlage der Neugestaltungsgrundsätze den Plan auf über die gemeinschaftlichen und öffentlichen Anlagen, insbesondere über die Einziehung,

Änderung oder Neuausweisung öffentlicher Wege und Straßen sowie über die wasserwirtschaftlichen, bodenverbessernden und landschaftsgestaltenden Anlagen (§ 41 Abs. 1 FlurbG).

Maßnahmen, die zum Schutz und zur Pflege von Denkmälern erforderlich sind und die dem Zweck der Flurbereinigung dienen, können in den Plan aufgenommen und nach Maßgabe der Finanzierungsrichtlinien im Rahmen der Flurbereinigung gefördert werden.

9 – Der Vorstand der Teilnehmergemeinschaft beteiligt bei der Aufstellung des Planes möglichst frühzeitig die Stellen der Denkmalpflege und des Denkmalschutzes; dabei soll angestrebt werden, dass schon im Planungsstadium die Erfordernisse der Denkmalpflege und des Denkmalschutzes hinreichend bekannt sind und bei der Aufstellung des Planes im möglichen Umfange beachtet werden können. Es soll erreicht werden, dass bei der Erörterung des Planes nach § 41 Abs. 2 FlurbG schwerwiegende Zielkonflikte mit den Belangen der Denkmalpflege und des Denkmalschutzes nicht mehr bestehen.

Das Landesamt für Denkmalpflege und der Heimatpfleger sind an der Aufstellung des Planes insbesondere zu beteiligen,
- soweit in den Plan Anlagen aufgenommen werden, deren Errichtung die Beseitigung, Veränderung oder Verlegung von Bau- oder Bodendenkmälern oder von Objekten erfordert, die in die Denkmalliste aufgenommen sind, oder
- soweit in der Nähe von Bau- oder Bodendenkmälern Anlagen errichtet, verändert oder beseitigt werden sollen.

Das Landesamt für Denkmalpflege und der Heimatpfleger sind bei den Terminen entweder gleichzeitig vertreten oder beauftragen einen gemeinsamen Vertreter mit der Wahrnehmung ihrer Interessen; dies gilt auch für die Beteiligung bei der Aufstellung des Dorferneuerungsplans (vgl. Nr. 7) sowie bei der Erörterung des Planes nach § 41 Abs. 2 FlurbG (vgl. Nr. 10).

10 – Der Vorstand der Teilnehmergemeinschaft beteiligt das Landesamt für Denkmalpflege und den Heimatpfleger als Träger öffentlicher Belange bei der Erörterung des Planes nach § 41 Abs. 2 FlurbG (vgl. auch Nr. 30 der LMBek vom 7. Juli 1977, LMBl S.201).[1)]

Mit der Ladung zum Anhörungstermin nach § 41 Abs. 2 FlurbG erhalten das Landesamt für Denkmalpflege und der Heimatpfleger einen Auszug aus dem Plan über die gemeinschaftlichen und öffentlichen Anlagen, in dem die Planungen enthalten sind, die diese Stellen berühren; insbesondere sind in dem Auszug die vorgesehenen Beseitigungen, Veränderungen oder Verlegungen von Bau- und Bodendenkmälern und die geplanten Anlagen in der Nähe von Bau- oder Bodendenkmälern sowie die vorgesehenen Veränderungen am Gebäudebestand kenntlich zu machen. Ggf. sind Ablichtungen geeigneter Unterlagen zur Verdeutlichung der Festsetzungen beizugeben. Bei der Übersendung des Auszugs aus dem Plan ist ferner darauf hinzuweisen, dass weitere Einzelheiten den bei der Flurbereinigungsdirektion oder an anderer Stelle ausliegenden Planunterlagen entnommen werden können.

Falls von den Stellen der Denkmalpflege und des Denkmalschutzes gegen den Plan über die gemeinschaftlichen und öffentlichen Anlagen Einwendungen erhoben werden, müssen diese zur Vermeidung des Ausschlusses im Anhörungstermin nach § 41 Abs. 2 FlurbG vorgebracht werden. Das Landesamt für Denkmalpflege und der Heimatpfleger sollen ihre Einwendungen aufeinander abstimmen und möglichst zu einer Stellungnahme zusammenfassen.

Nach Abschluss des Anhörungstermins legt der Vorsitzende des Vorstands die Planunterlagen einschließlich der Niederschrift zum Anhörungstermin der Flurbereinigungsdirektion zur Planfeststellung vor. Im Vorlagebericht ist zu den nicht im Termin behobenen Einwendungen der Stellen der Denkmalpflege und des Denkmalschutzes Stellung zu nehmen.

VI. Planfeststellung, Plangenehmigung

11 – Bestehen zwischen dem Landesamt für Denkmalpflege bzw. dem Heimatpfleger und der Teilnehmergemeinschaft in sachlicher oder rechtlicher Hinsicht auch nach dem Anhörungstermin nach § 41 Abs. 2 FlurbG noch wesentliche Meinungsverschiedenheiten, so versucht die Flurbereinigungsdirektion, diese mit der Höheren Denkmalschutzbehörde auszuräumen. Gelingt dies nicht, hat die Flurbereinigungsdirektion vor der Feststellung des Planes darüber dem Staatsministerium für Ernährung, Landwirtschaft und Forsten zu berichten und dessen Entscheidung abzuwarten.

---

1) **Amtl. Anm.:** nichtamtlicher Hinweis: nunmehr PlanR-LE, Bekanntmachung – 27.01.2003, AllMBl S. 31

12 – Die Flurbereinigungsdirektion stellt nach § 41 Abs. 3 FlurbG den Plan über die gemeinschaftlichen und öffentlichen Anlagen fest, sie entscheidet dabei auch über die verbliebenen Einwendungen. Die Planfeststellung ist eine einheitliche Sachentscheidung, in der alle in Betracht kommenden Belange gewürdigt und abgewogen werden. Durch sie wird die Zulässigkeit des Vorhabens einschließlich der notwendigen Folgemaßnahmen auch im Hinblick auf die Belange der Denkmalpflege und des Denkmalschutzes festgestellt.

Durch die Planfeststellung werden insbesondere folgende behördliche Entscheidungen ersetzt:
- die Erlaubnis nach Art. 6, 7, 10 Abs. 1 und Art. 15 DSchG und
- die Genehmigung oder Zustimmung für Errichtung, Änderung, Abbruch oder Beseitigung baulicher Anlagen (Art. 82 und 103 BayBO).

13 – Die Flurbereinigungsdirektion kann den Plan nach § 41 Abs. 4 FlurbG genehmigen, wenn mit Einwendungen von Seiten der Träger öffentlicher Belange nicht zu rechnen ist oder Einwendungen nicht erhoben oder nachträglich ausgeräumt werden.

14 – Das Landesamt für Denkmalpflege und der Heimatpfleger werden von der Flurbereinigungsdirektion durch Übersendung eines Abdruckes des Beschlusstextes über den Erlass des Planfeststellungsbeschlusses bzw. der Plangenehmigung unterrichtet.

VII. Durchführung der Baumaßnahmen

15 – Im Planfeststellungsbeschluss oder in der Erlaubnis nach Art. 7 DSchG enthaltene Auflagen und Bedingungen zum Schutz eines Denkmals sind in die Baubeschreibung aufzunehmen.

Bei Arbeiten, die nach Auskunft des Landesamts für Denkmalpflege Bau- oder Bodendenkmäler berühren werden, ist der Arbeitsablauf baubetrieblich so einzuleiten, dass eine Unterbrechung der Arbeiten durch die Bergung der Denkmäler weitgehend vermieden werden kann. Die Erfüllung dieser Auflagen ist durch die Flurbereinigungsdirektion zu überwachen.

16 – Werden bei der Durchführung von Baumaßnahmen Bau- oder Bodendenkmäler aufgefunden, so haben die Teilnehmergemeinschaft und der Auftragnehmer nach Art. 8 DSchG folgende Pflichten:
1. Der Fund ist unverzüglich dem Landesamt für Denkmalpflege oder der unteren Denkmalschutzbehörde anzuzeigen, gleichgültig, ob die Arbeiten mit oder ohne Planfeststellung oder Erlaubnis nach Art. 7 DSchG durchgeführt werden.
2. Die aufgefundenen Gegenstände und der Fundort sind bis zum Ablauf einer Woche nach Abgabe der Anzeige unverändert zu belassen, es sei denn, zwingende Gründe des öffentlichen Wohls gebieten die Fortsetzung der Arbeiten oder die Untere Denkmalschutzbehörde, der der Fund angezeigt wurde, gibt die Gegenstände vorher frei oder gestattet die Fortsetzung der Arbeiten. Nach Ablauf der Wochenfrist können die Arbeiten wieder aufgenommen werden.
3. Besteht die Gefahr, dass aufgefundene Gegenstände abhanden kommen, so sind sie unverzüglich der Unteren Denkmalschutzbehörde zur Aufbewahrung zu übergeben.

17 – Stillstandskosten und sonstige Mehrkosten wegen angeordneter Sicherungsmaßregeln (einschließlich notwendiger Planungsänderungen) sind grundsätzlich vom Bauherrn zu tragen und aus Baumitteln zu bestreiten.

18 – Bei Bodenaltertümern wird es sich in der Regel um Schatzfunde nach § 984 BGB handeln. Danach erwirbt das Eigentum an dem Fund zur Hälfte der Grundstückseigentümer und zur Hälfte der Finder. Entdecker ist auch bei vergebenen Bauarbeiten nach § 4 Nr. 9 VOB/B der Auftraggeber, also die Teilnehmergemeinschaft oder der Bauherr, in dessen Auftrag sie baut (z.B. die Gemeinde). Besitzeinweisung und Bauerlaubnis berechtigen den Bauherrn zur Bergung der Fundgegenstände. Sonst ist die Zustimmung der Grundstückseigentümer zur Entfernung einzuholen, sofern nicht der Fall des Art. 8 Abs. 5 DSchG gegeben ist.

Die Ablösung der Miteigentumsrechte soll der Finanzverwaltung übertragen werden.

19 – Im übrigen ist nach den Bestimmungen der gemeinsamen Bekanntmachung vom 25. Februar 1969 (LBMl S. 31)[1]) über kulturhistorische Funde bei staatlichen Baumaßnahmen zu verfahren.

---

1) **Amtl. Anm.:** nichtamtlicher Hinweis: aufgehoben durch Bekanntmachung vom 01.10.1986, LMBl. S. 173

VIII. Bodenordnung und Regelung der Rechtsverhältnisse

20 – Die Bodenordnung im Rahmen der Flurbereinigung kann eine wirksame Maßnahme sein, um Ziele der Denkmalpflege und des Denkmalschutzes zu verwirklichen. Die Erhaltung der Bau- und Bodendenkmäler ist daher durch Maßnahmen der Bodenordnung zu unterstützen. Grundstücke, auf denen sich Denkmäler befinden, sollen mit entsprechendem Umgriff im öffentlichen Eigentum bzw. im Eigentum von Verbänden oder Organisationen, deren Ziel der Schutz und die Pflege von Bau- und Bodendenkmälern ist, ausgewiesen werden, wenn dies von den Stellen der Denkmalpflege und des Denkmalschutzes befürwortet wird.

Die Flächen für Anlagen, die der Denkmalpflege und dem Denkmalschutz dienen, sollen durch Verwendung von freihändig erworbenem Land aufgebracht werden; erforderlichenfalls können diese Flächen auch nach § 40 FlurbG bereitgestellt werden.

Die Maßnahmen der Bodenordnung zur Erhaltung von Denkmälern können nach Maßgabe der Richtlinien für die Förderung und Finanzierung der Flurbereinigung gefördert werden. Sie sollen vor allem gefördert werden, wenn sich die Gemeinden, Landkreise und Bezirke im Rahmen ihrer Leistungsfähigkeit in angemessenem Umfang an den Kosten beteiligen.

21 – Die rechtlichen Verhältnisse an den Grundstücken, auf denen sich Bau- oder Bodendenkmäler befinden, werden im Flurbereinigungsplan geregelt, der vom Vorstand der Teilnehmergemeinschaft aufgestellt wird. Soweit diese Grundstücke im öffentlichen Eigentum oder im Eigentum von Verbänden oder Organisationen, deren Ziel der Schutz und die Pflege von Bau- und Bodendenkmälern ist, neu ausgewiesen werden, können Regelungen über Schutz-, Pflege- und Unterhaltungsmaßnahmen in den Flurbereinigungsplan aufgenommen werden. Diese Regelungen sind auf Vorschlag und im Einvernehmen mit dem Landesamt für Denkmalpflege festzulegen.

22 – Das Landesamt für Denkmalpflege, die Untere Denkmalschutzbehörde und der Heimatpfleger erhalten Abschriften aller von der Teilnehmergemeinschaft im Flurbereinigungsplan zum Schutz und zur Pflege von Bau- und Bodendenkmälern getroffenen Vereinbarungen und Festsetzungen.

D2.I.1c VwV Vollzug DSchG

Vollzug des Denkmalschutzgesetzes und baurechtlicher Vorschriften[1]

Vom 27. Juli 1984 (KWMBl. I 1984 S. 561 MABl. 1984 S. 421)
(BayVV Gliederungsnummer 2242-WK)[2]

Gemeinsame Bekanntmachung der Bayerischen Staatsministerien des Innern und für Unterricht und Kultus[3] vom 27. Juli 1984 Nr. II B 7-4121-0.27 und Nr. IV/2b-7/96 982

An die Regierungen
die unteren Bauaufsichtsbehörden
die unteren Denkmalschutzbehörden
das Bayerische Landesamt für Denkmalpflege
die Gemeinden
die Landkreise
die Bezirke

nachrichtlich an
die Bezirksheimatpfleger
die Landbauämter
die Universitätsbauämter
die Autobahndirektionen
die Straßenbauämter
das Straßen- und Wasserbauamt Pfarrkirchen
die Wasserwirtschaftsämter
das Talsperren-Neubauamt Nürnberg
die Kreis- und Stadtheimatpfleger

Inhaltsübersicht

1. Denkmalbegriff und Denkmalliste, Nähe von Baudenkmälern
2. Ausnahmen und Befreiungen
3. Ermessensentscheidungen und Nebenbestimmungen
4. Entschädigungspflicht
5. Finanzielle Förderung
6. Beteiligung der kommunalen Gebietskörperschaften an den Kosten der Denkmalpflege
7. Ordnungswidrigkeiten
8. Baumaßnahmen im ländlichen Bereich
9. Wohnungsbau-, Modernisierungs- und Städtebauförderung
10. Materielle Einzelprobleme
10.1 Fenster
10.2 Flurdenkmäler
10.3 Fußgängerzonen und verkehrsberuhigte Bereiche
11. Beteiligung des Landesamts für Denkmalpflege
12. Regelung des Verfahrens im Allgemeinen und Behördensprechtag
13. Erlaubnisverfahren nach dem Denkmalschutzgesetz für Denkmäler und Anlagen in der Nähe von Baudenkmälern
14. Baugenehmigungs- und Zustimmungsverfahren
15. Bodenverkehrsgenehmigungsverfahren
16. Bauleitplanverfahren
17. örtliche Bauvorschriften
18. Anordnung von Baumaßnahmen, Nutzungs-, Abbruch- und Erhaltungsgeboten nach dem Bundesbaugesetz; Anordnungen nach Art. 63 Abs. 5 und 6, Art. 82 BayBO; Anordnungen nach Art. 4, 15 Abs. 3 DSchG
19. Verfahren nach dem Städtebauförderungsgesetz
20. Planfeststellungsverfahren
21. Flurbereinigung und Dorferneuerung
22. Verfahren zur Erhaltung von Bodendenkmälern im Sinn des Art. 1 Abs. 4 DSchG
22.1 Erlaubnisverfahren
22.2 Genehmigungsverfahren

---

1) Fortgeltung ab 1.1.2016 gem. VwVWBek v. 31.5.2016 (AllMBl. S. 1555).
2) **Amtl. Anm.:** Die baurechtlichen Vorschriften sind zum Teil überholt, insbesondere gilt nunmehr das Baugesetzbuch (BauGB), nicht mehr das Bundesbaugesetz (BBauG)
3) **Amtl. Anm.:** jetzt: Bayerisches Staatsministerium für Wissenschaft, Forschung und Kunst

22.3	Verfahren bei Anzeigen	23.	Erhaltung von eingetragenen beweglichen Denkmälern
22.4	Auswertung von Funden		
22.5	Denkmäler, die gottesdienstlichen Zwecken dienen	24.	Besonderheiten für Baudenkmäler zu gottesdienstlichen Zwecken
22.6	Eigentumsverhältnisse	25.	Sonstige Bestimmungen

Beim Vollzug des Gesetzes zum Schutz und zur Pflege der Denkmäler (Denkmalschutzgesetz - DSchG) vom 25. Juni 1973 (GVBl S. 328), zuletzt geändert durch Gesetz vom 7. September 1982 (GVBl S. 722), ist Folgendes zu beachten:

1. Denkmalbegriff und Denkmalliste, Nähe von Baudenkmälern

1.1

Denkmäler sind alle Sachen, die unter die Definition des Art. 1 DSchG fallen. Die Anwendbarkeit der Schutzbestimmungen des Gesetzes hängt nur bei beweglichen Denkmälern von der Eintragung in die Denkmalliste ab (Art. 3 Abs. 1 DSchG), nicht dagegen bei Bau- und Bodendenkmälern. Die Denkmalliste dient im Bereich der Bau- und Bodendenkmäler vor allem der Erleichterung des Gesetzesvollzugs. Baudenkmäler im Sinn des DSchG sind auch die sogenannten Ensembles (vgl. Art. 1 Abs. 3 DSchG).

Um einen einheitlichen Gesetzesvollzug zu gewährleisten, sind die Behörden verpflichtet, sich an die Denkmalliste zu halten. Von der Liste darf in Bezug auf die Denkmaleigenschaft nur im Einvernehmen mit dem Landesamt für Denkmalpflege abgewichen werden. Solange für einzelne Bereiche die Denkmalliste nicht vorliegt, ist bei der Beurteilung der Denkmaleigenschaft zunächst von den vom Landesamt erstellten Entwürfen der Liste auszugehen. Soweit Denkmäler in der Liste nicht enthalten sind und soweit bei Bodendenkmälern weder ein Listenentwurf noch ein ausreichendes Inventar vorliegt, holen in Zweifelsfällen die mit den Verfahren befassten Behörden - in dringenden Fällen fernmündlich - eine Stellungnahme des Landesamts für Denkmalpflege darüber ein, ob beabsichtigt ist, das Objekt in die Liste einzutragen.

Die Denkmalliste steht jedermann zur Einsicht offen. Im Interesse aller Beteiligten wird die Denkmalliste laufend fortgeschrieben.

Die Bauaufsichtsbehörden und die unteren Denkmalschutzbehörden teilen dem Landesamt für Denkmalpflege Abbrüche oder sonstige Zerstörungen von Denkmälern mit.

1.2

Art. 6 Abs. 1 Nr. 1 in Verbindung mit Absatz 2 Satz 1 DSchG schützt Baudenkmäler u. a. vor unkontrollierten Veränderungen. Damit sind nicht nur Eingriffe in die Substanz der Bauwerke angesprochen, sondern z.B. auch Wandverkleidungen, Dacheindeckungen, Türen, Fenster. Bei Veränderungen soll angestrebt werden, dass Baustoffe verwendet werden, die den bereits vorhandenen Materialien entsprechen oder mit der vorhandenen Substanz vergleichbar sind.

1.3

Vor unkontrollierten Beeinträchtigungen durch Veränderungen in ihrer Umgebung sind Baudenkmäler durch Art. 6 Abs. 1 und 2 DSchG geschützt. „Anlagen " in der Nähe von Baudenkmälern sind nicht nur bauliche Anlagen im Sinn der Bayerischen Bauordnung, sondern auch Anlagen anderer Art, z.B. Straßen. Anlagen liegen dann „in der Nähe " von Baudenkmälern, wenn ihre Errichtung, Änderung oder Beseitigung Auswirkungen auf Baudenkmäler oder auf das Erscheinungsbild von Baudenkmälern haben kann.

2. Ausnahmen und Befreiungen

Baudenkmäler entsprechen oft nicht den Anforderungen des geltenden Baurechts. Wenn bei genehmigungspflichtigen Instandsetzungen, Umbauten oder Nutzungsänderungen die Vorschriften des Baurechts ausnahmslos beachtet werden müssten, könnten Baudenkmäler oft nicht in ihrer historischen Form erhalten werden. Deshalb sieht Art. 72 Abs. 3 Nr. 1 BayBO vor, dass zur Erhaltung und weiteren Nutzung von Baudenkmälern Ausnahmen von baurechtlichen Vorschriften zugelassen werden können, wenn nicht erhebliche Gefahren für Leben oder Gesundheit zu befürchten sind. Unter den Voraussetzungen des Art. 72 Abs. 5 BayBO kann auch von zwingenden baurechtlichen Vorschriften befreit werden. Ausnahmen sollen bei Vorliegen der gesetzlichen Voraussetzungen dann zugelassen werden, wenn die Ausnahme zur Erhaltung oder sachgerechten Nutzung des Baudenkmals beiträgt und dadurch nicht andere überragende Interessen unzumutbar beeinträchtigt werden; entsprechendes gilt für Befreiungen.

Ausnahmen oder Befreiungen können z.B. in Betracht kommen von Vorschriften über Abstandsflächen (Art. 6, 7 BayBO), über Herstellungs- und Unterhaltungsverpflichtungen (Art. 8, 62 BayBO), über Aufenthaltsräume und Wohnungen (Art. 58 bis 61 BayBO) sowie von Vorschriften der Versammlungsstättenverordnung. Können Herstellungs- und Unterhaltspflichten nicht wahrgenommen werden, ist in erster Linie auf die in den einschlägigen Vorschriften enthaltenen Ersatz- und Ablösungsbestimmungen zurückzugreifen. Für Kinderspielplätze wird eine Befreiung nur selten in Betracht kommen können. Ausnahmen und Befreiungen von gemeindlichen Bauvorschriften nach Art. 91 Abs. 1 und 2 BayBO bedürfen des Einvernehmens der Gemeinde (Art. 72 Abs. 6 BayBO).

Wegen der Beachtung der Belange der Denkmalpflege und der Gewährung von Ausnahmen bei Anwendung der Arbeitsstättenverordnung wird auf das Schreiben des Staatsministeriums für Arbeit und Sozialordnung an die Gewerbeaufsichtsämter vom 26. November 1980 - Nr. IX 321/189/80 hingewiesen.

3. Ermessensentscheidungen und Nebenbestimmungen

Soweit Entscheidungen im Ermessen der unteren Denkmalschutzbehörde oder der unteren Bauaufsichtsbehörde stehen, sind alle für und gegen die Erhaltung oder Veränderung des Denkmals sprechenden Gründe sorgfältig abzuwägen. Dabei soll den Denkmälern im Hinblick auf Art. 141 der Verfassung grundsätzlich besonderer öffentlicher Schutz gewährt werden. Die Zulässigkeit von Nebenbestimmungen zum Verwaltungsakt richtet sich nach Art. 36 BayVwVfG. Nebenbestimmungen sollen den Schutz der Denkmäler sicherstellen. Gerade bei der Restaurierung oder Instandsetzung von Bau- und Bodendenkmälern ist erfahrungsgemäß damit zu rechnen, dass unbekannte Details zutage treten oder sonstige Tatsachen im Hinblick auf Erhaltungszustand, Konstruktion und Sanierungsmöglichkeiten bekannt werden. Um den erhöhten Anforderungen an die Planung bei Vorhaben zu entsprechen, die denkmalpflegerische Fragen berühren, kann im Einzelfall die Entscheidung nach Art. 15 Abs. 5 DSchG ausgesetzt werden; so können z.B. erforderliche Gutachten, Aufmaße und Befunduntersuchungen abgewartet werden.

Nach pflichtgemäßem Ermessen kann nach Art. 36 Abs. 2 Nr. 5 BayVwVfG in die Entscheidung ein Auflagenvorbehalt aufgenommen werden, um im Zeitpunkt der Entscheidung nicht absehbare Belange des Denkmalschutzes nach Bekanntwerden entsprechender Umstände verfahrensrechtlich zu sichern.

4. Entschädigungspflicht

Im Baugenehmigungs- und Erlaubnisverfahren bleibt unberücksichtigt, ob einem Eigentümer oder sonst dinglich Verfügungsberechtigten Erhaltungsmaßnahmen für ein Denkmal nach Art. 4 Abs. 1 DSchG zumutbar sind (BayVGH vom 12.6.1978, BayVBl 1979, S. 118). Im Übrigen liegen das Eigentum beschränkende Maßnahmen des Denkmalschutzes weitgehend im Bereich der Sozialbindung des Eigentums; die Pflicht des Eigentümers, denkmalschützerische Maßnahmen zu dulden, hält sich damit grundsätzlich im Rahmen von Art. 103 Abs. 2 und Art. 158 der Verfassung sowie Art. 14 des Grundgesetzes (so ausdrücklich BayVerfGH vom 15.5.1981, BayVBl 1981, S. 429).
Sollte im Einzelfall trotzdem eine Entschädigungspflicht eintreten, so ist Art. 20 DSchG zu beachten. Steuervorteile und erreichbare Zuwendungen sind in angemessenem Umfang auf eine Entschädigung anzurechnen. Nimmt die Bauaufsichts- oder Denkmalschutzbehörde an, dass eine Maßnahme zu einer Verpflichtung des Entschädigungsfonds nach Art. 21 DSchG führen könnte, so ist über die Regierung

und das Landesamt für Denkmalpflege unter Beigabe der erforderlichen Unterlagen die vorherige Weisung des Staatsministeriums für Unterricht und Kultus einzuholen (vgl. auch KMS vom 13.10.1983 Nr. IV/2b-7/142 522).
Soweit eine Beeinträchtigung von Denkmälern durch die Versagung von Genehmigungen nach anderen Gesetzen verhindert werden kann, ohne dass Entschädigungsansprüche entstehen, sind diese Möglichkeiten auszunutzen.

5. Finanzielle Förderung

Für eine Reihe von Maßnahmen im Bereich von Denkmälern kommt eine direkte oder indirekte öffentliche Förderung oder Finanzierung in Betracht. Direkt wirken u. a. Zuwendungen des Landesamts für Denkmalpflege und der Gebietskörperschaften sowie die zahlreichen Formen der Wohnungsbauförderung, der Investitionsförderung, der Städtebauförderung, der Förderung der Modernisierung sowie Zuschüsse der Landesstiftung. Indirekt wirken die Steuervorteile z.B. aufgrund des Einkommensteuerrechts.
Einzelheiten enthalten der „Wegweiser" der Bayerischen Staatsregierung zu staatlichen Förderungs- und Finanzierungsmöglichkeiten und verschiedene Veröffentlichungen des Staatsministeriums für Unterricht und Kultus und des Landesamts für Denkmalpflege.
Die jeweils zuständigen Behörden, insbesondere auch die unteren Bauaufsichts- und Denkmalschutzbehörden, weisen die Maßnahmeträger und Bauherren frühzeitig auf die Förderungsmöglichkeiten hin, die erfahrungsgemäß in zahlreichen Fällen den Entschluss zur Durchführung von Maßnahmen im Sinn des Denkmalschutzes günstig beeinflussen können. Vor allem gilt das bei Anträgen und Verfahren, die auf eine Beeinträchtigung von Denkmälern hinauslaufen können.
Die verschiedenen Planungs-, Erlaubnis- und Genehmigungsverfahren sind im Übrigen eng mit dem Förderungsverfahren abzustimmen. Die Vorprüfungs- und Bewilligungsstellen und die Genehmigungsbehörden sollen so bald als möglich unter Beteiligung des Landesamts für Denkmalpflege untereinander Verbindung aufnehmen. Etwaige Bedenken sollen frühzeitig geklärt werden, bevor viel Zeit und erhebliche Mittel auf die Planung und Vorbereitung solcher Vorhaben verwendet werden.
Um Zweifel über die Reichweite der Entscheidung in förderungsrechtlicher und steuerrechtlicher Hinsicht auszuschließen, ist in den Baugenehmigungs- und Erlaubnisbescheiden kenntlich zu machen, wenn die Entscheidung von der Stellungnahme des Landesamts für Denkmalpflege abweicht.

6. Beteiligung der kommunalen Gebietskörperschaften an den Kosten der Denkmalpflege

Nach Art. 22 Abs. 2 DSchG beteiligen sich die Gemeinden, Landkreise und Bezirke im Rahmen ihrer Leistungsfähigkeit in angemessenem Umfang an den Kosten des Denkmalschutzes und der Denkmalpflege, insbesondere an den Kosten der Instandsetzung, Erhaltung, Sicherung und Freilegung von Denkmälern sowie an den Kosten der Inventarisierung.

7. Ordnungswidrigkeiten

Der Rahmen für Geldbußen ist durch Art. 23 DSchG und Art. 89 BayBO weit gespannt. Die höchstzulässige Geldbuße beträgt *500.000 DM*[1]. Im Fall unerlaubter Beseitigung eines Baudenkmals *1.000.000 DM*[2]. Im Hinblick auf die Bedeutung, die die Erhaltung der Geschichtszeugnisse des Landes für die ganze Bevölkerung hat, ist dieser Rahmen bei Geldbußen zu beachten, zumal kleinere Geldbußen häufig von vornherein in die Kosten eines Vorhabens einkalkuliert und von den Betroffenen auf andere Personen abgewälzt werden. Muss die Bedeutung eines Falls genau ermittelt werden, so ist das Landesamt für Denkmalpflege zu beteiligen.

---

1) **Amtl. Anm.:** entspricht 255.645,94 €
2) **Amtl. Anm.:** entspricht 511.291,88 €

8. Baumaßnahmen im ländlichen Bereich

Schwierigkeiten beim Vollzug des Denkmalschutzgesetzes im Rahmen von Baumaßnahmen im ländlichen Bereich können am besten dadurch ausgeräumt werden, dass die einzelnen Bauvorhaben so frühzeitig wie möglich - also auf jeden Fall, sobald eine Bauvoranfrage gestellt ist - in Besprechungen erörtert werden, zu denen alle Beteiligten herangezogen werden sollen. Vor allem soll bei den Behördensprechtagen des Landesamts für Denkmalpflege unter Zuziehung des Amts für Landwirtschaft und gegebenenfalls anderer Fachbehörden angestrebt werden, die entscheidungserheblichen Fragen zu klären. Dadurch können Misshelligkeiten vermieden werden, die dadurch entstehen, dass verschiedene Behörden unterschiedliche Aussagen machen.

Die Bauaufsichts- und Denkmalschutzbehörden sind daher gehalten, den Ämtern für Landwirtschaft und gegebenenfalls sonst noch zu beteiligenden Fachbehörden die Termine der Sprechtage des Landesamts für Denkmalpflege mitzuteilen.

9. Wohnungsbau-, Modernisierungs- und Städtebauförderung

Soweit Modernisierungs- und Sanierungsmaßnahmen nicht baugenehmigungspflichtig sind, bedarf es für Maßnahmen an oder in der Nähe von Baudenkmälern einer Erlaubnis nach Art. 6 Abs. 1 DSchG.

Sollen bei denkmalgeschützten Bauvorhaben Wohnungsbau-, Modernisierungs- oder Städtebauförderungsmittel eingesetzt werden, ist rechtzeitig zu prüfen, ob das Bauvorhaben mit den Erfordernissen des Denkmalschutzes übereinstimmt.

Auf Nummer 5 letzter Absatz wird hingewiesen.

10. Materielle Einzelprobleme

10.1
Fenster

Wegen des Einbaus von Einscheibenfenstern in historische Gebäude wird auf die gemeinsame Bekanntmachung der Staatsministerien des Innern und für Unterricht und Kultus vom 23. März 1977 (MABl S. 315, KMBl S. 112) hingewiesen.[1]

10.2
Flurdenkmäler

Flurdenkmäler (Steinkreuze, Bildstöcke u. a.) sind auch Bindeglieder zwischen Landschaft und menschlicher Kultur und müssen als religiöse und geschichtliche Zeugnisse geschützt werden. Regelmäßig handelt es sich um Baudenkmäler im Sinn des Art. 1 DSchG und um bauliche Anlagen im Sinn der Bayerischen Bauordnung. Für alle Restaurierungsmaßnahmen, bauliche oder gestalterische Veränderungen, die Beseitigung oder die Versetzung eines Flurdenkmals, für die weder ein Planfeststellungsverfahren noch ein Genehmigungsverfahren nach der Bayerischen Bauordnung durchzuführen ist, muss eine Erlaubnis nach dem Denkmalschutzgesetz eingeholt werden (Art. 15 in Verbindung mit Art. 6 Abs. 1 und 3 DSchG).

10.3
Fußgängerzonen und verkehrsberuhigte Bereiche

Fußgängerzonen und die gemäß § 42 StVO ausgestalteten verkehrsberuhigten Bereiche (Zeichen 325 und 326) werden häufig in der Nähe von Einzeldenkmälern oder in gestalterisch besonders empfindlichen Altstadtgebieten eingerichtet, die ganz oder teilweise als Ensembles im Sinn des Denkmalschutzgesetzes anzusehen sind. Sie verlangen besondere Rücksichtnahme auf das historische Orts-, Platz- und Straßenbild. Das gilt insbesondere für bauliche und gestalterische Veränderungen des

---

1) **Amtl. Anm.:** Aufgehoben durch Nr. 25 der Bekanntmachung des Bayerischen Staatsministeriums des Innern vom 07. Dezember 2001 (AllMBL S. 767), siehe Bekanntmachung des Bayerischen Staatsministeriums für Wissenschaft, Forschung und Kunst vom 23.04.2002 Nr. XII/4-K 4640/3-12/19 385 (KWMBl 2002 S. 158).

Straßenkörpers, z.B. der Fahrbahndecke oder des Fahrbahnniveaus, wie auch für die Errichtung von Anlagen im Straßenraum (z.B. Beleuchtungskörper, Blumenkästen).

Für bauliche oder gestalterische Veränderungen an Straßen, die selbst Denkmal sind oder sich auf den Bestand oder das Erscheinungsbild von Denkmälern auswirken können, ist eine denkmalrechtliche Erlaubnis erforderlich (Art. 15 in Verbindung mit Art. 6 Abs. 1 DSchG). Das gleiche gilt, soweit die Errichtung von anderen Anlagen, wie z.b. Gartenanlagen, Brunnen, Beleuchtungskörpern und Pflanzenbehältern, in der Nähe von Denkmälern nicht baugenehmigungspflichtig ist.

Die Vorschriften über Werbeanlagen sind gerade auch im Umkreis von Fußgängerzonen und verkehrsberuhigten Bereichen sorgfältig zu beachten.

11. Beteiligung des Landesamts für Denkmalpflege

11.1

Das Landesamt für Denkmalpflege ist zu hören in den Verfahren
- nach dem Denkmalschutzgesetz und in den folgenden Verfahren, soweit im "Einzelfall Bau- oder Bodendenkmäler betroffen werden
- nach der Bayerischen Bauordnung,
- zur Bauleitplanung und zum Erlass von örtlichen Bauvorschriften,
- zur Genehmigung des Bodenverkehrs,
- zur Anordnung von Baumaßnahmen, Nutzungs-, Abbruch- und Erhaltungsgeboten nach §§ 39 b bis 39 e BBauG,
- nach dem Städtebauförderungsgesetz,
- bei Veränderungen sowie Konservierungs- und Restaurierungsmaßnahmen an staatseigenen oder vom Staat verwalteten Denkmälern (Art. 12 Abs. 2 Satz 3 Nrn. 4 und 5 DSchG),
- in Straßen-, wasser-, flurbereinigungs-, gewerbe- und immissionsschutzrechtlichen Verfahren und
- in Förderungs- oder Finanzierungsverfahren.

11.2

Eine Beteiligung des Landesamts für Denkmalpflege ist entbehrlich,
- wenn das Landesamt bereits zu einem früheren Zeitpunkt eine Stellungnahme zu der Maßnahme abgegeben und bei gleicher Sachlage auf eine weitere Beteiligung verzichtet hat; im Übrigen ist davon auszugehen, dass das Landesamt an seine Stellungnahme nur im Rahmen der zeitlichen Geltungsdauer einer Baugenehmigung (Art. 78 BayBO) gebunden ist,
- wenn das Landesamt für Denkmalpflege für eine Gruppe von Maßnahmen - gegebenenfalls im Einvernehmen mit anderen beteiligten Behörden - Richtlinien aufgestellt hat und von diesen Richtlinien nicht abgewichen werden soll,
- wenn gemeindliche Gestaltungsvorschriften im Einvernehmen mit dem Landesamt für Denkmalpflege erlassen wurden und in einem Erlaubnis- oder Genehmigungsverfahren von diesen Vorschriften nicht abgewichen werden soll; das gilt nicht, wenn Denkmäler selbst betroffen sind,
- wenn bei untergeordneten Änderungen an baulichen Anlagen eine Beeinträchtigung des Baudenkmals ausgeschlossen erscheint; eine untergeordnete Änderung ist nicht mehr anzunehmen bei einer wesentlichen Änderung der äußeren Gestaltung, z.B. einer Änderung der Fassade, der Fenster, der Höhenentwicklung, der Farbgebung sowie einer Ausweitung von Werbeanlagen und bei Eingriffen in die Denkmalsubstanz im Innern,
- wenn dies durch eine sonstige Richtlinie des Staatsministeriums des Innern oder des Staatsministeriums für Unterricht und Kultus ausdrücklich festgelegt wird.

Eine besondere Eilbedürftigkeit rechtfertigt es nicht, von der Beteiligung des Landesamts abzusehen. Sofern mit der Entscheidung nicht bis zum nächsten Behördensprechtag gewartet werden kann, ist der Vorgang dem Landesamt für Denkmalpflege unmittelbar zu übersenden und gegebenenfalls eine telefonische Äußerung einzuholen.

12. Regelung des Verfahrens im Allgemeinen und Behördensprechtag

Die an Verwaltungsverfahren beteiligten Behörden und Stellen sind gehalten, im Wege der Beratung Verständnis für die Belange des Denkmalschutzes zu wecken. Sie entscheiden in eigener Zuständigkeit und sehen von einer Beteiligung des Landesamts für Denkmalpflege ab, wenn die Beeinträchtigung von Denkmälern bereits aufgrund anderer gesetzlicher Vorschriften als des Denkmalschutzgesetzes verhindert oder unterbunden werden kann (insbesondere nach §§ 29 ff. BBauG oder dem Stiftungsrecht).

Darüber hinaus ist anzustreben, die Belange des Denkmalschutzes und der Denkmalpflege so frühzeitig wie möglich in die Planungen und Verfahren einzuführen. Bereits im Vorfeld von Maßnahmen soll der Träger oder Bauherr von Amts wegen beraten werden, um spätere Schwierigkeiten zu vermeiden.

Zur Vereinfachung und Beschleunigung von Verwaltungsverfahren und behördeninterner Verfahren und Planungen im Geltungsbereich dieser Bekanntmachung hält das Landesamt für Denkmalpflege bei den unteren Bauaufsichtsbehörden im Abstand von höchstens vier Wochen Behördensprechtage ab. Neben den Gebietsreferenten des Landesamts nehmen teil Vertreter der Bauaufsichtsbehörde und der unteren Denkmalschutzbehörde, der Heimatpfleger sowie Vertreter jener Behörde, deren Maßnahme oder Verfahren durch das Landesamt zu beurteilen ist.

Die untere Bauaufsichts- oder - außerhalb bauaufsichtlicher Verfahren - die untere Denkmalschutzbehörde stellt die Tagesordnung auf, sorgt für die Vollständigkeit der Antragsunterlagen und bereitet diese so weit auf, dass über das Verfahren möglichst an einem Behördensprechtag entschieden werden kann. Sie bereitet auch etwaige Ortstermine vor. Ferner nimmt sie die Stellungnahme des Landesamts zu Protokoll und übersendet dem Landesamt eine Ausfertigung des Protokolls, soweit nicht im Einzelfall etwas anderes vereinbart wird. Dem Landesamt für Denkmalpflege bleibt vorbehalten, einzelne Fälle einer genaueren Prüfung zu unterziehen und um Aktenvorlage oder um Ortseinsicht zu bitten.

Die Entscheidungen sind jeweils in Abdruck dem Landesamt für Denkmalpflege zuzuleiten.

13. Erlaubnisverfahren nach dem Denkmalschutzgesetz für Denkmäler und Anlagen in der Nähe von Baudenkmälern

Soweit Maßnahmen im Sinn des Art. 6 Abs. 1 DSchG nicht bereits einer baurechtlichen Genehmigung oder Zustimmung bedürfen, ist eine Erlaubnis nach dem Denkmalschutzgesetz erforderlich (Art. 15 DSchG). Das Landesamt für Denkmalpflege ist zu hören, es sei denn, dass seine Beteiligung nicht erforderlich ist. Will die untere Denkmalschutzbehörde von der Stellungnahme des Landesamts auch nur in einzelnen Punkten abweichen, so hat sie die Weisung der höheren Denkmalschutzbehörde einzuholen (Art. 15 Abs. 2 Satz 2 DSchG).

Will die untere Denkmalschutzbehörde von der Stellungnahme des Landesamts für Denkmalpflege abweichen, ist diesem gegebenenfalls Gelegenheit zu geben, notwendige Nebenbestimmungen, insbesondere zur Dokumentation und Sicherung der Denkmäler, einzubringen. Im Erlaubnisbescheid ist auf das fehlende Einvernehmen mit dem Landesamt für Denkmalpflege und die negativen Rechtsfolgen nach § 82 i und § 82 k der Einkommensteuer-Durchführungsverordnung oder im Förderungsverfahren hinzuweisen. Dem Landesamt für Denkmalpflege ist ein Abdruck des Erlaubnisbescheids zu übersenden.

14. Baugenehmigungs- und Zustimmungsverfahren

14.1

Soweit in den Fällen des Art. 6 Abs. 1 Nrn. 1 und 2 DSchG eine Baugenehmigung erforderlich ist (Art. 65 bis 68 BayBO), entfällt nach Art. 6 Abs. 3 Satz 1 DSchG die Erlaubnis nach dem Denkmalschutzgesetz. Es findet dann nur das Baugenehmigungsverfahren statt. Das Landesamt für Denkmalpflege als Träger öffentlicher Belange wird in diesem Verfahren aufgrund des Art. 71 Abs. 1 Satz 2 BayBO angehört (vgl. Bekanntmachung vom 2.2.1976, MABl S. 66).

Bei Maßnahmen an Baudenkmälern (Art. 6 Abs. 3 in Verbindung mit Art. 6 Abs. 1 Nr. 1 DSchG) sind Belange des Denkmalschutzes regelmäßig betroffen, so dass das Landesamt für Denkmalpflege zu beteiligen ist, sofern nicht besondere Umstände ein abweichendes Verfahren rechtfertigen. Nach Art. 1 Abs. 3 DSchG gehören alle Teile eines Ensembles, auch soweit sie allein kein Einzelbaudenkmal nach Art. 1 Abs. 2 DSchG darstellen, zu den Baudenkmälern. Auf Art. 66 Abs. 3 Satz 2 BayBO wird ausdrücklich hingewiesen. Die Befreiung der Instandsetzungsmaßnahmen von der Genehmigungspflicht nach Art. 66 Abs. 5 BayBO lässt die Erlaubnispflicht nach Art. 6 DSchG unberührt.

Das Landesamt für Denkmalpflege braucht - unbeschadet der Nummer 11.2 - nicht beteiligt zu werden,
- wenn das Vorhaben den Festsetzungen eines Bebauungsplans im Sinn des § 30 BBauG entspricht und das Landesamt für Denkmalpflege an der Aufstellung des Bebauungsplans beteiligt gewesen ist; das Landesamt ist jedoch auch in diesem Fall anzuhören, wenn es möglich erscheint, dass die Baugenehmigung nach Art. 74 Abs. 1 BayBO, Art. 6 Abs. 3 in Verbindung mit Absatz 2 DSchG versagt oder unter einschlägigen Nebenbestimmungen erteilt wird; das ist insbesondere dann der Fall, wenn durch die äußere Gestaltung des Vorhabens eine Beeinträchtigung von Baudenkmälern möglich erscheint, oder wenn die Beseitigung oder Änderung eines Baudenkmals beantragt wird,
- wenn es sich um eine Maßnahme innerhalb eines Ensembles handelt, die kein einzelnes Baudenkmal (Art. 1 Abs. 2 DSchG) betrifft und eine Beeinträchtigung des Ensembles ausgeschlossen ist, so z.B. bei Änderungen im Innern von Gebäuden, die keine Baudenkmäler sind.

Vor unkontrollierten Beeinträchtigungen durch Veränderungen in ihrer Umgebung sind Baudenkmäler durch Art. 6 Abs. 1 und 2 DSchG geschützt.

14.2

Bauanträge, bei denen das Landesamt für Denkmalpflege zu beteiligen ist, sind vorab auf ihre Vereinbarkeit mit den Vorschriften der Baugesetze zu überprüfen, sofern dies nicht zu erheblichen Verzögerungen führt. Steht aufgrund dieser Vorprüfung fest, dass der Bauantrag abzulehnen ist, wird sich regelmäßig die Beteiligung des Landesamts für Denkmalpflege erübrigen. Der Ablehnungsbescheid ist entsprechend baurechtlich zu begründen. Es wird in der Regel zweckmäßig sein, dem Bauantrag, der dem Landesamt für Denkmalpflege zugeleitet wird, eine Stellungnahme über die baurechtliche Lage beizufügen.

Ist das Landesamt für Denkmalpflege zu beteiligen, wird zur Beschleunigung des Verfahrens häufig eine weitere Ausfertigung der Bauvorlagen zu verlangen sein (§ 1 Abs. 2 Satz 2 BauVerfV). Im Lageplan (§ 1 Abs. 1 Nr. 1, § 2 Abs. 2 BauVerfV) sollen die vorhandenen Baudenkmäler (Einzelbaudenkmäler oder Ensembles), auch diejenigen in der Nähe des Baugrundstücks, besonders gekennzeichnet werden. Ist in Genehmigungsverfahren für Baudenkmäler oder für Anlagen in der Nähe von Baudenkmälern (vgl. Art. 6 Abs. 1 DSchG) der weitere Umgriff um die zur Genehmigung anstehende bauliche Anlage von Bedeutung, so wird die Bauaufsichtsbehörde in der Regel an den Lageplan die erhöhten Anforderungen nach § 2 Abs. 1 Satz 2 BauVorlV stellen. Soweit es für die Beurteilung der Genehmigungsfähigkeit erforderlich ist, sind Bestandspläne des Denkmals zu verlangen. Bei Maßnahmen an Baudenkmälern oder in der Nähe von Baudenkmälern werden oft Fotos über den Zustand des Objekts und seiner Umgebung zur Beschleunigung des Verfahrens beitragen. Gibt das Landesamt für Denkmalpflege die erbetene Stellungnahme nicht innerhalb von zwei Monaten ab, so kann davon ausgegangen werden, dass es gegen die beantragte Maßnahme keine Einwendungen erhebt. Das gilt nicht, soweit das Landesamt für Denkmalpflege unter Angabe von Gründen Fristverlängerung erbeten hat.

14.3

Will die Bauaufsichtsbehörde bei der Baugenehmigung von der Stellungnahme des Landesamts für Denkmalpflege abweichen, so hat sie das Landesamt für Denkmalpflege unverzüglich davon zu unterrichten. Besitzt das Kulturdenkmal eine für das ganze Land oder einzelne Landesteile herausragende Bedeutung, kann das Landesamt für Denkmalpflege innerhalb eines Monats die Regierung um eine Entscheidung anrufen. Die Regierung hat innerhalb von zwei Monaten zu entscheiden. In der Baugenehmigung ist gegebenenfalls auf das fehlende Einvernehmen mit dem Landesamt für Denkmalpflege und die negativen Rechtsfolgen nach § 82 i und § 82 k der Einkommensteuer-Durchführungsverordnung und im Förderungsverfahren hinzuweisen.

14.4

Ist für ein Vorhaben auch die stiftungsaufsichtliche Genehmigung nach Art. 31 Abs. 1 Nr. 4 des Stiftungsgesetzes erforderlich, so ist es in der Regel zweckmäßig, über den Bauantrag erst zu entscheiden, wenn feststeht, dass die stiftungsaufsichtliche Genehmigung erteilt wird.

14.5

Ist für Abgrabungen, durch die Bodendenkmäler betroffen werden können, eine denkmalschutzrechtliche Erlaubnis erforderlich, so darf eine zugleich benötigte Baugenehmigung erst erteilt werden, wenn diese Erlaubnis vorliegt.

14.6

Dem Landesamt für Denkmalpflege ist ein Abdruck der Baugenehmigung zu übersenden.

14.7

Die Regelungen nach den Nummern 14.1 bis 14.6 gelten auch, wenn ein Vorbescheid (Art. 75 BayBO) beantragt wird, sowie bei der Erteilung einer Teilbaugenehmigung (Art. 76 BayBO). Entsprechendes gilt für das Zustimmungsverfahren (Art. 86 BayBO).

15. Bodenverkehrsgenehmigungsverfahren

Das Landesamt für Denkmalpflege ist zu beteiligen, wenn Baudenkmalgrundstücke von der Teilung des Grundstücks betroffen werden oder Baudenkmäler in der Nähe des von der Teilung betroffenen Grundstücks liegen und es möglich erscheint, dass
– im Fall des § 19 Abs. 1 Nr. 2 BBauG - Teilung innerhalb der im Zusammenhang bebauten Ortsteile - infolge der Teilung ein Grundstück entstehen würde, auf dem die mit der Teilung bezweckte Nutzung unter dem Gesichtspunkt des Schutzes von Baudenkmälern unzulässig wäre,
– im Fall von § 19 Abs. 1 Nr. 3 Alternative 3 BBauG - Teilung im Außenbereich zum Zweck der Bebauung - oder von § 19 Abs. 1 Nr. 3 Alternative 4 BBauG - Teilung im Außenbereich zur Vorbereitung einer Bebauung - die Teilung oder die mit ihr bezweckte Nutzung mit einer geordneten städtebaulichen Entwicklung unter dem Gesichtspunkt des Schutzes von Baudenkmälern nicht vereinbar wäre, oder die Teilung eine aus diesem Grund unzulässige Bebauung vorbereiten soll,
– im Fall des § 19 Abs. 1 Nr. 4 BBauG - räumlicher Geltungsbereich einer Veränderungssperre - überwiegende Belange des Denkmalschutzes der Zulassung einer Ausnahme nach § 14 Abs. 2 Satz 1 BBauG entgegenstehen.

Im Hinblick auf § 19 Abs. 3 Satz 3 BBauG unterrichtet die für die Entscheidung über den Antrag auf Teilungsgenehmigung zuständige Behörde das Landesamt für Denkmalpflege unverzüglich von den einschlägigen Anträgen unter Angabe des Grundstücks und, falls bekannt, der beabsichtigten Nutzung. Sie setzt dem Landesamt für Denkmalpflege unter Hinweis auf die Folgen des Fristablaufs eine Frist von zwei Wochen zur Äußerung; geht innerhalb dieser Frist keine Stellungnahme ein, so ist ohne diese zu entscheiden.

16. Bauleitplanverfahren

Bei der Aufstellung der Bauleitpläne sind auch die erhaltenswerten Ortsteile sowie Bauten, Straßen und Plätze von geschichtlicher, künstlerischer oder städtebaulicher Bedeutung und die Gestaltung des Orts- und Landschaftsbildes zu berücksichtigen (§ 1 Abs. 6 BBauG, vgl. auch § 10 Abs. 1 StBauFG hinsichtlich der Pflicht, Gebäude und sonstige Anlagen kenntlich zu machen, die bei der Durchführung der Sanierung ganz oder teilweise beseitigt werden müssen oder die erhalten bleiben sollen). Bei der Abwägung der öffentlichen und privaten Belange nach § 1 Abs. 7 BBauG müssen die Gemeinden beachten, dass Art. 141 Abs. 1 und 2 der Verfassung in besonderem Maße zur Berücksichtigung des Denkmalschutzes und der Denkmalpflege verpflichten. Die Bauleitplanung soll auch der Erhaltung von Ensembles erhöhte Aufmerksamkeit widmen.

Die Genehmigungsbehörde prüft, ob die Gemeinde bei der Aufstellung eines Bauleitplans ihr Planungsermessen im Rahmen der Gesetze ausgeübt und die zu berücksichtigenden Belange des Denkmalschutzes und der Denkmalpflege in die Überlegungen einbezogen und richtig gewichtet hat. Auf eine frühzeitige Beteiligung des Landesamts für Denkmalpflege im Bauleitplanverfahren ist hinzuwirken. Auf die Planungshilfen für die Bauleitplanung (Bek. vom 30.7.1982, MABl S. 517) wird hingewiesen.

17. Örtliche Bauvorschriften

Die Gemeinden können dem Anliegen des Denkmalschutzes auch durch den Erlass örtlicher Bauvorschriften nach Art. 91 BayBO - insbesondere nach Absatz 1 Nr. 2 -Rechnung tragen. Die frühzeitige Beteiligung des Landesamts für Denkmalpflege ist anzustreben.

18. Anordnung von Baumaßnahmen, Nutzungs-, Abbruch- und Erhaltungsgeboten nach dem Bundesbaugesetz; Anordnungen nach Art. 63 Abs. 5 und 6, Art. 82 BayBO; Anordnungen nach Art. 4, 15 Abs. 3 DSchG

Für das Verfahren gelten die oben genannten allgemeinen Verfahrensregelungen und die Grundsätze für das baurechtliche Genehmigungsverfahren entsprechend. Die Erhaltungssatzung nach § 39 h BBauG ist inzwischen von manchen Gemeinden mit Erfolg zur Erhaltung des Stadtbilds und der Stadtstruktur eingesetzt worden. Sie erlaubt über den Schutz von Einzeldenkmälern hinaus einen flächenhaften Schutz von Bauquartieren. Auch das Instandsetzungs- und Modernisierungsgebot kann für denkmalschützerische Aufgaben angewendet werden.

Bei dem Erlass von Abbruch- oder Beseitigungsgeboten für Denkmäler oder Teilen von ihnen gilt für die Beteiligung des Landesamts für Denkmalpflege das zum Baugenehmigungsverfahren Ausgeführte entsprechend. Das gleiche gilt für derartige Maßnahmen in der Nähe von Denkmälern und innerhalb oder in der Nähe von Ensembles. Anordnungen nach Art. 4 DSchG zu erlassen, liegt im pflichtgemäßen Ermessen der unteren Denkmalschutzbehörde. Das Landesamt für Denkmalpflege kann Anregungen geben.

19. Verfahren nach dem Städtebauförderungsgesetz

Das Landesamt für Denkmalpflege ist auch im Sanierungsverfahren nach dem Städtebauförderungsgesetz bei der Durchführung vorbereitender Untersuchungen (§ 4 Abs. 4 StBauFG) zu beteiligen. Die Genehmigung über die förmliche Festlegung des Sanierungsgebiets nach § 5 Abs. 2 StBauFG darf nur erteilt werden, wenn das Landesamt für Denkmalpflege bei den vorbereitenden Untersuchungen ausreichend beteiligt worden ist. Bei der Neugestaltung des förmlich festgelegten Sanierungsgebiets durch Bebauungspläne im Verfahren nach dem Städtebauförderungsgesetz ist auf die Erhaltung von Bauten, Straßen, Plätzen oder Ortsteilen von geschichtlicher, künstlerischer oder städtebaulicher Bedeutung Rücksicht zu nehmen; u. a. bleiben landesrechtliche Vorschriften über den Schutz und die Erhaltung von Baudenkmälern unberührt (§ 10 Abs. 1 Satz 2 StBauFG).

20. Planfeststellungsverfahren

Der Konzentrationswirkung der Planfeststellung, z.B. nach § 18 b Abs. 1 FStrG, Art. 38 Abs. 1 BayStrWG in Verbindung mit Art. 75 Abs. 1 BayVwVfG, § 31 Abs. 1 WHG in Verbindung mit Art. 83 Abs. 1 BayWG und Art. 75 Abs. 1 BayVwVfG, § 21 Abs. 1 WaStrG, § 9 Abs. 1 LuftVG, entspricht im Planfeststellungsverfahren die umfassende Beteiligung aller betroffenen oder zuständigen Behörden. Im Planfeststellungsverfahren sind deshalb auch die denkmalschutzrechtlichen Belange zu würdigen. Die planende Behörde soll schon in einem frühen Verfahrensstadium mit dem Landesamt für Denkmalpflege Kontakt aufnehmen und es über die Planungen unterrichten.

Werden Bau- oder Bodendenkmalgrundstücke von dem Vorhaben betroffen, so hat die planende Behörde dem Landesamt für Denkmalpflege bei der Ausarbeitung von Plänen für das Planfeststellungsverfahren eine Übersichtskarte im Maßstab 1 : 25000 (wenn vorhanden auch 1 : 5000) zu übersenden,

D2.I.1c VwV Vollzug DSchG

aus der die Planung ersichtlich ist. Im Planfeststellungsverfahren holt die Planfeststellungsbehörde auch die Stellungnahme des Landesamts für Denkmalpflege ein, benachrichtigt es vom Erörterungstermin und übersendet ihm den Planfeststellungsbeschluss.

Bei Maßnahmen, die nicht planfeststellungspflichtig sind oder nur in geringem Umfang Grund und Boden beanspruchen - vor allem Hochbaumaßnahmen -, besteht die Unterrichtungspflicht im Sinn des Satzes 1 in Grabungsschutzgebieten (Art. 7 Abs. 2 DSchG) uneingeschränkt, sonst nur, wenn die planende Behörde weiß oder vermutet oder den Umständen nach annehmen muss, dass sich auf dem in Aussicht genommenen Grundstück Bodendenkmäler oder sonstige Denkmäler befinden.

Mit dieser Unterrichtung soll dem Landesamt für Denkmalpflege Gelegenheit gegeben werden, nach Möglichkeit innerhalb von zwei Monaten zu prüfen und mitzuteilen, ob Bodendenkmäler berührt werden, gegebenenfalls Vorschläge für eine räumliche Verlegung oder zeitliche Verschiebung der Maßnahme zu unterbreiten oder die Bergung der Bodendenkmäler einzuleiten.

21. Flurbereinigung und Dorferneuerung

Auf die Gemeinsame Bekanntmachung der Staatsministerien des Innern, für Unterricht und Kultus und für Ernährung, Landwirtschaft und Forsten vom 6. Juni 1978 (MABl 1979 S. 11, LMBl S. 204) über Flurbereinigung und Denkmalpflege und auf die Dorferneuerungsrichtlinien vom 1. Oktober 1983 (LMBl S. 275) wird hingewiesen.

22. Verfahren zur Erhaltung von Bodendenkmälern im Sinn des Art. 1 Abs. 4 DSchG

22.1

Erlaubnisverfahren

Das Erlaubnisverfahren richtet sich nach Art. 15 Abs. 1 und 2 DSchG; es ist das gleiche wie das unter Nr. 13 Dargelegte. Der Antrag auf Erteilung einer Erlaubnis zur Durchführung von Maßnahmen nach Art. 7 Abs. 1 oder 2 DSchG, die nicht nach Art. 7 Abs. 3 DSchG erlaubnisfrei sind, ist bei der Gemeinde einzureichen, die den Antrag der Unteren Denkmalschutzbehörde vorlegt. Die Untere Denkmalschutzbehörde beteiligt den zuständigen Heimatpfleger und das Landesamt für Denkmalpflege, gegebenenfalls erneut die Gemeinde. Sollen Grabungen oder Erdarbeiten in Höhlen vorgenommen werden, so hat die Untere Denkmalschutzbehörde außerdem das Geologische Landesamt und das Bergamt zu hören. Das Erlaubnisverfahren findet auch statt, wenn Maßnahmen nach Art. 7 Abs. 4 DSchG durchgeführt werden sollen, sofern nicht für diese Maßnahmen eine Baugenehmigung erforderlich ist. Wegen der Berücksichtigung von Bodendenkmälern in Planfeststellungsverfahren vgl. Nummer 20.

22.2

Genehmigungsverfahren

Für Grabungen auf fremden Grundstücken ist neben der Erlaubnis eine Genehmigung zur Inanspruchnahme des fremden Eigentums nach Art. 7 Abs. 5 DSchG erforderlich. Voraussetzung ist ein Antrag desjenigen, der die Grabungen durchführen will. Die Gemeinde und das Landesamt für Denkmalpflege werden in gleicher Weise beteiligt wie im Erlaubnisverfahren (Art. 15 Abs. 1 und 2 DSchG). Auch die Vorlagepflicht ist die gleiche wie im Erlaubnisverfahren. Eine Grabung auf einem fremden Grundstück darf nur dann zugelassen werden, wenn das Landesamt für Denkmalpflege zuvor festgestellt hat, dass ein besonderes öffentliches Interesse an der Grabung besteht. Die Entscheidung der unteren Denkmalschutzbehörde soll einen Ausspruch über die Entschädigungspflicht enthalten.

22.3

Verfahren bei Anzeigen

Wird der Fund von Bodendenkmälern angezeigt (Art. 8 Abs. 1 DSchG), so hat die Untere Denkmalschutzbehörde, sofern nicht Art. 8 Abs. 3 DSchG anwendbar ist, sicherzustellen, dass die aufgefundenen Gegenstände und der Fundort bis zum Ablauf von einer Woche unverändert belassen werden (Art. 8 Abs. 2 DSchG). Außerdem hat die Untere Denkmalschutzbehörde sofort das Landesamt für

Denkmalpflege - möglichst fernmündlich - unter Angabe des Fundorts und unter möglichst genauer Beschreibung der aufgefundenen Gegenstände um Stellungnahme zu bitten, ob die Gegenstände vor Ablauf der Wochenfrist freigegeben werden sollen, ob die Fortsetzung der Arbeiten gestattet werden kann oder ob eine Entscheidung nach Art. 8 Abs. 4 DSchG ergehen soll. Eine solche Entscheidung muss immer dann ergehen, wenn die aufgefundenen Gegenstände oder der Fundort länger als eine Woche nach Erstattung der Anzeige unverändert belassen werden sollen. Ferner hat die untere Denkmalschutzbehörde dem zuständigen Heimatpfleger mitzuteilen, innerhalb welcher Frist er sich zu den Fragen der Freigabe der Gegenstände, der Fortsetzung der Arbeiten und zur Durchführung weiterer Maßnahmen (Art. 8 Abs. 4 DSchG) äußern kann (Art. 13 Abs. 1 Satz 2 DSchG). Art. 8 DSchG gilt auch bei baurechtlich genehmigten Vorhaben.

22.4

Auswertung von Funden
Am Verfahren nach Art. 9 DSchG sind Gemeinde und Heimatpfleger nicht beteiligt. Die Entscheidung der Unteren Denkmalschutzbehörde ergeht aufgrund einer Anregung des Landesamts für Denkmalpflege.

22.5

Denkmäler, die gottesdienstlichen Zwecken dienen
Das Verfahren nach den Nummern 22.1 bis 22.4 ist auch durchzuführen, wenn durch Entscheidungen über Bodendenkmäler Denkmäler betroffen sind, die unmittelbar gottesdienstlichen Zwecken dienen (Art. 26 Abs. 2 DSchG).

22.6

Eigentumsverhältnisse
Bei Bodenaltertümern wird es sich gelegentlich um Schatzfunde nach § 984 BGB handeln. Nach dieser Vorschrift erwirbt das Eigentum an dem Fund je zur Hälfte der Grundstückseigentümer und der Finder. Entdecker ist auch bei vergebenen Bauarbeiten der Bauherr.

23. Erhaltung von eingetragenen beweglichen Denkmälern

Das Erlaubnisverfahren für die in Art. 10 Abs. 1 DSchG aufgeführten Maßnahmen an beweglichen Denkmälern, die nach Art. 2 Abs. 2 DSchG in die Denkmalliste eingetragen sind, richtet sich nach Art. 15 Abs. 1 und 2 DSchG. Die Einschaltung des Heimatpflegers ist nur erforderlich, wenn sein Aufgabenbereich betroffen ist.

24. Besonderheiten für Baudenkmäler zu gottesdienstlichen Zwecken

Sollen Entscheidungen getroffen werden, die sich auf Baudenkmäler beziehen, die unmittelbar gottesdienstlichen Zwecken der Kirchen oder anerkannten Religionsgemeinschaften dienen, hat die Untere Denkmalschutzbehörde nach Art. 26 Abs. 2 Satz 2 DSchG der zuständigen kirchlichen Oberbehörde, also dem zuständigen Ordinariat oder dem Evangelisch-Lutherischen Landeskirchenrat, Gelegenheit zu geben, etwa zu berücksichtigende kirchliche Belange festzustellen. Wegen der Einzelheiten des Verfahrens wird die Bauaufsichts- und Denkmalschutzbehörden auf das KMS vom 16. Mai 1979 Nr. IV/2-7/34849 hingewiesen.
Die sich aus der Reform der Liturgie der römisch-katholischen Kirche ergebenden Forderungen sind enthalten in Art. 253 bis 280 der Institution Generalis Missalis Romani (amtliche deutsche Übersetzung im Messbuch - Für die Bistümer des deutschen Sprachgebrauchs - authentische Ausgabe I - allgemeine Einführung S. 19* bis 69*) und in dem Rundschreiben der Heiligen Kongregation für den Klerus an

die Vorsitzenden der Bischofskonferenzen für die Sorge um die kunstgeschichtlichen Werte der Kirche vom 11. April 1971 (abgedruckt im Archiv für katholisches Kirchenrecht 140, 1971, 173 bis 175; nichtamtliche deutsche Übersetzung im Pfarramtsblatt 1972 S. 336-338). Das Entscheidungsrecht der kirchlichen Oberbehörden erstreckt sich nicht auf baurechtliche Fragen.

25. Sonstige Bestimmungen

25.1

Auf die Vorschriften des Kommunal- und Stiftungsrechts über die Genehmigungspflicht bestimmter Vorgänge (Art. 75 der Gemeindeordnung, Art. 69 der Landkreisordnung, Art. 67 der Bezirksordnung, Art. 31 Abs. 1 Nr. 4, Art. 31 Abs. 4 und Art. 38 Abs. 1 des Stiftungsgesetzes) wird hingewiesen.

25.2

Die Gemeinsame Bekanntmachung der Staatsministerien des Innern und für Unterricht und Kultus vom 26. November/24. September 1973 (MABl S. 1039, KMBl 1974 S. 222), geändert durch Gemeinsame Bekanntmachung vom 18. Oktober 1976 (MABl S. 870, KMBl I S. 624) wird aufgehoben.

Denkmalpflegerische Maßnahmen an kirchlichen Gebäuden im Zusammenhang mit der Durchführung von Arbeiten, die der staatlichen Baulast unterfallen[1]

Vom 03. Mai 1990 (KWMBl. I 1990 S. 153)
(BayVV Gliederungsnummer 2242-WK)

Gemeinsame Bekanntmachung der Bayerischen Staatsministerien der Finanzen, des Innern, für Unterricht und Kultus und für Wissenschaft und Kunst[2] vom 3. Mai 1990 Az.: D/4-K 4640-7c/25 266

Bei der Finanzierung von denkmalpflegerischen Maßnahmen an kirchlichen Gebäuden, die Baudenkmäler sind, im Zusammenhang mit der Durchführung von Arbeiten, die der staatlichen Baulast unterfallen, wird nach Absprache zwischen den Staatsministerien der Finanzen, des Innern, für Unterricht und Kultus und für Wissenschaft und Kunst künftig wie folgt verfahren:

1. Der Freistaat Bayern trägt - ohne Anerkennung einer Rechtspflicht - nach Maßgabe des Einzelfalls bis zu 50 v. H. der Kosten für die aus denkmalpflegerischen Gründen notwendige Instandsetzung von Fresken, Stuck, Grabdenkmälern, Altären (Altartisch mit Aufbau), Gestühl, Kanzel, Taufstein und Beichtstühlen, soweit diese fest eingebaut sind. Satz 1 gilt nicht, soweit für ein bestimmtes kirchliches Gebäude aufgrund besonderer baulastrechtlicher Regelungen, insbesondere eines Vertrags oder eines Baulasttitels, etwas anderes bestimmt ist. Ein darüber hinausgehender Einsatz staatlicher Mittel der Denkmalpflege (Entschädigungsfonds des Staatsministeriums für Wissenschaft und Kunst, Zuschussmittel des Landesamts für Denkmalpflege) kommt angesichts des vom Freistaat Bayern getragenen Aufwands nicht in Betracht.
2. Zur Finanzierung der erwähnten - ohne Anerkennung einer Rechtspflicht erfolgenden - zusätzlichen staatlichen Leistungen werden aus dem Haushalt des Staatsministeriums für Unterricht und Kultus bei Kap. 05 53 Tit. 791 01 bis zu *5 Mio. DM*[3] jährlich bereitgestellt. Außerdem steht aus dem Haushalt des Staatsministeriums für Wissenschaft und Kunst für diesen Zweck aus Kap. 15 74 TG 75 1 Mio. DM zur Verfügung. Die Zuweisung der Mittel erfolgt in jedem Falle bei Kap. 15 74 TG 75.
3. Die zur Finanzierung des denkmalpflegerischen Mehraufwands notwendigen, im Einzelplan 05 Kap. 05 53 Tit. 791 01 und Einzelplan 15 Kap. 15 74 TG 75 ausgewiesenen Mittel werden von den Landbauämtern über die Regierungen beim Staatsministerium für Unterricht und Kultus beantragt. Den Anträgen sind vollständige Kosten- und Finanzierungspläne beizufügen.
4. Das Staatsministerium für Unterricht und Kultus weist die bei Kap. 05 53 Tit. 791 01 bis zu *5 Mio. DM*[3] jährlich zur Verfügung stehenden Mittel dem Staatsministerium für Wissenschaft und Kunst zu, das über die Mittelvergabe einvernehmlich mit dem Staatsministerium für Unterricht und Kultus entscheidet. Die Mittelbewilligung erfolgt durch das Staatsministerium für Wissenschaft und Kunst im Einvernehmen mit dem Staatsministerium für Unterricht und Kultus.
5. Das Staatsministerium für Wissenschaft und Kunst erlässt den Bewilligungsbescheid gegenüber dem Eigentümer/Maßnahmeträger. Abdruck erhalten das Staatsministerium für Unterricht und Kultus, die Regierung, das Landesamt für Denkmalpflege, das Landbauamt sowie die zuständige Diözese bzw. die Landeskirche. Gleichzeitig werden die bewilligten Mittel der Regierung zur Bewirtschaftung zugewiesen.
6. Die denkmalpflegerischen Arbeiten, die im Rahmen der jeweiligen staatlichen Baupflichtmaßnahme anfallen, werden von den Landbauämtern abgewickelt. Sie holen die ggf. erforderlichen gesetzlichen Genehmigungen und Erlaubnisse, z.B. die Erlaubnis nach dem Denkmalschutzgesetz, ein. Sie stellen den denkmalpflegerischen Mehraufwand einvernehmlich mit dem Landesamt für Denkmalpflege und dem kirchlichen Rechtsträger fest. Sie beteiligen das Landesamt für Denkmalpflege im Rahmen des Erlaubnisverfahrens.

---

1) Fortgeltung ab 1.1.2016 gem. VwVWBek v. 31.5.2016 (AllMBl. S. 1555).
2) **Amtl. Anm.:** jetzt: Bayerisches Staatsministerium für Bildung und Kultus, Wissenschaft und Kunst
3) **Amtl. Anm.:** entspricht 2.556.459,40 €

7. Die Landbauämter bewirtschaften die für die Durchführung der Maßnahmen benötigten finanziellen Mittel und rechnen diese ab. Sie legen nach Beendigung der Arbeiten den Regierungen und dem kirchlichen Rechtsträger einen Abschlußbericht vor.

Grundsätze für die Inventarisation der Kunst- und Geschichtsdenkmäler Bayerns[1]

Vom 06. September 1990 (KWMBl. I 1990 S. 324)
(BayVV Gliederungsnummer 2242-WK)

Bekanntmachung des Bayerischen Staatsministeriums für Wissenschaft und Kunst[2] vom 6. September 1990 Az.: D/4-K 4603-7c/34 872

I. Vorbemerkung

Die von Georg Hager entwickelten bayerischen Grundsätze der Inventarisation wurden im Ministerialblatt für Kirchen- und Schulangelegenheiten vom 9. April 1904 veröffentlicht und zuletzt 1971 überarbeitet.

Nach den Grundsätzen von 1904 sind inzwischen 103 Bände der Reihe „Die Kunstdenkmäler von Bayern" (Großinventare) bearbeitet worden, darunter neun Bände für den ehemaligen bayerischen Regierungsbezirk Pfalz. Zuletzt ist 1972 der Band „Landkreis Dillingen a. d. Donau" erschienen. Einschließlich der seit 1892 herausgegebenen Oberbayern-Hefte liegen die nicht mehr greifbaren Bände dieser Reihe nun auch wieder in dem 1982/84 hergestellten Reprint des Oldenbourg-Verlages vor. Die großen Lücken der Inventarisation in Mittelfranken, Oberfranken und Schwaben wurden durch die seit 1958 erschienenen 34 Bände der Reihe „Bayerische Kunstdenkmale" (Kurzinventare) geschlossen, die damit ihr Ziel erreicht hat und nicht weitergeführt wird.

Auf den Ergebnissen der Großinventare wie der Kurzinventare fußt die moderne Erfassung der bayerischen Denkmäler in Listen. Die Listenerfassung geht streng von der Definition des Denkmals nach Art. 1 Denkmalschutzgesetz aus. Danach wurden seit dem Erlass des Bayerischen Denkmalschutzgesetzes, von 1973 die ca. 110.000 Baudenkmäler und ca. 10.000 archäologischen Geländedenkmäler in den Denkmallisten erfasst und einschließlich der Beschreibung der Ensembles in den Bänden I-VII der Reihe „Denkmäler in Bayern" 1985/86 veröffentlicht.

Die wissenschaftliche Erfassung der archäologischen Geländedenkmäler (obertägige Bodendenkmäler) in der Reihe B der „Materialhefte zur bayerischen Vorgeschichte" konnte noch nicht abgeschlossen werden. Mit der Inventarisation der Bodendenkmäler durch die Abteilung archäologische Denkmalpflege des Landesamtes ist ein neuer Anfang gemacht worden.

Dass die „klassische" Inventarisation der Bau- und Kunstdenkmäler seit bald zwei Jahrzehnten stagnierte, hängt mit der durch das Denkmalschutzgesetz notwendigen Listenerfassung zusammen. Diese Erfassung erfolgte auf der Grundlage des neu definierten Denkmalbegriffs, wie er heute auch der Inventarisation zugrunde gelegt wird, allerdings mit der Maßgabe, dass auch untergegangene oder nur überlieferungsgeschichtlich bedeutende Monumente Berücksichtigung finden können. Die Weiterführung der Inventarisation soll nicht nur die bisher mit den begrenzten Mitteln der Kurzinventare bearbeiteten Lücken in Oberfranken, Mittelfranken und Schwaben schließen, sondern auch als Neubeginn in Oberbayern erfolgen.

Nachstehend werden die vom Landesamt für Denkmalpflege unter Beteiligung des Landesdenkmalrats erarbeiteten Grundsätze für die Inventarisation der Kunst- und Geschichtsdenkmäler Bayerns neu veröffentlicht. Sie lösen die am 9. April 1904 im Ministerialblatt für Kirchen- und Schulangelegenheiten veröffentlichten Grundsätze für die Inventarisation der Kunstdenkmäler Bayerns ab.

II. Grundsätze für die Inventarisation der Kunst- und Geschichtsdenkmäler Bayerns

1. Allgemeine Grundsätze

Gemäß Art. 12 Abs. 2 Satz 3 Nr. 3 des Gesetzes zum Schutz und zur Pflege der Denkmäler (Denkmalschutzgesetz) hat das Landesamt für Denkmalpflege die Aufgabe, die „Inventare" zu erstellen und

---
1) Fortgeltung ab 1.1.2016 gem. VwVWBek v. 31.5.2016 (AllMBl. S. 1555).
2) **Amtl. Anm.:** jetzt: Bayerisches Staatsministerium für Bildung und Kultus, Wissenschaft und Kunst

D2.I.1e VwV Grundsätze für die Inventarisation

fortzuführen. Unter Inventarisation versteht man die vollständige und präzise Erfassung der Denkmäler mit wissenschaftlichen Methoden und ihre Beschreibung durch Text, Abbildungen, Pläne usw. aufgrund allgemeiner oder auf den konkreten Einzelfall bezogener wissenschaftlicher Untersuchungen. Der materielle Bestand der aus der Geschichte ererbten Gegenstände ist ebenso zu erforschen und darzustellen wie die Traditionen, die schriftlich, bildlich oder auch mündlich zu diesen Gegenständen fassbar sind.

Die Inventarisation der Kunst- und Geschichtsdenkmäler hat als fundamentale Bestandserfassung die Denkmäler bewusst zu machen und damit ihre Erhaltung zu ermöglichen. Gegenstände werden als Denkmäler bewusst, wenn sich ihre geschichtlichen Aussagen und Überlieferungen mit ihrer anschaulichen Erscheinung so verbinden lässt, dass ihre Bedeutung erkennbar wird. Inventarisation eröffnet damit eine Chance, die Liebe zur monumentalen Überlieferung, zu den Denkmälern zu wecken. Sie ist Grundlage des Denkmalschutzes und eine Voraussetzung für die praktische Bau- und Kunstdenkmalpflege.

Mit Ausnahme der in einer eigenen Reihe zu inventarisierenden Bodendenkmäler sind in der Reihe „Die Kunstdenkmäler von Bayern" alle Denkmäler gemäß der Definition des Art. 1 Abs. 1 Denkmalschutzgesetz aufzunehmen, die gemäß Art. 3 Abs. 1 Denkmalschutzgesetz geschützt sind. Der im Reihentitel beibehaltene Begriff „Kunstdenkmal" ist also im weitesten Sinn zu verstehen. Selbstverständlich werden nicht nur kirchliche und profane Kunstdenkmäler, sondern sämtliche Gattungen von Geschichtsdenkmälern aufgenommen. Dabei ist Vollständigkeit des Inventars anzustreben. Öffentliche Sammlungen werden im Allgemeinen nicht einbezogen und hier nur unter Umständen auf das in Zusammenhang mit den Denkmälern der Region besonders Wichtige hingewiesen. Auch abgegangene Baudenkmäler sind Gegenstand der Darstellung, soweit sie zum Verständnis der erhaltenen Baudenkmäler beitragen; somit sind Hinweise auf zerstörte, nicht mehr bestehende Objekte, zum Beispiel Klöster, Kirchen, Burgen und Befestigungsanlagen, unter Angabe der Literatur und etwaiger alter Abbildungen geboten.

Im Allgemeinen gilt für die Bearbeitung der Grundsatz: Das Inventar ist nicht eine rein beschreibende Aufzählung, sondern eine wissenschaftliche Quellensammlung. Die Arbeit beruht auf gewissenhafter - wenn möglich selbständiger - wissenschaftlicher Untersuchung. Eine weit ausholende Untersuchung und eine erschöpfende Darstellung können nicht beabsichtigt sein, doch muss das Inventar für weitere Untersuchungen die nötige Orientierung und die entsprechenden Anhaltspunkte bieten. Dabei erfolgt die Inventarisation im Benehmen mit den betroffenen Kommunen.

2.
Anordnung des Stoffes

Die Bearbeitung wie die Veröffentlichung erfolgt nach Regierungsbezirken, innerhalb dieser nach Landkreisen bzw. Städten. Innerhalb der Landkreise hält sich das Inventar an die alphabetische Folge der Ortsnamen. Bei größeren Städten und Landkreisen kann mit Rücksicht auf die Handlichkeit des Inventars und die Möglichkeiten der Bearbeitung eine Teilung in mehrere Bände erfolgen, wobei die topographische Abgrenzung nach Möglichkeit die geschichtlichen Strukturen berücksichtigen sollte. Grundeinheit der Darstellung ist jeweils der durch seine Geschichte identifizierte Ort.

Der Ort wird zunächst als eine Gesamtheit ins Auge gefasst und in seiner historisch gewachsenen Struktur beschrieben. Innerhalb des Ortes werden an erster Stelle die kirchlichen, dann die profanen Denkmäler behandelt. Sind mehrere Kirchen an einem Ort, so geht derjenige Bau voraus, mit welchem die Anfänge und die älteste Geschichte des Ortes verknüpft ist, also in der Regel die Hauptkirche. Bauliche Annexe, wie Kreuzgänge, Klostergebäude, Kapellen bei einer Kirche werden in dem Zusammenhang, zu dem sie gehören, behandelt. Bei den profanen Denkmälern wird zunächst die Ortsbefestigung dargestellt. Dann folgen die öffentlichen Gebäude, geordnet nach ihrer Bedeutung, dann die Privatbauten, dann die öffentlichen Denkmäler wie Brunnen, Flurdenkmäler usw.

Bei der jedem Band vorangestellten historischen Einleitung handelt es sich nicht etwa um eine möglichst umfassende Darstellung der Lokalgeschichte, sondern um die Darstellung einer denkmalkundlichen Gesamtstruktur vor dem Hintergrund der jeweiligen territorialgeschichtlichen Entwicklung unter Berücksichtigung der Siedlungsverhältnisse, der Handels- und Verkehrsverhältnisse usw., wobei auch die den äußeren Rahmen des Bandes bildende moderne Kreis- bzw. Gemeindeeinteilung in ihrem

Verhältnis zu den in den Denkmälern zum Ausdruck kommenden, geschichtlichen Zusammenhängen besonders zu würdigen ist.

3.
Quellennachweise

Das Denkmälerinventar ist weder ein Repertorium von Schriftquellen noch eine Regestensammlung. Die Fragestellungen vor dem Objekt bestimmen, welche Quellen aufgesucht werden; nur in seltenen Fällen werden ganze Quellenkomplexe systematisch durchzusehen sein. Besondere Aufmerksamkeit ist der Erschließung der Bildquellen (alte Ansichten und Pläne, vor allem auch alte Stadtpläne) zuzuwenden. Pläne von Baudenkmälern sind auszuwerten und zu verzeichnen, insoweit sie wesentliche Vorgänge oder Zustände dokumentieren. Das gleiche gilt von alten Darstellungen durch Malerei, Graphik, Photographie.

Der Text des Inventars wird also begleitet von einem Apparat aus Zusammenstellungen und Anmerkungen. Der Behandlung des Gegenstandes selbst wird der listenmäßige Nachweis der Schrift- und Bildquellen sowie der Literatur vorangestellt; beides wird jeweils chronologisch, die Literatur nach Erscheinungsjahr, angeordnet. Bei diesen Nachweisen muss die Auffindbarkeit in Archiv und Bibliothek gewährleistet sein. Dem dienen bei den Schriftquellen die Angabe von Standort und Signatur, ebenso bei den Bildquellen, bei denen die Maße genannt werden, soweit es sich nicht um Reproduktionsgraphik handelt. Die Literatur wird nach allgemeinen bibliographischen Regeln angegeben: Verfassername, Titel, Erscheinungsort, Erscheinungsjahr. Bei Zeitschriftenveröffentlichungen folgt nach dem Titel des jeweiligen Beitrags der Titel der Zeitschrift, Jahrgangszahl, Jahr und Seiten. Für öfter zu nennende Literatur können Abkürzungen und Siglen verwendet oder auch Schlagworte angegeben werden, meist der Name des Verfassers und ein dem Titel entnommenes Schlagwort. Sämtliche Abkürzungen und Siglen sind im Abkürzungsverzeichnis aufzuführen und aufzulösen.

Soweit eine Quelle oder eine Literaturstelle unmittelbar zu einem Argument zu zitieren ist, kann dies in Anmerkungen erfolgen, welche die Seiten begleiten. Dies ist insbesondere dann der Fall, wenn auf eine abweichende Meinung oder Interpretation hinzuweisen ist.

4.
Beschreibung

Die Darstellung des einzelnen Baudenkmals beginnt mit seiner Benennung. Benannt wird das Baudenkmal wenn irgend möglich mit dem historischen Namen, der meist auch die Funktion anzeigt, welche den Denkmalcharakter mitbegründet. Bei kirchlichen Gebäuden ist möglichst der Titulus (Weihetitel) zu nennen, ferner die Konfession und die Eigenschaft der Kirche (Pfarrkirche, Filialkirche, Nebenkirche usw.).

Der Beschreibung eines Baudenkmals werden die baugeschichtlichen Angaben vorausgestellt. Vor allem bei größeren Denkmalkomplexen wird es sich empfehlen, vorab, gegebenenfalls regestenmäßig, die Überlieferung zur Baugeschichte aus den Quellen darzustellen. Die analytische und würdigende Beschreibung des Baudenkmals, auch als Quelle seiner eigenen Geschichte, beginnt dann mit einer Charakterisierung seiner Lage und seiner Gesamtgestalt, die auch durch einen Lageplan illustriert werden kann. Mit der Analyse der Gesamtgestalt wird der weitere Verlauf der Beschreibung im Einzelnen programmiert. Es empfiehlt sich hierbei, die überlieferten historischen Namen der Bauteile zu verwenden. Stehen solche Benennungen nicht zur Verfügung, so sollten den Bauteilen treffende Bezeichnungen erteilt werden, was ebenfalls in einem Planschema erläutert werden kann. In der Legende solcher Planschemata oder Lagepläne sollten Gebäudeteile (gekennzeichnet etwa durch Großbuchstaben) und Höfe (durch römische Ziffern) deutlich unterschieden werden. Ob die Beschreibung im Einzelnen dann mit der Außenerscheinung oder mit einem bestimmenden Innenraum ansetzt, wird vom Charakter des Baudenkmals und seiner Geschichte selbst nahegelegt. Wo Funktionen Raumfolgen erzeugt haben, werden diese das Nacheinander der Behandlung bestimmen, wo Komplexe oder Räume hierarchisch aufgebaut sind, wird der Text diese Hierarchie nachzeichnen. Da die Beschreibung nie Selbstzweck, sondern Bedeutungsanalyse oder doch wenigstens deren Vorbereitung ist, kann Belangloses übergangen, Bedeutung durch zusätzliche Angaben anschaulich gemacht werden.

D2.I.1e VwV Grundsätze für die Inventarisation

Die Schlüsse, welche für die Bedeutung des Denkmals aus der Verbindung von geschichtlicher Überlieferung und Befund zu ziehen sind, werden in einer Bauanalyse erfolgen, sobald die Bedeutung des Baudenkmals dies erfordert. Diese historische Bauanalyse klärt nicht nur - soweit möglich - die immanenten Entstehungsvorgänge, sondern stellt sie zugleich in den allgemeinen architektur- und kunstgeschichtlichen Zusammenhang. Die klare Darstellung dieser Zusammenhänge, die keiner Wertung bedarf, ist die Würdigung dieser Bedeutung.

Was für die Darstellung der baulichen Substanz gilt, gilt im Grunde auch für die Darstellung der Ausstattung, die historisch und inhaltlich Bestandteil des beschriebenen Bauwerks ist. Es muss allerdings bewusst bleiben und bewusst gemacht werden, dass die Trennung von baulicher Substanz und historisch zugehöriger Ausstattung zunächst lediglich die eines notwendigen Ordnungsschemas ist, welches die vorgefundene Wirklichkeit nur in Grenzfällen spiegelt. Man wird ansetzen bei den fest mit der Bausubstanz verbundenen Ausstattungskomplexen, die zwar mobilen, aber an einen Ort fixierten Ausstattungsgegenstände folgen lassen und mit den nur in bewegter Funktion erscheinenden Ausstattungsstücken schließen.

Die Beschreibung der Ausstattung und Einrichtung geht im Allgemeinen von den bei der Wirkung des Inneren am meisten mitsprechenden Teilen aus und schreitet der Übersichtlichkeit halber in der Regel in einer bestimmten Reihenfolge voran: z.B. Stukkaturen, Deckengemälde, Altäre, Sakramentshäuschen, Kanzel, Taufstein, Orgel, Chorgestühle, Beichtstühle, Skulpturen und Gemälde, die nicht in Verbindung mit Altären stehen, Glasgemälde, Epitaphien, Grabsteine, Glocken und kunstgewerbliche Gegenstände. Ausnahmen von dieser Reihenfolge können zweckdienlich sein. Bei Kirchen mit vielen Seitenkapellen zum Beispiel kann es sich empfehlen, die Ausstattung der einzelnen Kapellen zusammen zu behandeln.

Bei Teilen einer ehem. historischen Ausstattung, die nicht mehr am ursprünglichen Ort vorhanden sind, ist ebenfalls eine kurze Angabe angezeigt, gegebenenfalls mit Nachweis des jetzigen Aufbewahrungsortes und mit Beigabe einer Abbildung.

Insgesamt darf nie aus dem Auge verloren werden, dass eine wohlüberlegte wissenschaftliche Beschreibung der Denkmäler in Wort und Bild das Hauptanliegen des Inventars ist. Dabei mag die Beschreibung knapper gehalten sein, wenn sie mit der Abbildung, die auch wissenschaftliche Mitteilung ist, alles Sachliche klar darstellen kann. Bei den Beschreibungen muss ein Schema und eine unzweideutige Nomenklatur eingehalten werden, ohne dass die Individualität des Bearbeiters völlig untergehen soll.

Die Ausführlichkeit der Beschreibung bemisst sich nach der Bedeutung des Denkmals. Bei der Baubeschreibung einer Dorfkirche oder der Beschreibung eines Grabsteines können unter Umständen schon sehr kurze Angaben genügen. Im Allgemeinen muss die Beschreibung klar, übersichtlich und knapp im Ausdruck sein. Sie soll das Charakteristische des Denkmals, das künstlerisch besonders Wirksame betonen. Allein durch Art und Umfang der Beschreibung wird auf die Einschätzung des Denkmals hingewiesen. Der Frage nach dem entwerfenden und ausführenden Künstler ist mit besonderem Bedacht nachzugehen oder da, wo diese Frage zwecklos erscheinen muss, doch wenigstens die Einreihung in einen kunstgeschichtlichen Zusammenhang zu versuchen. Restaurierungen sollen erwähnt und kurz charakterisiert werden.

5.
Behandlung der Ausstattung

Unter „historischer Ausstattung" als Gegenstand der Inventarisation ist alles zu verstehen, was mit einem Bauwerk fest verbunden und damit baulich und architektonisch Teil der Bau- und Raumausstattung eines Gebäudes ist. Dies können z.B. funktionale Elemente eines Baudenkmals sein, wie Fenster, Türen, Böden, Treppen usw. oder aber auch dekorative Teile, wie Vertäfelungen und Bemalungen. Aber auch bewegliche Gegenstände können historische Ausstattungsstücke sein, wenn sie integrale Bestandteile einer historischen Raumkonzeption sind, z.B. als Teil einer Erstausstattung oder einer dieser gleichzusetzenden historisch abgeschlossenen Neuausstattung oder Umgestaltung. In allen diesen Fällen müssen die festen oder beweglichen Ausstattungsstücke eine historisch belegbare Einheit mit dem Bauwerk bilden; das bedeutet, dass die Entfernung solcher historischen Ausstattungsstücke den Denkmalcharakter und damit die historische Aussage des Baudenkmals schmälert.

Bewegliche Gegenstände, die nicht „historische Ausstattungsstücke" sind, können ebenfalls Gegenstand der Inventarisation sein, wenn sie auf Antrag des Berechtigten oder in besonders wichtigen Fällen in die Liste der beweglichen Denkmäler gemäß Art. 1 Abs. 2 Denkmalschutzgesetz aufgenommen sind oder bei denen es sich um eingetragenes Kulturgut im Sinn des Gesetzes zum Schutz deutschen Kulturguts gegen Abwanderung handelt.

Bei der Inventarisation von Kirchen als Kultraum wird auf die gottesdienstliche Zweckbestimmung besondere Rücksicht genommen. Die Aufnahme kirchlicher Gegenstände in ein Inventar darf die liturgische Zweckbestimmung nicht beeinträchtigen.

6.
Behandlung der Inschriften

Gegenstand der Inventarisation sind auch Inschriften. Daher sind Bezeichnungen wie In- und Aufschriften, Zeichen, Marken, Zahlen und Signaturen genau zu notieren, gegebenenfalls zu kopieren; Inschriften und Aufschriften allerdings nur insoweit, als sie zur Geschichte und Bedeutung des Denkmals beitragen - dies kann allerdings auch einmal von einem langen Epitaphtext gelten. Bei Jahreszahlen empfiehlt sich in der Regel die Beisetzung der aufgelösten Jahres- und Monatsdaten in Klammern; bei Angaben nach dem römischen Kalender ist sie unbedingt nötig, zum Beispiel VI. cal. Jan. MDCCV (=27. Dezember 1704). Abbildungen von Inschriften berücksichtigen Alter, Schriftart wie geschichtliche Aussagekraft.

Bauinschriften und Signaturen aus allen Epochen werden stets im Wortlaut mitgeteilt. Gibt man Grabinschriften nicht im Wortlaut wieder, so müssen im Interesse der genealogischen Forschung nicht nur das Jahr, sondern auch der Tag des Todes genannt werden.

Das Inventar wird Corpuswerke wie die „Deutschen Inschriften" und den „Deutschen Glockenatlas" nicht ersetzen, sondern diese gegebenenfalls als Quelle benutzen.

Bei den Goldschmiedearbeiten sind die Beschauzeichen und Meistermarken sorgfältig zu beachten und möglichst zu dokumentieren.

Wappen, die nicht sicher bestimmt werden können oder von der in maßgebenden gedruckten Wappenbüchern angegebenen Figuration abweichen, sind zu beschreiben.

7.
Photographien, Pläne und Karten

Abbildungen sollten in möglichst großer Zahl und in einem dem Gegenstand angemessenen Format wiedergegeben werden, nötigenfalls unter Beigabe von vergrößerten Ausschnitten. Dabei werden die kunstgeschichtlich wichtigen wie auch solche Denkmäler, in welchen sich die lokale Eigenart der Gegend widerspiegelt, berücksichtigt. Die kleinen, aber signifikanten Verschiedenheiten, die der Inventarisator zum Beispiel beim Studium gleichartiger Objekte - bei Dorfkirchen - im Grundriss, im Aufbau und in den Einzelformen findet, sollen in typischen Beispielen im Bild vorgestellt werden. Städtebaulich wichtige Gesamtsituationen wie etwa wichtige Straßenzüge sollen möglichst auch in Luftbildern dokumentiert werden. Wichtige, versteckt liegende Bauteile, wie zum Beispiel baugeschichtlich bedeutende Dachstühle, sind in den Abbildungen besonders zu berücksichtigen. Farbabbildungen sind dann zu wählen, wenn allein durch Farbwiedergabe Sachinformationen - z.B. Materialgegebenheiten - dargestellt werden können.

Grundrisse, Schnitte und Details sind möglichst getreu anzulegen und mit genauen Maßangaben (Maßleiste) zu versehen; abgebildet werden in jedem Fall Umzeichnungen. Verformungsgerechte Aufmaße sind nur in besonderen Fällen eine wissenschaftliche Basis der Inventarisation. Bei den Gesamtgrundrissen und Gesamtschnitten wird ein einheitlicher Reproduktionsmaßstab von 1:400 bzw. 1:200 angestrebt, nötigenfalls unter Verwendung von eingefalteten Blättern oder Tafeln nach einheitlichen Standardmaßen. Dabei sind die Abbildungen der Grundrisse möglichst so auszurichten, dass der obere Teil nach Norden weist. Ein Nordpfeil wird immer eingezeichnet. Die notwendigen bauanalytischen Informationen können durch Schraffuren der Schnittflächen gegeben werden. Dabei gilt dann die Regel, dass die ältesten Entstehungsperioden dunkler, die jüngeren heller erscheinen sollen.

Lagepläne werden im Maßstab 1: 1000 wiedergegeben. Bei Lageplänen von Höhenburgen ist eine Darstellung des Geländereliefs nicht zu entbehren. Die Analyse eines wichtigen, später veränderten

D2.I.1e VwV Grundsätze für die Inventarisation

Bauwerks (auch Altares usw.) kann es angezeigt erscheinen lassen, eine Rekonstruktionszeichnung des alten Bestandes beizugeben.

Alte Ortsansichten, alte Pläne, auch Stadtpläne und Siegel, können als notwendige zusätzliche Illustration abgebildet werden.

Unter Umständen empfiehlt es sich, auf geeignete Abbildungen in der Literatur hinzuweisen, besonders dann, wenn eine Abbildung im Inventar unterbleibt. Bei wichtigen Denkmälern genügt aber der Verweis auf Abbildungen in der Literatur nicht, denn alles Wesentliche sollte im Inventar selbst abgebildet sein.

Jedem Band wird eine Übersichtskarte des betreffenden Gebiets in geeignetem Maßstab beigegeben.

8.
Register

Jedem Band wird ein Generalregister (Orte, Objekte, Personen, Ikonographie) beigegeben, außerdem ein Abbildungsverzeichnis.

9.
Äußere Form

Die bisherige Form der Bände der Reihe „Die Kunstdenkmäler von Bayern" wird mit dem entsprechenden Format, Einband, Titelei sowie in der Kombination von (durchgehend nummerierten) Abbildungen und Text beibehalten; der Satz ist zweispaltig.

Die entsprechend der oben dargelegten Anordnung des Stoffes gegliederten Bände erscheinen gesondert und werden wie bisher im Rahmen der einzelnen Regierungsbezirke nach der Erscheinungsfolge fortlaufend nummeriert. Sie sind einzeln käuflich.

10.
Datenschutz

Die Inventarisation erfolgt im Rahmen der nach dem Bayerischen Datenschutzgesetz geltenden Vorschriften zum Schutz personenbezogener Daten. „Bewegliche historische Ausstattungsstücke" im Sinne von Art. 1 Abs. 2 Denkmalschutzgesetz und bewegliche Gegenstände, die nicht „historische Ausstattungsstücke" sind, dürfen nur mit Einwilligung des Eigentümers oder des sonstigen Berechtigten (Betroffenen) in ein Inventar aufgenommen werden. Eine Einwilligung ist nicht erforderlich, wenn in besonders wichtigen Fällen ein berechtigtes öffentliches Interesse an der Inventarisation des betreffenden Gegenstandes besteht und durch die Inventarisation schutzwürdige Belange des Betroffenen nicht beeinträchtigt werden. In strittigen Fällen entscheidet der Landesdenkmalrat.

Die Einwilligung bedarf der Schriftform. Der Betroffene ist in geeigneter Weise über die Bedeutung der Einwilligung aufzuklären.

11.
Auskunft

Gemäß Art. 16 Abs. 2 Denkmalschutzgesetz sind Eigentümer und Besitzer von Baudenkmälern und von eingetragenen beweglichen Denkmälern sowie sonstige Berechtigte verpflichtet, dem Landesamt für Denkmalpflege alle zum Vollzug der Inventarisation erforderlichen Auskünfte zu erteilen.

12.
Betretung

Eine Betretung zum Zwecke der Inventarisation von Baudenkmälern durch Angehörige des Landesamts für Denkmalpflege erfolgt stets einvernehmlich mit dem Eigentümer oder Besitzer oder sonstigen Berechtigten.

III.

Diese Bekanntmachung tritt am 1. Oktober 1990 in Kraft.

Verwaltungsverfahren bei der Inanspruchnahme des Entschädigungsfonds nach dem Gesetz zum Schutz und zur Pflege der Denkmäler (Denkmalschutzgesetz – DSchG)

(2242.1.2-K)

Bekanntmachung des Bayerischen Staatsministeriums für Wissenschaft, Forschung und Kunst vom 13. Mai 2011 Az.: B 4-K 5133.0-12c/1 260 KWMBl. 2011 S. 102

1. Der Entschädigungsfonds

[1]Der Entschädigungsfonds ist ein staatliches Sondervermögen ohne eigene Rechtspersönlichkeit, das von der Obersten Denkmalschutzbehörde, dem Staatsministerium für Wissenschaft, Forschung und Kunst, verwaltet wird. [2]Seine finanzielle Ausstattung richtet sich nach Art. 21 DSchG; sie wird zu gleichen Teilen vom Freistaat und den Kommunen getragen. [3]Der Fonds dient der Befriedigung von Entschädigungsansprüchen, die aus Enteignungen (Art. 18 DSchG) oder sonstigen wesentlichen materiellen Einwirkungen auf das Eigentum (Art. 20 DSchG) entstehen, sowie der Abgeltung eines unzumutbaren Sonderopfers, das sich aus der Erhaltung eines Baudenkmals gemäß Art. 4 DSchG ergibt.

2. Das Verwaltungsverfahren im Vollzug des Art. 4 Abs. 1 DSchG

2.1 Zentrale Bedeutung des Datenbogens

[1]Wesentliches Instrument des Verwaltungsverfahrens bei der Inanspruchnahme des Entschädigungsfonds ist der sog. Datenbogen. [2]Er enthält alle für das Entschädigungsfondsverfahren relevanten Informationen zum Baudenkmal, zur vorgesehenen Maßnahme, zu den zwingend erforderlichen Antragsunterlagen, zum chronologischen Ablauf des Verfahrens sowie zu den Zuständigkeiten der beteiligten Behörden. [3]Die aktuelle Version des Datenbogens sowie sonstige Unterlagen zum Verfahren sind auf der Internetseite des Staatsministeriums für Wissenschaft, Forschung und Kunst unter http://www.stmwfk.bayern.de/Kunst/Denkmaleigentuemer.aspx#Entschaedigungsfonds abrufbar.

2.2 Die Verwaltungsabläufe und Zuständigkeiten bei der Inanspruchnahme des Entschädigungsfonds

2.2.1 Das Landesamt für Denkmalpflege wählt in Zusammenarbeit mit der Unteren Denkmalschutzbehörde und im Einvernehmen mit dem Staatsministerium für Wissenschaft, Forschung und Kunst geeignete Objekte aus.

2.2.2 Das Landesamt für Denkmalpflege erfasst mit Unterstützung durch die betroffene Gemeinde und die Untere Denkmalschutzbehörde die Stammdaten, die relevanten Kostengrößen und den Finanzierungsvorschlag (Teil I des Datenbogens) und übermittelt diese dem Staatsministerium für Wissenschaft, Forschung und Kunst.

2.2.3 [1]Das Staatsministerium für Wissenschaft, Forschung und Kunst erteilt die Freigabe zur Antragstellung (Teil II des Datenbogens) und leitet die Teile I und II des Datenbogens an die Untere Denkmalschutzbehörde weiter. [2]Der Denkmaleigentümer und das Landesamt für Denkmalpflege erhalten hiervon nachrichtlich eine Kopie. [3]Erforderlichenfalls wird vor Freigabe des Datenbogens ein Finanzierungsgespräch durchgeführt.

2.2.4 Die Untere Denkmalschutzbehörde bearbeitet unter Mitwirkung des Denkmaleigentümers die Antragstellung mit Erklärung des Denkmaleigentümers (Teil III des Datenbogens) und setzt diese parallel in Lauf:

    2.2.4.1 Ein Exemplar von Teil III des Datenbogens betreffend den denkmalfachlichen Teil wird mit den erforderlichen Unterlagen an das Landesamt für Denkmalpflege übermittelt.

    2.2.4.2 [1]Ein weiteres Exemplar von Teil III des Datenbogens betreffend die sog. Zumutbarkeitsprüfung (Überprüfung der finanziellen und wirtschaftlichen Verhältnisse des Denkmaleigentümers) wird mit den erforderlichen Unterlagen an das Staatsministerium für Wissenschaft, Forschung und Kunst übermittelt. ²Der Unteren Denkmalschutzbehörde bleibt es freigestellt, dabei eine eigene Stellungnahme zur Zumutbarkeit beizufügen.

2.2.5 Das Landesamt für Denkmalpflege schließt die Bearbeitung nach Antragstellung mit Übersendung des abschließenden Prüfvermerks (Teil IV) des Datenbogens an das Staatsministerium für Wissenschaft, Forschung und Kunst ab.

2.2.6 Das Staatsministerium für Wissenschaft, Forschung und Kunst entscheidet abschließend über den Antrag und legt Art (Zuschuss und/oder Darlehen) und konkrete Höhe der Zuwendung verbindlich fest.

2.2.7 ¹Die Untere Denkmalschutzbehörde prüft nach Abschluss der Maßnahme die Schlussrechnung in rechnerischer und baufachlicher Hinsicht und übersendet eine Ausfertigung des geprüften Verwendungsnachweises an das Landesamt für Denkmalpflege. ²Dieses prüft den Verwendungsnachweis abschließend in denkmalfachlicher Hinsicht, stellt insbesondere die anerkennungsfähigen Kosten fest und ermittelt ggf. die Höhe der zustehenden Zuwendungen; es macht etwaige Rückforderungsansprüche geltend.

2.2.8 ¹Für Zuwendungen aus Mitteln des Entschädigungsfonds sind die einschlägigen Bestimmungen der Bayerischen Haushaltsordnung (BayHO) sowie die ergänzenden Verwaltungsvorschriften (VV) entsprechend anzuwenden. ²Auf die nachfolgenden Regelungen der VV zu Art. 44 BayHO wird ausdrücklich hingewiesen:
– Nr. 1.3 in Verbindung mit Nr. 1.4
 Genehmigung des vorzeitigen Maßnahmebeginns,
– Nr. 2.6
 Berücksichtigung von Vorsteuererstattungen bei der Ermittlung der zuwendungsfähigen Kosten,
– Nr. 8.4
 Jahresfrist für die Rücknahme oder den Widerruf eines Zuwendungsbescheides.

2.2.9 ¹Die Inanspruchnahme des Entschädigungsfonds erfolgt subsidiär. ²Bei der Beurteilung, inwieweit ein unzumutbares Sonderopfer vorliegt, sind steuerliche Vorteile und Zuwendungen anderer Finanzierungsgeber – insbesondere der öffentlichen Hand – zu berücksichtigen. ³Der Entschädigungsfonds ist aufgrund seiner gesetzlichen Vorgaben weder zur Vermögensmehrung des Zuwendungsempfängers noch zur Realisierung wirtschaftlicher Ziele geeignet. ⁴Unter bestimmten Voraussetzungen werden die Zuwendungsbescheide um eine Wertausgleichsklausel ergänzt sowie um die Verpflichtung des Zuwendungsempfängers, zugunsten des Freistaats Bayern eine beschränkte persönliche Dienstbarkeit zu bestellen.

2.3 Nachfinanzierungsverfahren

¹Soweit in Ausnahmefällen die Untere Denkmalschutzbehörde aufgrund veränderter und unvorhersehbarer Sachverhalte eine Nachfinanzierung für erforderlich hält, hat sie diese unverzüglich und unmittelbar beim Staatsministerium für Wissenschaft, Forschung und Kunst zu beantragen. ²Der Antrag der Unteren Denkmalschutzbehörde ist auf die veränderten Sachverhalte zu beschränken. ³Hierbei wird es sich in der Regel um Aussagen zur Höhe der Kosten (Kostenberechnung), deren Finanzierung (Finanzierungsplan) und ggf. um Feststellungen zu den wirtschaftlichen und finanziellen Verhältnissen des Zuwendungsempfängers (Zumutbarkeitsprüfung) handeln.

3. Das Verwaltungsverfahren aufgrund von Anordnungen nach Art. 4 Abs. 2 DSchG sowie bei unmittelbaren Maßnahmen nach Art. 4 Abs. 3 DSchG

¹Soweit die Untere Denkmalschutzbehörde Anordnungen nach Art. 4 Abs. 2 DSchG bzw. unmittelbare Maßnahmen nach Art. 4 Abs. 3 DSchG in Erwägung zieht und hierfür eine Beteiligung des Entschädigungsfonds für notwendig erachtet, hat sie vor Einleitung entsprechender Schritte das Einvernehmen mit dem Staatsministerium für Wissenschaft, Forschung und Kunst herzustellen. ²Hierzu sind dem Staatsministerium für Wissenschaft, Forschung und Kunst folgende Unterlagen vorzulegen:
– Im Einvernehmen mit dem LfD ausgearbeitetes Sicherungsprojekt,
– Kostenunterlage,

D2.I.1f VwV Inanspruchnahme Entschädigungsfonds 576

- Entwurf der vorgesehenen Anordnung nach Art. 4 Abs. 2 DSchG bzw. der vorgesehenen Duldungsanordnung nach Art. 4 Abs. 3 DSchG,
- Darstellung der finanziellen und wirtschaftlichen Verhältnisse des Denkmaleigentümers, verbunden mit einem Vorschlag der Unteren Denkmalschutzbehörde hinsichtlich des dem Eigentümer zumutbaren Eigenanteils.

[3]Auf die vorherige Darstellung der finanziellen und wirtschaftlichen Verhältnisse des Denkmaleigentümers kann ausnahmsweise bei besonderer Eilbedürftigkeit verzichtet werden. [4]In diesem Fall ist sie von der Unteren Denkmalschutzbehörde baldmöglichst nachzureichen; in der vorgesehenen Anordnung nach Art. 4 Abs. 2 DSchG bzw. der vorgesehenen Duldungsanordnung nach Art. 4 Abs. 3 DSchG ist dann festzulegen, dass die Untere Denkmalschutzbehörde die Entscheidung darüber, inwieweit dem Denkmaleigentümer eine finanzielle Beteiligung an der Maßnahme zuzumuten ist, erst nachträglich treffen wird.

4. Schlussbestimmungen

4.1 Inkrafttreten

Diese Bekanntmachung tritt am 1. Juli 2011 in Kraft.

4.2 Außerkrafttreten

Mit Ablauf des 30. Juni 2011 tritt die Bekanntmachung des Staatsministeriums für Wissenschaft, Forschung und Kunst über das Verwaltungsverfahren bei der Inanspruchnahme des Entschädigungsfonds nach dem Gesetz zum Schutz und zur Pflege der Denkmäler vom 24. Januar 2000 (KWMBl I S. 37) außer Kraft.

Bayerisches Staatsministerium für Wissenschaft, Forschung und Kunst
Vollzug des DschG
hier: Prüfung der Zumutbarkeit im Erlaubnisverfahren nach Art. 6 DSchG

Sehr geehrte Damen und Herren,
mit seiner Entscheidung vom 27.09.2007 hat der Bayerische Verwaltungsgerichtshof die Voraussetzungen konkretisiert, unter denen der Abbruch eines Baudenkmals wegen wirtschaftlicher Unzumutbarkeit der Erhaltung zu erlauben ist. Das Gericht hat klargestellt, dass Art. 6 Abs. 2 Satz 1 des Gesetzes zum Schutz und zur Pflege der Denkmäler – Denkmalschutzgesetz – DSchG – (BayRS 2242-1-WFK), zuletzt geändert durch § 9 des Gesetzes vom 20. Dezember 2007 (GVBl S. 958) so ausgelegt und angewendet werden kann, dass den aus Art. 14 GG folgenden Anforderungen an ein Inhalt und Schranken des Grundeigentums bestimmendes Gesetz entsprochen wird. Die Entscheidung ist auf der Internetseite der Landesanwaltschaft Bayern (www.landesanwaltschaft.bayern.de/entscheidungen.htm) abrufbar.
Auf der Grundlage diese Entscheidung werden zur Behandlung von Abbruchanträgen nach Art. 6 Abs. 1 DSchG folgende Hinweise gegeben:

1. Unzumutbarkeit als Ausnahmefall

Denkmalrechtliche Erhaltungs- und Instandsetzungsgebote bestimmen den Inhalt und die Schranken des Eigentums (Art. 14 Abs. 1
Satz 2 GG). Als Inhalts- und Schrankenbestimmungen unterliegen sie besonderen verfassungsrechtlichen Anforderungen; in der Regel sind sie rechtmäßig, sofern die Beschränkung des Eigentumsgrundrechts verhältnismäßig ist. Die Verhältnismäßigkeit ist nur dann nicht mehr gewährleistet, wenn der Eigentümer unzumutbar belastet wird. Das Bundesverfassungsgericht hat in seiner Entscheidung vom 02. März 1999 den hohen Rang des Denkmalschutzes betont. Aufgrund der gesteigerten Sozialbindung des Eigentums, die aus der Situationsgebundenheit des Grundstückes in Lage und Beschaffenheit folgt, muss der Eigentümer es grundsätzlich hinnehmen, dass ihm durch ein Beseitigungsverbot möglicherweise eine rentablere Nut- zung des Grundstücks verwehrt wird. Art. 14 Abs. 1 GG schützt nicht die einträglichste Nutzung des Eigentums (BVerfGE 100, 226, 242 f.). Anders liegt es aber, wenn ausnahmsweise für ein geschütztes Baudenkmal „keinerlei sinnvolle Nutzungsmöglichkeit" mehr besteht:

> „Wenn selbst ein dem Denkmalschutz aufgeschlossener Eigentümer von einem Baudenkmal keinen vernünftigen Gebrauch machen und es praktisch auch nicht veräußern kann, wird dessen Privatnützigkeit nahezu vollständig beseitigt. Nimmt man die gesetzliche Erhaltungspflicht hinzu, so wird aus dem Recht eine Last, die der Eigentümer allein im öffentlichen Interesse zu tragen hat, ohne dafür die Vorteile einer privaten Nutzung genießen zu können. Die Rechtsposition des Betroffenen nähert sich damit einer Lage, in der sie den Namen "Eigentum" nicht mehr verdient. Die Versagung einer Beseitigungsgenehmigung ist dann nicht mehr zumutbar." (BVerfGE 100, 226, 243)

Sofern im Ausnahmefall nachweislich weder eine Nutzbarkeit noch eine realistische Veräußerungsmöglichkeit bestehen, ist eine Zumutbarkeitsprüfung durchzuführen, die sich an den unten (Ziff. 2. bis 4.) beschriebenen Gesichtspunkten zu orientieren hat.
Von vornherein ausgeschlossen ist das Vorbringen einer Unzumutbarkeit bei juristischen Personen, die mittelbar oder unmittelbar mindestens mehrheitlich im Staatsbesitz stehen. Maßgeblich ist nicht die privatrechtliche Organisationsform, denn Art. 14 GG schützt nicht das Privateigentum, sondern das Eigentum Privater (BVerfGE 61,
82, 108). Diese Feststellung gilt nach ständiger Rechtsprechung des BVerfG auch für staatliches Handeln in privatrechtlich organisierter Form (BVerfGE 45, 63, 80) und für Unternehmen mit staatlichen Mehrheitsbeteiligungen (BVerfG NJW 1980, 1093). Beim derzeitigen Stand der Privatisierung sind die Unternehmen des Konzerns der Deutschen Bahn AG nicht grundrechtsfähig (BayVGH, U. vom 3.8.2004, 8 BV 03.275 und BVerwG, U. vom 4.5.2006, 9 C 3/05).

D2.I.1g VwV Zumutbarkeit nach Denkmalschutzgesetz

Im Übrigen kann der Einwand der Unzumutbarkeit der Erhaltung aufgrund der Umstände des Einzelfalles eingeschränkt oder ausgeschlossen sein (s.u. 4.).

2. Mitwirkungs- und Darlegungslast des Eigentümers, Wirtschaftlichkeitsberechnung

Der Eigentümer trägt eine sich aus den Erhaltungs- und Nutzungsverpflichtungen der Art. 4 und 5 DSchG ergebende <u>Mitwirkungslast</u>. Daher sind die unter 1. genannten Voraussetzungen (fehlende Nutzung/Nutzbarkeit, fehlende Veräußerbarkeit) vom Eigentümer darzulegen und nachzuweisen. Im Zuge des Nachweises, dass keine Verkaufsmöglichkeit besteht, sind Belege für eine über einen längeren Zeitraum erfolgte Vermarktung des Objektes vorzulegen. Eine Verkaufsmöglichkeit ist auch bei einer Wertminderung jedenfalls zumutbar, die etwa 10 % des Verkehrswertes des Grundstücks beträgt (BayObLG, BayVBl. 1999, 251).

Die <u>Prüfung der Zumutbarkeit</u> durch die Denkmalschutzbehörde hat nur zu erfolgen, wenn sich der Eigentümer (vorläufig) auf eine bestimmte denkmalverträgliche Nutzung mit oder ohne bauliche Veränderung festlegt. Wird allein die Beseitigung des Baudenkmals begehrt, so besteht <u>kein</u> Anlass für eine eingehende Zumutbarkeitsprüfung. In diesen Fällen genügt die Mitteilung des Landesamtes für Denkmalpflege, dass aufgrund der Bedeutung des Denkmals im Fall einer nachgewiesenen Unzumutbarkeit grundsätzlich die Inanspruchnahme öffentlicher Fördermittel in Frage kommt. Dieser Hinweis ist in die den Erlaubnisantrag ablehnende Entscheidung aufzunehmen.

Die Darlegungs- und Beweislast für die Unzumutbarkeit der Denkmalerhaltung liegt beim Eigentümer, d.h., der Eigentümer hat eine <u>Wirtschaftlichkeitsberechnung</u> vorzulegen, aus der sich die wirtschaftliche Unzumutbarkeit des Denkmalerhaltes ergibt. Die Gegenüberstellung von Sanierungs- und Neubaukosten ist nach der aktuellen Entscheidung des BayVGH nicht zulässig. Die Berechnung ist durch die Untere Denkmalschutzbehörde darauf zu überprüfen, ob sie die wesentlichen entscheidungsrelevanten Punkte enthält und ggf. entsprechend zu ergänzen.

Schema: Wirtschaftlichkeitsberechnung

a) Aufstellung der mit den Denkmalbehörden abgestimmten <u>notwendigen</u> Maßnahmen und Kosten (insbesondere: Notsicherungsmaßnahmen).
b) Davon sind aus Rechtsgründen folgende Kosten <u>abzuziehen</u>:
   – Kosten und Folgekosten von unterlassenem Bauunterhalt durch den Eigentümer und seine Rechtsvorgänger,
   – bau- und sicherheitsrechtlich veranlasste Kosten (BVerwG, Beschl. vom 11.04.1989, NJW 1989, 2638)
   – Abzug der möglichen Steuervorteile bei Instandsetzung (aus Gesamtkosten nach a)),
   – Abzug möglicher Zuwendungen (Entschädigungsfonds, Denkmalfördermittel, Fördermittel der Bayerischen Landesstiftung)
   – Abzug des Werts von Kompensationsmaßnahmen (s.u. 3., „Herbeiführung der Zumutbarkeit")
   → Zwischenergebnis = Basiskosten
c) Hinzurechnung der anteiligen Finanzierungs- und Bewirtschaftungskosten für die Basiskosten
d) Gegenüberstellung der Basiskosten (zzgl. c)) mit den aus dem Objekt zu erzielenden Einnahmen unter Berücksichtigung des Wertzuwachses des Objekts durch die Sanierung
   → Ergebnis = anteiliger Verlust oder Gewinn

Die Zumutbarkeit setzt nicht voraus, dass mit dem Denkmal eine Rendite erzielt werden kann; ausreichend ist eine „Schwarze Null". In der Berechnung ist <u>nicht</u> auf die zivilrechtlichen <u>Buchgrundstücke</u> abzustellen, da ansonsten die Wirtschaftlichkeitsberechnung durch eine nachträgliche Schaffung an sich unrentabler Grundstücke beeinflusst werden könnte (OVG Rheinland-Pfalz, B. vom 2.7.2008, 1 A 10430/08.OVG). Anzusetzen sind bei einem größeren Areal vielmehr die Erträge aller Grundstücke, die mit dem Denkmal eine <u>wirtschaftliche oder funktionale Einheit</u> bilden (s.u. 4.).

Wenn sich als Ergebnis der Wirtschaftlichkeitsberechnung eine dauerhafte Unterdeckung abzeichnet, muss die untere Denkmalschutzbehörde im Rahmen des Erlaubnisverfahrens ggf. in einem <u>Zwischenverfahren</u> klären, ob die erforderlichen Zuschussmittel (Entschädigungsfonds, Denkmalfördermittel,

Fördermittel der Bayerischen Landesstiftung) bewilligt oder verbindlich zugesagt werden können. Anfragen hierzu sind an das Landesamt für Denkmalpflege bzw. die Oberste Denkmalschutzbehörde als mittelverwaltende Stelle des Entschädigungsfonds zu richten. Bei umfangreicheren Ermittlungen kann das Verfahren nach Art. 15 Abs. 5 DSchG zur Vermeidung von Untätigkeitsklagen auf die Dauer von bis zu zwei Jahren ausgesetzt werden.

3. Herbeiführung der Zumutbarkeit

Die Bestimmung in Art. 141 Abs. 2 der Bayerischen Verfassung (BV) verpflichtet Staat, Gemeinden und Körperschaften des öffentlichen Rechts, die Denkmäler der Kunst, der Geschichte und der Natur sowie die Landschaft zu schützen und zu pflegen. Diese Vorschrift ist nach der Rechtsprechung des BayVerfGH für alle Träger staatlicher Gewalt bindendes objektives Verfassungsrecht. Demzufolge sind die Vollzugsbehörden verpflichtet, auch bei Vorliegen eines Abbruchantrages primär den Erhalt eines Baudenkmals zu verfolgen. Bei einem rechnerisch negativen Saldo der Wirtschaftlichkeitsberechnung ist daher zu prüfen, ob eine der nachfolgend genannten Kompensationsmöglichkeiten angeboten werden kann (nach *Martin*, in: Martin/Krautzberger (Hrsg.), Handbuch Denkmalschutz und Denkmalpflege, 2. Auflage München 2006, Kap. G Rn.118):

– Reduzierung der fachlichen Anforderung der Denkmalpflege, z. B. durch Verzicht auf bestimmte kostenintensive Standards
– teilweise Ausweitung der Nutzungsmöglichkeiten z. B. durch Erweiterung des Baurechts auf dem Denkmalgrundstück oder an anderer Stelle
– Dispense von bau- und anderen öffentlich-rechtlichen Vorschriften,
– teilweise Gestattung von Aufstockung, Ausbauten und Anbauten am Baudenkmal,
– teilweise Aufgabe des Baudenkmals und Beschränkung auf die Erhaltung des unverzichtbaren Bestandes,
– sonstiges Entgegenkommen von Behörden in technischen oder administrativen Fragen,
– Angebot der Übernahme des Eigentums des Denkmals bzw. Grundstückes auf die öffentliche Hand.

Die verbindliche Zusicherung einer der o.g. Maßnahmen ist ausreichend; einer Einverständniserklärung des Eigentümers bedarf es nicht.

4. Abwägende Berücksichtigung zusätzlicher Umstände

Auch wenn sich nach dem Ergebnis der geprüften Wirtschaftlichkeitsberechnung eine dauerhafte Unterdeckung ergibt, kann unabhängig von einer Herbeiführung der Zumutbarkeit die Abbrucherlaubnis ermessensfehlerfrei versagt werden, wenn besondere Umstände des Einzelfalles für eine erweiterte Zumutbarkeitslast sprechen bzw. eine Berufung auf Unzumutbarkeit völlig ausschließen. Dies ist z.B. der Fall, wenn der Eigentümer das Grundstück in Kenntnis oder fahrlässiger Unkenntnis der Denkmaleigenschaft und des grundsätzlichen Instandsetzungsbedarfes erworben hat. Wer ein solches Risiko bewusst eingeht, kann seiner Inanspruchnahme nicht entgegenhalten, seine Haftung müsse aus Gründen des Eigentumsschutzes begrenzt sein. Denn das freiwillig übernommene Risiko mindert die Schutzwürdigkeit des Eigentümers. Die Zumutbarkeit kann ferner davon beeinflusst werden, ob der Eigentümer Vorteile aus dem Risiko – etwa durch einen reduzierten Kaufpreis oder durch Schenkung – erzielt hat (BVerfGE 102, 1, 21 f.).

Allerdings darf auch in solchen Fällen nicht das gesamte sonstige Vermögen des Eigentümers beansprucht werden. Zur Finanzierung einer Deckungslücke herangezogen werden können jedoch die Erträge von Grundvermögen, das mit dem Denkmal in funktionalem oder wirtschaftlichem Zusammenhang steht:

„Dem Eigentümer ist nicht zumutbar, unbegrenzt für die Sanierung einzustehen, das heißt auch mit Vermögen, das in keinem rechtlichen oder wirtschaftlichen Zusammenhang mit dem sanierungsbedürftigen Grundstück steht. Dagegen kann es zumutbar sein, Vermögen zur Sanierung einzusetzen, das zusammen mit dem sanierungsbedürftigen Grundstück eine funktionale Einheit darstellt, etwa wenn dieses Bestandteil eines land- oder forstwirtschaftlichen Betriebes oder sons-

tigen Unternehmens ist. Dies gilt insbesondere für Grundvermögen, das zusammen mit dem sanierungsbedürftigen Grundstück eine solche Einheit bildet." (BVerfGE 102, 1, 22 f.)
Umgekehrt kann die Zumutbarkeitsschwelle im Einzelfall niedriger anzusetzen sein, wenn etwa das mit dem Denkmal bebaute Grundstück den wesentlichen Teil des Vermögens des Pflichtigen und die Grundlage seiner privaten Lebensführung darstellt, und er das Grundstück nach Durchführung der Sanierung wirtschaftlich nicht mehr halten könnte (BVerfGE 102, 1, 21).
Entscheidend ist die <u>Abwägung zwischen der Bedeutung des Denkmals</u> einerseits <u>und dem Grad der Eigentumsbeeinträchtigung</u> andererseits. Auch hier ist die Verpflichtung aus Art. 141 Abs. 2 BV zu beachten. Ist die Bedeutung eines gefährdeten Denkmals hoch, spricht dies für eine weitergehende Inanspruchnahme des Eigentümers. Generalisierende Aussagen sind nicht möglich.

5. Fassung des Erlaubnisbescheids

Die denkmalrechtliche Erlaubnis ist im Grundsatz ein dinglicher Verwaltungsakt mit Wirkung für und gegen Rechtsnachfolger. Da die Zumutbarkeitsprüfung aber personenbezogene Umstände einbezieht, ist bei erfolgter Rechtsnachfolge zu prüfen, ob die Erlaubnis gem. Art. 48 BayVwVfG zurückzunehmen ist. Hierauf sollte im Erlaubnisbescheid hingewiesen werden.
Bei der Herbeiführung von Kompensationsmaßnahmen ist eine vertragliche Vereinbarung der Beteiligten zweckmäßig, welche die dies- bezüglichen Einzelheiten, ihre Bedeutung im Rahmen der anstehen- den Entscheidung und den einvernehmlichen Ansatz ihres Wertes enthält.

6. Unterrichtung des Landesamtes für Denkmalpflege

Das Landesamt für Denkmalpflege führt nach Art. 12 Abs. 2 Nr. 3
DSchG die Denkmalliste fort. Zu diesem Zweck ist dem Landesamt für Denkmalpflege bei Erteilung von Abbrucherlaubnissen ein Abdruck der Entscheidung sowie nach erfolgtem Abbruch eine Mitteilung über den Vollzug der Erlaubnis zuzuleiten.
Um Beachtung dieser Vollzugshinweise wird gebeten.

Wirtschaftlichkeitsprüfung, Zumutbarkeit mit Prüfungsverfahren
(s. Nr. 3.3.3)[1])

1) Normative Grundlagen:

1.1
Verfassung des Freistaates Bayern

(in der Fassung der Bekanntmachung vom 15. Dezember 1998 [BayRS 100-1-I])

Art. 141
(1) ¹Der Schutz der natürlichen Lebensgrundlagen ist, auch eingedenk der Verantwortung für die kommenden Generationen, der besonderen Fürsorge jedes einzelnen und der staatlichen Gemeinschaft anvertraut. ²Tiere werden als Lebewesen und Mitgeschöpfe geachtet und geschützt. ³Mit Naturgütern ist schonend und sparsam umzugehen. ⁴Es gehört auch zu den vorrangigen Aufgaben von Staat, Gemeinden und Körperschaften des öffentlichen Rechts, Boden, Wasser und Luft als natürliche Lebensgrundlagen zu schützen, eingetretene Schäden möglichst zu beheben oder auszugleichen und auf möglichst sparsamen Umgang mit Energie zu achten, die Leistungsfähigkeit des Naturhaushaltes zu erhalten und dauerhaft zu verbessern, den Wald wegen seiner besonderen Bedeutung für den Naturhaushalt zu schützen und eingetretene Schäden möglichst zu beheben oder auszugleichen, die heimischen Tier- und Pflanzenarten und ihre notwendigen Lebensräume sowie kennzeichnende Orts- und Landschaftsbilder zu schonen und zu erhalten.
(2) Staat, Gemeinden und Körperschaften des öffentlichen Rechts haben die Aufgabe, die Denkmäler der Kunst, der Geschichte und der Natur sowie die Landschaft zu schützen und zu pflegen, herabgewürdigte Denkmäler der Kunst und der Geschichte möglichst ihrer früheren Bestimmung wieder zuzuführen, die Abwanderung deutschen Kunstbesitzes ins Ausland zu verhüten.

1.2

Art. 6 Maßnahmen an Baudenkmälern
(1) ¹Wer
1. Baudenkmäler beseitigen, verändern oder an einen anderen Ort verbringen oder
2. geschützte Ausstattungsstücke beseitigen, verändern, an einen anderen Ort verbringen oder aus einem Baudenkmal entfernen will, bedarf der Erlaubnis.

²Der Erlaubnis bedarf auch, wer in der Nähe von Baudenkmälern Anlagen errichten, verändern oder beseitigen will, wenn sich dies auf Bestand oder Erscheinungsbild eines der Baudenkmäler auswirken kann. ³Wer ein Ensemble verändern will, bedarf der Erlaubnis nur, wenn die Veränderung eine bauliche Anlage betrifft, die für sich genommen ein Baudenkmal ist, oder wenn sie sich auf das Erscheinungsbild des Ensembles auswirken kann.
(2) ¹Die Erlaubnis kann im Fall des Abs. 1 Satz 1 Nrn. 1 und 2 versagt werden, soweit gewichtige Gründe des Denkmalschutzes für die unveränderte Beibehaltung des bisherigen Zustands sprechen. ²Im Fall des Absatzes 1 Satz 2 kann die Erlaubnis versagt werden, soweit das Vorhaben zu einer Beeinträchtigung des Wesens, des überlieferten Erscheinungsbilds oder der künstlerischen Wirkung eines Baudenkmals führen würde und gewichtige Gründe des Denkmalschutzes für die unveränderte Beibehaltung des bisherigen Zustands sprechen.
(3) ¹Ist eine Baugenehmigung oder an ihrer Stelle eine bauaufsichtliche Zustimmung oder abgrabungsaufsichtliche Genehmigung erforderlich, entfällt die Erlaubnis. ²Ist in den Fällen des Art. 18 Abs. 2 der Bayerischen Bauordnung (BayBO) keine Baugenehmigung oder bauaufsichtliche Zustimmung, jedoch eine durch die Denkmaleigenschaft bedingte Abweichung nach Art. 63 Abs. 1 Satz 1 BayBO erforderlich, schließt die Erlaubnis nach diesem Gesetz die Zustimmung im Einzelfall nach Art. 18 Abs. 2 BayBO und die Abweichung nach Art. 63 Abs. 1 Satz 1 BayBO ein.

---

1) Fundstelle: https://media.w-goehner.de/1.233%20-%20Eigentumsrecht%20-%20Zumutbarkeit%20der%20Erhaltung%20-%20Pr%C3%BCfverfahren.pdf.

D2.I.1h VwV Wirtschaftlichkeitsprüfung

(4) Bei Entscheidungen nach den Abs. 1 bis 3 sind auch die Belange von Menschen mit Behinderung und von Menschen mit sonstigen Mobilitätsbeeinträchtigungen zu berücksichtigen.

1.3
Rechtsprechungs-Grundlagen:

- BVerfG, Beschluss vom 2. März 1999, Az.: 1 BvL 7/91, juris / EzD 1.1 Nr. 7 / DSI 2005/I, 63 ff. (mit Anm. W. K. Göhner) / Jahrbuch des BLfD 2002/2003 S. 137 ff. (Abhandlung von W. K. Göhner)
- BayVGH, Urteil vom 27. September 2007, Az.: Az.: 1 B 00.2474, juris / BayVBl 2008, 141-148 / DSI 2007/IV, 93 ff. (mit Anm. J. Spennemann, http://www.dnk.de/_uploads/beitrag-pdf/e56d03a888279222f48f9a41cba2c5bc.pdf) / Schönere Heimat 2007/IV, 241 f. (mit Anm. W. Eberl) / BayVBl 2008, 148 f. (mit Anm. D. Martin) / EzD 1.1 Nr. 18 (Anm. W. Eberl, S. 18-20) / VGHE BY 60, 268-288 / BRS 71 Nr. 200 (2007) / http://www.blfd.bayern.de/medien/urteil_2_2_5.pdf (mit Anm. W. K. Göhner)
- BayVGH, Urteil vom 18. Oktober 2010, Az.: 1 B 06.63, http://media.w-goehner.de/BayVGH_-_Urteil_v._18.10.2010_-_1_B_06.63_-_neutrale_Fassung_G_1.pdf
- BayVGH, Urteil vom 12. August 2015, Az.: 1 B 12.79, BayVBl 2016, 20 ff. (mit Anm. J. Spennemann, http://www.w-goehner.de/rechtsprechungsuebersicht/direktlink.php?id=127)

2) **Baudenkmal i. S. v. Art. 1 Abs. 1, 2 Satz 1 DSchG:**

2.1
Denkmalfähigkeit:

Sache
- von Menschen geschaffen
- aus vergangener Zeit
- kein Bodendenkmal (Art. 1 Abs. 4, Abs. 2 Satz 1 DSchG)

2.2
Denkmalbedeutung,

aus
- geschichtlichen,
- künstlerischen, – städtebaulichen,
- wissenschaftlichen oder
- volkskundlichen

Gründen.

2.3
Denkmalwürdigkeit:

2.3.1) Feststellung erfolgt durch Sachverständige = in Bayern nach Art. 12 Abs. 1 Satz 1 DSchG durch das BLfD

2.3.2) Die Erhaltung des besagten Objekts ist aus dem, das öffentliche bzw. allgemeine Interesse gesetzlich definierenden Katalog der Bedeutungsarten (s. Nummer 2.2) erforderlich und damit im Interesse der Allgemeinheit

2.3.3) Gründe der Denkmalbedeutung erreichen „gewisses im Bewußtsein der Öffentlichkeit verankertes Maß"

2.3.4) kein Entfall der Denkmaleigenschaft nach Instandsetzung, Sanierung und Modernisierung = „Verbleib eines erkennbaren Baudenkmals" bzw. „Schäden haben an den für die Denkmaleigenschaft relevanten Bauwerksteilen noch kein Ausmaß erreicht, so daß die Sanierung einer Neuerrichtung des Gebäudes gleichkommt"

3) Sprechen „gewichtige" Gründe des Denkmalschutzes für die unveränderte Beibehaltung des bisherigen Zustandes:

3.1
Diese ergeben sich in aller Regel aus der die Denkmaleigenschaft begründenden Bedeutung des Bauwerks, Art. 1 Abs. 1, 2 Satz 1 DSchG

3.1.1) „gesteigerte" Bedeutung nicht erforderlich: die Denkmal begründenden Faktoren sind i. d. R. so gewichtig, dass Versagung einer Abbrucherlaubnis in Betracht kommt.
3.1.2) Eine Abwägung zwischen für und wider die Erlaubniserteilung sprechenden Gründe erfolgt hier nicht.

3.2
Muss Erlaubnis erteilt werden, weil es wegen des Zustandes des Gebäudes oder aus anderen Gründen „ tatsächlich" unmöglich ist, das Baudenkmal zu erhalten?:

3.2.1) Gebäude wird in absehbarer Zeit verfallen und als Ruine nicht erhaltungswürdig sein oder
3.2.2) bei Sanierung würde nur so wenig Substanz erhalten bleiben, daß die Identität des Bauwerks verloren ginge oder
3.2.3) eine den Anforderungen von Art. 5 DSchG entsprechende Nutzung kommt nicht in Betracht.

3.3
Wurde seitens des Antragstellers die wirtschaftliche Unzumutbarkeit der Erhaltung des Baudenkmals ausreichend belegt?

3.3.1 Maßstab
– Auslegung von Art. 6 Abs. 2 Satz 1 DSchG in Entsprechung der Anforderungen aus Art. 14 GG an ein Inhalt und Schranken des Grundeigentums bestimmenden Gesetzes.
– Prüfung, ob dem Denkmaleigentümer die unveränderte Beibehaltung des bisherigen Zustandes mit den Erhaltungs- und Nutzungspflichten gem. Art. 4, 5 DSchG zuzumuten ist, muss dem Grunde nach im Erlaubnisverfahren erfolgen.
– Abzustellen ist auf den „für Denkmalbelange aufgeschlossenen Eigentümer"
– Erwartung an diesen Denkmaleigentümer ist, dass er das Denkmal nicht nur als Belastung betrachtet, sondern das Baudenkmal i. R. d. Zumutbaren zu erhalten versucht.

3.3.2 Nachweispflichten
– Eigentümer muss Nutzungskonzept mit dem eigentlichen Ziel der Denkmalerhaltung und sinnvollen Nutzung erstellen.
– Eigentümer die Wirtschaftlichkeit dieses konstruktiv am Denkmalerhalt orientierten Nutzungskonzepts berechnen.
– Spätester Zeitpunkt: mündliche Gerichtsverhandlung.

3.3.3 Prüfungsverfahren[1)2)]:
a) Aufstellung der mit dem Bayerischen Landesamt für Denkmalpflege und der örtlich zuständigen Unteren Denkmalschutzbehörde vor Maßnahmenbeginn abgestimmten, zur Erhaltung und sinnvollen Nutzung des Denkmals notwendigen Maßnahmen und Kosten (ohne Grunderwerbskosten) = Nutzungs- und Instandsetzungskonzept (Kostengliederung in Anlehnung an DIN 276).
b) Davon sind aus Rechtsgründen je nach den Umständen des Einzelfalls folgende Positionen abzuziehen:
– Kosten und Folgekosten von unterlassenem Bauunterhalt durch den Eigentümer und seine Rechtsvorgänger (Mindestwert: jährliche Instandhaltungskosten nach nachstehendem Buchstaben c) ab Entstehen der Instandhaltungsverpflichtung nach Art. 4 BayDSchG; Höchstwert: gutachtliche Ermittlung im Einzelfall),
– bauordnungsrechtlich veranlasste Kosten (Art. 54 Abs. 2 und 4 BayBO),

---
1) Vollzugsschreiben des Bayerischen Staatsministeriums für Wissenschaft, Forschung und Kunst vom 14. Januar 2009, Nr. B 4-K 5111.0-12c/ 31828 (07), http://www.denkmalnetzbayern.de/uploads/6f1599352732aed3026cf667ca16ac9d.pdf.
2) Urteilsanmerkung Dr. Jörg Spennemann, BayVBl 2016, 23-25, zu BayVGH, Urteil vom 12. August 2015, Az.; 1 B 12.79, BayVBl 2016, 20-23.

- in Aussicht gestellte Zuwendungen (z. B. Entschädigungsfonds, Denkmalpflegefördermittel, Förderung der Bayerischen Landesstiftung), ohne dass es auf die Stellung eines Antrages durch den Eigentümer ankäme,
- der Wert von angebotenen Kompensationsmaßnahmen zur Herbeiführung der Zumutbarkeit (z. B. teilweise Gestattung von Aufstockung, Ausbauten, An- und Neubauten oder Teilabbrüchen),
- Leistung durch eine Versicherung für eingetretene Schäden am Schutzobjekt,
- eine aufgrund der Denkmaleigenschaft eingeräumte Kaufpreisreduktion. → Zwischenergebnis = Basiskosten

c) Ermittlung der Finanzierungs- und Bewirtschaftungskosten für die Basiskosten bei Bedarf über einen Prognosezeitraum von 12-15 Jahren. Neben Zinsleistungen (nicht Tilgung) sind dies laufende Instandhaltungskosten (in Anlehnung an § 28 Abs. 2 Satz 1 Nr. 1 II. BV) und Abschreibungen (in Anlehnung an § 25 Abs. 2 II. BV), bei Vermietung ggf. Mietausfallwagnis und Verwaltungskosten. Nicht zu berücksichtigen sind sonstige, nutzerabhängige Betriebskosten (Verbrauchskosten wie Heizung, Warmwasser).
→ Zwischenergebnis = Finanzierungs- und Bewirtschaftungskosten

d) Gegenüberstellung der Finanzierungs- und Bewirtschaftungskosten (c) mit den aus dem Objekt zu erzielenden Erträgen (ortsübliche Miete oder Gebrauchsvorteile unter Zugrundelegung der nach Sanierung erzielbaren Nutzfläche) unter Hinzurechnung der möglichen Steuervorteile der Instandsetzung (§§ 7i, 7h, 10f, 10g, 11a und 11b EStG); bei fehlenden Angaben kann der Höchststeuersatz zugrunde gelegt werden.

Unabhängig von der Dauer des gewählten Prognosezeitraums gilt, dass die Erträge aus dem Denkmal dessen Kosten nicht jederzeit ausgleichen müssen. In der Anfangsphase (während notwendiger Umbau- und Restaurierungsarbeiten) wird es regelmäßig dazu kommen, dass die Kosten höher als die Erträge sind; umgekehrt geht die Zinsbelastung aufgrund der Darlehenstilgung stetig zurück.
→ Ergebnis = negativer / positiver / ausgeglichener Saldo

3.5
Sollte der Eigentümer geltend machen, dass er die bei der Berechnung der Baufinanzierung angenommenen Zinskonditionen nicht erhalten werde (mangelnde Kreditwürdigkeit) oder Steuererleichterungen nicht geltend machen könne, muss er sich zudem bis zum Nachweis des Gegenteils auf die grundsätzliche Verkaufsmöglichkeit verweisen lassen.

3.6
Im Falle eines anteiligen Verlusts als Ergebnis der Wirtschaftlichkeitsberechnung:

- ZWINGEND vor abschließender Ermessensentscheidung
- Vorlage über BLfD an BayStMBKWK (BayStMBW) mit exakter Forderung hinsichtlich eines ggf. (zusätzlich) erforderlichen finanziellen Ausgleichs für den Fall, daß der Staat trotz berechneter Unzumutbarkeit die Zumutbarkeit dennoch herstellen wollen würde!!

3.7
**erst JETZT: Abschließende Ermessensentscheidung
(dabei an Art. 141 Bay. Verf., Art. 3 Abs. 2 DSchG gebundene Entscheidung!).**

Empfehlungen zu Ensembles D2.I.1i

Empfehlungen des Bayerischen Landesdenkmalrates für Baumaßnahmen innerhalb oder in der Nähe von Ensembles im Sinne des Denkmalschutzgesetzes sowie in der Nähe von Einzelbaudenkmälern vom 14. Februar 1977

Stand: 3.2016
Fundstelle: Eberl/Martin/Spennemann, Kommentar zum Bayerischen Denkmalschutzgesetz, 7. Auflage 2016, Anhang 9

Nach Art. 1 Abs. 2 des Bayer. Denkmalschutzgesetzes (DSchG) sind Baudenkmäler bauliche Anlagen oder Teile davon aus vergangener Zeit, deren Erhaltung wegen ihrer geschichtlichen, künstlerischen, städtebaulichen, wissenschaftlichen oder volkskundlichen Bedeutung im Interesse der Allgemeinheit liegt. Zu den Baudenkmälern kann nach Art. 1 Abs. 3 DSchG auch eine Mehrheit von baulichen Anlagen (Ensembles) gehören, und zwar auch dann, wenn nicht jede einzelne dazugehörige bauliche Anlage für sich genommen ein Baudenkmal darstellt, das Orts-, Platz- oder Straßenbild aber insgesamt erhaltenswürdig ist.

Nach Art. 141 der Bayerischen Verfassung und den Grundgedanken des Denkmalschutzgesetzes sollen Baudenkmäler und damit auch Ensembles soweit wie möglich lebendig erhalten werden. Veränderungen sind deshalb nicht ausgeschlossen. Bei Baumaßnahmen (Neubauten und bauliche Änderungen) innerhalb oder in der Nähe von Ensembles und von Einzelbaudenkmälern ist auf den Maßstab und den Charakter Rücksicht zu nehmen (Art. 6 Abs. 1 Nr. 3, Abs. 2 DSchG).

Die nachstehende Aufzählung von Kriterien soll Städteplanern und Architekten, Baugenehmigungs- und Denkmalschutzbehörden helfen, als wichtige Voraussetzung für jede Planung und Beurteilung von Baumaßnahmen in einem Ensemble sich über die wesentlichen Merkmale des Vorhandenen Klarheit zu verschaffen. Da aber solche Hinweise nicht vollständig sein können, entbinden sie nicht von der Verpflichtung zur eigenverantwortlichen Beobachtung, Erfassung und Würdigung des Bestandes.

1 Ensembles

Ensembles zeichnen sich durch besondere Eigenarten aus. Jeder Planung müssen daher gesicherte Erkenntnisse über diese Eigenheiten vorausgehen. Als Grundlage hierfür kann die Beschreibung des Ensembles in der Denkmalliste und in den Inventaren des Landesamtes für Denkmalpflege benützt werden.

Der Ausdruck eines Ensembles wird von charakteristischen Merkmalen bestimmt. Diese gilt es jeweils zu erkennen, zu würdigen und sinnvoll in die Planung einzuführen. Solche Merkmale sind u.a.:

1.1
Städtebauliche Merkmale

1.1.1 Städtebauliche Struktur

Landschaftliche Einbindung; Ortsbild, Ortssilhouette (Höhenentwicklung); Umfang und Begrenzung des Ensembles; Art der Einbindung in das Gelände; Straßenschema, Viertelbildung; Maßstäblichkeit der Bebauung; Verhältnis der Baumassen zueinander, zu herausragenden Baudenkmälern und Blickpunkten und zu charakteristischen Vegetationsbereichen;

1.1.2 Nutzungsstruktur

Art der bestehenden Nutzung (Eigentümlichkeiten, Schwerpunkte); Zuschnitt, Anordnung und Größe der Grundstücke und Maß der bestehenden Nutzung; Gruppierung der Gebäude nach der Nutzungsart (z.B. Wohnhaus, Geschäfte, Scheunen, Ställe u.ä.);

1.1.3 Ensemblegrundriss und Straßenraum

Art des Bebauungsschemas (nach einheitlichem Plan angelegt, historisch gewachsen usw.); regional oder örtlich übliche Bauweise; Geschoßzahl; Straßenraum und Platzwände (Krümmung, Verengung, Ausweitung), Vor-und Rücksprünge der Baukörper aus der Bauflucht; Dominanten im Ensemble;

D2.I.1i Empfehlungen zu Ensembles

1.1.4 Anordnung und Stellung von Gebäuden und Gebäudeteilen

Offene oder geschlossene Bauweise, Gebäudeabstände; Dächer (First- und Traufrichtung); Hofbildung, Feuergassen; Arkaden und Laubengänge; Vor- und Hausgärten;

1.1.5 Bewuchs und Wasser

Grüngürtel und Grünflächen (Parks); Alleen und alleenartige Auffahrten zu Gebäuden; Gärten; Baumgruppen und Einzelbäume; Stadtbäche bzw. – flüsse; Uferausbildung und Art der Befestigung.

2 Bauliche Merkmale und historische Aspekte

2.1 Gestaltwirksame konstruktive Merkmale des Gebäudes (Bauart)

Holzfachwerk mit oder ohne Auskragungen; Blockwerk, Werksteinmauerwerk; Bruchsteinmauerwerk (verputzt oder verbandelt); Ziegelmauerwerk (verputzt oder unverputzt); Pfeilerausbildung, Stützpfeiler, Arkadenausbildung, Schwibbögen; Bedachung (Dachfuß, Dachvorsprung);

2.2 Fassaden

Fassadenbreite und -höhe, Geschoßzahl und – höhe; Gebäudehöhen, Verhältnis von Wand zu Öffnung, Öffnungsproportion; Achsenabstände, horizontale und vertikale plastische Gliederung (z.B. Gesimse, Pilaster, Konsolen, Rustika, Attika, Sockel), Fassadenrelief; Fenster- und Türumrahmungen, Leibung oder Putzbündigkeit; Fenster, Fenstersprossen, Fensterläden, Fenstergitter, Tor- und Türblätter, Material und Anstrich;
Oberflächenbehandlung und Farbgestaltung (z.B. Sichtmauerwerk, Steinbehandlung, Putzart, Verkleidung); figürlicher und ornamentaler Schmuck, plastisch oder gemalt; charakteristisches Zubehör (z.B. Hausmadonnen, historische Ausleger, Werbeanlagen, Sonnenschutz, Hauslaternen);

2.3 Dächer, Dachlandschaft

Gliederung der Bedachung; Dachform und -neigung (z.B. Satteldach, Walmdach, Krüppelwalmdach, Zeltdach, Grabendach); Verhältnis und Anschluß zwischen Dach und Baukörper; Dachhaut (Material und Farbe); Dachentwässerung (z.B. Regenrinnen, Fallrohre, Kessel, Wasserspeier); Dachaufbauten (z.B. Zwerchhäuser, Gauben, Kamine, Köpfe, Blitzableiter, Windfahnen);

2.4 Alter, Nutzung

Mutmaßliches Alter; erkennbare Änderungsabläufe in der Baugestalt; erkennbarer Nutzungswechsel;

2.5 Außenanlagen

Boden (befestigt oder unbefestigt); Trennung oder Nichttrennung in Fahrbahn und Gehweg, Breite von Fahrbahn und Gehweg; Material, Maßstäblichkeit und Verlegungsart des Bodenbelages; Art der Überwindung von Höhenunterschieden (z.B. Treppen, Rampen); Einfriedungen (Mauern, Hecken); Zugänge, Zäune, Geländer, Einfahrten und Tore; Akzente im Freiraum (z.B. Denkmäler, Brunnen, Steinpoller, Beleuchtung).

2.6 Einzelbaudenkmäler

Wesen, überliefertes Erscheinungsbild und künstlerische Wirkung von Einzelbaudenkmälern lassen sich in sinngemäßer Anwendung der unter Ziff. 1 aufgeführten Merkmale bestimmen.

3 Besondere Einzelprobleme

3.1 Bei Baumaßnahmen innerhalb oder in der Nähe eines Ensembles und in der Nähe eines Einzelbaudenkmals ist darauf zu achten, daß die Baumaßnahmen Rücksicht auf die oben dargestellten Charakteristika nehmen. Wenn sich auch wegen der großen Vielfalt der bestehenden Ensembles generelle Aussagen darüber, welche Charakteristika bei einer Baumaßnahme im Einzelfall berücksichtigt werden sollen, nicht machen lassen, werden im allgemeinen doch bestimmte Gestaltungsformen regelmäßig mit der vorhandenen historischen Substanz schwer zu vereinbaren sein.

3.1.1 Eine historische Dachlandschaft wird durch Flachdächer in der Regel beeinträchtigt. Dächer sollten entsprechend gestaltet werden, so wie es die vorgegebene Ortsstruktur anbietet.

3.1.2 Sofern die Möglichkeit besteht, ortsgebundene, dem historischen, baulichen und handwerklichen Charakter entsprechende Materialien zu verwenden, sollen ortsfremde Materialien nicht gebraucht werden. Die Fassadengestaltung soll die im Ortsbild üblichen Techniken berücksichtigen.

3.1.3 Alle alten Bauten sind wesentlich durch gegliederte Fensteröffnungen charakterisiert. Hier wirken teilungslose Fenster fast immer als Störung.

3.1.4 Fassadenelemente und Fassadenverkleidungen, die mit dem charakteristischen Ortsbild nicht in Einklang zu bringen sind, sollten nach Möglichkeit nicht zugelassen werden. Strukturfremde Veränderungen, wie z.B. Ladeneinbauten und Reklameeinrichtungen, sollten nur in einer dem Ortsbild entsprechenden Form möglich sein.

3.1.5 Hochhäuser haben, selbst wenn sie außerhalb eines Ensembles errichtet werden, in der Regel eine das Ensemble beeinträchtigende Wirkung. Die Bauhöhe, die Baumasse und die Gestaltung neuer Gebäude sollte sich nach dem Ortsbild richten; auf eine Verbindung zu den übrigen Teilen des Ensembles sollte geachtet werden.

3.1.6 Für Wege und Straßen und vor allem für Plätze sollten ungegliederte, „tote" Beläge nach Möglichkeit nicht verwendet werden, wenn die schützenswerte Umgebung Pflasterung oder eine anders geartete Oberflächengestaltung verlangt.

3.2 Bei Baumaßnahmen innerhalb von Ensembles kann neben der Beschreibung und Bewertung der einzelnen denkmalwürdigen Gebäude und der Merkmale des Ensembles auch ein Überblick über die ortsgeschichtliche und gestaltbildende Entwicklung des betreffenden Gebietes notwendig werden, der zum Verständnis für die baulichen und Nutzungsmerkmale beiträgt. Bei Baumaßnahmen in diesen Bereichen kann es sich empfehlen, gemäß Bauvorlagenverordnung zusätzliche Unterlagen (wie z.B. Straßen- und Platzabwicklungen, Massenmodelle, Bestandspläne) zur Entscheidungshilfe anzufordern.

Bayerisches Archivgesetz (BayArchivG)

Vom 22. Dezember 1989 (GVBl. S. 710)
(BayRS 2241-1-WK)
zuletzt geändert durch § 16 a G zur Ausführung des Gesetzes zur Abschaffung des Bayerischen Senates vom 16. Dezember 1999 (GVBl. S. 521)

Nichtamtliche Inhaltsübersicht

Abschnitt I
Allgemeines
Art. 1 Geltungsbereich
Art. 2 Begriffsbestimmungen
Art. 3 Abgrenzung zu sonstigen gesetzlichen Rechten

Abschnitt II
Staatliche Archive
Art. 4 Aufgaben der staatlichen Archive
Art. 5 Ehrenamtliche Archivpfleger
Art. 6 Anbietung
Art. 7 Übernahme
Art. 8 Auftragsarchivierung
Art. 9 Verwaltung und Sicherung des Archivguts

Art. 10 Benützung der staatlichen Archive
Art. 11 Schutzrechte

Abschnitt III
Archive sonstiger öffentlicher Stellen
Art. 12 Archiv des Bayerischen Landtags
Art. 13 Kommunale Archive
Art. 14 Andere öffentliche Archive

Abschnitt IV
Schlußbestimmungen
Art. 15 Ermächtigungen
Art. 16 Ausnahmen vom Geltungsbereich
Art. 17 Inkrafttreten

Der Landtag des Freistaates Bayern hat das folgende Gesetz beschlossen, das nach Anhörung des Senats hiermit bekanntgemacht wird:

Abschnitt I
Allgemeines

Artikel 1 Geltungsbereich
Dieses Gesetz gilt für die Archivierung von Unterlagen in den staatlichen Archiven und in Archiven sonstiger öffentlicher Stellen in Bayern.

Artikel 2 Begriffsbestimmungen
(1) ¹Archivgut sind alle archivwürdigen Unterlagen einschließlich der Hilfsmittel zu ihrer Nutzung, die bei Behörden, Gerichten und sonstigen öffentlichen Stellen oder bei natürlichen Personen oder bei juristischen Personen des Privatrechts erwachsen sind. ²Unterlagen sind vor allem Akten, Urkunden und andere Einzelschriftstücke, Karten, Pläne, Bild-, Film- und Tonmaterial und sonstige Datenträger sowie Dateien einschließlich der zu ihrer Auswertung erforderlichen Programme. ³Zum Archivgut gehört auch Dokumentationsmaterial, das von den Archiven ergänzend gesammelt wird.
(2) Archivwürdig sind Unterlagen, die für die wissenschaftliche Forschung, zur Sicherung berechtigter Belange Betroffener oder Dritter oder für Zwecke der Gesetzgebung, Rechtsprechung oder Verwaltung von bleibendem Wert sind.
(3) Archivierung umfaßt die Aufgabe, das Archivgut zu erfassen, zu übernehmen, auf Dauer zu verwahren und zu sichern, zu erhalten, zu erschließen, nutzbar zu machen und auszuwerten.

Artikel 3 Abgrenzung zu sonstigen gesetzlichen Rechten
Gesetzliche Einsichts-, Mitteilungs- und Vorlagerechte bleiben unberührt.

Abschnitt II
Staatliche Archive

Artikel 4 Aufgaben der staatlichen Archive
(1) Die staatlichen Archive sind die staatlichen Fachbehörden für alle Fragen des Archivwesens.
(2) ¹Die staatlichen Archive haben die Aufgabe, das Archivgut der Behörden, Gerichte und sonstigen öffentlichen Stellen des Freistaates Bayern nach Maßgabe dieses Gesetzes zu archivieren. ²Diese Auf-

gabe erstreckt sich auch auf Archivgut der Rechtsvorgänger des Freistaates Bayern und der Funktionsvorgänger der in Satz 1 genannten Stellen, das diese oder die staatlichen Archive übernommen haben.
(3) [1]Die staatlichen Archive archivieren in den in diesem Gesetz vorgesehenen Fällen auch Archivgut sonstiger öffentlicher Stellen. [2]Sie können ferner Archivgut weiterer öffentlicher Stellen auf Grund von Vereinbarungen übernehmen; Art. 6 bis 11 gelten, soweit die Vereinbarungen oder Rechtsvorschriften nichts anderes bestimmen.
(4) [1]Die staatlichen Archive können auf Grund von Vereinbarungen oder letztwilligen Verfügungen auch privates Archivgut archivieren, soweit daran ein öffentliches Interesse besteht. [2]Für dieses Archivgut gelten nur Art. 9 und 10 mit der Maßgabe, daß besondere Vereinbarungen mit den Eigentümern oder besondere Festlegungen in den letztwilligen Verfügungen unberührt bleiben. [3]Soweit dem Betroffenen Schutzrechte gegenüber der bisher speichernden Stelle zustehen, richten sich diese nunmehr auch gegen die staatlichen Archive.
(5) [1]Die staatlichen Archive beraten die Behörden, Gerichte und sonstigen öffentlichen Stellen des Freistaates Bayern bei der Verwaltung und Sicherung ihrer Unterlagen. [2]Sie beraten die Rechts- und Stiftungsaufsichtsbehörden bei allen Archivgut betreffenden rechts- und stiftungsaufsichtlichen Entscheidungen. [3]Sie beraten und unterstützen außerdem nichtstaatliche Archiveigentümer bei der Sicherung und Nutzbarmachung ihres Archivguts, soweit daran ein öffentliches Interesse besteht (Archivpflege).

Artikel 5 Ehrenamtliche Archivpfleger
(1) Die staatlichen Archive werden bei der Erfüllung ihrer Aufgaben nach Art. 4 Abs. 5 Sätze 2 und 3 von ehrenamtlichen Archivpflegern unterstützt.
(2) [1]Sie haben über die ihnen bekanntgewordenen Angelegenheiten Verschwiegenheit zu bewahren; das gilt nicht für Mitteilungen im amtlichen Verkehr und über Tatsachen, die offenkundig sind oder ihrer Bedeutung nach keiner Geheimhaltung bedürfen. [2]Sie dürfen die Kenntnis der nach Satz 1 geheimzuhaltenden Angelegenheiten nicht unbefugt verwerten. [3]Sie haben auf Verlangen des staatlichen Archivs amtliche Schriftstücke, Zeichnungen, bildliche Darstellungen und Aufzeichnungen jeder Art über dienstliche Vorgänge herauszugeben, auch soweit es sich um Wiedergaben handelt. [4]Diese Verpflichtungen bestehen auch nach Beendigung des Ehrenamts fort. [5]Die Herausgabepflicht trifft auch die Hinterbliebenen und die Erben.

Artikel 6 Anbietung
(1) [1]Alle Behörden, Gerichte und sonstigen öffentlichen Stellen des Freistaates Bayern haben dem zuständigen staatlichen Archiv die Unterlagen zur Übernahme anzubieten, die sie zur Erfüllung ihrer Aufgaben nicht mehr benötigen. [2]Dies ist in der Regel 30 Jahre nach Entstehung der Unterlagen anzunehmen, soweit durch Rechtsvorschriften oder Verwaltungsvorschriften der obersten Staatsbehörden nichts anderes bestimmt ist. [3]Anzubieten sind auch Unterlagen, die
1. personenbezogene Daten enthalten, einschließlich datenschutzrechtlich gesperrter Daten,
2. unter einem besonderen gesetzlichen Geheimnisschutz stehen oder sonstigen Geheimhaltungsvorschriften unterliegen.
[4]Von der Anbietungspflicht ausgenommen sind Unterlagen, deren Offenbarung gegen das Brief-, Post- oder Fernmeldegeheimnis verstoßen würde.
(2) Durch Vereinbarung zwischen den staatlichen Archiven und der anbietenden Stelle oder dem für die anbietende Stelle zuständigen Staatsministerium kann
1. auf die Anbietung von Unterlagen von offensichtlich geringer Bedeutung verzichtet werden,
2. der Umfang der anzubietenden gleichförmigen Unterlagen, die in großer Zahl erwachsen, im einzelnen festgelegt werden und
3. die Auswahl der anzubietenden maschinenlesbar gespeicherten Informationen einschließlich der Form der Datenübermittlung im einzelnen festgesetzt werden.
(3) Den Vertretern der staatlichen Archive ist Einsicht in die angebotenen Unterlagen und in die Findmittel der Registraturen zu gewähren.
(4) Entscheidet das zuständige staatliche Archiv nicht innerhalb von sechs Monaten über die Übernahme angebotener Unterlagen, ist die anbietende Stelle zu deren weiterer Aufbewahrung nicht verpflichtet.

D2.II.1 Bayerisches Archivgesetz

Artikel 7 Übernahme
(1) ¹Das zuständige staatliche Archiv übernimmt die von ihm im Benehmen mit der anbietenden Stelle als archivwürdig bestimmten Unterlagen. ²Unterlagen, deren Archivwürdigkeit verneint worden ist, sollen von der anbietenden Stelle vernichtet werden.
(2) Vor der Übernahme von Unterlagen im Sinn von Art. 6 Abs. 1 Satz 3 muß das zuständige staatliche Archiv durch geeignete Maßnahmen oder entsprechende Festlegungen sicherstellen, daß schutzwürdige Belange Betroffener oder Dritter und überwiegende Interessen des Gemeinwohls auch nach der Archivierung angemessen berücksichtigt werden.
(3) ¹Das zuständige staatliche Archiv kann archivwürdige Unterlagen bereits vor Ablauf besonderer Aufbewahrungsfristen endgültig übernehmen, wenn sie älter als 30 Jahre sind. ²Die Aufbewahrungsfristen werden in diesem Fall durch die Aufbewahrung im Archiv gewahrt.

Artikel 8 Auftragsarchivierung
(1) ¹Das zuständige staatliche Archiv kann auch Unterlagen übernehmen, deren besondere Aufbewahrungsfristen noch nicht abgelaufen sind und bei denen das Verfügungsrecht den abgebenden Stellen vorbehalten bleibt (Auftragsarchivierung). ²Für die Unterlagen gelten die bisher für sie maßgebenden Rechtsvorschriften fort. ³Die Verantwortung des zuständigen staatlichen Archivs beschränkt sich auf die in Art. 9 Abs. 1 Satz 1 bestimmten Maßnahmen.
(2) Für die Anbietung, die Entscheidung über die Archivwürdigkeit und die Übernahme der Unterlagen nach Ablauf der Aufbewahrungsfristen gelten Art. 6 und 7 entsprechend.

Artikel 9 Verwaltung und Sicherung des Archivguts
(1) ¹Die staatlichen Archive haben die ordnungs- und sachgemäße dauernde Aufbewahrung und Benützbarkeit des Archivguts und seinen Schutz vor unbefugter Benützung oder Vernichtung durch geeignete technische, personelle und organisatorische Maßnahmen sicherzustellen. ²Die staatlichen Archive haben das Verfügungsrecht über das Archivgut und sind befugt, das Archivgut nach archivwissenschaftlichen Gesichtspunkten zu ordnen, durch Findmittel zu erschließen sowie Unterlagen, deren Archivwürdigkeit nicht mehr gegeben ist, zu vernichten. ³Sollen solche Unterlagen in größerem Umfang vernichtet werden, muß das Benehmen mit der abgebenden Stelle hergestellt werden. ⁴Die staatlichen Archive können, soweit dies unter archivischen Gesichtspunkten vertretbar oder geboten ist, mit Zustimmung der abgebenden Stelle die im Archivgut enthaltenen Informationen in anderer Form archivieren und die Originalunterlagen vernichten.
(2) Die Verknüpfung personenbezogener Daten durch das Archiv ist nur zulässig, wenn schutzwürdige Belange Betroffener oder Dritter nicht beeinträchtigt werden.

Artikel 10 Benützung der staatlichen Archive
(1) Das in den staatlichen Archiven verwahrte Archivgut steht nach Maßgabe der folgenden Absätze und der Benützungsordnung Behörden, Gerichten und sonstigen öffentlichen Stellen, natürlichen und juristischen Personen auf Antrag für die Benützung zur Verfügung.
(2) ¹Das in den staatlichen Archiven verwahrte Archivgut kann benützt werden, soweit ein berechtigtes Interesse an der Benützung glaubhaft gemacht wird und nicht Schutzfristen entgegenstehen. ²Ein berechtigtes Interesse ist insbesondere gegeben, wenn die Benützung zu amtlichen, wissenschaftlichen, heimatkundlichen, familiengeschichtlichen, rechtlichen, unterrichtlichen oder publizistischen Zwecken oder zur Wahrnehmung von berechtigten persönlichen Belangen erfolgt. ³Die Zulassung zur Benützung ist zu versagen oder von Auflagen abhängig zu machen, wenn und soweit
1. Grund zu der Annahme besteht, daß Interessen der Bundesrepublik Deutschland oder eines ihrer Länder gefährdet würden,
2. Grund zu der Annahme besteht, daß schutzwürdige Belange Betroffener oder Dritter entgegenstehen,
3. Gründe des Geheimnisschutzes es erfordern,
4. der Erhaltungszustand des Archivguts gefährdet würde oder
5. durch die Benützung ein nicht vertretbarer Verwaltungsaufwand entstünde.

(3) ¹Soweit durch Rechtsvorschriften oder nach Maßgabe des Absatzes 4 nichts anderes bestimmt ist, bleibt Archivgut, mit Ausnahme bereits bei ihrer Entstehung zur Veröffentlichung bestimmter Unterlagen, für die Dauer von 30 Jahren seit seiner Entstehung von der Benützung ausgeschlossen. ²Archivgut, das sich auf natürliche Personen bezieht (personenbezogenes Archivgut), darf erst 10 Jahre

nach dem Tod des Betroffenen benützt werden. ³Ist der Todestag nicht oder nur mit unvertretbarem Aufwand festzustellen, endet die Schutzfrist 90 Jahre nach der Geburt des Betroffenen. ⁴Archivgut, das besonderen Geheimhaltungsvorschriften unterliegt, darf frühestens 60 Jahre nach seiner Entstehung benützt werden; das gleiche gilt für die Entschädigungsakten des Landesentschädigungsamts und die Rückerstattungsakten der Wiedergutmachungsbehörde Bayern. ⁵Für Archivgut, das Rechtsvorschriften des Bundes über Geheimhaltung im Sinn der §§ 8, 10 und 11 des Bundesarchivgesetzes unterliegt, gelten die Schutzfristen des § 5 des Bundesarchivgesetzes. ⁶Die Schutzfristen gelten nicht für Maßnahmen nach Art. 9 Abs. 1 Sätze 2 und 4.
(4) ¹Mit Zustimmung der abgebenden Stelle können die Schutzfristen im einzelnen Benützungsfall oder für bestimmte Archivgutgruppen verkürzt werden, wenn durch Rechtsvorschriften nichts anderes bestimmt ist und kein Grund zu der Annahme besteht, daß schutzwürdige Belange Betroffener oder Dritter entgegenstehen. ²Bei personenbezogenem Archivgut ist eine Verkürzung nur zulässig, wenn der Betroffene eingewilligt hat oder wenn die Benützung zur Erreichung des beabsichtigten wissenschaftlichen Zwecks, zur Behebung einer bestehenden Beweisnot oder aus sonstigen im überwiegenden Interesse der abgebenden Stelle oder eines Dritten liegenden Gründen unerläßlich ist und sichergestellt ist, daß schutzwürdige Belange des Betroffenen oder Dritter nicht beeinträchtigt werden. ³Die Schutzfristen können mit Zustimmung der abgebenden Stelle um höchstens 30 Jahre verlängert werden, wenn dies im öffentlichen Interesse liegt.
(5) ¹Die Benützung von Archivgut durch Stellen, bei denen es erwachsen ist oder die es abgegeben haben, ist auch innerhalb der Schutzfristen der Absätze 3 und 4 zulässig. ²Diese Schutzfristen gelten jedoch, wenn das Archivgut hätte gesperrt werden müssen.

Artikel 11 Schutzrechte
(1) ¹Vorschriften des Datenschutzrechts über den Auskunftsanspruch des Betroffenen bleiben unberührt. ²An Stelle der Auskunft kann das Archiv Einsicht in die Unterlagen gewähren.
(2) ¹Rechtsansprüche Betroffener auf Berichtigung sind in der Weise zu erfüllen, daß zu berichtigende Unterlagen um eine Richtigstellung ergänzt werden. ²Ist dies nicht möglich, sind die Unterlagen besonders zu kennzeichnen.
(3) ¹Der Betroffene kann verlangen, daß Unterlagen, die sich auf seine Person beziehen, eine Gegendarstellung beigefügt wird, wenn er glaubhaft macht, durch eine falsche Tatsachenbehauptung beeinträchtigt zu sein. ²Dies gilt nicht für Feststellungen, die in einer rechtskräftigen gerichtlichen oder in einer bestandskräftigen behördlichen Entscheidung enthalten sind. ³Nach dem Tod des Betroffenen kann die Beifügung einer Gegendarstellung von den Erben sowie von dem Ehegatten, den Kindern oder den Eltern verlangt werden, wenn sie ein berechtigtes Interesse daran geltend machen können.
(4) ¹Unterlagen sind zu vernichten, wenn sie zum Zeitpunkt der Abgabe an das Archiv von der abgebenden Stelle hätten vernichtet werden müssen. ²Unterlagen sind nicht zu vernichten, wenn die sich aus anderen Vorschriften ergebenden Vernichtungspflichten erst nach der Abgabe an das Archiv entstehen. ³Bis 60 Jahre nach ihrer Entstehung dürfen diese Unterlagen nur benützt werden, wenn die Benützung dem Vorteil des Betroffenen zu dienen bestimmt ist oder der Betroffene eingewilligt hat.

Abschnitt III
Archive sonstiger öffentlicher Stellen

Artikel 12 Archiv des Bayerischen Landtags
(1) ¹Für das Archiv des Landtags gelten die Bestimmungen des Abschnitts II sinngemäß. ²Der Landtag regelt die Einzelheiten der Benützung.
(2) Sofern der Landtag kein eigenes Archiv unterhält, hat er Unterlagen, die er zur Erfüllung seiner Aufgaben nicht mehr benötigt, dem zuständigen staatlichen Archiv zur Übernahme anzubieten.

Artikel 13 Kommunale Archive
(1) Die Gemeinden, Landkreise und Bezirke und die sonstigen kommunalen Körperschaften, Anstalten und Stiftungen des öffentlichen Rechts und ihre Vereinigungen regeln die Archivierung der bei ihnen erwachsenen Unterlagen in eigener Zuständigkeit.
(2) Für Unterlagen, die unter einem besonderen gesetzlichen Geheimnisschutz stehen oder sonstigen Geheimhaltungsvorschriften unterliegen, sowie für personenbezogene Daten einschließlich datenschutzrechtlich gesperrter Daten gelten Art. 6 Abs. 1 Satz 3, Art. 7 Abs. 1 Satz 2 und Abs. 2,

D2.II.1 Bayerisches Archivgesetz

Art. 9 Abs. 1 Satz 1 und Abs. 2, Art. 10 Abs. 2 Sätze 1 bis 3 Nrn. 1 bis 3, Abs. 3 Sätze 2 bis 6, Abs. 4 und 5 sowie Art. 11 sinngemäß.

(3) ¹Landkreise und Bezirke, die keine eigenen Archive unterhalten, haben Unterlagen, die sie zur Erfüllung ihrer Aufgaben nicht mehr benötigen, dem zuständigen staatlichen Archiv zur Übernahme anzubieten. ²Das Eigentum am Archivgut bleibt unberührt.

Artikel 14 Andere öffentliche Archive

(1) ¹Soweit die staatlichen Hochschulen und die der Aufsicht des Staates unterstehenden sonstigen Körperschaften, Anstalten und Stiftungen des öffentlichen Rechts sowie ihre Vereinigungen die bei ihnen erwachsenen Unterlagen in einem eigenen Archiv, in einem als Gemeinschaftseinrichtung betriebenen öffentlichen Archiv oder in einem Archiv einer sonstigen öffentlichen Stelle im Sinn dieses Abschnitts archivieren, regeln sie die Einzelheiten der Archivierung in eigener Zuständigkeit. ²Sie erlassen Benützungsordnungen. ³Art. 13 Abs. 2 gilt entsprechend.

(2) ¹Die staatlichen Hochschulen, Körperschaften, Anstalten, Stiftungen des öffentlichen Rechts und ihre Vereinigungen, die nicht nach Absatz 1 archivieren, haben Unterlagen, die sie zur Erfüllung ihrer Aufgaben nicht mehr benötigen, dem zuständigen staatlichen Archiv zur Übernahme anzubieten. ²Das Eigentum am Archivgut bleibt unberührt.

Abschnitt IV
Schlußbestimmungen

Artikel 15 Ermächtigungen

Die Staatsregierung wird ermächtigt, durch Rechtsverordnung
1. die Benützung der staatlichen Archive, vor allem die Zulassung, den Ausschluß und das Verhalten in den Archiven zu regeln¹⁾ und
2. die Maßnahmen zur Sicherung der in Art. 10 Abs. 2 Satz 3 Nrn. 1 bis 5 aufgezählten Belange im einzelnen festzulegen.

Artikel 16 Ausnahmen vom Geltungsbereich

Dieses Gesetz gilt nicht für die öffentlich-rechtlichen Religionsgemeinschaften, für den Bayerischen Rundfunk, für die Anstalt des öffentlichen Rechts „Zweites Deutsches Fernsehen" und für die Bayerische Landeszentrale für neue Medien sowie für öffentlich-rechtliche Unternehmen mit eigener Rechtspersönlichkeit, die am Wettbewerb teilnehmen, und deren Zusammenschlüsse mit Ausnahme von Zweckverbänden.

Artikel 17 Inkrafttreten

Dieses Gesetz tritt am 1. Januar 1990 in Kraft.

---

1) Die Archivbenützungsordnung ist abgedruckt als Nr. D2.II.1a.

Benützungsordnung für die staatlichen Archive Bayerns (Archivbenützungsordnung – ArchivBO)[1)]

Vom 16. Januar 1990 (GVBl. S. 6)
(BayRS 2241-1-1-WK)
zuletzt geändert durch § 10 V zur Anpassung von Verordnungen an den Euro im Geschäftsbereich des Bayerischen Staatsministeriums für Wissenschaft, Forschung und Kunst (EuroAnpV-WFK) vom 6. Juli 2001 (GVBl. S. 371)

Es erlassen auf Grund
1. des Art. 15 des Bayerischen Archivgesetzes (BayArchivG) die Bayerische Staatsregierung
2. des Art. 25 Abs. 1 Satz 1 Nr. 1 des Kostengesetzes das Bayerische Staatsministerium für Unterricht und Kultus im Einvernehmen mit dem Bayerischen Staatsministerium der Finanzen

folgende Verordnung:

Abschnitt I
Allgemeines

§ 1 Geltungsbereich
(1) Diese Verordnung gilt für die Benützung des in den staatlichen Archiven verwahrten Archivguts.
(2) Für die Stelle, bei der das Archivgut erwachsen ist oder die es abgegeben hat, und deren Funktionsnachfolger gilt Abschnitt II dieser Verordnung nur dann, wenn das Archivgut hätte gesperrt werden müssen oder wenn seine Vernichtung auf Grund des Art. 11 Abs. 4 Satz 2 BayArchivG unterblieben ist.
(3) [1]Bei der Benützung nichtstaatlichen Archivguts gehen Vereinbarungen mit Eigentümern und von diesen getroffene Festlegungen den Regelungen dieser Verordnung vor. [2]Für die Benützung des Geheimen Hausarchivs gilt § 11 des Übereinkommens zwischen dem Bayerischen Staate und dem vormaligen Bayerischen Königshaus vom 24. Januar 1923 (Beilagen Band XI zu Landtagsverhandlungen 1922/1923 S. 498 bis 503, Nr. 3298).
(4) Die für die Benützung von Archivgut getroffenen Bestimmungen gelten für die Benützung von Findmitteln, sonstigen Hilfsmitteln und Reproduktionen entsprechend.

Abschnitt II
Benützung

§ 2 Benützungsberechtigte
(1) Das Archivgut steht nach Maßgabe des Bayerischen Archivgesetzes und dieser Benützungsordnung Behörden, Gerichten und sonstigen öffentlichen Stellen sowie natürlichen und juristischen Personen für die Benützung zur Verfügung.
(2) Minderjährige können zur Benützung zugelassen werden, wenn die Zustimmung des gesetzlichen Vertreters vorliegt.

§ 3 Benützungszweck
[1]Das Archivgut kann benützt werden, soweit ein berechtigtes Interesse an der Benützung glaubhaft gemacht wird. [2]Ein berechtigtes Interesse ist insbesondere gegeben, wenn die Benützung zu amtlichen, wissenschaftlichen, heimatkundlichen, familiengeschichtlichen, rechtlichen, unterrichtlichen oder publizistischen Zwecken oder zur Wahrnehmung von berechtigten persönlichen Belangen erfolgt.

§ 4 Benützungsantrag
(1) Die Benützung ist beim staatlichen Archiv schriftlich zu beantragen.
(2) [1]Im Benützungsantrag sind der Name, der Vorname und die Anschrift des Benützers, gegebenenfalls der Name und die Anschrift des Auftraggebers, sowie das Benützungsvorhaben, der überwiegende Benützungszweck und die Art der Auswertung anzugeben. [2]Ist der Benützer minderjährig, hat er dies anzuzeigen. [3]Für jedes Benützungsvorhaben ist ein eigener Benützungsantrag zu stellen.
(3) Der Benützer hat sich zur Beachtung der Benützungsordnung zu verpflichten.
(4) Der Benützer hat sich auf Verlangen auszuweisen.

---
1) Änderungen vor dem 1.1.2000 sind nicht in Fußnoten nachgewiesen.

D2.II.1a Archivbenützungsordnung

(5) Bei schriftlichen oder mündlichen Anfragen kann auf einen schriftlichen Benützungsantrag verzichtet werden.

§ 5 Benützungsgenehmigung

(1) ¹Die Benützungsgenehmigung erteilt das staatliche Archiv. ²Sie gilt nur für das laufende und das darauffolgende Kalenderjahr, für das im Benützungsantrag angegebene Benützungsvorhaben und für den angegebenen Benützungszweck.

(2) ¹Die Benützungsgenehmigung ist zu versagen oder von Auflagen abhängig zu machen, wenn und soweit
1. Grund zu der Annahme besteht, daß Interessen der Bundesrepublik Deutschland oder eines ihrer Länder gefährdet würden,
2. Grund zu der Annahme besteht, daß schutzwürdige Belange Betroffener oder Dritter entgegenstehen,
3. Gründe des Geheimnisschutzes es erfordern,
4. der Erhaltungszustand des Archivguts gefährdet würde,
5. durch die Benützung ein nicht vertretbarer Verwaltungsaufwand entstünde.

²Im Fall von Satz 1 Nr. 1 holt das staatliche Archiv vor der Erteilung der Benützungsgenehmigung die Zustimmung der Generaldirektion der Staatlichen Archive Bayerns ein, die im Einvernehmen mit der abgebenden Stelle oder deren Funktionsnachfolger entscheidet.

(3) Die Benützungsgenehmigung kann ganz oder teilweise versagt oder mit Auflagen versehen werden, wenn
1. der Zweck der Benützung auf andere Weise erreicht werden kann, insbesondere durch Einsicht in Druckwerke oder Reproduktionen, und eine Benützung des Originals aus wissenschaftlichen oder rechtlichen Gründen nicht zwingend erforderlich ist,
2. das Archivgut zu amtlichen Zwecken, im Rahmen von Erschließungsarbeiten oder wegen einer gleichzeitigen anderweitigen Benützung benötigt wird,
3. der Benützer nicht die Gewähr für die Einhaltung der Benützungsordnung bietet.

(4) Wird die Benützung von Unterlagen nach Art. 11 Abs. 4 Satz 3 BayArchivG beantragt, so hat der Benützer die Einwilligung des Betroffenen beizubringen oder nachzuweisen, daß die Benützung dem Vorteil des Betroffenen zu dienen bestimmt ist.

(5) ¹Die Benützung kann auch auf Teile von Archivgut, auf anonymisierte Reproduktionen, auf die Erteilung von Auskünften oder auf besondere Zwecke, wie quantifizierende medizinische Forschung oder statistische Auswertung, beschränkt werden. ²Als Auflagen kommen insbesondere die Verpflichtung zur Anonymisierung von Namen bei einer Veröffentlichung und zur Beachtung schutzwürdiger Belange Betroffener oder Dritter sowie das Verbot der Weitergabe von Abschriften an Dritte in Betracht.

(6) Archivgut ist von der Benützung ausgeschlossen, solange es einer Schutzfrist unterliegt und eine Verkürzung der Schutzfrist nicht erfolgt ist.

(7) ¹Die Benützungsgenehmigung kann auch dann widerrufen werden, wenn Angaben im Benützungsantrag nicht mehr zutreffen oder die Benützungsordnung nicht eingehalten wird. ²Sie kann nachträglich mit Auflagen versehen werden.

§ 6 Verkürzung und Verlängerung von Schutzfristen

(1) ¹Der Antrag auf Verkürzung von Schutzfristen ist vom Benützer schriftlich bei dem das Archivgut verwahrenden staatlichen Archiv zu stellen. ²Bei personenbezogenem Archivgut nach Art. 10 Abs. 4 Satz 2 BayArchivG hat der Benützer die Einwilligung des Betroffenen beizubringen oder nachzuweisen, daß die Benützung zur Erreichung des beabsichtigten wissenschaftlichen Zwecks, zur Behebung einer bestehenden Beweisnot oder aus sonstigen im überwiegenden Interesse der abgebenden Stelle oder eines Dritten liegenden Gründen unerläßlich ist.

(2) ¹Über die Verkürzung und die Verlängerung von Schutzfristen entscheidet die Generaldirektion der Staatlichen Archive Bayerns. ²Diese holt die Zustimmung der abgebenden Stelle oder ihres Funktionsnachfolgers ein.

§ 7 Benützung in den staatlichen Archiven

(1) ¹Die Benützung erfolgt durch die Einsichtnahme in Findmittel, Archivgut und Reproduktionen in den dafür vorgesehenen Räumen der staatlichen Archive. ²Diese können die Benützung auch durch

Archivbenützungsordnung D2.II.1a

Beantwortung von schriftlichen oder mündlichen Anfragen, durch Abgabe von Reproduktionen oder durch Versendung von Archivgut ermöglichen.
(2) Mündliche oder schriftliche Auskünfte können sich auf Hinweise auf einschlägiges Archivgut beschränken.
(3) [1]Das Archivgut, die Reproduktionen, die Findmittel und die sonstigen Hilfsmittel sind mit größter Sorgfalt zu behandeln. [2]Eine Änderung des Ordnungszustands, die Entfernung von Bestandteilen und die Anbringung oder Tilgung von Vermerken sind unzulässig.
(4) [1]Das eigenmächtige Entfernen von Archivgut aus den für die Benützung vorgesehenen Räumen ist untersagt. [2]Das staatliche Archiv ist berechtigt, Kontrollen durchzuführen.
(5) [1]Die Verwendung von technischen Geräten bei der Benützung, wie Schreibmaschine, Diktiergerät, Computer oder beleuchtete Leselupe, bedarf besonderer Genehmigung. [2]Diese kann nur erteilt werden, wenn durch die Verwendung der Geräte weder Archivgut gefährdet noch der geordnete Ablauf der Benützung gestört wird.

§ 8 Reproduktionen
(1) [1]Die Anfertigung von Reproduktionen kann nur nach Maßgabe des § 5 erfolgen. [2]Reproduktionen werden durch die staatlichen Archive oder eine von diesen beauftragte Stelle hergestellt.
(2) Eine Veröffentlichung, Weitergabe oder Vervielfältigung von Reproduktionen ist nur mit vorheriger Zustimmung des staatlichen Archivs zulässig.
(3) Bei einer Veröffentlichung von Reproduktionen sind das verwahrende staatliche Archiv und die dort verwendete Archivsignatur anzugeben.

§ 9 Versendung von Archivgut
(1) [1]Auf die Versendung von Archivgut zur Benützung außerhalb des verwahrenden Archivs besteht kein Anspruch. [2]Sie kann in begründeten Ausnahmefällen erfolgen, insbesondere wenn das Archivgut zu amtlichen Zwecken bei öffentlichen Stellen oder für Ausstellungszwecke benötigt wird. [3]Die Versendung kann von Auflagen abhängig gemacht werden.
(2) Archivgut kann zu nichtamtlichen Zwecken nur an hauptamtlich verwaltete Archive versandt werden, sofern sich diese verpflichten, das Archivgut in den Benützerräumen unter Aufsicht nur dem Antragsteller vorzulegen, es archivfachlich einwandfrei zu verwahren, keine Reproduktionen anzufertigen und das Archivgut nach Ablauf der Ausleihfrist zurückzusenden.
(3) Eine Versendung von Archivgut für Ausstellungen ist nur möglich, wenn sichergestellt ist, daß das Archivgut wirksam vor Verlust und Beschädigung geschützt wird und der Ausstellungszweck nicht durch Reproduktionen oder Nachbildungen erreicht werden kann.

§ 10 Belegexemplar
[1]Von jeder Veröffentlichung, die zu einem erheblichen Teil unter Verwendung von Archivgut eines staatlichen Archivs angefertigt worden ist, ist diesem ein Exemplar kostenlos zu überlassen. [2]Entsprechendes gilt für die Veröffentlichung von Reproduktionen. [3]Auf die Abgabe kann in Ausnahmefällen verzichtet werden.

Abschnitt III
Benützungsgebühren

§ 11 Gebühren und Auslagen
(1) Für die Inanspruchnahme der staatlichen Archive werden Gebühren und Auslagen (Benützungsgebühren) erhoben.
(2) [1]Schuldner der Benützungsgebühren sind der Benützer und derjenige, in dessen Interesse die Inanspruchnahme erfolgt sowie derjenige, der die Schuld gegenüber dem Archiv schriftlich übernimmt. [2]Mehrere Schuldner haften als Gesamtschuldner.

§ 12 Höhe der Benützungsgebühren, Auslagen
(1) [1]Für die Vorlage oder Versendung von Archivgut, die Erteilung mündlicher oder schriftlicher Fachauskünfte, die Erstellung von Gutachten und für sonstige Tätigkeiten betragen die Gebühren bei Beanspruchung
1. eines Beamten
    des höheren Archivdienstes   neunundzwanzig €

D2.II.1a Archivbenützungsordnung

2. eines Beamten
   des gehobenen Archivdienstes — einundzwanzig €
3. eines Beamten
   des mittleren Archivdienstes — sechzehn €
4. eines Beamten
   des einfachen Dienstes — fünfzehn €

je Halbstunde Zeitaufwand. ²Die letzte angefangene Halbstunde des Zeitaufwands jeder Personengruppe wird als volle Halbstunde gerechnet. ³Das gleiche gilt, wenn der Zeitaufwand einer Gruppe eine Halbstunde nicht erreicht. ⁴Die Halbstundensätze gelten für andere, vergleichbare Archivbedienstete entsprechend.

(2) Für die Anfertigung von Reproduktionen werden Gebühren entsprechend den ortsüblichen gewerblichen Preisen erhoben.

(3) Neben den Gebühren nach den Absätzen 1 und 2 werden als Auslagen erhoben
1. die Postgebühren, die Kosten einer Versendung (z.B. für Verpackung und Versicherung) sowie die Fernsprechgebühren im Fernverkehr,
2. die Reisekosten nach den Reisekostenvorschriften und sonstige Aufwendungen bei Ausführung von Dienstgeschäften außerhalb der Dienststelle,
3. die anderen Behörden oder anderen Personen für ihre Tätigkeit zustehenden Beträge.

§ 13 Gebührenbefreiung

Gebühren nach § 12 Abs. 1 werden nicht erhoben bei Benützungen
1. durch Behörden des Freistaates Bayern,
2. von Archivgut durch Stellen, die dieses Archivgut abgegeben haben, oder deren Funktionsnachfolger,
3. für nachweisbar wissenschaftliche, heimatkundliche, familiengeschichtliche und unterrichtliche Zwecke,
4. in Amts- und Rechtshilfesachen für den Bund und die Länder der Bundesrepublik Deutschland,
5. für rechtliche Forschungen durch zentrale Stellen der öffentlich-rechtlichen Religionsgemeinschaften sowie der Anstalten und Stiftungen des öffentlichen Rechts, soweit die Benützung in eigener Sache erfolgt und Gegenseitigkeit gewährt wird.

§ 14 Fälligkeit, Vorschüsse

(1) Die Gebühren und Auslagen werden mit dem Tätigwerden der Archive fällig.
(2) Die Archive können einen angemessenen Vorschuß auf die Gebühren und Auslagen verlangen und von dessen Bezahlung ihre Tätigkeit abhängig machen.

Abschnitt IV
Schlußbestimmungen

§ 15 Inkrafttreten, Außerkrafttreten

(1) Diese Verordnung tritt am 1. Februar 1990 in Kraft.
(2) Gleichzeitig treten außer Kraft:
1. die Verordnung über die Erhebung von Benutzungsgebühren durch die Staatlichen Archive Bayerns – Archivgebührenordnung – ArchGebO – (BayRS 2241-3-K), geändert durch Verordnung vom 15. Juni 1987 (GVBl S. 236),
2. die Bekanntmachung des Bayerischen Staatsministeriums für Unterricht und Kultus über die Benützung der staatlichen Archive Bayerns (Benützungsordnung) vom 25. April 1955 (BayBSVK S. 1493).

Verleihung einer Denkmalschutzmedaille[1)]

Vom 18. Mai 1987 KWMBl. I 1987 S. 190
(BayVV Gliederungsnummer 2242-WK)

Bekanntmachung des Bayerischen Staatsministeriums für Wissenschaft und Kunst[2)] vom 18. Mai 1987
Az.: IV/2b-K 4521-7/18 194

1. Das Bayerische Staatsministerium für Wissenschaft und Kunst verleiht Personen oder Vereinigungen, die sich besondere Verdienste um den Denkmalschutz erworben haben, eine Medaille, die die Bezeichnung „Denkmalschutzmedaille" erhält.
2. Die Medaille wird in einer Stufe verliehen und grundsätzlich im Jahr bis zu 40mal vergeben. Sie ist kein Orden oder Ehrenzeichen im Sinne des Art. 118 Abs. 5 der Bayerischen Verfassung und auch nicht zum Tragen in der Öffentlichkeit bestimmt.
3. Über die Verleihung wird eine Urkunde ausgestellt, die gleichzeitig mit der Medaille ausgehändigt wird.
4. Die Bekanntmachung des Bayerischen Staatsministeriums für Unterricht und Kultus vom 21. Juli 1977 Nr. IV/2-7/99 817 (KMBl I S. 486) wird aufgehoben.

---

1) Fortgeltung ab 1.1.2016 gem. VwVWBek v. 31.5.2016 (AllMBl. S. 1555).
2) **Amtl. Anm.:** jetzt: Bayerisches Staatsministerium für Bildung und Kultus, Wissenschaft und Kunst

D2.III.2 Förderrichtlinien nichtstaatliche Museen

Richtlinien zu Vergabe staatlicher Zuwendungen an nichtstaatliche Museen in Bayern

Stand: April 2015

1. Zuwendungsfähige Maßnahmen

Staatliche Zuwendungen können von der Landesstelle für folgende Zwecke gewährt werden:
- Konzepte (z. B. Machbarkeitsstudien, Nutzungs- und Ausstellungskonzepte) Museumseinrichtung und Ausstellungsgestaltung (ausgenommen Sonder- und Wechselausstellungen)
- Schaffung geeigneter konservatorischer Bedingungen für die Präsentation und Verwahrung von Museumsgut in Ausstellungs- und Depoträumen, z. B. durch die Planung von Maßnahmen der Klimastabilisierung und Lichtschutzes sowie zur Einrichtung von Depots (präventive Konservierung)
- Konservierung und Restaurierung von Museumsgut (aktive Konservierung)
- Projekte im Bereich der Inventarisation und Dokumentation
- Didaktische Erschließung von Museumsbeständen (z. B. durch Infographik oder audiovisuelle Medien)
- Transferierung von Architekturobjekten in wissenschaftlich geleitete Freilichtmuseen
- Museumspädagogische Projekte, u. a. Planung und Einrichtung von museumspädagogischen Räumen
- Nachhaltige Projekte der Öffentlichkeitsarbeit
- Ergänzung und Abrundung bestehender Sammlungen durch Erwerb in begründeten Einzelfällen

Die Zuwendungen werden als Projektförderung im Wege der Anteilsfinanzierung für Investitionsmaßnahmen gewährt, die von dauerhaftem Nutzen für das Museum sind. Ausgaben für den laufenden Betrieb oder für Sonder- und Wechselausstellungen werden nicht gefördert. Ebenfalls nicht gefördert werden bauliche Maßnahmen, die Installation von Haustechnik sowie Sicherungseinrichtungen am Museumsgebäude.

Für die Vergabe der Fördermittel sind die Bedeutung und die Dringlichkeit des Projekts maßgebend.

2. Voraussetzungen für die Gewährung staatlicher Zuwendungen

Voraussetzungen für die Förderung einer Maßnahme im Rahmen der verfügbaren Haushaltmittel sind:
- gesicherte Trägerschaft
- gesicherte und ausreichende fachliche Leitung und Personalausstattung
- geordnete finanzielle Verhältnisse
- dauerhafte Verfügbarkeit einer aussagekräftigen und ausstellungsfähigen Sammlung
- auf Dauer angelegter Museumsbetrieb
- regelmäßige und ausreichende Öffnungszeiten
- Nutzbarkeit des Museums als öffentliche Bildungseinrichtung
- Herstellung des Einvernehmens mit der Landesstelle in allen wesentlichen Aspekten vor Beginn der geplanten Maßnahme
- zeitliche Bindung der Fördermittel von mindestens zehn Jahren

3. Zuwendungsverfahren

Anträge auf Gewährung einer Zuwendung sowie Auszahlungsanträge werden als PDF-Dateien zum Download auf www.museen-in-bayern.de unter Förderung bereitgestellt.

Zuwendungsantrag

Das Zuwendungsverfahren wird durch einen schriftlichen Antrag des Maßnahmeträgers – der in der Regel mit dem Museumsträger identisch ist – eingeleitet.

Dem Antrag sind alle für die Beurteilung des Vorhabens erforderlichen Unterlagen beizufügen, insbesondere die Beschreibung des Projekts, ein detaillierter Kosten- und Finanzierungsplan sowie die Terminplanung. Die Landesstelle kann für die fachliche Beurteilung weitere Unterlagen anfordern. Die Zuwendungsanträge sind der Landesstelle möglichst vor dem 30. Juni des laufenden Jahres vorzulegen.

Maßnahmebeginn

Mit der Maßnahme darf noch nicht begonnen worden sein. Eine Maßnahme gilt dann als bereits begonnen, wenn Lieferungs- oder Leistungsverträge abgeschlossen worden sind, die sich auf das Vorhaben beziehen.
Bei der Landesstelle kann die Zustimmung zum vorzeitigen Maßnahmebeginn beantragt werden. Diese Zustimmung greift der Entscheidung über die Bewilligung einer Zuwendung aus Mitteln der Landesstelle nicht vor; aus ihr kann daher keine Förderzusage abgeleitet werden. Ohne Zustimmung zum vorzeitigen Maßnahmebeginn ist eine Förderung bereits begonnener Maßnahmen ausgeschlossen.

Maßnahmedauer

Das Förderverfahren ist grundsätzlich an das jeweilige Haushaltsjahr gebunden. Für mehrjährige Projekte sind für jedes Jahr getrennte Anträge zu stellen.

Bewilligungsbescheid

Nach der fachlichen Prüfung des Antrags erhält der Antragsteller bei Verfügbarkeit ausreichender Haushaltsmittel einen schriftlichen Bewilligungsbescheid, in dem die Höhe der zuwendungsfähigen Kosten und der bewilligten Zuwendung festgesetzt sind. Der Antragsteller verpflichtet sich, die geförderte Maßnahme entsprechend den Festsetzungen, Bedingungen und Auflagen des Bescheids durchzuführen.
Veränderungen des geförderten Projekts, die sich auf die Gewährung der Zuwendung oder ihre Höhe auswirken können, sind der Landesstelle vom Antragsteller unverzüglich mitzuteilen.

Auszahlungsantrag

Der Auszahlungsantrag ist der Landesstelle bis spätestens 31. Oktober des jeweiligen Haushaltjahres unter Angabe der bis dahin angefallenen Kosten vorzulegen. Auch Aufwendungen, die innerhalb der nächsten zwei Monate anfallen, können im Auszahlungsantrag angegeben werden. Bei Nichteinhaltung der vorgenannten Frist verfällt der Anspruch auf Auszahlung des bewilligten Betrags.

Verwendungsnachweis

Der Verwendungsnachweis, in dem über die im Auszahlungsantrag angegebenen Aufwendungen unter Vorlage ausreichender Belege Rechnung zu legen ist, ist bei kommunalen Antragstellern bis zum 31. Oktober, bei sonstigen Antragstellern bis zum 30. April des folgenden Jahres einzureichen.
Geltend gemachte Eigenleistungen sind nachzuweisen. Bei Hilfskräften können derzeit Stundensätze bis zu 13,00 €, bei fachlich qualifizierten Kräften bis zu 15,50 € anerkannt werden. Bei nicht fristgerechter oder unvollständiger Vorlage des Verwendungsnachweises kann die Zuwendung ganz oder teilweise zurückgefordert werden.

Publizitätspflicht

Der Zuwendungsempfänger verpflichtet sich, auf die Förderung durch die Landesstelle für die nichtstaatlichen Museen im Auftrag des Freistaats Bayern am geförderten Produkt selbst (z. B. Ausstellungen, audiovisuelle Medien, Druckwerke) mit der Formulierung „Gefördert durch die Landesstelle für die nichtstaatlichen Museen in Bayern" unter Beifügung des Logos der Landesstelle dauerhaft hinzuweisen. Darüber hinaus ist auf die Förderung auch im Rahmen der Werbung und Öffentlichkeitsarbeit, insbesondere in Pressemitteilungen, Programmen und Publikationen im Internet, hinzuweisen. Das Logo ist in digitaler Form bei der Landesstelle zu beziehen.

D2.III.2 Förderrichtlinien nichtstaatliche Museen

Zusatzbestimmungen

Ergänzend gelten insbesondere die Art. 23 und 44 der Bayerischen Haushaltsordnung (BayHO), die Allgemeinen Nebenbestimmungen für Zuwendungen zur Projektförderung (ANBest-P), die Verwaltungsvorschriften für Zuwendungen des Freistaats Bayern an kommunale Körperschaften (VVK), die Allgemeinen Nebenbestimmungen für Zuwendungen zur Projektförderung an kommunale Körperschaften (ANBest-K) sowie die Art. 48, 49 und 49a des Bayerischen Verwaltungsverfahrensgesetzes (BayVwVfG).

Vollzug der Haager Konvention zum Schutz von Kulturgut bei bewaffneten Konflikten; hier: Anbringung der Kennzeichen der Konvention gemäß Art. 6, 16 und 17 der Haager Konvention

Bek. des Bayer. Staatsministeriums für Unterricht und Kultus, vom 16. Oktober 1984
(KMBl. I 1984 S. 641, MABl. 1985 S. 32)

An   die Regierungen
      die Kreisverwaltungsbehörden
An   die Bayer. Verwaltung der Staatl. Schlösser, Gärten und Seen
      das Bayer. Landesamt für Denkmalpflege
      die Bayer. Staatl. Sammlungen und Museen
nachrichtlich
an   die Gemeinden
     die Coburger Landesstiftung
     das Deutsche Museum
     das Germanische Nationalmuseum
     die Träger Nichtstaatlicher Museen
an   die Erzbischöflichen und Bischöflichen Ordinariate
     das Evang.-Luth. Landeskirchenamt.

Im Einvernehmen mit dem Bayer. Staatsministerium des Innern und dem Bayer. Staatsministerium der Finanzen wird folgendes bekanntgegeben:

1. **Allgemeines**
   Mit Gesetz vom 11. April 1967 in der Fassung des am 14. August 1971 in Kraft getretenen Änderungsgesetzes vom 10. August 1971 – BGBl II 1967 S. 1233 und 1971 S. 1025 – hat die Bundesrepublik Deutschland der Haager Konvention zum Schutz von Kulturgut bei bewaffneten Konflikten, ihren Ausführungsbestimmungen und dem Protokoll zugestimmt.
   Gemäß Art. 2 Abs. 1 Satz 1 dieses Gesetzes führen die Länder die Haager Konvention im Auftrag des Bundes aus. Der Bundesminister des Innern hat entschieden, daß die Kulturgutschutzkennzeichen angebracht werden können. Die Kennzeichen sind an die Regierungen ausgeliefert.

2. **Kennzeichnung der Baudenkmäler / Ortsbilder**
   2.1 Die Regierungen haben die Baudenkmalliste / Ortsbildliste erhalten. Sie haben die Betroffenen unterrichtet. Soweit angeregte Ergänzungen derzeit nicht vorgenommen werden können, sollen sie bei dem geplanten Nachfolgeprogramm in die Prüfung miteinbezogen werden.
   2.2 Die Kennzeichnung der Ortsbilder hat auf der Grundlage der an die Regierungen übermittelten Ortsbildliste zu erfolgen; d.h., die Ortsbilder sind entsprechend den in der Ortsbildliste genannten Umgrenzungen an geeigneten Zugängen/Straßeneinmündungen an baulichen Anlagen mit dem Kulturgutschutzkennzeichen zu versehen. Eine Anbringung der Schilder an Pfählen in Straßengrund ist u. a. wegen der bereits vorhandenen Vielzahl von Straßenverkehrsschildern etc. zu vermeiden.
   Außerdem sind innerhalb des Ortsbildes die in der Ortsbildliste bezeichneten besonders hervorragenden Baudenkmäler ebenfalls zu kennzeichnen. Den Gemeinden wird empfohlen, die Kennzeichen an den Rändern der Ortsbilder mit einem gemeindespezifischen Zusatzschild zu versehen, um deutlich zu machen, daß es sich um ein Ortsbild handelt, ebenso um die Ortsbildabgrenzung zu markieren. Staatliche Haushaltsmittel stehen für Zusatzschilder nicht zur Verfügung. Das Zusatzschild muß im Hinblick u. a. auch auf die Transparenz für die militärische Seite (s. Art. 7 der Haager Konvention) von der Form und dem möglichen Inhalt her für ganz Bayern einheitlich gestaltet sein, andererseits soll es jeder Gemeinde ermöglichen, das ihr eigene spezifische Ortsgepräge symbolhaft darzustellen. Dies kann, wie z. B. die Anbringung der Kulturgutschutzkennzeichen in Österreich und Belgien ganz allgemein gezeigt hat, für den Fremdenverkehr von Bedeutung sein.
   Das Zusatzschild für Ortsbilder besteht aus einem querrechteckigen Schild – blau auf weiß – mit jeweils stilisierter Silhouette des betreffenden Ortsgepräges (17,6 cm breit und 8 cm hoch). Unter

D2.IV.1 VwV zum Vollzug der Haager Konvention

dem Ortssymbol ist auf dem Schild die Bezeichnung „Denkmalort" anzubringen. Der verwendete Begriff „Denkmalort" entspricht dem rechtstechnischen Begriff des Art. 1c der Haager Konvention. Entsprechend der Farbgebung des Kennzeichens nach Art. 16 der Konvention soll die Farbe des Zusatzschildes cremeweiß gemäß RAL 9001 und die Farbe der Aufdrucke (Ortssymbol und Bezeichnung „Denkmalort") ultramarinblau nach RAL 5002 gehalten werden.

3. **Kennzeichnung der Museen**
Der Bundesminister des Innern hat zugestimmt, daß in Bayern die Kennzeichnung der Museen gleichzeitig mit den Baudenkmälern erfolgt. Die Kennzeichen sind aus dem für jede Regierung bestimmten Reservekontingent zu entnehmen.

Die Museumsliste und die Aufstellung über die für jeden Regierungsbezirk benötigten Kulturgutschutzkennzeichen für Museen und Sammlungen ist den Regierungen und den sonstigen beteiligten staatl. Dienststellen bekannt. Bei der Kennzeichnung ist von folgendem Grundsatz auszugehen:

Ist ein Baudenkmal bereits mit einem Kulturgutschutzkennzeichen versehen, muß in der Regel das darin befindliche Museum nicht mehr besonders gekennzeichnet werden.

Die Regierungen werden gebeten, die Träger der nichtstaatl. Museen – soweit diese in die 1. Kennzeichnungsaktion einbezogen sind – über die vorgesehene Kennzeichnung zu unterrichten. Es gilt insoweit das gleiche wie bei den Baudenkmälern.

Die Generaldirektion der Staatl. Naturwissenschaftlichen Sammlungen Bayerns, die Staatl. Museen und Sammlungen mit Außenstellen, das Bayer. Landesamt für Denkmalpflege und die Bayer. Verwaltung der Staatl. Schlösser, Gärten und Seen werden gebeten, ihre Außenstellen zu unterrichten.

4. **Genehmigungsverfahren gemäß Art. 17 Abs. 4 der Haager Konvention**
Die Kennzeichen dürfen nur dann zur Identifizierung von unbeweglichem Kulturgut verwendet werden, wenn zugleich eine von der zuständigen Behörde der Hohen Vertragspartei ausgestellte ordnungsgemäß datierte und unterzeichnete Genehmigung angebracht wird (s. Art. 17 Abs. 4 der Haager Konvention). Auf das in Anlage 1[1)] befindliche Muster wird verwiesen.

Im Einvernehmen mit dem Staatsministerium des Innern wird bestimmt, daß die Genehmigungsurkunden von den Kreisverwaltungsbehörden ausgestellt werden.

Für jedes Objekt werden 3 Urkundenformulare benötigt, und zwar:
1. Der Eigentümer/Träger des nach der Haager Konvention zu schützenden Objekts erhält die Genehmigung. Diese sollte als sicherungswürdiges Dokument entsprechend aufbewahrt werden.
2. Eine Zweitausfertigung sollte in eine witterungsbeständige Folie eingeschweißt und, soweit möglich, im Innern des schutzwürdigen Objekts an geeigneter Stelle (am besten wohl im Hausflur) angebracht werden.
3. Das dritte Exemplar verbleibt bei der ausstellenden Kreisverwaltungsbehörde.

5. **Auslieferung der Kennzeichen und der sonstigen Unterlagen sowie Anbringung der Kennzeichen gemäß Art. 6, 16 und 17 der Haager Konvention**
   5.1 Die Kulturgutschutzkennzeichen sind zusammen mit den Formularen für die Genehmigungsurkunden sowie einem eigenen Merkblatt für die Anbringung der Kennzeichen (s. das in Anlage 2[1)] befindliche Muster) vom Bundesamt für Zivilschutz unmittelbar an die Regierungen übermittelt worden. Die Regierungen verteilen die notwendigen Kontingente an die Kreisverwaltungsbehörden.
   5.2 Für den Bereich der Bayer. Verwaltung der Staatl. Schlösser, Gärten und Seen erfolgt die Auslieferung mit den von den Kreisverwaltungsbehörden ausgestellten Genehmigungsurkunden und dem o.g. Merkblatt an die Außenverwaltungen entsprechend einem Schreiben der Bayer. Verwaltung der Staatl. Schlösser, Gärten und Seen vom 10. Oktober 1983, das den Regierungen und den sonstigen beteiligten staatlichen Dienststellen bekannt ist.
   5.3 Für den übrigen staatlichen Bereich werden die Kennzeichen etc. nach entsprechender Benachrichtigung durch die Kreisverwaltungsbehörden von den grundbesitzverwaltenden Behörden abgeholt und an den staatlichen Gebäuden angebracht (VV zu Art. 64 BayHO). Ob und inwieweit hier eine denkmalpflegerische fachliche Beratung auf Kreisebene erfolgt,

---
[1)] Hinweis: Die Anlagen wurden aus drucktechnischen Gründen nicht aufgenommen.

bleibt der örtlichen Abstimmung vorbehalten. Es ist Sache der Regierung, ggf. Näheres zu bestimmen.

5.4 Die für die kommunalen Gebäude vorgesehenen Kennzeichen etc. werden nach Auslieferung durch die Kreisverwaltungsbehörden von den Kommunen angebracht (§ 1,2 ZSG).
Im übrigen gilt Ziffer 5.3.

5.5 Die Aushändigung der Kulturgutschutzkennzeichen an kirchliche Einrichtungen erfolgt ebenfalls über die Kreisverwaltungsbehörden. Das Nähere ist von den Regierungen mit den Erzbischöflichen und Bischöflichen Ordinariaten sowie dem Evang.-Luth. Landeskirchenamt in München abzustimmen.
Die Erzbischöflichen und Bischöflichen Ordinariate und das Evang.-Luth. Landeskirchenamt werden um Mitwirkung gebeten.

5.6 Die Aushändigung der Kulturgutschutzkennzeichen mit den sonstigen Unterlagen an private Eigentümer ist von den Kreisverwaltungsbehörden entsprechend den örtlichen Möglichkeiten zu veranlassen. Hierbei empfiehlt sich eine Zusammenarbeit mit den Kommunen.
Für die Kulturgutschutzkennzeichen wird kein Entgelt erhoben. Das Kulturgutschutzkennzeichen mit Genehmigungsurkunde und sonstigen Unterlagen darf jedoch nur dann ausgehändigt werden, wenn sich der Eigentümer zur Anbringung verpflichtet.
Im übrigen gilt Ziffer 5.3.

Zuständigkeitsgesetz (ZustG)

Vom 7. Mai 2013 (GVBl. S. 246)
(BayRS 2015-1-V)
zuletzt geändert durch § 1 Abs. 36 V zur Anpassung des Landesrechts an die geltende Geschäftsverteilung vom 26. März 2019 (GVBl. S. 98)
– Auszug –

Der Landtag des Freistaates Bayern hat das folgende Gesetz beschlossen, das hiermit bekannt gemacht wird:

Teil 1
Allgemeine Bestimmungen

Artikel 1 Auffangzuständigkeit

(1) ¹Soweit eine Zuständigkeit nicht anderweitig bestimmt ist, obliegen Ausführung und Vollzug der Gesetze und Verordnungen den Staatsministerien jeweils für ihren Geschäftsbereich. ²Fällt eine Aufgabe in den Geschäftsbereich mehrerer Staatsministerien, ist das schwerpunktmäßig betroffene Staatsministerium zuständig.

(2) ¹Soweit eine Zuständigkeit nicht anderweitig näher bestimmt ist, wird die Staatsregierung ermächtigt, die zur Ausführung und zum Vollzug zuständigen Behörden innerhalb der bestehenden Behördenorganisation durch Rechtsverordnung zu bestimmen. ²Die Staatsregierung kann diese Ermächtigung im Einzelfall durch Rechtsverordnung auf andere Stellen übertragen.

(3) ¹Rechtsverordnungen, für deren Erlass oder Änderung keine gesetzliche Ermächtigung mehr besteht, können von der Stelle, die zuletzt hierzu ermächtigt war, aufgehoben werden. ²Besteht die Stelle nicht mehr, so können sie vom fachlich zuständigen Staatsministerium aufgehoben werden.

Artikel 2 Änderung der Geschäftsbereiche der Staatsministerien

(1) Werden die Geschäftsbereiche der Staatsministerien neu abgegrenzt, gehen die in Gesetzen und Rechtsverordnungen bestimmten Zuständigkeiten auf das neu zuständige Staatsministerium über.

(2) Die einem Staatsministerium zugewiesenen Zuständigkeiten werden durch eine Änderung seiner Bezeichnung nicht berührt.

(3) ¹Im Fall des Abs. 1 wird die Staatsregierung ermächtigt, durch Rechtsverordnung in Gesetzen und Rechtsverordnungen die Bezeichnung des bisher zuständigen Staatsministeriums durch die Bezeichnung des neu zuständigen Staatsministeriums zu ersetzen und etwaige durch den Zuständigkeitsübergang veranlasste Anpassungen des Wortlauts der Vorschriften vorzunehmen. ²Im Fall eines Bezeichnungswechsels eines Staatsministeriums ohne Änderung seiner Zuständigkeit gilt Satz 1 entsprechend.

Teil 2
Einzelne Zuständigkeitsbestimmungen

Artikel 10 Kulturgutschutzgesetz

(1) Zuständig für die Entgegennahme der Zustimmung des Verleihers oder Deponenten nach § 6 Abs. 2 Satz 1 des Kulturgutschutzgesetzes (KGSG) ist im Fall der Leihe oder Deposition zugunsten einer Kulturgut bewahrenden Einrichtung
1. in staatlicher Trägerschaft die jeweilige Einrichtung selbst,
2. in nichtstaatlicher Trägerschaft das Landesamt für Denkmalpflege.

(2) Zuständig für die Erteilung von Genehmigungen nach § 24 KGSG sind die Staatsgemäldesammlungen.

(3) Zuständig für den Vollzug des Kulturgutschutzgesetzes in allen übrigen Fällen ist das Staatsministerium für Wissenschaft und Kunst.

Teil 3
Schlussvorschriften

Artikel 11 Inkrafttreten
Dieses Gesetz tritt am 1. Juni 2013 in Kraft.

Verfassung von Berlin

Vom 23. November 1995[1] (GVBl. S. 779)
(BRV 100-1)
zuletzt geändert durch Art. 1 13. ÄndG vom 22. März 2016 (GVBl. S. 114)
– Auszug –

Abschnitt II
Grundrechte, Staatsziele

Artikel 20 [Recht auf Bildung]
(1) [1]Jeder Mensch hat das Recht auf Bildung. [2]Das Land ermöglicht und fördert nach Maßgabe der Gesetze den Zugang eines jeden Menschen zu den öffentlichen Bildungseinrichtungen, insbesondere ist die berufliche Erstausbildung zu fördern.
(2) Das Land schützt und fördert das kulturelle Leben.

Artikel 21 [Freiheit von Kunst, Wissenschaft, Forschung, Lehre]
[1]Kunst und Wissenschaft, Forschung und Lehre sind frei. [2]Die Freiheit der Lehre entbindet nicht von der Treue zur Verfassung.

---

[1] Die Verfassung ist in ihrer ursprünglichen Fassung am 1.9.1950 (VOBl. I S. 933) auf Grundlage der Vorläufigen Verfassung von Groß-Berlin vom 13.8.1946 (VOBl. I S. 295) verkündet worden.

Gesetz zum Schutz von Denkmalen in Berlin (Denkmalschutzgesetz Berlin – DSchG Bln)

Vom 24. April 1995 (GVBl. S. 274)
(BRV 2130-12)
zuletzt geändert durch Art. 30 FormAnpassG vom 2. Februar 2018 (GVBl. S. 160)

Erster Abschnitt
Aufgaben, Gegenstand und Organisation des Denkmalschutzes

§ 1 Aufgaben
(1) Es ist Aufgabe von Denkmalschutz und Denkmalpflege, Denkmale nach Maßgabe dieses Gesetzes zu schützen, zu erhalten, zu pflegen, wissenschaftlich zu erforschen und den Denkmalgedanken und das Wissen über Denkmale zu verbreiten.
(2) Die Belange des Denkmalschutzes und der Denkmalpflege sind in die städtebauliche Entwicklung, Landespflege und Landesplanung einzubeziehen und bei öffentlichen Planungen und Maßnahmen angemessen zu berücksichtigen.

§ 2 Begriffsbestimmungen
(1) Denkmale im Sinne dieses Gesetzes sind Baudenkmale, Denkmalbereiche, Gartendenkmale sowie Bodendenkmale.
(2) [1]Ein Baudenkmal ist eine bauliche Anlage oder ein Teil einer baulichen Anlage, deren oder dessen Erhaltung wegen der geschichtlichen, künstlerischen, wissenschaftlichen oder städtebaulichen Bedeutung im Interesse der Allgemeinheit liegt. [2]Zu einem Baudenkmal gehören sein Zubehör und seine Ausstattung, soweit sie mit dem Baudenkmal eine Einheit von Denkmalwert bilden.
(3) [1]Ein Denkmalbereich (Ensemble, Gesamtanlage) ist eine Mehrheit baulicher Anlagen einschließlich der mit ihnen verbundenen Straßen und Plätze sowie Grünanlagen und Frei- und Wasserflächen, deren Erhaltung aus in Absatz 2 genannten Gründen im Interesse der Allgemeinheit liegt, und zwar auch dann, wenn nicht jeder einzelne Teil des Denkmalbereichs ein Denkmal ist. [2]Auch Siedlungen können Denkmalbereiche sein.
(4) [1]Ein Gartendenkmal ist eine Grünanlage, eine Garten- oder Parkanlage, ein Friedhof, eine Allee oder ein sonstiges Zeugnis der Garten- und Landschaftsgestaltung, deren oder dessen Erhaltung aus in Absatz 2 genannten Gründen im Interesse der Allgemeinheit liegt. [2]Zu einem Gartendenkmal gehören sein Zubehör und seine Ausstattung, soweit sie mit dem Gartendenkmal eine Einheit von Denkmalwert bilden.
(5) Ein Bodendenkmal ist eine bewegliche oder unbewegliche Sache, die sich im Boden oder in Gewässern befindet oder befunden hat und deren Erhaltung aus in Absatz 2 genannten Gründen im Interesse der Allgemeinheit liegt.

§ 3 Bodendenkmale
(1) [1]Wer ein Bodendenkmal entdeckt, hat die Arbeiten an der Fundstelle sofort einzustellen und die Entdeckung unverzüglich der unteren Denkmalschutzbehörde anzuzeigen. [2]Zur Anzeige verpflichtet sind der Entdecker und der Verfügungsberechtigte; wird das Bodendenkmal bei der Durchführung eines Bauvorhabens entdeckt, so ist auch der Bauleiter zur Anzeige verpflichtet. [3]Der Fund und die Fundstelle sind bis zum Ablauf von vier Werktagen nach der Anzeige in unverändertem Zustand zu belassen. [4]Die oberste Denkmalschutzbehörde kann diese Frist angemessen verlängern, wenn die sachgerechte Untersuchung oder die Bergung des Bodendenkmals dies erfordert. [5]Ist das Bodendenkmal bei laufenden Arbeiten entdeckt worden, soll die Frist von vier Werktagen nur überschritten werden, wenn der Betroffene hierdurch nicht wirtschaftlich unzumutbar belastet wird. [6]Die zuständige Denkmalbehörde ist unbeschadet des Eigentumsrechts berechtigt, den Bodenfund auszuwerten und, soweit es sich um bewegliche Bodendenkmale handelt, zu bergen und zur wissenschaftlichen Bearbeitung in Besitz zu nehmen, grundsätzlich jedoch nicht länger als sechs Monate vom Eingang der Anzeige an gerechnet.
(2) Bewegliche Bodendenkmale, deren Eigentümer nicht mehr zu ermitteln sind, werden mit der Entdeckung Eigentum des Landes Berlin.

(3) ¹Das Graben nach Bodendenkmalen bedarf unbeschadet sonstiger Erlaubnisse der Genehmigung der zuständigen Denkmalbehörde. ²Die Genehmigung ist zu versagen, wenn nicht Gewähr dafür gegeben ist, daß die Durchführung der Grabung dem Schutze und der Pflege der Bodendenkmale gerecht wird.
(4) ¹Abgegrenzte Flächen, in denen Bodendenkmale vorhanden sind oder vermutet werden, kann die zuständige Senatsverwaltung durch Rechtsverordnung zu Grabungsschutzgebieten erklären. ²In Grabungsschutzgebieten bedürfen Arbeiten, die Bodendenkmale zu Tage fördern oder gefährden können, der Genehmigung der zuständigen Denkmalbehörde. ³§ 13 gilt entsprechend. ⁴Eine bisherige land- und forstwirtschaftliche Nutzung bleibt ohne Genehmigung zulässig, sofern sie bodendenkmalverträglich ist.

§ 4 Denkmalliste
(1) ¹Denkmale sind nachrichtlich in ein öffentliches Verzeichnis (Denkmalliste) einzutragen. ²Bewegliche Bodendenkmale im Eigentum staatlicher oder kommunaler Museen und Sammlungen sind nur in den dort zu führenden Inventaren einzutragen.
(2) ¹Die Eintragung erfolgt von Amts wegen oder auf Anregung des Verfügungsberechtigten. ²Eintragungen in den Denkmallisten werden von Amts wegen oder auf Anregung des Verfügungsberechtigten gelöscht, wenn die Eintragungsvoraussetzungen entfallen sind. ³Dies gilt nicht, wenn die Wiederherstellung eines Denkmals angeordnet ist. ⁴Die Verfügungsberechtigten werden umgehend von der Eintragung sowie der Löschung unterrichtet.
(3) ¹Die Denkmallisten werden ortsüblich bekannt gemacht. ²Die Einsicht in die Denkmallisten ist jedermann gestattet.

§ 5 Denkmalfachbehörde
(1) Denkmalfachbehörde ist eine der zuständigen Senatsverwaltung nachgeordnete Behörde.[1]
(2) Der Denkmalfachbehörde obliegen insbesondere folgende Aufgaben:
1. Mitwirkung beim Vollzug dieses Gesetzes und nach Maßgabe weiterer einschlägiger Bestimmungen,
2. systematische Erfassung von Denkmalen (Inventarisierung) und Erstellen einer Denkmaltopographie sowie deren Veröffentlichung,
3. nachrichtliche Aufnahme von Denkmalen in ein Verzeichnis (Denkmalliste) und dessen Führung,
4. wissenschaftliche Untersuchungen der Denkmale und Unterhaltung denkmalfachlicher Sammlungen als Beitrag zur Landesgeschichte,
5. Beratung und Unterstützung der Eigentümer und Besitzer von Denkmalen bei Pflege, Unterhaltung und Wiederherstellung,
6. Hinwirken auf die Berücksichtigung von Denkmalen bei der städtebaulichen Entwicklung,
7. Herausgabe von Rundschreiben zur Pflege von Denkmalen,
8. fachliche Beratung und Erstattung von Gutachten in allen Angelegenheiten der Denkmalpflege,
9. Vergabe von Denkmalpflegezuschüssen,
10. Veröffentlichung und Verbreitung von denkmalfachlichen Erkenntnissen,
11. Vertretung öffentlicher Belange des Denkmalschutzes und der Denkmalpflege,
12. Wahrnehmung von Ordnungsaufgaben nach diesem Gesetz, soweit Aufgaben der Hauptverwaltung,
13. Entscheidung über die Zustimmung nach § 6 Abs. 5 Satz 1.
(3) Die Denkmalfachbehörde untersteht der Fachaufsicht der zuständigen Senatsverwaltung (oberste Denkmalschutzbehörde).

§ 6 Denkmalschutzbehörden
(1) Den Denkmalschutzbehörden als Sonderordnungsbehörden obliegt der Schutz der Denkmale im Sinne des § 2 Abs. 1.
(2) Oberste Denkmalschutzbehörde ist die zuständige Senatsverwaltung.
(3) Untere Denkmalschutzbehörden sind die Bezirksämter; sie sind für alle Ordnungsaufgaben nach diesem Gesetz zuständig, soweit nichts anderes bestimmt ist.

---

1) Die Bekanntmachung zur Errichtung des Landesdenkmalamts Berlin ist abgedruckt als Nr. D3.I.1a.

(4) ¹Der Stiftung Preußische Schlösser und Gärten Berlin-Brandenburg obliegen in bezug auf denkmalgeschütztes Stiftungsvermögen die Aufgaben einer unteren Denkmalschutzbehörde nach Absatz 3. ²Absatz 5 gilt entsprechend.
(5) ¹Die unteren Denkmalschutzbehörden entscheiden im Einvernehmen mit der Denkmalfachbehörde.[1] ²Das Einvernehmen gilt als hergestellt, wenn nicht innerhalb von vier Wochen eine Stellungnahme der Denkmalfachbehörde vorliegt. ³Kommt kein Einvernehmen zustande, so trifft die oberste Denkmalschutzbehörde als zuständige Behörde innerhalb von zwei Wochen die Entscheidung. ⁴Bei Gefahr im Verzug können die unteren Denkmalschutzbehörden vorläufig ohne Einvernehmen mit der Fachbehörde zum Schutze der Denkmale entscheiden. ⁵In diesen Fällen ist eine einvernehmliche Entscheidung mit der Fachbehörde unverzüglich nachzuholen. ⁶Satz 3 gilt entsprechend.
(6) Die Denkmalfachbehörde berichtet vor Einvernehmenserteilung der obersten Denkmalschutzbehörde regelmäßig über überwiegend Wohnzwecken (Neubau- oder Sanierungsmaßnahmen) dienende Vorhaben, für die eine denkmalrechtliche Genehmigungspflicht besteht und für die eine Erteilung des Einzeleinvernehmens erforderlich wird.

§ 7 Landesdenkmalrat
(1) ¹Der Landesdenkmalrat berät das zuständige Mitglied des Senats. ²In allen Angelegenheiten von grundsätzlicher Bedeutung ist er zu hören.
(2) ¹In den Landesdenkmalrat werden auf Vorschlag des zuständigen Mitglieds des Senats vom Senat für die Dauer von vier Jahren zwölf Mitglieder berufen. ²Der Landesdenkmalrat soll sich aus Vertretern der Fachgebiete der Denkmalpflege, der Geschichte und der Architektur sowie paritätisch aus sachberührten Bürgern und Institutionen Berlins zusammensetzen.
(3) ¹Die Mitglieder des Landesdenkmalrates sind ehrenamtlich tätig. ²Sie sind an Weisungen nicht gebunden.
(4) Der Landesdenkmalrat wählt aus seiner Mitte den Vorsitzenden und dessen Stellvertreter.
(5) Das Nähere regelt die Geschäftsordnung des Landesdenkmalrates, die vom Senat erlassen wird.

Zweiter Abschnitt
Allgemeine Schutzvorschriften

§ 8 Erhaltung von Denkmalen
(1) ¹Der Verfügungsberechtigte ist verpflichtet, ein Denkmal im Rahmen des Zumutbaren instand zu halten und instand zu setzen, es sachgemäß zu behandeln und vor Gefährdungen zu schützen. ²Mängel, die die Erhaltung des Denkmals gefährden, hat er der zuständigen Denkmalbehörde unverzüglich anzuzeigen.
(2) ¹Der Verfügungsberechtigte kann durch die zuständige Denkmalbehörde verpflichtet werden, bestimmte Maßnahmen zur Erhaltung des Denkmals durchzuführen. ²Kommt der Verfügungsberechtigte seiner Verpflichtung nach Absatz 1 Satz 1 nicht nach und droht hierdurch eine unmittelbare Gefahr für den Bestand eines Denkmals, kann die zuständige Denkmalbehörde die gebotenen Maßnahmen selbst durchführen oder durchführen lassen. ³Der Verfügungsberechtigte kann im Rahmen des Zumutbaren zur Erstattung der entstandenen Kosten herangezogen werden. ⁴Mieter, Pächter und sonstige Nutzungsberechtigte haben die Durchführung der Maßnahmen zu dulden.
(3) ¹Für Denkmale kann die Erstellung von Denkmalpflegeplänen durch den Verfügungsberechtigten von der zuständigen Denkmalbehörde angeordnet werden, sofern dies zur dauerhaften Erhaltung der Denkmale sowie zur Vermittlung des Denkmalgedankens und des Wissens über Denkmale erforderlich ist. ²Denkmale sind nach diesen Denkmalpflegeplänen im Rahmen des Zumutbaren zu erhalten und zu pflegen.

§ 9 Nutzung von Denkmalen
Denkmale sind so zu nutzen, daß ihre Erhaltung auf Dauer gewährleistet ist.

§ 10 Schutz der unmittelbaren Umgebung
(1) Die unmittelbare Umgebung eines Denkmals, soweit sie für dessen Erscheinungsbild von prägender Bedeutung ist, darf durch Errichtung oder Änderung baulicher Anlagen, durch die Gestaltung der

---
1) Die AV-Einvernehmen DSchG ist abgedruckt als Nr. D3.I.1b.

unbebauten öffentlichen und privaten Flächen oder in anderer Weise nicht so verändert werden, daß die Eigenart und das Erscheinungsbild des Denkmals wesentlich beeinträchtigt werden.
(2) Die unmittelbare Umgebung eines Denkmals ist der Bereich, innerhalb dessen sich die bauliche oder sonstige Nutzung von Grundstücken oder von öffentlichen Flächen auf das Denkmal prägend auswirkt.

Dritter Abschnitt
Maßnahmen des Denkmalschutzes; öffentliche Förderung; Verfahrensvorschriften

§ 11 Genehmigungspflichtige Maßnahmen

(1) [1]Ein Denkmal darf nur mit Genehmigung der zuständigen Denkmalbehörde
1. in seinem Erscheinungsbild verändert,
2. ganz oder teilweise beseitigt,
3. von seinem Standort oder Aufbewahrungsort entfernt oder
4. instand gesetzt und wiederhergestellt.

[2]Dies gilt auch für das Zubehör und die Ausstattung eines Denkmals. [3]Die Genehmigung nach Satz 1 ist zu erteilen, wenn Gründe des Denkmalschutzes nicht entgegenstehen oder ein überwiegendes öffentliches Interesse die Maßnahme verlangt.
(2) [1]Einer Genehmigung bedarf ferner die Veränderung der unmittelbaren Umgebung eines Denkmals, wenn diese sich auf den Zustand oder das Erscheinungsbild des Denkmals auswirkt. [2]Die Genehmigung ist zu erteilen, wenn die Eigenart und das Erscheinungsbild des Denkmals durch die Maßnahme nicht wesentlich beeinträchtigt werden.
(3) Bei Werbeanlagen sind entgegenstehende Gründe des Denkmalschutzes gemäß Absatz 1 Satz 3 oder eine wesentliche Beeinträchtigung gemäß Absatz 2 Satz 2 nicht anzunehmen, wenn sie für höchstens sechs Monate angebracht werden und der Werbeinhalt vorrangig im öffentlichen Interesse liegende Ziele verfolgt.
(4) [1]Die Genehmigung kann unter Bedingungen und Auflagen sowie unter dem Vorbehalt des Widerrufs oder befristet erteilt werden. [2]Gebietet es die besondere Eigenart eines Denkmals, kann die Genehmigung auch mit der Bedingung verbunden werden, daß bestimmte Arbeiten nur durch Fachleute oder unter der Leitung von Sachverständigen ausgeführt werden, die die zuständige Denkmalbehörde bestimmt.
(5) [1]Alle Veränderungen und Maßnahmen an Denkmalen sind zu dokumentieren. [2]Die Dokumentationspflicht obliegt dem Eigentümer, dem sonstigen Nutzungsberechtigten oder dem Veranlasser nach zumutbarer Maßgabe der zuständigen Denkmalbehörde.
(6) Die Denkmalbehörden berücksichtigen bei ihren Entscheidungen die Belange mobilitätsbehinderter Personen.

§ 12 Genehmigungsverfahren

(1) [1]Der Genehmigungsantrag ist der zuständigen Denkmalbehörde in Schriftform oder elektronisch und mit aus denkmalfachlicher Sicht prüffähigen Unterlagen einzureichen; bei bauordnungsrechtlich genehmigungspflichtigen Vorhaben ist der Antrag bei der Bauaufsichtsbehörde einzureichen. [2]Im Falle eines bauordnungsrechtlichen Genehmigungsverfahrens kann eine Genehmigung nach § 11 Abs. 1 und 2 auch gesondert beantragt werden. [3]Im Ausnahmefall kann die beantragte Genehmigung bis zu zwölf Monate ausgesetzt werden, soweit vorbereitende Untersuchungen am Denkmal oder seiner unmittelbaren Umgebung erforderlich sind. [4]Satz 2 gilt entsprechend für das Zustimmungsverfahren nach der Bauordnung für Berlin.
(2) [1]Die Genehmigung erlischt, wenn nicht innerhalb von zwei Jahren nach ihrer Erteilung mit der Ausführung begonnen oder wenn die Ausführung ein Jahr unterbrochen worden ist. [2]Die Fristen nach Satz 1 können auf schriftlichen oder elektronischen Antrag jeweils bis zu einem Jahr verlängert werden.
(3) [1]Durch die Erteilung von Genehmigungen auf Grund dieses Gesetzes werden Genehmigungen, die auf Grund anderer Rechtsvorschriften erforderlich sind, nicht ersetzt. [2]Wird im Falle eines bauordnungsrechtlichen Genehmigungs- oder Zustimmungsverfahrens eine Genehmigung nach § 11 Abs. 1 und 2 nicht gesondert beantragt, schließt die Baugenehmigung oder bauordnungsrechtliche Zustimmung die denkmalrechtliche Genehmigung ein. [3]Die Entscheidung ergeht im Einvernehmen mit der

zuständigen Denkmalbehörde. [4]Im bauaufsichtlichen Verfahren beteiligt die Bauaufsichtsbehörde die Denkmalschutzbehörde dann, wenn in der Denkmalliste eingetragene Denkmale betroffen sind. [5]Diese Regelung gilt entsprechend für Entscheidungen, die die unmittelbare Umgebung eines Denkmals betreffen (§ 10 Abs. 1).

§ 13 Wiederherstellung; Stillegung
(1) [1]Ist ein Denkmal ohne Genehmigung verändert und dadurch in seinem Denkmalwert gemindert worden oder ist es ganz oder teilweise beseitigt oder zerstört worden, so kann die zuständige Denkmalbehörde anordnen, daß derjenige, der die Veränderung, Beseitigung oder Zerstörung zu vertreten hat, den früheren Zustand wiederherstellt. [2]Die Denkmalbehörde kann die erforderlichen Arbeiten auf Kosten des Verpflichteten durchführen lassen, wenn die denkmalgerechte Wiederherstellung sonst nicht gesichert erscheint. [3]Sie kann von dem Verpflichteten einen angemessenen Kostenvorschuß verlangen. [4]Verfügungsberechtigte, Mieter, Pächter und sonstige Nutzungsberechtigte haben die Durchführung der Maßnahmen zu dulden.
(2) [1]Werden genehmigungspflichtige Maßnahmen ohne Genehmigung begonnen, so kann die zuständige Denkmalbehörde die vorläufige Einstellung anordnen. [2]Werden unzulässige Bauarbeiten trotz einer schriftlich oder mündlich verfügten Einstellung fortgesetzt, so kann die zuständige Denkmalbehörde die Baustelle versiegeln oder die an der Baustelle vorhandenen Baustoffe, Bauteile, Geräte, Maschinen und Bauhilfsmittel in amtlichen Gewahrsam bringen. [3]Die vorläufige Einstellung gilt für höchstens einen Monat.

§ 14 Auskunfts- und Duldungspflichten
(1) [1]Verfügungs- und Nutzungsberechtigte sind verpflichtet, zur Erfüllung der Aufgaben nach diesem Gesetz den Denkmalbehörden oder ihren Beauftragten auf Verlangen die erforderlichen Auskünfte zu erteilen und Unterlagen vorzulegen. [2]Notare, andere Personen und Stellen haben Urkunden, die sich auf ein Denkmal beziehen, den Denkmalbehörden vorzulegen und Auskünfte zu erteilen.
(2) [1]Die Verfügungs- oder Nutzungsberechtigten haben zu ermöglichen, daß die Beauftragten der Denkmalbehörden in Wahrnehmung der Aufgaben nach diesem Gesetz auf Verlangen Grundstücke, Gebäude und Räume zu angemessener Tageszeit betreten können. [2]Wohnungen dürfen gegen den Willen des Nutzungsberechtigten nur zur Verhütung einer dringenden Gefahr für ein Denkmal betreten werden. [3]Das Grundrecht der Unverletzlichkeit der Wohnung (Artikel 13 des Grundgesetzes, Artikel 19 der Verfassung von Berlin) wird insoweit eingeschränkt.
(3) Die zuständigen Denkmalbehörden und ihre Beauftragten sind berechtigt, Bodendenkmale zu bergen und die notwendigen Maßnahmen zur Klärung der Fundumstände sowie zur Sicherung weiterer auf dem Grundstück vorhandener Bodenfunde durchzuführen.
(4) Der Wechsel des Eigentums an einem Denkmal ist unverzüglich der unteren Denkmalschutzbehörde von dem Veräußerer und im Falle der Erbfolge von dem Erben anzuzeigen.

§ 15 Öffentliche Förderung
(1) Für Maßnahmen zur Erhaltung, Unterhaltung und Wiederherstellung von Bau-, Garten- und Bodendenkmalen sowie sonstigen Anlagen von denkmalpflegerischem Interesse können im Rahmen der im Haushaltsplan von Berlin bereitgestellten Mittel Darlehen oder Zuschüsse gewährt werden.
(2) [1]Die Gewährung eines Darlehens oder eines Zuschusses kann mit Auflagen und Bedingungen verbunden werden. [2]Auflagen und Bedingungen, die sich auf den Bestand oder das Erscheinungsbild der Anlagen beziehen, sind auf Ersuchen der Denkmalfachbehörde als Baulasten in das Baulastenverzeichnis nach der Bauordnung für Berlin einzutragen. [3]Das Nähere regelt die zuständige Senatsverwaltung durch Förderrichtlinien.[1)]

Vierter Abschnitt
Ausgleichspflichtige Eigentumsbeschränkung, Enteignung, Vorkaufsrecht

§ 16 Ausgleichspflichtige Eigentumsbeschränkung
(1) [1]Soweit durch die Anordnung von Maßnahmen nach § 8 und § 9 besondere Aufwendungen erforderlich werden, die in der Eigenschaft des Denkmals begründet sind und über das auch bei einem Denkmal wirtschaftlich zumutbare Maß hinausgehen, kann der Verfügungsberechtigte für die dadurch

---
1) Die Förderrichtlinie zur Erhaltung von Denkmalen ist abgedruckt als Nr. D3.III.1.

D3.I.1 Denkmalschutzgesetz Berlin

entstehenden Vermögensnachteile einen angemessenen Ausgleich in Geld verlangen. ²Unzumutbar ist eine wirtschaftliche Belastung insbesondere, soweit die Kosten der Erhaltung und Bewirtschaftung dauerhaft nicht durch die Erträge oder den Gebrauchswert des Denkmals aufgewogen werden können.
³Ein Anspruch auf Ausgleich besteht nicht, soweit der Verfügungsberechtigte oder sein Rechtsvorgänger die besonderen Aufwendungen durch mangelnde Instandhaltung selbst zu verantworten hat.
(2) Wird durch die Versagung einer nach § 11 Abs. 1 oder 2 erforderlichen Genehmigung oder durch sonstige behördliche Maßnahmen auf Grund dieses Gesetzes eine bisher rechtmäßig ausgeübte wirtschaftliche Nutzung eines Denkmals oder seiner unmittelbaren Umgebung wirtschaftlich unzumutbar erschwert, so kann ebenfalls ein angemessener Ausgleich in Geld verlangt werden.
(3) ¹§ 254 des Bürgerlichen Gesetzbuches gilt sinngemäß. ²Öffentliche Fördermaßnahmen und staatliche Begünstigungen sind auf den Ausgleich anzurechnen.
(4) ¹Würde der Ausgleich nach Absatz 1 oder 2 mehr als 50 vom Hundert des Verkehrswertes des Grundstücks oder des Verfügungsrechts betragen, so kann das Land Berlin die Übertragung des Eigentums oder sonstigen Verfügungsrechts verlangen. ²Kommt eine Einigung über die Übertragung nicht zustande, so kann das Land Berlin die Enteignung zu seinen Gunsten verlangen.

§ 17 Enteignung
(1) Kann eine Gefahr für den Bestand, die Eigenart oder das Erscheinungsbild eines Denkmals auf andere Weise nicht nachhaltig abgewehrt werden, so ist die Enteignung zugunsten des Landes Berlin zulässig.
(2) ¹Der Eigentümer von Zubehör und Ausstattung im Sinne von § 2 Abs. 2 Satz 2 und Abs. 4 Satz 2, der nicht zugleich Verfügungsberechtigter des Bau- oder Gartendenkmals ist, kann zur Aufrechterhaltung der Einheit von Denkmalwert verpflichtet werden, die Zubehör- und Ausstattungsstücke auch nach Beendigung seines Nutzungsrechts in dem Bau- oder Gartendenkmal zu belassen. ²Soweit ihm hierdurch wirtschaftlich nicht zumutbare Nachteile entstehen, kann er einen angemessenen Ausgleich in Geld verlangen. ³Eine Enteignung zugunsten des Verfügungsberechtigten des Bau- oder Gartendenkmals ist zulässig, wenn die Einheit von Denkmalwert auf andere Weise nicht sichergestellt werden kann.
(3) Für die Enteignung und Entschädigung, auch bei beweglichen Sachen, gelten die Vorschriften des Berliner Enteignungsgesetzes vom 14. Juli 1964 (GVBl. S. 737), geändert durch Artikel I des Gesetzes vom 30. November 1984 (GVBl. S. 1664), soweit in diesem Gesetz nicht etwas anderes bestimmt ist.

§ 18 *[aufgehoben]*

Fünfter Abschnitt
Bußgeldvorschriften

§ 19 Ordnungswidrigkeiten
(1) Ordnungswidrig handelt, wer vorsätzlich oder fahrlässig
1. entgegen § 3 Abs. 1 Satz 1 nach Entdeckung eines Bodendenkmals die Arbeiten an der Fundstelle nicht sofort einstellt oder die Entdeckung der zuständigen Behörde nicht unverzüglich anzeigt,
2. entgegen § 3 Abs. 1 Satz 3 den Fund oder die Fundstelle bis zum Ablauf von vier Werktagen nach Abgabe der Anzeige nicht in unverändertem Zustand beläßt, sofern die oberste Denkmalschutzbehörde der Fortsetzung der Arbeit nicht zugestimmt hat,
3. entgegen § 3 Abs. 3 Satz 1 ohne Einwilligung der zuständigen Denkmalbehörde nach Bodendenkmalen gräbt,
4. entgegen § 8 Abs. 2 einer von der zuständigen Denkmalbehörde zur Erhaltung des Denkmals getroffenen vollziehbaren Anordnung nicht nachkommt oder deren Durchführung nicht duldet,
5. entgegen § 8 Abs. 3 Satz 2 ein Gartendenkmal nicht erhält oder pflegt,
6. ohne die nach § 11 Abs. 1 oder Abs. 2 Satz 1 erforderliche Genehmigung eine dort genannte Handlung vornimmt oder eine gemäß § 11 Abs. 3 mit der Genehmigung verbundene Auflage oder Bedingung nicht erfüllt,
7. einer zur Wiederherstellung eines Denkmals von der zuständigen Denkmalbehörde erlassenen vollziehbaren Anordnung nach § 13 Abs. 1 Satz 1 zuwiderhandelt oder entgegen § 13 Abs. 1 Satz 4 die Durchführung der Maßnahmen nicht duldet,

8. entgegen § 14 Abs. 1 der Auskunfts- oder Vorlagepflicht nicht vollständig oder nicht richtig nachkommt oder entgegen § 14 Abs. 2 einem Beauftragten einer Denkmalbehörde das Betreten eines Grundstücks oder Besichtigen eines Denkmals nicht gestattet,
9. entgegen § 14 Abs. 4 den Eigentumswechsel nicht unverzüglich anzeigt.

(2) Die Ordnungswidrigkeit kann mit einer Geldbuße bis zu 500 000 Euro geahndet werden.

Sechster Abschnitt
Übergangs- und Schlußvorschriften

§ 20 Verwaltungsvorschriften
Die für den Denkmalschutz zuständige Senatsverwaltung erlässt die zur Ausführung des Gesetzes erforderlichen Verwaltungsvorschriften.

§ 21 Religionsgemeinschaften
(1) Entscheidungen und Maßnahmen der zuständigen Denkmalbehörde über Denkmale, die unmittelbar gottesdienstlichen Zwecken anerkannter Religionsgemeinschaften dienen, sind im Benehmen mit den zuständigen Behörden der Religionsgemeinschaften und unter Berücksichtigung der von diesen festgestellten gottesdienstlichen Belange zu treffen.
(2) § 16 Abs. 4 und § 17 finden auf Denkmale, die unmittelbar gottesdienstlichen Zwecken dienen, keine Anwendung.

§ 22 Überleitungsvorschrift
¹Die in dem Baudenkmalbuch und in dem Bodendenkmalbuch bislang eingetragenen Denkmale sowie die als in das Baudenkmalbuch eingetragen geltenden Denkmale gelten mit dem Inkrafttreten dieses Gesetzes als in die Denkmalliste nachrichtlich eingetragen. ²Bestands- und rechtskräftige Entscheidungen wirken gegenüber den Verfügungsberechtigten und Dritten fort.

§ 23 Inkrafttreten
(1) Dieses Gesetz tritt am Tage nach der Verkündung[1] im Gesetz- und Verordnungsblatt für Berlin in Kraft.
(2) Mit dem Inkrafttreten dieses Gesetzes tritt das Denkmalschutzgesetz Berlin vom 22. Dezember 1977 (GVBl. S. 2540), geändert durch Artikel I des Gesetzes vom 30. November 1981 (GVBl. S. 1470), außer Kraft.
(3) Die nach § 17 des Denkmalschutzgesetzes Berlin vom 22. Dezember 1977 (GVBl. S. 2540) erlassenen Rechtsverordnungen treten spätestens fünf Jahre nach Inkrafttreten dieses Gesetzes außer Kraft.

---

[1] Verkündet am 6.5.1995.

D3.I.1a Landesdenkmalamt Berlin

Errichtung des Landesdenkmalamtes Berlin
Bek. vom 2. August 1995 (ABl. S. 2833)

Mit Wirkung vom 1. Juli 1995 ist das Landesdenkmalamt Berlin als nachgeordnete Einrichtung der Senatsverwaltung für Stadtentwicklung und Umweltschutz institutionalisiert worden. Die Senatsverwaltung für Stadtentwicklung und Umweltschutz hat damit den Auftrag aus dem am 7. Mai 1995 in Kraft getretenen Denkmalschutzgesetz Berlin, das in § 5 die Einrichtung einer Denkmalfachbehörde vorsieht, vollzogen.

Das Landesdenkmalamt Berlin wird gebildet aus der Fachabteilung Bau- und Gartendenkmalpflege der Senatsverwaltung für Stadtentwicklung und Umweltschutz und dem Archäologischen Landesamt Berlin, das aus dem Geschäftsbereich der Senatsverwaltung für Kulturelle Angelegenheiten in den Geschäftsbereich der Senatsverwaltung für Stadtentwicklung und Umweltschutz übergeht.

Dienstsitz des Landesdenkmalamtes Berlin ist Lindenstraße Nr. 20-25, 10958 Berlin (Kreuzberg).

Die Zuständigkeiten der Obersten Denkmalschutzbehörde und der Fachaufsicht in Angelegenheiten des Denkmalschutzes obliegen weiterhin dem Referat II G der Senatsverwaltung für Stadtentwicklung und Umweltschutz (Anschrift w. o.).

AV-Einvernehmen Denkmalschutzgesetz

Ausführungsvorschriften zu § 6 Absatz 5 Satz 1 Denkmalschutzgesetz (DSchG Bln) über die Beteiligung des Landesdenkmalamtes an den Entscheidungen der unteren Denkmalschutzbehörden (AV-Einvernehmen)

Aufgrund des § 6 Absatz 2 Buchstabe a AZG in Verbindung mit § 20 DSchG Bln wird zur Ausführung des § 6 Absatz 5 Satz 1 in Verbindung mit § 5 Absatz 2 Nummer 13 DSchG Bln Folgendes bestimmt:

1. Einvernehmen nach § 6 Absatz 5 Satz 1 DSchG Bln

(1) Nach § 6 Absatz 5 Satz 1 DSchG Bln haben die unteren Denkmalschutzbehörden ihre Entscheidungen als Ordnungsbehörden im Einvernehmen mit dem Landesdenkmalamt zu treffen; entsprechend obliegt dem Landesdenkmalamt gemäß § 5 Absatz 2 Nummer 13 DSchG Bln die Entscheidung über die Zustimmung nach § 6 Absatz 5 Satz 1 DSchG Bln.

(2) Die Entscheidung über die Herstellung des Einvernehmens erfolgt grundsätzlich zu jeder Entscheidung der unteren Denkmalschutzbehörde im Einzelfall („Einzelfall-Einvernehmen"), soweit das Einvernehmen nicht vorab im Rahmen eines Denkmalpflegeplans für einzelne Maßnahmen oder durch allgemeine Vorgaben für eine Vielzahl von Fällen erteilt worden ist („pauschaliertes Einvernehmen") oder es durch Fristablauf gemäß § 6 Absatz 5 Satz 2 DSchG Bln als erteilt gilt.

2. Einzelfall-Einvernehmen

(1) Das Landesdenkmalamt trifft seine Entscheidungen über die Zustimmung grundsätzlich einzelfallbezogen
a) durch formularmäßige Bestätigung oder Mitzeichnung der von der unteren Denkmalschutzbehörde gefertigten Stellungnahme oder Protokolle gemeinsamer Besprechungen,
b) durch Bestätigung im elektronischen Genehmigungsverfahren oder
c) durch förmliches Schreiben an die untere Denkmalschutzbehörde.
Auf Anforderung der unteren Denkmalschutzbehörde und im Falle der Versagung des Einvernehmens ist sie in der Form des Absatzes 1 Satz 1 Buchstabe c) zu treffen.

(2) Die Verweigerung der Zustimmung ist zu begründen. Im Falle einer Ermessensentscheidung oder einer erforderlichen Interessenabwägung müssen in der Begründung die für die Abwägung maßgeblichen Gesichtspunkte aufgeführt werden.

3. Pauschaliertes Einvernehmen

(1) Das Einvernehmen mit dem Landesdenkmalamt ist hergestellt, wenn die Entscheidung der unteren Denkmalschutzbehörde in den in den nachfolgenden Absätzen 2 und 3 genannten Verfahren ergeht und den Vorgaben entspricht, die in den vom Landesdenkmalamt erstellten oder bestätigten
a) allgemeinen Rahmenvorgaben,
b) denkmalpflegerischen Gutachten oder
c) Denkmalpflegekonzeptionen, Erhaltungskonzepten oder Denkmalpflegeplänen enthalten sind.

(2) Die Regelungen zum pauschalierten Einvernehmen sind nur anwendbar bei
a) Anordnungen von Maßnahmen zur Erhaltung von Denkmalen nach § 8 Absatz 2 DSchG Bln,
b) Ersatzvornahmen nach § 8 Absatz 2 DSchG Bln,
c) Genehmigungen nach § 11 DSchG Bln und Entscheidungen über die Herstellung des Einvernehmens im bauordnungsrechtlichen Genehmigungs- oder Zustimmungsverfahren nach § 12 Absatz 3 Satz 3 DSchG Bln, soweit nicht ein Fall des Absatzes 3 gegeben ist,
d) Anordnungen der erforderlichen Untersuchungen nach § 12 Absatz 1 Satz 4 DSchG Bln,
e) Anordnungen der Wiederherstellung des früheren Zustandes nach § 13 Absatz 1 DSchG Bln,
f) Anordnungen der vorläufigen Einstellung der ungenehmigten Baumaßnahmen und andere Entscheidungen nach § 13 Absatz 2 DSchG Bln.

(3) Die Regelungen zum pauschalierten Einvernehmen sind in den Fällen des Absatzes 2 Buchstabe c) nicht anwendbar
a) bei Objekten, die
   i) vor 1870/71 errichtet worden sind,
   ii) von herausragender Bedeutung sind oder
   iii) aus Denkmalmitteln gefördert wurden oder werden,

D3.I.1b AV-Einvernehmen Denkmalschutzgesetz

b) bei Maßnahmen, die zum vollständigen oder teilweisen Verlust der Denkmaleigenschaft führen,
c) bei der Translozierung eines Denkmals oder
d) wenn die Entscheidung Ausgleichsansprüche nach § 16 Abs. 2 DSchG Bln begründen kann.

(4) Das pauschalierte Einvernehmen ist nicht erteilt, wenn die Entscheidung der unteren Denkmalschutzbehörden ganz oder teilweise von den Vorgaben nach Absatz 1 abweicht. Abweichend von Absatz 1 ist das pauschalierte Einvernehmen auch dann nicht erteilt, wenn die untere Denkmalschutzbehörde bei ihrer Entscheidung oder das Landesdenkmalamt vor der Entscheidung der unteren Denkmalschutzbehörde eine Entscheidung über die Herstellung des Einvernehmens im Einzelfall einfordert. In diesen Fällen gilt Ziffer 2 (Einzelfall-Einvernehmen).

4. Einvernehmen im Widerspruchsverfahren
(1) Für das Einvernehmen im Widerspruchsverfahren gelten die Ziffern 1 bis 3 entsprechend.
(2) Die Entscheidung des Landesdenkmalamtes im Rahmen des Einzelfall-Einvernehmens erfolgt durch förmliches Schreiben und ist zu begründen.

5. Beteiligung des Landesdenkmalamtes bei Verwaltungsstreitverfahren der Bezirke
Die unteren Denkmalschutzbehörden beteiligen in Verwaltungsstreitverfahren das Landesdenkmalamt. Das Landesdenkmalamt unterstützt die unteren Denkmalschutzbehörden durch Gutachten zur Denkmaleigenschaft, durch fachliche Stellungnahme zu Schriftsätzen und durch Teilnahme an Ortstermin und mündlicher Verhandlung.

6. Schlussvorschriften
(1) Diese Ausführungsvorschrift tritt am 01.07.2019 in Kraft.
(2) Die Ausführungsvorschrift tritt am 31.05.2021 außer Kraft.

Gesetz über die Sicherung und Benutzung von Archivgut des Landes Berlin (Archivgesetz des Landes Berlin – ArchGB)[1)]

Vom 14. März 2016 (GVBl. S. 96)
(BRV 224-3)

Das Abgeordnetenhaus hat das folgende Gesetz beschlossen:

§ 1 Anwendungsbereich
(1) Dieses Gesetz regelt die Sicherung und Benutzung von öffentlichem Archivgut und die Tätigkeit der öffentlichen Archive im Land Berlin.
(2) Soweit nach Berliner Landesrecht verfasste Stellen eigene Archive unterhalten und für diese Stellen keine besonderen Rechtsvorschriften gelten, sind die Bestimmungen dieses Gesetzes entsprechend anzuwenden.
(3) Dieses Gesetz gilt nicht für die öffentlich-rechtlichen Religions- und Weltanschauungsgemeinschaften, für die öffentlich-rechtlichen Rundfunkanstalten und für öffentlich-rechtliche Unternehmen mit eigener Rechtspersönlichkeit, die am wirtschaftlichen Wettbewerb teilnehmen, und deren Zusammenschlüsse.

§ 2 Organisation und Zuständigkeit im Archivwesen des Landes Berlin
(1) Die für kulturelle Angelegenheiten zuständige Senatsverwaltung ist verantwortlich für alle Grundsatzfragen der Archive des Landes Berlin.
(2) [1]Das Landesarchiv Berlin ist das zentrale Staatsarchiv des Landes Berlin. [2]Das Landesarchiv Berlin ist der für kulturelle Angelegenheiten zuständigen Senatsverwaltung als nichtrechtsfähige Anstalt nachgeordnet.
(3) [1]Die Bezirke können Heimatarchive für die Geschichte des Bezirkes einrichten. [2]Die Aufgaben des Landesarchivs Berlin nach § 3 sowie das Recht zur Übernahme von archivwürdigen Unterlagen auch der Bezirke durch das Landesarchiv Berlin nach den §§ 5 und 7 dieses Gesetzes bleiben davon unberührt.
(4) [1]Das Abgeordnetenhaus von Berlin und die juristischen Personen des öffentlichen Rechts, die der Aufsicht des Landes Berlin unterstehen, können entweder eigene Archive unterhalten, sofern diese den anerkannten Grundsätzen des Archivwesens entsprechen, oder Archivgut entsprechend § 5 Absatz 1 dem Landesarchiv Berlin zur Verfügung stellen. [2]Das Abgeordnetenhaus von Berlin ist berechtigt, durch eine Vereinbarung mit dem Landesarchiv Berlin die Übernahme und Benutzung archivwürdiger Unterlagen zu regeln.

§ 3 Aufgaben des Landesarchivs Berlin
(1) [1]Das Landesarchiv Berlin hat die Aufgabe, Unterlagen zu erfassen, zu bewerten und als Archivgut zu sichern und auf Dauer zu bewahren sowie die Erschließung zu gewährleisten und es für die Benutzung allgemein zugänglich zu machen. [2]Das Landesarchiv Berlin fördert die wissenschaftliche Forschung und die Öffentlichkeitsarbeit und wirkt an der Erforschung und der Vermittlung der Landesgeschichte mit.
(2) [1]Das Landesarchiv Berlin archiviert das aus den Geschäftsgängen aller Behörden, Gerichte und sonstigen Stellen des Landes Berlin sowie von deren Rechts- und Funktionsvorgängern hervorgegangene Archivgut. [2]Das Landesarchiv Berlin kann Archivgut privater Institutionen und natürlicher Personen archivieren oder sie bei der Wahrnehmung dieser Aufgaben unterstützen. [3]Das Landesarchiv Berlin ergänzt seine Bestände durch alles sonstige archivwürdige Material, an dessen Verwahrung und Erschließung ein öffentliches Interesse besteht.
(3) [1]Das Landesarchiv Berlin berät die Behörden, Gerichte und sonstigen Stellen des Landes Berlin bei der Verwaltung und Sicherung ihrer Unterlagen im Hinblick auf die spätere Archivierung. [2]Diese Stellen beteiligen das Landesarchiv Berlin bei der Einführung und Änderung technischer Systeme zur Erstellung und Speicherung elektronischer Unterlagen. [3]Die Beratungstätigkeit nach Satz 1 erstreckt sich auch auf die nichtöffentlichen Archive.

---

1) Dieses Gesetz tritt gem. § 11 Satz 1 am 25.3.2016 in Kraft. Bis zu diesem Zeitpunkt siehe das Archivgesetz des Landes Berlin 1993 v. 9.12.1993 (GVBl. S. 96).

(4) ¹Das Landesarchiv Berlin führt die Stadtchronik Berlins. ²Es führt die Aufgaben der audiovisuellen Stadtdokumentation und der Berlin-Information im Einvernehmen mit dem Presse- und Informationsamt des Landes Berlin fort. ³Durch Editionen, sonstige Publikationen, Ausstellungen, Führungen und andere geeignete Veranstaltungen fördert das Landesarchiv Berlin das Verständnis für die Geschichte Berlins.

(5) ¹Das Landesarchiv Berlin ist berechtigt, zum Zwecke der Erfüllung seiner Aufgaben personenbezogene Daten zu verarbeiten. ²Die Vorschriften des Berliner Datenschutzgesetzes in der Fassung vom 17. Dezember 1990 (GVBl. 1991 S. 16, 54), das zuletzt durch Gesetz vom 16. Mai 2012 (GVBl. S. 137) geändert worden ist, in der jeweils geltenden Fassung, bleiben unberührt.

§ 4 Archivgut

(1) Archivgut sind alle archivwürdigen Unterlagen wie Urkunden, Akten, Amtsbücher, Einzelschriftstücke, Film-, Bild- und Tonmaterial, Karten, Pläne, Karteien oder Teile davon und alle elektronischen Unterlagen, unabhängig von ihrer Speicherungsform sowie alle Hilfsmittel oder ergänzenden Daten, die für die Erhaltung oder das Verständnis dieser Informationen oder deren Benutzung notwendig sind.

(2) Archivwürdig sind Unterlagen, die für die wissenschaftliche Forschung, die Aufklärung und das Verständnis von Geschichte und Gegenwart bleibenden Wert haben, sowie solche, deren Aufbewahrung zur Sicherung berechtigter Belange oder zur Bereitstellung von Informationen für die Gesetzgebung, Rechtsprechung oder Verwaltung unerlässlich sind.

(3) Über die Archivwürdigkeit entscheidet das Landesarchiv Berlin.

§ 5 Aussonderung und Anbietung von Unterlagen

(1) ¹Alle Behörden, Gerichte und sonstigen Stellen des Landes Berlin sind verpflichtet, sämtliche Unterlagen, die zur Erfüllung ihrer Aufgaben nicht mehr benötigt werden, in der Regel spätestens 30 Jahre nach ihrer Entstehung auszusondern und unverändert anzubieten, soweit nicht Rechtsvorschriften andere Fristen bestimmen. ²Entstehung bezeichnet den Zeitpunkt der Vervollständigung einer Unterlage oder die letzte inhaltliche Bearbeitung einer Unterlage. ³Die Verpflichtung nach Satz 1 gilt auch für diejenigen Unterlagen von ehemals öffentlichen oder diesen gleichgestellten Stellen, die bis zum Zeitpunkt des Übergangs in eine Rechtsform des Privatrechts entstanden sind. ⁴Als Stellen des Landes im Sinne von Satz 1 gelten auch juristische Personen des Privatrechts, die nicht am wirtschaftlichen Wettbewerb teilnehmen und bei denen dem Land Berlin mehr als die Hälfte der Anteile oder der Stimmen zustehen. ⁵Diese Verpflichtung bezieht sich auch auf Unterlagen mit personenbezogenen Daten. ⁶§ 17 Absatz 4 des Berliner Datenschutzgesetzes bleibt dabei unberührt.

(2) Soweit gleichförmige Unterlagen, die in großer Zahl anfallen, archivwürdig sind, sind Art und Umfang des dem Landesarchiv Berlin zu übergebenden Archivgutes durch Vereinbarung der anbietenden Stelle mit dem Landesarchiv Berlin im Grundsatz festzulegen.

(3) Bei elektronischen Unterlagen sind das Format von Primär- und Metadaten sowie die Form der Übermittlung vorab zu vereinbaren.

(4) Von der Anbietungspflicht ausgenommen sind Unterlagen, deren Offenbarung gegen das Brief-, Post- oder Fernmeldegeheimnis verstoßen würde.

§ 6 Daten von ehemaligen Einrichtungen der DDR

(1) Wurden personenbezogene Daten aus ehemaligen Einrichtungen der DDR vor dem 3. Oktober 1990 nach ihrer Zweckbestimmung überwiegend für Verwaltungsaufgaben verarbeitet, die nach dem Grundgesetz von öffentlichen Stellen des Landes wahrzunehmen sind, so stehen sie derjenigen Stelle zu, die für die Verwaltungsaufgabe zuständig ist.

(2) Befinden sich die Daten im Gewahrsam nichtöffentlicher Stellen, so sind sie an die zuständige Stelle herauszugeben.

(3) ¹Sind die in Absatz 1 und 2 genannten Daten für den Verwaltungsvollzug nicht mehr erforderlich, ist zu prüfen, ob schutzwürdige Belange von Betroffenen die weitere Aufbewahrung bei der zuständigen Stelle erfordern. ²Ist dies nicht der Fall, sind die Daten dem Landesarchiv Berlin zu übergeben. ³Soweit das Landesarchiv Berlin die Übernahme ablehnt, sind die Daten zu vernichten. ⁴§ 17 Absatz 3 Satz 3 und 4 des Berliner Datenschutzgesetzes gilt insoweit nicht.

§ 7 Übernahme des Archivgutes

(1) ¹Das Landesarchiv Berlin übernimmt das Archivgut. ²Entscheidet es nicht innerhalb von zwölf Monaten über die Übernahme angebotener Unterlagen, so ist die anbietende Stelle zu deren weiterer Aufbewahrung nicht verpflichtet.

(2) ¹Das Landesarchiv Berlin kann in Ausnahmefällen im Auftrag öffentlicher Stellen Unterlagen aufbewahren. ²Speichernde Stelle für diese Unterlagen bleibt die abgebende Stelle. ³Die Regelungen zur Anbietungspflicht und zur Entscheidung über die Archivwürdigkeit und Übernahme der Unterlagen bleiben unberührt.

(3) Den Vertreterinnen und Vertretern des Landesarchivs Berlin ist zur Erfüllung ihrer Aufgaben Zutritt zu den Registraturen der Behörden, Gerichte und sonstigen Stellen des Landes Berlin und Einsicht in die angebotenen Unterlagen und die diesbezüglichen Findmittel der Registraturen zu gewähren.

(4) Das Landesarchiv Berlin darf das ihm gemäß § 2 Absatz 3 des Bundesarchivgesetzes vom 6. Januar 1988 (BGBl. I S. 62), das zuletzt durch Artikel 4 Absatz 38 des Gesetzes vom 7. August 2013 (BGBl. I S. 3154) geändert worden ist, in der jeweils geltenden Fassung,[1] von Behörden und sonstigen Stellen des Bundes, bundesunmittelbaren Körperschaften, Anstalten und Stiftungen angebotene Archivgut übernehmen.

§ 8 Sicherung des Archivgutes

(1) ¹Das Landesarchiv Berlin hat die erforderlichen technischen und organisatorischen Maßnahmen zu treffen, um die ordnungsgemäße und sachgemäße dauernde Aufbewahrung und Benutzbarkeit des übernommenen Archivgutes sowie seinen Schutz vor unbefugter Benutzung oder vor Vernichtung sicherzustellen. ²Gleiches gilt für die im Auftrag verwahrten Unterlagen. ³Bei der Aufbewahrung der Unterlagen sind auch die Regelungen zur Sicherung geheimhaltungsbedürftiger Unterlagen zu beachten. ⁴Die Verknüpfung personenbezogener Daten durch das Landesarchiv Berlin ist innerhalb der in § 9 genannten Schutzfristen nur zulässig, wenn schutzwürdige Belange betroffener Personen oder Dritter nicht beeinträchtigt werden.

(2) ¹Die öffentlichen Archive des Landes Berlin können untereinander sowie mit Archiven des Bundes und bundesunmittelbarer juristischer Personen des öffentlichen Rechts und anderer Bundesländer Archivgut austauschen, wenn dies im öffentlichen Interesse liegt, archivwissenschaftlichen Grundsätzen entspricht und schutzwürdige Belange Betroffener und Dritter nicht beeinträchtigt werden. ²In allen anderen Fällen ist übernommenes Archivgut, das im Eigentum des Landes Berlin steht, unveräußerlich.

(3) ¹Archivgut, dessen Archivwürdigkeit nicht mehr gegeben ist, ist zu vernichten oder zu löschen. ²Über die Vernichtung ist ein Nachweis zu fertigen und dauernd aufzubewahren.

§ 9 Benutzung des Archivgutes

(1) Jede Person hat auf Antrag das Recht, Archivgut nach Maßgabe dieses Gesetzes und der aufgrund dieses Gesetzes erlassenen Verwaltungsvorschriften zu benutzen.

(2) ¹Grundsätzlich darf Archivgut nach seiner Entstehung nicht vor Ablauf von zehn Jahren durch Dritte benutzt werden. ²Archivgut, das bundesrechtlichen oder besonderen Geheimhaltungsvorschriften unterliegt, darf frühestens 30 Jahre nach seiner Entstehung und nur dann zur Benutzung freigegeben werden, wenn ein öffentliches Interesse an der Geheimhaltung nicht entgegensteht.

(3) ¹Archivgut, das sich seinem wesentlichen Inhalt nach auf eine natürliche Person bezieht (personenbezogenes Archivgut), darf unbeschadet des Absatzes 2 Dritten nur mit der Einwilligung der Betroffenen zugänglich gemacht werden. ²Nach dem Tode der Betroffenen bedarf die Benutzung des Archivgutes bis zum Ablauf von zehn Jahren der Einwilligung der Angehörigen. ³Das Zustimmungsrecht wird von der überlebenden Ehegattin oder vom überlebenden Ehegatten oder der überlebenden Lebenspartnerin oder dem überlebenden Lebenspartner, falls eine solche oder ein solcher nicht vorhanden ist, wird es von den Abkömmlingen ersten Grades und, falls weder Ehegattin, Ehegatte, Lebenspartnerin oder Lebenspartner noch Abkömmlinge ersten Grades vorhanden sind, von den Eltern der Betroffenen ausgeübt. ⁴Ist das Todesjahr der Betroffenen dem Landesarchiv Berlin nicht bekannt, so endet die Schutzfrist hundert Jahre nach der Geburt. ⁵Ist auch das Geburtsjahr dem Landesarchiv Berlin nicht bekannt, so endet die Schutzfrist siebzig Jahre nach der Entstehung der Unterlage. ⁶Die Schutzfrist gilt nicht für die Benutzung durch die Betroffenen oder ihre Angehörigen.

---

1) Das Bundesarchivgesetz ist abgedruckt als Nr. C.III.1.

(4) ¹Die Schutzfristen können vom Landesarchiv Berlin verkürzt werden, wenn und soweit dies im überwiegenden öffentlichen Interesse liegt. ²Bei personenbezogenem Archivgut ist eine Verkürzung auch ohne Vorliegen eines überwiegenden öffentlichen Interesses zulässig, wenn die Betroffenen oder im Falle ihres Todes ihre Angehörigen im Sinne des Absatzes 3 Satz 3 eingewilligt haben. ³Kann die Einwilligung nicht eingeholt werden, so ist eine Verkürzung nur zulässig, wenn durch geeignete Maßnahmen gegenüber der Benutzerin oder dem Benutzer sichergestellt ist, dass die schutzwürdigen Belange der Betroffenen nicht beeinträchtigt werden. ⁴Für Personen der Zeitgeschichte können die Schutzfristen nach Absatz 2 Satz 1 und Absatz 3 im Hinblick auf Ereignisse von zeitgeschichtlicher Relevanz verkürzt werden, wenn die schutzwürdigen Belange der oder des Betroffenen angemessen berücksichtigt werden. ⁵Das Gleiche gilt für Archivgut, das sich auf die Tätigkeit natürlicher Personen in Ausübung öffentlicher Ämter bezieht.

(5) Ein überwiegendes öffentliches Interesse an der Benutzung von Archivgut vor Ablauf der Schutzfristen ist in der Regel dann gegeben, wenn die Person oder der historische Vorgang, auf die oder den in dem geschützten Archivgut Bezug genommen wird, von besonderer oder exemplarischer Bedeutung für die Erforschung der Geschichte oder das Verständnis der Gegenwart ist.

(6) ¹Die Schutzfristen nach Absatz 2 Satz 1 und Absatz 3 gelten nicht für Unterlagen, die bereits bei ihrer Entstehung zur Veröffentlichung bestimmt waren. ²Gleiches gilt für Archivgut, das bereits vor der Übergabe an das Landesarchiv Berlin einem Informationszugang nach dem Berliner Informationsfreiheitsgesetz vom 15. Oktober 1999 (GVBl. S. 561), das zuletzt durch Gesetz vom 23. Juni 2015 (GVBl. S. 285) geändert worden ist, in der jeweils geltenden Fassung, tatsächlich offen gestanden hat.

(7) ¹Die anbietende Stelle sowie deren Rechts- und Funktionsnachfolger sind befugt, Archivgut, das aus ihren Unterlagen ausgewählt worden ist, zu benutzen, wenn sie es zur Erfüllung ihrer Aufgaben wieder benötigen. ²Dies gilt nicht für personenbezogene Daten, die, wenn sie nicht übernommen worden wären, aufgrund einer Rechtsvorschrift hätten gesperrt oder gelöscht werden müssen; in diesen Fällen besteht die Benutzungsbefugnis nur nach Maßgabe der Absätze 3 bis 5.

(8) ¹Die Benutzung von Film-, Bild- und Tonmaterial, das im Landesarchiv Berlin verwahrt ist, unterliegt den Schutzfristen der Absätze 2 und 3 nur, soweit und solange daran Rechte Betroffener nach Maßgabe der §§ 22 und 23 des Gesetzes betreffend das Urheberrecht an Werken der bildenden Künste und der Photographie in der im Bundesgesetzblatt Teil III, Gliederungsnummer 440-3, veröffentlichten bereinigten Fassung, das zuletzt durch Artikel 3 § 31 des Gesetzes vom 16. Februar 2001 (BGBl. I S. 266) geändert worden ist, in der jeweils geltenden Fassung bestehen. ²Alles Weitere regelt die aufgrund des Absatzes 13 zu erlassende Benutzungsordnung.

(9) Die Benutzung ist zu versagen oder einzuschränken, soweit
1. Grund zu der Annahme besteht, dass das Wohl der Bundesrepublik Deutschland oder eines ihrer Länder gefährdet würde,
2. Grund zu der Annahme besteht, dass schutzwürdige Belange Dritter entgegenstehen,
3. der Erhaltungszustand des Archivgutes gefährdet würde,
4. Vereinbarungen mit derzeitigen oder früheren Eigentümerinnen oder Eigentümern entgegenstehen,
5. Berufs- oder besondere Amtsgeheimnisse im Sinne des § 203 Absatz 1 bis 3 des Strafgesetzbuchs oder andere Rechtsvorschriften über Geheimhaltung verletzt würden,
6. ein nicht vertretbarer Verwaltungsaufwand entstehen würde.

(10) ¹Die Entscheidung über die Versagung oder Einschränkung der Benutzung trifft das Landesarchiv Berlin. ²Die Entscheidung ist zu begründen.

(11) Die Benutzung von Unterlagen, die der Geheimhaltungspflicht nach § 203 Absatz 1 oder 3 des Strafgesetzbuchs zu einem früheren Zeitpunkt unterlegen haben, kann eingeschränkt oder versagt werden, soweit dies zur Wahrung schutzwürdiger Belange Betroffener erforderlich ist.

(12) Archivgut von Bundesbehörden beziehungsweise deren Rechts- und Funktionsvorgängern, das das Landesarchiv Berlin vom Bundesarchiv übernommen hat, unterliegt bei der Benutzung weiterhin den Vorschriften des Bundesarchivgesetzes in der jeweils geltenden Fassung.

(13) Die für kulturelle Angelegenheiten zuständige Senatsverwaltung wird ermächtigt, die Benutzung von Archivgut im Landesarchiv Berlin durch Ausführungsvorschriften zu regeln.¹⁾

---

1) Die Landesarchiv-Benutzungsordnung ist abgedruckt als Nr. D3.II.1a.

§ 10 Recht auf Auskunft und Gegendarstellung

(1) ¹Betroffenen ist auf ihren Antrag Auskunft über die im übernommenen Archivgut zu ihrer Person enthaltenen Daten zu erteilen, soweit diese nach archivfachlichen Kriterien verzeichnet sind. ²Die Auskunftserteilung unterbleibt, soweit die Daten nach einer Rechtsvorschrift oder wegen der überwiegenden berechtigten Interessen Dritter geheim gehalten werden müssen. ³In Zweifelsfällen ist vor Ablauf der Schutzfristen nach § 9 Absatz 2 das Benehmen mit der anbietenden Stelle herzustellen. ⁴Neben der Auskunft ist vom Landesarchiv Berlin auf Verlangen Akteneinsicht zu gewähren.

(2) ¹Auf Verlangen von Betroffenen, die die Richtigkeit von Tatsachenangaben in auf ihre Person bezogenem übernommenem Archivgut bestreiten, hat das Landesarchiv Berlin eine Gegendarstellung den Unterlagen hinzuzufügen; § 10 Absatz 2 und 3 des Berliner Pressegesetzes vom 15. Juni 1965 (GVBl. S. 744), das zuletzt durch Artikel VIII des Gesetzes vom 18. November 2009 (GVBl. S. 674) geändert worden ist, in der jeweils geltenden Fassung gilt entsprechend. ²Nach dem Tode der Betroffenen steht dieses Recht ihren Angehörigen zu; § 9 Absatz 3 Satz 3 gilt entsprechend.

(3) Aufgrund besonderer Rechtsvorschriften zu berichtigendes Archivgut ist um eine Richtigstellung zu ergänzen.

§ 11 Inkrafttreten, Außerkrafttreten

¹Dieses Gesetz tritt am Tage nach der Verkündung[1]) im Gesetz- und Verordnungsblatt für Berlin in Kraft. ²Gleichzeitig tritt das Archivgesetz des Landes Berlin vom 29. November 1993 (GVBl. S. 576), das zuletzt durch Artikel I § 19 des Gesetzes vom 15. Oktober 2001 (GVBl. S. 540) geändert worden ist, außer Kraft.

---

1) Verkündet am 24.3.2016.

D3.II.1a Landesarchiv-Benutzungsordnung

Ordnung für die Benutzung von Archivgut im Landesarchiv Berlin (Landesarchiv-Benutzungsordnung – LArchBO)

Vom 4. März 2008 (ABl. S. 1018)

Auf Grund des § 8 Abs. 10 des Archivgesetzes des Landes Berlin (ArchGB) vom 29. November 1993 (GVBl. S. 576), zuletzt geändert durch § 19 des Gesetzes vom 15. Oktober 2001 (GVBl. S. 540), wird bestimmt:

§ 1 – Benutzungsberechtigung, Benutzungsverhältnis

(1) Das Archivgut des Landesarchivs Berlin steht für jedermann auf Antrag und nach Maßgabe dieser Benutzungsordnung zur Benutzung bereit.

(2) Für die Benutzung von Archivgut, das von nachgeordneten Stellen des Bundes gemäß § 2 Abs. 3 und 4 des Bundesarchivgesetzes (BArchG) dem Landesarchiv Berlin übergeben worden ist, finden die §§ 4 und 5 BArchG Anwendung.

(3) Bei Benutzung von Archivgut privater Institutionen und natürlicher Personen gehen Vereinbarungen mit der Eigentümerin oder dem Eigentümer dieser Benutzungsordnung vor.

(4) Zwischen dem Landesarchiv Berlin und der Benutzerin oder dem Benutzer wird ein öffentlich-rechtliches Benutzungsverhältnis begründet.

§ 2 – Benutzungsvoraussetzungen

(1) Die Benutzung von Archivgut des Landesarchivs Berlin erfolgt auf Antrag und nach Einwilligung des Landesarchivs Berlin. Voraussetzung für die Benutzung von Archivgut ist die Anerkennung der Benutzungsordnung. Die Anerkennung erfolgt durch die Unterschrift der Benutzerin oder des Benutzers auf dem Benutzungsantrag.

(2) Der schriftliche Benutzungsantrag ist unter Verwendung des Formulars des Landesarchivs Berlin zu stellen. Der Antrag ist vollständig und sorgfältig auszufüllen.

(3) Bei schriftlichen und mündlichen Anfragen wird auf einen schriftlichen Benutzungsantrag verzichtet.

(4) Das Landesarchiv Berlin kann die Benutzerin oder den Benutzer auffordern, den amtlichen Personalausweis oder Reisepass vorzulegen.

(5) Die Einwilligung des Landesarchivs Berlin wird der Benutzerin oder dem Benutzer mündlich oder schriftlich mitgeteilt. Sie gilt für den angegebenen Benutzungszweck und das Benutzungsthema sowie für das laufende Kalenderjahr. Sie kann mit Auflagen erteilt werden.

(6) Die Benutzerin oder der Benutzer ist verpflichtet, bei der Benutzung die geltenden Vorschriften des Urheber- und Persönlichkeitsschutzes sowie die schutzwürdigen Belange Dritter zu beachten.

(7) Die Einwilligung kann versagt oder eingeschränkt werden, wenn
1. der Zweck der Benutzung durch die Einsichtnahme in Druckwerke oder Reproduktionen oder auf andere Weise erreicht werden kann oder
2. bei einer früheren Benutzung von Archivgut wiederholt oder schwerwiegend gegen Benutzungsbestimmungen verstoßen wurde.

(8) Unbeschadet der Regelungen gemäß §§ 48 und 49 des Verwaltungsverfahrensgesetzes (VwVfG) kann die Einwilligung auch widerrufen werden, wenn
1. die Angaben im Benutzungsantrag nicht oder nicht mehr zutreffen,
2. nachträglich Gründe bekannt werden, die zur Versagung oder Einschränkung der Benutzung geführt hätten,
3. wiederholt oder schwerwiegend gegen die Benutzungsbestimmungen verstoßen wird oder
4. das Urheber- oder Persönlichkeitsrecht verletzt oder sonstige schutzwürdige Belange Dritter nicht beachtet werden.

(9) Für die Mitwirkung anderer Personen als Beauftragte oder Hilfskräfte der Antragstellerin oder des Antragstellers ist von diesen ein gesonderter Benutzungsantrag zu stellen.

§ 3 – Benutzung

(1) Das Archivgut wird zur Benutzung im Original oder in Kopie im Landesarchiv Berlin vorgelegt oder als Kopie abgegeben. Zum Schutz des Archivgutes oder zur Wahrung schutzwürdiger Belange

Dritter können ausschließlich Auskünfte über seinen Inhalt erteilt werden. Über die Art der Benutzung entscheidet das Landesarchiv Berlin.
(2) Die Verkürzung von Schutzfristen gemäß § 8 Abs. 4 ArchGB ist von der Benutzerin oder dem Benutzer schriftlich zu beantragen und zu begründen. Bei personenbezogenem Archivgut sollen die Einverständniserklärungen der Betroffenen oder ihrer Angehörigen für die Einsichtnahme, die Abgabe von Reproduktionen und zur Veröffentlichung von der Antragstellerin oder dem Antragsteller vorgelegt werden.
(3) Die Benutzerin oder der Benutzer ist verpflichtet, das Archivgut in den Benutzungsräumen zu belassen, die innere Ordnung des Archivgutes zu bewahren, es nicht zu beschädigen, zu verändern oder in seinem Erhaltungszustand zu gefährden. Näheres regelt die Lesesaalordnung des Landesarchivs Berlin.
(4) Das Personal des Landesarchivs Berlin ist berechtigt, der Benutzerin oder dem Benutzer Weisungen zur Einhaltung der Benutzungsordnung zu erteilen, denen Folge zu leisten ist.

§ 4 – Ausschluss von der Benutzung
Eine Benutzerin oder ein Benutzer, die oder der fällige Gebühren oder Auslagen nicht bezahlt, Archivgut widerrechtlich beschädigt, aus dem Landesarchiv Berlin entfernt oder sonst in grober Weise oder wiederholt gegen archivrechtliche Vorschriften oder die Benutzungsbestimmungen verstößt, kann zeitweise oder auf Dauer von der Benutzung ausgeschlossen werden.

§ 5 – Reproduktionen
(1) Das Landesarchiv Berlin kann auf schriftlichen Antrag Reproduktionen von Archivgut anfertigen oder durch eine beauftragte Stelle anfertigen lassen. Ein Anspruch auf Anfertigung, insbesondere von Reproduktionen in größerem Umfang, besteht nicht. Näheres regelt die Lesesaalordnung.
(2) Reproduktionen werden nur angefertigt, soweit konservatorische oder rechtliche Gründe nicht entgegenstehen. Über das geeignete Reproduktionsverfahren entscheidet das Landesarchiv Berlin.
(3) Reproduktionen dürfen nur mit schriftlicher Einwilligung des Landesarchivs Berlin und nur zu dem genehmigten Zweck veröffentlicht, vervielfältigt, an Dritte weitergegeben oder in sonstiger Weise genutzt werden. Bei Veröffentlichungen von Reproduktionen sind als Quelle das Landesarchiv Berlin und die Archivsignatur anzugeben.
(4) Die Benutzerin oder der Benutzer hat die für die Erteilung der Einwilligung nach Absatz 3 und die Festsetzung der Gebühren nach § 7 erforderlichen Angaben zu machen und Nachweise vorzulegen.

§ 6 – Ausleihe
(1) Das Landesarchiv Berlin kann in begründeten Fällen und in beschränktem Umfang Archivgut an andere hauptamtlich verwaltete Archive ausleihen. Für die Einsichtnahme in dem auswärtigen Archiv findet § 2 Abs. 1 und 2 Anwendung. Im Übrigen unterliegt das Archivgut den Benutzungsbestimmungen des auswärtigen Archivs; ergänzend gilt die Benutzungsordnung des Landesarchivs Berlin.
(2) Die Weitergabe ausgeliehenen Archivgutes an Dritte ist nicht gestattet.
(3) Das Landesarchiv Berlin kann auf Antrag Reproduktionen von Filmen und Fotos an jedermann ausleihen.
(4) Archivgut kann für Ausstellungen an Einrichtungen ausgeliehen werden, die die Gewähr dafür bieten, dass das ausgeliehene Archivgut entsprechend den Anforderungen des Landesarchivs Berlin benutzt und geschützt wird.
(5) Die Leihfrist beträgt in der Regel vier Wochen. Sie kann in begründeten Fällen verlängert werden. Archivgut kann aus dienstlichen Gründen jederzeit zurückgefordert werden.
(6) Die Benutzerin oder der Benutzer ist verpflichtet, den Verlust oder die Beschädigung des ausgeliehenen Archivgutes unverzüglich dem Landesarchiv Berlin mitzuteilen. Für den Verlust oder die Beschädigung des ausgeliehenen Archivgutes haftet die Benutzerin oder der Benutzer, die oder der den Ausleihantrag gestellt hat.
(7) In den Fällen des Absatzes 1, 3 und 4 ist eine schriftliche Vereinbarung über die Einzelheiten der Ausleihe einschließlich der Gebührenerhebung zu schließen.
(8) Archivgut kann in begründeten Fällen an Behörden und sonstige öffentliche Stellen ausgeliehen werden.
(9) Spätestens mit Ablauf der Leihfrist ist das entliehene Archivgut unaufgefordert zurückzugeben oder die Verlängerung der Leihfrist schriftlich zu beantragen. Die Entscheidung über den Verlänge-

rungsantrag wird der Benutzerin oder dem Benutzer schriftlich mitgeteilt. Die Verpflichtung zur Rückgabe des Archivgutes besteht auch, wenn die schriftliche Benachrichtigung bis zum Ablauf der Leihfrist nicht vorliegt.

(10) Bei Überschreitung der Leihfrist wird die Rückgabe des Archivgutes schriftlich angemahnt. Die Mahnungen sind nach Maßgabe des anliegenden Gebührenverzeichnisses kostenpflichtig.

(11) Die Kosten der Restaurierung von beschädigtem Archivgut sind nach den geltenden gesetzlichen Vorschriften zu leisten. Darüber hinaus werden Bearbeitungsgebühren nach Maßgabe des anliegenden Gebührenverzeichnisses erhoben.

§ 7 – Gebühren und Auslagen

(1) Das Landesarchiv Berlin erhebt für die Benutzung von Archivgut, die von ihm erbrachten Leistungen und die Einräumung von Nutzungsrechten Gebühren und Auslagen gemäß dem anliegenden Gebührenverzeichnis zu dieser Benutzungsordnung in der jeweils geltenden Fassung.

(2) Auslagen werden zusätzlich zu den Gebühren und auch dann erhoben, wenn die Leistung gebührenfrei erfolgt.

(3) Gebühren werden nicht erhoben für einfache mündliche oder schriftliche Auskünfte.

(4) Die Gebühren nach Nummer 1 und Nummer 3 des Gebührenverzeichnisses werden nicht erhoben, wenn die Benutzung wissenschaftlichen und heimatkundlichen Zwecken, dem Unterricht oder der Klärung versorgungsrechtlicher Angelegenheiten dient und nicht in überwiegend privatem oder gewerblichem Interesse liegt. Für die Gebühren nach Nummer 1.2 und Nummer 4.1 des Gebührenverzeichnisses gilt dies nur, wenn der Ermittlungsaufwand den Zeitraum von zwei Stunden nicht überschreitet.

§ 8 – Inkrafttreten, Außerkrafttreten

Diese Benutzungsordnung tritt am 1. Mai 2008 in Kraft. Gleichzeitig tritt die Ordnung für die Benutzung von Archivgut des Landesarchivs Berlin (Landesarchiv-Benutzungsordnung – LArchBO) vom 7. Juli 1997 (ABl. S. 2817) außer Kraft.

Richtlinie über die Gewährung von Zuwendungen zur Erhaltung, Unterhaltung und Wiederherstellung von Denkmalen sowie sonstigen Anlagen von denkmalpflegerischem Interesse (Förderrichtlinie zur Erhaltung von Denkmalen)[1)]

Vom 01. Januar 2019

Auf Grund des § 6 Absatz 2 Buchstabe a des Allgemeinen Zuständigkeitsgesetzes (AZG) in Verbindung mit § 20 des Gesetzes zum Schutz von Denkmalen in Berlin (DSchG Bln) vom 24. April 1995 (GVBl. S. 274) erlässt die für den Denkmalschutz zuständige Senatsverwaltung zur Ausführung von § 15 DSchG Bln die folgenden Ausführungsvorschriften:

1 Zuwendungszweck

1.1 Das Land Berlin, vertreten durch das Landesdenkmalamt Berlin (Bewilligungsstelle), gewährt nach § 15 DSchG Bln sowie nach Maßgabe dieser Förderrichtlinie und der Ausführungsvorschriften zu § 44 Landeshaushaltsordnung Berlin (LHO) Zuwendungen für Maßnahmen zur Erhaltung, Unterhaltung und Wiederherstellung von Denkmalen sowie sonstigen Anlagen von denkmalpflegerischem Interesse (denkmalpflegerische Maßnahmen).
Handelt es sich bei der Zuwendung um eine Beihilfe im Sinne des Artikel 107 Absatz 1 des Vertrages über die Arbeitsweise der Europäischen Union (AEUV) wird die Beihilfe auf Grundlage der De-minimis-Verordnung[2)] oder der Allgemeine Gruppenfreistellungsverordnung[3)] (AGVO) freigestellt.

1.2 Die Zuwendungen werden nur im Rahmen verfügbarer Haushaltsmittel nach pflichtgemäßem Ermessen gewährt. Denkmalpflegerische Maßnahmen zur Sicherung und Erhaltung bedrohter Denkmalsubstanz genießen Priorität.

1.3 Auf die Zuwendung oder eine bestimmte Höhe der Zuwendung besteht kein Rechtsanspruch.

2 Gegenstand der Förderung

2.1 Zuwendungsfähig sind Ausgaben, die für denkmalpflegerische Maßnahmen im Sinne von Nummer 1.1 allein oder überwiegend aus Gründen der Denkmalpflege erforderlich werden (denkmalbedingte Mehraufwendungen).

2.2 Zu den denkmalbedingten Mehraufwendungen zählen u.a. Ausgaben für:
- vorbereitende Bau- und restauratorische Befunduntersuchungen,
- die Sicherung und Reparatur originaler Denkmalsubstanz, denkmalwerten Zubehörs und denkmalwerter Ausstattung,
- die Entwicklung und Anwendung vorbildlicher Erhaltungsmethoden,
- Restaurierungsmaßnahmen,
- besondere Baumaterialien und -techniken,
- Maßnahmen zur Regenerierung des denkmaltypischen Pflanzenbestandes,
- anteilige Gerüstkosten für verlängerte Standzeiten,
- die bau- bzw. grabungsbegleitende Dokumentation,
- Pflegewerke und Denkmalpflegepläne zur Erhaltung und Instandhaltung des Denkmals,
- anteilige Architekten- und Ingenieurhonorare,
- Veröffentlichungen über die geförderten Maßnahmen.

2.3 Zuwendungen werden gewährt für denkmalbedingte Mehraufwendungen.

---

1) https://www.berlin.de/landesdenkmalamt/service/rechtsvorschriften/.
2) Verordnung (EU) Nr. 1407/2013 der Kommission vom 18.12.2013 über die Anwendung der Artikel 107 und 108 des Vertrags über die Arbeitsweise der Europäischen Union auf De-minimis-Beihilfen (EU-Amtsblatt L 352/1 vom 24.12.2013).
3) Verordnung (EU) Nr. 651/2014 der Kommission vom 17.06.2014 zur Feststellung der Vereinbarkeit bestimmter Gruppen von Beihilfen mit dem Binnenmarkt in Anwendung der Artikel 107 und 108 des Vertrags über die Arbeitsweise der Europäischen Union, EU-Amtsblatt L187/1 vom 26. Juni 2014 in der jeweils geltenden Fassung.

D3.III.1 Förderrichtlinie zur Erhaltung von Denkmalen

2.4 Zuwendungen können auch gewährt werden bei einem Anspruch auf finanziellen Ausgleich nach § 16 Abs. 2 DSchG Bln infolge unzumutbarer Eigentumsbeschränkung aufgrund der Versagung einer Genehmigung oder einer sonstigen behördlichen Maßnahme bzw. zur Verhinderung eines solchen Anspruchs.

2.5 Nicht zuwendungsfähig sind:
- Rekonstruktionen, soweit es sich nicht um Sicherungs- und Ergänzungsmaßnahmen handelt,
- Erhaltungsaufwand aus unterlassener Bauunterhaltung und Grün-/Gartenpflege,
- haustechnische Maßnahmen, die nicht zum Schutz der Denkmalsubstanz erforderlich sind (z. B. Heizungsanlagen, Wasser- und Abwasserleitungen, Elektroinstallationen, Aufzüge usw.),
- Ausgaben für Erschließung und Genehmigungsverfahren.

3 Zuwendungsempfänger

3.1 Antragsberechtigt sind Eigentümerinnen und Eigentümer, sonstige dinglich Berechtigte, Bauunterhaltungs- oder Erhaltungspflichtige von Denkmalen.

3.2 Nicht antragsberechtigt sind der Bund und die Bundesländer sowie deren nachgeordnete Einrichtungen.

4 Zuwendungsvoraussetzungen

4.1 Die denkmalpflegerische Maßnahme muss im erheblichen Interesse von Denkmalschutz und Denkmalpflege stehen. Sie ist mit dem Landesdenkmalamt oder mit der von diesem zu benennenden bezirklichen Unteren Denkmalschutzbehörde während der gesamten Planungs- und Durchführungsphase abzustimmen.

4.2 Die Finanzierung der Gesamtmaßnahme muss gesichert sein. Die zur denkmalpflegerischen Beurteilung notwendigen Unterlagen müssen dem Landesdenkmalamt vorgelegt werden.

4.3 Die Maßnahme darf vor Erteilung des Zuwendungsbescheides noch nicht begonnen sein. Als Beginn gilt grundsätzlich der Abschluss eines der Ausführung zuzurechnenden Lieferungs- oder Leistungsvertrages. Das Landesdenkmalamt kann ausnahmsweise auf Antrag einem vorzeitigen Maßnahmenbeginn zustimmen. Der Antrag ist zu begründen. Die Zustimmung zum vorzeitigen Maßnahmenbeginn begründet keinen Rechtsanspruch auf eine Zuwendung, sofern diese nicht schriftlich zugesichert wurde.

4.4 Bei Zuwendungen im Sinne von Nummer 2.4 muss der Verfügungsberechtigte die Unzumutbarkeit der Eigentumsbeschränkung nachgewiesen haben.

4.5 Die denkmalpflegerische Maßnahme ist nur zuwendungsfähig, wenn der Antragsteller versichert, dass die Auftragsvergabe in Teillosen und nach Fachlosen erfolgt. Die Maßnahme darf nicht durch einen Generalübernehmer durchgeführt werden.

4.6 Eine Förderung von Unternehmen, die Rückforderungsansprüchen aufgrund eines früheren Beschlusses der Europäischen Kommission zur Feststellung der Unzulässigkeit einer Beihilfe und ihrer Vereinbarkeit dem Binnenmarkt nicht nachgekommen sind, ist ausgeschlossen.

5 Art und Umfang der Zuwendung

5.1 Zuwendungen werden als Projektförderung grundsätzlich im Wege der Anteilfinanzierung als Zuschüsse vergeben. In begründeten Einzelfällen kann das Landesdenkmalamt andere Finanzierungsarten wählen (Fehlbedarfsfinanzierung, Vollfinanzierung).

5.2 Die Zuwendung beträgt in der Regel höchstens bis zu 50 v. H. der denkmalbedingten Mehraufwendungen. Die Höhe der Zuwendung wird unter Abwägung der Interessen des Zuwendungsempfängers und des Landes Berlin durch das Landesdenkmalamt im Rahmen verfügbarer Haushaltsmittel nach pflichtgemäßem Ermessen festgesetzt. Hierbei hat sie die allgemeinen Instandsetzungsverpflichtungen des Antragstellers, seine finanzielle Leistungsfähigkeit, die wirtschaftliche Zumutbarkeit der Maßnahme, weitere Zuschüsse Dritter sowie die Bedeutung und den Zustand des Denkmals zu berücksichtigen.

5.3 Überschreitungen des Höchstsatzes sind ausnahmsweise zulässig, wenn
- das Objekt nicht nutzbar ist oder
- seine Nutzbarkeit erheblich eingeschränkt ist,
- die Maßnahme ausschließlich denkmalbedingten Mehraufwand darstellt oder
- nur durch eine höhere öffentliche Förderung eine akute Gefährdung des Denkmals abgewendet werden kann und an seiner Erhaltung besonderes denkmalpflegerisches Interesse besteht.

5.4 Zuwendungsfähig sind nur die dem Zuwendungsempfänger tatsächlich entstehenden denkmalbedingten Mehraufwendungen (zuwendungsfähige Ausgaben). Leistungen aus anderen öffentlichen Förderungsprogrammen (z. B. Städtebauförderung, Wohnungsmodernisierung) oder Zahlungen Dritter (z. B. Versicherungsleistungen, Zahlungen aus Baulasten, Spenden) sind anzurechnen, soweit sie auf die zuwendungsfähigen Ausgaben geleistet werden.

5.5 Verringern sich die zuwendungsfähigen Ausgaben, verringert sich auch die Zuwendung entsprechend der gewählten Finanzierungsart. Das Landesdenkmalamt kann die Zuwendung nachträglich erhöhen, wenn im Verlauf der Maßnahme unvorhersehbare, vom Zuwendungsempfänger nicht zu vertretende Umstände eintreten, die zusätzliche denkmalbedingte Mehraufwendungen verursachen.

5.6 Nicht zuwendungsfähig sind Eigenleistungen des Zuwendungsempfängers, die nicht zu Ausgaben führen. Ausgaben für das vom Zuwendungsempfänger selbst zur Verfügung gestellte Material können nur bei Vorlage des Kaufbelegs als zuwendungsfähige Ausgaben anerkannt werden. Abschreibungen für Abnutzung und kalkulatorische Kosten sind keine zuwendungsfähigen Ausgaben.

5.7 Ausgenommen von den Bestimmungen Nr. 5.6 sind Eigenleistungen von Fachbetrieben, Handwerkern und Restauratoren, die im Rahmen ihres Geschäftsbetriebes tätig werden; für diese werden die ortsüblichen Entgelte abzüglich eines pauschalisierten Gewinnanteils von 25 % anerkannt. Diese Regelung gilt auch für Eigenleistungen von Architekten, Ingenieuren und Baustatikern bis zu einem Höchstbetrag von 10 % der Gesamtkosten.

5.8 Zuwendungen im Sinne von Nummer 2.4 werden im Umfang des Ausgleichsanspruchs gewährt.

5.9 Abweichend von den Nrn. 5.1 – 5.8 kann das Landesdenkmalamt gem. Nr. 2.3 der AV zu § 44 LHO Bln pauschal feste Förderbeträge für zuwendungsfähige Ausgaben zuwenden (Festbetragsfinanzierung), die sich standardmäßig wiederholen und für die das Landesdenkmalamt Richtwerte in einem Kostenindex festgelegt hat.

Eine Förderung mit festen Beträgen kommt nicht in Betracht, wenn im Zeitpunkt der Bewilligung konkrete Anhaltspunkte dafür vorliegen, dass mit nicht nur unwesentlichen zusätzlichen Eigenmitteln oder Einsparungen zu rechnen ist.

6 Sonstige Zuwendungsbestimmungen

6.1 Wird für die Zuwendungsempfängerin oder den Zuwendungsempfänger erkennbar, dass sie oder er aufgrund von Verzögerungen bei der Durchführung der denkmalpflegerischen Maßnahmen die Zuwendung in dem im Zuwendungsbescheid genannten Haushaltsjahr ganz oder teilweise nicht mehr in Anspruch nehmen wird, hat sie oder er das Landesdenkmalamt unverzüglich darüber zu informieren. Das Landesdenkmalamt entscheidet nach pflichtgemäßem Ermessen entsprechend der jeweiligen Sach- und Haushaltslage, ob eine Verlängerung des Bewilligungszeitraums möglich ist oder ob der Zuwendungsbescheid ganz oder teilweise zu widerrufen ist.

6.2 Die Zuwendungsempfängerin oder der Zuwendungsempfänger hat das Landesdenkmalamt unverzüglich darüber zu informieren, wenn sich für die Zuwendung maßgebliche Umstände ändern, insbesondere wenn
- sie oder er abweichend vom verbindlichen Finanzierungsplan weitere Zuwendungen von öffentlicher oder privater Seite für die Maßnahme beantragt oder erhält,
- sie oder er feststellt, dass der Zuwendungszweck mit der bewilligten Zuwendung nicht zu erreichen ist,
- ein Insolvenzverfahren gegen sie oder ihn beantragt oder eröffnet wurde,
- die Verfügungsberechtigung über das geförderte Objekt sich geändert hat.

D3.III.1 Förderrichtlinie zur Erhaltung von Denkmalen

6.3 Zuwendungen nach Nummer 1.1 dieser Richtlinie werden, sofern die Verordnung über die Berücksichtigung der aktiven Förderung der Beschäftigung von Frauen und der Vereinbarkeit von Beruf und Familie bei der Gewährung freiwilliger Leistungen aus Landesmitteln (Leistungsgewährungsverordnung – LGV) vom 15.11.2011 Anwendung findet, nur unter der Bedingung der Durchführung von Maßnahmen der aktiven Förderung der Beschäftigung von Frauen i.S.d. § 4 LGV gewährt.

Zuwendungsempfängerinnen und Zuwendungsempfänger i.S.d. LGV weisen die Durchführung der Maßnahmen gemäß § 4 LGV durch eine entsprechende Erklärung im Rahmen des Verwendungsnachweises nach.

7 Verfahren

7.1 Antragsverfahren

Die Zuwendung ist beim Landesdenkmalamt zu beantragen. Die erforderlichen Antragsunterlagen sind beim Landesdenkmalamt erhältlich. Der Antrag muss alle zur Beurteilung der Förderfähigkeit erforderlichen Unterlagen enthalten. Dies sind:
- der Antrag,
- eine Beschreibung der geplanten Maßnahme, Fotos des Förderobjektes,
- bei Baumaßnahmen Baupläne, eine Leistungsbeschreibung sowie ein Zeitplan,
- ein Finanzierungsplan, der sämtliche Einnahmen und Ausgaben enthält, die im Zusammenhang mit der denkmalpflegerischen Maßnahme entstehen, insbesondere auch weitere beantragte und/oder bewilligte öffentliche oder private Fördermittel sowie eine Erklärung darüber, ob der Zuwendungsempfänger allgemein oder für das betreffende Vorhaben zum Vorsteuerabzug nach § 15 Umsatzsteuergesetz berechtigt ist,
- eine Erklärung, dass die Maßnahme noch nicht im Sinne von Nummer 4.3 begonnen wurde und auch vor der Bekanntgabe des Zuwendungsbescheides ohne vorherige Zustimmung der Bewilligungsbehörde nicht begonnen werden wird,
- bei Zuwendungen im Sinne von Nummer 2.4 den Sachverständigennachweis der Unzumutbarkeit der Eigentumsbeschränkung,
- die denkmalrechtliche Genehmigung,
- eine De-minimis-Erklärung, sofern eine Freistellung nach der De-minimis-Verordnung vorgesehen ist,
- bei juristischen Personen die Einwilligung in die Veröffentlichung in der zentralen Zuwendungsdatenbank im Internet von Name und Postanschrift des Zuwendungsempfängers oder der Zuwendungsempfängerin sowie Art, Höhe und Zweck der Zuwendung,
- die Identifikationsnummer, unter der der Antragsteller oder die Antragstellerin in der Transparenzdatenbank registriert ist,
- eine Begründung, wenn eine Ausnahme nach den unter Nr. 1.5.3.1 AV § 44 LHO genannten Voraussetzungen erfolgen soll.

Das Landesdenkmalamt kann darüber hinaus die Vorlage weiterer Unterlagen verlangen und im Falle einer Förderung nach Nr. 5.9 von einzelnen Antragsunterlagen absehen.

7.2 Bewilligungsverfahren

Die Zuwendungen für denkmalpflegerische Maßnahmen im Sinne von Nummer 1.1 werden durch Bewilligungsbescheid gewährt. Dieser enthält Angaben über die ermittelten zuwendungsfähigen Kosten, die Höhe des Fördersatzes, den Zuwendungshöchstbetrag sowie eine Frist für den Abruf der Fördermittel. Der Bescheid kann mit Bedingungen und Auflagen versehen werden. Insbesondere kann darin die Beteiligung des Landesdenkmalamtes, einer von dieser zu benennenden Unteren Denkmalschutzbehörde sowie von Fachleuten oder die Leitung durch Sachverständige bei Ausschreibung und Vergabe von Aufträgen, deren Ausführung denkmalpflegerische Sachkenntnis voraussetzt, vorgeschrieben werden.

Soweit es geboten scheint, kann das Landesdenkmalamt den Zuwendungsempfänger bzw. die Zuwendungsempfängerin durch eine Nebenbestimmung im Zuwendungsbescheid dazu verpflichten, Bedingungen und Auflagen, die sich auf den Bestand oder das Erscheinungsbild des Denkmals beziehen, als Baulasten in das Baulastenverzeichnis einzutragen.

7.3 Auszahlungsverfahren

Zuwendungen werden in der Regel nur nach Durchführung der zuwendungsfähigen Maßnahmen und nach Abnahme durch das Landesdenkmalamt bzw. der von ihr benannten Unteren Denkmalschutzbehörde ausgezahlt.

In besonders begründeten Ausnahmefällen, insbesondere bei hohen Fördersummen, können nach Vorlage von Zwischenverwendungsnachweisen bereits vor Abschluss der zuwendungsfähigen Maßnahmen Teilbeträge ausgezahlt werden.

7.4 Verwendungsnachweisverfahren

Der Zuwendungsempfänger bzw. die Zuwendungsempfängerin hat dem Landesdenkmalamt die zweckentsprechende Verwendung der Zuwendung – gegebenenfalls in Teilbeträgen – nachzuweisen. Der Verwendungsnachweis besteht aus einem Sachbericht, einem zahlenmäßigen Nachweis und einer tabellarischen Belegübersicht, in der die Ausgaben nach Art und in zeitlicher Reihenfolge getrennt aufgelistet sind (Belegliste). Der Verwendungsnachweis ist, wenn im Einzelfall nichts anderes bestimmt ist, spätestens sechs Monate nach Abschluss der geförderten Maßnahme beim Landesdenkmalamt einzureichen. Ist der Zuwendungszweck nicht bis zum Ablauf des Haushaltsjahres erfüllt, ist binnen vier Monaten des darauffolgenden Jahres dem Landesdenkmalamt ein Zwischennachweis über die erhaltenen Mittel vorzulegen.

7.5 Bei einer Zuwendung nach Nr. 5.9 können sich der Sachbericht auf eine Beschreibung der durchgeführten Maßnahme und der zahlenmäßige Nachweis auf die Vorlage einer einfachen Belegliste beschränken.

7.6. Zu beachtende Vorschriften:

Wird bei denkmalpflegerischen Maßnahmen im Sinne von Nummer 1.1 gegen den Zweck der Zuwendung oder die Auflagen des Bewilligungsbescheides bzw. gegen denkmalschutzrechtliche Belange verstoßen, so kann das Landesdenkmalamt den Bewilligungsbescheid ganz oder teilweise widerrufen. Für die Bewilligung, Auszahlung und Abrechnung der Zuwendung sowie für den Nachweis und die Prüfung der Verwendung und die gegebenenfalls erforderliche Aufhebung des Zuwendungsbescheides und die Rückforderung der gewährten Zuwendung gelten die Ausführungsvorschriften zu § 44 LHO sowie § 1 Absatz 1 des Gesetzes über das Verfahren der Berliner Verwaltung in Verbindung mit den §§ 48 bis 49 a Verwaltungsverfahrensgesetz (BUND), soweit nicht in dieser Förderrichtlinie Abweichungen zugelassen worden sind.

8 Geltungsdauer

Diese Verwaltungsvorschrift tritt am 01. Januar 2019 in Kraft. Sie tritt mit Ablauf des 31. Dezember 2023 außer Kraft.

D3.IV.1 Allgemeines Zuständigkeitsgesetz

Gesetz über die Zuständigkeiten in der Allgemeinen Berliner Verwaltung (Allgemeines Zuständigkeitsgesetz – AZG)

In der Fassung vom 22. Juli 1996[1] (GVBl. S. 302, ber. S. 472)
(BRV 2001-1)
zuletzt geändert durch Art. 1 Zwölftes ÄndG vom 25. September 2019 (GVBl. S. 610)
– Auszug –

1. Abschnitt
Gliederung und Aufgaben der Berliner Verwaltung

[...]

§ 4 Zuständigkeitsverteilung
(1) [1]Die Aufgaben der Hauptverwaltung außerhalb der Leitungsaufgaben werden im einzelnen durch die Anlage zu diesem Gesetz (Allgemeiner Zuständigkeitskatalog) bestimmt. [2]Alle dort nicht aufgeführten Aufgaben sind Aufgaben der Bezirke. [3]Im Vorgriff auf eine Katalogänderung kann der Senat durch Rechtsverordnung einzelne Aufgaben der Hauptverwaltung den Bezirken zuweisen.
(2) [1]Die Zuständigkeiten bei Polizeiaufgaben und Ordnungsaufgaben werden durch besonderes Gesetz mit zusammenfassendem Zuständigkeitskatalog geregelt. [2]Die Vorschriften der §§ 9 bis 13a über Bezirksaufsicht und Eingriffsrecht gelten auch für Ordnungsaufgaben der Bezirksverwaltungen.

Anlage
(zu § 4 Abs. 1 Satz 1)

Allgemeiner Zuständigkeitskatalog (ZustKat AZG)

Aufgaben der Hauptverwaltung außerhalb der Leitungsaufgaben
(Planung, Grundsatzangelegenheiten, Steuerung, Aufsicht)

[...]

Nr. 17 Wissenschaft, Forschung; Kunst und Kultur; kirchliche Angelegenheiten
(1) Wissenschaft und Forschung.
(2) Grundsatzangelegenheiten des Bibliotheks- und Archivwesens, Stiftung Zentral- und Landesbibliothek Berlin, Landesarchiv Berlin.
(3) Landesangelegenheiten der Kunst, der Theater, der Orchester, des Films und der Museen.
(4) Schutz und Rückgabe beweglicher Kulturgüter.
(5) Angelegenheiten der Religions- und Weltanschauungsgemeinschaften einschließlich der Genehmigung von Abgabebeschlüssen.

---

1) Neubekanntmachung des AZG v. 2.10.1958 (GVBl. S. 947, 1020) in der ab 19.11.1995 geltenden Fassung.

Verfassung des Landes Brandenburg

Vom 20. August 1992 (GVBl. I S. 298)
(Sa BbgLR 100-4)
zuletzt geändert durch Art. 1 Siebentes ÄndG vom 16. Mai 2019 (GVBl. I Nr. 16)
– Auszug –

1. Hauptteil:
Grundlagen

Artikel 2 (Grundsätze der Verfassung)
(1) Brandenburg ist ein freiheitliches, rechtsstaatliches, soziales, dem Frieden und der Gerechtigkeit, dem Schutz der natürlichen Umwelt und der Kultur verpflichtetes demokratisches Land, welches die Zusammenarbeit mit anderen Völkern, insbesondere mit dem polnischen Nachbarn, anstrebt.
[...]

2. Hauptteil:
Grundrechte und Staatsziele

4. Abschnitt:
Rechte der Sorben/Wenden

Artikel 25 (Rechte der Sorben/Wenden)
(1) ¹Das Recht des sorbischen/wendischen Volkes auf Schutz, Erhaltung und Pflege seiner nationalen Identität und seines angestammten Siedlungsgebietes wird gewährleistet. ²Das Land, die Gemeinden und Gemeindeverbände fördern die Verwirklichung dieses Rechtes, insbesondere die kulturelle Eigenständigkeit und die wirksame politische Mitgestaltung des sorbischen/wendischen Volkes.
(2) Das Land wirkt auf die Sicherung einer Landesgrenzen übergreifenden kulturellen Autonomie der Sorben/Wenden hin.
(3) Die Sorben/Wenden haben das Recht auf Bewahrung und Förderung der sorbischen/wendischen Sprache und Kultur im öffentlichen Leben und ihre Vermittlung in Schulen und Kindertagesstätten.
(4) ¹Im Siedlungsgebiet der Sorben/Wenden ist die sorbische/wendische Sprache in die öffentliche Beschriftung einzubeziehen. ²Die sorbische/wendische Fahne hat die Farben Blau, Rot, Weiß.
(5) ¹Die Ausgestaltung der Rechte der Sorben/Wenden regelt ein Gesetz. ²Dies hat sicherzustellen, dass in Angelegenheiten der Sorben/Wenden, insbesondere bei der Gesetzgebung, sorbische/wendische Vertreter mitwirken.

6. Abschnitt:
Bildung, Wissenschaft, Kunst und Sport

Artikel 34 (Kunst und Kultur)
(1) ¹Die Kunst ist frei. ²Sie bedarf der öffentlichen Förderung, insbesondere durch Unterstützung der Künstler.
(2) ¹Das kulturelle Leben in seiner Vielfalt und die Vermittlung des kulturellen Erbes werden öffentlich gefördert. ²Kunstwerke und Denkmale der Kultur stehen unter dem Schutz des Landes, der Gemeinden und Gemeindeverbände.
(3) Das Land, die Gemeinden und Gemeindeverbände unterstützen die Teilnahme am kulturellen Leben und ermöglichen den Zugang zu den Kulturgütern.

Gesetz über den Schutz und die Pflege der Denkmale im Land Brandenburg (Brandenburgisches Denkmalschutzgesetz – BbgDSchG)[1)]

Vom 24. Mai 2004 (GVBl. I S. 215)
(Sa BbgLR 557-1)

Abschnitt 1
Allgemeine Vorschriften

§ 1 Grundsätze

(1) Denkmale sind als Quellen und Zeugnisse menschlicher Geschichte und prägende Bestandteile der Kulturlandschaft des Landes Brandenburg nach den Bestimmungen dieses Gesetzes zu schützen, zu erhalten, zu pflegen und zu erforschen.

(2) [1]Das Land, Gemeinden und Gemeindeverbände, Behörden und öffentliche Stellen haben im Rahmen ihrer Zuständigkeit die Verwirklichung der Ziele des Denkmalschutzes und der Denkmalpflege zu unterstützen. [2]Sie haben die für Denkmalschutz und Denkmalpflege zuständigen Behörden bereits bei der Vorbereitung aller öffentlichen Planungen und Maßnahmen, die die Belange des Denkmalschutzes und der Denkmalpflege berühren können, zu unterrichten und anzuhören, soweit nicht eine weitergehende Form der Beteiligung vorgeschrieben ist.

(3) Die für Denkmalschutz und Denkmalpflege zuständigen Behörden wirken darauf hin, dass Denkmale in die Raumordnung, Landesplanung, städtebauliche Entwicklung und Landespflege einbezogen und sinnvoll genutzt werden.

(4) Denkmalschutz und Denkmalpflege berücksichtigen die Belange von Menschen mit Behinderung im Rahmen der geltenden Gesetze.

§ 2 Begriffsbestimmungen

(1) Denkmale sind Sachen, Mehrheiten von Sachen oder Teile von Sachen, an deren Erhaltung wegen ihrer geschichtlichen, wissenschaftlichen, technischen, künstlerischen, städtebaulichen oder volkskundlichen Bedeutung ein öffentliches Interesse besteht.

(2) Denkmale können sein:
1. bauliche Anlagen (Baudenkmale), technische Anlagen (technische Denkmale) oder Teile solcher Anlagen sowie gärtnerische Anlagen oder sonstige von Menschen gestaltete Teile von Landschaften mit ihren Pflanzen, Frei- und Wasserflächen (Gartendenkmale). Das Inventar ist, soweit es mit dem Denkmal eine Einheit von Denkmalwert bildet, Teil desselben;
2. Mehrheiten baulicher oder technischer Anlagen einschließlich der mit ihnen verbundenen Frei- und Wasserflächen, die in ihrer Gesamterscheinung, Struktur, Funktion oder in anderer Weise aufeinander bezogen sind, unabhängig davon, ob die einzelnen Anlagen für sich die Voraussetzungen des Absatzes 1 erfüllen (Denkmalbereiche). Denkmalbereiche sind insbesondere Zeugnisse der Siedlungs- und Produktionsgeschichte, des Städtebaus und der Garten- und Landschaftsgestaltung;
3. bewegliche Sachen, Sammlungen oder sonstige Mehrheiten beweglicher Sachen (bewegliche Denkmale); davon ausgeschlossen ist Archivgut, soweit es den dafür geltenden gesetzlichen Bestimmungen unterliegt, und
4. bewegliche und unbewegliche Sachen, insbesondere Reste oder Spuren von Gegenständen, Bauten und sonstigen Zeugnissen menschlichen, tierischen und pflanzlichen Lebens, die sich im Boden oder in Gewässern befinden oder befanden (Bodendenkmale).

(3) Dem Schutz dieses Gesetzes unterliegt auch die nähere Umgebung eines Denkmals, soweit sie für dessen Erhaltung, Erscheinungsbild oder städtebauliche Bedeutung erheblich ist (Umgebungsschutz).

§ 3 Denkmalliste

(1) [1]Denkmale sind nachrichtlich in ein öffentliches Verzeichnis (Denkmalliste) einzutragen. [2]Der Schutz nach diesem Gesetz ist nicht von der Eintragung der Denkmale in die Denkmalliste abhängig. [3]Die Eintragung beweglicher Denkmale und beweglicher Bodendenkmale öffentlich-rechtlicher Museen und Sammlungen in die Inventare ersetzt die Eintragung in die Denkmalliste.

---

1) Verkündet als Art. 1 G v. 24.5.2004 (GVBl. I S. 215); Inkrafttreten gem. Art. 3 dieses G am 1.8.2004.

(2) ¹Die Denkmalliste wird durch die Denkmalfachbehörde geführt. ²Eintragungen erfolgen von Amts wegen. ³Eintragungen sind zu löschen, wenn die Eintragungsvoraussetzungen entfallen sind. ⁴Eintragungen oder Löschungen können von Dritten angeregt werden.
(3) ¹Die Denkmalliste muss mindestens folgende Angaben über das Denkmal enthalten:
1. die Bezeichnung des Denkmals und Angaben zum Ort; bei Baudenkmalen, die aus mehreren baulichen Anlagen bestehen, und Gartendenkmalen ist die Begrenzung in einer Karte im geeigneten Maßstab anzugeben;
2. die Beschreibung des Denkmals und die Benennung des Schutzumfangs und
3. die wesentlichen Gründe der Eintragung.

²Die Denkmalliste ist mit der Bezeichnung des Denkmals und den Angaben zum Ort fortlaufend im Amtsblatt für Brandenburg bekannt zu machen; dies gilt nicht für bewegliche Denkmale und Bodendenkmale, soweit es für ihren Schutz erforderlich ist. ³Die Denkmalliste wird mit diesen Angaben von der Denkmalfachbehörde zusätzlich aktualisiert und in elektronischer Form veröffentlicht.
(4) ¹Die untere Denkmalschutzbehörde erhält die Denkmalliste für ihr Gebiet. ²Sie hat die Verfügungsberechtigten der Denkmale zu ermitteln und unverzüglich über die Eintragung oder Löschung zu unterrichten. ³Sind mehr als 20 Verfügungsberechtigte betroffen, können die Verfügungsberechtigten über die Eintragung oder Löschung durch eine Bekanntmachung im amtlichen Verkündungsblatt des Landkreises oder der kreisfreien Stadt unter Angabe der Stellen, bei denen die Denkmalliste eingesehen werden kann, unterrichtet werden.
(5) ¹Die Einsicht in die Denkmalliste ist jedermann gestattet. ²Soweit es sich um bewegliche Denkmale oder Bodendenkmale handelt, ist ein berechtigtes Interesse darzulegen.
(6) Soweit ein Denkmal aufgrund dieses Gesetzes in die Denkmalliste eingetragen wurde, hat die Denkmalfachbehörde auf Antrag des Verfügungsberechtigten die Eigenschaft als Denkmal durch Verwaltungsakt festzustellen.

§ 4 Denkmalbereiche
(1) ¹Denkmalbereiche können von den Gemeinden im Benehmen mit der Denkmalfachbehörde durch Satzung unter Schutz gestellt werden. ²Für den Inhalt der Satzung gilt § 3 Abs. 3 Satz 1 entsprechend.
(2) ¹Hat eine Gemeinde keine Satzung erlassen, kann die Denkmalschutzbehörde den Denkmalbereich durch eine ordnungsbehördliche Verordnung unter Schutz stellen, wenn eine Gefährdung der Substanz der Anlagen des Denkmalbereichs oder ihrer Gesamterscheinung, Struktur, Funktion oder des sie prägenden sonstigen Bezugs zu besorgen ist. ²Zuständig für den Erlass der Verordnung ist der Landrat. ³Bei kreisfreien Städten tritt an die Stelle der unteren Denkmalschutzbehörde die oberste Denkmalschutzbehörde. ⁴Die Verordnung ist aufzuheben, sobald die Gemeinde eine Satzung nach Absatz 1 erlassen hat.

§ 5 Grabungsschutzgebiete
Abgegrenzte Flächen, die bekannte oder nach begründeter Vermutung Bodendenkmale von besonderer Bedeutung bergen, an denen ein herausragendes wissenschaftliches Interesse besteht, können durch Rechtsverordnung[1] der Landesregierung zum Zweck der dauerhaften Bewahrung der Bodendenkmale vor Zerstörung oder bis zur ihrer wissenschaftlichen Untersuchung zu Grabungsschutzgebieten erklärt werden.

§ 6 Denkmalpflegepläne
¹Gemeinden können Denkmalpflegepläne aufstellen und fortschreiben. ²Der Denkmalpflegeplan enthält auf der Grundlage der Erfassung und Bewertung des Denkmalbestandes ein Planungs- und Handlungskonzept, wie die Erhaltung und Nutzung der Denkmale gewährleistet werden soll.

Abschnitt 2
Schutzbestimmungen

§ 7 Erhaltungspflicht
(1) Verfügungsberechtigte von Denkmalen haben diese im Rahmen des Zumutbaren[2] nach denkmalpflegerischen Grundsätzen zu erhalten, zu schützen und zu pflegen.

---
1) Siehe dazu z.B. die VO über das Grabungsschutzgebiet Seddin, abgedruckt als Nr. D4.I.1a.
2) Die VwV Zumutbarkeit Denkmalschutz ist abgedruckt als Nr. D4.I.1b.

D4.I.1 Brandenburgisches Denkmalschutzgesetz

(2) [1]Denkmale sind so zu nutzen, dass ihre Erhaltung auf Dauer gewährleistet ist. [2]Die bisher rechtmäßig ausgeübte oder eine der Lage und Beschaffenheit des Denkmals entsprechende Nutzung ist zulässig. [3]Denkmale sollen im Rahmen des für die Verfügungsberechtigten Zumutbaren der Öffentlichkeit zugänglich gemacht werden.

(3) Soweit in ein Denkmal eingegriffen wird, hat der Veranlasser des Eingriffs im Rahmen des Zumutbaren die Kosten zu tragen, die für die Erhaltung, fachgerechte Instandsetzung oder Bergung und Dokumentation des Denkmals anfallen.

(4) [1]Die Zumutbarkeit ist unter Berücksichtigung der durch die Denkmaleigenschaft begründeten sozialen Bindung des Eigentums und dessen Privatnützigkeit zu bestimmen. [2]Unzumutbar sind insbesondere in der Eigenschaft des Denkmals begründete besondere Belastungen, die zur Aufhebung der Privatnützigkeit führen, soweit sie durch Verwaltungsakte oder Maßnahmen nach diesem Gesetz entstehen. [3]Eine wirtschaftliche Belastung ist insbesondere unzumutbar, soweit die Kosten der Erhaltung und Bewirtschaftung dauerhaft nicht durch die Erträge oder den Gebrauchswert des Denkmals aufgewogen werden. [4]Eine unzumutbare Belastung liegt auch dann vor, soweit durch die Versagung einer Erlaubnis oder Maßnahmen nach diesem Gesetz eine bisher rechtmäßige oder zulässige, der Lage und Beschaffenheit des Denkmals entsprechende, insbesondere wirtschaftliche Nutzung des Denkmals unmöglich oder in einer Weise erschwert wird, so dass von dem Denkmal kein vernünftiger Gebrauch gemacht werden kann. [5]Können Verfügungsberechtigte oder Veranlasser Zuwendungen aus öffentlichen oder privaten Mitteln oder steuerliche Begünstigungen in Anspruch nehmen oder werden anderweitig Kompensationen eingeräumt, ist dies bei der Bestimmung der Zumutbarkeit zu berücksichtigen.

(5) [1]Die Unzumutbarkeit ist durch die Verfügungsberechtigten oder Veranlasser nachzuweisen. [2]Sie können sich nicht auf Belastungen durch erhöhte Erhaltungskosten berufen, soweit sie oder ihre Rechtsvorgänger die erhöhten Erhaltungskosten durch Unterlassen erforderlicher Erhaltungsmaßnahmen nach diesem Gesetz oder sonstigem öffentlichen Recht verursacht haben. [3]§ 254 des Bürgerlichen Gesetzbuches gilt sinngemäß.

(6) [1]Verfügungsberechtigte und Veranlasser haben in Verfahren nach diesem Gesetz Anspruch auf Beratung. [2]Das Land trägt zur Erhaltung und Pflege der Denkmale, insbesondere wenn Verfügungsberechtigte und Veranlasser wirtschaftlich unzumutbar belastet würden, nach Maßgabe dieses Gesetzes sowie der zur Verfügung stehenden Haushaltsmittel bei.

§ 8 Maßnahmen der Denkmalschutzbehörden

(1) Die Denkmalschutzbehörde hat nach pflichtgemäßem Ermessen diejenigen Maßnahmen zu ergreifen, die zum Schutz der Denkmale erforderlich sind.

(2) Kommen Verfügungsberechtigte oder Veranlasser ihren Pflichten nach § 7 nicht nach und tritt hierdurch eine Gefährdung des Denkmals ein, können sie im Rahmen des Zumutbaren von der Denkmalschutzbehörde verpflichtet werden, die zum Schutz des Denkmals erforderlichen Maßnahmen durchzuführen.

(3) Erfordert der Zustand eines Denkmals Maßnahmen zu seinem Schutz, ohne deren unverzügliche Durchführung es gefährdet würde, kann die Denkmalschutzbehörde diese Maßnahmen im Rahmen des Zumutbaren auf Kosten der Verfügungsberechtigten oder Veranlasser selbst durchführen oder durchführen lassen.

(4) [1]Wer ein Denkmal
1. widerrechtlich vorsätzlich oder fahrlässig beschädigt oder
2. dadurch beeinträchtigt, dass er Maßnahmen, die nach diesem Gesetz der Erlaubnis bedürfen, ohne die erforderliche Erlaubnis oder im Widerspruch zu ihr durchführt oder durchführen lässt,

hat auf Anordnung der Denkmalschutzbehörde den früheren Zustand wieder herzustellen oder das Denkmal auf andere seiner Eigenart entsprechende Weise instand zu setzen. [2]Die Denkmalschutzbehörde kann die erforderlichen Arbeiten auf Kosten des Verpflichteten selbst durchführen oder durchführen lassen, wenn die denkmalgerechte Wiederherstellung sonst nicht gesichert erscheint.

(5) [1]Verfügungsberechtigte oder Veranlasser sind zur Duldung von Maßnahmen nach den Absätzen 3 und 4 verpflichtet. [2]Dritte können von der Denkmalschutzbehörde zur Duldung verpflichtet werden, soweit dies für die Durchführung der Maßnahmen erforderlich ist.

§ 9 Erlaubnispflichtige Maßnahmen
(1) Einer Erlaubnis bedarf, wer
1. ein Denkmal entgegen dem Erhaltungsangebot des § 7 zerstören, beseitigen oder an einen anderen Ort verbringen,
2. ein Denkmal instand setzen, in seiner Substanz, seinem Erscheinungsbild oder in sonstiger Weise verändern,
3. die Nutzung eines Denkmals verändern,
4. durch die Errichtung oder Veränderung von Anlagen oder sonstige Maßnahmen die Umgebung eines Denkmals verändern oder
5. die bisherige Bodennutzung in Grabungsschutzgebieten oder von Grundstücken, von denen bekannt ist, dass sie Bodendenkmale bergen, verändern

will.
(2) Die Erlaubnis ist zu erteilen, soweit
1. die beantragte Maßnahme nach denkmalpflegerischen Grundsätzen durchgeführt werden soll oder
2. den Belangen des Denkmalschutzes entgegenstehende öffentliche oder private Interessen überwiegen und sie nicht auf andere Weise oder nur mit unverhältnismäßigem Aufwand berücksichtigt werden können.

(3) Alle Veränderungen und Maßnahmen an Denkmalen nach Absatz 1 sind nach Maßgabe der Denkmalschutzbehörde zu dokumentieren.
(4) [1]Die Erlaubnis kann mit Nebenbestimmungen verbunden werden. [2]Die Erlaubnis zur Zerstörung eines Denkmals kann mit der Nebenbestimmung verbunden werden, bestimmte Teile zu erhalten oder bei einer anderen baulichen Anlage wieder zu verwenden. [3]Weiter kann insbesondere bestimmt werden, dass Maßnahmen nur nach einem von der Denkmalschutzbehörde genehmigten Konzept oder bestimmte Arbeiten nur durch Fachleute oder unter der Leitung von Sachverständigen, deren Auswahl die Denkmalfachbehörde zustimmt, ausgeführt werden. [4]In die Nebenbestimmungen zu Maßnahmen an Bodendenkmalen sind Art und Ausmaß der erforderlichen Bergung und Dokumentation aufzunehmen.

§ 10 Nachforschungen
(1) [1]Wer nach Bodendenkmalen zielgerichtet mit technischen Hilfsmitteln suchen, nach Bodendenkmalen graben oder Bodendenkmale aus einem Gewässer bergen will, bedarf der Erlaubnis der Denkmalfachbehörde. [2]Dies gilt nicht für Nachforschungen, die von der Denkmalfachbehörde oder unter ihrer Mitwirkung vorgenommen oder veranlasst werden
(2) Die Erlaubnis ist zu erteilen, wenn Bodendenkmale oder Quellen für die Forschung nicht gefährdet werden oder ein überwiegendes öffentliches Interesse an der Nachforschung besteht.

§ 11 Funde
(1) [1]Funde sind Sachen, Mehrheiten von Sachen, Teile oder Spuren von Sachen, von denen anzunehmen ist, dass es sich um Denkmale (§ 2 Abs. 1) handelt. [2]Deren Entdeckung ist unverzüglich der Denkmalschutzbehörde anzuzeigen.
(2) [1]Anzeigepflichtig sind der Entdecker, der Verfügungsberechtigte des Grundstücks sowie der Leiter der Arbeiten, bei denen der Fund entdeckt wurde. [2]Die Anzeige durch eine dieser Personen befreit die übrigen.
(3) [1]Der Fund und die Fundstelle sind bis zum Ablauf einer Woche nach der Anzeige in unverändertem Zustand zu erhalten und in geeigneter Weise vor Gefahren für die Erhaltung des Fundes zu schützen. [2]Die Denkmalschutzbehörde kann die Frist um bis zu zwei Monate verlängern, wenn die Bergung und Dokumentation des Fundes dies erfordert. [3]Besteht an der Bergung und Dokumentation des Fundes aufgrund seiner Bedeutung ein besonderes öffentliches Interesse, kann die Frist auf Verlangen der Denkmalfachbehörde um einen weiteren Monat verlängert werden. [4]§ 7 Abs. 3 bleibt unberührt. [5]Innerhalb der in Satz 2 genannten Frist hat die Denkmalschutzbehörde dem Veranlasser die mit der Bergung und Dokumentation verbundenen Kosten mitzuteilen.
(4) Die Denkmalfachbehörde ist berechtigt, den Fund zur wissenschaftlichen Bearbeitung in Besitz zu nehmen.

§ 12 Schatzregal

(1) Bewegliche Denkmale und bewegliche Bodendenkmale, die herrenlos sind oder die so lange verborgen waren, dass ihr Eigentümer nicht mehr zu ermitteln ist, werden mit der Entdeckung Eigentum des Landes und sind unverzüglich an die Denkmalfachbehörde zu übergeben, wenn sie bei archäologischen Untersuchungen, in Grabungsschutzgebieten oder bei unerlaubten Nachforschungen entdeckt werden oder wenn sie für die wissenschaftliche Forschung von Wert sind.

(2) Dem Entdecker zufälliger Funde, die nach Absatz 1 Eigentum des Landes werden, ist durch die Denkmalfachbehörde eine angemessene Belohnung in Geld zu gewähren, es sei denn, bewegliche Bodendenkmale sind bei unerlaubten Nachforschungen entdeckt worden.

§ 13 Anzeigepflicht

(1) Verfügungsberechtigte haben Schäden oder Mängel, die an Denkmalen auftreten oder die ihre Erhaltung gefährden können, unverzüglich der Denkmalschutzbehörde anzuzeigen.

(2) Wird ein Grundstück mit einem in die Denkmalliste eingetragenen Denkmal veräußert, so hat der Veräußerer den Erwerber auf den bestehenden Schutz hinzuweisen und unverzüglich der Denkmalschutzbehörde den Eigentumswechsel anzuzeigen.

§ 14 Auskunftspflicht und Betretungsrecht

(1) Verfügungsberechtigte und Veranlasser sind verpflichtet, den nach diesem Gesetz zuständigen Behörden die zur Durchführung dieses Gesetzes erforderlichen Auskünfte zu erteilen.

(2) [1]Die mit dem Vollzug dieses Gesetzes beauftragten Personen sind berechtigt, nicht eingefriedete Grundstücke und nach vorheriger Benachrichtigung eingefriedete Grundstücke, Gebäude und Wohnungen zu betreten, um Denkmale festzustellen, zu besichtigen oder zu untersuchen, soweit es zur Erfüllung der sich aus diesem Gesetz ergebenden Aufgaben erforderlich ist. [2]Die Denkmalfachbehörde kann insbesondere verlangen, rechtzeitig vor Beginn eines Eingriffs Gelegenheit zur fachwissenschaftlichen Untersuchung von Denkmalen oder zu deren Bergung zu erhalten. [3]Hierzu sind ihr rechtzeitig alle einschlägigen Planungen sowie deren Änderungen bekannt zu geben. [4]Die Arbeiten der Denkmalfachbehörde haben so zu erfolgen, dass keine unzumutbaren Behinderungen bei der Durchführung des Vorhabens entstehen. [5]Das Betreten einer Wohnung ohne Einwilligung des Inhabers ist nur zulässig, wenn dies zur Verhütung einer dringenden Gefahr für ein Denkmal erforderlich ist. [6]Das Grundrecht auf Unverletzlichkeit der Wohnung (Artikel 13 des Grundgesetzes, Artikel 15 der Verfassung des Landes Brandenburg) wird insoweit eingeschränkt.

§ 15 Kennzeichnung der Denkmale

[1]Denkmale sollen gekennzeichnet werden. [2]Dabei soll von der obersten Denkmalschutzbehörde eine Plakette herausgegeben werden. [3]Verfügungsberechtigte haben die Anbringung von Kennzeichen und Erläuterungstafeln zu dulden.

Abschnitt 3
Organisation

§ 16 Denkmalschutzbehörden

(1) [1]Die Landkreise und kreisfreien Städte nehmen die Aufgaben der unteren Denkmalschutzbehörden als Pflichtaufgaben zur Erfüllung nach Weisung wahr. [2]Sie sind für die sich aus diesem Gesetz ergebenden Aufgaben zuständig, soweit dieses Gesetz nichts Anderes bestimmt.

(2) Die Stiftung Preußische Schlösser und Gärten Berlin-Brandenburg ist untere Denkmalschutzbehörde für die in ihrem Vermögen befindlichen baulichen und gärtnerischen Anlagen.

(3) Oberste Denkmalschutzbehörde ist das für Denkmalschutz zuständige Ministerium.

(4) [1]Die Denkmalschutzbehörden sind Sonderordnungsbehörden. [2]Die oberste Denkmalschutzbehörde ist Sonderaufsichtsbehörde.

(5) [1]Für den Vollzug der Aufgaben und auf das Aufsichtsrecht findet das Ordnungsbehördengesetz Anwendung, soweit dieses Gesetz nichts Anderes bestimmt. [2]Die Sonderaufsichtsbehörde kann anstelle der unteren Denkmalschutzbehörde auf deren Kosten tätig werden, wenn ihre Weisung innerhalb der bestimmten Frist nicht ausgeführt wurde. [3]Die untere Denkmalschutzbehörde ist davon unverzüglich zu unterrichten.

§ 17 Denkmalfachbehörde

(1) Denkmalfachbehörde ist das Brandenburgische Landesamt für Denkmalpflege und Archäologisches Landesmuseum.
(2) Die Denkmalfachbehörde hat insbesondere folgende Aufgaben:
1. Feststellung der Denkmaleigenschaft und systematische Erfassung des Denkmalbestandes (Inventarisation) sowie Führung der Denkmalliste,
2. Erforschung der Denkmale,
3. fachliche Beratung, Abgabe fachlicher Stellungnahmen auf Verlangen der Behörden, deren Belange durch Denkmalschutz und Denkmalpflege berührt sind, die Erstellung von Gutachten in allen Angelegenheiten der Denkmalpflege sowie fachlicher Publikationen,
4. Unterhaltung des Archäologischen Landesmuseums und fachwissenschaftlicher Sammlungen und
5. Berufung ehrenamtlicher Denkmalpfleger und Bodendenkmalpfleger.

(3) Die Denkmalfachbehörde ist bei der Erstellung von Gutachten nicht an fachliche Weisungen gebunden.
(4) Die Denkmalfachbehörde ist Träger öffentlicher Belange.

§ 18 Beirat und Beauftragte für Denkmalpflege

(1) [1]Die oberste Denkmalschutzbehörde beruft einen ehrenamtlichen Beirat für Denkmalpflege mit bis zu zehn Mitgliedern. [2]Er soll zu Grundsatzentscheidungen gehört werden, die Denkmalschutz und Denkmalpflege betreffen. [3]Er ist berechtigt, Empfehlungen auszusprechen. [4]Die Mitglieder des Beirats sind an Weisungen nicht gebunden.
(2) Dem Beirat gehören neben Vertretern der kommunalen Spitzenverbände Persönlichkeiten des öffentlichen Lebens und Vertreter der Fachwissenschaften an, die qualifizierte Kenntnisse der Denkmalpflege und des Denkmalschutzes besitzen oder zu den Belangen des Denkmalschutzes einen engen Bezug haben.
(3) Vertreter der Denkmalfachbehörde nehmen von Amts wegen an den Sitzungen des Beirats mit beratender Stimme teil.
(4) Das Nähere regelt die Geschäftsordnung des Beirats, die die oberste Denkmalschutzbehörde erlässt.
(5) Die unteren Denkmalschutzbehörden können einen ehrenamtlichen Beirat oder ehrenamtliche Beauftragte für Denkmalpflege berufen.

Abschnitt 4
Verfahrensbestimmungen

§ 19 Erlaubnisverfahren

(1) [1]Der Antrag auf Erteilung einer Erlaubnis nach § 9 ist schriftlich bei der Denkmalschutzbehörde einzureichen. [2]Dem Antrag sind alle für die Beurteilung des Vorhabens und die Bearbeitung des Antrags erforderlichen Unterlagen wie Pläne, Dokumentationen, Bestandsuntersuchungen, Fotografien, Gutachten oder Kosten- und Wirtschaftlichkeitsberechnungen beizufügen.
(2) [1]Die Denkmalschutzbehörde hat binnen zwei Wochen nach Eingang des Antrags zu prüfen, ob der Antrag vollständig ist. [2]Ist der Antrag unvollständig oder weist er sonstige erhebliche Mängel auf, fordert die Denkmalschutzbehörde den Antragsteller zur Behebung der Mängel innerhalb einer angemessenen Frist auf. [3]Werden die Mängel nicht innerhalb der Frist behoben, gilt der Antrag als zurückgenommen.
(3) [1]Sind die Antragsunterlagen vollständig, holt die Denkmalschutzbehörde eine Stellungnahme der Denkmalfachbehörde ein. [2]Gibt die Denkmalfachbehörde innerhalb eines Monats nach Zugang des Ersuchens keine Stellungnahme ab, gilt das Benehmen als hergestellt. [3]Will die Denkmalschutzbehörde von einer Stellungnahme der Denkmalfachbehörde abweichen, kann die Denkmalschutzbehörde innerhalb von zwei Wochen verlangen, dass der Vorgang der obersten Denkmalschutzbehörde vorgelegt wird. [4]Die oberste Denkmalschutzbehörde soll innerhalb eines Monats den Vorgang entscheiden.
(4) [1]Liegen für bestimmte erlaubnispflichtige Maßnahmen denkmalpflegerische Sammelgutachten der Denkmalfachbehörde vor, so entfällt die Beteiligung der Denkmalfachbehörde. [2]Die Denkmalschutzbehörde soll innerhalb eines Monats über den Antrag entscheiden.

(5) ¹Der Antrag auf Erteilung einer Erlaubnis nach § 10 ist schriftlich bei der Denkmalfachbehörde einzureichen. ²Absatz 1 Satz 2 und Absatz 2 gelten entsprechend. ³Die Denkmalfachbehörde soll innerhalb eines Monats über den Antrag entscheiden.
(6) ¹Eine Erlaubnis nach diesem Gesetz erlischt vier Jahre nach ihrer Erteilung. ²Die Frist kann auf schriftlichen Antrag einmalig um zwei Jahre verlängert werden.

§ 20 Bauordnungsrechtlich genehmigungspflichtige Vorhaben
(1) ¹Die bauordnungsrechtliche Genehmigung schließt die Erlaubnis nach § 9 ein. ²Die Bauaufsichtsbehörde entscheidet im Benehmen mit der Denkmalschutzbehörde. ³§ 19 Abs. 2 bis 4 bleibt unberührt. ⁴Im bauaufsichtlichen Verfahren beteiligt die Bauaufsichtsbehörde die Denkmalschutzbehörde, wenn in der Denkmalliste eingetragene Denkmale oder in Bauleitpläne übernommene Denkmale betroffen sind; dies gilt entsprechend für Entscheidungen, die die nähere Umgebung eines Denkmals betreffen.
(2) Für die Überwachung der Bauausführung nach den unter die Bestimmungen dieses Gesetzes fallenden Teilen der bauordnungsrechtlichen Genehmigung ist die untere Denkmalschutzbehörde zuständig.

§ 21 Denkmale, die der Religionsausübung dienen
¹Bei Entscheidungen über Denkmale, die der Religionsausübung dienen, haben die Denkmalschutzbehörde und die Denkmalfachbehörde die von den Kirchen und Religionsgemeinschaften festgestellten Belange der Religionsausübung zu beachten. ²In Streitfällen entscheidet die oberste Denkmalschutzbehörde im Benehmen mit der zuständigen kirchlichen Oberbehörde oder der zuständigen Stelle der betroffenen Religionsgemeinschaft.

§ 22 Gebühren und Bescheinigungen für steuerliche Zwecke
(1) Für die Denkmalschutzbehörden und die Denkmalfachbehörde sind Auszüge aus Büchern, Schriftstücken und Flurkarten des Liegenschaftskatasters, auch in elektronisch gespeicherter Form, frei von Gebühren und Auslagen.
(2) Bescheinigungen für die Erlangung von Steuervergünstigungen werden von der Denkmalschutzbehörde ausgestellt.

Abschnitt 5
Enteignung und Entschädigung, Ausgleich

§ 23 Enteignung
(1) Die Enteignung ist gegen Entschädigung zulässig, wenn auf andere zumutbare Weise nicht erreicht werden kann, dass
1. ein Denkmal in seiner Substanz, seiner Eigenart oder seinem Erscheinungsbild erhalten werden kann,
2. ein Denkmal der Allgemeinheit zugänglich gemacht werden kann, sofern hieran ein öffentliches Interesse besteht, oder
3. in einem Grabungsschutzgebiet planmäßige Nachforschungen betrieben werden können.

(2) ¹Die Enteignung erfolgt zugunsten des Landes oder einer anderen juristischen Person des öffentlichen Rechts. ²Zugunsten einer juristischen Person des Privatrechts ist die Enteignung dann zulässig, wenn der Enteignungszweck zu den satzungsmäßigen Aufgaben der juristischen Person des Privatrechts gehört und seine Erfüllung im Einzelfall gesichert erscheint.
(3) Für das Enteignungs- und Entschädigungsverfahren ist das Enteignungsgesetz des Landes Brandenburg anzuwenden.

§ 24 Ausgleich
(1) ¹Soweit Verwaltungsakte oder sonstige Maßnahmen nach diesem Gesetz zu einer unzumutbaren Belastung (§ 7 Abs. 4) führen würden, ist ein angemessener Ausgleich in Geld zu gewähren, sofern und soweit die Belastung nicht anderweitig ausgeglichen werden kann. ²Über den Ausgleich ist im Einvernehmen mit der obersten Denkmalschutzbehörde zugleich mit der belastenden Maßnahme zumindest dem Grunde nach zu entscheiden. ³Für die Bemessung des Ausgleichs ist das Enteignungsgesetz des Landes Brandenburg entsprechend anzuwenden.
(2) Absatz 1 gilt nicht für juristische Personen des öffentlichen Rechts mit Ausnahme der öffentlich-rechtlichen Religionsgemeinschaften.

§ 25 Berechtigte und Verpflichtete

(1) Entschädigung nach § 23 oder Ausgleich nach § 24 kann verlangen, wer in seinem Recht durch Enteignung oder Eigentumsbeschränkung beeinträchtigt wird und dadurch einen Vermögensnachteil erleidet.

(2) ¹Zur Leistung der Entschädigung nach § 23 oder des Ausgleichs nach § 24 ist das Land verpflichtet. ²Erfolgt eine Enteignung aufgrund eines Enteignungsverfahrens zugunsten einer juristischen Person des öffentlichen Rechts, die nicht Gebietskörperschaft ist, oder zugunsten einer juristischen Person des Privatrechts, so hat diese die Entschädigung zu tragen.

Abschnitt 6
Ordnungswidrigkeiten

§ 26 Ordnungswidrigkeiten

(1) Ordnungswidrig handelt, wer vorsätzlich oder fahrlässig
1. einer zur Erhaltung des Denkmals getroffenen vollziehbaren Anordnung nach § 8 Abs. 1 und 2 nicht nachkommt oder die Durchführung von Maßnahmen nach § 8 Abs. 3 und 4 nicht duldet,
2. Maßnahmen, die nach § 9 Abs. 1 und § 10 Abs. 1 der Erlaubnis bedürfen, ohne Erlaubnis oder abweichend von ihr durchführt oder durchführen lässt,
3. eine nach § 11 Abs. 1 erforderliche Anzeige nicht unverzüglich erstattet,
4. eine Fundstelle nach § 11 Abs. 3 nicht unverändert hält oder
5. eine nach § 14 Abs. 1 geforderte Auskunft nicht erteilt oder das Betreten eines Grundstücks, Gebäudes oder einer Wohnung nach § 14 Abs. 2 nicht duldet.

(2) Ordnungswidrig handelt, wer vorsätzlich unrichtige Angaben macht oder unrichtige Pläne oder Unterlagen vorlegt, um einen Verwaltungsakt nach diesem Gesetz zu erwirken oder zu verhindern.

(3) Ordnungswidrig handelt, wer wider besseres Wissen entgegen diesem Gesetz die Erlaubnis zur Zerstörung eines Denkmals erteilt.

(4) Ordnungswidrigkeiten können mit Geldbuße bis zu 500 000 Euro geahndet werden.

(5) ¹Bewegliche Gegenstände, auf die sich eine Ordnungswidrigkeit nach den Absätzen 1 bis 3 oder nach einer Verordnung nach § 27 Abs. 1 bezieht, können eingezogen werden. ²§ 23 des Gesetzes über Ordnungswidrigkeiten ist anzuwenden.

(6) Die Verfolgung der Ordnungswidrigkeiten verjährt in fünf Jahren.

(7) Verwaltungsbehörde im Sinne des § 36 Abs. 1 Nr. 1 des Gesetzes über Ordnungswidrigkeiten ist die untere Denkmalschutzbehörde.

§ 27 Verordnungsermächtigung für die Stiftung Preußische Schlösser und Gärten Berlin-Brandenburg

(1) ¹Die Stiftung Preußische Schlösser und Gärten Berlin-Brandenburg wird ermächtigt, zur Abwehr von Gefahren für die in ihrem Vermögen befindlichen baulichen und gärtnerischen Anlagen eine ordnungsbehördliche Verordnung zu erlassen.[1)] ²Ordnungswidrigkeiten nach dieser Verordnung können mit einer Geldbuße bis zu 10 000 Euro geahndet werden. ³Die Stiftung Preußische Schlösser und Gärten Berlin-Brandenburg vollstreckt die Geldbuße nach den Vorschriften des Verwaltungsvollstreckungsgesetzes für das Land Brandenburg. ⁴Die Stiftung kann mit der Landeshauptstadt Potsdam oder den Landkreisen durch eine öffentlich-rechtliche Vereinbarung regeln, dass Vollstreckungsaufgaben durch diese wahrgenommen werden.

(2) Zuständig für den Erlass der ordnungsbehördlichen Verordnung ist der Generaldirektor.

(3) Die ordnungsbehördliche Verordnung ist im Amtsblatt für Brandenburg zu verkünden.

Abschnitt 7
Überleitungsbestimmungen

§ 28 Überleitungsbestimmungen

(1) Soweit die nach § 9 der bis zum In-Kraft-Treten dieses Gesetzes geltenden Fassung des Brandenburgischen Denkmalschutzgesetzes geführten Verzeichnisse der Denkmale nach der Verordnung über

---

1) Die Ordnungsbehördliche Verordnung zur Abwehr von Gefahren für die im Vermögen der Stiftung Preußische Schlösser und Gärten Berlin-Brandenburg befindlichen baulichen und gärtnerischen Anlagen ist abgedruckt als Nr. D17.V.4.

D4.I.1 Brandenburgisches Denkmalschutzgesetz

das Verzeichnis der Denkmale[1] vom 30. April 1992 (GVBl. II S. 179) bekannt gemacht sind oder nach § 34 Abs. 1 der bis zum In-Kraft-Treten dieses Gesetzes geltenden Fassung des Brandenburgischen Denkmalschutzgesetzes als für die Führung des Verzeichnisses der Denkmale übernommen gelten, werden sie Bestandteil der Denkmalliste nach § 3.

(2) [1]Denkmale mit Gebietscharakter nach dem Gesetz zur Erhaltung der Denkmale in der Deutschen Demokratischen Republik (Denkmalpflegegesetz)[2] vom 19. Juni 1975 (GBl. I Nr. 26 S. 458), geändert durch Gesetz vom 3. Juli 1980 (GBl. I Nr. 20 S. 191), die in das Verzeichnis der Denkmale eingetragen waren, gelten als nach § 3 in die Denkmalliste eingetragen. [2]Die Eintragungen sind innerhalb von fünf Jahren nach In-Kraft-Treten dieses Gesetzes um die nach § 3 Abs. 3 erforderlichen Angaben zu ergänzen.

(3) Die Denkmalliste nach § 3 Abs. 3 Satz 2 ist spätestens sechs Monate nach In-Kraft-Treten dieses Gesetzes im Amtsblatt für Brandenburg erstmalig bekannt zu machen.

---

1) Aufgehoben mWv 1.8.2004 durch G v. 24.5.2004 (GVB I S. 215); siehe nunmehr das G zur Neuregelung des Denkmalschutzrechts im Land Brandenburg.
2) Aufgehoben mWv 21.8.1991 durch G v. 22.7.1991 (GVBl. S. 311).

Verordnung über das Grabungsschutzgebiet „Siedlungs- und Ritualraum Königsgrab Seddin"

Vom 12. Juli 2016 (GVBl.II/16, [Nr. 40])

Auf Grund des § 5 des Brandenburgischen Denkmalschutzgesetzes vom 24. Mai 2004 (GVBl. I S. 215) verordnet die Landesregierung:

§ 1 Erklärung zum Schutzgebiet
Die in § 2 näher bezeichnete Fläche im Landkreis Prignitz wird zum Grabungsschutzgebiet erklärt. Das Grabungsschutzgebiet trägt die Bezeichnung „Siedlungs- und Ritualraum Königsgrab Seddin".

§ 2 Schutzgegenstand
(1) Das Grabungsschutzgebiet hat eine Größe von rund 5 661 Hektar. Es umfasst Flächen in folgenden Fluren:

Gemeinde	Gemarkung	Flur
Groß Pankow (Prignitz)	Baek	3
Groß Pankow (Prignitz)	Hohenvier	1 bis 3
Groß Pankow (Prignitz)	Strigleben	2
Groß Pankow (Prignitz)	Tangendorf	2
Groß Pankow (Prignitz)	Klein Gottschow	4
Groß Pankow (Prignitz)	Groß Pankow	1, 2
Groß Pankow (Prignitz)	Helle	2 bis 4
Groß Pankow (Prignitz)	Retzin	1 bis 3
Groß Pankow (Prignitz)	Klein Linde	1, 2
Groß Pankow (Prignitz)	Kreuzburg	1, 2
Groß Pankow (Prignitz)	Rohlsdorf (R)	1 bis 3
Groß Pankow (Prignitz)	Wolfshagen	1 bis 11
Groß Pankow (Prignitz)	Seddin	1 bis 5
Groß Pankow (Prignitz)	Tacken	1.

Die Lage des Grabungsschutzgebietes ist in der als Anlage 1 beigefügten Übersichtskarte mit den Blattnummern 1 bis 3 im Maßstab 1 : 50 000 dargestellt.

(2) Die Grenze des Grabungsschutzgebietes ist in den in Anlage 2 aufgeführten Karten mit ununterbrochener roter Linie eingezeichnet; als Grenze gilt der innere Rand dieser Linie. Im Zusammenhang bebaute Ortslagen und ausgewiesene Gebiete mit bestehender landwirtschaftlicher Bebauung im Außenbereich sind nicht Gegenstand des Schutzgebietes. Die in Anlage 2 Nummer 1 aufgeführten 15 topografischen Karten im Maßstab 1 : 10 000 ermöglichen die Verortung im Gelände. Maßgeblich für den Grenzverlauf ist die Einzeichnung in den in Anlage 2 Nummer 2 mit den laufenden Blattnummern 1 bis 165 aufgeführten Liegenschaftskarten.

(3) Die Verordnung mit Karten kann beim Ministerium für Wissenschaft, Forschung und Kultur des Landes Brandenburg, oberste Denkmalschutzbehörde, in Potsdam sowie beim Landkreis Prignitz, untere Denkmalschutzbehörde, von jedermann während der Dienstzeiten kostenlos eingesehen werden.

§ 3 Schutzzweck
(1) Schutzzweck ist
1. die dauerhafte Erhaltung der im Boden und in den Gewässern liegenden beweglichen und unbeweglichen Bodendenkmale, insbesondere der Bestattungsplätze (Grabhügel, Flachgräberfelder), der unbefestigten und befestigten Siedlungen, der Wirtschafts-, Verkehrs- und Kultanlagen sowie der sonstigen menschlichen Zeugnisse, zum Beispiel von Religion und Krieg, insbesondere der Bronzezeit, aber auch der vorhergehenden und nachfolgenden Perioden;

2. die Erhaltung aller an und unter der Erd- oder Wasseroberfläche erhaltenen Reste und Spuren menschlicher Aktivitäten, wie Funde und Befunde einschließlich der zwischen ihnen bestehenden räumlichen und zeitlichen Kontexte;
3. die Erhaltung der auf der Geländeoberkante situierten oder leicht eingegrabenen großen Steine mit eingearbeiteten Schälchen (Schälchensteine) als besondere Zeugnisse der Religionsausübung;
4. die Erforschung komplexer menschlicher Daseins- und Organisationsformen am Rande der bronzezeitlichen Hochkulturen.

(2) Die Unterschutzstellung dient
1. wegen der besonders hohen Anzahl von sicht- und erkennbaren Bodendenkmalen, vor allem von raumprägenden Grabhügeln, gemeinsam mit den ausschließlich im Untergrund verborgenen Bodendenkmalen dem Schutz der räumlichen Beziehungen zwischen den Objekten. Darin eingeschlossen ist das Erscheinungsbild und die Raumwirkung der sicht- und erkennbaren Bodendenkmale;
2. der Nachvollziehbarkeit von Aufbau und Struktur der einzelnen Denkmalkomplexe (zum Beispiel Königsgrab, Burgwall Horst, Bestattungsplatz Teufelsberg).

(3) Die umfängliche Erhaltung von bronzezeitlichen raumbedeutsamen Bauwerken, die durch die Kenntnis abgegangener Strukturen ergänzt wird, ermöglicht es in einmaliger Weise, die räumlichen Bezüge und raumwirksamen Gestaltungsansätze der ehemals bestimmenden Akteure in dieser Region zu erforschen. Die einmalige Ausprägung und Lesbarkeit der archäologischen Ressourcen und der naturräumlichen Komponenten bedingen ein außerordentliches Forschungs- und Erkenntnispotenzial zum bronzezeitlichen Natur-, Sozial-, Wirtschafts-, Siedlungs-, Begräbnis- und Ritualraum.

§ 4 Erlaubnispflichtige Maßnahmen

(1) Im Grabungsschutzgebiet bedarf gemäß § 9 Absatz 1 Nummer 5 des Brandenburgischen Denkmalschutzgesetzes einer Erlaubnis, wer die bisherige Bodennutzung verändern will. Unter einer Veränderung der Bodennutzung ist jegliche Änderung der Nutzung von Flächen zu verstehen. Dazu zählen zum Beispiel Eingrabungen, Abgrabungen, Auffüllungen und Aufschüttungen, tiefergehende Bodenbearbeitung durch Tiefpflügen, die Umnutzung bisher land- oder forstwirtschaftlicher Flächen in Bauland oder die Umnutzung von Dauergrünland in Ackerland und von Dauergrün- und Ackerland in forstwirtschaftliche Flächen. Im Übrigen bleiben die Regelungen über erlaubnispflichtige Maßnahmen gemäß den §§ 9 und 10 des Brandenburgischen Denkmalschutzgesetzes unberührt. Unberührt bleibt auch die bisherige land-, forst- und fischereiwirtschaftliche Nutzung.

(2) Die bestehende Verkehrsinfrastruktur, das heißt Straßen gemäß § 1 Absatz 4 des Bundesfernstraßengesetzes beziehungsweise § 2 Absatz 2 des Brandenburgischen Straßengesetzes (insbesondere Fahrbahnen, Böschungen, Entwässerungsanlagen, Ver- und Entsorgungsleitungen/-anlagen sowie Alleenpflanzungen) sowie Eisenbahn, fällt nicht unter den Geltungsbereich der Grabungsschutzverordnung. Die bestehende Verkehrsinfrastruktur mit dem sich entwickelnden Verkehr genießt Bestandsschutz und wird in ihrer bestimmungsgerechten Nutzung nicht beeinträchtigt. Dies gilt insbesondere für die Unterhaltung, Überwachung und Grunderneuerung von Verkehrsinfrastruktur.

§ 5 Inkrafttreten

Diese Verordnung tritt am Tag nach der Verkündung in Kraft.

Anlagen (hier nicht wiedergegeben)
1. Anlage 1 – Übersichtskarte zu § 2 Absatz 1 der Verordnung über das Grabungsschutzgebiet Siedlungs- und Ritualraum Königsgrab Seddin, Blatt 1
2. Anlage 1 – Übersichtskarte zu § 2 Absatz 1 der Verordnung über das Grabungsschutzgebiet Siedlungs- und Ritualraum Königsgrab Seddin, Blatt 2
3. Anlage 1 – Übersichtskarte zu § 2 Absatz 1 der Verordnung über das Grabungsschutzgebiet Siedlungs- und Ritualraum Königsgrab Seddin, Blatt 3
4. Anlage 2 (zu § 2 Absatz 2)

Verwaltungsvorschrift des Ministeriums für Wissenschaft, Forschung und Kultur zur Prüfung der Zumutbarkeit im Rahmen von Erlaubnisverfahren und ordnungsrechtlichen Verfahren nach dem Brandenburgischen Denkmalschutzgesetz (VV Zumutbarkeit Denkmalschutz – BbgDSchG)

Vom 16. April 2009 (ABl./09, [Nr. 18], S.959)

1. Allgemeine Grundsätze[1)]

Das BbgDSchG regelt in § 7 Pflichten der Verfügungsberechtigten von Denkmalen und der Veranlasser von Eingriffen in Denkmale, die auf den Rahmen des Zumutbaren begrenzt sind. Der Begriff der Zumutbarkeit ist ein unbestimmter Rechtsbegriff, dessen behördliche Anwendung auf den konkreten Einzelfall vollständig gerichtlich überprüfbar ist. Bei der Anwendung des Begriffes auf die konkrete – unter einem Zumutbarkeitsvorbehalt stehende – Verpflichtung aus dem BbgDSchG sind die nachfolgend unter 2. und 3. dargestellten objektiven und subjektiven Kriterien zu prüfen. Das Prüfergebnis folgt aus einer Gesamtbetrachtung der für den Einzelfall heranziehbaren fachlichen Kriterien. Der Denkmalschutzbehörde ist dabei kein Ermessens- oder Beurteilungsspielraum eröffnet. § 7 Abs. 4 und 5 S. 2 benennt einzelne Kriterien, die nicht abschließend sind und jeweils auch nur für bestimmte Fallkonstellationen herangezogen werden können. Bei der Beurteilung der Zumutbarkeit findet eine Güterabwägung nicht statt, sodass z.B. eine Gewichtung der Bedeutung des Schutzobjektes kein relevantes Kriterium für den Prüfprozess ist.

Die unter dem Zumutbarkeitsvorbehalt stehenden Verpflichtungen nach dem BbgDSchG finden ihre verfassungsrechtliche Grundlage in der Sozialbindung des Eigentums gemäß Art. 14 Abs. 2 S. 2 GG. Die Reichweite der Sozialbindung des Eigentums entspricht für den Einzelfall dem Maß des Zumutbaren einer konkreten denkmalrechtlichen Verpflichtung. Eine wesentliche Voraussetzung zur Ermittlung der Grenze des Zumutbarkeitsrahmens ist daher eine Bewertung der Privatnützigkeit des von der Denkmaleigenschaft erfassten Eigentumsobjektes. Hierzu ist bei der Zumutbarkeitsprüfung eine schutzobjekt[2)]- bzw. grundstücksbezogene Betrachtungsweise vorrangig anzuwenden. Subjektive – auf der Person des Verfügungsberechtigten bzw. auf dessen Verhalten basierende – Aspekte sind nachrangig und können nur in den unter 3. beschriebenen Grenzen Eingang in die Prüfung finden. Juristische Personen des öffentlichen Rechts – mit Ausnahme der öffentlich-rechtlichen Religionsgemeinschaften – unterliegen nicht dem Grundrechtsschutz aus Art. 14 GG, sodass für diese kein Zumutbarkeitsmaßstab wie für private Eigentümer nach dem BbgDSchG zugrunde zu legen ist (s. a. § 24 Abs. 2). Dies gilt auch bei einer fiskalischen Betätigung oder wenn sie Träger einer privatrechtlichen Organisationsform (z.B. GmbH) sind.

Im Rahmen der schutzobjekt- bzw. grundstücksbezogenen Betrachtungsweise ist zu beurteilen, inwieweit Aufwendungen, die ausschließlich auf eine denkmalrechtliche Verpflichtung zurückzuführen sind, dazu führen, dass sich das von der Denkmaleigenschaft erfasste Eigentumsobjekt aus sich heraus wirtschaftlich nicht mehr trägt. Steht danach eine wirtschaftliche Nutzungsfähigkeit des Eigentumsobjektes in Frage, ist immer auch zu prüfen, ob dessen Privatnützigkeit dennoch durch eine realistische Veräußerungsmöglichkeit für den Verfügungsberechtigten gegeben ist. Dabei muss der Verfügungsberechtigte eine Wertminderung des mit einem Denkmal belegenen Grundstücks in einem verhältnismäßigen Rahmen hinnehmen.

Führen denkmalrechtlich bedingte Aufwendungen erst in Verbindung mit Aufwendungen aufgrund anderer öffentlich-rechtlicher Erfordernisse zu einer fehlenden wirtschaftlichen Tragfähigkeit, so dürfen die unwirtschaftlichen Aufwendungen nicht einseitig den Erfordernissen des Denkmalschutzes zugerechnet werden. In diesen Fällen ist zu prüfen, in welchem prozentualen Verhältnis die denkmalrechtlich bedingten Aufwendungen den Aufwendungen aufgrund anderer öffentlich-rechtlicher Erfordernisse gegenüberstehen. Überwiegen die denkmalrechtlich bedingten Aufwendungen in diesem

---

1) Im Folgenden sind unbenannte §§ solche des BbgDSchG.
2) Der Begriff des Schutzobjektes umfasst Denkmale und selbständige Bestandteile eines mehrgliedrigen Denkmals, die für sich die Voraussetzungen eines Denkmals nicht erfüllen.

D4.I.1b VwV Zumutbarkeit Denkmalschutz

Verhältnis nicht, können sie zur Begründung einer fehlenden wirtschaftlichen Tragfähigkeit nicht herangezogen werden.

Das Ergebnis der Zumutbarkeitsprüfung ist maßgeblich im denkmalrechtlichen Erlaubnisverfahren zur Bewertung der privaten Interessen im Rahmen der Abwägung mit den Belangen des Denkmalschutzes nach § 9 Abs. 2 Nr. 2 heranzuziehen. Sind die zur Wahrung der Belange des Denkmalschutzes bestehenden Verpflichtungen für den Betroffenen unzumutbar, so überwiegen die privaten Interessen regelmäßig die Belange des Denkmalschutzes. In diesen Fällen ist eine beantragte Erlaubnis durch die Denkmalschutzbehörde zu erteilen, sofern die unzumutbare Belastung nicht anderweitig ausgeglichen werden kann oder kein angemessener Ausgleich in Geld gewährt wird, § 24 Abs. 1. Der Ermessensspielraum der Denkmalschutzbehörde für Maßnahmen der Gefahrenabwehr nach § 8 Abs. 2 und 3 wird durch die Grenzen der Zumutbarkeit entsprechend eingeschränkt.

2. Objektive Kriterien

2.1 Schutzobjekte mit eigenem wirtschaftlichem Ertragswert

Bei Schutzobjekten, für die – ggf. nach einer Nutzbarkeitsprognose – ein Ertragswert nicht ausgeschlossen erscheint, ist zur Beurteilung der Zumutbarkeit einer Erhaltung oder eines denkmalrechtlich bedingten Sonderaufwandes eine schutzobjektbezogene Wirtschaftlichkeitsbetrachtung (vgl. Anlage 1) durchzuführen, die durch die Auswertung einer vom Verfügungsberechtigten[1]) abzufordernden Wirtschaftlichkeitsberechnung mit den unter 2.1.1 benannten inhaltlichen Mindestanforderungen erfolgt.

Ist das Schutzobjekt Teil einer wirtschaftlichen Einheit mit weiteren ertragsfähigen Objekten bzw. Flächen des betroffenen Grundstücks, die selbst nicht notwendig einem Schutzstatus unterfallen müssen, so sind diese in die Wirtschaftlichkeitsbetrachtung einzubeziehen. Werden Schutzobjekte vom Verfügungsberechtigten durch Grundstücksteilungen oder andere grundstücksbezogene Maßnahmen aus der wirtschaftlichen Einheit isoliert oder in ihrer wirtschaftlichen Nutzungsfähigkeit beschränkt, so ist die Einnahmesituation für das Schutzobjekt so anzunehmen, als wenn die isolierenden Maßnahmen nicht stattgefunden haben.

2.1.1
Inhaltliche Anforderungen an eine Wirtschaftlichkeitsberechnung

a) Kosten der Erhaltung und Bewirtschaftung des Schutzobjektes

Soweit zur Erhaltung bzw. wirtschaftlichen Nutzung eines Schutzobjektes neben den laufenden Instandhaltungskosten (s. u.) weitergehende Investitionen in das Schutzobjekt erforderlich werden, sind die voraussichtlichen Investitionskosten zu ermitteln und darzustellen. Hierfür ist eine konkrete Planung zugrunde zu legen. Dazu muss sich der Verfügungsberechtigte (vorläufig) auf eine bestimmte denkmalverträgliche Nutzung mit oder ohne bauliche Veränderungen festlegen, auch wenn dieser eine Beseitigung des Schutzobjektes anstrebt. Zur Darlegung der voraussichtlichen Sanierungskosten ist grundsätzlich die Vorlage einer detaillierten und fachtechnisch prüfbaren Kostenberechnung nach der DIN 276 in ihrer jeweils gültigen Fassung (notwendiger Mindeststandard der Aufgliederung nach Gewerken und Kosten) erforderlich.

Die voraussichtlichen Investitionskosten sind als jährliche Finanzierungskosten für das Investitionskapital auszuweisen. Hierbei ist ein marktüblicher Zinssatz für ein entsprechendes Kapitaldarlehen in Ansatz zu bringen (Fremdkapitalzinsen). Das gilt auch dann, wenn der Verfügungsberechtigte das Investitionskapital ohne eine Kreditaufnahme finanzieren kann (Eigenkapitalzinsen) oder Gründe in der Person des Verfügungsberechtigten vorliegen, die einer Kreditaufnahme im Einzelfall entgegenstehen (objektivierte Wirtschaftlichkeitsbetrachtung). Bei den Finanzierungskosten sind die Aufwendungen für die Darlehenstilgung nicht zu berücksichtigen, da diese eine Vermögensvermehrung zur Folge haben. Ebenso ist darauf zu achten, dass die Erwerbskosten für das Grundstück nicht mit ein-

---

1) Verfügungsberechtigt ist, wer (dingliche) Rechte an Denkmalen verändern, übertragen oder aufheben kann. Dazu gehören z.B. Eigentümer, Erbbauberechtigte oder Insolvenzverwalter. Im Folgenden wird mit der Verwendung des Begriffs Verfügungsberechtigter auch das weibliche Geschlecht erfasst.

bezogen werden, da diese Kosten unabhängig von denkmalrechtlichen Bindungen entstehen und sich nicht als Kosten der Erhaltung darstellen.

Als Kosten der Bewirtschaftung eines Denkmals kommen die laufenden Instandhaltungskosten, Rückstellungen für größere Reparaturen bzw. Substanzverlust, das Mietausfallwagnis, Verwaltungskosten und Betriebskosten in Betracht.

Vorbehaltlich anderer Nachweise des Verfügungsberechtigten für die Berechung der Bewirtschaftungskosten können die §§ 24 ff. der Verordnung über wohnungswirtschaftliche Berechungen (II. BV) in der jeweils gültigen Fassung analog herangezogen werden.

b) Erträge und Gebrauchsvorteile aus dem Schutzobjekt

Die darzustellenden Erträge bzw. Gebrauchsvorteile aus dem Schutzobjekt müssen nachhaltig erzielbar sein. Hierbei handelt es in erster Linie um zu erwartende Miet- und Pachtzinseinnahmen für realisierbare Wohn- und Gewerbeflächen im Schutzobjekt. Soweit Verfügungsberechtigte ihr Denkmal selbst nutzen wollen, sind als Gebrauchsvorteil fiktiv die erzielbaren Erträge aus dem Denkmal anzusetzen. Hierbei können im Rahmen der Bewirtschaftungskosten die Betriebskosten, jedoch keine Verwaltungskosten und kein Mietausfallwagnis Berücksichtigung finden.

Ist das Schutzobjekt Teil einer wirtschaftlichen Einheit mit weiteren ertragsfähigen Objekten bzw. Flächen des betroffenen Grundstücks (s.o. 2.1) so sind diesbezügliche Erträge unter Abzug der Investitions- und Bewirtschaftungskosten als Einnahmen in der Wirtschaftlichkeitsberechnung zu berücksichtigen.

c) Zuwendungen aus öffentlichen oder privaten Mitteln

Einmalige, verbindlich zugesagte staatliche oder private Zuwendungen und Zuschüsse für das Schutzobjekt sind in der Wirtschaftlichkeitsberechnung sanierungs- bzw. investitionskostenmindernd zu berücksichtigen. Kommt ein rechtsverbindlicher Zuwendungsbescheid, eine Zusicherung hierzu oder eine vertragliche Absprache – insbesondere mit privaten Förderstiftungen – nur dadurch nicht zustande, dass der Verfügungsberechtigte oder Veranlasser trotz Aufforderung keine entsprechenden Antragsunterlagen eingereicht oder andere Mitwirkungsakte in zurechenbarer Weise unterlassen hat, so muss er sich den Zuwendungsbetrag für den Zeitpunkt anrechnen lassen, an dem er bei ordnungsgemäßer Antragstellung. Mitwirkung die Mittel hätte in Anspruch nehmen können.

d) Steuerliche Begünstigungen

Die steuerlichen Begünstigungen umfassen alle Vorschriften, die für Aufwendungen an Schutzobjekten Steuervorteile vorsehen. Ein Steuervorteil entsteht, wenn sich infolge der Inanspruchnahme einer steuerlichen Begünstigung die festzusetzende Steuer mindern würde. Unerheblich ist, ob die Steuervorteile tatsächlich in Anspruch genommen werden. Die möglichen Steuervorteile sind auf der Einnahmeseite der Wirtschaftlichkeitsberechnung auszuweisen (vgl. Anlage 1 und 2).

Die Denkmalschutzbehörde beschränkt ihre Prüfung zur Berücksichtigung von steuerlichen Vorteilen auf die explizit für Denkmale vorgesehenen steuerlichen Begünstigungstatbestände in den §§ 7i, 10f, 10g und 11b EStG. Diese Beschränkung gilt auch dann, wenn daneben weitere steuerliche Begünstigungen in Anspruch genommen werden (z. B. Eigenheimzulage oder § 7 Abs. 4 EStG).

e) Anderweitige Kompensationen

Kompensationen sind alle rechtlichen und tatsächlichen Vorteile, die dem Verfügungsberechtigten zur Erleichterung des denkmalschutzrechtlichen Erhaltungsaufwandes eingeräumt werden, ohne dass er auf deren Durchsetzung bereits einen eigenständigen – von der Zumutbarkeitsbeurteilung losgelösten – Anspruch hätte. In der Wirtschaftlichkeitsberechung sind Kompensationen sanierungs- bzw. investitionskostenmindernd oder über zusätzliche Einnahmesituationen zu berücksichtigen.

f) Zurechnung erhöhten Erhaltungsaufwandes

Erhaltungskosten, die auf das pflichtwidrige Unterlassen von Instandhaltungsmaßnahmen am Schutzobjekt zurückzuführen sind, sind im Rahmen einer Wirtschaftlichkeitsbetrachtung von den erforderlichen Investitionskosten abzuziehen. Die Pflicht zu Erhaltungsmaßnahmen kann auch aus sonstigen öffentlichen Recht wie beispielsweise aus dem Gefahrenabwehrecht – insbesondere § 3 BbgBauO –

D4.I.1b VwV Zumutbarkeit Denkmalschutz

oder dem besonderen Städtebaurecht – insbesondere aufgrund von Sanierungs- und Erhaltungssatzungen sowie städtebaulichen Geboten gemäß § 177 BauGB – folgen und daher schon vor dem Wirksamwerden einer Erhaltungspflicht nach § 7 bestanden haben.

2.1.2
Bewertung der Unwirtschaftlichkeit

Ein unwirtschaftlicher Erhaltungsaufwand ist erst dann gegeben, wenn der Verfügungsberechtigte die Verpflichtung aus den mit dem Schutzobjekt erzielten Einnahmen nicht erfüllen kann, ohne sein sonstiges Vermögen anzugreifen. Die Wirtschaftlichkeit der Erhaltung ist anhand eines Prognosezeitraums zu betrachten, der sich an dem nach dem anwendbaren steuerlichen Begünstigungstatbestand geltenden Begünstigungszeitraum orientiert. Im Saldo müssen die Erträge aus dem Schutzobjekt die Kosten der Erhaltung und Bewirtschaftung in jedem Jahr des Prognosezeitraums übersteigen. Eine Baukostenvergleichsberechnung zwischen den Sanierungskosten für das Schutzobjekt und den Abbruch- und Neubaukosten für einen in Maßstab, Volumen und Nutzung vergleichbaren Neubau ist nicht geeignet, um die Zumutbarkeit der Erhaltung eines Schutzobjektes abschließend zu beurteilen.

2.2 Schutzobjekte ohne eigenen Ertragswert

Weisen Schutzobjekte für sich genommen keinen wirtschaftlichen Ertragswert auf – wie dies bei Bodendenkmalen in der Regel der Fall ist –, so muss auf die Ertragsfähigkeit des Bodens bzw. des von denkmalrechtlichen Bindungen tangierten Nutzungsvorhabens am Boden orientiert werden. Hierbei sind regelmäßig die Bruttoeinnahmen des investiven Gesamtprojektes dem Beitrag für den Denkmalschutz als betriebswirtschaftlichen Kostenfaktor gegenüberzustellen. Die Kriterien nach 2.1.1 c bis e sind bei der Bemessung des Beitrags für den Denkmalschutz entsprechend zu berücksichtigen.

3. Subjektive Kriterien

Die finanzielle Leistungsfähigkeit des Verpflichteten ist grundsätzlich kein geeignetes Kriterium zur Beurteilung der Zumutbarkeit. Eine Ausnahme gilt insoweit, als bei der Berücksichtigung von Möglichkeiten zur Inanspruchnahme steuerlicher Vergünstigungen (§ 7 Abs. 4 Satz 5) die Einkommensverhältnisse des Verfügungsberechtigten relevant werden können, s.o. 2.1.1 d.
Die Art und Weise des Erwerbs eines Schutzobjektes kann als subjektives Kriterium bei der Beurteilung der Zumutbarkeit heranzuziehen sein. Erfolgen unerlaubte Eingriffe in ein Schutzobjekt, die Maßnahmen zur Erhaltung, fachgerechten Instandsetzung oder zur Bergung und Dokumentation notwendig machen oder in ihrem Umfang erweitern, kann der Verfügungsberechtigte oder Veranlasser insoweit nicht die Unzumutbarkeit geltend machen, siehe auch § 8 Abs. 4.

4. Darlegungs- und Beweislast

Dem Verfügungsberechtigten obliegt die Darlegungs- und Beweislast für die Unzumutbarkeit seiner Erhaltungspflicht. Dies umfasst die Vorlage einer Wirtschaftlichkeitsberechnung mit den Anforderungen nach 2.1.1, die an einer erlaubnisfähigen und auf rentable Nutzungen ausgerichteten Investitionsplanung orientiert sein muss.
Hält der Verfügungsberechtigte sich objektiv für das Schutzobjekt anbietende Nutzungsformen für nicht realisierungsfähig (z.B. aufgrund fehlender Nutzungsinteressenten), so hat er dies durch erfolglos gebliebene Aktivitäten und Bemühungen um Vermarktung und Verwertung und ggf. durch Prognosen und Analysen zum potentiellen Nutzerkreis nachzuweisen. Ein fehlendes Nutzungs- bzw. Verwertungsinteresse des Verfügungsberechtigten ist für die Nutzungsprognose nicht relevant. Erst wenn er darlegt, dass trotz solcher Bemühungen das mit dem Denkmal belegene Grundstück nicht mit nennenswertem wirtschaftlichen Erfolg zu bewirtschaften sei, ist es Aufgabe der Denkmalschutzbehörde, zumutbare Alternativkonzepte aufzuzeigen.
Lässt sich eine wirtschaftlich auskömmliche Nutzung des Grundstücks unter Beibehaltung des Denkmals nicht darstellen, so bedarf es für die Annahme wirtschaftlicher Unzumutbarkeit auch des Nachweises, dass keine realistische Veräußerungsmöglichkeit für das Grundstück mehr existiert (s.o. 1).

Hierfür sind vom Verfügungsberechtigten Belege für eine über einen längeren Zeitraum erfolgte Vermarktung des Grundstücks vorzulegen.

5. In-Kraft-Treten
Diese Verwaltungsvorschrift tritt am Tag nach der Bekanntmachung im Amtsblatt für Brandenburg in Kraft.

Anlagen (hier nicht wiedergegeben)
1. Anlage 1 – Denkmalrechtliche Wirtschaftlichkeitsbetrachtung für ertragsfähige Schutzobjekte – Prüfschemata
2. Anlage 2 – Ermittlung des steuerlichen Vorteils zu §§ 7i, 10f, 10g, und 11b EStG

D4.I.2 VO zum Schutz von Kriegsstätten

Ordnungsbehördliche Verordnung zum Schutz von Kriegsstätten
Vom 31. März 2014 (GVBl.II/14, [Nr. 20])

Auf Grund des § 25 Absatz 1 in Verbindung mit § 30 Absatz 1 des Ordnungsbehördengesetzes in der Fassung der Bekanntmachung vom 21. August 1996 (GVBl. I S. 266) verordnet der Minister des Innern im Einvernehmen mit der Ministerin für Wissenschaft, Forschung und Kultur nach Kenntnisnahme durch den Ausschuss für Inneres des Landtages:

§ 1
Es ist verboten, auf Kriegsstätten nach
1. Kriegstoten einschließlich Leichenteilen,
2. Uniformen oder sonstigen Kleidungsstücken,
3. Erkennungsmarken oder sonstigen Gegenständen, die der Identifizierung dienen,
4. Nachlassgegenständen,
5. Auszeichnungen sowie
6. militärischem Gerät

zu suchen, Kriegstote sowie vorbezeichnete Gegenstände auszugraben oder in Besitz zu nehmen. Das Verbot erstreckt sich auch auf die Benutzung von Sonden und anderen technischen Hilfsmitteln, wenn hierdurch Kriegstote sowie vorbezeichnete Gegenstände zutage gefördert oder gefährdet werden können.

§ 2
(1) Als Kriegstote gelten
1. Personen, die in der Zeit vom 26. August 1939 bis 8. Mai 1945 während ihres militärischen oder militär-ähnlichen Dienstes gefallen oder tödlich verunglückt oder an den Folgen der in diesem Dienste erlittenen Gesundheitsschäden gestorben sind,
2. Zivilpersonen, die in der Zeit vom 26. August 1939 bis 8. Mai 1945 durch unmittelbare Kriegseinwirkung zu Tode gekommen oder an den Folgen der durch unmittelbare Kriegseinwirkung erlittenen Gesundheitsschäden gestorben sind,
3. sonstige in § 1 Absatz 1 des Gräbergesetzes aufgeführte Personengruppen.

(2) Kriegsstätten sind solche Gebiete, auf denen bis 8. Mai 1945 Kampfhandlungen stattgefunden haben und auf denen Kriegstote außerhalb ausgewiesener Begräbnisplätze bestattet wurden, oder in denen die in § 1 aufgeführten Gegenstände lagern.

(3) Die Kreisordnungsbehörden bestimmen durch ordnungsbehördliche Verordnungen räumlich umgrenzte Gebiete zu Kriegsstätten.

§ 3
Von dem Verbot nach § 1 können die Kreisordnungsbehörden Befreiung erteilen, wenn ein berechtigtes Interesse vorliegt. Die Befreiung kann nur erteilt werden, wenn gewährleistet ist, dass die beabsichtigte Such- oder Grabungsmaßnahme ordnungsgemäß durchgeführt und das öffentliche Interesse nicht beeinträchtigt wird. Vor Erteilung einer Befreiung ist das Benehmen mit dem Brandenburgischen Landesamt für Denkmalpflege und Archäologisches Landesmuseum herzustellen.

§ 4
(1) Ordnungswidrig handelt, wer gegen das Verbot des § 1 verstößt.
(2) Die Ordnungswidrigkeit kann mit einer Geldbuße geahndet werden.
(3) Zuständige Verwaltungsbehörde im Sinne des § 36 Absatz 1 Nummer 1 des Gesetzes über Ordnungswidrigkeiten istdie Kreisordnungsbehörde.
(4) Die durch eine Ordnungswidrigkeit nach Absatz 1 in Besitz genommenen Gegenstände können eingezogen werden.

§ 5
Die Vorschriften des Gräbergesetzes in der Fassung der Bekanntmachung vom 16. Januar 2012 (BGBl. I S. 98), das zuletzt durch Artikel 9 des Gesetzes vom 23. Juli 2013 (BGBl. I S. 2586) geändert worden ist, bleiben unberührt.

§ 6
Diese Verordnung tritt am Tag nach der Verkündung in Kraft.

D4.II.1 Brandenburgisches Archivgesetz

Gesetz über die Sicherung und Nutzung von öffentlichem Archivgut im Land Brandenburg (Brandenburgisches Archivgesetz– BbgArchivG)

Vom 7. April 1994 (GVBl. I S. 94)
(Sa BbgLR 557-5)
zuletzt geändert durch Art. 25 G zur Anpassung des bereichsspezifischen Datenschutzrechts an die VO (EU) 2016/679 vom 8. Mai 2018 (GVBl. I Nr. 8)

Der Landtag hat das folgende Gesetz beschlossen:

Abschnitt 1
Allgemeines

§ 1 Anwendungsbereich
(1) Dieses Gesetz regelt die Sicherung und Nutzung von öffentlichem Archivgut und die Tätigkeit der öffentlichen Archive im Land Brandenburg.
(2) Dieses Gesetz gilt nicht für die öffentlich-rechtlichen Religions- und Weltanschauungsgemeinschaften, für die öffentlich-rechtlichen Rundfunkanstalten und für öffentlich-rechtliche Unternehmen mit eigener Rechtspersönlichkeit, die am Wettbewerb teilnehmen, und deren Zusammenschlüsse.

§ 2 Begriffsbestimmungen
(1) [1]Öffentliches Archivgut ist Archivgut des Landes, Archivgut des Bundes, sofern und soweit es von einem öffentlichen Archiv übernommen wird, und kommunales Archivgut. [2]Öffentliches Archivgut sind auch archivwürdige Unterlagen, die die öffentlichen Archive zur Ergänzung ihres Archivgutes erwerben oder übernehmen.
(2) Archivgut des Landes sind alle archivwürdigen Unterlagen, die bei Verfassungsorganen, Behörden, Gerichten, juristischen Personen des öffentlichen Rechts oder deren Vereinigungen, bei deren Rechts- und Funktionsvorgängern oder sonstigen Stellen des Landes (Stellen des Landes) entstanden sind und zur dauernden Aufbewahrung von dem Brandenburgischen Landeshauptarchiv oder einem anderen öffentlichen Archiv übernommen oder diesem zur Nutzung überlassen werden.
(3) Kommunales Archivgut sind alle archivwürdigen Unterlagen, die bei Gemeinden oder Gemeindeverbänden, bei juristischen Personen des öffentlichen Rechts, die deren Aufsicht unterstehen, sowie bei deren Rechts- und Funktionsvorgängern (kommunale Stellen) entstanden sind und zur dauernden Aufbewahrung von einem kommunalen oder einem anderen öffentlichen Archiv übernommen oder diesem zur Nutzung überlassen werden.
(4) Zwischenarchivgut sind die von einem öffentlichen Archiv zur vorläufigen Aufbewahrung in ein Zwischenarchiv übernommenen Unterlagen, deren Aufbewahrungsfrist noch nicht abgelaufen und aus denen das Archivgut noch nicht ausgewählt worden ist.
(5) Unterlagen sind insbesondere Akten, Amtsbücher, Urkunden, Handschriften und andere Schriftstücke, Dateien, amtliche Druckschriften, Pläne, Karten, Plakate, Siegel, Petschafte, Bild-, Film-, Tondokumente, maschinenlesbare sowie sonstige Informationsträger einschließlich der zu ihrer Auswertung, Sicherung und Nutzung erforderlichen Hilfsmittel und Programme.
(6) Archivwürdig sind Unterlagen, die aufgrund ihrer rechtlichen, politischen, wirtschaftlichen, sozialen oder kulturellen Bedeutung für die Erforschung und das Verständnis von Geschichte und Gegenwart, für Gesetzgebung, Rechtsprechung und Verwaltung oder für die Sicherung berechtigter Belange Betroffener oder Dritter von bleibendem Wert sind.
(7) Öffentliche Archive sind alle Archive im Land Brandenburg, die von Stellen des Landes oder von Gemeinden und Gemeindeverbänden unterhalten werden und öffentliches Archivgut übernehmen.
(8) Archivfachliche Voraussetzungen für die Einrichtung und Unterhaltung eines öffentlichen Archivs sind:
1. die Betreuung durch hauptamtlich oder hauptberuflich tätiges Archivpersonal, das eine achivfachliche Ausbildung besitzt oder in sonstiger Weise fachlich geeignet ist, oder durch anderes geeignetes Personal, wenn eine fachliche Beratung durch ein öffentliches Archiv, in dem Archivfachpersonal vorhanden ist, erfolgt, und

2. das Vorhandensein geeigneter und ausreichender Magazin- und Diensträume, die den Brandschutz-, Datenschutz- und Sicherheitsvorschriften entsprechen.

Abschnitt 2
Erfassung, Übernahme, Verwahrung und Sicherung

§ 3 Aufgaben der öffentlichen Archive
(1) Die öffentlichen Archive haben die Aufgabe, das öffentliche Archivgut festzustellen, zu erfassen, zu übernehmen, auf Dauer zu verwahren, zu sichern und zu erhalten, zu erschließen, allgemein nutzbar zu machen, für die Benutzung bereitzustellen und auszuwerten.
(2) Die öffentlichen Archive beraten die anbietungspflichtigen Stellen bei der Verwaltung und Sicherung der Unterlagen.
(3) Die öffentlichen Archive nehmen Aufgaben im Rahmen der archivarischen Aus- und Fortbildung wahr.
(4) Die öffentlichen Archive wirken an der Auswertung des von ihnen verwahrten Archivgutes sowie an der Erforschung und Vermittlung insbesondere der brandenburgischen und deutschen Geschichte, der Heimat- und Ortsgeschichte mit und leiten dazu eigene Beiträge.

§ 4 Erfassung
(1) Die Stellen des Landes und die kommunalen Stellen sind verpflichtet, alle Unterlagen, die zur Erfüllung ihrer Aufgaben nicht mehr benötigt werden, dem zuständigen öffentlichen Archiv unverändert anzubieten und, soweit sie archivwürdig sind, zu übergeben. ²Unterlagen sind spätestens dreißig Jahre nach ihrer Entstehung anzubieten, soweit nicht Rechtsvorschriften oder Verwaltungsvorschriften oberster Landesbehörden längere Aufbewahrungsfristen festlegen.
(2) ¹Zur Übernahme anzubieten und abzuliefern sind auch Unterlagen, die
1. personenbezogene Daten enthalten, welche nach einer Rechtsvorschrift des Landes gelöscht oder vernichtet werden müßten oder nach Rechtsvorschriften des Bundes oder des Landes gelöscht werden könnten, sofern die Speicherung der Daten nicht unzulässig war oder
2. personenbezogene Daten im Sinne des Artikels 9 Absatz 1 der Verordnung (EU) 2016/679 des Europäischen Parlaments und des Rates vom 27. April 2016 zum Schutz natürlicher Personen bei der Verarbeitung personenbezogener Daten, zum freien Datenverkehr und zur Aufhebung der Richtlinie 95/46/EG (Datenschutz-Grundverordnung) (ABl. L 119 vom 4.5.2016, S. 1; L 314 vom 22.11.2016, S. 72) enthalten oder
3. einem Berufs- oder Amtsgeheimnis oder sonstigen Rechtsvorschriften über die Geheimhaltung unterliegen. Die nach § 203 Abs. 1 Nr. 1, 4 und 4a des Strafgesetzbuches geschützten Unterlagen einer Beratungsstelle dürfen nur in anonymisierter Form angeboten und übergeben werden.
(3) Von der Anbietungspflicht ausgenommen sind Unterlagen, deren Offenbarung gegen das Brief-, Post- oder Fernmeldegeheimnis verstoßen würde.
(4) ¹Juristische Personen des öffentlichen Rechts, die der Aufsicht des Landes unterstehen, und ihre Vereinigungen sind von der Anbietungspflicht befreit, wenn sie ein eigenes öffentliches Archiv unterhalten, das archivfachlichen Voraussetzungen im Sinne des § 2 Abs. 8 genügt, oder wenn die Unterlagen bei einer entsprechenden archivischen Gemeinschaftseinrichtung archiviert werden. ²Ob dieses öffentliche Archiv den archivfachlichen Voraussetzungen genügt, entscheidet die oberste Archivbehörde im Benehmen mit dem Archivträger.
(5) Die Landräte und die Oberbürgermeister sollen die Unterlagen, die im Rahmen ihrer Funktion als allgemeine untere Landesbehörde entstanden sind, dem zuständigen Kreis- oder Stadtarchiv anbieten und übergeben.
(6) Durch Vereinbarung zwischen dem zuständigen öffentlichen Archiv und der anbietenden Stelle oder, im Falle von Behörden, Gerichten und Stellen des Landes, der jeweils zuständigen obersten Landesbehörde kann
1. Art und Umfang der anzubietenden Unterlagen vorab festgelegt werden,
2. auf die Anbietung von Unterlagen von offensichtlich geringer Bedeutung verzichtet werden,
3. der Umfang der anzubietenden gleichförmigen Unterlagen, die in großer Zahl erwachsen, im einzelnen festgelegt werden.

(7) ¹Für maschinenlesbare Datenbestände sind Art und Umfang sowie die Form der Übermittlung der anzubietenden Daten vorab zwischen der anbietenden Stelle und dem zuständigen öffentlichen Archiv festzulegen. ²Datenbestände, die aus verarbeitungstechnischen Gründen vorübergehend vorgehalten werden, sind nicht anzubieten.

(8) Die anbietenden Stellen haben dem zuständigen öffentlichen Archiv auch Exemplare aller von ihnen herausgegebenen oder in ihrem Auftrag erscheinenden amtlichen Drucksachen und anderen Veröffentlichungen zur Übernahme anzubieten.

§ 5 Bewertung und Übernahme

(1) Das zuständige öffentliche Archiv entscheidet über die Archivwürdigkeit der angebotenen Unterlagen und über deren Übernahme in das Archiv.

(2) Dem zuständigen öffentlichen Archiv ist von der anbietenden Stelle Einsicht in alle vorhandenen Unterlagen sowie in die zugehörigen Findmittel und Programme zu gewähren.

(3) ¹Wenn das zuständige öffentliche Archiv die Archivwürdigkeit verneint oder innerhalb eines halben Jahres nach Anbietung nicht über die Archivwürdigkeit der angebotenen Unterlagen entscheidet, können die Unterlagen durch die anbietende Stelle vernichtet werden, wenn durch die Vernichtung schutzwürdige Belange Betroffener nicht beeinträchtigt werden. ²Vor einer Entscheidung des zuständigen öffentlichen Archivs oder vor Ablauf dieser Frist dürfen Unterlagen von der anbietenden Stelle ohne Zustimmung des zuständigen öffentlichen Archivs nicht vernichtet werden.

(4) Unterlagen nach § 4 Abs. 2 Nr. 2, die nicht von einem öffentlichen Archiv übernommen werden, sind zu löschen, wenn keine Notwendigkeit mehr besteht, die Daten im Interesse von Betroffenen weiter aufzubewahren.

(5) ¹Das zuständige öffentliche Archiv kann auch Zwischenarchivgut übernehmen. ²Die Aufbewahrung des Zwischenarchivgutes im zuständigen öffentlichen Archiv erfolgt im Auftrag der anbietenden Stelle oder ihres Rechts- oder Funktionsnachfolgers. ³Diese Stelle bleibt für die Unterlagen weiterhin verantwortlich und entscheidet über die Benutzung durch Dritte. ⁴Die Verantwortung des zuständigen öffentlichen Archivs beschränkt sich bis zur endgültigen Übernahme auf die notwendigen technischen und organisatorischen Maßnahmen zur Verwahrung und Sicherung dieser Unterlagen.

§ 6 Verwahrung und Sicherung

(1) ¹Öffentliches Archivgut ist im zuständigen öffentlichen Archiv aufzubewahren. ²In Ausnahmefällen kann mit Genehmigung der obersten Archivbehörde Archivgut des Landes aufgrund einer Vereinbarung in einem anderen als dem zuständigen öffentlichen Archiv aufbewahrt oder einem anderen als dem zuständigen öffentlichen Archiv übergeben werden, wenn dafür ein besonderer fachlicher Grund besteht, die archivfachlichen Voraussetzungen im Sinne des § 2 Abs. 8 gegeben sind und sichergestellt ist, daß schutzwürdige Belange Betroffener nicht und die Benutzung durch Betroffene und Dritte nicht erheblich beeinträchtigt werden.

(2) ¹Öffentliches Archivgut ist unveräußerlich. ²Unterlagen, bei denen keine Archivwürdigkeit besteht, sind vom zuständigen öffentlichen Archiv zu vernichten.

(3) ¹Die öffentlichen Archive haben die notwendigen organisatorischen, technischen und personellen Maßnahmen zu treffen, um die dauernde Aufbewahrung, Erhaltung und Benutzbarkeit des Archivgutes zu gewährleisten sowie seinen Schutz vor unbefugter Benutzung, vor Beschädigung oder Vernichtung sicherzustellen. ²Inbesondere sind geeignete Maßnahmen zu treffen, um vom Zeitpunkt der Übernahme an solche Unterlagen zu sichern, die personenbezogene Daten enthalten oder Rechtsvorschriften über Geheimhaltung unterliegen.

(4) ¹Für die Erfüllung der Aufgaben der öffentlichen Archive darf das Archivgut mittels maschinenlesbarer Datenträger erfaßt und gespeichert werden. ²Die Auswertung der gespeicherten Informationen ist nur zur Erfüllung der in diesem Gesetz genannten Zwecke zulässig.

(5) Die Verknüpfung personenbezogener Daten durch das zuständige öffentliche Archiv ist innerhalb der in § 10 genannten Schutzfristen nur zulässig, wenn die schutzwürdigen Belange Betroffener oder Dritter angemessen berücksichtigt werden.

Abschnitt 3
Benutzung

§ 7 Benutzung durch die abgebende Stelle
(1) Die abgebende Stelle hat das Recht, Archivgut, das aus ihren Unterlagen ausgewählt worden ist, jederzeit zu benutzen, wenn sie es zur Erfüllung ihrer Aufgaben benötigt.
(2) ¹Das gilt nicht für personenbezogene Daten, die aufgrund einer Rechtsvorschrift hätten gesperrt oder gelöscht werden müssen. ²In diesen Fällen besteht das Recht auf Benutzung nur nach Maßgabe des § 10, jedoch nicht zu dem Zweck, zu welchem die personenbezogenen Daten gespeichert worden sind.

§ 8 Benutzung durch Betroffene
(1) ¹Betroffenen ist auf Antrag Auskunft über die im Archivgut zu ihrer Person enthaltenen Daten zu erteilen, soweit das Archivgut durch Namen der Personen erschlossen ist. ²Ein weitergehender Auskunftsanspruch betroffener Personen nach Artikel 15 der Verordnung (EU) 2016/679 besteht nicht. ³Die Entscheidung über das bei der Auskunftserteilung zu verwendende Format trifft abweichend von Artikel 15 Absatz 3 Satz 3 der Verordnung (EU) 2016/679 das zuständige öffentliche Archiv. ⁴Anstelle der Auskunft ist durch das öffentliche Archiv Einsicht in die Unterlagen zu gewähren, soweit schutzwürdige Belange Dritter angemessen berücksichtigt werden können und keine Gründe für eine Einschränkung oder Versagung der Benutzung nach Maßgabe des § 11 bestehen. ⁵Die Versagung oder Einschränkung der Einsicht in die Unterlagen ist dem Antragsteller gegenüber schriftlich zu begründen.
(2) ¹Das öffentliche Archiv ist verpflichtet, den zum Archivgut gehörigen Unterlagen eine Gegendarstellung der betroffenen Person auf deren Verlangen beizufügen, wenn diese durch eine in den Unterlagen enthaltene Tatsachenbehauptung betroffen ist und ein berechtigtes Interesse an der Gegendarstellung glaubhaft macht. ²Nach ihrem Tod steht das Gegendarstellungsrecht deren Kindern, Eltern und der mit ihr durch Ehe, eingetragene Lebenspartnerschaft oder auf Dauer angelegte Lebensgemeinschaft verbunden gewesenen Person zu.
(3) ¹Die Gegendarstellung bedarf der Schriftform und muß von der betroffenen Person oder einer in Absatz 2 Satz 2 genannten Personen unterzeichnet sein. ²Sie muß sich auf Angaben über Tatsachen beschränken und darf keinen strafbaren Inhalt haben.
(4) ¹Ein durch Rechtsvorschriften geregelter Anspruch auf nachträgliche Berichtigung von Unterlagen wird durch die Übernahme der Unterlagen in ein öffentliches Archiv nicht eingeschränkt. ²Die Berichtigung hat in Form einer Gegendarstellung zu erfolgen. ³Weitergehende Ansprüche Betroffener aus Artikel 16 der Verordnung (EU) 2016/679 bestehen nicht. ⁴Die Artikel 18, 19 und 21 der Verordnung (EU) 2016/679 finden keine Anwendung. ⁵Abweichend von Artikel 20 der Verordnung (EU) 2016/679 entscheidet das zuständige Archiv über das Format, in dem die Daten bereitgestellt werden.
(5) Das Gegendarstellungsrecht gemäß der Absätze 2 und 4 gilt nicht für amtliche Niederschriften und Berichte über öffentliche Sitzungen der gesetzgebenden oder beschließenden Organe des Bundes, der Länder, Gemeinden und Gemeindeverbände und anderer juristischer Personen des öffentlichen Rechts sowie für Niederschriften und Urteile der Gerichte.

§ 9 Benutzung durch Dritte
(1) ¹Jede Person, die ein berechtigtes Interesse glaubhaft macht, hat das Recht, öffentliches Archivgut nach Maßgabe der Absätze 2 bis 3 sowie der §§ 10 und 11 zu benutzen, sofern durch dieses Gesetz oder durch Rechtsvorschrift nichts anderes bestimmt ist. ²Besondere Vereinbarungen mit Eigentümern von privatem Archivgut und testamentarische Bestimmungen bleiben unberührt.
(2) Ein berechtigtes Interesse ist insbesondere gegeben, wenn die Benutzung zu amtlichen, wissenschaftlichen, heimatkundlichen, familiengeschichtlichen, publizistischen, unterrichtlichen oder Bildungszwecken sowie zur Wahrnehmung berechtigter persönlicher Belange beantragt wird und schutzwürdige Belange betroffener Personen oder Dritter nicht beeinträchtigt werden oder der Zweck der Benutzung schutzwürdige Belange erheblich überwiegt.
(3) ¹Der Benutzer ist verpflichtet, von einem im Druck, maschinenschriftlich oder in anderer Weise vervielfältigten Werk, das er unter Verwendung von Archivgut eines öffentlichen Archivs verfaßt oder erstellt hat, nach Erscheinen des Werks unaufgefordert ein Belegexemplar unentgeltlich abzuliefern. ²Ist dem Benutzer die unentgeltliche Ablieferung eines Belegexemplars, insbesondere wegen der niedrigen Auflage oder der hohen Herstellungskosten, nicht zumutbar, kann er dem jeweiligen öffent-

lichen Archiv entweder ein Exemplar des Werks zur Herstellung einer Vervielfältigung für einen angemessenen Zeitraum überlassen oder eine Entschädigung bis zur Höhe des halben Ladenpreises verlangen. ³Wenn ein Ladenpreis nicht besteht, kann der Benutzer eine Entschädigung bis zur Höhe der halben Herstellungskosten des Belegexemplars verlangen.

§ 10 Schutzfristen
(1) Archivgut darf frühestens nach Ablauf von zehn Jahren nach Entstehung der Unterlagen benutzt werden.
(2) Archivgut, das besonderen Rechtsvorschriften über Geheimhaltung unterliegt, darf erst dreißig Jahre nach Entstehung der Unterlagen benutzt werden.
(3) ¹Archivgut, das sich nach seiner Zweckbestimmung oder nach seinem wesentlichen Inhalt auf eine natürliche Person bezieht (personenbezogenes Archivgut), darf frühestens zehn Jahre nach dem Tod der betroffenen Person benutzt werden. ²Ist das Todesjahr nicht oder nur mit unvertretbarem Aufwand feststellbar, endet die Schutzfrist neunzig Jahre nach der Geburt. ³Ist auch das Geburtsjahr dem Archiv nicht bekannt, endet die Schutzfrist für personenbezogenes Archivgut sechzig Jahre nach Entstehung der Unterlagen.
(4) Für die Benutzung von Archivgut, das dem Sozialgeheimnis unterliegende Daten enthält, gelten die Schutzfristen des § 5 des Bundesarchivgesetzes vom 6. Januar 1988 (BGBl. I S. 62), zuletzt geändert durch Gesetz vom 13. März 1992 (BGBl. I S. 506).
(5) ¹Die Schutzfristen nach den Absätzen 1 und 2 können im Einzelfall auf Antrag verkürzt werden, soweit das öffentliche Interesse und die §§ 11 und 12 dem nicht entgegenstehen. ²Die Benutzung kann dabei an Bedingungen und Auflagen gebunden werden.
(6) Die in den Absätzen 1 und 2 festgelegten Schutzfristen gelten nicht für Unterlagen und Archivgut von Stellen sowie von Parteien und Massenorganisationen der Deutschen Demokratischen Republik.
(7) Die in den Absätzen 1 bis 3 festgelegten Schutzfristen gelten nicht für Unterlagen, die bereits bei ihrer Entstehung zur Veröffentlichung bestimmt oder der Öffentlichkeit zugänglich waren.
(8) ¹Die in Absatz 3 festgelegten Schutzfristen gelten nicht für Archivgut, das die Tätigkeit von Personen der Zeitgeschichte und von Amtsträgern dokumentiert, soweit sie in Ausübung eines öffentlichen Amtes oder einer öffentlichen Funktion gehandelt haben und sofern sie nicht selbst Betroffene sind. ²Die schutzwürdigen Interessen Dritter sind angemessen zu berücksichtigen.
(9) Die Schutzfristen nach Absatz 3 können verkürzt werden, wenn
1. die betroffene Person oder nach ihrem Tod deren Kinder, Eltern oder die mit ihr durch Ehe, eingetragene Lebenspartnerschaft oder auf Dauer angelegte Lebensgemeinschaft verbunden gewesene Person in die Benutzung eingewilligt haben oder
2. die Benutzung zur Behebung einer bestehenden Beweisnot oder aus sonstigen im rechtlichen Interesse eines Dritten liegenden Gründen unerläßlich ist oder
3. die Benutzung für die Durchführung eines wissenschaftlichen Vorhabens erforderlich ist und wenn sichergestellt ist, daß schutzwürdige Belange der betroffenen Person und Dritter nicht beeinträchtigt werden, oder wenn das öffentliche Interesse an der Durchführung des wissenschaftlichen Vorhabens die schutzwürdigen Belange erheblich überwiegt.

(10) Vor Ablauf von Schutzfristen können die öffentlichen Archive Auskünfte aus dem Archivgut erteilen, soweit die §§ 11 und 12 dem nicht entgegenstehen.
(11) Die Schutzfristen können längstens um zwanzig Jahre verlängert werden, wenn dies im öffentlichen Interesse geboten ist.

§ 11 Einschränkung und Ausschluß der Benutzung
(1) Die Benutzung ist einzuschränken oder zu versagen, soweit
1. Grund zu der Annahme besteht, daß dem Wohl der Bundesrepublik Deutschland oder eines Landes wesentliche Nachteile entstehen,
2. schutzwürdige Belange Dritter entgegenstehen,
3. Rechtsvorschriften über Geheimhaltung verletzt würden,
4. der Erhaltungszustand des Archivgutes beeinträchtigt würde oder einer Benutzung entgegensteht,
5. durch die Benutzung ein nicht vertretbarer Verwaltungsaufwand entstehen würde oder
6. Vereinbarungen entgegenstehen, die mit Eigentümern aus Anlaß der Übernahme getroffen wurden.

(2) Nach § 203 Abs. 1 und 3 des Strafgesetzbuches geschützte Unterlagen aus einer Beratertätigkeit, die als Archivgut übernommen worden sind, dürfen vor Ablauf der Schutzfristen nur in anonymisierter Form benutzt werden.
(3) Die Benutzung kann an Bedingungen und Auflagen gebunden werden.

§ 12 Benutzung von Archivgut von Stellen des Bundes
(1) Für Archivgut, das gemäß § 2 Abs. 3 Satz 1 des Bundesarchivgesetzes von Stellen des Bundes dem Brandenburgischen Landeshauptarchiv oder einem anderen öffentlichen Archiv übergeben wurde, gelten § 2 Abs. 4 Satz 2 sowie die §§ 4 und 5 des Bundesarchivgesetzes entsprechend.
(2) Für Archivgut, das Rechtsvorschriften des Bundes über die Geheimhaltung im Sinne der §§ 8 bis 11 des Bundesarchivgesetzes unterliegt und das von anderen als den in § 2 Abs. 1 des Bundesarchivgesetzes genannten Stellen öffentlichen Archiven übergeben wurde, gelten § 2 Abs. 4 Satz 2 und § 5 des Bundesarchivgesetzes.

Abschnitt 4
Organisation und Zuständigkeiten

§ 13 Oberste Archivbehörde des Landes
(1) Oberste Archivbehörde ist das für das Archivwesen zuständige Landesministerium.
(2) Die oberste Archivbehörde übt die Dienst- und Fachaufsicht über das Brandenburgische Landeshauptarchiv aus.

§ 14 Brandenburgisches Landeshauptarchiv
(1) ¹Das Brandenburgische Landeshauptarchiv ist eine Einrichtung im Sinne von § 12 Abs. 1 des Landesorganisationsgesetzes vom 25. April 1991 (GVBl. S. 148)[1)] im Geschäftsbereich des für das Archivwesen zuständigen Landesministeriums. ²Es ist zuständig für das Archivgut des Landes.
(2) Das Brandenburgische Landeshauptarchiv ist auch zuständig für Unterlagen von Stellen des Bundes im Sinne von § 2 Abs. 3, 8 und 9 des Bundesarchivgesetzes.
(3) Das Brandenburgische Landeshauptarchiv übernimmt auch Archivgut anderer Herkunft, insbesondere
1. Unterlagen von Stellen gemäß § 1 Abs. 2, sofern diese kein eigenes Archiv unterhalten und die Unterlagen zur Übernahme anbieten,
2. Unterlagen von kommunalen Stellen, sofern diese kein eigenes Archiv unterhalten und die Unterlagen zur Übernahme anbieten,
3. Unterlagen natürlicher oder juristischer Personen des Privatrechts nach Einvernehmen mit den Eigentümern,
4. Unterlagen aufgrund letztwilliger Verfügungen oder Schenkungen.
(4) Das Brandenburgische Landeshauptarchiv kann für die obersten Landesbehörden Zwischenarchive gemäß § 2 Abs. 4 einrichten und unterhalten.
(5) ¹Das Brandenburgische Landeshauptarchiv nimmt Aufgaben der Archivberatung und Archivpflege wahr. ²Es berät und unterstützt
1. juristische Personen des öffentlichen Rechts, die der Aufsicht des Landes unterstehen, und ihre gemäß § 4 Abs. 4 eingerichteten Archive,
2. kommunale Stellen und ihre Archive und
3. natürliche und juristische Personen des Privatrechts und ihre Archive
bei der Sicherung und Nutzbarmachung ihres Archivgutes sowie bei der Aus- und Weiterbildung des in diesen Archiven tätigen Archivpersonals.

§ 15 Archivgut des Landtages
Der Landtag entscheidet in eigener Zuständigkeit, ob bei ihm entstandene Unterlagen, die zur Erfüllung der Aufgaben nicht mehr benötigt werden, von ihm selbst archiviert oder dem Brandenburgischen Landeshauptarchiv gemäß § 4 zur Übernahme angeboten werden.

§ 16 Kommunale Archive
(1) Die Gemeinden und Gemeindeverbände regeln die Archivierung ihres Archivgutes nach Maßgabe dieses Gesetzes in eigener Zuständigkeit.

---
1) Siehe nunmehr: LOG vom 24.5.2004 (GVBl. I S. 186).

D4.II.1 Brandenburgisches Archivgesetz

(2) Sie erfüllen diese Aufgabe durch
1. die Errichtung und Unterhaltung eigener Archive oder
2. die Errichtung und Unterhaltung einer für Archivierungszwecke geschaffenen archivischen Gemeinschaftseinrichtung oder
3. die Übergabe ihres Archivgutes an ein anderes öffentliches Archiv.

(3) [1]Die kommunalen Archive und archivischen Gemeinschaftseinrichtungen sollen den archivfachlichen Anforderungen im Sinne des § 2 Abs. 8 genügen. [2]Unterhalten Gemeinden und Gemeindeverbände keine eigenen Archive oder archivischen Gemeinschaftseinrichtungen, bieten sie ihre Unterlagen einem anderen öffentlichen Archiv zur Übernahme an. [3]Ist kein öffentliches Archiv zur Übernahme bereit, sind die Unterlagen vom Archiv des zuständigen Landkreises zu übernehmen. [4]Das Eigentum am Archivgut bleibt unberührt.

(4) Über die Verlängerung oder Verkürzung von Schutzfristen, über die Benutzung, deren Einschränkung oder Ausschluß sowie über den Erlaß einer Benutzungsordnung und die Erhebung von Gebühren entscheiden die Gemeinden und Gemeindeverbände in eigener Zuständigkeit.

(5) Die Gemeinden und Gemeindeverbände erlassen Archivordnungen durch Satzung.

Abschnitt 5
Schlußvorschriften

§ 17 Regelungsbefugnisse
(1) Das für das Archivwesen zuständige Mitglied der Landesregierung regelt durch Rechtsverordnung
1. die Benutzung der Archive des Landes (Benutzungsordnung),[1)]
2. die Erhebung von Gebühren bei der Benutzung der Archive des Landes (Gebührenordnung).

(2) Das für das Archivwesen zuständige Mitglied der Landesregierung regelt durch Runderlaß die Auslegung einzelner Regelungen dieses Gesetzes, insbesondere in organisatorischer Hinsicht.

(3) Das für das Archivwesen zuständige Mitglied der Landesregierung kann durch Rechtsverordnung dem Brandenburgischen Landeshauptarchiv andere, in sachlichem Zusammenhang mit dem Archivwesen stehende Aufgaben übertragen.

§ 18 Inkrafttreten, Außerkrafttreten
(1) Dieses Gesetz tritt am Tage nach der Verkündung[2)] in Kraft.

(2) Gleichzeitig treten, soweit sie nach Artikel 9 Abs. 1 des Einigungsvertrages als Landesrecht fortgelten, die folgenden Vorschriften außer Kraft:
1. Verordnung über das staatliche Archivwesen vom 11. März 1976 (GBl. I Nr. 10 S. 165),
2. Erste Durchführungsbestimmung zur Verordnung über das staatliche Archivwesen – Zuständigkeit der staatlichen Archive, Bestandsergänzung, Bewertung und Kassation – vom 19. März 1976 (GBl. I Nr. 10 S. 169),
3. Zweite Durchführungsbestimmung zur Verordnung über das staatliche Archivwesen – Benutzungsordnung – vom 16. März 1990 (GBl. I Nr. 21 S. 193),
4. Beschluß über die Erfassung und Auswertung der in der Deutschen Demokratischen Republik befindlichen Dokumente über die Zeit der Hitlerdiktatur vom 28. Mai 1964 – Auszug – (GBl. II Nr. 61 S. 575),
5. Beschluß über die Mikroverfilmung von Schrift- und Zeichnungsgut vom 19. September 1972 – Auszug – (GBl. II Nr. 57 S. 625),
6. Anordnung über die Verleihung der Titel „Oberarchivar", „Archivrat" und „Oberarchivrat" vom 1. April 1986 (GBl. I Nr. 17 S. 269).

---
1) Die Brandenburgische Landeshauptarchiv-Benutzungsordnung ist abgedruckt als Nr. D4.II.1a.
2) Verkündet am 12.4.1994.

# Verordnung über die Benutzung von Archivgut im Brandenburgischen Landeshauptarchiv (Brandenburgische Landeshauptarchiv-Benutzungsordnung – LHABenO)

Vom 17. Februar 2000 (GVBl. II S. 59)
(Sa BbgLR 557-6)
zuletzt geändert durch Art. 25 Elektronischer Rechtsverkehr-AnpassungsG vom 17. Dezember 2003 (GVBl. I S. 298)

Auf Grund des § 17 Abs. 1 Nr. 1 des Brandenburgischen Archivgesetzes vom 7. April 1994 (GVBl. I S. 94) verordnet der Minister für Wissenschaft, Forschung und Kultur:

§ 1 Arten der Benutzung
(1) Die Benutzung von Archivgut erfolgt in der Regel durch persönliche Einsichtnahme im Brandenburgischen Landeshauptarchiv.
(2) ¹An die Stelle der persönlichen Einsichtnahme kann auch die mündliche, schriftliche oder elektronische Auskunftserteilung sowie die Abgabe von Reproduktionen treten. ²Auskünfte können sich auf Hinweise zu einschlägigem Archivgut beschränken.

§ 2 Benutzungsgenehmigung
(1) ¹Die Benutzung von Archivgut erfolgt auf Antrag und nach Genehmigung des Brandenburgischen Landeshauptarchivs. ²Das Benutzungsverhältnis ist öffentlich-rechtlicher Natur.
(2) ¹Die Benutzungsgenehmigung ist schriftlich unter Verwendung der dafür vorgesehenen Formulare zu beantragen. ²Dabei hat der Antragsteller seinen Namen und seine Anschrift sowie den Benutzungszweck anzugeben und den Gegenstand der Nachforschungen möglichst genau zu bezeichnen. ³Er kann freiwillig seinen Beruf angeben. ⁴Handelt der Antragsteller im Auftrage Dritter, so hat er zusätzlich Namen und Anschrift dieser Person oder Stelle anzugeben.
(3) Der Antragsteller hat sich auf Verlangen auszuweisen.
(4) ¹Bei der Verwertung von Erkenntnissen aus Archivgut sind Persönlichkeits- und Urheberrechte sowie sonstige schutzwürdige Belange Betroffener und Dritter gemäß § 11 des Brandenburgischen Archivgesetzes zu berücksichtigen. ²Im Falle der Verletzung dieser Rechte und Belange haftet der Benutzer. ³Hierüber hat der Antragsteller eine schriftliche Erklärung abzugeben.
(5) ¹Das Brandenburgische Landeshauptarchiv darf die in Absatz 2 Satz 2 bis 4 genannten personenbezogenen Daten verarbeiten. ²Nach Ablauf des auf die Benutzung folgenden Kalenderjahres werden die jeweiligen Daten gelöscht, es sei denn, die jeweilige Sachlage lässt nach der Art der Benutzernachfrage eine Nutzung der betreffenden personenbezogenen Daten auch noch nach diesem Zeitpunkt erwarten, oder es liegt einer der in § 8 oder § 9 des Brandenburgischen Archivgesetzes genannten Fälle vor. ³Diese Datensätze sind zu kennzeichnen; die jeweils betroffenen Benutzer sind auf die verlängerten Fristen für die Zulässigkeit der Verarbeitung hinzuweisen.
(6) ¹Das Brandenburgische Landeshauptarchiv entscheidet nach Maßgabe der §§ 7 bis 9 des Brandenburgischen Archivgesetzes über den Antrag. ²Die Entscheidung wird dem Antragsteller mündlich, schriftlich oder elektronisch mitgeteilt. ³Die Einwilligung gilt nur für den angegebenen Benutzungszweck, den angegebenen Gegenstand der Nachforschungen und jeweils für das laufende Kalenderjahr; sie kann mit Nebenbestimmungen gemäß den §§ 10 Abs. 5 und 11 Abs. 3 des Brandenburgischen Archivgesetzes erteilt werden. ⁴§ 8 Abs. 1 Satz 3 des Brandenburgischen Archivgesetzes bleibt unberührt.
(7) Die Mitwirkung von Hilfskräften bei der Benutzung von Archivgut ist gesondert zu beantragen.

§ 3 Benutzung
(1) ¹Das Archivgut wird nach vorangegangener Beratung im Original oder als Reproduktion im Lesesaal des Brandenburgischen Landeshauptarchivs vorgelegt oder als Reproduktion ausgehändigt. ²Zum Schutz des Archivguts oder zur Wahrung schutzwürdiger Belange Dritter können auch ausschließlich Auskünfte über seinen Inhalt erteilt werden. ³Über die Art und Weise der Benutzung entscheidet das Brandenburgische Landeshauptarchiv unter Berücksichtigung der §§ 7 bis 12 des Brandenburgischen Archivgesetzes im Einzelfall.

(2) ¹Die Vorlage des Archivguts erfolgt im Rahmen der gegebenen Möglichkeiten des Brandenburgischen Landeshauptarchivs. ²Ein Anspruch auf Vorlage bestimmten Archivguts zu einem bestimmten Zeitpunkt besteht nicht.

(3) ¹Die Benutzer sind verpflichtet, das Archivgut in den Benutzungsräumen des Brandenburgischen Landeshauptarchivs zu belassen, seine innere Ordnung zu bewahren, es nicht zu beschädigen, zu verändern oder in seinem Erhaltungszustand zu gefährden. ²Insbesondere ist es untersagt, in dem Archivgut Stellen an- oder auszustreichen, Randbemerkungen oder andere Eintragungen zu machen oder Unterlagen durchzupausen.

(4) ¹Das Archiv unterstützt die Benutzer bei der Ermittlung des Archivguts und legt es vor. ²Ein Anspruch auf Unterstützung beim Lesen oder Übersetzen des Archivguts besteht nicht.

(5) ¹Die Verwendung technischer Geräte bei der Benutzung bedarf der Genehmigung. ²Diese kann versagt werden, wenn Grund zu der Annahme besteht, dass dadurch das Archivgut gefährdet würde, andere Benutzer gestört würden oder ein unvertretbarer Aufwand verursacht würde.

(6) Das Personal des Brandenburgischen Landeshauptarchivs ist berechtigt, den Benutzern Anweisungen zur Einhaltung der Benutzungs- und der Lesesaalordnung zu erteilen, denen Folge zu leisten ist.

(7) Näheres regelt die jeweils geltende Lesesaalordnung des Brandenburgischen Landeshauptarchivs.

§ 4 Verkürzung von Schutzfristen

(1) ¹Die Verkürzung von Schutzfristen gemäß den §§ 10 und 12 des Brandenburgischen Archivgesetzes ist schriftlich und unter Angabe von Gründen zu beantragen. ²Sie kann lediglich für einzelne Archivalieneinheiten oder fest umgrenzte Gruppen beantragt werden.

(2) ¹Über die Verkürzung entscheidet der Direktor des Brandenburgischen Landeshauptarchivs. ²Die Entscheidung ist dem Antragsteller schriftlich, bei Ablehnung unter Angabe der Gründe, mitzuteilen.

(3) Wird im Falle des § 10 Abs. 9 Nr. 1 des Brandenburgischen Archivgesetzes die schriftliche Einwilligung einer der zur Einwilligung berechtigten Personen vorgelegt, so kann auf die Schriftform des Antrages und bei positiver Entscheidung auch des Bescheides verzichtet werden.

§ 5 Reproduktionen

(1) Reproduktionen werden im Rahmen der gegebenen Möglichkeiten vom Brandenburgischen Landeshauptarchiv oder von einer von ihm beauftragten Stelle angefertigt, soweit konservatorische und urheberrechtliche Gründe nicht entgegenstehen und sichergestellt ist, dass schutzwürdige Belange Betroffener oder Dritter nicht beeinträchtigt werden.

(2) ¹Über das geeignete Reproduktionsverfahren entscheidet im Zweifelsfall das Brandenburgische Landeshauptarchiv. ²Ein Anspruch auf Anfertigung von Reproduktionen besteht nicht.

(3) Die Veröffentlichung von Reproduktionen von Archivgut aus dem Brandenburgischen Landeshauptarchiv bedarf der Genehmigung des Archivs.

§ 6 Ausleihe von Archivgut

¹In begründeten Ausnahmefällen kann zu amtlichen oder zu Ausstellungszwecken eine Benutzung durch Ausleihe von Archivgut stattfinden. ²Die Ausleihe bedarf einer besonderen Vereinbarung zwischen dem Brandenburgischen Landeshauptarchiv und dem Ausleiher.

§ 7 Gebühren

Die Berechnung von Gebühren und Auslagen für die Inanspruchnahme des Brandenburgischen Landeshauptarchivs richtet sich nach der Gebührenordnung für das Brandenburgische Landeshauptarchiv in der jeweils geltenden Fassung.

§ 8 Ausschluss von der Benutzung

Benutzer, die fällige Entgelte nicht zahlen, Archivgut beschädigen, aus dem Brandenburgischen Landeshauptarchiv entfernen oder sonst in grober Weise gegen Vorschriften des Brandenburgischen Archivgesetzes, der Benutzungs- oder der Lesesaalordnung verstoßen, können zeitweise oder auf Dauer von der Benutzung ausgeschlossen werden.

§ 9 In-Kraft-Treten

Diese Verordnung tritt am Tage nach der Verkündung in Kraft.

Fördergrundsätze des Ministeriums für Wissenschaft, Forschung und Kultur[1)]

Präambel

Das historische Erbe ist in besonderem Maße geeignet, kulturelle und regionale Identität zu fördern. Zudem ziehen neben den kulturhistorischen Höhepunkten viele Denkmäler die Besucherinnen und Besucher in die verschiedenen Regionen des Landes. Die Vielfalt der Fördervereine, die sich für die Erhaltung und Nutzung von Denkmalen einsetzen, zeugt von dem Potential, das Denkmäler im Hinblick auf bürgerschaftliches Engagement besitzen.

Das MWFK stellt nach Maßgabe des Haushaltes des Landes Projektfördermittel des Kapitel 06 810 Titel 893 13 zu diesem Zweck bereit.

Damit wird eine breite Fördermöglichkeit für die Sicherung und Erhaltung des kulturellen Erbes geschaffen. Mit den vorliegenden Fördergrundsätzen des Ministeriums für Wissenschaft, Forschung und Kultur (MWFK) sollen Inhalt und Verfahren der Förderung konkretisiert werden.

Das MWFK veröffentlicht jährlich eine Aufforderung zur Abgabe von Föderanträgen auf seiner Homepage und auf der Homepage des Brandenburgischen Landesamtes für Denkmalpflege und Archäologischen Landesmuseums (BLDAM).

Die nach dieser Richtlinie gewährten Förderungen stellen Beihilfen im Sinne von Art. 107 Abs. 1 des Vertrages über die Arbeitsweise der Europäischen Union (AEUV) dar, die nach Art. 53 der Allgemeinen Gruppenfreistellungsverordnung (EU) Nr. 651/2014 der Kommission vom 17. Juni 2014 (ABl. L 187/1 vom 26.06.2014) in der Fassung der Verordnung (EU) 2017/1084 der Kommission vom 14.06.2017 (ABl. L 156/1 vom 20.07.2017) (im Folgenden: AGVO) mit dem Binnenmarkt vereinbar und von der Anmeldepflicht gemäß Art. 108 Abs. 3 freigestellt sind. Die Definition wirtschaftlicher bzw. nichtwirtschaftlicher Tätigkeiten richtet sich nach der Bekanntmachung der Kommission zum Begriff der staatlichen Beihilfe im Sinne des Art. 107 Abs. 1 des Vertrages über die Arbeitsweise der Europäischen Union (ABl. C 262 vom 19.07.2016), insbesondere Ziffer 2 und Ziffer 7.2.1.)

1. Allgemeine Hinweise

Mit dem Ziel, landesweit für die bestehenden Bedarfe und das herausragende Engagement im Bereich der Denkmalpflege Fördermöglichkeiten zu schaffen, unterstützt das MWFK investive Projekte.

Anträge sind **bis zum 30. September d. J.** postalisch an das
Ministerium für Wissenschaft, Forschung und Kultur des Landes Brandenburg Referat 33 Dortustr. 36, 14467 Potsdam
zu richten. Das Antragsformular kann von der Webseite des MWFK unter www.mwfk.brandenburg.de abgerufen werden. Für die Fristwahrung zählt das Datum des Poststempels.

2. Zuwendungsempfänger

Zuwendungsempfänger können natürliche Personen sowie rechtsfähige juristische Personen des privaten Rechts und des öffentlichen Rechts sein.

3. Zuwendungszweck, Förderungsziel

3.1 Das Land Brandenburg gewährt nach Maßgabe

– dieser Förderkriterien,
– der allgemeinen haushaltsrechtlichen Bestimmungen, insbesondere der §§ 23, 44 LHO, der Verordnung (EU) Nr. 651/2014 der Kommission vom 17. Juni 2014 zur Feststellung der Vereinbarkeit bestimmter Gruppen von Beihilfen mit dem Binnenmarkt in Anwendung der Artikel 107 und 108 des Vertrags über die Arbeitsweise der Europäischen Union (AGVO)

Zuwendungen, die ausschließlich für investive Projekte der Denkmalpflege im Land Brandenburg zur Verfügung stehen.

[1)] https://bldam-brandenburg.de/wp-content/uploads/2019/07/FördergrundsätzeDenkmalmahilfe2020.pdf.

D4.III.1 MWFK Fördergrundsätze

Die Zuwendungen werden als Beihilfen für Kultur und die Erhaltung des kulturellen Erbes nach Maßgabe des Artikels 53 AGVO gewährt. Die Beihilfen müssen den Vorgaben der AGVO genügen. Ausgenommen von der Förderung sind Unternehmen, die einer Rückforderungsanordnung aufgrund eines früheren Beschlusses der Kommission zur Feststellung der Unzulässigkeit einer von demselben Mitgliedstaat gewährten Beihilfe und ihrer Unvereinbarkeit mit dem Binnenmarkt nicht nachgekommen sind und Unternehmen in Schwierigkeiten nach Art. 2 Nr. 18 AGVO.

3.2 Ein Anspruch auf Gewährung einer Zuwendung besteht nicht. Die Bewilligungsbehörde entscheidet auf Grund ihres pflichtgemäßen Ermessens im Rahmen der verfügbaren Haushaltsmittel.

3.3 Gegenstand der Förderung

Gefördert werden investive Projekte zur Erhaltung, Sicherung, Sanierung und Restaurierung unbeweglicher und beweglicher Denkmäler, archäologische Rettungs- und Forschungsgrabungen im Land Brandenburg sowie Ersatzvornahmen der Unteren Denkmalschutzbehörden als Mittel zur Vollstreckung denkmalrechtlicher Anordnungen.

4. Förderkriterien

Für die Auswahl der Projekte sind folgende Kriterien maßgeblich:
- geschichtliche, wissenschaftliche, technische, künstlerische, städtebauliche oder volkskundliche Bedeutung des Fördergegenstandes,
- Befürwortung durch die Untere Denkmalschutzbehörde und positive denkmalfachliche Bewertung des Vorhabens durch das Brandenburgische Landesamt für Denkmalpflege und Archäologisches Landesmuseum (BLDAM),
- Sicherung der Gesamtfinanzierung,
- angemessene Eigenbeteiligung in der Regel im Umfang von mindestens 20 % des Gesamtvolumens.

Gefördert werden können nur von den Denkmalbehörden anerkannte denkmalpflegerische Maßnahmen, die der Substanzerhaltung und Restaurierung von Kulturdenkmälern einschließlich ihrer wesentlichen Bestandteile dienen, sowie archäologische Rettungs- und Forschungsgrabungen. Renovierungsarbeiten sowie Umbau- und nutzungsbezogene Modernisierungsmaßnahmen sind nicht zuwendungsfähig.

Nicht förderfähig sind Ausgaben
- des Erwerbs eines Kulturdenkmals,
- einer Totalrekonstruktion,
- eines Neubaus in einem Denkmalbereich,
- für die Beschaffung von Finanzierungsmitteln (Darlehensfinanzierung etc.),
- für Maßnahmen in der Umgebung von Kulturdenkmälern,
- der laufenden Unterhaltung,
- für eigene Arbeitsleistung (unbare Leistungen),
- für Maßnahmen, die ausschließlich der Verschönerung dienen,
- für rentierliche nutzungsbedingte Aufwendungen sowie
- für Sachausgaben (ausgenommen Planungsausgaben, die unmittelbar mit dem Investitionsvorhaben in einem Zusammenhang stehen).

5. Art, Umfang und Höhe der Zuwendung

5.1. Die Zuwendung wird als nichtrückzahlbarer Zuschuss im Rahmen der Anteilfinanzierung als Projektförderung gewährt.

5.2. Zuwendungen werden in der Regel maximal bis zur Höhe von 50 Prozent der zuwendungsfähigen Gesamtausgaben gewährt. Zuwendungen an juristische Personen des öffentlichen Rechts können in der Regel bis zur Höhe von maximal 75 Prozent der zuwendungsfähigen Gesamtausgaben gewährt werden (vgl. Art. 53 Abs. 4 a AGVO). Zuwendungen für Ersatzvornahmen der Unteren Denkmalschutzbehörden werden in der Regel maximal bis zur Höhe von 50 Prozent der zuwendungsfähigen

Gesamtausgaben gewährt; diese werden als bedingt rückzahlbare Zuwendung gewährt. Für die Berechnung der Beihilfeintensität werden die Beträge vor Abzug von Steuern und sonstigen Abgaben herangezogen.

5.3. Die beantragte Zuwendung soll mindestens 8.000 € betragen.

5.4. Die in Art. 4 Abs. 1 lit. z AGVO bestimmte Anmeldeschwelle für Investitionsbeihilfen in Höhe von 150 Mio. Euro pro Projekt ist einzuhalten.

5.5. Die Zuwendung darf die nach den beihilfenrechtlichen Vorschriften der Europäischen Union maximal zulässige Beihilfeintensität oder den maximal zulässigen Beihilfebetrag bei Kumulierung verschiedener Förderungen nicht überschreiten. Auf die Kumulierungsvorschrift Art 8 AGVO wird verwiesen,

6. Bewilligungsverfahren

6.1. Die Entscheidung über eine Förderung erfolgt durch das MWFK. Die Vergabe der Mittel für investive Projekte erfolgt auf der Grundlage einer Förderempfehlung des BLDAM.

6.2. Bewilligungsbehörde ist das MWFK. Das MWFK kann die Bewilligung an das BLDAM übertragen.

6.3. Dem ausgefüllten Antragsvordruck sind eine Kopie der denkmalrechtlichen Erlaubnis bzw. der Baugenehmigung, ein Eigentumsnachweis sowie ein in Einnahmen und Ausgaben ausgeglichener Finanzierungsplan beizufügen. Der Antragsvordruck ist von der Homepage des BLDAM sowie des MWFK abrufbar. Falls erforderlich können weitere Unterlagen angefordert werden,

6.4. Der Durchführungszeitraum ist in der Regel auf das Bewilligungsjahr (Kalenderjahr) beschränkt.

6.5. Laufende oder bereits abgeschlossene Maßnahmen können nicht nachfinanziert werden. Mit den Vorhaben darf daher vor der Bewilligung noch nicht begonnen worden sein.

6.6. Auf die Veröffentlichungs- und Informationspflichten gemäß Art. 9 AGVO wird hingewiesen.

6.7. Erhaltene Förderungen können im Einzelfall gemäß Art. 12 AGV0 von der Europäischen Kommission geprüft werden.

7. Geltungsdauer der Fördergrundsätze

Diese Fördergrundsätze gelten für den Förderzeitraum bis zum 31.12.2025.

D4.IV.1 KGSG-Zuständigkeitsverordnung

Verordnung über die Zuständigkeit nach dem Kulturgutschutzgesetz für das Land Brandenburg (Kulturgutschutzgesetzzuständigkeitsverordnung – KGSGZustV)

Vom 13. März 2017 (GVBl. II Nr. 14)
(Sa BbgLR 554-4)

Auf Grund des § 3 Absatz 1 Satz 2 des Kulturgutschutzgesetzes vom 31. Juli 2016 (BGBl. I S. 1914) in Verbindung mit § 6 Absatz 2 des Landesorganisationsgesetzes vom 24. Mai 2004 (GVBl. I S. 186), der durch Artikel 2 des Gesetzes vom 10. Juli 2014 (GVBl. I Nr. 28 S. 2) geändert worden ist, verordnet die Landesregierung:

§ 1 Zuständige Behörde
Das für Kultur zuständige Ministerium ist zuständige Behörde im Sinne des § 3 Absatz 1 Satz 1 des Kulturgutschutzgesetzes vom 31. Juli 2016 (BGBl. I S. 1914).

§ 2 Inkrafttreten
Diese Verordnung tritt am Tag nach der Verkündung[1] in Kraft.

---

1) Verkündet am 17.3.2017.

Landesverfassung der Freien Hansestadt Bremen

In der Fassung der Bekanntmachung vom 12. August 2019[1] (Brem.GBl. S. 524)
(SaBremR 100–a–1)

– Auszug –

Erster Hauptteil
Grundrechte und Grundpflichten

Artikel 11 [Freiheit von Kunst und Wissenschaft]
(1) Die Kunst, die Wissenschaft und ihre Lehre sind frei.
(2) Der Staat gewährt ihnen Schutz und nimmt an ihrer Pflege teil.
(3) Der Staat schützt und fördert das kulturelle Leben.

---

1) Neubekanntmachung der Landesverfassung v. 21.10.1947 (Brem.GBl. S. 251) in der ab 8.6.2019 geltenden Fassung.

Bremisches Gesetz zur Pflege und zum Schutz der Kulturdenkmäler (Bremisches Denkmalschutzgesetz – BremDSchG)

Vom 18. Dezember 2018 (Brem.GBl. S. 631)

Der Senat verkündet das nachstehende, von der Bürgerschaft (Landtag) beschlossene Gesetz:

Abschnitt 1
Allgemeine Bestimmungen

§ 1 Denkmalpflege und Denkmalschutz
(1) Denkmalpflege und Denkmalschutz haben die Aufgabe, Kulturdenkmäler wissenschaftlich zu erforschen, zu pflegen, zu schützen und zu erhalten sowie auf ihre Einbeziehung in die städtebauliche Entwicklung, die Raumordnung und die Landespflege hinzuwirken.
(2) ¹Denkmalpflege und Denkmalschutz sind Angelegenheiten des Landes. ²Bei der Durchführung der Denkmalpflege und des Denkmalschutzes arbeiten die zuständigen Behörden des Landes und der Stadtgemeinden mit den Eigentümern von Kulturdenkmälern und den sonstigen Verfügungsberechtigten zusammen. ³Soweit das Land oder die Stadtgemeinden oder Einrichtungen, auf die das Land oder die Stadtgemeinden aufgrund Eigentum, finanzieller Beteiligung, Satzung oder sonstiger Bestimmungen, die deren Tätigkeit regeln, unmittelbar oder mittelbar einen beherrschenden Einfluss ausüben kann, nach § 9 Absatz 2 Verpflichtete sind, haben sich die zuständigen Behörden und Einrichtungen in besonderem Maße der Denkmalpflege und des Denkmalschutzes anzunehmen.

§ 2 Begriffsbestimmungen
(1) Kulturdenkmäler im Sinne dieses Gesetzes sind Sachen, Mehrheiten von Sachen oder Teile von Sachen, deren Erhaltung aus geschichtlichen, wissenschaftlichen, künstlerischen, technikgeschichtlichen, heimatgeschichtlichen oder städtebaulichen Gründen im öffentlichen Interesse liegt.
(2) Kulturdenkmäler im Sinne des Absatzes 1 können sein:
1. unbewegliche Denkmäler, wie Baudenkmäler, andere feststehende Denkmäler der Kunst, Kultur oder Technik und deren Inneres, Gartenanlagen und andere flächenhafte Anlagen einschließlich der mit ihnen verbundenen Frei- und Wasserflächen, jeweils auch als Sachgesamtheiten;
2. Mehrheiten unbeweglicher Sachen, die aufgrund eines übergeordneten Bezugs Kulturdenkmäler sind, ohne dass jeder einzelne Bestandteil die Voraussetzungen des Satzes 1 erfüllen muss (Ensembles), wie Orts-, und Platzgefüge, Siedlungen oder Straßenzüge;
3. bewegliche Denkmäler einschließlich Urkunden und Sammlungen;
4. Bodendenkmäler als mit dem Boden verbundene oder im Boden verborgene Sachen, Sachgesamtheiten und Spuren von Sachen, die von Menschen geschaffen oder bearbeitet wurden oder Aufschluss über menschliches Leben in vergangener Zeit geben.

(3) Zu einem Kulturdenkmal gehört auch das Zubehör, soweit es mit der Hauptsache eine kulturelle Einheit bildet.
(4) Dem Schutz dieses Gesetzes unterliegt auch die Umgebung der unbeweglichen Kulturdenkmäler im Sinne von Absatz 2 Nummer 1, 2 und 4.

§ 3 Geschützte Kulturdenkmäler
(1) ¹Kulturdenkmäler nach § 2 werden unter Denkmalschutz gestellt. ²Aufgrund der Unterschutzstellung unterliegen sie den Schutzvorschriften dieses Gesetzes.
(2) Kulturdenkmäler nach § 2 Absatz 2 Nummer 4 unterliegen der Schutzvorschrift des § 10 bereits vor der Unterschutzstellung.
(3) Die Belange des Denkmalschutzes und der Denkmalpflege sowie die Anforderungen des unmittelbar geltenden europäischen Rechts und der ratifizierten internationalen und europäischen Übereinkommen zum Schutz des materiellen kulturellen Erbes sind in die städtebauliche Entwicklung und die Landesplanung einzubeziehen und bei allen öffentlichen Planungen und Maßnahmen angemessen zu berücksichtigen.

§ 4 Denkmalschutzbehörden
(1) ¹Denkmalschutzbehörden für den Bereich der Stadtgemeinde Bremen sind das Landesamt für Denkmalpflege und die Landesarchäologie; für den Bereich Stadtgemeinde Bremerhaven werden die

Aufgaben dem Magistrat übertragen. ²Ist die Zuständigkeit nicht eindeutig bestimmbar oder wird sie bestritten, entscheidet die obere Denkmalschutzbehörde über die Zuständigkeit.

(2) Obere Denkmalschutzbehörde ist der Senator für Kultur.

(3) ¹Den Denkmalschutzbehörden nach Absatz 1 und 2 obliegt es, die unter Denkmalschutz gestellten Kulturdenkmäler zu schützen. ²Soweit gesetzlich nicht anders bestimmt, obliegt es den Denkmalschutzbehörden nach Absatz 1, zu diesem Zweck die notwendigen Maßnahmen zu ergreifen, um die Erfüllung der Pflichten nach diesem Gesetz zu gewährleisten. ³Die Denkmalschutzbehörden sind Träger öffentlicher Belange. ⁴Sie sind bei allen Planungen und Maßnahmen, die Belange des Denkmalschutzes und der Denkmalpflege berühren können, frühzeitig zu beteiligen.

(4) ¹Die obere Denkmalschutzbehörde entscheidet nach Anhörung der Denkmalfachbehörden. ²Die Denkmalschutzbehörden entscheiden im Einvernehmen mit den Denkmalfachbehörden; kommt kein Einvernehmen zu Stande, entscheidet die obere Denkmalschutzbehörde.

(5) ¹Die Denkmalschutzbehörden nach Absatz 1 und 2 dürfen Kontaktdaten der Personen nach § 9 Absatz 2 sowie weitere personenbezogene Daten verarbeiten, soweit dies zur Erfüllung ihrer Aufgaben nach diesem Gesetz erforderlich ist. ²An andere Behörden dürfen personenbezogene Daten gemäß Satz 1 übermittelt werden, wenn und soweit diese die Denkmalschutzbehörden nach diesem oder einem anderen Gesetz in ihre Aufgabenerfüllung einbeziehen und die personenbezogenen Daten auf Grundlage einer entsprechenden gesetzlichen Ermächtigung für die Erfüllung ihrer jeweiligen Aufgaben benötigen.

§ 5 Denkmalfachbehörden

(1) Denkmalfachbehörden sind das Landesamt für Denkmalpflege und die Landesarchäologie.

(2) ¹Den Denkmalfachbehörden obliegt es, die Kulturdenkmäler nach § 2 nach anerkannten wissenschaftlichen Standards zu erfassen, zu erforschen, zu dokumentieren und zu pflegen sowie ihre Erkenntnisse in geeigneter Form der Öffentlichkeit zu vermitteln. ²§ 4 Absatz 5 gilt entsprechend.

(3) Die Denkmalfachbehörden können zur Erfüllung ihrer Aufgaben Fachwerkstätten einrichten und betreiben.

§ 6 Denkmalrat

(1) ¹Für die Denkmalfachbehörden wird ein unabhängiger und sachverständiger Denkmalrat gebildet. ²Der Denkmalrat soll die Denkmalfachbehörden beraten und von diesen in allen Angelegenheiten von grundsätzlicher Bedeutung gehört werden.

(2) ¹Die Mitglieder des Denkmalrates werden von der oberen Denkmalschutzbehörde bestellt. ²Die obere Denkmalschutzbehörde wird ermächtigt, durch Rechtsverordnung das Nähere, insbesondere die Zusammensetzung des Denkmalrates, die Bestimmung des Vorsitzenden des Denkmalrates, die Anzahl der Mitglieder, die Amtszeit der Mitglieder und das Vorschlagsrecht für die Benennung der Mitglieder zu regeln.¹⁾

§ 7 Unterschutzstellung und Eintragung in die Denkmalliste

(1) ¹Die Unterschutzstellung der Kulturdenkmäler erfolgt von Amts wegen. ²Die zuständige Denkmalfachbehörde nimmt durch Bescheid die Unterschutzstellung vor; im Falle des Landeseigentums tritt an die Stelle eines Bescheides die Mitteilung an die zuständige Stelle des Landes.

(2) ¹Der Bescheid ist dem Eigentümer oder dem Erbbauberechtigten oder Nießbraucher bekannt zu geben. ²Ist dieser der zuständigen Denkmalfachbehörde nicht bekannt oder nicht zweifelsfrei durch oder aufgrund von öffentlichen Urkunden bestimmbar, steht der Bekanntgabe durch Bescheid eine öffentliche Bekanntmachung der Unterschutzstellung nach dem Bremischen Bekanntmachungsgesetz gleich. ³Widerspruch und Klage gegen die Unterschutzstellung haben keine aufschiebende Wirkung. ⁴Die Unterschutzstellung soll auf Ersuchen der Denkmalfachbehörde ins Grundbuch eingetragen werden. ⁵Die obere Denkmalschutzbehörde wird ermächtigt, durch Rechtsverordnung²⁾ die Einzelheiten des Verfahrens der Unterschutzstellung zu regeln.

(3) ¹Die obere Denkmalschutzbehörde wird ermächtigt, Kulturdenkmäler nach § 2 Absatz 2 Nummer 2 abweichend von Absatz 1 Satz 2 durch Rechtsverordnung unter Denkmalschutz zu stellen. ²Mit

---

1) Die Verordnung über die Zusammensetzung und die Tätigkeit des Denkmalrates ist abgedruckt als Nr. D5.I.1a.
2) Die Verordnung über die Unterschutzstellung von Kulturdenkmälern und das Eintragungs- und Löschungsverfahren ist abgedruckt als Nr. D5.I.1b.

D5.I.1 Bremisches Denkmalschutzgesetz

Behörden, deren Belange unmittelbar betroffen sind, ist Einvernehmen über die Unterschutzstellung im Wege der Rechtsverordnung herzustellen. ³Absatz 2 Satz 4 gilt entsprechend.
(4) Die nach Absatz 1 oder 3 unter Denkmalschutz gestellten Kulturdenkmäler werden nachrichtlich in die Denkmalliste eingetragen.
(5) ¹Die Denkmallisten dienen als Verzeichnis aller unter Denkmalschutz gestellten Kulturdenkmäler; sie werden bei den Denkmalfachbehörden geführt und enthalten Angaben zur Kennzeichnung des Kulturdenkmals, insbesondere zu Straße, Hausnummer, Liegenschaftskataster und baurechtlichen Festsetzungen, sowie Name und Anschrift der Personen nach § 9 Absatz 2. ²Ihr wesentlicher Inhalt wird ohne Name und Anschrift der Personen nach § 9 Absatz 2 in geeigneter Form der Öffentlichkeit zugänglich gemacht. ³Unabhängig hiervon können die Denkmallisten von jeder Person eingesehen werden; eine Einsichtnahme in die personenbezogenen Daten, insbesondere Name und Anschrift der Personen nach § 9 Absatz 2, ist jedoch nur zulässig, wenn dies zur Wahrung eines berechtigten Interesses erforderlich ist und kein schutzwürdiges, überwiegendes Interesse dieser Personen entgegensteht. ⁴Auf Verlangen erteilen die Denkmalfachbehörden und der Magistrat der Stadtgemeinde Bremerhaven Auskunft darüber, ob ein Kulturdenkmal besteht oder ein Verfahren zur Unterschutzstellung eingeleitet wurde.
(6) ¹Nach dem Verlust der Eigenschaft als Kulturdenkmal wird die Unterschutzstellung von Amts wegen durch die zuständige Denkmalfachbehörde aufgehoben. ²Die Vorschriften der Absätze 1 und 2 gelten für die Aufhebungsentscheidung entsprechend.

§ 8 Vorläufiger Schutz
(1) ¹Teilt die Denkmalfachbehörde dem Eigentümer oder dem Erbbauberechtigten oder Nießbraucher die Absicht der Einleitung eines Unterschutzstellungsverfahrens über ein Kulturdenkmal nach § 2 mit, unterliegt das Kulturdenkmal ab Zugang der Mitteilung vorläufig den Schutzvorschriften dieses Gesetzes (vorläufiger Schutz). ²Die Denkmalfachbehörde weist in ihrer Mitteilung auf den vorläufigen Schutz hin. ³§ 7 Absatz 2 Sätze 2 und 3 gelten entsprechend.
(2) Der vorläufige Schutz entfällt, wenn das Kulturdenkmal nicht binnen 6 Monaten nach der Mitteilung nach Absatz 1 unter Denkmalschutz gestellt wird.

Abschnitt 2
Allgemeine Schutzvorschriften

§ 9 Erhaltungspflicht
(1) ¹Kulturdenkmäler sind zu pflegen. ²Sie sind vor Gefährdung zu schützen, zu erhalten und, soweit notwendig, instand zu setzen. ³Maßnahmen nach Satz 1 und 2 sind fachgerecht durchzuführen.
(2) ¹Verpflichtet zu Maßnahmen in Erfüllung des Absatzes 1 sind der Eigentümer oder Erbbauberechtigte oder der Nießbraucher, neben diesen jeder, der die tatsächliche Gewalt über das Kulturdenkmal ausübt (sonstige Verfügungsberechtigte). ²Das Land und die Stadtgemeinden tragen zur Erfüllung der Maßnahmen nach Absatz 1 durch Zuschüsse nach Maßgabe der ihnen zur Verfügung stehenden Haushaltsmittel bei.
(3) ¹Soll in ein Kulturdenkmal eingegriffen werden, es insbesondere von seinem Standort entfernt oder ganz oder teilweise beseitigt oder der Zusammenhang einer Sachgesamtheit zerstört werden, trägt der Verursacher des Eingriffs alle Kosten, die für die Erhaltung, fachgerechte Instandsetzung, Bergung und wissenschaftliche Dokumentation anfallen. ²Mehrere Verursacher tragen die Kosten gesamtschuldnerisch.
(4) ¹Die Verpflichtungen nach Absatz 1 Satz 2 und Absatz 3 gelten nur, wenn und soweit eine Maßnahme hinsichtlich der Beeinträchtigung oder der Kosten für den Verpflichteten zumutbar ist. ²Unzumutbar ist eine Maßnahme insbesondere nicht, wenn
1. der Gebrauch des Kulturdenkmals für den Verpflichteten nur vorübergehend oder unter Berücksichtigung der Eigenart und der Bedeutung des jeweiligen Kulturdenkmals unwesentlich eingeschränkt wird oder
2. die Kosten der Maßnahme in einem angemessenen Verhältnis zur Eigenart und Bedeutung des jeweiligen Kulturdenkmals stehen und in diesem Rahmen durch den Gebrauchs- oder Verkehrswert des Kulturdenkmals oder im Fall von Absatz 3 durch den wirtschaftlichen oder sonstigen Nutzen des Eingriffs aufgewogen werden.

³Der Verpflichtete kann sich nicht auf Umstände berufen, die aus einer Unterlassung der Verpflichtungen nach Absatz 1 resultieren oder die sich aus einer Nutzung ergeben, die nicht der Eigenart und Bedeutung des jeweiligen Kulturdenkmals entspricht.
(5) ¹Bei öffentlichen Bauvorhaben sind Aufwendungen zum Schutz von Kulturdenkmälern sowie zur Herstellung der Barrierefreiheit Teil der Baukosten. ²Dies gilt auch für öffentliche Bauvorhaben in privatrechtlicher Trägerschaft.

§ 10 Genehmigungspflichtige Maßnahmen
(1) Ein nach §§ 3 und 8 geschütztes Kulturdenkmal darf nur mit Genehmigung der Denkmalschutzbehörde
1. zerstört oder beseitigt werden;
2. von seinem Standort entfernt werden;
3. in seinem Bestand oder Erscheinungsbild beeinträchtigt oder verändert werden;
4. wieder hergestellt oder instandgesetzt werden;
5. mit An- oder Aufbauten, Aufschriften oder Werbeeinrichtungen versehen werden.

(2) Der Genehmigung der Denkmalschutzbehörde bedürfen ferner Maßnahmen nach Absatz 1 in der Umgebung geschützter unbeweglicher Kulturdenkmäler.
(3) ¹Die Genehmigung nach Absatz 1 und 2 ist zu erteilen, wenn Belange des Denkmalschutzes nicht entgegenstehen oder ein überwiegendes öffentliches Interesse die Maßnahme verlangt. ²Ein öffentliches Interesse ist unter anderem gegeben, wenn die Zugänglichkeit für Menschen mit Behinderungen hergestellt oder verbessert wird.
(4) ¹Die Genehmigung kann unter Bedingungen oder Auflagen erteilt werden. ²Insbesondere kann die Genehmigung an die Bedingung geknüpft werden, dass die Ausführung der Arbeiten nur nach einem von der Denkmalschutzbehörde genehmigten Plan und unter Aufsicht einer Denkmalschutzbehörde oder eines von ihr benannten Sachverständigen erfolgt. ³Ist für die Prüfung der Genehmigungsfähigkeit oder für die Durchführung der genehmigten Maßnahmen die Hinzuziehung eines Sachverständigen notwendig, trägt der Antragsteller im Rahmen des Zumutbaren die dadurch entstehenden Kosten.
(5) Die Denkmalschutzbehörden beachten bei ihren Entscheidungen die Rechte von Menschen mit Behinderungen mit dem Ziel, die Barrierefreiheit im Sinne des Bremischen Behindertengleichstellungsgesetzes bei allen öffentlich zugänglichen Denkmälern möglichst zu erreichen.
(6) Wer eine Maßnahme im Sinne der Absätze 1 und 2 ohne Genehmigung der zuständigen Denkmalschutzbehörde beginnt oder eine genehmigte anders ausführt als in der Genehmigung vorgeschrieben wurde, hat auf Anordnung der Denkmalschutzbehörde den früheren Zustand wiederherzustellen oder das Kulturdenkmal auf eine andere von der zuständigen Denkmalschutzbehörde zu bestimmende Weise instand zu setzen.
(7) ¹Ist für eine Maßnahme nach Absatz 1 und 2 die Genehmigung durch eine Bauordnungsbehörde erforderlich, so entscheidet die Bauordnungsbehörde im Einvernehmen mit der Denkmalschutzbehörde. ²Bedingungen und Auflagen nach Absatz 4 werden Inhalt des Genehmigungsbescheids. ³Der Denkmalschutzbehörde obliegt hierbei die Überwachung des in ihren Aufgabenbereich fallenden Teils nach den Bestimmungen dieses Gesetzes.
(8) Die Denkmalfachbehörden können Eigentümer oder sonstige Verfügungsberechtigte von beweglichen Denkmälern einschließlich Urkunden und Sammlungen durch Bescheid von der Genehmigungspflicht nach Absatz 1 ganz oder teilweise befreien, soweit das Kulturdenkmal von einer geeigneten Institution fachlich betreut wird.

§ 11 Anzeigepflichten
(1) Eigentümer, Besitzer und sonstige Verfügungsberechtigte haben Schäden oder Mängel, die an geschützten Kulturdenkmälern auftreten und die ihre Erhaltung gefährden können, unverzüglich einer Denkmalschutzbehörde zu melden.
(2) Jeder Eigentumswechsel an einem geschützten Kulturdenkmal ist von dem bisherigen Eigentümer unverzüglich, spätestens bis zum Ablauf eines Monats nach dem Eigentumsübergang einer Denkmalfachbehörde anzuzeigen.
(3) Bei jedem Eigentumswechsel an einem geschützten Kulturdenkmal ist der bisherige Eigentümer verpflichtet, den neuen Eigentümer auf den bestehenden Denkmalschutz hinzuweisen.

§ 12 Sicherung der Erhaltung eines geschützten Kulturdenkmals

(1) ¹Wenn der Eigentümer oder der sonstige Verfügungsberechtigte nicht für die Erhaltung eines geschützten Kulturdenkmals sorgt, kann die zuständige Denkmalschutzbehörde ihm eine Frist zur Durchführung der erforderlichen Maßnahmen setzen; nach Ablauf der Frist kann sie die unabweisbar gebotenen Sicherungsmaßnahmen durchführen. ²Der Eigentümer oder der sonstige Verfügungsberechtigte ist zur Duldung dieser Maßnahmen verpflichtet.

(2) Der nach Absatz 1 Satz 1 zur Durchführung verpflichtete Eigentümer oder sonstige Verfügungsberechtigte kann zur Deckung der Kosten der unabweisbar gebotenen Sicherungsmaßnahmen im Rahmen des § 9 Absatz 4 herangezogen werden.

§ 13 Auskunfts- und Duldungspflichten

(1) Der Eigentümer und der sonstige Verfügungsberechtigte sind verpflichtet, Auskünfte zu erteilen, die zur Erfüllung der Aufgaben des Denkmalschutzes notwendig sind.

(2) ¹Denkmalschutzbehörden und Denkmalfachbehörden sind nach vorheriger Benachrichtigung der Eigentümer und der Besitzer berechtigt, Grundstücke und zur Abwehr einer dringenden Gefahr für ein Kulturdenkmal auch Wohnungen zu betreten, soweit dies zur Durchführung dieses Gesetzes notwendig ist. ²Sie dürfen geschützte Kulturdenkmäler und Anlagen, bei denen Anlass zu der Annahme besteht, dass sie nach § 3 zu schützen sein werden, besichtigen und die notwendigen Erfassungsmaßnahmen durchführen. ³Die Unverletzlichkeit der Wohnung nach Artikel 13 des Grundgesetzes wird insoweit eingeschränkt.

§ 14 Zugang zu Kulturdenkmälern

Geschützte Kulturdenkmäler sollen der Öffentlichkeit zugänglich gemacht werden, sofern es ihre Zweckbestimmung und die Wahrung der schutzwürdigen Belange der Eigentümer, der sonstigen Verfügungsberechtigten und der Nutzer erlauben.

Dritter Abschnitt
Ausgrabungen und Funde

§ 15 Funde

(1) Wer Anlass zu der Annahme hat, eine Sache entdeckt oder gefunden zu haben, die ein Kulturdenkmal oder Überreste oder Spuren eines solchen sein oder beinhalten kann, hat dies unverzüglich einer Denkmalfachbehörde mitzuteilen.

(2) ¹Diese Verpflichtung obliegt auch dem Eigentümer oder dem sonst Verfügungsberechtigten des Grundstücks, auf dem die Entdeckung oder der Fund erfolgt ist, sowie die leitende Person der Arbeiten, die zur Entdeckung oder zu dem Fund geführt haben. ²Die Mitteilung eines Verpflichteten befreit die Übrigen.

(3) ¹Die nach Absatz 1 und 2 Verpflichteten haben das Kulturdenkmal und die Fundstätte, wenn und soweit dies ohne Gefährdung der Allgemeinheit möglich ist, in unverändertem Zustand zu belassen und vor Gefahren für die Erhaltung zu schützen. ²Diese Verpflichtung erlischt nach Aufhebung durch die zuständige Denkmalfachbehörde, spätestens nach Ablauf einer Woche seit Zugang der Mitteilung nach Absatz 1.

(4) ¹Die zuständige Denkmalfachbehörde oder von ihr beauftragte Personen sind, auch nach Ablauf der Frist nach Absatz 3 Satz 2, berechtigt, die Fundstätte zu betreten und dort die gebotenen Maßnahmen für die Erhaltung, fachgerechte Instandsetzung, Bergung und wissenschaftliche Dokumentation der Funde durchzuführen. ²§ 13 Absatz 2 gilt entsprechend.

§ 16 Ausgrabungen

(1) ¹Wer nach Bodendenkmälern gräbt oder diese mit technischen Hilfsmitteln sucht, bedarf hierfür der schriftlichen Genehmigung der Landesarchäologie. ²Dies gilt entsprechend für das Suchen und Bergen von Kulturdenkmälern aus einem Gewässer. ³Wer ohne Genehmigung gräbt oder birgt, hat auf Anforderung der Landesarchäologie unverzüglich den früheren Zustand wiederherzustellen.

(2) ¹Die Genehmigung kann unter Bedingungen oder Auflagen erteilt werden. ²Die Auflagen können insbesondere die Ausführung der Grabung, die Mitteilung von gefundenen und entdeckten Sachen und deren Sicherung und Erhaltung betreffen. ³Wer die Bedingungen oder Auflagen nicht erfüllt, hat auf Anordnung der Landesarchäologie den früheren Zustand wiederherzustellen.

§ 17 Grabungsschutzgebiet
(1) ¹Die obere Denkmalschutzbehörde wird ermächtigt, abgegrenzte Gebiete, in denen Bodendenkmäler vermutet werden, durch Rechtsverordnung zu Grabungsschutzgebieten zu erklären. ²Die Behörden, deren Belange berührt werden, sind zu beteiligen.
(2) In Grabungsschutzgebieten bedürfen Arbeiten, die Bodendenkmäler gefährden können, der Genehmigung der oberen Denkmalschutzbehörde.
(3) ¹Die Denkmalschutzbehörden können in Grabungsschutzgebieten die wirtschaftliche Nutzung eines Grundstücks oder eines Grundstücksteils beschränken, auf dem sich ein geschütztes Kulturdenkmal befindet oder vermutet wird. ²Die Beschränkung ist auf Ersuchen der Denkmalschutzbehörde im Grundbuch einzutragen.

§ 18 Ablieferung
(1) Eigentümer und sonstige Verfügungsberechtigte eines gefundenen beweglichen Kulturdenkmals sind verpflichtet, es auf Verlangen der zuständigen Denkmalfachbehörde dieser oder einer von ihr beauftragten Person vorübergehend zur wissenschaftlichen Auswertung und Durchführung der wissenschaftlich gebotenen Maßnahmen für die Erhaltung, fachgerechte Instandsetzung, Bergung und wissenschaftliche Dokumentation zugänglich zu machen oder an sie auszuhändigen.
(2) ¹Nach Absatz 1 ausgehändigte Kulturdenkmäler sind an den Berechtigten zurückzugeben, sobald die gebotenen Maßnahmen durchgeführt sind, spätestens nach 12 Monaten seit der Ablieferung. ²Der Zeitraum kann angemessen verlängert werden, wenn die gebotenen Maßnahmen dies erfordern und eine Unterschutzstellung des Kulturdenkmals erfolgt ist.

§ 19 Schatzregal
(1) Bewegliche Kulturdenkmäler, die herrenlos sind oder die solange verborgen waren, dass ihr Eigentümer nicht mehr zu ermitteln ist, werden mit der Entdeckung Eigentum des Landes, wenn sie bei staatlichen Nachforschungen, in Grabungsschutzgebieten oder bei nicht genehmigten Grabungen oder Suchen entdeckt werden oder wenn sie einen hervorragenden wissenschaftlichen Wert besitzen.
(2) Das Land kann sie einer geeigneten Kulturgut bewahrenden Einrichtung überlassen oder sein Eigentum an den Finder, den Veranlasser eines Bodeneingriffs oder den Eigentümer des Grundstücks übertragen, auf dem der Fund erfolgt ist.

Abschnitt 4
Enteignung und Entschädigung

§ 20 Enteignung
(1) Die Enteignung ist zulässig zu Gunsten des Landes oder einer Stadtgemeinde, wenn und soweit auf andere Weise nicht sichergestellt werden kann, dass
1. ein geschütztes Kulturdenkmal in seinem Bestand oder Erscheinungsbild erhalten bleibt;
2. ein Kulturdenkmal nach § 2 Absatz 2 Nummer 4 ausgegraben, wissenschaftlich ausgewertet oder der Allgemeinheit zugänglich gemacht werden kann;
3. in einem Grabungsschutzgebiet planmäßige Nachforschungen betrieben werden können.
(2) Die Enteignung kann auf Zubehör, das mit der Hauptsache eine Einheit bildet, ausgedehnt werden.
(3) Ein beweglicher Bodenfund kann enteignet werden, wenn
1. Tatsachen vorliegen, nach denen zu befürchten ist, dass er wesentlich verschlechtert wird, und die Erhaltung nicht auf andere Weise sichergestellt werden kann,
2. nicht auf andere Weise sichergestellt werden kann, dass er für die Allgemeinheit zugänglich ist und hieran ein erhebliches Interesse besteht, oder
3. nicht auf andere Weise sichergestellt werden kann, dass er für die wissenschaftliche Forschung zur Verfügung gehalten wird.
(4) Für die Enteignung ist Entschädigung zu leisten.
(5) ¹Für das Enteignungs- und Entschädigungsverfahren und für die bei einer Enteignung zu leistende Entschädigung gelten die Vorschriften des Enteignungsgesetzes für die Freie Hansestadt Bremen. ²Antragsberechtigt ist die obere Denkmalschutzbehörde.

§ 21 Sonstige entschädigungspflichtige Maßnahmen

¹Soweit Maßnahmen auf Grund dieses Gesetzes enteignende Wirkung haben, ist eine angemessene Entschädigung zu zahlen. ²§ 20 Absatz 4 und 5 gilt entsprechend.

Abschnitt 5
Ordnungswidrigkeiten und Straftaten

§ 22 Ordnungswidrigkeiten

(1) Ordnungswidrig handelt, wer vorsätzlich oder fahrlässig
1. einer Verordnung, die aufgrund dieses Gesetzes erlassen wurde, zuwiderhandelt, soweit sie für einen bestimmten Tatbestand auf diese Bußgeldvorschrift verweist,
2. in § 10 Absatz 1 und 2 und § 16 Absatz 1 Satz 1 und 2 bezeichnete Handlungen ohne Genehmigung oder entgegen einer Auflage oder Bedingung nach § 10 Absatz 4 oder § 16 Absatz 2 Satz 1 vornimmt,
3. der Duldungspflicht nach § 12 Absatz 1 Satz 2 zuwiderhandelt,
4. der Anzeige- und Auskunftspflicht nach §§ 11 und 13 Absatz 1 nicht nachkommt oder entgegen § 13 Absatz 2 Satz 1 und 2 den Beauftragten der zuständigen Behörde das Betreten oder das Besichtigen nicht gestattet,
5. ein Kulturdenkmal, dessen Ablieferung nach § 18 Absatz 1 verlangt worden ist, beiseiteschafft, beschädigt oder zerstört,
6. der Anzeigepflicht nach § 15 Absatz 1 oder den Verpflichtungen nach § 15 Absatz 3 Satz 1 nicht nachkommt,
7. entgegen § 15 Absatz 4 der zuständigen Denkmalfachbehörde oder von ihr beauftragten Personen nicht gestattet, die Fundstätte zu betreten oder dort die gebotenen Maßnahmen durchzuführen.

(2) Ordnungswidrig handelt auch, wer wider besseres Wissen
1. unrichtige Angaben macht oder
2. unrichtige Pläne oder Unterlagen vorlegt,

um ein Tätigwerden der nach diesem Gesetz zuständigen Behörden zu erwirken oder zu verhindern.

(3) ¹Gegenstände, auf die sich eine Ordnungswidrigkeit bezieht oder die zur Vorbereitung oder Begehung einer Ordnungswidrigkeit verwendet worden sind, können eingezogen werden. ²§ 23 des Gesetzes über Ordnungswidrigkeiten findet Anwendung.

(4) ¹Ordnungswidrigkeiten können mit einer Geldbuße bis zu hunderttausend Euro, in besonders schweren Fällen bis zu fünfhunderttausend Euro geahndet werden. ²Zuständige Verwaltungsbehörden nach § 36 Absatz 1 Nummer 1 des Gesetzes über Ordnungswidrigkeiten sind die Denkmalschutzbehörden nach § 4 Absatz 1.

§ 23 Straftaten

(1) Wer vorsätzlich
1. ohne die nach § 10 Absatz 1 erforderliche Genehmigung handelt und dadurch ein Kulturdenkmal beschädigt oder zerstört oder
2. ohne die in § 16 Absatz 1 oder § 17 Absatz 2 erforderliche Genehmigung handelt und dadurch ein Kulturdenkmal von hervorragendem wissenschaftlichen Wert oder seinen Fundzusammenhang beschädigt oder zerstört,

wird mit Freiheitsstrafe von bis zu zwei Jahren oder Geldstrafe bestraft, wenn die Tat nicht nach anderen Vorschriften mit schwererer Strafe bedroht ist.

(2) Die zur Begehung einer Tat nach Absatz 1 verwendeten Gegenstände können eingezogen werden.

§ 24 Inkrafttreten, Außerkrafttreten

(1) Dieses Gesetz tritt am Tag nach seiner Verkündung[1)] in Kraft.
(2) Gleichzeitig tritt das Denkmalschutzgesetz vom 27. Mai 1975 (Brem.GBl. S. 265 – 2131-a-1), das zuletzt durch Artikel 2 § 5 des Gesetzes vom 17. Dezember 2002 (Brem.GBl. S. 605) geändert worden ist, außer Kraft.

---

1) Verkündet am 20.12.2018.

Verordnung über die Zusammensetzung und die Tätigkeit des Denkmalrates

Vom 30. April 2019 (Brem.GBl. S. 586)

Aufgrund des § 6 Absatz 2 Satz 2 des Bremischen Gesetzes zur Pflege und zum Schutz der Kulturdenkmäler (Bremisches Denkmalschutzgesetz – BremDSchG) vom 18. Dezember 2018 (Brem.GBl. S. 631) verordnet der Senator für Kultur als Obere Denkmalschutzbehörde:

§ 1 Aufgaben des Denkmalrates

¹Der Denkmalrat hat die Aufgabe, die Denkmalfachbehörden bei ihrer Tätigkeit zu beraten und zu unterstützen. ²Er soll in allen Angelegenheiten von grundsätzlicher Bedeutung und in solchen Einzelfällen gehört werden, die im Sinne des Denkmalschutzes herausragendes Gewicht haben. ³Es muss ferner gehört werden:
1. zur Vorbereitung der Unterschutzstellung durch Rechtsverordnung nach § 7 Absatz 3 Satz 1 des Denkmalschutzgesetzes,
2. zur Vorbereitung einer Rechtsverordnung nach § 17 Absatz 1 des Denkmalschutzgesetzes (Grabungsschutzgebiet),

und bei der Aufhebung dieser Unterschutzstellungen.

§ 2 Zusammensetzung des Denkmalrates

(1) ¹Der Denkmalrat besteht aus 17 Mitgliedern. ²Er soll sich aus Vertretern der für den Denkmalschutz und die Denkmalpflege bestimmenden Fachgebieten oder aus Personen zusammensetzen, die aufgrund ihres Wirkens in der Öffentlichkeit mit den Fragen des Denkmalschutzes und der Denkmalpflege vertraut sind.

(2) Die Obere Denkmalschutzbehörde bestellt als stimmberechtigte Mitglieder
1. je zwei Mitglieder der für Kultur und für das Bauwesen zuständigen Deputationen,
2. zwei Vertreterinnen oder Vertreter der Kirchen im Lande Bremen,
3. eine Vertreterin oder einen Vertreter der Architektenkammer Bremen,
4. eine Person mit ausgewiesener wissenschaftlicher oder vergleichbarer Expertise in Regionalgeschichte oder sonstigen denkmalbezogenen regionalen Angelegenheiten,
5. drei Historikerinnen oder Historiker, von denen eine oder einer im Bereich der Kunstgeschichte und eine oder einer in Bremerhaven tätig sein muss.

(3) Als Mitglieder ohne Stimmrecht gehören dem Denkmalrat an
1. eine Vertreterin oder ein Vertreter der für Kultur zuständigen senatorischen Behörde,
2. eine Vertreterin oder ein Vertreter der für das Bauwesen zuständigen senatorischen Behörde,
3. eine Vertreterin oder ein Vertreter der für das Inneres zuständigen senatorischen Behörde,
4. eine Vertreterin oder ein Vertreter des Magistrats der Stadt Bremerhaven,
5. die Leiterinnen oder Leiter der Denkmalfachbehörden nach § 5 des Denkmalschutzgesetzes.

(4) Die Obere Denkmalschutzbehörde kann über die Mitgliederzahl nach Absatz 1 hinaus bis zu drei mit der Denkmalpflege, Kunst oder Geschichte in Bremen besonders vertraute Persönlichkeiten als stimmberechtigte Mitglieder berufen.

(5) ¹Der Bestellung der Mitglieder nach Absatz 2 Nummer 1 geht eine entsprechende Wahl durch die jeweilige Deputation voraus. ²Die Mitglieder nach Absatz 2 Nummer 2 und 3 werden aufgrund von Vorschlägen der Kirchen oder der Architektenkammer, die Mitglieder nach Absatz 2 Nummer 4 und 5 aufgrund von Vorschlägen der Denkmalfachbehörden bestellt.

(6) Scheidet ein Mitglied während seiner Amtszeit aus, so ernennt die Obere Denkmalschutzbehörde nach Maßgabe der Absätze 1 bis 5 ein Ersatzmitglied, falls der Rest der Amtszeit des ausscheidenden Mitgliedes mehr als ein Jahr beträgt.

§ 3 Amtszeit der Mitglieder

(1) ¹Die Amtszeit der Mitglieder des Denkmalrates bestimmt sich nach der Wahlperiode der Bremischen Bürgerschaft. ²Ein Mitglied scheidet aus, sobald die Voraussetzung für seine Bestellung entfallen ist.

(2) Die Mitglieder des Denkmalrates bleiben bis zur Bestellung ihrer Nachfolger im Amt.

(3) Eine erneute Bestellung nach Ablauf der Amtszeit ist zulässig.

D5.I.1a Verordnung über den Denkmalrat

§ 4 Sitzungen
(1) ¹Die Leiterin oder der Leiter des Landesamtes für Denkmalpflege führt den Vorsitz im Denkmalrat. ²Sie oder er lädt zu den Sitzungen ein und stellt die vorläufige Tagesordnung auf.
(2) Der Denkmalrat tritt nach Bedarf zusammen.
(3) ¹Die Sitzungen des Denkmalrates sind nicht öffentlich. ²Zu den Sitzungen können sachkundige Personen als Beraterinnen oder Berater sowie die Betroffenen, insbesondere Eigentümerinnen und Eigentümer sowie sonstige Verfügungsberechtigte nach § 9 Absatz 2 Satz 1 des Denkmalschutzgesetzes, hinzugezogen werden.

§ 5 Beschlussfähigkeit
¹Der Denkmalrat ist beschlussfähig, wenn mindestens die Hälfte der stimmberechtigten Mitglieder anwesend ist. ²Er beschließt mit einfacher Mehrheit. ³Die Mitglieder nach § 2 Absatz 2 Nummer 1 bis 3 sowie Absatz 3 können durch andere Angehörige der entsendenden Stelle vertreten werden.

§ 6 Ehrenamtliche Tätigkeit
(1) ¹Die Mitwirkung der Mitglieder im Denkmalrat ist, soweit sie nicht in Vertretung für eine Behörde erfolgt, ehrenamtlich. ²Sie wird nicht vergütet.
(2) ¹Reisekosten für Mitglieder nach § 2 Absatz 2 und 4 werden nur auf Antrag und Nachweis erstattet, wenn und soweit eine im öffentlichen Dienst der Freien Hansestadt Bremen stehende Person sie von der Freien Hansestadt Bremen erstattet bekommen könnte. ²Im Übrigen wird eine Entschädigung für entstandenen Aufwand nicht gezahlt.
(3) Die Mitglieder nach Absatz 2 Nummer 2 und 4 sind an Weisungen nicht gebunden.

§ 7 Geschäftsführung
(1) Die Geschäftsführung des Denkmalrates obliegt dem Landesamt für Denkmalpflege.
(2) Über jede Sitzung des Denkmalrates ist eine Niederschrift anzufertigen.
(3) Die Obere Denkmalschutzbehörde kann eine Geschäftsordnung erlassen.

§ 8 Inkrafttreten
(1) Diese Verordnung tritt am Tage nach ihrer Verkündung[1] in Kraft.
(2) Gleichzeitig tritt die Verordnung über die Zusammensetzung und die Tätigkeit des Denkmalrates vom 26. März 1991 (Brem.GBl. S. 135) außer Kraft.

---

1) Verkündet am 19.9.2019.

Verordnung über die Unterschutzstellung von Kulturdenkmälern und das Eintragungs- und Löschungsverfahren

Vom 30. April 2019 (Brem.GBl. S. 582)

Aufgrund des § 7 Absatz 2 Satz 5 des Bremischen Gesetzes zur Pflege und zum Schutz der Kulturdenkmäler (Bremisches Denkmalschutzgesetz – BremDSchG) vom 18. Dezember 2018 (Brem.GBl. S. 631) verordnet der Senator für Kultur als Obere Denkmalschutzbehörde:

Abschnitt 1

§ 1 Schutzwirkung; Zuständigkeit

(1) ¹Kulturdenkmäler im Sinne des § 2 des Denkmalschutzgesetzes werden durch Bescheid (§ 7 Absatz 1 des Denkmalschutzgesetzes) oder durch Rechtsverordnung (§ 7 Absatz 3 des Denkmalschutzgesetzes) unter Denkmalschutz gestellt und anschließend in die Denkmalliste eingetragen. ²Die Rechtswirkungen der Unterschutzstellung werden durch den Bescheid (Unterschutzstellungsbescheid) oder die Rechtsverordnung (Unterschutzstellungsverordnung) begründet, soweit sie nicht nach § 3 Absatz 2 oder § 8 des Denkmalschutzgesetzes schon vorher eingetreten sind.
(2) ¹Für die Durchführung des Unterschutzstellungsverfahrens sind die Denkmalfachbehörden zuständig. ²Sie betreiben das Verfahren von Amts wegen.

§ 2 Unterschutzstellung durch Bescheid

(1) ¹Vor Erlass des Unterschutzstellungsbescheides prüft die Denkmalfachbehörde, ob ein Kulturdenkmal im Sinne des § 2 des Denkmalschutzgesetzes vorliegt. ²Sie hört hierzu den Eigentümer und nach Möglichkeit die sonstigen Verfügungsberechtigten, ferner das örtlich zuständige Ortsamt oder den Magistrat der Stadt Bremerhaven und, bei unbeweglichen Kulturdenkmälern, die für das Bauwesen zuständige senatorische Behörde an.
(2) ¹Mit der Bekanntgabe des Unterschutzstellungsbescheides nach § 7 Absatz 1 des Denkmalschutzgesetzes weist die Denkmalfachbehörde den Eigentümer oder sonstig Verfügungsberechtigten nach § 9 Absatz 2 Satz 1 des Denkmalschutzgesetzes auf ihre Rechte und Pflichten einschließlich ihrer Verpflichtung hin, geeignete Vorkehrungen gegen eigenmächtige Veränderungen durch Dritte zu treffen und die jeweiligen Besitzer des Kulturdenkmals von der Tatsache des Denkmalschutzes zu unterrichten. ²Die Denkmalfachbehörde bietet fachliche Beratung an.

§ 3 Unterschutzstellung durch Verordnung

(1) Sollen Ensembles unbeweglicher Kulturdenkmäler nach § 2 Absatz 2 Nummer 2 des Denkmalschutzgesetzes durch Rechtsverordnung nach § 7 Absatz 3 des Denkmalschutzgesetzes unter Denkmalschutz gestellt werden, so hört die Denkmalfachbehörde zur Frage der Denkmaleigenschaft nach § 2 des Denkmalschutzgesetzes zunächst das zuständige Ortsamt oder den Magistrat der Stadt Bremerhaven, ferner die für das Bauwesen zuständige senatorische Behörde und den Denkmalrat.
(2) Die Denkmalfachbehörde legt den unter Berücksichtigung der Ergebnisse der Anhörungen gefertigten Entwurf einer Unterschutzstellungsverordnung nebst Begründung einen Monat lang öffentlich zur Einsichtnahme aus.
(3) ¹Die Denkmalfachbehörde kündigt die Auslegung mindestens eine Woche vor ihrem Beginn unter Nutzung für eine möglichst breite Kenntnisnahme geeigneter Medien öffentlich an. ²In der Bekanntmachung weist sie darauf hin,
1. wo und wie lange der Entwurf der Verordnung ausgelegt ist,
2. dass etwaige Einwendungen der Eigentümer oder der sonstigen Verfügungsberechtigten nach § 9 Absatz 2 Satz 1 des Denkmalschutzgesetzes gegen die Bestimmungen der Denkmaleigenschaft nach § 2 des Denkmalschutzgesetzes bei der zuständigen Denkmalfachbehörde vorzubringen sind.
(4) ¹Nach Ablauf der Einwendungsfrist leitet die Denkmalfachbehörde den anhand der eingegangenen Einwendungen überarbeiteten Entwurf der Unterschutzstellungsverordnung zusammen mit den nicht berücksichtigten, von ihr mit einer Stellungnahme versehenen Einwendungen der oberen Denkmalschutzbehörde zu. ²Diese entscheidet über das weitere Verfahren und die Art der Erledigung der unberücksichtigten Einwendungen.

§ 4 Änderung, Aufhebung
Für die Änderung oder Aufhebung der Unterschutzstellungsverordnung gelten die §§ 2 und 3 entsprechend.

Abschnitt 2

§ 5 Eintragung in die Denkmalliste
(1) Die nach § 7 Absatz 1 oder Absatz 3 des Denkmalschutzgesetzes unter Denkmalschutz gestellten Kulturdenkmäler werden nachrichtlich in die Denkmallisten eingetragen und über das Internet öffentlich gemacht, sobald die Unterschutzstellung rechtsbeständig ist.
(2) ¹Der Eigentümer oder sonstig Verfügungsberechtigte nach § 9 Absatz 2 Satz 1 des Denkmalschutzgesetzes wird über die Eintragung unter Mitteilung ihres Inhalts und der Fundstelle in geeigneter Form informiert. ²Die Denkmalfachbehörde teilt die Eintragung eines unbeweglichen Kulturdenkmals unter Hinweis auf § 7 Absatz 4 des Denkmalschutzgesetzes die für das Bauwesen zuständige senatorische Behörde mit.

§ 6 Anlage der Denkmallisten
(1) Für jedes geschützte Kulturdenkmal ist ein Blatt anzulegen, das folgende Eintragungen enthalten soll:
1. die Kennzeichnung des Kulturdenkmals mit einer Darstellung seiner wesentlichen charakteristischen Merkmale unter Verwendung von Fotografien,
2. die Anschrift der Stelle, an der sich das Kulturdenkmal befindet,
3. bei unbeweglichen Kulturdenkmälern den Grundbuchauszug und einen Auszug aus dem Liegenschaftskataster,
4. Name und Anschrift des Eigentümers und nach Möglichkeit der sonstigen Verfügungsberechtigten nach § 9 Absatz 2 Satz 1 des Denkmalschutzgesetzes.

(2) Den Denkmallisten sind Katasterpläne im Maßstab 1: 1 000 beizufügen, auf denen die unbeweglichen Kulturdenkmäler kenntlich gemacht sind.
(3) Die Veröffentlichung der Denkmalliste im Internet enthält nicht die Eintragungen nach Absatz 1 Nummer 3 und 4.
(4) Die Einsichtnahme in die Denkmallisten umfasst nicht die Eintragungen nach Absatz 1 Nummer 3 und den Grundbuchauszug nach Absatz 1 Nummer 4.

§ 7 Löschung der Eintragung
¹Nach Aufhebung der Unterschutzstellung wird die Eintragung gelöscht. ²Die Löschung der Eintragung wird in gleicher Weise wie die Eintragung selbst dem Eigentümer sowie den sonstigen Verfügungsberechtigten bekannt gegeben.

§ 8 Inkrafttreten
(1) Diese Verordnung tritt am Tage nach ihrer Verkündung[1)] in Kraft.
(2) Gleichzeitig tritt die Verordnung über das Verfahren der Eintragung und Löschung von Kulturdenkmälern in den Denkmallisten vom 28. März 1991 (Brem.GBl. S. 133) außer Kraft.

---

1) Verkündet am 19.9.2019.

Gesetz über die Sicherung und Nutzung öffentlichen Archivguts im Lande Bremen (Bremisches Archivgesetz – BremArchivG –)

Vom 7. Mai 1991 (Brem.GBl. S. 159)
(Sa BremR 224–c–1)
zuletzt geändert durch Art. 1 ÄndG vom 2. April 2019 (Brem.GBl. S. 133)

Der Senat verkündet das nachstehende von der Bürgerschaft (Landtag) beschlossene Gesetz:

Abschnitt I
Archivgut des Landes und der Stadtgemeinde Bremen

§ 1 Aufgaben des Staatsarchiv
(1) ¹Das Staatsarchiv hat die Aufgabe, Unterlagen von Behörden, Gerichten und sonstigen Stellen des Landes und der Stadtgemeinde Bremen auf ihre Archivwürdigkeit hin zu werten und die als archivwürdig erkannten Teile als Archivgut zu übernehmen, zu verwahren und zu ergänzen, zu erhalten und instand zu setzen, zu erschließen und für die Benutzung bereitzustellen sowie zu erforschen und zu veröffentlichen. ²Diese Aufgabe erstreckt sich auch auf Unterlagen der Rechtsvorgänger des Landes und der Stadtgemeinde Bremen und der Funktionsvorgänger der in Satz 1 genannten Stellen.
(2) ¹Das Staatsarchiv archiviert auch archivwürdige Unterlagen anderer Herkunft, soweit sie der Ergänzung des nach Absatz 1 archivierten Archivguts dienen, insbesondere
1. nach Maßgabe des Bundesarchivgesetzes[1]) Unterlagen des Bundes,
2. im Einvernehmen mit den Eigentümern Unterlagen natürlicher oder juristischer Personen des Privatrechts.

²Entsprechend Satz 1 sammelt es auch archivwürdige Unterlagen.
(3) Das Staatsarchiv berät die Behörden, Gerichte und sonstigen Stellen des Landes und der Stadtgemeinde Bremen im Rahmen seiner Zuständigkeit bei der Verwaltung und Sicherung ihrer Unterlagen sowie bei der Führung elektronischer Akten gemäß §§ 6 und 7 des Gesetzes zur Förderung der elektronischen Verwaltung in Bremen.
(4) Das Staatsarchiv nimmt Aufgaben im Rahmen der archivarischen Aus- und Fortbildung wahr.
(5) ¹Das Staatsarchiv muß hauptamtlich von Personal betreut werden, das die Befähigung für eine Laufbahn des Archivdienstes besitzt oder sonst fachlich geeignet ist. ²Der Leiter oder die Leiterin muß die Befähigung für die Laufbahn des höheren Archivdienstes besitzen.

§ 2 Archivgut
(1) ¹Archivgut sind alle im Staatsarchiv befindlichen Unterlagen, die bei den im § 1 Abs. 1 genannten Stellen entstanden und archivwürdig sind. ²Unterlagen sind Aufzeichnungen unabhängig von ihrer Speicherform. ³Dazu gehören insbesondere Urkunden, Amtsbücher, Akten, Schriftstücke, amtliche Publikationen, Drucksachen, Karteien, Karten, Risse, Pläne, Plakate, Siegel, Bild-, Film- und Tondokumente. ⁴Unterlagen sind auch elektronische Aufzeichnungen sowie alle Hilfsmittel und ergänzenden Daten, die für die Erhaltung, das Verständnis dieser Informationen und deren Nutzung notwendig sind.
(2) ¹Archivwürdig sind Unterlagen, die für die Erforschung und das Verständnis der Geschichte, insbesondere der bremischen Geschichte, die Sicherung berechtigter Belange der Bürger und Bürgerinnen oder die Bereitstellung von Informationen für Gesetzgebung, Verwaltung oder Rechtsprechung von bleibendem Wert sind. ²Über die Archivwürdigkeit entscheidet das Staatsarchiv unter fachlichen Gesichtspunkten.
(3) Archivgut sind auch die nach § 1 Abs. 2 archivierten Unterlagen.

§ 3 Anbietung und Ablieferung von Unterlagen
(1) ¹Die Behörden, Gerichte und sonstigen Stellen des Landes und der Stadtgemeinde Bremen (anbietungspflichtige Stellen) haben alle Unterlagen, die zur Erfüllung ihrer Aufgaben nicht mehr benötigt werden, dem Staatsarchiv zur Übernahme anzubieten und die als archivwürdig bewerteten Unterlagen abzuliefern. ²Die Anbietung der Unterlagen erfolgt in der Regel nach Ablauf der Aufbewahrungsfristen. ³Alle Unterlagen sind dem Staatsarchiv spätestens dreißig Jahre nach ihrer Entstehung anzubieten,

---
1) Das Bundesarchivgesetz ist abgedruckt als Nr. C.III.1.

D5.II.1 Bremisches Archivgesetz

soweit keine anderen Rechtsvorschriften längere Aufbewahrungsfristen bei den anbietungspflichtigen Stellen festlegen. ⁴In besonderen Fällen können als archivwürdig bewertete Unterlagen auch vorzeitig als Archivgut übernommen werden.

(2) Als anbietungspflichtige Stellen des Landes und der Stadtgemeinde Bremen gelten auch
1. Stiftungen des Privatrechts, wenn das Land oder die Stadtgemeinde Bremen oder ein Rechtsvorgänger die Stiftung errichtet oder überwiegend das Stiftungsvermögen bereitgestellt hat, und
2. andere juristische Personen des Privatrechts, die nicht am wirtschaftlichen Wettbewerb teilnehmen und bei denen dem Land oder der Stadtgemeinde Bremen mehr als die Hälfte der Anteile oder der Stimmen zusteht.

²Der Pflicht zur Anbietung und Ablieferung unterliegen auch alle Unterlagen von ehemals öffentlichen oder diesen gleichgestellten Stellen, sofern die Unterlagen bis zum Zeitpunkt des Übergangs in eine Rechtsform des Privatrechts entstanden sind.

(3) Zur Übernahme anzubieten und abzuliefern sind auch Unterlagen, die
1. personenbezogene Daten im Sinne des Artikels 4 der Verordnung (EU) 2016/679 des Europäischen Parlaments und des Rates vom 27. April 2016 zum Schutz natürlicher Personen bei der Verarbeitung personenbezogener Daten, zum freien Datenverkehr und zur Aufhebung der Richtlinie 95/46/EG (Datenschutz-Grundverordnung) (ABl. L 119 vom 4. Mai 2016, S. 1, L 314 vom 22. November 2016, S. 72) enthalten, welche nach einer Rechtsvorschrift des Landes gelöscht werden müssten oder nach Rechtsvorschriften des Bundes oder des Landes gelöscht werden könnten, sofern die Speicherung der Daten nicht unzulässig war,
2. einem Berufs- oder Amtsgeheimnis oder sonstigen Rechtsvorschriften über Geheimhaltung unterliegen,
3. elektronische Daten enthalten, die einer laufenden Aktualisierung unterliegen, oder
4. besondere Kategorien personenbezogener Daten im Sinne des Artikels 9 Absatz 1 der Verordnung (EU) 2016/679 enthalten.

(4) Die Pflicht zur Anbietung und Ablieferung gilt auch für alle amtlichen Veröffentlichungen in jeder Erscheinungsform, die die anbietungspflichtigen Stellen herausgegeben haben oder die in ihrem Auftrag erschienen sind.

(5) ¹Durch Vereinbarung zwischen dem Staatsarchiv und der anbietungspflichtigen Stelle kann
1. auf die Anbietung bestimmter offensichtlich nicht archivwürdiger Unterlagen verzichtet werden,
2. der Umfang der anzubietenden und abzuliefernden gleichförmigen Unterlagen, die in großer Zahl entstehen, im Einzelnen festgelegt werden,
3. die Auswahl der anzubietenden elektronischen Aufzeichnungen einschließlich der Form der Datenübermittlung im Einzelnen festgesetzt werden.

Elektronische Aufzeichnungen, die aus verarbeitungstechnischen Gründen vorübergehend vorgehalten werden müssen, sind nicht anzubieten.

(6) Einzelheiten der Archivierung von Verschlusssachen, insbesondere die erforderlichen besonderen technischen und organisatorischen Maßnahmen, regelt der Senat durch Verwaltungsvorschrift.

(7) ¹Ab dem Zeitpunkt der Anbietung dürfen die angebotenen Unterlagen nicht mehr verändert werden. ²Zur Feststellung der Archivwürdigkeit ist dem Staatsarchiv auf Verlangen Einsicht in die angebotenen Unterlagen und die dazugehörigen Hilfsmittel zu gewähren. ³Entscheidet das Staatsarchiv nicht innerhalb eines halben Jahres über die Übernahme der angebotenen Unterlagen, erlischt deren Ablieferungspflicht.

(8) ¹Die übrigen juristischen Personen des öffentlichen Rechts, die der Aufsicht des Landes unterstehen, mit Ausnahme der Stadtgemeinde Bremerhaven, und für ihr Archivgut nicht entsprechend § 12 Absatz 1 Satz 1 Nummer 2 anderweitig Sorge tragen, bieten Unterlagen, die zur Erfüllung ihrer Aufgaben nicht mehr benötigt werden, dem Staatsarchiv zur Übernahme an. ²Absatz 1 Satz 2, 3 und 4, Absatz 2 Satz 2, Absätze 3 bis 6 und Absatz 7 Satz 3 gelten entsprechend.

§ 4 Verwahrung

(1) ¹Archivgut nach Maßgabe dieses Gesetzes ist auf Dauer sicher im Staatsarchiv zu verwahren; es ist in seiner Entstehungsform zu erhalten, sofern keine archivfachlichen Belange entgegenstehen. ²Archivgut ist vorbehaltlich des Absatzes 2 Satz 3 unveräußerlich.

(2) ¹Archivgut kann in einem anderen hauptamtlich oder hauptberuflich fachlich betreuten Archiv verwahrt werden, wenn dafür ein fachlicher Grund gegeben und sichergestellt ist, dass schutzwürdige Belange betroffener Personen nicht beeinträchtigt werden. ²Hierüber ist ein schriftlicher Vertrag abzuschließen. ³In begründeten Ausnahmefällen und unter den Voraussetzungen von Satz 1 kann Archivgut an andere öffentliche Archive unentgeltlich übereignet werden.
(3) ¹Das Staatsarchiv stellt die dauerhafte Erhaltung und Benutzbarkeit des Archivguts sowie seinen Schutz vor unbefugter Nutzung oder Vernichtung sicher. ²Es hat insbesondere technische und organisatorische Maßnahmen zur Sicherung solchen Archivguts zu treffen, das personenbezogene Daten enthält oder Geheimhaltungsvorschriften unterliegt (§ 3 Absatz 3).

§ 5 Rechte betroffener Personen bei der Verarbeitung personenbezogener Daten im Archivgut
(1) ¹Für personenbezogene Daten, die als Archivgut in das Staatsarchiv Bremen übernommen worden sind, ist das Staatsarchiv Bremen der Verantwortliche im Sinne der Verordnung (EU) 2016/679. ²Die Regelungen der Absätze 2 bis 11 gelten nicht für personenbezogene Daten, die das Staatsarchiv Bremen außerhalb des Archivguts verarbeitet.
(2) ¹Die Rechte einer betroffenen Person nach den Absätzen 3 bis 11 gelten, soweit das Archivgut durch Namen der Person erschlossen ist oder die betroffene Person Angaben macht, die das Auffinden des einschlägigen Archivguts mit vertretbarem Verwaltungsaufwand ermöglichen. ²Bei Archivgut im Sinne des § 1 Absatz 2 Satz 1 Nummer 2, das vor seiner Übernahme durch das Staatsarchiv nicht dem sachlichen Anwendungsbereich gemäß Artikel 2 der Verordnung (EU) 2016/679 angehört hat, kann durch Vereinbarung mit dem Eigentümer die Ausübung der Rechte nach den Absätzen 3 bis 11 anderer betroffener Personen als des Eigentümers vom Ablauf einer angemessenen Schutzfrist abhängig gemacht werden, wenn dies für die Übernahme als Archivgut unerlässlich ist.
(3) ¹Jeder Person ist auf Antrag eine Bestätigung darüber zu erteilen, ob von ihr personenbezogene Daten nach § 3 Absatz 3 Nummer 1 und 4 als Archivgut übernommen worden sind. ²Anstelle der Auskunft nach Artikel 15 Absatz 1 der Verordnung (EU) 2016/679 ist der betroffenen Person eine persönliche Einsichtnahme ihrer personenbezogenen Daten im Archivgut zu gewähren. ³Nimmt eine betroffene Person ihr Recht auf Einsichtnahme wahr, sind die §§ 8, 11 und 12 Absatz 2 der Bremischen Archivbenutzungsverordnung entsprechend anzuwenden. ⁴Unberührt von Satz 2 und Satz 3 bleibt das Recht auf Auskunft zur Verarbeitung personenbezogener Daten über Archivgut durch das Staatsarchiv Bremen.
(4) ¹Das Staatsarchiv kann zum Schutz berechtigter Belange Dritter oder wenn der Erhaltungszustand des Archivguts gefährdet erscheint oder aus anderen wichtigen Gründen der betroffenen Person eine andere Art der Benutzung des Archivguts als die Einsichtnahme ermöglichen, um eine Kenntnis ihrer personenbezogenen Daten zu gewährleisten. ²Einsichtgewährung oder Einräumung einer anderen Benutzungsart unterbleiben, soweit und solange
1. die öffentliche Sicherheit gefährdet oder dem Wohl des Bundes oder eines Landes ein Nachteil bereitet würde oder
2. die personenbezogenen Daten nach einer Rechtsvorschrift oder zum Schutz der Rechte Dritter geheim zu halten sind und deswegen das Interesse der betroffenen Person an der Kenntnis der personenbezogenen Daten zurücktreten muss.

³§ 9 Absatz 3 des Bremischen Ausführungsgesetzes zur EU-Datenschutz-Grundverordnung ist entsprechend anzuwenden.
(5) Die betroffene Person hat das Recht, eine Kopie des Archivguts, soweit es ihre personenbezogenen Daten enthält, anfertigen zu lassen, sofern das Archivgut hierfür geeignet ist und die Aufgabenerfüllung des Staatsarchivs nicht beeinträchtigt wird.
(6) ¹Die betroffene Person hat das Recht, über die geeigneten Garantien gemäß Artikel 46 der Verordnung (EU) 2016/679, insbesondere über die mit einer Archivgutnutzung nach § 7 verbundenen Bedingungen und Auflagen, unterrichtet zu werden. ²Abweichend von Artikel 15 Absatz 2 der Verordnung (EU) 2016/679 gilt diese Unterrichtung nur für personenbezogenes Archivgut, das vor Ablauf der Schutzfristen gemäß § 7 Absatz 3 und 4 übermittelt worden ist.
(7) ¹Zu unrichtigen, in der Richtigkeit bestrittenen oder unvollständigen personenbezogenen Daten im Archivgut hat eine betroffene Person das Recht, eine Gegendarstellung oder eine ergänzende Erklärung zu erstellen. ²Die Gegendarstellung oder die ergänzende Erklärung werden dem Archivgut in geeig-

neter Weise beigefügt. ³Weitergehende Ansprüche auf Berichtigung oder Vervollständigung personenbezogener Daten nach Artikel 16 der Verordnung (EU) 2016/679 bestehen nicht.
(8) ¹Die betroffene Person kann abweichend von Artikel 18 Absatz 1 Buchstabe a der Verordnung (EU) 2016/679 beantragen, eine Nutzung dieses Archivguts durch Dritte nach § 7 für vier Wochen auszusetzen, um während dieses Zeitraums die Gegendarstellung oder die ergänzende Erklärung zu erstellen. ²Im Übrigen bleibt Artikel 18 der Verordnung (EU) 2016/679 unberührt.
(9) Die Rechte nach den Absätzen 7 und 8 gelten nach dem Tod einer betroffenen Person auch für deren Ehegatten, eingetragene Lebenspartner, Kinder und Eltern, wenn diese ein berechtigtes Interesse geltend machen.
(10) Das Recht auf Datenübertragbarkeit nach Artikel 20 der Verordnung (EU) 2016/679 ist für Archivgut gemäß § 1 Absatz 2 Satz 1 Nummer 2 ausgeschlossen.
(11) ¹Anstelle des Widerspruchsrechts nach Artikel 21 Absatz 1 der Verordnung (EU) 2016/679 hat eine betroffene Person das Recht, aus Gründen, die sich aus ihrer besonderen Situation ergeben, einen Antrag zu stellen, die Schutzfrist für bestimmtes, sie betreffendes personenbezogenes Archivgut um höchstens 20 Jahre zu verlängern. ²Diesen Antrag kann eine betroffene Person auch für sie betreffendes personenbezogenes Archivgut stellen, das genetische oder biometrische Daten oder Daten zum Sexualleben im Sinne von Artikel 9 Absatz 1 der Verordnung (EU) 2016/679 enthält. ³Wenn zwingende schutzwürdige Gründe für eine Verarbeitung der Daten in Form einer Nutzung durch Dritte nicht die schutzwürdigen Belange der betroffenen Person erheblich überwiegen, hat das Staatsarchiv diesem Antrag stattzugeben. ⁴Im Fall von personenbezogenem Archivgut, das genetische Daten enthält, sind auch leibliche Kinder und Kindeskinder betroffener Personen zur Antragstellung befugt.

§ 6 Nutzung durch die abliefernde Stelle

(1) ¹Die abliefernde Stelle ist befugt, Archivgut, das aus ihren Unterlagen übernommen worden ist, zu nutzen, wenn sie es zur Erfüllung ihrer Aufgaben wieder benötigt. ²Dies gilt entsprechend für Archivgut, das aus Unterlagen von Rechts- und Funktionsvorgängern übernommen ist.
(2) ¹Die Art und Weise der Nutzung nach Absatz 1 wird zwischen der abliefernden Stelle und dem Staatsarchiv vereinbart. ²Dabei ist sicherzustellen, dass das Archivgut gegen Verlust, Beschädigung und unbefugte Benutzung geschützt wird sowie innerhalb eines angemessenen Zeitraums dem Staatsarchiv zurückgegeben wird.
(3) ¹Die Nutzungsbefugnis nach Absatz 1 und 2 gilt nicht für personenbezogene Daten, die anstelle der Übernahme aufgrund einer Rechtsvorschrift hätten gesperrt oder gelöscht werden müssen. ²In diesen Fällen besteht die Nutzungsbefugnis nur nach Maßgabe des § 7.

§ 7 Nutzung durch Dritte

(1) ¹Jeder, der ein berechtigtes Interesse glaubhaft macht, hat nach Maßgabe dieses Gesetzes das Recht, Archivgut, Reproduktionen und Findmittel auf Antrag zu nutzen, soweit aufgrund anderer Rechtsvorschriften nichts anderes bestimmt ist. ²Nutzungsrechte aufgrund anderer Rechtsvorschriften sowie besondere Vereinbarungen mit Eigentümern bei der Archivierung von Unterlagen natürlicher und juristischer Personen des Privatrechts bleiben unberührt.
(2) ¹Die Nutzung ist einzuschränken oder zu versagen, wenn
1. Grund zu der Annahme besteht, dass dem Wohl der Bundesrepublik Deutschland oder eines ihrer Länder wesentliche Nachteile entstehen,
2. Grund zu der Annahme besteht, dass schutzwürdige Belange betroffener Personen oder Dritter beeinträchtigt werden,
3. der Erhaltungszustand des Archivguts gefährdet erscheint,
4. ein nicht vertretbarer Verwaltungsaufwand zu erwarten ist oder
5. Rechtsvorschriften, insbesondere über Geheimhaltung, verletzt würden.

²Die Nutzung kann aus anderen wichtigen Gründen eingeschränkt oder versagt werden.
(3) ¹Archivgut darf regelmäßig nach Ablauf von 30 Jahren seit Entstehung der Unterlagen genutzt werden. ²Die Schutzfrist beträgt 60 Jahre seit Entstehung der Unterlagen für Archivgut, das besonderen Geheimhaltungsvorschriften unterliegt. ³Bezieht das Archivgut sich nach seiner Zweckbestimmung oder nach seinem wesentlichen Inhalt auf eine oder mehrere natürliche Personen (personenbezogenes Archivgut), so darf es unbeschadet der Sätze 1 und 2 frühestens 10 Jahre nach dem Tod der betroffenen Person oder der letztverstorbenen von mehreren betroffenen Personen genutzt werden; ist das Todes-

jahr dem Archiv nicht bekannt, endet die Schutzfrist 100 Jahre nach der Geburt der betroffenen Person oder der letztgeborenen von mehreren Personen. [4]Ist dem Archiv auch das Geburtsjahr nicht bekannt, gilt eine Schutzfrist von 60 Jahren seit Entstehung der Unterlagen. [5]Die festgelegten Schutzfristen können um höchstens 20 Jahre verlängert werden, wenn dies im öffentlichen Interesse geboten ist oder wenn schutzwürdige Belange des Betroffenen dies erfordern.
(4) [1]Die Schutzfristen nach Absatz 3 gelten nicht für solches Archivgut, das bereits bei der Entstehung der Unterlagen zur Veröffentlichung bestimmt oder das bereits vor der Übergabe an das Staatsarchiv der Öffentlichkeit rechtmäßigerweise tatsächlich zugänglich gemacht worden ist. [2]Die Schutzfristen für personenbezogenes Archivgut gelten nicht für Amtsträger in Ausübung ihrer Ämter und Personen der Zeitgeschichte, es sei denn, ihr schutzwürdiger Lebensbereich ist betroffen.
(5) [1]Die Schutzfristen können im Einzelfall auf sachlich begründeten Antrag verkürzt werden, wenn dies im öffentlichen oder in einem schwer wiegenden privaten Interesse liegt. [2]Ist personenbezogenes Archivgut vor Ablauf der Schutzfristen betroffen, ist darüber hinaus erforderlich, dass
1. die betroffenen Personen oder nach deren Tod ihre Angehörigen eingewilligt haben, es sei denn eine betroffene Person hat zu Lebzeiten der Nutzung nachweislich widersprochen. Die Einwilligung ist von dem überlebenden Ehegatten oder eingetragenen Lebenspartner, nach dessen Tod von seinen volljährigen Kindern, oder, wenn weder ein Ehegatte oder eingetragener Lebenspartner noch volljährige Kinder vorhanden sind, von den Eltern der betroffenen Person einzuholen,
2. die Nutzung zur Behebung einer bestehenden Beweisnot oder aus sonstigen im rechtlichen Interesse eines Dritten liegenden Gründen unerlässlich ist oder
3. die Nutzung für die Durchführung eines bestimmten Forschungsvorhabens erforderlich ist und sichergestellt ist, dass die schutzwürdigen Belange betroffener Personen nicht beeinträchtigt werden, oder das öffentliche Interesse an der Durchführung des Forschungsvorhabens die schutzwürdigen Belange der betroffenen Personen erheblich überwiegt. Soweit der Zweck und die Methode des Forschungsvorhabens dies zulassen, sind die Forschungsergebnisse ohne personenbezogene Angaben aus dem Archivgut zu veröffentlichen.
(6) Nach § 203 Absatz 1 und 3 des Strafgesetzbuchs geschützte Unterlagen aus einer Beratungstätigkeit, die als Archivgut übernommen worden sind, dürfen vor Ablauf der Schutzfristen für personenbezogenes Archivgut nach Absatz 3 Satz 3 und 4 nur in anonymisierter Form genutzt werden.
(7) [1]Um die Rechte betroffener Personen, Dritter oder öffentliche Belange zu schützen, und in anderen geeigneten Fällen kann die Nutzung von Archivgut an Bedingungen und Auflagen gebunden werden, insbesondere an eine Verpflichtung zur anonymisierten Verwertung. [2]Personenbezogenes Archivgut, das besondere Kategorien personenbezogener Daten nach Artikel 9 Absatz 1 der Verordnung (EU) 2016/679 enthält, kann durch Dritte in der Regel vor Ablauf der Schutzfristen nur genutzt werden, wenn die Verpflichtung der anonymisierten Verwertung vorgesehen ist.
(8) Die Verknüpfung personenbezogener Daten durch das Archiv ist innerhalb der Schutzfristen nur zulässig, wenn schutzwürdige Belange betroffener Personen Betroffener[1)] angemessen berücksichtigt werden.

§ 8 Veröffentlichung und Weitergabe von Archivalien sowie Findmitteln
(1) [1]Um der Öffentlichkeit den Zugang zu historischen und familienkundlichen Unterlagen zu ermöglichen oder zu erleichtern, ist das Staatsarchiv berechtigt, Archivgut, Reproduktionen von Archivgut und die dazu gehörigen Findmittel im Rahmen seiner gesetzlichen Aufgaben zu veröffentlichen. [2]Durch die Veröffentlichung dürfen keine überwiegenden schutzwürdigen Belange betroffener Personen oder Dritter beeinträchtigt werden; insoweit sind insbesondere auch die Art, die Form und die Zugänglichkeit der Publikation zu berücksichtigen. [3]Biometrische oder genetische Daten im Sinne von Artikel 9 Absatz 1 der Verordnung (EU) 2016/679 dürfen nicht veröffentlicht werden, wenn Belange betroffener Personen berührt sein könnten. [4]Im Fall genetischer Daten gilt dies auch für die Belange von leiblichen Kindern oder Kindeskindern betroffener Personen. [5]§ 7 gilt entsprechend.
(2) [1]Der Senator für Kultur kann auf begründeten Antrag nach Anhörung der Landesbeauftragten für den Datenschutz gestatten, dass Archiven, Museen und Forschungsstellen Vervielfältigungen von öffentlichem Archivgut nach § 2 Absatz 1 zur Geschichte von Opfergruppen der nationalsozialistischen Herrschaft sowie zu deren Aufarbeitung in der Nachkriegszeit zur Benutzung gemäß § 7 Absatz 1

---

1) Richtig wohl: „betroffener Personen".

überlassen werden. ²Eine Überlassung ist nur zulässig, wenn sichergestellt ist, dass bei der Benutzung der Vervielfältigungen § 7 sinngemäße Anwendung findet. ³Für die Überlassung von Kopien personenbezogenen Schriftguts an Stellen außerhalb der Europäischen Union gelten im Übrigen die Maßgaben des Kapitels V der Verordnung (EU) 2016/679.

§ 9 Befugnisse

(1) Der Senator für Kultur wird ermächtigt, durch Rechtsverordnung[1]) Einzelheiten der Nutzung des Archivguts, der Reproduktionen und der Findmittel des Staatsarchivs zu regeln, insbesondere das Antrags- und Genehmigungsverfahren und die Führung der entsprechenden Unterlagen, die Sorgfaltspflichten bei der Nutzung und die entsprechende Verpflichtung der Benutzer, die Versendung und Ausleihe von Archivgut und die Herstellung von Kopien und Reproduktionen.

(2) ¹Das Staatsarchiv erhebt Kosten. ²Die Höhe und Art der Kosten regelt die Kostenverordnung der Kulturverwaltung.

(3) Dem Staatsarchiv steht ein kostenloses Belegexemplar von Druckwerken, Publikationen und sonstigen Arbeiten zu, die unter wesentlicher Verwendung von Archivalien verfasst worden sind.

(4) ¹Abweichend von Artikel 9 Absatz 1 der Verordnung (EU) 2016/679 ist die Verarbeitung besonderer Kategorien personenbezogener Daten im Archivgut durch das Staatsarchiv zulässig, soweit dies für im öffentlichen Interesse liegende Archivzwecke erforderlich ist. ²Neben den Regelungen von § 4 Absatz 3 und § 7 Absatz 7 werden, falls nötig, weitere angemessene und spezifische Maßnahmen zum Schutz der Interessen der betroffenen Person getroffen.

Abschnitt II
Sonstiges öffentliches Archivgut

§ 10 Bremische Bürgerschaft

(1) Die Bürgerschaft entscheidet in eigener Zuständigkeit, ob bei ihr entstandene Unterlagen, die zur Erfüllung ihrer Aufgaben nicht mehr benötigt werden, von ihr selbst archiviert oder dem Staatsarchiv zur Übernahme angeboten werden (§ 3 Absatz 1 bis 6 und Absatz 7 Satz 3).

(2) ¹Sofern die Bürgerschaft ein eigenes Archiv unterhält, gelten die §§ 4 bis 7 entsprechend. ²Im Übrigen regelt sie die Einzelheiten der Benutzung in eigener Zuständigkeit.

§ 11 Archivgut der Stadtgemeinde Bremerhaven

(1) Die Stadtgemeinde Bremerhaven trägt für ihr Archivgut in eigener Zuständigkeit Sorge, indem sie es insbesondere verwahrt, erhält, erschließt, nutzbar macht und erforscht.

(2) ¹Sie erfüllt diese Aufgaben durch Errichtung und Unterhaltung eines eigenen Archivs. ²§ 1 Abs. 5 gilt entsprechend.

(3) ¹Archivwürdige Unterlagen, die zur Aufgabenerfüllung nicht mehr benötigt werden, sind in das Archiv zu übernehmen. ²§§ 2, 3, 4 Absatz 3, §§ 5 bis 7, 8 Absatz 1 und 9 Absatz 3 und 4 sowie § 13 gelten entsprechend. ³Über den Erlass einer Benutzungsordnung und die Erhebung von Kosten entscheidet die Stadtgemeinde Bremerhaven in eigener Zuständigkeit.

§ 12 Sonstiges öffentliches Archivgut

(1) ¹Die sonstigen der Aufsicht des Landes unterstehenden juristischen Personen des öffentlichen Rechts tragen für ihr Archivgut entsprechend § 11 Absatz 1 dadurch Sorge, daß sie
1. eigene Archive einrichten und unterhalten, die den archivfachlichen Anforderungen des § 1 Abs. 5 Satz 1 genügen,
2. das Archivgut einem anderen Archiv zur Übernahme anbieten, das die Verwahrung nach § 4 Abs. 3, die Rechte betroffener Personen nach § 5 und die Nutzung nach §§ 6 und 7 gewährleistet und hauptamtlich oder hauptberuflich von Personal betreut wird, das die Befähigung für eine Laufbahn des Archivdienstes besitzt oder sonst fachlich geeignet ist, oder
3. das Archivgut dem Staatsarchiv zur Übernahme anbieten (§ 3 Absatz 8).

²Der Senator für Kultur stellt im Einvernehmen mit den Aufsichtsbehörden fest, ob in den Fällen des Satzes 1 Nr. 1 und 2 die Archive den Anforderungen genügen.

(2) ¹Im Falle des Absatzes 1 Satz 1 Nummer 1 sind archivwürdige Unterlagen, die zur Aufgabenerfüllung nicht mehr benötigt werden, in diese Archive zu übernehmen. ²Im Übrigen gelten für diese

---

1) Die Bremische Archivbenutzungsordnung ist abgedruckt als Nr. D5.II.1a.

Archive §§ 2, 3, 4 Absatz 3, §§ 5 bis 7, 8 Absatz 1 und § 9 Absatz 3 und 4 sowie § 13 entsprechend. ³Über den Erlass einer Benutzungsordnung und die Erhebung von Kosten entscheidet der Träger des Archivs.

Abschnitt III
Übergangs- und Schlußvorschriften

§ 13 Archivgut von Stellen des Bundes, bundesrechtliche Geheimhaltungsvorschriften
¹Für Unterlagen, die das Staatsarchiv nach § 1 Absatz 2 Satz 1 Nummer 1 von Stellen des Bundes übernommen hat, gelten die entsprechenden Regelungen und Schutzfristen des Bundesarchivgesetzes.[1] ²Dies gilt auch für solches Archivgut, das Rechtsvorschriften des Bundes über Geheimhaltung unterliegt.

§ 14 Ausnahmen vom Anwendungsbereich
(1) Dieses Gesetz gilt nicht für die öffentlich-rechtlichen Religions- und Weltanschauungsgemeinschaften, für die öffentlich-rechtlichen Rundfunkanstalten sowie für öffentlich-rechtliche Unternehmen mit eigener Rechtspersönlichkeit, die am Wettbewerb teilnehmen, und deren Zusammenschlüsse.
(2) Bestehende Eigentums- und sonstige Rechtsverhältnisse am Archivgut werden durch dieses Gesetz nicht berührt.

§ 15 Inkrafttreten
(1) Dieses Gesetz tritt, soweit Absatz 2 nicht etwas anderes bestimmt, am Tage nach seiner Verkündung in Kraft.
(2) § 3 Abs. 5 und 6 und § 10 treten zwei Jahre nach der Verkündung in Kraft.

---

1) Das Bundesarchivgesetz ist abgedruckt als Nr. C.III.1.

Verordnung über die Benutzung des Staatsarchivs Bremen (Bremische Archivbenutzungsverordnung – BremArchivV)

Vom 30. Oktober 2013 (Brem.ABl. S. 1266)

Aufgrund des § 9 Absatz 1 des Bremischen Archivgesetzes vom 7. Mai 1991 (Brem.GBl. S. 159 – 224-c-1), das zuletzt durch das Gesetz vom 21. Mai 2013 (Brem.GBl. S. 166) geändert worden ist, wird verordnet:

Abschnitt 1
Allgemeines

§ 1 Geltungsbereich
¹Diese Verordnung gilt für das Staatsarchiv Bremen. ²Sie regelt die Benutzung von Archivgut, von Reproduktionen des Archivguts, von Findmitteln und von Bibliotheksgut.

§ 2 Nutzungsrecht
Nach Maßgabe des Bremischen Archivgesetzes und dieser Verordnung stehen Archivgut, Reproduktionen des Archivguts und Findmittel auf Antrag für die Benutzung zur Verfügung.

§ 3 Benutzungsarten
(1) Die Benutzung erfolgt
1. durch persönliche Einsichtnahme im Staatsarchiv,
2. durch persönliche, telefonische oder schriftliche Anfragen,
3. durch Anforderung von Reproduktionen von Archivgut,
4. durch Versendung von Archivgut zur Einsichtnahme an einem anderen Ort oder
5. durch Ausleihe von Archivgut für Ausstellungen und zu anderen Zwecken der Öffentlichkeitsarbeit.

(2) Die übliche Benutzungsart ist die persönliche Einsichtnahme im Staatsarchiv.
(3) ¹Über die Benutzungsart entscheidet das Staatsarchiv unter fachlichen Gesichtspunkten. ²Es besteht kein Rechtsanspruch auf eine bestimmte Benutzungsart.

§ 4 Benutzungsantrag
(1) ¹Der Benutzungsantrag ist in der Regel schriftlich zu stellen. ²Dabei sind Angaben zur Person zu machen und der Benutzungszweck sowie der Gegenstand der Nachforschungen möglichst genau anzugeben. ³Bei persönlicher Einsichtnahme ist für die schriftliche Antragstellung ein Vordruck zu verwenden.
(2) Wer Archivgut benutzen will, hat sich auf Verlangen auszuweisen.
(3) Für jeden Benutzungszweck und für jeden Gegenstand der Nachforschungen ist in der Regel ein gesonderter Antrag nach Absatz 1 zu stellen.
(4) Sollen andere Personen als Hilfskräfte oder Beauftragte zu den Arbeiten herangezogen werden, so haben diese eigene Anträge zu stellen.

§ 5 Benutzungsgenehmigung
(1) ¹Über den Benutzungsantrag entscheidet das Staatsarchiv nach Maßgabe von § 7 des Bremischen Archivgesetzes. ²Die Genehmigung ist beschränkt auf das Benutzungsvorhaben und den Benutzungszweck. ³Das Benutzungsverhältnis ist öffentlich-rechtlicher Natur.
(2) Die Benutzungsgenehmigung kann widerrufen werden, wenn
1. wiederholt oder schwerwiegend gegen das Bremische Archivgesetz, diese Verordnung oder ergänzende Bestimmungen (§ 16) verstoßen wird,
2. festgelegte Benutzungsbedingungen oder -auflagen nicht eingehalten werden oder
3. nachträglich Gründe bekannt werden, die zur Versagung geführt hätten.
(3) Bei Einschränkung, Versagung und Widerruf der Benutzungsgenehmigung sind die Gründe, auf Wunsch schriftlich, mitzuteilen.
(4) Zur weiteren Bearbeitung genehmigter Benutzungsanträge können auch Daten über den Ablauf der Benutzung, insbesondere über das benutzte Archivgut, verarbeitet werden.

§ 6 Benutzung von Archivgut unter Schutzfristen und von Verschlusssachen

(1) [1]Anträge nach § 7 Absatz 5 des Bremischen Archivgesetzes sind mit genauer Bezeichnung des Gegenstands der Nachforschungen, detaillierter Angabe des in Frage kommenden Archivguts und ausführlicher Begründung schriftlich an das Staatsarchiv zu richten. [2]Bei der Antragstellung ist ein Vordruck des Staatsarchivs zu verwenden.

(2) [1]Liegt bei personenbezogenem Archivgut keine Einwilligung nach § 7 Absatz 5 Satz 2 Nummer 1 des Bremischen Archivgesetzes vor, hat der Antragsteller das Vorliegen der Voraussetzungen nach § 7 Absatz 5 Satz 2 Nummer 2 oder 3 des Bremischen Archivgesetzes darzulegen. [2]Bei Forschungsvorhaben ist zu erläutern, warum schutzwürdige Belange der betroffenen Personen nicht beeinträchtigt werden oder warum das öffentliche Interesse an der Durchführung des Forschungsvorhabens die schutzwürdigen Belange erheblich überwiegt. [3]Hierzu können ergänzende Angaben und Unterlagen verlangt werden. [4]Bei Studien- und Prüfungsarbeiten ist eine Stellungnahme des betreuenden Hochschullehrenden beizufügen.

(3) [1]Für den Umgang mit Verschlusssachen gilt die Verschlusssachenanweisung für das Land Bremen in der jeweils geltenden Fassung. [2]Darüber hinaus dürfen im Staatsarchiv archivierte Verschlusssachen nur mit Zustimmung der abliefernden Stelle Dritten zugänglich gemacht werden.

§ 7 Rechtsschutzbestimmungen

(1) [1]Bei der Verwertung der aus dem Archivgut gewonnenen Erkenntnisse sind Urheber- und Persönlichkeitsrechte, insbesondere das Datenschutzrecht und andere schutzwürdige Belange, zu wahren. [2]Dies gilt insbesondere für die Fälle des § 7 Absatz 5 des Bremischen Archivgesetzes. [3]Auf Verlangen sind schriftliche Erklärungen darüber abzugeben, dass die Urheber- und Persönlichkeitsrechte gewahrt bleiben.

(2) Absatz 1 gilt auch für die Verwertung lediglich aus Findmitteln gewonnener Erkenntnisse.

Abschnitt 2
Benutzung im Staatsarchiv

§ 8 Benutzung von Archivgut und Findmitteln

(1) [1]Archivgut darf nur in den dafür bestimmten Räumen des Staatsarchivs während der Öffnungszeiten benutzt werden. [2]Im Interesse eines ungestörten Arbeitens soll im Lesesaal Ruhe herrschen.

(2) [1]Archivgut und Findmittel sind mit größter Sorgfalt zu behandeln. [2]Sie dürfen in ihrem Zustand nicht verändert werden. [3]Insbesondere ist es nicht gestattet, den Ordnungszustand des Archivguts zu verändern, Bestandteile des Archivguts zu entfernen, Vermerke im Archivgut anzubringen oder vorhandene zu tilgen sowie Archivgut als Schreib- oder Durchzeichnungsunterlage zu verwenden. [4]Den Anweisungen des Archivpersonals im Umgang mit dem Archivgut ist Folge zu leisten.

(3) [1]Das Archivpersonal kann die Verwendung technischer Geräte untersagen, wenn diese den Lesesaalbetrieb beeinträchtigen. [2]Das selbständige Herstellen von Reproduktionen jeglicher Art durch den Einsatz benutzereigener technischer Geräte ist grundsätzlich nicht zulässig. [3]Ausnahmen bedürfen der Genehmigung durch das Archivpersonal.

(4) Archivgut kann, sofern dies aus konservatorischen Gründen notwendig ist, als Reproduktion vorgelegt werden.

(5) [1]Die Benutzungszeiten und die Zeiten, zu denen Archivgut und Bibliotheksgut aus dem Magazin ausgehoben wird (Aushebezeiten), werden durch das Staatsarchiv bekannt gegeben. [2]In der Regel wird nur eine begrenzte Anzahl von Archivalien und Büchern gleichzeitig vorgelegt. [3]Weitere Einzelheiten regelt das Staatsarchiv.

§ 9 Benutzung der Bibliothek

Für die Benutzung der Bibliothek des Staatsarchivs gilt § 8 entsprechend.

§ 10 Benutzung fremden Archivguts

[1]Für die Benutzung von Archivgut, das von anderen Archiven übersandt wird, gelten die gleichen Bedingungen wie für das Archivgut des Staatsarchivs, sofern das übersendende Archiv nicht anderslautende Auflagen macht. [2]Gebühren und Auslagen tragen diejenigen, die die Versendung veranlasst haben.

§ 11 Beratung

(1) Während der Öffnungszeiten und nach den Möglichkeiten des Dienstbetriebs steht Fachpersonal zur Beratung zur Verfügung.
(2) Die Beratung erstreckt sich vornehmlich auf Hinweise auf das einschlägige Archivgut und die Literatur sowie auf die Vorlage der einschlägigen Findmittel.
(3) Ein Anspruch auf Unterstützung beim Lesen des Archivguts, der Findmittel und der Bücher besteht nicht.

§ 12 Anfertigung und Verwendung von Reproduktionen

(1) [1]Die Anfertigung von Reproduktionen zur Abgabe an Benutzerinnen und Benutzer ist nur in beschränktem Umfang möglich. [2]Ein Anspruch auf Anfertigung von Reproduktionen besteht nicht.
(2) [1]Über die Eignung von Archivgut, Findmitteln und Büchern für bestimmte Reproduktionsverfahren entscheidet das Archivpersonal. [2]Für die Qualität von Reproduktionen übernimmt das Staatsarchiv keine Gewährleistung.
(3) [1]Die Reproduktionen dürfen von Benutzerinnen und Benutzern nur mit schriftlicher Genehmigung des Staatsarchivs veröffentlicht, vervielfältigt, an Dritte weitergegeben oder zu gewerblichen oder geschäftlichen Zwecken verwendet werden. [2]Bei Veröffentlichung und Vervielfältigung von Reproduktionen sind das Staatsarchiv als Aufbewahrungsort und die Signatur des Archivguts anzugeben.

Abschnitt 3
Benutzung außerhalb des Staatsarchivs

§ 13 Schriftliche Auskünfte

(1) Bei schriftlichen Anfragen sind Benutzungszweck und Gegenstand der Nachforschungen genau anzugeben.
(2) Die schriftlichen Auskünfte des Staatsarchivs beschränken sich in der Regel auf Hinweise zu einschlägigen Findmitteln und einschlägigem Archivgut.
(3) Ein Anspruch auf Auskünfte, die eine beträchtliche Arbeitszeit erfordern, oder auf Beantwortung von wiederholten Anfragen innerhalb eines kürzeren Zeitraumes besteht nicht.

§ 14 Versendung von Archivgut

(1) [1]Auf Antrag kann in Ausnahmefällen Archivgut zur Benutzung an auswärtige Archive versandt werden. [2]Ein Anspruch auf Versendung von Archivgut besteht nicht. [3]Gebühren und Auslagen tragen diejenigen, die die Versendung veranlasst haben.
(2) [1]Die Versendung von Archivgut ist nur in beschränktem Umfang möglich und erfolgt stets befristet. [2]Die Frist kann auf Antrag verlängert werden.
(3) Die Benutzung des versandten Archivguts richtet sich nach den Vorschriften des Bremischen Archivgesetzes und dieser Verordnung.

§ 15 Ausleihe von Archivgut

(1) [1]Die Ausleihe von Archivgut für Ausstellungen und zu anderen Zwecken der Öffentlichkeitsarbeit ist unter bestimmten Bedingungen und Auflagen möglich, wenn der Ausleihezweck nicht durch Reproduktionen oder Nachbildungen erreicht werden kann. [2]Ein Anspruch auf Ausleihe von Archivgut besteht nicht.
(2) Über die Ausleihe ist in der Regel mit dem Entleiher ein Leihvertrag abzuschließen.

Abschnitt 4
Schlussbestimmungen

§ 16 Ergänzende Bestimmungen des Staatsarchivs

[1]Das Staatsarchiv kann zu dieser Verordnung ergänzende Bestimmungen treffen. [2]Insbesondere regelt es die Öffnungszeiten und das Hausrecht.

§ 17 Inkrafttreten, Außerkrafttreten

(1) Diese Verordnung tritt am Tage nach ihrer Verkündung[1] in Kraft.
(2) Gleichzeitig tritt die Bremische Archivbenutzungsverordnung vom 1. März 1993 (Brem.GBl. S. 99 – 224-c-2), die durch Artikel 16 des Gesetzes vom 16. Mai 2006 (Brem.GBl. S. 271) geändert worden ist, außer Kraft.

---

1) Verkündet am 12.11.2013.

D5.III.1 KGSG-Zuständigkeitsverordnung

Verordnung über die zuständigen Behörden nach dem Kulturgutschutzgesetz (Kulturgutschutzgesetzzuständigkeitsverordnung)

Vom 18. September 2018 (Brem.GBl. S. 428)

Auf Grund des § 3 Absatz 1 Satz 2 des Kulturgutschutzgesetzes vom 31. Juli 2016 (BGBl. I S. 1914), das durch Artikel 6 Absatz 13 des Gesetzes vom 13. April 2017 (BGBl. I S. 872) geändert worden ist, verordnet der Senat:

§ 1 [Zuständigkeit]
(1) Zuständige oberste Landesbehörde im Sinne des Kulturgutschutzgesetzes ist der Senator für Kultur.
(2) Zuständige Behörde im Sinne des Kulturgutschutzgesetzes ist der Senator für Kultur.

§ 2 [Inkrafttreten]
(1) Diese Verordnung tritt am Tag nach ihrer Verkündung[1] in Kraft.
(2) [1]Gleichzeitig treten die Ausführungsverordnung zum Gesetz zum Schutz deutschen Kulturgutes gegen Abwanderung vom 16. Juni 1958 (SaBremR 224-a-1) und die Verordnung über das Antragsrecht nach dem Gesetz zum Schutz deutschen Kulturgutes gegen Abwanderung vom 30. Mai 2006 (Brem.GBl. S. 347 – 224-a-2) außer Kraft, soweit Satz 2 nichts anderes bestimmt. [2]Die Ausführungsverordnung zum Gesetz zum Schutz deutschen Kulturgutes gegen Abwanderung ist weiter anzuwenden, soweit das Gesetz zum Schutz deutschen Kulturgutes gegen Abwanderung in der Fassung der Bekanntmachung vom 8. Juli 1999 (BGBl. I S. 1754), das zuletzt durch Artikel 2 des Gesetzes vom 18. Mai 2007 (BGBl. I S. 757, 2547) geändert worden ist, gemäß § 90 des Kulturgutschutzgesetzes fort gilt.

---

1) Verkündet am 26.9.2018.

Denkmalschutzgesetz (DSchG)[1]
Vom 5. April 2013 (HmbGVBl. S. 142)

Abschnitt I
Allgemeine Bestimmungen

§ 1 Aufgaben des Denkmalschutzes und der Denkmalpflege
(1) Es ist Aufgabe von Denkmalschutz und Denkmalpflege, die Denkmäler wissenschaftlich zu erforschen und nach Maßgabe dieses Gesetzes zu schützen und zu erhalten, sowie darauf hinzuwirken, dass sie in die städtebauliche Entwicklung, Raumordnung und Landespflege einbezogen werden.
(2) [1]Die Freie und Hansestadt Hamburg soll auch als Eigentümerin oder sonst Verfügungsberechtigte und als obligatorisch Berechtigte durch vorbildliche Unterhaltungsmaßnahmen an Denkmälern für den Wert des kulturellen Erbes in der Öffentlichkeit eintreten und die Privatinitiative anregen. [2]Dazu gehört auch die Verbreitung des Denkmalgedankens und des Wissens über Denkmäler in der Öffentlichkeit.

§ 2 Denkmalpflegerin oder Denkmalpfleger, Bodendenkmalpflegerin oder Bodendenkmalpfleger
Der Senat bestellt auf Vorschlag der zuständigen Behörde[2] eine Kunsthistorikerin oder einen Kunsthistoriker oder eine kunsthistorisch vorgebildete Architektin oder einen kunsthistorisch vorgebildeten Architekten als Denkmalpflegerin oder Denkmalpfleger und eine Archäologin oder einen Archäologen als Bodendenkmalpflegerin oder Bodendenkmalpfleger.

§ 3 Denkmalrat
(1) [1]Für die Zwecke des Denkmalschutzes und der Denkmalpflege wird der zuständigen Behörde der Denkmalrat als unabhängiger sachverständiger Beirat beigeordnet. [2]Der Denkmalrat besteht aus zwölf Mitgliedern. [3]Er soll sich zusammensetzen aus Vertreterinnen und Vertretern der Fachgebiete der Denkmalpflege, Geschichte und Architektur sowie aus in der Sache engagierten Bürgerinnen und Bürgern und Institutionen der Freien und Hansestadt Hamburg. [4]Frauen und Männer sollen zu gleichen Teilen berücksichtigt werden. [5]Die Leiterin oder der Leiter des Staatsarchivs nimmt mit beratender Stimme an den Sitzungen des Denkmalrats teil.
(2) [1]Die Mitglieder des Denkmalrates werden auf Vorschlag der zuständigen Behörde vom Senat ernannt. [2]Die zuständige Behörde hat Vorschläge der Fachverbände und des Landeskirchenamtes der Evangelisch-Lutherischen Kirche in Norddeutschland und des Erzbistums Hamburg einzuholen. [3]Die Amtsdauer beträgt drei Jahre. [4]Eine einmalige Wiederernennung ist zulässig. [5]Eine erneute dritte Ernennung ist frühestens drei Jahre nach dem Ausscheiden möglich. [6]Für die Berechnung der Amtszeit ist das Kalenderjahr maßgebend. [7]Scheidet ein Mitglied während der Amtszeit aus, so ernennt der Senat ein Ersatzmitglied, falls der Rest der Amtszeit des ausscheidenden Mitglieds mehr als ein Vierteljahr beträgt.
(3) Beamtete Mitglieder des Denkmalrates sind an Weisungen nicht gebunden.
(4) [1]Der Denkmalrat wählt aus seiner Mitte eine Vorsitzende oder einen Vorsitzenden und eine stellvertretende Vorsitzende oder einen stellvertretenden Vorsitzenden. [2]Er gibt sich eine Geschäftsordnung, die der Genehmigung der zuständigen Behörde bedarf. [3]Der Denkmalrat kann andere Sachverständige und die Bezirksämter hören.
(5) [1]Der Denkmalrat berät die zuständige Behörde. [2]Er nimmt Stellung zu grundsätzlichen und aktuellen Fragestellungen des Denkmalschutzes und der Denkmalpflege. [3]Der Denkmalrat ist berechtigt, Empfehlungen auszusprechen. [4]Der Senat berichtet alle zwei Jahre der Bürgerschaft über die Arbeit des Denkmalrates zu Denkmalschutz und Denkmalpflege. [5]Die Beschlüsse des Denkmalrates sollen auf der Internetseite der zuständigen Behörde unter Beachtung datenschutzrechtlicher Bestimmungen veröffentlicht werden.

§ 4 Gegenstand des Denkmalschutzes
(1) [1]Nach diesem Gesetz sind Baudenkmäler, Ensembles, Gartendenkmäler und Bodendenkmäler als Denkmäler geschützt. [2]Das Gleiche gilt für bewegliche Denkmäler, deren Verfügung über die Unterschutzstellung unanfechtbar geworden ist oder wenn sofortige Vollziehung angeordnet wurde.

---

1) Verkündet als Art. 1 G v. 5.4.2013 (HmbGVBl. S. 142); Inkrafttreten gem. Art. 10 dieses G am **1.5.2013**.
2) Vgl. die Anordnung zur Durchführung des Denkmalschutzgesetzes, abgedruckt als Nr. D6.I.1a.

(2) ¹Ein Baudenkmal ist eine bauliche Anlage oder ein Teil einer baulichen Anlage im Sinne des § 2 Absatz 1 der Hamburgischen Bauordnung vom 14. Dezember 2005 (HmbGVBl. S. 525, 563), zuletzt geändert am 20. Dezember 2011 (HmbGVBl. S. 554), in der jeweils geltenden Fassung, deren oder dessen Erhaltung wegen der geschichtlichen, künstlerischen oder wissenschaftlichen Bedeutung oder zur Bewahrung charakteristischer Eigenheiten des Stadtbildes im öffentlichen Interesse liegt. ²Zu einem Baudenkmal gehören auch sein Zubehör und seine Ausstattung, soweit sie mit dem Baudenkmal eine Einheit von Denkmalwert bilden.

(3) ¹Ein Ensemble ist eine Mehrheit baulicher Anlagen einschließlich der mit ihnen verbundenen Straßen und Plätze sowie Grünanlagen und Frei- und Wasserflächen, deren Erhaltung aus in Absatz 2 genannten Gründen im öffentlichen Interesse liegt, und zwar auch dann, wenn kein oder nicht jeder einzelne Teil des Ensembles ein Denkmal darstellt. ²Zu einem Ensemble gehören auch das Zubehör und die Ausstattung seiner Bestandteile, soweit sie mit den Bestandteilen des Ensembles eine Einheit von Denkmalwert bilden.

(4) ¹Ein Gartendenkmal ist eine Grünanlage, eine Garten- oder Parkanlage, ein Friedhof, eine Allee oder ein sonstiges Zeugnis der Garten- und Landschaftsgestaltung einschließlich der Wasser- und Waldflächen oder Teile davon, deren oder dessen Erhaltung aus in Absatz 2 genannten Gründen im öffentlichen Interesse liegt. ²Zu einem Gartendenkmal gehören auch sein Zubehör und seine Ausstattung, soweit sie mit dem Gartendenkmal eine Einheit von Denkmalwert bilden.

(5) Ein Bodendenkmal ist ein Überrest, eine bewegliche oder eine unbewegliche Sache, der oder die von Epochen und Kulturen zeugt, für die Ausgrabungen und Funde eine der Hauptquellen wissenschaftlicher Erkenntnis sind und deren Erhaltung aus in Absatz 2 genannten Gründen im öffentlichen Interesse liegt.

(6) Bewegliche Denkmäler sind alle nicht ortsfesten Sachen, die nicht unter die Absätze 2 bis 5 fallen und deren Erhaltung aus den in Absatz 2 genannten Gründen im öffentlichen Interesse liegt, insbesondere:
1. bewegliche Einzelgegenstände,
2. Sammlungen und sonstige Gesamtheiten von beweglichen Einzelgegenständen.

§ 5 Unterschutzstellung beweglicher Denkmäler

(1) ¹Die Unterschutzstellung beweglicher Denkmäler wird von der zuständigen Behörde durch Verwaltungsakt verfügt. ²Die zuständige Behörde ist in Fällen der Gefahr befugt, zur Sicherung der durch dieses Gesetz geschützten Interessen anzuordnen, dass bewegliche Denkmäler vorläufig in das Verzeichnis der beweglichen Denkmäler (§ 6 Absatz 4) eingetragen werden. ³Die Anordnung tritt außer Kraft, wenn die Unterschutzstellung nicht innerhalb von drei Monaten eingeleitet und nach weiteren sechs Monaten verfügt worden ist.

(2) Bewegliche Sachen werden als bewegliche Denkmäler nur unter Schutz gestellt, wenn sie von besonderer Bedeutung sind.

§ 6 Nachrichtliche Denkmalliste, konstitutives Verzeichnis beweglicher Denkmäler

(1) ¹Bei der zuständigen Behörde wird eine Denkmalliste für die Denkmäler im Sinne des § 4 Absätze 2 bis 5 geführt. ²In dieser Denkmalliste werden eine Identitätsnummer, die Belegenheit und eine Denkmalkurzbezeichnung aufgeführt. ³Der Schutz nach diesem Gesetz ist nicht von der Eintragung dieser Denkmäler in die Denkmalliste abhängig. ⁴Die Einhaltung der gesetzlichen Schutzpflichten kann von der bzw. dem Verfügungsberechtigten erst ab der Eintragung verlangt werden. ⁵Die Denkmalliste kann von jeder natürlichen und jeder juristischen Person eingesehen werden. ⁶Soweit es sich um eine Einsichtnahme im Hinblick auf die Bodendenkmäler handelt, ist ein berechtigtes Interesse darzulegen.

(2) ¹Die Eintragung erfolgt von Amts wegen oder auf Anregung der bzw. des Verfügungsberechtigten. ²Eintragungen in der Denkmalliste werden gelöscht, wenn die Eintragungsvoraussetzungen entfallen sind. ³Dies gilt nicht, wenn die Wiederherstellung eines Denkmals angeordnet ist.

(3) ¹Verfügungsberechtigte, deren Denkmäler bis zum 30. April 2013 noch nicht in die Denkmalliste eingetragen waren, werden von der Eintragung unterrichtet. ²Ist die Ermittlung der bzw. des Verfügungsberechtigten nicht oder nur mit unverhältnismäßigen Schwierigkeiten oder Kosten möglich, ist die Eintragung öffentlich bekannt zu machen. ³Ebenso kann die Eintragung oder Löschung öffentlich bekannt gemacht werden, wenn mehr als 20 Verfügungsberechtigte betroffen sind.

(4) ¹Bei der zuständigen Behörde wird gesondert ein konstitutives Verzeichnis der beweglichen Denkmäler geführt. ²In diesem Verzeichnis werden die Identitätsnummer und eine Denkmalkurzbezeichnung aufgeführt. ³Es kann von jeder natürlichen und jeder juristischen Person eingesehen werden.

Abschnitt II
Schutzbestimmungen und Genehmigungsverfahren

§ 7 Denkmalgerechte Erhaltung, Instandsetzung, Ersatzvornahme
(1) ¹Die Verfügungsberechtigten sind verpflichtet, das Denkmal im Rahmen des Zumutbaren denkmalgerecht zu erhalten, vor Gefährdungen zu schützen und instand zu setzen. ²Unzumutbarkeit ist insbesondere gegeben, soweit die Kosten der Erhaltung und Bewirtschaftung dauerhaft nicht durch die Erträge oder den Gebrauchswert des Denkmals aufgewogen werden können. ³Können die Verfügungsberechtigten Zuwendungen aus öffentlichen oder privaten Mitteln oder steuerliche Vorteile in Anspruch nehmen, so sind diese anzurechnen. ⁴Die Verfügungsberechtigten können sich nicht auf die Belastung durch erhöhte Erhaltungskosten berufen, die dadurch verursacht wurden, dass Erhaltungsmaßnahmen diesem Gesetz oder sonstigem öffentlichen Recht zuwider unterblieben sind.
(2) Die Freie und Hansestadt Hamburg trägt zu den Kosten der Erhaltung und Instandsetzung von Denkmälern nach Maßgabe der im Haushalt hierfür bereit gestellten Mittel bei.
(3) Bei allen Entscheidungen nach diesem Gesetz sind die berechtigten Interessen der Verfügungsberechtigten über das Denkmal, insbesondere die Belange von Menschen mit Behinderungen oder mit Mobilitätsbeeinträchtigungen, zu berücksichtigen.
(4) Die Verfügungsberechtigten haben der zuständigen Behörde das Auftreten offenkundiger Mängel anzuzeigen, welche die Erhaltung des Denkmals gefährden.
(5) Wird in ein Denkmal eingegriffen, es von seinem Standort entfernt oder beseitigt, so hat die Verursacherin oder der Verursacher des Eingriffes im Rahmen des Zumutbaren alle Kosten zu tragen, die für die Erhaltung und fachgerechte Instandsetzung, Bergung und wissenschaftliche Dokumentation des Denkmals anfallen.
(6) ¹Die Verfügungsberechtigten können durch die zuständige Behörde verpflichtet werden, bestimmte Maßnahmen zur Erhaltung des Denkmals durchzuführen. ²Kommen die Verfügungsberechtigten ihrer Verpflichtung nach Absatz 1 nicht nach, kann die zuständige Behörde die gebotenen Maßnahmen selbst durchführen oder durchführen lassen. ³Die Kosten der Maßnahmen tragen im Rahmen des Zumutbaren die Verfügungsberechtigten. ⁴Mieterinnen und Mieter, Pächterinnen und Pächter sowie sonstige Nutzungsberechtigte haben die Durchführung der Maßnahmen zu dulden.
(7) ¹Der Senat wird ermächtigt, durch Rechtsverordnung nähere Vorschriften über die Erhaltung von Bau- und Gartendenkmälern sowie Ensembles zu erlassen. ²Der Senat wird ferner ermächtigt, durch Rechtsverordnung die Verordnungsermächtigung nach Satz 1 für Festsetzungen im Rahmen von Bebauungsplänen in den Fällen auf die Bezirksämter weiter zu übertragen, in denen die örtlich zuständigen Bezirksversammlungen den Bebauungsplanentwürfen zugestimmt haben. ³Dabei besteht insbesondere die Möglichkeit, Ensembles baulich zu verdichten, wenn hierfür eine denkmalverträgliche Planung vorliegt.
(8) Bei Maßnahmen und Planungen ist die Verpflichtung zur Bewahrung des Kulturerbes gemäß dem Übereinkommen zum Schutz des Kultur- und Naturerbes der Welt vom 16. November 1972 (BGBl. 1977 II S. 215) zu berücksichtigen.
(9) Bescheide und sonstige Maßnahmen gelten auch für und gegen Rechtsnachfolgerinnen und Rechtsnachfolger.

§ 8 Umgebungsschutz
Die unmittelbare Umgebung eines Denkmals, soweit sie für dessen Erscheinungsbild oder Bestand von prägender Bedeutung ist, darf ohne Genehmigung der zuständigen Behörde durch Errichtung, Änderung oder Beseitigung baulicher Anlagen, durch die Gestaltung der unbebauten öffentlichen oder privaten Flächen oder in anderer Weise nicht dergestalt verändert werden, dass die Eigenart und das Erscheinungsbild des Denkmals wesentlich beeinträchtigt werden.

§ 9 Genehmigungsvorbehalt für Veränderungen von Denkmälern
(1) ¹Denkmäler dürfen ohne Genehmigung der zuständigen Behörde nicht ganz oder teilweise beseitigt, wiederhergestellt, erheblich ausgebessert, von ihrem Standort entfernt oder sonst verändert werden.

D6.I.1 Denkmalschutzgesetz Hamburg

²Einer Genehmigung für eine Standortveränderung beweglicher Denkmäler innerhalb des Geltungsbereichs dieses Gesetzes bedarf es nicht; die Verfügungsberechtigten sind jedoch verpflichtet, bei der zuständigen Behörde den jeweiligen Standort anzuzeigen.

(2) ¹Die beantragte Genehmigung darf nur versagt werden, wenn ihr überwiegende Gründe des Denkmalschutzes entgegenstehen. ²Sie ist zu erteilen, sofern überwiegende öffentliche Interessen dies verlangen, dabei sind insbesondere Belange des Wohnungsbaus, der energetischen Sanierung, des Einsatzes erneuerbarer Energien und die Belange von Menschen mit Behinderungen oder Mobilitätsbeeinträchtigungen zu berücksichtigen. ³Der Senat kann alle Entscheidungen selbst treffen. ⁴Entscheidet der Senat, ist die Frist des § 11 Absatz 1 während dieses Zeitraums gehemmt.

(3) ¹Die Genehmigung kann mit Nebenbestimmungen erteilt werden, soweit dies zum Schutz des Denkmals oder zur Dokumentation erforderlich ist. ²Insbesondere kann eine Genehmigung an die Bedingung geknüpft werden, dass die Ausführung nur nach einem von der zuständigen Behörde gebilligten Plan gemäß § 10, einer gebilligten denkmalpflegerischen Zielstellung gemäß § 10 Absatz 2 Satz 2 Nummer 3 oder unter Leitung einer oder eines von der zuständigen Behörde bestimmten Sachverständigen erfolgt.

(4) ¹Die Genehmigung der Beseitigung eines Denkmals und die Genehmigung der Entfernung eines Denkmals von seinem Standort können an die Bedingung der Wiedererrichtung des Denkmals an geeigneter Stelle und für eine seiner Eigenart entsprechenden Verwendung auf Kosten der Verfügungsberechtigten geknüpft werden. ²Die Wiedererrichtung kann auch auf einem Grundstück gefordert werden, das den über das Denkmal Verfügungsberechtigten nicht gehört.

§ 10 Denkmalpflegepläne, Denkmalpflegerische Zielstellung

(1) ¹Für Denkmäler kann die Erstellung von Denkmalpflegeplänen durch die oder den Verfügungsberechtigten von der zuständigen Behörde angeordnet werden, sofern dies zur dauerhaften Erhaltung der Denkmäler sowie zur Vermittlung des Denkmalgedankens und des Wissens über Denkmäler erforderlich ist. ²Denkmäler sind nach diesen Denkmalpflegeplänen im Rahmen des Zumutbaren zu erhalten und zu pflegen.

(2) ¹Der Denkmalpflegeplan gibt die Ziele und Erfordernisse des Denkmalschutzes und der Denkmalpflege sowie die Darstellungen und die Festsetzungen der Bauleitplanung wieder. ²Er kann insbesondere enthalten:
1. die Bestandsaufnahme und Analyse des Plangebietes unter denkmalfachlichen und denkmalschutzrechtlichen Gesichtspunkten,
2. die topographischen Angaben über Lage und Ausdehnung der Denkmäler und der Bodendenkmäler,
3. die denkmalpflegerischen Zielstellungen, unter deren Beachtung die Pflege und Erhaltung der Denkmäler jeweils zu verwirklichen ist.

§ 11 Entscheidung über einen Genehmigungsantrag

(1) ¹Wird ein Genehmigungsantrag nicht innerhalb von zwei Monaten nach Eingang des schriftlichen Antrags und Vorlage vollständiger Unterlagen im Sinne des Absatzes 2 bei der zuständigen Behörde beschieden, gilt die Genehmigung als erteilt. ²Wird die Antragstellerin oder der Antragsteller dahin beschieden, dass der Antrag noch nicht abschließend geprüft werden konnte, so verlängert sich die Frist nach Satz 1 um drei Monate.

(2) ¹Mit dem Genehmigungsantrag sind alle für die Beurteilung des Vorhabens und die Bearbeitung des Antrags erforderlichen Unterlagen einzureichen. ²Das können insbesondere Pläne, Dokumentationen, Fotografien, Gutachten, Nutzungskonzepte sowie Kosten- und Wirtschaftlichkeitsberechnungen sein. ³Die zuständige Behörde kann im Einzelfall die erforderlichen Unterlagen anfordern und verlangen, dass der Genehmigungsantrag durch vorbereitende Untersuchungen ergänzt wird.

(3) ¹Die Genehmigung erlischt, wenn nicht innerhalb von drei Jahren nach ihrer Erteilung mit der Ausführung begonnen oder die Ausführung länger als ein Jahr unterbrochen worden ist. ²Die Fristen nach Satz 1 können auf schriftlichen Antrag jeweils bis zu einem Jahr verlängert werden.

(4) Über den Eingang eines Genehmigungsantrages ist der Antragstellerin oder dem Antragsteller auf Verlangen eine Bescheinigung auszustellen.

§ 12 Änderungen im Verfügungsrecht
Änderungen im Verfügungsrecht über Denkmäler sind der zuständigen Behörde durch die oder den Verfügungsberechtigten, im Erbfall durch die Erbin, den Erben, die Testamentsvollstreckerin oder den Testamentsvollstrecker unverzüglich anzuzeigen.

§ 13 Wiederherstellung, Stilllegung
(1) ¹Ist ein Denkmal ohne Genehmigung verändert und dadurch in seinem Denkmalwert gemindert worden oder ist es ganz oder teilweise beseitigt oder zerstört worden, so soll die zuständige Behörde anordnen, dass derjenige, der die Veränderung, Beseitigung oder Zerstörung zu vertreten hat, den früheren Zustand wiederherstellt. ²Die zuständige Behörde soll die erforderlichen Arbeiten auf Kosten des Verpflichteten durchführen lassen, wenn die denkmalgerechte Wiederherstellung sonst nicht gesichert erscheint. ³Sie kann von dem Verpflichteten einen angemessenen Kostenvorschuss verlangen. ⁴Verfügungsberechtigte, Mieterinnen, Mieter, Pächterinnen, Pächter und sonstige Nutzungsberechtigte haben die Durchführung der Maßnahmen zu dulden.
(2) ¹Werden genehmigungspflichtige Maßnahmen ohne Genehmigung begonnen, so kann die zuständige Behörde die vorläufige Einstellung anordnen. ²Werden unzulässige Bauarbeiten trotz einer schriftlich oder mündlich verfügten Einstellung fortgesetzt, so kann die zuständige Behörde die Baustelle versiegeln oder die an der Baustelle vorhandenen Baustoffe, Bauteile, Geräte, Maschinen und Bauhilfsmittel in amtlichen Gewahrsam bringen.

§ 14 Genehmigungspflicht für Ausgrabungen
(1) ¹Wer Bodendenkmäler ausgraben, aus einem Gewässer bergen oder unter Einsatz von technischen Suchgeräten entdecken will, bedarf der Genehmigung der zuständigen Stelle. ²Die Genehmigung kann insbesondere gemäß § 7 Absatz 5 an Bedingungen oder Auflagen hinsichtlich der Ausführung der Ausgrabungen, der Dokumentation, des Fundverbleibes sowie der Konservierung und Restaurierung der aufzufindenden Überreste, Sachen oder Spuren geknüpft werden.
(2) ¹Beabsichtigte Änderungen der Bodennutzung an einem Grundstück, welches Bodendenkmäler enthält, sind von den Verfügungsberechtigten bei der zuständigen Stelle anzuzeigen. ²Nach Eingang der Anzeige darf die Änderung der Bodennutzung nicht vor Ablauf einer Frist von zwei Monaten vorgenommen werden. ³Die Änderung der Bodennutzung bedarf der Genehmigung, sofern sie die Bodendenkmäler beeinträchtigen kann. ⁴Ob eine Beeinträchtigung zu erwarten ist, entscheidet die zuständige Stelle. ⁵Absatz 1 Satz 2 gilt entsprechend.
(3) Absätze 1 und 2 gelten auch, wenn die Auffindung von Bodendenkmälern zwar nicht bezweckt wird, der Antragstellerin oder dem Antragsteller aber bekannt ist oder bekannt sein müsste, dass solche bei Erdarbeiten voraussichtlich entdeckt werden könnten.
(4) §§ 11 und 18 gelten entsprechend.
(5) Der Senat wird ermächtigt, durch Rechtsverordnung eine zuständige Stelle für die Ausübung der Bodendenkmalpflege zu bestimmen und dieser den Gebührenanspruch für diesen Bereich zu übertragen.

§ 15 Grabungsschutzgebiete
(1) Bestimmte abgegrenzte Flächen, in denen Bodendenkmäler vorhanden oder zu vermuten sind, können vom Senat durch Rechtsverordnung befristet oder auf unbestimmte Zeit zu Grabungsschutzgebieten erklärt werden, um die Bodendenkmäler zu erhalten.
(2) Der Senat wird ermächtigt, durch Rechtsverordnung die Verordnungsermächtigung nach Absatz 1 für Festsetzungen im Rahmen von Bebauungsplanverfahren für die Fälle auf die Bezirksämter weiter zu übertragen, in denen die örtlich zuständigen Bezirksversammlungen den Bebauungsplanentwürfen zugestimmt haben.

§ 16 Maßnahmen in Grabungsschutzgebieten
¹In Grabungsschutzgebieten bedürfen alle Maßnahmen, die Bodendenkmäler gefährden können, der Genehmigung der zuständigen Stelle. ²§ 9 Absatz 3, § 7 Absatz 5 und § 11 gelten entsprechend.

§ 17 Funde
(1) ¹Werden bei Erdarbeiten, Baggerungen oder anderen Gelegenheiten Sachen oder Sachteile gefunden, bei denen Anlass zu der Annahme besteht, dass es sich um bisher unbekannte Bodendenkmäler handeln kann, so haben die Finderin oder der Finder und die oder der Verfügungsberechtigte den Fund

D6.I.1 Denkmalschutzgesetz Hamburg

unverzüglich anzuzeigen und die zu seiner Sicherung und Erhaltung ergehenden Anordnungen zu befolgen. ²§ 9 Absatz 3 gilt entsprechend.

(2) ¹Die gleiche Verpflichtung obliegt der Leiterin oder dem Leiter der Arbeiten, bei denen der Fund gemacht worden ist. ²Zur Erfüllung der Anzeigepflicht genügt die Erstattung der Anzeige durch einen der Anzeigepflichtigen.

(3) ¹Denkmäler, die so lange im Boden verborgen gewesen sind, dass die Eigentümerin oder der Eigentümer nicht mehr zu ermitteln ist, werden mit der Entdeckung Eigentum der Freien und Hansestadt Hamburg. ²Der Fund ist unverzüglich der zuständigen Stelle anzuzeigen.

(4) Liegt kein Fall nach § 14 vor, dürfen die Arbeiten vor Ablauf von drei Tagen – Sonnabende, Sonn- und Feiertage nicht gerechnet – nach Anzeigeerstattung nicht fortgesetzt werden, es sei denn, die zuständige Stelle genehmigt die vorzeitige Fortsetzung.

§ 18 Überlassungspflicht
Bewegliche Funde, die unter die Anzeigepflicht nach § 17 Absätze 1 und 2 fallen, sind der zuständigen Stelle vorübergehend zur wissenschaftlichen Bearbeitung zu überlassen.

Abschnitt III
Enteignung und ausgleichspflichtige Maßnahmen

§ 19 Enteignungsgründe
Enteignungen im Rahmen dieses Gesetzes sind zulässig
1. zur Erhaltung eines gefährdeten Denkmals,
2. zur Entfernung eines Denkmals von seinem Standort und zur Wiedererrichtung eines Denkmals auf einem anderen geeigneten Grundstück gemäß § 9 Absatz 4,
3. zur Erhaltung oder Umgestaltung der Umgebung eines Denkmals, soweit sie aus zwingenden Gründen des Denkmalschutzes erforderlich sind,
4. zur Vornahme von Ausgrabungen von Bodendenkmälern.

§ 20 Begünstigte
¹Maßnahmen nach §§ 19, 21 und 22 sollen zu Gunsten der Freien und Hansestadt Hamburg getroffen werden. ²Sie dürfen zu Gunsten Dritter getroffen werden, wenn die Verwirklichung des Zwecks der Enteignung oder sonstigen Maßnahme erreicht und durch die Begünstigten dauerhaft gesichert wird.

§ 21 Ausgleichspflichtige Maßnahmen
¹Soweit Maßnahmen nach diesem Gesetz zu einer wirtschaftlich unzumutbaren, die Grenzen der Sozialbindung überschreitenden Belastung des Eigentums führen, ist ein angemessener Ausgleich in Geld zu gewähren, sofern und soweit die Belastung nicht in anderer Weise ausgeglichen werden kann. ²Über den Ausgleich ist durch die zuständige Behörde zugleich mit der belastenden Maßnahme zumindest dem Grunde nach zu entscheiden.

§ 22 Übertragungsanspruch der Freien und Hansestadt Hamburg
(1) ¹Die Freie und Hansestadt Hamburg kann von der durch eine ausgleichspflichtige Maßnahme nach diesem Gesetz betroffenen Eigentümerin oder von dem durch eine ausgleichspflichtige Maßnahme nach diesem Gesetz betroffenen Eigentümer die Übertragung des Eigentums verlangen, wenn der an die Eigentümerin oder den Eigentümer zu zahlende Ausgleich mehr als 50 vom Hundert des Wertes betragen würde. ²Die Übertragung eines Grundstücksteils kann verlangt werden, wenn die Teilung nach dem Baugesetzbuch zulässig ist. ³Der Übertragungsanspruch erlischt durch Verzicht der Eigentümerin oder des Eigentümers auf den Mehrbetrag.

(2) Kommt eine Einigung über die Übertragung nicht zustande, so kann das Eigentum durch Enteignung entzogen werden.

(3) Die Absätze 1 und 2 gelten entsprechend für Erbbauberechtigte.

§ 23 Verfahren
Soweit dieses Gesetz nichts anderes bestimmt, gelten die Vorschriften des Hamburgischen Enteignungsgesetzes in der Fassung vom 11. November 1980 (HmbGVBl. S. 305), zuletzt geändert am 18. Februar 2004 (HmbGVBl. S. 107), in der jeweils geltenden Fassung.

Abschnitt IV
Ausführungs- und Schlussbestimmungen

§ 24 Denkmäler, die der Religionsausübung dienen
(1) ¹Sollen Entscheidungen über Denkmäler getroffen werden, die unmittelbar gottesdienstlichen Zwecken der Kirchen oder anerkannter Religionsgemeinschaften dienen, beziehungsweise deren Gemeindeleben, so hat die zuständige Behörde die von der zuständigen kirchlichen Oberbehörde festgestellten liturgischen und gemeindlichen Belange und Erfordernisse zu berücksichtigen. ²Die Kirchen und die öffentlich-rechtlichen Religionsgemeinschaften sind im Verfahren zu beteiligen. ³Die zuständige Behörde entscheidet nur im Benehmen mit der zuständigen kirchlichen Oberbehörde.
(2) Der Vertrag zwischen der Freien und Hansestadt Hamburg und der Nordelbischen Evangelisch-Lutherischen Kirche (heutige Evangelisch-Lutherische Kirche in Norddeutschland) vom 29. November 2005 (HmbGVBl. 2006 S. 430) und der Vertrag zwischen dem Heiligen Stuhl und der Freien und Hansestadt Hamburg vom 29. November 2005 (HmbGVBl. 2006 S. 436) bleiben hiervon unberührt.

§ 25 Besichtigung von Denkmälern und Fundstellen
(1) ¹Bedienstete und Beauftragte der zuständigen Behörde dürfen nach vorheriger Benachrichtigung Grundstücke, zur Abwehr einer dringenden Gefahr für ein Denkmal auch Wohnungen, betreten, soweit es zur Durchführung dieses Gesetzes notwendig ist. ²Sie dürfen Denkmäler oder als Denkmal in Betracht kommende Sachen besichtigen und die notwendigen wissenschaftlichen Erfassungsmaßnahmen, insbesondere zur Inventarisation, durchführen. ³Im Falle einer Gefahr für das Denkmal ist das Betreten von Grundstücken auch ohne vorherige Benachrichtigung zulässig.
(2) Verfügungsberechtigte von Denkmälern oder als Denkmal in Betracht kommenden Sachen haben der zuständigen Behörde sowie ihren Beauftragten die zum Vollzug dieses Gesetzes erforderlichen Auskünfte zu erteilen.

§ 26 Einschränkung von Grundrechten
Durch dieses Gesetz wird das Grundrecht auf Unverletzlichkeit der Wohnung (Artikel 13 des Grundgesetzes) eingeschränkt.

§ 27 Ordnungswidrigkeiten
(1) Ordnungswidrig handelt, wer vorsätzlich oder fahrlässig
1. Maßnahmen, die nach § 8, § 9, § 14 oder § 16 der Genehmigung bedürfen, ohne Genehmigung oder abweichend von ihr durchführt oder durchführen lässt,
2. Anordnungen, Bedingungen oder Auflagen nach § 9 Absätze 3 und 4, § 10 Absatz 1, § 13 Absatz 1, § 14 oder § 17 Absätze 1 und 2 nicht erfüllt,
3. den ihr oder ihm nach § 7 Absatz 1, § 18 oder § 25 Absatz 2 obliegenden Pflichten nicht nachkommt,
4. im Falle des § 17 Absatz 4 die Arbeiten vorzeitig fortsetzt, ohne dass eine der dort genannten Zulässigkeitsvoraussetzungen vorliegt.
(2) Ordnungswidrig handelt, wer wider besseres Wissen unrichtige Angaben macht oder unrichtige Pläne oder Unterlagen vorlegt, um einen Verwaltungsakt nach diesem Gesetz zu erwirken oder zu verhindern.
(3) Ordnungswidrig handelt, wer einer ihm nach § 7 Absatz 4, § 12, § 14 Absatz 2 oder § 17 Absätze 1 bis 3 obliegenden Anzeigepflicht nicht nachkommt.
(4) Ordnungswidrig handelt, wer ein Denkmal im Sinne von § 4 fahrlässig zerstört.
(5) Die Ordnungswidrigkeit kann mit einer Geldbuße bis zu 500.000 Euro geahndet werden.
(6) Gegenstände, die durch ordnungswidrige Handlungen unter Verletzung des § 12 oder § 14 erlangt worden sind, können eingezogen werden.

§ 28 Fortführung der Denkmalliste
¹Das Verzeichnis der erkannten Denkmäler wird zusammen mit der bisherigen Denkmalliste als Denkmalliste fortgeführt. ²Es gilt als nach diesem Gesetz angelegt. ³Die in der bisherigen Denkmalliste eingetragenen beweglichen Denkmäler werden in das Verzeichnis der beweglichen Denkmäler überführt und gelten als rechtskräftig eingetragen. ⁴Die Denkmalliste wird spätestens bis zum 1. November 2013 öffentlich bekannt gemacht. ⁵Dies gilt nicht für Bodendenkmäler, soweit es für ihren Schutz erforderlich ist.

D6.I.1 Denkmalschutzgesetz Hamburg

§ 29 Verordnungsermächtigung
Der Senat wird ermächtigt, für Amtshandlungen nach diesem Gesetz Gebührenordnungen zu erlassen.

Anordnung zur Durchführung des Denkmalschutzgesetzes

Vom 8. April 2014
zuletzt geändert durch AO vom 25.9.2018 (Amtl. Anz. S. 2393)

(1) Zuständig für die Durchführung des Denkmalschutzgesetzes vom 5. April 2013 (HmbGVBl. S. 142) und der darauf gestützten Rechtsverordnungen in der jeweils geltenden Fassung ist, soweit dort oder nachstehend nichts anderes bestimmt ist, die Behörde für Kultur und Medien.
(2) Zuständige Behörde nach §§ 9 und 11 für das bezirksbezogene Denkmalschutzensemble Frank'sche Siedlung ist das Bezirksamt Hamburg-Nord.
(3) Zuständige Stelle für die Ausübung der Bodendenkmalpflege ist die Stiftung "Archäologisches Museum Hamburg und Stadtmuseum Harburg".

Hamburgisches Archivgesetz (HmbArchG)[1)]

Vom 21. Januar 1991 (HmbGVBl. S. 7)
(BS Hbg 224-8)
zuletzt geändert durch Art. 4 SicherheitsverbesserungsG vom 16. Juni 2005 (HmbGVBl. S. 233)

Der Senat verkündet das nachstehende von der Bürgerschaft beschlossene Gesetz:

§ 1 Aufgaben des Staatsarchivs

(1) [1]Das Staatsarchiv hat die Aufgaben, Unterlagen der Verfassungsorgane, Gerichte, Behörden und sonstigen Stellen der Freien und Hansestadt Hamburg und der ihrer Aufsicht unterstehenden juristischen Personen des öffentlichen Rechts auf ihre Archivwürdigkeit zu bewerten und die als archivwürdig festgestellten Teile als Archivgut zu übernehmen, zu verwahren, zu erhalten, zu erschließen und für die Benutzung bereitzustellen (Archivierung) sowie auszuwerten. [2]Diese Aufgaben erstrecken sich auch auf Unterlagen der Rechts- und Funktionsvorgänger der in Satz 1 genannten Stellen.
(2) Das Staatsarchiv kann auch Archivgut anderer Stellen archivieren, soweit daran ein öffentliches Interesse besteht.
(3) Das Staatsarchiv sammelt sonstiges Dokumentationsmaterial, soweit es als Ergänzung des Archivgutes dient.
(4) Das Staatsarchiv berät die in Absatz 1 genannten Stellen bei der Verwaltung und Sicherung ihrer Unterlagen im Hinblick auf die Archivierung nach Absatz 1 (Archivpflege) und kann diese Aufgabe auch gegenüber anderen Stellen (Absatz 2) wahrnehmen.
(5) Das Staatsarchiv wirkt durch eigene Beiträge an der Erforschung und Vermittlung der hamburgischen Geschichte mit.

§ 2 Archivgut

(1) [1]Archivgut sind alle archivwürdigen Unterlagen, die bei den in § 1 Absätze 1 und 2 genannten Stellen entstanden sind oder sich in ihrer Verfügungsbefugnis befinden. [2]Unterlagen sind alle Informationsträger wie Akten, Schriftstücke, Karteien, Dateien, Karten, Pläne, Bild-, Film-, Ton-, maschinenlesbare Datenträger und sonstige Aufzeichnungen, Drucksachen, Siegelstempel und sonstiges Dokumentationsgut einschließlich der Hilfsmittel zu ihrer Erschließung und Benutzung.
(2) [1]Archivwürdig sind Unterlagen, denen bleibender Wert für Gesetzgebung, Rechtsprechung, Verwaltung, Wissenschaft oder Forschung oder für die Sicherung berechtigter Belange von Einzelpersonen zukommt. [2]Über die Archivwürdigkeit von Unterlagen entscheidet das Staatsarchiv. [3]Die in § 1 Absatz 1 genannten Stellen unterstützen das Staatsarchiv bei dieser Entscheidung und machen ihm hierzu ihre Unterlagen zugänglich. [4]Archivwürdig sind auch Unterlagen, die aufgrund von anderen Rechtsvorschriften oder zur Rechtswahrung dauernd aufbewahrt werden müssen.
(3) Zwischenarchivgut sind die vom Staatsarchiv zur vorläufigen Aufbewahrung übernommenen Unterlagen, aus denen die archivwürdigen Teile noch nicht ausgewählt worden sind.

§ 3 Anbietung und Ablieferung

(1) [1]Die in § 1 Absatz 1 genannten Stellen sind verpflichtet, alle Unterlagen, die sie zur Erfüllung ihrer Aufgaben nicht mehr benötigen, fortlaufend auszusondern, dem Staatsarchiv anzubieten und ihm nach Feststellung der Archivwürdigkeit abzuliefern. [2]Unterlagen sollen spätestens 30 Jahre nach ihrer endgültigen Entstehung ausgesondert und angeboten werden, soweit sie nicht noch nachweislich im Geschäftsgang erforderlich sind oder soweit nicht Rechtsvorschriften andere Fristen bestimmen.
(2) [1]Anzubieten und bei festgestellter Archivwürdigkeit abzuliefern sind auch Unterlagen, die
1. personenbezogene Daten enthalten, die gesperrt sind oder die nach einer Rechtsvorschrift gelöscht werden müssten oder gelöscht werden könnten,
2. einem Berufs- oder besonderen Amtsgeheimnis oder sonstigen Rechtsvorschriften über Geheimhaltung unterliegen.

[2]Von der Anbietungspflicht ausgenommen bleiben Unterlagen, deren Offenbarung gegen das Brief-, Post- oder Fernmeldegeheimnis oder die Unverletzlichkeit der Wohnung verstoßen würde, sowie personenbezogene Daten, deren Speicherung unzulässig war oder die nach dienst- oder arbeitsrechtlichen Vorschriften zu löschen oder zu tilgen sind.

---

1) Inkrafttreten gem. Art. 54 der Verfassung der Freien und Hansestadt Hamburg v. 6.6.1952 (HmGVBl. S. 117) am **30.1.1991**.

(3) Daten verarbeitende Stellen und Staatsarchiv haben bei der Anbietung, Auswahl und Übernahme von Unterlagen mit personenbezogenen Daten, insbesondere solchen, die besonderen Geheimhaltungsvorschriften unterliegen, die schutzwürdigen Interessen Dritter zu berücksichtigen und die Datensicherung zu gewährleisten.
(4) Durch Vereinbarung zwischen dem Staatsarchiv und den in § 1 Absatz 1 genannten Stellen kann
1. auf die Anbietung von Unterlagen von offensichtlich geringer Bedeutung verzichtet werden,
2. der Umfang der anzubietenden gleichförmigen Unterlagen, die in großer Zahl anfallen, im Einzelnen festgelegt werden

und muss
3. die Auswahl der anzubietenden maschinenlesbar gespeicherten Informationen einschließlich der Form der Datenübermittlung im Einzelnen festgesetzt werden.
(5) [1]Eine Vernichtung oder Löschung von Unterlagen ist nur nach der Verneinung der Archivwürdigkeit zulässig; Absatz 2 Satz 2 bleibt unberührt. [2]Entscheidet das Staatsarchiv nicht innerhalb von sechs Monaten über die Archivwürdigkeit angebotener Unterlagen, können sie vernichtet oder gelöscht werden. [3]Für maschinenlesbare Unterlagen gilt eine Frist von vier Monaten.
(6) [1]Archivwürdige Unterlagen können bereits vor Ablauf der durch Rechts- oder Verwaltungsvorschriften bestimmten Aufbewahrungsfristen vom Staatsarchiv übernommen werden. [2]Die Pflicht zur Aufbewahrung wird durch das Staatsarchiv erfüllt. [3]Bis zum Ablauf der Aufbewahrungsfrist bleibt die abgebende Stelle Daten verarbeitende Stelle im Sinne des Hamburgischen Datenschutzgesetzes (HmbDSG) vom 5. Juli 1990 (Hamburgisches Gesetz- und Verordnungsblatt Seiten 133, 165, 226), zuletzt geändert am 30. Januar 2001 (Hamburgisches Gesetz- und Verordnungsblatt Seite 9).
(7) Für juristische Personen des öffentlichen Rechts, die der Aufsicht der Freien und Hansestadt Hamburg unterstehen, besteht die Pflicht zur Anbietung und Ablieferung an das Staatsarchiv nur dann, wenn sie kein eigenes Archiv unterhalten, das archivfachlichen Anforderungen genügt.
(8) Die Bürgerschaft entscheidet in eigener Zuständigkeit, ob bei ihr entstandene Unterlagen, die zur Erfüllung der Aufgaben nicht mehr benötigt werden, von ihr selbst archiviert oder dem Staatsarchiv zur Übernahme angeboten werden.

§ 4 Verwaltung des Archivguts
(1) [1]Das Staatsarchiv stellt die ordnungs- und sachgemäße Aufbewahrung und Benutzbarkeit des Archivguts und seinen Schutz vor Beschädigung, Vernichtung und unbefugter Benutzung sicher. [2]Es hat von der Übernahme an ebenso wie die abgebende Stelle die schutzwürdigen Interessen Dritter zu berücksichtigen; insbesondere hat es bei Unterlagen mit personenbezogenen Daten, die Vorschriften über die Verarbeitung und Sicherung dieser Unterlagen zu beachten, die für die abgebende Stelle gelten.
(2) Aufgrund einer schriftlichen Vereinbarung mit dem Staatsarchiv kann staatliches Archivgut bei einer anderen Stelle verwahrt werden, wenn dafür ein fachlicher Grund gegeben ist, den archivfachlichen Anforderungen genügt wird und die Einhaltung bestehender Rechtsvorschriften, insbesondere des Datenschutzes, gewährleistet ist.
(3) Soweit das Staatsarchiv gemäß § 1 Absatz 2 Archivgut privater Herkunft archiviert, kann es mit den Eigentümern Vereinbarungen treffen, die einen besonderen Umgang mit dem Archivgut entsprechend den Interessen der Eigentümer regeln.
(4) Die Verknüpfung personenbezogener Daten durch das Staatsarchiv ist vor Ablauf der in § 5 genannten Schutzfristen zulässig, wenn schutzwürdige Interessen Betroffener nicht beeinträchtigt werden.
(5) Soweit nicht Rechtsvorschriften über Löschung und Vernichtung personenbezogener Unterlagen zur Anwendung kommen, sind die nichtarchivwürdigen Unterlagen staatlichen Zwischenarchivguts so lange aufzubewahren, bis die abgebende Stelle oder deren Rechtsnachfolger sie zur Vernichtung freigegeben hat; erfolgt die Freigabe zur Vernichtung nicht innerhalb von 20 Jahren nach Übernahme, so können sie zurückgegeben werden.

§ 5 Benutzung des Archivguts
(1) Jeder hat das Recht, staatliches Archivgut auf Antrag zu amtlichen, wissenschaftlichen, heimatkundlichen oder publizistischen Zwecken sowie zur Wahrnehmung berechtigter persönlicher Interes-

D6.II.1 Hamburgisches Archivgesetz

sen zu benutzen, soweit in diesem Gesetz oder aufgrund dieses Gesetzes nichts anderes bestimmt wird und andere Gesetze nicht entgegenstehen.

(2) ¹Für die Benutzung gelten folgende Schutzvorschriften:
1. Soweit durch Rechtsvorschriften keine anderen Fristen bestimmt sind, ist die Benutzung des Archivguts mit Ablauf des 30. Jahres nach seiner endgültigen Entstehung zulässig. Diese Schutzfrist gilt nicht für Archivgut, das von vornherein zur Veröffentlichung bestimmt war.
2. Archivgut, das sich nach seiner Zweckbestimmung oder nach seinem wesentlichen Inhalt auf eine natürliche Person bezieht (personenbezogenes Archivgut), darf erst 10 Jahre nach dem Tod der Betroffenen benutzt werden. Ist das Todesjahr nicht oder nur mit unvertretbarem Aufwand festzustellen, endet die Schutzfrist 90 Jahre nach der Geburt der Betroffenen. Sind weder Todesjahr noch Geburtsjahr mit vertretbarem Aufwand festzustellen, endet die Schutzfrist für personenbezogenes Archivgut 60 Jahre nach seiner endgültigen Entstehung.
3. Unterliegt Archivgut besonderen Geheimhaltungsvorschriften, ist die Benutzung erst mit Ablauf des 60. Jahres nach seiner endgültigen Entstehung zulässig.
4. Für Archivgut, das Rechtsvorschriften des Bundes über Geheimhaltung im Sinne der §§ 8, 10 und 11 des Bundesarchivgesetzes[1)] unterliegt, gelten die Schutzfristen des § 5 des Bundesarchivgesetzes.
5. Die Schutzfristen für personenbezogenes Archivgut gelten nicht für Archivgut, das die Tätigkeit von Personen dokumentiert, soweit sie in Ausübung eines öffentlichen Amtes gehandelt haben und nicht selbst Betroffene sind. Hat die Tätigkeit in personenbezogenem Archivgut ihren Niederschlag gefunden, sind die schutzwürdigen Interessen Dritter angemessen zu berücksichtigen.

²Vor Ablauf von Schutzfristen kann das Staatsarchiv Auskunft aus dem Archivgut erteilen, soweit Absatz 5 im Übrigen nicht entgegensteht.

(3) Die in § 1 Absatz 1 genannten Stellen können die Schutzfristen für bestimmtes, bei ihnen entstandenes Archivgut um höchstens 20 Jahre verlängern, soweit dies aus Gründen des Gemeinwohls geboten ist.

(4) ¹Für einzelne Benutzungen oder Teile von Archivgut können die Schutzfristen verkürzt werden, soweit Absatz 5 im Übrigen nicht entgegensteht. ²Die Verkürzung bedarf im Falle des Absatzes 3 der Zustimmung der Stelle, bei der das Archivgut entstanden ist. ³Die Verkürzung der Schutzfristen für personenbezogenes Archivgut ist nur mit Einwilligung der Betroffenen oder ihrer Rechtsnachfolger zulässig oder wenn die Benutzung für ein wissenschaftliches Forschungsvorhaben oder zur Wahrnehmung berechtigter Belange von Personen oder Stellen notwendig ist und die schutzwürdigen Interessen Betroffener oder Dritter durch geeignete Maßnahmen angemessen berücksichtigt werden.

(5) ¹Die Benutzung ist durch das Staatsarchiv einzuschränken oder zu versagen, wenn
1. Grund zu der Annahme besteht, dass dem Wohl der Bundesrepublik Deutschland oder eines ihrer Länder wesentliche Nachteile erwachsen, oder
2. Grund zu der Annahme besteht, dass schutzwürdige Interessen Dritter beeinträchtigt werden, oder
3. der Erhaltungszustand des Archivguts entgegensteht oder
4. ein unverhältnismäßiger Verwaltungsaufwand entsteht oder
5. die Geheimhaltungspflicht nach § 203 Absätze 1 bis 3 des Strafgesetzbuches oder anderer Rechtsvorschriften über Geheimhaltung verletzt würden.

²Gesetzliche Informationsrechte und Vereinbarungen mit Eigentümern privaten Archivguts bleiben unberührt.

(6) Die Benutzung von Archivgut, das gemäß § 2 Absatz 3 Satz 1 des Bundesarchivgesetzes dem Staatsarchiv von Stellen des Bundes übergeben worden ist, richtet sich nach den Bestimmungen des Bundesarchivgesetzes.

(7) ¹Für Zwischenarchivgut bleibt die abgebende Stelle bis zum Ende der vorläufigen Aufbewahrung Daten verarbeitende Stelle im Sinne des Hamburgischen Datenschutzgesetzes. ²Im Übrigen richtet sich die Benutzung von Zwischenarchivgut nach den Bestimmungen dieses Gesetzes.

(8) ¹Einer Benutzung durch die Stellen, bei denen das Archivgut entstanden ist, stehen die Schutzfristen nur entgegen, wenn die Aufbewahrung im Staatsarchiv gesetzlich vorgeschriebene Sperrung, Ver-

---

1) Das Bundesarchivgesetz ist abgedruckt als Nr. C.III.1.

nichtung oder Löschung ersetzt. ²Ansonsten haben abgebende Stellen das Recht, Archivgut, das aus ihren Unterlagen ins Staatsarchiv gelangt ist, zu benutzen und auszuleihen.

(9) Das Staatsarchiv wird ermächtigt, durch Verwaltungsvorschrift (Benutzungsordnung)[1]) das Nähere über die Benutzung des Archivguts, insbesondere über das Antrags- und Genehmigungsverfahren, über die Vorlage von Archivgut, über die Sorgfaltspflicht bei der Benutzung und über die Herstellung von Reproduktionen zu regeln.

(10) Sofern die Bürgerschaft und die in § 3 Absatz 7 genannten Stellen eigene Archive unterhalten, regeln sie die Einzelheiten der Benutzung in eigener Zuständigkeit unter Beachtung der dafür anwendbaren Bestimmungen dieses Gesetzes.

(11) Die Freie und Hansestadt Hamburg hat Anspruch auf ein dem Staatsarchiv unentgeltlich und unaufgefordert zu überlassendes Belegexemplar von jeder im Druck, maschinenschriftlich oder auf andere Weise vervielfältigten Arbeit, für die die Auswertung des vom Staatsarchiv verwahrten Archivgutes von substantieller Bedeutung war.

§ 6 Auskunft und Gegendarstellung

(1) Das Recht des Betroffenen auf Auskunft (§ 18 HmbDSG) kann auch durch Gewährung von Einsicht in Archivgut erfüllt werden.

(2) Wird die Unrichtigkeit personenbezogener Angaben festgestellt, so ist dies berichtigend im Archivgut zu vermerken oder auf sonstige Weise so festzuhalten, dass der Hinweis bei einer Benutzung des Archivgutes nicht übersehen werden kann.

(3) Das Staatsarchiv ist verpflichtet, dem Archivgut eine Gegendarstellung des Betroffenen oder eines Hinterbliebenen hinzuzufügen, wenn die Richtigkeit von Angaben zur Person des Betroffenen bestritten und ein berechtigtes Interesse an der Gegendarstellung glaubhaft gemacht wird.

(4) Die Bestimmungen der Absätze 1 bis 3 gelten nur für Archivgut, für das das Staatsarchiv Daten verarbeitende Stelle im Sinne des Hamburgischen Datenschutzgesetzes ist.

§ 7 Ausnahmen vom Geltungsbereich

Dieses Gesetz gilt nicht für die öffentlich-rechtlichen Kreditinstitute.

---

1) Siehe dazu die Benutzungsordnung Staatsarchiv Hamburg, abgedruckt als Nr. D6.II.1a.

D6.II.1a Benutzungsordnung Staatsarchiv Hamburg

Verwaltungsvorschrift über die Benutzung von Archivgut im Staatsarchiv der Freien und Hansestadt Hamburg (Benutzungsordnung)

Vom 1. Juni 2004

Mitteilungen für die Verwaltung Nr. 6 vom 30. Juni 2004, S. 73

Auf Grund von § 5 Abs. 9 des Hamburgischen Archivgesetzes (HmbArchG) vom 21. Januar 1991 (Hamburgisches Gesetz- und Verordnungsblatt, S. 7), zuletzt geändert am 30. Januar 2001 (Hamburgisches Gesetz- und Verordnungsblatt, S. 16), wird bestimmt.

1. Geltungsbereich
Diese Benutzungsordnung regelt die Benutzung des vom Staatsarchiv der Freien und Hansestadt Hamburg (Staatsarchiv) verwalteten Archivguts (§ 2 Abs. 1 HmbArchG). Sie gilt auch für die Benutzung von Reproduktionen des Archivguts und entsprechend für die Benutzung der Unterlagen nach § 2 Abs. 3 HmbArchG (Zwischenarchivgut) und § 3 Abs. 6 HmbArchG (Vorarchivgut), der Findhilfsmittel und des Bibliotheksguts aus der Bibliothek des Staatsarchivs.

2. Arten der Benutzung
(1) Die Benutzung erfolgt grundsätzlich durch persönliche Einsichtnahme im Lesesaal des Staatsarchivs (Ziffer 6).
(2) Die Benutzung kann außerdem erfolgen durch
- die Abgabe von Reproduktionen des Archivguts (Ziffer 7),
- die Versendung des Archivgutes zur Einsichtnahme an ein anderes hauptamtlich geführtes Archiv im Inland (Ziffer 8),
- durch Ausleihe zu Ausstellungszwecken (Ziffer 9),
- die Ausleihe an öffentliche Stellen (Ziffer 10).

Über die Art der Benutzung entscheidet das Staatsarchiv.

3. Archivfachliche Beratung
Die Benutzenden werden archivfachlich beraten. Die Beratung bezieht sich vornehmlich auf die Möglichkeiten des Zugangs zum Archivgut. Ein Anspruch auf weitergehende Unterstützung (z.B. Auswertung von Findhilfsmitteln und Archivgut, Hilfe beim Lesen älterer Texte) besteht nicht.

4. Genehmigung der Benutzung
(1) Zwischen dem Staatsarchiv und den Benutzenden wird ein öffentlich-rechtliches Benutzungsverhältnis begründet.
(2) Die Benutzung ist beim Staatsarchiv grundsätzlich schriftlich unter Verwendung des hierfür bestimmten Vordruckes (Anlage 1) zu beantragen. Dabei sind insbesondere das Benutzungsvorhaben und der Benutzungszweck anzugeben. Im Falle der Vertretung einer anderen Person oder einer Einrichtung ist der schriftliche Nachweis der Vertretungsmacht beizufügen.
(3) Vor Einsichtnahme in Archivgut müssen minderjährige Antragstellerinnen und Antragsteller die Einwilligungserklärung ihres gesetzlichen Vertreters vorlegen. Für Schülergruppen stellt die betreuende Lehrkraft einen Sammelantrag.
(4) Der Antrag gilt nur für das angegebene Benutzungsvorhaben und den angegebenen Benutzungszweck.
(5) Über den Antrag entscheidet das Staatsarchiv. Die Genehmigung des Antrags kann mit Nebenbestimmungen verbunden werden (§ 5 Abs. 5 HmbArchG, § 36 Hamburgisches Verwaltungsverfahrensgesetz [HmbVwVfG]).

5. Benutzung vor Ablauf der Schutzfristen
(1) Für Archivgut, das den Schutzfristen nach § 5 HmbArchG unterliegt, ist die Benutzung gesondert schriftlich unter Verwendung des hierfür bestimmten Vordruckes zu beantragen (Anlage 2).
(2) Über die im Benutzungsantrag (Ziffer 4) genannten Angaben hinaus hat die Antragstellerin bzw. der Antragsteller entweder die schriftliche Einwilligungserklärung der Personen, auf die sich die Unterlagen beziehen, oder ihrer Rechtsnachfolger beizufügen oder im Antrag zu begründen, warum die

Einsichtnahme für ein wissenschaftliches Forschungsvorhaben oder zur Wahrnehmung berechtigter Belange notwendig ist (§ 5 Abs. 4 HmbArchG).
Wird die Benutzung von Archivgut, das gemäß § 2 Abs. 3 Satz 1 Bundesarchivgesetz (BArchG) von Stellen des Bundes dem Staatsarchiv abgeliefert worden ist, beantragt, hat die Antragstellerin bzw. der Antragsteller entweder die schriftliche Einwilligungserklärung der Personen, auf die sich die Unterlagen beziehen, beizufügen oder im Antrag zu begründen, warum die Benutzung für ein wissenschaftliches Forschungsvorhaben oder zur Wahrnehmung berechtigter Belange unerlässlich ist (§ 5 Abs. 5 BArchG).
Auf Verlangen des Staatsarchivs sind dem Antrag ergänzende Angaben und Unterlagen, bei Hochschularbeiten insbesondere Stellungnahmen der wissenschaftlich Betreuenden, beizufügen.
(3) Über den Antrag entscheidet das Staatsarchiv. Die Genehmigung des Antrags kann mit Nebenbestimmungen verbunden werden (§ 36 HmbVwVfG).
(4) Findhilfsmittel, die selbst den Schutzfristen nach § 5 HmbArchG unterliegen, können Benutzenden ohne einen besonderen Antrag (Absatz 1) vorgelegt werden, wenn die Einsichtnahme für ein wissenschaftliches Forschungsvorhaben notwendig ist. Um die schutzwürdigen Interessen Betroffener und Dritter angemessen zu berücksichtigen, müssen die Benutzenden die aus den Findhilfsmitteln erhobenen Einzelangaben zu natürlichen Personen anonymisieren, sobald es nach dem Zweck der Benutzung möglich ist. Die Benutzenden dürfen die erhobenen Einzelangaben nicht an Dritte weitergeben und müssen sie vor unbefugter Einnahme durch Dritte schützen

6. Benutzung in den Räumen des Staatsarchivs
(1) Das Archivgut wird grundsätzlich im Lesesaal während der Öffnungszeiten vorgelegt. Es ist den Benutzenden untersagt, Archivgut aus dem Lesesaal zu entfernen. Die Öffnungszeiten des Lesesaals sowie die Bestell- und Ausgabezeiten werden durch Aushang und auf andere geeignete Weise bekannt gegeben. Das Staatsarchiv kann die Anzahl der vorzulegenden Archivguteinheiten begrenzen.
(2) Die Benutzenden melden sich an jedem Benutzungstag bei der Aufsicht an und auch wieder ab.
(3) Das vorgelegte Archivgut ist mit größter Sorgfalt zu behandeln. Insbesondere ist es nicht gestattet,
- den Ordnungszustand zu verändern,
- Bestandteile zu entfernen,
- Markierungen und Anmerkungen anzubringen oder vorhandene zu tilgen,
- Archivgut als Schreib- oder Durchzeichnungsunterlage zu verwenden oder sich darauf zu stützen.

Die Anweisungen der Aufsicht müssen beachtet werden.
(4) Das Archivgut kann in Form von Reproduktionen vorgelegt werden, wenn dies zu seinem Schutz erforderlich ist und der Zweck der Benutzung durch die Auswertung der Reproduktionen zu erreichen ist. Über die Art der Vorlage entscheidet das Staatsarchiv.
(5) Die Verwendung technischer Geräte bedarf der Genehmigung durch die Lesesaalaufsicht. Diese Genehmigung kann widerrufen werden, insbesondere wenn Archivgut gefährdet oder der Lesesaalbetrieb beeinträchtigt wird.
(6) Mäntel, Taschen, Schirme u.ä. dürfen nicht mit in den Lesesaal gebracht werden.
(7) Das Staatsarchiv kann auch die Benutzung von Archivgut ermöglichen, das von anderen Archiven oder sonstigen Stellen zur Benutzung durch Dritte übersandt wurde. Soweit die versendende Stelle nichts anderes verfügt hat, gelten die Bestimmungen dieser Benutzungsordnung entsprechend.

7. Reproduktionen
(1) Auf Reproduktionen besteht kein Anspruch.
(2) Reproduktionen können auf Antrag und auf Kosten der Benutzenden vom Staatsarchiv oder einer von ihm beauftragten Stelle angefertigt werden. Das Staatsarchiv kann den Benutzenden genehmigen, die Reproduktionen in den Räumen des Staatsarchivs selbst herzustellen.
(3) Reproduktionen von Archivgut dürfen nur hergestellt werden, wenn das Staatsarchiv eine Gefährdung oder Beschädigung des Archivguts ausschließt. Es entscheidet über die jeweils geeigneten Reproduktionsverfahren.
(4) Reproduktionen dürfen nur unter Angabe der Herkunft aus dem Staatsarchiv und der von ihm festgelegten Signatur veröffentlicht, vervielfältigt oder an Dritte weitergegeben werden. Soweit das Staatsarchiv über Nutzungsrechte verfügt, dürfen Reproduktionen nur mit vorheriger Zustimmung des Staatsarchivs, nur zu dem angegebenen Zweck und unter Angabe der Herkunft aus dem Staatsarchiv

D6.II.1a Benutzungsordnung Staatsarchiv Hamburg 702

und der von ihm festgelegten Signatur veröffentlicht, vervielfältigt oder an Dritte weitergegeben werden.

(5) Werden Reproduktionen von Archivgut, das noch den Schutzfristen unterliegt, beantragt, müssen die Benutzenden dem Antrag eine Liste der zu reproduzierenden Schriftstücke beifügen. Sofern die Schutzfristen für das in Rede stehende Archivgut noch nicht verkürzt wurden, ist auch der Antrag i.S.d. Ziffer 5 (1) zu stellen.

Die Genehmigung des Antrags kann mit Nebenbestimmungen verbunden werden (§ 36 HmbVwVfG).

8. Versendung von Archivgut

Auf die Versendung von Archivgut besteht kein Anspruch. Die Versendung erfolgt nur in begründeten Ausnahmefällen, wenn der Benutzungszweck nicht durch Reproduktionen erreicht werden kann und die Benutzung in einem hauptamtlich verwalteten Archiv in der Bundesrepublik Deutschland erfolgt und dieses sich verpflichtet,

- das Archivgut der Antragstellerin oder dem Antragsteller nur in den Diensträumen unter ständiger fachlicher Aufsicht vorzulegen,
- es diebstahl- und feuersicher zu verwahren,
- keine Kopien oder Reproduktionen ohne vorherige Zustimmung des Staatsarchivs anzufertigen,
- das Archivgut nach Ablauf der vom Staatsarchiv bestimmten Ausleihfrist in der von ihm bestimmten Versendungsart zurückzusenden.

Archivgut, das Schutzfristen unterliegt, wird nicht versandt.

9. Ausleihe zu Ausstellungszwecken

Archivgut, das noch den Schutzfristen unterliegt, darf nicht ausgeliehen werden. Eine Ausleihe ist zudem nur möglich, wenn gewährleistet ist, dass das ausgeliehene Archivgut wirksam vor Verlust, Beschädigung und unbefugter Nutzung geschützt wird und der Ausstellungszweck nicht durch Reproduktionen erreicht werden kann. Das Staatsarchiv kann zur Sicherung des Archivguts Auflagen erteilen.

10. Benutzung durch eine öffentliche Stelle

(1) Soweit die Ausleihe ihre Grundlage nicht in einer gesetzlichen Bestimmung findet, besteht kein Anspruch auf Ausleihe.

(2) Wird das Archivgut einer öffentlichen Stelle ausgeliehen, ist diese verpflichtet, es vor Verlust, Beschädigung und unbefugter Nutzung zu schützen und es innerhalb eines angemessenen Zeitraums zurückzugeben. Die abgebende Stelle hat zudem sicherzustellen, dass der Ordnungszustand des Archivguts nicht verändert und insbesondere keine Unterlagen entfernt oder hinzugefügt werden.

11. Schlussbestimmungen

Diese Benutzungsordnung tritt am 1. Juni 2004 in Kraft. Die Benutzungsordnung vom 10. September 1993 wird aufgehoben.

Anordnung über die Zuständigkeiten auf dem Gebiet des Kulturgutschutzes vom 7. November 2017

Amtl. Anz. 2017, S. 1929

Auf Grund von § 3 Absatz 1 Satz 2 des Kulturgutschutzgesetzes (KGSG) vom 31. Juli 2016 (BGBl. I S. 1914), geändert am 13. April 2017 (BGBl. I S. 872, 889), und § 36 Absatz 2 Satz 1 des Gesetzes über Ordnungswidrigkeiten in der Fassung vom 19. Februar 1987 (BGBl. I S. 603), zuletzt geändert am 5. Juli 2017 (BGBl. I S. 2208, 2216), wird bestimmt:

I.
Zuständige Behörde nach Artikel 2 Absatz 2 Satz 1 Buchstaben a und b der Verordnung (EG) Nr. 116/2009 des Rates vom 18. Dezember 2008 über die Ausfuhr von Kulturgütern (ABl. EG Nr. L 39 S. 1) ist

die Behörde für Kultur und Medien.

II.
(1) Zuständig für die Durchführung des KGSG ist, soweit dort oder nachstehend nicht etwas anderes bestimmt ist,

die Behörde für Kultur und Medien.

(2) Ihr werden die Aufgaben der obersten Landesbehörde nach
1. § 4 Absatz 2 KGSG,
2. § 7 Absatz 1 Satz 1 und Absatz 3 Satz 1 KGSG,
3. § 8 Absatz 1, Absatz 2 Satz 2 und Absatz 3 KGSG,
4. § 9 Absatz 1 Satz 1, Absatz 2 Satz 2 und Absatz 3 KGSG,
5. § 10 Absätze 1 und 2, Absatz 3 Satz 1, Absatz 4 und Absatz 7 Satz 1 KGSG,
6. § 11 Absatz 2 Satz 2 KGSG,
7. § 12 Absatz 2 KGSG,
8. § 13 Absätze 1 und 3 KGSG,
9. § 14 Absatz 1 Satz 2, Absatz 2 Satz 1, Absatz 3 Satz 2, Absatz 4 und Absatz 6 Sätze 1 und 3 KGSG,
10. § 15 Absatz 1 Satz 1 und Absatz 2 KGSG,
11. § 17 Absatz 1 KGSG,
12. § 19 Absatz 1 Satz 1 und Absatz 3 KGSG,
13. § 22 Absatz 3 Sätze 1 und 3 KGSG,
14. § 23 Absatz 4 Sätze 2 und 4, Absatz 5 Satz 2, Absatz 6 Sätze 1 und 2 und Absatz 9 Satz 1 KGSG,
15. § 24 Absatz 6 Satz 1 und Absatz 7 KGSG,
16. § 25 Absatz 1 Satz 1, Absatz 4 Satz 2 und Absatz 5 KGSG,
17. § 26 Absatz 1 KGSG,
18. § 27 Absatz 1 und Absatz 2 Satz 2 KGSG,
19. § 69 Absatz 1 Satz 1 KGSG,
20. § 70 Absatz 2 KGSG,
21. § 73 Absatz 1 Satz 1 und Absatz 2 Satz 1 KGSG,
22. § 74 Absatz 1 Satz 1 KGSG und
23. § 75 Absatz 1 Satz 1 KGSG

übertragen.

III.
Zuständig für die Verfolgung und Ahndung von Ordnungswidrigkeiten sind in den Fällen des § 84 Absatz 1 Nummern 2 bis 4 KGSG

die Bezirksämter.

IV.
Fachbehörde nach §§ 42 und 44 bis 46 des Bezirksverwaltungsgesetzes vom 6. Juli 2006 (HmbGVBl. S. 404, 452), zuletzt geändert am 4. April 2017 (HmbGVBl. S. 92, 94), in der jeweils geltenden Fassung ist

die Behörde für Kultur und Medien.

D6.III.1 Kulturgutschutz-Zuständigkeitsanordnung

V.
Die Anordnung über die Zuständigkeiten auf dem Gebiet des Kulturgutschutzes vom 8. Dezember 2009 (Amtl. Anz. S. 2425) in der geltenden Fassung wird aufgehoben.

Verfassung des Landes Hessen

Vom 1. Dezember 1946[1] (GVBl. I S. 229, ber. GVBl. 1947 S. 106 u. GVBl. 1948 S. 68)
(FFN 10-1)
zuletzt geändert durch ErgänzungsG vom 12. Dezember 2018 (GVBl. S. 752)
– Auszug –

Erster Hauptteil
Die Rechte des Menschen

V.
Erziehung, Bildung und Denkmalschutz

Artikel 62 [Denkmal- und Landschaftsschutz]
[1]Die Denkmäler der Kunst, der Geschichte und Kultur sowie die Landschaft genießen den Schutz und die Pflege des Staates und der Gemeinden. [2]Sie wachen im Rahmen besonderer Gesetze über die künstlerische Gestaltung beim Wiederaufbau der deutschen Städte, Dörfer und Siedlungen.

---

[1] Die Verfassung wurde vorbereitet durch die am 30.6.1946 gewählte Verfassungsberatende Landesversammlung (vgl. WahlG v. 16.5.1946, GVBl. S. 139), auf die die Aufgaben des nach dem StaatsgrundG v. 22.11.1945 (GVBl. S. 23) von dem Ministerpräsidenten berufenen beratenden Landesausschusses gemäß G v. 18.6.1946 (GVBl. S. 167) übertragen wurden. Die Verfassung wurde am 29.10.1946 durch die Verfassungsberatende Landesversammlung beschlossen und in der Volksabstimmung am 1.12.1946 (vgl. G v. 14.10.1946, GVBl. S. 177, und G v. 30.10.1946, GVBl. S. 187) angenommen. Gemäß Art. 160 HV ist die Verfassung mit ihrer Annahme durch das Volk, also am **1.12.1946**, in Kraft getreten. Verkündet wurde sie am 11.12.1946 in der Nr. 34/35 des GVBl. mit Ausgabetag v. 18.12.1946.

D7.I.1 Hessisches Denkmalschutzgesetz

Hessisches Denkmalschutzgesetz (HDSchG)

Vom 28. November 2016 (GVBl. S. 211)
(FFN 76-17)

Inhaltsübersicht

§ 1	Aufgaben des Denkmalschutzes und der Denkmalpflege		§ 16	Auskunfts- und Duldungspflichten
§ 2	Begriffsbestimmung		§ 17	Zugang zu Kulturdenkmälern
§ 3	UNESCO-Welterbe		§ 18	Genehmigungspflichtige Maßnahmen
§ 4	Denkmalschutzbehörden		§ 19	Anzeigepflichtige Maßnahmen
§ 5	Denkmalfachbehörde		§ 20	Genehmigungsverfahren
§ 6	Landesdenkmalrat		§ 21	Funde
§ 7	Denkmalbeirat und ehrenamtliche Denkmalpflege		§ 22	Nachforschungen
			§ 23	Grabungsschutzgebiete
§ 8	Zuständigkeiten der Denkmalschutzbehörden		§ 24	Nutzungsbeschränkungen
			§ 25	Schatzregal
§ 9	Maßnahmen der Denkmalschutzbehörden		§ 26	Enteignung
§ 10	Denkmalverzeichnis		§ 27	Sonstige entschädigungspflichtige Maßnahmen
§ 11	Unbewegliche Kulturdenkmäler		§ 28	Bußgeldbestimmungen
§ 12	Bewegliche Kulturdenkmäler		§ 29	Staatskirchenverträge
§ 13	Erhaltungspflicht		§ 30	Aufhebung bisherigen Rechts
§ 14	Durchsetzung der Erhaltung		§ 31	Rechtsverordnungen
§ 15	Nutzung von Kulturdenkmälern		§ 32	Inkrafttreten

§ 1 Aufgaben des Denkmalschutzes und der Denkmalpflege

(1) Es ist die Aufgabe von Denkmalschutz und Denkmalpflege, die Kulturdenkmäler als Quellen und Zeugnisse menschlicher Geschichte und Entwicklung nach Maßgabe dieses Gesetzes zu schützen und zu erhalten sowie darauf hinzuwirken, dass sie in die städtebauliche Entwicklung, Raumordnung und den Erhalt der historisch gewachsenen Kulturlandschaft einbezogen werden.

(2) Bei der Erfüllung dieser Aufgaben wirken im Rahmen ihrer Leistungsfähigkeit das Land, die Gemeinden, die Gemeindeverbände, Ehrenamtliche in der Denkmalpflege sowie Eigentümerinnen, Eigentümer, Besitzerinnen und Besitzer von Kulturdenkmälern zusammen.

§ 2 Begriffsbestimmung

(1) Kulturdenkmäler im Sinne dieses Gesetzes sind bewegliche und unbewegliche Sachen, Sachgesamtheiten und Sachteile einschließlich Grünanlagen, an deren Erhalt aus künstlerischen, wissenschaftlichen, technischen, geschichtlichen oder städtebaulichen Gründen ein öffentliches Interesse besteht.

(2) [1]Bodendenkmäler sind Kulturdenkmäler, die Zeugnisse menschlichen, tierischen oder pflanzlichen Lebens von wissenschaftlichem Wert darstellen und die im Boden verborgen sind oder waren oder aus urgeschichtlicher Zeit stammen. [2]Die Oberste Denkmalschutzbehörde bestimmt durch Rechtsverordnung den Umfang, in dem Fossilien als Bodendenkmäler geschützt werden sollen. [3]Die Vorschriften des Naturschutzrechts bleiben unberührt.

(3) [1]Gesamtanlagen sind Kulturdenkmäler, die aus baulichen Anlagen einschließlich der mit ihnen verbundenen Grün-, Frei- und Wasserflächen bestehen und an deren Erhalt im Ganzen aus künstlerischen oder geschichtlichen Gründen ein öffentliches Interesse besteht. [2]Nicht erforderlich ist, dass jeder einzelne Teil der Gesamtanlage ein Kulturdenkmal darstellt.

(4) [1]Kulturdenkmäler, die sachenrechtlich unbeweglich sind, sind unbewegliche Kulturdenkmäler. [2]Kulturdenkmäler, die sachenrechtlich beweglich sind, sind bewegliche Kulturdenkmäler.

(5) Kulturdenkmäler sind auch die nach dem Kulturgutschutzgesetz vom 31. Juli 2016 (BGBl. I S. 1914) im hessischen „Verzeichnis national wertvollen Kulturgutes" eingetragenen Kulturgüter.

(6) Denkmalschutz ist hoheitliches Handeln, Denkmalpflege die Gesamtheit der staatlichen Hilfen für Eigentümerinnen und Eigentümer von Kulturdenkmälern und das Werben für Erhalt und die Pflege der Kulturdenkmäler.

§ 3 UNESCO-Welterbe
(1) Das UNESCO-Welterbe in Hessen steht unter dem besonderen Schutz des Landes.
(2) Die Denkmalfachbehörde nimmt die dem Land Hessen obliegenden Aufgaben im Zusammenhang mit dem UNESCO-Welterbe wahr, soweit Welterbestätten nach § 2 Kulturdenkmäler sind und Aufgaben nicht von der Obersten Denkmalschutzbehörde wahrgenommen werden.

§ 4 Denkmalschutzbehörden
(1) Oberste Denkmalschutzbehörde ist die für Denkmalschutz und Denkmalpflege zuständige Ministerin oder der hierfür zuständige Minister.
(2) ¹Untere Denkmalschutzbehörde ist in den kreisfreien Städten und in den kreisangehörigen Gemeinden, denen die Bauaufsicht übertragen ist, der Magistrat, in den Landkreisen der Kreisausschuss.
²Die Aufgaben des Denkmalschutzes obliegen den Gemeinden und Landkreisen zur Erfüllung nach Weisung.

§ 5 Denkmalfachbehörde
(1) Denkmalfachbehörde ist das Landesamt für Denkmalpflege Hessen.
(2) Die Denkmalfachbehörde erfüllt ihre Aufgaben nach § 1 Abs. 1 insbesondere, indem sie:
1. Eigentümerinnen, Eigentümer, Besitzerinnen und Besitzer von Kulturdenkmälern bei Pflege, Untersuchung und Wiederherstellung berät und unterstützt,
2. als Trägerin öffentlicher Belange das Interesse des Denkmalschutzes und der Denkmalpflege wahrnimmt,
3. Kulturdenkmäler systematisch inventarisiert,
4. das Denkmalverzeichnis des Landes Hessen führt,
5. Kulturdenkmäler wissenschaftlich untersucht und damit zur Erforschung der Landesgeschichte beiträgt,
6. Öffentlichkeitsarbeit leistet, um das Verständnis für Denkmalschutz und Denkmalpflege zu wecken und zu fördern.

§ 6 Landesdenkmalrat
(1) Die für Denkmalschutz und Denkmalpflege zuständige Ministerin oder der hierfür zuständige Minister beruft zu ihrer oder seiner Beratung den Hessischen Landesdenkmalrat.
(2) ¹Dem Hessischen Landesdenkmalrat sollen je eine Vertreterin oder ein Vertreter der mit Denkmalpflege und Denkmalschutz befassten Fachgebiete wie
1. Kunstgeschichte,
2. Archäologie,
3. Architektur,
4. Städtebau,
5. Geschichte,
6. Volkskunde und
7. bildende Künste

angehören. ²Ihm sollen ferner je eine Vertreterin oder ein Vertreter
1. des Hessischen Museumsverbandes,
2. des Hessischen Landesamtes für geschichtliche Landeskunde,
3. der Hochbauverwaltung des Landes Hessen,
4. der evangelischen Kirchen,
5. der katholischen Kirche,
6. der Kommunalen Spitzenverbände,
7. der Verbände der hessischen Haus- und Grundeigentümerinnen und -eigentümer,
8. der Architekten- und Stadtplanerkammer Hessen,
9. der Arbeitsgemeinschaft der Hessischen Handwerkskammern und
10. des Landesverbandes der jüdischen Gemeinden in Hessen

angehören, die qualifizierte Kenntnisse der Denkmalpflege und des Denkmalschutzes besitzen.
(3) Die im Hessischen Landtag vertretenen politischen Parteien entsenden je eine Vertreterin oder einen Vertreter mit beratender Stimme.

(4) Vertreter der für Denkmalschutz, Umweltschutz, Landschaftspflege, Naturschutz und Raumordnung zuständigen oberen Landesbehörden sollen zu den Sitzungen des Denkmalrates eingeladen werden.
(5) Das Nähere bestimmt die Geschäftsordnung des Hessischen Landesdenkmalrats, die die für Denkmalschutz und Denkmalpflege zuständige Ministerin oder der hierfür zuständige Minister im Benehmen mit dem Landesdenkmalrat erlässt.
(6) Den Denkmalschutz oder die Denkmalpflege betreffende Verwaltungsvorschriften sollen mit dem Hessischen Landesdenkmalrat beraten werden.

§ 7 Denkmalbeirat und ehrenamtliche Denkmalpflege
(1) Bei der Unteren Denkmalschutzbehörde wird nach Anhörung der Denkmalfachbehörde vom Kreisausschuss oder Magistrat ein sachverständiger, weisungsunabhängiger Denkmalbeirat berufen, der die Untere Denkmalschutzbehörde bei der Durchführung ihrer Aufgaben berät und unterstützt.
(2) [1]Die Untere Denkmalschutzbehörde kann sachkundige Ehrenamtliche in der Denkmalpflege im Benehmen mit der Denkmalfachbehörde bestellen. [2]Sie sind fachlich und organisatorisch der Unteren Denkmalschutzbehörde unterstellt. [3]Sie unterstützen die Denkmalschutzbehörden in der Denkmalpflege.

§ 8 Zuständigkeiten der Denkmalschutzbehörden
(1) Für Maßnahmen aufgrund dieses Gesetzes sind die Unteren Denkmalschutzbehörden zuständig, soweit dieses Gesetz nichts anderes bestimmt.
(2) [1]Bei Maßnahmen an Kulturdenkmälern, die im Eigentum des Bundes oder des Landes Hessen stehen, entscheidet die Oberste Denkmalschutzbehörde oder die von ihr bestimmte Behörde.[1]) [2]§ 13 Abs. 2 und die §§ 14, 26 und 27 finden auf Kulturdenkmäler im Eigentum des Landes Hessen keine Anwendung.

§ 9 Maßnahmen der Denkmalschutzbehörden
(1) [1]Denkmalschutzbehörden haben diejenigen Maßnahmen zu treffen, die ihnen nach pflichtgemäßem Ermessen erforderlich erscheinen, um Kulturdenkmäler zu schützen, zu erhalten und zu bergen sowie Gefahren von ihnen abzuwenden. [2]Sie haben bei allen Entscheidungen den berechtigten Interessen der Eigentümerinnen, Eigentümer, Besitzerinnen und Besitzer von Kulturdenkmälern Rechnung zu tragen. [3]Die Behörden haben bei allen Entscheidungen und Genehmigungen die Belange des Klima- und Ressourcenschutzes besonders zu berücksichtigen. [4]Bei öffentlich zugänglichen Denkmälern sind auch die Belange der Barrierefreiheit besonders zu berücksichtigen.
(2) Soweit ein Vorhaben nach diesem Gesetz einer Genehmigung bedarf, kann diese unter Bedingungen oder Auflagen erteilt werden.
(3) [1]Durch die Erteilung von Genehmigungen aufgrund dieses Gesetzes werden Genehmigungen, die aufgrund anderer Rechtsvorschriften erforderlich sind, nicht ersetzt. [2]Baugenehmigungen und bauordnungsrechtliche Zustimmungen schließen die denkmalschutzrechtliche Genehmigung ein.
(4) Wer eine Maßnahme, die nach diesem Gesetz der Genehmigung bedarf, ohne die erforderliche Genehmigung oder im Widerspruch zu den bei der Genehmigung erteilten Bedingungen oder Auflagen durchführt, ist auf Anordnung der Unteren Denkmalschutzbehörde verpflichtet, den alten Zustand wieder herzustellen oder das Kulturdenkmal auf andere Weise entsprechend den Bedingungen oder Auflagen der Unteren Denkmalschutzbehörde instand zu setzen.

§ 10 Denkmalverzeichnis
(1) [1]Kulturdenkmäler werden in das Denkmalverzeichnis des Landes Hessen eingetragen. [2]Der Inhalt des Denkmalverzeichnisses bestimmt sich nach den §§ 11 und 12.
(2) [1]Die Einsicht in das Denkmalverzeichnis ist jedermann gestattet. [2]Davon ausgenommen sind Angaben zum Eigentum und bei beweglichen Kulturdenkmälern auch zum Standort des Kulturdenkmals. [3]Die Daten des Denkmalverzeichnisses können über geeignete, öffentlich verfügbare elektronische Kommunikationsmittel bereitgestellt werden.

§ 11 Unbewegliche Kulturdenkmäler
(1) [1]Unbewegliche Kulturdenkmäler werden im Benehmen mit der Gemeinde erfasst und nachrichtlich in das Denkmalverzeichnis eingetragen. [2]Eigentümerinnen und Eigentümer sind zu unterrichten, wenn

---
1) Die Verordnung über Zuständigkeiten nach dem Hessischen Denkmalschutzgesetz ist abgedruckt als Nr. D7.I.1a.

ihr Kulturdenkmal erfasst wurde. ³Dies kann auf elektronischem Weg erfolgen. ⁴Der Schutz unbeweglicher Kulturdenkmäler ist nicht davon abhängig, dass sie in das Denkmalverzeichnis des Landes Hessen eingetragen sind.
(2) Die Öffentlichkeit wird in geeigneter Weise über den Bestand unbeweglicher Kulturdenkmäler unterrichtet, über Bodendenkmäler jedoch nur, wenn sie oberirdisch sichtbar sind.

§ 12 Bewegliche Kulturdenkmäler
(1) Als bewegliche Kulturdenkmäler können in das Denkmalverzeichnis eingetragen werden:
1. Zubehör eines unbeweglichen Kulturdenkmals, das mit diesem eine Sachgesamtheit nach § 2 Abs. 1 bildet,
2. Gegenstände, deren Zugehörigkeit zu einem bestimmten Ort historisch begründet ist und deren Verbleib an Ort und Stelle im öffentlichen Interesse liegt, und
3. Dokumente und Sammlungen, die die Kriterien des § 2 Abs. 1 erfüllen.

(2) ¹Eine bewegliche Sache wird durch Eintrag in das Denkmalverzeichnis Kulturdenkmal. ²National wertvolles Kulturgut nach § 2 Abs. 5 gilt als im Denkmalverzeichnis eingetragen.
(3) Vor einer Eintragung nach Abs. 1 ist die Eigentümerin oder der Eigentümer zu hören und von der Vornahme einer Eintragung unverzüglich zu unterrichten.
(4) ¹Eine Eintragung ist von Amts wegen zu löschen, wenn die Voraussetzungen für eine Eintragung nicht mehr vorliegen. ²Hiervon ist die Eigentümerin oder der Eigentümer unverzüglich zu unterrichten.

§ 13 Erhaltungspflicht
(1) Eigentümerinnen und Eigentümer, Besitzerinnen und Besitzer sowie Unterhaltungspflichtige von Kulturdenkmälern sind verpflichtet, diese im Rahmen des Zumutbaren zu erhalten und pfleglich zu behandeln.
(2) Das Land sowie die Gemeinden und Gemeindeverbände tragen hierzu durch Zuschüsse nach Maßgabe der verfügbaren Haushaltsmittel bei.[1])

§ 14 Durchsetzung der Erhaltung
(1) Kommt die Eigentümerin oder der Eigentümer, die Besitzerin oder der Besitzer oder kommen sonstige Unterhaltungspflichtige ihren Verpflichtungen nach § 13 Abs. 1 nicht nach und wird hierdurch das Kulturdenkmal gefährdet, können sie von der Unteren Denkmalschutzbehörde verpflichtet werden, erforderliche Erhaltungsmaßnahmen durchzuführen.
(2) ¹Erfordert der Zustand eines Kulturdenkmals zu seiner Instandhaltung, Instandsetzung oder zu seinem Schutz Maßnahmen, ohne deren unverzügliche Durchführung es gefährdet wäre, kann die Untere Denkmalschutzbehörde diejenigen Maßnahmen selbst durchführen, die zur Abwendung einer unmittelbaren Gefahr für den Bestand des Kulturdenkmals geboten sind. ²Die Eigentümerin oder der Eigentümer und die Besitzerin oder der Besitzer sind verpflichtet, solche Maßnahmen zu dulden. ³Die Eigentümerin oder der Eigentümer, die Besitzerin oder der Besitzer und sonstige Unterhaltungspflichtige können im Rahmen des Zumutbaren zur Erstattung der entstandenen Kosten herangezogen werden.

§ 15 Nutzung von Kulturdenkmälern
Werden Kulturdenkmäler nicht mehr entsprechend ihrer ursprünglichen Zweckbestimmung genutzt, sollen die Eigentümerinnen und Eigentümer eine Nutzung anstreben, die einen möglichst weitgehenden Erhalt der Substanz auf die Dauer gewährleistet.

§ 16 Auskunfts- und Duldungspflichten
(1) Die Eigentümerinnen und Eigentümer, die Besitzerinnen und Besitzer von Kulturdenkmälern sind verpflichtet, die zur Erfüllung der Aufgaben des Denkmalschutzes erforderlichen Auskünfte zu erteilen.
(2) ¹Denkmalschutzbehörden und Denkmalfachbehörde sind nach vorheriger Benachrichtigung der Eigentümerin oder des Eigentümers, der Besitzerin oder des Besitzers berechtigt, Grundstücke zu betreten und Kulturdenkmäler zu besichtigen, soweit es zur Erfüllung der Aufgaben des Denkmalschutzes erforderlich ist. ²Wohnungen dürfen gegen den Willen der Besitzerin oder des Besitzers nur zur Abwendung drohender Gefahr für Kulturdenkmäler betreten werden. ³Die Unverletzlichkeit der Wohnung nach Art. 13 des Grundgesetzes wird insoweit eingeschränkt.

---

1) Die Denkmalförderrichtlinien sind abgedruckt als Nr. D7.III.1.

§ 17 Zugang zu Kulturdenkmälern

¹Kulturdenkmäler sollen der Öffentlichkeit so weit wie möglich zugänglich gemacht werden, wenn der öffentliche Zutritt zugemutet werden kann. ²Die Denkmalfachbehörde soll in solchen Fällen Vereinbarungen über den freien Zutritt treffen; dies gilt insbesondere dann, wenn für die Erhaltung des Denkmals öffentliche Mittel aufgewendet werden oder aufgewendet worden sind.

§ 18 Genehmigungspflichtige Maßnahmen

(1) Der Genehmigung der Denkmalschutzbehörde bedarf, wer ein Kulturdenkmal oder Teile davon
1. zerstören oder beseitigen,
2. an einen anderen Ort verbringen,
3. umgestalten oder instand setzen,
4. mit Werbeanlagen versehen will.

(2) Der Genehmigung der Denkmalschutzbehörde bedarf ferner, wer in der Umgebung eines unbeweglichen Kulturdenkmals Anlagen errichten, verändern oder beseitigen will, wenn sich dies auf den Bestand oder das Erscheinungsbild des Kulturdenkmals auswirken kann.

(3) Die Genehmigung ist zu erteilen,
1. wenn Gründe des Denkmalschutzes dem Vorhaben nicht entgegenstehen,
2. wenn und soweit ihre Ablehnung der Eigentümerin oder dem Eigentümer wirtschaftlich unzumutbar wäre oder
3. wenn überwiegende öffentliche Interessen dies verlangen.

(4) ¹Eine Maßnahme in einer Gesamtanlage ist zu genehmigen, wenn sie diese in Substanz oder Wirkung nur unerheblich oder nur vorübergehend beeinträchtigt. ²Wenn das öffentliche Interesse an der beabsichtigten Maßnahme entgegenstehenden Gründen des Denkmalschutzes überwiegt, ist die Maßnahme zu genehmigen.

(5) Soweit in ein Kulturdenkmal eingegriffen wird, hat der Veranlasser des Eingriffs im Rahmen des Zumutbaren die Kosten zu tragen, die für die Erhaltung, fachgerechte Instandsetzung oder Bergung und Dokumentation des Denkmals anfallen.

§ 19 Anzeigepflichtige Maßnahmen

(1) Die Eigentümerinnen und Eigentümer, die Besitzerinnen und Besitzer haben Schäden und Mängel, die an Kulturdenkmälern auftreten und deren Denkmalwert oder Substanz beeinträchtigen, unverzüglich der Unteren Denkmalschutzbehörde anzuzeigen.

(2) Wird ein bewegliches Kulturdenkmal veräußert, so haben Veräußerin oder Veräußerer und Erwerberin oder Erwerber den Eigentumswechsel innerhalb eines Monats der Unteren Denkmalschutzbehörde anzuzeigen.

§ 20 Genehmigungsverfahren

(1) ¹Der Genehmigungsantrag ist schriftlich mit allen für die Beurteilung des Vorhabens und der Bearbeitung des Antrags erforderlichen Unterlagen einzureichen. ²Im Einzelfall kann verlangt werden, dass der Genehmigungsantrag durch vorbereitende Untersuchungen am Kulturdenkmal ergänzt wird.

(2) ¹Der Eingang des vollständigen Genehmigungsantrages nach Abs. 1 ist unter Angabe des Datums schriftlich zu bestätigen. ²Über den Genehmigungsantrag ist innerhalb von drei Monaten nach Eingang des vollständigen Genehmigungsantrages zu entscheiden; die Denkmalschutzbehörde kann diese Frist aus wichtigem Grund um bis zu drei Monate verlängern. ³Die Genehmigung gilt als erteilt, wenn über den Genehmigungsantrag nicht innerhalb der nach Satz 2 maßgeblichen Frist entschieden worden ist. ⁴Im Übrigen gilt § 42a des Hessischen Verwaltungsverfahrensgesetzes.

(3) Das Verfahren nach Abs. 1 Satz 1 kann über eine einheitliche Stelle nach Teil V Abschnitt 1a des Hessischen Verwaltungsverfahrensgesetzes abgewickelt werden.

(4) Soweit die besondere Eigenart eines Kulturdenkmales dies gebietet, kann verlangt werden, dass die Leitung oder Ausführung von Arbeiten, die besondere Erfahrungen und Kenntnisse voraussetzen, durch denkmalfachlich geeignete Personen erfolgt.

(5) ¹Die Unteren Denkmalschutzbehörden beteiligen die Denkmalfachbehörde an ihren Entscheidungen. ²Kommt zwischen Unterer Denkmalschutzbehörde und Denkmalfachbehörde kein Einvernehmen zustande, ist die Weisung der Obersten Denkmalschutzbehörde einzuholen.

(6) In Genehmigungsverfahren nach dem Bundes-Immissionsschutzgesetz entscheidet die für den Vollzug des Bundes-Immissionsschutzgesetzes zuständige Behörde im Benehmen mit der Denkmalfachbehörde.
(7) [1]Die Genehmigung erlischt, wenn nicht innerhalb von drei Jahren nach ihrer Erteilung mit der Ausführung begonnen oder die Ausführung drei Jahre unterbrochen worden ist. [2]Die Fristen nach Satz 1 können auf schriftlichen Antrag jeweils um bis zu zwei Jahre verlängert werden.
(8) [1]Für Maßnahmen, die Kulturdenkmäler nur in geringem Maß verändern, kann die Denkmalfachbehörde mit Unteren Denkmalschutzbehörden Verwaltungsvereinbarungen über eine Vereinfachung des Beteiligungsverfahrens nach Abs. 5 Satz 1 treffen. [2]Die fachliche Qualifizierung und personelle Ausstattung der Unteren Denkmalschutzbehörde muss Gewähr dafür bieten, dass die so übertragene Zuständigkeit fachgerecht erfüllt werden kann.

§ 21 Funde
(1) [1]Wer Bodendenkmäler entdeckt, hat dies unverzüglich der Denkmalfachbehörde anzuzeigen. [2]Die Anzeige kann auch gegenüber der Gemeinde oder der Unteren Denkmalschutzbehörde erfolgen; diese leiten die Anzeige unverzüglich der Denkmalfachbehörde zu.
(2) Anzeigepflichtig sind die Entdeckerin oder der Entdecker, die Eigentümerin oder der Eigentümer des Grundstücks sowie die Leiterin oder der Leiter der Arbeiten, bei denen die Sache entdeckt worden ist.
(3) [1]Der Fund und die Fundstelle sind bis zum Ablauf einer Woche nach der Anzeige im unveränderten Zustand zu erhalten und in geeigneter Weise vor Gefahren für die Erhaltung des Fundes zu schützen. [2]Die Denkmalfachbehörde soll der Fortsetzung der Arbeiten zustimmen, wenn deren Unterbrechung unverhältnismäßig hohe Kosten verursacht.
(4) Die Denkmalfachbehörde ist berechtigt, den Fund zu bergen, auszuwerten und zur wissenschaftlichen Bearbeitung vorübergehend in Besitz zu nehmen.

§ 22 Nachforschungen
Nachforschungen, insbesondere Grabungen, mit dem Ziel, Bodendenkmäler zu entdecken, bedürfen der Genehmigung der Denkmalfachbehörde.

§ 23 Grabungsschutzgebiete
(1) Die für Denkmalschutz und Denkmalpflege zuständige Ministerin oder der hierfür zuständige Minister kann durch Rechtsverordnung bestimmte abgegrenzte Gebiete befristet oder auf unbefristete Zeit zu Grabungsschutzgebieten erklären, wenn eine begründete Vermutung besteht, dass sie Bodendenkmäler bergen.
(2) [1]In Grabungsschutzgebieten bedürfen Arbeiten, die Bodendenkmäler gefährden können, der Genehmigung der Obersten Denkmalschutzbehörde. [2]Die bisherige land- und forstwirtschaftliche Nutzung bleibt im bisherigen Ausmaß unberührt.

§ 24 Nutzungsbeschränkungen
(1) Die Oberste Denkmalschutzbehörde kann die wirtschaftliche Nutzung eines Grundstücks oder eines Grundstücksteils beschränken, in dem sich Bodendenkmäler befinden.
(2) [1]Die Beschränkung nach Abs. 1 ist auf Ersuchen der Obersten Denkmalschutzbehörde im Grundbuch einzutragen. [2]Berechtigter ist das Land, vertreten durch die Denkmalfachbehörde.

§ 25 Schatzregal
(1) [1]Bodendenkmäler, die als bewegliche Sachen herrenlos oder so lange verborgen gewesen sind, dass ihre Eigentümerin oder ihr Eigentümer nicht mehr zu ermitteln ist, werden mit ihrer Entdeckung Eigentum des Landes, wenn sie
1. einen hervorragenden wissenschaftlichen Wert haben,
2. bei staatlichen Nachforschungen oder in Grabungsschutzgebieten entdeckt werden oder
3. bei unerlaubten Nachforschungen entdeckt werden.

[2]Die Finderin oder der Finder wird von Kosten und Aufwand der Überlassung freigestellt.
(2) [1]Erwirbt das Land Eigentum nach Abs. 1 Satz 1 Nr. 1 und 2, haben die Finderin oder der Finder einerseits, die Grundstückseigentümerin oder der Grundstückseigentümer andererseits je zur Hälfte Anspruch auf eine Fundprämie, wenn sie innerhalb von zwei Jahren einen Antrag bei der Denkmalfachbehörde stellen. [2]Die Höhe der Fundprämie bemisst sich entsprechend § 971 des Bürgerlichen

D7.I.1 Hessisches Denkmalschutzgesetz

Gesetzbuchs. ³Aufwendungen des Landes zur Sicherung und zum Erhalt der Funde sind dabei angemessen zu berücksichtigen. ⁴Über den Antrag entscheidet die Denkmalfachbehörde.

§ 26 Enteignung
(1) Die Enteignung ist zugunsten des Landes, eines Landkreises, einer Gemeinde oder einer rechtsfähigen Stiftung zulässig, soweit sie erforderlich ist, damit
1. ein Kulturdenkmal in seinem Bestand oder Erscheinungsbild erhalten bleibt,
2. ein Bodendenkmal wissenschaftlich ausgewertet oder der Allgemeinheit zugänglich gemacht werden kann,
3. in einem Grabungsschutzgebiet planmäßige Nachforschungen betrieben werden können.

(2) ¹Im Übrigen gelten die allgemeinen Vorschriften über die Enteignung. ²Antragsberechtigt ist die Denkmalfachbehörde.

§ 27 Sonstige entschädigungspflichtige Maßnahmen
(1) Soweit Anordnungen aufgrund dieses Gesetzes im Einzelfall zu einer unzumutbaren Belastung des Eigentums führen, hat das Land eine angemessene Entschädigung in Geld zu gewähren, sofern und soweit die Belastung nicht in anderer Weise ausgeglichen werden kann.

(2) ¹Die Grundsätze der Entschädigung bei der förmlichen Enteignung sind entsprechend anzuwenden. ²Enteignungsbegünstigt ist das Land, vertreten durch die Denkmalfachbehörde. ³Die Gemeinden und Gemeindeverbände sollen sich an der Entschädigung im Rahmen ihrer Leistungsfähigkeit beteiligen.

§ 28 Bußgeldbestimmungen
(1) Ordnungswidrig handelt, wer vorsätzlich oder fahrlässig
1. genehmigungspflichtige Maßnahmen entgegen § 18 Abs. 1 und 2, § 22 oder § 23 Abs. 2 Satz 1 ohne Genehmigung beginnt oder durchführt oder einer von der zuständigen Behörde mit der Genehmigung erteilten Bedingung oder Auflage zuwiderhandelt,
2. entgegen § 14 Abs. 2 Satz 2 Maßnahmen der Denkmalschutzbehörde zur Abwendung einer unmittelbaren Gefahr für den Bestand eines Kulturdenkmals nicht duldet,
3. der Auskunftspflicht nach § 16 Abs. 1 nicht nachkommt,
4. entgegen § 16 Abs. 2 Satz 1 und 2 den Beauftragten der zuständigen Behörde das Betreten von Grundstücken oder das Besichtigen von Kulturdenkmälern nicht gestattet,
5. entgegen § 19 Abs. 1 Schäden und Mängel nicht oder nicht unverzüglich anzeigt,
6. entgegen § 19 Abs. 2 den Eigentumswechsel eines beweglichen Kulturdenkmals nicht oder nicht rechtzeitig anzeigt,
7. entgegen § 21 Abs. 1 Satz 1 einen Fund nicht unverzüglich anzeigt,
8. entgegen § 21 Abs. 3 Satz 1 den Fund oder die Fundstelle nicht bis zum Ablauf einer Woche nach der Anzeige in unverändertem Zustand lässt,
9. den von der Denkmalfachbehörde erlassenen, vollziehbaren Anordnungen zur Bergung, Auswertung und zur wissenschaftlichen Bearbeitung nach § 21 Abs. 4 zuwiderhandelt oder
10. einer Nutzungsbeschränkung nach § 24 Abs. 1 zuwiderhandelt.

(2) ¹Ordnungswidrigkeiten nach Abs. 1 können mit einer Geldbuße bis zu fünfundzwanzigtausend Euro geahndet werden. ²Abweichend von Satz 1 können Ordnungswidrigkeiten nach Abs. 1 Nr. 1 im Falle der Zuwiderhandlung gegen § 18 Abs. 1 Nr. 1 und 3 mit einer Geldbuße bis zu fünfhunderttausend Euro geahndet werden.

(3) Verwaltungsbehörde im Sinne des § 36 Abs. 1 Nr. 1 des Gesetzes über Ordnungswidrigkeiten ist die zuständige Denkmalschutzbehörde.

(4) Ist eine Ordnungswidrigkeit nach Abs. 1 Nr. 1 begangen worden, können die zur Vorbereitung oder Begehung gebrauchten oder bestimmten Gegenstände eingezogen werden.

§ 29 Staatskirchenverträge

(1) ¹Art. 20 Satz 2 des Vertrages des Landes Hessen mit den Evangelischen Landeskirchen in Hessen vom 18. Februar 1960 (GVBl. S. 54)[1)] und Art. V Satz 2 des Vertrages des Landes Hessen mit den Katholischen Bistümern in Hessen vom 9. März 1963 (GVBl. I S. 102)[2)] bleiben unberührt. ²§ 18 Abs. 1 Nr. 3 und § 19 Abs. 2 finden insoweit keine Anwendung.
(2) Bei kircheneigenen Kulturdenkmälern ist die Kirchenleitung in den Verfahren nach den §§ 11 und 12 zu beteiligen.
(3) Bei Entscheidungen der Denkmalschutzbehörden sind bei Kulturdenkmälern, die der unmittelbaren Religionsausübung dienen, die von den Leitungen der Religionsgemeinschaften festgelegten religiösen Belange vorrangig zu berücksichtigen.

§ 30 Aufhebung bisherigen Rechts

Das Denkmalschutzgesetz in der Fassung vom 5. September 1986 (GVBl. I S. 270), zuletzt geändert durch Gesetz vom 30. November 2015 (GVBl. S. 523), wird aufgehoben.

§ 31 Rechtsverordnungen

Die für Denkmalschutz und Denkmalpflege zuständige Ministerin oder der hierfür zuständige Minister wird ermächtigt, durch Rechtsverordnung nähere Regelungen zu treffen über
1. den Umfang, in dem Fossilien als Bodendenkmäler nach § 2 Abs. 2 Satz 3 geschützt werden sollen,
2. die Übertragung einzelner Zuständigkeiten der Obersten Denkmalschutzbehörde auf andere Behörden nach § 8 Abs. 2 Satz 1,
3. die Erfassung der Kulturdenkmäler nach § 11 Abs. 1 Satz 1 und § 12 Abs. 1, 3 und 4,
4. Form und Führung des Denkmalverzeichnisses und seiner Auszüge nach § 10 Abs. 1 Satz 1,
5. die Unterrichtung der Öffentlichkeit, der Eigentümerinnen und Eigentümer nach § 10 Abs. 2, § 11 Abs. 1 Satz 2 und 3, § 11 Abs. 2, § 12 Abs. 3 und § 12 Abs. 4 Satz 2,
6. die nähere Ausgestaltung des Genehmigungsverfahrens nach § 20 und § 22 und
7. Grabungsschutzgebiete nach § 23 Abs. 1.

§ 32 Inkrafttreten

Dieses Gesetz tritt am Tag nach der Verkündung[3)] in Kraft.

---

1) Art. 20 des Vertrages des Landes Hessen mit den Evangelischen Landeskirchen in Hessen vom 18. Februar 1960 (GVBl. S. 54) hat folgenden Wortlaut:
„Die Kirchen werden der Erhaltung und Pflege denkmalswerter Gebäude nebst den dazugehörigen Grundstücken sowie denkmalswerter Gegenstände ihre besondere Aufmerksamkeit widmen. Sie werden Veräußerungen, Umgestaltungen und farbliche Instandsetzungen nur im Benehmen mit den Stellen der staatlichen Denkmalspflege vornehmen. Sie werden dafür sorgen, dass die Kirchengemeinden und sonstigen Verbände entsprechend verfahren. Im Übrigen finden auch auf kirchlichem Bereich die Vorschriften eines etwa zu erlassenden Denkmalsschutzes Anwendung."

2) Art. V des Vertrages des Landes Hessen mit den Katholischen Bistümern in Hessen vom 9. März 1963 (GVBl. I S. 102) hat folgenden Wortlaut:
„Die Bistümer werden der Erhaltung und Pflege denkmalswerter Gebäude nebst den dazugehörigen Grundstücken sowie denkmalswerter Gegenstände ihre besondere Aufmerksamkeit widmen. Sie werden Veräußerungen, Umgestaltungen und farbliche Instandsetzungen nur im Benehmen mit den Stellen der staatlichen Denkmalpflege vornehmen. Sie werden dafür sorgen, daß die Kirchengemeinden und sonstigen Verbände entsprechend verfahren. Im übrigen finden auch auf kirchlichem Bereich die Vorschriften eines etwa zu erlassenden Denkmalschutzgesetzes Anwendung."

3) Verkündet am 5.12.2016.

Verordnung über Zuständigkeiten nach dem Hessischen Denkmalschutzgesetz

Vom 21. Juni 2018 (GVBl. S. 341)
(FFN 76-19)

Aufgrund des § 31 Nr. 2 des Hessischen Denkmalschutzgesetzes vom 28. November 2016 (GVBl. S. 211) verordnet der Minister für Wissenschaft und Kunst:

§ 1 Zuständigkeiten des Landesamtes für Denkmalpflege Hessen
(1) ¹Bei Maßnahmen an Kulturdenkmälern im Eigentum des Bundes oder des Landes Hessen, die von der für den staatlichen Hochbau zuständigen Stelle des Landes Hessen durchgeführt werden, entscheidet das Landesamt für Denkmalpflege Hessen, soweit es der beabsichtigten Maßnahme zustimmt. ²Stimmt das Landesamt für Denkmalpflege Hessen einer Maßnahme nicht zu, legt es die Angelegenheit der Obersten Denkmalschutzbehörde zur Entscheidung vor.
(2) ¹Bei Maßnahmen an Kulturdenkmälern im Eigentum des Bundes, die der bauordnungsrechtlichen Zustimmung bedürfen und nicht von der für den staatlichen Hochbau zuständigen Stelle des Landes Hessen durchgeführt werden, entscheidet das Landesamt für Denkmalpflege Hessen, soweit es der beabsichtigten Maßnahme zustimmt. ²Stimmt das Landesamt für Denkmalpflege Hessen einer Maßnahme nicht zu, legt es die Angelegenheit der Obersten Denkmalschutzbehörde zur Entscheidung vor.

§ 2 Zuständigkeiten der für die Verwaltung des Kulturdenkmals zuständigen Behörde
¹Bei Maßnahmen an Kulturdenkmälern im Eigentum des Bundes oder des Landes Hessen, die nicht der Baugenehmigung oder der bauordnungsrechtlichen Zustimmung bedürfen und nicht von der für den staatlichen Hochbau zuständigen Stelle des Landes Hessen durchgeführt werden, entscheidet die für die Verwaltung des Kulturdenkmals zuständige Behörde im Einvernehmen mit dem Landesamt für Denkmalpflege Hessen. ²Kommt ein Einvernehmen nicht zustande, legt das Landesamt für Denkmalpflege Hessen die Angelegenheit der Obersten Denkmalschutzbehörde zur Entscheidung vor.

§ 3 Zuständigkeiten der Museumslandschaft Hessen Kassel und der Verwaltung der Staatlichen Schlösser und Gärten Hessen
¹Bei Maßnahmen nach § 18 des Hessischen Denkmalschutzgesetzes an Kulturdenkmälern im Eigentum des Bundes oder des Landes Hessen in den Zuständigkeitsbereichen der Museumslandschaft Hessen Kassel und der Verwaltung der Staatlichen Schlösser und Gärten Hessen entscheiden diese jeweils für ihren Bereich. ²Das Landesamt für Denkmalpflege Hessen ist zu beteiligen. ³Über Art und Umfang der Beteiligung wird eine Verwaltungsvereinbarung getroffen.

§ 4 Aufhebung von Rechtsvorschriften
Die Verordnung über Zuständigkeiten nach dem Denkmalschutzgesetz vom 15. August 2013 (GVBl. S. 534) wird aufgehoben.

§ 5 Inkrafttreten
Diese Verordnung tritt am Tag nach der Verkündung[1)] in Kraft.

---

1) Verkündet am 5.7.2018.

Hessisches Archivgesetz (HArchivG)[1)2)]

Vom 26. November 2012 (GVBl. S. 458)
(FFN 76-13)
zuletzt geändert durch Art. 14 Elftes G zur Verlängerung der Geltungsdauer und Änd. von Rechtsvorschriften vom 5. Oktober 2017 (GVBl. S. 294)

Teil 1
Allgemeine Bestimmungen

§ 1 Geltungsbereich

(1) ¹Dieses Gesetz regelt den Umgang mit öffentlichem Archivgut. ²Es soll das öffentliche Archivgut vor Beschädigung, Verlust, Vernichtung und Zersplitterung schützen, verfügbar halten und unter Anwendung moderner Technologien für die öffentliche Nutzung zugänglich machen. ³Es regelt den Datenschutz für das öffentliche Archivgut.
(2) Dieses Gesetz regelt auch die Archivierung der Unterlagen von ehemals öffentlichen oder diesen gleichgestellten Stellen, sofern die Unterlagen bis zum Zeitpunkt des Übergangs in eine Rechtsform des Privatrechts entstanden sind.
(3) ¹Dieses Gesetz gilt nicht für die Kirchen und andere öffentlich-rechtliche Religions- und Weltanschauungsgemeinschaften und deren Vereinigungen. ²Es gilt ferner nicht für die öffentlich-rechtlichen Rundfunkanstalten und für öffentlich-rechtliche Unternehmen mit eigener Rechtspersönlichkeit, die am wirtschaftlichen Wettbewerb teilnehmen, und deren Zusammenschlüsse und solche Zweckverbände, deren Zweck der Betrieb eines öffentlich-rechtlichen Unternehmens mit eigener Rechtspersönlichkeit ist, das am wirtschaftlichen Wettbewerb teilnimmt.

§ 2 Begriffsbestimmungen

(1) Archivwürdig im Sinne dieses Gesetzes sind Unterlagen, die aufgrund ihrer politischen, rechtlichen, wirtschaftlichen, sozialen und kulturellen Bedeutung für die Erforschung und das Verständnis von Geschichte und Gegenwart von bleibendem Wert sind.
(2) ¹Unterlagen im Sinne dieses Gesetzes sind Urkunden, Amtsbücher, Akten, Schriftstücke, amtliche Publikationen, Karteien, Karten, Pläne, Plakate, Siegel, Stempel, Bild-, Film- und Tonaufzeichnungen sowie alle anderen Informationsobjekte, auch digitale Aufzeichnungen, unabhängig von ihrer Speicherungsform. ²Dazu zählen auch alle Hilfsmittel und ergänzenden Daten, die für die Erhaltung, das Verständnis dieser Informationen und deren Nutzung notwendig sind.
(3) Öffentliches Archivgut sind alle archivwürdigen Unterlagen der Verfassungsorgane, Behörden, Gerichte, des Landtags und der sonstigen öffentlichen Stellen des Landes, der Städte, Gemeinden, Landkreise und kommunalen Verbände, ihrer Rechts- und Funktionsvorgänger sowie der sonstigen der Aufsicht des Landes unterstehenden juristischen Personen des öffentlichen Rechts und ihrer Vereinigungen einschließlich der Hochschulen, die zur dauernden Aufbewahrung von einem öffentlichen Archiv übernommen werden.
(4) Als öffentliches Archivgut gelten auch archivwürdige Unterlagen, die die öffentlichen Archive zur Ergänzung ihres Archivguts gesammelt, erworben oder übernommen haben.
(5) Öffentliche Archive im Sinne dieses Gesetzes sind die Archive, die für das Archivgut der in Abs. 3 und 6 genannten Stellen sowie ihrer Rechtsvorgänger zuständig sind und dieses nach Maßgabe dieses Gesetzes übernehmen, auf Dauer aufbewahren, sichern, erschließen und nutzbar machen.
(6) Als öffentliche Stellen des Landes gelten auch:
1. Stiftungen des Privatrechts, wenn das Land oder ein Rechtsvorgänger überwiegend das Stiftungsvermögen bereitgestellt hat, und
2. andere juristische Personen des Privatrechts, wenn sie nicht am wirtschaftlichen Wettbewerb teilnehmen und dem Land mehr als die Hälfte der Anteile oder der Stimmen zusteht.

(7) Die Archivierung umfasst die Aufgaben, Unterlagen zu erfassen, deren Archivwürdigkeit festzustellen, die archivwürdigen Unterlagen zu übernehmen und sachgemäß aufzubewahren, zu sichern,

---

1) Verkündet als Art. 1 G zur Neuregelung des Archivwesens und des Pflichtexemplarrechts v. 26.11.2012 (GVBl. S. 458).
2) Das G tritt am 1.1.2013 in Kraft, mit Ausnahme des § 21, der bereits am 6.12.2012 in Kraft getreten ist. Gem. § 22 Satz 2 **tritt das G mit Ablauf des 31.12.2022 außer Kraft.**

deren Integrität und Authentizität zu bewahren sowie sie zu erhalten, instand zu setzen, zu erschließen, verfügbar zu machen und für die Nutzung bereitzustellen.

Teil 2
Organisation und Aufgaben des Hessischen Landesarchivs

§ 3 Organisation des Hessischen Landesarchivs

(1) ¹Das Hessische Landesarchiv besteht aus dem Hauptstaatsarchiv Wiesbaden, dem Staatsarchiv Darmstadt und dem Staatsarchiv Marburg. ²Es bündelt zentrale archivfachliche und administrative Aufgaben. ³Das für das Archivwesen zuständige Ministerium übt die Rechts- und Fachaufsicht über das Hessische Landesarchiv aus.

(2) Kooperationspartner des Hessischen Landesarchivs sind der Landesbetrieb Archivschule Marburg – Hochschule für Archivwissenschaft (§ 5) und das Hessische Landesamt für geschichtliche Landeskunde (§ 6).

(3) Die vom Hessischen Landesarchiv zu erreichenden standortübergreifenden archivfachlichen Ziele werden zwischen dem für das Archivwesen zuständigen Ministerium und der Leiterin oder dem Leiter des Hessischen Landesarchivs im Rahmen einer Zielvereinbarung gemeinsam festgelegt.

§ 4 Aufgaben des Hessischen Landesarchivs

(1) ¹Das Hessische Landesarchiv hat die Aufgabe, die archivwürdigen Unterlagen des Landes zu archivieren. ²Es nimmt standortübergreifende Aufgaben des Archivwesens des Landes und der Archivverwaltung wahr.

(2) Aufgaben der Archivierung werden von Personen wahrgenommen, die eine archivfachliche Ausbildung besitzen oder in sonstiger Weise fachlich geeignet sind.

(3) ¹Das Hessische Landesarchiv berät die in § 2 Abs. 3 und 6 genannten Stellen im Rahmen seiner Zuständigkeit bei der Verwaltung und Sicherung ihrer Unterlagen im Hinblick auf die spätere Archivierung. ²Diese Stellen beteiligen das Hessische Landesarchiv bei der Einführung und Änderung technischer Systeme zur Erstellung und Speicherung digitaler Unterlagen. ³Die Beratungstätigkeit erstreckt sich auch auf die nicht staatlichen Archive im Rahmen der Archivpflege.

(4) Die Leiterin oder der Leiter des Hessischen Landesarchivs kann Verträge über die Archivierung von Unterlagen privater oder kommunaler Herkunft im Namen des Landes abschließen.

(5) Das Hessische Landesarchiv nimmt Aufgaben im Rahmen der Aus- und Fortbildung des archivarischen Fachpersonals wahr.

(6) Das Hessische Landesarchiv wirkt als Haus der Geschichte an der wissenschaftlichen Auswertung der von ihm aufbewahrten Unterlagen sowie an der Erforschung und Vermittlung der Geschichte des Landes mit.

Teil 3
Kooperationspartner des Hessischen Landesarchivs

§ 5 Archivschule Marburg – Hochschule für Archivwissenschaft

(1) ¹Das Land ist Träger der Archivschule Marburg – Hochschule für Archivwissenschaft. ²Sie ist ein Landesbetrieb nach § 26 der Hessischen Landeshaushaltsordnung in der Fassung der Bekanntmachung vom 15. März 1999 (GVBl. I S. 248), zuletzt geändert durch Gesetz vom 26. Juni 2013 (GVBl. S. 447), im Geschäftsbereich des für das Archivwesen zuständigen Ministeriums. ³Die Archivschule Marburg – Hochschule für Archivwissenschaft hat die Aufgabe, Archivarinnen und Archivare des gehobenen und höheren Dienstes für Bund und Länder nach hessischem Recht auszubilden. ⁴Sie führt Fortbildungsveranstaltungen und Weiterbildungsstudiengänge durch und betreibt archivwissenschaftliche Forschung.

(2) ¹Die Archivschule Marburg – Hochschule für Archivwissenschaft arbeitet mit dem Hessischen Landesarchiv auf der Grundlage von Kooperationsvereinbarungen zusammen. ²Die Qualität der Leistungen der Archivschule Marburg – Hochschule für Archivwissenschaft wird nach Maßgabe des für das Archivwesen zuständigen Ministeriums regelmäßig evaluiert.

§ 6 Hessisches Landesamt für geschichtliche Landeskunde

(1) ¹Das Land unterhält ein Hessisches Landesamt für geschichtliche Landeskunde mit Sitz in Marburg. ²Es hat die Aufgabe, Grundlagen der hessischen Geschichte zu erschließen und im Kontext überregionaler Forschung wissenschaftlich zu vermitteln. ³Es gibt eigene Schriften heraus und betreibt ein digitales landesgeschichtliches Informationssystem. ⁴Arbeitsgebiete sind insbesondere der Hessische Städteatlas und das Historische Ortslexikon.

(2) ¹Das Hessische Landesamt für geschichtliche Landeskunde arbeitet mit dem Hessischen Landesarchiv auf der Grundlage von Kooperationsvereinbarungen zusammen. ²Die wissenschaftliche Qualität der Leistungen wird nach Maßgabe des für das Archivwesen zuständigen Ministeriums regelmäßig evaluiert.

Teil 4
Archivische Verfahren

§ 7 Aufbewahrung im Rahmen laufender Fristen

(1) ¹Archivwürdige Unterlagen können vor Ablauf der festgelegten Aufbewahrungsfristen vom zuständigen Archiv übernommen werden. ²Das Verfügungsrecht liegt beim zuständigen Archiv.

(2) ¹Unabhängig von der Archivwürdigkeit können Unterlagen vor Ablauf der Aufbewahrungsfristen dem zuständigen Archiv zur befristeten Aufbewahrung als Zwischenarchivgut übergeben werden. ²Die abgebende Stelle bleibt weiterhin für die Unterlagen verantwortlich und entscheidet über die Benutzung durch Dritte.

(3) ¹Unterlagen, die allein zur Rechtssicherung aufgrund von Rechtsvorschriften dauernd aufzubewahren sind, können bei der aktenführenden Stelle verbleiben oder an das zuständige Archiv abgegeben werden. ²Die Einzelheiten werden in einer Vereinbarung geregelt.

§ 8 Anbietung von Unterlagen

(1) ¹Die in § 2 Abs. 3 und 6 genannten Stellen sind verpflichtet, alle Unterlagen, die zur Erfüllung ihrer Aufgaben nicht mehr benötigt werden und deren Aufbewahrungsfrist abgelaufen ist, unverzüglich auszusondern und dem zuständigen Archiv zur Archivierung anzubieten. ²Dies hat spätestens 30 Jahre nach Entstehung der Unterlagen zu erfolgen, soweit nicht Rechtsvorschriften andere Aufbewahrungsfristen bestimmen. ³Das zuständige Archiv hat binnen sechs Monaten über die Archivwürdigkeit angebotener Unterlagen zu entscheiden.

(2) Anzubieten sind auch Unterlagen, die besonderen Rechtsvorschriften über Geheimhaltung oder des Datenschutzes unterworfen sind oder die aufgrund besonderer Vorschriften hätten gelöscht oder vernichtet werden müssen.

(3) Die in § 2 Abs. 3 und 6 genannten Stellen dürfen nach Ablauf der Aufbewahrungsfristen Unterlagen nur vernichten oder Daten nur löschen, die das zuständige Archiv zur Vernichtung oder Löschung freigegeben hat oder wenn es nicht binnen sechs Monaten über die Archivwürdigkeit angebotener Unterlagen entschieden hat, und sofern kein Grund zur Annahme besteht, dass durch die Vernichtung oder Löschung schutzwürdige Belange von Betroffenen beeinträchtigt werden.

(4) Auf die Anbietung von offensichtlich nicht archivwürdigen Unterlagen und Daten wird im Einvernehmen mit dem zuständigen Archiv verzichtet.

(5) Die in § 2 Abs. 3 und 6 genannten Stellen bieten jeweils ein Exemplar der von ihnen herausgegebenen Veröffentlichungen, auch solcher in elektronischer Form, dem zuständigen Archiv zur Übernahme an.

(6) Die in § 2 Abs. 3 und 6 genannten Stellen können Unterlagen einem anderen öffentlichen Archiv anstelle des zuständigen Archivs mit dessen Einvernehmen zur Archivierung anbieten, wenn es im öffentlichen Interesse liegt.

§ 9 Digitales Archivgut

(1) Bei der Übernahme von digitalen Unterlagen sind Auswahlkriterien und technische Kriterien, insbesondere das Format von Primär- und Metadaten und die Form der Übermittlung, von dem zuständigen Archiv mit Zustimmung der abgebenden Stelle vorab festzulegen.

(2) Bei digitalen Unterlagen, die einer laufenden Aktualisierung unterliegen, legt das zuständige Archiv die Form der Anbietung und die Zeitabstände der Übergabe mit Zustimmung der abgebenden Stelle vorab fest.

§ 10 Feststellung der Archivwürdigkeit und Übernahme des Archivguts

(1) ¹Über die Archivwürdigkeit der angebotenen Unterlagen entscheidet das zuständige Archiv nach § 2 Abs. 1 unter Mitwirkung der anbietenden Stelle sowie unter den Gesichtspunkten der Zweckmäßigkeit und Wirtschaftlichkeit. ²Über die Archivwürdigkeit und Auswahl von gleichförmigen oder wiederkehrenden Unterlagen, die in großer Zahl anfallen, können schriftliche Vereinbarungen getroffen werden.

(2) Dem zuständigen Archiv ist Einsicht in anzubietende Unterlagen und die dazugehörigen Ordnungssysteme zu gewähren.

§ 11 Sicherung und Erschließung

(1) ¹Die öffentlichen Archive haben die notwendigen Maßnahmen zu treffen, um die dauernde Aufbewahrung, Erhaltung und Nutzbarkeit des Archivgutes sowie seinen Schutz vor unbefugter Nutzung oder vor Vernichtung sicherzustellen. ²Ausnahmsweise kann Archivgut in öffentlichen Archiven vernichtet oder gelöscht werden, wenn es für die Rechtssicherung und für die wissenschaftliche Forschung keine Bedeutung mehr hat.

(2) ¹Sofern es unter archivfachlichen Gesichtspunkten gerechtfertigt ist, können die öffentlichen Archive die im Archivgut enthaltenen Informationen auch in anderer Form archivieren und die Originalunterlagen ausnahmsweise löschen oder vernichten. ²Darüber ist ein Nachweis zu führen.

(3) ¹Die öffentlichen Archive sind verpflichtet, das Archivgut nach archivfachlichen Gesichtspunkten zu ordnen und durch Findmittel zu erschließen. ²Die Verknüpfung personenbezogener Daten durch das öffentliche Archiv ist innerhalb der in § 13 Abs. 1 und 2 genannten Schutzfristen nur zulässig, wenn schutzwürdige Belange betroffener Personen oder Dritter nicht beeinträchtigt werden.

(4) ¹Öffentliches Archivgut ist unveräußerlich und kann von Dritten nicht gutgläubig erworben werden. ²Eine Abgabe an andere öffentliche Archive ist ausnahmsweise zulässig, wenn sie im öffentlichen Interesse liegt und die Einhaltung der in diesem Gesetz für die Aufbewahrung und Nutzung von öffentlichem Archivgut getroffenen Bestimmungen gewährleistet ist.

Teil 5
Nutzung von Archivgut

§ 12 Recht auf Nutzung des öffentlichen Archivguts

(1) ¹Das Recht, öffentliches Archivgut zu nutzen, steht jeder Person zu, soweit durch Rechtsvorschriften nichts anderes bestimmt ist. ²Vereinbarungen zugunsten von Eigentümerinnen und Eigentümern privaten Archivguts bleiben unberührt.

(2) Der Zweck der Nutzung, der persönlicher, amtlicher, wissenschaftlicher, pädagogischer, publizistischer oder gewerblicher Art sein kann, muss dargelegt werden.

(3) Die Nutzung von archivierten Unterlagen, die Rechtsvorschriften des Bundes über Geheimhaltung unterliegen, richtet sich nach den Vorschriften des Bundesarchivgesetzes vom 10. März 2017 (BGBl. I S. 410).

(4) ¹Nutzer der öffentlichen Archive sind verpflichtet, von einem Werk, das unter wesentlicher Verwendung von Archivgut entstanden ist, unaufgefordert nach der Veröffentlichung ein Belegexemplar abzuliefern. ²Ist eine kostenfreie Ablieferung nicht zumutbar, kann entweder dem Archiv ein Exemplar des Werkes zur Erstellung einer Vervielfältigung überlassen werden oder eine Entschädigung bis zur Hälfte des Ladenpreises oder, wenn ein solcher Preis nicht besteht, bis zur Hälfte der Kosten des Belegexemplars verlangt werden.

§ 13 Schutzfristen

(1) ¹Für öffentliches Archivgut gilt im Regelfall eine Schutzfrist von 30 Jahren nach Entstehung der Unterlagen. ²Archivgut, das bei der Übernahme durch das öffentliche Archiv besonderen Geheimhaltungsvorschriften unterlegen hat, darf im Regelfall erst 60 Jahre nach Entstehung der Unterlagen genutzt werden. ³Dies gilt auch für Unterlagen, die aufgrund besonderer Vorschriften hätten gelöscht oder vernichtet werden müssen.

(2) ¹Unbeschadet der generellen Schutzfristen darf Archivgut, das sich seiner Zweckbestimmung oder seinem wesentlichen Inhalt nach auf eine oder mehrere natürliche Personen bezieht (personenbezogenes Archivgut), im Regelfall erst zehn Jahre nach dem Tod der betroffenen Person oder der letztverstorbenen von mehreren betroffenen Personen durch Dritte genutzt werden. ²Ist das Todesjahr nicht

festzustellen, endet die Schutzfrist 100 Jahre nach der Geburt der betroffenen Person oder der Geburt der letztgeborenen von mehreren Personen, deren Todesjahr nicht festzustellen ist. ³Ist weder Geburts- noch Todesjahr der betroffenen Person oder einer der betroffenen Personen mit vertretbarem Aufwand festzustellen, so endet die Schutzfrist 60 Jahre nach Entstehung der Unterlagen.
(3) Die Schutzfristen nach Abs. 1 und 2 gelten nicht für solches Archivgut, das bereits bei seiner Entstehung zur Veröffentlichung bestimmt war.
(4) ¹Die Schutzfristen nach Abs. 1 und 2 gelten auch bei der Nutzung durch öffentliche Stellen. ²Für die abgebenden Stellen gelten die Schutzfristen der Abs. 1 und 2 nur für Unterlagen, die bei ihnen aufgrund besonderer Vorschriften hätten gesperrt, gelöscht oder vernichtet werden müssen.
(5) ¹Die Schutzfristen können vom öffentlichen Archiv im Einzelfall auf Antrag der Nutzer verkürzt werden, wenn es im öffentlichen Interesse liegt. ²Bei personenbezogenem Archivgut ist dem Antrag auf Nutzung des Archivguts vor Ablauf der Schutzfristen stattzugeben, wenn
1. die Nutzung für ein bestimmtes Forschungsvorhaben erforderlich und sichergestellt ist, dass schutzwürdige Belange der betroffenen Personen oder Dritter nicht beeinträchtigt werden oder
2. das öffentliche Interesse an der Durchführung des Forschungsvorhabens die schutzwürdigen Belange erheblich überwiegt oder
3. die Nutzung zur Wahrnehmung berechtigter Belange im überwiegenden Interesse einer anderen Person oder Stelle unerlässlich ist und eine Beeinträchtigung schutzwürdiger Belange durch angemessene Maßnahmen ausgeschlossen wird.
(6) ¹Eine Nutzung personenbezogenen Archivguts ist unabhängig von den in Abs. 1 und 2 genannten Schutzfristen auch zulässig, wenn die Person, auf die sich das Archivgut bezieht, oder im Falle ihres Todes ihre Angehörigen zugestimmt haben. ²Die Einwilligung ist von dem überlebenden Ehegatten, der überlebenden Ehegattin, von dem eingetragenen Lebenspartner oder von der eingetragenen Lebenspartnerin, nach dem Tod der genannten Personen von den Kindern und, wenn weder Ehegatte, Ehegattin, eingetragener Lebenspartner oder eingetragene Lebenspartnerin noch Kinder vorhanden sind, von den Eltern der betroffenen Person einzuholen.
(7) ¹Vor Ablauf der Schutzfristen dürfen personenbezogene Angaben nur veröffentlicht werden, wenn die betroffenen Personen, im Falle ihres Todes ihre Angehörigen nach Abs. 6 eingewilligt haben oder dies für die Darstellung der Ergebnisse des bestimmten Forschungsvorhabens unerlässlich ist. ²Bei Amtspersonen in Ausübung ihres Amtes und bei Personen der Zeitgeschichte ist die Veröffentlichung zulässig, soweit diese einer angemessenen Berücksichtigung schutzwürdiger Belange nicht zuwiderläuft.

§ 14 Einschränkung der Nutzung von Archivgut in besonderen Fällen
(1) Die Nutzung von Archivgut ist einzuschränken oder zu versagen, wenn Grund zu der Annahme besteht, dass
1. dem Wohl der Bundesrepublik Deutschland oder dem Wohl eines ihrer Länder wesentliche Nachteile erwachsen,
2. schutzwürdige Belange Dritter beeinträchtigt werden,
3. der Erhaltungszustand des Archivguts gefährdet wird oder
4. durch die Nutzung ein nicht vertretbarer Verwaltungsaufwand entsteht.
(2) ¹Das für das Archivwesen zuständige Ministerium entscheidet über die Einschränkung oder Versagung der Nutzung des Archivguts des Hessischen Landesarchivs in den Fällen nach Abs. 1 Nr. 1. ²Das Hessische Landesarchiv entscheidet über die Einschränkung oder Versagung in den Fällen nach Abs. 1 Nr. 2 bis 4.

§ 15 Auskunfts- und Gegendarstellungsrecht
(1) ¹Einer betroffenen Person im Sinne von § 2 Abs. 1 des Hessischen Datenschutzgesetzes ist ohne Rücksicht auf die in § 13 Abs. 1 und 2 festgelegten Schutzfristen auf Antrag Auskunft über die im Archivgut zu ihrer Person enthaltenen Daten zu erteilen. ²Statt einer Auskunft kann das öffentliche Archiv Einsicht in die Unterlagen gewähren.
(2) ¹Das öffentliche Archiv ist verpflichtet, den zum öffentlichen Archivgut gehörigen Unterlagen eine Gegendarstellung der betroffenen Person beizufügen, wenn diese durch eine in den Unterlagen enthaltene Tatsachenbehauptung betroffen ist und ein berechtigtes Interesse an der Gegendarstellung

glaubhaft macht. ²Nach ihrem Tod steht dieses Recht den Angehörigen nach § 13 Abs. 6 zu. ³Weitergehende Pflichten nach Bundesrecht bleiben unberührt.
(3) ¹Die Gegendarstellung nach Abs. 2 bedarf der Schriftform und muss von der betroffenen Person oder ihren Angehörigen unterzeichnet sein. ²Sie muss sich auf Angaben über Tatsachen beschränken und darf keinen strafbaren Inhalt haben.
(4) Das Gegendarstellungsrecht nach Abs. 2 gilt nicht für amtliche Niederschriften und Berichte über öffentliche Sitzungen der gesetzgebenden oder beschließenden Organe des Bundes, der Länder, der Gemeinden und Gemeindeverbände und anderer juristischer Personen des öffentlichen Rechts sowie der Gerichte.

§ 16 Weitergabe von Vervielfältigungen öffentlichen Archivguts in besonderen Fällen
(1) Das für das Archivwesen zuständige Ministerium kann nach Anhörung des Hessischen Datenschutzbeauftragten gestatten, dass Archiven, Museen und Forschungsstellen des Auslandes Vervielfältigungen von öffentlichem Archivgut zur Geschichte der Juden unter der nationalsozialistischen Herrschaft, zur nationalsozialistischen Judenverfolgung und zu deren Aufarbeitung in der Nachkriegszeit sowie zur Geschichte des Schicksals einer Gruppe natürlicher Personen unter staatlicher Gewaltherrschaft zu archivischer Nutzung und wissenschaftlicher Forschung überlassen werden.
(2) ¹Die Gestattung ist nur zulässig, wenn sichergestellt ist, dass § 15 sowie bei der Nutzung der Vervielfältigungen die §§ 13 und 14 sinngemäße Anwendung finden. ²§ 17 des Hessischen Datenschutzgesetzes ist entsprechend anzuwenden.
(3) Im Einvernehmen mit der zuständigen obersten Bundesbehörde und dem Bundesarchiv dürfen Vervielfältigungen von Unterlagen nachgeordneter Stellen des Bundes überlassen werden.
(4) Ansprüche auf die Gestattung und Überlassung bestehen nicht.

Teil 6
Archivgut des Landtags, des Bundes, kommunales und sonstiges öffentliches Archivgut

§ 17 Archivgut des Landtags
(1) Der Hessische Landtag entscheidet, ob bei ihm entstandene archivwürdige Unterlagen von ihm selbst archiviert werden oder dem Hessischen Landesarchiv zur Übernahme angeboten werden.
(2) Sofern der Hessische Landtag ein eigenes Archiv unterhält, regelt er die Einzelheiten der Archivierung nach Maßgabe dieses Gesetzes.

§ 18 Archivgut des Bundes
¹Werden vom Hessischen Landesarchiv archivwürdige Unterlagen nachgeordneter Stellen des Bundes übernommen, so gelten sie als öffentliches Archivgut des Landes im Sinne dieses Gesetzes, soweit bundesrechtlich nichts anderes bestimmt ist. ²Für die Nutzung solcher Unterlagen gelten die Vorschriften des Bundesarchivgesetzes entsprechend.

§ 19 Kommunales Archivgut
Die Träger der kommunalen Selbstverwaltung, deren Verbände sowie kommunale Stiftungen regeln die Archivierung ihrer Unterlagen im Rahmen ihrer wirtschaftlichen Leistungsfähigkeit in eigener Zuständigkeit durch Satzung.

§ 20 Sonstiges öffentliches Archivgut
(1) Die in § 2 Abs. 3 genannten sonstigen der Aufsicht des Landes unterstehenden juristischen Personen des öffentlichen Rechts und ihre Vereinigungen einschließlich der Hochschulen und die in § 2 Abs. 6 genannten Stellen regeln die Archivierung der bei ihnen entstandenen Unterlagen in eigener Zuständigkeit in eigenen oder gemeinschaftlich getragenen fachlich geleiteten öffentlichen Archiven.
(2) Unterhalten die in Abs. 1 genannten Stellen eigene öffentliche Archive, so regeln sie die Archivierung ihres Archivgutes nach den in diesem Gesetz vorgegebenen Grundsätzen durch Satzung.
(3) ¹Nur sofern die Voraussetzungen des Abs. 1 nicht sichergestellt werden können und Vernichtung oder Zersplitterung der archivwürdigen Unterlagen drohen, sind die nicht mehr benötigten Unterlagen dieser Stellen dem Hessischen Landesarchiv anzubieten. ²In diesem Fall werden die archivwürdigen Unterlagen dieser Stellen als staatliches Archivgut behandelt.

Teil 7
Regelungsbefugnisse

§ 21[1) Ermächtigung zum Erlass von Rechtsverordnungen
(1) Die Landesregierung regelt durch Rechtsverordnung die Kostentragungspflicht
1. für Unterlagen, die aufgrund von Rechtsvorschriften dauernd aufzubewahren sind und an das Hessische Landesarchiv abgegeben werden,
2. für Zwischenarchivgut, das dem Hessischen Landesarchiv übergeben wird,
3. für die Übernahme von archivwürdigen digitalen Unterlagen durch das Hessische Landesarchiv, sofern diese nicht vorab archivtauglich konvertiert und aufbereitet sind,
4. bei Inanspruchnahme ressortspezifischer Dienstleistungen.

(2) Die für das Archivwesen zuständige Ministerin oder der hierfür zuständige Minister regelt durch Rechtsverordnung[2)
1. die Zuständigkeit des Hessischen Landesarchivs, des Hauptstaatsarchivs und der Staatsarchive,
2. die Nutzung des Archivguts des Hauptstaatsarchivs und der Staatsarchive, insbesondere das Verfahren, die Sorgfaltspflichten bei der Nutzung, die Ausleihe von Archivgut, die Herstellung von Kopien und Reproduktionen und die Einräumung von Nutzungsrechten.

Teil 8
Schlussbestimmungen

§ 22 Inkrafttreten, Außerkrafttreten
[1]Dieses Gesetz tritt am 1. Januar 2013 in Kraft. [2]Es tritt mit Ablauf des 31. Dezember 2022 außer Kraft. [3]Abweichend von Satz 1 tritt § 21 am Tage nach der Verkündung in Kraft.

---

1) § 21 ist bereits am 6.12.2012 in Kraft getreten, vgl. § 22 Satz 3.
2) Die Nutzungsordnung für die Hessischen Staatsarchive ist abgedruckt als Nr. D7.II.1a.

Nutzungsordnung für die Hessischen Staatsarchive

Satzung des Ministeriums für Wissenschaft und Kunst vom (StAnz. 2014 S. 49) (Hess. GültV 781)

Aufgrund des § 21 Abs. 2 Nr. 2 des Hessischen Archivgesetzes vom 26. November 2012 (GVBl. S. 458) verordnet die Ministerin für Wissenschaft und Kunst:

§ 1 Geltungsbereich
(1) ¹Diese Nutzungsordnung regelt die Nutzung des in den Hessischen Staatsarchiven (Hessisches Hauptstaatsarchiv, Hessisches Staatsarchiv Darmstadt und Hessisches Staatsarchiv Marburg) aufbewahrten Archivguts. ²Sie gilt auch für die Nutzung von Reproduktionen des Archivguts und für Archivgut, das den Staatsarchiven von Dritten zur allgemeinen Nutzung übergeben wurde. ³Sie gilt entsprechend für Archivgut, das von anderen Archiven oder sonstigen Stellen zur Nutzung übersandt wird, soweit die versendende Stelle nichts anderes verfügt hat. ⁴Weitergehende Rechtsvorschriften und besondere Vereinbarungen zugunsten von Eigentümern privaten Archivguts bleiben unberührt.
(2) Diese Nutzungsordnung gilt nicht für die elektronische Nutzung von Archivgut, das in digitaler Form veröffentlicht wurde.

§ 2 Nutzung
¹Archivgut wird grundsätzlich durch persönliche Einsichtnahme in dem Staatsarchiv genutzt, in dem das Archivgut aufbewahrt wird. ²Das Staatsarchiv kann die Nutzung auch durch Vorlage und Überlassung von Reproduktionen von Archivgut oder durch Ausleihe von Archivgut zu Ausstellungszwecken ermöglichen.

§ 3 Registrierung
Voraussetzung für die Nutzung von Archivgut ist die einmalige Registrierung und die Anlage eines Nutzerkontos in dem dafür bereitgestellten elektronischen Archivinformationssystem.

§ 4 Nutzungsantrag
(1) Die Nutzung ist für jedes Nutzungsvorhaben von der Nutzerin oder dem Nutzer bei dem aufbewahrenden Staatsarchiv zu beantragen.
(2) In dem Nutzungsantrag ist anzugeben:
1. Nachname, Vorname und Anschrift der Antragstellerin oder des Antragstellers,
2. Nachname, Vorname und Anschrift der Auftraggeberin oder des Auftraggebers, wenn die Nutzung im Auftrag erfolgt,
3. das Nutzungsvorhaben mit möglichst genauer zeitlicher und sachlicher Eingrenzung (Arbeitsthema),
4. die Art der Nutzung (persönlich, amtlich, wissenschaftlich, pädagogisch, publizistisch oder gewerblich); bei Nutzung zu wissenschaftlichen Zwecken ist außerdem die Art der geplanten Arbeit, bei Studien- und Prüfungsarbeiten zusätzlich die Hochschule anzugeben,
5. gegebenenfalls die Absicht der Veröffentlichung.
(3) Die Nutzerin oder der Nutzer hat sich auf Verlangen auszuweisen.
(4) Für die Nutzung digitaler Unterlagen, die im Rahmen eines automatisierten Online-Verfahrens bereitgestellt werden, bedarf es keines Nutzungsantrags.

§ 5 Nutzungsgenehmigung
(1) Das aufbewahrende Staatsarchiv erteilt die Nutzungsgenehmigung.
(2) ¹Die Nutzungsgenehmigung kann mit Bedingungen und Auflagen versehen werden. ²Dies gilt insbesondere, wenn gesetzliche Schutzfristen nach § 6 verkürzt werden oder wenn eine Vereinbarung mit der Eigentümerin oder dem Eigentümer privaten Archivguts vorliegt.
(3) ¹Bei der Verwertung der aus Archivgut gewonnenen Erkenntnisse sind die Rechte und schutzwürdigen Belange Betroffener und Dritter zu wahren. ²Im Falle der Verletzung dieser Rechte und Belange haftet die Nutzerin oder der Nutzer.
(4) Die Nutzung kann auf die Erteilung von Auskünften beschränkt werden.

(5) Das Staatsarchiv kann die Nutzung versagen, widerrufen oder nachträglich mit Auflagen versehen, wenn
1. die Nutzerin oder der Nutzer wiederholt oder schwerwiegend gegen archivrechtliche Bestimmungen verstoßen hat,
2. vom Nutzungszweck abweicht oder
3. erteilte Auflagen nicht eingehalten hat.

§ 6 Antrag auf Verkürzung von Schutzfristen
(1) Das Staatsarchiv teilt der Nutzerin oder dem Nutzer das Bestehen von Schutzfristen nach § 13 des Gesetzes unverzüglich mit.
(2) ¹Eine Verkürzung von Schutzfristen ist von der Nutzerin oder dem Nutzer bei dem aufbewahrenden Staatsarchiv unter Erläuterung der im Gesetz genannten Gründe mit einem gesonderten Formular zu beantragen. ²Der Bescheid des Staatsarchivs ist gegebenenfalls mit der Nutzungsgenehmigung zu verbinden.

§ 7 Nutzung in den Nutzungsräumen
(1) ¹Die Archivalien sind grundsätzlich in den dafür bestimmten Räumen des aufbewahrenden Staatsarchivs zu nutzen. ²Das Staatsarchiv ist berechtigt, Kontrollen durchzuführen.
(2) Öffnungszeiten der Nutzungsräume sowie sonstige Regelungen, die dem Schutz des Archivguts und einem geordneten Ablauf der Nutzung dienen, werden unter Berücksichtigung der örtlichen Gegebenheiten durch das Staatsarchiv festgelegt.
(3) Das Staatsarchiv berät die Nutzerin oder den Nutzer bei der Ermittlung einschlägiger Findmittel und Archivalien.
(4) ¹Die Nutzerin oder der Nutzer ist im Umgang mit den Archivalien zu äußerster Sorgfalt verpflichtet und haftet für jede Fahrlässigkeit. ²Insbesondere ist es nicht gestattet,
1. Archivalien sowie ihre Reihenfolge und Ordnung zu verändern,
2. Bestandteile des Archivguts zu entfernen,
3. Vermerke im Archivgut anzubringen oder vorhandene zu tilgen,
4. Archivgut als Schreib- oder Durchzeichnungsunterlage zu verwenden.
(5) ¹Die Verwendung technischer Geräte bei der Nutzung bedarf der Genehmigung. ²Diese kann versagt oder widerrufen werden, wenn dadurch das Archivgut gefährdet oder andere Nutzerinnen oder Nutzer gestört werden.
(6) Die Nutzungsräume müssen von Menschen mit Behinderungen barrierefrei erreicht werden können, soweit dies nicht mit unverhältnismäßigen Mehrkosten verbunden ist; andernfalls müssen die Staatsarchive die Möglichkeit der Nutzung durch den genannten Personenkreis mit organisatorischen Maßnahmen sicherstellen.

§ 8 Versendung und Ausleihe
(1) Die Versendung von Archivalien zur amtlichen Nutzung erfolgt im Rahmen der Amtshilfe.
(2) ¹Archivalien können zu Ausstellungszwecken ausgeliehen werden, wenn gewährleistet ist, dass das ausgeliehene Archivgut wirksam vor Verlust, Beschädigung und unbefugter Nutzung geschützt wird. ²Hierüber ist ein Leihvertrag abzuschließen.

§ 9 Reproduktionen
(1) ¹Die Nutzerin oder der Nutzer kann Reproduktionen von Archivgut durch das Staatsarchiv herstellen lassen, soweit archivrechtliche oder sonstige rechtliche Gründe nicht entgegenstehen. ²Ist das Staatsarchiv dazu technisch oder personell nicht in der Lage, kann es der Nutzerin oder dem Nutzer gestatten, Reproduktionen selbst herzustellen oder bei einer vom Staatsarchiv zu bestimmenden Stelle herstellen zu lassen. ³Das Staatsarchiv kann die Herstellung der Reproduktionen beaufsichtigen.
(2) ¹Reproduktionen von Archivgut dürfen nur hergestellt werden, soweit dabei eine Gefährdung oder Schädigung des Archivguts ausgeschlossen werden kann. ²Über die jeweils geeigneten Reproduktionsverfahren entscheidet das Staatsarchiv.
(3) Reproduktionen dürfen nur mit Zustimmung des Staatsarchivs, nur zu dem angegebenen Zweck und nur unter Angabe des Staatsarchivs und der von diesem festgelegten Signatur sowie gegebenenfalls unter Hinweis auf die dem Staatsarchiv zustehenden Veröffentlichungs- und Vervielfältigungsrechte veröffentlicht, vervielfältigt oder an Dritte weitergegeben werden.

(4) ¹Das Staatsarchiv kann ausnahmsweise die Herstellung von Reproduktionen von Archivgut gestatten, die schutzwürdige Belange Betroffener oder Dritter berühren oder noch der Schutzfrist unterliegen. ²Eine Weitergabe an Dritte ist nur zulässig, wenn diesen ebenfalls eine Nutzungsgenehmigung erteilt wurde. ³Das Staatsarchiv kann die Auflage machen, dass die Reproduktionen nach Abschluss des Nutzungsvorhabens zu vernichten oder ihm zurückzugeben sind.

§ 10 Nutzung durch abgebende Stellen

¹Für die Nutzung von Archivgut durch diejenigen Stellen, bei denen es entstanden ist oder die es abgegeben haben, finden die Vorschriften der §§ 2 bis 7, des § 8 Abs. 2 und des § 9 dieser Nutzungsordnung keine Anwendung, sofern es sich nicht um Unterlagen handelt, die bei ihnen aufgrund besonderer Vorschriften hätten gesperrt, gelöscht oder vernichtet werden müssen. ²Art und Weise der Nutzung werden im Einzelfall vereinbart.

§ 11 Aufhebung bisherigen Rechts

Die Benutzungsordnung für die Staatsarchive des Landes Hessen (Archivbenutzungsordnung – ArchivBO) vom 11. März 1997 (StAnz. S. 1300) wird aufgehoben.

§ 12 Inkrafttreten

Diese Verordnung tritt am Tage nach der Verkündung¹⁾ in Kraft.

---

1) Verkündet am 13.1.2014.

Richtlinie des Hessischen Ministeriums für Wissenschaft und Kunst für die Bewilligung von Zuwendungen für Kulturdenkmäler (Denkmalförderrichtlinie)

RL d. Ministeriums für Wissenschaft und Kunst vom 19.8.2017 – IV3 – 784/31.000 – (0077)
(StAnz. S. 850)
(Hess. GültV 76)

Bezug:
Erlass vom 10. September 2008 (StAnz. S. 2563)

1.
Grundsatz

Das Land Hessen trägt zur Erhaltung von Kulturdenkmälern gemäß § 13 Abs. 2 des Hessischen Denkmalschutzgesetzes (HD-SchG) in der Fassung vom 28. November 2016 (GVBl. Nr. 18 vom 5.12.2016, S. 211) bei, indem es Zuwendungen im Rahmen der zur Verfügung stehenden Haushaltsmittel bewilligt.
Die Förderung richtet sich nach den haushaltsrechtlichen Bestimmungen des Landes Hessen, insbesondere der Hessischen Landeshaushaltsordnung (LHO), den Vorläufigen Verwaltungsvorschriften zur Hessischen Landeshaushaltsordnung (VV-LHO) sowie den dazu ergangenen Richtlinien, insbesondere den
- Allgemeinen Nebenbestimmungen für die Verwendung der Zuwendungen des Landes sowie für den Nachweis und die Prüfung der Verwendung (Allgemeine Nebenbestimmungen für Zuwendungen zur Projektförderung [ANBest-P]).
- Allgemeinen Nebenbestimmungen für die Verwendung der Zuwendungen des Landes an Gebietskörperschaften und Zusammenschlüsse von Gebietskörperschaften sowie für den Nachweis und die Prüfung der Verwendung (Allgemeine Nebenbestimmungen für Zuwendungen zur Projektförderung an Gebietskörperschaften und Zusammenschlüsse von Gebietskörperschaften [ANBest.GK]).

Rechtsanspruch auf Förderung besteht nicht. Die Zuwendungen werden durch das Landesamt für Denkmalpflege Hessen (LfDH) bewilligt.
Die Förderung von Kulturdenkmälern dient der Allgemeinheit. Verhindert werden soll, dass die Förderung zur Spekulation ausgenutzt wird.

Beihilferechtliche Einordnung

Die auf der Grundlage dieser Richtlinien gewährten Zuwendungen sind keine Beihilfen im Sinne von Art. 107 Abs. 1 des Vertrages über die Arbeitsweise der Europäischen Union (AEUV).

2.
Zuwendungsempfänger

2.1. Zuwendungsempfänger können sein:
    2.1.1. Eigentümer oder Erbbauberechtigte des Kulturdenkmals (Erbbauvertrag auf mindestens 66 Jahre) oder Inhaber eines dinglich gesicherten Nutzungsrechts oder
    2.1.2. wenn sich das Kulturdenkmal im Eigentum einer Gebietskörperschaft befindet, im Besitz eines auf mindestens 25 Jahre abgeschlossenen Pachtvertrages oder
    2.1.3. bei Vorhaben kleineren Umfangs im Besitze eines auf mindestens 15 Jahre abgeschlossenen Nutzungsvertrages (zum Beispiel Miet- oder Pachtvertrag) oder
    2.1.4. Untere Denkmalschutzbehörden (UDSchB) zur Durchführung von Ersatzvornahmen nach § 14 HDSchG, wenn und soweit deren Haushaltsmittel hierfür erschöpft sind. In diesen Fällen ist in den Bedingungen für die Zuwendung sicherzustellen, dass dem Land gegenüber dem zum Bauunterhalt Verpflichteten ein Wertausgleichsanspruch (Ziff. 7) gesichert wird.

D7.III.1 Denkmalförderrichtlinie

2.2. Zuwendungen werden nicht gewährt an die Bundesrepublik Deutschland (einschließlich Sondervermögens), ein Bundesland, einen ausländischen Staat sowie deren Körperschaften und Anstalten. Satz 1 gilt nicht für Hessische Stiftungen, Hochschul- und Forschungseinrichtungen sowie hessische Landesbetriebe.

3.
Formelle Zuwendungsvoraussetzungen

3.1. Gegenstand der Förderung sind Kulturdenkmäler oder Teile von Kulturdenkmälern.
3.2. Die Maßnahme muss mit dem LfDH abgestimmt sein. Gesetzlich vorgeschriebene Genehmigungen bzw. Zustimmungen, insbesondere nach dem HDSchG, müssen vorliegen, begründen jedoch keinen Anspruch auf Zuwendung.
3.3. Die Gesamtfinanzierung des Vorhabens muss gesichert sein.
3.4. Zuwendungen zur Projektförderung dürfen nur für solche Vorhaben bewilligt werden, die noch nicht begonnen worden sind. Ist eine Maßnahme aufgrund zwingender Umstände unaufschiebbar, kann das Hessische Ministerium für Wissenschaft und Kunst (HMWK) einem vorzeitigen Beginn zustimmen; dies gilt nicht für kommunale Vorhaben. Die Zustimmung begründet keinen Rechtsanspruch auf Förderung. Entsprechende Anträge sind über das LfDH, das dazu eine Empfehlung ausspricht, an das HMWK zu leiten.
3.5. Die zur denkmalpflegerischen Beurteilung notwendigen Unterlagen müssen vorliegen (s.a. Ziffer 6.1). Dazu zählen insbesondere
   - eine Kostenschätzung mit Erläuterung der geplanten Leistungen sowie ggfs. Planunterlagen,
   - der Finanzierungsplan (aufgegliederte Berechnung der mit dem Zuwendungszweck zusammenhängenden Ausgaben mit einer Übersicht über die beabsichtigte Finanzierung einschließlich der Fördermittel anderer Stellen),
   - eine Erklärung, dass mit der Maßnahme noch nicht begonnen worden ist und
   - ein Antrag auf dem beim LfDH erhältlichen Vordruck.

4.
Materielle Zuwendungsvoraussetzungen

4.1. Gegenstand der Förderung sind Maßnahmen der Substanzerhaltung. In ihrem Bestand bedrohte Kulturdenkmäler haben bei der Förderung Vorrang vor anderen Maßnahmen.
4.2. Bezuschusst werden denkmalbedingte Aufwendungen, also solche, die allein oder überwiegend aus Gründen der Denkmalpflege erforderlich werden.
   4.2.1. Zu denkmalbedingten Aufwendungen zählen unter anderem auch anteilige Architekten- und Ingenieurhonorare, Gerüstkosten, Kosten vorbereitender Untersuchungen einschließlich Dokumentationen, Kosten restauratorischer Befunduntersuchungen und Sicherungen, Planungskosten, zum Beispiel für die Revitalisierung ungenutzter Kulturdenkmäler, Kosten für die Anwendung vorbildlicher Erhaltungsmethoden und Kosten bodendenkmalpflegerischer Untersuchungen einschließlich deren Dokumentation.
   4.2.2. Zu den denkmalbedingten Aufwendungen zählen weiter: Aufwendungen für die Wiederherstellung von teilzerstörten Kulturdenkmälern, wenn hierbei die originale Substanz gesichert wird, sowie Aufwendungen für die rekonstruierende Wiederherstellung, soweit untergegangene, aber für den Gesamtzusammenhang, in dem das Kulturdenkmal steht, unverzichtbare Teile eines noch bestehenden Kulturdenkmals ergänzt werden. Voraussetzung ist, dass der Umfang der Wiederherstellung im Verhältnis zum Umfang des Originals gering ist.
   4.2.3. Die Mehrwertsteuer zählt nur dann zum denkmalpflegerischen Aufwand, wenn der Zuschussempfänger keinen Vorsteuerabzug vornehmen kann.
4.3. Die nach diesen Richtlinien zu vergebenden Fördermittel dürfen nur eingesetzt werden, wenn eine Förderung aus anderen Programmen nicht ausreicht, um eine denkmalgerechte Erhaltung zu sichern.

4.4. Doppelförderung ist ausgeschlossen, Ergänzungsförderung unter den Voraussetzungen der Ziffer 4.6 zulässig.

4.5. Nicht förderungsfähig sind Kosten
- des Erwerbs eines Kulturdenkmals,
- einer Totalrekonstruktion,
- eines Neubaus in einer Gesamtanlage,
- für die Beschaffung von Finanzierungsmitteln,
- für Maßnahmen in der Umgebung von Kulturdenkmälern,
- laufender Unterhaltung, die vergleichbare Unterhaltungskosten nicht denkmalgeschützter Objekte nicht übersteigen,
- eigene Arbeitsleistung (Ausnahme: Ziff. 4.7)
- Maßnahmen, die ausschließlich der Verschönerung dienen und
- rentierliche nutzungsbedingte Aufwendungen.

4.6. Bei Zuwendungen, die geleistet werden müssen, um die Kosten des Erhalts im zumutbaren Rahmen zu halten (vgl. § 13 Abs. 1 HDSchG), um Maßnahmen der UDSchB nach § 14 zu ermöglichen, oder um Ansprüche nach § 27 HDSchG abzuwenden, kann im Einzelfall von den Voraussetzungen der Ziffer 4.1 bis 4.2 abgewichen werden.

4.7. Die vom Zuwendungsempfänger geleistete Eigenarbeitszeit wird nach einem von der Bewilligungsbehörde festgelegten Tarif bei der Berechnung der förderfähigen Aufwendungen der Maßnahme angerechnet. Sie ist als Eigenanteil im Finanzierungsplan nur berücksichtigungsfähig, wenn sie mehr als 150 Stunden beträgt. Sie ist durch eine Bestätigung des Architekten oder des Bauamts der Gemeinde oder der UDSchB glaubhaft zu machen. Das vom Zuwendungsempfänger selbst aufgewendete Material wird zum nachgewiesenen Einkaufspreis angerechnet. Der Einsatz von Geräten und Fahrzeugen von Privaten ist nur gegen Rechnung zuwendungsfähig. Bei Unternehmern, Handwerkern und Restauratoren, die bei Eigenleistungen im Rahmen ihres Geschäftsbetriebes tätig werden, werden die ortsüblichen Entgelte abzüglich eines pauschalierten Gewinnanteils von 25 vom Hundert anerkannt. Diese Regelung gilt auch für Architekten, Ingenieure und Baustatiker bis zu einem Höchstbetrag von 10 vom Hundert der Gesamtkosten der Maßnahme. Bei Eigenleistungen von Kommunen, zum Beispiel bei der Planung, Bauleitung und Durchführung der Baumaßnahme, kann der Tariflohn der eingesetzten Arbeitskräfte mit einem pauschalen Abzug von 25 vom Hundert in die Gesamtkostenberechnung einbezogen werden. Die Mindestleistungsgrenze von 150 Stunden pro Maßnahme gilt auch für die Gemeinde. Beim Einsatz gemeindeeigener Baufahrzeuge und Baumaschinen kann ein angemessener Stundensatz abzüglich eines Gemeindeanteils von 25 vom Hundert anerkannt werden.

5.
Art und Umfang der Zuwendung

5.1. Die Zuwendung wird in der Regel als Anteilfinanzierung gewährt (Nr. 2.2.1 der VV zu § 44 LHO).

5.2. Zuwendungsfähig ist der nachzuweisende denkmalbedingte Aufwand (Ziffer 4.2).

5.3. Die Höhe der Zuwendung richtet sich bei Maßnahmen privater und kirchlicher Eigentümer nach der Bedeutung des Kulturdenkmals und der Dringlichkeit des Falles, nach der Zahl der vorliegenden Anträge, den im Landeshaushalt ausgewiesenen Mitteln sowie nach der Leistungsfähigkeit der UDSchB und der Gemeinde. Zu berücksichtigen ist auch, ob der Antragsteller Steuervergünstigungen für die Maßnahme in Anspruch nehmen kann. Das LfDH entscheidet in jedem Einzelfall nach pflichtgemäßem Ermessen.

5.4. Eine nachträgliche Erhöhung der Zuwendung ist nur in begründeten Ausnahmefällen möglich, wenn im Verlauf der Maßnahme unvorhersehbare Erschwernisse auftreten, die nicht im Verantwortungsbereich des Zuwendungsempfängers liegen und zusätzlichen denkmalbedingten Aufwand verursachen. Das LfDH ist vor Eingehen entsprechender Verpflichtungen nach Maßgabe der Allgemeinen Nebenbestimmungen (Anlagen zu VV-LHO Nr. 5.1 zu § 44 LHO) zu informieren. Ein Anspruch auf eine Erhöhung der Zuwendung besteht nicht.

6. Verfahren

6.1 Antrag

6.1.1. Zuwendungsanträge sind unter Verwendung der beim LfDH erhältlichen Vordrucke dort bis spätestens zum 31. Januar des Jahres zu stellen. Die notwendigen Unterlagen (Ziffer 3.5), insbesondere der Finanzierungsplan, sind beizufügen. Verspätet eingehende Anträge können nur in Ausnahmefällen berücksichtigt werden; ein solcher Fall liegt in der Regel vor, wenn die Überschreitung der Frist unvermeidbar war und die Maßnahmen aus zwingenden denkmalpflegerischen und ordnungsrechtlichen Gründen unaufschiebbar sind.

6.1.2. Das LfDH erstellt aufgrund der zur Bewilligung vorgesehenen Anträge einen Maßnahmeplan für das laufende Haushaltsjahr. Er enthält
- alle Projekte, für die eine Zuwendung ab 30.000 Euro vorgesehen ist,
- eine Darstellung der regionalen Verteilung der Mittel auf die Bereiche der unteren Denkmalschutzbehörden und
- eine Liste der kommunalen Projekte.

Der Entwurf des Maßnahmeplans ist dem HMWK zur Abstimmung vorzulegen.

Nach erfolgter Abstimmung übersendet das HMWK ein Exemplar des Maßnahmeplans an das Ministerium der Finanzen/Bauberatungsstelle.

6.2 Bewilligung

6.2.1. Das LfDH bewilligt nach Maßgabe der zur Verfügung stehenden Haushaltsmittel und des abgestimmten Maßnahmeplans (Ziffer 6.1.2) die Zuwendung durch schriftlichen Bewilligungsbescheid. Dieser kann Bedingungen und Auflagen enthalten, insbesondere hinsichtlich der Beteiligung bei Ausschreibung und Vergabe von Arbeiten, die besondere denkmalpflegerische Sachkenntnis voraussetzen. Bei Zuwendungen, die geleistet werden müssen, um die Kosten des Erhalts im zumutbaren Rahmen zu halten oder um Ansprüche nach § 27 HDSchG abzuwenden (vgl. Ziff. 4.6) ist dies im Bewilligungsbescheid darzustellen und zu begründen.

Der Bewilligungsbescheid überträgt, soweit dies nach Ziff. 6.3.3 vorgesehen ist, dem LBIH die baufachliche Prüfung des Vorhabens.

Der Bewilligungsbescheid legt fest, wem gegenüber der Verwendungsnachweis zu führen ist. Die UDSchB, die Gemeinde und gegebenenfalls die Aufsichtsbehörden des Zuwendungsempfängers erhalten eine Durchschrift des Bewilligungsbescheides und, soweit erforderlich, die geprüften Antragsunterlagen.

Soweit nach Ziff. 6.3.3 eine baufachliche Prüfung vorgesehen ist, erhält der LBIH eine Durchschrift des Bewilligungsbescheids einschließlich der geprüften Antragsunterlagen.

Anträge, die im Rahmen dieser Richtlinien nicht bewilligt werden können, sind schriftlich abzulehnen.

6.2.2. Änderungen des Bewilligungsbescheides bedürfen der Schriftform.

6.2.3. Die bewilligte Zuwendung ist innerhalb der im Bewilligungsbescheid angegebenen Frist des laufenden Haushaltsjahres (Bewilligungszeitraum) abzurufen. Das LfDH kann die Frist auf Antrag verlängern. Einzelheiten regelt der Bewilligungsbescheid.

6.3 Verwendungsnachweis und Auszahlung

6.3.1. Die bewilligte Zuwendung wird durch das LfDH frühestens nach Bestandskraft des Bescheides ausgezahlt.

Soweit die denkmalbedingten Aufwendungen 10.000 Euro übersteigen und in den nächsten 2 Monaten entsprechende Zahlungen fällig sind, können Teilbeträge ausgezahlt werden.

6.3.2. Bei Zuwendungen bis 10 000 Euro erfolgt die Auszahlung, wenn die entsprechenden denkmalbedingten Aufwendungen entstanden und durch geprüften Verwendungsnachweis nachgewiesen sind.
Der Verwendungsnachweis ist auf den dem Bewilligungsbescheid beigefügten Formblättern zu führen, ihm ist ein Sachbericht einschließlich Fotografien beizufügen.
6.3.3. Die zuständige Stelle für die Prüfung des Verwendungsnachweises wird im jeweiligen Bewilligungsbescheid festgelegt.
Bei Maßnahmen privater Denkmaleigentümer mit einer vorgesehen Förderung von über 250.000 € erfolgt die baufachliche Prüfung des Verwendungsnachweises durch den LBIH.
Die jeweils geltenden Regelungen der Landeshaushaltsordnung (LHO) für Zuwendungen für Baumaßnahmen sind zu beachten.
Die denkmalfachliche Prüfung bleibt dem LfDH vorbehalten.

7.
Veräußerung eines geförderten Kulturdenkmals/Wertausgleich

7.1. Die Veräußerung eines mit mehr als 50.000 € geförderten Kulturdenkmals durch einen privaten Zuwendungsempfänger innerhalb von 15 Jahren nach Auszahlung der letzten Zuwendung ist dem LfDH unverzüglich anzuzeigen.
7.2. In den Bewilligungsbescheid wird ab einer Fördersumme von 200.000 € eine Wertausgleichsklausel aufgenommen, wenn die denkmalpflegerischen Mehraufwendungen eines privaten Zuwendungsempfängers mit mindestens 50 von 100 gefördert werden.
7.3. Zur Sicherung des Wertausgleichsanspruchs haben private Zuwendungsempfänger bei Zuwendungen von insgesamt mehr als 100.000 € auf ihre Kosten Sicherheiten bis zur Höhe des Zuwendungsbetrags zu bestellen und vor Auszahlung der Zuwendung nachzuweisen. Die Sicherheiten sind zurückzugeben, wenn der Wertausgleichsanspruch erfüllt wurde, spätestens jedoch nach 15 Jahren. Die Bewilligungsbedingungen sollen in diesen Fällen folgende Regelungen aufnehmen:
„Im Falle der Veräußerung des geförderten Kulturdenkmals durch den derzeitigen Eigentümer ist ein Betrag in Höhe von [...] an das Land Hessen, vertreten durch das Landesamt für Denkmalpflege Hessen, als Ausgleich für den dem Kulturdenkmal durch die gewährte Zuwendung zugeflossenen Wertzuwachs mit folgender Maßgabe zurückzuzahlen:
– *Wird das Kulturdenkmal innerhalb von 15 Jahren, beginnend mit dem Ablauf des Jahres, in dem die Zuwendung gewährt wurde, nicht verkauft, so entfällt die Pflicht, einen Wertausgleich zu leisten.*
– *Eine Abschreibung des Anspruchs findet jährlich mit 6 ⅔ % statt.*
– *Die zweckentsprechende Verwendung ist durch eine jederzeit fällige mit ... % verzinsliche Buchgrundschuld in Höhe der Landeszuwendung von ... € zu Gunsten des Landes Hessen, vertreten durch das Landesamt Denkmalpflege Hessen, zu sichern."*
Die Buchgrundschuld hat folgenden Wortlaut:
„Buchgrundschuld in Höhe von ... € zur Sicherung der zweckentsprechenden Verwendung der Landeszuwendung zur Erhaltung des Kulturdenkmals... und des Wertausgleichsanspruchs gemäß Ziffer... des Bewilligungsbescheids vom [Datum]. Die Buchgrundschuld ist jederzeit fällig und mit ... % zu verzinsen. Begünstigt ist das Land Hessen, vertreten durch das Hessische Ministerium für Wissenschaft und Kunst, dieses vertreten durch das Landesamt für Denkmalpflege Hessen."

8.
Schlussbestimmungen

Diese Richtlinien treten mit Wirkung vom 1. Oktober 2017 in Kraft. Meine Richtlinien vom 10. September 2008 (StAnz. S. 2563) hebe ich zu diesem Zeitpunkt auf.

D7.III.2 Verfassung Hessische Kulturstiftung

Verfassung der Hessischen Kulturstiftung[1)]

§ 1 Name, Rechtsform, Sitz
(1) Mit dem Namen „Hessische Kulturstiftung" wird eine Stiftung errichtet.
(2) Sie ist eine rechtsfähige Stiftung des bürgerlichen Rechts.
(3) Die Stiftung hat ihren Sitz in Wiesbaden.

§ 2 Stiftungszweck
(1) Zweck der Stiftung ist die Förderung und Bewahrung von Kunst und Kultur im Lande Hessen. Ihr obliegt insbesondere die Förderung von Museen, Bibliotheken und Archiven durch den Erwerb und die Sicherung besonders wertvoller Kulturgüter, Kunstgegenstände und Sammlungen mit herausragender Bedeutung.
Die Stiftung kann darüber hinaus bedeutsame Vorhaben der Dokumentation und Präsentation von Kunst und Geschichte fördern, soweit sie von besonderem Interesse sind sowie besondere Aufgaben künstlerischer Nachwuchsförderung wahrnehmen. Der Satzungszweck wird zudem durch die Beschaffung und Weitergabe von Mitteln an andere steuerbegünstigte Körperschaften oder juristische Personen des öffentlichen Rechtes zur Förderung von Kunst und Kultur im Land Hessen im Sinne des § 58 Nr. 1 AO verwirklicht. Sie verfolgt ausschließlich und unmittelbar gemeinnützige Zwecke im Sinne des Abschnitts „Steuerbegünstigte Zwecke" der Abgabenordnung in der jeweils geltenden Fassung. Die Stiftung ist selbstlos tätig und verfolgt nicht in erster Linie eigenwirtschaftliche Zwecke.

§ 3 Mittel der Stiftung, Zuwendungen
(1) Das Land Hessen hat die Stiftung im Zuge der Errichtung mit 21 Mio. DM (entspricht Euro 10 737 129) Stiftungskapital ausgestattet und das Stiftungskapital in den Folgejahren durch Zustiftungen erhöht.
(2) Das Land führt der Stiftung jährlich Zuwendungen nach Maßgabe des Landeshaushalts als verfügbare Stiftungsmittel zu.
(3) Das Stiftungsvermögen erhöht sich durch weitere Zustiftungen, die von sonstigen Förderern und dem Land hierzu bestimmt sind.
(4) Das Stiftungsvermögen ist in seinem Bestand ungeschmälert zu erhalten, um die Erfüllung des Stiftungszweckes langfristig sicherzustellen. Der Stiftungsrat kann beschließen, dass die Erträge des Stiftungsvermögens und Zuwendungen sonstiger Förderer nach Maßgabe der steuerrechtlichen Zulässigkeit dem Stiftungsvermögen zugeführt werden, wenn und solange dies erforderlich ist, um den steuerbegünstigten Zweck der Stiftung auch in Zukunft nachhaltig erfüllen zu können.
(5) Die Stiftung erfüllt ihre Aufgaben aus den Erträgen des Stiftungsvermögens, aus den Zuwendungen sonstiger Förderer und den Zuwendungen des Landes Hessen.
(6) Mittel der Stiftung dürfen nur für verfassungsmäßige Zwecke verwendet werden. Es darf keine Person durch Ausgaben, die dem Zwecke der Stiftung fremd sind oder durch unverhältnismäßig hohe Vergütungen begünstigt werden. Der Stifter erhält keine Zuwendungen aus Mitteln der Stiftung.
(7) Gegenstände, Werke, Güter oder Sammlungen, die die Stiftung erwirbt, werden im Rahmen der steuerrechtlichen Zulässigkeit grundsätzlich zur Verwirklichung kultureller Zwecke in das Eigentum des Landes übertragen. Die Entscheidung hierüber trifft der Stiftungsrat.

§ 4 Stiftungsorgane
(1) Organe der Stiftung sind
- der Stiftungsrat
- der Stiftungsvorstand

(2) Niemand darf Mitglied in beiden Stiftungsorganen sein.
Nach Beendigung ihrer Amtszeit nehmen die bestellten Mitglieder des Stiftungsrates ihre Amtsgeschäfte bis zur Bestellung ihrer Nachfolger wahr.

§ 5 Stiftungsrat
(1) Dem Stiftungsrat gehören der Ministerpräsident als Vorsitzender, der Minister für Wissenschaft und Kunst als stellvertretender Vorsitzender sowie der Minister der Finanzen und bis zu neun weitere

---
1) Fundstelle: https://www.hkst.de/de/stiftungsverfassung/.

Mitglieder an, bei deren Auswahl auch die Beteiligung privater Förderer an der Stiftungstätigkeit Ausdruck findet.
(2) Die Mitglieder des Stiftungsrates werden von der Landesregierung für die Dauer von fünf Jahren bestellt. Wiederbestellungen sind zulässig, ebenso vorzeitige Abberufungen aus wichtigem Grund. Wenn ein Mitglied des Stiftungsrates vor Ablauf seiner Amtszeit ausscheidet, erfolgt die Bestellung des Nachfolgers für den Rest der Amtszeit des ausgeschiedenen Mitgliedes des Stiftungsrates.

§ 6 Aufgaben des Stiftungsrats
(1) Der Stiftungsrat berät und entscheidet über alle Fragen, die zum Aufgabenbereich der Stiftung gehören. Insbesondere obliegt ihm die Entscheidung über die Verwendung der Stiftungsmittel, soweit es sich um Aufgaben handelt, die über die laufende Geschäftsführung hinausgehen.
(2) Der Stiftungsrat legt die Richtlinien für die Tätigkeit des Vorstands fest.
(3) Der Stiftungsrat hat ferner folgende Aufgaben:
1. Erlass einer Geschäftsordnung für die Stiftung;
2. Feststellung des Haushaltsplanes;
3. Genehmigung der Jahresrechnung und des Jahresberichts;
4. Entlastung des Vorstands;
5. Beschlussfassung über Anträge auf Änderung von Verfassung und Geschäftsordnung der Stiftung, Zusammenlegung und Auflösung der Stiftung gemäß § 10;
6. Beschlussfassung über die Wahl der Abschlussprüfer sowie die Wahl der Prüfer für außerordentliche Prüfungen.

(4) Die Tätigkeit im Stiftungsrat ist ehrenamtlich.
(5) An den Sitzungen kann der Vorstand beratend teilnehmen.

§ 7 Beschlussfassung des Stiftungsrats
(1) Beschlüsse des Stiftungsrats bedürfen der Mehrheit von drei Vierteln der abgegebenen Stimmen. Der Stiftungsrat ist beschlussfähig, wenn die Mitglieder ordnungsgemäß eingeladen und mehr als die Hälfte der gemäß § 5 Abs. 1 dem Stiftungsrat angehörenden Mitglieder, darunter der Vorsitzende oder der stellvertretende Vorsitzende, anwesend sind.
Abwesende Stiftungsratsmitglieder können an der Beschlussfassung des Stiftungsrates teilnehmen, indem sie schriftliche Stimmabgaben überreichen lassen. Die schriftlichen Stimmabgaben können durch andere Stiftungsratsmitglieder überreicht werden.
(2) Beschlüsse können auch außerhalb von Sitzungen durch Erklärungen der stimmberechtigten Mitglieder im schriftlichen Umlaufverfahren gefasst werden. Abs. 1 gilt entsprechend.

§ 8 Vorstand
(1) Der Vorstand der Stiftung besteht aus dem Vorsitzenden und mindestens einem weiteren Mitglied, die von der Landesregierung bestellt werden. Die Tätigkeit des Vorstands kann hauptamtlich oder ehrenamtlich bei Gewährung einer angemessenen Aufwandsentschädigung sein.
(2) Die Berufung erfolgt auf eine Dauer von bis zu fünf Jahren; eine vorzeitige Abberufung durch den Stiftungsrat aus wichtigem Grund ist zulässig.
(3) Der Vorstand verwaltet die Stiftung, führt die laufenden Geschäfte und sorgt für die Vorbereitung und Durchführung der Beschlüsse des Stiftungsrats. Er hat insbesondere den Jahresbericht vorzulegen sowie den Wirtschaftsplan und den Jahresabschluss, bestehend aus Bilanz, Gewinn- und Verlustrechnung, aufzustellen. Im übrigen bestimmen sich seine Befugnisse nach der Geschäftsordnung.
(4) Zur Erledigung der oben genannten Aufgaben wird eine Geschäftsstelle mit hauptamtlich tätigen Angestellten eingerichtet. Die Kosten trägt die Stiftung. Das Nähere regelt die Geschäftsordnung der Stiftung.
(5) Der Vorstand vertritt die Stiftung gerichtlich und außergerichtlich. Willenserklärungen des Vorstands sind verbindlich, wenn sie vom Vorsitzenden des Vorstands und einem Vorstandsmitglied abgegeben werden.

§ 9 Rechnungslegung und Prüfung
(1) Der Vorstand hat die zum Ende eines jeden Geschäftsjahres (Kalenderjahres) zu fertigenden Aufstellungen über die Einnahmen und Ausgaben der Stiftung und über ihr Vermögen (Wirtschaftsplan,

Jahresabschluss, bestehend aus Bilanz, Gewinn- und Verlustrechnung) durch einen öffentlich bestellten Wirtschaftsprüfer oder eine anerkannte Wirtschaftsprüfungsgesellschaft prüfen zu lassen.
(2) Der Landesrechnungshof hat ebenfalls das Recht zur Prüfung.

§ 10 Verfassungsänderung, Auflösung, Aufhebung der Stiftung
(1) Beschlüsse über Verfassungsänderungen und die Auflösung oder Zusammenlegung der Stiftung bedürfen der Mehrheit von drei Vierteln der Mitglieder des Stiftungsrats. Einer wesentlichen Änderung der Verhältnisse bedarf es dazu nicht.
(2) Bei Aufhebung oder Auflösung der Stiftung oder bei Wegfall steuerbegünstigter Zwecke fällt das Vermögen der Stiftung an das Land Hessen oder an eine andere steuerbegünstigte Körperschaft zwecks Verwendung für die Förderung von Kunst und Kultur im Land Hessen.

§ 11 Stiftungsaufsicht
Die Stiftung unterliegt der Stiftungsaufsicht nach Maßgabe des jeweiligen Stiftungsrechts.

§ 12 Schlussbestimmungen
Die vorliegende Verfassung tritt am 11.9.2017 in Kraft und ersetzt die bis dahin gültige Verfassung vom 1.8.2013.

Richtlinien für die Antragstellung der Hessischen Kulturstiftung[1]

Allgemein

- Alle Anträge sind an den Vorstand der Hessischen Kulturstiftung zu richten.
- Sie bedürfen der Schriftform.
- Förderanfragen müssen frühzeitig vor der Realisierung gestellt werden; eine Nachfinanzierung ist nicht möglich.

Bestandteile einer Förderanfrage

- Eine ausführliche Beschreibung des Projektes, Abbildungs- bzw. Dokumentationsmaterial, ein detaillierter und verbindlicher Kosten- und Finanzierungsplan, ggf. Gutachten (bei Ankäufen).
- Eine Vorlage für Finanzpläne steht auf der Webseite der Hessischen Kulturstiftung als Download zur Verfügung.

Hinweise für geplante Ankäufe

- Bei Anfragen zur Mitfinanzierung von Ankäufen soll die Sinnhaftigkeit der angestrebten Erwerbung in Bezug auf das Museumskonzept hervorgehen.
- Der Antragsteller bestätigt, dass Eigentumsverhältnisse und Provenienz geklärt sind.
- Bitte beachten Sie dazu die Bestimmungen des Kulturgutschutzgesetzes.
- Es werden zwei gutachterliche Stellungnahmen von unabhängigen und möglichst im aktiven Dienst stehenden, anerkannten Fachleuten über die besondere Bedeutung des Objektes/der Sammlung benötigt.
- Die Hessische Kulturstiftung behält sich vor, eigene Gutachten einzuholen; dies gilt insbesondere für die Prüfung der Preiswürdigkeit des angestrebten Ankaufs.
- Auktionserwerbe: Im Falle eines Ankaufs in einer Auktion muss das Limit eingehalten werden. Wird das Limit überschritten, trägt den zusätzlichen Aufwand der Antragsteller; der Zuschuss der Kulturstiftung bleibt unverändert. Kann unter dem Limit erworben werden, verpflichtet sich der Antragsteller zur anteiligen Rückerstattung des Förderbetrages.

Weitere Hinweise

Für Antragsteller aus dem Rhein-Main-Gebiet:
Bitte beachten Sie, dass Projekte entweder durch den Kulturfonds Frankfurt RheinMain oder die Hessische Kulturstiftung mitfinanziert werden können; eine Finanzierung durch beide Institutionen ist nicht möglich.
Die Hessische Kulturstiftung beteiligt sich in der Regel mit einem Zuschuss in Höhe von bis zu einem Drittel der Gesamtkosten.

Für Antragsteller aus der Region:
Bei Fördermaßnahmen in der Region kann die Stiftung Zuschüsse bis zu 50 % der Gesamtkosten gewähren.
Weitere Bedingungen sind abhängig vom Einzelfall und werden zusammen mit der Förderungszusage zugesandt.

---

[1] Fundstelle: https://www.hkst.de/de/downloads/.

Verordnung zur Benennung der zuständigen Behörde nach dem Kulturgutschutzgesetz

Vom 24. Oktober 2016 (GVBl. S. 186)
(FFN 75-3)

Aufgrund des § 3 Abs. 1 Satz 2 des Kulturgutschutzgesetzes vom 31. Juli 2016 (BGBl. I S. 1914) und des § 1 Abs. 1 des Gesetzes zur Bestimmung von Zuständigkeiten vom 3. April 1998 (GVBl. I S. 98), zuletzt geändert durch Gesetz vom 13. Dezember 2012 (GVBl. I S. 622), verordnet die Landesregierung

§ 1 [Zuständige Behörde]
Zuständige Behörde nach § 3 Abs. 1 Satz 1 des Kulturgutschutzgesetzes ist das Hessische Ministerium für Wissenschaft und Kunst.

§ 2 [Inkrafttreten]
Diese Verordnung tritt am Tag nach der Verkündung[1] in Kraft.

---

1) Verkündet am 7.11.2016.

Verfassung des Landes Mecklenburg-Vorpommern

Vom 23. Mai 1993 (GVOBl. M-V S. 372)
(GS Meckl.-Vorp. Gl. Nr.100-4)
zuletzt geändert durch Art. 1 ÄndG vom 14. Juli 2016 (GVOBl. M-V S. 573)
– Auszug –

1. Abschnitt:
Grundlagen

III.
Staatsziele

Artikel 16 (Förderung von Kultur und Wissenschaft)
(1) ¹Land, Gemeinden und Kreise schützen und fördern Kultur, Sport, Kunst und Wissenschaft. ²Dabei werden die besonderen Belange der beiden Landesteile Mecklenburg und Vorpommern berücksichtigt.
(2) Das Land schützt und fördert die Pflege der niederdeutschen Sprache.
[…]

Artikel 18 (Nationale Minderheiten und Volksgruppen)
Die kulturelle Eigenständigkeit ethnischer und nationaler Minderheiten und Volksgruppen von Bürgern deutscher Staatsangehörigkeit steht unter dem besonderen Schutz des Landes.

D8.I.1 Denkmalschutzgesetz M-V

Gesetz zum Schutz und zur Pflege der Denkmale im Lande Mecklenburg-Vorpommern (Denkmalschutzgesetz – DSchG M-V)

In der Fassung der Bekanntmachung vom 6. Januar 1998[1]) (GVOBl. M-V S. 12, ber. S. 247) (GS Meckl.-Vorp. Gl. Nr.224-2)
zuletzt geändert durch Art. 10 ÄndG vom 12. Juli 2010 (GVOBl. M-V S. 383)

Inhaltsübersicht

Erster Abschnitt
Allgemeine Vorschriften
§ 1 Aufgaben des Denkmalschutzes und der Denkmalpflege
§ 2 Begriffsbestimmungen

Zweiter Abschnitt
Behörden des Denkmalschutzes und der Denkmalpflege
§ 3 Denkmalschutzbehörden
§ 4 Denkmalfachbehörde
§ 5 Denkmalliste

Dritter Abschnitt
Maßnahmen für Denkmale
§ 6 Erhaltungspflicht
§ 7 Genehmigungspflichtige Maßnahmen
§ 8 Veräußerungs- und Veränderungsanzeige
§ 9 Auskunfts- und Duldungspflichten
§ 10 Denkmale der Kirchen und öffentlich-rechtlicher Religionsgemeinschaften

Vierter Abschnitt
Besondere Maßnahmen
§ 11 Fund von Denkmalen
§ 12 Nachforschungen
§ 13 Schatzregal
§ 14 Grabungsschutzgebiete

§ 15 Sonderregelung bei Maßnahmen zur Gewinnung von Bodenschätzen

Fünfter Abschnitt
Denkmalrechtliche Verfügungen, Zugang zu Denkmalen, Kennzeichnung, Entschädigung
§ 16 Allgemeine Maßnahmen der Denkmalbehörden
§ 17 Wiederherstellung des ursprünglichen Zustandes
§ 18 Zugang zu Denkmalen
§ 19 Kennzeichnung der Denkmale
§ 20 Durchsetzung der Erhaltung
§ 21 Enteignungen
§ 22 Vorkaufsrecht
§ 23 Entschädigung

Sechster Abschnitt
Denkmalförderung
§ 24 Finanzielle Zuwendungen
§ 25 Bescheinigung für steuerliche Zwecke

Siebter Abschnitt
Schlußvorschriften
§ 26 Ordnungswidrigkeiten
§ 27 Verwaltungsvorschriften
§ 28 Übergangsvorschriften
§ 29 Inkrafttreten

Erster Abschnitt
Allgemeine Vorschriften

§ 1 Aufgaben des Denkmalschutzes und der Denkmalpflege

(1) Aufgabe von Denkmalschutz und Denkmalpflege ist, die Denkmale als Quellen der Geschichte und Tradition zu schützen, zu pflegen, wissenschaftlich zu erforschen und auf eine sinnvolle Nutzung hinzuwirken.

(2) ¹Denkmalschutz und Denkmalpflege obliegen dem Land, den Landkreisen und Gemeinden. ²Die Landkreise und Gemeinden nehmen diese Aufgaben als Auftragsangelegenheiten nach Maßgabe dieses Gesetzes wahr.

(3) ¹Bei öffentlichen Planungen und Maßnahmen sind die Belange des Denkmalschutzes und der Denkmalpflege zu berücksichtigen. ²Bei der Abwägung ist eine Erhaltung und sinnvolle Nutzung der Denkmale und Denkmalbereiche anzustreben. ³Die für den Denkmalschutz und die Denkmalpflege zuständigen Behörden sind frühzeitig zu beteiligen.

§ 2 Begriffsbestimmungen

(1) Denkmale im Sinne dieses Gesetzes sind Sachen, Mehrheiten von Sachen und Teile von Sachen, an deren Erhaltung und Nutzung ein öffentliches Interesse besteht, wenn die Sachen bedeutend für die Geschichte des Menschen, für Städte und Siedlungen oder für die Entwicklung der Arbeits- und Wirt-

---
1) Neubekanntmachung des DenkmalschutzG v. 30.11.1993 (GVOBl. M-V S. 975) in der ab 1.1.1998 geltenden Fassung.

schaftsbedingungen sind und für die Erhaltung und Nutzung künstlerische, wissenschaftliche, geschichtliche, volkskundliche oder städtebauliche Gründe vorliegen.
(2) ¹Baudenkmale sind Denkmale, die aus baulichen Anlagen oder Teilen baulicher Anlagen bestehen. ²Ebenso zu behandeln sind Garten-, Friedhofs- und Parkanlagen sowie andere von Menschen gestaltete Landschaftsteile, wenn sie die Voraussetzungen des Absatzes 1 erfüllen. ³Historische Ausstattungsstücke sind wie Baudenkmale zu behandeln, sofern sie mit dem Baudenkmal eine Einheit von Denkmalwert bilden.
(3) ¹Denkmalbereiche sind Gruppen baulicher Anlagen, die aus den in Absatz 1 genannten Gründen erhaltenswert sind, unabhängig davon, ob die einzelnen baulichen Anlagen für sich Baudenkmale sind. ²Denkmalbereiche können Stadtgrundrisse, Stadt-, Ortsbilder und -silhouetten, Stadtteile und -viertel, Siedlungen, Gehöftgruppen, Straßenzüge, bauliche Gesamtanlagen, Produktionsstätten und Einzelbauten sein sowie deren engere Umgebung, sofern sie für deren Erscheinungsbild bedeutend sind. ³Mit dem Denkmalbereich wird das äußere Erscheinungsbild geschützt.
(4) Bewegliche Denkmale sind alle nicht ortsfesten Denkmale.
(5) ¹Bodendenkmale sind bewegliche oder unbewegliche Denkmale, die sich im Boden, in Mooren sowie in Gewässern befinden oder befanden. ²Als Bodendenkmale gelten auch
– Zeugnisse, die von menschlichen und mit diesem im Zusammenhang stehenden tierischen und pflanzlichen Leben in der Vergangenheit künden,
– Veränderungen und Verfärbungen in der natürlichen Bodenbeschaffenheit, die durch nicht mehr selbständig erkennbare Bodendenkmale hervorgerufen worden sind, sofern sie die Voraussetzungen des Absatzes 1 erfüllen.
(6) Auf Archivgut finden die Vorschriften des Gesetzes keine Anwendung.

Zweiter Abschnitt
Behörden des Denkmalschutzes und der Denkmalpflege

§ 3 Denkmalschutzbehörden
¹Denkmalschutzbehörden sind
1. das Ministerium für Bildung, Wissenschaft und Kultur als oberste Denkmalschutzbehörde und
2. die Landräte und Oberbürgermeister der kreisfreien und großen kreisangehörigen Städte als untere Denkmalschutzbehörden.

²Sofern nichts anderes bestimmt ist, sind die unteren Denkmalschutzbehörden für den Vollzug dieses Gesetzes zuständig. ³Sie arbeiten mit den am Denkmalschutz und der Denkmalpflege interessierten Verbänden, Bürgern und ehrenamtlichen Denkmalpflegern zusammen.

§ 4 Denkmalfachbehörde
(1) ¹Fachbehörde ist das Landesamt für Kultur und Denkmalpflege. ²Es berät und unterstützt die Gemeinden, Landkreise, kreisfreien Städte und großen kreisangehörigen Städte in der Denkmalpflege und dem Denkmalschutz. ³Es wirkt fachlich bei den Entscheidungen der unteren Denkmalschutzbehörden und der obersten Denkmalschutzbehörde mit.
(2) Die Denkmalfachbehörde nimmt im Rahmen der Denkmalpflege insbesondere folgende Aufgaben wahr:
1. Systematische Erfassung der Denkmale (Inventarisierung),
2. wissenschaftliche Untersuchung und Erforschung der Denkmale sowie Veröffentlichung und wissenschaftliche Behandlung der Fragen von Methodik und Praxis der Denkmalpflege,
3. Anleitung und Betreuung von Konservierung und Restaurierung von Denkmalen sowie fachliche Überwachung dieser Maßnahmen,
4. wissenschaftliche Ausgrabungen, Bergung und Restaurierung von Bodendenkmalen, Überwachung dieser Maßnahmen sowie die Erfassung der beweglichen Bodendenkmale,
5. Bewirtschaftung der ihnen vom Land bereitgestellten Mittel für Denkmalpflege,
6. allgemeine Vertretung der Interessen der Denkmalpflege bei Planungen und sonstigen Maßnahmen,
7. die Denkmalfachbehörde kann auf Vorschlag der unteren Denkmalschutzbehörden ehrenamtliche Denkmalpfleger ernennen.[1)]

---
1) Die VwV über die ehrenamtlichen Denkmalpfleger ist abgedruckt als Nr. D8.I.1a.

(3) ¹Aufgaben der Denkmalfachbehörde, die Bodendenkmale nach § 28 Abs. 1 des Bundesnaturschutzgesetzes betreffen, die zugleich die Voraussetzungen eines Naturdenkmals im Sinne des § 25 oder eines gesetzlich geschützten Geotops nach § 20 Abs. 2 des Naturschutzausführungsgesetzes erfüllen, nehmen jene im Einvernehmen mit der zuständigen Naturschutzbehörde wahr. ²Kommt das Einvernehmen nicht zustande, entscheidet die nächsthöhere Behörde in Benehmen mit der Naturschutzbehörde derselben Verwaltungsebene.

§ 5 Denkmalliste

(1) ¹Denkmale sind in die Denkmallisten einzutragen. ²Die Denkmallisten führen die unteren Denkmalschutzbehörden getrennt nach Bodendenkmalen, Baudenkmalen und beweglichen Denkmalen. ³Bewegliche Denkmale sind nur einzutragen, wenn dies wegen ihrer besonderen Bedeutung, die auch in einem historischen Ortsbezug liegen kann, angebracht erscheint. ⁴Werden bewegliche Denkmale in einer öffentlichen Sammlung betreut, so bedürfen sie nicht der Eintragung in die Denkmalliste. ⁵Der Eigentümer und die Gemeinde sollen vor der Eintragung des Denkmals in die jeweilige Denkmalliste angehört werden und sind von der Eintragung aller Denkmale in die jeweiligen Denkmallisten zu benachrichtigen. ⁶Veränderungen an den Denkmallisten dürfen nur nach Anhörung der Denkmalfachbehörde vorgenommen werden.

(2) ¹Der Schutz durch dieses Gesetz ist nicht davon abhängig, daß Denkmale in die Denkmallisten eingetragen sind. ²Die §§ 6, 7, 8 und 9 gelten jedoch für bewegliche Denkmale nur, wenn sie in die Denkmalliste eingetragen sind.

(3) ¹Die Ausweisung der Denkmalbereiche ergeht nach Anhörung der Denkmalfachbehörde und im Einvernehmen mit den Gemeinden durch Rechtsverordnung der unteren Denkmalschutzbehörde. ²Die Denkmalbereiche sind von der unteren Denkmalschutzbehörde ortsüblich bekannt zu machen.

(4) Die Eintragung ist von Amts wegen zu löschen, wenn die Eintragungsvoraussetzungen nicht mehr vorliegen.

(5) ¹Die Denkmallisten stehen jedermann zur Einsicht offen. ²Die Denkmallisten für Bodendenkmale und bewegliche Denkmale können nur von demjenigen eingesehen werden, der ein berechtigtes Interesse nachweist.

Dritter Abschnitt
Maßnahmen für Denkmale

§ 6 Erhaltungspflicht

(1) Eigentümer, Besitzer und Unterhaltungspflichtige von Denkmalen sind verpflichtet, diese im Rahmen des Zumutbaren denkmalgerecht instand zu setzen, zu erhalten und pfleglich zu behandeln.
(2) Das Land, die Landkreise sowie die Gemeinden können hierzu durch Zuwendungen beitragen.[1]
(3) Bei allen Entscheidungen nach diesem Gesetz sind die berechtigten Interessen der Eigentümer der Denkmale zu berücksichtigen.
(4) Werden Denkmale nicht mehr entsprechend ihrer ursprünglichen Zweckbestimmung genutzt, ist durch den Eigentümer eine Nutzung abzusichern, die eine möglichst weitgehende Erhaltung der Substanz auf die Dauer gewährleistet.
(5) Wird in ein Denkmal eingegriffen, so hat der Verursacher des Eingriffes alle Kosten zu tragen, die für die Erhaltung und fachgerechte Instandsetzung, Bergung und Dokumentation des Denkmals anfallen.

§ 7 Genehmigungspflichtige Maßnahmen

(1) ¹Der Genehmigung der unteren Denkmalschutzbehörde bedarf, wer
1. Denkmale beseitigen, verändern, an einen anderen Ort verbringen oder die bisherige Nutzung ändern will,
2. in der Umgebung von Denkmalen Maßnahmen durchführen will, wenn hierdurch das Erscheinungsbild oder die Substanz des Denkmals erheblich beeinträchtigt wird.

---

1) Die Richtlinie für die Bewilligung finanzieller Zuwendungen zur Erhaltung von Denkmalen in Mecklenburg-Vorpommern ist abgedruckt als Nr. D8.III.1.

²Vor der Entscheidung hat die untere Denkmalschutzbehörde die Denkmalfachbehörde zu hören. ³Der Genehmigung bedarf es nicht, wenn bei Vorhaben nach § 77 Abs. 1 der Landesbauordnung Mecklenburg-Vorpommern die Denkmalfachbehörde zugestimmt hat.
(2) ¹Der Antrag auf Erteilung einer Genehmigung ist schriftlich mit den zur Beurteilung des Vorhabens erforderlichen Unterlagen bei einer unteren Denkmalschutzbehörde einzureichen. ²Im Einzelfall kann verlangt werden, dass der Genehmigungsantrag durch vorbereitende Untersuchungen, insbesondere durch eine denkmalpflegerische Zielstellung gemäß Absatz 3 Nr. 1, ergänzt wird.
(3) Die Genehmigung ist zu erteilen,
1. bei Übereinstimmung der in Aussicht genommenen Maßnahmen mit einer von dem fachlich zuständigen Landesamt bestätigten, von dem Eigentümer oder Auftraggeber zu erstellenden denkmalpflegerischen Zielstellung der an dem Denkmal zu ergreifenden Maßnahmen und wenn sonstige Gründe des Denkmalschutzes oder der Denkmalpflege nicht entgegenstehen,
2. wenn ein überwiegendes öffentliches Interesse die Maßnahme verlangt.
(4) Im Übrigen kann die Genehmigung versagt werden, wenn und soweit gewichtige Gründe des Denkmalschutzes für die unveränderte Beibehaltung des bisherigen Zustandes sprechen.
(5) ¹Die Genehmigung kann mit Nebenbestimmungen erteilt werden, soweit dies zum Schutz des Denkmals erforderlich ist. ²Bei der Entscheidung sind die berechtigten Belange des Verpflichteten zu berücksichtigen.
(6) ¹Erfordert die genehmigungspflichtige Maßnahme nach anderen gesetzlichen Bestimmungen eine Planfeststellung, Genehmigung, Erlaubnis, Bewilligung, Zulassung oder Zustimmung, so ersetzt diese Entscheidung die Genehmigung nach Absatz 1. ²Die nach Satz 1 zuständigen Behörden haben vor der Erteilung einer Genehmigung das Einvernehmen mit der Denkmalfachbehörde herzustellen. ³Kann das Einvernehmen nicht binnen vier Wochen hergestellt werden, so entscheidet die zuständige oberste Landesbehörde innerhalb von vier Wochen abschließend.

§ 8 Veräußerungs- und Veränderungsanzeige
¹Wird ein Denkmal veräußert, so haben der frühere und der neue Eigentümer den Eigentümerwechsel unverzüglich, spätestens jedoch innerhalb eines Monats, der für die Führung der Denkmalliste fachlich zuständigen Behörde anzuzeigen. ²Die Anzeige eines Pflichtigen befreit den anderen.

§ 9 Auskunfts- und Duldungspflichten
(1) Eigentümer, Besitzer und sonstige Nutzungsberechtigte sind dazu verpflichtet, Auskünfte zu erteilen, die zur Erfüllung der Aufgaben des Denkmalschutzes und der Denkmalpflege notwendig sind.
(2) ¹Die unteren Denkmalschutzbehörden sowie die Denkmalfachbehörde oder ihre Vertreter sind berechtigt, Grundstücke und Wohnungen zu betreten sowie Prüfungen und Untersuchungen anzustellen, soweit dies für die Belange der Denkmalpflege und des Denkmalschutzes, insbesondere zur Eintragung in die Denkmalliste oder anderer Maßnahmen nach diesem Gesetz dringend erforderlich ist. ²Das Betreten von Wohnungen ist ohne Einwilligung des Eigentümers oder sonstiger Nutzungsberechtigter nur bei Gefahr im Verzuge zulässig.
(3) Das Grundrecht der Unverletzlichkeit der Wohnung (Artikel 13 des Grundgesetzes) wird durch dieses Gesetz eingeschränkt.

§ 10 Denkmale der Kirchen und öffentlich-rechtlicher Religionsgemeinschaften
(1) Die Kirchen und das Land tragen gemeinsam Verantwortung für den Schutz und Erhalt der kirchlichen Denkmale.
(2) ¹Die Kirchen stellen sicher, daß ihre Denkmale erhalten bleiben und der Allgemeinheit zugänglich gemacht werden, sofern hieran ein öffentliches Interesse besteht. ²Insoweit sind Enteignungen nach dem Denkmalschutzrecht unzulässig.
(3) ¹Bei Entscheidungen über Denkmale, die gottesdienstlichen, kultischen oder gleichartigen kirchlichen Zwecken unmittelbar dienen, berücksichtigen die Denkmalschutzbehörden die von den kirchlichen Oberbehörden festgestellten Belange. ²Die kirchliche Oberbehörde entscheidet im Benehmen mit der obersten Denkmalschutzbehörde, falls die untere Denkmalschutzbehörde oder die Denkmalfachbehörde die geltend gemachten Belange nicht anerkennt.

(4) Durch Vereinbarungen können den Kirchen Aufgaben des Denkmalschutzes übertragen werden.[1]

(5) [1]Das Land nimmt bei der Förderung nach dem Denkmalrecht, auch bei der Vergabe von Mitteln, Rücksicht auf die besonderen denkmalpflegerischen Aufgaben der Kirchen. [2]Es setzt sich dafür ein, daß die Kirchen auch von solchen Einrichtungen Hilfe erhalten, die auf nationaler und internationaler Ebene für die Kultur- und Denkmalpflege tätig sind.

Vierter Abschnitt
Besondere Maßnahmen

§ 11 Fund von Denkmalen

(1) [1]Wer Sachen, Sachgesamtheiten oder Teile von Sachen entdeckt, von denen anzunehmen ist, daß an ihrer Erhaltung gemäß § 2 Abs. 1 ein öffentliches Interesse besteht, hat dies unverzüglich anzuzeigen. [2]Anzeigepflicht besteht für
- den Entdecker,
- den Leiter der Arbeiten,
- den Grundeigentümer,
- zufällige Zeugen, die den Wert des Gegenstandes erkennen.

(2) [1]Die Anzeige hat gegenüber der unteren Denkmalschutzbehörde zu erfolgen. [2]Sie leitet die Anzeige unverzüglich an die Denkmalfachbehörde weiter.

(3) [1]Der Fund und die Fundstelle sind in unverändertem Zustand zu erhalten. [2]Die Verpflichtung erlischt fünf Werktage nach Zugang der Anzeige, bei schriftlicher Anzeige spätestens nach einer Woche. [3]Die untere Denkmalschutzbehörde kann die Frist im Rahmen des Zumutbaren verlängern, wenn die sachgerechte Untersuchung oder die Bergung des Denkmals dies erfordert.

(4) [1]Die Denkmalfachbehörde, die unteren Denkmalschutzbehörden mit Genehmigung der Denkmalfachbehörde sowie deren Beauftragte sind berechtigt, das Denkmal zu bergen und für die Auswertung und die wissenschaftliche Erforschung bis zu einem Jahr in Besitz zu nehmen. [2]Dabei sind alle zur Erhaltung des Denkmals notwendigen Maßnahmen zu treffen. [3]Die Denkmalfachbehörde kann die Frist um ein Jahr verlängern, wenn dies zur Erhaltung des Denkmals oder zu seiner wissenschaftlichen Erforschung erforderlich ist.

§ 12 Nachforschungen

Nachforschungen, insbesondere Grabungen oder der Einsatz von technischen Suchgeräten, mit dem Ziel, Denkmale, insbesondere Bodendenkmale, zu entdecken, bedürfen der Genehmigung der obersten Denkmalschutzbehörde.

§ 13 Schatzregal

Bewegliche Denkmale, die herrenlos sind oder die so lange verborgen gewesen sind, daß ihr Eigentümer nicht mehr zu ermitteln ist, werden mit der Entdeckung Eigentum des Landes, wenn sie bei staatlichen Nachforschungen oder in Grabungsschutzgebieten im Sinne des § 16[2] entdeckt werden oder wenn sie einen hervorragenden wissenschaftlichen Wert haben.

§ 14 Grabungsschutzgebiete

(1) Die untere Denkmalschutzbehörde kann im Benehmen mit der zuständigen Gemeinde bestimmte Grundstücke, die voraussichtlich Bodendenkmale enthalten, durch Eintragung in die Denkmalliste zu Grabungsschutzgebieten erklären.

(2) [1]In der Mitteilung an den Eigentümer und die Gemeinde gemäß § 5 Abs. 1 sind die Maßnahmen zu bezeichnen, die einer Genehmigung bedürfen. [2]Die Genehmigung erteilt die untere Denkmalschutzbehörde. [3]Auf die Genehmigung findet § 7 Abs. 2 bis 7 Anwendung.

§ 15 Sonderregelung bei Maßnahmen zur Gewinnung von Bodenschätzen

[1]In Gebieten, in denen nach den Zielen der Raumordnung und Landesplanung Maßnahmen nach dem Bundesberggesetz vorgesehen sind, ist rechtzeitig vor Beginn der Maßnahme der Denkmalfachbehörde Gelegenheit zur fachwissenschaftlichen Untersuchung von vermuteten Denkmalen, insbesondere von

---

1) Vgl. die Vereinbarung zwischen dem Land Mecklenburg-Vorpommern und der Evangelisch-Lutherischen Landeskirche Mecklenburg und der Pommerschen Evangelischen Kirche vom 03.05.1996 (ABl. M-V S. 499).
2) Richtig wohl: „§ 14".

Bodendenkmalen, oder zu deren Bergung zu geben. ²Hierzu sind der unteren Denkmalschutzbehörde rechtzeitig alle einschlägigen Planungen sowie deren Änderungen bekanntzugeben.

Fünfter Abschnitt
Denkmalrechtliche Verfügungen, Zugang zu Denkmalen, Kennzeichnung, Entschädigung

§ 16 Allgemeine Maßnahmen der Denkmalbehörden
Die unteren Denkmalschutzbehörden haben diejenigen Maßnahmen zu treffen, die ihnen nach pflichtgemäßem Ermessen erforderlich erscheinen, um Denkmale zu schützen, zu erhalten und zu bergen sowie Gefahren von ihnen abzuwenden.

§ 17 Wiederherstellung des ursprünglichen Zustandes
(1) ¹Wer eine Handlung, die nach diesem Gesetz der Genehmigung bedarf, ohne Genehmigung, unsachgemäß oder im Widerspruch zu den Auflagen durchführt, muß auf Verlangen der zuständigen unteren Denkmalschutzbehörde die Arbeiten sofort einstellen und den bisherigen Zustand wiederherstellen. ²Bei Gefahr im Verzug kann bis zur Entscheidung der unteren Denkmalschutzbehörde die Denkmalfachbehörde die Einstellung der Arbeiten anordnen. ³Die Baueinstellung nach den bauordnungsrechtlichen Vorschriften bleibt unberührt.
(2) Wer widerrechtlich ein Denkmal vorsätzlich oder fahrlässig beschädigt oder zerstört, ist auf Verlangen der unteren Denkmalschutzbehörde verpflichtet, das Zerstörte wiederherzustellen.
(3) Im übrigen finden die Vorschriften des Gesetzes über die öffentliche Sicherheit und Ordnung in Mecklenburg-Vorpommern Anwendung.

§ 18 Zugang zu Denkmalen
(1) Denkmale oder Teile derselben sollen im Rahmen des für den Eigentümer und sonstigen Nutzungsberechtigten Zumutbaren der Öffentlichkeit zugänglich gemacht werden.
(2) Die unteren Denkmalschutzbehörden sollen mit den Eigentümern und sonstigen Nutzungsberechtigten von Denkmalen Vereinbarungen über den Zutritt treffen.

§ 19 Kennzeichnung der Denkmale
¹Denkmale können gekennzeichnet werden. ²Das Nähere regelt die oberste Denkmalschutzbehörde durch Verwaltungsvorschrift. ³Eigentümer und sonstige Nutzungsberechtigte von Denkmalen haben die Anbringung von Kennzeichen und Erläuterungstafeln zu dulden.

§ 20 Durchsetzung der Erhaltung
(1) Kommen Eigentümer, Besitzer oder sonstige Unterhaltspflichtige ihren Verpflichtungen nach § 6 nicht nach und tritt hierdurch eine Gefährdung der Denkmale ein, können sie von der unteren Denkmalschutzbehörde verpflichtet werden, erforderliche Erhaltungsmaßnahmen im Rahmen des Zumutbaren durchzuführen.
(2) ¹Erfordert der Zustand eines Denkmals zu seiner Instandhaltung, Instandsetzung oder zu seinem Schutz Maßnahmen, ohne deren unverzügliche Durchführung es gefährdet würde, können die Denkmalschutzbehörden diejenigen Maßnahmen selbst durchführen oder einleiten, die zur Abwendung einer unmittelbaren Gefahr für den Bestand des Denkmals geboten sind. ²Eigentümer und Besitzer sind verpflichtet, solche Maßnahmen zu dulden. ³Eigentümer, Besitzer und sonstige Unterhaltungspflichtige können im Rahmen des Zumutbaren zur Erstattung der entstandenen Kosten herangezogen werden.

§ 21 Enteignungen
(1) Eine Enteignung von Denkmalen ist nach diesem Gesetz zulässig, wenn allein dadurch
1. ein Denkmal in seinem Bestand, seiner Eigenart oder seinem Erscheinungsbild erhalten werden kann,
2. ein Denkmal der Allgemeinheit zugänglich gemacht werden kann, sofern hieran ein öffentliches Interesse besteht, oder
3. in einem Grabungsschutzgebiet planmäßige Nachforschungen betrieben werden können.

(2) Im übrigen gilt das Enteignungsgesetz des Landes Mecklenburg-Vorpommern.

§ 22 Vorkaufsrecht
(1) ¹Der Gemeinde steht beim Kauf von Grundstücken, auf oder in denen sich Denkmale befinden, ein Vorkaufsrecht zu. ²Es darf nur ausgeübt werden, wenn dadurch die dauernde Erhaltung des Denkmals

ermöglicht werden soll. ³Das Vorkaufsrecht ist ausgeschlossen, wenn der Eigentümer das Grundstück an seinen Ehegatten, Lebenspartner oder an eine Person veräußert, die mit ihm in gerader Linie verwandt oder verschwägert oder in der Seitenlinie bis zum dritten Grad verwandt ist. ⁴Das Vorkaufsrecht steht der Gemeinde nicht zu beim Kauf von Rechten nach dem Wohnungseigentumsgesetz und bei Erbbaurechten.

(2) ¹Das Vorkaufsrecht kann nur binnen zwei Monaten nach Mitteilung des Kaufvertrages durch Verwaltungsakt gegenüber dem Veräußerer ausgeübt werden. ²Die §§ 504, 505 Abs. 2, §§ 506 bis 509 und 512 des Bürgerlichen Gesetzbuches sind anzuwenden. ³Nach Mitteilung des Kaufvertrages ist auf Ersuchen der Gemeinde zur Sicherung ihres Anspruchs auf Übereignung des Grundstücks eine Vormerkung in das Grundbuch einzutragen; die Gemeinde trägt die Kosten der Eintragung der Vormerkung und ihrer Löschung. ⁴Das Vorkaufsrecht ist nicht übertragbar. ⁵Bei einem Eigentumserwerb aufgrund der Ausübung des Vorkaufsrechts erlöschen rechtsgeschäftliche Vorkaufsrechte. ⁶Wird die Gemeinde nach Ausübung des Vorkaufsrechts im Grundbuch als Eigentümerin eingetragen, so kann sie das Grundbuchamt ersuchen, eine zur Sicherung des Übereignungsanspruches des Käufers im Grundbuch eingetragene Vormerkung zu löschen; sie darf das Ersuchen nur stellen, wenn die Ausübung des Vorkaufsrechts für den Käufer unanfechtbar ist.

(3) ¹Der durch das Vorkaufsrecht Verpflichtete hat der Gemeinde den Inhalt des mit dem Dritten abgeschlossenen Vertrags unverzüglich mitzuteilen; die Mitteilung des Verpflichteten wird durch die Mitteilung des Dritten ersetzt. ²Das Grundbuchamt darf bei Veräußerungen den Erwerber als Eigentümer in das Grundbuch eintragen, wenn ihm die Nichtausübung oder das Nichtbestehen des Vorkaufsrechts nachgewiesen ist. ³Besteht ein Vorkaufsrecht nicht oder wird es nicht ausgeübt, hat die Gemeinde auf Antrag eines Beteiligten darüber unverzüglich ein Zeugnis auszustellen. ⁴Das Zeugnis gilt als Verzicht auf die Ausübung des Vorkaufsrechts.

(4) ¹Die Gemeinde kann das Vorkaufsrecht zugunsten einer anderen juristischen Person ausüben; bei juristischen Personen des Privatrechts besteht diese Befugnis nur, sofern die dauernde Erhaltung der in oder auf einem Grundstück liegenden Baudenkmale oder ortsfesten Bodendenkmale zu den satzungsmäßigen Aufgaben der juristischen Person gehört und bei Berücksichtigung aller Umstände gesichert ist. ²Absatz 1 Satz 2 und 3 gilt entsprechend. ³Die Gemeinde kann das Vorkaufsrecht zugunsten eines anderen nur ausüben, wenn ihr die Zustimmung des Begünstigten vorliegt.

§ 23 Entschädigung

Haben Maßnahmen aufgrund dieses Gesetzes enteignende Wirkung, ist eine Entschädigung nach Maßgabe des § 5 des Enteignungsgesetzes zu leisten.

Sechster Abschnitt
Denkmalförderung

§ 24 Finanzielle Zuwendungen

¹Das Land, die Landkreise, die kreisfreien Städte, die großen kreisangehörigen Städte und Gemeinden können Zuwendungen zur Pflege von Denkmalen nach Maßgabe der jeweiligen Haushalte gewähren. ²Bei der Vergabe von Zuwendungen ist die Leistungsfähigkeit des Eigentümers zu berücksichtigen. ³Die Zuwendung setzt einen Antrag voraus.

§ 25 Bescheinigung für steuerliche Zwecke

Die Landkreise, kreisfreien Städte und großen kreisangehörigen Städte sind für die Erteilung von Bescheinigungen über Denkmale für steuerliche Zwecke zuständig.

Siebter Abschnitt
Schlußvorschriften

§ 26 Ordnungswidrigkeiten[1)]

(1) Ordnungswidrig handelt, wer vorsätzlich oder fahrlässig
1. eine nach § 8 oder § 11 Abs. 1 erforderliche Anzeige nicht unverzüglich erstattet,
2. Maßnahmen, die nach § 7 Abs. 1 und § 12 der Erlaubnis bedürfen, ohne Erlaubnis oder abweichend von ihr durchführt oder durchführen läßt,

---

1) Der Bußgeldkatalog ist abgedruckt als Nr. D8.I.1b.

3. entdeckte Bodendenkmale oder die Entdeckungsstätte nicht nach § 11 Abs. 3 in unverändertem Zustand erhält,
4. eine nach § 9 Abs. 1 geforderte Auskunft nicht erteilt,
5. seinen Verpflichtungen gemäß § 6 Abs. 1 Denkmale im Rahmen des zumutbaren denkmalgerecht instand zu setzen, zu erhalten und pfleglich zu behandeln, trotz vollziehbarer, diese Verpflichtungen konkretisierender Anordnung der zuständigen Behörden nicht nachkommt. Eine Geldbuße darf jedoch nur festgesetzt werden, wenn die Anordnung auf diese Bußgeldvorschrift verweist.

(2) ¹Die Ordnungswidrigkeiten können mit Geldbußen bis zu 150 000 Euro geahndet werden. ²Wird ohne Erlaubnis nach § 7 Abs. 1 Nr. 1 ein Denkmal zerstört, kann eine Geldbuße bis zu 1 500 000 Euro festgesetzt werden.

(3) Die Verfolgung der Ordnungswidrigkeit verjährt in fünf Jahren.

(4) Zuständige Behörde im Sinne des § 36 Abs. 1 Nr. 1 des Gesetzes über Ordnungswidrigkeiten ist die untere Denkmalschutzbehörde.

§ 27 Verwaltungsvorschriften

Das Ministerium für Bildung, Wissenschaft und Kultur erläßt die zur Ausführung dieses Gesetzes erforderlichen Verwaltungsvorschriften.

§ 28 Übergangsvorschriften

¹Die in den Listen der Bodenaltertümer nach den §§ 4 und 6 Abs. 1 der Verordnung zum Schutz und zur Erhaltung der ur- und frühgeschichtlichen Bodenaltertümer vom 28. Mai 1954 (GBl. Nr. 54 S. 547) erfaßten Denkmale unterliegen bis zum 31. Dezember 2006 den Bestimmungen des Gesetzes. ²Die Listen sind bis zu diesem Zeitpunkt von der Denkmalfachbehörde zu überprüfen und in Denkmallisten nach § 5 zu übernehmen. ³Diese Listen sind anschließend den unteren Denkmalschutzbehörden zu übergeben.

§ 29 (Inkrafttreten)

D8.I.1a VwV über die ehrenamtlichen Denkmalpfleger

Verwaltungsvorschrift über die ehrenamtlichen Denkmalpfleger (VwV ehrenamtliche Denkmalpfleger)
Vom 12. Mai 1997 (AmtsBl. M.-V. S. 511)

Nach § 4 Abs. 2 Nr. 11[1)] des Denkmalschutzgesetzes vom 30. November 1993 (GVOBl. M-V S. 975), geändert durch das Gesetz vom 3. Mai 1994 (GVOBl. M-V S. 559), erläßt das Kultusministerium folgende Verwaltungsvorschrift:

1. **Bestellung**
   1.1 In jedem Stadt- und Landkreis soll mindestens je ein ehrenamtlicher Denkmalpfleger für die Bau- und Kunstdenkmalpflege und für die Bodendenkmalpflege bestellt werden.
   Die ehrenamtlichen Denkmalpfleger werden von den fachlich zuständigen Denkmalfachbehörden auf Vorschlag der unteren Denkmalschutzbehörde bestellt, in deren Gebiet sie tätig werden.
   1.2 Die fachlich zuständige Denkmalfachbehörde kann ehrenamtliche Denkmalpfleger für bestimmte Fachgebiete bestellen.
   1.3 Die ehrenamtlichen Denkmalpfleger werden auf die Dauer von fünf Jahren widerruflich bestellt.
   1.4 Die ehrenamtlichen Denkmalpfleger erhalten bei der Bestellung einen Ausweis.
   1.5 Die ehrenamtlichen Denkmalpfleger werden gemäß § 83 Abs. 2 VwVfG M-V verpflichtet.
2. **Rechtsstellung**
   2.1 Die ehrenamtlichen Denkmalpfleger üben ihre Tätigkeit unentgeltlich aus.
   2.2 Die ehrenamtlichen Denkmalpfleger sind für die Denkmalschutz- und Denkmalfachbehörde tätig. Sie sind der fachlich zuständigen Denkmalfachbehörde zugeordnet und unterstehen deren Weisungen.
3. **Aufgaben**
   3.1 Zu den Aufgaben der ehrenamtlichen Denkmalpfleger gehören im Rahmen des Denkmalschutzgesetzes folgende Tätigkeiten:
   - Beratung und Unterstützung der Denkmalschutz- und Denkmalfachbehörde durch Weitergabe von Informationen und Anregungen zum Schutz und zur Pflege von Denkmalen,
   - Beobachtung von Planungen und Vorhaben, die die Belange der Denkmalpflege berühren,
   - Pflege von Kontakten zu Institutionen und Personen, die die Denkmalpflege unterstützen und fördern.
   3.2 Die ehrenamtlichen Denkmalpfleger dürfen hoheitliche Befugnisse nicht wahrnehmen.
   3.3 Die untere Denkmalschutzbehörde kann einem ehrenamtlichen Denkmalpfleger im Einvernehmen mit der zuständigen Denkmalfachbehörde einen Auftrag nach Nummer 3.1 erteilen. Die Denkmalfachbehörde kann ihr Einvernehmen versagen, wenn vorrangig Aufgaben der Denkmalfachbehörde zu erfüllen sind.
4. **Inkrafttreten**
   Diese Verwaltungsvorschrift tritt am Tage nach der Verkündung in Kraft.

---

1) Hinweis: Im DSchG M-V i.d.F. d. Bek. v. 6.1.1998 findet sich die Rechtsgrundlage für diese Verwaltungsvorschrift nunmehr in § 4 Abs. 2 Nr. 7.

Bußgeldkatalog für die Ahndung von Verstößen gegen das Denkmalschutzgesetz Mecklenburg-Vorpommern

Erlass des Ministeriums für Bildung, Wissenschaft und Kultur

Vom 20. Oktober 1999 (Mittl.bl. BM M-V S. 616)

Der nachfolgende Katalog dient der Vereinheitlichung der Bußgeldbeträge für Ordnungswidrigkeiten gemäß § 26 Denkmalschutzgesetz in der Fassung der Bekanntmachung vom 6. Januar 1998 (GVOBl. M-V S. 12, 247), geändert durch Artikel 4 des Gesetzes vom 21. Juli 1998 (GVOBl. M-V S. 647). Bei den angegebenen Beträgen handelt es sich lediglich um Richtwerte, von denen nach oben und unten abgewichen werden kann.
Bei der Festsetzung des Bußgeldes muß in jedem Fall eine Überprüfung der besonderen Umstände des Einzelfalls erfolgen. Dabei müssen die in § 17 Abs. 3, 4 des Gesetzes über Ordnungswidrigkeiten in der Fassung der Bekanntmachung vom 19. Februar 1987 (BGBl. I S. 602), zuletzt geändert durch Artikel 1 des Gesetzes vom 26. Januar 1998 (BGBl. I S. 156), festgelegten Grundsätze zur Höhe der Geldbuße berücksichtigt werden.

Hinweise zur Ahndung von Ordnungswidrigkeiten nach dem Denkmalschutzgesetz Mecklenburg-Vorpommern

1. Gesetzliche Grundlage für die Ahndung von Ordnungswidrigkeiten nach dem Denkmalschutzgesetz ist § 26 des Denkmalschutzgesetzes i. V. m. dem Gesetz über Ordnungswidrigkeiten.
2. Sachlich zuständig für die Verfolgung und Ahndung von Ordnungswidrigkeiten nach dem Denkmalschutzgesetz ist die untere Denkmalbehörde (§ 26 Abs. 4 des Denkmalschutzgesetzes). Die örtliche Zuständigkeit richtet sich nach § 37 des Gesetzes über Ordnungswidrigkeiten.
   Falls gleichzeitig Ordnungswidrigkeitentatbestände z. B. nach § 84 der Landesbauordnung Mecklenburg-Vorpommern erfüllt sein sollten, ist wegen der Mehrfachzuständigkeit die Regelung des § 39 des Gesetzes über Ordnungswidrigkeiten zu beachten.
3. Eine Ordnungswidrigkeit im Sinne des Denkmalschutzgesetzes ist eine rechtswidrige und vorwerfbare Handlung, die den Tatbestand mindestens eines der in § 26 Abs. 1 bis 5 des Denkmalschutzgesetzes aufgelisteten Tatbestände verwirklicht.
   Der Versuch einer Ordnungswidrigkeit nach dem Denkmalschutzgesetz kann nicht geahndet werden, da § 26 des Denkmalschutzgesetzes eine entsprechende Festsetzung nicht enthält (§ 13 Abs. 2 des Gesetzes über Ordnungswidrigkeiten).
4. Im Falle einer Beschädigung oder Zerstörung von Denkmalen könnte auch einer der Tatbestände des § 304 Strafgesetzbuch erfüllt sein. In diesem Fall hat die untere Denkmalschutzbehörde die Sache an die Staatsanwaltschaft abzugeben (§ 41 Abs. 1 des Gesetzes über Ordnungswidrigkeiten).
5. Die Verfolgung von Ordnungswidrigkeiten nach dem Denkmalschutzgesetz verjährt in fünf Jahren (§ 26 Abs. 3 des Denkmalschutzgesetzes).
6. Bei der Verfolgung von Ordnungswidrigkeiten gilt das Opportunitätsprinzip. Die Verfolgungsbehörde ist danach nicht stets verpflichtet, ein Bußgeldverfahren durchzuführen. Sie entscheidet hierüber nach pflichtgemäßem Ermessen (§ 47 Abs. 1 des Gesetzes über Ordnungswidrigkeiten).
7. Bei der Verfolgung und Ahndung von Ordnungswidrigkeiten ist das folgende Verfahren einzuhalten:
   Vor Erlass eines Bußgeldbescheides sind die Regelungen der §§ 53 ff. des Gesetzes über Ordnungswidrigkeiten zu beachten. Dem Betroffenen muss zumindest Gelegenheit gegeben worden sein, sich zu der Beschuldigung zu äußern (§ 55 des Gesetzes über Ordnungswidrigkeiten). Der Abschluss der Ermittlungen ist in den Akten zu vermerken (§ 61 des Gesetzes über Ordnungswidrigkeiten).
   Der Bußgeldbescheid muß die in § 66 des Gesetzes über Ordnungswidrigkeiten aufgezählten Angaben, Hinweise und Belehrungen enthalten. Eine nachvollziehbare und ausführliche Begrün-

D8.I.1b Bußgeldkatalog DSchG

dung des Bußgeldbescheides wird empfohlen, auch wenn diese gemäß § 66 Abs. 3 des Gesetzes über Ordnungswidrigkeiten nicht erforderlich ist.

8. Bei der Festlegung der Bußgeldhöhe sind folgende Grundsätze zu beachten:
Das gesetzliche Mindestmaß für die Geldbuße beträgt 10 Deutsche Mark (§ 17 Abs. 1 des Gesetzes über Ordnungswidrigkeiten). Das Höchstmaß beträgt 300 000 Deutsche Mark (§ 26 Abs. 2 Satz 1 des Denkmalschutzgesetzes). Im Fall einer Zerstörung des Denkmals nach § 7 Abs. 1 Buchstabe a des Denkmalschutzgesetzes kann eine Geldbuße bis zu 3 000 000 Deutsche Mark (§ 26 Abs. 2 Satz 2 des Denkmalschutzgesetzes) festgesetzt werden. Fahrlässiges Handeln kann gemäß § 17 Abs. 2 des Gesetzes über Ordnungswidrigkeiten im Höchstmaß nur mit der Hälfte des angedrohten Höchstbetrages der Geldbuße geahndet werden. Dieser beträgt bei fahrlässigem Handeln in den Fällen des § 26 Abs. 1 des Denkmalschutzgesetzes 150 000 Deutsche Mark (§ 17 Abs. 2 des Gesetzes über Ordnungswidrigkeiten).

Bei der Festlegung der Bußgeldhöhe sind in jedem Fall die Umstände des konkreten Einzelfalles zu bewerten. Die Richtwerte des beiliegenden Bußgeldkataloges sollen lediglich als Anhaltspunkte dienen. Es darf bei der Festsetzung des Bußgeldes keinesfalls nach einem starren Bemessungsschema vorgegangen werden.

Die Kriterien für die Bemessung der Bußgeldhöhe sind in § 17 Abs. 3 und 4 des Gesetzes über Ordnungswidrigkeiten festgelegt. Danach sind in erster Linie die beiden folgenden Kriterien Grundlage für die Zumessung der Geldbuße und müssen in jedem Fall bei der Bemessung berücksichtigt werden:

– die Bedeutung der Ordnungswidrigkeit
(§ 17 Abs. 3 Satz 1 des Gesetzes über Ordnungswidrigkeiten)
Dies ist gleichzusetzen mit der Schwere des Verstoßes gegen die Rechtsordnung. Bei der Bewertung ist der Grad der Gefährdung oder Beeinträchtigung des geschützten Rechtsguts zugrundezulegen. Es ist auch zu beachten, daß eine genehmigungsbedürftige Maßnahme, die zwar ohne Genehmigung durchgeführt wurde, aber genehmigungsfähig ist, das geschützte Rechtsgut in geringerem Umfang beeinträchtigt.

– der Vorwurf, der den Täter trifft
(§ 17 Abs. 3 Satz 1 des Gesetzes über Ordnungswidrigkeiten)
Bei diesem Bemessungskriterium sind besondere, in der Person des Täters liegende Umstände, die sein Verhalten mehr oder weniger vorwerfbar erscheinen lassen, zu berücksichtigen. So kann z. B. ein besonders leichtfertiges Handeln oder die Verletzung besonderer Berufspflichten den Tatvorwurf erschweren. Andererseits kann z. B. das Bemühen des Betroffenen, den eingetretenen Schaden wieder gutzumachen, oder eine Mitverursachung des Schadens durch andere Personen erleichternd gewertet werden.

Da es sich bei Geldbußen für Ordnungswidrigkeiten nach dem Denkmalschutzgesetz generell um hohe Beträge handeln wird, muss immer auch das Kriterium der

– wirtschaftlichen Leistungsfähigkeit des Täters
(§ 17 Abs. 3 Satz 2 des Gesetzes über Ordnungswidrigkeiten)
mitberücksichtigt werden. Zudem soll die Geldbuße

– den wirtschaftlichen Vorteil, den der Täter aus der Ordnungswidrigkeit gezogen hat, übersteigen
(§ 17 Abs. 4 des Gesetzes über Ordnungswidrigkeiten).
Falls der wirtschaftliche Vorteil nicht anderweitig zu ermitteln ist, kann er aus der Höhe der fiktiven Wiederherstellungs- bzw. Dokumentationskosten errechnet werden.

9. Gegen den Bußgeldbescheid ist der Rechtsbehelf des Einspruchs nach § 67 des Gesetzes über Ordnungswidrigkeiten möglich. Er ist innerhalb von zwei Wochen nach Zustellung bei der Behörde, die den Bußgeldbescheid erlassen hat, zu erheben. Die erlassende Behörde kann den Einspruch – z.B. bei Versäumung der Frist – als unzulässig verwerfen oder den Bußgeldbescheid nach Prüfung zurücknehmen. Tut sie dies nicht, so vermerkt sie die Gründe hierfür in den Akten und übersendet diese an die Staatsanwaltschaft. Die Verwaltungsbehörde sollte bereits bei der Abgabe der Verfahrensakte ihre weitere Beteiligung sowie die Beteiligung der zuständigen Denkmalfachbehörde am Hauptverfahren vor dem Amtsgericht ausdrücklich verlangen. Kommt es

daraufhin zu einem Gerichtsverfahren, wird die Verwaltungsbehörde an dem Verfahren beteiligt (§ 76 des Gesetzes über Ordnungswidrigkeiten).
10. Ist ein Rechtsbehelf nicht mehr gegeben, so wird der Bußgeldbescheid rechtskräftig. Die Vollstreckung erfolgt gemäß der §§ 89 ff. des Gesetzes über Ordnungswidrigkeiten i. V. m. den Regelungen des Verwaltungsverfahrens-, Zustellungs- und Vollstreckungsgesetzes des Landes Mecklenburg-Vorpommern in der Fassung der Bekanntmachung vom 10. August 1998 (GVOBl. M-V S. 743).

Archivgesetz für das Land Mecklenburg-Vorpommern (Landesarchivgesetz – LArchivG M-V)[1)]

Vom 7. Juli 1997 (GVOBl. M-V S. 282)
(GS Meckl.-Vorp. Gl. Nr.224-5)
zuletzt geändert durch Art. 1 G zur Anpassung datenschutzrechtlicher Vorschriften im Zuständigkeitsbereich des Ministeriums für Bildung, Wissenschaft und Kultur an die VO (EU) 2016/679 vom 8. Mai 2018 (GVOBl. M-V S. 172)

§ 1 Grundsatz und Geltungsbereich

(1) Dieses Gesetz regelt die Archivierung und Nutzung von Unterlagen in den öffentlichen Archiven in Mecklenburg-Vorpommern.

(2) [1]Öffentliche Archive dienen der Forschung und Bildung, der Verwaltung und Rechtssicherung. [2]Sie schützen das öffentliche Archivgut vor Vernichtung und Zersplitterung und sind der Öffentlichkeit für die Nutzung zugänglich.

(3) Dieses Gesetz gilt nicht für
1. öffentlich-rechtliche Religionsgemeinschaften und deren Vereinigungen,
2. öffentlich-rechtliche Rundfunkanstalten und die Medienanstalt Mecklenburg-Vorpommern,
3. öffentlich-rechtliche Unternehmen mit eigener Rechtspersönlichkeit, die am wirtschaftlichen Wettbewerb teilnehmen, und deren Zusammenschlüsse.

§ 2 Öffentliches Archivgut

(1) [1]Öffentliches Archivgut sind alle archivwürdigen Unterlagen, die zur dauernden Aufbewahrung von einem öffentlichen Archiv übernommen wurden und werden. [2]Dazu zählt auch Dokumentationsmaterial, das von einem öffentlichen Archiv ergänzend gesammelt wird.

(2) [1]Öffentliches Archivgut des Landes sind alle archivwürdigen Unterlagen, die bei Verfassungsorganen, Behörden, Gerichten und sonstigen Stellen des Landes, bei juristischen Personen des öffentlichen Rechts und ihren Vereinigungen, die der Aufsicht des Landes unterstehen, entstanden sind und zur dauernden Aufbewahrung in ein mecklenburg-vorpommersches staatliches Archiv übernommen worden sind, soweit es nicht in Archiven nach § 12 und § 13 archiviert ist. [2]Archivgut des Landes ist auch das Archivgut der Funktionsvorgänger in dem Satz 1 genannten Stellen. [3]Archivgut des Landes ist auch das Archivgut der ehemaligen staatlichen und wirtschaftsleitenden Organe, Kombinate, Betriebe, Genossenschaften und Einrichtungen auf dem Gebiet des jetzigen Landes Mecklenburg-Vorpommern aus der Zeit vom 8. Mai 1945 bis zum 2. Oktober 1990, soweit es in einem staatlichen Archiv archiviert ist.

(3) Unterlagen der SED, der übrigen Parteien und Massenorganisationen der ehemaligen Deutschen Demokratischen Republik sowie der mit ihnen verbundenen Organisationen und juristischen Personen, soweit sie bei einem Organisationsteil angefallen sind, der auf staatlicher Ebene Funktionsvorgänger des Landes oder einer kleineren Einheit war, werden wie Archivgut des Landes behandelt, soweit sie in den staatlichen Archiven des Landes archiviert sind.

(4) [1]Zwischenarchivgut sind die von einem öffentlichen Archiv zur vorläufigen Aufbewahrung übernommenen Unterlagen, deren Aufbewahrungsfrist (§ 6 Abs. 1 Satz 2) noch nicht abgelaufen und aus denen das Archivgut noch nicht ausgewählt worden ist. [2]Zwischenarchivgut sind insbesondere die von einem öffentlichen Archiv übernommenen Unterlagen, die nach anderen Rechtsvorschriften dauernd aufzubewahren sind. [3]Auf personenbezogene Daten in Zwischenarchivgut finden die jeweiligen datenschutzrechtlichen Vorschriften und Regelungen des Geheimnisschutzes Anwendung. [4]Durch Feststellung der Archivwürdigkeit wird Zwischenarchivgut zu öffentlichem Archivgut im Sinne dieses Gesetzes.

§ 3 Begriffsbestimmungen

(1) Öffentliche Archive im Land Mecklenburg-Vorpommern sind das Landesamt für Kultur und Denkmalpflege, die kommunalen Archive nach § 12 und die sonstigen öffentlichen Archive nach § 13.

(2) [1]Unterlagen im Sinne des Gesetzes sind insbesondere Akten, Urkunden, Schriftstücke, Karten, Pläne, Karteien, Siegel und Stempel, Bild-, Film- und Tonmaterial und Dateien sowie sonstige Infor-

---
1) Verkündet als Art. 1 G v. 7.7.1997 (GVOB. M-V S. 282); Inkrafttreten gem. Art. 3 dieses G am 24.7.1997.

mationsträger und die zu ihrer Erschließung und Nutzung erforderlichen Hilfsmittel. ²Dies umfasst auch Unterlagen, die Daten im Sinne des Artikels 9 Absatz 1 der Verordnung (EU) 2016/679 des Europäischen Parlaments und des Rates vom 27. April 2016 zum Schutz natürlicher Personen bei der Verarbeitung personenbezogener Daten, zum freien Datenverkehr und zur Aufhebung der Richtlinie 95/46/EG (Datenschutz-Grundverordnung) (ABl. L 119 vom 04.05.2016, S. 1, L 314, S. 72) enthalten.
(3) Archivwürdig sind Unterlagen, die nach Feststellung des zuständigen Archivs aufgrund ihrer rechtlichen, politischen, wirtschaftlichen, sozialen oder kulturellen Bedeutung für Wissenschaft und Forschung, für das Verständnis von Geschichte und Gegenwart, für die Gesetzgebung, Rechtsprechung und Verwaltung von bleibendem Wert sind.
(4) Personenbezogenes Archivgut sind Unterlagen, die sich nach ihrer Zweckbestimmung oder ihrem wesentlichen Inhalt auf eine natürliche Person (betroffene Person) beziehen.
(5) Entstehung im Sinne dieses Gesetzes bezeichnet den Zeitpunkt der letzten inhaltlichen Bearbeitung der Unterlagen.

§ 4 Organisation des staatlichen Archivwesens
¹Das Land unterhält für die Erfüllung der staatlichen Archivaufgaben im Sinne dieses Gesetzes das Landesamt für Kultur und Denkmalpflege als Landesoberbehörde. ²Oberste Archivbehörde ist das Ministerium für Bildung, Wissenschaft und Kultur.

§ 5 Aufgaben des staatlichen Archivs
(1) Das staatliche Archiv hat die Aufgabe, die archivwürdigen Unterlagen des Landes nach fachlichen Gesichtspunkten zu erfassen, zu übernehmen, dauerhaft zu sichern, durch Findmittel zu erschließen, aufzubereiten und für die Benutzung bereitzustellen (Archivierung).
(2) Das staatliche Archiv kann die ihm gemäß § 7 des Bundesarchivgesetzes,[1)] angebotenen archivwürdigen Unterlagen nachgeordneter Stellen des Bundes archivieren.
(3) Das staatliche Archiv kann auch andere als die in den Absätzen 1 und 2 genannten archivwürdigen Unterlagen von anderen öffentlichen Stellen sowie von privaten Stellen und Personen aufgrund von Vereinbarungen oder letztwilligen Verfügungen archivieren, wenn hierfür ein öffentliches Interesse besteht.
(4) ¹Das staatliche Archiv berät die in § 2 Abs. 2 Satz 1 genannten Stellen bei der Verwaltung und Sicherung ihrer Unterlagen im Hinblick auf die spätere Archivierung. ²Den Vertretern des staatlichen Archivs ist von der anbietenden Stelle Einsicht in alle vorhandenen Unterlagen sowie die dazugehörigen Findmittel und Programme zu gewähren, soweit dieses zum Zwecke der Feststellung der Archivwürdigkeit erforderlich ist. ³Das staatliche Archiv berät die kommunalen Archive (§ 12) und die sonstigen Archive (§ 13) bei der archivfachlichen Erfüllung ihrer Aufgaben.
(5) ¹Das Archiv erbringt aus dem von ihm verwahrten Archivgut Dienstleistungen für Forschung und Bildung. ²Es erteilt Auskünfte, berät und unterstützt Benutzer.
(6) Das staatliche Archiv wirkt an der Auswertung des von ihm verwahrten Archivgutes sowie an der Erforschung und Vermittlung insbesondere der mecklenburgisch-vorpommerschen Geschichte, der Heimat- und Ortsgeschichte mit und leistet dazu eigene Beiträge.

§ 6 Anbietung von Unterlagen
(1) ¹Die in § 2 Abs. 2 Satz 1 genannten Stellen des Landes bieten alle Unterlagen, die sie zur Erfüllung ihrer Aufgaben nicht mehr benötigen, dem staatlichen Archiv zur Übernahme an. ²Unabhängig davon sind alle Unterlagen 30 Jahre nach ihrer Entstehung anzubieten, soweit nicht Rechtsvorschriften andere Fristen bestimmen.
(2) ¹Die Pflicht zur Anbietung erstreckt sich auch auf Unterlagen, die
1. personenbezogene Daten enthalten, welche nach Artikel 17 Absatz 1 der Datenschutz-Grundverordnung oder nach einer Rechtsvorschrift des Landes gelöscht werden müßten oder nach Rechtsvorschriften des Bundes oder des Landes gelöscht werden könnten, sofern die Speicherung der Daten nicht unzulässig war, oder
2. einem Berufs- oder Amtsgeheimnis oder sonstigen Rechtsvorschriften über Geheimhaltung unterliegen.

---
1) Das Bundesarchivgesetz ist abgedruckt als Nr. C.III.1.

²Die gemäß § 203 Abs. 1 des Strafgesetzbuches geschützten Unterlagen einer Beratungsstelle dürfen nur in anonymisierter Form angeboten und übergeben werden. ³Von der Anbietungspflicht ausgenommen sind Unterlagen, deren Offenbarung gegen das Brief-, Post- oder Fernmeldegeheimnis verstoßen würde. ⁴Sieht die anbietungspflichtige Stelle im Einzelfall durch die Archivierung und Nutzung von Unterlagen nach Maßgabe dieses Gesetzes die Sicherheit des Bundes oder eines Landes gefährdet, so führt sie die Entscheidung der jeweiligen obersten Landesbehörde herbei. ⁵Diese kann für die Dauer der Gefährdung von der Anbietungspflicht befreien.

(3) Anzubieten und zu übergeben sind auch Unterlagen, die Daten im Sinne des Artikels 9 Absatz 1 der Datenschutz-Grundverordnung enthalten.

(4) Die in § 2 Abs. 2 Satz 1 genannten Stellen des Landes haben dem staatlichen Archiv auch ein Exemplar aller von ihnen herausgegebenen oder in ihrem Auftrag erscheinenden amtlichen Publikationen zur Übernahme anzubieten.

(5) Die in § 2 Abs. 2 Satz 1 genannten Stellen des Landes dürfen nur dann Unterlagen vernichten oder Daten löschen, wenn das staatliche Archiv die Übernahme abgelehnt oder nicht innerhalb von sechs Monaten über die Archivwürdigkeit angebotener Unterlagen entschieden hat.

(6) Von der Anbietung und von der Übergabe von Unterlagen kann nur im Einvernehmen mit dem staatlichen Archiv abgesehen werden, wenn diese wegen ihres offensichtlich geringen Quellenwertes nicht archivwürdig sind.

§ 7 Übernahme von Archivgut

(1) ¹Das staatliche Archiv übernimmt die von ihm als archivwürdig bestimmten Unterlagen von der anbietenden Stelle. ²Die Übernahme erfolgt anhand von Aussonderungsnachweisen, die von den anbietenden Stellen gefertigt werden.

(2) Lehnt das staatliche Archiv die Übernahme ab oder übernimmt es die angebotenen Unterlagen nicht innerhalb von sechs Monaten, so ist die anbietende Stelle zu deren weiterer Aufbewahrung nicht verpflichtet, sofern weder Rechtsvorschriften noch schutzwürdige Belange der betroffenen Personen dies verlangen.

(3) ¹Das staatliche Archiv kann archivwürdige Unterlagen bereits vor Ablauf der durch Rechtsvorschriften bestimmten Aufbewahrungsfristen im Einvernehmen mit der anbietenden Stelle übernehmen. ²Die Aufbewahrungsfristen werden in diesem Fall durch die Aufbewahrung im Archiv gewahrt.

(4) Werden maschinell lesbare Datenträger archiviert, so sind vor ihrer Übergabe von der anbietenden Stelle alle zur Verarbeitung und Nutzung der Daten notwendigen Informationen zu dokumentieren und dem Archiv zu übergeben.

§ 8 Verwaltung und Sicherung des Archivgutes

(1) ¹Das staatliche Archiv hat seine Aufgaben nach archivfachlichen Gesichtspunkten zu erfüllen. ²Es ist verpflichtet, das Archivgut durch angemessene Maßnahmen wirksam gegen unbefugte Nutzung zu sichern und den Schutz personenbezogener Daten oder solcher Unterlagen, die einem besonderen gesetzlichen Geheimnisschutz unterliegen, sicherzustellen. ³Es hat dabei die für die abgebenden Stellen geltenden Vorschriften einzuhalten und die notwendigen Maßnahmen zu treffen, um das Archivgut vor Beschädigung, Verlusten und Vernichtung zu schützen und seine Erhaltung, dauernde Aufbewahrung und Benutzbarkeit zu gewährleisten.

(2) ¹Soweit es unter archivfachlichen Gesichtspunkten vertretbar oder geboten ist, kann das Archiv die im Archivgut enthaltenen Informationen auch in anderer Form archivieren. ²Diese Verarbeitung und Nutzung darf nur zur Erfüllung der in diesem Gesetz genannten Zwecke erfolgen. ³Die Originalunterlagen können vernichtet werden. ⁴Darüber ist ein Nachweis zu führen.

(3) ¹Das staatliche Archiv ist befugt, Unterlagen, deren Archivwürdigkeit nicht mehr gegeben ist, auszusondern, sofern Aufbewahrungsfristen oder schutzwürdige Belange von betroffenen Personen oder Dritten nicht entgegenstehen. ²Über die Aussonderung ist ein Nachweis zu führen.

(4) Öffentliches Archivgut des Landes ist unveräußerlich.

§ 9 Nutzung des Archivgutes

(1) Jeder hat auf Antrag das Recht, das Archivgut nach Maßgabe dieses Gesetzes und der aufgrund dieses Gesetzes erlassenen Rechtsvorschriften zu nutzen.

(2) Die Nutzung nach Absatz 1 ist einzuschränken oder zu versagen, soweit
1. Grund zu der Annahme besteht, daß dem Wohl der Bundesrepublik Deutschland oder eines ihrer Länder wesentliche Nachteile erwachsen,
2. die Geheimhaltungspflicht nach § 203 Abs. 1 bis 3 des Strafgesetzbuches oder anderer Rechtsvorschriften verletzt würden,
3. Grund zu der Annahme besteht, daß schutzwürdige Belange betroffener Personen oder Dritter erheblich beeinträchtigt werden und das Interesse an der Nutzung nicht im Einzelfall überwiegt,
4. der Erhaltungszustand des Archivguts gefährdet würde,
5. durch die Nutzung ein nicht vertretbarer Verwaltungsaufwand entstehen würde,
6. Vereinbarungen mit gegenwärtigen oder früheren Eigentümern entgegenstehen.

§ 10 Schutzfristen

(1) [1]Unterliegt das Archivgut einem besonderen Amtsgeheimnis oder besonderen Rechtsvorschriften über die Geheimhaltung, darf es erst 30 Jahre nach Entstehung der Unterlagen genutzt werden. [2]Personenbezogenes Archivgut darf erst zehn Jahre nach dem Tod der betroffenen Person oder, wenn das Todesdatum nicht bekannt ist, 90 Jahre nach dessen Geburt genutzt werden. [3]Wenn beides nicht mehr feststellbar ist, darf das Archivgut erst 60 Jahre nach Entstehung der Unterlagen genutzt werden.

(2) Die Benutzung von Archivgut durch öffentliche Stellen, bei denen es entstanden ist oder die es abgegeben haben, ist auch innerhalb der Schutzfristen möglich; die Schutzfristen sind jedoch zu beachten, wenn das Archivgut hätte gesperrt, gelöscht oder vernichtet werden müssen.

(3) Die Schutzfristen nach Absatz 1 gelten nicht für
1. Unterlagen, die bei ihrer Entstehung zur Veröffentlichung bestimmt oder der Öffentlichkeit zugänglich waren,
2. personenbezogenes Archivgut, das die Tätigkeit von Personen dokumentiert, soweit sie in Ausübung eines öffentlichen Amtes gehandelt haben und ihre persönlichen Lebensverhältnisse nicht betroffen sind.

(4) [1]Die Schutzfristen können im Einzelfall oder für bestimmte Teile von Archivgut verkürzt werden, wenn Rechtsvorschriften nicht entgegenstehen. [2]Bei personenbezogenem Archivgut nach Absatz 1 Satz 2 ist im Einzelfall eine Verkürzung nur zulässig, wenn
1. die betroffene Person oder nach deren Tod der überlebende Ehegatte oder Lebenspartner, nach dessen Tod die Kinder oder, wenn keine Kinder vorhanden sind, die Eltern der betroffenen Person oder nach deren Tod der Partner einer auf Dauer angelegten Lebensgemeinschaft der betroffenen Person eingewilligt haben oder
2. die Nutzung zu wissenschaftlichen Zwecken unter den Voraussetzungen des § 9 des Landesdatenschutzgesetzes erfolgt oder
3. die Nutzung zur Wahrnehmung von Belangen, die im überwiegenden Interesse einer betroffenen Person oder Dritter liegen, unerlässlich ist und die Wahrung der schutzwürdigen Belange der betroffenen Person oder Dritter durch geeignete Maßnahmen sichergestellt ist.

(5) Für Archivgut, das nach § 6 Absatz 4 oder § 7 des Bundesarchivgesetzes von Stellen des Bundes dem staatlichen Archiv übergeben worden ist, gelten § 6 sowie die §§ 10 bis 14 des Bundesarchivgesetzes entsprechend.

§ 11 Rechtsansprüche der betroffenen Person

(1) [1]Der betroffenen Person ist auf Antrag ohne Rücksicht auf die in § 10 festgelegten Schutzfristen Auskunft über die im Archivgut zu ihrer Person enthaltenen Daten nach Artikel 15 der Datenschutz-Grundverordnung zu erteilen oder Einsicht in das auf sie bezogene Archivgut zu gewähren, soweit das Archivgut durch den Namen der Person erschlossen ist oder Angaben gemacht werden, die das Auffinden des Archivgutes oder der Angaben ermöglichen. [2]Dieses gilt nicht, soweit Geheimhaltungspflichten nach § 203 Abs. 1 bis 3 des Strafgesetzbuches oder anderer Rechtsvorschriften verletzt würden oder besondere Vereinbarungen mit gegenwärtigen oder früheren Eigentümern entgegenstehen.

(2) [1]Wer die Richtigkeit von Angaben zu seiner Person bestreitet, hat einen Anspruch darauf, daß den Unterlagen eine Gegendarstellung beigefügt wird, wenn er ein berechtigtes Interesse daran glaubhaft macht. [2]Nach dem Tod der betroffenen Person steht dieses Recht den Angehörigen nach § 10 Abs. 4 Nr. 1 in der dort genannten Folge zu. [3]Die Gegendarstellung bedarf der Schriftform und muß sich auf Angaben über Tatsachen beschränken. [4]Die Sätze 1 und 2 gelten nicht für Angaben, die in einer amt-

lichen Niederschrift über eine öffentliche Sitzung eines beschließenden Organs einer juristischen Person des öffentlichen Rechts oder eines Gerichts enthalten sind. [5]Ein weitergehendes Recht auf Berichtigung der Daten nach Artikel 16 der Datenschutz-Grundverordnung oder Einschränkung der Verarbeitung nach Artikel 18 der Datenschutz-Grundverordnung bestehen nicht.

§ 12 Kommunale Archive

(1) [1]Die kommunalen Körperschaften archivieren die bei ihnen sowie bei ihren Funktions- und Rechtsvorgängern entstandenen Unterlagen als pflichtige Selbstverwaltungsaufgabe. [2]Sie archivieren auch Unterlagen, die bei ihnen oder ihren Organen im übertragenen Wirkungskreis oder als untere staatliche Verwaltungsbehörde entstanden sind. [3]Die kommunalen Körperschaften regeln die Übernahme, Sicherung, Erschließung und Nutzung ihres Archivgutes nach archivfachlichen Gesichtspunkten im Sinne dieses Gesetzes in eigener Zuständigkeit. [4]§ 10 Abs. 1, 2 und 3 Satz 1 sowie Absatz 4 und § 11 gelten unmittelbar.
(2) [1]Sie erfüllen diese Aufgabe durch
1. die Unterhaltung eigener Archive oder
2. die Schaffung von oder die Beteiligung an Gemeinschaftsarchiven oder
3. das Anbieten und die Übergabe ihrer archivwürdigen Unterlagen an das staatliche Archiv, sofern dieses zur Übernahme bereit ist.

[2]Unterhalten kreisangehörige kommunale Körperschaften keine eigenen Archive oder sind sie nicht an Gemeinschaftsarchiven beteiligt und ist auch kein anderes öffentliches Archiv zur Übernahme bereit, so sind die archivwürdigen Unterlagen vom Archiv des zuständigen Landkreises zu übernehmen. [3]Die abgebende Körperschaft ist zu einer angemessenen Kostenbeteiligung verpflichtet.
(3) Die anbietenden kommunalen Körperschaften haben an den von dem staatlichen Archiv übernommenen archivwürdigen Unterlagen einen Anspruch auf Rückgabe für den Fall, daß ein eigenes Archiv nach Absatz 2 Nr. 1 oder ein Gemeinschaftsarchiv nach Absatz 2 Nr. 2 errichtet wird oder das staatliche Archiv das Archivgut nach § 8 Absatz 2und 3 vernichten oder aussondern wollen.
(4) Durch Satzung kann die Verpflichtung zur Ablieferung eines Belegexemplars entsprechend § 14 Nr. 2 vorgesehen werden.

§ 13 Sonstige öffentliche Archive

[1]Die staatlichen Hochschulen und die sonstigen der Aufsicht des Landes unterstehenden selbstverwaltungsberechtigten Körperschaften, Anstalten und Stiftungen des öffentlichen Rechts regeln die Archivierung der bei ihnen entstandenen Unterlagen in eigener Zuständigkeit und Verantwortung nach archivfachlichen Gesichtspunkten im Sinne dieses Gesetzes. [2]§ 12 Abs. 1 Satz 4 und Absatz 2 bis 4 gelten entsprechend.

§ 14 Verordnungsermächtigung

[1]Das Ministerium für Bildung, Wissenschaft und Kultur regelt durch Rechtsverordnung[1]) die Einzelheiten der Benutzung des staatlichen Archivs. [2]Dabei kann auch vorgesehen werden, daß Nutzer dem staatlichen Archiv kostenlos ein Belegexemplar von Publikationen, die unter Nutzung seines Archivguts entstanden sind, zum dauernden Verbleib oder zur Herstellung einer Vervielfältigung zu überlassen haben.

---

1) Die Archivbenutzungsverordnung ist abgedruckt als Nr. D8.II.1a..

Verordnung über die Benutzung des staatlichen Archivs in Mecklenburg-Vorpommern (Archivbenutzungsverordnung – ArchivBenutzVO M-V)

Vom 21. August 2006 (GVOBl. M-V S. 698)
(GS Meckl.-Vorp. Gl. Nr.224-5-3)
zuletzt geändert durch Art. 1 2. ÄndVO vom 28. Februar 2019 (GVOBl. M-V S. 120)

Aufgrund des § 14 Satz 1 des Landesarchivgesetzes vom 7. Juli 1997 (GVOBl. M-V S. 282), das durch Artikel 2 des Gesetzes vom 28. November 2005 (GVOBl. M-V S. 574) geändert worden ist, verordnet das Ministerium für Bildung, Wissenschaft und Kultur:

§ 1 Anwendungsbereich
¹Die Verordnung regelt die Benutzung des staatlichen Archivs im Landesamt für Kultur und Denkmalpflege. ²Das staatliche Archiv unterhält zwei Standorte in Schwerin und Greifswald.

§ 2 Benutzungsarten
(1) Die Benutzung des staatlichen Archivs erfolgt durch
1. persönliche Einsichtnahme (Direktbenutzung),
2. schriftliche Anfragen,
3. Anforderung von Reproduktionen von Archivgut,
4. Versendung von Archivgut zur Einsichtnahme an einem anderen Ort,
5. die Ausleihe von Archivgut zu Ausstellungszwecken.

(2) Die übliche Benutzungsart ist die persönliche Einsichtnahme in einem der Lesesäle des staatlichen Archivs.
(3) Über die Benutzungsart entscheidet das staatliche Archiv nach fachlichen Gesichtspunkten.

§ 3 Benutzungsantrag
(1) ¹Die Benutzung ist schriftlich zu beantragen. ²Die Antragstellung kann auch elektronisch erfolgen. ³Dabei sind Angaben zur Person (Name, Vorname, Anschrift) zu machen.
(2) Bei Beantragung der Nutzung von Akten, die einer Schutzfrist unterliegen (§ 10 Landesarchivgesetz) oder bei denen aus anderen Gründen die Zugänglichkeit eingeschränkt ist (§ 9 Absatz 2 Landesarchivgesetz), sind möglichst genaue Angaben zum Benutzungszweck und zum Gegenstand der Nachforschungen zu machen. Für jeden Gegenstand der Nachforschungen und jeden Benutzungszweck ist ein gesonderter Antrag zu stellen.
(3) Auf Verlangen hat sich der Benutzer auszuweisen.

§ 4 Benutzungsgenehmigung
(1) Über den Benutzungsantrag entscheidet das staatliche Archiv.
(2) Die Benutzungsgenehmigung kann unter Bedingungen und mit Auflagen erteilt werden.
(3) Die Benutzungsgenehmigung kann außer aus den in § 9 Abs. 2 des Landesarchivgesetzes genannten Gründen aus anderen wichtigen Gründen eingeschränkt oder versagt werden, insbesondere wenn
1. bei früherer Benutzung von Archivgut schwerwiegend gegen die Archivbenutzungsverordnung oder andere einschlägige Bestimmungen des staatlichen Archivs verstoßen worden ist,
2. der Ordnungszustand des Archivguts eine Nutzung nicht zulässt,
3. Archivalien aus dienstlichen Gründen oder wegen gleichzeitiger amtlicher oder anderweitiger Benutzung nicht verfügbar sind,
4. der mit der Nutzung des staatlichen Archivs erfolgte Zweck anderweitig, insbesondere durch Einsichtnahme in Druckwerke oder in Reproduktionen, hinlänglich erreicht werden kann,
5. ordnungsgemäß erhobene Gebühren nicht bezahlt wurden.
(4) Die Benutzungsgenehmigung kann widerrufen oder nachträglich mit Auflagen versehen werden, wenn
1. die Angaben im Benutzungsantrag nicht oder nicht mehr zutreffen,
2. Gründe bekannt werden, die zur Versagung der Benutzung geführt hätten,
3. der Benutzer wiederholt oder schwerwiegend gegen die Archivbenutzungsverordnung verstoßen hat,

4. Benutzungsbedingungen oder -auflagen nicht eingehalten wurden, Urheber- oder Persönlichkeitsschutzrechte oder andere schutzwürdige Belange Dritter nicht beachtet wurden.

§ 5 Antrag auf Verkürzung der Schutzfristen
(1) ¹Eine Verkürzung der Schutzfristen nach § 10 Abs. 4 des Landesarchivgesetzes ist schriftlich zu beantragen. ²Die Entscheidung über den Antrag trifft das staatliche Archiv.
(2) ¹Wird eine Verkürzung der Schutzfristen von Unterlagen beantragt, die sich auf eine natürliche Person beziehen (personenbezogenes Archivgut), so hat der Antragsteller über die in § 4 Abs. 2 genannten Angaben hinaus entweder die schriftliche Einwilligung des Betroffenen oder seiner Angehörigen beizufügen oder im Antrag eingehend zu begründen, warum eine Verkürzung der Schutzfrist unerlässlich ist und wie er die schutzwürdigen Belange der betroffenen Person und Dritter, zum Beispiel durch Anonymisierung, wahren wird. ²Der Benutzer hat eine Erklärung zur Wahrung von Persönlichkeitsrechten zu unterzeichnen.
(3) Auf Verlangen sind dem Antrag ergänzende Angaben und Unterlagen, bei Hochschulprüfungsarbeiten, insbesondere Stellungnahmen der akademischen Lehrer, gegebenenfalls Bürgschaften für den Benutzer, beizufügen.

§ 6 Belegexemplare
Von Arbeiten, die unter wesentlicher Verwendung von Archivgut des staatlichen Archivs verfasst worden sind, steht dem staatlichen Archiv ein kostenloses Belegexemplar zu.

§ 7 Arbeit im Benutzerraum
(1) Archivgut, Findhilfsmittel und Literatur aus der Dienstbibliothek dürfen nur im Benutzersaal während der Öffnungszeiten des jeweiligen Archivs benutzt werden.
(2) Für das Verhalten in den Benutzerräumen gelten die Vorschriften der Haus- und Benutzersaalordnungen des jeweiligen Archivs.

§ 8 Behandlung des Archivgutes
(1) ¹Das Archivgut ist mit größtmöglicher Sorgfalt zu behandeln. ²Es ist insbesondere nicht gestattet, auf Archivalien und Findhilfsmitteln Vermerke, Striche oder Zeichen anzubringen, Handpausen anzufertigen oder sonst irgend etwas zu tun, was ihren Überlieferungszustand verändern könnte.
(2) ¹An der Reihenfolge und Ordnung des Archivgutes sowie an ihrer Signierung und Verpackung darf nichts geändert werden. ²Auf Störungen in der Reihenfolge der Schriftstücke innerhalb einer Archivalieneinheit oder sonstige Unstimmigkeiten sowie auf Schäden und Verluste ist das Archivpersonal aufmerksam zu machen.

§ 9 Bestellung von Archivgut
(1) ¹Die Bestellung von Archivgut erfolgt auf den dafür vorgesehenen Bestellzetteln. ²Auf ihnen sind die Signaturen richtig und vollständig anzugeben.
(2) Es besteht kein Anspruch darauf, Archivalien in einer bestimmten Zeit oder größere Mengen von Archivgut gleichzeitig vorgelegt zu bekommen.
(3) ¹Anstelle von originalem Archivgut können, sofern dies aus konservatorischen oder organisatorischen Gründen notwendig ist, Reproduktionen vorgelegt werden. ²Die Entscheidung hierüber trifft das jeweilige Archiv.
(4) Vorbestellungen von Archivgut zur späteren Benutzung sind möglich.
(5) Das jeweilige Archiv kann Einzelheiten der Ausführung von Bestellungen durch Hausverfügung regeln.

§ 10 Rückgabe des Archivgutes
Beim Verlassen des jeweiligen Archivs sind alle benutzten Archivalien und Findhilfsmittel der Aufsicht im Benutzersaal zurückzugeben.

§ 11 Benutzung der Bibliothek
¹Die Hand- und Dienstbibliotheken des staatlichen Archivs können nur innerhalb des jeweiligen Archivs benutzt werden. ²Die §§ 12, 13 und 14 gelten entsprechend.

§ 12 Benutzung fremden Archivgutes
¹Für die Benutzung von Archivgut, das von anderen Archiven und Institutionen übersandt wird, gelten dieselben Bedingungen wie für das Archivgut des staatlichen Archivs, sofern die übersendende Stelle

nicht anderslautende Auflagen erteilt. ²Kosten und anfallende Gebühren tragen die Benutzer, die die Versendung veranlasst haben.

§ 13 Benutzung von technischen Hilfsmitteln
(1) Die Verwendung technischer Hilfsmittel ist im Zusammenhang mit der Benutzung von Archivgut grundsätzlich gestattet.
(2) Die Verwendung benutzereigener Geräte bedarf der Genehmigung durch das jeweilige Archiv und kann unter Angabe von Gründen versagt werden.
(3) ¹Archiveigene Lesegeräte stehen den Benutzern im Rahmen der Möglichkeiten zur Verfügung. ²Ein Anspruch auf ihre Benutzung besteht nicht.

§ 14 Anfertigung von Reproduktionen
(1) ¹Der Benutzer kann auf Antrag und auf eigene Kosten Reproduktionen durch das staatliche Archiv oder eine vom staatlichen Archiv beauftragte Stelle herstellen lassen, soweit das Archivgut keinen Schutzfristen unterliegt und schutzwürdige Belange von Betroffenen und Dritten nicht berührt werden. ²Ein Rechtsanspruch auf Reproduktionen besteht nicht.
(2) ¹Die Herstellung von Reproduktionen kann versagt oder eingeschränkt werden, wenn sich das Archivgut wegen seines Erhaltungszustandes oder seines Formats nicht zu Reproduktionen eignet. ²Über das jeweils geeignete Reproduktionsverfahren entscheidet das jeweilige Archiv.
(3) Eine Veröffentlichung, Weitergabe oder Vervielfältigung von Reproduktionen ist nur mit vorheriger Zustimmung des jeweiligen Archivs zulässig.
(4) Die Versandkosten für Reproduktionen trägt der Antragsteller.

§ 15 Beratung
(1) Das staatliche Archiv ist behilflich bei der Ermittlung der Archivalien und berät im Rahmen der personellen Möglichkeiten den Benutzer.
(2) Der Benutzer hat keinen Anspruch, beim Lesen oder Übersetzen der Archivalien unterstützt zu werden.

§ 16 Schriftliche Auskünfte
(1) Bei schriftlichen Anfragen sind Zweck und Gegenstand genau anzugeben.
(2) Die schriftlichen Auskünfte des staatlichen Archivs beschränken sich in der Regel auf Hinweise über Art, Umfang, Zustand und Benutzbarkeit des benötigten Archivgutes.
(3) Ein Anspruch auf Auskünfte, die einen beträchtlichen Arbeitszeitaufwand erfordern, oder auf Beantwortung von wiederholten Anfragen innerhalb eines kürzeren Zeitraums besteht nicht.

§ 17 Versendung von Archivgut
(1) ¹In begründeten Ausnahmefällen kann auf schriftlichen Antrag Archivgut zur nichtamtlichen Benutzung an andere Archive versandt werden. ²Ein Anspruch auf Versendung von Archivgut besteht nicht.
(2) Archivgut, das Benutzungsbeschränkungen unterliegt oder wegen seines hohen Wertes, seines Ordnungs- und Erhaltungszustandes, seines Formats oder aus anderen Sicherheits- oder konservatorischen Gründen versendungsunfähig ist, ist von der Versendung ausgeschlossen.
(3) Die Versendung setzt voraus, dass
1. der Benutzungszweck nicht durch Versendung von Reproduktionen erreicht werden kann,
2. das jeweilige Archiv gewährleistet, dass das Archivgut sicher verwahrt und die Benutzung durch den Antragsteller in seinen Benutzungsräumen nach Maßgabe dieser Archivbenutzungsverordnung erfolgt.
(4) ¹Die Versendung von Archivgut ist nur in beschränktem Umfang möglich und erfolgt stets befristet. ²Die Frist beträgt in der Regel vier Wochen. ³Sie kann auf Antrag verlängert werden.
(5) Aus dienstlichen Gründen kann versandtes Archivgut jederzeit zurückgefordert werden.
(6) Die Versand- und Versicherungskosten trägt der Antragsteller.

§ 18 Ausleihe von Archivgut
(1) ¹Auf die Ausleihe von Archivgut zu Zwecken der Öffentlichkeitsarbeit besteht kein Anspruch. ²Die Entscheidung über die Ausleihe wird vom Zustand und vom Wert des Archivguts abhängig ge macht. ³Sie ist darüber hinaus nur möglich, wenn gewährleistet ist, dass das ausgeliehene Archivgut wirksam vor Verlust, ⁴Beschädigung und unbefugter Benutzung geschützt wird und der Zweck der

D8.II.1a Archivbenutzungsverordnung

Leihe nicht durch Reproduktionen oder Nachbildungen erreicht werden kann. ⁵Das staatliche Archiv kann Auflagen erteilen, um die Sicherheit und Erhaltung des ausgeliehenen Archivguts zu gewährleisten. ⁶Die Herstellung von Reproduktionen von dem ausgeliehenen Archivgut durch den Entleiher oder Dritte bedarf der Zustimmung des jeweiligen Archivs.
(2) Über die Ausleihe ist mit dem Entleiher ein Leihvertrag abzuschließen.

§ 19 In-Kraft-Treten, Außer-Kraft-Treten

¹Diese Verordnung tritt am Tag nach ihrer Verkündung¹⁾ in Kraft. ²Mit dem In-Kraft-Treten dieser Verordnung tritt die Archivbenutzungsverordnung Mecklenburg-Vorpommern vom 3. August 1998 (GVOBl. M-V S. 789) außer Kraft.

---

1) Verkündet am 15.9.2006.

Richtlinie für die Bewilligung finanzieller Zuwendungen zur Erhaltung von Denkmalen in Mecklenburg-Vorpommern

Erlaß der Kultusministerin vom 29. Oktober 1994 (AmtsBl. M-V S. 1121)

Geänd. d. 1. ÄndRL v. 8.10.1998 (AmtsBl. M-V S. 1291)

Im Einvernehmen mit der Finanzministerin wird folgende Richtlinie erlassen:

1. **Zuwendungszweck, Rechtsgrundlage**
   1.1 Das Land gewährt nach Maßgabe dieser Richtlinien, den §§ 23 und 44 der Landeshaushaltsordnung (LHO), den Verwaltungsvorschriften zur LHO (VV/VV-K-LHO) und dem Gesetz zum Schutz und zur Pflege der Denkmale im Lande Mecklenburg-Vorpommern (Denkmalschutzgesetz – DSchG MV) in seiner jeweils gültigen Fassung Zuwendungen für den Schutz und die Pflege von Denkmalen als Zeugnisse der Vergangenheit und kulturellen Traditionen. Die Zuwendungen dienen der Sicherung, Erhaltung, Restaurierung und der teilweisen Rekonstruktion von Baudenkmalen, beweglichen Denkmalen und Bodendenkmalen.
   1.2 Ein Anspruch des Antragstellers auf Gewährung der Förderung besteht nicht. Die Bewilligungsbehörde entscheidet aufgrund ihres pflichtgemäßen Ermessens im Rahmen der verfügbaren Haushaltsmittel.
2. **Gegenstand der Förderung**
   2.1 Förderungen können für alle Arten von Denkmalen im Sinne des Denkmalschutzgesetzes von Mecklenburg-Vorpommern gewährt werden.
   2.2 Förderfähige Maßnahmen sind alle Arbeiten zur Sicherung, Erhaltung und Restaurierung von Denkmalen in ihrer Originalsubstanz.
   2.3 Förderfähige Maßnahmen sind auch Arbeiten zur Wiederherstellung von teilzerstörten Denkmalen, wenn dadurch die originale Substanz gesichert wird, sowie Arbeiten zur rekonstruierenden Wiederherstellung untergegangener Teile, wenn diese für das Verständnis oder das Erscheinungsbild des teilzerstörten Denkmals unverzichtbar sind. Der Umfang des wiederhergestellten Teile darf höchstens 50 % der Gesamtsubstanz des erhaltenen Originals ausmachen.
   2.4 Förderfähig sind auch Arbeiten zur Bergung und Sicherung wichtiger Denkmale. Planungskosten und Architektenhonorare sind nur insofern förderfähig, als sie durch Anforderungen der Denkmalschutzbehörden zusätzlich entstehen und in direktem Zusammenhang mit der beabsichtigten Maßnahme stehen.
   2.5 Nicht förderfähig sind:
   – Ausgaben für Erwerb und Erschließung des Denkmals,
   – Ausgaben für Beschaffung von Finanzierungsmitteln.
3. **Zuwendungsempfänger**
   3.1 Zuwendungsempfänger können Eigentümer, Besitzer oder Unterhaltungsberechtigte von Denkmalen sein. Zuwendungen werden nicht gewährt an den Bund (einschließlich Sondervermögen), an andere Bundesländer und an ausländische Staaten.
   3.2 Für die Weitergabe der Zuwendungen an Dritte sind die für den Zuwendungsempfänger maßgebenden Bestimmungen des Zuwendungsbescheides (einschließlich der Nebenbestimmungen), soweit zutreffend, auch dem Dritten aufzuerlegen.
4. **Zuwendungsvoraussetzungen**
   4.1 Zuwendungen dürfen nur für solche Vorhaben bewilligt werden, die noch nicht begonnen worden sind.
   4.2 Eine Förderung durch das Land soll nur erfolgen, wenn eine Beteiligung der Landkreise, kreisfreien Städte oder Gemeinden an der Finanzierung erfolgt.
   4.3 Zuwendungen werden grundsätzlich nur gewährt, wenn die zuwendungsfähigen Ausgaben
   – bei juristischen Personen des Privatrechts und des öffentlichen Rechts 20 000,00 DM
   – bei natürlichen Personen 10 000,00 DM
   übersteigen.

D8.III.1 Richtlinie finanzielle Zuwendungen

5. **Art und Umfang, Höhe der Zuwendungen**
   5.1 Die Förderung erfolgt als Projektförderung in der Form der Anteilfinanzierung. Die Zuwendungen werden als nicht rückzahlbare Zuschüsse gewährt. Sie können bis zu 50 % der denkmalbedingten Mehraufwendungen betragen. Die denkmalbedingten Mehraufwendungen ergeben sich aus den Gesamtausgaben der Maßnahmen ohne Ausgaben für Teilmaßnahmen, die nicht der Denkmalpflege dienen, abzüglich desjenigen Ausgabenanteils, der bei der Durchführung der Maßnahme ohnehin entstehen würde.
   5.2 Maßnahmen, die anderweitige Förderungen des Landes oder des Bundes mit gleichfalls denkmalpflegerischer Zielstellung erfahren, sind insgesamt nur mit bis zu 50 % der denkmalbedingten Mehraufwendungen förderfähig.
   5.3 Die Vergabe von Zuwendungen erfolgt nach der Notwendigkeit der Fördermaßnahmen sowie der kunst- und kulturgeschichtlichen Bedeutung des Denkmals. Die Bewilligungsbehörde kann im Einzelfall bei herausragendem Landesinteresse einen höheren als den in Ziffer 5.1 bzw. 5.2 genannten Höchstsatz festlegen.
   5.4 Der Eigenanteil kann in Form von eigener Arbeits- und Sachleistung erbracht werden. Für die eigene Arbeitsleistung des Zuwendungsempfängers und die Bereitstellung von Material aus eigenen Beständen können Zuwendungen nicht gewährt werden. Eigenarbeit kann nur auf die zuwendungsfähigen Ausgaben angerechnet werden, wenn sie eine Facharbeit ist und die entsprechende Sachkunde bei Antragstellung glaubhaft gemacht wird. Maßgeblich für den Wert der eigenen Arbeitsleistung ist der durchschnittliche Bruttoverdienst im Handwerk für die Arbeitsstunden, die ein Freischaffender oder Unternehmer für die Durchführung der beantragten Maßnahme ansetzt.

6. **Verfahren**
   6.1 Für die Bewilligung der Förderungen bedarf es eines schriftlichen Antrages. Der Vertreter hat seine Vertretungsberechtigung bei Antragstellung nachzuweisen.
   Dem Antrag sind folgende Unterlagen beizufügen:
   – Gesamtfinanzierungskonzept, detaillierte Maßnahmebeschreibung (siehe auch Punkt 18 der Anlage 1),[1)]
   – Maßnahmezeitplan,
   – detaillierter Kostenvoranschlag für die beabsichtigte Maßnahme,
   – Fotodokumentation (jetziger und früherer Zustand),
   – Schadensdokumentation (nach Möglichkeit Originalfotos, keine Kopien),
   – Lageplan auf topografischer Karte bzw. Stadtplan,
   – vom Landesamt für Denkmalpflege (Bodendenkmalpflege) bestätigte denkmalpflegerische Zielstellung,
   – Aussagen über die geplante Nutzung.
   6.2 Der Antrag auf Fördermittel von denkmalpflegerischen Maßnahmen soll bis zum 31. Oktober eines Jahres für das folgende Jahr eingereicht sein. Bewilligungsbehörden sind das Landesamt für Denkmalpflege und das Landesamt für Bodendenkmalpflege. Später eingereichte Anträge können durch die Bewilligungsbehörde allein schon deshalb abgelehnt werden.
   6.3 Maßnahmen an Objekten in kirchlichem Besitz müssen vor Antragstellung durch das zuständige Bauamt der Landeskirche bzw. den Baubeauftragten der Kirchen und Religionsgemeinschaften beurteilt werden. Diese Stellungnahme ist mit Antragstellung vorzulegen. An den Abstimmungen über Fördermaßnahmen im kirchlichen Bereich beteiligt das zuständige Landesamt die obersten Kirchenbehörden bzw. die obersten Stellen der Religionsgemeinschaften des Landes.
   6.4 Übersteigen die zuwendungsfähigen Ausgaben 150 000,00 DM, so müssen juristische Personen des Privatrechts und natürliche Personen vor Auszahlung des Zuschusses den Nachweis der dinglichen Sicherung für etwaige Rückforderungsansprüche in Höhe des Zuwendungsbetrages an rangbereiter Stelle sowie den Nachweis über den Abschluß einer ausreichenden Feuer- und Sturmschadenversicherung zum gleitenden Neuwert für das Gebäude führen. Die Bewilligungsstelle entscheidet über Ausnahmen.

---

1) Hinweis: Die Anlage konnte aus drucktechnischen Gründen nicht aufgenommen werden.

Richtlinie finanzielle Zuwendungen D8.III.1

6.5 Die Bewilligungsbehörden bewilligen die Zuwendung durch schriftlichen Bescheid. Die ANBest-K/P sowie die baufachlichen Ergänzungsbestimmungen zu den VV zu § 44 (ZBau § 44) sind unverändert zum Bestandteil des Zuwendungsbescheides zu machen. Der Zuwendungsbescheid kann weitere Nebenbestimmungen enthalten.

6.6 Der Verwendungsnachweis in Form eines Sachberichtes und eines zahlenmäßigen Nachweises ist innerhalb von sechs Monaten nach Erfüllung des Zuwendungszwecks, spätestens jedoch mit Ablauf des auf den Bewilligungszeitraum folgenden Monats, der Bewilligungsbehörde vorzulegen. Für Maßnahmen, deren Durchführung sich über ein Haushaltsjahr hinaus erstreckt, ist über die Verwendung der Zuwendung ein Zwischennachweis zu führen, der der Bewilligungsbehörde bis spätestens zwei Monate nach Ablauf des Haushaltsjahres vorzulegen ist. Das jeweilige Rechnungsprüfungsamt des Kreises, der kreisfreien Stadt und Gemeinde sowie gegebenenfalls die Rechnungsprüfungseinrichtungen der Kirchen und Religionsgemeinschaften prüfen zuvor anhand der originalen Rechnungs- und Zahlungsbelege die ordnungsgemäße Verwendung der Mittel. Zuwendungsempfänger, die keine eigene Prüfungseinrichtung unterhalten, haben die originalen Rechnungs- und Zahlungsbelege auch der Bewilligungsbehörde vorzulegen. Die abschließende Prüfung des Verwendungsnachweises erfolgt durch die Bewilligungsbehörde.

6.7 Für die Bewilligung, Auszahlung und Abrechnung der Zuwendung sowie für den Nachweis und die Prüfung der Verwendung und ggf. erforderliche Aufhebung des Zuwendungsbescheides und die Rückforderung der gewährten Zuwendung gelten die Allgemeinen Nebenbestimmungen für Zuwendungen zur Projektförderung (ANBest-K und P) gemäß den VV zu §§ 23 und 44 der LHO M-V, das Verwaltungsverfahrensgesetz (VwVfG M-V) sowie die baufachlichen Nebenbestimmungen zu den VV zu § 44 (ZBau § 44).

7. Inkrafttreten
Diese Richtlinie tritt mit Veröffentlichung in Kraft.

D8.III.2 Kulturförderrichtlinie

Richtlinie über die Gewährung von Zuwendungen im kulturellen Bereich in Mecklenburg-Vorpommern (Kulturförderrichtlinie – KultFöRL M-V)

Verwaltungsvorschrift des Ministeriums für Bildung, Wissenschaft und Kultur vom 5. Oktober 2017 – VII 430 – VV Meckl.-Vorp. Gl. Nr. 630 – 339
[geändert durch Verwaltungsvorschrift des Ministeriums für Bildung, Wissenschaft und Kultur vom 16. Januar 2018 – VII 430 –]

Das Ministerium für Bildung, Wissenschaft und Kultur erlässt im Einvernehmen mit dem Finanzministerium und nach Anhörung des Landesrechnungshofes folgende Verwaltungsvorschrift:

1 Rechtsgrundlage, Zuwendungszweck

1.1 Das Land Mecklenburg-Vorpommern gewährt nach Maßgabe dieser Verwaltungsvorschrift und der Verwaltungsvorschriften zu § 44 der Landeshaushaltsordnung Mecklenburg-Vorpommern sowie der Verordnung (EU) Nr. 651/2014 der Kommission vom 17. Juni 2014 zur Feststellung der Vereinbarkeit bestimmter Gruppen von Beihilfen mit dem Binnenmarkt in Anwendung der Artikel 107 und 108 des Vertrags über die Arbeitsweise der Europäischen Union (ABl. L 187 vom 26.6.2014, S. 1) Zuwendungen für die Förderung der kulturellen Grundversorgung und von kulturellen Projekten in Mecklenburg-Vorpommern.
1.2 Die Kulturförderung in Mecklenburg-Vorpommern erfolgt nach einem Drei-Säulen-Modell.
1.2.1 Die kulturelle Grundversorgung als erste Säule richtet sich auf den lokal und regional wirkenden Erwerb von kulturellen und künstlerischen Grundkompetenzen.
1.2.2 Projekte von überregionaler oder landesweiter Wirksamkeit und Bedeutung werden in der zweiten Säule gefördert.
1.2.3 Sonstige herausragende Projekte aus allen Genres sowie Projekte im Rahmen von Landesprogrammen im kulturellen Bereich werden in der dritten Säule gefördert
1.2.4 Näheres zu den Gegenständen der Förderung regelt die Anlage 1.
1.3 Ein Anspruch der Antragstellerin oder des Antragstellers auf Gewährung der Zuwendung besteht nicht. Vielmehr entscheidet die Bewilligungsbehörde aufgrund ihres pflichtgemäßen Ermessens im Rahmen der verfügbaren Haushaltsmittel.

2 Zuwendungsempfänger

2.1 Zuwendungsempfänger können juristische Personen des öffentlichen und privaten Rechts sowie natürliche Personen sein.
2.2 Ohne Ausnahme sind von der Förderung ausgeschlossen Zuwendungsempfänger, die einer Rückforderung aufgrund eines früheren Beschlusses der EU-Kommission zur Feststellung der Unzulässigkeit einer Beihilfe (Förderung) und ihrer Unvereinbarkeit mit dem Binnenmarkt nicht nachgekommen sind.

3 Zuwendungsvoraussetzungen

3.1 Zuwendungen werden nur für Vorhaben bewilligt,
a) die einer der unter Nummer 1.2 genannten Säulen zuzuordnen sind,
b) die einen räumlichen oder inhaltlichen Bezug zu Mecklenburg-Vorpommern aufweisen,
c) die von landesweiter oder besonderer künstlerischer oder kulturpolitischer Bedeutung sind und an denen ein erhebliches Landesinteresse besteht und
d) die vor Antragseingang beim Ministerium für Bildung, Wissenschaft und Kultur noch nicht begonnen worden sind. Mit Antragseingang gilt der vorzeitige Maßnahmebeginn als genehmigt; mit der Zustimmung zum vorzeitigen Maßnahmebeginn wird weder dem Grunde noch der Höhe nach ein Anspruch auf Bewilligung der Zuwendung begründet; die Antragstellerin oder der Antragsteller beginnt mit dem Projekt auf eigene Verantwortung; es bestehen keine Regressansprüche gegen das Land Mecklenburg-Vorpommern.
3.2 Zuwendungen sollen grundsätzlich nur bewilligt werden für Projekte,
a) die einer gleichberechtigten Teilhabe von Frauen und Männern Rechnung tragen,
b) die den Anforderungen des Landesbehindertengleichstellungsgesetzes und einer gleichberechtigten Teilhabe an der Gesellschaft Rechnung tragen (Inklusion),
c) die der Demokratieerziehung dienen,

d) die in Mecklenburg-Vorpommern durchgeführt werden oder deren Antragstellerinnen und Antragsteller eine Niederlassung oder Betriebsstätte in Mecklenburg-Vorpommern haben,
e) in deren Umsetzung wenigstens der Mindestlohn nach dem Vergabegesetz Mecklenburg-Vorpommern gezahlt wird,
f) bei denen sich die Zuwendungsempfänger angemessen an der Finanzierung beteiligen,
g) bei denen eine höchstmögliche Beteiligung Dritter an der Finanzierung des Projektes erfolgt.

3.3 Staatlich anerkannte Kinder- und Jugendkunstschulen, die als gemeinnützige Bildungseinrichtungen ein kontinuierliches außerschulisches oder unterrichtsbegleitendes Bildungsangebot bereitstellen und für jedermann zugänglich sind, können Zuwendungen erhalten, wenn sie folgendes Leistungsangebot erfüllen:
a) Kurse: in Semestern außerschulisch, aufeinander aufbauend, Individualförderung,
b) Workshops, Ferienangebote,
c) Projekte: interdisziplinär, genreübergreifend,
d) unterrichtergänzende Angebote: Schulprojekttage, Schulprojekte, Kooperation mit Schulen,
e) offene Angebote,
f) ästhetische Frühförderung,
g) individuelle Berufsorientierung und -vorbereitung.

Die überwiegende Zahl der hauptamtlich und nebenberuflich tätigen Lehrkräfte muss über einen Hochschulabschluss auf künstlerischem Gebiet oder einen gleichwertigen Abschluss verfügen. Gleichwertige Abschlüsse sind:
– die erste Staatsprüfung für Lehramt in musisch-künstlerischen Fächern oder
– ein ausgewiesener künstlerischer Schaffensprozess oder eine spartenspezifische Fachausbildung sowie eine pädagogische Befähigung oder ein Nachweis von langjährigen pädagogischen Erfahrungen.

3.4 Staatlich anerkannte Musikschulen

3.4.1 Staatlich anerkannte Musikschulen (nachfolgend Musikschulen genannt), die als gemeinnützige Bildungseinrichtungen auf der Grundlage der Rahmenlehrpläne und des Strukturplanes des Verbandes Deutscher Musikschulen organisiert sind und kontinuierlich musikalische Bildungsarbeit leisten sowie für jedermann zugänglich sind, können Zuwendungen erhalten. Gefördert werden Musikschulen durch Zuwendungen zu den als zuwendungsfähig anerkannten Personalausgaben von hauptamtlich und nebenberuflich tätigem pädagogischen Personal.

3.4.2 Die Musikschule soll regelmäßig die folgenden Bereiche eingerichtet haben:
a) Elementarbereich (Grundstufe); musikalische Früherziehung/musikalische Grundausbildung/Elementare Musikpädagogik,
b) Vokalunterricht sowie Instrumentalunterricht in den Bereichen Streich-, Blas-, Tasten-, Zupf- und Schlaginstrumente,
c) Ensemblespiel und -singen.

3.4.3 Die Leiterin oder der Leiter der Musikschule muss eine nach Ausbildung und Berufserfahrung geeignete Person sein, die vom Träger fest angestellt ist, über einen Hochschulabschluss im Fach Musik sowie über Befähigungen im Verwaltungs- und Kulturmanagement verfügt.

3.4.4 Unterricht wird durch hauptamtlich und nebenberuflich tätige Lehrkräfte mit musikpädagogischer Befähigung erteilt, die einen Hochschulabschluss oder eine entsprechende Ausbildung mit vergleichbaren Fähigkeiten und Erfahrungen oder einen langjährigen künstlerischen Schaffensprozess nachweisen können.

3.5 Öffentliche Bibliotheken

3.5.1 Hauptamtlich geleitete Bibliotheken in kommunaler oder privatrechtlicher Trägerschaft, die an der Landesstatistik teilnehmen und die Qualitätsstandards für öffentliche Bibliotheken erfüllen, können Zuwendungen erhalten. Die Qualitätsstandards für öffentliche Bibliotheken sind in Abhängigkeit von der Einwohnerzahl am Standort in den Anhängen der Anlagen 2c und 2d (Kriterienkatalog) festgelegt. Die Erfüllung der Qualitätsstandards ist im Rahmen der Antragstellung nachzuweisen, wobei mit Ausnahme eines Merkmals alle Qualitätsstandards zu erfüllen sind. Zwingend zu erfüllen ist die Erneuerungsquote.

3.5.2 Öffentliche Bibliotheken, die aus eigenen Mitteln nicht in der Lage sind, die Qualitätsstandards zu erfüllen und deshalb keinen Antrag zum Ankauf von Medien stellen oder dem landesweiten Onleiheverbund nicht beitreten können, kann einmalig eine Zuwendung als Anschubfinanzierung gewährt werden, um die Voraussetzungen zu schaffen, die Qualitätsstandards zu erfüllen. Vor Antragstellung ist die Vorhabenplanung mit der Fachstelle für öffentliche Bibliotheken und dem Ministerium für Bildung, Wissenschaft und Kultur abzustimmen. Der Träger der Bibliothek ist verpflichtet, seinerseits die Voraussetzungen dafür zu schaffen, dass die Bibliothek die Qualitätsstandards mindestens für fünf Kalenderjahre erfüllen kann.

3.6 Nicht förderfähig sind Projekte mit vorwiegend kommerziellem Charakter.

4 Art und Umfang, Höhe der Zuwendung

4.1 Art der Zuwendung

4.1.1 Die Zuwendungen werden im Rahmen der Projektförderung als Anteilfinanzierung oder Festbetragsfinanzierung in Form von nicht rückzahlbaren Zuschüssen gewährt. Eine Vollfinanzierung ist in begründeten Ausnahmefällen bei Vorliegen eines erheblichen Landesinteresses möglich und nur dann, wenn der Zuwendungsempfänger nicht in der Lage ist, das Projekt mitzufinanzieren.

4.1.2 Bei Projekten der kulturellen Grundversorgung (Nummer 1.2.1) erfolgt die Gewährung der Zuwendung bis zu einer Höhe von 30.000 Euro als Festbetragsfinanzierung, im Übrigen grundsätzlich als Anteilfinanzierung. Abweichend davon erfolgt die Gewährung der Zuwendung bei Musikschulen unabhängig von der Höhe der Zuwendung als Festbetragsfinanzierung. Der Festbetrag umfasst in der Regel höchstens den Umfang, in dem sich die Gemeinden und der Landkreis allein oder zusammen an den zuwendungsfähigen Ausgaben beteiligen, und entspricht höchstens 30 Prozent der als zuwendungsfähig anerkannten Personalausgaben. Staatlich anerkannte Kinder- und Jugendkunstschulen können bis zu einem Drittel – in Ausnahmefällen bis zu 50 Prozent – der zuwendungsfähigen Gesamtausgaben gefördert werden. Die Zuwendung an öffentliche Bibliotheken (Nummer 3.5.1) erfolgt als Festbetragsfinanzierung. Die Förderhöhe wird nach einem Verteilungsmodell berechnet. Dabei werden die Einwohnerzahl des Standortes der Bibliothek und der Erwerbungsetat pro Einwohner auf der Grundlage der Angaben für die Deutsche Bibliotheksstatistik berücksichtigt. Die Anschubfinanzierung (Nummer 3.5.2) erfolgt als Vollfinanzierung.

4.1.3 Bei Projekten von überregionaler oder landesweiter Wirksamkeit und Bedeutung (Nummer 1.2.2) erfolgt die Gewährung der Zuwendung bis zu einer Höhe von 30.000 Euro als Festbetragsfinanzierung, im Übrigen grundsätzlich als Anteilfinanzierung. Die Höhe der Zuwendung kann grundsätzlich bis zu 70 Prozent der zuwendungsfähigen Ausgaben betragen.

4.1.4 Bei sonstigen herausragenden Projekten aus allen Genres (Nummer 1.2.3) erfolgt die Gewährung der Zuwendung bis zu einer Höhe von 30.000 Euro als Festbetragsfinanzierung, im Übrigen grundsätzlich als Anteilfinanzierung. Die Höhe der Zuwendung kann grundsätzlich bis zu 50 Prozent der zuwendungsfähigen Ausgaben betragen.

4.1.5 Projekte nach den Nummern 1.2.1 und 1.2.2 können für einen Zeitraum von bis zu 24 Monaten gefördert werden. Projekte nach Nummer 1.2.3 werden grundsätzlich für einen Zeitraum von bis zu zwölf Monaten gefördert.

4.2 Bemessungsgrundlage

4.2.1 Personal- und Sachausgaben sowie Investitionen, die im direkten Zusammenhang mit dem Projekt entstehen, werden als zuwendungsfähige Ausgaben anerkannt. Zu den Sachausgaben zählen unter anderem Büro- und Arbeitsmaterial, Honorare, Telefon, Porto, Reisekosten gemäß Landesreisekostengesetz, Ausgaben für allgemein übliche Bewirtungen (zum Beispiel bei Jurysitzungen), wenn sie im Zusammenhang mit dem Projekt entstehen, anteilige Miet- und Betriebskosten. Investitionen als Hauptgegenstand des Projektes sind zuwendungsfähig, insbesondere Anschaffungen und Ausstattung einschließlich baulicher Nebenkosten im Zusammenhang mit der Installation und Inbetriebnahme. Bauliche Investitionen als Hauptgegenstand des Projektes sind nicht zuwendungsfähig.

4.2.2 Der zu erbringende Eigenanteil kann auch als unbare Leistung in Form von eigenen Arbeits- und Sachleistungen erbracht werden. Für den Wert der eigenen Arbeitsleistung ist nicht weniger als der Mindestlohn nach dem Vergabegesetz Mecklenburg-Vorpommern anzusetzen. Eigenarbeitsleistungen sind nachzuweisen.

4.2.3 Ausgaben, die innerhalb der folgenden Sätze liegen, werden unabhängig von der Höhe der Zuwendung ohne Vorlage weiterer Nachweise zum Antrag anerkannt:
a) Ausgaben für Verwaltungskosten (zum Beispiel Büromaterial, Telefonkosten, Porto) bis zu 7,5 Prozent der zuwendungsfähigen Gesamtausgaben,
b) Betriebs- und Nebenkosten für Büro- und Ausstellungsräume, Galerien, Veranstaltungsräume und dergleichen bis zu 3,50 Euro/m 2/Monat,
c) Honorarsätze entsprechend der jeweils aktuellen Empfehlung des Bundesverbandes freiberuflicher Kulturwissenschaftler.

Das Gebot der Sparsamkeit und Wirtschaftlichkeit bleibt unberührt.

4.2.4 Bei Maßnahmen, bei denen eine Kommune als koordinierender Zuwendungsgeber auftritt, können sich die zuwendungsfähigen Personalausgaben, als Ausnahme von Nummer 1.3 der Allgemeinen Nebenbestimmungen für Zuwendungen zur Projektförderung (ANBest-P), aus dem Tarifvertrag für den öffentlichen Dienst ableiten.

4.3 Zuwendungen des Landes werden grundsätzlich nur gewährt, wenn der Zuwendungsbetrag mindestens 3.000 Euro beträgt. Über begründete Ausnahmen entscheidet die Bewilligungsbehörde.

5 Sonstige Zuwendungsbestimmungen

5.1 Geförderte Investitionen unterliegen einer zeitlichen Zweckbindung von zehn Jahren, die durch tatsächliche zweckentsprechende Nutzung abgegolten wird. Ist der Zuwendungsempfänger durch Umstände, die er nicht zu vertreten hat, gehindert, die geforderte zweckentsprechende Nutzung zu gewährleisten, entscheidet das Ministerium für Bildung, Wissenschaft und Kultur unter Berücksichtigung der Gründe, ob die Zweckbestimmung durch die bisherige tatsächliche Nutzung gleichwohl als erfüllt angesehen werden kann. Bei einer dauerhaften Zweckentfremdung besteht eine Rückzahlungspflicht.

5.2 Die Inventarisierungs- und Nachweispflicht gemäß Nummer 4.2 der ANBest-P besteht erst ab einer Zuwendungshöhe von mehr als 30.000 Euro.

5.3 Aus einer einmaligen oder mehrmaligen Förderung erwächst kein Anspruch auf eine weitergehende oder anteilige Förderung in den Folgejahren.

5.4 Datenspeicherung

5.4.1 Die Erhebung der personenbezogenen Daten in den Antragsformularen erfolgt zur Prüfung der Zuwendungsvoraussetzungen und der ordnungsgemäßen Durchführung der Antragsverfahren.

5.4.2 Die Daten werden in einer Datenbank des Ministeriums für Bildung, Wissenschaft und Kultur zehn Jahre nach Abschluss des Verwaltungsvorgangs gespeichert. Die Postanschrift lautet:

Ministerium für Bildung, Wissenschaft und Kultur Mecklenburg-Vorpommern
19048 Schwerin.

Über diese Anschrift erhält die Antragstellerin oder der Antragsteller Auskünfte über die Verarbeitung personenbezogener Daten.

5.4.3 Die Daten stehen der Bewilligungsbehörde und den Prüfeinrichtungen des Landes und der Europäischen Union sowie den von diesen zu Prüfzwecken beauftragten Stellen zur Verfügung. Darüber hinaus können Angaben über alle gewährten Zuwendungen, Angaben über die einzelnen geförderten Vorhaben und die Zuwendungsempfänger sowie die Höhe der jeweils bereitgestellten Mittel einzeln oder insgesamt durch die Bewilligungsbehörde und die Europäische Union veröffentlicht werden.

5.5 Informationspflicht

Der Zuwendungsempfänger hat bei der Durchführung der Projekte in geeigneter Weise auf die Landesförderung hinzuweisen.

6 Verfahren

6.1 Antragsverfahren

6.1.1 Für die Gewährung einer Zuwendung bedarf es eines schriftlichen Antrags nach dem Muster der Anlagen 2a (Sammelantrag) oder 2b (Einzelantrag) sowie eines Finanzierungsplans nach dem Muster der Anlage 3, abweichend davon bei Bibliotheken (Nummer 3.5.1) eines schriftlichen Antrages nach dem Muster der Anlage 2c (Bibliotheken in Kommunen mit bis zu 20.000 Einwohnern) oder dem Muster der Anlage 2d (Bibliotheken in Kommunen mit mehr als 20.000 Einwohnern). Anträgen der staatlich anerkannten Kinder- und Jugendkunstschulen sind zudem die Anlagen 4a und 4b beizufügen. Die Antragstellung bei Musikschulen erfolgt nach dem Muster der Anlagen 5, 5a, 5b und 5c. Die

D8.III.2 Kulturförderrichtlinie

Landkreise, kreisfreien Städte und großen kreisangehörigen Städte können Sammelanträge nach dem Muster der Anlage 2a für Zuwendungen nach Nummer 1.2.1 für ihren Zuständigkeitsbereich stellen. Der vollständige Antrag ist beim Ministerium für Bildung, Wissenschaft und Kultur Mecklenburg-Vorpommern, 19048 Schwerin als Bewilligungsbehörde einzureichen. Die Anträge auf eine Projektförderung sollen bis zum 1. Oktober für Maßnahmen des folgenden Jahres bei der Bewilligungsbehörde vorliegen.

6.1.2 Für Anträge, die bis zum 31. Dezember 2017 für das Jahr 2018 gestellt werden, ist ein vorzeitiger Maßnahmebeginn zulässig.

6.1.3 Zu den Anträgen der Nummern 1.2.2 und 1.2.3 kann durch die Bewilligungsbehörde eine Stellungnahme der Kulturverwaltung zur Förderwürdigkeit des Projektes abgefordert werden. Ausgenommen davon sind Anträge der Landesverbände, Landesarbeitsgemeinschaften oder Landesprojekte ohne Zuordnung zu einer Gebietskörperschaft sowie Anträge der Landkreise sowie der kreisfreien und großen kreisangehörigen Städte. Beinhaltet der Antrag entweder kreisliche oder kommunale Finanzierungsanteile, wird entweder seitens des Kreises oder der Kommune die Förderwürdigkeit des Projektes grundsätzlich durch die Bestätigung des Finanzierungsplanes durch die finanziell beteiligte Gebietskörperschaft oder die finanziell beteiligten Gebietskörperschaften anerkannt.

6.1.4 Anträge, in denen die Gesamtfinanzierung nicht erkennbar sichergestellt ist, sind abzulehnen. Anträge, denen die erforderlichen begründenden Unterlagen nicht beiliegen, sind als nicht prüffähig anzusehen. Wenn die konkrete Aufforderung zur Nachlieferung unter angemessener Fristsetzung erfolglos bleibt, ist die Förderung allein aus diesem Grunde abzulehnen.

6.1.5 Bis zu einer Zuwendungshöhe von 30.000 Euro ist das Einreichen von begründenden Unterlagen bezüglich der Einnahmen und Ausgaben entbehrlich, soweit ein schlüssiger, nachvollziehbarer und rechnerisch richtiger Finanzierungsplan vorliegt. Die Bewilligungsbehörde kann in Einzelfällen auch bei einer Zuwendungshöhe über 30.000 Euro vom Einreichen begründender Unterlagen absehen.

6.1.6 Die Landkreise, kreisfreien Städte und großen kreisangehörigen Städte können Sammelanträge für Zuwendungen für Kleinprojekte in ihrem Zuständigkeitsbereich stellen, die im Einzelnen den Zuwendungsbetrag von 3.000 Euro nicht erreichen.

6.2 Bewilligungsverfahren

Die Bewilligung der Zuwendung erfolgt aufgrund eines schriftlichen Zuwendungsbescheides der Bewilligungsbehörde oder im Einzelfall durch einen öffentlich-rechtlichen Vertrag (Zuwendungsvertrag).

6.3 Auszahlungsverfahren

6.3.1 Die bewilligten Mittel sind mit der dem Zuwendungsbescheid beigefügten Mittelanforderung nach dem Muster der Anlage 6 bei der Bewilligungsbehörde anzufordern.

6.3.2 Unabhängig von der Höhe der Zuwendung erfolgt die Auszahlung der Mittel grundsätzlich abweichend von Nummer 1.4 der ANBest-P oder Nummer 1.3 der Allgemeinen Nebenbestimmungen für Zuwendungen zur Projektförderung an kommunale Körperschaften (ANBest-K), soweit diese voraussichtlich in den nächsten sechs Monaten nach Auszahlung für fällige Zahlungen im Rahmen des Zuwendungszwecks benötigt werden. Zur Vermeidung von Haushaltsrisiken kann durch die Bewilligungsbehörde in Einzelfällen davon abgewichen werden.

6.3.3 Die Zuwendung wird abweichend von Nummer 1.4.1 der ANBest-P oder abweichend von Nummer 1.3.1 der ANBest-K unabhängig von der Bereitstellung der Finanzierungsanteile anderer Zuwendungsgeber oder Dritter ausgezahlt. Der Eigenanteil ist entsprechend seinem Verhältnis zu den zuwendungsfähigen Gesamtausgaben bereitzustellen. Die Auszahlung eines Restbetrages in Höhe von bis zu 20 Prozent der bewilligten Zuwendung wird grundsätzlich von der Vorlage des Verwendungsnachweises des vorherigen Jahres oder der Verwendungsnachweise der vorherigen Jahre abhängig gemacht.

6.4 Verwendungsnachweisverfahren

Der Verwendungsnachweis ist bis zu einer Zuwendungshöhe von höchstens 20.000 Euro als einfacher Verwendungsnachweis gemäß Nummer 6.6 der ANBest-P zugelassen und – soweit im Zuwendungsbescheid keine abweichende Regelung getroffen wurde – spätestens sechs Monate nach Ablauf des Bewilligungszeitraumes bei der Bewilligungsbehörde einzureichen. Für den einfachen Verwendungsnachweis ist das Muster gemäß Anlage 7a zu verwenden. Bei Zuwendungen des Landes von mehr als

20.000 Euro ist ein vollständiger Verwendungsnachweis nach dem Muster gemäß Anlage 7b zu erbringen. Durch Musikschulen (Nummer 3.4) ist ein Verwendungsnachweis gemäß dem Muster der Anlage 7c zu erbringen. Tätigkeits- oder Geschäftsberichte (Sachbericht) sowie Presseberichte sind dem Verwendungsnachweis beizufügen. Bei Zuwendungen, die als Festbetrag bewilligt wurden, kann beim Verwendungsnachweis abweichend von Nummer 6.5 der ANBest-P auf die Vorlage von Originalbelegen verzichtet werden, wenn stattdessen eine Belegliste vorgelegt wird.

6.5 Weiterleitung von Zuwendungen durch Zuwendungsempfänger
Für Zuwendungen, die Landkreisen oder Kommunen gewährt und an weitere Zuwendungsempfänger weitergeleitet werden, gelten die Vorschriften der Nummer 12 der Verwaltungsvorschriften für Zuwendungen zur Projektförderung an kommunale Körperschaften (VV-K). Für Zuwendungen, die juristischen Personen des Privatrechts gewährt und an weitere Zuwendungsempfänger weitergeleitet werden, gelten die Vorschriften der Nummer 12 der Verwaltungsvorschriften zu § 44 der Landeshaushaltsordnung Mecklenburg-Vorpommern.

6.6 Zu beachtende Vorschriften
Für die Bewilligung, Auszahlung und Abrechnung der Zuwendung sowie für den Nachweis und die Prüfung der Verwendung und die gegebenenfalls erforderliche Aufhebung des Zuwendungsbescheides und die Rückforderung der gewährten Zuwendung gelten die Verwaltungsvorschriften zu § 44 der Landeshaushaltsordnung Mecklenburg-Vorpommern, soweit nicht in dieser Verwaltungsvorschrift Abweichungen zugelassen sind, und das Landesverwaltungsverfahrensgesetz.

7 Anlagen
Die Anlagen 1 bis 7c sind Bestandteil dieser Verwaltungsvorschrift.

8 Übergangsvorschrift
8.1 Für Zuwendungen, die bis zum Ablauf des 31. Dezember 2014 auf der Grundlage der Richtlinie über die Gewährung von Zuwendungen zur Projektförderung im kulturellen Bereich sowie nach § 96 des Bundesvertriebenengesetzes vom 26. Februar 2008 (AmtsBl. M-V S. 161), der Richtlinie über die Gewährung von Zuwendungen zur Förderung der Musikschulen in Mecklenburg-Vorpommern vom 5. Dezember 1996 (AmtsBl. M-V S. 1182) oder der Richtlinie über die Gewährung von Zuwendungen zur Projektförderung der Kinder- und Jugendkunstschulen in Mecklenburg-Vorpommern vom 24. Februar 2006 (AmtsBl. M-V S. 255) bewilligt worden sind, gelten deren Regelungen hinsichtlich der Abrechnung und der Verwendungsnachweisprüfung fort.
8.2 Für Zuwendungen, die auf der Grundlage der Kulturförderrichtlinie vom 14. Juli 2014 (AmtsBl. M-V S. 862), die durch die Verwaltungsvorschrift vom 23. September 2016 (AmtsBl. M-V S. 989) geändert worden ist, bewilligt worden sind, gelten deren Regelungen hinsichtlich der Abrechnung und Verwendungsnachweisprüfung fort.
8.3 Für Anträge, die bis zum 31. Dezember 2017 für das Jahr 2017 gestellt werden, ist die Kulturförderrichtlinie vom 14. Juli 2014 (AmtsBl. M-V S. 862), die durch die Verwaltungsvorschrift vom 23. September 2016 (AmtsBl. M-V S. 989) geändert worden ist, weiter anzuwenden.

9 Inkrafttreten, Außerkrafttreten
Diese Verwaltungsvorschrift tritt am Tag nach der Veröffentlichung in Kraft und am 31. Dezember 2022 außer Kraft. Mit dem Inkrafttreten dieser Verwaltungsvorschrift tritt die Kulturförderrichtlinie vom 14. Juli 2014 (AmtsBl. M-V S. 862), die durch die Verwaltungsvorschrift vom 23. September 2016 (AmtsBl. M-V S. 989) geändert worden ist, außer Kraft.

Anlage
(zu den Nummern 1.2.4 und 7)

Gegenstand der Förderung

Im Rahmen der kulturellen Grundversorgung nach Nummer 1.2.1 können grundsätzlich auch den Landkreisen, kreisfreien Städten und den kommunalen Gebietskörperschaften Zuwendungen für Bibliotheken, Kinder- und Jugendkunstschulen, Musikschulen, soziokulturelle Zentren sowie Einrichtungen des Films und der Medien sowie der Literaturhäuser gewährt werden.

D8.III.2 Kulturförderrichtlinie

- Bibliotheken können bei Erfüllung der Qualitätsstandards Zuwendungen für den Medienankauf erhalten; im Rahmen der Anschubfinanzierung können kleinere und mittlere Bibliotheken Zuwendungen für Medien und Technik erhalten.
- Kinder- und Jugendkunstschulen mit staatlicher Anerkennung können Zuwendungen erhalten.
- Projekte der Literaturhäuser können Zuwendungen erhalten.
- Musikschulen mit staatlicher Anerkennung können Zuwendungen erhalten.
- Soziokulturelle Einrichtungen können Zuwendungen erhalten für Projekte in soziokulturellen Zentren, Projekte soziokultureller Initiativen und Migrationsprojekte

Nach den Nummern 1.2.2 und 1.2.3 können Projekte aus folgenden Bereichen und mit folgenden inhaltlichen Schwerpunkten gefördert werden:

- Archive:
Restaurierung und Verfilmung von Archivgut, Verbesserung der technischen Ausstattung, Projekte der Landesverbände.
- Besondere Kulturprojekte:
Genre- und schwerpunktvernetzte Projekte, Kulturtourismus.
- Bibliotheken:
Fachstellentätigkeit der öffentlichen Bibliotheken, landesweite Onleihe und Projekte der Leseförderung.
- Bildende Kunst:
Projekte der Bildenden Kunst und des Kunsthandwerks, Projekte der Landesverbände, Ausstellungsförderung in den kommunalen und Vereinsgalerien, Katalogförderung, Projekte der Künstlerhäuser.
- Darstellende Kunst:
Beispielhafte Projekte, Projekte der Landesverbände, Eigeninszenierungen und kreative Projekte freier Theatergruppen sowie von Kinder- und Jugendtheatern.
- Heimatpflege, Niederdeutsche Sprache und Kulturarbeit:
Projekte des Niederdeutschen, Projekte zur Aufarbeitung der Landesgeschichte, Förderung der Landeskulturtage sowie Projekte der Heimatpflege, Projekte landesweit arbeitender Verbände und Institutionen, Pflege der Tanz- und Trachtenarbeit.
- Internationale Kulturarbeit:
Projekte und Initiativen mit Beteiligung ausländischer Künstlerinnen und Künstler in Mecklenburg-Vorpommern oder mit Beteiligung von Künstlerinnen und Künstlern aus Mecklenburg-Vorpommern im Ausland, Förderung von Beziehungen Partnerregionen.
- Kinder- und Jugendkunstschulen:
Projekte der Landesverbände.
- Kulturelle Jugendbildung:
Projekte im Rahmen der kulturellen Jugendbildung.
- Kulturerbe:
Ausstellungen und Projekte zur Backsteinarchitektur und zur Hanse, Projekte im Zusammenhang mit der „Europäischen Route der Backsteingotik", dem UNESCO-Weltkulturerbe und Bewerbungen hierzu, Projekte der Archäologie.
- Literatur:
Projekte der Literatur und der Entwicklung der Medienkompetenz.
- Museen und Ausstellungen:
Projekte der Museen von überregionalem Rang, Sammlungsbestand und wissenschaftliche Tätigkeit, Ausstellungsvorhaben, Vernetzung von Aktivitäten, Druckerzeugnisse, Restaurierung und Konservierung der Bestände, Erwerb von Kulturgut, Maßnahmen zur angemessenen Sicherung, Projekte von Landesverbänden im Museumswesen, Museumspädagogik.
- Musik:
Projekte der Landesverbände, landesweit wirksame Musikprojekte mit den Schwerpunkten junge Interpreten, Ur- und Erstaufführungen von zeitgenössischen Werken, Pflege der musikalischen Traditionen, Musikfeste unter dem Dach „Musikland Mecklenburg-Vorpommern".
- Soziokultur:
Projekte des Landesverbandes und soziokultureller Zentren von überregionalem Rang oder landesweiter Bedeutung.
- Projekte im Rahmen von Landesprogrammen im kulturellen Bereich

Landesverordnung über die zuständigen Behörden nach dem Kulturgutschutzgesetz (Kulturgutschutz-Zuständigkeitslandesverordnung – KGSZstLVO M-V)

Vom 4. Juli 2017 (GVOBl. M-V 2017, S. 183, GS Meckl.-Vorp. Gl. Nr. B 224-26-1)

Aufgrund des § 3 Absatz 1 Satz 2 des Kulturgutschutzgesetzes vom 31. Juli 2016 (BGBl. I S. 1914), das durch Artikel 6 Absatz 13 des Gesetzes vom 13. April 2017 (BGBl. I S. 872, 889) geändert worden ist, und § 14 Absatz 3 des Landesorganisationsgesetzes vom 14. März 2005 (GVOBl. M-V S. 98), das durch Artikel 8 Nummer 8 des Gesetzes vom 28. Oktober 2010 (GVOBl. M-V S. 615, 618) geändert worden ist, in Verbindung mit § 22 Absatz 3 Satz 3 des Kulturgutschutzgesetzes verordnet die Landesregierung:

§ 1 Zuständige Oberste Landesbehörde
Zuständige Behörde nach § 3 Absatz 1 Satz 1 des Kulturgutschutzgesetzes ist vorbehaltlich des § 2 das für Kultur zuständige Ministerium.

§ 2 Zuständigkeit für die Genehmigung der vorübergehenden Ausfuhr von nationalem Kulturgut
Die Zuständigkeit für die Genehmigung der vorübergehenden Ausfuhr von nationalem Kulturgut gemäß § 22 Absatz 3 Satz 1 des Kulturgutschutzgesetzes wird gemäß § 22 Absatz 3 Satz 3 des Kulturgutschutzgesetzes auf das Landesamt für Kultur und Denkmalpflege übertragen.

§ 3 Inkrafttreten
Diese Landesverordnung tritt am Tag nach der Verkündung in Kraft.

D9 Niedersächsische Verfassung

Niedersächsische Verfassung

Vom 19. Mai 1993 (Nds. GVBl. S. 107)
(GVBl Sb 100-1)
zuletzt geändert durch Art. 1 G über die Schuldenbremse in Niedersachsen vom 23. Oktober 2019 (Nds. GVBl. S. 288)
– Auszug –

Erster Abschnitt
Grundlagen der Staatsgewalt, Grundrechte und Staatsziele

Artikel 6 Kunst, Kultur und Sport
Das Land, die Gemeinden und die Landkreise schützen und fördern Kunst, Kultur und Sport.

Neunter Abschnitt
Übergangs- und Schlußbestimmungen

Artikel 72 Besondere Belange und überkommene Einrichtungen der ehemaligen Länder
(1) Die kulturellen und historischen Belange der ehemaligen Länder Hannover, Oldenburg, Braunschweig und Schaumburg-Lippe sind durch Gesetzgebung und Verwaltung zu wahren und zu fördern.
[...]

Niedersächsisches Denkmalschutzgesetz[1)]

Vom 30. Mai 1978 (Nds. GVBl. S. 517)
(GVBl. Sb 22510 01)
zuletzt geändert durch Art. 1 ÄndG vom 26. Mai 2011 (Nds. GVBl. S. 135)

Inhaltsübersicht

Erster Teil
Allgemeine Vorschriften
- § 1 Grundsatz
- § 2 Denkmalschutz und Denkmalpflege als öffentliche Aufgaben
- § 3 Begriffsbestimmungen
- § 4 Verzeichnis der Kulturdenkmale
- § 5 Wirkung der Eintragungen in das Verzeichnis

Zweiter Teil
Erhaltung von Kulturdenkmalen
- § 6 Pflicht zur Erhaltung
- § 7 Grenzen der Erhaltungspflicht
- § 8 Anlagen in der Umgebung von Baudenkmalen
- § 9 Nutzung von Baudenkmalen
- § 10 Genehmigungspflichtige Maßnahmen
- § 11 Anzeigepflicht

Dritter Teil
Ausgrabungen und Bodenfunde
- § 12 Ausgrabungen
- § 13 Erdarbeiten
- § 14 Bodenfunde
- § 15 Vorübergehende Überlassung von Bodenfunden
- § 16 Grabungsschutzgebiete
- § 17 Beschränkung der wirtschaftlichen Nutzung von Grundstücken
- § 18 Schatzregal

Vierter Teil
Denkmalbehörden
- § 19 Denkmalschutzbehörden
- § 20 Zuständigkeit der Denkmalschutzbehörden
- § 21 Landesamt für Denkmalpflege
- § 22 Beauftragte für die Denkmalpflege
- § 22a Beratende Kommissionen

Fünfter Teil
Maßnahmen des Denkmalschutzes, Verfahrensvorschriften
- § 23 Anordnungen der Denkmalschutzbehörden
- § 24 Genehmigungsverfahren
- § 25 Wiederherstellung des ursprünglichen Zustands
- § 26 Zusammenwirken der Denkmalbehörden
- § 27 Duldungs- und Auskunftspflichten
- § 28 Kennzeichnung von Kulturdenkmalen

Sechster Teil
Ausgleich und Enteignung
- § 29 Ausgleich
- § 30 Zulässigkeit der Enteignung
- § 31 Anwendung des Niedersächsischen Enteignungsgesetzes

Siebenter Teil
Zuschußmittel des Landes, Steuerbefreiung
- § 32 Zuschußmittel des Landes
- § 33 *[aufgehoben]*

Achter Teil
Straftaten und Ordnungswidrigkeiten
- § 34 Zerstörung eines Kulturdenkmals
- § 35 Ordnungswidrigkeiten

Neunter Teil
Schluß- und Übergangsvorschriften
- § 36 Kirchliche Kulturdenkmale
- § 37 Finanzausgleich
- §§ 38, 39 *[nicht wiedergegebene Änderungs- bzw. Aufhebungsvorschriften]*
- § 40 Übergangsvorschrift
- § 41 Inkrafttreten

[1)] Zu § 6 Abs. 3, § 10 Abs. 1 Nr. 1, Abs. 4 und Abs. 5 Satz 3 siehe § 5 NEFUG:
  1. Soll ein Kulturdenkmal ganz oder teilweise zerstört werden, um eine Unterkunft für Flüchtlinge oder Asylbegehrende zu errichten, so ist § 6 Abs. 3 nicht anzuwenden,
      a) soweit die überwiegende Wahrscheinlichkeit besteht, dass durch seine Anwendung die Errichtung einer Unterkunft für Flüchtlinge oder Asylbegehrende verzögert würde, und
      b) bis zum 31. Dezember 2019 der Antrag auf Erteilung einer Genehmigung nach § 10 Abs. 1 Nr. 1 oder einer Genehmigung oder Entscheidung nach § 10 Abs. 4 bei der zuständigen Behörde gestellt oder die Anzeige nach § 10 Abs. 5 Satz 3 beim Landesamt für Denkmalpflege eingereicht wurde.
  2. Der Veranlasser der beabsichtigten Zerstörung hat gegenüber der für die Erteilung der Genehmigung oder Entscheidung zuständigen Behörde oder, in den Fällen des § 10 Abs. 5 Sätze 1 und 2, gegenüber dem Landesamt für Denkmalpflege schriftlich die konkreten Tatsachen darzulegen, aus denen sich das Vorliegen der Voraussetzungen nach Nummer 1 ergibt.

D9.I.1 Niedersächsisches Denkmalschutzgesetz

Der Niedersächsische Landtag hat das folgende Gesetz beschlossen, das hiermit verkündet wird:

Erster Teil
Allgemeine Vorschriften

§ 1 Grundsatz
[1]Kulturdenkmale sind zu schützen, zu pflegen und wissenschaftlich zu erforschen. [2]Im Rahmen des Zumutbaren sollen sie der Öffentlichkeit zugänglich gemacht werden.

§ 2 Denkmalschutz und Denkmalpflege als öffentliche Aufgaben
(1) [1]Aufgabe des Landes ist es, für den Schutz, die Pflege und die wissenschaftliche Erforschung der Kulturdenkmale zu sorgen. [2]Bei der Wahrnehmung von Denkmalschutz und Denkmalpflege wirken das Land, die Gemeinden, Landkreise und sonstigen Kommunalverbände sowie die in der Denkmalpflege tätigen Einrichtungen und Vereinigungen und die Eigentümer und Besitzer von Kulturdenkmalen zusammen.
(2) Dem Land sowie den Gemeinden, Landkreisen und sonstigen Kommunalverbänden obliegt die besondere Pflicht, die ihnen gehörenden und die von ihnen genutzten Kulturdenkmale zu pflegen und sie im Rahmen des Möglichen der Öffentlichkeit zugänglich zu machen.
(3) In öffentlichen Planungen und bei öffentlichen Baumaßnahmen sind die Belange des Denkmalschutzes und der Denkmalpflege sowie die Anforderungen des UNESCO-Übereinkommens zum Schutz des Kultur- und Naturerbes der Welt vom 16. November 1972 (BGBl. 1977 II S. 213) rechtzeitig und so zu berücksichtigen, dass die Kulturdenkmale und das Kulturerbe im Sinne des Übereinkommens erhalten werden und ihre Umgebung angemessen gestaltet wird, soweit nicht andere öffentliche Belange überwiegen.

§ 3 Begriffsbestimmungen
(1) Kulturdenkmale im Sinne dieses Gesetzes sind Baudenkmale, Bodendenkmale, bewegliche Denkmaleund Denkmale der Erdgeschichte.
(2) Baudenkmale sind bauliche Anlagen (§ 2 Abs. 1 der Niedersächsischen Bauordnung), Teile baulicher Anlagen, Grünanlagen und Friedhofsanlagen, an deren Erhaltung wegen ihrer geschichtlichen, künstlerischen, wissenschaftlichen oder städtebaulichen Bedeutung ein öffentliches Interesse besteht.
(3) [1]Baudenkmal ist auch eine Gruppe baulicher Anlagen, die aus den in Absatz 2 genannten Gründen erhaltenswert ist, unabhängig davon, ob die einzelnen baulichen Anlagen für sich Baudenkmale sind. [2]Pflanzen, Frei- und Wasserflächen in der Umgebung eines Baudenkmals und Zubehör eines Baudenkmals gelten als Teile des Baudenkmals, wenn sie mit diesem eine Einheit bilden, die aus den in Absatz 2 genannten Gründen erhaltenswert ist.
(4) Bodendenkmale sind mit dem Boden verbundene oder im Boden verborgene Sachen, Sachgesamtheiten und Spuren von Sachen, die von Menschen geschaffen oder bearbeitet wurden oder Aufschluß über menschliches Leben in vergangener Zeit geben und aus den in Absatz 2 genannten Gründen erhaltenswert sind, sofern sie nicht Baudenkmale sind.
(5) Bewegliche Denkmale sind bewegliche Sachen und Sachgesamtheiten, die von Menschen geschaffen oder bearbeitet wurden oder Aufschluß über menschliches Leben in vergangener Zeit geben und die aus den in Absatz 2 genannten Gründen erhaltenswert sind, sofern sie nicht Bodendenkmale sind.
(6) Denkmale der Erdgeschichte sind Überreste oder Spuren, die Aufschluss über die Entwicklung tierischen oder pflanzlichen Lebens in vergangenen Erdperioden oder die Entwicklung der Erde geben und an deren Erhaltung aufgrund ihrer herausragenden wissenschaftlichen Bedeutung ein öffentliches Interesse besteht.

§ 4 Verzeichnis der Kulturdenkmale
(1) [1]Die Kulturdenkmale sind in ein Verzeichnis einzutragen, das durch das Landesamt für Denkmalpflege aufzustellen und fortzuführen ist. [2]Bewegliche Denkmale werden in das Verzeichnis nur eingetragen, wenn ihre besondere Bedeutung es erfordert, sie dem Schutz dieses Gesetzes zu unterstellen.
(2) [1]Die unteren Denkmalschutzbehörden und die Gemeinden führen für ihr Gebiet Auszüge aus dem Verzeichnis. [2]Jedermann kann Einblick in das Verzeichnis und die Auszüge nehmen. [3]Eintragungen

über bewegliche Denkmale und über Zubehör von Baudenkmalen dürfen nur die Eigentümer und die sonstigen dinglich Berechtigten sowie die von ihnen ermächtigten Personen einsehen.
(3) ¹Eine Eintragung ist im Verzeichnis zu löschen, wenn ihre Voraussetzungen entfallen sind. ²Ist die Eigenschaft als Baudenkmal nach Absatz 5 durch Verwaltungsakt festgestellt worden, so ist die Eintragung zu löschen, wenn der Verwaltungsakt unanfechtbar aufgehoben worden ist.
(4) ¹Vor der Eintragung eines Baudenkmals, eines Bodendenkmals oder eines unbeweglichen Denkmals der Erdgeschichte in das Verzeichnis ist die Gemeinde zu hören, auf deren Gebiet sich das Denkmal befindet. ²Die Gemeinde teilt dem Landesamt für Denkmalpflege Namen und Anschrift des Eigentümers des Denkmals nach Satz 1 mit. ³Das Landesamt für Denkmalpflege hört vor der Eintragung eines Baudenkmals dessen Eigentümer. ⁴Das Landesamt für Denkmalpflege unterrichtet die untere Denkmalschutzbehörde, die Gemeinde und den Eigentümer unverzüglich über die Neueintragung oder Löschung des Baudenkmals im Verzeichnis. ⁵Das Landesamt für Denkmalpflege unterrichtet die untere Denkmalschutzbehörde über die beabsichtigte Eintragung eines beweglichen Denkmals.
(5) Ist ein Baudenkmal nach dem 30. September 2011 in das Verzeichnis eingetragen worden, so hat das Landesamt für Denkmalpflege auf Antrag des Eigentümers durch Verwaltungsakt die Eigenschaft als Baudenkmal festzustellen.

§ 5 Wirkung der Eintragungen in das Verzeichnis

(1) ¹Die Anwendbarkeit der Schutzvorschriften dieses Gesetzes ist nicht davon abhängig, dass Kulturdenkmale in das Verzeichnis nach § 4 eingetragen sind. ²Die §§ 6, 10 und 11 gelten jedoch für bewegliche Denkmale nur, wenn sie in das Verzeichnis eingetragen sind.
(2) ¹Ist die Denkmalschutzbehörde nach § 4 Abs. 4 Satz 5 über die beabsichtigte Eintragung eines beweglichen Denkmals in das Verzeichnis der Kulturdenkmale unterrichtet worden, so kann sie gegenüber dem Eigentümer anordnen, dass das Denkmal vorläufig als eingetragen gilt. ²Absatz 1 Satz 2 gilt entsprechend. ³Die Anordnung wird unwirksam, wenn die Eintragung nicht innerhalb von sechs Monaten vorgenommen worden ist. ⁴Bei Vorliegen eines wichtigen Grundes kann diese Frist um bis zu drei Monate verlängert werden. ⁵Klagen gegen die Anordnung nach Satz 1 haben keine aufschiebende Wirkung.

Zweiter Teil
Erhaltung von Kulturdenkmalen

§ 6 Pflicht zur Erhaltung

(1) ¹Kulturdenkmale sind instand zu halten, zu pflegen, vor Gefährdung zu schützen und, wenn nötig, instandzusetzen. ²Verpflichtet sind der Eigentümer oder Erbbauberechtigte und der Nießbraucher; neben ihnen ist verpflichtet, wer die tatsächliche Gewalt über das Kulturdenkmal ausübt. ³Die Verpflichteten oder die von ihnen Beauftragten haben die erforderlichen Arbeiten fachgerecht durchzuführen.
(2) Kulturdenkmale dürfen nicht zerstört, gefährdet oder so verändert oder von ihrem Platz entfernt werden, daß ihr Denkmalwert beeinträchtigt wird.
(3)¹⁾ ¹Soll ein Kulturdenkmal ganz oder teilweise zerstört werden, so ist der Veranlasser der Zerstörung im Rahmen des Zumutbaren zur fachgerechten Untersuchung, Bergung und Dokumentation des Kulturdenkmals verpflichtet. ²Satz 1 gilt unabhängig davon, ob die Zerstörung einer Genehmigung nach diesem Gesetz bedarf. ³§ 10 Abs. 3 Sätze 2 und 3, § 12 Abs. 2 Sätze 2 bis 4 sowie § 13 Abs. 2 Sätze 2 und 3 bleiben unberührt.

---

1) Zu § 6 Abs. 3, § 10 Abs. 1 Nr. 1, Abs. 4 und Abs. 5 Satz 3 siehe § 5 NEFUG:
  1. Soll ein Kulturdenkmal ganz oder teilweise zerstört werden, um eine Unterkunft für Flüchtlinge oder Asylbegehrende zu errichten, so ist § 6 Abs. 3 nicht anzuwenden,
     a) soweit die überwiegende Wahrscheinlichkeit besteht, dass durch seine Anwendung die Errichtung einer Unterkunft für Flüchtlinge oder Asylbegehrende verzögert würde, und
     b) bis zum 31. Dezember 2019 der Antrag auf Erteilung einer Genehmigung nach § 10 Abs. 1 Nr. 1 oder einer Genehmigung oder Entscheidung nach § 10 Abs. 4 bei der zuständigen Behörde gestellt oder die Anzeige nach § 10 Abs. 5 Satz 3 beim Landesamt für Denkmalpflege eingereicht wurde.
  2. Der Veranlasser der beabsichtigten Zerstörung hat gegenüber der für die Erteilung der Genehmigung oder Entscheidung zuständigen Behörde oder, in den Fällen des § 10 Abs. 5 Sätze 1 und 2, gegenüber dem Landesamt für Denkmalpflege schriftlich die konkreten Tatsachen darzulegen, aus denen sich das Vorliegen der Voraussetzungen nach Nummer 1 ergibt.

§ 7 Grenzen der Erhaltungspflicht
(1) Erhaltungsmaßnahmen können nicht verlangt werden, soweit die Erhaltung den Verpflichteten wirtschaftlich unzumutbar belastet.
(2) Ein Eingriff in ein Kulturdenkmal ist zu genehmigen, soweit
1. der Eingriff aus wissenschaftlichen Gründen im öffentlichen Interesse liegt,
2. ein öffentliches Interesse anderer Art, zum Beispiel
    a) die nachhaltige energetische Verbesserung des Kulturdenkmals,
    b) der Einsatz erneuerbarer Energien oder
    c) die Berücksichtigung der Belange von alten Menschen und Menschen mit Behinderungen,
    das Interesse an der unveränderten Erhaltung des Kulturdenkmals überwiegt und den Eingriff zwingend verlangt oder
3. die unveränderte Erhaltung den Verpflichteten wirtschaftlich unzumutbar belastet.
(3) ¹Unzumutbar ist eine wirtschaftliche Belastung insbesondere, soweit die Kosten der Erhaltung und Bewirtschaftung nicht durch die Erträge oder den Gebrauchswert des Kulturdenkmals aufgewogen werden können. ²Kann der Verpflichtete Zuwendungen aus öffentlichen oder privaten Mitteln oder steuerliche Vorteile in Anspruch nehmen, so sind diese anzurechnen. ³Der Verpflichtete kann sich nicht auf die Belastung durch erhöhte Erhaltungskosten berufen, die dadurch verursacht wurden, daß Erhaltungsmaßnahmen diesem Gesetz oder sonstigem öffentlichem Recht zuwider unterblieben sind.
(4) ¹Absatz 1 und Absatz 2 Nr. 3 gelten nicht für das Land, die Gemeinden, die Landkreise und die sonstigen Kommunalverbände. ²Sie sind zu Erhaltungsmaßnahmen im Rahmen ihrer finanziellen Leistungsfähigkeit verpflichtet.

§ 8 Anlagen in der Umgebung von Baudenkmalen
¹In der Umgebung eines Baudenkmals dürfen Anlagen nicht errichtet, geändert oder beseitigt werden, wenn dadurch das Erscheinungsbild des Baudenkmals beeinträchtigt wird. ²Bauliche Anlagen in der Umgebung eines Baudenkmals sind auch so zu gestalten und instand zu halten, daß eine solche Beeinträchtigung nicht eintritt. ³§ 7 gilt entsprechend.

§ 9 Nutzung von Baudenkmalen
(1) ¹Für Baudenkmale ist eine Nutzung anzustreben, die ihre Erhaltung auf Dauer gewährleistet. ²Das Land, die Gemeinden, die Landkreise und die sonstigen Kommunalverbände sollen die Eigentümer und sonstigen Nutzungsberechtigten hierbei unterstützen.
(2) Ein Eingriff in ein Baudenkmal, der dessen Nutzbarkeit nachhaltig verbessert, kann auch dann genehmigt werden, wenn er den Denkmalwert wegen des Einsatzes zeitgemäßer Materialien oder neuer Modernisierungstechniken nur geringfügig beeinträchtigt.

§ 10[1)] Genehmigungspflichtige Maßnahmen
(1) Einer Genehmigung der Denkmalschutzbehörde bedarf, wer
1. ein Kulturdenkmal zerstören, verändern, instandsetzen oder wiederherstellen,
2. ein Kulturdenkmal oder einen in § 3 Abs. 3 genannten Teil eines Baudenkmals von seinem Standort entfernen oder mit Aufschriften oder Werbeeinrichtungen versehen,
3. die Nutzung eines Baudenkmals ändern oder
4. in der Umgebung eines Baudenkmals Anlagen, die das Erscheinungsbild des Denkmals beeinflussen, errichten, ändern oder beseitigen
will.

---

1) Zu § 6 Abs. 3, § 10 Abs. 1 Nr. 1, Abs. 4 und Abs. 5 Satz 3 siehe § 5 NEFUG:
   1. Soll ein Kulturdenkmal ganz oder teilweise zerstört werden, um eine Unterkunft für Flüchtlinge oder Asylbegehrende zu errichten, so ist § 6 Abs. 3 nicht anzuwenden,
      a) soweit die überwiegende Wahrscheinlichkeit besteht, dass durch seine Anwendung die Errichtung einer Unterkunft für Flüchtlinge oder Asylbegehrende verzögert würde, und
      b) bis zum 31. Dezember 2019 der Antrag auf Erteilung einer Genehmigung nach § 10 Abs. 1 Nr. 1 oder einer Genehmigung oder Entscheidung nach § 10 Abs. 4 bei der zuständigen Behörde gestellt oder die Anzeige nach § 10 Abs. 5 Satz 3 beim Landesamt für Denkmalpflege eingereicht wurde.
   2. Der Veranlasser der beabsichtigten Zerstörung hat gegenüber der für die Erteilung der Genehmigung oder Entscheidung zuständigen Behörde oder, in den Fällen des § 10 Abs. 5 Sätze 1 und 2, gegenüber dem Landesamt für Denkmalpflege schriftlich die konkreten Tatsachen darzulegen, aus denen sich das Vorliegen der Voraussetzungen nach Nummer 1 ergibt.

(2) Instandsetzungsarbeiten bedürfen keiner Genehmigung nach Absatz 1, wenn sie sich nur auf Teile des Kulturdenkmals auswirken, die für seinen Denkmalwert ohne Bedeutung sind.
(3) ¹Die Genehmigung ist zu versagen, soweit die Maßnahme gegen dieses Gesetz verstoßen würde. ²Die Genehmigung kann unter Bedingungen oder mit Auflagen erteilt werden, soweit dies erforderlich ist, um die Einhaltung dieses Gesetzes zu sichern. ³Insbesondere kann verlangt werden, daß ein bestimmter Sachverständiger die Arbeiten leitet, daß ein Baudenkmal an anderer Stelle wieder aufgebaut wird oder daß bestimmte Bauteile erhalten bleiben oder in einer anderen baulichen Anlage wieder verwendet werden.
(4) ¹Ist für eine Maßnahme eine Baugenehmigung oder eine die Baugenehmigung einschließende oder ersetzende behördliche Entscheidung erforderlich, so umfaßt diese die Genehmigung nach Absatz 1. ²Absatz 3 gilt entsprechend.
(5) ¹Maßnahmen nach Absatz 1 bedürfen keiner Genehmigung der Denkmalschutzbehörde, wenn sie an Kulturdenkmalen im Eigentum oder im Besitz des Bundes oder des Landes ausgeführt werden sollen und die Leitung der Entwurfsarbeiten und die Bauüberwachung dem Staatlichen Baumanagement Niedersachsen übertragen sind. ²Maßnahmen nach Absatz 1, die durch das Klosterkammer Hannover an Kulturdenkmalen im Eigentum oder Besitz einer von ihr verwalteten Stiftung ausgeführt werden, bedürfen ebenfalls keiner Genehmigung der Denkmalschutzbehörde. ³Maßnahmen nach den Sätzen 1 und 2 sind dem Landesamt für Denkmalpflege mit Planungsbeginn anzuzeigen.
(6) Bei Maßnahmen nach Absatz 1 an Kulturdenkmalen im Eigentum oder Besitz des Bundes oder des Landes, die nicht durch das Staatliche Baumanagement Niedersachsen betreut werden, ist der an die Denkmalschutzbehörde gerichtete Antrag auf Genehmigung zeitgleich auch dem Landesamt für Denkmalpflege zu übermitteln.

§ 11 Anzeigepflicht
(1) Wird ein eingetragenes bewegliches Denkmal veräußert, so haben der frühere und der neue Eigentümer den Eigentumswechsel unverzüglich der Denkmalschutzbehörde anzuzeigen.
(2) Sind Instandsetzungsarbeiten zur Erhaltung eines Kulturdenkmals notwendig oder droht ihm sonst eine Gefahr, so haben die Erhaltungspflichtigen, wenn sie die Arbeiten nicht ausführen oder die Gefahr nicht abwenden, dies unverzüglich der Denkmalschutzbehörde anzuzeigen.
(3) Die Anzeige eines Pflichtigen befreit die anderen.

Dritter Teil
Ausgrabungen und Bodenfunde

§ 12 Ausgrabungen
(1) ¹Wer nach Kulturdenkmalen graben, Kulturdenkmale aus einem Gewässer bergen oder mit technischen Hilfsmitteln nach Kulturdenkmalen suchen will, bedarf einer Genehmigung der Denkmalschutzbehörde. ²Ausgenommen sind Nachforschungen, die unter der Verantwortung einer staatlichen Denkmalbehörde stattfinden.
(2) ¹Die Genehmigung ist zu versagen, soweit die Maßnahme gegen dieses Gesetz verstoßen oder Forschungsvorhaben des Landes beeinträchtigen würde. ²Die Genehmigung kann unter Bedingungen und mit Auflagen erteilt werden. ³Insbesondere können Bestimmungen über die Suche, die Planung und Ausführung der Grabung, die Behandlung und Sicherung der Bodenfunde, die Dokumentation der Grabungsbefunde, die Berichterstattung und die abschließende Herrichtung der Grabungsstätte getroffen werden. ⁴Es kann auch verlangt werden, daß ein bestimmter Sachverständiger die Arbeiten leitet.

§ 13 Erdarbeiten
(1) Wer Nachforschungen oder Erdarbeiten an einer Stelle vornehmen will, von der er weiß oder vermutet oder den Umständen nach annehmen muß, daß sich dort Kulturdenkmale befinden, bedarf einer Genehmigung der Denkmalschutzbehörde.
(2) ¹Die Genehmigung ist zu versagen, soweit die Maßnahme gegen dieses Gesetz verstoßen würde. ²Die Genehmigung kann unter Bedingungen und mit Auflagen erteilt werden, soweit dies erforderlich ist, um die Einhaltung dieses Gesetzes zu sichern. ³§ 12 Abs. 2 Satz 3 und 4 und § 10 Abs. 4 gelten entsprechend.

§ 14 Bodenfunde

(1) ¹Wer in der Erde oder im Wasser Sachen oder Spuren findet, bei denen Anlaß zu der Annahme gegeben ist, daß sie Kulturdenkmale sind (Bodenfunde), hat dies unverzüglich einer Denkmalbehörde, der Gemeinde oder einem Beauftragten für die archäologische Denkmalpflege (§ 22) anzuzeigen. ²Anzeigepflichtig sind auch der Leiter und der Unternehmer der Arbeiten, die zu dem Bodenfund geführt haben, sowie der Eigentümer und der Besitzer des Grundstücks. ³Die Anzeige eines Pflichtigen befreit die übrigen. ⁴Nimmt der Finder an den Arbeiten, die zu dem Bodenfund geführt haben, auf Grund eines Arbeitsverhältnisses teil, so wird er durch Anzeige an den Leiter oder den Unternehmer der Arbeiten befreit.

(2) Der Bodenfund und die Fundstelle sind bis zum Ablauf von vier Werktagen nach der Anzeige unverändert zu lassen und vor Gefahren für die Erhaltung des Bodenfundes zu schützen, wenn nicht die Denkmalschutzbehörde vorher die Fortsetzung der Arbeiten gestattet.

(3) Die zuständige staatliche Denkmalbehörde und ihre Beauftragten sind berechtigt, den Bodenfund zu bergen und die notwendigen Maßnahmen zur Klärung der Fundumstände sowie zur Sicherung weiterer auf dem Grundstück vorhandener Bodenfunde durchzuführen.

(4) ¹Die Absätze 2 und 3 gelten nicht bei genehmigten Ausgrabungen (§ 12) und bei Arbeiten, die unter Verantwortung einer staatlichen Denkmalbehörde stattfinden. ²Die Denkmalschutzbehörde kann jedoch durch Auflagen in der Grabungsgenehmigung die Vorschriften für anwendbar erklären.

§ 15 Vorübergehende Überlassung von Bodenfunden

¹Eigentümer und Besitzer eines Bodenfundes sind verpflichtet, den Bodenfund auf Verlangen der zuständigen Denkmalschutzbehörde dieser oder einer von ihr benannten Stelle für längstens zwölf Monate zur wissenschaftlichen Auswertung, Konservierung oder Dokumentation zu überlassen. ²Reicht der Zeitraum zur Erfüllung der in Satz 1 genannten Zwecke im Einzelfall nicht aus, so kann er von der zuständigen Denkmalschutzbehörde angemessen verlängert werden.

§ 16 Grabungsschutzgebiete

(1) Das Landesamt für Denkmalpflege kann durch Verordnung abgegrenzte Flächen, in denen Kulturdenkmale von herausragender landes- oder kulturgeschichtlicher Bedeutung vorhanden sind oder vermutet werden, befristet oder unbefristet zu Grabungsschutzgebieten erklären.

(2) ¹In Grabungsschutzgebieten bedürfen alle Arbeiten, die Kulturdenkmale zutagefördern oder gefährden können, einer Genehmigung der Denkmalschutzbehörde. ²§ 13 Abs. 2 gilt entsprechend.

(3) ¹Wird durch die Versagung einer nach Absatz 2 Satz 1 erforderlichen Genehmigung die bisherige ordnungsgemäße land- oder forstwirtschaftliche Nutzung eines Grundstücks beschränkt, so hat das Land für die Dauer der Nutzungsbeschränkung für die dadurch verursachten wirtschaftlichen Nachteile einen angemessenen Ausgleich in Geld zu leisten, sofern nicht eine Ausgleichspflicht nach § 29 besteht. ²Der Ausgleich bemisst sich nach den durchschnittlichen Ertragseinbußen, gemessen an den Erträgen und Aufwendungen der bisherigen ordnungsgemäßen land- oder forstwirtschaftlichen Nutzung. ³Ersparte Aufwendungen sind anzurechnen. ⁴Über den Ausgleich entscheidet die für die Genehmigung zuständige Denkmalschutzbehörde nach Zustimmung der obersten Denkmalschutzbehörde.

§ 17 Beschränkung der wirtschaftlichen Nutzung von Grundstücken

Die untere Denkmalschutzbehörde kann die wirtschaftliche Nutzung eines Grundstücks oder eines Grundstücksteils beschränken, in dem sich ein Kulturdenkmal befindet.

§ 18 Schatzregal

¹Bewegliche Denkmale gemäß § 3 Abs. 5, die herrenlos oder so lange verborgen gewesen sind, dass ihr Eigentümer nicht mehr zu ermitteln ist, werden mit der Entdeckung Eigentum des Landes Niedersachsen, wenn sie bei staatlichen Nachforschungen oder in Grabungsschutzgebieten gemäß § 16 entdeckt werden oder wenn sie einen hervorragenden wissenschaftlichen Wert besitzen. ²Der Finder soll im Rahmen der verfügbaren Mittel des Landeshaushalts eine Belohnung erhalten. ³Über die Höhe entscheidet das Landesamt für Denkmalpflege unter Berücksichtigung der Umstände des Einzelfalls. ⁴Das Land kann sein Eigentum an dem beweglichen Denkmal auf den Eigentümer des Grundstücks übertragen, auf dem der Fund erfolgt ist.

Vierter Teil
Denkmalbehörden

§ 19 Denkmalschutzbehörden
(1) ¹Die Gemeinden, denen die Aufgaben der unteren Bauaufsichtsbehörde obliegen, im übrigen die Landkreise, nehmen die Aufgaben der unteren Denkmalschutzbehörde wahr. ²Oberste Denkmalschutzbehörde ist das Fachministerium.
(2) Die Aufgaben der unteren Denkmalschutzbehörden gehören zum übertragenen Wirkungskreis.
(3) Die oberste Denkmalschutzbehörde übt die Fachaufsicht über die unteren Denkmalschutzbehörden aus.
(4) ¹Die oberste Denkmalschutzbehörde kann anstelle einer unteren Denkmalschutzbehörde tätig werden oder anordnen, dass das Landesamt für Denkmalpflege an Stelle einer unteren Denkmalschutzbehörde tätig wird, wenn diese eine Weisung nicht innerhalb einer bestimmten Frist befolgt oder wenn Gefahr im Verzuge ist. ²Es hat die zuständige Denkmalschutzbehörde unverzüglich über die getroffene Maßnahme zu unterrichten.

§ 20 Zuständigkeit der Denkmalschutzbehörden
(1) ¹Soweit nicht durch Gesetz oder auf Grund eines Gesetzes etwas anderes bestimmt ist, sind die unteren Denkmalschutzbehörden zuständig. ²Betrifft die Durchführung dieses Gesetzes den Bereich einer Bundeswasserstraße oder des Küstengewässers, so ist abweichend von Satz 1 die oberste Denkmalschutzbehörde zuständig. ³Für Maßnahmen im Bereich des Küstengewässers ist das Einvernehmen mit der obersten Naturschutzbehörde erforderlich.
(2) ¹Die unteren Denkmalschutzbehörden stellen in Angelegenheiten auf dem Gebiet der Bodendenkmalpflege unverzüglich das Benehmen mit dem Landesamt für Denkmalpflege her. ²Die oberste Denkmalschutzbehörde befreit eine untere Denkmalschutzbehörde, die in ausreichendem Maß mit archäologischen Fachkräften besetzt ist, von dem Erfordernis der Herstellung des Benehmens. ³Archäologische Fachkräfte sind Personen, die nachgewiesen haben, dass sie durch ihre Ausbildung oder durch archäologische Tätigkeiten hinreichende Fachkenntnisse auf dem Gebiet der Bodendenkmalpflege erworben haben. ⁴Eine untere Denkmalschutzbehörde, die von dem Erfordernis der Herstellung des Benehmens befreit worden ist, hat der obersten Denkmalschutzbehörde Veränderungen in der Besetzung mit archäologischen Fachkräften unverzüglich mitzuteilen.
(3) ¹Die örtliche Zuständigkeit richtet sich bei beweglichen Bodenfunden nach dem Fundort. ²Bei Gefahr im Verzuge kann auch die Denkmalschutzbehörde Anordnungen erlassen, in deren Bezirk sich der Gegenstand befindet. ³Die zuständige Denkmalschutzbehörde ist unverzüglich zu unterrichten.

§ 21 Landesamt für Denkmalpflege
(1) ¹Das Landesamt für Denkmalpflege wirkt als staatliche Denkmalfachbehörde bei der Ausführung dieses Gesetzes mit. ²Es hat insbesondere die Aufgaben,
1. die Denkmalschutz-, Bau- und Planungsbehörden, Kirchen und andere, insbesondere Eigentümer und Besitzer von Kulturdenkmalen, fachlich zu beraten,
2. Kulturdenkmale zu erfassen, zu erforschen, zu dokumentieren und die Ergebnisse zu veröffentlichen sowie das Verzeichnis nach § 4 Abs. 1 aufzustellen und fortzuführen,
3. Restaurierungen und Grabungen durchzuführen,
4. wissenschaftliche Grundlagen für die Denkmalpflege zu schaffen,
5. zentrale Fachbibliotheken und Archive zu unterhalten.

(2) Die unteren Denkmalschutzbehörden stellen bei allen Maßnahmen, die für das Kulturerbe im Sinne des UNESCO-Übereinkommens zum Schutz des Kultur- und Naturerbes der Welt von nicht nur unerheblicher Bedeutung sind, das Benehmen mit dem Landesamt für Denkmalpflege her.

§ 22 Beauftragte für die Denkmalpflege[1)]
(1) ¹Die untere Denkmalschutzbehörde kann Beauftragte für die Bau- und Kunstdenkmalpflege und Beauftragte für die archäologische Denkmalpflege bestellen. ²Sie bestellt die Beauftragten im Einvernehmen mit dem Landesamt für Denkmalpflege. ³Die Beauftragten sind ehrenamtlich tätig.

---

1) Die Richtlinien zur Durchführung des § 22 des Niedersächsischen Denkmalschutzgesetzes (Beauftragte für die Denkmalpflege) sind abgedruckt als Nr. D9.I.1b.

(2) Die Beauftragten beraten und unterstützen die Denkmalschutzbehörden in allen Angelegenheiten des Denkmalschutzes und der Denkmalpflege.
(3) [1]Das Land ersetzt den Beauftragten die Kosten, die ihnen durch ihre Tätigkeit entstehen. [2]Die oberste Denkmalschutzbehörde wird ermächtigt, durch Verordnung nähere Vorschriften zu erlassen.

§ 22a Beratende Kommissionen
Die oberste Denkmalschutzbehörde kann für den Bereich der Bau- und Kunstdenkmalpflege eine Landeskommission für Denkmalpflege und für den Bereich der Bodendenkmalpflege eine Archäologische Kommission jeweils mit beratender Funktion für die oberste Denkmalschutzbehörde und die Denkmalfachbehörde berufen.

Fünfter Teil
Maßnahmen des Denkmalschutzes, Verfahrensvorschriften

§ 23 Anordnungen der Denkmalschutzbehörden
(1) Die Denkmalschutzbehörden treffen nach pflichtgemäßem Ermessen die Anordnungen, die erforderlich sind, um die Einhaltung der §§ 6 bis 17, 25, 27 und 28 sicherzustellen.
(2) [1]Wird ein Baudenkmal dadurch, daß es nicht genutzt wird, oder durch die Art seiner Nutzung gefährdet, so kann die Denkmalschutzbehörde anordnen, daß ein nach § 6 Abs. 1 Verpflichteter das Baudenkmal in bestimmter ihm zumutbarer Weise nutzt. [2]Dem Verpflichteten ist auf Antrag zu gestatten, das Baudenkmal in einer angebotenen anderen Weise zu nutzen, wenn seine Erhaltung dadurch hinreichend gewährleistet und die Nutzung mit dem öffentlichen Recht vereinbar ist.

§ 24 Genehmigungsverfahren
(1) [1]Der Antrag auf eine Genehmigung nach diesem Gesetz ist schriftlich mit den zur Beurteilung erforderlichen Unterlagen der Gemeinde zuzuleiten, bei beweglichen Denkmalen jedoch unmittelbar der Denkmalschutzbehörde. [2]Die Gemeinde leitet den Antrag unverzüglich mit ihrer Stellungnahme an die untere Denkmalschutzbehörde weiter, wenn sie deren Aufgaben nicht selbst wahrnimmt.
(2) [1]Eine Genehmigung nach diesem Gesetz erlischt, wenn nicht innerhalb von zwei Jahren nach ihrer Erteilung mit der Ausführung der Maßnahme begonnen oder wenn die Ausführung zwei Jahre unterbrochen worden ist. [2]Die Denkmalschutzbehörde kann die Frist verlängern. [3]In den Fällen des § 10 Abs. 4 richtet sich die Geltungsdauer nach den Vorschriften über die Baugenehmigung oder die sonstige Entscheidung, die die Genehmigung nach diesem Gesetz umfaßt.
(3) [1]Für Genehmigungen nach diesem Gesetz werden keine Gebühren und Auslagen erhoben. [2]Die Vorschriften über die Kosten der Baugenehmigungen und der sonstigen Entscheidungen, die Genehmigungen nach diesem Gesetz umfassen, bleiben unberührt.

§ 25 Wiederherstellung des ursprünglichen Zustands
(1) Wer diesem Gesetz zuwider in ein Kulturdenkmal oder in dessen Umgebung eingreift, hat auf Verlangen der Denkmalschutzbehörde den bisherigen Zustand wiederherzustellen.
(2) Wer widerrechtlich ein Kulturdenkmal vorsätzlich oder fahrlässig beschädigt oder zerstört, ist auf Verlangen der Denkmalschutzbehörde verpflichtet, das Zerstörte nach ihren Anweisungen zu rekonstruieren.

§ 26 Zusammenwirken der Denkmalbehörden
[1]Die Denkmalschutzbehörden werden vom Landesamt für Denkmalpflege bei der Erledigung ihrer Aufgaben unterstützt und beraten. [2]Sie haben dem Landesamt die Genehmigungsanträge für Maßnahmen von besonderer Bedeutung rechtzeitig anzuzeigen und in dem erforderlichen Umfang Auskunft und Akteneinsicht zu gewähren.

§ 27 Duldungs- und Auskunftspflichten
(1) [1]Bedienstete und Beauftragte der Denkmalbehörden dürfen nach vorheriger Benachrichtigung Grundstücke, zur Abwehr einer dringenden Gefahr für ein Kulturdenkmal auch Wohnungen, betreten, soweit es zur Durchführung dieses Gesetzes notwendig ist. [2]Sie dürfen Kulturdenkmale besichtigen und die notwendigen wissenschaftlichen Erfassungsmaßnahmen, insbesondere zur Inventarisation, durchführen. [3]Das Grundrecht der Unverletzlichkeit der Wohnung (Artikel 13 des Grundgesetzes) wird insoweit eingeschränkt.

(2) Eigentümer und Besitzer von Kulturdenkmalen haben den Denkmalbehörden sowie ihren Beauftragten die zum Vollzug dieses Gesetzes erforderlichen Auskünfte zu erteilen.

§ 28 Kennzeichnung von Kulturdenkmalen
(1) [1]Die Denkmalschutzbehörde kann Eigentümer und Besitzer von Bodendenkmalen und nicht genutzten Baudenkmalen verpflichten, die Anbringung von Hinweisschildern zu dulden, die die Bedeutung des Denkmals erläutern und auf seinen gesetzlichen Schutz hinweisen. [2]Die Schilder sind so anzubringen, daß sie die zulässige Bewirtschaftung des Grundstücks nicht erschweren.
(2) Eigentümer können Baudenkmale und Bodendenkmale mit einer von der obersten Denkmalschutzbehörde herausgegebenen Denkmalschutzplakette kennzeichnen, um auf den gesetzlichen Schutz des Denkmals hinzuweisen.

Sechster Teil
Ausgleich und Enteignung

§ 29 Ausgleich
(1) [1]Soweit Anordnungen aufgrund dieses Gesetzes im Einzelfall zu einer unzumutbaren Belastung des Eigentums führen, hat das Land einen angemessenen Ausgleich in Geld zu gewähren, sofern und soweit die Belastung nicht in anderer Weise ausgeglichen werden kann. [2]Für die Bemessung des Ausgleichs sind die Regelungen des Niedersächsischen Enteignungsgesetzes über die Entschädigung entsprechend anzuwenden. [3]Die Gemeinden und Landkreise sollen zu dem Ausgleichsaufwand beitragen, wenn und soweit durch die die Belastung auslösende Anordnung auch ihre örtlichen Belange begünstigt werden.
(2) Über den Ausgleich entscheidet die für die Anordnung zuständige Denkmalschutzbehörde nach Zustimmung der obersten Denkmalschutzbehörde zumindest dem Grunde nach zugleich mit der Anordnung, die die Belastung auslöst.

§ 30 Zulässigkeit der Enteignung
(1) [1]Eine Enteignung ist zulässig, soweit sie erforderlich ist, damit
1. ein Kulturdenkmal in seinem Bestand oder Erscheinungsbild erhalten bleibt,
2. Kulturdenkmale ausgegraben oder wissenschaftlich untersucht werden können,
3. in einem Grabungsschutzgebiet planmäßige Nachforschungen betrieben werden können.

[2]Die Enteignung kann auf Zubehör, das mit der Hauptsache eine Einheit von Denkmalwert bildet, ausgedehnt werden. [3]Enteignungsmaßnahmen können zeitlich begrenzt werden.
(2) [1]Ein beweglicher Bodenfund (§ 14 Abs. 1) kann enteignet werden, wenn
1. Tatsachen vorliegen, nach denen zu befürchten ist, daß er wesentlich verschlechtert wird,
2. nicht auf andere Weise sichergestellt werden kann, daß er für die Allgemeinheit zugänglich ist, und hieran ein erhebliches Interesse besteht oder
3. nicht auf andere Weise sichergestellt werden kann, daß er für die wissenschaftliche Forschung zur Verfügung gehalten wird.

[2]Der Enteignungsantrag kann innerhalb eines Jahres gestellt werden, nachdem der Bodenfund angezeigt oder bei Arbeiten nach § 14 Abs. 3 entdeckt worden ist.
(3) [1]Die Enteignung nach den Absätzen 1 und 2 ist zugunsten des Landes oder einer anderen juristischen Person des öffentlichen Rechts zulässig. [2]Zugunsten einer juristischen Person des Privatrechts ist die Enteignung zulässig, wenn der Enteignungszweck zu den satzungsmäßigen Aufgaben der juristischen Person gehört und seine Erfüllung im Einzelfall gesichert erscheint.

§ 31 Anwendung des Niedersächsischen Enteignungsgesetzes
(1) Für die Enteignung und Entschädigung, auch bei beweglichen Sachen, gelten die Vorschriften des Niedersächsischen Enteignungsgesetzes, soweit nicht in diesem Gesetz etwas anderes bestimmt ist.
(2) [1]Ist Gegenstand der Enteignung eine bewegliche Sache und soll nach dem Enteignungsbeschluß die Sache herausgegeben werden, so ist im Enteignungsbeschluß auch anzuordnen, an wen die Sache mit dem Eintritt der Rechtsänderung herauszugeben ist. [2]Die Ausführungsanordnung (§ 36 NEG) kann in diesem Falle schon vor der Zahlung der Entschädigung erlassen werden.
(3) [1]Ist zur Erhaltung oder wissenschaftlichen Auswertung eines beweglichen Denkmals oder eines beweglichen Bodenfundes (§ 14 Abs. 1) die sofortige Herausgabe dringend geboten, so kann die Ent-

eignungsbehörde im Beschluß über die vorzeitige Besitzeinweisung den Eigentümer oder Besitzer verpflichten, die Sache an einen bestimmten Empfänger herauszugeben. ²§ 35 Abs. 1 Satz 6 NEG findet keine Anwendung.
(4) ¹Sofern die Enteignung andere als die in § 3 NEG genannten Gegenstände betrifft, ist § 43 NEG nicht anzuwenden. ²In diesen Fällen kann die Entscheidung der Enteignungsbehörde über die Höhe der Entschädigung innerhalb eines Monats nach Zustellung durch Klage vor dem ordentlichen Gericht angefochten werden.

Siebenter Teil
Zuschußmittel des Landes, Steuerbefreiung

§ 32 Zuschußmittel des Landes[1)]
¹Das Land trägt, unbeschadet bestehender Verpflichtungen, zu den Kosten der Erhaltung und Instandsetzung von Kulturdenkmalen nach Maßgabe der im Haushaltsplan bereitgestellten Mittel bei. ²Zuschüsse des Landes können insbesondere mit der Auflage verbunden werden, ein Kulturdenkmal im Rahmen des Zumutbaren der Öffentlichkeit zugänglich zu machen oder Hinweisschilder anzubringen.

§ 33 *[aufgehoben]*

Achter Teil
Straftaten und Ordnungswidrigkeiten

§ 34 Zerstörung eines Kulturdenkmals
(1) Wer ohne die nach § 10 erforderliche Genehmigung und ohne Vorliegen der Voraussetzungen des § 7 ein Kulturdenkmal oder einen wesentlichen Teil eines Kulturdenkmals zerstört, wird mit Freiheitsstrafe bis zu zwei Jahren oder mit Geldstrafe bestraft.
(2) Reste eines Kulturdenkmals, das durch eine Tat nach Absatz 1 zerstört worden ist, können eingezogen werden.

§ 35 Ordnungswidrigkeiten
(1) Ordnungswidrig handelt, wer vorsätzlich oder fahrlässig
1. eine nach § 11 oder § 14 Abs. 1 erforderliche Anzeige nicht unverzüglich erstattet,
2. Maßnahmen, die nach § 10 Abs. 1, § 12 Abs. 1, § 13 Abs. 1 oder § 16 Abs. 2 der Genehmigung bedürfen, ohne Genehmigung oder abweichend von ihr durchführt oder durchführen läßt,
3. Auflagen nach § 10 Abs. 3, § 12 Abs. 2 oder § 13 Abs. 2 nicht erfüllt,
4. gefundene Gegenstände und die Fundstelle nicht gemäß § 14 Abs. 2 unverändert läßt.

(2) Ordnungswidrig handelt, wer wider besseres Wissen unrichtige Angaben macht oder unrichtige Pläne oder Unterlagen vorlegt, um einen Verwaltungsakt nach diesem Gesetz zu erwirken oder zu verhindern.
(3) Die Ordnungswidrigkeiten können mit Geldbußen bis zu 250 000 Euro geahndet werden.
(4) ¹Es können eingezogen werden:
1. Reste eines Kulturdenkmals, das durch eine ordnungswidrige Handlung zerstört worden ist,
2. Gegenstände, die durch ordnungswidrige Handlungen unter Verletzung des § 12 Abs. 1, § 13 Abs. 1, § 14 Abs. 1 und 2 oder § 16 Abs. 2 erlangt worden sind.

²§ 23 des Gesetzes über Ordnungswidrigkeiten ist anzuwenden.
(5) Die Verfolgung der Ordnungswidrigkeit verjährt in fünf Jahren.

[1)] Die Richtlinie über die Gewährung von Zuwendungen zur Erhaltung und Pflege von Kulturdenkmalen ist abgedruckt als Nr. D9.III.1.

Niedersächsisches Denkmalschutzgesetz D9.I.1

Neunter Teil
Schluß- und Übergangsvorschriften

§ 36 Kirchliche Kulturdenkmale
Die Verträge des Landes Niedersachsen mit den Evangelischen Landeskirchen in Niedersachsen vom 19. März 1955 (Nieders. GVBl. Sb. I S. 369) und vom 4. März 1965 (Nieders. GVBl. 1966 S. 4),[1] das Konkordat zwischen dem Heiligen Stuhle und dem Lande Niedersachsen vom 26. Februar 1965 (Nieders. GVBl. S. 192), zuletzt geändert durch Vertrag vom 29. Oktober 1993 (Nds. GVBl. 1994 S. 304),[2] sowie die zur Ausführung dieser Verträge geschlossenen Vereinbarungen bleiben unberührt.

§ 37 Finanzausgleich
Die Verwaltungskosten, die den Landkreisen und Gemeinden durch die Ausführung dieses Gesetzes entstehen, werden im Rahmen des kommunalen Finanzausgleichs gedeckt.

§§ 38, 39 *[nicht wiedergegebene Änderungs- bzw. Aufhebungsvorschriften]*

§ 40 Übergangsvorschrift
Das Verzeichnis der Baudenkmale nach § 94 der Niedersächsischen Bauordnung und die Denkmalliste nach § 5 des Denkmalschutzgesetzes für das Großherzogtum Oldenburg sind mit allen Eintragungen Bestandteile des Verzeichnisses der Kulturdenkmale nach § 4 dieses Gesetzes.

§ 41 Inkrafttreten
Dieses Gesetz tritt am 1. April 1979 in Kraft.

---

1) Art. 20 des Vertrages lautet: „Die Kirchen werden der Erhaltung und Pflege denkmalswichtiger Gebäude nebst den dazugehörenden Grundstücken und sonstiger Gegenstände ihre besondere Aufmerksamkeit widmen. Sie werden Veräußerungen und Umgestaltungen nur im Benehmen mit den Stellen der staatlichen Denkmalspflege vornehmen. Sie werden dafür sorgen, daß die Kirchengemeinden und sonstigen Verbände entsprechend verfahren."

2) § 13 der Anlage lautet: „Die Diözesen werden der Erhaltung und Pflege denkmalswerter Gebäude nebst den dazugehörenden Grundstücken und sonstiger Gegenstände ihre besondere Aufmerksamkeit widmen. Sie werden Veräußerungen oder Umgestaltungen nur im Benehmen mit den Stellen der staatlichen Denkmalspflege vornehmen. Sie werden dafür Sorge tragen, daß andere kirchliche Institutionen entsprechend verfahren."

D9.I.1a Verordnung über die Aufwandsentschädigung

Verordnung über die Aufwandsentschädigung der Beauftragten für die Bau- und Kunstdenkmalpflege und der Beauftragten für die archäologische Denkmalpflege[1)]

Vom 22. August 1979 (Nds. GVBl. S. 252)
(GVBl. Sb 22510)
zuletzt geändert durch Art. 1 ÄndVO vom 17. November 2005 (Nds. GVBl. S. 362)

Auf Grund des § 22 Abs. 3 Satz 2 des Niedersächsischen Denkmalschutzgesetzes vom 30. Mai 1978 (Nieders. GVBl. S. 517) wird verordnet:

§ 1 [Höhe der Aufwandsentschädigung]
(1) [1)]Die für das Gebiet oder Teilgebiet der Region Hannover oder eines Landkreises bestellten Beauftragten für die Bau- und Kunstdenkmalpflege und Beauftragten für die archäologische Denkmalpflege erhalten zur Abgeltung der mit dieser Tätigkeit verbundenen Aufwendungen eine Aufwandsentschädigung in Höhe von 110 Euro monatlich. [2)]Die für das Gebiet einer Gemeinde bestellten Beauftragten erhalten eine Aufwandsentschädigung in Höhe von 35 Euro monatlich.

(2) Ist ein Beauftragter sowohl für das Gebiet einer Gemeinde als auch für das Gebiet oder Teilgebiet der Region Hannover oder eines Landkreises bestellt, so erhält er nur die Aufwandsentschädigung nach Absatz 1 Satz 1.

§ 2 [Inkrafttreten]
Diese Verordnung tritt am 1. September 1979 in Kraft.

---

1) Änderungen vor dem 1.1.2006 sind nicht in Fußnoten nachgewiesen.

Richtlinie zur Durchführung des § 22 des Niedersächsischen Denkmalschutzgesetzes (Beauftragte für die Denkmalpflege)[1]

RL d. MWK v. 12.11.2013 – 35-57 707 (Nds. MBl. S. 904)
(VORIS 22510)
zuletzt geändert durch ÄndRdErl. vom 2. Oktober 2019 (Nds. MBl. S. 1467)

Bezug:
RdErl. v. 8.2.2006 (Nds. MBl. S. 133)
– VORIS 22510 –

§ 22 des Niedersächsischen Denkmalschutzgesetzes i.d.F. vom 30.5.1978 (Nds. GVBl. S. 517), zuletzt geändert durch Gesetz vom 26.5.2011 (Nds. GVBl. S. 135), sieht Beauftragte für die Bau- und Kunstdenkmalpflege und Beauftragte für die archäologische Denkmalpflege vor. Die Beauftragten sind ehrenamtlich tätig. Hinsichtlich ihrer Bestellung, ihrer Aufgaben und ihrer Arbeitsweise wird die nachstehende Richtlinie erlassen.

1. Bestellung

1.1

Es sollen nur solche Persönlichkeiten zu Beauftragten bestellt werden, die aufgrund ihrer besonderen Fach- und Ortskenntnis in der Lage sind, die in Nummer 2 aufgeführten Aufgaben zu erfüllen. Bei der Auswahl ist darauf zu achten, dass die Beauftragten ihre Tätigkeit neutral und ausschließlich den Zielen des Gesetzes dienend ausüben können.

1.2

Die Beauftragten können für das ganze Gebiet oder für einen Teil des Gebiets einer unteren Denkmalschutzbehörde bestellt werden.

1.3

Die Beauftragten werden gemäß § 22 des Niedersächsischen Denkmalschutzgesetzes von der unteren Denkmalschutzbehörde im Einvernehmen mit dem Landesamt für Denkmalpflege bestellt. Sie erhalten ein Bestellungsschreiben der unteren Denkmalschutzbehörde.

1.4

Die Bestellung wird für einen Zeitraum von vier Jahren ausgesprochen. Sie steht unter dem Vorbehalt des jederzeitigen Widerrufs. Wiederbestellung ist möglich.

1.5

Mit der Bestellung erhalten die Beauftragten eine Kopie der Richtlinie ausgehändigt. Sie erklären sich mit den übertragenen Aufgaben schriftlich einverstanden.

1.6

Die Beauftragten erhalten mit der Bestellung einen Ausweis, der sie legitimiert, im Rahmen der gesetzlichen Bestimmungen für die Denkmalbehörden beratend und unterstützend tätig zu sein (**Anlage**).

---

[1] Die **RL tritt mit Ablauf des 31. Dezember 2021 außer Kraft**; vgl. Nr. 4. Von einem Abdruck der Anlagen wurde aus drucktechnischen Gründen abgesehen.

D9.I.1b Richtlinie Beauftragte für Denkmalpflege

2. Aufgaben und Arbeitsweise der Beauftragten

2.1

Die Beauftragten haben beratende Funktion und sind ehrenamtlich tätig.

2.2

Sie sind bei der Ausübung ihrer Tätigkeit an die Weisungen der Denkmalschutzbehörden gebunden; sie wirken in allen Fachfragen auch mit dem Landesamt für Denkmalpflege zusammen. Es ist zu unterscheiden zwischen den Aufgaben der Beauftragten für die Bau- und Kunstdenkmalpflege und den Aufgaben der Beauftragten für die archäologische Denkmalpflege.

2.3

Die Aufgaben der Beauftragten für die Bau- und Kunstdenkmalpflege sind:
2.3.1 Benachrichtigung der unteren Denkmalschutzbehörden, sofern die Gefährdung eines Baudenkmals bekannt wird, sowie Hinweise auf Planungen oder sonstige Maßnahmen, die eine Gefährdung eines Baudenkmals zur Folge haben können,
2.3.2 Tätigkeiten nach § 27 des Niedersächsischen Denkmalschutzgesetzes, sofern eine Denkmalbehörde sie ausdrücklich beauftragt, insbesondere in Fällen der akuten Gefährdung eines Baudenkmals,
2.3.3 Unterstützung aller Maßnahmen der Denkmalbehörden, insbesondere bei der Beratung von Denkmaleigentümerinnen und Denkmaleigentümern oder Denkmalbesitzerinnen und Denkmalbesitzern, bei Maßnahmen zur Erfassung, Erforschung und Erhaltung von Baudenkmalen sowie bei der Öffentlichkeitsarbeit,
2.3.4 Zusammenwirken mit Institutionen, Verbänden und Personen, die mit Bau- und Kunstdenkmalpflege befasst sind oder ihre Ziele fördern,
2.3.5 Information der Öffentlichkeit über Denkmalschutz und Denkmalpflege, insbesondere im Zusammenwirken mit regionalen Institutionen und Organisationen, die die Erhaltung von Kulturdenkmalen zum Ziel haben,
2.3.6 Berichterstattung gegenüber der unteren Denkmalschutzbehörde über wahrgenommene Aufgaben.

2.4

Die Aufgaben der Beauftragten für die archäologische Denkmalpflege sind:
2.4.1 Benachrichtigung der unteren Denkmalschutzbehörden, sofern die Gefährdung eines Bodendenkmals bekannt wird, sowie Hinweis auf Planungen oder sonstige Maßnahmen, die eine Gefährdung eines Bodendenkmals zur Folge haben können, Überprüfung und Registrierung von Bodendenkmalen und Fundstellen im Gelände und Dokumentation der Ergebnisse,
2.4.2 Tätigkeiten nach § 27 des Niedersächsischen Denkmalschutzgesetzes, sofern eine Denkmalbehörde sie ausdrücklich beauftragt, insbesondere in Fällen akuter Gefährdung eines Bodendenkmals,
2.4.3 Beobachtung von Erdaufschlüssen, die archäologische Ergebnisse und Funde erwarten lassen,
2.4.4 Mitwirkung bei der Durchführung des Niedersächsischen Denkmalschutzgesetzes, insbesondere des § 14 Abs. 1 und 3 (Bodenfunde), des § 15 (vorübergehende Überlassung von Bodenfunden) sowie bei der Durchführung von Rettungsgrabungen im Auftrag einer Denkmalbehörde,
2.4.5 Zusammenwirken mit Institutionen, Verbänden und Personen, die mit archäologischer Denkmalpflege befasst sind oder ihre Ziele fördern,
2.4.6 Unterstützung aller Maßnahmen der Denkmalbehörden durch Aufklärung der Öffentlichkeit, insbesondere in den Medien, durch Ausstellungen und Vorträge,
2.4.7 Berichterstattung gegenüber der unteren Denkmalschutzbehörde über wahrgenommene Aufgaben.

3. Entschädigung

Die Höhe der Aufwandsentschädigung ist in der Verordnung über die Aufwandsentschädigung der Beauftragten für die Bau- und Kunstdenkmalpflege und der Beauftragen für die archäologische Denkmalpflege vom 22.8.1979 (Nds. GVBl. S. 252), zuletzt geändert durch Verordnung vom 17.11.2005 (Nds. GVBl. S. 362), geregelt.[1] Zuständig für die Durchführung dieser Verordnung und die Bewirtschaftung der Mittel ist das Landesamt für Denkmalpflege.

4. Schlussbestimmungen

Dieser RdErl. tritt am 1.1.2014 in Kraft und mit Ablauf des 31.12.2021 außer Kraft. Der Bezugserlass tritt mit Ablauf des 31.12.2013 außer Kraft.

---

[1] Abgedruckt als Nr. D9.I.1a.

… D9.II.1 Niedersächsisches Archivgesetz

Gesetz über die Sicherung und Nutzung von Archivgut in Niedersachsen[1])
(Niedersächsisches Archivgesetz – NArchG)

Vom 25. Mai 1993 (Nds. GVBl. S. 129)
(GVBl. Sb 22560)
zuletzt geändert durch Art. 3 G zur Neuordnung des niedersächsischen Datenschutzrechts vom 16. Mai 2018 (Nds. GVBl. S. 66)

Der Niedersächsische Landtag hat das folgende Gesetz beschlossen, das hiermit verkündet wird:

§ 1 Aufgaben des Niedersächsischen Landesarchivs

(1) ¹Die Aufgabe, aus dem Schriftgut der Behörden, Gerichte und sonstigen Stellen des Landes das Archivgut zu ermitteln, zu übernehmen, zu verwahren, zu erhalten, instand zu setzen, zu erschließen und nutzbar zu machen, obliegt dem Niedersächsischen Landesarchiv mit Sitz in Hannover und weiteren Standorten in Aurich, Bückeburg, Oldenburg, Osnabrück, Stade und Wolfenbüttel (Landesarchiv). ²Es nimmt an der Veröffentlichung und wissenschaftlichen Auswertung des Archivgutes teil.
(2) Die Aufgabe nach Absatz 1 betrifft auch das Schriftgut
1. der Stiftungen privaten Rechts, wenn das Land oder einer seiner Rechtsvorgänger überwiegend das Stiftungsvermögen bereitgestellt hat, und
2. anderer juristischer Personen des Privatrechts, wenn sie nicht am Wettbewerb teilnehmen und dem Land mehr als die Hälfte der Anteile oder der Stimmen zusteht.

(3) § 7 Abs. 1 bleibt unberührt.
(4) ¹Das Landesarchiv nimmt auch Schriftgut anderer Herkunft an, soweit dies im öffentlichen Interesse liegt. ²Es sammelt sonstige Unterlagen zur Ergänzung des Archivgutes.

§ 2 Begriffsbestimmungen

(1) Schriftgut sind schriftlich geführte oder auf maschinenlesbaren Datenträgern gespeicherte Akten mit Anlagen, Urkunden und andere Einzelschriftstücke, Karten, Pläne, Zeichnungen, Risse und Plakate, zudem Siegel und Stempel, Bild-, Film- und Tonaufzeichnungen, Karteien sowie Dateien einschließlich der Ordnungen und Verfahren, um das Schriftgut auswerten zu können.
(2) Archivgut ist das Schriftgut, das von bleibendem Wert für die Erfüllung öffentlicher Aufgaben, für die Sicherung berechtigter privater Interessen oder für die Forschung ist.

§ 3 Ermittlung und Übernahme des Archivgutes

(1) ¹Die in § 1 Abs. 1 Satz 1 und Abs. 2 genannten Stellen haben sämtliches Schriftgut, dessen Aufbewahrungsfrist abgelaufen ist oder das aus sonstigen Gründen ausgesondert werden soll, dem Landesarchiv in regelmäßigen Abständen im Originalzustand zur Übernahme anzubieten. ²Dazu gehört auch Schriftgut, das nach Rechtsvorschriften des Bundes der Geheimhaltung unterliegt, und Schriftgut, das besondere Kategorien personenbezogener Daten im Sinne des Artikels 9 Abs. 1 der Verordnung (EU) 2016/679 (Datenschutz-Grundverordnung) enthält. ³Spätestens 30 Jahre nach der letzten inhaltlichen Bearbeitung ist jegliches Schriftgut zur Übernahme anzubieten. ⁴Satz 1 gilt nicht für den Landtag.
(2) ¹Daten in automatisierten Dateien sind in Form einer Abbildung zur Übernahme anzubieten. ²Der Zeitpunkt der Herstellung, die Form der Datenübermittlung und eine etwaige Auswahl der Daten sind vorab zwischen dem Landesarchiv und der dateiführenden Stelle zu vereinbaren.
(3) ¹Daten, die unzulässig gespeichert sind, dürfen nicht angeboten werden. ²Sind solche Daten dem Landesarchiv übermittelt worden, so sind sie dort auf Ersuchen der übermittelnden Stelle zu löschen.
(4) ¹Das Landesarchiv stellt fest, welches Schriftgut Archivgut nach § 2 Abs. 2 ist. ²Es kann die Pflicht, Schriftgut anzubieten, einschränken.
(5) Das Landesarchiv kann bereits aus Schriftgut, dessen Aufbewahrungsfrist noch nicht abgelaufen ist, das Archivgut ermitteln.
(6) ¹Die in § 7 Abs. 1 Satz 1 genannten Einrichtungen können ihr Schriftgut dem Landesarchiv zur Übernahme anbieten. ²Die §§ 3a, 3b und 4 Satz 2 sowie die §§ 5 bis 6a sind anzuwenden. ³Die Ein-

---
[1]) Siehe auch die Verwaltungsvorschriften zum Niedersächsischen Archivgesetz abgedruckt als Nr. D9.II.1b.

richtungen regeln ihre Rechte und Pflichten hinsichtlich des Archivguts durch Vereinbarung mit dem Landesarchiv.

(7) ¹Private sowie Religionsgemeinschaften, die als Körperschaft des öffentlichen Rechts anerkannt sind, können ihr Schriftgut dem Landesarchiv anbieten. ²In Vereinbarungen dieser Personen und Religionsgemeinschaften mit dem Landesarchiv kann von den §§ 5 und 6 abgewichen werden.

§ 3a Löschung personenbezogener Daten in Schriftgut

Der im öffentlichen Interesse liegende Archivzweck (Artikel 17 Abs. 3 Buchst. d der Datenschutz-Grundverordnung) steht einer Löschung von in Schriftgut enthaltenen personenbezogenen Daten nach Artikel 17 Abs. 1 Buchst. a der Datenschutz-Grundverordnung nicht mehr entgegen, wenn

1. die in § 1 Abs. 1 Satz 1 und Abs. 2 genannten Stellen das Schriftgut dem Landesarchiv angeboten haben und das Landesarchiv
   a) festgestellt hat, dass es sich nicht um Archivgut handelt, oder
   b) die Feststellung, ob es sich um Archivgut handelt, nicht innerhalb von sechs Monaten nach dem Angebot getroffen hat

   oder
2. das Landesarchiv entschieden hat, dass dieses Schriftgut nicht anzubieten ist (§ 3 Abs. 4 Satz 2).

§ 3b Verarbeitung besonderer Kategorien personenbezogener Daten

¹Die Verarbeitung besonderer Kategorien personenbezogener Daten im Sinne des Artikels 9 Abs. 1 der Datenschutz-Grundverordnung ist zulässig. ²Sie berühren stets schutzwürdige Interessen der betroffenen Person im Sinne des § 5 Abs. 2 Satz 5.

§ 4 Sicherung des Archivgutes

¹Archivgut ist auf Dauer und sicher zu verwahren, zu erhalten und vor unbefugter Nutzung, vor Beschädigung oder Vernichtung zu schützen. ²Archivgut, dem ein bleibender Wert nach § 2 Abs. 2 nicht mehr zukommt, ist zu vernichten, sofern Aufbewahrungsfristen sowie Rechte von Personen oder Religionsgemeinschaften nach § 3 Abs. 7 Satz 1 nicht entgegenstehen.

§ 5 Nutzung des Archivgutes

(1) ¹Jede Person hat nach Maßgabe dieser Vorschrift und im Rahmen der Benutzungsordnung[1)] das Recht, auf Antrag Archivgut im Landesarchiv zu wissenschaftlichen Zwecken oder bei sonst berechtigtem Interesse zu nutzen. ²Die Nutzerinnen und Nutzer sind verpflichtet, von Werken, die sie unter wesentlicher Verwendung von Archivgut verfaßt haben, dem Landesarchiv, welches das Archivgut verwahrt, ein Exemplar kostenfrei abzuliefern. ³§ 12 Abs. 2 bis 5 des Niedersächsischen Pressegesetzes gilt entsprechend.

(2) ¹Archivgut darf erst 30 Jahre nach der letzten inhaltlichen Bearbeitung des Schriftgutes genutzt werden. ²Archivgut, das besonderen gesetzlichen Geheimhaltungs-, Sperrungs-, Löschungs- oder Vernichtungsvorschriften des Landes unterlegen hat, darf erst 50 Jahre nach der letzten inhaltlichen Bearbeitung des Schriftgutes genutzt werden. ³Archivierte Niederschriften von Sitzungen der Landesregierung oder Verschlußsachen dürfen nur genutzt werden, wenn die Vertraulichkeit oder Geheimhaltung aufgehoben worden ist. ⁴Ist das nach den Sätzen 1 bis 3 geschützte Archivgut zu einer betroffenen Person geführt und ist deren Geburts- oder Sterbedatum bekannt oder mit vertretbarem Aufwand aus diesem Archivgut zu ermitteln, so darf es frühestens 10 Jahre nach dem Tode dieser Person oder, falls das Sterbedatum nicht feststellbar ist, 100 Jahre nach deren Geburt genutzt werden. ⁵Im übrigen sind schutzwürdige Interessen betroffener Personen, soweit sie ohne besonderen Aufwand erkennbar sind, angemessen zu berücksichtigen.

(3) ¹Für die Nutzung von Archivgut, das dem Sozialgeheimnis unterliegende Daten enthält, gelten die Schutzfristen nach den §§ 11 und 12 des Bundesarchivgesetzes. ²Für die Nutzung von Archivgut, das nach anderen Rechtsvorschriften des Bundes der Geheimhaltung unterliegt oder das Stellen des Bundes dem Landesarchiv nach § 7 des Bundesarchivgesetzes oder entsprechenden archivrechtlichen Vorschriften des Bundes übergeben haben, gelten die Fristen des Absatzes 2.

(4) Das Landesarchiv kann die Nutzung von Archivgut auch nach Ablauf der Schutzfristen aus wichtigem Grund einschränken oder versagen, insbesondere wenn

---

1) Die Benutzungsordnung für das Niedersächsische Landesarchiv ist abgedruckt als Nr. D9.II.1a.

D9.II.1 Niedersächsisches Archivgesetz

1. Grund zu der Annahme besteht, daß dem Wohle des Bundes oder eines Landes Nachteile bereitet würden,
2. der Erhaltungszustand des Archivgutes dies erfordert.

(5) ¹Die Benutzungsordnung kann für bestimmte Arten von Archivgut abweichend von Absatz 2 Satz 1 kürzere Schutzfristen festlegen, wenn öffentliche Interessen oder schutzwürdige Interessen betroffener Personen nicht entgegenstehen. ²Das Landesarchiv kann im Einzelfall eine Nutzung von Archivgut vor Ablauf der Schutzfristen zulassen, wenn

1. kein Grund zu der Annahme besteht, daß Interessen nach Satz 1 entgegenstehen, oder
2. die Nutzung zur Durchführung eines wissenschaftlichen Forschungsvorhabens oder zur Erfüllung der öffentlichen Aufgaben von Presse und Rundfunk erforderlich ist und schutzwürdige Interessen betroffener Personen durch geeignete Maßnahmen hinreichend gewahrt werden.

(6) Archivgut, das schon bei seiner Entstehung als Schriftgut zur Veröffentlichung bestimmt war, unterliegt keinen Schutzfristen.

(7) ¹Weitergehende gesetzliche Rechte auf Nutzung bleiben unberührt. ²Die Nutzung von Archivgut durch die Einrichtungen oder Stellen, von denen es übernommen worden ist, unterliegt keinen Einschränkungen nach diesem Gesetz; dies gilt entsprechend in den Fällen des § 3 Abs. 7.

§ 6 Recht auf Auskunft und Gegendarstellung

(1) ¹Die Erteilung einer Auskunft nach Artikel 15 der Datenschutz-Grundverordnung ist abzulehnen, soweit und solange

1. das Archivgut nicht erschlossen ist,
2. die betroffene Person keine Angaben macht, die das Auffinden der Daten ermöglichen,
3. der für die Erteilung der Auskunft erforderliche Aufwand außer Verhältnis zu dem geltend gemachten Informationsinteresse steht,
4. Grund zu der Annahme besteht, dass die Auskunft die öffentliche Sicherheit gefährden oder sonst dem Wohl des Bundes oder eines Landes Nachteile bereiten würde, oder
5. die Auskunft dazu führen würde, dass ein Sachverhalt, der nach einer Rechtsvorschrift oder wegen der Rechte und Freiheiten einer anderen Person geheim zu halten ist, aufgedeckt wird.

²Die Ablehnung ist zu begründen. ³Die Ablehnung nach Satz 1 Nr. 4 oder 5 muss nicht begründet werden, soweit durch die Mitteilung der Gründe der mit der Auskunftsverweigerung verfolgte Zweck gefährdet würde. ⁴Soweit die Ablehnung nach Satz 3 nicht begründet wird, sind die Gründe dafür aktenkundig zu machen. ⁵Wird die Auskunft nach Satz 1 Nr. 1, 2 oder 3 abgelehnt, so ist § 9 Abs. 4 des Niedersächsischen Datenschutzgesetzes nicht anwendbar. ⁶Weitergehende Ansprüche nach Artikel 15 der Datenschutz-Grundverordnung bestehen nicht.

(2) ¹Besteht nach Artikel 15 der Datenschutz-Grundverordnung ein Anspruch auf Auskunft, so kann anstelle der Auskunft Einsichtnahme in das Archivgut gewährt werden, wenn der Erhaltungszustand des Archivgutes dies erlaubt. ²Ist das Archivgut in maschinenlesbaren Dateien gespeichert, so wird die Einsichtnahme in das Archivgut nur in eine Abbildung gewährt.

(3) ¹Macht eine betroffene Person glaubhaft, daß das Archivgut eine falsche Tatsachenbehauptung enthält, die sie nicht nur unerheblich in ihren Rechten beeinträchtigt, so kann die betroffene Person verlangen, daß dem sie betreffenden, erschlossenen Archivgut eine von ihr eingereichte Gegendarstellung beigefügt wird. ²Die Gegendarstellung muss sich auf Tatsachen beschränken und soll die Beweismittel aufführen. ³Kann die betroffene Person die Beeinträchtigung ihrer Rechte nicht ausreichend glaubhaft machen, so ist bei dem Archivgut zu vermerken, daß sie die Tatsachenbehauptung bestreitet.

§ 6a Ausschluss von Rechten und Pflichten nach der Datenschutz-Grundverordnung

Neben den Rechten aus § 6 bestehen Rechte betroffener Personen nach Artikel 16 Satz 1 (Berichtigung) und den Artikeln 18 (Einschränkung der Verarbeitung), 20 (Datenübertragbarkeit) und 21 (Widerspruch) sowie die Mitteilungspflicht nach Artikel 19 (über Berichtigung oder Löschung personenbezogener Daten oder eine Einschränkung der Verarbeitung) der Datenschutz-Grundverordnung bezüglich des Archivguts nicht.

§ 7 Archivgut des Landtages, der kommunalen Körperschaften und sonstiger Einrichtungen

(1) ¹Der Landtag, die kommunalen Körperschaften sowie die sonstigen der Aufsicht des Landes unterstehenden juristischen Personen des öffentlichen Rechts und deren Vereinigungen sind verpflichtet,

ihr Archivgut zu sichern. ²Dazu unterhält der Landtag ein eigenes Archiv oder bietet sein Schriftgut nach § 3 Abs. 6 dem Landesarchiv zur Übernahme an. ³Im übrigen können die in Satz 1 genannten Einrichtungen zur Sicherung ihres Archivgutes eigene oder gemeinsame Archive unterhalten oder ihr Schriftgut dem Archiv einer anderen in Satz 1 genannten Einrichtung oder nach § 3 Abs. 6 dem Landesarchiv zur Übernahme anbieten.
(2) Dieses Gesetz gilt nicht für öffentlich-rechtliche Rundfunkanstalten sowie für öffentlich-rechtliche Unternehmen, die am Wettbewerb teilnehmen.
(3) ¹Soweit die in Absatz 1 Satz 1 genannten Einrichtungen Archive unterhalten oder die Abgabe ihres Archivgutes an Archive einer anderen in Absatz 1 Satz 1 genannten Einrichtung geregelt haben, haben sie ihr Schriftgut diesen Archiven zur Übernahme anzubieten. ²Die §§ 3a, 3b und 4 Satz 1 sowie die §§ 5 bis 6a gelten entsprechend. ³Soweit Hochschulen des Landes Archive unterhalten, gelten auch § 3 Abs. 1 bis 5 und § 4 Satz 2 entsprechend mit der Maßgabe, daß an die Stelle des Landesarchivs das Hochschularchiv tritt. ⁴Im übrigen regeln die in Absatz 1 Satz 1 genannten Einrichtungen die Angelegenheiten ihrer Archive in eigener Zuständigkeit.

§ 8 Inkrafttreten
(1) Dieses Gesetz tritt vierzehn Tage nach seiner Verkündung[1] in Kraft.
(2) *[nicht wiedergegebene Aufhebungsvorschrift]*

---

1) Verkündet am 4.6.1993.

D9.II.1a Benutzungsordnung Landesarchiv

Benutzungsordnung für das Niedersächsische Landesarchiv

Erl. d. StK v. 23. Juni 2008 – 201-56222/1 – (Nds. MBl. S. 674)
(– VORIS 22560 –)

Bezug:
Bek. v. 1.8.2003 (Nds. MBl. S. 558)
– VORIS 22560 –

1. Grundlagen, Geltungsbereich

1.1

Diese Ordnung regelt auf der Grundlage des NArchG vom 25.5.1993 (Nds. GVBl. S. 129), geändert durch Artikel 1 des Gesetzes vom 5.11.2004 (Nds. GVBl. S. 402), die Benutzung des im Niedersächsischen Landesarchiv verwahrten und erschlossenen Archivgutes (siehe Nummern 2 und 3) durch

1.1.1 persönliche Einsichtnahme in das originale oder in Reproduktion vorgelegte Archivgut einschließlich der Findmittel und sonstigen archivischen Hilfsmittel, die das Archivgut erschließen (siehe Nummer 3),
1.1.2 Anfertigung von Kopien oder fotografischen oder digitalen Reproduktionen des Archivgutes (siehe Nummer 4) einschließlich der Einräumung von Nutzungsrechten daran,
1.1.3 Versendung von Archivgut zur Einsichtnahme in einem anderen Archiv (siehe Nummer 5),
1.1.4 Ausleihe von Archivgut zu Ausstellungszwecken (siehe Nummer 6) oder
1.1.5 schriftliche Auskünfte zu Archivgut (siehe Nummer 7).

1.2

Für die Benutzung von Archivgut, das von anderen Archiven oder Instituten übersandt wurde, gelten die gleichen Bedingungen wie für das Archivgut des Landesarchivs, sofern die übersendende Stelle nicht anderslautende Auflagen macht.

2. Benutzung

2.1

Wer Archivgut benutzen will, hat hierzu schriftlich, im Fall von Nummer 1.1.1 unter Verwendung eines dafür vorgesehenen Vordrucks, Angaben
2.1.1 zur Person, ggf. auch zur Person einer Auftraggeberin oder eines Auftraggebers oder Beauftragten oder Hilfskräften, die hinzugezogen werden sollen,
2.1.2 zum jeweiligen Thema und Zweck der Nachforschungen,
2.1.3 ggf. zur Begründung einer Verkürzung der Schutzfristen (§ 5 Abs. 5 Satz 2 NArchG)
zu machen und auf Verlangen sich und Beauftragte oder Hilfskräfte auszuweisen.

2.2

[1]Über die Benutzung entscheidet das im Landesarchiv jeweils zuständige Staatsarchiv unter Beachtung der gesetzlichen Pflichten zur Sicherung und Erhaltung des Archivgutes (§ 4 Satz 1 NArchG) und zur Wahrung schutzwürdiger Belange Betroffener (§ 5 Abs. 2 Sätze 4 und 5 sowie Abs. 5 Satz 2 Nr. 2 NArchG). [2]Die Benutzung kann unter Bedingungen und mit Auflagen zugelassen werden. [3]Die Genehmigung ist auf das jeweilige Kalenderjahr beschränkt.

2.3

Die Benutzung erfolgt in Abhängigkeit von den personellen und sächlichen Kapazitäten des Landesarchivs; auf eine bestimmte Art, Form oder einen bestimmten Umfang der Benutzung besteht kein Rechtsanspruch.

2.4

Jede Benutzerin und jeder Benutzer wird zur Ermittlung einschlägiger Archivbestände und Findmittel von einer zugewiesenen archivischen Fachkraft beraten.

2.5

[1]Archivgut ist mit größter Sorgfalt zu behandeln. [2]Es ist deshalb nicht zulässig,
2.5.1 auf dem Archivgut und in den Findmitteln Notizen oder Zeichen irgendwelcher Art anzubringen,
2.5.2 sonstige Veränderungen an dem Archivgut und den Findmitteln vorzunehmen,
2.5.3 Handpausen zu fertigen,
2.5.4 an der Ordnung des Archivgutes, insbesondere an der Reihenfolge der Schriftstücke innerhalb einer Archivalieneinheit, sowie an der Signierung und Verpackung oder an sonstigen Bestandteilen etwas zu verändern,
2.5.5 Archivgut, Findmittel oder sonstige archivische Hilfsmittel aus den für die Einsichtnahme oder zur Nutzung von archiveigenen technischen Geräten bestimmten Räumen des jeweiligen Staatsarchivs (Benutzerräume) zu entfernen,
2.5.6 Archivgut als Schreibunterlage oder zu sonstigen Zwecken zu verwenden.

2.6

[1]Wer gegen die Benutzungsordnung verstößt, kann von der weiteren Benutzung ausgeschlossen werden. [2]Weitergehende Ansprüche wegen missbräuchlichen Verhaltens bleiben unberührt.

3. Persönliche Einsichtnahme

3.1

[1]Archivgut, Findmittel sowie sonstige archivische Hilfsmittel zur Erschließung von Archivgut sind jeweils unter Angabe der Signaturen zu bestellen. [2]Sie dürfen nur in den jeweiligen Benutzungsräumen benutzt werden.

3.2

Findmittel werden nur insoweit vorgelegt, wie sie Archivgut nachweisen, das uneingeschränkt zugänglich ist oder bei dem unterstellt werden kann, dass die gesetzlichen Schutzfristen auf Antrag verkürzt werden können.

3.3

[1]Benutzereigene technische Geräte dürfen nur mit Zustimmung des im Landesarchiv jeweils zuständigen Staatsarchivs benutzt werden. [2]Für die Herstellung von Archivgutreproduktionen ist ihr Einsatz unzulässig.

3.4

[1]In den Benutzungsräumen hat die Unterhaltung zu unterbleiben; Essen, Trinken, Rauchen und die Benutzung von Mobiltelefonen sind dort nicht gestattet. [2]Garderobe, Taschen und andere Behältnisse sind außerhalb der Benutzungsräume in den dafür vorgesehenen Räumen oder Schließfächern zu verwahren.

3.5

[1]Vor dem Verlassen des jeweiligen Staatsarchivs sind das benutzte Archivgut sowie die sonstigen Arbeitsmittel des jeweiligen Staatsarchivs der Aufsicht in den Benutzungsräumen zurückzugeben. [2]Auf Verlangen ist dieser Einsicht in mitgebrachte Taschen, andere Behältnisse oder Unterlagen zu

D9.II.1a Benutzungsordnung Landesarchiv

gewähren. ³Benutztes Archivgut und sonstige Arbeitsmittel können für die Dauer von höchstens zwei Wochen zur weiteren Benutzung bereitgehalten werden.

4. Kopien und Reproduktionen von Archivgut

4.1

¹Kopien und fotografische oder digitale Reproduktionen von Archivgut sowie Siegelabgüsse, Siegelabdrucke, Faksimiles und sonstige Nachbildungen zum persönlichen Gebrauch der Benutzerin oder des Benutzers können auf Antrag vom jeweiligen Staatsarchiv hergestellt werden. ²Die Herstellung kann versagt oder eingeschränkt werden, insbesondere wenn das Archivgut aufgrund seines Erhaltungszustandes oder seines Formats für das zur Verfügung stehende Kopier- oder Reproduktionsverfahren (§ 4 Satz 1 NArchG) nicht geeignet ist oder wenn andernfalls schutzwürdige Interessen Betroffener nicht gewahrt werden können (§ 5 Abs. 2 Sätze 4 und 5 sowie Abs. 5 Satz 2 Nr. 2 NArchG).

4.2

Kopien und fotografische oder digitale Reproduktionen von Findmitteln werden nur hergestellt und abgegeben, wenn das darin erschlossene Archivgut abschließend geordnet und verzeichnet sowie uneingeschränkt zugänglich ist.

4.3

¹Kopien und sonstige Reproduktionen von Archivgut können grundsätzlich nur den Anforderungen als Arbeits- oder Gebrauchskopie genügen. ²Sollen sie in digitaler Form geliefert werden, ist das gewünschte Format anzugeben. ³Ein Online-Versand ist ausgeschlossen. ⁴Die Kompatibilität der gelieferten Datenträger und Daten mit der individuellen IT-Ausstattung einer Bestellerin oder eines Bestellers kann nicht garantiert werden.

4.4

¹Jede bildliche Veröffentlichung oder Vervielfältigung von Kopien oder Reproduktionen nach Nummer 4.1 bedarf der schriftlichen Erlaubnis des im Landesarchiv jeweils zuständigen Staatsarchivs. ²Bei der Publikation sind das im Landesarchiv jeweils verwahrende Staatsarchiv und die vollständige Archivsignatur anzugeben.

5. Versendung von Archivgut zur Einsichtnahme in einem anderen Archiv

5.1

Archivgut kann im begründeten Ausnahmefall auf schriftlichen Antrag zur privaten Benutzung an hauptamtlich geführte öffentliche Archive des Inlandes befristet versandt werden, wenn

5.1.1 der Benutzungszweck nicht auf andere Weise, z.B. durch die Herstellung und Abgabe von Reproduktionen, erreicht werden kann,

5.1.2 das Archivgut versendungsfähig hergerichtet ist,

5.1.3 das aufnehmende Archiv bereit ist, das Archivgut sicher zu verwahren, die Benutzung in seinen Benutzungsräumen nach Maßgabe dieser Benutzungsordnung zuzulassen und das Archivgut unter denselben Sicherheitsvorkehrungen und auf dem gleichen Weg wie bei der Übersendung zurückzuschicken und

5.1.4 die Benutzerin oder der Benutzer die Kosten der vom Landesarchiv für erforderlich gehaltenen Art der Versendung, ggf. unter Wertangabe nach dem aktuellen Wert des Archivgutes, einschließlich der zur Herrichtung des Archivguts notwendigen Kosten vorweg erstattet.

5.2
Von der Versendung ausgeschlossen ist

5.2.1 Archivgut, das Benutzungsbeschränkungen unterliegt,
5.2.2 Archivgut, das wegen seines hohen Wertes, seines Ordnungs- und Erhaltungszustandes, seines Formats oder aus anderen Sicherheits- oder konservatorischen Gründen versendungsunfähig ist, oder
5.2.3 Archivgut, das noch nicht abschließend verzeichnet ist, sowie
5.2.4 Findmittel.

5.3

[1]Die Herstellung von Reproduktionen aus versandtem Archivgut ist nicht zulässig. [2]Das versandte Archivgut kann jederzeit zurückgefordert werden.

6. Ausleihe von Archivgut zu Ausstellungszwecken

[1]Archivgut kann zu Ausstellungszwecken ausgeliehen werden, soweit nicht der Ausstellungszweck bereits durch die Herstellung und Abgabe von Reproduktionen oder Nachbildungen des Archivgutes erreicht werden kann. [2]Über die Ausleihe ist zwischen dem verwahrenden Staatsarchiv und der oder dem Entleihenden ein Leihvertrag abzuschließen.

7. Schriftliche Auskünfte

Schriftliche Auskünfte auf Anfragen beschränken sich in der Regel auf Hinweise über einschlägiges Archivgut.

8. Gebühren, Auslagen, Entgelte

Ergänzend zu den in der AllGO festgelegten Gebühren und Auslagen für Amtshandlungen und Leistungen nach den Nummern 2 bis 7 sind für weitergehende Leistungen des Landesarchivs Entgelte nach der **Anlage** zu entrichten.

9. Schlussbestimmungen

[1]Dieser Erl. tritt am 1.7.2008 in Kraft. [2]Gleichzeitig wird die Bezugsbekanntmachung aufgehoben.

D9.II.1a Benutzungsordnung Landesarchiv

Anlage

Entgeltordnung für das Niedersächsische Landesarchiv

Nummer	Gegenstand	Kosten EUR
1.	**Analoge Fotoarbeiten bzw. Kopien**	
1.1	Grundentgelt je Auftrag gemäß den Nummern 1.2 bis 1.4	5,00
1.2	Mikrofilmnegativ (Rollfilm 35 mm) je Aufnahme	0,20
1.3	Duplizierung von Mikrofilmen auf Diazo-Rollfilm je lfd. m (nur im Staatsarchiv Bückeburg)	1,00
1.4	Duplizierung von Mikrofiche (nur im Staatsarchiv Bückeburg)	2,00
1.5	Ausdrucke aus EDV-Findbüchern je Seite	0,50
1.6	Ausleihe von Farbmakrofiche oder von Farbektachromen Eine eventuell zu erteilende Nutzungs- oder Veröffentlichungsgenehmigung wird nach Nummer 4 gesondert berechnet. Bei Verlust werden die tatsächlichen Wiederbeschaffungskosten in Rechnung estellt.	10,00
1.7	Schwarzweiß-Kopien über Lese-Rückvergrößerungsgeräte etc. (Reader-Printer)	
1.7.1	DIN A 4 und Folio je Kopie	0,50
1.7.2	desgleichen DIN A 3 je Kopie	0,80
1.7.3	bei Selbstherstellung durch den Benutzer DIN A 4 und Folio je Kopie	0,30
1.7.4	desgleichen DIN A 3 je Kopie	0,50
1.8	Zuschläge bei besonderem Herstellungsaufwand je angefangene Viertelstunde der aufgewandten Arbeitszeit	11,00
2.	**Digitalisierung**	
2.1	Schwarzweiß-Buchscanner-Kopie ca. 300 dpi (abhängig von der Vorlagengröße) je Ausdruck (Arbeitskopie)	
2.1.1	DIN A 4	0,50
2.1.2	DIN A 3	0,80
2.2	Grundentgelt je Auftrag (Aufnahmeleistung einschließlich Konfektionierung auf Datenträgern, z.B. CD-ROM bzw. DVD) gemäß den Nummern 2.3.1 bis 2.3.3	12,00
2.3	Digitalaufnahme/Dateiscan (zur Weiterverarbeitung auf Datenträgern, z.B. CD-ROM bzw. DVD)	
2.3.1	Digitale Aufnahme über Graustufen-Buchscanner ca. 300 dpi (abhängig von der Vorlagengröße)	0,50
2.3.2	Digitale Aufnahme über mobile Digitalspiegelreflexkamera oder Flachbettscanner (TIF- oder JPEG-Format) je Aufnahme	1,00
2.3.3	Digitale Aufnahme über Großformat-Reprokamera (TIF-Format) je Aufnahme	5,00
2.4	Farbausdrucke (Arbeitskopie)	
2.4.1	DIN A 4	4,00
2.4.2	DIN A 3	8,00
2.5	Zuschläge bei besonderem Herstellungsaufwand je angefangene Viertelstunde der aufgewandten Arbeitszeit	11,00
3.	**Handwerkliche Leistungen und Zuschläge bei besonderem Personalaufwand (z.B. Anfertigung von Siegelabgüssen, Binde- und Restaurierungsarbeiten)**	
3.1	Berechnung nach Aufwand je angefangene Viertelstunde zuzüglich Material	11,00

Benutzungsordnung Landesarchiv D9.II.1a

Nummer	Gegenstand		Kosten EUR
4.	**Nutzungs- und Veröffentlichungsgenehmigungen** (Erlaubnis zur Veröffentlichung oder Vervielfältigung von Reproduktionen von Archivgut zu gewerblichen oder geschäftlichen Zwecken. Ansprüche Dritter aus Urheber-, Verwertungs- und Lizenzrechten sind gesondert abzugelten.)		
4.1	in Büchern, Broschüren, Zeitschriften und Zeitungen je nach Art und Auflage		
	a)	bis 5 000 Exemplare	40,00
	b)	bis 10 000 Exemplare	100,00
	c)	für jede weiteren 1 000 Exemplare	10,00
	bis zu einem Höchstbetrag von		500,00
4.2	auf Plakaten und Ansichtskarten		das Doppelte des Entgelts nach Nummer 4.1
4.3	bei Neuauflagen und Nachdrucken		die Hälfte des Entgelts nach Nummer 4.1
4.4	für die Verwendung im Film oder Fernsehen		je angefangene Minute 100,00
4.5	für die Verwendung auf Datenträgern		wie Nummer 4.1
	Bei gleichzeitiger Verwendung in gedruckten Publikationen ermäßigt sich das Entgelt für die Verwendung auf Datenträgern auf die Hälfte.		
4.6	Einblendung in Onlinedienste, Internetpräsentationen und vergleichbare Medien je Reproduktion		
	a)	für bis zu einem Monat	40,00
	b)	für sechs Monate	100,00
	c)	für ein Jahr	150,00
4.7	Erlaubnis zur Vervielfältigung von Siegelabgüssen, Siegelabdrucken, Faksimiles und sonstigen Nachbildungen von Archivgut		
	a)	bei einer Auflage bis 100 Stück	40,00
	b)	bei einer Auflage über 100 bis 500 Stück	80,00
	c)	bei einer Auflage über 500 Stück je weitere angefangene 10 Stück	10,00
4.8	Einräumung von persönlichen Nutzungsrechten an EDV-gespeicherten Erschließungsdaten		nach Vereinbarung

Studentinnen und Studenten, Schülerinnen und Schüler und Anspruchberechtigte nach dem SGB II und dem SGB III können auf Antrag von der Entrichtung der Grundentgelte gemäß den Nummern 1.1 bzw. 2.2 befreit werden. Die Stundensätze richten sich nach dem RdErl. des MF v. 15.4.2008 (Nds. MBl. S. 509) in der jeweils geltenden Fassung.

D9.II.1b VwV Niedersächsisches Archivgesetz

Verwaltungsvorschriften zum Niedersächsischen Archivgesetz

RdErl. d. StK v. 24.10.2006 – 201-56 201 – (Nds. MBl. 2006 Nr. 38, S. 959)
– VORIS 22560 –

Bezug:
a) RdErl. v. 10.1.1995 (Nds. MBl. S. 167)
   – VORIS 22560 02 00 02 001 –
b) RdErl. v. 18.12.1995 (Nds. MBl. 1996 S. 292)
   – VORIS 22560 02 00 02 003 –
c) RdErl. v. 3.11.1970 (Nds. MBl. S. 1302)
   – VORIS 22560 00 00 02 005 –

I.

Bei der Anwendung des NArchG vom 25.5.1993 (Nds. GVBl. S. 129), geändert durch Artikel 1 des Gesetzes vom 5.11.2004 (Nds. GVBl. S. 402), sind folgende Erläuterungen zu beachten:

1. Zu § 1 Abs. 1 Satz 1

Das Landesarchiv übernimmt und verwaltet das Archivgut nach dem archivischen Provenienzprinzip. Zur Wahrung dieses Prinzips gilt die Vorschrift in Fällen von Organisationsänderungen (z. B. bei Umorganisation staatlicher Behörden, bei Kommunalisierung von bisher staatlichen Aufgaben oder bei Übernahme von bisher kommunal verwalteten Aufgaben durch das Land) mit folgenden Maßgaben: Ist übergebenes Schriftgut durch die neue Verwaltung inhaltlich bearbeitet worden, wird es zu gegebener Zeit von dem für diese zuständigen Archiv bewertet und in seinen archivwürdigen Teilen als Archivgut übernommen. Wird solches Schriftgut dagegen inhaltlich nicht weiter bearbeitet, obliegt diese Aufgabe dem vor der Umorganisation zuständigen Archiv.

2. Zu § 1 Abs. 3

Die Vorschrift stellt insbesondere klar, dass der Entscheidung des LT, ein eigenes Archiv zu unterhalten oder sein Schriftgut nach § 3 Abs. 6 dem Landesarchiv anzubieten, Vorrang vor der möglichen Einstufung der Landtagsverwaltung als sonstige Stelle des Landes (§ 1 Abs. 1 Satz 1) und der damit verbundenen Anbietungspflicht nach § 3 Abs. 1 Satz 1 zukommt.

3. Zu § 3 Abs. 1 Satz 1

3.1 Für die in § 1 Abs. 1 Satz 1 und Abs. 2 genannten anbietungspflichtigen Stellen sind im Landesarchiv zuständig
3.1.1 für die obersten Landesbehörden und zentralen Fachbehörden das Hauptstaatsarchiv Hannover;
3.1.2 für die übrigen in § 1 Abs. 1 NArchG genannten Stellen
a) in der Region Hannover sowie in den Landkreisen Diepholz, Hameln-Pyrmont, Hildesheim, Holzminden und Nienburg (Weser)
   das Hauptstaatsarchiv Hannover;
b) in den Landkreisen Aurich, Leer und Wittmund sowie der Stadt Emden
   das Staatsarchiv Aurich;
c) im Landkreis Schaumburg
   das Staatsarchiv Bückeburg;
d) in den Landkreisen Ammerland, Cloppenburg, Friesland, Oldenburg, Wesermarsch und Vechta sowie den Städten Delmenhorst, Oldenburg (Oldenburg) und Wilhelmshaven
   das Staatsarchiv Oldenburg;
e) in den Landkreisen Emsland, Grafschaft Bentheim und Osnabrück sowie der Stadt Osnabrück
   das Staatsarchiv Osnabrück;
f) in den Landkreisen Celle, Cuxhaven, Harburg, Lüchow-Dannenberg, Lüneburg, Osterholz, Rotenburg (Wümme), Soltau-Fallingbostel, Stade, Uelzen und Verden

das Staatsarchiv Stade;
g) in den Landkreisen Gifhorn, Göttingen, Goslar, Helmstedt, Northeim, Osterode am Harz, Peine und Wolfenbüttel sowie den Städten Braunschweig, Salzgitter und Wolfsburg
das Staatsarchiv Wolfenbüttel.

3.2 Zum anbietungspflichtigen Schriftgut gehören auch alle amtlichen Publikationen (Gutachten, Studien, Veröffentlichungsreihen, Zeitschriften, Mitteilungsblätter, Kartenwerke u. Ä.), soweit sie – auch in elektronsicher Form – von Dienststellen der niedersächsischen Landesverwaltung herausgegeben werden oder in deren Auftrag einmalig oder laufend erscheinen. Sie werden dem im Landesarchiv jeweils zuständigen Staatsarchiv – mit ihrem Erscheinen – kostenlos zur Verfügung gestellt.

3.3 Für das Anbietungsverfahren insgesamt gelten die folgenden Regeln. Sofern das im Landesarchiv jeweils zuständige Staatsarchiv nicht auf die Anbietung verzichtet hat (§ 3 Abs. 4 Satz 2), übersenden die anbietungspflichtigen Stellen – ggf. auf elektronischem Weg – Verzeichnisse über das anzubietende Schriftgut nach dem Muster der Anlage 1. Bei gleichförmigem Massenschriftgut (z. B. Prozessakten der Gerichte, Einheitswertakten der Finanzämter, Krankenakten der Landeskrankenhäuser) können die anbietungspflichtigen Stellen die Verzeichnisse nach dem Muster der Anlage 2 fertigen. Für die Anbietung von elektronisch geführtem oder verwaltetem Schriftgut gelten die Bestimmungen der Nummer 5. Das im Landesarchiv jeweils zuständige Staatsarchiv kann bei der Schriftgutbewertung selbst Einsicht in das angebotene Schriftgut und die dazugehörigen Findmittel der Registraturen nehmen.

3.4 Das im Landesarchiv jeweils zuständige Staatsarchiv meldet der anbietungspflichtigen Stelle, welches Schriftgut von ihm als Archivgut übernommen wird. Die anbietungspflichtige Stelle liefert das Archivgut zusammen mit einem Abgabeverzeichnis oder einem nach dem Muster der Anlage 1 gefertigten Verzeichnis ab; Nummer 3.3 Satz 3 gilt entsprechend.

3.5 Die Kosten der erforderlichen Verpackung und Verschnürung des Archivgutes und des Transportes oder der postalischen Versendung zu dem im Landesarchiv jeweils zuständigen Staatsarchiv trägt die anbietungspflichtige Stelle. Bei elektronischen Unterlagen gilt dies entsprechend für die Kosten der Konvertierung bzw. Migration in das vom Landesarchiv vorgegebene Speicherformat und Speichermedium sowie für die Übermittlung dieser Unterlagen an das Landesarchiv.

3.6 Das im Landesarchiv jeweils zuständige Staatsarchiv bestätigt die Übernahme unter Rücksendung einer Ausfertigung des Abgabeverzeichnisses und Angabe der archivischen Bestandssignatur.

4. Zu § 3 Abs. 1 Satz 3

4.1 Unterliegt das zur Übernahme angebotene Schriftgut einer mehr als 30-jährigen Aufbewahrungsfrist, so wahrt das im Landesarchiv jeweils zuständige Staatsarchiv diese Frist, wenn es dem Schriftgut bleibenden Wert nach § 2 Abs. 2 zuerkannt (§ 3 Abs. 4 Satz 1) und es als Archivgut übernommen hat. Ist dem Schriftgut kein bleibender Wert zuerkannt worden, so stellt die anbietungspflichtige Stelle durch befristete Aufbewahrung selbst sicher, dass dieses Schriftgut erst nach Erlöschen des für die Fristdefinition jeweils maßgeblichen Rechts- oder Verwaltungsinteresses vernichtet wird.

4.2 Unbeschadet der Anbietungspflicht kann die Übernahme des Archivgutes im Einzelfall auf begrenzte Zeit ausgesetzt werden, wenn die Nutzung nach § 5 Abs. 7 Satz 2 nach der Beurteilung des Landesarchivs einen vertretbaren Umfang überschreiten würde oder dem Landesarchiv ausreichende Kapazitäten für eine sofortige Übernahme fehlen.

5. Zu § 3 Abs. 2 Satz 1

Werden Registraturen automatisiert verwaltet oder wird Schriftgut in Form automatisierter Dateien geführt (= elektronische Unterlagen), beachten die anbietungspflichtigen Stellen die Vorgaben des Landesarchivs zum Speicherformat und zum Speichermedium und liefern die erforderlichen Registraturdaten bzw. die Metadaten der jeweiligen elektronischen Unterlagen in leicht lesbarer Form. Die Abbildung einer automatisierten Datei kann in einem Papierausdruck, automatisiert hergestellten Mikroformen oder in einer Zweitausfertigung der automatisierten Datei bestehen. Unterliegen elektronische Unterlagen, wie z. B. Datenbanken, einer fortlaufenden Bearbeitung und Aktualisierung und werden deshalb im eigentlichen Sinne nicht geschlossen, kann das Landesarchiv die Abgabe einer Kopie dieser Unterlagen zu einem bestimmten Stichtag verlangen.

6. Zu § 3 Abs. 4 Satz 1

6.1 Das im Landesarchiv jeweils zuständige Staatsarchiv trifft die Feststellung nach § 3 Abs. 4 Satz 1 spätestens mit Ablauf des vierten Monats nach der Anbietung (§ 3 Abs. 1 Satz 1), andernfalls sind die anbietungspflichtigen Stellen ihrer Pflicht in diesem Falle ledig.

6.2 Hat das im Landesarchiv jeweils zuständige Staatsarchiv die Feststellung nach § 3 Abs. 4 Satz 1 im Hinblick auf Verschlusssachen getroffen, so setzt die anbietungspflichtige Stelle vor der Übernahme des Archivgutes durch das Landesarchiv im Wege eines Herabstufungsverfahrens innerhalb eines angemessenen Zeitraumes die Frist fest, nach deren Ablauf die Geheimhaltung aufgehoben und die Benutzung des Archivgutes nach § 5 Abs. 2 Satz 3 grundsätzlich zugelassen ist.

7. Zu § 3 Abs. 4 Satz 2

Der Umfang der Anbietungspflicht ist auf das Notwendige zu begrenzen. Das im Landesarchiv jeweils zuständige Staatsarchiv soll daher bei den anbietungspflichtigen Stellen insbesondere frühzeitig das Archivgut feststellen, Archivierungskonzepte erarbeiten und bei der Entwicklung übergreifender Archivierungsmodelle unterstützend mitwirken.

8. Zu § 3 Abs. 6 Satz 2 und Abs. 7 Satz 2

Für die Vereinbarungen gelten die Muster der Anlagen 3 und 4. Bei der Auslegung bereits bestehender Vereinbarungen sind die in diesen Anlagen niedergelegten Grundsätze zu beachten, sofern sie nach deren Wortlaut anwendbar sind.

9. Zu § 4

Wenn das im Landesarchiv jeweils zuständige Staatsarchiv elektronische Unterlagen (= automatisiert geführte Dateien i. S. von § 3 Abs. 2) übernommen und diese archivfachlich erschlossen hat, leitet es diese zusammen mit den erforderlichen Metadaten zur zentralen Langzeitspeicherung an das IZN weiter. Unter Beachtung der dafür jeweils maßgeblichen Standards verwahrt das IZN das aus elektronischen Unterlagen bestehende Archivgut des Landesarchivs sicher, authentisch, vollständig und dauerhaft nutzbar und gewährleistet seine Nutzung durch das Landesarchiv sowie seine Benutzerinnen und Benutzer auf der Basis aktueller Hard- und Software. Bei der Übernahme elektronischer Unterlagen, insbesondere solcher, die mit einer digitalen Signatur i. S. des Signaturgesetzes in der jeweils geltenden Fassung versehen sind, ist das Landesarchiv ab der Übernahme lediglich zur Sicherung der in den Unterlagen enthaltenen Informationen, einschließlich derjenigen zur Dokumentation aller für eine digitale Signatur maßgeblichen Komponenten, verpflichtet.

10. Zu § 5 Abs. 2 Satz 4

10.1 Archivgut ist in der Regel dann zur Person Betroffener geführt, wenn die Betroffenen in der maßgeblichen Bezeichnung des Archivgutes namentlich benannt werden und tatsächlich als Person wesentlicher Gegenstand des jeweiligen Inhalts sind (vgl. hierzu auch Nummer 11 Satz 3).

10.2 Ist weder das Geburts- noch das Sterbedatum der Betroffenen bekannt oder mit vertretbarem Aufwand aus dem Archivgut, dessen Benutzung begehrt wird, zu ermitteln, so ist die mit dieser Vorschrift beabsichtigte Differenzierung der Schutzfristen nach § 5 Abs. 2 Sätze 1 bis 3 nicht möglich. Die dort genannten Schutzfristen gelten dann als ausreichend, um auch die schutzwürdigen Interessen der Betroffenen zu wahren.

11. Zu § 5 Abs. 2 Satz 5

Sind schutzwürdige Interessen Betroffener erkannt worden, so reicht das Ermessen von der Feststellung, dass die genannten Interessen bereits durch die Schutzfristen nach § 5 Abs. 2 Sätze 1 bis 3 gewahrt sind, bis dahin, dass vor der allgemeinen Nutzung des Archivgutes zehn Jahre nach dem Tod der Betroffenen oder, falls das Sterbedatum nicht feststellbar ist, 100 Jahre nach deren Geburt vergangen sein müssen. Der Entscheidung selbst ist der Grad der Schutzwürdigkeit der Interessen Betroffener zugrunde zu legen. Die Interessen Betroffener können unterschiedlich schutzwürdig sein, je nachdem, ob im Archivgut der Individual-, der Privat- und Vermögens- oder der Intimbereich berührt wird.

12. Zu § 5 Abs. 4 Nr. 1 und § 6 Abs. 3 Nr. 1

Archivgut, das außerhalb des Sicherheitsbereichs entstanden ist, kann kaum jemals zu Gefährdungen i. S. der o. g. Vorschriften führen. Falls Zweifel bestehen, ob die Nutzung von Archivgut (§ 5) oder die Auskunft aus Archivgut an Betroffene bzw. die Einsichtnahme in Archivgut durch sie (§ 6) dem Wohl des Bundes oder eines Landes Nachteile bereiten würde, wird empfohlen, Stellungnahmen derjenigen Behörden der Gefahrenabwehr, der Strafverfolgung oder des Verfassungsschutzes einzuholen, von denen das Archivgut übernommen wurde.

13. Zu § 5 Abs. 5 Satz 2 Nr. 1

13.1 Die geforderte Gewissheit, dass öffentliche Interessen oder schutzwürdige Interessen Betroffener einer Nutzung von Archivgut vor Ablauf der gesetzlichen Schutzfristen nicht entgegenstehen, kann durch Prüfung des Entstehungszusammenhangs, der Bezeichnung oder des Inhalts des Archivgutes gewonnen werden. Insbesondere Archivgut, das Organisationsregelungen, allgemeine Richtlinien oder Angelegenheiten betrifft, die normalerweise Routinecharakter haben und ohne Verarbeitung persönlicher Daten behandelt werden, kann die Voraussetzung der Vorschrift erfüllen.

13.2 Unter Berücksichtigung dieser Gesichtspunkte entscheidet das im Landesarchiv jeweils zuständige Staatsarchiv im Einzelfall nach pflichtgemäßem Ermessen, ob und zu welchem Zeitpunkt vor Ablauf der gesetzlichen Schutzfristen die Nutzung von bestimmtem Archivgut zugelassen werden kann. Bei der Entscheidung über den Zeitpunkt ist zu berücksichtigen, in welchem Maße die geforderte Gewissheit, dass öffentliche Interessen oder schutzwürdige Interessen Betroffener nicht entgegenstehen, durch objektive Sachverhalte gestützt wird.

14. Zu § 5 Abs. 5 Satz 2 Nr. 2

14.1 Die der wissenschaftlichen Forschung sowie Presse und Rundfunk grundsätzlich eingeräumte Möglichkeit, zur Nutzung von Archivgut vor Ablauf der gesetzlichen Schutzfristen zugelassen zu werden, gründet in dem für sie geltenden besonderen Grundrechtsschutz.

14.2 Wissenschaftlich ist ein Forschungsvorhaben, wenn Personen, die in einem einschlägigen Hochschulstudium ausreichend vorgebildet sind, auf der Grundlage eines von ihnen verarbeiteten Forschungsstandes und ausgehend von einer begründeten Fragestellung weiterführende Erkenntnisse zu gewinnen versuchen. Die ausreichende Vorbildung kann u. a. auch durch Zeugnisse von Hochschullehrerinnen und -lehrern nachgewiesen werden. Eine ausreichende Vorbildung kann im Einzelfall auch im Selbststudium erworben sein; dem Nachweis dienen in diesem Fall insbesondere einschlägige wissenschaftliche Publikationen.

14.3 Presse und Rundfunk erfüllen grundsätzlich öffentliche Aufgaben. Dies wird für die Presse durch das Niedersächsische Pressegesetz, für die öffentlich-rechtlichen Rundfunkanstalten durch die Staatsverträge und Landesgesetze sowie für die privaten Rundfunkanstalten durch das NMedienG klargestellt.

14.4 Die Freiheit von Presse und Rundfunk ist grundsätzlich geschützt. Sie ist jedoch nicht schrankenlos, sondern durch die für die Presse geltende gesetzliche Sorgfaltspflicht sowie durch die für die Rundfunkanstalten gesetzlich festgelegten Programmgrundsätze, Bestimmungen über unzulässige Sendungen und Vorschriften über die Datenverarbeitung für journalistisch-redaktionelle Zwecke eingeschränkt. Beispielsweise ist der Presse gesetzlich aufgegeben, alle Nachrichten vor ihrer Verbreitung mit der nach den Umständen gebotenen Sorgfalt auf Inhalt, Herkunft und Wahrheit zu prüfen. Sie ist verpflichtet, Druckwerke von strafbarem Inhalt freizuhalten. Der Rundfunk ist in seinen Sendungen zur Wahrheit verpflichtet. Insbesondere die Informationssendungen haben den anerkannten journalistischen Grundsätzen zu entsprechen. Sie sind gründlich und gewissenhaft zu recherchieren. Für die privaten Rundfunkanstalten in Niedersachsen gelten bei der Datenverarbeitung für journalistisch-redaktionelle Zwecke die Vorschriften des NDSG über das Datengeheimnis und über die Datensicherung.

14.5 Die folgenden Maßnahmen sind zur Wahrung schutzwürdiger Interessen Betroffener geeignet und im Hinblick auf die beruflichen und gesetzlichen Sorgfaltspflichten des Benutzerkreises in der Regel auch hinreichend:
a) Die schriftliche Erklärung der Benutzerin oder des Benutzers, dass sie oder er aus dem Archivgut gewonnene Kenntnisse über schutzwürdige Daten Betroffener nur im Rahmen des genehmigten Antrags (§ 5 Abs. 1 Satz 1) und lediglich in einer Weise verwenden wird, die keinen Rückschluss auf einzelne Betroffene zulässt.
b) Die ergänzende schriftliche Erklärung der Benutzerin oder des Benutzers, dass sie oder er solche Kenntnisse Dritten nicht übermitteln wird.
c) Die Beschränkung der Nutzung auf Teile des Archivgutes.
d) Die Auflage, auf die Herstellung von Reproduktionen oder Schnellkopien des Archivgutes zu verzichten.

14.6 Das im Landesarchiv jeweils zuständige Staatsarchiv entscheidet im Einzelfall nach pflichtgemäßem Ermessen, ob, zu welchem Zeitpunkt vor Ablauf der gesetzlichen Schutzfristen und unter welchen der in Nummer 14.5 genannten Bedingungen und Auflagen die Nutzung von bestimmtem Archivgut zugelassen werden kann. Bei der Entscheidung über den Zeitpunkt ist zu berücksichtigen, mit welchem Grad an Sicherheit die schutzwürdigen Interessen Betroffener gewahrt werden.

15. Zu § 5 Abs. 7

15.1 Bei jeglicher Art der Nutzung, für die grundsätzlich der Weg der Einsichtnahme in den Benutzerräumen des im Landesarchiv jeweils zuständigen Staatsarchivs, ausnahmsweise und soweit dafür die Voraussetzungen bestehen auch der Verfilmung oder der sonstigen Reproduzierung sowie der Ausleihe offen steht, finden die Verfahrensregeln des § 5 Abs. 1 Satz 1 Anwendung.

15.2 Im Fall der Ausleihe bleibt das alleinige Verfügungsrecht des im Landesarchiv jeweils zuständigen Staatsarchivs über das Archivgut unberührt. Die Ausleihe ist zu befristen. Die nach der Vorschrift Nutzungsberechtigten haben während der Ausleihe die Sicherung des Archivgutes nach § 4 Satz 1 zu gewährleisten.

15.3 Die Nutzung des Archivgutes oder aus diesem entnommener personenbezogener Daten unterliegt außerhalb des durch das NArchG geregelten Bereichs den für den Umgang mit entsprechendem Schriftgut oder mit personenbezogenen Daten geltenden gesetzlichen Bestimmungen.

16. Zu § 5 Abs. 7 Satz 1

Ein weitergehendes gesetzliches Recht auf Nutzung haben beispielsweise die Ermittlungsbehörden und die Strafgerichte.

17. Zu § 5 Abs. 7 Satz 2

Die Freiheit von Nutzungseinschränkungen nach diesem Gesetz gilt sinngemäß auch für unmittelbare Rechts- oder Funktionsnachfolger der genannten Einrichtungen oder Stellen.

18. Zu § 6 Abs. 1 Satz 2

Bei der pflichtgemäßen Wahrnehmung seines Ermessens hat das im Landesarchiv jeweils zuständige Staatsarchiv insbesondere die Frage zu entscheiden, ob die Auskunft schriftlich oder mündlich, mit vollem Zitat oder in einer den Sachverhalt umschreibenden Weise erteilt wird.
Die Entscheidung über die Art der Auskunft hat vor allem sicherzustellen, dass die in § 6 Abs. 3 genannten Sachverhalte, bei deren Vorliegen die Auskunft zu versagen ist, beachtet werden.

19. Zu § 7 Abs. 1 Satz 1

Die in dieser Vorschrift genannte Sicherungspflicht für Archivgut ist analog zu den für das Landesarchiv unmittelbar geltenden Bestimmungen in § 4 und § 1 Abs. 1 zu verstehen. Die Art der jeweiligen Aufgabenerfüllung muss daher grundsätzlich den dort formulierten Vorgaben genügen.

20. Zu § 7 Abs. 1 Satz 3

Die Vorschrift korrespondiert mit der Bestimmung über die Zuständigkeit des Landesarchivs in § 1 Abs. 1 Satz 1 und legt fest, dass das Archivgut im Bereich der mittelbaren Landesverwaltung nach der in § 7 Abs. 1 Satz 1 definierten Sicherungspflicht primär von Archiven zu übernehmen ist, die von den jeweiligen Verwaltungsträgern selbst unterhalten werden oder mit denen diese zusammenarbeiten. Eine Übernahme von Archivgut der in § 7 Abs. 1 Satz 1 genannten Einrichtungen in das im Landesarchiv nach § 3 Abs. 6 jeweils zuständige Staatsarchiv kann daher nur in Ausnahmefällen in Frage kommen, z. B. weil andernfalls unersetzliches wertvolles Archivgut unterzugehen droht oder deutliche Lücken in der archivischen Überlieferung entstehen. Eine derartige Übernahme setzt außerdem voraus, dass ausreichende Magazinkapazitäten vorhanden sind und von der abgebenden Einrichtung ein Entgelt gezahlt wird, das alle durch die Bearbeitung und Unterbringung des jeweiligen Archivgutes anfallenden Kosten abdeckt.

21. Zu § 7 Abs. 3 Satz 1

I.
Die Vorschrift enthebt die in § 7 Abs. 1 Satz 1 genannten Einrichtungen, die eigene Archive unterhalten oder die Abgabe ihres Archivgutes an Archive einer anderen in Absatz 1 Satz 1 genannten Einrichtung geregelt haben, der Notwendigkeit, allein schon zur Erfüllung der in § 17 Abs. 2 Satz 2 NDSG vorgeschriebenen Voraussetzungen für die Abgabe von Archivgut an das zuständige Archiv Satzungen zu erlassen.

II.
Soweit die Landkreise, Gemeinden und die der Aufsicht des Landes unterstehenden anderen Körperschaften, Anstalten und Stiftungen des öffentlichen Rechts sowie deren Vereinigungen nach § 7 Abs. 1 Satz 3 eigene oder gemeinsame Archive unterhalten, wird empfohlen, nach Abschnitt I Nrn. 1 sowie 10 bis 21 zu verfahren. Soweit Hochschulen des Landes Archive unterhalten, wird empfohlen, außerdem nach Abschnitt I Nrn. 3.2 bis 7 zu verfahren.

III.
Die Bezugserlasse werden aufgehoben.
An
das Landesarchiv
die übrigen Dienststellen der Landesverwaltung
die anbietungspflichtigen Stiftungen und übrigen juristischen Personen des Privatrechts
Nachrichtlich:
An die
Landkreise, Gemeinden und der Aufsicht des Landes unterstehenden anderen Körperschaften, Anstalten und Stiftungen des öffentlichen Rechts sowie deren Vereinigungen

Anlagen (nichtamtliches Verzeichnis)[1]
Anlage 1: Muster 1
Anlage 2: Muster 2
Anlage 3: Muster Vereinbarung (§ 3 Abs. 6 Satz 2 des Niedersächsischen Archivgesetzes – NArchG –)
Anlage 4: Muster Vereinbarung (§ 3 Abs. 7 Satz 2 des Niedersächsischen Archivgesetzes – NArchG –)

---

1) Hier nicht abgedruckt.

D9.III.1 Richtlinie Zuwendungen für Kulturdenkmale

Richtlinie über die Gewährung von Zuwendungen zur Erhaltung und Pflege von Kulturdenkmalen

– Im Einvernehmen mit dem MF, dem MI und dem MW –
RL d. MWK v. 11.12.2018 – 35-57701/4 (Nds. MBl. 2019 S. 312)
(VORIS 22510)

1. Zuwendungszweck, Rechtsgrundlage

1.1

Das Land gewährt Zuwendungen für Maßnahmen, die der Erhaltung und Pflege von Kulturdenkmalen dienen.

Die Gewährung der Zuwendung erfolgt nach Maßgabe des § 32 des Niedersächsischen Denkmalschutzgesetzes (im Folgenden: NDSchG), der §§ 23 und 44 LHO einschließlich der dazu ergangenen Verwaltungsvorschriften (VV/VV-Gk) und der §§ 48, 49 und 49a VwVfG i.V.m. § 1 Abs. 1 NVwVfG sowie unter Beachtung der Verordnung (EU) Nr. 651/2014 der Kommission vom 17.6.2014 zur Feststellung der Vereinbarkeit bestimmter Gruppen von Beihilfen mit dem Binnenmarkt in Anwendung der Artikel 107 und 108 des Vertrags über die Arbeitsweise der Europäischen Union – sog. Allgemeine Gruppenfreistellungsverordnung, im Folgenden: AGVO – (ABl. EU Nr. L 187 S. 1, Nr. L 283 S. 65), geändert durch Verordnung (EU) 2017/1084 der Kommission vom 14.6.2017 (ABl. EU Nr. L 156 S. 1), und der Verordnung (EU) Nr. 1407/2013 der Kommission vom 18.12.2013 über die Anwendung der Artikel 107 und 108 des Vertrags über die Arbeitsweise der Europäischen Union auf De-minimis-Beihilfen (ABl. EU Nr. L 352 S. 1) – im Folgenden: De-minimis-Verordnung – in der jeweils geltenden Fassung sowie dieser Richtlinie.

1.2

Eine Beteiligung der Gebietskörperschaften an der Denkmalförderung ist anzustreben.

1.3

Ein Anspruch des Antragstellers auf Gewährung der Zuwendung besteht nicht, vielmehr entscheidet die Bewilligungsbehörde aufgrund ihres pflichtgemäßen Ermessens nach Maßgabe der verfügbaren Haushaltsmittel.

2. Gegenstand der Förderung

2.1

Gefördert werden die im Rahmen von Sicherungs-, Instandsetzungs- und Unterhaltungsmaßnahmen an Kulturdenkmalen allein oder überwiegend aus Gründen der Denkmalpflege erforderlichen Ausgaben (denkmalbedingte Aufwendungen).
Zu den förderfähigen Ausgaben gehören insbesondere auch
- Ausgaben für die Wiederherstellung von teilzerstörten Kulturdenkmalen, wenn hierbei auf ausreichende originale Substanz zurückgegriffen wird,
- Ausgaben für den denkmalgerechten Ersatz von Bauteilen,
- Kosten einer baugeschichtlichen oder restauratorischen Untersuchung und Dokumentation,
- Architekten- und Ingenieurhonorare,
- Ausgaben für die Darstellung der denkmalpflegerischen Bedeutung eines Kulturdenkmals,
- Ausgaben für die Erforschung und Erhaltung des archäologischen Erbes.

2.2

Nicht gefördert werden
- der Erwerb eines Kulturdenkmals,
- Maßnahmen, bei denen die Voraussetzungen für den Einsatz von Städtebauförderungsmitteln vorliegen.

3. Zuwendungsempfängerinnen und Zuwendungsempfänger

3.1

Eine Zuwendung kann erhalten
- die oder der Erhaltungspflichtige eines Kulturdenkmals (§ 6 NDSchG),
- eine für die Erhaltungspflichtige oder den Erhaltungspflichtigen tätige juristische oder natürliche Person.

3.2

Zuwendungen werden nicht gewährt an das Land Niedersachsen, den Bund (einschließlich Sondervermögen), ein anderes Bundesland, einen ausländischen Staat sowie deren jeweilige Körperschaften, Anstalten und Stiftungen des öffentlichen Rechts. Gleiches gilt für juristische Personen des Privatrechts, an denen eine der in Satz 1 genannten Gebietskörperschaften bzw. Institutionen zu mehr als 25 % beteiligt ist.

3.3

Unternehmen bzw. Einrichtungen, die einer Rückforderungsanordnung aufgrund eines früheren Beschlusses der Europäischen Kommission zur Feststellung der Unzulässigkeit einer von demselben Mitgliedstaat gewährten Beihilfe und ihrer Unvereinbarkeit mit dem Binnenmarkt nicht nachgekommen sind, dürfen keine Einzelbeihilfen gewährt werden (Artikel 1 Nr. 4a AGVO). Eine Zuwendung ist in den Fallgruppen des Artikels 1 Abs. 2 bis 5 AGVO ausgeschlossen.

4. Zuwendungsvoraussetzungen

4.1

Die Maßnahme muss den fachlichen Anforderungen der Denkmalbehörden entsprechen, insbesondere sind die denkmalfachlichen Auflagen in der Baugenehmigung oder der Genehmigung gemäß dem NDSchG zu beachten.

4.2

Zuwendungen, die als Beihilfen nach der AGVO gewährt werden, müssen den Voraussetzungen des Kapitels I AGVO (insbesondere den Anmeldeschwellen des Artikels 4 AGVO) und den Voraussetzungen des Artikels 53 AGVO genügen.

4.3

Zuwendungen, die als De-minimis-Beihilfe ausgesprochen werden, müssen die Voraussetzungen der De-minimis-Verordnung einhalten (insbesondere Geltungsbereich, Höchstgrenze, Erfordernis der transparenten Beihilfe, Kumulierung und Überwachung).

5. Art und Umfang, Höhe der Zuwendung

5.1

Die Zuwendung wird als nicht rückzahlbarer Zuschuss in Form einer Festbetragsfinanzierung zur Projektförderung gewährt. In begründeten Ausnahmefällen kann die Zuwendung auch als Fehlbedarfs- oder Anteilsfinanzierung gewährt werden.

5.2

Der Festbetrag soll in der Regel bis zu 30 % der gemäß Nummer 2.1 förderfähigen Ausgaben betragen. In begründeten Ausnahmefällen darf die Zuwendung höher sein. Zuwendungen an Gebietskörperschaften sollen nur bewilligt werden, wenn die Zuwendung im Einzelfall mehr als 25 000 EUR beträgt. Im Übrigen liegt die Mindestgrenze grundsätzlich bei 3 000 EUR.

5.3

Sofern es sich bei der Zuwendung um eine Beihilfe nach der AGVO handelt, darf der Beihilfebetrag nicht höher sein als die Differenz zwischen den beihilfefähigen Kosten und dem Betriebsgewinn der Investition. Der Betriebsgewinn wird vorab, auf der Grundlage realistischer Projektionen oder über einen Rückforderungsmechanismus von den beihilfefähigen Kosten abgezogen. Der Betreiber der Infrastruktur darf einen angemessenen Gewinn für den betreffenden Zeitraum einbehalten. Alternativ kann bei Beihilfen von nicht mehr als 2 Mio. EUR der Beihilfehöchstbetrag auf 80 % der beihilfefähigen Kosten festgesetzt werden (Artikel 53 Abs. 6 bis 8 AGVO).

5.4

Die Zuwendung darf nach Artikel 8 AGVO kumuliert werden mit anderen staatlichen Beihilfen, sofern diese Maßnahmen unterschiedliche bestimmbare beihilfefähige Kosten betreffen, sowie mit anderen Beihilfen für dieselben, sich teilweise oder vollständig überschneidenden beihilfefähigen Kosten, jedoch nur, wenn durch diese Kumulierung der höchste nach der AGVO für diese Beihilfen geltende Beihilfebetrag nicht überschritten wird.

6. Sonstige Zuwendungsbestimmungen

6.1

Die Zuwendungsempfängerin oder der Zuwendungsempfänger hat die Landesförderung mit der jeweils gültigen Wort-Bild-Marke des Landes Niedersachsen öffentlich kenntlich zu machen.

6.2

Auf die Berichterstattungspflichten des Niedersächsischen Landesamtes für Denkmalpflege als Bewilligungsbehörde nach den Artikeln 9, 11 und 12 AGVO wird hingewiesen. Informationen über jede Einzelbeihilfe von über 500 000 EUR werden auf einer ausführlichen Beihilfe-Website veröffentlicht. Erhaltene Förderungen können im Einzelfall von der Europäischen Kommission geprüft werden.

7. Anweisungen zum Verfahren

7.1

Für die Bewilligung, Auszahlung und Abrechnung der Zuwendung sowie für den Nachweis und die Prüfung der Verwendung und die ggf. erforderliche Aufhebung des Zuwendungsbescheides und die Rückforderung der gewährten Zuwendung gelten die VV/VV-Gk zu § 44 LHO, soweit nicht in dieser Richtlinie Abweichungen zugelassen worden sind.

7.2

Bewilligungsbehörde ist das Niedersächsische Landesamt für Denkmalpflege. Die untere und die oberste Denkmalschutzbehörde erhalten jeweils eine Durchschrift des Zuwendungsbescheides.

7.3

Anträge sind unter Beifügung der für die denkmalpflegerische Beurteilung erforderlichen Unterlagen sowie eines Kosten- und Finanzierungsplans über die untere Denkmalschutzbehörde beim Niedersächsischen Landesamt für Denkmalpflege zu stellen. Formblätter sind bei der unteren Denkmalschutzbehörde erhältlich. Kirchengemeinden reichen den Antrag auf ihrem Dienstweg beim Niedersächsischen Landesamt für Denkmalpflege ein.

7.4

Die jeweilige Auswahl der zu fördernden Vorhaben und die Festlegung der Fördersummen für Baudenkmale im Einzelfall erfolgen grundsätzlich durch den Qualitätszirkel des Niedersächsischen Landesamtes für Denkmalpflege.

7.5

Es wird ein einfacher Verwendungsnachweis nach Nummer 6.6 ANBest-P und ANBest-Gk zugelassen.

8. Schlussbestimmungen

Dieser RdErl. tritt am 1.1.2019 in Kraft und mit Ablauf des 31.12.2023 außer Kraft.

Verordnung über Zuständigkeiten im Bereich des Kulturgutschutzes (ZustVO-Kulturgutschutz)

Vom 29. August 2017 (Nds. GVBl. S. 274)
(VORIS 22510)

Aufgrund des § 5 Abs. 1 Satz 1 des Niedersächsischen Gesetzes über Verordnungen und Zuständigkeiten vom 22. Oktober 2014 (Nds. GVBl. S. 291) wird verordnet:

§ 1

(1) Die Staatskanzlei ist zuständig für die Aufgaben nach dem Kulturgutschutzgesetz (KGSG) in Bezug auf Kulturgut, das Archivgut im Sinne des § 2 Abs. 2 des Niedersächsischen Archivgesetzes ist (archivisches Kulturgut), soweit nicht eine Behörde des Bundes zuständig ist.

(2) Das für Kultur zuständige Ministerium ist zuständig für die Aufgaben nach dem Kulturgutschutzgesetz in Bezug auf nicht archivisches Kulturgut, soweit weder eine Behörde des Bundes noch nach Absatz 3 das Landesamt für Denkmalpflege zuständig ist.

(3) Das Landesamt für Denkmalpflege ist in Bezug auf nicht archivisches Kulturgut
1. zuständig für die Genehmigung der vorübergehenden Ausfuhr von nationalem Kulturgut nach § 22 KGSG,
2. zuständig für die Genehmigung der Ausfuhr von Kulturgut nach § 24 KGSG,
3. zuständige Behörde für das Benehmen nach § 27 Abs. 1 KGSG,
4. zuständig für die Sicherstellung von Kulturgut und die damit in Zusammenhang stehenden Aufgaben nach den §§ 33 bis 35 und 37 bis 39 KGSG und
5. zuständig für die Zusammenarbeit mit den Zollbehörden nach § 81 Abs. 1, 3 und 5 KGSG, soweit ein Zusammenhang mit einer Aufgabe nach den Nummern 1 bis 4 besteht.

(4) Das Landesamt für Denkmalpflege unterstützt das für Kultur zuständige Ministerium bei der Erfüllung von dessen Aufgaben nach § 61 KGSG.

§ 2

Diese Verordnung tritt am Tag nach ihrer Verkündung[1] in Kraft.

---

1) Verkündet am 5.9.2017.

Verfassung für das Land Nordrhein-Westfalen

Vom 28. Juni 1950 (GV. NRW. S. 127)
(SGV. NRW. 100)
zuletzt geändert durch Art. 1 ÄndG vom 11. April 2019 (GV. NRW. S. 202)
– Auszug –

Zweiter Teil
Von den Grundrechten und der Ordnung des Gemeinschaftslebens

Dritter Abschnitt
Schule, Kunst und Wissenschaft, Sport, Religion und Religionsgemeinschaften

Artikel 18 [Kultur, Kunst, Wissenschaft und Sport]
(1) Kultur, Kunst und Wissenschaft sind durch Land und Gemeinden zu pflegen und zu fördern.
(2) Die Denkmäler der Kunst, der Geschichte und der Kultur, die Landschaft und Naturdenkmale stehen unter dem Schutz des Landes, der Gemeinden und Gemeindeverbände.
[…]

D10.I.1 Denkmalschutzgesetz Nordrhein-Westfalen

Gesetz zum Schutz und zur Pflege der Denkmäler im Lande Nordrhein-Westfalen[1]) (Denkmalschutzgesetz – DSchG)

Vom 11. März 1980 (GV. NRW. S. 226)
(SGV. NRW. 224)
zuletzt geändert durch Art. 5 G zum Schutz der Natur in Nordrhein-Westfalen und zur Änd. anderer Vorschriften vom 15. November 2016 (GV. NRW. S. 934)

Nichtamtliche Inhaltsübersicht

§ 1	Aufgaben des Denkmalschutzes und der Denkmalpflege
§ 2	Begriffsbestimmungen
§ 3	Denkmalliste
§ 4	Vorläufiger Schutz
§ 5	Unterschutzstellung von Denkmalbereichen
§ 6	Verfahren bei der Unterschutzstellung von Denkmalbereichen
§ 7	Erhaltung von Denkmälern
§ 8	Nutzung von Baudenkmälern und ortsfesten Bodendenkmälern
§ 9	Erlaubnispflichtige Maßnahmen
§ 10	Veräußerungs- und Veränderungsanzeige
§ 11	Schutz der Bodendenkmäler
§ 12	Erlaubnisvorbehalt
§ 13	Ausgrabungen
§ 14	Grabungsschutzgebiete
§ 15	Entdeckung von Bodendenkmälern
§ 16	Verhalten bei der Entdeckung von Bodendenkmälern
§ 17	Schatzregal
§ 18	*[aufgehoben]*
§ 19	Sonderregelung bei Maßnahmen zur Gewinnung von Bodenschätzen
§ 20	Denkmalbehörden
§ 21	Zuständigkeit der Denkmalbehörden
§ 22	Denkmalpflege
§ 23	Beiräte
§ 24	Beauftragte für Denkmalpflege
§ 25	Denkmalpflegeplan
§ 26	Erlaubnisverfahren
§ 27	Wiederherstellung des ursprünglichen Zustandes
§ 28	Auskunfts- und Betretungsrecht
§ 29	Kostentragung und Gebührenfreiheit
§ 30	Enteignung
§ 31	Übernahme von Denkmälern
§ 32	(aufgehoben)
§ 33	Entschädigung
§ 34	*[aufgehoben]*
§ 35	Leistungen
§ 36	Denkmalförderungsprogramm
§ 37	Städtebauförderung, Wohnungsmodernisierung
§ 38	Denkmäler, die der Religionsausübung dienen
§ 39	Schutz bei Katastrophen
§ 40	Bescheinigungen für steuerliche Zwecke
§ 41	Bußgeldvorschriften
§ 42	Verwaltungsvorschriften
§ 43	Inkrafttreten, Berichtspflicht

Der Landtag hat das folgende Gesetz beschlossen, das hiermit verkündet wird:

§ 1 Aufgaben des Denkmalschutzes und der Denkmalpflege

(1) ¹Denkmäler sind zu schützen, zu pflegen, sinnvoll zu nutzen und wissenschaftlich zu erforschen. ²Sie sollen der Öffentlichkeit im Rahmen des Zumutbaren zugänglich gemacht werden.

(2) Denkmalschutz und Denkmalpflege obliegen dem Land, den Gemeinden und Gemeindeverbänden nach näherer Bestimmung dieses Gesetzes.

(3) ¹Bei öffentlichen Planungen und Maßnahmen sind die Belange des Denkmalschutzes unter der Denkmalpflege angemessen zu berücksichtigen.[2]) ²Die für den Denkmalschutz und die Denkmalpflege zuständigen Behörden sind frühzeitig einzuschalten und so mit dem Ziel in die Abwägung mit anderen Belangen einzubeziehen, daß die Erhaltung und Nutzung der Denkmäler und Denkmalbereiche sowie eine angemessene Gestaltung ihrer Umgebung möglich sind. ³Ihrerseits wirken Denkmalschutz und Denkmalpflege darauf hin, daß die Denkmäler in die Raumordnung und Landesplanung, die städtebauliche Entwicklung und die Landespflege einbezogen und einer sinnvollen Nutzung zugeführt werden.

---

1) Siehe auch die Verwaltungsvorschrift zur Ausführung des DSchG, abgedruckt als Nr. D10.I.1d.
2) Vgl. den Runderlass zur Berücksichtigung des Bodendenkmalschutzes bei der Umweltverträglichkeitsprüfung in Verfahren zur Zulassung oder Genehmigung von Abgrabungen und in bergrechtlichen Planfeststellungsverfahren, abgedruckt als Nr. D10.I.1e.

§ 2 Begriffsbestimmungen

(1) ¹Denkmäler sind Sachen, Mehrheiten von Sachen und Teile von Sachen, an deren Erhaltung und Nutzung ein öffentliches Interesse besteht. ²Ein öffentliches Interesse besteht, wenn die Sachen bedeutend für die Geschichte des Menschen, für Städte und Siedlungen oder für die Entwicklung der Arbeits- und Produktionsverhältnisse sind und für die Erhaltung und Nutzung künstlerische, wissenschaftliche, volkskundliche oder städtebauliche Gründe vorliegen. ³Die Vorschriften des Landesnaturschutzgesetzes bleiben unberührt.

(2) ¹Baudenkmäler sind Denkmäler, die aus baulichen Anlagen oder Teilen baulicher Anlagen bestehen.[1)] ²Ebenso zu behandeln sind Garten-, Friedhofs- und Parkanlagen sowie andere von Menschen gestaltete Landschaftsteile, wenn sie die Voraussetzungen des Absatzes 1 erfüllen. ³Historische Ausstattungsstücke sind wie Baudenkmäler zu behandeln, sofern sie mit dem Baudenkmal eine Einheit von Denkmalwert bilden.

(3) ¹Denkmalbereiche sind Mehrheiten von baulichen Anlagen, und zwar auch dann, wenn nicht jede dazugehörige einzelne bauliche Anlage die Voraussetzungen des Absatzes 1 erfüllt. ²Denkmalbereiche können Stadtgrundrisse, Stadt-, Ortsbilder und -silhouetten, Stadtteile und -viertel, Siedlungen, Gehöftgruppen, Straßenzüge, bauliche Gesamtanlagen und Einzelbauten sein sowie deren engere Umgebung, sofern sie für deren Erscheinungsbild bedeutend ist. ³Hierzu gehören auch handwerkliche und industrielle Produktionsstätten, sofern sie die Voraussetzungen des Absatzes 1 erfüllen.

(4) Bewegliche Denkmäler sind alle nicht ortsfesten Denkmäler.

(5) ¹Bodendenkmäler sind bewegliche oder unbewegliche Denkmäler, die sich im Boden befinden oder befanden. ²Als Bodendenkmäler gelten auch Zeugnisse tierischen und pflanzlichen Lebens aus erdgeschichtlicher Zeit, ferner Veränderungen und Verfärbungen in der natürlichen Bodenbeschaffenheit, die durch nicht mehr selbständig erkennbare Bodendenkmäler hervorgerufen worden sind, sofern sie die Voraussetzungen des Absatzes 1 erfüllen.

(6) Auf Archivgut finden die Vorschriften dieses Gesetzes keine Anwendung.

§ 3 Denkmalliste

(1) ¹Denkmäler sind getrennt nach Baudenkmälern, ortsfesten Bodendenkmälern und beweglichen Denkmälern in die Denkmalliste einzutragen; bewegliche Denkmäler sind nur einzutragen, wenn dies wegen ihrer besonderen Bedeutung, die auch in einem historisch begründeten Ortsbezug liegen kann, angebracht erscheint. ²Mit der Eintragung oder der vorläufigen Unterschutzstellung unterliegen sie den Vorschriften dieses Gesetzes. ³Werden bewegliche Denkmäler von einer öffentlichen Einrichtung betreut, so bedürfen sie nicht der Eintragung in die Denkmalliste; sie unterliegen gleichwohl den Vorschriften dieses Gesetzes. ⁴Die Vorschriften der §§ 1 Abs. 3, 11, 13 bis 17, 19, 28 und 29 gelten unabhängig von der Eintragung der Bodendenkmäler in die Denkmalliste.

(2) ¹Die Denkmalliste wird von der Unteren Denkmalbehörde geführt. ²Die Eintragung erfolgt im Benehmen mit dem Landschaftsverband von Amts wegen oder auf Antrag des Eigentümers oder des Landschaftsverbandes.

(3) Über die Eintragung ist ein Bescheid zu erteilen.

(4) Die Eintragung ist von Amts wegen zu löschen, wenn die Eintragungsvoraussetzungen nicht mehr vorliegen.

(5) ¹Die Denkmalliste steht hinsichtlich der Eintragung von Baudenkmälern und ortsfesten Bodendenkmälern jedermann zur Einsicht offen. ²Hinsichtlich der Eintragung von beweglichen Denkmälern ist die Einsicht nur dem Eigentümer und den sonst dinglich Berechtigten oder von ihnen besonders Ermächtigten gestattet.

(6) Der für die Denkmalpflege zuständige Minister wird ermächtigt, durch Rechtsverordnung[2)] die näheren Bestimmungen über Form und Führung der Denkmalliste sowie das Eintragungs- und Löschungsverfahren zu treffen.

§ 4 Vorläufiger Schutz

(1) Ist damit zu rechnen, daß ein Denkmal in die Denkmalliste eingetragen wird, so soll die Untere Denkmalbehörde anordnen, daß das Denkmal vorläufig als eingetragen gilt.

---

1) Der RdErl. zur Denkmalplakette des Landes Nordrhein-Westfalen ist abgedruckt als Nr. D10.I.1c.
2) Die Verordnung über die Führung der Denkmalliste ist abgedruckt als Nr. D10.I.1a.

(2) ¹Die Anordnung ist den Eigentümern oder den sonstigen Nutzungsberechtigten zuzustellen. ²Sie verliert ihre Wirksamkeit, wenn nicht innerhalb von sechs Monaten das Verfahren zur Eintragung in die Denkmalliste eingeleitet wird.
(3) Bis zum 1. Januar 1985 gilt Absatz 2 mit der Maßgabe, daß die Frist von sechs Monaten entfällt.

§ 5 Unterschutzstellung von Denkmalbereichen
(1) ¹Denkmalbereiche werden durch Satzung der Gemeinde, die der Genehmigung der Oberen Denkmalbehörde bedarf, unter Schutz gestellt. ²Mit der Unterschutzstellung unterliegt der Denkmalbereich den Vorschriften dieses Gesetzes.
(2) ¹In der Satzung ist das Gebiet zu bezeichnen, in dem Maßnahmen gemäß § 9 erlaubnispflichtig sind. ²Es ist anzugeben, aus welchen Gründen das Gebiet als Denkmalbereich festgesetzt wird. ³Dabei sollen Pläne oder zeichnerische, photographische oder photogrammetrische Darstellungen der zu schützenden Silhouette, der baulichen Abfolge der Stadt- oder Ortsbilder, Gesamtanlagen oder Einzelbauten mit der für ihr Erscheinungsbild notwendigen Umgebung (Freiräume, Freiflächen, Sichtbezüge) beigefügt werden. ⁴Der Plan oder die Darstellung ist zum Bestandteil der Satzung zu erklären. ⁵Der Satzung ist das Gutachten des Landschaftsverbandes gemäß § 22 Abs. 3 nachrichtlich beizufügen.
(3) Die Genehmigung darf nur versagt werden, wenn
a) die Satzung nicht ordnungsgemäß zustande gekommen ist,
b) die Satzung diesem Gesetz, den auf Grund dieses Gesetzes erlassenen oder sonstigen Rechtsvorschriften widerspricht oder
c) die Festlegungen zur Erfüllung der Ziele dieses Gesetzes nicht ausreichen.
(4) ¹Erläßt die Gemeinde innerhalb eines angemessenen Zeitraumes keine entsprechende Satzung, so fordert die Obere Denkmalbehörde sie auf, die Satzung innerhalb von drei Monaten vorzulegen. ²Nach Ablauf der Frist kann die Obere Denkmalbehörde Denkmalbereiche durch ordnungsbehördliche Verordnung unter Schutz stellen. ³Die Verordnung ist aufzuheben, sobald eine rechtsverbindliche Satzung vorliegt.

§ 6 Verfahren bei der Unterschutzstellung von Denkmalbereichen
(1) ¹Die Gemeinde hat den Entwurf der Satzung zur Unterschutzstellung von Denkmalbereichen für die Dauer eines Monats öffentlich auszulegen. ²Ort und Dauer der Auslegung sind mindestens eine Woche vorher ortsüblich mit dem Hinweis darauf bekanntzumachen, daß Bedenken und Anregungen während der Auslegungsfrist vorgebracht werden können.
(2) ¹Nach Ablauf der Auslegungsfrist sind der Entwurf der Satzung sowie die vorgebrachten Bedenken und Anregungen mit dem Landschaftsverband zu erörtern. ²Soweit den Bedenken und Anregungen nicht entsprochen wird, teilt die Gemeinde ihre Stellungnahme hierzu den Einsendern schriftlich mit. ³Bei der Vorlage der Satzung zur Genehmigung durch die Obere Denkmalbehörde sind die nichtberücksichtigten Bedenken und Anregungen mit einer Stellungnahme der Gemeinde beizufügen.
(3) ¹Die Gemeinde hat die genehmigte Satzung öffentlich auszulegen. ²Sie hat unter Hinweis auf die Genehmigung Ort und Zeit der Auslegung ortsüblich bekanntzumachen. ³Mit der Bekanntmachung tritt die Satzung in Kraft.
(4) Denkmalbereiche können auch in einem Bebauungsplan festgesetzt werden; auf diese Festsetzungen sind die Vorschriften des Bundesbaugesetzes anzuwenden.

§ 7 Erhaltung von Denkmälern
(1) ¹Die Eigentümer und sonstigen Nutzungsberechtigten haben ihre Denkmäler instand zu halten, instand zu setzen, sachgemäß zu behandeln und vor Gefährdung zu schützen, soweit ihnen das zumutbar ist. ²Für die Zumutbarkeit ist auch zu berücksichtigen, inwieweit Zuwendungen aus öffentlichen Mitteln oder steuerliche Vorteile in Anspruch genommen werden können. ³Die Eigentümer und sonstigen Nutzungsberechtigten können sich nicht auf Belastungen durch erhöhte Erhaltungskosten berufen, die dadurch verursacht worden sind, daß Erhaltungsmaßnahmen diesem Gesetz oder sonstigem öffentlichen Recht zuwider unterblieben sind.
(2) Soweit die Eigentümer und sonstigen Nutzungsberechtigten den Verpflichtungen nach Absatz 1 nicht nachkommen, kann die Untere Denkmalbehörde nach deren Anhörung die notwendigen Anordnungen treffen.

§ 8 Nutzung von Baudenkmälern und ortsfesten Bodendenkmälern
(1) Baudenkmäler und ortsfeste Bodendenkmäler sind so zu nutzen, daß die Erhaltung der Substanz auf Dauer gewährleistet ist.
(2) ¹Wird ein Baudenkmal oder ortsfestes Bodendenkmal nicht oder auf eine die erhaltenswerte Substanz gefährdende Weise genutzt und ist dadurch eine Schädigung zu befürchten, so kann die Untere Denkmalbehörde Eigentümer und sonstige Nutzungsberechtigte verpflichten, das Baudenkmal oder das ortsfeste Bodendenkmal in bestimmter, ihnen zumutbarer Weise zu nutzen. ²Den Verpflichteten ist auf Antrag zu gestatten, das Baudenkmal in einer angebotenen anderen Weise zu nutzen, wenn seine Erhaltung dadurch hinreichend gewährleistet und die Nutzung mit dem öffentlichen Recht vereinbar ist.

§ 9 Erlaubnispflichtige Maßnahmen
(1) Der Erlaubnis der Unteren Denkmalbehörde bedarf, wer
a) Baudenkmäler oder ortsfeste Bodendenkmäler beseitigen, verändern, an einen anderen Ort verbringen oder die bisherige Nutzung ändern will,
b) in der engeren Umgebung von Baudenkmälern oder ortsfesten Bodendenkmälern Anlagen errichten, verändern oder beseitigen will, wenn hierdurch das Erscheinungsbild des Denkmals beeinträchtigt wird, oder
c) bewegliche Denkmäler beseitigen oder verändern will.
(2) Die Erlaubnis ist zu erteilen, wenn
a) Gründe des Denkmalschutzes nicht entgegenstehen oder
b) ein überwiegendes öffentliches Interesse die Maßnahme verlangt.
(3) ¹Erfordert eine erlaubnispflichtige Maßnahme nach anderen gesetzlichen Bestimmungen eine Planfeststellung, Genehmigung, Erlaubnis, Bewilligung, Zulassung oder Zustimmung, so haben die dafür zuständigen Behörden die Belange des Denkmalschutzes und der Denkmalpflege entsprechend diesem Gesetz in angemessener Weise zu berücksichtigen. ²Im Falle einer bauaufsichtlichen oder immissionsschutzrechtlichen Genehmigung oder Zustimmung kann die Erlaubnis nach Absatz 1 auch gesondert beantragt werden.

§ 10 Veräußerungs- und Veränderungsanzeige
(1) ¹Wird ein Denkmal veräußert, so haben der frühere und der neue Eigentümer den Eigentumswechsel unverzüglich, spätestens jedoch innerhalb eines Monats, der Unteren Denkmalbehörde anzuzeigen. ²Die Anzeige eines Pflichtigen befreit den anderen.
(2) Wird ein bewegliches Denkmal an einen anderen Ort verbracht, so hat der Eigentümer oder sonstige Nutzungsberechtigte dies der Unteren Denkmalbehörde innerhalb eines Monats anzuzeigen.

§ 11 Schutz der Bodendenkmäler
Die Gemeinden, Kreise und Flurbereinigungsbehörden haben die Sicherung der Bodendenkmäler bei der Bauleitplanung, der Landschaftsplanung und der Aufstellung von Flurbereinigungsplänen zu gewährleisten.

§ 12 Erlaubnisvorbehalt
Für Eingriffe in Bodendenkmäler gilt § 9 entsprechend.

§ 13 Ausgrabungen
(1) ¹Wer nach Bodendenkmälern graben oder Bodendenkmäler aus einem Gewässer bergen will, bedarf hierzu der Erlaubnis der Oberen Denkmalbehörde. ²Ausgenommen sind Nachforschungen, die unter der Verantwortung des Landes, des Landschaftsverbandes oder der Stadt Köln (§ 22 Abs. 5) stattfinden.
(2) Die Erlaubnis ist zu erteilen, wenn die beabsichtigte Grabung oder Bergung Bodendenkmäler oder die Erhaltung von Quellen für die Forschung nicht gefährdet.
(3) ¹Die Erlaubnis kann mit Auflagen und unter Bedingungen erteilt werden, die die Planung und Ausführung der Grabung oder Bergung, die Leitung durch vorgebildete Fachkräfte, die Behandlung und Sicherung der Bodenfunde, die Dokumentation der Grabungsfunde, die Berichterstattung und die abschließende Herrichtung der Grabungsstätte betreffen. ²Sie kann auch unter der Bedingung erteilt werden, daß die Ausführung nach einem von der Oberen Denkmalbehörde gebilligten Plan erfolgt.

§ 14 Grabungsschutzgebiete

(1) [1]Die Obere Denkmalbehörde kann bestimmte Grundstücke, die nachweislich oder nach der Überzeugung von Sachverständigen Bodendenkmäler enthalten, durch ordnungsbehördliche Verordnung im Benehmen mit dem Landschaftsverband oder der Stadt Köln (§ 22 Abs. 5) für drei Jahre zu Grabungsschutzgebieten erklären; die Frist kann angemessen verlängert werden, soweit die Bedeutung der Bodendenkmäler dies erfordert. [2]Wenn in dem betreffenden Gebiet dem Bergrecht unterliegende Mineralien anstehen, ist das Einvernehmen mit dem Landesoberbergamt Nordrhein-Westfalen herbeizuführen.

(2) [1]In der Verordnung sind die Maßnahmen zu bezeichnen, die einer Erlaubnis bedürfen. [2]Die Erlaubnis erteilt die Obere Denkmalbehörde. [3]Auf die Erlaubnis findet § 9 Abs. 2 bis 4 Anwendung.

§ 15 Entdeckung von Bodendenkmälern

(1) [1]Wer in oder auf einem Grundstück ein Bodendenkmal entdeckt, hat dies der Gemeinde oder dem Landschaftsverband unverzüglich anzuzeigen. [2]Die Gemeinde hat unverzüglich den Landschaftsverband zu benachrichtigen. [3]Dieser unterrichtet die Obere Denkmalbehörde.

(2) [1]Zur Anzeige verpflichtet sind auch der Eigentümer und die sonstigen Nutzungsberechtigten sowie der Leiter der Arbeiten, bei denen das Bodendenkmal entdeckt worden ist, sobald sie von der Entdeckung erfahren. [2]Absatz 1 gilt entsprechend. [3]Die Anzeige eines Verpflichteten befreit die übrigen.

§ 16 Verhalten bei der Entdeckung von Bodendenkmälern

(1) Die zur Anzeige Verpflichteten haben das entdeckte Bodendenkmal und die Entdeckungsstätte in unverändertem Zustand zu erhalten.

(2) [1]Die Verpflichtung gemäß Absatz 1 erlischt drei Werktage nach Zugang der Anzeige, bei schriftlicher Anzeige spätestens eine Woche nach deren Absendung. [2]Die Obere Denkmalbehörde kann die Frist von drei Werktagen verlängern, wenn die sachgerechte Untersuchung oder die Bergung des Bodendenkmals dies erfordert. [3]Ist ein Bodendenkmal bei laufenden Arbeiten entdeckt worden, so soll die Frist von drei Werktagen nur überschritten werden, wenn der Betroffene hierdurch nicht wirtschaftlich unzumutbar belastet wird.

(3) Die Verpflichtung nach Absatz 1 erlischt vor Ablauf von drei Werktagen mit
a) dem Abschluß der Untersuchung oder Bergung durch den Landschaftsverband oder die Stadt Köln (§ 22 Abs. 5) oder
b) der Freigabe durch die Obere Denkmalbehörde im Benehmen mit dem Landschaftsverband oder der Stadt Köln (§ 22 Abs. 5).

(4) [1]Das Land und der Landschaftsverband oder die Stadt Köln (§ 22 Abs. 5) sind berechtigt, das Bodendenkmal zu bergen, auszuwerten und für wissenschaftliche Erforschung bis zu sechs Monaten in Besitz zu nehmen. [2]Dabei sind alle zur Erhaltung des Bodendenkmals notwendigen Maßnahmen zu treffen. [3]Die Obere Denkmalbehörde kann die Frist verlängern, wenn dies zur Erhaltung des Bodendenkmals oder für seine wissenschaftliche Erforschung erforderlich ist.

§ 17 Schatzregal

(1) [1]Bewegliche Denkmäler und bewegliche Bodendenkmäler sowie Funde von besonderer wissenschaftlicher Bedeutung, die herrenlos sind oder die solange verborgen waren, dass der Eigentümer nicht mehr zu ermitteln ist, werden mit der Entdeckung Eigentum des Landes. [2]Sie sind unverzüglich an die Untere Denkmalbehörde oder das Denkmalpflegeamt zu melden und zu übergeben.

(2) [1]Denjenigen, die ihrer Ablieferungspflicht nachkommen, soll eine angemessene Belohnung in Geld gewährt werden, die sich am wissenschaftlichen Wert des Fundes orientiert. [2]Ist die Entdeckung bei unerlaubten Nachforschungen gemacht worden, sollte von der Gewährung einer Belohnung abgesehen werden. [3]Über die Gewährung der Belohnung und ihre Höhe entscheidet im Einzelfall die Oberste Denkmalbehörde im Einvernehmen mit dem örtlich zuständigen Denkmalpflegeamt.

§ 18 *[aufgehoben]*

§ 19 Sonderregelung bei Maßnahmen zur Gewinnung von Bodenschätzen

(1) Auf Bodendenkmäler in Gebieten, in denen nach den Zielen der Raumordnung und Landesplanung bergbauliche Maßnahmen oder Maßnahmen nach dem Abgrabungsgesetz vorgesehen sind, finden – soweit die Gebiete hierfür in Anspruch genommen werden – mit Beginn dieser Maßnahme die §§ 14, 25 und 30 keine Anwendung.

(2) ¹Rechtzeitig vor Beginn der Maßnahmen ist dem Landschaftsverband oder der Stadt Köln (§ 22 Abs. 5) Gelegenheit zur fachwissenschaftlichen Untersuchung von vermuteten Bodendenkmälern oder zu deren Bergung zu geben. ²Hierzu sind dem Landschaftsverband oder der Stadt Köln (§ 22 Abs. 5) rechtzeitig alle einschlägigen Planungen sowie deren Änderungen bekanntzugeben. ³Die erforderlichen Arbeiten sind so vorzunehmen, daß keine unzumutbaren Behinderungen bei der Durchführung der Maßnahmen entstehen.
(3) Bei der Zulassung bergrechtlicher Betriebspläne haben die Bergbehörden das Benehmen mit dem Landschaftsverband oder der Stadt Köln (§ 22 Abs. 5) herbeizuführen.
(4) Während des Abbaues ist dem Landschaftsverband oder der Stadt Köln (§ 22 Abs. 5) die Möglichkeit einzuräumen, alle Abbaukanten und Bodenaufschlüsse laufend auf zutage tretende Bodendenkmäler zu überprüfen, diese archäologisch zu untersuchen und zu bergen.

§ 20 Denkmalbehörden
(1) Denkmalbehörden sind
1. Oberste Denkmalbehörde:
   der für die Denkmalpflege zuständige Minister;
2. Obere Denkmalbehörde:
   die Regierungspräsidenten für die kreisfreien Städte, im übrigen die Oberkreisdirektoren als untere staatliche Verwaltungsbehörden;
3. Untere Denkmalbehörden:
   die Gemeinden.

(2) Die Kreise sind zur Beratung der Unteren Denkmalbehörden verpflichtet, soweit diese nicht Große oder Mittlere kreisangehörige Städte sind.
(3) ¹Die Denkmalbehörden sind Sonderordnungsbehörden. ²Die ihnen nach diesem Gesetz obliegenden Aufgaben gelten als solche der Gefahrenabwehr.

§ 21 Zuständigkeit der Denkmalbehörden
(1) Soweit nicht durch Gesetz oder auf Grund eines Gesetzes etwas anderes bestimmt ist, sind die Unteren Denkmalbehörden für den Vollzug dieses Gesetzes zuständig.
(2) ¹Örtlich zuständig ist die Denkmalbehörde, in deren Bezirk sich das Denkmal befindet. ²Im Zweifel entscheidet die nächsthöhere Denkmalbehörde über die Zuständigkeit. ³Bei Bodendenkmälern richtet sich die örtliche Zuständigkeit nach der Entdeckungsstätte; bei Gefahr im Verzuge kann auch die Denkmalbehörde Anordnungen erlassen, in deren Bezirk sich das Bodendenkmal befindet.
(3) Ist der Bund oder das Land Nordrhein-Westfalen als Eigentümer oder Nutzungsberechtigter eines Denkmals betroffen, entscheidet anstelle der Unteren Denkmalbehörde der Regierungspräsident.
(4) ¹Die Unteren und Oberen Denkmalbehörden treffen ihre Entscheidungen im Benehmen mit dem Landschaftsverband. ²Das Benehmen gilt als hergestellt, wenn der Denkmalbehörde nicht innerhalb von drei Monaten eine Äußerung des Landschaftsverbandes vorliegt. ³Will die Denkmalbehörde von der Äußerung des Landschaftsverbandes abweichen, so hat der Landschaftsverband das Recht, unmittelbar die Entscheidung der Obersten Denkmalbehörde herbeizuführen. ⁴§ 22 Abs. 5 gilt entsprechend.

§ 22 Denkmalpflege
(1) ¹Die Denkmalpflege obliegt den Gemeinden und Gemeindeverbänden als Selbstverwaltungsaufgabe. ²§ 20 bleibt unberührt.
(2) Die Landschaftsverbände beraten und unterstützen die Gemeinden und Kreise in der Denkmalpflege und wirken fachlich bei den Entscheidungen der Denkmalbehörden mit.
(3) Die Landschaftsverbände nehmen im Rahmen der Denkmalpflege durch Denkmalpflegeämter insbesondere folgende Aufgaben wahr:
1. Fachliche Beratung und Erstattung von Gutachten in allen Angelegenheiten des Denkmalschutzes und der Denkmalpflege,
2. wissenschaftliche Untersuchung und Erforschung der Denkmäler sowie deren Veröffentlichung und wissenschaftliche Behandlung der Fragen von Methodik und Praxis der Denkmalpflege,
3. Konservierung und Restaurierung von Denkmälern sowie fachliche Überwachung dieser Maßnahmen,

D10.I.1 Denkmalschutzgesetz Nordrhein-Westfalen

4. wissenschaftliche Ausgrabungen, Bergung und Restaurierung von Bodendenkmälern, Überwachung dieser Maßnahmen sowie Erfassung der beweglichen Bodendenkmäler,
5. Bewirtschaftung der ihnen vom Land bereitgestellten Mittel für die Denkmalpflege,
6. Wahrnehmung der Interessen der Denkmalpflege bei Planungen und sonstigen Maßnahmen der Gemeinden und Gemeindeverbände oder anderer öffentlicher Stellen als Träger öffentlicher Belange,
7. Beratung bei der Vorbereitung von Erhaltungs- und Gestaltungssatzungen.

(4) Die Denkmalpflegeämter sind bei der Erstellung von Gutachten an fachliche Weisungen nicht gebunden; sie sind berechtigt, ihre Gutachten an diejenigen Personen, Behörden und sonstigen Stellen zu übermitteln, die ein berechtigtes Interesse nachweisen.

(5) Für ihr Gebiet nimmt die Stadt Köln anstelle des Landschaftsverbandes Rheinland die Aufgaben der Bodendenkmalpflege wahr.

§ 23 Beiräte

(1) Zur Vertretung der Belange der Denkmalpflege können bei der Obersten Denkmalbehörde ein Landesdenkmalrat gebildet sowie die anerkannten Denkmalpflegeorganisationen angehört werden.

(2) [1]Bei jeder Unteren Denkmalbehörde ist ein Ausschuß ihrer Vertretung für die Aufgaben nach diesem Gesetz zu bestimmen. [2]Die Vertretung bestimmt durch Satzung, ob ein Denkmalausschuß gebildet oder welchem anderen Ausschuß diese Aufgabe zugewiesen wird. [3]In der Satzung soll die Möglichkeit vorgesehen werden, daß an Beratungen von Aufgaben nach diesem Gesetz zusätzlich für die Denkmalpflege sachverständige Bürger mit beratender Stimme teilnehmen.

§ 24 Beauftragte für Denkmalpflege

(1) Die Untere Denkmalbehörde kann im Benehmen mit dem Landschaftsverband ehrenamtliche Beauftragte für Denkmalpflege bestimmen.

(2) Werden für ein Gemeindegebiet mehrere ehrenamtliche Beauftragte für Denkmalpflege berufen, so sollen deren Aufgabenbereiche nach regionalen oder fachlichen Gesichtspunkten abgegrenzt werden.

(3) [1]Der Beauftragte für Denkmalpflege wird für die Dauer von fünf Jahren berufen. [2]Die Wiederberufung ist zulässig.

(4) [1]Die ehrenamtlichen Beauftragten für Denkmalpflege werden gutachtlich tätig. [2]Sie haben insbesondere folgende Aufgaben:
1. Vermittlung von Informationen, Hinweisen und Auskünften an den Ausschuß gemäß § 23 Abs. 2, die Untere Denkmalbehörde und den Landschaftsverband,
2. Beobachtung der örtlichen Vorhaben, Planungen, Vorgänge und Presseberichterstattung, von denen die Interessen der Denkmalpflege berührt werden, sowie
3. Pflege von Verbindungen zu Institutionen und Personen, die der Denkmalpflege Verständnis entgegenbringen oder ihr förderlich sein können.

§ 25 Denkmalpflegeplan

(1) Die Gemeinden sollen Denkmalpflegepläne aufstellen und fortschreiben.

(2) [1]Der Denkmalpflegeplan gibt die Ziele und Erfordernisse des Denkmalschutzes und der Denkmalpflege sowie die Darstellungen und Festsetzungen in der Bauleitplanung nachrichtlich wieder. [2]Er enthält
1. die Bestandsaufnahme und Analyse des Gebietes der Gemeinde unter siedlungsgeschichtlichen Gesichtspunkten,
2. die Darstellung der Bau- und Bodendenkmäler, der Denkmalbereiche, der Grabungsschutzgebiete sowie – nachrichtlich – der erhaltenswerten Bausubstanz und
3. ein Planungs- und Handlungskonzept zur Festlegung der Ziele und Maßnahmen, mit denen der Schutz, die Pflege und die Nutzung von Denkmälern im Rahmen der Stadtentwicklung verwirklicht werden sollen.

§ 26 Erlaubnisverfahren

(1) Der Antrag auf Erteilung einer Erlaubnis nach diesem Gesetz ist schriftlich mit den zur Beurteilung des Vorhabens erforderlichen Unterlagen bei der zuständigen Denkmalbehörde einzureichen.

(2) ¹Eine Erlaubnis nach diesem Gesetz erlischt, wenn nicht innerhalb von zwei Jahren nach ihrer Erteilung mit der Durchführung des Vorhabens begonnen oder wenn die Durchführung zwei Jahre unterbrochen worden ist. ²Die Frist kann verlängert werden.

§ 27 Wiederherstellung des ursprünglichen Zustandes
(1) Wer eine Handlung, die nach diesem Gesetz der Erlaubnis bedarf, ohne Erlaubnis, unsachgemäß oder im Widerspruch zu Auflagen durchführt, muß auf Verlangen der Unteren Denkmalbehörde die Arbeiten sofort einstellen und den bisherigen Zustand wiederherstellen.
(2) Wer widerrechtlich ein Denkmal vorsätzlich oder fahrlässig beschädigt oder zerstört, ist auf Verlangen der Unteren Denkmalbehörde verpflichtet, das Zerstörte wiederherzustellen.
(3) Im übrigen finden die Vorschriften des Ordnungsbehördengesetzes Anwendung.

§ 28 Auskunfts- und Betretungsrecht
(1) Eigentümer und sonstige Nutzungsberechtigte von Denkmälern sind verpflichtet, den Denkmalbehörden und den Landschaftsverbänden die zur Durchführung dieses Gesetzes erforderlichen Auskünfte zu erteilen.
(2) ¹Die Denkmalbehörden und Denkmalpflegeämter sind berechtigt, nicht eingefriedete Grundstücke und, nach vorheriger Benachrichtigung, eingefriedete Grundstücke und Gebäude und Wohnungen zu betreten, um Denkmäler festzustellen, zu besichtigen oder zu untersuchen, soweit es zur Erfüllung der sich aus diesem Gesetz ergebenden Aufgaben erforderlich ist. ²Die Denkmalbehörden und Denkmalpflegeämter können insbesondere verlangen, rechtzeitig vor Beginn eines Eingriffs Gelegenheit zur fachwissenschaftliehen Untersuchung von Denkmälern oder zu deren Bergung zu erhalten. ³Hierzu sind ihnen rechtzeitig alle einschlägigen Planungen sowie deren Änderungen bekanntzugeben. ⁴Die Arbeiten der Denkmalpflegeämter und Unteren Denkmalbehörden haben so zu erfolgen, dass keine unzumutbaren Behinderungen bei der Durchführung des Vorhabens entstehen.
(3) ¹Das Betreten von Wohnungen ist ohne Einwilligung des Eigentümers oder sonstigen Nutzungsberechtigten nur bei Gefahr im Verzuge oder auf Grund richterlicher Anordnung zulässig. ²Für das Verfahren gelten die Vorschriften des Gesetzes über das Verfahren in Familiensachen und in den Angelegenheiten der freiwilligen Gerichtsbarkeit entsprechend. ³Das Grundrecht der Unverletzlichkeit der Wohnung (Artikel 13 des Grundgesetzes) wird insoweit eingeschränkt.
(4) Bei allen Maßnahmen ist Rücksicht auf die Betroffenen zu nehmen; für die durch die Ausübung dieser Rechte entstehenden Schäden ist Ersatz zu leisten.

§ 29 Kostentragung und Gebührenfreiheit
(1) ¹Wer einer Erlaubnis nach § 9 Abs. 1 oder einer Entscheidung nach § 9 Abs. 3 bedarf oder in anderer Weise ein eingetragenes Denkmal oder ein eingetragenes oder vermutetes Bodendenkmal verändert oder beseitigt, hat die vorherige wissenschaftliche Untersuchung, die Bergung von Funden und die Dokumentation der Befunde sicherzustellen und die dafür anfallenden Kosten im Rahmen des Zumutbaren zu tragen. ²In der Erlaubnis nach § 9 Abs. 1 oder der Entscheidung nach § 9 Abs. 3 wird das Nähere durch Nebenbestimmungen, in anderen Fällen durch Verwaltungsakt der unteren Denkmalbehörde geregelt.
(2) ¹In den Fällen des Absatzes 1 kann bestimmt werden, dass der oder die Betroffene die voraussichtlichen Kosten im Voraus zu zahlen hat. ²Zahlt der oder die Betroffene die voraussichtlichen Kosten der Erlaubnis nicht fristgerecht, so können sie im Verwaltungszwangsverfahren beigetrieben werden.
(3) Für weitere Amtshandlungen nach diesem Gesetz werden Gebühren nicht erhoben; dies gilt nicht für Entscheidungen nach den §§ 13, 14 und 40.

§ 30 Enteignung
(1) Baudenkmäler und ortsfeste Bodendenkmäler können enteignet werden, wenn allein dadurch
a) ein Denkmal in seinem Bestand, seiner Eigenart oder seinem Erscheinungsbild erhalten werden kann,
b) ein Denkmal der Allgemeinheit zugänglich gemacht werden kann, sofern hieran ein öffentliches Interesse besteht, oder
c) in einem Grabungsschutzgebiet planmäßige Nachforschungen betrieben werden können.
(2) Das Enteignungsrecht steht dem Land oder einer anderen juristischen Person des öffentlichen Rechts zu; es steht ferner einer juristischen Person des Privatrechts zu, wenn und soweit der Enteignungszweck zu den in der Satzung niedergelegten Aufgaben gehört.

D10.I.1 Denkmalschutzgesetz Nordrhein-Westfalen

(3) ¹Das Landesenteignungs- und -entschädigungsgesetz (EEG NRW) ist anzuwenden. ²Über die Zulassung der Enteignung entscheidet die Oberste Denkmalbehörde.

§ 31 Übernahme von Denkmälern
¹Der Eigentümer kann die Übernahme eines Denkmals durch die Gemeinde verlangen, wenn und soweit es ihm mit Rücksicht auf seine Pflicht zur Erhaltung des Denkmals auf Grund einer behördlichen Maßnahme nach diesem Gesetz wirtschaftlich nicht zuzumuten ist, das Denkmal zu behalten oder es in der bisherigen oder einer anderen zulässigen Art zu nutzen.[1] ²Im übrigen finden die Bestimmungen des § 30 entsprechende Anwendung.

§ 32 *[aufgehoben]*

§ 33 Entschädigung
¹Soweit der Vollzug dieses Gesetzes enteignende Wirkung hat, ist eine angemessene Entschädigung in Geld zu gewähren. ²Das Landesenteignungs- und -entschädigungsgesetz (EEG NRW) ist anzuwenden.

§ 34 *[aufgehoben]*

§ 35 Leistungen[2]
(1) ¹Leistungen nach diesem Gesetz werden aus Mitteln des Landes, der Gemeinden und Gemeindeverbände erbracht. ²Die Förderung der Pflege von Denkmälern setzt den Antrag des Eigentümers voraus.
(2) ¹Die Förderung erfolgt in Form von Zuschüssen, Darlehen und Zinszuschüssen. ²Die Leistungsfähigkeit des Eigentümers wird bei Festsetzung der Beteiligung bzw. Förderung des Landes berücksichtigt.
(3) ¹Landesmittel werden gewährt als
1. Pauschalzuweisungen an die Gemeinden und Gemeindeverbände zur Förderung privater Denkmalpflegemaßnahmen,
2. Einzelzuschüsse zur Förderung von Denkmälern, die im Eigentum von Gemeinden oder Gemeindeverbänden stehen,
3. Einzelzuschüsse für Denkmäler, die im Eigentum von Kirchen oder Religionsgemeinschaften stehen,
4. Einzelzuschüsse für größere private Denkmalpflegemaßnahmen.

²Die Höhe der Pauschalzuweisungen an die Gemeinden soll sich an der Bedeutung des Denkmälerbestandes und am Umfang der Denkmalpflegemaßnahmen ausrichten.
(4) Es können auch Denkmalpflegeorganisationen, gemeinnützige Träger und Einzelpersonen gefördert werden, die denkmalpflegerische Aufgaben wahrnehmen.
(5) Führt die Beteiligung öffentlicher Hände an den Kosten des Denkmalschutzes und der Denkmalpflege zu einer Wertsteigerung des Denkmals, so haben Eigentümer und Nutzungsberechtigte den diesbezüglichen Aufwand zu ersetzen, soweit ihnen dieses zugemutet werden kann.

§ 36 Denkmalförderungsprogramm
(1) ¹Die Regierungspräsidenten bereiten jährlich im Benehmen mit den Landschaftsverbänden und, soweit die Bodendenkmalpflege der Stadt Köln betroffen ist, mit dieser das Denkmalförderungsprogramm für das folgende Jahr vor. ²Das Programm enthält die Aufstellung aller beabsichtigten Maßnahmen sowie deren Kosten und Finanzierung.
(2) ¹Die Regierungspräsidenten legen das vorbereitete Denkmalförderungsprogramm der Obersten Denkmalbehörde vor. ²Diese beteiligt die Kirchen und Religionsgemeinschaften wegen der Einbeziehung ihrer Denkmäler. ³Sie stellt das Denkmalförderungsprogramm auf.

§ 37 Städtebauförderung, Wohnungsmodernisierung
¹Baudenkmäler und Denkmalbereiche können auch nach den Vorschriften des Bundes und des Landes über den Einsatz von Städtebau- und Wohnungsmodernisierungsmitteln erhalten, erneuert und einer funktionsgerechten Nutzung zugeführt werden. ²Die Landschaftsverbände wirken hierbei im Rahmen ihrer Aufgaben als Träger öffentlicher Belange mit.

---

1) Der RdErl. zum Verfahren bei Übernahmeverlangen gemäß § 31 DSchG ist abgedruckt als Nr. D10.I.1b.
2) Die Richtlinien über die Gewährung von Zuwendungen für Denkmalschutz und Denkmalpflege sind abgedruckt als Nr. D10.III.3.

§ 38 Denkmäler, die der Religionsausübung dienen

¹Mit den Kirchen und Religionsgemeinschaften soll die Zusammenarbeit bei Schutz und Pflege ihrer Denkmäler fortgesetzt werden. ²Bei Entscheidungen über diese Denkmäler haben die Denkmalbehörden die von den Kirchen und Religionsgemeinschaften festgestellten Belange der Religionsausübung zu beachten.

§ 39 Schutz bei Katastrophen

(1) ¹Der Kultusminister wird ermächtigt, durch Rechtsverordnung im Einvernehmen mit dem Innenminister die zum Schutz der Denkmäler für den Fall von Katastrophen erforderlichen Vorschriften zu erlassen. ²Dabei können insbesondere der Eigentümer und die sonstigen Nutzungsberechtigten verpflichtet werden,

a) den Aufbewahrungsort von Denkmälern zu melden,
b) Denkmäler mit den in internationalen Verträgen vorgesehenen Kennzeichen versehen zu lassen,
c) Denkmäler zu bergen, besonders zu sichern, bergen oder besonders sichern zu lassen oder sie zum Zwecke der vorübergehenden Verwahrung an Bergungsorten auf Anordnung der Denkmalbehörde abzuliefern,
d) die wissenschaftliche Erfassung von Denkmälern oder sonstige zu ihrer Dokumentierung, Sicherung oder Wiederherstellung von der Denkmalbehörde angeordnete Maßnahmen zu dulden.

(2) Soweit in der Rechtsverordnung eine Ablieferungsfrist vorgesehen wird, ist anzuordnen, daß die abgelieferten Sachen unverzüglich den Berechtigten zurückzugeben sind, sobald die weitere Verwahrung an einem Bergungsort zum Schutz der Denkmäler nicht mehr erforderlich ist.

§ 40 Bescheinigungen für steuerliche Zwecke

¹Bescheinigungen für die Erlangung von Steuervergünstigungen werden von der Unteren Denkmalbehörde im Benehmen mit dem Landschaftsverband ausgestellt. ²Sie dürfen nur erteilt werden, wenn das Denkmal in die Denkmalliste eingetragen ist oder gemäß § 4 Abs. 1 und 2 als vorläufig eingetragen gilt.

§ 41 Bußgeldvorschriften

(1) Ordnungswidrig handelt, wer vorsätzlich oder fahrlässig
1. eine Anzeige nach §§ 10 oder 15 Abs. 1 Satz 1 oder Abs. 2 Satz 1 nicht oder nicht rechtzeitig erstattet,
2. Maßnahmen, die nach § 9 Abs. 1, §§ 12, 13 Abs. 1 Satz 1 oder § 14 Abs. 2 Satz 1 der Erlaubnis bedürfen, ohne Erlaubnis oder abweichend von ihr durchführt oder durchführen läßt,
3. entdeckte Bodendenkmäler oder die Entdeckungsstätte nicht nach § 16 Abs. 1 unverändert läßt,
4. einer nach § 39 erlassenen Rechtsverordnung zuwiderhandelt, sofern die Rechtsverordnung für einen bestimmten Tatbestand auf diese Bußgeldvorschrift verweist.

(2) ¹Die Ordnungswidrigkeiten können mit Geldbußen bis zu 250 000 Euro geahndet werden. ²Wird ohne Erlaubnis nach § 9 Abs. 1 Buchstabe a ein Baudenkmal beseitigt, kann eine Geldbuße bis zu 500 000 Euro festgesetzt werden.

(3) Die Verfolgung der Ordnungswidrigkeit verjährt in fünf Jahren.

(4) Zuständige Behörde im Sinne des § 36 Abs. 1 Nr. 1 des Gesetzes über Ordnungswidrigkeiten ist die Untere Denkmalbehörde.

§ 42 Verwaltungsvorschriften

Der für die Denkmalpflege zuständige Minister erläßt die zur Ausführung dieses Gesetzes erforderlichen Verwaltungsvorschriften.

§ 43 Inkrafttreten, Berichtspflicht

¹Dieses Gesetz tritt am 1. Juli 1980 in Kraft. ²Die §§ 3 Abs. 6, 5, 6, 34 Abs. 9, 39 und 42 treten am Tage nach der Verkündung[1]) in Kraft. ³Die Landesregierung berichtet dem Landtag bis zum 31. Dezember 2018 über die Notwendigkeit und Zweckmäßigkeit dieses Gesetzes.

---

1) Verkündet am 29.3.1980.

D10.I.1a Denkmallisten-Verordnung

Verordnung über die Führung der Denkmalliste (Denkmallisten-Verordnung)[1]

Vom 13. März 2015 (GV. NRW. S. 430)
(SGV. NRW. 224)
zuletzt geändert durch Art. 1 ÄndVO vom 2. März 2016 (GV. NRW. S. 196)

Auf Grund des § 3 Absatz 6 des Denkmalschutzgesetzes vom 11. März 1980 (GV. NRW. S. 226, ber. S. 716), der durch § 51 des Gesetzes vom 20. Juni 1989 (GV. NRW. S. 366) geändert worden ist, verordnet das Ministerium für Wohnen, Bauen, Stadtentwicklung und Verkehr des Landes Nordrhein-Westfalen:

§ 1 Form der Denkmalliste

(1) ¹Die Denkmalliste gliedert sich in folgende Teile:
1. Teil A: die Liste der Baudenkmäler,
2. Teil B: die Liste der ortsfesten Bodendenkmäler,
3. Teil C: die Liste der beweglichen Denkmäler und
4. Teil D: die Liste der Denkmalbereiche, die durch Satzung, Bebauungsplan oder ordnungsbehördliche Verordnung den Vorschriften des Denkmalschutzes unterliegen.

²Die Denkmalbereiche sollen mindestens in ihren Begrenzungen digitalisiert und georeferenziert werden. ³Sie sind in der Liste zu führen.

(2) ¹Die Denkmalliste wird in digitaler Form mit in jedem Teil der Liste fortlaufender Nummerierung geführt. ²Für jedes Denkmal ist ein eigener Datensatz anzulegen.

(3) ¹Für Altdaten, die vor Inkrafttreten dieser Verordnung erstellt wurden, ist eine schrittweise Digitalisierung des Bestandes im Rahmen der personellen und finanziellen Möglichkeiten der Unteren Denkmalbehörden anzustreben. ²Dabei gewährleisten die die Denkmallisten führenden Stellen soweit möglich, dass der analoge Altdatenbestand bis zum Jahr 2020 in digitaler Form veröffentlicht wird.

§ 2 Inhalt der Denkmalliste

(1) Die Denkmalliste ist aktuell zu halten und muss folgende Angaben enthalten:
1. die eindeutige Nummerierung des Denkmals, bestehend aus einer Kombination des amtlichen Gemeindeschlüssels und einer von der Gemeinde vergebenen laufenden Nummer,
2. die Kurzbezeichnung des Denkmals,
3. die lagemäßige Bezeichnung des Denkmals mit direkter Georeferenzierung (Koordinate im Koordinatenreferenzsystem ETRS89/UTM) oder mindestens der Zuordnung zum Flurstück oder der Adresse (Gemeinde, Straßenname und Hausnummernbezeichnung) oder der Grundbuchbezeichnung,
4. die Darstellung der wesentlichen charakteristischen Merkmale des Denkmals in Text, Bild und Plan; die Bildauswahl, sowie bei ortsfesten Bau- und Bodendenkmälern die Auswahl des Planmaterials, soll mit parzellenscharfer Abgrenzung und mit Blick auf die Anforderungen unter Nummer 3 und 5 erfolgen und diese hinreichend unterstützen,
5. die Begründung der Denkmaleigenschaft anhand der gesetzlichen Tatbestandsmerkmale gemäß § 2 Absatz 1 des Denkmalschutzgesetztes des Landes Nordrhein-Westfalen vom 11. März 1980 (GV. NRW. S. 226, ber. S. 716), das zuletzt durch das Gesetz vom 16. Juli 2013 (GV. NRW. S. 488) geändert worden ist, und
6. den Tag der Eintragung des Denkmals.

(2) Bei Denkmalbereichen kann anstelle der Angaben nach Absatz 1 auf die Satzung, den Bebauungsplan oder die Verordnung Bezug genommen werden.

(3) Der Denkmalliste können nachrichtliche Angaben beigefügt werden.

(4) Die Untere Denkmalbehörde unterrichtet das zuständige Denkmalpflegeamt über jede Eintragung und Fortschreibung.

(5) Soweit der inhaltliche und räumliche Umfang des Denkmals sowie die Begründung der Denkmaleigenschaft in ihren wesentlichen Aussagen unverändert bleiben, sind Ergänzungen und Präzisierungen des Eintragungstextes auch ohne Verwaltungsakt möglich.

---

[1] Die VO **tritt mit Ablauf des 31.12.2020 außer Kraft**; vgl. § 8 Satz 2.

§ 3 Eintragungsverfahren

(1) [1]Die Untere Denkmalbehörde teilt ihre Absicht, ein Denkmal in die Denkmalliste einzutragen oder einen Antrag auf Eintragung abzulehnen, dem zuständigen Denkmalpflegeamt mit. [2]Eine Äußerung des Eigentümers oder Nutzungsberechtigten ist dem zuständigen Denkmalpflegeamt mitzuteilen. [3]In Fällen des § 3 Absatz 2 Satz 2 des Denkmalschutzgesetzes erfolgt die Mitteilung nach Satz 1 innerhalb einer angemessenen Frist, spätestens jedoch innerhalb von drei Monaten nach Antragstellung.

(2) [1]Beabsichtigt die Untere Denkmalbehörde eine von der Äußerung des Denkmalpflegeamtes abweichende Entscheidung zu erlassen, so teilt sie dies dem Denkmalpflegeamt unverzüglich unter Angabe von Gründen im Sinne des § 2 Absatz 1 des Denkmalschutzgesetzes mit. [2]Ersucht das Denkmalpflegeamt nicht innerhalb von zwei Monaten ab Mitteilung nach Satz 1 um die Entscheidung der Obersten Denkmalbehörde (§ 21 Absatz 4 Satz 3 Denkmalschutzgesetz NRW), so entscheidet die Untere Denkmalbehörde.

§ 4 Denkmäler des Landes Nordrhein-Westfalen und des Bundes

(1) [1]Ist das Land Nordrhein-Westfalen oder der Bund Eigentümer oder Nutzungsberechtigter eines Denkmals oder von Teilen eines Denkmals, führt die jeweils zuständige Bezirksregierung das Verfahren nach § 3 anstelle der Unteren Denkmalbehörde durch. [2]Bei der Sachverhaltsaufklärung und der Anhörung der Beteiligten kann sie sich der Hilfe der Unteren Denkmalbehörden bedienen. [3]Die Bezirksregierung erteilt den Bescheid gemäß § 3 Absatz 3 des Denkmalschutzgesetzes.

(2) Die Untere Denkmalbehörde ist von beabsichtigten Eintragungen zu unterrichten.

(3) Die Bezirksregierung teilt der Unteren Denkmalbehörde mit, dass die Eintragung in die Denkmalliste vorzunehmen ist.

§ 5 Veröffentlichung

(1) [1]Die Denkmalliste wird von der für die Führung zuständigen Unteren Denkmalbehörde zur Nutzung amtlich bereitgestellt und verbreitet. [2]Durch die Bereitstellung wird die Einsicht in die Denkmalliste sowie die Erteilung von Auskünften und Auszügen ermöglicht. [3]Insbesondere sollen hierzu Geodatendienste nach § 3 Absatz 3 des Geodatenzugangsgesetzes vom 17. Februar 2009 (GV. NRW. S. 84) eingesetzt werden. [4]Die Unversehrtheit des Originaldatenbestandes ist ständig zu gewährleisten. [5]Die Nutzung der bereitgestellten Denkmalliste darf nur unter Einhaltung der Nutzungsbedingungen mit Zustimmung der zuständigen Behörde erfolgen, die auch die Urheber- und Leistungsschutzrechte an den Inhalten der Denkmalliste innehat.

(2) Die die Denkmallisten führenden Stellen gewährleisten die Erleichterung des Informationszugangs, beispielsweise durch
1. die Benennung von Ansprechpartnern und
2. die Einrichtung öffentlich zugänglicher Informationsnetze und Datenbanken.

(3) Soweit die Veröffentlichung einzelner Datensätze der digitalen Denkmallisten nachteilige Auswirkungen hat auf
1. die internationalen Beziehungen, die Verteidigung oder bedeutsame Schutzgüter der öffentlichen Sicherheit oder
2. die Durchführung eines laufenden Gerichtsverfahrens, den Anspruch einer Person auf ein faires Verfahren oder die Durchführung strafrechtlicher, ordnungswidrigkeitenrechtlicher oder disziplinarrechtlicher Ermittlungen

ist von einer Veröffentlichung dieser Datensätze abzusehen.

(4) [1]Ebenso ist von einer Veröffentlichung abzusehen, wenn diese den Zustand und die Erhaltung des Denkmals und seiner Bestandteile im Sinne der §§ 2 und 7 des Denkmalschutzgesetzes beeinträchtigt. [2]Die Regelung hierzu erfolgt im Rahmen der Benehmensherstellung mit den Denkmalpflegeämtern gem. § 3 Absatz 2 des Denkmalschutzgesetzes. [3]Nutzer dieser Datensätze haben ihr berechtigtes Interesse nachzuweisen.

(5) [1]Soweit durch die Veröffentlichung der digitalen Denkmallisten personenbezogene Daten offenbart und dadurch die Interessen der Betroffenen erheblich beeinträchtigt würden, ist von der Veröffentlichung dieser Datensätze im Einzelfall abzusehen, es sei denn, die Betroffenen haben eingewilligt oder es überwiegt ein erhebliches öffentliches Interesse an der Veröffentlichung. [2]Die Wahrung von Rechten Dritter (zum Beispiel Bildrechte, Autorenrechte) bleibt von der Denkmallistenverordnung unberührt.

(6) Nach Maßgabe dieser Rechtsverordnung dürfen neben den für die Führung der Denkmalliste zuständigen Behörden in deren Auftrag auch andere behördliche Stellen Aufgaben nach Absatz 1 und 2 wahrnehmen.

§ 6 Löschung
Für die Löschung gelten § 2 Absatz 4, § 3 und § 4 entsprechend.

§ 7 Interkommunale Zusammenarbeit
Bei der Umsetzung dieser Verordnung sollen die Möglichkeiten der interkommunalen Zusammenarbeit genutzt werden.

§ 8 Inkrafttreten, Außerkrafttreten
[1]Diese Verordnung tritt am Tag nach der Verkündung[1]) in Kraft. [2]Sie tritt mit Ablauf des 31. Dezember 2020 außer Kraft.

---

1) Verkündet am 12.5.2015.

Verfahren bei Übernahmeverlangen gemäß § 31 DSchG

RdErl. d. Ministers für Landes- und Stadtentwicklung vom 16. März 1984 (MBl. NW. S. 854)

Die Regelung des § 31 Denkmalschutzgesetz – DSchG – vom 11. März 1980 (GV. NW. S. 226/ SGV.NW. 224) hat in einzelnen Gemeinden die Befürchtung ausgelöst, die Unterschutzstellung eines Denkmals könne für sie finanzielle Folgewirkungen haben, die geeignet seien, in den kommunalen Selbstverwaltungsbereich einzugreifen. Dies hat dazu geführt, daß Gebäude deren Denkmalwert unumstritten ist, noch nicht unter Schutz gestellt worden sind.

Um derartigen Befürchtungen entgegenzutreten und die bisher im allgemeinen zügig vorgenommene Unterschutzstellung denkmalwerter Objekte nicht zu verzögern, wird das Verfahren bei Übernahmeverlangen gem. § 31 DSchG geregelt. Hierbei ist von folgenden Grundsätzen auszugehen:

- Einerseits muß jede Gemeinde bereit sein, finanzielle Aufwendungen für den Schutz der Denkmäler in ihrem Gebiet zu leisten (Art. 18 Verfassung für das Land Northein-Westfalen, § 1 Abs. 2 DSchG). Hierbei ist jedoch zu berücksichtigen, daß die Gemeindefinanzen gesund bleiben müssen (§ 8 GO) und die stetige Aufgabenerfüllung der Gemeinde gesichert sein muß (§ 62 GO).
- Andererseits hat das Land eine besondere Erhaltungs-, Nutzungs- und Erforschungspflicht gegenüber Denkmälern, die bedeutend sind für die allgemeine, die Kultur-, die Wirtschafts- oder die Baugeschichte des Landes unter besonderer Berücksichtigung ihrer landschaftlichen Ausprägung (Art. 18 Verfassung für das Land Nordrhein-Westfalen, § 1 Abs. 2 DSchG).

Ich bitte daher folgendes zu beachten:

1. Die Gemeinden werden gebeten, dem Minister für Landes- und Stadtentwicklung unverzüglich auf dem Dienstwege zu berichten, wenn Denkmaleigentümer von ihnen die Übernahme eines Denkmal gem. § 31 DSchG verlangen und die Gemeinde das Übernahmeverlangen zwar für berechtigt hält, sie aber der Auffassung ist, die Übernahme des Denkmals sei ihr nicht zuzumuten. Die Gründe für die Unzumutbarkeit sind darzulegen. Dabei ist insbesondere auf die Finanzkraft der Gemeinde im Verhältnis zu den durch die Übernahme des Denkmals entstehenden Kosten und Folgekosten sowie sonstigen aus der Denkmaleigenschaft folgenden Verpflichtungen abzustellen.
2. Ist das Übernahmeverlangen des Denkmaleigentümers berechtigt und ist der Gemeinde die Übernahme des Denkmals nicht zuzumuten, so wird das Land – vertreten durch den Minister für Landes- und Stadtentwicklung – in einer Vereinbarung mit der Gemeinde regeln, wie diese die aus § 31 DSchG folgende Übernahmepflicht erfüllt.
   In der Vereinbarung ist festzulegen, daß bei einem Erwerb des Denkmals durch die Gemeinde das Land die Gemeinde durch Zuwendung zum Erwerb sowie zur Erhaltung und Nutzung des Denkmals so weit unterstützt, daß der Gemeinde die Übernahme zugemutet werden kann. Will die Gemeinde das Denkmal nicht auf Dauer behalten, so wird das Land die Gemeinde auf deren Wunsch bei der Suche nach einem geeigneten Erwerber des Denkmals unterstützen. Ausnahmsweise kann auch das Land das Denkmal erwerben und die Gemeinde von der Übernahmepflicht gem. § 31 DSchG freistellen.

Im Einvernehmen mit dem Innen- und Finanzminister.

D10.I.1c Denkmalplakette

Denkmalplakette des Landes Nordrhein-Westfalen

RdErl. d. Ministers für Stadtentwicklung, Wohnen und Verkehr vom 5. Mai 1988 (MBl. NW. S. 696)

1. Nach Inkrafttreten des Denkmalschutzgesetzes am 1. Juli 1980 sind bis Ende 1987 rund 46.000 Denkmäler unter Schutz gestellt worden. Damit haben neben den Gemeinden und den Landschaftsverbänden insbesondere die Denkmaleigentümer großes Verständnis und hohe Verantwortung für die Bewahrung des kulturellen Erbes in Nordrhein-Westfalen bewiesen. Als Anerkennung für die im allgemeinen Interesse übernommenen Verpflichtungen verleiht das Land Nordrhein-Westfalen dem Eigentümer eines Denkmals eine Denkmalplakette nebst Urkunde nach Maßgabe der folgenden Bestimmungen:

2. Die Plakette besteht aus emailliertem Stahlblech in Schildform mit einer Höhe von 134 mm und einer Breite von 113 mm. Sie trägt im unteren Feld das farbige NRW-Wappenzeichen und im oberen Feld in schwarzer Schrift auf weißem Grund das Wort „Denkmal" (Anlage 1).[1]
Die Plakette kann auf Wunsch der zuständigen Gemeinde auch in Form eines rechteckigen Denkmalschildes verliehen werden. Das Schild besteht ebenfalls aus emailliertem Stahlblech mit einer Höhe von 210 mm und einer Breite von 297 mm. Es zeigt auf der linken Seite auf hellgrauem Untergrund die Denkmalplakette des Landes; die rechte Seite ist für erläuternde Hinweise zum Denkmal vorgesehen, die von der zuständigen Gemeinde einzutragen sind (Anlage 2).
Die Urkunde zeigt am linken Rand in einem Band in den Landesfarben die Denkmalplakette des Landes und enthält folgenden Text: (Vorname, Name und Anschrift des Denkmaleigentümers) erhält diese Urkunde in Verbindung mit einer Denkmalplakette des Landes Nordrhein-Westfalen für das Denkmal (Kurzbezeichnung des Denkmals) in Anerkennung der Verpflichtung, das Denkmal im Interesse der Allgemeinheit zu erhalten und so zur Bewahrung des kulturellen Erbes in Nordrhein-Westfalen beizutragen (Anlage 3). Der Denkmaleigentümer und das Denkmal sind von der zuständigen Gemeinde einzutragen.

3. Die Denkmalplakette des Landes nebst Urkunde wird von der zuständigen Gemeinde dem Denkmaleigentümer oder dessen Beauftragten in angemessener Form mit der Bitte überreicht, sie sichtbar am Denkmal anzubringen. Hierbei wird er von der Gemeinde beraten und erforderlichenfalls unterstützt.
Die Denkmalplakette des Landes für Denkmäler des Bundes oder des Landes wird vom Regierungspräsidenten überreicht.

4. Die Denkmalplakette sollte an Denkmäler außen an gut sichtbarer Stelle mit dem mitgelieferten Befestigungsmaterial angebracht werden. Bei räumlich ausgedehnten Denkmälern, beispielsweise Burganlagen mit mehreren Zugängen, können mehrere Plaketten an geeigneten Stellen befestigt werden.

5. Mit der Übergabe geht die Denkmalplakette in das Eigentum des Denkmaleigentümers über.

6. Die von der Gemeinde benötigten Denkmalplaketten können einschließlich des Befestigungsmaterials und der Urkunde mit dem Anforderungsschreiben (Anlage 4) beim zuständigen Regierungspräsidenten angefordert werden. Die Kosten einschließlich der Versandkosten werden vom Land Nordrhein-Westfalen getragen.

---

[1] Hinweis: Die Anlagen konnten aus drucktechnischen Gründen nicht aufgenommen werden.

Verwaltungsvorschrift zur Ausführung des Gesetzes zum Schutz und zur Pflege der Denkmäler im Lande Nordrhein-Westfalen (VV zum DSchG)

RdErl. d. Ministeriums für Bauen, Wohnen, Stadtentwicklung und Verkehr v. 11.4.2014 (MBl. NRW S. 280) (Stand: 25.4.2017)

Aufgrund der durch § 42 Denkmalschutzgesetz vom 11. März 1980 (GV. NW. 1980 S. 226, ber. S. 716), zuletzt geändert durch § 51 EEG NW v. 20.6.1989 (GV. NW. S. 366), dem für die Denkmalpflege zuständigen Minister erteilten Ermächtigung zum Erlass von Verwaltungsvorschriften zur Ausübung des Denkmalschutzgesetzes werden die nachstehenden VV zum DSchG bekannt gegeben:

Zu § 3 Denkmalliste

1

Die Bestimmungen des § 3 DSchG betreffen die Rechtswirkungen der Unterschutzstellung von Denkmälern und ihre Reichweite im Rahmen des gesetzlichen Vollzuges. Bodendenkmäler sind aufgrund ihrer fachlichen Besonderheiten einer Sonderregelung unterworfen. Bodendenkmäler geben sich im Gegensatz zu Baudenkmälern in der Regel oberirdisch nicht zu erkennen. Ihre Identifizierung ist daher meist nur durch gezielte Prospektion oder durch nach fachlichen Standards der Archäologie und Paläontologie durchgeführte Ausgrabungen möglich. Infolgedessen befinden sich Bodendenkmäler mehrheitlich noch unerkannt im Boden. Die Mehrzahl der tatsächlich vorhandenen Bodendenkmäler ist aus diesem Grund noch nicht förmlich unter Schutz gestellt. Aufgrund dieser fachlichen Erwägungen ist für die Bodendenkmalpflege eine Vorwirkung des Denkmalschutzes für nicht eingetragene, aber vermutete Bodendenkmäler von großer Bedeutung. Dies betrifft vermutete Bodendenkmäler bei Planungen und Maßnahmen, die nur über diese Vorwirkung des Denkmalschutzes in einem praxisgerechten Umfang in die Abwägung zur Entscheidung einbezogen werden können. Dies umfasst etwa den Fernstraßenbau des Bundes in der Auftragsverwaltung durch das Land, Planungen der Deutschen Bahn AG zum Ausbau des Schienennetzes oder Planungsvorhaben zur Sicherstellung der Rohstoff- und Energieversorgung. Um der Besonderheit von Bodendenkmälern Rechnung zu tragen, die man in einer Vielzahl von Fällen gerade nicht auf Anhieb erkennen und durch Eintragen in die Denkmalliste schützen kann, ist mit der Anpassung des § 3 DSchG die gesetzliche Grundlage geschaffen worden. Die Änderung wurde schließlich durch eine oberverwaltungsgerichtliche Rechtsprechung notwendig, die nach alter Gesetzeslage aufgrund des konstitutiven Unterschutzstellungsverfahrens nicht eingetragene Denkmaler als nicht abwägungsrelevant bei denkmalrechtlichen Abwägungsverfahren einstufte (OVG Münster, Urteil vom 20.09.2011, Az. 10 A 2611/09).

2

Mit der Änderung soll sichergestellt werden, dass die Vorschriften der §§ 1 Abs. 3, 11, 13 bis 17, 19, 28 und 29 DSchG unabhängig von der Eintragung der Denkmäler in die Denkmalliste gelten. Voraussetzung dabei ist, dass vermutete, nicht eingetragene Bodendenkmäler nur dann Berücksichtigung in den Genehmigungsverfahren, Planfeststellungsverfahren und in der Bauleitplanung finden, wenn konkrete, wissenschaftlich begründete Anhaltspunkte für deren Vorhandensein vorliegen. Dazu ist eine wissenschaftlich fundierte Begründung nötig, die je nach den konkreten Umständen etwa durch Fundstücke (Oberflächenfunde wie Ziegel, Keramik, Werkzeuge), Bodenveränderungen oder Luftbilder sowie durch Vergleiche mit erforschten Situationen und Analogieschlüsse erfolgen kann. Lässt etwa eine Luftbild- oder Laserscan-Aufnahme das Vorhandensein eines Bodendenkmals oder einer Reihe von Bodendenkmälern (z.B. bronzezeitliche Grabhügel oder römische Burgus-Anlagen) in Verbindung mit Analogieschlüssen zu bereits bekannten Fundplätzen klar erkennen, ist eine genaue Vermessung oder terrestrische Prospektion zur Begründung des vermuteten Bodendenkmals nicht notwendig. Diese Konkretisierung wird erst im Falle einer Eintragung des Bodendenkmals in die Denkmalliste oder im Zusammenhang mit einer Planung oder Umweltverträglichkeitsprüfung relevant.

3

Das Gesetz ordnet an, dass in den genannten Vorschriften unter „Denkmälern" und „Bodendenkmälern" auch nicht eingetragene Bodendenkmäler zu verstehen sind und dass in § 1 Abs. 3 DSchG „die Belange des Denkmalschutzes und der Denkmalpflege" auch auf den Schutz nicht eingetragener Bodendenkmäler gerichtet sind.

§ 1 Abs. 3 DSchG bezieht sich auf den Umgang mit Denkmälern bei öffentlichen Planungen und Maßnahmen. Demnach sind die „Belange des Denkmalschutzes und der Denkmalpflege" auch auf den Schutz nicht eingetragener Bodendenkmäler gerichtet. Dies bezieht sich auf alle Verfahrensarten und auf alle Vorhabenträger. § 11 DSchG betrifft den Umgang mit ortsfesten Bodendenkmälern von Kommunen und Behörden als Planungsträger, insbesondere in der Bauleitplanung durch die Gemeinden, der Landschaftsplanung durch die Kreise und kreisfreien Städte und der Flurbereinigung durch die Flurbereinigungsbehörde. §§ 13-19 DSchG regeln Fallgruppen der Ausgrabung, Entdeckung und Ablieferung von Bodendenkmälern.

Das mit Neufassung des § 28 DSchG erweiterte Betretungsrecht gilt nun auch für nicht eingetragene Denkmäler. Mit der Nennung des neu eingeführten § 29 DSchG zur Kostentragung und Gebührenfreiheit sind vermutete Bodendenkmäler auch hinsichtlich der Kostentragung von notwendigen archäologischen Maßnahmen zur wissenschaftlichen Untersuchung, Bergung von Funden und Dokumentation zu berücksichtigen.

Zu § 17 Schatzregal

1

Ziel des § 17 DSchG ist es, bedeutende Funde und bewegliche Denkmäler und Bodendenkmäler zu erhalten, für die wissenschaftliche Forschung zu erschließen und sie nach Möglichkeit der Öffentlichkeit in Museen, Sammlungen und Ausstellungen zugänglich zu machen. Der staatliche Eigentumserwerb stellt sicher, dass die Funde jederzeit der wissenschaftlichen Forschung und der Allgemeinheit als Teil des gemeinschaftlichen kulturellen Erbes zur Verfügung stehen. Ziel des § 17 DSchG ist es zudem, dem illegalen Handel solcher Funde vorzubeugen. Das Gesetz sieht nunmehr ein sogenanntes „umfassendes" Schatzregal vor, das den Eigentumserwerb durch das Land mit einer differenzierten Betrachtung der Fundbedeutung und unabhängig von den Fundumständen formuliert. Das Land erlangt mit der Entdeckung originär Eigentum, ein Verwaltungsakt ist dazu nicht notwendig. Es ist zudem für den Eigentumserwerb nicht notwendig, dass das Land durch staatliches Handeln den Besitz begründet oder die Funde faktisch in Besitz nimmt. Auch bei illegalen und ohne Genehmigung nach § 13 DSchG durchgeführten Ausgrabungen, sogenannten Raubgrabungen, entdeckte Funde im Sinne von § 17 DSchG gehen in das Eigentum des Landes über. Entsprechend des Sachverhaltes in Anwendung des § 984 BGB bezüglich des Eigentumserwerbes macht sich ein Entdecker eines Fundes gem. § 246 StGB strafbar, wenn er den Fund in Kenntnis der gesetzlichen Regelung und mit der Absicht unterschlägt, das Eigentum daran zu behalten.

2

Der Eigentumserwerb des Landes aufgrund des Schatzregals betrifft bewegliche Denkmäler und bewegliche Bodendenkmäler sowie Funde von besonderer, wissenschaftlicher Bedeutung, die herrenlos sind oder deren Eigentümer nicht mehr zu ermitteln ist.

Bewegliche Denkmäler sind alle nicht ortsfesten Denkmäler (§ 2 Abs. 4 DSchG).

Bewegliche Bodendenkmäler sind solche nicht ortsfesten Denkmäler, die sich im Boden oder in einem Gewässer befinden oder befanden (§ 2 Abs. 5 Satz 1 DSchG). Darunter fallen archäologische und paläontologische Funde und (bewegliche) Fundkomplexe, die den Anforderungen der §§ 2 Abs. 1 und 3 Abs. 1 DSchG genügen und in die Denkmalliste eingetragen sind oder die Eintragungsvoraussetzungen erfüllen. Nach § 3 Abs. 1 Satz 2 DSchG ist eine Eintragung in die Denkmalliste allerdings nur bei einer besonderen wissenschaftlichen Bedeutung notwendig. Eine Eintragung ist auch in solchen Fällen nicht notwendig, wenn bewegliche Denkmäler von einer öffentlichen Einrichtung betreut werden (§ 3 Abs. 1 Satz 4 DSchG). Eine Eintragung beweglicher Bodendenkmäler in die Denkmalliste ist

im Gesetzesvollzug seit 1980 selten erfolgt, weil die großen Quantitäten des Fundmaterials aus Ausgrabungen von öffentlichen Einrichtungen betreut werden (die Archäologie-Museen) und die übrigen Funde, auch Lesefunde ehrenamtlicher Mitarbeiter und von Sondengängern, das Kriterium der besonderen Bedeutung wegen des fehlenden Fundkontextes häufig nicht erfüllen. Die gemeldeten Zufalls- oder Lesefunde werden soweit nötig und sinnvoll, wissenschaftlich erfasst, ausgewertet und bearbeitet.
Unter die Regelung des § 17 entfällt nur ein geringer Teil dieser Funde, eben der Teil mit besonderer Bedeutung gem. §§ 2 Abs. 1 und 3 Abs. 1 DSchG und insbesondere der Teil mit nachvollziehbarem Fundkontext.
Funde von besonderer wissenschaftlicher Bedeutung sind Sachen, die aus wissenschaftlichen Gründen besonders bedeutend sind, ohne dass es sich um bewegliche Denkmäler oder Bodendenkmäler handeln muss. Für die Annahme einer wissenschaftlichen Bedeutung reicht grundsätzlich jede Art von wissenschaftlichem Interesse aus, das auf einen Erkenntniszuwachs ausgerichtet ist. Ein Fund ist von wissenschaftlichem Interesse, wenn er z.b. als Gegenstand der naturwissenschaftlichen, prähistorischen, archäologischen, kunsthistorischen oder historischen Forschung in Betracht kommt. Eine besondere wissenschaftliche Bedeutung liegt vor, wenn der Fund besonders wichtige Erkenntnisse für die Wissenschaft erbringen kann. Beispielsweise sind Funde aus archäologischen oder paläontologischen Ausgrabungen aufgrund des wissenschaftlich dokumentierten Fundkontextes Funde von besonderer wissenschaftlicher Bedeutung, auch wenn sie im Einzelfall nicht die Voraussetzungen für bewegliche Bodendenkmäler nach § 2 Abs. 5 Satz 1 DSchG erfüllen. Entscheidend ist, dass diesen Funden dauerhaft eine wissenschaftliche Aussagekraft innewohnt, die etwa aus Forschungsinteresse von Bedeutung ist. Funde aus Untersuchungen historischer Bausubstanz, z.B. Depotfunde, die keinen originären Zusammenhang mit dem Bau selbst aufweisen (z.B. Münzdepots als Verbergefunde) und deren ursprüngliche Eigentümer oder deren Rechtsnachfolger nicht mehr zu ermitteln sind, unterliegen ebenfalls der Definition des Fundes von besonderer wissenschaftlicher Bedeutung.
Herrenlos bedeutet in diesem Sinne, dass Eigentum entweder nie bestanden hat (dies trifft etwa für paläontologische Funde zu) oder aufgegeben wurde oder anderweitig erloschen ist (z.B. bei Depot-, Grab- und Hortfunden). Insofern handelt es sich bei den Bestimmungen des § 17 DSchG auch nicht um Enteignung, da diese bestehendes Eigentum voraussetzen würde.
Verborgen bedeutet in diesem Zusammenhang, dass die Erlangung der tatsächlichen Sachherrschaft ernsthaft erschwert ist. Der klassische Dachboden- oder Kellerfund fällt daher nicht unter das Schatzregal, da seinem Auffinden eine große Wahrscheinlichkeit zukommt und in der Regel der aktuelle oder seinerzeitige Eigentümer noch zu ermitteln ist. Auch Funde, die im Bereich einer von einem generellen Besitzwillen getragenen Sachherrschaft entdeckt werden, fallen nicht unter das Schatzregal, auch wenn sie verborgen oder ihr Vorhandensein nicht bekannt war. Dies können etwa sakrale Ausstattungsgegenstände aus Gebäuden, Räumen und Grundstücken einer Kirchengemeinde oder eines Klosters sein.
Ortsfeste, unbewegliche Denkmäler (gem. § 2 Abs. 4 und 5 DSchG) sind vom Schatzregal nicht betroffen. Hier ist nach § 94 BGB der Zusammenhang mit dem Grundstück entscheidend; sie sind wesentliche Grundstücksbestandteile und stehen im Eigentum des Grundstückseigentümers.

3

Entdeckung ist nicht nur das zutage fördern und bergen eines verborgenen Fundes, sondern auch das Auffinden eines obertägig (z.B. durch Pflugtätigkeit auf dem Acker) zufällig zutage liegenden und sichtbaren Fundes. Die Entdeckung betrifft sogenannte Zufallsfunde, die von neuen, bis dahin unbekannten Fundstellen stammen, ebenso wie Funde aus geplanter und gezielter Suche (z.B. planmäßige Begehungen, Ausgrabungen, Sondengänger-Funde, Schatzsuchen).
Bei einer archäologischen Ausgrabung gilt als Entdecker das zuständige Denkmalpflegeamt, das die Ausgrabung als Grundlage einer Genehmigung nach § 13 DSchG gefordert hat. Dies gilt auch für erlaubte Begehungen durch ehrenamtliche Mitarbeiter, die auf Grundlage einer Genehmigung nach § 13 DSchG tätig werden. Die hier auftretenden Funde fallen bei vorliegender Bedeutung im Sinne von § 2 Abs. 1 DSchG unter die Schatzregalregelung, da diese unabhängig von den Fundumständen gilt.
Das Schatzregal regelt für den Fall des § 984 BGB lediglich die Rechtsfolge des originären Eigentumserwerbs abweichend. Nicht der Entdecker und der Eigentümer der Muttersache erwerben Eigentum, sondern das Land. Wer Entdecker ist, wird dadurch nicht geändert. Eine solche Änderung wäre

auch aus Gründen der Gesetzgebungskompetenz nicht möglich. Entdecker bleibt derjenige, der nach dem BGB Entdecker ist. Am Begriff des Entdeckers hat sich durch das Schatzregal insofern nichts geändert.

4

Die Bestimmung der besonderen wissenschaftlichen Bedeutung gehört aus denkmalrechtlicher Sicht zu den Aufgaben der Denkmalpflege. Diese Aufgaben sind gemäß § 22 DSchG den Landschaftsverbänden und den dort organisierten Denkmalpflegeämtern zugeordnet. Bei der besonderen wissenschaftlichen Bedeutung von Funden ist ein hoher Maßstab anzulegen, damit sie den Zielsetzungen des Schatzregals entsprechen.

Einzelne Keramikfragmente, Knochen, bearbeitete Steine oder Ziegelfragmente, die als Lesefunde ohne Fundkontext vorgelegt werden, erfüllen in der Regel weder die Anforderungen an ein bewegliches Bodendenkmal noch das Kriterium der besonderen wissenschaftlichen Bedeutung. Anders kann es sein, wenn das einzelne Fundobjekt Teil eines Fundkomplexes von mehreren tausend Einzelfunden einer Ausgrabung oder einer bekannten oder neu entdeckten Fundstelle ist und infolgedessen mit einer klaren wissenschaftlichen Aussage verbunden werden kann, etwa in chronologischer oder typologischer Hinsicht.

Letzteres könnte im Falle von z.B. seltener römischer Importkeramik der Fall sein: um dies zu beurteilen, ist die Sichtung des Materials durch das örtlich zuständige Denkmalpflegeamt nötig.

Kriterien für die besondere wissenschaftliche Bedeutung sind einzeln oder in Kombination insbesondere die folgenden

– Das Objekt gilt als Leit- oder Referenzfund einer Epoche oder Kultur
– Das Objekt gilt als „missing link" zur Beantwortung einer besonderen wissenschaftlichen Fragestellung
– Es handelt sich um ein einmaliges oder in seiner wissenschaftlichen Aussagekraft bedeutendes, äußerst seltenes Vorkommen eines bestimmten Fundtyps in einer bestimmten Region
– Das Objekt ist typologisch und/oder von seinem kunstgeschichtlich-antiquarischen Wert so einzigartig, das an seiner öffentlichen Präsentation ein besonderes Interesse besteht
– Das Objekt erfordert aus konservatorischen Gründen eine besondere Aufbewahrung, die nur durch die öffentliche Hand sichergestellt werden kann
– Das Objekt ermöglicht langfristige wissenschaftliche Untersuchungen, die nur am Original möglich sind

Die zuständige Obere Denkmalbehörde kann durch Verwaltungsakt feststellen, ob die Voraussetzungen des § 17 Abs. 1 Satz 1 DSchG vorliegen. Über die Eigenschaft des Fundes als bewegliches Denkmal, bewegliches Bodendenkmal oder sonstiger Fund von besonderer wissenschaftlicher Bedeutung, legt das zuständige Denkmalpflegeamt gem. § 22 Abs. 3 Nr. 1 DSchG ein Gutachten vor. Im Übrigen gilt § 21 Abs. 4 Satz 1 DSchG.

In den Fällen der Abtretung von Fundkonvoluten aus archäologischen Untersuchungen gilt für die Funde, die nicht unter die Bestimmungen des § 17 DSchG fallen, weiterhin die Eigentumsregelung auf Grundlage des § 984 BGB. Solche Funde können etwa Funde sein, die nicht eindeutig der Grabung oder archäologischen Untersuchung zugeordnet werden können (z.B. aufgrund verspäteter Ablieferung oder aufgrund Ablieferung durch Dritte). Im Rahmen der Fundübernahme und Sichtung durch die Denkmalpflegeämter ist zu entscheiden, welche Funde unter die Bestimmungen des § 17 DSchG fallen.

5

Die Schatzfundregelung geht bezüglich des Verhaltens bei der Entdeckung nicht über die übrigen gesetzlichen Bestimmungen gem. §§ 15 und 16 DSchG NRW hinaus. Besteht bei dem Entdecker der Verdacht, dass es sich bei dem Fund oder der Fundstelle um ein bewegliches oder ortsfestes Bodendenkmal handeln könnte, ist dies unverzüglich der Gemeinde oder dem Landschaftsverband anzuzeigen. Diese Verpflichtung gilt unabhängig davon, ob es sich bei dem Entdecker um einen denkmalpflegerischen Laien oder einen ehrenamtlichen Mitarbeiter der Bodendenkmalpflege handelt. Dies gilt im Zweifelsfall auch (wie bislang) beim kleinsten Keramikfragment, wenn die Vermutung naheliegt, dass der Fund bedeutend im Sinne des DSchG ist.

Die Verpflichtung zur Ablieferung des Fundes oder der Funde gem. § 17 Abs. 2 DSchG und damit auch der Bergung (Aufsammlung) der Funde besteht nur insoweit, als dass das entdeckte Bodendenkmal gem. § 16 Abs. 1 DSchG in möglichst unverändertem Zustand zu erhalten ist. Das Aufsammeln weniger freiliegender oder unmittelbar sichtbarer Keramikscherben oder eines einzelnen Fundobjektes (z.B. einer Münze, einer Fibel, eines Knochens oder Fossilien) bewegt sich im gesetzlichen Rahmen, das Freilegen und Ausgraben weiterer Funde jedoch nicht.

Auch ist dem Entdecker nicht zuzumuten, unbillige Härten im Zusammenhang mit der Ablieferung des oder der Funde in Kauf zu nehmen. In der Regel wird die Untere Denkmalbehörde oder das Denkmalpflegeamt die Fundmeldung entgegennehmen, die Fundstelle besichtigen und dabei gegebenenfalls die wissenschaftliche Untersuchung des Fundortes veranlassen.

Insofern sieht das Gesetz keine Verpflichtung zur Fundbergung und eine damit verbundene entschädigungslose Übernahme der Kosten einer Fundbergung vor, soweit diese mit einem Bodeneingriff verbunden ist

Das Aufsammeln eines entdeckten Fundes dürfte in der Regel keine Kosten verursachen. Für Entdecker eines Schatzfundes ergibt sich aus den gesetzlichen Regelungen keine generelle Pflicht zur aufwendigen Bergung eines Fundes und damit zur Übernahme von Kosten. Eine gesetzliche Pflicht zur Fundbergung und Übernahme der Kosten der Fundbergung und Ablieferung ergibt sich nur in den Fällen des § 29 Abs. 1 DSchG.

Die Formulierung „Sie sind unverzüglich an die Untere Denkmalbehörde oder das Denkmalpflegeamt zu melden und zu übergeben" bedeutet nach § 121 Abs. 1 BGB ein Handeln „ohne schuldhaftes Zögern".

6

Der im Gesetzestext formulierte staatliche Eigentumserwerb nennt als künftigen Eigentümer das Land. Da die Funde in das Eigentum des Landes NRW übergehen, hat das Land damit auch grundsätzlich für Magazinierung, Restaurierung und Konservierung der Funde aufzukommen.

Das Land Nordrhein-Westfalen ist weder Träger der archäologischen Fachmuseen noch der Denkmalpflegeämter. Insofern besteht für das Land Nordrhein- Westfalen auch die Möglichkeit, die unter das Schatzregal fallenden Funde per Vertrag im Einzelfall den Landschaftsverbänden und der Stadt Köln sowie weiteren Kommunen mit einer Stadtarchäologie und entsprechend leistungsfähigen Museen auf privatrechtlichem Wege durch Eigentumsübertragung zu überantworten.

7

Eine Regelung des Fundverbleibes –etwa durch Leihvertrag mit dem Denkmalpflegeamt bzw. Museum- zugunsten von ehrenamtlichen MitarbeiterInnen der Bodendenkmalpflege ist auch weiterhin im Rahmen des § 17 DSchG möglich und wird im Einzelfall zwischen dem Entdecker und dem örtlich zuständigen Denkmalpflegeamt geregelt. Dies betrifft auch die Tätigkeit von Sondengängern, die auf der Grundlage einer Genehmigung nach § 13 DSchG NRW tätig sind.

In Einzelfallbetrachtung kann seitens der Denkmalpflegeämter bei den Landschaftsverbänden und der Stadt Köln, die vom Land dazu ermächtigt werden, entschieden werden, ob bei Zufallsfunden
- es sich um einen Schatzfund nach § 17 DSchG handelt, dessen wissenschaftliche Bedeutung eine Überführung in ein öffentliches Museum (oder Archiv) erfordert,
- in welcher Höhe eine Belohnung gezahlt wird,
- der Besitz der Funde zugunsten der Entdecker geregelt werden kann.

8

Zuständig für die Zahlung der Belohnung ist der Eigentümer der Funde. Dies ist nach Gesetz das Land. In den Fällen, in denen die besondere wissenschaftliche Bedeutung eines Fundes eine Belohnung rechtfertigt, wird dies einschließlich der Bemessungsgrundlage der Belohnung in einer schriftlichen Begründung der Obersten Denkmalbehörde im Einvernehmen mit dem örtlich zuständigen Denkmalpflegeamt festgehalten. Dies ist auch aus haushaltsrechtlichen Gründen und im Interesse der Rechtssicherheit der Entscheidung notwendig.

D10.I.1d VwV Denkmalschutzgesetz

Die Bemessung der Belohnung erfolgt durch Einzelfallentscheidung, die den wissenschaftlichen Aussagewert eines Fundes, sowie seine antiquarische und kunstgeschichtliche Bedeutung zu berücksichtigen hat. Dabei kann insbesondere eine Rolle spielen, ob der Fund ein Novum im Sinne eines einzigartigen Belegs einer bestimmten Fundgattung oder eines Typus darstellt, oder durch eine von der Serie abweichende andersartige Materialität herausragt. Bei der Bemessung der Belohnung kann, insbesondere bei exzeptionellen Einzelobjekten, als Orientierungshilfe auch der Versicherungswert eines Fundes (etwa im Leihverkehr zwischen Museen) herangezogen werden, wobei sich die Belohnung dann in einem zu bestimmenden prozentualen Anteil dieses Versicherungswertes bewegen wird.

Von einer Bagatellgrenze für die Belohnung ist abzusehen, da ohnehin nur bewegliche Denkmäler, bewegliche Bodendenkmäler und Funde von besonderer wissenschaftlicher Bedeutung unter das Schatzregal fallen und insofern „Bagatellfunde" nicht betroffen sind.

Über die Gewährung der Belohnung und ihre Höhe entscheidet im Einzelfall die Oberste Denkmalbehörde im Einvernehmen mit dem örtlich zuständigen Denkmalpflegeamt. Die Regelung trennt bewusst die Zuständigkeiten zur Ermittlung der Denkmaleigenschaft und wissenschaftlichen Bedeutung einerseits und der Wertermittlung zur Festlegung der Belohnung andererseits. Die Einzelfallregelung im Zusammenhang mit der Soll-Bestimmung der Vorschrift besagt, dass in der Regel eine Belohnung zu zahlen ist und nur in begründeten Ausnahmefällen darauf verzichtet wird.

9

Eine besondere Situation entsteht, wenn die wissenschaftliche Bedeutung eines entdeckten Fundes erst zu einem späteren Zeitpunkt, also nach Rückgabe an den Entdecker ersichtlich wird. Hier sind grundsätzlich zwei Fälle zu unterscheiden. Für den Fall, dass die Bedeutung des Fundes zunächst nicht erkannt oder zu einem späteren Zeitpunkt erkannt wird, gilt dennoch der Eigentumserwerb des Landes. Für die Fälle, in denen die Entscheidung über das Vorliegen der Voraussetzungen des Schatzregals durch einen Verwaltungsakt der Oberen Denkmalbehörde getroffen worden ist, müsste dieser Verwaltungsakt gegebenenfalls geändert bzw. aufgehoben werden. Unter den Voraussetzungen der §§ 48 ff. VwVfG kann ein solcher Verwaltungsakt zwar aufgehoben werden. Die sich ergebenden Folgen, insbesondere ein finanzieller Ausgleich, dürften in der Regel jedoch eher eine andere Lösung nahelegen. Dies bleibt letztlich dem Land überlassen. In solchen Fällen könnte eine wissenschaftliche Dokumentation und Erfassung der Funde nach § 16 Abs. 4 DSchG erfolgen. Der Besitz an den Funden verbliebe beim Entdecker. In Fällen, in denen sich durch verfeinerte Methoden und wissenschaftliche Erkenntnisse die Auffassung darüber wandelt, was die „besondere wissenschaftliche Bedeutung eines Fundes" ausmacht, kann nicht im Nachhinein der Eigentumsanspruch des Landes geltend gemacht werden, weil es auf die fachliche Expertise und Bewertung zum Zeitpunkt des Entdeckens ankommt.

Zu § 28 Auskunfts- und Betretungsrecht

1

Das Betretungsrecht erstreckt sich auf die Denkmalbehörden und Denkmalpflegeämter. Damit ist geregelt, dass für ehrenamtliche Mitarbeiter der Denkmalpflege kein Betretungsrecht besteht. Dies wäre im Sinne der Gleichstellung Privater auch nicht begründbar. Unbenommen bleibt die Möglichkeit einer privatrechtlichen Einigung zwischen Grundstückseigentümern und Nutzungsberechtigten, Denkmalbehörden und Denkmalpflegeämtern, dass ortskundige ehrenamtliche Mitarbeiter an der Betretung und Besichtigung des Denkmals teilnehmen. Dies ist im Interesse einer effizienten Denkmalpflege ausdrücklich zu begrüßen, da ehrenamtliche Mitarbeiter der Denkmalpflege oftmals in besonderem Maß über Ortskenntnisse sowie Kontakte zu Eigentümern verfügen und für die Denkmalbehörden und amtliche Denkmalpflege eine wirksame Unterstützung darstellen.

2

Die Unteren Denkmalbehörden sind die für den Denkmalschutz in ihrem Gemeindegebiet zuständigen Vollzugsbehörden. Die neue gesetzliche Regelung sieht nun aus fachlichen Erwägungen auch für die Denkmalpflegeämter bei den Landschaftsverbänden und der Stadt Köln ein Betretungsrecht vor. Das

Betretungsrecht der Denkmalpflegeämter sollte nach vorheriger Information der örtlich zuständigen Unteren Denkmalbehörde wahrgenommen werden.

3

Die Regelung bezieht sich im Kontext des geänderten § 3 Abs. 1 DSchG sowohl auf eingetragene wie auf vermutete Bodendenkmäler. Sie bezieht sich aufgrund der Formulierung in § 28 Abs. 2 Satz 1 DSchG „...um Denkmäler festzustellen..." auch auf vermutete oder noch nicht förmlich unter Schutz gestellte Baudenkmäler. Durch die Begrenzung auf den Fall der denkmalschutzrechtlichen Erforderlichkeit wird der Rahmen der Sozialbindung des Eigentums durch die Vorschrift nicht überschritten.

4

§ 28 Abs. 2 DSchG sieht vor, dass nicht eingefriedete Grundstücke auch ohne vorherige Benachrichtigung betreten werden können, um Denkmäler festzustellen, zu besichtigen oder zu untersuchen. Im Sinne eines geregelten Gesetzesvollzugs und eines auskömmlichen Miteinanders von Denkmalbehörden, Denkmalpflegeämtern und Eigentümern empfiehlt sich in der Praxis eine vorherige Benachrichtigung der Eigentümer.

5

§ 28 Abs. 2 Satz 2 und 3 DSchG betreffen die Möglichkeit, rechtzeitig vor Beginn eines bereits angezeigten oder zu erwartenden Eingriffs in Denkmäler die Auswirkungen dieser Eingriffe zu prüfen oder abzuschätzen. Bei großflächigen Planungsmaßnahmen unterliegen die Denkmalbehörden und Denkmalpflegeämter im Vorfeld der Planung teilweise einem erheblichen Zeitdruck, besonders im Bereich der Bodendenkmalpflege. Archäologische Prognoseflächen müssen in solchen Fällen mitunter sehr kurzfristig prospektiert und Aussagen zum archäologischen und paläontologischen Potential getätigt werden. Mit der Regelung soll gewährleistet werden, dass die Denkmalpflege ihre begrenzten Personalressourcen strategisch einsetzen kann und nicht durch den Zeitplan der Planungen bestimmt wird.

Zu § 29 Kostentragung und Gebührenfreiheit

1

Die Pflicht zur Erhaltung des Denkmals stellt den Rechtsgrund für die Regelung der Kostentragung dar. Sie obliegt dem Veranlasser oder Vorhabenträger der durch § 29 Abs. 1 DSchG ausgelösten Veränderung eines Denkmals. Diese Rechtsauslegung wird für die Bodendenkmalpflege gestützt durch das von der Bundesrepublik Deutschland ratifizierte Übereinkommen zum Schutz des archäologischen Erbes von 1992 (Konvention von La Valetta/Malta). Nach Art. 6 der Konvention sind die Vorhabenträger von groß angelegten privaten und öffentlichen Erschließungsmaßnahmen an den Kosten der notwendigen archäologischen Dokumentation ebenso wie die öffentliche Hand zu beteiligen. Aus der mit der Ratifizierung durch die Bundesrepublik Deutschland eingegangenen völkerrechtlichen Verpflichtung folgt für die Länder eine Umsetzungspflicht durch entsprechende Ausgestaltung der Ländergesetze. Dies ergibt sich auch aus dem allgemeinen Grundsatz der Bundestreue der Länder. Mit der Neuregelung des § 29 DSchG setzt das Land NRW die Konvention von La Valetta/Malta konsequent in die Landesgesetzgebung um. Die Rechtsauslegung gilt gleichermaßen für Bau- wie für Bodendenkmäler, denn in der grundsätzlichen Intention der gesetzlichen Regelung sind beide gleich zu behandeln. Dem Begünstigten einer denkmalrechtlichen Erlaubnis, die mit einer Veränderung oder Zerstörung eines Denkmals verbunden ist, wird durch die Kostentragungspflicht eine Kompensation abverlangt, um den dem Denkmal zugefügten Schaden durch wissenschaftliche Untersuchung und Dokumentation wenigstens teilweise auszugleichen.

2

Die Höhe der zu tragenden Kosten ist durch die Zumutbarkeit begrenzt. Der Begriff der Zumutbarkeit ist bislang für archäologische Maßnahmen noch nicht durch eine entsprechende Rechtsprechung hinterlegt. Eine spezifische Zumutbarkeitsregelung zur Kostentragung erscheint aufgrund der heterogenen

Fallkonstellationen auch nicht sinnvoll. Es gilt vielmehr, die jeweils unterschiedliche Situation des Einzelfalls zu betrachten. Bestimmende Determinanten für die Zumutbarkeit im Einzelfall ergeben sich dann aus der wissenschaftlichen Bedeutung des Denkmals oder archäologischen sowie paläontologischen Fundplatzes, aus der wirtschaftlichen Situation des Vorhabenträgers und aus der Art des Vorhabens. Hier ist etwa zu differenzieren, ob es sich bei dem Vorhaben um ein rein privates Vorhaben handelt (typisch wäre die Errichtung eines Eigenheims), ein gemischt privat und wirtschaftlich getragenes Vorhaben oder eine rein wirtschaftliche oder gewerbliche Nutzung, bei der eine Umlage der Grabungs- und Dokumentationskosten auf die Endabnehmer oder Kunden möglich ist.

3

Als Gegenstand der gesetzlichen Kostentragung sind die wissenschaftliche Untersuchung, die Bergung von Funden und die Dokumentation der Befunde genannt. Der Begriff der wissenschaftlichen Untersuchung umfasst für archäologische und paläontologische Maßnahmen jegliche Arten der Prospektion, Sondierung und insbesondere der Ausgrabung von Fundplätzen. Im Rahmen von Prospektionsmaßnahmen (etwa bei Oberflächen-Begehungen), vor allem jedoch bei Ausgrabungen erfolgt die Bergung des spezifisch archäologischen oder paläontologischen Fundmaterials. Dazu können auch technisch aufwendige Blockbergungen größerer Fundkomplexe gehören. Als signifikante Beispiele sind hier die Blockbergungen der bandkeramischen Brunnenanlagen aus Kückhoven oder Düren-Arnoldsweiler im Rheinland zu nennen. Die Dokumentation der Befunde umfasst die Einmessung sowie textliche, zeichnerische und fotografische Dokumentation der Befunde während der laufenden Ausgrabungen und das Abfassen der Grabungsberichte gemäß den Richtlinien der Denkmalpflegeämter. Nicht eingeschlossen in die gesetzliche Kostentragung ist die abschließende wissenschaftliche Auswertung und Publikation der Ausgrabung.

4

Die neue Regelung betrifft im Sinne der Gleichbehandlung der Vorhabenträger auch unter Schutz gestellte Baudenkmäler. Auch derjenige, der ein Baudenkmal verändert oder beseitigt, soll für die Kosten zur Dokumentation des Befundes, im Falle eines Baudenkmals also des erhaltenen Baubestandes und der im Denkmal innewohnenden Informationen in zumutbarem Umfang herangezogen werden. Dabei dürfte es sich etwa um Verfahren der zeichnerischen, fotografischen oder digitalen Dokumentation des Bestandes (etwa im Rahmen einer analogen oder digitalen Bauaufnahme oder Teil-Bauaufnahme) sowie der Entnahme von Materialproben oder besonders signifikanten Einbauten handeln.

5

Der Umfang und die spezifischen Anforderungen an die wissenschaftliche Untersuchung und Dokumentation werden im Erlaubnisverfahren nach § 9 Abs. 1 DSchG oder Entscheidungsverfahren nach § 9 Abs. 3 DSchG durch Nebenbestimmungen geregelt. Im Rahmen der denkmalrechtlichen Verfahren und der damit verbundenen Benehmensherstellung zwischen den für den Vollzug zuständigen Unteren Denkmalbehörden und den Denkmalpflegeämtern besteht für letztere die Gelegenheit, ihre fachliche Expertise einzubringen. Dabei werden insbesondere Methode und Umfang der Ausgrabung und Dokumentation, technische oder konservatorische Anforderungen an die Durchführung der Ausgrabung und Fundbergung sowie der Bauforschung oder restauratorisch- konservatorischen Untersuchung formuliert. Dies können z.B. besondere Anforderungen an die konservatorische Behandlung organischer Funde aus Feuchtbodengebieten sein.
Die Kostenregelung bezieht sich auch auf andere Eingriffe in Denkmäler, etwa unbeabsichtigte Eingriffe bei Erdarbeiten oder bei der Umsetzung von Planungs- oder Abgrabungsmaßnahmen. Damit ist noch einmal verdeutlicht, dass sich die Kostenregelung auch auf vermutete Bodendenkmäler erstreckt. Näheres zu Umfang und Durchführung der wissenschaftlichen Untersuchung, Bergung von Funden und Dokumentation der Befunde wird durch Verwaltungsakt der unteren Denkmalbehörde oder Erlaubnis der Oberen Denkmalbehörde nach § 13 DSchG geregelt.

6

Die Regelung, dass der Vorhabenträger die wissenschaftliche Untersuchung, die Bergung von Funden und die Dokumentation der Befunde sicherzustellen und die dafür anfallenden Kosten im Rahmen des Zumutbaren zu tragen hat, lässt offen, ob er die notwendigen Arbeiten selbst durchführen lässt oder ob er lediglich zu den Kosten heranzuziehen ist und die notwendigen Arbeiten durch das Denkmalpflegeamt durchgeführt werden. Die Denkmalpflegeämter werden mit eigenem oder mit zusätzlich eingestelltem Personal insbesondere dann selbst tätig, wenn aufgrund eines bestehenden Forschungsinteresses, der Notwendigkeit bestimmter Spezialkenntnisse, Methoden und Erfahrungen nur sie imstande sind, den erforderlichen wissenschaftlichen Standard zu gewährleisten.

7

Durch die Bestimmung des § 29 Abs. 2 DSchG ist die Möglichkeit für die Landschaftsverbände und die Stadt Köln gegeben, im Sinne der Planungssicherheit eigener wissenschaftlicher Untersuchungen und Dokumentationen einen vorausschauenden Personaleinsatz, zeitnahes Bearbeiten der Fälle und gegebenenfalls zeitnahe Personalverstärkung organisieren zu können.

Zu § 43 Inkrafttreten, Berichtspflicht

Die regelmäßige Berichterstattung und Evaluation zu den Aufgaben, der Organisation und den Verfahren von Denkmalschutz und Denkmalpflege wird als notwendig erachtet. Damit soll sichergestellt werden, dass das nordrhein-westfälische Denkmalschutzgesetz auch künftig ein zeitgemäßes, effizientes und wirksames Instrument zur Umsetzung von Denkmalschutz und Denkmalpflege ist.

Berücksichtigung des Bodendenkmalschutzes bei der Umweltverträglichkeitsprüfung in Verfahren zur Zulassung oder Genehmigung von Abgrabungen und in bergrechtlichen Planfeststellungsverfahren (Gewinnung nicht-energetischer oberflächennaher Rohstoffe)

Gemeinsamer Runderlass des Ministeriums für Bauen, Wohnen, Stadtentwicklung und Verkehr – V B 5 – 56.01 -, d. Ministeriums für Wirtschaft, Energie, Industrie, Mittelstand und Handwerk u. d. Ministeriums für Klimaschutz, Umwelt, Landwirtschaft, Natur- und Verbraucherschutz vom 1. Februar 2016 (MBl. NRW S. 107)

1 Grundsätze

Eingetragene sowie nicht eingetragene Bodendenkmäler und Gebiete, die von den Ämtern für Bodendenkmalpflege der Landschaftsverbände bzw. der Stadt Köln (im Folgenden: „Ämter für Bodendenkmalpflege") als archäologisch bedeutende Fundplätze oder Landschaften eingestuft sind (im Folgenden kurz: Bodendenkmäler), sind als Gegenstand der Umweltverträglichkeitsprüfung nach § 2 Absatz 1 Satz 2 Nummer 3 UVPG unter dem Begriff der Kulturgüter und sonstigen Sachgüter erfasst. Für vermutete Bodendenkmäler hat das Amt deren Vorhandensein konkret darzutun. Das Vorhandensein eines Bodendenkmals muss ernsthaft angenommen werden können. Eine derartige, wissenschaftlich abgesicherte Beweisführung kann je nach den konkreten Umständen etwa durch Fundstücke (Oberflächenfunde wie Ziegel, Keramik, Werkzeuge), Bodenveränderungen oder Luftbilder sowie durch Vergleiche mit erforschten Situationen und Analogieschlüsse erfolgen. Entsprechendes gilt auch in Verfahren zur Zulassung oder Genehmigung von Abgrabungen oder in bergrechtlichen Planfeststellungsverfahren.

Im Rahmen ihrer Aufgaben nach § 22 Absatz 2 und 3, insbesondere Absatz 3 Nummer 6 in Verbindung mit § 1 Absätze 2 und 3 DSchG NRW, werden die Ämter für Bodendenkmalpflege in Verfahren zur Zulassung oder Genehmigung von Abgrabungen und in bergrechtlichen Planfeststellungsverfahren als zuständige Denkmalbehörden für die Belange nach § 2 Absatz 1 Satz 2 Nummer 3 UVPG tätig. Auf die besondere Regelung in § 19 Absatz 3 DSchG NRW für die Zulassung bergrechtlicher Betriebspläne wird hingewiesen. Die Aufgaben der Unteren Bodenschutzbehörden zur Erfassung von Böden als „Archiv der Natur- und Kulturgeschichte" nach § 2 Absatz 2 Nummer 2 bleiben unberührt.

2 Verfahren

2.1 Vorprüfung

Die in amtlichen Listen oder Karten verzeichneten Bodendenkmäler sind ausdrücklich als Nutzungs- und Schutz-Kriterium für die Vorprüfung des Einzelfalls nach § 3c UVPG in Verbindung mit Anlage 2 Punkt 2.3.11 zum UVPG anzuwenden. Amtliche Listen und Karten sind
- die Denkmallisten sowie
- die Funddatenbanken der Ämter für Bodendenkmalpflege in Verbindung mit deren fachlicher Bewertung, die denkmalfähige archäologische Fundplätze und archäologisch bedeutende Landschaften ausweisen. Aus der fachlichen Bewertung ergibt sich, ob diese Fundplätze konkret bedeutende Funde/Befunde erwarten lassen.

Archäologisch bedeutende Landschaften sind solche, die nachweislich oder nach der Überzeugung von Sachverständigen als historische Kulturlandschaften und -landschaftsteile von besonders charakteristischer Eigenart eine Mehrheit von Bodendenkmälern enthalten.

Die Daten werden maßnahmebezogen von den Ämtern für Bodendenkmalpflege zur Verfügung gestellt. Dementsprechend sind die Auswirkungen des Vorhabens auf Bodendenkmäler in den Fällen zu untersuchen, für die nach § 3c in Verbindung mit Anlage 2 UVPG eine Vorprüfung durchzuführen ist. Dazu verwendet die zuständige Behörde die oben genannten Daten aus dem jeweiligen Archiv bei dem zuständigen Amt für Bodendenkmalpflege. In Zweifelsfällen bietet es sich an, das für die Begutachtung und Bewertung von Bodendenkmälern zuständige Amt für Bodendenkmalpflege zu beteiligen.

2.2 Grunderfassung, Ermittlung von Inhalt und Umfang der beizubringenden Unterlagen (Scoping)

Bei der Aufnahme des Verfahrens nach § 5 UVPG (Scoping) beteiligt die zuständige Behörde neben den anderen in ihrem Aufgabengebiet berührten Behörden auch das zuständige Amt für Bodendenkmalpflege. Für bergrechtliche Verfahren wird auf § 18 Satz 2 UVPG und § 52 Absatz 2a Satz 2 BBergG hingewiesen. Die Bergbehörde soll auch das zuständige Amt für Bodendenkmalpflege beteiligen.

Das Amt für Bodendenkmalpflege hat das Vorhandensein eines vermuteten Bodendenkmals hinreichend konkret darzutun (siehe 1).

Die für das UVP-Verfahren zuständige Behörde hat dann in Abstimmung mit dem Amt für Bodendenkmalpflege und dem Vorhabenträger Umfang und Standard der weiteren Ermittlungen zur Konkretisierung des Bodendenkmals und zur Feststellung der Auswirkungen des Vorhabens auf das Bodendenkmal festzulegen (§ 5 Satz 2 und 3 UVPG). Für bergrechtliche Verfahren gilt Entsprechendes (§ 52 Absatz 2a Satz 2 BBergG).

Im Rahmen der Obliegenheit zur Mitwirkung im Verfahren hat der Vorhabenträger die zur Festlegung notwendige Grunderfassung der Bodendenkmäler in den betroffenen Flächen durch das zuständige Amt für Bodendenkmalpflege zu ermöglichen, soweit er Eigentümer oder Verfügungsberechtigter ist. Bei der Grunderfassung der Bodendenkmäler handelt es sich grundsätzlich um non-destruktive Untersuchungen (Begehungen). In Einzelfällen können, bedingt durch Bodenaufträge, Sondagen erforderlich werden. Für durch Sondagen verursachte Schäden wird Ersatz geleistet.

Soweit es dem Vorhabenträger unmöglich oder unzumutbar ist, die Durchführung der Grunderfassung im Verfahren zu gewährleisten, ist in der Zulassung eine Nebenbestimmung zu treffen, die das Betretungsrecht auf Grundlage des § 28 DSchG NRW die Ermittlung, Bewertung und Sicherung der Bodendenkmäler regelt.

2.3 UVP

Es ist Aufgabe des Vorhabenträgers, die notwendigen und zumutbaren Maßnahmen durchzuführen, um den festgelegten Anforderungen an die Vorlage der Unterlagen (§ 6 UVPG) zu den Auswirkungen auf die Bodendenkmäler zu genügen. Für bergrechtliche Verfahren gilt Entsprechendes (§ 57a Absatz 2, § 57c BBergG, § 2 UVP-V-Bergbau). Der Vorhabenträger kann sich im Verfahren der Sach- und Fachkunde des zuständigen Amtes für Bodendenkmalpflege bedienen und/oder es beauftragen.

2.4 Vertragliche Vereinbarungen

Vertragliche Vereinbarungen über Art, Umfang und Ausgestaltung der notwendigen Maßnahmen des Bodendenkmalschutzes im Vorfeld der Abgrabung sind zulässig. Wenn Antragsteller und zuständiges Fachamt zu einer schriftlichen Vereinbarung für den Einzelfall kommen, so sollte diese inhaltlich in den Nebenbestimmungen der Genehmigungen aufgenommen werden.

3 Kosten

Die Kosten für die Grunderfassung nach 2.2 und gegebenenfalls anfallende Entschädigungen der Grundstücksverfügungsberechtigten oder Wiederherstellungsmaßnahmen trägt das zuständige Amt für Bodendenkmalpflege. Die Kosten für die Maßnahmen nach 2.3 trägt der Vorhabenträger.

4 Inkrafttreten

Dieser Erlass tritt am Tag nach seiner Verkündung in Kraft. Er tritt am 31. Dezember 2020 außer Kraft.

Gesetz über die Sicherung und Nutzung öffentlichen Archivguts im Lande Nordrhein-Westfalen (Archivgesetz Nordrhein-Westfalen – ArchivG NRW)

Vom 16. März 2010 (GV. NRW. S. 188)
(SGV. NRW. 221)
zuletzt geändert durch Art. 1 ÄndG vom 16. September 2014 (GV. NRW. S. 603)

Erster Teil
Allgemeines

§ 1 Geltungsbereich
(1) Dieses Gesetz gilt für die Archivierung von Unterlagen
1. des Landes Nordrhein-Westfalen,
2. der Träger der kommunalen Selbstverwaltung, deren Verbände sowie kommunalen Stiftungen nach Maßgabe des § 10,
3. anderer der Aufsicht des Landes unterstehenden juristischen Personen des öffentlichen Rechts nach Maßgabe des § 11.

(2) ¹Dieses Gesetz gilt auch für die Archivierung der Unterlagen von ehemals öffentlichen bzw. diesen gleichgestellten Stellen, sofern die Unterlagen bis zum Zeitpunkt des Übergangs in eine Rechtsform des Privatrechts entstanden sind. ²Ebenso gilt es für Unterlagen anderer Stellen oder Unterlagen von natürlichen oder juristischen Personen, an deren Archivierung ein öffentliches Interesse besteht.

(3) Dieses Gesetz gilt nicht für die öffentlich-rechtlichen Religions- und Weltanschauungsgemeinschaften, öffentlich-rechtliche Rundfunkanstalten, die Landesanstalt für Medien sowie für öffentlich-rechtliche Unternehmen, die am wirtschaftlichen Wettbewerb teilnehmen, und deren Zusammenschlüsse.

§ 2 Begriffsbestimmungen
(1) Unterlagen nach § 1 sind Urkunden, Amtsbücher, Akten, Schriftstücke, amtliche Publikationen, Karteien, Karten, Risse, Pläne, Plakate, Siegel, Bild-, Film- und Tondokumente und alle anderen, auch elektronischen Aufzeichnungen, unabhängig von ihrer Speicherungsform, sowie alle Hilfsmittel und ergänzenden Daten, die für die Erhaltung, das Verständnis dieser Informationen und deren Nutzung notwendig sind.

(2) Öffentliche Archive im Sinne dieses Gesetzes sind alle Archive im Land Nordrhein-Westfalen, die von den in § 1 Absatz 1 genannten Stellen unterhalten werden und die mit der Archivierung der dort entstandenen Unterlagen sowie der Unterlagen ihrer Rechtsvorgänger betraut sind.

(3) Archivgut sind alle, gegebenenfalls nach Ablauf der Verwahrungs- bzw. Aufbewahrungsfristen in das Archiv übernommenen archivwürdigen Unterlagen im Sinne des § 1 Absatz 1 und Absatz 2.

(4) ¹Zwischenarchivgut sind Unterlagen, deren Verwahrungs- bzw. Aufbewahrungsfristen noch nicht abgelaufen sind, deren Archivwürdigkeit noch nicht festgestellt wurde und die vom zuständigen Archiv vorläufig übernommen wurden. ²Das Verfügungsrecht verbleibt bei der abliefernden Stelle.

(5) ¹Vorarchivgut sind Unterlagen, die dauerhaft aufzubewahren sind, oder deren Verwahrungs- bzw. Aufbewahrungsfristen noch nicht abgelaufen sind und die als archivwürdig bewertet und übernommen worden sind. ²Das Verfügungsrecht liegt bei dem zuständigen Archiv. ³Es gelten die Normen des Archivgesetzes.

(6) ¹Archivwürdig sind Unterlagen, denen ein bleibender Wert für Wissenschaft und Forschung, historisch-politische Bildung, Gesetzgebung, Rechtsprechung, Institutionen oder Dritte zukommt. ²Über die Archivwürdigkeit entscheidet das zuständige Archiv unter Zugrundelegung fachlicher Kriterien.

(7) Archivierung umfasst die Aufgaben Unterlagen zu erfassen, zu bewerten, zu übernehmen und das übernommene Archivgut sachgemäß zu verwahren, zu ergänzen, zu sichern, zu erhalten, instand zu setzen, zu erschließen, zu erforschen, für die Nutzung bereitzustellen sowie zu veröffentlichen.

Zweiter Teil
Staatliches Archivwesen

§ 3 Organisation und Aufgaben des Landesarchivs Nordrhein-Westfalen
(1) Das Landesarchiv Nordrhein-Westfalen ist eine Einrichtung des Landes im Geschäftsbereich der für das Archivwesen zuständigen obersten Landesbehörde.
(2) ¹Das Landesarchiv hat die Aufgabe, das Archivgut von Behörden, Gerichten und sonstigen öffentlichen Stellen des Landes nach Maßgabe dieses Gesetzes zu archivieren. ²Diese Aufgabe erstreckt sich auch auf Archivgut der Rechtsvorgänger des Landes Nordrhein-Westfalen und der Funktionsvorgänger der in Satz 1 genannten Stellen.
(3) ¹Das Landesarchiv kann auch Archivgut anderer Herkunft übernehmen, an dessen Archivierung ein öffentliches Interesse besteht. ²Dies gilt insbesondere für Archivgut von privatrechtlich organisierten, ganz oder mehrheitlich der öffentlichen Hand gehörenden Einrichtungen, die nicht am wirtschaftlichen Wettbewerb teilnehmen.
(4) ¹Im Rahmen der elektronischen Archivierung kann das Landesarchiv Serviceleistungen für andere staatliche und kommunale Kultur- und Gedächtniseinrichtungen in Nordrhein-Westfalen übernehmen. ²§§ 9 Absatz 1, 10 Absatz 2 und 11 Absatz 1 bleiben unberührt.
(5) Das Landesarchiv wirkt bei der Festlegung von landesweit gültigen Austauschformaten zur Archivierung elektronischer Dokumente mit.
(6) ¹Im Rahmen seiner Zuständigkeit berät das Landesarchiv die Behörden, Gerichte und sonstigen öffentlichen Stellen des Landes bei der Verwaltung, Aufbewahrung und Sicherung ihrer Unterlagen. ²Die obersten Landesbehörden stellen sicher, dass die anbietenden Stellen in ihrem Geschäftsbereich die in Absatz 4 genannten Austauschformate beachten. ³Das gilt sowohl bei der Planung, vor der Einführung und bei wesentlichen Änderungen von IT-Systemen, die zu nach § 2 Absatz 1 i.V.m. § 4 Absatz 1 anzubietenden elektronischen Dokumenten führen. ⁴Soweit hiervon ausnahmsweise abgewichen werden soll, ist bereits vor der geplanten Nutzung anderer Formate und Techniken Einvernehmen mit dem Landesarchiv zu erzielen, um die spätere Übernahme des Archivgutes sicherzustellen. ⁵Dies entfällt, wenn Formate oder Techniken eingesetzt werden, die nach einem Verfahren nach Artikel 91c Absatz 2 GG (Länderübergreifende Standards) abgestimmt sind.
(7) Das Landesarchiv nimmt Aufgaben im Rahmen der archivarischen Aus- und Fortbildung wahr.

§ 4 Anbietung und Übernahme
(1) ¹Die Behörden, Gerichte und sonstigen Stellen des Landes haben dem Landesarchiv alle Unterlagen zur Übernahme anzubieten, die sie zur Erfüllung ihrer Aufgaben nicht mehr benötigen. ²Die Anbietung erfolgt grundsätzlich nach Ablauf der Verwahrungs- bzw. Aufbewahrungsfristen. ³Unabhängig davon sind alle Unterlagen spätestens dreißig Jahre nach ihrer Entstehung dem Landesarchiv anzubieten, sofern keine anderen Rechtsvorschriften längere Aufbewahrungsfristen bei den anbietungspflichtigen Stellen festlegen. ⁴Dem Landesarchiv ist auf Verlangen zur Feststellung der Archivwürdigkeit Einsicht in die Unterlagen und die dazu gehörigen Hilfsmittel und ergänzenden Daten, die für das Verständnis dieser Information und deren Nutzung notwendig sind, zu gewähren. ⁵Elektronische Unterlagen, die einer laufenden Aktualisierung unterliegen, sind ebenfalls zur Archivierung anzubieten.
(2) Anzubieten und zu übergeben sind auch Unterlagen, die
1. personenbezogene Daten enthalten, die nach einer Vorschrift des Landes- oder Bundesrechts gelöscht werden müssten oder gelöscht werden könnten, sofern die Speicherung der Daten nicht unzulässig war,
2. einem Berufs- oder besonderen Amtsgeheimnis oder sonstigen Rechtsvorschriften über die Geheimhaltung unterliegen. Die nach § 203 Absatz 1 Nummer 1, 2, 4 oder 4a des Strafgesetzbuchs geschützten Unterlagen der Beratungsstellen dürfen nur in anonymisierter Form angeboten und übergeben werden.

(3) Das Landesarchiv regelt die Anbietung und Übernahme von Unterlagen im Benehmen mit den anbietungspflichtigen Stellen.
(4) Das Landesarchiv kann Unterlagen von Stellen des Bundes übernehmen, soweit das Bundesarchivgesetz dies zulässt und ein öffentliches Interesse des Landes hieran vorhanden ist.
(5) ¹Wird über angebotene Unterlagen nicht innerhalb von sechs Monaten vom Landesarchiv entschieden, entfällt die Verpflichtung zur weiteren Aufbewahrung. ²Die als archivwürdig bewerteten

Unterlagen sind innerhalb eines Jahres zu übergeben. ³Nicht archivwürdige Unterlagen sind vorbehaltlich Satz 4 durch die anbietende Stelle zu vernichten, wenn weder Rechtsvorschriften noch schutzwürdige Belange Betroffener entgegenstehen. ⁴Die anbietende Stelle kann mit Zustimmung der für sie zuständigen obersten Landesbehörde Unterlagen, die vom Landesarchiv als nicht archivwürdig bewertet wurden, an andere öffentliche Archive abgeben. ⁵Das Landesarchiv ist zuvor von der abliefernden Stelle zu unterrichten. ⁶Diese Möglichkeit besteht nicht für die in § 4 Absatz 2 genannten Unterlagen.

§ 5 Verwahrung und Sicherung
(1) Archivgut ist unveräußerlich.
(2) ¹Archivgut ist auf Dauer sicher zu verwahren. ²Es ist in seiner Entstehungsform zu erhalten, sofern keine archivfachlichen Belange entgegenstehen. ³Es ist nach archivfachlichen Erkenntnissen zu bearbeiten und vor unbefugter Nutzung, vor Beschädigung oder Vernichtung zu schützen. ⁴Das Landesarchiv hat geeignete technische und organisatorische Maßnahmen zur Sicherung solcher Unterlagen zu ergreifen, die personenbezogene Daten enthalten oder einem besonderen gesetzlichen Geheimnisschutz unterliegen. ⁵In besonders begründeten Einzelfällen kann es Unterlagen, die als Archivgut übernommen wurden und deren Archivwürdigkeit nicht mehr gegeben ist, vernichten, wenn öffentliches Interesse oder berechtigte Interessen Betroffener nicht entgegenstehen.
(3) Rechtsansprüche Betroffener auf Löschung unzulässig gespeicherter personenbezogener Daten bleiben unberührt.
(4) ¹Bestreitet ein Betroffener die Richtigkeit personenbezogener Daten im Archivgut und wird die Unrichtigkeit festgestellt, hat er einen Berichtigungsanspruch. ²Lässt sich weder die Richtigkeit noch die Unrichtigkeit der Daten feststellen, sind diese zu anonymisieren oder zu sperren; das Landesarchiv kann jedoch verlangen, dass an die Stelle der Anonymisierung oder Sperrung eine Gegendarstellung des Betroffenen tritt, soweit dadurch dessen schutzwürdige Belange angemessen berücksichtigt werden.

§ 6 Nutzung
(1) Jeder hat nach Maßgabe dieses Gesetzes und der hierzu ergangenen Benutzungsordnung das Recht, Archivgut auf Antrag zu nutzen, soweit aufgrund anderer Rechtsvorschriften nichts anderes bestimmt wird.
(2) ¹Die Nutzung ist ganz oder für Teile des Archivguts zu versagen, wenn
1. Grund zu der Annahme besteht, dass das Wohl der Bundesrepublik Deutschland oder eines ihrer Länder gefährdet würde,
2. es wegen überwiegenden berechtigten Interessen einer dritten Person geheim gehalten werden muss,
3. schutzwürdige Belange Betroffener oder Dritter beeinträchtigt würden,
4. die Geheimhaltungspflicht nach § 203 Absatz 1 Nummer 1, 2, 4 oder 4a des Strafgesetzbuchs oder anderer Rechtsvorschriften über Geheimhaltung verletzt würden,
5. der Erhaltungszustand des Archivguts eine Nutzung nicht zulässt,
6. ein nicht vertretbarer Verwaltungsaufwand entstehen würde.

²Im Falle der nur teilweisen Nutzungsversagung, kann die Nutzung zusätzlich auch an Auflagen gebunden werden. ³Die Nutzung kann auch im Übrigen aus wichtigem Grund an Auflagen gebunden werden. ⁴Gesetzliche Zugangsrechte und Vereinbarungen mit Eigentümern privaten Archivguts bleiben unberührt. ⁵Die Entscheidung zu Satz 1 Nummer 1 und Nummer 2 trifft das Landesarchiv im Einvernehmen mit der abliefernden Stelle.
(3) ¹Betroffenen ist auf Antrag nach Maßgabe des Absatzes 2 aus dem Archivgut Auskunft zu erteilen oder Einsicht in dieses zu gewähren, soweit es sich auf ihre Person bezieht. ²Die Entscheidung hierüber trifft das Landesarchiv. ³Die Sätze 1 und 2 gelten für Rechtsnachfolger mit der Maßgabe des § 7 Absatz 6 Nummer 2. ⁴Rechtsnachfolger im Sinne dieses Gesetzes sind Ehegatten oder Partner einer eingetragenen Lebensgemeinschaft, nach deren Tod Kinder, ansonsten die Eltern des Betroffenen.
(4) ¹Die abliefernde Stelle bzw. ihre Funktions- und Rechtsnachfolger haben das Recht, Archivgut, das aus ihren Unterlagen gebildet wurde, jederzeit zu nutzen. ²Dies gilt nicht für personenbezogene Daten, die aufgrund einer Rechtsvorschrift hätten gesperrt oder gelöscht werden müssen.

(5) Nutzer sind verpflichtet, von einem Medienwerk, das unter wesentlicher Verwendung von Archivgut des Landesarchivs verfasst oder erstellt wurde, nach Erscheinen dem Landesarchiv unaufgefordert ein Belegexemplar unentgeltlich abzuliefern.

§ 7 Schutzfristen
(1) ¹Die Nutzung des Archivguts (§ 6) ist zulässig nach Ablauf einer Schutzfrist von dreißig Jahren seit Entstehung der Unterlagen. ²Die Schutzfrist beträgt sechzig Jahre seit Entstehung der Unterlagen, für Archivgut, das besonderen Geheimhaltungsvorschriften unterliegt. ³Für Archivgut, das sich nach seiner Zweckbestimmung oder nach seinem wesentlichen Inhalt auf eine oder mehrere natürliche Personen bezieht (personenbezogenes Archivgut) endet die Schutzfrist jedoch nicht vor Ablauf von
1. zehn Jahren nach dem Tod der betroffenen Person oder der letztverstorbenen von mehreren betroffenen Personen, deren Todesjahr dem Landesarchiv bekannt ist,
2. hundert Jahren nach der Geburt der betroffenen Person oder der Geburt der letztgeborenen von mehreren Personen, deren Todesjahr dem Landesarchiv nicht bekannt ist, und
3. sechzig Jahren nach Entstehung der Unterlagen, wenn weder das Todes- noch das Geburtsjahr der betroffenen Person oder einer der betroffenen Personen dem Landesarchiv bekannt sind.

(2) Die Verknüpfung personenbezogener Daten durch das Archiv ist innerhalb der Schutzfristen nur zulässig, wenn schutzwürdige Belange Betroffener angemessen berücksichtigt werden.

(3) ¹Die Schutzfristen nach Absatz 1 gelten nicht für solche Unterlagen, die schon bei ihrer Entstehung zur Veröffentlichung bestimmt oder der Öffentlichkeit zugänglich waren. ²Für personenbezogenes Archivgut betreffend Amtsträger in Ausübung ihrer Ämter sowie Personen der Zeitgeschichte gelten die Schutzfristen des Absatzes 1 nur, sofern deren schützenswerte Privatsphäre betroffen ist.

(4) ¹Für Unterlagen, die das Landesarchiv nach § 4 Absatz 4 dieses Gesetzes von Stellen des Bundes übernommen hat, gelten die entsprechenden Schutzfristen des Bundesarchivgesetzes in der jeweiligen gültigen Fassung. ²Dies gilt auch für solches Archivgut, das Rechtsvorschriften des Bundes über Geheimhaltung unterliegt.

(5) ¹Die in Absatz 1 festgelegten Schutzfristen gelten auch bei der Nutzung durch öffentliche Stellen. ²Für die abliefernden Stellen bzw. ihre Funktions- und Rechtsnachfolger gelten diese Schutzfristen nur für Unterlagen, bei denen die Ablieferung eine aufgrund Rechtsvorschrift gebotene Sperrung, Löschung oder Vernichtung ersetzt hat.

(6) ¹Die Nutzung von Archivgut, das Schutzfristen nach Absatz 1 und 4 unterliegt, kann vor deren Ablauf auf Antrag genehmigt werden. ²Bei personenbezogenem Archivgut ist dies nur zulässig, wenn
1. die Betroffenen in die Nutzung eingewilligt haben,
2. im Falle des Todes der Betroffenen deren Rechtsnachfolger in die Nutzung eingewilligt haben, es sei denn, ein Betroffener hat zu Lebzeiten der Nutzung nachweislich widersprochen, oder die Erklärung der Einwilligung wäre nur höchstpersönlich durch die Betroffenen möglich gewesen.
3. die Nutzung zu benannten wissenschaftlichen Zwecken oder zur Wahrnehmung eines rechtlichen Interesses erfolgt und dabei sichergestellt wird, dass schutzwürdige Belange Betroffener nicht beeinträchtigt werden,
4. dies im überwiegenden öffentlichen Interesse liegt.

(7) ¹Das Landesarchiv kann in besonders begründeten Fällen auf Antrag nach Ablauf der Schutzfristen die Überlassung von Vervielfältigungen von Archivgut an Archive, Museen und Forschungsstellen zum Zwecke der archivischen Nutzung und wissenschaftlichen Forschung zulassen. ²Vorher kann dies nur für Archive, Museen und Forschungsstellen zugelassen werden, wenn diese einen besonderen Auftrag zur Dokumentation des Schicksals einer Gruppe natürlicher Personen unter nationalsozialistischer Herrschaft haben. ³Die Wahrung schutzwürdiger Belange der Betroffenen oder Dritter ist sicherzustellen. ⁴Die Überlassung von Archivgut nach den Sätzen 1 und 2 bedarf der Genehmigung der für das Archivwesen zuständigen obersten Landesbehörde. ⁵Die Übermittlung ins Ausland ist nur zulässig, wenn ein angemessenes Datenschutzniveau gewährleistet ist. ⁶Vor der Entscheidung über die Angemessenheit des Datenschutzniveaus ist die Landesbeauftragte für den Datenschutz und Informationsfreiheit zu hören. ⁷Fehlt es an einem angemessenen Datenschutzniveau, so ist die Übermittlung nur zulässig, wenn die empfangende Stelle ausreichende Garantien hinsichtlich des Schutzes der informationellen Selbstbestimmung bietet.

§ 8 Veröffentlichung
¹Das Landesarchiv ist berechtigt, Archivgut sowie die dazugehörigen Findmittel unter Wahrung der schutzwürdigen Belange Betroffener zu veröffentlichen. ²§ 6 Absatz 2 sowie § 7 Absatz 1 bis 4 gelten entsprechend.

§ 9 Archivgut des Landtags
(1) Der Landtag entscheidet in eigener Zuständigkeit, ob bei ihm entstandene Unterlagen, die zur Erfüllung der Aufgaben nicht mehr benötigt werden, von ihm selbst archiviert oder dem Landesarchiv zur Übernahme angeboten werden.
(2) ¹Sofern der Landtag ein eigenes Archiv unterhält, regelt er die Einzelheiten der Benutzung in eigener Zuständigkeit. ²Im Übrigen gelten die §§ 5 bis 8 entsprechend.

Dritter Teil
Archive sonstiger öffentlicher Stellen

§ 10 Kommunale Archive
(1) Die Träger der kommunalen Selbstverwaltung, deren Verbände sowie kommunale Stiftungen tragen dafür Sorge, ihr Archivgut in eigener Zuständigkeit zu archivieren.
(2) ¹Sie erfüllen diese Aufgaben durch
1. Errichtung und Unterhaltung eigener Archive oder Übertragung auf eine für Archivierungszwecke geschaffene Gemeinschaftseinrichtung oder
2. Übergabe ihres Archivguts zur Archivierung in einem anderen öffentlichen, nichtstaatlichen Archiv.

²Im Rahmen der elektronischen Archivierung ist die Nutzung von Serviceleistungen nach Maßgabe von § 3 Absatz 4 zulässig.
(3) Die Archive und Gemeinschaftseinrichtungen müssen archivfachlichen Anforderungen entsprechen, indem sie
1. hauptamtlich oder hauptberuflich von Personal betreut werden, das die Befähigung für eine Laufbahn des Archivdienstes besitzt oder sonst fachlich geeignet ist, oder
2. von einer Dienststelle fachlich beraten werden, bei der eine Archivarin oder ein Archivar mit der Befähigung für eine Laufbahn des Archivdienstes tätig ist.

(4) Unterlagen, die zur Aufgabenerfüllung nicht mehr benötigt werden, sind dem Archiv anzubieten.
(5) §§ 2 und 3 Absatz 5 und 6, § 4 Absatz 1 Satz 4 und 5 und Absatz 2 und §§ 5 bis 8 gelten entsprechend.
(6) Die kommunalen Archive können Unterlagen von anderen Stellen oder von natürlichen oder juristischen Personen übernehmen.

§ 11 Andere öffentliche Archive
(1) ¹Die anderen der Aufsicht des Landes unterstehenden juristischen Personen des öffentlichen Rechts regeln die Archivierung und Nutzung der bei ihnen entstandenen Unterlagen in eigener Zuständigkeit in eigenen, gemeinschaftlich getragenen oder fachlich geleiteten anderen Archiven. ²Die für kommunale Archive in Bezug genommenen Regelungen dieses Gesetzes gelten entsprechend.
(2) ¹Nur sofern die Voraussetzungen des Absatzes 1 nicht sichergestellt werden können und eine Vernichtung oder Zersplitterung der archivwürdigen Unterlagen drohen, sind die nicht mehr benötigten Unterlagen dieser Stellen dem Landesarchiv anzubieten. ²Archivwürdige Unterlagen dieser Stellen werden im Landesarchiv als staatliches Archivgut archiviert.
(3) § 4 Absatz 5 gilt entsprechend.

Vierter Teil
Schlussbestimmungen

§ 12 Ermächtigungen
Die zuständige oberste Landesbehörde regelt durch Rechtsverordnung Einzelheiten der Nutzung des Landesarchivs einschließlich der für die Nutzung des Archivguts zu erhebenden Gebühren und Auslagen in einer Benutzungs- und Gebührenverordnung.

§ 13 Inkrafttreten, Berichtspflicht
¹Dieses Gesetz tritt am 1. Mai 2010 in Kraft. ²Die Landesregierung berichtet dem Landtag bis zum 31. Dezember 2019 und danach alle fünf Jahre über die mit diesem Gesetz gemachten Erfahrungen.

D10.II.1a Archivnutzungs- und Gebührenordnung

Verordnung über die Nutzung und die Gebührenerhebung des Landesarchivs Nordrhein-Westfalen (Archivnutzungs- und Gebührenordnung Nordrhein-Westfalen – ArchivNGO NRW)

Vom 29. Mai 2015 (GV. NRW. S. 620)
(SGV. NRW. 221)

Auf Grund des § 12 des Archivgesetzes Nordrhein-Westfalen vom 16. März 2010 (GV. NRW. S. 188) verordnet das Ministerium für Familie, Kinder, Jugend, Kultur und Sport:

§ 1 Geltungsbereich
Diese Verordnung gilt für das Landesarchiv Nordrhein-Westfalen.

§ 2 Nutzungsrecht
Nach Maßgabe des Archivgesetzes Nordrhein-Westfalen vom 16. März 2010 (GV. NRW. S. 188), das zuletzt durch Gesetz vom 16. September 2014 (GV. NRW. S. 603) geändert worden ist, und dieser Verordnung stehen Archivgut, Vervielfältigungen und Findmittel auf Antrag jedermann für die Nutzung zur Verfügung.

§ 3 Nutzungsarten
(1) Die Nutzung erfolgt grundsätzlich durch die persönliche Einsichtnahme im verwahrenden Archiv.
(2) Das Landesarchiv Nordrhein-Westfalen kann auf Antrag abweichend von Absatz 1 unter fachlichen Gesichtspunkten folgende Nutzungsarten zulassen:
1. schriftliche Anfragen,
2. Anforderung von Vervielfältigungen von Archivgut,
3. Versendung von Archivgut zur Einsichtnahme an einem anderen Ort,
4. Ausleihe von Archivgut zu Ausstellungszwecken und
5. Zugriff auf digitale Archivalien über Rechnernetzwerke.

§ 4 Nutzung von Archivgut, Vervielfältigungen und Findmitteln
(1) Die Nutzung richtet sich nach den §§ 6 und 7 des Archivgesetzes Nordrhein-Westfalen.
(2) [1]Anträge nach § 7 Absatz 6 des Archivgesetzes Nordrhein-Westfalen sind mit genauer Bezeichnung des Themas der Arbeit, detaillierter Angabe des in Frage kommenden Archivguts und ausführlicher Begründung schriftlich an die zuständige Abteilung des Landesarchivs zu richten. [2]Von der antragstellenden Person können Empfehlungen angefordert werden, die geeignet sind, den Antrag zu begründen.
(3) [1]Für den Umgang mit Verschlusssachen (VS) gilt der Runderlass des Innenministeriums „VS-Anweisung" vom 9. April 2001 (MBl. NRW. S. 666), der durch Runderlass vom 13. Juni 2004 (MBl. NRW. S. 610) geändert worden ist. [2]Darüber hinaus dürfen im Landesarchiv archivierte Verschlusssachen nur mit Zustimmung der abliefernden Stelle Dritten zugänglich gemacht werden.

§ 5 Nutzungsvoraussetzungen
(1) [1]Die Genehmigung der Nutzung erfolgt auf Antrag, der schriftlich beim Landesarchiv zu stellen ist. [2]Hierbei ist separat für jedes Nutzungsvorhaben Folgendes anzugeben:
1. der Zweck und der Gegenstand der Nutzung in möglichst präziser zeitlicher und sachlicher Eingrenzung,
2. der Name, der Vorname und die Anschrift der antragstellenden Person oder der beauftragenden Person, wenn die Nutzung im Auftrag einer oder eines Dritten erfolgt, oder
3. im Falle der Vertretung der Name, der Vorname und die Anschrift der Vertreterin oder des Vertreters unter Nachweis der Vertretungsvollmacht. Im Falle der Antragstellung durch juristische Personen, Vereinigungen und Behörden gilt § 12 Absatz 1 Nummer 3 und 4 Verwaltungsverfahrensgesetz für das Land Nordrhein-Westfalen in der Fassung der Bekanntmachung vom 12. November 1999 (GV. NRW. S. 602), das zuletzt durch Artikel 1 des Gesetzes vom 20. Mai 2014 (GV. NRW. S. 294) geändert worden ist, für die Leitungen, Vertretungen und Beauftragten entsprechend.

[3]Die antragstellende Person ist verpflichtet, diese Angaben in zutreffender Art und Weise und der Wahrheit entsprechend zu machen und sich auf Verlangen auszuweisen. [4]Ansonsten kann die Geneh-

migung widerrufen werden. [5]Vor Einsichtnahme in Archivgut müssen minderjährige antragstellende Personen die Einwilligungserklärung ihres gesetzlichen Vertreters oder ihrer gesetzlichen Vertreterin vorlegen. [6]Für Schülergruppen stellt die betreuende Lehrkraft einen Sammelantrag.

(2) Das Landesarchiv ist berechtigt, die Nutzung von Archivgut von der Vorlage eines auf die Nutzerin oder den Nutzer ausgestellten Nutzungsausweises abhängig zu machen.

(3) Abweichend von Absatz 2 kann bei Nutzungen nach § 3 Absatz 2, insbesondere bei schriftlichen Anfragen, auf die Ausstellung eines Nutzungsausweises verzichtet werden.

(4) [1]Über den Nutzungsantrag entscheidet das Landesarchiv, das die Genehmigung an Bedingungen knüpfen und mit Auflagen versehen kann. [2]Auf eine bestimmte Art, Form oder einen bestimmten Umfang der Nutzung besteht kein Anspruch. [3]Nutzungsgenehmigungen sind fünf Kalenderjahre ab Erteilung der Genehmigung gültig.

(5) [1]Die Nutzungsgenehmigung kann außer aus den in § 6 Absatz 2 des Archivgesetzes Nordrhein-Westfalen genannten Gründen eingeschränkt oder versagt werden, wenn
1. die antragstellende Person bei früherer Nutzung von Archivgut schwerwiegend gegen die Archivnutzungsordnung verstoßen oder festgelegte Nutzungsbedingungen oder -auflagen nicht eingehalten hat,
2. der Ordnungszustand des Archivguts oder Vereinbarungen mit Eigentümerinnen oder Eigentümern von Archivgut dies erfordern,
3. Archivgut aus dienstlichen Gründen oder wegen gleichzeitiger anderweitiger Nutzung nicht verfügbar ist,
4. die personellen und sachlichen Kapazitäten des Landesarchivs vorübergehend eine Nutzung nicht zulassen oder
5. der mit der Nutzung verfolgte Zweck anderweitig, insbesondere durch Einsichtnahme in Druckwerke oder andere Veröffentlichungen oder in Reproduktionen erreicht werden kann.

[2]Bei Versagung der Nutzungsgenehmigung sind die Gründe – auf Antrag schriftlich – mitzuteilen.

(6) [1]Die nutzende Person ist zu verpflichten, alle Bestimmungen des Landesarchivs zu beachten und Nutzungsbedingungen oder Nutzungsauflagen einzuhalten. [2]Zudem ist sie verpflichtet, Urheber- oder Persönlichkeitsrechte sowie andere schutzwürdige Belange Dritter zu beachten. [3]Auf Verlangen hat sie darüber eine schriftliche Erklärung abzugeben.

§ 6 Einsichtnahme im Lesesaal
(1) Für das Verhalten während der Arbeit in den Lesesälen, die Behandlung der Archivalien, Vervielfältigungen und Findmittel sowie die Bestellung und Rückgabe von Archivalien gelten die Vorschriften der Lesesaalordnung des Landesarchivs.

(2) Die Hand- und die Dienstbibliothek des Landesarchivs können nur innerhalb des Lesesaals genutzt werden, wobei Einzelheiten der Nutzung der Dienstbibliothek vom Landesarchiv geregelt werden.

(3) [1]Für die Nutzung von Archivalien, die von anderen Archiven oder Instituten übersandt werden, gelten die gleichen Bedingungen wie für die Archivalien des Landesarchivs Nordrhein-Westfalen, sofern die übersendende Stelle nicht anderslautende Auflagen macht. [2]Kosten und anfallende Gebühren tragen diejenigen, die die Versendung veranlasst haben.

(4) Die Verwendung nutzereigener Geräte bedarf der Genehmigung durch das Landesarchiv und darf nicht zur Störung anderer Personen führen.

§ 7 Beratung
[1]Zur Beratung steht während der Dienststunden Fachpersonal zur Verfügung. [2]Die Beratung bezieht sich auf nutzungsrelevante Abläufe, Bestände, Findmittel sowie den Umgang mit Archivgut. [3]Ein Anspruch auf weitergehende Unterstützung (zum Beispiel beim Lesen und Auswerten der Findmittel und Archivalien) besteht nicht.

§ 8 Schriftliche Auskünfte
(1) Bei schriftlichen Anfragen sind Zweck und Gegenstand der Anfrage genau anzugeben.

(2) Die schriftlichen Auskünfte des Landesarchivs beschränken sich in der Regel auf Hinweise auf einschlägige Findmittel und Bestände.

(3) Ein Anspruch auf Auskünfte, die eine beträchtliche Arbeitszeit erfordern, oder auf Beantwortung von wiederholten Anfragen besteht nicht.

§ 9 Versendung

(1) ¹Auf die Versendung von Archivgut zur Einsichtnahme außerhalb des Lesesaals der das betreffende Archivgut verwahrenden Abteilung des Landesarchivs besteht kein Rechtsanspruch. ²Die Entscheidung über die Versendung liegt beim Landesarchiv.

(2) ¹Die Versendung kann auf begründeten Antrag hin in Ausnahmefällen und nur in sehr beschränktem Umfang zur Nutzung in hauptamtlich verwaltete Archive des Inlands erfolgen, sofern diese sich verpflichten, das Archivgut in den Diensträumen unter ständiger fachlicher Aufsicht nur der antragstellenden Person vorzulegen, es diebstahl- und feuersicher zu verwahren, keine Kopien oder Reproduktionen anzufertigen und das Archivgut nach Ablauf der vom Landesarchiv bestimmten Ausleihfrist, die vier Wochen nicht überschreiten soll, in der von diesem bestimmten Versendungsart zurückzusenden. ²Die Ausleihfrist kann auf Antrag verlängert werden.

(3) ¹Über die Art der Versendung entscheidet das Landesarchiv, wobei eine Sendung höchstens zehn Archivalieneinheiten umfassen soll. ²Die Kosten tragen diejenigen, die die Versendung veranlasst haben.

(4) ¹Abweichend von Absatz 2 ist die Versendung an die Eigentümerin oder den Eigentümer des Archivguts zulässig. ²Eigentümer im Sinne von Satz 1 ist auch jeder Miteigentümer zum Bruchteil oder zur gesamten Hand.

(5) Aus wichtigen Gründen können versandte Archivalien jederzeit zurückgefordert werden.

(6) Das Landesarchiv hat bei Versendung von Archivgut die Empfängerin oder den Empfänger zur Beachtung der Vorschriften dieser Verordnung zu verpflichten.

(7) Von der Versendung ausgeschlossen sind
1. Archivalien, die
   a) Nutzungsbeschränkungen unterliegen,
   b) wegen ihres hohen Wertes, ihres Ordnungs- und Erhaltungszustandes, wegen ihres Formates oder aus anderen Sicherheits- oder konservatorischen Gründen versendungsunfähig sind,
   c) häufig genutzt werden oder
   d) noch nicht ausreichend verzeichnet sind, und
2. Findmittel.

§ 10 Ausleihe

(1) ¹Auf die Ausleihe von Archivalien zu Zwecken der Öffentlichkeitsarbeit, insbesondere für Ausstellungen, besteht kein Rechtsanspruch. ²Die Entscheidung über die Ausleihe trifft das Landesarchiv, das für die Sicherheit des ausgestellten Archivguts notwendige Auflagen und Bedingungen festlegt. ³Eine Ausleihe ist nur zulässig, sofern der Ausstellungszweck nicht durch Vervielfältigungen erfüllt werden kann. ⁴§ 4 gilt entsprechend. ⁵Für die Versendung von Archivalien zur Ausleihe gelten die Bestimmungen des § 9.

(2) Der Antrag auf Genehmigung zur Ausleihe ist zu begründen.

(3) Über die Ausleihe ist zwischen dem Leihgeber und dem Entleiher ein Leihvertrag nach dem vom Landesarchiv vorgegebenen Muster abzuschließen.

§ 11 Vervielfältigungen

(1) Zur Nutzung außerhalb des Landesarchivs können nutzende Personen auf Antrag und auf eigene Kosten Vervielfältigungen von uneingeschränkt für die Nutzung freigegebenen Archivalien in den Werkstätten des Landesarchivs anfertigen lassen.

(2) ¹Ein Anspruch auf Herstellung von Vervielfältigungen besteht nicht. ²Insbesondere besteht kein Anspruch auf Durchführung größerer Aufträge zu Lasten anderer Nutzer oder des Dienstbetriebes im Landesarchiv.

(3) Die Genehmigung für die Anfertigung einer Vervielfältigung in den Werkstätten des Landesarchivs kann versagt werden, wenn
1. Überformate entstehen,
2. das Interesse anderer nutzender Personen beeinträchtigt ist oder
3. der Dienstbetrieb im Landesarchiv beeinträchtigt ist.

(4) ¹Vervielfältigungen dürfen nur hergestellt werden, wenn dies ohne Beschädigung der Archivalien möglich ist. ²Über das Reproduktionsverfahren, die Zielformate, die zu verwendenden Datenträger und den Versendungsweg entscheidet das Landesarchiv.

(5) ¹Vervielfältigungen dürfen nur mit schriftlicher Genehmigung des Landesarchivs weiter vervielfältigt, an Dritte weitergegeben oder veröffentlicht werden. ²Dabei sind der Aufbewahrungsort und die Archivsignatur des Originals anzugeben. ³Auf die dem Landesarchiv zustehenden Vervielfältigungs-, Weitergabe und Veröffentlichungsrechte ist hinzuweisen.

§ 12 Gebühren und Auslagen
(1) Das Landesarchiv Nordrhein-Westfalen erhebt für die von ihm erbrachten Leistungen sowie für die Nutzung seiner Einrichtungen Verwaltungs- und Nutzungsgebühren sowie Auslagen nach dieser Verordnung.
(2) Die Verwaltungs- und Nutzungsgebühren werden nach den Sätzen des als **Anlage** beigefügten Gebührenverzeichnisses erhoben.
(3) ¹Von der Erhebung von Verwaltungs- und Nutzungsgebühren sowie von Auslagen kann auf formlosen Antrag abgesehen werden, wenn dies aus Gründen der Billigkeit, insbesondere zur Vermeidung sozialer Härten, geboten erscheint. ²Dasselbe gilt für Amtshandlungen des Landesarchivs, wenn diese dem öffentlichen Interesse dienen.
(4) ¹Auslagen für die von der nutzenden Person beantragten oder sonst verursachten Leistungen, insbesondere für Verpackung, Wertversicherung, Einschreib- oder Eilsendungen, Porto (ausgenommen Standard- und Kompaktbriefe) und Vervielfältigungen sind zu erstatten. ²Entstandene Auslagen sind auch dann zu erstatten, wenn Verwaltungs- und Nutzungsgebühren nach dieser Verordnung nicht zu entrichten sind.

§ 13 Ergänzende Bestimmungen des Landesarchivs
Das Landesarchiv kann zu dieser Verordnung ergänzende Bestimmungen treffen.

§ 14 Inkrafttreten
Diese Verordnung tritt am Tag nach der Verkündung[1]) in Kraft.

---

[1]) Verkündet am 2.9.2015.

D10.II.1a Archivnutzungs- und Gebührenordnung

Anlage

Gebührenverzeichnis

1	Verwaltungsgebühren		
1.1	Beglaubigung	je Seite	2,50 €
1.2	Archivierung von öffentlichem Archivgut unter Eigentumsvorbehalt		
1.2.1	Bewertung, Erschließung und konservatorisch-restauratorische Bearbeitung von öffentlichem Archivgut unter Eigentumsvorbehalt		Die Gebühr richtet sich nach den zum Zeitpunkt der Leistung geltenden Richtwerten für die Berücksichtigung des Verwaltungsaufwandes bei der Festlegung der nach dem Gebührengesetz für das Land Nordrhein-Westfalen zu erhebenden Verwaltungsgebühren, Auslagenersatz nach Aufwand
1.2.2	Übernahme und Verwahrung von öffentlichem Archivgut unter Eigentumsvorbehalt		Auslagenersatz nach Aufwand
1.3	Prüfung und gegebenenfalls Erteilung einer Veröffentlichungsgenehmigung (bei gewerblicher Verwertung, die nicht ausschließlich wissenschaftlichen oder schulischen Zwecken dient)	je angefangene 30 Minuten	30,00 € Ansprüche Dritter aus Urheber-, Verwertungs- oder Lizenzrechten sind gesondert abzugelten
2	Nutzungsgebühren		
2.1	Anfertigung von Vervielfältigungen von Archivgut im Landesarchiv		
2.1.1	Selbstausdrucke (Papier) im Lesesaal (ohne Grundgebühr)	DIN A 4, schwarz/weiß	0,30 €
		DIN A 3, schwarz/weiß	0,50 €
		DIN A 4, Farbe	2,20 €
		DIN A 3, Farbe	3,50 €
2.1.2	Grundgebühr für reprographische Leistungen, die vom Landesarchiv erbracht werden		3,00 € (zuzüglich Gebühren pro einzelner reprographischer Leistung)
2.1.3	Grundgebühr für Speichermedien für digitale reprographische Leistungen, die vom Landesarchiv erbracht werden		3,00 €
2.1.4	Grundgebühr für die Datenübermittlung für digitale reprographische Leistungen, die vom Landesarchiv erbracht werden		3,00 €
2.1.5	Einzelne reprographische Leistungen, die vom Landesarchiv erbracht werden	DIN A 4, schwarz/weiß	0,50 €
		DIN A 3, schwarz/weiß	0,70 €
		DIN A 4, Farbe	2,40 €
		DIN A 3, Farbe	3,70 €
		Anfertigung digitaler Nutzungskopien von analogen Vorlagen, je Datei	0,50 €

		Anfertigung digitaler Nutzungskopien von analogem audiovisuellem Archivgut (Film, Video, Ton) je angefangener zehn Minuten Abspielzeit	15,00 €
		Anfertigung digitaler Nutzungskopien von digitalen Vorlagen	0,50 € pro Datei
		Zuschläge für erhöhten Arbeitsaufwand (zum Beispiel aus bestandserhalterischen Gründen, bei Überformaten oder bei umfangreichen Bearbeitungen digitalen Materials) oder bei Ausführung der Reproduktionsarbeiten durch gewerbliche Fachbetriebe	Gebühr nach Aufwand: je angefangene 30 Minuten 30 € zuzüglich Fremdkosten
2.2	Einsichtnahme von Archivgut im Lesesaal des verwahrenden Archivs		
2.2.1	Einsichtnahme im Lesesaal des verwahrenden Archivs		gebührenfrei
2.2.2	Einsichtnahme in Archivgut im Lesesaal des verwahrenden Archivs bei besonderem Aufwand (zum Beispiel durch den Einsatz von besonderen Geräten oder bei besonderem Nutzungsaufwand)	je angefangener Tag	25,00 €
2.3	Schriftliche oder mündliche Auskünfte		
2.3.1	die weniger als 30 Minuten Arbeitszeit in Anspruch nehmen		gebührenfrei
2.3.2	die mehr als 30 Minuten Arbeitszeit in Anspruch nehmen	je angefangene 30 Minuten (nach Ablauf der 30 Minuten gemäß 2.3.1)	30,00 €
2.4	Vorbereitung und begleitende Arbeiten bei Foto- und Filmaufnahmen im Landesarchiv	je angefangene 30 Minuten	30,00 €
2.5	Archivalienversand	je angefangene 30 Minuten	30,00 €
2.6	Bereitstellung von Archivgut für die Ausleihe zu Ausstellungszwecken		Gebühr nach Aufwand: je angefangene 30 Minuten 30 €
2.7	Ausleihe von Archivgut zu Ausstellungszwecken	je Ausstellungsmonat	100,00 €

D10.III.1 Kulturfördergesetz Nordrhein-Westfalen

Gesetz zur Förderung und Entwicklung der Kultur, der Kunst und der kulturellen Bildung in Nordrhein-Westfalen (Kulturfördergesetz NRW)

Vom 18. Dezember 2014 (GV. NRW. S. 917)
(SGV. NRW. 224)
zuletzt geändert durch Art. 24 ZuständigkeitsbereinigungsG vom 23. Januar 2018 (GV. NRW. S. 90)

Inhaltsübersicht

Teil 1
Allgemeine Bestimmungen
§ 1 Geltungsbereich
§ 2 Kulturförderung als Aufgabe von Land und Gemeinden

Teil 2
Ziele, Schwerpunkte und Grundsätze der Kulturförderung
§ 3 Ziele der Kulturförderung
§ 4 Schwerpunkte der Kulturförderung
§ 5 Grundsätze der Kulturförderung

Teil 3
Handlungsfelder der Kulturförderung
§ 6 Förderung der kulturellen Infrastruktur
§ 7 Förderung der Künste
§ 8 Erhalt des kulturellen Erbes
§ 9 Förderung der kulturellen Bildung
§ 10 Förderung der Bibliotheken
§ 11 Förderung der Freien Szene und der Soziokultur
§ 12 Förderung der Kultur- und Kreativwirtschaft
§ 13 Förderung der Breitenkultur
§ 14 Kultur und gesellschaftlicher Wandel
§ 15 Kultur und Strukturwandel
§ 16 Förderung interkommunaler Kooperation
§ 17 Experimente

Teil 4
Landeseigene Kulturaufgaben
§ 18 Aufgaben des Landes im föderalen Bundesstaat und international

§ 19 Eigene Einrichtungen und Beteiligungen des Landes
§ 20 Kunst am Bau
§ 21 Sonstige Aktivitäten des Landes

Teil 5
Kulturförderplan
§ 22 Zweck und Inhalt
§ 23 Verfahren

Teil 6
Berichtswesen und Qualitätssicherung
§ 24 Kulturförderbericht
§ 25 Landeskulturbericht
§ 26 Evaluation der Förderungen
§ 27 Regelmäßiger Dialog über Ziele und Wirksamkeit der Kulturförderung des Landes

Teil 7
Förderverfahren
§ 28 Förderverfahren
§ 29 Formen der Förderung
§ 30 Fördervereinbarungen
§ 31 Jurys und Sachverständige
§ 32 Antragstellung und Beratung

Teil 8
Schlussbestimmungen
§ 33 Übergangsbestimmung
§ 34 Inkrafttreten

Teil 1
Allgemeine Bestimmungen

§ 1 Geltungsbereich

(1) ¹Dieses Gesetz regelt Grundlagen für die Förderung und Entwicklung der Kultur, der Kunst und der kulturellen Bildung (Kulturförderung) in Nordrhein-Westfalen. ²Das Gesetz legt Ziele, Schwerpunkte und Grundsätze der Kulturförderung fest. ³Es definiert die Handlungsfelder und schafft Instrumente der Kulturförderung des Landes.

(2) Dieses Gesetz gilt für die Kulturförderung durch das Land sowie nach Maßgabe des § 2 Absatz 1 und 3 und des § 25 Absatz 2 Satz 2 bis 4 auch für die Gemeinden und Gemeindeverbände.

(3) ¹Kulturelle Aufgaben werden, soweit sie durch andere Landesgesetze geregelt sind, durch dieses Gesetz nicht berührt. ²Das schließt eine ergänzende Förderung freiwilliger Aufgaben auf Grundlage dieses Gesetzes nicht aus.

§ 2 Kulturförderung als Aufgabe von Land und Gemeinden/Gemeindeverbänden

(1) ¹Kultur und Kunst sind durch Land und Gemeinden gemäß Artikel 18 Absatz 1 der Verfassung für das Land Nordrhein-Westfalen zu pflegen und zu fördern. ²Bei der Wahrnehmung dieser Aufgabe ergänzen sich Land und Gemeinden wechselseitig in gleichberechtigtem partnerschaftlichem Zusammenwirken und beziehen hierbei die frei-gemeinnützigen Träger der Kultur mit ein.

(2) ¹Das Land pflegt und fördert die Kultur nach Maßgabe der Regelungen der Teile 2 bis 7. ²Es nimmt eigene Kulturaufgaben nach dem Teil 4 wahr und unterstützt die kulturellen Aktivitäten in den Gemeinden und Gemeindeverbänden nach Maßgabe der vom Land zu definierenden landeskulturpolitischen Ziele. ³Es fördert insbesondere Maßnahmen von regionaler, landesweiter, nationaler oder internationaler Bedeutung, sofern und soweit die Ziele der in Betracht gezogenen Maßnahme ohne Landesförderung nicht oder nicht in ausreichendem Maße erreicht werden können. ⁴Es regt neue Entwicklungen in Kultur, Kunst und kultureller Bildung an und gibt Anstöße zur Erprobung entsprechender Maßnahmen. ⁵Es trägt mit seiner Förderung zur Pflege und Weiterentwicklung der kulturellen Infrastruktur in Nordrhein-Westfalen bei. ⁶Dabei soll ein bedarfsgerechtes Angebot in allen Regionen angestrebt werden, das die Belange der kulturellen Vielfalt besonders berücksichtigt.

(3) ¹Die Gemeinden und Gemeindeverbände nehmen die Aufgabe der Kulturförderung und -pflege in ihrem Gebiet im Rahmen ihrer Selbstverwaltung in eigener Verantwortung wahr. ²Sie schaffen dabei gemäß § 8 Absatz 1 der Gemeindeordnung innerhalb der Grenzen ihrer Leistungsfähigkeit die für die kulturelle Betreuung ihrer Einwohner erforderlichen öffentlichen Einrichtungen. ³Bei der Wahrnehmung dieser Selbstverwaltungsaufgabe berücksichtigen sie die in Teil 2 genannten Ziele, Grundsätze und Schwerpunkte. ⁴Von den Mitwirkungspflichten des § 25 Absatz 2 Satz 2 bis 4 abgesehen, bleibt das Recht der kommunalen Selbstverwaltung durch die Regelungen dieses Gesetzes unberührt.

Teil 2
Ziele, Schwerpunkte und Grundsätze der Kulturförderung

§ 3 Ziele der Kulturförderung

Ziele der Kulturförderung sind:
1. die schöpferische Entfaltung des Menschen zu ermöglichen, sei es durch eigenes künstlerisches Schaffen, sei es durch Teilhabe an kulturellen oder künstlerischen Angeboten,
2. den in Nordrhein-Westfalen lebenden und arbeitenden Künstlerinnen und Künstlern eine freie künstlerische Entfaltung zu ermöglichen,
3. in der Gesellschaft zu Offenheit und Verständnis für künstlerische Ausdrucksformen und kulturelle Vielfalt beizutragen und die Menschen zur kritischen Auseinandersetzung mit Kultur und Kunst zu befähigen und
4. die gesellschaftliche und strukturelle Entwicklung in den Gemeinden und Regionen mitzugestalten. Sie soll insbesondere den Zusammenhalt in der Gesellschaft fördern und dazu beitragen, die Qualität und Attraktivität des Landes und der Gemeinden zu verbessern und nach innen und außen sichtbar zu machen.

§ 4 Schwerpunkte der Kulturförderung

(1) ¹Die Produktion und Präsentation der Künste in ihrer Breite und Vielfalt stehen im Zentrum der Kulturförderung. ²Dabei kommt herausragenden künstlerischen Leistungen, insbesondere der Gegenwartskunst, eine besondere Bedeutung zu.

(2) ¹Der Erhalt des kulturellen Erbes ist ein Schwerpunkt der Kulturförderung. ²Die erhaltenswerte Substanz an kulturellen Werken und Zeugnissen soll gepflegt, erforscht und nutzbar gemacht werden, das Geschichtsbewusstsein gestärkt, das kulturelle Gedächtnis lebendig gehalten und gepflegt werden.

(3) ¹Kulturelle Bildung initiiert und unterstützt die Begegnung und die Auseinandersetzung mit Kultur und Kunst. ²Durch kulturelle Bildungsangebote sollen die kulturelle kreative Betätigung und die Nutzung des Kulturangebotes als Bestandteile lebenslangen Lernens gestärkt werden. ³Ein Schwerpunkt liegt dabei auf der Förderung der kreativen Aktivitäten von Kindern und Jugendlichen. ⁴Sie sollen die Möglichkeit haben, ihre Wahrnehmungs- und Ausdrucksfähigkeit, ihren ästhetischen Eigensinn und ihre künstlerischen Talente zu erproben und weiterzuentwickeln.

D10.III.1 Kulturfördergesetz Nordrhein-Westfalen

§ 5 Grundsätze der Kulturförderung

(1) ¹Die Kulturförderung soll dem gesellschaftlichen Wandel Rechnung tragen. ²Neue Formen künstlerischer Produktionen sowie Veränderungen in der Wahrnehmung und Nutzung von kulturellen Angeboten sollen Berücksichtigung finden.

(2) Die Kulturförderung soll das zivilgesellschaftliche und ehrenamtliche Engagement innerhalb und außerhalb von Vereinen und Verbänden unterstützen und einbeziehen.

(3) ¹Durch die Kulturförderung sollen Einrichtungen, Programme und Maßnahmen unterstützt werden, die geeignet sind, auch Menschen zu erreichen, die aufgrund ihrer Herkunft, ihres Alters, ihres Geschlechts oder aufgrund einer Behinderung bisher nicht oder in nicht ausreichendem Maß am kulturellen Leben teilhaben können. ²Dabei soll die kulturelle Interaktion zwischen Bevölkerungsgruppen verschiedener Ethnien, Religionen oder Weltanschauungen gefördert und weiterentwickelt werden.

(4) Die Förderung soll die Zusammenarbeit verschiedener Träger der Kulturarbeit unterstützen, wenn diese Synergien erzeugt oder die Qualität der Arbeit steigert.

(5) In allen strukturpolitischen Entwicklungsplanungen ist zu prüfen, ob Belange der Kultur und Kunst als Faktoren der Strukturentwicklung berührt sind und berücksichtigt werden sollen.

(6) Bei der Kulturförderung sollen die Bezüge zu anderen Politikfeldern, insbesondere zur schulischen Bildung sowie zur Kinder- und Jugendarbeit, beachtet und die Zusammenarbeit gestärkt werden.

(7) Die Kulturförderung soll auf Nachhaltigkeit und Planungssicherheit ausgerichtet sein, um Kulturentwicklung als langfristigen Prozess zu unterstützen.

Teil 3
Handlungsfelder der Kulturförderung

§ 6 Förderung der kulturellen Infrastruktur

(1) ¹Das Land fördert die kulturelle Infrastruktur in Nordrhein-Westfalen als Grundlage einer sich fortentwickelnden Kulturlandschaft. ²Zu diesem Zweck fördert es Kulturorganisationen und öffentlich zugängliche Kultureinrichtungen, welche die kulturelle Infrastruktur in Nordrhein-Westfalen prägen, insbesondere Theater, Orchester, Festivals, Tanz-, Schauspiel- und Musik-Ensembles, soziokulturelle Zentren, Museen, Kunstvereine, Kunsthallen, Filmwerkstätten, öffentliche Bibliotheken, archivische Einrichtungen und Musikschulen. ³Das Land kann vom Fördernehmer als Fördervoraussetzung ein auf den Fördergegenstand bezogenes, gemeindliches oder gemeindeübergreifendes Strukturentwicklungskonzept verlangen.

(2) Das Land fördert Verbände und kulturfachliche Büros, die die Interessen von Künstlerinnen, Künstlern und Kultureinrichtungen überörtlich bündeln und wahrnehmen und mit dem Land im Bereich der Kulturförderung zusammenwirken.

§ 7 Förderung der Künste

(1) ¹Das Land fördert die professionelle Produktion und Präsentation künstlerischer Werke insbesondere in den folgenden Sparten:
1. Darstellende Kunst,
2. Musik,
3. Bildende Kunst,
4. Medienkunst,
5. Literatur und
6. Film.

²Das Land fördert auch spartenübergreifende Projekte sowie die Produktion und Präsentation digitaler Kunstformen.

(2) ¹Das Land fördert Künstlerinnen und Künstler mit dem Ziel, künstlerische Potentiale zu entdecken und zu entwickeln. ²Im Rahmen der individuellen Künstlerförderung vergibt das Land unter anderem Stipendien, lobt Preise aus, kauft Werke an und fördert die Produktion und Präsentation künstlerischer Werke.

(3) ¹Das Land fördert Arbeits- und Studienaufenthalte sowie die Präsentation künstlerischer Werke von nordrhein-westfälischen Künstlerinnen und Künstlern im Ausland. ²Das Land fördert nachhaltig angelegte internationale Kooperationen von in Nordrhein-Westfalen ansässigen Künstlerinnen und Künstlern.

§ 8 Erhalt des kulturellen Erbes

(1) ¹Das Land fördert den Erhalt und die Pflege des materiellen und immateriellen kulturellen Erbes. ²Es unterstützt Kultureinrichtungen in ihrer Aufgabe, Kulturgüter zu sammeln, zu bewahren, zu erschließen, zu erforschen, auszustellen oder auf andere Art öffentlich zugänglich zu machen.

(2) Das Land unterstützt Kultureinrichtungen bei der Digitalisierung von analogem Kulturgut, bei der Übernahme von originär digitalem Kulturgut, bei der Bereitstellung der Digitalisate für die öffentliche Nutzung sowie bei der digitalen Langzeitarchivierung.

§ 9 Förderung der kulturellen Bildung

(1) ¹Das Land fördert kulturelle Bildung, um im partnerschaftlichen Zusammenwirken mit den Aktivitäten der Gemeinden und Gemeindeverbände sowie mit frei-gemeinnützigen Kulturträgern zur Entwicklung einer vielfältigen und ausgewogenen Angebotsstruktur beizutragen und gleichzeitig eine qualitätsvolle Vermittlungsarbeit zu erreichen. ²Das Land schafft dabei durch Förderprogramme Anreize für Gemeinden und freie Träger, Angebote für die kulturelle Bildung zu entwickeln und zu stärken.

(2) ¹Das Land fördert Kultureinrichtungen als Orte der kulturellen Bildung und der kulturellen Kommunikation. ²Es unterstützt insbesondere ihre Zusammenarbeit mit Schulen und mit Einrichtungen der Kinder- und Jugendarbeit.

(3) ¹Das Land fördert die kulturelle Bildung im Rahmen von lokalen und regionalen Netzwerken. ²Es wirkt durch seine Förderung auf die Abstimmung von Förderzielen und -programmen und eine den örtlichen Gegebenheiten entsprechende Kooperation von Kultur und Bildung insbesondere in der Kinder- und Jugendarbeit sowie in der Schule hin.

(4) ¹Landeseigene Kultureinrichtungen sind dazu verpflichtet, Aufgaben der kulturellen Bildung wahrzunehmen. ²Sonstige institutionelle Förderungen und die Förderung von Projekten kann das Land mit der Auflage verbinden, dass in ihrem Rahmen auch ein angemessenes Angebot der kulturellen Bildung realisiert wird.

§ 10 Förderung der Bibliotheken

(1) ¹Das Land fördert die öffentlichen Bibliotheken in ihrer Funktion als Orte des lebenslangen Lernens, der Information, der Kommunikation und der Kultur. ²Das Land unterstützt die öffentlichen Bibliotheken insbesondere bei der Vermittlung von Informations- und Medienkompetenz, der Leseförderung, der Entwicklung neuer Dienstleistungen und der Modernisierung der technischen Infrastruktur. ³Das Nähere regelt das für Kultur zuständige Ministerium in einer Förderrichtlinie.

(2) Das Land unterhält eine zentrale Fachstelle für öffentliche Bibliotheken, welche die Aufgabe hat, Konzepte und Programme zur Sicherung und zum Ausbau öffentlicher Bibliotheken zu entwickeln und zu vermitteln sowie insbesondere kleinere Bibliotheken in allen bibliotheksfachlichen Fragen zu informieren, zu beraten und zu unterstützen.

§ 11 Förderung der Freien Szene und der Soziokultur

(1) Im Bereich der Förderung der Künste (§ 7) und der kulturellen Bildung (§ 9), der Kultur- und Kreativwirtschaft (§ 12), der Vorhaben, die einen Beitrag zur gesellschaftlichen Entwicklung (§ 14) oder zum strukturellen Wandel (§ 15) leisten und der Experimente (§ 17) fördert das Land insbesondere auch künstlerische Vorhaben, die in den Arbeits- und Organisationsformen der Freien Szene realisiert werden.

(2) Das Land unterstützt beispielgebende Vorhaben von soziokulturellen Zentren und sonstigen Einrichtungen, die im Bereich der Soziokultur tätig sind und die einen Beitrag zur Teilhabe aller an der Kultur leisten.

§ 12 Förderung der Kultur- und Kreativwirtschaft

(1) ¹Das Land fördert beispielgebende künstlerische und kulturelle Vorhaben, die einen Beitrag zur Entwicklung der Kultur- und Kreativwirtschaft leisten. ²Es fördert insbesondere künstlerische Vorhaben, die auf einen Transfer von Kreativ-Kompetenzen zwischen Künstlerinnen beziehungsweise Künstlern und Kultur- und Kreativwirtschaft abzielen.

(2) Das Land fördert Vorhaben, die die Arbeitsbedingungen von Künstlerinnen und Künstlern strukturell verbessern oder ihre Vermarktungschancen in der Kultur- und Kreativwirtschaft erhöhen.

§ 13 Förderung der Breitenkultur
(1) Das Land fördert in Zusammenarbeit mit den die Breitenkultur landesweit vertretenden Verbänden nichtprofessionelle kulturelle Aktivitäten sowie modellhafte Vorhaben, bei denen nichtprofessionelle und professionelle Künstlerinnen und Künstler zusammen arbeiten.
(2) [1]Das Land unterstützt nichtprofessionelle Aktivitäten insbesondere im Bereich der Musik. [2]Gefördert werden die Qualifizierung von Laienmusikern, das Vorantreiben neuer Entwicklungen, herausragende Projekte im Laienmusikbereich und die Nachwuchsarbeit durch Musikorganisationen.

§ 14 Kultur und gesellschaftlicher Wandel
[1]Das Land entwickelt und realisiert spezielle Programme der Kunst- und Kulturförderung zu gesellschaftlich bedeutsamen Themen. [2]Es fördert Vorhaben, die geeignet sind, einen Beitrag zum gesellschaftlichen Diskurs und zur gesellschaftlichen Entwicklung zu leisten.

§ 15 Kultur und Strukturwandel
Das Land fördert künstlerische und kulturelle Vorhaben, die zur strukturellen Entwicklung Nordrhein-Westfalens, insbesondere zur Stadtentwicklung, Regionalentwicklung oder zur wirtschaftlichen Entwicklung, insbesondere zur Entwicklung des Tourismus im nationalen oder internationalen Standortwettbewerb, einen Beitrag leisten.

§ 16 Förderung interkommunaler Kooperation
(1) [1]Das Land fördert die regional angelegte interkommunale Zusammenarbeit, die dem Erfahrungsaustausch, der Durchführung gemeinsamer Kunst- und Kulturprojekte und der kulturellen Profilierung der Regionen dient. [2]Ziel ist es, organisatorische und finanzielle Synergien zu erschließen und das kulturelle Angebot insbesondere in den Kreisen und kleineren Gemeinden zu stärken.
(2) Das Land fördert die landesweit angelegte interkommunale Zusammenarbeit, die dem Erfahrungsaustausch und der Durchführung gemeinsamer Kunst- und Kulturprojekte dient.
(3) Das Land unterstützt gemeindeübergreifende Kooperationen und Kulturentwicklungsplanungen, die der Erhaltung und Weiterentwicklung der kulturellen Infrastruktur, der Verbesserung der Auslastung, der Sicherung der Qualität und der Verbesserung der Wirtschaftlichkeit dienen.

§ 17 Experimente
Das Land unterstützt in Einzelfällen experimentelle Kulturprojekte, auch wenn sie keinem der vorgenannten Handlungsfelder zuzuordnen sind.

Teil 4
Landeseigene Kulturaufgaben

§ 18 Aufgaben des Landes im föderalen Bundesstaat und international
[1]Das Land nimmt die kulturpolitischen Interessen des Landes nach außen sowohl auf Bundes- als auch auf europäischer und internationaler Ebene wahr. [2]Es setzt sich insbesondere in den zuständigen Gremien dafür ein, die rechtlichen Rahmenbedingungen für die Kultur und die Kulturschaffenden weiterzuentwickeln und zu verbessern. [3]Es beteiligt sich an den gemeinsam getragenen Kultureinrichtungen im föderalen Bundesstaat.

§ 19 Eigene Einrichtungen und Beteiligungen des Landes
(1) Zur Erfüllung kultureller Aufgaben, die im Landesinteresse liegen, kann das Land Gesellschaften, Stiftungen und sonstige Vereinigungen gründen und unterhalten oder sich an solchen beteiligen.
(2) [1]Das Land unterhält das Landesarchiv Nordrhein-Westfalen. [2]Dieses hat nach Maßgabe des Archivgesetzes Nordrhein-Westfalen vom 16. März 2010 (GV. NRW. S. 188), das zuletzt durch Artikel 2 des Gesetzes vom 29. Januar 2013 (GV. NRW. S. 31) geändert worden ist, die Aufgabe, das Archivgut von Behörden, Gerichten und sonstigen öffentlichen Stellen des Landes sowie ihrer Rechts- und Funktionsvorgänger zu archivieren.
(3) Die Universitäts- und Landesbibliotheken Bonn, Düsseldorf und Münster nehmen im Auftrag und nach Weisung des Landes arbeitsteilig landesbibliothekarische Aufgaben wahr, insbesondere solche nach dem Pflichtexemplargesetz Nordrhein-Westfalen vom 29. Januar 2013 (GV. NRW. S. 31).

§ 20 Kunst am Bau
(1) Das Ministerium stellt bei ausgewählten Neu- und Umbauvorhaben des Landes die erforderlichen Mittel für Kunst-am-Bau-Projekte zur Verfügung.

(2) ¹Die Durchführung des Projektes obliegt dem jeweiligen Bauherrn. ²Soweit kulturfachliche Fragen betroffen sind, erfolgt sie in Zusammenarbeit mit dem Ministerium oder mit der von ihm benannten Stelle. ³Die Auswahl der Bauvorhaben und die Auswahl der Künstlerinnen und Künstler erfolgen in transparenten Verfahren und beziehen die künftigen Nutzer mit ein. ⁴Die ausgewählte Künstlerin oder der ausgewählte Künstler soll möglichst frühzeitig in den Planungsprozess einbezogen werden.
(3) Das Ministerium soll das Verfahren im Einvernehmen mit dem Finanzministerium und dem für Städtebau zuständigen Ministerium in einer Richtlinie regeln.

§ 21 Kulturmarketing und sonstige Aktivitäten des Landes
(1) Das Land kann zur Darstellung der Qualität und Vielfalt und zur Imagebildung des Kulturlandes Nordrhein-Westfalen sowie zur Stärkung des Kulturtourismus nach Nordrhein-Westfalen im In- und Ausland Werbe- und Marketingmaßnahmen durchführen.
(2) Das Land kann über die in den §§ 18 bis 21 Absatz 1 genannten Aufgaben hinausgehend eigene Kulturveranstaltungen und sonstige Maßnahmen im kulturellen Bereich durchführen, wenn sie im Interesse des Landes liegen.

Teil 5
Kulturförderplan

§ 22 Zweck und Inhalt
(1) ¹Die Kulturförderung des Landes erfolgt auf der Grundlage eines für die Dauer von fünf Jahren geltenden Kulturförderplans. ²Er soll so gefasst sein, dass er ein hohes Maß an Transparenz und Planungssicherheit schafft.
(2) Der Kulturförderplan konkretisiert für die Förderperiode die Ziele der Kulturförderung, zeigt Entwicklungsperspektiven auf, benennt die Bereiche, in denen besondere Schwerpunkte gesetzt werden sollen, und macht nähere Angaben zu den Handlungsfeldern und zu den geplanten Ausgaben vorbehaltlich der Bereitstellung entsprechender Mittel durch den Haushaltsgesetzgeber.
(3) ¹Der Kulturförderplan berücksichtigt wesentliche kulturelle Entwicklungen in den Gemeinden und Gemeindeverbänden. ²Er bezieht dabei die Ergebnisse, Feststellungen und Empfehlungen ein, die sich aus Maßnahmen der Qualitätssicherung im Sinne des Teils 6 – insbesondere aus dem Landeskulturbericht nach § 25 – ergeben.

§ 23 Verfahren
(1) Das Ministerium stellt den Kulturförderplan zu Beginn der Legislaturperiode im Einvernehmen mit dem Landtag auf.
(2) ¹Die kommunalen Spitzenverbände sowie Organisationen und Verbände aus Kultur, Kunst und kultureller Bildung sind anzuhören. ²Künstlerinnen und Künstler werden im Rahmen von Dialogveranstaltungen (§ 27) ebenfalls einbezogen.

Teil 6
Berichtswesen und Qualitätssicherung

§ 24 Kulturförderbericht
Das Ministerium erstellt und veröffentlicht jährlich einen Kulturförderbericht, in dem die wesentlichen Fördermaßnahmen der Kulturförderung des Landes in ihrer Gesamtheit und ihren Zusammenhängen dargestellt werden.

§ 25 Landeskulturbericht
(1) ¹Einmal in jeder Legislaturperiode legt das Ministerium einen Landeskulturbericht vor, der zur Umsetzung des zu Beginn der Legislaturperiode aufgestellten Kulturförderplans, zur Angebots- und Nachfrageentwicklung und zur Lage der Kultur in Nordrhein-Westfalen insgesamt berichtet und Stellung nimmt. ²Der Bericht soll mögliche Schlussfolgerungen für künftige Schwerpunkte der Kulturförderung darstellen.
(2) ¹Das Ministerium kann zur Vorbereitung Sachverständigen-Gutachten in Auftrag geben und Forschungsaufträge erteilen. ²Die Gemeinden und Gemeindeverbände unterstützen die Erstellung des Landeskulturberichtes, indem sie dem Land die für den Bericht erforderlichen Daten und Informationen zur Verfügung stellen, die bei ihnen bereits vorhanden sind oder die sie im Rahmen der ihnen

obliegenden Aufgaben zu erheben beabsichtigen. ³Die Darstellung und Übermittlung dieser Daten erfolgt nach Vorgabe des Ministeriums in Abstimmung mit den kommunalen Spitzenverbänden.
⁴Daten, für welche die Voraussetzungen des Satzes 2 nicht erfüllt sind, kann das Land in Abstimmung mit den kommunalen Spitzenverbänden selbst oder durch eine von ihm beauftragte Stelle erheben, sofern das Land die dafür anfallenden Kosten trägt.
(3) Das Ministerium leitet den Landeskulturbericht dem Landtag zu.

§ 26 Evaluation der Förderungen
¹Das Land überprüft regelmäßig die Zweckmäßigkeit und Wirksamkeit seiner Fördermaßnahmen. ²Es kann Fördernehmer im Zuwendungsbescheid oder Fördervertrag verpflichten, an Evaluationsmaßnahmen nach Satz 1 in einer der jeweiligen Förderung angemessenen Art und Weise mitzuwirken.

§ 27 Regelmäßiger Dialog über Ziele und Wirksamkeit der Kulturförderung des Landes
In regelmäßigen Abständen soll ein Dialog mit den Kulturschaffenden und -verantwortlichen über die Ziele und die Wirksamkeit der Kulturförderung des Landes stattfinden.

Teil 7
Förderverfahren

§ 28 Förderverfahren
(1) Das Förderverfahren richtet sich nach dem Haushalt und nach den haushaltsrechtlichen Vorschriften des Landes, insbesondere den §§ 23 und 44 der Landeshaushaltsordnung und den dazu ergangenen Verwaltungsvorschriften und Förderrichtlinien.
(2) ¹Das Ministerium kann im Einvernehmen mit dem Finanzministerium und darüber hinaus, soweit Kommunen als Fördernehmer betroffen sind, mit dem für Kommunales zuständigen Ministerium, sowie gemäß § 44 Absatz 1 Satz 4 der Landeshaushaltsordnung mit dem Landesrechnungshof, allgemeine Förderrichtlinien[1]) sowie Förderrichtlinien zu den Handlungsfeldern der §§ 6 bis 17 erlassen.
²Diese sind so zu gestalten, dass das Verfahren unter Beachtung der Grundsätze der Wirtschaftlichkeit und der Sparsamkeit auf möglichst unbürokratische und einfache Weise gestaltet wird und zugleich den bestmöglichen Einsatz der Fördermittel im Sinne der Zielsetzungen des § 3 sicherstellt.

§ 29 Formen der Förderung
Förderungen sind möglich durch Zuwendungsbescheid, Zuwendungsvertrag im Sinne des § 54 Verwaltungsverfahrensgesetz Nordrhein-Westfalen, Fördervereinbarung gemäß § 30 dieses Gesetzes und fachbezogene Pauschalen gemäß § 29 des Haushaltsgesetzes sowie nach § 30 des Haushaltsgesetzes.

§ 30 Fördervereinbarungen
¹Das Ministerium kann mit Gemeinden und Gemeindeverbänden, auch mit solchen, die sich in der Haushaltssicherung gemäß § 76 der Gemeindeordnung für das Land Nordrhein-Westfalen befinden, im Rahmen ihrer finanziellen Möglichkeiten zur mittel- bis langfristigen Erhaltung vorhandener kommunaler Kultureinrichtungen zeitlich befristete Fördervereinbarungen abschließen, in denen der Betrieb und die Entwicklung einer Einrichtung sowie die dazu erforderlichen beiderseitigen Finanzierungsbeiträge zwischen Land und Gemeinde vereinbart werden. ²Das Ministerium kann eine solche Fördervereinbarung mit einer Gemeinde oder einem Gemeindeverband auch zum Erhalt einer nichtkommunalen, aber von der Gemeinde oder dem Gemeindeverband langfristig geförderten Kultureinrichtung abschließen, wenn die Einrichtung das beantragt und sie vom Land institutionell gefördert wird. ³Die zuwendungsrechtlichen und haushaltsrechtlichen Regelungen zum Förderungsrahmen sind zu beachten.

§ 31 Jurys und Sachverständige
¹Die für Kultur zuständigen Behörden sollen zur Entscheidungsfindung bei der Verleihung von Auszeichnungen, Preisen und Stipendien sowie zum Erwerb von Kunstwerken und sonstigen bedeutsamen Kulturgütern Jurys oder externe Sachverständige hinzuziehen. ²Das gilt auch für Fördermaßnahmen im Rahmen von Förderprogrammen des Landes, wenn für die Entscheidungsfindung regelmäßig wiederkehrend eine Auswahl aus einer Mehrzahl von Bewerbungen getroffen werden muss. ³Die Jurys

---

1) Siehe dazu die Allgemeine Richtlinie zur Förderung von Projekten und Einrichtungen auf dem Gebiet der Kultur, der Kunst und der kulturellen Bildung, abgedruckt als Nr. D10.III.2.

sollen geschlechtsparitätisch besetzt werden. [4]Mitglieder der Jurys sollen auch Künstlerinnen und Künstler sein. [5]Es soll eine regelmäßige Rotation der Mitglieder sichergestellt werden.

§ 32 Antragstellung und Beratung
[1]Die Bezirksregierungen beraten die Kulturschaffenden bei der Antragstellung. [2]Sie bieten regelmäßig Informationsveranstaltungen für Zuwendungsempfängerinnen und Zuwendungsempfänger zum Zuwendungsverfahren an.

Teil 8
Schlussbestimmungen

§ 33 Übergangsbestimmung
Abweichend von §§ 22 Absatz 1, 23 Absatz 1 wird der erste Kulturförderplan unmittelbar nach Inkrafttreten dieses Gesetzes erarbeitet und gilt dann bis zur Veröffentlichung des nächsten Kulturförderplans in der folgenden Legislaturperiode gemäß §§ 22 und 23.

§ 34 Inkrafttreten
Dieses Gesetz tritt am Tag nach der Verkündung[1)] in Kraft.

---

1) Verkündet am 23.12.2014.

D10.III.2 Allgemeine Förderrichtlinie Kultur

Allgemeine Richtlinie zur Förderung von Projekten und Einrichtungen auf dem Gebiet der Kultur, der Kunst und der kulturellen Bildung

RdErl. d. Ministeriums für Familie, Kinder, Jugend, Kultur und Sport – 422-03.0 v. 30.12.2014
(MBl. NRW. 2014 S. 862)

Diese Richtlinie wird gemäß § 28 Absatz 2 des Kulturfördergesetzes NRW im Einvernehmen mit dem Finanzministerium und dem Ministerium für Inneres und Kommunales sowie gemäß § 44 Absatz 1 Satz 4 der Landeshaushaltsordnung mit dem Landesrechnungshof erlassen. Sie ist im Geltungsbereich des Gesetzes nach § 1 Kulturfördergesetz NRW anzuwenden.

1 Zuwendungszweck, Rechtsgrundlage

1.1 Zuwendungszweck
Zuwendungszweck ist die Förderung von Kultur, Kunst und kultureller Bildung durch das Land Nordrhein-Westfalen.

1.2 Rechtsgrundlage
Die Kulturförderung ist auf der Grundlage des Kulturfördergesetzes NRW vorzunehmen. Die zuwendungsrechtliche Umsetzung der Förderungen des Landes aufgrund des Kulturfördergesetzes NRW erfolgt grundsätzlich auf der Grundlage der §§ 23 und 44 Landeshaushaltsordnung einschließlich der dazu erlassenen Verwaltungsvorschriften. Ein Rechtsanspruch auf Förderung besteht nicht; vielmehr entscheidet die Bewilligungsbehörde aufgrund ihres pflichtgemäßen Ermessens im Rahmen der verfügbaren Haushaltsmittel.

1.3 Fachbezogene Pauschalen und Förderung gemeinnütziger Zwecke durch Glücksspieleinnahmen
Die Förderrichtlinie gilt gemäß §§ 29 Absatz 6, 30 Absatz 3 des Haushaltsgesetzes nicht für die im jährlichen Haushaltsplan geregelten fachbezogenen Pauschalen (§ 29 Haushaltsgesetz) und die Weiterleitung von Konzessionseinnahmen aus Glücksspielen (§ 30 Haushaltsgesetz).

2 Gegenstand der Förderung
Gefördert werden Maßnahmen der im Teil 3 des Kulturfördergesetzes NRW benannten Handlungsfelder:
a) Förderung der kulturellen Infrastruktur (§ 6 Kulturfördergesetz NRW),
b) Förderung der Künste (§ 7 Kulturfördergesetz NRW),
c) Erhalt des kulturellen Erbes (§ 8 Kulturfördergesetz NRW),
d) Förderung der kulturellen Bildung (§ 9 Kulturfördergesetz NRW),
e) Förderung der Bibliotheken (§ 10 Kulturfördergesetz NRW),
f) Förderung der Freien Szene und der Soziokultur (§ 11 Kulturfördergesetz NRW),
g) Förderung der Kultur- und Kreativwirtschaft (§ 12 Kulturfördergesetz NRW),
h) Förderung der Breitenkultur (§ 13 Kulturfördergesetz NRW),
i) Kultur und gesellschaftlicher Wandel (§ 14 Kulturfördergesetz NRW),
j) Kultur und Strukturwandel (§ 15 Kulturfördergesetz NRW),
k) Förderung interkommunaler Kooperation (§ 16 Kulturfördergesetz NRW),
l) Experimente (§ 17 Kulturfördergesetz NRW).

3 Zuwendungsempfängerin / Zuwendungsempfänger
Zuwendungsempfängerinnen und Zuwendungsempfänger sind
a) die Gemeinden und Gemeindeverbände,
b) sonstige juristische Personen des öffentlichen und privaten Rechts, Personenverbünde und Einzelpersonen, soweit sie in einem der im Teil 3 des Kulturfördergesetzes NRW genannten Handlungsfelder tätig sind.

4 Art und Umfang, Höhe der Zuwendung

4.1 Zuwendungsarten
Das Land fördert Kultur, Kunst und kulturelle Bildung
a) bei Zuwendungsempfängerinnen nach Nummer 3 a) durch Projektförderungen und
b) bei sonstigen Zuwendungsempfängerinnen und Zuwendungsempfängern durch institutionelle Förderungen und durch Projektförderungen.

4.2 Finanzierungsart
Das Land kann Zuwendungen grundsätzlich in Form von Anteilsfinanzierungen, Fehlbedarfsfinanzierungen oder Festbetragsfinanzierungen bewilligen. Die Zuwendung kann in Form der Festbetragsfinanzierung gewährt werden, wenn die Einnahmen- und Ausgabenpositionen des Kosten- und Finanzierungsplans aufgrund besonderer Erfahrungswerte verlässlich und nachvollziehbar begründet geschätzt werden können.
Unabhängig davon wird die Förderung grundsätzlich in Form einer Festbetragsfinanzierung gewährt, wenn die Zuwendung des Landes nicht mehr als 50 vom Hundert der Gesamtausgaben ausmacht und die Zuwendungshöhe nicht mehr als 50.000 Euro beträgt.

4.3 Bemessungsgrundlage

a) Anerkennung bürgerschaftlichen Engagements
Bürgerschaftliches Engagement in Form von freiwilligen, unentgeltlichen Arbeiten kann bei der Förderung nach dieser Richtlinie auf Grundlage der Richtlinie zur Berücksichtigung von bürgerschaftlichem Engagement bei der Gewährung von Zuwendungen im Zuständigkeitsbereich des Ministeriums für Familie, Kinder, Jugend, Kultur und Sport – 112 (BdH) – 14-01-01 – in der jeweils gültigen Fassung (SMBl. NRW. 631) als fiktive Ausgabe in die Bemessungsgrundlage einbezogen werden.

b) Zuwendungsfähige Ausgaben
Bei Projektförderung von Zuwendungsempfängern nach Nummer 3 b) können in begründeten Einzelfällen auch allgemeine Ausgaben als zuwendungsfähig anerkannt werden, wenn sie dem jeweiligen Projekt zugerechnet werden können.

4.4 Sponsoringmittel
Die Bewilligungsbehörde kann für den Einzelfall bestimmen, dass für den Projekt-Zweck eingeworbene Sponsoringmittel bei der Bemessung einer Zuwendung außer Betracht bleiben, soweit der Zuwendungsempfängerin oder dem Zuwendungsempfänger ein aus eigenen Mitteln zu erbringender Eigenanteil in Höhe von 10 vom Hundert der zuwendungsfähigen Gesamtausgaben verbleibt und Bundes- oder EU-Recht nicht entgegensteht.

4.5 Versicherungsverbot
Gemäß Nr. 1.4 ANBest-I der VV zu § 44 LHO dürfen Zuwendungsempfängerinnen und Zuwendungsempfänger Risiken für Schäden an Personen, Sachen und Vermögen nur versichern, soweit eine Versicherung gesetzlich vorgeschrieben ist.
Ausnahmen hierzu sind im Zuwendungsbereich Kulturförderung aus Gründen der wirtschaftlichen und sparsamen Mittelverwendung möglich, wenn unabhängig von der Förderhöhe oder dem Fördersatz die Zuwendungsempfängerin bzw. der Zuwendungsempfänger im Einzelfall nachvollziehbar begründet, dass der Abschluss einer Versicherung die wirtschaftlichere Lösung ist.

5 Verfahren
Das Land fördert auf schriftlichen Antrag, der in der Regel bei der zuständigen Bewilligungsbehörde einzureichen ist. Bewilligungsbehörde ist in der Regel die zuständige Bezirksregierung. Die kulturfachliche Förderentscheidung trifft das für Kultur zuständige Ministerium, soweit das Ministerium diese Entscheidung nicht an die Bewilligungsbehörde oder eine andere Stelle delegiert hat.

6 Inkrafttreten / Außerkrafttreten
Diese Richtlinie tritt am 1. Januar 2015 in Kraft.
Sie tritt mit dem Außerkrafttreten des noch aufzustellenden ersten Kulturförderplans außer Kraft, spätestens aber nach fünf Jahren. Die Geltungsdauer kann im Einvernehmen mit dem Finanzministerium und dem Ministerium für Inneres und Kommunales verlängert werden, wenn noch kein neuer Kulturförderplan aufgestellt ist.

D10.III.3 Förderrichtlinien Denkmalpflege

Richtlinien über die Gewährung von Zuwendungen für Denkmalschutz und Denkmalpflege (Förderrichtlinien Denkmalpflege)[1)]

RdErl. d. Ministeriums für Heimat, Kommunales, Bau und Gleichstellung des Landes Nordrhein-Westfalen v. 16. Mai 2019— 525 — (MBl. NRW. S. 211)
(SMBl. NRW 224)

1 Zuwendungszweck, Rechtsgrundlage

1.1 Zuwendungszweck

Ziel der Landesregierung ist es, durch Denkmalschutz und Denkmalpflege das baukulturelle, archäologische und paläontologische Erbe Nordrhein-Westfalens zu erhalten.

Das Land gewährt nach §§ 35 und 36 des Denkmalschutzgesetzes vom 11. März 1980 (GV. NRW. S. 226, ber. S. 716) in der jeweils geltenden Fassung Landesmittel als Zuwendungen für den Erhalt, die Pflege, die sinnvolle Nutzung, die wissenschaftliche Erforschung und die öffentliche Präsentation von Denkmälern.

1.2 Rechtsgrundlagen

Das Land Nordrhein-Westfalen gewährt die Zuwendungen für Maßnahmen im Bereich des Denkmalschutzes und der Denkmalpflege auf Antrag nach Maßgabe dieser Förderrichtlinie sowie den §§ 23 und 44 der Landeshaushaltsordnung (im Folgenden LHO genannt) in der Fassung der Bekanntmachung vom 26. April 1999 (GV. NRW. S. 158) und des Runderlasses des Finanzministeriums „Verwaltungsvorschriften zur Landeshaushaltsordnung" vom 30. September 2003 (MBl. NRW. S. 1254) jeweils in der jeweils geltenden Fassung.

Die Bewilligungsbehörde entscheidet aufgrund ihres pflichtgemäßen Ermessens im Rahmen des von der Obersten Denkmalbehörde aufgestellten Denkmalförderungsprogrammes. Die Förderung erfolgt ohne Rechtsanspruch im Rahmen der verfügbaren Haushaltsmittel.

Aus gewährten Zuwendungen kann nicht auf eine künftige Förderung geschlossen werden.

2 Gegenstand der Förderung

Gefördert werden Maßnahmen, die zum Erhalt und Instandsetzung der denkmalwerten Substanz eines Objektes nach § 2 des Denkmalschutzgesetzes sowie sonstiger archäologischer Stätten, deren Erforschung, Erfassung, Sicherung und Präsentation erforderlich sind. Den Gemeinden können zur Förderung denkmalpflegerischer Maßnahmen Dritter Pauschalmittel zur eigenen Bewirtschaftung zugewiesen werden.

Teil 1

3 Pauschalzuweisungen an Gemeinden und Gemeindeverbände zur Förderung von Denkmalpflegemaßnahmen

3.1 Zuwendungsempfänger

Zuwendungsempfänger sind Gemeinden und Gemeindeverbände. Diese sind gemäß Nummer 12 der Verwaltungsvorschriften für Zuwendungen an Gemeinden zu § 44 LHO, Teil II der Verwaltungsvorschriften zur LHO (im Folgenden VVG genannt) zur Weiterleitung der Fördermittel berechtigt und gewähren aus den ihnen zur Verfügung gestellten Mitteln Zuschüsse zur Förderung kleinerer privater Denkmalpflegemaßnahmen an natürliche und juristische Personen.

[1)] Der RdErl. tritt **am 30.6.2024 außer Kraft**, vgl. Nr. 7.

3.2 Zuwendungsvoraussetzung

Voraussetzung für die Gewährung von Pauschalzuweisungen ist die Veranschlagung von komplementären kommunalen Haushaltsmitteln.

3.3 Art und Umfang, Höhe der Zuwendung

3.3.1 Zuwendungsart

Die Zuwendungen werden im Wege der Projektförderung gewährt.

3.3.2 Finanzierungsart

Die Zuwendung wird als Festbetragsfinanzierung gewährt.

3.3.3 Form der Zuwendung

Die Mittel werden Gemeinden und Gemeindeverbänden als Pauschalzuweisungen zur Förderung kleinerer Denkmalpflegemaßnahmen Dritter zugewiesen.

3.3.4 Bemessungsgrundlage

3.3.4.1

Die Gewährung von Pauschalmitteln an Gemeinden und Gemeindeverbände richtet sich nach der Größe des Denkmalbestandes, dem Umfang der denkmalpflegerischen Maßnahmen in der Gemeinde und in dem Gemeindeverband sowie der jeweiligen haushälterischen Situation der einzelnen Kommune.

3.3.4.2

Die von Seiten des Landes zur Verfügung gestellten Pauschalmittel sind grundsätzlich in gleicher Höhe durch die Gemeinde beziehungsweise den Gemeindeverband im jeweiligen Haushalt zu verstärken. Gemeinden, die ein Haushaltssicherungskonzept gemäß § 76 Absatz 2 der Gemeindeordnung für das Land Nordrhein-Westfalen in der Fassung der Bekanntmachung vom 14. Juli 1994 (GV. NRW. S. 666) oder einem Haushaltssanierungsplan gemäß § 6 des Stärkungspaktgesetzes vom 9. Dezember 2011 (GV. NRW. S. 662) jeweils in der jeweils geltenden Fassung aufzustellen haben, erhalten eine Erhöhung der landesseitigen Pauschalmittel um 20 Prozent. Gemeinden mit einem überdurchschnittlichen Denkmalbestand pro Einwohner erhalten eine Erhöhung der landesseitigen Pauschalmittel um 10 Prozent. Der insgesamte Fördersatz kann somit bis zu 80 Prozent betragen. Die Fördersätze pro Gemeinde werden jährlich durch das für Denkmalschutz zuständige Ministerium veröffentlicht.

3.3.4.3

Zweckgebundene Geldspenden können als Komplementärmittel eingesetzt werden, soweit gemäß Nummer 2.3.3 VVG zu § 44 LHO ein kommunaler Eigenanteil in Höhe von 10 Prozent verbleibt.

3.3.4.4

Abweichend von Nummer 1.1 VVG sollen Zuwendungen nur bewilligt werden, wenn die Zuwendung im Einzelfall mehr als 1 000 Euro beträgt.

3.3.4.5

Die Zuwendung ist zusammen mit den kommunalen Verstärkungsmitteln nach Maßgabe des Absatzes 2 an den Endbegünstigten weiterzuleiten. Hierfür ist folgende Nebenbestimmung entsprechend des jeweiligen Fördersatzes nach Absatz 2 in den Zuwendungsbescheid mit aufzunehmen:
Die Zuwendungsempfängerin oder der Zuwendungsempfänger hat die mit der Zuwendung gewährten Landesmittel

a) in gleicher Höhe mit eigenen kommunalen Mitteln (bei einem Fördersatz von 50 Prozent),
b) mit kommunalen Mitteln in der Höhe von einem Viertel der Landesmittel (Fördersatz 80 Prozent),
c) mit kommunalen Mitteln in der Höhe von drei Siebteln der Landesmittel (Fördersatz 70 Prozent) oder
d) mit kommunalen Mitteln in der Höhe von zwei Dritteln der Landesmittel (Fördersatz 60 Prozent)

zu verstärken und an den Endbegünstigten weiterzuleiten.

3.4 Verfahren

Das Verwaltungsverfahren soll entsprechend dem E-Government-Gesetz Nordrhein-Westfalen vom 8. Juli 2016 (GV. NRW. S. 551) in der jeweils geltenden Fassung weitgehend elektronisch durchgeführt werden.

3.4.1

Der Antrag auf Bewilligung von Pauschalmitteln ist bei der zuständigen Bewilligungsbehörde (Bezirksregierung) in der Regel bis zum 1. Oktober des dem Denkmalförderungsprogramm vorausgehenden Jahres zu stellen.

3.4.2

Abweichend von Nummer 1.4 der Anlage 1 zu Nummer 5.1 VVG zu § 44 der Landeshaushaltsordnung – Allgemeine Nebenbestimmungen für Zuwendungen zur Projektförderung an Gemeinden (im Folgenden ANBest-G genannt) erfolgt die Auszahlung der Zuwendung automatisch zum 31. Juli des Bewilligungsjahres. Soweit die Bestandskraft des Zuwendungsbescheids nach dem 31. Juli eintritt, erfolgt die Auszahlung zum Zeitpunkt der Bestandskraft.
Bedingt hierdurch gelten folgende Abweichungen von den ANBest-G:

3.4.2.1

Abweichend von Nummer 9.3.1 ANBest-G kann ein Widerruf mit Wirkung für die Vergangenheit auch in Betracht kommen, soweit die Zuwendungsempfängerin oder der Zuwendungsempfänger den ausgezahlten Betrag nicht innerhalb des Durchführungszeitraums zur Erfüllung des Zuwendungszwecks verwendet.

3.4.2.2

Abweichend von Nummer 9.5 Satz 1 ANBest-G können für die Zeit von der Auszahlung bis zur zweckentsprechenden Verwendung ebenfalls Zinsen in Höhe von 5 Prozentpunkten über dem Basiszinssatz gemäß § 49a Absatz 4 in Verbindung mit Absatz 3 Satz 1 des Verwaltungsverfahrensgesetzes für das Land Nordrhein-Westfalen in der Fassung der Bekanntmachung vom 12. November 1999 (GV. NRW. S. 602) in der jeweils geltenden Fassung verlangt werden, wenn ausgezahlte Beträge nicht innerhalb des Durchführungszeitraums zur Erfüllung des Zuwendungszwecks verwendet worden sind und der Zuwendungsbescheid nicht zurückgenommen oder widerrufen wird.
Auf die Abweichungen gemäß Satz 1 und Nummer 3.4.2.1 ist im Zuwendungsbescheid hinzuweisen.

3.4.3

Die Gemeinden und Gemeindeverbände bewilligen Zuschüsse an Dritte aus den Ihnen zur Verfügung gestellten Pauschalmitteln nach den Vorgaben von Teil 2 dieser Richtlinie in Verbindung mit der VV zu § 44 LHO. Die durch die Gemeinde und durch den Gemeindeverband aus diesen Mitteln gewährten Zuschüsse an Dritte müssen im Einzelfall mindestens 200 Euro betragen und dürfen den Betrag von 10 000 Euro nicht überschreiten.

Anträge sind schriftlich vor Maßnahmebeginn bei der Unteren Denkmalbehörde einzureichen.

Teil 2

4 Förderung von denkmalpflegerischen Einzelprojekten

4.1 Zuwendungsempfänger

Zuwendungsempfänger sind Gemeinden und Gemeindeverbände, Kirchen oder Religionsgemeinschaften sowie private (juristische und natürliche) Personen.

4.2 Zuwendungsvoraussetzung

Zuwendungen dürfen nur bewilligt werden, wenn das zu fördernde Objekt gemäß § 3 des Denkmalschutzgesetzes in die Denkmalliste eingetragen ist oder dessen vorläufiger Schutz gemäß § 4 des Denkmalschutzgesetzes angeordnet wurde und die endgültige Unterschutzstellung bis zum Abschluss der Maßnahme voraussichtlich erfolgen wird. Maßnahmen der wissenschaftlichen Erforschung sowie kommunale Maßnahmen der Denkmalerfassung und der Präsentation müssen grundsätzlich entsprechende Objekte beinhalten oder der Vorbereitung einer Entscheidung nach dem Denkmalschutzgesetz dienen. Bei Baumaßnahmen muss eine Erlaubnis nach § 9 des Denkmalschutzgesetzes vorliegen.

4.3 Art und Umfang, Höhe der Zuwendung

4.3.1 Zuwendungsart

Die Zuwendungen werden im Wege der Projektförderung als nicht rückzahlbare Zuschüsse zu den zuwendungsfähigen Ausgaben gewährt.

4.3.2 Finanzierungsart

Die Zuwendung wird grundsätzlich als Anteilsfinanzierung mit Höchstbetragsregelung gewährt. Bei durch den Bund kofinanzierten Projekten kann in Ausnahmefällen entsprechend der Regelungen des Bundes für die Kofinanzierung eine Zuwendung in Form der Fehlbedarfsfinanzierung mit Höchstbetragsregelung gewährt werden.

4.3.3 Form der Zuwendung

Die Mittel werden als Einzelzuschüsse für denkmalpflegerische Maßnahmen gewährt.

4.3.4 Bemessungsgrundlage

Förderfähig sind die denkmalbedingten Aufwendungen für Baudenkmäler und bewegliche Denkmäler sowie Ausgaben für Bauvoruntersuchungen, wissenschaftliche Erforschung und Erfassung sowie Präsentation.

D10.III.3 Förderrichtlinien Denkmalpflege

4.3.5 Höhe der Zuwendung

4.3.5.1

Die Höhe der Zuwendung beträgt für Gemeinden und Gemeindeverbände, Kirchen oder Religionsgemeinschaften bis zu 30 Prozent und für Private bis zu 50 Prozent der zuwendungsfähigen Ausgaben.

4.3.5.2

Eigene Arbeit- und Sachleistungen des Antragstellers in Form von freiwilligen, unentgeltlichen Leistungen können als fiktive Ausgabe in die Bemessungsgrundlage einbezogen werden. Bei freiwilligen unentgeltlichen Arbeiten können 15 Euro je Arbeitsstunde angesetzt werden. Die freiwilligen, unentgeltlichen Arbeiten von Architekten und Ingenieuren sind mit dem Mindestwert der Honorarzone bei den anzurechnenden Kosten nach der Honorarordnung für Architekten und Ingenieure vom 10. Juli 2013 (BGBl. I S. 2276) anzusetzen. Freiwillige, unentgeltliche Arbeiten von Fachfirmen werden auf der Grundlage der DIN 276:2018-12 „Kosten im Bauwesen" in Verbindung mit den Kostenwerten des Baukosteninformationsdienstes mit dem anteiligen Wert von 70 Prozent in die Bemessungsgrundlage einbezogen. Die Anrechnung erfolgt unter der Bedingung, dass die Zuwendung nicht die Summe der tatsächlichen Ausgaben überschreitet.

4.3.5.3

Zweckgebundene Geldspenden können zur Erbringung des Eigenanteils eingesetzt werden, bei Gemeinden und Gemeindeverbänden soweit gemäß Nummer 2.3.3 VVG zu § 44 LHO ein Eigenanteil von 10 Prozent der zuwendungsfähigen Ausgaben verbleibt.

4.4 Verfahren

4.4.1

Anträge sind schriftlich mit Formblatt vor Maßnahmebeginn in der Regel bis zum 1. Oktober des dem Denkmalförderungsprogramms vorausgehenden Jahres bei der zuständigen Bewilligungsbehörde (Bezirksregierung) einzureichen. Der Unteren Denkmalbehörde (Gemeinde) ist eine Kopie des Antrags einzureichen. Dem Antrag sind die zur Prüfung der beabsichtigten Maßnahme erforderlichen Unterlagen (wie zum Beispiel Kostenvoranschläge, Leistungsbeschreibungen, Planzeichnungen, Finanzierungspläne) beizufügen.

4.4.2

Gemäß § 36 des Denkmalschutzgesetzes bereitet die Bezirksregierung das Denkmalförderungsprogramm im Benehmen mit dem Landschaftsverband für das jeweils folgende Jahr vor. Der Programmvorschlag ist der Obersten Denkmalbehörde, die das Denkmalförderungsprogramm aufstellt, bis zu einem von ihr benannten Termin vorzulegen.

4.4.3

Bewilligungsbehörden sind die Bezirksregierungen. Eine Durchschrift des Zuwendungsbescheides ist dem Landschaftsverband sowie der Unteren Denkmalbehörde zuzuleiten.

Teil 3

5 Zuwendungen für Aufgaben der Bodendenkmalpflege

5.1 Zuwendungsempfänger

Zuwendungsempfänger sind der Landschaftsverband Rheinland, der Landschaftsverband Westfalen-Lippe und die Stadt Köln.

5.2 Art und Umfang, Höhe der Zuwendung

5.2.1 Zuwendungsart

Die Zuwendungen werden im Wege der Projektförderung gewährt.

5.2.2 Finanzierungsart

Die Zuwendung wird für Maßnahmen in Form der Anteilfinanzierung mit Höchstbetragsregelung gewährt. Der Fördersatz beträgt maximal 80 Prozent je Einzelprojekt des Jahresprogramms.

5.2.3 Form der Zuwendung

Die Mittel werden als Zuweisung gewährt.

5.2.4 Bemessung der Zuwendung

Zuwendungsfähig sind die in der Anlage aufgeführten Ausgaben.

5.3 Sonstige Zuwendungsbestimmungen

Neben den einschlägigen Bestimmungen der ANBest-G ist den Zuwendungsempfängern zusätzlich aufzugeben:

5.3.1

Abweichungen vom durch die Oberste Denkmalbehörde bekanntgegebenen Jahresprogramm nach § 36 Denkmalschutzgesetz, die im Laufe des Haushaltsjahres notwendig werden und zu neuen Einzelprojekten führen, bedürfen der Zustimmung der Obersten Denkmalbehörde. Ein entsprechender Antrag ist der Bewilligungsbehörde vorzulegen.

5.3.2

Die von den Ämtern für Bodendenkmalpflege geführten monatlichen Grabungskalender sind der Bewilligungsbehörde und der Obersten Denkmalbehörde am Monatsanfang zur Kenntnis zu geben.

5.3.3

Befunde und Funde von besonderer Bedeutung sind der Bewilligungsbehörde und der Obersten Denkmalbehörde unverzüglich anzuzeigen.

5.3.4

Auf Anforderung sind der Bewilligungsbehörde und der Obersten Denkmalbehörde Projektdaten, □ergebnisse, und □erfahrungen zu geförderten Maßnahmen zur Verfügung zu stellen.

5.3.5

Die Zuwendungsempfängerinnen und Zuwendungsempfänger sind verpflichtet, sich an Landesausstellungen über die Ergebnisse der geförderten Maßnahmen zu beteiligen. Dazu sind bei der Organisation der Landesausstellungen gegebenenfalls Funde, Ergebnisberichte, wissenschaftliche Studien, Abbildungsmaterial und -vorlagen sowie Modelle zur Verfügung zu stellen.

5.3.6

Die Zuwendungsempfängerinnen und Zuwendungsempfänger legen der Bewilligungsbehörde bis zum 30. September des auf die Bewilligung folgenden Jahres einen Verwendungsnachweis auf Grundlage des Grundmusters 3 der Anlage 4 zu Nummer 10.3 der VVG zu § 44 LHO mit dem Sachbericht und dem dazu gehörenden zahlenmäßigen Nachweis vor.

5.3.7

Die von ihnen als Erstempfängerin oder Erstempfänger geprüften Verwendungsnachweise der Letztempfänger der Zuwendungen sind dem Verwendungsnachweis nach Nummer 7.1 ANBest-G beizufügen.

5.4 Verfahrensvorschriften

5.4.1 Antragsverfahren

5.4.1.1 Antragstellung und Antragsunterlagen

Anträge zur Förderung bodendenkmalpflegerischer Maßnahmen sind unter Beifügung des entsprechenden Jahresprogramms bis zum 1. November des dem Bewilligungszeitraum vorausgehenden Jahres in zweifacher Ausfertigung nach Grundmuster 1 der Anlage 2 zu Nummer 3.1 VVG zu § 44 LHO der Bezirksregierung Köln beziehungsweise Münster vorzulegen. Als Bestandteil des Antrags sind eine schriftliche Projektbeschreibung sowie ein Finanzierungsplan des beabsichtigten Jahresprogramms vorzulegen.

Die Gesamtkosten der Maßnahmen sind summarisch auszuweisen.

Ausgrabungen und Sonderprojekte, Konservierungs- und Restaurierungsmaßnahmen sowie Veröffentlichungen werden in einer gesonderten Programmliste zusammengefasst.

5.4.1.2 Antragsweg

Auf Grundlage der vorgelegten Jahresprogramme bereiten die Bezirksregierungen das Förderprogramm für das jeweils folgende Jahr vor. Der Programmvorschlag ist der Obersten Denkmalbehörde bis zu einem durch diese festgelegten Termin von der Bewilligungsbehörde vorzulegen. Das Förderprogramm wird in einer gemeinsamen Besprechung der Fördernehmerinnen und Fördernehmer und der Bewilligungsbehörde mit dem für Denkmalschutz zuständigen Ministerium abgestimmt.

5.4.2 Bewilligungsverfahren

5.4.2.1

Bewilligungsbehörden sind die Bezirksregierungen Köln und Münster.

5.4.2.2 Auszahlung der Mittel

Die Auszahlung der Mittel erfolgt quartalsweise.

5.4.3 Weiterleitung der Mittel

Die Gemeinden und Gemeindeverbände sind gemäß Nummer 12 VVG zu § 44 LHO zur Weiterleitung der Fördermittel berechtigt.

Teil 4

6 Sonstige Zuwendungsbestimmungen

6.1
§ 35 Absatz 5 des Denkmalschutzgesetzes findet Anwendung.

6.2
Ausnahmen von dieser Richtlinie bedürfen der Zustimmung des für Denkmalschutz zuständigen Ministeriums.

6.3
Auf Bautafeln und in Publikationen, wie beispielsweise Plakaten und Broschüren, ist die finanzielle Beteiligung des Landes in geeigneter Weise öffentlich kenntlich zu machen. So sind das Landeswappen in der jeweils gültigen Wort-Bild-Marke des für Denkmalschutz zuständigen Ministeriums sowie der entsprechende Hinweis aufzunehmen: „Gefördert vom Ministerium für Heimat, Kommunales, Bau und Gleichstellung des Landes Nordrhein-Westfalen".

7 Inkrafttreten und Außerkrafttreten
Der Runderlass tritt am 1. Juli 2019 in Kraft und am 30. Juni 2024 außer Kraft.

Anlage

Zuwendungsfähige Ausgaben Bodendenkmalpflege

1
Im Zusammenhang mit Ausgrabungen:

1.1
Ausgaben für befristet eingestellte Mitarbeiterinnen und Mitarbeiter, soweit diese nicht durch die Arbeitsverwaltung finanziert werden und sie ausschließlich und zusätzlich in den geförderten Projekten tätig sind.

1.2
Ausgaben für befristet eingestellte studentische Hilfskräfte bei archäologischen Ausgrabungen, Prospektionen, zur Dokumentation und Auswertung, soweit diese ausschließlich und zusätzlich in den geförderten Projekten tätig sind.

1.3
Ausgaben für Werkverträge mit Dritten im Zusammenhang mit archäologischen Maßnahmen.

1.4
Ausgaben für den Einsatz von für archäologische Grabungen notwendigem technischem Gerät, wie zum Beispiel Mieten für Großgeräte, wie Bagger oder Lastwagen oder entsprechende Leasingkosten.

1.5
Ausgaben zum Ankauf von grabungsspezifischen Verbrauchsmaterialien, wie zum Beispiel Werkzeuge, Folien, Zeichenmaterialien und Ähnliches und technischen Geräten zur Prospektion, Vermessung und Dokumentation. Gegenstände, deren Anschaffungskosten 410 Euro ohne Umsatzsteuer übersteigt, sind zu inventarisieren und bis Ablauf der Zweckbindungspflicht ausschließlich für weitere Maßnahmen gemäß dieser Förderrichtlinie zu verwenden. Die Zweckbindungsfrist beträgt fünf Jahre.

2
Im Zusammenhang mit sonstigen bodendenkmalpflegerischen Maßnahmen:

2.1
Ausgaben für Luftbildaufnahmen- und andere Prospektionsmaßnahmen.

D10.III.3 Förderrichtlinien Denkmalpflege

2.2
Ausgaben für die wissenschaftliche Untersuchung und Erforschung von Bodendenkmälern und Funden.

2.3
Ausgaben für die Fundbearbeitung und Fundaufbewahrung, einschließlich Mieten für zeitlich befristet angemietete Lagerräume.

2.4
Ausgaben zur Konservierung und Restaurierung von beweglichen Bodendenkmälern.

2.5
Ausgaben zur Konservierung und Restaurierung von ortsfesten Bodendenkmälern.

2.6
Ausgaben für Veröffentlichungen auf dem Gebiet der Bodendenkmalpflege.

2.7
Ausgaben für Entschädigungen und Belohnungen in der Umsetzung von § 17 des Denkmalschutzgesetzes.

3
Im Zusammenhang mit Sonderprojekten:

3.1
Ausgaben der Planung und Durchführung wissenschaftlicher Fachtagungen.

3.2
Ausgaben der Planung und Durchführung archäologischer und paläontologischer Ausstellungen.

3.3
Ausgaben für naturwissenschaftliche Untersuchungen und Gutachten, wie zum Beispiel Geophysik, Materialanalysen und naturwissenschaftliche Datierungsverfahren.

3.4
Ausgaben für paläontologische Forschungen.

3.5
Ausgaben für Digitalisierungsprojekte von Bodendenkmaldaten.

3.6
Ausgaben für Maßnahmen zur Öffentlichkeitsarbeit und Präsentation von Bodendenkmälern wie zum Beispiel Beschilderungen, Schutzbauten, archäologische Wanderwege und Rundtouren.

3.7
Ausgaben für bodendenkmalpflegerische Maßnahmen der Stadtarchäologien im Sinne der vorgenannten Fördertatbestände.

4
Bei der Bemessung der Zuwendung sind die Interessen des Landes und des Zuwendungsempfängers sorgfältig abzuwägen. Dabei sind insbesondere folgende Kriterien zu berücksichtigen:

4.1
Bedeutung des Denkmals,

4.2
Notwendigkeit, Dringlichkeit und Zweckmäßigkeit der Maßnahme und

4.3
Vorteile und Belastungen des Zuwendungsempfängers aus dem Denkmal.

5
Bei der Bemessung der Zuwendungen für studentische Hilfskräfte und bei wissenschaftlichen Untersuchungen sind Personalkosten zugrunde zu legen, die sich an den Richtlinien der Tarifgemeinschaft über die Arbeitsbedingungen der wissenschaftlichen und studentischen Hilfskräfte vom 23. Juni 2008 in der jeweils geltenden Fassung orientieren. Die Höhe der Förderung bei wissenschaftlichen Mitarbeitern richtet sich nach dem Tarifvertrag für den öffentlichen Dienst (TVöD) und dessen Entgeltordnung (VKA).

Verordnung über Zuständigkeiten im Bereich des Kulturgutschutzes (ZustVO-Kulturgutschutz NRW)

Vom 30. April 2019 (GV. NRW. S. 231)
(SGV. NRW. 224)

Aufgrund des § 3 Abs. 1 Satz 2 des Gesetzes zur Neuregelung des Kulturgutschutzrechts[1] vom 31. Juli 2016 (BGBl. I S. 1914), zuletzt geändert durch Art. 6 Abs. 13 des Gesetzes zur Reform der strafrechtlichen Vermögensabschöpfung vom 13. April 2017 (BGBl. I S. 872) und des § 5 Abs. 3 des Landesorganisationsgesetzes NRW vom 10. Juli 1962 (GV. NRW. S. 421), zuletzt geändert durch Art. 2 des sechsten Änderungsgesetzes vom 01. Oktober 2013 (GV. NRW. S. 566) wird verordnet:

§ 1 [Zuständige Behörde]
Das für Kultur zuständige Ministerium ist zuständige oberste Landesbehörde und zuständige Behörde für die Aufgaben nach dem Kulturgutschutzgesetz.

§ 2 [Inkrafttreten, Außerkrafttreten]
¹Diese Verordnung tritt am Tag nach ihrer Verkündung[2] in Kraft. ²Gleichzeitig tritt die Verordnung über Zuständigkeiten und das Antragsrecht nach dem Gesetz zum Schutz deutschen Kulturgutes gegen Abwanderung vom 18. Mai 2004 (GV. NRW. S. 248) außer Kraft.

---

1) Richtig wohl: „§ 3 Abs. 1 Satz 2 des Gesetzes zum Schutz von Kulturgut (Kulturgutschutzgesetz - KGSG)".
2) Verkündet am 31.5.2019.

Verfassung für Rheinland-Pfalz

Vom 18. Mai 1947 (VOBl. S. 209)
(BS Rh-Pf 100–1)
zuletzt geändert durch Art. 1 38. ÄndG vom 8. Mai 2015 (GVBl. S. 35)
– Auszug –

Erster Hauptteil
Grundrechte und Grundpflichten

III. Abschnitt
Schule, Bildung und Kulturpflege

Artikel 40 [Kultur, Schutz der geistigen Arbeit, Denkmal- und Landschaftspflege, Sport]
(1) Das künstlerische und kulturelle Schaffen ist durch das Land, die Gemeinden und Gemeindeverbände zu pflegen und zu fördern.
[...]
(3) ¹Der Staat nimmt die Denkmäler der Kunst, der Geschichte und der Natur sowie die Landschaft in seine Obhut und Pflege. ²Die Teilnahme an den Kulturgütern des Lebens ist dem gesamten Volke zu ermöglichen.
[...]

Denkmalschutzgesetz (DSchG)

Vom 23. März 1978 (GVBl. S. 159)
(BS Rh-Pf 224-2)
zuletzt geändert durch Art. 3 BibliotheksG-ÄndG vom 3. Dezember 2014 (GVBl. S. 245)

Inhaltsübersicht

Erster Abschnitt
Grundsätze
- § 1 Aufgabe des Denkmalschutzes und der Denkmalpflege
- § 2 Pflicht zur Erhaltung und Pflege

Zweiter Abschnitt
Kulturdenkmäler

Erster Unterabschnitt
Allgemeines
- § 3 Begriff des Kulturdenkmals
- § 4 Unbewegliche und bewegliche Kulturdenkmäler, Umgebungsschutz
- § 5 Denkmalzonen
- § 6 Auskünfte
- § 7 Betreten von Grundstücken

Zweiter Unterabschnitt
Geschützte Kulturdenkmäler
- § 8 Geschützte Kulturdenkmäler, Unterschutzstellung
- § 9 Öffentliche Auslegung
- § 10 Denkmalliste
- § 11 Einstweiliger Schutz
- § 12 Anzeige- und Hinweispflichten
- § 13 Genehmigung von Veränderungen, Anzeige von Instandsetzungen
- § 13a Genehmigungsverfahren
- § 14 Wiederherstellung und Erhaltung, Ersatzvornahme
- § 15 Freier Zugang zu Kulturdenkmälern

Dritter Abschnitt
Funde
- § 16 Begriff des Fundes
- § 17 Anzeige
- § 18 Erhaltung
- § 19 Wissenschaftliche Bearbeitung
- § 20 Schatzregal
- § 21 Genehmigung von Nachforschungen, Anzeige von Arbeiten, Kostenerstattung
- § 22 Grabungsschutzgebiete

Vierter Abschnitt
Besondere Bestimmungen für Kirchen und Religionsgemeinschaften
- § 23 [Besondere Bestimmungen für Kirchen und Religionsgemeinschaften]

Fünfter Abschnitt
Organisation
- § 24 Denkmalschutzbehörden
- § 25 Denkmalfachbehörde
- § 25a Denkmalschutz in Archivangelegenheiten
- § 25b Denkmalschutz in Bibliotheksangelegenheiten
- § 26 Landesbeirat für Denkmalpflege
- § 27 Ehrenamtliche Denkmalpfleger
- § 28 Anerkannte Denkmalpflegeorganisationen

Sechster Abschnitt
Finanzhilfen des Landes
- § 29 Förderungsgrundsätze

Siebenter Abschnitt
Enteignung, ausgleichspflichtige Maßnahmen, Vorkaufsrecht
- § 30 Enteignung
- § 31 Ausgleichspflichtige Maßnahmen
- § 32 Vorkaufsrecht

Achter Abschnitt
Ordnungswidrigkeiten
- § 33 [Ordnungswidrigkeiten]

Neunter Abschnitt
Übergangs- und Schlußbestimmungen
- § 34 Übergangsbestimmung für geschützte Denkmäler und zum Denkmalbuch
- § 35 Gebührenfreiheit
- § 36 Durchführungsvorschriften
- § 37 Schutz von Kulturdenkmälern bei bewaffneten Konflikten und bei Katastrophenfällen
- § 38 Aufhebung und Änderung von Rechtsvorschriften
- § 39 Inkrafttreten

D11.I.1 Denkmalschutzgesetz Rheinland-Pfalz

Erster Abschnitt
Grundsätze

§ 1 Aufgabe des Denkmalschutzes und der Denkmalpflege

(1) Aufgabe des Denkmalschutzes und der Denkmalpflege ist es, die Kulturdenkmäler (§ 3) zu erhalten und zu pflegen, insbesondere deren Zustand zu überwachen, Gefahren von ihnen abzuwenden und sie zu bergen.

(2) Aufgabe des Denkmalschutzes und der Denkmalpflege ist es auch, die Kulturdenkmäler wissenschaftlich zu erforschen und die Ergebnisse der Öffentlichkeit, insbesondere für Zwecke der Bildung und Erziehung, zugänglich zu machen.

(3) Denkmalschutz und Denkmalpflege wirken darauf hin, daß die Kulturdenkmäler in die Raumordnung und Landesplanung, die städtebauliche Entwicklung und den Naturschutz und die Landschaftspflege einbezogen und einer sinnvollen Nutzung zugeführt werden.

(4) Bei der Wahrnehmung der Aufgaben von Denkmalschutz und Denkmalpflege wirken die Denkmalschutzbehörden und die Denkmalfachbehörde mit den Eigentümern von Kulturdenkmälern, den sonstigen über Kulturdenkmäler Verfügungsberechtigten und den Besitzern von Kulturdenkmälern sowie den Gemeinden und Gemeindeverbänden nach Maßgabe der Bestimmungen dieses Gesetzes in möglichst partnerschaftlicher Weise zusammen.

§ 2 Pflicht zur Erhaltung und Pflege

(1) ¹Eigentümer, sonstige Verfügungsberechtigte und Besitzer sind verpflichtet, die Kulturdenkmäler im Rahmen des Zumutbaren zu erhalten und zu pflegen. ²Weitergehende Bestimmungen dieses Gesetzes bleiben unberührt.

(2) ¹Die Zumutbarkeit ist unter Berücksichtigung der durch die Eigenschaft als Kulturdenkmal begründeten Situationsgebundenheit im Rahmen der Sozialbindung des Eigentums und dessen Privatnützigkeit zu bestimmen. ²Unzumutbar ist insbesondere eine wirtschaftliche Belastung durch Erhaltungskosten, wenn diese dauerhaft nicht durch die Erträge oder den Gebrauchswert des Kulturdenkmals aufgewogen werden; in diesem Fall kann die Erhaltungspflicht auf die unveränderte Belassung des Kulturdenkmals beschränkt werden, wenn und soweit die Eigenart und Bedeutung des Kulturdenkmals dies auch unter Berücksichtigung der Belange der nach Absatz 1 Verpflichteten gebietet. ³Die Unzumutbarkeit ist durch die nach Absatz 1 Verpflichteten nachzuweisen. ⁴Die nach Absatz 1 Verpflichteten können sich nicht auf die Belastungen durch erhöhte Erhaltungskosten berufen, die dadurch verursacht wurden, dass Erhaltungsmaßnahmen diesem Gesetz oder sonstigem öffentlichem Recht zuwider unterblieben sind.

(3) ¹Das Land, der Bund, die Gemeinden und Gemeindeverbände und alle Körperschaften, Anstalten und Stiftungen des öffentlichen Rechts haben bei ihren Maßnahmen und Planungen, insbesondere bei der Bauleitplanung, die Belange des Denkmalschutzes und der Denkmalpflege sowie die Verpflichtung zur Bewahrung des Kulturerbes gemäß dem UNESCO-Übereinkommen zum Schutz des Kultur- und Naturerbes der Welt vom 16. November 1972 zu berücksichtigen. ²Bei Maßnahmen und Planungen, die Belange des Denkmalschutzes oder der Denkmalpflege berühren, ist die Denkmalfachbehörde von Beginn an zu beteiligen.

(4) Bauliche, technische und wirtschaftliche Maßnahmen, die Kulturdenkmäler in ihrem Bestand, ihrem Erscheinungsbild oder ihrem wissenschaftlichen Wert gefährden oder beeinträchtigen können, sind auf den unbedingt notwendigen Umfang zu beschränken; Absatz 1 Satz 2 gilt entsprechend.

Zweiter Abschnitt
Kulturdenkmäler

Erster Unterabschnitt
Allgemeines

§ 3 Begriff des Kulturdenkmals

(1) Kulturdenkmäler sind Gegenstände aus vergangener Zeit,
1. die
   a) Zeugnisse, insbesondere des geistigen oder künstlerischen Schaffens, des handwerklichen oder technischen Wirkens oder historischer Ereignisse oder Entwicklungen,

b) Spuren oder Überreste menschlichen Lebens oder
c) kennzeichnende Merkmale der Städte und Gemeinden
sind und
2. an deren Erhaltung und Pflege oder wissenschaftlicher Erforschung und Dokumentation aus geschichtlichen, wissenschaftlichen, künstlerischen oder städtebaulichen Gründen ein öffentliches Interesse besteht.
(2) Als Kulturdenkmäler gelten Gegenstände aus vergangener Zeit, die Zeugnisse, Spuren oder Überreste der Entwicklungsgeschichte der Erde oder des pflanzlichen oder tierischen Lebens sind und an deren Erhaltung und Pflege oder wissenschaftlicher Erforschung und Dokumentation ein öffentliches Interesse im Sinne von Absatz 1 Nr. 2 besteht.

§ 4 Unbewegliche und bewegliche Kulturdenkmäler, Umgebungsschutz
(1) [1]Unbewegliche Kulturdenkmäler sind insbesondere:
1. ortsfeste Einzeldenkmäler und Bauwerke,
2. Denkmalzonen (§ 5).

[2]Denkmalzonen können Gegenstände umfassen, die keine Kulturdenkmäler, jedoch für das Erscheinungsbild der Gesamtheit von Bedeutung sind. [3]Ausstattungsstücke, Freiflächen und Nebenanlagen sind Teil des unbeweglichen Kulturdenkmals, soweit sie mit diesem aus Gründen des Denkmalschutzes und der Denkmalpflege eine Einheit bilden. [4]Gegenstand des Denkmalschutzes ist auch die Umgebung eines unbeweglichen Kulturdenkmals, soweit sie für dessen Bestand, Erscheinungsbild oder städtebauliche Wirkung von Bedeutung ist.
(2) [1]Bewegliche Kulturdenkmäler sind insbesondere:
1. bewegliche Einzelgegenstände,
2. Sammlungen und sonstige Gesamtheiten von beweglichen Einzelgegenständen.

[2]Im Falle des Satzes 1 Nr. 2 gilt Absatz 1 Satz 2 entsprechend.
(3) Auf unbewegliche Kulturdenkmäler ist in den Geobasisinformationen des amtlichen Vermessungswesens hinzuweisen.

§ 5 Denkmalzonen
(1) Denkmalzonen sind insbesondere:
1. bauliche Gesamtanlagen (Absatz 2),
2. kennzeichnende Straßen-, Platz- und Ortsbilder (Absatz 3 Satz 1) sowie planmäßige Quartiere und Siedlungen (Absatz 3 Satz 2),
3. kennzeichnende Ortsgrundrisse (Absatz 4),
4. historische Park-, Garten- und Friedhofsanlagen (Absatz 5),
5. Kulturstätten (Absatz 6).

(2) Bauliche Gesamtanlagen sind insbesondere Gebäudegruppen, die sich durch ihre Größe oder Vielfalt oder die Vielgestaltigkeit zugehöriger Elemente herausheben, Burg-, Festungs- und Schlossanlagen, Stadt- und Landwehren, Abteien und Klöster einschließlich der mit ihnen verbundenen Grün-, Frei- und Wasserflächen.
(3) [1]Kennzeichnende Straßen-, Platz- und Ortsbilder sind solche, deren Erscheinungsbild in seiner Gesamtheit eine bestimmte Epoche oder Entwicklung oder eine charakteristische Bauweise mit einheitlicher Stilart oder unterschiedlichen Stilarten veranschaulicht. [2]Planmäßige Quartiere und Siedlungen sind einheitlich gestaltete Anlagen, die auf einem gemeinsamen Konzept beruhen.
(4) Ein kennzeichnender Ortsgrundriß ist gegeben, wenn die Anordnung der Baulichkeiten nach ihrem Grundriß für eine bestimmte Epoche oder eine Entwicklung charakteristisch ist, insbesondere im Hinblick auf Ortsformen, Straßenführungen und Festungsanlagen.
(5) Historische Park-, Garten- und Friedhofsanlagen sind Werke der Gartenbaukunst oder Zeugnisse des Totengedenkens, deren Lage sowie architektonische und pflanzliche Gestaltung von der Funktion der Anlage als Lebensraum und Selbstdarstellung früherer Gesellschaften und der von ihnen getragenen Kultur Zeugnis geben.
(6) Kulturstätten sind umgrenzbare Teile der Erdoberfläche mit sichtbaren Werken oder Gestaltungsspuren menschlicher Kultur sowie Aufschlüsse von Kulturdenkmälern im Sinne des § 3 Abs. 2.

D11.I.1 Denkmalschutzgesetz Rheinland-Pfalz

§ 6 Auskünfte
Eigentümer, sonstige Verfügungsberechtigte und Besitzer haben den Denkmalschutzbehörden und der Denkmalfachbehörde sowie ihren Beauftragten die zur Erfüllung ihrer Aufgaben erforderlichen Auskünfte zu erteilen.

§ 7 Betreten von Grundstücken
(1) ¹Die Denkmalschutzbehörden, die Denkmalfachbehörde und ihre Beauftragten sind berechtigt, zur Vorbereitung und zur Durchführung der nach diesem Gesetz zu treffenden Maßnahmen Grundstücke zu betreten, Vermessungen und Untersuchungen vorzunehmen sowie Fotografien anzufertigen. ²Wohnungen dürfen gegen den Willen des Eigentümers nur zur Verhütung dringender Gefahr für Kulturdenkmäler betreten werden; das Grundrecht der Unverletzlichkeit der Wohnung (Artikel 13 des Grundgesetzes) wird insoweit eingeschränkt.

(2) Eigentümer, sonstige Verfügungsberechtigte und Besitzer sind vor dem Betreten der Grundstücke zu benachrichtigen, es sei denn, daß die Benachrichtigung nur durch öffentliche Zustellung vorgenommen werden kann oder bei Gefahr im Verzug eine rechtzeitige Benachrichtigung nicht möglich wäre.

Zweiter Unterabschnitt
Geschützte Kulturdenkmäler

§ 8 Geschützte Kulturdenkmäler, Unterschutzstellung
(1) Geschützte Kulturdenkmäler sind:
1. die unbeweglichen Kulturdenkmäler und
2. die durch Verwaltungsakt unter Schutz gestellten beweglichen Kulturdenkmäler.

(2) ¹Bewegliche Kulturdenkmäler werden nur unter Schutz gestellt, wenn
1. sie von besonderer Bedeutung sind oder
2. der Eigentümer die Unterschutzstellung anregt.

²Kulturdenkmäler, die sich in staatlichen oder anderen von der obersten Denkmalschutzbehörde bezeichneten Sammlungen oder in öffentlichen Archiven befinden, werden nicht unter Schutz gestellt.

(3) Soweit es zur Klarstellung erforderlich ist, soll die Eigenschaft als unbewegliches Kulturdenkmal
1. bei Denkmalzonen durch Rechtsverordnung und
2. im Übrigen durch Verwaltungsakt

festgestellt werden.

(4) ¹Über die Unterschutzstellung nach Absatz 1 Nr. 2 und die Feststellung nach Absatz 3 entscheidet die untere Denkmalschutzbehörde von Amts wegen oder auf Antrag der Denkmalfachbehörde; die Entscheidung ergeht im Benehmen mit der Denkmalfachbehörde. ²Will die untere Denkmalschutzbehörde von der Äußerung der Denkmalfachbehörde abweichen oder deren Antrag ablehnen, so hat sie dies der Denkmalfachbehörde mitzuteilen; diese hat das Recht, die Angelegenheit der oberen Denkmalschutzbehörde vorzulegen. ³Die obere Denkmalschutzbehörde kann über die Angelegenheit selbst entscheiden oder sie an die untere Denkmalschutzbehörde zurückverweisen.

(5) Vor der Feststellung nach Absatz 3 sind der Eigentümer und die Gemeinde, in deren Gebiet sich die Schutzmaßnahme auswirkt, zu hören; im Falle des Absatzes 3 Nr. 1 geschieht dies gemäß § 9.

(6) ¹Der Verwaltungsakt, durch den die Unterschutzstellung nach Absatz 1 Nr. 2 oder die Feststellung nach Absatz 3 Nr. 2 verfügt wird, ist dem Eigentümer des Kulturdenkmals bekanntzugeben. ²Ist die Ermittlung des Eigentümers nicht oder nur mit unverhältnismäßigen Schwierigkeiten oder Kosten möglich, ist der Verwaltungsakt öffentlich bekanntzumachen.

(7) Die Absätze 3 bis 6 gelten entsprechend für die Aufhebung der betreffenden Entscheidungen.

§ 9 Öffentliche Auslegung
(1) ¹Der Entwurf einer Rechtsverordnung nach § 8 Abs. 3 Nr. 1 ist in den Gemeinden, in deren Gebiet sich die Schutzmaßnahme auswirkt, bei der Gemeindeverwaltung einen Monat zur Einsicht öffentlich auszulegen; ist das Gebiet einer Ortsgemeinde berührt, erfolgt die Auslegung bei der Verbandsgemeindeverwaltung. ²Zusammen mit der Rechtsverordnung soll eine Karte über das Gebiet der Denkmalzone ausgelegt werden.

(2) ¹Ort und Zeit der Auslegung sind mindestens eine Woche vorher öffentlich bekanntzumachen; dabei ist darauf hinzuweisen, daß jeder, dessen Belange durch die Rechtsverordnung berührt werden, spätestens bis zwei Wochen nach Ablauf der Auslegungsfrist bei der unteren Denkmalschutzbehörde oder der Gemeindeverwaltung, im Falle des Absatzes 1 Satz 1 zweiter Halbsatz bei der Verbandsgemeindeverwaltung Bedenken und Anregungen schriftlich oder zur Niederschrift vorbringen kann. ²Bedenken und Anregungen können bis zwei Wochen nach Ablauf der Auslegungsfrist auch von den anerkannten Denkmalpflegeorganisationen (§ 28) vorgebracht werden.

(3) Von der Auslegung kann abgesehen werden, wenn die Personen, Behörden und Stellen, deren Belange von der Rechtsverordnung berührt werden, bekannt sind und ihnen unter Einräumung einer Frist von zwei Wochen Gelegenheit zur Einsicht in den Entwurf sowie zum Vorbringen von Bedenken und Anregungen gegeben wird.

§ 10 Denkmalliste

(1) ¹Geschützte Kulturdenkmäler (§ 8 Abs. 1) werden in die Denkmalliste eingetragen. ²Die Denkmalliste ist ein nachrichtlich geführtes Verzeichnis, mit dem Rechtswirkungen nicht verbunden sind. ³Sie wird von der Denkmalfachbehörde erstellt und fortgeführt. ⁴Eintragung und Löschung erfolgen von Amts wegen; sie können auch vom Eigentümer, von der Gemeinde, in deren Gebiet das Kulturdenkmal gelegen ist, oder vom Landesbeirat für Denkmalpflege angeregt werden. ⁵Eintragung und Löschung erfolgen im Benehmen mit der unteren Denkmalschutzbehörde; diese hat zuvor die Gemeinde, in deren Gebiet das Kulturdenkmal gelegen ist, zu hören. ⁶Die Eintragung ist zu löschen, wenn die Eigenschaft als Kulturdenkmal nicht oder nicht mehr vorliegt oder die Unterschutzstellung aufgehoben ist; dies gilt nicht, wenn die Wiederherstellung des Kulturdenkmals verfügt ist.

(2) Die untere Denkmalschutzbehörde führt einen Auszug der Denkmalliste für ihr Gebiet; sie unterrichtet die Eigentümer von der Eintragung und deren Löschung.

(3) ¹Die Einsicht in die Denkmalliste ist jedem gestattet. ²Das Verzeichnis geschützter beweglicher Kulturdenkmäler ist gesondert zu führen; die Einsicht ist jedem gestattet, der ein berechtigtes Interesse darlegt.

§ 11 Einstweiliger Schutz

(1) ¹Die untere Denkmalschutzbehörde kann bestimmen, daß Gegenstände, mit deren Unterschutzstellung nach § 8 Abs. 1 Nr. 2 zu rechnen ist, als geschützte Kulturdenkmäler gelten, wenn zu befürchten ist, daß sonst der Zweck der Unterschutzstellung nicht erreicht würde. ²§ 8 Abs. 4 und 6 gilt entsprechend.

(2) ¹Die einstweilige Unterschutzstellung erfolgt auf eine Dauer von längstens sechs Monaten. ²Sie kann einmal um höchstens drei Monate, mit Zustimmung der oberen Denkmalschutzbehörde um höchstens sechs Monate verlängert werden. ³Die einstweilige Unterschutzstellung ist aufzuheben, wenn nicht mehr damit zu rechnen ist, daß der einstweilig geschützte Gegenstand nach § 8 Abs. 1 Nr. 2 geschützt wird.

(3) Einstweilig geschützte Gegenstände werden für die Dauer ihrer einstweiligen Unterschutzstellung in die Denkmalliste (§ 10) eingetragen.

§ 12 Anzeige- und Hinweispflichten

(1) ¹Eigentümer, sonstige Verfügungsberechtigte und Besitzer haben Schäden und Mängel, die die Erhaltung von geschützten Kulturdenkmälern gefährden könnten, unverzüglich der unteren Denkmalschutzbehörde anzuzeigen; diese gibt der Denkmalfachbehörde von der Anzeige unverzüglich Kenntnis. ²Die gleiche Anzeigepflicht gilt, soweit die nach Satz 1 Verpflichteten an einem Gegenstand Besonderheiten feststellen, die dessen Eigenschaft als Kulturdenkmal begründen.

(2) ¹Der Eigentümer eines geschützten Kulturdenkmals hat die Absicht, dieses zu veräußern, rechtzeitig der unteren Denkmalschutzbehörde anzuzeigen. ²Vor Abschluß des Kaufvertrages hat der Eigentümer den Erwerber darauf hinzuweisen, daß der zu verkaufende Gegenstand ein geschütztes Kulturdenkmal ist. ³Ist die Veräußerung erfolgt, so hat der Veräußerer dies unter Angabe des Erwerbers unverzüglich der unteren Denkmalschutzbehörde mitzuteilen. ⁴Absatz 1 Satz 1 Halbsatz 2 gilt entsprechend.

(3) Im Erbfall soll der Erbe den Eigentumsübergang unverzüglich der unteren Denkmalschutzbehörde anzeigen.

§ 13 Genehmigung von Veränderungen, Anzeige von Instandsetzungen

(1) ¹Ein geschütztes Kulturdenkmal darf nur mit Genehmigung
1. zerstört, abgebrochen, zerlegt oder beseitigt,
2. umgestaltet oder sonst in seinem Bestand verändert,
3. in seinem Erscheinungsbild nicht nur vorübergehend beeinträchtigt oder
4. von seinem Standort entfernt

werden. ²Ausstattungsstücke (§ 4 Abs. 1 Satz 3) eines unbeweglichen Kulturdenkmals dürfen nur mit Genehmigung nicht nur vorübergehend entfernt werden. ³In der Umgebung (§ 4 Abs. 1 Satz 4) eines unbeweglichen Kulturdenkmals darf eine bauliche Anlage nur mit Genehmigung errichtet, verändert oder beseitigt werden.

(2) Die Genehmigung nach Absatz 1 wird nur erteilt, wenn
1. Belange des Denkmalschutzes nicht entgegenstehen oder
2. andere Erfordernisse des Gemeinwohls oder private Belange diejenigen des Denkmalschutzes überwiegen und diesen überwiegenden Interessen nicht auf sonstige Weise Rechnung getragen werden kann.

(3) ¹Die Genehmigung nach Absatz 1 kann mit Nebenbestimmungen versehen werden. ²Auflagen und Bedingungen können zum Ziel haben, den Eingriff in das Kulturdenkmal auf ein Mindestmaß zu beschränken oder nach Beendigung der Maßnahme den ursprünglichen Zustand wiederherzustellen. ³Insbesondere kann durch Auflagen sichergestellt werden, daß beim Abbruch oder bei der Zerlegung eines unbeweglichen Kulturdenkmals das Kulturdenkmal wieder errichtet wird oder bestimmte Teile geborgen oder bei einer anderen baulichen Anlage wieder verwendet werden. ⁴Sofern es hierfür erforderlich ist, kann Sicherheitsleistung verlangt werden; dies gilt nicht für juristische Personen des öffentlichen Rechts. ⁵Nebenbestimmungen zur Bergung und zur Wiederverwendung sollen Art und Ausmaß der erforderlichen Maßnahmen angeben. ⁶Soweit die besondere Eigenart, die Bedeutung des Kulturdenkmals oder die Schwierigkeit der Maßnahme es gebietet, kann im Einzelfall durch Auflagen sichergestellt werden, dass die Leitung oder die Durchführung von Arbeiten, die besondere Erfahrungen oder Kenntnisse voraussetzen, durch denkmalfachlich geeignete Personen erfolgt.

(4) ¹Die Instandsetzung eines geschützten Kulturdenkmals ist, soweit sie nicht nach Absatz 1 Satz 1 der Genehmigung bedarf, unter genauer Beschreibung der geplanten Maßnahme der unteren Denkmalschutzbehörde anzuzeigen. ²Die Instandsetzungsmaßnahmen dürfen frühestens nach Ablauf von zwei Monaten nach Abgabe der Anzeige begonnen werden; die untere Denkmalschutzbehörde kann im Einvernehmen mit der Denkmalfachbehörde vor Ablauf der Frist die Durchführung der Maßnahmen gestatten. ³Bei Gefahr im Verzug können die unbedingt notwendigen Instandsetzungsmaßnahmen ohne die Anzeige nach Satz 1 oder ohne Einhaltung der Frist nach Satz 2 Halbsatz 1 begonnen werden; die Anzeige ist unverzüglich nachzuholen. ⁴Die Instandsetzung ist zu untersagen, soweit überwiegende Belange des Denkmalschutzes oder der Denkmalpflege entgegenstehen oder solange die Beschreibung nach Satz 1 nicht vorgelegt ist. ⁵Von der Untersagung ist abzusehen, soweit sich der Betroffene bereit erklärt, die Maßnahme nach den Vorschlägen der Denkmalfachbehörde auszuführen. ⁶Die Entscheidung nach Satz 4 oder Satz 5 trifft die untere Denkmalschutzbehörde im Benehmen mit der Denkmalfachbehörde; § 13a Abs. 3 Satz 4 und 5 gilt entsprechend.

§ 13a Genehmigungsverfahren

(1) ¹Der Antrag auf Erteilung einer Genehmigung nach § 13 Abs. 1 ist schriftlich bei der unteren Denkmalschutzbehörde einzureichen. ²Dem Antrag sind alle für die Beurteilung des Vorhabens und die Bearbeitung des Antrags erforderlichen Unterlagen, insbesondere Pläne, Dokumentationen, Fotografien, Gutachten sowie Kosten- und Wirtschaftlichkeitsberechnungen beizufügen.

(2) ¹Die untere Denkmalschutzbehörde soll unverzüglich nach Eingang des Antrags prüfen, ob der Antrag vollständig und ob ein Erörterungstermin mit dem Antragsteller erforderlich ist. ²Fehlende Angaben und Unterlagen sind innerhalb von zwei Wochen nach Eingang des Antrags oder unmittelbar nach dem Erörterungstermin zu benennen und unter Setzung einer angemessenen Frist nachzufordern. ³Der Antrag kann zurückgewiesen werden, wenn er unvollständig ist oder erhebliche Mängel aufweist und der Antragsteller der Nachforderung nicht fristgerecht nachkommt.

(3) ¹Die Entscheidung über den Antrag trifft die untere Denkmalschutzbehörde im Benehmen mit der Denkmalfachbehörde; § 31 Abs. 1 Satz 2 bleibt unberührt. ²Zur Herstellung des Benehmens legt die untere Denkmalschutzbehörde der Denkmalfachbehörde den vollständigen Antrag sowie ihren Ent-

scheidungsvorschlag vor. ³Wenn die Denkmalfachbehörde sich nicht innerhalb von zwei Monaten nach Zugang der Unterlagen äußert, gilt das Benehmen als hergestellt. ⁴Will die untere Denkmalschutzbehörde von der Äußerung der Denkmalfachbehörde abweichen, so hat sie dies der Denkmalfachbehörde mitzuteilen; diese hat das Recht, die Angelegenheit der oberen Denkmalschutzbehörde vorzulegen. ⁵Die obere Denkmalschutzbehörde kann über die Angelegenheit selbst entscheiden oder sie an die untere Denkmalschutzbehörde zurückverweisen.
(4) Entscheidet die untere Denkmalschutzbehörde nicht spätestens vor Ablauf von drei Monaten seit Eingang des vollständigen Antrags über die Genehmigung nach § 13 Abs. 1, gilt diese als erteilt, wenn nicht vor Ablauf der Frist die zuständige Denkmalschutzbehörde oder die Denkmalfachbehörde dem Antragsteller gegenüber widersprochen hat.
(5) ¹Eine Genehmigung nach § 13 Abs. 1 erlischt, wenn nicht innerhalb von drei Jahren nach ihrer Erteilung mit der Durchführung der Maßnahme begonnen wurde oder wenn die Durchführung ein Jahr unterbrochen worden ist. ²Die Fristen nach Satz 1 können jeweils auf schriftlichen Antrag um bis zu zwei weitere Jahre verlängert werden. ³Die Verlängerung kann mit neuen Nebenbestimmungen verbunden werden.

§ 14 Wiederherstellung und Erhaltung, Ersatzvornahme
(1) ¹Wer ein geschütztes Kulturdenkmal beschädigt, hat nach Anordnung der unteren Denkmalschutzbehörde die betreffenden Maßnahmen einzustellen und den ursprünglichen Zustand wiederherzustellen. ²Entsprechendes gilt, wenn eine Maßnahme nach § 13 Abs. 1 oder Abs. 4 Satz 1 ohne die erforderliche Genehmigung oder Anzeige oder unter Abweichung von der der Anzeige beigefügten Beschreibung durchgeführt wird oder durchgeführt worden ist.
(2) ¹Eigentümer und sonstige Verfügungsberechtigte, die die Erhaltung eines geschützten Kulturdenkmals dadurch gefährden, daß sie im Rahmen des Zumutbaren vorhandene Schäden oder Mängel nicht beseitigen oder keine Vorsorge zur Verhinderung von Schäden und Mängeln treffen, haben nach Anordnung der unteren Denkmalschutzbehörde die erforderlichen Erhaltungsmaßnahmen durchzuführen. ²Andere Berechtigte können zur Duldung verpflichtet werden.
(3) ¹Für die Durchführung der Maßnahmen nach den Absätzen 1 und 2 kann die untere Denkmalschutzbehörde eine angemessene Frist setzen. ²Wird eine Anordnung nach Absatz 1 oder 2 nicht, im Falle des Satzes 1 nicht innerhalb der Frist, befolgt, kann die untere Denkmalschutzbehörde die erforderlichen Maßnahmen nach Maßgabe der Bestimmungen des Landesverwaltungsvollstreckungsgesetzes von einem Dritten durchführen lassen oder selbst durchführen. ³Bei Gefahr im Verzug kann die untere Denkmalschutzbehörde unmittelbar tätig werden; das gleiche gilt, wenn der Eigentümer oder sonstige Verfügungsberechtigte nicht rechtzeitig ermittelt werden kann.
(4) ¹Über die Anordnungen nach den Absätzen 1 und 2 Satz 1 und die Durchführung nach Absatz 3 Satz 2 entscheidet die untere Denkmalschutzbehörde im Benehmen mit der Denkmalfachbehörde; § 13a Abs. 3 Satz 4 und 5 gilt entsprechend. ²Im Falle des Absatzes 3 Satz 3 ist die Denkmalfachbehörde unverzüglich zu benachrichtigen.

§ 15 Freier Zugang zu Kulturdenkmälern
¹Die untere Denkmalschutzbehörde soll mit den Eigentümern, sonstigen Verfügungsberechtigten und Besitzern Vereinbarungen über den freien Zugang zu unbeweglichen Kulturdenkmälern treffen, soweit diese hierfür geeignet sind. ²Der Zugang zu öffentlich zugänglichen Kulturdenkmälern soll im Rahmen des wirtschaftlich Zumutbaren, soweit dies mit Eigenart und Bedeutung des jeweiligen Kulturdenkmals vereinbar ist, barrierefrei im Sinne des § 2 Abs. 3 des Landesgesetzes zur Gleichstellung behinderter Menschen ermöglicht werden.

Dritter Abschnitt
Funde

§ 16 Begriff des Fundes
Funde im Sinne dieses Gesetzes sind Gegenstände, von denen bei ihrer Entdeckung anzunehmen ist, daß sie Kulturdenkmäler (§ 3) sind oder als solche gelten.

§ 17 Anzeige
(1) ¹Funde (§ 16) sind unverzüglich der Denkmalfachbehörde mündlich oder schriftlich anzuzeigen. ²Die Anzeige kann auch bei der unteren Denkmalschutzbehörde, der Verbandsgemeindeverwaltung

oder der Gemeindeverwaltung erfolgen; diese leiten die Anzeige unverzüglich der Denkmalfachbehörde weiter.
(2) Anzeigepflichtig sind der Finder, der Eigentümer des Grundstückes, sonstige über das Grundstück Verfügungsberechtigte, der Besitzer des Grundstücks und der Leiter der Arbeiten, bei deren Durchführung der Fund entdeckt wurde; die Anzeige durch eine dieser Personen befreit die übrigen.

§ 18 Erhaltung
(1) [1]Der Fund und die Fundstelle sind bis zum Ablauf einer Woche nach Erstattung der Anzeige in unverändertem Zustand zu erhalten und soweit zumutbar, in geeigneter Weise vor Gefahren für die Erhaltung des Fundes zu schützen; die schriftliche Anzeige ist mit der Abgabe erstattet. [2]Auf Antrag kann die Denkmalfachbehörde die Frist nach Satz 1 erster Halbsatz verkürzen; sie soll der Fortsetzung der Arbeiten, die zur Erhaltung des Fundes oder der Fundstelle unterbrochen werden mußten, zustimmen, wenn die Unterbrechung unverhältnismäßig hohe Kosten verursachen würde.
(2) [1]Bewegliche Funde sind der Denkmalfachbehörde unverzüglich zur Aufbewahrung zu übergeben, wenn die Gefahr besteht, daß sie abhanden kommen. [2]§ 17 Abs. 1 Satz 2 gilt entsprechend.
(3) § 17 Abs. 2 findet entsprechend Anwendung.

§ 19 Wissenschaftliche Bearbeitung
(1) Eigentümer eines Grundstückes, sonstige über ein Grundstück Verfügungsberechtigte und Besitzer eines Grundstückes, auf dem ein Fund entdeckt wurde, haben die zur sachgemäßen Bergung des Fundes und zur Klärung der Fundumstände notwendigen Maßnahmen zu dulden.
(2) Die Denkmalfachbehörde ist berechtigt, bewegliche Funde zur wissenschaftlichen Bearbeitung vorübergehend in Besitz zu nehmen.

§ 20 Schatzregal
(1) Funde, die herrenlos sind oder die so lange verborgen waren, dass ihr Eigentümer nicht mehr zu ermitteln ist, werden mit der Entdeckung Eigentum des Landes, wenn sie von besonderer wissenschaftlicher Bedeutung sind oder bei staatlichen Nachforschungen oder in Grabungsschutzgebieten (§ 22) entdeckt werden.
(2) [1]Der Finder soll im Rahmen der verfügbaren Mittel des Landeshaushalts eine Belohnung erhalten. [2]Über die Höhe entscheidet die Denkmalfachbehörde unter Berücksichtigung der Umstände des Einzelfalls.

§ 21 Genehmigung von Nachforschungen, Anzeige von Arbeiten, Kostenerstattung
(1) [1]Nachforschungen, insbesondere Geländebegehungen mit Schatzsuchgeräten sowie Ausgrabungen, mit dem Ziel, Kulturdenkmäler zu entdecken, bedürfen der Genehmigung der unteren Denkmalschutzbehörde. [2]Sie trifft die Entscheidung im Einvernehmen mit der Denkmalfachbehörde; wird kein Einvernehmen erzielt, kann die untere Denkmalschutzbehörde von der Stellungnahme der Denkmalfachbehörde abweichen, soweit die obere Denkmalschutzbehörde zustimmt. [3]§ 13 Abs. 3 Satz 1 bis 4 und § 13a Abs. 4 gelten entsprechend. [4]Nachforschungen in der Verantwortung der Denkmalfachbehörde bedürfen keiner Genehmigung nach diesem Gesetz.
(2) Erd- und Bauarbeiten, bei denen zu vermuten ist, daß Kulturdenkmäler entdeckt werden, sind der Denkmalfachbehörde rechtzeitig anzuzeigen.
(3) [1]Die Träger öffentlicher oder privater Bau- oder Erschließungsvorhaben oder von Vorhaben zum Abbau von Rohstoffen oder Bodenschätzen, deren Gesamtkosten jeweils 500 000,00 EUR übersteigen, können als Veranlasser im Rahmen des Zumutbaren zur Erstattung der Kosten erdgeschichtlicher oder archäologischer Nachforschungen und Ausgrabungen einschließlich der Dokumentation der Befunde verpflichtet werden. [2]Diese Entscheidung einschließlich der Festsetzung und Anforderung des Erstattungsbetrages, der in der Regel 1 v.H. der Gesamtkosten der Vorhaben nicht überschreiten soll, erfolgt durch die Denkmalfachbehörde. [3]Das für Denkmalpflege zuständige Ministerium erlässt die zur Durchführung dieser Regelung erforderliche Verwaltungsvorschrift.

§ 22 Grabungsschutzgebiete
(1) [1]Abgegrenzte Gebiete können durch Rechtsverordnung zu Grabungsschutzgebieten erklärt werden, wenn eine begründete Vermutung besteht, daß sie Kulturdenkmäler bergen. [2]§ 6 gilt entsprechend; § 7 gilt mit der Maßgabe entsprechend, daß Absatz 2 nur auf bebaute oder umfriedete Grundstücke Anwendung findet, es sei denn, daß die nach § 7 Abs. 1 geplanten Maßnahmen Veränderungen an dem

Grundstück bewirken können. ³Für den Erlass der Rechtsverordnung gelten § 8 Abs. 4 und § 9 entsprechend.
(2) Durch Rechtsverordnung kann auch einstweiliger Schutz begründet werden; § 8 Abs. 4 und § 11 Abs. 1 Satz 1 und Abs. 2 finden sinngemäß Anwendung.
(3) Vorhaben in Grabungsschutzgebieten, die verborgene Kulturdenkmäler gefährden können, bedürfen der Genehmigung der unteren Denkmalschutzbehörde; § 13 Abs. 3 Satz 1 bis 4, § 13a Abs. 4 und § 21 Abs. 1 Satz 2 gelten entsprechend.
(4) Auf Grabungsschutzgebiete ist in den Geobasisinformationen des amtlichen Vermessungswesens hinzuweisen.

Vierter Abschnitt
Besondere Bestimmungen für Kirchen und Religionsgemeinschaften

§ 23 [Besondere Bestimmungen für Kirchen und Religionsgemeinschaften]
(1) ¹Bei Kulturdenkmälern, die dem Gottesdienst oder sonstigen Kulthandlungen zu dienen bestimmt sind, haben die Denkmalschutzbehörden und die Denkmalfachbehörde auf die kultischen und seelsorgerischen Belange der Kirchen und Religionsgemeinschaften vorrangig Rücksicht zu nehmen. ²§ 30 findet keine Anwendung.
(2) ¹Maßnahmen nach § 13 Abs. 1 und 4 Satz 1 führen die Kirchen und Religionsgemeinschaften sowie die ihrer Aufsicht unterstehenden juristischen Personen an den Kulturdenkmälern, über die sie verfügungsberechtigt sind, im Benehmen mit der unteren Denkmalschutzbehörde und der Denkmalfachbehörde durch. ²Das gleiche gilt für Nachforschungen, Arbeiten und Vorhaben (§ 21 Abs. 1 und 2, § 22 Abs. 3) auf den Grundstücken der Kirchen und Religionsgemeinschaften sowie der ihrer Aufsicht unterstehenden juristischen Personen. ³Die §§ 6, 7, 12, 14, 25a Abs. 2 und § 30 finden keine Anwendung.
(3) ¹Absatz 2 gilt nur, wenn die Kirche oder Religionsgemeinschaft über eine von der obersten Denkmalschutzbehörde anerkannte Stelle verfügt, die die Aufgaben des Denkmalschutzes und der Denkmalpflege wahrnimmt. ²Die Anerkennung erfolgt, wenn Ausstattung und Organisation dieser Stelle sowie die Anwendung interner Vorschriften der Kirche oder Religionsgemeinschaft über Anzeigepflichten, Genehmigungsvorbehalte und Eingriffsmöglichkeiten Gewähr für die Erhaltung und Pflege der Kulturdenkmäler bieten. ³Verfügt eine Kirche oder Religionsgemeinschaft nicht über eine eigene nach Satz 1 anerkannte Stelle, kann sie sich mit Genehmigung der obersten Denkmalschutzbehörde der anerkannten Stelle einer anderen Kirche oder Religionsgemeinschaft bedienen; die Genehmigung ist unter den Voraussetzungen des Satzes 2 zu erteilen. ⁴Die Anerkennung oder die Genehmigung kann zurückgenommen werden, wenn eine ihrer Voraussetzungen nicht vorgelegen hat oder später nicht nur vorübergehend weggefallen ist.
(4) ¹§ 20 findet keine Anwendung, sofern Kulturdenkmäler von gottesdienstlicher oder sonstiger kultischer Bestimmung in Sachen entdeckt werden, die im Eigentum der Kirchen oder Religionsgemeinschaften stehen und ihren unmittelbaren Zwecken gewidmet sind. ²Soweit § 20 gegenüber den Kirchen und Religionsgemeinschaften Anwendung findet, werden diese Kulturdenkmäler den Kirchen oder Religionsgemeinschaften auf Antrag als Dauerleihgabe überlassen.
(5) Orden und religiöse Genossenschaften gelten als Kirchen im Sinne der Absätze 1 bis 4.

Fünfter Abschnitt
Organisation

§ 24 Denkmalschutzbehörden
(1) Die Denkmalschutzbehörden sind für die Durchführung dieses Gesetzes zuständig, soweit nichts anderes bestimmt ist.
(2) Denkmalschutzbehörden sind
1. das für Denkmalpflege zuständige Ministerium (oberste Denkmalschutzbehörde),
2. die Aufsichts- und Dienstleistungsdirektion (obere Denkmalschutzbehörde),
3. die Kreisverwaltung und die Stadtverwaltung der kreisfreien Stadt (untere Denkmalschutzbehörde); die Landkreise und die kreisfreien Städte nehmen die Aufgabe als Auftragsangelegenheit wahr.

(3) Soweit in diesem Gesetz nichts anderes bestimmt ist, ist die untere Denkmalschutzbehörde zuständig.
(4) Sind für eine Maßnahme mehrere untere Denkmalschutzbehörden örtlich zuständig, bestimmt die gemeinsame nächsthöhere Denkmalschutzbehörde eine von ihnen zur zuständigen unteren Denkmalschutzbehörde.
(5) ¹Ist eine zuständige untere Denkmalschutzbehörde selbst als Eigentümer, sonstiger Verfügungsberechtigter oder Besitzer betroffen, kann die obere Denkmalschutzbehörde sich für zuständig erklären. ²Sie entscheidet im Benehmen mit der Denkmalfachbehörde.

§ 25 Denkmalfachbehörde
(1) ¹Die Denkmalfachbehörde nimmt die fachlichen Angelegenheiten des Denkmalschutzes und der Denkmalpflege wahr. ²Es gehört insbesondere zu ihrer Aufgabe:
1. bei der Durchführung dieses Gesetzes nach Maßgabe der einzelnen Bestimmungen mitzuwirken,
2. die Denkmalschutzbehörden und die Eigentümer von Kulturdenkmälern zu beraten,
3. das Verständnis der Öffentlichkeit für Denkmalschutz und Denkmalpflege zu fördern,
4. Maßnahmen des Denkmalschutzes und der Denkmalpflege vorzuschlagen,
5. Kulturdenkmäler systematisch aufzunehmen und wissenschaftlich auszuwerten,
6. das Führen der Denkmalliste,
7. Gutachten zu Fragen des Denkmalschutzes und der Denkmalpflege zu erstellen,
8. nach verborgenen Kulturdenkmälern zu forschen,
9. denkmalfachliche Bescheinigungen einschließlich Bescheinigungen zur Vorlage beim Finanzamt auszustellen.

(2) Die Denkmalfachbehörde ist nicht zuständig für Kulturdenkmäler nach § 8 Abs. 2 Satz 2.
(3) ¹Denkmalfachbehörde ist die Generaldirektion Kulturelles Erbe. ²Sie ist dem für Denkmalpflege zuständigen Ministerium unmittelbar nachgeordnet.

§ 25a Denkmalschutz in Archivangelegenheiten
(1) Bei Unterlagen von bleibendem Wert (§ 1 Abs. 1 Satz 3 des Landesarchivgesetzes), die bewegliche Kulturdenkmäler sind, ist die Landesarchivverwaltung die zuständige Denkmalfachbehörde.
(2) ¹Die Denkmalschutzbehörden können auf Antrag der Landesarchivverwaltung bei Unterlagen von bleibendem Wert, die bewegliche Kulturdenkmäler und vor mehr als 30 Jahren entstanden sind, darüber hinaus einen besonderen kulturellen Wert haben oder für die Wissenschaft von besonderer Bedeutung sind und die im Eigentum von natürlichen oder juristischen Personen des bürgerlichen Rechts stehen, die Anordnung treffen, daß sie vorübergehend bis zu einem Jahr zur wissenschaftlichen oder archivfachlichen Bearbeitung von öffentlichen Archiven in Besitz genommen werden, wenn zu besorgen ist, daß diese Unterlagen einer angemessenen archivischen Nutzung entzogen werden sollen. ²Die Rechte Betroffener und Dritter auf Persönlichkeitsschutz sind dabei zu wahren. ³Sind Unterlagen in ihrer Erhaltung gefährdet, kann auch angeordnet werden, daß sie in öffentlichen Archiven verwahrt werden, bis die Eigentümer die erforderlichen Vorkehrungen zu ihrer Erhaltung getroffen haben.

§ 25b Denkmalschutz in Bibliotheksangelegenheiten
Für historische Buchbestände oder körperliche Medienwerke, die bewegliche Kulturdenkmäler sind und für die § 25a keine Anwendung findet, ist das Landesbibliothekszentrum Rheinland-Pfalz die zuständige Denkmalfachbehörde.

§ 26 Landesbeirat für Denkmalpflege
(1) ¹Der Landesbeirat für Denkmalpflege berät die oberste Denkmalschutzbehörde und die Denkmalfachbehörde. ²Er gibt Anregungen und Empfehlungen und erstellt Gutachten. ³Der Landesbeirat soll sich auch besonderer Anliegen der Öffentlichkeit im Rahmen des Denkmalschutzes und der Denkmalpflege annehmen.
(2) ¹Dem Landesbeirat für Denkmalpflege sollen Sachverständige für die Fachgebiete des Denkmalschutzes und der Denkmalpflege, Vertreter der anerkannten Denkmalpflegeorganisationen sowie Vertreter anderer von Denkmalschutz und Denkmalpflege berührter Bereiche, insbesondere Vertreter der Kirchen, der kommunalen Gebietskörperschaften und der Eigentümer angehören. ²Die Zahl der Mitglieder soll nicht mehr als 20 betragen. ³Die Mitglieder werden von dem für Denkmalpflege zuständigen Ministerium auf die Dauer von vier Jahren berufen. ⁴Die Mitglieder sind ehrenamtlich tätig.

(3) ¹Der Landesbeirat für Denkmalpflege wählt aus seiner Mitte den Vorsitzenden und seinen Stellvertreter auf die Dauer von vier Jahren. ²Der Landesbeirat gibt sich eine Geschäftsordnung, die der Genehmigung des für Denkmalpflege zuständigen Ministeriums bedarf.
(4) Das für Denkmalpflege zuständige Ministerium regelt das Nähere, insbesondere über die Berufung und die Entschädigung der Mitglieder, durch Rechtsverordnung;[1] hinsichtlich der Entschädigung der Mitglieder ergeht die Rechtsverordnung im Einvernehmen mit dem für den Landeshaushalt zuständigen Ministerium.

§ 27 Ehrenamtliche Denkmalpfleger

¹Die unteren Denkmalschutzbehörden und die Denkmalfachbehörde können zu ihrer Beratung und Unterstützung sowie zur Wahrnehmung bestimmter Aufgaben ehrenamtliche Denkmalpfleger berufen. ²Das für Denkmalpflege zuständige Ministerium bestimmt das Nähere, insbesondere über die Berufung und Entschädigung der ehrenamtlichen Denkmalpfleger, durch Rechtsverordnung;[2] hinsichtlich der Entschädigung ergeht die Rechtsverordnung im Einvernehmen mit dem für den Landeshaushalt zuständigen Ministerium.

§ 28 Anerkannte Denkmalpflegeorganisationen

(1) ¹Rechtsfähige Organisationen, die sich satzungsgemäß mit Aufgaben des Denkmalschutzes und der Denkmalpflege, der Ortsbildpflege oder der Stadterneuerung in Rheinland-Pfalz befassen, werden von dem für Denkmalpflege zuständigen Ministerium anerkannt, wenn sie nach ihrer bisherigen Tätigkeit Gewähr für eine sachgerechte Aufgabenerfüllung bieten und sich verpflichten, ihre Arbeitsergebnisse den Denkmalschutzbehörden und der Denkmalfachbehörde offenzulegen. ²Die Anerkennung erfolgt auf schriftlichen Antrag. ³Die Anerkennung ist zurückzunehmen, wenn festgestellt wird, daß eine der Voraussetzungen nicht vorgelegen hat oder später weggefallen ist.
(2) ¹Anerkannte Denkmalpflegeorganisationen können die nach diesem Gesetz erforderlichen Maßnahmen bei den Denkmalschutzbehörden oder der Denkmalfachbehörde anregen. ²Auf ihr Verlangen sind sie zu der angeregten Maßnahme zu hören.

Sechster Abschnitt
Finanzhilfen des Landes

§ 29 Förderungsgrundsätze

(1) Das Land fördert Maßnahmen des Denkmalschutzes und der Denkmalpflege im Rahmen der verfügbaren Mittel des Landeshaushalts.[3]
(2) Das Land fördert anerkannte Denkmalpflegeorganisationen (§ 28), gemeinnützige Träger und Einzelpersonen, die Aufgaben des Denkmalschutzes und der Denkmalpflege wahrnehmen, entsprechend ihrer Leistung im Rahmen der verfügbaren Mittel des Landeshaushalts.

Siebenter Abschnitt
Enteignung, ausgleichspflichtige Maßnahmen, Vorkaufsrecht

§ 30 Enteignung

(1) Die Enteignung ist zulässig, soweit auf andere zumutbare Weise nicht erreicht werden kann, daß
1. ein geschütztes Kulturdenkmal in seinem Bestand oder seinem Erscheinungsbild erhalten bleibt oder wissenschaftlich ausgewertet werden kann oder
2. in einem Grabungsschutzgebiet planmäßige Nachforschungen betrieben werden können.

(2) Die Enteignung erfolgt zugunsten des Landes, eines Landkreises oder einer kreisfreien Stadt, einer Verbandsgemeinde oder verbandsfreien Gemeinde oder einer Ortsgemeinde in dieser Reihenfolge.
(3) Im übrigen findet bei unbeweglichen Kulturdenkmälern und bei Grabungsschutzgebieten das Landesenteignungsgesetz Anwendung.

---

1) Die Landesverordnung über die Berufung und Entschädigung der Mitglieder des Landesbeirats für Denkmalpflege ist abgedruckt als Nr. D11.I.1b.
2) Die Landesverordnung über Aufgaben, Berufung und Entschädigung ehrenamtlicher Denkmalpfleger ist abgedruckt als Nr. D11.I.1a.
3) Die VwV Zuwendungen des Landes Rheinland-Pfalz zur Erhaltung von nichtstaatlichen Kulturdenkmälern ist abgedruckt als Nr. D11.III.1.

§ 31 Ausgleichspflichtige Maßnahmen

(1) ¹Soweit durch Maßnahmen aufgrund dieses Gesetzes im Einzelfall Einschränkungen der bisherigen rechtmäßigen Nutzung des Eigentums oder Pflichten zur Erhaltung und Pflege eines Kulturdenkmals zu einer die Grenzen der Sozialbindung überschreitenden Belastung führen, hat das Land einen angemessenen Ausgleich in Geld zu gewähren, sofern und soweit die Belastung nicht in anderer Weise ausgeglichen werden kann. ²Über den Ausgleich ist im Einvernehmen mit der Denkmalfachbehörde zugleich mit der belastenden Maßnahme zumindest dem Grunde nach zu entscheiden; dabei sind vorrangig vertragliche Regelungen anzustreben.

(2) Im Falle des Ausgleichs in Geld finden bei unbeweglichen Gegenständen die Bestimmungen des zweiten Abschnitts des Landesenteignungsgesetzes entsprechende Anwendung.

§ 32 Vorkaufsrecht

(1) ¹Wird ein Grundstück, auf dem sich ein unbewegliches Kulturdenkmal (§ 4 Abs. 1) befindet, verkauft, steht der Gemeinde, bei überörtlicher Bedeutung auch dem Lande, ein Vorkaufsrecht zu. ²Das Vorkaufsrecht des Landes geht dem Vorkaufsrecht der Gemeinde im Range vor. ³Das für Denkmalpflege zuständige Ministerium übt das Vorkaufsrecht zugunsten des Landes aus. ⁴Das Vorkaufsrecht darf nur ausgeübt werden, wenn das Wohl der Allgemeinheit dies rechtfertigt, insbesondere wenn dadurch die Erhaltung eines unbeweglichen Kulturdenkmals ermöglicht werden soll. ⁵Das Vorkaufsrecht ist ausgeschlossen, wenn der Eigentümer das Grundstück an seinen Ehegatten oder Lebenspartner oder an eine Person verkauft, die mit ihm in gerader Linie verwandt oder verschwägert oder in der Seitenlinie bis zum dritten Grad verwandt ist.

(2) ¹Die untere Denkmalschutzbehörde leitet eine Anzeige nach § 12 Abs. 2 Satz 1, die ein Grundstück betrifft, auf dem sich ein unbewegliches Kulturdenkmal befindet, unverzüglich an die Gemeinde weiter. ²Teilt der Eigentümer der Gemeinde nach Abschluß des Kaufvertrages dessen Inhalt schriftlich mit, so kann die Gemeinde nur binnen zwei Monaten das Vorkaufsrecht ausüben. ³Unterläßt der Eigentümer diese Mitteilung, so kann die Gemeinde ihn bis zum Ablauf eines Monats nach Eingang der Anzeige nach Satz 1 hierzu auffordern; der Eigentümer ist verpflichtet, dieser Aufforderung unverzüglich Folge zu leisten. ⁴Nach Eingang der Mitteilung gilt die gleiche Zweimonatsfrist wie in Satz 2. ⁵Unterläßt die Gemeinde die fristgerechte Aufforderung, so erlischt ihr Vorkaufsrecht für diesen Verkaufsfall. ⁶Die §§ 463 und 464 Abs. 2, die §§ 465 bis 468, 471 und 1098 Abs. 2 und die §§ 1099 bis 1102 des Bürgerlichen Gesetzbuches sind anzuwenden. ⁷Das Vorkaufsrecht ist nicht übertragbar. ⁸Die Sätze 1 bis 7 gelten für das Vorkaufsrecht des Landes entsprechend.

Achter Abschnitt
Ordnungswidrigkeiten

§ 33 [Ordnungswidrigkeiten]

(1) ¹Ordnungswidrig handelt, wer vorsätzlich oder fahrlässig
1. entgegen § 6 den Denkmalschutzbehörden, der Denkmalfachbehörde oder ihren Beauftragten nicht die für die Erfüllung ihrer Aufgaben erforderlichen Auskünfte erteilt oder wider besseres Wissen unrichtige Angaben macht oder unrichtige Pläne oder Unterlagen vorlegt, um einen Verwaltungsakt nach diesem Gesetz zu erwirken oder zu verhindern,
2. entgegen § 12 Abs. 1 oder Abs. 2 Anzeige-, Hinweis- oder Mitteilungspflichten nicht oder nicht rechtzeitig erfüllt,
3. entgegen § 13 Abs. 1 Satz 1 Nr. 1 ohne Genehmigung geschützte Kulturdenkmäler zerstört, abbricht, zerlegt oder beseitigt,
4. entgegen § 13 Abs. 1 Satz 1 Nr. 2 ohne Genehmigung geschützte Kulturdenkmäler umgestaltet oder sonst in ihrem Bestand verändert,
5. entgegen § 13 Abs. 1 Satz 1 Nr. 3 ohne Genehmigung geschützte Kulturdenkmäler in ihrem Erscheinungsbild nicht nur vorübergehend beeinträchtigt,
6. entgegen § 13 Abs. 1 Satz 1 Nr. 4 ohne Genehmigung geschützte Kulturdenkmäler von ihrem Standort entfernt,
7. entgegen § 13 Abs. 1 Satz 2 ohne Genehmigung Ausstattungsstücke eines unbeweglichen Kulturdenkmals nicht nur vorübergehend entfernt,

8. entgegen § 13 Abs. 1 Satz 3 ohne Genehmigung in der Umgebung eines unbeweglichen Kulturdenkmals bauliche Anlagen errichtet, verändert oder beseitigt,
9. entgegen § 13 Abs. 4 Satz 1 ohne Anzeige oder in Abweichung von der der Anzeige beigefügten Beschreibung ein geschütztes Kulturdenkmal instandsetzt,
10. entgegen § 17 Funde nicht unverzüglich anzeigt,
11. entgegen § 18 den Pflichten zur Erhaltung des Fundes nicht nachkommt,
12. entgegen § 21 Abs. 1 ohne Genehmigung Nachforschungen mit dem Ziel, Kulturdenkmäler zu entdecken, durchführt,
13. entgegen § 21 Abs. 2 Erd- oder Bauarbeiten, bei denen zu vermuten ist, daß Kulturdenkmäler entdeckt werden, nicht oder nicht rechtzeitig anzeigt,
14. entgegen § 22 Abs. 3 ohne Genehmigung in Grabungsschutzgebieten Vorhaben durchführt, die verborgene Kulturdenkmäler gefährden können.

²Ordnungswidrig im Sinne des Satzes 1 Nr. 3 bis 8, 12 oder 14 handelt auch, wer vorsätzlich oder fahrlässig von einer erteilten Genehmigung abweicht, wenn diese Abweichung einer erneuten Genehmigung bedurft hätte. ³In den Fällen des Satzes 1 Nr. 3 bis 9 ist von der Verfolgung als Ordnungswidrigkeit abzusehen, soweit eine Unterrichtung des Eigentümers nach § 10 Abs. 2 noch nicht erfolgt ist und er auch nicht in sonstiger Weise Kenntnis von der Eigenschaft als geschütztes Kulturdenkmal hatte oder haben musste.

(2) Die Ordnungswidrigkeit kann im Falle des Absatzes 1 Satz 1 Nr. 3 und 4 mit einer Geldbuße bis zu eine Million Euro geahndet werden; in den übrigen Fällen wird die Ordnungswidrigkeit mit einer Geldbuße bis zu einhundertfünfundzwanzigtausend Euro geahndet.

(3) Die Verfolgung der Ordnungswidrigkeit verjährt in fünf Jahren.

(4) ¹Gegenstände, auf die sich eine Ordnungswidrigkeit bezieht oder die zur Vorbereitung oder Begehung einer Ordnungswidrigkeit verwendet worden sind, können eingezogen werden. ²§ 23 des Gesetzes über Ordnungswidrigkeiten findet Anwendung.

(5) Verwaltungsbehörde im Sinne des § 36 Abs. 1 Nr. 1 des Gesetzes über Ordnungswidrigkeiten ist die untere Denkmalschutzbehörde.

Neunter Abschnitt
Übergangs- und Schlußbestimmungen

§ 34 Übergangsbestimmung für geschützte Denkmäler und zum Denkmalbuch
¹Die bis zum Ablauf des 9. Dezember 2008 nach § 8 Abs. 1 des Denkmalschutz- und -pflegegesetzes vom 23. März 1978 (GVBl. S. 159) unter Schutz gestellten Kulturdenkmäler gelten als abschließend festgestellt im Sinne des § 8 Abs. 3. ²Insoweit führt die untere Denkmalschutzbehörde für ihren Bereich das Denkmalbuch nach § 10 des Denkmalschutz- und -pflegegesetzes vom 23. März 1978 (GVBl. S. 159) zum Nachweis weiter.

§ 35 Gebührenfreiheit
(1) ¹Amtshandlungen der Denkmalschutzbehörden und der Denkmalfachbehörde nach diesem Gesetz sind frei von landesrechtlich geregelten Gebühren. ²Dies gilt nicht für Anordnungen der unteren Denkmalschutzbehörden nach § 14 Abs. 1 und 2 sowie für die Erstellung von Gutachten und die Ausstellung von Bescheinigungen durch die Denkmalfachbehörde nach § 25 Abs. 1 Satz 2 Nr. 7 und 9.

(2) Auszüge aus der Liegenschaftsbeschreibung, der Liegenschaftskarte und den Schriftstücken des Liegenschaftskatasters sind für die Denkmalschutzbehörden und die Denkmalfachbehörde frei von landesrechtlich geregelten Gebühren.

§ 36 Durchführungsvorschriften
Die zur Durchführung dieses Gesetzes erforderlichen Verwaltungsvorschriften erläßt das für Denkmalpflege zuständige Ministerium im Benehmen mit den Ministerien, deren Geschäftsbereich berührt wird.

§ 37 Schutz von Kulturdenkmälern bei bewaffneten Konflikten und bei Katastrophenfällen
¹Das für Denkmalpflege zuständige Ministerium wird ermächtigt, die für den Schutz von Kulturdenkmälern bei bewaffneten Konflikten und bei Katastrophenfällen notwendigen Bestimmungen durch Rechtsverordnung im Einvernehmen mit dem für den Katastrophenschutz zuständigen Ministerium zu

treffen. ²Insbesondere können Eigentümer, sonstige Verfügungsberechtigte und Besitzer verpflichtet werden,
1. Kulturdenkmäler mit den in internationalen Verträgen vorgesehenen Kennzeichen versehen zu lassen,
2. Kulturdenkmäler im Rahmen des Zumutbaren besonders zu sichern oder die Sicherung zu dulden,
3. bewegliche Kulturdenkmäler zur vorübergehenden Aufbewahrung in Bergungsorten abzuliefern oder die Abholung dazu zu dulden.

§ 38 Aufhebung und Änderung von Rechtsvorschriften
(1) *[nicht wiedergegebene Aufhebungsvorschriften]*
(2) *[nicht wiedergegebene Änderungsvorschrift]*
(3) ¹Kulturdenkmäler, die in das Verzeichnis nach Artikel 8 oder in die Denkmalliste nach Artikel 10 des Gesetzes, den Denkmalschutz betreffend (für den ehemaligen Regierungsbezirk Rheinhessen) eingetragen sind, gelten als geschützte Kulturdenkmäler im Sinne dieses Gesetzes. ²Sind sie am 10. Dezember 2008 in das Denkmalbuch nach § 10 des Denkmalschutz- und -pflegegesetzes vom 23. März 1978 (GVBl. S. 159) eingetragen, gelten sie als abschließend festgestellt im Sinne des § 8 Abs. 3; § 34 Satz 2 gilt entsprechend.
(4) Artikel 25 des Vertrages des Landes Rheinland-Pfalz mit den Evangelischen Landeskirchen in Rheinland-Pfalz vom 31. März 1962 (GVBl. S. 173, BS Anhang I 20)¹⁾ bleibt unberührt.

§ 39 Inkrafttreten
Dieses Gesetz tritt am 1. Mai 1978 in Kraft.

---

1) Art. 25 hat folgenden Wortlaut: „Die Kirchen werden ihre denkmalwerten Gebäude nebst den dazugehörenden Grundstücken und sonstigen historisch bedeutsamen Gegenständen nach ihren Kräften erhalten und sachgemäß pflegen. Sie werden Veräußerungen oder Änderungen sowie die innere Ausgestaltung nur im Benehmen mit der staatlichen Denkmalpflege vornehmen. Sie werden dafür sorgen, daß die Kirchengemeinden und die der kirchlichen Aufsicht unterstehenden Verbände entsprechend verfahren."

Landesverordnung über Aufgaben, Berufung und Entschädigung ehrenamtlicher Denkmalpfleger

Vom 22. März 1982 (GVBl. S. 121)
zuletzt geändert durch G vom 20.10.2010 (GVBl. S. 319)

Aufgrund des § 27 Satz 3 des Landesgesetzes zum Schutz und zur Pflege der Kulturdenkmäler (Denkmalschutz- und -pflegegesetz – DSchPflG –) vom 23. März 1978 (GVBl. S. 159, BS 224-2) wird hinsichtlich des § 6 im Einvernehmen mit dem Minister der Finanzen, verordnet:

§ 1 Aufgaben
Die ehrenamtlichen Denkmalpfleger beraten und unterstützen die Kreisverwaltungen und Verwaltungen der kreisfreien Städte als untere Denkmalschutzbehörden und das Landesamt für Denkmalpflege als Denkmalfachbehörde. Sie treten für die Belange des Denkmalschutzes und der Denkmalpflege ein. Ihnen können bestimmte Aufgaben übertragen werden, insbesondere
1. die Erkundung, Erforschung, Überwachung und Betreuung von Kulturdenkmälern,
2. Beobachtung von Vorgängen, die denkmalpflegerische Bedeutung haben können, wie Abrisse, Umbauten, Gebäudeveränderungen, Erdbewegungen und Grabungen,
3. Meldung von Vorgängen, die den Verdacht des Verstoßes gegen Vorschriften des Denkmalschutzes und der Denkmalpflege begründen,
4. Unterrichtung der berufenden Behörde über Planungsvorhaben,
5. Annahme und Weiterleitung von Fundanzeigen,
6. Sammlung von landes- und heimatkundlichen Veröffentlichungen sowie von Presseberichten aus dem Bereich des Denkmalschutzes und der Denkmalpflege und
7. Abgabe von Stellungnahmen zu Fragen und Vorgängen des Denkmalschutzes und der Denkmalpflege.

§ 2 Berufung
(1) Die unteren Denkmalschutzbehörden und die Denkmalfachbehörde können ehrenamtliche Denkmalpfleger berufen. Die Berufung durch die untere Denkmalschutzbehörde erfolgt im Benehmen mit der Denkmalfachbehörde.
(2) Die Berufung kann auch für einzelne Fachgebiete und für bestimmte örtliche Bereiche erfolgen.
(3) Soweit ehrenamtlichen Denkmalpflegern bestimmte Aufgaben im Sinne des § 3 Abs. 2 des Beamtenstatusgesetzes übertragen sind, werden sie nach den Vorschriften des Beamtenrechts zu Ehrenbeamten des Landes, im Falle der Berufung durch die Verwaltungen der kreisfreien Städte zu kommunalen Ehrenbeamten ernannt.

§ 3 Voraussetzung für die Berufung
Die zu berufende Person soll persönlich und fachlich geeignet sein. Sie soll insbesondere
1. Kenntnisse oder Erfahrungen in der praktischen Arbeit des Denkmalschutzes und der Denkmalpflege besitzen,
2. die einschlägigen Rechts- und Verwaltungsvorschriften kennen,
3. ihren Wohnsitz in dem örtlichen Bereich haben, in dem sie als ehrenamtlicher Denkmalpfleger tätig werden soll und
4. volljährig sein.

§ 4 Ausübung der Tätigkeit
(1) Die ehrenamtlichen Denkmalpfleger sind bei der Ausübung ihrer Tätigkeit an die Weisungen der berufenden Stelle gebunden.
(2) Die ehrenamtlichen Denkmalpfleger berichten der berufenden Stelle auf Anforderung unverzüglich, im Übrigen in angemessenen Zeitabständen.

§ 5 Abberufung, Entlassung und Verabschiedung
(1) Der ehrenamtliche Denkmalpfleger kann, sofern er nicht zum Ehrenbeamten berufen ist, jederzeit abberufen werden. Er ist abzuberufen, wenn er es beantragt. Für die Abberufung ist die Behörde zuständig, welche die Berufung verfügt hat.

(2) Die Entlassung und Verabschiedung der zu Ehrenbeamten ernannten Denkmalpfleger richtet sich nach den Vorschriften des Beamtenrechts.

§ 6 Entschädigung

(1) Den ehrenamtlichen Denkmalpflegern wird eine pauschale Aufwandsentschädigung von 60,00 EUR monatlich gewährt.

(2) Sie erhalten als Reisekostenvergütung
1. Fahrkostenerstattung oder, wenn die Benutzung eines regelmäßig verkehrenden Beförderungsmittels nicht möglich oder nicht zumutbar ist, Wegstrecken- und Mitnahmeentschädigung,
2. Tage- und Übernachtungsgeld

in entsprechender Anwendung der Bestimmungen des Landesreisekostengesetzes (LRKG) vom 24. März 1999 (GVBl. S. 89, BS 2032-30) in der jeweils geltenden Fassung. Anstelle der Reisekostenvergütung nach Satz 1 kann in entsprechender Anwendung des § 15 LRKG eine Pauschvergütung festgesetzt werden.

§ 7 Inkrafttreten[1]

Diese Verordnung tritt am Tage nach der Verkündung in Kraft.

---

1) Verkündet am 16. 4. 1982

Landesverordnung über die Berufung und Entschädigung der Mitglieder des Landesbeirats für Denkmalpflege

Vom 30. Dezember 1978 (GVBl. 1979 S. 13)
geändert durch VO vom 12.8.2001 (GVBl. S. 190)

Aufgrund des § 26 Abs. 4 des Landesgesetzes zum Schutz und zur Pflege der Kulturdenkmäler (Denkmalschutz- und -pflegegesetz – DSchPflG –) vom 23. März 1978 (GVBl. S. 159, BS 224-2) wird, hinsichtlich des § 5 im Einvernehmen mit dem Minister der Finanzen, verordnet:

§ 1 Berufung

(1) Zu Mitgliedern des Landesbeirats für Denkmalpflege beruft das für Denkmalpflege zuständige Ministerium

1. bis zu acht Sachverständige für die Fachgebiete des Denkmalschutzes und der Denkmalpflege; darunter sollen mindestens je zwei Vertreter der Kunstwissenschaft und der Altertumswissenschaft sein;
2. auf Vorschlag der anerkannten Denkmalpflegeorganisationen (§ 28 des Denkmalschutz- und -pflegegesetzes) zwei Vertreter dieser Organisationen;
3. auf Vorschlag der für Rheinland-Pfalz zuständigen Evangelischen Landeskirchen und katholischen (Erz-)Diözesen je zwei Vertreter der beiden Kirchen;
4. auf Vorschlag der Landesverbände der Gemeinden, Städte und Landkreise drei Vertreter der kommunalen Gebietskörperschaften;
5. auf Vorschlag der für Rheinland-Pfalz zuständigen Organisationen der Grundeigentümer zwei Vertreter der Grundeigentümer und
6. einen von der Architektenkammer Rheinland-Pfalz vorgeschlagenen Vertreter.

(2) Eine Wiederberufung der Mitglieder ist zulässig.

§ 2 Abberufung

Das für Denkmalpflege zuständige Ministerium kann ein Mitglied des Landesbeirats abberufen, wenn die Stelle, die das Mitglied vorgeschlagen hat, die Abberufung beantragt. Beruht die Berufung des Mitglieds auf dem Vorschlag mehrerer Stellen, so müssen diese die Abberufung gemeinsam beantragen.

§ 3 Ausscheiden

(1) Ein Mitglied scheidet aus dem Landesbeirat aus, wenn
1. der Zeitraum, für den das Mitglied berufen ist (Amtszeit), endet,
2. das Mitglied dem für Denkmalpflege zuständigen Ministerium gegenüber schriftlich auf die Mitgliedschaft verzichtet oder
3. das Mitglied abberufen wird.

(2) Scheidet ein Mitglied aus, wird ein neues Mitglied nach § 1 berufen. Wird während der Amtszeit die Berufung eines neuen Mitglieds erforderlich, so wird es nur für den Rest der Amtszeit berufen. Das Gleiche gilt, wenn die Mitgliedschaft durch Tod endet.

§ 4 Teilnahme an Sitzungen

Vertreter der obersten und der oberen Denkmalschutzbehörden sowie der Denkmalfachbehörde können mit beratender Stimme an den Sitzungen des Landesbeirats teilnehmen.

§ 5 Entschädigung

Die Mitglieder des Landesbeirats erhalten für ihre Teilnahme an Sitzungen des Landesbeirats außerhalb ihres Wohnorts und des Orts ihrer beruflichen Tätigkeit
1. Fahrkostenerstattung oder, wenn die Benutzung eines regelmäßig verkehrenden Beförderungsmittels nicht möglich oder nicht zumutbar ist, Wegstrecken- und Mitnahmeentschädigung,
2. Tage- und Übernachtungsgeld

in entsprechender Anwendung der Bestimmungen des Landesreisekostengesetzes vom 24. März 1999 (GVBl. S. 89, BS 2032-30) in der jeweils geltenden Fassung.

§ 6 In-Kraft-Treten[1]
Diese Verordnung tritt am Tage nach der Verkündung in Kraft.

---

1) Verkündet am 5.2.1979.

Landesarchivgesetz (LArchG)

Vom 5. Oktober 1990 (GVBl. S. 277)
zuletzt geändert durch G vom 11. Februar 2020 (GVBl. S. 42)

Inhaltsübersicht

Erster Abschnitt
Öffentliches Archivwesen

- § 1 Öffentliches Archivgut
- § 2 Öffentliche Archive
- § 3 Nutzung öffentlichen Archivguts
- § 4 Rechte des Betroffenen

Zweiter Abschnitt
Staatliche Archive

- § 5 Organisation und Zuständigkeit der Landesarchivverwaltung Rheinland-Pfalz
- § 6 Aufgaben der Landesarchivverwaltung
- § 7 Anbietungspflicht
- § 8 Übernahme, Verwahrung
- § 8 a Verarbeitung besonderer Kategorien personenbezogener Daten
- § 9 Verwaltung
- § 10 Ehrenamtliche Archivpfleger
- § 11 Archivgut des Landtags

Dritter Abschnitt
Schlussbestimmungen

- § 12 Ausnahmen vom Geltungsbereich
- § 13 Inkrafttreten

Erster Abschnitt
Öffentliches Archivwesen

§ 1 Öffentliches Archivgut

(1) ¹Unterlagen der Behörden, Gerichte und sonstigen öffentlichen Stellen des Landes, der kommunalen Gebietskörperschaften und der sonstigen, der Aufsicht des Landes unterstehenden juristischen Personen des öffentlichen Rechts und ihrer Vereinigungen, die für deren Aufgaben nicht mehr benötigt werden, sind in öffentlichen Archiven auf Dauer als Archivgut aufzubewahren, zu sichern, zu erschließen, nutzbar zu machen und zu erhalten, wenn sie bleibenden Wert haben; dies gilt auch für Unterlagen von Funktions- oder Rechtsvorgängern. ²Den in Satz 1 genannten Stellen stehen die von ihnen errichteten juristischen Personen des Privatrechts und ihre Vereinigungen gleich, die öffentliche Aufgaben erfüllen und nicht am Wettbewerb teilnehmen. ³Bleibenden Wert haben Unterlagen, denen für Gesetzgebung, Verwaltung oder Rechtsprechung, für die Erforschung oder das Verständnis der Geschichte oder für die Sicherung berechtigter Belange der Bürger Bedeutung zukommt. ⁴Soweit sie darüber hinaus einen besonderen kulturellen Wert haben, für die Wissenschaft von erheblicher Bedeutung sind oder wenn Rechts- oder Verwaltungsvorschriften dies bestimmen, sind Unterlagen unverändert aufzubewahren.

(2) Unterlagen sind unabhängig von ihrer Speicherungsform alle bei den in Absatz 1 genannten Stellen angefallenen Informationen, insbesondere Schriftstücke, Akten, Karten, Pläne, Siegel, Dateien, Bild-, Film- und Tonmaterialien, soweit sie Bestandteil des Vorgangs sind.

(3) ¹Archivgut kann nur an Träger anderer hauptamtlich und fachlich betreuter Archive übereignet werden, wenn dies wegen der Herkunft oder des Zusammenhanges geboten oder die Gegenseitigkeit gewährleistet ist. ²Im Übrigen ist Archivgut unveräußerlich. ³Eine widerrufliche Verwahrung in einem anderen hauptamtlich und fachlich betreuten öffentlichen Archiv ist zulässig, wenn ein fachlicher Grund besteht.

(4) Rechtsvorschriften, rechtskräftige Entscheidungen der Gerichte und bestandskräftige Entscheidungen der Behörden, nach denen Unterlagen zu vernichten oder zu löschen sind, bleiben nach Maßgabe von § 7 Abs. 2 unberührt.

§ 2 Öffentliche Archive

(1) ¹Das Land unterhält für die Erfüllung aller staatlichen Archivaufgaben die Landesarchivverwaltung. ²Sie hat das Archivgut der öffentlichen Stellen des Landes und nach Maßgabe der Absätze 2 und 3 der kommunalen Gebietskörperschaften sowie der sonstigen in § 1 Abs. 1 Satz 1 und 2 genannten juristischen Personen zu archivieren.

(2) ¹Die kommunalen Gebietskörperschaften, deren Verbände und deren Stiftungen des öffentlichen Rechts regeln die Archivierung der bei ihnen anfallenden Unterlagen in eigener Zuständigkeit als

Pflichtaufgabe der Selbstverwaltung nach den in diesem Gesetz vorgegebenen Grundsätzen. ²Sie können zu diesem Zweck
1. eigene oder gemeinsame Archive unterhalten,
2. ihr Archivgut der Landesarchivverwaltung mit dessen Zustimmung zu Eigentum übergeben oder
3. ihre Unterlagen der Landesarchivverwaltung zur Archivierung, Verwahrung und Verwaltung anbieten und gegen eine angemessene Kostenbeteiligung zu diesem Zwecke übergeben.
³Soweit eigene oder gemeinsame Archive nicht über hauptberufliches Personal verfügen, können ehrenamtliche Archivpfleger bestellt werden, die sich von der Landesarchivverwaltung laufend beraten lassen sollen; § 10 Abs. 2 gilt entsprechend.

(3) ¹Die sonstigen in § 1 Abs. 1 Satz 1 und 2 genannten juristischen Personen können mit Zustimmung des für das Archivwesen zuständigen Ministeriums eigene fachlich betreute Archive unterhalten; diese unterstehen der Fachaufsicht der Landesarchivverwaltung. ²Die §§ 7, 8, 8 a und 9 Abs. 1 bis 3 gelten für sie entsprechend. ³Die Freiheit der Wissenschaft und Forschung bleibt unberührt.

§ 3 Nutzung öffentlichen Archivguts

(1) ¹Jeder, der ein berechtigtes Interesse darlegt, hat das Recht, öffentliches Archivgut nach Maßgabe der Rechtsvorschriften und der Landesarchiv-Benutzungsverordnung[1]) zu nutzen. ²Die Darlegung eines berechtigten Interesses ist nicht erforderlich, soweit für Unterlagen vor Übergabe an das öffentliche Archiv bereits ein Zugang nach dem Landestransparenzgesetz vom 27. November 2015 (GVBl. S. 383, BS 2010-10) in der jeweils geltenden Fassung gewährt worden ist.

(2) Die Benutzung ist einzuschränken oder zu versagen, soweit
1. Grund zur Annahme besteht, dass das Wohl der Bundesrepublik Deutschland oder eines ihrer Länder gefährdet würde, oder
2. Grund zur Annahme besteht, dass schutzwürdige Belange Betroffener oder Dritter entgegenstehen, oder
3. der Erhaltungszustand des Archivguts gefährdet würde, oder
4. die Geheimhaltungspflicht nach § 203 Abs. 1 bis 3 des Strafgesetzbuches oder andere Rechtsvorschriften über Geheimhaltung verletzt würden, oder
5. Vereinbarungen entgegenstehen, die mit Eigentümern aus Anlass der Übernahme getroffen wurden.

(3) ¹Archivgut darf erst 30 Jahre nach Entstehen der Unterlagen benutzt werden. ²Soweit es sich auf natürliche Personen bezieht, darf es erst zehn Jahre nach deren Tod, oder, wenn das Todesjahr dem Archiv nicht bekannt ist, erst 100 Jahre nach der Geburt des Betroffenen benutzt werden; wenn weder das Jahr der Geburt noch das Jahr des Todes des Betroffenen bekannt ist, gilt eine Frist von 60 Jahren nach Entstehung der Unterlagen. ³Die Sperrfristen nach den Sätzen 1 und 2 gelten nicht für Unterlagen, die bereits bei ihrer Entstehung zur Veröffentlichung bestimmt waren oder für die die Voraussetzungen des Absatzes 1 Satz 2 vorliegen. ⁴Unterlagen, die aufgrund von Rechtsvorschriften geheim zu halten sind, dürfen erst 60 Jahre nach ihrer Entstehung benutzt werden. ⁵Die Sperrfristen nach den Sätzen 1, 2 und 4 können um höchstens 20 Jahre verlängert werden, wenn dies unter Anlegung strengster Maßstäbe im öffentlichen Interesse geboten ist.

(4) ¹Soweit Rechtsvorschriften nicht entgegenstehen, ist es zulässig, die Sperrfristen nach Absatz 3 auf Antrag verkürzt werden, wenn
1. die abgebende Stelle und bei personenbezogenem Archivgut der Betroffene oder nach dessen Tod sein Ehegatte oder Lebenspartner, seine Kinder oder seine Eltern eingewilligt haben, wobei die Existenz eines vorrangig Benannten alle anderen von der Entscheidung ausschließt, oder
2. die Benutzung zur Wahrnehmung der Aufgaben des Landtags, der Organe des Landtags und der Abgeordneten sowie der Landesregierung erforderlich ist und überwiegende schutzwürdige Interessen Betroffener und Dritter nicht entgegenstehen, oder
3. die Benutzung für ein wissenschaftliches Forschungs- oder Dokumentationsvorhaben einschließlich der Schaffung der wissenschaftlichen Infrastruktur oder zur Wahrnehmung berechtigter Belange unerlässlich ist und wichtige öffentliche Belange oder überwiegende schutzwürdige Interessen Betroffener und Dritter nicht entgegenstehen.

---

[1]) Die Landesarchiv-Benutzungsverordnung ist abgedruckt als Nr. D11.II.1a.

²Satz 1 gilt nicht für die Sperrfrist nach Absatz 3 Satz 4, soweit die Geheimhaltungspflicht auf Rechtsvorschriften des Bundes beruht.
(5) Die Regelungen der Absätze 3 und 4 gelten nicht für Stellen, die das Archivgut abgeliefert haben, wenn sie es zur Erfüllung ihrer Aufgaben wieder benötigen, soweit es sich nicht um Archivgut handelt, das vor der Ablieferung aufgrund besonderer Rechtsvorschriften hätte gesperrt, vernichtet oder gelöscht werden müssen.
(6) Die Verknüpfung personenbezogener Daten ist nur zulässig, wenn schutzwürdige Belange Betroffener oder Dritter nicht beeinträchtigt werden.
(7) Die Bestimmungen der Absätze 1 bis 4 und 6 sowie des § 4 gelten entsprechend für privates Archivgut in öffentlichen Archiven, unbeschadet besonderer Vereinbarungen zugunsten des Eigentümers.
(8) Die kommunalen Gebietskörperschaften und die sonstigen in § 1 Abs. 1 Satz 1 und 2 genannten juristischen Personen regeln die Benutzung ihrer Archive gemäß den Bestimmungen der §§ 1 bis 4 und § 9 Abs. 3 durch Satzung.

§ 4 Rechte des Betroffenen
(1) ¹Der Betroffene kann Auskunft oder Einsicht verlangen, soweit sich Archivgut auf ihn bezieht und § 3 Abs. 2 nicht entgegensteht. ²Der Antragsteller hat glaubhaft darzulegen, dass er Betroffener ist, und Angaben zu machen, die das Auffinden des ihn betreffenden Archivguts ohne unangemessenen Aufwand ermöglichen. ³Rechtsansprüche Betroffener auf Löschung der sie betreffenden personenbezogenen Daten bleiben unberührt. ⁴Ein weitergehender Auskunftsanspruch nach Artikel 15 der Verordnung (EU) 2016/679 des Europäischen Parlaments und des Rates vom 27. April 2016 zum Schutz natürlicher Personen bei der Verarbeitung personenbezogener Daten, zum freien Datenverkehr und zur Aufhebung der Richtlinie 95/46/EG (Datenschutz-Grundverordnung) (ABl. EU Nr. L 119 S. 1) in der jeweils geltenden Fassung besteht nicht. ⁵Ein Widerspruchsrecht nach Artikel 21 der Datenschutz-Grundverordnung gegen die Verarbeitung gespeicherter Daten besteht nicht.
(2) ¹Über den Anspruch auf Berichtigung oder Löschung personenbezogener Daten entscheidet die Stelle, bei der die archivierten Unterlagen entstanden sind. ²Wird von dieser Stelle oder durch gerichtliche Entscheidung festgestellt, dass personenbezogene Angaben unrichtig sind, so wird diesen eine Berichtigung beigefügt. ³Sie sind nur dann zu löschen, wenn ihre Speicherung unzulässig war. ⁴Macht der Betroffene die Unrichtigkeit personenbezogener Angaben glaubhaft, so ist ihnen unbeschadet der Beachtung der Sperrfristen gemäß § 3 Abs. 3 seine Gegendarstellung beizufügen; dies ist ausgeschlossen bei rechtskräftigen gerichtlichen oder bestandskräftigen behördlichen Entscheidungen. ⁵Weitergehende Ansprüche Betroffener aus den Artikeln 16 und 18 der Datenschutz-Grundverordnung bestehen nicht. ⁶Eine Mitteilungspflicht der Landesarchivverwaltung nach Artikel 19 der Datenschutz-Grundverordnung besteht nicht. ⁷Ein Recht auf Datenübertragbarkeit nach Artikel 20 der Datenschutz-Grundverordnung besteht nicht.
(3) Nach dem Tod des Betroffenen stehen die Ansprüche nach den Absätzen 1 und 2 bei Nachweis eines berechtigten Interesses dem Ehegatten oder Lebenspartner, den Kindern oder den Eltern zu, wobei die Existenz eines vorrangig Benannten alle anderen von der Entscheidung ausschließt.

Zweiter Abschnitt
Staatliche Archive

§ 5 Organisation und Zuständigkeit der Landesarchivverwaltung Rheinland-Pfalz
(1) Die Landesarchivverwaltung Rheinland-Pfalz besteht aus dem Landeshauptarchiv Koblenz und dem Landesarchiv Speyer.
(2) ¹Das Landeshauptarchiv Koblenz ist zuständig für die obersten Landesbehörden. ²Die übrigen Zuständigkeiten der beiden Standorte werden von dem für das Archivwesen zuständigen Ministerium durch Organisationserlass festgelegt.
(3) Oberste Aufsichtsbehörde ist das für das Archivwesen zuständige Ministerium.

§ 6 Aufgaben der Landesarchivverwaltung
(1) Die Landesarchivverwaltung erfüllt ihre Aufgaben unter Beachtung der archivfachlichen Anforderungen.

(2) Die Landesarchivverwaltung kann, soweit das Bundesarchivgesetz[1)] dies zulässt, Archivgut des Bundes verwahren oder übernehmen, wenn hierfür ein öffentliches Interesse des Landes besteht.

(3) ¹Die Landesarchivverwaltung kann auf Antrag der zuständigen Stelle Archivgut der Kirchen und Religionsgemeinschaften, der öffentlich-rechtlichen Rundfunkanstalten, der Parteien und Verbände sowie Archivgut von natürlichen und juristischen Personen des Privatrechts verwahren oder übernehmen, wenn hierfür ein öffentliches Interesse besteht und die Deckung der Kosten des entstehenden Aufwands gesichert ist. ²§ 1 Abs. 1 bleibt unberührt.

(4) Die Landesarchivverwaltung fördert die Erforschung und das Verständnis der deutschen Geschichte und der Landesgeschichte insbesondere durch Veröffentlichungen und Ausstellungen.

(5) ¹Die Landesarchivverwaltung berät die Behörden, Gerichte und sonstigen Stellen des Landes bei der Verwaltung und Sicherung ihrer Unterlagen und ist von diesen bei der Einführung neuer oder wesentlicher Änderung bestehender Speicherformen für elektronische Unterlagen zu beteiligen. ²Sie soll die der Aufsicht des Landes unterstehenden juristischen Personen des öffentlichen Rechts und deren Archive beraten. ³Sie kann auch Private bei der Verwaltung ihrer Archive unterstützen, soweit ein öffentliches Interesse besteht.

(6) Die für die Rechts- und Stiftungsaufsicht zuständigen Landesbehörden sind verpflichtet, alle öffentliches Archivgut betreffenden Entscheidungen im Benehmen mit der Landesarchivverwaltung zu treffen.

§ 7 Anbietungspflicht

(1) ¹Die öffentlichen Stellen des Landes haben alle Unterlagen, die sie zur Erfüllung ihrer Aufgaben einschließlich der Wahrung der Sicherheit der Bundesrepublik Deutschland oder eines ihrer Länder nicht mehr benötigen, in der Regel spätestens 30 Jahre nach ihrer Entstehung, der Landesarchivverwaltung unverändert und mit einem Aktenverzeichnis bzw. einem aussagekräftigen Verzeichnis aller angegebenen Vorgänge versehen anzubieten. ²Gleiches gilt für die in § 1 Abs. 1 Satz 1 und 2 genannten kommunalen Gebietskörperschaften und sonstigen juristischen Personen, die keine eigenen Archive nach § 2 Abs. 2 oder 3 unterhalten. ³Für Akten, die Gerichts- oder Verwaltungsverfahren sowie Dienstverhältnisse betreffen, beginnt die Ablieferungsfrist erst mit deren Beendigung, sofern nicht durch Rechts- oder Verwaltungsvorschriften längere Aufbewahrungsfristen vorgeschrieben sind.

(2) Anzubieten sind auch Unterlagen, die

1. nach den Bestimmungen des Landesdatenschutzgesetzes vernichtet oder gelöscht werden könnten oder müssten, sofern die Speicherung der Daten nicht unzulässig war, oder
2. nach gesetzlichen oder sonstigen Vorschriften geheim zu halten sind oder einem Amts- oder Berufsgeheimnis unterliegen oder
3. besondere Kategorien personenbezogener Daten im Sinne des Artikels 9 Abs. 1 der Datenschutz-Grundverordnung enthalten.

(3) Elektronische Unterlagen sind der Landesarchivverwaltung anzubieten.

(4) Durch Vereinbarung zwischen der Landesarchivverwaltung und der ablieferungspflichtigen Stelle können Unterlagen von offensichtlich geringer Bedeutung von der Anbietungspflicht ausgenommen oder gleichförmige Unterlagen, die in großer Zahl anfallen, nur in geringer Anzahl angeboten werden.

§ 8 Übernahme, Verwahrung

(1) Die Landesarchivverwaltung hat binnen sechs Monaten im Benehmen mit der anbietenden Stelle zu entscheiden, welche der angebotenen Unterlagen bleibenden Wert haben und deshalb zu übernehmen sind.

(2) ¹Die Landesarchivverwaltung kann auch Unterlagen in Verwahrung nehmen, die aufgrund von Rechts- oder Verwaltungsvorschriften noch unverändert aufzubewahren sind und besonderer Bestimmung durch die abgebende Stelle unterliegen. ²Die Bestimmungen der §§ 3, 4, 8 a und 9 finden entsprechende Anwendung; über die Benutzung, Einsichtnahme und Auskunftserteilung entscheidet die Landesarchivverwaltung im Einvernehmen mit der abgebenden Stelle.

§ 8 a Verarbeitung besonderer Kategorien personenbezogener Daten

¹Die Verarbeitung besonderer Kategorien personenbezogener Daten im Sinne des Artikels 9 Abs. 1 der Datenschutz-Grundverordnung ist für im öffentlichen Interesse liegende Archivzwecke zulässig. ²Bei der Verarbeitung dieser Daten sind angemessene und spezifische Maßnahmen zur Wahrung der

---

1) Das Bundesarchivgesetz ist abgedruckt als Nr. C.III.1.

Interessen der betroffenen Person vorzusehen. ³Diese Maßnahmen sind in dem Verzeichnis von Verarbeitungstätigkeiten nach Artikel 30 der Datenschutz-Grundverordnung darzustellen.

§ 9 Verwaltung
(1) ¹Das Archivgut im Sinne des § 1 Abs. 1 ist ordnungs- und sachgemäß auf Dauer aufzubewahren, zu erhalten und zu erschließen. ²Die Landesarchivverwaltung soll Unterlagen ohne besonderen kulturellen oder urkundlichen Wert in Form von technischen Vervielfältigungen archivieren oder ihren gesamten Inhalt in geeigneter Weise speichern. ³Sie ist befugt, Unterlagen, denen ein bleibender Wert nach § 1 Abs. 1 nicht mehr zukommt, im Einvernehmen mit der abgebenden Stelle zu vernichten. ⁴Über die Vernichtung ist ein Nachweis zu führen und dauernd aufzubewahren.
(2) Das Archivgut ist durch organisatorische, technische und personelle Maßnahmen vor unbefugter Benutzung, Beschädigung und Verlust zu schützen.
(3) Bei Unterlagen, die Rechtsvorschriften des Bundes über Geheimhaltung unterliegen, sind von der Übernahme an die schutzwürdigen Belange Betroffener zu berücksichtigen; insbesondere sind bei Unterlagen mit personenbezogenen Daten die Vorschriften über die Verarbeitung und Sicherung dieser Unterlagen zu beachten, die für die abgebende Stelle gelten.
(4) ¹Über die Verlängerung und die Verkürzung der Sperrfristen gemäß § 3 Abs. 3 Satz 5 und Abs. 4 entscheidet die Landesarchivverwaltung, in Fällen von grundsätzlicher Bedeutung im Einvernehmen mit dem für das Archivwesen zuständigen Ministerium. ²Das Nähere über die Benutzung, insbesondere die Zulassung, die Sorgfaltspflichten, den Ausschluss, die Ausleihe und Versendung sowie die Vervielfältigungen von Archivgut und die Belegexemplarpflicht regelt das für das Archivwesen zuständige Ministerium durch Rechtsverordnung.

§ 10 Ehrenamtliche Archivpfleger
(1) Die Landesarchivverwaltung kann ehrenamtliche Archivpfleger zur Unterstützung ihrer Aufgaben bestellen.
(2) ¹Die ehrenamtlichen Archivpfleger sind verpflichtet, über die ihnen bei Wahrnehmung ihrer Aufgaben bekannt gewordenen Angelegenheiten gegenüber Dritten Verschwiegenheit zu bewahren und dürfen diese Kenntnisse nicht unbefugt verwerten. ²Sie haben auf Verlangen Schriftstücke und sonstige Gegenstände, in deren Besitz sie durch ihre Tätigkeit gelangt sind, an die Landesarchivverwaltung herauszugeben. ³Diese Verpflichtungen bestehen auch nach Beendigung des Ehrenamts fort.

§ 11 Archivgut des Landtags
(1) Das Archivgut des Landtags wird im Landtagsarchiv aufbewahrt; der Landtag kann dem Landeshauptarchiv Unterlagen zur Verwahrung übergeben oder zur Übernahme anbieten.
(2) Der Landtag regelt die Benutzung des Landtagsarchivs unter Berücksichtigung seiner verfassungsrechtlichen Stellung sowie der Grundsätze der §§ 1 bis 4 und des § 9 Abs. 3.

Dritter Abschnitt
Schlussbestimmungen

§ 12 Ausnahmen vom Geltungsbereich
Dieses Gesetz gilt nicht für die Kirchen und die öffentlich-rechtlichen Religionsgemeinschaften, für die öffentlich-rechtlichen Rundfunkanstalten, die Anstalt des öffentlichen Rechts „Zweites Deutsches Fernsehen" sowie für öffentlich-rechtliche Unternehmen mit eigener Rechtspersönlichkeit, die am Wettbewerb teilnehmen und für deren Zusammenschlüsse.

§ 13 Inkrafttreten
Dieses Gesetz tritt am 1. Januar 1991 in Kraft.

Landesarchiv-Benutzungsverordnung (LArchBVO)

Vom 8. Dezember 2004 (GVBl. 2005 S. 1)
geändert durch Verordnung vom 14.04.2015 (GVBl. S. 36)

Aufgrund des § 9 Abs. 4 Satz 2 des Landesarchivgesetzes vom 5. Oktober 1990 (GVBl. S. 277), zuletzt geändert durch Artikel 140 des Gesetzes vom 12. Oktober 1999 (GVBl. S. 325), BS 224-10, wird verordnet:

§ 1 Geltungsbereich

Diese Verordnung regelt die Benutzung des in den Landesarchiven verwahrten, erschlossenen Archivguts. Die Bestimmungen gelten für die Benutzung von Vervielfältigungen, Findmitteln und sonstigen Hilfsmitteln entsprechend.

§ 2 Benutzungsarten

(1) Archivgut oder dessen für die Benutzung bestimmte Vervielfältigung ist grundsätzlich durch persönliche Einsichtnahme im verwahrenden Landesarchiv zu benutzen (§ 4). Die Benutzung kann auch erfolgen durch:
1. schriftliche oder in Textform gestellte Anfrage, auf die schriftlich oder in Textform Auskunft erteilt wird (§ 5),
2. Ausfertigung und Übereignung von Vervielfältigungen (§ 6),
3. Versendung von Archivgut (§ 7),
4. Ausleihe von Archivgut (§ 8).

(2) Die Benutzung von Archivgut durch die abliefernde Stelle regelt § 13.

§ 3 Benutzungsgenehmigung

(1) Die Benutzungsgenehmigung ist für jedes Vorhaben schriftlich beim verwahrenden Landesarchiv zu beantragen. Dabei sind Name, Anschrift und Staatsangehörigkeit der Antragstellerin oder des Antragstellers und, wenn die Benutzung im Auftrag Dritter erfolgen soll, auch der Auftraggeberin oder des Auftraggebers anzugeben; die erhobenen Daten werden nach den §§ 5, 12 bis 19 und 33 des Landesdatenschutzgesetzes automatisiert verarbeitet. Darüber hinaus sind der Zweck der Benutzung und der Gegenstand der Nachforschungen möglichst genau zu bezeichnen. Die Antragstellerin oder der Antragsteller hat sich auf Verlangen auszuweisen und gegebenenfalls die Bevollmächtigung der Auftraggeberin oder des Auftraggebers nachzuweisen.

(2) Über die Benutzungsgenehmigung entscheidet das verwahrende Landesarchiv. Die Zuständigkeit des für das Archivwesen zuständigen Ministeriums nach § 9 Abs. 4 Satz 1 des Landesarchivgesetzes (LArchG) bleibt unberührt.

(3) Die Benutzungsgenehmigung gilt nur für das angegebene Vorhaben sowie den angegebenen Benutzungszweck und wird grundsätzlich für das laufende Kalenderjahr erteilt. Sie kann mit Nebenbestimmungen verbunden und auf Antrag verlängert werden.

(4) Die Benutzungsgenehmigung ist einzuschränken oder zu versagen, wenn einer der in § 3 Abs. 2 LArchG genannten Gründe vorliegt; eine Entscheidung gemäß § 3 Abs. 2 Nr. 1 LArchG bedarf der Zustimmung des für das Archivwesen zuständigen Ministeriums.

(5) Die Benutzungsgenehmigung ist zu versagen, wenn eine Sperrfrist nach § 3 Abs. 3 LArchG nicht abgelaufen ist und auch nicht gemäß § 3 Abs. 4 LArchG verkürzt werden kann. Ist der Ablauf einer Frist nach § 3 Abs. 3 Satz 2 LArchG dem Landesarchiv nicht bekannt und auch nicht anhand der Find- und sonstigen Hilfsmittel des Landesarchivs feststellbar, hat die Antragstellerin oder der Antragsteller die ihr oder ihm bekannten Daten zur Ermittlung des Sachverhaltes beizubringen.

(6) Eine bereits erteilte Benutzungsgenehmigung kann widerrufen, zurückgenommen oder nachträglich eingeschränkt werden, wenn Gründe bekannt werden, die zu einer Versagung oder Einschränkung nach den Absätzen 3 bis 5 geführt hätten.

(7) Die Benutzungsgenehmigung kann versagt werden, wenn die Antragstellerin oder der Antragsteller zuvor gegen die Benutzungsverordnung oder das Landesarchivgesetz erheblich verstoßen hat oder aus anderen Gründen anzunehmen ist, dass für deren Einhaltung keine Gewähr geboten wird.

(8) Die Gründe für die Versagung oder Einschränkung der Benutzungsgenehmigung werden der oder dem Betroffenen schriftlich mitgeteilt.

§ 4 Benutzung im verwahrenden Landesarchiv

(1) Das verwahrende Landesarchiv berät die Benutzerin oder den Benutzer bei der Ermittlung des Archivguts.

(2) Archivgut, Schutzmedien, archiveigene Find- und sonstige Hilfsmittel sowie Bücher und Zeitschriften dürfen grundsätzlich nur in den dafür bestimmten Räumen des verwahrenden Landesarchivs benutzt werden. Die Interessen anderer Benutzerinnen und Benutzer sind angemessen zu berücksichtigen.

(3) Findmittel werden grundsätzlich nur insoweit vorgelegt, als sie Archivgut nachweisen, das uneingeschränkt zugänglich ist.

(4) Ist eine für die Benutzung bestimmte Vervielfältigung von Archivgut vorhanden, darf nur diese benutzt werden, wenn nicht die Vorlage des Originals für ein Forschungsvorhaben unentbehrlich ist.

(5) Archivgut ist mit größter Sorgfalt zu behandeln. Es ist insbesondere untersagt,
1. den Ordnungszustand des Archivguts selbständig zu verändern oder Teile zu entnehmen,
2. auf Archivgut, in Büchern und Findmitteln Striche oder Zeichen irgendwelcher Art anzubringen oder Tilgungen vorzunehmen,
3. Archivgut als Schreibunterlage zu verwenden oder Handpausen anzufertigen.

Beschädigungen und Fehler in der Reihenfolge der Schriftstücke sollen dem Archivpersonal gemeldet werden.

(6) Einzelheiten der Benutzung, insbesondere bezüglich der Bestellung von Archivgut, des Verhaltens im Benutzersaal und der Verwendung benutzereigener technischer Geräte, können durch eine Hausordnung (§ 12) geregelt werden. Für die Benutzung fremden oder besonders wertvollen Archivguts können besondere Bestimmungen getroffen werden.

§ 5 Schriftliche oder in Textform erteilte Auskünfte

(1) Auf eine schriftlich oder in Textform gestellte Anfrage wird schriftlich oder in Textform Auskunft erteilt, die in der Regel Hinweise auf das erschlossene einschlägige Archivgut sowie auf die entsprechenden Findmittel enthält. Ist eine kurzfristige Beantwortung nicht möglich, wird ein Zwischenbescheid erteilt. Ein Anspruch auf Auskünfte, die eine unverhältnismäßig lange Arbeitszeit erfordern, oder auf Beantwortung von wiederholten Anfragen innerhalb eines kürzeren Zeitraums besteht nicht.

(2) An Gerichte, Behörden und sonstige öffentlich-rechtliche Stellen werden schriftliche Auskünfte, sofern sie zur Klärung von Rechts- oder Verwaltungsangelegenheiten erbeten werden, im Rahmen der Amtshilfe erteilt.

§ 6 Vervielfältigungen

(1) Vervielfältigungen und digitalisierte oder fotografische Reproduktionen von für die Benutzung freigegebenem Archivgut werden, soweit dies der Dienstbetrieb zulässt, grundsätzlich durch Bedienstete der Landesarchivverwaltung angefertigt. Fotokopien am Lesedrucker können auch durch Benutzerinnen oder Benutzer angefertigt werden.

(2) Das verwahrende Landesarchiv entscheidet über das jeweils geeignete Reproduktionsverfahren unter Berücksichtigung der für das Archivgut schonendsten Art der Vervielfältigung sowie der Geräteausstattung. Die Interessen anderer Benutzerinnen und Benutzer sind angemessen zu berücksichtigen.

(3) Die Herstellung von Fotokopien und digitalen oder fotografischen Reproduktionen ist zu versagen, wenn sich das Archivgut wegen seines Erhaltungszustands, seines Formats oder aus anderen Gründen nicht zur Reproduktion eignet.

§ 7 Versendung von Archivgut

(1) Auf schriftlichen Antrag kann uneingeschränkt zur Benutzung freigegebenes Archivgut in begründeten Einzelfällen, in denen der Benutzungszweck weder durch persönliche Benutzung bei dem verwahrenden Landesarchiv noch durch Übersendung von Reproduktionen erreicht werden kann, zur Benutzung an hauptamtlich verwaltete auswärtige Archive oder, wenn solche am Ort nicht vorhanden sind, an wissenschaftliche Bibliotheken, an hauptamtlich verwaltete öffentliche Dienststellen oder an Gerichte versandt werden, sofern sich diese verpflichten,

1. das Archivgut in den Diensträumen unter ständiger fachlicher Aufsicht nur der Benutzerin oder dem Benutzer vorzulegen,
2. das Archivgut den üblichen konservatorischen Anforderungen entsprechend sowie diebstahl- und feuersicher zu verwahren,
3. das Archivgut nach Ablauf der vom verwahrenden Landesarchiv bestimmten Benutzungsfrist in der von diesem bestimmten Versendungsart zurückzusenden und
4. keine Kopien oder Reproduktionen von dem Archivgut anzufertigen.

Die Benutzungsfrist soll sechs Wochen nicht überschreiten; sie kann auf Antrag verlängert werden. Die Versendung von Archivgut an Privatpersonen – ausgenommen Eigentümerinnen und Eigentümer – ist nicht zulässig.

(2) Die Versendung von Archivgut ins Ausland ist nur mit Zustimmung des für das Archivwesen zuständigen Ministeriums zulässig.

(3) Von der Versendung ausgeschlossen sind
1. Archivgut, das wegen seines Erhaltungszustands, wegen seines Formats oder aus anderen Sicherheits- oder konservatorischen Gründen versendungsunfähig ist, sowie
2. archivalische Findmittel.

(4) Aus dienstlichen Gründen kann versandtes Archivgut jederzeit zurückgefordert werden.

(5) Das verwahrende Landesarchiv kann die Versendung mit Bedingungen oder Auflagen verbinden; insbesondere kann eine Versicherung wertvollen Archivguts gegen Beschädigung oder Verlust verlangt werden.

(6) Die Kosten der Versendung und gegebenenfalls der Versicherung trägt die Benutzerin oder der Benutzer.

(7) Die weitere Benutzung des versandten Archivguts richtet sich nach den Bestimmungen dieser Verordnung.

(8) Die Versendung von Archivgut zur amtlichen Benutzung erfolgt nach Maßgabe der Absätze 1 bis 7 im Rahmen der Amtshilfe.

§ 8 Ausleihe von Archivgut

(1) Uneingeschränkt zur Benutzung freigegebenes Archivgut kann zu Zwecken der Öffentlichkeitsarbeit, insbesondere für Ausstellungen ausgeliehen werden, wenn der Ausstellungszweck nicht durch Reproduktionen oder Nachbildungen erreicht werden kann und gewährleistet ist, dass das ausgeliehene Archivgut wirksam vor Verlust, Beschädigung oder unbefugter Benutzung geschützt wird. Auf die Ausleihe zu diesem Zweck besteht kein Anspruch. Die Herstellung von Reproduktionen von ausgestelltem Archivgut bedarf der Zustimmung des verwahrenden Landesarchivs.

(2) Leihgaben aus Depositalbeständen bedürfen der Zustimmung der Eigentümerin oder des Eigentümers.

(3) Über die Ausleihe ist mit der Entleiherin oder dem Entleiher ein Leihvertrag abzuschließen.

(4) Im Übrigen gelten § 7 Abs. 2, 3 Nr. 2 und Abs. 5 bis 7 entsprechend; im Fall der Ausleihe durch Versendung gilt außerdem § 7 Abs. 3 Nr. 1 entsprechend.

§ 9 Verwendung zu anderen als privaten Zwecken

Jede über den ausschließlich privaten Gebrauch hinausgehende Verwendung von Archivgut, insbesondere für Publikationen, geschäftliche und gewerbliche Zwecke, ist gesondert nach § 3 genehmigungspflichtig.

§ 10 Veröffentlichungen

(1) Bei der Benutzung von Archivgut in Veröffentlichungen ist jeweils die Herkunft durch Angabe von verwahrendem Landesarchiv, Bestand, Nummer und Seite genau und eindeutig zu bezeichnen.

(2) Die Benutzerin oder der Benutzer ist verpflichtet, Veröffentlichungen, in denen Archivgut verwertet worden ist, dem verwahrenden Landesarchiv bibliographisch anzuzeigen.

§ 11 Gebühren und Auslagen

Verwaltungs- und Benutzungsgebühren sowie Auslagen für die Inanspruchnahme der Landesarchive richten sich nach dem Landesgebührengesetz vom 3. Dezember 1974 (GVBl. S. 578, BS 2013-1) und der Landesverordnung über die Gebühren im Bereich der Landesarchivverwaltung (Besonderes Gebührenverzeichnis) vom 9. Mai 2003 (GVBl. S. 74, BS 2013-1-21) in den jeweils geltenden Fassungen.

§ 12 Hausordnung
Örtliche und organisatorische Besonderheiten können die Landesarchive ergänzend durch Hausordnung regeln.

§ 13 Benutzung durch die abliefernde Stelle
(1) Die abliefernde Stelle hat das Recht, das von ihr selbst abgelieferte Archivgut jederzeit zu benutzen, wenn sie es zur Erfüllung ihrer Aufgaben benötigt; die Bestimmungen dieser Verordnung finden insoweit keine Anwendung. Satz 1 gilt nicht, soweit es sich um Archivgut handelt, das vor der Ablieferung aufgrund besonderer Rechtsvorschriften hätte gesperrt, vernichtet oder gelöscht werden müssen.
(2) Absatz 1 gilt entsprechend für Archivgut, das vom Rechts- oder Funktionsvorgänger oder von der nachgeordneten Stelle einer die Benutzung ersuchenden Behörde abgeliefert wurde.
(3) Die Art und Weise der Nutzung nach Absatz 1 wird zwischen der abliefernden Stelle und dem verwahrenden Landesarchiv im Einzelfall vereinbart. Dabei ist sicherzustellen, dass das Archivgut gegen Verlust, Beschädigung und unbefugte Benutzung geschützt und innerhalb eines angemessenen Zeitraums unverändert zurückgegeben wird.

§ 14 In-Kraft-Treten
(1) Diese Verordnung tritt am Tage nach der Verkündung in Kraft.
(2) Gleichzeitig wird die Benutzungsordnung für die Landesarchive in der Fassung vom 12. Dezember 1983 aufgehoben.

D11.III.1 Zuwendungen für nicht staatliche Kulturdenkmäler

Zuwendungen des Landes Rheinland-Pfalz zur Erhaltung von nicht staatlichen Kulturdenkmälern

Verwaltungsvorschrift des Ministeriums für Bildung, Wissenschaft, Weiterbildung und Kultur vom 25. November 2015 (Amtsbl. S. 268) (9811/04 007/50)

Im Benehmen mit dem Ministerium der Finanzen, dem Ministerium des Innern und für Sport und dem Rechnungshof Rheinland-Pfalz wird gemäß § 29 Abs. 1 und § 36 des Denkmalschutzgesetzes (DSchG) vom 23. März 1978 (GVBl. S. 159), zuletzt geändert durch Artikel 3 des Gesetzes vom 3. Dezember 2014 (GVBl. S. 245), BS 224-2, Folgendes bestimmt:

1 Rechtsgrundlagen, Zuwendungszweck, Zuständigkeit

1.1 Rechtsgrundlagen
Das Land gewährt aufgrund des § 29 Abs. 1 DSchG nach Maßgabe dieser Verwaltungsvorschrift, den §§ 7, 23 und 44 der Landeshaushaltsordnung (LHO) sowie den hierzu ergangenen Verwaltungsvorschriften Zuwendungen zu Maßnahmen, die der Erhaltung und Pflege von Kulturdenkmälern dienen.

1.2 Zuwendungszweck
Die Zuwendungen sollen Eigentümerinnen, Eigentümer oder sonstige dinglich Berechtigte bei der Erfüllung der sich nach § 2 DSchG aus der Sozialbindung des Eigentums ergebenden Pflichten unterstützen.

1.3 Zuständigkeit
Zuständig für die Durchführung des Zuwendungsverfahrens ist die Denkmalfachbehörde gemäß § 25 Abs. 3 Satz 1 DSchG (Bewilligungsbehörde).

1.4 Ermessensentscheidung
Ein Rechtsanspruch auf Gewährung einer Zuwendung besteht nicht. Die Bewilligungsbehörde entscheidet nach pflichtgemäßem Ermessen im Rahmen der verfügbaren Haushaltsmittel. Die Grundsätze der Sparsamkeit und Wirtschaftlichkeit sowie das Subsidiaritätsprinzip sind zu berücksichtigen.

1.5 Beauftragter für den Haushalt; Landeskonservator
Zu den Aufgaben der oder des Beauftragten für den Haushalt nach § 9 LHO und der hierzu erlassenen Verwaltungsvorschrift gehören insbesondere die Überwachung der Regelungen dieser Verwaltungsvorschrift und der haushaltsrechtlichen Vorschriften. Die Leitung der Direktion Landesdenkmalpflege überwacht in Abstimmung mit der oder dem Beauftragten für den Haushalt die Vergleichbarkeit, die regionale Ausgewogenheit sowie die landesweit vergleichbare Ausübung des Ermessens im Rahmen der Förderentscheidung nach Nummer 8.

Widerspricht die oder der Beauftragte für den Haushalt einem Entscheidungsvorschlag der Direktion Landesdenkmalpflege und kann keine Einigung erzielt werden, findet das Verfahren nach Nummer 5.4 zu § 9 LHO der Verwaltungsvorschrift zum Vollzug der Landeshaushaltsordnung (VV-LHO) Anwendung.

Die oder der Beauftragte für den Haushalt kann ihre oder seine Aufgaben auf fachlich geeignete Personen übertragen, die im Übrigen nicht im Bewilligungsverfahren beteiligt sind.

2 Zuwendungsempfängerin und Zuwendungsempfänger
Zuwendungen kann erhalten, wer als Eigentümerin, Eigentümer, sonstige dinglich Berechtigte oder sonstiger dinglich Berechtigter oder mit deren oder dessen Zustimmung Maßnahmen nach Nummer 3.1 durchführt.

Den kommunalen Gebietskörperschaften, Zweckverbänden und Kirchen als Zuwendungsempfänger gleichgestellt sind Körperschaften, Anstalten und Stiftungen des öffentlichen Rechts.

3 Zuwendungsgegenstand, Genehmigungen, Maßnahmenbeginn

3.1 Zuwendungsgegenstand
Gefördert werden Maßnahmen
– an Kulturdenkmälern im Sinne der §§ 3 bis 5 DSchG,
– die den denkmalpflegerischen Erfordernissen entsprechen,

- mit der Denkmalfachbehörde abgestimmt sind und
- an deren Durchführung das Land nach § 23 LHO ein erhebliches Interesse hat.

Bei Maßnahmen an beweglichen Kulturdenkmälern, die noch nicht nach § 8 Abs. 2 DSchG geschützt sind, muss die jeweilige Eigentümerin oder der jeweilige Eigentümer der Unterschutzstellung schriftlich zugestimmt haben. Maßnahmen an beweglichen Kulturdenkmälern können nur gefördert werden, wenn diese überwiegend in Rheinland-Pfalz aufbewahrt oder betrieben werden.

Förderfähig sind weiterhin Durchführungen von Fortbildungsveranstaltungen, die in unmittelbarem Zusammenhang mit der Erhaltung oder energetischen Ertüchtigung von Kulturdenkmälern stehen.

3.2 Genehmigungen
Notwendige Genehmigungen oder Zustimmungen (Baugenehmigung, denkmalrechtliche Genehmigung nach § 13 Abs. 1 DSchG, sonstige öffentlich-rechtliche Genehmigungen) müssen vorliegen; bei Instandsetzungsmaßnahmen nach § 13 Abs. 4 DSchG muss die dort geforderte Anzeige erfolgt sein.

3.3 Maßnahmenbeginn
Die Maßnahme darf grundsätzlich vor Bewilligung der Zuwendung nicht begonnen sein. Ist eine Entscheidung über die Bewilligung noch nicht möglich, kann die Bewilligungsbehörde bei Maßnahmen, die aus sachlichen oder wirtschaftlichen Gründen keinen Aufschub dulden, einen vorzeitigen Maßnahmenbeginn gemäß Teil I Nr. 1.3 und Teil II Nr. 1.3 zu § 44 Abs. 1 LHO der VV-LHO zulassen. Eine kursorische Vorprüfung ist ausreichend. Die Zulassung eines vorzeitigen Maßnahmenbeginns und die Gründe hierfür sind zu dokumentieren. Die Zustimmung zum vorzeitigen Maßnahmenbeginn begründet keinen Rechtsanspruch auf eine Zuwendung. Planungen und Untersuchungen gelten nicht als Beginn des Vorhabens, es sei denn, sie sind alleiniger Zweck der Zuwendung. Das Gleiche gilt für die Einholung von Vergleichsangeboten, die im Rahmen des Antragsverfahrens vorgelegt werden.

4 Antrag

4.1 Schriftlicher Antrag
Die Gewährung einer Zuwendung bedarf grundsätzlich eines schriftlichen Antrags. Der Antrag muss alle Angaben enthalten, die zur denkmalpflegerischen Beurteilung der beabsichtigten Maßnahmen erforderlich sind.

Für den Fall, dass das für die Denkmalpflege zuständige Ministerium Antragsvordrucke herausgibt, sind diese zu verwenden.

4.2 Antragsfrist
Der Antrag ist bis zum 31. Oktober des Jahres vor dem geplanten Beginn der Maßnahme bei der Bewilligungsbehörde einzureichen (Ausschlussfrist). Bei Maßnahmen, die der Notsicherung eines Kulturdenkmals dienen, ist eine Überschreitung der Antragsfrist unschädlich. Die Bewilligungsbehörde kann in Einzelfällen Ausnahmen zulassen. Die Gründe hierfür sind zu dokumentieren.

4.3 Unterlagen
Dem Antrag sind folgende Unterlagen beizufügen:
- Beschreibung der geplanten Gesamtmaßnahme mit Ausweisung der denkmalbedingten Maßnahmen
- Darstellung der vorhandenen Schäden (ggf. mit Fotos)
- Planzeichnungen, ggf. Fotos, soweit erforderlich
- Gutachten, soweit erforderlich
- notwendige bau-, denkmalrechtliche und sonstige öffentlich-rechtliche Genehmigungen für die geplante Maßnahme bzw. eine Erklärung, dass die entsprechenden Anträge gestellt sind
- Kosten- und Finanzierungsplan
  a) Kostenberechnungen der Gesamtmaßnahmen nach DIN 276. Bei kleineren Maßnahmen können anstelle von Kostenberechnungen auch Angebote oder Kostenvoranschläge vorgelegt werden. Soweit die Verdingungsordnung für Bauleistungen (VOB) oder die Verdingungsordnung für Leistungen (VOL) nach Teil I Anlage 3 Nr. 3.1 zu § 44 Abs. 1 LHO der VV-LHO nicht angewendet werden müssen, sollen mindestens drei Vergleichsangebote über die jeweilige (Teil-)Maßnahme vorgelegt werden. Soweit die Vergleichsangebote im Antragsverfahren noch nicht vorgelegt werden können, sind sie spätestens mit dem Verwendungsnachweis vorzulegen.

D11.III.1 Zuwendungen für nicht staatliche Kulturdenkmäler

b) Leistungsbeschreibungen
c) ggf. Berechnung der denkmalbedingten Mehraufwendungen
d) ggf. Zuwendungsbescheide oder Zusicherungen von Leistungen Dritter
e) Erklärung über die Vorsteuerabzugsberechtigung
f) Nachweis zur Sicherung der Gesamtfinanzierung der Maßnahmen (weitere öffentliche und private Zuwendungen, Eigenmittel usw.)
g) Darstellung der in den letzten 15 Jahren erhaltenen öffentlichen Zuwendungen für das Kulturdenkmal
   – bei juristischen Personen des Privatrechts ein Nachweis über die Vertretungsbefugnis
   – in Fällen der Nummer 5.2.3 die Wirtschaftlichkeitsberechnung
   – in Fällen der Nummer 5.2.4 der Nachweis der fehlenden wirtschaftlichen Leistungsfähigkeit (Einkommen und Vermögen)
   – Erklärung der Antragstellerin oder des Antragstellers, ob beabsichtigt ist, die Möglichkeit einer erhöhten steuerlichen Sonderabschreibung in Anspruch zu nehmen
   – ggf. weitere, im begründeten Einzelfall von der Bewilligungsbehörde für erforderlich gehaltene Unterlagen
   – Erklärungen der Antragstellerin oder des Antragstellers über die Richtigkeit und Vollständigkeit der Angaben sowie über den noch nicht erfolgten Maßnahmenbeginn

4.4 Anträge kommunaler Gebietskörperschaften
Kommunale Gebietskörperschaften, auch soweit sie an einer antragstellenden juristischen Person beteiligt sind, müssen ihre Einnahmequellen ausschöpfen (§ 94 der Gemeindeordnung – GemO –).
Die Pläne müssen veranschlagungs- und ausführungsreif sein (vgl. § 10 Abs. 2 der Gemeindehaushaltsverordnung – GemHVO –).
Neben den in Nummer 4.3 genannten Unterlagen sind bei Anträgen kommunaler Gebietskörperschaften zusätzlich beizufügen:
– eine Übersicht über die Haushalts- und Finanzlage (Teil II Anlage 1 zu § 44 Abs. 1 LHO der VV-LHO),
– eine Beurteilung der dauernden Leistungsfähigkeit (Berechnung der sogenannten freien Finanzspitze) gemäß Anlage 3 Muster 14 der Verwaltungsvorschrift über Produktrahmenplan und Kontenrahmenplan mit Zuordnungsvorschriften für die kommunale Haushaltswirtschaft und Muster zur Gemeindeordnung und Gemeindehaushaltsverordnung (VV Gemeindehaushaltssystematik – VV-GemHSys –) vom 23. November 2006 (MinBl. 2007 S. 16; 2011 S. 182)
– Rats- bzw. Ausschussbeschluss über die Ausführung der Maßnahme.

Die Finanzierung (vgl. Nummer. 7.6) ist durch eine positive Stellungnahme der zuständigen Kommunalaufsichtsbehörde über die finanzielle Leistungsfähigkeit zur Erbringung des finanziellen Eigenanteils einschließlich der nicht zuwendungsfähigen Kosten nach dem Muster Teil II Anlage 2 zu § 44 Abs. 1 LHO der VV-LHO nachzuweisen. Die Aufsichtsbehörde hat bei der Abgabe der kommunalaufsichtlichen Stellungnahme die an andere Förderprogramme gerichteten Zuwendungsanträge sowie die bereits in Ausführung befindlichen Vorhaben bei ihrer Bewertung mit einzubeziehen.

4.5 Antragsprüfung, ZBau
Die Prüfung des Antrags erfolgt durch die Bewilligungsbehörde. Das Ergebnis der Antragsprüfung einschließlich der Feststellung der zuwendungsfähigen Ausgaben und der Höhe der Zuwendung ist in einem Prüfvermerk festzustellen. Dabei sind die Gründe für die Entscheidung zu dokumentieren.
Die Antragsprüfung hat unter Berücksichtigung von baufachlichen Kriterien insbesondere auch im Hinblick auf die Plausibilität der durchzuführenden Maßnahmen und der dargestellten Kosten zu erfolgen. Überschreiten die Zuwendungen von Bund und Land in der Summe die in Teil I Nr. 6.1 und Teil II Nr. 6.1 zu § 44 Abs. 1 LHO der VV-LHO festgesetzten Beträge oder erachtet die Bewilligungsbehörde dies als erforderlich, finden die baufachlichen Ergänzungsbestimmungen für Zuwendungen (ZBau) – Teil I Anlage 1 zu § 44 Abs. 1 LHO der VV-LHO – Anwendung. Die Aufgaben der Bauverwaltung nach der ZBau werden vom Landesbetrieb Liegenschafts- und Baubetreuung wahrgenommen. Bei Maßnahmen, die in mehreren Abschnitten durchgeführt werden sollen, ist der Zuwendungsbedarf für die Gesamtkonzeption maßgebend.

4.6 Mehrere Zuwendungsgeber – Abstimmungsverfahren
Soll eine Maßnahme am Kulturdenkmal durch mehrere öffentliche Zuwendungsgeber gefördert werden, ist Teil I Nr. 1.4 und Teil II Nr. 1.4 zu § 44 Abs. 1 LHO der VV-LHO anzuwenden.

5 Zuwendungsfähige Ausgaben

5.1 Denkmalbedingte Mehraufwendungen
Zuwendungsfähige Ausgaben sind grundsätzlich Aufwendungen für Kulturdenkmäler, die im Rahmen von Sicherungs-, Instandhaltungs- und Unterhaltungsmaßnahmen allein oder überwiegend aus Gründen der Denkmalpflege erforderlich werden, soweit sie den üblichen Aufwand bei vergleichbaren nicht denkmalwerten Objekten übersteigen (denkmalbedingte Mehraufwendungen) sowie Aufwendungen für Bauaufnahmen, restauratorische Untersuchungen und Gutachten, die auf Verlangen einer Denkmalschutz- oder der Denkmalfachbehörde anzufertigen und überwiegend aus Gründen des Denkmalschutzes erforderlich sind.

Zur Feststellung der Höhe der denkmalbedingten Mehraufwendungen kann das für die Denkmalpflege zuständige Ministerium konkretisierende Regelungen erlassen.

5.2 Sonstige Aufwendungen
Über die denkmalbedingten Mehraufwendungen (vgl. Nummer 5.1) hinaus können in folgenden begründeten Einzelfällen weitere Ausgaben als zuwendungsfähig anerkannt werden:

5.2.1 Maßnahmen an nicht nutzbaren Kulturdenkmälern, z. B. Ruinen, Befestigungen, Flurdenkmälern, Grabmälern, sonstigen Kleindenkmälern usw.

5.2.2 Maßnahmen an Sakralbauten, die allein oder überwiegend aus Gründen der Denkmalpflege erforderlich werden (denkmalbedingte Aufwendungen).

5.2.3 Notsicherungsmaßnahmen an Kulturdenkmälern, deren Unterhaltung der Eigentümerin oder dem Eigentümer wirtschaftlich nicht zugemutet werden kann. Die Antragstellerin oder der Antragsteller hat eine Wirtschaftlichkeitsberechnung vorzulegen, die die Unzumutbarkeit belegt. Das für die Denkmalpflege zuständige Ministerium kann hierzu Regelungen erlassen.

5.2.4 Notsicherungsmaßnahmen an Kulturdenkmälern, zu deren Durchführung die Eigentümerin oder der Eigentümer wirtschaftlich nicht in der Lage ist. Die fehlende wirtschaftliche Leistungsfähigkeit ist von der Eigentümerin oder dem Eigentümer zu belegen. Das für die Denkmalpflege zuständige Ministerium kann hierzu Regelungen erlassen.

5.2.5 Ausgaben für die Wiederherstellung von teilzerstörten Kulturdenkmälern, wenn hierbei auf originale Substanz zurückgegriffen wird oder Ausgaben für die rekonstruierende Wiederherstellung, soweit damit untergegangene, aber unverzichtbare Teile eines noch bestehenden Kulturdenkmals ergänzt werden.

5.2.6 Ist das Interesse des Landes an der Durchführung der beantragten Maßnahmen an Kulturdenkmälern besonders hoch, kann das für die Denkmalpflege zuständige Ministerium im Einzelfall weitere Ausnahmen zulassen.

Die Handhabung der Ausnahmetatbestände nach den Nummern 5.2.1 bis 5.2.6 hat restriktiv zu erfolgen. In allen Fällen sind die Gründe für eine Anerkennung von Aufwendungen über die denkmalbedingten Mehraufwendungen hinaus zu dokumentieren.

5.3 Nicht zuwendungsfähige Ausgaben
Nicht zuwendungsfähig sind folgende Ausgaben:
- Kosten des Erwerbs von Kulturdenkmälern
- Erschließungskosten und Kosten für die Beschaffung von Finanzierungsmitteln
- Einsatz von Fahrzeugen und Geräten von privaten Dritten
- reine Verschönerungsmaßnahmen ohne denkmalrelevanten Charakter
- nicht denkmalrelevante, regelmäßig wiederkehrende Unterhaltungskosten (z.B. Strom, Heizung)
- rentierliche nutzungsbedingte Aufwendungen
- Totalrekonstruktion oder Neubauten in Gesamtanlagen
- rein nutzungsbedingte gebäudetechnische Ausstattung (Haustechnik, Sanitär usw.)
- Maßnahmen an Kulturdenkmälern, die Museumsgut sind oder werden sollen
- nicht denkmalrelevante energetische Ertüchtigungsmaßnahmen

5.4 Berücksichtigung von Eigenleistung

Eigenleistungen müssen im Kosten- und Finanzierungsplan sowohl auf der Kosten- als auch auf der Finanzierungsseite dargestellt werden. Sie können nach den folgenden Maßgaben anerkannt werden:

5.4.1 Bei gemeinnützigen Vereinen, deren alleiniger Vereinszweck die Erhaltung eines oder mehrerer Denkmäler ist, kann der Fördersatz nach Nummer 7.3 erhöht werden, wenn durch den Verein Arbeitsleistungen in nicht unerheblichem Umfang, mindestens aber 200 Arbeitsstunden, geleistet werden. Der durch die Erhöhung des Fördersatzes errechnete Zuwendungsbetrag muss in einem angemessenen Verhältnis zur erbrachten Arbeitsleistung stehen. Die Arbeitsleistungen sind durch unterschriebene Stundennachweise glaubhaft zu machen, ggf. durch eine Architektin oder einen Architekten zu bestätigen und der Bewilligungsbehörde vorzulegen.

5.4.2 Das von der Zuwendungsempfängerin oder dem Zuwendungsempfänger selbst aufgewendete Material zum Einkaufspreis angerechnet.

5.4.3 Bei Unternehmerinnen, Unternehmern, Handwerkerinnen, Handwerkern, Restauratorinnen und Restauratoren, die Eigenleistungen im Rahmen ihres Geschäftsbetriebes erbringen, werden die ortsüblichen Entgelte abzüglich eines Gewinnanteiles von 30 v. H. anerkannt. Diese Regelung gilt auch für Architektinnen, Architekten, Ingenieurinnen und Ingenieure bis zu einem Höchstbetrag von 10 v. H. der Gesamtkosten der Maßnahmen.

5.4.4 Bei Eigenleistungen von kommunalen Gebietskörperschaften und Zweckverbänden kann der gezahlte und nachgewiesene Tariflohn der eingesetzten Arbeitskräfte mit einem pauschalen Abzug von 30 v. H. in die Gesamtkosten der Maßnahme einbezogen werden. Beim Einsatz gemeindeeigener Baufahrzeuge und -maschinen kann der ortsübliche Stundensatz abzüglich eines Eigenanteils von 30 v. H. anerkannt werden.

5.5 Erhöhung der Maßnahmenkosten

Stellt sich heraus, dass der Zuwendungszweck mit der bewilligten Zuwendung nicht zu erreichen ist, hat die Bewilligungsbehörde zu prüfen, ob das Vorhaben eingeschränkt, umfinanziert oder notfalls eingestellt wird oder ob die Zuwendung ausnahmsweise erhöht werden kann. Ein Rechtsanspruch auf Nachfinanzierung besteht nicht. Die Antragstellerin oder der Antragsteller ist entsprechend zu beraten. Die Regelung zur Verbindlichkeit der Einzelansätze aus dem Kosten- und Finanzierungsplan nach Teil I Anlage 3 Nr. 1.2 Satz 3 und Teil II Anlage 3 Nr. 1.2 Satz 2 zu § 44 Abs. 1 LHO der VV-LHO findet innerhalb der zuwendungsfähigen Kosten keine Anwendung, sofern der Zweck der Zuwendung vollständig erhalten bleibt und die erzielten Einsparungen zur Deckung von Mehrkosten dienen.

5.6 Zuwendungen für Fortbildungsveranstaltungen

Zuwendungsfähig sind weiterhin die tatsächlich entstandenen Ausgaben für die Durchführung von Fortbildungsveranstaltungen. Für die Berechnung von Reisekosten ist das Landesreisekostengesetz anzuwenden.

5.7 Umsatzsteuer

Die Umsatzsteuer zählt nicht zu den zuwendungsfähigen Aufwendungen, soweit die Zuwendungsempfängerin oder der Zuwendungsempfänger dafür vorsteuerabzugsberechtigt ist.

6 Leistungsform, Zuwendungs- und Finanzierungsart

6.1 Leistungsform der Zuwendung

Die Zuwendung wird grundsätzlich als bedingt rückzahlbarer (vgl. Nummer 11.1) und zweckgebundener Zuschuss oder Zuweisung bewilligt.

6.2 Zuwendungs- und Finanzierungsart

Die Zuwendung erfolgt als Projektförderung und wird als Anteilsfinanzierung mit Höchstbetrag bewilligt. Soweit eine Anteilsfinanzierung nicht geeignet erscheint, erfolgt die Bewilligung als Fehlbedarfsfinanzierung mit Höchstbetrag. Die Nummern 4.6 und 7.3 bleiben unberührt. Soweit die Zuwendung im Einzelfall nicht mehr als 5 v.H. der zuwendungsfähigen Ausgaben und höchstens 30.000 Euro beträgt, kann ausnahmsweise eine Bewilligung als Festbetragsfinanzierung erfolgen.

7 Höhe der Zuwendung

7.1 Fördersatz
Die Höhe der Zuwendung richtet sich im Einzelfall nach
- dem Landesinteresse an der Ausführung des Vorhabens,
- der Bedeutung des Objektes oder der Veranstaltung,
- den im jeweiligen Förderbereich gemäß Nummer 8.1 zur Verfügung stehenden Landesmitteln,
- der finanziellen Leistungsfähigkeit der Antragstellerin oder des Antragstellers sowie
- den Vorteilen und Belastungen der Zuwendungsempfängerin oder des Zuwendungsempfängers aus dem Kulturdenkmal einschließlich möglicher steuerlicher Vergünstigungen und weiterer Fördermöglichkeiten.

Soweit die Zuwendungsempfängerin oder der Zuwendungsempfänger beabsichtigt, die Möglichkeit einer erhöhten steuerlichen Sonderabschreibung in Anspruch zu nehmen, kann ein angemessener Abschlag bei der Bemessung des Fördersatzes erfolgen.

7.2 Höchstfördersatz
In der Regel beträgt der Fördersatz
- bei Zuwendungen an Private bis zu 50 v. H.,
- bei kommunalen Gebietskörperschaften, Zweckverbänden und Kirchen bis zu 33,33 v. H. der zuwendungsfähigen Kosten.

7.3 Ausnahmen vom Höchstfördersatz
In den in den Nummern 5.2.1, 5.2.3 bis 5.2.6, 5.4.1 und 5.6 genannten Fällen können die Fördersätze – in Ausnahmefällen bis zu einer Vollfinanzierung – überschritten werden, soweit die Finanzierung der Gesamtmaßnahme nicht auf andere Weise sichergestellt werden kann. Die Begründung hierfür ist zu dokumentieren.

7.4 Kleinbetragsregelung
Zuwendungen werden in der Regel nur gewährt, wenn die zuwendungsfähigen Ausgaben
- bei kommunalen Gebietskörperschaften, Zweckverbänden und Kirchen als Eigentümer oder sonstig dinglich Berechtigten 15.000 Euro
- bei sonstigen Eigentümerinnen, Eigentümern oder sonstig dinglich Berechtigten 1.500 Euro

übersteigen. Ausnahmen von dieser Regelung sind zu begründen.
Diese Regelung gilt nicht für Fortbildungsveranstaltungen gemäß Nummer 5.6.

7.5 Interessen Dritter
Liegt die beantragte Maßnahme auch im Interesse von Dritten, soll die Förderung davon abhängig gemacht werden, dass diese sich angemessen an den zuwendungsfähigen Ausgaben beteiligen.

7.6 Gesicherte Finanzierung
Die vollständige Finanzierung des Vorhabens muss unter Einbeziehung der Eigenmittel, der Zuwendung des Landes und Mittel von dritter Seite gesichert sein. Bei kommunalen Antragstellern gilt dies auch für die Folgekosten.

8 Förderbereiche, Auswahlkriterien

8.1 Förderbereiche
Die zur Verfügung stehenden Haushaltsmittel werden nach folgender Priorität in die aufgeführten Förderbereiche unterteilt:
8.1.1 Einzelveranschlagte Maßnahmen gemäß Haushaltsplan
8.1.2 Maßnahmen unter Entscheidungsvorbehalt des für Denkmalpflege zuständigen Ministeriums
8.1.3 Verbundförderungen und Kofinanzierungen
8.1.4 Großprojekte (Zuwendungssumme im Einzelfall über 30.000 Euro) und
8.1.5 Kleinförderungen (Zuwendungssumme im Einzelfall unter 30.000 Euro).
Bei den Kleinförderungen sind über einen Betrachtungszeitraum von jeweils drei Jahren die regionale Ausgewogenheit der Zuwendungen (Landkreise und kreisfreie Städte), die sich an der Denkmaldichte der betreffenden Gebiete orientiert, sowie die Berücksichtigung aller Denkmaltypen sicherzustellen.

D11.III.1 Zuwendungen für nicht staatliche Kulturdenkmäler 898

Innerhalb des für die Kleinförderungen vorgesehenen Zuwendungsbudgets ist eine Reserve für unvorhersehbare und unabweisbare Maßnahmen zu bilden. Diese Reserve kann zu Beginn des vierten Quartals des Haushaltsjahres aufgelöst werden. Auf Nummer 8.3 wird verwiesen.

8.2 Auswahlkriterien

Überschreitet die Summe der beantragten Fördermittel die verfügbaren Haushaltsmittel, prüft die Bewilligungsbehörde, inwieweit durch Reduzierung der denkmalpflegerischen Anforderungen, der Fördersätze oder sonstiger zuwendungsreduzierender Maßnahmen weitere Projekte gefördert werden können.

Ist dies nicht möglich oder reichen die Haushaltsmittel auch nach diesen Maßnahmen nicht aus, um alle grundsätzlich förderfähigen Anträge zu bewilligen, ist bis sechs Wochen nach behördeninterner Bekanntgabe des für Denkmalpflegezuwendungen zur Verfügung stehenden Budgets für das jeweilige Haushaltsjahr die Rangfolge der vorgesehenen Bewilligungen im Rahmen eines Bewertungsverfahrens je Förderbereich nach folgenden Kriterien festzustellen:

- Landesinteresse an der Ausführung des Vorhabens,
- Bedeutung des Kulturdenkmals,
- Dringlichkeit und Notwendigkeit der Maßnahme,
- Zweckmäßigkeit der Maßnahme,
- Bewertung der Maßnahme im Hinblick auf die Erhaltung der historischen Substanz,
- Bewertung des denkmalpflegerischen Interesses an der Maßnahme,
- finanzielle Leistungsfähigkeit der Antragstellerin oder des Antragstellers,
- mögliche steuerliche Vergünstigungen und weitere Fördermöglichkeiten,
- weitere für die Auswahlentscheidung erhebliche Kriterien im Ermessen der Bewilligungsbehörde.

Der gesamte Entscheidungsprozess ist zu dokumentieren.

8.3 Förderentscheidung

8.3.1 Für den jeweiligen Förderbereich werden Maßnahmen entsprechend der Rangfolge bewilligt. Die grundsätzlich bewilligungsfähigen Maßnahmen, die im Zeitpunkt der Entscheidung ausschließlich aufgrund nicht ausreichend vorhandener Haushaltsmittel unberücksichtigt bleiben, werden auf einer Nachrückerliste geführt. Für diese Fälle gilt der vorzeitige Maßnahmenbeginn nach Nummer 3.3 als genehmigt.

8.3.2 Überschreitet der Zuwendungsbetrag einschließlich Ko- und Verbundfinanzierung insgesamt den Betrag von 250.000 Euro, ist die vorherige Zustimmung des für die Denkmalpflege zuständigen Ministeriums einzuholen.

8.3.3 Bei Maßnahmen, die in mehreren Abschnitten durchgeführt werden, ist eine Gesamtkonzeption zu erarbeiten und vorzulegen.

9 Zuwendungsbescheid, Ablehnungsbescheid

Der Zuwendungsbescheid oder ein an dessen Stelle tretender öffentlich-rechtlicher Zuwendungsvertrag muss insbesondere enthalten:

- nach Teil I Nr. 4 und 5 und Teil II Nr. 4 und 5 zu § 44 Abs. 1 LHO der VV-LHO:
- Zuwendungsempfängerin oder Zuwendungsempfänger, Bezeichnung des Zuwendungszwecks (konkret geförderte Maßnahmen), Zuwendungsart, Finanzierungsform und Finanzierungsart, Höhe der zuwendungsfähigen Ausgaben mit Darstellung der Gesamtfinanzierung, bei Anteilsfinanzierung Höhe des Fördersatzes, Höchstbetrag der Zuwendung, Bewilligungs- und Durchführungszeitraum, Zweckbindungsfrist, Allgemeine und besondere Nebenbestimmungen, insb. Teil I Anlage 3 (ANBest-P) und Teil II Anlage 3 (ANBest-K) zu § 44 Abs. 1 LHO der VV-LHO, Frist zur Vorlage des Verwendungsnachweises bzw. zum Mittelabruf, Regelungen zur Auszahlung der Zuwendung, ggf. Regelungen zur Sicherung von Ansprüchen des Landes (vgl. Nummern 11.1 und 11.2), Rechtsbehelfsbelehrung
- Bezeichnung des Kulturdenkmals
- besondere denkmalpflegerische Festsetzungen bei der Ausführung der Arbeiten
- nach Teil I Anlage 3 Nr. 3 und Teil II Anlage 3 Nr. 3 zu § 44 Abs. 1 LHO der VV-LHO ggf. Hinweise für die Vergabe von Aufträgen und Einhaltung der Vergabevorschriften
- Soweit die Verdingungsordnung für Bauleistungen (VOB) oder die Verdingungsordnung für Leistungen (VOL) nach Teil I Anlage 3 Nr. 3.1 zu § 44 Abs. 1 LHO der VV-LHO nicht ange-

wendet werden müssen, eine Auflage, dass mindestens drei Vergleichsangebote über die jeweilige (Teil-)Maßnahme vorzulegen sind
- Regelungen zu Publizitätspflichten (vgl. Nummer 11.3)
- Hinweis auf das Prüfungsrecht des Landesrechnungshof nach § 91 Abs. 1 LHO
- Ggf. einen Auflagenvorbehalt bzgl. der Bauausführung zur Umsetzung der denkmalfachlichen Vorgaben

Nicht bewilligungsfähige Anträge werden unverzüglich abgelehnt. Grundsätzlich bewilligungsfähige Anträge, die aufgrund nicht ausreichend zur Verfügung stehender Haushaltsmittel nicht bewilligt werden können, erhalten eine Zwischennachricht im Sinne der Nummer 8.3.1 und spätestens bis zum 15. November des Jahres eine abschließende Entscheidung.

10 Verwendungsnachweis, Mittelabruf, Rücknahme, Widerruf

10.1 Vorlage des Verwendungsnachweises und Mittelabruf

Der Verwendungsnachweis ist bis zum von der Bewilligungsbehörde im Zuwendungsbescheid festgelegten Zeitpunkt, spätestens jedoch sechs Monate nach Abschluss der Maßnahme vorzulegen.

Der Mittelabruf erfolgt grundsätzlich mit Vorlage des Verwendungsnachweises oder eines Zwischennachweises (Erstattungsprinzip). In Ausnahmefällen können die Regelungen nach Teil I Anlage 3 Nr. 1.4 und Teil II Anlage 3 Nr. 1.3 zu § 44 Abs. 1 LHO der VV-LHO angewandt werden. Die Zuwendung soll nicht vor Bestandskraft des Zuwendungsbescheides ausgezahlt werden.

Der Zuwendungsbescheid kann mit einer auflösenden Bedingung für den Fall einer verspäteten Vorlage des Verwendungsnachweises oder des Mittelabrufs versehen werden.

10.2 Gegenstand der Verwendungsnachweisprüfung

Gegenstand der Verwendungsnachweisprüfung sind
- der Sachbericht,
- der zahlenmäßige Nachweis,
- die Belegliste und
- ggf. die Belege.

Anstelle eines Sachberichts kann auch eine Fotodokumentation vorgelegt werden oder eine Vor-Ort-Kontrolle durch die Bewilligungsbehörde oder durch die untere Denkmalschutzbehörde stattfinden. Das Ergebnis der Begutachtung ist hinreichend zu dokumentieren.

10.2.1 Bei Gesamtförderungen (einschließlich Ko- und Verbundfinanzierung) unter 100.000 Euro wird
- das Erreichen des Förderzwecks,
- die zwecksentsprechende Verwendung der Mittel,
- die fristgerechte Mittelverwendung,
- die Einhaltung von denkmalfachlichen und haushaltsrechtlichen Auflagen und Bedingungen und
- die Einhaltung der Vergabevorschriften bzw. Vergabeauflagen im Rahmen der Prüfung des Verwendungsnachweises unter Verzicht einer Prüfung der Einzelbelege festgestellt. Ergeben sich aufgrund dieser Prüfung Beanstandungen, hat eine vertiefte Prüfung unter Hinzuziehung der Einzelbelege stattzufinden. Im Übrigen sollen stichprobenartig vertiefte Verwendungsnachweisprüfungen unter Hinzuziehung der Einzelbelege stattfinden.

10.2.2 Bei Gesamtförderungen ab 100.000 Euro ist der Verwendungsnachweis unter Hinzuziehung der Einzelbelege zu prüfen.

10.2.3 Das Ergebnis des Abstimmungsverfahrens nach Nummer 4.6 bleibt hiervon unberührt.

10.2.4 Das Ergebnis der Verwendungsnachweisprüfung ist in einem Prüfvermerk hinreichend zu dokumentieren.

10.3 Rücknahme, Widerruf

Soweit Gründe für eine Rücknahme oder den Widerruf des Zuwendungsbescheides vorliegen, sind die Vorschriften des § 44 LHO und der hierzu erlassenen Verwaltungsvorschriften sowie § 1 Abs. 1 des Landesverwaltungsverfahrensgesetzes in Verbindung mit den §§ 48, 49 und 49a des Verwaltungsverfahrensgesetzes anzuwenden.

D11.III.1 Zuwendungen für nicht staatliche Kulturdenkmäler

11 Sonstige Regelungen

11.1 Wertausgleich bei Veräußerung des Kulturdenkmals
Wird das Kulturdenkmal innerhalb von 20 Jahren nach Erlass des Zuwendungsbescheides erstmalig verkauft, kann das Land von der Zuwendungsempfängerin oder dem Zuwendungsempfänger oder dessen Rechtsnachfolgerin oder Rechtsnachfolger einen angemessenen Ausgleich für den Wertzuwachs verlangen, der durch die Gewährung der Zuwendung entstanden ist. Die Höhe des Ausgleichs setzt die Bewilligungsbehörde fest. Hierbei soll auch die Höhe des erzielten Kaufpreises sowie aus dem Verkauf resultierende ertrags- und umsatzsteuerliche Belastungen des oder der Ausgleichspflichtigen berücksichtigt werden.

Darüber hinaus hat das Land in den Fällen einer Zuwendung nach den Nummern 5.2.3 bis 5.2.6 oder nach Nummer 7.3 regelmäßig einen Rückzahlungsanspruch gegen die Zuwendungsempfängerin oder den Zuwendungsempfänger oder dessen Rechtsnachfolgerin oder Rechtsnachfolger in Höhe der über die grundsätzlich zulässige Höchstförderung nach den Nummern 5.1, 5.2.1 oder 5.2.2 in Verbindung mit Nummer 7.2 hinaus gewährten Zuwendungen, soweit das Kulturdenkmal innerhalb von 20 Jahren nach Erlass des Zuwendungsbescheides erstmalig verkauft wird. Wenn dieser Betrag in einem groben Missverhältnis zum erzielten Kaufpreis steht, kann die Bewilligungsbehörde nach pflichtgemäßem Ermessen den Rückzahlungsanspruch in angemessenem Umfang reduzieren. Die Gründe hierfür sind zu dokumentieren.

Der nach Absatz 1 zugrunde gelegte Wertzuwachs sowie der Rückzahlungsanspruch nach Absatz 2 vermindern sich jährlich linear um 5 v.H., gerechnet vom Jahr der Investition. Soweit es nach den Umständen des Einzelfalls angemessen ist, kann die Bewilligungsbehörde eine kürzere Frist bis zum erstmaligen Verkauf des Denkmals und dementsprechend eine höhere lineare jährliche Verminderung des jeweiligen Anspruches festlegen. Hierbei soll insbesondere die voraussichtliche Nutzungsdauer der geförderten Maßnahmen berücksichtigt werden.

Eine entsprechende Nebenbestimmung ist im Zuwendungsbescheid aufzunehmen. Hierauf kann in den Fällen des Absatzes 1 verzichtet werden, soweit durch die Gewährung der Zuwendung kein Wertzuwachs am Denkmal zu erwarten ist.

Die Ansprüche sind grundsätzlich grundbuchmäßig zu sichern.

11.2 Freier Zugang
In geeigneten Fällen kann die Bewilligungsbehörde die Gewährung einer Zuwendung vom freien Zugang zum Kulturdenkmal (§ 15 DSchG) abhängig machen. Dieser Anspruch kann durch Eintragung einer beschränkten persönlichen Dienstbarkeit gesichert werden.

11.3 Publizitätspflichten
Die Zuwendungsempfängerin oder der Zuwendungsempfänger hat sicherzustellen, dass – soweit vorhanden – auf sämtlichen projektbezogenen Publikationen und auf Bauschildern und Bautafeln auf die Förderung durch das Land hingewiesen wird. Die Bewilligungsbehörde kann hierzu einen zu übernehmenden Text festlegen sowie die Verwendung des Landeswappens oder anderer Grafiken vorschreiben.

12 Inkrafttreten, Übergangsbestimmung
Diese Verwaltungsvorschrift tritt am 1. Januar 2016 in Kraft.
In Nummer 4.2 Satz 1 tritt für Bewilligungen des Jahres 2016 an die Stelle des 31. Oktober des Jahres vor dem geplanten Beginn der Maßnahme der 31. Januar 2016.

Errichtung „Generaldirektion Kulturelles Erbe"

Rundschreiben des Ministeriums für Bildung, Wissenschaft, Jugend und Kultur vom 2. Februar 2007 (9815 Az.: 53 006/50)

1. Bezeichnung und rechtliche Stellung

Mit Wirkung vom 1. Januar 2007 wird die
Generaldirektion Kulturelles Erbe (GDKE)
errichtet.

In ihr sollen das Landesamt für Denkmalpflege, das Landesmuseum Koblenz, das Landesmuseum Mainz und das Rheinische Landesmuseum Trier zusammengeführt werden. Der Aufbau erfolgt in mehreren Stufen.

In der ersten Stufe wird die „Generaldirektion Kulturelles Erbe" durch die Zusammenführung des Landesamts für Denkmalpflege einschließlich „Burgen, Schlösser, Altertümer" und dem Landesmuseum Koblenz errichtet.

Die „Generaldirektion Kulturelles Erbe" ist eine dem Ministerium für Bildung, Wissenschaft, Jugend und Kultur unmittelbar nachgeordnete staatliche Behörde.

2. Aufgaben

Die Aufgaben der in Ziffer 1 genannten Einrichtungen, Landesamt für Denkmalpflege einschließlich „Burgen, Schlösser, Altertümer" und Landesmuseum Koblenz, werden in der „Generaldirektion Kulturelles Erbe" fortgeführt und zwar in den folgenden Direktionen:

- Direktion Landesmuseum Koblenz
- Direktion „Burgen, Schlösser, Altertümer"
- Direktion Bau- und Kunstdenkmalpflege
- Direktion Archäologie mit Außenstellen Mainz, Koblenz und Speyer

Durch zentrale Steuerung und Koordination soll die gemeinsame Verantwortung für das kulturelle Erbe des Landes Rheinland-Pfalz gestärkt, die Zusammenarbeit optimiert und die Effektivität durch Synergien gesteigert werden. Es soll ein neuer Arbeitsbereich „Marketing" aufgebaut und die Vernetzung mit dem Tourismus intensiviert werden.

Die „Generaldirektion Kulturelles Erbe" wird insbesondere folgende Aufgaben wahrnehmen:

- Entwicklung einer übergreifenden Sammlungsstrategie für die kulturellen Einrichtungen des Landes
- Integrierte Planung, Steuerung und Umsetzung von Arbeitsschwerpunkten im Rahmen abgestimmter Zielvorhaben
- Gemeinsame Betreuung aller Direktionen in einer „Stabsstelle zentrale Serviceeinheit" in Bezug auf Verwaltung, wissenschaftliche und technische Koordination
- Steuerung der Ressourcen hinsichtlich kulturpolitischer Schwerpunktsetzungen
- Zentrales Marketing
- Vereinheitlichte Publikationen unter einem gemeinsamen Corporate Identity
- Zusammenarbeit mit dem Tourismus

Die Abstimmung der gemeinsamen Vorhaben aller Direktionen erfolgt in einer Konferenz der Generaldirektion, sie findet in der Regel vierteljährlich statt.

Die Abstimmung von Vorhaben mehrerer an einem Standort angesiedelter Direktionen erfolgt in einer Standortkonferenz, sie findet mindestens zweimal jährlich statt.

3. Leitung, Sitz, Haushalt

Die „Generaldirektion Kulturelles Erbe" wird von einer Generaldirektorin/einem Generaldirektor geleitet. Diese/dieser wird vom Ministerpräsidenten auf Vorschlag des zuständigen Ministeriums ernannt. Ihr/ihm obliegt die zentrale Steuerung gemeinsamer Aufgaben und die Koordination abgestimmter Projekte. Der Sitz der Generaldirektorin/des Generaldirektors ist in Mainz.

Die Direktorinnen und Direktoren der Direktionen werden von dem für Kultur zuständigen Ministerium ernannt.

Die „Stabsstelle zentrale Serviceeinheit" umfasst die Arbeitsbereiche Verwaltung, Marketing und Koordination. Sie hat ihren Sitz in Koblenz mit einer Außenstelle in Mainz.

D11.III.2 Errichtung Generaldirektion Kulturelles Erbe

Bis zur Errichtung eines eigenen Kapitels „Generaldirektion Kulturelles Erbe" im Rahmen der Aufstellung des nächsten Doppelhaushaltes im Einzelplan 09 werden die Personal-, Sach- und Investitionskosten des GDKE aus Mitteln der Kapitel 09 53 und 09 54 gedeckt. Die erforderlichen Mittel werden der „Generaldirektion Kulturelles Erbe" durch das für Kultur zuständige Ministerium zur Bewirtschaftung zugewiesen.

4. Inkrafttreten und Aufheben von Vorschriften

Dieses Rundschreiben tritt mit Wirkung vom 1. Januar 2007 in Kraft. Gleichzeitig werden das Rundschreiben des Kultusministeriums vom 10. 10. 1988 (Amtsblatt des Kultusministeriums Nr. 8/1988, Seite 461) sowie das Rundschreiben des Kultusministeriums vom 2. Mai 1978 (Amtsblatt, Seite 463) geändert durch Rundschreiben vom 26. Januar 1982 (Amtsblatt, Seite 197) aufgehoben.

Landesverordnung über Zuständigkeiten nach dem Kulturgutschutzgesetz

Vom 14. Februar 2017 (GVBl. S. 26)

Aufgrund des § 3 Abs. 1 Satz 2 des Kulturgutschutzgesetzes vom 31. Juli 2016 (BGBl. I S. 1914) in Verbindung mit § 7 Abs. 1 Satz 1 und Abs. 2 Satz 1 des Verkündungsgesetzes vom 3. Dezember 1973 (GVBl. S. 375), geändert durch Artikel 23 des Gesetzes vom 7. Februar 1983 (GVBl. S. 17), BS 114-1, verordnet die Landesregierung:

§ 1
Zuständige Behörde nach § 3 Abs. 1 Satz 1 in Verbindung mit § 6 Abs. 2 Satz 1, § 10 Abs. 6 Satz 2, § 14 Abs. 7, § 33 Abs. 1 und 4, den §§ 34 und 35 Abs. 1, § 37 Abs. 1 Satz 1 und Abs. 2, § 39 Satz 3, § 46 Abs. 1, den §§ 47, 61, 64 und 78 Abs. 1 bis 3, § 81 Abs. 1 und 3 und § 86 Abs. 1 des Kulturgutschutzgesetzes vom 31. Juli 2016 (BGBl. I S. 1914) in der jeweils geltenden Fassung ist das für die kulturellen Angelegenheiten zuständige Ministerium.

§ 2
Diese Verordnung tritt am Tage nach der Verkündung in Kraft.

D12 Verfassung Saarland

Verfassung des Saarlandes

Vom 15. Dezember 1947 (Amtsbl. S. 1077)
(BS Saar Nr. 100-1)
zuletzt geändert durch Art. 1 G zur Umsetzung der grundgesetzlichen Schuldenbremse und zur Haushaltsstabilisierung vom 10. April 2019 (Amtsbl. I S. 446)
– Auszug –

I. Hauptteil
Grundrechte und Grundpflichten

3. Abschnitt
Erziehung, Unterricht, Volksbildung, Kulturpflege, Sport

Artikel 34   [Kultur; Denkmalschutz]
(1) Kulturelles Schaffen genießt die Förderung des Staates.
(2) ¹Die Denkmäler der Kunst, der Geschichte und der Natur sowie die Landschaft genießen den Schutz und die Pflege des Staates. ²Die Teilnahme an den Kulturgütern ist allen Schichten des Volkes zu ermöglichen.

Saarländisches Denkmalschutzgesetz[1)]
Vom 13. Juni 2018 (Amtsbl. I S. 358)

Inhaltsübersicht

Abschnitt 1:
Allgemeine Bestimmungen
§ 1 Aufgaben des Denkmalschutzes und der Denkmalpflege
§ 2 Begriffsbestimmungen; Geltungsbereich

Abschnitt 2:
Schutzbestimmungen
§ 3 Schutz von Kulturdenkmälern; Verordnungsermächtigungen
§ 4 Denkmalliste

Abschnitt 3:
Erhalt und Nutzung; Genehmigungspflicht
§ 5 Erhalt und Nutzung von Baudenkmälern
§ 6 Veränderung von Baudenkmälern, Kulturdenkmälern nach § 2 Absatz 1 Satz 4 und Denkmalbereichen
§ 7 Veränderung von beweglichen Kulturdenkmälern
§ 8 Ausgrabung und Veränderung von Bodendenkmälern
§ 9 Grabungsschutzgebiet

Abschnitt 4:
Verfahrensvorschriften
§ 10 Genehmigungsverfahren
§ 11 Nutzungsbeschränkung
§ 12 Duldungspflicht
§ 13 Veränderungs- und Veräußerungsanzeige
§ 14 Einsichtsrecht
§ 15 Vorkaufsrecht

Abschnitt 5:
Funde
§ 16 Funde
§ 17 Ablieferung
§ 18 Schatzregal

Abschnitt 6:
Enteignung und Entschädigung
§ 19 Enteignung
§ 20 Enteignende Maßnahmen

Abschnitt 7:
Denkmalbehörden
§ 21 Denkmalbehörden
§ 22 Zuständigkeit der Denkmalbehörden
§ 23 Aufgabenwahrnehmung durch die Denkmalbehörden
§ 24 Beteiligung der Kommunen
§ 25 Landesdenkmalrat; Verordnungsermächtigung
§ 26 Denkmalbeauftragte

Abschnitt 8:
Übergangs- und Schlussvorschriften
§ 27 Örtliche Erhalt- und Gestaltungsvorschriften
§ 28 Ordnungswidrigkeiten
§ 29 Grundrechtsbeschränkung
§ 30 Kirchliche Kulturdenkmäler
§ 31 Schutz im Katastrophenfall
§ 32 Übergangsvorschriften
§ 33 Inkrafttreten, Außerkrafttreten

Abschnitt 1
Allgemeine Bestimmungen

§ 1 Aufgaben des Denkmalschutzes und der Denkmalpflege

(1) ¹Kulturdenkmäler sind als Zeugnisse menschlicher Geschichte und örtlicher Eigenart zu schützen, zu pflegen, sinnvoll zu nutzen und wissenschaftlich zu erforschen. ²Sie sollen der Öffentlichkeit im Rahmen des Zumutbaren zugänglich gemacht werden.
(2) Bei öffentlichen Planungen und öffentlichen Baumaßnahmen sind die Belange des Denkmalschutzes und der Denkmalpflege rechtzeitig und so einzubeziehen, dass die Kulturdenkmäler erhalten werden und ihre Umgebung angemessen gestaltet wird, soweit nicht andere öffentliche Belange überwiegen.
(3) Den juristischen Personen des öffentlichen Rechts obliegt in besonderem Maße, die ihnen gehörenden Kulturdenkmäler zu pflegen.
(4) Das Land trägt zu den Kosten der Erhaltung und Instandsetzung von Kulturdenkmälern nach Maßgabe der im Haushaltsplan bereitgestellten Mittel bei.

---

1) Verkündet als Art. 3 G v. 13.6.2018 (Amtsbl. I S. 358); Inkrafttreten gem. § 33 Abs. 2 dieses G am 1.8.2018, § 25 Abs. 4 tritt am 6.7.2018 in Kraft, vgl. § 33 Abs. 1.

D12.I.1 Saarländisches Denkmalschutzgesetz

§ 2 Begriffsbestimmungen; Geltungsbereich

(1) ¹Kulturdenkmäler sind Sachen, Teile oder Mehrheiten von Sachen aus zurückliegenden und abgeschlossenen Epochen, an deren Erhalt aus geschichtlichen Gründen, insbesondere künstlerischen, wissenschaftlichen oder städtebaulichen Gründen, ein öffentliches Interesse besteht. ²Diese können von Menschen geschaffen oder natürlich entstanden sein. ³Kulturdenkmäler im Sinne dieses Gesetzes sind bewegliche Kulturdenkmäler, Baudenkmäler und Bodendenkmäler. ⁴Kulturdenkmäler im Sinne dieses Gesetzes sind auch Baudenkmäler und Bodendenkmäler, die als „Kulturerbe" in die „Liste des Erbes der Welt" nach Artikel 11 Absatz 2 Satz 1 des Übereinkommens zum Schutz des Kultur- und Naturerbes der Welt vom 16. November 1972 (BGBl. 1977 II S. 213, 215) eingetragen sind.

(2) ¹Baudenkmäler sind

1. Kulturdenkmäler, die aus baulichen Anlagen im Sinne der Landesbauordnung vom 18. Februar 2004 (Amtsbl. S. 822), zuletzt geändert durch das Gesetz vom 13. Juli 2016 (Amtsbl. I S. 714; 2017 I S. 280), in der jeweils geltenden Fassung, oder Teilen baulicher Anlagen bestehen (Einzeldenkmäler) oder

2. Kulturdenkmäler bestehend aus Mehrheiten baulicher Anlagen, die als Gruppe räumlich und geschichtlich zusammenhängen, da sie

   a) auf der Grundlage einer Gesamtkonzeption entstanden sind (Gesamtanlagen),

   b) eine historisch oder städtebaulich-gestalterisch gewachsene Einheit darstellen (Ensembles) oder

   c) historisch oder städtebaulich zusammenhängende Siedlungsstrukturen oder Erscheinungsbilder darstellen (Denkmalbereich) unabhängig davon, ob die dazugehörigen einzelnen baulichen Anteile oder Teile von ihnen für sich Einzeldenkmäler sind; darunter

   – Ortskerne, Quartiere und Siedlungen,

   – Straßen-, Platz- und Ortsbilder sowie Ortsgrundrisse oder

   – Grün-, Frei- und Wasserflächen, Wirtschaftsflächen und -anlagen,

   oder

3. Garten-, Park- und Friedhofsanlagen, soweit es sich um Kulturdenkmäler handelt, die nicht unter Absatz 5 fallen.

²Zu einem Baudenkmal gehören auch sein Zubehör, seine Ausstattung sowie seine Grün-, Frei- und Wasserflächen, soweit sie mit dem Baudenkmal eine Einheit von Denkmalwert bilden.

(3) Gegenstand des Denkmalschutzes ist auch die Umgebung eines Baudenkmals oder eines oberirdisch sichtbaren ortsfesten Bodendenkmals, soweit sie für dessen Bestand, Erscheinungsbild oder städtebauliche Wirkung erheblich ist, sowie die zu einem Kulturdenkmal nach Absatz 1 Satz 4 gehörenden, bei der Organisation der Vereinten Nationen für Erziehung, Wissenschaft und Kultur (UNESCO) angemeldeten Pufferzonen, die das unmittelbare Umfeld des Kulturdenkmals, wesentliche Sichtachsen und andere Gebiete oder Merkmale umfassen, die für seine angemessene Erhaltung erforderlich sind.

(4) Bodendenkmäler sind Kulturdenkmäler sowie aus den in Absatz 1 Satz 1 genannten Gründen erhaltenswerte Überreste oder Spuren menschlichen, tierischen und pflanzlichen Lebens, die sich im Erdboden oder auf dem Grund eines Gewässers befinden oder befunden haben.

(5) Bewegliche Kulturdenkmäler sind alle nicht ortsfesten Kulturdenkmäler.

(6) Die Vorschriften dieses Gesetzes finden auf Archive, soweit sie unter das Saarländische Archivgesetz vom 23. September 1992 (Amtsbl. S. 1094), zuletzt geändert durch das Gesetz vom 13. Oktober 2015 (Amtsbl. I S. 790), in der jeweils geltenden Fassung fallen, keine Anwendung.

Abschnitt 2
Schutzbestimmungen

§ 3 Schutz von Kulturdenkmälern; Verordnungsermächtigungen

(1) Baudenkmäler, Bodendenkmäler, Kulturdenkmäler nach § 2 Absatz 1 Satz 4 sowie die in § 2 Absatz 4 genannten erhaltenswerten Überreste und Spuren menschlichen, tierischen und pflanzlichen Lebens sind unmittelbar durch dieses Gesetz geschützt.

(2) Bewegliche Kulturdenkmäler im Sinne des § 2 Absatz 5 werden durch Verwaltungsakt unter Schutz gestellt, wenn sie nicht im Eigentum einer Einrichtung in öffentlich-rechtlicher Trägerschaft stehen.

(3) ¹Die Oberste Denkmalbehörde wird ermächtigt, durch Rechtsverordnung im Benehmen mit der betreffenden Gemeinde Denkmalbereiche unter Schutz zu stellen. ²In der Rechtsverordnung sind
1. ihr Geltungsbereich zu beschreiben und in einer Karte darzustellen, die Bestandteil der Rechtsverordnung ist, und
2. der Schutzgegenstand näher zu beschreiben.

³Die Rechtsverordnung kann Vorschriften über die Gestaltung baulicher Anlagen und anderer Anlagen und Einrichtungen einschließlich der zu verwendenden Materialien und der anzuwendenden Techniken und über die Bepflanzung nicht bebauter Flächen enthalten. ⁴Auf Veranlassung der Obersten Denkmalbehörde ist der Entwurf der Rechtsverordnung für die Dauer eines Monats in der Gemeinde öffentlich auszulegen. ⁵Ort und Dauer der Auslegung sind mindestens eine Woche vorher ortsüblich mit dem Hinweis darauf bekannt zu machen, dass Anregungen während der Auslegungsfrist bei der Gemeinde oder bei der Obersten Denkmalbehörde vorgebracht werden können. ⁶Das Land erstattet der Gemeinde die durch die Beteiligung der Öffentlichkeit nachweislich entstandenen Kosten. ⁷Die Oberste Denkmalbehörde prüft die fristgerecht vorgebrachten Anregungen und teilt das Ergebnis den Betroffenen mit, soweit den Anregungen nicht entsprochen wird.
(4) ¹Die Oberste Denkmalbehörde wird ermächtigt, durch Rechtsverordnung im Benehmen mit der betreffenden Gemeinde abgegrenzte Gebiete befristet oder unbefristet zu Grabungsschutzgebieten zu erklären, wenn begründeter Anlass zur Annahme besteht, dass sie Bodendenkmäler bergen. ²Den betroffenen Grundstückseigentümerinnen und -eigentümern ist der Erlass der Rechtsverordnung schriftlich mitzuteilen.

§ 4 Denkmalliste
(1) ¹Beim Landesdenkmalamt wird eine Denkmalliste geführt, in die die Kulturdenkmäler getrennt nach beweglichen Kulturdenkmälern, Baudenkmälern, Bodendenkmälern und Denkmalbereichen nachrichtlich eingetragen werden. ²Die Denkmalliste enthält auch eine Aufstellung der Grabungsschutzgebiete.
(2) ¹Die Eintragung von Baudenkmälern und ortsfesten Bodendenkmälern und deren Löschung erfolgt nach Anhörung des Landesdenkmalrates und der betroffenen Gemeinde. ²Die Eintragung ist, sofern nicht die gesamte Sache Denkmalwert hat, hinsichtlich der vom Denkmalschutz erfassten Teile räumlich und gegenständlich abzugrenzen. ³Die Eigentümerinnen und Eigentümer sind vor der Eintragung unter Darlegung der fachlichen Gründe anzuhören und von der Eintragung sowie deren Löschung zu unterrichten. ⁴Anhörung und Unterrichtung dürfen nur unterbleiben, wenn ihre Durchführung unzumutbar ist, insbesondere wenn die Eigentümerin oder der Eigentümer nur mit unverhältnismäßig hohem Aufwand festgestellt werden kann.
(3) ¹Die Denkmalliste und ihre Fortschreibungen sind hinsichtlich der Baudenkmäler, Denkmalbereiche und Grabungsschutzgebiete im Amtsblatt des Saarlandes bekannt zu machen und in geeigneter Weise elektronisch bereitzustellen. ²Die Fortschreibungen sind spätestens ein halbes Jahr nach deren Eintragung bekannt zu machen und in geeigneter Weise elektronisch bereitzustellen. ³Die Gemeinden halten für ihren Zuständigkeitsbereich eine Teildenkmalliste der Baudenkmäler, Denkmalbereiche und Grabungsschutzgebiete zur Einsicht bereit.

Abschnitt 3
Erhalt und Nutzung; Genehmigungspflicht

§ 5 Erhalt und Nutzung von Baudenkmälern
(1) ¹Eigentümerinnen und Eigentümer sowie die sonstigen Nutzungsberechtigten haben die Baudenkmäler zu erhalten, instand zu setzen, sachgemäß zu behandeln und vor Gefährdung zu schützen, soweit dies wirtschaftlich zumutbar ist. ²Für die wirtschaftliche Zumutbarkeit ist auch zu berücksichtigen, inwieweit Zuwendungen aus öffentlichen Mitteln oder steuerliche Vorteile in Anspruch genommen werden können. ³Eigentümerinnen und Eigentümer sowie sonstige Nutzungsberechtigte können sich nicht auf Belastungen durch erhöhte Erhaltungskosten berufen, die dadurch verursacht worden sind, dass Erhaltungsmaßnahmen diesem Gesetz oder sonstigem öffentlichen Recht zuwider unterblieben sind. ⁴Die wirtschaftliche Unzumutbarkeit ist von der oder dem Verpflichteten glaubhaft zu machen. ⁵Sollte eine Erhaltungsmaßnahme nicht möglich sein, so ist die Belassung zu prüfen.

(2) ¹Eigentümerinnen und Eigentümer sowie die sonstigen Nutzungsberechtigten sollen die Baudenkmäler möglichst entsprechend ihrer ursprünglichen Zweckbestimmung oder in einer anderen Weise nutzen, die die Erhaltung der Substanz auf Dauer gewährleistet. ²Nutzungsänderungen sind dem Landesdenkmalamt anzuzeigen.

§ 6 Veränderung von Baudenkmälern, Kulturdenkmälern nach § 2 Absatz 1 Satz 4 und Denkmalbereichen

(1) Baudenkmäler und Kulturdenkmäler nach § 2 Absatz 1 Satz 4 dürfen, unabhängig von den Regelungen der Landesbauordnung, nur mit Genehmigung
1. zerstört oder beseitigt,
2. an einen anderen Ort verbracht,
3. in ihrem Bestand verändert,
4. in ihrem Erscheinungsbild verändert,
5. mit An- oder Aufbauten, Aufschriften oder Werbeeinrichtungen versehen

werden.

(2) ¹Der Genehmigung bedarf auch, wer in der Umgebung eines Baudenkmals Anlagen, die das Erscheinungsbild des Baudenkmals nicht nur vorübergehend beeinträchtigen, errichten, anbringen, ändern oder beseitigen will. ²Der Genehmigung bedürfen auch Veränderungen
1. in einer Pufferzone nach § 2 Absatz 3,
2. in der Umgebung eines Baudenkmals,

wenn die Veränderungen die angemessene Erhaltung des Kulturdenkmals nach § 2 Absatz 1 Satz 4 oder den Bestand, das Erscheinungsbild oder die städtebauliche Wirkung des Baudenkmals nicht nur vorübergehend beeinträchtigen können.

(3) Veränderungen des Erscheinungsbildes von Denkmalbereichen bedürfen der Genehmigung.

§ 7 Veränderung von beweglichen Kulturdenkmälern

¹Wer ein unter Schutz gestelltes bewegliches Kulturdenkmal zerstören, beseitigen, verändern oder an einen anderen Ort verbringen will, bedarf der Genehmigung. ²Instandsetzungsarbeiten sind genehmigungsfrei.

§ 8 Ausgrabung und Veränderung von Bodendenkmälern

(1) Wer nach Bodendenkmälern graben, Bodendenkmäler aus einem Gewässer bergen oder mit technischen Hilfsmitteln zielgerichtet nach Bodendenkmälern suchen will, bedarf hierzu der Genehmigung.

(2) Der Genehmigung bedarf auch, wer zu einem anderen Zweck Erdarbeiten vornehmen will, obwohl sie oder er weiß oder annehmen muss, dass sich dort Bodendenkmäler befinden.

(3) Bei Bodendenkmälern, die ganz oder zum Teil über der Erdoberfläche erkennbar sind, bedürfen Maßnahmen im Sinne von § 6 Absatz 1 und 2 der Genehmigung.

§ 9 Grabungsschutzgebiet

¹In Grabungsschutzgebieten bedürfen sämtliche Arbeiten, bei denen Bodendenkmäler zutage gefördert oder gefährdet werden können, der Genehmigung. ²Die land- und forstwirtschaftliche Nutzung bleibt im bisherigen Ausmaß und der bisherigen Art und Weise erlaubt.

Abschnitt 4
Verfahrensvorschriften

§ 10 Genehmigungsverfahren

(1) ¹Die Genehmigung zur Veränderung von Baudenkmälern und Denkmalbereichen ist schriftlich beim Landesdenkmalamt zu beantragen. ²Dem Antrag sind alle für die Beurteilung der Maßnahme und die Bearbeitung des Antrags erforderlichen Unterlagen, insbesondere Pläne, Fotografien, Dokumentationen, Kosten- und Wirtschaftlichkeitsberechnungen, beizufügen. ³Das Landesdenkmalamt kann, soweit dies im Einzelfall erforderlich ist, vorbereitende Untersuchungen und Gutachten, ausgenommen solche über den Denkmalwert, verlangen. ⁴Fehlende Unterlagen, Untersuchungen und Gutachten sollen innerhalb von sechs Arbeitstagen nach Eingang des Antrags angefordert werden. ⁵Der Antragstellerin oder dem Antragsteller ist die Bearbeitungsfähigkeit des Antrags mitzuteilen.

(2) Die Genehmigung ist zu erteilen, wenn Gründe des Denkmalschutzes nicht entgegenstehen oder andere öffentliche oder private Interessen überwiegen, denen nicht auf sonstige Weise Rechnung getragen werden kann.

(3) ¹Die Genehmigung kann unter Bedingungen, Auflagen, dem Vorbehalt des Widerrufs oder befristet erteilt werden. ²Insbesondere kann bestimmt werden, dass die Arbeiten nur nach einem vom Landesdenkmalamt genehmigten Plan und unter seiner Aufsicht oder der Aufsicht einer oder eines von ihr benannten Sachverständigen ausgeführt werden und zu dokumentieren sind.

(4) ¹Die Genehmigung gilt als erteilt, wenn sie nicht innerhalb von zwei Monaten nach Eingang des vollständigen Antrags versagt wird. ²Diese Frist kann um bis zu einem Monat verlängert werden, wenn zur Erteilung der Genehmigung die Entscheidung einer anderen Behörde erforderlich ist.

(5) ¹Erfordert eine Maßnahme nach § 6 Absatz 1 bis 3 eine Baugenehmigung, eine die Baugenehmigung einschließende oder ersetzende behördliche Entscheidung oder eine bauaufsichtliche Zustimmung gemäß § 21 der Landesbauordnung, so schließt diese die Genehmigung nach § 6 Absatz 1 bis 3 ein. ²Absatz 3 gilt entsprechend. ³Die Entscheidung erfolgt im Einvernehmen mit dem Landesdenkmalamt, wenn in der Denkmalliste eingetragene Baudenkmäler, ihre Umgebung oder Denkmalbereiche betroffen sind. ⁴Dem Landesdenkmalamt obliegt die Überwachung des in seinen Aufgabenbereich fallenden Teils der Entscheidung nach Satz 1 nach den Bestimmungen dieses Gesetzes.

(6) ¹Für die Genehmigung zur Veränderung von beweglichen Kulturdenkmälern nach § 7 gelten die Absätze 1 bis 4 entsprechend. ²Für die Genehmigung zur Ausgrabung von Bodendenkmälern nach § 8 Absatz 1 oder bei Arbeiten in Grabungsschutzgebieten nach § 9 sowie für die Genehmigung zur Veränderung von Bodendenkmälern oder Erdarbeiten nach § 8 Absatz 2 und 3 gelten die Absätze 1 bis 5 entsprechend.

§ 11 Nutzungsbeschränkung
¹Die wirtschaftliche Nutzung eines Grundstücks oder eines Grundstücksteils kann beschränkt werden, wenn sich dort Bodendenkmäler von geschichtlicher Bedeutung befinden. ²Die in Satz 1 genannte öffentliche Last ist auf Ersuchen des Landesdenkmalamtes im Grundbuch und im Baulastenverzeichnis nach § 83 der Landesbauordnung einzutragen.

§ 12 Duldungspflicht
¹Eigentümerinnen und Eigentümer sowie die sonstigen Nutzungsberechtigten haben die Anbringung von Hinweisschildern durch das Landesdenkmalamt zu dulden. ²Die Hinweisschilder können inhaltlich sowohl Kennzeichnung als auch Erklärung des Kulturdenkmals sein.

§ 13 Veränderungs- und Veräußerungsanzeige
(1) ¹Die Veräußerung eines Baudenkmals, eines beweglichen Kulturdenkmals oder eines Bodendenkmals ist von der Veräußerin oder dem Veräußerer unter Angabe der Erwerberin oder des Erwerbers innerhalb eines Monats nach Eigentumsübergang dem Landesdenkmalamt anzuzeigen. ²Im Erbfall sind die Erbinnen oder Erben oder die Testamentsvollstreckerin oder der Testamentsvollstrecker zur Anzeige des Eigentumswechsels verpflichtet.

(2) ¹Die Absicht der Veräußerungen von Baudenkmälern, die im Eigentum von Körperschaften, Anstalten und Stiftungen des öffentlichen Rechts stehen, sind rechtzeitig dem Landesdenkmalamt anzuzeigen. ²Das Landesdenkmalamt kann verlangen, dass eine beschränkte persönliche Dienstbarkeit (§ 1090 des Bürgerlichen Gesetzbuchs) eingetragen wird.

§ 14 Einsichtsrecht
Eigentümerinnen und Eigentümern ist auf Verlangen Einsicht in die bei den Denkmalbehörden über ihr Baudenkmal vorhandenen Unterlagen zu gewähren.

§ 15 Vorkaufsrecht
(1) ¹Den Gemeinden steht beim Kauf von Grundstücken, auf oder in denen sich Baudenkmäler oder Bodendenkmäler befinden, die in die Denkmalliste eingetragen sind, ein Vorkaufsrecht zu. ²Es darf nur ausgeübt werden, wenn das Wohl der Allgemeinheit dies rechtfertigt, insbesondere wenn dadurch die dauernde Erhaltung des Kulturdenkmals ermöglicht werden soll. ³Das Vorkaufsrecht ist ausgeschlossen, wenn die Eigentümerin oder der Eigentümer das Grundstück an ihren Ehegatten oder seine Ehegattin oder eine Person, mit der sie oder er in einer eingetragenen Lebenspartnerschaft lebt, verkauft. ⁴Gleiches gilt für einen Verkauf an Personen, die mit der Eigentümerin oder dem Eigentümer

D12.I.1 Saarländisches Denkmalschutzgesetz

in gerader Linie verwandt oder verschwägert oder in der Seitenlinie bis zum dritten Grad verwandt sind.

(2) ¹Das Vorkaufsrecht kann zugunsten einer anderen juristischen Person des öffentlichen Rechts ausgeübt werden, wenn dies der dauerhaften Erhaltung des Kulturdenkmals dient. ²Die Ausübung des Vorkaufsrechts zugunsten einer juristischen Person des Privatrechts ist zulässig, wenn die dauernde Erhaltung des Kulturdenkmals zu den satzungsgemäßen Aufgaben der juristischen Person gehört und bei Berücksichtigung aller Umstände gesichert erscheint. ³Die Ausübung des Vorkaufsrechts zugunsten einer oder eines anderen setzt deren oder dessen Zustimmung voraus.

(3) ¹Das Vorkaufsrecht kann nur binnen zweier Monate nach Mitteilung des Kaufvertrags ausgeübt werden. ²Veräußerin oder Veräußerer und Erwerberin oder Erwerber haben der Gemeinde den Inhalt des geschlossenen Vertrags unverzüglich nach dessen Abschluss mitzuteilen. ³Die §§ 463 bis 467, § 469 Absatz 1, die §§ 471, 1098 Absatz 1 Satz 2 und die §§ 1099 bis 1102 des Bürgerlichen Gesetzbuchs sind anzuwenden.

(4) ¹Das Vorkaufsrecht geht unbeschadet bundesrechtlicher Vorschriften allen anderen Vorkaufsrechten im Rang vor und bedarf nicht der Eintragung im Grundbuch. ²Bei einem Eigentumserwerb aufgrund der Ausübung des Vorkaufsrechts erlöschen rechtsgeschäftliche Vorkaufsrechte.

(5) ¹Dem Land steht beim Kauf von unter Schutz gestellten beweglichen Kulturdenkmälern ein Vorkaufsrecht zu. ²Es darf nur ausgeübt werden, wenn das Wohl der Allgemeinheit dies rechtfertigt, insbesondere wenn die Kulturdenkmäler der Öffentlichkeit zugänglich gemacht oder in ihrer Gesamtheit erhalten werden sollen. ³Absatz 1 Satz 3, Absatz 2 und Absatz 3 Satz 1 gelten entsprechend; die §§ 463 bis 467, § 469 Absatz 1 und § 471 des Bürgerlichen Gesetzbuchs sind anzuwenden.

Abschnitt 5
Funde

§ 16 Funde

(1) ¹Wer Sachen oder Teile von Sachen findet, bei denen vermutet werden kann, dass an ihrer Erhaltung oder Untersuchung ein öffentliches Interesse besteht, hat dies unverzüglich dem Landesdenkmalamt anzuzeigen. ²Anzeigepflichtig sind auch die Leiterin oder der Leiter der Arbeiten, die zu dem Fund geführt haben, sowie die Grundstückseigentümerin oder der Grundstückseigentümer und die sonstigen Nutzungsberechtigten. ³Die Kenntnis von der Anzeige einer oder eines Pflichtigen befreit die Übrigen. ⁴Die Anzeige kann auch gegenüber den Denkmalbeauftragten erfolgen. ⁵Diese haben die Anzeige unverzüglich an das Landesdenkmalamt weiterzuleiten.

(2) ¹Der Fund und die Fundstelle sind bis zum Ablauf von sechs Arbeitstagen nach Eingang der Anzeige beim Landesdenkmalamt unverändert zu lassen und vor Gefahren zu schützen, wenn nicht das Landesdenkmalamt vorher die Fortsetzung der Arbeiten gestattet. ²Die Fortsetzung der Arbeiten ist zu gestatten, wenn ihre Unterbrechung unzumutbare Kosten verursachen würde und das Landesdenkmalamt hierfür keinen Ersatz leisten will.

(3) Das Landesdenkmalamt und die von ihm Beauftragten sind berechtigt, bewegliche Funde zu bergen und zur wissenschaftlichen Bearbeitung vorübergehend in Besitz zu nehmen.

(4) Besteht ein besonderes öffentliches Interesse an einer Grabung, so können Grundstückseigentümerinnen und -eigentümer sowie sonstige Nutzungsberechtigte verpflichtet werden, die Grabung zuzulassen.

(5) Die Träger größerer öffentlicher oder privater Bau- oder Erschließungsvorhaben oder Vorhaben zum Abbau von Rohstoffen oder Bodenschätzen haben als Veranlasser im Rahmen des Zumutbaren die Kosten für Grabungen, die konservatorische Behandlung und die Dokumentation der Funde und Befunde zu übernehmen.

§ 17 Ablieferung

(1) ¹Wenn zu befürchten ist, dass sich der Zustand eines Fundes verschlechtert, die Gefahr des Abhandenkommens besteht oder er der Öffentlichkeit oder der wissenschaftlichen Forschung verloren geht, kann das Land die Ablieferung eines Fundes gegen angemessene Entschädigung verlangen. ²Macht das Land von diesem Recht keinen Gebrauch, geht es auf den Landkreis oder den Regionalverband Saarbrücken, dann auf die Gemeinde über. ³Mit der Ablieferung erlangt die berechtigte Körperschaft das Eigentum an dem Fund.

(2) Der Ablieferungsanspruch ist ausgeschlossen, wenn ein Ablieferungsangebot der Eigentümerin oder des Eigentümers nicht innerhalb von drei Monaten angenommen worden ist.
(3) Über die Voraussetzungen einer Ablieferung entscheidet auf Antrag einer oder eines Beteiligten das Landesdenkmalamt.
(4) ¹Die Entschädigung bemisst sich nach dem Verkehrswert des Fundes zum Zeitpunkt der Ablieferung; im Fall der wissenschaftlichen Bearbeitung des Fundes durch das Landesdenkmalamt ist der Zeitpunkt der Inbesitznahme maßgebend, wenn der Fund nicht vor dem Ablieferungsverlangen zurückgegeben worden ist. ²Mit Einverständnis des Ablieferungspflichtigen kann die Entschädigung in anderer Weise als durch Geld geleistet werden. ³Einigen sich die oder der Ablieferungspflichtige und die berechtigte Körperschaft nicht über die Höhe der Entschädigung, setzt das Ministerium für Wirtschaft, Arbeit, Energie und Verkehr als Enteignungsbehörde die Entschädigung fest.

§ 18 Schatzregal
Funde, die herrenlos sind oder die so lange verborgen waren, dass ihre Eigentümerin oder ihr Eigentümer nicht mehr zu ermitteln ist, werden mit der Entdeckung Eigentum des Landes, wenn sie bei staatlichen Nachforschungen, in Grabungsschutzgebieten oder bei nicht genehmigten Grabungen entdeckt worden sind oder wenn sie einen wissenschaftlichen Wert haben.

Abschnitt 6
Enteignung und Entschädigung

§ 19 Enteignung
(1) Kann eine Gefahr für den Bestand oder die Beschaffenheit oder das Erscheinungsbild eines in die Denkmalliste eingetragenen Kulturdenkmals auf andere Weise nicht nachhaltig abgewehrt werden, so ist die Enteignung zugunsten des Landes oder einer anderen juristischen Person des öffentlichen oder privaten Rechts zulässig.
(2) Die Enteignung wird vom Ministerium für Wirtschaft, Arbeit, Energie und Verkehr als Enteignungsbehörde durchgeführt.
(3) ¹Für die Enteignung von unbeweglichen Sachen oder damit verbundenen Rechten finden die §§ 93 bis 103 und 106 bis 122 des Baugesetzbuchs in der Fassung der Bekanntmachung vom 3. November 2017 (BGBl. I S. 3634) in der jeweils geltenden Fassung entsprechende Anwendung. ²Für das Verfahren zur Enteignung beweglicher Sachen oder damit verbundener Rechte gelten § 107 Absatz 1 Satz 1 bis 3, § 108 Absatz 1 und 3, die §§ 110 und 111, § 112 Absatz 1 und 3 sowie § 113 Absatz 1 Satz 1, Absatz 2 Nummer 1 bis 4 Buchstabe c) und 5 bis 7 des Baugesetzbuchs sinngemäß; für die Entschädigung gilt § 17 Absatz 4 entsprechend.

§ 20 Enteignende Maßnahmen
(1) ¹Kann aufgrund einer auf diesem Gesetz beruhenden Maßnahme die bisher rechtmäßig ausgeübte Nutzung einer Sache nicht mehr fortgesetzt werden und wird hierdurch die wirtschaftliche Nutzbarkeit insgesamt erheblich beschränkt, so hat das Land eine angemessene Entschädigung zu leisten. ²Das Gleiche gilt, wenn die Maßnahme in sonstiger Weise enteignend wirkt.
(2) ¹Bei unbeweglichen Sachen finden die §§ 93 bis 103 des Baugesetzbuchs entsprechende Anwendung. ²Bei beweglichen Sachen gilt § 17 Absatz 4 entsprechend. ³Zuständig für die Festsetzung der Entschädigung ist das Ministerium für Wirtschaft, Arbeit, Energie und Verkehr als Enteignungsbehörde. ⁴Die Anordnung der Maßnahme und die Festsetzung der Entschädigung haben gleichzeitig zu erfolgen.
(3) ¹Würde eine entschädigungspflichtige Maßnahme dazu führen, dass die Eigentümerin oder der Eigentümer das Eigentum nicht mehr wirtschaftlich zumutbar nutzen kann, so kann sie oder er statt der Entschädigung nach Absatz 1 vom Land die Übernahme des Eigentums gegen angemessene Entschädigung verlangen. ²Absatz 2 Satz 1 bis 3 gilt entsprechend.

Abschnitt 7
Denkmalbehörden

§ 21 Denkmalbehörden
(1) Oberste Denkmalbehörde ist das für Denkmalschutz und Denkmalpflege zuständige Ministerium für Bildung und Kultur.
(2) Das Landesdenkmalamt ist eine dem Ministerium nachgeordnete Behörde im Sinne des § 7 des Landesorganisationsgesetzes in der Fassung vom 27. März 1997 (Amtsbl. S. 410), zuletzt geändert durch das Gesetz vom 16. Mai 2018 (Amtsbl. I S. 254) und durch das Gesetz vom 18. April 2018 (Amtsbl. I S. 332), in der jeweils geltenden Fassung.
(3) Bei beweglichen Kulturdenkmälern, die national wertvolle oder landes- oder ortsgeschichtlich bedeutsame Archive darstellen oder wesentliche Teile derselben sind, ist das Landesarchiv die alleinige zuständige Denkmalbehörde.

§ 22 Zuständigkeit der Denkmalbehörden
(1) Die Oberste Denkmalbehörde nimmt die ihr durch dieses Gesetz zugewiesenen Aufgaben wahr.
(2) ¹Das Landesdenkmalamt ist als Fach- und Vollzugsbehörde für Fragen des Denkmalschutzes und der Denkmalpflege zuständig. ²In den Fällen des § 25 Absatz 3 Satz 2 dieses Gesetzes entscheidet das Landesdenkmalamt nach Anhörung des Landesdenkmalrates.
(3) ¹Das Landesdenkmalamt entscheidet bei Erhaltungs- und Umnutzungsmaßnahmen an überregional bedeutenden Baudenkmälern und Abbruchanträgen in Abstimmung mit der Obersten Denkmalbehörde. ²Kommt eine Einigung nicht zustande, entscheidet die Oberste Denkmalbehörde nach erneuter Anhörung des Landesdenkmalrates.

§ 23 Aufgabenwahrnehmung durch die Denkmalbehörden
(1) Der Vollzug dieses Gesetzes sowie der aufgrund dieses Gesetzes erlassenen Rechtsverordnungen obliegt den Denkmalbehörden.
(2) ¹Die Denkmalbehörden haben diejenigen Maßnahmen zu treffen, die ihnen nach pflichtgemäßem Ermessen erforderlich erscheinen, um Kulturdenkmäler zu schützen, zu erhalten und Gefahren von ihnen abzuwenden. ²Sie können insbesondere anordnen, dass bei widerrechtlicher Beeinträchtigung oder Beschädigung eines Kulturdenkmals der vorherige Zustand wiederherzustellen oder das Kulturdenkmal auf eine andere vorgeschriebene Weise zu behandeln ist.
(3) Die Denkmalbehörden können zur Erfüllung ihrer Aufgaben Sachverständige oder sachverständige Stellen heranziehen.
(4) ¹Bedienstete und Beauftragte der Denkmalbehörden sind berechtigt, Grundstücke und nach vorheriger Benachrichtigung Gebäude zu betreten, Untersuchungen vorzunehmen und Fotografien anzufertigen, soweit dies zur Durchführung dieses Gesetzes, insbesondere zur Inventarisation, erforderlich ist. ²Das Betreten von Wohnungen ist nur bei Tag zulässig. ³Das Betreten von Betriebs- und Geschäftsräumen ist nur während der üblichen Betriebs- und Geschäftszeiten zulässig. ⁴Das Betreten von Wohnungen und Betriebs- und Geschäftsräumen ist gegen den Willen der Eigentümerin, des Eigentümers oder sonstiger Nutzungsberechtigter nur bei Gefahr in Verzug oder aufgrund einer richterlichen Anordnung zulässig.
(5) Den Bediensteten oder Beauftragten der Denkmalbehörden sind zur Erfüllung ihrer Aufgaben nach diesem Gesetz die erforderlichen Auskünfte zu erteilen.
(6) Gegen Entscheidungen der Denkmalbehörden findet ein Vorverfahren nach den §§ 68 ff. der Verwaltungsgerichtsordnung in der Fassung der Bekanntmachung vom 19. März 1991 (BGBl. I S. 686), zuletzt geändert durch das Gesetz vom 8. Oktober 2017 (BGBl. I S. 3546), in der jeweils geltenden Fassung statt.

§ 24 Beteiligung der Kommunen
(1) Die Kommunen werden durch die Oberste Denkmalbehörde regelmäßig über die Entwicklungen des Denkmalschutzes und der Denkmalpflege informiert.
(2) Die Kommunen können gegenüber den Denkmalbehörden Stellungnahmen zu den in ihrem Gebiet befindlichen Denkmälern abgeben.
(3) ¹Die Denkmalbehörden informieren und beraten im Rahmen ihrer Aufgabenwahrnehmung im Einzelfall die betroffenen Kommunen. ²Die Kommunen erhalten Gelegenheit, sich hierzu zu äußern.

§ 25 Landesdenkmalrat; Verordnungsermächtigung

(1) ¹Der Landesdenkmalrat berät die Oberste Denkmalbehörde und das Landesdenkmalamt. ²Er beobachtet den Denkmalschutz und die Denkmalpflege im Saarland und fördert deren Entwicklung durch Stellungnahmen, Anregungen und Empfehlungen.

(2) ¹Im ersten Jahr einer jeden Legislaturperiode erstattet er der Landesregierung einen Bericht über die Situation des Denkmalschutzes und der Denkmalpflege im Saarland. ²Dieser Bericht wird von der Obersten Denkmalbehörde veröffentlicht.

(3) ¹Der Landesdenkmalrat wird über die Entwicklung des Denkmalschutzes und der Denkmalpflege im Saarland durch die Oberste Denkmalbehörde regelmäßig informiert. ²Vor der Eintragung von Baudenkmälern und unbeweglichen Bodendenkmälern in die Denkmalliste (§ 4), der Bescheidung eines Antrags auf Zerstörung oder Beseitigung und vor der Löschung eines Eintrags, vor der Unterschutzstellung beweglicher Kulturdenkmäler nach § 3 Absatz 2 sowie dem Erlass von Rechtsverordnungen nach diesem Gesetz ist der Landesdenkmalrat anzuhören.

(4) Die Oberste Denkmalbehörde wird ermächtigt, durch Rechtsverordnung das Nähere über die Anzahl der Mitglieder, die Zusammensetzung, die Amtszeit und die Geschäftsführung des Landesdenkmalrates sowie über eine Entschädigung der Mitglieder des Landesdenkmalrates zu regeln.

§ 26 Denkmalbeauftragte

(1) ¹Die Oberste Denkmalbehörde kann zur Unterstützung und Beratung der Denkmalbehörden Personen, die Kenntnisse und Erfahrungen in Denkmalschutz und Denkmalpflege besitzen, für die Dauer von fünf Jahren widerruflich zu Denkmalbeauftragten bestellen. ²Wiederbestellung ist zulässig. ³Die Bestellung soll für einzelne Fachgebiete und für bestimmte örtliche Bereiche erfolgen.

(2) Zu den Aufgaben der Denkmalbeauftragten gehören insbesondere
1. die Beobachtung von Vorgängen, die die Belange von Denkmalschutz und Denkmalpflege berühren können – wie Veränderungen an baulichen Anlagen, die Beseitigung baulicher Anlagen und Erdbewegungen – und die Unterrichtung der Denkmalbehörden darüber,
2. die Annahme und Weiterleitung von Fundanzeigen (§ 16 Absatz 1),
3. die Unterstützung des Landesdenkmalamtes bei der Erfassung der Kulturdenkmäler.

(3) ¹Die Denkmalbeauftragten sind ehrenamtlich tätig. ²Sie unterstehen den Weisungen der Denkmalbehörden. ³Sie sind Beauftragte im Sinne des § 23 Absatz 4 und 5 dieses Gesetzes.

(4) ¹Das Land ersetzt den Denkmalbeauftragten die Kosten, die ihnen durch ihre Tätigkeit entstehen. ²Der Kostenersatz kann pauschaliert werden.

Abschnitt 8
Übergangs- und Schlussvorschriften

§ 27 Örtliche Erhalt- und Gestaltungsvorschriften

¹Die Gemeinden können durch Satzung zur Verwirklichung der mit diesem Gesetz verfolgten Ziele Vorschriften über den Erhalt und die Gestaltung baulicher Anlagen und anderer Anlagen und Einrichtungen einschließlich der zu verwendenden Materialien und der anzuwendenden Techniken sowie über die Bepflanzung nicht bebauter Flächen erlassen. ²Örtliche Erhalt- und Gestaltungsvorschriften sind in Abstimmung mit dem Landesdenkmalamt zu erlassen.

§ 28 Ordnungswidrigkeiten

(1) Ordnungswidrig handelt, wer vorsätzlich oder fahrlässig
1. Maßnahmen, die nach § 6 Absatz 1 bis 3, §§ 7 bis 9 der Genehmigung bedürfen, ohne Genehmigung oder abweichend von ihr durchführt oder durchführen lässt,
2. vollziehbare Auflagen oder Bedingungen nach § 10 Absatz 3 nicht, nicht richtig, nicht vollständig oder nicht rechtzeitig erfüllt,
3. die Beschränkung der wirtschaftlichen Nutzung eines Grundstücks (§ 11) nicht oder nicht vollständig einhält,
4. eine gemäß § 13 Absatz 1 und § 16 Absatz 1 erforderliche Anzeige nicht oder nicht rechtzeitig erstattet,
5. gefundene Gegenstände und die Fundstelle nicht gemäß § 16 Absatz 2 unverändert lässt,
6. eine nach § 23 Absatz 5 geforderte Auskunft nicht, nicht richtig, nicht rechtzeitig oder nicht vollständig erteilt,

7. einer aufgrund dieses Gesetzes erlassenen Rechtsverordnung oder einer Örtlichen Gestaltungsvorschrift zuwiderhandelt, sofern die Rechtsverordnung oder die Satzung für einen bestimmten Tatbestand auf diese Bußgeldvorschrift verweist.

(2) Ordnungswidrig handelt auch, wer wider besseren Wissens unrichtige Angaben macht oder unrichtige Pläne oder Unterlagen vorlegt, um einen Verwaltungsakt nach Maßgabe dieses Gesetzes zu erwirken oder zu verhindern.

(3) [1]Die Ordnungswidrigkeit kann mit einer Geldbuße bis zu 250.000 Euro geahndet werden. [2]Wird ohne Genehmigung nach § 6 Absatz 1 sowie §§ 7 bis 9 ein Kulturdenkmal vorsätzlich zerstört, kann eine Geldbuße bis zu 500.000 Euro festgesetzt werden. [3]Reste eines Kulturdenkmals, das durch eine ordnungswidrige Handlung zerstört worden ist, können eingezogen werden. [4]§ 23 des Gesetzes über Ordnungswidrigkeiten in der Fassung der Bekanntmachung vom 19. Februar 1987 (BGBl. I S. 602), zuletzt geändert durch das Gesetz vom 27. August 2017 (BGBl. I S. 3295), in der jeweils geltenden Fassung ist anzuwenden. [5]Die Verfolgung der Ordnungswidrigkeit verjährt in fünf Jahren. [6]Verwaltungsbehörde im Sinne des § 36 Absatz 1 Nummer 1 des Gesetzes über Ordnungswidrigkeiten ist die Oberste Denkmalbehörde.

§ 29 Grundrechtseinschränkung

Die Grundrechte der Unverletzlichkeit der Wohnung (Artikel 13 des Grundgesetzes, Artikel 16 der Saarländischen Verfassung), der freien Entfaltung der Persönlichkeit (Artikel 2 Absatz 1 des Grundgesetzes, Artikel 2 der Saarländischen Verfassung) und des Eigentums (Artikel 14 des Grundgesetzes, Artikel 18 der Saarländischen Verfassung) werden durch dieses Gesetz eingeschränkt.

§ 30 Kirchliche Kulturdenkmäler

(1) [1]Bei Entscheidungen über Kulturdenkmäler, die der Religionsausübung dienen, sind die von den Kirchen und Religionsgemeinschaften festgestellten religiösen Belange zu beachten. [2]Erkennt das Landesdenkmalamt die geltend gemachten religiösen Belange nicht an, entscheidet die zuständige kirchliche Oberbehörde oder die entsprechende Stelle der betroffenen Religionsgemeinschaft im Benehmen mit der Obersten Denkmalbehörde.

(2) Für klösterliche Verbände gilt Absatz 1 entsprechend.

§ 31 Schutz im Katastrophenfall

Die Oberste Denkmalbehörde wird ermächtigt, die für den Schutz von Kulturdenkmälern bei bewaffneten Konflikten und bei Katastrophenfällen notwendigen Bestimmungen durch Rechtsverordnung im Einvernehmen mit dem für Katastrophenschutz und zivile Verteidigung zuständigen Ministerium zu treffen.

§ 32 Übergangsvorschriften

(1) Die im Zeitpunkt des Inkrafttretens dieses Gesetzes im Landesdenkmalamt tätigen Beamtinnen, Beamten und Tarifbeschäftigten einschließlich der zu ihrer Berufsausbildung dort Beschäftigten werden dem Landesdenkmalamt als nachgeordnete Behörde angegliedert.

(2) [1]Die Amtszeit der nach § 6 des bisherigen Saarländischen Denkmalschutzgesetzes berufenen Mitglieder des Landesdenkmalrats wird ohne Unterbrechung fortgeführt. [2]Der Landesdenkmalrat tritt bis zur nächsten turnusmäßigen Wahl an die Stelle eines Landesdenkmalrates nach § 25 dieses Gesetzes, soweit nicht mindestens 2/3 der Mitglieder des Landesdenkmalrates sich gegen einen Übergang dieser Form aussprechen. [3]Im Falle der Amtsniederlegung bleibt der bisherige Landesdenkmalrat bis zur Aufnahme der Geschäfte des neu berufenen Landesdenkmalrates bestehen und nimmt die gesetzlichen Aufgaben wahr. [4]Eine Neuwahl muss in diesem Fall spätestens einen Monat nach Inkrafttreten dieses Gesetzes erfolgen, der neue Landesdenkmalrat mindestens zwei Monate nach Inkrafttreten dieses Gesetzes erstmals zusammentreten.

(3) [1]Die Denkmalliste nach § 6 des bisherigen Saarländischen Denkmalschutzgesetzes wird als Denkmalliste nach § 4 dieses Gesetzes weitergeführt. [2]Die bereits erfolgten Eintragungen bleiben unverändert bestehen.

(4) Die zum Inkrafttreten dieses Gesetzes berufenen Denkmalbeauftragten bleiben als solche auch weiterhin berufen und nehmen die ihnen gesetzlich erteilten Aufgaben bis zur nächsten turnusmäßigen Berufung wahr.

§ 33 Inkrafttreten, Außerkrafttreten

(1) § 25 Absatz 4 tritt am Tag nach der Verkündung[1] in Kraft.
(2) ¹Im Übrigen tritt dieses Gesetz am 1. August 2018 in Kraft. ²Gleichzeitig tritt das Saarländische Denkmalschutzgesetz vom 19. Mai 2004 (Amtsbl. S. 1498), zuletzt geändert durch das Gesetz vom 13. Oktober 2015 (Amtsbl. I S. 790), außer Kraft.

---

[1] Verkündet am 5.7.2018.

Saarländisches Archivgesetz (SArchG)

Vom 23. September 1992 (Amtsbl. S. 1094)
(BS Saar 224-9)
zuletzt geändert durch Art. 7 G zur Anpassung des bereichsspezifischen Datenschutzrechts an die VO (EU) 2016/679 vom 22. August 2018 (Amtsbl. I S. 674)

Abschnitt I
Allgemeine Vorschriften

§ 1 Geltungsbereich
(1) Dieses Gesetz regelt die Tätigkeit der Archive
1. des Landes,
2. der Gemeinden und Gemeindeverbände,
3. der sonstigen der Aufsicht des Landes unterstehenden juristischen Personen des öffentlichen Rechts.

(2) Dieses Gesetz gilt nicht für die öffentlich-rechtlichen Religionsgemeinschaften, Rundfunkanstalten und öffentlich-rechtliche Unternehmen, die am Wettbewerb teilnehmen.

§ 2 Archivgut
(1) Archivgut sind alle archivwürdigen Unterlagen einschließlich der Hilfsmittel zu ihrer Nutzung, die bei Verfassungsorganen, Behörden, Gerichten, Gemeinden und Gemeindeverbände und sonstigen öffentlichen Stellen sowie bei natürlichen oder juristischen Personen des privaten Rechts anfallen; hierzu zählen insbesondere Urkunden, Akten, Amtsbücher, Karten, Pläne, Plakate, Bild-, Film- und Tonmaterial, elektronische Informationsträger, auf diesen gespeicherte Informationen und Programme zu ihrer Auswertung sowie andere Träger von Informationen.

(2) [1]Öffentliches Archivgut ist unveräußerlich. [2]In Ausnahmefällen ist eine Abgabe an andere öffentliche Archive zulässig, wenn diese im öffentlichen Interesse liegt und die Einhaltung der in diesem Gesetz getroffenen Regelungen für die Archivierung gewährleistet ist.

(3) [1]Archivwürdig sind Unterlagen, die auf Grund ihrer politischen, wirtschaftlichen, sozialen oder kulturellen Bedeutung für die Erforschung und das Verständnis von Geschichte und Gegenwart, für Gesetzgebung, Rechtsprechung und Verwaltung sowie für die berechtigten Belange der Öffentlichkeit von bleibendem Wert sind. [2]Als archivwürdig gelten auch solche Unterlagen, deren Archivierung durch Rechtsvorschrift angeordnet ist. [3]Über die Archivwürdigkeit der Unterlagen entscheiden die Archive, nachdem die unter § 2 Absatz 1 Satz 1 genannten Stellen diese dem jeweils zuständigen Archiv angeboten haben.

§ 3 Archivierung
(1) [1]Archivierung beinhaltet die Aufgabe, das Archivgut auf Dauer zu übernehmen, instandzusetzen, sachgemäß zu verwahren, zu erfassen, zu erschließen und für die Bedürfnisse der Gesetzgebung, der Verwaltung, der Rechtspflege, der Forschung sowie für Informationsinteressen der Öffentlichkeit bereitzuhalten und auszuwerten. [2]Die Archive wirken an der Erforschung der Geschichte ihres Archivsprengels mit.

(2) Mit Zustimmung der abgebenden Stelle können Archive die im Archivgut enthaltenen Informationen in anderer Form archivieren und die Originalunterlagen vernichten, soweit dies unter archivarischen Gesichtspunkten vertretbar oder geboten ist; für die neugeschaffenen Aufzeichnungen gelten dieselben Regelungen dieses Gesetzes, die auf die Originalunterlagen Anwendung finden würden.

(3) [1]Archivgut, dessen Archivwürdigkeit nicht länger gegeben ist, da seine Bedeutung für die Rechtswahrung oder für die wissenschaftliche Forschung nicht mehr erkennbar ist, kann in öffentlichen Archiven vernichtet oder gelöscht werden. [2]Über Vernichtung oder Löschung ist ein Nachweis zu führen.

§ 4 Speicherung, Datenschutz
(1) Durch geeignete technische und organisatorische Maßnahmen ist das Archivgut einschließlich der seiner Erschließung dienenden Hilfsmittel vor unbefugter Nutzung, Beschädigung oder Vernichtung zu sichern sowie der Schutz personenbezogener Daten oder solcher Unterlagen, die einem besonderen gesetzlichen Geheimnisschutz unterliegen, sicherzustellen.

(2) Zur besseren Erschließung darf das Archivgut mittels elektronischer Datenträger erfasst und gespeichert werden; die Verarbeitung der gespeicherten Informationen ist nur zur Erfüllung der in diesem Gesetz genannten Zwecke zulässig.
(3) Im Übrigen bleiben die Bestimmungen des Saarländischen Datenschutzgesetzes unberührt.

§ 5 *[aufgehoben]*

Abschnitt II
Landesarchiv

§ 6 Organisation
Das Landesarchiv ist eine Einrichtung des Landes im Geschäftsbereich von Ministerpräsidentin/Ministerpräsident und Staatskanzlei.

§ 7 Aufgaben
(1) Dem Landesarchiv obliegt die Archivierung des Archivguts der Verfassungsorgane, Behörden, Gerichte und sonstigen öffentlichen Stellen des Landes einschließlich ihrer Rechts- und Funktionsvorgänger.
(2) Das Landesarchiv übernimmt gemäß § 2 Abs. 3 des Gesetzes über die Sicherung und Nutzung von Archivgut des Bundes vom 6. Januar 1988 die archivwürdigen Unterlagen von nachgeordneten Stellen des Bundes, die ihren Sitz im Saarland haben.
(3) Das Landesarchiv kann auf Grund von Vereinbarungen Archivgut weiterer öffentlicher Stellen des Bundes, anderer Länder, von Kommunen, Anstalten und Körperschaften des öffentlichen Rechts archivieren.
(4) [1]Das Landesarchiv kann auf Grund von Vereinbarungen oder letztwilligen Verfügungen privates Archivgut archivieren, soweit daran ein öffentliches Interesse besteht. [2]Dabei können hinsichtlich der Benutzung des Archivguts von den Bestimmungen dieses Gesetzes abweichende Regelungen getroffen werden.
(5) [1]Das Landesarchiv wirkt an der Auswertung der von ihm aufbewahrten Quellen sowie an der Erforschung und öffentlichen Vermittlung der Geschichte des Saarlandes und der Nachbarregionen mit. [2]Es fördert das Verständnis für die Landesgeschichte insbesondere durch Veröffentlichungen, Ausstellungen, Führungen und andere diesem Zweck dienende Veranstaltungen und Präsentationen.
(6) Das Landesarchiv berät die Träger anderer Archive im Land auf deren Wunsch bei der Erfüllung ihrer Aufgaben, soweit daran ein öffentliches Interesse besteht, und wirkt bei der Ausbildung öffentlicher Archivare mit.

§ 8 Aussonderung und Anbietung
(1) [1]Die Verfassungsorgane, Behörden, Gerichte und die sonstigen öffentlichen Stellen des Landes haben, soweit sie nicht nach den Vorschriften dieses Gesetzes ein eigenes Archiv unterhalten, alle Unterlagen im Sinne von § 2 Absatz 1, die bei der Erfüllung ihrer Aufgaben oder der ihrer Rechts- und Funktionsvorgänger angefallen sind und die sie zur Erfüllung ihrer laufenden Dienstgeschäfte nicht mehr benötigen, auszusondern und dem Landesarchiv zur Übernahme anzubieten; Unterlagen sind spätestens 30 Jahre nach ihrer Entstehung auszusondern und anzubieten, soweit nicht eine längere Aufbewahrung durch gesetzliche Vorschriften zugelassen oder ausnahmsweise für die Wahrnehmung dienstlicher Aufgaben erforderlich ist. [2]Die öffentlichen Stellen nach Satz 1 übergeben von allen von ihnen herausgegebenen Druckschriften nach Erscheinen kostenlos ein Belegexemplar dem Landesarchiv. [3]Diese Verpflichtung gilt für elektronische Publikationen entsprechend. [4]Bei Unterlagen, die in elektronischer Form gespeichert und laufend aktualisiert werden, steht dem Landesarchiv das Recht zu, die Anbietung jährlich zu verlangen.
(2) [1]Anzubieten sind auch solche Unterlagen, die
1. personenbezogene Daten, einschließlich besonderer Kategorien personenbezogener Daten im Sinne des Artikel 9 Absatz 1 der Verordnung (EU) 2016/679, enthalten, die aufgrund einer Rechtsvorschrift gelöscht werden müssten oder gelöscht werden könnten, sofern die Verarbeitung der Daten nicht unrechtmäßig war,
2. einem Berufs- oder besonderen Amtsgeheimnis oder sonstigen Rechtsvorschriften über die Geheimhaltung unterliegen.

²Die nach § 203 Abs. 1 Nr. 1, 4 oder 4a des Strafgesetzbuchs geschützten Unterlagen der Gesundheitsbehörden und von Beratungsstellen dürfen nur in anonymisierter Form angeboten werden.
(3) Das Landesarchiv kann die ablieferungspflichtige Stelle von der Anbietung solcher Unterlagen, die im Hinblick auf ihre offensichtlich geringe Bedeutung für die Aufgaben des Landesarchivs ohne Belang sind, befreien.

§ 9 Übernahme

(1) ¹Das Landesarchiv entscheidet binnen eines halben Jahres im Benehmen mit der anbietenden Stelle, ob es sich um archivwürdige Unterlagen handelt. ²Die anbietende Stelle hat dem Landesarchiv Einblick in die angebotenen Unterlagen sowie die sie erschließenden Hilfsmittel zu gewähren.
(2) ¹Das Landesarchiv kann die Landesbehörden bei der Einrichtung und Organisation ihrer Registraturen beraten. ²Es berät die Behörden insbesondere bei der Sicherung ihrer elektronischen Akten in Hinblick auf deren spätere Archivierung. ³Bei der Einführung elektronischer Registraturen ist das Landesarchiv zu beteiligen.
(3) Bei umfangreichen Sammlungen von Unterlagen und bei gespeicherten maschinenlesbaren Informationen ist das Benehmen zwischen der anbietenden Stelle und dem Landesarchiv dadurch herzustellen, dass Art, Umfang und Form des zu übernehmenden Archivguts vorab im Grundsatz festgelegt werden.
(4) ¹Archivwürdige Unterlagen sind vom Landesarchiv zu übernehmen; § 8 Abs. 2 gilt entsprechend. ²Unterlagen, die vom Landesarchiv nicht übernommen werden, sind von der anbietenden Stelle spätestens nach Ablauf der Frist des Absatzes 1 Satz 1 entsprechend den gesetzlichen Vorschriften zu löschen.
(5) ¹Die abgebende Behörde oder Stelle hat darauf zu achten, dass die angebotenen Akten sich in einem geordneten Zustand befinden. ²Sie hat mit den abzugebenden Akten eine Auflistung mitzuliefern. ³Sie trägt die Kosten für Verpackung und Versand. ⁴Bei Archivierung elektronischer Unterlagen ist die abgebende Stelle verpflichtet, die zur Verarbeitung und Nutzung der Daten notwendigen Informationen zu dokumentieren und dem Landesarchiv zu übergeben.
(6) ¹Stehen der Übernahme schutzwürdige Belange Betroffener entgegen, denen durch die Einschränkung der Nutzung nach § 11 Abs. 7 nicht hinreichend Rechnung getragen werden kann, sind die Unterlagen zu anonymisieren. ²Ergibt eine Prüfung der anbietenden Stelle und des Landesarchivs, dass diesen Belangen auch durch Anonymisierung der Daten nicht hinreichend Rechnung getragen werden kann oder kann in dieser Frage keine Einigung erzielt werden, so unterbleibt die Übernahme. ³Absatz 3 Satz 2 bleibt unberührt.

§ 10 Nutzung durch die abliefernde Stelle

(1) Die abliefernde Stelle hat das Recht, Archivgut aus ihren Beständen jederzeit zu nutzen.
(2) ¹Das Nutzungsrecht erstreckt sich nicht auf personenbezogene Daten, die auf Grund einer Rechtsvorschrift hätten gesperrt oder gelöscht werden müssen. ²In diesen Fällen besteht das Nutzungsrecht nur nach Maßgabe des § 11, jedoch nicht zu dem Zweck, zu welchem die personenbezogenen Daten ursprünglich verarbeitet worden sind.

§ 11 Nutzung

(1) ¹Jedermann ist berechtigt, Archivgut im Sinne des § 2 aus einer mehr als 30 Jahre zurückliegenden Zeit zu amtlichen, wissenschaftlichen oder publizistischen Zwecken sowie zur Wahrnehmung berechtigter persönlicher Belange zu nutzen, sofern durch dieses Gesetz oder aufgrund einer Rechtsvorschrift nichts anderes bestimmt ist. ²Besondere Vereinbarungen mit den Eigentümern von Archivgut, das nicht dem Saarland gehört, und testamentarische Bestimmungen bleiben hiervon unberührt.
(2) ¹Archivgut, das besonderen Geheimhaltungs- und Schutzvorschriften unterliegt, darf erst 60 Jahre nach seiner Entstehung zur Nutzung durch Dritte freigegeben werden. ²Hierzu gehören insbesondere Verschlusssachen und Unterlagen, die dem Steuergeheimnis, dem Bankgeheimnis, dem Sozialgeheimnis oder der ärztlichen Schweigepflicht unterliegen.
(3) ¹Unbeschadet der Schutzfrist nach Absatz 2 darf Archivgut, das sich auf eine natürliche Person bezieht (personenbezogenes Archivgut), ohne Einwilligung des Betroffenen erst zehn Jahre nach seinem Tode durch Dritte benutzt werden. ²Ist der Todestag nicht oder nur mit unvertretbarem Aufwand feststellbar, endet die Schutzfrist 90 Jahre nach der Geburt des Betroffenen. ³Kann auch das Geburtsdatum nicht ermittelt werden, endet die Schutzfrist 60 Jahre nach Schließung der Unterlagen.

(4) Die Schutzfristen nach den Absätzen 1 und 3 gelten nicht für Unterlagen, die bei ihrer Entstehung zur Veröffentlichung bestimmt waren.

(5) ¹Ist das Archivgut aktenmäßig zusammengefasst, so bestimmen sich die Schutzfristen nach dem Datum des jüngsten Schriftstückes der Akte. ²§ 24 Absatz 2 in Verbindung mit § 8 Absatz 2 des Saarländischen Datenschutzgesetzes vom 16. Mai 2018 (Amtsbl. I S. 254) ist zu berücksichtigen.

(6) ¹Die festgelegten Schutzfristen können im Einverständnis mit der abgebenden Stelle für wissenschaftliche Forschungen im Einzelfall verkürzt werden. ²Beim Landesarchiv können die festgelegten Schutzfristen für wissenschaftliche Forschungen im Einzelfall im Einverständnis mit der Staatskanzlei verkürzt werden. ³Bei personenbezogenem Archivgut ist eine Verkürzung nur zulässig, wenn
1. die Betroffenen eingewilligt haben,
2. die Benutzung für die Durchführung eines bestimmten Forschungsvorhabens erforderlich ist und schutzwürdige Belange der Betroffenen nicht beeinträchtigt werden oder
3. das öffentliche Interesse an der Durchführung des Forschungsvorhabens die schutzwürdigen Belange des Betroffenen überwiegt.

⁴Personenbezogene Daten dürfen in Forschungsergebnissen nur veröffentlicht werden, wenn
1. die Betroffenen eingewilligt haben oder
2. dies für die Darstellung von Forschungsergebnissen unerlässlich ist.

(7) Die festgelegten Schutzfristen können im Einvernehmen mit der abgebenden Stelle um höchstens 20 Jahre verlängert werden, wenn dies im öffentlichen Interesse liegt.

(8) Die Benutzung von Archivgut kann eingeschränkt oder versagt werden, soweit
1. es besonderen gesetzlichen Geheimhaltungsvorschriften unterliegt,
2. das Wohl der Bundesrepublik Deutschland oder eines ihrer Länder gefährdet wäre,
3. schutzwürdige Belange Dritter entgegenstehen,
4. die Erhaltung des Archivgutes gefährdet würde,
5. sie einen nicht vertretbaren Verwaltungsaufwand verursachen oder
6. die Aufgaben des Landesarchivs in einem unvertretbaren Maß erschweren würde.

(9) Für die Benutzung von bundeseigenem Archivmaterial gelten die bundesrechtlichen Vorschriften.

(10) Die Nutzung des Archivgutes erfolgt durch persönliche Einsichtnahme, durch schriftliche Auskunft oder auf elektronischem Weg.

(11) ¹Vervielfältigungen von Archivgut nach § 2 Absatz 1 zur Geschichte der Juden unter der nationalsozialistischen Gewaltherrschaft, zur nationalsozialistischen Judenverfolgung sowie zu deren Aufarbeitung in der Nachkriegszeit können anderen Archiven, Museen oder Forschungsstellen zur archivischen Nutzung überlassen werden. ²Eine Überlassung ist nur zulässig, wenn sichergestellt ist, dass bei der Benutzung der Vervielfältigungen § 11 Absatz 1 bis 3, Absatz 6 und Absatz 8 Nr. 1 bis 3 sinngemäße Anwendung findet.

§ 12 Benutzungs- und Gebührenordnung

Die Ministerpräsidentin/der Ministerpräsident wird ermächtigt, durch Rechtsverordnung[1)] die Art der Benutzung des Archivguts im Einzelnen zu regeln sowie im Einvernehmen mit dem Ministerium für Finanzen und Europa Gebühren für die Benutzung festzusetzen; dabei kann auch bestimmt werden, dass Benutzer dem Landesarchiv kostenlos ein Belegexemplar von Druckwerken, die unter Nutzung seines Archivguts entstanden sind, zu überlassen haben.

§ 13 Weitere Aufgaben

Die Landesregierung kann dem Landesarchiv durch Verordnung weitere als in diesem oder anderen Gesetzen genannte Aufgaben des Landes übertragen, die in sachlichem Zusammenhang mit dem Archivwesen des Landes oder der Erforschung der Geschichte des Saarlandes und seiner Nachbarregionen stehen.

---

1) Die Verordnung über die Benutzung von Archivgut beim Landesarchiv ist abgedruckt als Nr. D12.II.1a; die Verordnung über den Erlass des Besonderen Gebührenverzeichnisses für das Landesarchiv ist abgedruckt als Nr. 12.II.1c.

D12.II.1 Saarländisches Archivgesetz

Abschnitt III
Archive sonstiger öffentlicher Stellen des Landes

§ 14 Archiv des Landtags

(1) ¹Das Landtagsarchiv ist ein Staatliches Archiv besonderer Art und dient der Verwahrung und Betreuung des Archivguts des Landtags. ²§ 7 Abs. 4, §§ 10 und 11 gelten für das Archiv des Landtags sinngemäß. ³Das Landtagspräsidium regelt die Einzelheiten der Nutzung des Landtagsarchivs in einer Benutzungsordnung.

(2) Unterlagen, die der Landtag zur Erfüllung seiner Aufgaben nicht mehr benötigt, bietet das Landtagsarchiv dem Landesarchiv zur Übernahme an.

§ 15 Kommunale und sonstige öffentliche Archive

(1) ¹Die Gemeinden, die Landkreise, der Regionalverband Saarbrücken und die Zweckverbände regeln die Archivierung der bei ihnen anfallenden Unterlagen in eigener Zuständigkeit durch Satzung (Archivsatzung). ²Sie tragen dabei durch eine angemessene personelle und sachliche Ausstattung der kommunalen Archive dafür Sorge, dass die Übernahme, Erhaltung und Erschließung des Archivmaterials nach archivfachlichen Gesichtspunkten im Sinne dieses Gesetzes gesichert ist. ³Ebenso ist zu gewährleisten, dass die Öffentlichkeit nach Maßgabe dieses Gesetzes angemessenen Zugang zum Archivgut erhält.

(2) § 7 Absatz 4, § 10 und § 11 gelten entsprechend.

(3) ¹Soweit keine kommunalen Archive bestehen, sind Unterlagen, die zur Aufgabenerfüllung nicht mehr benötigt werden, dem Landesarchiv zur Übernahme anzubieten. ²Das Eigentum am Archivgut bleibt unberührt. ³Für Archivierung, Verwahrung und Verwaltung dieser Unterlagen wird dem Landesarchiv seitens der abgebenden Körperschaft eine angemessene Kostenbeteiligung gewährt.

(4) Hochschulen und Kammern sind nach Maßgabe der Absätze 1 bis 3 berechtigt, eigene Archive zu unterhalten.

(5) ¹Sonstige Körperschaften, Anstalten und Stiftungen des öffentlichen Rechts können Archive errichten, wenn dies im öffentlichen Interesse liegt; die Errichtung bedarf der Genehmigung der Staatskanzlei. ²Die Absätze 1 bis 3 gelten entsprechend.

§ 16 *[aufgehoben]*

Abschnitt IV

§ 17 Inkrafttreten

Dieses Gesetz tritt am 1. Januar 1993 in Kraft.

Verordnung über die Benutzung von Archivgut beim Landesarchiv (Archivbenutzungsverordnung – ArchBO)

Vom 10. Dezember 2001 (Amtsbl. S. 43)
(BS Saar)

Auf Grund des § 12 des Saarländischen Archivgesetzes (SArchG) vom 23. September 1992 (Amtsbl. S. 1094) verordnet der Ministerpräsident:

§ 1 Benutzungsberechtigung
Das Archivgut steht nach Maßgabe des Saarländischen Archivgesetzes und dieser Verordnung auf Antrag jedermann zur Benutzung zur Verfügung.

§ 2 Benutzungsarten
(1) Die Benutzung erfolgt
a) durch persönliche Einsichtnahme im Landesarchiv,
b) durch mündliche, fernmündliche oder schriftliche Anfragen,
c) durch Anforderung von Reproduktionen von Archivgut,
d) durch Versendung von Archivgut zur Einsichtnahme an einem anderen Ort,
e) durch Ausleihe von Archivgut für Ausstellungen.
(2) Die übliche Benutzungsart ist die persönliche Einsichtnahme im Landesarchiv.

§ 3 Benutzungsantrag
(1) [1]Die Benutzungsgenehmigung ist schriftlich beim Landesarchiv zu beantragen. [2]Im Antrag ist folgendes anzugeben:
1. Name, Vorname und Anschrift des Antragstellers oder der Antragstellerin,
2. Name, Vorname und Anschrift des Auftraggebers oder der Auftraggeberin, wenn die Benutzung im Auftrag eines oder einer Dritten erfolgt,
3. der Benutzungszweck, der Gegenstand der Nachforschungen und die beabsichtigte Auswertung; bei Benutzung zu wissenschaftlichen Zwecken ist die Art der geplanten Arbeit, bei Studien- und Prüfungsarbeiten die Hochschule anzugeben,
4. die Art der vorgesehenen Veröffentlichung.
[3]Weitere persönliche Angaben (Geburtsjahr, Beruf) können vom Benutzer oder der Benutzerin auf freiwilliger Basis erhoben werden. Bei persönlicher Einsichtnahme ist für die schriftliche Antragstellung ein Vordruck zu verwenden.
(2) Bei Nutzungen nach § 2 Abs. 1 Buchstabe b) bis e), insbesondere bei schriftlichen oder mündlichen Anfragen, kann auf einen schriftlichen Antrag gemäß Absatz 1 verzichtet werden.
(3) [1]Der Antrag gilt nur für das laufende Kalenderjahr, das angegebene Nutzungsvorhaben und den angegebenen Nutzungszweck. [2]Wechselt der Nutzer oder die Nutzerin Nutzungsvorhaben oder Nutzungszweck, ist ein erneuter Antrag zu stellen.
(4) Der Benutzer oder die Benutzerin hat sich auf Verlangen auszuweisen.
(5) Sollen andere Personen als Hilfskräfte oder Beauftragte zu den Arbeiten herangezogen werden, so ist jeweils ein eigener Antrag zu stellen.
(6) Mit dem Antrag verpflichtet sich der Benutzer oder die Benutzerin, die Vorschriften dieser Verordnung sowie ergänzende Bestimmungen des Landesarchivs (§ 12) einzuhalten.
(7) Die Angaben im Antrag und Daten über den Ablauf der Benutzung, besonders über das benutzte Archivgut, können für die Zwecke des Landesarchivs weiter verarbeitet werden.

§ 4 Benutzungsgenehmigung
(1) Über den Benutzungsantrag entscheidet der Leiter oder die Leiterin des Landesarchivs.
(2) Die Benutzungsgenehmigung kann mit Bedingungen und Auflagen erteilt werden.
(3) Die Benutzungsgenehmigung kann eingeschränkt oder versagt werden, wenn
a) bei früherer Benutzung von Archivgut wiederholt oder schwerwiegend gegen diese Verordnung oder ergänzende Bestimmungen des Landesarchivs (§ 12) verstoßen oder festgelegte Benutzungsbedingungen oder -auflagen nicht eingehalten worden sind,

b) der Erhaltungszustand des Archivguts oder Vereinbarungen mit Eigentümern von Archivgut dies erfordern,
c) Archivgut aus dienstlichen Gründen oder wegen gleichzeitiger amtlicher oder anderweitiger Nutzung nicht verfügbar ist,
d) der mit der Nutzung verfolgte Zweck anderweitig, insbesondere durch Einsichtnahme in Druckwerke oder andere Veröffentlichungen oder in Reproduktionen erreicht werden kann,
e) die Benutzung einen nicht vertretbaren Verwaltungsaufwand verursachen würde.

(4) Die Benutzungsgenehmigung kann widerrufen werden, wenn
a) wiederholt oder schwerwiegend gegen diese Verordnung oder ergänzende Bestimmungen des Landesarchivs (§ 12) verstoßen wird oder festgelegte Nutzungsbedingungen oder -auflagen nicht eingehalten werden,
b) nachträglich Gründe bekannt werden, die zur Versagung geführt hätten,
c) Urheber- oder Persönlichkeitsschutzrechte oder andere schutzwürdige Belange Dritter nicht beachtet werden.

(5) Bei Einschränkung, Versagung oder Widerruf der Benutzungsgenehmigung sind die Gründe – auf Wunsch schriftlich – mitzuteilen.

§ 5 Durchführung der Benutzung

(1) [1]Die Archivbenutzung findet grundsätzlich nur in dem hierfür bestimmten Arbeitsraum (Benutzersaal) unter fachlicher Aufsicht statt. [2]Für das Verhalten im Benutzersaal gelten die Vorschriften der Benutzersaalordnung des Landesarchivs (§ 12).

(2) [1]Der Benutzer oder die Benutzerin ist verpflichtet, das Archivgut im Benutzersaal zu belassen, die innere Ordnung des Archivguts zu bewahren, es nicht zu beschädigen, zu verändern oder in seinem Erhaltungszustand zu gefährden. [2]Das gleiche gilt entsprechend für Findmittel jeder Art und Bibliotheksgut.

(3) [1]Die Durchführung der Benutzung bleibt dem Benutzer oder der Benutzerin überlassen. [2]Die Beratung durch das Personal des Archivs beschränkt sich grundsätzlich auf den Nachweis der einschlägigen, im Landesarchiv vorhandenen Archivalien. [3]Der Benutzer oder die Benutzerin hat keinen Anspruch auf umfassende Hilfe beim Lesen oder Übersetzen der Archivalien.

(4) Der Benutzer oder die Benutzerin haftet für den Verlust oder jede vorsätzliche oder fahrlässige Beschädigung von Archivalien.

(5) [1]Die Archivbücherei steht Benutzern oder Benutzerinnen zur Verfügung, soweit dienstliche Interessen nicht entgegenstehen. [2]Sie ist eine Präsenzbibliothek.

(6) [1]Die Benutzung privater technischer Hilfsmittel im Zusammenhang mit der Archivalienbenutzung ist grundsätzlich gestattet, soweit die Archivalien nicht gefährdet und die Ordnung im Benutzersaal nicht gestört wird. [2]Das Landesarchiv kann dazu auch eigene Räume oder Kabinen zur Verfügung stellen.

§ 6 Benutzung fremden Archivguts

[1]Für die Benutzung von Archivalien, die von anderen Archiven oder Instituten übersandt werden, gelten dieselben Bedingungen wie für das Archivgut des Landesarchivs, sofern die übersendende Stelle nicht anderslautende Auflagen macht. [2]Gebühren und Auslagen tragen diejenigen, die die Versendung veranlasst haben.

§ 7 Öffnungszeiten des Benutzersaales

(1) Die Öffnungszeiten werden durch das Landesarchiv gesondert festgesetzt und bekannt gegeben.
(2) Der Benutzersaal kann aus besonderem Anlass zeitweilig geschlossen werden.

§ 8 Anfertigung von Reproduktionen

(1) [1]Auf schriftlichen Antrag stellt das Landesarchiv oder eine von ihm beauftragte Stelle Reproduktionen von Archivalien her, sofern nicht fachliche Gründe entgegenstehen. [2]Über das jeweils geeignete Reproduktionsverfahren entscheidet das Landesarchiv. [3]Ein Anspruch auf die Anfertigung von Reproduktionen besteht nicht.

(2) Auf besonderen Antrag können einzelne fotografische Reproduktionen durch den Benutzer oder die Benutzerin selbst angefertigt werden, sofern nicht fachliche Gründe entgegenstehen.

(3) ¹Reproduktionen dürfen nur für den im Benutzungsantrag bezeichneten Zweck unter Angabe der Herkunft aus dem Landesarchiv verwendet werden. ²Bestehende Urheberrechte, auch des Landesarchivs, sind zu wahren.
(4) Für die Veröffentlichung von Archivalienreproduktionen ist die vorherige Genehmigung des Landesarchivs erforderlich.

§ 9 Schriftliche Auskünfte
Schriftliche Auskünfte auf Anfragen beschränken sich grundsätzlich auf die Mitteilung von Art, Umfang, Zustand und Benutzbarkeit einschlägiger Archivalien im Landesarchiv.

§ 10 Versand und Ausleihe von Archivalien
(1) Zum Versand geeignete Archivalien können in Ausnahmefällen zur Benutzung ausgeliehen werden, wenn Benutzung und Aufbewahrung unter vergleichbaren Bedingungen wie im Landesarchiv erfolgen und der Nutzungszweck nicht durch Versendung von Reproduktionen erreicht werden kann.
(2) Zur Ausstellung geeignete Archivalien können ausgeliehen werden, wenn die Ausstellungsbedingungen fachlichen Anforderungen entsprechen und der Ausstellungszweck nicht durch Verfügungstellung von Reproduktionen erreicht werden kann.
(3) ¹Die Entscheidung über Versand und Ausleihe sowie über die jeweilige Dauer fällt der Leiter oder die Leiterin des Landesarchivs unter fachlichen Gesichtspunkten. ²Ein Anspruch auf Versand oder Ausleihe besteht nicht.
(4) Über die Ausleihe ist zwischen dem Landesarchiv und dem Entleiher oder der Entleiherin ein Leihvertrag abzuschließen.
(5) Die Anfertigung von Reproduktionen am fremden Nutzungsort bedarf der vorherigen Einwilligung des Landesarchivs.
(6) Die jeweils anfallenden Kosten trägt der Besteller oder die Bestellerin.

§ 11 Ablieferungspflicht
¹Von Veröffentlichungen, die unter Nutzung des Archivgutes des Landesarchivs entstanden sind, steht dem Landesarchiv ein kostenloses Belegexemplar zu. ²Stellt dies im Einzelfall eine unzumutbare Härte dar, kann das Landesarchiv auf das Belegexemplar verzichten bzw. einvernehmlich einen Ankauf zu einem reduzierten Preis tätigen. ³Ist für die Benutzung eines Depositums mit dem Eigentümer oder der Eigentümerin die Abgabe eines Belegexemplars vereinbart, steht diesem oder dieser das Exemplar zu.

§ 12 Ergänzende Bestimmungen
¹Das Landesarchiv kann zu dieser Verordnung ergänzende Bestimmungen treffen. ²Insbesondere regelt es die Öffnungszeiten sowie den Schutz des Archiv- und Bibliotheksguts bei der Benutzung und den Ablauf der Benutzung durch eine Benutzersaalordnung.[1]

§ 13 Gebühren und Auslagen
Die Erhebung von Verwaltungs- und Benutzungsgebühren sowie von Auslagen für die Benutzung des Landesarchivs richtet sich nach der Gebührenordnung für die Benutzung des Landesarchivs in der jeweils geltenden Fassung.

§ 14 In-Kraft-Treten
(1) Diese Verordnung tritt am Tage nach ihrer Verkündung[2] in Kraft.
(2) Gleichzeitig tritt die Benutzungsordnung für das Landesarchiv Saarbrücken vom 27. März 1986 (GMBl. Saar S. 225) außer Kraft.

---
1) Die Benutzersaalordnung des Landesarchivs Saarbrücken ist abgedruckt als Nr. D12.II.1b.
2) Verkündet am 9.12.2001.

D12.II.1b Benutzersaalordnung Landesarchiv

Benutzersaalordnung des Landesarchivs Saarbrücken[1)]

Auf Grund des § 12 der Verordnung über die Benutzung von Archivgut beim Landesarchiv (Archivbenutzungsordnung – ArchBO) vom 10. Dezember 2001 (Amtsbl. 2002, S. 43) wird für den Benutzersaal des Landesarchivs folgende Ordnung erlassen:

1) Der Benutzersaal des Landesarchivs ist montags bis freitags von 8.30 bis 16 h geöffnet. Eine Verlängerung der Öffnungszeit ist im Einzelfall nach Voranmeldung möglich.
2) Mäntel, Aktentaschen, Koffer und dergl. sind vor dem Betreten des Benutzersaales in der Garderobe bzw. den Schließfächern abzulegen. Der Schließfachschlüssel darf nicht außer Haus mitgenommen werden; er ist bei zeitweiligem Verlassen des Gebäudes bei der Aufsicht zu hinterlegen.
3) Der Benutzer stellt bei seinem erstmaligen Besuch mit Formular des Landesarchivs einen Antrag auf Archivbenutzung. Der Antrag ist vollständig auszufüllen und zu unterschreiben. Mit der Unterschrift erkennt der Benutzer die Benutzungsordnung und die Benutzersaalordnung des Landesarchivs an. Ändert der Benutzer sein Thema oder nach Beginn eines neuen Kalenderjahres ist ein neuer Antrag zu stellen.
4) Archivalien sind mit Formularen des Landesarchivs zu bestellen, die vollständig auszufüllen und zu unterschreiben sind. Für jedes Archivale ist ein eigenes Bestellzettelpaar erforderlich. Unmittelbar aufeinander folgende Signaturen können ebenfalls mit nur einem Bestellzettelpaar angefordert werden.
5) Die der Benutzung dienenden Archivfindmittel sind dem Benutzer ohne Bestellzettel zugänglich. Sie sind bei dem Aufsichtspersonal anzufordern.
6) Die Archivalien werden zu bestimmten Bestellzeiten, die vom Archiv besonders festgesetzt werden, ausgehoben und vorgelegt. Außerhalb dieser Zeiten besteht kein Anspruch auf Vorlage.
7) Grundsätzlich wird nur eine begrenzte Anzahl von Archivalien gleichzeitig vorgelegt.
8) Vorbestellungen von Archivalien zur späteren Benutzung sind möglich.
9) Die vorgelegten Findmittel und Archivalien sind sorgfältig zu behandeln. Die vorgegebene Reihenfolge der Schriftstücke darf nicht verändert werden. Beim Bemerken von Unstimmigkeiten oder Schäden ist sofort die Aufsicht zu verständigen. Es ist insbesondere verboten, Archivalien als Schreibunterlage zu benutzen, den Arm auf sie zu stützen, beim Umblättern die Finger anzufeuchten, in den Archivalien Einträge, Nachzeichnungen verblasster Stellen oder Radierungen vorzunehmen, Siegel abzutrennen, Briefmarken herauszulösen oder sonstige Teile zu entnehmen oder herauszuschneiden.
10) Das Archiv kann den Arbeitsplatz im Benutzersaal zuweisen und aus fachlichen Gründen die ausschließliche Benutzung bestimmter Schreibutensilien oder von Buchstützen vorschreiben.
11) Rauchen, Essen und Trinken sowie störende Unterhaltung sind untersagt. Für Pausen steht das Foyer zur Verfügung.
12) Die Benutzung ist grundsätzlich Sache des Benutzers. Das Personal des Landesarchivs kann im Einzelfall beraten und Hilfestellung geben.
13) Die vorgelegten Archivalien dürfen nur vom Besteller selbst eingesehen werden. Für die Mitbenutzung durch andere Personen ist eine besondere Erlaubnis einzuholen.
14) Bei Beendigung der Benutzung sind die Archivalien der Aufsicht zurückzugeben. Dabei ist mitzuteilen, ob ihre Benutzung beendet ist oder später fortgesetzt werden soll. Archivalien werden nur zwei Wochen lang zur weiteren Benutzung zurückgelegt; danach ist eine erneute Bestellung erforderlich.
15) Reproduktionen von Archivalien können mit besonderem Formular des Landesarchivs bestellt werden, wenn die Vorlagen dazu geeignet sind. Die Signaturen und die zu reproduzierenden Teile sind eindeutig anzugeben.
16) Im Einzelfall und mit vorheriger Genehmigung des Archivs können Benutzer selbst fotografische Reproduktionen für den im Benutzungsantrag genannten Zweck anfertigen, sofern nicht fachliche Gründe entgegenstehen.

[1)] Fundstelle: https://www.google.com/url?sa=t&rct=j&q=&esrc=s&source=web&cd=1&ved=2ahUKEwivpuSR84vjAhW QbsAKHSp3DfQQFjAAegQIABAB&url=https%3A%2F%2Fwww.saarland.de%2Fdokumente%2Fthema_landesarchiv %2FBenutzersaalordnung.pdf&usg=AOvVaw3Eln9e5JNHPsj0BNugKgQ_.

17) Die Benutzung technischer Hilfsmittel im Benutzersaal ist gestattet (Laptop, Schreibmaschine, Diktiergerät etc.), sofern nicht fachliche Gründe entgegenstehen oder andere Benutzer gestört werden. Das Landesarchiv kann die Benutzung separater Kabinen anordnen.
18) Technische Geräte (Lesegerät, Computer etc.), die das Landesarchiv zur Verfügung stellt, sind schonend zu behandeln. Vor der erstmaligen Benutzung erfolgt eine Einweisung durch die Benutzersaalaufsicht.
19) Die Archivbibliothek ist eine Präsenzbibliothek. Der im Benutzersaal aufgestellte Teil kann frei benutzt werden. Die Bücher sind nach Gebrauch sorgfältig zurückzustellen. Bücher aus dem magazinierten Teil der Bibliothek sind zur Benutzung im Benutzersaal mit besonderem Bestellzettel anzufordern.
20) Den Anweisungen des Archivpersonals ist Folge zu leisten. Es ist berechtigt, Kontrollen durchzuführen.

D12.II.1c Verordnung Gebührenverzeichnis Landesarchiv

Verordnung über den Erlass des Besonderen Gebührenverzeichnisses für das Landesarchiv

Vom 28. Mai 2002 (Amtsbl. S. 1075),
zuletzt geändert durch Verordnung vom 7. Dezember 2010 (Amtsbl. I S. 1453)

Auf Grund des § 5 Abs. 2 des Gesetzes über die Erhebung von Verwaltungs- und Benutzungsgebühren im Saarland (SaarlGebG) vom 24. Juni 1964 (Amtsbl. S. 629), zuletzt geändert durch Gesetz vom 7. November 2001 (Amtsbl. S. 2158), in Verbindung mit § 12 des Saarländischen Archivgesetzes (SArchG) vom 23. September 1992 (Amtsbl. S. 1094) verordnet der Ministerpräsident im Einvernehmen mit dem Ministerium für Finanzen und Bundesangelegenheiten:

§ 1 Allgemeines
(1) Das Landesarchiv erhebt für die von ihm erbrachten Dienstleistungen und für die Benutzung seiner Einrichtungen Verwaltungs- und Benutzungsgebühren sowie Auslagen nach dieser Verordnung.
(2) Die Gebühren werden nach dem anliegenden Besonderen Gebührenverzeichnis für das Landesarchiv (GebVerzLArch) erhoben.
(3) Als Auslagen werden die Aufwendungen für Porto, Verpackung, Wertsendungen, Nachnahmeverfahren, Einschreib- und Eilsendungen sowie für spezielle Materialien erhoben.
(4) Das Landesarchiv kann eine Vorauszahlung der Gebühren und Auslagen verlangen.

§ 2 Kostenschuldner/Kostenschuldnerin
(1) Schuldner oder Schuldnerin der Gebühren und Auslagen ist derjenige oder diejenige,
1. der oder die die Einrichtung in Anspruch nimmt,
2. in dessen oder deren Interesse die Inanspruchnahme erfolgt oder
3. der oder die die Schuld gegenüber der Einrichtung schriftlich übernimmt.

(2) Mehrere Schuldner oder Schuldnerinnen haften als Gesamtschuldner oder Gesamtschuldnerinnen.

§ 3 Gebührenbefreiung
(1) In den Fällen der Nummern 1, 2.1 und 5.1 des Besonderen Gebührenverzeichnisses kann von der Erhebung der Gebühr bei wissenschaftlichen, heimatkundlichen und familiengeschichtlichen Forschungen abgesehen werden, wenn deren Ergebnisse allgemein verbreitet und gewerbsmäßige Zwecke damit nicht verfolgt werden. § 3 des Gesetzes über die Erhebung von Verwaltungs- und Benutzungsgebühren im Saarland bleibt unberührt.
(2) Im Einzelfall kann von der Gebührenerhebung für Projekte abgesehen werden, die dem Landesarchiv unmittelbar dienen. Bei Gemeinschaftsprojekten des Landesarchivs mit anderen Trägern werden keine Gebühren erhoben.

§ 4 In-Kraft-Treten
Diese Verordnung tritt am Tage nach ihrer Verkündung in Kraft.

Anlage (zu § 1 Abs. 2)
Besonderes Gebührenverzeichnis für das Landesarchiv (GebVerzLArch)
in der Fassung vom 7. Dezember 2010

Nr.	Gegenstand	Gebühren in Euro
1	**Benutzung im Landesarchiv** Benutzung von Findmitteln, Archivalien und Bibliotheksgut im Benutzersaal des Landesarchivs	
	für 1 Tag	2,50
	für 1 Woche	10,50
	für 1 Monat	25,00
2	**Schriftliche Auskünfte**	
2.1	Schriftliche Fachauskünfte, die Ermittlung und Einsichtnahme in Archivalien erfordern, einschließlich Ermittlung von Vorlagen bei Bestellungen von Kopien, je angefangene halbe Stunde Arbeitszeit	28,00
2.2	Anfertigung von Gutachten, je angefangene halbe Stunde	38,00
2.3	Anfertigung von Abschriften und Auszügen aus Archivgut, Übertragungen in moderne Schrift und Übersetzungen, je angefangene halbe Stunde	38,00
3	**Ausleihe von Archivgut**	
	Ausleihe von Archivalien zur auswärtigen Benutzung, pro Sendung zuzüglich Versandauslagen	10,00
4	**Anfertigung von Reproduktionen** (Gebühren zzgl. Porto und Verpackungskosten)	
4.1	Mindestgebühr für reprografische Leistungen (außer Papierkopien bei Barzahlung und Selbstabholung)	5,00
4.2	Anfertigung von Fotokopien (Normalkopierer), Schwarzweiß-Buchscanner-Kopien, Rückvergrößerungen von 35 mm-Mikrofilm und von anderen Filmformen mittels Reader-Printer oder Computerausdrucke, je Seite	
	DIN A4	0,25
	DIN A3	0,35
4.3	Farbkopien, Farbausdrucke auf Normalpapier, je Seite	
	DIN A4	2,50
	DIN A3	4,00
4.4	Anfertigung von schwarz-weiß Mikrofilmaufnahmen (Schrittschaltkamera, 35 mm-Mikrofilm)	
	je Aufnahme (bis 2 Vorlagenseiten)	0,40
4.5	Digitale Reproduktionen in Druckqualität, je Datei, bei einer Vorlagengröße	
	bis DIN A3	2,00
	über DIN A3	5,00
4.6	Scan vom schwarz-weiß Mikrofilm oder Mikrofiche in Graustufen, 300 dpi je Datei (= Seite)	0,35
4.7	Bearbeitungsgebühr für Verwaltungsaufwand im Falle einer Auftragsvergabe an externe Dienstleister (zuzüglich zu deren Herstellungskosten)	10,00
	Für Schüler, Auszubildende und Studierende ermäßigen sich die Gebühren 4.2 bis 4.6 um 50 %.	
5	**Nutzung von Archivalienreproduktionen**	
5.1	Publikationen im Druck oder auf elektronischen Speichermedien (CD-ROM) je Reproduktion bei einer Auflage	
	bis 1000 Exemplare	25,00
	über 1000 Exemplare	30,00
	Bei Nachdrucken, Neuauflagen etc. ermäßigen sich die Gebühren um die Hälfte. Bei gleichzeitiger Publikation im Druck und auf CD-ROM wird ein Nachlass von 50 % auf die Gebühr für die gedruckte Ausgabe gewährt. Die Gebühren beziehen sich nur auf die Wiedergabe einzelner Archivalienreproduktionen. Bei Veröffentlichungen, die überwiegend Reproduktionen von Archivalien des Landesarchivs vorsehen, wird die Gebühr besonders festgesetzt.	

D12.II.1c Verordnung Gebührenverzeichnis Landesarchiv

Nr.	Gegenstand	Gebühren in Euro
5.2	Audiovisuelle Nutzung einmalige Wiedergabe, je Reproduktion, je angefangene 30 Sek. Bei Wiederholungen ermäßigt sich die Gebühr um die Hälfte. Einblendung in Online-Dienste, je Reproduktion je Woche je Monat je Vierteljahr	100,00 25,00 35,00 75,00

Richtlinie für die Gewährung von Zuwendungen des Landes aus Mitteln der Denkmalpflege zur Erhaltung und Instandsetzung von Kulturdenkmälern (Denkmalförderrichtlinie - DFRL -)

Vom 15. April 2002 (GMBl. S. 279), geändert durch 3. VwV v. 13.5.2008

1. Zuwendungszweck, Rechtsgrundlage

Das Land gewährt nach Maßgabe dieser Richtlinie und der Verwaltungsvorschriften zu § 44 LHO Zuwendungen zur Erhaltung und Instandsetzung von Kulturdenkmälern. Mit diesen Zuwendungen trägt das Land zu den Ausgaben der Erhaltung und Instandsetzung von Kulturdenkmälern nach § 1 Abs. 4 SDschG bei.

Ziel ist es, Kulturdenkmäler gemäß § 1 SDSchG als Zeugnisse menschlicher Geschichte und örtlicher Eigenart zu erhalten; insbesondere soll ihr Zustand gepflegt und ggf. wiederhergestellt werden. Erforderlichenfalls sind Kulturdenkmäler zu bergen.

Ein Anspruch des Antragstellers auf Gewährung der Zuwendung besteht nicht, vielmehr entscheidet das Ministerium für Umwelt als Bewilligungsbehörde im Rahmen der verfügbaren Haushaltsmittel auf Grund seines pflichtgemäßen Ermessens.

2. Gegenstand der Förderung

2.1 Gefördert werden Maßnahmen, die unmittelbar dazu dienen, Kulturdenkmäler im Sinne des § 2 Abs. 1 SDschG denkmalgerecht zu erhalten oder instand zu setzen (denkmalbezogene Maßnahmen), soweit sie den Bestimmungen des Denkmalschutzes unterliegen.
Hierzu zählen u.a.:
- a) bauliche Aufwendungen an charakteristischen Bauteilen wie Fassaden, Dachdeckungen, Gewölben, Decken, Fußböden, Fenster, Türen und Treppen,
- b) Aufwendungen, die sich aus der Anwendung besonderer Materialien ergeben, wie z. B. Edelhölzer, Kupfer, sonderformatige Steine bzw. aus der Anwendung historisch bedingter Handwerkstechniken,
- c) Konservierung und Restaurierung an Werken der architekturbezogenen Kunst und beweglichen denkmalwerten Ausstattung,
- d) Rekonstruktion archäologischer Objekte,
- e) Leistungen zur Sicherung wirtschaftlich nicht genutzter Denkmale, wie z. B. Mahnmale, Standbilder, Kleinarchitektur, Stadtmauern, Ruinen usw.,
- f) Notsicherung stark gefährdeter Objekte oder gefährdeter sichtbarer Bodendenkmale,
- g) Maßnahmen zum Schutz von Denkmalen vor Witterungseinflüssen, fremdem Zutritt und Zugriff (Überdachung, Schaffung von Räumlichkeiten zur Unterbringung von Denkmalen, insbesondere Kleinarchitektur, geschützte Ausstattung, Geräte, Maschinen usw.),
- h) Regenerierungsmaßnahmen am objekttypischen Pflanzenbestand im Interesse der Erhaltung und Wiederherstellung von Denkmalen der Landschafts- und Gartengestaltung und
- i) die Pflege und Kultivierung von historischen Parkanlagen,
- j) Aufmaße, Dokumentationen, Prospektionen u.ä.

Nicht gefördert werden Maßnahmen im Sinne von Satz 1, die ausschließlich der laufenden Unterhaltung des Kulturdenkmales dienen.

2.2 Einzelne Teilmaßnahmen, Gewerke oder Bauabschnitte im Sinne der Nr. 2.1 dieser Richtlinie werden nur dann gefördert, wenn sichergestellt ist, dass auch die übrigen, nicht geförderten Maßnahmen denkmalfachlich sinnvoll sind und ein schlüssiges Gesamtkonzept mit gesicherter Finanzierung vorgelegt wird. Eine Anfinanzierung von Vorhaben, deren Finanzierung nicht gesichert ist, ist unzulässig.

2.3 Wurden an dem Kulturdenkmal Instandsetzungsarbeiten ohne oder abweichend von der Beteiligung des Landesdenkmalamtes im Sinne der Nr. 4.1 durchgeführt, so können weitere Maßnahmen nur dann gefördert werden, wenn das Kulturdenkmal in seinen früheren Zustand zurückversetzt oder auf eine andere vorgeschriebene Weise instand gesetzt wurde.

2.4 Wurde an dem Kulturdenkmal eine Maßnahme durchgeführt, die eine Ordnungswidrigkeit gem. § 20 SDSchG darstellt, können weitere Maßnahmen nur dann gefördert werden, wenn das Ord-

D12.III.1 Denkmalförderrichtlinie

nungswidrigkeitenverfahren abgeschlossen und die rechtswidrig durchgeführten Maßnahmen entsprechend der Nr. 2.3 dieser Richtlinie beseitigt sind.

3. Zuwendungsempfänger

3.1 Eine Zuwendung kann auf Antrag erhalten
 – der Eigentümer des Kulturdenkmals oder
 – ein durch Zustimmung des Eigentümers Berechtigter,

4. Zuwendungsvoraussetzungen

4.1 Voraussetzung für die Gewährung eines Zuschusses ist:
 – das Objekt muss die Voraussetzungen als Kulturdenkmal gemäß § 2 SDschG erfüllen
 – die Genehmigung der Maßnahme gem. § 8 Abs. 1 SDschG, bzw. die Vorlage eines Bauscheins gemäß § 8 Abs. 8, bzw. bei genehmigungsfreien und anzeigepflichtigen Maßnahmen gemäß § 8 Abs. 9 und 10 SDschG die Abstimmung mit dem Landesdenkmalamt,
 – die Antragstellung gem. Antragsformular vor Beginn der Maßnahme und
 – die Abnahme der Arbeiten durch das Landesdenkmalamt.

4.2 Eine Zuwendung wird nur gewährt, wenn die Zuwendung einen Betrag von 500 EUR übersteigt (Bagatellgrenze) und mit der Maßnahme nach Bestandskraft des Zuwendungsbescheides bzw. nach Erteilung der Zustimmung zum vorzeitigen Maßnahmebeginn begonnen wird.

4.3 Natürliche Personen und juristische Personen des privaten Rechts als Zuwendungsempfänger haben zur Sicherung eines etwaigen Erstattungsanspruchs des Landes bei einer Gesamtzuwendung des Landes von mehr als 25.000,00 € die Eintragung einer vorrangigen Buchgrundschuld in Höhe der Landeszuwendung zugunsten des Saarlandes zu veranlassen. Ist dies nicht möglich, sind andere, gleich geeignete Sicherheiten (z.B. Bankbürgschaft) vorzulegen. Diese Sicherheiten sind durch eine § 49 a Abs. 3 Satz 1 SVwVfG entsprechende Verzinsungsregelung zu ergänzen. Die Sicherheiten müssen bis zu einem Zeitpunkt, der mindestens 12 Jahre nach dem Termin zur Vorlage des Verwendungsnachweises liegt, gelten. Zahlungen dürfen erst erfolgen, wenn der Zuwendungsempfänger die Erfüllung dieser Auflage nachgewiesen hat.

4.4 Es können nur Kulturdenkmäler gefördert werden, deren Standort sich im Saarland befindet. Bewegliche Kulturdenkmäler können nur gefördert werden, wenn sie überwiegend im Saarland aufbewahrt bzw. betrieben werden.

4.5 Jedes Denkmal kann nur einmal je Haushaltsjahr gefördert werden.

5. Art und Umfang, Höhe der Zuwendung

5.1 Zuwendungsart
 Die Zuwendung erfolgt in Form der Projektförderung.

5.2 Finanzierungsart
 Die Zuwendung wird als Teilfinanzierung gewährt.
 Eine Vollfinanzierung durch das Land kann gewährt werden, wenn eine wirtschaftliche Nutzung des Kulturdenkmales nicht möglich ist (bei sog. Nur-Denkmälern, z.B. bei Ruinen).

5.3 Form der Zuwendung
 Die Zuwendung erfolgt grundsätzlich in Form eines Zuschusses bzw. einer Zuweisung.

5.4 Bemessungsgrundlage
 Die Gewährung der Zuwendung erfolgt aufgrund der Bedeutung des Kulturdenkmals, des Grades seiner Gefährdung (Dringlichkeit der erforderlichen Maßnahmen), des Landesinteresses an der Durchführung der Maßnahme aus denkmalfachlicher Sicht (u.a. Sicherung, unmittelbare Erhaltung), de Möglichkeit zur Inanspruchnahme anderer finanzwirksamer öffentlich-rechtlicher Vergünstigungen und nach Maßgabe der im Haushalt des Landes bereitgestellten Haushaltsmittel (Ermessenskriterien). Die zuwendungsfähigen Ausgaben werden ermittelt auf der Grundlage eines Kostenvoranschlages oder der/des günstigsten Leistungsangebote/s.

5.4.1 Fördersatz
 a) Der Fördersatz bei Zuwendungen für Kulturdenkmäler, die auch aus Denkmalpflegemitteln des Bundes oder anderer überregionaler Mittelgeber gefördert werden (Projekte von nationaler Bedeutung) darf nicht höher sein, als der jeweilige Fördersatz der übrigen Zuwendungsgeber. Auch muss der in Nr. 5.6.2 festgelegte Eigenanteil erbracht werden.

b) Die Verteilung der Mittel erfolgt für die Groß- und Kleinprojekte (Nr. 7.1.2 b)) jeweils nach einem linearen Fördersatz auf der Basis der zuwendungsfähigen Aufwendungen (denkmalbedingte Kosten). Die Höhe des jeweiligen Zuschusses richtet sich nach den im Landeshaushalt jeweils verfügbaren Haushaltsmittel und der Anzahl der förderfähigen Anträge, jedoch maximal 50 v. H. der zuwendungsfähigen Ausgaben. Die Bewilligungsbehörde teilt jedes Jahr nach dem in Nr. 7.1.1 vorgegebenen spätesten Antragstermin 01. März dem Landesdenkmalamt die Grenzwerte der zuwendungsfähigen Ausgaben für Groß- und Kleinprojekte sowie die Aufteilung der vorhandenen Haushaltsmittel auf die Groß- und Kleinprojekte mit. Auf dieser Grundlage erstellt das Landesdenkmalamt je einen Maßnahmenplan für die Groß- und Kleinprojekte.

c) Eine Förderung bis zu 100 v. H. der zuwendungsfähigen Ausgaben ist in Einzelfällen zulässig, wenn
- der Zuwendungsempfänger an der Erfüllung des Zwecks kein oder ein nur geringes wirtschaftliches Interesse hat, das gegenüber dem Landesinteresse nicht ins Gewicht fällt,
- die Erfüllung des Zwecks in dem notwendigen Umfang nur bei Übernahme sämtlicher zuwendungsfähiger Ausgaben durch das Land möglich ist,
- das Denkmal nicht gewerblich oder zur Gewinnerzielung genutzt wird,
- der Antragsteller nachweist, dass er nicht über die zum Erhalt des Kulturdenkmales erforderlichen Eigenmittel verfügt und diese auch nicht in Eigenleistung erbringen kann,
- nur dadurch der Erhalt des Kulturdenkmales gewährleistet werden kann und ein besonderes Landesinteresse an der Erhaltung des Kulturdenkmales besteht.

5.5 Zuwendungsfähige Ausgaben

5.5.1 Zuwendungsfähig sind nur solche Ausgaben, die unter Anlegung eines strengen Maßstabes bei einer sparsamen, zweckmäßigen und wirtschaftlichen Durchführung denkmalbezogener Maßnahmen entstehen (denkmalbezogene Ausgaben). Hierzu können auch solche Aufwendungen zählen, durch die ein Kulturdenkmal wieder seiner ursprünglichen Nutzung zugeführt werden kann oder durch die eine ersatzweise Nutzung mit weitgehender Erhaltung seiner Substanz und Eigenart auf Dauer ermöglicht wird.

Neben Aufwendungen an Kulturdenkmälern zählen hierzu auch Aufwendungen für Maßnahmen
- im Bereich eines Denkmalschutzgebietes nach § 2 Abs 6 SDSchG und
- in der Umgebung eines Kulturdenkmales von besonderer Bedeutung, soweit sie den Bestimmungen des Denkmalschutzes unterliegen,
- der Bauaufnahme, einer statischen Untersuchung, Studie, Dokumentation oder eines sonstigen Gutachtens (einschließlich der Ausgaben, die sich aus der Nutzung der dafür notwendigen Hilfsmittel und Geräte ergeben), wenn diese auf Verlangen der Denkmalschutzbehörden anzufertigen sind und in einem unmittelbaren zeitlichen und sachlichen Bezug zu denkmalbezogenen Maßnahmen baulicher Art stehen,
- zur Wiederherstellung von teilzerstörten Kulturdenkmälern, wenn hierbei die ursprüngliche Substanz erhalten und gesichert wird, sowie Aufwendungen für rekonstruierende Wiederherstellungen - soweit es sich um untergegangene, aber für den Gesamtzusammenhang des Kulturdenkmals unverzichtbare Teile handelt -, durch die ein noch bestehendes Kulturdenkmal ergänzt wird. Voraussetzung ist, dass der Umfang der Wiederherstellung im Verhältnis zum Umfang der noch vorhandenen Teile des Kulturdenkmales gering ist. Der Bedarf ist eingehend zu begründen.

Zu den zuwendungsfähigen Ausgaben gehören auch die
- Gerüstausgaben einer restauratorischen Untersuchung sowie
- Architekten- und Ingenieurhonorare bis max. 20 v.H. der sonstigen zuwendungsfähigen Ausgaben.

Die Umsatzsteuer zählt nur dann zu den zuwendungsfähigen Ausgaben, wenn der Zuwendungsempfänger nicht zum Vorsteuerabzug berechtigt ist.

D12.III.1 Denkmalförderrichtlinie

Nicht zuwendungsfähig sind die Ausgaben für gesetzlich vorgeschriebene Genehmigungen und den Erwerb eines Kulturdenkmales sowie Ausgaben für die Beseitigung nicht denkmalgerechter Arbeiten. Grundlage für die Festsetzung der zuwendungsfähigen Ausgaben ist die Anlage 6 (Nichtzuwendungsfähige Kosten bei Hochbaumaßnahmen) der VV zu § 44 LHO.

5.5.2 Anerkennung von Eigenleistungen
Eigenleistungen sind nur in Höhe der nachgewiesenen Materialausgaben zuwendungsfähig.

5.6 Mehrfachförderung

5.6.1 Der Zuwendungsempfänger hat einen Eigenanteil von mindestens 25 v.H. der zuwendungsfähigen Ausgaben zu erbringen. Auf die Erbringung eines Eigenanteiles kann in den Fällen der Nr. 5.4.1 c) ganz oder teilweise verzichtet werden.

5.6.2 Werden auch Zuwendungen von Dritten oder aus anderen Förderprogrammen des Landes gewährt, so verringert sich die Zuwendung
 – bei einer Anteilfinanzierung anteilig mit etwaigen Zuwendungen anderer Zuwendungsgeber und den vorgesehenen eigenen und sonstigen Mitteln des Zuwendungsempfängers,
 – bei einer Vollfinanzierung um den vollen in Betracht kommenden Betrag.
Dies gilt (mit Ausnahme der Vollfinanzierung) nur, wenn sich der Eigenanteil des Zuwendungsempfängers auf weniger als 25 v.H. der zuwendungsfähigen Ausgaben reduzieren würde (Nr. 5.6.1).
Die öffentlichen Mittel dürfen insgesamt die zuwendungsfähigen Ausgaben nicht übersteigen. Im Übrigen gilt Nr. 2 ANBest-P/ANBest-P-GK.

5.6.3 Ist eine Kirchengemeinde Zuwendungsempfängerin, so gelten von dem zuständigen Bistum bzw. der zuständigen Landeskirche bereitgestellte Mittel als Eigenmittel der Kirchengemeinde.

6. Sonstige Zuwendungsbestimmungen

6.1 Die Zuwendung wird anteilig gekürzt, wenn eine Teilmaßnahme ohne Zustimmung nach Nr. 6.3 nicht ausgeführt wird.

6.2 Können nicht durch den Zuwendungsempfänger zu vertretende Ausgabensteigerungen bei einzelnen Gewerken oder Teilmaßnahmen nicht durch Einsparungen bei anderen Gewerken oder Teilmaßnahmen ausgeglichen werden, so kann mit vorheriger Zustimmung der Bewilligungsbehörde auf die Ausführung einzelner Teilmaßnahmen oder Gewerke verzichtet werden, soweit hiergegen keine denkmalfachlichen Bedenken bestehen.

6.3 Ansprüche, die sich aus der Zuwendung ergeben, sind, soweit im Zuwendungsbescheid nicht ausdrücklich etwas anderes bestimmt ist, nicht auf Dritte übertragbar.

6.4 Der Zuwendungsempfänger hat innerhalb eines Zeitraumes von 10 Jahren, gerechnet vom Eingangsdatum des Verwendungsnachweises beim Ministerium für Umwelt, jede bauliche und sonstige Veränderung an dem geförderten Kulturdenkmal vorab von der Bewilligungsbehörde genehmigen zu lassen. Werden innerhalb dieses Zeitraumes ohne diese Genehmigung andere Maßnahmen an dem geförderten Kulturdenkmal durchgeführt, kann der Zuwendungsbescheid mit Wirkung für die Vergangenheit widerrufen werden. Der Zuwendungsbescheid soll mit Wirkung für die Vergangenheit widerrufen werden, wenn sich die Veränderung auf geförderte Teile des Kulturdenkmals erstreckt und hierfür eine denkmalrechtliche Erlaubnis gemäß § 8 SDSchG nicht erteilt wurde und aus denkmalfachlicher Sicht nicht erteilt werden kann.

6.5 Bei einer Übertragung des Eigentums an
 – dem geförderten Kulturdenkmal innerhalb eines Zeitraumes von 10 Jahren, gerechnet vom Eingangsdatum des Verwendungsnachweises beim Ministerium für Umwelt,
 – geförderten technischen Einrichtungen, Einrichtungsgegenständen, Geräten und Maschinen innerhalb eines Zeitraumes von 5 Jahren, gerechnet vom Eingangsdatum des Verwendungsnachweises beim Ministerium für Umwelt,
müssen vom Erwerber die mit der Zuwendung verbundenen Verpflichtungen übernommen werden (z.B. durch Festschreibung im notariellen Kaufvertrag). Die Übertragung des Eigentums ist der Bewilligungsbehörde unverzüglich anzuzeigen. Erfolgt eine Eigentumsübertragung ohne entsprechende vertragliche Verpflichtung des Neueigentümers, so kann der Zuwendungsempfänger zur Rückzahlung der Zuwendung und zum Wertausgleich verpflichtet werden.

6.7 Mit Hilfe der Zuwendungen erworbene oder hergestellte Gegenstände sind für die Dauer von 5 Jahren gerechnet vom Eingangsdatum des Verwendungsnachweises beim Ministerium für Umwelt, dem Zuwendungszweck entsprechend einzusetzen. Ist ein zweckentsprechender Einsatz nicht mehr möglich, so ist der Restwert dem Ministerium für Umwelt anteilig zu erstatten.

7. Verfahren

7.1.1 Antragsverfahren

Der vollständige Zuwendungsantrag ist bis spätestens 1. März des Jahres vor Beginn der Maßnahme (Antragsjahr) beim Ministerium für Umwelt –Referat A/4- zu stellen. Maßgebend ist der Posteingang beim Ministerium für Umwelt (Datum des Eingangsstempels). Der Antrag ist in zweifacher Ausfertigung zu stellen. Beide Ausfertigungen sind mit einer Originalunterschrift des Antragstellers zu versehen. Dem Antrag sind beizufügen:
- ein Maßnahmenkatalog,
- die Genehmigung der Maßnahme (§ 8 Abs. 1 SDSchG), bzw. die Vorlage eines Bauscheins (§ 8 Abs. 8 SDSchG), bzw. bei genehmigungsfreien und anzeigepflichtigen Maßnahmen (§ 8 Abs. 9 und 10 SDSchG) die Abstimmung mit dem Landesdenkmalamt,
- gewerkebezogene Kostenanschläge,
- eine Vollmacht des Eigentümers zur Druchführung der Maßnahme, falls der Antragsteller nicht selbst Eigentümer ist,
- Gegebenenfalls eine Haushaltsunterlage bau (HU-Bau), sofern die Betragsgrenze nach Nummer 6.2 VV zu § 44 LHO/VV-P-GK (derzeit 250.000.-€ bzw. 375.000,-€) überschritten wird.

7.1.2 Das Landesdenkmalamt erstellt aufgrund der zur Bewilligung vorgesehenen Anträge nach Maßgabe der verfügbaren Haushaltsmittel und unter Berücksichtigung der Ermessenskriterien möglichst bis zum 30. April des Antragsjahres einen Maßnahmenkatalog.

Dieser enthält
- alle Maßnahmen, die auch durch den Bund oder andere bedeutende Mittelgeber gefördert werden (Großprojekte von nationaler Bedeutung),
- eine Liste der Großprojekte sowie eine Liste der Kleinprojekte und
- Maßnahmen von besonderem Landesinteresse

unter Angabe
- der voraussichtlichen zuwendungsfähigen Ausgaben
- der sich ergebenden Zuwendungshöhe.

Nach der Entscheidung über die zu fördernden Maßnahmen übersendet das Landesdenkmalamt bis spätestens 31. Mai des jeweiligen Jahres dem Referat A/4 die zur Erstellung der Zuwendungsbescheide erforderlichen Prüfberichte.

7.2 Zustimmung zum vorzeitigen Maßnahmenbeginn

Die Bewilligungsbehörde kann auf Antrag für Maßnahmen, die aus dringenden sachlichen oder wirtschaftlichen Gründen keinen Aufschub bis zum Erlass des Zuwendungsbescheides dulden, die Zustimmung zum vorzeitigen Maßnahmenbeginn erteilen. Die Zustimmung muss in diesem Fall schriftlich erfolgen.

7.3 Bewilligungsverfahren

Die Zuwendungsbescheide werden den Zuwendungsempfängern im Zeitraum 01. Juni bis 15. Juli zugestellt.

7.4 Anforderungs- und Auszahlungsverfahren

7.4.1 Die Maßnahme ist bis zum 31. Januar des auf das Antragsjahr folgenden Jahres abzuschließen (Bewilligungszeitraum). Sind Teilzahlungen nach Nr. 7.4 möglich, erlischt der Anspruch des Zuwendungsempfängers auf nicht innerhalb des Bewilligungszeitraumes abgerufene Mittel mit Ausnahme des Sicherheitseinbehalts in Höhe von 5 v. H. der Zuwendung. Die Bewilligungsbehörde kann den Bewilligungszeitraum in begründeten Fällen auf schriftlichen Antrag einmalig bis zum 30. Juni des auf das Antragsjahr folgenden Jahres verlängern.

7.4.2 Die Auszahlung erfolge grundsätzlich nach Abschluss der Maßnahme und Prüfung des Verwendungsnachweises.

7.4.3 Das Ministerium für Umwelt –Referat A/4- kann als zusätzliche Sicherheit im Rahmen der Nr. 7 VV zu § 44 LHO / VV-P-GK und Nr. 1 ANBest-P / ANBest-P-GK die Teilzahlungen auf 95 v.H. der Zuwendung begrenzen und die Auszahlung des Restbetrages von der Vorlage und Prüfung des Verwendungsnachweises abhängig machen.

D12.III.1 Denkmalförderrichtlinie

7.5 Verwendungsnachweisverfahren

7.5.1 Der Verwendungsnachweis ist bis spätestens 30. April (bei Verlängerung des Bewilligungszeitraumes nach Nr. 7.4.1 bis spätestens 30. September) des beim Antragsjahr folgenden Jahres bei der Bewilligungsbehörde einzureichen. Dabei sind Originalbelege gewerkebezogen geordnet sowie ein Zahlungsnachweis beizufügen. Der Zuwendungsempfänger muss schriftlich erklären, dass die angegebenen zuwendungsfähigen Ausgaben tatsächlich entstanden sind. Erfolgt die Vorlage des Verwendungsnachweises nicht fristgerecht, erlischt der Zuwendungsbescheid in allen seinen Rechtswirkungen (Verfristung). In diesem Fall sind evtl. bereits ausgezahlte Zuwendungen zurückzufordern.

7.5.2 Das Landesdenkmalamt prüft, ob der Verwendungsnachweis auch aus fachlicher Sicht vollständig ist, die im Zuwendungsbescheid festgesetzten zuwendungsfähigen Ausgaben tatsächlich in der angegebenen Höhe entstanden sind, der zahlenmäßige Nachweis sachlich und rechnerisch richtig ist, die Maßnahme im vollen der Bewilligung zugrunde liegenden Umfang denkmalgerecht durchgeführt, die Zuwendung zweckentsprechend verwendet, der genehmigte Ausgabenplan eingehalten und die Maßnahme nicht unerlaubt vorzeitig begonnen wurde sowie ob Auflagen und andere Nebenbestimmungen eingehalten wurden, der Zuwendungszweck insgesamt erreicht wurde und die Förderung auch nachträglich gerechtfertigt ist. Hierbei genügt eine Prüfung des zahlenmäßigen Nachweises, einschließlich einer Überprüfung der eingereichten Belege. Die Maßnahmenausführung ist vor Ort zu prüfen. Das Landesdenkmalamt setzt die tatsächlich zuwendungsfähigen Ausgaben fest. Wurden Teilzahlungen gewährt, prüft das Landesdenkmalamt auch die rechtzeitige zweckentsprechende Verwendung der ausgezahlten Mittel.

7.5.3 Verwendungsnachweise von Gebietskörperschaften und deren Zusammenschlüssen werden regelmäßig nur darauf geprüft, ob sie vollständig sind, offensichtliche Unrichtigkeiten ersichtlich sind oder sich aus den Angaben im Verwendungsnachweis Anhaltspunkte für Unregelmäßigkeiten ergeben. Eine vollständige Prüfung (ggfls. mit Einsichtnahme in Bücher, Belege usw.) braucht nur in Einzelfällen zu erfolgen. Das Ministerium für Umwelt ist jedoch jederzeit hierzu berechtigt. Die Verantwortung für die sachliche und rechnerische Richtigkeit und Vollständigkeit der Angaben im Verwendungsnachweis liegt beim Zuwendungsempfänger bzw. den dort verantwortlichen Personen. Die sachliche und rechnerische Richtigkeit der Angaben im Verwendungsnachweis im Sinne der Nrn. 12 bis 15 VV zu § 70 LHO ist vom Zuwendungsempfänger festzustellen.

7.5.4 Nach Abschluss seiner Prüfung erstellt das Landesdenkmalamt einen Prüfvermerk. 7.5.5 Übersteigen die tatsächlich zuwendungsfähigen Ausgaben den im Zuwendungsbescheid festgesetzten Betrag, so bleibt die Zuwendung unverändert.

7.5.6 Unterschreiten die tatsächlich zuwendungsfähigen Ausgaben den im Zuwendungsbescheid festgesetzten Betrag, so wird die Zuwendung gemäß Nr. 2.1 ANBest-P/ANBest-P-GK dem sich aus dem Zuwendungsbescheid ergebenden Fördersatz entsprechend festgesetzt. Im Falle einer Festbetragsfinanzierung gilt Nr. 2.4 ANBest-P/ANBest-P-GK.

7.5.7 Ein Änderungs- oder Abrechnungsbescheid ergeht nur dann, wenn das Ergebnis der Verwendungsnachweisprüfung von den Festsetzungen des Zuwendungsbescheides abweicht und dies eine Änderung des Zuwendungsbescheides erforderlich macht. In allen anderen Fällen gilt die Schlusszahlung als Abrechnung und Abschluss des Zuwendungsverfahrens.
In den Fällen der Nr. 7.5.6 ergeht grundsätzlich kein Änderungs- oder Abrechnungsbescheid. Entspricht der vom Landesdenkmalamt nach Nr. 7.5.2. und Nr. 7.5.5 ermittelte Betrag der tatsächlich zuwendungsfähigen Ausgaben dem vom Zuwendungsempfänger im Verwendungsnachweis angegebenen Betrag, so findet Nr. 2.1 ANBest-P / ANBest-P-GK unmittelbare Anwendung, sofern nicht ausdrücklich etwas anderes bestimmt wird. Es ergeht dann auch in Fällen der Nr. 7.5.7 kein Änderungs- oder Abrechnungsbescheid. Nr. 2.3 ANBest-P findet dann keine Anwendung.

7.6 Zu beachtende Vorschriften
Für die Bewilligung, Auszahlung und Abrechnung der Zuwendung sowie für den Nachweis und die Prüfung der Verwendung und die ggf. erforderliche Aufhebung des Zuwendungsbe-

scheides und die Rückforderung der gewährten Zuwendung gelten die VV / VV-P-GK zu § 44 LHO, soweit nicht in dieser Förderrichtlinie Abweichungen zugelassen sind.

8. Schluss- und Übergangsbestimmungen

Diese Förderrichtlinie tritt am 01. Januar 2002 in Kraft. Sie ist auch für bereits vorliegende Anträge anzuwenden.

Gesetz über die Stiftung Saarländischer Kulturbesitz (SSKG)
Vom 24. April 2013 (Amtsbl. I S. 108)

Der Landtag hat folgendes Gesetz beschlossen, das hiermit verkündet wird:

§ 1 Name, Rechtsform und Sitz der Stiftung
¹Die Stiftung Saarländischer Kulturbesitz ist eine rechtsfähige Stiftung des öffentlichen Rechts. ²Sie hat ihren Sitz in Saarbrücken.

§ 2 Stiftungszweck
(1) Die Stiftung Saarländischer Kulturbesitz fördert Kunst und Kultur, Bildung, Wissenschaft und Forschung, indem sie insbesondere die ihr übertragenen Kunst- und Kulturgüter bewahrt und pflegt sowie der Allgemeinheit zugänglich und nutzbar macht.
(2) ¹Die Stiftung verwirklicht ihren Zweck in erster Linie durch den Betrieb eigener Museen und vergleichbarer Einrichtungen. ²Sie ist berechtigt, den Betrieb anderer Museen, Ausstellungsgalerien oder Kultureinrichtungen zu übernehmen oder mit solchen Einrichtungen zu kooperieren.
(3) ¹Die Stiftung führt Dauer- und Sonderausstellungen mit eigenen Exponaten oder Leihgaben durch. ²Durch eine zeitgemäße Kunstvermittlung kommuniziert die Stiftung die Inhalte ihrer Sammlungen und Sonderausstellungen. ³Hierzu zählen Vorträge, Workshops und museumspädagogische Projekte.
(4) Die Stiftung kann im Rahmen ihres Museumsbetriebes Ausstellungskataloge sowie Monographien und Publikationen herausgeben.
(5) ¹Die Stiftung erfasst, beschreibt und erforscht die ihr anvertrauten Kunst- und Kulturgüter sowie deren kunsthistorischen Kontext. ²Die Einrichtungen der Stiftung stehen sowohl für interne als auch externe Forschungen zur Verfügung, auch in Kooperation mit anderen Institutionen und Einrichtungen.
(6) Die Stiftung ist berechtigt, Kunst- und Kulturgüter zu erwerben oder als Zuwendungen Dritter anzunehmen.
(7) Die Stiftung kann zur Erfüllung ihrer Aufgaben eigene Gesellschaften errichten oder sich an Gesellschaften beteiligen.

§ 3 Gemeinnützigkeit
(1) ¹Die Stiftung verfolgt ausschließlich und unmittelbar gemeinnützige Zwecke im Sinne des Abschnitts „Steuerbegünstigte Zwecke" der Abgabenordnung. ²Der Vorstand ist verpflichtet, die Gemeinnützigkeit regelmäßig in Abstimmung mit dem zuständigen Finanzamt zu überprüfen und sicherzustellen. ³Die Stiftung ist selbstlos tätig und verfolgt nicht in erster Linie eigenwirtschaftliche Zwecke.
(2) ¹Mittel der Stiftung dürfen nur für die satzungsmäßigen Zwecke verwendet werden. ²Das Saarland als Stifter erhält keine Zuwendungen aus Mitteln der Stiftung.
(3) Es darf keine Person durch Ausgaben, die dem Zweck der Stiftung fremd sind, oder durch unverhältnismäßig hohe Vergütungen begünstigt werden.

§ 4 Stiftungsvermögen
(1) Das Stiftungsvermögen besteht aus stiftungseigenen Museen, Liegenschaften, Kunst- und Kulturgütern sowie sonstigem Vermögen.
(2) Die Stiftung ist berechtigt, Zustiftungen anzunehmen.
(3) Vermögensumschichtungen sind zulässig.

§ 5 Finanzierung
(1) Die Stiftung finanziert sich aus eigenen Mitteln, Zuschüssen und Spenden sowie aus Zuwendungen des Landes nach Maßgabe des Haushaltsgesetzes.
(2) Die Zuwendungen des Landes in Form institutioneller Förderungen und Projektförderungen sind nach Maßgabe der haushaltsrechtlichen Vorschriften zu verwenden.
(3) ¹Die Stiftung ist berechtigt, Zuwendungen, Spenden (Geld- oder Sachleistungen) und Zuwendungen von Todes wegen anzunehmen. ²Diese Leistungen sind unter Berücksichtigung etwaiger von der oder dem Zuwendenden getroffener Auflagen zur Erfüllung des Stiftungszwecks zu verwenden.

§ 6 Organe
(1) Organe der Stiftung sind
1. das Kuratorium und
2. der Vorstand.

(2) Zur Beratung der Organe wird ein Beirat gebildet.

(3) ¹Bei der Erfüllung ihrer Aufgaben haben die Mitglieder der Organe die Grundsätze der Sparsamkeit und Wirtschaftlichkeit zu beachten. ²Die einschlägigen Vorschriften der Landeshaushaltsordnung sind entsprechend anzuwenden.

(4) ¹Eine gleichzeitige, stimmberechtigte Mitgliedschaft in beiden Organen ist nicht möglich. ²Vertreterinnen und Vertreter des Ministeriums für Finanzen und Europa und des Ministeriums für Inneres und Sport können weder Mitglieder in den Organen noch im Beirat sein.

(5) ¹Die Mitglieder des Kuratoriums und des Beirates sind ehrenamtlich tätig. ²Die Zahlung von pauschalen Vergütungen für Arbeits- und Zeitaufwand (Tätigkeitsvergütungen) ist in angemessener Höhe zulässig. ³Sie bedarf einer Regelung in der Satzung.

(6) ¹Für Mitglieder der Organe und des Beirates gilt das Saarländische Reisekostengesetz entsprechend. ²Das Nähere regelt eine vom Kuratorium zu erlassende Reisekosten- und Spesenordnung. ³Die Erstattung von Auslagen im Übrigen bedarf einer Regelung in der Satzung.

(7) Die Haftung der Kuratoriums- und Beiratsmitglieder gegenüber der Stiftung ist auf Vorsatz und grobe Fahrlässigkeit beschränkt.

§ 7 Zusammensetzung, Berufung und Amtszeit des Kuratoriums
(1) ¹Die Ministerin oder der Minister für Bildung und Kultur ist Vorsitzende bzw. Vorsitzender des Kuratoriums (Kuratorin bzw. Kurator). ²Darüber hinaus gehören dem Kuratorium an:
1. die Stellvertreterin oder der Stellvertreter der Kuratorin bzw. des Kurators,
2. mindestens neun und höchstens zwölf weitere Mitglieder.

³Im Kuratorium sollen Personen mit kunst- oder kulturwissenschaftlichem und ökonomischem Hintergrund in einem ausgewogenen Verhältnis vertreten sein. ⁴Mitglieder des Kuratoriums dürfen nicht im Dienst der Stiftung stehen.

(2) ¹Die Stellvertreterin oder der Stellvertreter der Kuratorin bzw. des Kurators und die weiteren Mitglieder werden auf Vorschlag der Ministerin oder des Ministers für Bildung und Kultur durch die Landesregierung für die Dauer von fünf Jahren berufen. ²Bei vorzeitigem Ausscheiden kann für den Rest der Amtszeit eine neue Berufung erfolgen. ³Diese hat zu erfolgen, wenn anderenfalls die in Absatz 1 geregelte Mindestzahl von elf Mitgliedern unterschritten wäre. ⁴Wiederholte Berufungen sind möglich. ⁵Eine vorzeitige Abberufung aus wichtigem Grund ist zulässig.

(3) Vertreterinnen oder Vertreter des Ministeriums für Finanzen und Europa und des Ministeriums für Inneres und Sport können an den Sitzungen des Kuratoriums teilnehmen.

(4) Die oder der Vorsitzende des Beirates kann an den Sitzungen des Kuratoriums teilnehmen.

(5) Die oder der Vorsitzende des Personalrates der Stiftung kann an den Sitzungen des Kuratoriums teilnehmen.

§ 8 Aufgaben des Kuratoriums
(1) ¹Das Kuratorium beschließt über alle grundsätzlichen Fragen, die zum Aufgabenbereich der Stiftung gehören. ²Es überwacht die Tätigkeit des Vorstandes, kann ihm Weisungen erteilen und jederzeit Auskunft und Bericht sowie Vorlage der Geschäftsunterlagen verlangen.

(2) Das Kuratorium beschließt insbesondere über
1. die Errichtung von Gesellschaften (§ 2 Absatz 7),
2. den Erwerb, die Veräußerung und die Belastung von Grundstücken sowie den Neu- und Umbau von stiftungseigenen Gebäuden (§ 4),
3. die Zustimmung zu Vermögensumschichtungen betreffend Kunst- und Kulturgüter (§ 4 Absatz 3),
4. die Annahme von Zuwendungen mit Auflagen (§ 5 Absatz 3),
5. die Reisekosten- und Spesenordnung (§ 6 Absatz 6),
6. die Bestellung und Abberufung sowie die Einstellung und Entlassung des Vorstandes (§ 9),
7. die Einräumung einer Einzelvertretungsbefugnis der Vorstandsmitglieder (§ 10 Absatz 1),
8. die Zustimmung zur Geschäftsordnung des Vorstandes (§ 10 Absatz 3),

9. die Ernennung, Einstellung und Entlassung der Leiterinnen und Leiter der Stiftungseinrichtungen (§§ 10 Absatz 4, 12 Absatz 1),
10. die Satzung zum Wirtschaftsplan, den Wirtschaftsplan und den Finanzplan (§ 13 Absatz 2),
11. die Bestellung der Wirtschaftsprüferin oder des Wirtschaftsprüfers bzw. der Wirtschaftsprüfungsgesellschaft zur Prüfung des Jahresabschlusses (§ 13 Absatz 4),
12. die Feststellung des Jahresabschlusses und die Verwendung des Bilanzgewinnes (§ 13 Absatz 5),
13. die Entlastung des Vorstandes (§ 13 Absatz 5),
14. die Stiftungssatzung und deren Änderung (§ 14),
15. die Festsetzung allgemein gültiger Entgelte.

§ 9 Zusammensetzung, Bestellung und Abberufung des Vorstandes
(1) Der Vorstand besteht aus zwei Personen, einem kunst- und kulturwissenschaftlichen Vorstand und einem Verwaltungsvorstand.
(2) ¹Die Vorstandsmitglieder werden vom Kuratorium für die Dauer von höchstens 5 Jahren bestellt und erhalten entsprechend befristete Anstellungsverträge. ²Wiederholte Bestellungen und Vertragsverlängerungen sind möglich.
(3) ¹Die Amtszeit endet durch Zeitablauf oder wenn das Kuratorium das Vorstandsmitglied aus wichtigem Grund abberuft. ²Ein wichtiger Grund liegt auch vor, wenn der dem Vorstandsamt zu Grunde liegende Anstellungsvertrag endet oder eine Freistellung von der vertraglichen Leistungspflicht aus dem Anstellungsvertrag erfolgt.

§ 10 Aufgaben des Vorstandes
(1) ¹Der Vorstand führt die laufenden Geschäfte und vertritt die Stiftung gerichtlich und außergerichtlich. ²Die Vorstandsmitglieder vertreten die Stiftung gemeinsam. ³Das Kuratorium kann für festgelegte Aufgabenbereiche oder im Einzelfall Einzelvertretungsbefugnis erteilen. ⁴In Fällen des § 181 Bürgerliches Gesetzbuch wird die Stiftung durch die Kuratorin oder den Kurator und das nicht betroffene Vorstandsmitglied vertreten.
(2) Beschränkungen der Befugnisse des Vorstandes im Innenverhältnis sind vom Kuratorium in der Satzung zu regeln.
(3) Die interne Geschäftsverteilung sowie den Geschäftsgang regelt der Vorstand in einer Geschäftsordnung, die der Zustimmung des Kuratoriums bedarf.
(4) Ein Vorstandsmitglied kann auf Beschluss des Kuratoriums im Rahmen der ihm übertragenen Aufgaben zugleich eine Einrichtung der Stiftung leiten.
(5) ¹Der Vorstand nimmt in der Regel an den Sitzungen des Kuratoriums beratend teil. ²Er ist verpflichtet, das Kuratorium über alle wesentlichen Angelegenheiten zu unterrichten.

§ 11 Zusammensetzung, Bestellung und Aufgaben des Beirates
(1) ¹Der Beirat besteht aus mindestens sechs und höchstens zehn kunst- und kulturwissenschaftlich sachverständigen Mitgliedern, wobei auch landeskundliche Kompetenz vertreten sein sollte. ²Die Mitglieder werden von der Ministerin oder dem Minister für Bildung und Kultur berufen. ³Der Beirat wählt aus seiner Mitte eine Vorsitzende oder einen Vorsitzenden sowie eine Stellvertreterin oder einen Stellvertreter.
(2) ¹Die Amtszeit der Beiratsmitglieder beträgt fünf Jahre; wiederholte Berufungen sind zulässig. ²Die Mitglieder des Beirates können jederzeit aus wichtigem Grund von der Ministerin oder dem Minister für Bildung und Kultur abberufen werden. ³Scheidet ein Mitglied vorzeitig aus, kann für den Rest seiner Amtszeit ein Ersatzmitglied berufen werden.
(3) Der Beirat berät die Organe in allen den Stiftungszweck betreffenden Fragen.

§ 12 Personal
(1) ¹Die bei der Stiftung tätigen Beschäftigten sind Beschäftigte der Stiftung. ²Über Einstellung, Eingruppierung und Entlassung entscheidet der Vorstand, soweit diese Entscheidung nicht dem Kuratorium obliegt. ³Über die Ernennung, Einstellung und Entlassung der Leiterinnen und Leiter der Stiftungseinrichtungen entscheidet das Kuratorium. ⁴Der Verwaltungsvorstand ist Dienstvorgesetzter des Stiftungspersonals.
(2) ¹Auf das Personal der Stiftung sind die für die Tarifbeschäftigten des Landes jeweils geltenden Tarifverträge und sonstigen Bestimmungen entsprechend anzuwenden. ²Es gilt das Besserstellungsverbot.

§ 13 Rechnungslegung und -prüfung

(1) Das Wirtschaftsjahr der Stiftung ist das Kalenderjahr.

(2) ¹Die Stiftung hat rechtzeitig vor Beginn eines jeden Jahres, spätestens bis zum 1. Oktober, eine Satzung zum Wirtschaftsplan zu erlassen sowie einen Wirtschaftsplan und einen Finanzplan aufzustellen. ²Der Wirtschaftsplan umfasst den Investitionsplan, den Finanzplan, den Erfolgsplan und die Stellenübersicht. ³Er bildet die Grundlage für die Verwaltung aller Erträge und Aufwendungen. ⁴Teil VI (§§ 105 – 112) der Landeshaushaltsordnung ist zu beachten. ⁵Die Satzung zum Wirtschaftsplan, der Wirtschaftsplan und der Finanzplan bedürfen der Zustimmung des Ministeriums für Finanzen und Europa.

(3) ¹Die Stiftung erstellt eine mittelfristige Investitions- und Finanzplanung für fünf Jahre. ²Diese Planung ist im Zusammenhang mit der Aufstellung des Wirtschaftsplans jährlich durchzuführen. ³Sie bedarf der Zustimmung des Ministeriums für Finanzen und Europa.

(4) Der Jahresabschluss und der Lagebericht sind entsprechend den für große Kapitalgesellschaften geltenden Vorschriften des Dritten Buches des Handelsgesetzbuches aufzustellen und zu prüfen.

(5) ¹Der geprüfte Jahresabschluss und der Lagebericht sind dem Kuratorium zusammen mit dem Prüfungsbericht vorzulegen. ²Die Vorlagen und der Prüfungsbericht sind jedem Kuratoriumsmitglied auszuhändigen. ³Dem Vorstand ist vor Zuleitung Gelegenheit zur Stellungnahme zu geben. ⁴Die Jahresabschlussprüferin oder der Jahresabschlussprüfer soll an den Verhandlungen über den Jahresabschluss teilnehmen. ⁵Das Kuratorium beschließt innerhalb der ersten sechs Monate des Wirtschaftsjahres über den Jahresabschluss, die Ergebnisverwendung einschließlich der Verlustabdeckung und über die Entlastung des Vorstands für das vorangegangene Wirtschaftsjahr.

§ 14 Satzung

(1) ¹Die Stiftung gibt sich eine Satzung,¹⁾ die vom Kuratorium beschlossen wird und der Zustimmung der Landesregierung bedarf. ²Das Gleiche gilt für Änderungen der Satzung.

(2) Die Satzung regelt die nähere Ausgestaltung der Stiftung.

§ 15 Stiftungsaufsicht

Die Stiftung untersteht der Rechtsaufsicht des Ministeriums für Inneres und Sport.

§ 16 Aufhebung der Stiftung

Bei Aufhebung der Stiftung oder bei Wegfall steuerbegünstigter Zwecke fällt das Vermögen der Stiftung Saarländischer Kulturbesitz an das Land Saarland, das es ausschließlich und unmittelbar für gemeinnützige Zwecke zu verwenden hat, die dem Stiftungszweck nach § 2 nahe kommen.

§ 17 Übergangsvorschriften

(1) ¹Mit Inkrafttreten dieses Gesetzes endet die Amtszeit der amtierenden Organ- und Beiratsmitglieder. ²Die Mitglieder des Kuratoriums und des Beirats führen ihre Aufgaben fort, bis die Neubesetzung erfolgt ist.

(2) ¹Die Regelungen des § 13 Absatz 4 und 5 sind spätestens für das Wirtschaftsjahr 2014 anzuwenden. ²Für die vorangehenden Wirtschaftsjahre, letztmalig für das Wirtschaftsjahr 2013, ist die Vorlage einer von einem öffentlich bestellten Wirtschaftsprüfer, einer öffentlich bestellten Wirtschaftsprüferin oder einer anerkannten Wirtschaftsprüfungsgesellschaft geprüften Jahresrechnung zulässig.

§ 18 Inkrafttreten, Außerkrafttreten

¹Dieses Gesetz tritt am Tag nach der Verkündung²⁾ in Kraft. ²Gleichzeitig tritt das Gesetz zur Errichtung einer Stiftung Saarländischer Kulturbesitz vom 7. November 1979 (Amtsbl. S. 1005), zuletzt geändert durch Gesetz vom 27. November 2002 (Amtsbl. S. 2587), außer Kraft.

---

1) Die Satzung der Stiftung Saarländischer Kulturbesitz ist abgedruckt als Nr. D12.III.2a.
2) Verkündet am 16.5.2013.

Satzung der Stiftung Saarländischer Kulturbesitz
Vom 31. Mai 2016 (Amtsbl. I S. 497)

Aufgrund des § 14 des Gesetzes über die Stiftung Saarländischer Kulturbesitz vom 24. April 2013 (Amtsbl. S. 108), nachfolgend Stiftungsgesetz, gibt sich die Stiftung folgende Satzung:

§ 1 Stiftungszweck, Aufgaben
(1) Die Stiftung Saarländischer Kulturbesitz, nachfolgend Stiftung, hat den gesetzlichen Zweck, Kunst und Kultur, Bildung, Wissenschaft und Forschung zu fördern, indem sie insbesondere die ihr übertragenen Kunst- und Kulturgüter bewahrt und pflegt sowie der Allgemeinheit zugänglich und nutzbar macht.
(2) ¹Die Stiftung führt zur Verwirklichung dieses Stiftungszwecks inhaltlich und verwaltungstechnisch folgende Museen:
1. Saarlandmuseum (Moderne Galerie und Alte Sammlung)
2. Museum für Vor- und Frühgeschichte, Römische Villa Nennig
3. Deutsches Zeitungsmuseum.

²Sie bewahrt, pflegt und ergänzt die ihr übertragenen Sammlungen.
(3) ¹Die Stiftung entwickelt ihre Sammlungen nach wissenschaftlichen und künstlerischen Kriterien kontinuierlich weiter. ²Ihre wissenschaftliche und museumspädagogische Arbeit dokumentiert die Stiftung in Publikationen. ³Mit Hilfe einer zeitgemäßen Kunstvermittlung und Öffentlichkeitsarbeit erschließt sie die Inhalte ihrer Sammlungen und Sonderausstellungen für die Öffentlichkeit. ⁴Ihre Museen, Archive und Bibliotheken bilden die Basis sowohl für die eigene Forschung als auch für die Forschungen Dritter zu den betreffenden Themen. ⁵In Verfolgung ihrer musealen und wissenschaftlichen Arbeit kooperiert die Stiftung mit anderen Institutionen, Museen und Hochschulen.

§ 2 Gemeinnützigkeit
(1) ¹Die Stiftung verfolgt ausschließlich und unmittelbar gemeinnützige Zwecke im Sinne des Abschnitts „Steuerbegünstigte Zwecke" der Abgabenordnung. ²Zweck der Stiftung ist die Förderung von Kunst und Kultur, Bildung, Wissenschaft und Forschung. ³Die Stiftung ist selbstlos tätig und verfolgt nicht in erster Linie eigenwirtschaftliche Zwecke. ⁴Der Vorstand ist verpflichtet, die Gemeinnützigkeit regelmäßig in Abstimmung mit dem zuständigen Finanzamt zu überprüfen und sicherzustellen.
(2) ¹Mittel der Stiftung dürfen nur für die satzungsmäßigen Zwecke verwendet werden. ²Das Saarland als Stifter erhält keine Zuwendungen aus Mitteln der Stiftung.
(3) Es darf keine Person durch Ausgaben, die dem Zweck der Stiftung fremd sind, oder durch unverhältnismäßig hohe Vergütungen begünstigt werden.

§ 3 Vermögen, Mittelverwendung
(1) ¹Die Stiftung ist verpflichtet, das Stiftungsvermögen im Rahmen des § 4 Stiftungsgesetz zu erhalten. ²Restitutionen im Sinne der „Gemeinsamen Erklärung der Bundesregierung, der Länder und der kommunalen Spitzenverbände zur Auffindung und Rückgabe NS-verfolgungsbedingt entzogenen Kulturgutes, insbesondere aus jüdischem Besitz" vom Dezember 1999 sind möglich.
(2) ¹Das Vermögen der Stiftung ist zu inventarisieren. ²Der Vorstand berichtet dem Kuratorium jährlich über die Aktualisierung der Inventarliste.
(3) ¹Zur Stärkung des Stiftungsvermögens und zur Kofinanzierung einzelner Vorhaben bemüht sich die Stiftung um weitere Zustiftungen und Zuwendungen. ²Zu diesem Zweck tritt der Vorstand insbesondere an potentielle Sponsorinnen und Sponsoren sowie Stifterinnen und Stifter heran und bemüht sich um Projektförderungen durch Dritte.
(4) Bei Auflösung oder Aufhebung der Stiftung oder bei Wegfall steuerbegünstigter Zwecke fällt das Vermögen der Stiftung an das Bundesland Saarland, das es ausschließlich und unmittelbar für gemeinnützige, mildtätige oder kirchliche Zwecke zu verwenden hat, die dem Stiftungszweck nach § 1 Abs. 1 nahe kommen.
(5) ¹Die Stiftung veröffentlicht über ihre Tätigkeit einen Jahresbericht, den der Vorstand vorlegt. ²Die Veröffentlichung soll zu Beginn des dritten Quartals des Folgejahres sichergestellt werden und kann auch ausschließlich auf elektronischem Wege erfolgen.

(6) ¹Die Plan-Gewinn- und Verlustrechnung der Stiftung sowie die Satzung zum Wirtschaftsplan (§ 13 Abs. 2 Satz 1 Stiftungsgesetz) sind im Amtsblatt des Saarlandes zu veröffentlichen. ²Der Wirtschaftsplan kann in den Räumlichkeiten der Stiftung eingesehen werden.

§ 4 Kuratorium

(1) Das Kuratorium nimmt die ihm durch § 8 Stiftungsgesetz übertragenen Aufgaben und eingeräumten Befugnisse wahr.

(2) ¹Das Kuratorium wird von der Kuratorin/dem Kurator nach Bedarf, jedoch mindestens zweimal jährlich, zu einer Sitzung einberufen. ²Die Sitzungen sind nicht öffentlich.

(3) ¹Mitarbeiterinnen und Mitarbeiter der Stiftung sowie des Ministeriums für Bildung und Kultur können im Einvernehmen mit der Kuratorin/dem Kurator an den Sitzungen teilnehmen, sofern das Kuratorium nicht widerspricht. ²Mit der Zustimmung des Kuratoriums kann die Kuratorin/der Kurator Sachverständige zu Sitzungen des Kuratoriums hinzuziehen. ³Die Sachverständigen sind von der Kuratorin/dem Kurator zur Verschwiegenheit zu verpflichten.

(4) ¹Der Vorstand erstellt zu den Sitzungen nach Absprache mit der Kuratorin/dem Kurator die vorbereitenden Unterlagen (Einladung, Tagesordnung sowie schriftliche Vorlagen). ²Die Mitglieder des Kuratoriums sind schriftlich unter Mitteilung von Tagesordnung, Sitzungsbeginn und Sitzungsort mit einer Frist von mindestens zwei Wochen einzuladen. ³Die Einladung kann auch per Fax oder E-Mail erfolgen. ⁴Die für die Sitzung erforderlichen Unterlagen sind zwei Wochen vor dem Sitzungstermin zu übersenden; bei verspäteter Übersendung beschließt das Kuratorium auf Antrag eines Mitglieds über eine Vertagung der Beschlussfassung. ⁵Die Vorlagen sollen Beschlussvorschläge enthalten. ⁶In Eilfällen kann die Einladung auch mündlich oder telefonisch unter Mitteilung von Tagesordnung, Sitzungsbeginn und Sitzungsort übermittelt und die Einladungsfrist abgekürzt werden. ⁷Die Entscheidung hierüber trifft die Kuratorin/der Kurator nach pflichtgemäßem Ermessen.

(5) ¹Das Kuratorium kann Beschlüsse auch ohne Einberufung einer Sitzung im Wege schriftlicher sowie EDV-gestützter Abstimmung (schriftlicher Beschluss) fassen

1. bei besonderer Eilbedürftigkeit auf Anordnung der Kuratorin/des Kurators
2. auf Beschluss des Kuratoriums in einer vorangegangenen Sitzung oder
3. im Einzelfall, sofern nicht mehr als zwei Mitglieder des Kuratoriums diesem Verfahren widersprechen.

²Das Ergebnis eines schriftlichen Beschlusses ist den Kuratoriumsmitgliedern unverzüglich mitzuteilen. ³Die Beschlüsse sind der nächsten regulären Sitzungsniederschrift beizufügen.

(6) ¹Das Kuratorium ist beschlussfähig, wenn alle Mitglieder ordnungsgemäß geladen sind und wenigstens die Hälfte der Mitglieder anwesend ist. ²Bei Beschlussunfähigkeit kann zur Beratung derselben Gegenstände mit einer Frist von einer Woche erneut geladen werden; in dieser Sitzung ist die Beschlussfähigkeit unabhängig von der Zahl der anwesenden Mitglieder gegeben.

(7) ¹Ein Beschlussvorschlag ist angenommen, wenn er mehr Ja-Stimmen als Nein-Stimmen auf sich vereint. ²Bei Stimmengleichheit entscheidet die Stimme der Kuratorin/des Kurators. ³In den Fällen des Abs. 5 kommt der Beschluss zustande, wenn alle Mitglieder ordnungsgemäß über die Abstimmung informiert wurden und wenigstens die Hälfte der Mitglieder an der Stimmabgabe teilnimmt.

(8) Die Kuratorin/der Kurator führt die Beschlüsse des Kuratoriums bezüglich der Vertragsverhältnisse der Mitglieder des Vorstands aus; insoweit vertritt sie/er die Stiftung.

(9) ¹Über die Sitzungen des Kuratoriums ist ein von der Kuratorin/dem Kurator zu unterzeichnendes Protokoll anzufertigen. ²In diesem sind Ort und Tag der Sitzung, die Teilnehmerinnen und Teilnehmer, die Gegenstände der Tagesordnung, der wesentliche Inhalt der Verhandlungen und die Beschlüsse wiederzugeben. ³Der Vorstand soll der Kuratorin/dem Kurator binnen zwei Wochen das Protokoll der Sitzung zuleiten. ⁴Nach Unterzeichnung durch die Kuratorin/den Kurator ist das Protokoll vom Vorstand an die Kuratoriumsmitglieder, die Vorsitzende/den Vorsitzenden des Beirats sowie an die nach § 7 Abs. 3 Stiftungsgesetz genannten Ministerien zu übermitteln. ⁵Das Protokoll bedarf der Genehmigung des Kuratoriums.

§ 5 Mitwirkungsverbot der Kuratoriumsmitglieder

(1) Mitglieder des Kuratoriums dürfen an Sitzungen des Kuratoriums weder beratend noch entscheidend mitwirken, wenn der zu treffende Beschluss

D12.III.2a Satzung der Stiftung Saarländischer Kulturbesitz

1. ihnen selbst,
2. einer oder einem ihrer Angehörigen,
3. einer von ihnen kraft Gesetzes oder kraft Vollmacht vertretenen natürlichen oder juristischen Person

einen unmittelbaren Vorteil oder Nachteil bringen kann.

(2) Das Mitwirkungsverbot gilt auch, wenn das Mitglied des Kuratoriums
1. Angehöriger einer Person ist, die eine natürliche oder juristische Person, der die Entscheidung einen unmittelbaren Vorteil oder Nachteil bringen kann, in der betreffenden Angelegenheit vertritt,
2. bei einer natürlichen oder juristischen Person oder einer Vereinigung, der die Entscheidung einen unmittelbaren Vorteil oder Nachteil bringen kann, gegen Entgelt beschäftigt ist und nach den tatsächlichen Umständen, insbesondere der Art seiner Beschäftigung, ein Interessenwiderstreit anzunehmen ist,
3. Mitglied des Vorstandes, des Aufsichtsrats oder eines gleichartigen Organs einer juristischen Person oder einer Vereinigung ist, der die Entscheidung einen unmittelbaren Vorteil oder Nachteil bringen kann
4. in anderer als öffentlicher Eigenschaft in der Angelegenheit ein Gutachten abgegeben hat oder sonst tätig geworden ist.

(3) ¹Ob ein Interessenwiderstreit vorliegt, entscheidet im Streitfall das Kuratorium. ²Die von der Entscheidung Betroffenen dürfen an der Beratung und Abstimmung nicht teilnehmen.

(4) ¹Angehörige im Sinne des Abs. 1 Nr. 2 und des Abs. 2 Nr. 1 sind:
1. die/der Verlobte,
2. die Ehegattin/der Ehegatte oder die eingetragene Lebenspartnerin/der eingetragene Lebenspartner,
3. Verwandte und Verschwägerte gerader Linie,
4. Geschwister,
5. Kinder der Geschwister,
6. Ehegattinnen/Ehegatten oder eingetragene Lebenspartnerinnen/eingetragene Lebenspartner der Geschwister und Geschwister der Ehegattinnen/Ehegatten oder der eingetragenen Lebenspartnerinnen/eingetragenen Lebenspartner,
7. Geschwister der Eltern,
8. Personen, die durch ein auf längere Dauer angelegtes Pflegeverhältnis mit häuslicher Gemeinschaft wie Eltern und Kind miteinander verbunden sind (Pflegeeltern und Pflegekinder).

²Angehörige sind die in Satz 1 aufgeführten Personen auch dann, wenn
1. in den Fällen der Nummern 2, 3 und 6 die die Beziehung begründende Ehe oder eingetragene Lebenspartnerschaft nicht mehr besteht;
2. in den Fällen der Nummern 3 bis 7 die Verwandtschaft oder Schwägerschaft durch Annahme als Kind erloschen ist;
3. im Falle der Nummer 8 die häusliche Gemeinschaft nicht mehr besteht, sofern die Personen weiterhin wie Eltern und Kind miteinander verbunden sind.

(5) ¹Ein Beschluss, der unter Verletzung der Abs. 1 und 2 gefasst wurde, ist unwirksam. ²Er gilt jedoch ein Jahr nach der Beschlussfassung als von Anfang an gültig zustande gekommen, es sei denn, dass vor Ablauf der Frist die Kuratorin/der Kurator dem Beschluss widersprochen oder die Rechtsaufsicht den Beschluss beanstandet hat.

§ 6 Vorstand

(1) ¹Die Vorstandsmitglieder entscheiden in allen Angelegenheiten, soweit das Kuratorium nicht zuständig ist. ²Der Vorstand trägt in geeigneter Weise dafür Sorge, dass das Kuratorium seinen Aufgaben nachkommen kann. ³Er bereitet die Beschlüsse des Kuratoriums vor und führt sie aus.

(2) Der Vorstand erörtert den Entwurf des Wirtschaftsplanes und des Jahresabschlusses mit dem Ministerium für Finanzen und Europa, mit dem Zuwendungsgeber und der Rechtsaufsicht.

(3) ¹Die Geschäftsbereiche der Vorstandsmitglieder sowie Organisation und Geschäftsverteilung innerhalb der Stiftung ergeben sich aus der Geschäftsordnung des Vorstands, die der vorherigen Zustimmung des Kuratoriums bedarf. ²Änderungen der Geschäftsordnung des Vorstands bedürfen der Zustimmung des Kuratoriums.

(4) Zu den laufenden Geschäften gehören insbesondere
1. die mit der Verwaltung der Stiftung und der Führung ihrer Museen verbundenen regelmäßig wiederkehrenden Geschäfte,
2. die mit der Durchführung und Abwicklung von Aufträgen verbundenen Rechtsgeschäfte.

(5) ¹Der Vorstand kann einzelne Aufgaben, insbesondere laufend wiederkehrende Geschäfte bis zu einer Wertgrenze von 10.000,00 Euro, an Mitarbeiterinnen oder Mitarbeiter teilweise oder vollständig übertragen. ²Die Übertragung ist schriftlich zu dokumentieren.

(6) ¹Abweichungen von mehr als 10 % der aggregierten Positionen der Gewinn- und Verlustrechnung innerhalb des Wirtschaftsplans bedürfen der Kenntnisnahme des Kuratoriums. ²Eventuelle Kostenerhöhungen müssen gegenfinanziert sein. ³Für die nachfolgenden Geschäfte bedarf der Vorstand stets, auch im Rahmen des Wirtschaftsplans, der Zustimmung des Kuratoriums
1. alle Geschäfte, die zu einer Ausgabe von mehr als 100.000,00 Euro verpflichten, es sei denn, das Kuratorium hat eine besondere Ermächtigung erteilt;
2. der Abschluss von Darlehensverträgen und die Übernahme von Bürgschaften;
3. die Annahme von Erbschaften oder Schenkungen, sofern sie mit erheblichen Folgekosten verbunden sind;
4. der Abschluss von Verträgen mit einer Vertragsdauer von mehr als 10 Jahren oder einer Miete oder Pacht, wenn diese die Summe von 50.000,00 Euro pro Jahr überschreiten oder wenn von den ortsüblichen Miet- oder Pachtbedingungen abgewichen werden soll;
5. die Führung von Rechtsstreitigkeiten von besonderer Bedeutung;
6. der Abschluss von Vergleichen, von Abfindungsvereinbarungen und der Erlass von Forderungen, soweit diese einen Betrag von 50.000,00 Euro überschreiten;
7. der Abschluss von Arbeitsverträgen entsprechend der Entgeltgruppe 14 TV-L und höher;
8. alle sonstigen Geschäfte, für die sich das Kuratorium die Beschlussfassung vorbehält.

(7) ¹Der Vorstand ist nach Information der Kuratorin/des Kurators, im Verhinderungsfalle mit der Stellvertreterin/dem Stellvertreter, berechtigt, Geschäfte und Rechtshandlungen, die durch das Kuratorium beschlossen werden müssen, ohne Zustimmung des Kuratoriums vorzunehmen, wenn Gefahr in Verzug ist oder die Belange der Stiftung ein sofortiges Handeln erfordern. ²Das Kuratorium ist im Nachgang unverzüglich zu unterrichten.

§ 7 Mitwirkungsverbot der Vorstandsmitglieder

(1) ¹Für das Verbot der Mitwirkung eines Mitglieds des Vorstands wegen Interessenwiderstreites gilt § 5 entsprechend. ²An die Stelle des betroffenen Vorstandsmitglieds tritt die Kuratorin/der Kurator.

(2) ¹Im Falle eines Interessenwiderstreites informiert das betroffene Vorstandsmitglied unverzüglich das jeweils andere Mitglied auch darüber, zu welchem Gegenstand ein Interessenwiderstreit vorliegt. ²Der Vorstand entscheidet daraufhin gemeinsam, wie dieser dem Kuratorium unverzüglich offengelegt wird.

§ 8 Beirat der Stiftung

(1) ¹Der Beirat der Stiftung berät und unterstützt das Kuratorium und den Vorstand bei der Wahrnehmung ihrer Aufgaben. ²Er unterbreitet hierzu Stellungnahmen, Empfehlungen und Vorschläge.

(2) Der Beirat kann sich eine Geschäftsordnung geben.

(3) Der Beirat wird von der/dem Vorsitzenden nach Bedarf, jedoch mindestens einmal jährlich, zu einer Sitzung einberufen.

(4) ¹Die Kuratorin/der Kurator ist berechtigt, jederzeit an Beiratssitzungen teilzunehmen. ²Ein Vorstandsmitglied nimmt mit beratender Stimme an den Sitzungen teil.

(5) ¹Über die Sitzungen des Beirats ist eine Niederschrift zu erstellen. ²Diese soll vom Vorsitzenden unterzeichnet und den Mitgliedern des Beirats, dem Vorstand und dem Kuratorium spätestens bis zur nächsten Sitzung des Beirats übermittelt werden.

(6) ¹Die Tätigkeit als Mitglied des Beirats und sonstige ehrenamtliche Tätigkeit für die Stiftung wird grundsätzlich unentgeltlich geleistet. ²Anspruch auf Aufwandsentschädigung, Auslagenersatz und Sitzungsgeld entsteht, soweit gesetzlich nichts anderes bestimmt ist, nur im Rahmen dieser Satzung.

(7) ¹Die Mitglieder des Beirats erhalten für die Wahrnehmung ihres Mandats auf Antrag eine Aufwandsentschädigung in Höhe von 300,00 Euro je teilgenommener Sitzung. ²Sie umfasst den Ersatz der notwendigen Auslagen mit Ausnahme der Reisekosten. ³Mitglieder, die aufgrund einer hauptbe-

ruflichen Stellung im öffentlichen Dienst Mitglieder des Beirats sind, erhalten keine Aufwandsentschädigung.
⁴Auf Antrag sind den Beiratsmitgliedern die entstandenen Reisekosten im Rahmen des Saarländischen Reisekostengesetzes (SRKG) zu erstatten.
⁵Die vom Kuratorium erlassene Reisekosten- und Spesenordnung findet auf Mitglieder des Beirats entsprechende Anwendung.

§ 9 Beratungsgremien
¹Für einzelne Einrichtungen der Stiftung können gesonderte Beratungsgremien gebildet werden. ²Hierüber entscheidet das Kuratorium. ³Im Einzelfall kann eine entsprechende Anwendung der Regelungen des § 8 Abs. 7 vereinbart werden.

§ 10 Ausschüsse
(1) Das Kuratorium kann Ausschüsse einrichten.
(2) Die entstandenen Reisekosten sowie die notwendigen Auslagen werden den Mitgliedern auf Antrag nach dem SRKG erstattet.
(3) ¹Im Einzelfall kann den Ausschussmitgliedern auf Beschluss des Kuratoriums eine Aufwandsentschädigung gewährt werden. ²Für Mitglieder der Organe bzw. Gremien der Stiftung oder im öffentlichen Dienst beschäftigte Ausschussmitglieder ist die Gewährung einer Aufwandsentschädigung ausgeschlossen.

§ 11 Verschwiegenheitspflicht
Die Mitglieder des Vorstands, des Kuratoriums, des Beirats und die Mitglieder der nach den § 9 und § 10 gebildeten Beratungsgremien und Ausschüsse sind während ihrer Amtszeit und nach ihrem Ausscheiden zur Verschwiegenheit über die Angelegenheiten der Stiftung verpflichtet.

§ 12 Inkrafttreten, Übergangsvorschrift
(1) ¹Diese Satzung tritt am Tage nach ihrer Veröffentlichung[1] im Amtsblatt des Saarlandes in Kraft. ²Das Datum der Beschlussfassung des Kuratoriums sowie das Datum der Zustimmung der Landesregierung sind mit zu veröffentlichen.
(2) Die Regelung des § 3 Abs. 5 ist spätestens für das Jahr 2018 anzuwenden.

---

1) Veröffentlicht am 30.6.2016.

Zweite Verordnung über Zuständigkeit nach dem Gesetz zum Schutz deutschen Kulturgutes gegen Abwanderung
Vom 20. September 1961 (Amtsbl. S. 563)

Auf Grund der §§ 3 Abs. 1, 5 Abs. 2, 11 Abs. 1 und 2 und 12 Abs. 2 des Gesetzes zum Schutz deutschen Kulturgutes gegen Abwanderung vom 6. August 1955 (Bundesgesetzbl. I, S. 501)[1)] verordnet die Landesregierung:

§ 1
(1) Zuständige oberste Landesbehörde im Sinne des § 2 Abs. 1 des Gesetzes ist der Minister für Kultus, Unterricht und Volksbildung.
(2) Zuständige oberste Landesbehörde im Sinne des § 11 Abs. 1 des Gesetzes ist der Ministerpräsident.

§ 2
Die Befugnis, das Antragrecht im einzelnen durch Rechtsverordnung zu regeln, wird, soweit es sich um Kunstwerke und anderes Kulturgut im Sinne des Ersten Abschnitts des Gesetzes handelt, auf den Minister für Kultus, Unterricht und Volksbildung, soweit es sich um Archivgut im Sinne des Zweiten Abschnitts des Gesetzes handelt, auf den Ministerpräsidenten übertragen.

§ 3
Das Vorschlagsrecht des Landes gemäß § 5 Abs. 2 Satz 3 des Gesetzes wird durch den Minister für Kultus, Unterricht und Volksbildung, das Vorschlagsrecht gemäß § 12 Abs. 2 des Gesetzes durch den Ministerpräsidenten ausgeübt.

§ 4
(1) Diese Verordnung tritt mit dem Tage ihrer Veröffentlichung in Kraft.
(2) Mit dem gleichen Tag tritt die Verordnung über Zuständigkeiten nach dem Gesetz zum Schutz deutschen Kulturgutes gegen Abwanderung vom 12. November 1958 (Amtsbl. S. 1527) außer Kraft.

---

1) Zwar bezieht sich die Verordnung noch auf die alte Rechtslage vor Inkrafttreten des KGSG am 6. August 2016 (abgedruckt als Nr. C.I.2), sie bildet allerdings immer noch die Rechtsgrundlage für die Zuständigkeit des Ministeriums für Bildung und Kultur des Saarlandes. Eine neue Landesverordnung zur Umsetzung des KGSG ist derzeit in Planung.

D12.IV.2 Verordnung Antragsrecht nach KgSchG

Verordnung über das Antragsrecht gemäß § 3 Abs. 1 und § 11 Abs. 2 des Gesetzes zum Schutz deutschen Kulturgutes gegen Abwanderung vom 6. August 1955 (BGBl. I S. 501)

Vom 18. Dezember 1958 (Amtsbl. S. 1527)

Auf Grund der §§ 3 und 11 des Gesetzes zum Schutz deutschen Kulturgutes gegen Abwanderung vom 6. August 1955 (Bundesgesetzbl. I, S. 501)[1)] in Verbindung mit § 2 der VO über Zuständigkeiten nach dem Gesetz zum Schutz deutschen Kulturgutes gegen Abwanderung vom 12. November 1958 (Amtsbl. S. 1527) wird verordnet:

§ 1
Zum Antrag auf Eintragung von Kunstwerken und anderem Kulturgut — einschließlich Bibliotheksgut — in das „Verzeichnis national wertvollen Kulturgutes" gemäß § 3 Abs. 1 des Gesetzes zum Schutz deutschen Kulturgutes gegen Abwanderung vom 6. August 1955 (Bundesgesetzbl. I, S. 501) und auf Eintragung von Archiven, archivarischen Sammlungen, Nachlässen und Briefsammlungen in das „Verzeichnis national wertvoller Archive" gemäß § 11 Abs. 2 des Gesetzes sind die Eigentümer und die Besitzer solcher Kulturgüter berechtigt.

§ 2
Der Antrag ist an den Minister für Kultus, Unterricht und Volksbildung als zuständige oberste Landesbehörde zu richten und muß eine genaue Bezeichnung der Gegenstände, deren Eintragung beantragt wird, sowie Angaben über den Eigentümer, den Besitzer und den Aufenthalt der Gegenstände zur Zeit der Antragstellung enthalten.

§ 3
Diese Verordnung tritt mit dem Tage der Verkündung in Kraft.

---

1) Zwar bezieht sich die Verordnung noch auf die alte Rechtslage vor Inkrafttreten des KGSG am 6. August 2016 (abgedruckt als Nr. C.I.2), sie bildet allerdings immer noch die Rechtsgrundlage für die Zuständigkeit des Ministeriums für Bildung und Kultur des Saarlandes. Eine neue Landesverordnung zur Umsetzung des KGSG ist derzeit in Planung.

Verordnung über Anträge auf Eintragung von Archivbeständen in das „Verzeichnis national wertvollen Archivgutes"

Vom 24. Oktober 1961 (Amtsbl. S. 603)

Auf Grund der §§ 11 Abs. 2, 3 Abs. 1 des Gesetzes zum Schutz deutschen Kulturgutes gegen Abwanderung vom 6. August 1955 (Bundesgesetzbl. I S. 501),[1] und des § 2 der Zweiten Verordnung über Zuständigkeiten nach dem Gesetz zum Schutz deutschen Kulturgutes gegen Abwanderung vom 20. September 1961 (Amtsbl. S. 563) wird verordnet:

§ 1
Zum Antrag auf Eintragung von Archiven, Archivaliensammlungen, Nachlässen und Briefsammlungen in das „Verzeichnis national wertvollen Archivgutes" sind der Eigentümer und der Besitzer berechtigt.

§ 2
Der Antrag ist an den Ministerpräsidenten zu richten und muß eine genaue Bezeichnung der Gegenstände, deren Eintragung beantragt wird, sowie Angaben über den Eigentümer, den Besitzer und den Lagerort der Gegenstände z. Z. der Antragstellung enthalten.

§ 3
Diese Verordnung tritt mit dem Tage ihrer Veröffentlichung in Kraft.

---

1) Zwar bezieht sich die Verordnung noch auf die alte Rechtslage vor Inkrafttreten des KGSG am 6. August 2016 (abgedruckt als Nr. C.I.2), sie bildet allerdings immer noch die Rechtsgrundlage für die Zuständigkeit des Ministeriums für Bildung und Kultur des Saarlandes. Eine neue Landesverordnung zur Umsetzung des KGSG ist derzeit in Planung.

Verfassung des Freistaates Sachsen

Vom 27. Mai 1992 (SächsGVBl. S. 243)
(BS Sachsen 100-1)
zuletzt geändert durch Art. 1 Verfassungsänderungsgesetz vom 11. Juli 2013 (SächsGVBl. S. 502)
– Auszug –

1. Abschnitt:
Die Grundlagen des Staates

Artikel 5 [Bürger, Minderheiten]
[...]
(2) Das Land gewährleistet und schützt das Recht nationaler und ethnischer Minderheiten deutscher Staatsangehörigkeit auf Bewahrung ihrer Identität sowie auf Pflege ihrer Sprache, Religion, Kultur und Überlieferung.
[...]

Artikel 6 [Sorben]
(1) ¹Die im Land lebenden Bürger sorbischer Volkszugehörigkeit sind gleichberechtigter Teil des Staatsvolkes. ²Das Land gewährleistet und schützt das Recht auf Bewahrung ihrer Identität sowie auf Pflege und Entwicklung ihrer angestammten Sprache, Kultur und Überlieferung, insbesondere durch Schulen, vorschulische und kulturelle Einrichtungen.
[...]

Artikel 11 [Kultur, Wissenschaft, Sport]
[...]
(2) ¹Die Teilnahme an der Kultur in ihrer Vielfalt und am Sport ist dem gesamten Volk zu ermöglichen. ²Zu diesem Zweck werden öffentlich zugängliche Museen, Bibliotheken, Archive, Gedenkstätten, Theater, Sportstätten, musikalische und weitere kulturelle Einrichtungen sowie allgemein zugängliche Universitäten, Hochschulen, Schulen und andere Bildungseinrichtungen unterhalten.
(3) ¹Denkmale und andere Kulturgüter stehen unter dem Schutz und der Pflege des Landes. ²Für ihr Verbleiben in Sachsen setzt sich das Land ein.

10. Abschnitt:
Die Kirchen und Religionsgemeinschaften

Artikel 112 [Sonderausschüsse]
[...]
(2) ¹Die Baudenkmale der Kirchen und Religionsgemeinschaften sind, unbeschadet des Eigentumsrechtes, Kulturgut der Allgemeinheit. ²Für ihre bauliche Unterhaltung haben die Kirchen und Religionsgemeinschaften daher Anspruch auf angemessene Kostenerstattung durch das Land nach Maßgabe der Gesetze.

Gesetz zum Schutz und zur Pflege der Kulturdenkmale im Freistaat Sachsen (Sächsisches Denkmalschutzgesetz – SächsDSchG)

Vom 3. März 1993 (SächsGVBl. S. 229)
(BS Sachsen 46-1)
zuletzt geändert durch Art. 2 G über Zuständigkeiten im Schornsteinfeger- und Denkmalschutzrecht vom 2. August 2019 (SächsGVBl. S. 644)

Der Sächsische Landtag hat am 22. Januar 1993 das folgende Gesetz beschlossen:

Inhaltsübersicht

I. Abschnitt
Aufgabe und Gegenstand von Denkmalschutz und Denkmalpflege
§ 1 Aufgabe
§ 2 Gegenstand des Denkmalschutzes

II. Abschnitt
Organisation des Denkmalschutzes
§ 3 Denkmalschutzbehörden
§ 3a Denkmalfachbehörden
§ 4 Zuständigkeit der Denkmalschutzbehörden
§ 5 (aufgehoben)
§ 6 Denkmalrat
§ 7 Ehrenamtliche Beauftragte für Denkmalpflege

III. Abschnitt
Schutzvorschriften
§ 8 Erhaltungspflicht
§ 9 Nutzung, Zugang
§ 10 Verzeichnis der Kulturdenkmale
§ 11 Maßnahmen der Denkmalschutzbehörden
§ 12 Genehmigungspflichtige und anzeigepflichtige Vorhaben an Kulturdenkmalen
§ 13 Genehmigungsverfahren
§ 14 Genehmigungspflicht für Bodeneingriffe, Nutzungsänderungen und Nachforschungen; Kostenerstattungspflicht
§ 15 Auskunfts- und Duldungspflichten
§ 16 Anzeigepflichten
§ 17 Vorkaufsrecht
§ 18 Kulturdenkmale, die der Religionsausübung dienen

§ 19 Sammlungen
§ 20 Funde
§ 21 Denkmalschutzgebiete
§ 22 Grabungsschutzgebiete
§ 23 Archäologische Reservate
§ 24 Schutz bei Katastrophen

IV. Abschnitt
Schatzregal, Entschädigung, Enteignung
§ 25 Schatzregal
§ 26 Entschädigung
§ 27 Voraussetzungen der Enteignung
§ 28 Gegenstand der Enteignung
§ 29 Entschädigungsgrundsätze
§ 30 Entschädigungsberechtigter und Entschädigungsverpflichteter
§ 31 Bemessung der Entschädigung
§ 32 Enteignungsbehörde und Enteignungsantrag
§ 33 Verfahren bei der Enteignung von Grundstücken
§ 34 Verfahren bei der Enteignung beweglicher Sachen

V. Abschnitt
Straftaten und Ordnungswidrigkeiten
§ 35 Straftaten
§ 36 Ordnungswidrigkeiten

VI. Abschnitt
Schlußbestimmungen
§ 37 [aufgehoben]
§ 38 Übergangsvorschriften
§ 39 Aufhebung von Vorschriften
§ 40 Inkrafttreten

I. Abschnitt
Aufgabe und Gegenstand von Denkmalschutz und Denkmalpflege

§ 1 Aufgabe
(1) Denkmalschutz und Denkmalpflege haben die Aufgabe, die Kulturdenkmale zu schützen und zu pflegen, insbesondere deren Zustand zu überwachen, auf die Abwendung von Gefährdungen und die Bergung von Kulturdenkmalen hinzuwirken und diese zu erfassen und wissenschaftlich zu erforschen.
(2) ¹Diese Aufgabe wird vom Freistaat Sachsen und im Rahmen ihrer Leistungsfähigkeit von den Gemeinden und den Landkreisen erfüllt. ²Sie wirken dabei mit Eigentümern und Besitzern von Kulturdenkmalen zusammen.

(3) Die Belange des Denkmalschutzes und der Denkmalpflege sind bei allen öffentlichen Planungen und Maßnahmen angemessen zu berücksichtigen.
(4) Die Belange von Menschen mit Behinderungen oder mit Mobilitätsbeeinträchtigungen sind zu berücksichtigen.

§ 2 Gegenstand des Denkmalschutzes

(1) Kulturdenkmale im Sinne dieses Gesetzes sind von Menschen geschaffene Sachen, Sachgesamtheiten, Teile und Spuren von Sachen einschließlich ihrer natürlichen Grundlagen, deren Erhaltung wegen ihrer geschichtlichen, künstlerischen, wissenschaftlichen, städtebaulichen oder landschaftsgestaltenden Bedeutung im öffentlichen Interesse liegt.
(2) Zu einem Kulturdenkmal gehören auch Zubehör und Nebenanlagen, soweit sie mit der Hauptsache eine Einheit von Denkmalwert bilden.
(3) Gegenstand des Denkmalschutzes sind auch
1. die Umgebung eines Kulturdenkmals, soweit sie für dessen Bestand oder Erscheinungsbild von erheblicher Bedeutung ist,
2. Denkmalschutzgebiete (§ 21), Grabungsschutzgebiete (§ 22) und archäologische Reservate (§ 23),
3. Reste von Menschen und von anderen Lebewesen, die sich in historischen Gräbern und Siedlungen befinden.
(4) Gegenstand des Denkmalschutzes können auch Orte zu geschichtlichen Ereignissen sein.
(5) Kulturdenkmale im Sinne dieses Gesetzes können insbesondere sein
a) Bauwerke,
b) Siedlungen und Ortsteile, Straßen- oder Platzbilder oder Ortsansichten von besonderer städtebaulicher oder volkskundlicher Bedeutung,
c) Werke der Garten- und Landschaftsgestaltung, historische Landschaftsformen wie Dorffluren, Haldenlandschaften,
d) Werke der Produktions- und Verkehrsgeschichte,
e) Orte und Gegenstände zu wissenschaftlichen Anlagen oder Systemen,
f) Steinmale,
g) unbewegliche und bewegliche archäologische Sachzeugen wie Reste von Siedlungs- und Befestigungsanlagen, Grabanlagen, Höhlen, Wüstungen, Kult- und Versammlungsstätten und andere Reste von Gegenständen und Bauwerken,
h) Werke der bildenden Kunst und des Kunsthandwerks,
i) Sammlungen.

II. Abschnitt
Organisation des Denkmalschutzes

§ 3 Denkmalschutzbehörden

(1) Denkmalschutzbehörden sind
1. das Staatsministerium des Innern als oberste Denkmalschutzbehörde,
2. die Landesdirektion Sachsen als obere Denkmalschutzbehörde,
3. die Landkreise und Kreisfreien Städte und die in Absatz 2 genannten Gemeinden als untere Denkmalschutzbehörden.
(2) ¹Städten, die aufgrund von § 2 Abs. 2 des Gesetzes zur Neugliederung des Gebietes der Landkreise des Freistaates Sachsen (Sächsisches Kreisgebietsneugliederungsgesetz – SächsKrGebNG) vom 29. Januar 2008 (SächsGVBl. S. 102) die Kreisfreiheit verloren haben, ist auf Antrag die Aufgabe der unteren Denkmalschutzbehörde zu übertragen. ²Gemeinden mit überdurchschnittlich großem Bestand an Kulturdenkmalen, denen die Aufgaben der unteren Bauaufsichtsbehörden übertragen sind und die für die Aufgaben des Denkmalschutzes ausreichend über geeignete Fachkräfte verfügen, können auf ihren Antrag durch die oberste Denkmalschutzbehörde zu unteren Denkmalschutzbehörden erklärt werden. ³Die Erklärung kann widerrufen werden, wenn die Gemeinde dies beantragt, wenn ihre Zuständigkeit als untere Bauaufsichtsbehörde endet oder wenn die untere Denkmalschutzbehörde dauernd nicht ausreichend mit geeigneten Fachkräften besetzt ist. ⁴Die Erklärungen über die Zuständigkeit sind im Sächsischen Gesetz- und Verordnungsblatt bekanntzumachen.

(3) ¹Die den Landkreisen, Kreisfreien Städten und den Gemeinden, die nach Absatz 2 zur unteren Denkmalschutzbehörde erklärt wurden, übertragenen Aufgaben der unteren Denkmalschutzbehörde sind Weisungsaufgaben. ²Das Weisungsrecht ist nicht beschränkt. ³Weisungsfrei sind
1. die Erteilung von Bescheinigungen für die Erlangung von Steuervergünstigungen nach § 4 Abs. 4 und
2. die Bewilligung von Zuwendungen zur Erhaltung und Pflege von Kulturdenkmalen nach § 8 Abs. 2.
⁴Fachaufsichtsbehörden sind die in Absatz 1 Nr. 1 und 2 genannten Behörden.

§ 3a Denkmalfachbehörden

(1) Fachbehörden für alle Fragen des Denkmalschutzes und der Denkmalpflege sind das Landesamt für Denkmalpflege und das Landesamt für Archäologie.¹⁾
(2) Das Landesamt für Denkmalpflege ist die zuständige Fachbehörde für alle Aufgaben, die nicht dem Landesamt für Archäologie zugewiesen sind, insbesondere für Bau- und Kunstdenkmale, Anlagen der Garten- und Landschaftsgestaltung, Werke der Produktions- und Verkehrsgeschichte, Sammlungen.
(3) Das Landesamt für Archäologie ist zuständige Fachbehörde für
1. unbewegliche archäologische Sachzeugen
   a) unterhalb der Erdoberfläche außerhalb von Gebäuden, insbesondere Fundamente von Vorgängerbauten, Grablegen, sonstige archäologische Funde,
   b) unter der Bodenfläche im Innern von baulichen Anlagen, zum Beispiel Gebäuden und Gebäuderuinen,
   c) unter der Wasseroberfläche im Bereich des Gewässerbettes,
2. bewegliche archäologische Sachzeugen und Sammlungen solcher Sachzeugen.

§ 4 Zuständigkeit der Denkmalschutzbehörden

(1) Soweit nicht etwas Abweichendes bestimmt ist, ist die untere Denkmalschutzbehörde zuständig.
(2) ¹Die untere Denkmalschutzbehörde entscheidet im Einvernehmen mit der zuständigen Fachbehörde.²⁾ ²Kommt kein Einvernehmen zustande, so entscheidet die obere Denkmalschutzbehörde. ³Die obere und die oberste Denkmalschutzbehörde entscheiden im Benehmen mit der zuständigen Fachbehörde.
(3) ¹Erscheint bei Gefahr im Verzug ein rechtzeitiges Tätigwerden der zuständigen Denkmalschutzbehörde nicht erreichbar, so können die Fachbehörden oder, falls auch die zuständige Fachbehörde nicht rechtzeitig tätig werden kann, die Polizei die erforderlichen vorläufigen Maßnahmen treffen. ²Die zuständige Behörde ist unverzüglich zu unterrichten.
(4) ¹Bescheinigungen für die Erlangung von Steuervergünstigungen werden von den unteren Denkmalschutzbehörden erteilt. ²Das Staatsministerium des Innern kann Gegenstand, Voraussetzungen und Verfahren, Empfängerkreis sowie Art, Umfang und Nachweis der zu bescheinigenden Aufwendungen durch Rechtsverordnung regeln; davon ausgenommen sind Anerkennungen nach § 32 Abs. 2 des Grundsteuergesetzes (GrStG) vom 7. August 1973 (BGBl. I S. 965), das zuletzt durch Artikel 6 des Gesetzes vom 1. September 2005 (BGBl. I S. 2676, 2681) geändert worden ist, in der jeweils geltenden Fassung.

§ 5 *[aufgehoben]*

§ 6 Denkmalrat

(1) ¹Bei der obersten Denkmalschutzbehörde wird ein Denkmalrat gebildet. ²Der Denkmalrat soll von der obersten Denkmalschutzbehörde in allen Fragen von grundsätzlicher Bedeutung gehört werden. ³Für die Verwendung von staatlichen Denkmalpflegefördermitteln kann die oberste Denkmalschutzbehörde vom Denkmalrat Vorschläge einholen.

---

1) Vgl. die Gemeinsame Verwaltungsvorschrift des Sächsischen Staatsministeriums des Innern und des Sächsischen Staatsministeriums für Wissenschaft und Kunst zur Zuständigkeit des Landesamtes für Denkmalpflege und des Landesamtes für Archäologie abgedruckt als Nr. D13.I.1f.
2) Vgl. die Verwaltungsvorschrift des Sächsischen Staatsministeriums des Innern zur Herstellung des Einvernehmens gemäß § 4 Abs. 2 SächsDSchG zwischen den unteren Denkmalschutzbehörden und dem Landesamt für Denkmalpflege Sachsen abgedruckt als Nr. D13.I.1e.

D13.I.1 Sächsisches Denkmalschutzgesetz

(2) Sind bei der Behandlung von Fragen des Denkmalschutzes und der Denkmalpflege ethnische oder konfessionelle Gruppen oder besondere Denkmalarten betroffen, hat der Denkmalrat einen Vertreter der betroffenen Gruppen mit beratender Stimme beizuziehen.

(3) [1]Der Denkmalrat besteht aus dreizehn von der obersten Denkmalschutzbehörde auf die Dauer von fünf Jahren berufenen, ehrenamtlich tätigen Mitgliedern. [2]Er entscheidet unabhängig und ist nicht weisungs- und entscheidungsgebunden.

(4) [1]In den Sitzungen führt der Staatsminister des Innern oder ein von ihm Beauftragter den Vorsitz. [2]Die oberste Denkmalschutzbehörde erläßt eine Geschäftsordnung[1)] für den Denkmalrat, die auch das Berufungsverfahren und das Vorschlagsrecht regelt. [3]Die Geschäftsordnung kann bestimmen, daß der Denkmalrat Fachausschüsse bildet, an die Aufgaben delegiert werden können.

§ 7 Ehrenamtliche Beauftragte für Denkmalpflege

(1) Die unteren Denkmalschutzbehörden und die Fachbehörden stützen sich in ihrer Tätigkeit auf die fachliche Mitarbeit von ehrenamtlichen Beauftragten für Denkmalpflege.

(2) [1]Die ehrenamtlichen Beauftragten beraten und unterstützen die in Absatz 1 genannten Behörden. [2]Die oberste Denkmalschutzbehörde regelt die Berufung und die Aufgaben der ehrenamtlichen Beauftragten durch Verwaltungsvorschrift.[2)]

(3) [1]Die ehrenamtlichen Beauftragten für Denkmalpflege werden von der unteren Denkmalschutzbehörde im Einvernehmen mit den Fachbehörden auf die Dauer von fünf Jahren berufen. [2]Die Berufung kann wiederholt werden.

(4) [1]Die oberste Denkmalschutzbehörde kann mit Zustimmung des Staatsministeriums für Finanzen durch Rechtsverordnung[3)] die Entschädigung und den Reisekostenersatz für die ehrenamtlichen Beauftragten für Denkmalpflege regeln. [2]Dabei können Durchschnittssätze festgelegt werden.

III. Abschnitt
Schutzvorschriften

§ 8 Erhaltungspflicht

(1) Eigentümer und Besitzer von Kulturdenkmalen haben diese pfleglich zu behandeln, im Rahmen des Zumutbaren denkmalgerecht zu erhalten und vor Gefährdung zu schützen.

(2) [1]Der Freistaat Sachsen trägt hierzu durch Zuwendungen nach Maßgabe der dafür zur Verfügung stehenden Haushaltsmittel bei. [2]Das Staatsministerium des Innern regelt Gegenstand, Voraussetzungen und Verfahren, Empfängerkreis sowie Art, Umfang und Höhe der Zuwendungen durch Verwaltungsvorschrift.[4)] [3]Bewilligungsbehörden sind die unteren Denkmalschutzbehörden, soweit nicht durch die Förderzuständigkeitsverordnung SMI vom 8. Februar 2012 (SächsGVBl. S. 150), die zuletzt durch die Verordnung vom 22. Februar 2016 (SächsGVBl. S. 102) geändert worden ist, in der jeweils geltenden Fassung, etwas anderes geregelt ist. [4]Für Zuwendungen an Städte, Landkreise und Gemeinden, die untere Denkmalschutzbehörde sind, ist die Landesdirektion Sachsen Bewilligungsbehörde. [5]Die notwendigen Haushaltsmittel werden den Bewilligungsbehörden zur Bewirtschaftung zugewiesen.

§ 9 Nutzung, Zugang

(1) Werden Kulturdenkmale nicht mehr entsprechend ihrer ursprünglichen Zweckbestimmung genutzt, sollen Eigentümer und Besitzer eine Nutzung anstreben, die eine möglichst weitgehende Erhaltung der Substanz auf die Dauer gewährleistet.

(2) Kulturdenkmale oder Teile derselben sollen der Öffentlichkeit im Rahmen des Zumutbaren zugänglich gemacht werden.

---

1) Die Verwaltungsvorschrift des Sächsischen Staatsministerium des Innern über die Geschäftsordnung für den Denkmalrat ist abgedruckt als Nr. D13.I.1c.
2) Die Verwaltungsvorschrift des Sächsischen Staatsministeriums des Innern über die ehrenamtlichen Beauftragten für Denkmalpflege und zur Aufhebung einer Verwaltungsvorschrift ist abgedruckt als Nr. D13.I.1b.
3) Die Denkmalpflegeentschädigungsverordnung ist abgedruckt als Nr. D13.I.1a.
4) Die Verwaltungsvorschrift des Sächsischen Staatsministeriums des Innern über die Gewährung von Zuwendungen zur Erhaltung und Pflege von sächsischen Kulturdenkmalen und zur Aus- und Fortbildung der Denkmalpflege ist abgedruckt als Nr. D13.III.1.

§ 10 Verzeichnis der Kulturdenkmale

(1) ¹Die Kulturdenkmale sollen nachrichtlich in öffentliche Verzeichnisse (Kulturdenkmallisten) aufgenommen werden.[1]) ²Der Denkmalschutz nach diesem Gesetz ist nicht von der Aufnahme eines Kulturdenkmals in ein Verzeichnis abhängig.

(2) ¹Die Eintragung erfolgt von Amts wegen durch die Fachbehörden im Benehmen mit der Gemeinde, in der das Kulturdenkmal gelegen ist. ²Der Eigentümer oder die Gemeinde können die Eintragung anregen.

(3) ¹Der Eigentümer ist von der Eintragung zu unterrichten. ²Auf Antrag des Eigentümers hat die Denkmalschutzbehörde durch Verwaltungsakt über die Eigenschaft als Kulturdenkmal zu entscheiden. ³Die Einsicht in die Kulturdenkmallisten ist jedermann gestattet. ⁴Eintragungen über bewegliche Kulturdenkmale und über Zubehör (§ 2 Abs. 2) dürfen nur die Eigentümer und die sonstigen dinglich Berechtigten sowie die von ihnen ermächtigten Personen einsehen.

(4) Den Gemeinden, den unteren und der oberen Denkmalschutzbehörde werden Auszüge der Kulturdenkmallisten übermittelt.

(5) Die oberste Denkmalschutzbehörde regelt das Nähere durch Verwaltungsvorschrift.

§ 11 Maßnahmen der Denkmalschutzbehörden

(1) Die Denkmalschutzbehörden haben zur Wahrnehmung ihrer Aufgaben diejenigen Maßnahmen zu treffen, die ihnen nach pflichtgemäßem Ermessen erforderlich erscheinen.

(2) Die Denkmalschutzbehörden können insbesondere anordnen, daß bei widerrechtlicher Beeinträchtigung, Beschädigung oder Zerstörung eines Kulturdenkmales der vorherige Zustand nach ihrer Anweisung wiederherzustellen ist.

(3) Die Vorschriften der §§ 14, 15 und 17 des Sächsischen Polizeibehördengesetzes vom 11. Mai 2019 (SächsGVBl. S. 358, 389), in der jeweils geltenden Fassung, finden sinngemäß Anwendung.

§ 12 Genehmigungspflichtige und anzeigepflichtige Vorhaben an Kulturdenkmalen

(1) ¹Ein Kulturdenkmal darf nur mit Genehmigung der Denkmalschutzbehörde
1. wiederhergestellt oder instand gesetzt werden,
2. in seinem Erscheinungsbild oder seiner Substanz verändert oder beeinträchtigt werden,
3. mit An- und Aufbauten, Aufschriften oder Werbeeinrichtungen versehen werden,
4. aus einer Umgebung entfernt werden,
5. zerstört oder beseitigt werden.

²Abweichend von Satz 1 Nr. 1 und 2 sind der Denkmalschutzbehörde die Wiederherstellung oder Instandsetzung von Kulturdenkmalen, die aufgrund außergewöhnlicher Ereignisse mit überörtlicher Wirkung, insbesondere Naturkatastrophen, zerstört oder beschädigt wurden, sowie geringfügige Vorhaben schriftlich anzuzeigen. ³Ausgenommen von Satz 2 sind Kulturdenkmale im Sinne des § 2 Abs. 5 Buchst. g. ⁴Ein geringfügiges Vorhaben an einem Kulturdenkmal ist die Beseitigung von Schäden und Mängeln an einzelnen Teilen des Kulturdenkmales zur Herstellung eines denkmalverträglichen Zustandes; es umfasst insbesondere die Ausbesserung von Bauteilen nach Schädigung oder üblicher Abnutzung. ⁵Die Denkmalschutzbehörde hat den Eingang der Anzeige unverzüglich schriftlich zu bestätigen. ⁶Mit der Durchführung der Maßnahme nach Satz 2 kann begonnen werden, wenn die Denkmalschutzbehörde nicht innerhalb von drei Wochen nach Eingang der Anzeige bei der Denkmalschutzbehörde schriftlich gegenüber dem Anzeigenden erklärt, dass ein Genehmigungsverfahren durchzuführen ist. ⁷Die Entscheidung, ob die Anzeige genügt oder ein Genehmigungsverfahren durchzuführen ist, obliegt der Denkmalschutzbehörde.

(2) ¹Bauliche oder garten- und landschaftsgestalterische Anlagen in der Umgebung eines Kulturdenkmals, soweit sie für dessen Erscheinungsbild von erheblicher Bedeutung sind, dürfen nur mit Genehmigung der Denkmalschutzbehörde errichtet, verändert oder beseitigt werden. ²Andere Vorhaben in der Umgebung eines Kulturdenkmals bedürfen dieser Genehmigung, wenn sich die bisherige Grundstücksnutzung ändern würde. ³Die Genehmigung ist zu erteilen, wenn das Vorhaben das Erscheinungsbild des Kulturdenkmals nur unerheblich oder nur vorübergehend beeinträchtigen würde oder wenn überwiegende Gründe des Gemeinwohls Berücksichtigung verlangen.

(2a) Die Genehmigung nach Absatz 1 Satz 1 oder Absatz 2 Satz 1 und 2 soll erteilt werden, wenn es sich um eine Maßnahme des öffentlichen Hochwasserschutzes handelt, für die überwiegende Gründe

---
1) Vgl. die VwV Kulturdenkmallisten, abgedruckt als Nr. D13.I.1d.

des Gemeinwohls vorliegen, und die Erhaltung von für das kulturelle Erbe bedeutenden Kulturdenkmalen nicht gefährdet wird.
(3) Bedarf ein Vorhaben der Baugenehmigung oder bauordnungsrechtlichen Zustimmung, tritt an die Stelle der Genehmigung nach diesem Gesetz die Zustimmung der Denkmalschutzbehörde gegenüber der Bauaufsichtsbehörde.

§ 13 Genehmigungsverfahren

(1) ¹Der Genehmigungsantrag ist schriftlich bei der zuständigen Denkmalschutzbehörde (§ 4) einzureichen. ²Bei Vorhaben nach § 12 Abs. 3 gilt der Genehmigungsantrag als mit dem Antrag auf Baugenehmigung oder bauordnungsrechtliche Zustimmung gestellt.
(2) ¹Mit dem Genehmigungsantrag sind alle für die Beurteilung des Vorhabens und der Bearbeitung des Antrags erforderlichen Unterlagen, insbesondere Pläne, Dokumentationen, Fotografien, Gutachten, Kosten- und Wirtschaftlichkeitsberechnungen, einzureichen. ²Die Denkmalschutzbehörde kann im Einzelfall die erforderlichen Unterlagen anfordern und verlangen, daß der Genehmigungsantrag durch vorbereitende Untersuchungen ergänzt wird.
(3) Bei Kulturdenkmalen im Sinne von § 2 Abs. 5 Buchst. a bis c, f und g, soweit es sich um unbewegliche Kulturdenkmale handelt, ist insbesondere die zuständige Naturschutzbehörde rechtzeitig zu beteiligen.
(4) ¹Entscheidet die zuständige Denkmalschutzbehörde nicht innerhalb von zwei Monaten nach Eingang des Antrags über die Genehmigung, so gilt diese als erteilt, wenn nicht die zuständige Behörde die Entscheidung über einen Genehmigungsantrag unter Berücksichtigung der berechtigten Interessen des Antragsstellers aussetzt. ²Eine Aussetzung kann höchstens auf zwei Jahre festgesetzt werden, soweit dies zur Klärung der Belange des Denkmalschutzes, insbesondere für vorbereitende Untersuchungen erforderlich ist.
(5) ¹Die Genehmigung erlischt, wenn nicht innerhalb von drei Jahren nach ihrer Erteilung mit der Ausführung begonnen oder die Ausführung länger als zwei Jahre unterbrochen worden ist. ²Die Fristen nach Satz 1 können auf schriftlichen Antrag jeweils um bis zu zwei Jahre verlängert werden.

§ 14 Genehmigungspflicht für Bodeneingriffe, Nutzungsänderungen und Nachforschungen; Kostenerstattungspflicht

(1) ¹Der Genehmigung der Denkmalschutzbehörde bedarf, wer
1. Erdarbeiten, Bauarbeiten oder Gewässerbaumaßnahmen an einer Stelle, von der bekannt oder den Umständen nach zu vermuten ist, daß sich dort Kulturdenkmale befinden, ausführen will,
2. die bisherige Bodennutzung von Grundstücken, von denen bekannt ist, daß sie im Boden Kulturdenkmale bergen, ändern will.

²§ 12 Abs. 3 und § 13 gelten entsprechend.
(2) ¹Nachforschungen, insbesondere Grabungen, mit dem Ziel, Kulturdenkmale zu entdecken, bedürfen der Genehmigung der zuständigen Fachbehörde. ²§ 13 Abs. 1 Satz 1 und Abs. 2 bis 5 gilt entsprechend.
(3) ¹Die Träger größerer öffentlicher oder privater Bauvorhaben oder Erschließungsvorhaben oder Vorhaben zum Abbau von Rohstoffen oder Bodenschätzen als Veranlasser können im Rahmen des Zumutbaren zur Erstattung der Kosten archäologischer Ausgrabungen, der konservatorischen Sicherung der Funde und der Dokumentation der Befunde verpflichtet werden. ²Die Höhe des Erstattungsbetrages kann durch öffentlich-rechtlichen Vertrag mit der zuständigen Fachbehörde geregelt werden. ³Kommt kein Vertrag zustande, erfolgt die Festsetzung durch die obere Denkmalschutzbehörde.

§ 15 Auskunfts- und Duldungspflichten

(1) Eigentümer und Besitzer von Kulturdenkmalen sind verpflichtet, Auskünfte zu erteilen, die zur Erfüllung der Aufgaben des Denkmalschutzes erforderlich sind.
(2) ¹Die Denkmalschutzbehörden und ihre Beauftragten sind berechtigt, nach vorheriger Benachrichtigung der Eigentümer und Besitzer
1. Grundstücke zu betreten,
2. Kulturdenkmale zu besichtigen,
3. wissenschaftliche Erfassungsmaßnahmen durchzuführen, insbesondere Einsicht in Archive und Sammlungen zu nehmen,

soweit dies zur Erfüllung der Aufgaben des Denkmalschutzes erforderlich ist. ²Wohnungen dürfen gegen den Willen des Eigentümers oder Besitzers nur zur Abwendung dringender Gefahren für Kulturdenkmale betreten werden. ³Die Unverletzlichkeit der Wohnung nach Artikel 13 des Grundgesetzes und Artikel 30 der Verfassung des Freistaates Sachsen wird insoweit eingeschränkt.

§ 16 Anzeigepflichten
(1) Eigentümer und Besitzer haben
1. Änderungen der bisherigen Nutzung von Kulturdenkmalen,
2. Schäden und Mängel, die an Kulturdenkmalen auftreten und die ihre Erhaltung gefährden können,
unverzüglich einer Denkmalschutzbehörde anzuzeigen.
(2) Wird ein Kulturdenkmal veräußert, so haben der Veräußerer und der Erwerber den Eigentumswechsel innerhalb eines Monats einer Denkmalschutzbehörde anzuzeigen.
(3) Die Anzeigen nach Absätzen 1 und 2 sind unverzüglich an die zuständige Fachbehörde weiterzuleiten.

§ 17 Vorkaufsrecht
(1) ¹Wird ein Grundstück, auf dem sich ein unbewegliches Kulturdenkmal befindet, verkauft, steht der Gemeinde, bei überörtlicher Bedeutung des Kulturdenkmals auch dem Freistaat Sachsen ein Vorkaufsrecht zu. ²Der Staatsbetrieb Zentrales Flächenmanagement Sachsen ist für die Ausübung des Vorkaufsrechts für den Freistaat Sachsen zuständig. ³Es geht dem Vorkaufsrecht der Gemeinde im Range vor.
(2) ¹Das Vorkaufsrecht darf nur ausgeübt werden, wenn dadurch die Erhaltung eines Kulturdenkmals ermöglicht werden soll. ²Das Vorkaufsrecht ist ausgeschlossen, wenn der Eigentümer das Grundstück an seinen Ehegatten, an seinen Partner einer eingetragenen Lebenspartnerschaft oder an eine andere Person verkauft, die mit ihm in gerader Linie verwandt oder verschwägert oder in einer Seitenlinie bis zum dritten Grad verwandt ist.
(3) ¹Der durch das Vorkaufsrecht Verpflichtete hat der Gemeinde den Inhalt des mit dem Dritten abgeschlossenen Vertrages unverzüglich mitzuteilen; die Mitteilung des Verpflichteten wird durch die Mitteilung des Dritten ersetzt. ²Bei Kulturdenkmalen mit überörtlicher Bedeutung leitet die Gemeinde die Mitteilung unverzüglich an die zuständige Behörde des Freistaates weiter; der Verpflichtete kann die Mitteilung an die Landesbehörde selbst vornehmen. ³Die Frist nach Absatz 4 Satz 1 beginnt in diesem Fall mit dem Zugang der Mitteilung bei der Landesbehörde.
(4) ¹Das Vorkaufsrecht kann nur binnen zwei Monaten nach Mitteilung des Kaufvertrages ausgeübt werden. ²Die §§ 463 bis 469 Abs. 1 und § 471 des Bürgerlichen Gesetzbuches (BGB) sind anzuwenden. ³Das Vorkaufsrecht ist nicht übertragbar. ⁴Bei einem Eigentumserwerb aufgrund der Ausübung des Vorkaufsrechts erlöschen rechtsgeschäftliche Vorkaufsrechte.

§ 18 Kulturdenkmale, die der Religionsausübung dienen
(1) Die Denkmalschutzbehörden haben bei Kulturdenkmalen, die der Religionsausübung dienen, die gottesdienstlichen Belange, die von der oberen Kirchenbehörde oder der entsprechenden Stelle der betroffenen Religionsgemeinschaft festzustellen sind, vorrangig zu beachten.
(2) Entscheidungen und Maßnahmen der Denkmalschutzbehörden bei Kulturdenkmalen, die in kirchlichem Eigentum stehen, ergehen im Benehmen mit der oberen Kirchenbehörde oder der entsprechenden Stelle der betroffenen Religionsgemeinschaft.
(3) ¹§§ 11 und 12 finden keine Anwendung auf Kulturdenkmale, die in kirchlichem Eigentum stehen und dem Gottesdienst dienen, soweit die Kirchen im Einvernehmen mit der obersten Denkmalschutzbehörde eigene Vorschriften zum Schutz dieser Kulturdenkmale erlassen. ²Vor der Durchführung von Vorhaben im Sinne des § 12 Abs. 1 ist mit der zuständigen Fachbehörde Einvernehmen herzustellen. ³Ergibt sich weder mit ihr noch mit der oberen Denkmalschutzbehörde eine Einigung, so entscheidet die oberste Denkmalschutzbehörde im Benehmen mit der obersten Kirchenbehörde.
(4) Die §§ 27 bis 34 sind auf kircheneigene Kulturdenkmale und sonstige Kulturdenkmale, die der Religionsausübung dienen, nicht anwendbar.

§ 19 Sammlungen
¹Von den Genehmigungspflichten nach diesem Gesetz sind Kulturdenkmale ausgenommen, die von einer staatlichen Sammlung verwaltet werden. ²Die oberste Denkmalschutzbehörde kann andere

D13.I.1 Sächsisches Denkmalschutzgesetz

Sammlungen von den Genehmigungspflichten widerruflich ausnehmen, soweit sie fachlich betreut werden.

§ 20 Funde
(1) ¹Wer Sachen, Sachgegenstände, Teile oder Spuren von Sachen entdeckt, von denen anzunehmen ist, daß es sich um Kulturdenkmale handelt, hat dies unverzüglich einer Denkmalschutzbehörde anzuzeigen. ²Der Fund und die Fundstelle sind bis zum Ablauf des vierten Tages nach der Anzeige in unverändertem Zustand zu erhalten und zu sichern, sofern nicht die zuständige Fachbehörde mit einer Verkürzung der Frist einverstanden ist.
(2) ¹Anzeigepflichtig sind der Entdecker, der Eigentümer und der Besitzer des Grundstückes sowie der Leiter der Arbeiten, bei denen die Sache entdeckt wurde. ²Nimmt der Finder an den Arbeiten, die zu einem Fund geführt haben, aufgrund eines Arbeitsverhältnisses teil, so wird er durch die Anzeige an den Leiter oder Unternehmer der Arbeiten befreit.
(3) Die Gemeinden sind verpflichtet, die ihnen bekannt werdenden Funde unverzüglich der zuständigen Fachbehörde mitzuteilen.
(4) Die zuständige Fachbehörde oder ihre Beauftragten sind berechtigt, die Funde zu bergen, auszuwerten und zur wissenschaftlichen Bearbeitung in Besitz zu nehmen.

§ 21 Denkmalschutzgebiete
(1) ¹Die Gemeinden können im Benehmen mit den Fachbehörden oder auf deren Vorschlag Gebiete, insbesondere Straßen-, Platz- oder Ortsbilder, Ortsgrundrisse, Siedlungen, Ortsteile, Gebäudegruppen, Produktionsanlagen, an deren Erhaltung aus geschichtlichen, künstlerischen, wissenschaftlichen, städtebaulichen oder landschaftsgestalterischen Gründen ein besonderes öffentliches Interesse besteht, sowie deren Umgebung, soweit sie für deren Erscheinungsbild bedeutend ist, durch Satzung unter Schutz stellen (Denkmalschutzgebiete). ²Die Satzung bedarf der Genehmigung der nach § 112 Abs. 1 der Gemeindeordnung für den Freistaat Sachsen (SächsGemO) in der Fassung der Bekanntmachung vom 18. März 2003 (SächsGVBl. S. 55, 159), in der jeweils geltenden Fassung, zuständigen Rechtsaufsichtsbehörde. ³Für die übertragene Aufgabe gewährt der Freistaat Sachsen den Landkreisen 0,01 EUR jährlich je Einwohner.
(2) ¹Die bisherige land- und forstwirtschaftliche Nutzung im Denkmalschutzgebiet bleibt unberührt. ²Veränderungen an dem geschützten Bild des Denkmalschutzgebietes bedürfen der Genehmigung der Denkmalschutzbehörde. ³Die Genehmigung ist zu erteilen, wenn die Veränderung das Bild des Denkmalschutzgebietes nur unerheblich oder nur vorübergehend beeinträchtigen würde. ⁴Die Denkmalschutzbehörde hat vor ihrer Entscheidung die Gemeinde zu hören. ⁵§ 13 gilt entsprechend.
(3) ¹In der Satzung oder in einem der Satzung als Bestandteil beigefügten Plan ist das Gebiet zu bezeichnen, in dem Vorhaben gemäß Absatz 2 genehmigungspflichtig sind. ²Der Satzung ist eine Begründung der geschichtlichen, künstlerischen, wissenschaftlichen, städtebaulichen und landschaftsgestalterischen Merkmale beizufügen, die den Erlaß der Satzung rechtfertigt. ³Dabei sollen alle Pläne sowie zeichnerische, photographische und photogrammetrische Darstellungen verwendet werden.
(4) ¹Erläßt die Gemeinde auf einen Vorschlag der zuständigen Fachbehörde innerhalb eines Jahres keine entsprechende Satzung, so fordert die obere Denkmalschutzbehörde sie auf, die Satzung innerhalb von drei Monaten vorzulegen. ²Nach Ablauf der Frist kann die obere Denkmalschutzbehörde Denkmalschutzgebiete durch Rechtsverordnung unter Schutz stellen. ³Die Verordnung ist aufzuheben, sobald eine rechtsverbindliche Satzung vorliegt.

§ 22 Grabungsschutzgebiete
(1) ¹Die untere Denkmalschutzbehörde wird ermächtigt, Gebiete, die begründeter Vermutung nach Kulturdenkmale von besonderer Bedeutung bergen, durch Rechtsverordnung zu Grabungsschutzgebieten zu erklären. ²§ 21 Abs. 3 findet entsprechende Anwendung.
(2) ¹In Grabungsschutzgebieten dürfen Nachforschungen und Arbeiten, durch die verborgene Kulturdenkmale zutage gefördert oder gefährdet werden können, nur mit Genehmigung der Denkmalschutzbehörde vorgenommen werden. ²§ 13 Abs. 1 Satz 1 und Abs. 2 bis 5 und § 21 Abs. 2 Satz 1 gelten entsprechend.

§ 23 Archäologische Reservate
(1) ¹Die oberste Denkmalschutzbehörde wird ermächtigt, Gebiete, die begründeter Vermutung nach Kulturdenkmale von besonderer Bedeutung bergen, an denen ein besonderes übergreifendes wissen-

schaftliches Interesse besteht, durch Rechtsverordnung zu archäologischen Reservaten zu erklären. ²§ 21 Abs. 3 findet entsprechende Anwendung.
(2) ¹In archäologischen Reservaten sind Nachforschungen und Arbeiten, durch die verborgene Kulturdenkmale zutage gefördert oder gefährdet werden können, verboten. ²Die Denkmalschutzbehörde kann Befreiung erteilen, wenn die Befreiung auch unter Würdigung der Belange des Eigentümers oder Besitzers mit den Denkmalschutzbelangen vereinbar ist und
1. Gründe des Wohls der Allgemeinheit die Befreiung erfordern oder
2. das Verbot zu einer offenbar nicht beabsichtigten Härte führen würde.
(3) ¹In archäologischen Reservaten bedürfen Änderungen der bisherigen Grundstücksnutzung der Genehmigung der Denkmalschutzbehörde. ²§ 13 Abs. 1 Satz 1, Abs. 2 bis 5 und § 21 Abs. 2 Satz 1 gelten entsprechend.

§ 24 Schutz bei Katastrophen
(1) ¹Die oberste Denkmalschutzbehörde wird ermächtigt, durch Rechtsverordnung die zum Schutz der Kulturdenkmale für den Fall von Katastrophen erforderlichen Vorschriften zu erlassen. ²Dabei können insbesondere die Eigentümer und Besitzer verpflichtet werden,
1. den Aufbewahrungsort von Kulturdenkmalen zu melden,
2. Kulturdenkmale mit den in internationalen Verträgen vorgesehenen Kennzeichen versehen zu lassen,
3. Kulturdenkmale zu bergen, besonders zu sichern oder sie zum Zwecke der vorübergehenden Verwahrung an Bergungsorten auf Anordnung der Denkmalschutzbehörde abzuliefern,
4. die wissenschaftliche Erfassung von Kulturdenkmalen oder sonstige zu ihrer Dokumentierung, Sicherung oder Wiederherstellung von der Denkmalschutzbehörde angeordnete Maßnahmen zu dulden.

³Soweit in der Rechtsverordnung eine Ablieferungsfrist vorgesehen wird, ist anzuordnen, daß die abgelieferten Sachen unverzüglich den Berechtigten zurückzugeben sind, sobald die weitere Verwahrung an einem Bergungsort zum Schutz der Kulturdenkmale nicht mehr erforderlich ist.
(2) Die Ermächtigung nach Absatz 1 kann von der obersten Denkmalschutzbehörde durch Rechtsverordnung auf die nachgeordneten Denkmalschutzbehörden übertragen werden.

IV. Abschnitt
Schatzregal, Entschädigung, Enteignung

§ 25 Schatzregal
(1) Bewegliche Kulturdenkmale, die herrenlos oder so lange verborgen gewesen sind, daß ihr Eigentümer nicht mehr zu ermitteln ist, werden mit der Entdeckung Eigentum des Freistaates Sachsen und sind unverzüglich an die zuständige Fachbehörde zu melden und zu übergeben.
(2) ¹Der Finder hat Anspruch auf eine angemessene Belohnung. ²Über die Höhe entscheidet die Fachbehörde im Einvernehmen mit der obersten Denkmalschutzbehörde.

§ 26 Entschädigung
(1) ¹Soweit Maßnahmen aufgrund dieses Gesetzes enteignende Wirkung haben, ist eine angemessene Entschädigung zu leisten. ²Die Vorschriften über die Entschädigung bei förmlicher Enteignung (§§ 29 bis 31) sind entsprechend anzuwenden.
(2) Kommt eine Einigung über die Entschädigung nicht zustande, so entscheidet die obere Denkmalschutzbehörde.

§ 27 Voraussetzungen der Enteignung
(1) Die Enteignung ist zulässig, soweit die Erhaltung eines Kulturdenkmals oder seines Erscheinungsbildes, die Erhaltung eines Denkmalsschutzgebietes oder die Erhaltung eines Kulturdenkmals in einem geschützten archäologischen Reservat auf andere zumutbare Weise nicht gesichert werden kann.
(2) Die Enteignung ist außerdem zulässig
a) bei Funden, soweit auf andere Weise nicht sicherzustellen ist, daß ein Kulturdenkmal wissenschaftlich ausgewertet werden kann oder allgemein zugänglich ist,
h) bei Kulturdenkmalen, wenn die nachrichtliche Erfassung nach § 10 auf andere Weise nicht möglich ist oder den Auskunfts- und Duldungspflichten nach § 15 nicht nachgekommen wird.

(3) Zum Zwecke von planmäßigen Nachforschungen ist die Enteignung zulässig, wenn eine begründete Vermutung dafür besteht, daß durch die Nachforschung Kulturdenkmale entdeckt werden.
(4) § 92 des Baugesetzbuches gilt entsprechend.

§ 28 Gegenstand der Enteignung
Durch die Enteignung können
a) das Eigentum oder andere Rechte an Grundstücken oder beweglichen Sachen entzogen oder belastet werden,
b) Rechte entzogen werden, die zum Erwerb, zum Besitz oder zur Nutzung von Grundstücken oder beweglichen Sachen berechtigen, oder die den Verpflichteten in der Benutzung von Grundstücken oder beweglichen Sachen beschränken,
c) Rechtsverhältnisse begründet werden, die Rechte der in Buchstabe b bezeichneten Art gewähren.

§ 29 Entschädigungsgrundsätze
(1) Für die Enteignung ist eine angemessene Entschädigung in Geld zu leisten.
(2) Die Entschädigung wird gewährt
a) für den durch die Enteignung eintretenden Rechtsverlust,
b) für andere durch die Enteignung eintretende Vermögensnachteile.
(3) [1]Vermögensvorteile, die dem Entschädigungsberechtigten (§ 30) infolge der Enteignung entstehen, sind bei der Festsetzung der Entschädigung zu berücksichtigen. [2]Hat bei der Entstehung eines Vermögensnachteils ein Verschulden des Entschädigungsberechtigten mitgewirkt, so gilt § 254 BGB entsprechend.
(4) Für die Bemessung der Entschädigung ist der Zeitpunkt maßgebend, in dem die Enteignungsbehörde über die Enteignung entscheidet.
(5) Dinglich Berechtigte, die durch die Enteignung in ihren Rechten betroffen werden, sind, soweit sie nicht unmittelbar entschädigt werden, nach Maßgabe der Artikel 52 und 53 des Einführungsgesetzes zum Bürgerlichen Gesetzbuch auf die Entschädigung des Eigentümers angewiesen.

§ 30 Entschädigungsberechtigter und Entschädigungsverpflichteter
(1) Entschädigung kann erlangen, wer in seinem Recht durch Enteignung beeinträchtigt wird und dadurch einen Vermögensnachteil erleidet.
(2) [1]Zur Leistung der Entschädigung ist der Enteignungsbegünstigte verpflichtet. [2]Die Ansprüche des Berechtigten sind gegen den Freistaat zu richten. [3]Die Entschädigung wird je zur Hälfte vom Freistaat und von den kommunalen Aufgabenträgern nach § 1 Abs. 2 getragen. [4]Die Entschädigungslast der kommunalen Aufgabenträger wird bei der Verwendung der Mittel des Ausgleichstocks im Rahmen des kommunalen Finanzausgleichs als außergewöhnliche Belastung anerkannt.

§ 31 Bemessung der Entschädigung
(1) Die Entschädigung ist unter gerechter Abwägung der Interessen der Allgemeinheit und der Beteiligten zu bemessen.
(2) [1]Bei der Entschädigung für den Rechtsverlust ist der Verkehrswert zu berücksichtigen. [2]Ein Preis, der mit Rücksicht auf ungewöhnliche oder persönliche Verhältnisse zu erzielen wäre, bleibt außer Betracht.
(3) Für Vermögensnachteile, die nicht schon durch die Entschädigung nach Absatz 2 abgegolten sind, ist eine angemessene Entschädigung zu leisten, die nicht über den Betrag hinausgehen darf, der erforderlich ist, um die infolge der Enteignung eintretenden Vermögensnachteile abwenden zu können.

§ 32 Enteignungsbehörde und Enteignungsantrag
[1]Die Enteignung wird von der oberen Denkmalschutzbehörde (Enteignungsbehörde) durchgeführt. [2]Bei ihr ist der Enteignungsantrag zu stellen.

§ 33 Verfahren bei der Enteignung von Grundstücken
Ist Gegenstand der Enteignung ein Grundstück, ein Recht an einem Grundstück oder ein Recht, das zum Erwerb, zum Besitz oder zur Nutzung eines Grundstückes berechtigt oder das den Verpflichteten in der Benutzung von Grundstücken beschränkt, gelten für das Verfahren die §§ 106 bis 122 des Baugesetzbuches entsprechend, soweit in diesem Gesetz nichts Abweichendes bestimmt ist.

§ 34 Verfahren bei der Enteignung beweglicher Sachen

(1) Ist Gegenstand der Enteignung eine bewegliche Sache, ein Recht an einer beweglichen Sache oder ein Recht, das zum Erwerb, zum Besitz oder zur Nutzung der beweglichen Sache berechtigt oder den Verpflichteten in der Nutzung der beweglichen Sache beschränkt, so gelten die nachfolgenden Bestimmungen.

(2) Für das Enteignungsverfahren gelten § 107 Abs. 1 Satz 1 bis 3, § 108 Abs. 1 und Abs. 2, §§ 110, 111 und 112 Abs. 1 und Abs. 3 Nr. 1 bis 3 des Baugesetzbuches entsprechend.

(3) ¹Für den Enteignungsbeschluß gelten § 113 Abs. 1 Satz 1, Abs. 2 Nr. 1 bis 4c und 5 bis 7 des Baugesetzbuches entsprechend. ²Der Enteignungsbeschluß muß außerdem den zur Herausgabe nach dem Eintritt der Rechtsänderung Verpflichteten und die Höhe der Entschädigungen mit der Angabe, von wem und an wen sie zu leisten sind, bezeichnen.

(4) ¹Der im Enteignungsbeschluß geregelte neue Rechtszustand tritt anstelle des bisherigen Rechtszustandes, sobald der Enteignungsbeschluß unanfechtbar geworden ist. ²Der neue Rechtszustand tritt auch ein, wenn noch über die Höhe der Entschädigung gestritten wird.

(5) Soll nach dem Inhalt des Enteignungsbeschlusses der Enteignungsbegünstigte den Besitz an der Sache erhalten, so haben die Eigentümer und Besitzer ihm mit Eintritt der Rechtsänderung die Sache herauszugeben.

(6) ¹Ist zur Erhaltung, wissenschaftlichen Erfassung oder Auswertung eines Kulturdenkmals die sofortige Herausgabe an den Antragsteller dringend geboten, kann die Enteignungsbehörde durch Beschluß den Eigentümer oder Besitzer verpflichten, die Sache an den Antragsteller herauszugeben. ²Die Anordnung ist nur zulässig, wenn über sie in einer mündlichen Verhandlung verhandelt worden ist. ³§ 116 Abs. 1 Satz 3 bis 5, Abs. 2 und Absätze 4 bis 6 des Baugesetzbuches gelten entsprechend.

V. Abschnitt
Straftaten und Ordnungswidrigkeiten

§ 35 Straftaten
(1) Wer
1. ohne die nach § 12 Abs. 1 Nr. 5 erforderliche Genehmigung ein Kulturdenkmal oder einen wesentlichen Teil eines Kulturdenkmals zerstört, oder
2. ohne die nach § 14 Abs. 2 erforderliche Genehmigung Grabungen mit dem Ziel, Kulturdenkmale zu entdecken, durchführt,

wird mit Freiheitsstrafe bis zu zwei Jahren oder Geldstrafen bestraft.

(2) Die fahrlässige Begehung einer Tat nach Absatz 1 wird mit Freiheitsstrafe bis zu einem Jahr oder Geldstrafe bestraft.

(3) Reste eines Kulturdenkmals, das durch eine Tat nach Absatz 1 zerstört worden ist, können eingezogen werden.

§ 36 Ordnungswidrigkeiten
(1) Ordnungswidrig handelt, wer vorsätzlich oder fahrlässig
1. ohne Genehmigung der Denkmalschutzbehörde die in § 12 Abs. 1 Nr. 1 bis 4, Abs. 1 Nr. 5, zweite Alternative und Abs. 2 Sätze 1 und 2, § 14 Abs. 1, § 14 Abs. 2 (soweit die Tat nicht nach § 35 mit Strafe bedroht ist), § 21 Abs. 2 Satz 2, § 22 Abs. 2 Satz 1, § 23 Abs. 3 Satz 1 bezeichneten Handlungen vornimmt oder den in Genehmigungen enthaltenen vollziehbaren Auflagen zuwiderhandelt,
2. den ihn nach §§ 16, 20 Abs. 1 und 2 treffenden Pflichten zuwiderhandelt,
3. den Maßnahmen der Denkmalschutzbehörden nach § 4 Abs. 3, § 11 Abs. 1 und 2 zuwiderhandelt, sofern die Behörde auf diese Bußgeldvorschrift verweist,
4. den Vorschriften einer nach § 21 Abs. 4 Satz 2, § 22 Abs. 1 Satz 1, § 23 Abs. 1 Satz 1, § 24 Abs. 1 Satz 1 erlassenen Rechtsverordnung zuwiderhandelt, soweit die Rechtsverordnung auf diese Bußgeldvorschrift verweist,
5. den Vorschriften einer nach § 21 Abs. 1 erlassenen Satzung zuwiderhandelt, soweit die Satzung für einen bestimmten Tatbestand auf diese Bußgeldvorschrift verweist,
6. die in § 23 Abs. 2 Satz 1 bezeichneten Handlungen ohne Befreiung vornimmt.

D13.I.1 Sächsisches Denkmalschutzgesetz

(2) Die Ordnungswidrigkeit kann mit einer Geldbuße bis zu 125 000 EUR, in besonders schweren Fällen bis zu 500 000 EUR geahndet werden.
(3) Gegenstände, auf die sich eine Ordnungswidrigkeit nach Absatz 1 Nr. 1 und 3 bis 6 bezieht, können eingezogen werden.
(4) Die Verfolgung der Ordnungswidrigkeit verjährt in fünf Jahren.
(5) Verwaltungsbehörde im Sinne von § 36 Abs. 1 Nr. 1 des Gesetzes über Ordnungswidrigkeiten ist die untere Denkmalschutzbehörde.

VI. Abschnitt
Schlußbestimmungen

§ 37 *[aufgehoben]*

§ 38 Übergangsvorschriften
(1) Die zentrale Denkmalliste, die Bezirksdenkmallisten und die Kreisdenkmallisten einschließlich der Nachträge und der vorläufigen Unterschutzstellungen nach §§ 7 Abs. 2, 8 Abs. 2, 9 Abs. 2 und 13 Satz 2 des Denkmalpflegegesetzes der DDR vom 19. Juni 1975 (GBl. I Nr. 26 S. 458) sowie die Liste der Bodenaltertümer einschließlich der Nachträge nach § 6 Abs. 1 der Verordnung der DDR zum Schutze und zur Erhaltung der ur- und frühgeschichtlichen Bodenaltertümer vom 28. Mai 1954 (GBl. I Nr. 54 S. 547) gelten, soweit diese Listen das Gebiet des Freistaates Sachsen betreffen, als vorläufiges Verzeichnis der Kulturdenkmale (§ 10) für das jeweilige Gemeindegebiet solange weiter, bis das Verzeichnis nach § 10 für das Gemeindegebiet erstellt ist.
(2) Die Denkmalschutzbehörde kann einzelne Objekte in den in Absatz 1 genannten Denkmallisten löschen, wenn bei ihnen die Voraussetzungen nach § 2 nicht vorliegen.

§ 39 Aufhebung von Vorschriften
[hier nicht wiedergegeben]

§ 40 Inkrafttreten
Dieses Gesetz tritt am Tag nach seiner Verkündung[1] in Kraft.

---

1) Verkündet am 16.3.1993.

Verordnung des Sächsischen Staatsministeriums des Innern über die Entschädigung und den Reisekostenersatz für die ehrenamtlichen Beauftragten für Denkmalpflege (Denkmalpflegeentschädigungsverordnung)

Vom 4. April 2015 (SächsGVBl. S. 291)
(BS Sachsen 46-1.1/2)

Aufgrund von § 7 Absatz 4 Satz 1 des Sächsischen Denkmalschutzgesetzes vom 3. März 1993 (SächsGVBl. S. 229), das zuletzt durch Artikel 4 des Gesetzes vom 2. April 2014 (SächsGVBl. S. 234) geändert worden ist, wird mit Zustimmung des Staatsministeriums der Finanzen verordnet:

§ 1 Gegenstand der Förderung

(1) [1]Ehrenamtliche Beauftragte für Denkmalpflege erhalten eine Entschädigung und Reisekostenersatz in Form einer jährlichen Pauschale. [2]Die Höhe der Pauschale richtet sich nach den jährlich bereitgestellten Haushaltsmitteln. [3]Sie darf einen Höchstbetrag von 200 Euro nicht überschreiten.

(2) Mit der Pauschale sind alle notwendigen Aufwendungen, die den ehrenamtlichen Beauftragten für Denkmalpflege im Zusammenhang mit ihrer Tätigkeit entstehen, abgegolten.

(3) Voraussetzung für die Auszahlung der Pauschale ist die Vorlage eines Tätigkeitsberichtes gemäß § 2 Absatz 4.

§ 2 Verfahren

(1) Die unteren Denkmalschutzbehörden melden bis zum 30. April des jeweiligen Haushaltsjahres die Anzahl der berufenen ehrenamtlichen Beauftragten für Denkmalpflege an die obere Denkmalschutzbehörde.

(2) Die oberste Denkmalschutzbehörde erteilt der oberen Denkmalschutzbehörde bis zum 30. April des jeweiligen Haushaltsjahres die Ermächtigung zur Bewirtschaftung des Haushaltstitels 0323/671 31-7.

(3) [1]Die obere Denkmalschutzbehörde teilt die zur Bewirtschaftung zugewiesenen Haushaltsmittel durch die Gesamtzahl der im Freistaat Sachsen gemeldeten ehrenamtlichen Beauftragten für Denkmalpflege. [2]Diesen Quotienten multipliziert sie mit der Zahl der von der jeweiligen unteren Denkmalschutzbehörde gemeldeten ehrenamtlichen Beauftragten für Denkmalpflege. [3]Das Produkt dieser Rechnung ist der auf die jeweilige untere Denkmalschutzbehörde entfallende Anteil. [4]Die obere Denkmalschutzbehörde erteilt der jeweiligen unteren Denkmalschutzbehörde bis zum 30. Juni des jeweiligen Haushaltsjahres die Ermächtigung zur Bewirtschaftung der auf sie entfallenden Haushaltsmittel.

(4) [1]Die ehrenamtlichen Beauftragten für Denkmalpflege legen bis zum 15. Oktober der unteren Denkmalschutzbehörde einen Tätigkeitsbericht für den Zeitraum vom 1. Oktober des Vorjahres bis zum 30. September des laufenden Jahres vor (Anlage). [2]Ist die Berufung des ehrenamtlichen Beauftragten für Denkmalpflege nach dem 1. Oktober des Vorjahres erfolgt oder ist vor dem 30. September des laufenden Jahres der Zeitraum der Berufung abgelaufen oder wurde sie widerrufen, so umfasst der Tätigkeitsbericht den Zeitraum, für den der ehrenamtliche Beauftragte für Denkmalpflege berufen war. [3]Voraussetzung für die Auszahlung der Pauschale ist ein Tätigkeitsbericht über einen zusammenhängenden Zeitraum von mindestens drei Monaten. [4]Der Tätigkeitsbericht gibt Auskunft über die Erfüllung der Aufgaben gemäß § 7 Absatz 2 des Sächsischen Denkmalschutzgesetzes.

(5) [1]Die untere Denkmalschutzbehörde teilt die ihr zur Bewirtschaftung zugewiesenen Haushaltsmittel durch die Zahl der von ihr berufenen ehrenamtlichen Beauftragten für Denkmalpflege, die einen Tätigkeitsbericht nach Absatz 4 vorgelegt haben. [2]Der Quotient hieraus ist die Pauschale gemäß § 1 Absatz 1. [3]Die untere Denkmalschutzbehörde zahlt die Pauschalen bis zum 30. November an die zuwendungsberechtigten ehrenamtlichen Beauftragten für Denkmalpflege aus.

(6) Die unteren Denkmalschutzbehörden erstatten der oberen Denkmalschutzbehörde bis zum 31. Januar des folgenden Jahres Bericht über die zweckentsprechende Verwendung der Haushaltsmittel, insbesondere über die Berechnung der Pauschale, über die ausgezahlten Beträge und in zusammengefasster Form über die Tätigkeitsberichte der ehrenamtlichen Beauftragten für Denkmalpflege.

§ 3 Inkrafttreten und Außerkrafttreten

[1]Diese Verordnung tritt am Tag nach ihrer Verkündung[1]) in Kraft. [2]Gleichzeitig tritt die Denkmalpflegeentschädigungsverordnung vom 8. Dezember 1995 (SächsGVBl. S. 431), die durch Artikel 12 § 7 des Gesetzes vom 12. Dezember 2008 (SächsGVBl. S. 866) geändert worden ist, außer Kraft.

Anlage
(zu § 2 Absatz 4)

Tätigkeitsbericht (Muster)
ehrenamtlicher Beauftragter/ehrenamtliche Beauftragte für Denkmalpflege

Name, Adresse
Telefon, E-Mail
IBAN/BIC

untere Denkmalschutzbehörde
Berichtszeitraum
Tätigkeitsbericht

	Datum/Tätigkeit
Aufsuchen bestimmter Kulturdenkmale, Gründe hierfür	
Beratungen mit Denkmalschutz- oder Denkmalfachbehörden sowie Denkmaleigentümern	
Unterstützung der Denkmalschutz- und/oder Denkmalfachbehörden	
Informationsveranstaltungen gestaltet/unterstützt (zum Beispiel Tag des offenen Denkmals, PEGASUS und Ähnliches)	
Archivrecherchen (zum Beispiel Stadt- beziehungsweise Staatsarchiv, Kirchenarchive, Heimatsammlungen)	
Sonstiges	

Datum, Unterschrift

Ehrenamtlicher Beauftragter/ehrenamtliche Beauftragte für Denkmalpflege

(nicht von dem ehrenamtlichen Beauftragten/der ehrenamtlichen Beauftragten für Denkmalpflege auszufüllen)

Untere Denkmalschutzbehörde

Voraussetzungen für Auszahlung der Pauschale

☐ erfüllt

☐ nicht erfüllt

Begründung:

Datum, Unterschrift
Untere Denkmalschutzbehörde

---

1) Verkündet am 29.4.2015.

Verwaltungsvorschrift des Sächsischen Staatsministeriums des Innern über die ehrenamtlichen Beauftragten für Denkmalpflege und zur Aufhebung einer Verwaltungsvorschrift (VwV Ehrenamtliche Beauftragte für Denkmalpflege)

Vom 4. April 2015 (SächsABl. 2015 Nr. 17, S. 534)

I. Berufung

1. Zur Unterstützung und Beratung der unteren Denkmalschutzbehörden und der Denkmalfachbehörden werden ehrenamtliche Beauftragte für Denkmalpflege bestellt. Die ehrenamtlichen Beauftragten für Denkmalpflege werden von der unteren Denkmalschutzbehörde im Einvernehmen mit den Denkmalfachbehörden berufen. Eine Pflicht zur Übernahme einer Tätigkeit als ehrenamtlicher Beauftragter für Denkmalpflege besteht nicht.
2. In jeder unteren Denkmalschutzbehörde soll mindestens je ein ehrenamtlicher Beauftragter für Denkmalpflege berufen werden
   a) für den Fachbereich Bau- und Kunstdenkmalpflege einschließlich technische Denkmale und
   b) für den Fachbereich Archäologie.
   Die Berufung kann aus wichtigem Grund widerrufen werden.
3. Ehrenamtliche Beauftragte für Denkmalpflege können auch berufen werden für das Gebiet einer unteren Denkmalschutzbehörde nach § 3 Absatz 2 des Sächsischen Denkmalschutzgesetzes vom 3. März 1993 (SächsGVBl. S. 229), das zuletzt durch Artikel 4 des Gesetzes vom 2. April 2014 (SächsGVBl. S. 234) geändert worden ist.
4. Die ehrenamtlichen Beauftragten für Denkmalpflege werden auf die Dauer von fünf Jahren berufen.
5. Die ehrenamtlichen Beauftragten für Denkmalpflege erhalten bei der Berufung einen Ausweis (Anlage).[1)] Dieser ist zurückzugeben, wenn die Berufung abgelaufen ist oder widerrufen wird.
6. Die ehrenamtlichen Beauftragten für Denkmalpflege werden nach § 1 des Verpflichtungsgesetzes vom 2. März 1974 (BGBl. I S. 469, 547), das durch § 1 Nummer 4 des Gesetzes vom 15. August 1974 (BGBl. I S. 1942) geändert worden ist, in der jeweils geltenden Fassung, bei Übernahme ihrer Aufgaben verpflichtet.

II. Rechtsstellung der ehrenamtlichen Beauftragten für Denkmalpflege

1. Die nach Ziffer I berufenen Personen sind ehrenamtlich tätig. Sie sind Beauftragte der Denkmalschutzbehörden und Denkmalfachbehörden (vergleiche § 7, § 15 Absatz 2 und § 20 Absatz 4 des Sächsischen Denkmalschutzgesetzes). Sie haben ihre Tätigkeit gewissenhaft und unparteiisch auszuüben und sind zur Verschwiegenheit über die ihnen bei Ausübung ihrer Tätigkeit bekannt gewordenen Angelegenheiten verpflichtet. Der Umfang der Verschwiegenheitspflicht bestimmt sich nach § 1 des Gesetzes zur Regelung des Verwaltungsverfahrens- und Verwaltungszustellungsrechts für den Freistaat Sachsen vom 19. Mai 2010 (SächsGVBl. S. 142), das durch Artikel 3 des Gesetzes vom 12. Juli 2013 (SächsGVBl. S. 503) geändert worden ist, in Verbindung mit § 84 des Verwaltungsverfahrensgesetzes in der Fassung der Bekanntmachung vom 23. Januar 2003 (BGBl. I S. 102), das zuletzt durch Artikel 3 des Gesetzes vom 25. Juli 2013 (BGBl. I S. 2749) geändert worden ist, in den jeweils geltenden Fassungen.
2. Die ehrenamtlichen Beauftragten für Denkmalpflege sind für die Denkmalschutzbehörden und die Denkmalfachbehörden tätig. Sie werden durch die Denkmalfachbehörde fachlich angeleitet, für deren Fachbereich sie berufen wurden. Sie üben ihre Tätigkeit regelmäßig außerhalb ihrer beruflichen Arbeitszeit aus.

III. Allgemeine Aufgaben, Information

1. Die ehrenamtlichen Beauftragten für Denkmalpflege beraten und unterstützen die Denkmalschutzbehörden, indem sie ihnen ihre fachlichen Kenntnisse zugänglich machen, fachbezogene Informationen aus ihrem Bereich vermitteln und das allgemeine Verständnis für die Anliegen von Denkmalpflege und Denkmalschutz fördern.

---

1) Die Anlage konnte aus drucktechnischen Gründen nicht aufgenommen werden.

D13.I.1b VwV Ehrenamtliche Beauftragte für Denkmalpflege

2. Die ehrenamtlichen Beauftragten für Denkmalpflege beobachten in ihrem Bereich alle Planungen, Vorhaben und Vorgänge, von denen die Belange der Denkmalpflege und des Denkmalschutzes berührt sein können, im Hinblick auf die Wahrung dieser Belange. Hierzu gehört auch die Beobachtung der örtlichen und überörtlichen Informationsmedien. Hierzu gehören vor allem Presse, Rundfunk und Fernsehen.
3. Die ehrenamtlichen Beauftragten für Denkmalpflege unterrichten in erster Linie die Denkmalschutzbehörden und die Denkmalfachbehörden über alle Beobachtungen in ihrem Bereich, insbesondere wenn eine denkmalschutzrechtliche Maßnahme erforderlich sein könnte. Sie geben den Denkmalschutzbehörden sonstige zweckdienliche Auskünfte, Hinweise und Anregungen.
4. Die ehrenamtlichen Beauftragten für Denkmalpflege erhalten darüber hinaus im Einzelfall Aufträge der Denkmalschutzbehörden sowie der Denkmalfachbehörden.
5. Bei Gefahr im Verzug für ein Kulturdenkmal sollen die ehrenamtlichen Beauftragten für Denkmalpflege die zuständige untere Denkmalschutzbehörde unterrichten, um ihr ein rechtzeitiges Tätigwerden zu ermöglichen. Erscheint dies nicht erreichbar, sollen sie die zuständige Denkmalfachbehörde oder, falls auch diese nicht rechtzeitig tätig werden kann, die Polizei unterrichten, um dieser ein Tätigwerden nach § 4 Absatz 3 des Sächsischen Denkmalschutzgesetzes zu ermöglichen.

IV. Entscheidungen, gesetzliche Aufgaben

1. Bei allen Fragen, zu deren Klärung die Sachkenntnis der Denkmalschutzbehörden und die Sach- und Fachkenntnis der Denkmalfachbehörden insbesondere wissenschaftlicher und konservatorischer Art eingesetzt werden müssen, haben die ehrenamtlichen Beauftragten für Denkmalpflege die Denkmalschutzbehörden und die Denkmalfachbehörden unverzüglich zu informieren. Die ehrenamtlichen Beauftragten für Denkmalpflege sind nicht befugt, für die Denkmalfachbehörden eine Erklärung nach § 4 Absatz 2 des Sächsischen Denkmalschutzgesetzes abzugeben.
2. Die ehrenamtlichen Beauftragten für Denkmalpflege sind berechtigt, von Eigentümern und Besitzern von Kulturdenkmalen freiwillig erteilte Auskünfte entgegenzunehmen und an die zuständige Denkmalschutzbehörde weiterzuleiten.
3. Die ehrenamtlichen Beauftragten für Denkmalpflege sind befugt, nach vorheriger Benachrichtigung und mit Einwilligung der Eigentümer und Besitzer von Kulturdenkmalen soweit erforderlich
    a) Grundstücke zu betreten,
    b) Kulturdenkmale zu besichtigen,
    c) mit entsprechendem Auftrag einer Denkmalfachbehörde wissenschaftliche Erfassungsmaßnahmen durchzuführen, insbesondere Einsicht in Archive und Sammlungen zu nehmen.
4. Die ehrenamtlichen Beauftragten für Denkmalpflege sind befugt, mit Einwilligung der Eigentümer oder Besitzer und soweit sie dazu von einer Denkmalfachbehörde ermächtigt sind und dies ohne Grabungsarbeiten möglich ist, Funde von Kulturdenkmalen zu bergen und zur wissenschaftlichen Bearbeitung für die zuständige Denkmalfachbehörde in Besitz zu nehmen (Notbergung).
5. Die ehrenamtlichen Beauftragten für Denkmalpflege sind nicht befugt, eigenständig Grabungen durchzuführen. Sie haben Funde, Dokumentationen und alle sonstigen bei der Wahrnehmung ihrer Aufgaben in ihren Besitz gelangten Gegenstände an die zuständige Denkmalfachbehörde zu übergeben.
6. Die Durchsetzung der Auskunfts- und Duldungspflicht nach Ziffer IV Nummer 2 und 3 und der Fundsicherungsarbeiten nach Ziffer IV Nummer 4 gegen den Willen des Eigentümers oder Besitzers obliegt der zuständigen Denkmalschutzbehörde.
7. Die Ausübung der den ehrenamtlichen Beauftragten für Denkmalpflege zustehenden Befugnisse kann beträchtliche rechtliche und finanzielle Folgen haben. Die ehrenamtlichen Beauftragten für Denkmalpflege haben sich deshalb mit der Ausübung dieser Befugnisse auf die unter den gegebenen Umständen notwendigen Maßnahmen zu beschränken. Das von ihnen beabsichtigte Vorgehen haben sie möglichst vorher der zuständigen Denkmalschutzbehörde oder einer Denkmalfachbehörde mitzuteilen. Falls eine vorherige Benachrichtigung einer Denkmalschutzbehörde nicht möglich ist, haben sie die zuständige Denkmalschutzbehörde unverzüglich über das Veranlasste zu unterrichten.

V. Verbindungen mit nahestehenden Institutionen und Personen

1. Die ehrenamtlichen Beauftragten für Denkmalpflege pflegen Verbindungen mit Institutionen und Personen, die der Denkmalpflege Verständnis entgegenbringen oder ihr förderlich sein können, insbesondere mit
   a) Behörden und Dienststellen. Hierzu gehören insbesondere die Ämter der Landkreise, Kreisfreien Städte und Gemeinden, das Landesamt für Straßenbau und Verkehr (LASuV) einschließlich seiner Niederlassungen, das Sächsische Landesamt für Umwelt, Landwirtschaft und Geologie (LfULG) einschließlich seiner Außenstellen sowie die Flurbereinigungsbehörden,
   b) Schulen und Einrichtungen der Erwachsenenbildung,
   c) Kirchgemeinden,
   d) Museen und Sammlungen,
   e) den öffentlichen Archiven,
   f) den im Naturschutzdienst tätigen Personen,
   g) den Informationsmedien und
   h) den Vereinen.
2. Die Pflege der Verbindungen mit nahestehenden Institutionen und Personen nach Ziffer V Nummer 1 kann insbesondere im Austausch von fachlichen Informationen, von Informationsmaterial sowie in Vorträgen oder Führungen bestehen.

VI. Hinweise

1. Die ehrenamtlichen Beauftragten für Denkmalpflege sind bei der Wahrnehmung ihrer Aufgaben gegen Arbeitsunfälle nach § 2 Absatz 1 Nummer 10 a des Siebten Buches Sozialgesetzbuch – Gesetzliche Unfallversicherung – (Artikel 1 des Gesetzes vom 7. August 1996, BGBl. I S. 1254), das zuletzt durch Artikel 2 Absatz 22 des Gesetzes vom 1. April 2015 (BGBl. I S. 434) geändert worden ist, in der jeweils geltenden Fassung, versichert.
2. Verletzt ein ehrenamtlicher Beauftragter für Denkmalpflege bei der Ausübung seiner hoheitlichen Aufgaben eine Amtspflicht, die ihm einem Dritten gegenüber obliegt, so richtet sich die Haftung für den dem Dritten entstandenen Schaden nach § 839 BGB in Verbindung mit Artikel 34 des Grundgesetzes (unmittelbare Haftung durch den Dienstherrn, Rückgriff gegen den Beauftragten nur bei vorsätzlicher oder grob fahrlässiger Amtspflichtverletzung).

VII. Inkrafttreten und Außerkrafttreten

1. Diese Verwaltungsvorschrift tritt am Tag nach ihrer Veröffentlichung in Kraft. Gleichzeitig tritt die Verwaltungsvorschrift des Sächsischen Staatsministeriums des Innern über ehrenamtliche Beauftragte für Denkmalpflege vom 15. September 1993 (SächsABl. 1994 S. 2), zuletzt enthalten in der Verwaltungsvorschrift vom 6. Dezember 2013 (SächsABl. SDr. S. S 808), außer Kraft.
2. Die Verwaltungsvorschrift des Sächsischen Staatsministeriums des Innern zur Verordnung über die Entschädigung und den Reisekostenersatz für ehrenamtliche Beauftragte für Denkmalpflege vom 10. Juni 2004 (SächsABl. S. 702), die durch Ziffer XXVI der Verwaltungsvorschrift vom 1. März 2012 (SächsABl. S. 336) geändert worden ist, zuletzt enthalten in der Verwaltungsvorschrift vom 6. Dezember 2013 (SächsABl. SDr. S. S 808), tritt außer Kraft.

# D13.I.1c VwV Geschäftsordnung Denkmalrat

Verwaltungsvorschrift des Sächsischen Staatsministerium des Innern über die Geschäftsordnung für den Denkmalrat
(VwV GeschO Denkmalrat)

Vom 15. September 1993 (SächsAbl. 1994 S. 5),
zuletzt geändert durch die Verwaltungsvorschrift vom 23. Juni 2017 (SächsAbl. S. 955)

Aufgrund von § 6 Abs. 4 Satz 2 des Gesetzes zum Schutz und zur Pflege der Kulturdenkmale im Freistaat Sachsen (Sächsisches Denkmalschutzgesetz – SächsDSchG) vom 3. März 1993 (SächsGVBl. S. 229) erläßt das Sächsische Staatsministerium des Innern als oberste Denkmalschutzbehörde folgende Geschäftsordnung für den Denkmalrat:

1 Aufgabe

1.1 Beim Sächsischen Staatsministerium des Innern wird ein Denkmalrat gebildet. Der Denkmalrat soll vom Sächsischen Staatsministerium des Innern in allen Fragen von grundsätzlicher Bedeutung gehört werden. Das Sächsische Staatsministerium des Innern kann vom Denkmalrat Vorschläge in sonstigen den Denkmalschutz und die Denkmalpflege betreffenden wichtigen Angelegenheiten einholen.

1.2 Auf Verlangen des Sächsischen Staatsministeriums für Wissenschaft und Kunst gibt das Sächsische Staatsministerium des Innern dem Denkmalrat Gelegenheit zur Äußerung. Der Denkmalrat kann auch ohne Aufforderung durch das Sächsische Staatsministerium des Innern zur Angelegenheit der Denkmalpflege Stellung nehmen.

2 Zusammensetzung

2.1 Vorsitzender des Denkmalrates ist der Staatsminister des Innern oder ein von ihm Beauftragter.
2.2 Die Mitglieder des Denkmalrates werden vom Sächsischen Staatsministerium des Innern im Benehmen mit dem Landesamt für Denkmalpflege und dem Landesamt für Archäologie berufen. Die Staatsministerien des Innern und für Wissenschaft und Kunst sowie die Fachbehörden haben ein Vorschlagsrecht. Es werden berufen:
a) ein Vertreter der Evangelisch-Lutherischen Landeskirche Sachsens,
b) ein Vertreter der katholischen Kirche,
c) zwei Vertreter der Kommunalen Landesverbände,
d) ein Vertreter der Universitäten,
e) zwei Kulturdenkmaleigentümer oder zwei Vertreter einer Vereinigung von Kulturdenkmaleigentümern,
f) ein Vertreter der Wirtschaft,
g) ein Mitglied eines Heimatschutzverbandes.

2.3 Als Mitglieder des Denkmalrates werden aufgrund ihres Amtes vom Sächsischen Staatsministerium des Innern berufen:
a) der/die Landeskonservator/Landeskonservatorin des Landesamtes für Denkmalpflege,
b) der/die Landesarchäologe/Landesarchäologin des Landesamtes für Archäologie,
c) der Landesdirektionspräsident,
d) ein Vertreter der staatlichen Hochbauverwaltung.

Als stellvertretende Mitglieder werden die Stellvertreter im Amt berufen.

2.4 Die Mitglieder des Denkmalrates sind ehrenamtlich tätig. Für ihre Tätigkeit gelten die §§ 82 bis 87 des Vorläufigen Verwaltungsverfahrensgesetzes (SächsVwVfG) vom 21. Januar 1993 (SächsGVBl. S. 74).

2.5 Die Berufung erfolgt auf die Dauer von fünf Jahren, sie kann zweimal wiederholt werden. Aus wichtigem Grund kann die Berufung widerrufen werden. Beruht die Mitgliedschaft auf einem öffentlichen Amt oder einem Amt bei der entsendenden Stelle, so endet sie spätestens mit dem Ablauf der Amtszeit.

2.6 Personen, die in besonderer Weise auf dem Gebiet der Denkmalpflege Verdienste erworben haben, können als Ehrenmitglieder vom Staatsministerium des Innern berufen werden. Die Staatsministerien des Innern und für Wissenschaft und Kunst sowie die Fachbehörden haben ein Vorschlagsrecht.

Das Ehrenmitglied hat kein Stimmrecht bei der Einberufung des Denkmalrates nach Nummer 4.3 Satz 2 und bei den Beschlüssen nach Nummer 6.

3 Fachausschüsse

3.1 Der Denkmalrat kann Fachausschüsse bilden für die Fachbereiche
a) Bau- und Kunstdenkmalpflege,
b) Archäologie,
c) technische Denkmale.

3.2 Der Denkmalrat kann die Beschlußfassung über Angelegenheiten, die sich nur auf einen der Fachbereiche der Denkmalpflege beziehen, allgemein oder im Einzelfall dem zuständigen Fachausschuß übertragen. Unbeschadet einer solchen Übertragung hat der Denkmalrat einen Beschluß zu fassen, wenn die Mehrheit des Fachausschusses dies beschließt oder das Sächsische Staatsministerium des Innern es verlangt.

3.3 Die Fachausschüsse können zu den Beratungen einzelner Angelegenheiten sachkompetente Personen mit beratender Stimme hinzuziehen.

4 Einberufung

4.1 Die Sitzungen des Denkmalrates werden vom Vorsitzenden einberufen. Das Sächsische Staatsministerium für Wissenschaft und Kunst ist zu verständigen.

4.2 Der Denkmalrat kann einberufen werden, wenn mindestens zehn Mitglieder berufen sind.

4.3 Jährlich soll mindestens eine Sitzung stattfinden. Ein Drittel der Mitglieder des Denkmalrates können verlangen, daß eine Sitzung einberufen wird.

4.4 Die Einberufung soll mindestens 14 Tage vor der Sitzung unter Angabe der Tagesordnungspunkte erfolgen. Die Tagesordnung bestimmt der Vorsitzende. Ein Drittel der Mitglieder des Denkmalrates, ferner das Sächsische Staatsministerium für Wissenschaft und Kunst können verlangen, daß weitere Punkte auf die Tagesordnung gesetzt werden.

4.5 Nummer 4.1, Nummer 4.3 Satz 2 und Nummer 4.4 gelten für die Fachausschüsse entsprechend.

5 Sitzung

5.1 Der Vorsitzende leitet die Sitzung. Die Sitzung ist nicht öffentlich. Der Vorsitzende kann im Einzelfall die Öffentlichkeit zulassen.

5.2 Der Vorsitzende lädt, falls erforderlich oder auf Verlangen des Sächsischen Staatsministeriums für Wissenschaft und Kunst weitere Sachverständige oder sonstige Personen, insbesondere Betroffene, zu der Sitzung ein.

5.3 Bei der Behandlung von Fragen des Denkmalschutzes und der Denkmalpflege, durch welche ethnische oder konfessionelle Gruppen oder besondere Denkmalarten betroffen sind, hat der Vorsitzende einen Vertreter dieser Gruppen mit beratender Stimme beizuziehen.

5.4 Vertreter des Sächsischen Staatsministeriums für Wissenschaft und Kunst haben das Recht, an der Sitzung teilzunehmen.

5.5 Über die Sitzung ist eine Niederschrift anzufertigen. Darin sind die Namen des Vorsitzenden, der anwesenden Mitglieder und weiteren Sitzungsteilnehmern sowie die behandelten Gegenstände, die gestellten Anträge und die gefaßten Beschlüsse festzuhalten. Die Niederschrift ist vom Vorsitzenden und, soweit ein Schriftführer hinzugezogen worden ist, auch von diesem zu unterzeichnen. Die Mitglieder erhalten eine Ausfertigung der Sitzungsniederschrift.

6 Beschlüsse

6.1 Der Denkmalrat oder ein Ausschuß ist beschlußfähig, wenn mehr als die Hälfte der Mitglieder anwesend ist.

6.2 Bei der Abstimmung entscheidet die einfache Mehrheit. Bei Stimmengleichheit entscheidet die Stimme des Vorsitzenden, der zuletzt abstimmt.

6.3 Außerhalb der Sitzungen können Beschlüsse im Umlaufverfahren gefaßt werden. Dabei ist Einstimmigkeit erforderlich.

7 Laufende Geschäfte

Die laufenden Geschäfte führt das Sächsische Staatsministerium des Innern.

8 Schlußbestimmung

Die Geschäftsordnung tritt am Tage nach ihrer Veröffentlichung in Kraft.

Verwaltungsvorschrift des Sächsischen Staatsministeriums des Innern für die Erfassung von Kulturdenkmalen in öffentlichen Verzeichnissen (VwV Kulturdenkmallisten)[1)]

Vom 8. September 2016 (SächsABl. S. 1236)

I.
Anwendungsbereich

1. Diese Verwaltungsvorschrift regelt die nachrichtliche Erfassung von Kulturdenkmalen in öffentlichen Verzeichnissen (Kulturdenkmallisten) gemäß § 10 des Sächsischen Denkmalschutzgesetzes vom 3. März 1993 (SächsGVBl. S. 229), das zuletzt durch Artikel 4 des Gesetzes vom 2. April 2014 (SächsGVBl. S. 234) geändert worden ist, in der jeweils geltenden Fassung.
2. Das Landesamt für Denkmalpflege und das Landesamt für Archäologie Sachsen führen jeweils eine Kulturdenkmalliste, in die mit Ausnahme von Nummer 3 alle Kulturdenkmale gemäß § 2 Absatz 1 des Sächsischen Denkmalschutzgesetzes aufgenommen werden sollen.
3. Bewegliche Kulturdenkmale, die zu einer staatlichen oder kommunalen Sammlung gehören, werden in der Regel nicht in die Kulturdenkmallisten aufgenommen.
4. Die Erfassung von Kulturdenkmalen, die sowohl durch das Landesamt für Denkmalpflege als auch durch das Landesamt für Archäologie Sachsen betreut werden, wird einvernehmlich zwischen dem Landesamt für Denkmalpflege und dem Landesamt für Archäologie Sachsen geregelt. Eine Erfassung von Kulturdenkmalen, die Zuständigkeiten beider Fachbehörden berühren (zum Beispiel Burganlagen, Kirchen), ist in beiden Erfassungssystemen möglich.

II.
Ermittlung der Kulturdenkmaleigenschaft

1. Die Ermittlung der Kulturdenkmaleigenschaft erfolgt im Einzelfall durch Feststellung der gesetzlichen Tatbestände anhand objektiver Merkmale. Voraussetzung für die Denkmaleigenschaft eines Objektes ist dessen Denkmalfähigkeit und Denkmalwürdigkeit.
2. Denkmalfähigkeit bedeutet, dass das Objekt mindestens eine geschichtliche, künstlerische, wissenschaftliche, städtebauliche oder landschaftsgestaltende Bedeutung haben muss. Ein denkmalfähiges Objekt ist denkmalwürdig, wenn ein öffentliches Erhaltungsinteresse an ihm besteht.
3. Die Denkmalwürdigkeit von Bauwerken mit geschichtlicher Bedeutung hängt nicht von vorrangig ästhetischen Gesichtspunkten, sondern vom Bestehen eines öffentlichen Interesses an der Erhaltung des im Schutzobjekt verkörperten besonderen Aussagewerts, Erinnerungswerts oder Assoziationswerts ab. Eine geschichtliche Bedeutungskategorie ist nicht allein auf übergeordnete oder besonders bedeutsame Entwicklungen oder Verhältnisse beschränkt, sondern sie umfasst vielmehr auch Gegenstände des Denkmalschutzes, die nur für die regionale, Heimat- oder Stadtgeschichte von Bedeutung sind und diese dokumentieren. Der Schutzgrund der künstlerischen Bedeutung erfordert ein gesteigertes Maß an ästhetischer oder gestalterischer Qualität. Für den Schutzgrund der städtebaulichen Bedeutung ist es nicht ausreichend, wenn ein Gebäude die Gliederung und das Erscheinungsbild eines Ortskerns oder Stadtkerns, eines Ortsteils oder Stadtteils, einer Straße oder eines Platzes oder die ländliche Siedlungsstruktur (mit)prägt. Städtebauliche Gründe sind nur gegeben, wenn das Objekt zu einer stadtgeschichtlichen oder stadtentwicklungsgeschichtlichen Unverwechselbarkeit führt, die entweder auf eine einheitliche Planung zurückzuführen oder aus anderen Gründen im Laufe der Zeit zustande gekommen ist.
4. Die Denkmalwürdigkeit ist ein Korrektiv zur Denkmalfähigkeit. Aus der Vielzahl grundsätzlich denkmalfähiger Objekte sollen nur diejenigen ausgewählt werden, die auch denkmalwürdig sind. Dabei gilt der Kenntnis- und Wissensstand eines sachverständigen Fachmannes als Beurteilungsmaßstab. Um rein individuelle Vorlieben oder private Interessen für oder gegen die Denkmaleigenschaft abzugrenzen, ist deshalb Voraussetzung, dass die Denkmaleigenschaft einer Sache und die Notwendigkeit ihrer Erhaltung in das Bewusstsein der Bevölkerung eingegangen ist oder

---

[1)] Die Vorschrift tritt mit Ablauf des 31.12.2021 außer Kraft; vgl. das Sächsische Gültigkeitsverzeichnis für Verwaltungsvorschriften (www.revosax.sachsen.de).

mindestens von einem breiten Kreis von Sachverständigen geteilt wird. Gesichtspunkte können dabei insbesondere sein:
a) Seltenheitswert,
b) Alter,
c) dokumentarischer und exemplarischer Wert,
d) Maß der Originalität und Integrität. Hierbei ist zu beachten, dass im Laufe der Zeit eingetretene Veränderungen selbst von denkmalpflegerischem Wert sein können.
5. Ohne Belang für die Ermittlung der Kulturdenkmaleigenschaft sind:
a) Erhaltungszustand (zum Beispiel vernachlässigtes Gebäude),
b) Erhaltungsmöglichkeit, zum Beispiel aufgrund eines Konflikts mit anderen Interessen (zum Beispiel Verkehrsplanung),
c) Bereitstehen von Finanzmitteln für die Erhaltung des Kulturdenkmales.

III.
Gliederung und Inhalt der Kulturdenkmallisten

1. Die Kulturdenkmallisten werden für jede Gemeinde gesondert angelegt.
2. Sie bestehen jeweils aus den unbeweglichen Kulturdenkmalen (Teil 1) sowie den beweglichen Kulturdenkmalen (Teil 2). Im Zweifel ist ein Kulturdenkmal in Teil 1 zu erfassen (Auffangtatbestand).
3. Die Kulturdenkmallisten sind nach folgender Gliederung zu erstellen:
a) Benennung von Landkreis/Kreisfreier Stadt, Gemeinde und gegebenenfalls Ortsteil,
b) Ausgewiesene oder zur Ausweisung vorgeschlagene Denkmalschutzgebiete, Grabungsschutzgebiete und archäologische Reservate,
c) Teil 1 Unbewegliche Kulturdenkmale,
d) Teil 2 Bewegliche Kulturdenkmale.
4. Teil 1 und Teil 2 der Kulturdenkmalliste des Landesamtes für Denkmalpflege sind jeweils wie folgt zu untergliedern:
a) Lagebeschreibung (in der Regel Straße und Hausnummer, gegebenenfalls Gemarkung, Flur, Flurstücksnummer),
b) Bezeichnung des Objektes (gegebenenfalls Bauwerksname),
c) Angaben über etwaigen zusätzlichen Schutz (gegebenenfalls Sachgesamtheit),
d) Kurzcharakteristik und Denkmaltext (fachlich-konservatorische Begründung),
e) Kartierung auf Grundlage der automatisierten Liegenschaftskarte (ALK) oder anderer geeigneter Geobasisdaten des Freistaates Sachsen.
5. Teil 1 der Kulturdenkmalliste des Landesamtes für Archäologie Sachsen ist wie folgt zu untergliedern:
a) Lagebeschreibung (gegebenenfalls Straße, Hausnummer, Gemarkung, Flur, Flurstücksnummer, geographische Lagekoordinaten),
b) Bezeichnung des Objektes (gegebenenfalls Denkmalname),
c) Angaben über etwaigen zusätzlichen Schutz (gegebenenfalls Sachgesamtheit),
d) Kurzcharakteristik und Denkmaltext (fachlich-konservatorische Begründung),
e) Kartierung auf Grundlage der automatisierten Liegenschaftskarte (ALK) oder anderer geeigneter Geobasisdaten des Freistaates Sachsen.
6. Teil 2 der Kulturdenkmalliste des Landesamtes für Archäologie Sachsen ist wie folgt zu untergliedern:
a) Angabe über Besitzer (Name, Adresse) und Aufbewahrungsort (Sammlung/Museum),
b) Fundstelle, wenn bekannt (Lagebezeichnung, geographische Lagekoordinaten),
c) Bezeichnung des Objektes oder der Sachgesamtheit,
d) Angaben über etwaigen zusätzlichen Schutz (gegebenenfalls Kulturgutschutz),
e) Kurzcharakteristik und Denkmaltext (Inventar-/Sammlungsnummer oder Sammlungsbezeichnung, fachlich-konservatorische Begründung).
7. Bei der fachlich-konservatorischen Begründung sind die wesentlichen bisher bekannten Merkmale des jeweiligen Objektes oder der Sachgesamtheit zu nennen, die zur Erfüllung der Tatbestandsmerkmale des Kulturdenkmalbegriffes erforderlich sind. Hierbei können Kurzbeschrei-

bungen und Abkürzungen verwendet werden. Eine ausschließliche Wiederholung von Gesetzesbegriffen ist zu vermeiden.

IV.
Verfahren

1. Das zuständige Landesamt erarbeitet einen Entwurf der Kulturdenkmalliste einschließlich fachlich-konservatorischer Begründungen. Das zuständige Landesamt für Denkmalpflege stützt sich dabei insbesondere auf Beobachtungen, auf bereits erfolgte Untersuchungen und Dokumentationen, auf Begehungen, auf Fachliteratur und auf Nachforschungen in Archiven. An den Begehungen können weitere Personen, insbesondere Behördenmitarbeiter, teilnehmen. Das zuständige Landesamt wirkt auf eine vertrauensvolle Zusammenarbeit mit dem Denkmaleigentümer hin.
2. Über die Aufnahme eines Kulturdenkmals in den Entwurf der Kulturdenkmalliste entscheidet das zuständige Landesamt im Benehmen mit der Gemeinde, in der sich das Kulturdenkmal befindet.
3. Das zuständige Landesamt leitet die im Benehmen mit der Gemeinde abgestimmte Kulturdenkmalliste der unteren Denkmalschutzbehörde zu.
4. Die Kulturdenkmallisten sind fortzuschreiben. Die unteren Denkmalschutzbehörden wirken daran mit.

V.
Bekanntmachung der Kulturdenkmallisten

1. Über die Aufnahme eines Objektes in eine der Kulturdenkmallisten ist der Eigentümer von der unteren Denkmalschutzbehörde schriftlich zu benachrichtigen, wenn die Anschrift des Eigentümers der Behörde bekannt ist oder von ihr mit vertretbarem Aufwand festgestellt werden kann.
2. Die Benachrichtigung ist kein Verwaltungsakt und daher entsprechend formlos zu gestalten. Der Eigentümer ist unter Hinweis auf § 10 des Sächsischen Denkmalschutzgesetzes darüber zu informieren, dass
   a) die Kulturdenkmalliste beim zuständigen Landesamt, bei der unteren Denkmalschutzbehörde oder bei der Gemeinde eingesehen werden kann, Eintragungen über bewegliche Kulturdenkmale jedoch nur die Eigentümer und sonstigen dinglich Berechtigten sowie die von ihnen ermächtigten Personen einsehen dürfen,
   b) die Eintragung von Amts wegen erfolgt ist durch das zuständige Landesamt im Benehmen mit der Gemeinde, in der das Kulturdenkmal gelegen ist,
   c) der Denkmalschutz nach dem Sächsischen Denkmalschutzgesetz nicht von der Aufnahme eines Kulturdenkmals in die Kulturdenkmalliste abhängig ist und
   d) die Denkmalschutzbehörde auf Antrag des Eigentümers durch Verwaltungsakt über die Eigenschaft als Kulturdenkmal zu entscheiden hat.
3. Die untere Denkmalschutzbehörde übersendet die Kulturdenkmallisten auf Anfrage gemeindeweise zusammengestellt den betroffenen Behörden und Stellen, insbesondere
   a) der oberen Denkmalschutzbehörde,
   b) den Gemeinden,
   c) dem Landesamt für Steuern und Finanzen,
   d) dem Staatsbetrieb Sächsisches Immobilien- und Baumanagement,
   e) dem Landesamt für Umwelt, Landwirtschaft und Geologie,
   f) dem Staatsbetrieb Sachsenforst,
   g) dem Staatsbetrieb Landestalsperrenverwaltung,
   h) dem Landesamt für Straßenbau und Verkehr,
   i) dem Sächsischen Oberbergamt,
   j) dem Staatsbetrieb Geobasisinformation und Vermessung Sachsen sowie
   k) den oberen Kirchenbehörden und entsprechenden Stellen der anderen Religionsgemeinschaften, soweit Kulturdenkmale in deren Eigentum stehen.

Das Landesamt für Denkmalpflege und das Landesamt für Archäologie Sachsen informieren sich bei Bedarf gegenseitig über ihre jeweiligen Kulturdenkmallisten.

4. Nach Übersendung gemäß Nummer 3 macht die Gemeinde die Kulturdenkmalliste des Landesamtes für Denkmalpflege unverzüglich ortsüblich bekannt. Für die Bekanntmachung gilt Nummer 2 entsprechend.

VI.
Elektronisches Datenverarbeitungssystem

1. Das zuständige Landesamt führt die Kulturdenkmalliste in einem elektronischen Datenverarbeitungssystem. Verantwortlichkeiten und Arbeitsprozesse bei der Erstellung, Nutzung und Aktualisierung von Inhalten sind schriftlich festzulegen.
2. Den Denkmalschutzbehörden kann ein Zugriff auf die digitalen Kulturdenkmalkarten und die Kulturdenkmallisten gewährt werden. Neben den unteren Denkmalschutzbehörden kann dieser Zugriff auch den unteren Naturschutzbehörden gewährt werden, wenn dies für denkmalpflegerische Belange in Planungsverfahren relevant ist. Die Zahl der Nutzer ist auf das notwendige Maß zu beschränken. Der Abruf von Daten durch die unteren Denkmalschutz- und Naturschutzbehörden ist auf die Daten der Kulturdenkmale ihres eigenen Zuständigkeitsbereichs beschränkt.
3. Für die Nutzung ist ein Login mit Anmelde- und Passwort der berechtigten Personen einzurichten.
4. Die Pflege der digitalen Kulturdenkmalkarten und Kulturdenkmallisten ist dem zuständigen Landesamt vorbehalten. Die untere Denkmalschutzbehörde ist verpflichtet, die Kulturdenkmalliste ihres Zuständigkeitsbereiches in einem festgelegten Aktualisierungsrhythmus zu kontrollieren. Sie übermittelt ergänzende oder zu korrigierende Daten bezüglich der in ihrem Zuständigkeitsbereich gelegenen Kulturdenkmale dem zuständigen Landesamt.
5. Den Behörden gemäß Ziffer V Nummer 3 Buchstabe a und c bis j kann der Zugriff auf die digitalen Kulturdenkmalkarten und Kulturdenkmallisten über das Internet gestattet werden, sobald hierfür die erforderlichen technischen und datenschutzrechtlichen Voraussetzungen geschaffen sind. Nummer 2 Satz 2 und 3 sowie Nummer 3 gelten entsprechend. Bei einer Gestattung der Nutzung kann auf eine Übersendung der Kulturdenkmalliste gemäß Ziffer V Nummer 3 verzichtet werden.
6. Die datenschutzrechtlichen Bestimmungen des Freistaates Sachsen sind zu beachten. Stellen außerhalb der Landesverwaltung, die die digitalen Kulturdenkmalkarten und Kulturdenkmallisten nutzen können, sind auf die Einhaltung der datenschutzrechtlichen Bestimmungen des Freistaates Sachsen zu verpflichten.
7. Das zuständige Landesamt soll jeder Person Einblick in die Kulturdenkmalliste über öffentlich zugängliche Netze anbieten. Im Übrigen wird auf die Vorschriften des Sächsischen E-Government-Gesetzes vom 9. Juli 2014 (SächsGVBl. S. 398), das durch die Verordnung vom 4. April 2015 (SächsGVBl. S. 374) geändert worden ist, in der jeweils geltenden Fassung, verwiesen.

VII.
Übergangsbestimmung

Mit der Übersendung der Kulturdenkmalliste nach Ziffer V Nummer 3 an die Gemeinde tritt diese an die Stelle der vorläufigen Kulturdenkmalverzeichnisse nach § 38 Absatz 1 des Sächsischen Denkmalschutzgesetzes.

VIII.
Inkrafttreten und Außerkrafttreten

Diese Verwaltungsvorschrift tritt am Tag nach der Veröffentlichung[1] in Kraft. Gleichzeitig tritt die VwV Kulturdenkmallisten vom 15. September 1993 (SächsABl. 1994 S. 6), zuletzt enthalten in der Verwaltungsvorschrift vom 1. Dezember 2015 (SächsABl. SDr. S. S 348), außer Kraft.

---

1) Veröffentlicht am 29.9.2016.

D13.I.1e VwV-Einvernehmen nach § 4 Abs. 2 SächsDSchG

Verwaltungsvorschrift des Sächsischen Staatsministeriums des Innern zur Herstellung des Einvernehmens gemäß § 4 Abs. 2 SächsDSchG zwischen den unteren Denkmalschutzbehörden und dem Landesamt für Denkmalpflege Sachsen (VwV-Einvernehmen)

Vom 12. März 2001 (SächsABl. S. 427)

Zur Beschleunigung und Vereinfachung des denkmalschutzrechtlichen Genehmigungs- und Zustimmungsverfahrens wird im Einvernehmen mit dem Sächsischen Staatsministerium für Wissenschaft und Kunst folgende Verwaltungsvorschrift erlassen:

I.

Für denkmalschutzrechtliche Genehmigungen und Zustimmungen wird das Einvernehmen gemäß § 4 Abs. 2 des Gesetzes zum Schutz und zur Pflege der Kulturdenkmale im Freistaat Sachsen (Sächsisches Denkmalschutzgesetz — SächsDSchG) vom 3. März 1993 (SächsGVBl. S. 229), geändert durch Artikel 2 des Aufbaubeschleunigungsgesetzes vom 4. Juli 1994 (SächsGVBl. S. 1261), in der jeweils geltenden Fassung zwischen der unteren Denkmalschutzbehörde und dem Landesamt für Denkmalpflege, mit Ausnahme der in Ziffer II. genannten Fallgruppen, im Voraus erteilt.

Eine Stellungnahme des Landesamtes für Denkmalpflege für die denkmalschutzrechtliche Genehmigung nach § 12 Abs. 1 SächsDSchG und die Zustimmung nach § 12 Abs. 3 SächsDSchG ist nur noch für die Fallgruppen nach Ziffer II. erforderlich, für alle anderen Fallgruppen trifft die untere Denkmalschutzbehörde die Entscheidung.

II.

1. Für die nachfolgend genannten Fallgruppen bedarf es weiterhin einer Stellungnahme des Landesamtes für Denkmalpflege, um das Einvernehmen gemäß § 4 Abs. 2 SächsDSchG herzustellen:
   a) Werke der bildenden Kunst, des Kunsthandwerks und Sammlungen,
   b) Bauten, die der Religionsausübung dienen oder dienten
      aa) Kloster, Stift, Annex,
      bb) Dom, Kirche, Synagoge,
   c) Herrschaftsbauten
      aa) Schlossanlage, Herrenhaus, Annex,
      bb) Burg, Festung,
      cc) Parlamentsgebäude,
   d) Öffentliche Bauten (auch bei Nutzungsänderung)
      aa) Rathaus, Museum, Theater, Festhalle,
      bb) Bildungseinrichtungen,
      cc) Bauten der Justiz,
   e) Banken und Kaufhäuser,
   f) Bauten und Anlagen der Industrie und Technik
      aa) Industrie- und Gewerbebauten und deren Ausstattung, auch Bergbau-, Wasserbau- und Energieversorgungsbauten,
      bb) Verkehrsbauten,
   g) Anlagen der Garten- und Landschaftsgestaltung
      aa) Park, öffentliche Anlage, Allee,
      bb) Friedhof,
   h) Wohngebäude- und Nebengebäude vor 1870,
   i) Villenanlagen,
   j) Abbruch eines Kulturdenkmales, sofern mehr als 50 vom Hundert der Substanz des Kulturdenkmales betroffen ist.
2. Für nachfolgend genannte Fallgruppen gilt die Einschränkung nach Ziffer II. nicht:
   a) für die Errichtung von Werbeanlagen,
   b) für die Errichtung von Telekommunikationseinrichtungen,
   c) für Maßnahmen in Denkmalschutzgebieten nach § 21 SächsDSchG, ausgenommen die Fallgruppen nach II. 1. Buchst. a bis j.

III.
Den unteren Denkmalschutzbehörden wird auf Antrag durch das Sächsische Staatsministerium des Innern die Berechtigung übertragen, die denkmalschutzrechtliche Genehmigung oder Zustimmung nach dieser Verwaltungsvorschrift zu erteilen, sofern die Besetzung mit geeigneten Fachkräften gewährleistet ist. Die Entscheidung erfolgt im Benehmen mit dem Landesamt für Denkmalpflege.

Die Übertragung kann widerrufen werden, wenn die untere Denkmalschutzbehörde nicht dauernd ausreichend mit geeigneten Fachkräften besetzt wird.

IV.
Die Entscheidung nach Ziffer I. und II. Nummer 2 dieser Verwaltungsvorschrift ist dem Landesamt für Denkmalpflege innerhalb von vier Wochen in Mehrfertigung zu übersenden.

V.
Diese Verwaltungsvorschrift tritt zum 2. April 2001 in Kraft.

D13.I.1f Abgrenzungserlass Zuständigkeit

Gemeinsame Verwaltungsvorschrift des Sächsischen Staatsministeriums des Innern und des Sächsischen Staatsministeriums für Wissenschaft und Kunst zur Zuständigkeit des Landesamtes für Denkmalpflege und des Landesamtes für Archäologie (Abgrenzungserlass)

Vom 18. Juni 2003 (SächsABl. S. 650)

I. Zuständigkeit

1. Das Landesamt für Archäologie ist zuständige konservatorische Fachbehörde für
   a) unbewegliche archäologische Sachzeugen
      aa) unterhalb der Erdoberfläche außerhalb von Gebäuden, insbesondere Fundamente von Vorgängerbauten, Grablegen, sonstige archäologische Funde,
      bb) unter der Bodenfläche im Innern von baulichen Anlagen (zum Beispiel Gebäude, Gebäuderuinen),
      cc) unter der Wasseroberfläche im Bereich des Gewässerbettes (vergleiche § 7 SächsWG),
   b) bewegliche archäologische Sachzeugen und Sammlungen solcher Sachzeugen.
2. Das Landesamt für Denkmalpflege ist die zuständige konservatorische Fachbehörde für alle konservatorischen Aufgaben, die nicht dem Landesamt für Archäologie zugewiesen sind, insbesondere für Bau- und Kunstdenkmale, Anlagen der Garten- und Landschaftsgestaltung, Werke der Produktions- und Verkehrsgeschichte, Sammlungen (ausgenommen solche von archäologischen Sachzeugen,) Archive und so weiter.
   Beide Ämter sind jeweils gemäß der Einteilung unter 1. und 2. allein zuständige konservatorische Fachbehörde für alle anfallenden Aufgaben.
3. Zur Herstellung vertrauensvoller Arbeitsbeziehungen unterrichten sich beide Landesämter umfassend über künftige Vorhaben von beidseitigem Interesse.
4. Ergeben sich Schnittstellen zwischen den Zuständigkeiten beider Landesämter, so zum Beispiel bei Grabungen innerhalb von Gebäuden oder wenn Gebäuderuinen über den Boden hinausragen, setzt sich das nach den Nummern 1. oder 2. zuständige Landesamt mit dem anderen Landesamt rechtzeitig vorher ins Benehmen hinsichtlich der Festlegungen des weiteren Vorgehens, das heißt, es soll eine Anhörung des fachlichen Rates des anderen Amtes erfolgen.
5. Ist die Zuständigkeit beider Ämter berührt und wird keine Einigkeit über die Vorgehensweise zwischen beiden Landesämtern erzielt, so ist die Sache durch das Landesamt für Archäologie dem Staatsministerium für Wissenschaft und Kunst und durch das Landesamt für Denkmalpflege dem Staatsministerium des Innern unverzüglich vorzulegen.
   Die Staatsministerien entscheiden im Einvernehmen. Ist diese nicht zu erzielen, richtet sich das weitere Vorgehen nach § 16 der Geschäftsordnung der Sächsischen Staatsregierung in der Fassung der Bekanntmachung vom 14. November 1999 (SächsABl. S. 1003).
6. Sofern den Denkmalschutzbehörden konkrete Abgrenzungskonflikte zwischen den Landesämtern, die diesen Erlass betreffen, bekannt werden, haben sie unverzüglich das Sächsische Staatsministerium des Innern als oberste Denkmalschutzbehörde schriftlich zu benachrichtigen.
7. Die Denkmalschutzbehörden werden angewiesen, in diesem Sinne zu verfahren.

II. In-Kraft-Treten

Diese Verwaltungsvorschrift tritt am Tage nach ihrer Veröffentlichung in Kraft.

Archivgesetz für den Freistaat Sachsen (SächsArchivG)

Vom 17. Mai 1993 (SächsGVBl. S. 449)
(BS Sachsen 290-1)
zuletzt geändert durch Art. 25 Gesetz zur Anpassung landesrechtlicher Vorschriften an die Datenschutz-Grundverordnung vom 26. April 2018 (SächsGVBl. S. 198)

Inhaltsübersicht

Erster Abschnitt
Allgemeines
§ 1 Geltungsbereich
§ 2 Begriffsbestimmungen

Zweiter Abschnitt
Staatliches Archivwesen
§ 3 Organisation des staatlichen Archivwesens
§ 4 Aufgaben des Sächsischen Staatsarchivs
§ 5 Anbietung und Übernahme
§ 6 Rechtsansprüche betroffener Personen
§ 7 Deposita
§ 8 Verwaltung und Sicherung des Archivgutes
§ 9 Benutzung des Archivgutes
§ 10 Schutzfristen

§ 11 Übermittlung von Vervielfältigungen von Archivgut in besonderen Fällen

Dritter Abschnitt
Archive sonstiger öffentlicher Stellen
§ 12 Archiv des Landtages
§ 13 Kommunale Archive
§ 14 Archive von Hochschulen und Akademien
§ 15 Andere öffentliche Archive

Vierter Abschnitt
Schlußbestimmungen
§ 16 Verordnungsermächtigung
§ 17 Besondere Kategorien personenbezogener Daten
§ 18 Einschränkung eines Grundrechts
§ 19 Inkrafttreten

Der Sächsische Landtag hat am 22. April 1993 das folgende Gesetz beschlossen:

Erster Abschnitt
Allgemeines

§ 1 Geltungsbereich
(1) Dieses Gesetz regelt die Archivierung von Unterlagen im Sächsischen Staatsarchiv und in den Archiven der der Aufsicht des Freistaates Sachsen unterstehenden juristischen Personen des öffentlichen Rechts sowie die Archivierung von Unterlagen im Archiv des Sächsischen Landtages nach Maßgabe des § 12 Abs. 2.
(2) Dieses Gesetz gilt nicht für die öffentlich-rechtlichen Religionsgemeinschaften, die öffentlich-rechtlichen Rundfunkanstalten und die öffentlich-rechtlichen Unternehmen, die am wirtschaftlichen Wettbewerb teilnehmen, sowie deren Zusammenschlüsse.

§ 2 Begriffsbestimmungen
(1) ¹Archivgut sind alle in das Archiv übernommenen archivwürdigen Unterlagen mit den zu ihrer Nutzung nötigen Hilfsmitteln. ²Archivwürdige Unterlagen entstehen beim Landtag, bei Gerichten, Behörden und sonstigen öffentlichen Stellen, bei natürlichen Personen oder bei juristischen Personen des Privatrechts. ³Zum Archivgut zählt auch Dokumentationsmaterial, das von den Archiven ergänzend gesammelt wird.
(2) Unterlagen sind unabhängig von ihrer Speicherungsform alle Aufzeichnungen, insbesondere Urkunden, Amtsbücher, Akten, Einzelschriftstücke, Karten, Risse, Pläne, Medaillen, Bilder, Filme, Tonaufzeichnungen.
(3) Archivwürdig sind Unterlagen, denen ein bleibender Wert für Gesetzgebung, Rechtsprechung, Regierung und Verwaltung, für Wissenschaft und Forschung oder für die Sicherung berechtigter Belange betroffener Personen und Institutionen oder Dritter zukommt.
(4) Das Archivieren beinhaltet das Erfassen und Bewerten von Unterlagen und das Übernehmen, Verwahren, Erhalten, Erschließen sowie Nutzbarmachen und Auswerten von Archivgut.
(5) Als Entstehung gilt der Zeitpunkt der letzten Bearbeitung der Unterlagen.

Zweiter Abschnitt
Staatliches Archivwesen

§ 3 Organisation des staatlichen Archivwesens
(1) Der Freistaat Sachsen unterhält für die Erfüllung aller staatlichen Archivaufgaben das Sächsische Staatsarchiv.
(2) Oberste Aufsichtsbehörde für das staatliche Archivwesen ist das Staatsministerium des Innern.
(3) Die oberste Aufsichtsbehörde kann die Erfüllung einzelner Aufgaben des Sächsischen Staatsarchivs durch öffentlich-rechtliche Vereinbarung auf andere Archive öffentlich-rechtlicher Trägerschaft übertragen, wenn dies besonderen historischen Interessen entspricht.

§ 4 Aufgaben des Sächsischen Staatsarchivs
(1) Das Sächsische Staatsarchiv ist Fachbehörde für alle Aufgaben des Archivwesens.
(2) [1]Das Sächsische Staatsarchiv archiviert die Unterlagen der Gerichte, Behörden und sonstigen öffentlichen Stellen des Freistaates Sachsen nach Maßgabe dieses Gesetzes. [2]Diese Aufgabe erstreckt sich auch auf die Unterlagen der Rechtsvorgänger des Freistaates Sachsen und der Funktionsvorgänger der in Satz 1 genannten Stellen sowie aus der Zeit vom 8. Mai 1945 bis zum 2. Oktober 1990 auf die Unterlagen der ehemaligen staatlichen oder wirtschaftsleitenden Organe, der Kombinate, Betriebe, Genossenschaften, Einrichtungen und Parteien, gesellschaftlichen Organisationen und juristischen Personen, soweit diese Unterlagen nicht nach § 13 Abs. 1 Satz 2 durch kommunale Archive archiviert werden. [3]Es archiviert auch das Archivgut der ehemaligen Deutschen Zentralstelle für Genealogie.
(3) [1]Das Sächsische Staatsarchiv kann, soweit das Gesetz über die Sicherung und Nutzung von Archivgut des Bundes (Bundesarchivgesetz – BArchG) vom 6. Januar 1988 (BGBl. I S. 62), zuletzt geändert durch Gesetz vom 27. Juni 2013 (BGBl. I S. 1888), in der jeweils geltenden Fassung,[1]) es zulässt, Unterlagen von Stellen des Bundes und Archivgut des Bundes übernehmen, wenn hierfür ein öffentliches Interesse des Freistaates Sachsen besteht. [2]Die Benutzung des Archivgutes richtet sich nach den Bestimmungen dieses Gesetzes, soweit Rechtsvorschriften des Bundes nichts anderes bestimmen.
(4) [1]Das Sächsische Staatsarchiv kann auch von anderen als den in § 5 Abs. 1 genannten Stellen oder Personen Archivgut aufgrund von besonderen Rechtsvorschriften, Vereinbarungen oder letztwilligen Verfügungen übernehmen. [2]Die §§ 7 und 8 gelten in diesen Fällen sinngemäß, sofern die Rechtsvorschriften, Vereinbarungen oder letztwilligen Verfügungen nichts anderes bestimmen.
(5) [1]Im Rahmen seiner Zuständigkeit berät das Sächsische Staatsarchiv die Gerichte, Behörden und sonstigen öffentlichen Stellen des Freistaates Sachsen bei der Verwaltung und Sicherung ihrer Unterlagen. [2]Dieses ist bei der Einführung neuer oder wesentlicher Änderung bestehender Systeme der Informationstechnologie anzuhören, wenn diese Bezüge zur Archivierung elektronischer Unterlagen enthalten.
(6) [1]Das Sächsische Staatsarchiv berät nichtstaatliche Archive. [2]Wenn ein öffentliches Interesse gegeben ist, kann das Sächsische Staatsarchiv private Eigentümer von Archivgut beraten.
(7) Das Sächsische Staatsarchiv nimmt Aufgaben im Rahmen der archivarischen Aus- und Fortbildung wahr.
(8) Das Staatsministerium des Innern kann dem Sächsischen Staatsarchiv weitere Aufgaben übertragen, die in sachlichem Zusammenhang mit dem Archivwesen oder der wissenschaftlichen Forschung stehen.

§ 5 Anbietung und Übernahme
(1) [1]Die Gerichte, Behörden und sonstigen öffentlichen Stellen des Freistaates Sachsen (anbietungspflichtige Stellen) haben dem Sächsischen Staatsarchiv alle Unterlagen zur Übernahme anzubieten, die sie zur Erfüllung ihrer Aufgaben nicht mehr benötigen. [2]Abweichend von Satz 1 sind die Unterlagen jedoch spätestens 30 Jahre nach ihrer Entstehung dem Sächsischen Staatsarchiv anzubieten, sofern nicht durch Bundes- oder Landesrecht oder Verwaltungsvorschriften der obersten Bundes- oder Staatsbehörden längere Aufbewahrungsfristen bestimmt werden. [3]Abweichend von Satz 1 sind elektronische Unterlagen, die einer laufenden Aktualisierung unterliegen, ebenfalls anzubieten. [4]Näheres regeln das Sächsische Staatsarchiv und die fachlich zuständige Behörde einvernehmlich.

---

1) Das Bundesarchivgesetz ist abgedruckt als Nr. C.III.1.

(2) ¹Soweit Bundes- oder Landesrecht nichts anderes bestimmt, erstreckt sich die Anbietungspflicht auch auf Unterlagen, die dem Datenschutz oder dem Geheimschutz unterliegen und die Daten im Sinne des Artikels 9 Absatz 1 der Verordnung (EU) 2016/679 des europäischen Parlaments und des Rates vom 27. April 2016 zum Schutz natürlicher Personen bei der Verarbeitung personenbezogener Daten, zum freien Datenverkehr und zur Aufhebung der Richtlinie 95/46/EG ABl. L 119 vom 4.5.2016, S. 1, L 314 vom 2.11.2016, S. 72), in der jeweils geltenden Fassung, enthalten, und auf Unterlagen, die personenbezogene Daten enthalten, welche nach Bundes- oder Landesrecht oder der Verordnung (EU) 2016/679 gelöscht, vernichtet oder in der Verarbeitung eingeschränkt werden müssten oder könnten oder in der Verarbeitung eingeschränkt worden sind. ²Soweit die Speicherung der Daten unzulässig war, ist dieses besonders zu kennzeichnen.

(3) ¹Werden gemäß Absatz 1 anbietungspflichtige Stellen in eine nichtstaatliche Trägerschaft überführt oder deren Aufgaben auf eine nichtstaatliche Stelle übertragen, haben sie alle Unterlagen, die zum Wirksamwerden der Änderung vorhanden sind, unverzüglich zu erfassen und dem Sächsischen Staatsarchiv ein Verzeichnis dieser Unterlagen zu übermitteln. ²Die Unterlagen sind dem Sächsischen Staatsarchiv anzubieten, sobald sie zur Erfüllung der Aufgaben nicht mehr benötigt werden. ³Absatz 1 Satz 3 und 4 sowie die Absätze 6 und 7 gelten entsprechend.

(4) Zur Anbietung sind auch alle Personen und Stellen im Freistaat Sachsen verpflichtet, die die tatsächliche Verfügungsgewalt über Unterlagen im Sinne von § 4 Abs. 2 Satz 2 besitzen.

(5) ¹Die anbietungspflichtigen Stellen sind verpflichtet, die von ihnen herausgegebenen Veröffentlichungen unmittelbar nach Erscheinen einfach an das Sächsische Staatsarchiv abzugeben.

(6) ¹Das Sächsische Staatsarchiv entscheidet in den Fällen des Absatzes 1 und 2 innerhalb von sechs Monaten über die Archivwürdigkeit der Unterlagen. ²Zur Feststellung der Archivwürdigkeit ist den Bediensteten des Sächsischen Staatsarchivs Einsicht in die Unterlagen und die dazugehörigen Registraturhilfsmittel zu gewähren. ³Nach Ablauf dieser Frist entfällt die Verpflichtung zur weiteren Aufbewahrung.

(7) ¹Wird die Archivwürdigkeit bejaht, hat die anbietende Stelle die Unterlagen anhand von Ablieferungsnachweisen innerhalb von sechs Monaten an das Sächsische Staatsarchiv zur Übernahme zu übergeben. ²Wird die Archivwürdigkeit verneint, so hat die anbietende Stelle die Unterlagen zu vernichten, wenn weder Rechtsvorschriften noch schutzwürdige Belange betroffener Personen entgegenstehen. ³Über die Vernichtung ist ein Nachweis zu fertigen, der 30 Jahre aufzubewahren ist.

(8) ¹Das Sächsische Staatsarchiv kann Unterlagen bereits vor Ablauf der für die abgebende Stelle jeweils geltenden Aufbewahrungsfrist übernehmen, soweit Rechtsvorschriften nicht entgegenstehen. ²Die durch Rechts- oder Verwaltungsvorschriften festgelegten Aufbewahrungsfristen werden auch durch die Aufbewahrung im Archiv eingehalten.

(9) ¹Das Sächsische Staatsarchiv kann auf die Anbietung von Unterlagen ohne bleibenden Wert verzichten und für diese unbefristete Vernichtungsgenehmigungen erteilen. ²Absatz 7 Satz 2 und 3 gilt entsprechend. ³Das fachlich zuständige Staatsministerium kann im Einvernehmen mit dem Sächsischen Staatsarchiv durch Verwaltungsvorschrift Art und Umfang der anzubietenden Unterlagen bestimmen.

(10) Das Sächsische Staatsarchiv hat nach der Übernahme ebenso wie die abgebende Stelle die schutzwürdigen Belange betroffener Personen zu berücksichtigen; insbesondere hat es bei Unterlagen mit personenbezogenen Daten bei der Erfüllung seiner Aufgaben die Vorschriften über die Sicherung dieser Unterlagen zu beachten, die für die abgebende Stelle gelten.

§ 6 Rechtsansprüche betroffener Personen

(1) ¹Rechtsansprüche betroffener Personen gemäß Artikel 15 der Verordnung (EU) 2016/679 beschränken sich auf eine Auskunft über die im Archivgut zu ihrer Person enthaltenen Daten, wenn das Archivgut durch Namen der Personen erschlossen ist. ²Die Auskunft kann auch in Form der Einsicht in das Archivgut oder durch Aushändigung einer Kopie gewährt werden.

(2) ¹Wird die Richtigkeit personenbezogener Daten von der betroffenen Person bestritten, hat sie das Recht zu verlangen, dass dem Archivgut ihre Gegendarstellung beigefügt wird, wenn die betroffene Person ein berechtigtes Interesse daran glaubhaft macht. ²Nach ihrem Tod steht dieses Recht den Angehörigen nach § 10 Absatz 4 Satz 2 zu. ³Weitergehende Rechte auf Berichtigung gemäß Artikel 16 der Verordnung (EU) 2016/679, auf Löschung gemäß Artikel 17 der Verordnung (EU) 2016/679 und auf Einschränkung der Verarbeitung gemäß Artikel 18 der Verordnung (EU) 2016/679 bestehen

nicht. ⁴Eine Mitteilungspflicht des Sächsischen Staatsarchivs gemäß Artikel 19 der Verordnung (EU) 2016/679 besteht nicht.
(3) Ein Recht auf Datenübertragbarkeit gemäß Artikel 20 der Verordnung (EU) 2016/679 und ein Widerspruchsrecht betroffener Personen gegen die Archivierung sie betreffender Daten gemäß Artikel 21 Absatz 1 der Verordnung (EU) 2016/679 bestehen nicht.

§ 7 Deposita

(1) ¹Die in § 13 aufgeführten Stellen können ihr Archivgut dem Sächsischen Staatsarchiv als Depositum unter Wahrung des Eigentums zur Übernahme anbieten. ²Das gleiche gilt für öffentlich-rechtliche Religionsgemeinschaften und ihre Untergliederungen sowie für natürliche und juristische Personen des Privatrechts. ³Zwischen dem Eigentümer des Archivgutes und dem Sächsischen Staatsarchiv ist ein Depositalvertrag abzuschließen.
(2) Das Sächsische Staatsarchiv ist zur Übernahme nicht verpflichtet.
(3) Depositalgut unterliegt den gleichen Bestimmungen wie das öffentliche Archivgut, sofern nicht durch Depositalverträge etwas anderes bestimmt wird.

§ 8 Verwaltung und Sicherung des Archivgutes

(1) Das Sächsische Staatsarchiv hat das Verfügungsrecht über das Archivgut und ist verpflichtet, das Archivgut nach archivwissenschaftlichen Erkenntnissen zu bearbeiten und einer ordnungsgemäßen Benutzung zugänglich zu machen.
(2) ¹Durch die Feststellung der Archivwürdigkeit und die Übernahme der Unterlagen gemäß § 5 Abs. 7 erfolgt ihre Widmung zu öffentlichem Archivgut. ²Die Widmung begründet eine hoheitliche Sachherrschaft, die durch bürgerlich-rechtliche Verfügungen nicht berührt wird. ³Das Sächsische Staatsarchiv kann von dem Besitzer die Herausgabe des öffentlichen Archivgutes verlangen.
(3) ¹Das Archivgut ist in seiner Entstehungsform zu erhalten, soweit nicht archivfachliche Belange entgegenstehen. ²Es ist nachhaltig vor Schäden, Verlust, Vernichtung oder unbefugter Nutzung zu schützen.
(4) Archivgut ist ein Bestandteil des Landeskulturgutes; seine Veräußerung ist verboten.

§ 9 Benutzung des Archivgutes

(1) Jedermann hat vorbehaltlich der Rechte aus § 6 nach Maßgabe der aufgrund von § 16 Nr. 1 erlassenen Rechtsverordnungen[1] das Recht, das Archivgut des Freistaates Sachsen zu nutzen.
(2) ¹Die Benutzung ist einzuschränken oder zu versagen, wenn
1. Grund zur Annahme besteht, daß das Wohl der Bundesrepublik Deutschland oder eines ihrer Länder gefährdet würde,
2. Grund zur Annahme besteht, daß schutzwürdige Belange betroffener Personen oder Dritter entgegenstehen,
3. Rechtsvorschriften über Geheimhaltung verletzt würden,
4. der Erhaltungszustand des Archivgutes entgegensteht,
5. ein nicht vertretbarer Arbeitsaufwand entstehen würde oder
6. Vereinbarungen mit gegenwärtigen oder früheren Eigentümern entgegenstehen.

²Die Nutzung kann aus anderen Gründen eingeschränkt oder versagt werden. ³Die Entscheidung trifft das Sächsische Staatsarchiv.
(3) Der Benutzer ist verpflichtet, ein Belegexemplar eines Werkes, das er unter wesentlicher Verwendung von Archivgut des Sächsischen Staatsarchivs verfaßt oder erstellt hat, unentgeltlich an das Sächsische Staatsarchiv abzugeben.

§ 10 Schutzfristen

(1) ¹Die Benutzung von Archivgut ist unbeschadet § 9 Abs. 2 erst nach Ablauf von Fristen (Schutzfristen) zulässig. ²Für die Benutzung von Archivgut gelten folgende Schutzfristen:

---

[1] Die Verordnung des Sächsischen Staatsministeriums des Innern über die Benutzung der staatlichen Archive ist abgedruckt als Nr. D13.II.1a. Die Verordnung des Sächsischen Staatsministeriums des Innern über die Benutzungsgebühren des Sächsischen Staatsarchivs ist abgedruckt als Nr. D13.II.1b.

1. eine allgemeine Schutzfrist von 30 Jahren nach Entstehung der Unterlagen,
2. eine Schutzfrist von 60 Jahren nach Entstehung der Unterlagen, die sich nach ihrer Zweckbestimmung auf einen durch ein Berufsgeheimnis, ein besonderes Amtsgeheimnis oder einen durch sonstige Rechtsvorschrift über Geheimhaltung geschützten Lebenssachverhalt beziehen, und
3. eine Schutzfrist von
   a) 10 Jahren nach dem Tod der Person oder
   b) 100 Jahren nach der Geburt der Person, wenn das Todesjahr nur mit unverhältnismäßigem Aufwand feststellbar ist, oder
   c) 60 Jahren nach der Entstehung der Unterlagen, wenn weder das Todesjahr noch das Geburtsjahr feststellbar ist,

für Archivgut, das sich seiner Zweckbestimmung oder seinem wesentlichen Inhalt nach auf eine oder mehrere natürliche Personen bezieht (personenbezogenes Archivgut). ³Für Archivgut, das Rechtsvorschriften des Bundes über die Geheimhaltung unterliegt, gelten § 11 Absatz 3 und § 12 Absatz 3 des Bundesarchivgesetzes entsprechend.
(2) ¹Die Schutzfristen nach Absatz 1 gelten nicht für solche Unterlagen, die bereits bei ihrer Entstehung zur Veröffentlichung bestimmt waren. ²Die Schutzfristen nach Absatz 1 Satz 2 Nr. 1 und 2 gelten nicht für Archivgut nach § 4 Abs. 2 Satz 2. ³Für Amtsträger in Ausübung ihrer Ämter und absolute Personen der Zeitgeschichte, soweit nicht ihr schutzwürdiger privater Lebensbereich betroffen ist, gilt die Schutzfrist des Absatzes 1 Satz 2 Nr. 3 nicht. ⁴Entsprechendes gilt auch für Mitarbeiter der in § 4 Abs. 2 Satz 2 genannten Stellen.
(3) ¹Die in Absatz 1 festgelegten Schutzfristen gelten auch bei der Benutzung durch öffentliche Stellen. ²Für die abgebenden öffentlichen Stellen gelten die Schutzfristen des Absatzes 1 nur für Unterlagen, die bei ihnen aufgrund besonderer Vorschriften hätten in der Verarbeitung eingeschränkt, gelöscht oder vernichtet werden müssen.
(4) ¹Eine Benutzung personenbezogenen Archivgutes ist unabhängig von den in Absatz 1 genannten Schutzfristen zulässig, wenn die Person, auf die sich das Archivgut bezieht, eingewilligt hat. ²Nach dem Tod der Person ist die Einwilligung von dem überlebenden Ehegatten oder eingetragenen Lebenspartner, nach dessen Tod von den geschäftsfähigen Kindern der betroffenen Person und, wenn weder ein Ehegatte noch Kinder vorhanden sind, von den Eltern der betroffenen Person zu erklären.
(5) ¹Die Schutzfristen nach Absatz 1 Satz 2 Nr. 1 und 2 können im Einzelfall verkürzt werden, wenn es im öffentlichen Interesse liegt. ²Bei personenbezogenem Archivgut ist eine Verkürzung nur zulässig, wenn die Benutzung für ein konkretes Forschungsvorhaben oder zur Wahrnehmung berechtigter Belange einer anderen Person oder öffentlichen Stelle erforderlich ist und wenn das öffentliche Interesse an der Durchführung des Forschungsvorhabens oder die berechtigten Belange einer anderen Person oder öffentlichen Stelle die schutzwürdigen Belange der Person, auf die sich das Archivgut bezieht, überwiegen. ³Soweit der Forschungszweck es zulässt, sind die Forschungsergebnisse ohne personenbezogene Angaben aus dem Archivgut zu veröffentlichen.

§ 11 Übermittlung von Vervielfältigungen von Archivgut in besonderen Fällen
(1) ¹Das Sächsische Staatsarchiv kann Archiven, Museen und Forschungsstellen, die zu dem Zweck unterhalten werden, das Schicksal natürlicher Personen unter staatlicher Gewaltherrschaft darzustellen und zu erforschen, Vervielfältigungen von Archivgut vor Ablauf der Schutzfristen übermitteln, wenn ein besonderes öffentliches Interesse an der Übermittlung besteht. ²Die Übermittlung ist nur zulässig, wenn die empfangende Stelle ausreichende Garantien hinsichtlich des Schutzes des Persönlichkeitsrechts und der Ausübung der damit verbundenen Rechte bietet und sich in einer schriftlichen Vereinbarung mit dem Sächsischen Staatsarchiv verpflichtet, die §§ 6 und 10 entsprechend anzuwenden.
(2) Die Übermittlung bedarf der Zustimmung des Sächsischen Staatsministeriums des Innern.

Dritter Abschnitt
Archive sonstiger öffentlicher Stellen

§ 12 Archiv des Landtages
(1) ¹Der Sächsische Landtag unterhält ein eigenes Archiv. ²Er ist für die Archivierung der Unterlagen des Landtages, seiner Ausschüsse und sonstigen Gremien sowie seiner Verwaltung zuständig.

[3]§ 3 Abs. 2 gilt nicht. [4]Für die Unterlagen des Sächsischen Datenschutzbeauftragten gelten § 4 Abs. 2 und § 5 Abs. 1.

(2) [1]Für das Archiv des Sächsischen Landtages gelten § 5 Abs. 2 und 10, §§ 6, 8 bis 10 und § 11 Abs. 1 und 2 Satz 2 sinngemäß. [2]Die Einzelheiten der Archivierung und Benutzung regelt der Sächsische Landtag in eigener Zuständigkeit.

(3) Der Sächsische Landtag kann Archivgut und bei ihm entstandene Unterlagen, die er zur Erfüllung seiner Aufgaben nicht mehr benötigt, dem Sächsischen Staatsarchiv zur Übernahme anbieten.

§ 13 Kommunale Archive

(1) [1]Die kommunalen Träger der Selbstverwaltung, deren Verbände sowie kommunale Stiftungen archivieren ihr Archivgut im Sinne von § 2 einschließlich des von ihnen übernommenen Archivgutes nach § 4 Abs. 2 zur allgemeinen Nutzung in eigener Zuständigkeit. [2]Die Archive der Landkreise und Gemeinden sind auch zuständig für die Archivierung der vom 8. Mai 1945 bis zum 2. Oktober 1990 entstandenen Unterlagen der staatlichen oder wirtschaftsleitenden Organe, Kombinate, Betriebe, Genossenschaften und Einrichtungen der Kreise, Städte und Gemeinden.

(2) [1]Die kommunalen Träger der Selbstverwaltung, deren Verbände sowie kommunale Stiftungen unterhalten zu diesem Zweck eigene oder gemeinsame Archive in öffentlich-rechtlicher Form, die den archivfachlichen Anforderungen hinsichtlich Personal, Räumen und Ausstattung entsprechen müssen. [2]Die Archive sind durch Bedienstete mit einer archivfachlichen Ausbildung zu führen.

(3) [1]Unterhalten kreisangehörige kommunale Körperschaften keine eigenen oder gemeinsamen Archive, übernimmt das zuständige Archiv des Landkreises archivwürdige Unterlagen und Archivgut. [2]Die abgebende Körperschaft ist zum Kostenausgleich verpflichtet. [3]Das Eigentum am Archivgut bleibt unberührt.

(4) [1]§ 4 Abs. 4 und 5 Satz 2, § 5 Abs. 1 bis 3 und 5 bis 10 sowie §§ 6 bis 11 gelten entsprechend. [2]Die Rechtsträger der Archive erlassen eine Archivsatzung.

§ 14 Archive von Hochschulen und Akademien

(1) Die staatlichen Hochschulen und die Sächsische Akademie der Wissenschaften zu Leipzig verwahren, erhalten und erschließen ihr Archivgut im Sinne von § 2 zur allgemeinen Nutzung in eigener Zuständigkeit.

(2) § 13 Abs. 2 und 4 gilt entsprechend.

§ 15 Andere öffentliche Archive

(1) [1]Die sonstigen der Aufsicht des Freistaates Sachsen unterstehenden juristischen Personen des öffentlichen Rechts können mit Zustimmung des Staatsministeriums des Innern eigene fachlich geleitete Archive oder zusammen mit anderen juristischen Personen des öffentlichen Rechts oder anderen öffentlichen Archiven gemeinsame Archive unterhalten, die der Fachaufsicht des Sächsischen Staatsarchivs unterstehen. [2]Sofern sie keine eigenen oder gemeinsamen Archive unterhalten, haben sie die zur Erfüllung ihrer Aufgaben nicht mehr benötigten Unterlagen dem Sächsischen Staatsarchiv nach Maßgabe des § 5 zur Übernahme anzubieten. [3]Das Eigentum am Archivgut bleibt unberührt.

(2) § 13 Abs. 2 und 4 gilt entsprechend

Vierter Abschnitt
Schlußbestimmungen

§ 16 Verordnungsermächtigung

Das Staatsministerium des Innern regelt durch Rechtsverordnung
1. die Benutzung des Sächsischen Staatsarchivs einschließlich der dafür zu erhebenden Gebühren und Auslagen sowie
2. die Anbietung und Übernahme elektronischer Unterlagen sowie
3. eine Ablieferungspflicht von Belegexemplaren von im Freistaat Sachsen hergestellten oder herausgegebenen Medaillen an das Münzkabinett der staatlichen Kunstsammlungen in Dresden. Dabei ist vorzusehen, daß das Münzkabinett dem Ablieferungspflichtigen auf Antrag bis zur Hälfte des Ladenpreises oder mangels eines solchen der Herstellungskosten erstattet, wenn für ihn die unentgeltliche Abgabe insbesondere wegen der hohen Herstellungskosten und der geringen Auflage im Einzelfall unzumutbar ist.

§ 17 Besondere Kategorien personenbezogener Daten
Die §§ 5, 6 und 9 bis 11 finden auch Anwendung auf die besonderen Kategorien personenbezogener Daten gemäß Artikel 9 Absatz 1 der Verordnung (EU) 2016/679.

§ 18 Einschränkung eines Grundrechts
Das Recht auf informationelle Selbstbestimmung (Artikel 2 Abs. 1 in Verbindung mit Artikel 1 Abs. 1 des Grundgesetzes, Artikel 33 der Verfassung des Freistaates Sachsen) wird durch dieses Gesetz eingeschränkt.

§ 19 Inkrafttreten
(1) Dieses Gesetz tritt am Tage nach seiner Verkündung[1] in Kraft.
(2) Gleichzeitig tritt die Verordnung über das staatliche Archivwesen der DDR vom 11. März 1976 (GBl. I Nr. 10 S. 165) außer Kraft.

---

1) Verkündet am 14.6.1993.

D13.II.1a Sächsische Archivbenutzungsverordnung

Verordnung des Sächsischen Staatsministeriums des Innern über die Benutzung der staatlichen Archive (Sächsische Archivbenutzungsverordnung – SächsArchivBenVO)

Vom 24. Februar 2003 (SächsGVBl. S. 79)

Aufgrund von § 16 Nr. 2 in Verbindung mit § 9 des Archivgesetzes für den Freistaat Sachsen (SächsArchivG) vom 17. Mai 1993 (SächsGVBl. S. 449), das zuletzt durch Artikel 1 des Gesetzes vom 25. Juni 1999 (SächsGVBl. S. 398) geändert worden ist, wird verordnet:

§ 1 Art der Benutzung

(1) Archivgut wird grundsätzlich durch persönliche Einsichtnahme im verwahrenden Archiv benutzt. Dem Anspruch auf Archivgutnutzung kann durch Vorlage von Reproduktionen entsprochen werden.

(2) Das Archiv kann auch mündliche oder schriftliche Auskünfte erteilen. Diese beschränken sich grundsätzlich auf Hinweise zu Art, Umfang und Benutzbarkeit des einschlägigen Archivgutes.

(3) Das Archiv kann die Benutzung auch durch persönliche Einsichtnahme außerhalb des Archivs, durch Ausleihe für Ausstellungen sowie durch Abgabe von Reproduktionen ermöglichen.

§ 2 Benutzungsverhältnis und Benutzungsgenehmigung

(1) Das Benutzungsverhältnis ist öffentlich-rechtlicher Natur.

(2) Die Benutzung des Archivs ist genehmigungsbedürftig. Die Benutzungsgenehmigung ist schriftlich bei dem Archiv zu beantragen.
Im Antrag sind anzugeben:
1. der Name und der Vorname sowie die Anschrift des Antragstellers,
2. im Falle der Vertretung der Name und der Vorname sowie die Anschrift des Vertreters unter Nachweis der Vertretungsmacht; in den Fällen des § 12 Abs. 1 Nr. 3 und 4 des Verwaltungsverfahrensgesetzes (VwVfG) in der Fassung der Bekanntmachung vom 23. Januar 2003 (BGBl. I S. 102), in der jeweils geltenden Fassung, in Verbindung mit § 1 des Vorläufigen Verwaltungsverfahrensgesetzes für den Freistaat Sachsen (SächsVwVfG) vom 21. Januar 1993 (SächsGVBl. S. 74), das zuletzt durch § 17 des Gesetzes vom 31. März 1999 (SächsGVBl. S. 161, 163) geändert wurde, in der jeweils geltenden Fassung (juristische Personen, Vereinigungen und Behörden) gilt Entsprechendes,
3. der Name und der Vorname von Personen, die den Antragsteller bei der persönlichen Einsichtnahme unterstützen,
4. das Benutzungsvorhaben mit zeitlicher und sachlicher Eingrenzung.

Änderungen, die zwischen der Antragstellung und dem Abschluss des Benutzungsvorhabens eintreten und welche Angaben nach Satz 3 sowie § 3 betreffen, hat der Antragsteller dem Archiv unverzüglich mitzuteilen.

(3) Wird der Zugang zu Unterlagen mit personenbezogenen Daten beantragt, für welche die Schutzfristen des § 10 Abs. 1 Satz 3 und 4 SächsArchivG noch nicht abgelaufen sind, haben sich die in Absatz 2 Satz 3 genannten Personen auszuweisen, in anderen Fällen besteht diese Verpflichtung auf Verlangen des Archivs. In den Fällen des § 6 Abs. 1 Satz 2, Abs. 3 Satz 2 SächsArchivG ist der Antrag schriftlich zu begründen.

(4) Unbeschadet der Regelungen gemäß § 1 des SächsVwVfG in Verbindung mit §§ 48 und 49 des VwVfG kann die Benutzungsgenehmigung auch widerrufen werden, wenn
1. die Angaben im Antrag auf Benutzungsgenehmigung nicht oder nicht mehr zutreffen,
2. nachträglich Gründe bekannt werden, die zur Versagung der Benutzungsgenehmigung geführt hätten,
3. wiederholt oder schwerwiegend gegen die Benutzungsbestimmungen verstoßen wird, oder
4. das Urheber- oder das Persönlichkeitsrecht verletzt oder sonst schutzwürdige Belange Dritter nicht beachtet werden.

§ 3 Verkürzung der Schutzfristen

Eine Verkürzung der Schutzfristen gemäß § 10 Abs. 4 und 5 SächsArchivG ist schriftlich beim Archiv zu beantragen. Der Antrag ist zu begründen, wobei das Forschungsvorhaben einschließlich seiner

Träger und seine öffentliche, insbesondere wissenschaftliche, Bedeutung und die Art der benötigten personenbezogenen Daten darzulegen sind.

§ 4 Einsichtnahme im Archiv
(1) Zur persönlichen Einsichtnahme wird Archivgut grundsätzlich nur in den dafür vorgesehenen Räumen (Benutzerräume) des Archivs vorgelegt.
(2) Die Öffnungszeiten der Benutzerräume sowie Regelungen, die insbesondere einem geordneten Ablauf der Benutzung oder dem Schutz des Archivgutes dienen, legt das Archiv in Benutzerraum-Ordnungen näher fest.
(3) Das Archiv kann auch die Einsichtnahme in Archivgut ermöglichen, das von anderen Archiven übersandt wird. Soweit mit dem versendenden Archiv nichts anderes vereinbart wurde, gelten die Bestimmungen dieser Verordnung entsprechend.

§ 5 Einsichtnahme außerhalb des Archivs
(1) Das Archiv kann in begründeten Ausnahmefällen und in beschränktem Umfang die persönliche Einsichtnahme auch in anderen hauptamtlich geleiteten Archiven ermöglichen. Dort muss sichergestellt sein, dass das Archivgut nur in den Diensträumen, die den archivfachlichen Anforderungen entsprechen, verwahrt und nur unter archivfachlicher Aufsicht eingesehen wird. Reproduktionen dürfen nur mit Zustimmung des versendenden Archivs angefertigt werden.
(2) Über die Art der Versendung und der Rücksendung entscheidet das versendende Archiv.
(3) Aus wichtigen Gründen kann das versandte Archivgut jederzeit zurückgefordert werden.
(4) Das Archiv kann die Benutzung audiovisueller Medien wie Lauffilme und Tonträger abweichend von Absatz 1 an anderer geeigneter Stelle ermöglichen, wenn es über die technischen Mittel nicht selbst verfügt.
(5) Die Versendung von Archivgut an Behörden und sonstige öffentliche Stellen im Geltungsbereich des Grundgesetzes zur Einsichtnahme durch diese erfolgt nur in begründeten Ausnahmefällen. Die Absätze 2 und 3 gelten entsprechend.

§ 6 Ausleihe für Ausstellungen
(1) Auf die Ausleihe von Archivgut für Ausstellungen besteht kein Anspruch.
(2) Die Ausleihe ist nur möglich, wenn der Ausstellungszweck nicht durch Reproduktionen erreicht werden kann und wenn gesichert ist, dass das ausgeliehene Archivgut nach den Anforderungen des Archivs nachhaltig vor Schäden, Verlust, Vernichtung oder unbefugter Benutzung geschützt wird. Reproduktionen dürfen nur mit Zustimmung des verleihenden Archivs angefertigt werden.
(3) Die Einzelheiten sind in einem öffentlich-rechtlichen Leihvertrag zu regeln.

§ 7 Abgabe von Reproduktionen
(1) Das Archiv kann auf schriftlichen Antrag Reproduktionen von Archivgut herstellen, wie zum Beispiel Kopien, Filme, audiovisuelle und elektronische Medien. Über die geeigneten Reproduktionsverfahren entscheidet das Archiv.
(2) § 2 Abs. 2 und § 3 gelten entsprechend.
(3) Reproduktionen dürfen nur mit schriftlicher Zustimmung des Archivs und nur zu dem genehmigten Zweck veröffentlicht, vervielfältigt, an Dritte weitergegeben oder in sonstiger Weise genutzt werden. Bei Veröffentlichungen von Reproduktionen sind mindestens das Archiv und der Hersteller der Reproduktion anzugeben.

§ 8 In-Kraft-Treten
Diese Verordnung tritt am Tage nach ihrer Verkündung in Kraft.

Verordnung des Sächsischen Staatsministeriums des Innern über die Benutzungsgebühren des Sächsischen Staatsarchivs (Sächsische Archivgebührenverordnung – SächsArchivGebVO)

Vom 23. Mai 2006 (SächsGVBl. 2006 Nr. 7, S. 163)
geänd. durch Art. 2, Abs. 12 der Verordnung vom 5. April 2019 (SächsGVBl. S. 245)

Es wird verordnet aufgrund von
1. § 16 Nr. 1 des *Archivgesetzes für den Freistaat Sachsen* (SächsArchivG) vom 17. Mai 1993 (SächsGVBl. S. 449), das zuletzt durch Artikel 2 des Gesetzes vom 5. Mai 2004 (SächsGVBl. S. 148) geändert worden ist,
2. § 27 Abs. 1 Satz 1 und Abs. 3 Satz 2 des *Verwaltungskostengesetzes des Freistaates Sachsen* (SächsVwKG) in der Fassung der Bekanntmachung vom 17. September 2003 (SächsGVBl. S. 698) im Einvernehmen mit dem Staatsministerium der Finanzen:

§ 1 Allgemeines
(1) Das Sächsische Staatsarchiv erhebt für die Benutzung seiner Einrichtungen und für die von ihm erbrachten Leistungen Benutzungsgebühren und Auslagen nach dieser Verordnung.
(2) Die Benutzungsgebühren werden nach den Sätzen des Verzeichnisses über die Benutzungsgebühren des Sächsischen Staatsarchivs (Gebührenverzeichnis) gemäß Anlage erhoben. Mit der Benutzungsgebühr werden Amtshandlungen, die mit der Erbringung der Leistung in engem Zusammenhang stehen, abgegolten.

§ 2 Schuldner
(1) Schuldner der Benutzungsgebühren und Auslagen ist derjenige,
1. der das Sächsische Staatsarchiv in Anspruch nimmt,
2. in dessen Interesse die Inanspruchnahme erfolgt oder
3. der die Benutzungsgebühren und Auslagen gegenüber dem Sächsischen Staatsarchiv schriftlich übernimmt oder für die Schuld eines anderen kraft Gesetzes haftet.
(2) Mehrere Schuldner haften als Gesamtschuldner.

§ 3 Entstehen, Fälligkeit, Vorschuss
(1) Die Benutzungsgebühren und Auslagen entstehen mit der Inanspruchnahme der Leistungen des Sächsischen Staatsarchivs oder mit der Benutzung seiner Einrichtungen.
(2) Die Benutzungsgebühren und Auslagen werden mit der Bekanntgabe der Kostenentscheidung an den Schuldner fällig, wenn das Sächsische Staatsarchiv nicht einen späteren Zeitpunkt bestimmt.
(3) Das Sächsische Staatsarchiv kann eine Vorauszahlung der Benutzungsgebühren und Auslagen verlangen.

§ 4 Befreiung, Nichterhebung und Ermäßigung
(1) § 12 des *Sächsischen Verwaltungskostengesetzes* vom 5. April 2019 (SächsGVBl. S. 245), in der jeweils geltenden Fassung, findet keine Anwendung, soweit sich aus den folgenden Absätzen nichts anderes ergibt.
(2) Von der Zahlung der Benutzungsgebühren sind Behörden und Gerichte des Freistaates Sachsen befreit. Sonstige öffentliche Stellen, die nach § 5 Absatz 1 des *Archivgesetzes für den Freistaat Sachsen* verpflichtet sind, dem Sächsischen Staatsarchiv Unterlagen anzubieten (anbietungspflichtige öffentliche Stellen), sind von der Zahlung der Benutzungsgebühren befreit, soweit Unterlagen benutzt werden, die sie oder ihre Funktionsvorgänger dem Sächsischen Staatsarchiv zur Archivierung übergeben haben.
(3) Von der Zahlung der Benutzungsgebühren und Auslagen sind kommunale Körperschaften des öffentlichen Rechts, die der Rechtsaufsicht des Freistaates Sachsen unterstehen, befreit, wenn sie die betreffende öffentlich-rechtliche Leistung bei der Wahrnehmung von Pflichtaufgaben nach Weisung in Anspruch nehmen und nicht berechtigt sind, die Benutzungsgebühren und Auslagen einem Dritten aufzuerlegen oder auf Dritte umzulegen.
(4) Von der Zahlung der Benutzungsgebühren nach Nummer 2 des Gebührenverzeichnisses sind Gerichte und Staatsanwaltschaften auf dem Gebiet der Bundesrepublik Deutschland befreit.

(5) Von der Zahlung der Benutzungsgebühren nach Nummer 3 des Gebührenverzeichnisses sind anbietungspflichtige öffentliche Stellen des Freistaates Sachsen befreit.

(6) Benutzungsgebühren nach Nummer 1 des Gebührenverzeichnisses werden nicht erhoben, wenn es sich um ein wissenschaftliches oder heimatkundliches Benutzungsvorhaben handelt und gewerbsmäßige Zwecke nicht verfolgt werden. Von einer Gebührenerhebung nach Nummer 1 des Gebührenverzeichnisses kann außerdem im Einzelfall abgesehen werden, wenn die Erhebung eine besondere Härte bedeuten würde oder sonstige Gründe der Billigkeit vorliegen.

(7) Benutzungsgebühren nach Nummer 5 des Gebührenverzeichnisses werden nicht erhoben, wenn die Veröffentlichung wissenschaftlichen oder heimatkundlichen Zwecken dient und gewerbsmäßige Zwecke nicht verfolgt werden. Die Gebühren nach Nummer 5 des Gebührenverzeichnisses werden um die Hälfte ermäßigt, wenn die Veröffentlichung wissenschaftlichen oder heimatkundlichen Zwecken dient oder sonst im öffentlichen Interesse liegt und gewerbsmäßige Zwecke nicht überwiegen.

§§ 5 und 6 (aufgehoben)

§ 7 In-Kraft-Treten
Diese Verordnung tritt am Tage nach ihrer Verkündung in Kraft. Gleichzeitig tritt die Verordnung des Sächsischen Staatsministeriums des Innern über die Benutzungsgebühren der staatlichen Archive (*Sächsische Archivgebührenverordnung – SächsArchGebVO*) vom 8. Februar 1996 (SächsGVBl. S. 82), geändert durch Artikel 6 der Verordnung vom 12. Dezember 2001 (SächsGVBl. 2002 S. 3, 4), außer Kraft.

Anlage
(zu § 1 Abs. 2 Satz 1)

Gebührenverzeichnis

Nr.	Gegenstand	Gebührensatz in EUR
1	Mündliche oder schriftliche Auskünfte, die über Hinweise zu Art, Umfang und Benutzbarkeit des einschlägigen Archivgutes hinausgehen, einschließlich der dazu erforderlichen Ermittlungen, sowie Ermittlung von Archivgut für die Durchführung von Reproduktionsaufträgen und für sonstige Nutzungszwecke, je angefangene Viertelstunde Für erfolglose Ermittlungen werden ebenfalls Gebühren erhoben.	12,00
2	Versendung von Archivgut für die Einsichtnahme außerhalb des Archivs, je Sendung	18,00
3	Ausleihe von Archivgut für Ausstellungen, je Archivalieneinheit	18,00
4	Reproduktionen	
4.1	Grundgebühr, je Auftrag oder Inanspruchnahme	2,50
4.2	Reproduktionen auf Normalpapier	
4.2.1	schwarz-weiß	
4.2.1.1	von losen planliegenden Vorlagen, je Reproduktion	
	A4	0,25
	A3	0,50
4.2.1.2	von fest formierten oder nicht planliegenden Vorlagen, je Reproduktion	
	A4	0,60
	A3	1,20
4.2.1.3	von verfilmten oder digitalisierten Vorlagen, je Reproduktion auf Bestellung	
	A4	0,60
	A3	1,20

D13.II.1b Sächsische Archivgebührenverordnung

	in Selbstbedienung	
	A4	0,15
	A3	0,30
4.2.2	farbig, je Reproduktion	
	A4	2,00
	A3	4,00
4.3	Reproduktionen auf Spezialpapier in Fotoqualität	
4.3.1	schwarz-weiß, je Reproduktion	
	A5	6,50
	A4	8,50
	A3	13,00
4.3.2	farbig, je Reproduktion	
	A5	8,50
	A4	11,00
	A3	16,50
4.4	Reproduktionen, Ausgabe als Datei, je Reproduktion	
	niedrigauflösend, Format jpeg	0,60
	hochauflösend, Format jpeg	3,00
	hochauflösend, Format tiff	4,50
	zuzüglich je Datenträger	2,50
4.5	Diapositive, farbig, ungerahmt, je Aufnahme	
	24 x 36 mm	7,50
	60 x 60 mm	8,50
	90 x 120 mm	13,50
	130 x 180 mm	17,50
4.6	Mikrofilm, Rollfilm 35 mm, je Aufnahme	0,35
4.7	Mikrofilmkopie auf Rollfilm 35 mm, je Meter	1,30
4.8	Reproduktionen von audiovisuellem Archivgut	
4.8.1	Reproduktionen von Schallarchivalien, je angefangene Viertelstunde Laufzeit in Formaten zur privaten Nutzung (wie beispielsweise Audiokassette)	15,00
	in sendetauglichen Formaten (wie beispielsweise DATKassette, CD-A)	30,00
4.8.2	Reproduktionen von Laufbildarchivalien, je angefangene Viertelstunde Laufzeit	
	in Formaten zur privaten Nutzung (wie beispielsweise VHSKassette)	20,00
	in semiprofessionellen Formaten (wie beispielsweise S-VHSKassette)	30,00
	in sendetauglichen Formaten (wie beispielsweise Betacam SP)	40,00
4.9	Zuschlag für besonders vereinbarte Terminaufträge, je Einzelfall	30,00
4.10	Zuschlag für Sonderleistungen und erhöhten Arbeitsaufwand, je angefangene Viertelstunde	8,50

5	Veröffentlichung von Archivgut	
5.1	Veröffentlichung von Archivalien in Druckwerken oder auf elektronischen Speichermedien, je Reproduktion	
	Auflage	
	bis 5 000	40,00
	bis 50 000	80,00
	über 50 000	160,00
5.2	Veröffentlichung von Archivalien in audiovisuellen Medien (Hörfunk, Fernsehen, Kino)	
5.2.1	je Reproduktion von Dokumenten, Fotos und Ähnlichem	
	lokale Ausstrahlung	25,00
	regionale Ausstrahlung	50,00
	nationale oder internationale Ausstrahlung	100,00
5.2.2	je angefangene Wiedergabeminute bei audiovisuellem Archivgut	
	lokale Ausstrahlung	50,00
	regionale Ausstrahlung	100,00
	nationale oder internationale Ausstrahlung	200,00
5.2.3	Wiederholungen innerhalb von 48 Stunden sind kostenfrei. Danach wird für jede weitere Wiederholung die Hälfte der Gebühr nach Nummer 5.2 erhoben.	
5.3	Veröffentlichung von Archivalien im Internet und anderen Online-Diensten, je Reproduktion von Dokumenten, Fotos und Ähnlichem oder angefangener Wiedergabeminute bei audiovisuellem Archivgut	
	bis sechs Monate	50,00
	über sechs Monate	100,00

D13.III.1 VwV-Denkmalförderung

Verwaltungsvorschrift des Sächsischen Staatsministeriums des Innern über die Gewährung von Zuwendungen zur Erhaltung und Pflege von sächsischen Kulturdenkmalen und zur Aus- und Fortbildung der Denkmalpflege (VwV-Denkmalförderung)

Vom 20. Dezember 1996

zuletzt geändert durch VwV vom 1. Februar 2016 (SächsABl. S. 192)

1 Zuwendungszweck, Rechtsgrundlage

1.1 Der Freistaat gewährt in Übereinstimmung mit Artikel 11 der Verfassung des Freistaates Sachsen und auf Grundlage des Gesetzes zum Schutz und zur Pflege der Kulturdenkmale im Freistaat Sachsen (Sächsisches Denkmalschutzgesetz – SächsDSchG) vom 3. März 1993 (SächsGVBl. S. 229) nach Maßgabe dieser Verwaltungsvorschrift und der Vorläufigen Verwaltungsvorschrift für die Bewilligung staatlicher Zuwendungen nach § 44 Abs. 1 der Vorläufigen Sächsischen Haushaltsordnung (Vorl.VV zu § 44 SäHO) Zuwendungen zu Maßnahmen, die dem Schutz und der Pflege von Kulturdenkmalen und der Aus- und Fortbildung in der Denkmalpflege dienen.

1.2 Die Zuwendung bei Maßnahmen zum Schutz und der Pflege von Kulturdenkmalen soll den Eigentümer oder den Besitzer bei der Erfüllung der sich nach § 8 SächsDSchG aus der Sozialbindung des Eigentums ergebenden Erhaltungspflichten unterstützen.

Die Zuwendung zu Maßnahmen der Aus- und Fortbildung soll fachlich und inhaltlich richtige denkmalpflegerische Maßnahmen an Kulturdenkmalen sichern.

Ein Anspruch auf Gewährung einer Zuwendung besteht nicht.

Vielmehr entscheidet die Bewilligungsbehörde aufgrund ihres pflichtgemäßen Ermessens im Rahmen der verfügbaren Haushaltsmittel.

2 Gegenstand der Förderung

2.1 Eine Zuwendung kann bewilligt werden für Maßnahmen zum Schutz und zur Pflege eines Kulturdenkmales, für Maßnahmen an Objekten im Sinne des § 2 des SächsDSchG, in einem Denkmalschutzgebiet, einem Grabungsschutzgebiet oder einem archäologischen Reservat gemäß §§ 21, 22 und 23 SächsDSchG und für Maßnahmen der Aus- und Fortbildung in der Denkmalpflege.

2.2 Hierin sind insbesondere eingeschlossen:

2.2.1 behutsame Maßnahmen zur Pflege und zur Bewahrung der Eigenschaften eines Kulturdenkmales, eines Denkmalschutzgebietes, eines Grabungsschutzgebietes oder eines archäologischen Reservates (im Weiteren allgemein als Denkmal bezeichnet) – Instandhaltung –; ausbessernde Maßnahmen an einem Denkmal, die sich auf einen eingegrenzten Bereich beziehen und in bezug auf Eingriffe an der Originalität schonend sind – Reparatur –;

2.2.2 (dokumentierende) Maßnahmen zur Freilegung unterlegter Fassungen an einem Denkmal, um einerseits in (Teil)Bereichen den Geschichtswert des Denkmales entweder weitreichender zu erfassen beziehungsweise dort erst aufzudecken oder ursprünglichere Fassungen freizulegen, um die ästhetische Perzeption des Denkmales erst wieder zu gewinnen oder nachdrücklich zu erhöhen;

2.2.3 Maßnahmen, um verlorengegangene, verdeckte oder unscheinbar gewordene ästhetische Eigenschaften an einem Denkmal zu erneuern; diese Maßnahmen sind auf die ästhetische Ganzheit des Denkmales im Sinne seiner künstlerisch sichtbaren Geschlossenheit oder seiner gewachsenen Vielschichtigkeit ausgerichtet – Renovierung –;

2.2.4 Maßnahmen, um an einem Denkmal Verletzungen, ästhetische Verunstaltungen oder frühere Fehlinterpretationen zu berichtigen und das Denkmal – unter weitestreichender Wahrung seiner Originalität – durch das Schließen und die Korrektur der die Gesamterscheinung beeinträchtigenden Fehlstellen zu bewahren; durch vorangegangene Analyse am Denkmal drohende Gefahren für den Bestand eindämmen und seine Geschichtlichkeit erhalten – Restaurierung –;

2.2.5 umfangreichere Maßnahmen an einem Denkmal, um die Eigenschaften des Denkmales unter weitgehender Wahrung der Originalität bei begrenzten Erneuerungen zu bewahren – Instandsetzung –;

2.2.6 tiefgreifende und umfassende Gesamtmaßnahmen an einem Denkmal, um dessen langfristige Erhaltung zu gewähren, verbunden mit der Wiederherstellung von Bauteilen, des (Bau)Gefüges und mit dem Ziel, die ästhetische Gesamtheit des Denkmales wiederzugewinnen – Sanierung –;

2.2.7 Maßnahmen, um originale Spuren als erhaltenswertes Gut an einem Denkmal langzeitlich zu sichern. Die Offenheit und die fragmentarische Erhaltung der Form sowie das Ablesen der Geschichtlichkeit bestimmen die Maßnahmen – Konservierung –;

2.2.8 Maßnahmen, um auffallende Lücken im Bestand eines Denkmales zu schließen. Die Vollform des Denkmales wird nicht angestrebt – Ergänzung –;

2.2.9 Maßnahmen, um die vorhandene, stark beeinträchtigte Wirkung eines Denkmales zu beheben (Gesamtheit, Ensemble). Die Maßnahme wurde notwendig, um das nicht gegebene Erschließen der offenen, verletzten Form der verbliebenen Stücke zu erreichen – Vervollständigung –;

2.2.10 rückbildende Maßnahmen zum Wiederherstellen, Maßnahmen zur Wiederkehr eines früheren Zustandes an einem Denkmal, wobei der Denkmalwert nicht berührt wird, sondern Verunstaltungen beseitigt werden – Apokatastase –; gleichfalls Maßnahmen der rekonstruierenden Wiederherstellung, sofern damit Teile eines bestehenden Denkmales ergänzt werden;

2.2.11 Maßnahmen, die (bei möglicher gradueller Demontage des Vorhandenen) das Zusammenfügen der vorhandenen, originalen Teile und das ablesbare Schließen kleiner Fehlstellen beinhalten, um das verbliebene Denkmal in einen erkennbaren Zusammenhang zu stellen, wobei kein vollständiges Denkmal entsteht – Anastylose –;

2.2.12 Maßnahmen, um die durch Bergung aus einem anderen Denkmal gewonnenen und wiederverwendbaren (Bau)Teile in einen neuen ganzheitlichen oder fragmentarischen Zusammenhang in einem bestehenden Denkmal oder in (an) einem anderen Gebäude zu stellen – Spoliencharakter/Lapidariumgedanke –;

2.2.13 Maßnahmen, um ein zerstörtes Denkmal wiederzugewinnen, wenn hierbei das Denkmal in seiner Grundstruktur, in wesensbestimmenden Teilen noch vorhanden ist und der Denkmalwert sich durch ästhetische Werte, Symbolwerte, Werte im städtebaulichen Kontext oder Geschichtswerte definiert;

2.2.14 Maßnahmen, um ein Denkmal oder Teile desselben nachzubilden, damit der vorhandene Denkmalwert gewahrt bleibt – Kopie –;

2.2.15 archäologische Maßnahmen, um Bodendenkmale auszugraben, freizulegen und zu sichern;

2.2.16 Maßnahmen, um ein Denkmal an einen anderen Ort innerhalb der Kulturlandschaft zu versetzen – Translozierung –; nur bei nachweisbar drohendem Verlust des Denkmales als letzte Rettung anzuwenden;

2.2.17 Maßnahmen an einem Objekt, das nicht Kulturdenkmal ist, an dem aber zum Schutz des Erscheinungsbildes eines Kulturdenkmales oder eines Denkmalschutzgebietes denkmaladäquate Maßnahmen durchzuführen sind;

2.2.18 Aus- und Fortbildungsmaßnahmen der Denkmalpflege (Seminare für Handwerker, Architekten, Ingenieure, Kunsthistoriker und andere in der Denkmalpflege tätige Berufe) sind grundsätzlich an einen Teilnehmerkreis gerichtet, der eine abgeschlossene Berufsausbildung oder eine abgeschlossene Fach- oder Hochschulausbildung nachweisen kann.

3 Zuwendungsempfänger

3.1 Eine Zuwendung kann bewilligt werden dem
– Eigentümer,
– Besitzer oder
– Bauunterhaltspflichtigen

eines Objektes, an dem insbesondere Maßnahmen nach Nummer 2.2.1 bis 2.2.17 durchgeführt werden und Kosten nach Nummer 5.4.1 entstehen;

im Fall der Nummer 5.4.4 jedoch nur juristischen Personen des öffentlichen Rechts und juristischen Personen des Privatrechts, die als gemeinnützig anerkannt sind;

Einrichtungen, die in ihrem Aus- und Fortbildungsprofil theoretisch-wissenschaftliche und technisch-praktische Seminare in der Denkmalpflege anbieten und Maßnahmen nach Nummer 2.2.18 durchführen und denen Kosten nach Nummer 5.4.2 entstehen.

3.2 Zuwendungen werden nicht gewährt
- dem Bund,
- anderen Ländern und
- ausländischen Staaten;

ausgenommen hiervon sind Untergliederungen der Genannten, soweit sie juristische Personen des Privatrechts oder des öffentlichen Rechts sind und den Genannten nicht die Mehrheit im Sinne von § 53 Haushaltsgrundsätzegesetz gehört. Wird die Bauunterhaltspflichtigkeit eines Kulturdenkmales, eines Denkmalschutzgebietes, eines Grabungsschutzgebietes, archäologischen Reservates oder von Teilen der drei letztgenannten für einen längeren Zeitraum durch Vertragsbindung (Mindestübernahme der Bauunterhaltspflichtigkeit 12 bis 18 Jahre) an andere außer den zuerst oben genannten übertragen, so können für diese Zuwendungen bewilligt werden.

3.3 Soweit für öffentlich-rechtliche Körperschaften Sonderregelungen in dieser Verwaltungsvorschrift getroffen werden, so gilt dies auch für deren Untergliederungen sowie für juristische Personen des Privatrechts, die von diesen Körperschaften mehrheitlich kontrolliert werden.

4 Zuwendungsvoraussetzungen

4.1 Genehmigung der Maßnahmen

Die Maßnahmen an Kulturdenkmalen müssen denkmalpflegerischen Anforderungen und Zielen der Denkmalpflege, wie sie sich insbesondere in den Zielen von § 1 Abs. 1 und § 8 Abs. 1 SächsDSchG wiederfinden, folgen, sich auf den Gegenstand des Denkmalschutzes im Sinne der §§ 2, 21, 22 und 23 SächsDSchG beziehen und mit der denkmalschutzrechtlichen Genehmigung gemäß § 12 SächsDSchG übereinstimmen.

Notwendige Genehmigungen und Zustimmungen (zum Beispiel Baugenehmigung, denkmalschutzrechtliche Genehmigungen) müssen vor Beginn der Maßnahmen vorliegen.

Einrichtungen, die Aus- und Fortbildungsseminare in der Denkmalpflege ausrichten, haben gegenüber dem Zuwendungsgeber für die zuwendungsfähige Maßnahme den Nachweis zu führen, dass sie personell, inhaltlich, finanziell, organisatorisch und räumlich befähigt sind, Aus- und Fortbildungsseminare auszurichten, die den wissenschaftlich-fachlichen Ansprüchen der Lehre der Denkmalpflege entsprechen und den derzeitigen Stand der Lehre wiedergeben.

4.2 Baubeginn/Maßnahmebeginn

Die Maßnahme darf vor der Bewilligung der Zuwendung nicht begonnen sein. Ist eine Entscheidung über die Bewilligung noch nicht möglich, kann das Staatsministerium des Innern im Einzelfall bei Maßnahmen, die aus schwerwiegenden sachlichen oder wirtschaftlichen Gründen keinen Aufschub dulden, nach Maßgabe Nummer 1.3 der Vorl.VV zu § 44 SäHO einen vorzeitigen Baubeginn/Maßnahmebeginn zulassen.

Das Staatsministerium des Innern ermächtigt die Bewilligungsbehörde, bei Maßnahmen im Sinne von Nummer 2.2.1 bis 2.2.7, die Genehmigung zum vorzeitigen Baubeginn zu erteilen. Die Zustimmung zum vorzeitigen Baubeginn ersetzt nicht die Baugenehmigung oder denkmalschutzrechtliche Genehmigung und begründet keinen Rechtsanspruch auf eine Zuwendung.

4.3 Schwellenwerte

Zuwendungen werden grundsätzlich nur gewährt, wenn die zuwendungsfähigen Kosten
- bei juristischen Personen des Privatrechts und des öffentlichen Rechts als auch sonstigen 5 000 EUR,
- bei natürlichen Personen 1 500 EUR

übersteigen.

5 Art und Umfang, Höhe der Zuwendungen

5.1 Zuwendungsart

Die Zuwendung wird im Rahmen der Projektförderung gewährt.

5.2 Finanzierungsart

Die Finanzierung erfolgt als Anteilfinanzierung mit Höchstbetrag.

5.3 Form der Zuwendung

Die Zuwendung wird als ein nicht rückzahlbarer Zuschuss gewährt.

5.4 Bemessungsgrundlage
Zuwendungsfähig sind:
- 5.4.1 Aufwendungen im Sinne von Nummer 2.2.1 bis 2.2.17
  - an Kulturdenkmalen,
  - bei Maßnahmen im Bereich eines Denkmalschutzgebietes,
  - bei Maßnahmen im Bereich eines Grabungsschutzgebietes,
  - bei Maßnahmen im Bereich eines archäologischen Reservates,

  die im Rahmen von Instandhaltungs-, Reparatur-, Renovierungs-, Restaurierungs-, Instandsetzungs-, Sanierungs-, Konservierungs-, Ergänzungs-, Vervollständigungs-, Wiederherstellungs-, Zusammenfügungs-, Bergungs- und Einbau-, Wiederherstel-lungs-, Nachbildungs- und Umsetzungsmaßnahmen an Kulturdenkmalen allein oder überwiegend aus Gründen der Denkmalpflege erforderlich werden, soweit sie den üblichen Aufwand bei vergleichbaren nicht geschützten Objekten übersteigen
  - denkmalbedingte Mehraufwendungen -.

  Zu den denkmalbedingten Mehraufwendungen gehören auch die anteiligen Planungskosten (Architekten- und Ingenieurhonorare) und die Kosten einer restauratorischen Untersuchung. Die letztgenannten Kosten sind nur insofern förderfähig, als sie durch Anforderungen der Denkmalschutzbehörde oder der Landesoberbehörden für Denkmalschutz und Denkmalpflege zusätzlich entstanden sind und in direktem Zusammenhang mit der beabsichtigten Maßnahme stehen.

- 5.4.2 Aufwendungen im Sinne von Nummer 2.2.18 bei Aus- und Fortbildungsseminaren
  Personalkosten:
  - anteilige Personalkosten für die Vorbereitung und Durchführung der Seminare;
  Sachkosten:
  - anteilige Kosten für Mietzins (Betriebskosten),
  - Honorare und Reisekosten der Dozenten,
  - auf die Seminare bezogene Lehrmittel (Ausrüstung/Werkzeuge), die mit der Durchführung der Seminare im Zusammenhang stehen, insbesondere Demonstrationen, Verbrauchsmaterialien, Bücher, Skripte, Fotomaterialien,
  - auf die Seminare bezogene Sachkosten, wie Telefon- und Portogebühren, Büromaterialien für die Vorbereitung und Durchführung,
  - Publikationen der Aus- und Fortbildungsveranstaltungen (Seminarangebot).

- 5.4.3 Aufwendungen einer Bauaufnahme (Genauigkeitsstufe III, auf Anforderung IV, nach den Empfehlungen für Bauaufnahmen), einer restauratorischen Analyse, einer statischen, (infrarot)thermographischen, photogrammetrischen, bauphysikalischen, dendrochronologischen, archäologischen (stratigraphischen) Untersuchung oder eines sonstigen Fachgutachtens, die auf Verlangen der Denkmalschutzbehörde oder den Landesoberbehörden für Denkmalschutz und Denkmalpflege anzufertigen sind und in unmittelbarem, direktem Zusammenhang mit der Maßnahme stehen, können auf die denkmalbedingten Mehraufwendungen angerechnet werden.
  Diese Kosten sind jedoch nicht zuwendungsfähig, wenn derartige Maßnahmen aus anderen Gründen (zum Beispiel Baurecht, Umweltrecht) verlangt werden.
  Gleichfalls sind in besonderen Ausnahmen Planungskosten förderfähig, wenn vor allem durch sie der (rechtliche) Schutz eines Kulturdenkmales nachgewiesen werden kann; die Kosten müssen auf Veranlassung der Denkmalschutzbehörde oder der Landesoberbehörden für Denkmalschutz und Denkmalpflege zurückgehen.

- 5.4.4 Kosten des Erwerbs eines Grundstücks, das begründeter Vermutung nach ein archäologisches Kulturdenkmal birgt, welches durch die anderweitige Nutzung des Grundstücks gefährdet ist. Eine Förderung erfolgt jedoch nur insoweit, als das auf dem Grundstück befindliche archäologische Kulturdenkmal keine bestimmungsgemäße Nutzung zulässt und der Eigentümer durch das archäologische Kulturdenkmal keine anderweitigen wirtschaftlichen Vorteile erlangt.

- 5.4.5 Nicht zuwendungsfähig sind unter anderem auch:
  Maßnahmen an Kulturdenkmalen, Denkmalschutzgebieten, Grabungsschutzgebieten, archäologischen Reservaten, wenn an demselben Objekten in zeitlichem Zusammenhang den Denk-

malwert beeinträchtigende Maßnahmen durchgeführt werden; hier insbesondere auch Entkernung von Gebäuden oder andere den Denkmalwert reduzierende Maßnahmen. Kosten des Erwerbs eines Kulturdenkmales.

5.4.6 Anrechnung von Eigenleistungen bei Maßnahmen an Kulturdenkmalen

Eigenarbeit wird auf die zuwendungsfähigen Kosten angerechnet, wenn sie eine Facharbeit ist und die entsprechende Sachkunde bei Antragstellung nachgewiesen wird.

Die vom Zuwendungsempfänger geleistete Eigenarbeitszeit wird nach einem von der Bewilligungsbehörde festgelegten Tarif bei den Gesamtkosten der Maßnahme angerechnet. Sie ist nur zuwendungsfähig, wenn sie mehr als 150 Stunden beträgt. Sie ist durch eine Bestätigung des Architekten glaubhaft zu machen.

Das vom Zuwendungsempfänger selbst aufgewendete Material wird zum nachgewiesenen Einkaufspreis angerechnet. Der Einsatz von Geräten und Fahrzeugen von Privaten ist nicht zuwendungsfähig.

Bei Unternehmern, Handwerkern und Restauratoren, die bei Eigenleistungen im Rahmen ihres Geschäftsbetriebes tätig werden, werden die ortsüblichen Entgelte abzüglich eines pauschalierten Gewinnanteils von 25 vom Hundert anerkannt. Diese Regelung gilt auch für Architekten, Ingenieure und Baustatiker bis zu einem Höchstbetrag von 10 vom Hundert der Gesamtkosten der Maßnahme.

Bei Eigenleistungen von Kommunen, zum Beispiel bei der Planung, Bauleitung und Durchführung der Baumaßnahme, kann der Tariflohn der eingesetzten Arbeitskräfte mit einem pauschalen Abzug von 25 vom Hundert in die Gesamtkostenberechnung einbezogen werden. Die Mindestleistungsgrenze von 150 Stunden pro Maßnahme gilt auch für die Gemeinde. Beim Einsatz gemeindeeigener Baufahrzeuge und Baumaschinen kann ein angemessener Stundensatz abzüglich eines Gemeindeanteils von 25 vom Hundert anerkannt werden.

5.4.7 Anrechnung von Leistungen Dritter

Leistungen aus anderen öffentlichen Förderprogrammen oder von Dritten vermindern die Zuwendungen, soweit sie auf die zuwendungsfähigen Kosten geleistet werden und zusammen mit der Zuwendung diese Kosten übersteigen.

Wenn die Bewilligungsbehörde die begründete Vermutung hat, dass eine Förderung auch durch Dritte möglich ist, kann dem Antragsteller aufgegeben werden, ein ernsthaftes Bemühen um anderweitige Förderung nachzuweisen.

5.5 Höhe der Zuwendung

Fördersatz:

Der Fördersatz beträgt bei Zuwendungen bis zu 60 vom Hundert des denkmalbedingten Mehraufwandes/der Aufwendungen für Aus- und Fortbildungsseminare. In begründeten Ausnahmefällen kann dieser Fördersatz überschritten werden, sofern ein dringendes Staatsinteresse dies erfordert.

6 Sonstige Zuwendungsbestimmungen

6.1 In Ergänzung zu beziehungsweise unter Abweichung von der Vorl.VV zu § 44 SäHO sowie den Allgemeinen Nebenbestimmungen für Zuwendungen zur Projektförderung (ANBest-P) und den Allgemeinen Nebenbestimmungen für Zuwendungen zur Projektförderung an kommunale Körperschaften (ANBest-K) sind in den Zuwendungsbescheid folgende Nebenbestimmungen aufzunehmen:

6.2 Abweichend von § 44 SäHO ist der Zuwendungsbescheid zu widerrufen, wenn der Zweck der Zuwendung nicht erreicht wird, insbesondere eine Teilmaßnahme nicht ausgeführt wurde. Eine Rückforderung gemäß der Vorl.VV zu § 44 SäHO erfolgt im Regelfall anteilig.

6.3 Ansprüche aus dem Zuwendungsbescheid können nicht auf Dritte übertragen werden.

6.4 Ermäßigt sich der denkmalbedingte Mehraufwand einer durchgeführten Teilmaßnahme, kann von einer Rückforderung abgesehen werden, wenn der Zuwendungsempfänger nachweist, dass die zuwendungsfähigen Kosten der Gesamtmaßnahme insgesamt den der Bewilligung zugrundegelegten Betrag erreichen.

6.5 Der Zuwendungsbescheid kann widerrufen werden, wenn der Antragsteller Nebenbestimmungen (Bedingungen, Befristungen, Auflagen, Widerrufsvorbehalte) der denkmalschutzrechtlichen Genehmigung nicht einhält.

6.6 Zur Sicherung des Zugangs zu einem Kulturdenkmal für die Öffentlichkeit soll in geeigneten Fällen die Zuwendung von der Eintragung einer Dienstbarkeit im Grundbuch abhängig gemacht werden. Dies gilt nicht für Kulturdenkmale, die dem Gottesdienst dienen.

6.7 Wenn bei Überschreitung des Regelfördersatzes nicht auszuschließen ist, dass die dafür maßgeblichen Gründe nachträglich entfallen, ist im Zuwendungsbescheid zu bestimmen, dass bei Wegfall der für die Überschreitung maßgeblichen Gründe sich die Zuwendung vermindert. Zur Sicherung eines etwaigen Rückforderungsanspruchs sollen von privaten Zuwendungsempfängern vor Auszahlung Sicherheiten bis zur Höhe des den Regelfördersatz übersteigenden Betrags verlangt werden (zum Beispiel Bankbürgschaft, Grundschuld). Die Sicherheiten sind zurückzugeben, wenn eine nachträgliche Änderung der für die Überschreitung maßgeblichen Gründe auszuschließen ist, unabhängig hiervon spätestens nach zehn Jahren.

6.8 Bei Zuwendungen zum Erwerb von Grundstücken mit Kulturdenkmalen ist im Zuwendungsbescheid die zulässige Grundstücksnutzung zu bestimmen und für den Fall eines Verstoßes hiergegen die Rückforderung der Zuwendung vorzubehalten.
Zur Sicherung der Nutzungsbeschränkung ist vor Auszahlung die Eintragung einer Dienstbarkeit im Grundbuch zu verlangen.

6.9 Die Bewilligungsbehörde behält sich vor, Bedingungen, Befristungen, Auflagen später zu ändern, aufzuheben, zu ergänzen oder neu aufzunehmen.

7 Verfahren

7.1 Antragsverfahren

Anträge auf Gewährung einer Zuwendung zur Erhaltung und Pflege eines Kulturdenkmales sind bei der Bewilligungsbehörde und der unteren Denkmalschutzbehörde, Anträge auf Gewährung einer Zuwendung für Aus- und Fortbildungsseminare in der Denkmalpflege sind bei der Bewilligungsbehörde unter Verwendung der dort erhältlichen Vordrucke sowie unter Beifügung der geforderten Unterlagen vor Beginn der geplanten Maßnahme bei der Bewilligungsbehörde einzureichen.
Nachfolgend genannte und anliegende Vordrucke[1] sind Bestandteil der Verwaltungsvorschrift:
– Antrag auf Gewährung einer Zuwendung zur Erhaltung und Pflege eines Kulturdenkmales,
– Anlage A, Beschreibung der denkmalpflegerischen Zielsetzung,
– Anlage B, Antrag – Kostenanschlag –,
– Antrag auf Gewährung einer Zuwendung für Aus- und Fortbildungsseminare in der Denkmalpflege.

Eine Überschreitung der Antragsfrist ist für den Antragsteller unschädlich, wenn nach Prüfung durch die Bewilligungsbehörde festgestellt wird, dass bei Unterlassen der eingeleiteten Maßnahmen Verluste an dem Kulturdenkmal, dem Denkmalschutzgebiet, dem Grabungsschutzgebiet oder dem archäologischen Reservat drohen – Gefahrenabwehr –.

7.2 Bewilligungszeitraum

Die Zuwendung wird für einen bestimmten Zeitraum bewilligt; dies ist das jeweilige Haushaltsjahr. Jedoch kann der Bewilligungszeitraum bei entsprechender Zeitdauer des Vorhabens weitere Jahre umfassen.

7.3 Bewilligungsverfahren

7.3.1 Bewilligungsbehörde
Bewilligungsbehörde für Maßnahmen zum Schutz und zur Pflege von Kulturdenkmalen gemäß § 3 der Förderzuständigkeitsverordnung SMI vom 8. Februar 2012 (SächsGVBl. S. 150), die zuletzt durch Artikel 1 der Verordnung vom 24. Juni 2015 (SächsGVBl. S. 410) geändert worden ist, in der jeweils geltenden Fassung, ist das Landesamt für Denkmalpflege. Die Bewilligungsbehörde entscheidet bei Maßnahmen an Kulturdenkmalen im Sinne des § 2 Absatz 5 Buchstabe g des Sächsischen Denkmalschutzgesetzes sowie bei Maßnahmen in einem Grabungsschutzgebiet oder einem archäologischen Reservat im Einvernehmen mit dem Landesamt für Archäologie. Kommt kein Einvernehmen gemäß Satz 2 zustande, so entscheidet das Staatsministerium des Innern im Benehmen mit dem Staatsministerium für Wissenschaft und Kunst.

---

[1] Von einem Abdruck der Anlagen wurde aus drucktechnischen Gründen abgesehen.

D13.III.1 VwV-Denkmalförderung

Bewilligungsbehörde für Maßnahmen der Aus- und Fortbildung in der Denkmalpflege ist das Staatsministerium des Innern.

Die Bewilligungsbehörde bewilligt – nach Ermittlung der zuwendungsfähigen Kosten – den Zuwendungshöchstbetrag unter Angabe der ermittelten zuwendungsfähigen Kosten und des Fördersatzes.

Die Bewilligungsbehörde ermittelt und bewilligt – im Falle der Nummer 5.4.2 – den Zuwendungsbetrag aus den zuwendungsfähigen Kosten. Der Auszahlungstermin der Zuwendung für Seminare im jeweiligen Haushaltsjahr ist der 1. Juli des Bewilligungsjahres.

7.3.2 Genehmigungen bei Maßnahmen an Kulturdenkmalen
Der Genehmigung des Staatsministeriums des Innern bedürfen:
- eine Erhöhung des Fördersatzes über 85 vom Hundert;
- Kosten für die Planung/den Entwurf/das Gutachten zum (rechtlichen) Schutz eines Kulturdenkmales, Denkmalschutzgebietes, Grabungsschutzgebietes, archäologischen Reservates.

Die Bewilligungsbehörde hat dem Staatsministerium des Innern eine Liste der Zuwendungsvorschläge für das entsprechende Haushaltsjahr, die den Betrag von 125 000 EUR übersteigen, spätestens vier Wochen nach Ausreichung der Haushaltsmittel, Zuwendungsvorschläge für Verpflichtungsermächtigungen kommender Haushaltsjahre vier Wochen vor Kassenschluss, vorzulegen. Der Betrag von 125 000 EUR schließt Zuwendungen vorangegangener Haushaltsjahre ein. In der Liste ist die jährliche Trennung zwischen Zuwendungen vorangegangener Haushaltsjahre und der entsprechend im Haushaltsjahr neu vorgesehenen Zuwendungen vorzunehmen. Das Staatsministerium des Innern behält sich vor, einzelne Zuwendungsvorschläge vor Ausreichung des Zuwendungsbescheides zu prüfen.

Bei Maßnahmen, die in mehreren Abschnitten oder Bewilligungszeiträumen an einem Kulturdenkmal, Denkmalschutzgebiet, Grabungsschutzgebiet oder einem archäologischen Reservat durchgeführt werden sollen, ist der auf der Grundlage einer Gesamtkonzeption zu errechnende Gesamtzuwendungsbedarf maßgebend.

7.3.3 Ergibt sich nach Vorlage des Nachweises der entstandenen zuwendungsfähigen Kosten ein gegenüber dem Zuwendungshöchstbetrag verminderter Zuwendungsbetrag, wird dieser durch weiteren Bescheid festgesetzt.

7.4 Anforderungs- und Auszahlungsverfahren
Die Auszahlung erfolgt nach Vorlage des Verwendungsnachweises. Die Bewilligungsbehörde kann anteilig Teilzahlungen leisten, soweit der Zuwendungsempfänger erklärt, dass er die Auszahlung voraussichtlich innerhalb von zwei Monaten für fällige Zahlungen im Rahmen des Zuwendungszwecks benötigt. Die Teilauszahlung soll einen Betrag von 2 500 EUR nicht unterschreiten (Ausnahmen ergeben sich nach Nummer 4.3 – Schwellenwert 1 500 EUR –) und einen Betrag von mehr als 80 vom Hundert des gesamten Zuschusses nicht übersteigen.

7.5 Verwendungsnachweisverfahren
Die Verwendung der Zuwendung ist der Bewilligungsbehörde innerhalb von sechs Monaten nach Abschluss der Maßnahme beziehungsweise nach Ablauf des Bewilligungszeitraumes auf dem vorgeschriebenen Vordruck nachzuweisen.

7.6 Für die Bewilligung, Auszahlung und Abrechnung der Zuwendung sowie für den Nachweis und die Prüfung der Verwendung und die gegebenenfalls erforderliche Aufwendung des Zuwendungsbescheides und die Rückforderung der gewährten Zuwendung gelten die Vorl.VV zu § 44 SäHO, soweit nicht in dieser Förderrichtlinie Abweichungen zugelassen worden sind.

8 Inkrafttreten
Diese Verwaltungsvorschrift tritt am 1. Juli 1997 in Kraft.
Die Verwaltungsvorschrift des Sächsischen Staatsministeriums des Innern für die Gewährung von Zuwendungen zur Erhaltung und Pflege von Kulturdenkmalen (VwV-Denkmalförderung) vom 27. Dezember 1993 (SächsABl. 1994 S. 209) tritt gleichzeitig außer Kraft.

Verordnung der Sächsischen Staatsregierung und des Sächsischen Staatsministeriums für Wissenschaft und Kunst über Zuständigkeiten nach dem Kulturgutschutzgesetz (Sächsische Kulturgutschutzgesetz-Zuständigkeitsverordnung – SächsKGSGZustVO)

Vom 22. Juni 2017 (SächsGVBl. S. 368)

Es verordnet auf Grund
– des § 3 Absatz 1 Satz 2 des Kulturgutschutzgesetzes vom 31. Juli 2016 (BGBl. I S. 1914) die Staatsregierung und
– des § 24 Absatz 7 Satz 2 des Kulturgutschutzgesetzes vom 31. Juli 2016 (BGBl. I S. 1914) in Verbindung mit § 16 Absatz 1 Satz 2 Nummer 1 des Sächsischen Verwaltungsorganisationsgesetzes vom 25. November 2003 (SächsGVBl. S. 899) das Staatsministerium für Wissenschaft und Kunst:

§ 1 Zuständigkeiten im Geschäftsbereich des Staatsministeriums für Wissenschaft und Kunst

(1) Das Staatsministerium für Wissenschaft und Kunst ist zuständige oberste Landesbehörde und zuständige Behörde nach dem Kulturgutschutzgesetz für Kulturgut außer Archivgut nach § 2 Absatz 2.

(2) Abweichend von Absatz 1 wird die Zuständigkeit für die Genehmigung der Ausfuhr von Kulturgut nach § 24 des Kulturgutschutzgesetzes, außer für Archivgut nach § 2 Absatz 2, auf den Staatsbetrieb Staatliche Kunstsammlungen Dresden übertragen.

§ 2 Zuständigkeiten im Geschäftsbereich des Staatsministeriums des Innern

(1) Das Staatsministerium des Innern ist zuständige oberste Landesbehörde und zuständige Behörde nach dem Kulturgutschutzgesetz für Archivgut nach Absatz 2.

(2) Archivgut im Sinne dieser Verordnung sind Archivgut und archivwürdige Unterlagen im Sinne von § 2 Absatz 1 und 2 des Archivgesetzes für den Freistaat Sachsen vom 17. Mai 1993 (SächsGVBl. S. 449), das zuletzt durch das Gesetz vom 18. Dezember 2013 (SächsGVBl. 2014 S. 2) geändert worden ist, in der jeweils geltenden Fassung.

(3) Abweichend von Absatz 1 wird die Zuständigkeit gemäß § 6 Absatz 2 des Kulturgutschutzgesetzes bei Leih- oder Depositalverträgen des Sächsischen Staatsarchivs auf das Sächsische Staatsarchiv übertragen.

§ 3 Inkrafttreten, Außerkrafttreten

¹Diese Verordnung tritt am Tag nach der Verkündung[1] in Kraft. ²Gleichzeitig tritt die Sächsische Kulturgutschutzverordnung vom 15. November 2006 (SächsGVBl. S. 498) außer Kraft.

---

1) Verkündet am 27.7.2017.

Verfassung des Landes Sachsen-Anhalt

Vom 16. Juli 1992 (GVBl. LSA S. 600)
(BS LSA 100.3)
zuletzt geändert durch Art. 1 G zur Parlamentsreform 2014 vom 5. Dezember 2014 (GVBl. LSA S. 494)
– Auszug –

Präambel
In freier Selbstbestimmung gibt sich das Volk von Sachsen-Anhalt diese Verfassung. Dies geschieht in Achtung der Verantwortung vor Gott und im Bewußtsein der Verantwortung vor den Menschen mit dem Willen,
[…]
die kulturelle und geschichtliche Tradition in allen Landesteilen zu pflegen.
[…]

2. Hauptteil.
Bürger und Staat

Dritter Abschnitt:
Staatsziele

Artikel 36 Kunst, Kultur und Sport
(1) Kunst, Kultur und Sport sind durch das Land und die Kommunen zu schützen und zu fördern.
(2) Die heimatbezogenen Einrichtungen und Eigenheiten der einzelnen Regionen innerhalb des Landes sind zu pflegen.
(3) Das Land und die Kommunen fördern im Rahmen ihrer finanziellen Möglichkeiten die kulturelle Betätigung aller Bürger insbesondere dadurch, daß sie öffentlich zugängliche Museen, Büchereien, Gedenkstätten, Theater, Sportstätten und weitere Einrichtungen unterhalten.
(4) Das Land sorgt, unterstützt von den Kommunen, für den Schutz und die Pflege der Denkmale von Kultur und Natur.
[…]

Artikel 37 Kulturelle und ethnische Minderheiten
(1) Die kulturelle Eigenständigkeit und die politische Mitwirkung ethnischer Minderheiten stehen unter dem Schutz des Landes und der Kommunen.
(2) Das Bekenntnis zu einer kulturellen oder ethnischen Minderheit ist frei; es entbindet nicht von den allgemeinen staatsbürgerlichen Pflichten.

Denkmalschutzgesetz des Landes Sachsen-Anhalt

Vom 21. Oktober 1991 (GVBl. LSA S. 368, ber. 1992 S. 210)
(BS LSA 2242.1)
zuletzt geändert durch Art. 2 Drittes InvestitionserleichterungsG vom 20. Dezember 2005
(GVBl. LSA S. 769)

Der Landtag von Sachsen-Anhalt hat das folgende Gesetz beschlossen, das hiermit verkündet wird:

I. Abschnitt
Grundsätze und Ziele des Denkmalschutzes und der Denkmalpflege

§ 1 Grundsätze

(1) ¹Es ist die Aufgabe von Denkmalschutz und Denkmalpflege, die Kulturdenkmale als Quellen und Zeugnisse menschlicher Geschichte und prägende Bestandteile der Kulturlandschaft nach den Bestimmungen dieses Gesetzes zu schützen, zu erhalten, zu pflegen und wissenschaftlich zu erforschen. ²Der Schutz erstreckt sich auf die gesamte Substanz eines Kulturdenkmals einschließlich seiner Umgebung, soweit diese für die Erhaltung, Wirkung, Erschließung und die wissenschaftliche Forschung von Bedeutung ist.
(2) ¹Bei der Wahrnehmung dieser Aufgaben wirken das Land und die kommunalen Gebietskörperschaften sowie Eigentümer und Besitzer von Kulturdenkmalen zusammen. ²Ihnen obliegt zugleich die besondere Pflicht, die ihnen gehörenden oder von ihnen genutzten Kulturdenkmale zu erhalten.
(3) Bei öffentlichen Planungen und Baumaßnahmen sind die Belange des Denkmalschutzes und die Denkmalpflege rechtzeitig zu berücksichtigen, so daß die Kulturdenkmale möglichst erhalten bleiben und ihre Umgebung angemessen gestaltet werden kann.
(4) Kulturdenkmale sollen im Rahmen des Möglichen und Zumutbaren der Öffentlichkeit zugänglich gemacht werden.

§ 2 Begriffsbestimmung

(1) ¹Kulturdenkmale im Sinne dieses Gesetzes sind gegenständliche Zeugnisse menschlichen Lebens aus vergangener Zeit, die im öffentlichen Interesse zu erhalten sind. ²Öffentliches Interesse besteht, wenn diese von besonderer geschichtlicher, kulturell-künstlerischer, wissenschaftlicher, kultischer, technisch-wirtschaftlicher oder städtebaulicher Bedeutung sind.
(2) Kulturdenkmale im Sinne dieses Gesetzes sind:
1. Baudenkmale,
    die aus baulichen Anlagen oder Teilen baulicher Anlagen bestehen. Dazu gehören auch Garten-, Park- und Friedhofsanlagen, andere von Menschen gestaltete Landschaftsteile, produktions- und verkehrsbedingte Reliefformen sowie Pflanzen-, Frei- und Wasserflächen. Ausstattungsstücke und Zubehör sind, sofern sie mit einem Baudenkmal eine Einheit von Denkmalwert bilden, wie diese zu behandeln;
2. Denkmalbereiche
    als Mehrheiten baulicher Anlagen. Denkmalbereiche können historische Kulturlandschaften, die in der Liste des Erbes der Welt der UNESCO gemäß Artikel 11 Abs. 2 Satz 1 des Übereinkommens vom 23. November 1972 zum Schutz des Kultur- und Naturerbes der Welt (Bekanntmachung vom 2. Februar 1977, BGBl. II S. 213) aufgeführt sind, Stadtgrundrisse, Stadt- und Ortsbilder sowie -silhouetten, Stadtteile und -viertel, Siedlungen, Gehöftgruppen, Straßenzüge, bauliche Gesamtanlagen und Einzelbauten, einschließlich deren Umgebung, sein, wenn das Bauwerk zu ihr in einer besonderen historischen, funktionalen oder ästhethischen Beziehung steht. Hierzu gehören auch handwerkliche und industrielle Produktionsstätten;
3. archäologische Kulturdenkmale
    als Reste von Lebewesen, Gegenständen und Bauwerken, die im oder auf dem Boden, im Moor und unter Wasser erhalten geblieben sind und die von der Geschichte des Menschen Zeugnis ablegen. Insbesondere sind dies Siedlungen und Wüstungen, Befestigungsanlagen aller Art, Landwehren und markante Grenzverläufe, Produktionsstätten wie Ackerfluren und Werkplätze, Glashütten, Öfen, Steinbrüche, Pingen, Halden, Verkehrsanlagen, Be- und Entwässerungssyste-

D14.I.1 Denkmalschutzgesetz Sachsen-Anhalt

me, Gräberfelder, Grabanlagen, darunter Grabhügel und Großsteingräber, Höhlen, Kultstätten, Denkmale der Rechtsgeschichte und Überreste von Bauwerken sowie Steinmale und Schälchensteine;
4. archäologische Flächendenkmale,
in denen Mehrheiten archäologischer Kulturdenkmale vorhanden sind;
5. bewegliche Kulturdenkmale
und Bodenfunde als Einzelgegenstände und Sammlungen, wie Werkzeuge, Geräte, Hausrat, Gefäße, Waffen, Schmuck, Trachtenbestandteile, Bekleidung, Kultgegenstände, Gegenstände der Kunst und des Kunsthandwerkes, Münzen und Medaillen, Verkehrsmittel, Maschinen und technische Aggregate, Teile von Bauwerken, Skelettreste von Menschen und Tieren, Pflanzenreste und andere Hinterlassenschaften;
6. Kleindenkmale
wie Meilensteine, Obelisken, Steinkreuze, Grenzsteine und andere.

II. Abschnitt
Organisation und Zuständigkeiten der Denkmalbehörden

§ 3 Oberste Denkmalbehörde

[1]Das für den Denkmalschutz zuständige Ministerium ist die oberste Denkmalbehörde. [2]Es übt die Fachaufsicht über die obere Denkmalschutzbehörde (§ 4 Abs. 2 Satz 1) aus. [3]Darüber hinaus übt das für den Denkmalschutz zuständige Ministerium die Dienst- und Fachaufsicht über das Denkmalfachamt (§ 5 Abs. 1) aus.

§ 4 Denkmalschutzbehörden

(1) Die Denkmalschutzbehörden treffen nach pflichtgemäßem Ermessen die Anordnungen, welche die Durchsetzung dieses Gesetzes gewährleisten.
(2) [1]Obere Denkmalschutzbehörde ist das Landesverwaltungsamt. [2]Es übt die Fachaufsicht über die unteren Denkmalschutzbehörden aus. [3]Es kann an deren Stelle tätig werden, wenn Gefahren für die Erhaltung eines Denkmals bestehen oder wenn eine Weisung innerhalb einer bestimmten Frist nicht befolgt wird. [4]Die zuständige untere Denkmalschutzbehörde ist unverzüglich darüber zu unterrichten.
(3) [1]Städte und Gemeinden, denen die Aufgaben der unteren Bauaufsichtsbehörden übertragen sind, im übrigen die Landkreise und kreisfreien Städte, nehmen die Aufgaben der unteren Denkmalschutzbehörde wahr. [2]Die Aufgaben der unteren Denkmalschutzbehörde gehören zum übertragenen Wirkungskreis. [3]Die unteren Bauaufsichtsbehörden sind in allen Fällen, in denen Belange des Denkmalschutzes und der Denkmalpflege berührt werden, zum Zusammenwirken mit den zuständigen Denkmalschutzbehörden verpflichtet.
(4) [1]Den Kirchenbauämtern und den Kulturstiftungen des Landes können die Rechte und Pflichten der unteren Denkmalschutzbehörden für von ihnen betreute oder verwaltete Kirchen und andere Kulturdenkmale von der obersten Denkmalbehörde auf Antrag übertragen werden.[1]) [2]Die Denkmalschutzbehörden sind von diesen Entscheidungen zu unterrichten.

§ 5 Denkmalfachamt

(1) Denkmalfachamt ist das Landesamt für Denkmalpflege und Archäologie (Landesmuseum für Vorgeschichte).
(2) [1]Das Denkmalfachamt nimmt Aufgaben im Rahmen seiner Zuständigkeit für die archäologischen und nichtarchäologischen Kulturdenkmale wahr. [2]Diese Aufgaben sind insbesondere:
1. wissenschaftliche Erfassung, Erforschung und Dokumentation des Bestandes an Kulturdenkmalen in Sachsen-Anhalt;
2. Führung der nachrichtlichen Denkmalverzeichnisse;
3. Abgabe von fachlichen Stellungnahmen auf Verlangen der Behörden sowie Erteilung von Gutachten in allen Angelegenheiten von Denkmalschutz und -pflege;
4. fachliche Unterstützung und Beratung für die Denkmalschutzbehörden, Eigentümer, Besitzer und andere Verfügungsberechtigte von Denkmalen;

---

[1]) Der Runderlass zur Übertragung der Funktion einer unteren Denkmalschutzbehörde auf Kulturstiftungen ist abgedruckt als Nr. D14.I.3; der Runderlass zur Übertragung der Aufgaben der unteren Denkmalschutzbehörde auf das Bistum Magdeburg ist abgedruckt als Nr. D14.I.4.

5. fachliche Weiterbildung der unteren Denkmalschutzbehörden und der ehrenamtlichen Beauftragten;
6. Ausführung beziehungsweise Mitwirkung bei Restaurierungs- und Konservierungsarbeiten und Durchführung von wissenschaftlichen Ausgrabungen oder deren fachliche Überwachung;
7. Schaffung wissenschaftlicher Grundlagen für die Denkmalpflege sowie die Veröffentlichung wissenschaftlicher Ergebnisse und Erfahrungen über Denkmalbestand und -pflege;
8. Förderung des Verständnisses der Öffentlichkeit für Denkmalschutz und Denkmalpflege;
9. Sicherung von Bodendenkmalen und Funden;
10. Erfassung archäologischer Bodenfunde sowie Sammlung, Erfassung und Bewahrung von archäologischen Kulturdenkmalen im Landesmuseum für Vorgeschichte;
11. Unterhaltung von eigenen wissenschaftlichen Fachbibliotheken und Facharchiven;
12. musterhafte Ausarbeitung von Vorschlägen für Maßnahmen an Kulturdenkmalen und von Fachplanungen.

(3) ¹Das Denkmalfachamt hat bei Gutachten und Bewertungen nur fachliche Gesichtspunkte zu berücksichtigen. ²Es ist berechtigt, fachliche Gutachten, Stellungnahmen und andere Ausarbeitungen an Behörden und Institutionen zu übermitteln, deren Aufgaben oder Vorhaben davon berührt sind.

§ 6 Ehrenamtliche Beauftragte und Denkmalräte

(1) Durch die unteren Denkmalschutzbehörden sollen im Einvernehmen mit dem Denkmalfachamt ehrenamtliche Beauftragte bestellt werden, die als Sachverständige die bestellende Behörde unterstützen.[1]

(2) Ehrenamtliche Beauftragte für archäologische Denkmalpflege können auch durch das Denkmalfachamt bestellt werden.

(3) ¹Die oberste Denkmalbehörde beruft nach Anhörung des Denkmalfachamtes den ehrenamtlichen tätigen Denkmalrat.[2] ²Ihm sollen Sachverständige für die Fachgebiete des Denkmalschutzes und der Denkmalpflege, Vertreter anerkannter Denkmalpflegeorganisationen sowie Vertreter anderer von Denkmalschutz und -pflege im Sinne dieses Gesetzes berührter Bereiche angehören.

(4) ¹Der Denkmalrat bei dem für den Denkmalschutz zuständigen Ministerium ist bei Grundsatzentscheidungen, die den Denkmalschutz und die Denkmalpflege betreffen, zu hören. ²Er ist berechtigt, Anregungen und Empfehlungen auszusprechen.

(5) Einzelheiten der Tätigkeit der ehrenamtlichen Beauftragten[3] und des Denkmalrates[4] sowie die Kostenerstattung können durch Verordnung der obersten Denkmalbehörde geregelt werden.

§ 7 Mitwirkung von Einrichtungen und Vereinigungen

(1) Eingetragenen Vereinen und anderen juristischen Personen, die nach ihrer Satzung und nicht nur vorübergehend die Ziele des Denkmalschutzes und der Denkmalpflege fördern, können mit deren Einverständnis
1. die Betreuung bestimmter durch dieses Gesetz geschützter Kulturdenkmale,
2. bestimmte Aufgaben der Denkmalforschung und Erfassung
sowie sonstige geeignete Aufgaben widerruflich übertragen werden, sofern sie die Gewähr für die sachgerechte Erfüllung der Aufgabe bieten.

(2) ¹Die Entscheidung über die Beauftragung trifft die oberste Denkmalbehörde. ²Das für den Denkmalschutz zuständige Ministerium wird ermächtigt, das Verfahren durch Verordnung zu regeln.

§ 8 Zuständigkeiten

(1) ¹Soweit dieses Gesetz nichts anderes bestimmt, sind die unteren Denkmalschutzbehörden zuständig. ²Sie entscheiden im Benehmen mit dem Denkmalfachamt. ³Die obere Denkmalschutzbehörde entscheidet nach Anhörung des Denkmalfachamtes.

---

1) Die Richtlinien zur Durchführung des § 6 des Denkmalschutzgesetzes des Landes Sachsen-Anhalt; Bestellung der ehrenamtlichen Beauftragten sind abgedruckt als Nr. D14.I.1c.
2) Der RdErl. Zusammensetzung, Berufung und Organisation des Denkmalrates ist abgedruckt als Nr. D14.I.1d.
3) Die Verordnung über Tätigkeit und Entschädigung ehrenamtlicher Beauftragter für die Denkmalpflege und für archäologische Denkmalpflege ist abgedruckt als Nr. D14.I.1a.
4) Die Verordnung über die Tätigkeit und die Kostenerstattung der Mitglieder des Denkmalrates ist abgedruckt als Nr. D14.I.1b.

(2) ¹Die Gemeinden sollen nach Anhörung des Denkmalfachamtes Denkmalpflegepläne aufstellen und fortschreiben. ²Der Denkmalpflegeplan enthält die Aufgaben der Denkmalpflege sowie Ziele und Erfordernisse des Denkmalschutzes.
(3) Vorhaben, die innerhalb von Gemeinde-, Gebiets-, Verkehrs- und anderen Planungen Kulturdenkmale nach § 2 berühren, sind den Denkmalfachämtern zur Stellungnahme vorzulegen.
(4) *[aufgehoben]*
(5) ¹Sollen Entscheidungen über Kulturdenkmale getroffen werden, die unmittelbar gottesdienstlichen Zwecken der Kirchen oder anerkannter Religionsgemeinschaften dienen, so haben die zuständigen Denkmalschutzbehörden die von den kirchlichen Oberbehörden festgestellten kirchlichen Belange zu berücksichtigen. ²Die Kirchen sind am Verfahren zu beteiligen.

III. Abschnitt
Schutz und Erhaltung

§ 9 Erhaltungspflicht
(1) ¹Die Kulturdenkmale unterliegen dem Schutz dieses Gesetzes. ²Sie sind so zu nutzen, daß ihre Erhaltung auf Dauer gesichert ist. ³Das Land und die kommunalen Gebietskörperschaften sollen die Eigentümer, Besitzer und sonstigen Verfügungsberechtigten von Kulturdenkmalen dabei unterstützen.
(2) ¹Die Eigentümer, Besitzer und anderen Verfügungsberechtigten von Kulturdenkmalen sind verpflichtet, diese im Rahmen der wirtschaftlichen Zumutbarkeit nach denkmalpflegerischen Grundsätzen zu erhalten, zu pflegen, instandzusetzen, vor Gefahren zu schützen und, soweit möglich und zumutbar, der Öffentlichkeit zugänglich zu machen. ²Bei der Zugänglichmachung der im Eigentum von Land oder Kommunen stehenden Kulturdenkmale ist den Belangen von behinderten Menschen Rechnung zu tragen. ³Kulturdenkmale, deren Sinn und Nutzung öffentlicher Bildung dient, sind schrittweise barrierefrei zu gestalten, es sei denn, das öffentliche Erhaltungsinteresse an dem Denkmal überwiegt.
(3) ¹Wer bei Arbeiten oder bei anderen Maßnahmen in der Erde oder im Wasser Sachen oder Spuren von Sachen findet, bei denen Anlaß zu der Annahme gegeben ist, daß sie Kulturdenkmale sind (archäologische und bauarchäologische Bodenfunde), hat diese zu erhalten und der zuständigen unteren Denkmalschutzbehörde anzuzeigen. ²Der Bodenfund und die Fundstelle sind bis zum Ablauf von einer Woche nach der Anzeige unverändert zu lassen und vor Gefahren für die Erhaltung der Bodenfunde zu schützen. ³Das Denkmalfachamt und von ihm Beauftragte sind berechtigt, die Fundstelle nach archäologischen Befunden zu untersuchen und Bodenfunde zu bergen.
(4) Das Land und die kommunalen Gebietskörperschaften tragen zur Erhaltung der Kulturdenkmale nach Absatz 2 unter Berücksichtigung der verfügbaren Haushaltsmittel durch Zuwendungen bei.
(5) Die Denkmalschutzbehörde kann durch Anordnung abgegrenzte Flächen, in denen archäologische Kulturdenkmale vorhanden sind oder begründete Anhaltspunkte für ihr Vorhandensein existieren, befristet zu Grabungsschutzgebieten erklären.
(6) ¹Kommen Eigentümer, Besitzer und andere Verfügungsberechtigte ihren Verpflichtungen nach diesem Gesetz nicht nach, können die unteren Denkmalschutzbehörden gefahrenabwendende Maßnahmen anordnen oder selbst durchführen. ²Die Eigentümer, Besitzer und Verfügungsberechtigten sind zur Duldung solcher Maßnahmen verpflichtet.
(7) Die unteren Denkmalschutzbehörden können von den Eigentümern, Besitzern und sonstigen Verfügungsberechtigten die Erstattung der nach Absatz 6 entstandenen Kosten verlangen.
(8) Wer ein Kulturdenkmal beschädigt, hat nach Anordnung der Denkmalschutzbehörden die betreffenden Maßnahmen einzustellen und den früheren Zustand wiederherzustellen oder das Kulturdenkmal auf eine andere vorgeschriebene Weise instandzusetzen.

§ 10 Grenzen der Eingriffe in Kulturdenkmale
(1) ¹Eingriffe im Sinne dieses Gesetzes sind Veränderungen in der Substanz oder Nutzung von Kulturdenkmalen, die deren Denkmalqualität erheblich beeinträchtigen können oder zur Zerstörung eines Kulturdenkmals führen. ²Alle Eingriffe in ein Kulturdenkmal sind auf das notwendige Mindestmaß zu beschränken.

(2) Ein Eingriff in ein Kulturdenkmal ist zu genehmigen, wenn
1. der Eingriff aus nachgewiesenen wissenschaftlichen Gründen im öffentlichen Interesse liegt;
2. ein überwiegendes öffentliches Interesse anderer Art den Eingriff verlangt oder
3. die unveränderte Erhaltung des Kulturdenkmals den Verpflichteten unzumutbar belastet.

(3) Sind als Folge eines Eingriffes erhebliche Beeinträchtigungen eines Kulturdenkmals im Sinne des Absatzes 1 zu erwarten, so ist der Eingriff unzulässig, wenn bei der Abwägung aller Anforderungen die Belange des Denkmalschutzes und der Denkmalpflege vorgehen.

(4) [1]Erhaltungsmaßnahmen können nicht verlangt werden, wenn die Erhaltung den Verpflichteten unzumutbar belastet. [2]Unzumutbar ist eine wirtschaftliche Belastung insbesondere dann, wenn die Kosten der Erhaltung nicht durch die Erträge oder den Gebrauchswert des Kulturdenkmals aufgewogen und andere Einkünfte des Verpflichteten nicht herangezogen werden können.

(5) [1]Die wirtschaftliche Unzumutbarkeit ist durch den Verpflichteten glaubhaft zu machen. [2]Kann der Verpflichtete Zuwendungen aus öffentlichen oder privaten Mitteln oder steuerliche Vorteile in Anspruch nehmen, sind diese anzurechnen. [3]Der Verpflichtete kann sich nicht auf die Belastung durch erhöhte Erhaltungskosten berufen, die dadurch verursacht wurden, daß Erhaltungsmaßnahmen diesem Gesetz oder sonstigen öffentlichen Recht zuwider unterblieben sind.

(6) Eingriffe in ein Kulturdenkmal, die es seiner Denkmalqualität berauben oder zu seiner Zerstörung führen, dürfen nur genehmigt werden, wenn alle Möglichkeiten einer Erhaltung ausgeschöpft wurden.

§ 11 Vorkaufsrecht

(1) [1]Wird ein Grundstück, auf dem sich ein unbewegliches, geschütztes Kulturdenkmal befindet, verkauft, steht der Gemeinde, bei überörtlicher Bedeutung auch dem Land, ein Vorkaufsrecht zu. [2]Das Vorkaufsrecht des Landes geht dem Vorkaufsrecht der Gemeinde im Range vor. [3]Die obere Denkmalschutzbehörde übt das Vorkaufsrecht zugunsten des Landes aus. [4]Das Vorkaufsrecht darf nur ausgeübt werden, wenn das Wohl der Allgemeinheit dies rechtfertigt, insbesondere wenn dadurch ein unbewegliches geschütztes Kulturdenkmal erhalten wird oder erhebliche Schäden an diesem beseitigt werden. [5]Das Vorkaufsrecht ist ausgeschlossen, wenn der Eigentümer das Grundstück an seinen Ehegatten, seinen Eingetragenen Lebenspartner oder an eine Person verkauft, die mit ihm in gerader Linie verwandt oder verschwägert oder in der Seitenlinie bis zum dritten Grad verwandt ist.

(2) [1]Die untere Denkmalschutzbehörde leitet eine Anzeige nach § 17, die ein Grundstück betrifft, auf dem sich ein unbewegliches geschütztes Kulturdenkmal befindet, unverzüglich an die Gemeinde weiter. [2]Teilt der Eigentümer der Gemeinde nach Abschluß des Kaufvertrages dessen Inhalt schriftlich mit, so kann die Gemeinde nur binnen zwei Monaten das Vorkaufsrecht ausüben. [3]Unterläßt der Eigentümer diese Mitteilung, so kann die Gemeinde ihn bis zum Ablauf eines Monats nach Eingang der Anzeige nach Satz 1 hierzu auffordern. [4]Der Eigentümer ist verpflichtet, dieser Aufforderung unverzüglich Folge zu leisten. [5]Nach Eingang der Mitteilung gilt die gleiche Zweimonatsfrist wie in Satz 2. [6]Unterläßt die Gemeinde die fristgerechte Aufforderung, so erlischt das Vorkaufsrecht für diesen Verkaufsfall. [7]Die §§ 504, 505 Abs. 2, §§ 506 bis 509, 512, 1098 Abs. 2 und §§ 1099 bis 1102 des Bürgerlichen Gesetzbuches sind anzuwenden. [8]Die Gemeinde kann das Vorkaufsrecht zugunsten einer anderen Person des öffentlichen Rechts ausüben oder zugunsten einer juristischen Person des Privatrechts, wenn die dauernde Erhaltung der in oder auf einem Grundstück liegenden Kulturdenkmale zu den satzungsgemäßen Aufgaben der juristischen Person gehört und bei Berücksichtigung aller Umstände gesichert ist. [9]Die Gemeinde kann das Vorkaufsrecht zugunsten eines anderen nur äußern, wenn ihr die Zustimmung des Begünstigten vorliegt. [10]Die Sätze 1 bis 8 gelten für das Vorkaufsrecht des Landes entsprechend.

§ 12 Schatzregal, Ablieferungspflicht

(1) [1]Bewegliche Kulturdenkmale, die herrenlos sind oder die solange verborgen gewesen sind, daß ihr Eigentümer nicht mehr zu ermitteln ist, werden mit der Entdeckung Eigentum des Landes, wenn sie bei staatlichen Nachforschungen oder in Grabungsschutzgebieten entdeckt werden oder wenn sie einen hervorragenden wissenschaftlichen Wert haben. [2]Denjenigen, die ihrer Ablieferungspflicht nachkommen, kann eine angemessene Belohnung in Geld gewährt werden, die sich am wissenschaftlichen Wert des Fundes orientiert.

(2) Für alle übrigen Kulturdenkmale gilt:
1. Das Land und die kommunalen Gebietskörperschaften sind berechtigt, innerhalb von sechs Monaten nach der Entdeckung die Ablieferung eines in ihrem Gebiet zutage getretenen beweglichen Fundes gegen angemessene Entschädigung zu verlangen. Das Ablieferungsbegehren bedarf der Schriftform.
2. Die Ablieferung kann verlangt werden, wenn Tatsachen vorliegen, nach denen anzunehmen ist, daß sich der Erhaltungszustand des Fundes andernfalls wesentlich verschlechtern wird oder er der wissenschaftlichen Erforschung verlorengeht.
3. Das bewegliche Kulturdenkmal ist an die Körperschaft abzuliefern, die die Ablieferung als Erste verlangt; haben mehrere die Ablieferung gleichzeitig verlangt, ist die Reihenfolge der Nummer 1 Satz 1 maßgebend. Im Ablieferungsverlangen ist auf diese Regelung hinzuweisen. Mit der Ablieferung erlangt die berechtigte Körperschaft das Eigentum an dem Fund.
4. Die Körperschaft, die in den Besitz des beweglichen Kulturdenkmals gelangt ist, hat die in der Reihenfolge nach Nummer 1 Satz 1 bevorrechtigten Körperschaften unverzüglich von der Ablieferung zu informieren. Die berechtigte Körperschaft kann dann innerhalb von einem Monat die Übereignung des Fundes verlangen. Der geleistete Aufwand für Entschädigung und Erhaltungsmaßnahmen ist auszugleichen.
5. Die Entschädigung ist in Geld zu leisten. Sie bemißt sich nach dem Verkehrswert des beweglichen Kulturdenkmals zum Zeitpunkt der Ablieferung. Im Falle der wissenschaftlichen Bearbeitung des beweglichen Kulturdenkmals durch das zuständige Denkmalfachamt ist der Zeitpunkt der Inbesitznahme maßgebend. Einigen sich der Ablieferungspflichtige und die berechtigte Körperschaft nicht über Höhe der Entschädigung, so setzt die berechtigte Körperschaft die Entschädigung fest. Geht das Eigentum auf eine andere Körperschaft über, tritt diese an die Stelle der berechtigten Körperschaft. Die Entschädigung kann mit Einverständnis des Ablieferungspflichtigen in anderer Weise als durch Geld geleistet werden.

§ 13 Vorübergehende Überlassung
Eigentümer und Besitzer von Bodenfunden oder Sammlungen davon sind auf Verlangen der unteren oder oberen Denkmalschutzbehörde verpflichtet, den Bodenfund oder die Sammlung der Behörde oder einer von ihr benannten Stelle zur wissenschaftlichen Auswertung, Konservierung oder Dokumentation befristet zu überlassen.

IV. Abschnitt
Verfahrensvorschriften

§ 14 Genehmigungspflichten
(1) Einer Genehmigung durch die zuständige Denkmalschutzbehörde bedarf, wer ein Kulturdenkmal
1. instandsetzen, umgestalten oder verändern,
2. in seiner Nutzung verändern,
3. durch Errichtung, Wegnahme oder Hinzufügung von Anlagen in seiner Umgebung im Bestand und Erscheinungsbild verändern, beeinträchtigen oder zerstören,
4. von seinem Standort entfernen,
5. beseitigen oder zerstören

will.

(2) [1]Erd- und Bauarbeiten, bei denen begründete Anhaltspunkte bestehen, daß Kulturdenkmäler entdeckt werden, bedürfen der Genehmigung der unteren Denkmalschutzbehörde und sind rechtzeitig anzuzeigen. [2]Wenn die untere Denkmalschutzbehörde nicht innerhalb von zwei Wochen widerspricht, gilt die Genehmigung als erteilt. [3]Verstoßen die Maßnahmen gegen dieses Gesetz, ist die Genehmigung zu versagen. [4]In Grabungsschutzgebieten bedürfen alle Arbeiten, die Kulturdenkmale zutage fördern oder gefährden könnten, einer Genehmigung der zuständigen unteren Denkmalschutzbehörde. [5]Eine gegebene land- und forstwirtschaftliche Nutzung bleibt im bisherigen Umfang ohne weitere Genehmigung zulässig, sofern sie nicht zur Gefährdung der Denkmalsubstanz beiträgt.

(3) [1]Wer Nachforschungen anstellen, insbesondere nach Kulturdenkmalen graben will, bedarf der Genehmigung der unteren Denkmalschutzbehörde. [2]Die Genehmigung kann mit Auflagen verbunden

werden. ³Ausgenommen sind Nachforschungen, die in der Verantwortung des Denkmalfachamtes stattfinden.
(4) ¹Die Genehmigung ist schriftlich zu erteilen. ²Innerhalb von Denkmalbereichen sind die Schutzziele entsprechend der unterschiedlichen Denkmalwertigkeit der darin gelegenen baulichen Anlagen zu differenzieren und in dieser Abgestuftheit bei der Erteilung von Genehmigungen, Auflagen und Bedingungen entsprechend zu berücksichtigen.
(5) Genehmigungen nach den Absätzen 1 bis 3 sind im Benehmen mit dem Denkmalfachamt zu erteilen, soweit das Vorhaben nicht dem Inhalt eines Denkmalpflegeplans nach § 8 Abs. 2 entspricht.
(6) ¹Vor Zustellung der Genehmigung darf mit den Maßnahmen nicht begonnen werden. ²Sie dürfen nur so ausgeführt werden, wie sie genehmigt worden sind.
(7) ¹Eine nach diesem Gesetz erteilte Genehmigung erlischt, wenn nicht innerhalb von drei Jahren nach der Erteilung mit der Ausführung der Maßnahme begonnen wurde. ²Die zuständige untere Denkmalschutzbehörde kann diese Frist verlängern.
(8) ¹Ist für eine Maßnahme eine Baugenehmigung oder eine die Baugenehmigung einschließende oder ersetzende behördliche Entscheidung erforderlich, so umfaßt diese die Genehmigung nach Absatz 1; Absatz 4 gilt entsprechend. ²Das Denkmalfachamt ist an den Verfahren zu beteiligen.
(9) ¹Die untere Denkmalschutzbehörde kann verlangen, dass der Eigentümer oder der Veranlasser von Veränderungen und Maßnahmen an Kulturdenkmalen diese dokumentiert. ²Art und Umfang der Dokumentation sind im Rahmen von Auflagen festzulegen. ³Die Veranlasser von Veränderungen und von Maßnahmen an Denkmalen können im Rahmen des Zumutbaren zur Übernahme der Dokumentationskosten verpflichtet werden.
(10) Muß ein Kulturdenkmal aus zwingenden Gründen zerstört oder weggenommen werden, bedarf dies der Genehmigung durch die obere Denkmalschutzbehörde.
(11) ¹Eine Genehmigung nach den Absätzen 1 bis 3 und 10 gilt als erteilt, wenn die Denkmalschutzbehörde nicht innerhalb von zwei Monaten nach Eingang des Antrags entschieden hat. ²Die Frist beginnt auch im Falle fehlender oder unvollständiger Antragsunterlagen mit dem Eingang des Antrags, wenn die Denkmalschutzbehörde es unterläßt, dem Anragsteller innerhalb von fünf Arbeitstagen nach Eingang des Antrags schriftlich unter Aufzählung der fehlenden Antragsunterlagen mitzuteilen, dass die Frist erst mit Eingang der noch fehlenden Antragsunterlagen beginnt. ³Die Denkmalschutzbehörde kann das Verfahren für einen weiteren Monat aussetzen, wenn dadurch die Ablehnung eines Antrages vermieden werden kann.

§ 15 Antragstellung
(1) ¹Der Antrag auf Genehmigung ist schriftlich bei der zuständigen Denkmalschutzbehörde zu stellen. ²Alle für die Bearbeitung erforderlichen Unterlagen sind beizufügen. ³Die oberste Denkmalbehörde wird ermächtigt, durch Verordnung[1]) Vorschriften über Umfang, Inhalt und Form der beizufügenden Unterlagen zu erlassen.
(2) ¹Der Antragsteller ist dafür verantwortlich, daß die von ihm veranlaßte Maßnahme dem Denkmalrecht entspricht. ²Er hat Projektbearbeiter und Unternehmer zu bestellen, die eine den Zielen dieses Gesetzes entsprechende Durchführung nach Ausbildung und Berufserfahrung sicherstellen.
(3) Die zuständige Denkmalschutzbehörde kann verlangen, daß für bestimmte Arbeiten die Unternehmer benannt werden.

§ 16 Auskunfts- und Duldungspflichten
(1) ¹Bedienstete und Beauftragte der Denkmalschutzbehörden und des Denkmalfachamtes dürfen nach vorheriger Benachrichtigung Grundstücke, zur Abwendung dringender Gefahr für ein Kulturdenkmal auch Wohnungen, betreten, soweit es zur Durchführung dieses Gesetzes erforderlich ist. ²Sie dürfen Kulturdenkmale besichtigen und die notwendigen wissenschaftlichen Erfassungsmaßnahmen, insbesondere zur Inventarisation, durchführen. ³Das Grundrecht auf Unverletzlichkeit der Wohnung (Artikel 13 des Grundgesetzes) wird insoweit eingeschränkt.
(2) Eigentümer, Besitzer und Verfügungsberechtigte von Kulturdenkmalen haben den Denkmalschutzbehörden und dem Denkmalfachamt sowie ihren Beauftragten die zum Vollzug dieses Gesetzes erforderlichen wahrheitsgemäßen Auskünfte zu erteilen.

---

1) Die Verordnung über Umfang, Inhalt und Form des Antrags auf denkmalrechtliche Genehmigung ist abgedruckt als Nr. D14.I.1e.

(3) ¹Die zuständige Denkmalschutzbehörde kann Eigentümer, Besitzer und Verfügungsberechtigte von Kulturdenkmalen verpflichten, diese zum Zeichen ihres gesetzlichen Schutzes und zur Förderung ihrer geistigen Erschließung kennzeichnen zu lassen. ²Sie haben die Anbringung von Kennzeichen und Interpretationstafeln zu dulden und diese vor Gefährdungen zu schützen. ³Die Kennzeichen und Tafeln dürfen die zulässige Nutzung nicht beeinträchtigen. ⁴Die Kennzeichnung von Denkmalbereichen obliegt der Gemeinde als Eigentümer der Verkehrs- und Freiflächen.

(4) Bestehen begründete Anhaltspunkte, daß in einem Grundstück archäologische Kulturdenkmale von wesentlicher Bedeutung vorhanden sind, so ist das Denkmalfachamt berechtigt, dort nach archäologischen Kulturdenkmalen zu forschen, Ausgrabungen vorzunehmen, Bodenfunde zu bergen und die notwendigen Maßnahmen zur Klärung der Fundumstände sowie zur Sicherung weiterer auf dem Grundstück vorhandener Bodenfunde durchzuführen.

(5) ¹Die Denkmalschutzbehörde kann die wirtschaftliche Nutzung eines Grundstückes oder eines Grundstückteiles, in dem sich ein Kulturdenkmal befindet, beschränken. ²Entschädigungen werden nach Maßgabe von § 19 Abs. 4 gewährt.

§ 17 Anzeigepflicht

(1) ¹Vor der Veräußerung eines Kulturdenkmals hat dies der Eigentümer unverzüglich der zuständigen Denkmalschutzbehörde anzuzeigen. ²Der Veräußerer ist verpflichtet, den neuen Eigentümer auf den bestehenden Denkmalschutz hinzuweisen.

(2) ¹Eigentümer, Besitzer und Verfügungsberechtigte von Kulturdenkmalen haben Schäden und Mängel, die den Denkmalwert und die Denkmalsubstanz beeinträchtigen oder gefährden, unverzüglich der zuständigen Denkmalschutzbehörde anzuzeigen. ²Dies gilt insbesondere für Schäden, die durch Feuer, Wasser oder andere unvorhersehbare Ereignisse eingetreten sind.

(3) Bodenfunde sind entsprechend § 9 Abs. 3 durch den Finder, Verfügungsberechtigten oder den Leiter der Arbeiten unverzüglich gegenüber der unteren Denkmalschutzbehörde anzuzeigen.

§ 18 Denkmalverzeichnis

(1) ¹Das Denkmalverzeichnis ist nachrichtlich. ²Es werden von dem Denkmalfachamt getrennte Listen für Baudenkmale, bewegliche Kulturdenkmale, archäologische Kulturdenkmale und Grabungsschutzgebiete geführt. ³Die Aufnahme erfolgt auf der Grundlage des § 2 nach Anhörung der unteren Denkmalschutzbehörde. ⁴Der Schutz durch dieses Gesetz ist nicht davon abhängig, daß Kulturdenkmale in das Verzeichnis eingetragen sind.

(2) ¹Die Feststellung der Denkmaleigenschaft nach § 2 Abs. 1 durch das Denkmalfachamt ist dem Eigentümer, Besitzer oder Verfügungsberechtigten mitzuteilen. ²Diese Aufgabe obliegt der zuständigen unteren Denkmalschutzbehörde, die auch einen Auszug aus dem Denkmalverzeichnis für ihr Gebiet führt. ³Auf Antrag des Eigentümers, Besitzers oder Verfügungsberechtigten hat die untere Denkmalschutzbehörde durch Verwaltungsakt über die Eigenschaft als Kulturdenkmal innerhalb eines Monats zu entscheiden.

(3) ¹Die Einsicht in das Denkmalverzeichnis ist jedermann gestattet. ²Die Liste der beweglichen Kulturdenkmale dürfen nur die Eigentümer beziehungsweise die sonstigen dinglich Berechtigten oder von diesen ermächtigte Personen einsehen.

(4) Eintragungen in das Denkmalverzeichnis sind zu löschen, wenn nach Feststellung des Denkmalfachamtes die Voraussetzungen entfallen sind.

V. Abschnitt
Enteignung und Entschädigung

§ 19 Enteignung und Entschädigung

(1) Die Enteignung eines Kulturdenkmals ist zulässig, soweit sie erforderlich ist, um
1. ein Kulturdenkmal in seinem Bestand oder Erscheinungsbild zu erhalten,
2. Kulturdenkmale auszugraben und wissenschaftlich untersuchen zu können,
3. in einem Grabungsschutzgebiet planmäßige Nachforschungen betreiben zu können.

(2) Antragsberechtigt ist die obere Denkmalschutzbehörde.

(3) ¹Die Enteignung ist zulässig zugunsten des Landes, einer kommunalen Gebietskörperschaft oder einer anderen juristischen Person öffentlichen Rechts oder einer rechtsfähigen Stiftung, wenn der Stif-

tungszweck auf Denkmalschutz und Denkmalpflege ausgerichtet ist. ²Im übrigen gelten die Vorschriften des Enteignungsgesetzes des Landes Sachsen-Anhalt.
(4) ¹Soweit der Vollzug dieses Gesetzes im Einzelfall eine über den Rahmen der Sozialbindung des Eigentums (Artikel 14 Abs. 2 des Grundgesetzes) hinausgehende enteignende Wirkung hat, hat das Land eine angemessene Entschädigung in Geld zu gewähren. ²Beihilfen und gewährte Steuervorteile, die auf die Denkmaleigenschaft zurückzuführen sind, sind in angemessenem Umfang auf die Entschädigung anzurechnen.
(5) Das Land und die kommunalen Gebietskörperschaften, soweit durch die zugrundeliegende Maßnahme auch deren örtliche Belange begünstigt werden, sollen die Entschädigung gemeinsam tragen.

VI. Abschnitt
Finanzierung

§ 20 Finanzierung
(1) Das Land Sachsen-Anhalt trägt, unbeschadet bestehender Verpflichtungen, zu den Kosten der Erhaltung und Instandsetzung von Kulturdenkmalen nach Maßgabe der im Haushalt bereitgestellten Mittel bei.
(2) ¹Von der obersten Denkmalbehörde werden Zuschüsse bereitgestellt, die nach Anhörung des Denkmalfachamtes je nach Dringlichkeit und unter Berücksichtigung der Leistungsfähigkeit der Eigentümer und Verfügungsberechtigten Zuschüsse für die Konservierung, Instandsetzung und Restaurierung von Kulturdenkmalen auf Antrag bewilligt werden können. ²Ein angemessener Anteil dieser Mittel kann für besondere Vorhaben des Denkmalfachamtes zur Verfügung gestellt werden.
(3) Bescheinigungen für die Erlangung von Steuervorteilen werden von den zuständigen unteren Denkmalschutzbehörden auf Antrag erteilt.
(4) Das Land soll anerkannte Denkmalpflege-Organisationen, gemeinnützige Träger und Einzelpersonen, die Aufgaben des Denkmalschutzes und der Denkmalpflege wahrnehmen, entsprechend ihrer Leistungen im Rahmen der verfügbaren Mittel des Landeshaushaltes fördern.
(5) ¹Für Amtshandlungen nach diesem Gesetz werden Kosten erhoben, wenn durch Dritte Leistungen in Anspruch genommen werden, die über den Umfang dieses Gesetzes hinausgehen. ²Das für den Denkmalschutz zuständige Ministerium wird ermächtigt, die Kosten durch gesonderte Gebührenordnung nach Maßgabe des Verwaltungskostengesetzes des Landes Sachsen-Anhalt vom 27. Juni 1991 (GVBl. LSA S. 154) festzulegen.
(6) Die Verwaltungskosten, die den Landkreisen und Gemeinden durch die Ausführung dieses Gesetzes entstehen, werden im Rahmen des kommunalen Finanzausgleiches gedeckt.

VII. Abschnitt
Straftaten und Ordnungswidrigkeiten

§ 21 Zerstörung eines Kulturdenkmals
(1) Wer vorsätzlich ohne die nach § 14 Abs. 1 und 2 erforderliche Genehmigung ein Kulturdenkmal oder einen wesentlichen Teil eines Kulturdenkmals zerstört oder in seiner Denkmaleigenschaft wesentlich beeinträchtigt, wird mit einer Freiheitsstrafe bis zu zwei Jahren oder mit einer Geldstrafe bestraft.
(2) Kulturdenkmale und Reste von Kulturdenkmalen, die infolge strafbarer oder ordnungswidriger Handlungen wesentlich beschädigt oder zerstört wurden, können vorbehaltlich der Rechte Dritter eingezogen werden.

§ 22 Ordnungswidrigkeiten
(1) Ordnungswidrig handelt, wer vorsätzlich oder fahrlässig
1. entgegen § 9 Abs. 3 Satz 1 einen Bodenfund nicht anzeigt und die Fundstelle bis zum Ablauf einer Woche nicht im unveränderten Zustand beläßt;
2. entgegen § 9 Abs. 6 Satz 2 Maßnahmen der Denkmalschutzbehörden und des Denkmalfachamtes zur Abwendung einer Gefahr für den Bestand des Denkmals nicht duldet;
3. entgegen § 13 den zuständigen Denkmalbehörden Bodenfunde oder Sammlungen zu wissenschaftlichen oder restauratorischen Zwecken nicht vorübergehend überläßt;

D14.I.1 Denkmalschutzgesetz Sachsen-Anhalt

4. genehmigungspflichtige Maßnahmen entgegen § 14 Abs. 1 und 2 ohne Genehmigung beginnt oder ausführt oder einer von der zuständigen Behörde mit der Genehmigung erteilten Auflage zuwiderhandelt;
5. der Auskunftspflicht nach § 16 Abs. 2 nicht nachkommt oder entgegen § 16 Abs. 1 den Beauftragten der zuständigen Denkmalschutzbehörde bzw. des Denkmalfachamtes das Betreten von Grundstücken oder Besichtigen von Denkmalen nicht gestattet;
6. entgegen § 16 Abs. 5 einer Nutzungsbeschränkung zuwiderhandelt;
7. entgegen § 17 Abs. 1 Satz 1 und Abs. 2 Satz 1 seinen Anzeigepflichten nicht nachkommt.

(2) Ordnungswidrigkeiten können mit einer Geldbuße bis zu 500 000 Euro geahndet werden.
(3) Zuständige Behörde im Sinne des § 36 Abs. 1 Nr. 1 des Gesetzes über Ordnungswidrigkeiten ist die untere Denkmalschutzbehörde.
(4) [1]§ 21 Abs. 2 gilt entsprechend. [2]§ 23 des Gesetzes über Ordnungswidrigkeiten ist anzuwenden.

VIII. Abschnitt
Übergangs- und Schlußbestimmungen

§ 23 *[aufgehoben]*

§ 24 Inkrafttreten

[1]Dieses Gesetz tritt am Tag nach seiner Verkündung[1)] in Kraft. [2]Ausgenommen davon ist § 19, der erst mit dem Enteignungsgesetz des Landes Sachsen-Anhalt in Kraft tritt.[2)]

---

1) Verkündet am 28.10.1991.
2) In Kraft seit dem 2.5.1994.

Verordnung über Tätigkeit und Entschädigung ehrenamtlicher Beauftragter für die Denkmalpflege und für die archäologische Denkmalpflege

Vom 3. Februar 1994 (GVBl. LSA S. 203)
(BS LSA 2242.2)
zuletzt geändert durch Anl. Nr. 290 Viertes RechtsbereinigungsG vom 19. März 2002
(GVBl. LSA S. 130)

Auf Grund des § 6 Abs. 5 in Verbindung mit § 3 Satz 1 des Denkmalschutzgesetzes des Landes Sachsen-Anhalt vom 21. Oktober 1991 (GVBl. LSA S. 368), geändert durch § 97 Abs. 3 des Verwaltungsverfahrensgesetzes für das Land Sachsen-Anhalt vom 18. August 1993 (GVBl. LSA S. 412), in Verbindung mit dem Beschluß der Landesregierung über den Aufbau der Landesregierung Sachsen-Anhalts und die Abgrenzung der Geschäftsbereiche in der Fassung vom 14. August 1991 (MBl. LSA S. 447), zuletzt geändert durch den Beschluß vom 9. Februar 1993 (MBl. LSA S. 623), wird verordnet:

§ 1 Tätigkeit

(1) ¹Die ehrenamtlichen Beauftragten für Denkmalpflege und für archäologische Denkmalpflege beraten und unterstützen die bestellende Behörde. ²Die Beauftragten treten für die Belange des Denkmalschutzes und der Denkmalpflege ein.
(2) Die Aufgaben der Beauftragten für Denkmalpflege sind unter anderem:
1. Benachrichtigung der unteren Denkmalschutzbehörden, sofern die Gefährdung eines Bau- oder Kunstdenkmals bekannt wird, sowie Hinweise auf Planungen oder sonstige Maßnahmen, die eine Gefährdung eines Bau- oder Kunstdenkmals zur Folge haben können.
2. Unterstützung bei der Erfüllung von Aufgaben der bestellenden Denkmalbehörde, wie Erfassung und Kennzeichnung des Bestandes,
3. Information der Öffentlichkeit über Aufgaben und Ziele von Denkmalschutz und Denkmalpflege durch Vorträge, Ausstellungen und Werbung um Unterstützung.

(3) Die Aufgaben der Beauftragten für archäologische Denkmalpflege sind unter anderem:
1. Benachrichtigung der unteren Denkmalschutzbehörde, sofern die Gefährdung eines archäologischen Denkmals bekannt wird, sowie Hinweise auf Planungen oder sonstige Maßnahmen, die eine Gefährdung eines archäologischen Denkmals zur Folge haben können. Überprüfung und Registrierung archäologischer Denkmale und Fundstellen im Gelände und Dokumentation der Ergebnisse,
2. Unterstützung bei der Erfüllung der Aufgaben der bestellenden Behörde wie Erfassung und Kennzeichnung des Bestandes sowie Beobachtung von Erdaufschlüssen, die archäologische Ergebnisse und Funde erwarten lassen,
3. Information der Öffentlichkeit über Aufgaben und Ziele von Denkmalschutz und Denkmalpflege durch Vorträge, Ausstellungen und Werbung um Unterstützung.

§ 2 Ausübung der Tätigkeit

(1) Die Beauftragten sind ehrenamtlich tätig.
(2) Die Beauftragten werden entsprechend ihrer Bestellung für einen Landkreis oder den Teil eines Landkreises oder einer kreisfreien Stadt tätig.
(3) Die Beauftragten berichten der bestellenden Stelle auf Anforderung unverzüglich, im übrigen in angemessenen Zeitabständen, mindestens jedoch einmal im Quartal.

§ 3 Entschädigung

(1) Die für einen Landkreis oder eine kreisfreie Stadt bestellten Beauftragten erhalten zur Abgeltung der mit dieser Tätigkeit verbundenen Aufwendungen eine monatliche Aufwandsentschädigung von 112 DM.
(2) Sind die Beauftragten nur für einen Teil eines Landkreises oder einer kreisfreien Stadt bestellt, ermäßigt sich die monatliche Aufwandsentschädigung des Absatzes 1 auf die Hälfte.

§ 4 Sprachliche Gleichstellung
Personen- und Funktionsbezeichnungen in dieser Verordnung gelten jeweils in weiblicher und männlicher Form.

§ 5 Inkrafttreten
Diese Verordnung tritt am Tage nach ihrer Verkündung[1] in Kraft.

---

1) Verkündet am 14.2.1994.

Verordnung über die Tätigkeit und die Kostenerstattung der Mitglieder des Denkmalrates

Vom 18. August 1994 (GVBl. LSA S. 940)
(BS LSA 2242.3)
zuletzt geändert durch § 1 ÄndVO vom 11. März 1998 (GVBl. LSA S. 156)

Auf Grund des § 6 Abs. 5 in Verbindung mit § 3 Satz 1 des Denkmalschutzgesetzes des Landes Sachsen-Anhalt vom 21. Oktober 1991 (GVBl. LSA S. 368), zuletzt geändert durch Artikel 2 des Gesetzes zum Enteignungsgesetz des Landes Sachsen-Anhalt und zur Änderung des Denkmalschutzgesetzes und des Wassergesetzes vom 13. April 1994 (GVBl. LSA S. 508), in Verbindung mit dem Beschluß der Landesregierung über den Aufbau der Landesregierung Sachsen-Anhalt und die Abgrenzung der Geschäftsbereiche in der Fassung vom 24. März 1994 (MBl. LSA S. 915), geändert durch Abschnitt I des Beschlusses vom 22. Juli 1994 (MBl. LSA S. 1954), wird verordnet:

§ 1 Tätigkeit
(1) [1]Der Denkmalrat berät und unterstützt die oberste Denkmalbehörde des Landes in allen Fragen des Denkmalschutzes und der Denkmalpflege. [2]Der Denkmalrat ist bei Grundsatzentscheidungen, die den Denkmalschutz und die Denkmalpflege betreffen, zu hören. [3]Er ist berechtigt, Anregungen und Empfehlungen auszusprechen.
(2) Die Mitglieder des Denkmalrates sind ehrenamtlich tätig.

§ 2 Kostenerstattung
(1) [1]Die Mitglieder des Denkmalrates erhalten für die Teilnahme an den Sitzungen des Denkmalrates außerhalb ihres Wohnortes und des Ortes ihrer beruflichen Tätigkeit Reisekostenvergütung nach dem Bundesreisekostengesetz in der Fassung vom 13. November 1973 (BGBl. I S. 1621), zuletzt geändert durch Artikel 28 des Jahressteuergesetzes 1997 vom 20. Dezember 1996 (BGBl. I S. 2049). [2]Fahrkosten werden nach § 5 Abs. 1 Satz 1 Alternative 2 des Bundesreisekostengesetzes gewährt.
(2) Andere Kostenerstattungen sind auf Leistungen nach Absatz 1 anzurechnen.

§ 3 Inkrafttreten
Diese Verordnung tritt am Tage nach ihrer Verkündung[1)] in Kraft.

---

1) Verkündet am 29.8.1994.

Richtlinien zur Durchführung des § 6 des Denkmalschutzgesetzes des Landes Sachsen-Anhalt; Bestellung der ehrenamtlichen Beauftragten

RdErl. des MK vom 5. Juli 1994 (MBl. LSA S. 2122)

Geänd. d. Rd.Erl. des MK vom 1.10.1994 (MBl. LSA S. 2532)

Nach § 6 des Denkmalschutzgesetzes des Landes Sachsen-Anhalt vom 21.10.1991 (GVBl. LSA S. 368), zuletzt geändert durch Art. 2 des Gesetzes zum Enteignungsgesetz des Landes Sachsen-Anhalt und zur Änderung des Denkmalschutzgesetzes und des Wassergesetzes vom 13.4.1994 (GVBl. LSA S. 508), werden ehrenamtliche Beauftragte bestellt. Hinsichtlich ihrer Bestellung werden folgende Richtlinien erlassen:

1. **Bestellung**

    1.1 Als ehrenamtliche Beauftragte können nur Persönlichkeiten bestellt werden, die auf Grund ihrer besonderen Fach- und Ortskenntnisse in der Lage sind, die in § 1 der Verordnung über Tätigkeit und Entschädigung ehrenamtlicher Beauftragter für die Denkmalpflege und für archäologische Denkmalpflege vom 3.2.1994 (GVBl. LSA S. 203) aufgeführten Aufgaben zu erfüllen.

    Bei der Auswahl dieser Personen ist darauf zu achten, daß sie ihre Tätigkeit neutral und ausschließlich den Zielen des Gesetzes folgend, ausüben werden.

    Personen, die in einer kommunalen oder einer Landesbehörde tätig sind, können nicht als Beauftragte bestellt werden, wenn Aufgaben, die das Denkmalschutzgesetz des Landes Sachsen-Anhalt betreffen, zu ihren dienstlichen Verpflichtungen gehören, oder wenn sie in Einrichtungen tätig sind, die archäologische Aufgaben des Landes Sachsen-Anhalt betreffen.

    1.2 Die Bestellung nach § 6 Abs. 1 und 2 des Denkmalschutzgesetzes des Landes Sachsen-Anhalt wird für einen Zeitraum von vier Jahren ausgesprochen. Sie kann jederzeit von der bestellenden Behörde widerrufen werden. Nach Ablauf des jeweiligen Bestellungszeitraumes ist eine Wiederbestellung möglich.

    1.3 Die Denkmalfachämter prüfen, ob die vorgeschlagenen Personen den Anforderungen der Nr. 1.1. gerecht werden und ob eine Begrenzung der Aufgaben oder der örtlichen Zuständigkeit erfolgen soll. Die unteren Denkmalschutzbehörden und die Denkmalfachämter sind verpflichtet, die Bestellung zu widerrufen, wenn die ausgeführte Tätigkeit der Beauftragten nicht den verbindlich formulierten Aufgaben des Beauftragten entspricht. Die Denkmalfachbehörden können gegenüber den unteren Denkmalschutzbehörden Empfehlungen aussprechen.

    1.4 Mit der Bestellung erhält der Beauftragte ein Bestellungsschreiben nach dem Muster der Anlage 1[1)] und eine Aufstellung der ihm übertragenen Aufgaben. Die Denkmalfachämter erarbeiten einen Aufgabenkatalog für die Beauftragten. Die Festlegung der Aufgaben für jeden Beauftragten erfolgt durch die bestellende Behörde. Sie basiert auf § 1 der Verordnung über Tätigkeit und Entschädigung ehrenamtlicher Beauftragter für die Denkmalpflege und für archäologische Denkmalpflege. Sollten Aufgaben und/oder Zuständigkeiten begrenzt werden, so ist dies in den jeweiligen Aufstellungen entsprechend auszuführen. Der Beauftragte hat hinsichtlich seiner Aufgabenstellung und Zuständigkeit schriftlich sein Einverständnis zu erklären.

    1.5 Der Beauftragte erhält mit seiner Bestellung einen Ausweis, der ihn legitimiert, im Rahmen der ihm übertragenen Aufgaben für die zuständigen unteren Denkmalschutzbehörden und/oder Denkmalfachämter beratend und unterstützend tätig zu sein (Anlage 2). Die Ausweise werden von der zuständigen bestellenden Behörde fortlaufend numeriert. Der Empfang des Ausweises ist vom Beauftragten zu quittieren. Nach Beendigung der Tätigkeit des Beauftragten, ist der Ausweis an die bestellende Behörde zurückzugeben.

---

1) Hinweis: Die Anlagen konnten aus drucktechnischen Gründen nicht aufgenommen werden. Sie sind abgedruckt in: MBl. LSA 1994 S. 2123 f.

2. **Sprachliche Gleichstellung**
Personen- und Funktionsbezeichnungen gelten jeweils in weiblicher und männlicher Form.
3. **Inkrafttreten**
Dieser RdErl. tritt mit seiner Veröffentlichung in Kraft.

D14.I.1d VwV Denkmalrat

Zusammensetzung, Berufung und Organisation des Denkmalrates
RdErl. des MK vom 25.4.2014 (MBl. LSA. S.242)

1. Regelungsgegenstand
Dieser RdErl. regelt die Zusammensetzung, Berufung, Organisation und die Aufgaben des gemäß § 6 Abs. 3 des Denkmalschutzgesetzes des Landes Sachsen-Anhalt vom 21.10.1991 (GVBl. LSA S. 368), zuletzt geändert durch Artikel 2 des Gesetzes vom 20.12.2005 (GVBl. LSA S. 769, 801), von der obersten Denkmalbehörde berufenen Denkmalrates.

2. Zusammensetzung
2.1 Der auf Vorschlag des Denkmalfachamtes von der obersten Denkmalbehörde berufene ehrenamtlich tätige Denkmalrat setzt sich aus folgenden Mitgliedern zusammen:
a) Bis zu acht Sachverständige für die Fachgebiete des Denkmalschutzes, der Archäologie und der Denkmalpflege, z. B. Kunsthistoriker, Archäologen, Architekten, Ingenieure oder Techniker, Denkmalpfleger, Historiker und andere,
b) einen im Denkmalrecht kundigen Vertreter,
c) einen Vertreter aus dem Handwerk oder aus der praktischen Denkmalpflege und
d) bis zu vier Vertreter von mit dem Denkmalschutz befassten Organisationen im Sinne von § 7 des Denkmalschutzgesetzes des Landes Sachsen-Anhalt.

2.2 Die angesprochenen Stellen und Institutionen sollen Vertreter namentlich benennen.

3. Amtszeit
3.1 Die Mitglieder des Denkmalrates werden für die Dauer von fünf Jahren berufen. Eine Wiederberufung ist zulässig.
3.2 Die Mitglieder des Denkmalrates bleiben bis zur Berufung ihrer Nachfolger im Amt.

4. Abberufung
Ein Mitglied des Denkmalrates kann durch die oberste Denkmalbehörde abberufen werden, wenn die Stelle, die das Mitglied vorgeschlagen hat, die Abberufung beantragt.

5. Ende der Mitgliedschaft
5.1 Ein Mitglied scheidet aus:
a) mit Ablauf der Amtszeit,
b) nach schriftlichem Verzicht auf weitere Mitgliedschaft gegenüber der obersten Denkmalbehörde.

5.2 Scheidet ein Mitglied während der Amtszeit aus, so wird ein von der betreffenden vorschlagenden Stelle benanntes neues Mitglied von der obersten Denkmalbehörde berufen, falls der Rest der Amtszeit des ausscheidenden Mitglieds mehr als ein Jahr beträgt.

6. Leitung des Denkmalrates
6.1 Der Denkmalrat wählt aus seiner Mitte einen Vorsitzenden und einen Stellvertreter.
6.2 Die Wahl des Vorsitzenden und des Stellvertreters erfolgt mit einfacher Mehrheit der anwesenden Mitglieder. Stimmenthaltungen werden nicht berücksichtigt. Auf Antrag eines Mitgliedes finden geheime Wahlen statt.

7. Sitzungen
7.1 Der Denkmalrat tritt mindestens halbjährlich zu einer Sitzung zusammen.
7.2 Der Vorsitzende beruft den Denkmalrat unter Angabe von Ort, Zeit und der Tagesordnung schriftlich ein. Die Einladung soll den Mitgliedern und der obersten Denkmalbehörde rechtzeitig zugehen.
7.3 Der Denkmalrat ist auf Antrag von einem Drittel seiner Mitglieder innerhalb von drei Wochen einzuberufen.
7.4 Auf Verlangen der obersten Denkmalbehörde ist der Denkmalrat unverzüglich einzuberufen.
7.5 Zu den Sitzungen können durch den Vorsitzenden sachkundige Personen als Berater sowie Betroffene eingeladen werden.
7.6 Vertreter der obersten Denkmalbehörde, der oberen Denkmalschutzbehörde sowie der Landesarchäologe und der Landeskonservator können mit beratender Stimme an den Sitzungen teilnehmen.

8. Beschlussfähigkeit
Der Denkmalrat beschließt mit einfacher Mehrheit der anwesenden Mitglieder.

9. Aufgaben des Denkmalrates

9.1 Der Denkmalrat berät die oberste Denkmalbehörde bei Grundsatzangelegenheiten des Denkmalschutzes, der Archäologie und der Denkmalpflege oder bei Einzelfällen von Landesinteresse. Er hat das Recht, seine Empfehlungen und Stellungnahmen über die Pressestellen, das Landesamt für Denkmalpflege und Archäologie oder die oberste Denkmalbehörde der Öffentlichkeit zugänglich zu machen. Die Denkmalbehörden sind verpflichtet, die Empfehlungen des Denkmalrates bei ihren Entscheidungen zu berücksichtigen. Der Denkmalrat ist berechtigt, Publikationen herauszugeben, die sich mit fachlichen Problemen von Denkmalschutz und Denkmalpflege befassen.

9.2 Der Denkmalrat hat die Aufgabe, die Preisträger des Denkmalpreises der obersten Denkmalbehörde vorzuschlagen.

10. Sitzungsleitung und Niederschrift

10.1 Der Vorsitzende leitet die Sitzung. Die Sitzungen sind nicht öffentlich. Der Vorsitzende kann die Öffentlichkeit über die Ergebnisse unterrichten.

10.2 Über jede Sitzung ist eine Niederschrift anzufertigen, die von dem Vorsitzenden zu unterzeichnen ist. Die Niederschrift ist den Mitgliedern des Denkmalrates und der obersten Denkmalbehörde zuzusenden.

11. Geschäftsführung

Die Führung der laufenden Geschäfte des Denkmalrates wird von der obersten Denkmalbehörde wahrgenommen.

12. Sprachliche Gleichstellung

Personen- und Funktionsbezeichnungen in diesem RdErl. gelten jeweils in männlicher und weiblicher Form.

13. Inkrafttreten

Dieser RdErl. tritt am Tag nach seiner Veröffentlichung in Kraft.

D14.I.1e Denkmalantragsverordnung

Verordnung über Umfang, Inhalt und Form des Antrags auf denkmalrechtliche Genehmigung (Denkmalantragsverordnung des Landes Sachsen-Anhalt – DenkmAVO LSA)

Vom 27. August 2018 (GVBl. LSA 2018, 294)

Aufgrund des § 15 Abs. 1 Satz 3 in Verbindung mit § 3 Satz 1 des Denkmalschutzgesetzes des Landes Sachsen-Anhalt vom 21. Oktober 1991 (GVBl. LSA S. 368), zuletzt geändert durch Artikel 2 des Gesetzes vom 20. Dezember 2005 (GVBl. LSA S. 769, 801), in Verbindung mit Abschnitt II Nr. 1 des Beschlusses der Landesregierung über den Aufbau der Landesregierung Sachsen-Anhalt und die Abgrenzung der Geschäftsbereiche vom 24. Mai/7. Juni 2016 (MBl. LSA S. 369), geändert durch Beschluss vom 20. September 2016 (MBl. LSA S. 549), wird verordnet:

§ 1 Zuständige Behörde

Anträge auf denkmalrechtliche Genehmigung gemäß § 14 Abs. 1 bis 4 in Verbindung mit § 15 Abs. 1 Satz 1 und 2 des Denkmalschutzgesetzes des Landes Sachsen-Anhalt sind grundsätzlich an die zuständige untere Denkmalschutzbehörde zu richten. Anträge zur Genehmigung von Denkmalzerstörungen sind gemäß § 14 Abs. 10 des Denkmalschutzgesetzes des Landes Sachsen-Anhalt an die obere Denkmalschutzbehörde zu richten.

§ 2 Antragsunterlagen

(1) Die Genehmigung nach § 14 Abs. 1 bis 4 und 10 und § 15 Abs. 1 des Denkmalschutzgesetzes des Landes Sachsen-Anhalt ist unter Verwendung von amtlichen Formularen schriftlich zu beantragen. Die amtlichen Formulare sind beim Landesverwaltungsamt im Internet abrufbar.
(2) Die Vorlage vollständiger, prüfbarer Antragsunterlagen ist Voraussetzung für die Durchführung des Genehmigungsverfahrens und den Beginn der Bearbeitungsfrist des § 14 Abs. 11 des Denkmalschutzgesetzes des Landes Sachsen-Anhalt. Gemäß § 15 Abs. 2 des Denkmalschutzgesetzes des Landes Sachsen-Anhalt sind die Antragsteller dafür verantwortlich, dass die von ihnen beantragte Maßnahme dem Denkmalrecht entspricht.
(3) Neben der Unterschrift des Antragstellers sind soweit zutreffend auch jene von Miteigentümern des Kulturdenkmals sowie des Entwurfsverfassers der geplanten Baumaßnahme zu leisten.
(4) Die zuständige Behörde kann die Vorlage weiterer Unterlagen verlangen.

§ 3 Qualifizierte Denkmalbereiche

(1) Gemäß § 1 in Verbindung mit § 14 Abs. 4 des Denkmalschutzgesetzes des Landes Sachsen- Anhalt kann das Denkmalfachamt im Benehmen mit der zuständigen unteren Denkmalschutzbehörde Denkmalbereiche (§ 2 Abs. 2 Nr. 2 des Denkmalschutzgesetzes des Landes Sachsen-Anhalt) qualifizieren, indem es konstitutive Merkmale des Denkmalwerts benennt sowie Bereiche oder baulichen Gegebenheiten innerhalb des Denkmalbereichs beschreibt, an denen Baumaßnahmen ohne Beeinträchtigung des Denkmalwerts erfolgen können.
(2) Das Denkmalfachamt veröffentlicht die Gesamtheit der qualifizierten Denkmalbereiche. Die Veröffentlichung soll die Angaben des Absatzes 1 enthalten sowie eine Karte jedes qualifizierten Denkmalbereichs.

§ 4 Vereinfachtes Verfahren

(1) Abweichend von § 2 kann der Antragsteller um eine denkmalrechtliche Genehmigung im vereinfachten Verfahren nachsuchen, sofern die Baumaßnahme innerhalb eines qualifizierten und veröffentlichten Denkmalbereichs nach § 3 erfolgen und die Maßnahme nicht an einem eingetragenen Baudenkmal durchgeführt soll sowie eine Beeinträchtigung des Denkmalwerts ausgeschlossen werden kann. Die Genehmigung ist schriftlich zu beantragen. Die beabsichtigte Baumaßnahme ist im Antrag zu erläutern sowie der Ausschluss einer Beeinträchtigung des Denkmalwerts anhand der konstitutiven Merkmale des Denkmalbereichs zu begründen.
(2) Die Prüfung des Antrags im vereinfachten Verfahren erstreckt sich allein auf die Möglichkeit einer Beeinträchtigung des Denkmalbereichs. Der Antrag ist abzulehnen, wenn die konstitutiven Merkmale des Denkmalbereichs durch die Maßnahme tangiert sind oder aus anderen Gründen eine Beeinträchtigung des Denkmalwerts nicht auszuschließen ist. Ein ablehnender Bescheid im vereinfachten Ver-

fahren stellt keine abschließende Sachentscheidung der zuständigen Behörde dar, dem Antragsteller steht dazu das Verfahren nach § 2 offen.

§ 5 Sprachliche Gleichstellung
Personen- und Funktionsbezeichnungen in dieser Verordnung gelten jeweils in weiblicher und männlicher Form.

§ 6 Inkrafttreten
Diese Verordnung tritt am Tag nach der Verkündung in Kraft.[1)]

---

1) Verkündet am 27.8.2018.

Gesetz zur Neuordnung der Landesverwaltung

Vom 17. Dezember 2003 (GVBl. LSA S. 352)

– Auszug –

Artikel 2 Landesamt für Denkmalpflege und Archäologie (Landesmuseum für Vorgeschichte)

(1) Zum 1. Januar 2004 wird im Geschäftsbereich des Kultusministeriums ein Landesamt für Denkmalpflege und Archäologie (Landesmuseum für Vorgeschichte) errichtet.

(2) Mit Ablauf des 31. Dezembers 2003 werden das Landesamt für Denkmalpflege und das Landesamt für Archäologie (Landesmuseum für Vorgeschichte) aufgelöst. Ihre Aufgaben gehen auf das Landesamt für Denkmalpflege und Archäologie (Landesmuseum für Vorgeschichte) über.

(3) Die Beschäftigten der aufgelösten Landesämter werden Beschäftigte des neu errichteten Landesamtes. Artikel 1 § 4 Abs. 1 Satz 2 gilt entsprechend.

Artikel 14 In-Kraft-Treten

(1) Dieses Gesetz tritt vorbehaltlich des Absatzes 2 am 1. Januar 2004 in Kraft.

(2) Artikel 4 Nr. 2 tritt hinsichtlich des § 2 Abs. 3 des Gesetzes zur Ausführung des Bundessozialhilfegesetzes am 1. Juli 2004 in Kraft.

Übertragung der Funktion einer unteren Denkmalschutzbehörde auf Kulturstiftungen

RdErl. des MK vom 22.1.2004 – 63-0577-kst (MBl. LSA S. 258)

1. Der Kulturstiftung Dessau-Wörlitz, der Stiftung Schlösser, Burgen und Gärten des Landes Sachsen-Anhalt und der Stiftung zum Erhalt der Dome, Kirchen und Klöster des Landes Sachsen-Anhalt werden gemäß § 4 Abs. 4 des Denkmalschutzgesetzes des Landes Sachsen-Anhalt vom 21.10.1991 (GVBl. LSA S. 368, 1992 S. 310), zuletzt geändert durch Art. 12 des Gesetzes vom 17.12.2003 (GVBl. LSA S. 352, 355), widerruflich die Funktion einer unteren Denkmalschutzbehörde übertragen.
2. Dieser RdErl. tritt am Tage nach seiner Veröffentlichung in Kraft.

An
das Landesverwaltungsamt,
das Landesamt für Denkmalpflege und Archäologie, an die Landkreise und kreisfreien Städte,
an die Gemeinden, denen die Funktion einer unteren Bauaufsichts- und Denkmalschutzbehörde übertragen wurde,
das Bistum Magdeburg

D14.I.4 Bistum Magdeburg als untere Denkmalschutzbehörde

Übertragung der Aufgaben der unteren Denkmalschutzbehörde auf das Bistum Magdeburg

RdErl. des MK vom 5.3.2003- 63.1-0577-kath.b

Aufgrund des Antrages des Bistums Magdeburg werden die Aufgaben der unteren Denkmalschutzbehörde nach § 4 Abs. 4 des Denkmalschutzgesetzes des Landes Sachsen-Anhalt vom 21.10.1991 (GVBL LSA S. 368), zuletzt geändert durch Art. 2 des Gesetzes vom 13.8.2002 (GVBl. LSA S. 358), dem Bistum Magdeburg übertragen.

In der Anlage[1] wird die Vereinbarung zwischen dem Land Sachsen-Anhalt und dem Bistum Magdeburg bekannt gegeben, die am 1.2.2003 durch Unterzeichnung durch den Kultusminister und durch den Generalvikar wirksam geworden ist.

An die
Denkmalschutzbehörden,
das Landesamt für Denkmalpflege, das Landesamt für Archäologie

§ 1 Funktionsübertragung einer unteren Denkmalschutzbehörde

(1) Das Bistum Magdeburg ist Rechtsträger seiner diözesanen Verwaltungsbehörde, dem Bischöflichen Ordinariat Magdeburg. Eine Hauptabteilung innerhalb des Bischöflichen Ordinariates Magdeburg ist die Hauptabteilung Bau. Diese ist Kirchenbauamt im Sinne des § 4 Abs. 4 Satz 1 Denkmalschutzgesetz.

(2) Das Bistum Magdeburg und das Kultusministerium sind sich darüber einig, dass i. S von § 4 Abs. 4 DenkmSchG die Rechte und Pflichten der unteren Denkmalschutzbehörde dem Bischöflichen Ordinariat Magdeburg (Kirchenbauamt) übertragen werden.

(3) Die Übertragung der Rechte und Pflichten erstreckt sich auf Kulturdenkmale im Eigentum und in der Nutzung der Katholischen Kirche im Bereich des Bistums Magdeburg, soweit diese im Land Sachsen-Anhalt gelegen sind.

§ 2 Geltungsbereich

(1) Gegenstand dieser Vereinbarung sind alle Kulturdenkmale gemäß § 2 Abs. 2 DenkmSchG, die ganz oder überwiegend durch die Katholische Kirche, einschließlich der zu ihr gehörenden Orden und religiösen Genossenschaften sowie anderer kirchlicher und karitativer Einrichtungen und Verbände und sonstiger Rechtspersonen öffentlichen oder privaten Rechts, genutzt werden.

(2) Das Kirchenbauamt ist bei Mehrheiten von baulichen Anlagen, die zusammen ein Kulturdenkmal i. S. des Denkmalschutzgesetzes bilden, zuständig, wenn dieses Kulturdenkmal insgesamt überwiegend kirchlich genutzt wird oder wenn die Denkmalbelange sich überwiegend auf den kirchlich genutzten Anlagenteil beziehen.

(3) Zuständigkeitskonflikte zwischen dem Kirchenbauamt und kommunalen unteren Denkmalschutzbehörden sollen einvernehmlich beigelegt werden; ist dies nicht möglich, entscheidet die oberste Denkmalbehörde.

§ 3 Denkmalliste kirchlicher Kulturdenkmale

(1) Im Wege der Unterrichtung wird das Kirchenbauamt dem Kultusministerium eine Denkmalliste derjenigen Kulturdenkmale übergeben, für die das Kirchenbauamt als untere Denkmalschutzbehörde zuständig ist.

(2) Diese Denkmalliste ist eine offene Liste, sie soll in regelmäßigen Abständen aktualisiert werden.

§ 4 Personelle und sachliche Ausstattung

(1) Das Bistum Magdeburg sichert zu, dass das Kirchenbauamt sachlich und personell vergleichbar mit den unteren Denkmalschutzbehörden ausgestattet ist.

(2) Die personelle Ausstattung ist zurzeit des Abschlusses dieser Vereinbarung:
    1,0 Stelle Bauingenieur, Dipl.-Ing. (FH),
    1,0 Stelle Maschinenbauingenieur und Patentingenieur,
    1,0 Stelle Bauingenieur, Dipl.-Ing. (FH),

---

1) Hier nicht wiedergegeben.

1,0 Stelle Technischer Zeichner (Elektro und Bau).
(3) Die rechtliche Begleitung der Verfahren Wird gewährleistet.

§ 5 Verfahren
(1) Die Wahrnehmung der Aufgaben des Kirchenbauamtes als untere Denkmalschutzbehörde erfolgt im Wege der Übertragung; die Verfahren werden selbständig und in eigener Verantwortung geführt.
(2) Die Rechte und Pflichten des Kirchenbauamtes als untere Denkmalschutzbehörde bestimmen sich nach dem jeweils geltenden weltlichen Recht und unter besonderer Berücksichtigung staatskirchenrechtlicher Bestimmungen, insbesondere des Vertrages zwischen dem Hl. Stuhl und dem Land Sachsen-Anhalt vom 15. Januar 1998.
(3) Die katholische Kirche ist zur Erfüllung der ihr mit dieser Vereinbarung übertragenen Rechte und Pflichten vom Verbot des Insichgeschäftes befreit.
(4) In Achtung vor dem kirchlichen Selbstverwaltungsrecht sind die Verfahrensakten isoliert und getrennt von sonstigen Verwaltungsvorgängen zu führen und aufzubewahren.
(5) Das Kultusministerium sichert zu, dass das Kirchenbauamt gleichberechtigt zu den kommunalen unteren Denkmalschutzbehörden behandelt wird. Dies betrifft u.a. die Zustellung von Runderlassen, Verwaltungsvorschriften und anderen Normen und Informationen, wie sie auch andere Denkmalbehörden erhalten.
(6) Die Fachaufsicht wird durch die obere Denkmalschutzbehörde (Regierungspräsidium) ausgeübt, in deren Zuständigkeitsbereich sich das jeweilige Kulturdenkmal befindet.

§ 6 Finanzielle Entlastung
Das Kultusministerium erkennt die Entlastung öffentlicher Verwaltung durch diese Übertragung an. Unter Berücksichtigung eigener kirchlicher Anliegen und Interessen behalten sich beide Seiten vor, sich zu einem späteren Zeitpunkt über die, mit den kommunalen unteren Denkmalschutzbehörden vergleichbaren Kosten und deren Erstattung zu verständigen.

§ 7 Geltungsdauer
(1) Diese Vereinbarung gilt zunächst zwei Jahre und verlängert sich um jeweils ein weiteres Jahr, sofern nicht einer der Vereinbarungsparteien diese Vereinbarung 9 Monate vor Ablauf des Vertragsjahres kündigt.
(2) Während des Vereinbarungszeitraumes aufgenommene Verwaltungsverfahren werden unter Beibehaltung der Zuständigkeit bis zu ihrem Abschluss fortgesetzt; insoweit und nur für diese Verfahren ist die Wirksamkeit dieser Vereinbarung durch den Abschluss der Verwaltungsverfahren auflösend bedingt.

§ 8 In-Kraft-Treten
Diese Vereinbarung tritt am 1.2.2003 in Kraft.

Archivgesetz Sachsen-Anhalt (ArchG LSA)

Vom 28. Juni 1995 (GVBl. LSA S. 190)
(BS LSA 2243.1)

zuletzt geändert durch Art. 11 G zur Anpassung des Datenschutzrechts in LSA an das Recht der EU[1] vom 18. Februar 2020 (GVBl. LSA S. 25)

Abschnitt 1
Allgemeine Bestimmungen

§ 1 Zweck und Geltungsbereich
(1) [1]Dieses Gesetz regelt den Umgang mit öffentlichem Archivgut in Sachsen-Anhalt. [2]Es soll das öffentliche Archivgut vor Vernichtung und Zersplitterung schützen und seine öffentliche Benutzung gewährleisten.
(2) Dieses Gesetz gilt nicht für
1. die öffentlich-rechtlichen Religionsgemeinschaften und deren Vereinigungen,
2. die öffentlich-rechtlichen Rundfunkanstalten,
3. die öffentlich-rechtlichen Unternehmen mit eigener Rechtspersönlichkeit, die am wirtschaftlichen Wettbewerb teilnehmen, und deren Zusammenschlüsse,
4. solche Zweckverbände, deren Zweck der Betrieb eines öffentlich-rechtlichen Unternehmens mit eigener Rechtspersönlichkeit ist, das am wirtschaftlichen Wettbewerb teilnimmt.

§ 2 Begriffsbestimmungen
(1) [1]Öffentliches Archivgut sind alle archivwürdigen Unterlagen, die bei
1. den Verfassungsorganen, Behörden, Gerichten und sonstigen öffentlichen Stellen des Landes Sachsen-Anhalt,
2. den Gemeinden, Verbandsgemeinden und Landkreisen sowie bei sonstigen kommunalen Zusammenschlüssen oder
3. den sonstigen der Aufsicht des Landes unterstehenden juristischen Personen des öffentlichen Rechts und deren Zusammenschlüssen

sowie bei deren Rechts- und Funktionsvorgängern entstanden sind und zur dauernden Aufbewahrung von einem öffentlichen Archiv übernommen werden. [2]Den in Satz 1 genannten Stellen stehen die von ihnen errichteten juristischen Personen des Privatrechts, die öffentliche Aufgaben erfüllen und nicht am Wettbewerb teilnehmen, gleich.
(2) Als öffentliches Archivgut gelten auch Unterlagen oder dokumentarische Materialien, die von öffentlichen Archiven zur Ergänzung ihres Archivgutes angelegt, erworben oder diesen zur dauernden Verwahrung und Nutzung überlassen worden sind.
(3) [1]Unterlagen im Sinne dieses Gesetzes sind unabhängig von ihrer Speicherungsform alle Aufzeichnungen und sonstigen Informationsobjekte. [2]Hierzu zählen insbesondere Akten, Dateien, Urkunden, Amtsbücher, Einzelschriftstücke, Druckschriften, Karten, Pläne, Zeichnungen, Risse, Plakate, Siegel, Stempel, Bild-, Film- und Tonaufzeichnungen sowie verfügbare Hilfsmittel und Programme, die zur Nutzung und dauerhaften Erhaltung der Unterlagen erforderlich sind.
(4) Archivwürdig sind Unterlagen, denen für die Gesetzgebung, Rechtsprechung, Regierung und Verwaltung, für die Wissenschaft und Forschung, für das Verständnis von Geschichte und Gegenwart, zur Rechtswahrung oder zur Sicherung berechtigter privater Interessen bleibender Wert zukommt.
(5) Archivieren ist das Ermitteln, Bewerten, Übernehmen, Verwahren auf Dauer, Sichern, Erhalten, Instandsetzen, Erschließen sowie Nutzbarmachen und Auswerten von Archivgut.
(6) Öffentliche Archive sind das Landesarchiv Sachsen-Anhalt, die Archive, die vom Landtag oder von Hochschulen errichtet sind, sowie die Kommunalarchive und die Archive von Stellen im Sinne des Absatzes 1 Satz 1 Nr. 3.

---

1) **Amtl. Anm.:** Die Artikel 1, 5 Nr. 3 und Artikel 7 dieses Gesetzes dienen der Umsetzung der Artikel 32 bis 34, 41 bis 49 und 53 der Richtlinie (EU) 2016/680 des Europäischen Parlaments und des Rates vom 27. April 2016 zum Schutz natürlicher Personen bei der Verarbeitung personenbezogener Daten durch die zuständigen Behörden zum Zwecke der Verhütung, Ermittlung, Aufdeckung oder Verfolgung von Straftaten oder der Stafvollstreckung sowie zum freien Datenverkehr und zur Aufhebung des Rahmenbeschlusses 2008/977/JI des Rates (ABl. L 119 vom 4.5.2016, S. 89; L 127 vom 23.5.2018, S. 9).

§ 3 Landesarchivgut

(1) ¹Öffentliches Archivgut ist Landesarchivgut, wenn es bei einer der in § 2 Abs. 1 Satz 1 Nr. 1 genannten Stellen entstanden ist, oder wenn es sich um archivwürdige Unterlagen handelt, die in deren Eigentum übergegangen oder diesen zur Nutzung überlassen worden sind. ²Landesarchivgut ist auch sonstiges Archivgut, das in die Zuständigkeit des früheren Staatsarchivs Magdeburg fiel. ³Landesarchivgut sind ferner archivwürdige Unterlagen, die das Landesarchiv Sachsen-Anhalt von anderen als den in Satz 1 genannten öffentlichen Stellen oder von natürlichen Personen oder von juristischen Personen des privaten Rechts übernommen oder erworben haben, sofern es sich nicht um Depositalgut handelt.

(2) ¹Die in Wahrnehmung staatlicher Aufgaben entstandenen archivwürdigen Unterlagen der SED, der übrigen Parteien und Massenorganisationen der Deutschen Demokratischen Republik sowie der mit diesen verbundenen Organisationen und juristischen Personen werden wie Landesarchivgut behandelt, soweit sie bei einem Organisationsteil anfielen oder archiviert wurden, der über die Orts- und Kreisebene, grundsätzlich aber nicht über die Ebene des heutigen Landes hinausging. ²Satz 1 gilt, sobald die dort genannten Unterlagen im Landesarchiv Sachsen-Anhalt archiviert sind.

§ 4 Kommunales und sonstiges öffentliches Archivgut

(1) ¹Öffentliches Archivgut ist kommunales Archivgut, wenn es bei einer der in § 2 Abs. 1 Satz 1 Nr. 2 genannten Stellen entstanden ist. ²Kommunales Archivgut ist auch Archivgut, das in die Zuständigkeit der früheren Kreis- und Stadtarchive fiel.

(2) Öffentliches Archivgut ist sonstiges öffentliches Archivgut, wenn es bei einer der in § 2 Abs. 1 Satz 1 Nr. 3 genannten Stelle entstanden ist.

§ 5 Depositalgut

(1) ¹Natürliche Personen sowie juristische Personen des öffentlichen oder privaten Rechts können ihr Archivgut einem öffentlichen Archiv als Depositum unter Wahrung des Eigentums anbieten. ²Zwischen Eigentümern des Archivgutes und dem jeweiligen öffentlichen Archiv ist ein Depositalvertrag abzuschließen.

(2) Deposita unterliegen den gleichen Bestimmungen wie öffentliches Archivgut, sofern nicht durch den jeweiligen Depositalvertrag etwas anderes bestimmt wird.

§ 6 Rechtsansprüche betroffener Personen

(1) ¹Rechtsansprüche betroffener Personen gemäß Artikel 15 der Verordnung (EU) 2016/679 des Europäischen Parlaments und des Rates vom 27. April 2016 zum Schutz natürlicher Personen bei der Verarbeitung personenbezogener Daten, zum freien Datenverkehr und zur Aufhebung der Richtlinie 95/46/EG (Datenschutz-Grundverordnung) (ABl. L 119 vom 4.5.2016, S. 1; L 314 vom 22.11.2016, S. 72; L 127 vom 23.5.2018, S. 2) beschränken sich auf Auskunft über die im erschlossenen Archivgut enthaltenen, sie betreffenden personenbezogenen Daten. ²Die Auskunft ist auf Antrag zu erteilen, soweit
1. das Archivgut personenbezogen erschlossen ist oder die betroffenen Personen Angaben machen, die das Auffinden der Daten ermöglichen, und
2. der für die Erteilung der Auskunft erforderliche Aufwand nicht außer Verhältnis zu dem geltend gemachten Informationsinteresse steht.

³Das öffentliche Archiv bestimmt das Verfahren, insbesondere die Form der Auskunftserteilung nach pflichtgemäßem Ermessen. ⁴Anstelle der Auskunft kann Einsichtnahme in das Archivgut gewährt werden, wenn der Erhaltungszustand des Archivgutes dies erlaubt. ⁵Ist das Archivgut in maschinenlesbaren Dateien gespeichert, so kann nur Einsicht in eine Abbildung gewährt werden.

(2) ¹Die Auskunft wird nicht gewährt, soweit
1. sie die öffentliche Sicherheit gefährden oder sonst dem Wohle der Bundesrepublik Deutschland oder eines ihrer Länder Nachteile bereiten würde oder
2. personenbezogene Daten oder die Tatsache ihrer Speicherung nach einer Rechtsvorschrift oder ihrem Wesen nach, insbesondere wegen der überwiegenden berechtigten Interessen Dritter, sofern diese der Auskunftserteilung nicht zugestimmt haben, geheim gehalten werden müssen.

²§ 11 Abs. 3 und 4 des Datenschutz-Grundverordnungs-Ausführungsgesetzes Sachsen-Anhalt findet entsprechende Anwendung.

(3) Weitergehende Rechtsansprüche betroffener Personen auf Auskunft gemäß Artikel 15 der Verordnung (EU) 2016/679 bestehen nicht.
(4) ¹Machen betroffene Personen glaubhaft, daß das Archivgut eine falsche Tatsachenbehauptung enthält, die sie nicht nur unerheblich in ihren Rechten beeinträchtigt, so können sie verlangen, daß dem sie betreffenden erschlossenen Archivgut eine von ihnen eingereichte Gegendarstellung beigefügt wird. ²Ein Gegendarstellungsrecht besteht nicht für amtliche Niederschriften und Berichte über öffentliche Sitzungen rechtsetzender oder beschließender Kollegialorgane. ³Gegendarstellungen müssen sich auf Tatsachen beschränken und sollen die Beweismittel anführen. ⁴Im Übrigen bestehen weitergehende Rechte betroffener Personen auf Berichtigung gemäß Artikel 16 der Verordnung (EU) 2016/679 nicht.
(5) ¹Rechte betroffener Personen auf Löschung gemäß Artikel 17 der Verordnung (EU) 2016/679 oder auf Einschränkung der Verarbeitung gemäß Artikel 18 der Verordnung (EU) 2016/679 bestehen bei archivierten personenbezogenen Daten nicht. ²Eine Mitteilungspflicht gemäß Artikel 19 der Verordnung (EU) 2016/679 besteht für öffentliche Archive nicht. ³Das Recht auf Datenübertragbarkeit gemäß Artikel 20 der Verordnung (EU) 2016/679 und ein Widerspruchsrecht betroffener Personen gegen die Archivierung sie betreffender Daten gemäß Artikel 21 Abs. 1 der Verordnung (EU) 2016/679 bestehen nicht.

Abschnitt 2
Landesarchiv Sachsen-Anhalt

§ 7 Landesarchiv Sachsen-Anhalt
(1) ¹Das Landesarchiv Sachsen-Anhalt hat die Aufgabe, das Landesarchivgut zu archivieren. ²Abweichend von Satz 1 können der Landtag sowie die Hochschulen ihr Archivgut in eigenen Archiven archivieren; diese Archive stehen, soweit keine entgegenstehenden Regelungen getroffen werden, dem Landesarchiv Sachsen-Anhalt gleich.
(2) ¹Das Landesarchiv Sachsen-Anhalt kann Archivgut anderer Herkunft annehmen, sofern das im öffentlichen Interesse liegt. ²Es sammelt sonstige Unterlagen zur Ergänzung des Archivgutes.
(3) Das Landesarchiv Sachsen-Anhalt ist berechtigt, Veröffentlichungen und wissenschaftliche Auswertungen des Archivgutes selbst vorzunehmen.
(4) Das Landesarchiv Sachsen-Anhalt berät im Rahmen seiner Möglichkeiten Kommunalarchive und Archive sonstiger öffentlicher Stellen auf deren Anforderung.

Abschnitt 3
Archivgut

§ 8 Verwahrung und Sicherung
(1) ¹Das Landesarchiv Sachsen-Anhalt hat das Verfügungsrecht über das Landesarchivgut und ist verpflichtet, dieses nach archivwissenschaftlichen Erkenntnissen zu bearbeiten und der Benutzung zugänglich zu machen. ²Die Zugänglichmachung kann unter Wahrung schutzwürdiger privater und öffentlicher Belange auch durch die Präsentation von digitalisiertem Archivgut und von Erschließungsdaten im Internet erfolgen.
(2) ¹Archivgut ist Kulturgut und als solches unveräußerlich. ²Das Landesarchiv Sachsen-Anhalt hat es auf Dauer sicher zu verwahren und vor Schäden, Verlust, Vernichtung oder unbefugter Nutzung zu schützen.
(3) Landesarchivgut kann in Ausnahmefällen auf Grund eines widerruflichen Depositalvertrages in einem anderen öffentlichen Archiv verwahrt werden.
(4) Eine Übereignung von Landesarchivgut an Archive des Bundes und der Länder ist nur zulässig, wenn dieses fachlich geboten und Gegenseitigkeit gewährleistet ist.

§ 9 Grundsätze der Anbietung und Übernahme
(1) ¹Die in § 2 Abs. 1 Satz 1 Nr. 1 genannten Stellen haben alle Unterlagen, sobald sie diese zur Erfüllung ihrer öffentlichen Aufgaben nicht mehr benötigen, unverzüglich, spätestens 30 Jahre nach der letzten inhaltlichen Bearbeitung, dem Landesarchiv Sachsen-Anhalt im Originalzustand zur Übernahme anzubieten und, wenn es sich um archivwürdige Unterlagen handelt, als Archivgut zu übergeben. ²Dateien sollen in einem Dateiformat übergeben werden, das das für Archivwesen zuständige Minis-

terium im Einvernehmen mit dem für Informations- und Kommunikationstechnologie zuständigen Ministerium bestimmt. ³Ist durch Rechtsvorschriften oder durch Verwaltungsvorschriften oberster Landesbehörden eine längere als dreißigjährige oder eine dauernde Aufbewahrung bestimmt, wird der Zeitpunkt des Anbietens und der Übergabe durch Vereinbarung zwischen den in § 2 Abs. 1 Satz 1 Nr. 1 genannten Stellen und dem Landesarchiv Sachsen-Anhalt geregelt.

(2) ¹Anzubieten und zu übergeben sind auch Unterlagen, die
1. a) dem § 30 der Abgabenordnung oder dem § 35 des Ersten Buches Sozialgesetzbuch – Allgemeiner Teil – unterliegen,
   b) anderen als den in Buchstabe a genannten Rechtsvorschriften des Bundes oder des Landes über Geheimhaltung unterliegen oder gelöscht, vernichtet oder in der Verarbeitung eingeschränkt werden müssten oder könnten oder in der Verarbeitung eingeschränkt worden sind oder
   c) besondere Kategorien personenbezogener Daten im Sinne des Artikels 9 Abs. 1 der Verordnung (EU) 2016/679 enthalten;
2. personenbezogene Daten aus Einrichtungen der Deutschen Demokratischen Republik enthalten, deren Verarbeitung nicht zulässig ist und die bis zur Entscheidung über die Übernahme durch das Landesarchiv Sachsen-Anhalt von den anbietungspflichtigen Stellen weiterhin in der Verarbeitung einzuschränken sind.

²Das Landesarchiv Sachsen-Anhalt hat von der Übernahme an ebenso wie die abgebende Stelle die schutzwürdigen Belange betroffener Personen zu berücksichtigen.

§ 9a Ausnahmen, Verfahren, Auskunft

(1) Von der Anbietungspflicht sind Unterlagen ausgenommen,
1. deren Speicherung, unzulässig gewesen ist,
2. deren Offenbarung gegen das Brief-, Post- oder Fernmeldegeheimnis verstoßen würde, es sei denn, es liegt ein Fall des § 9 Abs. 2 Satz 1 Nr. 2 vor,
3. die gelöscht oder vernichtet werden müssten und die
   a) ausschließlich zum Zwecke der Datenschutzkontrolle, der Datensicherung oder zur Sicherstellung des ordnungsgemäßen Betriebes einer Datenverarbeitungsanlage gespeichert wurden,
   b) im Rahmen optisch-elektronischer Beobachtung nur vorübergehend gespeichert wurden,
   c) den Kernbereich privater Lebensgestaltung betreffen oder
   d) in Ausübung von Befugnissen zur heimlichen Informationsbeschaffung entstanden sind und
      aa) bei denen sich nachträglich herausstellt, dass die Voraussetzungen für die Ausübung dieser Befugnisse nicht vorgelegen haben,
      bb) die für den damit verfolgten Zweck nicht mehr benötigt werden, sofern es sich um Bildaufzeichnungen oder Aufzeichnungen des nicht öffentlich gesprochenen Wortes handelt, oder
      cc) die im Rahmen von Maßnahmen nach den §§ 98a, 99, 100a, 100c bis 100i, 110a sowie 163d bis 163f der Strafprozessordnung erhoben worden sind,
4. die dem Wahlgeheimnis unterliegen,
5. die nach statistikrechtlichen Vorschriften zu anonymisieren sind oder
6. für deren Archivierung besondere Rechtsvorschriften des Bundes oder des Landes etwas anderes bestimmen.

(2) ¹Sofern andere Rechtsvorschriften die Löschung personenbezogener Daten oder die Vernichtung von solchen Unterlagen vorsehen, die personenbezogene Daten enthalten, ist diese bei den anbietungspflichtigen Stellen auszusetzen, solange eine fristgerechte Entscheidung gemäß Absatz 4 über die Archivwürdigkeit aussteht. ²In den Fällen des Satzes 1 dürfen personenbezogene Daten von den anbietungspflichtigen Stellen ohne Einwilligung der betroffenen Personen nur zu Zwecken der Anbietung oder Übergabe an das Landesarchiv Sachsen-Anhalt verarbeitet oder genutzt werden.

(3) ¹Das Landesarchiv Sachsen-Anhalt entscheidet im Benehmen mit der anbietenden Stelle, ob die angebotenen Unterlagen archivwürdig sind. ²Wird die Archivwürdigkeit bejaht, so müssen die Unterlagen vom Archiv übernommen werden.

(4) Wird die Archivwürdigkeit verneint oder wird innerhalb von zwölf Monaten eine Entscheidung nicht getroffen, so kann die anbietende Stelle die Unterlagen nach Ablauf der Aufbewahrungsfristen vernichten.

(5) [1]Schon vor dem Zeitpunkt des Anbietens der Unterlagen ist Beschäftigten des Landesarchivs Sachsen-Anhalt zur Erfassung und Sicherung archivwürdiger Unterlagen Auskunft und Einsicht in alle Unterlagen und Hilfsmittel der Registraturen der in § 2 Abs. 1 Satz 1 Nr. 1 genannten Stellen zu gewähren, sofern nicht Belange des Geheim- oder Persönlichkeitsschutzes entgegenstehen. [2]Geheimhaltungsvorschriften des Landes stehen der Einsichtnahme insoweit nicht entgegen. [3]Das Landesarchiv Sachsen-Anhalt hat durch geeignete sachliche und personelle Maßnahmen sicherzustellen, dass Belange des Geheim- und Persönlichkeitsschutzes nicht beeinträchtigt werden.

§ 9b Laufend aktualisierte Datenbestände in automatisierten Verfahren ohne Historisierungsfunktion

(1) An die Stelle der Anbietung und der Übergabe nach § 9 tritt bei Aufzeichnungen in solchen automatisierten Verfahren, die einer laufenden Aktualisierung unterliegen, die Pflicht, regelmäßig, jedoch höchstens jährlich einen aktuellen Datenbestand anzubieten und nach Feststellung der Archivwürdigkeit eine Kopie dieses Datenbestandes dem Landesarchiv Sachsen-Anhalt zu übergeben.

(2) Absatz 1 gilt nicht für Unterlagen
1. im Sinne des § 9a Abs. 1 Nrn. 2 bis 6,
2. die anstelle von Akten geführt werden und eine vollständige Historisierung aufweisen, indem sie
   a) im Datenbestand selbst alle Änderungen nachweisen oder
   b) einen vollständigen Änderungsnachweis bis zu einer Übernahme durch das Landesarchiv Sachsen-Anhalt außerhalb des Datenbestandes führen,
3. die ausschließlich der Unterstützung der allgemeinen Bürotätigkeit, insbesondere der Textverarbeitung, Vorgangsverwaltung, Terminüberwachung und der Führung von Adress-, Telefon- oder vergleichbaren Verzeichnissen dienen, nur vorübergehend vorgehalten werden und bei denen offensichtlich ist, dass die verarbeiteten Daten nicht archivwürdig sind, oder
4. bei denen das Landesarchiv Sachsen-Anhalt allgemein oder im Einzelfall im Benehmen mit den in § 2 Abs. 1 Satz 1 Nr. 1 genannten Stellen von der Übergabe eines kopierten aktuellen Datenbestandes abgesehen hat.

(3) Ob und in welchen zeitlichen Abständen, zu welchem Zeitpunkt und in welcher Form kopierte aktuelle Datenbestände oder Änderungsnachweise übergeben werden, legt das Landesarchiv Sachsen-Anhalt im Benehmen mit den in § 2 Abs. 1 Satz 1 Nr. 1 genannten Stellen fest.

(4) Stellt sich erst nach Übergabe eines kopierten aktuellen Datenbestandes oder eines Änderungsnachweises an das Landesarchiv Sachsen-Anhalt heraus, dass personenbezogene Daten betroffener Personen unzulässig gespeichert wurden oder die Voraussetzungen für die Erhebung in Ausübung von Befugnissen zur heimlichen Informationsbeschaffung nicht vorlagen, müssen diese Daten auf Antrag betroffenen Personen oder auf Anzeige der abgebenden Stelle im Archivbestand gelöscht werden.

§ 9c Evaluierung

(1) Die Auswirkungen des § 9b für die Gemeinden, Verbandsgemeinden und Landkreise werden nach einem Erfahrungszeitraum von drei Jahren nach Inkrafttreten des § 9b durch die Landesregierung unter Mitwirkung der Kommunalen Spitzenverbände auf ihre Kostenneutralität hin überprüft.

(2) Die Landesregierung unterrichtet den Landtag schriftlich über das Ergebnis der Überprüfung.

§ 10 Benutzung[1)]

(1) [1]Das Recht, öffentliches Archivgut nach Maßgabe dieses Gesetzes zu nutzen, steht jeder Person auf Antrag zu, soweit durch Rechtsvorschrift nichts anderes bestimmt ist. [2]Weitergehende gesetzliche Rechte und besondere Vereinbarungen zugunsten von Eigentümern privaten Archivguts bleiben unberührt. [3]Die Nutzer sind verpflichtet, von Werken, die sie unter wesentlicher Verwendung von Landesarchivgut verfassen, dem Landesarchiv Sachsen-Anhalt ein Exemplar kostenfrei abzuliefern; § 11 Abs. 3 bis 5 des Landespressegesetzes gilt entsprechend.

---

1) Die Benutzungsordnung des Landesarchivs Sachsen-Anhalt ist abgedruckt als D14.II.1a.

(2) Die Nutzung ist nicht zulässig, soweit
1. Grund zu der Annahme besteht, daß das Wohl der Bundesrepublik Deutschland oder eines ihrer Länder gefährdet würde, oder
2. Grund zu der Annahme besteht, daß schutzwürdige Belange betroffener Personen oder Dritter entgegenstehen, oder
3. der Erhaltungszustand des Archivgutes gefährdet würde oder
4. ein nicht vertretbarer Verwaltungsaufwand entstehen würde.

(3) ¹Öffentliches Archivgut darf durch Dritte regelmäßig erst nach Ablauf von 30 Jahren nach der letzten inhaltlichen Bearbeitung der Unterlagen genutzt werden. ²Öffentliches Archivgut, das sich nach seiner Zweckbestimmung oder seinem wesentlichen Inhalt auf natürliche Personen bezieht, darf erst 30 Jahre nach dem Tode der betroffenen Personen durch Dritte genutzt werden; ist das Todesjahr nicht oder nur mit unvertretbarem Aufwand festzustellen, endet die Schutzfrist 110 Jahre nach der Geburt der betroffenen Personen. ³Kann auch das Geburtsjahr nicht oder nur mit unvertretbarem Aufwand festgestellt werden, endet die Schutzfrist 60 Jahre nach der Entstehung der Unterlagen. ⁴Archivgut nach § 9 Abs. 2 Satz 1 Nr. 1 darf erst 60 Jahre nach Entstehen genutzt werden. ⁵Die Schutzfristen der Sätze 1 bis 4 entfallen für solche Unterlagen, die bereits bei ihrer Entstehung zur Veröffentlichung bestimmt waren. ⁶Die Schutzfrist des Satzes 1 gilt nicht für die Unterlagen, die vor dem 3. Oktober 1990 entstanden sind.

(4) ¹Die Schutzfrist nach Absatz 3 Satz 1 kann verkürzt werden, sofern Absatz 2 dem nicht entgegensteht. ²Die Schutzfristen nach Absatz 3 Satz 2 und 3 können verkürzt werden,
1. wenn die Einwilligung der betroffenen Personen vorliegt;
2. wenn die Benutzung des Archivgutes
   a) für ein benanntes wissenschaftliches Forschungsvorhaben oder
   b) zur Wahrung berechtigter Interessen, die im überwiegenden Interesse einer anderen Person oder Stelle liegen, unerläßlich ist und die schutzwürdigen Interessen betroffener Personen durch angemessene Maßnahmen hinreichend gewahrt werden;
3. für Archivgut über Personen der Zeitgeschichte und Amtsträger in Ausübung ihres Amtes, wenn die schutzwürdigen Interessen der betroffenen Personen angemessen berücksichtigt werden.

³Die Schutzfristen nach Absatz 3 Satz 1 und 4 können um höchstens 30 Jahre verlängert werden, soweit dies im öffentlichen Interesse liegt.

(4a) ¹Schon vor Ablauf der Schutzfristen nach Absatz 3 Satz 1 bis 4 sind Unterlagen, die vor ihrer Übergabe an das Landesarchiv Sachsen-Anhalt bereits einem gesetzlichen Informationszugang offen gestanden haben, der Nutzung zugänglich zu machen, soweit dem besondere Verfahrensvorschriften nicht entgegenstehen. ²Die Entscheidung über den Informationszugang nach Satz 1 trifft das Landesarchiv Sachsen-Anhalt im Benehmen mit der abgebenden Stelle.

(5) Die Verknüpfung personenbezogener Daten während der Schutzfristen nach Absatz 3 ist nur zulässig, wenn schutzwürdige Belange betroffener Personen angemessen berücksichtigt werden.

(6) ¹Die Nutzung von Archivgut durch die Stellen, von denen es übernommen worden ist, unterliegt keinen Einschränkungen nach diesem Gesetz. ²Satz 1 gilt nicht für solche Unterlagen, die bei den abgabepflichtigen Stellen auf Grund gesetzlicher Vorschriften zu löschen oder zu vernichten waren. ³Weitergehende gesetzliche Rechte zur Nutzung bleiben unberührt.

(7) ¹Das Landesarchiv Sachsen-Anhalt kann in begründeten Fällen auf Antrag vor Ablauf der Schutzfristen gemäß Absatz 3 an Archive, Bibliotheken und Museen sowie Forschungs- und Dokumentationsstellen Vervielfältigungen von Archivgut überlassen, wenn diese einen gesetzlichen Auftrag zur Dokumentation, wissenschaftlichen Erforschung und Darstellung des Schicksals einer Gruppe natürlicher Personen unter nationalsozialistischer Herrschaft wahrnehmen. ²Bei der zweckgebundenen Nutzung der überlassenen Vervielfältigungen ist die Wahrung schutzwürdiger Belange betroffener Personen oder Dritter gemäß den Absätzen 2 bis 4 von der aufnehmenden Einrichtung oder Stelle zu gewährleisten.

Abschnitt 4
Kommunalarchive und Archive sonstiger öffentlicher Stellen

§ 11 Kommunale Archive
(1) [1]Die in § 2 Abs. 1 Satz 1 Nr. 2 genannten Stellen archivieren ihr Archivgut in eigener Verantwortung und Zuständigkeit. [2]Hierbei handelt es sich um eine Aufgabe des eigenen Wirkungskreises. [3]Sofern die in Satz 1 genannten Stellen kein eigenes Archiv unterhalten, bieten sie ihre Unterlagen gemeinsamen Archiven oder als Depositum anderen kommunalen Archiven oder dem Landesarchiv Sachsen-Anhalt zur Archivierung an.
(2) [1]Die in § 2 Abs. 1 Satz 1 Nr. 2 genannten Stellen regeln das Verfahren der Anbietung und Übernahme des kommunalen Archivgutes in eigener Zuständigkeit. [2]§ 8 Abs. 2, § 9 Abs. 2 sowie §§ 9a und 9b gelten entsprechend. [3]Für die Nutzung des kommunalen Archivgutes gilt § 10 entsprechend.
(3) Kommunale Archive können ihren Archivbestand durch notwendige Kopien aus dem Landesarchivgut (§ 3 Abs. 2) erweitern.

§ 12 Sonstige öffentliche Archive
(1) [1]Sonstiges öffentliches Archivgut kann von den in § 2 Abs. 1 Satz 1 Nr. 3 genannten Stellen in eigenen Archiven archiviert werden. [2]Sofern die in Satz 1 genannten Stellen kein eigenes Archiv unterhalten, bieten sie ihre Unterlagen gemeinsamen Archiven oder dem Landesarchiv Sachsen-Anhalt zur Archivierung an.
(2) § 11 Abs. 1 Satz 2 und Abs. 2 gelten entsprechend.

§ 13 Herausgabeverpflichtung
Befindet sich Archivgut in einem nicht zuständigen Archiv eines anderen Rechtsträgers, ist es an das zuständige Archiv auf Verlangen herauszugeben.

Abschnitt 5
Schlußvorschriften

§ 14 Einschränkung von Grundrechten
Durch dieses Gesetz wird das Recht auf Schutz personenbezogener Daten im Sinne des Artikels 6 Abs. 1 der Verfassung des Landes Sachsen-Anhalt und Artikel 2 Abs. 1 des Grundgesetzes und das Grundrecht des Brief-, Post- und Fernmeldegeheimnisses (Artikel 10 des Grundgesetzes) eingeschränkt.

§§ 15–16 *[aufgehoben]*

§ 17 Inkrafttreten
Dieses Gesetz tritt am Tage nach seiner Verkündung[1]) in Kraft.

---

1) Verkündet am 4.7.1995.

Benutzungsordnung des Landesarchivs Sachsen-Anhalt

Die Benutzungsordnung regelt die Benutzung in den Lesesälen des Landesarchivs Sachsen-Anhalt (LASA) auf der Grundlage des Archivgesetzes Sachsen-Anhalt (ArchG LSA), zuletzt geändert durch Gesetz vom 3. Juli 2015 (GVBl. LSA S. 314). Zusätzlich können standortspezifische Lesesaalordnungen in Kraft sein.

§ 1 Zugang zu Archivgut
(1) Die Benutzung von Archivgut steht gemäß § 10 Abs. 1 ArchG LSA jeder Person auf Antrag zu, soweit durch Rechtsvorschrift nichts anderes bestimmt ist.
(2) Für die Benutzung von Depositalgut können abweichende Regelungen gelten.
(3) Die Benutzung ist mit dem dafür vorgesehenen Formular zu beantragen. Die Genehmigung des Benutzungsantrags gilt für das laufende Kalenderjahr in allen Lesesälen des Landesarchivs.
(4) Die Benutzungserlaubnis kann entzogen werden, wenn eine Benutzerin oder ein Benutzer wiederholt oder schwerwiegend gegen diese Benutzungsordnung oder eine standortspezifische Lesesaalordnung verstößt oder erteilte Auflagen nicht einhält.
(5) Frei aufgestellte Findhilfsmittel, die Online-Recherche und weitere Findhilfsmittel auf Lesesaal-PCs sowie der Freihandbereich der Dienstbibliotheken können auch ohne Antrag genutzt werden.
(6) Die Öffnungszeiten der Lesesäle werden durch Aushang in den Dienstgebäuden und auf der Homepage des Landesarchivs bekannt gegeben.

§ 2 Bestellung von Archivgut
(1) Archivgut ist mit dem dafür vorgesehenen Bestellschein zu bestellen. Für jede Archivguteinheit ist ein Bestellschein auszufüllen. Es ist möglich, Archivgut für einen bestimmten Benutzungstag per E-Mail, Brief oder Telefon unter Angabe der Signatur formlos vorzubestellen.
(2) Für die Bestellung zur Vorlage am selben Tag können in den einzelnen Lesesälen besondere Bestellzeiten gelten. Die Bestellzeiten werden in den Lesesälen durch Aushang und auf der Homepage des Landesarchivs bekannt gegeben.
(3) Eine pauschale Begrenzung der Anzahl des an einem Benutzungstag vorlegbaren Archivgutes besteht nicht. Jedoch kann in Abhängigkeit von verfügbaren Personalressourcen im Einzelfall eine Begrenzung erforderlich werden.

§ 3 Vorlage von Archivgut
(1) Die Vorlage von Archivgut erfolgt in der Regel noch am Tag der Bestellung, sofern dieses im Rahmen der Bestellzeiten bestellt wurde und der Vorlage keine der in den folgenden Absätzen genannten Ausschlussgründe entgegenstehen.
(2) Archivgut kann nicht vorgelegt werden, wenn es aus dienstlichen Gründen oder wegen anderweitiger Benutzung zum Bestellzeitpunkt nicht verfügbar ist oder sein Erhaltungs- bzw. Ordnungszustand eine Benutzung nicht zulässt. Das Landesarchiv bemüht sich in solchen Fällen, die Benutzbarkeit zeitnah z. B. durch Restaurierungs- oder Erschließungsarbeiten herzustellen. Es teilt der Benutzerin oder dem Benutzer mit, in welchem zeitlichen Rahmen dies voraussichtlich erfolgen kann.
(3) Vor einer Einsichtnahme in Archivgut, das noch allgemeinen oder personenbezogenen Schutzfristen gemäß ArchG LSA unterliegt, ist ein Antrag auf Zugang zu Archivgut vor Ablauf von Schutzfristen mit dem dafür vorgesehenen Formular zu stellen.
(4) Aus Gründen der Bestandserhaltung wird Archivgut in Form von Nutzungsmedien (Mikrofilme oder Digitalisate, ggf. auch Literatur) vorgelegt, sofern diese verfügbar sind. Die Einsichtnahme in das Original kann beim Vorliegen von Nutzungsmedien nur gewährt werden, wenn dies erforderlich ist, um das Benutzungsanliegen zu erreichen.
(5) Es besteht kein Anspruch darauf, Archivgut über den Tag der ersten Vorlage hinaus zu reservieren. Bei Bedarf kann Archivgut aber für einen Zeitraum von längstens vier Wochen für eine weitere Benutzung bereitgehalten werden, sofern dem nicht dienstliche Belange oder Benutzungswünsche Dritter entgegenstehen.
(6) Für die Vorlage von Depositalgut können abweichende Regelungen gelten.

§ 4 Umgang mit Archiv- oder Bibliotheksgut
(1) Archiv- oder Bibliotheksgut, Findhilfsmittel und Nutzungsmedien dürfen nicht aus dem Lesesaal entfernt werden. Archivgut ist bei der Benutzung mit aller Sorgfalt zu behandeln, um Beschädigungen

D14.II.1a Benutzungsordnung Landesarchiv

zu vermeiden. Bei der Benutzung besonders empfindlicher Objekte kann das Landesarchiv festlegen, dass geeignete Schutzhandschuhe zu tragen sind.
(2) Darüber hinaus ist es verboten,
1. den Ordnungszustand von Archivgut und Findhilfsmitteln zu verändern,
2. Bestandteile von Archivgut und Findhilfsmitteln zu entfernen,
3. inhaltliche Veränderungen des Archivguts vorzunehmen,
4. Archivgut als Schreibunterlage zu verwenden oder Durchzeichnungen anzufertigen.

(3) Beschädigungen von Archiv- oder Bibliotheksgut, Findhilfsmitteln und Nutzungsmedien, die von Benutzerinnen oder Benutzern festgestellt werden oder die während einer Benutzung neu entstehen, sind der Lesesaalaufsicht unverzüglich anzuzeigen.

§ 5 Verhalten im Archivgebäude, Haftung

(1) Überbekleidung, Taschen und Mappen sowie Schirme dürfen in den Lesesaal nicht mitgeführt werden. Das Essen und Trinken ist im Lesesaal nicht gestattet.
(2) Andere Benutzerinnen und Benutzer dürfen nicht gestört werden. Das Telefonieren im Lesesaal ist nicht zulässig.
(3) Für Schäden am Eigentum von Benutzerinnen oder Benutzern haftet das Land nur bei Vorsatz und grober Fahrlässigkeit. Die Benutzung von Schließfächern im Garderobenbereich erfolgt auf eigene Gefahr.

§ 6 Reproduktionen

(1) Die Anfertigung von Reproduktionen durch das Landesarchiv ist auf den dafür vorgesehenen Formularen zu beantragen. Sofern das Archivgut hierfür geeignet ist, können Reproduktionen auf Antrag von Benutzerinnen oder Benutzern an den vom Archiv bereitgestellten Geräten selbst angefertigt werden. Die Anfertigung von Reproduktionen ist gebührenpflichtig und nur zulässig, wenn durch sie der Erhaltungszustand des Archivguts nicht gefährdet wird. Nähere Informationen werden in den Lesesälen und auf der Homepage des Landesarchivs bekannt gegeben.
(2) Es ist nicht zulässig, mit eigenem Gerät Reproduktionen von Archivgut anzufertigen. Die Benutzung der bildaufzeichnenden Funktion von Geräten aller Art (Kameras, Scanner, Mobiltelefone oder -computer) ist im Lesesaal nicht erlaubt.

§ 7 Gebühren

Für gebührenpflichtige Amtshandlungen, die Benutzung von Archivgut sowie für sonstige Leistungen des Landesarchivs im Rahmen der Archivgutbenutzung werden Gebühren und Auslagen nach Maßgabe der Allgemeinen Gebührenordnung des Landes Sachsen-Anhalt (AllGO) vom 10. Okt. 2012 (GVBl. LSA S. 336) in der jeweils gültigen Fassung erhoben.

§ 8 Inkrafttreten

Diese Benutzungsordnung tritt am 1. Juli 2016 in Kraft. Gleichzeitig treten die bisherigen Benutzungsordnungen der Abteilungen Magdeburg, Merseburg und Dessau des Landesarchivs Sachsen-Anhalt außer Kraft.

Beschluß der Landesregierung über die Stiftung des öffentlichen Rechts „Kulturstiftung Dessau-Wörlitz" in Dessau

MBl. LSA 1994, S. 1914
Geändert durch Beschluß vom 19.11.1996 (MBl. LSA 1996, S. 2436, MBl. LSA 1998, S. 1286)

Auf Grund des § 24 des Stiftungsgesetzes vom 13.9.1990 (GBl. I S. 1483) wird beschlossen:
1. Als rechtsfähige Stiftung des öffentlichen Rechts im Sinne des Stiftungsgesetzes besteht die „Kulturstiftung Dessau-Wörlitz".
2. Die Stiftung hat die aus der <u>Anlage</u> ersichtliche Satzung.[1] Stiftungsbehörde ist das Kultusministerium des Landes Sachsen-Anhalt.
3. Mit Beteiligung des Landtages gemäß Artikel 92 Abs. 1 der Verfassung des Landes Sachsen-Anhalt i. V. m. § 64 der Landeshaushaltsordnung des Landes Sachsen-Anhalt wird der Stiftung das Eigentum an den in den Zuordnungsbescheiden der Oberfinanzdirektion Magdeburg, Vermögenszuordnungsstelle Halle, vom 26.1.1993, vom 1.2.1993, vom 2.2.1993, vom 12.2.1993, vom 19.2.1993, vom 15.3.1993 und vom 25.3.1993 genannten Flurstücken übertragen. Das Land Sachsen-Anhalt wird die Stiftung im Rahmen seiner Möglichkeiten in gleicher Weise auch mit ihrem weiteren angestammten Vermögen ausstatten.
4. Bis zur Bestellung der satzungsmäßigen Organe wird die Stiftung für eine Übergangszeit durch einen Stiftungsbeauftragten vertreten, den die Stiftungsbehörde bestellt. Das Ministerium der Finanzen und das Kultusministerium werden beauftragt, die Möglichkeiten der Einrichtung einer Geschäftsstelle beim Stiftungsbeauftragten zu prüfen.
5. Der Beschluß tritt am Tage seiner Veröffentlichung in Kraft.

---

[1] Die aktuelle Fassung der Satzung der Kulturstiftung Dessau-Wörlitz ist abgedruckt als Nr. D14.III.1a. Vom Abdruck der hier als Anlage erwähnten alten Fassung wurde abgesehen.

Satzung der Kulturstiftung Dessau-Wörlitz

Bek. im MBl. LSA Nr. 17/2016 vom 2.5.2016

Die vom Kuratorium der Kulturstiftung Dessau-Wörlitz am 16.11.2015 beschlossene und vom Kultusministerium am 19.2.2016 genehmigte Satzung der Kulturstiftung Dessau-Wörlitz wurde im Ministerialblatt des Landes Sachsen-Anhalt Nr. 17/2016 vom 2.5.2016 bekannt gemacht.

Präambel

Die Kulturstiftung Dessau-Wörlitz wurde im Jahre 1918 als Joachim-Ernst-Stiftung durch Prinzregent Aribert von Anhalt errichtet. Ihren jetzigen Namen erhielt sie 1947.
In Folge der Bodenreform hatte sie ihre umfangreichen Liegenschaften verloren. 1994 wurde sie als öffentlich-rechtliche Stiftung mit Sitz in Dessau wiederbelebt.
Sie bewahrt, pflegt, restauriert, erforscht und vermittelt das von Leopold III. Friedrich Franz, Fürst und Herzog von Anhalt-Dessau, gestaltete historische Gartenreich Dessau-Wörlitz, auf wissenschaftlicher Grundlage. Diese Kulturlandschaft, seit 2000 mit dem Rang eines Weltkulturerbes der UNESCO, als ein Muster praktizierter Aufklärung in Deutschland, mit den Bauten, Gartenanlagen und Liegenschaften, die sich in ihrem Eigentum oder Besitz befinden, bildet eine einzigartige Verbindung von Geist und Natur. Insbesondere gehören dazu Schloss Wörlitz mit dem gleichnamigen Landschaftspark, Schloss und Park Oranienbaum, Schloss und Park Luisium, Schloss und Garten Großkühnau, Schloss Mosigkau mit dem dazugehörigen barocken Schlossgarten und der Waldpark Sieglitzer Berg. Die weitere satzungsgemäße Aufgabe der Erhaltung und Ausgestaltung des Denkmalensembles in Mosigkau fiel der Stiftung durch die Zusammenlegung mit der Stiftung Schloss Mosigkau Ende 2004 zu. Diese war am 2. April 1780 durch Testament der Anna Wilhelmine von Anhalt-Dessau als Hochadliges Fräuleinstift Mosigkau errichtet und im Jahr 1950 in eine öffentlich-rechtliche Stiftung umgewandelt worden.

§ 1 Name, Rechtsform und Sitz der Stiftung

(1) Die Stiftung trägt den Namen „Kulturstiftung Dessau-Wörlitz".
(2) Sie ist eine staatliche Stiftung des öffentlichen Rechts und hat ihren Sitz in Dessau-Roßlau.

§ 2 Stiftungszweck

(1) Zweck der Kulturstiftung ist die Erhaltung, Pflege und Wiederherstellung der denkmalgeschützten historischen Kulturlandschaft Gartenreich Dessau-Wörlitz mit UNESCO-Welterbestatus. Hierzu zählen insbesondere die ihr anvertrauten historischen Garten- und Parkanlagen, die Schlösser und historischen Gebäude mit ihren umfangreichen Kunstsammlungen und authentischen Ausstattungen von höchster Qualität sowie die baulichen und natürlichen Gestaltungselemente im Gartenreich Dessau-Wörlitz auf einer Fläche von 142 qkm.
(2) Zweck der Kulturstiftung ist weiterhin die Erschließung und Erforschung des Gartenreiches Dessau-Wörlitz in Kooperation mit universitären und außeruniversitären Bildungseinrichtungen sowie die qualitätsvolle Vermittlung der Forschungsergebnisse.
(3) Der Kulturstiftung obliegen auch die Sicherung eines qualitätsvollen kulturellen Bildungsangebotes sowie eine angemessene touristische Vermittlung.

§ 3 Gemeinnützigkeit

(1) Die Kulturstiftung verfolgt ausschließlich und unmittelbar gemeinnützige Zwecke im Sinne der Abgabenordnung.
(2) Sie ist selbstlos tätig und verfolgt nicht in erster Linie eigenwirtschaftliche Zwecke. Die Mittel der Kulturstiftung dürfen nur für ihren satzungsmäßigen Zweck verwendet werden. Es dürfen keine Personen oder Institutionen durch Ausgaben, die dem Stiftungszweck fremd sind, oder durch Unverhältnismäßig hohe Vergütungen oder sonstige Vermögenszuwendungen begünstigt werden.

§ 4 Stiftungsvermögen

(1) Das Stiftungsvermögen bilden insbesondere die unbeweglichen und beweglichen Vermögensgegenstände der ehemaligen Landeseinrichtung „Staatliche Schlösser und Gärten Wörlitz, Oranienbaum und Luisium" sowie die unbeweglichen und beweglichen Vermögensgegenstände der in 2004 zugelegten Stiftung Schloss Mosigkau und das Schloss Großkühnau mit dazugehörigem Garten.
(2) Die Kulturstiftung kann Zustiftungen mit Zustimmung der Stiftungsbehörde annehmen.

(3) Die Kulturstiftung hat ihr Vermögen im Einklang mit den Rechtsvorschriften und dem in Stiftungsgeschäft und Stiftungssatzung zum Ausdruck kommenden Stifterwillen nach den Regeln ordentlicher Wirtschaftsführung zu verwalten. Die Verwaltung dient der dauernden und nachhaltigen Erfüllung des Stiftungszwecks. Das Kuratorium ist verpflichtet, im Falle des Verkaufes einzelner Teile des Stiftungsvermögens den Erlös dem Stiftungsvermögen zuzuführen.

(4) Dem Stiftungsvermögen sind dessen Erträge, soweit diese nicht zur Erfüllung der Stiftungsaufgaben benötigt werden, sowie Zuwendungen und sonstige Einnahmen sofern sie nicht anderweitig zweckgebunden sind, zuzuführen.

(5) Bei der Verwendung der Grundstücke des Stiftungsvermögens soll das Kuratorium den Belangen der Allgemeinheit Rechnung tragen soweit die Anforderungen der UNESCO und das finanzielle Interesse der Kulturstiftung dies zulassen.

§ 5 Stiftungsmittel
Die Kulturstiftung finanziert die Erfüllung ihres Stiftungszwecks insbesondere aus
1. Erträgen des Stiftungsvermögens,
2. Gebühren, Entgelten sowie Spenden,
3. Zuwendungen des Landes und des Bundes sowie
4. sonstigen dazu bestimmten Zuwendungen und Einnahmen.

§ 6 Organe der Kulturstiftung
Organe der Kulturstiftung sind das Kuratorium und der Vorstand.

§ 7 Kuratorium
(1) Das Kuratorium besteht aus folgenden Mitgliedern:
1. der Kultusministerin/dem Kultusminister des Landes Sachsen-Anhalt,
2. den für die Geschäftsbereiche Städtebau und Verkehr, Finanzen, Wirtschaft, Landwirtschaft und Umwelt des Landes Sachsen-Anhalt zuständigen Ministerinnen/Ministern des Landes Sachsen-Anhalt
3. einem Mitglied, das vom Bund entsandt wird,
4. der Oberbürgermeisterin/dem Oberbürgermeister der Stadt Dessau-Roßlau,
5. der Bürgermeisterin/dem Bürgermeister der Stadt Oranienbaum-Wörlitz.

(2) Die Präsidentin/der Präsident des Landesverwaltungsamtes, die Landeskonservatorin/der Landeskonservator des Landes Sachsen-Anhalt, zwei weiteren am anhaltischen Kulturleben besonders interessierte Persönlichkeiten, die vom Kuratorium vorgeschlagen und für die Dauer von 4 Jahren durch die/den Kuratoriumsvorsitzende/n berufen werden, und die/der Vorsitzende der Gesellschaft der Freunde des Dessau-Wörlitzer Gartenreiches e. V. nehmen als Mitglieder mit beratender Stimme an den Kuratoriumssitzungen teil.

(3) Den Vorsitz im Kuratorium führt die Kultusministerin/der Kultusminister. Die Stellvertretung liegt bei dem von der Bundesrepublik Deutschland entsandten Mitglied.

(4) Für jedes Mitglied ist eine Vertretung zu bestellen. Ist ein Kuratoriumsmitglied verhindert und wird nicht vertreten, so kann eine Person mit Sitzungsvollmacht zu den Sitzungen entsandt werden.

(5) Die Tätigkeit der Mitglieder im Kuratorium ist ehrenamtlich und unentgeltlich.

(6) Die Einberufung des Kuratoriums erfolgt textförmig durch die Vorsitzende/den Vorsitzenden unter Mitteilung der Tagesordnung und Übersendung der Sitzungsunterlagen mit Beschlussvorschlägen. Die Ladungsfrist beträgt drei Wochen. Die/der Kuratoriumsvorsitzende kann den Vorstand beauftragen in ihrem/seinem Namen und mit ihrer/seiner Vollmacht die Mitglieder des Kuratoriums zu den Sitzungen einzuladen und die Sitzungsunterlagen mit Beschlussvorschlägen zu versenden.

(7) Zur Vorbereitung der Sitzungen wird eine Arbeitsgruppe eingesetzt.

(8) Das Nähere regelt die Geschäftsordnung des Kuratoriums.

§ 8 Aufgaben des Kuratoriums
(1) Das Kuratorium beschließt über alle grundsätzlichen Angelegenheiten der Kulturstiftung, soweit sie nicht dem Vorstand übertragen sind. Das Kuratorium beschließt insbesondere über:
1. den jährlichen Haushaltsplan der Kulturstiftung,
2. Satzungsänderungen und die Geschäftsordnung des Kuratoriums,

D14.III.1a Satzung der Kulturstiftung Dessau-Wörlitz

3. die Bestellung der Direktorin/des Direktors als Vorstand und den Abschluss sowie die Verlängerung des Anstellungsvertrags mit der Direktorin/dem Direktor,
4. den Widerruf der Bestellung der Direktorin/des Direktors, die Kündigung des Anstellungsvertrags der Direktorin/des Direktors sowie sonstige, die Direktorin/den Direktor betreffende personalrechtliche Maßnahmen,
5. die Einstellung und Höhergruppierung der Beschäftigten ab der Entgeltgruppe E 13 TV-L,
6. die Vermögens- und Grundstücksangelegenheiten, insbesondere Veräußerung und/oder Belastung von für die Erreichung des Zweckes der Kulturstiftung wesentlichen Vermögensgegenständen der Kulturstiftung,
7. die Entlastung des Vorstands auf der Grundlage der Rechnungsprüfung,
8. die Verwendung von rücklagefähigen Überschüssen der Kulturstiftung sowie die Bewilligung über- und außerplanmäßiger Ausgaben,
9. die Annahme von Zustiftungen,
10. die Berufung der Mitglieder des Wissenschaftlichen Beirates.

(2) Die Beschlüsse des Kuratoriums kommen mit einfacher Mehrheit der abgegebenen Stimmen zustande. Das Kuratorium ist beschlussfähig, wenn einschließlich der/des Vorsitzenden oder deren Stellvertretung mehr als die Hälfte der Mitglieder anwesend sind. Bei Stimmengleichheit entscheidet die Stimme der/des Vorsitzenden. Das Kuratorium tritt mindestens zweimal jährlich zusammen. Die Beschlüsse des Kuratoriums nach Nr. 1. bis 9. Bedürfen der Zustimmung der in § 7 Abs. 1 Nr. 1. bis 3. Genannten Kuratoriumsmitglieder.

(3) Das Kuratorium überwacht die Ausführung seiner Beschlüsse durch den Vorstand und dessen Geschäftsführung.

(4) Das Nähere, insbesondere die Aufgabenverteilung zwischen Kuratorium und Vorstand, regelt die Geschäftsordnung des Kuratoriums.

§ 9 Vorstand

(1) Als Vorstand der Kulturstiftung wird eine Direktorin/ein Direktor nach internationaler Ausschreibung durch das Kuratorium bestellt.
(2) Die Bestellung erfolgt für höchstens 5 Jahre.
(3) Eine Wiederbestellung und Verlängerung des Anstellungsvertrags für weitere fünf Jahre ist einmalig ohne öffentliche Ausschreibung möglich.
(4) Der Vorstand führt die laufenden Geschäfte der Kulturstiftung. Er führt die Beschlüsse des Kuratoriums aus und bereitet die Sitzungen des Kuratoriums vor. Er ist für die Geschäftsführung dem Kuratorium gegenüber verantwortlich. Er übt die personalrechtlichen Befugnisse aus und vertritt die Kulturstiftung gerichtlich und außergerichtlich.
(5) Das Nähere regelt die Geschäftsordnung des Kuratoriums.

§ 10 Wissenschaftlicher Beirat

(1) Das Kuratorium und der Vorstand werden bei der Erfüllung ihrer Aufgaben durch den wissenschaftlichen Beirat unterstützt. Dieser besteht aus bis zu zehn Mitgliedern. In den wissenschaftlichen Beirat können vom Kuratorium Mitglieder berufen werden, die sich durch besondere wissenschaftliche Leistungen und durch besondere Kenntnisse und Erfahrungen der in § 2 ausgewiesenen Stiftungszwecke oder auf dem Gebiet der Denkmalpflege ausgezeichnet haben.
(2) Die Beiratsmitglieder werden durch das Kuratorium für die Dauer von vier Jahren berufen.
(3) Die Tätigkeit im Beirat ist ehrenamtlich.
(4) Das Nähere regelt die Geschäftsordnung des Kuratoriums.

§ 11 Bedienstete

(1) Für die Dienst- und Arbeitsverhältnisse der Bediensteten der Kulturstiftung sind die für die Tarifbeschäftigten des Landes Sachsen-Anhalt geltenden Vorschriften zu vereinbaren.
(2) Mit Einwilligung des Kuratoriums können mit einzelnen Bediensteten von den unter Absatz 1 genannten Vorschriften abweichende Vereinbarungen getroffen werden.
(3) Intern nicht besetzbare freie Stellen sind öffentlich, ab Entgeltgruppe E13 TV-L mindestens landesweit auszuschreiben.

§ 12 Haushalts- und Wirtschaftsführung, Rechnungsprüfung

(1) Für das Haushalts-, Kassen- und Rechnungswesen sowie für die Rechnungslegung der Kulturstiftung finden die für die Landesverwaltung geltenden Bestimmungen entsprechende Anwendung.
(2) Gemäß § 111 Abs. 1 LHO prüft der Landesrechnungshof Sachsen-Anhalt die Haushalts- und Wirtschaftsführung der Kulturstiftung und die bestimmungsgemäße Verwendung der Mittel.
(3) Die Jahresrechnung wird gemäß § 109 Abs. 2 LHO durch den Landesrechnungshof geprüft.

§ 13 Satzungsänderungen

(1) Die Satzung und ihre Änderung bedürfen der Genehmigung der Stiftungsbehörde und sind von ihr im Ministerialblatt für das Land Sachsen-Anhalt zu veröffentlichen.
(2) Beschlüsse über Satzungsänderungen bedürfen der Zustimmung der in § 7 Abs. 1 Nrn. 1. bis 3. genannten Mitglieder des Kuratoriums.

§ 14 Auflösung der Kulturstiftung und Vermögensrückfall

(1) Der Beschluss über die Selbstauflösung der Kulturstiftung bedarf der Zustimmung der Mitglieder des Kuratoriums gemäß § 7 Abs. 1 Nrn. 1. bis 3. sowie der Genehmigung durch die Stiftungsbehörde.
(2) Bei der Auflösung oder Aufhebung der Kulturstiftung oder bei Wegfall ihres bisherigen Zweckes fällt das Stiftungsvermögen an diejenigen zurück, die es in die Kulturstiftung eingebracht haben.
(3) Sonstiges Vermögen fällt an das Land.

§ 15 Dienstsiegel

Die Kulturstiftung Dessau-Wörlitz führt ein Dienstsiegel mit dem Namen und dem Markenzeichen der Kulturstiftung.

§ 16 In-Kraft-Treten

Diese Satzung tritt am Tage nach ihrer Veröffentlichung im Ministerialblatt für das Land Sachsen-Anhalt in Kraft.

Beschluss der Landesregierung zur Errichtung der Stiftung Schlösser, Burgen und Gärten des Landes Sachsen-Anhalt
MBl. LSA 1996, S. 157

Auf Grund des § 24 Abs. 2 Satz 1 des Stiftungsgesetzes vom 13.9.1990 (GBl. I S. 1483) wird beschlossen:

1. Als rechtsfähige Stiftung des öffentlichen Rechts im Sinne des Stiftungsgesetzes wird die „StiftungSchlösser, Burgen und Gärten des Landes Sachsen-Anhalt" mit Sitz im Schloß Leitzkau errichtet.
2. Zweck der Stiftung ist es, bedeutende Kulturdenkmale des Landes Sachsen-Anhalt zu erhalten und zubewahren sowie diese eine ihrer Bedeutung angemessenen Nutzung zuzuführen.
3. Das Vermögen der Stiftung besteht aus den Grundstücken, die das Land nach Maßgabe der Landeshaushaltsordnung des Landes Sachsen-Anhalt (LHO) vom 30.4.1995 (GVBl. LSA S. 35), zuletzt geändert durch Art. 2 des Gesetzes zur Anpassung des Abgeordnetengesetzes Sachsen-Anhalt und der Landeshaushaltsordnung des Landes Sachsen-Anhalt an das Pflege-Versicherungsgesetz vom 14.12.1994 (GVBl. LSA S. 1042), übereignet. Zum Zeitpunkt der Gründung der Stiftung bilden die in Anlage 2 aufgeführten landeseigenen Liegenschaften das Stiftungsvermögen.
4. Für das Haushalts-, Kassen- und Rechnungswesen sowie für die Rechnungslegung finden die für dieLandesverwaltung geltenden Vorschriften entsprechende Anwendung. Gemäß § 111 Abs. 1 LHO prüft der Landesrechnungshof des Landes Sachsen-Anhalt die Haushalts- und Wirtschaftsführung der Stiftung sowie die bestimmungsgemäße Verwendung der Mittel.
5. Die Stiftung erhält die aus der Anlage 1 ersichtliche Satzung.
6. Stiftungsbehörde ist das Kultusministerium.
7. Dieser Beschluß tritt am Tage nach seiner Veröffentlichung im MBl. LSA in Kraft.

Anlage 1

Satzung der Stiftung Schlösser, Burgen und Gärten des Landes Sachsen-Anhalt

§ 1 Name, Rechtsform und Sitz
Unter dem Namen „Stiftung Schlösser, Burgen und Gärten des Landes Sachsen-Anhalt" ist eine rechtsfähige Stiftung des öffentlichen Rechts errichtet. Der Sitz der Stiftung ist das Schloß Leitzkau.

§ 2 Stiftungszweck
(1) Zweck der Stiftung ist es, bedeutsame Liegenschaften in Sachsen-Anhalt, insbesondere in bezug auf ihre historische, kunsthistorische, denkmalpflegerische und landschaftsprägende Bedeutung, zu verwalten. Hierzu gehört es insbesondere, die Liegenschaften baulich zu betreuen, sowie sie der Öffentlichkeit zugänglich zu machen oder einer ihrer Bedeutung gerecht werdenden Nutzung zuzuführen. Die Stiftung ist berechtigt, mit Dritten Nutzungsverträge abzuschließen, soweit sie dem Stiftungszweck nicht entgegenstehen. Das Nähere regelt eine Geschäftsordnung, die vom Stiftungsrat erlassen wird.
(2) Die Stiftung verfolgt ausschließlich und unmittelbar gemeinnützige Zwecke im Sinne der Abgabenordnung.
(3) Die Zuständigkeit der Denkmalfachämter und Denkmalschutzbehörden bleibt unberührt.

§ 3 Stiftungsvermögen
(1) Das Vermögen der Stiftung besteht aus landeseigenen Grundstücken, die das Land mit dem gesetzlichen Zubehör in das Eigentum der Stiftung überträgt.
(2) Zustiftungen zur Vermehrung des Stiftungsvermögens darf die Stiftung unter der Voraussetzung des § 105 Abs. 1 i. V. m. § 40 LHO annehmen.

§ 4 Treuhänderische Verwaltung
Die Stiftung kann die treuhänderische Verwaltung von kulturhistorisch wertvollen Denkmalen, die sich im Eigentum oder Besitz von Kommunen befinden, übernehmen. Die Kommunen tragen die aus der treuhänderischen Verwaltung entstehenden Kosten. Der Umfang der Verwaltung ist im Einzelfall durch Vertrag zu regeln.

§ 5 Stiftungsmittel
(1) Die zur Erfüllung des Stiftungszweckes erforderlichen Mittel zur Deckung der einmaligen und laufenden Kosten erhält die Stiftung vor allem

1. aus Erträgen des Stiftungsvermögens,
2. aus Gebühren, Entgelten, Zuwendungen des Landes Sachsen-Anhalt im Rahmen des jeweiligen Haushaltes sowie
3. aus sonstigen Einnahmen.

(2) Die Stiftung ist berechtigt, Zuwendungen Dritter, insbesondere des Bundes und anderer Gebietskörperschaften, anzunehmen, um sie für den Stiftungszweck zu verwenden. Zur Erreichung des Stiftungszwecks sollen soweit wie möglich Arbeitsfördermittel in Anspruch genommen werden, um Arbeitslosen sinnvolle Arbeitsmöglichkeiten zu eröffnen.

§ 6 Satzungsänderungen

Satzungsänderungen bedürfen der Zustimmung der Mehrheit des Stiftungsrates und der Genehmigung des Kultusministeriums und des Ministeriums der Finanzen.

§ 7 Organe

Organe der Stiftung sind:
1. der Stiftungsrat,
2. der Vorstand,
3. der Beirat.

§ 8 Stiftungsrat

(1) Der Stiftungsrat besteht aus bis zu acht stimmberechtigten Mitgliedern, und zwar
1. einer Person, die das Kultusministerium vertritt, als vorsitzendes Mitglied, das doppelte Stimmrecht hat,
2. je einer Person, die das Ministerium der Finanzen, das Ministerium des Innern und das Ministerium für Wirtschaft und Technologie vertritt,
3. weiteren Personen zur Vertretung von Zuwendungsgebern und Kommunen.

Die Mitglieder, die Ministerien vertreten, werden durch diese benannt. Die übrigen Mitglieder werden auf Vorschlag des Stiftungsrates von der Landesregierung benannt. Die Mitglieder können sich vertreten lassen. Der Landeskonservator oder die Landeskonservatorin gehört dem Stiftungsrat mit beratender Stimme an.

(2) Beschlüsse im Stiftungsrat kommen mit einfacher Mehrheit der abgegebenen Stimmen, zustande. Der Stiftungsrat ist beschlußfähig, wenn mehr als die Hälfte der satzungsgemäßen Mitglieder anwesend sind.

(3) Wenn der Stiftungsrat nichts anderes beschließt, können der Vorstand und das vorsitzende Mitglied des Beirates an den Sitzungen teilnehmen.

§ 9 Aufgaben des Stiftungsrates

(1) Der Stiftungsrat überwacht die Ausführung seiner Beschlüsse durch den Vorstand sowie dessen Geschäftsführung.

(2) Der Stiftungsrat beschließt über alle grundsätzlichen Angelegenheiten der Stiftung, soweit sie nicht dem Vorstand übertragen sind. Der Stiftungsrat beschließt insbesondere den Haushalts- und Stellenplanentwurf und die Geschäftsordnung der Stiftung sowie über die Einstellung und Beförderung der Arbeitnehmer ab der Vergütungsgruppe IIa BAT.

(3) Das Nähere regelt die Geschäftsordnung.

§ 10 Der Vorstand

(1) Ein Direktor oder eine Direktorin wird als Vorstand der Stiftung nach Anhörung des Beirats auf Vorschlag des Stiftungsrates durch das Kultusministerium berufen.

(2) Der Vorstand leitet die Stiftung, führt die Beschlüsse des Stiftungsrats aus und bereitet dessen Sitzungen vor. Er vertritt die Stiftung gerichtlich und außergerichtlich. Das Nähere regelt die Geschäftsordnung.

§ 11 Beirat

Der Stiftungsrat beruft einen Beirat, der sich aus bis zu acht sachverständigen Personen zusammensetzt und den Stiftungsrat und den Vorstand berät. Der Beirat wählt ein vorsitzendes Mitglied. Dem Beirat sollen insbesondere Vertreter der Denkmalpflege, Kunstgeschichte, Architektur, Restaurierung, des Museumswesens, des Finanzwesens sowie der Kulturpolitik angehören. Das Nähere regelt die Geschäftsordnung.

§ 12 Bedienstete

Auf die Arbeits- und Dienstverhältnisse sind die für den öffentlichen Dienst des Landes Sachsen-Anhalt geltenden Vorschriften anzuwenden.

D14.III.2 Errichtung der Stiftung Schlösser, Burgen und Gärten

§ 13 Dienstsiegel
Die Stiftung führt ein Dienstsiegel mit dem Landeswappen und dem Namen der Stiftung.

§ 14 Haushalts- und Wirtschaftsprüfung
(1) Für das Haushalts-, Kassen- und Rechnungswesen sowie für die Rechnungslegung der Stiftung finden die für die Landesverwaltung geltenden Bestimmungen entsprechende Anwendung.
(2) Gemäß § 111 Abs. 1 LHO prüft der Landesrechnungshof des Landes Sachsen-Anhalt die Haushalts- und Wirtschaftsführung der Stiftung und die bestimmungsgemäße Verwendung der Mittel.
(3) Die nach § 109 Abs. 2 LHO durchzuführende jährliche Prüfung wird durch die Rechnungsprüfungsämter des Landesrechnungshofes vorgenommen.

§ 15 Beendigung der Stiftung und Vermögensrückfall
(1) Der Beschluß über die Selbstauflösung bedarf der Zustimmung aller Mitglieder des Stiftungsrates und der Genehmigung des Kultusministeriums.
(2) Bei der Auflösung oder Aufhebung der Stiftung oder bei Wegfall ihres bisherigen Zweckes fällt das Stiftungsvermögen an diejenigen zurück, die ihr Eigentum in die Stiftung eingebracht haben. Das sonstige Stiftungsvermögen fällt an das Land zurück.

Anlage 2

Landeseigene Liegenschaften, die in das Stiftungsvermögen übertragen werden

Ort	Liegenschaft
Regierungsbezirk Magdeburg	
Pansfelde	Burg Falkenstein
Letzlingen	Jagdschloß Letzlingen
Ermsleben	Konradsburg
Regierungsbezirk Halle	
Eckartsberga	Burg
Halle	Moritzburg
Regierungsbezirk Dessau	
Leitzkau	Schloß
Plötzkau	Schloß

Richtlinie über die kumulierte Anwendung von Förderprogrammen

Gem. RdErl. des MK, MS, MRLU und MWV vom 24. November 1997 (MBl. LSA S. 1938)

– Im Einvernehmen mit dem MF –

I.
Ausgaben für eine Maßnahme, die gleichzeitig die Zuwendungsvoraussetzungen nach
1. den Richtlinien über die Gewährung von Zuwendungen für die Erhaltung und Pflege von Kulturdenkmalen (RdErl. des MK vom 13.10.1997, MBl. LSA S. 1847)[1],
2. der Richtlinie über die Gewährung von Zuwendungen zur Dorferneuerung im Rahmen der Gemeinschaftsaufgabe „Verbesserung der Agrarstruktur und des Küstenschutzes" (RdErl. des ML vom 2.12.1991, MBl. LSA 1992 S. 95) i.V.m. RdErl. des ML vom 30.1.1996 (MBl. LSA S. 392),
3. der Richtlinie über die Gewährung von Zuwendungen für die Förderung städtebaulicher Sanierungs- und Entwicklungsmaßnahmen (RdErl. des MRS vom 9.10.1991, MBl. LSA S. 939, zuletzt geändert durch RdErl. des MWV vom 16.6.1997, MBl. LSA S. 1409) i.V.m. RdErl. des MRS vom 9.3.1993 (MBl. LSA S.1098),
4. der Richtlinie über die Gewährung von Zuwendungen für die Förderung städtebaulicher Sanierungsmaßnahmen im ländlichen Bereich (RdErl. des MRS vom 24.8.1992, MBl. LSA S. 1417),
5. der Richtlinie über die Gewährung von Zuwendungen für die Förderung des städtebaulichen Denkmalschutzes, Sicherung und Erhaltung historischer Stadtkerne (RdErl. des MRS vom 24.9.1991, MBl. LSA S. 707),
6. der Richtlinien über die Gewährung von Zuwendungen zur Förderung der Durchführung von allgemeinen Maßnahmen zur Arbeitsbeschaffung nach §§ 91 bis 96 des Arbeitsförderungsgesetz (RdErl. des MS vom 7.7.1997, MBl. LSA S. 1366) oder
7. der Richtlinie über die Gewährung von Zuwendungen für die Durchführung von Projekten gemäß § 249h des Arbeitsförderungsgesetzes im Bereich der Verbesserung der Umwelt, der sozialen Dienste und Jugendhilfe, der Erhöhung des Angebotes im Breitensport und in der Durchführung denkmalpflegerischer Maßnahmen, der städtebaulichen Erneuerungsmaßnahmen und städtebaulichen Denkmalschutzes und der Arbeiten zur Verbesserung des Wohnungsumfeldes (RdErl. des MS vom 6.11.1997, MBl. LSA S. 1897)

erfüllt, können kumulativ gemäß dieser Richtlinie gefördert werden. Es muß ein erhebliches Landesinteresse an der Förderung der Maßnahme aus mehreren Förderprogrammen bestehen.
Bei Gebietskörperschaften ist ein Eigenanteile von 10 v.H. zu sichern.
Es gilt das in den Richtlinien jeweils festgelegte Antragsverfahren.
Die Antragstellenden haben im Finanzierungsplan die bei den Zuwendungsgebern jeweils beantragte Summe auszuweisen. Bei einer kumulativen Förderung ist sicherzustellen, daß die zuwendungsfähigen Gesamtausgaben übereinstimmen. Die Zuwendungsgeber leiten die Ergebnisse ihrer Verwendungsnachweisprüfung den weiteren beteiligten Zuwendungsgebern zu.

II.
Dieser Gem. RdErl. tritt am Tage seiner Veröffentlichung in Kraft.

---

1) Hinweis: Die Richtlinie von 1997 wurde mittlerweile mehrfach ersetzt. Die aktuelle Fassung ist abgedruckt als Nr. D14.III.4.

D14.III.4 Denkmalpflegerichtlinie Sachsen-Anhalt

Richtlinie über die Gewährung von Zuwendungen zur Förderung von Maßnahmen zur Erhaltung, Pflege und Erschließung von Kulturdenkmalen (Denkmalpflegerichtlinie Sachsen-Anhalt)

Erl. der StK vom 27.7.2017 – StK-63-57002

1. Zuwendungszweck, Rechtsgrundlagen

1.1 Das Land Sachsen-Anhalt gewährt auf der Grundlage
   a) der Verordnung (EU) Nr. 651/2014 der Kommission vom 17.6.2014 zur Feststellung der Vereinbarkeit bestimmter Gruppen von Beihilfen mit dem Binnenmarkt in Anwendung der Artikel 107 und 108 des Vertrags über die Arbeitsweise der Europäischen Union (ABl. L 187 vom 26.6.2014, S. 1),
   b) der §§ 23 und 44 der Landeshaushaltsordnung des Landes Sachsen-Anhalt (LHO) vom 30.4.1991 (GVBl. LSA S. 35), zuletzt geändert durch Artikel 1 des Gesetzes vom 22.3.2017 (GVBl. LSA S. 55), der dazu ergangenen Verwaltungsvorschriften (VV-LHO, RdErl. des MF vom 1.2.2001, MBl. LSA S. 241, zuletzt geändert durch RdErl. vom 28.1.2013, MBl. LSA S. 73), der Verwaltungsvorschriften für Zuwendungen an Gebietskörperschaften und Zusammenschlüsse von Gebietskörperschaften in der Rechtsform einer juristischen Person des öffentlichen Rechts (VV-Gk, Anlage 2 zur VV Nr. 5.1 zu § 44 LHO) sowie des Zuwendungsrechtsergänzungserlasses (RdErl. des MF vom 6.6.2016, MBl. LSA S. 383) in der jeweils geltenden Fassung,
   c) des § 20 Abs. 1 des Denkmalschutzgesetzes des Landes Sachsen-Anhalt vom 21.10.1991 (GVBl. LSA S- 368, 1992 S. 310), zuletzt geändert durch Artikel 2 des Gesetzes vom 20.12.2005 (GVBl. LSA S. 769, 801),

sowie nach Maßgabe dieser Richtlinie Zuwendungen für Maßnahmen, die dem Erhalt der Pflege und der Erschließung von Kulturdenkmalen gemäß § 2 des Denkmalschutzgesetzes des Landes Sachsen-Anhalt dienen. Kulturdenkmale gehören zur Infrastruktur des Landes Sachsen-Anhalt. Die Erschließung umfasst Arbeiten, die ausschließlich mit der späteren Nutzung im Zusammenhang stehen.

Ein Anspruch auf Gewährung der Zuwendung besteht nicht, die Bewilligungsbehörde entscheidet auf Grund ihres pflichtgemäßen Ermessens im Rahmen der verfügbaren Haushaltsmittel.

2. Gegenstand der Förderung

2.1 Mit den Zuwendungen sollen die Ausgaben gefördert werden, die im Rahmen von Sicherungs-, Bergungs-, Instandsetzungs-, Erschließungs- und Erhaltungsmaßnahmen an (beweglichen und unbeweglichen) Kulturdenkmalen allein oder überwiegend aus Gründen der Denkmalpflege erforderlich werden (denkmalbedingte Ausgaben). Dies kann auch Maßnahmen der Nutzbarmachung einschließen, wenn hierdurch der Erhalt eines gefährdeten Kulturdenkmals gesichert werden kann.

2.2 Entsprechendes gilt für Ausgaben, die für Maßnahmen im Umfeld eines Kulturdenkmals oder innerhalb einer historischen Kulturlandschaft erforderlich werden und unmittelbaren Einfluss auf den Schutz, die Erhaltung oder die Erschließung eines Kulturdenkmals oder einer historischen Kulturlandschaft haben.

2.3 Bei der Entscheidung über die Bewilligung einer Zuwendung besteht an dem Projekt eine besondere Priorität, wenn
   a) das Kulturdenkmal oder das Vorhaben lässt sich den jeweiligen landespolitischen Schwerpunkten zuordnen,
   b) die Zuwendung wird dafür verwendet, akute Gefahren (z.B. Einsturzgefahr) von dem Kulturdenkmal abzuwenden,
   c) durch die Zuwendung wird eine nachhaltige Nutzung des Kulturdenkmals ermöglicht, oder
   d) das Projekt hat Modellcharakter. Modellcharakter hat ein Projekt dann, wenn es eine Vorbildwirkung für andere Maßnahmen entfaltet (z.B. besondere Art und Weise der Sanierung, Erhaltung, Nutzung des Kulturdenkmals); die Maßnahme eine besondere Öffentlichkeitswirksamkeit im Bereich des Denkmalschutzes, der Denkmalpflege oder der Archäologie entfaltet. Dies ist z.B. der Fall, wenn das Projekt selbst zur Verbreitung des Gedankens der

Denkmalpflege oder der Archäologie beiträgt oder es durch geeignete Maßnahmen öffentlichkeitswirksam verbreitet wird.

2.4 Folgende Maßnahmen an Kulturdenkmalen können anerkannt werden:
   a) Arbeiten an Kulturdenkmalen, die deren Erhalt, Sicherung und Erschließung, auch touristisch, dienen,
   b) Sicherungen gegen Zerstörungen (Feuer, Blitz, Wasser) und Einwirkungen (Sachbeschädigung) durch Unbefugte (Sicherung gegen Einbruch),
   c) Arbeiten an Parkanlagen, Gärten und historischen Kulturlandschaften, wenn denkmalpflegerische oder denkmalschützende Belange erfüllt werden,
   d) Maßnahmen im Sinne von Wiederherstellungen und Rekonstruktionen an Kulturdenkmalen,
   e) Erwerb von Kulturdenkmalen oder Grundstücken, wenn durch den Ankauf als Voraussetzung die Erhaltung oder Sanierung des Kulturdenkmals gesichert werden kann,
   f) Gutachten und Dokumentationen,
   g) baugeschichtliche und restauratorische Untersuchungen und Dokumentationen,
   h) wirksame Öffentlichkeitsarbeit, die dem Erhalt des Kulturdenkmals verpflichtet ist,
   i) Maßnahmen, die im Denkmalumfeld erforderlich sind und im Sinne des Umgebungsschutzes Einfluss auf das Erscheinungsbild des Denkmals haben,
   j) Darstellung der denkmalpflegerischen Bedeutung eines archäologischen Kulturdenkmals,
   k) Dokumentation vor der Zerstörung eines Kulturdenkmals, an dem ein erhebliches Landesinteresse besteht,
   l) bau- und erkundungsbegleitende archäologische Maßnahmen,
   m) Arbeiten zu Denkmalen oder Flächendenkmalen, Denkmalpflegepläne und Stadt- oder Raumkataster,
   n) notwendige Vorarbeiten für Baumaßnahmen,
   o) Sicherung und Erhalt von beweglichen Kulturdenkmalen,
   p) Publikationen.

3. Zuwendungsempfänger

3.1 Zuwendungen können erhalten:
   a) der Erhaltungspflichtige eines Kulturdenkmals gemäß § 9 des Denkmalschutzgesetzes des Landes Sachsen-Anhalt,
   b) der Erhaltungspflichtige im Sinne des Umgebungsschutzes gemäß § 1 Abs. 1 des Denkmalschutzgesetzes des Landes Sachsen-Anhalt, soweit die Maßnahme in unmittelbarer Beziehung zu einem Kulturdenkmal steht,
   c) natürliche oder juristische Personen, die Vorhaben entsprechend Nummer 2.4 realisieren wollen.

3.2 Nicht rechtsfähige Personen haben eine verantwortliche Person zu benennen, die für die zweckentsprechende Verwendung der Zuwendung haftet.

3.3 Eine Förderung von Landeseinrichtungen ist ausgeschlossen.

4. Zuwendungsvoraussetzungen

4.1 Die Bewilligungsbehörde prüft in jedem Einzelfall, ob die Förderung eine potenzielle Beihilfe nach den Artikeln 107 und 108 des Vertrags über die Arbeitsweise der Europäischen Union (AEUV) darstellt. Förderungen nach dieser Richtlinie, die Beihilfen nach der Verordnung (EU) Nr. 651/2014 darstellen, werden unter Anwendung der Verordnung (EU) Nr. 651/2014 als Einzelbeihilfe gewährt.

4.2 Es muss sich um ein Kulturdenkmal nach § 2 des Denkmalschutzgesetzes des Landes Sachsen-Anhalt handeln. Die Maßnahme muss im Interesse von Denkmalschutz und Denkmalpflege liegen. Die Maßnahmen nach Nummer 2.4 müssen den Anforderungen der zuständigen Denkmalschutzbehörden entsprechen, insbesondere sind deren denkmalfachliche Auflagen in der Baugenehmigung oder der Genehmigung nach § 14 des Denkmalschutzgesetzes des Landes Sachsen-Anhalt Voraussetzung für die Bewilligung.

4.3 Die Maßnahme darf vor der Bewilligung der Zuwendung nicht begonnen sein. Als Maßnahmebeginn sind dabei unter anderem der Abschluss eines dem Projekt zuzuordnenden Leistungs- oder Liefervertrages sowie die Erteilung verbindlicher Zusagen zu verstehen. Ist eine Entscheidung der Bewilligungsbehörde noch nicht möglich, kann die Bewilligungsbehörde auf Antrag bei

Maßnahmen, die aus sachlichen oder wirtschaftlichen Gründen keinen Aufschub dulden, nach Maßgabe der Nummer 1.3 der VV zu § 44 LHO in Verbindung mit Abschnitt 6 des Zuwendungsrechtsergänzungserlasses einen vorzeitigen Maßnahmebeginn zulassen. Die Zustimmung zum vorzeitigen Maßnahmebeginn begründet keinen Rechtsanspruch auf eine Zuwendung.

5. Art, Umfang und Höhe der Zuwendung

5.1 Die Zuwendung wird im Wege der Anteils-, Festbetrags- oder Fehlbedarfsfinanzierung als nicht rückzahlbarer Zuschuss zur Projektförderung bewilligt.

5.2 Die Zuwendung beträgt bis zu 49 v.H. der für die Maßnahmen nach Nummer 2.4 zuwendungsfähigen Ausgaben. Gebietskörperschaften und Zusammenschlüsse von Gebietskörperschaften in der Rechtsform einer juristischen Person des öffentlichen Rechts als Eigentümerin eines Kulturdenkmals haben sich an der Finanzierung angemessen zu beteiligen, so dass sie Zuwendungen nach Nummer 2 2.2 VV-Gk nur zur Teilfinanzierung erhalten können-

5.3 In besonders begründeten Ausnahmefällen kann die Zuwendung höher liegen. Diese Ausnahmeregelung kann nur zur Anwendung kommen, wenn an den Maßnahmen ein erhebliches denkmalpflegerisches Landesinteresse besteht und das Ziel auf anderem Wege nicht erreichbar ist. Eine Eigenbeteiligung des Antragstellers von mindestens 10 v.H. an den notwendigen Aufwendungen ist grundsätzlich erforderlich.

5.4 Bei der Bemessung des Eigenanteils können Eigenarbeitsleistungen nach Maßgabe der im Zuwendungsrechtsergänzungserlass benannten Kriterien und Pauschalwerte anerkannt werden. Höhe und Umfang der Eigenarbeitsleistungen sind sowohl im Finanzierungsplan, im Bewilligungsbescheid als auch im Verwendungsnachweis ausdrücklich auszuweisen. Die Eigenarbeitsleistungen dürfen nur auf den Eigenanteil der Zuwendungsempfangenden angerechnet werden. Die Zuwendung darf die tatsächlich getätigten zuwendungsfähigen Ausgaben des Projekts nicht übersteigen.

5.5 Zuwendungsfähige Ausgaben sind nur die in direktem Zusammenhang mit dem Projekt entstehenden Personal- und Sachausgaben sowie Investitionen; ausgenommen sind Ausgaben für Stammpersonal und sonstigen anteiligen Verwaltungsaufwand. Für die Anerkennung von zuwendungsfähigen Personalausgaben können zur Verfahrensvereinfachung grundsätzlich die Pauschalwerte des Zuwendungsrechtsergänzungserlasses zur Anwendung kommen.

6. Sonstige Zuwendungsbestimmungen

6.1 Ein Bauschild mit dem Hinweis auf die Mitfinanzierung durch das Land ist für die Öffentlichkeit sichtbar anzubringen. Bei Berichten der Zuwendungsempfänger gegenüber den Medien soll auf die Förderung durch das Land hingewiesen werden.

6.2 Den Zuwendungsempfängern ist in angemessener Form im Zuwendungsbescheid aufzuerlegen, die öffentliche Zugänglichkeit des Kulturdenkmals zu gewährleisten, sofern durch diese Auflage nicht in höherwertige Rechte eingegriffen wird. Dieses ist insbesondere der Fall, wenn Eigentumsrechte oder in das Recht der Unverletzlichkeit der Wohnung eingegriffen werden könnte. Angemessenheit liegt in der Regel vor, wenn die Kulturdenkmale der Öffentlichkeit gewidmet sind.

7. Anweisungen zum Verfahren

7.1 Bewilligungsbehörde ist das Landesverwaltungsamt. Es entscheidet nach Anhörung des Denkmalfachamtes.

7.2 Kirchengemeinden reichen den Antrag über die zuständige untere Denkmalschutzbehörde und das regional zuständige Kirchenbauamt, soweit ein solches besteht, beim Landesverwaltungsamt ein.

7.3 Zuwendungsanträge zur Erhaltung von Kulturdenkmalen sind unter Beifügung der denkmalrechtlichen Genehmigung sowie der für die Beurteilung erforderlichen Unterlagen über die untere Denkmalschutzbehörde bis zum 1.8. für das kommende Haushaltsjahr zu stellen.

7.4 Unter Berücksichtigung der in Nummer 1 genannten Rechtsgrundlagen kann das für Kultur zuständige Ministerium Ausnahmen zulassen, soweit die unter Nummer 4.1 aufgeführten beihilferechtlichen Vorschriften eingehalten werden. Die sich aus der Rechtsgrundlagen nach Nummer 1 ergebenden Beteiligungspflichten bleiben unberührt.

7.5 Die Antragsvordrucke sind beim Landesverwaltungsamt erhältlich oder können über das Internet (http://www.kultur.sachsen-anhalt.de oder http://www.landesverwaltungsamt.sachsen-anhalt.de) abgerufen werden.

7.6 Für die Bewilligung, Auszahlung und Abrechnung der Zuwendung sowie für den Nachweis und die Prüfung der Verwendung und die gegebenenfalls erforderliche Aufhebung des Zuwendungsbescheides und die Rückforderung der gewährten Zuwendung gelten die VV zu § 44 LHO sowie die VV-Gk, soweit nicht in dieser Richtlinie Abweichungen zugelassen worden sind.

8. Sprachliche Gleichstellung
Personen- und Funktionsbezeichnungen in diesem Erl. gelten jeweils in männlicher und weil weiblicher Form.

9. Inkrafttreten, Außerkrafttreten
Dieser Erl. tritt am Tag nach der Veröffentlichung in Kraft und am 31.12.2022 außer Kraft.

D14.IV.1 KGSG-Zuständigkeitsverordnung

Verordnung über Zuständigkeiten nach dem Kulturgutschutzgesetz (KGSG-ZustVO)

Vom 22. November 2016 (GVBl. LSA S. 351)
(BS LSA 224.2)

Aufgrund des § 3 Abs. 1 Satz 2 des Kulturgutschutzgesetzes vom 31. Juli 2016 (BGBl. I S. 1914) in Verbindung mit § 16 Abs. 1 des Organisationsgesetzes Sachsen-Anhalt vom 27. Oktober 2015 (GVBl. LSA S. 554), geändert durch § 11 Abs. 2 des Gesetzes vom 10. Dezember 2015 (GVBl. LSA S. 627), wird verordnet:

§ 1 [Zuständigkeiten]

Zuständige Behörden im Sinne des § 3 Abs. 1 Satz 2 des Kulturgutschutzgesetzes sind
1. das für Archivwesen zuständige Ministerium für Archive aller Art mit Archivalien auf allen Trägern gemäß Anhang I Kategorie A 12 und
2. das für Kulturgutschutz zuständige Ministerium für alle übrigen Kulturgüter gemäß Anhang I Kategorie A

der Verordnung (EG) Nr. 116/2009 des Rates vom 18. Dezember 2008 über die Ausfuhr von Kulturgütern (kodifizierte Fassung) (ABl. L 39 vom 10.2.2009, S. 1).

§ 2 [Inkrafttreten]

¹Diese Verordnung tritt am Tag nach der Verkündung[1]) in Kraft. ²Gleichzeitig tritt die Kulturgutschutzverordnung des Landes Sachsen-Anhalt vom 27. Juni 2008 (GVBl. LSA S. 274) außer Kraft.

---

1) Verkündet am 28.11.20106.

Verordnung zur Übertragung von Verordnungsermächtigungen im Bereich der Justiz

Vom 28. März 2008 (GVBl. LSA S. 137)
(BS LSA 300.20)
zuletzt geändert durch § 1 Vierte ÄndVO vom 22. Mai 2018 (GVBl. LSA S. 62)

– Auszug –
[…]

§ 1 [Ermächtigungen zum Erlass von Rechtsverordnungen]
Die Landesregierung überträgt die ihr nach folgenden Vorschriften zustehenden Ermächtigungen zum Erlass von Rechtsverordnungen auf das für Justiz zuständige Ministerium:
[…]
3a. § 88 Satz 2 des Kulturgutschutzgesetzes,
[…]

D15 Verfassung Schleswig-Holstein

Verfassung des Landes Schleswig-Holstein

In der Fassung vom 2. Dezember 2014[1]) (GVOBl. Schl.-H. S. 344, ber. 2015 S. 41)
(GS Schl.-H. II, Gl.Nr. 100-1)
zuletzt geändert durch Art. 1 ÄndG vom 19. Dezember 2016 (GVOBl. Schl.-H. S. 1008)
– Auszug –

Abschnitt 1
Land und Volk

Artikel 6 Nationale Minderheiten und Volksgruppen
[...]
(2) ¹Die kulturelle Eigenständigkeit und die politische Mitwirkung nationaler Minderheiten und Volksgruppen stehen unter dem Schutz des Landes, der Gemeinden und Gemeindeverbände. ²Die nationale dänische Minderheit, die Minderheit der deutschen Sinti und Roma und die friesische Volksgruppe haben Anspruch auf Schutz und Förderung.

Artikel 13 Schutz und Förderung der Kultur
(1) Das Land schützt und fördert Kunst und Wissenschaft, Forschung und Lehre.
[...]
(3) Die Förderung der Kultur einschließlich des Sports, der Erwachsenenbildung, des Büchereiwesens und der Volkshochschulen ist Aufgabe des Landes, der Gemeinden und Gemeindeverbände.

---

1) Neubekanntmachung der Verfassung idF v. 13.5.2008 (GVOBl. Schl.-H. S. 223) in der ab 11.12.2014 geltenden Fassung.

Gesetz zum Schutz der Denkmale (Denkmalschutzgesetz)[1]

Vom 30. Dezember 2014 (GVOBl. Schl.-H. 2015 S. 2)
(GS Schl.-H. II, Gl.Nr. 224-11)

Der Landtag hat folgendes Gesetz beschlossen:

Inhaltsübersicht:

Gliederung
Präambel

Abschnitt 1
Allgemeine Bestimmungen
- § 1 Denkmalschutz und Denkmalpflege
- § 2 Begriffsbestimmungen, Anwendungsbereich
- § 3 Denkmalschutzbehörden
- § 4 Öffentliche Planungen und Maßnahmen, Welterbe
- § 5 Vertrauensleute
- § 6 Denkmalrat und Denkmalbeiräte
- § 7 Datenschutz

Abschnitt 2
Schutz von Denkmalen
- § 8 Schutz von unbeweglichen Kulturdenkmalen
- § 9 Unterschutzstellung von beweglichen Kulturdenkmalen
- § 10 Ausweisung von Schutzzonen

Abschnitt 3
Umgang mit Denkmalen
- § 11 Handhabung des Gesetzes
- § 12 Genehmigungspflichtige Maßnahmen
- § 13 Verfahren bei genehmigungspflichtigen Maßnahmen
- § 14 Kostenpflicht bei Eingriffen
- § 15 Funde
- § 16 Erhaltung des Denkmals
- § 17 Maßnahmen der Denkmalschutzbehörden

Abschnitt 4
Ordnungswidrigkeiten und Straftaten
- § 18 Ordnungswidrigkeiten
- § 19 Straftaten

Abschnitt 5
Enteignung
- § 20 Vorübergehende Inbesitznahme eines Kulturdenkmals
- § 21 Enteignung

Abschnitt 6
Schlussvorschriften
- § 22 Gebühren
- § 23 Staatsverträge mit Religionsgemeinschaften
- § 24 Übergangsvorschriften
- § 25 Inkrafttreten

Präambel

Grundlage für die Gestaltung der Zukunft ist die Erinnerung an die Vergangenheit. Sie stützt sich auf Orte, bewegliche und unbewegliche Objekte und immaterielle Zeugnisse wie Sprache, Brauchtum, traditionelle Handwerkstechniken oder Musik. Aufgabe des Denkmalschutzes und der Denkmalpflege ist es, diesem Grundbedürfnis des Einzelnen und der Gesellschaft nach Erinnerung zu dienen. Dies setzt die Zusammenarbeit von Behörden und Eigentümerinnen und Eigentümern, aber auch von anderen Betroffenen, z.B. Nutzerinnen und Nutzern oder ehrenamtlich Tätigen voraus. Denkmale sind materielle Zeugen menschlichen Wirkens. Sie dokumentieren historische Ereignisse und Entwicklungen, künstlerische Leistungen, technische Errungenschaften, soziale Lebenswirklichkeiten, unabhängig davon ob diese heute positiv oder negativ bewertet werden. Sie sind Teil des heutigen Lebensraumes und der heutigen Kultur. Durch Denkmale schützt und vertieft die Gesellschaft ihre Identität sowie Toleranz und Solidarität mit verschiedenen Gruppierungen, einschließlich den Minderheiten. Denkmalschutz und Denkmalpflege ermöglichen es künftigen Generationen, Geschichte zu erfahren, wahrzunehmen, zu interpretieren und zu hinterfragen. Erkenntnisse über Denkmale müssen daher öffentlich zugänglich sein. Daher ist es der Gesellschaft ein Anliegen, den überlieferten Denkmalbestand zu erhalten. Eine angemessene Nutzung begünstigt die langfristige Erhaltung. Jede Nutzung muss sich an der Substanzerhaltung orientieren.

---

1) Siehe bis zum Inkrafttreten dieses G das Denkmalschutzgesetz 2012.

D15.I.1 Denkmalschutzgesetz Schleswig-Holstein

Abschnitt 1
Allgemeine Bestimmungen

§ 1 Denkmalschutz und Denkmalpflege

(1) ¹Denkmalschutz und Denkmalpflege liegen im öffentlichen Interesse. ²Sie dienen dem Schutz, der Erhaltung und der Pflege der kulturellen Lebensgrundlagen, die auch eingedenk der Verantwortung für die kommenden Generationen der besonderen Fürsorge jedes Einzelnen und der Gemeinschaft anvertraut sind. ³Mit diesen Kulturgütern ist im Rahmen einer nachhaltigen Ressourcennutzung schonend und werterhaltend umzugehen.

(2) ¹Es ist Aufgabe von Denkmalschutz und Denkmalpflege, Denkmale nach Maßgabe dieses Gesetzes zu erfassen, wissenschaftlich zu erforschen und zu dokumentieren und das Wissen über Denkmale zu verbreiten. ²Dabei wirken Denkmalschutzbehörden und Eigentümerinnen und Eigentümer, Besitzerinnen und Besitzer und die sonst Verfügungsberechtigten zusammen.

(3) ¹Das Land, die Kreise und die Gemeinden fördern diese Aufgabe. ²Das Land, die Kreise und die Gemeinden und alle Körperschaften und Stiftungen des öffentlichen Rechts haben sich ihren Denkmälern in besonderem Maße anzunehmen und diese vorbildlich zu pflegen.

§ 2 Begriffsbestimmungen, Anwendungsbereich

(1) Denkmale im Sinne dieses Gesetzes sind Kulturdenkmale und Schutzzonen.

(2) ¹Kulturdenkmale sind Sachen, Gruppen von Sachen oder Teile von Sachen aus vergangener Zeit, deren Erforschung oder Erhaltung wegen ihres besonderen geschichtlichen, wissenschaftlichen, künstlerischen, technischen, städtebaulichen oder die Kulturlandschaft prägenden Wertes im öffentlichen Interesse liegen. ²Kulturdenkmale können beweglich und unbeweglich sein. ³Sie sind insbesondere Baudenkmale, archäologische Denkmale und Gründenkmale. ⁴Nach diesem Gesetz sind

1. Baudenkmale bauliche Anlagen oder Teile oder Mehrheiten von baulichen Anlagen oder Sachgesamtheiten;
2. archäologische Denkmale solche, die sich im Boden, in Mooren oder in einem Gewässer befinden oder befanden und aus denen mit archäologischer Methode Kenntnis von der Vergangenheit des Menschen gewonnen werden kann; hierzu gehören auch dingliche Zeugnisse wie Veränderungen und Verfärbungen in der natürlichen Bodenbeschaffenheit sowie Zeugnisse pflanzlichen und tierischen Lebens, wenn aus ihnen mit archäologischer Methode Kenntnis von der Vergangenheit des Menschen gewonnen werden kann;
3. Gründenkmale von Menschen gestaltete Garten- und Landschaftsteile, wenn sie die Voraussetzungen des Satzes 1 erfüllen; Gründenkmale können insbesondere Garten-, Park- und Friedhofsanlagen einschließlich der dazugehörigen Wasser- und Waldflächen sein; sie können außerdem Alleen und Baumreihen sein;
4. bewegliche Kulturdenkmale Einzelgegenstände, Sammlungen und sonstige Gesamtheiten beweglicher Einzelgegenstände, die für die Geschichte und Kultur Schleswig-Holsteins eine besondere Bedeutung haben, nationales Kulturgut darstellen oder aufgrund internationaler Empfehlungen zu schützen sind.

⁵Zu einem Kulturdenkmal können auch sein ortsfestes Zubehör und seine Ausstattung gehören.

(3) ¹Schutzzonen sind Welterbestätten, soweit sie nicht als Kulturdenkmale geschützt sind, sowie Denkmalbereiche und Grabungsschutzgebiete. ²Nach diesem Gesetz sind

1. Welterbestätten die gemäß Artikel 11 Absatz 2 des Übereinkommens zum Schutz des Kultur- und Naturerbes der Welt vom 16. November 1972 (BGBl. II 1977 S. 215) in die „Liste des Erbes der Welt" eingetragenen Stätten, soweit sie dort nicht ausschließlich als Naturerbe eingetragen sind,
2. Pufferzonen definierte Gebiete um eine Welterbestätte zum Schutz ihres unmittelbaren Umfeldes, wesentlicher Sichtachsen und weiterer wertbestimmender Merkmale,
3. Denkmalbereiche historische Kulturlandschaften, kulturlandschaftliche Einheiten oder Mehrheiten von Sachen oder Kulturdenkmalen, die durch ihr Erscheinungsbild oder durch ihre Beziehung zueinander von besonderer geschichtlicher, wissenschaftlicher, künstlerischer, technischer, städtebaulicher oder die Kulturlandschaft prägender Bedeutung sind; Denkmalbereiche können auch

a) aus Sachen bestehen, die einzeln die Voraussetzungen des Satzes 2 nicht erfüllen
b) insbesondere Siedlungsstrukturen, Orts- oder Stadtgrundrisse, Stadt-, Ortsbilder und -silhouetten, Stadtteile und -viertel, Siedlungskerne oder Siedlungen sein,
4. Grabungsschutzgebiete abgegrenzte Bezirke, in denen archäologische Denkmale bekannt oder zu vermuten sind.

§ 3 Denkmalschutzbehörden

(1) ¹Der Denkmalschutz obliegt dem Land, den Kreisen und den kreisfreien Städten. ²Die Kreise und kreisfreien Städte nehmen diese Aufgabe als Aufgabe zur Erfüllung nach Weisung wahr.
(2) ¹Denkmalschutzbehörden sind:
1. das für Kultur zuständige Ministerium als oberste Denkmalschutzbehörde,
2. das Landesamt für Denkmalpflege Schleswig-Holstein und das Archäologische Landesamt Schleswig-Holstein als obere Denkmalschutzbehörden,
3. die Landrätinnen oder Landräte für die Kreise und die Bürgermeisterinnen oder Bürgermeister für die kreisfreien Städte als untere Denkmalschutzbehörden.

²Die Aufgaben der oberen Denkmalschutzbehörden werden für den Bereich der Hansestadt Lübeck von deren Bürgermeisterin oder Bürgermeister wahrgenommen.
(3) Die unteren Denkmalschutzbehörden sind für den Vollzug dieses Gesetzes zuständig, soweit nicht durch Gesetz oder aufgrund eines Gesetzes etwas anderes bestimmt ist.
(4) ¹Die oberen Denkmalschutzbehörden sind zugleich Fachaufsichtsbehörden über die unteren Denkmalschutzbehörden. ²Die oberen und unteren Denkmalschutzbehörden haben die jeweils zuständige Denkmalschutzbehörde über alle Vorgänge zu unterrichten, die deren Eingreifen erfordern. ³Die unteren Denkmalschutzbehörden haben der obersten einmal jährlich über ihren Mitteleinsatz für die Aufgaben des Denkmalschutzes und der Denkmalpflege, insbesondere den Personaleinsatz, zu berichten.
(5) ¹Das Landesamt für Denkmalpflege Schleswig-Holstein ist zuständig für den Schutz und die Pflege der Kulturdenkmale und Schutzzonen mit Ausnahme der archäologischen Kulturdenkmale, Grabungsschutzgebiete, archäologischen Denkmalbereiche und archäologischen Welterbestätten. ²Das Archäologische Landesamt Schleswig-Holstein ist zuständig für die archäologischen Kulturdenkmale, Grabungsschutzgebiete, archäologische Denkmalbereiche und archäologische Welterbestätten.
(6) Die oberste Denkmalschutzbehörde kann durch Verordnung[1]) Zuständigkeiten nach diesem Gesetz auf die oberen oder die unteren Denkmalschutzbehörden übertragen, wenn dies für die Erledigung bestimmter Aufgaben zweckmäßiger ist.

§ 4 Öffentliche Planungen und Maßnahmen, Welterbe

(1) Die Belange des Denkmalschutzes und der Denkmalpflege sowie die Anforderungen des europäischen Rechts und der in Deutschland ratifizierten internationalen und europäischen Übereinkommen zum Schutz des materiellen kulturellen Erbes sind in die städtebauliche Entwicklung, Landespflege und Landesplanung einzubeziehen und bei allen öffentlichen Planungen und Maßnahmen angemessen zu berücksichtigen.
(2) ¹Die juristische Person, die für die Verwaltung der Welterbestätte zuständig ist, richtet eine Welterbekoordination ein und benennt eine offizielle Welterbebeauftragte oder einen offiziellen Welterbebeauftragten für die Belange der Welterbestätte. ²Die juristische Person hat integrierte Planungs- und Handlungskonzepte in Form von Managementplänen aufzustellen und fortzuschreiben. ³Kommt sie ihrer Verpflichtung zur Aufstellung oder Fortschreibung des Managementplans auch nach einer von der zuständigen oberen Denkmalschutzbehörde gesetzten angemessenen Frist nicht nach, wird der Managementplan ersatzweise von der zuständigen oberen Denkmalschutzbehörde erstellt oder fortgeschrieben.
(3) ¹Die Denkmalschutzbehörden und der oder die Welterbebeauftragte sind Träger öffentlicher Belange. ²Sie sind bei allen öffentlichen Planungen und Maßnahmen, die Belange des Welterbes, des Denkmalschutzes und der Denkmalpflege berühren können, so frühzeitig zu beteiligen, dass die in Absatz 1 genannte[2]) Belange sowie die Belange der Welterbestätte, ihrer Pufferzonen und ihrer we-

---

1) Der Erlass einer entsprechenden Verordnung ist derzeit in Planung. Ab ihrer Veröffentlichung wird sie zugänglich sein unter: https://www.schleswig-holstein.de/DE/Landesregierung/LD/Service/Grundlagen/_documents/Gesetzliches.html.
2) Richtig wohl: „genannten".

sentlichen Sichtachsen in die Abwägung mit anderen Belangen eingestellt und die Erhaltung und Nutzung der Denkmale sowie eine angemessene Gestaltung ihrer Umgebung sichergestellt werden können. [3]Welterbestätten sind einschließlich ihrer Umgebung in ihrem außergewöhnlichen universellen Wert zu erhalten.

§ 5 Vertrauensleute
[1]Die oberen Denkmalschutzbehörden können im Einvernehmen mit den Kreisen und kreisfreien Städten ehrenamtliche Vertrauensleute für Kulturdenkmale bestellen. [2]Das Nähere regelt die oberste Denkmalschutzbehörde durch Verordnung.[1)]

§ 6 Denkmalrat und Denkmalbeiräte
(1) [1]Die oberste Denkmalschutzbehörde bildet zur Beratung der Denkmalschutzbehörden einen Denkmalrat. [2]Der Denkmalrat ist unabhängig. [3]Er ist vor der Entscheidung über einen Widerspruch gegen eine Maßnahme nach § 9 und vor der Ausweisung einer Schutzzone nach § 10 Absatz 1 zu hören. [4]Der Denkmalrat kann sich zu Einzelfällen sowie zu grundsätzlichen und aktuellen Fragestellungen des Denkmalschutzes und der Denkmalpflege äußern und ist berechtigt, Empfehlungen auszusprechen. [5]Die Beschlüsse des Denkmalrates zu grundsätzlichen Fragen werden auf der Internetseite der obersten Denkmalschutzbehörde veröffentlicht.

(2) Die Kommunen und die unteren Denkmalschutzbehörden können im Benehmen mit den oberen Denkmalschutzbehörden ehrenamtliche Denkmalbeiräte bilden.

(3) [1]Die Mitglieder des Denkmalrates sind ehrenamtlich tätig. [2]Das Nähere über die Berufung, Amtsdauer, Entschädigung, Zusammensetzung und Geschäftsführung des Denkmalrates regelt die oberste Denkmalschutzbehörde durch Verordnung.[2)]

§ 7 Datenschutz
[1]Die Denkmalschutzbehörden dürfen personenbezogene Daten verarbeiten, soweit dies zur Erfüllung der ihnen zugewiesenen Aufgaben erforderlich ist. [2]Darüber hinaus dürfen die Denkmalschutzbehörden die zur jeweiligen Aufgabenerledigung erforderlichen personenbezogenen Daten an die Kommunen und unteren Bauaufsichtsbehörden übermitteln.

Abschnitt 2
Schutz von Denkmalen

§ 8 Schutz von unbeweglichen Kulturdenkmalen
(1) [1]Unbewegliche Kulturdenkmale sind gesetzlich geschützt. [2]Sie sind nachrichtlich in ein Verzeichnis (Denkmalliste) einzutragen. [3]Der Schutz der Kulturdenkmale ist nicht von der Eintragung in die Denkmalliste abhängig. [4]Die Denkmalliste ist nicht abschließend. [5]Sie ist regelmäßig zu überprüfen, zu ergänzen und zu bereinigen. [6]Die oberen Denkmalschutzbehörden führen die Denkmallisten für ihren jeweiligen Zuständigkeitsbereich.

(2) [1]Die Denkmallisten sollen elektronisch geführt werden. [2]Sie sind im Umfang der Verordnung nach Satz 4 öffentlich bekannt zu machen. [3]Insbesondere sollen Angaben zur Belegenheit des Grundstücks, eine kurze Beschreibung des Kulturdenkmals sowie eine kurze Begründung der Denkmaleigenschaft in die Denkmalliste aufgenommen werden. [4]Die oberste Denkmalschutzbehörde legt durch Verordnung[3)] fest, welche Daten in den Denkmallisten nach Absatz 1 zu verarbeiten und welche dieser Daten zu veröffentlichen sind.

(3) [1]Von der Eintragung sind die Eigentümerinnen und Eigentümer unverzüglich zu benachrichtigen. [2]Können sie nicht oder nur mit unverhältnismäßigem Aufwand ermittelt werden, gilt die Veröffentlichung der Eintragung in der Denkmalliste als öffentliche Benachrichtigung. [3]Ebenso kann die Eintragung oder Löschung öffentlich bekannt gemacht werden, wenn mehr als 20 Personen betroffen sind. [4]Benachrichtigt werden auch die Kommunen, in deren Gebiet das Kulturdenkmal liegt.

§ 9 Unterschutzstellung von beweglichen Kulturdenkmalen
(1) [1]Die Unterschutzstellung beweglicher Kulturdenkmale wird von den oberen Denkmalschutzbehörden von Amts wegen oder auf Antrag der Eigentümerinnen oder Eigentümer durch Verwaltungsakt

---
1) Die Landesverordnung über die Vertrauensleute für Kulturdenkmale ist abgedruckt als Nr. D15.I.1b.
2) Die Landesverordnung über den Denkmalrat ist abgedruckt als Nr. D15.I.1a.
3) Vgl. hierzu die Landesverordnung über die Denkmallisten für Kulturdenkmale, abgedruckt als Nr. D15.I.1e.

verfügt. ²Die Eintragung ist zu löschen, wenn ihre Voraussetzungen nicht mehr vorliegen. ³Die Einhaltung der gesetzlichen Schutzpflichten für bewegliche Kulturdenkmale kann von den Eigentümerinnen oder Eigentümern, den Besitzerinnen oder Besitzern oder den sonst Verfügungsberechtigten erst ab der Eintragung in die Denkmalliste der beweglichen Kulturdenkmale verlangt werden.

(2) ¹Die Denkmalliste der beweglichen Kulturdenkmale[1)] wird gesondert von der übrigen Denkmalliste geführt. ²Sie darf nur von den Eigentümerinnen und Eigentümern, den sonst dinglich Berechtigten und den von ihnen ermächtigten Personen eingesehen werden. ³Die oberste Denkmalschutzbehörde legt durch Verordnung fest, welche Daten in den Denkmallisten nach Absatz 1 zu verarbeiten und welche dieser Daten zu veröffentlichen sind.

(3) ¹Die obere Denkmalschutzbehörde kann anordnen, dass ein bewegliches Kulturdenkmal, mit dessen Eintragung in die Denkmalliste der beweglichen Kulturdenkmale zu rechnen ist, vorläufig als in die Liste eingetragen im Sinne dieses Gesetzes gilt, wenn die Gefahr einer Verschlechterung oder Ortsveränderung droht. ²Die Anordnung verliert ihre Wirksamkeit, wenn nicht spätestens binnen drei Monaten die endgültige Eintragung erfolgt.

§ 10 Ausweisung von Schutzzonen
(1) ¹Die oberen Denkmalschutzbehörden können im Benehmen mit den betroffenen unteren und der obersten Denkmalschutzbehörden sowie den betroffenen Kommunen Denkmalbereiche und Grabungsschutzgebiete durch Verordnung ausweisen. ²In ihr sind Ausmaß, Bestandteile, Schutzziel und -zweck sowie die zur Erreichung des Schutzzwecks erforderlichen Genehmigungsvorbehalte festzulegen. ³Näheres zum Verfahren kann die oberste Denkmalschutzbehörde durch Verordnung regeln.[2)]

(2) Vom Welterbekomitee anerkannte Welterbestätten in ihren vom Welterbekomitee anerkannten Grenzen gelten als Schutzzonen, soweit sie nicht als Kulturdenkmale geschützt sind.

(3) Abweichend von § 62 des Landesverwaltungsgesetzes gelten Verordnungen über Denkmalbereiche und Grabungsschutzgebiete unbefristet.

(4) Die Festlegung einer Schutzzone durch Verordnung ist nachrichtlich in der Denkmalliste zu vermerken.

(5) Die Festlegung von Schutzzonen ist zu veröffentlichen und den zuständigen Planungs- und Bauaufsichtsbehörden mitzuteilen.

Abschnitt 3
Umgang mit Denkmalen

§ 11 Handhabung des Gesetzes
¹Bei allen Maßnahmen ist auf die berechtigten Belange der Verpflichteten Rücksicht zu nehmen. ²Die Denkmalschutzbehörden sollen sie im Rahmen ihrer Möglichkeiten unterstützen und beraten.

§ 12 Genehmigungspflichtige Maßnahmen
(1) Der Genehmigung der unteren Denkmalschutzbehörde bedürfen
1. die Instandsetzung, die Veränderung und die Vernichtung eines Kulturdenkmals,
2. die Überführung eines Kulturdenkmals von heimatgeschichtlicher oder die Kulturlandschaft prägender Bedeutung an einen anderen Ort,
3. die Veränderung der Umgebung eines unbeweglichen Kulturdenkmals, wenn sie geeignet ist, seinen Eindruck wesentlich zu beeinträchtigen.

(2) Der Genehmigung der oberen Denkmalschutzbehörde bedürfen
1. alle Maßnahmen in Denkmalbereichen und in deren Umgebung, die geeignet sind, die Denkmalbereiche wesentlich zu beeinträchtigen; Maßnahmen nach Absatz 1 bleiben davon unberührt,
2. alle Maßnahmen in Grabungsschutzgebieten und Welterbestätten, die geeignet sind, diese zu beeinträchtigen oder zu gefährden,
3. Eingriffe in den Bestand eines Denkmals zum Zweck der Erforschung,
4. die Anwendung archäologischer Methoden, die geeignet sind, Kulturdenkmale aufzufinden, an Stellen, von denen bekannt ist oder den Umständen nach zu vermuten ist, dass sich dort Kulturdenkmale befinden,

---

1) Die Landesverordnung über die Denkmallisten für Kulturdenkmale ist abgedruckt als Nr. D15.I.1e.
2) Die Landesverordnung über das Verfahren zur Ausweisung von Denkmalbereichen und Grabungsschutzgebieten ist abgedruckt als Nr. D15.I.1c.

5. das Verwenden von Mess- und Suchgeräten, die geeignet sind, Kulturdenkmale aufzufinden, ohne dazu nach anderen Rechtsvorschriften befugt zu sein,
6. Nachforschungen, Erdarbeiten oder taucherische Bergungen an Stellen, von denen bekannt ist oder den Umständen nach zu vermuten ist, dass sich dort Kulturdenkmale befinden, ohne dazu nach anderen Rechtsvorschriften befugt zu sein, oder
7. die ganze oder teilweise Inbesitznahme eines durch Grabung oder durch taucherische Bergung zu Tage getretenen Kulturdenkmals.

(3) [1]Absatz 1 und 2 gelten nicht für Maßnahmen der oberen Denkmalschutzbehörden und ihrer Beauftragten. [2]Berührt eine Maßnahme Genehmigungspflichten nach Absatz 1 und 2, ist die obere Denkmalschutzbehörde allein zuständig.

§ 13 Verfahren bei genehmigungspflichtigen Maßnahmen

(1) [1]Die zuständige Denkmalschutzbehörde prüft innerhalb von vier Wochen, ob der Antrag unvollständig ist oder sonstige erhebliche Mängel aufweist. [2]Ist das der Fall, fordert sie die Antragstellerin oder den Antragsteller zur Behebung der Mängel innerhalb einer angemessenen Frist auf. [3]Werden die Mängel nicht innerhalb der Frist behoben, gilt der Antrag als zurückgewiesen. [4]Die Genehmigung gilt als erteilt, wenn die zuständige Denkmalschutzbehörde nicht innerhalb von drei Monaten nach Eingang der vollständigen Antragsunterlagen bei der Denkmalschutzbehörde einen Bescheid erlassen hat. [5]Die Frist ruht während der Untersuchung des Denkmals oder seiner Umgebung nach Absatz 6. [6]Die Genehmigung erlischt, wenn mit der Maßnahme nach diesem Absatz nicht innerhalb dreier Jahre nach Erteilung der Genehmigung begonnen worden oder eine begonnene Maßnahme länger als ein Jahr unterbrochen ist, es sei denn, in anderen Rechtsvorschriften ist etwas anderes bestimmt; die Frist von einem Jahr kann auf Antrag um bis zu zwei Jahre verlängert werden.

(2) [1]Die Genehmigung kann versagt werden, soweit dies zum Schutz der Denkmale erforderlich ist. [2]Sie ist zu erteilen, wenn Gründe des Denkmalschutzes nicht entgegenstehen und der Status als Welterbestätte nicht gefährdet ist oder ein überwiegendes öffentliches Interesse die Maßnahme notwendig macht. [3]Die öffentlichen und die privaten Belange sind miteinander und untereinander abzuwägen.

(3) [1]Maßnahmen an Baudenkmalen, die die Eigentümerin oder der Eigentümer zum Zeitpunkt des Maßnahmebeginns in Unkenntnis der Denkmaleigenschaft veranlasst hat, gelten als genehmigt. [2]Grob fahrlässige Unkenntnis steht der Kenntnis gleich. [3]Bei Vorhaben, deren energiewirtschaftliche Notwendigkeit und deren vordringlicher Bedarf gesetzlich festgelegt sind, ist die Genehmigung zu erteilen. [4]Für die Belange von Menschen mit Behinderung, von älteren Menschen sowie von anderen Personen mit Mobilitätsbeeinträchtigung sind bei öffentlich zugänglichen Denkmalen angemessene Vorkehrungen zu treffen. [5]Bei allen anderen Denkmalen sind diese Belange besonders zu berücksichtigen. [6]Bei Maßnahmen aus Gründen der Gefahrenabwehr bei überregionalen Infrastrukturen gilt die Genehmigung als erteilt. [7]Maßnahmen nach Satz 6 sind zu dokumentieren und die untere Denkmalschutzbehörde ist unverzüglich zu informieren.

(4) Die Genehmigung kann mit Bedingungen oder Auflagen versehen werden.

(5) Die oberste Denkmalschutzbehörde wird ermächtigt, für bestimmte Gebiete, Denkmale oder Genehmigungstatbestände durch Verordnung[1]) festzulegen, dass die untere Denkmalschutzbehörde vor Erteilung der Genehmigung die Zustimmung der oberen Denkmalschutzbehörde einzuholen hat.

(6) [1]Soweit es zur Entscheidung über die Genehmigung erforderlich ist, kann die zuständige Denkmalschutzbehörde verlangen, dass ihr die Untersuchung des Denkmals oder seiner Umgebung ermöglicht wird. [2]Hält es die Behörde für diese Untersuchung im Einzelfall für nötig, Sachverständige oder sachverständige Stellen heranzuziehen, hat die Antragstellerin oder der Antragsteller im Rahmen des Zumutbaren die hierdurch entstehenden Kosten zu tragen.

§ 14 Kostenpflicht bei Eingriffen

[1]Wird in ein Denkmal eingegriffen oder ist ein Eingriff beabsichtigt oder liegen zureichende Anhaltspunkte dafür vor, dass in ein Denkmal eingegriffen werden wird, hat die Verursacherin oder der Verursacher des Eingriffes die Kosten im Rahmen des Zumutbaren zu tragen, die für die Untersuchung, Erhaltung und fachgerechte Instandsetzung, Bergung, Dokumentation des Denkmals sowie die Veröffentlichung der Untersuchungsergebnisse anfallen. [2]Soweit die Höhe der Kostentragung seitens der

---

1) Die Landesverordnung über die Einführung des Zustimmungsvorbehalts bei Genehmigungsverfahren betreffend Gründenkmale ist abgedruckt als Nr. D15.I.1d.

Verursacherin oder des Verursachers nicht einvernehmlich in einem öffentlich-rechtlichen Vertrag geregelt wird, wird sie in einem Bescheid der zuständigen oberen Denkmalschutzbehörde festgesetzt.

§ 15 Funde

(1) [1]Wer Kulturdenkmale entdeckt oder findet, hat dies unverzüglich unmittelbar oder über die Gemeinde der oberen Denkmalschutzbehörde mitzuteilen. [2]Die Verpflichtung besteht ferner für die Eigentümerin oder den Eigentümer und die Besitzerin oder den Besitzer des Grundstücks oder des Gewässers, auf oder in dem der Fundort liegt, und für die Leiterin oder den Leiter der Arbeiten, die zur Entdeckung oder zu dem Fund geführt haben. [3]Die Mitteilung einer oder eines der Verpflichteten befreit die übrigen. [4]Die nach Satz 2 Verpflichteten haben das Kulturdenkmal und die Fundstätte in unverändertem Zustand zu erhalten, soweit es ohne erhebliche Nachteile oder Aufwendungen von Kosten geschehen kann. [5]Diese Verpflichtung erlischt spätestens nach Ablauf von vier Wochen seit der Mitteilung.

(2) [1]Bewegliche Kulturdenkmale, die herrenlos sind oder die so lange verborgen gewesen sind, dass ihre Eigentümerinnen oder Eigentümer nicht mehr zu ermitteln sind, werden mit der Entdeckung Eigentum des Landes, wenn sie

1. bei staatlichen Nachforschungen oder
2. in Grabungsschutzgebieten im Sinne des § 2 Absatz 3 Nummer 4 oder
3. bei nicht genehmigten Grabungen oder Suchen

entdeckt werden oder

4. einen hervorragenden wissenschaftlichen Wert besitzen.

[2]Mit Ausnahme der Fälle des Absatzes 2 Nummern 1 und 3 hat die Finderin oder der Finder Anspruch auf eine angemessene Belohnung. [3]Über die Höhe entscheidet die oberste Denkmalschutzbehörde. [4]Absatz 4 findet keine Anwendung.

(3) Ein gefundenes oder ausgegrabenes bewegliches Kulturdenkmal ist der oberen Denkmalschutzbehörde unbeschadet des Eigentumsrechts auf Verlangen befristet zur wissenschaftlichen Bearbeitung auszuhändigen.

(4) [1]Das Land, der Kreis und die Gemeinde, in deren Gebiet ein bewegliches Kulturdenkmal entdeckt oder gefunden ist, haben in dieser Reihenfolge das Recht, die Ablieferung zu verlangen. [2]Bei Funden im Gebiet der Hansestadt Lübeck steht dieses Recht der Hansestadt Lübeck und, wenn diese von ihrem Recht keinen Gebrauch macht, dem Land zu. [3]Die Ablieferung kann nur verlangt werden, wenn Tatsachen vorliegen, nach denen zu befürchten ist, dass der Erhaltungszustand des Gegenstandes verschlechtert wird oder der Gegenstand der wissenschaftlichen Forschung verlorengeht. [4]Die Ablieferung kann nicht mehr verlangt werden, wenn

1. seit der Mitteilung drei Monate verstrichen sind,
2. die Eigentümerinnen oder Eigentümer den Erwerbsberechtigten nach Satz 1 und 2 die Ablieferung des Kulturdenkmals, bevor über die Ablieferungspflicht entschieden ist, angeboten und die Erwerbsberechtigten das Angebot nicht binnen drei Monaten angenommen haben.

[5]Die obere Denkmalschutzbehörde entscheidet auf Antrag einer oder eines Beteiligten, ob die Voraussetzungen der Ablieferung vorliegen.

§ 16 Erhaltung des Denkmals

(1) Eigentümerinnen und Eigentümer, Besitzerinnen und Besitzer sowie die sonst Verfügungsberechtigten haben Denkmale im Rahmen des Zumutbaren zu erhalten, sachgemäß zu behandeln und vor Gefährdung zu schützen.

(2) Wer ein Denkmal vorsätzlich oder grob fahrlässig beschädigt, ist unabhängig von der Verhängung einer Geldbuße zum Ersatz des von ihm verursachten Schadens verpflichtet.

(3) [1]Ein Eigentümerwechsel ist der oberen Denkmalschutzbehörde unverzüglich mitzuteilen. [2]§ 90 Absatz 3 der Gemeindeordnung bleibt unberührt.

§ 17 Maßnahmen der Denkmalschutzbehörden

(1) [1]Die Denkmalschutzbehörden haben zur Wahrnehmung ihrer Aufgaben diejenigen Maßnahmen zu treffen, die ihnen nach pflichtgemäßem Ermessen erforderlich scheinen. [2]Handlungen, die geeignet sind, ein Denkmal zu schädigen oder zu gefährden, können untersagt werden. [3]Im Einzelfall können die Denkmalschutzbehörden mit der Eigentümerin oder dem Eigentümer zur Pflege des Denkmals

D15.I.1 Denkmalschutzgesetz Schleswig-Holstein

einen öffentlich-rechtlichen Vertrag über Abweichungen von Genehmigungstatbeständen oder Verfahren nach den durch dieses Gesetz oder aufgrund dieses Gesetzes ergangenen Vorschriften schließen.
(2) Kommen die Eigentümerinnen und Eigentümer, Besitzerinnen und Besitzer oder die sonst Verfügungsberechtigten ihren Verpflichtungen nach diesem Gesetz nicht nach, kann die obere Denkmalschutzbehörde auf deren Kosten die notwendigen Anordnungen treffen.
(3) Wer eine nach diesem Gesetz genehmigungspflichtige Maßnahme ohne Genehmigung der zuständigen Denkmalschutzbehörde beginnt oder eine genehmigte Maßnahme unsachgemäß durchführt, hat auf Anordnung der zuständigen Denkmalschutzbehörde und auf seine Kosten den alten Zustand wiederherzustellen oder das Kulturdenkmal auf andere geeignete Weise instand zu setzen.
(4) [1]Eigentümerinnen und Eigentümer, Besitzerinnen und Besitzer und die sonst Verfügungsberechtigten haben den Denkmalschutzbehörden und ihren Beauftragten die Besichtigung von Denkmalen zu gestatten und ihnen Auskunft zu geben, soweit dies zur Durchführung des Denkmalschutzes und Denkmalpflege erforderlich ist. [2]Das Gleiche gilt, wenn ein Kulturdenkmal vermutet wird. [3]Wohnungen dürfen gegen den Willen der unmittelbaren Besitzerinnen und Besitzer nur zur Verhinderung einer dringenden Gefahr für Kulturdenkmale betreten werden. [4]Das Grundrecht der Unverletzlichkeit der Wohnung (Artikel 13 des Grundgesetzes) wird insoweit eingeschränkt.
(5) [1]Die obere Denkmalschutzbehörde kann die wirtschaftliche Nutzung eines Grundstücks oder eines Grundstückteils beschränken, auf dem sich Denkmale befinden. [2]Die bisherige Nutzung bleibt unberührt. [3]Die Beschränkung nach Satz 1 ist auf Ersuchen der oberen Denkmalschutzbehörde im Grundbuch einzutragen. [4]Macht die obere Denkmalschutzbehörde von dieser Möglichkeit Gebrauch, entfällt für Eigentümerinnen und Eigentümer die Mitteilungspflicht nach § 16 Absatz 3.

Abschnitt 4
Ordnungswidrigkeiten und Straftaten

§ 18 Ordnungswidrigkeiten
(1) Ordnungswidrig handelt, wer vorsätzlich oder fahrlässig
1. einer Verordnung, die aufgrund dieses Gesetzes erlassen wurde, zuwiderhandelt, soweit sie für einen bestimmten Tatbestand auf diese Bußgeldvorschrift verweist und nicht nach § 19 mit Strafe bewehrt ist,
2. die in § 12 bezeichneten Handlungen ohne Genehmigung vornimmt, soweit diese Handlungen nicht nach § 19 mit Strafe bewehrt sind,
3. den Mitteilungs- und Auskunftspflichten des § 15 Absatz 1 Satz 1 und 2 und des § 17 Absatz 4 Satz 1 und 2 zuwiderhandelt,
4. ein Kulturdenkmal, dessen Ablieferung gemäß § 15 Absatz 4 verlangt worden ist, beiseiteschafft, beschädigt oder zerstört.

(2) Ordnungswidrig handelt auch, wer wider besseres Wissen
1. unrichtige Angaben macht oder
2. unrichtige Pläne oder Unterlagen vorlegt,

um ein Tätigwerden der Denkmalschutzbehörden nach Maßgabe dieses Gesetzes zu erwirken oder zu verhindern.
(3) [1]Gegenstände, auf die sich eine Ordnungswidrigkeit bezieht oder die zur Vorbereitung oder Begehung einer Ordnungswidrigkeit verwendet worden sind, können eingezogen werden. [2]§ 23 des Gesetzes über Ordnungswidrigkeiten findet Anwendung.
(4) [1]Ordnungswidrigkeiten können mit einer Geldbuße bis zu hunderttausend Euro, in besonders schweren Fällen bis zu fünfhunderttausend Euro geahndet werden. [2]Zuständige Verwaltungsbehörde nach § 36 Absatz 1 Nummer 1 des Gesetzes über Ordnungswidrigkeiten sind die Landrätinnen oder Landräte und die Bürgermeisterinnen oder Bürgermeister der kreisfreien Städte.

§ 19 Straftaten
(1) Wer vorsätzlich
1. ohne die nach § 12 Absatz 1 Nummer 1 erforderliche Genehmigung ein Kulturdenkmal beschädigt oder zerstört oder
2. die in § 12 Absatz 2 Nummer 4 bis 7 genannten Handlungen vornimmt, ohne die dafür erforderliche Genehmigung zu haben,

wird mit Freiheitsstrafe bis zu zwei Jahren oder Geldstrafe bestraft, wenn die Tat nicht in anderen Vorschriften mit schwererer Strafe bedroht ist.
(2) Die zur Begehung einer Tat nach Absatz 1 verwendeten Geräte sollen eingezogen werden.

Abschnitt 5
Enteignung

§ 20 Vorübergehende Inbesitznahme eines Kulturdenkmals
(1) ¹Die obere Denkmalschutzbehörde kann ein Kulturdenkmal bis zur Dauer von einem Monat in Besitz nehmen, wenn auf andere Weise von ihm eine Schädigung nicht abgewendet werden kann. ²Wird innerhalb dieser Frist das Enteignungsverfahren eingeleitet, kann die Besitznahme bis zum Abschluss desselben verlängert werden.
(2) Die Anordnung ist den Beteiligten zuzustellen.
(3) ¹Die Eigentümerin oder der Eigentümer des Kulturdenkmals ist für die durch den Besitzentzug entstehenden Vermögensnachteile zu entschädigen. ²Über Art und Höhe der Entschädigung entscheidet die obere Denkmalschutzbehörde nach Anhörung der Beteiligten.

§ 21 Enteignung
(1) Die Enteignung von Kulturdenkmalen ist zulässig, wenn auf andere Weise eine Gefahr für deren Erhaltung nicht zu beseitigen ist.
(2) Die Enteignung erfolgt zugunsten des Landes, des Kreises oder der Gemeinde, in dessen oder in deren Zuständigkeitsbereich sich das Kulturdenkmal befindet.
(3) Bei unbeweglichen Kulturdenkmalen findet das für die Enteignung von Grundeigentum geltende Landesrecht Anwendung.
(4) Bei beweglichen Kulturdenkmalen finden die §§ 1, 2, 4, 5, 7, 8, 11, 12, 24 bis 37, 39, 57 des Gesetzes über die Enteignung von Grundeigentum vom 11. Juni 1874 (GS. S. 221) in der Fassung der Bekanntmachung vom 31. Dezember 1971 (GVOBl. Schl.-H. S. 182), zuletzt geändert durch Artikel 11 des Gesetzes vom 15. Juni 2004 (GVOBl. Schl.-H. S. 153), entsprechende Anwendung.

Abschnitt 6
Schlussvorschriften

§ 22 Gebühren
¹Entscheidungen und Eintragungen nach diesem Gesetz sind gebührenfrei. ²Das gilt auch für Beratungen der Eigentümerinnen und Eigentümer, der Besitzerinnen und Besitzer oder der sonst Verfügungsberechtigten.

§ 23 Staatsverträge mit Religionsgemeinschaften
Unbeschadet der Regelungen in Staatskirchenverträgen zwischen dem Land Schleswig-Holstein mit Kirchen oder Religionsgemeinschaften und abweichend von § 12 Absatz 1 Nummern 1 und 2 werden alle Maßnahmen an Kulturdenkmalen im Eigentum der Kirchen oder Religionsgemeinschaften, insbesondere Instandsetzung, Veränderung und Vernichtung, nur im Benehmen mit der oberen Denkmalschutzbehörde vorgenommen.

§ 24 Übergangsvorschriften
(1) ¹Die vor dem Inkrafttreten dieses Gesetzes in das Denkmalbuch eingetragenen Kulturdenkmale gelten als nach Inkrafttreten dieses Gesetzes in die Denkmalliste eingetragen. ²Denkmalbereiche und Grabungsschutzgebiete, die vor dem Inkrafttreten dieses Gesetzes durch Verordnung festgelegt wurden, gelten nach Inkrafttreten dieses Gesetzes unverändert fort.
(2) Einfache Kulturdenkmale gemäß § 1 Absatz 2 des Denkmalschutzgesetzes in der Fassung vom 12. Januar 2012 (GVOBl. Schl.-H. S. 83), Zuständigkeiten und Ressortbezeichnungen ersetzt durch Artikel 5 der Verordnung vom 4. April 2013 (GVOBl. Schl.-H. S. 143), gelten als Kulturdenkmale für die Dauer einer Abschreibung gemäß §§ 7i, 10f, 10g und 11b Einkommensteuergesetz,

D15.I.1 Denkmalschutzgesetz Schleswig-Holstein

1. wenn die Bescheinigungsbehörde bis zum Tag vor dem Inkrafttreten des Gesetzes
   a) einen entsprechenden Grundlagenbescheid (Bescheinigung für das Finanzamt) für Baumaßnahmen an Kulturdenkmalen erteilt hat,
   b) die Erteilung eines solchen Grundlagenbescheides gemäß § 108a Landesverwaltungsgesetz schriftlich zugesichert hat oder
2. wenn die für die Erteilung eines solchen Grundlagenbescheides erforderlichen Voraussetzungen für eine solche Zusicherung objektiv vorliegen.

(3) [1]Vorhaben von überregionaler Bedeutung, deren Planfeststellung oder Plangenehmigung vor dem Inkrafttreten dieses Gesetzes bei der zuständigen Behörde beantragt wurden, werden nach den bis dahin geltenden Vorschriften des Denkmalschutzgesetzes in der Fassung vom 12. Januar 2012 zu Ende geführt. [2]Dies gilt nur dann nicht, wenn der Träger des Vorhabens dies bei der zuständigen Planfeststellungsbehörde beantragt.

§ 25 Inkrafttreten

[1]Dieses Gesetz tritt am Tag nach seiner Verkündigung[1)] in Kraft. [2]Gleichzeitig tritt das Denkmalschutzgesetz vom 12. Januar 2012 (GVOBl. Schl.-H. S. 83)[2)], Zuständigkeiten und Ressortbezeichnungen ersetzt durch Artikel 5 der Verordnung vom 4. April 2013 (GVOBl. Schl.-H. S. 143), außer Kraft.

---

1) Verkündet am 29.1.2015.
2) **Amtl. Anm.:** GS Schl.-H. II, Gl.Nr. 224-1

Landesverordnung über den Denkmalrat (Denkmalratsverordnung)[1]

Vom 10. Juni 2015 (GVOBl. Schl.-H. S. 152)
(GS Schl.-H. II, Gl.Nr. 224-11-1)

Aufgrund § 6 Absatz 3 Satz 2 des Denkmalschutzgesetzes vom 30. Dezember 2014 (GVOBl. Schl.-H. 2015 S. 2) verordnet das Ministerium für Justiz, Kultur und Europa:

§ 1 Aufgaben
¹Der Denkmalrat hat die Aufgabe, die Denkmalschutzbehörden zu beraten. ²Der Denkmalrat ist unabhängig. ³Er kann sich zu Einzelfällen sowie zu grundsätzlichen und aktuellen Fragestellungen des Denkmalschutzes und der Denkmalpflege äußern und ist berechtigt, Empfehlungen auszusprechen und diese öffentlich zu machen.

§ 2 Zusammensetzung
(1) ¹Der Denkmalrat besteht aus achtzehn Mitgliedern, die aufgrund ihrer wissenschaftlichen oder fachlichen Tätigkeit oder ihres allgemeinen Wirkens in der Öffentlichkeit besondere Kenntnisse und Erfahrungen in Fragen des Denkmalschutzes und der Denkmalpflege erworben haben. ²Jeweils die Hälfte der Mitglieder sollen Frauen und Männer sein.
(2) ¹Als Mitglieder beruft die oberste Denkmalschutzbehörde
1. je zwei Mitglieder auf Vorschlag:
   a) der oberen Denkmalschutzbehörden,
   b) der Arbeitsgemeinschaft der kommunalen Landesverbände,
   c) der Evangelisch-Lutherischen Kirche in Norddeutschland,
2. je ein Mitglied auf Vorschlag:
   a) der Arbeitsgemeinschaft des Grundbesitzes e.V.,
   b) der in Schleswig-Holstein tätigen Interessengemeinschaften Bauernhaus und Interessengemeinschaften Baupflege,
   c) der Schleswig-Holsteinischen Landwirtschaftskammer,
   d) des Verbandes Schleswig-Holsteinischer Haus-, Wohnungs- und Grundeigentümer e.V.,
   e) des Verbandes der norddeutschen Wohnungsunternehmen,
   f) der Handwerkskammer Schleswig-Holstein,
   g) des Verbandes der Restauratoren e.V.,
3. eine Heimatforscherin oder einen Heimatforscher auf Vorschlag des Schleswig-Holsteinischen Heimatbundes,
4. eine Architektin oder einen Architekten auf Vorschlag der Architekten- und Ingenieurkammer Schleswig-Holstein,
5. ein Mitglied aus dem Bereich der Wirtschaft auf gemeinsamen Vorschlag der IHK Schleswig-Holstein – Arbeitsgemeinschaft der Industrie- und Handelskammern zu Flensburg, zu Kiel und zu Lübeck und der Vereinigung der Unternehmensverbände in Hamburg und Schleswig-Holstein,
6. zwei weitere Mitglieder aus dem Bereich der Kulturwissenschaften oder der Organisationen, die sich mit Denkmalschutz und Denkmalpflege befassen; eines dieser Mitglieder soll über Kenntnisse aus dem Bereich der Gartendenkmalpflege und/oder dem Kulturlandschaftsschutz verfügen.

²Die im Schleswig-Holsteinischen Landtag vertretenen Fraktionen können jeweils ein Mitglied mit beratender Stimme entsenden.
(3) Die in Absatz 2 Satz 1 genannten Stellen sollen mindestens doppelt so viele Personen vorschlagen, wie jeweils auf ihren Vorschlag zu berufen sind.
(4) Stellvertreterinnen oder Stellvertreter werden nicht berufen.

§ 3 Tätigkeitsperiode
(1) ¹Die Tätigkeitsperiode des Denkmalrates beträgt fünf Jahre. ²Sie beginnt mit der ersten Sitzung.
(2) Nach Ablauf der Tätigkeitsperiode führt der Denkmalrat die Geschäfte bis zum Zusammentritt des neu berufenen Denkmalrates weiter.

---

1) **Die VO tritt mit Ablauf des 30.6.2020 außer Kraft**, vgl. § 11 Satz 2. Die aktuelle Fassung ist abrufbar unter: https://www.schleswig-holstein.de/DE/Landesregierung/LD/Service/Grundlagen/_documents/Gesetzliches.html.

§ 4 Berufung, Abberufung

(1) ¹Die Mitglieder des Denkmalrates werden für die Tätigkeitsperiode des Denkmalrates berufen. ²Wiederberufung ist zulässig. ³Sie sind ehrenamtlich tätig.

(2) ¹Mitglieder können nach § 98 des Landesverwaltungsgesetzes aus dem Denkmalrat abberufen werden. ²Vor der Abberufung sind das betroffene Mitglied und die Stelle, die es nach § 2 Absatz 2 vorgeschlagen hat, zu hören.

(3) Scheidet ein Mitglied aus dem Denkmalrat aus, ist ein neues Mitglied nach § 2 für die verbleibende Tätigkeitsperiode des Denkmalrates zu berufen.

§ 5 Sitzungen

(1) ¹Der Denkmalrat wird zu seiner ersten Sitzung von der obersten Denkmalschutzbehörde einberufen. ²Seine Mitglieder werden auf die nach §§ 95 und 96 des Landesverwaltungsgesetzes für ehrenamtliche Tätigkeit im Verwaltungsverfahren geltenden Grundsätze verpflichtet. ³Der Denkmalrat wählt aus seiner Mitte eine Vorsitzende oder einen Vorsitzenden und eine Vertreterin oder einen Vertreter der oder des Vorsitzenden.

(2) Zu den weiteren Sitzungen wird der Denkmalrat von der oder dem Vorsitzenden nach Bedarf einberufen.

(3) ¹Der Denkmalrat soll mindestens zweimal jährlich tagen. ²Mindestens einmal jährlich erstatten die oberen Denkmalschutzbehörden dem Denkmalrat einen Bericht. ³Der Denkmalrat erstattet der obersten Denkmalschutzbehörde in der Regel jährlich einen Bericht.

(4) ¹Die oder der Vorsitzende setzt die Tagesordnung fest. ²Fragen, die dem Denkmalrat von der obersten Denkmalschutzbehörde zugeleitet werden, müssen auf die Tagesordnung der nächsten Sitzung gesetzt werden. ³Mitglieder des Denkmalrates können Anträge an die Tagesordnung stellen. ⁴Diese müssen zwei Wochen vor Beginn der Sitzung bei dem Vorsitzenden Mitglied des Denkmalrates eingegangen sein. ⁵Bei Feststellung der Tagesordnung zu Beginn einer jeden Sitzung wird eine Entscheidung darüber getroffen, ob der Antrag zur Beratung angenommen wird.

(5) ¹Die Sitzungen des Denkmalrates sind nicht öffentlich. ²An den Sitzungen nehmen die Leiterinnen und Leiter der oberen Denkmalschutzbehörden mit beratender Stimme teil. ³Darüber hinaus können weitere, von der obersten Denkmalschutzbehörde und der obersten Bauaufsichtsbehörde beauftragte Mitarbeiterinnen oder Mitarbeiter mit beratender Stimme teilnehmen. ⁴Der Denkmalrat kann weitere Sachverständige oder sonstige Personen, die von Maßnahmen des Denkmalschutzes und der Denkmalpflege betroffen sind, sowie Gäste zu den Sitzungen hinzuziehen. ⁵Der Ombudsmann für Denkmalschutz hat das Recht, als Gast an den Sitzungen des Denkmalrates teilzunehmen. ⁶Er hat Rede-, aber kein Stimmrecht.

(6) Die oder der Vorsitzende eröffnet, leitet und schließt die Sitzungen; sie oder er ist für die Ordnung verantwortlich.

§ 6 Beschlussfassung

(1) ¹Der Denkmalrat ist beschlussfähig, wenn alle Mitglieder ordnungsgemäß geladen und mindestens die Hälfte seiner stimmberechtigten Mitglieder anwesend sind. ²Beschlüsse können auch im schriftlichen Verfahren gefasst werden, wenn kein Mitglied widerspricht. ³Stimmenthaltungen werden nicht mitgezählt.

(2) ¹Beschlüsse des Denkmalrates werden mit Stimmenmehrheit gefasst. ²Bei Stimmengleichheit gibt die Stimme der oder des Vorsitzenden den Ausschlag.

(3) Für Wahlen durch den Denkmalrat gilt § 104 des Landesverwaltungsgesetzes.

§ 7 Ausschüsse

Der Denkmalrat kann die Erledigung der Aufgaben nach § 1 und § 6 Denkmalschutzgesetz im Einzelfall oder allgemein durch die Geschäftsordnung (§ 10) Ausschüssen übertragen.

§ 8 Entschädigung

(1) ¹Mitglieder, die nicht im öffentlichen Dienst stehen, erhalten anlässlich der Teilnahme an Sitzungen und Besichtigungen eine Entschädigung in Höhe des Tagegeldes für mindestens 24-stündige Abwesenheit sowie Reisekostenvergütung (ohne Tagegeld) nach Maßgabe des Bundesreisekostengesetzes. ²Darüber hinaus werden Entschädigungen oder Vergütungen nicht gezahlt.

(2) Mitglieder, die im öffentlichen Dienst stehen, erhalten Reisekostenvergütung nach den für ihr Hauptamt geltenden Vorschriften.

(3) Andere Personen, die zu den Sitzungen hinzugezogen werden, erhalten eine Reisekostenvergütung nach dem Bundesreisekostengesetz.

§ 9 Geschäftsführung
(1) Die Geschäfte des Denkmalrates werden bei der obersten Denkmalschutzbehörde geführt, die für die Sitzungen eine Protokollführerin oder einen Protokollführer bestimmt.
(2) Über jede Sitzung des Denkmalrates ist eine Niederschrift nach § 105 des Landesverwaltungsgesetzes anzufertigen.
(3) Beschlüsse zu grundsätzlichen und aktuellen Fragen müssen in der Beschlussfassung als solche bezeichnet werden.

§ 10 Geschäftsordnung
[1]Der Denkmalrat kann seine inneren Angelegenheiten durch eine Geschäftsordnung regeln. [2]Sie bedarf der Genehmigung der obersten Denkmalschutzbehörde.

§ 11 Inkrafttreten, Außerkrafttreten
[1]Diese Verordnung tritt am 1. Juli 2015 in Kraft. [2]Sie tritt mit Ablauf des 30. Juni 2020 außer Kraft.

VO über Vertrauensleute

Landesverordnung über die Vertrauensleute für Kulturdenkmale[1)]
Vom 10. Juni 2015 (GVOBl. Schl.-H. S. 154)
(GS Schl.-H. II, Gl.Nr. 224-11-2)

Aufgrund § 5 des Denkmalschutzgesetzes vom 30. Dezember 2014 (GVOBl. Schl.-H. 2015 S. 2) verordnet das Ministerium für Justiz, Kultur und Europa:

§ 1 Bestellung
(1) Die Vertrauensleute für Kulturdenkmale nach § 5 Denkmalschutzgesetz werden von der oberen Denkmalschutzbehörde im Einvernehmen mit den Kreisen und kreisfreien Städten, in deren Gebiet sie tätig werden sollen, bestellt.
(2) [1]Die zu bestellenden Personen müssen persönlich und fachlich geeignet sein. [2]Sie sollen insbesondere
1. Kenntnisse oder Erfahrungen in Denkmalschutz und Denkmalpflege besitzen,
2. ihren Wohnsitz nach Möglichkeit in dem örtlichen Bereich haben, in dem sie als Vertrauensleute für Kulturdenkmale tätig werden sollen, und
3. volljährig sein.
(3) [1]Bei der Bestellung sind der örtliche Tätigkeitsbereich und die Kulturdenkmale, für die die Bestellung erfolgt, festzulegen. [2]Die oberen Denkmalschutzbehörden können gemeinsame Vertrauensleute bestellen.
(4) [1]Die Bestellung als Vertrauensperson für Kulturdenkmale erfolgt schriftlich. [2]Die Vertrauensperson erhält zur Wahrnehmung ihrer Aufgaben einen Ausweis zum Nachweis ihrer Legitimation.

§ 2 Amtsdauer
(1) [1]Die Vertrauensleute werden für die Dauer von fünf Jahren bestellt. [2]Wiederbestellung ist zulässig.
(2) [1]Die Vertrauensleute können jederzeit aus wichtigem Grund von der oberen Denkmalschutzbehörde, die sie bestellt hat, abberufen werden. [2]Vor der Abberufung sind die betroffenen Vertrauensleute und der Kreis oder die kreisfreie Stadt, in deren Gebiet sie tätig sind, zu hören.

§ 3 Ausübung der Tätigkeit
(1) [1]Die Vertrauensleute sind ehrenamtlich tätig. [2]Soweit in dieser Verordnung nichts anderes geregelt ist, gelten die §§ 93 bis 99 des Landesverwaltungsgesetzes.
(2) Die Vertrauensleute sind bei der Ausübung ihrer Tätigkeit an Weisungen der Denkmalschutzbehörden nicht gebunden.

§ 4 Entschädigung
(1) [1]Die obere Denkmalschutzbehörde kann im Rahmen der von ihrem Träger bereitgestellten Haushaltsmittel den Vertrauensleuten eine Aufwandsentschädigung bis zum Höchstbetrag von 300,00 Euro im Jahr gewähren. [2]Mit ihr sind alle notwendigen Aufwendungen, die den Vertrauensleuten im Zusammenhang mit ihrer Tätigkeit entstehen, abgegolten. [3]Dies gilt auch für entgangenen Arbeitsverdienst.
(2) [1]Das Nähere wird durch Verwaltungsvorschriften geregelt. [2]Sie werden erlassen
1. von der obersten Denkmalschutzbehörde für die von einer oberen Denkmalschutzbehörde des Landes bestellten Vertrauensleute und
2. von der Bürgermeisterin oder dem Bürgermeister der Hansestadt Lübeck für die von ihr oder ihm bestellten Vertrauensleute.

§ 5 Inkrafttreten, Außerkrafttreten
[1]Diese Verordnung tritt am 1. Juli 2015 in Kraft. [2]Sie tritt mit Ablauf des 30. Juni 2020 außer Kraft.

---

1) **Die VO tritt mit Ablauf des 30.6.2020 außer Kraft**, vgl. § 5 Satz 2. Die aktuelle Fassung ist abrufbar unter: https://www.schleswig-holstein.de/DE/Landesregierung/LD/Service/Grundlagen/_documents/Gesetzliches.html

Landesverordnung über das Verfahren zur Ausweisung von Denkmalbereichen und Grabungsschutzgebieten[1)]

Vom 10. Juni 2015 (GVOBl. Schl.-H. S. 156)
(GS Schl.-H. II, Gl.Nr. 224-11-5)

Aufgrund § 10 Absatz 1 Satz 3 des Denkmalschutzgesetzes vom 30. Dezember 2014 (GVOBl. Schl.-H. 2015 S. 2) verordnet das Ministerium für Justiz, Kultur und Europa:

§ 1 [Verfahren bei Erlass einer Verordnung]

(1) [1]Vor Erlass einer Verordnung nach § 10 Absatz 1 Denkmalschutzgesetz ist den Kommunen, in deren Zuständigkeitsbereich der Denkmalbereich oder das Grabungsschutzgebiet liegt, sowie den zuständigen unteren Denkmalschutzbehörden ein Entwurf der Verordnung mit Begründung und Übersichtskarte zur Stellungnahme innerhalb einer angemessenen Frist, wenigstens aber sechs Wochen, zuzuleiten. [2]Die obere Denkmalschutzbehörde prüft die fristgemäß vorgebrachten Stellungnahmen.

(2) [1]Der Entwurf der Verordnung, seine Begründung und eine Übersichtskarte sind für die Dauer eines Monats öffentlich auszulegen. [2]Ort und Dauer der Auslegung sind mindestens eine Woche vorher ortsüblich bekannt zu machen mit dem Hinweis darauf, wo Anregungen schriftlich, zur Niederschrift oder elektronisch vorgebracht werden können. [3]Der Verordnungsentwurf mit Begründung und Karte soll daneben in geeigneten Fällen über das Internet der Öffentlichkeit zugänglich gemacht werden; in diesem Fall ist die Internetadresse in die Bekanntmachung nach Satz 2 aufzunehmen.

(3) Die obere Denkmalschutzbehörde prüft die fristgemäß vorgebrachten Anregungen und führt einen Erörterungstermin durch oder teilt das Ergebnis den Beteiligten, die Stellungnahmen abgegeben haben, und der betroffenen Kommune schriftlich mit.

(4) Wird der Entwurf einer Rechtsverordnung räumlich oder sachlich erheblich erweitert, ist das Verfahren nach den Absätzen 1 bis 3 zu wiederholen.

(5) [1]Die obere Denkmalschutzbehörde hat den Entwurf der Verordnung mit Begründung und Übersichtskarte sowie einer Übersicht der wesentlichen Anregungen und Stellungnahmen und dem dazugehörigen Votum der obersten Denkmalschutzbehörde zur Herstellung des Benehmens zuzuleiten. [2]Der Entwurf der Verordnung mit Begründung und Übersichtskarte ist danach der zuständigen unteren Denkmalschutzbehörde sowie den betroffenen Kommunen zur Herstellung des Benehmens zuzuleiten.

(6) Die Verordnung ist nachrichtlich in der Denkmalliste zu vermerken und den zuständigen Planungs- und Bauaufsichtsbehörden mitzuteilen.

§ 2 [Verfahren bei Änderung oder Aufhebung einer Verordnung]

[1]§ 1 ist bei Änderung oder Aufhebung einer Rechtsverordnung entsprechend anzuwenden. [2]Bei einer räumlich oder sachlich nicht erheblichen Änderung einer Rechtsverordnung kann das Verfahren nach § 1 ersetzt werden, indem den von der Änderung berührten Behörden, Gemeinden sowie den von der Änderung betroffenen Eigentümern und sonstigen Berechtigten Gelegenheit zur Stellungnahme gegeben wird.

§ 3 [Räumlicher Geltungsbereich]

[1]Die Abgrenzung des räumlichen Geltungsbereichs ist in der Verordnung zu beschreiben und in Karten darzustellen, die als Bestandteil der Verordnung im Gesetz- und Verordnungsblatt zu veröffentlichen sind und bei den zuständigen Denkmalschutzbehörden eingesehen werden können; diese Stellen haben Ausfertigungen der Karten aufzubewahren. [2]Die Karten müssen mit hinreichender Bestimmtheit erkennen lassen, welche Grundflächen zum Geltungsbereich gehören; im Zweifel gelten die Flächen als nicht betroffen.

§ 4 [Inkrafttreten, Außerkrafttreten]

[1]Diese Verordnung tritt am 1. Juli 2015 in Kraft. [2]Sie tritt mit Ablauf des 30. Juni 2020 außer Kraft.

---

1) **Die VO tritt mit Ablauf des 30.6.2020 außer Kraft**, vgl. § 4 Satz 2. Die aktuelle Fassung ist abrufbar unter: https://www.schleswig-holstein.de/DE/Landesregierung/LD/Service/Grundlagen/_documents/Gesetzliches.html.

Landesverordnung über die Einführung des Zustimmungsvorbehalts bei Genehmigungsverfahren betreffend Gründenkmale[1]

Vom 10. Juni 2015 (GVOBl. Schl.-H. S. 155)
(GS Schl.-H. II, Gl.Nr. 224-11-4)

Aufgrund des § 13 Absatz 5 des Denkmalschutzgesetzes vom 30. Dezember 2014 (GVOBl. Schl.-H. 2015 S. 2) verordnet das Ministerium für Justiz, Kultur und Europa:

§ 1 [Zustimmungsersuchen]
Vor der Erteilung einer Genehmigung nach § 12 Absatz 1 Nummer 1 Denkmalschutzgesetz hat die untere Denkmalschutzbehörde die Zustimmung der oberen Denkmalschutzbehörde einzuholen, wenn Gründenkmale betroffen sind.

§ 2 [Inkrafttreten, Außerkrafttreten]
[1]Die Verordnung tritt am 1. Juli 2015 in Kraft. [2]Sie tritt mit Ablauf des 30. Juni 2020 außer Kraft.

---

1) Die VO **tritt mit Ablauf des 30.6.2020 außer Kraft**, vgl. § 2 Satz 2. Die aktuelle Fassung ist abrufbar unter: https://www.schleswig-holstein.de/DE/Landesregierung/LD/Service/Grundlagen/_documents/Gesetzliches.html.

Landesverordnung über die Denkmallisten für Kulturdenkmale[1)]

Vom 10. Juni 2015 (GVOBl. Schl.-H. S. 157)
(GS Schl.-H. II, Gl.Nr. 224-11-6)

Aufgrund § 8 Absatz 2 Satz 4 und § 9 Absatz 2 Satz 3 des Denkmalschutzgesetzes vom 30. Dezember 2014 (GVOBl. Schl.-H. 2015 S. 2) verordnet das Ministerium für Justiz, Kultur und Europa:

§ 1 Zuständigkeit
Die oberen Denkmalschutzbehörden (§ 3 Absatz 2 Satz 1 Nummer 2 Denkmalschutzgesetz) führen die Denkmallisten der unbeweglichen Kulturdenkmale und die Denkmallisten der beweglichen Kulturdenkmale tagesaktuell für ihren jeweiligen Zuständigkeitsbereich (§ 8 Absatz 1 Satz 6, § 9 Absatz 1 Satz 1, Absatz 2 Denkmalschutzgesetz).

§ 2 Denkmalliste der unbeweglichen Kulturdenkmale
(1) Für die Denkmalliste der unbeweglichen Kulturdenkmale nach § 8 Denkmalschutzgesetz sind die folgenden Daten zu verarbeiten:
1. die Bezeichnung des Kulturdenkmals,
2. seine Objektnummer,
3. die Beschreibung der wesentlichen Merkmale des Kulturdenkmals einschließlich des Zubehörs und der Ausstattung, soweit vorhanden,
4. die Begründung des Denkmalwertes,
5. die Bezeichnung des Umfangs des Denkmalschutzes,
6. die Bezeichnung des Ortes, an dem sich das Kulturdenkmal befindet (Anschrift oder Koordinatenbezeichnungen, gegebenenfalls auch Darstellung in digitalen Karten),
7. die Grundbuchbezeichnung, sofern sie noch nicht in einer Datenbank erfasst oder ihre Verarbeitung notwendig ist,
8. die Angabe der zuständigen unteren Denkmalschutzbehörde,
9. die Namen und Anschriften der Eigentümerinnen und Eigentümer, sofern sie noch nicht in einer Datenbank erfasst sind,
10. der Tag, an dem das Kulturdenkmal in die Liste aufgenommen wurde, und der Tag einer Veränderung (Aktualisierung) oder Löschung,
11. bei Grundbucheintragung der Beschränkung der wirtschaftlichen Nutzung gemäß § 17 Absatz 5 Satz 3 Denkmalschutzgesetz der Tag des Eintragungsersuchens und der Eintragung ins Grundbuch.

(2) Bei der Festlegung einer Schutzzone sind nach § 10 Absatz 4 Denkmalschutzgesetz in der Denkmalliste der unbeweglichen Kulturdenkmale folgende Daten zu vermerken:
1. die Bezeichnung der Schutzzone,
2. die Beschreibung der wesentlich für die Erkenntnisse und Bewertung erforderlichen Merkmale der Schutzzone (Ausmaß und Bestandteile),
3. die Beschreibung des Schutzzieles und des Schutzzweckes,
4. die Kommunen und unteren Denkmalschutzbehörden, in deren Zuständigkeitsbereich die Schutzzone liegt,
5. den Hinweis auf die Veröffentlichung der jeweiligen Verordnung.

(3) Die Denkmalliste nach Absatz 1 gliedert sich in
1. Schutzzonen
   a) Denkmalbereiche,
   b) Grabungsschutzgebiete,
   c) Welterbestätten mit Pufferzonen,
2. Archäologische Denkmale,
3. Baudenkmale
   a) Sachgesamtheiten,
   b) Mehrheit von baulichen Anlagen,

[1)] **Die VO tritt mit Ablauf des 30.6.2020 außer Kraft**, vgl. § 6 Satz 2. Die aktuelle Fassung ist abrufbar unter. https://www.schleswig-holstein.de/DE/Landesregierung/LD/Service/Grundlagen/_documents/Gesetzliches.html.

D15.I.1e VO Denkmallisten für Kulturdenkmale

    c) Bauliche Anlagen,
    d) Teile von baulichen Anlagen,
4. Gründenkmale (von Menschen gestaltete Garten- und Landschaftsteile),
5. Sonstige Kulturdenkmale.

§ 3 Denkmalliste der beweglichen Kulturdenkmale
Für die Denkmalliste nach § 9 Absatz 1 Denkmalschutzgesetz sind die folgenden Daten zu verarbeiten:
1. die Angaben nach § 2 Absatz 1 Nummer 1 bis 6, 8 bis 9, den unbeweglichen Kulturdenkmalen entsprechend,
2. der Hinweis auf die Verfügung, mit der die Eintragung des Kulturdenkmals in die Denkmalliste oder ihre Veränderung oder Löschung angeordnet wird.

§ 4 Aktualisierung überführter Angaben
Angaben zu Denkmalen, die gemäß § 24 Denkmalschutzgesetz in die Denkmalliste überführt worden sind, werden in ihrer Veröffentlichung gemäß § 5 laufend ergänzt und angepasst.

§ 5 Veröffentlichungspflicht
[1]Für unbewegliche Kulturdenkmale sind die Angaben gemäß § 2 Absatz 1 Nummer 1 bis 6 an geeigneter Stelle zu veröffentlichen (§ 8 Absatz 2 Satz 1 und 3 Denkmalschutzgesetz). [2]Sie sind einmal im Jahr zu einem vorher bekanntgegebenen Stichtag zu aktualisieren. [3]Sie sind den unteren Denkmalschutzbehörden mindestens einmal im Quartal zur Kenntnis zu geben. [4]Angaben zu Zubehör und Ausstattung gemäß § 2 Absatz 1 Nummer 3 können hiervon ausgenommen werden. [5]Angaben zu beweglichen Kulturdenkmalen werden nur auf Antrag der Eigentümerinnen und Eigentümer im Umfang der § 3 in Verbindung mit § 2 Absatz 1 Nummer 1 bis 5 veröffentlicht.

§ 6 Inkrafttreten, Außerkrafttreten
[1]Diese Verordnung tritt am 1. Juli 2015 in Kraft. [2]Sie tritt mit Ablauf des 30. Juni 2020 außer Kraft.

Gesetz über die Sicherung und Nutzung öffentlichen Archivgutes in Schleswig-Holstein (Landesarchivgesetz – LArchG)

Vom 11. August 1992 (GVOBl. Schl.-H. S. 444, ber. S. 498)
(GS Schl.-H. II, Gl.Nr. 224-5)
zuletzt geändert durch Art. 8 G zur Anpassung des Datenschutzrechts an die VO (EU) 2016/679 und zur Umsetzung der RL (EU) 2016/680 vom 2. Mai 2018 (GVOBl. Schl.-H. S. 162)

Nichtamtliche Inhaltsübersicht

Erster Teil
Allgemeine Bestimmungen
- § 1 Grundsatz
- § 2 Geltungsbereich
- § 3 Begriffsbestimmungen

Zweiter Teil
Landesarchiv
- § 4 Organisation und Aufgaben des Landesarchivs
- § 5 Beratung und Einsicht in Registraturen
- § 6 Anbietung
- § 7 Übernahme
- § 8 Verwaltung des Archivguts
- § 9 Nutzung des Archivguts
- § 10 Schiedsausschuss
- § 11 Schutzrechte
- § 12 Unterlagen von Stellen des Bundes, bundesrechtliche Geheimhaltungsvorschriften
- § 13 Rechtsverordnungen

Dritter Teil
Sonstige öffentliche Archive
- § 14 Archiv des Schleswig-Holsteinischen Landtags
- § 15 Kommunale Archive
- § 16 Sonstige öffentliche Archive
- § 17 Aufsicht
- § 18 Inkrafttreten

Der Landtag hat das folgende Gesetz beschlossen:

Erster Teil
Allgemeine Bestimmungen

§ 1 Grundsatz
¹Öffentliche Archive dienen der Forschung und Bildung, der Verwaltung und Rechtssicherung und ermöglichen die Auseinandersetzung mit Geschichte, Kultur und Politik. ²Sie schützen das öffentliche Archivgut gegen Vernichtung und Zersplitterung und sind der Öffentlichkeit für die Nutzung zugänglich. ³Sie bilden das öffentliche Gedächtnis eines Landes.

§ 2 Geltungsbereich
(1) ¹Die Archivierung ist Aufgabe
1. des Landes,
2. der Kreise,
3. der Gemeinden,
4. der Ämter,
5. der Zweckverbände mit Ausnahme der in Absatz 2 Nr. 3 genannten Zweckverbände sowie
6. aller sonstigen der Aufsicht des Landes unterstehenden Träger der öffentlichen Verwaltung.

²Die Kreise, Gemeinden, Ämter, Zweckverbände und die sonstigen der Aufsicht des Landes unterstehenden Träger der öffentlichen Verwaltung nehmen diese Aufgabe eigenverantwortlich wahr.

(2) Dieses Gesetz gilt nicht für
1. die öffentlich-rechtlichen Religions- und Weltanschauungsgemeinschaften und ihre Dienste, Werke und Einrichtungen,
2. die öffentlich-rechtlichen Rundfunkanstalten und die Unabhängige Landesanstalt für das Rundfunkwesen sowie
3. öffentlich-rechtliche Unternehmen mit eigener Rechtspersönlichkeit, die am Wettbewerb teilnehmen, und deren Zusammenschlüsse sowie Zweckverbände nach § 15 Abs. 3 des Gesetzes über kommunale Zusammenarbeit und nach dem Sparkassengesetz.

D15.II.1 Landesarchivgesetz Schleswig-Holstein

§ 3 Begriffsbestimmungen

(1) Archivgut sind alle archivwürdigen Unterlagen, die in ein Archiv übernommen sind, und sonstiges Dokumentationsmaterial, das von einem Archiv als Ergänzung seines Archivgutes gesammelt wird.

(2) Unterlagen im Sinne dieses Gesetzes sind insbesondere Akten, Urkunden, Schriftstücke, Karten, Pläne, Karteien, Bild-, Film- und Tonmaterial und sonstige Informationsträger einschließlich der darauf befindlichen Informationen und der zu ihrer Ordnung, Nutzung und Auswertung erforderlichen Hilfsmittel.

(3) [1]Archivwürdig sind Unterlagen, die nach Feststellung der zuständigen Archivbehörde für
1. Wissenschaft oder Forschung,
2. das Verständnis der Gegenwart und der Geschichte,
3. Zwecke der Gesetzgebung, Verwaltung oder Rechtsprechung oder
4. die Sicherung berechtigter Belange betroffener Personen oder Dritter

von bleibendem Wert sind. [2]Archivwürdig sind auch Unterlagen, die aufgrund von anderen Rechtsvorschriften oder zur Rechtswahrung dauernd aufbewahrt werden müssen.

(4) Archivierung umfaßt die Aufgabe, archivwürdige Unterlagen nach fachlichen Gesichtspunkten zu erfassen, zu übernehmen, als Archivgut dauernd zu verwahren, zu sichern, zu erschließen, aufzubereiten und für die Benutzung bereitzustellen.

(5) Entstehung im Sinne dieses Gesetzes bezeichnet den Zeitpunkt der Vervollständigung einer Unterlage oder des letzten organischen Zuwachses von Unterlagen.

Zweiter Teil
Landesarchiv

§ 4 Organisation und Aufgaben des Landesarchivs

(1) [1]Das bestehende Landesarchiv Schleswig-Holstein wird als Landesoberbehörde mit Sitz in Schleswig im Geschäftsbereich des für Kultur zuständigen Ministeriums des Landes Schleswig-Holstein errichtet. [2]Es führt die bisherige Bezeichnung „Landesarchiv Schleswig-Holstein" (Landesarchiv). [3]Seine Zuständigkeit erstreckt sich auf das ganze Land.

(2) Das Landesarchiv hat die Aufgabe, die archivwürdigen Unterlagen der Behörden und Gerichte des Landes, ihrer besonderen Organisationseinheiten sowie ihrer Funktionsvorgänger und der Rechtsvorgänger des Landes zu archivieren.

(3) [1]Das Landesarchiv kann auch archivwürdige Unterlagen anderer Verfügungsberechtigter, insbesondere privater Personen, archivieren. [2]Die Beteiligten können durch Vertrag regeln, ob die Vorschriften dieses Gesetzes angewandt werden sollen oder ob andere Pflichten und Rechte für die Vertragsparteien gelten. [3]Schutzwürdige Belange betroffener Person[1]) dürfen nicht beeinträchtigt werden.

(4) Soweit daran ein öffentliches Interesse besteht, ergänzt das Landesarchiv seine Bestände durch sonstiges Dokumentationsmaterial.

(5) [1]Das Landesarchiv erbringt aus seinen Quellenbeständen als Informationszentrum Dienstleistungen für Forschung und Bildung. [2]Es erteilt Auskünfte, berät und unterstützt Benutzerinnen und Benutzer.

(6) [1]Das Landesarchiv soll durch eigene Maßnahmen die Auseinandersetzung mit der Geschichte des Landes Schleswig-Holstein fördern. [2]Es kann zu diesem Zweck auch eigene Forschungsvorhaben durchführen oder sich an anderen Forschungsvorhaben beteiligen.

(7) Das Landesarchiv trägt zur Qualifizierung ehren-, neben- und hauptamtlicher Mitarbeiterinnen und Mitarbeiter von Archiven bei.

(8) Es erfüllt weitere Aufgaben, die in sachlichem Zusammenhang mit dem Archivwesen des Landes stehen.

§ 5 Beratung und Einsicht in Registraturen

(1) [1]Das Landesarchiv hat die in § 4 Abs. 2 genannten Stellen bei der Verwaltung und Sicherung ihrer Unterlagen im Hinblick auf die spätere Archivierung zu beraten. [2]Es kann den Landtag, die in § 2 Abs. 1 Nr. 2 bis 6 genannten Träger der öffentlichen Verwaltung und die in § 4 Abs. 3 genannten anderen Verfügungsberechtigten bei der Verwaltung und Sicherung ihrer Unterlagen im Hinblick auf die spätere Archivierung beraten.

---

1) Wortlaut amtlich.

(2) ¹Schon vor dem Zeitpunkt des Anbietens der Unterlagen nach § 6 Abs. 1 ist den Vertreterinnen und Vertretern des Landesarchivs zur Erfassung und Sicherung archivwürdiger Unterlagen Einsicht in alle Unterlagen und Hilfsmittel der Registraturen der in § 4 Abs. 2 genannten Stellen zu gewähren. ²Geheimhaltungsvorschriften des Landes stehen der Einsichtnahme nicht entgegen. ³Bei Unterlagen, die sich auf eine natürliche Person beziehen, besteht das Recht auf Einsicht nicht, soweit schutzwürdige Interessen einzelner entgegenstehen. ⁴Die erforderlichen Auskünfte sind zu erteilen. ⁵Das Landesarchiv hat durch geeignete sachliche und personelle Maßnahmen sicherzustellen, daß Gesichtspunkte des Geheimschutzes nicht beeinträchtigt werden.

§ 6 Anbietung
(1) ¹Die Behörden und Gerichte des Landes Schleswig-Holstein und ihre besonderen Organisationseinheiten haben dem Landesarchiv alle Unterlagen, die sie zur Erfüllung ihrer Aufgaben nicht mehr benötigen, unverzüglich zur Übernahme anzubieten. ²Unterlagen sind spätestens 30 Jahre nach ihrer Entstehung anzubieten, soweit nicht Rechtsvorschriften andere Fristen bestimmen.
(2) ¹Anzubieten sind auch Unterlagen, die personenbezogene Daten, deren Verarbeitung eingeschränkt ist oder nach einer Rechtsvorschrift gelöscht werden müßten oder könnten, enthalten oder besonderen Geheimhaltungsvorschriften unterliegen sowie Schriftgut, das besondere Kategorien personenbezogener Daten im Sinne von Artikel 9 Absatz 1 der Verordnung (EU) 2016/679[1)] enthält, soweit dies zur Erfüllung von Aufgaben nach diesem Gesetz erforderlich ist. ²§ 12 des Landesdatenschutzgesetzes gilt entsprechend. ³Ausgenommen sind Unterlagen, deren Offenbarung gegen das Brief-, Post- oder Fernmeldegeheimnis verstoßen würde. ⁴Unberührt bleiben die Rechtsvorschriften über die Löschung unzulässig erhobener oder weiterverarbeiteter Daten oder Unterlagen.
(3) ¹Die Anbietungspflicht umfaßt auch die Akten, die die einzelnen Entnazifizierungsverfahren betreffen und nach § 15 Abs. 1 Satz 1 des Gesetzes zur Beendigung der Entnazifizierung vom 17. März 1951 (GVOBl. Schl.-H. S. 85) nach Weisung des Innenministers in Verwahrung zu nehmen waren. ²§ 3 Abs. 3 des Gesetzes über die Sammlung des Schleswig-Holsteinischen Landesrechts vom 4. April 1961 (GVOBl. Schl.-H. S. 47) ist auf diese Akten nicht anzuwenden.
(4) Das Landesarchiv kann im Benehmen mit der anbietenden Stelle
1. die Auswahl und die Form der Übergabe maschinenlesbar gespeicherter Informationen festlegen,
2. den Umfang der anzubietenden gleichförmigen Unterlagen, die in großer Zahl erwachsen, festlegen und
3. auf das Anbieten von Unterlagen von offensichtlich geringer Bedeutung verzichten.
(5) Ausnahmsweise können im Einvernehmen mit dem Landesarchiv Unterlagen nach Maßgabe der Absätze 1, 2 und 4 einem sonstigen öffentlichen Archiv angeboten werden, wenn die Einhaltung der in den §§ 7, 8, 9 und 11 getroffenen Bestimmungen gewährleistet ist.

§ 7 Übernahme
(1) Das Landesarchiv übernimmt die von ihm als archivwürdig festgestellten Unterlagen.
(2) Lehnt das Landesarchiv die Übernahme ab oder übernimmt es angebotene Unterlagen nicht innerhalb eines Jahres, so ist die anbietende Stelle zu deren weiterer Aufbewahrung nicht verpflichtet.
(3) ¹Archivwürdige Unterlagen können bereits vor Ablauf der durch Rechtsvorschriften bestimmten Aufbewahrungsfristen vom Landesarchiv endgültig übernommen werden. ²Die Aufbewahrungsfristen werden in diesem Fall durch die Aufbewahrung im Landesarchiv gewahrt.
(4) Das Landesarchiv kann im Einvernehmen mit der abgebenden Stelle auch Unterlagen übernehmen, für die noch keine Anbietungspflicht besteht und über deren Archivwürdigkeit noch keine Feststellung getroffen worden ist.

§ 8 Verwaltung des Archivguts
(1) ¹Das Landesarchiv hat die ordnungs- und sachgemäße Aufbewahrung und Benutzbarkeit seines Archivguts sowie dessen Schutz vor unbefugter Nutzung, Beschädigung oder Vernichtung durch geeignete organisatorische und personelle Maßnahmen sicherzustellen. ²Es hat von der Übernahme an im Rahmen dieses Gesetzes die schutzwürdigen Belange betroffener Personen oder Dritter zu berücksichtigen.

---

1) **Amtl. Anm** · Verordnung (EU) 2016/679 des Europäischen Parlaments und des Rates vom 27. April 2016 zum Schutz natürlicher Personen bei der Verarbeitung personenbezogener Daten, zum freien Datenverkehr und zur Aufhebung der Richtlinie 95/46/EG (Datenschutz-Grundverordnung) (ABl. L 119 S. 1, ber. 2016 ABl. L 314 S. 72).

D15.II.1 Landesarchivgesetz Schleswig-Holstein

(2) ¹Das Landesarchiv ist verpflichtet, das Archivgut nach archivfachlichen Gesichtspunkten zu ordnen und durch Findmittel zu erschließen. ²Die Verknüpfung personenbezogener Daten durch das Landesarchiv ist nur zulässig, wenn schutzwürdige Belange betroffener Personen oder Dritter nicht beeinträchtigt werden.

(3) Soweit es unter archivfachlichen Gesichtspunkten vertretbar oder geboten ist, kann das Landesarchiv im Benehmen mit der abgebenden Stelle die im Archivgut enthaltenen Informationen auch in anderer Form archivieren und die Originalunterlagen vernichten.

(4) ¹Unterlagen, bei denen die Voraussetzungen für die Archivwürdigkeit nicht oder nicht mehr vorliegen, sind zu vernichten, soweit nicht die abgebende Stelle erklärt, daß die Voraussetzungen für eine Einschränkung der Verarbeitung an Stelle der Löschung vorliegen. ²In diesem Falle sind die Unterlagen von der abgebenden Stelle auf ihre Kosten zurückzunehmen.

(5) Soweit Verfahrensakten der Gerichte und Staatsanwaltschaften betroffen sind, ist in den Fällen der Absätze 3 und 4 das Einvernehmen erforderlich.

(6) Das Landesarchiv kann Archivgut mit Ausnahme der Unterlagen nach § 6 Abs. 3 an andere öffentliche Archive abgeben, wenn dies fachlich geboten ist und wenn die Einhaltung der in den §§ 9 und 11 getroffenen Bestimmungen gewährleistet bleibt.

(7) ¹Bei Unterlagen nach § 7 Abs. 4 bleibt das Verfügungsrecht über die Unterlagen bei der abgebenden Stelle, die auch über die Nutzung entscheidet. ²Die Verantwortung des Landesarchivs beschränkt sich auf die in Absatz 1 bestimmten Maßnahmen.

(8) ¹Die Verarbeitung besonderer Kategorien personenbezogener Daten im Sinne von Artikel 9 Absatz 1 Verordnung (EU) 2016/679 ist zulässig, soweit dies im Einzelfall zur Erfüllung von Aufgaben nach diesem Gesetz erforderlich ist. ²§ 12 des Landesdatenschutzgesetzes gilt entsprechend.

§ 9 Nutzung des Archivguts

(1) ¹Alle Personen haben das Recht, das Archivgut nach Maßgabe dieses Gesetzes und der auf seiner Grundlage erlassenen Rechtsvorschriften zu nutzen. ²Weitergehende gesetzliche Rechte bleiben unberührt.

(2) Die Nutzung des Archivgutes ist einzuschränken oder zu versagen, soweit
1. die Geheimhaltungspflicht nach § 203 Abs. 1 bis 3 des Strafgesetzbuches oder andere Rechtsvorschriften verletzt würden,
2. Grund zu der Annahme besteht, daß das Wohl der Bundesrepublik Deutschland oder eines ihrer Länder gefährdet wird,
3. Grund zu der Annahme besteht, daß schutzwürdige Belange betroffener Personen oder Dritter entgegenstehen,
4. dadurch der Erhaltungszustand des Archivguts gefährdet würde,
5. ein nicht vertretbarer Verwaltungsaufwand entstehen würde oder
6. besondere Vereinbarungen mit privaten Eigentümern getroffen werden.

(3) ¹Soweit durch Rechtsvorschriften nichts anderes bestimmt ist, bleibt Archivgut für die Dauer von zehn Jahren seit Entstehung der Unterlagen von der Nutzung ausgeschlossen. ²Unterliegt das Archivgut einem besonderen Amtsgeheimnis oder besonderen Rechtsvorschriften über Geheimhaltung, darf es erst dreißig Jahre nach Entstehung der Unterlagen genutzt werden. ³Archivgut, das sich nach seiner Zweckbestimmung oder seinem wesentlichen Inhalt auf eine natürliche Person bezieht (personenbezogenes Archivgut), darf in jedem Falle erst zehn Jahre nach deren Tod oder, wenn das Todesdatum nicht bekannt oder nur mit unvertretbarem Aufwand feststellbar ist, neunzig Jahre nach deren Geburt genutzt werden. ⁴Ist weder ein Todes- noch ein Geburtsdatum feststellbar, endet die Schutzfrist für personenbezogenes Archivgut sechzig Jahre nach Entstehung der Unterlagen.

(4) ¹Schutzfristen nach Absatz 3 gelten nicht für
1. Unterlagen, die bei ihrer Entstehung zur Veröffentlichung bestimmt oder der Öffentlichkeit zugänglich waren, sowie
2. die Nutzung des Archivguts durch die Stellen, bei denen die Unterlagen entstanden sind oder die sie abgegeben haben, wenn sie das Archivgut für die Erfüllung ihrer Aufgaben wieder benötigen. Dies gilt nicht für Archivgut, das vor der Ablieferung hätte in der Verarbeitung eingeschränkt, vernichtet oder gelöscht werden müssen,
3. die Nutzung des Archivguts zu wissenschaftlichen Zwecken unter den Voraussetzungen und nach dem Verfahren des § 13 des Landesdatenschutzgesetzes.

4. personenbezogenes Archivgut, das die Tätigkeit von Personen dokumentiert, soweit sie in Ausübung eines öffentlichen Amtes gehandelt haben und ihre persönlichen Lebensverhältnisse nicht betroffen sind. In diesem Fall endet die Schutzfrist zehn Jahre nach Entstehung der Unterlagen. Hat die Tätigkeit in personen-bezogenem Archivgut ihren Niederschlag gefunden, sind die schutzwürdigen Interessen Dritter angemessen zu berücksichtigen.

(5) Das Landesarchiv kann die Schutzfristen im Einzelfall oder für bestimmte Teile von Archivgut verkürzen, wenn Rechtsvorschriften nicht entgegenstehen.

(6) Bei personenbezogenem Archivgut ist im Einzelfall der Nutzung eine Verkürzung nur zulässig, wenn
1. die betroffenen Personen oder nach deren Tod die überlebende Ehegattin oder der überlebende Ehegatte, die überlebende eingetragene Lebenspartnerin oder der überlebende eingetragene Lebenspartner, nach deren oder dessen Tod die Kinder oder wenn weder eine Ehegattin oder ein Ehegatte, eine eingetragene Lebenspartnerin oder ein eingetragener Lebenspartner noch Kinder vorhanden sind, die Eltern eingewilligt haben oder
2. die Nutzung zu wissenschaftlichen Zwecken oder zur Wahrnehmung von Belangen, die im überwiegenden Interesse betroffener Personen oder Dritter liegen, unerlässlich ist und die Wahrung der schutzwürdigen Belange der betroffenen Personen oder Dritter durch geeignete Maßnahmen sichergestellt ist.

§ 10 Schiedsausschuß

(1) ¹Gegen die Entscheidung des Landesarchivs über die Nutzung von Archivgut kann binnen eines Monats beim Landesarchiv Widerspruch eingelegt werden. ²Über den Widerspruch entscheidet ein Schiedsausschuß binnen drei Monaten. ³Das Recht, durch Klage die Verweigerung der Nutzung des Archivguts anzufechten, bleibt unberührt.

(2) ¹Der Schiedsausschuß wird beim Landesarchiv gebildet und besteht aus drei Mitgliedern, die von dem für Kultur zuständige[1]) Ministerium des Landes Schleswig-Holstein[2]) für drei Jahre berufen werden. ²Jeweils ein Mitglied soll über besondere Fachkenntnisse auf dem Gebiet des Archivwesens, des Datenschutzes und der wissenschaftlichen Forschung oder der Archivbenutzung zu wissenschaftlichen Zwecken verfügen. ³Dem Schiedsausschuß gehört mindestens eine Frau an.

(3) Das für Kultur zuständigen[1]) Ministerium des Landes Schleswig-Holstein[3]) regelt das Nähere über die Zusammensetzung und das Verfahren des Schiedsausschusses durch Verordnung.

§ 11 Schutzrechte

(1) ¹Das Recht der betroffenen Person auf Auskunft gemäß Artikel 15 der Verordnung (EU) 2016/679 über die im Archivgut zu ihrer Person enthaltenen Daten oder auf Einsicht in das Archivgut, das sich auf sie bezieht, besteht nicht, soweit
1. eine Nutzung nach § 9 Absatz 2 Nummer 1, 2 oder 6 einzuschränken oder zu versagen wäre,
2. Grund zu der Annahme besteht, dass schutzwürdige Belange Dritter entgegenstehen,
3. das Archivgut nicht erschlossen ist,
4. die betroffene Person keine Angaben macht, die das Auffinden der Daten ermöglichen,
5. der für die Erteilung der Information erforderliche Aufwand außer Verhältnis zu dem geltend gemachten Informationsinteresse steht,
6. Grund zu der Annahme besteht, dass die Erteilung der Information die öffentliche Sicherheit oder Ordnung gefährden oder sonst dem Wohl des Bundes oder eine[1]) Landes schwere Nachteile bereiten würde und die Interessen des Verantwortlichen an der Nichterteilung der Information die Interessen der betroffenen Person überwiegen, oder
7. die personenbezogenen Daten oder die Tatsache ihrer Verarbeitung nach einer Rechtsvorschrift oder wegen der Rechte und Freiheiten anderer Personen geheim zu halten sind.

²Eine Ablehnung nach Satz 1 Nummer 6 oder 7 muss nicht begründet werden, soweit durch die Mitteilung der Gründe der mit der Auskunftsverweigerung verfolgte Zweck gefährdet würde. ³Soweit die Ablehnung nach Satz 2 nicht begründet wird, sind die Gründe dafür aktenkundig zu machen. ⁴Weitergehende Ansprüche nach Artikel 15 der Verordnung (EU) 2016/679 bestehen nicht. ⁵Rechte be-

---

1) Wortlaut amtlich.
2) Richtig wohl: „dem für Kultur zuständigen Ministerium des Landes Schleswig-Holstein".
3) Richtig wohl: „Das für Kultur zuständige Ministerium des Landes Schleswig-Holstein".

troffener Personen nach Artikel 16 Satz 1 und den Artikeln 18, 20 und 21 der Verordnung (EU) 2016/679 und die Mitteilungspflicht nach Artikel 19 der Verordnung (EU) 2016/679 bestehen nicht.
(2) [1]Wird festgestellt, daß personenbezogene Angaben unrichtig sind, so ist dies in den Unterlagen zu vermerken oder auf sonstige Weise festzuhalten. [2]Bestreiten betroffene Personen die Richtigkeit personenbezogener Angaben, so ist ihnen die Möglichkeit einer Gegendarstellung einzuräumen. [3]Das Landesarchiv ist verpflichtet, die Gegendarstellung den Unterlagen hinzuzufügen. [4]Nach dem Tode der betroffenen Personen steht dieses Recht dem Personenkreis nach § 9 Abs. 6 Satz 1 Nr. 1 zu.
(3) Rechtsansprüche betroffener Personen auf Löschung unzulässig gespeicherter personenbezogener Daten bleiben unberührt.

§ 12 Unterlagen von Stellen des Bundes, bundesrechtliche Geheimhaltungsvorschriften
(1) Für Unterlagen, die nach § 7 des Bundesarchivgesetzes vom 10. März 2017 (BGBl. I S. 410), geändert durch Artikel 10 Absatz 3 des Gesetzes vom 31. Oktober 2017 (BGBl. I S. 3618) von Stellen des Bundes dem Landesarchiv übergeben werden, gelten § 6 Absatz 3 Satz 1 sowie die §§ 10 bis 14 des Bundesarchivgesetzes entsprechend.
(2) Für Unterlagen, die den Rechtsvorschriften des Bundes über die Geheimhaltung im Sinne des § 6 des Bundesarchivgesetzes unterliegen, und die von anderen als den in öffentlichen Stellen des Bundes nach § 5 Absatz 1 Satz 1 des Bundesarchivgesetzes genannten Stellen dem Landesarchiv übergeben werden, gelten §§ 5 und 10 bis 13 des Bundesarchivgesetzes entsprechend.

§ 13 Rechtsverordnungen
Das für Kultur zuständige Ministerium des Landes Schleswig-Holstein regelt durch Verordnung
1. die Nutzung des Archivguts, insbesondere das Antrags- und Genehmigungsverfahren, die Sorgfaltspflichten bei der Nutzung und die Herstellung von Kopien und Reproduktionen, sowie
2. die unentgeltliche Abgabe eines Belegexemplares jeder unter maßgeblicher Benutzung von Archivgut des Landesarchivs hergestellten, vervielfältigten Arbeit. Hierbei sind die Belastung mindernde Ausgleichsleistungen oder Maßnahmen vorzusehen, wenn die unentgeltliche Abgabe für die oder den Verpflichteten nicht zumutbar ist.

Dritter Teil
Sonstige öffentliche Archive

§ 14 Archiv des Schleswig-Holsteinischen Landtags
(1) [1]Der Schleswig-Holsteinische Landtag entscheidet in eigener Zuständigkeit, ob bei ihm entstandene Unterlagen, die zur Erfüllung der Aufgaben nicht mehr benötigt werden, von ihm selbst archiviert oder dem Landesarchiv zur Archivierung angeboten werden. [2]Im Falle der Anbietung ist das Landesarchiv zur Übernahme der archivwürdigen Unterlagen verpflichtet.
(2) [1]Sofern der Schleswig-Holsteinische Landtag ein eigenes Archiv unterhält, gelten die §§ 8, 9 und 11 sinngemäß. [2]Die Präsidentin oder der Präsident des Landtags regelt die Einzelheiten der Benutzung durch Satzung.

§ 15 Kommunale Archive
(1) [1]Die Kreise, Gemeinden, Ämter und Zweckverbände regeln die Archivierung und Nutzbarmachung der bei ihnen entstandenen Unterlagen in eigener Verantwortung, insbesondere Antrags- und Genehmigungsverfahren sowie Zugangsbedingungen. [2]Sie können zu diesem Zweck
1. eigene Archive errichten und unterhalten oder
2. zusammen mit anderen kommunalen Körperschaften Gemeinschaftsarchive schaffen oder sich daran beteiligen oder
3. ihre Unterlagen dem Landesarchiv – sofern dieses zur Übernahme bereit ist – oder einem sonstigen öffentlichen Archiv anbieten und übergeben. Die Kreise mit eigenem Archiv sind zur Übernahme des ihnen von den Gemeinden und Ämtern angebotenen Archivguts verpflichtet. Einzelheiten der Archivierung und Rückgabe, insbesondere die Kostenbeteiligung der abgebenden kommunalen Körperschaft, werden durch öffentlich-rechtlichen Vertrag geregelt.

[3]Die anbietenden Kreise, Gemeinden, Ämter und die Zweckverbände haben an den von dem Landesarchiv übernommenen archivwürdigen Unterlagen einen Anspruch auf Rückgabe für den Fall, daß ein eigenes Archiv oder ein Gemeinschaftsarchiv nach Satz 2 Nr. 1 oder 2 errichtet wird.

(2) ¹Archivwürdige Unterlagen, die zur Aufgabenerfüllung nicht mehr benötigt werden, sind im Falle des Absatzes 1 Satz 2 Nr. 1 oder 2 in das Archiv zu übernehmen oder im Falle des Absatzes 1 Satz 2 Nr. 3 dem Landesarchiv oder dem sonstigen öffentlichen Archiv anzubieten und zu übergeben. ²§ 6 Abs. 2 und 4 und § 7 Abs. 3 gelten entsprechend.
(3) ¹Für die Verwaltung und Sicherung von Archivgut in einem Archiv nach Absatz 1 Satz 2 Nr. 1 oder 2, die Geltendmachung von Schutzrechten und die Benutzung des Archivguts gelten § 8 Absatz 1, 2, 4, 5, 8 und 9, § 9 sowie die §§ 11 und 12 Abs. 2 entsprechend. ²Durch Satzung kann eine Verpflichtung zur Ablieferung eines Belegexemplars bestimmt werden. ³§ 13 Nr. 2 gilt entsprechend.

§ 16 Sonstige öffentliche Archive
(1) ¹Die sonstigen der Aufsicht des Landes unterstehenden Körperschaften ohne Gebietshoheit, Anstalten und Stiftungen des öffentlichen Rechts haben die bei ihnen entstandenen Unterlagen nach Maßgabe des § 6 Abs. 1, 2 und 4 dem Landesarchiv anzubieten. ²Das Landesarchiv ist zur Übernahme der archivwürdigen Unterlagen verpflichtet. ³Einzelheiten der Archivierung und Rückgabe, insbesondere die Kostenbeteiligung der anbietenden Körperschaft, Anstalt oder Stiftung, werden durch öffentlich-rechtlichen Vertrag geregelt.
(2) ¹Absatz 1 findet keine Anwendung, wenn die betreffenden Körperschaften, Anstalten und Stiftungen
1. eigene Archive errichten und unterhalten oder
2. zusammen mit anderen Körperschaften, Anstalten oder Stiftungen Gemeinschaftsarchive schaffen oder sich daran beteiligen oder
3. zusammen mit Privaten Gemeinschaftsarchive schaffen oder sich daran beteiligen und nach Feststellung des Landesarchivs das jeweilige Archiv archivfachlichen Anforderungen genügt oder
4. ihre Unterlagen einem sonstigen öffentlichen Archiv anbieten und übergeben.

²Die nach Absatz 1 anbietenden Stellen haben gegenüber dem Landesarchiv einen Anspruch auf Rückgabe der archivwürdigen Unterlagen für den Fall, daß die Unterlagen einem eigenen Archiv oder einem Gemeinschaftsarchiv nach Satz 1 Nr. 1 oder 2 übergeben werden.
(3) ¹Archivwürdige Unterlagen, die zur Aufgabenerfüllung nicht mehr benötigt werden, sind im Falle des Absatzes 2 Satz 1 Nr. 1 oder 2 in das Archiv zu übernehmen oder im Falle des Absatzes 2 Satz 1 Nr. 3 dem Landesarchiv oder einem sonstigen öffentlichen Archiv anzubieten und zu übergeben. ²§ 6 Abs. 2 und 4 und § 7 Abs. 3 gelten entsprechend.
(4) ¹Für die Verwaltung und Sicherung von Archivgut in einem Archiv nach Absatz 2 Satz 1 Nr. 1, 2 oder 3, die Geltendmachung von Schutzrechten und die Benutzung des Archivguts gelten § 8 Abs. 1, 2, 4 und 5, § 9 sowie die §§ 11 und 12 Abs. 2 entsprechend. ²Durch Satzung kann eine Verpflichtung zur Ablieferung eines Belegexemplars bestimmt werden. ³§ 13 Nr. 2 gilt entsprechend.

§ 17 Aufsicht
Die Aufsicht über das Landesarchiv führt das für Kultur zuständige Ministerium des Landes Schleswig-Holstein als oberste Archivbehörde.

§ 18 Inkrafttreten
¹Dieses Gesetz tritt mit Ausnahme der §§ 15 und 16 am Tage nach seiner Verkündung[1] in Kraft. ²§ 15 tritt am 1. Januar 2000, § 16 tritt am 1. Januar 1995 in Kraft.

---

1) Verkündet am 13.8.1992.

Gesetz für die Bibliotheken in Schleswig-Holstein (Bibliotheksgesetz – BiblG)[1)]

Vom 30. August 2016 (GVOBl. Schl.-H. S. 791)
(GS Schl.-H. II 221-38)

Inhaltsübersicht:

Präambel

Abschnitt 1
Allgemeine Bestimmungen
§ 1 Zweck und Begriffsbestimmung
§ 2 Allgemeine Aufgaben von Bibliotheken

Abschnitt 2
Bibliotheken in Schleswig-Holstein
§ 3 Öffentliche Bibliotheken
§ 4 Wissenschaftliche Bibliotheken
§ 5 Schulbibliotheken und Bibliotheken für den Dienstgebrauch

§ 6 Schleswig-Holsteinische Landesbibliothek
§ 7 Finanzierung und Benutzungsentgelt
§ 8 Datenschutz und Belegexemplare

Abschnitt 3
Pflichtexemplare
§ 9 Anbietungspflicht und Pflichtbibliotheken
§ 10 Verfahren der Anbietung und Ablieferung
§ 11 Verordnungsermächtigung
§ 12 Ordnungswidrigkeiten

Präambel

Die Bibliotheken im Land Schleswig-Holstein im Sinne dieses Gesetzes sind für alle Menschen frei zugänglich und gewährleisten damit flächendeckend in besonderer Weise das Grundrecht, sich aus allgemein zugänglichen Quellen ungehindert unterrichten zu können. Bibliotheken sind Partner für Bildung, Kultur, Wissenschaft und lebenslanges Lernen. Sie zählen damit zum Kernbereich der öffentlichen Daseinsvorsorge. Sie sind Standortfaktor und im Rahmen der Sozialraum- und Stadtentwicklungsplanung sowie bei Maßnahmen zur Förderung digitaler Infrastruktur und digitaler Angebote im Bereich von Bildung und Kultur zu berücksichtigen.

Bibliotheken gehören neben den Schulen und Hochschulen zu den wichtigsten Bildungseinrichtungen des Landes und bilden in ihrer Gesamtheit einen herausragenden Bestandteil der kulturellen Infrastruktur in Schleswig-Holstein. Dieses Gesetz soll die bibliothekarische Grundversorgung in Schleswig-Holstein und damit den bedarfsgerechten und bürgerorientierten Erhalt und Ausbau der Bibliotheken, wie im Landesentwicklungsplan vorgesehen, sicherstellen. Es konkretisiert die besondere Bedeutung der Bibliotheken in Schleswig-Holstein für die Pflege von Bildung, Kultur und Wissenschaft, die Verwirklichung von Grundrechten, die demokratische Willensbildung und für das Miteinander von Kulturen. Das Gesetz betont die Stellung der Bibliotheken in der digitalen Gesellschaft als unverzichtbare Partner für die kulturelle Bildung. Die Bibliotheken im Land sind nach Maßgabe dieses Gesetzes angehalten, untereinander und mit anderen Einrichtungen der Bildung, Kultur und Wissenschaft – auch im Hinblick auf zukunftsorientierte Ansprüche und Handlungsfelder wie Integration, Digitalisierung und Inklusion – zu kooperieren. Dies gilt auch für ihre Träger im Rahmen einer interkommunalen Zusammenarbeit.

Abschnitt 1
Allgemeine Bestimmungen

§ 1 Zweck und Begriffsbestimmung

(1) Zweck dieses Gesetzes ist es, die bestehende Bibliotheksstruktur in Schleswig-Holstein zu sichern und die Grundlagen für deren Weiterentwicklung zu schaffen.
(2) ¹Eine Bibliothek im Sinne dieses Gesetzes ist jede vom Land, den Gemeinden und Gemeindeverbänden gemäß Artikel 13 Absatz 3 der Verfassung des Landes Schleswig-Holstein[2)] sowie von den unter der Aufsicht des Landes stehenden juristischen Personen unterhaltene Einrichtung, die unter archivarischen, ökonomischen und synoptischen Gesichtspunkten Bücher und andere Medienwerke

---
1) Verkündet als Art. 1 G v. 30.8.2016 (GVOBl. Schl.-H. S. 791); Inkrafttreten gem. Art. 3 dieses G am 30.9.2016.
2) Abgedruckt als Nr. D15.

für die Benutzerinnen und Benutzer sammelt, ordnet und zugänglich macht. ²Für Bibliotheken in privater Trägerschaft und Bibliotheken gemeinnütziger Träger gilt dieses Gesetz, soweit es besonders bestimmt ist.
(3) ¹Medienwerke sind alle Darstellungen in Schrift, Bild und Ton, die in körperlicher Form verbreitet oder in unkörperlicher Form der Öffentlichkeit zugänglich gemacht werden, soweit sie Text enthalten oder mit einem Text verbunden sind. ²Medienwerke in körperlicher Form sind alle Darstellungen auf Papier, elektronischen Datenträgern und anderen Trägern. ³Medienwerke in unkörperlicher Form sind alle Darstellungen in öffentlichen Netzen.

§ 2 Allgemeine Aufgaben von Bibliotheken
(1) ¹Die Bibliotheken in Schleswig-Holstein dienen der Erfüllung von Aufgaben im Bereich von Kultur und Bildung sowie von Wissenschaft und Forschung. ²Sie bewahren schriftliches Kulturgut, unterstützen mit ihren Beständen das Angebot anderer Kultur-, Wissenschafts- und Bildungseinrichtungen und tragen zum Miteinander von Kulturen bei.
(2) ¹Bibliotheken in Schleswig-Holstein sind Dienstleister der modernen Wissensgesellschaft, die Wissen als Allgemeingut versteht, an dem jedes Mitglied der Gesellschaft teilhaben und mitwirken kann. ²Sie stärken die Lese-, Medien- und Informationskompetenz ihrer Nutzerinnen und Nutzer durch geeignete Maßnahmen sowie durch Zusammenarbeit mit anderen Einrichtungen der Kultur und Bildung und untereinander. ³Sie leisten Beiträge zur Bewahrung des kulturellen Erbes und zum Erhalt der Regional- und Minderheitensprachen.
(3) ¹Das Land, die Gemeinden und die Gemeindeverbände gewährleisten in gemeinsamer Verantwortung und gegenseitiger Verpflichtung die bibliothekarische Grundversorgung der Öffentlichkeit. ²Dies umfasst insbesondere die Förderung der allgemeinen, beruflichen, wissenschaftlichen und kulturellen Bildung.
(4) ¹Bibliotheken in Schleswig-Holstein wirken bei der Erfüllung regionaler und überregionaler Aufgaben, bei der Entwicklung neuer Dienstleistungen, im Rahmen von konsortionalen Erwerbungen, bei der Fernleihe sowie bei der Aus-, Fort- und Weiterbildung in bibliothekarischen Berufen zusammen. ²Sie sollen mit Schulen und anderen Bildungseinrichtungen zusammenarbeiten und sie gemeinsam mit den zuständigen Fachministerien beim Aufbau lernspezifischer Angebote unterstützen.
(5) ¹Bibliotheken richten sich mit ihren Angeboten an alle Mitglieder der Gesellschaft. ²Sie sollen die besonderen Bedürfnisse von Kindern und Jugendlichen sowie von Menschen mit Behinderung berücksichtigen und dabei nach Möglichkeit die gleichberechtigte Teilhabe, die soziale Inklusion und Barrierefreiheit fortentwickeln.
(6) Um ihre Aufgaben erfüllen zu können, müssen Öffentliche und wissenschaftliche Bibliotheken nachfolgende Kriterien erfüllen:
1. regelmäßige Öffnungszeiten,
2. einen angemessenen Medienetat,
3. eine angemessene Personalausstattung hinsichtlich Anzahl und fachlicher Qualifikation,
4. eine geeignete Räumlichkeit inklusive Mobiliar und IT-Ausstattung und
5. die Erschließung und Veröffentlichung der Medienbestände in Katalogen, die lokal oder über öffentliche Netze zur Verfügung gestellt werden.

Abschnitt 2
Bibliotheken in Schleswig-Holstein

§ 3 Öffentliche Bibliotheken
(1) ¹Öffentliche Bibliotheken sind Bibliotheken in Rechtsträgerschaft der Gemeinden und Kreise. ²Sie sind bei der Auswahl ihrer Medien unabhängig und an Weisungen nicht gebunden. ³Sie sollen in besonderer Weise der Lese- und Lernförderung von Kindern und Jugendlichen, der Förderung der schulischen, beruflichen und kulturellen Bildung insbesondere in Zusammenarbeit mit Kultur-, Wissenschafts- und Bildungseinrichtungen dienen. ⁴Sie vermitteln Medien- und Informationskompetenz. ⁵Bibliotheken in privater Trägerschaft und Bibliotheken anderer gemeinnütziger Träger können mit Zustimmung der zuständigen Gemeinde die Funktion einer Öffentlichen Bibliothek erfüllen. ⁶Dazu zählen auch die Bibliotheken in der Trägerschaft der Dansk Centralbibliotek for Sydslesvig e.V.
(2) Öffentliche Bibliotheken sollen hauptamtlich von bibliothekarischen Fachkräften geführt werden.

(3) ¹In Abstimmung untereinander gewährleisten die Gemeinden und Gemeindeverbände durch das System der Öffentlichen Bibliotheken, dass alle Einwohnerinnen und Einwohner in angemessener räumlicher Nähe und unter zumutbaren zeitlichen Bedingungen Zugang zu einer Öffentlichen Bibliothek haben. ²Soweit Standbibliotheken nicht eingerichtet sind, können Fahrbibliotheken vorgehalten werden.

(4) Der Büchereiverein sowie die von ihm unterhaltene Büchereizentrale mit Dienstleistungs- und Fachstellenfunktionen unterstützen das Land bei der Erfüllung seiner Aufgaben zur Förderung des Öffentlichen Bibliothekswesens gemäß Artikel 13 Absatz 3 der Landesverfassung.[1)]

§ 4 Wissenschaftliche Bibliotheken

(1) ¹Wissenschaftliche Bibliotheken in Schleswig-Holstein sind Bibliotheken in direkter Trägerschaft des Landes und Bibliotheken der unter der Rechtsaufsicht des Landes stehenden Hochschulen oder Forschungseinrichtungen, deren Bestände besonders auf die Bedürfnisse von Wissenschaft, Forschung und Lehre ausgerichtet sind. ²Sie stehen unbeschadet ihrer besonderen Aufgaben für Forschung, Lehre und Studium allen Menschen für die private und berufliche wissenschaftliche Bildung zur Verfügung. ³Dazu zählen auch die Bibliothek des Nordfriisk Instituut und die Bibliothek der Ferring-Stiftung auf Föhr.

(2) Die Bibliotheken und Forschungseinrichtungen an den Hochschulen wirken bei der freien und ungehinderten Verbreitung und Zugänglichmachung wissenschaftlicher Arbeiten (Open Access) mit und unterstützen die mit ihnen verbundenen Einrichtungen bei der Verfolgung dieses Ziels.

(3) ¹Die Deutsche Zentralbibliothek für Wirtschaftswissenschaften – Leibniz-Informationszentrum Wirtschaft sammelt und erschließt weltweit erscheinende wirtschaftswissenschaftliche Literatur. ²Sie erfüllt unbeschadet anderer gesetzlicher Bestimmungen ihren überregionalen Versorgungsauftrag in besonderer Weise durch digitale und vernetzte Dienstleistungen.

(4) ¹Die Bibliothek der Hansestadt Lübeck hat als wissenschaftliche Stadtbibliothek regionalbibliothekarische Funktionen und steht in der Trägerschaft der Stadt Lübeck. ²Sie ist organisatorisch mit den Öffentlichen Bibliotheken desselben Trägers verbunden und gemeinsam zuständig für die Versorgung mit Medienwerken.

(5) ¹Die Eutiner Landesbibliothek hat als regionale Forschungsbibliothek spezialbibliothekarische Funktionen hinsichtlich der historischen Reiseliteratur, der Geschichte Ostholsteins und des Literatur- und Informationsspektrums des 18. Jahrhunderts. ²In Trägerschaft der „Stiftung Eutiner Landesbibliothek" nimmt sie gleichermaßen bibliothekarische Aufgaben wahr und betreibt wissenschaftliche Forschungsarbeit.

§ 5 Schulbibliotheken und Bibliotheken für den Dienstgebrauch

(1) ¹Die an den öffentlichen Schulen bestehenden Schulbibliotheken widmen sich vorrangig den Bedürfnissen der Lernenden und Lehrenden an den jeweiligen Schulen. ²Sie dienen in Zusammenarbeit mit anderen Öffentlichen und wissenschaftlichen Bibliotheken im besonderen Maße der Lese- und Lernförderung sowie der Vermittlung von Medien- und Informationskompetenz. ³Die Bestimmungen des Schulgesetzes bleiben unberührt.

(2) ¹Bibliotheken für den Dienstgebrauch, der Verwaltung und der Gerichte sowie des Schleswig-Holsteinischen Landtags stehen für die Allgemeinheit nur dann zur Verfügung, wenn die gewünschten Medienwerke in anderen Bibliotheken des Landes nicht vorhanden sind und dienstliche Belange nicht beeinträchtigt werden. ²Im Übrigen entscheidet die Leitung der jeweiligen Dienststelle über den Zugang zur Bibliothek.

§ 6 Schleswig-Holsteinische Landesbibliothek

(1) ¹Die Schleswig-Holsteinische Landesbibliothek ist eine Landesoberbehörde mit Sitz in Kiel im Geschäftsbereich des für Kultur zuständigen Ministeriums und wird als öffentlich zugängliche Einrichtung geführt. ²Ihre Zuständigkeit erstreckt sich auf das ganze Land.

(2) Die Schleswig-Holsteinische Landesbibliothek hat als wissenschaftliche Regionalbibliothek die Aufgabe, Medienwerke sowie weiteres Kulturgut mit Bezug zur Geschichte und Landeskunde des Landes Schleswig-Holstein und seiner Nachbargebiete, insbesondere Dänemarks, zu sammeln, zu archivieren, zu erschließen, nachhaltig zu erhalten, bibliographisch nachzuweisen und der Öffentlichkeit zugänglich zu machen.

---

1) Abgedruckt als Nr. D15.

§ 7 Finanzierung und Benutzungsentgelt
(1) Die Bibliotheken werden von ihren Trägern finanziert.
(2) Das Land Schleswig-Holstein stellt in gemeinsamer Verantwortung mit den Gemeinden und Gemeindeverbänden gemäß Artikel 13 Absatz 3 der Verfassung des Landes Schleswig-Holstein[1]) aus dem Finanzausgleichsgesetz Mittel zur Förderung des Öffentlichen Bibliothekswesens über den Büchereiverein zur Verfügung.
(3) ¹Die Vorort-Nutzung der Bestände der Bibliotheken ist kostenfrei, sofern nicht lizenz- oder urheberrechtliche Bestimmungen entgegenstehen. ²Für die Inanspruchnahme darüber hinausgehender Leistungen können die Träger angemessene und sozial ausgewogene Benutzungsentgelte festlegen.

§ 8 Datenschutz und Belegexemplare
(1) ¹Bibliotheken dürfen zur Erschließung und Verzeichnung ihrer Bestände personenbezogene Daten verarbeiten und über öffentliche Netze zur Verfügung stellen. ²Soweit es sich dabei um Nachlässe und anderes nicht veröffentlichtes Material handelt, finden die Vorschriften des Landesarchivgesetzes vom 11. August 1992 (GVOBl. Schl.-H. S. 444, ber. S. 498), zuletzt geändert durch Artikel 9 des Gesetzes vom 3. Januar 2005 (GVOBl. Schl.-H. S. 21), Zuständigkeiten und Ressortbezeichnungen zuletzt ersetzt durch Verordnung vom 4. April 2013 (GVOBl. Schl.-H. S. 143), entsprechende Anwendung.
(2) ¹Bibliotheken können in ihren Benutzungsbestimmungen die unentgeltliche Abgabe oder Übermittlung eines Belegexemplares jedes unter maßgeblicher Präsenznutzung von Altbestand, Nachlässen oder anderen besonderen Beständen hergestellten oder vervielfältigten Medienwerks verlangen. ²Ist die kostenfreie Ablieferung, insbesondere wegen einer niedrigen Auflage oder hoher Herstellungskosten, nicht zumutbar, gilt § 10 Absatz 2 entsprechend.

Abschnitt 3
Pflichtexemplare

§ 9 Anbietungspflicht und Pflichtbibliotheken
(1) Von jedem Medienwerk, das im Geltungsbereich dieses Gesetzes verbreitet oder öffentlich zugänglich gemacht wird, ist unabhängig von seiner Herstellungsart oder seiner Wiedergabeform jeweils ein Exemplar unaufgefordert und unmittelbar nach Beginn der Verbreitung oder öffentlichen Zugänglichmachung den Pflichtbibliotheken (Absatz 4) anzubieten und auf deren Verlangen unentgeltlich und auf eigene Kosten abzuliefern oder zu übermitteln (Pflichtexemplar).
(2) Anbietungspflichtig ist, wer berechtigt ist, ein Medienwerk zu verbreiten oder öffentlich zugänglich zu machen und den Sitz, eine Betriebsstätte oder den Hauptwohnsitz im Geltungsbereich dieses Gesetzes hat.
(3) Der Anbietungspflicht dieses Gesetzes unterliegen nicht
1. Veröffentlichungen, die ausschließlich amtliche Mitteilungen enthalten,
2. Pressemitteilungen, Newsletter und Pressespiegel,
3. Medienwerke, die ausschließlich gewerblichen oder geschäftlichen Zwecken wie der Kundeninformation, der Information und Instruktion von Mitarbeiterinnen und Mitarbeitern oder der Verkehrsabwicklung dienen, und
4. Filmwerke sowie Rundfunksendungen, soweit sie nicht als körperliche Werke publiziert werden.

(4) Die Aufgabe der Sammlung der Pflichtexemplare nehmen die Universitätsbibliothek Kiel, die Schleswig-Holsteinische Landesbibliothek und die Bibliothek der Hansestadt Lübeck gemeinsam wahr.
(5) Von den Pflichtbibliotheken ist in gegenseitiger Absprache sicherzustellen, dass von den in Schleswig-Holstein hergestellten oder veröffentlichten Medienwerken wenigstens ein Pflichtexemplar gesammelt, erschlossen und in geeigneter Form auf Dauer gesichert und für die Allgemeinheit nutzbar gehalten wird, soweit an dessen Sicherung ein öffentliches Interesse besteht.
(6) ¹Mit der Ablieferung eines Medienwerkes auf einem elektronischen Datenträger oder eines Medienwerkes in unkörperlicher Form erhalten die Pflichtbibliotheken das Recht, das Werk zu speichern, zu vervielfältigen und in eine andere Form zu bringen oder diese Handlungen in ihrem Auftrag vornehmen zu lassen, soweit dies notwendig ist, um das Medienwerk in die Sammlung aufzunehmen, zu

---
[1]) Abgedruckt als Nr. D15.

erschließen und für die Benutzung bereitstellen zu können sowie seine Erhaltung und Benutzbarkeit dauerhaft zu sichern. ²Entgegenstehende technische Maßnahmen sind vor der Ablieferung aufzuheben.
(7) Mit der Ablieferung eines Medienwerkes in unkörperlicher Form erhalten die Pflichtbibliotheken das Recht, das Werk in ihren Räumen zugänglich zu machen.

§ 10 Verfahren der Anbietung und Ablieferung
(1) Medienwerke in körperlicher Form sind den Pflichtbibliotheken binnen eines Monats seit Beginn der Verbreitung, Medienwerke in unkörperlicher Form sind den Pflichtbibliotheken binnen einer Woche seit dem Beginn der öffentlichen Zugänglichmachung anzubieten.
(2) Für Medienwerke in körperlicher Form gewährt die die Ablieferung verlangende Bibliothek auf Antrag einen angemessenen Zuschuss zu dem anzubietenden Medienwerk (maximal in Höhe der Selbstkosten), wenn die unentgeltliche Ablieferung wegen hoher Herstellungskosten oder einer geringen Auflage eine unzumutbare Belastung darstellen würde.
(3) ¹Medienwerke in unkörperlicher Form werden unter Einhaltung der von der Deutschen Nationalbibliothek für Pflichtexemplare festgelegten technischen Standards und Verfahren zur Abholung bereitgestellt oder an die zuständige Pflichtbibliothek übermittelt. ²Abzuliefern sind auch alle Elemente, Software und Werkzeuge, die in ein abzulieferndes Medienwerk in unkörperlicher Form eingebunden sind oder die zu seiner Darstellung, Speicherung, Benutzung und Langzeitsicherung benötigt werden, mit Ausnahme von Standardsoftware.
(4) Bei periodischen Medienwerken genügt eine Anbietung beim erstmaligen Erscheinen und am Beginn jedes Kalenderjahres zum laufenden Bezug.
(5) ¹Kommen die Anbietungspflichtigen ihrer Angebotspflicht nicht nach, sind die Pflichtbibliotheken nach einem Monat zur Mahnung und nach fruchtlosem Ablauf eines weiteren Monats berechtigt, die Medienwerke auf Kosten der Anbietungspflichtigen anderweitig zu beschaffen. ²Nach Ablauf eines Monats nach dem Beginn der öffentlichen Zugänglichmachung können die Pflichtbibliotheken ein frei zugängliches unkörperliches Medienwerk in ihren Bestand übernehmen und im Rahmen ihres gesetzlichen Auftrags nutzen.
(6) ¹Die Pflichtbibliotheken können auf die Anbietung solcher Medienwerke verzichten, an deren Sammlung, Inventarisierung und bibliographischen Aufzeichnung kein öffentliches oder wissenschaftliches Interesse besteht. ²Ein Anspruch auf Aufnahme in eine Sammlung einer zuständigen Stelle besteht nicht.
(7) ¹Die Anbietungspflichtigen haben den Pflichtbibliotheken in jedem Fall, also auch, wenn keine Ablieferung erfolgt, unentgeltlich die zu ihrer Aufgabenerfüllung notwendigen Auskünfte auf Verlangen zu erteilen. ²Kommen sie dieser Pflicht nicht nach, sind die Pflichtbibliotheken nach Ablauf eines Monats seit Beginn der Verbreitung oder öffentlichen Zugänglichmachung berechtigt, die Informationen auf Kosten der Anbietungspflichtigen anderweitig zu beschaffen.

§ 11 Verordnungsermächtigung
¹Näheres zur Zuständigkeit der Pflichtbibliotheken, zur Durchführung des Verfahrens, zur Anbietungspflicht, zur Entschädigung und zu Ausnahmen von der Anbietungspflicht regelt das zuständige Ministerium durch Verordnung. ²Die Pflicht zur Anbietung und Übermittlung von unkörperlichen Medienwerken beginnt erst mit dem Erlass der Verordnung nach Satz 1.

§ 12 Ordnungswidrigkeiten
(1) ¹Ordnungswidrig handelt, wer vorsätzlich gegen die Verpflichtungen für körperliche Medienwerke aus §§ 9 und 10 verstößt. ²Die Ordnungswidrigkeit kann mit einer Geldbuße bis zu 5.000 Euro geahndet werden.
(2) Zuständige Verwaltungsbehörde nach § 36 Absatz 1 Nummer 1 des Gesetzes über die Ordnungswidrigkeiten sind die Landrätinnen und Landräte und die Bürgermeisterinnen und Bürgermeister der kreisfreien Städte.

Gesetz zur Umwandlung der Kulturstiftung des Landes Schleswig-Holstein in eine Stiftung des öffentlichen Rechts

Vom 30. Mai 1995 (GVOBl. Schl.-H. S. 221)
(GS Schl.-H. II 224-7)
zuletzt geändert durch Art. 12 LVO zur Anpassung von Rechtsvorschriften an geänderte Zuständigkeiten der obersten Landesbehörden und geänderte Ressortbezeichnungen vom 16. Januar 2019 (GVOBl. Schl.-H. S. 30)

Nichtamtliche Inhaltsübersicht

§ 1 Umwandlung, Errichtung und Rechtsform
§ 2 Stiftungszweck
§ 3 Stiftungskapital und Stiftungsmittel
§ 4 Organe
§ 5 Mitglieder des Stiftungsrates
§ 6 Aufgaben des Stiftungsrates
§ 7 Mitglieder des Vorstandes
§ 8 Aufgaben des Vorstandes
§ 9 Satzung
§ 10 Aufsicht
§ 11 [Vorübergehende Geschäftsführung]
§ 12 Inkrafttreten

§ 1 Umwandlung, Errichtung und Rechtsform

(1) Unter Umwandlung der im Jahre 1984 als rechtsfähige Stiftung des bürgerlichen Rechts gegründeten Kulturstiftung des Landes Schleswig-Holstein wird mit demselben Namen eine rechtsfähige Stiftung des öffentlichen Rechts errichtet.
(2) Der Sitz der Stiftung ist Kiel.

§ 2 Stiftungszweck

(1) ¹Die Stiftung hat den Zweck,
1. Kulturgüter und Kunstgegenstände von herausragender Bedeutung für das Land Schleswig-Holstein zu sichern,
2. Veranstaltungen und Publikationen von besonderem Interesse für die Kultur, Kunst oder Geschichte des Landes Schleswig-Holstein zu ermöglichen oder selbst durchzuführen,
3. neue Formen und Entwicklungen auf den Gebieten von Kultur und Kunst zu fördern,
4. Maßnahmen zur Entwicklung und Stärkung der kulturellen Infrastruktur im Lande zu unterstützen.

²Mit Mitteln der Stiftung erworbene Gegenstände, Werke oder Güter werden Eigentum des Landes.
(2) Die Stiftung kann aus ihren Mitteln auch Zuwendungen geben an
1. öffentliche oder gemeinnützige Einrichtungen, die im Sinne des Stiftungszwecks nach Absatz 1 tätig sind,
2. sonstige gemeinnützige Organisationen, die sich im Interesse des Landes der Erwerbung und Bewahrung wertvoller Kulturgüter und Kunstgegenstände widmen, Kultur- und Kunstveranstaltungen im Sinne von Absatz 1 durchführen oder neue Formen und Entwicklungen auf den Gebieten von Kultur und Kunst gemäß Absatz 1 fördern,
3. Einzelpersonen, die im Auftrag der Kulturstiftung entsprechend dem Stiftungszweck nach Absatz 1 tätig werden.

(3) Die Stiftung verfolgt ausschließlich und unmittelbar gemeinnützige Zwecke im Sinne der §§ 51 bis 68 der Abgabenordnung.

§ 3 Stiftungskapital und Stiftungsmittel

(1) Das Stiftungskapital besteht aus dem Vermögen der bisherigen Stiftung in Höhe von 15,6 Mio DM und erhöht sich um die Beträge und Vermögenswerte, die der Stiftung als Zustiftung zugeführt werden.
(2) Die Stiftung erfüllt ihre Aufgaben aus den Erträgen des Stiftungskapitals und aus Zuwendungen.

§ 4 Organe

Organe der Stiftung sind
1. der Stiftungsrat und
2. der Vorstand.

D15.III.1 Kulturstiftung Schleswig-Holstein

§ 5 Mitglieder des Stiftungsrates
(1) ¹Der Stiftungsrat besteht aus der Ministerin oder dem Minister für Bildung, Wissenschaft und Kultur als Vorsitzender oder Vorsitzendem sowie sechs weiteren Mitgliedern, davon zwei Mitglieder, die der Schleswig-Holsteinische Landtag für eine Amtszeit von vier Jahren entsendet. ²Sie sollen mit dem kulturellen Leben in Schleswig-Holstein verbunden sein. ³Von den weiteren Mitgliedern müssen drei Frauen und drei Männer sein.

(2) ¹Die weiteren Mitglieder werden von dem Ministerium für Bildung, Wissenschaft und Kultur des Landes Schleswig-Holstein für eine Amtszeit von vier Jahren bestellt. ²Die Wiederbestellung ist zulässig.

§ 6 Aufgaben des Stiftungsrates
(1) Der Stiftungsrat nimmt den Jahresbericht entgegen, beschließt den Haushaltsplan, entlastet den Vorstand, erläßt die Satzung und entscheidet über Satzungsänderungen.

(2) ¹Der Stiftungsrat berät den Vorstand in allen Stiftungsangelegenheiten. ²Das Nähere regelt die Satzung.

§ 7 Mitglieder des Vorstandes
(1) ¹Der Vorstand der Stiftung besteht aus drei Mitgliedern. ²Ihm gehören an:
1. die Staatssekretärin oder der Staatssekretär im Ministerium für Bildung, Wissenschaft und Kultur, als Vorsitzende oder Vorsitzender,
2. zwei weitere Mitglieder.

(2) ¹Die Mitglieder werden von dem Ministerium für Bildung, Wissenschaft und Kultur des Landes Schleswig-Holstein bestellt, davon ein Mitglied auf Vorschlag des Stiftungsrates. ²Die Amtszeit der Vorstandsmitglieder beträgt vier Jahre. ³Die Wiederbestellung ist zulässig.

§ 8 Aufgaben des Vorstandes
(1) Der Vorstand führt die Geschäfte der Stiftung und bedient sich hierzu einer Geschäftsstelle.

(2) Die Geschäftsstelle erledigt für den Vorstand insbesondere folgende Aufgaben:
1. Ausführung der Beschlüsse des Stiftungsrates und des Vorstandes,
2. die Verwaltung des Stiftungsvermögens,
3. die Aufstellung und Ausführung des jährlichen Haushaltsplanes und
4. die Erstellung eines Tätigkeitsberichts und einer Jahresrechnung.

(3) Die oder der Vorstandsvorsitzende vertritt die Stiftung gerichtlich und außergerichtlich.

§ 9 Satzung
(1) ¹Die Satzung regelt die innere Organisation der Stiftung. ²Sie enthält insbesondere nähere Bestimmungen über
1. die Bestellung und Abberufung der Mitglieder des Stiftungsrates und des Vorstandes,
2. die Aufgaben und Befugnisse des Stiftungsrates und des Vorstandes,
3. den Stiftungszweck,
4. das Stiftungsvermögen und
5. die angemessene Berücksichtigung von Frauen bei der Verwendung der Stiftungsmittel.

(2) Die Satzung bedarf der Genehmigung der Aufsichtsbehörde.

§ 10 Aufsicht
Aufsichtsbehörde ist der Innenminister oder die Innenministerin¹⁾ des Landes Schleswig-Holstein.

§ 11 [Vorübergehende Geschäftsführung]
Die Geschäfte von Stiftungsrat und Vorstand werden bis zu ihrer Konstituierung von den Organen der bisherigen Stiftung wahrgenommen.

§ 12 Inkrafttreten
Dieses Gesetz tritt am Tage nach seiner Verkündung²⁾ in Kraft.

---

1) Richtig wohl „das Innenministerium"; siehe Art. 67 Änd. v. 24.10.1996 (GVOBl. Schl.-H. S. 652, 661).
2) Verkündet am 22.6.1995.

Landesverordnung über die zuständige Behörde nach dem Kulturgutschutzgesetz (Kulturgutschutz-Zuständigkeitsverordnung – KGSGZustVO)

Vom 11. Oktober 2016 (GVOBl. Schl.-H. S. 842)
(GS Schl.-H. II, Gl.Nr. B 244-2-2)

Aufgrund des § 3 Absatz 1 Satz 2 des Kulturgutschutzgesetzes vom 31. Juli 2016 (BGBl. I S. 1914) verordnet die Landesregierung:

§ 1 [Zuständigkeit nach dem Kulturgutschutzgesetz]
Die für Kultur zuständige oberste Landesbehörde ist sowohl die zuständige Behörde als auch die zuständige oberste Landesbehörde nach dem Kulturgutschutzgesetz vom 31. Juli 2016 (BGBl. I S. 1914).

§ 2 [Inkrafttreten]
Diese Verordnung tritt am Tage nach ihrer Verkündung[1] in Kraft.

---

[1] Verkündet am 27.10.2016.

Verfassung des Freistaats Thüringen

Vom 25. Oktober 1993 (GVBl. S. 625)
(BS Thür 100-1)
zuletzt geändert durch Art. 1 Viertes ÄndG vom 11. Oktober 2004 (GVBl. S. 745)
– Auszug –

Erster Teil
Grundrechte, Staatsziele und Ordnung des Gemeinschaftslebens

Dritter Abschnitt
Bildung und Kultur

Artikel 30 [Kultur; Kunst und Brauchtum]
(1) Kultur, Kunst, Brauchtum genießen Schutz und Förderung durch das Land und seine Gebietskörperschaften.
(2) ¹Die Denkmale der Kultur, Kunst, Geschichte und die Naturdenkmale stehen unter dem Schutz des Landes und seiner Gebietskörperschaften. ²Die Pflege der Denkmale obliegt in erster Linie ihren Eigentümern. ³Sie sind der Öffentlichkeit im Rahmen der Gesetze unter Beachtung der Rechte anderer zugänglich zu machen.
[...]

Thüringer Gesetz zur Pflege und zum Schutz der Kulturdenkmale (Thüringer Denkmalschutzgesetz – ThürDSchG –)

In der Fassung der Bekanntmachung vom 14. April 2004[1)] (GVBl. S. 465, ber. 562)
(BS Thür 224-1)
zuletzt geändert durch Art. 2 Thüringer VerwaltungsreformG 2018 vom 18. Dezember 2018 (GVBl. S. 731)

Inhaltsübersicht

Erster Abschnitt
Allgemeine Vorschriften
- § 1 Aufgabe der Denkmalpflege und des Denkmalschutzes
- § 2 Kulturdenkmale
- § 3 Denkmalpflegepläne
- § 4 Denkmalbuch
- § 5 Eintragungsverfahren

Zweiter Abschnitt
Erhaltung von Kulturdenkmalen
- § 6 Öffentliche Planungen und Maßnahmen
- § 7 Erhaltungspflicht
- § 8 Anzeigepflichten
- § 9 Auskunfts- und Duldungspflichten
- § 10 Zugang zu Kulturdenkmalen
- § 11 Durchsetzung der Erhaltung

Dritter Abschnitt
Schutz von Kulturdenkmalen
- § 12 Allgemeine Maßnahmen der Denkmalschutzbehörden
- § 13 Erlaubnis
- § 14 Erlaubnisverfahren
- § 15 Beseitigung widerrechtlicher Maßnahmen

Vierter Abschnitt
Zusätzliche Vorschriften für Bodendenkmale
- § 16 Zufallsfunde
- § 17 Schatzregal
- § 18 Nachforschungen
- § 19 Archäologische Schutzgebiete
- § 20 Nutzungsbeschränkungen
- § 21 Ablieferung

Fünfter Abschnitt
Kosten
- § 21a Kosten

Sechster Abschnitt
Denkmalbehörden
- § 22 Denkmalschutzbehörden
- § 23 Zuständigkeiten
- § 24 Denkmalfachbehörde
- § 25 Denkmalrat
- § 26 Ehrenamtliche Mitarbeiter

Siebenter Abschnitt
Enteignung, Entschädigung und Ordnungswidrigkeiten
- § 27 Enteignung
- § 28 Sonstige entschädigungspflichtige Maßnahmen
- § 29 Bußgeldbestimmungen

Achter Abschnitt
Verfahrens- und Ausführungsbestimmungen
- § 30 Vorkaufsrecht
- § 31 Steuerbescheinigungen
- § 32 Religionsgemeinschaften
- § 33 (aufgehoben)
- § 34 Ausführungsvorschriften

Neunter Abschnitt
Übergangs- und Schlussbestimmungen
- § 34a Übergangsbestimmung
- § 35 Gleichstellungsbestimmung
- § 36 (In-Kraft-Treten)

Erster Abschnitt
Allgemeine Vorschriften

§ 1 Aufgabe der Denkmalpflege und des Denkmalschutzes

(1) ¹Denkmalpflege und Denkmalschutz haben die Aufgaben, Kulturdenkmale als Quellen und Zeugnisse menschlicher Geschichte und erdgeschichtlicher Entwicklung zu schützen und zu erhalten sowie darauf hinzuwirken, dass sie in die städtebauliche und dörfliche Entwicklung sowie in die Raumordnung und Landschaftspflege einbezogen werden. ²Dabei obliegt dem Denkmalschutz die hoheitlichrechtliche Aufgabe und Verantwortung, der Denkmalpflege die fachliche Beratung und Fürsorge für den hoheitlichen Denkmalschutz.

(2) Bei der Erfüllung dieser Aufgaben wirken im Rahmen ihrer Leistungsfähigkeit das Land, die Gemeinden und Gemeindeverbände sowie Eigentümer und Besitzer von Kulturdenkmalen zusammen.

---
1) Neubekanntmachung des ThürDSchG v. 7.1.1992 (GVBl. S. 17, 550) in der ab 1.5.2004 geltenden Fassung.

D16.I.1 Thüringer Denkmalschutzgesetz

(3) Die Belange von Menschen mit Behinderungen oder mit Mobilitätsbeeinträchtigungen sind zu berücksichtigen.

§ 2 Kulturdenkmale

(1) ¹Kulturdenkmale im Sinne dieses Gesetzes sind Sachen, Sachgesamtheiten oder Sachteile, an deren Erhaltung aus geschichtlichen, künstlerischen, wissenschaftlichen, technischen, volkskundlichen oder städtebaulichen Gründen sowie aus Gründen der historischen Dorfbildpflege ein öffentliches Interesse besteht. ²Kulturdenkmale sind auch Denkmalensembles (Absatz 2) und Bodendenkmale (Absatz 7).
(2) ¹Denkmalensembles können sein:
1. bauliche Gesamtanlagen (Absatz 3),
2. kennzeichnende Straßen-, Platz- und Ortsbilder (Absatz 4),
3. kennzeichnende Ortsgrundrisse (Absatz 5),
4. historische Park- und Gartenanlagen (Absatz 6),
5. historische Produktionsstätten und -anlagen.

²Nicht erforderlich ist, dass jeder einzelne Teil des Denkmalensembles ein Kulturdenkmal darstellt.
(3) Bauliche Gesamtanlagen sind insbesondere Gebäudegruppen, einheitlich gestaltete Quartiere und Siedlungen und historische Ortskerne einschließlich der mit ihnen verbundenen Pflanzen, Frei- und Wasserflächen.
(4) Ein kennzeichnendes Straßen-, Platz- oder Ortsbild ist insbesondere gegeben, wenn das Erscheinungsbild der Anlage für eine bestimmte Epoche oder Entwicklung oder für eine charakteristische Bauweise mit auch unterschiedlichen Stilarten kennzeichnend ist.
(5) Ein kennzeichnender Ortsgrundriss ist gegeben, wenn das Erscheinungsbild der Anlage für eine bestimmte Epoche oder Entwicklung charakteristisch ist, insbesondere im Hinblick auf Orts- und Siedlungsformen, Straßenführungen, Parzellenstrukturen und Festungsanlagen.
(6) ¹Historische Park- und Gartenanlagen sind Werke der Gartenbaukunst, deren Lage sowie architektonische und pflanzliche Gestaltung von der Funktion der Anlage als Lebensraum und Selbstdarstellung früherer Gesellschaftsformen und der von ihr getragenen Kultur Zeugnis geben. ²Dazu zählen auch Tier- und botanische Gärten, soweit sie eine eigene historische und architektonische Gesamtgestaltung besitzen.
(7) Bodendenkmale sind bewegliche oder unbewegliche Sachen, bei denen es sich um Zeugnisse, Überreste oder Spuren menschlicher Kultur (archäologische Denkmale) oder tierischen oder pflanzlichen Lebens (paläontologische Denkmale) handelt, die im Boden verborgen sind oder waren.

§ 3 Denkmalpflegepläne

(1) Im Einvernehmen mit der Denkmalfachbehörde sollen die Gemeinden für Denkmalensembles nach § 2 Abs. 3 bis 5 Denkmalpflegepläne aufstellen.
(2) ¹Der Denkmalpflegeplan gibt die Ziele und Erfordernisse des Denkmalschutzes und der Denkmalpflege sowie die Darstellungen und die Festsetzungen für die Bauleitplanung wieder. ²Er enthält:
a) die Bestandsaufnahme und Analyse des Plangebietes unter denkmalfachlichen und denkmalschutzrechtlichen Gesichtspunkten,
b) die topographischen Angaben über Lage und Ausdehnung der Denkmalensembles und der Bodendenkmale in Schrift und Plan,
c) die denkmalpflegerischen Zielstellungen, unter deren Beachtung die Pflege und Erhaltung der Denkmalensembles und Bodendenkmale jeweils zu verwirklichen ist.

§ 4 Denkmalbuch

(1) ¹Unbewegliche Kulturdenkmale werden nachrichtlich in ein öffentliches Verzeichnis (Denkmalbuch) aufgenommen; Bodendenkmale werden im Denkmalbuch registriert, wenn sie oberirdisch sichtbar oder von besonderer Bedeutung sind. ²Der Schutz unbeweglicher Kulturdenkmale und der Bodendenkmale ist nicht davon abhängig, dass sie in das Denkmalbuch eingetragen sind.
(2) Bewegliche Kulturdenkmale sind in das Denkmalbuch einzutragen, wenn es sich bei ihnen
1. um Zubehör eines Baudenkmals handelt, das mit der Hauptsache aus künstlerischen, geschichtlichen und sonstigen Gründen eine Einheit bildet, oder
2. um Gegenstände der bildenden Kunst handelt, deren Zugehörigkeit zu einem bestimmten Ort historisch begründet ist und deren Verbleib an Ort und Stelle im öffentlichen Interesse liegt.

(3) Von der Eintragung beweglicher Kulturdenkmale sind Gegenstände ausgenommen, die von einer staatlichen Sammlung verwaltet werden.

§ 5 Eintragungsverfahren

(1) ¹Das Denkmalbuch wird von der Denkmalfachbehörde von Amts wegen geführt. ²Der Eigentümer, die untere Denkmalschutzbehörde, die Gemeinde sowie ein der Denkmalpflege verpflichteter Verband oder Verein können die Eintragung anregen. ³Vor der Eintragung sind die Eigentümer zu hören; über die erfolgte Eintragung erhalten sie eine Benachrichtigung. ⁴Bei der Ermittlung der Eigentümer leisten die Gemeinden Amtshilfe. ⁵Die Gemeinden sollen vor Eintragungen in das Denkmalbuch gehört werden. ⁶Eintragungen sind zu löschen, wenn die gesetzlichen Voraussetzungen nicht mehr vorliegen.
(2) Die Unterrichtung erfolgt bei Denkmalensembles (§ 2 Abs. 2) durch Bekanntmachung im Thüringer Staatsanzeiger sowie durch ortsübliche Bekanntmachung.
(3) ¹Die unteren Denkmalschutzbehörden und die Gemeinden führen für ihr Gebiet Auszüge aus dem Denkmalbuch. ²Die Einsicht in das Denkmalbuch und seine Auszüge ist hinsichtlich der unbeweglichen Kulturdenkmale jedem gestattet. ³Hinsichtlich der Eintragung von beweglichen Kulturdenkmalen ist die Einsicht nur dem Eigentümer und den sonst dinglich Berechtigten oder von ihnen besonders Ermächtigten gestattet. ⁴Die Vorschriften des Datenschutzes bleiben unberührt.
(4) ¹Unbewegliche eingetragene Kulturdenkmale sind im Liegenschaftskataster nachzuweisen. ²Leistungen der Kataster- und Vermessungsbehörden zum Nachweis der unbeweglichen Kulturdenkmale im Liegenschaftskataster sind frei von Gebühren und Auslagen. ³Im Übrigen bleiben die §§ 2 und 3 des Thüringer Verwaltungskostengesetzes vom 7. August 1991 (GVBl. S. 285-321-) in der jeweils geltenden Fassung unberührt.

Zweiter Abschnitt
Erhaltung von Kulturdenkmalen

§ 6 Öffentliche Planungen und Maßnahmen

¹Bei öffentlichen Planungen und Maßnahmen sind die Belange des Denkmalschutzes und der Denkmalpflege angemessen zu berücksichtigen. ²Die für den Denkmalschutz und die Denkmalpflege zuständigen Behörden sind so frühzeitig zu beteiligen, dass die Erhaltung und Nutzung von Kulturdenkmalen sowie eine angemessene Gestaltung ihrer Umgebung möglich sind.

§ 7 Erhaltungspflicht

(1) ¹Eigentümer und Besitzer von Kulturdenkmalen sind verpflichtet, diese im Rahmen des Zumutbaren denkmalgerecht zu erhalten und pfleglich zu behandeln. ²Unzumutbar ist eine Belastung insbesondere, soweit die Kosten der Erhaltung und Bewirtschaftung nicht durch Erträge oder den Gebrauchswert des Kulturdenkmals aufgewogen werden können. ³Der Verpflichtete kann sich nicht auf die Belastung durch erhöhte Erhaltungskosten berufen, die dadurch verursacht wurden, dass Erhaltungsmaßnahmen entgegen den Bestimmungen dieses Gesetzes oder sonstiger öffentlich-rechtlicher Vorschriften unterblieben sind.
(2) Das Land, die Kreise sowie die Gemeinden und Gemeindeverbände tragen nach Maßgabe der verfügbaren Haushaltsmittel zur Pflege und Erhaltung der Kulturdenkmale durch Zuschüsse in angemessenem Umfang bei.[1)]
(3) Werden Kulturdenkmale nicht mehr entsprechend ihrer ursprünglichen Zweckbestimmung genutzt, sollen die Eigentümer eine Nutzung anstreben, die eine möglichst weit gehende Erhaltung der Substanz auf die Dauer gewährleistet.
(4) Wird in ein Kulturdenkmal eingegriffen, so hat der Verursacher des Eingriffes alle Kosten zu tragen, die für die Erhaltung und fachgerechte Instandsetzung, Bergung und Dokumentation des Kulturdenkmals anfallen.

§ 8 Anzeigepflichten

(1) Eigentümer und Besitzer haben Schäden und Mängel, die an Kulturdenkmalen auftreten und ihren Denkmalwert und ihre Substanz beeinträchtigen, unverzüglich der Denkmalschutzbehörde anzuzeigen.

---

1) Die Denkmalförderrichtlinie ist abgedruckt als Nr. D16.III.3.

(2) ¹Wird ein bewegliches eingetragenes Kulturdenkmal veräußert, so haben Veräußerer und Erwerber den Eigentumswechsel innerhalb eines Monats der Denkmalfachbehörde über die Denkmalschutzbehörde anzuzeigen. ²Die Veräußerungsanzeige für unbewegliche Kulturdenkmale nach § 30 bleibt unberührt.
(3) ¹Bauarchäologische Zufallsfunde und Münzfunde sind ebenfalls anzeigepflichtig. ²§ 16 gilt entsprechend.

§ 9 Auskunfts- und Duldungspflichten
(1) Eigentümer und Besitzer von Kulturdenkmalen sind verpflichtet, die zur Erfüllung der Aufgaben des Denkmalschutzes und der Denkmalpflege erforderlichen Auskünfte zu erteilen.
(2) ¹Denkmalschutzbehörden und Denkmalfachbehörde sind nach vorheriger Benachrichtigung der Eigentümer und Besitzer berechtigt, Grundstücke zu betreten und Kulturdenkmale zu besichtigen, soweit es zur Erfüllung der Aufgaben des Denkmalschutzes erforderlich ist. ²Wohnungen dürfen gegen den Willen des Besitzers nur zur Abwendung drohender Gefahr für Kulturdenkmale betreten werden. ³Die Unverletzlichkeit der Wohnung nach Artikel 13 des Grundgesetzes wird insoweit eingeschränkt.

§ 10 Zugang zu Kulturdenkmalen
¹Kulturdenkmale oder Teile derselben sollen der Öffentlichkeit soweit wie möglich zugänglich gemacht werden, wenn der öffentliche Zutritt zugemutet werden kann. ²Dabei sind die Rechte von Menschen mit Behinderungen oder mit Mobilitätsbeeinträchtigungen zu berücksichtigen. ³Die Denkmalfachbehörde soll mit dem Eigentümer solcher Denkmale Vereinbarungen über den Zutritt treffen; dies gilt insbesondere dann, wenn für die Erhaltung des Denkmals öffentliche Mittel aufgewendet werden oder aufgewendet worden sind.

§ 11 Durchsetzung der Erhaltung
(1) Kommen Eigentümer oder Besitzer ihren Verpflichtungen nach § 7 nicht nach und tritt hierdurch eine Gefährdung des Kulturdenkmals ein, können sie von den Denkmalschutzbehörden verpflichtet werden, erforderliche Erhaltungs- und Instandsetzungsmaßnahmen durchzuführen.
(2) ¹Erfordert der Zustand eines Kulturdenkmals zu seiner Instandhaltung, Instandsetzung oder zu einem Schutz Maßnahmen, ohne deren unverzügliche Durchführung es gefährdet würde, können die Denkmalschutzbehörden diejenigen Maßnahmen selbst durchführen, die zur Abwendung einer unmittelbaren Gefahr für den Bestand des Kulturdenkmals geboten sind. ²Eigentümer und Besitzer sind verpflichtet, solche Maßnahmen zu dulden. ³Eigentümer, Besitzer und sonstige Unterhaltungspflichtige werden im Rahmen des Zumutbaren zur Erstattung der entstandenen Kosten herangezogen.

Dritter Abschnitt
Schutz von Kulturdenkmalen

§ 12 Allgemeine Maßnahmen der Denkmalschutzbehörden
(1) ¹Die Denkmalschutzbehörden haben diejenigen Maßnahmen zu treffen, die nach pflichtgemäßem Ermessen erforderlich sind, um Kulturdenkmale zu erhalten, zu bergen und zu bewahren sowie Gefahren von ihnen abzuwenden. ²Sie haben bei allen Entscheidungen den berechtigten Interessen der Eigentümer oder Besitzer von Kulturdenkmalen Rechnung zu tragen. ³Bei den dem Gottesdienst gewidmeten Gegenständen (res sacrae) sind religiöse Belange vorrangig zu berücksichtigen. ⁴Sofern staatlicher Denkmalschutz und liturgische Interessen der Religionsgemeinschaften in Konflikt geraten, haben in der Interessensabwägung liturgische Belange Vorrang.
(2) Soweit ein Vorhaben nach diesem Gesetz einer Erlaubnis bedarf, kann diese unter Bedingungen, Auflagen, Befristungen und Widerrufsvorbehalt erteilt werden.
(3) ¹Durch die Erteilung von Erlaubnissen auf Grund dieses Gesetzes werden Genehmigungen, die auf Grund anderer Rechtsvorschriften erforderlich sind, nicht ersetzt. ²Baugenehmigungen und bauordnungsrechtliche Zustimmungen schließen die denkmalschutzrechtliche Erlaubnis ein; sie bedürfen insoweit der Zustimmung der Denkmalschutzbehörde.

§ 13 Erlaubnis

(1) Einer Erlaubnis der Denkmalschutzbehörde bedarf,
1. wer ein Kulturdenkmal oder Teile davon
   a) zerstören, beseitigen oder an einen anderen Ort verbringen,
   b) umgestalten, instand setzen oder im äußeren Erscheinungsbild verändern oder
   c) mit Werbe- oder sonstigen Anlagen versehen will,
2. wer in der Umgebung eines unbeweglichen Kulturdenkmals Anlagen errichten, verändern oder beseitigen will, wenn sich dies auf den Bestand oder das Erscheinungsbild des Kulturdenkmals auswirken kann,
3. wer Erdarbeiten an einer Stelle vornehmen will, von der bekannt ist oder vermutet wird oder den Umständen nach anzunehmen ist, dass sich dort Kulturdenkmale befinden.

(2) ¹Die Erlaubnis kann versagt werden, soweit gewichtige Gründe des Denkmalschutzes für die unveränderte Beibehaltung des bisherigen Zustandes sprechen. ²Im Falle des Absatzes 1 Nr. 2 kann die Erlaubnis darüber hinaus nur versagt werden, soweit das Vorhaben zu einer Beeinträchtigung des Wesens, des überlieferten Erscheinungsbildes oder der künstlerischen Wirkung eines Kulturdenkmals führen würde und gewichtige Gründe des Denkmalschutzes für die unveränderte Beibehaltung des bisherigen Zustandes sprechen.

(3) Der Inhaber einer Erlaubnis nach Absatz 1 Nr. 3 ist im Rahmen des Zumutbaren verpflichtet, die Kosten für die denkmalfachliche Begleitung der Erdarbeiten, für die Sicherung und Behandlung von Funden und für die Dokumentation der Denkmalfachbehörde zu erstatten.

§ 14 Erlaubnisverfahren

(1) ¹Der Erlaubnisantrag ist der zuständigen Denkmalschutzbehörde schriftlich mit allen für die Beurteilung des Vorhabens und der Bearbeitung des Antrags erforderlichen Unterlagen einzureichen. ²Die Denkmalschutzbehörde prüft den Antrag innerhalb von zwei Wochen auf Vollständigkeit und teilt dem Antragsteller den Eingang des Antrags mit. ³Ist der Antrag unvollständig oder weist er sonstige erhebliche Mängel auf, fordert die Denkmalschutzbehörde den Antragsteller zur Behebung der Mängel innerhalb einer angemessenen Frist auf. ⁴Werden die Mängel innerhalb der Frist nicht behoben, gilt der Antrag als zurückgenommen. ⁵Die Denkmalschutzbehörde kann verlangen, dass der Antrag durch denkmalpflegerische Zielstellungen oder vorbereitende Untersuchungen am Kulturdenkmal ergänzt wird. ⁶Die Kosten dieser vorbereitenden Untersuchungen hat der Antragsteller zu tragen.

(2) Soweit die besondere Eigenart, die Bedeutung des Kulturdenkmals oder die Schwierigkeit der Maßnahme es erfordert, soll die Leitung oder Ausführung der vorbereitenden Untersuchung oder die Durchführung von Arbeiten, die besondere Erfahrungen und Kenntnisse voraussetzen, durch denkmalfachlich geeignete Personen zur Auflage einer Erlaubnis gemacht werden.

(3) ¹Die untere Denkmalschutzbehörde entscheidet über einen Erlaubnisantrag nach Anhörung[1]) der Denkmalfachbehörde innerhalb einer Frist von drei Monaten nach Vorlage der vollständigen Antragsunterlagen; die Denkmalschutzbehörde kann diese Frist gegenüber dem Antragsteller aus wichtigem Grund um bis zu zwei Monate verlängern. ²Der Antrag gilt als genehmigt, wenn über ihn nicht innerhalb der nach Satz 1 maßgeblichen Frist entschieden worden ist. ³Die fachliche Stellungnahme der Denkmalfachbehörde ist grundsätzlich innerhalb von sechs Wochen gegenüber der unteren Denkmalschutzbehörde zu erteilen. ⁴Diese ist an die fachliche Stellungnahme der Denkmalfachbehörde gebunden. ⁵Sofern die Gemeinden einen Denkmalpflegeplan erstellt haben (§ 3), entscheidet die untere Denkmalschutzbehörde über die Erlaubnisanträge allein. ⁶Die Denkmalfachbehörde kann wegen der Bedeutung des Objekts und des Vorhabens im Einzelfall die fachliche Beteiligung verlangen. ⁷Entsprechendes gilt für die fachliche Beteiligung im Falle des § 12 Abs. 3.

(4) ¹Die Erlaubnis erlischt, wenn nicht innerhalb von drei Jahren nach ihrer Erteilung mit der Ausführung begonnen oder die Ausführung ein Jahr unterbrochen worden ist. ²Die Fristen nach Satz 1 können auf schriftlichen Antrag jeweils um bis zu einem Jahr verlängert werden.

(5) Die Stiftung Thüringer Schlösser und Gärten übt die Rechte und Pflichten der unteren Denkmalschutzbehörde für von ihr betreute oder verwaltete Kulturdenkmale aus.

---

1) Vgl. dazu die Verwaltungsvorschrift zu einem verkürzten Verfahren entsprechend § 14 Abs. 3 ThürDSchG zwischen den Unteren Denkmalschutzbehörden und dem Thüringischen Landesamt für Denkmalpflege und Archäologie, abgedruckt als Nr. D16.I.1d.

§ 15 Beseitigung widerrechtlicher Maßnahmen

[1]Wer eine Maßnahme, die nach diesem Gesetz der Erlaubnis oder Genehmigung bedarf, ohne die erforderliche Genehmigung oder im Widerspruch zu den bei der Genehmigung erteilten Auflagen durchführt, ist auf Anordnung der Denkmalschutzbehörde verpflichtet, den alten Zustand wiederherzustellen oder das Kulturdenkmal auf andere Weise entsprechend den Auflagen der Denkmalschutzbehörde instandzusetzen. [2]Die Denkmalschutzbehörden können die Einstellung der Maßnahmen anordnen.

Vierter Abschnitt
Zusätzliche Vorschriften für Bodendenkmale

§ 16 Zufallsfunde

(1) [1]Wer Bodendenkmale entdeckt oder findet, hat dies unverzüglich der Denkmalfachbehörde anzuzeigen. [2]Die Anzeige kann auch gegenüber der Gemeinde oder der unteren Denkmalschutzbehörde erfolgen; diese leiten die Anzeige unverzüglich der Denkmalfachbehörde zu.

(2) [1]Anzeigepflichtig sind der Entdecker, der Eigentümer, Besitzer oder sonst Verfügungsberechtigte des Grundstücks sowie der Leiter der Arbeiten, bei deren Durchführung die Sache entdeckt worden ist. [2]Die Anzeige durch eine dieser Personen befreit die Übrigen.

(3) [1]Der Fund und die Fundstelle sind bis zum Ablauf einer Woche nach der Anzeige im unveränderten Zustand zu erhalten und in geeigneter Weise vor Gefahren für die Erhaltung des Fundes zu schützen. [2]Die Denkmalfachbehörde soll der Fortsetzung der Arbeiten zustimmen, wenn ihre Unterbrechung unverhältnismäßig hohe Kosten verursacht und der wissenschaftliche Wert des Fundes oder der Befunde dies zulässt.

(4) Die Denkmalfachbehörde ist berechtigt, den Fund zu bergen, auszuwerten und zur wissenschaftlichen Bearbeitung vorübergehend in Besitz zu nehmen.

§ 17 Schatzregal

Bewegliche Kulturdenkmale, die herrenlos oder so lange verborgen gewesen sind, dass ihr Eigentümer nicht mehr zu ermitteln ist, werden mit der Entdeckung Eigentum des Landes, wenn sie bei staatlichen Nachforschungen, in archäologischen Schutzgebieten oder bei ungenehmigten Nachforschungen entdeckt wurden, oder wenn sie einen hervorragenden wissenschaftlichen Wert besitzen.

§ 18 Nachforschungen

[1]Nachforschungen, insbesondere Grabungen mit dem Ziel, Bodendenkmale zu entdecken, bedürfen der Genehmigung der Denkmalfachbehörde. [2]Die Grabungsgenehmigung kann bestimmen, wer Unternehmer der Grabung sein soll. [3]§ 16 Abs. 4 gilt sinngemäß.

§ 19 Archäologische Schutzgebiete

(1) [1]Die oberste Denkmalschutzbehörde kann durch Rechtsverordnung bestimmte abgegrenzte Gebiete befristet oder auf unbefristete Zeit zu Archäologischen Schutzgebieten erklären, wenn dies erforderlich ist, damit die in ihnen enthaltenen Bodendenkmale

1. dauerhaft vor Zerstörung bewahrt oder
2. bis zu einer wissenschaftlichen Untersuchung

vor Eingriffen in den Boden gesichert werden. [2]Die Ausweisung eines Archäologischen Schutzgebietes ist nur zulässig, wenn eine begründete Vermutung besteht, dass es Bodendenkmale von erheblicher Bedeutung birgt.

(2) In Archäologischen Schutzgebieten bedürfen Arbeiten, die Bodendenkmale aus ur- und frühgeschichtlicher Zeit gefährden können, der Erlaubnis der obersten Denkmalschutzbehörde.

§ 20 Nutzungsbeschränkungen

(1) [1]Die oberste Denkmalschutzbehörde kann die wirtschaftliche Nutzung eines Grundstücks oder eines Grundstücksteils beschränken, in dem sich Bodendenkmale von wissenschaftlicher oder geschichtlicher Bedeutung befinden. [2]Berechtigter ist das Land, vertreten durch die Denkmalfachbehörde.

(2) Die Beschränkung nach Absatz 1 ist auf Ersuchen der obersten Denkmalschutzbehörde im Grundbuch einzutragen.

(3) ¹Soll eine Grabung auf einem fremden Grundstück erfolgen, so kann der Eigentümer verpflichtet werden, die Grabung zuzulassen, wenn die Denkmalfachbehörde. entsprechend der Angemessenheit der Aufwendungen festgestellt hat, dass ein besonderes öffentliches Interesse an der Grabung besteht. ²Der Inhaber der Grabungsgenehmigung oder der Unternehmer der Grabung nach § 18 Satz 2 hat dem Eigentümer den durch die Grabung entstehenden Schaden zu ersetzen.

§ 21 Ablieferung

(1) Das Land, die untere Denkmalschutzbehörde und die Gemeinde, in deren Gebiet Funde (bewegliche Bodendenkmale) gemacht worden sind, haben in dieser Reihenfolge das Recht, die Ablieferung gegen eine angemessene Entschädigung zu verlangen.

(2) Die Ablieferung kann verlangt werden, wenn Tatsachen vorliegen, nach denen zu befürchten ist, dass der Erhaltungszustand des Fundes verschlechtert wird oder dieser der Öffentlichkeit oder wissenschaftlichen Forschungen verloren geht.

(3) Die Ablieferung kann nicht mehr verlangt werden, wenn
1. seit der Anzeige nach § 16 Abs. 1 drei Monate verstrichen sind; dies gilt nicht, wenn der Erwerbsberechtigte (Absatz 1) innerhalb dieser Frist sich gegenüber dem Eigentümer das Recht, die Ablieferung zu verlangen, vorbehalten hat;
2. der Eigentümer dem Erwerbsberechtigten die Ablieferung des Fundes, bevor über die Ablieferungspflicht entschieden ist, angeboten und der Erwerbsberechtigte das Angebot nicht binnen drei Monaten angenommen hat.

(4) Die untere Denkmalschutzbehörde entscheidet auf Antrag eines Beteiligten, ob die Voraussetzungen der Ablieferung vorliegen.

Fünfter Abschnitt
Kosten

§ 21a Kosten

¹Für Erlaubnisse nach diesem Gesetz werden keine Gebühren und Auslagen erhoben. ²Die Bestimmungen über die Kosten der Baugenehmigung bleiben unberührt.

Sechster Abschnitt
Denkmalbehörden

§ 22 Denkmalschutzbehörden

(1) Oberste Denkmalschutzbehörde ist das für Denkmalschutz, Denkmalpflege und Archäologie zuständige Ministerium.

(2) ¹Untere Denkmalschutzbehörden sind die kreisfreien Städte und Landkreise jeweils im übertragenen Wirkungskreis. ²Kreisangehörigen Gemeinden mit mehr als 30 000 Einwohnern und mit besonders hohem und wertvollem Denkmalbestand kann die oberste Denkmalschutzbehörde die Zuständigkeit als untere Denkmalschutzbehörde verleihen, wenn eine qualifizierte personelle Ausstattung langfristig gewährleistet ist.[1]) ³Die Aufgaben des Denkmalschutzes obliegen den Landkreisen und Gemeinden als Aufgabe des übertragenen Wirkungskreises.

(3) ¹Bei der unteren Denkmalschutzbehörde soll nach Anhörung der Denkmalfachbehörde vom Landkreis oder der kreisfreien Stadt ein sachverständiger, weisungsunabhängiger Beirat berufen werden, der die Denkmalschutzbehörde bei der Durchführung ihrer Aufgaben unterstützt. ²Die ehrenamtlichen Mitarbeiter (§ 26) sind von Amts wegen Mitglieder des Beirats.

§ 23 Zuständigkeiten

(1) Für Maßnahmen auf Grund dieses Gesetzes sind die unteren Denkmalschutzbehörden zuständig, soweit dieses Gesetz nichts anderes bestimmt.

(2) ¹Bei Maßnahmen an Kulturdenkmalen, die im Eigentum des Bundes oder des Landes stehen sowie in den in diesem Gesetz bestimmten Fällen, entscheidet die oberste Denkmalschutzbehörde nach Anhörung der Denkmalfachbehörde. ²§ 7 Abs. 2 sowie die §§ 11, 27 und 28 finden auf Kulturdenkmale des Landes keine Anwendung.

---

1) Die Thüringer Verordnung zur Verleihung der Zuständigkeit als untere Denkmalschutzbehörde ist abgedruckt als Nr. D16.I.1a.

§ 24 Denkmalfachbehörde[1]

(1) ¹Denkmalfachbehörde ist das Landesamt für Denkmalpflege und Archälogie.[2] ²Es ist Träger des Museums für Ur- und Frühgeschichte Thüringens.

(2) ¹Die Denkmalfachbehörde ist der obersten Denkmalschutzbehörde unmittelbar nachgeordnet. ²Sie haben zur Erfüllung der in § 1 Abs. 1 genannten Ziele insbesondere folgende Aufgaben:
1. Mitwirkung bei denkmalschutzrechtlichen Erlaubnis- und sonstigen Verfahren, an denen die Beteiligung der Denkmalfachbehörden vorgesehen ist;
2. Beratung und Unterstützung der Eigentümer und Besitzer von Kulturdenkmalen bei Pflege, Unterhaltung und Wiederherstellung (Denkmalpflege);
3. systematische Aufnahme der Kulturdenkmale (Inventarisation);
4. Führung des Denkmalbuches;
5. wissenschaftliche Untersuchung der Kulturdenkmale als Beitrag zur Erforschung der Landesgeschichte;
6. Erarbeitung methodischer Grundlagen auf dem Gebiet der Restaurierung und Konservierung;
7. Stellungnahme als Träger öffentlicher Belange in förmlichen Verfahren nach Bundes- und Landesrecht;
8. Öffentlichkeitsarbeit, um das Verständnis für Denkmalschutz und Denkmalpflege zu wecken und zu fördern;
9. Ausstellen von denkmalschutzrechtlichen Steuerbescheinigungen;
10. Bewilligung der Zuwendungen des Landes nach § 7 Abs. 2 und
11. Bodendenkmalpflege einschließlich Paläontologie.

(3) ¹Das Landesamt für Archäologie ist zuständige Denkmalfachbehörde für alle Bereiche der Bodendenkmalpflege einschließlich der Paläontologie. ²Es ist gleichzeitig Träger des Museums für Ur- und Frühgeschichte Thüringens.

§ 25 Denkmalrat

(1) Die oberste Denkmalschutzbehörde beruft zu ihrer Beratung einen Denkmalrat.

(2) Dem Denkmalrat sollen insbesondere Vertreter der mit Denkmalpflege und Denkmalschutz befassten Fachgebiete wie Kunstgeschichte, Vorgeschichte, Architektur, Städtebau, Restaurierung, Geschichte, Volkskunde und bildende Künste, des Museumsverbandes, der staatlichen Hochbauverwaltung, der öffentlich-rechtlichen Religionsgemeinschaften, der kommunalen Spitzenverbände, des Haus- und Grundbesitzervereins und weiterer Verbände auf Landesebene angehören, die qualifizierte Kenntnisse der Denkmalpflege und des Denkmalschutzes besitzen.

(3) Der Landtag entsendet drei Abgeordnete.

(4) Über Stimmrecht verfügen nur die von der obersten Denkmalschutzbehörde berufenen und die vom Landtag entsandten Mitglieder.

(5) Vertreter der für Umweltschutz, Städtebau, Landschaftspflege, Naturschutz und Raumordnung zuständigen oberen Landesbehörden sowie der Beauftragte für Menschen mit Behinderungen sollen zu den Sitzungen des Denkmalrates eingeladen werden.

(6) Das Nähere bestimmt die Satzung des Denkmalrates,[3] die die oberste Denkmalschutzbehörde erlässt.

§ 26 Ehrenamtliche Mitarbeiter

(1) ¹Die Denkmalfachbehörde kann ehrenamtliche Mitarbeiter für die Bau- und Kunstdenkmalpflege sowie die Archäologie bestellen. ²Die ehrenamtlichen Mitarbeiter sind fachlich und organisatorisch der Denkmalfachbehörde unterstellt. ³Sie werden im Benehmen mit der unteren Denkmalschutzbehörde, in deren Gebiet sie tätig werden sollen, bestellt.

(2) Die ehrenamtlichen Mitarbeiter beraten und unterstützen die Denkmalfachbehörde und die Denkmalschutzbehörden in allen Angelegenheiten des Denkmalschutzes und der Denkmalpflege.

---

1) Vgl. auch das Thüringer Gesetz über die Errichtung der „Stiftung Thüringer Schlösser und Gärten", abgedruckt als Nr. D16.III.4.
2) Die Anordnung über die Organisation der gemeinsamen Verwaltung des Landesamtes für Denkmalpflege und Archäologie und des Landesarchivs ist abgedruckt als Nr. D16.I.1c.
3) Die Satzung des Thüringer Landesdenkmalrates ist abgedruckt als Nr. D16.I.1b.

(3) Das Land ersetzt den ehrenamtlichen Mitarbeitern die Kosten, die ihnen durch ihre Tätigkeit entstehen.

Siebenter Abschnitt
Enteignung, Entschädigung und Ordnungswidrigkeiten

§ 27 Enteignung
(1) Die Enteignung ist zugunsten des Landes, eines Landkreises, einer Gemeinde oder einer rechtsfähigen Stiftung zulässig, soweit sie erforderlich ist, damit:
1. ein Kulturdenkmal in seinem Bestand oder Erscheinungsbild erhalten bleibt,
2. ein Bodendenkmal (§ 2 Abs. 7) wissenschaftlich ausgewertet oder der Allgemeinheit zugänglich gemacht werden kann,
3. in einem Archäologischen Schutzgebiet (§ 19) planmäßige Nachforschungen betrieben werden können.

(2) Für die Enteignung und Entschädigung gelten die Bestimmungen des Thüringer Enteignungsgesetzes vom 23. März 1994 (GVBl. S. 329) in der jeweils geltenden Fassung.

§ 28 Sonstige entschädigungspflichtige Maßnahmen
(1) ¹Stellt eine Maßnahme auf Grund dieses Gesetzes eine wirtschaftliche Belastung für den Privateigentümer oder sonst dinglich Berechtigten dar, die über die Sozialbindung des Eigentums (Artikel 14 Abs. 2 Grundgesetz) hinausgeht und daher unzumutbar ist, ist eine angemessene Entschädigung in Geld zu leisten. ²Führen Maßnahmen dazu, dass der Privateigentümer das Eigentum insgesamt nicht mehr wirtschaftlich zumutbar nutzen kann, so kann er stattdessen die Übernahme des Eigentums gegen angemessene Entschädigung verlangen.
(2) ¹Die Grundsätze der Entschädigung bei der förmlichen Enteignung sind entsprechend anzuwenden. ²Enteignungsbegünstigt und zur Entschädigung verpflichtet ist das Land.

§ 29 Bußgeldbestimmungen
(1) Ordnungswidrig handelt, wer vorsätzlich oder fahrlässig
1. erlaubnispflichtige Maßnahmen entgegen § 13, § 18 Satz 1 oder § 19 Abs. 2 ohne Erlaubnis beginnt oder durchführt oder einer von der zuständigen Behörde mit der Erlaubnis erteilten Auflage zuwiderhandelt;
2. entgegen § 11 Abs. 2 Satz 2 Maßnahmen der Denkmalschutzbehörde zur Abwendung einer unmittelbaren Gefahr für den Bestand eines Kulturdenkmals nicht duldet;
3. der Auskunftspflicht nach § 9 Abs. 1 nicht nachkommt oder entgegen § 9 Abs. 2 Satz 1 den Beauftragten der zuständigen Behörde das Betreten von Grundstücken oder Besichtigen von Kulturdenkmalen nicht gestattet;
4. entgegen § 8 Abs. 2 den Eigentumswechsel eines beweglichen eingetragenen Kulturdenkmals nicht oder nicht rechtzeitig anzeigt;
5. einer Einstellungsanordnung nach § 15 Satz 2 zuwiderhandelt;
6. entgegen § 16 Abs. 1 Satz 1 einen Fund nicht unverzüglich anzeigt;
7. entgegen § 16 Abs. 3 den Fund oder die Fundstelle nicht bis zum Ablauf einer Woche nach der Anzeige in unverändertem Zustand lässt;
8. den von der Denkmalfachbehörde erlassenen, vollziehbaren Anordnungen zur Bergung, Auswertung und zur wissenschaftlichen Bearbeitung nach § 16 Abs. 4 zuwiderhandelt;
9. einer Nutzungsbeschränkung nach § 20 Abs. 1 zuwiderhandelt.

(2) ¹Ordnungswidrigkeiten nach Absatz 1 Nr. 1, mit Ausnahme der Zuwiderhandlungen nach § 13 Abs. 1 Nr. 1 Buchst. a, sowie Ordnungswidrigkeiten nach Absatz 1 Nr. 2 bis 9 können mit einer Geldbuße bis zu einhundertfünfzigtausend Euro geahndet werden. ²Ordnungswidrigkeiten nach Absatz 1 Nr. 1 können im Falle der Zuwiderhandlung gegen § 13 Abs. 1 Nr. 1 Buchst. a mit einer Geldbuße bis zu fünfhunderttausend Euro geahndet werden.

(3) ¹Verwaltungsbehörde im Sinne des § 36 Abs. 1 Nr. 1 des Gesetzes über Ordnungswidrigkeiten (OWiG) ist die untere Denkmalschutzbehörde. ²Abweichend von Satz 1 ist die oberste Denkmalschutzbehörde zuständig, wenn gegen eine Maßnahme dieser Behörde verstoßen wird.

(4) ¹Ist eine Ordnungswidrigkeit nach Absatz 1 Nr. 1 begangen worden, so können die zur Vorbereitung oder Begehung gebrauchten oder bestimmten Gegenstände eingezogen werden. ²§ 19 OWiG ist anzuwenden.

Achter Abschnitt
Verfahrens- und Ausführungsbestimmungen

§ 30 Vorkaufsrecht

(1) ¹Der Gemeinde steht beim Kauf von Grundstücken, auf oder in denen sich Kulturdenkmale befinden, ein öffentlich-rechtliches Vorkaufsrecht zu. ²Das Vorkaufsrecht darf ausgeübt werden, wenn das Wohl der Allgemeinheit dies rechtfertigt, insbesondere, wenn dadurch die dauernde Erhaltung eines Kulturdenkmals ermöglicht werden soll. ³Das Vorkaufsrecht ist ausgeschlossen, wenn der Eigentümer das Grundstück an seinen Ehegatten oder an eine Person veräußert, die mit ihm in gerader Linie verwandt oder verschwägert oder in der Seitenlinie bis zum dritten Grad verwandt ist.
(2) ¹Das Vorkaufsrecht kann nur binnen zwei Monaten nach der Mitteilung des Kaufvertrages ausgeübt werden. ²Die §§ 463 bis 469 Abs. 1 und § 471 des Bürgerlichen Gesetzbuchs sind anzuwenden. ³Das Vorkaufsrecht ist nicht übertragbar. ⁴Nach Mitteilung des Kaufvertrages ist auf Ersuchen der Gemeinde ihr zur Sicherung des Anspruchs auf Übereignung des Grundstücks eine Vormerkung in das Grundbuch einzutragen; die Gemeinde trägt die Kosten der Eintragung der Vormerkung und ihrer Löschung. ⁵Bei einem Eigentumserwerb auf Grund der Ausübung des Vorkaufsrechts erlöschen rechtsgeschäftliche Vorkaufsrechte. ⁶Wird die Gemeinde nach Ausübung des Vorkaufsrechts im Grundbuch als Eigentümerin eingetragen, so kann sie das Grundbuchamt ersuchen, eine zur Sicherung des Übereignungsanspruchs des Käufers im Grundbuch eingetragene Vormerkung zu löschen; sie darf das Ersuchen nur stellen, wenn die Ausübung des Vorkaufsrechts für den Käufer unanfechtbar ist.
(3) ¹Der durch das Vorkaufsrecht Verpflichtete hat der Gemeinde den Inhalt des mit dem Dritten abgeschlossenen Vertrags unverzüglich mitzuteilen; die Mitteilung des Verpflichteten wird durch die des Dritten ersetzt. ²Das Grundbuchamt darf bei Veräußerungen den Erwerber als Eigentümer in das Grundbuch nur eintragen, wenn ihm die Nichtausübung oder das Nichtbestehen des Vorkaufsrechts nachgewiesen ist. ³Besteht ein Vorkaufsrecht nicht oder wird es nicht ausgeübt, hat die Gemeinde auf Antrag eines Beteiligten darüber unverzüglich ein Zeugnis auszustellen. ⁴Das Zeugnis gilt als Verzicht auf die Ausübung des Vorkaufsrechts.
(4) ¹Die Gemeinde kann das Vorkaufsrecht zugunsten einer anderen juristischen Person des öffentlichen Rechts ausüben. ²Absatz 1 Satz 2 und 3 gelten entsprechend. ³Die Ausübung des der Gemeinde zustehenden Vorkaufsrechts zugunsten einer juristischen Person des Privatrechts ist zulässig, wenn die dauernde Erhaltung des auf oder in dem Grundstück liegenden Kulturdenkmals zu den satzungsmäßigen Aufgaben der juristischen Person gehört und bei Berücksichtigung aller Belange gesichert erscheint. ⁴Die Gemeinde kann das Vorkaufsrecht zugunsten eines anderen nur ausüben, wenn ihr die notariell beglaubigte Zustimmung des Begünstigten vorliegt.

§ 31 Steuerbescheinigungen

Bescheinigungen für die Erlangung von Steuervergünstigungen werden nach Maßgabe der einschlägigen Steuergesetze und nur nach vorheriger Abstimmung der Maßnahme von der Denkmalfachbehörde ausgestellt.

§ 32 Religionsgemeinschaften

Bei Entscheidungen und Maßnahmen der Denkmalschutzbehörden über Kulturdenkmale im Eigentum oder Besitz der Kirchen oder anderer Religionsgemeinschaften sind die in Artikel 9 des Staatsvertrags des Freistaats Thüringen mit den Evangelischen Kirchen in Thüringen vom 15. März 1994 (GVBl. S. 509) und in Artikel 18 des Staatsvertrags zwischen dem Heiligen Stuhl und dem Freistaat Thüringen vom 11. Juni 1997 (GVBl. S. 266) getroffenen Regelungen zu beachten oder entsprechend anzuwenden.

§ 33 (aufgehoben)

§ 34 Ausführungsvorschriften
¹Die oberste Denkmalschutzbehörde wird ermächtigt, durch Rechtsverordnung Zuständigkeiten auf nachgeordnete Behörden zu übertragen. ²Sie erlässt ferner die zur Ausführung dieses Gesetzes erforderlichen Verwaltungsvorschriften.

Neunter Abschnitt
Übergangs- und Schlussbestimmungen

§ 34a Übergangsbestimmung
(1) Die unteren Denkmalschutzbehörden erhalten zum Ausgleich der Mehrbelastungen für die Aufgabenwahrnehmung nach § 21 Abs. 4 in den Jahren 2008 und 2009 einen angemessenen finanziellen Ausgleich.
(2) Ab dem Jahr 2010 erfolgt die Kostenerstattung nach Absatz 1 innerhalb der nach dem Thüringer Finanzausgleichsgesetz zu regelnden Auftragskostenpauschale.

§ 35 Gleichstellungsbestimmung
Status- und Funktionsbezeichnungen in diesem Gesetz gelten jeweils in männlicher und weiblicher Form.

§ 36 (In-Kraft-Treten)

Thüringer Verordnung zur Verleihung der Zuständigkeit als untere Denkmalschutzbehörde

Vom 2. Juni 1994 (GVBl. S. 640)

Aufgrund des § 22 Abs. 3 Satz 2 des Thüringer Denkmalschutzgesetzes vom 7. Januar 1992 (GVBl. S. 17) verordnet der Minister für Wissenschaft und Kunst:

§ 1
Den Städten Altenburg, Eisenach, Gotha, Mühlhausen und Nordhausen wird die Zuständigkeit als untere Denkmalschutzbehörde verliehen.

§ 2
Diese Verordnung tritt am 30. Juni 1994 in Kraft.

Satzung des Thüringer Landesdenkmalrates

Erlaß des TMWK vom 27. Oktober 1993 (ThürStAnz. S. 2297)

Geänd. d. ÄndSatzg v. 15.1.2001 (ThürStAnz S. 334)

Das Thüringer Ministerium für Wissenschaft, Forschung und Kunst bildet auf der Grundlage des Thüringer Denkmalschutzgesetzes (ThDSchG) vom 07.01.1992 § 25 Abs. 1 und Abs. 5 einen Landesdenkmalrat und erlässt folgende Satzung:

§ 1 Name und Aufgaben

(1) Der Denkmalrat führt die Bezeichnung „Thüringer Landesdenkmalrat".

(2) Der Thüringer Landesdenkmalrat berät und unterstützt das Thüringer Ministerium für Wissenschaft, Forschung und Kunst in allen Fragen des Denkmalschutzes und der Denkmalpflege. Er nimmt insbesondere zu grundsätzlichen Fragen und zu denkmalpflegerischen Vorhaben von grundsätzlicher Bedeutung Stellung. Er ist vor Erlass von Ausführungsvorschriften zum Denkmalschutzgesetz zu hören.

§ 2 Mitglieder

(1) Mitglieder sind:
1. Je ein Vertreter der Fachgebiete, der über qualifizierte Kenntnisse der Denkmalpflege und des Denkmalschutzes verfügt:
   Kunstgeschichte,
   Ur- und Frühgeschichte,
   Architektur,
   Städtebau,
   Geschichte,
   Volkskunde,
   Bildende Künste,
   Restaurierung.
2. Je ein Vertreter folgender Einrichtungen, der über qualifizierte Kenntnisse der Denkmalpflege und des Denkmalschutzes verfügt:
   Staatliche Hochbauverwaltung,
   Evangelische Kirchen,
   Katholische Bistümer,
   Landesverband der Jüdischen Gemeinden,
   Gemeinde- und Städtebund Thüringen,
   Thüringischer Landkreistag,
   Museumsverband Thüringen e.V.,
   Arbeitsgemeinschaft der Thüringer Handwerkskammern,
   Arbeitsgemeinschaft der Thüringer Industrie- und Handelskammern,
   Architektenkammer Thüringen
   Sparkassen-Kulturstiftung Hessen-Thüringen
3. Je ein von den im Thüringer Landtag vertretenen Fraktionen entsandter Vertreter.

(2) Die Mitglieder gemäß Abs. 1 Ziff. 1 und 2 haben volles Stimmrecht; die Mitglieder gemäß Abs. 1 Ziff. 3 wirken an der Meinungsbildung beratend mit.

(3) Die Mitglieder gemäß Abs. 1 Ziff. 1 und 2 werden vom Thüringer Ministerium für Wissenschaft, Forschung und Kunst berufen. Vor der Berufung der Mitglieder gemäß Abs. 1 Ziff. 2 gibt das Thüringer Ministerium für Wissenschaft, Forschung und Kunst den Einrichtungen Gelegenheit, einen Vertreter vorzuschlagen.

(4) Scheidet ein Mitglied vorzeitig aus, wird ein neues Mitglied nach Maßgabe von Abs. 1 Ziff. 3 entsandt oder von Abs. 3 berufen.

(5) Die Berufung erfolgt für die Dauer einer Legislaturperiode des Thüringer Landtages. Endet die Legislaturperiode, setzt der Thüringer Landesdenkmalrat bis zur Neukonstituierung seine Tätigkeit fort.

D16.I.1b Satzung des Thüringer Landesdenkmalrates

§ 3 Teilnahme
(1) An den Sitzungen wirken Vertreter nachfolgender Behörden mit:
- Thüringer Ministerium für Wissenschaft, Forschung und Kunst,
- Thüringisches Landesamt für Denkmalpflege, Bau- und Kunstdenkmalpflege,
- Thüringisches Landesamt für Archäologische Denkmalpflege,
- Thüringer Landesverwaltungsamt – Obere Denkmalschutzbehörde,
  - Umwelt- und Landesplanung,
  - Bau- und Wohnungswesen

und, sofern durch die Lage eines Kulturdenkmales betroffen:
- Untere Denkmalschutzbehörden,
- Stadt oder Gemeinde.

Das Thüringer Ministerium für Wissenschaft, Forschung und Kunst kann im Einzelfall die Teilnahme weiterer beratender Personen oder Institutionen veranlassen. Über die Teilnahme von Gästen entscheidet im Übrigen der Thüringer Landesdenkmalrat.

(2) Das Thüringer Ministerium für Wissenschaft, Forschung und Kunst und der Vorsitzende können Sachverständige zu den Sitzungen laden.

§ 4 Sitzungen
(1) Sitzungen finden nach Bedarf statt. In jedem Kalenderhalbjahr soll mindestens eine Sitzung stattfinden. Die voraussichtlich regulären Sitzungstermine werden durch den Vorsitzenden in Abstimmung mit dem Thüringer Ministerium für Wissenschaft, Forschung und Kunst zu Beginn des Kalenderjahres festgelegt.

(2) Auf Antrag von mindestens vier stimmberechtigten Mitgliedern (§ 2 Abs. 1 Ziff. 1 und 2) oder auf Antrag von mindestens zwei beratenden Mitgliedern (§ 2 Abs. 1 Ziff. 3) oder auf besonderen Wunsch des Thüringer Ministeriums für Wissenschaft, Forschung und Kunst ist umgehend eine Sitzung einzuberufen.

(3) Die Einladung zu den Sitzungen erfolgt mit einer Ladungsfrist, die nicht kürzer als zwei Wochen sein soll. In der Einladung sind diejenigen Angelegenheiten zu bezeichnen, die in der Sitzung behandelt werden sollen.

(4) Auf Antrag von mindestens vier Mitgliedern oder auf Wunsch des Thüringer Ministeriums für Wissenschaft, Forschung und Kunst muß eine Angelegenheit zum nächstmöglichen Zeitpunkt in einer Sitzung behandelt werden.

(5) Über die Sitzungen sind Niederschriften zu fertigen, in denen das wesentliche Ergebnis der Beratungen aufgezeichnet ist. Die Niederschrift ist den in §§ 2 und 3 genannten Mitgliedern und Stellen innerhalb von vier Wochen nach der Sitzung zuzustellen.

(6) Die Sitzungen sind nicht öffentlich. Der Vorsitzende unterrichtet die Öffentlichkeit in geeigneter Weise über die Ergebnisse der Sitzung. Der gemäß § 2 Abs. 1 Ziff. 2 und 3 bestellten Mitglieder weisen bei einer Übermittlung von Sitzungsniederschriften an die sie entsendende Stelle ausdrücklich auf die Nichtöffentlichkeit der Sitzungen hin.

§ 5 Wahlen
(1) Wahlen erfolgen mit einfacher Mehrheit der anwesenden Mitglieder. Stimmenthaltungen werden nicht berücksichtigt.
(2) Der Vorsitzende wird mit Stimmenmehrheit der anwesenden Mitglieder gewählt.
(3) Auf Antrag eines stimmberechtigten Mitgliedes finden geheime Wahlen statt.

§ 6 Vorstand
(1) Der Vorstand besteht aus dem Vorsitzenden, den beiden Stellvertretern und zwei Beisitzern.
(2) Für den Vorsitzenden sind zwei Stellvertreter zu wählen, die nach der Reihenfolge der Wahl den Vorsitzenden im Verhinderungsfall vertreten.
(3) Der Vorstand übernimmt zwischen den Sitzungen des Landesdenkmalrates die Aufgaben nach § 1 (Abs. 2) dieser Satzung.

§ 7 Arbeitsgruppen

Der Thüringer Landesdenkmalrat kann zur Vorbereitung eines Votums Arbeitsgruppen bilden, die sowohl problem- als auch objektbezogen tätig werden können. Die Arbeitsgruppen haben dem Thüringer Landesdenkmalrat über ihre Tätigkeit zu berichten.

§ 8 Geschäftsführung

Der Vorsitzende führt die Geschäfte des Thüringer Landesdenkmalrates. Die Geschäftsstelle des Thüringer Landesdenkmalrates ist das Thüringische Ministerium für Wissenschaft, Forschung und Kunst.

§ 9 Reisekosten

(1) Die Tätigkeit der Mitglieder ist ehrenamtlich.

(2) Mitglieder im Sinne von § 2 Abs. 1 Ziff. 1 und 2 (mit Ausnahme der Vertreter staatlicher Stellen) und Mitglieder im Sinne von § 3 Abs. 1, letzter Absatz und § 3 Abs. 2 sowie Mitglieder von Arbeitsgruppen im Sinne § 7 erhalten für ihre Teilnahme an Sitzungen Reisekosten nach Maßgabe der für die Beamten des Freistaats Thüringen geltenden reistekostenrechtlichen Vorschriften.

Die Abrechnungen sind dem Thüringer Ministerium für Wissenschaft, Forschung und Kunst. einzureichen.

Anordnung über die Organisation der Gemeinsamen Verwaltung des Landesamts für Denkmalpflege und Archäologie und des Landesarchivs

ThürStAnz Nr. 5/2017 S. 153

1 Allgemeines

1.1 Die Gemeinsame Verwaltung des Landesamts für Denkmalpflege und Archäologie und des Landesarchivs (im Folgenden: Gemeinsame Verwaltung) ist organisatorisch dem Landesamt für Denkmalpflege und Archäologie zugeordnet.

1.2 Diese Anordnung regelt das Zusammenwirken der Gemeinsamen Verwaltung mit dem Landesamt für Denkmalpflege und Archäologie und dem Landesarchiv sowie die personellen Zuständigkeiten in der Gemeinsamen Verwaltung.

1.3 Für die Mitarbeiterinnen und Mitarbeiter der Gemeinsamen Verwaltung finden ergänzend zu dieser Anordnung die Geschäftsordnung des Landesamts für Denkmalpflege und Archäologie sowie die sonstigen für dessen Bediensteten geltenden innerbehördlichen Regelungen Anwendung.

2 Aufgaben

2.1 Die Gemeinsame Verwaltung ist zuständig für die Wahrnehmung folgender Aufgaben des Landesamts für Denkmalpflege und Archäologie und des Landesarchivs:
- Personalangelegenheiten
- Haushaltsangelegenheiten
- Rechtsangelegenheiten
- Angelegenheiten des Inneren Dienstes
- Bewirtschaftung und Verwendungsnachweisprüfung der Fördermittel und die Erteilung steuerrechtlich relevanter Bescheinigungen
- IT-Angelegenheiten des Landesamts für Denkmalpflege und Archäologie.

Bei der Wahrnehmung dieser Aufgaben arbeitet die Leiterin oder der Leiter der Gemeinsamen Verwaltung mit der Leiterin oder dem Leiter des Landesamts für Denkmalpflege und Archäologie und der Leiterin oder dem Leiter des Landesarchivs eng zusammen und verkehrt direkt mit ihnen.

2.2 Darüber hinaus nimmt die Gemeinsame Verwaltung sonstige ihr durch die für die Denkmalpflege und Archäologie zuständige oberste Landesbehörde und die für das staatliche Archivwesen zuständige oberste Landesbehörde (im Folgenden: fachlich zuständige oberste Landesbehörde) zugewiesene Aufgaben wahr.

3 Personelle Zuständigkeiten

3.1 Die Leiterin oder der Leiter der Gemeinsamen Verwaltung wird im Benehmen mit der Leiterin oder dem Leiter des Landesamts für Denkmalpflege und Archäologie und der Leiterin oder dem Leiter des Landesarchivs durch die für die Denkmalpflege und Archäologie zuständige oberste Landesbehörde bestellt.

3.2 Dienstvorgesetzte oder Dienstvorgesetzter der Leiterin oder des Leiters und der Mitarbeiter und Mitarbeiterinnen der Gemeinsamen Verwaltung ist die Leiterin oder der Leiter des Landesamts für Denkmalpflege und Archäologie. Im Übrigen sind die Mitarbeiter und Mitarbeiterinnen der Gemeinsamen Verwaltung dem Leiter der Gemeinsamen Verwaltung unterstellt.

3.3 Die Leiterin oder der Leiter des Landesamts für Denkmalpflege und Archäologie und die Leiterin oder der Leiter des Landesarchivs haben in den sie betreffenden Angelegenheiten gegenüber der Leiterin oder dem Leiter der Gemeinsamen Verwaltung ein fachliches Weisungsrecht. Widerspricht die Leiterin oder der Leiter der Gemeinsamen Verwaltung der Weisung und kann eine Einigung nicht erzielt werden, entscheidet die jeweils fachlich zuständige oberste Landesbehörde.

4 Beauftragter für den Haushalt

4.1 Die Leiterin oder der Leiter der Gemeinsamen Verwaltung ist die oder der Beauftragte für den Haushalt des Landesamts für Denkmalpflege und Archäologie und des Landesarchivs.

4.2 Widerspricht die oder der Beauftragte für den Haushalt einem Vorhaben und kommt auf Ebene der Dienststellen keine Einigung zustande, so entscheidet die jeweils fachlich zuständige oberste Landesbehörde.

4.3 Im Übrigen gelten im Verhältnis der oder des Beauftragten für den Haushalt zum Landesamt für Denkmalpflege und Archäologie und zum Landesarchiv § 9 der Thüringer Landeshaushaltsordnung sowie die dazu erlassenen Verwaltungsvorschriften in der jeweils gültigen Fassung.

5 Inkrafttreten

Diese Anordnung tritt mit Wirkung vom 13. Juli 2016 in und mit Ablauf des 31. Dezember 2021 außer Kraft. Gleichzeitig tritt die Anordnung zur Organisation der gemeinsamen Verwaltung von Einrichtungen im Geschäftsbereich des Thüringer Ministeriums für Wissenschaft, Forschung und Kunst vom 10. Oktober 2002 (ThürStAnz Nr. 45/2002 S. 2711) außer Kraft.

Verwaltungsvorschrift zu einem verkürzten Verfahren entsprechend § 14 Abs. 3 ThürDSchG zwischen den Unteren Denkmalschutzbehörden und dem Thüringischen Landesamt für Denkmalpflege und Archäologie

Vom 21. Juni 2013, 5 3/5692 (ABl. TMBWK 2013, S. 222)

geändert durch Verwaltungsvorschrift vom 30.03.2017 (ThürStAnz 2017, S. 627)

A. Verfahren

In den nachfolgend formulierten Fallgruppen soll bei Beachtung bestimmter denkmalfachlicher Mindeststandards die gesetzlich in § 14 Abs. 3 ThürDSchG vorgeschriebene Anhörung vereinfacht und verkürzt werden. Durch sie wird den Denkmalschutzbehörden für bestimmte Kategorien bzw. Fallgruppen von Kulturdenkmalen und Maßnahmen (Gewerke) die Möglichkeit gegeben, die Anfrage in verkürzter und standardisierter Form an die Fachbehörde zu richten.

Das dabei anzuwendende Verfahren ist folgendermaßen zu gestalten:

Die Untere Denkmalschutzbehörde richtet in den im nachstehenden Katalog aufgeführten Fällen die gemäß § 14 Abs. 3 ThürDschG vorgeschriebene Anfrage in verkürzter und standardisierter Form brieflich oder per Fax an das Landesamt für Denkmalpflege und Archäologie. Als Begründung für die Anwendung des verkürzten Verfahrens genügt die Angabe der einschlägigen Ordnungsziffer aus dem nachstehenden Fallkatalog.

Der Entscheidungsvorschlag der Unteren Denkmalschutzbehörde wird beigelegt.

Das Landesamt erteilt bei Anwendung des verkürzten Verfahrens sein fachliches Einverständnis innerhalb einer Woche nach Eingang der Anfrage durch Mitzeichnung und Stempel.

Äußert sich das Landesamt innerhalb einer Woche nach Eingang der Anfrage nicht, gilt das Einverständnis als erteilt.

B. Katalog der Fallgruppen und Fälle, in denen das verkürzte Verfahren anzuwenden ist

Fassaden

An Fassaden von nicht als Einzeldenkmal ausgewiesenen Gebäuden im Denkmalensemble:

1.1 Maßnahmen, die der Reinigung von Backstein- und Klinkerfassaden oder Instandsetzung von Anstrichen und Putzen an Putz- und Stuckfassaden dienen und bei denen die Fassaden mit allen ihren gestalterischen Details in ihrer überlieferten Substanz einschließlich der Oberflächenästhetik material- und handwerksgerecht repariert werden.

1.2 Maßnahmen zur Wiederherstellung zerstörter bzw. fehlender Gestaltungs- oder Gliederungselemente im Sinne einer Komplettierung des Gesamterscheinungsbildes bei Stuck- und Putzfassaden von Gebäuden nach 1880, wenn die notwendigen Details eindeutig am Bau oder durch Quellen belegt sind.

1.3 Bei geplanten gestalterischen Veränderungen, wie z. B. Balkonanlagen und Fluchttreppen, wenn diese dem Gebäudetyps entsprechen und nicht die Hauptansichtsseiten (Schaufassaden) betreffen.

Werbeanlagen, Schaukästen und Warenautomaten

2.1 Werbung für Leistungen, die im Gebäude erbracht werden.

2.2 Werbeanlagen und Verkaufsautomaten, die sich in ihrer gestalterischen Qualität den Anforderungen des Straßen- oder Siedlungsbildes, d. h. sich der Architektur des Bauwerkes oder der baulichen Gesamtanlage nach Maßstab, Werkstoff, Form und Farbe anpassen.

2.3 Werbeanlage, die Öffnungen, Gesimse oder sonstige architektonische Gliederungen oder Teile des Bauschmuckes nicht verdecken oder überschneiden.

2.4 An der Fassade aufgebrachte Werbebilder, -schriftzüge u.ä., die in Form hinterleuchteter, angestrahlter oder unbeleuchteter Einzelbuchstaben, Schriftzüge oder Symbole gestaltet werden, wobei vorzugsweise auf die Wandfläche gemalte Werbeaussagen in handwerklich guter Ausführung und zurückhaltender Farbgebung verwendet werden sollten.

2.5 Für Schrifttafeln, Ausleger u. ä. gilt Ziff. 2.4. sinngemäß.
2.6 Werbeanlagen, bei denen es sich nicht um Leuchttransparente handelt (hierzu zählen auch Leuchtkästen mit einzelnen Buchstaben oder Symbolen sowie grelle Farben, blinkende oder schwellende Lichtwerbeanlagen).,
2.7 Werbeanlagen, die solitär und nicht gehäuft angebracht werden; dies gilt auch für Verkaufsautomaten und deren Kombination mit Werbeanlagen.
2.8 Werbeanlagen, die sich auf die konstruktiven Flächen des Erdgeschosses beschränken.
2.9 Werbeanlagen, die nicht über mehrere Fassadenabschnitte übergreifen.
2.10 Werbeanlagen und Warenautomaten, bei denen das technische Zubehör nicht sichtbar angeordnet wird.
2.11 Zeitlich begrenzte Werbungen für kulturelle, politische sportliche, religiöse o. ä. Veranstaltungen oder Werbung an Baugerüsten.
2.12 Schaukästen für im Gebäude ansässige Betriebe oder Vereine und Gruppierungen.
2.13 In der Umgebung von eingetragenen Denkmalen bzw. an Gebäuden in Denkmalensembles, die kein Einzeldenkmal sind, kann im Sinne des Antragstellers von den o. g. Grundsätzen abgewichen werden, wenn die Werbeanlagen stadt- bzw. ortsbildbildverträglich gestaltet sind und die Wirkungsmöglichkeit des Denkmalensembles bzw. des / der Einzeldenkmale in der unmittelbarer Umgebung nicht gravierend beeinträchtigt werden.

Fenster

Bei Einzeldenkmalen unter der Maßgabe, dass an Kulturdenkmalen bei bauzeitlichen Fenstern grundsätzlich die Reparaturfähigkeit bzw. Nachrüstbarkeit geprüft wurde und
3.1 bei überlieferten Fenstern, mit Ausnahme von Fenstern mit künstlerischer Gestaltung (Glasmalerei), die erhalten und handwerksgerecht repariert werden,
3.2 bei Einfachfenstern, wenn sie durch eine zusätzliche, neue Ebene (Umbau zum Kastendoppelfenster oder Verbundfenster) umgebaut werden und der äußere Flügel unverändert erhalten bleibt,
3.3 bei vorhandenen Kastendoppelfenstern, wenn sie durch Veränderung der Verglasung der inneren Flügel oder durch zusätzliche Dichtungen wärme- und schallschutztechnisch verbessert werden bzw. wenn im Ausnahmefall bei Kastendoppelfenstern die innere Ebene durch neue Fenster ersetzt wird und wenn hierdurch unabweisbar erhöhte Anforderungen an Schall und Wärmeschutz erfüllt werden können,
3.4 wenn die mangelnde Reparaturfähigkeit der Originalfenster und Wirtschaftlichkeit des Neueinbaus nachgewiesen wurde,
3.5 wenn die auszutauschenden Fenster keine künstlerische Gestaltung (Glasmalerei, Bleiverglasung) aufweisen und nachweislich nicht bauzeitlich sind bzw. nach 1940 entstanden sind,
3.6 wenn die ursprünglichen Abmessungen, Proportionen und die ursprüngliche Gestaltung (Gliederung, Fensterteilung, Sprossung, Profile) sowie die ursprüngliche Konstruktion (Anzahl der Öffnungsflügel, Funktion der Beschläge) wiederholt werden,
3.7 wenn ein identisches bzw. zeittypisches Material wie bei den Originalfenstern zum Einsatz kommt und bei den auszutauschenden Fenstern gegebenenfalls prägende Beschläge wieder verwendet werden,
3.8 wenn die vorgesehene Farbgebung bzw. die Oberflächengestaltung den dokumentierten Ergebnissen restauratorischer Befunduntersuchungen oder / und einem abgestimmten Farbgestaltungskonzept für das Gebäude entspricht.
An Gebäuden im Denkmalensemble, die nicht als Einzeldenkmal ausgewiesen sind,
3.9 wenn sich beim Austausch von Fenstern die Neubaufenster hinsichtlich Gliederung, Profilierung sowie Format und Sprossenbreite die bauzeitliche Fassadenarchitektur einordnen.

Dacheindeckung

4.1 Bei technisch zwingend erforderlichen Neueindeckungen einschließlich Dachklempnerarbeiten, wenn diese form- und materialgleich (Form, Material, Oberfläche, Verlegeart usw.) zu einer nachgewiesenen historischen Dacheindeckung und ohne Verwendung von Surrogaten erfolgt.

4.2 Zum historischen Gebäudebestand gehörende und für das Erscheinungsbild und die Funktion des Kulturdenkmales wesentliche Dachaufbauten wie Gaupen, Zwerchhäuser, Schornsteine, Brandmauern usw., wenn diese in den historischen Formen erhalten bzw. handwerksgerecht aufgearbeitet und saniert werden.

Dachausbau

Für Bauten in Denkmalensembles, die nicht als Einzeldenkmal ausgewiesen sind, wenn
5.1 das Dach keinen prägenden Anteil an der Denkmaleigenschaft hat, weil die Dachkonstruktion nicht mehr bauzeitlich ist, beispielsweise durch Neuerrichtung nach Brandschäden seit 1940,
5.2 keine negativen Auswirkungen auf das Erscheinungsbild des Gebäudes und das Gesamterscheinungsbild des Denkmalensembles auftreten werden,
5.3 der Dachausbau und die Dämmmaßnahmen nach den geltenden Regeln der Handwerkskunst durchgeführt werden.

Neubauten im Denkmalensemble

Neubauten, die gem. § 34 BauGB errichtet werden und sich in das Erscheinungsbild des Ensembles einfügen, und örtliche Gestaltungssatzungen beachten.

Einfriedungen (Mauern und Zäune)

Einfriedungen, die Teil eines Kulturdenkmals sind und
7.1 die in der rezenten Form handwerksgerecht durch einen Fachbetrieb mit denkmalfachlicher Eignung (vgl. § 14 Abs. 2 ThürDSchG) repariert werden bzw. die bei denen die Maßnahme auf Grundlage einer Fachplanung mit Bestands- und Zustandserfassung sowie Leistungsbeschreibung durch einen denkmalfachlich qualifizierten Fachplaner erfolgt,
7.2 bei Mauern darüber hinaus die chemische und physikalische Verträglichkeit der zur Reparatur vorgesehenen Mörtel mit den vorhandenen historischen Baustoffen durch eine Mörtelanalyse und eine darauf aufbauende Auswahl des Reparaturmörtels nachgewiesen ist.

Ephemere Anlagen

Bei ephemeren Anlagen, wenn
8.1 ihre Standzeit nur befristet ist und nicht länger als 12 Monate beträgt und
8.2 sie nicht die Sichtbeziehung auf ein Kulturdenkmal größtenteils verhindern sowie
8.3 völlig reversibel sind und
8.4 sie die Kulturdenkmale in ihrer Umgebung nicht beschädigen.

Telekommunikationseinrichtungen / Antennen

9.1 Bei Anlagen, die aus dem öffentlichen Straßenraum bei normalen Betrachtungsabständen am Gebäude optisch nicht vordergründig wahrzunehmen sind, also nicht in den öffentlichen Raum hineinwirken, sondern z. B. hofseitig oder in Blockinnenbereichen errichtet werden,
9.2 Anlagen, die von öffentlich zugänglichen Standorten mit Blickbeziehungen auf eine charakteristische Ortsansicht nicht wahrnehmbar sind.

Stadtbodengestaltungen

Bei Straßenbaumaßnahmen, wenn die Belange der Archäologie berücksichtigt werden und die vorgesehene Oberflächenausbildung und -gestaltung ohne Einschränkung einem mit der Denkmalfachbehörde abgestimmten Stadtbodenkonzept entspricht.
Diese Regelung tritt am Tag der Veröffentlichung in Kraft, sie ist befristet bis zum 31. Dezember 2022.

Thüringer Gesetz über die Sicherung und Nutzung von Archivgut (Thüringer Archivgesetz – ThürArchivG –)[1)]

Vom 29. Juni 2018 (GVBl. S. 308)

Inhaltsübersicht

§ 1	Geltungsbereich		§ 12	Feststellung der Archivwürdigkeit und Übernahme
§ 2	Öffentliches Archivgut		§ 13	Normierte Bewertungsverfahren
§ 3	Archivgut des Landes und des Bundes		§ 14	Aufbewahrung im Rahmen laufender Fristen
§ 4	Kommunales Archivgut, Kommunale Archive		§ 15	Datenschutz, Sicherung und Erschließung
§ 4a	Archivgut der Hochschulen		§ 16	Benutzung von Archivgut
§ 5	Sonstiges öffentliches Archivgut		§ 17	Schutzfristen
§ 6	Öffentliche Archive		§ 18	Einschränkung der Benutzung in besonderen Fällen
§ 7	Aufgaben öffentlicher Archive		§ 19	Auskunfts- und Berichtigungsrecht
§ 8	Organisation des staatlichen Archivwesens, Zuständigkeit und Aufgaben		§ 20	Ausnahmen vom Geltungsbereich
§ 9	Aufsicht		§ 21	Gleichstellungsbestimmung
§ 10	Archivpflege		§ 22	Inkrafttreten, Außerkrafttreten
§ 11	Aussonderung und Anbietung von Unterlagen			

Der Landtag hat das folgende Gesetz beschlossen:

§ 1 Geltungsbereich

Dieses Gesetz regelt den Umgang mit öffentlichem Archivgut in Thüringen.

§ 2 Öffentliches Archivgut

(1) [1]Öffentliches Archivgut sind alle archivwürdigen Unterlagen der in § 3 Abs. 1 und § 4 Abs. 1 genannten öffentlichen Stellen, die zur dauernden Aufbewahrung von einem öffentlichen Archiv übernommen werden. [2]Als öffentliches Archivgut gelten auch archivwürdige Unterlagen sowie dokumentarische Materialien, die von öffentlichen Archiven zur Ergänzung ihres Archivgutes angelegt, erworben oder übernommen worden sind. [3]Durch die Feststellung der Archivwürdigkeit und die Übernahme der Unterlagen gemäß § 7 Abs. 1 erfolgt ihre Widmung zu öffentlichem Archivgut. [4]Die Widmung begründet eine hoheitliche Sachherrschaft, die durch bürgerlich-rechtliche Verfügungen nicht berührt wird.

(2) Archivwürdig sind
1. Unterlagen, denen insbesondere aufgrund ihres rechtlichen, politischen, wirtschaftlichen, sozialen und kulturellen Wertes besondere Bedeutung zukommt
    a) als Quellen für die Erforschung oder das Verständnis von Geschichte und Gegenwart, auch im Hinblick auf künftige Entwicklungen, oder
    b) für die Sicherung berechtigter Belange der Bürger, Institutionen oder Dritter oder
    c) durch bleibenden Wert für die Gesetzgebung, Regierung, Verwaltung oder Rechtsprechung oder
2. Unterlagen, die nach der Richtlinie über die Aufbewahrung von Schriftgut in der Verwaltung des Freistaats Thüringen dauerhaft aufzubewahren sind,
3. Unterlagen der Strafverfolgungsbehörden, die Staatsschutzdelikte nach den §§ 81 bis 83, 84 bis 90, 90a Abs. 3, den §§ 90b, 91, 94, 96 Abs. 1, den §§ 97a bis 100a, 105, 106, 109d bis 109f, 129, 129a des Strafgesetzbuches und § 20 des Vereinsgesetzes betreffen. Unterlagen nach § 2 Abs. 2 Nr. 3 sind dauerhaft im Landesarchiv aufzubewahren.

(3) [1]Unterlagen im Sinne dieses Gesetzes sind Aufzeichnungen jeder Art, unabhängig von der Art ihrer Speicherung. [2]Dazu zählen insbesondere Urkunden, Amtsbücher, Akten, Schriftstücke, Karten, Pläne, Plakate, Siegel, Petschafte, Stempel, Amtsdrucksachen, amtliche Veröffentlichungen, Daten-, Bild-, Film-, Tonaufzeichnungen, digitale Aufzeichnungen sowie alle anderen Informationsobjekte ein-

---

[1)] Siehe bis zum 8.8.2018 das Thüringer Archivgesetz vom 23.4.1992.

schließlich der Hilfsmittel und ergänzenden Daten, die für die Erhaltung, Ordnung, Benutzung und Auswertung notwendig sind.

(4) ¹Öffentliches Archivgut ist unveräußerlicher Bestandteil des Landeskulturguts. ²Eine Abgabe an andere öffentliche Archive ist zulässig, wenn sie im öffentlichen Interesse liegt und die Grundsätze dieses Gesetzes für die Aufbewahrung und Benutzung von öffentlichem Archivgut beachtet werden.

§ 3 Archivgut des Landes und des Bundes

(1) Als öffentliches Archivgut des Landes werden alle archivwürdigen Unterlagen bestimmt, die bei den Verfassungsorganen, Behörden, Gerichten und sonstigen Stellen des Landes, bei deren Funktions- und Rechtsvorgängern sowie bei sonstigen der Aufsicht des Landes unterstehenden juristischen Personen des öffentlichen Rechts und ihrer Vereinigungen entstanden sind und vom Landesarchiv nach Maßgabe dieses Gesetzes archiviert werden.

(2) ¹Die in Wahrnehmung staatlicher Aufgaben entstandenen Unterlagen der SED, der übrigen Parteien und Massenorganisationen der ehemaligen DDR sowie der mit ihnen verbundenen Organisationen und juristischen Personen, soweit sie bei einem Organisationsteil angefallen sind, der auf staatlicher Ebene Funktionsvorgänger des Landes oder einer kleineren Einheit war, werden wie Archivgut des Landes behandelt. ²Dies gilt, sobald die in Satz 1 genannten Unterlagen im Landesarchiv archiviert werden.

(3) ¹Werden vom Landesarchiv Unterlagen nachgeordneter Stellen des Bundes übernommen, so gelten sie als öffentliches Archivgut des Landes im Sinne dieses Gesetzes, soweit bundesrechtlich nichts anderes bestimmt ist. ²Für die Benutzung solcher Unterlagen gelten die Vorgaben der §§ 6 und 10 bis 14 des Bundesarchivgesetzes vom 10. März 2017 (BGBl. I S. 410) in der jeweils geltenden Fassung.

§ 4 Kommunales Archivgut, Kommunale Archive

(1) Als kommunales Archivgut werden alle archivwürdigen Unterlagen bestimmt, die bei Gemeinden, Landkreisen, bei juristischen Personen des öffentlichen Rechts, die deren Aufsicht unterstehen, sowie bei deren Funktions- und Rechtsvorgängern entstanden sind.

(2) ¹Die in Absatz 1 genannten Stellen regeln die Archivierung ihrer Unterlagen in eigener Verantwortung und Zuständigkeit. ²Die Gemeinden und Landkreise nehmen diese Aufgaben als Pflichtaufgaben im eigenen Wirkungskreis wahr. ³Die Aufgaben der kommunalen Archive werden unter Beachtung der Grundsätze dieses Gesetzes durch Satzung bestimmt.

(3) Die in Absatz 1 genannten Stellen tragen durch eine angemessene personelle und sachliche Ausstattung der kommunalen Archive dafür Sorge, dass sie archivfachlichen Anforderungen entsprechen und die Erhaltung des Archivguts und dessen öffentliche Nutzung gesichert sind.

(4) ¹Sofern Gemeinden kein öffentliches Archiv unterhalten, bieten sie ihre Unterlagen anderen kommunalen Archiven oder dem zuständigen Kreisarchiv zur Archivierung an. ²Sind diese nicht zu einer Übernahme bereit, sind die Unterlagen vom Landesarchiv zu übernehmen. ³Das Eigentum an dem Archivgut bleibt unberührt. ⁴Die abgebende Körperschaft ist zum Kostenausgleich verpflichtet. ⁵Ein Rücknahmerecht wird durch die Übergabe nicht berührt.

(5) ¹Unterlagen nach § 3 Abs. 2 werden kein kommunales Archivgut. ²Sie sind vom Landesarchiv zu übernehmen.

§ 4a Archivgut der Hochschulen

(1) ¹Die staatlichen Hochschulen des Landes können eigene öffentliche Archive unterhalten und zu diesem Zweck ihr Archivgut in eigener Verantwortung und Zuständigkeit archivieren. ²Die Aufgaben werden nach den in diesem Gesetz vorgegebenen Grundsätzen durch Satzung bestimmt. ³§ 3 Abs. 2 findet keine Anwendung.

(2) Sofern die staatlichen Hochschulen kein eigenes öffentliches Archiv unterhalten, bieten sie ihre Unterlagen dem Landesarchiv zur Archivierung an.

§ 5 Sonstiges öffentliches Archivgut

¹Die sonstigen der Aufsicht des Landes unterstehenden juristischen Personen des öffentlichen Rechts und ihre Vereinigungen können ihr Archivgut in eigener Verantwortung und Zuständigkeit archivieren. ²Die von ihnen zu diesem Zweck unterhaltenen öffentlichen Archive bestimmen ihre Aufgaben nach den in diesem Gesetz vorgegebenen Grundsätzen durch Satzung. ³Sofern sie kein eigenes Archiv unterhalten, bieten sie ihre Unterlagen dem Landesarchiv zur Archivierung an. ⁴In den Fällen des § 3 Abs. 2 findet § 5 keine Anwendung.

§ 6 Öffentliche Archive

Öffentliche Archive im Sinne dieses Gesetzes sind alle Archive, die für das Archivgut von öffentlichen Stellen des Landes, von sonstigen seiner Aufsicht unterstehenden öffentlichen Stellen sowie von Gemeinden und Landkreisen zuständig sind.

§ 7 Aufgaben öffentlicher Archive

(1) ¹Die öffentlichen Archive haben die Aufgabe, die archivwürdigen Unterlagen der in den §§ 3 und 4 Abs. 1 genannten öffentlichen Stellen zu übernehmen. ²Sie erfassen, verwahren, erhalten und erschließen die von ihnen übernommenen archivwürdigen Unterlagen und stellen sie zur Benutzung bereit (Archivierung). ³Zur Ergänzung der übernommenen archivwürdigen Unterlagen können sie auch archivwürdige Unterlagen anderer Herkunft und sonstiges Dokumentationsmaterial erwerben, soweit daran ein besonderes öffentliches Interesse besteht.

(2) ¹Im Rahmen ihrer Zuständigkeit beraten die öffentlichen Archive die öffentlichen Stellen bei der Verwaltung und Sicherung ihrer Unterlagen im Hinblick auf die spätere Archivierung. ²Das Landesarchiv berät die Kommunalarchive, Archive sonstiger öffentlicher Stellen sowie nichtstaatliche Archive auf deren Anforderung (Archivberatungsstelle).

(3) ¹Die öffentlichen Archive wirken an der Erforschung und Vermittlung der von ihnen aufbewahrten archivalischen Quellen mit. ²In diesem Sinne wird das Landesarchiv als Stätte landesgeschichtlicher Forschung wirksam. ³Das Landesarchiv soll Vereine und Organisationen mit historischer oder kultureller Zielsetzung nach Maßgabe seiner Möglichkeiten unterstützen.

§ 8 Organisation des staatlichen Archivwesens, Zuständigkeit und Aufgaben

(1) ¹Das öffentliche Archiv des Landes ist das Landesarchiv. ²Es besteht aus den Abteilungen Staatsarchiv Altenburg, Staatsarchiv Gotha, Staatsarchiv Greiz, Staatsarchiv Meiningen, Staatsarchiv Rudolstadt und Hauptstaatsarchiv Weimar.

(2) Der Thüringer Landtag unterhält ein eigenes Archiv und regelt die Archivierung und Benutzung der bei ihm entstandenen archivwürdigen Unterlagen eigenständig nach Maßgabe dieses Gesetzes.

(3) Das Landesarchiv ist zuständig für:
1. Archivgut von Behörden, Gerichten und sonstigen öffentlichen Stellen des Landes,
2. Archivgut von nachgeordneten Stellen des Landes und von sonstigen der Aufsicht des Landes unterstehenden juristischen Personen des öffentlichen Rechts und ihrer Vereinigungen,
3. Archivgut von nachgeordneten Stellen des Bundes sowie von Gemeinden, Landkreisen und kommunalen Verbänden, sofern es ihm angeboten und von ihm übernommen wird.

(4) Das Landesarchiv nimmt Aufgaben im Rahmen der Aus- und Fortbildung des archivarischen Fachpersonals wahr.

(5) Für die Archivierung elektronischer Unterlagen der nach § 3 Abs. 1 und 3 genannten öffentlichen Stellen unterhält das Landesarchiv ein Digitales Magazin.

(6) ¹Das Landesarchiv wirkt bei der Festlegung von landesweit gültigen Übernahme- und Austauschformaten zur Archivierung elektronischer Daten mit. ²Die landesweit gültigen Übernahme- und Austauschformate werden in Form einer Rechts- und Verwaltungsvorschrift durch das für das zentrale E-Government und die Informationstechnik zuständige Ministerium unter Einbindung der für das staatliche Archivwesen zuständigen obersten Landesbehörde und im Benehmen mit dem Landesarchiv festgelegt.

(7) Bei der Planung, vor der Einführung und bei wesentlichen Änderungen von IT-Systemen, die zu nach § 2 Abs. 3 in Verbindung mit § 11 Abs. 1 anzubietenden elektronischen Dokumenten führen, ist rechtzeitig das Benehmen mit dem Landesarchiv herzustellen, insbesondere um sicherzustellen, dass die in der Verwaltungsvorschrift nach Absatz 6 genannten Formate beachtet und Schnittstellen zum Digitalen Magazin des Landesarchivs berücksichtigt werden.

(8) Die Kosten für die Übertragung digitaler Daten und die Erstellung von Schnittstellen tragen die abgebenden Stellen.

(9) Die Landesregierung kann dem Landesarchiv andere als die in diesem Gesetz oder in anderen Rechtsvorschriften genannten Aufgaben übertragen, wenn sie in sachlichem Zusammenhang mit dem Archivwesen des Landes und der Erforschung der Landesgeschichte stehen.

§ 9 Aufsicht

(1) ¹Oberste Archivbehörde des Landes ist die für das staatliche Archivwesen zuständige oberste Landesbehörde. ²Das Landesarchiv ist ihr dienst- und fachaufsichtlich unmittelbar unterstellt.
(2) Die für das staatliche Archivwesen zuständige oberste Landesbehörde regelt durch Rechtsverordnung[1]) die Benutzung des Landesarchivs einschließlich der für die Nutzung des Archivguts zu erhebenden Gebühren und Auslagen in einer Gebührenverordnung.
(3) Bei den kommunalen Archiven regelt sich die Aufsicht nach den allgemeinen Bestimmungen über die Kommunalaufsicht.

§ 10 Archivpflege

¹Die Archivpflege als verantwortliches Handeln zum Schutz der archivalischen Quellen für die Orts- und Landesgeschichte wird vom Freistaat Thüringen unterstützt. ²Die öffentlichen Archive, insbesondere das Landesarchiv, können auch nichtstaatliche Archiveigentümer bei der Sicherung und Nutzbarmachung ihres Archivgutes beraten, soweit daran ein öffentliches Interesse besteht.

§ 11 Aussonderung und Anbietung von Unterlagen

(1) ¹Die in § 3 Abs. 1 und § 4 Abs. 1 genannten öffentlichen Stellen sind verpflichtet, alle Unterlagen, die zur Erfüllung ihrer Aufgaben nicht mehr erforderlich sind und deren Aufbewahrungsfristen abgelaufen sind, auszusondern und dem zuständigen öffentlichen Archiv zur Übernahme anzubieten. ²Dies sollte im Regelfall unmittelbar nach Ablauf der Aufbewahrungsfristen, spätestens jedoch 30 Jahre nach Schließung der Unterlagen erfolgen. ³Ist durch Rechtsvorschriften oder Verwaltungsvorschriften eine längere als eine dreißigjährige oder eine dauernde Aufbewahrung bestimmt, wird der Zeitpunkt des Anbietens und der Übergabe zwischen den in § 3 Abs. 1 und 3 und § 4 Abs. 1 genannten Stellen und dem öffentlichen Archiv vereinbart. ⁴Die in § 3 Abs. 2 genannten Stellen sind verpflichtet, die dort genannten Unterlagen dem Landesarchiv unverzüglich vollständig anzubieten und sie auf Anforderung herauszugeben.

(2) ¹Bei elektronischen Unterlagen, die an das Landesarchiv übergeben werden sollen, legt das Landesarchiv unter den Voraussetzungen des Absatzes 1 in Verbindung mit § 8 Abs. 6 und 7 den Zeitpunkt und die Form der Übermittlung vorab fest. ²Hat das Landesarchiv den bleibenden Wert dieser Unterlagen festgestellt, hat die aufbewahrende Stelle nach erfolgreicher und bestätigter Abgabe an das Landesarchiv sämtliche bei sich verbliebenen Kopien zu löschen. ³Über die Löschung ist ein Nachweis zu fertigen, der 30 Jahre aufzubewahren ist. ⁴Elektronische Unterlagen, die einer laufenden Aktualisierung unterliegen, sind im Benehmen mit der abgebenden Stelle zu bestimmten, vorab festzulegenden Stichtagen ebenfalls anzubieten. ⁵Der Zeitabstand zwischen den Stichtagen soll ein Jahr nicht unterschreiten.

(3) ¹Anzubieten sind auch Unterlagen,
1. die besonderen Rechtsvorschriften über Geheimhaltung oder über den Datenschutz unterworfen sind,
2. die personenbezogene Daten enthalten, welche nach Rechtsvorschriften des Bundes oder des Landes oder nach Artikel 17 Abs. 1 der Verordnung (EU) 2016/679 des Europäischen Parlaments und des Rates vom 27. April 2016 zum Schutz natürlicher Personen bei der Verarbeitung personenbezogener Daten, zum freien Datenverkehr und zur Aufhebung der Richtlinie 95/46/EG (Datenschutz-Grundverordnung) (ABl. L 119 vom 4.5.2016, S. 1; L 314 vom 22.11.2016, S. 72) in der jeweils geltenden Fassung gesperrt, gelöscht oder vernichtet werden müssten oder könnten,
3. die Informationen enthalten, deren Verarbeitung nach Artikel 9 Abs. 1 der Verordnung (EU) 2016/679 untersagt ist.

²Die Anbietungspflicht gilt für § 11 Abs. 3 Satz 1 Nr. 2 3. Alternative nur, wenn die Voraussetzungen von Artikel 17 Abs. 3 Buchst. d der Verordnung (EU) 2016/679 und für § 11 Abs. 3 Satz 1 Nr. 3 nur, wenn die Voraussetzungen von Artikel 9 Abs. 2 Buchst. j der Verordnung (EU) 2016/679 vorliegen. ³Ihre Verarbeitung ist vorbehaltlich den Bedingungen und Garantien des Artikels 89 Abs. 1 der Verordnung (EU) 2016/679 gestattet. ⁴Unberührt bleiben gesetzliche Vorschriften über die Löschung oder Vernichtung unzulässig erhobener oder verarbeiteter Daten oder Unterlagen. ⁵Soweit die Speicherung der Daten unzulässig war, ist dieses besonders zu kennzeichnen. ⁶Unberührt bleiben gesetzliche Vorschriften über die Verarbeitung von Daten, die durch einen Eingriff in den Schutzbereich des Arti-

---

1) Die Thüringer Verordnung über die Benutzung der Staatsarchive ist abgedruckt als Nr. D16.II.1a.

kels 10 des Grundgesetzes erlangt wurden. [7]Soweit anzubietende Unterlagen Daten enthalten, die Verfügungsbeschränkungen unterliegen, ist die verpflichtete Stelle gehalten, die herausgebende Stelle um die Zustimmung zur Anbietung zu ersuchen.
(4) Die als archivwürdig bewerteten Unterlagen sind innerhalb eines Jahres an das zuständige öffentliche Archiv zu übergeben.
(5) Die in § 3 Abs. 1 und § 4 Abs. 1 genannten öffentlichen Stellen dürfen Unterlagen nur vernichten oder Daten nur löschen, wenn das zuständige öffentliche Archiv die Übernahme abgelehnt oder nicht innerhalb eines Jahres über die Archivwürdigkeit angebotener Unterlagen entschieden hat.
(6) Von dem Anbieten und Vorlegen von Unterlagen kann im Einvernehmen mit dem zuständigen öffentlichen Archiv abgesehen werden, wenn diese wegen ihres offensichtlich geringen Quellenwertes nicht archivwürdig sind.
(7) Ausgesonderte Unterlagen sind im Regelfall zu vernichten, sofern kein Grund zu der Annahme besteht, dass durch die Vernichtung schutzwürdige Belange von Betroffenen beeinträchtigt werden.
(8) [1]Die in § 3 Abs. 1 und § 4 Abs. 1 genannten öffentlichen Stellen sind verpflichtet, ein Exemplar der von ihnen herausgegebenen oder in ihrem Auftrag erscheinenden amtlichen Druckschriften und amtlichen Veröffentlichungen dem zuständigen öffentlichen Archiv unmittelbar nach Erscheinen zur Verfügung zu stellen. [2]Sofern die Veröffentlichung in elektronischer Form erscheint, erfolgt die Abgabe in dieser Form. [3]Die abgebende Stelle räumt dem öffentlichen Archiv das Recht ein, die Daten zu speichern, zu vervielfältigen und zu verändern, sofern dies zur dauerhaften Archivierung notwendig ist. [4]Ebenso wird das Recht zur öffentlichen Zugänglichmachung eingeräumt, sofern der Herausgeber dies nicht ausdrücklich einschränkt oder untersagt. [5]Von der Abgabepflicht nach unmittelbarem Erscheinen nach Satz 1 ausgeschlossen sind
1. Veröffentlichungen, die lediglich zur Information von Presse, Rundfunk und Fernsehen bestimmt sind,
2. Informationsmaterialien geringen Umfangs und von zeitlich begrenzter Dauer.

[6]Diese nach Satz 5 Nr. 1 und 2 ausgenommenen Unterlagen sind unter der Maßgabe des Absatzes 1 dem öffentlichen Archiv anzubieten.

§ 12 Feststellung der Archivwürdigkeit und Übernahme
(1) [1]Über die Archivwürdigkeit der angebotenen Unterlagen und über die Übernahme in das öffentliche Archiv entscheiden die öffentlichen Archive im Benehmen mit der anbietenden Stelle. [2]In den Fällen des § 3 Abs. 2 sowie den Fällen, in denen eine dauerhafte Aufbewahrung in Rechtsvorschriften oder Vereinbarungen geregelt ist, bedarf es der Feststellung der Archivwürdigkeit nicht. [3]Das öffentliche Archiv ist seinerseits berechtigt, Unterlagen mit offensichtlich geringem Quellenwert auszuscheiden, wenn öffentliche Interessen oder berechtigte Interessen Dritter nicht entgegenstehen.
(2) [1]Vertretern des zuständigen öffentlichen Archivs ist die Einsicht in die zur Archivierung angebotenen Unterlagen und in die Findmittel der Registraturen zu gewähren. [2]Bei digitalen Unterlagen ist ein lesender Zugriff ausschließlich auf die dem zuständigen öffentlichen Archiv zur Archivierung angebotenen Unterlagen mit Einblick in die fachliche und technische Dokumentation zu gewähren.
(3) Die Bewertungskriterien im Sinne des § 2 Abs. 2 sind in entsprechenden Verwaltungsvorschriften zu regeln.
(4) [1]Das öffentliche Archiv hat von der Übernahme an ebenso wie die abgebende Stelle die schutzwürdigen Belange Betroffener zu berücksichtigen und von der Anbietung an die maßgeblichen Rechtsvorschriften des Bundes und des Landes über die Geheimhaltung sowie die Regelungen des Thüringer Sicherheitsüberprüfungsgesetzes vom 17. März 2003 (GVBl. S. 185) in der jeweils geltenden Fassung und der Verschlusssachenanweisung für den Freistaat Thüringen vom 17. Juni 2011 in der Fassung vom 2. Dezember 2016 (ThürStAnz Nr. 52/2016 S. 1624) zu beachten. [2]Amtsträger und für den öffentlichen Dienst Verpflichtete in öffentlichen Archiven unterliegen allen für die Bediensteten der abgebenden Stellen geltenden Geheimhaltungsvorschriften.
(5) [1]Archivgut, dem nach archivfachlicher Prüfung ein bleibender Wert nach § 2 Abs. 2 nicht mehr zukommt, ist zu vernichten, sofern Rechtsvorschriften, Aufbewahrungsfristen oder Rechte Dritter nicht entgegenstehen. [2]Darüber ist ein Nachweis zu führen.

§ 13 Normierte Bewertungsverfahren

¹Bei der Bewertung von Unterlagen kann durch Vereinbarung zwischen dem zuständigen öffentlichen Archiv und der anbietenden öffentlichen Stelle oder der jeweils zuständigen obersten Landesbehörde ein normiertes Bewertungsverfahren durchgeführt werden. ²Dabei kann von gleichförmigen oder wiederkehrenden Unterlagen, die in großer Zahl anfallen, eine exemplarische Auswahl getroffen werden.

§ 14 Aufbewahrung im Rahmen laufender Fristen

(1) ¹Die in § 3 Abs. 1 und § 4 Abs. 1 genannten öffentlichen Stellen haben die bei ihnen entstehenden Unterlagen innerhalb der durch Rechts- oder Verwaltungsvorschriften vorgegebenen Aufbewahrungsfristen zu verwahren und zu sichern. ²Darüber hinausgehende Festlegungen über die Aufbewahrung sind im Benehmen mit dem zuständigen öffentlichen Archiv zu treffen.

(2) ¹Archivwürdige Unterlagen können vor Ablauf entsprechender Fristen von dem zuständigen öffentlichen Archiv übernommen werden. ²Dies gilt insbesondere für Unterlagen, die gemäß § 2 Abs. 2 Nr. 1 Buchst. c oder Nr. 2 dauernd aufzubewahren sind.

(3) ¹Archivwürdige Unterlagen, deren Aufbewahrungsfrist noch nicht abgelaufen ist, können dem zuständigen öffentlichen Archiv zur befristeten Aufbewahrung als Zwischenarchivgut angeboten werden. ²Die Aufbewahrung des Zwischenarchivguts erfolgt im Auftrag der abgebenden Stellen oder ihrer Rechts- und Funktionsnachfolger. ³Die abgebende Stelle oder deren Rechts- oder Funktionsnachfolger bleibt für die Unterlagen und die Entscheidungen über die Nutzung durch Dritte weiterhin verantwortlich.

(4) ¹Für die Abgabe elektronischer Unterlagen nach Absatz 3 gelten die Voraussetzungen nach § 8 Abs. 6 und 7. ²Mit der erfolgreichen und bestätigten Abgabe an das öffentliche Archiv sind elektronische Unterlagen mit Ausnahme der zugehörigen Metadaten in den Systemen der abgebenden Stellen zu löschen. ³Über die Löschung ist ein Nachweis zu fertigen, der 30 Jahre aufzubewahren ist.

§ 15 Datenschutz, Sicherung und Erschließung

(1) ¹Durch geeignete technische und organisatorische Maßnahmen ist das Archivgut einschließlich der seiner Erschließung dienenden Hilfsmittel vor unbefugter Nutzung zu sichern sowie der Schutz personenbezogener Daten oder solcher Unterlagen, die einem besonderen gesetzlichen Geheimnisschutz unterliegen, sicherzustellen. ²Maßnahmen nach Satz 1 sind geeignet, wenn sie mindestens die Anforderungen der Artikel 32 und 89 der Verordnung (EU) 2016/679 erfüllen.

(2) Die öffentlichen Archive haben die notwendigen Maßnahmen zu treffen, um die dauernde Aufbewahrung, Erhaltung und Benutzbarkeit des Archivguts sowie seinen Schutz vor Beschädigung oder Vernichtung zu gewährleisten.

(3) Die öffentlichen Archive sind verpflichtet, die von ihnen archivierten Unterlagen als öffentliches Archivgut nach archivwissenschaftlichen Gesichtspunkten zu ordnen und durch Findmittel zu erschließen.

(4) Zur besseren Erschließung darf das Archivgut elektronisch erfasst und gespeichert werden; die Auswertung der gespeicherten Informationen ist nur zur Erfüllung der in diesem Gesetz genannten Zwecke zulässig.

(5) Die Verknüpfung personenbezogener Daten durch das öffentliche Archiv ist innerhalb der in § 17 genannten Schutzfristen nur zulässig, wenn schutzwürdige Belange betroffener Personen oder Dritter nicht beeinträchtigt werden.

(6) Der Zugang zu unzulässig erhobenen Daten wird ausschließlich gewährt, wenn die Benutzung der Rehabilitierung Betroffener, der Wiedergutmachung oder dem Zweck gemäß § 17 Abs. 5 Satz 2 Nr. 1 dient.

(7) Im Übrigen bleiben die Bestimmungen des Thüringer Datenschutzgesetzes unberührt.

(8) ¹Die öffentlichen Archive sind berechtigt, Archivgut sowie die dazugehörigen Findmittel unter Wahrung schutzwürdiger Belange betroffener Personen und Dritter zu veröffentlichen. ²Sofern das Archivgut den Schutzfristenregelungen nach § 17 Abs. 1 Satz 2 bis 4, Abs. 3 und 6 oder den Beschränkungen nach § 18 unterliegt, sind diese bei der Veröffentlichung entsprechend zu berücksichtigen.

§ 16 Benutzung von Archivgut

(1) ¹Jeder hat nach Maßgabe dieses Gesetzes das Recht, Archivgut in öffentlichen Archiven auf Antrag zu nutzen, soweit nicht Schutzfristen, Einschränkungen in besonderen Fällen oder andere Rechtsvor-

schriften entgegenstehen. ²Vereinbarungen zugunsten nichtöffentlicher Eigentümer von Archivgut bleiben unberührt.
(2) ¹Die Benutzung ist schriftlich zu beantragen. ²Die Benutzungsgenehmigung erteilt das verwahrende öffentliche Archiv.
(3) ¹Der Nutzer ist verpflichtet, von einem Werk, das er unter wesentlicher Verwendung von Archivgut verfasst oder erstellt hat, nach Veröffentlichung des Werkes dem verwahrenden öffentlichen Archiv unaufgefordert einen Beleg in der veröffentlichten Form unentgeltlich abzuliefern. ²Ist dem Nutzer die unentgeltliche Ablieferung eines Belegexemplares insbesondere wegen der niedrigen Auflage oder der hohen Herstellungskosten nicht zumutbar, kann er dem verwahrenden öffentlichen Archiv entweder ein Exemplar des Werkes zur Herstellung einer Vervielfältigung für einen angemessenen Zeitraum überlassen oder eine Entschädigung bis zur Höhe des halben Ladenpreises verlangen. ³Wenn ein Ladenpreis nicht besteht, kann der Nutzer eine Entschädigung bis zur Höhe der halben Herstellungskosten des Belegexemplares verlangen. ⁴Eine elektronische Ablieferung ist ebenfalls möglich.
(4) ¹Öffentliche Archive berücksichtigen bei der Ausgestaltung der Rechte von Nutzern und der Bereitstellung von öffentlichen Informationen über Archivgut die Belange von Menschen mit Behinderungen. ²Sie gestalten die Zugänglichkeit zu Gebäuden und Archivgut schrittweise barrierefrei entsprechend den geltenden Vorschriften.

§ 17 Schutzfristen
(1) ¹Archivgut wird im Regelfall 30 Jahre nach Entstehung der Unterlagen für die Benutzung freigegeben. ²Archivgut, das sich nach seiner Zweckbestimmung oder nach seinem wesentlichen Inhalt auf eine oder mehrere natürliche Personen bezieht oder die schützenswerte Privatsphäre berührt (personenbezogenes Archivgut), darf erst zehn Jahre nach dem Tod der betreffenden Person benutzt werden. ³Ist das Todesjahr nicht oder nur mit hohem Aufwand feststellbar, endet die Schutzfrist 100 Jahre nach der Geburt der betroffenen Person. ⁴Kann auch deren Geburtsjahr nicht oder nur mit unvertretbarem Aufwand festgestellt werden, endet der Schutz 60 Jahre nach Entstehung der Unterlagen.
(2) ¹Die Schutzfrist nach Absatz 1 Satz 1 gilt nicht für solche Unterlagen, die bereits bei ihrer Entstehung zur Veröffentlichung bestimmt waren oder für Unterlagen, für die vor der Übergabe an das Landesarchiv bereits ein Zugang oder eine Veröffentlichung nach anderen gesetzlichen Vorschriften vorlag. ²Außerdem findet sie auf Unterlagen im Sinne des § 3 Abs. 2 sowie der staatlichen Verwaltungsbehörden der ehemaligen DDR, die nicht personenbezogen sind, keine Anwendung.
(3) ¹Archivgut, das besonderen Geheimhaltungsvorschriften unterliegt, darf erst 60 Jahre nach seiner Schließung benutzt werden. ²Für personenbezogenes Archivgut, das besonderen Geheimhaltungs- und Schutzfristen unterliegt, beträgt die Schutzfrist, wenn das Todesjahr betroffener Personen feststellbar ist, 30 Jahre nach dem Tod beziehungsweise 130 Jahre nach der Geburt bei nicht zu ermittelndem Todesjahr. ³Sind weder Geburts- noch Todesjahr zu ermitteln, darf das Archivgut erst 90 Jahre nach dessen Schließung benutzt werden.
(4) ¹Die in den Absätzen 1 und 3 festgesetzten Schutzfristen gelten auch für die Benutzung durch öffentliche Stellen. ²Die Benutzung von Archivgut durch öffentliche Stellen nach § 3 Abs. 1 und § 4 Abs. 1, bei denen es entstanden ist, die es abgegeben haben oder die an deren Stelle fachlich oder aufgabenbezogen zuständig sind, ist auch innerhalb der Schutzfristen möglich; die Schutzfristen sind jedoch zu beachten, wenn das Archivgut aufgrund besonderer Vorschriften hätte gesperrt, gelöscht oder vernichtet werden müssen.
(5) ¹Die Schutzfristen können vom verwahrenden öffentlichen Archiv im Einzelfall auf Antrag des Nutzers verkürzt werden, wenn besondere schutzwürdige Belange nicht entgegenstehen. ²Bei personenbezogenem Archivgut ist eine Verkürzung der Schutzfristen zulässig, wenn:
1. die Benutzung für ein bestimmtes Forschungsvorhaben erforderlich ist und schutzwürdige Belange der betroffenen Person oder Dritter nicht beeinträchtigt werden oder das öffentliche Interesse an der Durchführung des Forschungsvorhabens die schutzwürdigen Belange erheblich überwiegt;
2. die Benutzung zur Wahrnehmung berechtigter Belange wie zum Zweck der Strafverfolgung, der Rehabilitierung von Betroffenen, Vermissten und Verstorbenen, der Wiedergutmachung, der Hilfeleistung nach dem Häftlingshilfegesetz, dem Schutz des Persönlichkeitsrechtes, der Aufklärung von Verwaltungsakten oder der Aufklärung des Schicksals Vermisster und ungeklärter Todesfälle erforderlich ist.

³Die Forschungsergebnisse nach Satz 2 Nr. 1 sind ohne personenbezogene Angaben aus dem Archivgut zu veröffentlichen, es sei denn, es handelt sich um Amtsträger in Ausübung ihrer Ämter oder Personen der Zeitgeschichte, sofern deren schützenswerte Privatsphäre nicht betroffen ist. ⁴Für Archivgut, welches besonderen Geheimhaltungsvorschriften unterliegt oder für das ein besonderes Schutzbedürfnis gegeben ist, ist zusätzlich das Einvernehmen mit der abgebenden Stelle herzustellen.

(6) ¹Eine Benutzung personenbezogenen Archivguts ist unabhängig von den festgelegten Schutzfristen auch zulässig, wenn es sich um den Betroffenen selbst handelt oder wenn die Person, auf die sich das Archivgut bezieht, oder im Falle ihres Todes, ihre Angehörigen zugestimmt haben. ²Die Einwilligung ist durch den Benutzer von den Angehörigen einzuholen. ³Für die Erteilung der Einwilligung befugte Angehörige sind:
1. der Ehegatte,
2. der eingetragene Lebenspartner,
3. sofern der Ehegatte oder eingetragene Lebenspartner verstorben ist oder ein solcher nicht vorhanden ist, die Kinder der betroffenen Person,
4. wenn weder Personen nach Nummer 1 oder 2 noch nach Nummer 3 vorhanden sind, die Eltern der betroffenen Person. Die Zustimmung der Angehörigen setzt die mutmaßliche Einwilligung der Betroffenen voraus.

⁴Sind überwiegende schutzwürdige Belange Dritter zu wahren, ist gemäß § 19 Abs. 1 Satz 1 zu verfahren. ⁵Absatz 5 Satz 4 gilt entsprechend.

(7) Die festgelegten Schutzfristen können durch das verwahrende öffentliche Archiv um höchstens 20 Jahre verlängert werden, wenn dies im öffentlichen Interesse liegt; davon bleiben die in Absatz 3 festgelegten Schutzfristen unberührt.

§ 18 Einschränkung der Benutzung in besonderen Fällen

(1) Die Benutzung von Archivgut ist einzuschränken oder zu versagen, wenn Grund zu der Annahme besteht, dass
1. dem Wohl der Bundesrepublik Deutschland oder dem Wohl eines ihrer Länder wesentliche Nachteile erwachsen,
2. schutzwürdige Belange betroffener Personen oder Dritter beeinträchtigt werden,
3. Rechtsvorschriften über Geheimhaltung verletzt würden,
4. der Erhaltungszustand des Archivgutes beeinträchtigt würde,
5. durch die Benutzung ein nicht vertretbarer Verwaltungsaufwand entstünde,
6. Vereinbarungen mit gegenwärtigen oder früheren Eigentümern entgegenstehen oder
7. aus anderen wichtigen Gründen, insbesondere aufgrund der Verfolgung sachwidriger Interessen.

(2) Die Benutzung von archivierten Unterlagen, die Rechtsvorschriften des Bundes über Geheimhaltung unterliegen, richtet sich nach den Regelungen des Bundesarchivgesetzes in der jeweils geltenden Fassung.

(3) Die für das staatliche Archivwesen zuständige oberste Landesbehörde entscheidet über die Einschränkung oder Versagung der Benutzung des Archivguts des Landesarchivs in den Fällen nach Absatz 1 Nr. 1. Das Landesarchiv entscheidet über die Einschränkung oder Versagung in den Fällen nach Absatz 1 Nr. 2 bis 7.

§ 19 Auskunfts- und Berichtigungsrecht

(1) ¹Einer betroffenen Person ist, ohne Rücksicht auf die in § 17 Abs. 1 festgelegten Schutzfristen, auf Antrag Auskunft über die im Archivgut zu ihrer Person enthaltenen Daten zu erteilen, soweit diese erschlossen sind. ²Ein Auskunftsanspruch nach Artikel 15 der Verordnung (EU) 2016/679 besteht nicht. ³Die Entscheidung hierüber und über das dabei zu verwendende Format trifft das öffentliche Archiv. ⁴Artikel 20 der Verordnung (EU) 2016/679 gilt insoweit nicht. ⁵Statt einer Auskunft kann das Archiv Einsicht in die Unterlagen gewähren. ⁶Für die Sätze 1 und 5 gilt § 17 Abs. 5 Satz 4 entsprechend.

(2) ¹Das öffentliche Archiv ist verpflichtet, den zum Archivgut gehörigen Unterlagen eine Gegendarstellung der betroffenen Person auf deren Verlangen beizufügen, wenn diese durch eine in den Unterlagen enthaltene Tatsachenbehauptung betroffen ist und ein berechtigtes Interesse an der Gegendarstellung glaubhaft macht. ²Weitergehende Ansprüche der betroffenen Person aus Artikel 16 der Verordnung (EU) 2016/679 und aus Artikel 17 der Verordnung (EU) 2016/697, insbesondere auf Lö-

schung von Daten, sowie aus Artikel 18 der Verordnung (EU) 2016/679 auf Einschränkung der Verarbeitung der Daten, bestehen nicht. ³Nach ihrem Tod steht das Gegendarstellungsrecht den Angehörigen gemäß § 17 Abs. 6 zu. ⁴Weitergehende Pflichten nach Bundesrecht bleiben unberührt.

(3) ¹Die Gegendarstellung nach Absatz 2 bedarf der Schriftform und muss von der betroffenen Person oder ihren Angehörigen unterzeichnet sein. ²Sie muss sich auf Angaben über Tatsachen beschränken und darf keinen strafbaren Inhalt haben.

(4) ¹Ein durch besondere Rechtsvorschriften geregelter Anspruch auf nachträgliche Berichtigung von Unterlagen oder Löschung wegen unzulässiger Datenverarbeitung wird durch die Übernahme der Unterlagen in ein öffentliches Archiv nicht berührt. ²Ein Widerspruchsrecht nach Artikel 21 Abs. 1 der Verordnung (EU) 2016/679 gegen die Archivierung rechtmäßig gespeicherter personenbezogener Daten besteht nicht.

(5) Das Gegendarstellungsrecht gemäß Absatz 2 gilt nicht für amtliche Niederschriften und Berichte über öffentliche Sitzungen der gesetzgebenden oder beschließenden Organe des Bundes, der Länder, Gemeinden und Gemeindeverbände und anderer juristischer Personen des öffentlichen Rechts sowie der Gerichte.

(6) Eine Mitteilungspflicht des öffentlichen Archivs nach Artikel 19 der Verordnung (EU) 2016/679 gegenüber allen Empfängern, denen personenbezogene Daten offengelegt wurden, besteht nicht.

§ 20 Ausnahmen vom Geltungsbereich
Dieses Gesetz gilt nicht für:
1. öffentlich-rechtliche Religionsgemeinschaften und deren Vereinigungen;
2. öffentlich-rechtliche Rundfunkanstalten;
3. öffentlich-rechtliche Unternehmen mit eigener Rechtspersönlichkeit, die am wirtschaftlichen Wettbewerb teilnehmen, und deren Zusammenschlüsse;
4. solche Zweckverbände, deren Zweck der Betrieb eines öffentlich-rechtlichen Unternehmens mit eigener Rechtspersönlichkeit ist, das am wirtschaftlichen Wettbewerb teilnimmt.

§ 21 Gleichstellungsbestimmung
Status- und Funktionsbezeichnungen in diesem Gesetz gelten jeweils in männlicher und weiblicher Form.

§ 22 Inkrafttreten[1]), Außerkrafttreten
¹Dieses Gesetz tritt mit dem 14. Tag nach Ablauf des Tages in Kraft, an dem es im Gesetz- und Verordnungsblatt für den Freistaat Thüringen verkündet worden ist.[2]) ²Gleichzeitig treten außer Kraft:
1. das Thüringer Archivgesetz vom 23. April 1992 (GVBl. S. 139), zuletzt geändert durch Gesetz vom 2. Juli 2016 (GVBl. S. 228), und
2. die Thüringer Verordnung über das Antragsrecht nach dem Gesetz zum Schutz deutschen Kulturgutes gegen Abwanderung vom 30. März 1995 (GVBl. S. 164).

---

1) **Amtl. Anm.:** Gemäß Artikel 85 Abs. 2 der Verfassung des Freistaats Thüringen
2) Verkündet am 26.7.2018.

Thüringer Verordnung über die Benutzung der Staatsarchive (Thüringer Archiv-Benutzungsordnung)
Vom 26. Februar 1993 (GVBl. S. 225)

Aufgrund des § 9 Abs. 2 Nr. 2 des Thüringer Archivgesetzes vom 23. April 1992 (GVBl. S. 139) verordnet der Minister für Wissenschaft und Kunst:

§ 1 Art der Benutzung
(1) Archivgut wird im Regelfall durch persönliche Einsichtnahme im verwahrenden Archiv benutzt (Direktbenutzung).
(2) An die Stelle der Direktbenutzung kann auch der Auskunftsdienst in Form von schriftlichen oder mündlichen Auskünften treten. Die Beantwortung von Anfragen kann sich auf Hinweise zu einschlägigem Archivgut beschränken.
(3) Die Staatsarchive können die Benutzung nach § 6 auch durch Versendung oder durch Ausleihe von Archivgut an andere öffentliche Stellen ermöglichen. Ein Rechtsanspruch auf Versendung und Ausleihe besteht nicht.
(4) Die Benutzung kann auch durch Vorlage von Reproduktionen erfolgen und durch die Abgabe von Kopien nach § 7 ergänzt werden. Ein Rechtsanspruch auf Abgabe von Kopien besteht nicht.
(5) Die für die Benutzung von Archivgut getroffenen Bestimmungen gelten für die Benutzung von Findmitteln, sonstigen Hilfsmitteln und Reproduktionen entsprechend.

§ 2 Benutzungsantrag
(1) Die Benutzungsgenehmigung ist schriftlich beim verwahrenden Staatsarchiv zu beantragen.
(2) Im Benutzungsantrag (Anlage 1)[1] ist folgendes anzugeben:
1. Name, Vorname, Beruf, Staatsangehörigkeit und Anschrift des Antragstellers,
2. Name und Anschrift des Auftraggebers, wenn die Nutzung im Auftrag eines Dritten erfolgt,
3. Benutzungszweck (Thema der Arbeit) mit möglichst präziser zeitlicher und sachlicher Eingrenzung; bei wissenschaftlicher Benutzung ist die Art der wissenschaftlichen Arbeit anzugeben,
4. Art der vorgesehenen Veröffentlichung.

(3) Der Benutzer hat sich auf Verlangen auszuweisen.
(4) Der Benutzer hat sich zur Beachtung der Benutzungsordnung zu verpflichten und zu erklären, daß er bei der Verwertung von Erkenntnissen aus Archivalien die Persönlichkeits- und Urheberrechte sowie andere berechtigte Interessen Dritter beachten wird und daß er für die schuldhafte Verletzung dieser Rechte einsteht (Anlage 1).
(5) Der Antrag gilt nur für das laufende Kalenderjahr und den angegebenen Benutzungszweck. Bei Änderungen des Benutzungszweckes oder des Forschungsgegenstandes ist erneut ein Antrag zu stellen.
(6) Wünscht ein Benutzer andere Personen als Hilfskräfte oder Beauftragte zu seinen Arbeiten heranzuziehen, so ist von diesen jeweils ein Antrag entsprechend der Anlage 1 zu stellen.
(7) Der Benutzer ist nach der Bestimmung des § 16 Abs. 4 ThürArchivG zur Abgabe von Belegexemplaren verpflichtet.

§ 3 Benutzungsgenehmigung
(1) Die Benutzungsgenehmigung erteilt nach den Bestimmungen des § 16 Abs. 1 bis 3 ThürArchivG das verwahrende Staatsarchiv.
(2) Das Ministerium für Wissenschaft und Kunst kann nach § 9 Abs. 3 ThürArchivG außer aus den in § 18 Abs. 1 ThürArchivG genannten Gründen die Nutzung aus anderen wichtigen Gründen einschränken oder versagen, insbesondere wenn
1. der Benutzer wiederholt oder schwerwiegend gegen die Benutzungsordnung oder gegen die Lesesaalordnung verstoßen hat oder ihm erteilte Auflagen nicht einhält,
2. der Ordnungszustand des Archivguts eine Nutzung nicht zuläßt,
3. Archivalien aus dienstlichen Gründen oder wegen gleichzeitiger amtlicher oder anderweitiger Benutzung nicht verfügbar sind,

---
[1] Hinweis: Die Anlagen konnten aus drucktechnischen Gründen nicht aufgenommen werden.

4. der Nutzungszweck anderweitig, insbesondere durch Einsichtnahme in Druckwerke oder in Reproduktionen hinlänglich erreicht werden kann.

(3) Die Benutzungsgenehmigung kann mit Nebenbestimmung versehen werden. Als Auflage kommen dabei insbesondere die Verpflichtung zur Anonymisierung von Namen bei einer Veröffentlichung und zur Beachtung schutzwürdiger Belange Betroffener oder Dritter in Betracht sowie die Verpflichtung, keine Kopien oder Abschriften an Dritte weiterzugeben.

(4) Die Benutzungsgenehmigung kann widerrufen oder nachträglich mit Auflagen versehen werden, wenn Gründe bekannt werden, die zur Versagung der Benutzung geführt hätten oder der Benutzer wiederholt oder schwerwiegend gegen die Benutzungsordnung verstoßen oder ihm erteilte Benutzungsauflagen nicht eingehalten hat.

§ 4 Antrag auf Verkürzung der Schutzfristen

(1) Eine Verkürzung der Schutzfristen nach § 17 Abs. 5 ThürArchivG wird vom Benutzer beim verwahrenden Staatsarchiv beantragt. Die Entscheidung über den Antrag trifft das Ministerium für Wissenschaft und Kunst.

(2) Wird eine Verkürzung der Schutzfristen von Unterlagen beantragt, die sich auf eine natürliche Person beziehen (personenbezogenes Archivgut), so hat der Antragsteller über die in § 2 Abs. 1 genannten Angaben hinaus entweder die schriftliche Einwilligung des Betroffenen oder seiner Angehörigen beizufügen oder im Antrag eingehend zu begründen, warum eine Verkürzung der Schutzfrist unerläßlich ist und wie er die schutzwürdigen Belange der betroffenen Person und Dritter, zum Beispiel durch Anonymisierung, wahren wird. Der Benutzer hat eine Erklärung zur Wahrung von Persönlichkeitsrechten zu unterzeichnen (Anlage 2).

(3) Soll bei einer Benutzung zu wissenschaftlichen Zwecken von der Anonymisierung personenbezogener Angaben abgesehen werden, so hat der Antragsteller anzugeben, welche Personen oder welchen Personenkreis er zu nennen beabsichtigt. Außerdem hat er zu begründen, worin das wissenschaftliche Interesse an der Namensnennung besteht und warum das Forschungsvorhaben sonst nicht durchgeführt werden kann.

(4) Auf Verlangen sind dem Antrag ergänzende Angaben und Unterlagen, bei Hochschulprüfungsarbeiten insbesondere Stellungnahmen der akademischen Lehrer, gegebenenfalls Bürgschaften für den Benutzer, beizufügen.

§ 5 Benutzung des Archivguts in den Benutzerräumen

(1) Die Archivalien, Findbehelfe und Bücher dürfen nur in den dafür bestimmten Räumen der Archive benutzt werden. Das eigenmächtige Entfernen von Archivgut aus den Benutzerräumen ist verboten. Das Staatsarchiv ist berechtigt, Kontrollen durchzuführen.

(2) Öffnungszeiten der Benutzerräume sowie sonstige Regelungen, die dem Schutz des Archivguts und einem geordneten Ablauf der Benutzung dienen, werden unter Berücksichtigung der örtlichen Gegebenheiten in der Hausordnung des Staatsarchivs festgelegt.

(3) Das Archiv ist behilflich bei der Ermittlung und Vorlage der Archivalien und Findmittel und berät insoweit den Benutzer. Der Benutzer hat keinen Anspruch, beim Lesen oder Übersetzen der Archivalien unterstützt zu werden.

(4) Der Benutzer ist im Umgang mit den Archivalien und Findmitteln zu größtmöglicher Sorgfalt verpflichtet und haftet für jede Fahrlässigkeit. Insbesondere ist es nicht gestattet,
1. die Reihenfolge und Ordnung der Archivalien zu verändern; vor allem bei der Benutzung von losen Akten ist äußerste Sorgfalt geboten,
2. Bestandteile des Archivguts wie Blätter, Zettel, Umschläge, Siegel, Stempelabdrucke und Briefmarken zu entfernen,
3. Vermerke im Archivgut anzubringen oder vorhandene zu tilgen,
4. Archivgut als Schreib- oder Durchzeichnungsunterlage zu verwenden.

(5) Festgestellte Mängel im Ordnungs- und Erhaltungszustand der Archivalien sind dem Archivpersonal mitzuteilen.

(6) Die Verwendung technischer Geräte bei der Benutzung bedarf der Genehmigung. Diese kann versagt werden, wenn dadurch das Archivgut gefährdet oder andere Benutzer gestört werden.

(7) Das Staatsarchiv ermöglicht auch die Vorlage von Archivgut, das von anderen Archiven oder sonstigen Stellen zur Benutzung durch Dritte übersandt wird. Soweit die versendende Stelle nichts anderes verfügt hat, gelten die Bestimmungen dieser Verordnung entsprechend.

§ 6 Versendung und Ausleihe von Archivgut

(1) Auf die Versendung und Ausleihe von Archivgut zur Einsichtnahme außerhalb des Benutzerraumes des verwahrenden Staatsarchivs besteht kein Anspruch.

(2) Auf begründeten Antrag können in Ausnahmefällen Archivalien zu Forschungszwecken an hauptamtlich verwaltete auswärtige Archive versandt werden, sofern dort eine ordnungsgemäße Benutzung und Aufbewahrung gewährleistet sind. Diese sind verpflichtet, das Archivgut in den Diensträumen unter ständiger fachlicher Aufsicht nur dem Antragsteller vorzulegen, es diebstahl- und feuersicher zu verwahren sowie das Archivgut nach Ablauf der vom Staatsarchiv bestimmten Ausleihfrist, in der von diesem bestimmten Versendungsart zurückzusenden. Die Ausleihfrist soll sechs Wochen nicht überschreiten, kann aber auf Antrag auch verlängert werden.

(3) Vor der Versendung ist zu prüfen, ob der Benutzungszweck nicht durch die Übersendung von Reproduktionen erreicht werden kann.

(4) Die Versand- und Versicherungskosten trägt der Antragsteller.

(5) Die Versendung von Archivalien zur amtlichen Benutzung durch Landesbehörden erfolgt im Rahmen der Amtshilfe.

(6) Aus dienstlichen Gründen können versandte Archivalien jederzeit zurückgefordert werden.

(7) Auf die Ausleihe von Archivalien zu Ausstellungszwecken besteht kein Anspruch. Die Entscheidung über eine mögliche Ausleihe wird vom substantiellen Zustand der Archivalien abhängig gemacht. Sie ist darüber hinaus nur möglich, wenn gewährleistet ist, daß das ausgeliehene Archivgut wirksam vor Verlust, Beschädigung und unbefugter Benutzung geschützt wird und der Ausstellungszweck nicht durch Reproduktionen oder Nachbildungen erreicht werden kann. Die Staatsarchive können Auflagen erteilen, um die Sicherheit und Erhaltung des zu Ausstellungszwecken ausgeliehenen Archivguts zu gewährleisten. Die Herstellung von Reproduktionen von ausgestelltem Archivgut durch den Leihnehmer oder Dritte bedarf der Zustimmung des verwahrenden Staatsarchivs.

(8) Über die Ausleihe zu Ausstellungszwecken ist zwischen dem Leihgeber und dem Leihnehmer ein Leihvertrag abzuschließen.

§ 7 Reproduktionen und Nachbildungen von Archivgut

(1) Benutzer können auf Antrag und eigene Kosten Reproduktionen von Archivalien in den Werkstätten des Archivs herstellen lassen, soweit die Archivalien keinen Schutzfristen unterliegen und schutzwürdige Belange von Betroffenen und Dritten nicht berührt werden.

(2) Reproduktionen von Archivgut dürfen nur hergestellt werden, soweit dabei eine Gefährdung oder Schädigung des Archivguts ausgeschlossen werden kann. Dies gilt insbesondere für Siegelabgüsse und Siegelabdrücke sowie für Schnellkopien. Über die jeweils geeigneten Reproduktionsverfahren entscheidet das verwahrende Staatsarchiv. Aufnahmefilme und sonstige Reproduktionsvorlagen mit Ausnahme der zur unmittelbaren Abgabe bestimmten Bildträger verbleiben dem Staatsarchiv.

(3) Reproduktionen dürfen nur mit Zustimmung des verwahrenden Staatsarchivs, nur zu dem angegebenen Zweck und nur unter Angabe des verwahrenden Staatsarchivs und der von diesem festgelegten Signatur sowie unter Hinweis auf die dem Staatsarchiv zustehenden Veröffentlichungs- und Vervielfältigungsrechte vervielfältigt oder an Dritte weitergegeben werden.

§ 8 Benutzung durch abgebende Stellen

Für die Benutzung von Archivgut durch Behörden, Gerichte und sonstige Stellen des Landes, bei denen es entstanden ist oder die es abgegeben haben, finden die Bestimmungen dieser Benutzungsordnung keine Anwendung, sofern es sich nicht um Schriftgut handelt, das bei ihnen aufgrund besonderer Bestimmungen hätte gesperrt, gelöscht oder vernichtet werden müssen. Die Art und Weise der Benutzung wird zwischen der abgebenden Stelle und dem verwahrenden Staatsarchiv entsprechend den festgelegten Regelungen im Einzelfall vereinbart. Dabei ist sicherzustellen, daß das Archivgut gegen Verlust, Beschädigung und unbefugte Benutzung geschützt und innerhalb eines angemessenen Zeitraums zurückgegeben wird.

§ 9 Inkrafttreten

Diese Verordnung tritt am ersten Tage des auf die Verkündung folgenden Kalendermonats in Kraft.

Abgabe amtlicher Veröffentlichungen an Bibliotheken und das Hauptstaatsarchiv

Verwaltungsvorschrift des Thüringer Kultusministeriums vom 19. November 2008 (ABl. TKM 19, Nr. 1, S. 3)

Im Einvernehmen mit der Staatskanzlei und den Ministerien wird folgendes erlassen:

1. Alle Behörden, Dienststellen und Einrichtungen des Landes haben von allen durch sie herausgegebenen oder in ihrem Auftrag einmalig oder laufend erscheinenden amtlichen Veröffentlichungen unentgeltlich je ein Exemplar unmittelbar nach ihrem Erscheinen unaufgefordert abzugeben:
   a) an:
      die Thüringer Universitäts- und Landesbibliothek in Jena,
      die Bibliothek des Thüringer Landtages in Erfurt,
      das Thüringische Hauptstaatsarchiv in Weimar,
   b) an:
      die Deutsche Nationalbibliothek,
      die Staatsbibliothek zu Berlin – Preußischer Kulturbesitz,
      die Bayerische Staatsbibliothek in München und
      die Bibliothek des Deutschen Bundestages in Berlin
   c) darüber hinaus auf Anforderung für Zwecke des Internationalen Amtlichen Schriftentausches bis zu 5 unentgeltliche Exemplare an die Staatsbibliothek zu Berlin – Preußischer Kulturbesitz.
2. Sofern die Veröffentlichung in elektronischer Form erscheint, erfolgt die Abgabe in dieser Form entsprechend den Standards der Deutschen Nationalbibliothek. Diese kann auch in einem unentgeltlichen Zugriff auf Speichermedien erfolgen.
3. Mit der Abgabe der elektronischen Form räumt die abgebende Stelle der sammelnden Bibliothek das Recht ein, die Daten zu speichern, zu vervielfältigen und zu verändern, soweit dies zur dauerhaften Archivierung notwendig ist.
   Ebenso wird das Recht zur öffentlichen Zugänglichmachung eingeräumt, sofern der Herausgeber dies nicht ausdrücklich einschränkt oder untersagt.
4. Von der Abgabe sind ausgeschlossen:
   – Veröffentlichungen, die lediglich zur Information von Presse, Rundfunk und Fernsehen bestimmt sind,
   – Informationsmaterialien geringen Umfangs und von zeitlich begrenzter Geltungsdauer.
   Von der Abgabe nach Nr. 1 c sollen solche amtlichen Veröffentlichungen ausgenommen werden, bei denen die Kosten des Einzelexemplars unverhältnismäßig hoch sind und deren Abgabe deshalb eine nicht vertretbare Etatbelastung verursachen würde.
   Wissenschaftliche Veröffentlichungen der oder aus den Hochschulen gelten nicht als amtliche Veröffentlichungen.
   In Zweifelsfällen entscheidet das zuständige Ministerium im Benehmen mit dem Kultusministerium über die Abgabepflicht.
5. Die der Aufsicht des Landes unterstehenden Körperschaften, Anstalten und Stiftungen des öffentlichen Rechts werden gebeten, auf Anfrage der Bibliothek amtliche Publikationen in elektronischer Form nach Maßgabe des Erlasses zur Verfügung zu stellen.
6. Der Erlass des TMWFK vom 25. September 1996 betreffend Abgabe amtlicher Druckschriften an Bibliotheken und das Hauptstaatsarchiv wird aufgehoben.

Thüringer Gesetz über die Errichtung der Kulturstiftung des Freistaats Thüringen (KultStiftG)

Vom 19. Mai 2004 (GVBl. S. 515)

zuletzt geändert durch Art. 4 G zur Neustrukturierung der Familienförderung und zu Änderungen bei Stiftungen vom 18. Dezember 2018 (GVBl. S. 813, 815)

Der Landtag hat das folgende Gesetz beschlossen:

§ 1 Errichtung

Unter dem Namen „Kulturstiftung des Freistaats Thüringen" wird eine rechtsfähige Stiftung des öffentlichen Rechts mit Sitz in Erfurt errichtet.

§ 2 Stiftungszweck

(1) [1]Zweck der Stiftung ist die Förderung und Bewahrung von Kunst und Kultur in Thüringen. [2]Ihr obliegt insbesondere die Förderung zeitgenössischer Kunst und Kultur der in Thüringen lebenden Künstlerinnen und Künstler durch Stipendien und Projekte. [3]Die Stiftung kann darüber hinaus bedeutsame Vorhaben der Dokumentation und Präsentation von Kunst und Geschichte fördern. [4]Des Weiteren können der Erwerb und die Sicherung besonders wertvoller Kulturgüter, Kunstgegenstände und Sammlungen mit herausragender Bedeutung durch die Museen, Bibliotheken und Archive unterstützt werden.

(2) Die Stiftung kann die Geschäftsbesorgung für Vorhaben und Projekte im Sinne des Stiftungszwecks für Dritte übernehmen.

§ 3 Stiftungsvermögen

(1) Die Stiftung erfüllt ihre Aufgaben aus den Erträgen des Stiftungsvermögens, aus Zuwendungen des Landes nach Maßgabe des Landeshaushaltes sowie aus Zuwendungen Dritter, soweit sie nicht dem Stiftungsvermögen zuzuführen sind.

(2) [1]Das Land stattet die Stiftung mit dem ihm zustehenden Kapitalanteil aus dem Liquidationsvermögen der Stiftung Kulturfonds nach Abzug eventuell noch zu begleichender Verbindlichkeiten aus der Liquidation aus. [2]Soweit die Liegenschaften der Stiftung Kulturfonds von den Vertragsparteien des Staatsvertrags über die Neuordnung der Rechtsverhältnisse der Stiftung Kulturfonds verwertet werden, wird der Anteil Thüringens ebenfalls an die Stiftung ausgezahlt. [3]Das Stiftungsvermögen kann sich durch Zustiftungen von privaten oder öffentlichen Förderern erhöhen.

(3) [1]Das Stiftungsvermögen ist in seinem Wert ungeschmälert zu erhalten, um die Erfüllung des Stiftungszwecks langfristig sicherzustellen. [2]Die Erträge des Stiftungsvermögens dürfen nur zur Verwirklichung des Stiftungszwecks und zur Erhöhung des Stiftungsvermögens verwendet werden.

(4) Die Stiftung kann durch einen Förderverein unterstützt werden.

§ 4 Satzung

[1]Die Stiftung gibt sich eine Satzung, die vom Stiftungsrat mit einer Mehrheit von sechs Stimmen beschlossen wird und der Zustimmung beider Landesvertreter bedarf. [2]Die Satzung ist durch das für Kunst zuständige Ministerium zu genehmigen. [3]Für Satzungsänderungen gilt diese Regelung entsprechend.

§ 5 Stiftungsorgane

Organe der Stiftung sind:
1. der Stiftungsrat,
2. der Vorstand sowie
3. das Kuratorium.

§ 6 Stiftungsrat

(1) Der Stiftungsrat besteht aus acht Mitgliedern, und zwar
1. dem für Kunst zuständigen Minister als Vorsitzenden,
2. einem von dem für Kunst zuständigen Minister benannten Bediensteten des für Kunst zuständigen Ministeriums,
3. je einem Vertreter des Gemeinde- und Städtebundes Thüringen und des Thüringischen Landkreistags,

4. dem Vorsitzenden des Kuratoriums sowie
5. drei Vertretern des öffentlichen Lebens.

(2) ¹Die Mitglieder nach Absatz 1 Nr. 5 werden von der Landesregierung im Benehmen mit dem für Kunst zuständigen Ausschuss des Thüringer Landtags für die Dauer von fünf Jahren berufen. ²Wiederberufungen sind ebenso zulässig wie die vorzeitige Abberufung aus wichtigem Grund.
(3) ¹Bis zur Wahl eines Kuratoriumsvorsitzenden nach § 9 Abs. 2 ist der Stiftungsrat auch ohne diesen beschlussfähig. ²Bei Stimmengleichheit entscheidet die Stimme des Vorsitzenden des Stiftungsrats.
(4) Der Vorstand nimmt beratend an den Sitzungen teil.
(5) Die Mitglieder des Stiftungsrats sind ehrenamtlich tätig.
(6) Das Nähere regelt die Satzung.

§ 7 Aufgaben des Stiftungsrats
(1) ¹Der Stiftungsrat entscheidet auf Vorschlag des Kuratoriums über die Förderung von Vorhaben im Sinne des § 2 Abs. 1 Satz 3 und 4. ¹Der Stiftungsrat entscheidet, soweit nicht der Vorstand nach § 8 Abs. 4 zuständig ist, auf Vorschlag des Kuratoriums über die Förderung von Vorhaben. ²Ferner entscheidet er über alle Fragen von grundsätzlicher oder besonderer wirtschaftlicher Bedeutung sowie über den Wirtschaftsplan.
(2) Der Stiftungsrat überwacht die Ausführung seiner Beschlüsse durch den Vorstand sowie dessen Geschäftsführung und entlastet den Vorstand nach Prüfung der Jahresrechnung.
(3) Das Nähere regelt die Satzung.

§ 8 Vorstand
(1) Der Vorstand der Stiftung besteht aus dem Geschäftsführer.
(2) ¹Die Berufung des Vorstands erfolgt durch den Stiftungsrat für mindestens drei, jedoch höchstens fünf Jahre. ²Die Berufung kann aus wichtigem Grund widerrufen werden. ³Erneute Berufungen sind möglich.
(3) ¹Der Vorstand führt die laufenden Geschäfte der Stiftung und vertritt die Stiftung gerichtlich und außergerichtlich. ²Er trifft für den Fall seiner Verhinderung Vorsorge durch Erteilung einer entsprechenden Vollmacht. ³Die Erteilung einer Generalvollmacht bedarf der vorherigen Zustimmung des Stiftungsrats. ⁴Im Übrigen werden die Befugnisse des Vorstands durch die Satzung bestimmt.
(4) ¹Der Vorstand entscheidet auf Vorschlag des Kuratoriums über die Förderung von Vorhaben, wenn die beabsichtigte Förderung jeweils einen in der Satzung festzulegenden Betrag nicht übersteigt. ²Die beantragte Förderhöhe ist insoweit unbeachtlich.

§ 9 Kuratorium
(1) ¹Das Kuratorium besteht aus bis zu zwölf unabhängig tätigen Sachverständigen verschiedener Kunst- und Kulturbereiche. ²Die Mitglieder des Kuratoriums werden vom Stiftungsrat mit einer Mehrheit von fünf Stimmen für die Dauer von drei Jahren gewählt. ³Vorschlagsberechtigt sind die einschlägigen Kunst- und Kulturverbände Thüringens sowie das für Kunst zuständige Ministerium. ⁴Einmalige Wiederwahl ist zulässig.
(2) Das Kuratorium wählt aus seiner Mitte einen Vorsitzenden für die Dauer von drei Jahren.
(3) ¹Das Kuratorium berät den Stiftungsrat und den Vorstand in allen den Stiftungszweck betreffenden Fragen. ²Es unterbreitet dem Vorstand beziehungsweise dem Stiftungsrat Vorschläge für die zu fördernden Vorhaben. ³Das Kuratorium zieht zur Beratung der Fördervorschläge mindestens einen Vertreter der zuständigen Fachabteilung des für Kunst zuständigen Ministeriums bei.
(4) Die Mitgliedschaft im Kuratorium ist ehrenamtlich.
(5) Das Nähere regelt die Satzung.

§ 10 Wirtschaftsführung
(1) ¹Vor Beginn eines jeden Geschäftsjahrs hat der Vorstand einen Wirtschaftsplan aufzustellen. ²Dieser bildet die Grundlage für die Einnahmen und Ausgaben. ³Geschäftsjahr ist das Kalenderjahr.
(2) ¹Innerhalb von sechs Monaten nach Ablauf des Geschäftsjahrs hat der Vorstand den Jahresabschluss zu erstellen und mit dem Prüfbericht des Rechnungsprüfers, der Vermögensübersicht sowie dem Tätigkeitsbericht der Rechtsaufsichtsbehörde vorzulegen. ²Das Nähere regelt die Satzung.
(3) Die Haushalts- und Wirtschaftsführung der Stiftung unterliegt der Prüfung durch den Rechnungshof.

(4) ¹Im Übrigen gelten die Rechtsvorschriften des Landes über das Haushalts-, Kassen- und Rechnungswesen sowie die hierzu ergangenen Verwaltungsvorschriften. ²Für die Arbeitnehmer der Stiftung finden die für die Arbeitnehmer des Landes geltenden Regelungen entsprechende Anwendung.

§ 11 Aufsicht
Die Stiftung unterliegt der Rechtsaufsicht des für Kunst zuständigen Ministeriums.

§ 12 Aufhebung der Stiftung
¹Die Stiftung kann nur durch Gesetz aufgehoben werden. ²Im Fall der Aufhebung der Stiftung fällt deren Vermögen an das Land zurück und ist für gemeinnützige kulturelle Zwecke, in erster Linie entsprechend den Stiftungszwecken, zu verwenden.

§ 13 Gleichstellungsbestimmung
Status- und Funktionsbezeichnungen in diesem Gesetz gelten jeweils in männlicher und weiblicher Form.

§ 14 In-Kraft-Treten
Dieses Gesetz tritt am 1. Januar 2005 in Kraft.

Richtlinie zur Förderung von Kultur und Kunst

In der Neufassung vom 17. August 2015 (ThürStAnz S. 1479 ff, mit Datum vom 06.11.2015 geändert)

1. Zuwendungszweck, Rechtsgrundlage

1.1 Der Freistaat Thüringen gewährt gemäß §§ 23 und 44 Thüringer Landeshaushaltsordnung (ThürLHO), nach Maßgabe dieser Verwaltungsvorschrift sowie den Verwaltungsvorschriften zu § 44 ThürLHO unter Beachtung der Verordnung (EU) Nr. 651/2014 der Kommission vom 17. Juni 2014 zur Feststellung der Vereinbarkeit bestimmter Gruppen von Beihilfen mit dem Binnenmarkt in Anwendung der Art. 107 und 108 des Vertrages über die Arbeitsweise der Europäischen Union sowie der Verordnung (EU) Nr. 1407/2013 der Kommission vom 18. Dezember 2013 über die Anwendung der Artikel 107 und 108 des Vertrages über die Arbeitsweise der Europäischen Union auf De-minimis-Beihilfen Zuwendungen für die Durchführung von Projekten der Kultur und der Kunst, für Geschäftsstellen und Investitionen sowie für die individuelle Künstlerförderung. Bei Einsatz von Mitteln aus dem Europäischen Fonds für regionale Entwicklung gelten darüber hinaus die einschlägigen Verordnungen der Europäischen Union zur Strukturfondsförderung in der jeweils geltenden Fassung.

1.2 Zweck der Zuwendung ist die Finanzierung kultureller Einrichtungen und Projekte sowie die Unterstützung von Einzelpersonen. Zur Erreichung der Zielstellung wird als Hauptindikator die Anzahl der geförderten Einrichtungen, Projekte und Personen erfasst.

1.3 Zur Erfüllung des in Nummer 1.2 genannten Zuwendungszwecks soll pro Vorhaben mindestens eines der folgenden allgemeinen Leistungsziele umgesetzt werden:
- Schaffung bzw. Konsolidierung der kulturellen Infrastruktur
  Indikator: Anzahl der geförderten Vorhaben
- Förderung kultureller Bildung und Teilhabe
  Indikator: Anzahl der Teilnehmer
- Erhalt des kulturellen Erbes und identifikationsstiftende Wirkung
  Indikator: Anzahl der geförderten Vorhaben
- Förderung des künstlerischen Nachwuchses sowie Aufbau und Erweiterung von Fachkompetenz
  Indikator: Anzahl der geförderten Personen
- Förderung künstlerischer und kultureller Vielfalt (z.B. Kreativität, Originalität, Authentizität) und Interkulturalität
  Indikator: Anzahl der geförderten Vorhaben
- Erhöhung der öffentlichen Wirkung (z.B. überregionale Ausstrahlung,) oder Verbesserung der touristischen Vermarktung (z.B. Einbindung in touristisches Gesamtkonzept, herausragende Einzelvermarktung)
  Indikatoren: Besucherzahlen, Presseresonanz, Übernachtungszahlen
- Schaffung und Ausbau barrierefreier Zugänge
  Indikator: Anzahl der zusätzlichen barrierefreien Zugänge
- Ausgleich regionaler Benachteiligung
  Indikator: Anzahl kultureller Veranstaltungen in der Region im Vergleich zu anderen Regionen des Landes
- Bildung oder Aufrechterhaltung von Netzwerken
  Indikator: Zahl der an einem Netzwerk beteiligten Einrichtungen und / oder Mitglieder im Vergleich zum Vorjahr
- Einbindung / Anerkennung ehrenamtlichen Engagements
  Indikator: Anzahl der geförderten Vorhaben

1.4 Die Zuwendungen werden als Beihilfen für Kultur und die Erhaltung des kulturellen Erbes nach Maßgabe des Artikels 53 AGVO gewährt. Die Beihilfen müssen den Vorgaben der AGVO genügen.

1.5 Bewilligungsbehörde ist die für Kultur zuständige Oberste Landesbehörde. Ein Rechtsanspruch des Antragstellers auf Gewährung der Zuwendung besteht nicht. Vielmehr entscheidet die Bewilligungsbehörde auf Grund ihres pflichtgemäßen Ermessens im Rahmen der verfügbaren Haushaltsmittel.

D16.III.2 Richtlinie zur Förderung von Kultur und Kunst

2. Gegenstand der Förderung
2.1 Gefördert werden
- 2.1.1 kulturelle, künstlerische und kulturgeschichtliche Projekte
  Dies sind zeitlich befristete Vorhaben von überregionaler oder beispielgebender Bedeutung mit Schwerpunkten in den Bereichen Archive, Bibliotheken, Bildende Kunst, Brauchpflege, Darstellende Kunst, Gedenkstätten, Jugendkultur, Landes- und Kulturgeschichte, Literatur, Museen, Musik, Soziokultur, Spartenübergreifendes.
  Darüber hinaus können auch Projekte zur Bewahrung und Aneignung des kulturellen Erbes und zur Ausbildung des künstlerischen Nachwuchses gefördert werden.
- 2.1.2 Bau- und Sanierungsmaßnahmen, Erhaltung, Erneuerung, Erweiterung und Verbesserung der Ausstattung von kulturellen Einrichtungen
  Gefördert werden beispielsweise Theater, Museen, Galerien, Jugendkunstschulen, Orchester, Musikschulen, öffentliche Bibliotheken, soziokulturelle Zentren, Kulturhäuser, Kultur- und Begegnungsstätten.
- 2.1.3 Stipendien
- 2.1.4 Erweiterung des Medienbestandes in öffentlichen Bibliotheken bzw. der Sammlungen in Museen und Galerien
- 2.1.5 Tätigkeit und Ausstattung der Geschäftsstellen von kulturellen Verbänden mit überörtlicher oder vernetzender Wirkung oder sonstigen Trägern freier Kulturarbeit, die kulturpolitisch bedeutsame Maßnahmen durchführen.

2.2 Nicht gefördert werden
- Maßnahmen, die gewerblichen Zwecken dienen
- Karnevalsprojekte
- Fertigung und Beschaffung von Einheitskleidung
- Stadt- / Gemeindejubiläen und -feste
- Herstellungskosten für kommerzielle Publikationen, Medien und Tonträger
- Kunst im öffentlichen Raum

3. Zuwendungsempfänger
3.1 Antragsberechtigt sind
- natürliche Personen
- als gemeinnützig anerkannte juristische Personen (z. B. eingetragene Vereine, Gesellschaften, Stiftungen)
- Kultureinrichtungen in kommunaler Trägerschaft
- Gebietskörperschaften
- sonstige Träger nicht-kommerzieller kultureller Projekte

Antragsberechtigt ist nur, wer seinen Sitz bzw. Wohnsitz in Thüringen hat oder wessen Projekt einen besonderen Bezug zu Thüringen nachweist.
Die Weiterleitung der Förderung an Dritte kann im Rahmen der Bestimmungen von § 44 ThürLHO von der Bewilligungsbehörde zugelassen werden. Näheres regelt der Bewilligungsbescheid.

3.2 Einem Unternehmen, das einer Rückforderungsanordnung aufgrund eines früheren Beschlusses der Kommission zur Feststellung der Unzulässigkeit einer Beihilfe und ihrer Unvereinbarkeit mit dem Binnenmarkt nicht nachgekommen ist, dürfen keine Einzelbeihilfen gewährt werden.

3.3 Eine Zuwendung ist in den Fallgruppen des Artikels 1 Abs. 2 bis 5 AGVO ausgeschlossen.

4. Zuwendungsvoraussetzungen
Voraussetzung für eine Zuwendung ist, dass
- 4.1 an der Durchführung des Vorhabens ein erhebliches Landesinteresse besteht. Kulturelle und kulturgeschichtliche Projekte müssen von überregionaler Bedeutung oder beispielgebend sein. Künstlerische Projekte müssen sich durch Innovation, künstlerische Eigenständigkeit, Kreativität, Originalität und Authentizität auszeichnen. Bau- und andere Investitionsmaßnahmen (Ziffer 2.1.2) müssen kulturellen Zwecken dienen und für die kulturelle Infrastruktur bedeutsam sein.
- 4.2 bei Antragstellung mit dem Vorhaben noch nicht begonnen wurde. Will der Antragsteller mit dem Vorhaben vor der Bewilligung der Zuwendung beginnen (vorzeitiger Maßnahmebeginn), so bedarf dies grundsätzlich der vorherigen Zustimmung der Bewilligungsbehörde.

4.3 die jeweilige kommunale Gebietskörperschaft (Gemeinde, Stadt oder Landkreis) das Vorhaben befürwortet. Ausgenommen davon sind Anträge zur Gewährung von Stipendien, Anträge von Landesarbeitsgemeinschaften, überregionalen Gesellschaften und Verbänden sowie Anträge ohne örtlichen Bezug. Darüber hinausgehende Ausnahmen können von der Bewilligungsbehörde im Einzelfall gewährt werden.
4.4 der Nachweis erbracht wird, dass die Gesamtfinanzierung des Vorhabens gesichert ist.
4.5 der Zuwendungsempfänger über eine ordnungsgemäße Geschäftsführung verfügt und in der Lage ist, die Verwendung der Mittel bestimmungsgemäß nachzuweisen.

5. Art und Umfang, Höhe der Zuwendungen

5.1 Die Zuwendung wird im Wege der Projektförderung als nicht rückzahlbarer Zuschuss zu den zuwendungsfähigen Ausgaben gewährt. Zuwendungsfähig sind alle unmittelbar mit dem Vorhaben entstehenden Ausgaben. In Hochbaumaßnahmen sind die Kostengruppen nach DIN 276 maßgeblich.
5.2 Die Zuwendung wird je nach Lage im Einzelfall und gegebenenfalls in Abstimmung mit weiteren Zuwendungsgebern als Anteil- oder Fehlbedarfsfinanzierung gewährt.
In begründeten Ausnahmefällen ist eine Vollfinanzierung möglich.
Zuwendungen bis einschließlich 8.000 EURO können in geeigneten Fällen als Festbetragsfinanzierung gewährt werden.
Stipendien und Geschäftsstellenförderungen werden unabhängig von der Höhe der Zuwendung grundsätzlich als Festbetragsfinanzierung vergeben.
5.3 Zuwendungen an Gebietskörperschaften werden auch gewährt, wenn die zuwendungsfähigen Ausgaben 7.500 EURO nicht übersteigen.
5.4 In geeigneten Fällen kann eine Verwaltungskostenpauschale nach entsprechender Einzelfallprüfung gewährt werden. Die Höhe der Pauschale bemisst sich an dem Umfang der zuwendungsfähigen Ausgaben und soll 5 % nicht übersteigen.
Als geeignete Fälle gelten Förderungen an Gebietskörperschaften oder an Einrichtungen und Vereine, die weder institutionell noch im Rahmen einer Geschäftsstellenförderung unterstützt werden.
5.5 Bei der Feststellung der zuwendungsfähigen Kosten sind die Voraussetzungen des Artikels 53 AGVO und die gemeinsamen Bestimmungen des Kapitel I, insbesondere die Anmeldeschwellen des Artikels 4 Abs. 1 lit. z AGVO (Investitionsbeihilfen bis 100 Mio. EUR pro Projekt, Betriebsbeihilfen bis 50 Mio. EUR pro Unternehmen und Jahr) einzuhalten.
5.6 Die Zuwendung darf nach Artikel 8 AGVO nicht mit anderen staatlichen Beihilfen – einschließlich Beihilfen nach der Verordnung (EU) Nr. 1407/2013 der Kommission vom 18. Dezember 2013 über die Anwendung der Artikel 107 und 108 des Vertrages über die Arbeitsweise der Europäischen Union auf De-minimis-Beihilfen (ABl. L 352 vom 24. Dezember 2013, S. 1) – kumuliert werden, es sei denn, die andere Beihilfe bezieht sich auf unterschiedliche bestimmbare beihilfefähige Kosten, oder es wird die höchste nach der AGVO für diese Beihilfen geltende Beihilfeintensität bzw. der höchste nach der AGVO für diese Beihilfen geltende Beihilfebetrag nicht überschritten.

6. Besondere Zuwendungsbestimmungen

6.1 Förderung von Geschäftsstellen

Geschäftsstellen werden grundsätzlich im Rahmen einer Festbetragsfinanzierung gefördert. Voraussetzungen dafür sind:
– Wahrnehmung von Aufgaben von überregionaler oder besonderer kultureller Bedeutung für den Freistaat Thüringen
– befürwortendes Votum des zuständigen Fachbeirats
– Vorlage der Jahresabschlüsse der der Antragstellung vorangehenden drei Jahre

Der geforderte Umfang des Verwendungsnachweises wird im Bewilligungsbescheid geregelt. Es sind aber **mindestens** folgende Unterlagen gegenüber der Bewilligungsbehörde vorzulegen:
– geprüfter Jahresabschluss über den Förderzeitraum
– Zusammenfassung aller Einnahmen und Ausgaben des Trägers im Abrechnungszeitraum

D16.III.2 Richtlinie zur Förderung von Kultur und Kunst

- Einzelnachweis aller im Rahmen der Geschäftsstellenförderung bezuschussten Ausgaben
- Sachbericht mit Aussagen zu Aktivitäten im Abrechnungszeitraum

6.2 Ausschreibungen
Für Projekte, für die gesonderte Fördervoraussetzungen und –bedingungen gelten (z.B. Sonderprogramme für Musikschulen), können gesonderte Ausschreibungen und ggf. Antragsformulare veröffentlicht werden.

6.3 Stipendien
Für die Vergabe von Stipendien werden gesonderte Fördervoraussetzungen und –bedingungen ausgeschrieben. Die Stipendiaten müssen die ordnungsgemäße Verwendung der Fördermittel ausschließlich anhand eines Sachberichtes nachweisen. Es ist kein zahlenmäßiger Nachweis erforderlich.

7. Verfahren

7.1 Antragsverfahren
7.1.1 Der Antrag auf Förderung ist schriftlich auf anliegendem Vordruck bei der Bewilligungsbehörde einzureichen.
7.1.2 Antragsfrist ist im Regelfall
- der 31.3. des Vorjahres für Zuwendungen über 50.000 EUR
- der 31.10. des Vorjahres für Zuwendungen bis 50.000 EUR

Gebietskörperschaften, deren Haushalt bei Ablauf der Antragsfrist noch nicht bestätigt ist, müssen diese Antragsfristen einhalten, stellen aber den Antrag „unter Vorbehalt der Bestätigung ihres Haushaltes".
7.1.3 Anträge mit den Schwerpunkten Bildende Kunst oder Museen sind der Bewilligungsbehörde in doppelter Ausführung vorzulegen.

7.2 Bewilligungsverfahren
Zur Entscheidung über den Antrag werden durch die Bewilligungsbehörde regelmäßig Fachbeiräte konsultiert.
Die Bewilligung der Zuwendung erfolgt durch einen schriftlichen Bescheid.
Im Falle der Gewährung einer De-minimis-Beihilfe darf der Gesamtbetrag aller „Deminimis"- Beihilfen, den der Antragsteller innerhalb von drei Steuerjahren erhalten hat, den Schwellenwert von 200.000 EUR nicht überschreiten. Hierzu ist mit dem Antrag eine vollständige Übersicht über die in den vorangegangenen zwei Steuerjahren sowie im laufenden Steuerjahr erhaltenen „De-minimis"-Beihilfen vorzulegen (vgl. Ziffern IV „Projektbeschreibung" und V „Anlagen" des Antragsformulars).

7.3 Auszahlungsverfahren
Die Zuwendung wird vom Zuwendungsempfänger durch Mittelabruf bei der Bewilligungsbehörde, gegebenenfalls auch in Raten, angefordert. Die Auszahlung erfolgt durch die Bewilligungsbehörde.

7.4 Verwendungsnachweisverfahren / Controlling
Der Verwendungsnachweis ist gegenüber der Bewilligungsbehörde entsprechend den Regelungen des Bewilligungsbescheides zu führen. Er umfasst einen zahlenmäßigen Nachweis und einen Sachbericht, soweit diese Richtlinie keine abweichenden Regelungen (Ziffer 6) getroffen hat.
Im Nachweis muss für Zwecke der Zielerreichungskontrolle zwingend auf mindestens eines der unter Nr. 1.3 dieser Verwaltungsvorschrift genannten Kriterien eingegangen werden.
Wird der Verwendungsnachweis nicht ordnungsgemäß geführt oder nicht rechtzeitig vorgelegt, so kann der Zuwendungsbescheid widerrufen und die Zuwendung zurückgefordert werden. Außerdem kann der Zuwendungsempfänger von der Bewilligung weiterer Zuwendungen so lange ausgeschlossen werden, bis der Verwendungsnachweis erbracht ist.
Die geförderten Maßnahmen werden einem Controlling gemäß den Verwaltungsvorschriften zu § 23 ThürLHO unterzogen.
Erhaltene Förderungen können im Einzelfall gemäß Artikel 12 AGVO von der Europäischen Kommission geprüft werden.

7.5 Zu beachtende Vorschriften
Für die Bewilligung, Auszahlung und Abrechnung der Zuwendung sowie für den Nachweis und die Prüfung der Verwendung und die ggf. erforderliche Aufhebung des Zuwendungsbescheids und die Rückforderung der gewährten Zuwendung gelten die VV zu § 44 ThürLHO.

7.6 Auf die Berichterstattungspflichten der für Kultur zuständigen Obersten Landesbehörde als bewilligende Einrichtung gemäß Artikel 11 AGVO wird hingewiesen.

7.7 Aufgrund europarechtlicher Vorgaben werden ab dem 01.07.2016 gewährte Einzelbeihilfe über 500.000 EUR veröffentlicht, vgl. Artikel 9 AGVO.

8. Inkrafttreten, Befristung
Diese Richtlinie tritt zum 01.01.2014 in Kraft und mit Ablauf des 31.12.2020 außer Kraft.

D16.III.3 Denkmalförderrichtlinie

Richtlinie für die Bewilligung von Zuwendungen für Denkmalschutz und Denkmalpflege (Denkmalförderrichtlinie)

Vom 08. Dezember 2003 (ThürStAnz S. 2682, ber. ThürStAnz 2004 S. 376)
Geändert durch Verwaltungsvorschrift vom 06.06.2016 (ThürStAnz 2016 S. 915)

1. Zuwendungszweck, Rechtsgrundlage

Das Land gewährt Zuwendungen zur Erhaltung von Kulturdenkmalen nach Maßgabe des § 7 Abs. 2 des Thüringer Denkmalschutzgesetzes (ThDSchG) vom 7. Januar 1992 (GVBl. S.17, 550) in seiner jeweils geltenden Fassung, §§ 23, 44 der Thüringer Landeshaushaltsordnung (ThürLHO), sowie der §§ 48, 49, 49a Thüringer Verwaltungsverfahrensgesetz (ThürVwVfG) und den dazu ergangenen Verwaltungsvorschriften sowie unter Beachtung der Verordnung (EU) Nr. 651/2014 der Kommission vom 17. Juni 2014 zur Feststellung der Vereinbarkeit bestimmter Gruppen von Beihilfen mit dem Binnenmarkt in Anwendung der Art. 107 und 108 des Vertrages über die Arbeitsweise der Europäischen Union sowie der Verordnung (EU) Nr. 1407/2013 der Kommission vom 18. Dezember 2013 über die Anwendung der Artikel 107 und 108 des Vertrages über die Arbeitsweise der Europäischen Union auf De-minimis-Beihilfen.

2. Gegenstand der Förderung

Gegenstand der Förderung sind Kulturdenkmale einschließlich Denkmalensembles oder Teile von Kulturdenkmalen und der Umgebungsschutzbereich, wenn die erforderlichen Maßnahmen in unmittelbarem Zusammenhang mit dem Denkmal stehen.

2.1. Förderfähig sind Maßnahmen, die der Sicherung, Erhaltung und Pflege von Kulturdenkmalen dienen. Bezuschusst werden können denkmalpflegerische Aufwendungen. Hierzu zählen u. a. auch:
- Wissenschaftliche Untersuchungen, Zielstellungen, Studien, Projekte, die im direkten Zusammenhang mit der Erhaltung des Kulturdenkmals stehen;
- Leistungen zur Sicherung wirtschaftlich nicht genutzter Denkmale, wie z. B. Stadtmauern, Ruinen, Mahnmale, Standbilder, Kleinarchitektur usw.;
- Aufwendungen für die Wiederherstellung von teilzerstörten Kulturdenkmalen, wenn hierbei die originale Substanz gesichert wird und Aufwendungen für die rekonstruierende Wiederherstellung, soweit untergegangene, aber für das Verständnis oder die Erscheinung unverzichtbare Teile eines noch bestehenden Kulturdenkmals ergänzt werden sowie Aufwendungen für die Rekonstruktion archäologischer Denkmale. Voraussetzung ist, dass der Umfang der Wiederherstellung jeweils in angemessenem Verhältnis zum Original steht. Der Bedarf ist eingehend zu begründen.
- Regenerierungsmaßnahmen am objekttypischen Pflanzenbestand im Interesse der Erhaltung und Wiederherstellung von Denkmalen der Landschafts- und Gartengestaltung, insbesondere die Pflege und Kultivierung historischer Parkanlagen;

2.2. Förderfähig ist weiterhin die Durchführung von Fortbildungsveranstaltungen, die in unmittelbarem Zusammenhang mit der Erhaltung von Kulturdenkmalen stehen.

2.3. Nicht förderfähig sind:
- Kosten für den Erwerb eines Kulturdenkmals,
- Kosten für die Beschaffung von Finanzierungsmitteln,
- Eigene Arbeitsleistung des Zuwendungsberechtigten,
- Kosten eines Neubaus in der Gesamtanlage,
- Maßnahmen die ausschließlich der Verschönerung dienen und nicht auch Ortsbild pflegend sind, rentierliche nutzungsbedingte Aufwendungen und laufende Unterhaltungskosten,
- Kosten einer Totalrekonstruktion mit Ausnahme ur- und frühgeschichtlicher Denkmale,
- Kosten für die nicht denkmalbezogene, nutzungsbedingte gebäudetechnische Ausstattung,
- Erhaltungsaufwand aus unterlassener Bauunterhaltung

3. Zuwendungsempfänger

3.1 Zuwendungsempfänger können Eigentümer und Besitzer von Kulturdenkmalen im Sinne von § 2 ThürDSchG sowie nach Maßgabe von Nr. 2.2. in der Denkmalpflege tätige natürliche oder juristische Personen sein.

3.2 Zuwendungen werden nicht gewährt an die Bundesrepublik Deutschland (einschließlich Sondervermögen) und andere Bundesländer sowie deren Körperschaften, Anstalten und Stiftungen des Öffentlichen Rechts.

3.3 Einem Unternehmen, das einer Rückforderungsanordnung aufgrund eines früheren Beschlusses der Kommission zur Feststellung der Unzulässigkeit einer Beihilfe und ihrer Unvereinbarkeit mit dem Binnenmarkt nicht nachgekommen ist, dürfen keine Einzelbeihilfen gewährt werden.

4. Zuwendungsvoraussetzungen

4.1 Zuwendungen dürfen nur für solche Vorhaben bewilligt werden, die noch nicht begonnen worden sind. Ist im Einzelfall durch die Denkmalfachbehörde einem vorzeitigen, förderunschädlichen Maßnahmebeginn zugestimmt worden, ersetzt diese Zustimmung nicht die bau- oder denkmalschutzrechtliche Genehmigung und begründet keinen Rechtsanspruch auf eine Zuwendung, sofern diese nicht schriftlich zugesichert wurde.

4.2 Die Maßnahme muss mit der zuständigen Denkmalfachbehörde abgestimmt sein. Gesetzlich vorgeschriebene Genehmigungen bzw. Zustimmungen, insbesondere nach dem Thüringer Denkmalschutzgesetz und der Thüringer Bauordnung in ihrer jeweils geltenden Fassung müssen vorliegen.

4.3 Die Gesamtfinanzierung des Vorhabens muss gesichert sein.

4.4 Die zur denkmalpflegerischen Beurteilung notwendigen Unterlagen müssen vorliegen, insbesondere ein Antrag gemäß Anlage.[1]

4.5 Die nach diesen Richtlinien zu bewilligenden Zuwendungen dürfen nur vergeben werden, soweit die Eigenmittel des Trägers der Maßnahme sowie die Förderung aus anderen Programmen nicht ausreichen, um die Kosten zu decken. Ausnahmen sind zulässig bei Bodendenkmalen oder Denkmalen ohne wirtschaftliche Nutzung, z. B. Ruinen, Stadtmauern, Standbildern usw.

5. Art und Umfang, Höhe der Zuwendungen

5.1 Art der Förderung
Die Förderung erfolgt als Projektförderung in Form einer Anteilsfinanzierung. Die Zuwendungen werden als nichtrückzahlbare Zuschüsse gewährt.

5.2 Zuwendungsfähige Ausgaben
Gefördert werden die reinen denkmalpflegerischen Mehraufwendungen. Diese ergeben sich aus den Gesamtausgaben der Maßnahmen ohne Ausgaben für Teilmaßnahmen, die nicht der Denkmalpflege dienen, abzüglich desjenigen Ausgabenanteils, der bei der Durchführung der Maßnahme ohnehin entstehen würde. Zu den denkmalbedingten Mehraufwendungen gehören auch anteilige Architekten- und Ingenieurhonorare, Gerüstkosten für verlängerte Standzeiten und Aufwendungen einer restauratorischen Untersuchung. Soweit der denkmalpflegerische Mehraufwand nicht eindeutig ermittelbar ist, sind die zuwendungsfähigen Ausgaben von der Denkmalfachbehörde zu schätzen.

5.3 Berücksichtigung von Eigenleistungen
Der Eigenanteil kann in Form von eigenen Sach- und Arbeitsleistungen (Eigenleistungen) erbracht werden. Der Wert der eigenen Arbeitsleistung ist mit 10 € pro Stunde anzusetzen. Für die eigene Arbeitsleistung und Bereitstellung von Material aus eigenen Beständen kann eine Zuwendung nicht gewährt werden. Eigenleistungen können nur zur Berechnung der zuwendungsfähigen Gesamtausgaben herangezogen werden. Die Fördersumme darf hierbei im Ergebnis den Betrag nicht überschreiten, der nach Abzug der Eigenleistungen von den Gesamtkosten verbleibt bzw. den Betrag der tatsächlichen Ausgaben nicht übersteigen. Leistungen durch eigene Mitarbeiter können zuwendungsrechtlich als Fremdleistungen anerkannt werden und in die Förderung einbezogen werden, wenn und soweit die hierdurch entstehenden Kosten durch Rechnungen nachgewiesen werden.

5.4 Erhöhung der Zuwendung
Eine nachträgliche Erhöhung der Zuwendung ist nur in begründeten Ausnahmefällen möglich. Sie kommt nur dann in Betracht, wenn im Verlauf der Maßnahme unvorhersehbare Erschwernisse auftreten, die nicht im Verantwortungsbereich des Zuwendungsempfängers liegen und zusätzlichen denkmalbedingten Aufwand verursachen. Die Denkmalfachbehörde ist vor Eingehen entsprechender Verpflichtungen nach Maßgabe der Allgemeinen Nebenbestimmungen (Nr. 5 ANBest-GK, ANBest-P) zu informieren. Ein Rechtsanspruch auf einmalige oder zusätzliche Zuwendung besteht nicht.

---

1) Die Anlage konnte aus drucktechnischen Gründen nicht aufgenommen werden.

6. Verfahren

6.1 Antragsfrist
Die Anträge sind bei der zuständigen Unteren Denkmalschutzbehörde bis zum 30. September des laufenden Haushaltsjahres für das folgende Haushaltsjahr (Kalenderjahr) einzureichen. Anträge von Kirchgemeinden sind innerhalb dieser Frist über die zuständigen Kirchenbauämter bei den Unteren Denkmalschutzbehörden einzureichen. Verspätet eingehende Anträge können nur in Ausnahmefällen berücksichtigt werden. Ein solcher Fall liegt in der Regel vor, wenn die Überschreitung der Frist unvermeidbar war und die Maßnahme aus dringenden denkmalpflegerischen Gründen unaufschiebbar ist. Sollen die verspätet beantragten Maßnahmen für spätere Bewilligungszeiträume vorgemerkt werden, entbindet dies nicht von einer erneuten, fristgerechten Antragstellung.

6.2 Form und Inhalt der Anträge
6.2.1 Die Antragsformulare sind entsprechend den Mustervordrucken (s. Anlage) vollständig auszufüllen und in zweifacher Ausfertigung einzureichen.

6.2.2 Dem Antrag sind Anlagen mit folgenden Angaben beizufügen:
- kurze Vorstellung des Objektes (Standort, Nutzung, Eigentümer, Benachrichtigung über die Eintragung, bei Objekten der architekturbezogenen Kunst und beweglichen Kunstgütern der Nachweis der Denkmaleigenschaft)
- vorhandene Schäden (mit Farbfotos belegen)
- vorgesehene Instandsetzung, Sanierung- bzw. Restaurierungsmaßnahmen
- betreuendes Architekturbüro/zuständige Kirchenbauämter
- Stand der Vorbereitung des Vorhabens (Vorlage einer denkmalpflegerischen Zielstellung, Abstimmung mit unterer Denkmalschutzbehörde, Vorlage von Schadensanalysen, Projektunterlagen, Kostenermittlungen usw.)
- finanzielle Aufwendungen für die einzelnen Teilleistungen
- Nachweis über die Finanzierung des Gesamtvorhabens oder der Teilleistung (einschließlich der beantragten Zuwendung)
- Nachweis eines Bauablaufplanes bei Fortführungsmaßnahmen

6.3 Vorprüfung der Anträge:
Die Unteren Denkmalschutzbehörden prüfen die Anträge auf ihre Vollständigkeit und im Hinblick auf die Einhaltung der Antragsfrist innerhalb von 2 Wochen. Bei Unvollständigkeit ist der Antragsteller unter Fristsetzung um entsprechende Nachlieferungen zu bitten. Verspätet eingegangene Anträge sind mit einem Vermerk zu den (ggf. besonderen) Umständen, auf denen die Verspätung beruht, zu versehen und an die Denkmalfachbehörde zur Entscheidung weiter zu reichen.

6.4. Auswahlverfahren
6.4.1. Die Unteren Denkmalschutzbehörden geben die von Ihnen vorgeprüften und mit den Gebietsreferenten der Denkmalfachbehörde vorausgewählten Anträge mit einer Stellungnahme bis spätestens zum 15. November des laufenden Jahres für das kommende Jahr an die Denkmalfachbehörde weiter. Diese erstellt Maßnahme- bzw. Objektlisten, welche auch Zuwendungen des Bundes, von Stiftungen oder anderen Zuwendungsgebern ausweisen. Die Listen werden dem das für Denkmalschutz, Denkmalpflege und Archäologie zuständige Ministerium bis spätestens zum 15. Januar des laufenden Förderjahres zur Bestätigung vorgelegt.

6.4.2 Ein Rechtsanspruch auf Gewährung einer Zuwendung besteht nicht. Die zuständige Denkmalfachbehörde entscheidet in jedem Einzelfall nach Rücksprache mit den Unteren Denkmalschutzbehörden der Landkreise, kreisfreien Städte und großen kreisangehörigen Gemeinden nach pflichtgemäßem Ermessen im Rahmen der verfügbaren Haushaltsmittel.

Aus den gewährten Zuwendungen können keine Rückschlüsse auf eine künftige Förderung im bisherigen oder anderen Umfang geschlossen werden. Ferner steht der Bescheid unter dem Vorbehalt der jederzeitigen Änderung oder des Widerrufs aus zwingenden Gründen gemäß § 36 Abs. 2 Nr. 3 i.V.m. § 49 Abs. 2 Nr. 1 ThürVwVfG.

Bei der Entscheidung über die Förderung und Festlegung der Zuwendungshöhe ist sowohl den Bedingungen des Denkmals als auch den beim Zuwendungsempfänger gegebenen Voraussetzungen Rechnung zu tragen. Folgende Kriterien sind u.a. zu berücksichtigen:

- Bedeutung und Zustand des Objektes
- die zur Verfügung stehenden Landesmittel
- Art der Maßnahme / Dringlichkeit der erforderlichen Leistungen
- Möglichkeiten der Förderung durch andere Zuwendungsgeber
- Belastungen des Eigentümers aufgrund der Pflicht zur Erhaltung des Denkmals

6.4.3 Nicht bewilligte Anträge werden durch schriftlichen Bescheid unverzüglich abgelehnt.

6.5. Bewilligung

6.5.1 Die Bewilligung der Zuwendung erfolgt durch einen schriftlichen Bescheid. Dieser enthält Angaben über die ermittelten zuwendungsfähigen Ausgaben und den genauen Verwendungszweck der Fördermittel, Art und Höhe der Zuwendung, die Finanzierungsform, die Finanzierungsart sowie den Bewilligungszeitraum. Weiterhin wird mit dem Bescheid bekannt gegeben, wo die Zwischen- und Verwendungsnachweise vorzulegen sind. Er kann Bedingungen und Auflagen enthalten, insbesondere hinsichtlich der Beteiligung bei der Ausschreibung und Vergabe von Arbeiten, die besondere denkmalpflegerische Sachkenntnis voraussetzen. Dem Bewilligungsbescheid sind gleichzeitig die geltenden Nebenbestimmungen zur Beachtung beigefügt.

6.5.2 Die jeweils zuständige Untere Denkmalschutzbehörde erhält eine Gesamtübersicht der bewilligten Fördermittel und geförderten Objekte ihres Verantwortungsbereiches.

6.6. Mittelabruf, Auszahlung und Verwendungsnachweisprüfung

6.6.1 Für die Gewährung, Auszahlung und Abrechnung der Zuwendung, für Nachweis und Prüfung der Verwendung gelten die Verwaltungsvorschriften zu den §§ 23 und 44 ThürLHO, für gegebenenfalls erforderliche Aufhebung des Zuwendungsbescheides und die Rückforderung der gewährten Zuwendung gelten die Bestimmungen der §§ 49 und 49a sowie § 48 des ThürVwVfG.

6.6.2 Der Zuwendungsgeber ist berechtigt, Bücher, Belege und sonstige Geschäftsunterlagen anzufordern und zu prüfen sowie die ordnungsgemäße Verwendung der Zuwendung durch örtliche Erhebungen zu prüfen oder durch Beauftragte prüfen zu lassen (§ 44 Abs. 1 Satz 3 ThürLHO). Daneben kontrollieren die Unteren Denkmalschutzbehörden die Einhaltung der denkmalpflegerischen Forderungen und bestätigen dies auf dem Verwendungsnachweis.
Die Prüfungsrechte des Rechnungshofs (§ 91 ThürLHO) oder seiner mit der Prüfung beauftragten Rechnungsprüfungsstellen (§ 88 Abs. 1 ThürLHO) bleiben hiervon unberührt.

6.7. Sonstiges

Der Beihilfempfänger muss den schriftlichen Antrag mit allen erforderlichen Inhalten vor Beginn der Arbeiten für das Vorhaben oder die Tätigkeit gestellt haben.
Aufgrund europarechtlicher Vorgaben werden ab dem 01.07.2016 gewährte Einzelbeihilfe über 500.000 EUR veröffentlicht, vgl. Artikel 9 AGVO.
Erhaltene Förderungen können im Einzelfall gemäß Artikel 12 AGVO von der Europäischen Kommission geprüft werden.

7. Kosten

Für Bewilligungen und andere im Zusammenhang mit dieser Richtlinie ergehende Verfügungen, einschließlich solcher im Widerspruchsverfahren, werden keine Gebühren erhoben.

8. Inkrafttreten

Diese Richtlinie tritt am 01.01.2004 in Kraft und gilt bis 31.12.2008, sofern sie nicht sechs Monate vor Ablauf verlängert wird.
Gleichzeitig tritt die Vorläufige Richtlinie für die Bewilligung von Zuwendungen für Denkmalschutz und Denkmalpflege vom 18.12.1992 (GABl 1/1993 S.8) außer Kraft.

Thüringer Gesetz über die Errichtung der „Stiftung Thüringer Schlösser und Gärten"

Vom 10. März 1994 (GVBl. S. 284)
geändert durch G vom 1.8.2009 (GVBl. S. 585)

Der Landtag hat das folgende Gesetz beschlossen:

§ 1 Errichtung, Rechtsstellung
Unter dem Namen „Stiftung Thüringer Schlösser und Gärten" wird eine rechtsfähige Stiftung des öffentlichen Rechts mit Sitz in Rudolstadt errichtet. Die Stiftung entsteht mit Inkrafttreten dieses Gesetzes.

§ 2 Stiftungszweck
(1) Zweck der Stiftung ist es, die kulturhistorisch bedeutsamen Liegenschaften, insbesondere in bezug auf ihre historische, kunsthistorische, denkmalpflegerische und landschaftsprägende Bedeutung, zu verwalten. Hierzu gehört es insbesondere, die Liegenschaften baulich zu betreuen sowie sie der Öffentlichkeit zugänglich zu machen oder einer ihrer Bedeutung gerecht werdenden Nutzung zuzuführen. Das Nähere regelt die Satzung.
(2) Die Zuständigkeit der Denkmalfachbehörden bleibt unberührt.

§ 3 Stiftungsvermögen
(1) Das Vermögen der Stiftung besteht aus landeseigenen Grundstücken, die in der Anlage 1 zu diesem Gesetz aufgeführt sind. Das Eigentum an diesen Grundstücken ist auf die Stiftung zu übertragen, es geht mit Inkrafttreten dieses Gesetzes auf die Stiftung über.
(2) Mit bestandskräftiger Zuordnung zum Landesvermögen gilt für die in Anlage 2 aufgeführten Grundstücke Absatz 1 Satz 2 entsprechend. Die weiteren in der Anlage 2 aufgeführten Grundstücke können die Eigentümer der Stiftung übertragen. Darüber hinaus können der Stiftung nach entsprechendem Beschluß des Stiftungsrats weitere Grundstücke nur im Rahmen des Stiftungszwecks (§ 2 Abs. 1) übertragen werden (Anlage 3).
(3) Das Eigentum am Denkmalensemble Schloss und Park Wilhelmsthal, wie in Anlage 3 bezeichnet, wird vom Land an die Stiftung Thüringer Schlösser und Gärten übertragen und geht am 1. Juli 2009 über.
(4) Die bisherigen Eigentümer sollen angemessene Beiträge zur Verwaltung der Liegenschaften leisten.

§ 4 Rückübertragung
(1) Der Stiftung übertragene Grundstücke können in begründeten Ausnahmefällen an die bisherigen Eigentümer zurückübertragen werden, sofern sichergestellt ist, daß diese die Liegenschaften einem in § 2 Abs. 1 genannten Zweck zuführen.
(2) Im Falle der Rückübertragung ist der Anspruch der Stiftung auf Ersatz der auf die Liegenschaft gemachten Aufwendungen mit den nach § 3 Abs. 3 geleisteten Beiträgen zu verrechnen.

§ 5 Zuwendungen
(1) Zur Erfüllung des Stiftungszwecks erhält die Stiftung jährliche Zuwendungen des Landes. Diese Zuwendungen werden im Rahmen der jeweiligen Haushalte bewilligt und dienen zur Abdeckung des jährlichen Fehlbedarfs der Stiftung.
(2) Die Stiftung ist berechtigt, Zuwendungen Dritter, insbesondere des Bundes und von Gebietskörperschaften, anzunehmen, um sie für den Stiftungszweck zu verwenden. Das Land wird der Stiftung Denkmalpflegemittel, die der Bund für bedeutende Kulturdenkmale zur Verfügung stellt, zuwenden.

§ 6 Satzung
Die Stiftung gibt sich eine Satzung, die einstimmig vom Stiftungsrat beschlossen wird. Satzungsänderungen werden mit einer Mehrheit von mindestens vier Stimmen vom Stiftungsrat beschlossen und bedürfen der Genehmigung des Ministeriums für Wissenschaft und Kunst.

§ 7 Organe der Stiftung
Organe der Stiftung sind der Stiftungsrat und der Direktor.

§ 8 Stiftungsrat
(1) Der Stiftungsrat besteht aus bis zu acht Mitgliedern, und zwar
1. einem Vertreter des Ministeriums für Wissenschaft und Kunst als Vorsitzenden,
2. einem Vertreter des Finanzministeriums,
3. einem Vertreter des Ministeriums für Wirtschaft und Verkehr,
4. dem Landeskonservator,
5. zwei Vertretern des Arbeitskreises (§ 11),
6. Vertretern von Zuwendungsgebern, die auf Beschluß des Stiftungsrats Mitglied werden.

Die Mitglieder können sich vertreten lassen.
(2) Beschlüsse im Stiftungsrat kommen mit einfacher Mehrheit der abgegebenen Stimmen zustande. Der Stiftungsrat ist beschlußfähig, wenn mehr als die Hälfte der Mitglieder anwesend sind.
(3) In Haushalts- und Stellenangelegenheiten bedürfen die Beschlüsse des Stiftungsrats der Zustimmung der Vertreter des Ministeriums für Wissenschaft und Kunst und des Finanzministeriums.
(4) Der Direktor der Stiftung und der Vorsitzende des Beirats nach § 12 nehmen beratend an den Sitzungen teil.

§ 9 Aufgaben des Stiftungsrats
(1) Der Stiftungsrat beschließt über alle grundsätzlichen Angelegenheiten der Stiftung, soweit sie nicht durch dieses Gesetz dem Direktor übertragen sind. Er beschließt insbesondere über den Haushalts- und Stellenplanentwurf und die Geschäftsordnung der Stiftung sowie über die Einstellung, Beförderung und Entlassung der Arbeitnehmer ab der Gehaltsgruppe III des Bundesangestelltentarifvertrages. Das Nähere regelt die Satzung.
(2) Der Stiftungsrat überwacht die Ausführung seiner Beschlüsse durch den Direktor sowie dessen Geschäftsführung.

§ 10 Der Direktor
(1) Der Direktor wird nach Anhörung des Beirats auf Vorschlag des Stiftungsrats durch das Ministerium für Wissenschaft und Kunst berufen.
(2) Der Direktor leitet die Stiftung, führt die Beschlüsse des Stiftungsrats aus und bereitet dessen Sitzungen vor. Er vertritt die Stiftung gerichtlich und außergerichtlich. Das Nähere regelt die Satzung.

§ 11 Arbeitskreis
Zur Wahrnehmung ihrer Interessen bilden Vertreter der Landkreise, Städte und Gemeinden, zu deren Gebietskörperschaft eine Liegenschaft der Stiftung gehört, einen Arbeitskreis, der den Stiftungsrat und den Direktor berät. Der Arbeitskreis wählt einen Vorsitzenden. Das Nähere regelt die Satzung.

§ 12 Beirat
Der Stiftungsrat beruft einen Beirat, der sich aus bis zu acht sachverständigen Persönlichkeiten zusammensetzt und den Stiftungsrat und den Direktor berät. Der Beirat wählt einen Vorsitzenden. Dem Beirat sollen insbesondere Vertreter der Denkmalpflege, Kunstgeschichte, Architektur, Restaurierung, des Museumswesens sowie der Kulturpolitik angehören. Die erstmalige Berufung des Beirats wird durch das Ministerium für Wissenschaft und Kunst vorgenommen. Das Nähere regelt die Satzung.

§ 13 Beschäftigte
Auf die Arbeitnehmer der Stiftung sind die für Arbeitnehmer geltenden Tarifverträge und sonstigen Bestimmungen des Freistaats anzuwenden.

§ 14 Dienstsiegel
Die Stiftung führt ein Dienstsiegel.

§ 14a Eigenwirtschaftliche Tätigkeit
Die Stiftung ist berechtigt, in begründeten Ausnahmefällen im Rahmen des Stiftungszwecks jeweils eigenwirtschaftlich in Form von Gesellschaften mit eigener Rechtspersönlichkeit tätig zu werden. § 8 Abs. 3 gilt entsprechend.

§ 15 Aufsicht, Haushalt, Rechnungsprüfung
(1) Die Stiftung untersteht der Aufsicht des Ministeriums für Wissenschaft und Kunst.

D16.III.4 Stiftung Thüringer Schlösser und Gärten

(2) Für das Haushalts-, Kassen- und Rechnungswesen sowie für die Rechnungslegung gelten die Bestimmungen der Thüringer Landeshaushaltsordnung (LHO), insbesondere die §§ 23, 44, 44 a und 105 LHO und die dazu ergangenen Verwaltungsrichtlinien.

(3) Soweit ein Wirtschaften nach Einnahmen und Ausgaben nicht zweckmäßig ist, kann der Stiftungsrat beschließen, daß die Wirtschaftsführung aufgrund eines Wirtschaftsplans nach den Regeln der kaufmännischen doppelten Buchführung zu erfolgen hat (§ 110 LHO); hierzu ist die Genehmigung des Finanzministeriums erforderlich.

(4) Der Thüringer Rechnungshof prüft die Haushaltsführung der Stiftung gemäß § 91 LHO.

§ 16 Aufhebung
Die Stiftung kann nur durch Gesetz aufgehoben werden. Im Fall der Aufhebung fällt das eingebrachte Vermögen an die Eigentümer zurück, die ihr Eigentum in die Stiftung eingebracht haben.

§ 17 Inkrafttreten
Dieses Gesetz tritt am Tage nach der Verkündung[1] in Kraft.

Anlage 1
(Zu § 3 Abs. 1)

Landeseigene Grundstücke (Liegenschaften), die mit Errichtung der Stiftung in das Stiftungsvermögen übergehen

Erfurt	Peterskirche Erfurt
	Flurstück 1/14
	Flur 156
	Gemarkung Erfurt-Mitte
Eisenach	Burgruine Brandenburg
	Flurstück 185 a
	Flur 2
	Gemarkung Lauchröden
Hildburghausen	Veste Heldburg
	Flurstücke 2931, 2931/2, 2932, 2936, 3009
	Gemarkung Heldburg
Rudolstadt	Schwarzburg
	Flurstücke 341, 366/343, 344 bis 363
	Flur 4
	Gemarkung Schwarzburg
	Jagdschloß Paulinzella
	Flurstück 32
	Flur 1
	Gemarkung Paulinzella
Pößneck	Burg Ranis
	Flurstück 6
	Flur 11
	Gemarkung Ranis
Schleusingen	Bertholdsburg
	Flurstücke 79/1, 79/2, 79/3, 80, 81/1, 81/2
	Flur 17
	Gemarkung Schleusingen

---

[1] Verkündet am 17. 3. 1994.

Anlage 2
(Zu § 3 Abs. 2)

Grundstücke (Liegenschaften),
die nach der Vermögenszuordnung in das Stiftungsvermögen übergehen oder der Stiftung übertragen werden

Altenburg	Schloßkomplex einschließlich Mauritianum und Lindenaumuseum
Apolda	Wasserburg Kapellendorf
Arnstadt	Burgruinen Ehrenstein und Liebenstein
Artern	Klosterruine St. Wigbert, Göllingen
	Sachsenburg Oldisleben
Bad Salzungen	Schloß und Park Altenstein, Bad Liebenstein
Erfurt	Schloß und -park Molsdorf
Gera	Kloster Mildenfurth, Wünschendorf
	Osterburg, Weida
Gotha	Schloß und -park Friedenstein
	Klosterruine Georgenthal
	Burgruine Mühlburg, Mühlberg
	Burgruine Burg Gleichen, Wandersleben
Greiz	Sommerpalais mit Park
Hildburghausen	Kloster Veßra einschließlich Fachwerkhaus Suhl-Heinrichs
Jena	Altes Schloß und Gut Dornburg
Meiningen	Schloß und -park Elisabethenburg
	Ruine Henneburg, Henneberg
Rudolstadt	Schloßkomplex Heidecksburg
	Klosterruine Paulinzella
Schleiz	Schloß Burgk
Schmalkalden	Schloß Wilhelmsburg
Schmölln	Posterstein
Sömmerda	Runneburg, Weißensee
Sondershausen	Schloßkomplex Sondershausen einschließlich Fürstengruft
Weimar	Bastille, Hofdamenhaus und Schlossvorplatz, Gemarkung Weimar, Flur 37 Flurstücke 149 (noch zu vermessende Teilfläche), 150, 151 und 152 (noch zu vermessende Teilfläche)
	Burgruine Oberschloss Kranichfeld

Anlage 3
(zu § 3 Abs. 2 Satz 3 und Abs. 3)

Grundstücke (Liegenschaften),
die nach entsprechendem Beschluss des Stiftungsrats oder durch Gesetz im Rahmen des Stiftungszwecks übertragen wurden

Dornburg	Rokokoschloss, Renaissanceschloss, Parkanlagen, Nebengebäude, Weinberg Gemarkung Dornburg lfd. Nr. 1, Flur 1 Flurstück 1042
Weimar	Kirms-Krackow-Haus mit Teehaus und Garten Gemarkung Weimar Flur 37 Flurstücke 98 und 106
Wilhelmsthal	Denkmalensemble Schloss und Park Wilhelmsthal, Gemarkung Eckhardtshausen Flur 10 Flurstücke 757/1, 757/11 und 757/13

D16.IV.1 Beschluss Zuständigkeit einzelner Ministerien

Zuständigkeit der einzelnen Ministerien nach Artikel 76 Abs. 2 Satz 1 der Verfassung des Freistaats Thüringen[1)]

Beschluss der Thüringer Landesregierung
Vom 31. März 2015 (GVBl. S. 10)
zuletzt geändert durch Beschluss vom 11.12.2018 (GVBl. S. 824)

1.
Soweit dieser Beschluss die Geschäftsbereiche der Ministerien neu abgrenzt, gehen die in Gesetzen und Rechtsverordnungen einem Ministerium zugewiesenen Verordnungsermächtigungen oder Zuständigkeiten auf das nach der Neuabgrenzung zuständige Ministerium über. Die einem Minister, einer Ministerin oder einem Ministerium in Rechtsvorschriften zugewiesenen Ermächtigungen oder Zuständigkeiten werden von einer Änderung der Ressortbezeichnung nicht berührt.

2.
Die Landesregierung führt im Dienstverkehr die Bezeichnung:
Thüringer Landesregierung.
Sie setzt sich zusammen aus:
dem Thüringer Ministerpräsidenten,
dem Thüringer Minister für Kultur, Bundes- und Europaangelegenheiten und Chef der Staatskanzlei,
dem Thüringer Minister für Inneres und Kommunales,
der Thüringer Ministerin für Bildung, Jugend und Sport,
dem Thüringer Minister für Migration, Justiz und Verbraucherschutz,
der Thüringer Finanzministerin,
dem Thüringer Minister für Wirtschaft, Wissenschaft und Digitale Gesellschaft,
der Thüringer Ministerin für Arbeit, Soziales, Gesundheit, Frauen und Familie,
der Thüringer Ministerin für Umwelt, Energie und Naturschutz,
der Thüringer Ministerin für Infrastruktur und Landwirtschaft.
Die Staatskanzlei und die Ministerien führen im Dienstverkehr folgende Bezeichnungen:
02 Thüringer Staatskanzlei,
03 Thüringer Ministerium für Inneres und Kommunales,
04 Thüringer Ministerium für Bildung, Jugend und Sport,
05 Thüringer Ministerium für Migration, Justiz und Verbraucherschutz,
06 Thüringer Finanzministerium,
07 Thüringer Ministerium für Wirtschaft, Wissenschaft und Digitale Gesellschaft,
08 Thüringer Ministerium für Arbeit, Soziales, Gesundheit, Frauen und Familie,
09 Thüringer Ministerium für Umwelt, Energie und Naturschutz,
10 Thüringer Ministerium für Infrastruktur und Landwirtschaft.

3.
Der Ministerpräsident übt die ihm aufgrund der Verfassung des Freistaats Thüringen sowie die ihm kraft Gesetzes zustehenden Rechte aus. Hoheits- und Verwaltungsakte ergehen unter der Bezeichnung
Der Thüringer Ministerpräsident.
Der Ministerpräsident bedient sich zur Führung seiner Geschäfte und der laufenden Geschäfte der Landesregierung der Staatskanzlei.

02 Geschäftsbereich der Thüringer Staatskanzlei
Der Thüringer Minister für Kultur, Bundes- und Europaangelegenheiten und Chef der Staatskanzlei ist außerdem zuständig für
[...]
21. Staatsarchive, Öffentliche Bibliotheken, Digitalisierung von Kulturgut, Deutsche Digitale Bibliothek,

---

[1)] Obwohl nicht direkt auf das KGSG (abgedruckt als Nr. C.I.2) bezogen, regelt der Beschluss laut den Thüringer Behörden die Zuständigkeit auf dem gesamten Gebiet des Kulturgutschutzes.

25. die Rechtsaufsicht über die der Staatskanzlei unterstellten Stiftungen des öffentlichen Rechts im Kulturbereich und die Betreuung der Stiftung Schloss Friedenstein Gotha, der Kulturstiftung Meiningen, die Vertretung und Mitwirkung bei der Kulturstiftung der Länder (Stiftung bürgerlichen Rechts, Staatsvertrag), der Stiftung Deutsches Zentrum Kulturgutverluste (Stiftung bürgerlichen Rechts), der Stiftung Preußischer Kulturbesitz (Staatsvertrag), der Stiftung Haus der Geschichte der Bundesrepublik Deutschland (Staatsvertrag),
28. allgemeine Kulturförderung, Kunstförderung, Kulturlastenausgleich,
29. Denkmalpflege und Denkmalschutz, Archäologie, UNESCO-Weltkulturerbe, immaterielles Welterbe, Weltdokumentenerbe, Europäisches Kulturerbesiegel und Haager Konvention Kulturgutschutz, Zentralstelle des Landes nach dem Kulturgüterrückgabegesetz, Provenienzforschung,

4.
Dieser Beschluss tritt mit Ausnahme der Zuständigkeiten, die bereits am 16. Dezember 2014 sowie am 6. Januar 2015 in Kraft getreten sind, mit Wirkung vom 24. März 2015 in Kraft.

D17.I.1 Anzahl Objekte nach der Haager Konvention

Anzahl der in der Bundesrepublik Deutschland nach der Haager Konvention zum Schutz von Kulturgut bei bewaffneten Konflikten zu schützenden Objekte (ohne Denkmäler der Vor- und Frühgeschichte, Museen, Bibliotheken und Archive)

Beschl. der KMK vom 26. Juni 1998

(Neufassung des KMK-Beschlusses v. 18.9.1981)

Land	Objekte einschl. Ensembles[1]
Baden-Württemberg	1.360
Bayern	1.600
Berlin	600
Brandenburg	400
Bremen	80
Hamburg	240
Hessen	800
Mecklenburg-Vorpommern	300
Niedersachsen	960
Nordrhein-Westfalen	1.280
Rheinland-Pfalz	800
Saarland	160
Sachsen	700
Sachsen-Anhalt	400
Schleswig-Holstein	400
Thüringen	400

---

1) Die genannten Zahlen sind als Höchstgrenzen für jedes Bundesland zu verstehen. Das Bundesamt für Bevölkerungsschutz und Katastrophenhilfe führt eine zentrale Datei, in der alle geschützten Objekte erfasst sind. Das schweizerische Inventar der Kulturgüter von nationaler und regionaler Bedeutung ist abrufbar unter: https://www.babs.admin.ch/de/aufgabenbabs/kgs/inventar.html#dokumente.

UNESCO-Weltkulturerbe
Fortschreibung der deutschen Tentativliste und Verfahren zur Nominierung von Welterbestätten

Beschl. der KMK vom 04. März 2010

1. Die Kultusministerkonferenz bestätigt die Nominierungen auf der „Vorläufigen Liste der Kultur- und Naturgüter, die in den Jahren 2000 bis 2010 von der Bundesrepublik Deutschland zur Aufnahme in die UNESCO-Liste des Kultur- und Naturerbes der Welt angemeldet werden sollen" (Tentativliste) gem. Beschluss des 283. Plenums vom 22./23.10.1998. Den Ländern ist ein bilateraler Tausch der Positionen auf der Liste freigestellt. Das Sekretariat wird gebeten, Änderungen in der zeitlichen Reihung der Nominierungen als Folge von bilateral vereinbartem Tausch, durch Einreihung von auf Wiedervorlage gehaltenen Anmeldungen gem. Ziff. 5 des Beschlussvorschlages sowie Beschlüssen des Welterbekomitees und der Kultusministerkonferenz den Ländern durch zeitnahe Aktualisierungen der Liste bekannt zu geben.
2. Nominierungsanträge der Länder gemäß „Vorläufiger Liste ..." sind als Ausschlussfrist spätestens am 15. Dezember des Vorjahres der Nominierung im Sekretariat der Kultusministerkonferenz zum Anmeldestichtag 1. Februar einzureichen, sofern auf die freiwillige Vorprüfung („Completeness-Check") durch das Welterbezentrum mit den in Nr. 127 und Nr. 168 der „Richtlinien für die Durchführung des Übereinkommens zum Schutz des Kultur- und Naturerbes der Welt" (WHC – 08/01, Januar 2008) genannten Fristen verzichtet wurde.
3. Nominierungsanträge, die nicht fristgerecht eingereicht oder im Verfahren zurückgezogen werden oder von der UNESCO zurückgewiesen worden sind, können erst bei einer weiteren Fortschreibung der Liste berücksichtigt werden. Dies gilt für Nominierungen ab dem Anmeldestichtag 01.02.2012.
4. Zum Anmeldestichtag 01.02.2011 sollen folgende Anträge eingereicht werden:
   (1) Das Markgräfliche Opernhaus Bayreuth – Einzigartiges Monument barocker Theaterkultur
   (2) Schwetzingen – Kurfürstliche Sommerresidenz
5. Nominierungen, die gemäß Nr. 159 der „Richtlinien ..." vom Welterbekomitee auf Wiedervorlage („Referral") gelegt und von den Ländern in der vorgesehenen 3-Jahres-Frist nachgebessert worden sind, werden dem Welterbezentrum zum nächstmöglichen Anmeldestichtag vorgelegt.
6. Zur Fortschreibung der Tentativliste werden die Länder bis zum Herbst 2012 um Vorlage von jeweils zwei Vorschlägen pro Land auf dem von der UNESCO bereitgestellten „Tentative List Submission Format" gebeten. Bei Vorschlägen aus unterrepräsentierten Kategorien (z. B. ländliche Architektur) können mehr als zwei Vorschläge gemacht werden. Maßgeblich für die Definition der unterrepräsentierten Kategorien sind die GAP-Reports von IUCN und ICOMOS. Der Kulturausschuss der Kultusministerkonferenz wird beauftragt, im Jahre 2013 diese Vorschläge von einer Expertengruppe evaluieren zu lassen und das Ergebnis der Kultusministerkonferenz zur Beschlussfassung vorzulegen.
7. Das Sekretariat wird gebeten, das Auswärtige Amt über die Beschlussfassung zu unterrichten.

D17.I.3 Fortschreibung der deutschen Liste Weltkulturerbe

UNESCO-Weltkulturerbe
Fortschreibung der deutschen Liste[1)]

Beschl. der KMK vom 12.06.2014

1. Die Kultusministerkonferenz bekennt sich zu ihrer besonderen Verantwortung für das Kulturerbe der deutschen Länder und fühlt sich verpflichtet, das nominierte und eingeschriebene Welterbe nachhaltig zu schützen und zu nutzen. Deutschland gehört mit 38 Welterbestätten zu den 5 Staaten mit den meisten Eintragungen auf der Welterbeliste mit derzeit insgesamt 981 Statten in 160 Staaten. Die Kultusministerkonferenz wird sich daher dafür einsetzen, die Idee und das Ziel der Welterbekonvention zu starken und zu einem weltweiten verantwortungsvollen Umgang mit dem Kultur- und Naturerbe der Menschheit beizutragen. Vor diesem Hintergrund hat die Kultusministerkonferenz 2010 ein neues Verfahren zur Fortschreibung der „Vorschlagsliste der Bundesrepublik Deutschland für die Nominierungen zur Liste des Kultur- und Naturerbes der Welt" (Tentativliste) beschlossen, das sich durch Transparenz und den Nachweis des außergewöhnlichen universellen Wertes und Erfüllung der Kriterien der ICOMOSLückenstudie „Filling the gaps" auszeichnet. Dass Deutschland ein reiches Kulturerbe von herausragender Bedeutung besitzt, zeigen auch die bei der Kultusministerkonferenz eingereichten 31 Antrage der Länder. Gemeinsame Aufgabe aller Länder ist es daher, die Zeugnisse auf nationaler, regionaler und lokaler Ebene zu erhalten und zu schützen.

2. Die Kultusministerkonferenz dankt dem von ihr eingesetzten Fachbeirat für die Evaluierung der von den Ländern eingereichten Bewerbungen zur Fortschreibung der deutschen Tentativliste und schließt sich seinen Ausführungen an. Sie beschließt die Tentativliste für die Bundesrepublik Deutschland mit den folgenden Kulturgütern in der vom Fachbeirat empfohlenen Reihung für eine Einschreibung in die Welterbeliste ab 2016, die das Kriterium des außergewöhnlichen universellen Wertes nachweisen und die Kriterien der ICOMOS-Lückenstudie „Filling the gaps"erfüllen:
   - Hohlen der ältesten Eiszeitkunst
   - Jüdischer Friedhof Altona Königstrase
   - Wasserbau und Wasserkraft, Trinkwasser und Brunnenkunst in Augsburg
   - Künstlerkolonie Mathildenhohe Darmstadt
   - Die SchUM-Stadte Speyer, Worms und Mainz
   - Alte Synagoge und Mikwe in Erfurt – Zeugnisse von Alltag, Religion und Stadtgeschichte zwischen Kontinuität und Wandel
   - Alpine und voralpine Wiesen- und Moorlandschaften (Historische Kulturlandschaften im Werdenfelser Land, Ammergau, Staffelseegebiet und Murnauer Moos, Landkreis Garmisch-Partenkirchen)

Des Weiteren werden die folgenden Kulturguter aufgenommen, die den außergewöhnlichen universellen Wert erfüllen:
   - Gebaute Traume – Die Schlosser Neuschwanstein, Linderhof und Herrenchiemsee des Bayerischen Konigs Ludwig II.
   - Residenzensemble Schwerin – Kulturlandschaft des romantischen Historismus

Die Kultusministerkonferenz begrüßt, dass der Fachbeirat eine Vielzahl von Möglichkeiten und Chancen aufgezeigt hat, wie die weiteren 22 Antrage, die aktuell für die Fortschreibung der Tentativliste nicht vorgeschlagen worden sind, durch zusätzliche Forschung oder Präzisierungen weiterentwickelt oder im Rahmen serieller Nominierungen oder durch Antragstellungen bei anderen Programmen, wie Weltdokumentenerbe, Immaterielles Kulturerbe und Europäisches Kulturerbe-Siegel, berücksichtigt werden können.

[1)] https://www.kmk.org/fileadmin/Dateien/pdf/Themen/Kultur/2014_06_12-Unesco-Weltkulturerbe_Fortschreibung.pdf.

Empfehlung der Kultusministerkonferenz zur Durchführung des Europäischen Übereinkommens zum Schutz archäologischen Kulturguts vom 6. Mai 1969

Beschl. der KMK vom 5. November 1976

Die Bundesrepublik Deutschland hat dem Europäischen Übereinkommen zum Schutz archäologischen Kulturguts vom 6. Mai 1969 zugestimmt (Gesetz vom 17. Oktober 1974 – BGBl. II S. 1285 –). Das Übereinkommen verfolgt das Ziel, das archäologische Kulturgut zu erhalten und zu erforschen.

A. Zur Durchführung der Artikel 1 bis 3 des Übereinkommens hält die Kultusministerkonferenz folgende gesetzgeberische Maßnahmen für unerläßlich, soweit nicht bereits ausreichende Landesvorschriften bestehen:
  I. 1. Eine Definition der geschützten Gegenstände, durch die archäologisches Kulturgut erfaßt wird (Artikel 1).
     2. Schutzbestimmungen für Bodendenkmale und Fundorte (Artikel 2 Buchst. a) sowie für die Ausweisung von Grabungsschutzgebieten (Artikel 2 Buchst. b).
     3. Durch Sanktionen geschützte Genehmigungsvorbehalte für Ausgrabungen mit der Möglichkeit, entsprechende Bedingungen und Auflagen zu erteilen.
  II. Bestehende Gesetze sind daraufhin zu überprüfen, ob sie den Anforderungen der Artikel 1 bis 3 genügen.
  III. Die Kultusministerkonferenz nimmt Artikel 8 des Übereinkommens zum Anlaß, den Ländern die Prüfung zu empfehlen, ob ein Schatzregal landesrechtlich zu schaffen ist (vgl. § 23 des baden-württembergischen Denkmalschutzgesetzes vom 25. Mai 1971, § 18 Abs. 3 des Hamburgischen Denkmalschutzgesetzes, § 19 Abs. 1 des bremischen Denkmalschutzgesetzes).

B. Ferner empfiehlt die Kultusministerkonferenz, Verwaltungsvorschriften zu erlassen.
  I. Die Information der Wissenschaft und der Öffentlichkeit über archäologisches Kulturgut ist durch folgende Maßnahmen zu fördern:
     1. Veröffentlichung der Ergebnisse der Ausgrabungen und Entdeckungen (Artikel 4 Abs. 1).
     2. Austausch von Informationen (Artikel 5 Buchst. b).
     3. Bildungspolitische Maßnahmen in der Öffentlichkeit (Artikel 5 Buchst. d).
  II. Archäologisches Kulturgut ist wissenschaftlich zu erfassen, insbesondere zu inventarisieren (Artikel 4 Absatz 2).
  III. Museen und ähnliche Einrichtungen haben
     1. am Kulturaustausch mitzuwirken durch Weitergabe von archäologischem Kulturgut zu wissenschaftlichen und bildungspolitischen Zwecken (Artikel 5 Buchst. a, Artikel 6 Absatz 1),
     2. dem Erwerb von archäologischem Kulturgut, das aus unzulässigen Grabungen stammt oder aus amtlichen Grabungen entwendet worden ist, entgegenzuwirken (Artikel 6 Absatz 2, Artikel 5 Buchst. d Artikel 7).

D17.II.1 Kriegsbedingt verlagerte Kulturgüter

Gemeinsame Länderposition zur Frage der kriegsbedingt verlagerten Kulturgüter

Beschl. der KMK vom 12. April 1996

Das Thema der kriegsbedingt verlagerten Kulturgüter ist eines der zentralen kulturpolitischen Themen in den Beziehung zu den ost- und mitteleuropäischen Staaten. Es liegt genau an der Schnittstelle zwischen der außenpolitischen Zuständigkeit des Bundes und der Kulturhoheit der Länder. Eine der wesentlichen Aufgaben der Kultusministerkonferenz muß es sein, die Voraussetzungen dafür zu schaffen, daß Bund und Länder diese Verhandlungen gemeinsam führen können. Die Ländergemeinschaft steht in einer besonderen Verantwortung ihren eigenen Interessen wie auch den Partnerstaaten gegenüber. Die Verhandlungen sind schwierig und langwierig; eine Prinzipien- und Strategiediskussion ist dringend erforderlich. Hier kann die Ländergemeinschaft durch eine politische Position, die die Bundesposition ergänzt und konstruktive Anstöße gibt, eine wichtige Initiative ergreifen.

Die kulturpolitischen Eckpunkte einer solchen Länderposition können wie folgt umschrieben werden:

- Die Rechtsposition der Bundesrepublik auf Rückführung ist eindeutig. Ein reines Beharren auf dieser Rechtsposition ohne darüber hinausgehende Strategie und Angebote wird jedoch nicht weiterführen.
- Der Kunstraub der Nationalsozialisten war beispiellos. Besonders Osteuropa war davon betroffen, viele Kulturgüter sind unwiederbringlich zerstört. Die Anerkennung der eigenen, deutschen Geschichte darf sich nicht in Lippenbekenntnissen erschöpfen. Es muß ein offeneres und besseres Verhandlungsklima geschaffen werden.
- Im Umgang mit den noch in der Bundesrepublik befindlichen Kulturgütern aus Ländern Ost- und Mitteleuropas zeigt sich die Glaubwürdigkeit der eigenen Position. Diese Kulturgüter dürfen vor dem Hintergrund der eigenen Geschichte nicht als Verhandlungsmasse betrachtet werden, was sie sowohl der Qualität als auch der Quantität nach gar nicht sein können; sie sollten zügig und ohne Vorbehalte zurückgegeben werden.
- Eine offene und konstruktive Lösung der Problematik könnte durch das Angebot einer verstärkten Kulturkooperation in den Partnerstaaten befördert werden. Diese Politik der Gesten und Kulturkooperation könnte zu einer Bewältigung dieses schwierigen historischen Erbes führen, die beispielhaft für die neue Etappe in den Beziehungen zu diesen Staaten ist. Erste gemeinsame Projekte könnten das Spektrum der Möglichkeiten in kleineren Schritten aufzeigen.
- Zeitlich vorrangiges Ziel muß die Sicherung und Zugänglichmachung der Kulturgüter vor Ort sein, um zu verhindern, daß sie ein zweites – und letztes – Mal verloren gehen.
- Das Thema der kriegsbedingt verlagerten Kulturgüter muß als zentrales Thema der auswärtigen Kulturpolitik entsprechend wahrgenommen werden. Die Länder spielen hier über ihre Beteiligung an den bilateralen Kulturabkommen eine wichtige Rolle.
- Zu bestimmten Staaten oder Fragestellungen sollten sich die Länder Beratungskapazität sichern.
- Die staatenspezifisch jeweils unterschiedlichen Gegebenheiten – in Rußland, Polen, Ukraine usw. – müssen berücksichtig werden.
- Die Dokumentation der bundesdeutschen Kulturgutverluste 50 Jahre nach Kriegsende in zufriedenstellender Form abzuschließen, liegt im Interesse der betroffenen Institutionen, der Länder und des Bundes.

Ergänzung der Länderposition zur Frage der kriegsbedingt verlagerten Kulturgüter

Beschl. der KMK vom 8. Mai 2003

Die Kultusministerkonferenz stellt fest, dass
- die Gemeinsame Länderposition zur Frage der kriegsbedingt verlagerten Kulturgüter vom 12. April 1996 Grundlage für das weitere Verfahren ist,
- diese Gemeinsame Länderposition durch die Politik der Bundesregierung nur in Teilen umgesetzt werden konnte und die Rückführungsverhandlungen noch nicht zu abschließenden Vereinbarungen geführt haben,
- die notwendige enge Abstimmung mit den Ländern bzw. den zuständigen Länderbeauftragten und den ebenfalls betroffenen Kommunen stärker als bisher vom Bund berücksichtigt werden sollte,
- die zwischenzeitlich erfolgte Beteiligung des Bundes an der Verwaltungsvereinbarung über die Koordinierungsstelle für Kulturgutverluste sich sehr positiv ausgewirkt hat und bittet den Bund, die zukünftige Zusammenarbeit sowohl durch das Einbringen der Leistungen der Koordinierungsstelle in die Rückführungsverhandlungen als auch durch eine erforderliche Aufgabenabstimmung zu verbessern.

Vor diesem Hintergrund
- begrüßen die Länder alle konstruktiven Schritte, die geeignet sind, für die Rückführungsverhandlungen ein gegenseitiges Vertrauensklima zu schaffen und positive Erfahrung zu fördern,
- erklären die Länder erneut ihre Bereitschaft, kriegsbedingt verlagerte Kulturgüter, die sich unrechtmäßig in ihrem Besitz befinden, zurückzugeben,
- sprechen sich die Länder nachdrücklich dafür aus, die deutsche völkerrechtliche Position sobald wie möglich durch eine Rückgabe eindeutig kriegsbedingt verlagerter Kulturgüter auch zu dokumentieren,
- sollte die Aufnahme bilateraler regionaler Verhandlungen der Länder – in Abstimmung mit dem Bund – für Teilbereiche der kriegsbedingt verlagerten Kulturgüter möglich sein.

D17.III.1 Erklärung Washingtoner Holocaust-Konferenz

Erklärung der Bundesregierung, der Länder und der kommunalen Spitzenverbände zur Auffindung und zur Rückgabe NS-verfolgungsbedingt entzogenen Kulturgutes, insbesondere aus jüdischem Besitz[1]

Vom 9. Dezember 1999

Die Bundesrepublik Deutschland hat nach dem Zweiten Weltkrieg unter den Voraussetzungen der alliierten Rückerstattungsregelungen, des Bundesrückerstattungsgesetzes und des Bundesentschädigungsgesetzes begründete Ansprüche wegen des verfolgungsbedingten Entzugs von Kulturgütern erfüllt sowie die entsprechenden Verfahren und Institutionen zur Verfügung gestellt, damit die sonstigen Rückerstattungsverpflichteten von den Berechtigten in Anspruch genommen werden konnten. Die Ansprüche standen in erster Linie den unmittelbar Geschädigten und deren Rechtsnachfolgern oder im Fall erbenloser oder nicht in Anspruch genommenen jüdischen Vermögens den in den Westzonen und in Berlin eingesetzten Nachfolgeorganisationen zu. Die materielle Wiedergutmachung erfolgte im Einzelfall oder durch Globalabfindungsvergleiche. Das Rückerstattungsrecht und das allgemeine Zivilrecht der Bundesrepublik Deutschland regeln damit abschließend und umfassend die Frage der Restitution und Entschädigung von NS-verfolgungsbedingt entzogenem Kulturgut, das insbesondere aus jüdischem Besitz stammt.

In der DDR war die Wiedergutmachung von NS-Unrecht nach alliiertem Recht über gewisse Anfänge nicht hinausgekommen. Im Zuge der deutschen Vereinigung hat sich die Bundesrepublik Deutschland zur Anwendung der Grundsätze des Rückerstattungs- und Entschädigungsrechts verpflichtet. NS-verfolgungsbedingt entzogenes Kulturgut wurde nach den Bestimmungen des Vermögensgesetzes und des NS-Verfolgtenentschädigungsgesetzes zurückgegeben oder entschädigt. Dank der globalen Anmeldung seitens der Conference on Jewish Material Claims against Germany, Inc. (JCC) als der heutigen Vereinigung der Nachfolgeorganisationen sind im Beitrittsgebiet gelegene Ansprüche im Hinblick auf Kulturgüter jüdischer Geschädigter geltend gemacht worden. Wie früher in den alten Bundesländern wurde auch hier soweit wie möglich eine einzelfallbezogene materielle Wiedergutmachung und im übrigen eine Wiedergutmachung durch Globalvergleich angestrebt.

I.

Die Bundesrepublik Deutschland hat – ungeachtet dieser materiellen Wiedergutmachung – auf der Washingtoner Konferenz über Holocaust-Vermögen am 3. Dezember 1998[2] erneut ihre Bereitschaft erklärt, auf der Basis der verabschiedeten Grundsätze und nach Maßgabe ihrer rechtlichen und tatsächlichen Möglichkeiten nach weiterem NS-verfolgungsbedingt entzogenen Kulturgut zu suchen und gegebenenfalls die notwendigen Schritte zu unternehmen, eine gerechte und faire Lösung zu finden. In diesem Sinne wird der Stiftungsratsbeschluss der Stiftung Preußischer Kulturbesitz vom 4. Juni 1999 begrüßt.

Die Bundesregierung, die Länder und die kommunalen Spitzenverbände werden im Sinne der Washingtoner Erklärung in den verantwortlichen Gremien der Träger einschlägiger öffentlicher Einrichtungen darauf hinwirken, dass Kulturgüter, die als NS-verfolgungsbedingt entzogen identifiziert und bestimmten Geschädigten zugeordnet werden können, nach individueller Prüfung den legitimierten früheren Eigentümern bzw. deren Erben zurückgegeben werden. Diese Prüfung schließt den Abgleich mit bereits erfolgten materiellen Wiedergutmachungsleistungen ein. Ein derartiges Verfahren ermöglicht es, die wahren Berechtigten festzustellen und dabei Doppelentschädigungen (z.B. durch Rückzahlungen von geleisteten Entschädigungen) zu vermeiden.

Den jeweiligen Einrichtungen wird empfohlen, mit zweifelsfrei legitimierten früheren Eigentümern bzw. deren Erben über Umfang sowie Art und Weise einer Rückgabe oder anderweitige materielle Wiedergutmachung (z.B. gegebenenfalls in Verbindung mit Dauerleihgaben, finanziellem oder materiellem Wertausgleich) zu verhandeln, soweit diese nicht bereits anderweitig geregelt sind (z.B. durch Rückerstattungsvergleich).

---

[1] Quelle: https://www.kulturgutverluste.de/Webs/DE/Stiftung/Grundlagen/Gemeinsame-Erklaerung/Index.html. Zur Umsetzung dieser Erklärung erließ die BKM eine Handreichung (Neufassung 2019), abrufbar unter: https://www.kulturgutverluste.de/Webs/DE/Recherche/Handreichung/Index.html;jsessionid=958B88171589C6BE9C88F70B8EAD6456.m0.

[2] Siehe dazu die Grundsätze der Washingtoner Konferenz in Bezug auf Kunstwerke, die von den Nationalsozialisten beschlagnahmt wurden, abgedruckt als A.III.5.

II.

Die deutschen öffentlichen Einrichtungen wie Museen, Archive und Bibliotheken haben schon in der Vergangenheit die Suche nach NS-verfolgungsbedingt entzogenem Kulturgut unterstützt:
1. durch Erschließung und Offenlegung ihrer Informationen, Forschungsstände und Unterlagen,
2. durch Nachforschungen bei konkreten Anfragen und eigene Recherchen im Falle von aktuellen Erwerbungen,
3. durch eigene Suche im Rahmen der Wahrnehmung der Aufgaben der jeweiligen Einrichtung,
4. durch Hinweise auf die Geschichte von Kulturgütern aus NS-verfolgungsbedingt entzogenem Besitz in den Sammlungen, Ausstellungen und Publikationen.

Diese Bemühungen sollen – wo immer hinreichend Anlass besteht – fortgeführt werden.

III.

Darüber hinaus prüfen Bundesregierung, Länder und kommunale Spitzenverbände im Sinne der Washingtoner Grundsätze ein Internet-Angebot einzurichten, das folgende Bereiche umfassen sollte:
1. Möglichkeiten der beteiligten Einrichtungen, Kulturgüter ungeklärter Herkunft zu veröffentlichen, sofern NS-verfolgungsbedingter Entzug vermutet wird.
2. Eine Suchliste, in die jeder Berechtigte die von ihm gesuchten Kulturgüter eintragen und damit zur Nachforschung für die in Frage kommenden Einrichtungen und die interessierte Öffentlichkeit ausschreiben kann.
3. Informationen über kriegsbedingte Verbringung NS-verfolgungsbedingt entzogener Kulturgüter in das Ausland.
4. Die Schaffung eines virtuellen Informationsforums, in dem die beteiligten öffentlichen Einrichtungen und auch Dritte ihre Erkenntnisse bei der Suche nach NS-verfolgungs-bedingt entzogenen Kulturgütern eingeben können, um Parallelarbeiten zu gleichen Themen (z.B.: Bei welcher Auktion wurden jüdische Kulturgüter welcher Sammlung versteigert?) auszuschließen und im Wege der Volltextrecherche schnell zugänglich zu machen.

IV.

Diese Erklärung bezieht sich auf die öffentlich unterhaltenen Archive, Museen, Bibliotheken und deren Inventar. Die öffentlichen Träger dieser Einrichtungen werden aufgefordert, durch Beschlussfassung in ihren Gremien für die Umsetzung dieser Grundsätze zu sorgen. Privatrechtlich organisierte Einrichtungen und Privatpersonen werden aufgefordert, sich den niedergelegten Grundsätzen und Verfahrensweisen gleichfalls anzuschließen.

D17.III.2 Kommission NS-verfolgungsbedingt entzogenes Kulturgut

Absprache zwischen Bund, Ländern und kommunalen Spitzenverbänden zur Einsetzung einer Beratenden Kommission im Zusammenhang mit der Rückgabe NS-verfolgungsbedingt entzogenen Kulturguts, insbesondere aus jüdischem Besitz

Beschl. der KMK vom 05. Dezember 2002 i.d.F. vom 08. Dezember 2016

(1) Für den Fall, dass im Zusammenhang mit der Rückgabe NS-verfolgungsbedingt entzogenen Kulturgutes, insbesondere aus jüdischem Besitz, in Einzelfällen der Anspruchsteller und der über das Kulturgut Verfügende eine Mediation wünschen, wird eine unabhängige Beratende Kommission gebildet, die im Bedarfsfall gemeinsam angerufen werden kann. Die Anrufung kann auf Seiten des über das Kulturgut Verfügenden durch öffentliche Einrichtungen erfolgen, für die die Washingtoner Prinzipien von 1998[1] sowie die Gemeinsame Erklärung von Bund, Ländern und kommunalen Spitzenverbänden zu deren Umsetzung von 1999[2] unmittelbar gelten, sowie durch private kulturgutbewahrende Einrichtungen in Deutschland, die sich durch entsprechende Erklärung bei Antragstellung diesen Grundsätzen bindend unterwerfen. Ebenso ist eine Anrufung auf Seiten des über das Kulturgut Verfügenden durch Privatpersonen möglich, die ebenfalls eine solche verbindliche Erklärung abgeben.

(2) Die Kommission soll in jedem Verfahrensstadium auf eine gütliche Einigung hinwirken. Im Ergebnis ihrer Tätigkeit kann die Kommission Empfehlungen aussprechen, die mit ihrer Begründung veröffentlicht werden. Es wird erwartet, dass sowohl öffentliche Einrichtungen wie auch Private diese Empfehlungen befolgen.

(3) Die Kommission besteht aus bis zu zehn geeigneten Persönlichkeiten mit juristischem, ethischem, kulturellem und historischem Sachverstand, die kein herausgehobenes politisches Amt bekleiden. Die Kommissionsmitglieder werden von der Beauftragten der Bundesregierung für Kultur und der Medien im Einvernehmen mit der Kultusministerkonferenz und den kommunalen Spitzenverbänden für eine Zeitdauer von zehn Jahren (bei Neuberufung) berufen. Die Kommissionsmitglieder werden ehrenamtlich tätig.

(4) Die Kommission gibt sich eine Verfahrensordnung, die öffentlich bekanntgemacht wird.

(5) Die Stiftung Deutsches Zentrum Kulturgutverluste unterstützt die Beratende Kommission als Geschäftsstelle für organisatorische Aufgaben. Ein geeigneter Mitarbeiter/eine geeignete Mitarbeiterin nimmt die Aufgaben eines Geschäftsführers/einer Geschäftsführerin wahr.

---

1) Abgedruckt als A.III.5.
2) Abgedruckt als D17.III.1.

Satzung der Stiftung „Deutsches Zentrum Kulturgutverluste"[1)]

§ 1 Name, Rechtsform, Sitz

Die Stiftung führt den Namen "Deutsches Zentrum Kulturgutverluste". Sie ist eine von Bund, Ländern und kommunalen Spitzenverbänden errichtete rechtsfähige Stiftung des bürgerlichen Rechts und hat ihren Sitz in Magdeburg.

§ 2 Stiftungszweck

(1) Zweck der Stiftung ist die Förderung von Kunst und Kultur, Wissenschaft und Forschung im Hinblick auf Kulturgutverluste sowie die damit zusammenhängende Förderung des internationalen Austauschs, der Toleranz und des Völkerverständigungsgedankens. Die Stiftung ist national und international der zentrale Ansprechpartner in Deutschland zu Fragen der Umsetzung der „Grundsätze der Washingtoner Konferenz in Bezug auf Kunstwerke, die von den Nationalsozialisten beschlagnahmt wurden" (Washingtoner Prinzipien)[2)] und der „Erklärung der Bundesregierung, der Länder und der kommunalen Spitzenverbände zur Auffindung und Rückgabe NSverfolgungsbedingt entzogenen Kulturguts, insbesondere aus jüdischem Besitz" (Gemeinsame Erklärung).[3)]

(2) Schwerpunkt der Tätigkeit der Stiftung ist die Beratung und Unterstützung von Kultur- und Wissenschaftseinrichtungen im Bund, den Ländern und den Kommunen insbesondere beim Umgang mit Kulturgütern, die im Zusammenhang mit Verfolgungsmaßnahmen in der Zeit des Nationalsozialismus entzogen oder in Folge des Zweiten Weltkrieges verlagert wurden oder abhandengekommen sind. Die Stiftung setzt sich für gerechte und faire Lösungen in den Fällen NS-verfolgungsbedingt entzogener Kulturgüter ein. In den Fällen kriegsbedingt verlagerter oder abhanden gekommener Kulturgüter berät und unterstützt die Stiftung in Abstimmung mit den jeweils federführenden obersten Bundesbehörden die genannten Einrichtungen bei der Herbeiführung völkerrechtskonformer Lösungen.

(3) Sie führt die Aufgaben der Koordinierungsstelle Magdeburg und der Arbeitsstelle für Provenienzforschung zusammen und baut diese aus. Einzelheiten zur Überführung dieser Aufgaben werden im Finanzierungsabkommen zwischen Bund, Ländern und kommunalen Spitzenverbänden geregelt.

(4) Der Stiftungszweck wird insbesondere unmittelbar und mittelbar verwirklicht durch:

1. die Initiierung, Begleitung, Stärkung und Förderung der Provenienzforschung in öffentlichen Einrichtungen auf Bundes-, Landes- und kommunaler Ebene in Deutschland, vor allem im Rahmen einer antragsgebundenen Projektförderung,
2. die Beratung öffentlicher Einrichtungen in Deutschland zu Fragen der Gestaltung von gerechten und fairen Lösungen unter möglichem Einschluss von Restitutionen und materiellen Ausgleichen,
3. die Weiterleitung und Vermittlung von Anfragen an zuständige Stellen in Bund, Ländern und Kommunen,
4. ein Angebot für privat getragene Einrichtungen und Privatpersonen, um diese bei der eigenen Suche nach NS-Raubkunst und Fragen einer gerechten und fairen Lösung zu unterstützen, wenn sie den Washingtoner Prinzipien und der Gemeinsamen Erklärung folgen und an der Unterstützung im Einzelfall ein öffentliches Interesse besteht,
5. die Unterstützung der nationalen und internationalen Vernetzung bei der Umsetzung des Stiftungszwecks,
6. Kooperationen mit der universitären und außeruniversitären Forschungslandschaft, insbesondere mit einschlägigen Professuren, wie auch den Einsatz für den Auf- und Ausbau entsprechender Forschungsverbünde unter Einbeziehung der betroffenen Einrichtungen,
7. die Zusammenarbeit mit gemeinnützig tätigen Vereinigungen von Provenienzforscherinnen und -forschern in Deutschland, die im Sinne des Stiftungszwecks tätig sind und an deren Unterstützung ein öffentliches Interesse besteht,
8. Maßnahmen der Fort- und Weiterbildung, Tagungen und Veranstaltungen,
9. Presse- und Öffentlichkeitsarbeit, Dokumentationen und wissenschaftliche Publikationen.

(5) Die Stiftung unterhält mehrsprachige, öffentlich zugängliche Datenbanken zu ihren Aufgabengebieten.

---

1) https://www.kulturgutverluste.de/Webs/DE/Stiftung/Grundlagen/Satzung/Index.html.
2) Abgedruckt als A.III.5.
3) Abgedruckt als D17.III.1.

(6) Die Stiftung unterstützt die unabhängige „Beratende Kommission im Zusammenhang mit der Rückgabe NS-verfolgungsbedingt entzogener Kulturgüter, insbesondere aus jüdischem Besitz" durch die Übernahme von organisatorischen Aufgaben. Die Empfehlungen der Kommission können durch die Stiftung für diese veröffentlicht und dokumentiert werden.
(7) Die Stiftung kann im Rahmen einer Geschäftsbesorgung Aufgaben auf dem Gebiet des Kulturgutschutzes mit Zustimmung aller Länder und des Bundes wahrnehmen.
(8) Auf die Förderung durch Stiftungsmittel besteht kein Rechtsanspruch. Die Leistungen der Stiftung richten sich nach Maßgabe der ihr zur Verfügung stehenden Mittel. Die Stifter erhalten keine Zuwendungen aus Mitteln der Körperschaft.

§ 3 Selbstlosigkeit, Ausschließlichkeit und Unmittelbarkeit
(1) Die Stiftung verfolgt ausschließlich, unmittelbar und mittelbar gemeinnützige Zwecke im Sinne des Abschnitts „Steuerbegünstigte Zwecke" der Abgabenordnung (AO).
(2) Die Stiftung ist selbstlos tätig. Sie verfolgt nicht in erster Linie eigenwirtschaftliche Zwecke.
(3) Mittel der Stiftung dürfen nur für die satzungsmäßigen Zwecke verwendet werden. Es darf keine Person durch Ausgaben, die dem Zweck der Stiftung fremd sind, oder durch unverhältnismäßig hohe Vergütungen begünstigt werden.
(4) Die Stiftung erfüllt ihre Aufgaben selbst oder durch eine Hilfsperson im Sinne des § 57 Absatz 1 Satz 2 AO, sofern sie nicht im Wege der Mittelbeschaffung gemäß § 58 Nummer 1 AO tätig wird. Die Stiftung kann zur Verwirklichung des Stiftungszwecks Zweckbetriebe unterhalten.

§ 4 Stiftungsvermögen
(1) Die Stiftung ist mit einem Grundstockvermögen ausgestattet, dessen Höhe im Stiftungsgeschäft näher bestimmt ist.
(2) Zur Erfüllung des Stiftungszwecks erhält die Stiftung eine jährliche Zuwendung nach Maßgabe der gemeinsamen Finanzierungsvereinbarung von Bund, Ländern und kommunalen Spitzenverbänden in der jeweils geltenden Fassung.
(3) Das Stiftungsvermögen kann durch Zustiftungen (Geldbeträge, Rechte und sonstige Gegenstände) der Stifter sowie Dritter erhöht werden. Zuwendungen Dritter dürfen nicht mit Auflagen verbunden sein, die die Erfüllung des Stiftungszwecks beeinträchtigen. Werden Zuwendungen nicht ausdrücklich zum Vermögen gewidmet, so dienen diese ausschließlich und unmittelbar der Erfüllung des Stiftungszwecks.
(4) Zuwendungen Dritter können auch mit der Maßgabe erbracht werden, dass aus diesen Mitteln eine unselbständige Stiftung oder ein Sonderfonds gebildet wird, die im Rahmen der allgemeinen Aufgabenstellung der Stiftung zweckgebunden sind (§ 58 Nummer 3 AO); hierzu bedarf es der Zustimmung des Stiftungsrats.
(5) Das Vermögen der Stiftung ist grundsätzlich in seinem Bestand zu erhalten. Ein Rückgriff auf das Stiftungsvermögen ist nur zulässig, wenn der Stiftungszweck anders nicht zu verwirklichen ist und der Bestand der Stiftung nicht gefährdet erscheint, insbesondere das Stiftungsvermögen in den folgenden Jahren auf seinen vollen Wert wieder aufgefüllt werden kann. Es darf nur veräußert oder belastet werden, wenn von dem Erlös gleichwertiges Vermögen erworben wird. Das Stiftungsvermögen kann zur Werterhaltung beziehungsweise zur Stärkung seiner Ertragskraft umgeschichtet werden.
(6) Die Stiftung ist nicht befugt, Kredite aufzunehmen.

§ 5 Verwendung der Stiftungsmittel
(1) Die Erträge des Stiftungsvermögens und die ihm nicht zuwachsenden Zuwendungen sind zur Erfüllung des Stiftungszwecks zu verwenden.
(2) Die Stiftung kann die zweckgebundenen Mittel, die nicht aus den Zuwendungen nach Artikel 5 des Finanzierungsabkommens in der jeweils gültigen Fassung stammen, ganz oder teilweise einer Rücklage zuführen, soweit dies erforderlich ist, um ihre steuerbegünstigten satzungsmäßigen Zwecke nachhaltig erfüllen zu können, und soweit für die Verwendung der Rücklage konkrete Ziel- und Zeitvorstellungen bestehen.
(3) Freie Rücklagen dürfen gebildet werden, soweit die Vorschriften des steuerlichen Gemeinnützigkeitsrechts dies zulassen. Sie können dem Stiftungsvermögen zugeführt werden.

§ 6 Organe und Gremien der Stiftung

(1) Organe der Stiftung sind:
1. der Stiftungsrat,
2. der Vorstand.

(2) Als beratendes Gremium wird ein Kuratorium gebildet.

(3) Die Mitglieder der Stiftungsorgane und -gremien sind mit Ausnahme des hauptamtlichen Vorstandsmitglieds ehrenamtlich für die Stiftung tätig. Ein Anspruch auf Ersatz der ihnen entstandenen Auslagen und Aufwendungen kann entsprechend der für die unmittelbare Bundesverwaltung geltenden Bestimmungen geltend gemacht werden. Dies gilt nicht für Vertreter oder Vertreterinnen des Bundes, der Länder und der kommunalen Spitzenverbände.

§ 7 Stiftungsrat

(1) Der Stiftungsrat besteht aus 15 Mitgliedern. Ihm gehören an:
1. zwei Vertreter oder Vertreterinnen des oder der Beauftragten der Bundesregierung für Kultur und Medien sowie je ein Vertreter oder eine Vertreterin des Auswärtigen Amtes und des Bundesministeriums der Finanzen,
2. acht durch die Ständige Konferenz der Kultusminister der Länder in der Bundesrepublik Deutschland benannte Vertreter oder Vertreterinnen der Länder, die in einem Dreijahresrhythmus durch Vertreter oder Vertreterinnen anderer Länder ersetzt werden; alle Länder sollen gleichmäßig bei der Entsendung berücksichtigt werden,
3. je ein Vertreter oder eine Vertreterin des Deutschen Städtetages, des Deutschen Städte- und Gemeindebundes und des Deutschen Landkreistages.

Eine Stellvertretung ist möglich. Bei den Mitgliedern nach Absatz 1 Nummer 2 entstammen die Stellvertreter oder Stellvertreterinnen den Ländern, die kein ordentliches Mitglied entsenden; bei der Benennung findet Absatz 1 Nummer 2 entsprechend Anwendung.

(2) Den Vorsitz im Stiftungsrat nimmt ein Vertreter oder eine Vertreterin des oder der Beauftragten der Bundesregierung für Kultur und Medien, die Stellvertretung im Stiftungsratsvorsitz ein Vertreter oder eine Vertreterin der Länder wahr.

(3) Der oder die Vorsitzende des Kuratoriums nimmt beratend an den Sitzungen des Stiftungsrats teil. Gleiches gilt für einen Vertreter oder eine Vertreterin des Sitzlandes, soweit dieses nicht mit Stimmrecht im Stiftungsrat vertreten ist.

(4) Die Amtszeit der Mitglieder des Stiftungsrats beginnt mit der konstituierenden Sitzung des Stiftungsrates. Solange von einem Entsendungsrecht kein Gebrauch gemacht wird, bleibt dieser Stiftungsratssitz unbesetzt.

(5) Jedes Mitglied kann sein Amt durch schriftliche Erklärung gegenüber dem oder der Vorsitzenden des Stiftungsrats niederlegen. Ein Mitglied, das als Inhaber eines öffentlichen Amtes oder einer Funktion entsandt ist, scheidet mit Beendigung dieses Amtes oder der Funktion aus dem Stiftungsrat aus. Scheidet ein Stiftungsratsmitglied vor Ablauf der Amtszeit aus, ist unverzüglich ein neues Mitglied für den Rest der Amtsperiode zu entsenden.

§ 8 Aufgaben des Stiftungsrats

(1) Dem Stiftungsrat obliegt die Entscheidung in allen Angelegenheiten, die für die Stiftung und ihre Entwicklung von grundsätzlicher oder besonderer Bedeutung sind. Er beaufsichtigt die Stiftung unter den Gesichtspunkten der Rechtmäßigkeit, Zweckmäßigkeit und Wirtschaftlichkeit. Seine Aufgaben sind insbesondere:
1. die Beschlussfassung über den Wirtschaftsplan (einschließlich Stellenplan),
2. die Festlegung von Leitlinien und Förderrichtlinien für die Arbeit der Stiftung,
3. die Bestimmung der Schwerpunkte der Stiftungsarbeit,
4. die Berufung und Abberufung des Vorstandes und des Kuratoriums,
5. die Einrichtung und Berufung von Fachbeiräten,
6. die Kontrolle der gewissenhaften und sparsamen Verwaltung des Stiftungsvermögens und der sonstigen Mittel,
7. die Entgegennahme der Jahresrechnung, die Auswahl eines Rechnungsprüfers oder einer Rechnungsprüferin und die Entlastung des Vorstands,
8. die Billigung des Jahresberichts über die Tätigkeit der Stiftung,

9. Personalentscheidungen, soweit sie nicht dem Vorstand vorbehalten sind. Näheres regelt die Geschäftsordnung,
10. der Beschluss über die Annahme von Schenkungen, Erbschaften, Zustiftungen sowie den Erwerb und die Veräußerung von Vermögensgegenständen von erheblicher Bedeutung,
11. der Abschluss von Rechtsgeschäften, die aufgrund des Vertragsgegenstandes, der Vertragsdauer oder anderer Umstände von erheblicher Bedeutung sind.

(2) Der Stiftungsrat gibt dem Vorstand mit einer Mehrheit von mindestens 12 Stimmen der Mitglieder eine Geschäftsordnung. Er kann dem Vorstand Weisungen erteilen und überwacht die Geschäftsführung der Stiftung. Er kann vom Vorstand jederzeit Auskunft und Bericht sowie die Vorlage der Akten und Bücher verlangen.

§ 9 Beschlussfassung des Stiftungsrats

(1) Die Mitglieder nach § 7 Absatz 1 Nummer 1 führen jeweils zwei Stimmen, die Mitglieder gemäß § 7 Absatz 1 Nummer 2 und 3 jeweils eine Stimme. Beschlüsse werden, soweit nicht die Satzung eine andere Regelung vorsieht, mit einer Mehrheit von mindestens 12 Stimmen der Mitglieder gefasst. Bei Stimmengleichheit gibt die Stimmabgabe des oder der Vorsitzenden den Ausschlag. Entscheidungen über Haushalts-, Finanz- und Personalangelegenheiten bedürfen der Zustimmung aller Vertreter oder Vertreterinnen gemäß § 7 Absatz 1 Nummer 1. Dies gilt auch für Entscheidungen über sonstige Angelegenheiten, wenn diese erhebliche finanzielle Auswirkungen haben können. Entscheidungen über Personalangelegenheiten bedürfen zusätzlich der Zustimmung aller Vertreter und Vertreterinnen nach § 7 Absatz 1 Nummer 2. Sofern dauerhafte finanzielle Beiträge aller Länder erbracht werden, bedürfen Entscheidungen über Haushalts- und Finanzangelegenheiten ebenfalls zusätzlich der Zustimmung aller Vertreter und Vertreterinnen nach § 7 Absatz 1 Nummer 2.
(2) Der Stiftungsrat entscheidet in der Regel in Sitzungen, die der Vorstand im Auftrag des oder der Vorsitzenden nach Bedarf, jedoch in der Regel zweimal im Jahr, einberuft. Auf Antrag von mindestens einem Drittel der Mitglieder muss eine Sitzung einberufen werden.
(3) Die Einladung zur Stiftungsratssitzung erfolgt schriftlich oder in Textform unter Angabe der Tagesordnung, wobei zwischen dem Tag der Absendung der Ladung und dem Tag der Sitzung – beide nicht mitgezählt – 14 Tage liegen müssen. Auf Form und Frist zur Ladung kann durch Beschluss von mindestens 12 Stimmen der Mitglieder des Stiftungsrats verzichtet werden. Der Stiftungsrat ist beschlussfähig, wenn zu der Sitzung ordnungsgemäß eingeladen wurde, die anwesenden Mitglieder mindestens 12 Stimmen führen und mindestens sechs Vertreter oder Vertreterinnen der Länder anwesend sind.
(4) An den Sitzungen des Stiftungsrats nehmen die Vorstandsmitglieder mit Rederecht teil, soweit der Stiftungsrat im Einzelfall nichts anderes beschließt. Der Vorstand ist berechtigt, Anträge zu stellen. Der Stiftungsrat kann Gäste zu seinen Sitzungen einladen. Die Sitzung leitet der oder die Stiftungsratsvorsitzende, im Verhinderungsfalle sein oder ihr Stellvertreter oder seine oder ihre Stellvertreterin.
(5) Eine Beschlussfassung im schriftlichen oder in Textform gestalteten Umlaufverfahren ist zulässig, wenn alle Mitglieder des Stiftungsrats diesem Verfahren schriftlich oder in Textform zustimmen.
(6) Weitere Regelungen über den Geschäftsgang des Stiftungsrats kann eine Geschäftsordnung treffen, die vom Stiftungsrat mit einer Mehrheit von 12 Stimmen der Mitglieder erlassen wird.
(7) Über die Sitzungen des Stiftungsrats ist eine Niederschrift anzufertigen. Beschlüsse sind im Wortlaut festzuhalten. Über im Umlaufverfahren gefasste Beschlüsse ist in der jeweils nächsten Sitzung zu informieren und die Beschlüsse sind in die Niederschrift aufzunehmen. Die Stiftungsratsmitglieder und ihre Stellvertreter oder Stellvertreterinnen sowie der oder die Vorsitzende des Kuratoriums erhalten Abschriften der Sitzungsniederschriften.

§ 10 Vorstand

(1) Der Vorstand besteht aus bis zu zwei Mitgliedern. Ein Vorstandsmitglied nimmt sein Amt hauptamtlich wahr. Wird ein zweites Vorstandsmitglied berufen, kann dieses nur ehrenamtlich tätig sein. Das ehrenamtliche Vorstandsmitglied kann nach Maßgabe eines Beschlusses des Stiftungsrats eine angemessene Aufwandsentschädigung für entstandene Aufwendungen erhalten. Der Vorstand wird vom Stiftungsrat mit einer Mehrheit von 16 Stimmen für die Dauer von fünf Jahren berufen und von dem oder der Stiftungsratsvorsitzenden bestellt. Die Mitglieder des Vorstands können nicht gleichzeitig Mitglieder des Stiftungsrats oder des Kuratoriums sein. Die Wiederbestellung ist zulässig.

Im Falle des vorzeitigen Ausscheidens von Mitgliedern des Vorstands sind die Nachfolger nur für die restliche Amtszeit zu bestellen. Die Mitglieder des Vorstands führen ihr Amt bis zum Amtsantritt ihrer Nachfolger weiter. Im Falle der vorzeitigen Abberufung durch den Stiftungsrat hat das Mitglied des Vorstands das Amt mit sofortiger Wirkung niederzulegen. Bis zum Amtsantritt des Nachfolgers kann das Amt kommissarisch von einem oder einer Bediensteten der Stiftung nach Benennung durch den Stiftungsrat weitergeführt werden.

(2) Die Geschäftsverteilung innerhalb des Vorstands sowie die Vertretung der Vorstandsmitglieder regelt der Stiftungsrat in einer Geschäftsordnung. Das hauptamtliche Vorstandsmitglied führt die laufenden Geschäfte der Stiftung unbeschadet der Rechte der anderen Organe. In Zweifelsfragen entscheidet der oder die Vorsitzende des Stiftungsrats. Das hauptamtliche Vorstandsmitglied vertritt die Stiftung gerichtlich und außergerichtlich.

(3) Die Stiftung wird gegenüber dem Vorstand durch den Vorsitzenden oder die Vorsitzende des Stiftungsrats vertreten.

(4) Der Stiftungsrat kann ein Mitglied des Vorstands aus wichtigem Grund abberufen. Hierzu bedarf es eines Beschlusses mit einer Mehrheit von 16 Stimmen im Stiftungsrat.

(5) Der Vorstand beruft die Sitzungen der Stiftungsgremien im Einvernehmen mit dem oder der jeweiligen Vorsitzenden ein, bereitet diese vor, nimmt an ihnen ohne Stimmrecht teil und führt ihre Beschlüsse aus.

(6) Der Vorstand stellt die Entwürfe des Wirtschaftsplans sowie der mittelfristigen Finanzplanung auf und erstellt die Jahresrechnung und den Jahresbericht.

§ 11 Kuratorium

(1) Das Kuratorium besteht aus mindestens neun, höchstens elf anerkannten Persönlichkeiten, insbesondere auch aus dem Ausland. Sie werden vom Stiftungsrat berufen.

(2) Die Mitglieder des Kuratoriums werden auf die Dauer von fünf Jahren bestellt. Die Wiederbestellung ist zulässig. § 7 Absatz 4 Satz 1 und Absatz 5 gelten entsprechend. Mitglieder des Kuratoriums können aus wichtigem Grund vom Stiftungsrat abberufen werden.

(3) Das Kuratorium wählt für die Dauer der Amtszeit aus seiner Mitte jeweils eine Person zum oder zur Vorsitzenden und zum oder zur stellvertretenden Vorsitzenden. Die Wiederwahl ist zulässig.

(4) Das Nähere wird in einer vom Stiftungsrat zu beschließenden Geschäftsordnung festgelegt.

§ 12 Rechte und Pflichten des Kuratoriums

(1) Das Kuratorium berät und unterstützt den Stiftungsrat und den Vorstand bei ihrer Tätigkeit. Es erörtert die inhaltlichen Schwerpunkte der Stiftungstätigkeit und gibt hierzu Empfehlungen ab.

(2) Das Kuratorium trifft mindestens einmal im Jahr zu einer ordentlichen Sitzung zusammen. Eine außerordentliche Sitzung ist einzuberufen, wenn mindestens ein Drittel der Mitglieder oder der Stiftungsrat dies verlangen. Die Stiftungsratsmitglieder können, der Vorstand soll an den Sitzungen des Kuratoriums beratend teilnehmen.

(3) Für die Einberufung des Kuratoriums gelten § 9 Absatz 3 Satz 1 sowie Absatz 4 entsprechend. Das Kuratorium ist beschlussfähig, wenn zu der Sitzung ordnungsgemäß eingeladen wurde und mindestens die Hälfte der Mitglieder anwesend ist.

§ 13 Zusammenwirken mit anderen kulturellen und wissenschaftlichen Einrichtungen

Die Stiftung erfüllt ihre Aufgaben in engem Zusammenwirken mit anderen kulturellen und wissenschaftlichen Einrichtungen im In- und Ausland.

§ 14 Haushalt, Rechnungsprüfung

(1) Für die Aufstellung und Ausführung des Wirtschaftsplans gelten die Bestimmungen der Bundeshaushaltsordnung (BHO) und der Tarifvertrag für den öffentlichen Dienst, Bereich Bund, entsprechend.

(2) Das Geschäftsjahr der Stiftung ist das Kalenderjahr. Innerhalb der ersten fünf Monate eines jeden Jahres hat der Vorstand eine Jahresrechnung für das abgelaufene Kalenderjahr aufzustellen. Die Rechnung kann jährlich durch einen Wirtschaftsprüfer, eine Wirtschaftsprüferin oder eine Wirtschaftsprüfungsgesellschaft geprüft werden, die vom Stiftungsrat bestellt werden. Sie haben nach Vorgaben zu prüfen, die vom Stiftungsrat im Einvernehmen mit dem Bundesrechnungshof zu erlassen sind.

(3) Die Haushalts- und Wirtschaftsführung der Stiftung unterliegt der Prüfung durch den Bundesrechnungshof gemäß § 104 Absatz 1 Nummer 4 BHO. Die Rechnungshöfe der Länder sind ebenfalls zu dieser Prüfung berechtigt, sofern die Länder Anteile finanzieller Art oder nach Artikel 5 Absatz 4 der gemeinsamen Finanzierungsvereinbarung von Bund, Ländern und kommunalen Spitzenverbänden erbracht haben.

§ 15 Satzungsänderung
(1) Der Stiftungsrat kann Änderungen der Satzung beschließen, wenn sie den Stiftungszweck nicht berühren und die ursprüngliche Gestaltung der Stiftung nicht wesentlich verändern oder die Erfüllung des Stiftungszwecks erleichtern.
(2) Beschlüsse über Änderungen nach Absatz 1 bedürfen der Zustimmung aller Vertreter und Vertreterinnen des Bundes und der Länder. Eine Beschlussfassung im Umlaufverfahren ist nicht möglich.
(3) Beschlüsse über Änderungen der Satzung bedürfen der Genehmigung der Stiftungsbehörde. Sie sind mit einer Stellungnahme der zuständigen Finanzbehörde anzuzeigen.

§ 16 Zweckerweiterung, Zweckänderung, Zusammenlegung, Auflösung
(1) Der Stiftungsrat kann der Stiftung einen weiteren Zweck geben, wenn das Vermögen oder die Erträge der Stiftung nur teilweise für die Verwirklichung des Stiftungszwecks benötigt werden, der neue Zweck mit dem ursprünglichen Zweck verwandt ist und dessen dauernde und nachhaltige Verwirklichung ohne Gefährdung des ursprünglichen Zwecks gewährleistet erscheint.
(2) Der Stiftungsrat kann die Änderung des Stiftungszwecks, die Zusammenlegung mit einer anderen Stiftung oder die Auflösung der Stiftung beschließen, wenn der Stiftungszweck unmöglich wird oder sich die Verhältnisse seit Errichtung der Stiftung derart geändert haben, dass die dauernde und nachhaltige Erfüllung des Stiftungszwecks nicht mehr sinnvoll erscheint. Die Beschlüsse dürfen die Steuerbegünstigung der Stiftung nicht beeinträchtigen.
(3) Beschlüsse nach Absatz 1 und 2 bedürfen der Zustimmung aller Vertreter oder Vertreterinnen des Bundes und der Länder. Eine Beschlussfassung im Umlaufverfahren ist nicht möglich.
(4) Beschlüsse über Zweckerweiterung, Zweckänderung, Zusammenlegung oder Auflösung werden erst nach Genehmigung der Stiftungsbehörde wirksam. Sie sind mit einer Stellungnahme der zuständigen Finanzbehörde anzuzeigen.

§ 17 Stiftungsbehörde
(1) Die Stiftung unterliegt der staatlichen Aufsicht nach Maßgabe des jeweils im Land Sachsen-Anhalt geltenden Stiftungsrechts.
(2) Der Stiftungsbehörde sind Änderungen in der Zusammensetzung der Stiftungsorgane sowie Haushaltsplan, Jahresrechnung und Tätigkeitsbericht unaufgefordert vorzulegen.

§ 18 Anfallberechtigung
Im Falle der Auflösung oder Aufhebung der Stiftung oder bei Wegfall des gemeinnützigen Zwecks fällt deren Vermögen je zur Hälfte an die Kulturstiftung des Bundes und die Kulturstiftung der Länder mit der Auflage, es unmittelbar und ausschließlich zugunsten selbstloser gemeinnütziger kultureller Zwecke zu verwenden, die dem bisherigen Stiftungszweck möglichst nahe kommen.

§ 19 Inkrafttreten
Die Satzung tritt mit Bekanntgabe der Anerkennungsurkunde in Kraft.

Abkommen zur Errichtung der Kulturstiftung der Länder[1)]

Vom 4. Juni 1987, i.d.F. v. 25.10.1991

Die Länder Baden-Württemberg, Bayern, Berlin, Bremen, Hamburg, Hessen, Niedersachsen, Nordrhein-Westfalen, Rheinland-Pfalz, Saarland und Schleswig-Holstein errichten zur Förderung und Bewahrung von Kunst und Kultur nationalen Ranges mit Wirkung vom 1. Januar 1988 die „Kulturstiftung der Länder".

Die vertragschließenden Länder verpflichten sich zur Beteiligung an der Kulturstiftung der Länder nach Maßgabe der in Abschnitt II vereinbarten Satzung. Die Länder Brandenburg, Mecklenburg-Vorpommern, Sachsen, Sachsen-Anhalt und Thüringen sind bis zum 31. Dezember 1994 von der Zahlung von Mitteln für die Stiftung befreit. Die übrigen Länder entrichten nach Maßgabe der jeweils geltenden Haushaltsgesetze an die Kulturstiftung der Länder die Mittel der gemeinsamen Finanzierungen (vgl. Teil II der Liste der Vorhaben gem. § 2 Abs. 2 Nr. 4 der Stiftungssatzung) und jährlich mindestens 10 Millionen DM für die Durchführung laufender Aufgaben. Die Anteile der einzelnen Länder werden nach dem Königsteiner Schlüssel ermittelt. Die Länder können auch das Stiftungsvermögen durch Zustiftungen aufstocken. Für die Zeit ab 1. Januar 1995 sind die Mittel und die jeweiligen Anteile der Länder neu festzulegen; die Zahlungsverpflichtung der an der Errichtung der Stiftung beteiligten Länder von insgesamt mindestens 10 Millionen DM bleibt erhalten.

Das Abkommen kann von jedem Land durch schriftliche Erklärung gegenüber den übrigen Ländern zum Schluß eines Kalenderjahres mit einer Frist von 2 Jahren gekündigt werden, erstmals zum 31. Dezember 1997. Zum Zeitpunkt der Aufhebung der Stiftung bestehende vertragliche Verpflichtungen zur Versorgung von Mitgliedern des Vorstandes der Stiftung werden von den Ländern nach dem Königsteiner Schlüssel getragen.

Die Bundesrepublik Deutschland (Bund) kann nach Maßgabe eines mit den Ländern zu schließenden Abkommens an der Stiftung mitwirken.

Die Zuwendungen der Länder werden über den Haushalt des Sekretariats der Ständigen Konferenz der Kultusminister der Länder zur Verfügung gestellt.

---

1) Quelle: http://www.kulturstiftung.de/errichtungsabkommen/.

Abkommen über die Mitwirkung des Bundes an der Kulturstiftung der Länder

Vom 4. Juni 1987, i.d.F. v. 25.11.1993 (GMBl. 1992, 99)[1)]

Die Bundesrepublik Deutschland (Bund) und die Länder Baden-Württemberg, Bayern, Berlin, Bremen, Hamburg, Hessen, Niedersachsen, Nordrhein-Westfalen, Rheinland-Pfalz, Saarland, Schleswig-Holstein (Länder) schließen folgendes Abkommen:

§ 1

(1) Der Kulturstiftung der Länder obliegt die Förderung von überregional und international bedeutsamen Kunst- und Kulturvorhaben als eigene Aufgabe. In die Förderung werden folgende Vorhaben einbezogen:

I.
1. Musikförderung
   a) Projekte des Deutschen Musikrates e.V.
      Musikförderungsprogramm:
      Laienmusizieren (Deutsche Chor- und Laienorchesterwettbewerbe)
      Zeitgenössische Musik
      Deutscher Musikwettbewerb (hinsichtlich der Stipendien vgl. II.)
      Musik-Almanach
   b) Bundesweite Veranstaltungen und sonstige Projekte zentraler Einrichtungen und Verbände auf dem Gebiet der Musik
   c) Arbeitsgemeinschaft der Volksmusikverbände
   d) Arbeitsgemeinschaft Deutscher Chorverbände
2. Förderung der bildenden Kunst und der Museen
   a) Kunstfonds e.V., Bonn
   b) Kunst- und Kulturausstellungen
   c) Bundesverband Bildender Künstler
   d) Deutscher Werkbund
   e) Deutscher Museumsbund
3. Förderung der Literatur und des Theaters
   a) Literaturfonds e.V., Darmstadt
   b) Kulturwerk Deutscher Schriftsteller, Freier Deutscher Autorenverband und sonstige Literaturverbände und -einrichtungen
   c) Bund Deutscher Amateurtheater (Geschäftsstelle und Projekte)
   d) Internationales Theatertreffen
   e) Arbeitsgemeinschaft Literarischer Gesellschaften
   f) [entfällt]
4. Filmförderung
   a) Filmfestspiele Mannheim
   b) Filmfestspiele Oberhausen
5. Denkmalschutz
   a) Deutsche Burgenvereinigung
   b) Arbeitsgemeinschaft Friedhof und Denkmal
6. Internationale Veranstaltungen und Projekte von bundesweiter Bedeutung im Inland in den Bereichen Kunst und Kultur
7. Fonds Soziokultur e.V., Hagen
8. Fonds Darstellende Künste e.V., Essen

---

1) Die Länder Brandenburg, Mecklenburg-Vorpommern, Sachsen, Sachsen-Anhalt und Thüringen traten bei durch Abkommen vom 25. Oktober 1991/26. Februar 1992 (GMBl. S. 99).

II.
1. Zentrum Bundesrepublik Deutschland des Internationalen Theaterinstituts e.V. (Geschäftsstelle und Projekte)
2. Sektion Bundesrepublik Deutschland der Internationalen Gesellschaft der Bildenden Künste e.V. (Geschäftsstelle und Projekte)
3. Deutsche Akademie für Sprache und Dichtung
4. Stipendien für den Deutschen Musikwettbewerb

(2) Die vorstehende Liste der Vorhaben kann durch einen Beschluß des Stiftungsrates der Kulturstiftung der Länder in seiner erweiterten Zusammensetzung geändert und ergänzt werden.

§ 2
(1) Zur Erfüllung der in § 1 genannten Aufgaben stellt der Bund Mittel nach Maßgabe des jeweils geltenden Haushaltsgesetzes des Bundes zur Verfügung.
(2) Der Bund kann der Stiftung weitere Mittel zuwenden.

§ 3
(1) Die Mitwirkung des Bundes im einzelnen ergibt sich aus dem Abkommen zur Errichtung der Kulturstiftung der Länder vom 4. Juni 1987. Bei der Entscheidung über die Aufstellung des Wirtschaftsplanes wird der Bund – unabhängig von der Einheit des Wirtschaftsplanes – nicht in die alleinige Zuständigkeit der Länder einwirken.
(2) Die Länder wirken durch die Kulturstiftung der Länder in den Gremien des „Haus der Geschichte der Bundesrepublik Deutschland" sowie der „Kunst- und Ausstellungshalle" in der Bundeshauptstadt mit, sofern ihre Mitwirkung nicht in anderer Form geregelt ist.

§ 4
Mitglieder im Stiftungsrat der Kulturstiftung der Länder in erweiterter Zusammensetzung sind drei Mitglieder der Bundesregierung. Vertretung ist zulässig.

§ 5
(1) Das Abkommen kann vom Bund und jedem Land durch eine schriftliche Erklärung gegenüber den übrigen Parteien des Abkommens zum Schluß eines Kalenderjahres mit einer Frist von zwei Jahren gekündigt werden, erstmals zum 31. Dezember 1997.
(2) Das Abkommen ist aufgehoben, wenn der Bund oder mindestens sechs Länder gekündigt haben, und zwar zu dem Zeitpunkt, zu dem die letzte Kündigung wirksam wird.
(3) Das Abkommen ist ebenfalls aufgehoben, wenn die „Kulturstiftung der Länder" aufgehoben ist.

§ 6
Das Abkommen tritt mit Wirkung vom 1. Januar 1988 in Kraft.

Satzung der Kulturstiftung der Länder

Vom 4. Juni 1987, genehmigt am 17. November 1987; zuletzt geändert am 22. Juni 2016 durch Beschluss des Stiftungsrates – insbesondere Spezifizierung des Stiftungszwecks in § 2 Abs. 2, genehmigt am 19. April 2017.[1]

Die Stiftung erhält folgende Satzung:

§ 1 Name, Sitz, Rechtsform
(1) Die Stiftung führt die Bezeichnung „Kulturstiftung der Länder".
(2) Sie ist eine rechtsfähige Stiftung des bürgerlichen Rechts und hat ihren Sitz in Berlin.

§ 2 Stiftungszweck
(1) Zweck der Stiftung ist die Förderung und Bewahrung von Kunst und Kultur nationalen Ranges.
(2) Der Stiftungszweck wird insbesondere verwirklicht durch
1. die Förderung des Erwerbs für die deutsche Kultur besonders wichtiger und bewahrungswürdiger Kulturgüter, vor allem wenn deren Abwanderung ins Ausland verhindert werden soll oder wenn sie aus dem Ausland zurückerworben werden sollen, z. B. durch finanzielle und/oder ideelle Unterstützung gemeinnütziger und öffentlich zugänglicher kultureller Einrichtungen;
2. die Förderung von und die Mitwirkung bei Vorhaben der Dokumentation und Präsentation deutscher Kunst und Kultur, z. B. durch die Unterstützung von Ausstellungsvorhaben, Restaurierungsprojekten, die Herausgabe von Publikationen eigener Förderungen; es werden nur Projekte bzw. kulturelle Einrichtungen unterstützt, die entweder auch gemeinnützig oder Körperschaften des öffentlichen Rechts sind (§ 58 Nr. 2 AO);
3. die Förderung zeitgenössischer Formen und Entwicklungen von besonderer Bedeutung auf dem Gebiet von Kunst und Kultur, z. B. durch die Unterstützung von Preisvergaben;
4. die Förderung von überregional und international bedeutsamen Kunst- und Kulturvorhaben, z. B. durch die Unterstützung von den Ländern ausgewählter kultureller Einrichtungen; es werden nur Projekte bzw. kulturelle Einrichtungen unterstützt, die entweder auch gemeinnützig oder Körperschaften des öffentlichen Rechts sind (§ 58 Nr. 2 AO).

(3) Die Kulturstiftung verfolgt ausschließlich und unmittelbar gemeinnützige Zwecke im Sinne des Abschnitts „Steuerbegünstigte Zwecke" der Abgabenordnung. Sie ist selbstlos tätig und verfolgt nicht in erster Linie eigenwirtschaftliche Zwecke.

§ 3 Regionale Ausgewogenheit
Bei der Förderung von Kunst und Kultur durch die Stiftung soll eine regionale Ausgewogenheit angestrebt werden; dies gilt nicht für die Verwirklichung des Stiftungszwecks nach § 2 Abs. (2) Nr. 2.

§ 4 Mittel der Stiftung
(1) Das Stiftungsvermögen besteht nach dem Stande vom 1. Oktober 1991 aus Wertpapieren und Barmitteln im Gesamtwert von rd. 500.000 DM sowie aus der Geschäftsausstattung. Zusätzlich zum Stiftungsvermögen kann ein Sondervermögen gebildet werden, das ausschließlich für die Vergabe von Darlehen zur Erfüllung satzungsgemäßer Aufgaben genutzt werden darf. Über die Bildung und die Auflösung dieses Sondervermögens entscheidet der Stiftungsrat.
(2) Die Stiftung erhält zur Erfüllung ihrer Aufgaben Mittel der Länder nach Maßgabe des Abkommens zur Errichtung der Kulturstiftung der Länder in der jeweils geltenden Fassung.
(3) Die Stiftung kann Zuwendungen des Bundes erhalten.
(4) Die Stiftung soll sich um einmalige und laufende Zuwendungen Dritter bemühen.
(5) Die Stiftung kann durch einen Förderverein unterstützt werden.
(6) Zur Erfüllung des Stiftungszweckes dürfen nur die Erträge des Stiftungsvermögens sowie die jährlichen Mittel der Länder und Spenden Dritter herangezogen werden, soweit die Mittel nicht als Zustiftungen zur Vermehrung des Stiftungsvermögens bestimmt sind.
(7) Die Mittel der Stiftung dürfen nur für satzungsgemäße Zwecke verwendet werden. Es darf keine Person durch Ausgaben, die dem Stiftungszweck fremd sind, oder durch unverhältnismäßig hohe Vergütungen begünstigt werden.

---
1) Quelle: https://www.kulturstiftung.de/satzung/.

(8) Den durch die Stiftung Begünstigten steht aufgrund dieser Satzung ein Rechtsanspruch auf Leistungen nicht zu.

§ 5 Stiftungsorgane
Organe der Kulturstiftung sind
1. der Stiftungsrat,
2. der Vorstand,
3. das Kuratorium.

§ 6 Stiftungsrat
(1) Der Stiftungsrat besteht aus jeweils einem Mitglied der Landesregierungen der an der Stiftung beteiligten Länder sowie ein bis zwei Mitgliedern der Bundesregierung. Diese kann auch Staatssekretäre/Staatssekretärinnen als Mitglieder bestellen. Vertretung ist zulässig.
(2) An den Sitzungen des Stiftungsrates können die Mitglieder des Vorstandes sowie die oder der Kuratoriumsvorsitzende und deren oder dessen Stellvertreterin oder Stellvertreter beratend teilnehmen.
(3) Den Vorsitz des Stiftungsrates hat die Regierungschefin oder der Regierungschef des Landes inne, das den Vorsitz in der Ministerpräsidentenkonferenz führt; sie oder er kann sich durch ein anderes Mitglied der Landesregierung vertreten lassen. Die Stellvertretung hat das von der Landesregierung des Landes bestellte Mitglied, das den Vorsitz in der Ministerpräsidentenkonferenz in dem vergangenen Jahr geführt hat. Sofern diese Länder nicht an der Stiftung beteiligt sind, verlängert sich die Amtszeit der oder des bisherigen Vorsitzenden und der oder des stellvertretenden Vorsitzenden des Stiftungsrates um den entsprechenden Zeitraum.
(4) Die Mitglieder des Stiftungsrates werden von den jeweiligen Regierungen bestellt.
(5) Der Stiftungsrat berät und entscheidet über alle Fragen, die zum Aufgabenbereich der Stiftung gehören, soweit es sich nicht um die Führung der laufenden Geschäfte handelt.
(6) Der Stiftungsrat entscheidet über die Aufstellung des Wirtschaftsplanes.
(7) Der Stiftungsrat erlässt eine Geschäftsordnung für die Stiftung.

§ 7 Beschlußfassung des Stiftungsrates
(1) Der Stiftungsrat entscheidet einstimmig. Jedes Mitglied des Stiftungsrates mit Stimmrecht hat eine Stimme.
(2) Beschlüsse gemäß §§ 2 Abs. 2 Nr. 1 bis 3, 12 und über Änderungen dieser Satzung bedürfen nur der Stimmen der Mitglieder der Länder.
(3) Beschlüsse können auch außerhalb von Sitzungen gefasst werden, wenn sich alle stimmberechtigten Mitglieder daran schriftlich beteiligen. Die Beschlussfassung erfolgt einstimmig. Bei mehr als drei Stimmenthaltungen kommt kein Beschluss zustande.

§ 8 Vorstand
(1) Der Stiftungsrat bestellt den Vorstand. Dieser besteht aus zwei Personen: der Generalsekretärin oder dem Generalsekretär und deren oder dessen Stellvertreterin oder Stellvertreter.
(2) Die Generalsekretärin oder der Generalsekretär führt die laufenden Geschäfte der Stiftung, bereitet die Beschlüsse des Stiftungsrates vor und führt sie aus.
(3) Jedes Mitglied des Vorstandes vertritt die Stiftung gerichtlich und außergerichtlich allein. Im Innenverhältnis ist das stellvertretende Mitglied gehalten, nur im Falle der Verhinderung der Generalsekretärin oder des Generalsekretärs tätig zu werden.
(4) Die Mitglieder des Vorstandes können eine angemessene Vergütung erhalten, die vom Stiftungsrat festgelegt wird. Sie haben darüber hinaus Anspruch auf Ersatz der aus dienstlicher Veranlassung entstandenen notwendigen Ausgaben.

§ 9 Kuratorium
(1) Das Kuratorium besteht aus bis zu 15 Förderern und bis zu 15 Sachverständigen.
(2) Die Mitglieder des Kuratoriums werden vom Stiftungsrat auf 5 Jahre berufen; Wiederberufung ist zulässig. Die Mitglieder des Kuratoriums können aus wichtigem Grunde abberufen werden.
(3) Das Kuratorium kann zur Erfüllung einzelner Aufgaben auch Nichtmitglieder beratend hinzuziehen.
(4) Das Kuratorium wählt die Vorsitzende oder den Vorsitzenden und eine Stellvertreterin oder einen Stellvertreter.

(5) Das Kuratorium fasst seine Beschlüsse mit der Mehrheit der abgegebenen Stimmen. Es ist beschlussfähig, wenn die Hälfte der Mitglieder anwesend ist.
(6) Die Mitglieder des Kuratoriums werden ehrenamtlich tätig.

§ 10 Aufgaben des Kuratoriums
(1) Das Kuratorium berät den Stiftungsrat bei der Erfüllung seiner Aufgaben, insbesondere bei der Festlegung von Förderungsschwerpunkten für die Arbeit der Stiftung.
(2) Die Mitglieder des Stiftungsrates sind berechtigt, an den Sitzungen des Kuratoriums ohne Stimmrecht teilzunehmen.

§ 11 Ausgleich der Zuwendungen
Soweit Mittel der Stiftung für den Erwerb besonders wichtiger und bewahrungswürdiger Zeugnisse deutscher Kultur aufgewendet werden, ist ein angemessener Ausgleich zwischen den Ländern durch den Einsatz von Erwerbungsmitteln anzustreben.

§ 12 Aufhebung der Stiftung
(1) Die Kulturstiftung soll vom Stiftungsrat aufgehoben werden, wenn mindestens sechs Länder das Abkommen über die Errichtung der Kulturstiftung gekündigt haben, die Kündigung des sechsten Landes wirksam geworden ist und die verbleibenden Mittel die weitere nachhaltige Erfüllung des Stiftungszwecks nicht mehr sicherstellen.
(2) Bei Aufhebung der Stiftung oder bei Wegfall steuerbegünstigter Zwecke fällt das Vermögen an die Länder Baden-Württemberg, Bayern, Berlin, Bremen, Hamburg, Hessen, Niedersachsen, Nordrhein-Westfalen, Rheinland-Pfalz, Saarland und Schleswig-Holstein in dem Verhältnis, in dem sie zu seiner Bildung beigetragen haben. Sie haben es ausschließlich und unmittelbar für ähnliche gemeinnützige Zwecke im Sinne dieser Satzung zu verwenden.

§ 13 Rechnungslegung und Prüfung
(1) Der Rechnungshof des Landes Berlin prüft die Haushalts- und Wirtschaftsführung der Stiftung.
(2) Die Generalsekretärin oder der Generalsekretär hat unbeschadet der Prüfung nach Abs. (1) die zum Ende eines jeden Geschäftsjahres (Kalenderjahres) zu fertigenden Aufstellungen über die Einnahmen und Ausgaben der Stiftung und über ihr Vermögen durch einen öffentlich bestellten Wirtschaftsprüfer oder eine anerkannte Wirtschaftsprüfungsgesellschaft prüfen zu lassen.

§ 14 Ruhen des Stimmrechts und des Vorsitzes im Stiftungsrat
(1) Solange ein Land mit Ausnahme der Mittel der gemeinsamen Finanzierungen (vgl. Teil II der Liste der Vorhaben gemäß § 2 Abs. (2) Nr. 4.) keine Zahlungen nach Abschnitt I des Abkommens über die Errichtung der Kulturstiftung der Länder an die Stiftung entrichtet, ruht das Stimmrecht des von diesem Land bestellten Mitgliedes des Stiftungsrates im Stiftungsrat. Führt dieses Land während dieser Zeit den Vorsitz in der Ministerpräsidentenkonferenz, verlängert sich die Amtszeit der oder des bisherigen Vorsitzenden und der oder des stellvertretenden Vorsitzenden des Stiftungsrates (§ 6 Abs. (3)) um den entsprechenden Zeitraum.
(2) Absatz (1) findet auf die Länder Brandenburg, Mecklenburg-Vorpommern, Sachsen, Sachsen-Anhalt und Thüringen bis zum 31. Dezember 1994 keine Anwendung.

Staatsvertrag über die Errichtung einer „Stiftung Preußische Schlösser und Gärten Berlin-Brandenburg"

Vom 23. August 1994 (GVBl. Bbg I 1995 S. 2)

Das Land Berlin und das Land Brandenburg sind wie folgt übereingekommen:

Artikel 1 Errichtung
(1) Das Land Berlin und das Land Brandenburg errichten die rechtsfähige Stiftung öffentlichen Rechts mit dem Namen „Stiftung Preußische Schlösser und Gärten Berlin-Brandenburg".
(2) Die Stiftung hat ihren Sitz in Potsdam.
(3) Die Stiftung führt ein Dienstsiegel.

Artikel 2 Aufgaben und Vermögen
(1) Die Stiftung hat die Aufgabe, die ihr übergebenen Kulturgüter zu bewahren, unter Berücksichtigung historischer, kunst- und gartenhistorischer und denkmalpflegerischer Belange zu pflegen, ihr Inventar zu ergänzen, der Öffentlichkeit zugänglich zu machen und die Auswertung dieses Kulturbesitzes für die Interessen der Allgemeinheit insbesondere in Wissenschaft und Bildung zu ermöglichen. Das Nähere regelt die Satzung.
(2) Der Stiftung sind zur Wahrnehmung der in Absatz 1 genannten Aufgaben folgende Grundstücke und Gebäude einschließlich ihres Inventars, soweit die vertragschließenden Länder verfügungsberechtigt sind, unentgeltlich zu übereignen oder, solange dies nicht möglich sein sollte, zur unentgeltlichen Nutzung zu übertragen:

1. im Land Brandenburg
Park Sanssouci (289 ha) mit den Schlössern Sanssouci, Neues Palais, Charlottenhof, Bildergalerie, Neue Kammern, Orangerie, Drachenhaus, Belvedere, Römische Bäder, Chinesisches Teehaus sowie Parkarchitekturen und -gebäuden,
Neuer Garten einschließlich des Heiligen Sees (146 ha) mit Marmorpalais, Schloß Cecilienhof, Meierei, Orangerie und diversen Gartenarchitekturen und -gebäuden,
Park Babelsberg (114 ha) mit Schloß Babelsberg einschließlich Küchengebäude, Dampfmaschinenhaus, Flatowturm, Gerichtslaube, Kleines Schloß, Matrosenhaus, Havelhaus sowie diversen Nebengebäuden,
historische Gebäude in der Stadt Potsdam: Jagdschloß Stern, ehemaliger Marstall des Stadtschlosses, Dampfmaschinenhaus (Moschee), Kopfbau zum Langen Stall, Schloß Lindstedt, Belvedere auf dem Pfingstberg, Thiemann-Haus,
Schloß und Park Rheinsberg (27 ha) einschließlich aller Nebengebäude, Wasserflächen und Brücken, Schloß und Park Sacrow (38 ha),
Schloß und Park Caputh (5 ha),
Schloß und Park Königs Wusterhausen (5 ha) einschließlich Nebenanlagen,
2. im Land Berlin
Schloß Charlottenburg mit den Nebengebäuden Belvedere, Mausoleum und Schinkelpavillon, Jagdschloß Grunewald,
Pfaueninsel (76 ha) mit Schloß und Parkgebäuden,
Schloß Glienicke und Parkgebäude.

Die Stiftung ist berechtigt und auf übereinstimmenden Wunsch der vertragschließenden Länder verpflichtet, das Eigentum an weiteren Grundstücken und Gebäuden nebst Inventar zu erwerben. Das Eigentum an das Schloß Charlottenburg und das Schloß Glienicke umgebenden Schloßgärten sowie die Zuständigkeit für ihre Verwaltung ist der Stiftung erst zu einem von den Vertragsparteien noch zu bestimmenden Zeitpunkt zu übertragen. Die Nutzung der Schloßgärten und Parkanlagen auch als Erholungsgebiete ist weiterhin zu gewährleisten. Das Nähere regelt die Satzung.

(3) Die Stiftung kann zu den in Absatz 1 genannten Zwecken vertraglich die Verwaltung weiterer Schlösser und Gärten in den Ländern Berlin und Brandenburg übernehmen. Die Stiftung kann öffentliche Träger von bedeutenden historischen und kulturhistorischen Schloß-, Park- und Gartenanlagen in Berlin und Brandenburg auf Wunsch beraten. Die Zuständigkeit der Denkmalschutzbehörden wird hiervon nicht berührt.

(4) Jedes der vertragschließenden Länder kann Zuständigkeiten für Bau- und Gartendenkmalschutz und -pflege der auf seinem Gebiet liegenden im Vermögen der Stiftung befindlichen Gebäude und Gartenanlagen auf die Stiftung übertragen.

(5) Hinsichtlich der von der Stiftung gemäß Absatz 3 verwalteten Schlösser und Gärten sowie hinsichtlich der Schloßgärten Charlottenburg und Glienicke – solange diese noch nicht gemäß Absatz 2 Satz 3 übertragen sind – treffen die zuständigen Denkmalschutzbehörden ihre Entscheidungen im Benehmen mit der Stiftung.

(6) Bei der Vergabe von Schloßräumen und Freiflächen ist den denkmalpflegerischen und konservatorischen Belangen Rechnung zu tragen. Die Vergabe wird auf eine Nutzung durch die obersten Organe des Bundes, der vertragschließenden Länder bzw. der Bundeshauptstadt Berlin beschränkt. Der Stiftungsrat kann Ausnahmen zulassen. Das Nähere über Vergabe und Nutzungsgebühren regeln Vergaberichtlinien des Stiftungsrates, deren Erlaß nicht gegen sämtliche Stimmen des Bundes oder eines Landes erfolgen kann.

Artikel 3 Finanzierung

Zur Erfüllung ihrer Aufgaben erhält die Stiftung nach Maßgabe der jeweiligen Haushaltspläne Zuschüsse des Landes Berlin und des Landes Brandenburg. Die Stiftung wird im Rahmen ihrer Zweckbestimmung Zuwendungen des Bundes und Dritter entgegennehmen. Das Nähere regelt ein Finanzierungsabkommen.[1)]

Artikel 4 Rechtsaufsicht

(1) Die Stiftung unterliegt der Rechtsaufsicht der für kulturelle Angelegenheiten zuständigen obersten Landesbehörde des Sitzlandes (Aufsichtsbehörde). Diese übt die Aufsicht im Einvernehmen mit der für kulturelle Angelegenheiten zuständigen obersten Landesbehörde Berlins aus. Für Umfang und Mittel der Aufsicht sind die im Sitzland für landesunmittelbare Körperschaften, Anstalten und Stiftungen des öffentlichen Rechts geltenden Vorschriften maßgebend.

(2) Die Übernahme weiterer Aufgaben im Rahmen des Artikels 2 Abs. 3 bedarf der Genehmigung der Aufsichtsbehörde, die im Einvernehmen mit der für kulturelle Angelegenheiten zuständigen obersten Landesbehörde Berlins entscheidet.

Artikel 5 Organe

Organe der Stiftung sind
1. der Stiftungsrat,
2. der Generaldirektor.

Artikel 6 Aufgaben des Stiftungsrates

(1) Der Stiftungsrat erläßt eine Satzung nach Maßgabe dieses Vertrages.[2)] Die Satzung bedarf der Zustimmung der Aufsichtsbehörde, die im Einvernehmen mit der für kulturelle Angelegenheiten zuständigen obersten Landesbehörde Berlins entscheidet. Entsprechendes gilt für Satzungsänderungen, die durch den Stiftungsrat vorgenommen werden können.

(2) Der Stiftungsrat kann Richtlinien beschließen, nach denen die Stiftung zu verwalten ist. Er kann dem Generaldirektor Weisungen erteilen und kann von ihm jederzeit Auskunft und Bericht verlangen. Der Stiftungsrat überwacht die Geschäftsführung der Stiftung.

(3) Der Stiftungsrat entscheidet über
1. die jährlichen und mehrjährigen Arbeits- und Veranstaltungsprogramme,
2. die Feststellung des Haushaltsplans und der Finanzplanung,
3. die Einstellung und Entlassung des Generaldirektors und seines ständigen Vertreters nach den dienstrechtlichen Vorschriften,
4. die Entlastung des Generaldirektors,
5. alle nicht nach Artikel 9 dem Generaldirektor obliegenden Geschäfte.

(4) Der Zustimmung des Stiftungsrates bedürfen
1. die Übernahme weiterer Aufgaben im Rahmen des Artikels 2 Abs. 3,
2. Erwerb, Veräußerung und Belastung von Grundstücken.

Die Satzung kann weitere Rechtsgeschäfte an die vorherige Zustimmung des Stiftungsrates binden.

---

1) Das Abkommen über die gemeinsame Finanzierung der „Stiftung Preußische Schlösser und Gärten Berlin-Brandenburg" ist abgedruckt als Nr. D17.V.2.
2) Die Satzung der Stiftung Berlin-Brandenburg ist abgedruckt als Nr. D17.V.3.

Artikel 7 Zusammensetzung des Stiftungsrates
(1) Dem Stiftungsrat gehören an
1. drei Vertreter Berlins,
2. drei Vertreter Brandenburgs,
3. drei Vertreter des Bundes.

Die in Nummer 1 genannten Mitglieder werden vom Senat von Berlin entsandt und abberufen, die in Nummer 2 genannten von der Regierung des Landes Brandenburg. Im Falle der Verhinderung können die Mitglieder des Stiftungsrates von mit Vollmacht versehenen Angehörigen der Verwaltung der sie entsendenden Gebietskörperschaft vertreten werden.
(2) Das Land Berlin, das Land Brandenburg und der Bund haben jeweils drei Stimmen.

Artikel 8 Verfahren im Stiftungsrat
(1) Der Stiftungsrat wählt aus seiner Mitte alternierend für die Dauer von zwei Jahren den Vertreter eines Landes zum Vorsitzenden sowie dessen Stellvertreter aus dem anderen vertragschließenden Land.
(2) Der Stiftungsrat gibt sich eine Geschäftsordnung. Sie kann Abstimmungen auch im schriftlichen Verfahren vorsehen, jedoch nur mit der Maßgabe, daß im Einzelfall die Zustimmung aller Mitglieder des Stiftungsrates zu dieser Abstimmungsart erforderlich ist.
(3) Der Stiftungsrat tritt mindestens einmal jährlich zu einer ordentlichen Sitzung zusammen. Auf Antrag von jeweils mindestens drei Mitgliedern muß der Stiftungsrat zu weiteren Sitzungen zusammentreten.
(4) Der Stiftungsrat ist beschlußfähig, wenn je zwei Vertreter des Landes Berlin, des Landes Brandenburg und des Bundes anwesend oder vertreten sind. Er faßt Beschlüsse mit der einfachen Mehrheit der abgegebenen Stimmen.
(5) Entscheidungen des Stiftungsrates nach Artikel 6 Abs. 3 Nr. 2 und 4 sowie über den Inhalt der Satzung können nur mit Zustimmung von zwei Dritteln der Mitglieder des Stiftungsrates getroffen werden, wobei Beschlüsse gegen sämtliche Stimmen eines vertragschließenden Landes oder des Bundes nicht möglich sind. Die Stimmen der im Stiftungsrat vertretenen Gebietskörperschaften können bei diesen Entscheidungen nur einheitlich abgegeben werden.

Artikel 9 Generaldirektor
(1) Dem Generaldirektor obliegt die Führung der laufenden Geschäfte. Er vertritt die Stiftung gerichtlich und außergerichtlich. Er hat die Beschlüsse des Stiftungsrates auszuführen.
(2) Der Generaldirektor und sein ständiger Vertreter werden vom Stiftungsrat mit mindestens zwei Dritteln der Stimmen seiner Mitglieder gewählt. Eine Entscheidung gegen die Stimmen eines vertragschließenden Landes ist nicht möglich. Sie sind zu Beamten auf Lebenszeit zu berufen. In Ausnahmefällen ist auch ein privatrechtlicher Dienstvertrag zulässig.
(3) Der Generaldirektor nimmt an den Sitzungen des Stiftungsrates beratend teil. Er ist verpflichtet, den Stiftungsrat über alle wichtigen Angelegenheiten zu unterrichten.
(4) Stellung und Aufgaben des Generaldirektors und seines ständigen Vertreters regelt die Satzung.

Artikel 10 Personal
(1) Die Stiftung hat das Recht, Beamtenverhältnisse zu begründen, und ist Arbeitgeber ihrer Angestellten und Arbeiter.
(2) Planstellen für Beamte dürfen nur in dem Umfange eingerichtet werden, als sie für eine dauernde Tätigkeit zur Erfüllung hoheitsrechtlicher Aufgaben erforderlich sind.
(3) Für die Beamten der Stiftung mit Ausnahme derer, die bei Errichtung der Stiftung aus einem Beamtenverhältnis zum Land Berlin übernommen werden, gilt das Beamtenrecht des Sitzlandes; für die aus einem Beamtenverhältnis zum Land Berlin übernommenen Beamten gilt das Beamtenrecht Berlins.
(4) Oberste Dienstbehörde, Dienstbehörde und Ernennungsbehörde ist für den Generaldirektor und seinen ständigen Vertreter der Stiftungsrat. Diese Aufgabe – mit Ausnahme der in Artikel 6 Abs. 3 Nr. 3 genannten – nimmt für den Stiftungsrat der Vorsitzende wahr. Oberste Dienstbehörde, Dienstbehörde und Ernennungsbehörde für die übrigen Beamten der Stiftung, Personalstelle für die Angestellten, Arbeiter und Auszubildenden der Stiftung sowie Personalwirtschaftsstelle ist der Generaldirektor.

(5) Für die Arbeitsverhältnisse der Angestellten und Arbeiter sowie die Vertragsverhältnisse der Auszubildenden der Stiftung mit Ausnahme derer, die bei Errichtung der Stiftung aus einem Beschäftigungsverhältnis zum Land Berlin übernommen werden, sind die im Sitzland jeweils geltenden Regelungen maßgebend; für die aus einem Beschäftigungsverhältnis zum Land Berlin übernommenen Arbeitnehmer und Auszubildenden gelten die bisher maßgebenden Regelungen weiter. Die Stiftung tritt in die Rechte und Pflichten aus den zum Zeitpunkt ihrer Errichtung bestehenden Arbeitsverhältnissen und Berufsausbildungsverhältnissen
1. der beim Land Berlin – Verwaltung der Staatlichen Schlösser und Gärten – beschäftigten Angestellten, Arbeiter und Auszubildenden,
2. der beim Land Brandenburg – Stiftung Schlösser und Gärten Potsdam-Sanssouci – beschäftigten Angestellten, Arbeiter und Auszubildenden

unter Wahrung des Besitzstandes hinsichtlich der materiellen Arbeitsbedingungen ein.
(6) Für die Bediensteten der Stiftung gilt das Personalvertretungsrecht des Sitzlandes.

Artikel 11 Haushalt
(1) Für das Haushalts-, Kassen- und Rechnungswesen sowie für die Rechnungslegung der Stiftung und die Rechnungsprüfung bei der Stiftung finden die für die Verwaltung des Sitzlandes geltenden Bestimmungen entsprechende Anwendung; zuständiger Rechnungshof ist der des Sitzlandes. Er unterrichtet den Bundesrechnungshof und den Rechnungshof von Berlin, deren Rechte nach § 91 der jeweiligen Haushaltsordnungen unberührt bleiben. Der Rechnungshof des Sitzlandes soll insbesondere bei den in Berlin gelegenen Schlössern und Gärten mit dem Rechnungshof von Berlin zusammenarbeiten.
(2) Der Haushaltsplan der Stiftung ist alljährlich rechtzeitig vor Beginn des Haushaltsjahres von dem Generaldirektor im Entwurf aufzustellen und vom Stiftungsrat festzustellen. Er bedarf der Genehmigung der Aufsichtsbehörde; Artikel 4 Abs. 1 Satz 2 gilt entsprechend.

Artikel 12 Beirat
(1) Für die Beratung des Stiftungsrates und des Generaldirektors in wichtigen Fragen wird ein Beirat aus sachverständigen Persönlichkeiten gebildet. Das Nähere regelt die Satzung.
(2) Die Mitglieder des Beirates werden vom Stiftungsrat berufen. Der Vorsitzende des Beirates nimmt mit beratender Stimme an den Sitzungen des Stiftungsrates teil.

Artikel 13 Vertragsdauer
(1) Dieser Staatsvertrag gilt für unbestimmte Zeit. Er kann zum Schluß des Haushaltsjahres mit einer Frist von einem Jahr gekündigt werden, frühestens zum 31. Dezember 1999. Zu dem Zeitpunkt, zu dem eine Kündigung wirksam wird, ist die Stiftung aufgelöst.
(2) Wird die Stiftung aufgelöst, so werden ihre Bediensteten jeweils in den Dienst des Landes übernommen, in dem ihre Beschäftigungsstelle liegt. Soweit das Personal der Stiftung nicht bestimmten Schlössern und Gärten zugeordnet war, wird es nach besonderer Vereinbarung der vertragschließenden Länder anteilig in deren Dienst übernommen.
(3) Die gemäß Artikel 2 Abs. 2 der Stiftung übereigneten Grundstücke und Gebäude, einschließlich ihres Inventars, sind in das Eigentum jeweils des Landes zurückzuführen, von dem die Stiftung sie erworben hat. Das sonstige Vermögen steht anteilig den vertragschließenden Ländern zu.
(4) Bilden die vertragschließenden Länder ein gemeinsames Land, gehen die Rechte und Pflichten aus diesem Vertrag auf das neue Land über.[1)]

Artikel 14 Schlußbestimmung
(1) Die Organe der Stiftung sind innerhalb von drei Monaten nach Inkrafttreten des Staatsvertrages zu bilden.
(2) Bis sie handlungsfähig sind, wird die Funktion des Generaldirektors durch den Generaldirektor der Stiftung Schlösser und Gärten Potsdam-Sanssouci wahrgenommen. Die Funktion des Stiftungsrates wird gemeinsam von den für kulturelle Angelegenheiten zuständigen obersten Landesbehörden der vertragschließenden Länder wahrgenommen.

---

1) Protokollnotiz zu Artikel 13 Abs. 4: Bilden die vertragschließenden Länder ein gemeinsames Land, bedürfen Erlaß oder Änderung von Vergaberichtlinien nach Artikel 2 Abs. 6 Satz 4 der Zustimmung Berlins. Das gemeinsame Land gewährleistet eine angemessene Vertretung Berlins im Stiftungsrat.

Artikel 15 Inkrafttreten
Dieser Staatsvertrag tritt am ersten Tag des auf den Austausch der Ratifikationsurkunden folgenden Monats in Kraft.

Abkommen über die gemeinsame Finanzierung der „Stiftung Preußische Schlösser und Gärten Berlin-Brandenburg"

Vom 23. August 1994 (GVBl. Bbg I 1995 S. 2)

Die Bundesrepublik Deutschland (im folgenden Bund genannt)
vertreten durch den Bundesminister des Innern,
das Land Berlin,
vertreten durch den Regierenden Bürgermeister,
das Land Brandenburg,
vertreten durch den Ministerpräsidenten,
schließen das nachstehende Abkommen zur Ausführung des Artikels 3 des Staatsvertrages über die Errichtung der „Stiftung Preußische Schlösser und Gärten Berlin-Brandenburg":

Artikel 1
(1) Die Vertragschließenden verpflichten sich, nach Maßgabe ihrer Haushaltspläne der „Stiftung Preußische Schlösser und Gärten Berlin-Brandenburg" die zum Ausgleich des Stiftungshaushalts erforderlichen Mittel zur Verfügung zu stellen.

(2) Den Vertragschließenden wird gemäß Artikel 2 (6) des Staatsvertrages über die Errichtung einer „Stiftung Preußische Schlösser und Gärten Berlin-Brandenburg" ein Nutzungsrecht bei der Vergabe von Schloßräumen und Freiflächen eingeräumt.

Artikel 2
Im Haushaltsjahr 1994 wird die Stiftung nach Maßgabe der im Bundeshaushalt und der in den Haushalten der Länder Berlin und Brandenburg vorgesehenen Zuwendungen finanziert.
Ab dem Haushaltsjahr 1995 tragen der Bund 37 v. H., das Land Brandenburg 43 v. H. und das Land Berlin 20 v. H. des Zuwendungsbedarfs der Stiftung.

Artikel 3
An Archiv- und Sammlungsgegenständen, die mit Bundeszuwendungen beschafft werden, wird der Bund in Höhe seines Finanzierungsanteils Miteigentümer.
Die Inventarisierung, die zeitliche Bindung, der Wertausgleich, die Einräumung dinglicher Rechte richten sich nach den Vorl. VV zur LHO sowie den ANBest-I.

Artikel 4
Mit Zustimmung der anderen Vertragschließenden kann der Bund oder ein Land über seinen jeweiligen Finanzierungsanteil hinausgehende Leistungen erbringen. Dieser Zustimmung bedarf es nicht, wenn auf Grund einer Vereinbarung mit der „Stiftung Preußische Schlösser und Gärten Berlin-Brandenburg" Leistungen zur Abgeltung der Kosten von einzelnen Projekten gewährt werden und hierdurch keine Folgekosten entstehen.

Artikel 5
Es gilt das Haushaltsrecht des Sitzlandes. Der Rechnungshof des Sitzlandes prüft die Haushalts- und Wirtschaftsführung. Er unterrichtet den Bundesrechnungshof und den Rechnungshof von Berlin, deren Rechte nach § 91 der jeweiligen Haushaltsordnungen unberührt bleiben.
Der Rechnungshof des Sitzlandes soll insbesondere bei den in Berlin gelegenen Schlössern und Gärten mit dem Rechnungshof von Berlin zusammenarbeiten.

Artikel 6
(1) Dieses Abkommen wird auf die Dauer von 6 Jahren ab Inkrafttreten geschlossen.
(2) Spätestens zwei Jahre vor Ablauf des Finanzierungsabkommens oder bei einer wesentlichen Veränderung der Geschäftsgrundlage werden die Vertragschließenden über die weitere Finanzierung der „Stiftung Preußische Schlösser und Gärten Berlin-Brandenburg" verhandeln.

Artikel 7
Das Abkommen tritt mit Wirkung vom 1. Januar 1994 in Kraft.

Satzung der Stiftung Preußische Schlösser und Gärten Berlin-Brandenburg

Vom 18. Februar 1998 (ABl. S. 3030)
zuletzt geändert durch Beschluss des Stiftungsrates vom 05.05.2011 (ABl. Berlin S. 2744)

Der Stiftungsrat der Stiftung Preußische Schlösser und Gärten Berlin-Brandenburg (im Folgenden: Stiftung) erlässt gemäß Artikel 6 Abs. 1 des Staatsvertrages vom 23. August 1994 über die Errichtung einer "Stiftung Preußische Schlösser und Gärten Berlin-Brandenburg" (im Folgenden: Staatsvertrag) die nachstehende Satzung.

§ 1 Aufgaben der Stiftung

(1) Die Stiftung hat gemäß Artikel 2 des Staatsvertrages die Aufgabe, die ihr übergebenen Kulturgüter zu bewahren, unter Berücksichtigung historischer, kunst- und gartenhistorischer und denkmalpflegerischer Belange zu pflegen, ihr Inventar zu ergänzen, der Öffentlichkeit zugänglich zu machen und die Auswertung dieses Kulturbesitzes für die Interessen der Allgemeinheit, insbesondere in Wissenschaft und Bildung, zu ermöglichen. Ihr obliegen nach den Gesetzen von Berlin und von Brandenburg die Aufgaben der unteren Denkmalschutzbehörde bezüglich des denkmalgeschützten Stiftungsvermögens.

(2) Zu den Aufgaben der Stiftung gehören insbesondere

1. die bauliche und gärtnerische Unterhaltung und Sanierung der Liegenschaften und der Kulturdenkmale unter Beachtung der Anforderungen des Denkmalschutzes und der Denkmalpflege;
2. eine denkmalverträgliche Nutzung der Kulturdenkmale, insbesondere als Museum, durch die Öffentlichkeit zu ermöglichen. Es sind Einrichtungen zu unterhalten, die der Betreuung der Besucher dienen;
3. die wissenschaftliche und publizistische Aufarbeitung und Dokumentation des Kulturdenkmalbestandes sowie die Öffentlichkeitsarbeit.

(3) Die Stiftung verfolgt ausschließlich und unmittelbar gemeinnützige Zwecke im Sinne des Abschnitts "Steuerbegünstigte Zwecke" der Abgabenordnung in der jeweils geltenden Fassung. Die Stiftung ist selbstlos tätig und verfolgt nicht in erster Linie eigenwirtschaftliche Zwecke. Die Mittel der Stiftung sind nur im Sinne des Stiftungszwecks zu verwenden. Es darf keine Person durch Ausgaben, die dem Zweck der Stiftung fremd sind oder durch unverhältnismäßig hohe Vergütungen begünstigt werden.

(4) Bei Auflösung oder Aufhebung der Stiftung oder bei Wegfall steuerbegünstigter Zwecke fällt das Vermögen an das Land Berlin und das Land Brandenburg, die es unmittelbar und ausschließlich für gemeinnützige, mildtätige oder kirchliche Zwecke zu verwenden haben. Die jeweilige Übertragung erfolgt an das Bundesland, von dem die Stiftung das Vermögen erhalten hat. Im Übrigen erfolgt eine anteilige Vermögensübertragung. Bilden die beiden Bundesländer ein gemeinsames Bundesland, gehen die Rechte und Pflichten auf das neue Land über.

§ 2 Nutzung der Kulturgüter

(1) Bei der Durchführung der Aufgaben der Stiftung nach § 1 Abs. 1 hat die Stiftung der Erhaltung und Pflege der Kulturgüter den Vorrang zu geben.

(2) Im Rahmen ihrer Verpflichtung zur Bewahrung und Pflege der Schlossgärten und Parkanlagen gewährleistet die Stiftung die weitere Nutzung auch als Erholungsgebiet. Der Generaldirektor erlässt hierzu Parkordnungen, die der Erhaltung der Anlagen einerseits und der Benutzung durch die Öffentlichkeit andererseits Rechnung tragen.

(3) Eintrittsgeld für die Benutzung der Schlossgärten und Parkanlagen wird grundsätzlich nicht erhoben; dies gilt nicht für Veranstaltungen. Ausnahmeregelungen bestimmt der Stiftungsrat. Für den Besuch der in den Schlossgärten und Parkanlagen befindlichen museal genutzten Gebäude kann ein Benutzungsentgelt verlangt werden; der Generaldirektor erlässt hierzu eine Benutzungsentgeltordnung.

§ 3 Aufgaben des Stiftungsrates

(1) Gemäß Artikel 6 des Staatsvertrages entscheidet der Stiftungsrat über
1. die jährlichen und mehrjährigen Arbeits- und Veranstaltungsprogramme,
2. die Feststellung des Haushaltsplanes und der Finanzplanung,
3. die Einstellung und Entlassung des Generaldirektors und seines ständigen Vertreters nach den dienstrechtlichen Vorschriften,

D17.V.3 Satzung der Stiftung Berlin-Brandenburg

4. die Entlastung des Generaldirektors,
5. alle nicht nach Artikel 9 des Staatsvertrags und § 4 dieser Satzung dem Generaldirektor obliegenden Geschäfte,
6. die Satzung und Satzungsänderungen.

(2) Der vorherigen Zustimmung des Stiftungsrates bedürfen
1. die Übernahme weiterer Aufgaben im Rahmen des Artikels 2 Abs. 3 des Staatsvertrages,
2. Erwerb, Veräußerung und Belastung von Grundstücken.

(3) Einstellung und Entlassung der Abteilungsleiter sowie des Stiftungskonservators sind im Einvernehmen mit dem Stiftungsrat vorzunehmen.

§ 4 Stellung und Aufgaben des Generaldirektors und seines ständigen Vertreters

(1) Gemäß Artikel 9 Abs. 1 des Staatsvertrages obliegt dem Generaldirektor die Führung der laufenden Geschäfte. Er vertritt die Stiftung gerichtlich und außergerichtlich. Er hat die Beschlüsse des Stiftungsrates auszuführen.

(2) Zu den laufenden Geschäften des Generaldirektors gehören insbesondere:
1. Die mit der Verwaltung der Stiftung verbundenen, regelmäßig wiederkehrenden Geschäfte.
2. Die mit der Durchführung und Abwicklung von Dauerverträgen verbundenen Rechtsgeschäfte.

(3) Zu den laufenden Geschäften des Generaldirektors gehören nicht:
1. Alle Geschäfte, die die Stiftung außerhalb ihrer etatisierten Ausgaben zu einer Ausgabe von mehr als 170.000,- EUR im Einzelfall verpflichten.
2. Die Annahme von Erbschaften und Schenkungen, sofern Folgekosten für die Stiftung entstehen, die im laufenden oder in einem künftigen Haushaltsjahr Ausgaben von mehr als 35.000,- EUR zur Folge haben.
3. Der Abschluss von Darlehensverträgen, die Übernahme von Bürgschaften und der Abschluss von Gewährverträgen.
4. Der Abschluss und die Kündigung von Miet- und Pachtverträgen mit einer Vertragsdauer von mehr als zehn Jahren oder einer Miete oder Pacht, wenn diese die Grenze von 35.000,- EUR pro Jahr überschreitet oder wenn von den ortsüblichen Miet- oder Pachtbedingungen abgewichen werden soll. Hiervon ausgenommen sind Dienst- oder Werkdienstwohnungen.
5. Die Führung von Rechtsstreitigkeiten von besonderer Bedeutung sowie der Abschluss von Abfindungsvereinbarungen und der Erlass von Forderungen, soweit der Betrag 35.000,- EUR überschritten wird; der Abschluss von Vergleichen, soweit der Betrag von 50.000,- EUR überschritten wird.
6. Alle sonstigen Geschäfte, über die der Stiftungsrat sich die Beschlussfassung vorbehält.

(4) Der Direktor der Generalverwaltung ist der ständige Vertreter des Generaldirektors

(5) Der Generaldirektor ist verpflichtet, den Stiftungsrat über alle wichtigen Angelegenheiten zu unterrichten und ihm über alle Angelegenheiten der Stiftung Auskunft zu erteilen. Er nimmt an den Sitzungen des Stiftungsrates und des Beirates beratend teil (Artikel 9 des Staatsvertrages)

(6) Der Generaldirektor und sein ständiger Vertreter sind auf der Grundlage eines mit dem Stiftungsratsvorsitzenden geschlossenen Dienstvertrages für die Stiftung tätig und erhalten eine angemessene Vergütung.

§ 5 Haushaltsplan, Rechnungslegung, Prüfung

(1) Für das Haushalts-, Kassen- und Rechnungswesen sowie für die Rechnungslegung der Stiftung finden die für die Verwaltung des Sitzlandes geltenden Bestimmungen entsprechende Anwendung.

(2) Der Generaldirektor legt dem Stiftungsrat rechtzeitig vor Beginn eines Haushaltsjahres einen Haushalts- und Stellenplan vor, der vom Stiftungsrat festzustellen und von der Aufsichtsbehörde zu genehmigen ist.

(3) Der Generaldirektor legt dem Stiftungsrat den Jahresabschluss für das abgelaufene Haushaltsjahr vor. Der Jahresabschluss sowie die Haushalts- und Wirtschaftsführung sind – unbeschadet der Prüfungsrechte der Rechnungshöfe – von einem unabhängigen Wirtschaftsprüfungsunternehmen zu prüfen, das auf der Grundlage einer Beschlussfassung des Stiftungsrates zu beauftragen ist.

§ 6 Beirat

(1) Der Beirat hat die Aufgabe, den Stiftungsrat und den Generaldirektor in allen wichtigen Fragen zu beraten.

(2) Der Beirat besteht aus mindestens sechs, höchstens zwölf Mitgliedern, die auf denjenigen Gebieten sachverständig sind, auf denen die Stiftung Aufgaben zu erfüllen hat.
(3) Die Mitglieder des Beirates werden jeweils für vier Jahre vom Stiftungsrat berufen. Der Generaldirektor kann Vorschläge unterbreiten. Es sollen zur Hälfte Frauen berufen werden. Eine Wiederberufung ist zulässig. Mitglieder des Beirates können jederzeit aus wichtigem Grund, insbesondere wenn sie den mit ihrer Mitgliedschaft im Beirat zusammenhängenden Aufgaben nicht nachkommen, vom Stiftungsrat abberufen werden. Eine Stellvertretung ist nicht zulässig. Scheidet ein Mitglied vorzeitig aus, so wird für die verbleibende Amtsdauer des ausgeschiedenen Mitglieds ein neues Mitglied berufen.
(4) Der Beirat kann im Rahmen seiner Beratungsaufgaben von sich aus dem Stiftungsrat und dem Generaldirektor Stellungnahmen, Empfehlungen und Vorschläge unterbreiten.
(5) Die Mitglieder des Beirates sind ehrenamtlich tätig. Sie erhalten eine Erstattung der Reisekosten entsprechend den Vorschriften des Bundesreisekostengesetzes.
(6) Der Beirat ist beschlussfähig, wenn mindestens die Hälfte seiner Mitglieder anwesend ist. Er fasst Beschlüsse mit den Stimmen der Mehrheit seiner anwesenden Mitglieder. Seine Vorsitzende oder seinen Vorsitzenden und deren oder dessen Stellvertreter/in wählt er aus seiner Mitte mit einer Mehrheit von zwei Dritteln der Stimmen seiner anwesenden Mitglieder.
(7) Der Beirat wird von seiner oder seinem Vorsitzenden oder stellvertretenden Vorsitzenden einberufen und tritt mindestens einmal jährlich zusammen. Bei Bedarf oder auf schriftlich begründeten Antrag von mindestens einem Drittel seiner Mitglieder tritt er zu weiteren Sitzungen zusammen.
(8) Beschlüsse des Beirates werden dem Stiftungsrat und dem Generaldirektor schriftlich zur Kenntnis gegeben. Der Generaldirektor kann mit beratender Stimme an den Sitzungen des Beirates teilnehmen.
(9) Der Beirat gibt sich eine Geschäftsordnung, die der Zustimmung des Stiftungsrates bedarf.

§ 7 Schlussbestimmung; Inkrafttreten
Diese Satzung tritt am Tag nach ihrer Veröffentlichung in Kraft.

D17.V.4 Stiftungsanlagenverordnung

Ordnungsbehördliche Verordnung zur Abwehr von Gefahren für die im Vermögen der Stiftung Preußische Schlösser und Gärten Berlin-Brandenburg befindlichen baulichen und gärtnerischen Anlagen (Stiftungsanlagenverordnung – StiftAnlVO)

Vom 21. September 2006 (ABl. S. 691)

Auf Grund des § 27 Abs. 1 des Brandenburgischen Denkmalschutzgesetzes in der Fassung der Bekanntmachung vom 24. Mai 2004 (GVBl. I S. 215) verordnet der Generaldirektor der Stiftung Preußische Schlösser und Gärten Berlin-Brandenburg:

§ 1 Geltungsbereich

(1) Diese Verordnung gilt für die baulichen und gärtnerischen Anlagen der folgenden im Vermögen der Stiftung Preußische Schlösser und Gärten Berlin-Brandenburg (im Weiteren: Stiftung) befindlichen Liegenschaften in der Landeshauptstadt Potsdam sowie in den Städten Königs Wusterhausen und Rheinsberg:

Landeshauptstadt Potsdam:
a) Schlösser- und Parkanlagen Sanssouci, Neuer Garten, Pfingstberg, Babelsberg, Lindstedt und Sacrow;
b) Jagdschloss Stern mit zugehöriger Gartenanlage (Jagdhausstraße 32), ehemaliger Pferdestall mit zugehöriger Nutzfläche (Jagdhausstraße 33), Kastellanshaus mit Wirtschaftsgebäude und zugehöriger Gartenanlage (Jagdhausstraße 32 b); Gartenland westlich des Kastellanshauses;
c) Hofmarschallhaus mit zugehöriger Gartenanlage (Allee nach Sanssouci 5);
d) Marstall (Breite Straße 1 a);
e) Dampfmaschinenhaus „Moschee" (Breite Straße 28);
f) Villa des Gärtners J. L. Heydert (Hofgärtnerhaus „Thiemannhaus") mit Wirtschaftsgebäude (Gartenhaus), Pavillon und Gartenanlage (Friedrich-Ebert-Straße 83);
g) Kopfbau Langer Stall (Werner-Seelenbinder-Straße 7).

Stadt Königs Wusterhausen:
Schloss Königs Wusterhausen

Stadt Rheinsberg:
Schloss und Schlosspark Rheinsberg

(2) Zu den Bestandteilen der gärtnerischen Anlagen gehören auch die Einfriedungen, Werke der bildenden Kunst, die Bepflanzung der Grundstücke, Straßen und Wege, die historische Straßenpflasterung und -möblierung sowie die Wegeführung der befestigten und unbefestigten Wege, die Seen und Wasserläufe mit ihren historischen Uferlinien und den dazugehörigen Brücken und Übergängen sowie den landschaftlich gestalteten Uferzonen.

(3) Die Flurstücke, die ganz oder teilweise innerhalb des Geltungsbereichs der Verordnung liegen, sind in der als Anlage 1 dieser Verordnung beigefügten Flurstücksliste aufgeführt. Ferner ist der Geltungsbereich dieser Verordnung in den als Anlage 2 beigefügten Plänen mit ununterbrochener roter Linie gekennzeichnet.

§ 2 Gegenstand und Zweck

Die in § 1 genannten baulichen und gärtnerischen Anlagen der Stiftung sind Denkmale im Sinne des Brandenburgischen Denkmalschutzgesetzes. Die in § 1 Abs. 1 Buchstabe a bezeichneten Liegenschaften unterliegen darüber hinaus dem Schutz der Denkmalbereichssatzung Berlin-Potsdamer Kulturlandschaft. Mit den nachfolgenden Regelungen soll sichergestellt werden, dass die baulichen und gärtnerischen Anlagen nach denkmalpflegerischen Grundsätzen erhalten, geschützt, gepflegt und so genutzt werden, dass ihre Erhaltung auf Dauer gewährleistet ist und Beeinträchtigungen ihres Erscheinungsbildes vermieden werden.

§ 3 Benutzung der Anlagen

(1) Die Stiftung macht die in § 1 genannten baulichen und gärtnerischen Anlagen für Besucher zum Zweck der Erholung, der bürgerschaftlichen Begegnung und der kulturellen Bildung zugänglich. Bei

der Nutzung ist jedes Verhalten untersagt, das geeignet ist, die baulichen und gärtnerischen Anlagen zu beschädigen, zu verschmutzen oder anderweitig zu beeinträchtigen. Insbesondere ist es untersagt:
a) mit Kraftfahrzeugen, außer mit Krankenfahrstühlen, oder Fahrrädern zu fahren oder diese mitzuführen oder abzustellen,
b) Inlineskates oder Skateboard zu fahren,
c) Hunde, mit Ausnahme von Blindenführ- und Behindertenbegleithunden, oder andere Haustiere frei laufen zu lassen oder auf die gekennzeichneten Liegewiesen mitzunehmen oder in Gewässern baden zu lassen,
d) auf bauliche oder Bestandteile gärtnerischer Anlagen, wie Bäume oder Objekte bildender Kunst, zu klettern,
e) zu reiten,
f) Ball- oder andere Sportspiele zu betreiben,
g) zu angeln, zu baden, Boot zu fahren oder Modellboote fahren zu lassen,
h) Feuer zu entzünden oder zu unterhalten,
i) zu lagern, zu zelten oder anderweitig im Park zu übernachten,
j) Schlitten oder Ski zu fahren und die Wasserflächen bei Eis zu betreten,
k) Pflanzen oder Teile davon zu entfernen, mitzunehmen oder sonst zu beschädigen,
l) Unrat jeglicher Art, insbesondere Lebensmittelreste, Zigarettenkippen, Papier, Glas, Konserven oder sonstige Verpackungsmaterialien oder andere Abfälle wegzuwerfen oder zurückzulassen,
m) Handzettel, Flugblätter, Werbeprospekte oder andere Druckerzeugnisse abzulegen oder zu verteilen oder andere Werbeaktionen durchzuführen,
n) Werbetafeln aufzustellen, Plakate oder Schilder anzubringen,
o) Handel oder Gewerbe zu treiben,
p) Demonstrationen durchzuführen.

(2) Hundehalter und -führer haben dafür Sorge zu tragen, dass ihre Hunde die Gebäude und Gartenanlagen nicht verunreinigen. Sie haben den Kot ihrer Hunde unverzüglich zu beseitigen. Dies gilt nicht für blinde Hundeführer.

(3) Anderweitige Beeinträchtigungen liegen vor, wenn nicht nur kurzfristig das Erscheinungsbild der baulichen und gärtnerischen Anlagen gestört oder verändert wird oder eine vorübergehende Störung oder Veränderung des Erscheinungsbildes zu einer Häufung entsprechender Handlungen führen kann (Wiederholungsgefahr).

§ 4 Ausnahmen

Der Generaldirektor kann auf Antrag Ausnahmen von den Bestimmungen dieser Verordnung zulassen. Die Ausnahmen können unter Bedingungen und Befristungen erteilt und mit Auflagen verbunden werden. Anträge auf Zulassung von Ausnahmen sind schriftlich zu stellen.

§ 5 Ordnungswidrigkeiten

(1) Ordnungswidrig handelt, wer vorsätzlich oder fahrlässig entgegen § 3 Abs. 1 eine untersagte Handlung vornimmt.
(2) Ordnungswidrig handelt auch, wer vorsätzlich oder fahrlässig entgegen § 3 Abs. 2 den Hundekot nicht unverzüglich beseitigt.
(3) Ordnungswidrig handelt außerdem, wer vorsätzlich oder fahrlässig gegen die nach § 4 erteilte Ausnahmezulassung oder gegen die darin enthaltenen Bedingungen verstößt.
(4) Die Ordnungswidrigkeit kann mit einer Geldbuße bis zu 10.000 Euro geahndet werden, soweit sie nicht nach Bundes oder Landesrecht als Straftat oder Ordnungswidrigkeit geahndet wird.
(5) Zuwiderhandlungen gegen § 3 Abs. 1 Buchstabe p sind nach § 26 Nr. 2 Versammlungsgesetz mit Strafe bedroht.

§ 6 Inkrafttreten

Diese Verordnung tritt am Tag nach der Verkündung im Amtsblatt für Brandenburg in Kraft.

D17.V.4 Stiftungsanlagenverordnung

Anlage 1 zur ordnungsbehördlichen Verordnung der Stiftung Preußische Schlösser und Gärten Berlin-Brandenburg

Liste der Flurstücke, die ganz oder teilweise innerhalb des Geltungsbereichs der Verordnung liegen

Bezeichnung/Lage	Gemarkung	Flur	Flurstück
Park Sanssouci			
Park Sanssouci	Potsdam	22	1
Park Sanssouci	Potsdam	22	2
Park Sanssouci	Potsdam	22	3/8
Park Sanssouci	Potsdam	22	4
Park Sanssouci	Potsdam	22	5
Park Sanssouci	Potsdam	22	6/2
Park Sanssouci	Potsdam	22	8
Park Sanssouci	Potsdam	22	9
Park Sanssouci	Potsdam	22	10
Park Sanssouci	Potsdam	22	142/1
Park Sanssouci	Potsdam	22	142/2
Park Sanssouci	Potsdam	23	216/1
Park Sanssouci	Potsdam	23	216/2
Park Sanssouci	Potsdam	23	230
Park Sanssouci	Potsdam	23	243
Park Sanssouci	Potsdam	23	244
Park Sanssouci	Potsdam	23	253
Park Sanssouci	Potsdam	23	254
Park Sanssouci	Potsdam	23	255
Park Sanssouci	Potsdam	23	256
Park Sanssouci	Potsdam	23	257
Park Sanssouci	Potsdam	23	259
Park Sanssouci	Potsdam	23	261
Park Sanssouci	Potsdam	23	262
Park Sanssouci	Potsdam	23	263
Park Sanssouci	Potsdam	23	273/2
Park Sanssouci	Potsdam	23	274
Park Sanssouci	Potsdam	23	275
Park Sanssouci	Potsdam	23	276
Park Sanssouci	Potsdam	23	293/1
Park Sanssouci	Potsdam	23	300/2
Park Sanssouci	Potsdam	24	1
Park Sanssouci	Potsdam	24	2
Park Sanssouci	Potsdam	24	3
Park Sanssouci	Potsdam	24	4
Park Sanssouci	Potsdam	24	5
Park Sanssouci	Potsdam	24	19/1
Park Sanssouci	Potsdam	24	19/2

Park Sanssouci	Potsdam	24	21
Park Sanssouci	Potsdam	24	22
Park Sanssouci	Potsdam	24	23
Park Sanssouci	Potsdam	24	24
Park Sanssouci	Potsdam	24	25
Park Sanssouci	Potsdam	24	26
Park Sanssouci	Potsdam	24	27
Park Sanssouci	Potsdam	24	30
Park Sanssouci	Potsdam	24	32
Park Sanssouci	Potsdam	24	33
Park Sanssouci	Potsdam	24	34
Park Sanssouci	Potsdam	24	35
Park Sanssouci	Potsdam	24	36
Park Sanssouci	Potsdam	24	37
Park Sanssouci	Potsdam	24	38
Park Sanssouci	Potsdam	24	39
Park Sanssouci	Potsdam	24	45
Park Sanssouci	Potsdam	24	48
Park Sanssouci	Potsdam	24	50
Park Sanssouci	Potsdam	24	53
Park Sanssouci	Potsdam	24	54
Park Sanssouci	Potsdam	24	55
Park Sanssouci	Potsdam	24	56
Park Sanssouci	Potsdam	24	57
Park Sanssouci	Potsdam	24	58
Park Sanssouci	Potsdam	24	59
Park Sanssouci	Potsdam	24	60
Park Sanssouci	Potsdam	24	61
Park Sanssouci	Potsdam	24	62
Park Sanssouci	Potsdam	24	63
Park Sanssouci	Potsdam	24	64
Park Sanssouci	Potsdam	24	65
Park Sanssouci	Potsdam	24	66
Park Sanssouci	Potsdam	26	1
Park Sanssouci	Potsdam	26	2
Park Sanssouci	Potsdam	26	3
Park Sanssouci	Potsdam	26	4
Park Sanssouci	Potsdam	26	6/2
Park Sanssouci	Potsdam	26	944
Park Sanssouci	Potsdam	26	6/4
Park Sanssouci	Potsdam	26	945
Park Sanssouci	Potsdam	26	737
Park Sanssouci	Potsdam	26	738

D17.V.4 Stiftungsanlagenverordnung

Park Sanssouci	Potsdam	26	10
Park Sanssouci	Potsdam	27	103/1
Park Sanssouci	Potsdam	27	103/2
Park Sanssouci	Potsdam	27	133
Park Sanssouci	Potsdam	27	134
Park Sanssouci	Potsdam	27	141
Park Sanssouci	Potsdam	27	142/1
Park Sanssouci	Potsdam	27	142/2
Park Sanssouci	Bornstedt	1	1
Park Sanssouci	Bornstedt	1	2
Park Sanssouci	Bornstedt	1	3/2
Park Sanssouci	Bornstedt	1	7
Park Sanssouci	Bornstedt	1	28/2
Park Sanssouci	Bornstedt	1	132
Park Lindstedt			
Park Lindstedt	Bornim	6	35
Park Lindstedt	Bornim	6	36
Neuer Garten			
Neuer Garten	Potsdam	1	92
Neuer Garten	Potsdam	1	316
Neuer Garten	Potsdam	1	407/2
Neuer Garten	Potsdam	1	417
Neuer Garten	Potsdam	1	701
Neuer Garten	Potsdam	1	702
Neuer Garten	Potsdam	1	709
Neuer Garten	Potsdam	1	710
Neuer Garten	Potsdam	1	878
Neuer Garten	Potsdam	2	125
Neuer Garten	Potsdam	2	126
Neuer Garten	Potsdam	2	127
Neuer Garten	Potsdam	2	130
Neuer Garten	Potsdam	2	132
Neuer Garten	Potsdam	2	133
Neuer Garten	Potsdam	2	134
Neuer Garten	Potsdam	2	135
Neuer Garten	Potsdam	2	354
Neuer Garten	Potsdam	2	356
Neuer Garten	Potsdam	2	361
Neuer Garten	Potsdam	2	363
Neuer Garten	Potsdam	2	365
Neuer Garten	Potsdam	2	368
Neuer Garten	Potsdam	2	370
Neuer Garten	Potsdam	2	373

Neuer Garten	Potsdam	2	398
Neuer Garten	Potsdam	2	488
Neuer Garten	Potsdam	2	489
Neuer Garten	Potsdam	2	495
Neuer Garten	Potsdam	2	496
Neuer Garten	Potsdam	2	501
Neuer Garten	Potsdam	2	506
Neuer Garten	Potsdam	2	507
Neuer Garten	Potsdam	2	508
Neuer Garten	Potsdam	2	849
Neuer Garten	Potsdam	2	850
Park Babelsberg			
Park Babelsberg	Babelsberg	19	1/1
Park Babelsberg	Babelsberg	19	1/2
Park Babelsberg	Babelsberg	19	2
Park Babelsberg	Babelsberg	19	3
Park Babelsberg	Babelsberg	19	166
Park Babelsberg	Babelsberg	19	167
Park Babelsberg	Babelsberg	19	5
Park Babelsberg	Babelsberg	19	168
Park Babelsberg	Babelsberg	19	169
Park Babelsberg	Babelsberg	19	8/2
Park Babelsberg	Babelsberg	19	23
Park Babelsberg	Babelsberg	19	24
Park Babelsberg	Babelsberg	19	25/3
Park Babelsberg	Babelsberg	19	165
Park Babelsberg	Babelsberg	21	1
Park Babelsberg	Babelsberg	21	2
Park Babelsberg	Babelsberg	21	3
Park Babelsberg	Babelsberg	21	4
Park Babelsberg	Babelsberg	21	5
Park Babelsberg	Babelsberg	21	6
Park Babelsberg	Babelsberg	21	7
Park Babelsberg	Babelsberg	21	8
Park Babelsberg	Babelsberg	21	9
Park Babelsberg	Babelsberg	21	10
Park Babelsberg	Babelsberg	21	11
Park Babelsberg	Babelsberg	21	12
Park Babelsberg	Babelsberg	21	13
Park Babelsberg	Babelsberg	21	14
Park Babelsberg	Babelsberg	21	15
Park Babelsberg	Babelsberg	21	16
Park Babelsberg	Babelsberg	21	17

D17.V.4 Stiftungsanlagenverordnung

Park Babelsberg	Babelsberg	21	18
Park Babelsberg	Babelsberg	21	19
Park Babelsberg	Babelsberg	21	20/1
Park Babelsberg	Babelsberg	21	21
Park Babelsberg	Babelsberg	21	22/1
Park Babelsberg	Babelsberg	21	23
Park Babelsberg	Babelsberg	21	24
Park Babelsberg	Babelsberg	21	25
Park Babelsberg	Babelsberg	21	28
Park Babelsberg	Babelsberg	21	34
Park Babelsberg	Babelsberg	21	41
Park Babelsberg	Babelsberg	21	42
Park Sacrow			
Park Sacrow	Sacrow	1	117
Park Sacrow	Sacrow	1	118/11
Park Sacrow	Sacrow	1	118/12
Park Sacrow	Sacrow	1	118/13
Park Sacrow	Sacrow	1	118/14
Am Stern			
Am Stern	Drewitz	7	613
Am Stern	Drewitz	7	614
Am Stern	Drewitz	7	623
Am Stern	Drewitz	7	625
Am Stern	Drewitz	7	626
Am Stern	Drewitz	7	627
Stadt Potsdam			
Stadt Potsdam	Potsdam	6	31
Stadt Potsdam	Potsdam	23	301
Stadt Potsdam	Potsdam	23	1081
Stadt Potsdam	Potsdam	25	234/4
Stadt Potsdam	Potsdam	25	553/1
Königs Wusterhausen			
Schloss Königs Wusterhausen	Königs Wusterhausen	8	77
Rheinsberg			
Park Rheinsberg	Rheinsberg	10	20
Park Rheinsberg	Rheinsberg	10	21
Park Rheinsberg	Rheinsberg	10	22
Park Rheinsberg	Rheinsberg	10	23
Park Rheinsberg	Rheinsberg	10	24/5
Park Rheinsberg	Rheinsberg	10	24/6
Park Rheinsberg	Rheinsberg	10	24/7
Park Rheinsberg	Rheinsberg	10	30
Park Rheinsberg	Rheinsberg	10	31/2

Vertrag über die gemeinnützige Verwendung der gemäß § 20b Parteiengesetz der DDR in Verbindung mit Buchstabe d) Satz 3 Anlage II Kapitel II Sachgebiet A Abschnitt III des Einigungsvertrages unter treuhänderischer Verwaltung stehenden Kunstwerke der Parteien und der mit ihnen verbundenen Organisationen, juristischen Personen und Massenorganisationen der DDR

Vom 18. Mai 1995 (GVOBl. M-V 1996 S. 290)

Die Bundesanstalt für vereinigungsbedingte Sonderaufgaben, Anstalt des öffentlichen Rechts,
vertreten durch den Vorstand
– im Einvernehmen mit der Unabhängigen Kommission zur Überprüfung des Vermögens der Parteien und Massenorganisationen der DDR –
und
das Land Berlin,
vertreten durch den Regierenden Bürgermeister
das Land Brandenburg,
vertreten durch den Ministerpräsidenten
das Land Mecklenburg-Vorpommern
vertreten durch den Ministerpräsidenten
das Land Sachsen-Anhalt,
vertreten durch den Ministerpräsidenten
der Freistaat Sachsen,
vertreten durch den Ministerpräsidenten
der Freistaat Thüringen,
vertreten durch den Ministerpräsidenten
– nachstehend „Land/Länder" genannt –
schließen folgenden

Vertrag:

Präambel

Die Bundesanstalt für vereinigungsbedingte Sonderaufgaben ist mit den Ländern übereingekommen, diesen die nach Buchstabe d) Satz 3 der Anlage II Kapitel II Sachgebiet A Abschnitt III des Einigungsvertrages zugunsten gemeinnütziger Zwecke zu verwendenden Kunstgegenstände der Parteien und der mit ihnen verbundenen Organisationen, juristischen Personen und Massenorganisationen der DDR zu Eigentum zu übertragen.

Im Vorgriff auf die Eigentumsübertragung der Kunstgegenstände der Parteien und der mit ihnen verbundenen Organisationen, juristischen Personen und Massenorganisationen werden die Kunstgegenstände, über deren endgültige Zuordnung nach Buchstabe d) Sätze 2 bis 4 der Anlage II Kapitel II Sachgebiet A Abschnitt III des Einigungsvertrages noch nicht abschließend entschieden werden konnte, den Ländern leihweise überlassen. Es ist beabsichtigt, den Ländern die leihweise überlassenen Kunstgegenstände unverzüglich zu Eigentum zu übertragen, soweit sie nach Buchstabe d) Satz 3 der Anlage II Kapitel II Sachgebiet A Abschnitt III des Einigungsvertrages zugunsten gemeinnütziger Zwecke zu verwenden sind.

Die Vertragsschließenden stimmen darin überein, daß die Länder die Kunstgegenstände, die sie nach diesem Vertrag zu Eigentum oder als Leihgabe erhalten haben, im erforderlichen und üblichen Umfang auch Dritten zur Durchführung von Ausstellungen und zu Forschungszwecken unter Berücksichtigung konservatorischer Notwendigkeiten und der jeweiligen Interessenlage der Länder leihweise überlassen.

Artikel 1 Betroffene Kunstgegenstände

I) Von diesem Vertrag betroffen sind die Kunstgegenstände, die in den Anlagen 1 bis 4 aufgelistet sind.[1]

II) Die Bundesanstalt für vereinigungsbedingte Sonderaufgaben haftet nicht für Sach- oder Rechtsmängel der Kunstgegenstände.

Artikel 2 Aufteilungsgrundsatz

Die Kunstgegenstände werden dem Land zu Eigentum übertragen bzw. leihweise überlassen, auf dessen Gebiet sie von der Bundesanstalt für vereinigungsbedingte Sonderaufgaben bzw. ihren Beauftragten aufgefunden wurden. Für die Zuordnung der Kunstgegenstände auf die jeweiligen Länder ist hierbei allein der in den Anlagen angegebene ursprüngliche Standort der Kunstgegenstände ausschlaggebend.

Artikel 3 Eigentumsübertragung

I) Die Bundesanstalt für vereinigungsbedingte Sonderaufgaben bietet den Ländern die Eigentumsübertragung folgender Kunstgegenstände an:
 - dem Land Berlin die Kunstgegenstände nach Anlage 1a,
 - dem Land Brandenburg die Kunstgegenstände nach Anlage 1b,
 - dem Land Mecklenburg-Vorpommern die Kunstgegenstände nach Anlage 1c,
 - dem Land Sachsen-Anhalt die Kunstgegenstände nach Anlage 1d,
 - dem Freistaat Sachsen die Kunstgegenstände nach Anlage 1e,
 - dem Freistaat Thüringen die Kunstgegenstände nach Anlage 1f.

II) Die jeweiligen Länder nehmen dieses Angebot an.

III) Die Bundesanstalt für vereinigungsbedingte Sonderaufgaben und die Länder kommen überein, daß die Kunstgegenstände von den Ländern bis zum 28. Februar 1995 übernommen werden.

IV) Soweit sich die Kunstgegenstände im Besitz der Bundesanstalt für vereinigungsbedingte Sonderaufgaben befinden, vereinbaren die Bundesanstalt für vereinigungsbedingte Sonderaufgaben und das jeweilige Land hiermit als Besitzkonstitut einen unentgeltlichen Verwahrungsvertrag. Soweit eine Übergabe der Kunstgegenstände an die Länder nicht möglich ist, ist die Bundesanstalt für vereinigungsbedingte Sonderaufgaben berechtigt, die Kunstgegenstände bei einem geeigneten Dritten zu hinterlegen.

Die Bundesanstalt für vereinigungsbedingte Sonderaufgaben macht für im Rahmen dieses Verwahrungsvertrages bis zum 28. Februar 1995 einschließlich getätigte Aufwendungen keinen Aufwendungsersatz gemäß § 693 BGB gelten, soweit den Ländern die Annahme der Kunstgegenstände nicht möglich ist. Die Bundesanstalt für vereinigungsbedingte Sonderaufgaben haftet aus diesem Verwahrungsvertrag nur für Vorsatz und grobe Fahrlässigkeit.

V) Soweit ein Dritter im Besitz der Kunstgegenstände ist, tritt die Bundesanstalt für vereinigungsbedingte Sonderaufgaben hiermit
 - dem Land Berlin die Kunstgegenstände nach Anlage 2a,
 - dem Land Brandenburg die Kunstgegenstände nach Anlage 2b,
 - dem Land Mecklenburg-Vorpommern die Kunstgegenstände nach Anlage 2c,
 - dem Land Sachsen-Anhalt die Kunstgegenstände nach Anlage 2d,
 - dem Freistaat Sachsen die Kunstgegenstände nach Anlage 2e,
 - dem Freistaat Thüringen die Kunstgegenstände nach Anlage 2f

den Anspruch auf Herausgabe der Kunstgegenstände ab. Die Bundesanstalt für vereinigungsbedingte Sonderaufgaben tritt die Rechte aus bestehenden Leihverträgen an die jeweiligen Länder ab.

Die Länder nehmen diese Abtretung an. Die Bundesanstalt für vereinigungsbedingte Sonderaufgaben übergibt den jeweiligen Ländern die Leihverträge in beglaubigter Kopie.

VI) Die jeweiligen Länder benennen bis zum 30. September 1994 einen Ort zur Übergabe der Kunstgegenstände. Die Bundesanstalt für vereinigungsbedingte Sonderaufgaben transportiert die Kunstgegenstände gemäß Artikel 3, die sich in ihrem Besitz befinden, auf eigene Kosten bis zum 28. Februar 1995 an den von den jeweiligen Ländern zu bestimmenden Ort in den neuen Bundesländern oder Berlin.

---

1) Hinweis: Die im Vertrag erwähnten Anlagen befinden sich als Original im Kultusministerium.

Für die Beschädigung, Zerstörung, Veränderung oder den Verlust von Kunstgegenständen während oder aus Anlaß des Transportes haftet die Bundesanstalt für vereinigungsbedingte Sonderaufgaben nur für Vorsatz und grobe Fahrlässigkeit.

Artikel 4 Restitution/Herausgabe an den Berechtigten

Die Länder verpflichten sich, die Rückübertragung von Kunstgegenständen, die sie durch diesen Vertrag zu Eigentum erhalten, auf den Berechtigten nach Maßgabe des 2. Abschnitts des Vermögensgesetzes in der Fassung der Bekanntmachung vom 3. August 1992 (BGBl. I S. 1446) zu dulden. Darüber hinaus verpflichten sich die Länder, diejenigen Kunstgegenstände, die entgegen der Annahme zum Zeitpunkt der Übertragung an die Länder nicht im Eigentum der Parteien und Massenorganisationen stehen, an die jeweils Berechtigten herauszugeben. Die Länder verpflichten sich weiterhin, die Bundesanstalt für vereinigungsbedingte Sonderaufgaben in den Fällen der Sätze 1 und 2 von etwaigen Schadensersatzansprüchen Dritter wegen Verschlechterung oder Untergangs, die ab dem 1. März 1995 eintreten, freizustellen.

Artikel 5 Leihvertrag

I) Die Bundesanstalt für vereinigungsbedingte Sonderaufgaben schließt mit den jeweiligen Ländern folgende Leihverträge ab:
Die Bundesanstalt für vereinigungsbedingte Sonderaufgaben stellt
– dem Land Berlin die Kunstgegenstände nach Anlage 3a,
– dem Land Berlin die Kunstgegenstände nach Anlage 3b,
– dem Land Mecklenburg-Vorpommern die Kunstgegenstände nach Anlage 3c,
– dem Land Sachsen-Anhalt die Kunstgegenstände nach Anlage 3d,
– dem Freistaat Sachsen die Kunstgegenstände nach Anlage 3e,
– dem Freistaat Thüringen die Kunstgegenstände nach Anlage 3f
als Dauerleihgabe zur Verfügung.

II) Die Bundesanstalt für vereinigungsbedingte Sonderaufgaben wird den jeweiligen Ländern die in den Anlagen 3a bis 3f aufgelisteten Kunstgegenstände unverzüglich zu Eigentum übertragen, soweit sie nach Buchstabe d) Satz 3 der Anlage II Kapitel II Sachgebiet A Abschnitt III des Einigungsvertrages zu gemeinnützigen Zwecken zu verwenden sind.

III) Die Länder verpflichten sich, der Bundesanstalt für vereinigungsbedingte Sonderaufgaben jederzeit auf Anfrage über den jeweiligen Standort der Kunstgegenstände Auskunft zu geben.

Artikel 6 Beendigung des Leihvertrages

Aus wichtigem Grund kann der Verleiher den Leihvertrag kündigen und hat Anspruch auf vorzeitige Rückgabe. Als wichtiger Grund gilt insbesondere der Bescheid einer zuständigen Behörde, wonach der Restitutions- bzw. Herausgabeanspruch eines Dritten festgestellt wird.

Artikel 7 Hin- und Rücktransport

Der Verleiher sorgt für den Hin- und Rücktransport der Leihgaben; er erteilt die gegebenenfalls notwendigen Aufträge und trägt die Kosten einschließlich der Verpackungskosten.

Artikel 8 Freistellungserklärung

Der Entleiher stellt den Verleiher von allen Ansprüchen Dritter wegen der Beschädigung, Zerstörung, Veränderung oder des Verlustes der Leihgabe frei.

Artikel 9 Mitteilungspflichten und Nutzungsrechte

I) Der Entleiher ist verpflichtet, den Verleiher unverzüglich von jeder Veränderung oder Beschädigung zu benachrichtigen oder den Verlust der Leihgabe anzuzeigen.

II) Der Entleiher ist berechtigt, die Leihgabe wie seine eigenen Sammlungsgegenstände zu behandeln, das heißt auch, selbst zu restaurieren und fotografisch zu reproduzieren. Rechte Dritter bleiben hiervon unberührt.

Artikel 10 Leihgabe an das Deutsche Historische Museum

Dem Deutschen Historischen Museum werden
– vom Land Berlin die Kunstgegenstände nach Anlage 4a,
– vom Land Brandenburg die Kunstgegenstände nach Anlage 4b,
– vom Land Mecklenburg-Vorpommern die Kunstgegenstände nach Anlage 4c,
– vom Land Sachsen-Anhalt die Kunstgegenstände nach Anlage 4d,

D17.VI.1 Kunstwerke DDR

- vom Freistaat Sachsen die Kunstgegenstände nach Anlage 4e,
- vom Freistaat Thüringen die Kunstgegenstände nach Anlage 4f

leihweise bis einschließlich Mai 1995 für ein Ausstellungsvorhaben überlassen. Die Länder empfehlen dem Deutschen Historischen Museum nachdrücklich, die Urheber der Kunstgegenstände in angemessener Form vorab über das Ausstellungsvorhaben zu informieren.

Artikel 11 Finanzzuweisungen

I) Im Vorgriff auf das gemäß Anlage II Kapitel II Sachgebiet A Abschnitt III Buchstabe d) Satz 3 des Einigungsvertrages im Beitrittsgebiet gemeinnützig zu verwendende Vermögen weist die Bundesanstalt für vereinigungsbedingte Sonderaufgaben, zweckgebunden entsprechend dem Finanzantrag der Länder vom 19. August 1994 (Anlage 6) für Maßnahmen im Zuge der Übernahme und Aufbewahrung der Kunstgegenstände nach diesem Vertrag,

- dem Land Berlin   269.348,10 DM
- dem Land Brandenburg   534.710,79 DM
- dem Land Mecklenburg-Vorpommern   397.877,96 DM
- dem Freistaat Sachsen   984.067,12 DM
- dem Land Sachsen-Anhalt   593.827,88 DM
- dem Freistaat Thüringen   541.353,15 DM

zu.

II) Die Auszahlung der nach Absatz 1 zugewiesenen Gelder erfolgt gemäß dem Finanzantrag der Länder vom 19. August 1994 unmittelbar an die von den Ländern mit den konservatorischen Maßnahmen beauftragten Träger der Einrichtungen Kunstfonds des Freistaates Sachsen, Burg Beeskow und Dokumentationsstelle Halle. Die Länder ermächtigen die Bundesanstalt für vereinigungsbedingte Sonderaufgaben die gemäß Absatz 1 zugewiesenen Gelder mit befreiender Wirkung an die Träger der vorgenannten Einrichtungen auszuzahlen.

Artikel 12 Salvatorische Klausel

Sollten einzelne Vertragsbestimmungen dieses Vertrages unwirksam sein, so bleibt die Wirksamkeit der anderen Vertragsbestimmungen unberührt.

Artikel 13 Bindungswirkung

Dieser Vertrag wird unmittelbar zwischen der Bundesanstalt für vereinigungsbedingte Sonderaufgaben und den einzelnen Ländern, die ihn abschließen, wirksam, ohne daß es der Annahme durch alle Länder bedarf. Der Vertrag begründet nur vertragliche Beziehungen zwischen der Bundesanstalt für vereinigungsbedingte Sonderaufgaben und dem einzelnen Land. Mit dem Abschluß dieses Vertrages sind alle Ansprüche bezüglich der gemeinnützigen Verwendung der Kunstgegenstände der ehemaligen Parteien und Massenorganisationen abschließend geregelt.

Artikel 14 Gerichtsstand

Der Gerichtsstand für alle Streitigkeiten aus diesen Verträgen ist Berlin.

Bericht und Empfehlungen der Kultusministerkonferenz zur Erhaltung und Pflege jüdischen Kulturguts in Deutschland

Beschl. d. KMK vom 6. Dezember 1996

Die Erhaltung und Pflege jüdischen Kulturguts in Deutschland ist auch für die Denkmalpflege eine Aufgabe und Verpflichtung von hohem fachlichen und politischen Stellenwert. Um die damit zusammenhängenden Fragen und Probleme aufzuarbeiten, hat der seinerzeitige Unterausschuß Museen und Denkmalpflege nach Besprechung und Abstimmung mit Vertretern verschiedener jüdischer Institutionen eine gemeinsame Arbeitsgruppe „Jüdisches Kulturgut" eingesetzt.

An der Arbeitsgruppe wirkten Vertreter folgender Institutionen mit: Stiftung „Neue Synagoge Berlin – Centrum Judaicum", Berlin; Institut für die Geschichte der deutschen Juden, Hamburg; Berlin Museum, Jüdische Abteilung. Nach Teilung des Unterausschusses Museen und Denkmalpflege in zwei selbständige Unterausschüsse gehörten der Arbeitsgruppe Vertreter der Länder Baden-Württemberg (Vorsitz), Berlin und Sachsen, von seiten des Unterausschusses Museen der Vertreter des Landes Brandenburg an.

Die Arbeitsgruppe hat sich insbesondere mit den nach den Denkmalschutzgesetzen der Länder geschützten Zeugnissen der jüdischen Geschichte in Deutschland befaßt und dabei folgende Sachkomplexe behandelt: Erfassung und Inventarisierung jüdischer Kulturdenkmale, insbesondere ehemaliger Synagogen, jüdischer Friedhöfe, Mikwen usw.; Pflege und Betreuung jüdischer Friedhöfe; Dokumentation jüdischer Grabstätten und Grabsteine; Gesichtspunkte, die bei der Erhaltung, Restaurierung und Nutzung von Baudenkmälern, die zum jüdischen Kulturgut zählen, zu beachten sind. Zu den genannten Themen hat die Arbeitsgruppe jeweils Empfehlungen erarbeitet, die sich an alle Landesstellen richten, die mit der Erhaltung und Pflege jüdischen Kulturguts befaßt sind.

Mit dem Empfehlungsentwurf hat sich inzwischen auch der Zentralrat der Juden in Deutschland einverstanden erklärt.

1. Erfassung jüdischer Kulturdenkmale

Als vorrangige Aufgabe befaßte sich die Arbeitsgruppe mit der Frage, inwieweit die Kulturdenkmale, die zum jüdischen Kulturgut zählen, in den einzelnen Ländern bekannt, erfaßt und dokumentiert sind, und ob insoweit ein Nachholbedarf besteht.

Eine bei den Ländern durchgeführte Erhebung ergab, daß in nahezu allen Ländern Erfassungen, Dokumentationen und Inventarisationen von jüdischen Kulturdenkmalen existieren. Gerade in der letzten Zeit hat im Zuge einer verstärkten Inventarisation von Kulturdenkmalen auch die Erfassung zum jüdischen Kulturgut gehörender Kulturdenkmale erhebliche Fortschritte gemacht. Allerdings sind die Zusammenstellungen jüdischer Kulturgüter in den einzelnen Ländern, was Form, Umfang, Inhalt und Kategorien der erfaßten Objekte betrifft, sehr unterschiedlich. Spezielle Erfassungen jüdischer Kulturgüter beschränken sich in einigen Ländern auf Friedhöfe und Synagogen (zum Teil auch einschließlich von Mikwen und Gemeindehäusern). In einigen Ländern ist es möglich, aus den vorhandenen Denkmallisten entsprechende Listen über Kulturdenkmale, die zum jüdischen Kulturgut zählen, einschließlich der Denkmalbegründung zusammenzustellen. Wegen der Einzelheiten wird auf das in der Anlage beigefügte Verzeichnis der Erfassungen von Kulturdenkmalen, die zum jüdischen Kulturgut zählen, verwiesen.

Neben diesen Erfassungen gibt es eine Reihe von monographischen Arbeiten und Dokumentationen über jüdisches Kulturgut in einzelnen Regionen oder Ländern. Als vorbildlich betrachtet die Arbeitsgruppe das Werk „Zeugnisse jüdischer Kultur" (siehe Vermerk auf beiliegendem Verzeichnis), das für die neuen Länder erschienen ist und das durchaus als Modell für ähnliche Ausarbeitungen in den alten Ländern gelten könnte.

Zusammenfassend läßt sich sagen, daß eine Fülle von Material, Dokumentationen und Übersichten zu diesem Problemkreis vorliegen, aber keine gesamtdeutsche Übersicht nach einheitlichen Kriterien. Angesichts der Kulturhoheit der Länder, die auch unterschiedliche Verhältnisse im Stand sowie in der Art und Weise der Erfassung von Kulturdenkmalen zur Folge hat, aber auch angesichts der Unterschiedlichkeiten hinsichtlich des Bestandes an jüdischem Kulturgut in den einzelnen Ländern, fehlen die Voraussetzungen für eine nach einheitlichen Kriterien und Methoden erfolgende bundesweite Er-

D17.VI.2 Erhaltung und Pflege jüdischen Kulturguts

fassung von Kulturdenkmalen, die zum jüdischen Kulturgut zählen. Eine solche bundesweit einheitliche Erfassung ist jedoch auch nicht erforderlich. Wichtig und entscheidend ist vielmehr, daß die in den einzelnen Ländern vorhandenen Möglichkeiten ausgeschöpft werden, jüdische Kulturdenkmale möglichst vollständig zu erfassen und unter den bestehenden gesetzlichen und faktischen Rahmenbedingungen optimal zu pflegen und zu erhalten. Dies sollte in engem Kontakt mit den jeweils zuständigen israelitischen Religionsgemeinschaften geschehen.

Als erste Empfehlung spricht sich die Arbeitsgruppe dafür aus, daß in allen Ländern – soweit noch nicht vorhanden aber möglich – Verzeichnisse über Kulturdenkmale, die zum jüdischen Kulturgut zählen, erstellt oder, soweit erforderlich, vervollständigt werden.

2. Pflege jüdischer Friedhöfe

Die Friedhöfe der ehemaligen jüdischen Gemeinden in Deutschland bedürfen einer ständigen Pflege und Betreuung. In den alten Ländern wird diese Betreuung auf der Grundlage einer Absprache zwischen Bund, Ländern und Vertretern jüdischer Organisationen in Deutschland vom 21.6.1957 durchgeführt. Die Mittel für die Betreuungs- und Pflegemaßnahmen werden nach dieser Absprache vom Bund und von den Ländern je zur Hälfte aufgebracht. Nach dem Inhalt der Absprache müssen die Betreuungsmaßnahmen den religiösen Überzeugungen und der jahrtausendealten Tradition des Judentums Rechnung tragen. Danach ist der jüdische Friedhof eine Stätte der Totenruhe. Die Ruhe der Toten gilt als unantastbar. Der jüdische Friedhof muß daher als eine in die Landschaft eingefügte Gesamtheit dauernd erhalten bleiben. Dazu gehören nach der erwähnten Absprache: Erhaltung einer sicheren Einfriedung mit verschließbarem Tor, ordnungsmäßige Unterhaltung der Zugangswege und der Hauptwege auf dem Friedhof, regelmäßiges Schneiden des Grases und Beseitigung des Unkrautes. Umgefallene Grabsteine sind wieder aufzurichten. Eine individuelle Pflege des Einzelgrabes bleibt den Angehörigen des Verstorbenen bzw. den jüdischen Stellen überlassen. Einzelfragen sind in Verbindung mit den zuständigen jüdischen Stellen zu klären.

Die Arbeitsgruppe empfiehlt den neuen Ländern, soweit noch nicht geschehen, der Absprache vom 21.6.1957 über die praktische Durchführung der Betreuung verwaister jüdischer Friedhöfe beizutreten.

3. Dokumentation jüdischer Grabstätten

Die teils sehr alten Grabsteine auf den jüdischen Friedhöfen unterliegen einem natürlichen Verwitterungsprozeß. Dieser Prozeß hat sich durch die zunehmende Luftverschmutzung in den letzten Jahren stark beschleunigt. Unter der Verwitterung leiden vor allem Grabinschriften, die wesentlicher Träger der historischen und religiösen Aussagekraft jüdischer Friedhöfe sind. Da eine Restaurierung und Konservierung sämtlicher Grabsteine im Hinblick auf ihre große Zahl und die zur Verfügung stehenden konservatorischen Möglichkeiten sowie aus denkmalpflegerischen und religiösen Gesichtspunkten nicht möglich ist, ist die Dokumentation der Grabsteine und Grabinschriften eine vorrangige und vordringliche Aufgabe. Nur auf diese Weise kann der Geschichts- und Kulturwert alter jüdischer Friedhöfe für die Nachwelt überliefert werden. Solche Dokumentationen bilden auch die Grundlage für die Erforschung der Geschichte der ehemaligen jüdischen Gemeinden und sollen das Wissen um deren Schicksal lebendig erhalten. Sie sind damit auch ein wichtiges heimatgeschichtliches Anliegen der Kommunen.

Jüdische Friedhöfe beanspruchen unsere Aufmerksamkeit als Quellen für die jüdische Geschichte unter zwei Gesichtspunkten. Zum einen sind die Grabdenkmäler kunsthistorische Zeugnisse, wobei nicht nur die nach ästhetischen Maßstäben herausgehobenen Grabstätten zu berücksichtigen sind, sondern auch die weniger bedeutenden, die oft in hohem Maße aussagekräftig sind. Zum anderen sind die Grabinschriften wesentliche Quellen für die jüdische Geschichte. Dies gilt in besonderem Maße für die Zeit vor 1875, weil erst ab dieser Zeit mit der Einrichtung von Standesämtern Geburt, Heirat und Tod amtlich beurkundet wurden. Die Grabinschriften vor dieser Zeit sind somit steinerne Urkunden von einzigartigem historischem Wert, weil für Juden eine den Kirchenbüchern in der christlichen Kirche vergleichbare Quellenkategorie nicht existiert. Aber auch für die Zeit, in der es Standesämter gibt, sind die Grabinschriften wertvolle historische Quellen, weil sie über die amtlichen Urkunden hinausgehende Aussagen enthalten.

Wie die von der Arbeitsgruppe durchgeführte Erhebung ergeben hat, liegen bereits in einer Anzahl von Fällen wissenschaftliche Dokumentationen jüdischer Grabsteine vor. Häufig sind daran Privatinitiativen oder Fördervereine, die sich der christlich-jüdischen Verständigung widmen, beteiligt.

Die Arbeitsgruppe appelliert an die Länder, die Maßnahmen zur Dokumentation jüdischer Friedhöfe zu verstärken und alle Initiativen auf privater und kommunaler Basis für die Dokumentation jüdischer Friedhöfe zu unterstützen.

4. Erhaltung und Restaurierung der Baudenkmäler, die zum jüdischen Kulturgut zählen
In den Ländern wird seit der gesetzlichen und organisatorischen Stärkung des Denkmalschutzes in den letzten beiden Jahrzehnten das jüdische Kulturgut mit derselben Intensität und nach denselben Maßstäben betreut, wie die übrigen Kulturdenkmale. Bei jüdischem Kulturgut können jedoch besondere Probleme und Schwierigkeiten auftauchen. Dies gilt insbesondere für diejenigen ehemaligen Synagogen, die die Verwüstung des nationalsozialistischen Unrechtsregimes in mehr oder weniger zerstörter Form überstanden haben. Da diese Synagogen nur in den seltensten Fällen wieder für den Gottesdienst einer jüdischen Gemeinde genutzt werden können, ergeben sich Probleme, welcher sinnvollen und angemessenen Nutzung eine solche Synagoge nach ihrer Restaurierung und Instandsetzung zugeführt werden soll.

In vielen Fällen ist eine restaurierte Synagoge der geeignete Standort für die Einrichtung eines Dokumentationszentrums des jüdischen Glaubens und der Geschichte der Juden des jeweiligen Ortes. Gleichzeitig kann eine solche Synagoge in geeigneten Fällen auch ein Ort der Begegnung zwischen Juden und Christen und für einen deutsch-israelischen Austausch werden.

Aber auch andere, der einstigen Zweckbestimmung der Synagoge adäquate Nutzungen lassen sich finden. Schon von alters her war die Synagoge nicht bloß Ort des Gebetes, sondern Stätte des gesamten Gemeindelebens, Versammlungs- und Lehrhaus. Deshalb lassen sich nahezu alle Aufgaben der Kultur- und Bildungsarbeit mit gutem Grund in einer Synagoge unterbringen.

In den Fällen, in denen sich Nutzungen der oben dargestellten Art nicht finden lassen oder nicht möglich sind, sollten jedoch die Bemühungen der Denkmalpflege um die Erhaltung einer ehemaligen Synagoge nicht aufgegeben werden. Vielmehr sollte die Denkmalpflege auch in diesen Fällen unter Ausnutzung aller rechtlichen und faktischen Möglichkeiten dazu beitragen, die substanzielle Erhaltung der uns überlieferten Synagogen zu sichern. Durch die Fürsorge für die Erhaltung ehemaliger Synagogen eröffnet die Denkmalpflege auch zukünftigen Generationen die Möglichkeit, sich mit der deutsch-jüdischen Geschichte in angemessener Form zu befassen.

Die Arbeitsgruppe spricht die Empfehlung an die Denkmalpflege der Länder aus, die Bemühungen um die Erhaltung und Restaurierung jüdischer Kulturdenkmale, insbesondere der ehemaligen Synagogen fortzusetzen und sich für eine angemessene Nutzung einzusetzen. Als angemessene Nutzung kommen insbesondere Dokumentationszentren des jüdischen Glaubens und der Geschichte der Juden des jeweiligen Ortes, aber auch Begegnungsstätten zwischen Christen und Juden sowie alle anderen Aufgaben der Kultur- und Bildungsarbeit in Betracht.

Aber auch dort, wo solche Nutzungen nicht möglich oder durchsetzbar sind, sollte die substanzielle Erhaltung der überlieferten Synagogen ein Hauptziel der Landesdenkmalpflege sein.

D17.VI.2 Erhaltung und Pflege jüdischen Kulturguts

Anhang

Verzeichnis von Kulturdenkmalen, die zum jüdischen Kulturgut zählen
(Stand: 07.12.1994)

Land	Verzeichnisse vorh.	mögl.	Objekte	Informationsgehalt
BW	ja Friedh. und Synagogen	nein übrige Baudenkmäler, da aus dem Gesamtbestand der Baudenkmäler mit vertretbarem Aufwand nicht ausscheidbar	Friedhöfe Synagogen	Belegungsdatum, Zahl der Grabsteine, Erhaltungszustand, Dokumentationshinweise; z.T. umfassende Dokumentation Umfassende Dokumentation
BY	ja		sämtl. bekannte jüdische Kulturdenkmale (Friedhöfe, Synagogen, Mikwen, Gemeindehäuser, Judenhäuser usw.)	stichwortartige Darstellung entspr. den allg. Denkmallisten. Arbeitsheft „Denkmäler jüd. Kultur in BY".
BE	nein (außer die bek. Frh.)	nein		
BB	nein	ja	Friedhöfe, Synagogen, Badehäuser	Lokalisierung (Liste)
HB	Nur ein Friedhof als denkmalgeschütztes Kulturgut vorhanden			Dokumentation der historisch relevanten Grabsteine in Wort und Bild
HH	ja Friedhöfe (begonnen) und Baudenkmäler der jüdischen Gemeinde	nein übrige Denkmäler	Friedhöfe Baudenkmale, die zur jüdischen Gemeinde gehören, wie Synagogen, Schulen, Wohnstifte u.s.f.	Standard der üblichen Inventarisation
HE	ja Friedhof und Synagoge	nein übrige Baudenkmäler, da aus dem Gesamtbestand der Baudenkmäler mit vertretbarem Aufwand nicht ausscheidbar	Friedhöfe Synagogen	Lokalisierung Umfassende Dokumentation (Privatarbeit über Mikwen in Arbeit)
MV	ja		Friedhöfe Baudenkmäler	Lokalisierung
NI	ja		Friedhöfe Synagogen, Mikwe Gemeindehaus	Lokalisierung
NW	ja ja	 ja	Friedhöfe Synagogen sonst. Gebäude	Lokalisierung (landesweit) tlw. umfassende Dokumentation auf Gemeindeebene Lokalisierung Lokalisierung

Erhaltung und Pflege jüdischen Kulturguts D17.VI.2

Land	Verzeichnisse vorh.	mögl.	Objekte	Informationsgehalt
RP	ja		Friedhöfe	Lokalisierung (Liste)
SL	ja Friedhöfe	ja Baudenkmäler	Friedhöfe Baudenkmäler	Lokalisierung Denkmalbegründung
SN	teilweise	ja	Baudenkmäler Gedenkstätten, Synagogen	Lokalisierung
ST	ja		Friedhöfe Synagogen sonst. Gebäude	Lokalisierung (Liste) mit Denkmalbegründungen
SH	nein	ja	Friedhöfe Synagogen	Teilweise Auflistung – der Grabsteine – des Inhalts der Synagogen
TH	ja Friedhöfe Synagogen		Friedhöfe Synagogen	Lokalisierung (Liste) Lokalisierung Denkmalbegründung

Im Jahr 1992 ist im Tourist-Verlag, Berlin, eine Dokumentation „Zeugnisse jüdischer Kultur" für die Länder BB, BE, MV, ST, und TH erschienen, die Kurzbeschreibungen auch der zum jüdischen Kulturgut zählenden Kulturdenkmale (Baudenkmale, Friedhöfe) enthält.

BW	=	Baden-Württemberg	NI	=	Niedersachsen
BY	=	Bayern	NW	=	Nordrhein-Westfalen
BE	=	Berlin	RP	=	Rheinland-Pfalz
BB	=	Brandenburg	SL	=	Saarland
HB	=	Bremen	SN	=	Sachsen
HH	=	Hamburg	ST	=	Sachsen-Anhalt
HE	=	Hessen	SH	=	Schleswig-Holstein
MV	=	Mecklenburg-Vorpommern	TH	=	Thüringen

D17.VI.3 Volontariat in der Denkmalpflege

Grundsätze für die Beschäftigung von Volontären/Volontärinnen in der Denkmalpflege[1]

Beschl. d. KMK vom 26. Juni 1998

1. **Ziel**
   Das Volontariat befähigt zur selbständigen wissenschaftlichen Tätigkeit in der Denkmalpflege (Bau-, Kunst- und Gartendenkmalpflege, Restaurierung, archäologische Denkmalpflege).
2. **Zugang**
   Voraussetzung für ein wissenschaftliches Volontariat ist ein abgeschlossenes wissenschaftliches Hochschulstudium. Die Stellen werden in der Regel öffentlich ausgeschrieben.
3. **Dauer**
   Das Volontariat dauert in der Regel zwei Jahre.
4. **Ausbildungsplan**
   Für das Volontariat ist durch die ausbildende Stelle ein verbindlicher Ausbildungsplan aufzustellen. Durch den Ausbildungsplan ist zu gewährleisten, dass Fachkenntnisse und Fähigkeiten zur selbständigen Tätigkeit in den verschiedenen fachlichen Aufgaben der Denkmalpflege erworben werden können.
   Der Ausbildungsplan soll außerdem Kenntnisse über Grundlagen des Denkmalrechts, den Vollzug des Denkmalschutzgesetzes, die Verwaltung sowie die Organisation und Aufgaben der vom Denkmalschutz betroffenen Behörden und Körperschaften vermitteln.
   Für die ordnungsgemäße Durchführung des Ausbildungsplans ist ein/eine Betreuer/Betreuerin verantwortlich, die von der ausbildenden Stelle benannt wird.
   Durch zeitliche Gliederung sollen in Abstimmung zwischen der ausbildenden Stelle und dem/der Volontär/Volotärin Ausbildungsschwerpunkte vereinbart werden.
   Entsprechend der Struktur und Ausstattung der ausbildenden Stelle können Teilabschnitte des Volontariats in einschlägigen anderen Fachbehörden oder Ämtern absolviert werden.
   Zum Abschluß des Volontariats wird ein Zeugnis über den Inhalt der Ausbildungsabschnitte sowie die Fähigkeiten des/der Volontärs/Volontärin ausgehändigt, das von allen Fachämtern für Denkmalpflege und archäologische Denkmalpflege in der Bundesrepublik Deutschland als Qualifikationsnachweis anerkannt wird.
5. **Rechtsstellung und Vergütung**
   Die Volontäre/Volontärinnen stehen in einem Vertragsverhältnis, das durch den Abschluss eines Volontärvertrages begründet wird. Für die Volontäre/Volontärinnen gelten das Dienstrecht des höheren Dienstes und die Geschäftsordnung der ausbildenden Stelle.
   Die Volontäre/Volontärinnen können für die Erledigung allgemeiner Dienstaufgaben herangezogen werden, soweit dieses im Rahmen der Einübung praktischer Fähigkeiten entsprechend dem Berufsbild in der Denkmalpflege dienlich ist und dem Ausbildungsplan weder zeitlich noch inhaltlich entgegensteht.
   Die Volontäre/Volontärinnen sind hinsichtlich der Teilnahme an Fortbildungsveranstaltungen und Fachtagungen sowie der Möglichkeit zu eigener wissenschaftlicher Arbeit den übrigen wissenschaftlichen Mitarbeitern der ausbildenden Stelle gleichgestellt.
   Die Vergütung der Volontäre/Volontärinnen richtet sich nach den jeweiligen landesrechtlichen Regelungen.
6. **Schlussbestimmungen**
   Diese Grundsätze werden Bestandteil des Volontärvertrages.

---

[1] Quelle: http://www.dnk.de/_uploads/media/219_1998_KMK_Volontaere.pdf.